T0369595

Fowler's Dictionary of Modern English Usage

Fowler's
Dictionary of Modern English Usage

FIRST EDITION

H. W. Fowler

FOURTH EDITION

Edited by

Jeremy Butterfield

OXFORD
UNIVERSITY PRESS

Great Clarendon Street, Oxford, OX2 6DP,
United Kingdom

Oxford University Press is a department of the University of Oxford.
It furthers the University's objective of excellence in research, scholarship,
and education by publishing worldwide. Oxford is a registered trade mark of
Oxford University Press in the UK and in certain other countries

First edition 1926
Second edition 1965
Third edition 1996
Fourth edition 2015

Published in the United States of America by Oxford University Press
198 Madison Avenue, New York, NY 10016, United States of America

British Library Cataloguing in Publication Data
Data available

Library of Congress Control Number: 2014945276

ISBN 978-0-19-966135-0
ebook ISBN 978-0-19-106494-4

Printed and bound in Great Britain by Bell and Bain Ltd, Glasgow

To my beloved parents,
who gave me my first copy of *Fowler* when I was
at the Royal Grammar School, Guildford.

Conflicting views

Ours is a Copious Language, and Trying to Strangers.

MR PODSNAP IN DICKENS'S *OUR MUTUAL FRIEND*, 1865

Grammar is like walking. You have to think about it when you start but if you have to go on thinking about it you fall over. It should come as second nature.

ALICE THOMAS ELLIS IN *THE SPECTATOR*, 1989

Arguments over grammar and style are often as fierce as those over Windows versus Mac, and as fruitless as Coke versus Pepsi and boxers versus briefs.

PROFESSOR JACK LYNCH, *THE ENGLISH LANGUAGE: A USER'S GUIDE*, 2007

Time changes all things; there is no reason why language should escape this universal law. (Le temps change toute chose; il n'y a aucune raison pour que la langue échappe à cette loi universelle.)

FERDINAND DE SAUSSURE, *COURSE IN GENERAL LINGUISTICS*, 1959 (1916)

Dislikes

First (for I detest your ridiculous and most pedantic neologism of 'firstly').

THOMAS DE QUINCEY, 1847

Comments on *hopefully* by members of a usage panel, as reported in 1985:

I have fought this for some years, will fight it till I die. It is barbaric, illiterate, offensive, damnable, and inexcusable.

I don't like chalk squeaking on blackboards either.

'Hopefully' is useful or it would not be used so universally.

'Grounded' meaning a withdrawal of privileges is a word I dislike. It's off the television (*Roseanne* notably) but now in common use. (I just heard it on *Emmerdale Farm*, where they probably think it's dialect.) I would almost prefer 'gated', deriving from Forties public school stories in *Hotspur* and *Wizard*. Other current dislikes: 'Brits'; 'for starters'; 'sorted'; and (when used intransitively) 'hurting'.

ALAN BENNETT IN *LONDON REVIEW OF BOOKS*, 4 JAN. 1996

A revision for the twenty-first century

This new, fourth edition of *Fowler's Dictionary of Modern English Usage* has been thoroughly revised and updated to reflect how English speakers the world over use the language now, in the early twenty-first century. It offers detailed, reasoned guidance on thousands of points of grammar, spelling, punctuation, syntax, style, appropriate word choice, and pronunciation. It presents the facts of disputed or controversial usages and illuminates them with up-to-date examples, thereby enabling readers to make informed choices for themselves about their own usage.

In order to make the book relevant to modern users, my editing has consisted of three major tasks. To take editorial decisions, I have drawn on my observation and knowledge of contemporary usage issues derived from my experience as a teacher, translator, author, and former Editor-in-Chief of dictionaries.

First, the addition of over 250 new entries. These entries discuss words and phrases that have been coined or that have become more widespread since the previous edition. Many of them reflect the staggering changes in the way we communicate: *blog, to google, hashtag, homepage, online, phablet, selfie, social media.* Many, in contrast, are not new but raise usage or style issues not previously covered: *achingly* (pretentious? clichéd?), *ad nauseam* (misspelt as *-eum*), *to address* (overused?), *brainstorming* (not, contrary to urban myth, politically incorrect), *challenging* (meaning exactly what?), *epicentre* (misused?), *the problem is, is,* to name just a few.

Some of the new entries also reflect changed attitudes towards (or 'around' as many now say) language dealing with race, gender, disability, sexuality, and so forth: *ageism, conjoined twins, the language of disability, Indigenous Australians.*

Secondly, I examined each entry to see whether the points raised were still valid. In many cases, naturally, they were. That was particularly true of more straightforward matters such as spelling and alternative plural forms—although even here some surprises emerged, such as changing conventions for plurals of Latin-derived words ending in *-um,* which can cause so much head-scratching.

But in less cut-and-dried areas, many of the conventions that applied at the time of the previous edition, nearly twenty years ago, have changed, and I have updated entries accordingly, e.g. *between you and I, hopefully,* or the much debated use of *they, their,* etc. after singular noun phrases and pronouns such as *every student, everybody, everyone.*

Thirdly, I have modernized, where appropriate, the style and tone of voice of entries. Sometimes this involved rephrasing dated or literary wording, or language that is 'lexicographerspeak'; sometimes it meant removing a tone which was socially or linguistically outdated. Most visibly for the reader, because *Fowler* is a book that has always elucidated points of usage by well-chosen examples, I have carefully selected and added hundreds of examples of words being used in their modern contexts. To do this, I have drawn on a great variety of contemporary British, US, and international sources, ranging from the *Yorkshire Post* and the *Daily Telegraph,* to *Socialist Worker* and *Private Eye,* from *The Times of India* and the *Australian Broadcasting Corporation,* to *Scotland on Sunday* and *CNN* news.

These examples are all drawn from the unparalleled resource that is the *Oxford English Corpus.*

The Oxford English Corpus

The use I have made of the *Oxford English Corpus* marks a watershed in the life of this book. Since many readers will be unfamiliar with the term 'corpus', it is worth explaining what this possibly funereal-sounding Latin word means in modern lexicography and linguistics. A corpus can be defined as 'a collection of written or spoken texts in machine-readable form, assembled for the purpose of linguistic research'. But such a definition is abstract, and raises questions such as 'How does a corpus work?', 'What are the practical benefits', and 'What does it contain?' To answer the first, the corpus allows users to analyse *all* the examples of a given word contained in it. For instance, the noun *challenge* appears in nearly a quarter of a million different sentences. These sentences can be read on screen, and are exhaustively analysed using linguistic software.

For this book, the practical benefits of using a corpus included establishing how often competing forms of a word are used, e.g. *geographic(al)*, or *website* versus *web site*. Corpus analysis also shows whether a word is more frequent in one variety of English than another: British English favours *educationalist* whereas *educationist* is widely used in Indian English. Lexically, it makes it possible to tease out differences between similar words through the word associations revealed by the data (e.g. *optimal/optimum*, *repertoire/repertory*). The corpus also brings to light previously unsuspected uses, malapropisms such as to be *clambering* to do something instead of *clamouring*, or misspellings such as to take a *peak* at something instead of *peek*.

As regards contents, the *Oxford English Corpus* contains over 2.5 billion words, consisting of twenty-first century texts from the year 2000 onwards, and is continuously updated. It is based mainly on texts collected from pages on the World Wide Web supplemented by printed texts to make it truly comprehensive. All types of English are included, from literary novels and specialist journals to everyday newspapers and magazines, and from Hansard to the language of blogs, emails, and social media.

And, the *Oxford English Corpus* reflects the international reach of English, comprising as it does not merely texts from the UK and the United States, but also Ireland, Australia, New Zealand, the Caribbean, Canada, India, South Africa, Singapore, Malaysia, the Philippines, and Hong Kong.

The Web

This preface was written shortly after the twenty-fifth anniversary of the World Wide Web, and the Web has enormously benefited the editing in several ways.

It has allowed remote online access to the *Oxford English Corpus*, the benefits of which have already been summarized. In my reviewing of entries, the information I gleaned from online searches proved invaluable in establishing contemporary relevance. In particular, online discussion groups, blogs, and forums for and by copy editors, copywriters, learners, and word buffs provided fresh perspectives on issues that continue to cause puzzlement or controversy.

Lastly, the World Wide Web provides unparalleled access to a panoply of scholarly resources that previous editors would find mind-boggling: from the complete works of any classic author you care to name, to online dictionaries of all kinds, to long-forgotten books which may hold the key to a word's historical development. In particular, it has been a joy to be able to consult the *Oxford English Dictionary* online throughout this revision.

Making the fullest use of this book

It sounds almost crass to point this out, but the main use of a dictionary—which is what this is, albeit a dictionary of usage—is as an alphabetically ordered look-up resource. If you have a query about the difference between *imply* and INFER, you go straight to the relevant entry; similarly for the spelling of SIZEABLE, SIZABLE; if you have doubts about whether 'the man whom they claimed is a member of a dissident faction' passes grammatical muster, you go to WHO AND WHOM; if you find yourself swithering between 'If it *was* up to me' and 'If it *were* up to me', the entry on the SUBJUNCTIVE MOOD may be instructive.

But if you use the book only as a look-up of last resort, a sort of linguistic emergency service, you will unwittingly deprive yourself of at least half its pleasure and usefulness. The book covers, as it has since Henry Fowler created it, issues to do with every feature of English, including etymology (*forlorn hope*), very similar words (*flagrant* versus *blatant*), changing meanings (*nonplussed*), changes in the acceptability of words (*shag*), pronunciation (*chorizo, macho*), and bugbears, such as *-ize* verbs, *split infinitives*, and avoiding the passive, which, like Broadway hit musicals, just run and run.

And it also includes unexpected information. For example, Fowler included numerous technical terms from grammar, rhetoric, and poetry, many of which have been retained. They can provide an insight into mechanisms of language that we use without thinking and without naming, e.g. *hendiadys, litotes, personification*. There are several lengthy articles that explain a rule or feature governing innumerable different words (RECESSIVE ACCENT, DOUBLING OF CONSONANTS WITH SUFFIXES). A comprehensive web of cross-references guides you from one entry to others on the same topic, or related topics. There is also more than occasional humour, Fowlerian (*mot juste*) or other (*misprints*).

Previous editors' examples

Previous editors did not pluck their conclusions out of thin air: they too had their own evidence, of disparate kinds. For Henry Fowler, it consisted partly of the files he had access to as an Oxford University Press lexicographer. But he was clearly also an avid collector of journalistic examples, often of ill-advised usage, hundreds of which he used to illustrate his discussions in the original edition. Those that illustrate a point still relevant for today's speakers of English have been kept.

For his 1965 revision, much of Sir Ernest Gowers' evidence came from a rather different source: the morass of official documents he had to wade through in his distinguished civil service career. To his eagle eye for cant and jargon we owe, for example, the entry on *officialese*, which has been retained and updated.

In preparing the third edition, in the pioneering days of computerized language analysis, Robert Burchfield created a personal database of quotations, drawn from language of the 1980s and 1990s. To his industry this current edition owes the many hundreds of examples drawn from literary authors of all stripes, such as Chinua Achebe, Peter Ackroyd, Peter Carey, J. M. Coetzee, Kingsley Amis, Raymond Carver, Iris Murdoch, and Vikram Seth.

Prescriptive or descriptive?

It is usually only literary giants—Shakespeare, Milton, Byron, etc.—whose names stand for their entire work. Henry Fowler is one of that select non-literary band who have achieved such status (Baedeker, Bradshaw, Debrett's, Hansard, Wainwright). Apart from being a metonym—people refer to 'Fowler', meaning the book—he has become a common noun: one can talk of 'the latest Fowler', 'a Fowler for today', and even 'a Fowler of Politics'. The publication of Henry Fowler's original 1926 edition as an *Oxford World's Classic* highlights its legendary status as the most famous book about English usage ever written.

All this suggests Fowler's almost superhuman status as an arbiter of 'correct' English. And because of that people have taken it for granted that he laid down cast-iron rules to be adhered to absolutely. That belief is far from the truth. He was, paradoxically, both descriptive and prescriptive. On the one hand, his analysis of authentic English usage is often both penetratingly accurate and commonsensical (he considered the ban on prepositions at the end of a sentence 'a superstition'). On the other hand, his training as a classical scholar and his career as a schoolmaster meant that he had an ingrained attachment to prescriptive rules.

This tension between a descriptive and a prescriptive approach is something that any compiler of a modern usage dictionary inevitably feels. My method has been to assess critically the statements made by the previous troika of authors/editors, and present their views tempered by contemporary evidence so that readers can make their own judgements. However, like many commentators on usage, to an extent I want to have my cake and eat it, to square the circle of descriptivism and prescriptivism. As a lexicographer and editor I favour the former; as a language-user I have my own preferences, tastes, habits, and bugbears, as all previous editors had. *Fowler* would not be *Fowler* without them.

Acknowledgements

It gives me great pleasure to thank the team at Oxford University Press who have been instrumental in the creation of this revised edition. In the first place, thanks go to my Commissioning Editor, Rebecca Lane, who saw the merits of my plan for the book, which then led to the Delegates appointing me as the editor. Throughout the process of revising the text, I have been able to count on unstinting support and encouragement from my dedicated editor, Joanna Harris.

This revised edition of *Fowler* draws widely on the evidence of contemporary usage obtained from the Oxford English Corpus (which I explain in detail in the Preface). That corpus is maintained by Dr Pete Whitelock, whom I should like to thank for his always prompt and helpful replies to my queries. Angus Stevenson of the dictionaries department suggested several interesting usages to investigate. I am also indebted to Dr Donald Watt, who painstakingly reviewed all my edits and made innumerable valuable suggestions, stylistic and factual. Bernadette Mohan has meticulously proofread the text in its entirety to ensure that its contents are presented error-free and in a consistent style. Thanks are also due to Clare Jones, Bethan Lee, and Cornelia Haase for their crucial role in turning electronic files into an elegantly produced book, while its marketing and PR have been deftly and efficiently handled by Phil Henderson and Nicola Burton.

Finally, outside the Press, I should like to thank colleagues and friends too numerous to mention with whom, over the years, I have discussed knotty points of English usage; and in particular my partner, who has always been my sternest critic.

Dedication, 1926

To the memory of my brother

FRANCIS GEORGE FOWLER, M.A. CANTAB.

who shared with me the planning of this book,
but did not live to share the writing.

I think of it as it should have been, with its prolixities docked, its dullnesses enlivened, its fads eliminated, its truths multiplied. He had a nimbler wit, a better sense of proportion, and a more open mind, than his twelve-year-older partner; and it is a matter of regret that we had not, at a certain point, arranged our undertakings otherwise than we did.

In 1911 we started work simultaneously on the *Pocket Oxford Dictionary* and this book; living close together, we could, and did, compare notes; but each was to get one book into shape by writing its first quarter or half; and so much only had been done before the war. The one in which, as the less mechanical, his ideas and contributions would have had much the greater value had been assigned, by ill chance, to me. In 1918 he died, aged 47, of tuberculosis contracted during service with the B.E.F. in 1915–16.

The present book accordingly contains none of his actual writing; but, having been designed in consultation with him, it is the last fruit of a partnership that began in 1903 with our translation of Lucian.

H. W. F.

Key to the Pronunciation

The pronunciation system is that of the International Phonetic Alphabet (IPA) and, except where otherwise specified, is based on the pronunciation, widely called 'Received Pronunciation' or RP, of educated people in southern England. The necessary adjustments have been made when standard American English pronunciations are given.

The symbols used, with typical examples, are as follows:

Consonants

b, d, f, h, k, l, m, n, p, r, s, t, v, w, and *z* have their usual English values. Other symbols are used as follows:

ɡ (**g**et)	ŋ (ri**ng**)	ʒ (deci**s**ion)
tʃ (**ch**ip)	θ (**th**in)	j (**y**es)
dʒ (**j**ar)	ð (**th**is)	
x (lo**ch**)	ʃ (**sh**e)	

Vowels

Short vowels	*Long vowels*	*Diphthongs*
a (c**a**t)	ɑː (**ar**m)	eɪ (d**ay**)
ɛ (b**e**d)	ɛː (h**air**)	ʌɪ (m**y**)
ə (**a**go)	iː (s**ee**)	ɔɪ (b**oy**)
ɪ (s**i**t)	ɔː (s**aw**)	əʊ (n**o**)
ɒ (h**o**t)	əː (h**er**)	aʊ (h**ow**)
ʌ (r**u**n)	uː (t**oo**)	ɪə (n**ear**)
ʊ (p**u**t)		ʊə (p**oor**)
i (happ**y**)		

(ə) before /l/, /m/, or /n/ indicates that the syllable may be realised with a syllabic **l**, **m**, or **n**, rather than with a vowel or consonant, e.g. /ʌm'bɪlɪk(ə)l/ rather than /ʌm'bɪlɪkəl/ The main or primary stress of a word is shown by a superior ' placed immediately before the relevant syllable. When a word also has a secondary stress this is indicated by an inferior ˌ placed immediately before the relevant syllable.

The mark ˜ (called a tilde) indicates a nasalized sound, as in the following sounds that are not natural in English:

æ̃ (t**im**bre)	ɑ̃ (él**an**)	ɔ̃ (garç**on**)

Abbreviations and Symbols

†	obsolete
→	becomes
*	unacceptable construction, spelling, etc.
*	precedes a reconstructed etymological formation
?	precedes a questionable or contentious use
~	varies freely with; by comparison with
ʌ	indicates the omission of a word

SMALL CAPITALS refer the reader to the article so indicated, for further information.

a, ante	before, not later than
abbrev.	abbreviation, abbreviated as
acc.	accusative
adj.	adjective
adv.	adverb
advt	advertisement
AmE	American English
arch.	archaic
Aust.	Australian
aux.	auxiliary
AV	Authorized Version (of the Bible)
BEV	Black English Vernacular (US)
BrE	British English
c.	*circa*
c.	century, centuries
Canad.	Canadian
cf.	compare
colloq.	colloquial
conj.	conjunction
const.	construed (with)
d.	died
dat.	dative
det.	determiner
dial.	dialect, -al
EU	European Union
e.g.	*exempli gratia*, 'for example'
ELT	English Language Teaching
Eng.	English
esp.	especially
et al.	*et alii*, 'and others'
exc.	except
f.	from
fem.	feminine
fig.	figuratively
Fr.	French
Ger.	German
gen.	genitive
Gk	Greek
ibid.	*ibidem*, 'in the same book or passage'
idem	'the same'
i.e.	*id est*, 'that is'
IE	Indo-European
Ir.	Irish
It.	Italian
L, Lat.	Latin
lit.	literally
math.	mathematical
MDu.	Middle Dutch
ME	Middle English
MLG	Middle Low German
mod.	modern
modE	modern English
modF	modern French
mus.	music
n., n.pl.	noun, plural noun
NAmer.	North American
naut.	nautical
NIr.	Northern Irish
nom.	nominative
obs.	obsolete
obsolesc.	obsolescent
occas.	occasional(ly)
OE	Old English
OF	Old French
OProvençal	Old Provençal
orig.	originally
pa.t.	past tense

pa.pple	past participle
perh.	perhaps
pers.	person
Pg.	Portuguese
pl.	plural
poet.	poetic
ppl	participial
pple	participle
prep.	preposition, prepositional
pres.	present
prob.	probably
RP	Received Pronunciation (in BrE)
SAfr.	South African
Sc.	Scottish
sc.	*scilicet*, 'understand' or 'supply'
sing.	singular
Sp.	Spanish
SPE	Society for Pure English
spec.	specifically
s.v.	*sub voce*, 'under the word'
t.	tense
theol.	theological
tr.	translation (of)
trans.	transitive
UK	United Kingdom
ult.	ultimately
UN	United Nations
US	United States
usu.	usually
v., vs.	verb, verbs
vol.	volume
WGmc	West Germanic

Bibliographical Abbreviations

Alford	Henry Alford, *The Queen's English*, 1864
Amer. N. & Q.	*American Notes & Queries*
Amer. Speech	*American Speech*
Ann.	*Annual*
Baldick	C. Baldick, *The Concise Oxford Dictionary of Literary Terms*, 1990
BMJ	*British Medical Journal*
Bodl. Libr. Rec.	*Bodleian Library Record*
Bull. Amer. Acad. Arts & Sci.	*Bulletin of the American Academy of Arts and Sciences*
Burchfield	R. Burchfield, *The Spoken Word: a BBC Guide*, 1981
CGEL	*A Comprehensive Grammar of the English Language*, ed. R. Quirk et al., 1985
Chr. Sci. Monitor	*Christian Science Monitor*
Chron.	*Chronicle*
COCA	M. Davies, *The Corpus of Contemporary American English: 450 million words, 1990-present*, 2008–. Available online at http://corpus.byu.edu/coca/.
COD	*The Concise Oxford Dictionary*, 8th edn, 1990; 9th edn, 1995
COHA	M. Davies, *The Corpus of Historical American English: 400 million words, 1810–2009*, 2010–. Available online at http://corpus.byu.edu/coha/.
Conc. Scots Dict.	*Concise Scots Dictionary*
Crystal	D. Crystal, *A First Dictionary of Linguistics and Phonetics*, 1980
DARE	*Dictionary of American Regional English*, ed. F. G. Cassidy et al., 2 vols. (A–H), 1985, 1991
Dict.	*Dictionary (of)*
Dict. Eng. Usage	*Dictionary of English Usage*
Eccles. Hist.	*Ecclesiastical History*
Encycl.	*Encyclop(a)edia*
European Sociol. Rev.	*European Sociological Review*
Fowler	H. W. and F. G. Fowler, *The King's English*, 1906
Garner	Bryan A. Garner, *A Dictionary of Modern Legal Usage*, 1987
Gaz.	*Gazette*
Gimson	A. C. Gimson, *An Introduction to the Pronunciation of English*, 3rd edn, 1980
Hartmann and Stork	R. R. K. Hartmann and F. C. Stork, *Dictionary of Language and Linguistics*, 1973
Hart's Rules	*New Hart's Rules: The Handbook of Style for Writers and Editors*, 2005

Internat.	*International*
Jespersen	Otto Jespersen, *A Modern English Grammar on Historical Principles*, i–vii, 1909–49
Jones	Daniel Jones, *An English Pronouncing Dictionary*, 1917
Jrnl	*Journal (of)*
Jrnl RSA	*Journal of the Royal Society of Arts*
London Rev. Bks	*London Review of Books*
Lyons	J. Lyons, *Semantics*, 2 vols., 1977
Mag.	*Magazine*
MEU	*Modern English Usage*, 1926
Mitchell	Bruce Mitchell, *Old English Syntax*, 2 vols., 1985
MWCDEU	*Merriam-Webster Concise Dictionary of English Usage*, 2002
N&Q	*Notes & Queries*
NEB	*New English Bible*
New SOED	*The New Shorter Oxford English Dictionary*, 2 vols., 1993
NODWE	*New Oxford Dictionary for Writers and Editors*, 2005
NY Rev. Bks	*New York Review of Books*
NYT	*New York Times*
OCELang.	*The Oxford Companion to the English Language*, ed. Tom McArthur, 1992
OCELit.	*The Oxford Companion to English Literature*, ed. Margaret Drabble, 5th edn, 1985
ODCIE	*Oxford Dictionary of Current Idiomatic English*, ed. A. P. Cowie et al., 2 vols, 1975, 1983
ODEE	*Oxford Dictionary of English Etymology*, 1966
ODNB	*Oxford Dictionary of National Biography*
ODO	*Oxford Dictionary Online*
OEC	*Oxford English Corpus*
OED	*The Oxford English Dictionary*, issued in parts 1884–1928; as 12 vols., 1933
OED 2	*Oxford English Dictionary*, 2nd edn, 20 vols., 1989
OEDS	*A Supplement to the Oxford English Dictionary*, 4 vols., 1972–86
OGEU	*The Oxford Guide to English Usage*, 2nd edn, 1993
OMEU	*The Oxford Miniguide to English Usage*, 1983
Oxf. Dict. Eng. Gramm.	*The Oxford Dictionary of English Grammar*, 1994
Parl. Aff.	*Parliamentary Affairs*
POD	*The Pocket Oxford Dictionary*
Poutsma	Hendrik Poutsma, *A Grammar of Late Modern English*, 5 vols., 1926–9
Publ. Amer. Dial. Soc.	*Publications of the American Dialect Society*
Q	*Quarterly*
Quirk	R. Quirk et al., *A Grammar of Contemporary English*, 1972
Reg.	*Register*
Rep.	*Report*
Rev.	*Review (of)*

Sci. Amer.	*Scientific American*
Smith	Egerton Smith, *The Principles of English Metre*, 1923
Tel.	*Telegraph*
TES	*The Times Educational Supplement*
THES	*The Times Higher Educational Supplement*
TLS	*The Times Literary Supplement*
Trans. Philol. Soc.	*Transactions of the Philological Society*
Tulloch	S. Tulloch, *The Oxford Dictionary of New Words*, 1991
Visser	F. Th. Visser, *An Historical Syntax of the English Language*, parts i–iii, 4 vols., 1963–73
Wales	Katie Wales, *A Dictionary of Stylistics*, 1989
Walker	John Walker, *A Critical Pronouncing Dictionary and Expositor of the English Language*, 1791; 4th edn 1806
WDEU	*Webster's Dictionary of English Usage*, 1989
Webster's Third	*Webster's Third New International Dictionary*, 1961
Wells	J. C. Wells, *Longman Pronunciation Dictionary*, 1990

For convenience, the dates assigned to the works of Shakespeare are those given in the Bibliography of the *OED*. The texts of the individual works are cited from the original-spelling edition of Stanley Wells and Gary Taylor, OUP, 1986.

All examples from the Bible are cited from the Authorized Version of 1611 (quoted from the 'exact reprint' with an introduction by Alfred W. Pollard, OUP, 1985).

a-[1]**,** a prefix denoting lack of something or negation, represents Greek ἀ- before a consonant and becomes *an-* (Greek ἀν-) before a vowel. It occurs (*a*) in words representing Greek compounds, mostly adopted through French or Latin, in which the prefix is wholly or partially obscured, as *abyss, adamant, amethyst, amorphous, anarchy, anomalous*; (*b*) in terms of the arts or sciences, having Greek bases, but coming into English through medieval or modern Latin, as *abranchiate* (having no gills), *anaesthesia* (absence of sensation), *anorexia* (want of appetite), *apetalous* (without petals), *aphasia* (loss of speech); (*c*) in words formed in the 19c. on Greek elements, as *agnostic, aseptic.* In the last century or so, privative *a-*, most commonly with the pronunciation /eɪ/, has come to be attached to a limited number of adjectives in general use, as *ahistoric* (1937), *ahistorical* (1957), *amoral* (1882), *apolitical* (1952), *asocial* (1883), and *atypical* (1885), and to their derivatives (*amorality*, etc.). But it is far from being a free-forming prefix.

a-[2]**.** In origin a preposition, it is recorded from 1523 onwards in many literary works, (*a*) with *be*: engaged in (*She is a taking of her last farewell*—Bunyan; *'twas the Bishops or Judges a coming*—Leigh Hunt); (*b*) with a verb of motion: to, into (*Simon Peter sayde vnto them: I goo a fysshynge*—Tyndale; *We were able to set the loan a going again*—Jefferson). Now interpreted as a prefix joined to an *-ing* word, it has enjoyed a modest revival, imparting as it often does an element of humour, informality or whimsicality to the present participle or gerund that it precedes. Probably the best known modern example—and also the most frequent in the *OEC*—is *the times they are a-changing* from the 1964 song and album title of the same name by Bob Dylan. But there are plenty of other modern examples: *Kris Kirk ... plans to return, a-brandishing the manuscript* [of his book] *by the end of March—Melody Maker*, 1988; *Nobody has told them about these employment opportunities that are going a-begging—Guardian*, (Trinidad), 2005; *Back then, ladies wore parasols and long, pretty, lacy dresses, and men would go a-courting in a very nice way that didn't involve alcohol at all—OEC*, 2005.

-a. Now being printed more and more to represent the sound that replaces *of* in rapid (especially popular or informal) speech, as in *kinda* (= kind of), *loadsa, sorta.* Examples: *These guys were a pleasant surprise and impressed the hell outa me—ChartAttack*, 2000 (Canad.); *I'se a real credit, she said, loadsa times*—N. Virtue, 1988 (NZ).

Cf. also *-a* = *have, 've* (as a colloquial shortening) in *coulda* (= could have), *shoulda, woulda*; and *-a* = *to* in *gonna* (= going to), *gotta* (= got to), and *wanna* (= want to).

a, an. **1** *History.* In origin, *a* (and its by-form *an*), which is usually called the indefinite article, but now, by many grammarians, an indefinite or central determiner, is a version of OE *ān* 'one'. It largely split off in function from the numeral about 1150, though in some circumstances the two are still interchangeable (e.g. *the Smiths have two daughters and a son*) or are hardly distinguishable in meaning (*he gave me a glass of water*).

2 *Pronunciation.* In most circumstances *a* is pronounced /ə/ (uh) and *an* is pronounced /ən/ (uhn), but, when emphasized, as in slow dictation, /eɪ/ and /an/ respectively. Public speakers, particularly broadcasters, regularly use the emphatic form /eɪ/ of *a* when there is absolutely no call for it: *she has a* (pause) *difficult task ahead of her.* It is only a short step from this to the unacceptable *she has a* (pause) *embarrassing task ahead of her.*

3 *A* or *an*? (*a*) *Before words beginning with vowels.* Before all normal vowels or diphthongs *an* is obligatory (*an actor, an eagle, an illness, an Old Master, an uncle*).

Before a syllable beginning in its written form with a vowel but pronounced with a consonantal sound, *a* is used (*a eulogy, a unit, a use*; *a one, a once-only*). Before all consonants except silent *h*, *a* is customary: *a book, a history, a home, a household name, a memorial service, a puddle, a young man*; but, with silent *h, an hour, an honour.*

(*b*) Before words beginning with *h.* Opinion is divided over the form to use before *h*-words in which the first syllable is unstressed: the standard modern approach is to use *a* (never *an*) together with an aspirated *h* (*a habitual, a heroic, a historical, a Homeric, a hypothesis*), but not to demur if others use *an* with minimal or nil aspiration given to the following *h* (*an historic* /ən (h)ɪs'tɒrɪk/, *an horrific* /ən (h)ɒ'rɪfɪk/, etc.).

It is impossible to say how many people use *an* before such words in speech, although Wells (3rd edn, 2008) shows that only six per cent of British English speakers favour *an historic*. Writing, perhaps predictably, seems more conservative, and at the present time (2015), the *OEC* provides clear evidence for the use of *an* before HABITUAL, HEREDITARY, HISTORIAN, HISTORIC(AL), *horrific*, and *horrendous*. It is used most often with *historic*, and least often with *horrendous*: see also HORRID 3.

(*c*) Three special cases: *an hotel* (with no aspiration in the second word) is now old-fashioned (E. Waugh and 1930s), but by no means extinct (*Encounter*, 1987; A. Brink, 1988); in *humble*, the *h* was originally mute and the pronunciation /'ʌmb(ə)l/ prevailed until the 19c. but is now obsolete: it should therefore be preceded by *a*, not *an*; American English *herb*, being pronounced with silent *h*, is always preceded by *an*, but the same word in British English, being pronounced with an aspirated *h*, by *a*.

4 *With single letters and groups of letters pronounced as letters.* Be guided by the pronunciation: *a B road, a CFC refrigerant, a KLM flight, a TUC leader*; but *an A road, an FA cup final, an MCC ruling, an OUP book, an SAS unit*, on the assumption that these will not be mentally expanded to 'a Football Association cup final', 'a Marylebone Cricket Club ruling', etc. Acronyms beginning with a consonant are preceded by *a* not *an*: *a NATO* (pronounced /'neɪtəʊ/) *conference.*

5 Position of *a, an.* The indefinite article normally precedes the word or words it determines (*a popular history*). However, it follows the adjectives *many, such,* and *what* (*many a year, such a family, what an awful nuisance!*). It also follows any adjective preceded by *as* or *how* (*Iris Murdoch is as good a writer as Virginia Woolf*; *he did not know how tiresome a person she would be*), and often an adjective preceded by *so* (*so bold a move deserved success*), but *such a bold move* is more usual. In some circumstances the positioning is optional: either before or after an adjective preceded by *too* (*too strict a regime,* or *a too strict regime*), and before or after the adverbs *quite* and *rather* (*at quite an early hour* or *at a quite early hour; it's rather a hard puzzle* or *it's a rather hard puzzle*).

6 *Special uses.* The indefinite article has a number of other idiomatic uses: *his duties as* (*a*) *judge* (optionally omitted); *he owns a Van Gogh* (a painting by Van Gogh); *an eleventh-century Aldhelm* (an 11c. MS of one of Aldhelm's works); *one of my older records, a Smetana* (a composition by Smetana); *a village Bradman* (a Bradman-like cricketer); *Jon broke a rib* (used with parts of the body when there is more than one); *half an hour, once a fortnight, fifty miles an hour, £15,000 a year* (in measure phrases); *I once knew a Lucy Jones* (a person called Lucy Jones); *a Mr Armitage called while you were out* (a person called Mr Armitage unknown to the speaker). In fixed phrases like *a knife, fork, and spoon*, the indefinite article is not repeated; but if emphasis is required, or if the sequence requires *an* as well as *a* (*a minute, an hour, or a day*) omission is not desirable.

7 Unacceptable *a* in the standard language but what of the future? There are signs that *a* is intruding into the proper territory of *an* in American English of various kinds. Two scholars presented substantial evidence of this phenomenon in both the unscripted and scripted speech of American politicians, entertainers, etc., pronounced both as /eɪ/ and as /ə/ (*a apple, a interesting, a ultimate*, etc.). Also in representations of the speech of African Americans (e.g. *He had a old Ford somebody gave him*—M. Golden, 1989; *My old dad lost one of his legs, had it bit off by a alligator this time he's fishing the rim canal*—E. Leonard, 1994). This is not the same as the emphatic *a* of 2 above.

AAVE. An initialism for AFRICAN AMERICAN VERNACULAR ENGLISH.

abacus. In its meaning of a calculating device, this Latin word has the plural *abacuses*. In its architectural meaning, denoting the flat slab on top of a capital, the Latin plural *abaci* /-SAI/ is widely used. See -US 1.

abbreviations. **1** For abbreviations other than shortened forms, which are dealt with below, see ACRONYMS and CONTRACTIONS.

2 *Shortened words.* These are words such as *ad* or *bike* the beginning or ending of which has been dropped in general use. It is not necessary to use an apostrophe to indicate the dropped part, i.e. *cello*, not **'cello*. The practice of shortening ('curtailing') ordinary words was condemned in the 18c. Thus Addison in the *Spectator* (1711): 'It is perhaps this Humour of speaking no more than we needs must which has so miserably curtailed some of our Words ... as in *mob., rep., pos., incog.* and the like.' In his *Proposal for Correcting, Improving, and Ascertaining the English Tongue* (1712), Swift proposed the publication of an annual *index expurgatorius* 'to ... condemn those barbarous mutilations of vowels and syllables [including the curtailments mentioned by Addison]'. Nowadays this method of word formation is considered standard. Some of the words formerly condemned have survived and thrived, while others have withered away. Examples (showing the date of first record of the shortened form in the *OED*):

(*a*) *Now obsolete or obsolescent*

brig(antine) 1720
coster(monger) 1851
phiz (physiognomy) 1688
rep(utation) 1705
spats (spatterdashes) 1802

(*b*) *In current use but with varying degrees of informality*

ad(vertisement) 1841
bike (bicycle) 1882
bra(ssière) 1936
(omni)*bus* 1832
cab(riolet) 1827
(violon)*cello* 1876
cinema(tograph) 1909
cox(swain) 1869
deb(utante) 1920
dynamo(-electric machine) 1882
(in)*flu*(enza) 1839
fridge (refrigerator) 1935
gym(nasium, -nastics) 1871
incog(nito) 1700
(women's, etc.) *lib*(eration) 1970
mike (microphone) 1927
mob(ile vulgus) 1688
pants (pantaloons) 1840
(tele)*phone* 1884
photo(graph) 1860
polio(myelitis) 1931
pram (perambulator) 1884
prefab(ricated building) 1937
prep(aration) 1862
pro(fessional) 1866
pub(lic house) 1859
quad(rangle) 1820
quotes (quotation marks, quotations) 1888
rep(resentative n.) 1896
rhino(ceros) 1884
spec(ulation) 1794
specs (spectacles) 1826
Strad(ivarius) 1884
taxi(meter cab) 1907
telly (television) 1942
turps (turpentine) 1823
typo(graphical) 1816
vet(erinary surgeon) 1862
viva (voce) 1891
zoo(logical garden) 1847

3 *Abbreviations and contractions.* For guidance on when to use a full point, see FULL STOP 2.

abdication. For confusion of *abrogation* with this, see ABROGATION.

abductor. So spelt, not *-er*. See -OR.

abetter, -or. In legal language, *abettor* is the standard and recommended form, and is also widely used in non-legal contexts. *Abetter* is occasionally used for someone who merely encourages someone in an activity, e.g. *a warrant for his arrest as an abetter of the prince was issued—ODNB*, 2009. See -OR.

abjure, adjure. Despite the dire warnings of usage commentators not to confuse them, these verbs are so far removed from the realms of ordinary vocabulary that such warnings seem largely irrelevant. *Abjure* (from French *abjurer*, Latin *abjūrāre* 'to deny on oath') means 'to renounce on oath' (*he had abjured, he thought, all superstition*—I. Murdoch, 1985) and *to abjure one's country* (or *realm*) is to swear to abandon it for ever. It is also used in the weakened sense 'to renounce' (*Are faculty members willing to abjure e-mail in communicating with their students and colleagues?—The Nation*, 2002). By contrast, *adjure* (from Fr. *adjurer*, L *adjūrāre* 'to swear to something') means 'to request earnestly' with or (now) more frequently without an oath, and is usually followed by a direct object and a *to*-infinitive, e.g. *They were all talking at once, adjuring each other to have fresh cups of tea*—L. A. G. Strong, 1948.

-able, -ible.

1 Origins.
2 Meaning.
3 Spelling problems.
4 Both endings in use.
5 Forms differ in meaning.
6 Cognate forms.
7 List of the main words ending in *-able*.
8 List of the main words ending in *-ible*.
9 Negative forms of adjectives ending in *-able* or *-ible*.

1 *Origins.* Originally, English words ending in *-able* owed their form to the Latin termination *-ābilis* or to the Old French *-able* (or both) by the addition of *-bilis* to verbs in *-āre*, Fr. *-er*, as *amāre, amābilis* ('to love, lovable'), *mūtāre, mūtābilis* ('to change, changeable'). This method of formation in Latin was extended to verbs with other stems, e.g. *capere, capābilis* → *capable*, and to nouns, as *favor, favōrābilis* → *favourable*. The *-able* suffix is a living element that can be added to nouns or verbs with English or French roots whether or not a Latin word in *-ābilis* exists: *clubbable* (Dr Johnson), *forgivable* (16c.), even *unputdownable* (1947).

Words ending in *-ible* are a closed set which cannot be added to. They reflect Fr. *-ible*, L *-ībilis*, from *-i-*, *-ī-*, a connective or stem-vowel of L verbs in *-ēre, -ere, -īre* + *-bilis*, e.g. medieval Latin *audībilis* (from L *audīre* 'to hear') → *audible*.

2 *Meaning. -able* is a living suffix and may be added to any transitive verb to make an adjective meaning 'capable of being —*ed*', e.g. *bear* → *bearable, conceive* → *conceivable, manage* → *manageable*. Other *-able* words are formed from nouns (e.g. *actionable*). In many common words the meaning of *-able* is active not passive, e.g. *agreeable* (willing to agree), *comfortable* (able to give comfort), *viable* (able to live). Many common words containing the suffixes *-able* or *-ible* have no matching verb or noun, e.g. *affable, amenable, delectable, feasible*, and *plausible*.

3 *Spelling problems.* The spelling of the source-word changes in various circumstances:

(i) With some exceptions, words ending in silent *-e* lose the *e* when *-able* is added, e.g. *adorable, excusable, removable, usable*. A few words retain the *e* when its loss could create ambiguity or obscure the root: e.g. *giveable, hireable, likeable, liveable, rateable, saleable* (see 7 below).

(ii) Words ending in a consonant + *y* change *y* to *i* before *-able*, e.g. *dutiable, pliable* (from *ply*), *rectifiable, undeniable*; but *employable, enjoyable, payable*, in which a vowel precedes *y*. An exception: *flyable*.

(iii) Words ending in *-ce* or *-ge*, retain the *e* to indicate the 'soft' sound of *c* or *g*, e.g. *(un)bridgeable, changeable, chargeable, noticeable, peaceable, serviceable*.

(iv) Words ending in *-ee* retain both letters: *agreeable, foreseeable*.

(v) Many verbs of more than two syllables ending in *-ate* lose this ending in the corresponding adjectives in *-able*: *appreciable* (not **appreciatable*), *calculable, demonstrable, educable, tolerable*. When the verb has only two syllables the ending has to be retained to fully convey the verb's meaning, *debatable, locatable*).

(vi) In words of English formation, a final consonant is usually doubled before *-able* when it is also doubled in the present participle: *biddable, forgettable, regrettable*.

(vii) Words of more than one syllable ending in *-fer* double the *r* when the stress is on the final syllable, but do not when the stress is earlier in the word: *conferrable, deferrable, preferable, insufferable* (but in *transferable* the stress is variable on the first two syllables). *Infer* makes *inferable* with variant *inferrable*, and *refer* makes *referable* with variant *referrable*.

4 *Both endings in use.* Some words have historically had two forms. In the following list the standard modern form comes first:

collapsible	collapsable
confusable	confusible
connectable	connectible
deductible	deductable
detectable	detectible
discussable	discussible
extendable	extendible
ignitable	ignitible
preventable	preventible

5 *Forms differ in meaning.* Some adjectives differ in meaning in their *-able* and *-ible* forms:

contractable: liable to be contracted or acquired, as a disease or a habit

contractible: capable of contracting or drawing together, contractile
impassable: that cannot be traversed, closed (of a mountain pass, etc.)
impassible: incapable of feeling or emotion; incapable of suffering injury; (theol.) not subject to suffering
passable: that can pass muster; that can be traversed (of a mountain pass, etc.)
passible: (theol.) capable of feeling or suffering (from late L *passībilis*, from L *patī*, *pass-* to suffer)

See also COLLECTABLE, COLLECTIBLE.

6 *Cognate forms.* Some words in *-able* stand alongside cognate words of similar formation: *solvable* may be preferred in some contexts because *soluble* is frequently used to mean 'that can be dissolved'; *submersible* is competing with *submergible* in the language of the oil industry; a mistake is often called *uncorrectable* (*uncorrectable bureaucratic ineptitude should be criminal—OEC*, 2004), because *incorrigible* has become ethical in sense.

7 List of the main words ending in *-able*. For convenience a list of the most common words in *-able* follows.

*many printing houses in the UK and abroad omit the medial *-e-* in words so marked.

abominable, acceptable, accountable, actionable, adaptable, adjustable, administrable, adorable, advisable, agreeable, alienable, allocable, allowable, amenable, amiable, amicable, analysable, applicable, appreciable, approachable, arable, arguable, arrestable, ascribable, assessable, attainable, attributable, available

bankable, bearable, believable, biddable, *blameable, breakable, bribable, bridgeable

calculable, capable, certifiable, changeable, chargeable, clubbable, collectable, comfortable, conceivable, conductable, conferrable, confinable, conformable, confusable (see 4), connectable, consolable, contestable, contractable (see 5), convictable, copiable, correctable, creatable, creditable, culpable, curable

datable, debatable, declinable, deferrable, definable, demonstrable, dependable, deplorable, desirable, despicable, detachable, detectable, detestable, developable, dilatable, dispensable, disposable, disputable, dissolvable, drivable, durable, dutiable

eatable, educable, endorsable, enforceable, equable, evadable, excisable, excitable, excludable, excusable, expandable, expendable, extendable (see 4), extractable

fashionable, finable, flammable, forceable (see 5), foreseeable, forgettable, forgivable, frameable

gettable, *giveable

*hireable

ignitable (see 4), illimitable, imaginable, imitable, immovable, immutable, impalpable, impassable (see 5), impeccable, imperturbable, implacable, impregnable, impressionable, improvable, incapable, incurable, indefatigable, indescribable, indictable, indispensable, indistinguishable, indubitable, inferable, inflammable, inflatable, inimitable, inseparable, insufferable, intolerable, intractable, irreconcilable, irrefutable, irreplaceable, irrevocable

justifiable

knowledgeable

laughable, leviable, *likeable, *liveable, losable, lovable

machinable, malleable, manageable, manoeuvrable, marriageable, measurable, mistakable, movable, mutable

*nameable, noticeable

objectionable, obtainable, offerable, operable, opposable

palatable, passable (see 5), payable, peaceable, penetrable, perishable, permeable, persuadable, pleasurable, preferable, prescribable, presentable, processable, profferable, pronounceable, provable

*rateable, readable, receivable, recognizable, reconcilable, rectifiable, refusable, registrable, regrettable, reliable, removable, reputable, retractable

*saleable, scalable, serviceable, *sizeable, solvable (see 6), statable, storable, sufferable, suitable, superannuable

teachable, *timeable, tolerable, traceable, tradable, transferable, tuneable

unconscionable, uncorrectable (see 6), undeniable, unexceptionable, unflappable, unget-at-able, unknowable, unmistakable, unpronounceable, unscalable, *unshakeable, unspeakable, untouchable, usable

viable

washable

8 List of the main words ending in *-ible.* A list of some of the most frequently used words in *-ible*:

accessible, adducible, admissible, audible

collapsible (see 4), collectible, combustible, compatible, comprehensible, connectible (see 4), contemptible, contractible (see 5), convertible, credible

defensible, destructible, diffusible, digestible, dirigible, discernible, discussible (see 4), dismissible, divisible,

edible, educible, eligible, exhaustible, expansible, expressible, extendible (see 4), extensible

fallible, feasible, flexible, forcible (see 5)

gullible

horrible

impartible, impassible (see 5), implausible, inaccessible, incompatible, inadmissible, incomprehensible, incorrigible (see 6), incredible, indelible, indestructible, indigestible, indivisible, ineligible, infallible, inflexible, intangible, intelligible, invincible, invisible, irascible, irreducible, irrepressible, irresistible, irresponsible, irreversible

legible

negligible

omissible, ostensible

passible (see 5), perceptible, perfectible, permissible, persuasible, plausible, possible

reducible, reprehensible, reproducible, resistible, responsible, reversible, risible

sensible, submergible (see 6), submersible (see 6), suggestible, suppressible, susceptible

transfusible

vendible, visible

9 Negative forms of adjectives ending in *-able* or *-ible.* These adjectives are frequent as negatives, and complex rules govern the choice of *in-* or *un-* or some other element. A simple contrast is shown in the pairs *conceivable/inconceivable* and *bearable/unbearable.* In other negative formations the matter was settled in ancient times by the assimilation of L *in-* to the initial letter of the stem of the word. Thus the negative forms of *illimitable, implacable, incredible, incurable,* and *irrefutable,* for example, were settled in Latin long before these words were adopted in English.

able-bodied, abled. It is best to avoid using *able-bodied* to mean 'not having a physical disability', since many people with disabilities object to its use in this way. A better word choice is *non-disabled. Abled,* meaning 'not disabled', is a revival of an obsolete 16c. word, and has been recorded in print in the US since the 1980s. It is now occasionally used in the phrases *differently abled* and *less abled* as a more positive alternative to *disabled. They were gentle ... kids, who took endless pains to guard against what they referred to as 'the exploitation of the differently abled'*—A. Maupin, 1992; *Getting about for less abled residents isn't easy—Bolton Evening News,* 2003. See also DISABILITY, THE LANGUAGE OF.

ableism, meaning 'discrimination in favour of the abled' (i.e. against people with disabilities), is first recorded in the US from the early 1980s. There is a corresponding adjective and noun **ableist**: *The cover design appears to be rather male-dominated, white, ableist—Rouge,* 1990. Spelling both words with *-ei-* is preferable to the spellings *ablism* and *ablist*: at first glance they could make it look as if *ab-* sounds as it does in *abdomen,* and, presumably for that reason, are rather rare.

able to. Used with the verb *to be,* and followed by a *to*-infinitive in the active voice, this semi-auxiliary is a natural part of the language, whether with an animate or, to some extent, with an inanimate subject (*I have not been able to write for several days*—G. Vidal, 1955; *a yarn about not being able to keep a job*—K. Amis, 1978; *By his proceeding to the beach ... the next phase of the attack was able to proceed—New Yorker,* 1986). Attributing ability to inanimate subjects, however, is not always advisable and seems altogether too forced when the following infinitive is in the passive voice (*No evidence that an air rifle was able to be fired—Times* (heading of Law Report), 1988). In general it is better to use the modal verb *can/could* with passive infinitives, or express the sentence actively.

ablution. From the 16c. onwards *ablution(s)* has been used for the process of washing the body, or parts of the body, as a religious rite. The word was drawn into lay use in the 18c. as a somewhat light-hearted term for 'the washing or cleansing of one's person', and continues to be used humorously in that way, particularly in the phrase *perform one's ablutions.* It is also used as a formal or literary word, e.g. *Morse waited with keen anticipation until his morning ablutions were complete*—C. Dexter, 1989. For much of the 20c. its major serious use was in the armed services in the UK, where *ablutions* was the customary word for the process of washing oneself or for the building (also called the *ablution(s) block*) set aside for this purpose. This use is now rather dated, but occasionally still found, especially in South African writing, e.g. *There are also not sufficient ablution facilities at the area's beaches*—*Economist* (Namibia), 2002.

abode. In the meaning 'a dwelling place', *abode* is falling into disuse except in the fixed expressions: *(of) no fixed abode*, used of someone without a permanent address; *place of abode*, meaning where someone habitually lives, and *right of abode*, especially as applied to citizens of Hong Kong who sought the right to settle in Britain after 1997. It has not entirely gone from literature in its ordinary use: *The house, standing at the edge of a fair-sized tract of woodland and once, perhaps, the abode of gamekeepers*—K. Amis, 1974. Outside literature, it is often used humorously or ironically, preceded by a possessive such as *my* and an adjective, especially in the combination *humble abode*, e.g. *I will be hosting a soiree at my humble abode on the night in question*—weblog, 2004; *I couldn't help thinking that the brochure writer, in a previous incarnation as an estate agent, might also have described a cardboard box as an ideal palatial under-bridge abode*—*www.divernet.com*, 2004.

abolishment, abolition. Both entered the language in the 16c. and for two centuries they coexisted as synonyms (used of authority, laws, sins, faith, guilt, and other abstract concepts) with approximately equal currency. The choice of *abolition* by those working for the abandonment, first of slavery, and then of capital punishment, ensured the relative supremacy of this member of the pair. *Abolishment* is occasionally still used in more neutral and ad hoc uses emphasizing the process rather than the result, but it is nearly 30 times less frequent in the *OEC* than *abolition*: *But there are fears the service may be scrapped before it has a chance to be extended due to the abolishment of Argyll and Clyde Health Board by ministers*—*Scotland on Sunday*, 2005.

aboriginal, aborigines. *Aborigines*, the earlier of the two words, comes from the Latin *ab orīgine*, 'from the beginning', and initially referred to the native inhabitants of Latium. From the 16c. onwards it came to mean the original inhabitants of any country, and from the 18c. the ethnic groups living in a country before European colonists arrived. The singular form *Aborigine*, first recorded in Australia in 1829, has become established, despite being criticized on etymological grounds as an inappropriate back-formation. *Aboriginal* is a later word (1650), formed from *ab* + *orīgine* + *-al*. In Australian contexts, a capital letter *A* should be used for both words.

Australian Aborigines prefer to be known as **Indigenous Australians**, and this phrase is becoming more and more standard. Both *Aboriginal* and *Aborigine* are used as nouns in Australian sources, *Aborigine* being the commoner of the two as a noun, while *Aboriginal* is much commoner than it as an adjective (e.g. *Aboriginal art, communities, people*, etc.) *Aboriginal* is the term used by the Australian government, but is disliked by Indigenous Australians themselves. It goes without saying that the abbreviated form **Abo** is nowadays offensive.

about. 1 *Meaning 'approximately'.* In the meaning 'roughly, approximately' (e.g. *about half, fifty, nine o'clock, ten per cent, 186,000 miles a second*) *about* is the usual British English word; *around* is also used, but is much more common in American English (e.g. *the convention adjourned around four o'clock; around fifty people came to the party*). *Round about* is more informal, and is largely confined to British English.

2 *'to be all about'.* Since the 1930s, the phrase *to be (all) about* something has frequently been used to mean 'to be chiefly concerned with' and even 'to have as its aim', e.g. *You do the Hokey Cokey and you turn around, That's what it's all about; Love and war were about winning, not fair play*—A. Price, 1982). The phrase *what it's all about (really)* is a bit of a cliché and should only be used in informal contexts. *They like the feeling that they have had to fight other men for possession. That is what it is all about, really*—A. Brookner 1984.

3 *Tending to replace 'of'.* Dwight Bolinger (*World Englishes*, 1988, vii. 238–9) records many instances of a tendency in informal English for *about* to be used to replace *of*: *We're more aware about it; the Vietnamese are disdainful about Chinese cooking; the issue about how such things are monitored.* These uses, brought about by a process called 'reiconization', are still lurking at the edge of acceptability.

4 *'be about to do'.* With a following *to*-infinitive (transitive, intransitive, or passive), *be about* denotes intention: *she was about to mash the potatoes; direct negotiations are about to resume; Macbeth's tyranny was about to be opposed.* The more idiomatic negative use, *not be about to,* indicating determination not to do something, should only be used informally: *I'm not about to foist something on the general public just for the sake of releasing something—Record Mirror,* 1982. In more formal styles, it is better to use one of several alternatives such as *do not intend to* (or, more emphatically, *have no intention of*), *am not likely to,* etc.

above. Old grumblings about the use of *above* to mean 'more than' are shown to be out of order by the continuous record of the use since the 16c.: e.g. *It was neuer Acted: or if it was, not aboue once*—Shakespeare *Hamlet; it is above a week since I saw Miss Crawford*—Austen, 1814; *he doesn't look a day above forty.* Nevertheless either *more than* or *over* is the more usual and natural expression in such contexts.

abridgement, abridgment. The first is the preferred British form, and is given first in dictionaries. In the US *abridgment* is given first in dictionaries, but the spelling *abridgement* is as frequently used in practice. See MUTE E. See also -MENT.

abrogation. *Abrogation* refers to the repeal or abolition of a right, law or custom, e.g. *the political disenfranchisement of the working class and the systematic abrogation of its democratic rights—OEC,* 2004. **Abdication** of something means the act of giving up an office or of some abstraction such as a duty, principle, and above all, responsibility. *?Abrogation of responsibility* is quite frequently used instead of the more established collocation *abdication of responsibility.* Whether and when dictionaries will acknowledge this as legitimate remains to be seen. Examples: *?Failing to act to help victims on their presentation to the emergency department represents a singular abrogation of responsibility—BMJ,* 2001; *That points to a shocking abdication of parental responsibility—OEC,* 2002.

absent. The use of this word as a preposition meaning 'in the absence of, without' is first recorded in 1944 in US legal writing, and by the 1970s had become more general in the US: *Absent such an appeal, the constitutional issues were conclusively determined against Ender—NY Law Jrnl,* 1972; *Finally, absent an agreement, one must ask what the likely terms of political debate would be in 1988—Dædalus,* 1987; *Absent any major change in government programs, many companies have no clear idea how they will pay for them—Chicago Tribune,* 1989.

absolute adjectives. See ADJECTIVE 4.

absolute comparative. *CGEL* 7.85 draws attention to the existence of comparatives used where no explicit comparison is made though it may be implied. Thus *senior* retains its comparative force in *A is senior to B,* but cannot be used in a *than*-clause. We can say *A is older than B,* but we cannot say **A is senior than B.* There is a wide range of adjectives with a comparative form that can be used in contexts where the comparison is not made explicit: the *better*-class hotels, the *Greater* London area, *higher* education, the *major* political parties, an *older* man, a *prior* claim, of *superior* quality, the *younger* generation. Such implied comparisons are a feature of advertising language: *higher* mileage, a *smoother* finish, etc.

absolute construction. 1 *Definition and examples.* 'Absolute phrases' or 'absolute constructions' are grammatically independent of the following clause. They may be verbless, but usually contain a verb in its present or past participial form referring to a noun or pronoun. Examples: Given Didi's condition, *he performed an heroic feat in Israel*—D. Athill, 1986; that done, *they drove the animal through a side gate*—E. O'Brien, 1988; The washing up finished, *Jennifer called through the echoey building*—F. Weldon, 1988; Our business done, *we were now kinder to each other—New Yorker,* 1991. While use of absolute phrases is a highly literary device, a handful of absolute phrases are common enough in conversation or non-literary writing, e.g. *all things considered, all told, God willing, other things being equal, present company* *excepted, that being so, weather/time permitting.*

2 Fowler (1926) and Gowers (1965) objected strongly to a comma coming between the noun and the participle in sentences such as *The King, having read his speech from the throne, their Majesties retired,* which according to them should be punctuated *The King having read his speech from the throne, their Majesties retired.*

3 Sometimes absolute phrases containing a participle in *-ing* or *-ed* have no explicit grammatical subject; the subject appears in the attached clause: *Looking at Jim, I remembered the first time I had seen him—Encounter,* 1988. (It was 'I' who was looking at Jim.). But if the subject of the absolute phrase is not expressed, and is different from that of the main clause, the result is an 'unattached participle'. Picking up my Bible, *the hill seemed the only place to go just then*—J. Winterson, 1985; Packing to leave, *her fingertips had felt numb on contact with her belongings*—M. Duckworth, 1986. For further examples see UNATTACHED PARTICIPLES.

4 *CGEL* 15.59 points out that in formal scientific writing, unrelated constructions have become institutionalized 'where the implied subject is to be identified with the *I, we,* and *you* of the writer(s) or reader(s)': When treating patients with language retardation ... *the therapy consists of* [etc.]; To check on the reliability of the first experiment, *the experiment was replicated with a second set of subjects.*

absolutely! Originally an exclamation conveying emphatic and sincere agreement with what someone has just said (e.g. *'Is such really the state of matters between you and Rivers?'—'Absolutely, sir!'*—C. Brontë *Jane Eyre,* 1847), it has recently been robbed of its original meaning by massive overuse. It is ironic that in 1996 Burchfield could describe it as 'a pleasingly old-world variation of "yes, quite so"', for it is no exaggeration to say that, at least in Britain, it has altogether ousted 'yes' from the speech of middle-class media persons and pundits. Read, listen to or watch any interview, and it is sure to crop up, usually several times. It is enthusiastically bludgeoning 'yes' to death.

Does it matter that it is so overused when 'yes' would do just as well? Apart from the fact that it raises some people's blood pressure to heart-attack levels, possibly not. It is undergoing, or has already undergone, the same erosion of meaning that has reduced 'awesome' to the status of 'nice'; such erosion is a natural feature of language. A word of caution is in order, though. People who use the word too freely may be ridiculed, as President Obama was on *www.cnn.com* for replying *'Absolutely!'* when asked by a Pakistani journalist if he read Urdu poetry. The word can, in fact, suggest absolute insincerity.

Despite its current apogee, *absolutely* as an exclamation is first recorded from 1825, and is found in *Jane Eyre,* as already noted. But its potential pariah status was confirmed as long ago as 1993 by its inclusion in the *Banished Words of the Year* list.

absolute possessives. Under this term are included the possessive pronouns *hers, his, its, ours, theirs,* and *yours,* and also (except in the archaic adjectival use, as *mine/thine eyes*) *mine* and *thine.* None of the *-s* forms takes an apostrophe. The ordinary uses are straightforward (except for *its*; see below): *the house is hers, his, ours, mine,* etc.; *I met a friend of yours, hers,* etc. Matters become more complicated when two or more possessives refer to a single noun that follows the last of them. In such cases the *-s* and *-ne* forms are incorrect. The correct forms are shown in *your and our and his efforts* (not *yours* and *ours*); *either my or your informant must have lied* (not *mine*); *her and his strong contempt* (not *hers*). Rearrangement of the pronouns removes any risk of error: thus *his efforts and yours and ours, either your informant or mine must have lied,* etc. *Its* is the only pronoun in the series that normally cannot be used predicatively or in the double possessive construction: thus *its tail is red,* but not **this tail is its* nor **a mate of its. CGEL* 6.29 n. points out, however, that independent *its* is occasionally found, e.g. *History has its lessons and fiction its; She knew the accident was either her husband's fault or the car's: it turned out to be not his but its.* In such cases strong emphasis is placed on the contrasted pronouns.

absolve. Formerly pronounced either /ab'z-/ or /ab's-/, but the pronunciation with /-z-/ now seems to be dominant, presumably under the influence of *resolve.* Its normal constructions are of three kinds: (not common) followed by a phrase or clause led by *for*; (both common) followed by a phrase or clause led by either *from* or *of*. Examples: (*a*) *One's conscience may be pretty well absolved for not admiring this man*—Miss Mitford, 1817; *We may perhaps absolve Ford for the language of the article*—R. Burlingame, 1949 (*WDEU*); (*b*) *absolve me from all spot of sin*—J. Agee, 1950; *Having thus absolved himself from the duty of making the essential discriminations*—F. R. Leavis, 1952; (*c*) *it absolved him of all responsibility*—L. A. G. Strong, 1948; *Dollar was absolved of personal liability for the line's debts*—*Time*, 1950 (*WDEU*).

absorbedly. Four syllables. See -EDLY.

abstract nouns. **1** Abstract nouns denote ideas, qualities, or states rather than concrete objects. They are words such as *difference, equality, justice, love, quality, size*, and *truth*.

2 While past writers on usage have insisted that a concrete word is always preferable to an abstract one, their proposition is highly debatable. What is clear, however, is that using abstract nouns instead of the verbs from which they come often leads to turgid writing that will easily tire, not to say baffle or infuriate, readers. Gowers (1965) called it 'abstractitis' and provided the following example, among others, *Participation by the men in the control of the industry is non-existent*, which he said should be rewritten as *The men have no part in the control of the industry*. Here is a more recent example from a Scottish government organization: *Specific considerations will need to be given to what assistance minority groups will require to fully participate and contribute to the design, development and delivery of policies and services.* To restore this terminally ill sentence to some semblance of health, drastic surgery is required, starting with removal of the unnecessary abstract nouns: *considerations* (let us pass over the fact that it is plural), *design, development*, and *delivery*. My suggested rewrite is: *We need to think about how we can help minority groups play a full part in developing and delivering policies and services.* (I have removed 'designing' as superfluous, since you can hardly develop something you have not designed beforehand.)

It is sad to realize that, despite the tireless campaigning work of organizations such as the Plain English Campaign over the last few decades, ingrained, almost hereditary habits of bureaucratic wordiness, repetition, and lack of clarity mislead some officials into producing such claptrap.

abstruse, obtuse. These two are confused surprisingly often, usually with *obtuse* being used when *abstruse* is presumably meant. Topics, subjects, theories, etc. which are *abstruse* (from Latin *abstrūsus* 'concealed, hidden') are rather obscure or difficult to understand, e.g. *an abstruse philosophical inquiry*. Someone who is *obtuse* is annoyingly insensitive or slow to understand, e.g. *He wondered if the doctor was being deliberately obtuse.* To use *obtuse* to mean 'obscure, difficult', though often done, is not recommended, since some people will consider it a rank mistake, despite its being recognized in some dictionaries. Examples: (abstruse) *lectures on a series of abstruse topics, not excluding Roman laxatives and prophylactics*—*Daily Tel.*, 2007; *The language is abstruse and esoteric, almost incomprehensible, (the "discourse" inaccessible except to the initiates)*—*www.freeindia.com*, 2004; (obtuse) *There is a crispness to Imelda Staunton that has the positive snap of a headmistress dealing with some rather obtuse children*—*Scotland on Sunday*, 2004; *Henry III was equally politically obtuse in his dealings with Henry of Navarre*—*Canadian Journal of History*, 2000; (obtuse used dubiously) *While many academics shelter themselves beneath obtuse writing and inaccessible subject matter, Gould had the confidence to address the world with clarity and common sense*—*Human Nature Review*, 2002.

abysmal, abyssal. Of the respective base-nouns, *abysm* 'bottomless gulf, deep immeasurable space' has retreated into obsolescence except in reflections of Shakespeare's line in *The Tempest* (1612), *What seest thou els in the dark-backward and Abisme of Time? Abyss*, on the other hand, is a customary word, whether literal or figurative, for '[a place, etc., of] immeasurable depth'. A person facing defeat in an election or humiliation of some other kind, for example, is often said to be 'staring into the abyss'.

The derivatives *abysmal* and *abyssal* have moved in opposite directions. Residual uses of *abysmal* applied to gorges, precipices, deep space, etc., can be found (*the abysmal depths of interstellar space*—P. W. Merrill, 1938; *the abysmal depths of the ocean*—T. Barbour, 1944), but the word is mostly used in figurative contexts:

(*a*) = bottomless, fathomless (*Contemplate with despair the abysmal depths of your incapacity*—A. Burgess, 1987); (*b*) = extremely bad (*Guatemala's abysmal human rights record*—*NY Times*, 1984; *the abysmal quality of what is produced* [in Romania]—*NY Rev. Bks*, 1989).

Abyssal, once also used figuratively, is now only in restricted use as a technical term in oceanography, 'belonging to one of the deepest levels of the ocean' (*the ocean basin floor . . . is called the abyssal floor*—A. C. and A. Duxbury, 1984).

Academe. In ancient Greece, Ἀκαδήμεια was the proper name of a garden near Athens sacred to the hero Academus. In the 4c. BC it was the site of a philosophical school established there by Plato. Shakespeare modified the Greek name to the three-syllable *Achademe* in *Love's Labour's Lost* and used it to mean 'a place of learning'. Milton's line *The olive-grove of Academe, Plato's retirement* (*Paradise Regained*, IV. 244) also used the three-syllable form of the word, but applied it specifically to Plato's philosophical school. Later writers followed Shakespeare's lead, and, particularly since the publication of Thackeray's *Pendennis* in 1849 (*the least snugly sheltered arbour among the groves of Academe*), the word *Academe* (frequently but not invariably with an initial capital) has been modishly used by many writers to mean 'the academic community, the world of university scholarship', notably in the phrase *the groves of Academe* (cf. *Atque inter silvas Academi quaerere verum*—Horace, *Ep.* 2. 2. 45). Mary McCarthy's novel *The Groves of Academe* (1952) helped to establish the currency of the expression. It is a tangled story, but it is clear that *Academe* (or *academe*) has now slipped away from its Greek original, and has passed into general use as an acceptable expression (*One of the most remarkable pieces of hostile reviewing ever seen in academe*—Jonathan Clark, 1989). More recently (first recorded in 1946), it has been joined by **Academia** (or **academia**) in the same sense (*Businessmen liked to adopt the language of academia*—A. Sampson, 1971).

academic. The central uses of this word (first recorded in the late 16c.), i.e. relating to education and scholarship, remain firm, but a little more than a century ago (first noted 1886) it developed a depreciatory range of meanings as well, 'unpractical, merely theoretical, having no practical applications', e.g. *All the discussion, Sirs, is—academic. The war has begun already*—H. G. Wells, 1929; *The strike vote . . . was dismissed as 'largely academic' by Merseyside Health Authority*—*Times*, 1990.

Academy. *The Academy, the Garden, the Lyceum, the Porch*, and *the Tub* are names used for the five chief schools of Greek philosophy, their founders, adherents, and doctrines: *the Academy*, Plato, the Platonists, and Platonism; *the Garden*, Epicurus, the Epicureans, and Epicureanism; *the Lyceum*, Aristotle, the Aristotelians, and Aristotelianism; *the Porch* (or *the Painted Porch*, Gk στοὰ ποικίλη), Zeno, the Stoics, and Stoicism; *the Tub*, Diogenes (who lived in extreme poverty, legend has it, in a tub), the Cynics, and Cynicism.

accent. 1 The noun is stressed on the first syllable and the verb (meaning 'to lay stress on, to emphasize') on the second. But the participial adjective *accented* has first-syllable stress. See NOUN AND VERB ACCENT, PRONUNCIATION and SPELLING.

2 In general use, an accent is 'an individual, local, regional or national mode of pronunciation' (*Liverpool accent, German accent, upper-class accent*)'. Examples: *She had . . . the accent of a good finishing school*—J. Braine, 1957; *My mother came from Nashville, Tennessee, and try as she would she couldn't obliterate her accent*—Lord Hailsham, 1981. It is also used to mean the position of the stress in a word, and a sign put on a word in writing to mark a feature of its pronunciation; *You must pronounce this all as one word with the accent on the first syllable*—C. S. Lewis, 1955; *using an acute accent* (*voilá*) *instead of the correct grave accent* (*voilà*)—*OEC*, 2005.

There are other special meanings in art and music. The meaning relating to pronunciation is the earliest one, and has given rise to extended uses, in which accent means 'a distinctive feature or emphasis': *After 1926 the accent was to lie on the development of technical education*—R. Pethybridge, 1990; *In the eastern area, the food is heavier, with more of an accent on mutton and pork*—*Countries and their Culture*, 2004. This use is common in advertising and marketing: *Accent is on comfort when you step in for a relaxing drink.*

accent, accentuate. In figurative senses (= to emphasize a particular feature), *accentuate* is now very much the commoner of the two verbs, but *accent* is far from extinct, particularly when fashion, decoration, or design is the topic. Examples: (accent) *The great piers . . . are accented at the cardinal points by shafts of dark lias*—R. J. King, 1877; *warm beige walls accented by graceful tiles with leafy patterns and dark-wood tables*—*Boston Globe*, 2011; (accentuate) *I observed a severe grey skirt, the waist accentuated by a leather belt*—W. Golding, 1967; *The villagey feeling was accentuated by the use of tile-hanging*—M. Girouard, 1977; *Collingwood also has a rather learned look, accentuated by steel spectacles*—R. Cobb, 1985.

In the literal sense 'to place an accent on a syllable or word', the only word used (of the two) is *accent* (e.g. *'begin' is accented on the second syllable*).

accept, except. Though clearly distinct in meaning, in fast speech *accept* is often pronounced /ɪk'sɛpt/. As a result poor spellers may occasionally set down the wrong word. David Crystal reported in his book *Who Cares About English Usage?* (1984) that a number of English undergraduates presented with the pair of sentences *Shall we accept/except his invitation to dinner?* chose *except* not *accept*. But the confusion is ancient: Queen Elizabeth I is known to have done the same in a letter.

acceptance, acceptation. 1 The first of these, though coming later into the language, has gradually driven out most uses of the second during the last four centuries, except that *acceptation* is still much the more usual of the two in the rather highbrow meaning 'the particular sense, or the generally accepted meaning, of a word or phrase'. So we find *acceptance* as the usual noun for accepting death, facts, ideas, homosexuality, offers, reality, responsibility, and all manner of other things. Nevertheless, *acceptation* occasionally crops up still in this verbal sense, but cannot be recommended. Examples: (= acceptance) *The negotiating policy of leaders of leftist parties and trade unions only resulted in the acceptation of these leaders into the old elite*—weblog, 2003; (= meaning) *he is not a citizen in the ordinary acceptation of the word*—*The American Conservative*, 2004.

2 The tsunami of illiteracy unleashed by the Internet has either created or helped spread the bizarre use of **acceptation* to mean 'exception', especially in the phrase **with the acceptation of*, e.g. **However, in your case I will make an acceptation*—*OEC*; *I do not believe I am the acceptation to 'the rule'*—weblog, 2012.

accepter, acceptor. In general contexts the word is normally spelt *accepter* (*he is no accepter of conventions; the sketch about the ungracious award accepter*), but in specialized senses in law and science *acceptor* is the standard and recommended form: *the Bill of Exchange . . . is an order written by the drawer and addressed to the acceptor*—J. E. T. Rogers, 1868; *the ionization energy of donors is less than that of acceptors*—*Physical Review*, 1949; *another possible electron acceptor such as sulphate or perhaps even nitrate may be reduced*—*Forestry*, 1986. See -ER AND -OR; -OR.

access, accession. 1 *As nouns.* Fowler (1926) distinguished between these two in detail in order to prevent their being confused. There is, however, no evidence in the *OEC* that they are ever confused.

2 *As verbs.* Since the 1890s, *accession* has been used as a verb meaning 'to enter in the accessions register of a library' (*the new books have been promptly accessioned*—G. M. Jones, 1892). In more recent times (first recorded 1975), *access* (perhaps as a back-formation) has occasionally been used in the same sense (*the Lowestoft Hoard had to be accessed*—*TLS*, 1978).

Since the early 1960s, *access* has been used in computer language to mean 'to obtain or retrieve (data or a file); to gain access to (a system or network)', e.g. *Each time you access a website, you retrieve information from the appropriate computer, wherever in the world that computer might be*—B. Robson and O. K. Baek, 2009. This use is part of the everyday vocabulary of the field, and bothers nobody. Closely related to this use is the metaphor of the brain as computer in the meaning 'to bring (a fact, word, etc.) to mind', e.g. *when the speaker is temporarily unable to access the word in Spanish*—*Amer. Speech*, 1987.

The relatively recent meaning (1978) that some people dislike (on the grounds that it is an example of 'verbing') is 'to approach or enter a place' in more generalized contexts, such as *The kitchen may be accessed from the dining room*. If you wish to shun it, there are synonyms aplenty to hand: *reach*, *approach, enter,* etc. Alternatively, you could rephrase.

accessary, accessory. 1 The first of these two spellings is virtually defunct, and the second is the standard in all contexts and all varieties of English. But it was not always so. They were given separate entries in the *OED* because their derivations differ. Moreover, in meaning, both as nouns and as adjectives, they mostly ran on separate tracks until about 1900. The *-ary* form traditionally tended to imply complicity in an offence, acting as (or one who acts as) a subordinate in a crime, while the *-ory* form was mostly reserved for general contexts where someone or something contributed in a subordinate way. In the course of the 20c. *accessory* took over in all contexts both as a noun and as an adjective. Examples: *As the one person who knew of their illegalities I felt that I was becoming an accessory after the fact*—S. Unwin, 1960; *if he buried the captain, as he says, he's an accessory*—R. Macdonald, 1971; *accessory ideas associated with the principal idea*—M. Cohen, 1977. As a noun, *accessory* is widely used (usually in the plural) for the smaller articles of dress (gloves, handbag, etc.) or the extras in a motor vehicle (fog lights, radio, etc.). Examples: *Accessories ... may be considered essential to an outfit*—A. Lurie, 1981; *auto accessories.*

2 Both words were frequently pronounced with the main stress on the first syllable until the early part of the 20th century, but now /ak'sɛsəri/ is the standard pronunciation. A common mistake is to pronounce *accessory* with initial /as-/ as if it were spelt 'assessory'.

accessible. Is correctly spelled *-ible,* not *-able.* See -ABLE, -IBLE 8.

accessorize. Denounced by Burchfield as 'what looked like being one of the least lovable words of the 20c.', and despised by some because it is one of the modernish *-ize* verbs, *accessorize* first sashayed onto the linguistic catwalk as long ago as 1934. It seems to be here to stay: an essential part of the vocabulary of fashion, interior design and related fields, it has both transitive and intransitive uses: (transitive) *The Sultan has accessorized himself with epaulettes, medals and several strings of pearls—Times,* 1989; (intransitive) *Earth tone nylon covers of seats in a car easily accessorize with any hue—Toronto Star,* 1984.

accessory. See ACCESSARY, ACCESSORY.

accidently. This non-standard form, used instead of *accidentally,* is recorded as early as 1611 and is still encountered occasionally in print: e.g. *When I have accidently collided with it*—B. Rubens, 1985; *Julie Kohler (Moreau) loses her groom on the steps of the church when he is accidently shot by a group of men fooling about with a gun—Listener,* 1987. But it is very much a minority form.

acclimate, acclimatize. Both words mean 'to become or to cause to become accustomed to a new climate', literally or metaphorically. *Acclimate* is the slightly older form, being first recorded from 1792, and *acclimatize* from 1836. In the *OEC* data they occur more or less equally (if one lumps the uncommon *-ise* spelling in with *acclimatize*). In most countries *acclimatize* is the preferred form, except in the US, where there is a marked preference for *acclimate.* In biology each word is used in a very precise technical sense: if an organism *acclimatizes,* it responds physiologically or behaviourally to changes in a complex of environmental factors; if an organism *acclimates,* it responds to a change in a single environmental factor. The derivatives **acclimation** and **acclimatization** follow the pattern of their parent verbs in their general meaning, and in their technical meanings. Examples: (acclimatize) *They also argue that the more English becomes institutionalized as the world's main medium of international expression the more native and non-native users will need to learn to acclimatize to each other's ways of using it—Concise Oxford Companion to the English Language,* 2000 (BrE); *Staff should be acclimatized and trained in new technologies and methodologies—First Monday Jrnl.,* 2001 (AmE); (acclimate) *'I'll drop in after dinner,' Dick promised. 'First I must get acclimated.'*—F. Scott Fitzgerald, 1934 (AmE); *but as they are acclimated and toughened to the native condition they suffer far less than we do*—F. Lloyd Wright, 1954 (AmE); *As with the photosynthetic apparatus, stomata can acclimate to long-term variation in CO2 supply—Integrative and Comparative Biology,* 2002 (AmE).

accommodate, accommodation. Two of the English words most often misspelt, they require two *c*s and two *m*s. The verb *accommodate* is followed by *to* when it means 'to adapt' (*He would easily have accommodated his body to the rule of never* *turning his head on his shoulders*—R. Graves, 1938; *The principles of natural justice have to be accommodated to the nature of the body deciding it*—High Court transcripts, 2005 (Aust.)) and with *with* in its rather rarer meaning of 'to equip, supply, oblige' (e.g. *New issue stamp dealers will be only too pleased to accommodate you with Malawi's latest pre-neolithic nonet*—*Stamp and Coin Mart*, 1994. *Accommodations* (in the plural), once common in the UK for 'lodgings, living premises', is now more or less restricted to American English (e.g. *overnight accommodations*).

accompanist. Now the standard form of the word for 'a person who plays a musical accompaniment'. The secondary form **accompanyist** (also first recorded in the 19c.), used e.g. by Dickens in *Oliver Twist*, has fallen out of favour, although it is occasionally encountered.

accomplice, accomplish. The most widespread pronunciation of both words is now with /-kʌm-/ not /-kɒm-/, though the first thirteen editions of Daniel Jones's *English Pronouncing Dictionary* (1917–67), presumably correctly reflecting the mood of that time, gave precedence to the second of these two pronunciations, which is still occasionally heard.

accord. The standard construction is 'of one's own accord', as in *Of his owne accord he went vnto you* (2 Cor. (AV) 8: 17) and *her face, of its own accord, folded into a false, obedient smile*—E. O'Brien, 1989. It is therefore somewhat surprising that the construction 'on one's own accord', following the obsolete use illustrated in *On mine owne accord, Ile off* (Shakespeare, *Winter's Tale*, 1611) with *on* as the head of the phrase is well represented in the *OEC*, often in the most surprising places, e.g. *And commanders in Iraq, on their own accord, are already moving troops from their combat ranks to the training teams*—*New York Times*, 2006. It is impossible to say whether this is a survival or a solecism.

according as. This subordinating conjunction is nowadays generally used to mean 'depending on whether', in contexts where two or more alternatives present themselves: e.g. *Llanabba Castle presents two quite different aspects, according as you approach it from the Bangor or the coast road*—E. Waugh, 1928; *Its quality differs with its color, according as it is white, red, yellow, or bluish*—*A tribute to Hinduism*, 2003. Even in that use, i.e. as an alternative to 'depending on whether, according to whether', it has a literary or somewhat archaic feel. Historically it also expressed dependence on some other condition (e.g. *everyone contributes according as he or she is able*); this meaning still occasionally appears, but sounds even more formal than the first: e.g. *a company which has demonstrated its willingness to switch and change according as the market dictates*—*OEC*, 2002.

account. *On account of* is a slightly formal compound preposition meaning 'because of' (e.g. *He remained miserable and ashamed, largely on account of his appetite which continued to torment him*—A. Brookner, 1988), and first recorded in 1625. The following variants of it are non-standard, or informal: (*a*) the non-standard *on accounts of* shown in *they giv' it the name, on accounts of Old Harmon living solitary there* (Dickens, *Our Mutual Friend*, Victorian working-class context); and (*b*) its use with and without *of* and *on* as in the following examples: *I was feeling kind of down, on account that tooth of mine was giving me the devil*—P. G. Wodehouse, 1936; *Account of you think you're tough you're going up to State Prison where you'll have to prove it*—E. Leonard, 1994 (AmE); *It took us until dinner, twelve hours to crank out six-two pizzas, on account we couldn't get the ingredients right the first few times*—*OEC*, 2005 (AmE).

accoutrement. Throughout the English-speaking world this spelling is much more frequent than **accouterment**, which occurs mostly in North American English, but even there is less frequent than the *-tre-* form.

accumulative, cumulative. In the meaning 'gathering or growing by gradual increase', these two adjectives have been competing since the 17c., but *cumulative* can now be declared a very convincing winner. Currently *it* is much more likely both in general contexts (*cumulative dose, effect, impact, total*, etc.) and in more specialized areas of legal sentencing, dividends, reference library indexes, errors, voting, etc. *Accumulative* is still occasionally used, but in a ratio of 1:35 in the *OEC*; similarly, **accumulatively** is an unusual choice for **cumulatively**. *Accumulative* is also occasionally used in its other meaning of 'acquisitive': *Fijians are not accumulative. A good example of this is the farming of ginger and dalo. When* *the price went up, the production went down*—*Aust. Jrnl. of Anthropology*, 2002.

accused. *The accused*, meaning a person who has been accused in law, is an everyday use and a legal one. *The* or *an accused woman, person, banker, teacher*, etc., in which individuals are only generically identified, are also routinely acceptable in non-legal contexts. However, expressions like *the accused thief* or *the accused rapist*, appear quite regularly in slightly amateurish journalism, but never in law, since identification with the crime is in question by the very use of the term *accused*. *Alleged* would be a better word here.

acerb, acerbic. The first of these is the earlier, being first recorded in *Othello* (1622) in its literal meaning of 'sour, bitter', while *acerbic* dates to 1853. *Acerb* is now, as the *OED* puts it, 'chiefly US and literary', and shows up just once in the *OEC* (*acerbic* appears 1,716 times). There are earlier examples from modern literature, e.g. *Many of his acerb remarks about wives and marriage may or may not apply to his own*—D. M. Frame, 1964; *The acerb after effects of the tragic act of love*—J. Updike, 1978.

The misspelling *ascerbic* turns up in print from time to time—perhaps modelled on *ascetic*—but has no validity.

Achilles heel, Achilles tendon. The presence or absence of an apostrophe in these two expressions is not a matter of rule, but of custom. Consistency in a given publication is desirable, whichever form is chosen. *NODWE* recommends leaving the apostrophes out.

achingly. *Achingly* means literally 'in an aching manner; so as to cause continuous dull pain', e.g. *My eyes*—*dry now, achingly dry*—*flashing a wretched hostility back into his*—R. Broughton, 1873. Its use as an intensifier modifying an adjective and meaning 'acutely, intensely' is not new: *It is too achingly brilliant*—*it wants repose*—*New Monthly Magazine*, 1883. Nowadays, it is quite widely used, particularly in arts journalism, to modify adjectives such as *sad, poignant, tender, melancholic*, even *beautiful*, where it retains a link with its literal meaning, and the metaphor is dormant rather than dead: *It is hysterically funny and achingly sad, but without a hint of sentimentality*—*Scotland on Sunday*, 2005; *The chief narrator, Rosamond, is an achingly lonely old woman, who lost her one great love when she was in her twenties*—*ABC Radio*, 2008 (Aust.). To use it to intensify words such as *hip, trendy, fashionable* is a mannerism of a certain superficial and gushy style of journalistic writing. That raises—at least in my literal mind—the question whether being fashionable, hip etc. causes physical discomfort for the person who is, or the journalist who wants to be. Jesting apart, achingly seems to be following the pattern of *awfully, dreadfully, terribly*, etc. and is used as an intensifier, with no reference whatsoever to its literal meaning.

acid rain. A classic example of a term that was in use for a surprisingly long period (first recorded 1845) in specialist contexts before becoming a standard item of modern ecological and environmentalist vocabulary, familiar to most people.

acid test. See POPULARIZED TECHNICAL TERMS.

acknowledgement. In most printed work this is the preferred spelling in British English, whereas the form without *-e-* (*-ledgment*) is more usual in American English. The choice is a matter of convention, not of correctness.

acoustics. *Acoustics* is construed as a singular noun when used to mean 'the science of sound' (e.g. *Acoustics is a branch of physics*), and as a plural when used to mean 'the acoustic properties (of a building)' (e.g. *the acoustics of the church hall are not impressive*).

acqu. See AQU-, ACQU-.

acquaintanceship. Categorized by Fowler as a 'needless variant' for *acquaintance*, this word has a respectable pedigree, and dates to at least 1640, but in current use is very much a minority taste. Strictly speaking it refers to the state of being acquainted with someone or something, not to the person or people with whom you are acquainted, so in the next example *acquaintance* would have been better: *Aunt Kate of Hungerford or some other member of her wide acquaintanceship of old ladies*—P. Norman, 1979. Here is a more recent and typical example: *health problems not unconnected with a lifetime's intimate acquaintanceship with alcohol*—*Sunday Herald*, 2000.

acronym. 1 (From *acro-*, Greek ἀκρο-, combining form of ἄκρος 'topmost' + *-onym* after *homonym.*) This term, first used in 1943, denotes abbreviations formed from the initial letters of other words and pronounced as a single word, such as *NATO* (as distinct from *B-B-C*). A word was clearly needed for this prolific method of modern word-formation. Examples of familiar modern acronyms include: *Aids* (*a*cquired *i*mmune *d*eficiency *s*yndrome), *Captcha* (*c*ompletely *a*utomatic *p*ublic *T*uring test to tell *c*omputers and *h*umans *a*part), *PIN* (*p*ersonal *i*dentification *n*umber), and *WASP* (*W*hite *A*nglo -*S*axon *P*rotestant). Many words of this kind, especially those that are the names of organizations, start off with uniform capitals and full stops, and only become word-like acronyms after constant use: thus U.N.E.S.C.O. → UNESCO → Unesco. Others (e.g. ASH) are deliberately contrived to lend themselves to being pronounced as words and thereby become acronyms. Some acronyms were written with uniform lower-case letters virtually from the beginning: *laser* (*l*ight *a*mplification by *s*timulated *e*mission of *r*adiation), and *radar* (*r*adio *d*etection *a*nd *r*anging).

2 In everyday use, *acronym* is often applied to abbreviations that are technically initialisms, since they are pronounced as separate letters (e.g. *EU* = European Union, *DVD* = digital versatile disc).

3 For guidance on when to use a full point, see FULL STOP 2.

4 While acronyms and initialisms that everyone knows are useful shorthand, less well-known ones are a barrier to communication and become another form of jargon. For example, the initialism *SEO* (search engine optimization) is immediately understood by people in the Internet world but will be meaningless to many others. It is sound advice to avoid using such words unless you are addressing people in the same specialist or technical field as you. Even if you have explained the full form of the term, people less familiar with it than you have to expand it mentally every time they encounter it, as if they were translating from another language. The use of these abbreviations has become so widespread, and been so often criticized, that they are known as *TLAs*, 'three-letter acronyms', even though many of them are technically initialisms.

action (verb). Use of this to mean 'to take action on' will undoubtedly upset, not to say enrage, some people; it is widely stigmatized as an example of 'verbing', of gratuitously converting nouns to verbs. Burchfield (1996) acidly recommended that 'the word is best left at present to the tight-lipped language of business managers', while the *OED* notes 'especially in business jargon'. But it is hardly a novel creation: it was used in a legal meaning by Fielding in his 1734 translation of *Don Quixote,* while the anathematized use dates at least as far back as 1960.

Oxford English Corpus data suggests it may be more common in British than in American English, and shows that requests, changes, and decisions are typically *actioned,* and not only in business, e.g. *Could the Minister explain what she is trying to hide by not actioning two requests from the Health Committee—New Zealand Parliamentary Debates,* 2004. While it has the stale whiff of bureaucracy or HR-speak about it, in its favour it can be argued that it is shorter than 'put into action, put into effect' and the like. On the other hand , 'act on' would do just as well in the example above, while the use of *action* in the next can only be described as tragically laughable: *Dismissal will be actioned when the balance of probabilities suggests that an employee has committed a criminal act—Daily Tel.,* 1981.

activate, actuate. These two verbs are differentiated rather clearly in modern use, despite having been interchangeable for much of their history. *Activate* is the term generally used to mean 'make something active or operative' (e.g. *fumes from cooking are enough to activate the alarm*) and specifically 'convert a substance, molecule, etc. into a reactive form' (e.g. *a DNA-repair enzyme that is activated by visible light*). *Actuate,* by contrast, is much less often encountered in technical contexts, though in practice devices, diaphragms, forces, pinions, pistons, and so on, as shown in 18c. and 19c. examples in the *OED,* can still be actuated by this or that instrument or agent, e.g. *The button is a switch actuating motorized stopdown of the diaphragm—Popular Photography,* 2000. *Actuate* is chiefly used as a synonym for 'motivate', with abstract qualities like anger, greed, jealousy, etc., e.g. *the defendants were actuated by malice.* While *activate* can be used in this way (*Are they activated by concern for public morality?—Essays & Studies,* 1961), *actuate* is generally preferred.

active. For the grammatical term, see PASSIVE VOICE.

actually. It was not Fowler but Gowers (1965) who listed this adverb under 'meaningless' words, which is something of a slur. Though a few people overuse it conversationally with a reduced meaning, and it can be an irritating verbal tic, most people, as Burchfield (1996) accepted, usefully oil the wheels of conversation with it in ways that are broadly defined below.

As an ordinary adverb modifying verbs, it means 'in fact, in reality' as in *Often it wasn't actually a railway station but a special stopping place in the middle of nowhere*—*New Yorker*, 1987. As a sentence adverb, it is used (*a*) to emphasize that something someone has done or said is surprising, a use which is far from new, e.g. *I had some dispositions to be a scholar and had actually learned my letters*—Goldsmith, 1762; (*b*) to express a contradictory or unexpected opinion, or to correct someone else or oneself, e.g. *except that instead of going into the technological future I had to go back in time. Actually, I don't really mean that, back in time*—J. Barnes, 1989; *'I told you, I've got problems at work.' 'Actually, you didn't.'*—S. Mackay, 1981; (*c*) to introduce a new topic or add information, e.g. *He had a thick Cockney accent—he sounded like my granddad, actually.* It can also be used to introduce advice, e.g. *Actually, it might be a good idea not to travel from Gatwick in the summer this year.*

actuate. See ACTIVATE, ACTUATE.

acuity, acuteness. *Acuity* (first recorded 1543) has long vied with *acuteness* (1627) in literal and figurative contexts. In current use, the dividing line between them is fairly sharp, but they overlap slightly in one area of meaning. *Acuity* denotes 'sharpness or keenness of thought, vision, or hearing'. In the *OEC* data it appears far more frequently than *acuteness*, and typically appears in the phrases *visual/mental/psychological/intellectual acuity* and *acuity of vision*. *Acuteness* refers to the severity or suddenness of a disease, illness, or problem; and to mental sharpness or perceptiveness. It is in this second meaning that it works as a synonym for *acuity*, with which it alternates in the collocation *acuteness/acuity of ... observation*. Examples: (acuity) *People that I know who like to read poetry with acuity and intelligence*—A. Hecht, 1981; *almost drowsy, but with no loss of mental acuity*—I. Asimov, 1982; *being able to see 6/12 on a visual acuity chart*—*Nursing Times*, 1986; *I think it's scientific in at least the acuity of the observations and descriptions made upon these objects*—*OEC*, 2004; (acuteness) *A case study is useful in illustrating the acuteness of the problems facing first-time buyers in York*—*OEC*, 2002; *The steadiness of our minds and the acuteness of our intellects are not accidental happenings*—*Hinduism Today*, 2001; *Lady Mary evoked the art and interiors of the houses she had known as a child with the acuteness of observation and lack of sentimentality that characterised her own personality*—*Daily Tel.*, 2010.

acumen. The Victorian pronunciation was /əˈkjuːmən/, stressed on the second syllable. This still seems to be the dominant pronunciation in American English, but it has given way to /ˈakjʊmən/, stressed on the first syllable, in British English.

ad, a frequent abbreviation of *advertisement* or *advertising* (so *small ad, adman*, etc.), first recorded in 1841 and now in very widespread use. Of the three forms *ad, advert, advertisement,* it is by far the most common. While some dictionaries still label it 'informal', it would to my mind be truer to say that both it and *advert* are the standard forms in speech, while *advertisement* is slightly formal. In the *OEC ad* is more than three times as frequent as *advertisement.*

AD should be placed—in recognition of what it stands for (*anno Domini*, in the year of Our Lord)—before the numerals it relates to, i.e. AD 44 (not 44 AD). It is standard practice for convenience, however, to write 'the third century AD' to correspond to 'the third century BC'. In print, AD is often put in small capitals, and is usually printed without full points, but with a space between it and the numeral. Note that the fashionably dechristianized alternative CE (for 'Common Era') is often used (following the date), along with BCE ('before Common Era'). This device seems to satisfy the demands of political correctness despite the fact that it is merely a disguised continuation of the same system. Cf. BC.

adagio. (Mus.) slow; as noun, plural *adagios*. See -O(E)S 4.

adaptation, adaption. For Swift, Dickens, and others less celebrated, using *adaption* to mean 'adaptation, the action of adapting' was perfectly acceptable. At no time, however, has it seriously challenged *adaptation*, which in the *OEC* is at least fifty times more likely to occur. The revised (2011) *OED* labels *adaption* 'nonstandard' which is perhaps a little severe: it turns up from time to time in good sources: e.g. *But I daresay you'll display your usual power of adaption*—P. Lively, 1987; *the first such adaption of the second half of the play*—*Oxford Companion to Shakespeare*, 2001. The derivatives **adaptational**, **adaptationism**, and **adaptationist** are much more frequently used than the shorter forms.

adapter, adaptor. The spelling with *-er* is more than three times as common as that with *-or* in both meanings of the word ('device', 'person who adapts something'), although in an ideal world it would be useful to restrict *adaptor* to the device and *adapter* to the much less used meaning 'a person who adapts something or to something'. See -ER AND -OR; -OR.

addendum. This word raises two questions: what its plural is, and whether *addenda* should be used as a singular. **1** *Addendum* is the neuter gerundive of the Latin verb *addere*, and translates literally as 'something to be added'. It typically refers to (i) an item of additional information, often omissions, at the end of a book to correct or clarify the contents, or (ii) to an additional clause modifying an agreement. The etymologically correct Latin plural *addenda* is much more often used than the English plural *addendums*, which cannot, however, be said to be wrong, but rather, like the plural *aquariums*, is a sign of how far the word has become part of English. Examples: *Included in the work are several addenda that provide useful information about historical events and locations mentioned in McPherson's narrative*—*Alabama Review*, 2000; *Instead it* [*sc.* the General Assembly] *gets bogged down in motions and amendments, addendums and deliverances, overtures and the like*—*Scotland on Sunday*, 2002.

2 *Addenda*, being a plural form, should not be used as a singular to refer to a single item: *addendum* is preferable. Despite the singular use of *addenda* having a long history, it is likely to be viewed askance by good editors: **This section takes the form of an addenda or an appendix*—*Early Modern Literary Studies*, 2003.

address (verb). People in the business of not really meaning what they say love this verb. Although it seems at first hearing to promise forceful action, it can justifiably be criticized for being massively overused. Its stablemate is 'issue', which is similarly overworked to the point of near collapse. When someone—usually a politician, public servant, or business spokesperson—undertakes to *address an issue*, it is often unclear to what exactly they are committing. Will they merely note it in passing as something to be dealt with at an unspecified future date, analyse it in depth, pass the buck to their minions, or actually do something to resolve it as soon as humanly possible? Anyone seriously intending action on an 'issue' would be well-advised to avoid the woolly cliché and to specify the exact measures they intend taking—produce the figures, set up an inquiry, sack the people concerned, and so forth. Or simply put their head over the parapet and say that they will *resolve, deal with*, or *sort out* the question.

addresses. It is now customary to use as little punctuation as possible in addresses. Thus (omitting commas at the end of lines):

> The College Secretary
> St Peter's College
> Oxford OX1 2DL

and (omitting the comma after the house number):

> 44 High Street

The postal code can be put on the same line as the town, or below it.

-ade. Nearly all words of two or more syllables ending in *-ade* are derived from French (some being drawn into that language from other Romance languages). The majority have passed through a stage of being pronounced with final /-ɑːd/, but are now normally pronounced with /-eɪd/, e.g. *accolade, arcade, balustrade, brigade, brocade, cascade, cavalcade, crusade, esplanade, lemonade, marmalade, masquerade, palisade, parade, serenade*, and *tirade*. A small *group*, e.g. *fanfaronnade, fusillade, glissade, pomade, promenade*, and *rodomontade*, are still commonly pronounced with either /-eɪd/ or /-ɑːd/; and *aubade, ballade, charade*, and *façade*, always have /-ɑːd/.

adequate. **1** In its meaning 'sufficient', *adequate* is most commonly used without a complement (*There is an adequate supply of food in the flooded area*). When it has one, this is either *for* or *to* (*Their earnings are adequate for/to their needs*). It is also used idiomatically to mean 'barely sufficient': *The standard rapidly sinks to a level which is, at best, adequate but at worst incompetent.*

2 Arguments that *adequate* is an absolute are as invalid and contrary to usage as similar arguments for *unique*. Language is rarely as absolute as purists would like, and it is natural to find *adequacy* graded by adverbs and with comparatives and superlatives: *We are seeking a more adequate return on our investments; The work done is fairly adequate; The most adequate description yet released of the horror of the hijacking; some very adequate salaries.*

adherence, adhesion. Both words were adopted from French in the 17c., and ultimately come from the Latin verb *adhaerēre, adhaes-*, which gives us 'to adhere'. *Adherence* now mostly appears in figurative senses relating to beliefs, principles, and rules. *Adhesion* has tended more and more to imply physical contact between surfaces, e.g. the grip of wheels on road or rail, the sticking together of two surfaces. *Adhesion* also has a technical medical sense, 'a mass of fibrous connective tissue joining two surfaces that are normally separate'. The distinction between the two is almost universally observed in the *OEC* data. Nevertheless, *adherence* is sometimes used literally (e.g. *adherence of petals and sepals*), and *adhesion* is used figuratively (e.g. *his blind adhesion to the failed ideology of socialism*—weblog, 2005), but may sound odd.

ad hoc, Latin, literally 'to this', has been used in English since the 17c. to mean 'for a particular purpose; in response to a specific need or demand' (*an ad hoc committee is to be set up*). It should be printed in roman, as two separate words, with no hyphen. It is also used to imply lack of planning or system, in which case it can be modified by adverbs like *very* or *fairly* (e.g. *The arrangement seems extremely ad hoc to them*). Only one derivative has achieved a more than tenuous foothold in the lexicon; **adhocracy**, meaning bureaucracy devoid of planning or forethought. The use of ad hoc measures with no long-term strategy is labelled **adhocism**, but the word is rarely used.

ad idem, = Latin, literally 'to the same (thing)', has continued to appear sporadically in English printed work since the 16c., and is printed in italics. Its only extant meaning is 'in agreement', and it occasionally appears in legal language, but Garner's *Dictionary of Legal Usage* puts it on a list of 'forbidden words'. Since only a few lawyers and Latinists will know what it means, it should be used very sparingly.

adieu. **1** Should one ever need the plural of this literary word, both *adieus* and *adieux* are correct, although the first is more frequent. The singular in pronounced /əˈdjuː/ (uh-**dyoo**) and both plurals are *pronounced* /-z/. See -x.

2 *Adieu* has been wordjacked, especially in the US, and is being held hostage in the phrase '*without further adieu', an illiteracy for 'without further ado'. Hopes for its release are rapidly fading.

adjacent, adjoining. **1** *Adjacent to* is correct, but **adjoining to* is wrong, as in *fertile unappropriated soil in or *adjoining to the principal slave countries.* This is because *adjoining* comes from the verb *adjoin*, which requires no preposition, e.g. *the dining room adjoins a conservatory.*

2 These two words do not mean the same, but they share one meaning, so they should be used with care in order to create unambiguous statements. *Adjacent* can mean either 'near' or 'touching', whereas *adjoining* invariably denotes immediate contact, as its link with 'join' suggests. *Adjacent angles* in a triangle are separated by the length of one side of the triangle, and *adjacent tables* are next to each other, but with a space between. However, while an *adjacent parcel of land* sometimes describes one that is merely nearby, it often refers to one which is joined. Similarly, an *adjacent room* may, for example, be across a corridor, or it may share a common wall or walls. That is where the ambiguity arises, and in many cases it would be clearer to use *adjoining*. (unambiguous) examples: *With no time to reconsider, I slipped into the adjoining bathroom to disrobe—www.travelintelligence.net,* 2003; *Within a few minutes the runaway animal which had broken loose from a field adjoining the* *railway line was taken back home—Stamford Mercury*, 2007; (ambiguous examples) *The accommodation is completed by two adjacent rooms which are off a corridor to the right of the hall—Sunday Business Post*, 2003; *a country immediately adjacent to their own—Contemporary Review*, 2002. Are the rooms and countries mentioned near each other, or joined in some way?

adjective.

1 As name of a part of speech.
2 Position of adjectives.
3 Comparison.
4 'Absolute' adjectives.
5 Hyphenation.
6 Compound adjectives.
7 Adjectives used as adverbs.
8 Adjectives as nouns.
9 Transferred epithets.

1 *As name of a part of speech.* The italicized words in 'a *black* cat' and 'a body *politic*', used as an addition to the name of a thing to describe the thing more fully or definitely, were usually called *noun adjectives* from the 15c. to the 18c. The term *noun adjective* (as distinguished from *noun substantive*) was not recognized as being one of the primary parts of speech. Joseph Priestley, in *The Rudiments of English Grammar* (1761), was perhaps the first English grammarian to recognize the *adjective* as an independent part of speech, though some earlier writers had used the term in this way.

Since the mid-19c., some writers have used the word *modifier* to signify 'a word, phrase, or clause which modifies another'. Within this terminology, the italicized words in 'the *black* cat', 'a body *politic*', and 'the *city* council' are all modifiers. In traditional grammar, *home* in *home counties* and *city* in *city council* are called attributive uses of the nouns *home* and *city*.

An adjective has three forms, traditionally called a positive (*hot*), a comparative (*hotter*), and a superlative (*hottest*). In some modern grammars (e.g. *CGEL*), the base form is called the *absolute*, not the *positive*, form.

2 *Position of adjectives.* (*a*) Most adjectives can be used in two positions: both before the noun, i.e. attributively (a *black* cat, a *gloomy* outlook) and after it, i.e. predicatively, normally separated by a verb (the cat is *black*, the outlook seems *gloomy*).

(*b*) Some adjectives are normally restricted to following the noun in predicative position, e.g. *afraid* (*he is afraid* but not **the afraid boy*), *answerable, rife, tantamount*, etc. Conversely, numerous adjectives are restricted to preceding the noun in attributive position, either always, e.g. *main* as in *the* main *reason*, not **this reason is* main; or in certain meanings: e.g. *he is a* big *eater* not **as an eater he is* big; *the* sheer *richness of his material* not **the richness of his material is* sheer. So also *mere repetition, pure fabrication, a tall order, the whole occasion*, etc.

(*c*) A few adjectives (technically 'postpositive'), usually denoting status, exceptionally come immediately after the noun, e.g. *the body politic, court martial, poet laureate, postmaster-general, president elect.*

These are different from cases in which an adjective just happens to follow the noun it governs (e.g. *The waiter ... picked up our dirty glasses in his fingertips, his eyes impassive—Encounter*, 1987); or when the natural order is reversed for rhetorical effect (e.g. *before the loving hands of the Almighty cradled him in bliss eternal*—N. Williams, 1992).

3 *Comparison.* Adjectives of one or two syllables (monosyllabic, disyllabic) normally have comparative and superlative forms ending in *-er* and *-est* (*soft, softer, softest*). Adjectives of more than two syllables (polysyllabic) are generally preceded by *more* and *most* (*more frightening, a most remarkable woman*). For special effect, a polysyllabic adjective is sometimes used in an unexpected *-er* or *-est* form: e.g. *'Curiouser and curiouser!' cried Alice*—L. Carroll, 1865; *one of the generousest creatures alive*—Thackeray, 1847/8; *Shelby Metcalf, the winningest coach in Southwest Conference basketball history—Chicago Tribune*, 1990. See also -ER, -EST.

4 *'Absolute' adjectives.* Because of their meaning and function, certain adjectives cannot be modified by adverbs such as *largely, more, quite, too*, or *very* to denote that they have more of the quality concerned. These adjectives include *equal, impossible, perfect, supreme, total, unique*; (see also ADEQUATE). There are exceptions, usually literary, e.g. *All animals are equal but some animals are more equal than others*—G. Orwell, 1945. Absolute adjectives can, however, be modified by adverbs denoting an extreme such as *absolutely, completely* and *utterly*, since that is consistent with their meaning: *The ... ghosts ... made the place absolutely impossible—Harper's Mag.*, 1884.

5 *Hyphenation.* It is absolutely unnecessary to insert a hyphen between an adverb ending in *-ly* and an adjective it qualifies. It is therefore correct to write *a highly competitive market, a newly adopted constituency* (not **a highly-competitive market,* etc.). When the adverb does not end in *-ly,* however, a hyphen is required if the adjective comes before the noun, but not if it comes after: *a well-known woman, ill-defined criteria,* but *this woman is well known, the criteria are ill defined.*

6 *Compound adjectives.* These proliferated in the 20c., and will no doubt be a fertile source of new adjectives. There are several types: (*a*) noun + adjective: *accident-prone* (1926), *acid-free* (1930), *child-proof* (1956), *computer-literate* (1976), *future-proof* (1983), *user-friendly* (1976);

(*b*) noun + past participle: *computer-aided* (1962), *custom-built* (1925), *hand-operated* (1871);

(*c*) noun + participle in *-ing*: *data-handling* (1964), *pressure-reducing* (1934), *stress-relieving* (1938).

A new kind of compound adjective emerging in technical and scientific work is the type *landscape ecological principles* (= the principles of landscape ecology). From the starting-point *landscape ecology* (the name of an academic subject), some writers are unwisely tempted into converting the second noun into an adjective to produce *landscape ecological principles.* Similarly, from *physical geography* (name of subject) emerge such phrases as *physical geographical studies.* In all such cases it is better to use an *of-* or *in-* construction: *studies in physical geography, research in environmental psychology, students of historical geography,* etc.

7 *Adjectives used as adverbs.* (*a*) In formal written work, adjectives are not often used as adverbs. But some adjectives are regularly used as adverbs informally, often in fixed expressions such as *come clean, hold tight, drive slow.* To these may be added *real* and *sure,* which in the UK are often taken to be tokens of informal North American speech (*That was* real *nice; I* sure *liked seeing you*).

(*b*) Some adjectives have corresponding adverbs that are identical, e.g. *fast, late, straight,* and the type *monthly, weekly,* etc. So you can say *He left in the late afternoon* or *He left late in the afternoon,* and this is acceptable in any kind of writing. Other examples in which the adverb and the adjective have the same form are: *clean, close, deep, fine, straight,* and *wide.*

Adverbs without *-ly* and those with *-ly* often occur in close proximity: *'I play straight, I choose wisely, Harry' he assured me*—John Le Carré, 1989.

8 *Adjectives as nouns.* For many centuries English adjectives have been put to service as nouns while remaining in use as adjectives. Thus (*a*), all of which can be used as count nouns:

	first recorded as adj.	*first recorded as noun*
ancient	1490	1541
classic	1613	1711
classified	1889	1961
daily	1470	1832 (newspaper)
explosive	1667	1874
intellectual	1398	1599

(*b*) adjectives preceded by *the* and used as uncount nouns to indicate 'that which is—' or 'those who are—':

beautiful	1526	the beautiful	1756
poor	1200	the poor	1230
sublime	1604	the sublime	1679
unemployed	1600	the unemployed	1782

But see DISABILITY, THE LANGUAGE OF, 1.

9 *Transferred epithets.* A curiosity of English is the way in which an adjective can be made to qualify a person or thing other than the noun it relates to grammatically. Examples: *'It's not your* stupid *place,' she says. 'It's anyone's place.'*—P. Lively, 1987 (the person addressed, not the place, is stupid); *I will be sitting quietly at the kitchen table stirring an* absent-minded *cup of coffee*—*Chicago Tribune,* 1989 (the person, not the coffee, is absent-minded). The traditional name for this phenomenon is 'transferred epithet' or 'hypallage'.

On other aspects of the behaviour of adjectives, see ABSOLUTE COMPARATIVE; ADVERB; DOUBLE COMPARISON; PARTS OF SPEECH. See also FUN and MAGIC, used as quasi-adjectives.

adjoining. See ADJACENT, ADJOINING.

adjudicator. Regularly spelt with final *-or.*

adjunct. This grammatical term is used in various ways by different grammarians. In this book it is used in accordance with the *OED* definition: 'A word or group of words amplifying or modifying the meaning of another word or group of words in a sentence', as also defined by David Crystal (1980): 'A term used in grammatical theory to refer to an optional or secondary element in a construction; an adjunct may be removed without the structural identity of the rest of the construction being affected'.

adjure. See ABJURE.

administer, administrate. **1** *administrate.* In the meaning 'manage and be responsible for the running of' something, inspires fear and loathing in editors or others alert to the intricacies of English usage. That consummate wordsmith Bill Bryson (1984) bans it *tout court*: 'administer not administrate'. Others doubt its very existence, or despise it as an upstart back-formation.

They need not fret that *administrate* will smother *administer*, which is dozens of times more frequent in *OEC* data. Nor is it a recent interloper, being first recorded in 1538, and deriving directly from Latin (*administer*, from French, was first recorded in 1385). Its detractors argue that it is long-winded, but it has the same number of syllables as, and only two letters more than, *administer*. For the charge of being unnecessary to stick, *administrate* must be proved to perform exactly like *administer* in the meaning concerned. Some meagre scraps of evidence suggest that it does not, e.g. *the machinery of such aid is still primed by administrators eager to go out and administrate—Times*, 1981; *a bureaucracy in disarray in which all the members, both administrators and administrated, are complicit—Senses of Cinema*, 2005.

Those examples aptly convey connotations of bureaucracy, of *administrate* being what administrators do, which *administer* could not. But when opportunities for such neat wordplay do not justify its use, the prosecution case strengthens, and *administrate* begins to look guilty of identity theft in e.g. *The lab is administrated and maintained by Schools of Library and Information Sciences and Visual Arts—OEC*, 2000, where *administer* works equally well. Even intransitively, meaning 'to do administrative work' (e.g. *Sometimes we get caught up in the business end of operating a studio, teaching and administrating, serving on committees and doing public relations—Dance Magazine*, 2000), *administrate* is unnecessary, as the next example proves: *Yeats ... propagandised, speechified, fundraised, administered, and politicked*—Seamus Heaney, 1978. The jury has returned a unanimous verdict of guilty.

2 *administer.* In medical contexts *administer to* is often used instead of *minister to* (an injured person, etc.). This has attracted criticism, but now looks pretty well established. It goes back to the 17c. and is presumably influenced by the transitive use in *administer morphine, antibiotics, medication*, etc. Examples: *American doctors, being vastly rich, have better things to do with their leisure time than administer to patients at weekends—Times*, 1994; *Padre Pro went about clandestinely, and in disguise, celebrating Mass, hearing confession and administering to the sick—Sunday Business Post*, 2001.

admission, admittance. Like many other word pairs, these two have competed for several centuries (*admission* being first recorded in 1494, *admittance* in 1589) without ever establishing totally independent territories. In the meaning corresponding to *admit* = 'to acknowledge or accept as true', *admission* is the word to use, not *admittance*. Where they get in each other's way is in meanings related to 'the action of admitting, letting in, to a place'.

Admission is the dominant word of the two: it alone has a countable use (*There are more admissions in the sciences this year*), and it is the only one to have developed attributive uses (*admission charge, fee, money, officer, policy, process, ticket*), and elliptical uses thereof (*Admission £1*). The tutor, secretary, etc., dealing with admissions to colleges and universities is called the *admissions tutor, secretary, officer*, etc. *Admission* is the usual word for the action of being received into an office or position (*he gained admission to the Society of Antiquaries*). *Admission* is also the word used for the admitting of a crime, guilt, etc., a confession.

Admittance hangs on determinedly, especially as the word used on notices on entrances (e.g. *No admittance except on official business*) but also as an unusual alternative in meanings where *admission* is required: *The DTI's lack of admittance of negligence in this affair is a travesty of justice—Times*, 1988.

admit. **1** *Admit* was once freely interchangeable in most senses with the phrasal verb *admit of*. Nowadays *admit of* is restricted to the meaning 'allow as possible, leave room for', e.g. *a hypothesis admits by its nature of being opposable; his truthfulness admits of no exceptions; it seems to admit of so many interpretations; the* *circumstances will not admit of delay*. Even in these senses, the construction seems old-fashioned.

2 Some critics object to the use of the phrase *admit to* (= confess to, acknowledge), e.g. *Senior Ministry of Defence officials yesterday admitted to a catalogue of errors in the development of a new light anti-tank weapon—Times*, 1989. There are no defensible grounds for this objection, which seems to have been first raised by Gowers (1965). The construction is unexceptionable, and widespread, particularly with a following *-ing* form, e.g. *After Columbine, it seemed strange that so few commentators admitted to remembering the rage of their youth—Art in America*, 2000.

ad nauseam. The correct spelling of this Latin phrase is with *-eam* at the end. Some people write it with *-eum*, perhaps influenced by the fact that the phrase *ad infinitum* ends in *-um*, or perhaps because the *-am* is often pronounced /-əm/ (-uhm). Whatever the reason, if you go to the trouble of using a Latin phrase in the first place, it is best to spell it correctly.

-ado. The older three-syllable and multisyllable English words ending in *-ado* are often assumed to be direct adoptions of Spanish or Portuguese words. Many of them are in fact either (*a*) affected refashionings of French words in *-ade* (thus *ambuscado*, found in Shakespeare and in many other writers, is a refashioning of *ambuscade*, from French *embuscade*); or (*b*) adaptations (*-ado* being 'felt' to be a Spanish or Portuguese ending) of *-ada* in the original language (e.g. *tornado* from Sp. *tronada* thunderstorm). A number of *-ado* words remain firmly in the language: (normally pronounced with /-ɑːdəʊ/: *aficionado, amontillado, avocado, bravado, desperado, incommunicado;* (with /-eɪdəʊ/) *bastinado, tornado*. Others are archaic or obsolete (if pronounced, they would normally have /-ɑːdəʊ/), e.g. *ambuscado, barricado, grenado, scalado. Mikado*, always with /-ɑːdəʊ/, is unconnected, being from Japanese (from *mi* 'august, honourable' + *kado* 'door').

adopted, adoptive. When parents adopt a child, the child, traditionally, is said to be *adopted*, and those taking the child into their family *adoptive*. Usage has partly eroded this useful distinction and the two words are now occasionally used interchangeably. In wider use, *adopted* is the word usually applied to a new area, country, town, etc. that a person has chosen to live in, but the *OED* and other dictionaries cite examples where *adoptive* is used instead (*adoptive country, home, his adoptive England*, etc.). The distinction between *adopted* and *adoptive* appears to be somewhat elastic.

adrift. This 17c. adverb (in origin a phrase = 'in a drifting condition') acquired a new range of senses in the language of late-20c. sports commentators, namely 'short or wide of (a target), behind (a competitor)': *For most of the game St Mary 's struggled and they were 10 points adrift midway through the second period—Sligo Weekender*, 2002. First recorded in this sporting sense from 1971, the metaphor has spread to more general contexts: *pay audits on progress towards equal pay, which is still 17% adrift for full-timers and 38% for part-timers—Guardian*, 2008.

adult. 1 Now usually pronounced /ˈadʌlt/ in RP and /əˈdʌlt/ in American English, but there is variation among speakers throughout the English-speaking world, and the American pronunciation is gaining ground in the UK. It is worth recalling that the *OED* (in 1884) and Daniel Jones (in 1917) gave priority to /əˈdʌlt/.

2 Since the late 1950s, changing social attitudes have caused the word *adult* to be used euphemistically in the sense 'sexually explicit', applied to certain categories of films, magazines, shows, etc.

adumbrate. This Latinate word (L *adumbrāre* 'to overshadow'; cf. L *umbra* 'shadow') first enriched the language in the 16c. In its meaning of 'to represent in outline' it is highly formal or learned, donning a legal wig in contexts such as *If the Court pleases, we in general adopt the propositions adumbrated by our learned friend—High Court of Australia*, transcripts, 2004, but even there sounds faintly ridiculous. Elsewhere it puts on academicals: e.g. *an emergent issue, perhaps most clearly adumbrated towards the end of the book—Aust. Jrnl of Anthropology*, 2001. When not attired in either of those ways, it is best left to its antique slumbers.

advance. 1 *advance, advanced. Advance* is one of a class of nouns that has been used so frequently as a modifier before another noun (*advance copy, guard, information, notice, payment,* etc.) that it has effectively become an adjective, and this quasi-adjectival use is recorded in the *OED* from 1842 onwards: e.g. *The shrill unearthly shriek of the engineer's whistle thrilled in our ears, as the advance warning of our coming*—*American Agriculturist,* 1842; *Good advance publicity means sales*—D. L. Sayers, 1932.

For the most part it steers clear of *advanced,* which means 'far on in development': e.g. *advanced technology, an advanced degree, at his advanced age.* The two words are sometimes confused, however, as I discovered on spotting a sign informing road users about impending roadworks and entitled **advanced notice,* even though the simple metal panel looked anything but technologically sophisticated. Although **advanced notice* seems to be the most common collision of the two words, confusion also occasionally travels in the other direction, with e.g. **advance cell technology* for *advanced cell technology.*

2 *advance, advancement. Advance* is much the commoner word of the two: e.g. *a new advance on the capital city* (approach to), *the advance of knowledge* (progress), *an advance of £10* (paid before the due time), *the advance of old age* (onset), *seats booked in advance* (before the game or performance), and so on. *Advancement* is far from extinct: e.g. *1985/6 was another year of great advancement for Glaxo Inc.* (progress); *the structure of the department allows for speedy advancement* (promotion); *the advancement of the main aims of the EC* (furtherance). But there are not many contexts in which *advancement* can be used in the general sense of progress, except in *of*-phrases of a type that call to mind Francis Bacon's title *The Advancement of Learning* (1605). *The advance of new ideas* means their increasing effect, whereas *the advancement of new ideas* means the process of encouraging and supporting them.

adventurous, adventuresome, venturesome, venturous illustrate how rich in synonyms English is, historically, but how some fall by the wayside, or retreat into genteel retirement, only rarely appearing in public these days. First recorded in *c.*1374, 1731, 1661, and 1565 respectively, they are listed as headwords here in order of rapidly decreasing frequency, *adventurous* being nearly 30 times more frequent than its closest rival *adventuresome.* The other two are occasionally used in, as Burchfield put it, 'a somewhat self-conscious manner': *For the venturesome investor, Europe may be, eventually, a better growth opportunity than the U.S.*—*Business Economics,* 2002 (AmE); *The very venturous Huxley who was said to have become a Muslim in order to divorce her husband quickly*—J. Huxley, 1986.

adverb.

1 General.
2 Sentence adverbs.
3 Formation of adverbs.
4 Adverbial uses of nouns of time, e.g. *nights, Tuesdays.*
5 Position of adverbs.
6 Same spelling as adjectives.
7 The type *to* + adverb + infinitive.

1 *General.* The term *adverb* covers a wide variety of words, and is the least satisfactory of the conventional word categories applied to English. The principal adverb uses answer the question 'how?' or 'in what manner?', many of these being formed by the addition of the suffix *-ly* to adjectives (e.g. *carefully, quickly, steadily, well*); 'when?' or 'how often?' (e.g. *soon, regularly, yesterday*); 'where?' (e.g. *downstairs, here, outside*); and 'to what extent?' (e.g. *extremely, hardly, somewhat*). For a more detailed analysis of types of adverb, and for further terminology, the reader is referred to a standard grammar such as Greenbaum's *Oxford English Grammar* (1996), 141–52.

2 *Sentence adverbs.* See HOPEFULLY; SENTENCE ADVERB.

3 *Formation of adverbs.* Large numbers of adverbs and adverbial phrases are formed by adding *-ly* to adjectives, as in *regularly, steadily,* and *quickly.* Other adverbs are identical with adjectives (*fast, well*), and members of a third type are formed by adding other elements such as *-ward(s), -ways* and *-wise* to nouns, as in *homewards, edgeways,* and *clockwise* (some of these are also adjectives). In the 20c. the range of adverbs ending in *-wise* increased enormously, with many new ad hoc (and often criticized) formations, e.g. *foodwise* (1923). See -WISE, -WAYS.

4 *Adverbial use of nouns of time.* Some adverbs of time end in *-s,* e.g. *always, nowadays.* Days of the week and other time words can also be used in a similar way, but usage varies across the English-speaking world. While days of the week can be used in this way in British English, e.g. *I'm free Mondays and Saturdays*, the following uses are not typical of it: *nights* (= at night, each night), in origin an adverbial genitive found already in *Beowulf*: *I lay awake* nights *for a week sweating about this four hundred and fifty dollars—New Yorker*, 1987; *We nip off to her place* afternoons—R. Hall, 1978 (NZ); Tuesday night, *the board approved the addition of a new subsection—Chicago Tribune*, 1987; *I was to be offered an option of taking her to live with me* summers—S. Bellow, 1987; *Noriega ... said* Monday *the U.S. Southern Command in Panama ... threatens the Central American nation—USA Today*, 1988. None of these examples, all taken from NZ and US sources, would be the norm in the UK. The same notions would be expressed in a different manner, e.g. *at night, in the afternoons, on Tuesdays and Thursdays, On Tuesday night, on Monday, every summer.*

5 *Position of adverbs.* Adverbs that modify single words such as adjectives, nouns, and other adverbs generally precede them as closely as possible (*often late; very large; quite a while; too modestly*). The placement of adverbs in clauses and sentences follows standard rules: e.g. (*a*) (between auxiliaries) *a car dealer who could* certainly *have afforded to hire somebody;* (*b*) (between an auxiliary and a main verb) *Roosevelt's financial policy was* roundly *criticized in 1933; he had* inadvertently *joined a lonely-hearts club;* (*c*) (adverb does not separate a verb from its object) *he* dutifully *observes all its quaint rules; They aim to set each subject* briefly *into context; Did he hear her* correctly?; *This alarmed me* greatly.

But there are many reasons for altering the position of the adverb (change of meaning, emphasis, rhythm, etc.): e.g. *there is little chance that the student will function* effectively *after he returns to China* (i.e. *effectively* is not between the auxiliary and the main verb).

6 *Same spelling as an adjective.* See ADJECTIVE 7.

7 For the type *to* + adverb + infinitive, see SPLIT INFINITIVE.

adversary. Stress on the first syllable.

adverse, averse. The use of the phrase **adverse to* for *averse to* is quite common, and should be avoided, e.g. **he is not adverse to an occasional cigar* (read *averse to*). *Adverse* is used to mean: 'unfavourable' (an *adverse balance of trade, adverse circumstances, adverse weather conditions*); 'hostile' (*adverse criticism, an adverse reaction*); 'harmful' (*the adverse effects of drugs*). *Averse to* means 'disliking or opposing something', and is often used with a negative word, e.g. *as a former CIA director, he is not averse to secrecy.* While it is true that *adverse to* was once used to mean the same thing (*the whole Parliamentary tradition as built up in this country ... is adverse to it*—Winston Churchill, 1942), it would nowadays be considered a mistake.

advert. An abbreviation of *advertisement* first recorded in 1814 and in continuous use since the second half of the 19c., though it has never been common in American English, While some dictionaries still label it 'informal', it would to my mind be truer to say that both it and *ad* are the standard forms in speech, while *advertisement* is slightly formal. In British English, at any rate, it is nearly twice as common in the *OEC* data as the full form.

advertise. So spelt, not *-ize*. See -ISE 1.

advertisement. Always pronounced in RP with the main stress on the second syllable, but, as Walter Nash noted in *English Usage* (1986), the stress is placed on the third syllable in many regional varieties of English.

advertising, language of. All linguistic means of persuasion are exploited to the limit by advertising copywriters, who, ideally, are the poets of marketing. The linguistic strategies involved are too numerous and complex to be discussed in full here, so a summary is offered instead. In a study of the use of language to influence and persuade people, the American scholar Dwight Bolinger (*Language, the Loaded Weapon*, 1980) describes several techniques which advertisers share with other persuaders in manipulating language to their own ends. These may be summarized as (*a*) literalism, in which an assertion is made that is literally true but will normally be understood in special ways that the advertiser intends (e.g. *Dentists recommend Colgate* suggests that all dentists recommend it, whereas only two need be found to justify the statement made), (*b*) euphemism, in which less favourable aspects are made to sound more appealing (e.g. something that is average may be described as *standard* and a small quantity of a product may be described as *handy version* or *fun size*), and uninteresting concepts are made to sound more interesting (e.g. *crafted* instead of *made, ultra-pure* instead of *clean* or *fresh, executive* instead of *more expensive*), (*c*) use of jaunty vocabulary and slogans (e.g. *Drinka pinta milka day; The future's bright, the future's Orange; Vorsprung durch Technik; Because you're worth it*), and (*d*) the use of special syntax to associate the customer with a product (e.g. *Aren't you glad you use Dial?* and *Put a tiger in your tank*) both of which make an assumption to flatter and reassure the customer. See also EUPHEMISM; SLOGAN.

advise, advice. 1 The verb *advise* can never be spelt *-ize*. See -ISE 1.

2 It should not be necessary to say that *advise* is a verb meaning 'to offer advice (to), to recommend' (*he advises the Japanese about nutritional matters; they advised her not to pursue the matter further*), and that *advice* is a noun meaning principally 'an opinion given or offered as to future action' (*to take advice from an accountant; an advice note*), but the two spellings are often confused.

3 Both words are used in a special way, particularly in business and commercial writing. (*a*) The verb means 'to inform' (*please advise us when the goods have been dispatched*). Some people regard using it in this way as a heinous example of commercialese; it can certainly come across as rather starchy and formal, especially in the phrase *please be advised that* and often could easily be replaced by 'tell' or 'let know'. However, when it conveys the idea of informing officially, it seems more apt. (*b*) The noun means 'a formal notice of transaction' (*the firm sent advice that the goods had been dispatched*).

advisedly. Pronounced as four syllables. See -EDLY.

adviser, advisor. Both forms occur throughout the English-speaking world and the *-or* form is recognized as a variant by many dictionaries. Despite impressions that the *-er* form is predominantly British and *-or* American, in the *OEC* data *adviser* is nearly three times as common across all varieties of English, and so the traditional spelling still predominates, but particularly in Britain. Examples: (adviser) *An adviser to Charles V, Fosca seeks to advise the world*—L. Appignanesi, 1988; *the Service would never forgive me a mucky divorce, dear—not its legal adviser, it couldn't*—J. le Carré, 1989; (advisor) *The goose . . . shuffled off to see if she could find some advisors*—J. Winterson, 1985; *He was working as an advisor on governmental agricultural schemes*—L. Ingalls, 1986 (US).

-ae, -as, as plurals of nouns in *-a*. Most English nouns in *-a* are from Latin (or Latinized Greek) nominative feminine singular nouns, which have in Latin the plural ending *-ae*. But some have a different Latin origin: *subpoena* is not nominative; *comma* and *drama* are neuter; *addenda, data*, and *stamina* are plural. With all such words a plural form in *-ae* is impossible, though sometimes found, e.g. the incorrect **subpoenae*. Other words ending in *-a* are not from Latin at all, e.g. *indaba* is from Zulu, *sofa* from Arabic, and *swastika* from Sanskrit.

Of those words able to form genuinely Latinate plurals in *-ae*, some retain it in all uses (*algae, larvae*); some alternate with *-as* (usually *antennae* in British English, but *antennas* = aerials; *formulas* in general work, *formulae* in scientific; *lacunae* or *lacunas; nebulae* or *nebulas*); and some always have *-as* (*areas, ideas, villas*). See also LATIN PLURALS.

æ, œ. 1 Joined together as shown, æ and œ are called ligatures. Although printed until the 19c., and occasionally beyond, in Latin and Greek words such as *Aeneid, Aeschylus, Caesar, Oedipus*, and in English words derived from Latin and Greek such as *formulae, phoenix*, they are now used only when a source with them has to be reproduced exactly, and in the following cases: (*a*) in Old English words (*Ælfric, Cædmon*); (*b*) in Danish, Icelandic, and Norwegian words; and (*c*) in the relevant vowels of the IPA system.

2 *Spelling.* Since the late 19c. there has been a marked drift away from *ae* and *oe* to simple *e* in words derived from Greek and Latin. The movement has been relatively slow in British English: *oecology* and *oeconomy* have become *ecology* and *economy*, and *mediaeval* is now mostly printed as *medieval;* but *oe* is retained in e.g. *Oedipus* (or *Œdipus*), *oesophagus,* and the 20c. word *oestrogen.* In American English the substitution has proceeded apace, resulting in the dominance of e.g. *esophagus* and *estrogen* (but *Oedipus*). Further differences between British English and American English spelling are commented on in the relevant entries throughout the book, e.g. *aegis, aeon, diarrhoea,* etc.

See also FETID; FOETUS.

aegis. Is by far the preferred spelling throughout the English-speaking world. The variant **egis**, recognized in US dictionaries, is almost never used in the *OEC* data. A Google search for 'under the aegis of' suggests *aegis* is hundreds of times more frequent.

aeon. This spelling is preferred to **eon** in British English, but not by a huge margin. Elsewhere in the English-speaking world *eon* is preferred, especially in scientific writing, and when denoting a major period of geological time, e.g. *the late Precambrian eon.* For more on *aeon,* see TIME.

aerie, aery (nest of bird of prey). Use EYRIE.

aesthete, aesthetic. Normally pronounced /ˈiːsθiːt/ and /iːsˈθɛtɪk/ (**ees**-theet and ees-**thet**-ik) in RP, and spelt with initial *ae-* even in US English, but pronounced with the first syllable as /ɛs-/. The recognized US variants **esthete**, **esthetic** are rarely used in practice, according to the *OEC* data. See Æ, Œ. See also ASCETIC.

aet., aetat. (with full points). Abbreviations of Latin *aetatis* 'of or at the age of', are very rarely used in English now, but are often encountered on portraits, Latin inscriptions on gravestones, and older printed matter. They should be printed in roman.

affect, effect **1** These two words are often confused. To avoid this most widespread of mistakes, it may help to remember that *effect* is most common as a noun meaning 'a result or consequence', and therefore, if your sentence requires a noun it probably requires *effect*: *In England, at any rate, education produces no effect whatsoever*—Oscar Wilde. Memorizing this ironic sentence, with all its letter *e*s, may also help.

Effect is also the correct choice in such phrases as *to take effect, to good effect, personal effects* and *sound effects.*

Affect is most common as a verb meaning 'to make a difference to': *Bodily exercise indirectly affects all the organs of the body; These measures chiefly affect* [i.e. are directed at] *drug-pushers; It will not affect* [i.e. have a bearing on] *his chances of promotion.*

2 As a noun, *affect* survives only as a technical term in psychology, meaning 'an emotion or a desire, especially as influencing behaviour', e.g. *By triggering affect and emotion, intolerant behaviors are set in motion.* Unlike the verb, it is stressed on the first syllable, /ˈafɛkt/.

3 *Affect* in the sense 'assume (a character), pretend to have or feel or do something' (*As he reached the pick-up point, he should affect to slow down as if hunting for a car*—J. le Carré, 1989) is a quite separate verb of different origin.

4 As a verb, *effect* means 'to bring about, to cause, to have as a result', as in *to effect changes, to effect a cure, to effect a rescue.* Examples: *A single glass of brandy may effect* (i.e. bring about) *his recovery; The prisoner effected* (i.e. made good) *his escape; Britain acting alone does not possess the power or legitimacy to directly effect change on the scale required*—*Daily Tel.*, 2007.

5 Examples of mistaken uses: *the judge postponed sentence because he was angered by the victim's injuries and did not want emotion to* effect *his decision*—*Times,* 1989 (read *affect*); *the affect of Aids on a South African township community*—*BBC,* press release, 2004 (read *effect*).

affinity. The only issue that this word supposedly raises is this: is it correct to use it to mean 'a natural liking for and understanding of someone or something', followed by the preposition *for* (e.g. *Shevek felt a kind of affinity for the man*—U. Le Guin, 1974)? According to Fowler (1926), and some later commentators, it has to imply a two-way relationship between people or things, whereas in the example above the relationship is clearly one-way. Dictionaries, sensibly, give little credence to this egregious example of the etymological fallacy.

The appropriate preposition to follow *affinity* will select itself automatically according to the meaning being conveyed and the syntax of the sentence. When the word implies similarity between people or things, or a sympathy based on common interests, it can be followed by *between, with,* or *to*: *the affinity between Britain and most of her former colonies; Beckett . . . stresses that he wrote the little book on order, not out of any deep affinity with Proust*—M. Esslin, 1980; (as Mr Darcy notes) *Whatever bears affinity to cunning is despicable—Pride and Prejudice,* Jane Austen. If the meaning to be activated is 'a liking or fondness for someone or something', or an 'aptitude or talent for something', *for* is the natural choice, as it also is when *affinity* means that one foodstuff goes well with another, and in science. Examples: *The conductor's unexpected affinity for English music is demonstrated by* Cockaigne—*OEC,* 2003; *Even if you're not a fan of grapefruit solo, you'll love the recipe below, which takes advantage of its natural affinity for avocados and shellfish—Shape Magazine,* 2004; *Newcastle disease virus has an affinity for red blood cells, allowing it to spread throughout the host's body—OEC,* 2002.

affirmative. From its use in US signalling and radio communication, where, for the sake of clarity, it is used instead of 'yes', *affirmative* has made a cautious entrance in ordinary prose. Thus (military) *'Roger, you say a boat full of bad guys and machine guns. Is this for real? Over.' 'That's affirmative, son.'*—T. Clancy, 1987; and (non-military) *'You awake over there?' Affirmative.'*—T. O'Brien, 1976. Cf. NEGATIVE.

affirmative action. This term originated in the US in the 19c., when it meant action taken by government to affirm a particular policy. In the 1930s, again in the US, it developed its current meaning of active measures taken by employers, colleges, etc., to improve opportunities for members of minority groups, women, etc. Though still used more in the US than elsewhere, the term is not confined to there: e.g. *Entebra takes a positive view of Sarkozy for advocating affirmative action to help immigrant youths find work—Sunday Times,* 2005. In Britain the term 'positive discrimination' is more widely used and more generally understood by the public.

affix. A grammatical term that includes prefixes like *post-* in *postscript,* suffixes like *-ward* in *windward,* and the italicized elements in *un*-touch-*able*. The term is also used for infixes like Eliza Doolittle's abso-*blooming*-lutely.

afflict. See INFLICT.

aficionado. This word, borrowed from Spanish (= supporter, enthusiast), has the plural *aficionados,* not *-oes,* and is spelt with only one letter *f,* not two. It can be pronounced /əˌfɪsjəˈnɑːdəʊ/ or /əˌfɪʃjəˈnɑːdəʊ/ (uh-fis-yuh-**nah**-doh, uh-fish-yuh-**nah**-doh), but not /əˌfɪksjəˈnɑːdəʊ/ (uh-fix-yuh-**nah**-doh). The final *-o* of *aficionado* shows that it is masculine in Spanish; feminine *aficionada* can be used in English to refer to a woman.

afore-. A combining form used in words such as *aforementioned, aforesaid, aforenamed* and the fixed expression *malice aforethought.* No hyphen is needed. Such words have their natural home in legal documents and contracts, but also thrive in other habitats, such as discussions of the arts, e.g. *Both of the aforementioned critics singled out the two paintings—The Art Bulletin,* 2003. The use of *aforesaid* was derided by Fowler as 'pedantic humour', but it serves the useful purpose of expressing in one word what would otherwise take two or more.

a fortiori. Literally 'from yet firmer (argument)', i.e. with yet stronger reason, more conclusively, a term used first in logic and then generally, introducing a fact that, if another fact already accepted is true, must also and still more obviously be true (*It could not have been finished in a week;* a fortiori *not in a day*). Pronounced /eɪ fɔːtɪˈɔːrʌɪ/ (ay for-ti-**aw**-ry).

African American (both without and with a hyphen) as a noun and adjective is currently the most neutral term in the US to refer to Americans of African origin, though *black* (or *Black*) is also still widely used. *African American* has eclipsed **Afro-American**, which was first recorded in the 19c. and became widespread in the 1960s and 1970s, but is now mostly used in anthropological and cultural contexts.

African American Vernacular English. Is the most recent technical term to describe the variety of English used by many African Americans, briefly discussed here under BLACK ENGLISH.

aftermath. The original meaning of this agricultural word is 'a second or later mowing; the crop of grass which springs up after the first mowing in early summer'. It developed its figurative meaning in the 17c., to denote 'something unpleasant or unwelcome in itself, or something that follows on an unpleasant or unwelcome event (such as war or disease)'. *Depression is sometimes an immediate aftermath of completing a piece of work*—A. Storr, 1979; *In total, nine ambulances, four paramedics, a rapid response car and a rapid response doctor were needed to deal with the aftermath of the violence—Birmingham Post*, 2007. The phrase 'in the aftermath of' is a useful staple of news reporting (e.g. *in the aftermath of Hurricane Sandy*), to the extent that it tends to be overused: it fits somewhat awkwardly in contexts where the event preceding the aftermath can hardly be considered unpleasant or unwelcome, e.g. *?an odd mix of visuals Kahlua aimed at audiences in the United States in the aftermath of the brand's celebrity-driven launch—Art Bulletin*, 2000.

afterward, afterwards. The *OEC* data suggest that *afterwards* is the more commonly used form all over the Anglosphere, with the sole exception of the US. Even there it is still slightly more frequent than the form *afterward*, despite the fact that American dictionaries give preference to the latter.

age. **1** *It all started when he got diphtheria, at age eighteen—New Yorker*, 1991. The preferred British English equivalent of American *at age eighteen* is *at the age of eighteen.*

2 For near synonyms of *age*, see TIME.

aged. *Aged 66, the house had aged well*, etc., pronounced /eɪdʒd/, as one syllable; *an aged man*, etc., pronounced /ˈeɪdʒɪd/, as two syllables.

ageing, aging. The great Atlantic divide between North American and British English spelling here manifests itself unexpectedly. US dictionaries give preference to *aging*, with *ageing* as an alternative; British dictionaries do the reverse. The *OEC* data shows that in the US and Canada *aging* is massively more frequent, although *ageing* is very occasionally used. In Britain the opposite is true, and elsewhere the forms compete on more equal terms, *ageing* being the commoner of the two.

ageism, agism. The first appearance in the *OED* of *ageism*, meaning 'prejudice or discrimination on the grounds of a person's age', and of its related adjective **ageist**, dates from 1969. According to the *OEC* data, *ageism* is more common, but not hugely so, than its near synonym *age discrimination*. Spelling both words with *-gei-* is preferable to the spellings *agism* and *agist*: at first glance the latter could make it look as if *ag-* sounds as it does in *aggro*, and, presumably for that reason, are rather rare.

agenda. **1** This word comes from a Latin plural (= things to be done). It is nowadays always treated as singular, its plural being *agendas*. (The pseudo-Latin plural *agendae* is occasionally encountered, but it is wrong.) The singular form *agendum* is extremely rare and technically means a single agenda item, e.g. *I have never given the subject much investigation, but have left it as an agendum for some more convenient season*—M. F. Maury, 1849. Its use as a synonym of *agenda* has historical precedents but is unadvisable: presumably, it is based on the mistaken notion that because *agenda* is plural, a singular needs to be formed. Whatever the reasoning, it sounds exceptionally precious: e.g. *It's a dependable schedule; a new* Sonic Youth *album every two or three years, with a new agendum and nuances, but the same dynamics that they've had from the start—Stylus*, 2004.

2 In the 20c. *agenda* also developed the metaphorical meanings 'a plan of things to be done or problems to be addressed' and 'the underlying intentions or motives of a particular person or group', e.g *But for others, social and religious issues will dominate the agenda—Sunday Business Post*, 2004; *Sex was the hidden agenda at these discussions*—M. Atwood, 1987.

These uses of the word in certain collocations, such as *to set/dominate/follow the ... agenda, at the top of the agenda*, etc., are so overused as to have become rather clichéd, in the sense, as Orwell wrote, that 'They will construct your sentences for you—even think your thoughts for you'. For example, in *if shopping is on your agenda, visit the market in Estoi*, what does *if shopping is on your agenda* mean other than 'if you plan to go shopping'?

aggravate. A half a century ago, schoolmasters were insisting—perhaps some still do insist—that *aggravate* could properly be used only to mean 'to increase the seriousness of' (crime, grief, illness, misery, terror, etc.), a use first recorded in the late 16c. The meaning 'to annoy, exasperate' has existed since good Queen Bess's day, but it is an article of faith with some people that it 'should be left to the uneducated', as Fowler loftily put it in 1926. Because the criticized meaning is at least 400 years old, and because it is unlikely to be confused with the other meaning, there is no principled reason to avoid it, or the related adjective **aggravating**. The worst that can be said of either word is that, on the one hand, they may have a slightly informal, even dated, tang, and on the other, that they fail to capture the subtle gradations of peevishness expressed by synonyms like *annoy, irritate, exasperate, madden, infuriate*, and so forth. Choose from those if you wish to avoid the tut-tutting of unreconstructed pedants. Examples (meaning 'irritate') *Don't aggravate yourself. I'll be no trouble*—A. Lurie, 1965; *Do not aggravate them, be quiet, smile nicely*—P. Carey, 1982; *It was aggravating that he had to do so many little jobs himself*—M. Wesley, 1983; *Jane Fairfax aggravates her in all sorts of ways*—T. Tanner, 1986.

aggressor, not *aggresser*.

agism, agist. *See* AGEISM, AGISM.

agitator, not *agitater*.

ago. Strictly speaking, using *since* and *ago* next to each other as in *?It is 10 years ago since he died* says the same thing twice. If *ago* is used, many critics believe it is preferable to follow it with *that*, not *since*, i.e. *It is 10 years ago that he died.* Though first criticized as long ago as 1770, using the two words together seems, frankly, the most venial of faults, and in any case the *OEC* data suggests that for the most part people write . . . *ago that* . . . , and not . . . *ago since* . . .

agreement (in grammar).

1 Definition.
2 Problems with long subjects.
3 Nouns joined by *and*.
4 Noun subjects separated by *along with, as well as*, etc.
5 Collective nouns.
6 Indefinite pronouns.
7 Subject-complement agreement.
8 *one of those (. . .) who.*

1 *Definition.* Grammatical agreement (also called *concord*) is the correct relation to each other of different parts of a clause or sentence. In English it particularly concerns how the form of the verb agrees with its subject, e.g. *The house* was *small, and its walls* were *painted white*, rather than *were* and *was*.

2 *Problems with long subjects.* (*a*) Lengthy sentences in which the verb is separated from its singular subject by intervening words in the plural can cause the speaker or writer to put the verb in the plural, but this contravenes strict grammatical agreement: *The consequence of long periods of inactivity or situations in which patients cannot look after themselves* *are *often quite severe and long-lasting.* Here there are three options: change *consequence* to *consequences*, change *are* to *is*, or (probably best) recast the sentence more simply, e.g. *Long periods of inactivity . . . can often have quite severe and long-lasting consequences.*

(*b*) The phenomenon illustrated above is known as 'attraction' or 'proximity': it causes the verb to agree with a closely preceding noun or noun phrase rather than with the noun or noun phrase that is the true subject of the sentence. It also occurs with subjects which are not as lengthy as in the example in (*a*), and older literature abounds with examples: *The* outside *of her garments* were *of lawn* (Marlowe).

In all the following modern examples 'attraction' has occurred, and the verb should be singular: *Copyright *of Vivienne's papers* are *in the keeping of the Haigh-Wood family* (*Literary Review*, 1985); *the spread *of nuclear weapons and technology* are *likely to make the true picture very different* (*Dædalus*, 1991); **At least* one *in two churches* are *likely to be burgled next year* (*Times*, 1992).

3 *Nouns joined by 'and'.* (*a*) Two nouns joined by *and* normally form a plural subject and require a plural verb: Speed and accuracy do *not go hand in hand;* Fish and chips are *served in the evening.* But when the noun phrase is regarded as a single unit it can be followed by a singular verb: Tarring and feathering was *too good for Meakin as far as I was concerned;* Fish and chips is *my favourite meal.*

(*b*) This can extend to concepts that are distinct in themselves but are regarded as a single item in a particular sentence: *A certain* cynicism and resignation comes *along with the poverty of Italian comedy; the* usefulness and credibility *of such an arms control agreement* hinges *on* ... (Such constructions existed in Old and Middle English: examples are listed in Mitchell 1985 and Visser 1963.)

(*c*) Naturally, there are borderline cases in which both singular and plural concord is possible, and judgements will differ: The hurt and disbelief *of patients' friends and families* is/are *already quite real* (are *hurt and disbelief* 'a single unit'?); The extent and severity *of drug use in the United States* has/have *been a shock* ('*has*' is influenced by the singular complement '*shock*').

4 *Noun subjects separated by 'as well as, together with'* etc. Nouns separated by other linking words (e.g . *accompanied by, along with, as well as, not to mention, together with,* etc.) are followed by a singular verb if the first noun or noun phrase is singular. (The use of commas to separate these phrases from the grammatical subject indicates clearly that they do not form part of it.) Examples: *A very profitable* company *such as British Telecom,* along with *many other companies in the UK,* is *not prepared to pay a reasonable amount; Daddy had on the hairy tweed* jacket *with leather elbow patches* which, together with *his pipe,* was *his trade mark.* So too when the linking words are *or* or *nor: Every glance* or *smile* is *potent with meaning; Every run-out* or *lbw* is *similarly analysed; neither our mourning* nor *our rejoicing* is *as the world's is* (T. S. Eliot, 1935).

5 *Collective nouns.* (*a*) Collective nouns are words such as *BBC, committee, government, group,* which are singular in form but denote a group of people, animals, or objects. 'Notional agreement' affects this group and those dealt with in 6 and 7. 'Notional agreement' occurs when the verb agrees with the idea of plurality implicit in the grammatical subject, rather than with its grammatically singular form.

(*b*) Accordingly, in British English, collective nouns are followed by a singular verb when they are thought of as a single unit, and by a plural verb when they are considered as a collection of individuals: (singular) A group *of four young men, in denim overalls,* was *standing close to him; the* Oxford University Press publishes *many scholarly monographs each year;* (plural) *The* jury *retired at five minutes* past *five o'clock to consider* their *verdict; Let us hope that the* Ministry of Defence *are on our side this time.*

(*c*) In American English it is standard practice to use a singular verb with collective nouns: the government *routinely imposes differential taxes on hotels, bars ... and the like* (*Bull. Amer. Acad. Arts & Sci.,* 1987); *the* KGB uses *blackmail and intimidation* (*Chr. Sci. Monitor,* 1987).

(*d*) In noun phrases of the type 'a + *noun + of + plural noun', e.g. a group/band/ majority of consumers,* where the first singular noun acts as a sort of quantifier, the choice of singular or plural verb depends on whether the first, singular noun or the second, plural noun is regarded as the head of the phrase. Both options are used, and reflect the contrast between thinking of the set as a whole or its members individually, but the plural is very common: a fleet *of helicopters* was *flying low* (*New Yorker,* 1986); *a* handful *of bathers* were *bobbing about in the waves* (P. Roth, 1987); *you think of the States as a country where the* majority *of all the shareholdings* are *in the hands of women (Dædalus,* 1987); *a rich and detailed picture of a world in which a* multitude *of elements* were *intertwined* (*NY. Rev. Bks,* 1989).

6 *Indefinite pronouns.* In many constructions, these (*each, either, every, everybody, neither, nobody, none, no one,* etc.) govern a singular verb, but sometimes contextual considerations lead to the use of a plural verb: (singular) Neither *of these figures* illuminates *the case against Trident* (D. Steel, 1985); none *of her features* is *particularly striking* (D. Lodge, 1962); (plural) Neither *the Government* nor *the tribunal, surely,* want *to bear responsibility for* ... (*Daily Tel.,* 1987); None *of our fundamental problems* have *been solved* (*London Rev. Bks,* 1987).

Sometimes there is a clash of agreement within a given sentence: Everyone *was in* their *shirt-sleeves* (F. Tuohy, 1984); No one *in* their *senses* wants *to create instability* (D. Healey, 1985); *I really resent it when I call* somebody *who*'s *not home and* they *don't have an answering machine* (*Chicago Tribune,* 1988).

Constructions in which an indefinite pronoun is followed by a plural pronoun often result from the desire to avoid using 'his', because sexist, or 'his or her', because cumbersome: *Why would* anyone *plan* their *own funeral?; We don't want* anyone *to hurt* themselves; *It must have been* someone *who wanted to clear* their *conscience;* Nobody *wants to return to the car park and find that* their *car has been clamped.*

7 *Subject-complement agreement.* (*a*) When a subject and a complement of different number are separated by the verb *to be* (or verbs such as *seem, become,* etc.), the verb should agree with the number of the subject: (singular) *the only traffic* is *oxcarts and bicycles; The problem* is *the windows; The result* was *these awkward declarations; The view it obscured* was *pipes, fire escapes, a sooty-walled well; Our main problem* is *the older pesticides;* (plural) *These socials* were *a big deal to her; The house and garden* were a *powerful cauldron of heat and light; the March events in Poland* were *a natural stage in the evolution of communism.*

(*b*) In certain limited circumstances the verb correctly agrees with the complement: *Forty droschen* is *the price; More nurses* is *the next item on the agenda* (i.e. the subject of more nurses). But in the following example *is* would have been better than *are: ?Another legacy are injuries which could keep both* [players] *out of the big match.* Cf. BE 1.

8 *one of those (...) who.* With this phrase, and similar phrases such as *one of the things that,* the choice between singular and plural verb depends on whether the emphasis is on 'one' or on the plural noun or pronoun: (plural) *Lily had been* ... one of those *numerous people who* are *simply famous for being famous* (I. Murdoch, 1987); *That's* one of those *propositions that* become *harder to sustain the further they're explored* (K. Amis, 1988); *That's one of the* things *that* happen *to you—OEC,* 2005; (singular) *Perhaps you were* one of those *fellows who* sees *tricks everywhere* (P. Carey, 1985); *I am* one of those *people who* wants *others to do what I think they should* (J. Bakewell, 1988); *Yes,* one *of the things that* makes *the Lethal Weapon series special is the humor—DVD Verdict,* 2000. See also ONE 3.

See also COLLECTIVE NOUN; EITHER 4; NEITHER 4; THERE IS; WHEREABOUTS; and the entries for many personal and indefinite pronouns.

agriculturalist, agriculturist. Only ten years separate the birth of these 18c. word cousins denoting someone engaged in agriculture, *agriculturist* first having seen the light of day in 1778. Both are correct, but there is a US preference for the shorter form.

ahead of. This prepositional phrase has been used since the 18c. in the physical sense 'in front of' and from the 19c. in the figurative sense 'better than, superior to (in quality, performance, etc.)'. Its meaning in relation to time dates from the beginning of the 20c., with a use by George Bernard Shaw in *The Devil's Disciple,* III.78: *We are some minutes ahead of you already.* Shaw is also credited with an early use (in 1934) of the cliché *ahead of its* (or *one's*) *time,* in *On the Rocks* I.219: *Women and men who are ahead of their time. They alone can lead the present into the future. They are ghosts from the future.*

Since the 1980s, *ahead of,* with reference to time, has come to mean 'before', often, but not always, with the idea of 'in preparation for' or 'taking account of': *Some ISPs such as Wanadoo are investing in LLU but decline to reveal any significant detail because they don't want to give the game away ahead of a commercial launch—The Register,* 2005; *Discontent is growing ahead of next month's mid-term elections—Independent,* 2010. This use, which originated in American English, is rapidly becoming an irritating tic of newspaper or TV journalists. Their lexical wardrobes seem empty of sensible alternatives, from the straightforward *before* to the more meaningful *in preparation for, in advance of,* and so forth. Outside the media bubble the phrase can sound awkward and clichéd.

ahold. Apart from an isolated use in Shakespeare's *The Tempest* (1610), not recorded as an adverb before 1872; now used colloquially (alternating with **aholt**), especially in AmE, with verbs like *catch, get, lay, take.* (*A kid gets ahold of it* [*sc.* a firearm], *you have an immediate situation*—D. DeLillo, 1985; *'Come on, grab ahold,' he said, slapping hard on the side of the pumpkin—New Yorker,* 1988). But the more usual idioms are *to catch, get,* etc., *hold* (of something), with no *a-* prefixed.

-aholic. A suffix abstracted from *alcoholic* and used to form nouns and adjectives suggesting that a person is addicted to the object, activity, etc. given in the first element. First recorded in 1954, this suffix and its variants *-oholic* and *-holic* have proved to be a useful and productive word element, often reflecting contemporary social preoccupations. It is most common in *workaholic* (1968), *chocoholic* (1961), *spendaholic,* and the often newsworthy *sexaholic,* but also in such less common formations as *blogaholic, milkaholic,* and *rageaholic.* The suffix appears as *-holic* in words of two syllables ending in an *-er* sound, e.g. *sugarholic* (1965), *computerholic* (1977), while *-oholic* rather than *-aholic* is the commoner spelling in *chocoholic.*

aid. The noun was first recorded in the sense 'material (especially economic) help given by one country to another' in 1940 (*Christian aid, foreign aid, Marshall aid,* etc.), but became even more widely prevalent in 1984 and later years as the second element in the names of events, etc., organized to raise money for charitable causes (*Band Aid, Fashion Aid, Live Aid,* etc.). Such formations were triggered by *Band Aid,* the name of a rock music group formed by Bob Geldof in 1984 to raise money for the relief of famine in Ethiopia.

aide. A person who helps is occasionally called an *aid.* An *aide,* by contrast, is (*a*) an assistant to an important person, especially a political leader, e.g. *presidential aides, a former aide to Mr Brown;* (*b*) short for an *aide-de-camp,* a high-ranking officer in the armed services (e.g. *Brigadier Monson summoned his five closest aides for a working lunch*—N. Barber, 1984); (*c*) (mainly in American English) a person employed as an assistant or an ancillary worker, especially in a hospital or as a visitor to the home of an ill or elderly person (e.g. *There is domiciliary care . . . offered by 200 home helps, 18 aides and their organisers—Daily Tel.*, 1984; *Just before he died a nurse's aide brought his dinner tray into the room*—E. L. Doctorow, 1989).

ain't. **1** A controversial word. The use of *ain't* often arouses passions (for example, in comments to online dictionary entries) that one would never have dreamt such a seemingly inoffensive word could provoke. 'Do you hear? Don't say "ain't" or "dang" or "son of a buck" . . . You're not a pair of hicks!' scolds a mother to her children in a *New Yorker* short story.

In 1942 Eric Partridge remarked that using *ain't* for *isn't* is 'an error so illiterate that I blush to record it'. In 1961 *Webster's Third New International Dictionary* listed the word with a factual rather than a critical note ('though disapproved by many and more common in less educated speech, used orally in most parts of the US by many cultivated speakers especially in the phrase *ain't I*'), and found itself virtually placed in the stocks for this entry alone. Dictionaries of current English tend to hold the word, as it were, in a pair of tweezers. The label 'informal' is applied to it. None admits it to the sacred unqualified ranks of standard English. The reasons lie in the word's history.

2 *History and formation.* How did the word come about? And why do some people use it naturally, while others regard its use as a sign of irretrievable vulgarity or ignorance? As a contraction for *am, is, are, have + not,* its formation is irregular, which partly accounts for the stigma attached to it. It is an 18c. word, derived ultimately from the 17c. form *an't* used to stand for *aren't* and *am not.* It is not a reduced form of any logical ancestor. Properly speaking, the last element in a tag question of the type 'I am here, am I not?', if reduced, should be *amn't I,* as it often is in Scotland and Ireland. The word *ain't* has been recorded in the popular speech of London and elsewhere since 1778. It has been an undisputed element in Cockney speech since at least the time of Dickens (*'You seem to have a good sister.' 'She ain't half bad.'—Our Mutual Friend,* 1865).

3 *Current use.* It is a feature of the deliciously disrespectful rantings of the British TV character Lauren, with her signature phrase *coz I ain't* (*bleedin'*) *bovvered.* It also features widely in the language of comic strips and modern rap music (of US origin). The *OED* used to note that 'the contraction is also found as a (somewhat outmoded) upper-class colloquialism'. It has also been espoused in intellectual circles as an affectation, which tends to confuse the issue: e.g. *I've not the spirit to pack up and go without him. Ain't I a craven*—Virginia Woolf, 1938; *Still working the Cape Cod and Florida cycle. And it ain't too bad—Yale Alumni Magazine,* 1988.

It is enshrined in a number of common catchphrases: 'you ain't seen nothing yet'; 'if it ain't broke, don't fix it'; 'it ain't gonna happen'; 'it ain't over till it's over/till the fat lady sings'; and it is used in some classic songs: 'ain't she sweet; 'it ain't necessarily so'; 'Is you is or is you ain't my baby?'

It flourishes in certain varieties of US English, and in Black American Vernacular it has also acquired the meanings 'do not, does not, did not' (*Ain't you know Felo ben stay'n wid me?*). Because many people on both sides of the Atlantic regard it as incorrect, or even non-existent, it is often used (*a*) to emphasize a phrase or to make it more colourful, e.g. *Members receive further rider training and VIP access to motorbike sporting events. But it ain't cheap—Daily Tel.*, 2007. The headline to a news item about the closing of a salad bar with the wonderful name of 'Fritz That's It' ran as "Fritz That's It" ain't'; (*b*) to convey an informal style of speech or writing: General Alexander Haig once said of George Bush: *Anybody who has to spend all his time demonstrating his manhood has somehow got to know he ain't got it.*

4 For over 200 years *ain't* has been knocking at the door of standard English, but it is still a shunned outsider, pressing its grubby nose forlornly against the windows. In tag questions it has largely been thwarted by *aren't*. In ordinary speech and writing it stigmatizes the person using it as uneducated or socially suspect. But precisely because of its contentious status, it is widely used in popular catchphrases; to spice up or draw attention to a form of words; in informal speech; and for characterization in fiction.

air (verb). The meaning 'to broadcast' (first recorded 1943) was originally American English but is now quite frequent in British English too, e.g. *On Tuesday, several popular radio stations aired rare interviews with the prime minister—Daily Tel.*, 2011.

ait /eɪt/. The recommended spelling of a term (also **eyot**) for an islet, especially one on a river and specifically on the Thames. It comes from Old English *iggaþ*, from *īeg* 'island' + *-aþ*, which may have been a diminutive suffix.

aitch. **1** The letter H was written as **ache** by Shakespeare and his contemporaries, and answers to Middle English and Old French *ache*. The spelling *aitch* is first recorded from 1761.

2 English /h/ occurs only as an aspirated pre-vocalic fricative at the beginning of a syllable. The dropping of the sound (aitch-dropping) and its converse, the false insertion of initial /h/ ('arm' for *harm;* 'hill' for *ill*), were already noted by John Walker in his *Pronouncing Dictionary* (1791) as characterizing many types of popular regional speech. As the *OED* (1898) says: 'In recent times the correct treatment of initial *h* in speech has come to be regarded as a kind of shibboleth of social position.' It is perhaps worth pointing out that loss of /h/ is also a feature of RP in unaccented, non-initial contexts in connected speech, e.g. *I pushed him back* /ʌɪ ˈpʊʃt ɪm ˈbak/, and *I could have hated her* /ʌɪ kəd əv ˈheɪtɪd ə/; also at the beginning of a syllable after certain consonant groups, as in *exhaust, exhortation*, and in such suffixes as *-ham* in *Chatham, Clapham, Durham*, and *-herd* in *shepherd*.

See also HAITCH.

-al. **1** *As an adjectival suffix.* It is normally found in words of Latin or Greek origin: *oral* (L *ōrālis*, from *ōr-*, *ōs* 'mouth'); *hebdomadal* (late L *hebdomadālis*, from Gk ἑβδομάς (-αδ-), from ἑπτά 'seven') 'weekly'. Words of English origin (*house, path*, etc.) have never developed adjectives in *-al*. In L itself *-ālis* was added to existing adjectives, e.g. *annuālis* (from *annuus*), giving English *annual*. Fowler (1926) regarded *coastal* as a barbarism (properly *costal*, he thought, from L *costa*), but his hostility to the word has not been taken up by modern writers. See TIDAL.

On adjectives in *-ic*/*-ical* (e.g. *comic*/*comical, geographic*/*geographical, historic*/*historical*), see -IC(AL) and the individual words.

2 *As a suffix to nouns.* Fowler had no objection to older nouns ending in *-al* that had passed into common use, and that, for the most part, were not competing with virtually synonymous words ending in *-ation, -ion, -ment*, etc., e.g. *acquittal* (first recorded 1430), *arrival* (1384), *proposal* (1683), *refusal* (1474), *retrieval* (*ante* 1643). He expressed strong disapproval, however, of an upsurge of interest during the Victorian period (among historians and novelists) in *-al* nouns that did compete with synonymous words of different formation. Thus, he objected to *accusal* (used instead of *accusation*), *appraisal* (for *appraisement*), *bequeathal* (for *bequest*), *refutal* (for *refutation*), *retiral* (for *retirement*), etc. His judgement seems to have been sound. Such words are rarely encountered now, except that *appraisal* (a markedly literary word in the 19c.) and *retiral* (in Scotland) are now everyday words in the language of personnel departments (e.g. *promotion depends in large measure on the results of annual appraisals; to fill a vacancy due to retiral*). See also OVERTHROWAL. Few 20c. formations of this kind have become fixtures in the language, *misconstrual* (1950) being an exception.

à la. Adopted from French (= *à la mode*), despite being feminine in that language, when used in English to mean 'in the manner or style of' it does not vary according to the sex of the person mentioned (*giant landscape photocollages à la David Hockney; afternoon talk shows à la Oprah*). It is also used in front of place-names, street-names, etc. (*a regatta à la Henley; the BBC should give serious consideration to an autumn shuffle à la* 10 *Downing Street*—C. Freud, 1989).

à la carte. In its culinary meaning it refers to food dishes that can be ordered as separate items, rather than as part of a set meal, e.g. *an à la carte menu, eating à la carte. À la carte* is also a metaphor for choosing parts of something that is sold as a package, particularly in the entertainment industry, e.g. *Everyone understands where the music industry will end up some years down the line: selling songs à la carte to consumers with few or no restrictions.* It is also used more abstractly for selecting particular aspects of a belief system, policy, etc. that is usually considered as a whole, e.g. *It is not possible to be in favor of the death penalty à la carte. The state either claims the right to impose this doom or it does not.* This phrase can work as an elegant shorthand, and often the context, as in the previous example, clarifies its exact meaning. But if you use it without elaborating further what you mean, you risk being discourteous to readers and listeners who are not as familiar as you with the niceties of fine dining. As Fowler said, referring to the use of French words: 'Display of superior knowledge is as great a vulgarity as display of superior wealth.'

alarmed. In addition to its meaning of 'frightened, disturbed' as the past participle of the verb *alarm*, it has since at least as early as 1968 acquired the meaning of 'fitted with or protected by an alarm or alarms'. Such signs as 'This door is alarmed' still make me pause for a nanosecond at the incongruity of their message, and are an excellent everyday example of AMBIGUITY.

albeit. This conjunction is a reduced form of the phrase *all be it* (*that*) (= let it entirely be that), and means 'although, even though'. It should be written as one word, not as 'all be it', which you will occasionally find. It has been in continuous use since the time of Chaucer, and despite having a possibly archaic ring is used often enough in writing in two syntactic patterns: (*a*) more commonly, preceding an adjective, adverb, or non-finite clause, e.g. *It is an unwelcome, albeit necessary, restraint*—A. Storr, 1972; *'Jesus!' they said in Italian albeit in a conversational manner*—H. Secombe, 1981; *No wonder he landed the post of shadow arts minister, albeit briefly*—*Guardian*, 2005; (*b*) introducing a finite clause, generally without *that*, but occasionally (particularly in British English) with it, e.g. *Their voices, too, albeit the accent was provincial, were soft and musical*, 1878; *In most EU countries the central bank plays a role here, albeit that the supervision is often entrusted to another agency*—*OEC*, 2000 (BrE).

Some people dislike the use of *albeit* in type (*b*) constructions. It is certainly true that it can often be replaced by the more neutral (*al*)*though*. However, in the last example above, and in the next, it seems to me to have a more intense concessive force than that; it is equivalent to 'despite the fact that', and replacing it would subtly weaken the sentence: *In Iatmul a man is a master in his own house, albeit he has to fight for it against a wife practically as strong as he is*—M. Mead, 1949.

albino. Plural *albinos*. See -O(E)S 4.

Albion. Partly because of its late appearance as an entry in the *OED*, speculation about the origin of the word *Albion* and of the phrase *perfidious Albion* was once rife. *Albion* was known already to the Old English translator of Bede's *Ecclesiastical History*, and much earlier still to Pliny (in Latin) and to Ptolemy (in Greek). Etymologically, it answers ultimately to a reconstructed Indo-European form **albho-* (cf. Latin *albus* white), the allusion being to the white cliffs of Dover. The French phrase *la perfide Albion* is believed to have been first used by the Marquis de Ximenès (1726–1817).

alexandrine. In prosody, a line (usually iambic) of twelve syllables (the French *vers héroïque*), used in English, for example, as the last line of a Spenserian stanza (*All things decay in time and to their end do draw*) or as a variant in a poem of heroic couplets, rarely in a whole work. In Fr. the alexandrine is found, for example, in Alexandre de Bernay's dodecasyllabic version (late 12c.) of the great cyclic *Roman d'Alexandre* (e.g. *D'Alixandre vous vœil l'istorie rafreschir*). The most famous English example is Alexander Pope's couplet, *A needless Alexandrine ends the song, That, like a wounded snake, drags its slow length along.*

alga. Plural *algae*, pronounced /ˈaldʒiː/ or /-giː/.

alibi. **1** (Plural *alibis*). Originally, in legal language 'a plea that when an alleged act took place one was elsewhere' (from Latin *alibī* 'elsewhere, in another place', old locative case of *alius* 'another'). The earliest use of *alibi* in English (18c.) corresponded to that of the Latin: those under suspicion had to prove that they were *alibi* (elsewhere). From this use it rapidly hardened into a noun: an *alibi* was 'an instance of being *alibi*'. Example: *Just because the suspects had arranged a false alibi to account for their whereabouts ... they were not necessarily murderers*—T. Capote, 1966.

2 In the 20c. it developed a colloquial weakened meaning referring to any kind of excuse, pretext, or justification: *I have an alibi because I'm going to have a baby*—L. P. Hartley, 1951; *So far delivery has not lived up to expectations raised by the bold, soaring rhetoric, and the alibis are running out*—*Independent*, 2002. This colloquial use is first recorded in American sports writing, e.g. *Don't offer alibis for losing* [a game of tennis]—W. T. Tilden, 1922, and then in detective fiction. The corresponding sense of 'a person providing an alibi' has followed suit, e.g. *Tom and Maureen are my alibis*—C. Hare, 1949.

Since not long after its first appearance, this extended meaning has attracted criticism, and is still disliked by some. It is possibly more acceptable in US usage than in British, and has been used by distinguished writers.

3 By the usual process known as CONVERSION, the now dominant sense has generated an occasionally used informal verb meaning 'to provide with an alibi': *Aunt Primrose ... hadn't opportunity. She's alibied by Mrs Fitch*—J. Cannan, 1958; *There's got to be somebody to alibi us*—L. Duncan, 1978. Its forms are *alibis, alibiing, alibied.*

alien. From the 14c. to the 19c. inclusive, in the sense 'of a nature or character different *from*', *alien* was construed with *from* (e.g. *This uncouth style, so alien from genuine English*—Henry Reed, 1855). As the *OED* says, this sense gradually passed imperceptibly into 'of a nature repugnant, adverse or opposed *to*'. The crossover came at some point near the end of the 19c., and the construction with *to* is now routine, e.g. *Thinking, and certainly brooding, were quite alien to his character*—J. C. Oates, 1980). The older construction still occurs occasionally: *a reflection upon how far man has come to feel himself alien from the animal kingdom of which he is a member*—A. Storr, 1968.

-(al)ist. For such alternative forms as *educationist* and *educationalist*, see -IST 2.

alkali. Final syllable now universally pronounced /-ʌɪ/ (formerly often /-iː/). The more usual plural form is *alkalis* but the by-form *alkalies* is found in many standard textbooks.

all. **1** *all* or *all of.* The question whether to use *all* or *all of* has been debated since the 19c.; few debates in the history of usage can have been more pointless. *All* on its own can be used before singular or plural nouns: *all those years ago; all the time; all our stocks and shares; almost all his former colleagues.* In such cases *all of* is an option, whereas it is obligatory before pronouns standing alone (*all of it, all of us, all of its own*) and in certain idiomatic uses (e.g. *all of a sudden*). The construction with *of* is comparatively modern (first recorded *c.*1800), and is probably due to association with *none of, some of, little of, much of, few of, many of.* Examples: *All of those activities whose very virtue is that they enable you to think* [etc.]—H. Jacobson, 1983; *He will have to be all of these things*—A. Brookner, 1986; *'It's one of my limitations.' 'I haven't begun to list all of mine.'*—P. Roth, 1986; *At each stop, all of us visitors were greeted by a hail of celebratory statistics*—*New Yorker*, 1989.

2 There is also a common idiomatic use with numbers and quantities: *we had walked all of ten miles* = as many as; *It* *must have been all of fifteen minutes of . . . dull, homesick silence*—Mark Twain, 1883; *Even I, all of eight years old, couldn't stand another second of his shrieking—Me Three Magazine*, 1944 (AmE).

3 Since the 1960s *all's* (or *alls*) has been noted in informal American English in the sense 'all that' (it is probably a shortened form of *all as*): e.g. *So all's I need, pretty much, is a tie—New Yorker*, 1990; *Meanwhile, alls I hear about is how great the economy is doing—OEC*, 2004.

4 When *all* is the subject of the verb *to be* followed by a plural complement, the linking verb is expressed in the singular: *All I saw was fields*—N. Williams, 1985; *In some sense, all we have is the scores—incomplete and corrupted as they often are—New Yorker*, 1989.

5 See also ALL RIGHT; ALL THAT; ALL TOGETHER; ALL TOLD; ALREADY; BUT 9C. For *is all*, see IS 10. For *at all*, see AT 2.

all-around. An optional American English variant (*everything on this all-around Italian menu is good; the best all-around American city school; a good all-around player*) of *all-round* adjective, the latter being the only form used in British English.

allay. The inflexions are *allays, allaying, allayed.*

alleged, allegedly. *Alleged* is pronounced as two syllables, and *allegedly* as four. Their role is (*a*) in legal contexts, to distinguish an unproven accusation (i.e. an allegation) from a proven fact (*the victim of the alleged fraud; their alleged attackers*) or (*b*) to cast doubt on the genuineness of a statement or claim (*the alleged illness that prevented him from coming to the wedding; the alleged medical breakthrough*). The disclaiming qualification they provide is not needed in sentences in which the context already makes the situation clear: *An Iraqi prisoner has described how he was* [*allegedly*] *subjected to vicious beatings—Independent*, 2004. The disclaimer would be needed if the sentence was a direct statement not attributed to the victim: *An Iraqi prisoner was allegedly subjected to vicious beatings.*

allegory. Generally pronounced /ˈalɪg(ə)ri/ (**a**-li-g(uh)ri) in British English, stressing the first syllable only, but with a secondary stress in American English, /ˈaləˌgɔri/ (**a**-li-**gaw**-ri). 'A narrative of which the true meaning is to be got by translating its persons and events into others that they are understood to symbolize' (Fowler, 1926). 'A figurative narrative or description, conveying a veiled moral meaning, an extended metaphor' (*OCELit.*, 1985). The form flourished in medieval literature to the extent that 'every kind of serious realism was in danger of being choked to death by the vines of allegory' (E. Auerbach, *Mimesis*, 1953, ch. 10). Later allegorical works of signal importance included Spenser's *Faerie Queene* (1590–6), Bunyan's *Pilgrim's Progress* (1678–84), and Dryden's *Absalom and Achitophel* (1681). Allegorical elements are present in some modern writing, e.g. Virginia Woolf's *Between the Acts* (1941), which by means of a village pageant presents 'a communal image of rural England, past and present', or George Orwell's *Animal Farm* (1945).

allegro. Plural *allegros*. See -O(E)S 4.

alleluia. Latin form (from Greek), the Septuagint representation of Hebrew *hallēlu-yāh*, i.e. 'praise ye Jah' (or 'Jehovah'). In English, an exclamation meaning 'Praise the Lord', which occurs in many psalms and anthems. In AV spelt *Alleluia*; by Handel spelt **Hallelujah**. Both forms are acceptable in context. Pronounced /ˌalɪˈluːjə/; but with initial /ˌhal-/ for the form *Hallelujah*.

allergy. An early 20c. formation (first in German as *Allergie*) from Greek ἄλλ-ος 'other, different' + ἔργ-ον 'work', meaning 'sensitiveness to pollen, certain foods, antibiotics, etc.'. It acquired the figurative sense 'a feeling of antipathy to a person or thing' by the 1940s, exemplified in Auden's *Before the Diet of Sugar he was using razor blades And excited soon after with an allergy to maidenheads—For the Time Being*, 1944. Slightly earlier, the corresponding adjective **allergic** had come into general use, with varying degrees of informality. It is a classic example of how a technical term becomes part of general language, and, though disliked by Gowers (1965), is now standard. Allergies to anything disliked range from the understandable to the far-fetched: to colonels (*Punch*, 1942), all kinds of rationing (the European public, according to Koestler, 1951), opera on television

(*Observer*, 1958), even to negotiating with terrorists (*Times*, 1986), etc.

alley. Plural *alleys*.

alliteration. A consonance or agreement of sounds (not necessarily of letters) usually at the beginning of a word or syllable, as in *b*ig, *b*old, and am*b*er; *kn*ife, *gn*arled, and *n*ote. In the literature of the Germanic languages, alliteration could exist between all vowels indiscriminately: in Old English, for example, not only does *e*llen alliterate with *e*nde and *ēa*c with *ēa*ge, but *e*cg alliterates with *ī*ren and *ī*sig with *ū*tfūs.

Throughout the ages, in the literature of many countries, alliteration has been used for various special effects, whether for humour, as in Voltaire's 'Non, il n'est rien que Nanine n'honore'; for emphasis, as in Victor Hugo's 'La Marseillaise ailée et volant dans les balles, Les bombes, les obus, les tambours, les cymbales'; or for delicate effects of sound, as in Shakespeare's 'Full fathom five thy father lies'. It is not infrequent in Latin verse, as in Ennius' 'at tuba terribili sonitu taratantara dixit'.

In English literature, the systematic use of alliterative verse is associated with the medieval period, most memorably in poems like *Beowulf, Piers Plowman* (In a somere seyson whan softe was þe sonne), and *Sir Gawain and the Green Knight*. The great cycle of English alliterative verse ended with the poem *Flodden Field* (1513). In modern times the tradition has been revived in some of Auden's verse (With labelled luggage we alight at last, Joining joking at the junction on the moor, *The Exiles*, 1968).

Alliterative phrases abound in English, e.g. *to aid and abet, first and foremost, as good as gold, by fair means or foul, part and parcel, as right as rain.*

allot. Use *allotted, allotting,* but *allotment.*

allow. 1 In the American English informal phrase *allow as how,* the meaning is 'to state as an opinion, have to admit that': *She allowed as how my old friend J.J. was flying on Monday morning*—N. Thornburg, 1976; *He allowed as how she was faithful*—T. Morrison, 1981. This is not a standard construction in Britain (see *as how* at AS 7), but it is occasionally found in informal British writing.

2 In the sense 'to admit the truth of, concede', *allow* followed by a subordinate clause has been in continuous use since the 17c. and is still in standard use today: *I suppose it will be allowed us that marriage is a human society*—Milton, 1643; *He allowed that the old Pre-Raphaelites had ... exquisite merits*—Hawthorne, 1858; *What was their civilisation? Vast, I allow: but vile*—J. Joyce, 1922; *The book itself is still a work in progress, although Mary allows that she might part with it one day in the future*—*Raw Vision*, 2004.

3 For several centuries *allow* alternated in many meanings with the phrasal verb *allow of:* e.g. *His condition would not allow of* (= permit the occurrence of) *his talking earlier*, 1732; *Jortin is willing to allow of* (= to accept as valid) *other miracles*—J. R. Lowell, 1849. Constructions with *of* are nowadays rare and seem somewhat old-fashioned. They are, nevertheless, still part of the verb's syntactic repertoire in the meaning 'to permit the occurrence or existence of something', especially in the phrase 'allow of (no) exceptions'. Examples: *Culturally, it seems to allow also of other possibilities*—*Oxford Companion to the Body*, 2001; *The conflict between* [*the principle of capitalism and socialism is*] *irreconcilable and does not allow of any compromise*—Ludwig von Mises Institute, 2004; *The principle allows of no exceptions*—Schopenhauer, 2004.

all right. 'Is *alright* all right?' asks *MWCDEU*. For dozens of usage pundits, before and after Fowler, the answer is a dismissive 'no'. Having condemned it in a tract two years before, in 1926 Fowler declared categorically 'there are no such forms as *all-right, allright,* or *alright*'. Burchfield (1996) snottily wrote 'The ... inability to see that there is anything wrong with *alright* reveals one's background, upbringing, education, etc.' Journalists' style guides generally outlaw it, and the *Telegraph*, true to form, goes so far as to call it 'an abomination'.

In measured contrast to such hostility, the *OED* points out that '*alright* is frequent, although more widespread in non-literary printed sources (e.g. newspapers and journals) than in literary texts'. Apart from the weight of frequent use, there are arguments in favour of the one-word spelling: (*a*) the need to distinguish it from *all* as a pronoun (e.g. *He finished the crossword and got it all right*); (*b*) the analogy of *altogether, already,* etc., once written as two words before merging into one, and similarly needing to be distinguished from two-word forms (e.g. *We went back all together and all safe*); (*c*) its frequent pronunciation as a single word; (*d*) its arguably greater appropriateness (i) in set expressions, such as *doing alright, feeling alright, that's quite alright,* etc. and (ii) in its several discourse functions, such as signalling agreement (*'Alright, I'll do it'*), introducing an instruction to someone over whom you have authority (*'Alright, you can go now'*), as an informal greeting, etc.; and, debatably, (*e*) its legitimization, literarily in Molly Bloom's soliloquy (1922), and popularly in song titles such as 'Don't think twice it's alright' (1962), 'It's alright ma I'm only bleeding' (1965), 'The kids are alright' (1979), etc. It is also worth noting that its second-earliest citation in the *OED* as an adjective is the one-word form 'Where ever [*sic*] I goe both too and fro, You have my heart alright', although nearly all the *OED* citations, even in its discourse function, are of the two-word form.

The conclusion is: feel free to use it in business or personal writing, and in dialogue in fiction. But in any formal work, or any that is likely to be edited, its pariah status will ensure that it is dismembered either literally or metaphorically. Examples: (all right) *One advantage of the permissive society is that it's all right to live together before marriage—Woman's Own,* 1971; *It's all right for you . . . You won't have to do the post-mortem with these guys*—Len Deighton, 1974; *'Oh, all right', she said, 'go and be damned.'*—Graham Greene, 1980; (alright) *They've been bloody inscrutable alright*—P. Cave, 1979; *You'll be alright, love*—Chinua Achebe, 1987; *If you've got the ears to know what sounds good you're going to be pretty much alright—Guitarist,* 1992.

all-round. See ALL-AROUND.

all that. As a reinforced demonstrative adverb qualifying an adjective or adverb it is now found quite commonly in negative constructions: *The Spanish gypsies . . . hired to do the sweeping were not all that handy with a broom—Harper's Bazaar,* 1962; *I looked round the stock. It wasn't all that brilliant, I must admit*—J. Leasor, 1969. *All* is simply an intensifier in such constructions. Gowers (1965) cited examples of *all that* qualifying an adverb (e.g. *The figures show that even Lazards do not sell £2m. all that frequently*), and judged that the use was 'now well on its way to literary status'. It is now a standard construction. For the more debatable type *I was that angry,* see THAT (demonstrative adverb).

all together, altogether. These are often confused, because their meanings encroach on one another. *All together* means 'everyone or everything together', and the word *all* is usually removable without damaging the syntax or affecting the meaning: e.g. *One victim and five suspects, all together in a sealed room*—A. Morice, 1971; *we went back all together and all safe—Daily Tel.,* 2004.

Altogether is adverbial and can mean (*a*) 'entirely; in every way': e.g. *The idea of counselling in schools is not altogether new—Times,* 1970; *Martinez was not altogether unknown. But the antagonism of people in Chicago is insignificant. He has another ball game in mind altogether*—Saul Bellow, 1982; (*b*) 'in all, in total', e.g. *you owe me £400 altogether;* (*c*) 'considering everything', e.g. *The weather was bad and the hotel overcrowded. Altogether, it was a disappointing holiday.*

It is much more common for *all together* to be wrongly written for *altogether* than the other way round. Examples of wrong spelling: (should be *altogether*) **All together, IIASA received White House support through four administrations—Bull. Amer. Acad. Arts & Sci.,* 1987; **The federal government doesn't seem all together that bothered—CNN* transcripts, 2007; (should be *all together*) *It's really interesting how altogether we can feel like a human race, not any more any single country—CNN* transcripts, 2007.

all told. This fixed phrase = 'when all are counted; in all' is first recorded from 1850, e.g. *All told, those Celtic teams won the NBA title 11 times in 13 years—Basketball Scene Annual,* 1988. Originally a development of *tell* in the meaning 'to count', it has now made its natural way into contexts where counting is not present = 'taking all factors into account', e.g. *All told, I enjoyed life in the army.* This is perfectly standard, and not open to any sensible objection when speaking, but should you wish to avoid it in more formal writing, you could use *all in all* or *all things considered.*

allude, allusion. 1 The *-lu-* can be pronounced as either /ljuː/ (lyoo) or /luː/ (loo).

2 It has been claimed by some critics that to *allude* to someone or something can only properly mean to mention them 'indirectly or covertly', i.e. without mentioning their name, unlike *refer*, which means to mention them directly, i.e. by name. So, according to this view, if you *refer* to Julius Caesar you name him, whereas if you *allude* to him you identify him without naming him, e.g. 'the Roman dictator assassinated in 44 BC'. That use is clearly shown in *He would allude to her, and hear her discussed, but never mentioned her by name*—E. M. Forster, 1910. But in practice, *allude* is often used to mean 'refer', e.g. *He had star quality, an element often alluded to in Arlene's circle of show-biz friends*—Gore Vidal, 1978; *She tabled a letter alluding to fraud that caused alarm amongst her fellow councillors*—*OEC*, 2003 (Aust.). This use is well established and perfectly acceptable.

3 *Allusion* and *reference* should follow the same principle, *allusion* involving indirect mention and *reference* involving direct mention by name, but again in practice the distinction blurs at the edges. But, as Burchfield observed about both it and *allude*, 'indirectness is not always part of the sealed meaning of the two words, and the reference is sometimes ambiguously direct or indirect or just plainly direct', as can be seen in the following example: *She came across allusions to her family in the papers*—Vita Sackville-West, 1931; *Midway in the questioning ... he'd begun to notice the number of allusions to a particular November weekend*—Truman Capote, 1966; *She was ... annoyed that he could make her feel so uncomfortable by his veiled allusion to last night*—A. Murray, 1993.

ally. **1** *Pronunciation.* Originally stressed, both as noun and as verb, on the second syllable. As a noun it is now invariably stressed on the first. The verb is less straightforward, since either syllable can be stressed, i.e. /ˈalʌɪ/ or /əˈlʌɪ/ (**a**-ly, uh-**ly**) in British English, but stressing the second syllable is standard in American English. The first is probably commoner in most uses of the verb (e.g. *he allied his racing experience with his father's business acumen*); the second is still heard when *allied* is followed by *to* to mean 'in combination with' (e.g. *skilled craftsmanship allied to advanced technology*), or in the meaning is 'connected, related' (e.g. *members of the medical and allied professions*). When it describes members of an alliance, *allied* is stressed on the first syllable (e.g. *During the first three days of the land war in 1991, allied troops took some 30,000 Iraqi soldiers prisoner*).

2 *Capitalization.* By convention, the noun *Allies* and the adjective *Allied* are spelt with a capital letter when they refer to Britain and her allies in the First and Second World Wars.

Alma Mater. An affectionate title (= bounteous mother), once given by the Romans to several goddesses, especially to Ceres and Cybele, now applied to one's university or school seen as a 'fostering mother'. Generally pronounced /ˌalmə ˈmɑːtə/ (al-muh **mah**-tuh) in British English, also /ˈmeɪtə/ (**may**-tuh).

almanac. Normally so spelt except in traditional titles like 'The Oxford Almanack' and *Whitaker's Almanack.*

almoner. The *OED* (1884) and Daniel Jones (1917) gave preference to the pronunciation /ˈalmənə/, but /ˈɑːm-/ is now standard, doubtless on the analogy of *alms* /ɑːmz/. The word itself is now rarely used, except when referring to a specific role in Masonic lodges, (*medical*) *social worker* now being the term used to denote an official in British hospitals with certain duties concerning the welfare of patients.

almost. **1** Its occasional use as a quasi-adjective meaning 'close to being, not quite' (*an almost Quaker; his almost impudence of manner; an almost Prime Minister*) seems slightly forced, but it is not new (*OED* 1552–).

2 See MOST 9.

along. **1** *Along about* is an American English regionalism meaning 'approximately': *In the one case you start out with a friend along about eleven o'clock on a summer's night*—M. Twain, 1879; *'Nettie Bill got married along about the same time I got married to Jack,' Aunt Lou said*—M. Grimm, 1989.

2 *along of.* Used to mean 'owing to, on account of' (*A present from the Gentlemen, along o' being good!*—Kipling, 1906; *'The* *trouble I've had along of that lady's crankiness,' he confided*—N. Marsh, 1963), and '(together) with' (You *come along a me, Ginger*—J. Cary, 1940), *along of* is not standard.

alongside. *Alongside* is both an adverb (*Kevin came quickly alongside*) and a preposition (*the two vehicles were alongside each other*; *learning to read begins very early indeed, alongside learning to talk*). It has been used as a preposition with or without *of* for some two centuries and both constructions are still available; use with *of* is now less usual in British English, although it still occurs: *Margaret turned round to walk alongside of the girl in her feeble progress homeward*—L. Otis, 2002. It is more common in American English: *Certain plants thrive alongside of each other*—website, 2004 (AmE).

alot. This single-word spelling of *a lot* is now not uncommon. It goes without saying that it is non-standard, and to be avoided. Nevertheless, it illustrates rather strikingly how arbitrary the convention of spelling certain pairs of words together or separately can be. Examples: **My parents have been out* alot *the past 2 weeks*; **The recession has affected the advertising business* alot; **We still had* alot *of fun, just a different kind of fun*. Cf. AWHILE.

already. The adverb is spelt as one word (*I have lost a great deal of time already*) and of course is not to be confused with the two separate words *all ready* (*We are all ready to start now*, i.e. all of us are ready).

alright. See ALL RIGHT.

also. 1 The word is an adverb and is almost always used in that way: e.g. *Besides being an astronomer and mathematician, Grassi was also an architect*. Occasionally, it strays into the territory of conjunctions: e.g. *He has made a good impression. He writes well, he keeps to deadlines, and follows house rules. Also, he's an agreeable person./Remember your watch and money; also the tickets*. This use has attracted some criticism, so is perhaps best avoided, or at least not overused, in writing, though it is common enough in speaking.

Also is sometimes used as an 'additive conjunct' within a sentence, where *and also, and*, or *but also* would be in place: e.g. *Great attention has been paid to the history of legislation, also* [= and also] *to that of religion*.

2 The normal position is before the main verb and after any auxiliary or modal verbs: *It was also held to be the cause of the milder form of the illness known as AIDS-related complex—New York Review of Books*, 1986; *He also believes that a garden shouldn't be too manicured—Sunday Times*, 2004.

In most circumstances, it is pedantic and against natural usage to insist on having *also* immediately next to the word or phrase which it emphasizes. For example, to insist on *My brother also is coming* (i.e. as well as my sister, cousin, etc.), to distinguish it from *My brother is also coming* (i.e. as well as telephoning, driving, etc.).

alternate. 1 *As adjective*. In its regular meanings '(of two things) each following and succeeded by the other in a regular pattern' (e.g. *walls built of alternate layers of stone and timber*), and 'every other or every second' (e.g. *the congregation sang alternate verses; sprinklers may be used on alternate days only*), *alternate* is standard in all forms of English.

In the course of the 20c., in American English, *alternate* usurped some of the territory of *alternative* in its ordinary sense of 'available as another possibility or choice'. (In American English it is pronounced /ˈɔltərnət/, **awl**-tuhr-nit, stressing the first syllable). This use is disliked by many British speakers, and is less common in British English than in American. The Book of the Month Club offers 'alternate selections'. A route, a material, a lyric, etc., can be described as 'alternate' rather than (as in the UK) 'alternative': *An alternate way to make these rellenos is to stuff the meat mixture into whole green chiles—San Diego Union*, 1987. There are *alternate* (or *alternative*) *schools* in the US which offer a non-traditional curriculum.

2 *As noun*. Frequently used in American English, but far less in British English, to denote 'a person who acts as a deputy or substitute', especially in theatrical, sporting, and legal contexts: *I was fourth alternate in the Miss Teenage South Carolina pageant*—William Boyd, 1984; *Her alternate* [*sc.* dancer], *Pavlenko, was inconsistently brilliant—Dance Magazine*, 2002. In American English it is pronounced /ˈɔːltərnət/, **awl**-tuh-nit, stressing the first syllable, but in British English the second syllable is stressed.

3 *Alternate* is also a verb, pronounced /ˈɔːltəːneɪt/ or /ˈɒltəːneɪt/ (**awl**-tuh-nayt, **ol**-tuh-nayt) meaning 'to occur or do in turn, often repeatedly': *some adults who wish to alternate work with education; In a democratic system political parties expect to alternate in office*—P. Richards, 1988.

alternative. 1 *As noun.* The ultratraditionalist view that there can only be one of two (not more) alternatives because Latin *alter* means 'other (of two)' was always pedantic, was described by Gowers (1965) as a 'fetish', and is now utterly irrelevant. The word can still be used in this manner (e.g. *a fate compared to which death would have been a joyful alternative*), and the *OED* amply illustrates such traditional uses. But, beginning with an example from John Stuart Mill in 1848, it also shows the word in extended use meaning 'a choice between more than two things'. Gladstone is reported as saying in 1857 *My decided preference is for the fourth and last of these alternatives*, and nobody will bat an eyelid at the word being used to denote as many choices as the particular case offers.

2 *As adjective.* Since the late 1960s the adjective has increasingly been used to mean 'of or relating to activities that depart from or challenge traditional norms and practices, or that purport to do so': e.g. *alternative energy* (i.e. non-nuclear, not using fossil fuels), *alternative medicine* (i.e. mainly homoeopathic or holistic), *alternative society* (i.e. rejecting a traditional way of life), etc. This meaning is sometimes conveyed in American English by *alternate*, e.g. *alternate fuel, alternate therapy*, etc.

although, though. *Though* can always be used instead of *although*, but the reverse is not true. *Though* is slightly more frequent than *although*, and somewhat less formal. **1** Both words can introduce a subordinate clause: *He did well, although he did not win an outright majority*—*Economist*, 1981; *Though there was a tendency for students to factionalize, there were always students good about diplomacy*—*Christian Science Monitor*, 1982; *Although the defendant had undoubtedly committed an offence . . . , that was not an arrestable offence*—*Times*. Where they are interchangeable, however, *although* generally has a stronger concessive force, and is somewhat more usual at the beginning of a sentence.

2 In the following uses, *though* alone is possible: (*a*) as an adverb in medial or final position: *It is true, though, that one misses out on one's husband's early years of struggle*—*Times*, 1985; *'What a sad story!' said Maria. 'Isn't it, though?'*—G. Vidal, 1948; (*b*) in inverted constructions: *Young though he is, he doesn't look it;* (*c*) in the fixed expressions *as though* and *even though*: *Anderson is a borderline New Waver who looks as though she has been out in the rain upside down*—*Washington Post*, 1982; *He was by no means a dry, boring theoretician even though he wrote extraordinarily advanced books on dance*—Margot Fonteyn, 1980.

3 *Even although* is a well-established Scotticism with historical precedents, but is generally considered non-standard elsewhere, and even in Scotland may be considered wrong by some people: *?That's why I put Hearts favourites even although Hibs are playing some fantastic football*—*Scotland on Sunday*, 2005.

alto. Plural *altos*. See -O(E)S 6.

altogether. See ALL TOGETHER.

aluminium. The British English spelling harmonizes best with other names of elements, such as *magnesium, potassium, sodium*, etc., whereas the American English spelling *aluminum* is the one given to the word by its discoverer, Sir H. Davy, *c.*1812. *Aluminium* is stressed on the third syllable, and *aluminum* on the second.

alumnus. From Latin (= nursling), and pronounced /əˈlʌmnəs/ (uh-**lum**-nuhs), *alumnus* is better established in American than in British parlance, but is fast catching up in Britain as universities and schools are increasingly forced to encourage former pupils and students to supplement their funding. Although *alumnus* is a masculine noun in Latin, it can refer either to a male or to a female ex-student. The feminine **alumna** (/əˈlʌmnə/, uh-**lum**-nuh), plural *alumnae* (/əˈlʌmnʌɪ/, uh-**lum**-ny) also exists, but is rather less common than *alumnus*. The masculine plural form *alumni* (/əˈlʌmniː/, uh-**lum**-nee) is the one most generally used to refer to a mixed gathering, though occasionally *alumnae* is used to refer to gatherings of women only.

In both American English and British English, rival views on the pronunciation of Latin words in English mean that the masculine and feminine plural pronunciations are sometimes reversed.

alveolar. See DENTAL.

a.m. As an abbreviation of Latin *ante meridiem* 'before noon', it is always pronounced as /ˌeɪˈɛm/, and is normally written in the form *8.15 a.m.* (or in AmE *8:15 a.m.*), that is with a full point after each letter. Note that 12.30 a.m. = half an hour after midnight, and 12.30 p.m. = half an hour after noon. The abbreviation is sometimes used as a noun = the period before noon: *I arrived here this a.m.*

amateur. Dictionaries present an array of ways to pronounce this word, but /ˈamətə/ (**a**-muh-tuh) is now pretty standard and /ˈamətjʊə/ (**a**-muh-tyoo-uh) and /-ʧ-/ (**a**-muh-choo-uh) have become minority pronunciations.

ambidextrous. Not *-erous.*

ambience. Derived from French *ambiance* (a form also occasionally used in English) only a century ago (first recorded 1889) in the sense 'environment, surroundings, atmosphere', the word is now firmly established in the language to refer to the particular character and atmosphere of somewhere. Some people still affect the French pronunciation, but it is most often pronounced as /ˈambɪəns/. Its entrance into English was helped by the fact that the corresponding adjective *ambient* had been a part of the language since the late 16c. and had also been used absolutely. *Ambience* filled an obvious gap.

ambiguity. **1** *Ambiguity* in language denotes the possibility of more than one meaning being understood from what is heard or read. Intentional ambiguity can be effective, for example as a literary device or in advertising. Our concern here is with unintentional and misleading ambiguity that occurs in ordinary speech and writing, most often as a result of poor word order.

2 The early grammarians and writers on usage placed great emphasis on misconceptions arising from the wrong ordering of words. For example, William Cobbett (1823), Letter XXI: 'Of all the faults to be found in writing this [*sc.* the wrong placing of words] is one of the most common, and, perhaps, it leads to the greatest number of misconceptions.' He claimed to have 'noted down about two hundred errors in Doctor Johnson's Lives of the Poets'. Henry Alford (1864) wrote at length on the matter and quoted as one of his examples, *I with my family reside in the parish of Stockton, which consists of my wife and daughter.* Fowler (1906) said that 'A captious critic might find examples [of false ordering of words] on almost every page of almost any writer.' There is an air of unreality and implausibility about these old precepts and about the examples given in support. Nowadays skilled copy-editors or proofreaders are expected to remove such crudely ambiguous constructions at the pre-publication stage.

3 Nevertheless, some highly ambiguous—and often comical—phrasing does get into print, especially in ephemeral media such as websites and newspapers, and provides an easy target for satire in magazines such as *Private Eye*, online language forums such as Michael Quinion's *worldwidewords.org*, or BBC Radio 4's *The News Quiz*. The most common ambiguities arise from: (*a*) the association of a word or phrase with the wrong part of the sentence, e.g. *He* [*sc.* David Beckham] *also revealed that his sons Brooklyn, 13, Romeo, 10, and Cruz, seven, will stay in London to go to school along with his wife Victoria, 38, and their one-year-old daughter Harper—BBC Sport* website (as reported in *Private Eye*, no. 1333, Feb. 2013).

(*b*) the unclear application of a negative, e.g. *They did not go out to water the plants*, which can mean either they did not go out at all, or they did go out but not to water the plants; similarly with the type *We did not go to the shops because we were expecting visitors*, which can potentially mean we did not go to the shops, or the fact that we were expecting visitors was not the reason we went to the shops.

(*c*) from words that have more than one meaning or function, as in *Visiting friends can be tiresome;* the famous line *The peasants are revolting; The Minister appealed to her supporters; The dog is not allowed to run outside* (i.e. does this mean to run out of the house, or to run once it is outside?), and so forth.

(*d*) from false or unclear reference, as in *If the children don't like their toys, get rid of them; We only have two first editions* (and no other books?); *He specializes in selling old and valuable books* (two kinds of books?); *the meetings on Monday and Friday* (how many meetings on each day?).

(*e*) through ellipsis: e.g. *He loves his dog more than his children* (who loves whom most?).

4 In written work, ambiguity can be reduced in several ways: by changing the order of clauses, by supplying elements omitted through ellipsis, by restructuring the sentence altogether, or by the use of punctuation to mark the boundaries of clauses. In spoken English, potential ambiguity is often cancelled by a shift of intonation at the boundary of clauses.

5 Nevertheless, care is required, especially in contexts where backward reference (see ANAPHORA), ellipsis (see ELLIPSIS), and misrelated clauses (see UNATTACHED PARTICIPLES) are involved. If these matters are not attended to, ambiguity of various degrees of seriousness can certainly arise.

6 See AMPHIBOLY, AMPHIBOLOGY.

ambiguous, ambivalent. *Ambivalent* (first recorded 1916) is a Jungian word meaning 'entertaining contradictory emotions (as love and hatred) towards the same person or thing' and fairly quickly moved into literary and general use. Bertrand Russell used it in 1929, and C. S. Lewis called death ambivalent because it is 'Satan's great weapon and also God's great weapon'. The core of its meaning is being in two minds about someone or something. Attitudes, characters, feelings, reactions, relationships—anything judged to contain contradictions—can be described as *ambivalent*.

For the most part it is distinguished from *ambiguous*, which means rather '(of speech, words, etc.) having more than one possible meaning', and '(of events, etc.) not clear or decided'. Examples: (ambivalent) *Women can be extremely ambivalent about their own ambition and aggression at work*—*She*, 1989; *Aronson comes down hard on Camus's ambivalent response to French colonialism*—*The Nation*, 2004; *Carter is an ambivalent figure, a seemingly emotionless killer who weeps at the exploitation of his brother's daughter*—*Screen Online*, 2003; (ambiguous) *This remark may in isolation be ambiguous*—law report, 2003; *Reform is an ambiguous word*—*Business Week Magazine*, 2003; *This impression is reflected in the ambiguous results of the two statistical tests*—*Genetics Online*, 2005. In the following sentence, *ambivalent* would have been the better choice: *Booksellers are feeling ambiguous about marking or commemorating the anniversary of the attacks of September 11*—weblog, 2002. *Ambivalently* is also found, often where *ambiguously* would be more suitable: e.g. *The people who inhabit Gormenghast, ambivalently described as 'figures' and 'shapes', are poised between the two meanings*—M. H. Short et al., 1987.

ameba. See AMOEBA.

amen. Both /ˌɑːˈmɛn/ and /ˌeɪˈmɛn/ are heard.

amend, emend. The first of these is much the more usual word. It is used of the making of (minor) adjustments to a document, a motion, a parliamentary law, etc. in order to make it fairer or more accurate, or to reflect changing circumstances. *Emend* is the property mainly of textual scholars who propose improvements to and changes in the reading of texts and manuscripts so as to make them more intelligible or to remove errors.

America. To English speakers outside North America, the term *America* means first and foremost the USA, and *North America* is used to denote a larger geographical area including also Canada and Mexico. The terms *American* and *North American* are used correspondingly as adjectives and nouns. *Central America* refers to the countries in the narrow strip of land to the south of Mexico (including Guatemala, Nicaragua, and Panama), and *South America* to the region to the south of the Panama Canal, including Argentina, Brazil, Chile, Colombia, etc.

amid, amidst. **1** *Amid*, recorded as a preposition and adverb before the Norman Conquest, developed a secondary form *amides* by the 14c., and, by association with the form of superlatives, a further secondary form *amidst* (cf. *against, amongst*) in the 16c. *Amides* dropped out of use and *amid* and *amidst* survive only as prepositions.

2 Both words are used in all the regional varieties of English covered by *OEC* data. There is no easily perceived difference in meaning (at the time of writing the *OED* retains a distinction suggested in the first edition which is not borne out by actual use). There is, however, a major difference in frequency of use, *amid* outnumbering *amidst* by something more than four to one. *OEC* data suggests that *amid*, being often used in news articles, is more neutral in register than *amidst*, which can be somewhat more literary, and can have a poetic or archaic savour.

Some commentators have attempted to insist that either word must only be used with uncount nouns, not with plural nouns, but there is absolutely no historical, logical, or stylistic justification for such a claim. What is true, and important, however, is that they can be used in contexts in which *among* will not work, and that fact probably explains their continued use.

(*a*) In their shared meaning 'in the middle of, surrounded by' all three can be used with plural nouns (e.g. *set amid/amidst/among scenic rolling hills*); but only *amid* and *amidst* can be used with uncount nouns, e.g. *an oasis of calm amid the noise of Montmartre, amidst the chaos and violence.*

(*b*) Both *amid* and *amidst* also mean 'against a background of' (e.g. *amid fears/allegations/reports/speculation/controversy*) or 'to the accompaniment of' (e.g. *amid cheers/shouts and whistles/applause* etc.). In this meaning they can both be used with uncount and plural nouns in a way that *among* cannot.

Examples: (amid) *I . . . have often stood by the Frome at Woolbridge, enjoying the mellow manor house amid its water meadows*—*Times*, 1987; *'we shall enjoy strong, sustained growth and prosperity into the1980s,' he said amid Conservative cheers*—*Daily Tel.*, 1989; *Beijing has been trying to take some of the heat out of the economy since April, amid fears that the country's long-running boom was accelerating out of control*—*BBC News*, 2004; (amidst) *he returned here for more tests amidst rumors that he had Parkinson's disease*—*Washington Post*, 1984; *this woman, sitting with such modest dignity amidst my students and colleagues*—M. Frayn, 1989; *His election came amidst some controversy*—*Yorkshire Post Today*, 2003.

Amish. A sub-dialect of American English spoken by the Amish people, a strict sect of Mennonite followers of Jacob Amman or Amen (*fl.* 1693), the Swiss founder of the sect. Found in 28 US states, but with their largest populations in Pennsylvania, Ohio, and Indiana, the Amish people maintain an older style of life: horse and buggies for transport, no electricity in their homes, plain dress and so on. Old Order Amish speech is marginally distinctive in pronunciation (e.g. *house* is pronounced /hɑːs/ not /haʊs/), with many syntactic features that do not quite match those of neighbouring, non-Amish varieties of American English. For example, reflecting German usage, they do not use—have not adopted—the English progressive tense: they say *he works very hard* rather than *he is working very hard.*

amn't. A frequent variant in Irish and Scottish English of *aren't* used as part of the tag question *amn't I?* See BE 4.

amoeba. The standard spelling in both the UK and the US is *amoeba*; **ameba** is an accepted, but not common, variant in the US. The plural generally used in technical scientific writing is *amoebae; amoebas* is less common in scientific language, but widely used elsewhere. The spelling of the related adjective is much oftener **amoebic** than **amebic**.

amok, amuck. Of these two spellings, the first is nowadays the commoner, is given as the main spelling in many dictionaries, and is closer in form to the original Malay word *amoq*, meaning 'attacking in frenzy'. (The spelling *amock* also occurs but is not recognized by dictionaries.) There are two pronunciations: /əˈmɒk/ is recommended in many dictionaries, though the variant pronunciation /əˈmʌk/ is frequently heard, and is the one I would use. The phrase to *run amok/amuck* has both literal and metaphorical meanings, e.g. (literal) *Edward now wore the manic look of some animal transferred into the wrong environment, as though he might run amok, or bite*—Penelope Lively, 1990; (metaphorical) *It wasn't his fault that her feelings seemed to be running amok*—E. Rees, 1992. Occasionally, it is used in the phrase *amok with* in what looks like a mistake for *awash with*: *?the streets all amok with trash and the remains of cigarettes*—*OEC*, 2005.

among, amongst. 1 For uses of *among* and *between*, see BETWEEN 2.

2 The Old English antecedent *on gemang* yielded *onmang* before 1100, whence by regular phonetic gradation *amang, among*. By the 14c. the variant *amonges* had emerged (cf. AMID, AMIDST 1) and by the 16c., by form-association with superlatives, *among(e)st. Among* is now at least ten times commoner in the *OEC.*

3 There is no demonstrable difference of meaning or function between the two, except that *amongst* seems to be somewhat less common in American than in British English. An older view, favoured by Fowler, that *amongst* is commoner than *among* before a following vowel does not seem to be borne out by the evidence: Typical examples: (*among*) *the giants war among themselves*—J. M. Coetzee, 1977; *there were a lot of very young people among the temporary staff*—P. Fitzgerald, 1980; *Britain also has ... the lowest level of welfare expenditure among the countries of the European Community*—*Times*, 1985; (*amongst*) *the other guests served themselves discreetly and talked amongst themselves*—B. Rubens, 1987; *they stood on the edges of the lamplight amongst the wattles by the creek*—P. Carey, 1988; *If a settled view is formed amongst voters that the additional money on the NHS has been wasted progressive politics will be in trouble for decades*—*Independent*, 2007.

amoral. Used to mean 'not within the sphere of moral sense; not to be characterized as either good or bad', this word, first recorded in 1882, has largely ousted the slightly older words *non-moral* (*a*1866) and *unmoral* (1841). Many usage books caution against confusing this word with *immoral*, but in practice such confusion seems to be not that common. For examples, see IMMORAL.

amount, number. In most circumstances *amount* is used with uncount nouns to mean 'quantity' (e.g. *a reasonable amount of forgiveness, glue, resistance, straw*), i.e. nouns which normally have no plural; and *number* is used with plural nouns (e.g. *a certain number of boys, houses, jobs*, etc.). *Amount* is now fast invading the territory of *number*, sometimes, but by no means always, when the following plural noun is viewed as an aggregate or collection. This substitution is older than one might think: the *OED* notes it first in a quotation of 1801. Examples: *Fame had magnified the amount of the forces*—1849; *I have any amount of letters for you*—G. B. Shaw, 1893; *I expect you get a fair amount of road accidents on these winding roads?*—R. Billington, 1988; *Billy's had a tremendous amount of problems*—T. McGuane, 1989 (US); *But booksellers have less and less space for the amount of books that are being published*—*The Author*, 1990; *The amount of bulbs she would find between the stones next spring*—A. Huth, 1991. The loss of the distinction may be irritating to many, but it is beginning to look like an unstoppable process, akin to the widespread use of *less* instead of *fewer*.

ampersand. The name of the symbol '&' used as a space-saving device. H. W. Fowler used it extensively in print and writing and it is not uncommon in handwritten work. In print it survives mainly in the names of jointly owned firms, e.g. Marks & Spencer, and not always then, e.g. Faber and Faber Ltd. In origin it is a 19c. corruption of *'and* per se (= by itself) *and'*, the name of the character '&' as it appears at the end of the alphabet in primers and hornbooks, i.e. '& (standing) by itself, and'. The sign '&' itself seems to be a stylized version of Latin *et* 'and'.

amphiboly /amˈfɪbəli/, **amphibology** /ˌamfɪˈbɒlədʒi/. In rhetoric, a figure of speech signifying ambiguity that arises 'from the uncertain construction of a sentence or clause, of which the individual words are unequivocal' (*OED*). For example, the road sign *Slow Children*, meaning 'Slow down, Children in the vicinity', could perversely be taken to refer to the walking pace or the learning speed of children in the vicinity. A classic example occurs in Shakespeare's *Othello* III. i: Cassio. *Doest thou heare my honest friend?* Clowne. *No, I heare not your honest friend, I heare you.*

amphimacer. See CRETIC.

amuck. see AMOK.

amuse(d). See BEMUSE(D), AMUSE(D).

amusedly. Pronounced as four syllables. See -EDLY.

an (indefinite article). See A, AN.

an-. See A-[1].

anacoluthon. (Greek ἀνακόλουθον 'not following'.) The name given to a change or break in the grammatical construction of a sentence or phrase, e.g. (a recapitulatory pronoun in casual speech) *put little bits of bacon on which the fatter they are the better*—*The Victorian Kitchen*, BBC2, 1989 (cook speaking); (*is* omitted) *She's had five husbands and* ∧ *on the lookout for the sixth*—Oxford University examination script, 1989; (with an intervening pause) *he did not* *see—was prevented by the brightness of the sun from seeing—the traffic lights.* Instances of anacolutha occur at all periods from the Anglo-Saxon period onwards.

anacrusis. (Gk ἀνάκρουσις 'prelude, up-striking'.) In prosody, a syllable or syllables preceding the point at which the reckoning of the normal measure begins. It is a particular feature of Old English verse and that of the other Germanic peoples. In modern verse, where analysis is often disputed, anacrusis may account for the initial *Or* in

Or wás there a déarer one
Still, and a nearer one.
(Hood)

anaemia, anaemic. Usually spelt **anemia** and **anemic** in North American English. See Æ, Œ.

anaesthetic, anaesthetize. Usually spelt **anesthetic** and **anesthetize** in American English. See Æ, Œ.

analogous. The *g* in the final syllable is pronounced with a hard /-g-/ and not, as one hears all too often, /-dʒ-/. It should properly be used in contexts involving definite comparisons that justify the notion of analogy: *Terrorism is more analogous to a virulent, malignant illness, a plague that needs to be exposed, contained and then, yes, eradicated with the most precise surgical and other means—The Nation,* 2001. In practice, however, it does not always manage to keep its distance from the more general word *similar.* Originally confined largely to technical language, the word has spread rapidly into general use, and is usually complemented by *to,* or occasionally by *with*: *Some have suggested that the effort needed to defeat the terrorists is analogous to the cold war—Commonweal,* 2001.

analogy. 1 In the study of language *analogy* is the name given to the process by which the creation of words and phrases can be influenced by other words which seem like parallels, without going through all the stages that produced those precedents. This is a fundamental aspect of the way languages develop, and applies to all aspects of usage, including word-formation, spelling, inflection, meaning, collocation, and pronunciation. Thus, the inflection *bake, baked, baked* (instead of the historical *bake, book, baken*) is due to analogy with such words as *rake, raked, raked,* etc.

2 The process of analogy can be further illustrated by the way in which (*a*) new words are formed from native bases on the analogy of a pattern taken over from a foreign language, e.g. *starvation* (first recorded 1778) as the noun corresponding to the verb *starve* (Old English *steorfan*) by analogy with, for example, *vexation* (*c.*1400 from Old French), the noun corresponding to the verb *vex* (also Middle English from Old French from Latin *vexāre, -ātum*); and (*b*) the manner in which loanwords are made to fit into existing word patterns in English, e.g. *strive* (from OF *estriver*) taken into the native conjugation of *drive* (OE *drīfan*), the only verb of French origin to be so treated.

3 The same process can be seen at work in the emergence of new past participles and past tenses of some verbs, e.g. *dug* (16c., earlier *digged*) by analogy with *stuck;* and *dove* (19c., chiefly US) beside the traditional *dived* on the analogy of *strove* (from *strive*).

4 False analogies frequently produce irregular analogical formations in the language of children, e.g. 'I couldn't *of*' from recognizing that unstressed *have* and unstressed *of* are both pronounced /əv/ in informal English; and 'I am *being* have' from a false analysis of the imperative 'Behave yourself!'

5 It is easy to assemble a list of unintended casual errors arising from false analogies: *Thou shalt not make unto thee* any *craven image* (oral example, 1989, instead of *graven*); *The Most Eligible Batchelors of 1960* (*Observer Mag.*, 1988, after *batch* n.).

6 *Word-formation.* In the 20c., analogy has been at work in the identification and extraction of suitable final elements and regarding them as new suffixes for exploitation: e.g. -(*a*)*thon* (extracted from *marathon*) producing *talkathon, telethon, walkathon,* etc.; *-burger* (extracted from *hamburger*) producing *beefburger, cheeseburger, steakburger,* etc.; *-teria* (by an analysis of *cafeteria* as *café* + *-teria*) producing *Danceteria, washeteria,* etc.

7 The apparent arbitrariness of some 20c. processes of analogy in word formation should be judged against the performances of earlier centuries. It is salutary to bear in mind that a great many analogical formations can be said to be badly formed or at least 'irregularly formed', and that this has not stopped them from becoming part of the unquestioned core of the language, e.g. *chaotic* (from *chaos*, after the analogy of other Greek-derived words like *demotic, erotic, hypnotic*); *dilation* (from *dilate;* only *dilatation* is etymologically sound); *operatic* (from *opera*, after *dramatic*).

analyse. After a period of uncertainty (Dr Johnson, for example, used the form *analyze*), this verb has settled down as *analyse* in British English and *analyze* in American. Both forms are etymologically defensible.

analysis. 1 'The resolution or breaking up of anything complex into its various simple elements', in chemistry, grammar, etc. It is the opposite process to *synthesis*. Plural *analyses* /-iːz/.

2 The French phrase *en dernière analyse* has been drawn on in English to provide the common phrases *in the last* (or *final*) *analysis* (first recorded in 1877).

anapaest. /ˈanəpiːst/ or /-pɛst/ (prosody). AmE **anapest**. A metrical foot (⏑⏑–) consisting of two short or unstressed syllables followed by one long or stressed syllable: *I am monarch of all I survey*—William Cowper, 1781.

anaphora. 1 (First recorded in the 16c.) In rhetoric, the repetition of the same word or phrase in several successive clauses: e.g. *The voice of the Lord is powerfull; the voyce of the Lord is full of Maiestie; The voyce of the Lord breaketh the Cedars* (Ps. 29: 4–5).

2 (First recorded in the 20c.) In grammar, the use of a word which refers back to, or is a substitute for, a preceding word or group of words. In the sentence 'The city was deserted when it was overrun by the rebels', 'it' refers back to 'the city', i.e. is anaphoric. Cf. CATAPHORIC.

anastrophe. A term of rhetoric meaning 'inversion, or unusual arrangement, of the words or clauses of a sentence': e.g. *Day is done,* gone the sun—*New Yorker,* 1989; Beats there a heart amongst us so jaded ... *that it has failed to be touched ... by the sound of Roy Orbison?—The Face,* 1989.

anathema. 1 Derived from late Latin *anathema* 'an excommunicated person' and Gk ἀνάθεμα originally 'a thing devoted', but in later usage 'a thing devoted to evil, an accursed thing', it came into English in the 16c. initially in the broad sense 'the formal act, or formula, of consigning to damnation'. With the passage of time, this sense weakened until the word became freely used as a general weapon of ecclesiastical, and then of lay, rancour. Its plural is most commonly *anathemas* (*he knew no curses except the day-to-day anathemas of the Webfeet*—J. Mark, 1982), but in the specialized sense 'a thing devoted or consecrated to divine use' the singular form is normally pronounced, with shift of stress, /anəˈθiːmə/, plural *anathemata* /anəˈθiːmətə/.

2 Beginning in the 18c., *anathema* has also been used as a quasi-adjective meaning 'accursed, consigned to perdition' (*Saint Paul wished to become anathema himself, so he could thereby save his brethren*—Abraham Tucker, 1765). It is used in predicative position only (after a verb) and is arguably a kind of uncount noun (similar to *pleasure*). Note that it is not normally used in the plural, e.g. *taxes are anathema* [not *anathemas*] *to most people.* Examples: *The policy they embraced was however anathema to many Conservatives, who rightly saw in it the beginning of the end of British rule in India*—Roy Jenkins, 1988; *Waif look is anathema to fashion house*—headline in *Times*, 2007.

anchylosis. See ANKYLOSIS.

ancien régime. Printed in italics and with acute *e*.

ancillary. *Ancillary* derives ultimately from the Latin noun *ancilla*, 'handmaid'. *Ancilla* is the word used by the Virgin Mary in the Vulgate Bible when the Angel Gabriel announces the Incarnation to her: 'dixit autem Maria ecce ancilla Domini fiat mihi secundum verbum tuum'; 'And Mary said Behold the handmaid of the Lord; be it unto me according to thy word (AV, Luke 1:48)'. Its main modern meaning of 'providing necessary support to the essential operations of a central organization, especially a hospital', and its use as a noun, both date from the mid-20c. The standard pronunciation is /anˈsɪləri/ (an-**si**-luh-ri), but there is a tendency for people to add /i/ after the double *l*, and pronounce the word an-**si**-lee-uh-ri. As a result, it is often wrongly spelt **ancilliary*.

and. The simplest-looking words are often the most complicated, and *and* is no exception. **1** The normal function of this connective conjunction is, of course, to join sentence elements of the same kind: e.g. *Gavin and Stacey; first and foremost; the rules and regulations; she served quickly and efficiently; for ever and ever; an acute and wary sense of the ordinary.* It can imply progression (*faster and faster*), causation (*misbehave and you'll not get your pocket money*), great duration (*she ran and ran*), a large number or a great quantity (*miles and miles, piles and piles*), and addition (*four and four are eight*).

2 In practice *and* is often omitted for contextual effects of various kinds, especially between sequences of descriptive adjectives, which can be separated by commas or simply by spaces instead: (without *and* and using a comma or commas instead) *marginal, remote, troublesome, peculiar Europeans with unpronounceable names; factories outlined against a still, sunless sky;* (without *and* and without commas) *the teeming jerrybuilt dun-coloured traffic-ridden deafening city*—P. Lively, 1987; *he envied Jenkin his simple uncluttered uncomplicated innocent life*—I. Murdoch, 1987.

3 There is a persistent belief that it is grammatically wrong or poor style to begin a sentence with *And*, but this prohibition has been cheerfully ignored by standard authors from Anglo-Saxon times onwards. An initial *And* is a useful aid to writers as the narrative continues. The *OED* provides examples from the 9c. to the 19c., including one from Shakespeare's *King John:* Arthur. *Must you with hot Irons, burne out both mine eyes?* Hubert. *Yong Boy, I must.* Arthur. *And will you?* Hubert. *And I will.* It is also used for other rhetorical purposes, and sometimes just to introduce an improvised afterthought: *Tibba still pined and slavered for the school lunches. And little other care hath she.*—A. N. Wilson 1982; *I'm going to swim. And don't you dare watch*—G. Butler, 1983. It is also used in expressing surprise at, or asking the truth of, what one has already heard: *O John! and you have seen him! And are you really going?*—1884 in *OED*. Some grammar checkers flag *And* at the beginning of a sentence as something to be avoided, but the alternatives they suggest, such as 'in addition' and 'moreover' will not work in many cases, and would clearly be ridiculous in the examples just quoted.

4 *and all.* Another well-established use of *and* is in the phrase *and all.* Wright's *English Dialect Dictionary* gives prominence to this use, meaning 'and everything; also, besides, in addition'. In some of the examples it seems to lack any perceptible lexical sense and to be just a rhythmical device to eke out a sentence. Wright's 19c. evidence is drawn from almost every county and he also lists examples from dialectal contexts in the works of Tennyson, Gissing, Kipling, and others: (Scottish) *Woo'd and married an' a'*; (Westmorland) *when she saw me she wept, I wept ano'*; (West Yorkshire) *Whoy, we'n been up an darn anole;* (Lincolnshire) *He wants sendin' to Ketton* [Kirton-in-Lindsey prison], *an a-cat-o'-nine-tails an'-all.* The use has seeped out into more general use: *When I held her in my arms she was like a dying bird, so thin and all*—M. Doane, 1988; *We had a hell of a job pushing it, what with the sarnie-boards and all*—Caris Davis, 1989; *Isn't it amazing? He has a Ph.D. and all.*—J. Shute, 1992.

5 *there are kings and kings. There are maidens and there are maidens, but that wasn't one of his best* said a BBC cricket commentator wearily at the end of a barren over by the West Indian bowler Curtly Ambrose. He was using a construction first recorded in English in the 16c. 'expressing a difference of quality between things of the same name or class', as the *OED* expresses it. The use, the *Dictionary* says, is 'commonly called a French idiom' and refers to Molière's *il y a fagots et fagots* in *Le Médecin malgré lui* (1666), but the English evidence is earlier. The *OED* cites examples from the 16c. to the 19c., including *Alack, there be roses and roses, John!* (Browning, 1855). To which may be added the following 19c. and 20c. examples: *Well, as to that, of course there are kings and kings. When I say I detest kings, I mean I detest* bad *kings*—W. S. Gilbert, *The Gondoliers*, 1889;*There are ways to steal and there are ways to steal*—*NewYorker*, 1988; *There is homelessness and homelessness. The word has become a shibboleth for opposition politicians and the 'caring' media*—*Times*, 1991.

6 See also AGREEMENT 3; AND/OR; *and which* (WHICH 5); COMMA 3, 5; GOOD AND; *nice and* (NICE 2); TRY AND.

and/or, a formula to show that you can choose between the items it connects or choose both of them. In other words, it indicates three logical possibilities: a cocktail recipe stating 'add gin and/or vodka' logically means 'add gin or add vodka or add both'. First recorded in the mid-19c. in legal contexts, and still employed from time to time in legal documents, *and/or* has been criticized by pundits, mostly on aesthetic grounds, when used in non-legal writing.

Aesthetics apart, an example like *This paper discusses logics whose premisses and/or conclusions can contain ambiguous material—Journal of Semantics*, 2001 seems impeccable, because *and/or* clearly means 'the premises may contain ambiguous material, or the conclusions may, or they both may', and it signals that very concisely. In less logically precise contexts than that, however, it is inconsiderate to readers: it burdens them with the task of teasing out exactly what the three possibilities are. What are we to make, for example, of *Stalin, characteristically insensitive to Western public opinion and/or relying on the political ambiguity of these phrases in the existing context, signed it—The Oxford Companion to United States History*, 2001? The writer is asking the reader to decide what Stalin's motives were.

It is also sometimes unclear whether three possibilities are meant, or only two. The less ambiguous way of expressing three possibilities is to use 'X *or* Y *or both'*, while in many contexts, just '*or*' will do perfectly. Finally, *and/or* linking more than two items is to be avoided at all costs: *Social variation in language may be due to social class, ethnic origin, age, and/or sex* leaves it bafflingly unclear with which other factors 'sex' is associated.

anemia, anemic. The normal spelling in NAmer. English of *anaemia, anaemic.*

anemone. Because of its unusual sequence of *n-m-n* it is often pronounced as */ə'nɛnəmiː/, i.e. swapping round the second *m* and final *n*. In order to spell the word correctly, it may be helpful to remember Fowler's (1926) hint: '*an emine*(*nce*) not *an enemy* gives the order of consonants'.

anent. This ancient preposition (in origin a phrase, Old English *on efn, on emn* 'in line or company with, on a level with') survives in Scottish law ('in respect of or reference to'). In general English it is used to mean 'with respect to', but it often carries an air of affectation or of faint jokiness. It is also frequently used, with a tinge of pomposity, in letters to the editor (of a newspaper, dictionary, etc.). Examples: *Their arguments are anent What nanny really meant*—W. H. Auden, 1952; *Adamant you'll find me anent 'aficionado'*—O. Nash, 1961; *the consensus view of the reading public anent poetry: they, too, dislike it—TLS*, 1984; *His Lordship had been much influenced by averments anent section 74*—Lord Jauncey (a Scottish law lord), 1988; *a Dr Malcolm Carruthers had delivered a lecture to Edinburgh's Lister Institute anent the astonishing cardiac benefits of the kilt*—A. Coren, 1989.

anesthetic, anesthetize. The normal spelling in American English of *anaesthetic, anaesthetize.*

aneurysm. Correctly so spelt (not *aneurism*), with the *y* answering to the second upsilon in Gk εὐρύς 'wide'. Form-association with other words ending in *-ism* has led to the adoption of *aneurism* by many writers, but *aneurysm* is still the better form.

angle (noun[1]). In the meaning 'a particular way of approaching or considering an issue or problem', *angle* is first recorded from 1860, and was used by George Eliot in *Middlemarch* in 1872. Burchfield considered it 'lightweight' and 'best avoided in polished prose'. His objection seems generally unfounded, although there are some contexts in which *angle* suggests a lack of objectivity, or even underhandedness (*selling angle, propaganda angle*). Should you require a weightier word, several are to hand: *perspective, point of view, position, standpoint*, and *viewpoint.*

angle (noun[2]), **angler, angling.** An 'angle' was originally (in Old English) a fishing-hook. During the 15c. it came to be used as a verb meaning 'to fish with a hook and bait'; and, in the 16c., *angler* emerged in the sense 'one who fishes with a hook and line'. These derivatives stood alongside *fish* (verb), *fisher*, and *fisherman.*

The original noun *angle* fell into disuse in the 19c., but the verb *angle*, the noun *angler*, and the verbal noun *angling* remain, though only in carefully designated uses.

The verb *angle* has survived mainly in transferred senses. Politicians *angle* for votes; most of us, at one time or another, *angle* for a present, an invitation, a compliment, etc. Yet, the distinction is far from fixed, and it is also idiomatic *to fish for compliments* and *to fish* (not *angle*) *in troubled waters*.

In certain contexts *angling/fishing* are interchangeable, while in others they have their own restrictions. *Fishing*, which covers everything from jam-jars through rod-and-line to trawlers, can sometimes be too general a term. *Angling* refers to rod and line only. No one says 'I'm going angling tomorrow'; in such a sentence 'fishing' would always be used. *Fly-fishing* is idiomatic; *fly-angling* is not.

Coarse fishing means fishing in a river or pond for roach, rudd, perch, pike, and other freshwater fish by anglers equipped with tackle, groundbait, maggots, and floats.

An *angler* is one who fishes with rod and line; *fisher* survives only in the biblical phrase (Matt. 4: 19) 'I will make you fishers of men'; *fisherman* is a generic term for a person who fishes for sport or one who goes out to sea in a fishing boat to earn a living. *Angler* is often the preferred term in fishing magazines. It also has the advantage of not referring to gender.

Anglo (noun). Plural *Anglos*. For two centuries this term has been used in Canada to designate English-speaking, as distinct from French-speaking, Canadians. Since the 1930s, and especially in the southwestern States of America, an *Anglo* is an American with an English-speaking background, as distinct from a person whose first language is Spanish.

Anglo-. Used to form compound nouns and adjectives referring (*a*) to events or facts involving the two countries specified, e.g. *Anglo-American relations, Anglo-French cooperation, Anglo-Irish agreement*, etc. and (*b*) to people whose mother and father were of the different nationalities mentioned, e.g. *a venerable Anglo-Japanese journalist who was completely bilingual.* Some people in the large parts of the United Kingdom that are not England understandably view this first use in particular with some distaste, but it continues to be the standard formulation. Is there an alternative that avoids offending nationalist sensibilities? The obvious answer is to replace the *Anglo-* part with *British-*, e.g. *British-American, British-French,* (or with *English-*, if the reference is to England specifically and exclusively). The element *Brito-* has not achieved widespread currency, except in the somewhat specialized terms *Brito-Arctic* (relating to British territory in the Arctic) and *Britocentric* (having Britain as a centre), *-centricity*, and a few other compounds.

Anglo-Indian. This term was first used in the early 19c. to denote a person of mixed British and Indian descent. At a slightly later date it was introduced as a term for a British civil servant, businessman, memsahib, etc. who had lived for many years in India, but that use is now historical only. Nowadays *Anglo-Indian* can refer to people of dual heritage living in India or in the UK, although *British-Indian* is better since it avoids the taint of Anglocentrism.

angst, angsty. George Eliot is the first person, according to the *OED*, to have used the German word *Angst* (= fear) in English, albeit in inverted commas, in a letter of August 1849. Later (1922) it was used in a translation of Freud, then entered literary and philosophical language, and is now part of general language with the meaning 'a feeling of deep anxiety or dread, typically an unfocused one about the human condition or the state of the world in general', or, more trivially, as a synonym for any kind of anxiety. Examples: *Full of existential angst and loneliness, her paintings are able to evoke an empathetic response from the viewer—Art in America*, 2004; *A collective wail of middle-class angst went up from mainstream party leaders: what have we done?—Daily Tel.*, 2009; *John McCain has a proven record of working across the aisle to the extent that it's caused some angst amongst Republicans—CNN*, 2008.

Angst's offspring *angsty* is first recorded in *The Oxford Magazine* in 1956, and now seems set to follow its sire into literary, or pseudo-literary, use. What it lacks in specificity it attempts to make up for in pizzazz: *Rare is the teen who doesn't have at least one journal filled with shame-inducing pseudo-profundity, or a private collection of angsty song lyrics—Montreal Mirror*, 2005; *In the midst of all my angsty rambling last week, a ray of sunlight shone through the gloom*—weblog, 2005 (BrE).

ankylosis. This form, answering correctly to Greek ἀγκύλωσις 'stiffening of the joints', has now virtually driven out the once dominant form *anchylosis*.

annex, annexe. The verb is spelt *annex* in both British and American English. The normal spelling of the noun in American English is *annex*. In British English both spellings are correct, but *annexe* is somewhat more frequent. In legal and administrative writing, *annex*, denoting an addition to a document, with no final *e*, is the accepted convention.

anniversaries. The normal practice is to refer to the tenth, twentieth, thirtieth, etc. anniversary of an event, but some particular names have come to be applied to the more significant anniversaries. Among these are: (weddings) *silver* (25 years), *ruby* (40), *golden* (50), and *diamond* (60, sometimes 75); (public events) *centenary* /sən'tiːnəri/, /-'tɛnəri/ (100) (but in North America and some other English-speaking countries more usually *centennial;* so also in the relevant combinations that follow); *sesquicentenary* (150), *bicentenary* (200); (not recorded) *semiquincentenary* (250); *tercentenary* (or *tri-*) (300), *quatercentenary* [NB: not *quarter-*] (400), *quincentenary* (500), *sexcentenary* (600), *septcentenary* (700), *octocentenary* (800); (not recorded) *nonacentenary* (900); *millenary* (1,000).

annul. The base form of this verb ends with a single *-l*, as does *annuls*, but the *-l* is doubled to *-ll-* in *annulled* and *annulling*. The corresponding noun is *annulment*. The not uncommon and mistaken spelling **annull* is presumably influenced by the idea of making something null and void. See -LL-, -L-.

Annunciation /əˌnʌnsɪ'eɪʃən/, is now mostly restricted to meaning 'the announcement of the incarnation, made by the angel Gabriel to the Virgin Mary', in which case it is best written with an initial capital, especially if it refers to a painting, sculpture, etc. of the event, e.g. *Botticelli's Annunciation*. It is also occasionally used as a rather high-falutin' or archaizing synonym of *announcement*, e.g. *The forbidden, the transgressive, is always an annunciation—London Review of Books*, 2003. It should not be confused, as it sometimes is, with *enunciation*, 'the uttering or pronouncing of articulate sounds; manner of utterance', as has happened here: **the rich baritone voice and precise annunciation that characterise Gwynne's work.*

anorak. This word of Greenland Inuit origin has taken on a special, derogatory meaning in British English by being indelibly associated with people waiting around in cold weather (in anoraks, supposedly) to watch trains and aeroplanes or do other things the rest of the world can sneer at. Hence an *anorak* is a boring, studious, or socially inept person who, as the *OED* puts it, 'pursues an unfashionable and solitary interest with obsessive dedication'. The word is recorded as being first used in this way in 1984, and since then has become part of the vocabulary of put-downs, though very often it is used to highlight obsessive interest rather than social awkwardness: people will readily confess to being anoraks in a particular sphere. According to the *OEC* data, it is commonly used in sporting and political contexts. Examples: *I'll return to this book which anyone but a political anorak would find extremely tedious*—weblog, 2005; *David Wright wants to know why I keep referring to free-kicks as frees. Because there's four less [sic] letters to type and no hyphen, you nit-picking anorak. Honestly—Guardian, World Cup Reports*, 2002; *According to my (I am a wine anorak, and proud of it) wine file for 2002, I supped my way through about 180 different wines*—weblog, 2003.

Outside Britain, the equivalent word is *geek* or *nerd*.

anorexia has two related adjectives, **anorexic** and **anorectic**. The first came into English via French, and is now vastly more frequent. The second is slightly older, and comes directly from the Greek ἀνόρεκτος 'without appetite'. Nowadays it is found mostly in technical medical writing. Although it is a perfectly legitimate form, in non-specialist contexts it may strike some people as odd, so is probably best avoided for that reason.

another. For *one another* see EACH 2.

ante-, anti-. These two useful prefixes mean rather different things. The first, from Latin, means 'before, preceding, in front of' (*antenatal* 'happening or existing before birth', *antebellum* 'before a (specified) war', *antechamber* 'chamber or room leading to a more important one'). The second, which is much more frequent, come from the Greek ἀντί 'opposite' and means 'opposite; opposed to; against', e.g. *anti-hero* 'a person totally unlike a conventional hero'; *anti-American, anti-Semitism; anti-aircraft* (*gun*). When creating new words on this model, British English tends to use the hyphen much more than does American English, e.g. *anti-war sentiments* as opposed to *antiwar sentiments*. Both British English and American English keep the hyphen when the second element begins with a capital letter, e.g. *anti-American, anti-Semitic*.

In British English both prefixes are pronounced /ˈantɪ/, but in American English *anti-* is pronounced /ˈantaɪ/.

As the *OED* points out, the analogy for the limitless number of *anti-* formations seems to have been given by *Antichrist* and its adjective *anti-Christian*, which (with the analogous *antipope*) were almost the only examples in use before 1600. Shakespeare has no independent *anti-* compounds (though he did use 'fused' *anti-* words such as *antidote, antipathy*, and *antipodes*).

antenna. In the meaning 'a sensory organ found in pairs on heads of insects, crustaceans, etc.', the plural is *antennae*. In the sense '(radio) aerial', the plural is *antennas*.

antepenult. A term of prosody and phonology, 'preceding the penult; the last but two', as in '*al*titude' and '*heav*iness'.

antetype. See -TYPE.

Anthony. In standard English pronounced /ˈantəni/ with medial /t/ not /θ/ (th). But the pronunciation with medial /θ/ is common in US English, and heard increasingly often in British English, presumably as a result of the 'speak as you spell' school of thought.

anthropophagi. This learned word, familiar especially from Shakespeare's *Othello* (*And of the Cannibals, that each other eate, The Anthropophagie*), is plural in formation and means 'man-eaters, cannibals'. It comes via Latin from Greek ἀνθρωποφάγ-ος 'man-eating', from ἄνθρωπος 'man' + φαγεῖν 'to eat', and is pronounced in English as /anθrəˈpɒfəgʌɪ/ or /-dʒʌɪ/ (an-thruh-**po**-fuh-gy, or -jy).

anticipate. Here lies another of the great usage battlegrounds, where the conflict is all the more fraught for overlapping meanings that confuse the issue. **1** The two primary and never disputed meanings are (*a*) 'to be aware of (a thing) in advance and act accordingly', e.g. *I shall anticipate any such opposition by tendering my resignation now* (Angus Wilson); *Some unknown writer in the second century ... suddenly anticipated the whole technique of modern ... narrative* (C. S. Lewis); *Lecky has anticipated what the animal liberationists are now saying*—*Listener*, 1983; and (*b*) 'to forestall (a person) and take action before they do', e.g. *I'm sorry—do go on, I did not mean to anticipate you*—John Le Carré.

2 'To regard as probable; expect or predict' is the disputed meaning. The *ODO* gives it first billing, and it is the one which is the most common, e.g. *Wing mirrors were selling better than they had ever anticipated*—Margaret Drabble, 1987. Criticism has rained down on it since at least 1881, but the heavy artillery of Fowler, Burchfield, and many others has never succeeded in bombing it into submission.

Like *expect*, it can be followed by a noun or noun phrase (*She anticipated scorn on her return to the theatre*); by a *that*-clause (*It was anticipated that the rains would slow the military campaign*); and by another verb in the infinitive, when *anticipate* is passive, e.g. *Profits are not anticipated to show much improvement*. On the rare occasions when it is active and followed by an infinitive, it sounds distinctly unidiomatic: *?But we do anticipate to hear something today*. Unlike *expect*, it can be followed by an *-ing* form of the verb, e.g. *Here are some answers I anticipate receiving*.

3 Despite its wide currency, however, it can still irritate more traditional readers (and listeners), perhaps because it is a cumbersome word compared with the more straightforward alternative *expect*. It should in any case be avoided where it may be unclear which meaning is intended, as in *One would not expect Cleopatra to have suffered such a fate, nor did she herself anticipate it*—A. Fraser, 1988, which could mean either 'expect' or 'to be aware of (a thing) in advance and act accordingly'.

antistrophe. In rhetoric and grammar, the repetition of words in inverse order, e.g. *You must say what you mean and mean what you say*.

antithesis. **1** In rhetoric, 'an opposition or contrast of ideas, expressed by using as the corresponding members of two contiguous sentences or clauses, words which are the opposites of, or strongly contrasted with, each other: as he *must* increase, *but* I *must* decrease', *in* newness *of* spirit, *not in* oldness *of the* letter' (*OED*). Antithesis is a marked feature of Samuel Johnson's style: *The colours of life in youth and age appear different, as the face of nature in spring and winter; The old man pays regard to riches, and the youth reverences virtue; Marriage has many pains, but celibacy has no pleasures* (*Rasselas*, ch. 26).

2 In ordinary use, it can mean (i) 'a person or thing that is the direct opposite of someone or something else', in which case the preposition following it is generally *of*, although *to* is also used; and (ii) 'a contrast or opposition between two things', which meaning is followed by *between*. Examples: *This revolting creed was the antithesis of everything the Royal Navy stood for—History Today*, 2002; *Designed as the antithesis to the Oscars, the Golden Raspberry Award Foundation has been mocking Hollywood's below-par cinematic output for almost three decades—The Guardian (Film)*, 2009; *The two halves of the work therefore corresponded to his antithesis between faith and understanding*—H. Chadwick, 2001.

antitype. See -TYPE.

antonomasia. In rhetoric, (*a*) the substitution of an epithet or descriptive phrase for a proper name, e.g. *the Iron Duke* for 'the Duke of Wellington', *the Iron Lady* for 'Mrs Margaret Thatcher'; (*b*) the use of a proper name to express a general idea, e.g. *a Solomon* for 'a wise man', *a Cicero* for 'an orator'. The original Greek word meant literally 'name instead'.

anxious. It is as well to be aware that using *anxious* to mean 'eager' or 'keen' (e.g. *She's very anxious that you should like her*—A. N. Wilson, 1982) may displease some people, especially in the US. There, this use has been criticized by several usage authorities since the early 20c. The objection is based on the axiom that *anxious* (1623) should be restricted to meaning 'worried, nervous'; in other words, it should reflect a state of *anxiety* (first recorded in a 1525 work by Sir Thomas More). However, the contested meaning goes back to the 18c.: the phrase *anxious to please* appeared in Robert Blair's poem *The Grave* (1743), and Lord Nelson declared in 1794 that 'The General seems as anxious as any of us to expedite the fall of the place'. In this meaning, *anxious* is followed either by a *to*-infinitive, as in the last two examples, or a *that*-clause, e.g. *George III and the new prime minister, William Pitt, were particularly anxious that Fox should lose his seat—ODNB*, 2009.

In some examples there seem to be connotations of both eagerness and anxiety, e.g. *Punch was always anxious to oblige everybody*—Kipling, 1888. Many, however, suggest only eagerness: *All seemed pleased with the performance, and anxious for another of the same sort*—K. Amis, 1954; *You must be anxious to see your folk*—S. King, 1979.

The best that can be said is that for certain audiences it is wise to avoid using *anxious* to mean 'eager', despite the fact that it is historically well attested, was described by Fowler (1926) as a 'natural development', and is absolutely standard.

any. The main issues raised by *any* are (i) whether a following verb should be singular or plural and (ii) whether to write *any more* or *anymore, any way* or *anyway*, etc. These are dealt with in 1 and 2 respectively, while succeeding sections deal with less vexed questions. **1** (*a*) *Any, anybody*, and *anyone* (as well as other indefinite pronouns such as *everybody*) are now frequently, if controversially, followed by the plural forms *they, them, their, themselves*: e.g. *Can* any *illegal migrant entering the country be sure that* they *will not be deported?;* anybody/anyone *who wants to improve* their *writing may attend the course.* Popular usage, historical precedent, and concision lend weight to the use of the plural in such contexts, but many writers prefer to use *he or she*, or, unusually these days, *he* (*him, his, himself*). See AGREEMENT 6.

(*b*) *any of ... is/are, do/does*, etc? Is it correct to say *Are any of your children currently attending school?* or *Is any of your children currently attending school? Does any of us* or *do any of us really have the right not to forgive?* Both are correct but suggest or presuppose different things. *Are* etc. *any of* obviously suggests more than one, i.e. *some*, while *is* etc. *any of* can be seen as shorthand for *any single one of.*

Whether you plump for a singular or a plural verb, mixed constructions are best avoided: **I don't suppose there* is *any of us who* haven't *experience of something like that* should be *I don't suppose there* is *any of us who* hasn't *experience of something like that.*

2 *One word or two words?* (*a*) **anybody, anyone**. Always written as one word, these pronouns are interchangeable in most contexts (though *anyone* is about five times more frequent than *anybody*), e.g. *What they keep in those boxes is anybody's* (or *anyone's*) *guess; they were giving free beer to anyone* (or *anybody*) *who played; the little boy staring out of these pictures could be anyone* (or *anybody*).

(*b*) **any one** as two words means 'any single person or thing', as in *you can have any one you like* (*any you like* would include the possibility of more than one). Examples: *'We all realized this was bigger than any one of us,' Reilly said*—*Boston Globe*, 2009.

(*c*) **any more, anymore**. (i) Logically it would seem sensible to reserve the separated form for contexts in which the meaning is 'even the smallest amount' (*the boy had eaten two of the apples and refused to eat any more of them*) and the one-word form for the meaning 'any longer'. But things are not as neat as that.

By and large *any more* is used in all areas when the meaning required is 'even the smallest amount'. When the required meaning is 'any longer' there are geographical divisions. American English and other forms of English outside the UK tend to favour *anymore*, which is now being adopted by some British writers and publishing houses. The majority of authors and printers in the UK, however, still print *any more* for this second sense. Examples (all in negative contexts): (any more) *There's nothing for me in London, John, not any more*—M. Wesley, 1983 (BrE); *no one will know any more what history is*—T. Keneally 1985 (Aust.); (anymore) *he wasn't a schoolkid anymore*—M. du Plessis, 1983 (SAfr.); *You seldom hear about love anymore*—S. Bellow, 1987 (US); *No one bats an eyelid about tattoos and piercings anymore*—*Cherwell Magazine*, 2004 (BrE).

Contexts remain in which the words must be kept separate, e.g. *Mrs Carbuncle can't buy coal any more than the Fordyces can*—*New Yorker*, 1987. Perhaps it is unnecessary to point out that when *more* modifies a following adjective *any* has to be a separate word, e.g. *It doesn't get any more real than when the acrid smoke from a pile of green logs in a circular stone-flanked hearth doesn't escape from an Iron Age roundhouse*—*Birmingham Post*, 2007.

But even in such circumstances some writers obscure the meaning by allowing the two words to merge: *She was mysterious and wouldn't tell me anymore* (= anything else)—J. Winterson, 1985.

(ii) In American regional use, *anymore* is also used in positive constructions in the sense 'nowadays, now'. The *Dictionary of American Regional English* cites examples (beginning with one of 1859) from virtually every State, e.g. *We all use night-crawlers anymore; We put up quite a bit of hay here anymore; He's hard of hearing anymore.* Harry S. Truman is cited as saying, 'It sometimes seems to me that all I do anymore is to go to funerals'.

(*d*) **Anyhow** and **anyway**, always written as single words, are interchangeable as adverbs, though *anyway* is the more frequent in *OEC* data by a ratio of 16:1. Examples: *Anyhow I'm carving out a career there teaching the boss's daughter to read novels*—T. Keneally, 1985; *I'll prepare the list anyway, she decided, and a tentative date*—B. Rubens, 1987.

(*e*) **any way**. These adverbial uses of *anyway* are to be distinguished from the noun phrase *any way: someone approached me to ask if there was any way I could help; do it any way you like.*

(*f*) **anyplace**. A markedly American adverb (= UK *anywhere*) first recorded in the second decade of the 20c., e.g. *He's a fine man, and he can be a pastor anyplace*—*Boston Globe*, 2006. Even in American English, however, it is much less common than *anywhere*.

(*g*) **anytime**. Another characteristically American adverb (= at any time), e.g. *She said she would vote for him anytime*—*New Yorker*, 1987; *Anytime you can reduce the number of people or the number of processes, you make the market more efficient*—*Successful Farming Magazine*, 2004.

(*h*) **anyway**. See 2*d*-*e*, above.

(*i*) **any ways, anyways**. See ANYWAYS.

3 *As adverb. Any* can be correctly used as an adverb to emphasize a comparative adjective or adverb: *they are not treated like schoolgirls any longer; he can't play any better; she refuses to go any further.* In American English, and occasionally in British English, in informal contexts, it can stand alone with the sense 'at all': *We're used to responsibility. Doesn't worry us any*—A. Christie, 1937; *But it's not going to help any with my exams*—*New Yorker*, 1988.

4 *Any* in comparisons. A fine net of illogicality mars constructions of the types *this is the most brutal piece of legislation of any passed by this government* (read *this is a more brutal piece of legislation than any other passed by this government*), and *a better book than any written by this author* (read *any others*).

anyways, any ways. *Any ways* as an adverb = 'in any way, in any respect, at all', is used in the *Book of Common Prayer* (*All those who are any ways afflicted ... in mind, body, or estate*), in AV (*And if the people of the land doe any wayes hide their eyes from the men*), and in many literary contexts during the last four centuries. It seems to have dropped out of standard UK use now, though it survives in regional use. It is also encountered written as one word, *anyways* in informal American English, e.g. *So who promised this guy anything anyways?—Reader* (Chicago), 1983. The use of this alternative form of *anyway* to mean 'in any case, anyhow' was marked in the *OED* (1885) as 'dialect or illiterate'. In fact, it is part of North American informal or dialectal English, though not generally accepted as standard, and is often used in fiction as a means of characterization. The *OEC* data shows that it is not confined to North America, being quite often found also in informal British English, especially weblogs. *Anyways, I've been a bit too verbose so far so I'll break it down for you in 30 words—www.drownedinsound.com,* 2000 (BrE); *A lot of the automakers were about to go into a two-week shutdown anyways—CNN, Lou Dobs Tonight,* 2003.

aorist. (Greek ἀόριστος 'indefinite'.) One of the past tenses of the Greek verb, which takes its name from its denoting a simple past occurrence, with none of the limitations as to completion, continuance, etc., which belong to the other past tenses. It corresponds to the simple past tense in English, e.g. 'he died'.

apart from. As a complex preposition, meaning 'except for' and 'in addition to', standard in the UK from the early 17c. onwards, e.g. *the raven, who apart from anything else was much stronger in the air than the dove*—Julian Barnes, 1989; *apart from anything else, women politicians are constantly subjected to comment on their looks, criticism of their style and scepticism about their ability—Guardian,* 2010. An equivalent expression used in American English from the early 19c. alongside *apart from* is *aside from*, e.g. *There's little to do aside from what Virginia refers to as 'putting the farm to bed for the winter'—The New Farm,* 2004 (AmE). The *OEC* data suggests that, while *aside from* is now common throughout the *Anglosphere, apart from* continues to be widely used, even in American English, e.g. *Apart from him, I don't know of anybody who ever made any particular very important mark in the world*—L. Kirstein, 1986.

apartheid. There are several ways of pronouncing this Afrikaans word denoting a now—fortunately—defunct form of institutional white supremacism. The pronunciation /əˈpɑːtheɪt/ (uh-**part**-hayt) comes closest to the Afrikaans; but /əˈpɑːt(h)ʌɪd/ and /əˈpɑːt(h)ʌɪt/, with the *-h-* pronounced or silent, uh-**part**-hyd/-hyt, uh-**par**-tyd/-tyt, are also heard. No one pronunciation can be said to be more correct than any other.

apex. In scientific writing, such as botany and anatomy, the plural form *apices*, pronounced /ˈeɪpɪsiːz/ (**ay**-pi-seez) is the standard, e.g. *The ovary is formed when the two carpel apices meet—OEC,* 2002. In other contexts, *apexes* tends to be more used, e.g. *Kurdistan is one of the major apexes for military operations against the Iraq army—BBC* press release, 2003. See APICAL; -EX, -IX; LATIN PLURALS.

aphaeresis /əˈfɪərɪsɪs/. The taking away or suppression of a letter or syllable at the beginning of a word, e.g. *cute*, and *round* for *acute*, and *around*. See APHESIS.

aphesis. (Greek ἄφεσις 'a letting go'.) J. A. H. Murray's term for the gradual and unintentional loss of a short unaccented vowel at the beginning of a word; as in *squire* for *esquire, down* for *adown*. It is a special form of the phonetic process called *aphaeresis* for which, from its frequency in the history of the English language, a distinctive name is useful. The corresponding adjective is **aphetic**.

apical. The technical adjective derived from *apex* is pronounced either /ˈeɪpɪk(ə)l/ or /ˈapɪk(ə)l /.

apiece. This adverb, meaning 'to, for, or by each one of a group', immediately follows a noun or a number: e.g. *after buying his brothers a pint apiece* [*he*] *had to be content with half for himself*—M. Bragg, 1969; *These 145,000 highest earners have* *incomes that start at $1.6 million apiece*—*World Socialist,* 2005. It should always be written as one word, although its underlying meaning explains mistakes such as **We thought we'd charge $25 a piece*—*Raw Vision,* 2005. Conversely, the informal US adverbial phrase *a piece,* meaning 'a short distance' is written as two words, e.g. *A new shop in Manset [is] down the road a piece from Wilbur's place*—*Down East,* 1992. It is occasionally found written as one, e.g. **so we headed to another one down the road apiece*—*Urban Scrawl,* 2004, (NZ).

aplomb. Pronounced /ə'plɒm/, rhyming with *bomb.* The pronunciation /ə'plʌm/ like *plum* is not wrong but is now a minority one.

apocope. /ə'pɒkəpi/ (Gk ἀποκοπή 'a cutting off'.) The cutting off or omission of the last letter or syllable(s) of a word, e.g. *curio* for *curiosity, cinema* for *cinematograph;* and, in more ancient times, Old English *rīdan* → early Middle English *rīden* (two syllables) → later Middle English *rīde* (still two syllables) → modern English *ride* (one syllable).

apodosis /ə'pɒdəsɪs/. The main clause in a sentence (as contrasted with the introductory clause or *protasis* /'prɒtəsɪs/), especially in a conditional sentence, as 'If thine enemy hunger, *feed him'.* The *apodosis* is also called a matrix clause and the *protasis* a subordinate clause.

apology, apologia, apologue. *Apology* is the normal word for a regretful acknowledgement of fault or failure, an assurance that no offence was intended (*I owe you an apology; he made his apologies to the chairman and left the meeting early*). An *apologia* is a written defence or justification of the opinions or conduct of a writer, speaker, etc., the currency of the word being largely due to J. H. Newman's *Apologia pro Vita Sua,* 1864. An *apologue* is a moral fable, like Aesop's Fables or George Orwell's *Animal Farm* (1945).

apophthegm. A terse, pointed saying; a maxim. Pronounced /'apəθɛm/, despite the fact that leaving the *ph* silent conceals the derivation of the word from Gk ἀπόφθεγμα. In American English frequently spelt **apothegm**, a spelling that was the more usual in England till Johnson spelled *apophthegm* in his Dictionary.

aposiopesis /ˌəpɒsɪəʊ'piːsɪs/ or /ˌapəʊsʌɪəʊ'piːsɪs/. (Greek, noun of action, corresponding to a verb meaning 'to keep silent'.) A rhetorical artifice, in which the speaker (or writer) comes to a sudden halt, as if unable or unwilling to proceed. Such ellipses are often the result of an emotional state of mind, e.g. *'Well, I never'*—*said she*—*'what an audacious'*—*emotion prevented her from completing either sentence*—Thackeray, 1847/8. But there are many other kinds, e.g. *I haven't the foggiest* [*notion*]; *Of all the ...* [implying that 'this *is the worst*']; *What the ... !; She is in fact a*—. *But I refrain from saying the word.*

a posteriori. (Latin, = 'from what comes after'.) Pronounced /eɪ pɒˌstɛrɪ'ɔːrʌɪ/, with the initial *a* as in *hate* and the final *-i* as in *eye.* It is a phrase used to characterize reasoning or arguing from known facts to probable causes. 'The prisoners have weals on their backs, so they must have been whipped' is an example of a posteriori reasoning. Contrasted with A PRIORI.

apostrophe.

A History.
B Some golden rules.
C General.
D Possessives.
E Relinquishment of the apostrophe.

A *History.* The mark ' was introduced in English in the 16c. to indicate that a letter or letters had been omitted. The apostrophe before *s* became regulated as an indication of the singular possessive case towards the end of the 17c., and the apostrophe after *s* was first recorded as an indication of the plural possessive case towards the end of the 18c. Since then gross disturbances of these basic patterns have occurred in written and printed work, as will be evident from what follows. Such instability suggests that further disturbances may be expected in the 21c.

B *Some golden rules.*

1 An apostrophe is required before a possessive *s* in the singular (*the boy's hat, the water's edge*) and after a possessive *s* in the plural (*the boys' gymnasium, the ladies' maids, in four days' time*). Except that in the small group of words that do not end in *-s* in the plural, the plural possessive is indicated by *'s* (*children's shoes, men's boots, women's handbags, the oxen's hoofs*).

2 *It's* = 'it is' (see C2 below). *Its* (no apostrophe) is the possessive form of the pronoun *it* (see D5 below).

3 *Errant apostrophes.* From the 17c. onwards an apostrophe was often used in the plural number when the noun ended in a vowel, e.g. *grotto's, opera's, toga's.* Since the mid-19c., grammarians have condemned this use, but it continues to appear in signs and notices, especially in shop windows (*potato's 40p a lb, paddle boat's for hire*). Henry Alford (*The Queen's English*, 1864) reported, 'One not uncommonly sees outside an inn, that *"fly's"* and *"gig's"* are to be let.' This use is often called the greengrocers' (or grocers') apostrophe because of the frequency with which plural forms such as *apple's, cauli's*, and *orange's* appear in their shops.

4 For proper names ending in *-y*, use *s* (not *'s* or *-ies*) in the plurals (*the two Germanys, two bitter Januarys, three Hail Marys*).

5 *'s* is an informal shortened form in both speech and writing of *is* (*the joke's on him*), *has* (*he's got a knife*), and *us* (*let's go*). In informal speech only, or in writing representing it, the following can also be shortened to *'s: as* (*I'm sore's hell*), *does* (*What's he do*), *it is* (*'S that bloody comet*), and *that is* (*'By car?' ''Sright.'*).

6 For the mistake *Who's turn to deliver?* see WHO'S.

C *General.*

1 *Abbreviations.* Though once commonly used in the plural of abbreviations and numerals (*QC's, the 1960's*), the apostrophe is now best omitted in such circumstances: *MAs, MPs, the 1980s, the three Rs, in twos and threes*, Except that it is normally used in contexts where its omission might possibly lead to confusion , e.g. *dot your i's and cross your t's; there are three i's in inimical; the class of '61* (= 1961).

2 *Contractions.* Apostrophes in contractions of the type *I'll* = 'I will' should be joined close up to the letters on either side: *don't, haven't, isn't, shan't, won't; I'll, he'll, we'll; I'd, he'd, she'd; I've, you've; we're, they're; he's, she's, it's* (= it is).

Apostrophes are no longer needed in *cello, flu*, and *phone* (for *violoncello, influenza*, and *telephone*) as these are now established words in their own right.

3 *Special cases.* An apostrophe is correct in a small number of archaic words and some modern compounds to indicate that a letter has been omitted: *e'en* (even), *fo'c's'le* (forecastle), *ne'er-do-well, o'er* (over), *rock 'n' roll.*

4 When an abbreviation is used as a verb, e.g. to *OD* on chocolate, to *OK* a budget, to *KO* an opponent, an apostrophe is inserted before the verb inflections, e.g. *OD'ing, OD's, OD'd.*

5 For the use of *'d* for *-ed*, see -ED AND 'D.

6 *Miscellaneous.* No apostrophe in *Guy Fawkes Day. 's* in *St Elmo's fire, St George's Cross, St John's wort, (St) Valentine's Day. s'* in *All Saints' Day, April Fools' Day, Presidents' Day* (*q.v.*).

D *Possessives.*

1 For the ordinary uses, see B1 above.

2 Names ending in *-s*. Use *'s* for the possessive case in names and surnames whenever possible; in other words, whenever you would tend to pronounce the possessive form of the name with an extra *iz* sound, e.g. *Charles's brother, St James's Square, Thomas's niece, Zacharias's car.* It is customary, however, to omit the *'s* when the last syllable of the name is pronounced *iz* (/-ɪz/), as in *Bridges', Moses'. Jesus'* is an acceptable liturgical archaism.

3 *Classical names.* In classical names use *s'* (not *s's*): *Mars', Herodotus', Venus'.* Classical names ending in *-es* are usually written *-es'* in the possessive: *Ceres' rites, Xerxes' fleet;* similarly *Demosthenes', Euripides', Socrates', Themistocles'.*

4 *French names.* Those ending in *s* or *x* should always be followed by *'s* when used possessively in English, which is pronounced as a *z*, e.g. *Rabelais's* /ˈrabəleɪz/, *le Roux's* /lə ˈruːz/, *Dumas's* /ˈdjuːmɑːz/.

5 *Hers, its, ours*, etc. An apostrophe must not be used with the possessive pronouns *hers, its, ours, theirs, yours* or the possessive adjective *its.* But an apostrophe is required in possessive indefinite or impersonal pronouns: *anybody's game, each other's books, one's sister, somebody else's fault* (see ELSE 1), *someone's hat.*

6 *In place names and names of institutions.* Use an apostrophe before the *s* in *Arthur's Pass* (NZ), *Land's End, Lord's Cricket Ground, The Queen's College* (Oxford), *St John's* (Newfoundland), *St John's Wood* (London), *St Michael's Mount* (Cornwall). After the *s* in *Queens' College* (Cambridge). Do not use an apostrophe in *All Souls* (Oxford), *Bury St Edmunds, Earls Court, Golders Green, Johns Hopkins University* (Baltimore), *St Albans, St Andrews,*

St Kitts (Caribbean). Recent standard editions of local maps are the best guide to the correct spelling of the hundreds of names of this type. For institutions, it may be helpful to consult their website.

7 *Compound proper names and complex noun phrases.* These normally require an apostrophe only after the last element, e.g. *The Duke of Edinburgh's Award, Faber and Faber's address, the Queen of Holland's crown, Lewis and Short's Latin Dictionary, my aunt and uncle's place, a quarter of an hour's chat.*

8 There is no agreed solution to the problem of the types (*a*) *Hannah's [Jamie Lee Curtis] love interest,* in which the heroine Hannah in a TV film is played by an actress called Jamie Lee Curtis. The alternatives are (*b*) *Hannah [Jamie Lee Curtis]'s,* or (*c*) *Hannah's [Jamie Lee Curtis's].* My preference is for type (*c*), but it may seem over-fussy to some.

Some other examples (drawn from American sources of 1989–90) of multiple apostrophes (or their omission) which tend to be resolved in an ad hoc manner: *Wayne's daughter Kim's latex ear* (correct); *It [Burger King's] decision was not unexpected* (read *Its*); *A former boxer ignores Gillespie's (Carroll O'Connor) advice* (read *Gillespie's (Carroll O'Connor)'s*).

9 For the type *the sentence's structure,* see 'S AND -S' AND OF-POSSESSIVE.

10 For the type *a friend of my mother's,* see DOUBLE POSSESSIVE.

11 For the type *for appearances' sake, for Jesus' sake,* etc., see SAKE.

12 For the type *the Council's abolition* (= the abolition of the Council), see OBJECTIVE GENITIVE.

E *Relinquishment of the apostrophe.* Since about 1900, many business firms, institutions, and journals have abandoned apostrophes in their titles, e.g. *Barclays Bank, Citizens Advice Bureau, Diners Club, Farmers Weekly, Harrods, Mothers Pride Bread,—— Teachers Training College.*

Though occasionally disapproved of, the practice can be justified as an attributive rather than possessive use of the noun (i.e. *Barclays Bank* is attributive, implying association with *Barclays,* whereas *Barclays' Bank* is possessive, implying ownership by people called *Barclay*).

Some other names appear in various forms, with and without apostrophes, e.g. *Sainsburys/Sainsbury's.* This trend towards the dropping of the apostrophe in such names and titles seems certain to continue.

appal. The standard British spelling, whereas *appall* is more usual in American English. The derivative forms are *appalled* and *appalling* in both countries. See -LL-, -L-.

apparatus. (Plural *apparatuses*). In British English pronounced /apə'reɪtəs/, but elsewhere (especially in Australia and NZ) /-'rɑːtəs/ and in American English /-'radəs/. See -US 2.

apparent. The pronunciation /ə'parənt/ is now the most common one, with /ə'pɛːrənt/ (rhyming with *parent*) heard only occasionally, particularly in Scotland. The reverse was the case when the relevant section of the *OED* was issued in 1885.

appeal. In the US commonly used in legal language as a transitive verb = 'to appeal against', e.g. *The Justice Department is considering whether to appeal Hudson's ruling—Boston Globe,* 2010. The standard equivalent in Britain is to *appeal against* the verdict of a lower court. However, the transitive use appears not infrequently in UK sources, especially the news, and seems to be becoming more and more common, to the chagrin of some, me included, e.g. *We applied for leave to appeal Lord Justice Kennedy's ruling and leave was denied—Bolton Evening News, 2003.*

appear(ed). For its use (and also *seem(ed)*) with a perfect infinitive (e.g. *GEC appeared to have taken a firm grip on the project*), see PERFECT INFINITIVE 1.

appeasement. For centuries used without discreditable or humiliating overtones in the broad sense 'the act or process of giving satisfaction, pacification'. Even in 1920 Winston Churchill could say, with reference to Turkey, and merely as an expression of opinion worth examining, *Here again I counsel prudence and appeasement. Try to secure a really representative Turkish governing authority, and come to terms with it.* Since 1938, the word has acquired unfavourable overtones, because of its connection with the attempts at conciliation by concession made by Neville Chamberlain, the British Prime Minister, before the outbreak of war with Germany in 1939. It nowadays always carries the implication of making shameful or inadvisable concessions.

appendix. The recommended plural forms are *appendices* (in books and documents) and *appendixes* (in surgery and zoology). But this distinction, though a useful one, cannot be said to have been universally adopted. See -EX, -IX.

applicable. The traditional pronunciation, stressing the first syllable (recommended by Walker (1791), *OED* (1885), and Gimson (1977)) has largely been replaced in British English by second-syllable stress, which is the pronunciation the current *OED* puts first. In the US, dictionaries tend to put the traditional pronunciation first.

apposition. 1 *Definition. Apposition* is the placing of a noun or noun phrase beside another noun or noun phrase which shares the same grammatical function and refers to the same person or thing. In *A portrait of Benjamin Disraeli, the famous statesman, was recently sold,* the phrase *the famous statesman* is said to be in apposition to *Benjamin Disraeli.* The parallel elements are known as **appositives**. Apposition is a major feature of English, and there are many types.

In the sentence *Sir James Murray, the lexicographer, was born in Hawick,* the second element, *the lexicographer,* is in apposition to the first, *Sir James Murray.* Similarly, in the sentence *The highest mountain in New Zealand, Mount Cook, is called Aorangi by the Maoris,* the second element, *Mount Cook,* is in apposition to the first, *The highest mountain in New Zealand.* In both cases the second element syntactically duplicates the first. This is the most straightforward type of apposition in English.

2 *Punctuation.* Appositives may be either 'restrictive' (i.e. defining) or 'non-restrictive' (i.e. descriptive), although there is a certain amount of overlap between the two types. When apposition is non-restrictive, leaving out the information contained in the appositive does not make the sentence meaningless or ungrammatical. So, in *A portrait of Benjamin Disraeli, the famous statesman, was recently sold,* the appositive *the famous statesman* could be omitted. When apposition is restrictive, you do not separate the item in apposition with commas, but when it is non-restrictive, you do: (restrictive) the grammarian *Otto Jespersen; William* the Conqueror; the inventor and entrepreneur *James Dyson;* (non-restrictive) *he picked up the goods at the warehouse,* a huge complex of brightly painted buildings; *she loved the paintings of Claude Monet,* one of the leading exponents of impressionism.

3 The appositive element is placed first in the type 'title or descriptive label + personal name', e.g. Chancellor *Merkel of Germany;* singing sensation *Jonas Kaufmann;* distinctively coiffed pseudo-Scot *Donald Trump.* Originally US, this type of construction is now rapidly becoming adopted in all English-speaking countries, especially in newspapers.

4 Appositives can be introduced by *and* or *or*, e.g. *he worked in Duke Humfrey, a section of the Bodleian Library, and* arguably one of the most elegant rooms in the whole library; *their political interests lay in the Gulf, or* the Persian Gulf as it is often called.

appraisal. Censured by Fowler (1926) as an unnecessary invention, this word has now all but ousted **appraisement**, though the latter word was dominant in the 19c. and is still occasionally found, particularly in legal language. See -AL. The derivative **reappraisal** (used especially in the phrases *critical, radical, agonizing reappraisal*) is a 20c. formation.

appraise, apprise. Confusion of near-sounding words or 'minimal pairs' is an ever-present possibility. *Appraise* means 'to assess the value of (something or somebody)': *When a man is stripped of all worldly insignia, one can appraise him for what he is truly worth*—C. Chaplin, 1964; *The curtain of motion and colour had been momentarily lifted, so that the reality behind it could be appraised*—J. Fuller, 1983; *it was an interval at least long enough for him to appraise the situation*—Antonia Fraser, 1988. *Apprise* is a rather formal or bureaucratic word and means 'to inform, to give notice to', and occurs normally in the construction *apprise* (someone) *of* (something). It is common in the constructions *be apprised* and *keep someone apprised*: *Attlee asked the Chiefs of Staff to confirm that they were fully apprised of the shipping situation*—D. Fraser, 1982; *He was ... annoyed that I had not bothered to apprise him of the upsetting news sooner*—P. Bailey, 1986.

appreciate. 1 It is standard in British and US English to pronounce the *-ci-* as /ʃɪ/ (shi) not /sɪ/; the second would sound rather niminy-piminy.

2 Its normal use to mean 'esteem at full value, acknowledge with gratitude' (*I appreciate everything that you have done to help us*) is unobjectionable. So too is its use to express polite requests, e.g. *it would be appreciated if you would send your invoice in triplicate.* There is some justification, however, in Sir Ernest Gowers' suggestion that it is best to avoid using the construction *appreciate* followed by a *how* or a *that* clause, e.g. *I appreciate* (better *understand*) *how hard it is for you to make ends meet without a housing allowance; I appreciate* (better *realize*) *that you are disappointed by our failure to promote you.* In other contexts the notion of *sympathize* is also needed, e.g. *I appreciate* (better *sympathize with*) *your predicament.*

apprehend, comprehend. In the meanings in which they overlap, namely as synonyms of *understand,* these two words denote slightly different aspects of understanding. *Apprehend* means to grasp or perceive, not necessarily fully, the essence or importance of something, whereas *comprehend* means to understand in detail an argument or statement. Both can be followed by a simple object or by a *that*-clause. Examples: (apprehend) *She drew a breath, long enough to apprehend that he was about to step from one world into another*—I. Murdoch, 1962; *There are some natures too coarse to apprehend the mysteries*—G. Vidal, 1962; *As the mind apprehends and tries to make sense of the world, it develops ever-richer and more sophisticated concepts*—J. Wolff, 2003; (comprehend) *He wandered off, thinking I was round the bend, not comprehending my complete and luminous sanity*—W. Golding, 1959; *Speak more slowly so that we can comprehend everything you say*—B. Malamud, 1966; *To comprehend language fully, to assemble it correctly and to express it properly is a task that has no equal in human capability*—Anthony Smith, 1984.

apprise. In the sense 'to give notice to' always so spelt, not *-ize.* See APPRAISE; -ISE 1.

apricot. Mostly pronounced with initial /eɪ-/ in Britain, but mostly as /ˈaprɪkɒt/ in American English and sometimes in Scotland.

a priori. (Latin, = 'from what is before'.) Pronounced /eɪ prʌɪˈɔːrʌɪ/, with *a* as in *hate* and with both *is* as in *eye,* this phrase is used to characterize reasoning or arguing from causes to effects, deductively. *Because they were wearing handcuffs it was obvious that they had been taken into custody* and *Because I've failed I live on her money* are examples of a priori reasoning. Contrasted with A POSTERIORI.

apropos. /ˈaprəpəʊ/. Brought into English at the time of Dryden from French *à propos* 'with reference to', *apropos* is now always written as one word in English and without an accent. It can be used as an adjective; *Instead of answering me directly he said something (I didn't know at the time whether it was apropos or not), the significance of which I realised only later*—S. Themerson, 1951; but its main uses are (1) as a preposition, e.g. *Voltaire has something to say on English irregularity too, this time apropos Shakespeare*—N. Pevsner, 1956; *Her voice, as has been mentioned apropos that of Boudica, was not harsh*—Antonia Fraser, 1988; (2) with *of,* forming a compound preposition, e.g. *And then I thought, apropos of my last blog entry, about gender roles*—weblog, 2004 (AmE). *Apropos of nothing* (and informal variants such as *apropos of bugger all*) has become a cliché that means little more than 'unexpectedly, out of the blue' *Apropos of nothing she declared that love must be wonderful*—G. Clare, 1981; (3) occasionally, under the influence of *appropriate,* followed by *to,* e.g. *Is there not a passage in John Stuart Mill apropos to this?* Type (3) is not recommended.

apt. For a comparison of *apt to* with *liable to,* see LIABLE.

aqu-, acqu-. Words beginning with these letter combinations are sometimes misspelled, e.g. **acquatic* by mistake for *aquatic,* or **aquire* for *acquire.* To avoid such mistakes, it may help to remember that the first part of words relating to water, such as *aqualung, aquifer, aquarium, aquatic,* comes from Latin *aqua* 'water', which has no letter *c.* (*Aquiline* 'like an eagle' comes from Latin *aquila* 'eagle'). Words which are correctly spelled *acqu-,* such as *acquaint, acquiesce, acquit,* do not relate to water, and most of them were adopted in Middle English from Old French or Latin words beginning with *acqu-.*

aquarium. Plural *aquariums* or *aquaria*, but the first is rather more frequent. See -UM 3; LATIN PLURALS.

Arab, Arabian, Arabic. 1 These three adjectives refer to different aspects of the Arabian peninsula and its peoples. *Arab* means a member of the Semitic people now inhabiting large parts of the Middle East and North Africa, and is also used as an adjective before a noun, e.g. *the Arab people, the Arab spring, Arab philosophy; Arabian* refers to Arabia, the whole peninsula between the Red Sea and the Persian Gulf, including other states than Saudi Arabia, e.g. *the Arabian desert, fauna, camel;* and *Arabic* refers to the language, literature, or script of Arabic-speaking people, e.g. *Arabic alphabet, literature, numerals, script.*

2 *Arabic* is written with an initial capital in the expression *Arabic numerals* (the numbers 1, 2, 3, etc., as distinct from the Roman numerals I, II, III, etc.). It is written with a small initial in *gum arabic*, a type of gum exuded by African acacia trees.

3 The expression *the Arab street*, first recorded in the US in 1977, refers to popular opinion in Arab countries or communities, especially on political issues.

4 The expression *street Arab*, first recorded in 1853, and for about a century commonly applied to a homeless vagrant (especially a child) living in the streets of a city, is now regarded as ethnically offensive.

arbiter, arbitrator. Do these words mean the same? Though there is some overlap, they are used differently, and associate with different words. *Arbiter* has two closely related meanings: (*a*) 'a person who settles a dispute or has ultimate authority in a matter', in which meaning it is often modified by adjectives such as *final, independent, impartial*, e.g. *the Secretary of State is the final arbiter;* (*b*) 'a person whose views or actions have influence in a particular sphere', in which case it is often followed by *of* and a noun, e.g. *arbiter of fashion, morality, truth.* As Gowers (1965) put it, perhaps overstating the case, 'An arbiter makes decisions of his own accord and is accountable to no one for them'. In contrast, an *arbitrator* is 'an independent person or body officially appointed to settle a dispute' e.g. *the facts of the case are put to an independent arbitrator. Arbiter* could not replace *arbitrator* in this last example; what distinguishes *arbitrators* from *arbiters* are the legal or procedural rules to which *arbitrators* must adhere. To quote Gowers again, 'an arbiter acts arbitrarily; an arbitrator must not'. Examples: (arbiter) *The great nineteenth-century critic and arbiter of taste, John Ruskin*—L. Hudson, 1985; *Harley then insisted that the tournament director, who is the ultimate arbiter at professional tournaments, be summoned*—M. Hamer, 1991; (arbitrator) *Either party may apply to have the dispute referred to arbitration by the judge or by an outside arbitrator*—R. C. A. White, 1985; *Edward* [Edward I of England] *insisted on intervening in the succession dispute ... not as an impartial arbitrator, but as feudal overlord of Scotland*—*Oxford Companion to British History*, 2002. In the second example, *arbiter* could reasonably replace *arbitrator*, but the connotations of a complicated legal case would be lost.

arc (verb). The derivative forms are spelt *arced* and *arcing*, pronounced /ɑːkt/ and /ˈɑːkɪŋ/ respectively, i.e. with the medial *c* pronounced as /k/ despite the fact that it is followed by *e* and *i*.

archaeological, etc. In all varieties of English *archaeological, archaeologist*, and *archaeology* are much more common according to *OEC* data, even in North American English, where the forms in *archeolog-* are accepted variants. These forms are also used in a minority of cases outside North America.

archaism. 1 Archaisms are words and phrases that have fallen out of general use but are employed for special effect, normally in literature. These vary in effect from the gently old-fashioned or jokey (e.g. *erstwhile, gentlewoman, goodly, hence, lest, methinks, perchance, quoth*) to the unnatural or even unusable (e.g. *peradventure, whilom*).

2 Archaisms are most commonly found in allusive use in literature, e.g. *If Mimi's cup runneth over, it runneth over with decency rather than with anything more vital*—Anita Brookner, 1985 (an Old Testament allusion to Ps. 23: 5.) *The whole creation groaneth and travaileth in pain together*—Iris Murdoch, 1987; (a New Testament allusion to Rom. 8:22.). Archaic word forms also occur in titles, as in *The*

Compleat Girl (by Mary McCarthy, 1963, in allusion to Isaak Walton's *The Compleat Angler*), Whitaker's *Almanack* (which preserves an older spelling of almanac), and in fixed expressions such as *olde worlde*, e.g. *Charming stone built olde worlde cottage of immense character—Rhyl Journal & Advertiser*, 1976).

3 The prefix *a-* with a present participle (a centuries-old type of word formation) is having a new lease of life: *a-basking, a-changing*, etc. See A-[2].

4 Words that could usefully be paint-stripped from the fresh timber to which they cling in some modern writing include ALBEIT, ANENT, DERRING-DO, NAY, PERADVENTURE, PERCHANCE, QUOTH, SURCEASE, *twain*, UNBEKNOWN(ST), *yea, yesteryear*.

Everything depends on the skill with which such old words, spellings, and pieces of grammar are deposited in particular contexts. As Burchfield put it, perhaps a little *de haut en bas*, 'like Marcel Proust's famous madeleine cakes, they can conjure up rich memories of an older age. But they can also be as out of place as a donkey jacket worn at the Cenotaph on Remembrance Day'.

archetype. See -TYPE.

arctic. To be pronounced as /ˈɑːktɪk/ with the first *c* fully in place.

ardour. In American English normally spelled *ardor*. See -OUR AND -OR.

are, is. when one of these is required between a subject and a complement that differ in number (e.g. *these things ... a scandal*) the verb should normally follow the number of the subject (*are*, not *is, a scandal*). Similarly *The only difficulty in Finnish is* (not *are*) *the changes undergone by the stem*. see AGREEMENT 7; BE 1.

aren't I? See BE 4.

areola. /əˈriːələ/, plural *-lae* /-liː/ (uh-**ree**-uh-luh, -lee) (Anatomy) a circular pigmented area, especially that surrounding a nipple. The spellings **aureole** and **aureola** from a different word meaning 'a circle of light or brightness surrounding something, especially in art' or 'a corona round the sun or moon' are occasionally used in non-scientific or erotic contexts, and are accepted as variants by *ODO*, e.g. *breasts growing heavier and more malleable, the aureole around her nipple darkening.*

argot. See JARGON.

arguably. First recorded only as late as 1890, and not in the original *OED*, this adverb now seems indispensable. It is used as a sentence adverb (qualifying a whole clause or sentence) to mean 'as may be shown by argument or made a matter of argument', e.g. *Arguably, this is another kind of corruption, but it was in general a very long-range bribery, and it was invariably offered in the guise of friendship*—R. M. Sunter, 1986; *Arguably, Pip's search for Estella's true identity ... can be seen as a displaced search for his own identity—Essays & Studies*, 1987. It is frequently followed immediately by a comparative or a superlative adjective, e.g. *It is arguably one of our most successful companies—Sunday Times*, 2004; *Fibich was arguably worse off even than Hartmann, for he knew no one*—A. Brookner, 1988.

Arguably is most appropriate in contexts that are open to genuine argument and disagreement, as in the first three examples above. In general use, however, it implies little or no argument. In principle a way of investing the opinion being expressed with greater authority, it is often hardly more forceful in effect than 'possibly' or 'perhaps'. As such, it can be a useful safety net for those who are unsure of their facts or lack the courage of their conviction, as in the next example: *Meet the man with the surname everyone knows, Giorgio Armani, who arguably adorns more bodies worldwide than any other living designer—Clothes Show*, 1991.

***argumentum ad* —.** The phrase *argumentum ad* precedes a number of Latin nouns in the accusative case, such as *hominem*, to denote several types of argument used in philosophy, logic, or law. Of these, the best known is *argumentum ad hominem*, one which attacks the character of the person making an argument rather than the argument itself. When written in full it should be in italics; but when *ad hominem* is used on its own, it is printed in roman, e.g. 'an ad hominem argument'. Other types of argument include *argumentum ad crumenam* (purse), one touching the hearer's pocket; *argumentum ad baculum* (stick) or *argumentum baculinum*, threat of force instead of argument;

argumentum ad ignorantiam, one depending for its effect on the hearer's not knowing something essential; *argumentum ad populum*, one pandering to popular fashion; *argumentum ad verecundiam* (modesty), one to meet which requires the opponent to offend against decorum. Also *argumentum e* (or *ex*) *silentio*, an argument from silence: used of a conclusion based on lack of contrary evidence.

-arily. Under American influence, in the second half of the 20c., adverbs ending in *-arily* (e.g. *momentarily, necessarily, primarily, temporarily, voluntarily*) have come to be commonly pronounced by standard British English speakers with the main stress on *-ar-*. All such words were traditionally pronounced in RP with the main stress on the first syllable.

aristocrat, aristocratic. There are two ways of pronouncing *aristocrat*, a word derived from French *aristocrate*, coined during the French Revolution in 1789, and first mentioned in that form in English in the same year. You can emphasize either the first syllable /ˈarɪstəkrat/ (**a**-ris-tuh-krat) or the second /əˈrɪstəkrat/ (uh-**ris**-tuh-krat). The first is still the standard one in British English. The second is the standard American pronunciation, but is fast gaining ground in Britain too, particularly among transatlantic academics and pundits. Interestingly, it was once the standard in Britain, so it could be viewed as a revival rather than an intrusion. *Aristocratic* is generally pronounced emphasizing the fourth syllable in British English /ˌarɪstəˈkratɪk/ (a-ris-tuh-**kra**-tɪk), although some speakers also emphasize the second, /əˌristəˈkratɪk/ (uh-**ris**-tuh-**kra**-tik), which is standard in American English.

arithmetic(al), geometric(al) progression mean very different things. Arithmetical *progression* is an equal increase between the items in the progression, e.g. the numbers 1, 3, 5, 7, 9, etc., showing an increase of 2 in each case. A *geometrical increase* is larger, and is one in which the ratio between successive quantities is constant, as 1, 3, 9, 27. In other words, the first involves growth (or decline) at an unchanging rate and the second at an increasing rate. Both expressions have been commandeered in general language to express a rapid rate of increase—or decrease—and Fowler (1926) went to torturous lengths to castigate their inappropriate or mistaken use. The *OEC* provides no evidence for *arithmetic(al) progression* being used hyperbolically in the way Fowler criticized, and provides several examples of *geometric progression* which suggest that the writers understand perfectly what it really means.

armadillo. The plural form is *armadillos*. See -O(E)S 8.

armour. US *armor*. See -OUR AND -OR.

around, round. **1** As both adverb and preposition these words are interchangeable in some contexts but not in others. In general, British English favours *round* and American English *around*. In AmE *round* is generally regarded as informal or non-standard and is only standard in certain fixed expressions such as *all (the) year round* and *they went round and round in circles*.

2 *Around* is obligatory in both varieties of English in fixed expressions such as *around and about, all around* (*are signs of decay*), *she's been around*, and especially in phrasal verbs having the general meaning 'to behave in an aimless manner', as *fool around, mess around, play around, sit around, wait around*. In some of these *about* is also possible, but not *round*.

3 In BrE it is usual to say *winter comes round, the wheels go round, send the book round, show me round*, whereas in all these cases AmE would normally use *around*. In BrE contexts referring to surrounding (something or someone) *around* can replace *round*, as in *she put her arm round/around him; seated round/around the table; the cheerfulness round/around her*. There is, however, a general preference for *round* to be used for definite, specific movement, e.g. *she turned round; a bus came round the corner*, while *around* tends to be used in contexts which are less definite, e.g. *she wandered around for ages*, or for abstract uses, e.g. *a rumour circulating around the cocktail bars*.

4 BrE still tends to prefer *about* as a preposition meaning 'approximately', although *around* is also used, e.g. *there are about/around 100 in all; come about/around 4 o'clock*, whereas AmE generally prefers *around*.

The following are some typical examples from a wide variety of sources: (*around,* prep.) *Jesse ... moped around the house all summer*—Lee Smith, 1983 (US); *Coming around the farthest mark—New Yorker,* 1986; *around the time of his birth*—S. Bellow, 1987 (US); *the area around Waterloo*—R. Elms, 1988 (UK); *I wrapped a blanket around me*—L. Maynard, 1988 (US); *You know how to get all the people around the operating table*—K. Russell, 1988 (UK); *around that time*—Julian Barnes, 1989 (UK); *they stood grouped around their luggage*—M. Bracewell, 1989 (UK). (*round,* prep.) *it stood just round the corner from his father's house*—Van Wyck Brooks, *a*1961 (US); *a map rolled up round a broom handle*—J. Winterson, 1985 (UK); *He looked round the table as if daring anyone to smile*—D. Lodge, 1988 (UK). (*around,* adv.) *Sir William, whom I haven't gotten around to discussing*—R. Merton, 1985 (US); *Stay around till she gets back—New Yorker,* 1987; *Hartmann's sunny ... attitude was marvellous to have around*—A. Brookner, 1988 (UK); *The devices have been around awhile—USA Today,* 1988; *I went around to the front door—New Yorker,* 1989. (*round,* adv.) *in the end she talked me round*—N. Bawden, 1987 (UK); *the news had gotten round pretty fast—New Yorker,* 1988.

arouse, rouse. *Rouse* is almost always preferred in the literal sense of 'wake up' and with a person or animal as object. *Arouse* is chiefly used with the senses 'call into existence, occasion', with such abstract nouns as *suspicion, anger, passion, curiosity, resentment* as object of the active or subject of the passive. *Arouse* has also been used since 1948 in the meaning of excite sexually. Perhaps because of potential confusion with this sense, it is very rarely used transitively to mean 'wake up', and *rouse* would be more suitable in *I shook his arm, but failed to arouse him. Arouse* is occasionally used intransitively, e.g. *arousing from their slumbers the team headed for home.*

arpeggio. Plural *-os.* See -O(E)S 4.

arrant is historically the 'same word' as **errant**, i.e. a spelling variant, and Old French *errant,* from which they are both derived, is itself a product of two branches, Vulgar Latin *iterāre* 'to journey, travel' and Latin *errāre* 'to wander'. In English, these meanings have produced *arrant,* 'complete, utter, downright' (*arrant fool, knave, liar, nonsense,* etc.), and *errant,* 'roving in quest of adventure' (*knight errant*) and 'astray, straying from proper behaviour, erring in opinion' (*errant children, errant husband, an errant taste in dress*). The use of *errant* to mean 'complete, utter' as in *errant nonsense,* which is occasionally encountered, is etymologically correct but will strike most people as a mistake and is best avoided.

arrive. The absolute sense 'to achieve success or recognition', which is first recorded in 1889, is a borrowing from French *arriver,* condemned by Fowler. Since his day it has become a standard, not to say indispensable, part of English.

arsis. (Gk ἄρσις 'lifting, raising'.) In classical prosody there has been much dispute as to the exact meaning of this word and readers should turn to *The Oxford Classical Dictionary* for elucidation. But in modern English prosody, it means 'a stressed syllable or part of a metrical foot' (and thus = Latin *ictus*), as in Tennyson's 'The spléndour fálls on cástle wálls'. Cf. THESIS 2.

artefact, artifact. *Artefact* is the recommended and more common spelling of the word in British English. In American English it is merely a variant of *artifact,* which is much the more usual spelling (*The American Indian Gallery displays artifacts such as prehistoric tools and pottery from Ohio and southwestern tribes—Article Alley* website , 2005). Etymologically, *artefact* is the better form, as the word is derived from *arte,* ablative of Latin *ars* 'art' + *factum,* neuter past participle of *facere* 'to make', but *artifact,* perhaps formed by analogy with *artifice* and *artificial,* has been recorded in British as well as American sources since as far back as 1825.

artiste rhymes with *feast* and means 'a professional performer, especially a singer or dancer'. It is a separate borrowing from French and not, as some people seem to think, a feminine form of *artist,* which has the distinct meaning of someone who works in one of the fine arts. As a blog on *www.dailyartist.com* puts it, 'An artiste is something you don't want to be, that is, if you consider yourself an artist'. *Artiste,* which conveys no judgment that the performance is in fact artistic, is now regarded as at best an affectation and at worst an insult; usually a word such as *performer* would do just as well. Examples: *Distinguished people make a practice of visiting the opera, and pull rank so as to meet the artistes, especially attractive females*—R. Butters, 1991; *Bollywood might soon be a viable ticket to superstardom for these artistes*—*The Week* (India), 2004.

as.

1 *as . . . as me* or *I/him* or *he* etc.?
2 *as* = 'in the capacity or role of'.
3 Omission of *as*.
4 *as*, relative pronoun.
5 *as* = 'though'.
6 *as from, as of*.
7 *as how*.
8 *as if, as though*.
9 *as per*.
10 *as such*.
11 *as to, as for*.
12 *as* or *like*.
13 inelegant *as as*.
14 *equally as*.
15 *as regard(s)*.
16 *as far as*.
17 *as well as*.

1 *as . . . as me* or *I/him* or *he*, etc.? (*a*) In this common type of comparison, the first *as* is clearly an adverb, but, when no verb follows it, the second *as* can be interpreted either as a preposition or as a conjunction. How it is interpreted affects the choice between *me* and *I*, etc. Your alternatives are the subject pronoun, i.e. *as good* etc. *as I/we/he/she/they* and the object pronoun *as good* etc. *as me/us/him/her/them*.

In conversation and informal writing the second pattern is standard: to say or write 'they are faster than we' would in most circumstances sound positively precious and mealy-mouthed. The first pattern is available for formal or highly literary uses, or if you are obliged to avoid the carping of nitpicking purists.

Both patterns are grammatically sound. In *They're as good* etc. *as us* the second *as* can be regarded as a preposition, like *after* or *before*—and no one would write or say *after I, before she*, etc. In *as good as we*, the *as* can be considered a conjunction with the following verb left out, i.e. a case of ellipsis: = *they're as good as we are*. In fiction the subject and object pronouns are used equally. The following examples convey the formality of using the subject: *It was obvious that he had been consulted as well as I*—G. Greene, 1965; *he started to encounter kids as gifted as he, some even more so*—*New Yorker*, 1986.

(*b*) The potential ambiguity of *he loves me as much as my sister* (= either 'as much as my sister loves me' or 'as much as he loves my sister') is best avoided by including a verb in each part of the sentence: *he loves me as much as he loves my sister; he loves me as much as my sister does*.

Choosing the appropriate pronoun can avoid ambiguity, as in *I don't like George as much as them* (= I don't like George as much as I like them) against *I don't like George as much as they* (= I don't like George as much as they like him).

(*c*) In negative constructions the first (adverbial) *as* can be replaced by *so*: *not so good as us*. With *so*, it is unusual to use the *I/we/he/she/they* option.

2 *as* = 'in the capacity or role of'. In this meaning *as* is a preposition, and its uncontroversial use appears in these examples: *it is as a historian that he is best known; I hear you have found a job as a nanny*. But the *as*-clause can spell two kinds of danger: (*i*) it may be in the wrong place in the sentence: *As a voluntary, charitable project the Government is about to charge us some £30,000 VAT for extending our premises*—letter to *The Times*, 1988. The government is not 'a voluntary charitable project'. Similarly, in *As a 32-year career law enforcement professional, you know that I do not like being forced to release prisoners from jail*—*Chicago Tribune*, 1988, the 'law enforcement professional' is 'I', not 'you'. While both examples are easily understood, the grammatically dainty may turn their nose up at them, and it is a trivial matter to move the offending *as*-phrase to its correct position; (*ii*) a false antecedent is created, e.g. *As a medical student his call-up was deferred*—P. Fitzgerald, 1986. The 'call-up' was not 'a medical student', and the only solution is to recast the sentence: *Because he was a medical student, his call-up was deferred*.

3 Omission of *as*. (*a*) *The board appointed him CEO* or *as CEO? They declared the building surplus to requirements* or *as surplus to requirements?* There is a group of verbs to do with selecting, classifying, or viewing people and things in certain ways, such as *appoint, deem, describe, elect*, etc., which take an object (*him, the building* in the examples above) and an object complement (*CEO, surplus*), which may be a noun or an adjective. The question sometimes arises whether *as* should be used between the object and its complement. Such verbs fall into three groups: (i) *as* is not generally used, with one or two rare exceptions: *consider, declare, deem, proclaim, pronounce, reckon;* (ii) *as* is obligatory, although very occasionally omitted with some verbs: *accept, acknowledge, characterize, choose, class, count, define, describe, designate, label, nominate, regard;* (iii) both constructions are possible: *appoint, elect, rate, term*. Leaving *as* out after verbs which it normally follows or inserting it after those which it does not is unlikely to offend many people. However, it is worth noting that *consider* and *regard* are rather inflexible in this matter: *we regard you as a model pupil* but *we consider you a model pupil*. Examples of variation, all from the *OEC*: (count) *He also counts Hagel a friend; I still count her as a friend;* (label) *a campaign to label the film anti-Semitic; They were labelled as a Stone Age people;* (nominate) *when John Kerry was making his drive to be nominated the Presidential candidate of the Democratic Party; the Kremlin's intention to nominate Matvienko as its candidate*; (rate) *95 per cent of patients rated the service excellent; Only 7% rated their health as excellent.*

(*b*) *As* is sometimes dropped in informal conversation (*she used to come regular as clockwork; it was soft as butter*), but this is not a good practice in written English. It is also occasionally left out in standard similes (*he was good as gold;* (*as*) *old as the hills*).

4 *as,* relative pronoun. When preceded by *same* or *such*, constructions with *as* used as a relative pronoun are still for the most part standard: *We can expect the same number to turn up as came last year; such repairs as have been made to the house are most acceptable;* But it is not difficult to find contexts, especially in 19c. writing, where the same construction has a strong tinge of archaism: *there was such a scuffling, and hugging ... as no pen can depict*—Thackeray, 1847/8. In all other circumstances, the use of *as* as a relative pronoun is restricted to non-standard or regional speech both in British and in American English: *it's only baronets as cares about farthings*—Thackeray, 1847/8; *This is him as had a nasty cut over the eye*—Dickens, 1865; *There's plenty as would like this nice little flat, Mr. E.*—A. Burgess, 1963; *You're the kind as'll never know it*—R. Elms, 1988.

5 *as* = 'though' *As* is used in the same way as *though* in concessive clauses such as *much as I like them* and *good as they may seem,* in which a contrary statement follows: *good as they may seem, I have known much better ones.* In American English, and increasingly in British English, an initial *as* is added to the first clause, making it like a comparison. Despite having a long pedigree, this structure is largely a reintroduction into BrE and can still jar. These two examples show the difference: *As poor as they are, the fashion sense here blows my mind—Independent*, 2008; *There was a call waiting from Yordan. Late as it was, I reached him in Madrid*—B. Gordon, 1999.

6 *as from, as of.* The formula *as from* is used in contracts to indicate the date from which certain items or clauses are to take effect. This use is reasonable if it is retrospective: e.g. *The rate of payment is increased by 5% as from the 1st of September last.* For present and future dates the *as* is superfluous. Thus *your redundancy takes effect from today* (rather than *as from today*); *your membership of the Club will become valid on 1 January next* (rather than *as from 1 January next*).

Phrases of the type *as of now, as of today,* etc., first recorded in the work of Mark Twain in 1900, are now well established in standard English in the UK and elsewhere. It is worth noting, however, that some people dislike *as of now.* Examples: *I'm resigning from the committee as of now*—D. Karp, 1957; *As of last term, Oxford has a new centre for the performing arts—Oxford Mag.*, 1986; *As of today, I do not believe Tebbit has enough votes to win*—J. Critchley, 1990.

This use of *as of* has led to the widespread use of the rather illogical or tautological phrase *as of yet*, e.g. *I haven't sized up the market as of yet—Computer Technology Review*, 2000; *There are no plans as of yet for further expansion—OEC*, 2002. In the first example, a simple *yet* is enough; in the second, *so far* or *as yet* would be preferable.

7 *as how.* Is a UK and US dialectal conjunction meaning *that* and used to introduce a clause. Historically, it has been used in literature to convey an impression of less than refined speech. Nowadays, it appears most often in the phrases *being as how, seeing as how.* In US English in particular it can follow the verb *allow*, is not considered non-standard by *MWCDEU*, and is not uncommon. Examples: *Seeing as how the captain had been hauling him over the coals*—F. Marryat, 1833; *The doctors came and said as how it was caused all along of his way of life*—Bret Harte, 1871 (US); *Just across the border here into Texas, the folks figured as how it was the thing to do to join the Union*—1949 in *DARE; Chelsea allowed as how her father and she had gone outside*—*NYT*, 2008. See also BEING AS (HOW), BEING (THAT), SEEING.

8 *as if, as though.* (*a*) Historical strictures aimed at *as though* can be ignored. These two phrases are largely interchangeable, but *as if* is rather more frequent, and more natural in exclamations, e.g. *as if I would!*

(*b*) (i) When an *as if* clause indicates that something is hypothetical, uncertain, or not factually true, there is sometimes a choice between *were* or *was*, i.e. *as if I was/were* and *as if he/she/it was/were.* When the statement introduced by *as if* is very hypothetical or uncertain, the subjunctive form *were* is preferable. But when the uncertainty is less marked, or not present at all, the indicative form *was* should be used. Examples: (were) *It was rather as if the capital city were a vast pan*—A. N. Wilson, 1985; *It was as if Sally were disturbed in some way*—A. Brookner, 1986; *It isn't as if I were a novelist or a private detective*—*OEC*, 2004; (was) *There was a silence, as if he was searching for something to say*—A. Guinness, 1985; *And, as if this wasn't challenge enough*—*OEC*, 2000; *I'm not sure why he's so funny—though he's got decent material, it's not as if he's a comic genius*—*DVD Verdict*, 2003.

(ii) *As though* operates in a similar manner. Examples: (were) *He was looking at her as though she were for sale*—A. Thomas Ellis, 1985; *His body felt as though he were trembling, but he was not*—B. Moore, 1987; (was) *The Faithful had gone back to their chorus sheets as though nothing was happening at all*—J. Winterson, 1985; *He devoured all, exhausted, as though his life was in danger*—A. S. Byatt, 1987.

(iii) There is a further distinction. *As if* and *as though* are followed by the past tense when the verb refers to an unreal possibility, i.e. when the statement introduced by *as if* or *as though* is untrue or unlikely, e.g. *It's not as though he lived like a Milord*—E. Waugh, 1945; *Several groups . . . seem to be debating the issues at stake as if they had real consequences*—*OEC*, 2000. Conversely, the present tense is used when the statement is true or likely to be true, especially after verbs such as *appear, look, seem* or *sound*, e.g. *I suppose you get on pretty well with your parents. You look as if you do*—K. Amis, 1960; *He speaks as though even the rules which we freely invent are somehow suggested to us in virtue of their being right*—M. Warnock, 1965.

9 *as per.* This complex preposition, meaning 'in accordance with' (from the Latin preposition *per* meaning 'through, by, by means of') is more or less restricted to business letters and to such publications as DIY manuals (e.g. *as per instructions*), and can sound out of place in other contexts. Otherwise, it occurs most often in the informal phrases *as per usual, as per normal,* and humorous variants. Examples: *I shall accompany him, as per usual*—W. S. Gilbert, 1874; *As per usual somebody's nose was out of joint*—J. Joyce, 1922; *But we were able to mobilise fire engines as per normal*—*This is Wiltshire*, 2004. Humorous variants also occur, e.g. *She knew better, didn't she. As per always*—P. Bailey, 1986.

10 *as such. As such,* meaning 'in this capacity' or 'accordingly', is an established and valid expression, but it tends to be overused in contexts where it adds little meaning: (useful) *Euro-MPs are not against the Euro-quango as such*—*English Today*, 1985; (redundant) *Today, computers do little computing as such outside of specific areas. They are more concerned with manipulative tasks such as word processing*—*New Scientist*, 1987. In many cases, an expression such as *in principle* would serve better: instead of *there is no objection to the sale of houses as such,* write *there is no objection in principle to the sale of houses.*

11 *as to, as for.* (*a*) Some older uses of *as to* meaning 'with respect to, with reference to' (e.g. *As to myself, I am not satisfied*—D. Hartley, 1748) have given way to *as for* (e.g. *As for you, son, your mother will hear of this*). *As to* survives, however, when the noun governed is non-personal (e.g. *As to the matter raised at the Governing Body, my view is* . . .), and especially when the sense required is 'with regard to' (e.g. *correct as to colour and shape; the rates of postage vary both as to distance and weight*).

(*b*) In the meaning of 'with regard to' *as to* is frequently used before subordinate questions, as in *The Politics Fellow left no instructions as to whether you should write a second examination paper or not.* It is also used after certain preceding passive clauses, e.g. *I am not much troubled as to its outward appearance*—G. Gissing, 1903; *I am also simultaneously bemused ... as to why people should sunbathe indoors*—*The Face*, 1986.

(*c*) In most other circumstances, though, *as to* is best left unused, especially when other constructions are available or when its presence is simply unnecessary: *He asked his mother (as to) when he would be regarded as old enough to go to discos; Ms Jones raised the question as to whether a similar conflict will arise between the urban elites and the peasantry* (better *the question of whether*); *I brooded all the time as to whether I had hit the right note* (better *on whether*).

(*d*) *As for* sometimes implies a degree of scorn, e.g. *As for Smith minor, he can't even swim across the baths yet,* but not necessarily: *As for me, I was more than content with the description of me as a map of low desires*—H. Jacobson, 1986.

12 *as* or *like.* In general, *as* should be used before adverbs (*there are times, as now, when I could hate him*) and prepositions (*he acted well again, as in 'Henry V' last year*). *Like* should be used before nouns, noun phrases, and pronouns, and occasionally as a conjunction. Sometimes the choice between the two words affects the meaning: *let me discuss this with you as your father* is obviously not the same as *let me discuss this with you like your father.*

13 Inelegant *as as.* Fowler (1926) mentioned in passing the cacophonous confusion that arises when *as* is directly followed by another *as* with a different function, e.g. *Today, consumption is promoted as a prime leisure activity in itself, as well* as as *a way of marking social distinction—Class and Capital*, 2004. It seems to happen mostly when *as well as* collides with *as* meaning 'in its capacity of'. The solution is to recast the phrase, i.e. *Today, consumption is promoted not only as a prime leisure activity in itself, but also as a way of marking social distinction.* Reading aloud what one has written is the surest way to avoid such infelicities, which the eye accepts but the ear shuns.

14 *equally as.* For the debatable construction *equally as* (*good*, etc.), see EQUALLY.

15 *as regard(s).* See REGARD 1.

16 *as far as.* See FAR 4.

17 *as well as.* See WELL adv. A.

See also AS AND WHEN; AS ... AS, SO ... AS.

as and when. The Fowler brothers (1906) lumped this phrase together with 'if and when', considering both to be tautological. Gowers (1965) criticized it at vitriolic length, suggesting that a writer who uses it 'likes verbiage for its own sake'. According to his argument, therefore, in sentences where *as and when* is used either word on its own would convey exactly the same meaning. But for many modern examples the argument is debatable, to say the least.

I suspect that as a mandarin Gowers was frustrated by exposure to innumerable bureaucratic examples of its unnecessary use. The phrase certainly has a legalistic aura, reminiscent of other legal pairs such as 'aid and abet', 'goods and chattels', etc., and the *OEC* data shows that it is more frequent in legal discourse than any other kind. It is also most frequent in British English, and not very common in American English. Discussion and examples follow.

As and when seems to have three meanings or uses: (*a*) broadly, as a synonym of 'whenever', to suggest that event A, dependent on event B, will be (or was) repeated if event A happens (or happened), e.g. *Consumption occurs only as and when the body eats the bread and generates sensations the consumer feels—OEC*, 2005; *He paid all the bills and gave me cash as and when I needed it—OEC*, 2004; *as and when available, necessary, needed, required.* While it is possible to argue that 'whenever' would work just as well in these example, neither *as* nor *when* on its own would: they fail to convey the idea of an event being repeated at unpredictable intervals. (*b*) to mean 'when' or 'if', casting varying degrees of doubt on the event happening: *The correct procedure, as and when we win our case, is then to apply for a writ of mandamus—Listener*, 1979; *an inter-departmental task team ... set up to address evacuation of South Africa's missions in the region 'as and when this becomes necessary'—Daily Despatch*, 2003.

If 'when' or 'if' replaced *as and when* in the previous examples, the idea would be lost that an indeterminate and possibly long period of time will have to elapse before the event happens. (*c*) to mean 'as soon as possible', 'as soon as the opportunity arises/the information becomes available/etc.', often without a following clause (i.e. elliptically): *They confirmed the existing main roads as future main traffic arteries to be widened 'as and when'*—*Listener*, 1965; *Radio 4 will be broadcasting the results both over the airwaves and online. Details on their website as and when*—*OEC*, 2004; *We are making provisional bookings, but we are confirming them as and when we know the airfield's status*—*The Press*, York, 2000. This is an idiomatic phrase which can only be replaced by a paraphrase.

Finally, there are some very few instances where *as and when* truly appears unnecessary, e.g. *These types of drugs are most effective when taken regularly, rather than as and when symptoms are particularly painful*—*NHS Direct*, 2004 (replace with 'when').

Cf. IF AND WHEN

as ... as, so ... as. In simple comparisons, the normal construction in standard English is clearly *as* ... *as* (*as busy as a bee, as mad as a hatter, as soon as you can*). Quite commonly, however, in the 19c. and earlier, the antecedent could also be *so*, especially, but not only, in negative sentences: *You have never so much as answered me*—Scott, 1818; *No country suffered so much as England*—Macaulay, 1849; *When did a morning shine So rich in atonement as this?*—Tennyson, 1855. Nowadays *as* ... *as* is overwhelmingly the more common of the two, but *so* ... *as* is far from extinct. Examples: (*a*) *variations ... of a star as small as three kilometres across could be detected; there is not quite as much text as was expected; his porno movies can't be as much fun as we're led to believe they are;* (*b*) *It's here. So long as nobody disturbs it; she had seldom known anything so luxurious as this steam room.*

as bad or worse than. Criticism is aimed at this and at similar constructions like *as good or better than; as well or better than*, because *bad, good, well*, etc. grammatically require *as*, not *than*, in comparisons. This mixed construction has been a grammarian's bugbear since the 18c., but is common in speech, and does nothing to obscure meaning. Nevertheless, to use it, especially in writing, may well bring down upon you the wrath of logically fastidious persons. To help you avoid that dire fate, I offer three options. If we take as our model the sentence *we're sure they can judge a novel just as well if not better than us* (*London Rev. Bks*, 1987), they are (*a*) add the *as* and introduce commas, i.e. *just as well as, if not better than, us;* (*b*) add the *as* and place the comparative after the term of comparison, i.e. *just as well as us, if not better;* (*c*) insert the construction *at least as* before the relevant adjective or adverb and remove the comparative, i.e. *at least as well as us.* This last option may subtly change the meaning, and therefore cannot be applied indiscriminately.

ascendance, ascendancy, ascendant. **1** *Spelling.* The recommended spellings are *-ancy, -ant.* Although the forms **ascendency** and **ascendent** are still in use and given as alternatives by some dictionaries, they are about ten times less common in the *OEC* than the recommended forms. The variant *ascendance* is quite often used instead of *ascendancy,* but might cause some readers to scratch their heads.

2 *Meaning. Ascendancy,* as well as *ascendance,* means possession of dominant power or influence, and is used in such phrases as *to establish* (*the*) *ascendancy* (*over*), *to gain the ascendancy* (*over*), etc. Other than in technical astrological language, *ascendant* as a noun occurs in the idiom *in the ascendant.* Originally, this meant 'supreme, dominant', and that is the only meaning the *OED* currently recognizes as legitimate. However, by a natural association of the word with the corresponding verb *ascend* 'to rise', it is often used in a progressive or upward sense, to mean 'in the process of gaining control', and this meaning is recognized by the *ODO*, among others. Very often, in fact, the context does not make it clear which meaning is intended.

3 *Correct formulation.* Although *in the ascendant* is the standard and traditional form of the phrase, the *OEC* data shows, perhaps surprisingly, that *in the ascendancy* is used rather more often. Some people will no doubt continue to regard it as a mistake, but for others the distinction has already clearly been lost. Examples: unquestionable uses (ascendancy) *But* *even if the moderates regain the ascendancy, it may not be enough to persuade many of the protesters to return home*—*Daily Tel.*, 2012; (ascendant) *Pragmatism is in the ascendant. Letwin has suffered from his failure to sound an early alarm about the danger posed by the NHS reforms*—*New Statesman*, 2011; *Even when the Gestapo system was in the ascendant over much of Europe, ... Churchill had faith that it would one day be possible to defeat Nazism altogether*—*BBC History*, 2004; questionable uses (in the ascendancy) *Up to 1947 the left was in the ascendancy*—*Socialist Worker Online*, 2005; (ascendance) *Hegemony is distinct from coercion, which utilizes executive or legislative powers or police intervention to maintain the ascendance of the dominant elite*—*Sociology of Religion*, 2003.

ascension. Except in the technical language of astronomy, and as a Christian term (when it is always written with an initial capital), the use of *ascension* to refer to the physical action of ascending is now virtually extinct, **ascent** being the standard word. Consequently, a sentence such as the following sounds somewhat odd: *?our canal boat was making its biggest lock ascension of our week-long trip on the Erie Canal system in upstate New York*—*Boat Magazine*, (US) 2004.

ascetic. Presumably because its *-etic* ending is the same as in *aesthetic*, *ascetic* is sometimes wrongly used for it. e.g. **The fine art showcased in our inventory is rare not only because it possesses great ascetic value, but also because of the high demand for pieces by listed artists*—*Alhambra Coin Center* website (AmE). But the words have completely different origins and meanings. *Ascetic* comes ultimately from the Greek ἀσκητής (askeetees), meaning a Christian monk or hermit, and as an adjective originally described self-discipline in abstaining from all forms of indulgence for religious reasons, e.g. *The old Ascetick Christians found a Paradise in a Desert*—Sir T. Browne, *a*1682. Nowadays it is still often used in this strictly religious sense, and also more generally, to denote a way of life free from self-indulgence: *The Albigensians looked good because they lived the ascetic life the Church's shepherds should have been living*—*Catholic and Enjoying It* (weblog), 2009; *Senior advisers describe an ascetic lifestyle: one meal a day, working through lunch, and in the evenings on official papers*—*Guardian*, 2008.

Aesthetic comes from Ancient Greek αἰσθητικός 'of or relating to sense perception', from the verb αἰσθάνεσθαι 'to perceive'. It applies to the perception, appreciation, or criticism of what is beautiful, and is often applied to values, experiences, qualities and pleasures. Examples: *Henry's good-natured wit is an additional joy in an elegant body of work already delivering ample esthetic pleasure*—*Art in America*, 2005; *If you love the aesthetic qualities of black-and-white photography, you'll fall head-over-heels with what* Criterion's *achieved here*—*DVD Verdict*, 2004.

ascribe. For malapropistic use of this, see SUBSCRIBE.

as far as. See FAR 4.

as follows. The phrase *as follows* is not replaced by *as follow* even when the subject of the sentence is plural, because it is being used to refer forwards to what follows it (i.e. cataphorically): *His preferences are as follows ... ; his view is as follows ...* The reason for its fixed form is that it was originally an impersonal construction = 'as it follows'.

ashamedly. Pronounced as four syllables, /əˈʃeɪmɪdli/. See -EDLY.

Asian, Asiatic. 1 The standard and accepted adjective when referring to people is *Asian* rather than *Asiatic*, which has offensive connotations. However, *Asiatic* is standard in scientific and technical use, for example in biological and anthropological classifications, e.g. *Asiatic lion/lily/Greeks/peoples.*

2 In Britain *Asian* (as adjective and noun) is generally used to refer to people who come from (or whose parents came from) India, Pakistan, or elsewhere in South Asia, while in North America it refers to people from China, Japan, and other countries of East Asia. In the US, **Asian American** is the standard word to refer to people of Asian, particularly East Asian, descent.

3 In Daniel Jones (1917) the only pronunciation given for *Asia, Asiatic, Persia*(*n*), *version*, etc., was with medial /-ʃ-/ (sh). During the 20c. /-ʃ-/ was gradually overtaken by /-ʒ-/ (zh) in all such words, and the newer pronunciation is standard in American

English and the more common of the two in British English.

aside, a side. Written as one word, *aside* is an adverb meaning 'to or on one side' (*to put aside, to take aside,* etc.) or a noun meaning 'words spoken in a play for the audience to hear, but supposed not to be heard by the other characters'. In the sense 'on each side' it must be written as two words, e.g. *they were playing seven a side,* i.e. with seven players in each team, *a seven-a-side game*

aside from. See APART FROM.

as per. See AS 9.

assassinate. The traditional restriction of this word to mean 'to kill an important person for political reasons' (e.g. the assassination of Archduke Francis Ferdinand at Sarajevo in 1914) has been largely eroded. The word is now also often applied to the killing of any person who is regarded by the killer(s) as a legitimate political or sectarian target. In the course of the 20c., an older figurative meaning of the word, 'to destroy someone's reputation', was also revived. Examples: (political) *If the NLF* [National Liberation Front in Vietnam] *felt his death would serve a political purpose, he would be assassinated*—F. Fitzgerald, 1972; *Palestinian guerrillas sought for a second time in three months to assassinate King Hussein*—H. Kissinger, 1979; (figurative) *Those around Bush, many of whom came of age during Vietnam and almost none of whom served, have attempted to assassinate the character and insult the patriotism of anyone who disagrees with them—Whiskey Bar,* 2004, (AmE).

The same considerations apply to the corresponding noun **assassination**. Examples: (political) *the point-blank assassination of an off-duty detective at the dog track* [in Belfast]—*NewYorker,* 1994; *Assassinations of individual foreigners later escalated into massive bombings—Bull. Amer. Acad. Arts & Sci.,* 1994; (figurative) *The important thing is to end your character assassination of the manager with some magnanimity—Observer Sport Magazine,* 2004.

assignment. The main meaning of *assignment* is now the originally American English one of a task or piece of work allotted to a person. In law it also denotes a legal transfer of a right or property, or the document that effects the transfer. To refer to the action of assigning something to someone, technically either *assignment* or **assignation** (which is pronounced /asɪg'neɪʃən/) is possible, e.g. *assignment/assignation of copyright,* but in practice the first is far and away the commoner form, the second being confined to highly technical or formal documents. The dominant meaning of *assignation* is of course 'an agreement to meet, especially a secret meeting of lovers'.

assimilation. In phonetics, 'the influence exercised by one sound segment upon the articulation of another, so that the sounds become more alike, or identical' (D. Crystal, 1980). Thus, in connected speech there is a tendency, for example, for *lunch score* to be articulated as /'lʌntʃ ʃkɔː/, i.e. with the normal /s/ of *score* assimilated to the final sound of *lunch.* It is common for a final *n* to become *m* in connected speech under the influence of a following labial. Examples include 'o*m* probation', 'a millio*m* pounds', and 'have bee*m* put'. Assimilation accounts for the creation of such words from ancient times as Latin *illuminatio* 'illumination' from *in-* + *lumen, luminis,* and L *irrationalis* 'irrational' from *in-* + *rationalis.* Cf. DISSIMILATION.

assist. 1 The sense 'to be present (at a ceremony, entertainment, etc.)', now uncommon and sounding affected, is a Gallicism: *And assisted—in the French sense—at the performance of two waltzes* (Dickens).

2 The sentence *May I assist you to potatoes?* in Mrs Gaskell's *Wives and Daughters* (1864) is a genteel way of saying 'May I help you to potatoes?' In many contexts *help* and *assist* are interchangeable, but in general *help* is the word to prefer, since *assist* will sound more formal. The two verbs share the same constructions. Examples: (followed by *in* and gerund) *They assisted him in receiving and entertaining his guests* (Poutsma); (followed by object and *to*-infinitive) *Mr. A. is assisting his wife to show a book of photographic portraits to a girl on a visit* (Poutsma); (followed by object and complement) *a young man who assisted him with the management of the farm* (T. Capote, 1966).

association. See -CIATION 3.

assonance. As a term of prosody it means partial rhyming, either (*a*) a correspondence of vowels but not of consonants, as in the last line of Yeats's *Byzantium*, That dolphin-torn, that gong-tormented sea, or (*b*) a correspondence of consonants but not of vowels, as in Wilfred Owen's *Arms and the Boy* where *blade/blood, flash/flesh, heads/lads, teeth/death, apple/supple*, and *heels/curls* lie at the end of successive lines. Type *b* is also called *pararhyme* and *half-rhyme*.

assume, presume. **1** *Meaning*. Which word to choose becomes an issue only when the meaning is 'to suppose', and there is a following clause, with or without *that*, e.g. *I assume/presume (that) you are coming to the party*. Some usage writers, including Fowler, have attempted to impose distinctions based on the degree of tentativeness behind the assumption or presumption, but such distinctions are extremely hard to define precisely.

Fowler (1926) expressed the semantic difference as follows: 'in the sense *suppose*, the object-clause after *presume* expresses what the presumer really believes, till it is disproved, to be true; that after *assume*, what the assumer postulates, often as a confessed hypothesis'. This seems reasonable, and is borne out by the *ODO*, which defines *assume* in this meaning as 'suppose to be the case without proof' and *presume* as 'suppose that something is the case on the basis of probability'. The aspect of probability in *presume* is foregrounded, for instance, in collocations without a following clause, such as *to presume someone innocent until proved guilty; his presumed father; missing, presumed dead*. Similarly, it would have been rather strange if Stanley had said 'Doctor Livingstone, I assume'.

What is clear is that the construction *assume that* is far commoner than *presume that;* in the *OEC* the first is nearly fifteen times more frequent than the second. Accordingly, in conversation, *assume* feels like the natural alternative, while *presume* may draw attention to the action of presuming; as Burchfield put it, 'there is a faint suggestion of presumptuousness about *presume*'.

2 *Syntax*. The constructions available after the two verbs across all their meanings are very similar. *Assume* can be followed by a *to*-infinitive, a *that*-clause, or a direct object; *presume* occurs in the same three constructions but also with a direct object and complement, and intransitively with a *to*-infinitive. Some examples (principally given to illustrate the various constructions): (assume) *William assumes the willingness of the Assembly*—E. A. Freeman, 1869; *He was writing 'Gerontion', a dramatic monologue in which he assumes the persona of the 'little old man'*—P. Ackroyd, 1984; *When you're young you assume everybody old knows what they're doing*—M. Amis, 1987; *The political parties either assume that after independence all will be well with low taxes and high services, or predict absolute disaster*—*Guardian*, 2007. (presume) *Death is presumed from the person not being heard of for seven years*—*Law Rep.*, 1871; *Those who ... presumed that if he spent his time with me I must also ... be either rich or disingenuous*—L. Durrell, 1957; *I know that in law every man is presumed innocent until proved otherwise*—A. Maclean, 1971; *It is a reckless ambassador who would presume to preempt his chiefs*—H. Kissinger, 1979; *He looked surprised—almost annoyed—as if a servant had presumed too great a familiarity*—P. P. Read, 1981.

assuming (that) is sometimes used as a 'subordinator' to mean 'on the assumption that'. Since it is the participle of the verb *to assume*, it is open to the often tiresome objection that the subject of the sentence has to be capable of assuming things, whereas of course the conceptual subject of the phrase is the people involved. It can be followed by a noun (or noun phrase) or by a *that*-clause: *Assuming an average of three feet per step, this equates to patients walking around an extra three quarters of a mile each day*—*Medical News Today*, 2005; *Assuming that the museum is open on Monday, the car will pick us up at 10 a.m.* There is no doubt at all about the intended meanings here.

assure, assurance. *Assure* has never found public acceptance in the meaning of 'to secure the future payment of an amount with insurance'. It is used by some insurance offices and agents, especially when death is the event insured against (*the life assured*). Outside those circles, you *insure* your life and take out *life assurance* (or *insurance*).

assuredly. Pronounced as four syllables, /əˈʃʊərɪdli/. See -EDLY.

assure, ensure, insure. These three words have overlapping meanings and all have to do with aspects of certainty, assuredness, and security. The following sentences show the main uses. *Assure* means 'to give an assurance in order to remove doubt, etc., and can be followed by *of* or by a *that*-clause: *I assure you of my love; I assured him that he had not been overlooked.* It also has special uses in *to rest assured* (*rest assured that I will be at the station when the train arrives*) and as an adjective *assured*, meaning 'self-confident'. Mostly in British English, it can also mean 'to cover (someone's life) by insurance', e.g. *those who assure with this Company.*

Ensure means 'to make certain, guarantee', and is followed by a direct object, or by a *that*-clause *Security checks at airports should ensure that no firearms are carried by passengers; that will ensure your success.*

Insure means 'to protect yourself financially by insurance', e.g. *He was insured against theft or loss.* Also, chiefly in American English, it is used instead of *ensure*, e.g. *He kept saying that he would take her out on the day the show was going to be broadcast, to insure that she didn't see it—New Yorker,* 1992; *The revolution has done enough to insure that there is no return to the decrepit imperial system—Dædalus,* 1993. To use insure in this way is not technically wrong in British English, but it is a much less common variant, and may be seen by some as a mistake.

asterisk (*). Used conventionally: **1** As a guide to a footnote (placed at the end of the context requiring elucidation, and at the head of the footnote itself). Formerly, a group of three asterisks was placed thus (*⁎*) to draw attention to a particular passage in a book or journal.

2 Especially in books written before the second half of the 20c., as a device to indicate omitted letters, particularly in coarse slang words, e.g. *c**t, f**k.*

3 In etymologies, placed before a word or form not actually found, but of which the existence is inferred, e.g. *wander* f. OE *wandrian* = MLG, MDu *wanderen*, etc., ← WGmc. **wandrōjan.*

4 In modern linguistic writing, and in this book, placed before unacceptable forms or constructions that are cited to draw attention to what are the correct ones, as **childs* (for *children*), **Leave the room, kindly* (for *Kindly leave the room*).

5 *Asterisk* should be pronounced with an /-ɪsk/ sound at the end, to match the spelling, and not as though it were spelled *-ix. Asterix* is a character in a cartoon strip.

asthma. Pronounced /ˈasmə/ in British English, but /ˈazmə/ in American.

asthmatic. To describe people affected by asthma, it is desirable to avoid using *asthmatic* as a noun, e.g. *?In 1999, the auto maker found that asthmatics in Madison County visited the hospital far more often than others—BusinessWeek,* 2002. This is because the humanness of the people concerned should not, as it should not with other disabilities, be reduced to a single medical condition ('the disability is not the person'). The preferred formulation for the plural is 'people with asthma', e.g. '*Sometimes people with asthma will have difficulty controlling their health problems if there's mould in the building', says Patry—Montreal Mirror,* 2001.

astronaut. First recorded in 1928, it has settled down as the usual word for a person trained to travel in a spacecraft. **Cosmonaut** (1959) is the usual word for a Russian equivalent.

astronomical. The figurative use of the word to mean 'immense', especially of figures, distances, etc., may be viewed by some as a bit of a cliché, and is probably best restricted to informal contexts. First recorded in 1899, this use of the word turns up with great frequency in popular and journalistic work, especially applied to large sums of money, prices, wage increases, foreign debts, etc.

asylum. **1** Plural *-ums*. See -UM 1.

2 First established in the 19c. as the normal word for a hospital for psychiatrically disturbed patients (though much older in the general sense 'a sanctuary, a secure place of refuge'), *asylum* in this sense fell out of use in the 20c. Such places are now usually called 'hospitals', 'clinics', or 'units', preceded by a proper name. The dominant current meaning of the word occurs in *political asylum* (first recorded 1954), the condition of being, or permission to remain in a country as, a political refugee.

asyndeton /əˈsɪndɪt(ə)n/ (Gk, = 'unconnected'.) Unlinked coordination, especially words not joined by conjunctions, is an ordinary feature of the language, e.g. *his comfort, his happiness, his life depended* *on the goodwill of his friends; carefully, quietly, remorselessly, the cat stalked the bird.* Asyndeton is also a rhetorical device in literature: *Is this the Region, this the Soil, the Clime, . . . this the seat That we must change for Heav'n* (*Paradise Lost* i. 242–4); *Come back in tears, O memory, hope, love of finished years* (C. Rossetti).

at.

1 *at about.*
2 *at all.*
3 *at* or *in.*
4 *where . . . at.*

1 *at about.* Occasional objections since the 1930s to this use, on the grounds that it says the same thing twice, can safely be ignored. The *OED* illustrates the use (e.g. *at about seven o'clock in the evening; at about that rate*) from 1843 onwards in works by writers of the stature of George Borrow, Trollope, Virginia Woolf, D.H. Lawrence, and Evelyn Waugh.

2 *at all.* This phrase meaning 'in every way, in any way' has a variety of adverbial uses in standard English, e.g. (with negative construction) *I did not speak at all;* (interrogative) *did you speak at all?;* (conditional) *if you spoke at all.* In former standard use, the phrase was restricted to affirmative constructions with the meanings 'of all; altogether; only'. This use survives in Ireland and in some dialects in Britain and in the US: *And what at all have you got there?*—J. Barlow, 1895; *John Cusack is the finest dancer at all*—P. W. Joyce, 1910; *He is the greatest man at all*—*Dialect Notes,* 1916; *Use one statement at all*—1976 in *DARE; Was he the right man at all?*—J. Leland, 1987. Two oral examples of 1990 from speakers in Dublin (in both examples = altogether): *He felt very awkward in this company at all; I had a great time at all.*

3 *at* or *in.* With proper names of places *at* is 'particularly used of all towns, except the capital of our own country, and that in which the speaker dwells (if of any size), also of small and distant islands or parts of the world' (*OED*). This rule admits of many exceptions, some of them arising from the new perspectives afforded by air travel to 'small and distant islands or parts of the world'. In general terms, *in* has gained ground and *at* retreated somewhat.

The implication of *in* is that the subject has been, or is, physically in (the place referred to): *we stayed in Fiesole for two weeks; St Peter's College is in Oxford.* But the choice depends in part on the dimensions of the place referred to. Reference to a specific place normally requires *at* (*at the North Pole; the plane landed at Nadi in Fiji*); reference to an area, country, etc., requires *in* (*she grew up in Switzerland; in Ontario; in Acton*). Large cities are treated as areas (*Professor Miyake lives in Tokyo*) but can also be regarded as specific stopping-points on journeys (*the plane called at Tokyo on the way to Seoul*). A further distinction is provided by the pair of sentences *he is at Oxford* (= is a member of the University of Oxford) and *he is in Oxford* (= living in, visiting, the city of Oxford).

4 *where . . . at.* The tautologous regional use of *at* in such sentences as *Where does he live at? This is where I get off at* does not belong in the standard language. On the other hand the colloquial phrase *where it's at,* meaning 'the focus of fashion or style', swept into American English in the 1960s and thence into other forms of English. For example, David Lodge used the title 'Where It's At: California Language' for an article in *The State of the Language* (1980) about what was trendy language in California at that time. The expression should probably be avoided in more formal English, and in any case could sound somewhat dated.

-atable. For the types *demonstrable* (rather than the rare form *demonstratable*) and *debatable* (with *-atable*) see -ABLE, -IBLE 3 (v). Some of the forms that Fowler recommended in 1926, *incubatable, inculcatable,* and *inculpatable,* seem to have been figments of his imagination as there is no record of them in the *OED* or other large general dictionaries. The shorter form *inculpable,* on the other hand, has been in continuous use since the 15c.

ate (past tense of *eat*). The standard pronunciation is /ɛt/, rhyming with *yet,* but /eɪt/, rhyming with *date,* is also common and is equally acceptable. In American English /eɪt/ is standard.

atelier. This 19c. loanword from French (= workshop, studio) is nowadays anglicized enough to be generally pronounced /əˈtɛlɪeɪ/, (uh-**te**-li-ay). The pseudo-French pronunciation recommended by Fowler and Burchfield would now sound mannered, if not pretentious.

-athon, -thon. The popularity of this useful little suffix illustrates how English nonchalantly plays fast and loose with etymology. The *-athon* element has no meaning in the Greek from which it comes, but is merely part of the place name Marathon, where a decisive battle was fought in antiquity. Using the suffix in this way was described by Burchfield as 'barbarous', but no matter. It combines with verbs or nouns to denote an activity, especially a sporting one, carried out for an unusually prolonged time, very often as a fund-raising event, e.g. a *skipathon* by children to raise funds for their primary school.

Some words created by adding *-thon* disappear no sooner than the event so described has happened, e.g. a *haircut-a-thon* [*sic*], or a *blogathon*, but others have become established and recognized by dictionaries, such as *walkathon*, and (with reduction to *-thon*) *telethon*. The earliest words formed in this manner date from the 1930s, the first being *talkathon*, originally meaning a debate deliberately prolonged to prevent the progress of a bill.

Words created using *-(a)thon* do not require hyphens, and their plural is *-ons*. The word *'thon* is occasionally found as an informal shortening of *marathon* meaning a long-distance race.

-ati. This plural suffix, used to create nouns 'designating elite or prominent groups of people who are associated with what is specified by the stem word' was introduced into English in the word *illuminati* (1599). However, the several modern words containing the suffix take their inspiration from the slightly later *literati* (1620). The *-ati* part of that word seems to be an amalgam of the Latin and Italian masculine plural past participle, while the only word containing *-ati* introduced before the 19c., *illiterati* (1788) comes directly from Latin.

What sets modern *-ati* words apart from their predecessors is that the suffix can be added at will to stems which are not borrowed directly from either Latin or Italian, two topical examples being *bloggerati* and *twitterati*. Use of the suffix in this way started earlier than might be assumed, with the creation of *culturati* (= *culture* + *-ati*) in 1892, but it was only in the 20c. that the trend intensified, *glitterati* being first recorded in 1956. Since then this useful suffix has generated words that have become established, such as *technorati* and *digerati* (the elite of, or people who are very knowledgeable about, the digital technology world). Others that have not become fully established include, at one end of the social spectrum, *lagerati* (= 'lager louts') and *blazerati* (= 'blazer-wearing sports officials') at the other.

-ative, -ive. There has been a great deal of slipping and sliding in the use of these rival suffixes in some, but not all, of the words affected. The earliest English words in *-ative* entered the language in the Middle English period, some directly from French *-atif, -ative* and others from the participial stem *-āt-* in Latin verbs in *-āre*. Some others were simply formed in English on the model of existing adjectives in *-ative*. A number of them were joined by rival forms in *-ive* (i.e. with the *-at-* omitted), and in some cases the rivalry between the *-ative* and the *-ive* forms continues.

The pairs which have competing forms are treated at their alphabetical places. There follows a select list (from scores of words of this type) with the date when each was first recorded. A dash signifies that the *OED* has no record of the word in question.

-ative	*-ive*
affirmative 1509	—
anticipative 1664	—
argumentative 1642	argumentive (1668, once only)
assertative 1846	assertive 1562
authoritative 1605	authoritive (1645, once only)
contemplative 1340	—
demonstrative 1530	—
elucidative 1822	—
exploitative 1885	exploitive 1921
figurative 1398	—
interpretative 1569	interpretive1680
interrogative 1520	—
investigative 1803	—
preventative 1654–66	preventive 1639
qualitative 1607	qualitive (1846, once only)
quantitative 1581	quantitive1656
representative 1387–8	—
retardative 1847	retardive (1797, now rare)
talkative (q.v.) 1432–50	—
vegetative 1398	vegetive 1526

See also INTERPRETIVE; QUALITY 2; QUANTITATIVE.

ATM. To refer to an *ATM* as an 'ATM machine' is a classic, oft-quoted tautology. It is tautological because *ATM*, in its banking meaning, stands for 'automated teller machine'. But such repetition harms nobody.

-ato. Musical terms ending in *-ato* retain the Italianate pronunciation /ɑːtəʊ/, rhyming with British *tomato*, e.g. *obbligato, pizzicato, staccato*.

atop. Used since the 17c. as an adverb (also, less frequently, *atop of*) and preposition, it is now rare except as a preposition. As such, it is rather literary. Examples: *the half-drunk glass of the stuff that waited atop a pile of 'Smith's Weeklies'*—T. Keneally, 1980; *Now I am seated atop the piano, spinning*—Lee Smith, 1983; *her graying hair arranged into a crown atop her head*—M. Doane, 1988.

atrium. Once confined to Roman archaeology and architecture (referring to the open-roofed hall or central courtyard of a Roman house), this word is now more likely to be encountered in its modern architectural meaning of 'a central hall in a modern building, typically rising through several stories and having a glazed roof'. For both these meanings, the more common plural is *atria*, not *atriums*, and in the medical meaning, *atria* is the norm. The word is pronounced /ˈeɪtrɪəm/ the first syllable rhyming with *mate*, rather than *cat*. See LATIN PLURALS 1.

at this moment in time. This phrase (first recorded from 1972) is one of the most widely ridiculed and reviled of modern clichés, and comes very high on many people's list of pet hates. It goes without saying that when used instead of a simple 'now' it is long-winded and unnecessary: *So how and where is Pete at this moment in time?—Cherwell*, 2003. In official or business contexts it can typify the bombastic wordiness which Sir Bruce Fraser (1973) labelled 'pompo-verbosity': *A spokesman for PIAB said: 'Unfortunately, we are not releasing any statistical information just yet and therefore I regret I cannot give you any meaningful statistics at this moment in time'—BBC News, Business*, 2004.

But is it to be avoided in all situations? Possibly not. For instance, often it does not stand in for a simple 'now', but rather for more emphatic phrases such as 'at the moment, at present', in which case its wordiness is more pardonable: *Well at this moment in time you are definitely going about it the wrong way—BBC News, Business*, 2004. Moreover, it can be a useful emphasizing device, suggesting the flow of time in a way that 'now' cannot; suggesting, in fact, that while things are the way they are currently, they may well change in future: *I'm afraid there's no prospect of anything just at this moment in time*—Ruth Rendell, 1986; *But, I do want a husband and kids. But, not right now, I don't want to be distracted at this moment in time—Jet Magazine*, 2003.

Apart from its emphasizing role, *at this moment in time* also highlights a particular moment in a narrative of past events: *There were five similar* [flak] *towers ... but at this moment in time, they were only of passing interest*—C. Egleton, 1974. Of course, even in that example, it could be shortened too to 'at that moment' or 'just then', as it could in the next: *When the face* [of a wave] *is very steep, nearly vertical, it is referred to as a wall, since at this moment in time it is a wall of water—Paddles* Magazine, 1996.

The fact remains, though, that many people detest the phrase under any circumstances, so it is as well to avoid it in any kind of serious writing. And there is an ample stock of synonymous phrases that can replace it, e.g. *at the moment, at present, currently, just now*, and so forth.

attorney See BARRISTER, SOLICITOR.

attraction (grammar). See AGREEMENT 2.

attributive. **1** 'Attributive' is a technical grammar term used throughout this book. It refers to an adjective or noun that is placed immediately before a noun in order to describe a characteristic of that noun. Examples of attributive adjectives are *brown* and *daily* in *brown shoes* and *daily newspapers;* in the phrases *beauty contest, bedside lamp, grammar term*, the words *beauty, bedside* and *grammar* are all nouns being used in an attributive position, in other words, as if they were adjectives. Most adjectives can precede or follow a noun, e.g. *my shoes are brown*. When they follow a noun, linked by a verb such as *be, seem, look*, etc., they are termed 'predicative'. For more information on this distinction, see ADJECTIVE 2. Plural attributive nouns, once relatively rare, are now commonplace (*appointments book, customs duty, narcotics dealer, procedures manual*).

2 English permits the placing of more than one noun in a series: (two attributive nouns) *a museum conservation department; an Oxfordshire gentry family; a quality control manager;* (three or more attributive nouns) *a dilapidated South Side low-income apartment complex; Oxford City Football Club president JT; the undisputed Secret Service crossword king.*

3 For attributive adjectives, see ADJECTIVE 2.

4 *An historical note.* By 1400 a large class of compound nouns of the type *cherrystone* and *hall-door* had come into being, and before long such two-unit expressions became attached to other nouns, resulting in noun phrases like *coffee house conversation* (Hume, 1752) and *fellow-workman* (Coverdale, 1535). It was an easy step to the formation of more complex assemblages like *whoreson malt-horse drudge* (*Taming of the Shrew*, 1596), *tortoise-shell memorandum book* (Smollett, 1771), and many others. What has happened in the 20c. is that this ancient process has gathered momentum, especially in the hands of journalists and civil servants, to produce all too frequently phrases of the type *university block grant arrangements, rate support grant settlement, and Slav Bosnia Famine Witness Dr John Smith,* as well as eye-stretching comments of the kind (in a letter to *The Times* in July 1991) *the dilemma of trading off patient waiting time against treatment resource idle time.*

au. See À LA.

Aubretia, Aubrieta. Horticulture provides fertile ground for misspelling, there being no good reason why experts in the art and science of growing things should be equally skilled at spelling. *Aubretia* is named after a French botanist called Claude Aubriet, and the original spelling was *Aubrieta*, which is the plant's genus name. In non-technical use, however, the forms *Aubretia* and **Aubrietia** are now more usual.

***au courant*, au fait.** **1** These loanwords from French, both meaning 'acquainted or conversant with what is going on', joined the language in the mid-18c. and have been freely used by good writers since then. *Au fait* was often construed in the past with *of* (*I will put you au fait of all the circumstances of the case*—A. Granville, 1828), but is now almost always followed by *with* (*he was very keen to keep me au fait with his progress*—R. Cobb, 1985). Since it entered the language, *au courant* has been followed by either *of* or *with* (*They are quite eager to place me* au courant *of all their proceedings*—J. S. Mill, 1830; *It would have been wiser if the United States had been kept* au courant *of the negotiations from the very outset*—*Daily Tel.*, 1928; *keeping its public* au courant *with recent work*—D. Macdonald, *a*1961).

2 Print *au courant* in italic, but *au fait* in roman.

audience. Despite its etymological meaning, *audience* (ultimately from Latin *audīre* to hear), with the advent of films and of television, has securely established itself as a normal word for those watching a cinema or TV film.

audit (verb). British readers of American books or newspapers are still likely to be baffled by the 'new' use (first recorded in 1933) of the verb to mean 'to attend (a course or other form of instruction) in order to participate without the need to earn credits by writing papers' (*OED 2*), e.g. *She audited his undergraduate lectures; she waylaid him in the department office*—A. Lurie, 1974.

au fait. See AU COURANT, AU FAIT.

auger, augur. The spelling *auger* is quite often used by mistake for *augur*. An *auger* (from Old English *nafogār*, with loss of initial *n*) is a tool for boring holes. *Augur* (from Latin *augur* a soothsayer) is used occasionally to mean a prophet, but occurs more frequently as a verb, especially in the phrases *augur well* or *augur ill* (or *badly*) 'to have *good* or *bad* expectations *of, for*'. Examples: *Everything augured badly—they weren't meant to be together*—E. J. Howard, 1965; *The novel augured well for a successful career in fiction-writing*—J. Pope Hennessy, 1971; (*auger* wrongly used) *And recent elections don't auger well for Roh*—*Business Week*, 2002.

aught. By about 1300 Old English *āwiht* 'anything' had become *aught*. It remained in use for many centuries (e.g. *Excuse me, dear, if aught amiss was said*—Pope, 1702) but now survives mainly in the fixed expressions *for aught I know, for aught I care.* From about the same date it was also spelt *ought* (e.g. *Grieve not, my Swift, at ought* *our realm acquires*—Pope, 1728), and so became a homonym of the modal verb *ought* (which is from OE *āhte,* past tense of *āgan* 'to own'). The presence of the modal verb may have helped to drive *aught* into restricted use.

augur. See AUGER.

aural, oral. In standard English these are both pronounced /'ɔːrəl/, rhyming with *floral.* In some other varieties of English they are distinguished, by virtue of the fact that the second of the pair is pronounced /'ɒrəl/.

aureola, aureole. See AREOLA.

autarchy, autarky. The first (from Greek αὐταρχία) means 'absolute sovereignty'; the second (from Gk αὐτάρκεια) means 'self-sufficiency'. They have the same pronunciation in English, but should be carefully distinguished in spelling.

authentic, genuine. **1** Both words mean 'entitled to acceptance or belief, as being in accordance with fact', but *genuine* commonly (and *authentic* less commonly) has the additional nuance of 'not sham or feigned'. The distinction made by Fowler (1926) was that *'authentic* implies that the contents of a book, picture, account, or the like, correspond to facts and are not fictitious, and *genuine* implies that its reputed is its real author'. One rather implausible sentence he produced to illustrate his point was *The Holbein Henry VIII is both authentic and genuine;* it was valid, he claimed, because it really is a portrait of him and is by Holbein, not by another painter.

But such a fine distinction is not generally applicable: data, documents, a Chippendale chair, a signature, and much else can be described as either *authentic* or *genuine* without a perceptible shift of meaning. On the other hand, an authentic account of a series of events or of an unusual or complex experience is one that is convincing, one that can be believed (*Harrier was thrilled to detect genuine disappointment in her voice*—M. Bracewell, 1989). In such contexts *genuine* means 'real, not fake'. Hitler's alleged diaries, 'discovered' in the 1980s, sounded authentic but were found to be not genuine.

2 An especially important domain in which *authentic* has been used in recent years is that of 'early' music (i.e. before about 1700), where *authentic instruments* are those made and played according to the principles of the period in which the music was written; and so a violin (for example) can be an *authentic* baroque one, although it may be of modern manufacture and therefore not *genuine* or *original.* An increasingly common alternative is *period instruments,* first recorded in the 1920s but not widely used until the 1970s.

author (verb). **1** By the process of conversion (see CONVERSION) this 16c. verb came into being as a companion to the earlier noun (*The last foul thing Thou ever author'dst*—Chapman's *Iliad,* 1596). It has had a chequered career, used both transitively and intransitively, in literary works since then, but has come into widespread use, especially in newspapers and online, and often in transferred senses (of 'creative' acts or events in non-literary spheres, e.g. the cinema, sport). It is widely reviled by usage commentators, in part because of the general antipathy to 'verbing'; it is forbidden by the *AP Stylebook,* while the *Telegraph* style guide says 'the American habit of using it as a verb is to be studiously avoided'. Despite its stylistic leprosy, it is widely used, particularly in US English, from which half the *OEC* examples come: *this is the last building by the architecture firm that authored the Empire State*—*OEC,* 2004; *She authored numerous articles on Latin American photography, art and politics for various publications*—*Art in America,* 2005.

2 Authoring is a relatively recent addition to the language of computing, and means 'the process of creating multimedia documents for electronic publishing': *In order to profit from the possibilities of hypertext, teachers have to be provided with powerful authoring environments which allow them to create complex hypertexts*—*Literary and Linguistic Computing,* 1992.

authoress. A word of long standing, being first recorded in 1478, *authoress* has never come to the fore meaning a female author. Like many other female designations that stress gender irrelevantly, it is now largely *verboten.* The *OED*'s comment accurately reflects modern use: 'Now used only when sex is purposely emphasized; otherwise . . . *author* is now used of both sexes.' As the following examples suggest, it is only appropriate where an author's femaleness has already been made explicit in the surrounding co-text: *the hostess interviews Anne Rice, the authoress of those wacked-out vampire books*—*OEC*, 2003; *Potter struggled for eight years to make Orlando, which was adapted from Virginia Woolf's 1928 novel-length "love letter" to authoress Vita Sackville-West*—*OEC*, 2003. See -ESS; FEMININE DESIGNATIONS.

authoritarian, authoritative. Since these two are occasionally muddled, it is worth setting out how they differ in meaning and connotation. *Authoritarian* is generally used of people or their actions and has the negative meaning 'favouring or encouraging strict obedience to authority' (with overtones of excess); typical collocates include *regime, ruler, government, personality,* and *leadership. Authoritative* is generally used of things that people say or write, or the manner of their saying them (*voice* is a common collocate), and has the favourable meaning 'recognized as true or dependable'. Examples: (authoritarian) *The West was happy to bolster authoritarian governments that were not controlled by the Soviet Union to prevent them from turning communist*—*Foreign Affairs Magazine*, 2004; (authoritative) *He was cool, authoritative, and well spoken; a very authoritative article which looks at whether the Queen or the Governor General is Australia's head of State*—J. Ray, 2003.

automaton /ɔːˈtɒmət(ə)n/. The plural can be either *automata* or the slightly more frequent *automatons*. Scientific writing seems to prefer the first form. See LATIN PLURALS.

auxiliary verbs. An auxiliary verb is one that precedes another verb to form a particular tense or mood, for example *be* in *We* were *going, have* in *They* have *gone*, and *do* in Do *you mind?* Sometimes more than one auxiliary verb is used to form a tense, as in *We* will be *going* and *You* have been *warned*. Some verbs, such as *can, may,* and *would,* are called modal (or modal auxiliary) verbs, and others (notably *dare* and *need*), though less obviously auxiliary in function, are called semi-modal verbs because they behave in similar ways to auxiliary verbs (for example, you can say *dare not* and *need not*, which is characteristic of auxiliary verbs). See also DARE; MODAL VERB; NEED.

avail. 1 *Noun.* The noun poses no problems. It is used most frequently in the phrases *of no avail* (his efforts were of no avail), *to no avail/to little avail* (he tried the key but to no avail, etc.,), *without avail* (his effort was without avail).

2 *Standard uses.* Uncontroversial uses of the verb are common: (*a*) the intransitive use, which has an archaic or highly literary feel, e.g. *words avail very little with him;* (*b*) the transitive use, with a personal object, which is also archaic-sounding, e.g. *his good works availed him nothing;* (*c*) the standard pattern, with reflexive pronoun + *of*, e.g. *none of the English departments . . . avail themselves of such opportunities*—F. Tuohy, 1964; *I availed myself of the invitation to move about*—D. Lessing, 1979.

3 *Disputed uses.* In the 19c., when the adjective *available* acquired the meaning 'that may be availed of', the verb came to be used as an indirect passive: *Power . . . must be availed of, and not by any means let off and wasted*—Emerson, 1861. Fowler (1926) decried this use as 'wrong' *tout court*. The *OED* data suggests that it has very limited currency nowadays, Irish newspapers being a bastion of its use: *the wonderful system of drainage is being availed of*—*Daily Tel.*, 1927; *it is generally forgotten that the same process can always be availed of by a media organisation sued for defamation*—*Sunday Business Post*, 2003.

4 Some other easily avoidable and some frankly marginal constructions are shown in the following examples: (*a*) reflexive pronoun omitted: *I want to encourage other people within the police service who are also retiring under the severance scheme to avail of the opportunities for training*—*Guardian*, 2009; (*b*) passive use: *interested teachers can come and they will be availed this information*—*Times* (Zambia), 2004 (i.e. they will be provided with this information); (*c*) *avail* used transitively with a double object: *The association with this country has availed Koreans many advantages*—*Washington Post*, 1986.

Clearly the verb *avail* (with or without *of* and with or without a reflexive pronoun) is on the move, as it has been since Fowler first commented on the phenomenon. Purists can make up their own minds whether to follow the trend, or to stick to tradition.

avant-garde. From the 15c. onwards the noun had a single meaning in English, namely 'the foremost part of an army', but this use was taken over at some point in the 19c. by *vanguard.* The 20c. witnessed the revival of *avant-garde* with the transferred meaning 'the pioneers or innovators in any art in a particular period', and as an adjective referring to them. It continues to be used with great frequency, but still retains its quasi-French pronunciation /ˌavɑ̃ˈgɑːd/, not as yet /ˈavəntˌgɑːd/. It is printed with a hyphen, in roman type.

avenge, revenge (verbs). Is there a distinction between these verbs? A note of 1885 in the *OED* observed that 'the restriction of *avenge* and its derivatives to the idea of just retribution, as distinguished from the malicious retaliation of *revenge'* is not 'absolutely observed, although it largely prevails'. Webster's Third (1986 version) says that while both verbs are used in the sense 'to punish a person who has wronged one or someone close to one ... *avenge* more often suggests punishing a person when one is vindicating someone else than oneself or is serving the ends of justice', whereas *'revenge* more often applies to vindicating oneself, and usually suggests an evening up of scores or a personal satisfaction more than an achievement of justice'.

The distinctions are probably overstated and rarely observed, as the examples show. Examples: (avenge) *Edwy had the power to avenge himself upon Dunstan—OED,* 1861; *he avenged himself for Father's obstruction of all his efforts to nominate an heir*—P. Scott, 1962; *The ferocity and guile with which Absalom had avenged the rape of his sister*—D. Jacobson, 1970; *That brave god will leap down from his steed when he has to avenge his father's death*—K. Crossley-Holland, 1980; *Through characterization the novelist has the means to avenge himself on his enemies if, of course, he is willing to risk an action for libel*—P. D. James, 1993. (revenge) *He was father's partner, and father broke with him, and now he revenges himself*—Dickens, 1865; *murmurings ... that Ham's wife ... had decided to revenge herself upon the animals*—Julian Barnes, 1989; *It wasn't just that I could never revenge myself on him ... I felt the first dim recollection that my own life had lost all purpose.*—Simon Mason, 1990; *If I were to revenge myself upon you ... that would be an act of despair*—I. Murdoch, 1993; *He revenged the French attack on the Sussex coast in autumn 1515 by retaliating effectively in a series of devastating raids on Normandy*—*Oxf. Dict. of Nat. Biog.,* 2008.

aver. This formal word means 'to assert as a fact; to state positively, to affirm'. Just as assertion means rather more than mere statement, so *aver* means more than the neutral word *say.* Examples: *The shopman averring that it was a most uncommon fit*—Dickens, 1838; *It is passionately averred in Tortilla Flat that Danny alone drank three gallons of wine*—J. Steinbeck, 1935; *Belloc liked to aver that you belonged to the flower of the bourgeoisie if you knew the maiden names of your four great grand-mothers*—A. N. Wilson, 1984; *He was, she avers, 'a real Sweetie'*—Godfrey Smith, 1990.

averse, aversion. *Averse to* and *aversion to* are nowadays the standard, rather than the construction favoured by Dr Johnson, *averse from.* In a note of almost unprecedented length, the *OED* states that *averse to* and *aversion to* are justified because they express a mental relation analogous to that indicated by *hostile, contrary, repugnant, hostility,* etc. and naturally take the same construction. Historically, both *to* and *from* have been used, often by the same writers, but *averse to* and *aversion to* are now without question the more usual. Examples: (averse to) *Nor was he averse to being reminded of Calcutta*—A. Desai, 1988; *Vic wasn't averse to keeping Everthorpe guessing whether he and Robyn Penrose were having an affair*—D. Lodge, 1988; (averse from) *The British Parliament is averse from making further one-sided concessions*—*Daily Tel.,* 2009; (aversion to) *he had a lifelong aversion to British officialdom*—J. le Carré, 1989; (aversion from) *Dr Mainwaring's prescription had not cured her aversion from the prospect of becoming hopelessly senile in the company of people who knew her*—K. Amis, 1974. See also ADVERSE.

avid. Loanwords seldom take over all the meanings and constructions of the word in the original language. *Avid,* first recorded in English only in 1769, is no exception. The *Oxford Latin Dictionary* lists six main senses for Latin *auidus:* (1) greedy for gain, covetous; (2) having an immoderate appetite for food, greedy; (3) (of qualities, actions, etc.) voracious, greedy, insatiable; (4) eager, ardent; (5) ardently desirous (of), eager (for); (6) lustful, passionate. Despite the objections of some, including Kingsley

Amis, in English, *avid* has settled down in most contexts as a kind of medley of senses 3, 4, and 5 of the Latin word, that is, 'extremely, and usually praiseworthily, eager'. It is used attributively, or, if predicatively, is usually followed by *for* or by a *to*-infinitive. Examples: (attributively) *an avid collector of old coins; an avid reader; an avid interest in politics;* (predicatively), *The Africans are avid for advancement* (D. Lessing, 1968); *people in Eastern Europe are now avid to find out how democracy works.*

avocation. In the 17c. and 18c. (after Latin *āuocātio*) *avocation* was used in English to mean 'the calling away or withdrawal (of a person) from an employment, a distraction'. Since, however, the business which called one away could be of either minor or major importance, a nice balance of meanings developed. Already in the 17c. it came to mean (still its main sense) 'a hobby or minor occupation', or (with complete loss of the original Latin meaning) 'one's usual occupation, vocation, or calling'. It is worth noting that *The Economist* style guide bans this second meaning. Examples: (= hobby) *He understood the importance of organized political parties and pursued politics as a career, not simply an avocation—Oxford Companion to United States History*, 2001; *In England, Pigot pursued the usual avocations of the very rich, leasing grand houses in London, collecting pictures, buying a country estate, and entering the House of Commons—Oxf. Dict. of Nat. Biog.*, 2010; (= occupation, calling) *the consummate lumberjack, who had found his true avocation in working mahogany—Environmental History*, 2003; *A rancher by training and avocation, he studied agricultural management at the University of the Philippines—www.AsiaWeek.com*, 2000.

avoirdupois. Should you need to pronounce this word, the older pronunciation /ˌavədəˈpɔːɪz/ is standard in American English, while in British English it competes with /ˌavwɑːdjʊˈpwɑː/.

avouch, avow, vouch. *Avouch* was once a proud word of multiple meanings (eleven senses spread over a column and a half in the *OED*) and wide currency, e.g. *Thou hast auouched the Lord this day to be thy God*—(Deut. (AV) 26: 17); *Then my account I well may giue, And in the Stockes auouch it* (Autolycus in *The Winter's Tale*, IV iii. 22). It is now archaic in feel, but on the very rare occasions it is used, usually in somewhat elevated circumstances, it means 'guarantee, solemnly assert, maintain the truth of, vouch for' (*a miracle avouched by the testimony of . . . ; millions were ready to avouch the exact opposite*). *Avow*, still in common use, means declare (something) openly, admit (*avow one's belief, faith, etc.; avow oneself to be a vegetarian; the avowed aim of the government is to bring inflation down*). *Vouch* is restricted to the phrase *vouch for* (somebody or something) (*I can vouch for him, for his honesty; experts were produced to vouch for the authenticity of the painting*).

avuncular. A minor curiosity of the language is that this word, meaning 'of or resembling an uncle', lacks a feminine equivalent. In 1982, readers of William Safire's column in the *New York Times Magazine* suggested (several of them facetious) *amital* (Latin *amita* aunt), *auntique, auntsy, materteral* (Latin *matertera* maternal aunt), *tantative* (French *tante* aunt), *tantular*, and *tantoid*, but none of them has taken hold.

await, wait. *Await* is generally a transitive verb. It can mean, somewhat formally, 'to wait for, expect' (*he awaited his fate, I shall await your answer*) or 'to be in store for' (*a surprise awaits you*). It is occasionally used with an implied but not expressed object, e.g. *a warm welcome awaits* (i.e. you/us/them), but some people consider this incorrect. Far more stylistically suspect is the phrase *await and see* that you sometimes hear or see.

Wait, on the other hand, can be used transitively and intransitively in a wide range of meanings and idiomatic phrases (*wait a minute; you must wait your turn; he waited for an hour; wait till I come; wait and see;* etc.).

Wait also acquired (late 18c.) a quasi-transitive informal use in the type *Don't wait lunch for me* (= defer a meal)

awake, awaken, wake, waken. **1** *History.* The network of forms in Old English and Middle English for these four verbs amounts to a philological nightmare. From earliest times, they have been unstable and unpredictable in two main respects: (*a*) the choice of form for the past tense and past participle, depending on whether the verb was felt to belong to the strong conjugation (with pastness indicated by change of stem vowel) or to the weak conjugation (with past tense and past participle ending in *-ed, -ened*); (*b*) the likelihood that any of them could at most times and in the work of any given writer be used either intransitively to mean 'to arise from or come out of sleep' or causally (and transitively) 'to rouse (someone) from sleep'. To make things worse, the presence or absence of a following *up* seems to have been optional, especially since the 19c., after *wake* and *waken*. The complicated chain of events is set down under the respective entries in the *OED*.

2 *Forms*. In modern English *wake* and *awake* can be paired as strong verbs having a change of vowel, and *awaken* and *waken* can be paired as weak verbs. For the first pair, the past forms are *woke* and *awoke*, and the participial forms are *woken* and *awoken*. The second pair are regular, with past and participial forms *awakened* and *wakened*.

The forms *waked* and *awaked* occasionally occur, either by confusion, or as dialect forms and in the language of children.

3 *Awake, awaken*, and *waken* often have a tinge of formality or literariness not present in *wake*, which people use about four times as often as the others combined. All four verbs can be used both transitively and intransitively.

4 Examples of the more common uses of this quartet of verbs, set out in frequency order *wake, awaken, awake, waken*:

(*a*) *When do you usually wake* (*up*) *in the morning?; I wake* (*up*) *at about seven every morning; Wake up! It's morning; I woke* (*up*) *early this morning; I had woken* (*up*) *at dawn; I was woken* (*up*) *by the wind in the night; I woke* (*her*) *up at nine o'clock.*

(*b*) *We must awaken motorists to the danger of speeding on foggy motorways; the episode awakened her interest in impressionist painting; enough noise to awaken the dead.*

(*c*) *I awoke from a deep sleep;* (*somewhat literary*) *She awoke to the sound of driving rain; she awoke her sleeping child; the accident awoke old fears.*

(*d*) *We were wakened by the storm; when she fell asleep nothing would waken her.*

aware. The *OED* classes *aware* as a predicative adjective, i.e. one that can normally stand only after a noun or the verb *to be*. Its more usual constructions, which are still in use, are illustrated by the types (*a*) (followed by *of* + noun) *Arnan loked, and was aware of Dauid* (Coverdale, 1535); (*b*) (followed by a *that*-clause) *Are you aware that your friends are here?* (1885). In both constructions *aware* could be premodified by *very much* or by (*very*) *well*. In the 20c. it has started to be used attributively (e.g. *an aware person*, one who is alert to the possibilities of a given set of circumstances), or absolutely, preceded by an adverb in *-ly* (e.g. *he was environmentally aware all right, rather too much so*). Both uses are paralleled by a widening of the applications of the corresponding noun **awareness**. Examples: *it . . . succeeded in striking a* démodé *note in that aware community*—M. Allingham, 1938; *the painfully aware state that seems to have succeeded her earlier calm*—A. Brookner, 1985; *It's hoped the public awareness campaign will encourage youngsters to think twice about who they're chatting to online*—*The Register*, 2004.

away. Used with intensive force before adverbs (*away back, away down, away up*, etc.), originally in American English, since the early 19c.: *Perhaps away up in Canada*—J. Palmer, 1818; *Manufacturers of all good cars are away behind in their deliveries*—*NY Even. Post*, 1906. It now seems to be *yielding* in all major forms of English to the shorter form *way*: hence such common phrases as *way back* (*in the 1960s*), *way down south, way off course, way out here, way over there*. See WAY 1.

awesome has followed the route of words like *fantastic, tremendous*, etc., in acquiring its current favourable meaning of 'marvellous, great' which has all but exterminated its original meaning of 'full of awe, inspiring awe (usually with profoundly reverential implications)'. In the slang of a certain age group, in Britain almost as much as in the US, *awesome* has become such a generalized word of approval (like *cool* and *wicked*) that it can be used to refer to things as un-awe-inspiring as *Reading week was awesome: instead of doing any work I went on holidays*—weblog, 2004.

MWCDEU (2002) notes that in the meaning 'impressive, remarkable' the word 'has been part of the standard hyperbole of sports broadcasting and writing for several years', and cites supporting evidence, including the following: *The depth of quality on the Steeler squad is awesome—there is no apparent weakness anywhere*—A. Mount in *Playboy*, 1979.

Its current, widespread use as a blanket term of approval is first noted in the *Official Preppy Handbook* (1980), edited by L. Birnbach and others, where it was glossed as 'terrific, great', and was presumably a relative newcomer to the American slang scene. The *OED* Olympianly calls this 'a trivial use' and Burchfield sarcastically noted that 'in certain social groups the word has made its way into areas where it can be used of public or domestic experiences that seem as important to them as the experiences of religion'. Whether one chooses to use it in this weakened sense will depend on factors such as geography and an appreciation of the ludicrousness of certain words being uttered by people *d'un certain âge*. Further examples: (= impressive) *The roadside drinkers stare open-mouthed at the sight of the awesome Ford GT40—Today*, 1992; *If the English performances in Paris and Edinburgh had been executed by New Zealand they would be proclaimed as awesome and unstoppable—Rugby World and Post*, 1992; (= excellent, fantastic) *So I just had the most awesome weekend EVER!—OEC*, 2010; *I had meant to link to your (totally awesome!) article in my post—www.futuremovies.co.uk*, 2011.

awful. For nearly two hundred years this adjective has been used as 'a mere intensifier deriving its sense from the context = Exceedingly bad, great, long, etc.' (*OED*). Thus *an awful looking woman*; *an awful while since you have heard from me* (Keats); *an awful scrawl; what an awful duffer I am*, etc. For a similar period it has also served as an adverb (*it is awful hot, it is awful lonely here*—Trollope; *Aunt Polly's awful particular about this fence*—M. Twain), though this use is now non-standard in British English and markedly informal in American English. Side by side with these, and over a similar period, the adverb **awfully** has become established, especially in Britain, as a simple intensifying adverb = very, exceedingly, extremely. Examples: *You'll be awfully glad to get rid of me*— William Black, 1877; *I'm awfully glad you didn't run away*—J. B. Priestley, 1929; *You are awfully good to look after Elizabeth for us*—M. Binchy, 1982.

These are all natural semantic developments, paralleled by the development of similar intensifiers such as *dreadfully, horribly, terribly*, etc.

awhile, a while. 1 When used as a noun meaning 'a period of time' *while* is written separately from the indefinite article *a* that often precedes it (and obviously also when an adjective intervenes, as in the type *It's a long while since I last saw you*): *I moved away and looked at the T'ang Dynasty horses for a while—Encounter*, 1990; *I'm going away for a while*—B. Neil, 1993. This is by far the normal (and recommended) practice.

2 From the 14c. onwards, however, the word has also been used as the adverb: e.g. *Sailing awhile to the Southward*—Defoe, 1725; *Awhile she paused, no answer came*—Scott, 1810; *when he reached the street-sign he stopped awhile and stood beneath it*—C. Dexter, 1983; *They delayed awhile, but finally the dance was held—New Yorker*, 1990.

3 Writing *a* + *while* (noun) as one word has a long history. As the *OED* puts it: 'Improperly written together, when there is no unification of sense, and *while* is purely a [noun]'. Three historical examples are given, from Caxton (1489), John Yeats (1872), and Ouida (1882). It is easy to find further examples of this tendency, historical and modern: *For awhile explication was impossible*—G. Meredith, 1861; *He took awhile to die*—B. Ripley, 1987 (US).

4 The tendency towards writing the expression as one word in all circumstances is reinforced by the fact that in many contexts *awhile* could easily be replaced by *for a while* without loss of sense or rhythm: e.g. *Mrs Hardcastle was silent awhile, frowning to herself*—F. Kidman, 1988 (NZ); *I asked her one day, after she'd been home awhile, what she thought* [etc.]—M. Golden, 1989 (US); *She could wait awhile, it wouldn't kill her—New Yorker*, 1991.

axe. Thus spelt almost everywhere in English-speaking countries except the US, where it is often printed as *ax*.

axis. Plural *axes*, pronounced /ˈaksiːz/, **ak**-seez.

aye, ay. **1** The word meaning 'yes' appeared suddenly about 1575 and is of disputed origin. It is now always pronounced /ʌɪ/, rhyming with *eye*, and is normally spelt *aye*, especially in parliamentary language (*The ayes have it*), in nautical language in *Aye, aye, sir* (the correct reply on board ship on receipt of an order), and in some northern dialects in Britain, especially in Scotland (*Are you coming? Aye, I'm on my way.*).

2 The word meaning 'ever' was first recorded *c*1200 in the *Ormulum*, and is derived from Old Norse *ei, ey* (cognate with Old English *ā*), used in the same sense. It is normally pronounced /eɪ/, rhyming with *hay*, and spelt *aye*.

3 The spelling *ay* is occasionally used for both meanings.

azure. This 14c. loanword from French has fluctuated in pronunciation in the last two centuries between /ˈaʒ(j)ʊə/, /ˈaʒə/ (*OED*, 1885, Daniel Jones, 1917, but both cite other pronunciations as well), and /ˈeɪ-/ (given as a variant in *OED* and Jones). The initial sound is now usually /a-/, as in *cat*, not /eɪ-/, as in *pay*. The final sound varies between /-ʒjʊə/ rhyming with *pure* /pjʊə/ (the dominant pronunciation) and /-ə/.

bacillus. Plural *bacilli* /bəˈsɪlʌɪ/. See LATIN PLURALS; -US.

back.

- **1** *back of.*
- **2** *in back of.*
- **3** *in back.*
- **4** *the back of beyond.*

1 *back of.* As a prepositional phrase meaning 'behind, in the back of', *back of* has been used for three centuries, mostly in North America, and still persists there *(In the shade back of the jo-house*—E. Pound, 1949; *the old couple on Killiney Hill near Dublin who lived in a greenhouse back of the main house—OEC,* 2008), but also occurs occasionally in Britain (*No one could live there, back of the railways*—M. Laski, 1953.)

2 By contrast, *in back of* (modelled on *in front of*) is markedly American (*Should I or should I not go out to the swimming pool in back of my sister's condominium?*—A. Beattie, 1980; *an unmarked door in back of the humble pizzeria on the corner—OEC,* 2007).

3 *in back.* Used absolutely in AmE in the phrase *to get in back* 'to get into (one of) the back seat(s) of a car' ('*What luck,' she muses, sliding back in [the car]. 'Get in back, Herman.'*—B. Ripley, 1987).

4 The phrase *back o' behint* occurs in some English dialects, and *the back of beyond* throughout the English-speaking world, both of them in the sense 'a very remote or out-of-the-way place'.

back-formation. A word coined by J. A. H. Murray—from which derives the German *Rückbildung*—for the formation of a word from a longer word which has the appearance of being derived from it. So *burgle* (first recorded 1872) is a back-formation from the much older word *burglar* (15c.), *edit* (18c.) from *edition* (16c.) or *editor* (17c.), *lech* 'to behave lecherously' (1911) from *lecherous* (14c.) and related words, *reminisce* (verb) (1829) from *reminiscence* (16c.), and *televise* (1927) from *television* (1907). In the 20c. the type *window-shopping* (1922), yielding the verb *window-shop* (1951), was a potent model. Some back-formations had, and some still have, more than a tinge of jocularity, e.g. *buttle* 'to act as a butler' (1867) from *butler* (13c.). Whereas back-formations such as *diagnose* (from *diagnosis*), *extradite* (from *extradition*), *grovel* (16c.) (from *grovelling* (adverb) 'in a prone position', 14c.), *legislate* (from *legislation*), and *resurrect* (18c.) (from *resurrection*) sit comfortably and neutrally in the language, some people still persist in objecting to words such as *donate* (from *donation*), *enthuse* (from *enthusiasm*), and *liaise* (from *liaison*). Most Americans use *burglarize* and reject *burgle*; in Britain *burglarize* is often rejected as a 'vulgar Americanism', and *burgle* is used without constraints. The process of back-formation has a long history, and it will doubtless continue to generate new words in the years ahead.

backlog. The *OED* first recorded the word (with a hyphen) as meaning 'a large log placed at the back of the fire' (first noted in the 17c.). From the slow-burning nature of such logs, the metaphorical use 'a reserve supply, an accumulation' established itself from the last quarter of the 19c. onwards (*the contrast between the immediate emotion and the backlog of our considered view*—J. Bailey, 1976). In the 1930s the word also acquired the meaning 'arrears of unfulfilled orders, uncompleted cases, unfinished work, etc.' (*court cases of which there was a considerable back-log—Listener,* 1958; *the backlog of visitors granted temporary admission is now over 3,500—Daily Tel.,* 1986), and this third sense is now the dominant one. The word is never hyphenated now.

backslang. A kind of 19c. slang in which words are pronounced backwards, e.g. *cool* for *look*. *Yob* (first recorded in 1859) was originally *backslang* for *boy*, but now means 'hooligan'.

backward(s). 1 In most adverbial uses, *backward* and *backwards* are interchangeable, but usage varies subtly from person to person and from region to region. The *OEC* data suggest that *backwards* is used roughly twice as often as *backward* throughout the English-speaking world, and is the commoner form in all the varieties of English covered by the data. In the US, the two forms are more or less equally frequent, but in BrE there is a very marked preference for *backwards*, in the ratio of 5:1. In the fixed expressions *to bend* (or *lean*) *over backwards, backwards and forwards*, and *to know (something) backwards, backwards* is commoner, and *backward* is not used much except in AmE. Examples: (*a*) *Talk ran backward from the events of the morning*—A. Munro, 1987 (Canad.); *I walked backward to look at her in the sun*—E. L. Doctorow, 1989 (US); (*b*) *The government is clearly bending over backwards to bring the land plans to fruition*—*OEC*, 2004 (Aust.); *he hauled the cart out backwards*—J. M. Coetzee, 1983 (SAfr.); *the door kept swinging backwards and forwards*—A. Brookner, 1984 (UK).

2 As an adjective the only form used is *backward*: *he watched her walking away without a backward glance*—R. Sutcliff, 1954; *Getting involved with the blind in any way seemed like a backward step*—V. Mehta, 1987.

See FORWARD(S).

3 In addition to its directional meanings, *backward* has developed in informal use the meaning 'slow to learn', (applied especially to children). This is now considered offensive and should be replaced by more neutral and considerate terms such as *having learning difficulties*, cumbersome though these tend to be.

bacterium is the singular form, and *bacteria* its plural. See -UM 2. Mistaken uses of *bacteria* as a singular are regrettably common in newspapers: e.g. **A common gut bacteria may be a major cause of rheumatoid arthritis*—*Independent*, 1991; **the author reports that the bacteria for Legionnaires' disease has been found*—*Chicago Tribune*, 1995.

bad. 1 After the verb *feel*—*I feel bad* (about doing something) or *I feel bad* (= my health is not good at the moment)—*bad* is an adjective complement (meaning either 'guilty, ashamed' or 'unwell') rather than an adverb and completely unobjectionable even in quite formal English: *To be absolutely honest, what I feel really bad about is that I don't feel worse*—Michael Frayn, 1965. After *to be* and most other verbs, *badly* is required: *Things started to go badly for them; They sank seventeen ships and badly damaged eight more; Russia badly needed Finnish products; We are not too badly off.* In these cases, *bad* is used only informally or in dialect: *I only came cause she's so bad off*—L. Hellman, 1934.

2 In a slang (principally youth slang) use originating in US Black English, *bad* means the very opposite of its traditional meaning, i.e. 'formidable, very good, extremely impressive', applied to people and things. This use is first recorded from 1897, rather earlier than one might think, and was widely used in jazz circles, e.g. *Jazzmen often call a thing 'terrible' or 'bad' when they like it very much*—*New York Times*, 1959. In the meaning of 'impressive' *bad* even has special degrees of comparison: *badder, baddest*: *She said that part of the problem was that they often wanted to distinguish themselves by being badder than their rivals. Badder? Surely the comparative of bad is worse? But then worse has connotations of being less good at doing something*—*Spectator*, 1993. This is a good example of how one of the most basic words can be reinvented by speakers in a specific social group, rather as *wicked* and *mean* have been in the past.

bade, past tense of BID, is traditionally pronounced /bad/, rhyming with *bad*, but /beɪd/, rhyming with *spade*, is also heard.

badinage. Printed in roman and pronounced /ˈbadɪnɑːʒ/, **ba**-dee-nazh. Example: *Jean whose comical taunts and restless badinage had always stirred up what might otherwise have proved too quiet a scene*—I. Murdoch, 1987.

bafflegab. A scrumptious, treasurable word, mainly used in North American English, that deserves a more global presence. It was first recorded in 1952 and applies to abstruse technical terminology used as a means of persuasion or obfuscation, aka *gobbledegook*. The word was coined by Milton A. Smith, assistant general counsel for the American Chamber of Commerce, and is worth treasuring for its 'definition' by him as 'Multiloquence characterized by a consummate interfusion of circumlocution ... and other familiar manifestations of abstruse expatiation commonly utilized for promulgations implementing procrustean determinations by governmental bodies'.

baggage, luggage. To some British ears the word *baggage*, in its main meaning, may still have a residual American flavour, perhaps as a legacy of the *baggage trains* and *baggage wagons* of pioneering days in America. Fowler (1926) regarded *baggage* as an Americanism, and Gowers in 1965 pithily summed up the relationship between the two words as it was in his day: 'Englishmen travel by land with *luggage* and by sea and air with *baggage*. Americans, more sensibly, travel everywhere with *baggage*'. Since the arrival of mass air travel, however, *baggage* and *luggage* have acquired dual, and then multiple, nationality, and in some contexts are used interchangeably; in Britain *baggage handlers* might sometimes be forced to strike, thus preventing *luggage carousels* from disgorging their load. A British airline has the following advice on its website: 'To ensure a hassle-free experience at the airport, please familiarize yourself with baggage allowances and what you are permitted to take in your luggage' followed by a link titled 'Learn more about baggage'.

In fact, though the two words overlap to some extent in meaning, *baggage* generally connotes something heavier and bulkier and less easily transportable by hand. Those connotations may help explain why in many fixed collocations *baggage* far outweighs, as it were, *luggage*, e.g. *excess baggage, baggage claim, baggage handler*. But people refer to *hand luggage* much more than *hand baggage*. A few British railway stations still have *left-luggage offices*. In the US a person who looks after the checked baggage of passengers on a train is a *baggageman*. The same word is also used there for a baggage porter in a hotel.

In figurative uses, *baggage* is the usual word everywhere: *She was not an intellectual; her philosophical baggage was comparatively light.*—K. O. Morgan, 1990; *He was loudly proclaiming the need for a 'new' left that had the courage to throw off the ideological baggage of the past*—Logos Journal, 2004.

bail out, bale out. The spelling *bail* (ultimately from OF *bailler* 'to take charge of') is always used in contexts of securing the release of a person after an undertaking is given to guarantee his or her reappearance in court on an appointed day. Metaphorically, too, a person or a company, etc., may be *bailed out*, or released, from a difficulty, for example by the repayment of their debts. In the senses 'to scoop water out of a boat', or 'to make an emergency descent by parachute from an aircraft' the spelling *bale* (*out*) is now usual, as if the action were that of letting a bundle through a trapdoor, even though the word has a different origin (from OF *baille* bucket).

***baited breath.** For this mistaken spelling, see BATED BREATH.

balance. 1 *Balance* as a noun is about four centuries older than the verb, and has derived several metaphorical uses from its primary meaning of 'an apparatus for weighing'; for example in accounting (where the notions of *balancing the books* and *balance sheets* are ever-present) and in more abstract uses such as *the fragile balance between peace and war*. More than two centuries ago in the US, the word branched out from the accounting sense and came to mean 'something (other than money) left over' (*I'll bring the balance of our things; The balance of the penalty still has to be paid*). This extension of meaning has faced two centuries of disapproval, starting with Noah Webster, but has certainly not ended its run yet. The fate of the extended sense is, as it were, permanently weighed in the balance by a tiny few, but no longer hangs in the balance to those many who have not heard that there is a problem. In short, modern usage has confirmed this construction as largely acceptable, but should you prefer to avoid it, use the words *rest* or *remainder*.

2 The word occurs in a number of fixed or semi-fixed expressions such as *balance of nature, balance of power, balance of probabilities, in the balance, on balance, to maintain a balance, to redress the balance, to strike a balance, to tip the balance*, and to *upset the balance*. These are all established and acceptable uses.

baleful, baneful. These two highly literary words are little used in everyday language; *baleful* is slightly better known perhaps and rather more common than *baneful*. Since they overlap in meaning, they tend to be confused.

For centuries (originally from Old English *b(e)alu* 'evil, mischief') *baleful* has been a mostly literary word meaning either 'having an evil influence' or 'menacing', and is used in particular of people's presence or appearance: (*the baleful presence of his father in the house was like a constant reproach*—R. Hayman, 1981; *foghorns boom in still longer and lower choruses of baleful warning*—I. Banks, 1986.) It is used especially of eyes or looks (*he fixed his baleful eye on us*). Cf. the corresponding adverb in: *Two cultures glare balefully at each other with an antagonism that goes far beyond party politics*—*OEC*, 2004.

Baneful (from *bane*, poison, ultimately from Old English *bana* 'slayer') was first recorded in the 16c. and developed from its earlier meaning 'poisonous' to 'causing harm or ruin': *Defeat the scare of kidnappings, violence and other baneful evils that shake modern society*—Pope John Paul II, 1984; *the baneful memory of that night haunted her, sometimes tormented her*—I. Murdoch, 1987). It corresponds to the noun *bane* (*selfishness is the bane of my life*). *Baleful* is the more likely to be needed, especially with reference to looks and glances.

bale out. See BAIL OUT, BALE OUT.

balk. See BAULK.

ballad at first, a song intended as the accompaniment to a dance (cf. late Latin *ballare*, OProvençal *balar* 'to dance'), then, a light, simple song of any kind. Between the mid-16c. and the early 19c., a popular song printed as a broadsheet, celebrating or scurrilously attacking persons or institutions: Autolycus hawks such ballads in *The Winter's Tale*. Now, either a short sentimental or romantic composition, often in slow tempo, with each verse sung to the same melody, a pop song; or, much more encouragingly, a simple, spirited poem in short stanzas, such as *Sir Patrick Spens*, Keats's *La Belle Dame Sans Merci*, and Oscar Wilde's *The Ballad of Reading Gaol*. Ballads, both ancient and modern, frequently made use of a refrain. The *Lyrical Ballads* of Wordsworth and Coleridge manifest (as Margaret Drabble has it) 'their own interpretation and development of balladry'.

From *Sir Patrick Spens* (probably 17c.):

Late late yestreen I saw the new moone,
Wi the auld moone in hir arme,
And I feir, I feir, my deir master,
That we will cum to harme.

From *The Ballad of Reading Gaol* (1898):

I never saw a man who looked
With such a wistful eye
Upon that little tent of blue
Which prisoners call the sky,
And at every drifting cloud that went
With sails of silver by.

ballade /baˈlɑːd/ In the 14c. and 15c. a poem ('ful delectable to heryn and to see') of three or more stanzas in RHYME ROYAL, often contrasted (by Chaucer and his contemporaries) with a *rondel* and a *virelay*. A typical example is Chaucer's *Compleynt of Venus*. In general, a poem consisting of one or more triplets of seven- or (afterwards) eight-line stanzas, each ending with the same line as refrain, and (usually) an envoi. François Villon (*fl. c.*1460) wrote many French ballades, including the celebrated *Ballade des dames du temps jadis* with its refrain 'Mais où sont les neiges d'antan?'. The form was revived in England in the Victorian period, especially in the works of Swinburne, W. E. Henley, and Austin Dobson.

A 20c. example by J. C. Squire:

Ballade of the Poetic Life

The fat men go about the streets,
The politicians play their game,
The prudent bishops sound retreats
And think the martyrs much to blame;
Honour and love are halt and lame
And Greed and Power are deified,
The wild are harnessed by the tame;
For this the poets lived and died.

Shelley's a trademark used on sheets:
Aloft the sky in words of flame
We read 'What porridge had John Keats?
Why, Brown's! A hundred years the same!'
Arcadia's an umbrella frame,
Milton's a toothpaste; from the tide
Sappho's been dredged to rouge my Dame—
For this the poets lived and died.

And yet, to launch ideal fleets
Lost regions in the stars to claim,
To face all ruins and defeats,
To sing a beaten world to shame,
To hold each bright impossible aim
Deep in the heart; to starve in pride
For fame, and never know their fame—
For this the poets lived and died.

Envoi
Princess, inscribe beneath my name
'He never begged, he never sighed,
He took his medicine as it came'—
For this the poets lived—and died.

ball game. From the North American use of the term to mean 'baseball' has come a medley of phrases in which *ball game* means 'a state of affairs': *a different/ a new/a whole new/another,* etc., *ball game.* This extended use, first recorded in 1968, is now in danger of overuse even in countries where baseball is hardly played at all.

ballon d'essai /ba'lɔ̃ dɛ'seɪ/, plural *ballons d'essai.* See TRIAL BALLOON.

ballot (verb). The inflected forms are *balloted* and *balloting.* See -T-, -TT-.

balmy. In Britain the only current senses of the word are 'yielding balm' and 'deliciously fragrant, soothing' (used especially of the weather: *it was a warm, balmy afternoon*; compare also *those happy and balmy days for fathers, when they and their wishes were immediately obeyed*—G. Clare, 1981). Until the mid-20c. it was also used to mean 'weak-minded, insane' (*'I s'pose you're balmy on her,' he said resignedly*—R. Crompton, 1922; *people here must have gone balmy*—J. B. Priestley, 1929). This use is still current in the US, but in Britain it has given way to BARMY.

bambino /bam'biːnəʊ/. Plural *bambini* /-ni/. A colloquial word for a young (especially Italian) child. In origin it is a diminutive of Italian *bambo* 'silly'.

banal. Once pronounced /'beɪnəl/ or /'banəl/, and magnificently derided by Fowler (1926) as an unnecessary word 'imported from France by a class of writers whose jaded taste relished novel or imposing jargon', this word, nowadays pronounced /bə'nɑːl/ or /-nal/, is part of the normal vocabulary of English. The derivative *banality* /-'alɪti/ is common enough (*Regarding the trial of Adolf Eichmann, Hannah Arendt made a celebrated comment about the 'banality of evil'—OEC,* 2004), the adverb *banally* /-'ɑːlˌlɪ/ less so. In American English the words are commonly pronounced /'beɪnəl/, /beɪ'nalɪti/ and /'beɪnəli/, but there is much variation.

bandeau. Plural more often *bandeaux,* than *bandeaus,* both with the final letter pronounced /z/. See -X.

baneful. See BALEFUL.

banjo. Recommended plural *-os*; but see -O(E)S 2.

Bantu (plural the same or *Bantus*), referring to a large group of indigenous peoples of Central and northern Africa, became a strongly offensive term under the old apartheid regime in South Africa, especially when used to refer to a single individual. In standard current use in South Africa the term *black* or *African* is used as a collective or non-specific term for African peoples. The term *Bantu* continues, however, to be accepted as a neutral 'scientific' term outside South Africa to refer to the group of languages and their speakers collectively.

baptist(e)ry. Standard sources in Britain use *baptistery.* In the US *baptistry* appears to be the more frequently used of the two forms. Cf. Latin *baptistērium.*

barbarian, barbaric, barbarous. These words had their origins in people's ideas about foreign languages. The Greek word *barbaros* (Greek βάρβαρος 'non-Hellenic'), which is the ultimate source of all these words, meant someone who spoke words sounding like *ba ba.* To the Greeks, the *barbarians* were foreigners, and principally the Persians, but the word carried no derogatory overtones in itself. Over the centuries the non-Hellenic, non-Roman, or non-Christian peoples became regarded as enemies who violated and plundered the civilized world (*into that chaos came real barbarians like the Huns, who were ... destructively hostile to what they couldn't understand*—Kenneth Clark, 1969), and this gave rise to the unfavourable connotations of *barbarian* and associated words. By a normal process of sense-development the word came to be applied (16–17c.) to *any* person or group regarded as uncivilized or uncultivated. The corresponding adjective has had a matching history. It has been applied, principally, to slaves, foreign languages, foreigners, prehistoric man, etc., almost always with reference to past time. *Many survived the depredation of the barbarian incursion of the late third century from which Britain was spared*—G. Webster, 1991.

The noun *barbarian* is sometimes resurrected to refer to modern times: *Ancient civilisations were destroyed by the imported barbarians; we breed our own*—Dean Inge, 1922; *Twentieth-century barbarians cannot be transformed into cultured, civilized human beings until they acquire an appreciation and love for art*—*OEC*, 2003.

Since the 15c., *barbaric* has been applied to the customs, language, culture, etc., of foreign people, and in particular those regarded as backward or savage (*the noble savage . . . turns out to be a barbaric creature with a club and scalping knife*—H. J. Laski, 1920; *Some of the subsidiary practices* [in fox-hunting] *such as the 'blooding' of children are little short of barbaric*—*Independent*, 1998). From the 17c. onwards (Milton speaks of *barbaric pearl and gold*), the word has also been used of aesthetically attractive objects seen, or brought from, abroad: Lawrence of Arabia, for example, described the colourful garments of his Arabic companions as *splendid and barbaric.* In present-day use, however, the word is applied almost invariably to brutal or wicked physical treatment of people (e.g. rape, child abuse, kidnapping, murder) or unacceptable social behaviour (e.g. the hooliganism of football supporters): *As well as hare coursing, the equally barbaric practice of badger baiting continues in many areas undetected*—*OEC*, 2005. *Barbaric* is somewhat stronger and more specific than *barbarous*, which has a more general reference and is softened by its use in aesthetic as well as physical contexts: *Keynes called the gold standard a 'barbarous relic' and clearly explained its limits*—*OEC*, 2010; *The science of medicine is a barbarous jargon and the effects of our medicine on the human system are in the highest degree uncertain*—*OEC*, 2003.

barbarism, barbarity, barbarousness. *Barbarism* has the widest scope of reference, being applied to matters of taste as well as human behaviour, and it has a special meaning in relation to language (see BARBARISMS). *He took up a new job in Berlin on the very day in 1930 when the Reichstag election heralded unprecedented barbarism in Europe*—*New Scientist*, 1991; *I do not believe urban barbarism is about to engulf us*—*East Anglian Daily Times*, 1993. *Barbarity* and *barbarousness* are synonymous words for savage cruelty or extremely uncivilized behaviour, but *barbarousness* is very rarely used. *Barbarousness*, though not *barbarity,* can be used of a linguistically poor construction, formation, etc.

barbarisms. The word *barbarism* is commonly, and with strictly logical appropriateness, used to describe words that are badly formed, that is words that are formed in a manner that departs from the traditions of the language concerned. In the past, philologists applied the term with particular relish to heterogeneous combinations of Latin/Greek/English elements exhibited in such words as *breathalyser, helipad, impedance* (instead of **impedience*), *speedometer* (instead of **speedmeter*), *television* (Greek and Latin), and *triphibious*. The 'barbarisms' of earlier centuries for the most part escaped censure: e.g. false word-division (*adder* venomous snake, from Old English *nǣdre*); insertion of redundant letters (*bridegroom*, from Old English *brȳdguma,* from which *guma* man was assimilated to *groom*; and *daffodil,* from medieval Latin *affodilus*, akin to *asphodel*). In the present blizzard of word-creation, it is difficult to see how older standards of word-formation can be maintained, and objections to new creations can often seem pedantic and linguistically Luddite. Only a fraction of modern coinages are made after consultation with a philologist. See HYBRIDS; METANALYSIS.

barbecue. This 17c. word (from Haitian *barbacòa* 'a framework of sticks set upon posts'), once used mainly of large social entertainments in the open air at which animals like pigs or oxen were roasted whole, has long since become suburbanized and domesticated. As likely as not, a modern barbecue is an outdoor feast of steak, fish, or chicken cooked rapidly over hot charcoal. From jokey respellings of the word, e.g. *Bar-B-Q,* the word now often appears, especially in America, written as *barbeque*, but this is not standard in British English, although *ODO* now recognizes it. The diminutive form *barbie* is especially common in Aust. and NZ.

barely. Like HARDLY and SCARCELY, *barely,* in the sense 'only just', should normally be followed by *when* to introduce any succeeding clause: *Chance had barely begun to sip his drink when dinner was announced*—J. Kosinski, 1983. Only in very informal contexts is the use of *than* permissible: *Barely had her spirits fallen, leaving* *her to brood over the sea, than the pinch was repeated*—L. Bromfield, 1928.

baritone. Adopted in its musical sense from Italian *baritono* in the 17c. and therefore spelt with medial *-i-*, though many earlier writers (e.g. G. Eliot, Palgrave) preferred **barytone**. Contrast BARYTONE.

bark is sparingly used in literary contexts (by poets like William Cowper and Walter Scott and modern writers like Joyce Carol Oates) as a synonym for 'boat, ship'. The doublet **barque** (also derived, but through French, from Latin *barca* 'ship's boat') is a sailing vessel of specified rigging.

barmy, now usually so spelt in Britain (formerly also **balmy**), is a mainly British slang word applied to someone or something that is crazy (*probably gone barmy with shock, done his nut*—Maggie Gee, 1981; *barmy pressure groups like the League of Empire Loyalists*—A. Ryan, 1984). It can be regarded as a derivative of *barm,* the froth on fermenting malt liquor (cf. a now lost adjective **barmy-brained**, over-excited, flighty), but the evidence points rather to its being a respelt (and thus differentiated) form of **balmy**. The two words are pronounced identically, i.e. /'bɑːmi/ in RP. Since the 1980s the expression *barmy army* has been used informally to describe groups of political fanatics and, by extension, jingoistic sports supporters (especially of the English cricket team) and others: *We've had what feels like 900 years of Blair's barmy army now so we know how the system works*—*OEC*, 2005.

baroque /bə'rɒk/, rhyming with *rock*, US /bə'rəʊk/, rhyming with *coke*, was first applied to a florid style of architectural decoration, e.g. that of Francesco Borromini, which arose in Italy in the late Renaissance and became prevalent in Europe during the 18c. Later the term was extended to refer to profusion, oddity of combination, or abnormal features generally in other arts, including the visual arts (e.g. the sculpture of Bernini and the painting of Rubens), creative writing, and music (e.g. some of the work of J. S. Bach and Handel): *at Blenheim the English Baroque* [style of architecture] *culminates*—J. N. Summerson, 1953; *the conjunction of Christian and classical imagery* [in *Lycidas*] *is in accord with a baroque taste which did not please the eighteenth century*—T. S. Eliot, 1957. More recently, the word has come to be applied outside the artistic sphere with rather negative connotations as an elegant way of describing anything viewed as excessively complicated or convoluted, e.g. *The difficulty is that in practice it has led to an increasingly baroque system of a state retirement pension*—*OEC*, 2002; *The film cuts out some of the (rather baroque) complications of the novel*—*OEC*, 2004. With reference to the arts, *baroque* and ROCOCO are sometimes used rather loosely, without distinction. Both are written with initial letters not in capitals.

barque. See BARK.

barrage. Pronounced /'bɑːrɪdʒ/ in the 19c., and still so pronounced in American English in the first meaning, but now normally /'barɑːʒ/ in British English. **1** At first just an artificial bar across a river to control the level of the water, later a massive structure built across a body of water to allow extensive irrigation or to permit the creation of hydroelectric power.

2 In the First World War it came to be applied to a barrier of continuous artillery fire (*artillery barrage*) concentrated on a given area, and, in the 1939–45 war, also (*balloon barrage*) to a set of inflated balloons (called *barrage balloons*) placed in the air as a defence against low-flying hostile aircraft. The word is frequently used in a metaphorical sense, especially in phrases of the type *a barrage of questions, cheers, complaints, statements*, etc. In BrE it is pronounced the same as for the first meaning, i.e. /'barɑːʒ/, but in AmE the second syllable is stressed, /bə'rɑːʒ/.

barring. As a marginal preposition (in origin an absolute use of the present participle of the verb *bar*), *barring* has been in use since the late 15c. and is still frequent: *'we've finished here—barring accidents'—he held up crossed fingers*—G. Charles, 1971; *They're all fine, thank God. Barring himself, who's got the divil of a hangover this morning*—A. Lejeune, 1986. Cf. the similar use of *excepting* and *saving*.

barrister, solicitor. In British English a *barrister* (in full *barrister-at-law*) is a person called to the Bar and having the right of practising as an advocate in the higher courts; a *solicitor* is a member of the legal profession qualified to advise clients and instruct barristers but not to appear as an advocate except in certain lower courts. The processes of law are governed differently elsewhere: in the US, for example, an **attorney** (in full **attorney-at-law**) advises clients on business and other matters and may also represent them in court; clients are usually represented in court by a **counselor** (in full **counselor-at-law**) or a **trial lawyer**. An American **District Attorney** (or **DA**) is the prosecuting officer of a district. The **Attorney-General** is the chief legal officer in England, the US, and some other countries.

barytone. This doublet of BARITONE is now reserved for the sense in Greek grammar 'not having the acute accent on the last syllable'. It faithfully reproduces the medial υ of Greek βαρύτονος (from βαρύς 'heavy' + τόνος 'pitch, tone').

basalt. Now normally pronounced /ˈbasɔːlt/ with stress on the first syllable, but before about 1920 more regularly /bəˈsɔːlt/ with stress on the second syllable.

base, basis. The plural of both words is *bases,* that of *base* (/ˈbeɪ-sɪz/) rhymes with *cases,* while the second syllable of the plural of *basis* (/ˈbeɪ-siːz/) rhymes with *cheese.* Expressions such as *on a regular basis, on a daily basis,* and *on a voluntary basis* are sometimes frowned on when simpler adverbs (*regularly, daily, voluntarily*) are available, but the longer forms often make the point more effectively, can produce a better sentence balance, and are well established.

based (on). 1 One of the commonest of all phrasal verbs in the passive voice: *M's hypothesis is based on the known habits of bees; the typeface Baskerville is based on the typefaces of the eighteenth-century printer John Baskerville.* (The verb, of course, can also be used in the active voice: *M bases his hypothesis on* ...). This construction is to be distinguished from the participial use of *based* in *Cruise missiles are based on Sicilian soil* (where *based* stands by itself and is not part of a phrasal verb). The past participle *based* is very frequently used in combinations with preceding nouns: e.g. *community-based, computer-based, Edinburgh-based, evidence-based, land-based, rule-based, science-based, shore-based.*

2 Avoid using *based on* as an unattached participle without a clear antecedent (**The Prime Minister will be judged based on these events*: better ... *will be judged on criteria based on these events,* or ... *will be judged according to these events*). Avoid it especially in initial position: *Based upon the US Democratic Party's new policy, I'd appeal to the world via the UN to assist us in withdrawing troops from Iraq—Independent,* 2007. In recent usage **based around** has become a common and illogical construction, and should be avoided: *The article is based around a concept which occurred to him as he lay on a Scilly Isles beach in 2000—OEC,* 2003. See also UNATTACHED PARTICIPLES.

basically. A 20c. adverb, at first used sparingly as an emphasizer to mean 'essentially, fundamentally' (*the basically democratic quality which belongs to a hereditary despotism*—G. K. Chesterton, 1905), but now somewhat worn down by prodigious overuse as an adverb beginning and governing a sentence. Examples: *I know I'm attractive in a way, but basically I'm ugly*—L. Michaels, 1969; *Basically, I feel great, except for fatigue*—M. Ali, 1987; *Basically I see myself as a frank individual*—S. Bellow, 1988; *Basically, decay is just a process*—K. Russell, 1988. Sometimes it comes close to being a meaningless 'filler', and can often be dispensed with when succinct, tight prose is the goal.

Basic English is the name given by C. K. Ogden in 1929 to a simplified form of the English language that he invented, comprising a select vocabulary of 850 words and simplified syntax. He intended it to be used as an international auxiliary language. Despite much experimentation it did not succeed, perhaps partly because, as H. G. Wells said, 'it was more difficult to train English speakers to restrict themselves to the forms and words selected than to teach outsiders the whole of Basic'.

basis. See BASE.

bas-relief. Evelyn, Dr Johnson, and others went this way and that in their treatment of this word and of its Italian equivalent, *basso-rilievo.* Virtually all possible spellings and pronunciations, some Anglicized, some not, have been recorded. Anyone leaning towards French should write *bas-relief* (plural *bas-reliefs*) and pronounce it /barəljef/, and one leaning towards Italian should write *basso-rilievo* (plural *bassi-rilievi*) and pronounce it /basoriljɛvo/. In practice, however, *bas-relief* (plural *bas-reliefs*) is most commonly printed in roman and pronounced /ˈbas rɪˈliːf/; and the preferred form of the other word is *basso-relievo* (plural *-vos*), printed in italic and with a semi-Anglicized pronunciation /ˌbasəʊrɪˈljeɪvəʊ/.

bassinet (occasionally **bassinette**) /basɪˈnet/, a wicker cradle. The word is more or less confined to the US (*I walked right past the bassinet, not even realizing that my second child had already arrived—OEC*, 2008). Nine times out of ten it is written with the *-et* ending. In folk etymology it is falsely connected with the current French word *bercelonnette* (a diminutive of *berceau* 'cradle'); it is in fact a diminutive of French *bassin* 'basin'.

bated breath. The well-known IDIOM *with bated breath*, meaning 'in great suspense; very anxiously or excitedly' (*he waited for a reply to his offer with bated breath*), is often misspelt **with baited breath*. The phrase is first recorded in *The Merchant of Venice*, when Shylock sarcastically asks Antonio: *Shall I bend low and in a bondman's key, With bated breath and whispring humblenes, Say this. Bated* comes from the obsolete verb *bate*, a shortened form of *abate*, and 'to bate one's breath' originally meant to restrain one's breathing, and make it soft and gentle, as in the Shakespearean quotation. Since neither *bated* nor *bate* ever appears in other contexts, it is not surprising that some people replace the word they don't know with the more familiar *bait*—even if it is hard to imagine what exactly *baited breath* might be, other than distinctly fetid. The cause of the mistake is understandable, but the fishy spelling is, for the time being at least, incorrect. See also FOLK ETYMOLOGY.

bath, bathe (verb). **1** The British and the Americans use these verbs rather differently. In British English *to bath* /bɑːθ/ is 'to wash (someone) while immersing them in a bath' or 'to wash (oneself) while immersed in a bath'. In phrases like *she baths the baby three times a day/you can bath after me*, the verb is pronounced /bɑːθ(s)/ in RECEIVED PRONUNCIATION. Conversely, in BrE *to bathe* /beɪð/ means either 'to swim in a body of water, especially the sea' (*he preferred to bathe rather than just sun himself on the beach*), although usage in this meaning is now somewhat dated, or 'to apply liquid to (a wound, the skin, etc.) as a cleansing or soothing agent' (*the doctor bathed the wound with a saline solution*). US usage shows a marked preference for *bathe* (not *bath*) in the sense 'to wash (someone/oneself) in a bath' (*he often bathes before he goes to bed; they bathed* /beɪðd/ *the baby*). The various metaphorical extensions of *bathe* are used in all varieties of English: *bathed in sunshine, sweat*, etc.

2 In both BrE and AmE the idea is often expressed in a different way (*her daughter usually takes/has a bath after finishing her homework*).

bathetic. A 19c. word, first recorded in Coleridge, and formed from *bathos* by mistaken analogy with *pathos/pathetic*. It tends to be used in literary criticism and reviews of the arts (*a genuinely cheerful, pleasantly bathetic coda to a brilliant career—OEC*, 2003), as does the adverb **bathetically** (*Bathetically, I found myself thinking of Groucho Marx*—R. Adams, 1980). The unhappily formed variant **bathotic** (presumably modelled on *chaos/chaotic*) has practically vanished from use, though there are examples (1863–1952) in the *OED*.

bathroom. It is important to bear in mind that one of the primary meanings of *bathroom* in the US is 'lavatory' e.g. *I have to go to the bathroom*. The word alternates there in this sense with *restroom, washroom*, (colloquial) *john*, and numerous other synonyms. For a general description of the various synonyms of *lavatory*, see TOILET.

baulk, balk. 1 The pronunciation /bɔːlk/ is more frequent, but /bɔːk/ is not uncommon, doubtless because of the analogy of *stalk, talk, walk*. For the verb, *baulk* is the much more common spelling in Britain, although it does alternate with *balk* (*fears that the government may yet baulk at implementing the recommendations; purists may balk*). In all other varieties, writers prefer *balk*. Apart from its primary use, illustrated above, meaning 'to hesitate, refuse to go on', followed by *at*, the verb is also used adjectivally or in the passive to mean 'to thwart', in which case it is followed by *of*. Examples: *I gave her the number and hung up feeling baulked of my escape*—L. R. Banks, 1987; *Fenella had the feeling that they were simply mustering their strength* *again; they had been baulked of their prey and they had retired*—B. Wood, 1993.

2 For the noun in its main general senses 'stumbling-block, hindrance', *balk* now seems to be the dominant spelling in the US (*the series of small balks that were to delay the publication of* Dubliners—J. Updike, 1984), and *baulk* in the UK (*Bill was also in baulk, up-country somewhere*—J. le Carré, 1974). In its specialized senses, e.g. the *baulk line* in billiards and snooker, a length of sawn timber (*the gravediggers ... pulled the supporting baulks from beneath the coffin*—J. Wainwright, 1980), etc., *baulk* is the more usual spelling in Britain.

bay window, bow window, oriel. A *bay window* is one that protrudes outward from the line of a room in a rectangular, polygonal, or curved form, thus forming an alcove in a room; a *bow window* is a bay window in the shape of a curve. Sometimes, *bow window* is loosely used to refer to any of the shapes covered by *bay window*. An *oriel* is a large polygonal bay window projecting from the upper face of a wall and supported by a corbel or bracket.

-b-, -bb-. Single-syllable words consisting of a simple, short vowel (*a, e, i, o, u*) before *b* normally double the consonant before suffixes beginning with a vowel (*dab* + *-ed* → *dabbed, web* + *-ing* → *webbing, glib* + *-est* → *glibbest, shrub* + *-ery* → *shrubbery*) and before a final *-y* (*scab* + *-y* → *scabby, snob* + *-y* → *snobby*). The *b* is not doubled if the stem contains a diphthong (*dauber*) or a vowel + consonant (*entombed, numbed, barbed*). Words of more than one syllable ending in *b* (e.g. *Beelzebub, cherub, cobweb, hubbub, rhubarb, syllabub*) rarely add vowel-led suffixes; but if the vowel before the *b* is long there is no doubling, e.g. *cherubic*, but if it is short, there is, e.g. *cobwebby*, and *hobnobbed*. See SPELLING 6.

BC, before Christ, should always be placed after the numerals and printed in small capitals (55 BC). The abbreviation is first recorded in English in John Blair's *Chronology and History of the Ancient World* (1756), but was not widely adopted until the 19c. Cf. AD.

be.

1 *be* linking singular and plural.
2 *be* and *were* as subjunctives.
3 The case of the complement: *it's me/him/us* etc. versus *it's I/he/we*.
4 Paradigmatic forms.
5 Anxiety about placing an adverb or other word(s) between *to be* and a following participle.
6 Ellipsis of *be*.

1 Very often the subject of the verb *be* is singular and the complement plural, or vice versa, and in these cases the verb should agree with the subject: (singular subject, plural complement) *Gustave is other animals as well*—Julian Barnes, 1984; (plural subject, singular complement) *These huge biographies are usually a mistake nowadays*—N. Stone, 1985.But when the subject is a collective noun, the verb may be in the plural, following the usual pattern with such nouns: *Its prey are other small animals*—David Attenborough, 1987. When the subject is the relative pronoun *what*, the verb is singular: *What I'm really interested in ... is the objects in this house*—*New Yorker*, 1986. In accordance with the above rules, *aren't* should have replaced *isn't* in the following example: *whether certain ethnocentric attitudes in our own working class ...* isn't *also a hampering factor*—*Encounter*, 1987. Cf. AGREEMENT 7; WHAT 1, 2.

2 The irregular and defective verb *to be* now has two subjunctive forms, *be* (present subjunctive) and *were* (past subjunctive). They are the survivors of a system, too complex to be set down here, in Old English and Middle English. These subjunctive forms are rapidly disappearing from use, but are still quite often found in the following types of clause:

(*a*) replacing *if* or *whether*, at the head of a clause, with inversion of subject and verb: *We would much prefer to support specific projects,* be *they in management schools or in university laboratories*—*Journal of the Royal Society of Arts*, 1986; Were *this done, we would retain a separate Barwith skill*—*Times*, 1986.

(*b*) after *if* in hypothetical conditions: *If the truth be told, I never wanted to fly away with the sky-gods*—J. M. Coetzee, 1977; *If I were obliged to rough out a blueprint of the Church of the future, I would start with the need for good popular theology*—Gerald Priestland, 1982. However, the past indicative form *was* is often used instead of *were*, especially in conversational style: *I wouldn't tell the police if I was you*—*OEC*, 2002.

(*c*) in dependent clauses after verbs of advising and instructing such as *demand, insist, suggest*, etc.: *The Admiralty insisted that the case* be *clarified*—P. Wright, 1987; *In order to broaden the 'target audience' of your newsletter . . . I might suggest that such material* be *written at a lower level of readability—Underground Grammarian,* 1982; also after nouns and clauses of equivalent meaning: *It is important in today's vote that the principle itself* be *accepted—Times,* 1985; *the demand that the invention* be *used to benefit both the people and the land*—Dædalus, 1986.

(*d*) in certain fixed phrases such as *if I* were *you, as it* were, etc; and in fossilized optative-type formulas, e.g. be *that as it may, evil* be *to him who evil thinks, far* be *it from me, the powers that* be, *so* be *it, God* be *thanked,* be *it on your head.*

Note that in negative constructions of the type *be* + passive, it is usual to place *not* immediately before *be: Jim Wallis requests that he* not be *called a leader of the 'religious left'—OEC,* 2005.

The fading power of the subjunctive mood is underlined by the frequency with which *was* is used instead of *were* in sentences of the type *if I were/was you*: *I'd get out if I* was *you*—Maurice Gee, 1983; *if I* was *your husband I should view me with suspicion*—I. Murdoch, 1974.

If a reasonably high degree of formality is intended (see the examples above), the subjunctive forms of *be* are available. If formality is not essential, the ordinary indicative forms are acceptable. In some circumstances (see SUBJUNCTIVE MOOD) the option chosen genuinely reflects the presence, or alternatively the absence, of some degree of uncertainty, supposition, intention, etc.

3 The case of the complement: *it's me/him/us* etc. versus *it's I/he/we.* Dean Alford, the Victorian cleric and would-be authority on correct usage, (1864) joyfully rejected the famous old rule that a pronoun complement must be in the same case as the subject of the joining verb *to be. It's me,* like French *c'est moi,* had even then come to stay. In both speech and writing the type *it's me/that's him/it's her* is now virtually universal: *I suppose you knew it was me*—P. Wright, 1987. To use *I* instead of *me* in such contexts is markedly formal, not to say, to British ears at least, pretentious; when phoning a renowned American writer, and asking whether it was him at the other end of the line, I was perplexed to hear him say 'This is he'. The exception to this almost universal rule is that if the pronominal complement is immediately (or soon afterwards) followed by *who* (or *that*), the subject case is still frequently used in formal styles: *it was he who would be waiting on the towpath*—P. D. James, 1986. Contrast *it isn't me that Cheryl wants to see*—H. Kureishi, 1987: here *me* is effectively the object of *wants to see* not of *isn't.*

The formally correct nominative is also still found in fairly formal writing: *If anyone could write about the narcissistic personality, it was she—NY Rev. Bks,* 1987. But the objective case of the pronoun, which *OED* reports as 'common in colloquial lang. from end of 16th c.', has triumphed for the most part except when *who* or *that* is adjacent.

4 *Paradigmatic forms.* No special difficulties arise with the normal indicative forms, *am, is, are*; past tense *was, were*; participles *being, been.* In speech, reduced forms of *am, is,* and *are* (*'m, 's, 're*) are freely used, and these often make their way into written English (*I'm* = I am, *she's* = she is, *they're* = they are), though such reduction is impossible after a preceding sibilant consonant (*the moss is green,* not **the moss's green*) or affricate (*the church is cold,* not **the church's cold*).

There are two anomalous forms: *ain't* (see AIN'T); and *aren't* when used as a tag-question in the form *aren't I?*. The expected reduced form of *am I not?* is *amn't I?,* used in many modes of speech in Scotland and Ireland but not in standard southern British English.

Whatever the explanation for its origins, *aren't I?* is a regular and natural tag-question in standard BrE. An American scholar, John Algeo, has said (1995) that 'the expression is now in widespread use in America with no consciousness of a British origin', though he acknowledges that it might indeed be of British origin.

In informal contexts, the reduced forms *i'n't* and *i'nt* were once (18c.) commonly written for *isn't, is not*: the evidence is to be found in the *OED.* One hears, or one imagines one hears, some people saying /ɪnt/ to this day for *isn't* in such a sentence as *It isn't fair* /ɪt ɪnt fɛː/. But this pronunciation, and also the colloquialism *innit?* /ˈɪnɪt/ for *isn't it,* both lie outside the realm of standard English.

The charming forms *wast* (2nd person singular past tense) and *wert* (2nd person singular past subjunctive, and also, since the 16c., past indicative) are now used only as archaisms. Examples: *I would thou wert cold or hot*—Rev. 3:15; *Thou wer't borne a foole*—Shakespeare, *The Winter's Tale* 1611; *Oh, wert thou in the cauld blast*—Burns, *a*1796; *Hail to thee, blithe spirit! Bird thou never wert*—Shelley, 1820.

5 Anxiety about placing an adverb or other word(s) between *to be* and a following participle. Constructions of the type *she had to be humoured* and *they seemed to be looking in different directions* are, of course, common. In such constructions it is perfectly correct to place an adverb between *to be* and the following (past or present) participle: *he turned out to be* secretly *engaged to someone else; mosquitoes seemed to be* actively *circulating on the furniture.* To place such adverbs before *to be* (e.g. *he turned out* secretly *to be engaged to someone else*) because of a belief that by doing so you are avoiding a SPLIT INFINITIVE, is an unhappy example of HYPERCORRECTION. On the other hand, it is frequently necessary, for idiomatic reasons, to place the adverb after the participle in such constructions: *the injection always has to be given* slowly.

6 In certain contexts, forms of *to be* may be idiomatically omitted: e.g. *I am burning this and feeding the ash to the fruit tree,* where there is no need to insert *am* before *feeding.* Further examples of ellipses of forms of *to be* lie ready to hand, especially in informal circumstances: e.g. *There wasn't a normal person in that film. Perverts the lot!* [*sc.* They were all perverts!]; *What had happened, Lex had got the sack* [*sc.* was 'hat Lex]; *While playing upstairs, she heard knock on the door* [*sc.* While she was aying]; *Sorry I'm sure* [*sc.* I'm sorry I'm e]. However, when *be* is used as an aux- and a linking verb in the same sen- it must be repeated, because it p ns two different roles: In *The Bill w rtaken by the 1964 election* the wo as part of the passive construction taken, is an auxiliary. *Its postponen lcome* shows *was* being used as h. It is therefore not possible **The Bill was overtaken by th d its postponement welcome* ten to insert *was.*

bean. From its use (e lang term for a sovereign s emerged a range of inforn

(*they never had a bean, she never saved a bean*) meaning '(having) no money whatever'. Slang or very informal terms for 'money' keep slipping into and out of the language. Those that have gone include *chink* ('exceedingly common in the dramatists and in songs of the 17th c.'—*OED*), *dibs, oof* (Yiddish), *rhino,* and *tin.* Survivors (first used in the 20c., except where indicated) include *bread, dough* (1851), *lolly* (UK), *dosh* (UK), *mazuma* (Yiddish), *the needful* (1774), *readies* (bank notes), and *spondulicks* (1857).

beat. The old past participle *beat* has almost vanished from standard English, but it continues in non-standard and regional speech, especially in North America, e.g. *Just when you think you've beat it,* (i.e. drug addiction) *it comes back and threatens your life—CNN transcripts,* 2009; *Age hasn't mellowed me so much as it has beat me down—OEC,* 2003 (Canad.). In the expression 'can't be beaten' *beat* is standard in AmE, e.g. *Yes, the calm and peace of a graveyard can't be beat—OEC,* 2002. *Beat* is also standard in the participial adjectives *dead-beat* and *beat-up.* It may also lie somewhere in the background of the 1950s expressions *beat generation* and *beatnik,* under the influence of the noun *beat,* the strongly marked rhythm of jazz and popular music. Jack Kerouac (1922–69), the coiner of *beat generation,* at some point unpersuasively rationalized the first element of the phrase as a shortening of *beatitude.*

beau. The plural form is *beaux,* an old-fashioned form for an old-fashioned word, or, less commonly, *beaus.* See -X.

beau geste /bəʊ ˈʒɛst/. Especially since the appearance of P. C. Wren's *Beau Geste* (1924), the first of his Foreign Legion novels, this French expression, meaning 'a display of magnanimity, a fine gesture' has been knocking at the door of standard English, but has not managed to push its elegantly shod foot far across the threshold. Nevertheless, it makes occasional appearances: *Clyde, in a beau geste, allows a humble farmer to keep his cash—OEC,* 2004.

beau idéal or ***beau ideal.*** Pronounced as in French or Anglicized as /ˌbəʊ ʌɪˈdiːəl/, and printed in italic. In origin an abstract conception, the ideal Beautiful, *beau* being the noun and *idéal* the adjective. In English it is mainly used in the sense 'the highest conceived or conceivable type of beauty or excellence, the perfect type or model'. Most people who know the expression in English probably think of it as = *beau* (adjective) + *idéal* (noun), 'the beautiful ideal'. Examples: *He was my beau ideal of a writer*—*OEC*, 2004; *Shakespeare, literature's beau ideal of the man of the theater, was always putting plays and players into his work*—*OEC*, 2011.

beautician. Despite the existence of parallel forms like *academ/ician* (from *academ/y*) and *geometr/ician* (from *geometr/y*), this 20c. word (first recorded in the US in 1924) still retains for some people a slight flavour of etymological illegitimacy. Most words ending in *-ician* correspond to subject names ending in *-ic* or *-ics*: *arithmetic/arithmetician, music/musician, mathematics/mathematician.*

beautiful. 1 From 'the House Beautiful' in Bunyan's *Pilgrim's Progress* (where 'Beautiful' is to be regarded as a proper name) has flowed a host of imitative uses, in which the adjective is placed after the noun it qualifies. One of the earliest examples in the *OED* manages to make the allusion gruesomely comical: *God's Acre Beautiful or the Cemeteries of the Future* (W. Robinson, 1880). *The House Beautiful*, the title of a lecture Oscar Wilde gave in 1883, has become lexicalized to the extent that a British magazine is published under this name, while *The Body Beautiful* (first recorded in *Ladies' Home Jrnl*, 1917) has similarly entered the language (*today's obsession with the body beautiful*).

2 *the beautiful people.* Coined in the US in the 1960s, it originally applied to two separate groups of people: (*a*) the 'flower people' of the 1960s, hippies; (*b*) wealthy and fashionable people, the smart set. Other than in historical contexts, only the second meaning now survives, e.g. *It is a place where the beautiful people go to let their hair down*—*OEC*, 2011.

because (originally *by cause that* after Old French *par cause de*).

A Standard usage.
B *The reason is . . . because.*
C Ambiguous *because* after negating words.
D Other questionable *because*-clauses.
E *because* or *for.*

A 1 *Because* as a conjunction normally introduces a dependent clause expressing the cause, reason, or motive of the content of the main clause: *she wept because she loved him* (the *because*-clause, here following the main clause, answers the question 'why?'); *because we were running short of petrol, we began to look for a garage* (here the *because*-clause precedes the main clause); *I know he committed suicide, because his wife told me* (answering the question 'how do you know?', where the comma has an important structural function, to show that the question being answered is 'how do you know he committed suicide?' rather than 'why did he commit suicide?'); *she thinks I'm upset because you shouted at her* (answering the question 'why does she think that?'); (preceded by *just*) *'And all they are doing is sitting around on their high-priced butts drinking tea, just because they haven't had your scripts.' 'My word,' said Henry.* All these, including the last from Malcolm Bradbury's *Cuts* (1987), are well-regulated uses of the conjunction *because.*

2 It is also in order to use *because* after an introductory *it is, it's, that's, this is*: *It is only because he regarded it as absolutely necessary that he took such harsh measures; It doesn't hurt, and I can tell you why, it's because I've changed my work; 'That's because I'm so damned good at journalism,' she added; Mars looks especially good on this encounter . . . This is because the atmosphere obscures light rays.* All these examples are drawn from reputable sources, and reflect current use.

3 In some informal contexts, *because* can be safely omitted: *Tammy put a hymn book up in front of her face she was so embarrassed.* It can also be replaced by, or re-expressed in, another construction: *Being poor, he could not afford to buy books* (= because he was poor); *An experienced teacher, Mr Walton solved the problem quickly* (= because he is).

4 Also acceptable in informal use is the unadorned retort *Because,* with the implication that a fuller reply is being withheld for some reason: *'Why didn't you leave the bottle?' 'Because!' I said shortly. I wasn't going to explain my feelings on the matter.*—M. Carroll, 1968.

B *The reason is . . . because.* Opinion, learned and otherwise, is sharply divided over whether this construction is a serious offence, indictable in the high court of language, or merely a pardonable minor misdemeanour. (The presumed correct alternative is *the reason is ... that.*) H. W. Fowler certainly belonged to the first school when he objected to it in the first, 1926 edition, and his *fatwa* has been consistently pursued by subsequent editors. Burchfield (1996) went so far as to suggest that the formulation 'aches with redundancy', and it is true that *because* is logically redundant after *reason*. Nevertheless, many people seem prepared to put up with some degree of discomfort in order to use the construction. Redundancy is, after all, a regular component of idiom, and given that the construction is so common it is becoming harder to insist on replacing it. In the following example, in fact, it would weaken the statement considerably to replace *because* with *that*: *The minipill was developed for one reason alone: because it was believed to provide safe contraception*—*New Scientist*, 1970. However, *because of* should be avoided in this kind of construction: **The reason we have no light is because of a broken fuse* should read *The reason we have no light is that the fuse is broken.* See also REASON.

For acceptable uses of the phrase *the reason why*, see REASON WHY 2.

C Ambiguous *because* after negating words. Using *because* after a negative clause (e.g. *I do not play cards because I enjoy good company*), i.e. a clause containing a word such as *not* or *never*, or including a word in *un-*, etc. can technically cause ambiguity. It is not clear whether the example means (i) 'I do play cards, but not because ... ', or (ii) 'I do not play cards, and the reason is ... '. Often, the context will help make the meaning clear: *Very many people ... do not attend church because they are bored by ritualistic services; Her twin was told she was unlikely to have children because of her husband's low sperm count.*

When necessary, a judiciously placed comma will usually remove any ambiguity: *Very many people ... do not attend church, because they are bored by ritualistic services.* Alternatively, the order of the clauses can be reversed, although that will also reverse the emphasis: *Because they are bored by ritualistic services, very many people ... do not attend church.*

D Other questionable *because*-clauses, with varying degrees of questionableness, are: **1** *I know he committed suicide because the girl did not love him and his wife told me* (with a second *because* implied between *and* and *his wife*: an awkward mixture of two constructions).

2 In constructions with *why* and *because* placed in that order: *he was implying that why he knew that she had kept the promise was because he had been seeing Arnold; why I spoke sharply was because she was rude.* Such constructions are sometimes called pseudo-cleft sentences.

3 *Because* (or *just because*) at the head of a dependent clause governing a main clause: *Just because a fellow calls on a girl is no sign that she likes him*—G. Ade, 1897; *Because we don't explicitly ask these questions doesn't mean they aren't answered*—*New Yorker*, 1986. Such *because*-clauses, though common in speech, are awkward in written English because they demand too long an attention span before the onset of the main clause, and should be recast, e.g. *These questions are still answered even though we don't explicitly ask them.*

E *because* or *for*. *Because* is a subordinating and *for* a coordinating conjunction. The main standard uses of *because* are illustrated in section A above. *For* as a conjunction means 'seeing that, since': *Those houses ... ought not to be called houses, for they were unfit to be lived in*—*Daily Worker*, 1963. It always follows, and, as it were, acts as a kind of gloss on, or appendage to, a main clause. See FOR 1.

because of, as a prepositional phrase followed by a noun or noun phrase, is totally acceptable in most of its uses: *Three schools ... have been forced to close because of structural faults in their roofs; Hardy's legacy is somewhat hard to define because of its essential ambiguity.* It normally operates as a paraphrased equivalent of a notionally longer clause: *... because the roofs were found to have structural faults; ... because it is essentially ambiguous.* It should not be used, however, in constructions in which the word *reason* (or equivalent) appears in the main clause: *the reason we have no light is because of a broken fuse* (read *is that the fuse is broken*). Another example of the need to avoid REDUNDANCY.

because why? This phrase, used interrogatively (and frequently written in the form *Cause why* or *Cos why*), is chiefly dialectal (the *OED* cites evidence beginning in 1887) or in informal use. Examples: *'Cos* *why? 'Cos I'm going to German-eye.*—E. M. Forster, 1910; *I know a lot of people that rant on about their religion and it doesn't do any good. Because why? Because they're trying to convince themselves, maybe?*—S. Chaplin, 1961.

bed and breakfast (also **B & B, b & b**). From their appearance on signs outside places where such services are available, these terms have come to be used concretely of the accommodation building itself (*The Garth Woodside Mansion, where Mark Twain was a guest, now is a bed and breakfast*—*Chicago Tribune*, 1989), as well as of the services offered. The recommended way to write the abbreviation is with capitals and spaces, without full stops.

bedevil. The inflected forms are different in British and American English. In BrE the final *l* is doubled to give *bedevilled, bedevilling*, in AmE it is not: *bedeviled, bedeviling*. See -LL-, -L-; DOUBLING OF CONSONANTS WITH SUFFIXES.

bedizen. /bɪˈdʌɪz(ə)n/. A somewhat archaic verb ('to deck out gaudily'), now used only by the exquisitely literate. Examples: *He likes to think he's living in a palace full of bedizened captives waiting for him to arrive*—I. Murdoch, 1989; *Isn't life bedizened with jaunty contradictions*?—Julian Barnes, 1991.

Bedouin, a desert Arab. This usual English spelling of the word is derived from French. It contains, but ignores, the Arabic plural ending *-īn*. Some 19c. writers used the singular form *bedawy*, plural *bedawin* (and variants) as approximate equivalents of the Arabic forms of the word, but these spellings are no longer extant. The form *Bedu* is used in the same sense in more technical writing (*The Bedu had their own food with them in their saddle bags*—T. E. Lawrence, 1917).

beef, the flesh of an ox, a bull, or a cow, is normally a MASS NOUN; but a waiter might say 'two roast beefs', meaning 'two orders for roast beef'. The word is also used (plural *beeves*, US also *beefs* or *beef*) in the sense 'ox(en), especially when fattened, or their carcasses'. In the slang sense 'complaint, grievance', the only plural form is *beefs*.

been and gone and—. First observed by Dickens in popular speech in 1836, this 'amplification of the past participle of a verb, used to express surprise or annoyance at the act specified' (*OED*) is still used in light-hearted contexts in standard modern, mainly British, English, but sounds a trifle dated: *And what's more, he's been and gone and got it printed*—P. Bailey, 1986.

begin. See COMMENCE.

begrudge, grudge (verbs). These two words overlap in meaning, but not completely. To *begrudge someone something* (such as success or a reward) is to envy them for having it, whereas to *grudge something* is to resent the giving (by yourself or someone else) of something that you think you have a right to. Both words are commonly used in negative contexts. Examples best clarify the distinction, although the meanings overlap in practice: *I imagine you won't grudge me a glass of brandy first*—P. Fitzgerald, 1988; *Considering the responsible job they do, we should not begrudge them a good income*—*Daily Mail*, 2007.

beg the question. 1 In strict use, the English equivalent of Latin *petitio principii*, used in logic to mean the 'fallacy of founding a conclusion on a basis that as much needs to be proved as the conclusion itself' (Fowler, 1926). Gowers (1965) cited as an example, *capital punishment is necessary because without it murders would increase.*

2 In general use, the phrase has come to mean one of two things: (*a*) 'to bring a question to mind' (e.g. *I am not saying these drivers should be prosecuted, but if the new rules are not enforced, it begs the question what is the point of it?*—*Northern Echo*, 2007); (*b*) 'to evade a difficulty, to refrain from giving a straightforward answer'. Examples: *Let's ... beg the question of just who was in love with whom*—H. Jacobson, 1986;— *All of which begs the question, why did they do it?*—*OEC*, 2007. These meanings, in particular the first one, are very common, and are recognized in some dictionaries, but not in the *OED*. In precise English, some punctilious writers will prefer to avoid them in favour of the available alternatives: for (*a*) *raise, suggest, invite the question*, and for (*b*) *evade* or *avoid the question*. But to all intents and purposes the original meaning has been almost entirely lost, which is hardly surprising, considering that it would only ever be used in a very limited field of discourse.

behalf. The only use current in standard BrE is *on behalf of*, with two main senses, 'in the interest of or for the benefit of (another person, cause, etc.)', and 'as the agent or representative of (another)'. In American English *in behalf of* vies with *on behalf of* in the same two senses, though Garner (1987) insists that a distinction exists. *In behalf of*, he says, means 'in the interest or in defense of' (*he fought in behalf of a just man's reputation*); and *on behalf of* means 'as the agent of, as representative of' (*on behalf of the corporation, I would like to thank* . . .).

A new non-standard use (or rather a revival of an obsolete one), first noted in the 1980s, is a tendency to substitute *on behalf of* for *on the part of*, or just to use *behalf* instead of *part*: e.g. (a person interviewing a golfer) **That was an 11th-hour decision on your behalf* (read *part*); **His death was largely due to panic on his behalf* (= on his part). This use is to be avoided.

behemoth. The usual pronunciation now is /bɪˈhiːmɒθ/, stressing the second syllable.

behest. An ancient, somewhat formal, word, used especially in the phrase *at the behest* (*of*): e.g. *Van Dyck painted all five of the surviving royal children at the behest of their father*—A. Fraser, 1979; *The time and place were at her behest*—P. Lively, 1991.

beholden. Once the normal past participle of the verb *behold* (*These are stars beholden By your eyes in Eden*—E. Barrett Browning, 1850), *beholden* survives only in the sense 'attached, or obliged (to a person); under personal obligation for favours or services': *In his post as editor* . . . *he had shown himself beholden to no clique*—T. Keneally, 1980.

behoof. An ancient word, now virtually obsolete, meaning 'advantage': e.g. *it was surprising how many people would dredge up from their past some exotic Jewish ancestor for Sefton's behoof*—H. Jacobson, 1983.

behove. Now most often used exclusively in formal registers as a quasi-impersonal verb with *it* as a dummy subject, to mean 'it is incumbent upon or necessary for (a person) to do (something)': e.g. *What books does it behove me to read?; it behoves us to know as much as possible about local government.* In the UK it is pronounced to rhyme with *grove* and *rove*, and in the US it is spelt **behoove** and pronounced to rhyme with *move* and *prove*. It is also used to mean 'befit' (usually in negative contexts): e.g. *It ill behoves him to protest.*

being as (how), being (that). Used by many regional speakers, especially in the US, and jocularly by standard speakers, *being as* (*how*) and *being* (*that*) are not uncommon in casual conversation, but have not found acceptance in straightforward standard speech: *being as it's holiday time* . . . —Sue Cook, BBC Radio 4, 1977; *Being as how you can't be married, you'd better have him christened*—J. Bowen, 1986.

Being (*that*), in particular, was not always so restricted: the *OED* records numerous examples from literary sources, including: *I believe your newspapers* . . . *tell you all, but being there is nothing newer, I would do it too*—Lady Russell, 1692; *With whom he himself had no delight in associating, 'being that he was addicted unto profane and scurrilous jests'*—Scott, 1815. Cf. AS 7.

belabour (US **belabor**). In the senses, (*a*) to thrash, (physically) assail, and (*b*) to assail with words, recorded from 1600 and 1596 respectively. Examples: (*a*) *I got very mad as expected, and tried to belabour both of them*—A. Burgess, 1971; *and how they* [*sc.* Harpies] *belabour us, squawking, with their horrible claws and flapping wings*—F. Weldon, 1988. (*b*) *In the face of such overwhelming beauty it is not necessary to belabor the faithful with logic*—H. L. Mencken, 1923; *It was in vain that the fiery little George Augustus, and his wife, belaboured Walpole with their arguments*—C. Chenevix Trench, 1973. Since the last century, these two meanings have been joined by another, especially in American English: *belabor* is being used interchangeably with *labor* in the combination *to belabor* (*a point, a question, a theme*, etc.). Some dictionaries accept this use, but the *OED* has not yet done so, and many British speakers would consider it at best a novelty, at worst a mistake.

believe me, a phrase used to strengthen an assertion, is sometimes extended to the somewhat condescending form *believe you me.* Crashaw used *Beleeve mee* in this manner in 1646: the *OED* records his use and numerous others. The extended form *believe you me*, whose syntax is probably unique in standard modern speech, is first recorded in 1808. Modern examples: *And believe you me this aspect of the war effort is not being ignored*—N. Williams, 1985; *'Is that so?' 'It is, believe you me, young man.'*—P. Bailey, 1986.

belittle. It will probably come as a surprise to most readers of this book that the currency and acceptability of the verb *belittle* in the UK were ever in doubt. The word is first recorded in the late 18c. in America, and in its ordinary sense, 'to make (a person or an action) seem unimportant or of little value', became widely accepted in the UK only at some point in the 20c. Fowler (1926) and Gowers (1965) both rejected *belittle* and expressed a marked preference for *decry, depreciate, disparage, poohpooh*, etc. Predictably, their objections have not prevented the word from becoming a standard, useful part of the language, and it is now part of the long list of lost causes.

belly. The Old English word *bælig* meant 'a bag, skin-bag, purse, pod, husk'. By the 14c. *belly* had come to mean 'that part of the human body which lies between the breast and the thighs, and contains the intestines', i.e. the ordinary modern sense. Over the centuries, in its ordinary anatomical sense, the word has had mixed fortunes in the scale of mentionable words, and has still largely failed to displace *abdomen* (formal), *stomach* (the organ itself but also widely used of the surface area of that part of the body), or *tummy* (children's language, used by adults as a genteelism) in standard contexts. See GUTS.

beloved traditionally has two pronunciations, each determined by the word's role in the phrase. When used as a past participle (*beloved by all, was much beloved*), it has two syllables, /-ˈlʌvd/; as an adjective (*dearly beloved brethren; the beloved wife of*), or as a noun (*my beloved*), it normally has three, /-ˈlʌvɪd/. This distinction is, sadly, in danger of being forgotten, even by those, such as the clergy, who should know better. Cf. *aged, blessed, cursed.*

below. In business and technical writing, and on the Internet, *below* is often used as an adjective in the same way as *above* to refer the reader to tables, charts, illustrations, etc: *The below figure illustrates what happens to data being written on a disk when a shock occurs*—*OEC*, 2004. While this development can be seen as a reasonable extension of *below's* syntactic repertoire, on the analogy of *above*, it is not yet considered good style. The well-established pattern *the table, chart, illustration below* should be used instead.

bemuse(d), amuse(d). The meaning of this verb, often used as a past participle or adjective (*her bemused expression; he was bemused by what was happening*) appears to be in flux, at least in AmE. It was first recorded, according to the *OED*, by Pope in 1705, and then used by him again in 1734 in the line of poetry *Is there a Parson much be-mus'd in Beer*, (*'be-mus'd in'* being a pun on the name of the by then dead Poet Laureate Laurence Eusden, reputed to be a drunkard).

The original *OED* entry (1887) defines the meaning as 'to make utterly confused or muddled, as with intoxicating liquor; ... to stupefy', a definition which is highly dependent on that 1734 quotation. *ODO* defines the meaning more broadly as 'to puzzle, confuse, or bewilder', and Collins also uses the last two verbs for its definition. In BrE these are the meanings generally associated with the word, e.g. *slightly irritating, and indeed bemusing, metamathematical-cum-philosophical asides*—*London Rev. Bks*, 2003; *That comment bemused him, it was the last thing he had expected to hear*—A. Briggs, 2010 (UK); *Also, American audiences and Sassenachs will be bemused by the strong* [*sc.* Scottish] *accents*—*Film Inside_Out*, 2005 (UK).

However, *the American Heritage Dictionary of the English Language* (5th ed., 2012) includes a usage note that the word 'is sometimes used to mean "amused, especially when finding something wryly funny" as in *The stream of jokes from the comedian left the audience bemused, with some breaking out into guffaws.*' The note goes on to say that 78 per cent of the dictionary's usage panel reject this usage. Merriam-Webster's *Unabridged* dictionary mentions two other meanings which need not concern us here, and defines this 'amuse' meaning as 'to cause (someone) to have feelings of wry amusement especially from something that is surprising or perplexing'. It includes this quote from Scots author Ian Rankin, which does not clarify without more context whether the meaning is simply 'puzzled' or 'wryly amused': *He was young, sandy-haired, and seemed bemused by the whole scene being acted out before him*—I. Rankin, *Set in Darkness*, 2000. Their second example seems less ambiguous: *While he found himself bemused by the antics of his beer-swilling American schoolmates, Javier really didn't have time to waste ... Academics took up so much of his time*—B. Seaman, *Binge*, 2005. What is one to make of all this?

A representative selection of examples in *OEC* data fails to show *bemuse(d)* being used unambiguously to mean 'amuse(d)'. (Is *a bemused smile* a puzzled one or an amused one?) A quick scan of some of the books listed by Google ngrams for 1995–2000 similarly shows it mostly being used to mean 'confuse(d), perplex(ed)'. Examples of the 'amuse(d)' meaning do not leap out from COCA. However, a trawl of COHA data for the decade of 2000 soon reveals examples that could easily be interpreted as 'amused': *But it always bemused Brooks that she was better known for being the first African-American writer to win a Pulitzer Prize (in 1950) than for the poems themselves—Newsweek*, 2000; *Father Tim shoots a bemused glance at Babs, and they both laugh—Southern Review*, 2002. It is also clear from online discussion, and comments made on the Merriam-Webster website by members of the public that the 'amuse(d)' meaning is a topical issue. Merriam-Webster's Collegiate dictionary included that meaning as long ago as 2003; discussion of President Obama's behaviour during the 2008 election campaign often used the word in the newer meaning, e.g. *Mr. Obama maintained a placid and at times bemused demeanor ... as he parried the attacks.*

There can be no objection in principle to this extension of the word's meaning: such changes are facts of language. And after all, if something, particularly someone's behaviour, perplexes you, you may well react to it with a degree of quizzical, detached amusement. Presumably in AmE that aspect of the word is now taking precedence over the simply 'perplex(ed)' meaning. It is also possible, of course, that certain writers think *bemuse* is merely a synonym for *amuse*, but a more stylish one. Whatever underlies the change, the word is becoming problematic: if you use it in AmE, some people will interpret it one way, and some the other, so it becomes ambiguous; and those who cleave fast to the older meaning will be annoyed by the newer one.

benchmark, written as one word, without a hyphen, as both noun and verb, is a busy word with an interesting history. Originally it referred physically to a wedge-shaped incision made by surveyors in a vertical surface so that a bracket could be inserted to form a *bench* or support for surveying equipment at a fixed and reproducible height. By the 1880s it started to develop its current metaphorical meaning, 'a point of reference, a standard', e.g. *the pay settlement will set a benchmark for other employers and workers.* Since the 1960s, in computing it has been used to mean 'a program or set of programs used as a standard against which the performance of other programs ... is compared or evaluated' (*OED*). This meaning also created a verb, used both in IT and, much more often, in general contexts, meaning to 'evaluate (something) by comparison with a standard', e.g. *we are benchmarking our performance against external criteria.* In this meaning the preposition most often used before the standard mentioned is *against*, as in the previous example, but *to* is also occasionally used, e.g. *companies who wish to have a system benchmarked to one of these recognized standards.*

beneath. Over the centuries, *beneath, below,* and *under* have tended largely to overlap. It would appear that, by the end of the 19c., *beneath* had become somewhat restricted in use: a literary and slightly archaic equivalent of both *below* and *under*, and that is still the case. Fowler (1926) judged that, apart from the 'beneath contempt' sense, 'it is now a poetic, rhetorical, or emotional substitute for *under* or *below*'.

Be that as it may, *beneath* continues to be used in literary style with two meanings. Examples: **1** (in a lower position than) *Lowe dropped to his knees, as if to drive the knife upwards beneath Leiser's guard*—J. le Carré, 1965; *I watched a child drag a butterbox on wheels beneath the cold streaky sky*—T. Keneally, 1980; *drinking pre-lunch aperitifs beneath crystal chandeliers*—P. Lively, 1987; *his body was positively abloom beneath the riding mac*—T. Wolfe, 1987; (fig.) *The Dog Beneath the Skin*—W. H. Auden and C. Isherwood, 1935.

2 (not worthy of) *he considers such work beneath him; she had married beneath her* (i.e. to a man of lower social status).

Cf. UNDERNEATH.

benefited is the recommended spelling of the past tense and past participle of the verb *benefit*: see DOUBLING OF CONSONANTS 2; -T-, -TT-. Nevertheless the norm in some publications, e.g. *The New Yorker*, is *benefitted*.

Bengali /bɛn'gɔːli/. Like many other Indian words in the period of the Raj, once commonly spelt with final *-ee*, but now always with *-i*.

benign, benignant. *Benign* was adopted from French in the 14c., and is by far the more usual of the two. It is used principally in the medical sense of not life-threatening (e.g. a tumour), also to mean 'gracious, kindly' and 'exhibiting kindly feeling in look, gesture, or action'; and especially in transferred use of anything considered to be propitious (e.g. the aspects of the planets), or salubrious (e.g. the weather, the air). *Benignant* /bɪ'nɪgnənt/, formed in the late 18c. after *malignant*, has remained at the margin of the language, unlike the word on which it was modelled. It means 'gracious, kindly (especially to inferiors)' (*a benignant monarch*), or 'salutary, beneficial' (*the benignant authority of the new regime*). It is not normally used of medical conditions. Cf. MALIGN, MALIGNANT.

bereaved, bereft. When the verb *bereave* is used transitively to mean 'to rob, dispossess (someone) of (usually immaterial things, e.g. hope, ideas, senses)', its past tense and past participle are normally *bereft* (*I faltered helplessly, nearly bereft of speech*—W. Styron, 1979; *Without her, he felt bereft as a child at a boarding school*—A. N. Wilson, 1982). When this meaning is intended, it is incorrect to use *bereaved*, e.g. **Thus Boniface, bereaved of all his goods, remained in their custody three days*—*OEC* (undated). In contexts of death it normally has *bereaved* as its past tense and past participle, e.g. *She was bereaved of her husband, my grandfather, by a sudden case of appendicitis*—*OEC*, 2003. When an attributive adjective is called for, *bereaved* is normally used (*a bereaved wife*). Similarly when the context requires a collective noun (*the bereaved assembled for the funeral*). In some contexts the boundary between the two meanings is blurred, e.g. *Shirai sounds authentically bereft when she sings of how 'father and mother are long dead ... no one knows me here 'in the song* In der Fremde—*OEC*, 2000, where it is unclear from context if the intended meaning is 'grieving' or 'robbed of hope'.

See -T AND -ED.

Berkeley. Burchfield (1996) confidently assumed 'There can be few people who do not know that Berkeley Square in London is pronounced with the sound of *lark*, and Berkeley in California with the sound of *lurk*'. His assumption may no longer be true, so the point is worth reiterating.

berserk. *Berserk* may be pronounced either as /bə'zɜːk/ or /bə'sɜːk/, though the first is commoner.

At first a noun (written especially as *berserker, -ar, -ir*), adopted in the early 19c. from the language of the Icelandic sagas, meaning 'a Norse warrior who fought with frenzied fury' (*Out of terrible Druids and Berserkers, come at last Alfred and Shakspeare*—Emerson, 1837; *as though they were expecting another onslaught of rapacious Danes or shield-biting berserkers*—P. Theroux, 1983). In Icelandic the word was probably derived from ON *bern-, bjǫrn* bear (the animal) + *serkr* coat, sark, but some scholars derive the first element from ON *berr* bare (thus 'fighting in his bare shirt'), whence the 19c. English spelling (Carlyle, Emerson, and Charles Kingsley) *baresark*. Henry Kingsley and Kipling popularized its use as a quasi-adverb in the phrase *to go berserk*, to act in a frenzied manner, and the word is now mainly used thus: *a maladjusted Jamaican who goes berserk sometimes and screams and spits and bites*—E. Huxley, 1964; *I can better understand people who go berserk ... than people who just can't* bother *to keep a kid alive*—A. S. Byatt, 1985.

beseech. For the past tense and past participle, use either *beseeched*, thus following e.g. Shakespeare and Iris Murdoch (*Why had he not wept, screamed, fallen to his knees, beseeched, raged, seized Jean by the throat?*—*The Book and the Brotherhood*, 1987); or *besought*, in the tradition of Milton, or, to take a more modern example, Penelope Lively (*The Lord is praised and besought and worshipped*—*Moon Tiger*, 1987). The two forms are about equally common in the *OEC*. See -T AND -ED.

beside, besides. 1 *As adverb.* In modern English, *besides* is the only adverbial form of the two and as such it means 'in addition, as well' (*Besides, he is already* *married; he has a current account and two other accounts besides*).

2 *As preposition. Beside* is the correct form when the meaning required is 'alongside, at the side of' (*dangling his arms beside his hips; she knelt down beside him; she suggested that the other passengers wait beside the road for the bus; a cat is seated beside the fire*). *Beside* is also used to mean 'in comparison with' (*beside Locke modern logical positivists are shown to have made very modest contributions to philosophy*).

Beside is the normal form in fixed phrases (*beside the point, beside the question, beside the mark*), where the meaning is 'away from, wide of (a mark)', and in the fixed expression *to be beside oneself.* To use *besides* in such cases, as in **besides the question, *besides the point,* is incorrect.

3 *Besides* is the correct form when the meaning is 'in addition to, other than' (*there has to be one other besides myself; besides all those tanks they have 1,000 warplanes; They have nothing in common besides being terribly sexy—Eye Weekly*, Toronto, 2003). *Beside* should not be used to mean this, as in **Beside their homework, they have letters to write,* where *besides* is needed.

bespeak. The finite verb survives (*with a poise that bespeaks 38 years in the public eye—OEC,* 2011), with past tense *bespoke* (*She had no confidence in the stupid fashion which bespoke mincing and vapidity*—P. Carey, 1988) and past participle *bespoken.* The older variant participle *bespoke* lingers on only as an attributive adjective meaning 'made to order' (*bespoke suit, goods,* etc.) in contrast with *ready-made.* As in the examples above, *bespeak* is immediately followed by a noun or noun phrase. The following construction with *of,* on the analogy of speak, is wrong: **There was a chill in the air bespeaking of fall—OEC,* 2007.

bestir, though rarely used, is now always reflexive in the general meaning of 'to begin to move actively, to busy onself', e.g. *Almost uniquely, it seems, I bestirred myself on Thursday to visit my local polling station—OEC,* 2009. Occasionally people use it transitively, almost as if it were a synonym for *stir* or *stir up: The contemporary North American and European left is rarely bestirred by issues of labour and rights—OEC,* 2009. While the transitive use was normal until the 19c., (*No Mauell, you haue so bestir'd your valour*—Shakespeare, *King Lear,* 1605), such use today is likely to be judged incorrect or pretentious.

bet (verb). When Kingsley Amis chose *betted* rather than *bet* as the past participle of the verb *bet* in *Difficulties with Girls* (1988) (*I'd have betted you wouldn't be much good at taking somebody out*), he opted for what is now the far less common form, both in Britain and (even more so) in the US. For both the past tense and the past participle, *betted* is rather unusual, although it is correct, e.g. *Orders from the government, on which the company had betted heavily, fell flat—OEC,* 2004. But in some contexts it sounds distinctly strange, e.g. *?Interestingly, many of those who had betted on the horse earlier withdrew their money on seeing the unruly behaviour of the horse—OEC,* 2009. When a sum of money is stated immediately after the verb (*he bet me £50 that the secret ballot would confirm his view*), only *bet* can used.

bête noire. Whatever the sex or nature of the person or concept referred to, *bête noire* should be written and printed thus, and not as *bête noir.* The plural is *bêtes noires,* with both *s*'s silent (*TV advertisements were his* bêtes noires). The word is printed in roman.

bethink. The *ODO* accurately describes the verb *bethink oneself of* as '*formal or archaic* (*he bethought himself of the verse from the Book of Proverbs*).' Dictionaries for foreign learners of English have no entry for the word, but well-read native speakers will all be familiar with it from its frequent use down the ages: e.g. *bethink yourself wherein you may haue offended*—Shakespeare, 1605; *If they shall bethinke themselues ... and repent*—AV, 1611; *Rip bethought himself a moment*—W. Irving, 1820.

betimes. Formed along with *betime* in the 14c. and used for several centuries in various meanings, e.g. 'at an early time; in a short time, soon.' By the end of the 17c. *betime* was obsolete, while *betimes* has gradually become restricted to literary or archaizing use, especially to mean 'early; in good time', when it has a charming Pepysian ring, or, particularly in AmE, to mean 'sometimes'. Modern examples: (at an early hour) *Susan was required to check* *in by ten a.m. and, since the journey would take at least four hours, the girls were up betimes*—J. Bowen, 1986; (at times) *Fans Court ... employs top-grade ingredients for Cantonese and Szechuan, but these betimes vitiated by salty or oily sauces*—*Toronto Life*, 1983; (in a short time) *Tokyo ... Kyoto, Hiroshima ... —memorable visits ... doomed now to fade betimes from my lax memory as if logged in disappearing ink*—J. Barth, 1994 (AmE).

better. This word has numerous idiomatic uses (*to know better, go one better*, etc.) and a few somewhat debatable ones. **1** *had better* (often written as *'d better*). This modal idiom or semi-auxiliary is correctly used to mean 'would find it wiser to' (*You had better come and have a talk; 'She'd better go home,' she heard Miss Braithwaite* say—B. Rubens, 1987). In negative and interrogative contexts, the normal types are shown in *You'd better not come any closer* and *Hadn't we better go home now?*

2 In a wide range of informal circumstances (but never in formal contexts) the *had* or *'d* can be dispensed with. Thus the type *You had better come tomorrow* can informally be reduced to (*You*) *better come tomorrow*. This reduced construction (without preceding pronoun and without *had*) is shown in the following example: *When you're feeling censorious, better ask yourself which you'd choose*—P. D. James, 1986. (Further examples, from 1831 onwards, in the *OED*.) In practice, this use of an unsupported *better* is much more common in North America, Australia, and NZ than in Britain. Examples: *I think I better get the taxi ... so as to catch the last bus back*—P. Roth, 1979 (US); *Come on! ... We better go on*—E. Jolley, 1980 (Aust.); *'You better be right,' she said*—A. Munro, 1987 (Canad.); *'You better lay low, Glory'*—R. Scott, 1988 (NZ). Cf. NOT 12.

3 *better than* = more than. *MWCDEU* (2002) cites several modern American examples of this use, including *We were whistling along at slightly better than Mach 2*—(*Saturday Review*, 1979), but adds that 'it is not generally found in the more formal kinds of writing'. The *OED* cites this use from miscellaneous writers of the period 1587 to 1823 (Lamb), but it does not turn up very often in standard use in Britain now (*Better than 95 per cent of the nation's alcoholics are middle-class*—*Listener*, 1984).

4 *better half, better part* = larger portion. The *OED* gives examples from literary sources (Sidney, Wordsworth, etc.) from 1580 to 1805, and both expressions are still current, e.g. *for the better half of the last decade; for the better part of a year.* (Quite distinct, of course, from *my better half* = 'my husband' or especially 'my wife'.)

better, bettor, one who bets. If only to distinguish it from the preceding word, *bettor* seems preferable, but in practice *better* is the usual form in Britain and *bettor* in the US.

between (preposition).

1 *between you and I.*
2 *between* and *among.*
3 *between each, between every* followed by a singular noun.
4 *between + and.*
5 Repeated *between.*
6 *between 1914–18*

1 *Between you and I.* What follows is an attempt to explain the phenomenon of *between you and I.* Given its pariah grammatical status, however, it should of course be avoided in any kind of formal writing, (where, in any case, it is unlikely to occur, as explained at (*c*) below). (*a*) Few phrases are as likely to be tut-tutted by pedants and usage pundits as *between you and I.* Burchfield (1996) thundered that 'anyone who uses it now lives in a grammarless cavern in which no distinction is recognized between a grammatical object and a subject'. In his last phrase resides the purists' objection. According to traditional grammar, the pronoun *I* is only ever the subjective case, *me* only ever the objective case; *between*, being a preposition, takes prepositional objects, so the phrase must be *between you and me.* However, objections to that interpretation can be raised on two counts: (i) in actual use this subject/object case distinction is often flouted, not only for *I/me*, but for other personal pronouns; (ii) *between you and I* has a special interpersonal function, and has become to an extent institutionalized in this form.

(*b*) *Wobbly cases.* (i) The *OED* entry for *I* contains a category headed 'As object of a verb or preposition'. It then goes on to state 'used for the objective case after a verb or preposition when separated from the governing word by other words (esp. in coordinate constructions with another pronoun and *and*)'. The point about 'coordinate constructions with another pronoun' is significant. The *OED* lists many historical examples, such as Ben Jonson's *Musco has beene with my cosen and I all this day*, 1601, and *Vanbrugh's Between you and I*, 1697. The *OED* further notes: 'This has been common at various times (esp. towards the end of the 16th and in the 17th cent., and from the mid 20th cent. onwards); it has been considered ungrammatical since the 18th cent.' A Shakespearian example is *All debts are cleerd betweene you and I if I might but see you at my death*. It is also worth mentioning that *I* is used as an object in traditional south-west English speech, and in the Caribbean. The opposite phenomenon, namely the objective case being used when the subjective is strictly grammatical, is also common in everyday speech in phrases of the kind *Mary and me went, him and me went*, etc. Together, these two opposed uses illustrate the wobbliness of the grammatical rule. Cf. HE 1.

(*c*) *A conversational use. Between you and I* is a way of introducing, or commenting on, a confidential piece of information: *Jane, let's just keep this between you and I; And just between you and I, he means while they are actually —ing*. Because it is conversational, examples are infrequent in the *OEC*, and in *COCA*. In fact, *between you and me* is more often used in this fashion, e.g. *And, hey, just between you and me, we all secretly like Duran Duran, don't we?*

(*d*) *The hypercorrection theory*. According to this theory, use of *between you and I* is caused by anxiety over the *I/me* distinction. Since the conversational *me* as subject mentioned at (*b*) above is stigmatized, people avoid using *me*, so the theory goes, even where it is appropriate. The theory is impossible to prove, though there may be some support for it in the following. In the *OEC* data, *between you and me* is many times more frequent than *between you and I*, not only, as mentioned above, in its confidential use, but in its simple relational meaning, e.g. *But that might just be a difference between you and me*. The kinds of texts *where between you and I* is used in this relational way are classed as informal or non-standard, e.g. *'There's nothing between you and I anymore,' he groaned*.

2 *between* and *among*. The boundaries in the use of *between* and *among* are not clearly drawn. Many people, and usage guides, cling to the idea that *between* is used of two and *among* of many, but the *OED* maintains that 'In all senses, *between* has been, from its earliest appearance, extended to more than two ... It is still the only word available to express the relation of a thing to many surrounding things severally and individually, *among* expressing a relation to them collectively and vaguely.' As an example of correct usage it gives *a treaty between three countries*, where *among* would clearly be impossible. The *OED* further divides the uses of *between* into four main branches: of simple position; of intervening space; of relation to things acting conjointly or participating in action; of separation. These distinctions are needed to account for the wide fluctuations of usage over the last eight centuries.

The main present-day patterns can be fairly clearly discerned, I think, in the following examples: (two persons or things) *things that had happened a long time since—between Isaac and myself*—N. Williams, 1985; *a perfect cross between a serious documentary and a light-hearted travelogue*—*OEC*, 2009; (more than two persons, things, etc.) *there was one iron between fifteen of us*—D. Lodge, 1962; *dividing his time between engineering, mechanical inventions, and writing for periodicals*—G. S. Haight, 1968; *The death of his sister had changed things between Marcus, Ruth and Jacqueline*—A. S. Byatt, 1985; (number of events, groups, etc., less clearly defined) *Does he sigh between the chimes of the clock?*—J. M. Coetzee, 1977; *preventing the sharing of information and collaboration between research teams*—*OEC*, 2003; (borderline cases in which *among* should perhaps have been used, especially in the 1987 example) *I want to walk between the trees and smell them too*—E. Jolley, 1980; *a company has £25 million of profit to distribute between 10,000 workers*—*Times*, 1987; (*among* correctly used) *there's only us ... left among the wreckage*—S. Barstow, 1960; *there were a lot of very young people among the temporary staff*—P. Fitzgerald, 1980; *the day has not yet come when the giants war among themselves*—J. M. Coetzee, 1977; (*among* now sounding somewhat forced) *a conversation among Richard Smith, Sir Anthony Grabham, and Professor Cyril Chantler*—*Brit. Med. Jrnl*, 1989.

3 *between each, between every* followed by a singular noun. Traditionally, constructions of the type *twenty-two yards between each telegraph pole* and *he had a cup of coffee between each tutorial* have been regarded with suspicion or downright dislike (and have been replaced by, for example, *between each telegraph pole and the next* and *between tutorials*). Jespersen (*Mod. Eng. Gram.* vii) and other grammarians have had no difficulty in finding evidence in support of the condemned type: *Between each kiss her oaths of true loue swearing—The Passionate Pilgrime,* 1599; *pausing between every sentence*—G. Eliot, 1859; *a row of flower-pots were ranged, with wide intervals between each pot*—W. Collins, 1860; *staring at her furtively between each mouthful of soup*—M. Kennedy, 1924. This evidence must be respected and the constructions should be accepted, although they could conceivably be avoided in writing for readers of a morbidly punctilious turn of mind. It is worth noting that constructions of the type *between every two* are highly ambiguous as to 'between two' and 'between two pairs' and should be avoided; it is not clear, e.g. if *Decentralized nurse work stations are located between every two patient rooms* means that there is a work station between every patient room, or between each pair of patient rooms.

4 *between + and. Between* should be followed by *and,* not other words such as *or,* as in the following examples: **four days that could make the difference between life or death for Dad* (read '*and death*'). The same mistake occasionally occurs with other phrases, like *as opposed to, as against,* e.g. **Can the president drive a wedge between the Washington GOP* (= Republican) *community as opposed to those outside?—OEC,* 2009.

5 Repeated *between.* In long sentences, the reader or listener may have to wait a long time for the second term or element in a *between*-construction to be mentioned, e.g. *You need to decide between voting for a party which, against all advice, introduced the poll tax, a form of tax first used in the 14th century, and one that dislikes the rates system but has no alternative to offer.* The solution to the problem is not to insert a second *between* between *and* and *one.* Either let it stand, or recast the sentence entirely.

6 To use a dash to join two dates, as in *between 1914–18* is wrong because it treats the dash as if it were the word 'and'. Rewrite *from 1914 to 1918* or *between 1914 and 1918.*

betwixt as preposition and adverb is now archaic or obsolete in standard English. However, the alliterative combination *betwixt and between,* first recorded in 1832, is not uncommon in the meaning 'not fully or properly either of two things'. Examples: *Well, he's kind of caught betwixt and between—OEC,* 2001; *But, right now, I'm a little betwixt and between about whether we should continue with it, because we lost several good candidates—OEC,* 2006. *Betwixt* on its own lives on in some British and American dialects, and, perhaps surprisingly, in modern writing, often rather self-consciously, in the fields of the arts and humanities, e.g. *I start from the premise that it is betwixt materiality and language that the dancing body is produced—OEC,* 2003.

beware. Derived in Middle English from the verb *be* + the adjective *ware* = 'cautious', *beware* now has no inflected forms. It is used in the imperative, or with a modal auxiliary like *must* or *had better*: *Beware of the dog!*; *beware lest he overtake you*; *you must/had better beware or someone will attack you.* Use with a direct object, as in Shakespeare's *Beware the Ides of March* or Longfellow's *Beware the pine-tree's withered branch!* (1842), would still be acceptable in poetry but is not a feature of ordinary speech or writing. In current English, *of* is used as a link word: *Beware of flying elephants and risk-free bonds—Sunday Times,* 2005.

bi-. 1 This prefix, which was first used in contexts of time (*biweekly, bimonthly, biyearly,* etc.) in the 19c., is a cause of endless confusion. Some compounds can only ever mean 'occurring or continuing for two of the specified units of time', or 'appearing every two ... ', as in *bicentennial.* Some, however, such as *biweekly, bimonthly* and *biyearly,* can mean that, or they can mean 'occurring twice in the specified unit of time': e.g. is a *biweekly* newspaper available every two weeks or twice a week? Because ambiguity is usually present, and cannot be resolved by the devising of rules, it is always better to use unambiguous equivalents, e.g. *twice a week, twice-weekly; every two weeks,* *fortnightly; twice-yearly; every two years*; etc. See BIANNUAL; BICENTENARY.

2 *Bi* (without a hyphen) is an informal shortening of *bisexual*, first recorded in the 1960s: *The drama convincingly portrayed the myriad ways sexuality could be expressed between men whether gay, bi or straight*—*OEC*, 2008.

biannual. First recorded in 1877, it has mostly been used to mean 'half-yearly, twice a year'. By contrast, the much older word **biennial** (first recorded in 1621) has been traditionally used to mean 'existing or lasting for two years; changed every two years; occurring once in every two years'. The distinction is far from watertight. Except in contexts, such as the titles of conferences, where it is not unreasonable to assume that attendees know how often the event happens, it is as well to replace *biannual* with *half-yearly* or *twice-yearly*, and *biennial* with *two-yearly*.

bias. The recommended inflected forms of the verb are *biased, biasing*, and of the noun, *biases*. See -S-, -SS-.

Bible. Use an initial capital when it refers to the holy scriptures themselves (but *three bibles* = three copies of the Bible); use a small initial when the word is used in a transferred sense (*Wisden is the cricketers' bible*). The corresponding adjective *biblical* is always written with a small initial letter.

bicentenary, a noun meaning 'two-hundredth anniversary' and also a corresponding adjective, is pronounced *-teen-* more usually than *-ten-*. It is the usual term in BrE, whereas **bicentennial** is more usual in American English and elsewhere. See CENTENARY 2.

biceps. The form *biceps* works as both a singular and plural noun: *the biceps on his left arm; a pair of bulging biceps*. The singular *bicep* is a back-formation and is incorrect, as is the plural *bicepses*. See also FORCEPS.

bid. 1 In the playing-card and auction-room senses the past tense and past participle are both *bid* (*two no-trumps were bid; Granada bid for a franchise, which was duly awarded*—*OEC*, 2003.

2 In other senses, the past tense is usually spelt *bade* (*we bade him adieu; it bade fair to be the best holiday ever*) and pronounced /bad/, rhyming with *bad*. The *OEC* has a few examples of *bid* used instead in this meaning, perhaps in an attempt to avoid the slightly literary sound of *bade*, but most people would regard this is as wrong. The past participle is *bidden*, except that *bid* is used in a few set phrases, e.g. *Do as you are bid*.

3 When it is used—not very often nowadays—in the sense 'command', it governs a bare infinitive (*Why should he . . . keep me from my own And bid me sit in Canterbury, alone?*—T. S. Eliot, 1935). When used in a passive construction, a *to*-infinitive follows (*he was bidden to get on with it*). This use has largely been replaced by *tell* (someone) *to do* (something).

bide. Apart from archaistic, regional, and poetical uses, this long-standing word (in Old English and until the 19c. it meant 'to remain') is now idiomatic only in *to bide one's time* (past tense *bided*).

biennial. See BIANNUAL.

billet-doux. Pronounced /ˌbɪleɪˈduː/. The plural is *billets-doux*, pronounced /ˌbɪleɪˈduːz/.

billion. It is now best to work on the assumption that the word means 'a thousand million' in all English-speaking areas, unless there is direct contextual evidence to the contrary. In British English it has come to mean 'a thousand million', as it always has in American English, and its old BrE meaning of 'a million million' has been superseded in any kind of technical or economic writing. Despite that, many average British people have not yet caught up with the newer meaning, so in British contexts directed at non-experts it may be advisable to spell things out: *£8,000,000,000* or *£8,000 million*, rather than *£8 billion*. It is also important to realize that in major European languages, such as French and German, *billion* means 'a million million'. When preceded by a numeral, the plural is *billion* (unchanged: *three billion people*), but *billions* is used when it is followed by *of* (*billions of people*). Cf. MILLIARD; TRILLION.

bimonthly. See BI-.

binomial (noun). There are two principal uses: **1** The two-part technical Latin name of a plant or animal species: *Primula vulgaris* primrose, *Equus caballus* horse,

Homo sapiens man. Both parts should be printed in italic, with the generic name given an initial capital. After the first mention of a species, later references may be shortened, if there is no risk of confusion, by the abbreviation of the generic name to the initial capital alone, followed by a full point: *P. vulgaris, E. caballus.* (*New Hart's Rules.*)

2 The name given to two-part expressions joined by *and* (occasionally *or*) in which the order of words is fixed: (nouns) *bread and butter, cup and saucer, gin and tonic, by hook or by crook, ladies and gentlemen, law and order, odds and ends; Tweedledum and Tweedledee;* (adjs.) *fast and furious; spick and span;* (verbs) *to have and to hold, tried and tested.*

biopic. This informal word for a film biography, pronounced /ˈbʌɪəʊpɪk/ (**biy**-oh-pik), originated in America in the 1940s and is the standard journalistic word for films of this genre, although occasionally it is used with a somewhat condescending tone: *that old American favourite, the schmaltzy biopic—OEC,* 2003. Like the slightly later **docudrama**, it is an example of a frequently used modern PORTMANTEAU WORD.

bipolar disorder is a term that came into use in medical circles in the 1970s. It is now increasingly being used in non-specialist language to replace the stigmatizing and doubly negative term **manic depression** to denote 'a form of mental illness characterized by one or more episodes of mania typically accompanied by one or more episodes of major depression' (*OED*). The previous lack of public awareness and discussion of this condition has been largely remedied in recent years, in no small part because of the revelation by media personality Stephen Fry that the condition affects him.

bisect. See DISSECT.

bishopric. See SEE.

bite. In British English and American English, *bit* is the normal past tense form, and *bitten* the normal past participle. In the US (as reported in *DARE*), *bit* is recorded locally as past participle 'especially among males and lesser educated speakers' (*These apples are wormy, I think you got bit,* i.e. cheated).

bivouac (verb). The inflected forms are *bivouacked* and *bivouacking.* See -C-, -CK-.

biweekly. See BI-.

biyearly. See BI-.

black. 1 *Black* has been used to refer to African peoples and their descendants since at least the late 14c. Although the word has been in continuous use ever since, other terms have enjoyed prominence too. In the US **colored** was the term adopted in preference by emancipated slaves following the American Civil War. Then *colored* was itself superseded in the US in the early 20c. by **Negro** as the term preferred by prominent black American campaigners such as Booker T. Washington. In Britain, on the other hand, **coloured** was the most widely used and accepted term in the 1950s and early 1960s.

As a consequence of the civil rights and Black Power movements of the 1960s, *black* became the most widely used and accepted term in the 1960s and 1970s, replacing *Negro.* Adopted by Americans of African heritage to signify a sense of racial pride, it remains the most widely used and generally accepted term also in Britain today. In the US, the more formal **African American** replaced *black* in many contexts during the 1980s, but both are now generally acceptable. **Colo(u)red people**, common in the early part of the 20th century, is now regarded as offensive, both in the US and Britain. The phrase survives, however, in the full name of the NAACP, the National Association for the Advancement of Colored People. An inversion of the phrase, **people of color**, has gained some favour, especially in the US, but is also used to refer to other non-white ethnic groups, e.g. *a gathering spot for African Americans and other people of color interested in reading about their cultures. Black* is also occasionally used to refer to Indigenous Australians. See also AFRICAN AMERICAN; COLOURED; NIGGER.

2 It is generally considered inappropriate and offensive in Britain to call people of South Asian heritage *black.* Uncontroversial ways of describing them are to use the terms *Indian, Malay, Pakistani, Bangladeshi,* etc., as appropriate, or to use *Asian* or *British Asian* as a blanket term.

3 For a time it was thought appropriate to spell *black* with a capital initial as a racial term, but the normal preference now is for a small initial: *black Americans*.

black, blacken. *Black* is used when the meaning is deliberately to make something black (to *black* boots with blacking; to colour one's face black as camouflage, in order to play a role as a black person, etc.); and, in the British trade-union movement, to declare (something) to be *black*, i.e. to boycott it. *To black someone's eye*, meaning 'to hit (someone) in the eye so as to cause bruising' is a fixed phrase, in which *blacken* cannot replace *black*. (But if you successfully *black someone's eye*, it will undoubtedly be *blackened*). *Blacken* is more often used to imply an unintentional or fortuitous process (*the ceiling blackened with smoke*). Unlike *black*, it can be used intransitively (*his mood/the sky blackened*), and is more common as a past participle used as an adjective: *The scarred, blackened fields are testament to the violence inflicted on the earth in this kind of farming, OEC*, 2004. *Blacken* also has a special metaphorical use, 'to besmirch or tarnish', with reference to people's character, reputation, etc.

Black English. 1 The form of English spoken by many black people, especially as an urban dialect of the United States. A chance occurrence of the term in 1734 is recorded in the *OED*, but the recognition of Black English as a describable and distinctive form of American English did not emerge until the civil-rights movement in the 1960s.

2 As the previous editor of *Fowler's* remarked (R.W. Burchfield *The English Language*, 1985, p. 164), African American Vernacular English, or Black Vernacular English, as it is often called, makes many 'holes in the standard American syntactical cobweb: e.g. *all my black brother* (uninflected plural); *a novel base on* ... (loss of final consonant in *based*); *God didn't make no two people alike* (double negation)'. He made the important point that these are not casualties of an imperfect learning of standard American but features of a creolized form of English, shaped orally by some deep ancestral memory of patterns of speech brought many generations earlier by African slaves. William Labov's well-known work *The Social Stratification of English in New York City* (1965) demonstrated that Black English is not a fractured form of standard American English, but a powerfully alternative form of American speech, a variety that is richly imagistic and inventive.

blamable. See BLAMEABLE.

blame (verb). First used *c*.1200 to mean 'to find fault with' (e.g. *Thow blamest crist, and seistful bitterly, He mysdeparteth richesse temporal*—Chaucer), *blame* came to be used with *for* (*to blame someone for something*) in the 18c. (first recorded in Defoe, 1727) with the meaning 'to censure (a person) for (something)'. A century later a construction with *upon* or *on* (*to blame something on someone*) came into use, meaning 'to assign responsibility (for something) to (a person)'. While Fowler did not comment on the word, Gowers in his revision of 1965 described it as 'a needless variant' of *to blame* (someone) *for*, but such strictures are futile in the face of incontrovertible evidence of usage, and both constructions are now standard.

blameable is the preferred spelling in BrE, and *blamable* is standard for American English, for this word whose pedigree stretches back to the 14c. See -ABLE, -IBLE 7.

blanch, blench (verbs). People sometimes wonder whether to say *to blanch at* something or *to blench at* something. Both are correct, in different contexts, but the second can be slightly ambiguous, as explained below. **1** *Blanch* first recorded in the 14c. and related to French *blanc* 'white', has two main meanings. Referring to people, it means 'to turn pale, from fear, shock, and similar emotions'; and, referring to vegetables, almonds, etc., 'to prepare for further cooking by immersing briefly in boiling water'. The variant form *blench* has been used to mean 'to become pale' since the early 19c. It is, strictly speaking, incorrect to use *to blanch at* something to mean 'to recoil from', but it is a solecism few will nowadays notice. Examples: (blanch) *On his way out, Blair blanched visibly when he was introduced to Martin Rowson, the cartoonist who makes much of his living making the PM look foolish—Scotland on Sunday*, 2002; *Blanch the asparagus spears in boiling salted water for two minutes—Scotland on Sunday*, 2005; *Some parents may blanch at the prospect of forking out £15 for a large piece of curved plastic—*

Telegraph, 2006; (blench) *any sensible military planner would blench white at the thought—OEC*, 2011; *A shudder shook the boy's frame, and his face blenched—OEC* (undated).

2 Confusingly, there is also an originally separate verb *blench*. It started out in Old English and is still current with the meaning 'to make a sudden flinching movement out of fear or pain' (*many people blench when they enter a dentist's surgery*). If you use the structure *to blench at* it could in some contexts be interpreted to mean either 'to turn pale' or 'to flinch', e.g. *Many decent doctors blench at the crude and dishonest shroud-waving carried out in their name—Guardian*, 2008. In practice, as both actions suggest a similar state of mind, it does not greatly matter. But if you wish to be absolutely precise, you could use appropriate synonyms such as *turn pale* on the one hand, or, on the other, *flinch, recoil, baulk*, etc.

blank verse, verse without rhyme, 'especially the iambic pentameter or unrhymed heroic, the regular measure of English dramatic and epic poetry, first used by the Earl of Surrey (died 1547)' (*OED*). *Paradise Lost* and the greater part of Shakespeare's plays are written in blank verse.

blatant. 'Apparently invented by Spenser, and used by him as an epithet of the thousand-tongued monster begotten of Cerberus and Chimaera, the "blatant" or "blattant beast", by which he symbolized calumny' (*OED*). Except when used with allusion to Spenser, the word has (since the late 19c.) come to describe a wrong or inappropriate action performed unashamedly (*the blatant way in which he intruded, a blatant lie, a blatant piece of late tackling*), and overlaps in meaning with *flagrant* but has rather less of *flagrant*'s implications of offensiveness: *It was a blatant lie* means that the lie was obvious; *It was a flagrant lie* means that (when discovered) it was outrageous. *Blatant* typically modifies words such as *attempt, bias, discrimination, disregard, hypocrisy, lie, racism, rip-off, sexism*, and *violation*; It overlaps in meaning to a considerable extent with FLAGRANT.

blend (noun). For the linguistic term, see PORTMANTEAU WORDS.

blended, blent. The unvarying past tense and past participle of the verb *blend* in ordinary use is *blended* (*the sky blended in the distance with the sea; blended tea, wines*, etc.). Since the 20c. *blent* has been used only in literary works: *It was the memory of Saturday morning, blent with another emotion too vague to name*—S. Gibbons, 1937; and, probably most famously, in *A serious house on serious earth it is, In whose blent air all our compulsions meet*—P. Larkin, 1955.

blessed, blest. When used as an ATTRIBUTIVE adjective, always spelt *blessed* and pronounced as two syllables, /ˈblɛsɪd/: *the Blessed Virgin Mary, the Blessed Sacrament, every blessed night*. So too when used as a plural noun with *the* (*Isles of the blessed*), and in the biblical expression *blessed are the meek*. When used as a finite verb, the past tense and past participle are normally written as *blessed* and pronounced /blɛst/: *the bishop* (*had*) *blessed his wife and children before he died*. So too in the colloquial expression *blessed if I know*. The spelling *blest*, once common in all the above uses, is now mostly restricted to poetry and hymns (*Blest are the pure in heart*—J. Keble, Hymn 370 in *English Hymnal*). It is also used in the colloquial expression *Well I'm blest*.

blind. As with other words designating disabilities, such as *deaf*, it is better to avoid using the formulation *the* + nominalized adjective, i.e. *the blind*, to refer to groups of people in society with sight problems. Such use is quite rightly perceived as diminishing and limiting people's individual identity. Instead, use *blind people*, which is the wording now adopted by the British Royal National Institute of Blind People (RNIB) in its name.

bloc. A 20c. loanword from French, it is used, especially in politics and business, of 'a combination of persons, groups, parties, or nations formed to foster a particular interest' (*OED*). The phrase *bloc vote* is now often used instead of the traditional *block vote*. See also EN BLOC.

blog, an online diary or journal, is one of the cultural keywords of our time. *Blogs* have enabled countless millions of people to express themselves in public on personal or broader topics, and contributed, directly or indirectly, to political and social changes. (As a microcosmic example of that, my local Town Council was morally obliged to step down after a **blogger** tirelessly investigated some financial shenanigans in which they had engaged.) First recorded in this form before the turn of the millennium, *blog* is, morphologically speaking, rather like *cello*. The full form is, of course, the portmanteau word **weblog**, but it, like *violoncello*, tends only to be used in formal documents and manuals. In fact, in the *OEC* data *weblog* occurs in just over seven per cent of instances. *Blog* has given rise to many derivatives, of which the most common are the agent noun *blogger*, the verb *to blog*, and the verbal noun **blogging**. The next most common derivatives are *the* **blogosphere**, first recorded in 1999, to refer to 'The cultural or intellectual environment in which blogs are written and read; blogs, their writers, and readers collectively, especially considered as a distinct online network' (*OED*); and **blogroll** 'a list on a blog of hyperlinks to other blogs or websites'. In common with other abbreviations of its kind, *blog* requires no apostrophe before the *b-*. In derivatives and inflections, remember to double the *-g-*.: *blogged, blogger, blogged*. See also -G-, -GG-.

blond(e). 1 The two forms retain a trace of the grammatical gender they have in French, the language from which they were adopted. A *blonde* is in principle 'a *woman* with blonde hair'. A *blonde* person is 'a fair-haired *woman*'. By contrast a tall *blond* person usually = 'a tall blond (young) *man*'. But the distinction is not an absolute one in all English-speaking countries: e.g. (*blond*, of a woman) *The little girls whispered to each other, their blond heads shining in the rather dark room*—*New Yorker*, 1990; (*blond*, of a man) *Crews of all blond men who hardly ever spoke*—T. Findley, 1984 (Canad.); *His blond eye-lashes gave him a bemused look*—P. Fitzgerald, 1988 (UK); (*blonde*, of the hair of a woman, a doll) *her blonde plaits reaching half-way down her bony back*—C. Dexter, 1989 (UK); *lugging that doll of hers, a thing with blonde shiny hair*—A. Duff, 1990 (NZ); (*blonde*, of a man) *Brad glanced back to see two huge blonde men in black suits step from the elevator, one of them carrying a red metal toolkit*—*OEC*, 2003 (AmE). In the phrases *dizzy blonde* and *blonde moment*, based on stereotypical ideas of *blondes* (i.e. *blonde* women) as scatterbrained and empty-headed, *blonde* is much more usual than *blond*: e.g. *This morning I had a definite blonde moment, when I thought that the cord dangling from the ceiling in the bathroom turned the shower on. Actually, it was my room's emergency alarm*—*OEC*, 2005. *Blond* is also used to describe material of a light colour, particularly wood, from which an object is made: e.g. *Simple benches of blond wood are its sole furnishings*—*OEC*, 2000.

2 The German phrase *eine blonde Bestie* (Nietzsche) 'a person of the Nordic type' was rendered in English as 'blond(e) beast', but is now only of historical interest.

bloody. 1 In its original literal meaning 'like blood, smeared with blood, attended with much bloodshed, etc.', in use in the language as an adjective from earliest times, but since the 18c. diminishing in currency in these literal senses as the word came to be used as 'an intensifier: absolute, downright, utter', e.g. *All bloody rot; who says I'm drunk?*—George Moore, 1894. The first edition of the *OED* (1887) placed it in the realm of 'foul language', and as recently as 1995 the *Concise Oxford Dictionary* called it 'coarse slang'; and its numerous euphemisms, of which the best known are *bleeding, blooming*, and *ruddy*, testify to its former taboo status. Since then, however, it has seemed increasingly tame, and other words have taken on its former mantle of offensiveness. Its other meaning of 'unpleasant, perverse' now sounds rather dated, and is usually expressed by its derivative, *bloody-minded: Why go out of your way to be bloody about Archie when I'm trying to help him?*—A. Heckstall-Smith, 1954; *I like his mental resilience, his bloody-minded refusal to be written off*—*OEC*, 2008.

2 As an adverb it has been in use as an intensifier since the later part of the 17c., meaning 'absolutely, completely, utterly'. The *OED* rules out any connection with the oath *'s blood!*, and there is no foundation to the belief that it is a shortening of *by Our Lady*. The first edition of the *OED* instead attributed its use to 'the prevalent craving for impressive or graphic intensives seen in the use of ... *awfully* ... *devilish* ... *damned* ... *rattling*, etc.' Shaw was the first writer to put it on the stage, as it were, when he had Eliza Doolittle, in *Pygmalion* (1914), exclaim *Walk! Not bloody likely*. (Sensation). *I am going in a* *taxi*. No doubt he predicted the scandal that ensued. Since then, however, and particularly since the end of the 1939–45 war, the word has lost almost all traces of horridness. Characters in TV plays, for example, regularly use expressions like *serve you bloody right, you bloody well will do it or else* without attracting large quantities of hostile correspondence. These days, in conversation between friends it has become the most mild-mannered of oaths. Nevertheless, those attuned to the nuances of social interaction will know when to avoid it 'in polite society'.

3 These uses are recorded in American dictionaries, but are not properly part of American English. It is a pleasing myth that Australians use them more freely and vigorously than in other parts of the English-speaking world, and the colourful entry in the *Australian National Dictionary* (1988) appears to support it, with examples of use steeped in the language of pioneering adversity and 'ranging in force from mildly irritating to execrable': e.g. (adjective) *You must think yourself a damned clever bushman, talking about tracking a bloody dingo over bloody ground where a bloody regiment of newly-shod horses would scarcely leave a bloody track*—M. J. O'Reilly, 1944; (adverb) *Here* [*sc.* in Tobruk] *we bloody-well are; and here we bloody-well stay*—C. Wilmot, 1944.

bluebell. In southern England this is the wild hyacinth, *Scilla nutans*; in the north, and especially in Scotland, it is another name for the harebell, *Campanula rotundifolia*, with fewer, larger, and thinner-textured flowers than the other. Abroad, the word is applied to a number of blue flowers shaped somewhat like bells, including plants of the genera *Viorna, Veronica*, and *Wahlenbergia*.

Blue Book. (Should be written with initial capitals.) Specifically (*a*) *Brit* a parliamentary or Privy Council report, issued in a blue cover; (*b*) *US* a printed book giving personal details of government officials. (*New SOED*, 1993). See GREEN PAPER; WHITE PAPER.

bluish (not *blueish*) is the preferred spelling.

blurb, a brief descriptive paragraph of the contents of a book, printed on the jacket or wrapper to entice the reader to buy. The word is said to have been invented in 1907 by Gelett Burgess, an American writer, who appended the name Miss Blinda Blurb to a comic book embellished with a drawing of a young lady. Nowadays, the word *blurb* can apply also to other kinds of promotional material, such as for concerts, films, hotels, etc. The language used in *blurbs* tends to be predictable and repetitive, which is hardly surprising if one views the *blurb* as a distinct literary sub-genre. As a noun, the word has shed its previous informality, largely because there is no ready alternative. In American English, but rarely elsewhere, *blurb* can also be a verb (*this is the first time I have blurbed a whole line of books*), but this use is still informal.

boat. A *boat* is a 'small vessel propelled on water' by various means, and includes vessels used for fishing, for cargo, or to carry passengers. A *ship* is a large seagoing vessel, especially when part of a navy. A submarine, however, despite its designation HMS, is referred to as a *boat* rather than a *ship* (if the choice has to be made between these two).

boatswain. The originally nautical pronunciation /ˈbəʊsən/ is now general whether the word is written in full or as **bosun**.

bog(e)y, bogie. The latest editions of the Oxford dictionaries prefer *bogey* for the golfing term, *bogey* for the mischievous spirit, (with *bogy* as a variant), and *bogie* for the railway term. The golfing term is said to have originated in a name (*bogey-man*) given in 1890 on a golf course at Great Yarmouth by a Major Wellman to his 'well-nigh invincible opponent', namely the 'ground score'. To complete the picture, from the mid-19c. in Australian English *bogey* has had the informal meaning 'a spell of bathing or swimming'.

boggle (verb). In origin a 16c. verb formed from the noun *boggle*, a variant of *bogle*, a spectre of the kind such as horses are reputed to see, it now has both intransitive (*the mind boggles at the extent of the damage*) and transitive uses (*the suddenness of the collapse of Communism boggles the imagination*). The transitive uses still seem ever so slightly novel, despite their long history. The adjective **mind-boggling**, is first recorded in 1964 (A *lot of mind-boggling statistics—Punch*), and has been joined since the mid-1970s by the more colloquial reduced form **boggling**: *Serious* *damage can mean even more boggling bills—Which?,* 1990; *It's just boggling that they didn't decide to at least do one of these songs for the live album—OEC,* 2005.

bog-standard (usually spelt with a hyphen) is one of those informal but likeable compound adjectives that seem older than the dictionaries suggest. Largely confined to British use, it appears in the online version of the *OED*, with evidence starting from 1968. Its derogatory connotations wrongly lead many people to think that it is somehow connected to *bog*, the colloquial British word for a toilet. The most likely explanation, however, as Quinion (2004) suggests, is that is an alteration through mishearing of *box-standard* meaning 'basic, standard'. The noun *box standard* was known in the 1880s, and the adjective *box-standard* is first recorded as being used in early 1983 by the British inventor Sir Clive Sinclair.

bona fide(s). 1 As an adverbial phrase, *bona fide,* of Latin origin, means 'in good faith' and, when used at all, is normally pronounced in English contexts as /ˈbəʊnə ˈfʌɪdi/. It is first recorded in the mid-16c.

2 As the adjectival phrase *bon fide* (normally pronounced like the adverbial phrase) it means 'acting or done in good faith' and was first recorded in the late 18c.: *In particular, there was no evidence to support the conclusion that those payments were bona fide*—Ontario Superior Court of Justice, 2003.

3 The noun phrase *bona fides* is pronounced in English /ˈbəʊnə ˈfʌɪdiːz/ and was originally used as a singular (Latin *fidēs* faith) in legal contexts, with the meaning 'good faith, freedom from intent to deceive': e.g. *Bona fides is therefore opposed to fraud, and is a necessary ingredient in contracts*—1845 in *OED.* Mistakenly treated as a plural form of *bona fide* (assumed to be a singular noun although in Latin *fidē* was the ablative singular of nominative *fidēs*), the phrase has developed the different meaning of 'guarantees of good faith' or 'credentials'. From about the early 1940s onwards this new use and meaning has tended to dominate: e.g. *his bona fides were* (not *was*) *questioned,* and this use is perfectly acceptable (e.g. *All strangers whose bona fides ... are not completely verified must be immediately reported to your superior officer)* provided that the meaning intended is the plural one of 'guarantees of good faith' or 'credentials'.

4 The form **bone fide* is extremely common and used in all sorts of circles where it ought to be recognized as the mistake it is; sadly, it seems to pass largely unnoticed. Other manglings of the phrase include **bona fida* and **bona fidae.*

bon mot. Not italicized. In the singular pronounced /bɔ̃ məʊ/ and in the plural written *bons mots* and pronounced the same, or as /bɔ̃ məʊz/.

bonne bouche. In French 'a pleasing taste to the mouth' but in English 'a dainty mouthful or morsel' (which would be rendered in French as 'morceau qui fait ou donne bonne bouche'). Fowler (1926) resignedly remarked that such 'variation of meaning or form is no valid objection to the use of a phrase now definitely established'. Written in italics.

Book of Common Prayer, The. Until recently the official service book of the Church of England, it was originally compiled by Thomas Cranmer and others to replace the Latin services of the medieval Church. It first appeared in 1549, but the most familiar form now is the revised version of 1662. Like the Bible and the works of Shakespeare, it has contributed a great many familiar phrases to the language at large: e.g. *We haue erred and strayed from thy wayes, lyke loste shepe; Not waiyng* [weighing] *our merits, but pardonyng our offences.*

Between 1965 and 1971, Series 1, 2, and 3 of a revised Prayer-Book were issued as experimental forms of service, and in 1980 the Alternative Service Book was published. The aim of the revisers was to present the service book in up-to-date language. In the process some of the most memorable words and phrases in the Book of Common Prayer were replaced by others, and ancient and venerated points of accidence and syntax were removed. *Our Father, which art in heaven* became *Our Father in heaven; He ascended into heaven, and sitteth* became *He ascended into heaven, and is seated; Thereto I plight thee my troth* became *This is my solemn vow; With all my worldly goods I thee endow* became *All that I have I share with you.*

Anglicans are deeply divided about the merits of the two versions, but the BCP seems to be becoming marginalized by being mostly used only at restricted times or by special request (at weddings, funerals, etc.).

bored. The normal constructions are with *with* or with *by: they were bored with being left alone in the country; he became bored with Patrick; they were bored by the party political broadcasts before the general election.* A tendency has emerged in recent years, especially in non-standard English in Britain and abroad, to construe the verb with *of,* especially in conversation and on blogs, by analogy with *tired of.* The construction should be avoided in writing. Examples: *They* [*sc.* children] *use the preposition 'of' in an unorthodox way: 'I'm bored of this,' they say (taking the construction from 'tired of')*—I. Opie, 1993; *I soon became bored of office life, OEC,* 2009.

born(e). It is easy to forget that *born,* relating to birth, is a variant past participle of the verb *to bear,* and that *I was born on a Friday* means 'My mother bore me on a Friday'. *Born* is also used in figurative expressions such as *an indifference born of long familiarity.* In all other meanings, the past participle of *bear* is *borne* (*I have borne with this too long; He was borne along by the wind*), and this form is used with reference to birth when the construction is active, or when it is passive followed by *by* (the mother): *She has borne no children; Of all the children borne by her only one survived.*

bosom. Recorded from Old English onwards in the singular in the general sense 'the breast of a human being' and 'the enclosure formed by the breast and the arms' (*he clasped the fugitive to his bosom*; by extension, *in Abraham's bosom* (cf. Luke 16: 22) 'in the abode of the blessed dead'; *in the bosom of one's family* 'surrounded by their loving care and protection'). It has also come into use at various dates in technical and literary senses (of the sea, a sail, a recess round the eye of a millstone, etc.). It was not until the 20c. that the word came to be used colloquially in the plural (first recorded in 1959) to mean 'a woman's breasts': e.g. *She gave him a quick glimpse of fine bosoms as she bent to the door of the icebox*—I. Fleming, 1965. Care should be taken to avoid using the plural in contexts like the following, which may cause unintended humour: *The characters are fully rounded and indeed are also shown happy in the bosoms of their individual families—OEC* (undated).

botanic(al). Both forms are recorded from the mid-17c. onwards, but *botanical* is now much the more common of the two in Britain except in traditional names like the *Botanic Garden* in Oxford.

both.

1 *both . . . as well as.*
2 Redundant *both.*
3 Ambiguous constructions.
4 Need for symmetry in *both . . . and* phrases.
5 Used with more than two items.
6 *on both of our behalfs.*
7 *the both.*
8 *we both/both of us.*

1 *both . . . as well as.* This construction, though quite frequent, is one to be avoided, e.g. **And it's been very rewarding to see the response from all our partners both in North America, as well as in Europe—OEC,* 2007. *Both* should always be paired with *and,* such that the last example should read: *And it's been very rewarding to see the response from all our partners both in North America and in Europe.* Alternatively, *as well as* can stand on its own, without *both: And it's been very rewarding to see the response from all our partners in North America as well as in Europe.*

2 Redundant *both. Both,* as a conjunction, used together with *equally* is strictly speaking redundant, e.g. **both comparisons would be equally appropriate.* Although this type of construction is common in speaking, it should be avoided in more formal writing. A less common type of redundancy occurs when *bo*th follows the rather literary coordinating phrase *at one and the same time as,* e.g. **And as such it is a piece of theatre that is at one and the same time both profoundly disturbing and wonderfully enlightening—OEC,* 2004. Rewrite as: *And as such it is a piece of theatre that is at one and the same time profoundly disturbing and wonderfully enlightening* or *And as such it is a piece of theatre that is both profoundly disturbing and wonderfully enlightening.*

3 *Ambiguous constructions.* Because *both* is so flexible in use, its intended meaning can be unclear in some uses: (*a*) *We both won a prize* can mean either 'we won one prize between the two of us', or 'we won a prize each'. It is better to use *each* or to rephrase with a word such as *joint,* as appropriate: *We each won a prize/We won a joint prize.* (*b*) *You will see a tree at both ends of the road* is not so much ambiguous as counter-intuitive, since the tree can only be in one place. Rephrase as *You will see a tree [*or *trees] at each end of the road.*

4 Need for symmetry in *both ... and* phrases. A sentence of the kind *Her speech is detrimental both to understanding and peace* needs to be rephrased so that the two elements governed by *both* match each other: *Her speech is detrimental both to understanding and* to *peace,* where the word *to* has been inserted; or *Her speech is detrimental to both understanding and peace,* in which case *both* has moved to follow the preposition *to,* which governs both nouns. Acceptable constructions: *Being speechless is both a symptom and a cause of depression; its capacity to address both the internal and the international demands of the 1980s.*

5 *Used with more than two items.* If language behaved like a simple mathematical system, the illogicality of using *both* of more than two items would be immediately apparent. In practice, *both* is almost always used with two homogeneous words or phrases: *both the people and the land; both by day and by night; he both loves and hates his brother; both now and evermore* etc. From the 14c. onwards, however, it has also been used 'illogically' in conjunction with more than two objects: *both man and bird and beast* (Coleridge, 1798) and *both Chaucer and Shakespeare and Milton* (De Quincey, *c.*1839) form part of an array of examples presented in the *OED.* Nevertheless, unless you happen to be a writer who enjoys breaking the rules, it is best to use *both* to link only two words or phrases.

6 *on both of our behalfs.* Peter Carey's *Oscar and Lucinda* (1988) contains the sentence *I should not address you like this, even if I do hurt on your behalf, on both of our behalfs.* It just passes muster, but a prudent copy editor would have emended it to *on behalf of us both.* In general following *behalf* with an *of*-construction is less awkward and less likely to be ambiguous than one using a possessive pronoun.

7 *the both.* In spoken English, the use of *both* preceded by *the* is not uncommon: *Good morning from the both of us; I ordered a brandy for the both of us.* It is more frequently encountered in regional speech, as, for example, *the both of you* heard on *The Archers.* However, one's loyalty to the radio programme need not extend to aping its language: *the both* should not be used in formal prose.

8 *we both/both of us.* The various (subjective and objective) types that follow are all equally acceptable: (*a*) *you both look cross; we both felt happy; it suited them both;* (*b*) *there was not enough for both of them; everybody knows both of us; both of us had small flakes of snow clinging to us; we've both of us got standards.*

bottleneck. Since the late 19c., applied to 'a narrow or confined space where traffic may become congested', and then (first recorded in 1928) metaphorically, 'anything obstructing an even flow of production, etc., or impeding activity, etc.' (*OED*). Care should be taken to avoid unsuitable elaboration of the image, as in *breaking* or *ironing out a bottleneck,* and strictly speaking a *bottleneck* cannot be *big* or *extensive* or even *major* without producing a counter-intuitive effect: *A Parcel Force van ... had stopped to deliver to the shops, completely blocking the street, creating a huge bottleneck that no one could get out of*—news website, BrE 2005 [*OEC*].

bottom line. From its use in accountancy as 'the last line of a profit-and-loss account, showing the final profit (or loss)' (*OED*), this expression has come to be used, and then to be overworked, to mean 'the final analysis or determining factor; the point, the crux of the argument' (*OED*). These figurative uses are first recorded in the late 1960s, are now a bit of a cliché, and should be confined to informal speech or writing, e.g. *The bottom line is that we all love music and want to play it*—*New Musical Express,* 1992.

bounden is still used in *bounden duty* though not in *in duty bound.* For centuries it was the regular past participle of *bind.* It was also commonly used as an adjective

(= 'made fast in bonds'; also fig.), but only *bounden duty* survives.

bounteous. Like BEAUTEOUS and PLENTEOUS, a literary word. It means 'generously liberal, munificent' or '(of things), ample in size or amount, abundant'. The word is more likely to be encountered in the works of Johnson and Tennyson, for example, than in the work of any modern writer. But it is not extinct: *Old hounds patrolling the corridors, seeing that none of the condemned flee back to the air, the light, the bounteous world above*—J. M. Coetzee, 1990.

bourgeois. *When I was a boy—a* bourgeois *boy—it was applied to my social class by the class above it*; bourgeois *meant 'not aristocratic, therefore vulgar'. When I was in my twenties this changed. My class was now vilified by the class below it;* bourgeois *began to mean 'not proletarian, therefore parasitic,* reactionary'. (C. S. Lewis, *Studies in Words,* 2nd edn, 1967.) C. S. Lewis here neatly sums up the shift in meaning of this word caused by its appropriation by Marxists. In socialist political discourse, the word still has this meaning today. But in general use, it is a disparaging synonym for **middle-class**, as it has been since at least 1754, with connotations of philistinism, respectability and lack of imagination. *Bourgeois,* being originally French, has a feminine form, *bourgeoise,* as shown in the Aldous Huxley example that follows. That feminine form *bourgeoise* is rarely used as an adjective in the way exemplified, and is more often a noun, meaning 'a bourgeois woman' as in the second example. However, the *OEC* data suggests that often it is a misspelling of *bourgeois,* as in the final example. Examples: *How can you be so disgustingly bourgeoise, Pamela? So crass, so crawling?*—Aldous Huxley, 1939; *Marina Foïs is the lonely alcoholic bourgeoise in miniskirts*—*Montreal Mirror,* 2002; *Also bought a natty little pasta machine today hopelessly bourgeois! Fresh pasta here I come*—weblog, 2004 (BrE); **Nonetheless, Marx did indulge in the bourgeoise* (read *bourgeois*) *custom of hiring a household maid*—*OEC,* 2004 (AmE).

bourn(e). There are two distinct words, each of them spelt in the past and still sometimes today either with or without a final *-e.* One, meaning 'a small stream, a brook' (first recorded in the 14c.), survives in the south of England, used especially in the context of winter torrents of the chalk downs, and in the place-names *Bournemouth* and *Eastbourne*; it corresponds to the northern word *burn,* also = 'a small stream'. The other word (first recorded in the 16c.), which is a loanword from French, means 'the limit or terminus of a race, journey, or course; destination, goal'. In the well-known passage in Shakespeare's *Hamlet* (1602), *The dread of something after death, The vndiscouer'd country, from whose borne, No trauiler returnes,* the word probably means 'frontier, boundary'.

bowsprit. Pronounced /ˈbəʊsprɪt/.

bow window. See BAY WINDOW.

brace (noun). (= a pair). A collective noun having the same form in the singular (*a brace of pheasants*) and the plural (*two brace of pistols*). Plural uses are now rare.

brackets. Two marks of the form ( ), [ ], { }, < >, used to enclose an explanation, an aside, a pronunciation, an etymology, etc. ( ) are often called 'parentheses' or 'round brackets', [ ] 'square brackets', { } 'curly' or 'hooked brackets', and < > 'angle brackets'. In editing or describing documents it may be confusing if you use the general word when you mean a specific type of bracket. In particular, it is useful to remember that in American English *brackets* often means 'square brackets'.

Brahman Also formerly **Brahmin**. A member of the highest or priestly caste in the Hindu caste system. In American use, and occasionally elsewhere, *Brahmin* (with a letter *i,* and capital *B*) is often applied to 'a socially or culturally superior person, especially a member of the upper classes from New England' especially in the phrase *Boston Brahmins.*

brainstorm, brainstorming. An attendee on a course I was giving once rebuked me for using the word *brainstorming.* I should, so I was reprimanded, have used the phrase **thought shower**. This is an urban myth, much like the idea that Eskimos have dozens of words for 'snow'. The myth flourishes in the mistaken idea that *brainstorm(ing)* is offensive to people affected by epilepsy, but no organization in the field of epilepsy has a policy banning these words. You can therefore use them whenever you wish without the stigma of being thought politically incorrect, or having to use the preposterous *thought shower*.

brand-new. Correctly so spelt, with a hyphen, being (in the 16c.) formed from *brand* 'burning (wooden) torch' + *new* (i.e. fresh as from the furnace). Because the *-d-* is frequently not pronounced, the spelling *bran-new* was a common variant almost from the beginning, e.g. *Mr. and Mrs. Veneering were bran-new people in a bran-new house* (Dickens, 1865), but *brand-new* is the standard now.

bravado /brəˈvɑːdəʊ/ is an ostentatious display of courage or boldness, often concealing a felt timidity. **Bravery** is daring, valour, fortitude (as a good quality). **Bravura** /brəˈv(j)ʊərə/ is now virtually restricted to its musical sense, 'a passage or piece of music requiring great skill and spirit in its execution, written to tax the performer's powers' (*bravura songs, a bravura performance*).

brave. Apart from its ordinary sense ('courageous, daring'), the word has been used for some four centuries as a general epithet of admiration or praise (e.g. *O that's a braue man, hee writes braue verses, speakes braue words*—Shakespeare). Apparently this use began to fall out of currency towards the end of the 19c. (to judge from the *OED*), but it swept back into use in the 20c. (*a brave attempt, a brave step*, etc.), and, most notably, in Aldous Huxley's revival of Miranda's *O braue new world* (*Tempest*, v.i.183) in the title of his satirical novel *Brave New World* (1932).

bravo. It would be a brave person who would follow Fowler's advice (1926) to use *bravo* when applauding a male singer in an operatic performance, *brava* for a female singer, and *bravi* for the company. Gender and number distinctions have been abandoned in such circumstances, and *bravo* is the only cry of the three heard, if it is heard at all, in theatres now.

breach, breech. *Breach* is 'a breaking' (*in breach of his contract, breach of the peace, breach of promise* 'breaking of promise to marry', *step into the breach* 'give help in a crisis, etc.). *Breech* is principally, (*a*) in plural *breeches* 'short trousers', memorably in **Breeches Bible**, the Geneva Bible of 1560 with *breeches* for *aprons* in Gen. 3:7; and in **breeches-buoy**, a lifebuoy on a rope with canvas breeches for the user's legs; when used in the sense 'short trousers', normally pronounced /ˈbrɪtʃɪz/; (*b*) = buttocks, now used only with reference to a baby's position at or before birth (**breech birth**, with the baby's buttocks foremost); (*c*) the back part of a rifle or gun barrel (**breech-loading gun**, one loaded at the breech, not through the muzzle).

The two words are occasionally confused: e.g. *Following the picket line injunction, volunteers with trade union principles came forward to fill the breech*—*OEC*, 2000.

breakdown. Beside its primary meaning, 'a collapse, a failure of mechanical action or of health or of mental power', *breakdown* has been used since the 1930s to mean 'an analysis or classification (of figures, statistics, etc.). It is obviously important not to use this transferred sense in contexts in which it might have a tinge of ambiguity: e.g. *a breakdown* (better *an analysis*) *of engine failures in long-haul aircraft has not revealed any one main cause; a complete breakdown of our exports to dollar countries is not available at present.*

breakthrough. First used in the First World War to mean 'an advance of troops penetrating a defensive line', *breakthrough* has come to be used (since about the middle of the 20c.) of any significant advance in knowledge, achievement, etc. For a time it was an immensely popular vogue word, but it seems now to have joined the ranks of ordinary foot-soldier words, both in its literal and in its transferred senses. In fact, overuse has turned it into something of a cliché, such that it is routinely applied to advances which are not particularly significant. Reinforcements in the way of adjectives such as *major, big, real, significant, important, dramatic*, and *historic*, are often needed to bolster its flagging morale. It is often used attributively, as in *breakthrough technologies, products, drugs*, etc., i.e. technologies, products, etc. which are considered to constitute a breakthrough; and in *breakthrough record, film, role*, etc., i.e. records, films, etc. which are a turning point in an artist's career.

breech. See BREACH, BREECH.

brethren. This ancient plural of the word **brother** (first recorded *c*.1175) survives only in restricted use. It means 'fellow-members of a Christian society' (*dearly beloved brethren*); in particular the **Plymouth Brethren**

(who call themselves 'the Brethren'), a religious body recognizing no official order of ministers, and having no formal creed, which arose at Plymouth *c.*1830. A member of this body is called a **Plymouth brother**, and occasionally also a *Brethren* (*Uncle Bill was coming to the meeting as well, even though he wasn't a Brethren*—N. Virtue, 1988).

briar, brier. There are two distinct words, the first 'the white heath, *Erica arborea,* of southern Europe or a tobacco pipe made from its root', and the other (from Old English *brǣr*) meaning 'a prickly bush, especially of the wild rose'. The heath word is a 19c. loanword from French *bruyère.* There is widespread inconsistency in the spelling of both words, but the recommended spelling for each is *briar.*

bridegroom. The quirks of etymology are seen in the emergence of this word in the 16c. The Old English word was *brȳdguma* = *brȳd* 'bride' + *guma* 'man'. Had Middle English and Early Modern English *grome,* 'lad, groom' (itself of unknown etymology) not been substituted for the second element, the word would have come down to us as *bridegoom.*

brier. See BRIAR, BRIER.

brilliance, brilliancy. Like many other pairs having alternative endings, one tends to dominate, and it is *brilliance. Brilliancy* is not very frequent at all, and when used often has the literal meaning of 'intense brightness of light' or 'vividness of colour' rather than 'exceptional talent or intelligence'. It is also applied to a particularly spectacular game of chess. Examples: *These windows have a brilliancy and glow like no other process I've ever seen, short of traditional stained glass—Arts and Activities,* 2000; *On the 2nd Venus reaches its greatest brilliancy for this apparition: magnitude 4.5—Natural History,* 2005; *Artistic brilliancy is often delayed until later years because of traditional family businesses, or choices made in vocations which do not give satisfaction—Pattaya Mail,* 2001.

bring. 1 Partially distinguished from *take* according to movement towards the speaker (*bring*), or away from or accompanying the speaker (*take*): *take your raincoat with you and bring me a newspaper from the corner shop.* There are many circumstances, however, in which this simple distinction does not apply. When the standpoint of the speaker is unstable, there is a choice: *Shall I bring the camera?* is spoken in terms of the destination and *Shall I take the camera?* in terms of the starting point. In other varieties of English, and in some dialects, the pattern differs.

2 In regional speech in many areas in Britain and the US, the verb is conjugated *bring/brang/brung* (like *sing/sang/sung*) or even *bring/brung/brung,* but *brought* remains rock-solid for the past tense and past participle in standard English.

brinkmanship. Though viewed by Gowers (1965) somewhat stuffily as an undesirable neologism, this word, sadly enough, continues to be useful to journalists and politicians whenever two countries, groups, etc., come to the brink of war but do not engage in it. One of the products of nuclear confrontation between the Western powers and the USSR bloc in the 1950s, the word is attributed to the American politician Adlai Stevenson, who used it of the foreign policy of John Foster Dulles in 1956. *Brinkmanship* is also used in an extended sense to signify extreme risk taking in other spheres, as in *diplomatic/industrial/emotional brinkmanship.* For the formation, cf. *seamanship, statesmanship,* etc.

Brit, Brit-. A colloquial shortening of **Briton** or **Britisher**, first recorded in 1901, but not really in general use until the second half of the 20c., and sometimes employed with a suggestion of teasing or, occasionally, of hostility. In Australia and New Zealand, *Brit* is now challenging **Pom** as an everyday word for a British person, and has similar connotations. Elsewhere usage varies: the word sometimes has an edge to it, but it is also favoured simply as being shorter than *Briton* and *Britisher.* Nearly half of the examples of the word in the *OEC* are from British sources, but the word is used throughout the Anglosphere. Examples: *The average Brit spends 145 hours a year watching TV shows they're not interested in—OEC,* 2005 (BrE); *The military officers include Pakistanis, Bangladeshis, a Nigerian and a Brit—OEC,* 2004 (AmE); *Brit actor Gil Kolirin—OEC,* 2008 (Aust.). The **Britpop** and **Britart** movements of the 1990s, and the existence of the **Brit Awards**, may have helped make the word more current in general use. *Brit-*

as a prefix is liberally attached to a range of nouns, to denote 'music, art, design, etc., created by (young) British people and perceived as fashionable, innovative, or influential, especially on account of international attention or success' (*OED*), e.g. *Britrock, Britlit, Britfash, Britfilm.*

Britain, British, Briton. See ENGLAND, ENGLISH.

Briticism. This word for 'a phrase or idiom characteristic of Great Britain, but not used in the English of the United States or other countries' (*OED*) seems to have been modelled on *Gallicism, Scotticism,* etc. Some writers, including H. W. Fowler, favoured *Britishism,* but in scholarly work *Briticism* (or, more usually, *BrE, British English*) is now the more usual term of the two.

Britisher. A US word (first recorded in 1829) for a British subject. The *OEC* data suggests that it is not very much used. People in Britain might register surprise, or even be slightly affronted, if the word were used, since the regular word used in Britain for 'a native or inhabitant of Great Britain' is **Briton**, or to be slightly less formal, **Brit**.

Britishism. See BRITICISM.

Brito-. See ANGLO-.

broadcast (verb). For a short time in the 1920s it was not clear whether the past forms of the verb *broadcast* (in its airwaves sense) were to be *broadcasted* or *broadcast.* Learned arguments were displayed in a tract of the Society for Pure English (1924) and elsewhere, bearing on the interpretation of *broadcast* as a compound of *cast,* and comparing and contrasting the past forms of e.g. *forecast* and *roughcast.* In the event, the shorter form *broadcast* has prevailed, and is five times more frequent in *OEC* data than *broadcasted.* Many will consider the latter wrong, but it is recognized as valid in some BrE and AmE dictionaries, and there are sound linguistic reasons for its existence, discussed at PODCAST.

broccoli, now the only spelling (formerly also *brocoli*), is an Italian plural noun (singular *broccolo*), but is treated in English as a singular mass noun, like *spinach, spaghetti,* etc. (*Let it simmer until the broccoli is soft*).

brochure, pamphlet. Pronounced *brochure* /ˈbrəʊʃə/ (**broh**-shuh) or /brɒˈʃʊə/ (bro-**shoo**-uh), but in American English with the stress on the second syllable only. *Brochure,* first recorded in English in 1765, means literally 'a stitched work' (cf. French *brocher* 'to stitch'). In the sense 'a short printed work, i.e. a few leaves merely stitched together', it was once more or less synonymous with the much older word *pamphlet.* From about the 1920s, however, *brochure* has tended to be restricted to mean a small, often glossy, pamphlet or booklet containing pictures and information about a product or service, whereas a *pamphlet* continues to refer to a small unbound printed booklet, normally meant to be informative rather than promotional

broke(n). The regular past participle and adjective are, 'as any fule kno', *broken* (*the window had been broken during the night; a broken heart*). However, the archaic past participle *broke* lingers on as the (predicative) adjective *broke,* 'ruined, without money', and in the rather dated British *stony-broke.* The informal phrase *to go for broke,* meaning 'to make strenuous efforts, to go "all out"' (*I decided to go for broke and turn professional and see how I got on*), though originally from the US, is now also commonly used in the UK. The informal *if it ain't broke, don't fix it,* meaning if something is reasonably successful or effective, there is no need to change or replace it, also originated in the US, but now has global reach. While its homespun syntax may give it the appearance of being an ancient adage, the *OED* records its first appearance from as recently as 1977.

brow. See MISQUOTATIONS.

brunch. This PORTMANTEAU WORD formed from *br*(*eakfast* + *l*)*unch* made its way from British university slang into more general language throughout the 20c. First recorded in *Punch* in 1896, for half a century or so it used to be frequently written within inverted commas, but they became unnecessary some time ago.

brunet(te). In Britain, *brunette* as adjective and noun applies to females. In the US, the French masculine form *brunet* is occasionally applied without distinction to both men and women, but there too the word is most commonly applied to a girl or a woman. Examples: (brunette) *A pregnant brunette walks in off the street wearing black shorts*—T. Wolfe, 1965; (brunet) *tucked her blond locks under a series of brunet wigs*—G. D. Garcia, 1985.

bruschetta. In our new, foodie culture, *bruschetta* is one of the supposedly sophisticated breads supplanting more prosaic, homegrown fare. First recorded in print (in English) in 1954, by the pioneering food writer Elizabeth David, this 'Italian appetizer or side dish consisting of toasted bread spread with olive oil, usually seasoned and rubbed with garlic' (*OED*) is in origin a peasanty dish. If you are foolhardy enough to try saying the word *all'italiana,* pronounce it broo-**ske**-tuh, with a short pause before the *t* sound. However, since most people pronounce it broo-**she**-tuh, this pronunciation seems likely to predominate, and is already recognized as an alternative in most dictionaries. Remember, though, to spell the word with *-sch-* not *-sh-*.

brusque. English first borrowed this word from French—which had already borrowed it from Italian—in the 17c. By the 18c. it was so well established that the spelling was sometimes anglicized to **brusk**, which occasionally occurs nowadays, and which, although 'logical', has to be considered non-standard. Pronunciation depends on personal taste: the options are /brʌsk/, rhyming with *tusk,* also the recommended US pronunciation; /bruːsk/, rhyming with *roost,* and closest to the original French; or /brʊsk/, rhyming with *foot.*

Brythonic. See GAELIC.

buck, doe, hart, hind, roe, stag. The *OED* definitions make the distinctions sufficiently clear:

buck, the he-goat, *obsolete* . . . The male of the fallow-deer. (In early use perhaps the male of any kind of deer.) . . . The male of certain other animals resembling deer or goats, as the reindeer, chamois. In S. Africa (after Dutch *bok*) any animal of the antelope kind. Also, the male of the hare and the rabbit.

doe, the female of the fallow deer; applied also to the female of allied animals, as the reindeer . . . The female of the hare or rabbit.

hart, the male of the deer, especially of the red deer; a stag; specifically a male deer after its fifth year.

hind, the female of the deer, especially of the red deer; specifically a female deer in and after its third year.

roe, a small species of deer inhabiting various parts of Europe and Asia; a deer belonging to this species.

stag, the male of a deer, especially of the red deer; specifically a hart or male deer of the fifth year.

buffalo. Plural *-oes.* See -O(E)S 1.

buffet. Referring to refreshments, the word can be pronounced in British English as /ˈbʊfeɪ/, (**boo**-fay) or the more anglicized /ˈbʌfeɪ/ (**bu**-fay). When the meaning is 'a cupboard in a recess for china and glasses', the word is pronounced /ˈbʌfɪt/, rhyming with *muppet.* In American English, /bəˈfeɪ/, i.e. with the main stress on the second syllable, seems to be the standard pronunciation for all meanings.

bugger. The word is used as noun and verb with varying degrees of coarseness or vulgarity. In BrE, and many other varieties, but rather less so in American English, it can also be used quite light-heartedly. Senses: (noun) **1** A sodomite. **2** Something or someone unpleasant or undesirable (*Heard one old lady say, 'It's a bugger this dark!'* [i.e. the blackout]—Harrisson and Madge, 1940; *cheeky little bugger;* (said with a sympathetic voice) *poor buggers!; let's not play silly buggers* [= act foolishly]). **3** *bugger-all* 'nothing' (*I used to go and get her pension and do her shopping for her and I can tell you there was bugger-all left by the end of the* week—P. Barker, 1986). **4** A damn (*I don't give a bugger whether you won't or will*—Dylan Thomas, 1939). (Senses 3 and 4 uncommon in American English.)

(verb) **1** To commit buggery with. **2** Used as a swear word (*Bugger!; Bugger me!; Buggered if I know!; Well, I'll be buggered!*). **3** (in passive) To be tired out (*he was completely buggered after two nights without sleep*). **4** (with *up*) To ruin, spoil (*The rain buggered up the weekend for us*); **5** (with *off*) To go away (*he buggered off home after the lecture; bugger off!*). **6** (with *about, around*) To mess about (*it's not wise to bugger about with electricity*). (Senses 3, 4, 5, and 6 uncommon in AmE.)

There are still many circumstances, of course, in which such uses should be ruled out altogether, but the word is more acceptable as a swear word than it used to be, at least in BrE. Most of the uses listed above can be heard on radio and television, although they remain highly informal and should not normally be used outside the domain of casual conversation. The word remains somewhat more offensive in AmE.

bulk has a core meaning of 'the mass or size of something large' (*residents jump up and down on their rubbish to reduce its bulk*). As such it is often used with singular nouns (the *bulk* of paper or of a book or of a tree, etc., is its size). Some people object to the use of *bulk* followed by *of* + an ordinary noun in the plural to mean 'most': *the bulk of policemen, the bulk of brewers*, etc., but this usage has a long pedigree, including Addison and Hume, and is well established and generally uncontentious in modern English.

bullet points. People are often unsure how to write and punctuate bullet points. As bullet points are relatively recent, it is hardly surprising that there are no hard-and-fast rules. Also, much depends on:

- the writer's visual sensibility;
- the medium in which bullet points are being used (e.g. White Paper vs Powerpoint); and
- the intended audience (e.g. designers vs lexicographers).

The following advice is merely a rule of thumb.

1 For bullet points that are not complete sentences, you:

- need not begin with a capital letter
- can leave out any punctuation at the end of each bullet

But if you prefer to have punctuation:

- you can finish each bullet with a semi-colon;
- you can add 'and', if you wish, after the last-but-one bullet, as in this list; and
- you can put a full stop after your last bullet point.

It is important to make sure that the structure of your points is parallel, as in the previous two lists. The second one would not be parallel if it were

- finish each bullet with a semi-colon;
- you can add 'and', if you wish, after the last-but-one bullet, as in this list; and
- put a full stop after your last bullet point.

because the first and last points would be commands, while the middle one would not.

2 When your bullet points are complete sentences:

- It is generally advisable to finish each one with a full stop.
- You can leave full stops out if you want your text to have a very clean, uncluttered look.
- Even then, it is advisable to put a full stop after the last one.

You should bear in mind that in on-screen presentations with few complete sentences, punctuation at the end of bullet points may clutter the look. In other written material you should consider the overall look of the document, the number of bullet points, and their length. If you find your bullet points are getting rather long, you should assess them to see if they are actually making more than one point.

Finally, whichever style you choose, aim to be consistent.

bunch. As a collective noun, it has been used since the 16c. to signify a quantity, a collection, or a cluster of things (a *bunch of flowers, grapes, keys*, etc.). It is also commonly used to mean 'a company or group of people' (*the best of a bad bunch, the pick of the bunch*). The sporadic use of the type '*a bunch of* + persons' in earlier centuries (e.g. *a bunch of cherubs*) does not support the view that this construction has unlimited currency, at least in Britain. The type *a bunch of spectators ran on to the pitch* verges on slang; whereas if the plural noun is qualified by an adjective or other qualifier that indicates a feature or features held in common by them (*a bunch of corrupt politicians held the reins of power* [i.e. they had corruption in common]; *a bunch of weary runners crossed the line together an hour after the other competitors had finished* [i.e. they had weariness in common]), the informality is much less evident.

bunkum. This word meaning 'empty talk, nonsense' is one of the best-known American words to have spread to all English-speaking countries. Its origin is less well known. It is a respelling of *Buncombe,* the name of a county in N. Carolina. The phrase arose in America in the 1820s when the member of congress for that county needlessly delayed a vote near the close of a debate on the 'Missouri question'. Though begged to stop, he carried on, insisting that he was bound *to make a speech* *for Buncombe* in order to impress his constituents.

bureau. The plural *bureaux*, pronounced /ˈbjʊərəʊz/, is more frequent in BrE, but practically unknown in N. Amer. English, in which *bureaus* is preferred. See -X.

burger. A familiar shortening of *hamburger* and a fertile source of derived words and compounds. There are *burger bars, burger parlours*, etc., throughout the English-speaking world. As a terminal element, *-burger* (first recorded as such in 1939) has generated *beefburger, cheeseburger, veggieburger, lamburger, nutburger, porkburger*, and *steakburger*, among others.

burgle, burglarize. The first of these is a back-formation (first recorded in 1870) from *burglary*. It was at first thought to be facetious but is now the regular word in Britain (and in other English-speaking areas except N. America). AmE, from about the same date, seems to have mostly preferred *burglarize* (*He had a history of burglarizing homes—OEC*, 2003).

Burma. The military authorities in *Burma* have promoted the name **Myanmar** as the official name for their state since 1989; *Burma* is often preferred by people who oppose the current government and support the re-establishment of democracy.

burnt, burned. *Burnt* is the usual form in the past participle (*a thatched cottage was burnt down last week*) and as adjective (*burnt almond, a burnt offering*). In the past tense, *burned* is the more usual form (*she burned her hands while preparing the barbecue*), but *burnt* is also permissible in all English-speaking areas. Some writers detect a preference for one form or the other as between transitive and intransitive uses, but the evidence for such a distinction is unconvincing. However spelt, the word is normally pronounced /bɜːnt/, but *burned* as past tense and participial adjective may also be pronounced /bɜːnd/. See also -T AND -ED.

bus. The form *'bus* (with apostrophe) is now extinct. Inflected forms are: plural *buses*; as vb, present *buses*, past *bused*, present participle *busing*. See -S-, -SS-.

business. The regular word *business*, pronounced /ˈbɪznɪs/ with just two syllables, in its various senses stands apart from **busyness**, pronounced /ˈbɪzɪnɪs/, the ordinary abstract noun corresponding to *busy* (the state, etc., of being busy).

bust (participial adjective) the phrase *to go bust* 'to become insolvent', though widely used, is still slightly informal in tone, and in any formal writing should be replaced by *to go bankrupt*. On an historical note, its use is first recorded in a letter written by Rupert Brooke in 1913: The Blue Review *has gone bust, through lack of support.*

but.

1 Normal uses as a contrastive conjunction and preposition
2 Used at the beginning of a sentence.
3 Case after *but* = except.
4 *but that, but what.*
5 Two successive *but*-constructions.
6 *But . . . however.*
7 *cannot but* + bare infinitive.
8 *Always—but always.*
9 Miscellaneous uses.

1 *Normal uses as a contrastive conjunction and preposition. But* is a contrastive conjunction, so the words, phrases, or sentences linked by it must always display a clear contrast. Normal uses: *naughty but nice; nature is cruel but tidy; it was cool outside but even cooler inside; the answer is not to remove the parish system but to put more resources into it; he had many gifts and interests, but perhaps music was the greatest.*

But frequently means 'except (for)' when used as a preposition and 'except (that)' when used as a conjunction: (preposition) *the aftermath of the last economic crisis but one; everyone was pleased but John; There was little to be seen but a forest of brick chimneys.* (conjunction) *Claudia's eyes are closed but once or twice her lips twitch; I was willing enough, but I was ill-equipped; What else can we do but talk as if it were true?*

The contrast must never be neutralized by the placing of an additional circumstance in one of the contrasted elements. Fowler (1926) cites numerous examples of such partially cancelled contrasts, e.g. *In vain the horse kicked and reared, but he could not unseat his rider.* The objection to this sentence is as follows: if the horse kicked in vain, its failure to unseat the rider involves no contrast; either *in vain* or *but* must be dropped.

2 *Used at the beginning of a sentence.* The widespread public belief that *But* should not be used at the beginning of a sentence seems to be unshakeable. Yet it has absolutely no foundation in grammar or idiomatic usages, and examples are frequent in good literature, as shown in the examples lower down.

In certain kinds of compound sentences, *but* is used to introduce a balancing statement 'of the nature of an exception, objection, limitation, or contrast to what has gone before; sometimes, in its weakest form, merely expressing disconnection, or emphasizing the introduction of a distinct or independent fact' (*OED*). In such circumstances, *but* is most commonly placed after a semi-colon, but it can legitimately be placed at the beginning of a following sentence, and frequently is. Examples: *And went againe into the iudgement hall, & saith to Iesus, Whence art thou? But Iesus gaue him no answere.*—John (AV) 19: 9; *All Animals have Sense. But a Dog is an Animal.*—Locke, 1690; *Fare ye well. But list! sweet youths, where'er you go, beware.*—J. Wilson, 1816; *Of course they loved her, the two remaining ones, they hugged her, they had mingled their tears. But they could not converse with her.*—I. Murdoch, 1993.

Starting a sentence with *but*, as with *and*, is a matter not of grammar but of style. It is important to stress, however, that unless contextual dislocation is being deliberately sought as a rhetorical device, it is not desirable to litter the pages with constructions like *He is tired. But he is happy.*

3 Case after *but* = except. Because of the historical levelling of inflexions of nouns, the problem arises only with pronouns that show case: *Everyone but she can see the answer* vs. *Everyone but her can see the answer.* The best course would appear to be to use the subjective case when the *but*-construction lies within the subject area of a clause or sentence (*No one but she would dream of doing that*), and to use the objective case when the *but*-construction falls within the object area of a clause or sentence (*No one else may use my typewriter but her*). The formula is not watertight, however. For example, when a subject containing *but* is delayed, but is merely an emphatic repetition of the main subject, the case remains the same: *But no one understood it, no one but I*—J. M. Coetzee, 1977. When the clause contains the verb *to be,* it is nevertheless usual for a late-placed *but* to be followed by the objective case: *No one is fool enough to work the straights but me*—J. Fuller, 1983. After interrogatives the objective case is the more usual: *Who can have done that but him?*

Fowler's description of the problem is worth repeating: 'The question is whether *but* in this sense is a preposition, and should therefore always take an objective case (*No-one saw him but me,* as well as *I saw no-one but him*), or whether it is a conjunction, and the case after it is therefore variable (*I saw no-one but him,* i.e. but I did see *him; No-one saw him but I,* i.e. but *I* did see him).' He concluded that when the *but*-construction falls within the object area the objective case has prevailed (*No-one knows it but me*).

4 *but that* has many undisputed formal or literary (though somewhat fading) uses: e.g. (*a*) to introduce a consideration or reason to the contrary, = 'except for the fact that, were it not that' (formerly *that* was occasionally omitted): *And but she spoke it dying, I would not Beleeue her* lips—Shakespeare, 1611; *I too should be content to dwell in peace ... But that my country calls*—Southey, 1795; *He would not have set out for France by road but that he knew all flights had been cancelled*; (formulaic use without *that*) *it never rains but it pours.* (*b*) after *doubt*: *I do not doubt but that you are surprised*—Ruskin, 1870. (*c*) after *tell*: *How could he tell but that Mildred might do the same?—Blackwood's Mag.*, 1847.

The danger in *negative* and *interrogative* constructions of this kind is that a redundant *not* can inadvertently (and wrongly) be placed in the dependent clause: **I do not doubt but that you are not surprised; *Who knows but that the whole course of history might* not *have been changed?* It is usually better to rephrase: *Who knows: the whole course of history might have been different?*

In the past, *but what* was sometimes used in similar constructions, but these uses are now mainly found in informal or non-standard types of English: *Nor am I yet so old but what I can rough it still*—Trollope, 1862; *It's no telling but what I might have gone on to school like my own children have*—Lee Smith, 1983 (US); *I never bake a pan of brownies ... but what I think of him*—ibid.

5 Two successive *but*-constructions. It is more or less self-evident that it is not desirable to add a *but*-construction to an unrelated *but*-construction in the same sentence. An example (from Fowler, 1926) of the rejected construction: *I gazed upon him for some time, expecting that he might awake; but he did not, but kept on snoring.*

6 *But ... however.* It is advisable to avoid using *but* with a further contrasting word, such as *however, nevertheless, still,* and *yet*: (*But*) *one thing, however, had not changed, and that was ...* ; (*but*) *nevertheless they went on arguing.* Note, however, that *but still* is a standard idiom, especially informally: *It's late but still you did want me to stay.*

7 *cannot but* + bare infinitive. This construction has been in standard use since the 16c., but is now somewhat formal in feel. Examples: *The frailty of man without thee cannot but fall—Bk of Common Prayer,* 1549; *I cannot but be gratified by the assurance*—Jefferson, 1812. The use with *help* inserted between *cannot* and *but* is nowadays much more often used than the shorter construction, e.g. *she could not help but follow him into the big department store*—B. Rubens, 1987; *yet he could not help but admire Miss Leplastrier for the way she looked after the details*—P. Carey, 1988. The construction with *help* has not been found in print before the late 19c.: *She could not help but plague the lad*—H. Caine, 1894. See also HELP, 3.

8 *Always—but always. But* is often used after a pause to introduce a word that is being repeated for emphasis: e.g. *Nothing, but nothing, seems to work—OEC,* 2002; *My dad was an old Southern gentleman and he always—but always—wore a hat—OEC,* 2001.

9 *Miscellaneous uses.* (*a*) *but* at end of sentence. One of the most surprising and largely uncharted modern uses of *but* is as a qualifying adverb at the end of sentences. Taking a lead from the Scots and the Irish, not-quite-standard speakers in Australia, in some parts of South Africa, and perhaps elsewhere provide evidence of this construction which has not yet entered the standard English of England: e.g. *'He should have left the key with me,' she said. 'I'm his wife.' 'I didn't ask for it, but.'*—M. Richler, 1980 (Canad.); *'I been waiting round for years and years and I still don't know what it is, but.'*—M. Eldridge, 1984 (Aust.); *'That was a lovely cat, but'* [= that was a truly lovely cat]—R. Mesthrie, 1987 (SAfr.); *'She's lovely.' 'Isn't she but,' said Jimmy Sr.*—R. Doyle, 1991 (Ir.). (*b*) *not but eight* = only, merely eight. See NOT 9. (*c*) *all but* (adverbially) = everything short of, almost. Examples: *Man ... All but resembleth God ... All but the picture of his maiestie*—J. Bastard, 1598; *These were all but unknown to Greeks and Romans*—A. P. Stanley, 1862; *Edwin had persuaded his father to all but cut out his oldest son*—S. Chitty, 1981; *by the end of the war this attitude had all but disappeared*—P. Wright, 1987. (*d*) Used after an exclamation (*Ah, but, My, but,* etc.) to express some degree of opposition, surprise, etc. (a use first recorded in 1846): *Ah, but who built it, that we tiny creatures can walk in its arcades?*—M. Drabble, 1987; *My, but he was obliging—New Yorker,* 1987.

buy. 1 As noun, in such uses as *the best buy,* the word has been current since the third quarter of the 19c. Its currency was greatly assisted by the appearance in the second half of the 20c. of numerous consumer journals like *Which?*

2 As verb, the originally American sense 'to believe', first noted in 1926, is now well established in everyday speech (*He says he's heard it all before, and he doesn't buy it*) but is best avoided in more formal writing. See also VERBS IN -IE, -Y, AND -YE.

buy-in. Meaning 'agreement with, or acceptance of, a policy or suggestion' is another word so often bandied about in the business world that it has ended up nauseating even some of that world's less verbally challenged inhabitants. As a result, *Forbes* magazine included it in its 2012 list of the 32 most annoying items of business jargon. It sounds like a nice, dynamic word for obtaining support for an idea from people not involved in the discussion which generated that idea; sceptics would say that what it actually means is 'we've agreed on this; now you must do it.' As David Logan, a US professor of management and organization said: 'Asking for someone's "buy-in" says, "I have an idea. I didn't involve you because I didn't value you enough to discuss it with you. I want you to embrace it as if you were in on it from the beginning, because that would make me feel really good".'

buzz. See -Z-, -ZZ-.

by (preposition). Owing to its many different meanings, *by* can occasionally acquire an unwanted ambiguity in certain contexts. The absurdity and ambiguity of *he was knocked down by the town hall*, or of *In Poets' Corner where he* [*sc.* Dryden] *has been buried by Chaucer and Cowley* (G. E. B. Saintsbury, 1881) can be lessened in speech by a change of intonation, but in writing are better avoided altogether by choosing a different preposition, or by some other means, such as replacing *by* with *close to* or *in front of*. Fowler (1926) warned against the accidental, slovenly use of too many *bys* with different meanings in the same sentence, as in (a modern example): *Send stories* by *reporters* by *fax* by *the end of Friday*. Such sequences are more likely to occur in hurried forms of spoken English, or in writing which there has been no time to edit properly.

by and large. This adverbial phrase is first found in the 17c. in nautical (sailing ship) language meaning (to sail) 'to the wind (within six points) and off it' (*OED*). It very rapidly—the new use first recorded in 1706—slipped into general use in its current metaphorical sense, 'without entering into details, on the whole'.

by, by-, bye. Nearly all the words in this group are derived from *by* preposition or adverb, the main exception being *by-law* (a variant of the obsolete *byrlaw*, of Scandinavian origin, = local custom). Over the centuries, the main body of *by-* words has settled down into three groups: **1** *by and by* 'soon'; *by the by* 'by the way, incidentally'. (In *by the by*, the second *by* is a variant of *bye*, and spelling the phrase *by the bye* is accepted as a variant in *ODO* but not in the *OED*).

2 *bye* (in cricket and other games); *bye-bye* (familiar form of 'goodbye'); *bye-byes* (sleep).

3 *by-* as a prefix, meaning 'secondary, subordinate'. Hyphenation practice varies: *byline* (a line in a newspaper column giving the writer's name) tends to be written as one word, whereas *by-law*, and longer forms such as *by-election* and *by-product*, are hyphenated. The following list suggests recommended spellings: (with hyphen) *by-blow, by-election, by-form, by-lane, by-law, by-line, by-product, by-street*; (one word) *bygone, byline, byname* (a sobriquet), *bypass, bypath, byplay, byroad, bystander, byway, byword*. The *OED* gives the spelling *bye-law* as an acceptable variant, but not *bye-election*, which is best avoided.

by far and away. See FAR 6.

Byzantine. 1 Spelt with an initial capital when used of the architecture, art, politics, etc., of ancient Byzantium; but usually with a small initial when it means 'intricate, complicated' (*byzantine rules, complexity, bureaucracy*).

2 There can be few words of such byzantine complexity in their pronunciation. The recommended ones, as most dictionaries seem to agree, stress the second syllable: /bɪˈzantʌɪn/ (bi-**zan**-tyn) and /bʌɪˈzantʌɪn/ (by-**zan**-tyn). The following are also current: /bʌɪˈzantiːn/ (by-**zan**-teen), and with first-syllable stress /ˈbɪzantʌɪn/ (**bi**-zan-tyn) and /ˈbɪzantiːn/ (**bi**-zan-teen). Whichever one you choose, no doubt someone will find fault.

cabbalist(ic), cabbala, etc. In these, and also in the other derivatives of *cabbala* (= Hebrew oral tradition), *-bb-*, which reflects a doubled consonant in Hebrew, is the better spelling in English (not *-b-*).

cacao (plural *-os*), pronounced /kəˈkɑːəʊ/ or /-ˈkeɪəʊ/, and in origin a Spanish word derived from Nahuatl *cacauatl*, is 'a seed pod from which cocoa and chocolate are made, or the tree from which such seed pods are obtained'. Cf. COCOA.

cache, cachet. People sometimes confuse these two words in speaking and writing, using *cachet* when *cache* is required. Despite having five letters in common, and coming ultimately from the same French verb (*cacher*, but in two different meanings), in English they are completely unrelated. A *cache* of something is a 'collection of items of the same type stored in a hidden or inaccessible place' such as an *arms cache* or a *cache of gold*, and rhymes with *cash*. *Cachet* is 'prestige, high status; the quality of being respected or admired' and is pronounced /ˈkaʃeɪ/ (**ka**-shay). Despite being lambasted by Fowler ('should be expelled [from the language] as an alien'), *cachet* has since his time become perfectly naturalized and lost most of its charming French accent. Examples (correct use): *Several inmates seized a cache of grenades and other weapons and killed six security officers, including a high-ranking counterterrorism official—OEC*, 2011; *The department stores knew they had to offer something different, something perceived to have more cachet—N.Y. Times*, 2004; (*cachet* wrongly used for *cache*) **Egyptian excavators this week chanced upon a cachet of limestone reliefs—OEC*, 2005.

cacoethes /kakəʊˈiːθiːz/, a Latin (ultimately Greek) word meaning 'an urge to do something undesirable', was frequently used in elevated English prose until about the end of the 19c., especially in the phrases *cacoethes scribendi* 'an unhealthy passion for writing' (based on Juvenal's *tenet insanabile multos scribendi cacoethes*) and *cacoethes loquendi* 'an itch for speaking'. Both phrases are still occasionally used, but much less commonly than before.

cactus. Plural in general use *cactuses*, in botany *cacti* /ˈkaktʌɪ/, but the distinction is far from watertight.

caddie, caddy. The golf-attendant has *-ie*; so too the corresponding verb. The small container for holding tea has *-y*. *Caddie* was originally Scottish (from French *cadet*); *caddy* is from Malay *kātī*.

cadi /ˈkɑːdɪ/, a judge in a Muslim country. Plural *cadis*. The spelling with initial *c-* (not *k-*) is recommended.

cadre, used in the armed forces to mean 'a nucleus or small group (of servicemen) formed to be ready for expansion when necessary', is pronounced as /ˈkɑːdə/ or, in imitation of French, /ˈkɑːdrə/. When used to mean 'a group of activists in a communist or revolutionary party, or a member of such a group', it seems to be most commonly pronounced /ˈkeɪdə/.

caecum, Caesar, caesura, etc. Now always printed with *-ae-* as two separate letters, not ligatured. See Æ, Œ. Some of these words are regularly spelt with medial *-e-* in American English (e.g. *cecum, Cesarian, cesium*).

Caesarean, Caesarian. The dominant spelling is with *-ean*, especially in the medical term *Caesarean section* (US *Ces-*). The word is often written with a small initial *c*.

caesura. 1 In Greek and Latin prosody, the division of a metrical foot between two words, especially in certain recognized places near the middle of the line.

2 An obligatory feature of Old English verse like *Beowulf*: the caesura is indicated by a space in printed versions of the poems:

e.g. *under heofones hwealf healsittendra.* In later English verse, chiefly noticeable in long metres such as that of Tennyson's *Locksley Hall*: *Till the war-drum throbb'd no longer, // and the battle-flags were furl'd.* In post-medieval English verse, 'the term does not refer to anything in the *structure* of most English verse, ... and there is no reason to prefer it to "pause" or "syntactic break" in describing a line' (D. Attridge, 1982).

café is such a familiar word that it can be spelt without an accent, though spelling it with one is, of course, also correct. There are two ways of pronouncing it. Americans generally stress the second syllable /ka'feɪ/ (ka-**fay**) and British English speakers the first (**ka**-fay). British English speakers who stress the second syllable may run the risk of sounding bizarre or affected. Humorously, in British English it used to be, and still occasionally is, pronounced /keɪf/ (kayf). Informally, it can be written as *caff* and pronounced /kaf/. In American English the word also means a bar or nightclub. In recent years the word has started a new life in communications technology, in terms such as *Internet cafe* and *cybercafe.*

caffeine. Now always pronounced /'kafiːn/, but formerly (e.g. in Daniel Jones's *English Pronouncing Dictionary,* 1917) as three syllables, /'ka-fɪ-iːn/.

cagey, 'cautious and uncommunicative', was first recorded in America as recently as 1909, was not common in the UK until the mid-century, and is of unknown etymology. Sometimes spelt *cagy.*

calcareous, calcarious. The 'incorrect' form with final *-eous* is now standard. First recorded about 1790, the spelling with *-eous* was influenced by words in *-eous* from Latin *-eus.* The etymological sense of *calcareous* would be 'of the nature of a spur', whereas the word actually means 'of the nature or, or composed of, lime (-stone)', from Latin *calx, calcis* lime + *-arius.*

calculate. 1 *Calculate* makes *calculable*; *see* -ABLE, IBLE 6.

2 The meaning 'to suppose, reckon' is American in origin (first recorded in 1805) but has not at any stage become standard in American English, let alone elsewhere, and is generally annotated in modern dictionaries as American dialect: 'This use of the word ... is not sanctioned by English usage' (Webster, 1847); 'Formerly chiefly New England, now more widespread, somewhat old-fashioned' (*DARE,* 1985). The illustrative examples cited in the large American dictionaries are nearly all taken from regional sources, e.g. *Transactions of the Michigan Agricultural Society,* 1857, and *Report of the Maine Board of Agriculture,* 1882. A typical sentence: *I calculate it's pretty difficult to git edication down at Charleston*—C. Gilman, 1836. Nevertheless, it is used quite widely with a following clause, as in *Many executives ... calculate that their best interests lie in not conforming to factory regulations*—S. Box, 1992; *Hawk-eye, no white fool, calculated that the best thing was to collaborate with the French to minimize the bloodshed—OEC,* 2000 (BrE); *Sometimes they would calculate that they could penetrate these markets by collaborating on production in such countries as Japan, where manufacturing costs were also lower—OEC,* 2002 (AmE); *They calculated that Nehru's daughter could secure more votes than any of them at the coming elections—OEC,* 2003 (Indian). In all of these examples *calculate* can be seen to mean more than simply 'suppose or reckon'; instead, it suggests a very rational, 'calculated' decision, based on an appraisal of a situation, even though not on an arithmetical calculation.

calculus. The medical word ('a stone or concretion formed within the body') usually has plural *-li* /-lʌɪ/; the mathematical, usually *-luses.*

caldron. See CAULDRON.

calendar, an almanac, not *k-.*

calends, the first of the month in the ancient Roman calendar, not *k-.*

calf. For plural, etc., see -VE(D), -VES.

calibre (US *caliber*) is now always pronounced /'kalɪbə/; the variant /kə'liːbə/ has been discarded.

caliph. The transliteration of words of Arabic origin that have entered English through another language (in this case medieval French) normally leads to the emergence of a number of variant spellings and pronunciations. *Caliph* is now the dominant spelling in English (not *ka-, kha-, -if*) and /'keɪlɪf/ the dominant pronunciation, not /'kalɪf/.

calk (verb). See CAULK.

callus (plural *calluses*) means 'a hard thick area of skin or tissue'; the corresponding adjective **callous** is used to mean '(of skin) hardened or hard', but is much more frequently used in the non-literal meaning 'unfeeling, insensitive'. The spelling *callous* should not be used for the noun.

caloric. Once used as the name (corresponding to French *calorique*) given by Lavoisier to 'a supposed elastic fluid, to which the phenomena of heat were formerly attributed' (*OED*); now a regular adjective (pronounced /kəˈlɒrɪk/ meaning 'of or pertaining to heat'.

calorie. A word (first used in the 1860s) that stepped right outside physics laboratories (where it means 'a unit of quantity of heat') into widespread general currency as the 20c. proceeded. The general public have adopted what physicists call the *large calorie*, i.e. the amount needed to raise the temperature of 1 kilogram of water through 1°C, and use it as a measure of the energy value of foods. The word was formed arbitrarily in French from Latin *calor* 'heat'.

calyx. Plural generally *calyces* /-lɪsiːz/ (-li-seez), rarely *calyxes*.

camellia. The spelling with *-ll-* is standard, as is the pronunciation with medial /-iː-/.

camelopard, an archaic name for the giraffe, does not contain the word *leopard* and should not be spelt or pronounced as if it did. Pronounce /ˈkamɪləʊpɑːd/ or /kəˈmɛləpɑːd/.

cameo. Plural *-s*. See -O(E)S 5.

camomile, the literary and popular form of the word, answers to medieval Latin *camomilla*. The initial *ch* of the form *chamomile* answers to Lat. *chamaemelon* (Pliny) and Greek χαμαίμηλον 'earth apple' (from χαμαί 'on the ground' + μῆλον 'apple').

campanile. Pronounced /kampəˈniːleɪ/. Its plural in Italian is in *-i*, in English *-es*.

can (noun). See TIN.

can (modal auxiliary) has a wide range of uses. It usually expresses (*a*) possibility: *the data that can be gathered; anyone can make a mistake; manned spacecraft can now link up with other spacecraft in outer space; the virus can lie dormant in apparently normal skin; he can be very trying.* (*b*) ability: *his four-year-old son can ride a bicycle; at his peak Murray could read more than forty languages.* (*c*) permission: In informal circumstances, since the second half of the 19c., *can* has often been used in contexts of permission where *may* had earlier been obligatory: *Can I speak with the Count?*—Tennyson, 1879; *Father says you can come*—T. B. Reed, 1894; *No one can play the organ during service time without the consent of the Vicar*—*Church Times*, 1905. In everyday life, such informal uses of *can* now occur all the time: e.g. *can I speak to your supervisor, please?* But in any context where politeness or formality are overriding considerations, *may* is the better word: *May I come and stay with you?; May I have another whisky, please?* In past tense contexts, *could* (and not *might*) is more or less obligatory: e.g. *At that time only rectors could* (= were entitled to) *receive tithes.*

In some cases, the distinction between *can* and *may* crucially changes the meaning and needs to be preserved, e.g. *I'll drop in tomorrow, if I can* [= if I am able, if I have the time, etc.] and *I'll drop in tomorrow, if I may* [= if you will permit me, if that is convenient for you, etc.]. Cf. MAY AND MIGHT.

canard. Except in the realm of cookery (*canard sauvage*, etc.), where the French pronunciation of *canard* is retained, the word in its main English meaning, 'an unfounded rumour or story', is now pronounced either as /kəˈnɑːd/ or /ˈkanɑːd/.

candelabrum. Because of its Latin origin, the word should technically have *candelabra* as its plural, but *candelabra* has often been treated as a singular from the early 19c. onwards (Walter Scott spoke of *four silver candelabras* in *Ivanhoe*), and is now the more common singular, with *candelabras* as its plural.

cannon. **1** From the 16c. onwards, but no longer, the regular word for a piece of ordnance, to the types of which numerous exotic-sounding names were applied (*aspic, basilisk, culverin, serpentine*, etc.). Now, in military language, normally restricted to a shell-firing gun in an aircraft (a use first recorded in 1919).

2 Historically the word was used as an ordinary noun, with plural *cannons*; but also collectively (*Cannon to right of them, Cannon to left of them, Cannon in front of them Volley'd and thunder'd*—Tennyson, 1855).

3 *Cannon* should be carefully distinguished in spelling from *canon*, meaning (*a*) 'a rule' and (*b*) 'a member of a cathedral chapter'; confusion could be unfortunate.

cannot. 1 This is normally written as one word (rather than *can not*) and is often pronounced like the reduced form *can't*. One encounters *can not* occasionally in letters, examination scripts, etc.; the division seems more to do with custom ('I have always written it this way') than with emphasis. The reduced form *can't*, which now seems so natural, is relatively recent in origin. It does not occur in the works of Shakespeare, for example, and the earliest example of it given in the *OED* is one of 1706.

2 *Cannot* (or *couldn't*, etc.) is correctly used before *but* (see BUT 7); before the combination *help but* + infinitive (see HELP 3); and before the verb *help* + gerund (*I couldn't help thinking that he wasn't listening either*—B. Rubens, 1985). For constructions of the type *he can't hardly walk*, see HARDLY 4.

3 *can't seem* + infinitive = seem unable to. This construction is relatively recent (the first example in the *OED* is one of 1898). Examples: *Fitzgerald, who can't seem to tell anyone something without cadging a drink from them first, adds a great deal of humor to the picture*—*OEC*, 2000; *the kind of film you don't mind watching but can't seem to remember a few hours later*—*OEC*, 2003. It appears less in formal writing and more in informal written and spoken English.

can't. See CANNOT.

cant. In the 18c. and 19c., one of its primary meanings was 'the secret language or jargon used by gypsies, thieves, professional beggars, etc.' (*They talk'd to one another in Cant*—J. Stevens, 1707). During the same period, it was also applied contemptuously to the special phraseology of particular classes of (non-criminal, non-vagrant) persons (*All love—bah! that I should use the cant of boys and girls—is fleeting enough*—Dickens, 1839). These meanings are now confined to scholarly work or historical novels. Instead *cant* now usually means 'insincere pious or moral talk', e.g. *shameful surrender to the prevalent cant and humbug of the age*—*Daily Telegraph*, 1992. See JARGON.

cantatrice, 'a female singer', which is an early 19c. loanword from Italian or French (spelt the same in both languages), is now pronounced in an Italian manner as /ˈkantatriːʃeɪ/ or in a French manner as /kɑ̃tətriːs/ at choice. The French pronunciation is the more usual of the two in English.

canto. Plural *-os*. See -O(E)S.

canvas, canvass. 1 *Canvas* 'coarse cloth' is spelt with one *s*, with plural *canvases*. When used as a verb, 'to cover or line with canvas', it is conjugated as *canvasses, canvassed, canvassing* (but often *-s-* in American English).

2 *Canvass* 'to solicit votes' has the forms *canvassed, canvasser, canvasses*, and *canvassing*. The corresponding noun is also spelt *canvass*, plural *canvasses*. Historically both words come from the same French original, and it is only in the 20c. that *canvas* has become fairly consistently restricted to cloth, and *canvass* to voting.

caoutchouc. This strange-looking word, adopted in the 18c. from a Quechua word via Spanish and French, is pronounced /ˈkaʊtʃʊk/.

caper. See SINGULAR -S.

capercaillie, capercailzie. A Scottish word of Gaelic origin meaning 'wood-grouse'. 'The *lz* for l_3 [i.e. *l* followed by yogh] is a 16th c. Scots way of representing *l mouillé* . . . and is properly represented by *ly*' (*OED*). In fact, however, the prevailing spelling is *capercaillie* (not, as formerly, *capercailzie*), and the dominant pronunciation is /ˌkapəːˈkeɪli/.

capita, caput. See PER CAPITA.

capital. 1 adjective. In his edition of Fowler, Burchfield was amused to note 'A headmaster pointed out to me in 1990 that he had frequently encountered illiterate confusion of *capital* and *corporal* in contexts of the type *"My son could do with some capital punishment now and then"*'.

2 noun. *Capital*, the most important town or city of a country or region, is to be distinguished from *Capitol*, which is (*i*) a building in which an American legislative body meets, the best-known of which is the one in Washington, DC; and (*ii*) the hill in Rome where the geese saved the day.

capitalist. Many old-fashioned socialists, including Burchfield's father, regularly stressed the word on the second syllable, i.e. as /kə'pɪtəlɪst/, but nowadays the stress is normally placed on the first syllable of it and of *capitalism, capitalization*, and *capitalize*.

capitals. Apart from certain elementary rules that everyone knows and observes, such as that capitals are used to begin a new sentence after a full stop, for the initial letter of quoted matter (but see PUNCTUATION), and for proper names like *John Smith* (with rare exceptions like the idiosyncratic *e. e. cummings*) and those of the days and months, their present-day use shows wide variation from one publishing house to another, and even within the pages of the same book, newspaper, etc.

What follows is an abridged and slightly modified version of the relevant section in *New Hart's Rules*, pp. 88–100.

A Capital initials should be used for:

1 *Prefixes and titles forming part of a compound name*: *Sir Roger Tichborne, the Bishop of Oxford, the Duke of Wellington.* Also, *Her Majesty the Queen, the Prince of Wales, His Excellency the British Ambassador, His Holiness, Your Honour*—when the title of a particular person; but in a general sense lower case is correct: *every king of England from William I to Richard II; for king* is used here in a general sense, where *monarch* or *sovereign* would be equally correct.

2 *Parts of recognized geographical names*: (of countries or regions) *Northern Ireland* (as a political entity), but *northern England*, a plain description in general terms; similarly, *Western Australia, West Africa, South Africa, New England*, etc.; (names of straits, estuaries, etc.) *Firth of Clyde, Norfolk Broads, Straits of Gibraltar, Plymouth Sound, Thames Estuary*; (names of rivers) *River Plate* (Rio de la Plata), *East River* (New York), but *the Thames*, or *the river Thames*; (topographical and urban names) *Trafalgar Square, Addison's Walk* (in Magdalen College, Oxford), *Regent Street, London Road* (if official name), but *the London road* (that leading to London).

3 *Proper names of periods of time*: *Bronze Age, Stone Age, Dark Ages, Middle Ages, Renaissance; First World War, Second World War*, or *World War I, II*, but *the 1914–18 war, the 1939–45 war.*

4 *Proper names of institutions, movements*, etc.: *Christianity, Marxism, Buddhism, Islam, the Church of England, the (Roman) Catholic Church*; but lower case for the building or for a church in a general sense. *Church* and *State*—both capitalized when viewed as comparable institutions, also *the State* as a concept of political philosophy; *the Crown, Parliament, Congress* (US), *House of Commons* (*of Representatives*, US), *House of Lords, Ministry of Finance*, etc. Also, *HM Government*, or *the Government*, in official parlance and meaning a particular body of persons, the Ministers of the Crown and their staffs; but *the government* (lower case) is correct in general uses.

5 *Parties, denominations, and organizations, and their members*: *Air Force, Army, Navy* (as titles of particular organizations), *Conservative, Labour* (in British politics); *Socialist, Liberal Democrat, Christian Democrat* (European countries, etc.); *Republican, Democratic* (USA); and so on. But *socialist, republican, conservative, democratic*, etc., as normal adjectives when not party titles. Also, *Baptist, Congregationalist, Methodist, Presbyterian, Unitarian, Church of England, Anglican, Roman Catholic, Orthodox* (i.e. Eastern Orthodox), *Evangelical* (continental and US). But *congregational* (singing, polity), *unitarian* views of God, *orthodox* belief, *catholic* sympathies in non-denominational sense. The general rule is that capitalization makes a word more specific and limited in its reference: contrast *a Christian scientist* (man of science) and *a Christian Scientist* (member of the Church of Christ Scientist).

6 *Titles of office-holders*. In certain cases and certain contexts these are virtually proper names of persons: *HM the Queen, the Prime Minister, the Archbishop of Canterbury*. The extension of this principle depends on the context: *the President* (of the USA, of Magdalen College, Oxford, etc.). Similarly, *the Bishop of Hereford, the Dean of Christ Church*; and in a particular diocese, *the Bishop*, or within a particular cathedral or college, *the Dean* (referring to a particular individual, or at least a holder of a particular office: *the Bishop is* ex officio *chairman of many committees*). But in contexts like *when he became bishop, the bishops of the Church of England, appointment of bishops*—such instances are better printed in lower case, and the same applies to other office-holders.

7 *Names of ships, aircraft types, railway engines, trade names,* etc.: The *Cutty Sark,* HMS *Dreadnought*; the Königs, the fastest German battleships in 1916 (capitals but not italic for *types* of ships). The Spitfire, the Flying Fortress, the Dakotas of the 1939–45 war. These are types, since aircraft do not usually have individual names; but 'the US bomber Enola Gay which dropped the atom bomb over Hiroshima on 6 August 1945' (not italic as not official like a ship's name). *A Boeing, a Concorde, an Airbus* (airliners).

8 *Proprietary and brand names*: *A Ford Focus, a Renault Mégane* (trade names). *Anadin, Apple, Persil, Samsung,* etc. Initial capitals must always be used for proprietary names. A capital initial should strictly also be used when the reference is generic (e.g. *can you lend me a Biro?*), but in practice this is more common in the regulated world of published print than in general writing. Brand and company names also generally begin with a capital letter, e.g. *J Sainsbury, Tesco,* except those where the company itself has chosen otherwise, e.g. *eBay,* with the second letter in upper case, and the now defunct *bmi,* all lower case.

9 *Pronouns referring to the Deity*. These should begin with capitals only if specifically requested by an author: *He, Him, His, Me, Mine, My, Thee, Thine, Thou*; but even so it is better to use lower case *who, whom,* and *whose*. In religious writings, capitals are now either old-fashioned or a personal preference of some writers. The main trend is to use lower case in such circumstances.

B *Words derived from proper names.*

1 *Adjectives.* (i) Use a capital initial when usage favours it, and when connection with the proper name is still felt to be alive: *Christian, Dantesque, Hellenic, Homeric, Machiavellian, Platonic, Roman* (Catholic, Empire), *Shakespearian.* (ii) Use a lower-case initial when connection with the proper name is remote or conventional: *arabic* (letters), *french* (chalk, cricket, polish, windows), *italic* (script), *roman* (numerals), and when the sense is an attribute or quality suggested by the proper name: *chauvinistic, gargantuan, herculean, lilliputian, machiavellian* (intrigue), *quixotic, titanic.*

2 *Verbs.* (i) Use a capital initial when the sense of the verb is historical or cultural and has a direct reference to the proper name: *Americanize, Christianize, Europeanize, Hellenize, Latinize, Romanize.* (ii) Use a lower-case initial when the sense is an activity associated with but not referring directly to the proper name: *bowdlerize, galvanize, google, hoover, mercerize, pasteurize.* It should be noted that some brands are keen for verbs derived from their trade names to start with a capital in all contexts, but usage seems to favour lower case.

3 *Nouns.* Use a lower-case initial (i) When reference to the proper name is remote or allusive: *boycott, jersey* (garment), *mackintosh, morocco* (leather), *quisling, sandwich, suede, wellington* (boot). (ii) in names of scientific units: *ampere, joule, newton, volt, watt.* (iii) in names of metres: *alcaics, alexandrines, sapphics.*

See also BINOMIAL 1.

C Medial *capitals.* The uses we have discussed so far all concern the first letters of words. Use of capitals within words is confined exclusively to commercial usage, and has no other purpose or effect than to highlight or distinguish the name of a product, a process, etc.: e.g. *Cinema Scope, eBay, GeoSphere* (made from satellite photographs of the earth).

caption. Adopted in the 14c. from medieval Lat. *captiōn-em* 'taking, seizing', *caption* has had a continuous history since then in various legal senses. Towards the end of the 18c. it began to be used, chiefly in the US (corresponding to *heading* or *title* in the UK), to mean 'the heading of a chapter, section, or newspaper article'. Fowler (1926) called it 'rare in British use, and might well be rarer'. Despite his scornful disapproval, from about the 1920s it has gradually come to be used in all English-speaking areas for the title below an illustration, and, more recently, for a subtitle in cinematography and television. Despite its meaning, it has no direct connection with Latin *caput,* 'head'.

carafe. Formerly in Scotland used as a normal term for the crystal jug or decanter from which water at the table was served. In

Victorian England the word was commonly applied as, according to Fowler, a 'genteelism' for a glass water-bottle, over which a tumbler was placed, for use in a bedroom. In the course of the 20c., *carafe* came to be adopted as a normal English word for an open-necked container for serving wine at table.

carat. See CARET.

caravanserai. This word of Persian origin, for a kind of inn where companies of merchants or pilgrims travelling together in Middle Eastern countries or in North Africa put up, took a considerable time to settle down in its fixed present-day spelling. It was first noted by Hakluyt in 1599; the older spellings included *Carauan-sara, caravansery*, and *caravansary*. The standard pronunciation is /karəˈvansərʌɪ/, with stress on -van- and final syllable rhyming with *eye*.

carburettor. The standard spelling in British English, as against *carburetor* (with one *t*) in American English.

carcass, plural *carcasses*, are the forms recommended, not *-ase*(*s*).

care (verb). The modern colloquial expression *I couldn't care less* dates from the 1940s (*OED*: the first example is of a book title). More recent is the almost exclusively American English expression *I could care less*, which has more or less the same meaning (*My ordeal was over and I could care less what he did now*). Explaining why this affirmative phrase should mean the opposite of what it appears to mean is a popular pastime among those who care deeply about such matters, and the phrase itself has even been the butt of a British TV sketch. Logically, if you *couldn't care less* about something, the implication is that it is impossible for you to care less than you already do; but if you *could care less*, it is possible for you to care less, which does not make a great deal of sense. Perhaps the explanation for the affirmative version is simply that the original idiom has been poorly relayed, and people have just repeated the variant parrot-fashion: other idioms have suffered the same fate. On the other hand, the stress pattern is different: normally stress falls on *couldn't* in the first and the pronoun *I* in the second, which suggests an awareness of the switch and in some measure accounts for two apparently opposite constructions meaning the same thing.

careen (verb). In origin a nautical word (first recorded in Hakluyt, 1600) meaning 'to turn (a ship) over on one side for cleaning, caulking, or repairing', or, intransitively, '(of a ship) to lean over, to tilt when sailing on wind', *careen* carries a residual notion in non-nautical contexts of leaning or tilting. In a separate modern development in American English, since the 1920s, *careen* has rapidly become standard in the sense 'to rush headlong, to hurtle, especially with an unsteady motion', i.e. the speed is more central to the meaning than any latent notion of leaning or tilting. This modern meaning occurs much less often in British English, the broad sense being often covered by the verb *career*, whose similarity of sound has presumably fostered the new meaning of *careen*. Examples: *Bond chases him down, and they fight while careening down narrow mountain roads in a burning jeep full of explosives*—*OEC*, 2000 (AmE); (metaphorically) *I watched in horror as the events careen to their tragic conclusion through a series of tactical blunders*—*OEC*, 2001 (AmE).

caret is a mark (‸ ⁁) indicating a proposed insertion in printing or writing; *carat* is a unit of weight for precious stones; *carat* (US *karat*) is a measure of purity of gold, pure gold being 24 carat.

cargo. The plural can be spelt *cargoes* or *cargos*, although *cargoes* is far more common. See -O(E)S 2.

Caribbean. In the US and in the Caribbean itself, the word is pronounced just as often with the stress on the second syllable, /kəˈrɪbɪən/, as on the third, /ˌkarɪˈbiːən/. In Britain the standard pronunciation has the main stress on the third syllable.

caries is a Latin singular noun (*cariēs*) meaning decay. In its ordinary dental sense, it was formerly always pronounced as three syllables, /ˈkɛːrɪiːz/, in English, and this was the only pronunciation entered in Daniel Jones/ Gimson (up till the 14th edn., 1977). It now normally has two syllables, i.e. /ˈkɛəriːz/.

carillon. This word, though borrowed from French, is not usually pronounced in the quasi-French way /karijɔ̃/. Instead, it has been anglicized with three possible pronunciations: stressing the first syllable, i.e. /ˈkarɪljɒn/ or /ˈkarɪljən/ (**ka**-ril-yon or **ka**-ril-yuhn), and stressing the second syllable, /kəˈrɪljən/ (kuh-**ril**-yuhn).

caring (adjective). This by now well-established word is relatively recent, being first recorded from 1966. It has two broad meanings: (*a*) 'with reference to professional social work, care of the sick or elderly'; the phrase *the caring professions* is now a fixture in the language and the standard term. (*b*) 'compassionate, sensitive, empathetic'. Once something of a political hot potato, especially in the phrase *caring society*, so established is this meaning that even Her Majesty the Queen can be described by Prince William as an 'extremely caring grandmother'. *Caring (and) sharing* is, however, something of a cliché, and probably best avoided.

carnelian. See CORNELIAN.

carousel. 1 Historically, a tournament (first recorded 1650); then, a merry-go-round (1673, now chiefly US, where it is usually spelt, like the French original, *carrousel*); from about 1960, a moving conveyor system for delivering passengers' luggage at airports. It is pronounced /karəˈsɛl/, occasionally /-zɛl/.

2 It is, of course, to be carefully distinguished from *carousal* (revelry in drinking), which is pronounced /kəˈraʊzəl/, with the main stress on the second syllable.

carpet. See RUG, CARPET.

carrel. A *carrel* or *carol* was the name given in medieval English monasteries to a small enclosure or 'study' in a cloister. The word dropped out of use with the dissolution of the monasteries in the 16c.; but it was revived in the early 20c. to denote a private cubicle provided in a library for use by a reader (e.g. *The study cubicles in the college library at Ampleforth are still called 'carrels'—Medium Aevum*, 1960).

cartel. In its older senses, especially 'a written agreement relating to the exchange or ransom of prisoners' (a use first recorded in 1692), it was pronounced /ˈkɑːtəl/, with the stress on the first syllable. About the end of the 19c., after German *Kartell*, the stress was moved to the second syllable, i.e. /kɑːˈtɛl/, in the new, originally German, meaning 'an association of manufacturers or suppliers with the purpose of maintaining prices at a high level and restricting competition'.

case (nouns). There are two distinct nouns. **1** First recorded in English in the 13c. (from Old French *cas* and Latin *cāsus*), *case*[1] was at first 'a thing that befalls or happens, an occurrence'. From this abstract base sprang numerous extended meanings, especially (*a*) an instance or example of the occurrence or existence of something (*the most recent case of that kind of behaviour that he could recall*); (*b*) numerous technical senses in law (e.g. *This concluded the case for the prosecution*); (*c*) an instance of disease (*seven cases of cholera*); (*d*) in grammar, one of the varied forms of a word expressing its relationship to some other word in the vicinity (*the case-ending of the accusative singular of Latin nouns ending in* -iō *is* -iōnem).

2 Quite separately, *case*[2] entered English in the 13c. (from Norman French *casse* and Latin *capsa*), meaning a receptacle, a box, a bag, a covering, etc. The two words have stood side by side ever since, and perhaps the majority of speakers have always been unaware that the two are distinct words.

3 *In case* functions as a conjunction, e.g. *We put on thick jumpers, in case it was cold.* In American English, *in case* can also mean 'if' (i.e. as a shortening of the phrase *in the case that*): *In case it rains I can't go* (= If it should rain).

4 Fowler (1926) cited a pageful of examples in which removing the phrase containing *case*, or rewording, would improve the sentence: e.g. *Though this sort of thing proceeds from a genuine sentiment in the case of Burns* [omit *the case of*]; *His historical pictures were in many cases masterly* [Many of his]. It is still worth guarding against using *case*, especially the phrase *in the case of*, in a way that can make a sentence somewhat tortuous: *In every case except that of France the increase has been more rapid than in the case of the U.K.* would be punchier and 25 per cent shorter if rewritten as *In every country except France the increase has been more rapid than in the U.K.* Similarly, the phrase *it is not the case that* . . . sounds rather portentous, and while it may on occasion add spurious *gravitas*, it is often merely padding to be shortened or left out altogether: *It is not the case that the BBC will be excluded from Ofcom—Scotland on*

Sunday, 2002 could be rewritten either as '*it is not true to say that . . .* ' or '*The BBC will not be excluded . . .* '.

casein. Can be pronounced /ˈkeɪsiːn/, with two syllables, but the standard guides to pronunciation give precedence to the three-syllable form /ˈkeɪsɪɪn/.

cases.

1 Remaining cases in English.
2 Case after the verb *to be*.
3 After *as* and *than*.
4 After *but*.
5 After *not*.
6 'Case-switching'.

1 *Cases* are the functions of nouns, pronouns, and adjectives in sentences, as reflected in their endings or some other aspect of their form. The *cases* we are concerned with are: (*a*) subjective (or nominative): the function of subject of a verb or sentence (e.g. *house* in *The house was on fire*); (*b*) objective (or accusative): the function of object, after a transitive verb or preposition (e.g. *book* in *Give me the book* and *Look in the book*). Of less concern in English are (*c*) genitive (or possessive): the function of possession or ownership (e.g. *Jane's* and *my* in *Jane's umbrella is in my car*); (*d*) dative: the function of reference or relation (e.g. *me* in *Give me the book*).

Before the Norman Conquest, English nouns, pronouns, and adjectives had a range of forms distinguishing the nominative singular from the accusative, genitive, and dative (singular and plural). The nouns in particular fell into distinct groups according to their grammatical gender. The simplest of these patterns is shown in the Old English word for 'stone': *stān* nom. and acc., *stānes* gen., *stāne* dat., *stānas* nom. and acc. plural, *stāna* gen. plural, and *stānum* dat. plural. From the Conquest onwards, the case-endings rapidly disappeared except as signs of the possessive (singular and plural) of nouns and of the plural of nouns. Adjectives gradually became invariable. Pronouns alone were left with forms that distinguish *case*:

subjective	*objective*	*possessive*
I	me	my
he	him	his
she	her	her
we	us	our
they	them	their
who	whom	whose
whoever	whomever	

The main casualty of this process is that, because nouns form such a dominant part of the language, and because they do not change endings in the old accusative and dative positions, English speakers have partially lost an instinctive power to recognize *case* distinctions.

2 The verb *to be* can usefully be regarded as linking elements that are historically in the same case. In nouns and some pronouns, the *cases* before and after are normally indistinguishable: *Paris is the capital of France; what's yours is mine.* In constructions introduced by *It is* or *This* (or *That*) *is*, however, the objective forms of pronouns have become the norm in standard English, especially in short declarative sentences: thus *It's me* rather than *It is I; This* (or *That*) *is him* rather than *This* (or *That*) *is he.* Using the subjective pronoun, i.e. *It is I, This is he*, despite being grammatically sounder, would sound ridiculously pompous or affected in speech. In writing, however, greater care is often exercised: many writers prefer the subjective forms, especially when the pronoun is followed by a relative clause beginning with *who* or *that.* Examples: (subjective) *If I were he, I should keep an eye on that young man*—C. P. Snow, 1979; *This time it was I who took the initiative*—R. Cobb, 1985; *It is we who are inappropriate. The painting was here first*—P. Lively, 1987; (objective) *Too much of a bloody infidel, that's me*—T. Keneally, 1980; *Hugh stepped forward. 'It's me, don't be frightened'*—M. Wesley, 1983; *'So . . . ' says Jasper. 'That's him, the old fraud.'*—P. Lively, 1987.

3 After *as* and *than*. There is considerable variation, but broadly speaking when *as* or *than* are felt to be prepositions the objective *case* is used (*as happy as me*) and when they are felt to be conjunctions the subjective *case* is used (*as happy as I* with *am* understood). The subjective *case* would sound rather formal in speech, and even in writing there is a tendency towards the objective: the examples from Evelyn Waugh and Lord Hailsham below look decidedly old-fashioned. Examples: (*as* subjective) *I sensed that he was as apprehensive as I about our meeting*—J. Frame, 1985; *Numbed as she is, she's as alive as Amaral or you or I*—*New Yorker*, 1987; (*than* subjective) *I hope you had a more cheerful Christmas than we*—*E. Waugh*, 1955; *On the whole the men . . . are more formal and authoritarian in tone than* *she*—M. Butler, 1987; *He was eight years older than I, and planned to be everything that I, too, hoped to become in life*—Ld Hailsham, 1990. (*as* objective) *Jim would have run the farm as good as me*—M. Eldridge, 1984 (Aust.); *He seems to be as lonely as me, and to mind it more*—D. Lodge, 1991; (*than* objective) *I wanted you to be wiser than me, better than me*—M. Ramgobin, 1986 (SAfr.); *we're sure they can judge a novel just as well* [as] *if not better than us*—Julian Barnes, 1987.

See AS 1, THAN 6.

4 After *but*. The objective form of the pronoun is preferable, though in practice both types occur: (subjective) *But no one understands it, no one but I, who have sat in corners all my life watching him*—J. M. Coetzee, 1977; (objective) *No one is fool enough to work the straights but me*—J. Fuller, 1983.

For a fuller discussion of the problem, see BUT 3.

5 After *not*. Since this construction is common in speech, the objective *case* is the norm: *'Who made that mistake?' 'Not me!'*. In formal writing, the subjective forms of pronouns still (just) tend to be preferred: *it must be he who's made of india-rubber, not I*—A. Carter, 1984; *Who would be Scrooge enough to call such ideas humbug? Not I.*—*New Yorker*, 1986. But see NOT 7.

6 '*Case-switching*'. Change of the *case* of pronouns within the same clause or sentence is a marked feature of modern English. The nation is divided in its attitude to some of the types. Among the often criticized patterns are constructions of the type *This is strictly between you and I* (see BETWEEN 1) and *They asked Jim and I to do the job* (see I). Technically ungrammatical, and unacceptable in writing, but very common in informal speech, is the type *Me* (or *Myself*) *and Bill went to the pub* (i.e. at the head of a sentence or clause).

A number of other uses of objective forms are standard, though some are fairly informal; in none of the examples that follow, however, would the subjective form sound natural. Examples: (sentences led by *Me, I*) *Me, I don't trust cats*—G. Keillor, 1989; (*me* + pres. pple) *Me thinking I'd probably got some filthy fever in spite of the jabs*—Julian Barnes, 1989; (straightforwardly illogical, but seeming natural) *we sat down on either side of the radiogram, she with her tea, me with a pad and pencil*—J. Winterson, 1985; (with an exclamatory infinitive) *What! me fight a big chap like him?*; (*Me too* in response to another person's assertion) *'Let's talk about each other, that's all I am interested in at the moment.' 'Me too,' says Tom.*—P. Lively, 1987; (in reply to a question) *'What do you make of that, Tonio?' 'Me?' he said.*—B. Moore, 1987; (*Me neither*) *'Too bad I can't reach the curtain.' 'Me neither,' he said.*—*New Yorker*, 1987; (*silly me*) *'After Diana had told me what Irena was asking?' 'Of course. Silly me.'*—A. Lejeune, 1986. See also ME 2, WHO AND WHOM.

casino. Plural *casinos*. See -O(E)S 4.

casket. In America, and in some other English-speaking countries outside Britain, undertakers tend to use *casket* rather than *coffin*. In newspaper accounts of funerals in these countries, the words *casket* and *coffin* are often used interchangeably in the same column. In Britain the normal word is *coffin*, and *casket* is normally reserved for 'a small, often ornamental, box or chest for jewels, etc.', and sometimes 'a small wooden box for cremated ashes'.

The interchangeable nature of the two words in US newspapers was shown, for example, in accounts of the funeral of Ferdinand Marcos, former President of the Philippines, in October 1989: e.g. (caption) *Imelda Marcos kisses the casket containing the body of her late husband, Ferdinand Marcos*; (text) *Mr. Marcos' coffin, draped with a Philippines flag, was borne by 10 pallbearers* (both from the 15 Oct. issue 1989 of the *Chicago Tribune*).

cast (verb). This late Old English word of Scandinavian origin has competed for centuries with Anglo-Saxon *throw*, and its credentials include an array of 83 meanings in the *OED*. In current usage, however, it often sounds archaic or rhetorical, influenced by the New Testament *He that is without sin among you, let him first cast a stone*—John 8:7, and is largely restricted to a range of familiar phrases, idioms, and proverbs: *cast an eye over, cast a shadow over, cast a spell, cast lots, cast a vote, cast ashore, cast aside, Cast not a clout till May be out, be cast down* (downhearted), *cast accounts*, etc. In ordinary contexts of propelling with force, *throw* is the more natural word.

caste. From the 17c. to the 19c., the spelling of the word meaning 'one of the several hereditary classes into which society in India has from time immemorial been divided' (*OED*) wavered between *cast* and *caste*. The latter form has prevailed. It is derived from Spanish and Portuguese *casta* 'race, lineage, breed'. *Caste* is to be carefully distinguished from the noun *cast* in its multifarious meanings: *reflections of a moral cast, the cast* (= the actors) *of a play, a cast in dice,* and numerous senses in angling, hawking, sculpture, etc.

caster, castor. The two forms represent several words and overlap in usage: (i) *caster* is the only spelling for a few technical meanings; (ii) *castor* (a different word) is the only spelling for the oil; and both are used for the sugar (which is named after the type of pot with a perforated lid it was put in) and for the small swivelling wheel on the feet of furniture. Although you are never wrong if you use *castor* for the principal meanings, *caster* is recommended for the sugar, and *castor* for the small wheel.

The name **Castor** in Greek mythology, one of the twin sons (Castor and Pollux) of Tyndareus and Leda, now represented in the name of the constellation Gemini, is unrelated.

casualty. In the fifth edition of *The Concise Oxford Dictionary* (1964), where senses are arranged in historical order, the sense 'accident, mishap, disaster' is correctly placed first. In the eighth edition (1990), where the current senses are arranged in order of comparative familiarity and importance, the meaning 'a person killed or injured in a war or accident' is placed first, and the earliest historical sense 'an accident, mishap, or disaster' is placed last. The change in the ordering of senses is partly a matter of lexical technique, but in this case it also reflects a change in the currency of the respective meanings. Nonliteral uses of the now dominant meaning are common: *lower profits will become the first casualty of the new government's policy.*

catachresis. In grammar, 'improper use of words; application of a term to a thing which it does not properly denote'. In rhetoric, 'abuse or perversion of a trope or metaphor' (*OED*). The popular uses of *chronic* = habitual, inveterate (*a chronic liar*), *infer* = imply, suggest, and *refute* = deny, contradict (without argument), are examples of lexical catachresis. In the *OED*, catachrestic uses are preceded by the sign ¶. In poetry or highly formal prose, nonce-deviations from ordinary linguistic uses are examples of rhetorical catachresis: e.g. Dylan Thomas's phrase *Once below a time,* and W. H. Auden's coinage *metalogue* (modelled on *prologue* and *epilogue*), 'a speech delivered between the acts or scenes of a play', an artificial word not taken up by anyone else.

catacomb. The dominant pronunciation in standard British English is now /ˈkatəkuːm/. The older one, /-kəʊm/, the only pronunciation given by Daniel Jones in 1917, is now seldom heard in Britain but is customary in American English.

cataphoric (adjective). First (19c.) used of the action of an electric current, it is now (since the 1970s) used by grammarians of a reference to a succeeding word or group of words. In the sentence *After his discovery of New Zealand, Captain Cook went on to discover several Pacific islands, his* refers forward to *Captain Cook,* i.e. is cataphoric. There are numerous more complicated types of grammatical cataphora. Cf. ANAPHORA 2.

catchphrase. A phrase that catches on quickly and is repeatedly used with direct or indirect allusion to its first occurrence. The word is first recorded in the mid-19c. The adoption of catchphrases from popular songs, films, slogans, advertisements, etc. became a marked feature of the language in the 20c. Hundreds of catchphrases are gathered up in Eric Partridge's *Dictionary of Catch Phrases* (1977) and in Nigel Rees's *Dictionary of Popular Phrases* (1990). Examples: *Have a nice day* (origin disputed, but quickly established in the US in the early 1970s); *to laugh* (or *cry*) *all the way to the bank* (attributed to the American entertainer Liberace); *Here's one I made earlier* (first used in 1950s cookery programmes, but popularized by the BBC children's programme *Blue Peter,* 1963 onwards); *Not tonight, Josephine* ('probably arose through music-hall in Victorian times', N. Rees; not believed to have been said by Napoleon himself); *I'll get me coat* (from the BBC series *The Fast Show*); *economical with the truth* (1986, used by the Cabinet Secretary, Sir Richard Armstrong); *get a life* (early 1990s).

catch-22. Mainly used in the phrase *a catch-22 situation*, it does not strictly mean any ordinary difficulty or dilemma, but 'a dilemma or circumstance from which there is no escape because of mutually conflicting or dependent conditions'. It is the title of a novel by Joseph Heller (1961) featuring predicaments of this kind: '*There was only one catch, and that was catch-22, which specified that a concern for one's own safety in the face of dangers that were real and immediate was the process of a rational mind. Orr was crazy and could be grounded. All he had to do was ask; and as soon as he did, he would no longer be crazy and would have to fly more missions.*'

catchup, catsup. This word (first recorded in 1690) for a spicy sauce or condiment is now entirely replaced by *ketchup* in Britain. Of the various spellings of the word in the US, *ketchup* and *catsup* are the most common. The word is believed to be of Chinese origin via Malay.

category. To begin with, restricted to its original philosophical meaning, 'one of a possibly exhaustive set of classes among which all things might be distributed'; later (attributed to Kant) 'one of the a priori conceptions applied by the mind to sense-impressions'. These philosophical senses made their way imprecisely into general use from the 17c. onwards, and settled down with the broad meaning, 'a class, or division, in any general scheme of classification'. It was against this more general meaning that Fowler (1926) thundered: 'category should be used by no-one who is not prepared to state (1) that he does not mean *class*, & (2) that he knows the difference between the two'. His objection now seems quixotic, and *category*, like hundreds of other words that started life as technical terms, e.g. *acid test, limelight*, has become part of general language, as it has also in French, Italian, German, etc. See also POPULARIZED TECHNICAL TERMS.

cater (verb). The choice between *to* and *for* to link this verb with its complement depends on the meaning, and on the geographical variety of English: (*a*) *for* is used in the meaning 'provide people with food and drink at a social event or other gathering' (*my mother helped to cater for the party*); (*b*) both *for* and *to* are used when the meaning is 'provide with what is needed or required' (*the school caters for/to children with learning difficulties*). *To*, perhaps influenced by *pander*, is the norm in North American English; *for* is standard elsewhere; (*c*) when the meaning is 'take into account or make allowances for', *for* is obligatory (*the scheme caters for interest rate fluctuations*); (*d*) *to* is obligatory when the sense is 'try to satisfy (a need or demand)', as in *he catered to her every whim*. Further examples: *The following suggested items can be obtained from shops which cater for local Chinese communities*—*China Now*, 1978; *Gingerbread caters for all categories of single parents*—*Times*, 1980; *I saw the town of Mystic, ... today a town largely catering to tourists and day trippers from New York*—weblog, 2004 (Aust).

cater-cornered. This adjective and adverb meaning 'diagonal, diagonally', spelt in various ways (*cater-corner, catty-corner(ed), catacorner(ed), kitty-corner(ed)*, etc.), is in daily use in American English, but is virtually unknown in British English.

Catholic. When used with a small initial, *catholic* (like its Greek original καθολικός) means 'universal' (*science is truly catholic, catholic tastes*) or 'of universal human interest; having sympathies with, or embracing, all'. Swift, for example, declared of one of his works, *All my Writings ... for universal Nature, and Mankind in general. And of such Catholick Use I esteem this present Disquisition.* In a religious context, care must be taken to make the specific meaning clear. When spelt with an initial capital it refers to the Roman Catholic Church, although historically its range of reference is wider than this, embracing all Churches claiming to be descended from the ancient Christian Church. Although the meaning is clear in (for example) *Catholics and Protestants*, use *Roman Catholic* when there is any room for uncertainty.

catsup. See CATCHUP.

catty-cornered. See CATER-CORNERED.

Caucasian. The normal word, as noun and adjective, in American English (and increasingly elsewhere) for a white person (as distinct from an African American, a Japanese person, etc.). It avoids referring to skin colour or racial group, and is politically less sensitive than alternatives. It is also, as adjective and noun, the normal word used in all English-speaking countries for the people, language, etc., of the Caucasus.

cauldron. The normal spelling in British English, whereas *caldron* is the more usual form in American English.

caulk (verb). This word, meaning 'to stop up (the seams of a boat, etc.) with oakum, etc.', is normally so spelt in British English, and as *calk* in American English.

'cause. See 'COS.

causerie. Adopted in the early 19c. (first recorded 1827) from French in the sense 'a chat', it later came to be used to mean 'an informal essay, article, or talk, especially one on a literary subject and forming one of a series'. This later sense was taken from Sainte-Beuve's *Les Causeries du Lundi* (1851–62), which was published as a series of articles in two French newspapers. In the 20c., *causerie* has also been used in English for 'a discussion, an informal seminar'.

cavalcade. A classic example of a word that has discarded its original meaning. Ultimately derived from late Latin *caballicāre* 'to ride on horseback', from *caballus* 'horse', it was brought into English via French in the senses 'a march or raid on horseback' (1591, last recorded 1647) and 'a procession on horseback' (1644). Almost at once, in the 17c., *any* procession came to be called a *cavalcade*: the earliest examples are of theatrical devils and of cows. Noel Coward used the word as the title of a play in 1931: he might equally well have called it *Pageant*.

Its final element, *-cade*, has yielded a new formation, *motorcade* 'a procession of motor vehicles', first recorded in America in 1913, and now used in journalism across the English-speaking world. Compare -ATHON.

Cave, caveat. *Caveat*, both in legal use and in the general sense 'a warning, an admonition' is now regularly pronounced /ˈkaviːat/ with a short *a* in the first syllable, but until the mid-20c. was regularly pronounced /ˈkeɪviːat/. The dated British public-school slang word *Cave!* 'Beware!' is the Latin imperative of *cavēre* 'to take care, beware'. It is pronounced /ˈkeɪviː/, despite the short *a* of the original.

caviar(e). The spelling *caviar* is the more common of the two but both spellings are correct.

cayman is the recommended spelling of this word (= a S. American alligator-like reptile), not *caiman*.

-c-, -ck-. Until the 18c., words like *critic, epic*, and *music* were often written with final *-ck, -cke*, or *-que*. The present-day *-ic* forms became established in the 19c. In inflected forms that preserve the pronunciation /-k/ before the native suffixes *-ed, -er, -ing*, and *-y*, a *-k-* is added: *mimicked, picnicker, frolicking*, and *panicky*. Before the classical suffixes *-ian, -ism, -ist, -ity*, and *-ize*, the soft *c* is left by itself: *musician, criticism, publicist, electricity*, and *criticize*. See ARC, SOCCER, TALC, ZINC.

cease. Other than in formal language, this 14c. loanword from French has yielded to *stop*: we naturally say *to stop breathing* not *to cease breathing*, and *to stop work*, not *to cease work*. Fowler thought that *cease* ought to 'be allowed to go into honourable retirement', but it appears to have plenty of active life left for special uses, especially in the field of business, e.g. *cease trading, production, publication*, and in a few set phrases (notably *wonders will never cease*, and in the structure *never cease to amaze, amuse, surprise*, etc.). Unlike *stop*, it can be followed by a *to*-infinitive, often producing a better effect. We could not, for example, substitute *stop* for *cease* in sentences of the following type, with a personal subject, without effectively reversing the meaning: *Sherlock Holmes never ceased to analyse and respect the brilliance of his enemy, Moriarty*—*Observer*, 2004.

-ce, -cy. The hundreds of mostly abstract nouns ending in *-ce* or *-cy* fall into three main classes: (i) Those which now always end in *-ce*: *annoyance, credence, elegance, magnificence, obedience, silence*, etc. The majority of these have competed with matching forms in *-ancy* or *-ency* at some time in the past: e.g. *credency* (recorded once in 1648), *silency* (obsolete in 17c.). (ii) Those which now always end in *-cy*: *agency, diplomacy, infancy, obstinacy*, etc. Some of these too have had matching forms in *-ce* at some point in the (often quite recent) past: e.g. *obstinance*, marked 'rare' in the *OED* but probably obsolete. (iii) Those which exist in both forms, usually with clearly distinguishable meanings: *dependence*, the state of being dependent; *dependency*, (especially) a country or province controlled by another; *emergence*, a coming to light; *emergency*, a sudden state of danger; *excellence*, the state of excelling; *Excellency* (in *His* (etc.) *Excellency*), used mainly, but not exclusively, as a term of address, principally to ambassadors.

The facts for each word are set out in the *OED*.

In the lists that follow, those which once had a competing form are marked with a dagger; and those which continue to have a competing form (often with slightly different meanings) are marked with an asterisk:

-ance	*-ence*
admittance	†coincidence
avoidance	†innocence
*brilliance	†intelligence
forbearance	*permanence
*irrelevance	*persistence
	*prurience

-ancy	*-ency*
†buoyancy	†cogency
†constancy	†decency
†vacancy	†frequency

ceiling. 1 *Ceiling* has been used by government departments and administrators since the 1930s to mean 'an upper limit' (as in *a ceiling on prices*), and is sometimes contrasted with *floor*, which is a lower limit. As with *target*, care needs to be taken not to use it in contexts that are incongruous: a *ceiling* can be *reached*, for example, or *raised* or *lowered* or *adjusted*, or can be *high* or *low* or *unrealistic*, but it cannot (without absurd effect) be *extended* or *exceeded* or *increased*. It is also unwise to use it with words that are also associated with it in its literal use, such as *suspend*.

2 A **glass ceiling** has been used since the 1980s, originally in American English and increasingly in British English, to symbolize a notional barrier to professional advancement, especially affecting women and members of minorities: *For most top amateurs there is a glass ceiling on the professional circuit, and it does not take them long to hit it—Economist*, 1995. In church politics, the witty variation *stained-glass ceiling* is sometimes found: *Women and the Church ... welcomed the statistics but said that female clergy risked hitting a 'stained-glass ceiling'*.

celeb. There can, surely, be few words more indicative of our modern obsession with instant, if transient, fame than this truncated form of *celebrity*. Andy Warhol predicted that one day everyone would be world-famous for fifteen minutes; nowadays, it seems, being in the spotlight for even less time can guarantee immortality in our 'celeb culture'. As an abbreviation of *celebrity, celeb* is still markedly informal, and so should be avoided in formal writing.

celebrant. In British English a *celebrant* is a person who performs a rite, especially the Eucharist, a use first recorded in 1839. In the ordinary sense 'one who celebrates', i.e. at a party, an anniversary, etc., the word normally used is *celebrator*. In American English since the 1930s, *celebrant* has also been applied to a person celebrating anything (e.g. a birthday, a new appointment, a wedding anniversary), and the word is used alongside *celebrator* in this general sense, as it is very occasionally in British English. Examples: *The party had gone splendidly until just after midnight when the celebrant himself had been involved in a pathetic little bout of fisticuffs*—C. Dexter, 1989; (caption) *A St. Patrick's Day celebrant enjoys a Hydro-Bike Explorer ... on the Chicago River—Chicago Sun-Times*, 1994; *Pity the poor celebrants at T in the Park—OEC*, 2003 (BrE).

celibacy, celibate. Traditionally *celibate* refers to people such as priests, monks and nuns permanently abstaining from marriage and sexual relations for religious reasons, e.g. *Religious dress and grave goods were used to differentiate celibate priests and monks from ordinary secular men—OEC*, 2005. *Celibacy* is the state of being unmarried and refraining from sexual relations, e.g. *The vow of celibacy all* [Catholic] *priests have to take is blamed by some for the low numbers of candidates coming forward—OEC*, 2006. More recently, some speakers have started to use *celibate* to refer merely to abstaining from sexual intercourse not indefinitely but for a limited period, e.g. *I'd just as soon be alone and celibate than to* [*sic*] *be out in the clubs and the bars trying to 'hook up'—OEC*, 2008. Some people consider this incorrect, and it might be seen as belittling the sacrifice religious celibates make. On the other hand, it is arguably a useful extension of the adjective's original application, and expresses with a single word what would otherwise be a whole clause, i.e. in the last example above 'not have sex'.

cello, an abbreviation of *violoncello*, is now by custom normally written as shown, without a preceding apostrophe. Its plural is *cellos*.

Celsius designates a scale of temperature on which water freezes at 0° and boils at 100° under standard conditions. Named after a Swedish astronomer, Anders *Celsius* (1701–44), it contrasts with the Fahrenheit scale in which the freezing-point of water is 32° and the boiling-point 212°. Note that *centigrade* is a generic term for any such scale, and has been displaced by the more exact *Celsius* in weather reports and general usage.

Celt, Celtic. These two words are no longer spelt with initial *K*-. Except for the football club *Celtic* (in Glasgow), which is pronounced /ˈsɛltɪk/, both *Celt* and *Celtic* are pronounced with initial /k/ in standard English.

censer, censor, censure. A *censer* is a vessel in which incense is burnt. A *censor* is an official authorized to examine printed matter, films, news, etc., before public release, and to suppress any parts on the grounds of obscenity, a threat to security, etc. As a verb, *censor* 'to act as censor of', should be distinguished from *censure* 'to criticize harshly'.

centenary /sɛnˈtiːnərɪ/, less commonly /-ˈtɛnərɪ/. **1** As adjective and noun, the more usual term in Britain, and *centennial* /sɛnˈtɛnɪəl/ elsewhere. In all areas it means '(marking) the hundredth anniversary', '(celebration) of the hundredth anniversary'.

2 The recommended forms for longer intervals of the *centenary* (or *centennial*) kind are as follows: 150: sesquicentenary; 200: bicentenary; 300: tercentenary (or tri-); 400: quatercentenary; 500: quincentenary; 600: sexcentenary; 700: septcentenary; 800: octocentenary.

centigrade. Formerly the normal term for a scale of temperature in which the freezing-point of water is 0° and the boiling-point 100°, it has now been replaced in weather forecasts by CELSIUS.

centi-, hecto-. In the metric system *centi-* denotes division, and *hecto-* multiplication, by 100. Cf. DECA-, DECI-; KILO-, MILLI-.

centre (AmE **center**). The use of the verb with *(a)round* to mean 'to have something as a centre; to be mainly concerned with' was first recorded in the 1860s and has had a continuous history since then. It probably developed under the influence of the prepositional patterns associated with the verbs *gather* and *move*. The construction was widely attacked for much of the 20c. as being illogical: how can a centre be (*a*) round anything? The attacks have failed, to judge from the following examples: *The foremost problems in European politics ... will centre round the revision of the Treaty of Versailles*—A. L. Rowse, 1931; *That strange figure around whom this account properly centres*—W. Sansom, 1950; *There is the added enticement of a plot centred around a real historical event*—*Listener*, 1983. Those seeking a safety net are advised to use other constructions such as *to base on, to centre on, to revolve round.*

centrifugal, centripetal are both usually pronounced stressing the third syllable, namely /ˌsɛntrɪˈfjuːgəl/ and /ˌsɛntrɪˈpiːtəl/, *-petal* rhyming with *lethal*. The older pronunciations /sɛnˈtrɪfjʊgəl/ and /sɛnˈtrɪpɪtəl/ are now rarely heard.

century. 1 Each century as conventionally named by number (*the 5th, the 16th,* etc., *century*) contains only one year (500, 1600) beginning with the number that names it, and ninety-nine (401–499, 1501–1599) beginning with a number lower by one. Accordingly 763, 1111, 1300, 1990, belong to the 8th, 12th, 13th, and 20th centuries. For dates before the birth of Christ, 55 BC was in the first century BC, and 500–401 BC was in the fifth century BC. For a different method of reckoning in Italy, see TRECENTO.

2 Despite the above reckoning, in modern usage, 1 January 1800 is often counted as being the first day of the 19c., 1 January 2000 as the first day of the 21c., and so on.

cephalo-. In the range of words containing the element *cephalo-* (from Greek κεφαλή 'head'), there is much uncertainty about the pronunciation of the initial letter. When BSE (bovine spongiform encephalopathy) broke out, the broadcasting media invariably pronounced the third word as /ɛnˈkɛf-/. Many scientists also pronounce words like *cephalosporin* with initial /k-/, but just as frequently one hears an Anglicized /s-/, which is traditional in the numerous compound words containing this prefix, such as *cephalopod.*

ceremonial, ceremonious. *Ceremonial*, meaning 'with or concerning ritual or ceremony', is a neutral descriptive adjective (as in *ceremonial occasions, dress, robes, for ceremonial reasons*). *Ceremonious*, meaning 'having or showing a fondness for ceremony', is a more evaluative and judgemental word. The difference can be seen by contrasting *ceremonial entry* with *ceremonious entry*: A visitor may make *a ceremonious* [i.e. excessively fussy] *entry* into a room, but an army of occupation *a ceremonial* [i.e. one marked by normal ceremony] *entry* into the main square of a conquered city. Examples: *Dozens of Irish Guardsmen performed ceremonial duties at the royal wedding in April, some of whom had returned from Helmand only a matter of weeks earlier—OEC*, 2011; *On the far side of the hearth the headman was sitting with his legs crossed, his back very straight, ceremoniously smoking a hookah*—M. Connell, 1991.

certitude, certainty. If we leave aside special meanings in philosophy, both words imply the absence of doubt about the truth of something, but *certitude* is a subjective feeling of absolute conviction whereas *certainty* is, strictly speaking, verifiable. *Certitude* tends to be restricted to formal, especially religious, writing and has almost no countable usage, i.e. *a certitude* and *certitudes* hardly exist. Preferring *certitude* to *certainty* is a highly marked stylistic choice. Examples: (certainty) *He was filled with certainty, a deep, sure, clean conviction that engulfed him like a flood*—R. P. Warren, 1939; *He never had the absolute certainty that one day he'd get the boat*—R. Ingalis, 1987; (certitude) *We craved certitude and order, and Oxford gave us both*—Ved Mehta, 1993; *Moral certitude does not like to be disturbed, from whichever source it flows—OEC*, 2005.

cervical. With the advent of nationwide cervical screening and cervical smears, the word emerged from laboratories, where it was normally pronounced stressing the second syllable, /sə:ˈvʌɪkəl/ (sə-**viy**-kuhl), into wide public use. In medical use, and in the US, this is the dominant pronunciation. In non-technical use in Britain, the standard pronunciation /ˈsə:vɪkəl/ (**serv**-i-kuhl), stressing the first syllable, is being influenced by the medical one.

cesarean, or **cesarian,** the normal American English spellings of CAESAREAN.

ceteris paribus. This Latin phrase meaning 'other things being equal', is normally printed in italics and pronounced, according to taste, /ˌsɛtərɪs ˈparɪbəs/ or /ˌkɛtərɪs ˈparɪbəs/, the first syllable rhyming with *net*. For the first word, initial /si:t-/ (**seat**-) or /ˈkeɪt-/ (**kate**-) also occur. It is a stock example of the differing traditions of pronouncing Latin words in English.

ch. Words of French origin beginning with *ch* fall into two main groups: (*a*) those adopted in the medieval period or Renaissance, and (*b*) later borrowings. The earlier group are almost all now pronounced with initial /ʧ-/, e.g. *chafe* (14c.), *chain* (14c.), *chamber* (14c.), *chapel* (13c.), *charity* (12c.), *cherish* (14c.), *chief* (14c.), *choice* (13c.); and the later loan-words retain the /ʃ-/of the French original, e.g. *champagne* (17c.), *Chardonnay* (20c.), *château* (18c.), *chef* (19c.), *chic* (19c.), *chiffon* (18c.), *crêpe de chine* (19c.).

chagrin. The dominant standard pronunciation of the noun in British English is /ˈʃagrɪn/ and in American English /ʃəˈgrɪn/. The adjective *chagrined* is spelt with one *-n-*, and pronounced like the noun with the addition of final /-d/.

chair, chairperson. The term *chairman*, which combines connotations of power with grammatical gender bias, has been a keyword in feminist sensitivities about language. *Chairman* is first recorded from 1654, and *chairwoman* dates from as far back as 1699. But, as the *OED* notes, *chairwoman* was hardly a recognized name until the 19c., and even then it did not solve the problem of how to refer neutrally to the person chairing a committee, investigation, etc. Two gender-neutral alternatives emerged in the 1970s: *chairperson* (mainly applied to women, 1971) and *chair* (ditto, 1976), although *chair* was already in use to mean 'the authority invested in a chairman': *I was recently challenged for using 'chairman' to describe my position. My accuser went on to assert that I was being insensitive to the work of the Equal Opportunities Commission by not using 'chairwoman', 'chairperson', or 'chair'*—Ann Scully, *Times*, 1988. *Chair* seems to be more popular than *chairperson*, partly because it seems less contrived and less obviously gender-neutral. It is now de rigueur in all varieties of English to use this in preference to any term marked for gender.

chaise longue /ʃeɪz ˈlɒŋg/, a sofa with a backrest at only one end. Plural *chaises longues* (pronounced the same as the singular). In American English it has been transformed by folk etymology into the logical-seeming *chaise lounge*, which is the accepted and dominant form.

challenged. Among the more notorious formations due to the political correctness movement of the 1980s and 1990s are expressions containing *challenged* as second element. The use of this pattern in *physically challenged* was originally intended to give a more positive tone than words such as *disabled* or *handicapped*. Despite the laudable intention behind the promotion of *challenged* in this meaning, the word soon became the butt of people aiming to make fun of what they viewed as 'PC' language. Nowadays the only serious formations in general use are *physically-challenged* and *intellectually challenged* (= having learning difficulties). Otherwise *challenged* is regularly combined with a wide range of adverbs for humorous effect, with the meaning 'lacking in the quality or thing denoted by the adverb', e.g. *ethically-challenged* (= unscrupulous), *financially challenged* (= poor), *follicularly challenged* (= balding), *hygienically challenged* (= dirty), *vertically challenged* (= shorter than average), etc. See also DISABLED.

challenging (adjective). This is one of those vogue, positive words, like *issue*, that seem to be rapidly ousting their synonyms from the linguistic stage, presumably because the synonyms are seen as not dynamic enough. According to this 'all's for the best in the best of all possible worlds' mentality, anything is possible—if only one has a positive attitude and is prepared to challenge oneself always to do better. *Challenging* is, in fact, something of a Janus-faced word. In one direction it frowns towards the notion of difficulty, e.g. *a challenging time, year, experience*; in the other, it smiles towards ideas of excitement and mental or physical stimulation, e.g. *challenging work, a challenging task, job*. That it combines both meanings under one roof makes it useful when both aspects are indeed involved. Problems can arise, however, when it is trotted out to avoid calling a spade a spade. For example, reacting to nearly 500 complaints about the depiction of extreme violence in a popular crime drama, the BBC issued a statement including the wording 'We acknowledge that certain scenes may have been challenging'. This sounds like a coy and somewhat self-righteous euphemism for 'upset many viewers'. A good thesaurus will help any writer avoid the treacherous woolliness of this word.

Cham /kam/, an obsolete form of *khan*, a term formerly applied to the rulers of the Tartars and Mongols, and to the emperor of China, is used in English mainly with reference to Smollett's phrase *that great Cham of literature, Samuel Johnson*.

chamois. The name of the agile goat antelope is pronounced /ˈʃamwɑː/. Its plural is spelt the same but pronounced /-wɑːz/. In the phrase *chamois leather*, the word is normally pronounced /ˈʃamɪ/.

chamomile. See CAMOMILE.

champ at the bit. This phrase, meaning 'to be restlessly impatient or eager to do something' (e.g. *I'm champing at the bit to do it*) contains the verb *champ*, which describes extremely energetic munching. *Champ* used to be said especially of a horse which impatiently bites the bit in its mouth, but is nowadays rarely used in either meaning. First recorded in the US in the 19c., the graphic image *to champ at the bit* has become part of English worldwide. However, because of our dwindling familiarity with horses and equine terminology, *champ* is very often replaced with the more familiar *chomp*, e.g. *?You've done your background research. You're chomping at the bit to get started on your TV career*—*OEC*, 2004 (BrE). *Chomp at the bit* is in fact more common in *OEC* data than *champ at the bit* and is first recorded from 1645. Nevertheless, some purists will see it as an egregious mistake, even though it is registered in dictionaries.

chancellery, chancery. In British diplomatic use, the official term for the offices holding the general political section of an embassy or consulate is a *chancery*, but journalists frequently refer, for example, to the *chancelleries* of the great powers, thereby using the customary American English term.

chant(e)y. See SHANTY 2.

chap (= man, boy). The word is a shortening, first recorded in the late 16c., of *chapman*. It was not until the 19c. that its main meaning, 'a buyer, purchaser, customer', retreated into dialectal use, and the present-day British informal sense emerged, e.g. *a pleasant, interesting*, etc., *chap*. It now sounds rather dated, and has been largely replaced in British English by the native *bloke* or the American *guy*.

chaperone is recommended, not *chaperon*, for both noun and verb. Pronounced /ˈʃapərəʊn/.

char. This informal, somewhat dated, British English word is short for *charwoman* or *charlady* (a woman employed as a cleaner in houses or offices), whose occupation is *charring* (so spelt). The element *char* has nothing to do with charcoal or burning; it is a descendant of Old English *cierr* 'a turn', Middle English *char(e)* 'an occasional turn of work'. Until the 19c. it was often spelt *chare*. Now seldom heard: those who clean offices are normally called *cleaners*, as are those who work in private houses.

charabanc /ʃaˈrəˌbaŋ/ is now the only extant spelling of this 19c. loanword from French meaning 'an early form of (motor) coach'. The French word *char-à-banc* literally means 'benched carriage'. The word has largely fallen out of use, except humorously or knowingly, for, as the *Economist* remarked as far back as 1953, *But now the charabancs have all turned into coaches.*

character. Fowler (1926) argued the case for not using *character* in two sets of circumstances: (*a*) as a substitute for an abstract-noun termination, *-ness*, *-ty*, etc.: e.g. *Every housing site has its own unique character—Country Life*, 1972 (instead of *uniqueness* or . . . *is unique*); (*b*) in the construction *of a* [adjective] *character*: e.g. *These zones were to be of a different character from typical streets, with traffic levels that would vary according to their functions—Architecture Weekly*, 2004 (instead of simply *different* or . . . *were to differ from* . . .). The economies he recommended are desirable in formal written work.

charge (noun). *In charge of* has two constructions: Tom can be *in charge of* Dick, and Dick can be *in the charge of* Tom (with an inserted *the* now usual) or in Tom's charge (in which case *the* is implicit). In all cases, Tom is given authority over Dick. Examples: *She didn't think it unreasonable to put Sebastian in Rex's charge on the journey*—Evelyn Waugh, 1945; *Until they are 12 months old, the hound puppies are in the charge of the walkers who keep them at their homes—Leicester Mercury*, 1984; *In 1964, he was also put in charge of national defense—OEC*, 2008. However, the construction *in charge of* will be found with the meaning 'in the charge of' (as distinguished above) in writing of the earlier part of the 20c., and in these cases only the context can resolve any ambiguity: *The young prince was doing lessons at Ludlow in charge of* (= under the supervision of) *the Queen's brother, Lord Rivers*—Josephine Tey, 1951.

charisma. From Greek χάρισμα 'gift of grace', the word made its way from theology to sociology in 1922 when the German sociologist Max Weber (writing in German) used it to mean 'a gift or power of leadership or authority'. It was quickly adopted by other sociologists. Nowadays it is used as a synonym for 'influence' or 'authority' or even 'attraction' or 'charm' in various contexts, e.g.: *She presents well, has charm, charisma and vitality, but comes across as severely intellectual—Business*, 1991.

charismatic. The adjective *charismatic*, in addition to its religious meanings (as in *the charismatic movement*), has developed in line with *charisma* and can be used of a person, an achievement such as *performance*, or an abstraction such as *leadership, personality, presence*, or *quality*. There is also an adverb *charismatically*: *He had a charismatic quality about him that had long made him one of Europe's most eligible bachelors*—A. MacNeill, 1989; *She blossomed from a precocious teenager . . . into a charismatically attractive woman with towering talent.*—S. Stone, 1989.

charlatan. Pronounced with initial /ʃ-/ like *shark*, not /tʃ-/ like *cheap*.

chastise. A Latinate-looking word (first recorded in English in the 14c.) for which no demonstrable base has been found in classical Latin, medieval Latin, or medieval French. It is correctly so spelt, not with *-ize*. And, as the *OED* remarks, 'The word is too early to be a simple English formation from *chaste* adjective'.

chateau. Nowadays often written without the circumflex accent (that is, not *château*). The plural is very much more often *chateaux* than *chateaus*, since the word is generally used in contexts to do with France. See -X.

chatterati, (the). See CHATTERING CLASSES (THE); see also -ATI.

chattering classes, (the). This phrase was coined with parodic intent in 1980 by a right-leaning British political commentator to ridicule journalists and media people whose job is to comment on events, as well as liberal intellectuals who merely like talking about them. It is now well established, in Britain with those connotations, e.g. *A battle between Middle England—the sensible heart of the British middle classes—and Islington Person, the politically correct voice of the chattering classes—Daily Mail*, 1994. It, or its rather less common variant *the chattering class*, has since then permeated the Anglosphere, usually with clearly political overtones, e.g. *The Toronto chattering classes are abuzz with word of a new CBC show this fall—Frank Magazine*, 2004 (Canad.). But in some contexts it is merely a shorthand for the influential people in a particular group, albeit a less than complimentary one, e.g. *Six weeks from now, much of Hollywood's chattering class will descend on Toronto for the annual 10 days' orgy of new product—OEC*, 2005 (AmE). Given its potentially toxic connotations, it is best avoided when no venom is intended. The humorous variant **chatterati** seems to be typical of British English.

chauvinism. The original meaning, 'exaggerated or aggressive patriotism' (from the surname of Nicolas Chauvin of Rochefort, a Napoleonic veteran depicted in the French vaudeville *La Cocarde tricolore* (1831), is still occasionally used. But in English (though not in French) it has developed a range of extended uses signifying other kinds of excessive loyalty or prejudice, including *cultural chauvinism, ethnic* (and *racial*) *chauvinism, religious chauvinism*, and *female chauvinism*. The best known is, of course, *male chauvinism* (first recorded in 1935) and its corresponding noun (1940) and adjective (1969), *male chauvinist*. So well established are they now that they are often used in the simple forms *chauvinism* and *chauvinist*, usually without any danger of ambiguity because the context is all.

cheap, cheaply (adverbs). *Cheap* as an adverb can only be used to mean 'at a low price' and regularly follows the verb it qualifies as closely as possible, whereas *cheaply* has that meaning and also the meaning 'in low esteem': (cheap) *you can get them cheap at Woolworths*; (cheaply) *it's advisable to acquire one's first house as cheaply as possible; a tendency to treat religion cheaply*. *Cheap* is an adjective in the idiomatic phrases *to hold cheap* and *to come cheap*, e.g. *a pariah nation which holds life cheap—OEC*, 2010; *A gondolier doesn't come cheap—but punting down the canals is the very best way to explore—Best*, 1991. However, the *OEC* data suggests that people more often interpret it as an adverb, and replace it with *cheaply*, e.g.: *If a society holds human life so cheaply, is it any surprise that young people will also hold life cheaply and engage in violence?—OEC*, 2008.

check (draft on bank), **checkered** (e.g. *a checkered career*). The American English spellings of CHEQUE, CHEQUERED.

checkers. The American name for the game that is called *draughts* in Britain.

checkmate. A word of Persian origin (meaning 'the king is dead') via Old French *eschec mat*. *Mate* is the form normally used in chess, and *checkmate* in metaphorical contexts.

cheerful, cheery. For the ordinary notions 'full of cheer; cheering, gladdening', *cheerful* is the usual word. It can be applied to a person's appearance, disposition, etc., and also to concepts or things of pleasant aspect (*a cheerful conversation, greeting, group, time*, etc.). It can also mean 'not reluctant, not opposed' (*his cheerful acceptance of the inevitable*). *Cheery*, which Johnson called 'a ludicrous word', is more colloquial: it suggests that the person, mood, voice, etc., to whom or to which it is applied is in good spirits, lively.

cheers. The word has long been used in all English-speaking areas as a salutation before drinking. In a way that must be baffling to foreigners, it is also now popularly used in British English by a wide section of the population as an equivalent to 'thank you', or as an expression of good wishes before parting.

cheque is the standard spelling in British English for the banking sense of the word. Etymologically it is a variant of *check* meaning 'a device for checking the amount of an item'.

chequered is the standard spelling in British English for (*a*) the literal sense 'bearing a pattern of squares often alternately coloured'; (*b*) in the phrase *a chequered career*, i.e. one with varied fortunes.

cherub has plural *cherubim* when used to mean an angelic being; in transferred use, e.g. applied to a well-behaved small child, the natural plural is *cherubs*. The adjective *cherubic* is pronounced /tʃɪˈruːbɪk/.

chiaroscuro. Pronounced /kɪˌɑːrəˈskʊərəʊ/.

chiasmus /kʌɪˈazməz/, inversion in the second of two parallel phrases of the order followed in the first. If the two phrases are written one below the other, and lines are drawn between the corresponding terms, those lines make the Greek letter *chi*, a diagonal cross:

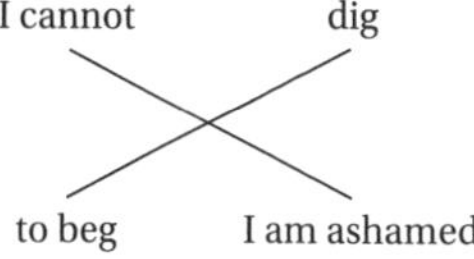

chic. See CH.

Chicano /tʃɪˈkɑːnəʊ/ (less commonly *chicano*, feminine **Chicana**), a word first recorded in 1947, borrowed from Mexican Spanish and derived from the Spanish word *mejicano*, meaning 'Mexican' to refer to Americans of Mexican descent. The word became current in the early 1960s, used by politically active groups. It is still in frequent use but has become less politicized. However, Mexican Americans with less militant political views might find the words offensive. **Hispanic** and **Latino** are more generic words denoting people in the US of Latin-American or Spanish descent.

chide. A verb that is possibly passing out of use. It started out in Old English as a weak verb with unchanged stem vowel in the past tenses. But in the 15c. and 16c. the conjugated forms *chide/chode/chidden* became common, and later *chide/chid/chided*. At present in standard English the dominant pattern is *chide/chided/chided*, but *chid* and *chidden* very occasionally turn up.

chiefest. A minor curiosity is that *chief*, used as a quasi-adjective from the 14c. onwards (*chief town, chief difficulty*, etc.), developed a superlative form *chiefest* at the beginning of the 15c. as it weakened in force from the absolute meaning of 'head' or 'supreme' to that of 'leading'. *Chiefest* is found in Shakespeare (*Within their chiefest Temple Ile erect A Tombe*, 1591), the 1611 AV (*And whosoeuer of you will bee the chiefest, shalbe seruant of all*—Mark 10: 44), and in many other classic sources until the mid-19c. It now occurs occasionally in modern texts, where, unless it is a self-conscious archaism, or a historical quote, it may well be regarded as a mistake, e.g.: *At heart I'm an arranger still, whose chiefest literary pleasure is to take a received melody . . .* —*OEC*, 2004.

chiffon. See CH.

childish, childlike. *Childish* can be used neutrally to mean simply 'like, or proper to, a child', but is more frequently used as a criticism of adults or their behaviour equivalent to 'silly, immature'. By contrast, *childlike* is more or less restricted to the favourable meaning 'having the good qualities of a child such as innocence, frankness, etc.' Examples: (childish) *I feel . . . my father's hand . . . Stroke out my childish curls*—E. Barrett Browning, 1856; *John observing his daughter, saw her now as more grown-up, less childish*—I. Murdoch, 1976; *She said suddenly with touching, childish fear, '. . . I don't want to be alone.'*—A. Newman, 1978; (childlike) *His childlike curiosity about life was held in check by childish timidity*—M. Holroyd, 1974; *She habitually wore an expression of childlike wonder*—R. West, 1977.

children's language. David Crystal (1986) estimated that 'by around 18 months, most children come to use a spoken vocabulary of about 50 words', but the choice of words differs from child to child. The common core of words usually includes *allgone, baby, bee(p)-beep, bye-bye, daddy, mama, nigh(t)-night*. By the third year a tattered form of grammar has been acquired (*this is him's car, her gave me* one, I happy, Me do it, want Teddy drink, I ride train? Wayne naughty*). Andrew Radford (1988) called such constructions 'small clauses' and compared them with similar constructions in informal adult speech. Children aged 2–3 do not use auxiliaries, inflexions, preposed *wh-* phrases, infinitival *to*, or numerous other obligatory elements of adult speech. In this form of reduced grammar *I can see a cow* becomes *see cow*, and a great many clauses are verbless (*Paula good girl*).

After the age of three a child's acquisition of language proceeds by leaps and bounds. Forms like *bringed* and *taked* are gradually discarded. An average child of three probably uses as many as 3,000 English words, including 'hard' words like *helicopter, calculator, penguin,* and *vacuum cleaner* (not perfectly pronounced but clear nevertheless) and 'difficult' concepts like *triangle*.

chilli is the right spelling in British English (more usually *chili* in American English) for the dried red pod of a capsicum. Plural *chillies*, AmE *chilies*. It is etymologically derived via Spanish from the Nahuatl word for the plant. It has no connection with the name of the S. American country Chile.

chimera /kʌɪˈmɪərə/ is the recommended spelling, not *chimaera*. It was adopted in the 14c. from Old French *chimere* (from Latin *chimaera*, Greek χίμαιρα 'she-goat, monster').

Chinaman. In 1926 Fowler could say that this word was in current use, but at some point between then and 1965 (Gowers), *Chinaman* acquired a derogatory edge, and is now practically extinct in British English (except as a term in cricket for a left-handed bowler's offbreak to a right-handed batsman). *Chink* (first recorded in 1901) is highly offensive slang for a Chinese.

chiropodist can justifiably be considered an early example of job title inflation. As the *OED* says, is 'a factitious [artificial] designation, apparently assumed in 1785', and immediately attacked for its 'absurdity and needless affectation'. It was judged to be a high-flying term for a 'corn-cutter'. It was derived either from Greek χείρ, χειρο- 'hand' + πούς, ποδ- 'foot' (to indicate that both hands and feet were the subject of attention), or from the Greek adjective χειροπόδης 'having chapped feet'. Despite the ridicule its creation inspired, the term now passes unremarked in ordinary use for one who treats the feet and their ailments. The related noun **chiropody**, the art of treating corns, defective nails, etc., first recorded a century later in 1886, is also now in standard use. The *ch-* in both words is pronounced as a *k* sound.

chivalry. Despite the fact that it first entered the language from French in the 14c., it and its derivatives are now always pronounced with initial /ʃ-/ not /ʧ-/, unlike most early loanwords beginning with *ch-* from French: see CH. The corresponding adjective **chivalric** is most often pronounced by medievalists with the main stress on the second syllable, but /ˈʃɪvəlrɪk/ is also widely used.

chlorine. Always pronounced /ˈklɔːriːn/ now (formerly also with final /-ɪn/).

chloroform. Pronounced either as /ˈklɒrəfɔːm/ or as /ˈklɔːr-/.

chock-full. From the 17c. onwards it alternated with *choke-full* and *chuck-full*, and the choice of headword became a vexatious matter for 19c. lexicographers. *Chock-full* has triumphed, possibly by association with the 19c. formation *chock-a-block* (used in the same sense).

chocoholic is the more common and recommended spelling for someone addicted to chocolate, but **chocaholic** is not wrong. See -AHOLIC.

choir. The dominant spelling from the time of its adoption from Old French in the 14c. until the close of the 17c. was *quire* (or *queere*, etc.), and it is still so spelt in the Book of Common Prayer. But *choir* (respelt on the model of Latin *chorus*) gained the ascendancy about 1700 and is now standard in all main senses, and in *choirboy, choir-stall*, etc. However, in cathedrals and minsters (e.g. Wells, York) *quire* is often retained as the standard spelling for the part eastward of the nave, in which the services are performed, generally separated from the rest of the building by a screen or screens. The paper term *quire* is unrelated: it is from Old French *quaer, quaier* (modern French *cahier*), ultimately from Latin *quaterni*, a set of four.

choler. As one of the 'four humours' (*sanguis, cholera, melancolia, phlegma*) of medieval physiology, it was supposed to cause irascibility of temper. It survives in poetic or archaistic use in the sense 'irascibility'. The corresponding adjective **choleric** 'irascible, angry' has fared slightly better, though it too has somewhat limited currency, being much more formal than either of its synonyms mentioned. Examples: (choler) *His face was improved by the flush of this momentary choler*—J. R. Ackerley, 1960; (choleric) [in medieval science] *the choleric man is hot and dry, after the nature of fire*—W. C. Curry, 1960; *Gold's demeanor at the Y was habitually unsociable, his countenance that of someone introverted and choleric*—J. Heller, 1979; *Her red face makes her look choleric, in a most unattractive way*—M. Forster, 1986.

cholesterol. This crucial word in modern health care suffers the indignity of being often misspelt. The most common misspelling seems to be *cholestorol* with *-orol* instead of *-erol*; nearly as common, by a process of METATHESIS, are spellings beginning with *chlo-*, e.g. *chloresterol, chlorestorol.*

chomp at the bit. For the use of *chomp at the bit* by mistake for *champ at the bit*, see CHAMP.

chorale. 1 Pronounced /kɔːˈrɑːl/. It originally referred to 'a stately hymn tune, especially one associated with the German Lutheran Church' and to musical compositions consisting of or resembling a harmonized version of a *chorale.* The final *-e* was apparently added in the 19c. soon after the adoption of the word from German *Choral(gesang)* in order to indicate that the main stress falls (as in German) on the second syllable. For this convention cf. *locale, morale.*

2 Since the 1940s used in America in the names of choirs that sing principally choral music (e.g. *the Collegiate Chorale, the Paul Hill Chorale*).

chord, cord. The musical *chord* and the spinal *cord* are no more than third cousins, both ultimately deriving in a very roundabout way from the same Latin word, *chorda.* Their relationship is as follows: **1** There are two distinct words spelt *chord*: (*a*) (in origin a shortening of *accord* respelt with initial *ch*) in music, a group of (usually three or more) notes sounded together, as a basis of harmony; (*b*) (a technical word in mathematics, engineering, etc.) a straight line joining the ends of an arc, the wings of an aeroplane, etc. From (*a*) came the idiomatic expression *to strike a chord* 'to recall something to one's memory'. This second *chord* is a 16c. refashioning of *cord* after the initial *ch* of its Latin original (*chorda*).

2 *Cord* = string, rope, rib of cloth, and in *spinal cord, umbilical cord, vocal cord*, etc., is descended from Middle English *corde,* adopted from Old French *corde* in the 14c., which is derived from Latin *chorda,* a string of a musical instrument. The anatomical expressions (*spinal cord, vocal cords*, etc.) are still occasionally spelt as *spinal chord, vocal chords*, etc., but these spellings are not recommended.

chorizo is a word English has borrowed from Spanish to denote 'a kind of highly spiced pork sausage' (a definition which singularly fails to do justice to its moreish deliciousness). British and American dictionaries suggest the pronunciation /tʃəˈriːzəʊ/ (chuh-**ree**-zoh) as the standard. You can also pronounce the *-z-* as an *s*: chuh-**ree**-soh. Some people, including famous cooks, pronounce the *z* as in *pizza*: /tʃəˈrɪtsəʊ/ (chuh-**rit**-soh). If you wish to make an impression by mimicking the pronunciation of the language from which a word comes, it is wise to make sure you choose the right language.

Christian name. Now that Britain is, *nolens volens,* a multicultural society, this traditional term for a person's first name is gradually giving way, especially on official forms, to *first name, forename,* or (as in American English) *given name.* A second name is usually called a *middle name.*

chronic in medical use describes a disease that is long-lasting (as opposed to *acute*). It has the same meaning, implying continuing severity, when used of other circumstances (*chronic unemployment, shortages,* etc.). An *acute* problem is intense but brief; a *chronic* problem is severe and likely to persist. *Traffic congestion has become so chronic in Britain's cities that vehicles travel at an average speed of just 8 mph—Back Street Heroes,* 1988.

The word is also used in informal British English to mean 'bad, intense, severe, objectionable'. Though Fowler tagged it 'illiterate', it is a colourful part of informal language, as in *it's chronic 'ere of a Saturday sometimes*—Kipling, 1904. The adjectival or adverbial phrase *something chronic* is also used informally: *Mark my words, next time you see her she'll have married an accountant, who she'll bully something chronic*—*OEC*, 2004.

chrysalis. Plural either *chrysalises* or (in learned work) *chrysalides* /krɪˈsalɪˌdiːz/, with four syllables and stress on the second.

chuffed. In standard southern British English it is now mostly used, somewhat slangily, to mean 'delighted, very pleased': *He was chuffed at this new monumental skive he had discovered*—A. Waugh, 1960; *You were pleased at the time. Chuffed in fact*—Paul Scott, 1977. In some other varieties of English in the UK the word sometimes has the opposite meaning 'displeased, disgruntled': *Don't let on they're after you, see, or she'll be dead chuffed, see? She don' like the law*—Celia Dale, 1964. The two meanings seem to reflect separate uses of dialectal *chuff* (adjective) listed in Joseph Wright's *Eng. Dialect Dict.*, (*a*) = proud, conceited; pleased, elated (various northern and Midlands counties, but not recorded in southern ones); (*b*) = ill-tempered, surly, cross (Lancs., Lincs., Berks., Kent, Devon, Cornwall, etc.).

The channel by which the dominant ('delighted') meaning entered standard English cannot be ascertained with any certainty.

chute. 1 A sloping channel or slide for conveying things to a lower level.

2 A slide into a swimming pool.

3 Short for *parachute*. As to the etymology, 'there appears to be a mixture of the French *chute* fall (of water, descent of a canal lock, etc.) and the English word *shoot*' (*OED*). In the 20c., however, the spelling *chute* has been almost always used in British English, rather than *shute* or *shoot*, for the three senses given here.

-ciation, -tiation. 1 The way in which nouns ending in *-ciation* or *-tiation* are pronounced divides standard speakers into those who are prepared to tolerate two successive /ʃ/ (sh) sounds, e.g. *initiation* /ɪˌnɪʃɪˈeɪʃn/ (i-nish-ee-**ay**-shuhn), and those who choose not to. The matter does not stop there, however, as the patterns are not always the same in the corresponding verbs (where they exist) ending in *-ciate*, *-tiate*.

2 Everyone comes out in favour of /s/ in the *-nci-* part of *denunciation, pronunciation*, and *renunciation*. Equally, everyone favours /ʃ/ in the *-iti-* part of *initiation* (and *initiate*) and *propitiation* (and *propitiate*).

3 For other common words in this group there is considerable fluctuation. Perhaps the least debatable distribution is as follows: (/ʃ/ dominant) *appreciate/-iation, consubstantiation, differentiate/-iation, negotiate/-iation, satiate/-iation, substantiate/-iation;* (/s/ dominant) *annunciation, associate/-iation, dissociate/-iation, emaciate/-iation, enunciate/-iation.*

cicada. Pronounced /sɪˈkɑːdə/, but /sɪˈkeɪdə/ is often encountered in various English-speaking countries including Britain and America.

cicatrice /ˈsɪkətrɪs/, (from French) and **cicatrix** (from Latin), plural *cicatrices* /sɪkəˈtrʌɪsiːz/, are both used for 'a mark or scar left by a healed wound; (in botany) a mark on a stem, etc., left when a leaf or other part becomes detached'.

cicerone, a guide who gives information to tourists about places of interest. This loanword from Italian can be pronounced, according to taste, either as /ʧɪʧəˈrəʊni/ or /sɪsəˈrəʊni/.

cigarette. The normal pronunciation in British English is with the main stress on the final syllable, but Walter Nash (1986) observed that people move the stress to the first syllable to suit the rhythm of a clause or sentence. Thus *Cígarettes are déar* but *I smóked a cigarétte*. Stressing the first syllable is an alternative pronunciation in American English.

cinema. Fowler (1926), writing at a time when the film industry was becoming established, needed half a column of argument to justify the spelling and pronunciation of the word compared with the rival form *kinema* /kʌɪˈniːmə/ (falsely stressed; cf. Greek κίνημα). *Cinema* /ˈsɪnɪmə/, of course, has triumphed, and has generated a formative prefix *cine-* (*cine-camera, -film*, etc.). *Cinematograph*, the original full form in English, has been entirely displaced by its abbreviation *cinema*.

Cingalese is an archaic form of *Sinhalese,* which remains as a language name, and also as the name of the majority of the population of Sri Lanka, but has been partially replaced by *Sri Lankan* as the general name for a native or inhabitant of the republic of *Sri Lanka* (until 1972 called *Ceylon*).

cinque. 1 Also *cinq.* The five on dice or cards is pronounced /sɪŋk/. *Ace, deuce, trey* /treɪ/, *cater* /ˈkeɪtə/, and *sice* /sʌɪs/, are the others of the series.

2 *Cinque Ports* /sɪŋk/ is the name for a group of ports (orig. five: Dover, Hastings, Hythe, Romney, and Sandwich; Rye and Winchelsea were added later) on the SE coast of England with ancient trading privileges.

Cinquecento. Pronounced /ˌʧɪŋkwɪˈʧɛntəʊ/. For its meaning see TRECENTO.

cinquefoil. Pronounced /ˈsɪŋkfɔɪl/ both in its botanical and its architectural sense.

cion. See SCION.

cipher. The preferred spelling (not *cy-*).

circuit is pronounced /ˈsəːkɪt/ and *circuitry* /ˈsəːkɪtrɪ/, but *circuitous* is pronounced /səːˈkjuːɪtəs/ with the *-ui-* treated as a diphthong.

circumbendibus. See FACETIOUS FORMATIONS.

circumcise. Like *exercise, televise,* and a few other words, always spelt with *-ise.* See -ISE 1.

circumlocution lacks a well-established adjective, though *-locutional* (first recorded 1865), *-locutionary* (1863), and *-locutory* (1659) are all used from time to time. Synonyms like *periphrastic* and *roundabout* are preferred.

circumstance. Debate about the merits of *in the circumstances* and *under the circumstances* continued for most of the 20c. The pedantic view is that since circumstances are, etymologically speaking, around (*circum*) us, we must be *in* them and not *under* them; but Fowler rightly rejected this argument as puerile and observed that 'under the same Circumstances' was recorded in 1665 in the *OED* and 'in (the) circumstances' not until much later (in fact 1856). On the other hand, some other usage guides (including *The Economist Style Guide*) continue to blacklist *under the circumstances.*

The *OED* distinction, 'Mere situation is expressed by "*in* the circumstances", action affected is performed "*under* the circumstances"', is a subtle one, and no more than a general guide. It is as well to bear in mind that the choice of *in* versus *under* is affected by the preceding adjectives or other qualifiers: so *in certain circumstances, in such circumstances, in present circumstances; under these circumstances, under no circumstances, she won't agree under any circumstances* are all idiomatic constructions.

cirrus has plural *cirri* /ˈsɪrʌɪ/. See -US.

civil partnership is 'a legally recognized relationship similar to but distinct from marriage, available in certain jurisdictions to same-sex couples' (*OED*). In the UK, a form of civil union was brought into force by the Civil Partnership Act of 2004. See also GAY MARRIAGE.

clad. See CLOTHE.

claim. There are three areas of difficulty with this word. The first concerns *claim + that,* and the second *claim + to.* The third concerns the expression *to claim responsibility.* There are five uses of the verb *to claim* that are beyond dispute: **1** Used transitively meaning 'to demand as one's due or right' (*the creditor claimed repayment*).

2 + certain kinds of *to*-infinitive phrases (*every townsman could claim to be tried by his fellow-townsmen; he claimed to be the next-of-kin*) (but see 6 (i) below).

3 + a *that*-clause (*he claimed that his offer was a generous one*) (but see 6 (ii) below).

4 In insurance = to make a claim (for an indemnity) (*Before deciding to claim for a small amount of damage,* etc.).

5 To assert and demand recognition of (an alleged right, attribute, etc.) (*the degree of accuracy that has been claimed for them; both sides claimed victory; the only living but distant relative claimed the title after the childless duke died*).

6 There are three areas of potential or actual dispute: (i) *claim to.* H. W. and F. G. Fowler in *The King's English* (1906) said that *claim* should not be followed by an infinitive except when the subject of *claim* is also that of the infinitive. 'Thus, *I claim to be honest,* but not *I claim this to be honest.*' They objected to sentences of the type *The constant failure to live up to what we claim to be our most serious convictions proves that we do not hold them at all* (*Daily Tel.*, *a*1906). Passive constructions such as **This central Asian wine was claimed to be drinkable for up to 10 years—Oxford Companion to Wine,* 2000 would also be rejected on the same principle. The weight of current usage, however, has all but overturned this rule, e.g. *levels of greed and selfishness that Labour once claimed to be the trademark of the Thatcher years—OEC,* 2007. It is principally on grounds of style that alternative constructions using *assert, contend, maintain,* etc., might be preferred.

(ii) *claim* + *that*-clause. There is an argument that *claim* should not be used as a mere synonym for *allege, assert, declare, maintain, say,* etc., but should contain an element of argued contention, e.g.: *He claimed that adding VAT to domestic fuel and power would help create a greener and cleaner world by stimulating the use of more energy efficiency measures—Environment Digest,* 1990. In line with that, the following would be considered inappropriate: *The Sun claims that the Stonebridge council estate in north London 'is Britain's tinderbox where Los Angeles-style riots could explode at any time'—New Statesman,* 1992.

(iii) *claim responsibility for.* In news reports, it is often said that a particular group *claimed responsibility for* (an attack, bombing, etc.). The objection is that the use of *claim* implies something laudable or desirable, whereas a terrorist attack is neither. Alternative expressions such as *accept* or *admit responsibility* or *declare that* (they were responsible) avoid these sensitivities, but *claim* is likely to remain by far the commonest verb used in this connection in the mass media.

clamant, used to mean 'clamorous, noisy', is either poetical (*This clamant word Broke through the careful silence—*Keats, 1818) or pompously journalistic (*A deliriously clamant crowd rightly thought a try inevitable—Times,* 1963). In some Scottish writing it is used, quite acceptably, to mean 'urgent' (*My appetite was a clamant, instant annoyance—*R. L. Stevenson, 1878; *Instead, from day one, they should have shouted from the rooftops the clamant need for the most radical reform—Scotland on Sunday,* 2005).

clamber, clamour. To *clamour* (or *clamor* in AmE) for something or to do something means to seek or demand something forcefully, e.g. *Facebook expects investors to clamour for a piece of the social-networking company—NZ Herald,* 2011; *Seekers after equality clamoured to be admitted to smoke-filled male haunts—The F Word,* 2001. To *clamber* means to climb, of course, and is sometimes wrongly used for *clamour*. Presumably this amusing malapropism arises from the idea of physically clambering somewhere to get a better view: **Now, it seems, there is a positive clambering to acknowledge her talents—Sunday Herald,* 2000; **Unfortunately, the included 64 MB of memory will have owners desperately clambering for additional storage space—Infopackets,* 2007.

clandestine. The recommended pronunciation in British and American stresses the second syllable, and has a short *i* in the third, /klanˈdɛstɪn/ (klan-**des**-tin). Alternatively, the first syllable can be stressed: /ˈklandɛstɪn/ (**klan**-des-tin). In AmE pronouncing the last syllable to rhyme with *tine* and *teen* is acceptable, but to British ears sounds odd.

classic, classical. *Classic* and *classical* have distinct meanings, which occasionally overlap. A not uncommon mistake is to use *classical* where *classic* is more appropriate. *Classical* is the normal word to refer to the arts and literature of ancient Greece and Rome (*a classical scholar, classical Latin, architecture of classical proportions*), and to other ancient cultures, such as Chinese culture. The Greek and Roman works studied, and the subject itself, are called (*the*) *Classics* with an initial capital letter. *Classical* is also applied to traditional forms of dance (*classical ballet*), and to serious or conventional music (i.e. that of Bach, Beethoven, Brahms, Mozart, etc.) as distinct from light or popular music; and in physics to the concepts which preceded relativity and quantum theory. *Classical* has come to be widely used in marketing circles to denote anything made in a supposedly traditional style: *Classical designs of branded* *clothing are on show—Shanghai Star*, 2003, but in this context *classic* is preferable.

Classic means (*a*) 'of acknowledged excellence' (*the classic textbook on the subject*); (*b*) 'very typical and representative of its kind' (*a classic example of money wasting*); (*c*) referring to a garment or design, 'of a simple, elegant style not greatly subject to changes in fashion' (*a classic little black dress*). Often *classical* is used when *classic* is more appropriate: a *classical* example is one taken from an ancient, especially Greek or Roman, culture, whereas a *classic* example is the most typical example of its kind. In the following example **In the UK, we have a classical example of why compensation does not make up for loss—OEC*, 2001, read *classic*.

clause. In a book like this, that by its nature cannot offer a full-scale presentation of English grammar, the terminology must needs be kept to basic essentials. In simple terms a *clause* is one level above a *phrase* which in turn is one level above a *word*. A main or principal clause is of the type *He arrived at Heathrow airport at 12 noon*. The sentence could continue with a subordinate clause, e.g. *because the plane was scheduled to depart at 2 o'clock*. The essential nature of a clause is that it should have a subject (*He; the plane*) and a predicate (*arrived at Heathrow airport*, etc.; *was scheduled*, etc.). The subject and predicate can be further divided into their *constituents*. Accordingly, *the plane* consists of the definite article or determiner (*the*) and a noun (*plane*); *at Heathrow airport* consists of a preposition (*at*) and a noun phrase (*Heathrow airport*); *was scheduled* consists of an auxiliary (*was*) and a main verb (*scheduled*), and can also be called a verb phrase. Modern grammars are studded with algebraic-looking strings of various types. The subordinate clause *because the plane was scheduled to depart at 2 o'clock* can be set out in a serial manner as

conj. + NP (det. + noun) + VP (aux. + main verb) + *to*-inf. + prep. phrase

or in diagrammatic form as illustrated.

Analyses of this kind will not be attempted in this book, but readers should be warned that they will find a forest of tree-diagrams and elaborate bracketings and abbreviations in most modern grammars. Those who quail before such analyses should at any rate be prepared to master such abbreviations as S (subject), V (verb), O (object), C (complement), and A (adverbial), e.g. *My son* [S] *considers* [V] *the price* [O] *quite reasonable* [C] *in the circumstances* [A].

clean, cleanly. *Clean*, spelt *clǣne* (with a final -*e*), was already an adverb (as well as an adjective) in OE, and has never ceased to be one. Modern examples: *the bullet went clean through his shoulder-blade; it went clean out of my mind; the car plunged clean over the cliff*. (In a sentence like *the room must be swept clean*, 'clean' can be analysed as an adjective standing as complement of the predicate.) It would be absurd to add -*ly* to *clean* in any of these examples.

For the 'absent -*ly*' syndrome, see CLEAR, CLEARLY.

clear, clearly. 1 Whenever a single-syllable adjective is used in an obviously adverbial role some people suffer from what might be called the 'absent -*ly*' or 'something-is-missing syndrome'. Because so many single-syllable adjectives (*apt, brief, damp*, etc.) are never used as adverbs,

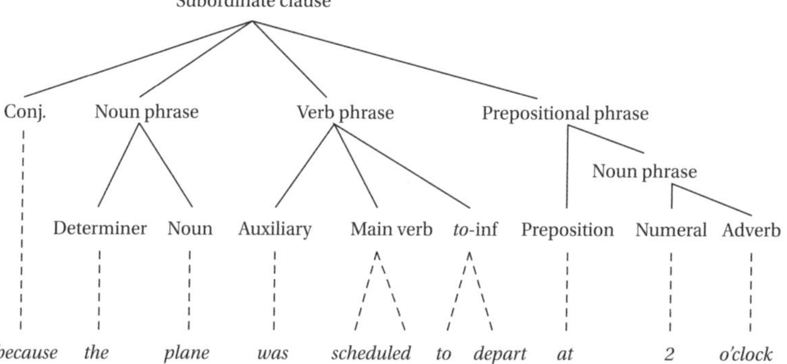

it is an easy step to believing that none can be used. But it would be absurd to substitute *clearly* for *clear* in such phrases as *go clear, keep clear, stand clear, stay clear, steer clear, loud and clear,* or in sentences like *the thieves got clear away.*

2 Nevertheless, it should be emphasized that the normal relationship between the two words is shown by the contrastive pair *a clear disappointment* (adjective)/*it is clearly a disappointment* (adverb).

3 *Clearly* is overwhelmingly the more usual adverbial form of the two. In the following examples it could not be replaced by *clear*: (as simple adverb) *the author writes clearly and concisely*; (used as intensifier) *he was clearly mad;* (as a sentence adverb) *Clearly the Minister of State should resign.*

cleave¹ (to split). A separate verb from CLEAVE², *cleave*¹ is a mostly literary word with unfixed past tenses. In the past tense *clave* is archaic; *clove, cleft,* and *cleaved* are all permissible, but *cleaved* is the more usual of the three, especially in scientific and technical contexts. The past participle is *cloven* or *cleaved* (especially in many technical uses). The adjective is *cloven* in some fixed expressions (*cloven-footed, cloven hoof*) and *cleft* in some others (*cleft palate, in a cleft stick*). See also CLEFT SENTENCE.

cleave² (to stick fast, adhere). A separate word from CLEAVE¹, *cleave*² is fairly regularly conjugated as *cleave/cleaved/cleaved,* except that the archaic variant *clave,* doubtless as an echo of the Bible, occurs occasionally. Biblical (AV) examples: *The Nobles held their peace, and their tongue cleaued to the roofe of their mouth* (Job 29: 10); *and Orpah kissed her mother in law, but Ruth claue vnto her* (Ruth 1: 14).

cleft. See CLEAVE¹.

cleft lip is the standard accepted term and should be used instead of *harelip,* which is likely to cause offence.

cleft sentence. In grammar, a *cleft sentence* is one 'derived from another by dividing the latter into two clauses, each with its own finite verb, so as to place emphasis on a particular component of the original sentence. *Bob always plays golf on Sundays* could be reworded as any of the following cleft sentences: *It is Bob who always plays golf on Sundays*; *It is golf that Bob always plays on Sundays*; *It is on Sundays that Bob always plays golf*' (*Oxford Dictionary of English Grammar*). Cleft sentences are a common feature of spoken and written English.

clematis. The standard pronunciation in British English is /ˈklɛmətɪs/, but the variant /kləˈmeɪtɪs/, with the main stress on the second syllable, is encountered often enough, and especially abroad. *Clematis* is the form usually used to denote the plural, with no change (e.g. *in fact clematis come in a variety of guises*). Alternatively, you can use the plural *clematises.* The form *clematii,* though not infrequenty encountered, is completely wrong.

clench, clinch. *Clinch* is a 16c. variant spelling of *clench* (from Old English (*be*) *clencan*) and since then has been treated as a separate word. We *clench* our teeth, fingers, or fist. We *clinch* an argument, bargain, etc.; lovers *clinch* (embrace), and so do boxers and wrestlers. A remark or statement that settles an argument is a *clincher.* Usually nails are *clinched* (not *clenched*) to make a *clinker-built* (also *clincher-built*) boat. Occasionally *clinch* is mistakenly used for *clench,* presumably because it is a more frequent word, as in **I clinched my teeth, *he clinched his fist,* etc.

clerestory. Pronounced /ˈklɪəˌstɔːri/.

clerk. Pronounced /klɑːk/ in British English and /klɜːrk/ in American English.

clever. Fowler (1926) wrote a splendidly prejudiced piece about the misuse of *clever,* 'especially in feminine conversation' in the sense of 'learned, well read, bookish, or studious'. Nowadays, while *clever* is normally a term of approval (= skilful, talented; quick to understand and learn), it can be used contextually in a negative sense, or sarcastically, implying slickness or mere ingenuity (*clever-clever, clever clogs, clever Dick, too clever by half,* etc.).

clew, clue. They are 'the same word' (from Old English *cliwen*), but *clew* has gradually become confined to two main uses, (*a*) a ball of thread in the legend of Theseus enabling him to find his way through a labyrinth; (*b*) as a nautical term = a lower or after corner of a sail; a set of small cords suspending a hammock. Since the 17c., *clue* has gone its own way and now has a wide range of uses in which its literal sense is obscured. It broadly means 'a piece of evidence' (in a treasure hunt, a detective novel, a crossword puzzle, etc.) putting one on the track of a discovery, a solution, etc.

cliché. A *cliché* is a phrase that has become meaningless with overuse; for example, it is now meaningless to wish someone *a nice day* because a once sincere intention has become an empty cliché. In the printing trade, French *cliché* was a stereotype block, which produced the same page over and over again. (It was the past participle of the verb *clicher* 'to stereotype', said to be imitative of the sharp contact of matrix and metal.) Dislike of threadbare, stereotyped expressions is a relatively recent phenomenon: the word *cliché* is first recorded in English in 1892.

He was, however, on the whole, taking all things into consideration, by and large, not to put too fine a point on it, reasonably well self-sufficient. So wrote Anthony Burgess, in a classic mocking of clichés, in *Inside Mr Enderby* (1963). Despite the fact that Nicholas Bagnall wrote a spirited book called *A Defence of Clichés* in 1985, familiar overworked expressions are more often than not mercilessly pilloried. Everyone will have his or her personal list of stock phrases that annoy the hell out of them (I know I have mine). Judging what is a cliché is to an extent subjective, but the common denominator must be that the phrases are wildly overused and, as one writer on clichés has put it, 'do your thinking for you'. Among clichés often ridiculed in Britain are: *at the end of the day, at this moment in time, draw a line under, explore every avenue, in this day and age, leave no stone unturned, a level playing-field, over the moon, situation* (preceded by a noun or phrase, e.g. *a crisis situation*), *take on board, think outside the box*, and *this is the 21st century.*

It should be noted that in the course of the 20c. the word *cliché* came to be applied to commonplace things of other kinds—visual images, stock situations, remarks in radio or TV shows (*Am I bovvered?*), ideas, attitudes, etc. When reviewing Bagnall's book, Burchfield said that 'clichés are a sad subject, really, always reminding us of the repetitiveness of things, the humdrumness that lies beyond and within the doorstep if one's imagination should weaken or one's sense of humour runs out'. But perhaps the wisest comments on clichés were by Christopher Ricks (1980): 'A cliché begins as heartfelt, and then its heart sinks.' 'The only way to speak of a cliché is with a cliché.'

client has extended its range dramatically in recent years. Previously, a person using the services of a professional—a lawyer, an architect, an accountant, etc.—was a *client.* A person using the services of a sex worker was traditionally also a *client.* Shops have *customers*; so too, probably, do car showrooms, but hairdressing salons call their customers *clients* rather than customers. Theatres, restaurants, and hotels have *patrons,* but takeaways are regarded as shops and have *customers.* In the world of privatized public transport, *passengers* are often referred to as *customers* or sometimes even as *clients.* In the interests of neutral description, social workers now have *clients* rather than the more judgemental *cases* or *patients.*

clientele. A body of *clients* is a *clientele* /ˌkliːɒn'tɛl/, no accent, not italic.

climacteric. 1 The older pronunciation with the main stress on *-ter-*, which was favoured by Johnson, Walker, and some 19c. lexicographers, and is given precedence by the *OED*, has now been mostly replaced by /klʌɪ'maktərɪk/.

2 It is used as adjective and noun to refer to 'a critical period or moment in history, a person's life or career, etc.' e.g. *At any rate the unprecedented success of the War Requiem marked a climacteric in Britten's career*—M. Kennedy, 1993; or to refer as the *OED* expresses it, to 'the period in middle age at which a person's reproductive or sexual capacity declines; *spec.* (in women) the menopause', e.g. *hot flushes or other climacteric symptoms.*

climactic is an adjective formed in English in the 19c. from *climax* on the model of *syntax/syntactic,* but not on Greek analogies. Fowler (1926) disliked it: 'It may fairly be demanded of the literary critics who alone have occasion for the adjective that they should mend it or end it.' It closely resembles *climatic*, of or relating to climate, also first recorded in the 19c. The two are quite often confused, *climactic* being more often wrongly used for *climatic* than the other way round. Examples: (correct) *My biggest reservations relate to the climactic battle scene*—*OEC*, 2005; *Life in such* *climatic extremes is lived on the edge*—OEC, 2002; (incorrect) **a climatic showdown at the villain's highly mechanized lair*—OEC, 2004; **despite the region's extremely harsh climactic conditions*—OEC, 2001.

climate. From its normal weather-related sense, *climate*, beginning in the 17c., developed a valuable metaphorical meaning, 'the mental, moral, etc., environment or attitude of a body of people in respect of some aspect of life, policy, etc., especially in *climate of opinion, of thought*': *To us he* [*sc.* Freud] *is no more a person Now but a whole climate of opinion*—W. H. Auden, 1940; *The whole climate of thought will be different*—G. Orwell, 1949.

climatic. See CLIMACTIC.

climax. From a Greek word meaning 'ladder' the term was originally (first in the 16c.) used in English in rhetoric as 'a figure in which a number of propositions or ideas are set forth so as to form a series in which each rises above the preceding in force or effectiveness of expression'. So, the biblical (1 Cor. 2: 9) (1) *Eye hath not seene,* (2) *nor eare heard,* (3) *neither haue entred into the heart of man, /the things which God hath prepared for them that loue him* proceeds through three progressive stages of strangeness. Wales (1989) cites an example of 1553 from the work of Thomas Wilson; *Of sloth cometh pleasure, of pleasure cometh spending, of spending cometh whoring, of whoring cometh lack, of lack cometh theft, of theft cometh hanging, and here an end for this world.*

Popular use of this technical term in the 18c. led to the ordinary current meanings, (*a*) the event or point of greatest intensity or interest; a culmination or apex; (*b*) 20c., the sexual sense. In both of these meanings it is also used as a verb.

clime is a literary or poetical word for a tract or region of the earth, often considered in relation to its distinctive climate, and has also been used metaphorically, as in the first example: *This inclement clime of human life*—Edward Young, 1742; *Every man of every clime*—W. Blake, 1783–94; *Where a sweet clime was breathed from a land Of fragrance ... and flowers*—Keats, 1820. Fowler (1926) suggested that to be acceptable in ordinary prose it must mean 'always region (often with reference to its characteristic weather), & never, like climate, the weather conditions themselves'. Nowadays, however, it largely occurs in fixed phrases—some would say clichés—such as *foreign climes, warmer climes, sunnier climes,* which combine the place and climate meanings.

cling. The principal parts were once *cling/clang/clung,* but *clang* as past tense withdrew into regional use in the 19c. The past tense now in standard English is always *clung.*

clique, 'a small group of people who spend time together and do not let others join them', is among the thousands of English words purloined from French. If English speakers use French words a lot, they usually alter the pronunciation: for example, it would be very affected indeed to pronounce *clairvoyant* as the French do. But it is better to say *clique* with the French-like pronunciation /kliːk/, (kleek), rather than /klɪk/, to avoid confusion with *click.* Nevertheless, the latter pronunciation is quite widespread, especially in AmE.

clitoris comes via New Latin from Greek. The standard plural is *clitorises; clitorides* replicates the Greek plural, and is also used, but is rather technical. *Clitori* is wrong.

clone, from Greek κλών 'twig', 'slip', came into English at the beginning of the 20c. in the technical language of botany (later in biology). Since about 1970 it has swept into popular use of a person or animal that strongly resembles its parent; and also of a person or thing whose behaviour, appearance, or activities are directly modelled on those of another (well-known) person or thing: e.g. — *is a typical Sloane Ranger clone*; *there were several Jaguar clones in the car park.*

close (verb) has a suggestion of formality or politeness when it is used in contexts in which *shut* might sound rather peremptory: *Close the door after you and we'll have a talk.* Private talks are usually held *behind closed doors.* But a child who has entered a room and carelessly left the door open will almost certainly be asked by its parent to *shut* (not *close*) *the door. Closed* has a life of its own. Some trade unions are *closed shops*; a gallery is often *closed* to the public on Mondays; the stock market *closed* one point up on the day's dealing; Albania used to be a *closed society*; Hebrew is *a closed book* (i.e. is unknown) to most people. In none of these examples would *shut* be possible.

close (adjective) is used in scores of collocations: *close contest, friend, proximity, resemblance, shave,* etc. Occasionally people mistakenly use *closed formation* for *close formation,* in the meaning 'very close together'. In Britain the season when something, especially the killing of game, is illegal is the *close season* but in the US it is the *closed season.*

close, closely. 1 No strict dividing line can be drawn between predicative uses of the adjective *close* (e.g. *the weather remained sultry and close*) and adverbial ones, e.g. *to stand, sit, lie,* etc., *close* (i.e. in immediate contact or proximity); with verbs of motion, as *come, bring,* etc., *close*; or with prepositions *by, to, beside,* etc. (*close by the wall; he came close to solving the problem; she sat close beside him*).

2 *Close* is a Middle English loanword from Old French. It was not until the mid-16c. that it acquired the native suffix *-ly* in printed work. Then *closely* gradually became the dominant form.

3 Despite the dominance overall of *closely,* there are some highly idiomatic phrases in which it should be avoided: *for close on 200 years; sticking close to his desk; the road runs close beside the river; stay close together; close on the heels of.* Examples (of *closely* infelicitously used): *The killings also come closely on the heels of the disbanding of the dreaded SOG (Special Operations Group)*—OEC, 2004; *Danny, needs to escape an asylum past guards and other inmates by sticking closely to the shadows*—OEC, 2007.

4 Some grammarians treat *close to,* as in *he was standing close to the door,* as a complex preposition.

closure. 1 The *closure* included by Fowler in his 1926 edition is a parliamentary term which he was at pains to distinguish from other ways of bringing a debate to an end (see 2). Much more relevant to most people nowadays is the meaning derived from psychoanalysis, namely 'a sense of personal resolution; a feeling that an emotionally difficult experience has been conclusively settled or accepted'. This formerly technical term has become part of general language in phrases such as *to achieve, bring, find, get, closure,* e.g. *His death will bring closure to all those traumatized no matter if they believe he is guilty or not*—OEC, 2002. It is in danger of becoming a rather woolly cliché.

2 Several names are used for the provision by which a debate in the House of Commons can be cut short in spite of the wish of a minority to continue it. The most important one is the *closure* (introduced in 1882), a decision by vote or under rules to put a question without further debate. The equivalent French word *clôture* (used in English without the circumflex) was occasionally used in the House of Commons instead of *closure,* but has fallen out of use there. It survives, however, in the procedures of some legislative bodies in the United States. A *gag rule* (or *gag law*) came into use in America at the end of the 18c. as a means of preventing or restricting discussion in a legislative body. The word *gag* was later adopted in the House of Commons, applied opprobriously to the action of a parliamentary majority in 'closuring' a debate. The *guillotine* (first recorded 1893), or closure by instalments, is a method used in the House of Commons for preventing obstruction or undue delays by fixing the dates and times at which specified stages of a bill must be voted on. The *kangaroo,* or *kangaroo closure,* is a UK term (first recorded in 1913) for a Parliamentary closure by which some amendments are selected for discussion and some excluded. The unselected (normally minor) items are then voted on without debate.

cloth. The aristocratic, Mitfordian pronunciation /klɔːθ/ lingers on, just, in the speech of a few elderly patricians, but has been almost entirely replaced in the standard language by /klɒθ/. The plural *cloths* is normally pronounced /klɒθs/ but modern dictionaries of pronunciation also record /klɒðz/.

clothe has *clad* beside *clothed* both as past tense and past participle. While *clothed,* however, is suitable in most contexts (except when *dressed* is more suitable as less formal), *clad* is (1) either somewhat more formal or literary, or (2) never used absolutely, but always with some specification of the kind of clothing, or qualified by an adverb (e.g. *ill-clad, insufficiently clad*), or (3) in technical use. Accordingly, *clad* cannot be substituted for *clothed* in *You* *were fed and clothed at my expense* or *When he was dressed he let us in*. But it stands unchallenged by *clothed* (or *dressed*) in literary contexts like Coleridge's *I guess, 'twas frightful there to see A lady so richly clad as she* and Milton's *'Tis Chastity, my brother, Chastity: She that has that, is clad in complete steel*; also, qualified by an adverb, *They are lightly clad in summer*; and in metallurgy, etc. (*steel clad with Ni* [*sc.* nickel] *on one side; clad with stainless steel*).

As a second element *-clad* is frequent in such compound adjectives as *ice-clad, ivy-clad, olive-clad* (hills), *snow-clad*.

clothes. Until about the end of the 19c. the more usual standard pronunciation seems to have been /kləʊz/, with ample authority from rhymes in 17c. and 18c. poets, including Shakespeare (*Then vp he rose, and dond his close—Hamlet*). Daniel Jones (1917) described this pronunciation as 'old-fashioned'. The spelling-pronunciation /kləʊðz/ has now almost entirely replaced it.

cloture. See CLOSURE 2.

cloud. First recorded in the US in the 1950s, *on cloud seven* or especially *on cloud nine*, meaning 'in a euphoric state', has become standard everywhere. Clouds are divided into classes. In Webster's Third (1961), *cloud nine* = a cumulonimbus cloud, i.e. a mountainous cumulus cloud, a thundercloud, the ninth highest in a ten-part classification (*stratus* is the tenth). According to William and Mary Morris (1988), the popularity of the phrase may be credited to an American radio show of the 1950s in which every time the hero was knocked unconscious—which was often—he was transported to *cloud nine*. There he could speak again.

cloven. See CLEAVE[1].

clue. See CLEW.

co-. Prefix of Latin origin. To illustrate the issue with words starting with this prefix, there are three potential ways of writing *cooperate* (*cooperate, co-operate, coöperate*), but the third, with the diaeresis ¨, has been abandoned

The form recommended nowadays is *cooperate* (also *cooperation, cooperative, uncooperative*), despite the clash of the two letter *o*s. (*Coordinate, coordination*, etc., are also the recommended spellings.)

The spellings recommended for other words containing the prefix *co-* are as follows: (*a*) Hyphen never used: (*coagulate, coalition, coefficient, cohabit, cohere, coincide, coition* (in most of which *co-* is hardly felt to be a prefix in English). (*b*) Hyphen best avoided, though sometimes used: *coed, coequal, coeval, coexist, coexistence, coordinate* (also *uncoordinated*), (common words in which the main element is transparent). (*c*) Scientific and technical words in scholarly work: *coaxial, cosec, cosecant, coseismal, cosine, cotangent* (clear to scientists, etc.).

Words commonly written with a hyphen include: (*a*) *co-respondent* (in divorce case) to avoid confusion with *correspondent*. (*b*) *co-actor, co-author* (noun and verb), *co-determination, co-driver, co-editor, co-education, co-host, co-latitude, co-parent, co-partner, co-pilot, co-signatory, co-star, co-tidal, co-worker* (hyphen used to avoid momentary perplexity on the part of the reader). (*c*) Others: *co-occur, co-occurrence, co-op, co-opt, co-own* (the two *o*s might otherwise be pronounced as /kuː/).

cobalt. The pronunciation recommended is /ˈkəʊbɔːlt/ not /-bɒlt/.

cobra. The pronunciations /ˈkəʊbrə/ and /ˈkɒbrə/ seem to be equally frequent in British English.

cocaine. In our drug-ridden world, the substance, pronounced /kəʊˈkeɪn/, is all too familiar. The relevant entry in the *OED* (1891) gave a three-syllabled pronunciation, equivalent in the IPA to /ˈkəʊkeɪˌʌɪn/, as the regular one, and described /kəʊˈkeɪn/ as 'vulgar'. Times have changed.

coccyx. Bone at base of spine. Pronounced /ˈkɒksɪks/. The plural is *coccyxes* or, rather rarely, *coccyges* /-ɪdʒiːz/.

cockscomb, coxcomb. Nowadays, the first spelling (formerly also written *cock's-comb*) is 'the crest or comb of a cock'; formerly also 'a jester's cap (shaped like a cock's comb)'. *Coxcomb*, a respelt version of the same word, means 'an ostentatiously conceited man, a dandy'. Any of the three spellings is likely to turn up in earlier literature for any of the meanings.

cocoa, originally a corruption, of CACAO, is now the only spelling for 'a powder made from crushed cacao seeds, often with other ingredients; a drink made from this'. So *cocoa bean, butter.*

codex. Plural *codices* /'kəʊdɪˌsiːz/. See -EX, -IX 2; LATIN PLURALS.

coed, co-ed. Normally without a hyphen. Its use as a noun meaning (*a*) a coeducational institution, (*b*) (especially US) a female student at such an institution, has become much less frequent as such institutions have become more common. The distinction is much less noteworthy than it was, for example, when Auden wrote *Enormous novels by co-eds Rain down on our defenceless heads* in *Nones* (1951). But the word remains in frequent use as an adjective, '(of an educational institution) open to or attended by both males and females'.

coffin. See CASKET.

cognate. 1 In philology, used (as adjective and noun) of a word in a given language having the same linguistic family or derivation as the corresponding word in another language, as English *father*, German *Vater*, Latin *pater*, all going back to the same Indo-European base **pətēr*. The term is also applied to languages derived from the same original language, e.g. Spanish, French, Italian, and Portuguese, all descended from Latin, are *cognate languages.*

2 *cognate object* (or *cognate accusative*). In grammar, an object that is related in origin and sense to the verb governing it (as in live *a good* life, die *a cruel* death, *he* fought *the good* fight, as distinct from *enjoy a good life, suffer a cruel death, win a hard fight*).

cognizance, cognizant, cognizable. 1 All three words are stressed on the first syllable, and have a short letter *i* /ɪ/. Sometimes the pronunciation /kɒg'nʌɪzəns/ is heard. These words were frequently pronounced with the *g* silent (/'kɒnɪzəns/, etc.) until well into the 20c., and the *OED* still lists such pronunciations as acceptable variants. It is recommended that the *g* be sounded, if only to make the words consistent with related words in which it has always been pronounced, as *cognate, cognition*, and *cognitive.*

2 Replacing the -*z*- with an -*s*- to spell *cognisance*, etc, is an acceptable though less common variant.

cognoscenti. This is the plural form of *cognoscente*, 'one who knows a subject thoroughly; a connoisseur: chiefly in reference to the fine arts'. It can be pronounced /ˌkɒgnə'ʃɛntiː/, kog-nuh-**shen**-tee, the first syllable rhyming with *cog*, or, more rarely, /ˌkɒnjə'ʃɛntiː/, kon-yuh-**shen**-tee. The singular is hardly ever used, but is sometimes mistakenly written when the plural is intended, as in **the giant table and chair plonked in a public place that has drawn high praise from the art cognoscente—OEC.*

coherent, cohesive. Both words come from a Latin root, *cohærēre* which is the ancestor of our word *cohere*, but their meanings are subtly different. *Coherent* means 'logical and consistent' and is applied to plans and strategies, and to speakers and their arguments. *Cohesive* means 'tending to stick together' and is generally used either physically (as with liquid mixtures, for example) or in a more abstract sense, to describe groups, communities, units, etc. To illustrate the difference, a *coherent* approach to an issue is one which is consistent and well considered; a *cohesive* approach is one which aims to promote greater unity among the people involved. Occasionally people use *cohesive* when *coherent* would be more appropriate, as in the final example below. Examples: (*coherent*) *The company lacks a coherent strategy for future success in online music sales—OEC*, 2004; *I'm still waiting to hear a coherent argument against gay marriage—OEC*, 2005; (*cohesive*) *The fate of the cohesive gel implant rests in the results of studies in the years ahead—Cosmetic Surgery Times*, 2003; *He was not able to show that they acted together as a cohesive political force*—T. Harris, 1993; *Living and travelling together in cohesive groups is a feature of nomadic peoples—OEC*, 2002; (*cohesive* instead of *coherent*) *?The lack of a cohesive strategy beggars belief—OEC*, 2000.

cohort. The use of this word to mean 'an assistant, a colleague, an accomplice' is likely still to cause purists 'wailing and gnashing of teeth' of biblical proportions, despite its over sixty years of existence. An excursion into the word's earlier history may help explain such a violent reaction. In the Roman army a *cohors* (accusative *cohortem*) was a body of infantry consisting of 300–600 men (in some units 500 to 1,000 men). Ten cohorts made a legion. Taken into English in the 15c., the word was quickly used of similar divisions in other armies (e.g. *the Cohort bright Of Watchfull Cherubim*—Milton, 1667; *The Assyrian came down like a wolf on the fold, And his cohorts were gleaming in purple and* gold—Byron, 1815), and then of any band of persons united in defence of a common cause (*My friends and my acquaintances . . . I had a numerous cohort of the latter*—Bolingbroke, 1719). The word acquired new meanings in the mid-20c. First, from the 1940s, it was applied in demography to a group of people having a common statistical characteristic, especially that of being born in the same year. As technical demographic jargon, the use lies out of reach of the general public and is doing no one any harm.

But more or less simultaneously it began to be used in American English to mean 'an assistant, a colleague, an accomplice': *The old poet had left, accompanied by two of his cohorts*—M. McCarthy, 1952; *Mr. Stratton consented, since it was four o'clock, to partake together with his cohort, of a sandwich and a glass of milk*—A. Cross, 1967. Before long the use turned up in the British press and in other contexts in Britain: *The impending trial of Bobby Seale, chairman of the Black Panther movement, and his eight cohorts in New Haven*—*Sunday Times*, 1970; *Brock and Emma had one wall, Bob, Johnny and their cohorts the other wall and centre aisle*—J. le Carré, 1989.

There are two threads to the explanation of how the word acquired this meaning, which can now hardly be regarded as new. On the one hand, it seems likely that *co-* was interpreted as the prefix used in *cooperate, cohabit, coincide*, etc, implying a general notion of 'with, together'. On the other, the use of *cohorts* in the plural was capable either of being understood as meaning 'a number of groups', or of being taken to mean 'a number of individual people in a single group'. The second interpretation seems to have prevailed over time, and so the singular was interpreted to mean 'assistant, colleague, etc.'

Whatever the explanation, this new meaning is now here to stay in all varieties of English. As Burchfield commented, it is 'a remarkable example of a descending scale of meaning (from "a tenth of a Roman legion" to "a single assistant")'. More portentously, he suggested: 'Our language becomes vulnerable when the majority of its speakers forget major sections of Western history, in this case the fighting arrangements of Roman armies.' But it could be argued (despite my own personal distaste for it) that the change in meaning of *cohort* is no more objectionable than the change of meaning of *decimate*, similarly derived from ancient warfare, whose evolution he described more soberly.

coiffeur, coiffure. *Coiffeur*, meaning a hairdresser, is pronounced /kwɑːˈfəː/ (feminine **coiffeuse** /-ˈfəːz/). *Coiffure*, meaning the way hair is arranged, is pronounced /kwɑːˈfjʊə/. As long-standing loanwords from French, *coiffeur* (1847), *coiffeuse* (1870), and *coiffure* (*a*1631), none of them needs italics in English.

colander, a word of long standing in the language (first recorded *c.*1450), is normally pronounced /ˈkʌləndə/. The variant form *cullender*, once common, is rarely encountered now.

coldslaw. See COLESLAW.

cold war (or **Cold War**). Wrongly written lower case by most people, it should properly have initial capitals (*the Cold War*) when referring to the years of suppressed hostilities between the USSR and the Western powers after the 1939–45 war. After the collapse of Soviet Communism, the phrase disappeared along with the concept it described. It survives, however, in the weakened sense of 'a state of rivalry and tension between two rival factions, persons, etc.', in which meaning lower case is appropriate, e.g. *Ultimately, however, the police could at best lower the temperature of the cold war between ghetto and suburb, not remove the sources of conflict*—*OEC*, 2000.

coleslaw, a dressed salad of sliced raw cabbage, carrot, onion, etc., is so spelt, the first element being *cole* 'cabbage'. *Coldslaw* is a respectably old (first recorded in 1794), but mistaken, US variant, due to FOLK ETYMOLOGY. *Coleslaw* is an anglicized version of Dutch *koolsla*, from *kool* 'cabbage' + *sla*, a reduced colloquial form of *salade*.

colic yields the adjective *colicky*. For the spelling, see -C-, -CK-.

coliseum, colosseum. A *colosseum* is a large stadium or amphitheatre (from medieval Latin neuter of Latin *colosseus* 'gigantic'), especially the one with a capital *C* in Rome. The variant *coliseum* is used, especially in America, for a large public building for sporting events, exhibitions, etc., and, with capital *C*, as the name of theatres (including the well-known one in London), cinemas, and dance-halls.

collaborate. This verb, and the corresponding noun **collaborator**, acquired the sinister connotation of traitorous cooperation with the enemy during the Second World War. Fortunately the original sense, namely, to work in conjunction with another or others, especially in a literary or artistic production, can still be used without risk of ambiguity.

collation. In the Roman Catholic Church a light meal allowed in lieu of supper on fasting days. Originally applied to the light repast or refection taken by the members of Benedictine monasteries at the close of the day, after the reading of Cassian's *Collationes Patrum* (= Lives of the Fathers). In lay circles, the word is seldom used except in *cold collation.*

colleague. Etymologically, the word means 'one chosen along with another, a partner in office'. At one time, as the *OED* says, it was 'strictly, said of those who stand in the same relationship to their electors, or to the office which they jointly discharge', as illustrated by a comment by Gladstone in 1851: *The treaty ... upon ... which, as a Colleague of your Lordship, I had the honour to be employed.* The *OED* rather snootily and old-fashionedly still also says 'not applied to partners in trade or manufacture', and Burchfield felt that the word was on 'a downward spiral' because 'trade unions speak of their *colleagues* ... fellow-strikers, fellow-prison officers, associates of any kind, now qualify for the term *colleagues*'. Despite his qualms, and the *OED*'s anachronistic restriction of the word, it is completely acceptable to refer to anyone with whom one works in any profession or business. For the looser sense Burchfield disliked, *fellow-* is a useful alternative, e.g. *fellow-pupils, fellow-members, fellow-writers.*

collectable, collectible. Both these words function as adjectives and nouns, and both are correct. In the *OEC* data, *collectible* is the more frequent of the two in total, and is the preferred form in North American English in both functions. In British English the data suggests a preference for *collectable* as the adjective, while for the noun the two forms are equally common. Examples: (collectable) *A beautiful boxed catalogue was published which will remain eminently collectable—Architecture Australia Magazine*, 2001; *In total the thieves stole more than 100 bone china, porcelain and pottery collectables from three display cabinets—www.thisiswiltshire.co.uk*, 2005; (collectible) *I recently bought a collectible comic book on eBay*—weblog, 2005 (BrE); *We like art and collectibles and antiques; anything silver, mahogany or in a gilded frame—Art Business News*, 2000 (AmE).

collective noun, a noun that is normally singular in form and denotes a collection or number of individuals. Apart from the names of individual animals, birds, etc. (*deer, grouse, sheep*, etc.), terms for groups of animals, birds, etc. (*a pride of lions, a gaggle of geese*, etc.), and the names of institutions, firms, and teams (*BBC, Marks & Spencer, Tottenham Hotspur*, etc.), there are some 200 collective nouns in common use in English (*choir, committee, flock, multitude*, etc.).

There are several main considerations. **1** In British English it is in order to use *either* a plural verb *or* a singular verb after most collective nouns, so long as attendant pronouns are made to follow suit: *when the jury* retires *to consider* its *verdict; when the jury* retire *to consider* their *verdict.* What is to be avoided is switching from plural to singular or vice-versa in the same sentence, e.g. *A family displaced by fighting prepares* [singular] *to return to their* [plural] *village—Independent*, 2006.

The same principle applies to all the main collectives like *army, audience, clan, committee, company, court, crew, folk, government, group, herd.* By contrast, in American English the choice is much more restricted. For such words the following verb and any attendant pronouns are usually in the singular.

2 The principle at work in BrE is that if the collective noun is thought of as a unit, a singular verb or pronoun follows naturally (*Mention the* family *and everyone is for* it, *however they define* it); but if the members of the group are thought of as individuals, a plural verb or pronoun is appropriate (*I looked at my* family *and I knew that* they *did not know what I had seen*).

3 Collective nouns that stand for a group of inanimate objects, e.g. baggage, china, cutlery, earthenware, linen, luggage, stoneware, are always treated as singular.

4 When a collective noun is followed by *of* + a plural noun or pronoun, the choice between a singular and a plural verb remains open, but in practice a plural verb is somewhat more common: *a large number of conductors want to hear the great artists*—*Dædalus*, 1986; *a handful of bathers were bobbing about in the waves*—P. Roth, 1987; *the current crop of bestsellers include a number of monuments to bad taste*—*The Face*, 1987. Contrast: *one group of disenchanted Levellers puts pen to paper*—M. Lasky, 1985; *a fleet of helicopters was flying low*—*New Yorker*, 1986; *a pool of sheep is assembled for each trials session*—*Daily Tel.*, 1987.

5 Particular cases: (*a*) *the United States, the United Nations, the Vatican, the Commons, the House of Lords, Congress* (US) are always treated as singular (e.g. *the United States* has *demanded a more open Japan*—*Dædalus*, 1987. (*b*) institutional names normally require a singular verb: *the CEGB* finds *it 25 per cent cheaper to buy in French electricity*—*Daily Tel.*, 1987. But not invariably: *MI5* were *living in the past*—P. Wright, 1987. (*c*) animal, bird, etc., names that are singular in form but are being used in the plural naturally require a plural verb (and plural pronouns): *five bison* were *grazing in a shaded part of the valley; several silverfish* were *scuttling across the floor to* their *hiding-place*.

See also AGREEMENT 5; PROPER TERMS.

college. The word has many long-established meanings: (*a*) a body of officials, membership of which is a privilege or honour, e.g. College of Cardinals, College of Arms, College of Physicians, etc., (*b*) an establishment for further education, normally part of a university as at Oxford, Cambridge, London, and elsewhere.

As time went on, especially in the US and Scotland, the name sometimes became interchangeable with *university*, but was applied mostly to any institution for higher education affiliated to a university.

In wider educational circles, *college* has been traditionally used in the names of some of the ancient public schools (notably Eton and Winchester). As the provision of secondary and tertiary education in Britain has increased and changed in recent years, the word has come to be applied to a much broader group of educational and professional institutions—*business colleges, teacher-training colleges, sixth-form colleges, secretarial colleges, military* and *naval colleges, colleges of agriculture*, and so on. One consequence is that a general phrase like *at college* has become somewhat elastic: it can mean at a university, pursuing a specific profession at any of the many different kinds of institution listed above, or merely doing post-GCSE (or, in Scotland, post-Standard Grade) work. Depending on the situation, it is often helpful to use a more specific phrase.

collide, collision. It is sometimes asserted that these two words are 'properly' restricted to circumstances involving a violent impact between two moving objects. There is no basis for such a belief. A car can *collide* with a tree, a bollard, or any other fixed object, as well as with another moving vehicle. Nevertheless there is a lot to be said for using *hit* instead in factual reports: [Two young men named] *died when their car hit a tree between Penzance and Land's End yesterday*—*Times*, 1990.

collocation. A term introduced in linguistics (though in much earlier use as a general word) by J. R. Firth to refer to the habitual co-occurrence of individual words. Thus *Tweedledum* goes with *Tweedledee, spick* with *span*, and *fish* with *chips*, and always in that order. A person killed in a traffic accident in Oxford in September 1988 was described by a witness not merely as a *bystander* but as an *innocent bystander*. *Bystanders* are almost always *innocent*. *Consequences* are often *far-reaching*; politicians are often *cautiously optimistic*; new medical discoveries often have *far-reaching implications*; *liars* are frequently called *habitual liars*. These are just elementary examples of an adhesive process which is part of the natural machinery of the language.

See BINOMIAL.

colloquial (usually abbreviated as *colloq.*) is a label used in some dictionaries and books on language to indicate a use that is normally restricted to informal (especially spoken) English. Since the publication of Webster's Third in 1961, in which the label *informal* was used instead (though much more sparingly), some other dictionary houses in Britain and abroad have followed that lead, maintaining that users interpret the label *colloq.* to mean 'derogatory'. In this book the two terms are used interchangeably, but are to be distinguished from *slang*, which denotes a greater degree of informality, and usually a stronger element of metaphor or imagery. See also SLANG.

colon. **1.** The name of this punctuation mark (:) comes from Latin *cōlon*, from Greek κῶλον 'limb', member or clause of sentence, portion of strophe. As a mark of punctuation (as distinct from a term in rhetoric) it was adopted in English in the 16c. Since then its use has been made subject to various (changing) rules, and nowadays it is probably the punctuation mark that is least used and least well understood in ordinary writing (as distinct from printing). Fowler (1926) expressed his own view of its function amusingly and helpfully: 'the colon ... has acquired a special function, that of delivering the goods that have been invoiced in the preceding words; it is a substitute for such verbal harbingers as *viz., scil., that is to say, i.e.*, etc.'

2 As if in echo of Fowler, the guidance given in *New Hart's Rules* runs as follows:

'The colon points forward: from a premiss to a conclusion, from a cause to an effect, from an introduction to a conclusion, from a general statement to an example. It fulfils the same function as words such as *namely, that is, as, for example, for instance, because, as follows*, and *therefore*. Material following a colon need not contain a verb or be able to stand alone as a sentence:

That is the secret of my extraordinary life: always do the unexpected

It is available in two colours: pink and blue.'

Note that in British English the word following a colon is not in capitals (unless it is a proper name), but in American English it is capitalized if it introduces a grammatically complete sentence:

Mr Smith had committed two sins: First, his publication consisted principally of articles reprinted from the London Review ...

3 It is regularly used to introduce examples, as:

Always remember the ancient maxim: Know thyself.

It is also used instead of a comma to introduce direct speech, especially that extending over more than one sentence:

Philips said: 'I'm embarrassed. Who wouldn't be embarrassed?'

4 A dash should not be added to a colon which is being used to introduce a list: *the following will be needed: a pen, pencil, rubber, and ruler.*

To which it should be added that a colon is also used between numbers in a statement of proportion (as in 10:1) and in biblical references (as in Gen. 4: 3). It also appears on most digital clocks and watches to mark off the hours from the minutes (as in 21:30).

Americans use a colon after the initial greeting in a letter

Dear Mr. Jones:

Thank you for ...

In British English a comma is customary in such contexts (or no punctuation at all):

Dear Mr Jones(,)

Thank you for ...

colossal. In its ordinary sense 'like a colossus, gigantic', it is a relatively recent formation in English (first recorded in 1712 and not listed in Johnson's Dictionary, 1755). The use of the word as a mere intensive = 'remarkable, splendid' (*a colossal blunder, the novel is simply superb, colossal*) is a Germanism. Like all intensives, it can cover a wide spectrum of values, and should be sparingly used. The *OED*'s earliest example of its use as an intensive is one of 1892.

colosseum. See COLISEUM.

colour. In British English the customary spellings for words related to *colour* are *colourable, colourant, coloured, colourful, colourist*, and *colourless*, but *coloration, colorific, colorimeter*, and *decolorize*. In American English all have *-or-*, not *-our-*.

coloured. **1** *Coloured* referring to skin colour is first recorded in the early 17c. and was adopted in the US by emancipated slaves as a term of racial pride after the end of the American Civil War. In Britain it was the accepted term until the 1960s, when it was superseded (as in the US) by *black*. The term *coloured* lost favour among black people during this period and is now widely regarded as offensive except in historical contexts.

2 The word was formerly used euphemistically by white people in Britain and elsewhere as a term meaning 'non-white', but is much less commonly heard now.

3 In South Africa the term *coloured* (also written *Coloured*) has a different history. It is used to refer to people of mixed-race parentage rather than, as elsewhere, to refer to African peoples and their descendants (i.e. as a synonym for *black*). Under apartheid it was imposed as an official racial designation. However, in modern use in South Africa the term is not generally considered offensive or derogatory.

columnist. Though the *n* in *column* is silent, the same letter is usually fully pronounced in *columnist.*

combat (noun). Pronounced /'kɒmbat/, but be prepared to encounter the somewhat old-fashioned pronunciation with initial /'kʌm-/. Similarly with the derivatives *combatant* and *combative.*

combat (verb). **1** If pronounced with the stress on the first syllable, the same variation of the stem vowel is found as in the noun. The inflected forms are *combated* and *combating.*

2 If pronounced with the stress on the second syllable (but this is not recommended except in American English), the pronunciation is /kəm'bat/ and the inflected forms are *combatted* and *combatting* (e.g. *It is obvious that covert action is only one instrument among many in combatting terrorism—Dædalus,* 1987).

combining form. A term, probably first used in the *OED* itself, for a linguistic form that normally occurs only in compounds or derivatives as a means of coining new words. It can be added at the beginning or end of a word. Examples: *electro-*, formally representing Greek ἠλεκτρό-, combining form of ἤλεκτρον 'amber', as in *electrodynamic, electromagnet,* etc.; *kilo-*, an arbitrary derivative of Greek χίλιοι 'a thousand', as in *kilogram, kilometre,* etc. Two combining forms can combine to form a new word: e.g. *leuco-* (Greek λευκός 'white') + *-cyte* (Greek κύτος 'receptacle') made *leucocyte* 'white blood cell'.

The connecting vowel in combining forms is normally *-o-* (Angl*o*phile, bar*o*meter, phil*o*logy, etc.) or *-i-* (alt*i*meter, hort*i*culture, etc.).

come (verb). **1** The slightly archaic or informal conversational use of *come* as in *four years ago come Christmas,* that is with a future event following as grammatical subject, is compared by the *OED* to a similar construction in French: *dix-huit ans viennent les Pâques* 'eighteen years old come Easter'; i.e. = let Easter come, when Easter shall come. The construction is first recorded in the early 15c., and has been in continuous use since then.

2 In standard English *come* is often followed by *and* as an introduction to a verb indicating the purpose of coming. This construction has been in continuous use since the Old English period: e.g. *Come, lovely nymph, and bless the silent hours*— Pope, 1704; *I wonder ... whether anyone will come and help me*—D. Potter, 1986. For further discussion of this construction, which some people condemn, see TRY AND.

Formerly in standard British English and still in American English and occasionally elsewhere *come* is followed by a bare infinitive, i.e. one without the word *to*, often for rhetorical or dramatic effect: e.g. *Quicke, quicke, wee'le come dresse you straight*—Shakespeare, 1598; *Come lie up close beside me*—E. Jolley, 1980 (Aust.); *We can sell this house, you can come live with* us—Lee Smith, 1983 (US); *Come let us say a prayer together and then we'll read some Tennyson*—J. Gardam, 1985 (UK).

come-at-able. See GET-AT-ABLE.

comedian. 1 In Shakespeare's *Twelfth Night* (1601), Olivia asks the disguised Viola, who has come to woo her on behalf of Orsino with a lover's speech ready to deliver, 'Are you a comedian?', meaning 'Are you a comic actor?'. At a slightly earlier date (1581), the word is recorded in the meaning 'writer of comic plays'; together these constitute the earliest records of the word.

2 In the course of the 19c., it developed its current meaning of a professional humorous entertainer, first on the stage and later on radio and television. The term can be used both of men (e.g. Michael McIntyre, Matt Lucas) and of women (e.g. Victoria Wood, Miranda Hart).

3 From about 1860 onwards a female comedian could also be called a *comedienne.* In our gender-conscious age, the term is still quite often used, but usually only in conjunction with the performer's name, or where her sex is otherwise relevant. It is spelt without an accent.

4 *Comedian* has also for centuries been used to mean 'a writer of comedies, a comic poet' but nowadays is mostly used of the classical writers Aristophanes, Menander, Plautus, and Terence, to distinguish them from the tragedians Aeschylus, Sophocles, and Euripides.

comedienne. See COMEDIAN 3.

comestibles has been sparingly used as a humorous or affected word for 'food' since the early 19c.

comic, comical. The broad distinction is that *comic* is used of literary compositions, songs, dramatic performances, performers, etc., whose main aim is comedy, as *comic actor, opera, poet, relief, scene, strip*; whereas *comical* is principally used to mean 'laughable, mirth-provoking' when the humour is unintended, as *comical attempt, behaviour, effect, face, sight*, etc. *Comic* is much the more frequent of the two words, and can also have the meaning of 'laughable' but is often taken to imply intention rather than effect. The following examples demonstrate the different nuances of these words in this meaning: (comic) *Both brothers laughed out loud at the deliberately comic delivery of his English phrases as they shook hands*—A. Grey, 1983; *Simply said, this anthology is too long. None of it lacks literary charm, that is certain; but much of it lacks any actual comic element*—*First Things Magazine*, 2005; (comical) *In reality, the relationship was a strained and sometimes comical mismatch, a 50-year-long saga of crossed purposes*—*Daily Tel.*, 1992; *He wiped his head, looking almost comical in his shorts and sandals*—N. Barber, 1992.

comma.

1 History.
2 Between adjectives preceding a noun.
3 In compound sentences; 'comma splice'.
4 To separate supplementary information.
5 In lists: the 'Oxford comma'.
6 To avoid ambiguity.
7 With noun phrases in apposition.
8 Other uses.

1 *History.* The word *comma* derives from Latin *comma*, Greek κόμμα 'piece cut off, short clause'. It was first used in English in the 16c., in imitation of the terminology of Greek rhetoric and prosody, to mean 'a phrase or group of words less than a colon'. As a mark of punctuation it was also introduced into English in the 16c. The following description reflects the *New Hart's Rules*, but with examples from different sources.

2 *Between adjectives preceding a noun.* (*a*) Generally, commas should be inserted between qualitative adjectives (i.e. those having a comparative form): *in hoarse, melancholy tones*; *a strong-willed, intellectual woman*; *a cold, damp, badly heated room*. They are not required with classifying adjectives (i.e. those that have no comparative form), e.g.: *French medieval lyric poets*; *annual economic forecasts*. When qualitative and classifying adjectives are used together, no comma is needed: *a small* (qualitative) *edible* (classifying) *fish*; *a distinguished* (qualitative) *foreign* (classifying) *diplomat*.

(*b*) But, by convention, in many contexts the comma can be omitted: (*i*) where the last adjective relates more closely to the noun than do the preceding ones, e.g. *abundant patriotic pageantry*; (*ii*) where the adjectives form a kind of unit: *a good little boy*; *a super-efficient liquid-cooled rear engine*.

(*c*) The comma can be replaced by *and* between a pair of adjectives to make a stronger effect: *a ruthless and manipulative woman* instead of *a ruthless, manipulative woman*. Where *and, but,* or *or* join two or more adjectives the comma is omitted: *a reluctant and limited step*; *solid but adventurous entrepreneurs*; *no extensive or protracted military intervention*.

3 In compound sentences; *'comma splice'*. A comma is customary in sentences containing two main statements joined by a conjunction such as *and, but, yet*, etc.: *The road runs close to the coast, and the railway line follows it closely*; *I believed, and therefore I spoke*; *this is one principle, but it is not the only one*. A common fault in writing is to use the 'comma splice'. This means using a comma to separate clauses, but not using a conjunction, as in **I like swimming very much, I go to the pool every day*. In this sentence, the comma should either be replaced by a semicolon, or retained and followed by *and*. The comma splice often mars professional or business writing, reducing it to the level of children's essays, e.g. *We had a holiday in Florence, it was very hot, we could hardly bear it* ...

4 *To separate supplementary information.* Commas are used in pairs (*a*) to separate elements in a sentence that are not part of the main statement: *There is no sense, as far as I can see, in this suggestion; It appears, however, that we were wrong; There were, to be sure, at least four pubs in the village;* (*b*) to separate a relative clause from its antecedent when the clause is a non-restrictive clause, i.e. one which by definition supplies extra information: *The book, which was on the table, was a gift.* Without the comma, the relative clause would serve to identify the book in question rather than give extra information about it: *The book that/which was on the table was a gift.*

5 In lists: the 'Oxford *comma*'. Where more than two words or phrases occur in sequence, a comma should precede the *and*. This is the so-called 'Oxford comma'. Examples: *an index of social, economic, and religious diversity; areas of natural beauty, architectural monuments, and sites of historical interest.*

The 'Oxford comma' is fervently debated by editors and other language stylists, but its use is generally a matter of individual house or editorial style. The important thing is to use it, or not use it, consistently. It should, in any case, be used where not to do so would create ambiguity or nonsense, as it would in the following examples: *tea, bread and butter, and cake* ('bread and butter' is the unit of meaning, not 'bread and butter and cake'); *New premises were opened by Marks & Spencer, Jaeger, and Currys* (leaving out the second comma in this example would make 'Jaeger and Currys' an implausible joint brand); in the made up *I should like to thank my parents, Sinead O'Connor, and the Pope*, leaving out the Oxford comma would give the writer a hilariously improbable parentage.

6 *To avoid ambiguity.* An important function of the comma is to avoid ambiguity or momentary misunderstanding: *In the valley below, the houses look very small* (the valley is not below the houses); *Mr Hogg said that he had shot, himself, as a small boy* (Mr Hogg is still alive).

7 *With noun phrases in apposition.* Omit the comma between nouns or noun phrases in apposition, e.g. *my friend judge Leonard; her daughter Mary.* Retain it when the noun is a parenthesis, e.g. *His father, Humphrey V. Roe, was not so fortunate.*

8 *Other uses.* (*a*) A comma usually separates adverbs such as *already, soon, however,* and *moreover* when used as the first word of a sentence. Examples: *Already, prints and posters have turned anguished, passionate paintings into mere features of the décor; Moreover, you were late home after school; Soon, some inner compulsion erupts into the pretty pictures.* (*b*) Omit the comma when giving house numbers in addresses: *44 High Street.* In recommended British style, omit the comma in dates; *27 July 1990* (not *July 27, 1990*). (*c*) The subject of a sentence should not be separated by a comma from the verb it governs: *The charm in Nelson's history, is the unselfish greatness* (read *history is the*); *The primary reason that utilities are expanding their non-regulated activities, is the potential of higher returns* (read *activities is the*). (*d*) A comma also separates complementary parts of a sentence*: Parliament is not dissolved, only prorogued; The question is, can this be done?* (*e*) Commas can introduce direct speech: *He then asked, 'Do you want to come?'.*

commando. Plural *commandos.* See -O(E)S 4.

commence. Families and neighbours are divided by the question of when to use *commence* and when to use *begin.* The main considerations are as follows: **1** *Begin* is a native word; *commence,* a French loanword, joined the language in the 14c. The two words have slugged it out for nearly seven centuries, and commence, in boxing parlance, is still well behind on points.

2 It is a sound rule to use *begin* in all ordinary contexts unless *start* is customary (*the engine started straight away; he starts work at 9 a.m.; the game started on time*). Commence 'has more formal associations with law (*to commence an action*) and procedures, combat (*hostilities commenced on 4 August*), divine service, and ceremonial, in which it continues earlier Anglo-French use' (*OED*). As a general rule it should be reserved for such contexts.

3 Until about the end of the 19c. both *begin* and *commence* were commonly used in constructions with a *to*-infinitive and with a gerund. In present-day English, *begin* is by far the more usual (*she began to cry/she began crying*). *WDEU* cites only three 20c. examples of *commence* + *to*-infinitive but the *OEC* data suggests that it is a not uncommon, if rather mannered, construction, e.g. *Remembering the advice of his father, Crusoe commenced to pray and to read from the Bible—OEC*, 2005. *Commence* with a gerund is found in Hemingway, and in over 600 examples in the *OEC*. Using it in preference to *start* or *begin* in either construction can strike the right note of formality or the false note of pomposity.

commentate is a predictable back-formation from the noun *commentator*. It was freely used from the late 18c. onwards in the broad sense 'to furnish with comments', but such uses are now rare. The word was revived in the 1950s in sports broadcasting in the sense 'to deliver an oral commentary, especially upon politics or sport, to act as a commentator', as a more precise replacement for *comment*. Some people dislike it, but it has a specific context and serves a useful purpose.

commercialese. A word first recorded from 1910, it was used by Partridge in *Usage and Abusage* and by Gowers in his edition of Fowler to satirize the stereotyped, pompous words and phrases once commonly used in business letters, but now largely extinct. Arcane expressions and abbreviations included *ult.* (last month), *inst.* (this month), *prox.* (next month), *even date* (today), and *same* (it). In the age of email, tweeting, Plain English, dress-down Fridays, and business suits obligatorily worn without ties, such formulations are as redundant as candle-snuffers. Yet some few words which once formed part of commercialese linger on, and are best avoided: *advise* (tell, inform), *as per* (in accordance with), *re* (about, concerning), *enclosed please find* (I enclose).

commiserate. For about three centuries only a transitive verb (e.g. *She did not exult in her rival's fall, but, on the contrary, commiserated her*—H. Ainsworth, 1871), under the influence of *condole with* and *sympathize with*, etc., it is now always construed with *with* (*We often commiserate with ourselves, feeling that no one has to go through what we are called to endure, and that no one understands—Evangelical Times*, 2005.)

commissionaire is the recommended spelling for a uniformed door-attendant, not *-ionnaire*.

committee. See COLLECTIVE NOUN.

commonality. Since the early 1950s, this word has been chiefly used in the sense 'community of function, structure, or purpose', rather than in any of its earlier meanings. Once restricted to technical writing (*Commonality can be increased when subjects are asked to predict common normative responses—Jrnl General Psychology*, 1971) it has, especially in the US, become a staple of writing styles, for instance in the military, humanities, social sciences, and human resources, where portentousness is highly esteemed for its own sake: *As a meditation on the commonality of death and sex and of the impotent struggle of goodness and taste against the wars that mankind seems addicted to,* The White Countess *has much to offer—Film Inside Out*, 2005. Those wanting to keep their prose closer to the ground might wish to replace it with *common ground, common features, connection, link*, or any of a dozen other, less high-falutin' words which can replace it in most contexts.

communal. The traditional British pronunciation, with the main stress on the first syllable, /ˈkɒmjʊn(ə)l/, is rapidly being eroded by the standard American pronunciation, stressing the second syllable, /kəˈmjuːn(ə)l/.

commune. The noun, pronounced /ˈkɒmjʊn/, and the verb, pronounced /kəˈmjuːn/, are regularly distinguished by the positioning of the main stress.

community. 1 *Community* is such a vogue word to refer to 'a group of people living in the same place or having a particular characteristic in common', e.g. *the gay, Bangladeshi, scientific, art community*, that it is in danger of becoming clichéd. Its appeal and its treacherousness are two sides of the same coin: its attraction is that it is often more 'touchy-feely' than alternatives; its danger resides in the fact that it implies a unity of ideas or purpose that may not in fact exist. Less emotionally mesmerizing alternatives include 'people', e.g. *gay people, Bangladeshi people*, or the appropriate noun, e.g. *scientists, artists*. The application of the word to specific groups within society has given it an indelible association with minority racial groups, such that phrases like *community leaders* and *community relations* tend to be a shorthand for 'leaders of specific religious groups' and 'relations between different ethnic groups'.

2 Used with the definite article, i.e. *the community*, the word refers to 'the people of a district or country considered collectively, especially in the context of social values and responsibilities'. In this sense it is synonymous with *society*, but arguably has the advantage of sounding less impersonal. In this meaning it is often used before other nouns (i.e. attributively) 'to denote a worker or resource designed to serve the people of a particular area'. Examples of this use in the UK are *police community support officers* (PCSOs), *community service* (unpaid work to be done by offenders instead of imprisonment), and *community home* (a home for young offenders).

commuter. This long-established American word and the related verb *commute* became established in the UK about the middle of the 20c. to refer to someone who travels regularly by rail or road to and from his or her place of work, especially a suburbanite travelling to and from a large city. A ticket used for this purpose on a train or bus is called a *commutation ticket* in the US and a *season ticket* in the UK.

compact. As a predicative adjective (e.g. *the new roadster is extremely compact*) and as a verb (e.g. *trampling on the lawn will also compact the soil*) it is normally pronounced /kəm'pakt/, with the stress on the second syllable. When used attributively, as in *compact disc*, the stress moves to the first syllable: /'kɒmpakt/. As a noun, (*a*) a case for face-powder, (*b*) an agreement, it is always stressed on the first syllable.

comparable. 1 The main stress in British English traditionally falls on the first syllable, /'kɒmpərəb(ə)l/. However, many speakers now place it on the second syllable, a pronunciation greeted by traditionalists with a sharp intake of breath.

2 Its uses with *to* and *with* correspond to the senses at COMPARE TO, COMPARE WITH.

comparatively. 1 This adverb, like *relatively*, has been regularly used with an immediately following adjective since at least the early 19c. (e.g. *A comparatively modern phraseology*—R. H. Barham, 1840). Direct comparison need not be in question: *comparatively* simply = 'fairly, somewhat', e.g.: *Emma ... was comparatively outgoing*—*Bodl. Libr. Rec.*, 1987.

2 Uses with the adjective *few* have sometimes been seen as more debatable. It has been argued that if a comparison is directly made (e.g. *There were many casualties but comparatively few* [of them] *were fatal*) the use is clearly unobjectionable. Gowers (1965) strongly objected to constructions of the type *casualties were comparatively few*, i.e. there were not many casualties. Logically, however, it is difficult to separate such uses from those in (1), especially as other qualifying adverbs are idiomatically used with *few* (*too few, very few*). As *CGEL* (5.24) expresses it, 'Being gradable, *many, much, few,* and *little* can be modified by intensifying adverbs: *too much, very few,* etc.'

comparatives (i.e. comparative adjectives). See ADJECTIVE 3, 4; -ER AND -EST.

compare to, compare with. It is important to bear in mind that this verb has two distinct meanings which partly determine which preposition is appropriate. *Compare to* is generally used to suggest that two things are similar, to liken them, or to draw an analogy between them, whereas *compare with* is used to weigh or balance one thing against another, by pointing out the similarities and differences. **1** In the meaning 'to liken', *compare is* normally construed with *to* (or in religious works sometimes *unto*): *Shall I compare thee to a Summers day?*—Shakespeare; *For who in the heauen can be compared vnto the Lord?*—Ps. (AV) 89: 6; *He compared the religions to different paths towards the peak of the same mountain.* In these examples, the likenesses are being stressed, even though in Shakespeare's sonnet the loved one is *more louely and more temperate.* Fowler (1926), illustrated the core of this meaning in the sentence *he compared me to Demosthenes* = he suggested that I was comparable to Demosthenes or put me in the same class.

2 In the meaning 'to weigh or balance one thing against another', *compare* may be construed either with *with* or with *to.* American English generally favours *to,* while in British English use is more evenly divided. Examples: (to) *Her novel was compared to the work of Daniel Defoe*; (with) *To compare Great things with small—Milton, 1667; He did not individually compare other women with her, but because she was* *the first, she was equal in his memory to the sum of all the others*—J. Berger, 1972.

3 When the past participial form *compared* precedes a subordinate clause or phrase, the preposition is either *to* or *with*, although usage seems to be moving in favour of *to*: (to) *This was a modest sum compared to what other people spent*—T. Wolfe, 1987; *Even allowing for that, it's well down, Vic. Compared to last year*—D. Lodge, 1988; (with) *The church looked dimly mysterious compared with the glare of the passage*—P. D. James, 1986; *the same daily burden . . . of everything being just slightly disappointing compared with what one knows one has inside oneself*—J. Updike, 1988.

4 In BrE, *with* is preferable when *compare* is intransitive: *His achievements do not compare with those of A. J. Ayer*—*Sunday Times*, 1988. In AmE, however, *compare to* is more common: *None of those birds compare to L.A. pigeons*—*LA Weekly*, 2004.

comparison, grammatical. See ADJECTIVE 3,4; ABSOLUTE COMPARATIVE; DOUBLE COMPARISON.

compendious means 'containing the substance within small compass, concise, succinct'. Like many words indicating size, however, it is somewhat extendible in meaning, and is often misleadingly applied to works that are more marked by their comprehensiveness than by their conciseness. Jespersen's *Essentials of English Grammar* (1933) is a compendious work; *A Comprehensive Grammar of the English Language* (1985), edited by Randolph Quirk et al., is not.

compendium. For the plural, both *compendiums* and *compendia* are possible. The first is the recommended form. See -UM 3.

compensate. 1 It provides a salutary reminder of one of the ways in which the language changes. The *OED* pointed out (in 1891) that /ˈkɒmpənseɪt/ 'is the pronunciation now usual in England, but appears to be quite recent; pronouncing dictionaries had until *c*.1850–70 only /kəmˈpɛnseɪt/, which is also that of the 18th c. poets. Tennyson has both.'

2 The use of *compensate* in the broad sense 'to offset a disability or frustration by development in another direction' is a standard example (also *over-compensate*) of a scientific term—in this case a Jungian one—making its way into popular use: e.g. *A young man afraid of marriage may compensate by specializing in dating and courting, becoming a 'man about* town'—J. E. Gordon, 1963.

competence. In 1926 Fowler opined that 'Neither *competence* nor *competency* has any sense in which the other cannot be used; the first form is gaining on the second' and wished that *competency* could be abandoned as a 'needless variant'. While it is true that *competence* is by far the commoner of the two, since Fowler's day *competency* has gone from strength to strength and developed a distinct personality.

Some dictionaries define both words as 'the ability to do something effectively or successfully', and in some contexts they are interchangeable, e.g. *These exams should test the students' competence/competency based on content drawn from all areas of the curriculum.* However, each word has specialist uses. For *competence* these are in the domains of linguistics, biology and medicine; for *competency*, they are in the fields of education, training and human resources. In particular, in business the concept of *core competency* has become something of a watchword.

Competence in the meaning discussed is usually an uncount noun with no plural form, while *competency* is a COUNT NOUN. When *competences* appears in the plural, one often has the impression that it is a misspelling of *competencies*.

complacent, complaisant. The first of these now has two main senses: (1) smugly self-satisfied. (2) calmly content. *Complaisant* also has two senses: (1) politely deferential. (2) willing to please, acquiescent. The two words form a minimal pair, in that they are distinguished in pronunciation by only one sound, medial /s/ in the first and medial /z/ in the second. They are etymological doublets in that they both ultimately derive from Latin *complacēre* to please, but they reached English by different medieval channels.

Historically, and even down to the 19c., the two words (and also their derivatives, *complacence* and *complacency* beside *complaisance* and *complaisancy*) became cross-linked and confused in some contexts. Burke, Scott, and Charlotte Brontë are cited in the *OED* as using *complacent* to mean 'obliging in manner, complaisant':

e.g. *Mr. Moore ... was ... a complacent listener to her* talk—C. Brontë, 1849. But the distinctions indicated above, i.e. the two senses of each word, are now clear-cut and should be observed.

compleat. A standard example of a 20c. revival of an older (16–18c.) spelling of *complete*. The title of Izaak Walton's *The Compleat Angler* (1653) was the principal model for the modern revival; *The Compleat Bachelor*—O. Onions (title of book), 1900; *She writes and sings and dances and plays I don't know how many instruments. The compleat girl.*—M. McCarthy, 1963.

complected. Used to mean 'complexioned, having a (specified) complexion', the word was first recorded in 1806 in the US, and is still more common there than elsewhere. *Complexioned* is more common in all varieties of English, including American, and to many British ears *complected* will sound jarringly American. Examples: *They told me the man they meant wasn't dark complected*—W. Faulkner, 1932; *George Gobbin was a tall dark-complected man in his late fifties*—J. D. MacDonald, 1977; *She was a good-looking, dark-complected lesbian—way out in the open about that*—M. Chabon, 1990.

complement. 1 In grammar, a relatively modern term (first recorded in 1874) for a word or phrase added to a verb to complete the predicate of a sentence. It is a term of wide application, and the way in which complements are classified varies from grammarian to grammarian. Some typical types (in each example the words in roman type form the complement): (adjectival) *the going looked* firm; the task seemed nice and easy; (adverbial) *she smiled at him* in a Mona Lisa way; *they remained* out of reach; *she spoke* clearly; (as subject complement) *he died* a happy man (= he was a happy man when he died); *he is* a solicitor; (as object complement) *he called his brother* an idiot. It makes for simplicity if a direct object is not regarded as a complement, but there is no agreement among grammarians about this. Readers should be prepared to meet and accept various interpretations of which part of the predicate of a sentence is to be regarded as a complement.

2 *Complement* and *compliment* are pronounced exactly the same, both as noun and as verb. As nouns they are pronounced /ˈkɒmplɪmənt/ with a *schwa* (an indistinct unstressed vowel sound) in the final syllable. The verbs are pronounced /ˈkɒmplɪmɛnt/ with a fully pronounced final syllable.

complementary, complimentary are often confused in writing, because they sound exactly the same in speech. *Complementary* can mean 'completing' or 'forming a complement', e.g. *Chelsea Theatre is a small yet dynamic new writing theatre enriched by a complementary programme of arts activities*—*OEC*, 2004. In collocations such as *complementary medicine, complementary therapy*, it refers to medical treatment that falls outside the scope of scientific medicine but supports it (e.g. acupuncture and osteopathy).

Complimentary also has two meanings, which may explain why the two words are often muddled. The first is 'expressing a compliment, praising', e.g. *Thank you very much for your highly complimentary comments.* The second meaning is 'given free of charge' as in *a complimentary copy, ticket, breakfast, drink, service*, etc. Examples of the words being muddled: (*complimentary* wrongly used) **There's a family of coated papers and a complimentary number of uncoated papers*—*Paper Focus*, 1989; **The efficacy of complimentary medicine is hotly disputed*—*OEC*, 2008; (*complementary* wrongly used) **With a complementary glass of champagne*—advertisement in a US newspaper, 1991. *He *has also been very complementary about the region's reputation for chef training, all vital ingredients in the restaurant equation*—*OEC*, 2005.

Similar confusion often happens (especially in advertisements) between the corresponding verbs, *complement* and *compliment*. As an aid to remembering the difference, a *complement completes* something, and *completes* is spelled with an *e*. If you pay someone a *compliment*, you are being *kind*, with an *i*, to them.

complex. 1 The noun is familiar, originally as a term derived from Jungian psychology, and first recorded as long ago as 1907, meaning 'a group of repressed feelings or thoughts which cause abnormal behaviour or mental states', usually with some prefixed defining word, e.g. *inferiority complex, Oedipus complex*, and *persecution complex*. It has become part of everyday language in the looser meaning of a fixed mental idea or obsession. Examples: *Both of them had a complex about economy and living within a budget*—Mary McCarthy, 1954.

2 But by far the most common use of *complex* as a noun is in the sense 'a group or network of buildings or systems', typically qualified by adjectives or nouns such as *housing, industrial, leisure, shopping, sports*, etc. that pinpoint the activities involved.

3 In British English, the first syllable of both noun and adjective is stressed, /ˈkɒmplɛks/. In American English the noun is pronounced the same, but the adjective is stressed on the second syllable, /kɑmˈplɛks/.

complexion. Spelt with an *-x-*, not *complection*. See -XION, -XIVE.

complexioned. See COMPLECTED.

compliment. See COMPLEMENT 2.

complimentary. See COMPLEMENTARY.

compline. The former variant spelling *complin* has now been abandoned. The pronunciation /ˈkɒmplɪn/ is now dominant, but the spelling-pronunciation /ˈkɒmplʌɪn/ is heard often enough.

compose. See COMPRISE.

composite. Pronounced /ˈkɒmpəzɪt/ in BrE. The older pronunciation (e.g. in Walker, 4th edn, 1806) /kəmˈpɒzɪt/ is still standard AmE. The spelling-pronunciation /ˈkɒmpəˌzʌɪt/, in which the final syllable rhymes with *light*, should be avoided.

compost. Both syllables have a fully pronounced short *o*, /ˈkɒmpɒst/.

compound. See NOUN AND VERB ACCENT.

compound (verb). In law, the primary meaning was once 'to condone (a liability or offence) in exchange for money; to settle by a payment of money'. *To compound a felony* therefore meant 'to forbear from prosecuting (a felony) in exchange for some consideration' and was an offence at law. In practice, the phrase *to compound a/the felony* is generally used to mean 'to make worse, to aggravate'. To criticize this extended meaning strikes me as overpedantic.

compound prepositions. (Also called *prepositional phrases* and **complex prepositions**.) **1** *Simple prepositions.* At an elementary level, *at, by, from, to*, etc., are simple prepositions (*he was at home, she sat by the fire*, etc.). There are approximately seventy of these, about half of which have two syllables (*above, below, until*, etc.) or more (*notwithstanding, underneath*).

2 *Marginal prepositions.* There is also a smaller group of marginal prepositions, i.e. words which operate in much the same way as simple prepositions, but which have affinities with some other word classes. These include *bar, barring, concerning, considering, given, granted, including*, and *pending* (e.g. *considering the difficulties at that time, you did very well; given the chance, he would like to earn more money*).

3 *Compound prepositions.* These fall into two subsets, the first consisting of two words (e.g. *according to, apart from, because of, contrary to, next to, out of, previous to, thanks to*), and the second consisting of three (e.g. *in accordance with, in consequence of, with regard to*). Examples: *according to him, inflation should soon fall to single figures; the church stands next to the village hall; in consequence of the baggage-handlers' action, no planes will leave Gatwick today.*

Fowler (1926) excluded marginal prepositions from consideration and strongly objected to the overuse of compound prepositions: 'taken as a whole, they are almost the worst element in modern English, stuffing up the newspaper columns with a compost of nouny abstractions'. His colourful view no longer seems to be supported by the facts.

comprehend. See APPREHEND.

comprise. **A.** For well over a hundred years, many critics, including Fowler, have bridled at certain uses of the verb *comprise*. Readers may find it helpful to have both the undisputed and disputed uses explained and illustrated, with alternatives. They can thus draw their own conclusions and make an informed choice.

1 *The undisputed use.* As Allen (2008) put it, 'Comprise has the whole as its subject and the parts as its object', as in *a full pack comprises 52 cards*. In this meaning *comprise* could be replaced by any of *consists of, is composed of*, or *is made up of*. Examples: *Love comprises among other* *things a desire for the well-being and spiritual freedom of the one who is loved*—M. Spark, 1984; *Our opposing team comprised school friends Arnie, 27, a teacher, and Danny, 26, a film director*—*Evening Standard*, 2007.

2 *Disputed uses.* (*a*) Some critics object to reversing the equation, and using *comprise* as the grammatical subject of the elements that make up the whole, rather than of the whole itself. The example in (**1**) would thus become *52 cards comprise a full pack.* But it has to be said that this use is long-established in English. The *OED* shows it without comment, and it would be absurd to censure Jane Austen posthumously or Garrison Keillor currently for using the word in this way. Should you desperately wish to avoid it, however, you could replace it with *constitute, make up,* or *form.* Examples: *Seven boys comprised the choir*—G. Keillor, 1985.

(*b*) *Comprise* used passively. This construction, formerly blackballed and still occasionally criticized today, is accepted by the *OED*, and has been around since at least 1874. Examples: *The Saxe-Coburg inheritance is comprised of the ducal palace and three castles*—*Daily Tel.*, 1991; *As this team of scientists was comprised entirely of men the experiment necessarily involved letting the male subjects design computerised images of their ideal women*—*Observer*, 2007. In the first example '*is comprised of*' could be rewritten as *comprises, consists of,* or *is made up of.* In the second '*was comprised entirely of*' could be reworded as *consisted entirely of, was composed entirely of,* or *was made up entirely of.*

(*c*) *comprise* + *of.* Not least because it is a verbal tic beloved of estate agents (i.e. *this property comprises of hall, living room* . . .), this is probably the most widely reviled, or at least ridiculed, use. It may well offend not only died-in-the-wool purists, but ordinary mortals with a residual sense of written style. Examples: *The target population of the study comprised of CANR bachelor's degree graduates from summer semester 1993 through spring semester 1998*—*OEC*, 2004; *The league comprises of eight teams*—*OEC*, 2004. In both examples *comprise(d)* on its own is preferable, or *consists/consisted of.*

B. For the difference between *comprise* and *include*, see INCLUDE.

C. *Comprise* is one of the small group of words ending in *-ise* where *-ize* is not acceptable. See also -ISE, -IZE.

comptroller, a rather grand-looking spelling of *controller*, was introduced about 1500 ('especially affected by official scribes', *OED*) by mistaken association with French *compte* 'calculation' or its source, late Latin *computus. Comptroller* is still retained in certain official designations, e.g. *Comptroller of the* (Royal) *Household, Comptroller of the Lord Chamberlain's Office*, and is correctly pronounced in the same way as *controller.*

computerate is a word to which Fowler could well have objected, on the grounds that it is a 'hybrid' of the English word *computer* and the suffix *-ate*, which is not now generally used to create new words. Despite his possible objections from beyond the grave, it is usefully shorter than *computer-literate*, which is an alternative that can be used to avoid upsetting purists, living or otherwise.

computerese. Computer terminology has become familiar to the English-speaking world in the last twenty years or so as the technological revolution has impinged on the lives of most people at work and home. Since North American organizations have led in this field, English has become the electronic lingua franca much as it has been the international medium of communication in air travel and other domains. Most recently, the rapid expansion of the *Internet* (or *World Wide Web*) has produced a vocabulary of its own, both at technical level and in everyday slang. Much of the technical jargon is based on initialisms of three or more letters, such as *http* (= *hypertext transfer protocol*), *ISP* (= *Internet service provider*), *www* (= *World Wide Web*, used in website addresses), *Wi-Fi* (= Wireless Fidelity, for transmission of data over wireless networks), and *VOIP* (*voice over Internet protocol*, a technology for making telephone calls over the Internet).

2 Other terminology is based on or adapted from words belonging to the core of English: people buy *hardware* and install *software* on it, and occasionally *freeware* (but they need to beware of *adware* and *malware*); their desk becomes a *workstation*; many computer programs are manipulated by using a *mouse* to make choices from a *menu*; computer symbols are *icons*;

a location on the *Internet* is a *site*, which is *accessed* by means of a *home page*, and the data is explored by *browsing* or *surfing* (usually with a *browser*). People communicate by *email* (= *electronic mail*) as distinct from *snail mail* (= the ordinary postal service), send aggressive messages by *flaming* (a revival of an old meaning), and break into other people's systems by *hacking*. Medical analogy is invoked to alert users to the dangers of computer *bugs* and *viruses*, some of which may be *macro-borne* (= communicated by copying an infected macro program). What is most interesting from the point of view of language is how little of this vocabulary has developed extended meanings in other contexts, leaving the world of computer jargon a closed environment, borrowing words from everyday language and signally failing to return them.

comrade. 1 As a form of address by a socialist or a communist to another, or as a prefix to such a person's surname (a use first recorded in English in 1884), the decline in its use as such mirrors the decline in socialist and communist politics in Britain.

2 It used to be pronounced /ˈkɒmreɪd/ in this political sense, and /-rɪd/ when used to mean an 'associate'. Ironically, the socialist pronunciation now seems to be the norm.

concave means 'having an outline or surface curved like the interior of a circle or sphere'. *Convex* means 'having an outline or surface curved like the ***exterior*** of a circle or sphere'.

concede. In electoral contests it is appropriate for the defeated candidate to *concede defeat*. But, as a graceful gesture to the winner, some candidates have been known to *concede victory*, thereby shifting the emphasis to the success of the other person.

concensus. For this common misspelling, see CONSENSUS.

concept. The philosophical sense of the word ('the product of the faculty of conception, an idea of a class of objects, a general notion'), first formulated in the 17c., remains in use. In non-philosophical circles, the word is widely used in the weakened sense of a general notion or idea, especially in contexts of marketing and design. Examples: *He was the man who invented the concept of a weekly news magazine*—D. Halberstam, 1979. Although some people object to the overuse of the extended meaning, there is room in the language for both sets of uses.

concerned. The idiomatic expression *as far as . . . is concerned*, e.g. *as* (or *so*) *far as Jim is concerned* = 'so far as regards Jim's case or interests' is well established and unobjectionable. Gowers (1965), however, pointed out examples where use of this phrase resulted in long-windedness which could be avoided by simply using a preposition: *The punishment does not seem to have any effect so far as the prisoners are concerned* (*read* on the prisoners); *The months of January, February, and part of March 1963 were disastrous as far as the building industry of this country was concerned* (*read* for the building industry); *The girl is entirely unknown as far as the larger cinema audiences are concerned* (*read* to the larger audiences). Such economies are worth making. For the criticized use of *as far as . . .* instead of *as far as . . . is concerned*, see FAR 4.

concert (noun and verb). See NOUN AND VERB ACCENT.

concerto. The pronunciation /kənˈtʃəːtəʊ/ and plural *concertos* are recommended, but /kənˈtʃɛːtəʊ/ and plural *concerti* (naturally in *concerti grossi*) are equally common in standard English. See -O(E)S 4

concessionaire is the recommended spelling (not *-ionnaire*) for the holder of a (trading) concession.

concessive. 1 In grammar, a concessive phrase or clause contains information that is surprising or unexpected in the light of the main clause. The main words introducing concessive constructions are *although* and *though*; others include *if, even if, even though, when,* and *while*. Examples; (clauses containing verbs) *Although she was only 14, she was admitted to the University of Oxford; He was awarded a First even though he failed to complete one of the papers; While I respect your right to absent yourself, I think you should have left a note saying where you were*; (introducing *-ing, -ed*, and verbless clauses) *While not seeming to mind, she suffered remorse in private; Even though given every chance, the filly came last in the Oaks; Though past the crawling stage, the baby could not yet stand up unsupported.*

2 Prepositions of concession include *in spite of, despite,* and *for all.* Examples: *In spite of his sprained ankle he could still ride a bicycle; despite this setback he had a successful career; for all his talent, he was unable to settle down.*

conch. Sir William Golding consistently pronounced the word as /kɒntʃ/ in a lecture that he gave on *The Lord of the Flies* at the University of Oxford in February 1990. His pronunciation seems to be now as common as the more traditional one of /kɒŋk/. The word is derived from Latin *concha,* Greek κόγχη 'shell'.

conciseness, concision. To any scholar familiar with the earliest meanings of the word *concision,* namely 'the action of cutting to pieces; mutilation' (first recorded 1382) and 'circumcision' (*Beware of dogs, beware of euill workers: beware of the concision*—Phil. (AV) 3: 2), where it is applied contemptuously to Judaizing Christians, the natural word for 'brevity of speech or writing' is *conciseness.* Fowler (1926) in fact condemned concision as a literary critics' word used by writers under French influence, 'and often requiring the reader to stop and think whether he knows its meaning'. It has been used to mean 'brevity of style' only since the late 18c. while *conciseness* is the earlier word in this meaning, being first recorded in 1659. Despite Fowler's dislike for *concision,* it is now the more usual of the two words in the meaning discussed, according to the *OEC* data, particularly in formal written registers. The choice between the two words depends on the formality of what you are writing, and on aesthetic balance with other words in the sentence. *Concision* is, of course, the more concise form.

concord. For *grammatical concord,* see AGREEMENT.

concordat. Pronounced in a fully Anglicized way, /kən'kɔːdat/.

concur. The inflected forms *concurred* and *concurring* retain the stem vowel /əː/ of *concur,* but *concurrent* has /ʌ/, i.e. is pronounced /kən'kʌrənt/.

condemn. 1 A word that is baffling to learners of English in that the final *n* is silent in the infinitive and in the inflected forms *condemned* and *condemning,* but is sounded in its derivatives (*condemnable, condemnation, condemnatory*).

2 See CONTEMN.

condom. J. C. Wells (1990) pointed out that the established pronunciation in Britain had been /'kɒndəm/, but that the spelling-pronunciation /'kɒndɒm/, with the same vowel sound in each syllable, became common with the spread of HIV in the 1980s.

conduct (noun and verb). See NOUN AND VERB ACCENT.

conduit. The dominant pronunciation in the UK is now the spelling-pronunciation /'kɒndjʊɪt/, with the variant final syllable /-dɪt/ occasionally heard. Pronouncing the first syllable /'kʌn-/ as my father and some standard speakers of his generation did, is now uncommon.

confederacy, confederation. See FEDERATION.

confer. The inflected forms are *conferred, conferring.* See DOUBLING OF CONSONANTS WITH SUFFIXES 2; -R-, -RR-.

conferrable. See -ABLE, -IBLE 6.

confidant, confidante. *Confidant* is now used of both men and women, and *confidante* properly only of women. *Confidant* is pronounced stressing the first syllable and making the last rhyme with *ant,* /'kɒnfɪdant/. *Confidante* can be pronounced in the same way, or stressing the last syllable, /ˌkɒnfɪ'dant/. It can also be pronounced in a somewhat more French manner, /ˌkɒnfɪ'dɑːnt/, making the last syllable rhyme with *aunt.* Both words made their way into English from French after 1700. The English spelling in *-ant(e)* is usually taken to be an attempt to represent the pronunciation of the French *-ent, -ente.* Walker (4th edn, 1806) commented: 'so universal is its use [i.e. the use of *confidant* pronounced in a French way] at present, that a greater mark of rusticity cannot be given than to place the accent on the first syllable, and to pronounce the last *dent* instead of *dant.*'

confine (noun and verb). See NOUN AND VERB ACCENT.

confiscate. 'As in other words of the same form, *compensate, concentrate,* *contemplate*, etc., the stress is now usually on the first syllable, but till *circa* 1864 the dictionaries had only *confíscate*' (*OED*).

conflict (noun and verb). See NOUN AND VERB ACCENT.

confusable words. For various types of words that are commonly confused (*hoards/hordes, reek/wreak, reign/rein*, etc.), see DIFFERENTIATION.

congeries. A collective name for 'a disorderly collection; a mass or heap' (from Latin *congeriēs*, from *congerere* 'to carry together'). Pronounced /kɒn'dʒɪəriːz/ (kon-**jiuh**-reez), with three syllables; the pronunciation with four syllables as /kɒn'dʒeriˌɪːz/ is old-fashioned. In the unlikely event the plural should ever be required, it is the same as the singular in form and pronunciation. Example: *Japan's most established party of government was formed in 1955 as a congeries of centre and conservative groupings with the encouragement of business—OEC*, 2003.

conifer. The pronunciations /'kɒnɪfə/ and /'kəʊn-/ are both heard, but the first of these seems much more common.

conjoined twins. The more accurate and correct term *conjoined twins* has supplanted the older term *Siamese twins* in all contexts other than informal conversation.

conjugal. The pronunciation recommended is /'kɒndʒʊgəl/, with the stress on the first syllable, not /kən'dʒuːgəl/.

conjugation. The inflection of verbs, or any class of verbs inflected in a specified way (*first conjugation, second conjugation, strong conjugation*, etc.). The word (from Latin *conjugātiō*) means 'yoking together'. Cf. DECLENSION.

conjunction. In grammar, a word used to connect clauses or sentences or words in the same clause. Conjunctions usually join like with like, i.e. a noun or its equivalent with another noun or its equivalent (*a rake* and *a hoe*; *she* and *Mr Ramsay*; *Nothing stirred in the drawing-room* or *in the dining-room* or *on the staircase*); an adjective with another adjective (*bright* and *breezy*; *crazy* but *nice*); an adverb with another adverb (*slowly* but *surely*); and so on.

In compound sentences, conjunctions fall into two main groups, subordinating conjunctions and coordinating conjunctions. Examples: (subordinating) as *the dinner isn't quite ready, let us have another drink*; *he went back to university* so that *he could complete his degree*; *I shan't go* if *you won't come with me*; though *she could not hear what was said, she could see that they were happy*; (coordinating, especially *and, but, for, nor, or*) *She would go back* and *look for it*; *He should have been a great philosopher*, but *he had made an unfortunate marriage; it did her husband good to be three thousand*, or *if she must be accurate, three hundred miles from his library*; For *in one moment if there were no breeze, his father would slap the pages of his book together.*

John Algeo (*Internat. Jrnl Lexicography*, 1988) pointed out that *whilst, now, and nor, but nor*, and one or two other coordinating conjunctions are found in BrE, but not in American English. Examples (cited by Algeo): *I would like to thank many friends and colleagues for their encouragement* whilst *I was writing this book*—Rosemary Jackson, 1981; Now *the socialists have adopted the expensive red rose as their emblem, may I suggest to Mrs Thatcher the simple blue forget-me-not—Times*, 1986; *But doctors prescribing the pills were not told of the maker's doubts*, and nor *was the Government's drug watchdog—Guardian*, 1986; *I am not a trained architect*, but nor *was Sir Edwin Lutyens—Sunday Times*, 1985.

Many of the more important conjunctions are treated in separate articles: see AND; BECAUSE; BUT; FOR; etc.

conjure. In the dominant sense 'to perform tricks which are seemingly magical', *conjure* is pronounced /'kʌndʒə/; but in the sense 'to beseech, to appeal solemnly to (a person)' it is pronounced /kən'dʒʊə/.

conjuror is the recommended spelling, not *conjurer*.

connection. 1 This is the recommended spelling, rather than *connexion*, which is still occasionally used, and is the more correct version from a purely etymological point of view. See -XION, -XIVE.

2 Fowler (1926) accepted the phrase *in connection with* only when it had 'a real meaning', e.g. *Buses ran in connection with the trains; The isolated phrase may sound offensive, but taken in connection with the context it was not so*. He intensely disliked its use as a compound preposition: 'vagueness and pliability [are] its only merits ... the average writer has not realized ... that ... laziness is mastering his style, or haziness his ideas'. He was right to criticize the long-windedness of a phrase beloved in particular of journalists, the legal profession and PC Plod. As a broad rule, if a simple preposition will do instead, use it: *inquiries in connection with the vandalizing of a local school* would be shorter and pithier as *inquiries into the vandalizing of a local school*.

connoisseur /kɒnəˈsəː/ was adopted in the 18c. from a now obsolete form of French *connaisseur* (from *connaître*, to know).

connote, denote. Both words mean broadly 'to signify' but that is where the similarity ends. A word *denotes* its primary meaning; it *connotes* attributes associated with the broad primary meaning. The primary meaning of the word *spring* is 'the season in which vegetation begins to appear, the first season of the year (in the northern hemisphere from March to May)'. But spring *connotes* fresh growth, young love, the sap rising in the blood, rebirth, freshness, and so on. The primary meaning of *dog* is 'any four-legged flesh-eating animal of the genus *Canis*, kept as a pet or for work or sport'. But the connotations of the word can include fidelity, obedience (especially a sheepdog), aggressiveness (especially a Rottweiler), etc.

conscience. Write *for conscience' sake*. But see SAKE.

conscientious. Notice the spelling with *-tious*, not *-scious*. Pronounced /kɒnʃɪˈɛnʃəs/, not /kɒnsɪ-/.

consensus. 1 It means 'general agreement' and should be carefully distinguished from *census* 'the official count of a population'. (One of the commonest misspellings at present is the writing of *concensus* for *consensus*.) The second element of *consensus* ultimately derives from Latin *sentīre, sens-* 'to feel', while *census* goes back to Latin *censēre* 'to assess'.

2 Since the mid-19c., *consensus* has been commonly used with a following of and noun (*consensus of opinion, evidence, authority*, etc.): some scholars have criticized these on the ground that they say the same thing twice, but they are an established part of the language. A century later, beginning in the 1960s, attributive uses (*consensus view, consensus politics*) came to the fore, and these uses are now, perhaps, dominant.

consequent, consequential. 1 The shorter word should normally be used when the sense is the simple and common one of 'resulting, following in time': *in the consequent confusion he vanished; The very rapid increase of trade, and the consequent influx of wealth. Consequential* is usually more appropriate when the context calls for a word meaning 'of the nature of a consequence or sequel', as in *two consequential amendments were passed; the widespread use of fossil fuels, and the consequential pollution of the atmosphere; Conservative MPs are hoping that she will take the opportunity of the consequential changes in the junior ranks to bring in some new faces—Times*, 1986.

2 Fowler's view (1926) that *consequential* does not mean 'of consequence' needs modification. It has meant 'self-important (of persons)' since the 18c.: He *here consider'd it essential To shew he could be consequential*—1816 in *OED; Pampered and consequential freedmen*—F. W. Farrar, 1875; *It is very odd to look at all these poor consequential idiots and remember that war might at any moment make real mincemeat of them*—S. T. Warner, 1942.

The *OED* (1891) also gave five examples between 1728 (Fielding) and 1821 (*He must withhold no consequential fact*—T. Campbell) used in the sense 'important, significant', and marked it 'obsolete'. But it is alive and well, though somewhat literary: *He considered his notebooks far more consequential than his published prose—TLS*, 1989; *The calibre of the Consultants seems to have varied gradually over time. They've grown older, and somewhat less consequential, in recent decades—Jacket Magazine*, 2003 (AmE); *If not, he must believe that the views of the then Shadow Home Secretary were more consequential than the views of the then British Government—London Rev. Books*, 2003.

3 *Consequential* has various technical meanings in law and insurance, especially *consequential damages, consequential loss*: the precise meaning of these terms may be found in specialized textbooks.

conservative. One of the hazards commentators on English usage face is that the passage of time will inevitably invalidate some of their judgements. Fowler (1926) vehemently rejected ('perhaps the most ridiculous of slipshod extensions') the use of this word to mean 'moderate, cautious, low', as in e.g. *at a conservative estimate.* This use, first recorded in America at the beginning of the 20c., is now widespread and standard in all English-speaking areas.

conservatory. In the sense of 'a school or academy of music' the English word is a 19c. Anglicized version of Italian *conservatorio.* In Italy the word originally applied to hospitals for the rearing of foundlings and orphans in which musical education was given. It was adopted in French as *conservatoire* (a form also used in English, e.g. the renamed Royal Conservatoire of Scotland), and in Germany as *Konservatorium. Conservatory,* in the sense 'a school of advanced standing specializing in one of the fine arts (as music, drama, or dance)' is especially common in the US, e.g. the New England Conservatory of Music (Boston), the Oberlin Conservatory of Music, and the American Conservatory Theater (San Francisco).

consider. 1 In the meaning 'regard as being', *consider* occurs in three typical constructions, two that are accepted and a third that is disputed by some usage writers: (1) with a noun or adjective complement in apposition to the object: *I consider them friends, I consider them friendly;* (2) with *to be* inserted between the object and its complement: *I consider them to be friends, I consider them to be friendly*; and (3) more controversially, with *consider* followed by *as,* possibly under the influence of words such as *regard* and *treat: I consider them as friends, I consider them as friendly.* Construction (2) is especially common in reflexive use when an adjective, rather than a noun, follows (*I consider myself to be well-informed*), and in passive constructions (*medicines that are considered to be safe during pregnancy*).

Since as long ago as 1917, various writers on usage, including Gowers (1965), have expressed reservations about the construction *consider as,* and would delete the *as* in sentences like *They considered him* (*as*) *a bad influence; I consider it* (*as*) *essential.* On the other hand, *CGEL* 16.47 sets down all three types *We consider him a genius/as a genius/to be a genius* as mere variants. Outside the confines of such simple sentences what is the position?

It is clear that all three constructions, with and without *as,* or using *to be,* are in use. *Consider as* has a long and distinguished history, having been used by writers such as Addison, Jane Austen, Adam Smith, and Charles Darwin. The choice nowadays does not seem to be based on particular rules, but rather on the nature of the surrounding words. Economy points in one direction and the rhythm of the sentence in another. Constructions with *as* seem to be the least favoured of the three and the least common.

Examples: (without *as*) *He is considered a rich man*—F. Marryat, 1842; *They were quite a trio, they decided, though each of the other two secretly considered herself the star*—F. Raphael, 1960; *The village boys . . . considered it a privilege to enjoy a stroll with him in the evenings*—M. Das, 1987; (with *as*) *Tungay considered the whole establishment, master and boys, as his natural enemies*—Dickens, 1850; *The patient improved considerably but could not be considered as cured*—M. Balint, 1968; (with *to be*) *he . . . considered himself to be a good sound Royalist*—R. D. Blackmore, 1869; *A determination to show people what she considered to be their proper place*—N. Mitford, 1949; *so progressives must consider all women to be clever!*—I. Murdoch, 1957.

2 When *as* is associated with the object complement and not with the verb *consider,* and has the meaning of 'in its quality as, in its capacity as', nobody can legitimately object: *Cologne Opera and San Francisco Ballet have both inspected the theatre and are considering it as* [= in its capacity as] *a venue*—*Times,* 1980.

3 *consider of,* 'think attentively or carefully of', first recorded in the 16c., is now distinctly archaic. Examples: *Let us consider of the Hesperides themselves*—Ruskin, 1860; *A General Court will be held at The Bank on Thursday . . . to consider of a Dividend*—*Times,* 1891.

considerable. The word is used in more grammatical patterns in the United States than in Britain. **1** *As adjective.* In the UK it is applied only to immaterial things, to abstractions: *I have given the matter considerable attention; he was a man of great energy and considerable ability; a considerable sum of money; he suffered considerable* *pain; a considerable number of people were queuing at the taxi-rank.* This is also the natural use of the adjective in American English, but it is also used (*a*) = great in size [usually qualifying mass nouns] (examples from American dictionaries): *silk fabric containing considerable gold or silver thread; certain pharmaceutical preparations similar to cerates, but containing considerable tallow; a house with a considerable barn in back; the product contains considerable salt.* Also, *One of them housed a dark, pungent hill of milo grain worth considerable money—a hundred thousand dollars*—T. Capote, 1966; and (*b*) absolutely (or as noun) = 'much, a great deal' (*During the last two years considerable has been written on the subject*).

2 *As noun.* Used informally in AmE = a good deal; a fair amount or quantity of (something). Examples: *Jim did considerable toward stirring up the farmers*—*Atlantic Monthly*, 1932; *It was a kind of mixed hound, with a little bird dog and some collie and maybe a considerable of almost anything else*—W. Faulkner, 1943; *he has done considerable for the community*—*Random House Dict.*, 1987.

3 *As adverb.* At first (17c. onwards) in use in Britain, but now obsolete or dialectal in this country. According to American dictionaries it is still current in AmE. Examples: *I presume I do have considerable more time for writing than you do*—O. W. Norton, 1862; *By-and-by she let it out that Moses had been dead a considerable long* time—M. Twain, 1884; *that speeded things up considerable*—1984 quoted in *MWCDEU.*

considerateness, consideration. The first of these is not much used and then only when an abstract noun corresponding to *considerate* is called for contextually and *considerateness*, as the more 'obvious' of the pair, comes to mind. In practice *considerateness* has only one current sense, 'thoughtfulness for others' (*your considerateness over the years has been greatly appreciated*), and it shares this sense with *consideration* (*consideration for others is one of his good points*). By contrast, *consideration* has a number of current senses, including (*a*) a circumstance taken into account, a reason considered; careful thought (*To have a doctor living nearby is a consideration of some weight with me; the topography of the village of Fetherhoughton may repay consideration*—H. Mantel, 1989); (*b*) a reward, remuneration (*pigs were sold to me for a trifling consideration*); (*c*) in several idiomatic phrases, especially *to take into consideration, under (active) consideration*, and *in consideration of. Consideration* is a blossoming word; *considerateness* is a wayside flower.

considering. 1 In origin an absolute use of the present participle or verbal substantive, it has been used for centuries as (*a*) (first recorded in the 14c.) a preposition, with a simple object = taking into account (*Considering the conditions, the horses galloped well*); (*b*) (15c.) with an object clause (*I should think you have every right to be cross, considering how much you have done for her*); (*c*) (18c.) elliptically (*We came out of it not too badly, considering*). This last use is somewhat informal, and in more formal style should be replaced by 'all things considered' or 'taking everything into account'. Modern examples: *It's odd that one boasts considering that no one is ever taken in by it*—V. Woolf, 1921; *Considering the stories I had heard of a maze of forgotten galleries, I had thought it advisable to imitate Theseus and Ariadne and take with me a large ball of string ... to mark my trail*—G. Household, 1981; *these were years of disappointment, even grief, for* [Ogden] *Nash, in what was, considering, a remarkably successful career in writing*—*NY Times Bk Rev.*, 1990.

2 See UNATTACHED PARTICIPLES.

consist. In most contexts *consist* is followed by *of* and means 'to have as its parts or elements' (*an ordinary fence, consisting of a ditch and a bank; Newton imagined light to consist of particles*). By contrast, when followed by *in*, it most often means 'have its essential features as specified' (*not everyone can tell in what the beauty of a figure consists; his term of office consisted in a series of ill-judged decisions*). Modern examples: (with *of*) *The stage itself ... consisted of a number of timber boards set on concrete blocks*—W. Trevor, 1976; *The group consisted of five string players and twosingers*—J. Simms, 1982; (with *in*) *the new monastery ... consists in a series of buildings, arranged hexagonally*—L. Mumford, 1944; *Part of my unease about my cousin consisted in a fear that he would succeed in life and I would fail*—I. Murdoch,1978.

consistency, consistence. Theoretically, the two words should be interchangeable in both meanings, i.e. 'consistent behaviour or treatment' and 'the way in which a substance holds together'. In practice *consistency* is now almost always used: in the *OEC* data it makes up over 99 per cent of examples. Fowler (1926) hoped that the *-cy* form would be used exclusively in the first meaning, and the *-ce* form in the second, but instead one has practically annihilated the other. On the rare occasions when people use *consistence,* they attach either meaning to it.

consistory. In its normal ecclesiastical senses at first pronounced /kɒnsɪˈstɔːri/, then /ˈkɒnsɪstəri/ until about the end of the 19c., with the main stress on the first syllable, but now always /kənˈsɪstəri/.

consolatory. Pronounced /kənˈsɒlətəri/.

console. The verb is pronounced /kənˈsəʊl/ and the noun (= panel, cabinet, etc.) /ˈkɒnsəʊl/.

consols (= government securities). Pronounced /ˈkɒnsəlz/.

consommé. Pronounced /kənˈsɒmeɪ/ and print in romans.

consort. The noun is stressed on the first syllable and the verb on the second. See NOUN AND VERB ACCENT 1.

consortium the last syllable is pronounced /-tɪəm/, i.e. with a *t* sound, in British English, but usually with an *sh* sound in American English /-ʃəm/. For some unknown reason, the Latinate plural *consortia* is more widely used in writing than *consortiums.* See -UM 3.

conspectus. Plural *conspectuses.* See -US 2.

conspicuity. Marked 'rare' in the *OED* (the usual word, of course, being *conspicuousness*), it has been given a new lease of life in road-safety contexts: *The word 'conspicuity' ... has become fashionable in road-safety circles ... in connection with the visibility of pedestrians after dark*—*Walk,* 1984; *This seems to be the first population based aetiological study investigating motorcycle conspicuity and risk of crash related injury and death*—*BMJ,* 2004.

conspicuous, in the sense 'attracting notice or attention', is commonly used (some think overused) in the phrase *conspicuous by its absence* (first recorded in 1859): *Pinkie Aurangzeb was conspicuous by her absence; and Rani was queen for a day*—S. Rushdie, 1983.

constable. Pronounced /ˈkʌnstəbəl/, but don't be surprised if you hear some standard speakers saying /ˈkɒn-/.

constitution(al)ist. See -IST, -ALIST.

construct, construe. 1 These related words are both used to denote grammatical function. For example, a word is *construed* or *constructed* with *on* when *on* is its regular complement, e.g. *insist on* and *rely on* (the *OED* abbreviates this to 'const. on'). The word has been used since the 14c., as the *OED* says, in a range of broader senses, to mean 'to analyse or trace the grammatical construction of a sentence; to take its words in such an order as to show the meaning of a sentence; *specifically* to do this in the study of a foreign and especially a classical language, adding a word for word translation; hence, loosely, to translate orally a passage in an ancient or foreign author'. It is often virtually a synonym of *translate* or *interpret.*

2 *Construct* alternates with *construe* when used passively, as in, '*different* is usually construed with/constructed with *from*'. In such contexts *construed* is now the more common of the two.

3 A curiosity worth noting is that at an early date *construe* (from Latin *construere* 'to pile together, build up') was stressed on the first syllable, and the final syllable was reduced to *-stre, -ster.* As a result, /ˈkɒnstə/ continued to be the pronunciation down to the 19c., even after *conster* had disappeared as a written form. Walker (1791) called this 'a scandal to seminaries of learning'. The main stress was moved to the second syllable at some indeterminable point in the first half of the 20c.

4 Examples of the commonest uses of *construe*: *He could not construe the simplest German poem without the help of a translation*—M. Baring, 1924; *His life could be construed ... as a series of delinquent approaches to virtue*—V. S. Pritchett, 1980; *She said nothing to me which could not be construed as loyal admiration*—P. Ackroyd, 1983; *He asked his interrogators to specify* *anything he had written or said which could be construed as anti-Soviet*—R. Owen, 1985.

constructive. 1 In lay language and in politics used especially in the sense 'having the quality of contributing helpfully': *a constructive approach; constructive criticism,* etc. It is the opposite of *destructive.*

2 In legal language it is often applied 'to what in the eye of the law amounts to the act or condition specified' (*OED*) and is current in the phrase *constructive dismissal,* whereby an employer alters an employee's conditions in such a way that continued employment becomes impossible.

construe. See CONSTRUCT.

consubstantiation. See -CIATION.

consummate. The verb is nowadays generally pronounced /'kɒnsjʊmeɪt/ (**kon**-syuh-mayt) stressing the first syllable, and occasionally /'kɒnsəmeɪt/, the second syllable rhyming with *some.* The adjective is stressed on the second syllable, /kən'sʌmət/ (kən-**sum**-ət).

consummation. For *a consummation devoutly to be wished,* see HACKNEYED PHRASES.

consumption. This long-standing term (first recorded in the 14c.) for 'wasting of the body by disease' (from 17c., 'a pulmonary disease, phthisis'), was replaced in the course of the 20c. by the more specific medical term *tuberculosis,* abbreviated as *TB.*

contact. The verb, meaning 'to get in touch with', surfaced in the US in the 1920s and was greeted with open hostility by purists for several decades. By 1990 it had settled down as a natural and essential part of the language, though those few who remember the controversy continue to avoid using it. The stress pattern has not yet settled down for good; most often both the noun and verb are stressed on the first syllable, but the normal pattern of stressing the second syllable for the verb and the first for the noun may be beginning to establish itself. See CONVERSION; NOUN AND VERB ACCENT.

contact clauses. This is Jespersen's term (*Mod. Eng. Gram.,* III, 1927), now widely used, for dependent clauses that are not formally joined by a relative pronoun or conjunction, e.g. *the man I saw last week; he has found the key you lost yesterday; there is a man below wants to speak to you.* As Jespersen pointed out, these have always been frequent in colloquial English but in the 18c. were opposed by Latinate scholars as such constructions do not occur in Latin. These constructions are often spoken of as clauses 'with omission of the relative pronoun', i.e. in the above examples, with omission of 'that/whom', 'that', and 'who'.

Jespersen cited a series of examples of contact clauses from the Old English period onwards, e.g. *Where is the thousand markes* ʌ *I gaue thee villaine*—Shakespeare, 1590; *Here she set up the same trade* ʌ *she had followed in Ireland*—I. Walton, 1653; *There are lots of vulgar people* ʌ *live in Grosvenor Square*—Wilde, 1893; *It was haste* ʌ *killed the yellowsnake*—Kipling, 1895; *There isn't a boy in your stables* ʌ *would give me up like that*—G. B. Shaw, 1901.

Further examples are listed in the *OED* e.g. *What is it* ʌ *makes me beat so low?*—Tennyson, 1850; *It may bee* ʌ *they will reuerence him*—(AV), 1611; *I fear* ʌ *They will* not—Tennyson, 1847. Grammarians are agreed that contact clauses are probably the product of a paratactic construction of two independent clauses, i.e. the loose running together of two independent clauses, rather than examples of the simple omission of a relative pronoun or conjunction.

See OMISSION OF RELATIVES.

contagious. A *contagious* disease is one transmitted by physical contact. It contrasts with an *infectious* disease or illness, transmitted by micro-organisms in the air or water. In non-literal uses, *contagious* tends to be used of both pleasant and unpleasant things (*corruption, folly, greed, guilt, panic,* and *suffering,* but also *delight, enthusiasm, laughter, sense of fun,* and *vigour*), whereas *infectious* is mainly restricted to pleasant or positive things (*enthusiasm, laugh, smile,* and *energy*).

contango. Plural *contangos.*

contemn. This literary word (= treat with contempt, scorn) is pronounced with the final *n* silent: /kən'tɛm/. The inflected forms of the verb are similarly pronounced with silent *n* (/kən'tɛmɪŋ/ and /kən'tɛmd/), but *contemner* may be pronounced with or without sounding the *n.*

contemporaneous. See CONTEMPORARY.

contemporary. 1 *Contemporary* has two meanings: (*a*) 'living or occurring at the same time' (*writers contemporary with the events they write of*); similarly with the corresponding noun (*the comic poet Alexis, a younger contemporary of Plato*). (*b*) 'existing or done at the present time' (as in *contemporary literature*) and hence 'up-to-date, modern' (as in *contemporary ideas, contemporary furnishings*). This second meaning might appear to be inconsistent with the first, but it is shorthand for 'contemporary with the present'. Further examples: *Contemporary curtains for contemporary colour schemes*—M. Drabble, 1963; *Before I always wanted something up to date, what they call contemporary*—J. Fowles, 1963.

2 Because of its two meanings, *contemporary* is ambiguous in theory, but rarely so in practice. Gowers (1965) mentioned the ambiguity of 'Twelfth Night *is to be produced with contemporary incidental music*', which does not make it clear whether the music is of Shakespeare's time or of ours. Some writers use parentheses to cancel any ambiguity, e.g. *contemporary incidental music* (*from the 16th century*). Another way to avoid misunderstanding is to use **contemporaneous**, first recorded in 1656, and only ever used in meaning (*a*). It is found surprisingly often, especially in historical contexts: *Built in the thirteenth and fourteenth centuries, they are contemporaneous with many of the great Gothic cathedrals of Europe*—S. Stewart, 1991

3 It is historically interesting that although *contemporary* is the original (1655) form, the by-form **co-temporary** (with or without hyphen) was used by many writers, including Dr Johnson, from the 17c. to the 19c. e.g. *Prudentius a Christian poet, cotemporary with Theodosius*—Fanny Burney, *a*1789; *Supported by cotemporary scholars*—Max Müller, 1861.

contemptible, contemptuous. 1 The first means 'to be despised, deserving contempt, despicable' (*there are few things in life more contemptible than child abuse*), the second (often followed by *of*) 'showing contempt, scornful' (*Saddam Hussein showed a contemptuous disregard for the feelings of hostages held in Baghdad; he is contemptuous of the laws governing human rights*).

2 In historical contexts, e.g. in the works of Shakespeare, *contemptible* will be encountered in the sense 'exhibiting or expressing contempt' (e.g. *The contemptible idea I always entertained of Cellarius*—Gibbon, 1762), but this meaning is now obsolete.

content (verb). *Content oneself with* (not *by*) is the right form of the phrase that means 'accept as adequate despite wanting more or better': e.g. *You should not content yourself with being a mere collector of insects; He contents himself with reporting the results of other scholars.*

content(ment). The two forms now mean almost the same, *contentment* having almost lost its verbal use (*The contentment of his wishes left him unhappy*) and meaning, like *content*, contented state. *Contentment* is the usual word, *content* surviving chiefly in *to one's heart's content* and as a poetic or rhetorical variant.

content(s), what is contained. The *OED* (1893) said 'The stress *contént* is historical, and still common among the educated, but *cóntent* is now used by many, especially by young people'. Fowler (1926) took the same view. But *content* (singular, as in *the cubic content*) and *contents* (plural, as in *the contents of the house will be sold at auction*) are now invariably pronounced with initial stressing, doubtless owing to a wish to differentiate the word from *content* = contentment.

contest. The noun (*a close contest*) is stressed on the first syllable, the verb (*he will not contest the seat at the next election*) on the second. See NOUN AND VERB ACCENT 1.

Continent. In the UK *the Continent* (note the capital *C*) still invariably means 'the mainland of Europe' as distinct from the British Isles, as a geographical and cultural designation not affected by Britain's membership of the European Union. A *continental breakfast* (small *c*) is a light breakfast of bread, rolls, coffee, etc. (as distinct from an 'English' or 'Scottish' cooked breakfast), and a *continental quilt* is a rather dated name for what is nowadays called a duvet.

continual, continuous. Since the mid-19c. it has been customary to regard *continual* as being applicable to events that occur frequently but with intervals between, and *continuous* to anything that happens or proceeds in an unbroken manner. In practice the distinction is not as neat as that.

Since it was first recorded in the 14c., *continual* has been used at all times to mean 'incessant, perpetual', and also, less strictly (*OED*), to mean 'repeated with brief intermissions'. *Continuous* is a more modern word (first recorded in 1673) than *continual*. It was first used in technical contexts in botany (of plants having their parts in immediate connection) and optics, and was not brought into general use until the 18c.

Fowler's judgement (1926), though somewhat cryptic, expresses the nice distinction between the two words: 'That is *-al* which either is always going on or occurs at short intervals and never comes (or is regarded as never coming) to an end. That is *-ous* in which no break occurs between the beginning and the (not necessarily or even presumably long-deferred) end.'

Continuous is used in physical contexts (such as lines, roads, etc.) and is preferred in technical contexts: e.g. *continuous assessment* (1959), *continuous creation* (1941), *continuous process* (1909, in industry, opposite of *batch process*), *continuous stationery* (1942), *continuous tenses* (1887, in grammar), and numerous others. The other principal use refers to time: *continuous* here means 'going on uninterruptedly' whereas *continual* means 'constantly or frequently recurring'. The following examples show how difficult it is to keep the two meanings apart: (continual) *The house and garden had seen their best days, and the decline was now continual, from season to season*—R. Frame, 1986; *His son was a continual source of amusement and delight to him*—E. Blair, 1990; *He singled out two big issues that should be addressed: 'The first is the continual underfunding of road and rail infrastructure'*—*Lloyd's List*, 2006; (continuous) *The correspondence between the two men was continuous throughout the next few months*—V. Brome, 1978; *The 1840s were years of continuous self-education for Philip Henry Gosse*—A. Thwaite, 1984.

To make your intended meaning absolutely clear, other words are sometimes preferable, e.g. (in place of *continual*) *constant, habitual, intermittent, recurrent, repeated,* and (in place of *continuous*) *ceaseless, constant, incessant, unbroken, uninterrupted.*

continually, continuously. Historically, *continually* (first recorded in the 14c.) was the earlier by far: *continuously* was not recorded until 1678. During the intervening three centuries, *continually* was used to mean both 'incessantly, constantly, all the time' and less strictly (*OED*) 'with frequent repetition, very frequently'. The arrival of *continuously* tended to restrict continually to this 'less strict' meaning of 'frequently'. In modern use *continually* can be defined as 'repeatedly; again and again' and *continuously* as 'without interruption'. To illustrate the distinction, the *OEC* data shows, for example, that water is generally described as flowing *continuously* rather than *continually,* since its source is never interrupted (*water flows continuously from the stone font into a pool in the floor*). On the other hand, people feel things *continually* (*continually amazed, frustrated, surprised*) and to perform actions (*continually interrupt, remind, stress, thwart*). The following examples clearly illustrate the difference; in every case replacing one word with the other would change the meaning, sometimes to ridiculous effect. Examples: (continually) *Among all our talks, we returned continually to an argument about science*—C. P. Snow, 1934; *You can't do that at ease with a man continually on the go to the cellar for another litre*—G. Greene, 1967; *He said that the business of the court ... was being continually held up by irrelevancies*—J. B. Morton, 1974; *The black coat lost its warmth and he shivered continually*—J. M. Coetzee, 1983; (continuously) *This lost energy must be continuously supplied by the engines*—C. E. Dole, 1971; *Clinical governance requires that the quality of medical care be continuously monitored*—*Bath Chronicle*, 2001. In the following example *continuously* seems to be wrongly used for *continually: The Chinese officials also continuously stated that they could put a stop to inflation at any time*—P. Lowe, 1989.

continuance, continuation. *Continuance,* first recorded in the 14c. is about six times less common than *continuation* (also 14c.) in the *OEC* data. It tends to be used when the context requires the meaning 'a state of continuing in existence or operation; the duration of an event or action' (i.e. a fact) rather than 'the act or an instance of continuing' (i.e. a process), which calls for *continuation.* Another distinction between them is that *continuance* suggests that there is no interruption in the state, whereas *continuation* can suggest a resumption of the process. Examples: (continuance) *At present in extremely short supply, these are the four basic tools for the continuance and improvement of the human race—OEC,* 2002; *The continuance of hunting is the bastion for the defence of every other legitimate country sport—Bristol Evening Post,* 2003; *He also denied that there was discontent brewing among party workers over Modi's continuance in the office—OEC,* 2004; (continuation) *The step-up in the air war might even jeopardize the continuation of the talks themselves—Newsweek,* 1972; *Tiering* [of dresses] *is a continuation of the peasant theme that has been with us for what seems like a long, long time—Detroit Free Press,* 1978; *It feels more like a natural continuation of the first movie—OEC,* 2006; *If, as Clausewitz said, war is the continuation of politics by other means, then in America litigation is often just the continuation of business by other means—OEC,* 2001.

continue should not be followed by *on* (adverb), although this is sometimes found in informal writing (*I continued on down the street*—A. Bergman, 1975) because it is a tautology. Use either *continue* (without *on*) or a verb of motion (such as *go, move,* etc.) with *on*. This use of the adverb should be distinguished from the preposition *on*, which has a linking role and is quite acceptable: *I fear that, if we continue on our present path, we are going to fail—Modern Age,* 2003.

continuous. See CONTINUAL.

continuously. See CONTINUALLY.

continuum. Plural *continua*. See -UM 2.

contract. The noun has initial stressing and the verb is stressed on the second syllable. See NOUN AND VERB ACCENT 1.

contractable, contractible. See -ABLE, -IBLE 3.

contractions. 1 Fowler (1926) used the word to mean an abbreviation consisting of the first and last letters of a word, e.g. *Mr* for *Mister, St* for *Saint,* as distinct from abbreviations like *Jun.* for *Junior, Capt.* for Captain. A full stop, he argued, was not needed for contractions but was desirable for abbreviations. This useful convention has been widely adopted, but (*a*) is occasionally awkward as when, for example, *Rev.* (with full stop) and *Revd* (without) (both = *Reverend*) are distinguished in this way, and (*b*) has been widely undermined by many publications abandoning the full stop for abbreviations as well as contractions.

2 Contractions of the type *I'm* (= *I am*) and *don't* (= *do not*) are exceedingly common in informal and online writing and increasingly found in various kinds of fairly formal contexts (e.g. in book reviews). The conventional forms of contractions have been subject to considerable fluctuation at various periods. Shakespeare, for example, used *Ile/I'le* for 'I will', *hee'l, shee'l, wee'l, you'l* for 'he, etc., will', and *I'ld, hee'ld,* etc., for 'I, etc., would'. But the *OED* records some of the most frequent modern colloquial contractions only from later periods: *ain't* 1778, *can't* 1706, *couldn't* 1882, *don't* 1670, *I've* 1885, *shan't* 1850, *shouldn't* 1848, *won't* 1660, and *wouldn't* 1836. Fluctuation in the use of the reduced forms is subject to all manner of social and stylistic assumptions which vary from one century to another.

contractual. The form **contractural** is sometimes used when *contractual* is meant. The existence of the suffixes *-ual* (*mutual, spiritual,* etc.) and *-ural* (*procedural, structural,* etc.) may account linguistically for this mistake. *Contractural* does in fact exist as a very precise medical term.

contralto. The plural is now almost invariably *contraltos,* and not (as in Italian) *contralti.* See -O(E)S 4.

contrary. 1 The placing of the main stress has fluctuated over the centuries: 'the poets, from Chaucer to Spenser and Shakespeare, use both *contráry* and *cóntrary.*' (*OED*). In standard English, initial stressing is now obligatory for the adjective and the noun, except that /kənˈtrɛːri/, rhyming with *Mary,* is customary for the adjective in the sense 'perverse, obstinately self-willed', probably under the influence of the nursery rhyme *Mary, Mary, quite contrary, How does your garden grow?* Second-syllable stressing is also usual in *contráriwise.*

2 The phrase *on the contrary* is properly used only in a statement intensifying a denial of what has just been stated or implied (e.g. *You say that war is inevitable; on the contrary I think the outstanding differences between the two countries can be settled by negotiation*). By contrast, the phrase *on the other hand* (= from another point of view) is usually directly or impliedly paired with *on the one hand* (= from one point of view) to indicate two contrasted sides of a subject, circumstances, considerations, points of view, etc.: *If men of eminence are exposed to censure on the one hand, they are as much liable to flattery on the other*—Addison, 1711.

3 *to the contrary.* In British English the phrase *to the contrary* following a noun or pronoun (e.g. *there is plenty of evidence to support this view and none to the contrary*) is normal, as it is in American and other forms of English. But *to the contrary* at the head of a sentence or as an aside (e.g. *To the contrary, it simply replaced one world-view with another*—*Art Journal*, Fall 2000; *Others assert, to the contrary, that responses to colours are the result of acquired knowledge of their cultural coding*—*OEC*, 2005) is largely, though not exclusively, AmE. In BrE such a sentence would normally begin *On the contrary*.

contrast. 1 The noun is pronounced with initial stress, and the verb with the stress on the second syllable. See NOUN AND VERB ACCENT 1.

In older literature you may encounter certain unfamiliar transitive uses of the verb, and also uses of the verb constructed with *by*, (e.g. *The brown and sun-tinged hermit and the pale decrepit elder contrast each other*—H. Fuseli, 1801–15; *The smooth slopes ... are contrasted by the aspect of the country on the opposite bank*—A. W. Kinglake, 1863). Nowadays the normal constructions are with *with* and with *and*: *Her sudden energy contrasted with Henry's sudden exhaustion*—J. Frame, 1970; *He is contrasting Adam in his state of innocence and us in our state of knowledge*—A. N. Wilson, 1983; *He has contrasted his position with the Government's*—*OEC*, 2009.

2 The noun can be followed by *to, with,* or *between: Captain Massingham's picture ... was in provocative contrast to all the soft and pretty comforts of his wife's bedroom*—M. Keane, 1981; *The light of intellectual processes in contrast with the darkness of the unconscious*—J. Hawkes, 1951; *Doing such a thing roused Wendy to angry thoughts of the contrast between the life she had once known and the one she was living now*—M. Laski, 1952; *Colour contrasts between brown stock bricks, red brick dressings, and white woodwork*—M. Girouard, 1977.

contribute. The standard pronunciation is with the main stress on the second syllable, /kən'trɪbjuːt/. Stressing the first syllable, /'kɒntrɪbjuːt/ is becoming increasingly common in British English, and is marked in some US dictionaries as a specifically British trend.

controversy. Traditional British English pronunciation places the stress on the first syllable, /'kɒntrəvəːsi/, as does American English. In Britain a variant with stress on the second syllable is becoming increasingly common, despite the strictures of purists. Early stress on words of more than three syllables is unusual in English (*excellency, matrimony*, and *presidency* are others), and so the shift is not surprising.

contumely. This rarely uttered word is stressed on the first syllable, and can have four syllables, /'kɒntjuːmɪli/, or three, /'kɒntjuːmli/.

conundrum. A 16c. word of unknown origin (not Latin, but possibly originating in some now-lost university joke). Plural *conundrums*. See -UM 1.

***convenance*, convenience.** The first is used mainly in the French phrase *mariage de convenance*, but *marriage of convenience* is much the more usual term in English.

conversant. The placing of the stress has changed over the centuries from the third syllable to the first and, most recently, to the second. Second-syllable stressing is recommended, /kən'vəːsənt/.

conversationalist, conversationist. Both terms have been in use since the early 19c., and neither can be faulted as formations. In practice, *conversationalist* is overwhelmingly the more common of the two.

conversazione. This now rather unusual word of Italian origin for 'a social gathering held by a learned or art society' is pronounced /ˌkɒnvəsatsɪ'əʊneɪ/. Its plural is either *conversaziones* (the more usual) or *conversazioni*, pronounced /ˌkɒnvəsatsɪˈəʊniː/.

converse. The verb (= engage in conversation) is pronounced with the stress on the second syllable, and the noun, in its archaic sense 'conversation', with the stress on the first. The adjective and noun *converse* = (something) opposite, which are both pronounced with initial stressing, are unrelated words.

conversion, in grammar, the process by which a word previously used as one part of speech is extended to another. It is a modern term (first recorded in 1928) for an ancient process. It is also called **zero-derivation**. **1** Historically, *conversion*, and especially the employment of nouns as hitherto unrecorded verbs, is exceedingly common. Examples (with the date of first use of the noun given first, and that of the verb second): *chair* (*a*1300, 1552), *distance* (*c*.1290, 1578), *elbow* (Old English, 1605, Shakespeare), *inconvenience* (*c*.1400, *a*1656), *magic* (*c*.1384, 1906), *napalm* (1942, 1950), *service* (*c*.1230, 1893), *silence* (*a*1225, 1603, Shakespeare), *telephone* (1835, 1877). In these examples the maximum interval is one of over 600 years (*service*) and the minimum 8 years (*napalm*), but doubtless more extreme examples exist.

2 Examples of the *conversion* of other parts of speech are less common, but they do exist: e.g. (adjective → verb) *dirty* (15.., 1591), *empty* (OE, 1526), *lower* (*c*.1200, 1659), *ready* (*c*.1205, *a*1340), *total* (*c*.1386, 1716); (noun or verb → adjective) *go, no go* (OE, 1910), *touch and go* (1655, 1812); (verb → noun) *call* (OE, *a*1300), *save* (*c*.1250, 1906); (miscellaneous) *but me no buts, the hereafter, a fun party, a must.*

3 In the 20c., resistance to such processes hardened, and examples such as the following are almost invariably regarded with alarm: *Another rival* ... *candidate* ... audibles *his allegations—Chicago Sun-Times*, 1988; *somebody had* blow-torched *into it the names of all the people who spoke for it—New Yorker*, 1989; *it is difficult to* example *one aircraft accident statistic where the cause has been reliably attributed to cigarette smoking*—letter to *Times*, 1989.

Among the most fiercely resisted *conversion*-verbs that came into prominence in the 20c. are *author, contact, critique, host, impact, interface, reference*, and *parent* (= to be a parent). See also VERBING.

convert. The noun has initial stress, and the verb is stressed on the second syllable. See NOUN AND VERB ACCENT 1.

convertible. Always so spelt, not *-able*. See -ABLE, -IBLE 7.

convex. See CONCAVE.

convict. The verb is stressed on the second syllable, and the noun on the first. See NOUN AND VERB ACCENT 1.

convince. This verb, which has been in use in English in various senses and constructions since the 16c., began to be used in the 1950s with *to* + infinitive to mean 'persuade', and was criticized by some usage pundits, though not by Gowers (1965). Examples: *He worked very hard personally to convince Ike to run*—D. Halberstam, 1979; *The miners tried to convince their colleagues to join them*—BBC World Service, 1991; *He wants to convince me to become his disciple*—B. Aldiss, 1993. It is a classic example of a change in construction that is acceptable to the many and repugnant to the few.

convolvulus. Plural *convolvuluses*. See -US 1. (If you wish to use *convolvuli* instead, pronounce the final syllable /-lʌɪ/.)

convoy. Until the early part of the 20c. the noun (stressed on the first syllable) and the verb (on the second syllable) were regularly distinguished. Now both words are stressed on the first syllable.

cony, coney (a rabbit). The recommended spelling for this archaic word, should you ever wish to give your historical novel a bit of period flavour, is *cony* (plural *conies*), not *coney* (plural *coneys*).

cooee, a sound used to attract attention, derived from an indigenous Australian language, is the universal spelling now for the interjection, the noun (*within cooee* (*of*), Aust. and NZ, = within hailing distance), and the rarely used verb.

cookie has settled down in this spelling (not *cooky*) in its various meanings, (Scottish, archaic) a plain bun, (US) a small sweet biscuit, (slang) a person. Also in the informal phrase *that's the way the cookie crumbles,* that's how things turn out. Since the 1980s *cookie* has probably become most familiar in all forms of English as a computing term for a set of data sent by the server of an Internet website to a user's browser to identify and track the user's future access to that website.

coolie. 'The usual modern form' (Fowler, 1926), not *cooly* or *coolee.* Mercifully, the world has changed to the point that the word is only encountered now in historical contexts.

coomb. The usual form (rather than *combe*) in Britain for a valley or hollow on the side of a hill or a short valley running up from the coast. In place names, however, *-combe* is the more usual form (*Ilfracombe, Winchcombe,* etc.).

cooperate, co-opt, coordinate. See CO-.

cope. The traditional construction with *with* has been in common use since the 16c.: e.g. *His being too unwell to cope with Dr. Johnson*—Mme D'Arblay, 1782; *Let the scholar measure his valour by his power to cope with intellectual giants*—Emerson, 1875; *There was pain later on but nothing his stubborn soul could not cope with*—W. Golding, 1979; *Like many religious professionals, I cope with festivals, but I can't really enjoy them*—L. Blue, 1985.

It now stands alongside absolute uses (= to manage) which were first recorded in the 1930s: e.g. *Angela rang the bell wildly for someone to come and cope*—E. Bowen, 1934; *it wasn't as if Marcia was an invalid or unable to cope, even if she was a bit eccentric*—B. Pym, 1977.

copula, copular. In grammar, used to denote a word that connects a subject and predicate. 'The term *copula* refers to the verb *be,* and *copular* verbs are those verbs (including *be* and *become*) which are functionally equivalent to the copula' (*CGEL* 2.16). Typical *copular* constructions are: *he* felt *annoyed, she* sounded *surprised, he never* became *Prime Minister, the outcome* remained *uncertain, it all* came *true, the weather* turned *cold*; and especially the type *Canberra* is *the capital of Australia.*

coquette, a woman who flirts. The more modern British pronunciation is /kɒ'kɛt/, the first syllable rhyming with *lock,* instead of the older /kəʊ'kɛt, which is standard American English. The same distinction applies to the related abstract noun *coquetry,* pronounced either as /'kɒkɪtri/ or as /'kəʊkɪtri/, and to the rarely used verb *coquet,* /kɒ'kɛt/, /kəʊ'kɛt/.

corbel (verb), to support or project on corbels, gives *corbelled, corbelling* (US *corbeled, corbeling*). See -LL-, -L-.

cord. See CHORD, CORD.

cordelier, a Franciscan friar of a strict order (wearing a knotted cord round the waist). Pronounced /kɔːdə'lɪə/.

cordon. On its own, *cordon* is always pronounced /'kɔːdən/, but when used with *bleu* or *sanitaire* it is commonly (?almost always) pronounced in a manner suggestive of its French origin: /kɔː(r)dɔ̃/.

core. *Rotten at the core* (*heart*) is a MISQUOTATION.

co-respondent. See CO-.

corn. In British English means 'wheat' or 'oats', in American English 'maize' (also commonly called *Indian corn,* or more rarely *Indian maize*).

cornelian, a variety of chalcedony of a deep dull red, flesh, or reddish white colour, is in origin a refashioning of 15c. French *corneline* (modern French *cornaline*). Later in the same century a by-form **carnelian** appeared in English, influenced by Latin *carno, carnem* flesh, *carneus* flesh-coloured. Although on etymological grounds cornelian is marginally the better form, *carnelian* is more commonly used.

cornucopia. From a late Latin modification of Latin *cornū* 'horn' + *cōpiae* 'of plenty'. Its plural in English is *cornucopias* (not *cornucopiae*).

corolla, a whorl or whorls of petals forming the inner envelope of a flower, has *corollas* as its plural in English. In origin it is a Latin diminutive of *corōna* 'crown'.

corona. In its several English meanings (in astronomy, anatomy, botany, etc.) based on Latin *corōna* 'crown', its plural is *coronae* /-niː/, rarely *coronas.* The Cuban cigar, the Corona, always has its plural in *-as.*

coronal. The adjective (of the skull; in astronomy and botany, of a corona) is pronounced /kə'rəʊnəl/, and the rare literary noun (= a circlet, a garland) /'kɒrənəl/. Under the influence of CORONARY, the adjective *coronal* is now sometimes stressed on the first syllable.

coronary. With the increasing frequency of the condition called (*a*) *coronary thrombosis* (often called merely *a coronary*), the word has become very familiar to the general public. It is pronounced /'kɒrənərɪ/ in British English; in American English the last two syllables rhyme with *Mary*.

coroneted. Spelt with one *-t-*, in accordance with the rule that unstressed syllables in verbs ending in *-t* are not doubled in their inflected forms (thus *benefited, targeted*, etc.). See -T-, -TT-.

corporal, corporeal. Neither word is common except in particular phrases. *Corporal* means 'of or relating to the human body', and is common in the phrase *corporal punishment* (though this type of punishment is now effectively banned in EU schools). In other possible contexts (used of beauty, deformity, etc.) it is now almost entirely replaced by *bodily* or *personal*. *Corporeal* means principally 'bodily, physical, material, as distinct from spiritual' (*that which is created is of necessity corporeal and visible and tangible*—Jowett, 1875; *the corporeal presence of Christ in the Sacrament*). Occasionally *corporeal punishment* is written by mistake for *corporal punishment*.

corps. Pronounced /kɔː/ in the singular, but /kɔːz/ in the plural, though the spelling is the same.

corpulence, corpulency. The first of these is by far the more frequent of the two words, though they both acquired the sense 'obesity' at a similar date and seemed to be variants of equal standing between the 16c. and the late 19c. In Hilary Mantel's *Fludd* (1989) the phrase *His Corpulence* is used satirically as a term of address to a bishop (cf. *His Eminence, His Excellency*). See -CE, -CY.

corpus. The standard plural, inherited directly from Latin, is *corpora*, which is almost always used in preference to *corpuses*. One of its most frequent uses in English language contexts now is for a representative group of English texts, spoken and (especially) written, running to many millions of words, and used as measurable evidence, especially for the currency and frequency of individual words and constructions. Among the best-known pioneering corpora of this kind were the Brown Corpus (1963–4), edited by W. Nelson Francis and H. Kučera, and updated in 1982; the corpus of the Survey of English Usage (University College London) (originated in the 1960s); and the COBUILD corpus (Collins-Birmingham University International Language Database), established by 1987. The Oxford English Corpus contains more than two billion words of 21st-century Englishes, including British, US, Canadian, Australian, Caribbean, New Zealand, and Indian.

corpuscle. Pronounced /'kɔːpʌsəl/. The variant /kɔː'pʌsəl/ seems to have died out.

corpus delicti. In roman type, not italics. In law, the facts and circumstances constituting a breach of the law, literally (in Latin) 'the body of a crime'. In lay use, the concrete evidence of a crime, especially the body of a murdered person. Those in the legal profession should avoid potentially making asses of themselves by writing either the often seen *corpus delecti*, or the less commonly spotted *corpus dilecti*, which respectively would translate from Latin as 'the body of the chosen [male] one' and 'the body of the loved [male] one'.

corral. This word of Spanish (and Portuguese) origin is pronounced /kɒ'rɑːl/. It is related to the South African word *kraal* (ultimately from the same Portuguese base) = a fenced village of huts.

correctitude, formed as a combination of *correct* + *rectitude* in the late 19c., does not mean the same as mere 'correctness of conduct or behaviour': it connotes self-conscious, probably self-important, correctness, and was memorably used by Churchill: *Lord Curzon ... soused him in sonorous correctitudes.* It is used nowadays in the ironic phrase *political correctitude*, and deserves to be more widely used in contexts such as *They decided last year that Mr Latham was an un-electable oddball and national embarrassment—struggling to exude the requisite correctitude to be considered aldermanic, much less prime ministerial*—*OEC*, 2005 (Aust.).

correctness. Linguistic correctness of some kind is clearly the *raison d'être* of any usage book. But that does not mean imposing one view of language, or an inflexible set of rules, both of which, in any case, would be impossible. It means helping writers, editors, and the general public avoid the kinds of mistake that come about through ignorance or inadvertence.

Obviously there are errors and errors, ranging from the crass spelling mistake of *We can't possibly know* everybodies *position* (from an advertisement in a computer journal called *DEC User*, 1988) to the inadvertent hilarity of an omitted hyphen in *For sale—four-poster bed, 101 years old. Perfect for* antique *lover* (from a report in the American magazine *People*, 1988). Schoolteachers derive a great deal of pleasure from the howlers of their pupils' essays. The type is well known: *Socrates died of an overdose of* wedlock; *The First World War, caused by the* assignation *of the* Arch-Duck *by an anarchist, ushered in a new* error *in the* anals *of human history.*

It is only when one moves into the world of fully adult writing that such mistakes become less forgivable. Had it existed, perhaps T. S. Eliot should have done Community Service for allowing *staid* (for *stayed*) to appear in the first edition (1939) of *The Family Reunion* (*You have staid in England, yet you seem Like someone who comes from a very long distance*). He could be joined in his stint behind the counter of a charity shop by the person who wrote to *the London Review of Books* in 1988 about barbed wire being *payed out from the saddle horn*. These might be said to belong to the sophisticated school of error. Possibly the most common type is that shown in a malapropistic setting down of words that are nearly right but not quite right. Phrases like *baited breath* (for *bated breath*), *wet the appetite* (*whet*), and *hare's breath* (*hair's breadth*) lie scattered about in newspapers like broken bottles. Keep the words *snook, intransitive, disquieted,* and *recoup* in mind when reading the sentences that follow: *I'm in no position to cock a snoot at these new acts* (*The Face*, 1986); *One, a head of English, could not explain the function of an intransigent verb* (letter to *Sunday Times*, 1988); *Our man came away profoundly disappointed. And not a little disquietened* (*Auckland* (NZ) *Star*, 1988); *No explanation has been given on how investors in the expedition will recuperate the $2.5 million cost of the adventure* (Associated Press report on salvaging relics from the Titanic, 1987). Such are typical casualties of the fast-moving newsprint world, or, of course, the Internet, where a feeble grasp of spelling and meaning often seems the rule rather than the exception. It is much more difficult to find errors of the same kind, and in such numbers, in copy-edited books put out by reputable publishers.

corrector. Spelt *-or*, not *-er*. See -OR.

correlative (adjective). 'Applied to words corresponding to each other, and regularly used together, each in one member of a compound or complex sentence: e.g. *either——or; so——as.*' (*OED*). A relatively modern term (first recorded in 1871), it is applied to clause-connecting words in English after the manner of similar words in Latin (*tantus——quantus, tam——quam, sic——ut*, etc.). Other common correlatives are *both——and, neither——nor, not only——but,* and *whether——or.* Correct and incorrect uses of correlatives are discussed under the relevant words.

correspond. In the meanings (*a*) 'to be analogous or similar' and (*b*) 'to agree in amount, position, etc.', *correspond* is usually followed by *to*: (*a*) *Our nature corresponds to our external condition*—J. Butler, 1736; *Gandhi's concept of Religion corresponds to his concept of Truth*—G. Richards, 1991. (*b*) *The degrees of condensation of the air correspond to the degrees of cold*—R. J. Sullivan, 1794; *The peaks in such a curve correspond to the scattering of the electron wave*—*Sci. Amer.*, 1976. When it means (*c*) 'to be in harmony or agreement' it can be followed by *to* or *with*; (*c*) *The prudence of the execution should correspond with the wisdom ... of the design*—*Junius Letters*, 1769; *There were two bedrooms to correspond with the rooms downstairs*—D. H. Lawrence, 1921. Had the *Junius* sentence been written now, it would probably appear as *correspond to the wisdom.* When the meaning is (*d*) 'to communicate by interchange of letters', it is followed by *with*, or used without a following preposition: (*d*) *Those who have a mind to correspond with me, may direct their Letters to the Spectator*—Addison, 1711; *My brother Michael ... and I corresponded about socialism and religion*—Tony Benn, 1979.

corrigendum. Plural (much commoner than the singular) *corrigenda*; see -UM 2.

corrupter. So spelt, not *-or*. See -OR.

corsage is still pronounced /kɔːˈsɑːʒ/ in a broadly French manner.

corset. In its ordinary meaning of 'a closely fitting undergarment worn by women to give shape and support to the figure', it is properly used in the singular. But Somerset Maugham (*Cakes and Ale*, 1930) is not the only person to have spoken of the garment in the plural. (*She did not put on her corsets again, but rolled them up*). The corresponding participial adjective *corseted* has only one *-t-*. See -T-, -TT-.

cortège. Printed in roman type with a grave accent. Pronounced /kɔːˈteɪʒ/.

Cortes, the national assembly of Spain or Portugal is usually pronounced /ˈkɔːtɛz/ in English. So too is *Cortés*, the 16c. Spanish conquistador.

cortex, the outer part of a bodily organ (*cerebral cortex, renal cortex*, etc.) has as its plural *cortices* /ˈkɔːtɪsiːz/. Cf. Latin *cortex, corticis* bark. See -EX, -IX.

coruscating is one of those glitteringly impressive words on which certain magpie writers, especially journalists, light in order to embellish their prose, often with scant regard for its meaning. It derives ultimately from the Latin coruscāre 'to vibrate, glitter, sparkle, gleam', and 'glittering' or 'sparkling', literally or metaphorically, is what it means in English, e.g. *She preserves the steely delicacy and coruscating wit of Wilde's writing—OEC*, 2005. It is therefore puzzling that, despite its relative rarity, it is commonly misused in phrases such as *coruscating attack, criticism, review* by mistake for the slightly less rare Latinate word *excoriating*. This is the participial adjective of the verb *excoriate*, of Latin origin, which in English has been used to mean literally 'strip the skin off' someone, and non-literally 'criticize them mercilessly', e.g. *Audiences are excoriated for not understanding what composers write—OEC*, 2004. Do not compound the stylistic felony by doubling *coruscating*'s single letter *r*, as noted in *The Guardian's Corrections and clarifications column* on March 23 2007: 'In the following article, Terry Eagleton's "corruscating [*sic*] review" of Richard Dawkins's book *The God Delusion* may have been withering or possibly even acidulous.' Other alternatives whose meaning would be clearer to reader and writer alike are *blistering, devastating*, and *scathing*.

coryphaeus /kɒrɪˈfiːəs/, (in ancient Greek drama) the leader of the chorus, has as plural *coryphaei* /kɒrɪˈfiːʌɪ/. See -US 1.

'cos. A frequent reduced form of *because*, first recorded in 1828, and used, like *'cause*, only in the representation of informal or regional speech: *that's why I seldom ever talk about paintings,'cos you always sound like a jerk*—Steve Martin (an American) in *The Face*, 1988; *I said 'Why exactly are you calling?' ''Cause your name's on my list?'—OEC*, 2005.

cosmonaut. See ASTRONAUT.

cosset (verb). The inflected forms are *cosseted, cosseting*, with a single -t-. See -T-, -TT-.

cosy as adjective meaning 'comfortable, etc.' and as noun meaning 'teapot-warmer' is always spelt with *-sy* in Britain and in most other English-speaking countries except the US, where the standard (but not invariable) spelling is *cozy*.

cot. 1 In the senses 'small bed for a baby' and 'hospital, naval, etc., bed', the word is Anglo-Indian in origin (Hindi *khāt* 'bedstead, hammock'). A *cot death* (US *crib death*) is a modern term (first recorded in 1970) for the unexplained death of a baby in its sleep.

2 In the sense 'a small house', it is a native word, corresponding to Old English *cot* in the same sense. It survived as a poetical and literary word until about the end of the 19c. (e.g. *A few humble fishermen's cots*—E. E. Napier, 1849). As a second element in *bell-cot, sheep-cot* it means a small structure for shelter or protection.

3 See COTE.

cote /kəʊt/. A native word (Old English *cote*) = *cot* 2 and for many centuries more widely used than it, e.g. *bell-cote, sheep-cote, swine-cote*. The forms *dovecote* and *dovecot* have both been used since the 15c.; the spelling *dovecote*, pronounced /ˈdʌvkɒt/, is now dominant and recommended.

cotemporary. See CONTEMPORARY 1.

co-tidal. See CO-.

cotillion (a dance). Spelt *-ion* in English, not quite reflecting the spelling of its

French original (*cotillon*). Pronounced /kəˈtɪljən/.

cottar, cotter, cottier. Three forms of a word used at various times in the past, principally in Scotland (usually spelt *cottar*, but also *cotter*) for 'a tenant occupying a cottage with or (late 18c.-19c.) without land attached to it; a married farm-worker who has a cottage as part of his contract' (*Conc. Scots Dict.*, 1985); and in Ireland (usually *cottier*) for a peasant renting and cultivating a smallholding under specified conditions of tenure. The word is best remembered, perhaps, in the title of Burns's poem 'The Cotter's Saturday Night'.

cotyledon. Pronounced /ˌkɒtɪˈliːd(ə)n/ (ko-ti-**lee**-duhn). *Plural cotyledons*; see -ON 3.

couch[1]. *Couch* is sometimes used as a synonym of *sofa*, a use that Fowler decried as a 'genteelism'. Technically, a sofa normally has a back and two arms, and a couch has often just one raised end and is designed in such a way that it is suitable for sleeping or reclining on. *Couch* is also the word used for 'a long padded seat with a headrest at one end', i.e. a psychiatrist's or doctor's couch. *Couch* is also a poetic or literary word for a bed. The distinction between a *couch* and a *bed* is brought out in these examples: *I've made a bed up for you on the couch*—M. Amis, 1973; *My brother and I share the verandah in the summer—what were two couches by day became our beds at night*—B. Mason, 1980. A *settee* is an upholstered seat with a back and usually with arms, designed so that two or more people can sit on it. (Those for whom such things matter will wish to know that *settee*, like *couch*, is considered non-U, while *sofa* is U.) An *ottoman* is 'an upholstered seat, usually square and without a back or arms, sometimes a box with a padded top'. A *divan* is 'a long, low, padded seat set against a room-wall; a backless sofa' or 'a bed consisting of a base and mattress, usually with no board at either end'.

couch[2], any of several weed-like grasses. Usually pronounced /kaʊtʃ/, but previously /kuːtʃ/. In origin it is a southern-counties variant of *quitch* (Old English *cwice*), which has the same meaning.

couchant. In heraldry pronounced /ˈkaʊtʃənt/. It is usually placed after the noun it governs (*two lions couchant*).

could is a modal auxiliary, formally the past tense indicative of CAN. In contexts of possibility, ability, and permission, it operates for the most part in the same way as *can*: (possibility, opportunity, risk, etc.) *the tide could swing decisively against him; it is difficult to imagine that a jury could find in his favour; pains that he thinks could be cancer; could he be making this up?; he's pleased, but his mood could change at any time*; (ability) *she could* [was able to] *remember it as if it were yesterday; all I could do was offer him a drink; she could not walk and think deeply at the same time; if only he could settle down and live like a normal person*; (permission, instead of may) *Could I come and see you next week?; Could I have breakfast now, please?* Cf. MAY AND MIGHT. *Could* is occasionally used as a past subjunctive, 'expressing an inclination in a conditional form' (*OED*): *I could wish our Royal Society would compile a Body of Natural History*—Addison, 1711; *I could not think of leaving you so soon*—Mrs Inchbald, 1786; *'I could hang up sheets, I guess.' But she's too busy to.*—*New Yorker*, 1987. The negative form is, of course, *could not*, frequently written in reduced form *(couldn't)*. For *I could(n't) care less*, see CARE (verb).

could of. An alteration of *could've* = could have, accurately reflecting how the phrase is pronounced, but displaying a disregard for grammar and meaning. It is the kind of mistake likely to be made by people who have heard the phrase but never read it, and is found depressingly often, especially on the Internet.

coulomb (unit of electric charge). Now pronounced /ˈkuːlɒm/.

coulter (a plough blade). Not *col-*.

council, counsel. 1 A *council* is an advisory or administrative body of people formally constituted and meeting regularly (*parish council, city council, county council*, etc.) or a meeting of such a body. A member of one is a *councillor* (in American English sometimes spelt *councilor*). *Council* is often used attributively of housing, etc., provided by a local council (*council flat, council housing*). Special uses of the word include *Privy Council*, a body of advisers appointed by the sovereign; and *the Queen* (or *King*) *in Council*, the Privy Council as issuing Orders in Council or receiving petitions, etc.

2 *Counsel* is advice (e.g. in set phrases, *counsel of despair, counsel of perfection, to keep one's own counsel*), especially that given formally; also, a barrister or other legal adviser (plural unchanged: *K. began the defence of his client with public sympathy but under immense difficulties against five prosecuting counsel*). A person trained to give advice on personal, social, or psychological problems is a counsellor (AmE frequently *counselor*), e.g. *marriage guidance counsellor*. A *Queen's* (or *King's*) *Counsel* in Britain is a counsel to the Crown, taking precedence over other barristers. A *counselor* (or *counsellor*) in America is a barrister; also called a *counselor-at-law*.

3 *Counsel* is used as a verb (= to give counsel), but *council* cannot be.

countable nouns. See COUNT NOUNS.

countenance, face, physiognomy, visage. *Face* is the ordinary name for the part; *countenance* is the face with reference to its expression; *physiognomy*, to the cast or form of a person's features, expression, etc. *Visage* is a literary word, used ornamentally for *face* without special significance.

counterproductive is familiar enough now to be spelt as one word. It is a modern word (first recorded in 1959) which has mushroomed in use to describe any action or series of actions having the opposite of the desired effect: *Security measures will be counterproductive if they provoke resentment—Independent*, 2006.

count nouns (or **countable nouns** or **countables**) are those that can form a plural or be used with an indefinite article, e.g. *ship, crisis, fellow-traveller, kindness* (= a kind act). They differ from **uncount** (or **non-count** or **uncountable**) **nouns**, which do not form plurals, e.g. *adolescence, heating, richness, warfare*; and from **mass nouns**, which form plurals only in the sense of 'a type of ... ' or 'a quantity of ... ', e.g. *bread, medicine, wine*. Some words are countable in one meaning and uncountable in another, e.g. *ice, iron, paper*. See also MASS NOUN.

countrified, countrify are the recommended spellings (not *countryfied*, etc.). See -FY.

couple. 1 See AGREEMENT 5 (d).

2 Phrases of the type 'a couple weeks later', i.e. with no *of* between *a couple* and *weeks*, are well established in American English (first recorded in 1925): *the universe would have collapsed back onto itself in a couple million years*—J. Updike, 1986; *in the next couple months we got to know each other like real buddies*—G. Keillor, 1989. This use sounds somewhat alien to British ears.

3 The structure 'a couple more + plural noun', i.e. where *couple* operates as a quasi-adjective, is common in all English-speaking countries: *We can end this chapter by looking at a couple more examples of Middle English writing*—C. L. Barber, 1965; *She had a couple more hits—OEC*, 2004; *'How's your work?' 'Nearly done. A couple more days.'*—Maurice Gee, 1992 (NZ).

4 *A couple of* = about two is used informally (*I'll just be a couple of minutes* = in approximately two minutes).

couplet (prosody), two successive lines of verse, usually rhyming and of the same metrical type, e.g.

> But most by Numbers judge a Poet's
> song,
> And smooth or rough, with them, is
> right or wrong;
>
> —Pope.

coupon. Now always pronounced /ˈkuːpɒn/, but until about the middle of the 20c. it was also commonly pronounced /kuːpɔ̃/ in a quasi-French manner.

course. The phrase *of course* has a useful role in the meaning 'as is/was to be expected, normal, obvious, well-known'. It assumes the reader's or listener's prior knowledge, understanding, or agreement (e.g. *as there were patches of fog about, the driving conditions were not, of course, ideal, but there was no obligation on the driver to stay at the depot*). Fowler (1926) rightly urged caution about using the phrase 'as the herald of an out-of-the-way fact that one has just unearthed from a book or reference, e.g. *Milton, of course, had the idea of his line from Tacitus; The House being in Committee, the Speaker would not, of course, under ordinary circumstances, have been present.*' To use it in that way can be irritatingly smug, superior, and patronizing.

courteous, courtesy. Pronounced with initial /ˈkəːt-/.

courtesan. Pronounced with initial /kɔːt/ and place the main stress on the final syllable.

courtier. Pronounced /ˈkɔːtɪə/.

court martial as a noun is spelt as two words without a hyphen, with plural preferably *courts martial*, although *court martials* is also acceptable. As a verb it is spelt with a hyphen, and has inflected forms *court-martialled, court-martialling* in British English, and *court-martialed, court-martialing* in American English.

Coventry. Pronounced /ˈkɒvəntri/.

covert (adjective). The traditional pronunciation /ˈkʌvət/ is still favoured by more conservative speakers in Britain, but the current American English pronunciation /ˈkəʊvəːt/ is gaining ground outside the US all the time. The American pronunciation is perhaps derived from the spelling (cf. *over*) but, more likely, is influenced by its opposite *overt*.

cow, cower. To *cow* (probably from Old Norse *kúga* 'oppress') someone is to intimidate them into doing something you wish them to do, and is a transitive verb (*the intellectuals had been cowed into silence*). To *cower* (from Middle Low German *kūren* 'lie in wait') is to crouch down in fear (*children cowered in terror as the shoot-out erupted*). It is intransitive, which means that it cannot be used in a passive construction. Occasionally *cower* is incorrectly used instead of *cow*: **Mr Howard is adamant Australia will not be cowered by the attacks, vowing to continue to work to defeat the scourge of terrorism—www.abc.net.au*, 2005.

cowrie, the shell of a mollusc, is so spelt, not *cowry*.

coxcomb. See COCKSCOMB, COXCOMB.

coxswain. Despite its spelling, the word is normally pronounced /ˈkɒksən/, with /ˈkɒksweɪn/ available as a pedantic or spelling-pronunciation alternative. In practice, however, the abbreviated form **cox** /kɒks/ is commoner than *coxswain* noun and verb.

coyote. Pronounced /ˈkɔɪəʊt/ with two syllables or /kɔɪˈəʊti/ with three.

cozy. See COSY.

crabbed (adjective), irritable, hard to decipher, etc. Pronounced /ˈkrabɪd/.

craft (verb). The verb (and its past participle adjective *crafted*) had a thin and fugitive life from its first recorded use in the 14c. until the second half of the 20c. Since then it has come into widespread use, especially in the language of advertising (*a beautifully crafted antique-pine replica*) and in literary and other criticism (*performances crafted out of a shared language*).

cranesbill is the recommended spelling of this name for several species of *Geranium*, not *crane's-bill*.

cranium, like several Latin words ending in *-um* borrowed into English, has a Latinate plural *crania* and an anglicized one, *craniums*. As with many of the analogous words, each form is appropriate to different styles of writing. *Crania* is better than *craniums* in scientific contexts, but both forms are used. In non-scientific contexts, *craniums* sounds more natural, but *crania* also occurs. Examples: (scientific) *The notion that teeth and crania are under different genetic control is in no way heretical—Paleobiology*, Fall 2002; *the well-known differences between Neandertal and human crania—American Scientist*, 2004; (non-scientific) *What Doctorow's people look like, act like, feel like is secondary to what they think. They're ambulatory intellects, walking craniums—New York Metro*, 2004; *I think a new record has been set for most exploding craniums in a single feature film—DVD Verdict*, 2007. See -UM 3.

crape, crêpe. The first is used for a band of black silk or ornamental silk worn as a sign of mourning, and the second, written with the accent and in roman, for other gauzelike fabrics having a wrinkled surface. There are some other special distinctions: (*a*) *crape fern*, a New Zealand fern; *crape hair*, artificial hair used in stage make-up; but (*b*) *crêpe de Chine, crêpe paper* (thin crinkled paper), and *crêpe Suzette* (dessert pancake).

crasis. In phonology, the running of two vowel sounds into one, as when *cocaine* (q.v.) and *codeine* (q.v.) became reduced, in the course of the 20c., from three syllables to two. The phenomenon is also shown in the medieval and Renaissance practice of reducing *to* to *t* or *t'* before an infinitive beginning with a vowel (*t'adorn, tamend, t'enjoy*, etc.) and *the* to *th* or *th'* before a word beginning with a vowel (*thage, themperor, th'infection, thother*, etc.). In Greek phonology it is 'the combination of the vowels of two syllables, especially at the end of one word and beginning of the next, into one long vowel or diphthong, as in κἀγώ for καὶ ἐγώ' (*OED*).

crayfish is the usual word in Britain for a small lobster-like freshwater crustacean. Americans call them *crawfish* as well as *crayfish*, and also use *crawfish* informally as a verb = 'to retreat from a position, to back out' (*he crawfished out of the issue by claiming that he didn't drink*). Australians and New Zealanders tend to abbreviate the word to *cray* (so *cray-fishing, cray-pot*, etc.). *Crayfish* is a classic example of how FOLK ETYMOLOGY works: originally the word had no connection with the word *fish* whatsoever, but is a 16c. alteration of the Middle English *crevis(se)*, borrowed from the Old French word for what in modern French is *écrevisse* 'crayfish'.

crèche is usually pronounced /krɛʃ/ in English, but /kreɪʃ/ (kraysh) is a common enough variant. The word is written in roman type, with or without the grave accent over the *-è-*. It is a mistake to write **crêche* with a circumflex, though Mrs Gaskell and other writers have done so. Nowadays, Microsoft Word will usually correct the mistake for you.

credence, credit, credibility. 1 With reference to believing something, *credence* traditionally had only one main meaning, namely 'belief, trustful acceptance', in other words, 'the state of believing something'. Fowler and Gowers were adamant that this was the only correct meaning, and indeed it is the only one in this sphere recognized in the *OED*. It is realized chiefly in the phrase *give* (or *lend*) *credence to*, which means 'to believe, put faith in', with a human subject (e.g. *the Western powers gave credence to Mikhail Gorbachev's views long before the Berlin Wall was demolished*). However, *credence* has also come to be widely used in the meaning they rejected, namely 'the likelihood of something being true; plausibility', a meaning recognized by many dictionaries, and it is in this sense that it overlaps with *credibility*. This second meaning is mainly realized in the phrases *lend credence* (with a non-human subject), *add credence*, and *gain credence*. Examples: *This seems to lend some credence to the argument that larger farms tend to make weaker contributions to the local economy—OEC*, 2003; *However, neither Heed nor Lee cite a single statistic to add credence to their claim—OEC*, 2004; *Martin Luther King's words gained credence from his actions—OEC*, 2005.

2 The phrase *to give credit to* was also once (16-19c.) frequently used to mean 'to give credence to', i.e. to believe, put faith in: e.g. *Charges like these may seem to deserve some degree of credit*—Gibbon, 1781. Nowadays the phrase is more likely to be used in the form *to give a person credit for (something)* = to attribute merit to a person for (something): *You chaps do tend to give the rest of us credit for perceptions about your work that we don't . . . always have*—J. Wain, 1953.

3 *Credibility* shares some of the meaning of both words in that belief lies at the heart of its meaning. It is used to mean (*a*) 'the condition of being credible or believable' (*Christianity rests on the credibility of the Gospel story*) in which case it overlaps with the second, newer meaning of *credence*; and (*b*) 'reputation, status' (*because of his crackdown on crime, he has gained credibility as a Chief Constable*). It is now much more commonly used in this second meaning. Further examples: *The Scots . . . give scant credibility to Walters' promise to move the exploration office to Glasgow—Sunday Times*, 1987; *Let's look at . . . this idea of selecting artists who have some sort of credibility—Art Line*, 1989.

4 Two special uses of *credibility* are *credibility gap*, meaning 'a disparity between facts and what is said or written about them'. The first use of this recorded in the *OED* is from 1966, in the *Guardian*. Note the inverted commas, indicating it was then a new phrase: *Official American statements are no longer taken on trust. . . . The phenomenon . . . is called the 'credibility gap'*. Second, chiefly in British English, *street credibility* (often shortened informally to *street cred*), meaning 'acceptability among fashionable young urban people': *Motor enthusiast David George has seen his Ford Granada gain street credibility with its very own TV career—Bolton Evening News*, 2005.

credible, creditable, credulous. *Credible* means (*a*) 'able to be believed, worthy of belief', with reference to people or statements, e.g.: *at a certain point his assertions ceased to be credible; it is not credible that he could have saved so much money on his earnings; I found him to be a credible witness*; (*b*) referring to alternatives, candidates, plans, deterrents, etc., it also has an extended meaning 'convincing, having substance', comparable to that of *credibility: He fought a remarkable re-election campaign . . . , recovering his popularity not least through his total control of the media, as well as the lack of a credible challenger*—J. Palmowski, 2003. *Creditable* means 'bringing credit or honour, deserving praise': *The company produced a creditable performance, particularly when compared with the results of many of its competitors*—*Daily Tel.*, 1992. *Credulous* means 'too ready to believe, gullible' as in *credulous public, audience, press,* etc. Examples: *There is a strong streak of the credulous in most Russians*—R. Owen, 1985. *No one, except the touchingly credulous American public, is surprised*—*OEC*, 2004.

credo. Pronounced /ˈkriːdəʊ/ or /ˈkreɪdəʊ/. Plural *credos*. See -O(E)S 6.

crenel, an indentation in the parapet of a tower. If so spelt it is pronounced /ˈkrɛnəl/. If written as *crenelle*, it is to be pronounced /krɪˈnɛl/. The corresponding verb is written with -ll- (*crenellated castles*); in American English often with -l- (*crenelated*).

creole. What earlier generations described as *broken English, bastard Portuguese*, and so on, are now seen as new languages (*pidgins* and *creoles*) which came into being because of the need for people with no language in common to communicate with each other in these adverse linguistic circumstances. A *creole* is 'a language formed from the contact of a European language (especially English, French, or Portuguese) with another (especially African) language'. Detailed scholarly work on *creoles*, especially since the mid-20c., has led to the discovery that they are rule-based and systematic, however opaque or dislocated they may seem to the uninitiated. John Holm (1988), for example, cites a text from an English-based creole called Ndjuka, spoken in the interior of Suriname in northern South America:

Mi be go a onti anga wan dagu fu mi. A be wan bun onti dagu.

'I had gone hunting with a dog of mine. He was a good hunting dog.'

The term *creole* is applied to a wide range of languages, including the original languages spoken by black slaves in the US (and partially surviving in the Black English Vernacular speech of lower-class blacks in urban communities in the US); English-based creoles like Krio (in Sierra Leone), Guyanese, and Gullah; French-based creoles in Haiti and the Ivory Coast, and Portuguese-based creoles in Brazil and Cape Verde. Intensive study of creoles continues: the bibliography of John Holm's *Pidgins and Creoles*, i (1988), for example, runs to twenty closely printed pages. The groundwork for it all was laid by the German scholar Hugo Schuchardt in a series of studies published in the 1880s and 1890s.

crêpe. See CRAPE, CRÊPE.

crescendo. Plural *crescendos*. See -O(E)S 3. In origin the word is an Italian musical direction, the gerund of *crescere* 'to increase, grow'. Its essential meaning is a gradual increase in loudness or intensity towards some unreached peak.

As a musical direction the word has been in use in English since the 18c.: from there it became applied to other progressive increases in force and effect, as in *The fear is that in a bid to deflect the rising crescendo of criticism about his own failure in the September 11 episode, Bush may well choose to open a new theatre of war*—*OEC*, 2004. From the early 1900s, apparently first in American English, *crescendo* developed further to mean the result rather than the process of increasing, and has been widely used as a synonym for *peak* or *climax*, notably in phrases such as *reach* (or *rise to*) *a crescendo*: *In the past week, as the date approached for the annual review of her detention order, international pressure reached a crescendo*—*Independent*, 2007. This newer use causes distress and anxiety among more sensitive editors, not to mention many musicians, but seems likely to prevail, since it is the more commonly required meaning. If you wish to avoid upsetting anyone, there are alternatives aplenty: *apogee, climax, culmination, peak, pinnacle,* and *summit*.

cretic /ˈkriːtɪk/. In prosody, a Greek (occasionally English) metrical foot containing one short or unstressed syllable between two long or stressed ones. The words *otiose* and *multitude* would neatly form such a foot. Blake's 'Spring' (*Songs of Innocence*) makes use of the measure: *Sound the Flute!/Now it's mute./Birds delight/Day and Night;/Nightingale/In the dale,/Lark in Sky,/Merrily*. It is also called *amphimacer* /am'fɪməsə/.

cretin. 1 From its first use in English in the late 18c. until about 1900 it seems to have been regularly pronounced /'kriːtɪn/, which is still the standard pronunciation in AmE, whereas /'krɛtɪn/ is now normal in BrE.

2 It was formerly used to refer to people who are physically deformed and have learning difficulties because of congenital thyroid deficiency. Because the condition affected people in certain valleys of the Swiss Alps, the word originated in Switzerland and derives through French *crétin*, from Swiss French *crestin* 'Christian' (from Latin *Christiānus*), here used to mean 'human being', to remind people that sufferers of the condition were fully human. Happily, it is no longer used in this medical sense. Its main meaning now (first recorded in the 1930s) is, of course, 'a fool, one who behaves stupidly'.

crevasse, crevice. A *crevasse* is a deep open crack or fissure in a glacier; in American English it is also used to mean a breach in a river embankment. A *crevice* is a narrow cleft or opening, especially one in the surface of anything solid, e.g. a rock or a building. Etymologically the words are doublets from the same Latin base (*crepātia*), from Latin *crepāre* 'to creak, rattle, crack'.

crick, rick, wrick. The earliest of these to appear was *crick* (as noun, 15c.); the corresponding verb meaning 'to produce a crick (in the neck, etc.)' is not recorded until the 19c. The noun is probably of onomatopoeic origin. *Rick* (as noun first recorded 1854, as verb 1798) and *wrick* (noun 1831, verb 1886) are much later words: they are apparently of dialect origin and have Low German affinities. *Crick* and *rick* are commonly used of strains or sprains of the neck, back, joints, etc., but *wrick* has dropped out of use.

cringe makes *cringing*. See MUTE E.

cripple has long been in use and is first recorded in Old English in the glosses added to the Latin of the *Lindisfarne Gospels* round AD 950. Despite its long history, it has now acquired offensive connotations and has been largely replaced by less demeaning terms such as 'person with disabilities'. Similar changes have affected **crippled**. See also DISABILITY, DISABLED.

crisis. Plural *crises* /'krʌɪsiːz/. See LATIN PLURALS 1.

criterion meaning 'a principle or standard by which something is judged', correctly has the plural *criteria*, as in Classical Greek (see -ON 1). Sadly, this plural is increasingly used as a singular, a use that is not only non-standard—at least for the moment—but will inflict considerable mental anguish on purists, e.g. *A *report . . . will tell councillors that the bidding criteria* has *significantly changed since the previous bid—Rochdale Observer*, 2002. The following examples illustrate correct uses of the singular and plural: *They award a green label to products that meet certain environmental criteria; Some possible criteria for this area of work are listed below*—J. Thorpe, 1989; *Thus stated, Hume's criterion is quite vague*—J. Losee, 2001. See also STRATUM.

criticism. In everyday use, *criticism* means 'finding fault, censure', but *literary criticism* and *textual criticism* are more in the realm of assessment or evaluation. The two senses, one adverse and the other evaluative, coexist without risk of ambiguity or cross-infection.

critique. Both noun and verb have attracted criticism by Fowler and by later usage writers. The noun, meaning 'a detailed analysis and assessment of something, especially a literary, philosophical, or political theory' (e.g. *a critique of Marxist historicism*) has in fact been around for a long time, being first recorded in a work of *a*1719 by Addison, albeit in its earlier meaning of 'review'. The verb, meaning 'evaluate (a theory or practice) in a detailed and analytical way; write a critique of' is almost as old-established, being first recorded in 1751.

Of the noun, Fowler (1926) said, 'there is some hope of its dying out', but gave no reason for his antipathy, merely suggesting that *review* and *criticism* should be used instead. But the word has not withered away, and is perfectly unobjectionable when it refers to a thoroughgoing analysis of something, as in *This emphasis on ideology appealed to New Left intellectuals as they developed a radical critique of the institutions of civil society—The Oxford Companion to Australian History,* 2001; *Hitchens carved out a reputation for barbed repartee, scathing critiques of public figures and a fierce intelligence—OEC,* 2011. *Critique* is indeed in such rude good health that it shows every sign of muscling in on *criticism* in its negative meaning of simple 'disapproval'. In the following examples you could easily replace it with *criticism,* and it can justifiably be viewed as somewhat pretentious. But at the same time these examples suggest that the dividing line between a 'detailed analysis' and mere negative criticism can often be a rather fuzzy one: *President Vladimir Putin has delivered a scathing critique of Western dominance of the global economy—OEC,* 2007; *Republicans' strategy is to counter critique with caricature—OEC,* 2004.

Some critics have objected to *critique* as a verb on the grounds that it is another example of a modern extension of a noun use, but the verb's antiquity invalidates this argument. As with the noun, it seems legitimate to use the word in contexts suggesting detailed analysis has happened, such as *Instead time should be spent critiquing the research design and the methodology section before accepting the research results—OEC,* 2001. Criticism is more valid, however, when the verb is used to mean more generally 'to judge critically, to make a critical assessment of or comment on (an action, person, etc.), not necessarily in writing'. Examples: *By the end of the Keating era, no-one could critique Aboriginal policy without being labelled racist—OEC,* 2004; *And yes, I like to critique the Times coverage of foreign affairs from time to time—OEC,* 2003.

crochet, in its ordinary handicraft sense, is pronounced /ˈkrəʊʃeɪ/ as noun and verb. The *t* remains silent in the other parts of the verb: *crocheted* /ˈkrəʊʃeɪd/, *crocheting* /ˈkrəʊʃeɪɪŋ/.

crocus (the flower). As plural, *crocuses, croci* /-kʌɪ/, and (used collectively) *crocus* are all in standard use, the most common being *crocuses. Croci* is confined to technical writing.

croquet. The noun and verb operate like CROCHET, with a silent *t* in the inflected forms of the verb.

crosier. See CROZIER.

cross. Daniel Jones (1917) gave priority to the now extremely rare and patrician pronunciation /krɔːs/. At some point in the first half of the 20c. the tide turned in favour of /krɒs/, and this is now the standard pronunciation. The same applies to *frost, loss, lost, off,* etc.

croup. Both the throat trouble and the rump (of a horse) are now regularly spelt *croup* and pronounced /kruːp/, though they are distinct words from unrelated etymological bases.

croupier. The pronunciation /ˈkruːpɪə/ is recommended, but /-pɪeɪ/, in imitation of the French original, is still widely used. Cf. DOSSIER.

crow. The past tense varies between *crowed* and (chiefly in the UK) *crew,* but the past participle is always *crowed*: *Roosters, still in the shed, crowed*—E. Jolley, 1985; *He burst into her bedroom as the cock crew, or would have crowed, had there been any cocks in Surbiton*—B. Rubens, 1987. The past tense *crew* is normally used only of the noise made by cocks, and not, for example, when the sense is 'boast'.

crown. *The Crown* is often used in the sense 'the office of the monarch as head of State'. In such contexts the pronouns appropriate to queen or king should not be used. Thus *the Crown can act only on the advice of its* (not *her,* not *his*) *Ministers; the country is unlikely to return to government by the Crown, for which* (not *whom*) *such an experiment would be fraught with peril.*

crozier is the recommended spelling, not *crosier.*

cruel makes *crueller, cruellest* (in American English often *crueler, cruelest*). See -LL-, -L-.

crumby, crummy. When the reference is to actual crumbs, as in *a crumby loaf* or *tablecloth,* use *crumby.* When the meaning is 'dirty, squalid, inferior, worthless', use *crummy.*

crystalline. The normal modern pronunciation is /ˈkrɪstəlʌɪn/, but the *OED* reports that some older writers (Milton, Gray, Shelley, and Palgrave), after Latin, used the pronunciation /krɪsˈtalɪn/.

cubic, cubical. *Cubic* is the form used in all senses, *cubical* only in that of 'shaped like a cube'. So *cubic content, equation, measure, metre,* etc.; but a *cubical box* or *stone. Cubic,* however, is sometimes used in the sense 'cube-shaped', for example of minerals crystallizing in cubes, as *cubic alum, saltpetre.* See -IC(AL).

cui bono? This Latin phrase, printed in italics, literally means 'to whom (is it) a benefit?' In English it can be defined as 'who stands to gain? (with the implication that this person is responsible)'. As Fowler (1926) pointed out, it should not be used to mean 'To what end?; What is the good?'

cuirass. Pronounced /kwɪˈras/.

cul-de-sac. Pronounced /ˈkʌldəˌsak/ or /ˈkʊl-/ and print in roman. Plural *culs-de-sac* (pronounced the same as the singular).

culinary. Pronounced /ˈkʌlɪn(ə)rɪ/ in British English and /ˈkjuːlɪnˌɛːrɪ/ or /ˈkʌl-/ in American English.

cullender. See COLANDER.

cult. In the meaning 'a particular form or system of religious worship', especially referring to ritual and ceremony, *cult* dates from the 17c. In the 19c., archaeologists applied the term to primitive practices which they did not think worthy of the name religion; as a result *cult* gained unfavourable connotations and is objected to by many whose activities are now described by it.

Cult has also developed extended meanings: (*a*) 'a devotion or homage to a person or thing', as in *personality cult, the cult of beauty, the Wordsworth cult,* and (*b*) in the 20c., 'a popular fashion followed by a specific section of society': *The eastern cult for junk food may be having a remarkable effect on the health and appearance of Japan's youngsters—Times,* 1986.

In a further extension, *cult* is commonly used attributively (before a noun) to denote someone or something with a special following, as in *cult classic, cult figure, cult film, cult status,* etc.

cultivable, cultivatable. Both words are used to mean 'capable of being cultivated', but the first is much more commonly used.

cultivated, cultured. Both words are used pretty much interchangeably to mean 'having refined taste and manners and a good education', but they part company in some other circumstances. *Cultivated* distinguishes a crop raised in a garden or gardens (*cultivated blackberries*) from one grown in a wild state. *Cultured* is used of pearls (also called *culture pearls*) grown under controlled conditions.

culture. Here is a word that seems to mean all things to all people. It is one of the 1,000 most commonly used English words, and there are well over 300,000 examples of it (including the plural form and compounds such as *culture-bound*) in the current Oxford English Corpus In many of these, *culture* is used generically, in its mass noun meaning of 'the arts and other manifestations of human intellectual achievement regarded collectively', e.g.: *For him spiritual and political ideas were becoming more and more inseparable in his concern with 'culture' as a whole*—R. Crawford, 1990.

In others it has a very specific reference, in its meaning of 'the ideas, customs, and social behaviour of a particular people or society', e.g. *Unofficial sources report that the two organisations aimed to research and develop Mongol culture—Amnesty,* 1992. In this meaning it is often preceded by a defining adjective or noun, as in *consumer culture, drugs culture, political culture, pop culture, yob culture, youth culture.* Examples: *It was, nonetheless, a film that tried to solicit an understanding of the emerging drug culture*—J. Parker, 1991; *Pop music and its link with youth culture should be an important field of study in media education—Action,* 1991.

Since as long ago as 1940, the previously mentioned meaning ('the ideas, customs, and social behaviour of a particular people or society') has been used in a more restricted way to refer to 'the philosophy, practices, and attitudes of an institution, business, or other organization' as in *corporate* or *organizational culture,* e.g. *Managers see their role as creating a culture in which the team can make a sound contribution to agreed goals—Management Accounting,* 1991. This meaning is now a standard part of the language, even though it has been something of a vogue word, and can at times be used rather vaguely.

Well-established 20c. compounds such as *culture clash, culture shock,* and *culture vulture,* were joined in the 1990s by *culture jamming* 'the subversion of advertising and other mass-media output (by parody, alteration, etc.) as a form of protest against consumerism, corporate culture, and the power of the media': *Beginning with spoof advertisements, culture-jamming has grown to encompass defacing billboards to alter their message and campaigns such as TV Turnoff Week and Buy Nothing Day*—*Times*, 2006.

cum. The Latin preposition meaning 'with, together with' has been used in English for several centuries in some fixed phrases (*cum grano salis*, with a grain of salt; *cum privilegio*, with privilege (of sole printing); etc.) and in many English place names, e.g. *Horton-cum-Studley*. In the 19c. it took on a fresh lease of life as a combining word used to indicate a dual nature or function, as in *kitchen-cum-dining-room*. Hyphens are nowadays optional. The productive nature of this use can be seen in numerous examples, e.g.: *'Do you work there?' Yes, as a sort of administrator cum priest.'*—J. Higgins, 1985; *Young designers get a pick-me-up from Vienna's coffee house cum design store*—*Metropolis Magazine*, 2003.

cumin is the standard and more common spelling nowadays, not **cummin**, and the pronunciation /ˈkjuːmɪn/ (**kyoo**-min) has replaced the older /ˈkʌmɪn/ (**kum**-min). The word is spelt with two *m*s in what was once its most familiar context, in the Bible, Matt. (AV) 23: 23 (*for yee pay tithe of mint, and annise, and cummine*), and this spelling is retained in later versions of the Bible. In general language it is acceptable but less common: the unlikely combination of etymology (Old English *cymen*, from Latin *cumīnum*) and modern cookery books jointly sanction the *cumin* spelling.

cumulative. See ACCUMULATIVE.

cumulus. Plural *cumuli* /-lʌɪ/. See -US.

cuneiform (from Latin *cuneus* wedge, medieval Latin *cuneiformis*) is now normally pronounced in British English as three syllables, i.e. /ˈkjuːnɪfɔːm/, with a four-syllable variant, /kjuːˈneɪɪfɔːm/. In American English the usual pronunciation is still with four syllables.

cupful. The recommended plural is *cupfuls*, but in American English, *cupsful* is accepted as a variant. *Cupful* is a measure of volume, and so *three cupfuls* is three times the quantity contained in a single cup; *three cups full* denotes the cups themselves, not their contents, as in *three cups full of water*.

cupola. Pronounced /ˈkjuːpələ/ (**kyoo**-puhluh). The plural is *cupolas*, not *cupolae*.

curaçao, a liqueur. Spelt *-çao* (not *-çoa*) and pronounced /kjʊərəˈsəʊ/, the last syllable rhyming with *no*, or /kjʊərəˈsaʊ/, to rhyme with *now*.

curare, a poisonous substance. Spelt with a final *-e* (not *-ara*), and pronounced /kjʊˈrɑːri/.

curator. In the sense 'keeper or custodian of a museum or other collection' pronounced /kjʊəˈreɪtə/, but in Scottish law (a ward's guardian) pronounced /ˈkjʊərətər/.

curb, kerb. In British English, *curb* as a noun means 'a check or restraint', and as a verb 'to restrain'. As a noun, it also means 'a strap fastened to a bit (on a horse)', and 'a fender round a hearth'. In American English, the spelling *curb* also means a stone edging to a pavement (*sidewalk*) or raised path, which in British English is spelt *kerb*.

curio is a 19c. abbreviation of curiosity. Plural *curios*. See -O(E)S 4.

curriculum. Plural very much more often *curricula* than *curriculums*. See -UM 3.

cursed, curst. The usual adjectival form is *cursed*, as in *I am weary of everyone in this cursed country*, is pronounced as two syllables (by contrast with the past tense and past participle of the verb *curse*, which are always one syllable). *Curst* is chiefly used (especially in verse) to show that the rare single-syllable pronunciation is meant, or, archaically, to denote the old sense 'cantankerous, shrewish'.

curtsy = a woman's or girl's formal greeting, should be spelt *-sy*, not *curtsey*. Plural *curtsies*. The verb is *curtsy, curtsied, curtsying*. Etymologically it is a variant (first recorded in the 16c.) of *courtesy*.

curvet = a horse's leap. Pronounced /kəːˈvet/. The inflections of the corresponding verb should, according to rule, double the *t* (*curvetted, curvetting*). See -T-, -TT-.

customer. See CLIENT.

cute. Starting out in the 18c. as an abbreviation of acute in the sense 'quick-witted, keen-witted, clever', it was for a while often written with an apostrophe as *'cute* (*'He will be a 'cute man yet,' resumed the locksmith*—Dickens, 1840). This sense ran into the sands in British English but not in American English. In AmE, beginning in the 1830s, a new informal use emerged, 'attractive, charming, pretty (often in a mannered or amusing way)'. In AmE the word is exceedingly common as a general term of approval, much like *nice,* and can be applied to ideas and activities as well as to people, e.g. *Yes, Lisa runs a little gym in West Palm. We all go there to work out. Isn't that cute?*—P. Booth, 1986 (AmE). Though now quite commonly used also in BrE, it usually refers to sexually attractive or desirable people, or, often with generous lashings of irony, to cuddly, lovable creatures, as epitomized by small, furry animals or infants of the human persuasion. Examples: *The scene where Gina McKee finally gets to sleep with the cute guy who then gets dressed and sets dinner for one is heartbreaking*—*OEC,* 2002 (BrE); *I fear, however, that it will be harder to get people to sympathise with black Africans than with cute fluffy foxes*—*OEC,* 2004 (BrE).

-cy. See -CE, -CY.

cyber-. A by-product of the word *cybernetics* is the use of the first element *cyber-*, usually not hyphenated, in a whole host of terms related to computers or to the Internet: *cybercafe* (a cafe equipped with terminals to access the Internet); *cybercrime* (criminal activity, such as identity fraud, conducted over the Internet); *cyberpunk* (a style of science fiction); *cybersex* (sexual arousal from computer images); *cybersquatting* (registering a well-known company, brand, or personal name as an Internet domain name, in the hope of selling it at a profit to the holder of the name); *cyberterrorism* (the unlawful, and often politically motivated, use of computers or information technology to cause disruption, fear, or financial loss); and, the most commonly used derived term, *cyberspace,* referring to the notional environment within which electronic communication via the Internet occurs.

cybernetics. A term introduced in 1948 by Norbert Wiener meaning 'the theory or study of communication and control in living organisms or machines' (cf. Greek κυβερνήτης 'steersman'). It spread rapidly to refer to organisms treated as if they were machines, to observed similarities between neural activity and the electronic devices of modern communications, and so on.

cycle. For *cycle* as a time-word, see TIME.

Cyclopean. *ODO* gives preference to /saɪklə'piːən/ rather than /sʌɪ'kləʊpɪən/, but both pronunciations are admissible.

Cyclops (in Greek mythology, a member of a race of one-eyed giants). The forms recommended are: for the singular *Cyclops* /'sʌɪklɒps/; for the plural *Cyclopes* /sʌɪ'kləʊpiːz/, or, in non-specialized or jocular contexts, *Cyclops* or the Anglicized form *Cyclopses.* The use of *Cyclop* as a singular is highly irregular.

Cymric, Welsh. Pronounced /'kɪmrɪk/. Cf. Welsh *Cymru* 'Wales'.

cynic, cynical. Except when there is direct reference to the sect of philosophers in ancient Greece called *Cynics,* and in the medical term *cynic spasm,* the adjective form is always *cynical. Cynic* is ultimately derived from Greek κυνικός 'doglike, currish'.

cynosure, meaning 'a centre of attraction or admiration', can be pronounced /'sɪnəzjʊə/ (**sin**-uh-zyoo-uh), or /'sʌɪnəzjʊə/ (**syn**-uh-zyoo-uh), and the last syllable in either case can also be pronounced as /-sjʊə/ (-syoo-uh). Its use in the phrase *the Cynosure of neighbouring eyes* from Milton's poem 'L'Allegro' (1632) has ensured that it and variants of it (*the cynosure of all eyes,* etc.) have remained in use in literary or florid writing ever since.

cypher. See CIPHER.

czar. See TSAR.

Czech. After much fluctuation (*Tshekh, Tsekh,* etc.) in the period after the 1840s, when it was first recorded, the word settled down in the 20c. in its current Polish form *Czech,* pronounced /ʧek/.

dactyl, a metrical foot (–⌣⌣) consisting of one long (or stressed) syllable followed by two short (or unstressed) syllables, as in the words *pottery* and *Julia*. Dactylic metres are common in Greek and Latin verse, but comparatively rare in English: *Cannon to right of them Cannon to left of them, Cannon in front of them Volley'd and thunder'd*—Tennyson, 1854.

dado /ˈdeɪdəʊ/ (the lower part of the wall of a room; the plinth of a column). Plural *dados*. See -O(E)S 6.

dahlia. Pronounced /ˈdeɪlɪə/ in British English and usually /ˈdaljə/ or /ˈdɑːlɪə/ in American English.

Dáil (in full *Dáil Éireann*), the lower house of parliament in the Republic of Ireland, is pronounced /dɔɪl/.

dais. A single syllable (/deɪs/) in English until the beginning of the 20c. but /ˈdeɪɪs/, i.e. two-syllabled, in Daniel Jones's *English Pronouncing Dictionary* (1917) and in most authorities since then.

Dame. See SIR.

dampen. This verb was regarded as 'chiefly US' by the *OED* (1894) and by the *COD* (7th edn, 1982), but it has now settled down as a fairly frequent variant of *damp* (verb) in the UK: *everyone ignored the snow that had failed to dampen the impact of John F. Kennedy's brilliant oratory*—J. Archer, 1979; *In 2005 a CAT scan on Tutankhamun dampened decades of speculation that the ancient king had been killed by foul play*—*OEC*, 2007 (BrE).

dangling participles. See UNATTACHED PARTICIPLES.

dare.

1 *Dare* as a semi-modal: special features.
2 *Dare* as an ordinary verb.
3 *Dare* as past tense.
4 Examples.
5 *How dare you, he,* etc.; *don't you dare.*
6 *I dare say.*
7 *Dare* (= challenge, defy) + object + *to*-infinitive.

1 *Dare* is what is called a semi-modal verb, because, like the modal verbs *can, may, should*, etc., it has certain special features, but unlike these fully modal verbs it can also behave like an ordinary verb. Its special features are: (*a*) use with a 'bare' infinitive, i.e. one without *to: I'm not sure that I dare answer*; (*b*) negatives and questions formed without *do*, e.g. *They dare not break in. They cannot break in*—T. S. Eliot, 1935; *dare I break in*? But in practice interrogative forms are normally confined to *how dare you, he, they*, etc., as discussed in 5 below; (*c*) a third person singular form *dare* without final *s*, e.g. as in Lord Alfred Douglas's famous line *I am the Love that dare not speak its name.*

2 *Dare* can also be an ordinary verb, with a following *to*-infinitive or a bare infinitive, or with no infinitive at all. As an ordinary verb it forms negatives and questions with *do*, and the third person singular is *dares: They would not dare to come; Do you dare to contradict me?; I don't dare to answer; He dares to answer; Tell me if you dare.* Some constructions sound more natural than others. For example, *I don't dare to answer* is perfectly grammatical, but *I dare not answer* is more idiomatic, at least in everyday English. In the present tense, *dare* behaves as a modal verb much more often than as an ordinary verb.

3 Because of its double status as an ordinary verb and as a semi-modal, *dare* can be used without inflection for past as well as present time: (present) *a person hardly dare think in this house;* (past) *She turned round. She dare not look at his face.* Formerly condemned (by the 1894 *OED* among others) as 'careless', it is now only literary or dated: Example: *'Yes, yes,' she stuttered, then 'thank you', as an afterthought. She* *dare not look at his face now*—M. Duckworth, 1960.

4 Examples: (modal) *He hates only because he dare not love*—J. M. Coetzee, 1977; *I dare not speak these dreams to any person*—Garrison Keillor, 1986; *No one dared defy the group by going out at the last moment*—Ian McEwan, 1986; (ordinary) *Marcus wouldn't dare to tell a lie like that unless it was true*—R. Hill, 1970; *I did not dare to look down*—B. Rubens, 1985; *How do they dare to be different?*—*New Yorker*, 1987 (This construction is needed to avoid the special meaning of *how dare they ... ?*); *She no longer dared to go into these shadowy apartments*—Anita Brookner, 1988.

5 Special uses: *how dare you, he, she,* etc. ... *?* and *don't* (*you*) *dare* ... Both these constructions are normally followed by a bare infinitive: *How dare you come in without knocking?*—R. Dahl, 1984; *How dare someone walk up my path and take my property?*—*Gloucestershire Echo*, 2007; *Now you sit down there and don't you dare even look at anybody till I get back*—Kingsley Amis, 1988.

6 *I dare say,* used to indicate that you believe that something is probably true, is often written as *I daresay*, and said with the main stress on *dare*. It is normally followed by a *that*-clause, often with *that* omitted: *Dare say you'd like a last look at uncle Caleb's old cottage*—Ted Walker, 1981; '*From time to time I clean. Mrs Pollypot she don't like cleaning.' 'I dare say not.'*—M. Wesley, 1983; *I daresay I'll come back to it, in the fullness of time*—Penelope Lively, 1987.

7 Finally, there is the use of *dare* with an object, meaning 'to challenge or defy someone (to do something)', followed by a *to*-infinitive: *She dared me to believe and take up her cause*—D. Malouf, 1985; *He looked round the table as if daring anyone to smile*—David Lodge, 1988.

darkling. Formed as an adverb in the 15c. from *dark* adjective + *-ling*, the adverbial suffix, it meant 'in the dark, in darkness', e.g. *O wilt thou darkling leaue me?*—Shakespeare, 1590. By confusion with the *-ing* of present participles, it later itself became a present participle (e.g. *His honest brows darkling as he looked towards me*—Thackeray, 1855), and, more commonly, an adjective, 'being in the dark, showing itself darkly, etc.': e.g. *Here like darkling nightingales they sit*—G. Meredith, 1859; *And we are here as on a darkling plain ... Where ignorant armies clash by night*—M. Arnold, 1867; *Jesus makes a primary act of conversion ... in seeing this darkling venture as the stumbling of ignorance away from reprobation and towards truth*—Geoffrey Hill, 1989.

darky. It goes without saying that this word, once used to refer insultingly to black people, especially those from the Southern US, is nowadays completely out of bounds. Though my country grandmother could use it fifty years ago in all innocence, not intending any slur or offence, social attitudes have, fortunately, evolved since then. The word still has restricted currency as a term of racial abuse in literature dealing with or describing that topic (e.g. *Was it something about not taking on the darkies as conductors?*—J. le Carré, 1983), but otherwise it is to be shunned.

dash. 1 There are, in formal printing at least, two types of dash: the en rule (–) and the em rule (—), also called the en dash and em dash. An en rule is twice the length of a hyphen, and an em rule is twice the length of an en rule. Most word-processing programs are able to distinguish the two lengths of rule, but in ordinary writing no distinction is usually made—and many people are not aware that one exists at all. The *New Hart's Rules* provides comprehensive guidance about using this punctuation mark. What follows is a summary.

The en rule (–) is used (*a*) to denote a span, e.g. 'folios 23–94'; (*b*) to specify a period of time, e.g. 'the 1939–45 war'; (*c*) between separate places or areas linked, for example, in a political context, e.g. 'the Rome–Berlin axis'; (*d*) between the names of joint authors to avoid confusion with the hyphen of a single double-barrelled name, e.g. 'the Temple–Hardcastle project' (that is, the joint project of Mr Temple and Mr Hardcastle); Lloyd–Jones, 1939 (as a citation; Lloyd-Jones, with a hyphen, would be a single double-barrelled name).

The longer em rule (—) is the more familiar in everyday use, and corresponds to what most people understand by the term dash. Its principal uses are: (*a*) a single dash used to introduce an explanation or expansion of what comes before, the explanatory statement usually being followed by a full stop, e.g *It is a kind of irony of history that I should write about the French Revolution in the very country where it has had the least impact—I mean England, of course* (The example is taken from *Encounter*, 1990.); and (*b*) a pair of dashes used to indicate asides and parentheses, forming a more distinct break than commas would: *Helen has only seen her father once in her adult life and—until her flight from Grassdale—her brother is a virtual stranger to her*—J. Sutherland, 1996).

The dash should not be added to a colon; use a simple colon, not :—, as a mark introducing a list or the like. Fowler (1926) insisted that after a second dash 'any stop that would have been used if the ... dashes and their contents had not been there should still be used'. He was right, but such a circumstance seldom arises.

2 In its first function mentioned above, of expanding on a preceding statement, the dash serves a useful function in informal or chatty emails or letters. But, it is distinctly overused in certain gushy genres of writing, such as marketing and advertising, and in the sloppier kind of academic writing, as a means of trying to connect disconnected thoughts. To see a printed page with too many dashes skateboarding across it is akin to looking at a beautiful face disfigured by acne.

3 The use of a dash to stand for a coarse word (e.g. *f*–) in reported speech is much less common than it used to be, because public acceptance of these words being spelt out is that much greater.

data /ˈdeɪtə/ **1** *Data* is in origin the Latin plural of *datum*. Fowler, writing as a classicist and long before the computer age, declared uncompromisingly that 'data is plural only', and pointed to the singular *datum*, which he conceded even in his day to be comparatively rare. In fact, for much of the time *data* appears in contexts in which a conscious choice between singular and plural is unnecessary: *Written sources provide systematic periodic data that can show trends and provide other relevant facts*—J. Waters et al., 1989.

In some technical contexts (such as *sense data* in philosophy, and in scientific or statistical research), in which the information is regarded as several items, the plural is still usual; but in general use there has been a marked tendency towards the singular since about 1970, under the influence of computing (see below).

2 After about 1970, the primary meaning of *data* passed to the domain of computing, in which the information concerned is normally regarded as a unit, so that *data* is treated as singular and used with words such as *its, this,* and *much*, rather than *their, these,* and *many* (which might now sound pedantic and even precious). This tendency has had a major influence on more general use. Examples: (singular) *This data is open to a variety of interpretations*—T. Harris, 1993; *This initial data is stored in the computer memory database*—*OEC*, 2002. The plural, however, also continues to be used, especially in scientific writing, to emphasize the plural implications of the word: *The data ... are mapped so that each class has, as far as possible, an equal number of countries*—P. M. Mather, 1991; *Clinical data are expected to show big drops in viral levels in patients*—*OEC*, 2003.

datable is so spelt, not *dateable*. See -ABLE, -IBLE 7.

date. 1 For *date, epoch*, etc., see TIME.

2 For dates, the recommended British style is *25 June 1990*, with no comma between month and year. Many newspapers, however, and most Americans prefer the style *June 25 1990* or *June 25, 1990*. The conventional way of setting down a date in numerals differs in Britain and America: thus *5/7/90* means 5 July 1990 in Britain, but 7 May 1990 in America.

3 See AD; BC.

davit. Being in origin an application of OF *daviot* (diminutive of *Davi* 'David') it was often in the past pronounced /ˈdeɪvɪt/, but the preferred pronunciation now is /ˈdavɪt/.

day and age. Burchfield said of this phrase that '[it] slid into the language in the 1940s (a film called *This Day and Age* was released in 1933 but is not certainly the source of the cliché), and is now used remorselessly by people who display little feeling for the language. It means no more than *nowadays* or *at the present time,* and the language would not be the poorer if it were to drop out of use'. But despite his Olympian strictures it is arguable that, overused or not, in some contexts it does mean rather more than he suggested: it conveys the speaker's surprise or even outrage about a state of affairs that he or she finds surprising, unsatisfactory, or retrograde. Examples: *He tries his hand at dating a real life woman, but in this day and age you need a medical report and a legal contract for even a single date*—*OEC*, 2001 (AmE); *you pop the DVD into the machine and settle back to be outraged and horrified, wondering how, in this day and age, such judicial failures can still occur*—*OEC*, 2004 (AmE).

days. See ADVERB 4.

D-Day, D-day. Originally the military code name (first recorded in 1918) for a particular day fixed for the beginning of an operation, specifically, and most famously, the day (6 June 1944) of the invasion of the Atlantic coast of German-occupied France by Allied forces. Nowadays it is used more generally to refer to any date on which a major event is due to occur, e.g. *Without a D-day, Saddam is left in the dark about the date of the impending attack*—*OEC*, 2003; *in light of the 1995 Disability Discrimination Act D-day of October 2004*—*OEC* (undated).

-d-, -dd-. Single-syllable words ending in *d* double it when adding suffixes beginning with vowels if the sound preceding *d* is that of a single short vowel: *laddish, redden, bidding, trodden, muddy*; but if the sound preceding *d* is a diphthong or double vowel or a vowel + *r*, the *d* is not doubled: *deaden, breeder, goodish, braided, harden.* Words of more than one syllable follow the rule for monosyllables if their last syllable is stressed or is itself a word (*forbidding, bedridden*), but otherwise do not double the *d* (*nomadic, wickedest, rigidity, periodical*).

de-. The prefix *de-* is still often called on to form new verbs (and derivatives). Twentieth-century examples (with date of first record indicated) include: *de-accession* (1972), *debark* (operate on dog to stop it from barking, 1943), *de-beak* (1937), *debrief* (1945), *decaffeinate* (1927), *decertify* (1918), *decriminalization* (1945), *de-emotionalize* (1942), *de-emphasize* (1938), *de-escalate* (1964), *deglamorize* (1938), etc. Note that a hyphen is usual when the second element begins with an *e*; in other cases it is optional. Cf. DIS-.

dead letter, apart from its theological and post-office uses, is a phrase for a regulation that still has a nominal existence but is no longer observed or enforced. Capital punishment can properly be called a *dead letter* in any country where the penalty remains on the statutes even though it has not been acted on for many years. The term cannot properly be applied to aspects of life that are simply passing out of fashion, e.g. quill pens, steam locomotives, hot-metal printing, since they were not brought into being by regulation in the first place.

deaf mute (adjective) is now regarded as offensive because it wrongly implies that people so described are unable to communicate. It should be avoided in favour of the neutral term *profoundly deaf.*

deal (noun). The phrase *a deal* used as a shorthand for *a good* or *great deal* in the sense 'an undefined, but considerable or large quantity' was much favoured by such writers as Shakespeare, Richardson, and Johnson, but is now mainly found in informal or dialectal writing or speech (*the decision saved him a deal of trouble*). *A great deal* and *a good deal* should not be used to mean 'a large number' of countable things, as in **A great deal of people have complained*; in these cases use *a great many.*

dean, doyen, though originally the same word (cf. French *doyen* from Latin *decānus*), meaning the senior member of a group, have become differentiated. *Dean* is the title of an ecclesiastical or academic officer; *doyen,* pronounced either /ˈdɔɪən/ (**doy**-yuhn), in an anglicized way, or in a quasi-French way as /ˈdwɑːjã/ , is a title of respect for 'the most senior or most prominent of a particular category or body of people'. The feminine form is **doyenne**, pronounced /ˈdɔɪɛn/ (**doy**-yen), /dɔɪˈɛn/ (doy-**yen**), or /dwɑːˈjɛn/ (dwah-**yen**).

Dear (as part of a formal greeting at the beginning of a letter). First introduced in the 15c., the beginning formula varied in the amount of elaboration: *Right dere and welbeloved; My most dere lorde and fader; Dearest broder,* etc. By the end of the 18c. it had settled down as part of the ordinary polite form of addressing an equal, ranging in increasing levels of informality and affection from *Dear Sir* and *Dear Madam* to *Dear Smith* (old-fashioned), to *Dear Mr/Miss/Mrs/Ms Jones,* to *Dear Ken/Mary,* etc., to *My dear Bill/Elizabeth,* etc., to *Dearest Margaret/Cedric,* etc. Increasingly now one receives circular letters beginning *Dear Customer, Dear Colleague,* etc., and formulas containing both the first and last names of the person addressed (*Dear Jeremy Butterfield*). The essential point is that the word *Dear* in itself is simply part of a letter-beginning formula, and no longer implies any particular or clear-cut level of intimacy or friendship.

dear, dearly (adverbs). With the verb *love* and in some other contexts where the meaning is 'very much' (*he loved her dearly; I would dearly like to join you on Friday*), *dearly* is usual and *dear* merely poetic (*The dear-loved peaceful seat*—Byron, 1807); but with *buy, cost, pay, sell,* etc., when the sense is 'at a high price, or great cost', *dearly* (*they paid dearly for their crimes*) and *dear* (*the recession has cost Britain dear*) are both available, though usually one or the other feels contextually more idiomatic.

debacle. Usually now written and printed without accents of the original French (*débâcle*), and in roman. Pronounced in an anglicized way, /deɪˈbɑːkəl/ day-**bah**-kuhl.

debar means 'to exclude from admission or from a right; prohibit from an action (*he was debarred from entering*)', by contrast with *disbar,* which can only mean 'to deprive (a barrister) of the right to practise; to expel from the Bar'.

debatable. So spelt. See -ABLE, -IBLE 6.

debauchee. Pronounced /dɪbɔːˈtʃiː/, with the main stress on the final syllable.

debouch. Pronounced /dɪˈbaʊtʃ/ to rhyme with 'pouch'.

debrief (verb) means 'to obtain information from (a person) on the completion of a mission or after a journey' and is first recorded in the *OED* shortly after the end of the Second World War. This verb started life in military circles but has since infiltrated other spheres of activity in all varieties of English. People are sometimes confused about who is the subject and who the object of *debriefing,* in other words who *debriefs* whom. It is the person responsible for and in charge of the task, mission, report, etc., who debriefs others: e.g. *Marine Corporal Wassef Ali Hassoun is safe in Germany this afternoon after being debriefed by his superior officers*—*OEC,* 2004. The use of the passive is common, as in this example.

debris. So spelt, without the accent of the original French (*débris*). The recommended pronunciation is /ˈdɛbriː/, but /ˈdeɪbriː/ is an acceptable alternative. In American English it is often pronounced /dəˈbriː/.

debut is usually spelt without the accent of the original French (*début*) in British English and pronounced /ˈdeɪbjuː/, **day**-byoo.

debutant /ˈdɛbjuːtɒ̃/ or /ˈdeɪ-/ is a man making his first public appearance, especially in sport or in artistic sphere, e.g. *a debutant director, goalkeeper.* The word is written without the accent of the original French (*débutant*).

debutante /ˈdɛbjʊtɑːnt/ or /ˈdeɪ-/ or /-tɒnt/ is (*a*) a female making her first public appearance, especially in sport; (*b*) a young woman making her social debut. The shortened form *deb* used to be freely used for sense (*b*), especially in spoken English, but has disappeared, together with the phenomenon it described. The word is written without the accent of the original French (*débutante*).

decade. Until the 19c. frequently spelt *decad* (pronounced /ˈdɛkəd/), but now always *decade.* The preferred pronunciation is /ˈdɛkeɪd/, but increasingly, and in unexpected quarters, one hears /dɪˈkeɪd/, rhyming with *decayed.*

decade names. To write decade names, you can use either words, i.e. *the sixties, the nineteen sixties,* or figures, *the 1960s.* If using figures, you should give them in full, as just shown, rather than *the 60s,* even though this is how you would say it. You do not need to put an apostrophe before the letter *s,* e.g. *the 1950s, the 1970s, the 1870s,* not *the 1950's,* etc. When you use the name of the decade to define and sum up a historical or cultural period, you should write it in words, and may use an initial capital letter, e.g. *Paris in the Twenties.* The numerical form simply indicates a time span, e.g. *the oyster blight of the 1920s.* See also NOUGHTIES.

deca-, deci-. In the metric system, *deca-* means multiplied, and *deci-* divided, by ten; *decalitre,* 10 litres, *decilitre,* $\frac{1}{10}$ litre; so with *gramme, metre,* etc.

deceptively belongs to a small set of words whose meaning is rather ambiguous. This happens because people use *deceptively* in two rather different ways. For example, is *a deceptively smooth surface* smooth or not? The answer is that it appears to be smooth, but in reality is not. So, in this case *deceptively* means something like 'apparently' or 'misleadingly'. But this is the reverse of its use, beloved by estate agents, in phrases such as *a deceptively spacious room.* If we follow the logic of the first example, this would mean that the room *looks* spacious, but in fact is not. And that is the exact opposite of the meaning intended. In this context, *deceptively* is being used to mean something like 'surprisingly', i.e. it is surprising how large the room is.

We can all easily understand what this sort of example is supposed to mean without going to the trouble of analysing it. But often what is being stated really is rather unclear. If you describe a runner as *deceptively fast,* is he or she fast while seeming slow, or slow while seeming to be fast? To avoid confusion, it is best not to use *deceptively* at all when it can create ambiguity, and reword, using *apparently, misleadingly, surprisingly,* etc., to make your point absolutely clear.

decided, decisive (adjectives). **1** Both words relate to decision and decision-making, but there are clear differences. Used of people, *decided* means 'having clear opinions' (*he found them vacillating; he left them decided*) and *decisive* means 'able to decide quickly' (*the constable, a decisive man, arrested the pickpocket immediately*). Used of circumstances, *decided* means 'definite, unquestionable' (*a decided advantage*) and *decisive* means 'deciding an issue, conclusive' (*a decisive superiority over its rival*). In some contexts either word can be used, but with different implications: a *decided victory* is one that is overwhelming, whereas a *decisive victory* is one that, whether overwhelming or not, has a definite effect on the course of a war. Managers are *decided* when they have a definite opinion on a subject, and *decisive* when they make decisions promptly and effectively.

2 The corresponding adverbs are **decidedly** (= unquestionably, undeniably) and **decisively** (= with conclusive effect). The first typically associates with adjectives, e.g. *decidedly different, odd, uncomfortable,* the second with verbs, e.g. *act, win, respond decisively.*

decimate. Once a key word in the battle between prescriptivists and descriptivists, *decimate* has changed meaning because the old one—fortunately—is no longer needed. In the Roman army, Latin *decimāre* meant 'to punish every tenth man chosen by lot'. 'Punish' sometimes meant 'put to death'. In strict terms, so prescriptivists would argue, *decimate* should mean 'to kill, destroy, or remove *one in every ten* of (something)', and it has been so used in English since the 17c. *Rhetorically* and *loosely,* as the *OED* expresses it, it has also been used from about the same time to mean 'to kill, destroy or remove *a large proportion* of'. The dispute between those who will and those who will not use *decimate* in its 'rhetorical or loose' sense has been resolved by usage. Examples of the disputed meaning abound and are acceptable: *On the deadly foot and mouth disease which had decimated large herds of animals, Mr Hakayobe said Government had taken measures to address the problem*—*OEC,* 2005; *The populations of dolphins and porpoises in the Black Sea have been decimated*—M. Donoghue et al., 1990.

A usage that is not generally accepted, however, is to use *decimate* to mean to physically overpower someone by a massive margin, as in this boxing context **And due to both size and skill, Foreman, Lewis, Bowe and Vitali Klitschko would have decimated him*—*OEC,* 2004 (AmE).

decisive. See DECIDED, DECISIVE.

declaredly. Pronounced /dɪˈklɛːrɪdli/ with four syllables. See -EDLY.

déclassé. Spelt with accents and printed in roman (fem. **déclassée**). The meaning is 'having fallen in social status'.

declension. In grammar, (*a*) the variation of the form of a noun, pronoun, or adjective, by which its grammatical case, number, and gender are identified; (*b*) the class in which a noun etc. is put according to the exact form of this variation. Cf. CONJUGATION.

décolletage, décolleté. The first means 'a low neckline of a woman's dress, etc.' or 'a woman's cleavage as revealed by a low neckline on a dress or top' and the second '(of a dress etc.) having a low neckline' and '(of a woman) wearing a dress with a low neckline'. Both are printed in roman, and are usually pronounced in a French way, /ˌdeɪkɒlɪˈtɑːʒ/ and /deɪˈkɒlteɪ/.

decor. The spelling *decor* (without accent) and pronunciation /ˈdɛkɔː/ (**dek**-aw) are standard nowadays. Spelling *décor* with an accent is also correct, as is the more French pronunciation /ˈdeɪkɔː/ (**day**-kaw).

decoy. By rule the noun should be pronounced /ˈdiːkɔɪ/ and the verb /dɪˈkɔɪ/, but opposite stressing also occurs.

decrease. The noun is pronounced /ˈdiːkriːs/ and the verb /dɪˈkriːs/. See NOUN AND VERB ACCENT 1.

decry, descry are distantly related in origin but now have widely different meanings. To *decry* something is to disparage or deplore it, e.g. *She decries the spread of tower blocks and the failure to turn derelict sites into green spaces—Evening Standard,* 2007. To *descry* is a very literary word meaning to catch sight of a person or thing in the distance, e.g. *Her thoughts were brought to an abrupt end, as she descried two figures on their way up the path*—J. Ashe, 1993; *While he clearly indicates productions he considers successful, I would be hard-pressed to descry a pattern among them—OEC,* 2000. The two should not be confused, as has happened in the next example: **I have some sympathy with people who descry this, and who argue that society's easy tolerance of single mothers . . . is actually fostering moral irresponsibility—OEC,* 2005.

deduction is the inferring of particular instances from a general law, as opposed to *induction,* the inference of a general law from particular instances.

deem is a fairly formal word (frequently used in legal language) for 'judge, consider'. It is followed by either a noun or adjective complement, or by a *to*-infinitive: *He deemed it* his duty *to abstain from voting; In Ireland what a man said was deemed* more important *than what he did; Because of your failure to reply you are deemed* to have withdrawn *from the project.* It is non-standard to insert *as* between *deem* and its complement, as in **It is important because many deem bikers as the missing link between early apes and modern humans—OEC,* 2004.

deep, deeply. *Deep* as adverb is deeply entrenched in the language. It is used literally (*the boat was stuck deep in the mud*), and in many transferred and figurative senses (*the card-players sat up deep into the night; still waters run deep*; etc.). In such types of sentence it would not be idiomatic to use *deeply. Deeply* is used especially before past participles (as in the first sentence of this entry) and also when the meaning is 'profoundly, thoroughly' (*I should like to consider the matter a little more deeply*) or 'intensely' (*he was deeply conscious of his shortcomings*).

deer. See COLLECTIVE NOUN.

defect. The pronunciations recommended are /ˈdiːfɛkt/ for the noun (= imperfection, blemish) and /dɪˈfɛkt/ for the verb (= abandon one's country or cause in favour of another). See NOUN AND VERB ACCENT 1.

defective, deficient. Some useful distinctions can be made. *Defective* tends mostly to mean 'faulty in quality, showing some definite fault, damage, etc., that impairs or cancels the efficiency of something' (*defective eyesight, hearing, measures, pronunciation, translation, valve, vehicle,* etc.); while *deficient* vies with *insufficient* to mean 'present in less than the quantity needed for effectiveness' (*deficient courage, diet, funds, water supply,* etc.). But there are many contexts in which the words converge in meaning, or are replaced by *insufficient, inadequate, faulty,* etc. Neither word is used now by professional people dealing with issues of mental health.

defence. The spelling in British English corresponding to AmE **defense**.

defer. The extended forms and derivatives are *deferred, deferring; deference* (respect), *deferral* (postponement), *deferment* (postponement).

deficient. See DEFECTIVE.

definite article. The use of the definite article *the* causes few difficulties to native speakers but is a major problem for foreign learners of the language. This is partly because many foreign languages, e.g. Russian, Chinese, Japanese, lack a definite article, and partly because the distribution of the definite article in English is a matter of some complexity. Some of the main types are outlined below. **1** *Names.* (*a*) In general, no definite article: *John Smith, High Street, Sutton Courtenay, Oxfordshire, England* (cf. *la France*); (religious festivals)

Christmas, Easter, Good Friday; (months, days of the week) *January, Monday*; (continents) *Africa, Asia*; (lakes, mountains) *Lake Windermere, Mt Everest*; (assorted place names) *Buckingham Palace, Magdalen College, Paddington Station, Windsor Castle*. (*b*) But there are many exceptions: (unmodified names) *the Bible, the Pentagon, the Parthenon, The Times*; (names with premodification) *the Bodleian Library, the British Broadcasting Corporation, the English Channel, the National Gallery, the North/the South Island* (of New Zealand); (with postmodification) *the House of Commons, the President of the United States*.

2 *Words*. In its ordinary use, the definite article *the* precedes a noun and implies a specific instance: e.g. *the cushion on the chair; he opened the door; the story is apocryphal*. It is also used as a guide to a particular place, person, etc., known by the speaker/hearer/reader to exist: e.g. *the earth, the Equator, the Church, the sky; the aristocracy, the working class; the French, the Chinese*. It is frequently used in a non-specific way to mean 'whichever one of its kind is or was convenient, open, etc.': *I go to the cinema once a year; he heard it on the radio; she took the train to London*. *The* is often used of a part of the body following a preposition (instead of a possessive pronoun): *he took me by the shoulder; a pat on the back; they pulled her by the hair; he kicked his opponent on the shin*. The definite article is not repeated before the second of a pair of nouns joined by *and*: *the laws and ordinances of the ancient Hebrews*. Names of illnesses (*flu, measles, mumps*, etc.) are normally used without the definite article, but examples with *the* also occur in standard sources: *Annie has got the mumps*—B. Trapido, 1982; *It was that hot summer you had the measles*—N. Bawden, 1987.

3 *Uncount nouns*. Mass or uncount nouns are normally construed without the definite article: *compelled by* guilt *to offer* atonement; *he couldn't stand* waste; *the important distinction between* narrative *and* dialogue; *the parents behaved with* dignity *and* grace. But many nouns can be used both as uncount nouns and count nouns: *instances of several claims to divine* illumination; *the Blackpool* illuminations.

4 *Omitted*. In a number of other circumstances the definite article is regularly omitted: (names of subjects of study) *his main interest was* philology; (meal names) *he had* breakfast *before catching the train*; (seasons) *snow on the ground and it is only* autumn; (places habitually visited) *he was taken to* hospital (BrE) *for the operation; he goes to* church *every Sunday*.

5 *Emphasis*. The definite article is also used for emphasis = the actual (person): *Not* the *Jeffrey Archer*.

See also THE.

definite, definitive. In most of their uses the distinction is clear-cut, but occasionally *definitive* is used when *definite* is more appropriate. Both refer to things that are said or written. *Definite* means 'clear and distinct', (as in *definite advantage, improvement, possibility*, etc.) whereas *definitive* means 'decisive, unconditional, final' as in *definitive answer, statement, diagnosis, conclusion*, etc. A *definitive version, work, study, account, guide*, etc., is a printed work that is regarded as the best authority on its subject and likely to remain so. Only *definitive* has connotations of authority and conclusiveness: a *definite answer* is one that is clear and specific, whereas a *definitive answer* is authoritative and dependable; *a definite no* is a firm refusal, whereas *a definitive no* is an authoritative judgement or decision that something is not the case. Examples of the wrong use of *definitive*: **It is thought that any definitive news will be announced this afternoon*; **He promised Farmer Boldwood a definitive answer*.

defriend. See UNFRIEND.

defuse, diffuse. The only thing that distinguishes *defuse* from *diffuse* in speaking is that its first vowel is a long *i*, /diːˈfjuːz/, rhyming with *tea*, as opposed to /dɪˈfjuːz/ with a short *i*. It is therefore hardly surprising that *diffuse* (correctly = to disperse) is often written instead of *defuse* in the latter's figurative meaning of 'to remove tension or potential danger from (a crisis, etc.)'. Examples of the mistaken use: **The Scott report is a time-bomb stealthy politicians and officials are trying to diffuse*—*Guardian*, 1995; **She is coping because she has learned that forgiveness is the only way to diffuse ire and hatred*—*Birmingham Evening Mail*, 2007.

Since this mistake is especially common in newspapers, we might suspect that close writing deadlines are the culprit.

dégagé /deɪˈɡɑːʒeɪ/. Print in roman with accents. It means 'without constraints, unconstrained (in manner or address), unconcerned (about fashion or dress)'.

degree. The phrase *to a degree* originally (in the 18c., e.g. in Sheridan's *The Rivals: Assuredly, sir, your father is wrath to a degree*) meant 'extremely'. The use survived in more florid English into the 20c. and was accepted by Fowler (1926) 'however illogical it seems'. But this meaning is now dated, and in current use *to a degree* means 'to some extent' rather than 'to a great extent' and this is what will be understood if the word *degree* is not qualified. To avoid any doubt, qualify the word *degree* in some way, as in *to a large degree, to a certain degree, to some degree, to an amazing degree,* etc., e.g. *All art is an abstraction to some degree*—Henry Moore, 1966).

deity. The traditional British pronunciation /ˈdiːɪti/ has now largely yielded to /ˈdeɪɪti/, but is still standard in American English. Similarly with the related words *deify, deification, deism,* etc. See -EITY.

déjà vu. Written with accents, in roman, and generally pronounced /deɪʒɑː ˈvuː/ (day-zhah **voo**). This idiomatic French phrase (literally 'already seen') has become a part of general language since its first appearance in the technical language of psychology in 1903 in the sense 'an illusory feeling of having already experienced a present situation'. Outside psychology, its normal sense now is 'a clear impression that something has been previously seen or experienced', especially in sentences of the type *he had a distinct feeling of* déjà vu. Two similarly formed French phrases have never become anglicized, and are tainted with pretentiousness: *déjà entendu* (first recorded 1965) and *déjà lu* (1960), a feeling that one may have heard a passage of music, etc./ read a passage, a poem, etc., elsewhere.

deliberate, deliberative (adjectives). *Deliberative* now most commonly means 'of, or appointed for the purpose of deliberation or debate' (*a deliberative assembly*). Much less commonly, it means 'characterized by deliberation' (*in his cooler and more deliberative moments*). In that meaning it overlaps somewhat with *deliberate,* in the latter's meaning of 'fully considered, careful', e.g. *Rather, a request is being made for a more* deliberate *approach to be adopted—Guardian* (Trinidad), 2005. What possibly distinguishes *deliberative* is the amount and depth of deliberation involved: *They take a very sober, thoughtful,* deliberative *look at a situation—CNN* transcripts, 2001.

delimit (verb). See LIMIT (verb) 2.

deliver, in addition to its established physical meanings to do with bringing and providing things, is often used to mean 'provide something that you have promised or that people expect of you' as in *the failure of successive governments to deliver economic growth* or *if you can't deliver improved sales figures, you're fired.* While this meaning is well established and was once a lively metaphor, it now runs the risk of being hackneyed and vague. Words you could use instead include *provide* and *supply.* Or you could rewrite your sentence to be more precise and specific about what you mean. *Deliver* has also developed a vogue intransitive use (without an object) equivalent to 'provide what is agreed or expected', e.g. *The foregoing is proof that local government is delivering at the regional level—Glasgow Herald,* 2003. It is shorthand for *deliver the goods,* a phrase used in the same sense from the mid-19c. This elliptical use is common in journalism because it encapsulates so much in a single word; for similar reasons it also features prominently in the language of business and management. Outside those spheres, and often even within them, it tends to sound contrived or even slick.

delusion, illusion overlap in meaning because both are to do with things wrongly believed or wrongly thought for various reasons. There is, however, a distinguishing principle: a *delusion* is a wrong belief regarded from the point of view of the person holding it (and has special uses in psychiatry, as in *delusions of grandeur*), whereas an *illusion* is a wrong belief or impression regarded externally. *Delusion,* unlike *illusion,* has a corresponding verb, **delude**, and the influence of this verb is sometimes implicit in the choice between *delusion* and *illusion.* The following examples will help to clarify these points: Examples: (delusion) *He suffered from the delusion that everything smelled of cats*—A. Koestler, 1947; *One of her recurrent delusions is that she is a* *mistress of dialects*—K. Tynan, 1961; *Ed continues to labour under the delusion that I'm a Liverpool fan—Guardian Unlimited*, 2003; (illusion) *in the world as we know it ... freedom is largely an illusion*—J. M. Roberts, 1975; *Alfred Crowther loved his first-born child, but he had no illusions about him*—B. T. Bradford, 1986.

de luxe is regularly so written and printed in Britain, and pronounced /də'lʌks/, less commonly /də'lʊks/; and as one word, *deluxe,* in America, pronounced /dɪ'ləks/ or /di:-/.

demagogic. This word and its derivative *demagogy* have resisted the general movement towards Anglicization: the second *g* remains /g/ not /ʤ/. Doubtless the main word of the group, *demagogue*, has had a bearing on the matter. See GREEK G.

demagogue. Sometimes spelt **demagog** in American English.

demand. You demand something *of* or (more commonly) *from* someone (*demanded ten pounds from him*); you make a demand *on* someone *for* something (*never-ending demands on him for his comments*).

demean. There are two verbs. The first, which was first recorded in the 14c. but is now somewhat archaic, is normally reflexive and means 'to behave, to conduct oneself (in a specified way)' (*The Prince Borghese certainly demeans himself like a kind and liberal gentleman*—N. Hawthorne, 1858). Cf. *demeanour.* The second, first recorded in 1601 and probably formed on the adjective *mean* after *debase,* is now dominant. Used transitively it means 'to lower in status, reputation, etc.' (*he simplified the argument without in any way demeaning it*); and, reflexively, 'to lower or humble oneself' (*he would not demean himself to accept such menial work*). Fowler's reservations (1926) about the second verb have long since been overcome by usage.

demi- (= half-). This prefix of French origin is effectively obsolete as a productive form, having been superseded by *half-* and *semi-,* and, for words of Greek origin, *hemi-*. It survives in a small number of current English words (some of them loanwords from French), e.g. *demigod, demi-monde, demi-pension, demi-sec, demisemiquaver, demitasse. Demijohn* is probably a corruption of French *dame-jeanne* Lady Jane; and *demiurge,* 'the creator of the universe' in the philosophy of Plato, represents Greek δημιουργός, literally 'public or skilled worker'. See SEMI-.

demise. Outside legal contexts used, somewhat euphemistically, as a synonym of death (of a person), failure (of a political movement, etc.), cessation (the shutting down of a newspaper, business premises, etc.). This figurative use is perfectly standard and acceptable, despite objections in some quarters. Example: *We were on our way to a funeral when we heard about Margaret Thatcher's demise* [i.e. her resignation]—V. Grove, 1990.

demo, abbreviation of *demonstration.* A 20c. word (first recorded 1936). Plural *demos.* See -O(E)S 6.

demonetize. Pronounced /diːˈmʌnɪtʌɪz/, not /-'mɒn-/.

demoniac /dɪ'məʊnɪak/, **demoniacal** /diːmə'nʌɪəkəl/ (adjectives). These two rather rare words are not clearly differentiated in meaning. The choice between them is largely governed by the rhythm of the sentence. The adjective, *demonic* /dɪ'monɪk/, has largely replaced them in the meaning 'of or pertaining to demons'.

demonstrable is usually pronounced stressing the second syllable /dɪ'mɒnstrəb(ə)l/ (di-**mon**-struh-b(uh)l), but can also be pronounced stressing the first, /'dɛmənstrəb(ə)l/ (**de**-muhn-struh-b(uh)l).

dengue (a tropical disease). Pronounced /'dɛŋgi/.

denote. See CONNOTE.

denouement, the final unravelling of a plot or complicated situation in a play, novel, etc. is usually printed in roman, without the accent of the original French (*dénouement*). Pronounced /deɪ'nuːmɑ̃/. It is quite often misspelt *denoument.*

dental. In phonetics, a consonant made by the tip of the tongue against the upper teeth, e.g. /θ/, /ð/, the speech sounds represented by English *th.* They are closely related to *alveolar* consonants made by the tip or blade of the tongue against the teeth-ridge (or alveolar ridge), e.g. the speech sounds represented by English *t, d, n, s, z.*

dent, dint, are variants of the same word (*dent* first recorded in Middle English, *dint* in Old English). At one time they both meant a blow or the mark or hollow made by such a blow. Now *dent* means **1** a slight mark or hollow in a surface, as one made by a blow, a collision, etc.; **2** a noticeable effect (*an overlong lunch made a dent in the afternoon*). *Dint* is mostly restricted to the phrase *by dint of,* by means of, but is sometimes used as a variant of *dent* 1, especially in the phrases *make a dint* and *put a dint* in something (= to have an effect on), e.g. *Anything that puts a dint in the plans of car bombers and armed insurgents has to be a good thing*—*OEC,* 2004.

denture(s) was originally a genteelism (first recorded in 1874) for *false teeth,* but is now standard in formal contexts.

denunciation. Pronounced /-sɪˈeɪʃən/, and see -CIATION.

depart has been used transitively since the 14c. (e.g. *The clergy were ordered to depart the kingdom,* 1839 in *OED; Mrs. J. Gargery had departed this life on Monday last*—Dickens, 1861). *MCWDEU* (2002) cites numerous recent US examples of transitive use, e.g. *one boiling morning in July, we departed my father's house*—*Harper's,* 1971. But, except in the formal or literary phrase *departed this life,* the construction no longer forms part of the standard language in Britain. One *departs from* (a place) or *departs for* (a destination).

department. See FIELD.

depend. In its main meanings, *depend* is followed by *on; upon* is markedly more formal and is used in less than 10 per cent of *OEC* examples, e.g. *Chlorine will kill bacteria in water, but it takes some time. The time needed depends on the concentration of chlorine*—*OEC,* 2004; *It was quite wrong to come to depend too much upon one's children*—P. Fitzgerald, 1979; *I'll have a damn good try . . . You can depend on that*—A. Price, 1982; The slightly archaic sense 'to hang down' continues to be called on, but only ever in literary contexts: *From a beam crossing the low ceiling depended a mobile, the property of Parker*—E. Bowen, 1968. When *it depends* is followed by an indirect question, *on* is more often used than omitted in writing, e.g. *it depends on what you mean by a minimum wage; it depends on how much it costs.* Fowler (1926) judged the omission of *on* to be 'slovenly' and 'indefensible', but his view now seems completely outmoded.

dependant, dependent. Until recently the only correct spelling of the noun in British English was *dependant,* as in *a single man with no dependants.* However, the variant *dependent* is also now standard, and is as common as *dependant* in the *OEC.* In American English *dependent* is the standard form for the noun. The adjective should always be spelled *-ent,* not *-ant,* e.g. *we are dependent on his goodwill.*

dependence, dependency. See -CE, -CY (iii).

deponent. In Latin grammar, applied to verbs that are passive in form but active in meaning, as *cōnor, cōnātus sum, cōnārī* ('to try'), *morior, mortuus sum, morī* ('to die').

depositary, depository. A *depositary* is a person or authority to whom something is entrusted, a trustee. A *depository* is a storage place for furniture, books, etc.; a source (normally a book or suchlike, occasionally a person) of wisdom, knowledge, etc.

depot. Printed in roman, without the accents of the original French (*dépôt*). Pronounced /ˈdɛpəʊ/.

deprecate, depreciate. 1 The two words are similar in form and in current use overlap somewhat in meaning and use, but their origin is different. *Deprecate* is from Latin *dēprecārī* 'to try to avert by prayer' and its primary current meaning is 'to express disapproval of (a person or thing)': *Style mavens generally deprecate the use of shudder quotes, but when dealing with a movement that is built on using common words in unconventional or undefined ways, they are unavoidable*—*OEC,* 2005. *Depreciate* is from Latin *dēpretiāre* ('to lower in value', from *pretium* price) and is in origin an antonym of *appreciate* in the meaning of 'increase in value'. In current use it means (*a*) (without an object) 'to become lower in value or price': *Bonds are hardly safe in the teeth of rising interest rates, and we've seen how quickly cash can depreciate in an inflationary environment*—*www.financialsense.com,* 2005; and (*b*) (with an object) 'to undervalue, to disparage', e.g. *Before this Wilde depreciated pity as a* *motive in art; now he embraced it*—R. Ellmann, 1969.

2 It is in this last meaning that the two words overlap, the intruder normally being *deprecate* in place of *depreciate: Dealers have felt a need to deprecate their own firms' values, to disassociate themselves from them*—A. Davidson, 1989; *A talent that results in giving exquisite pleasure to collectors of memorabilia is to be admired, not deprecated*—M. J. Staples, 1992. As a result *depreciate* is being more and more confined to its financial meaning in relation to currencies, share values, etc. A few die-hard Latinists have objected, and continue to object to this use of *deprecate* instead of *depreciate*, but it is now so well established as to be unassailable.

3 This intrusion on the part of *deprecate* is reflected in the derivative adjectives *self-deprecating* and *self-deprecatory* meaning 'disparaging oneself', and the noun *self-deprecation*, where the meanings are closer to *depreciate* than *deprecate*. Examples: *Sadly he declined, saying in a charmingly self-deprecatory way that he doubted he had any views worth hearing*—L. Kennedy, 1990; *She may arguably be the most successful female chef in Britain, but her modesty and self-deprecation is* [sic] *more akin to that of a fish-and-chip shop-owner*—*Scotsman*, 2007. These forms and uses are now fully established, although *self-depreciation* is also occasionally found: *She* [George Eliot] *wrote of her 'isolation' or 'excommunication' from the world and she was prone to morbid self-depreciation*—*Times*, 1996.

deprival. First recorded in 1611, it is still occasionally used instead of *deprivation* to describe the act of depriving someone of something. See -AL. Example: *It is difficult to regard that as other than a deprival of justice*—*OEC*, 2003.

deprivation. Pronounced /ˌdɛprɪ'veɪʃən/.

Derby(shire). Pronounced /'dɑːbɪ(ʃə)/ in standard British English. In AmE, /'dərbi-/ is customary for the several meanings of the word e.g. horserace [*Kentucky Derby*], a bowler hat.

de rigueur. Print in roman, and pronounce /də rɪ'gəː/. Occasionally misspelt as *de rigeur*, with the first *u* lacking.

derisive, derisory. Both words entered the language in the 17c. in the sense 'characterized by derision, scoffing, mocking'. *Derisive* also came to mean 'that causes derision, ridiculous' in the 1890s, and *derisory* followed suit in the 1920s. The two words are now for the most part kept separate, *derisive* being mostly used in the first sense (*derisive laughter, derisive remarks*, etc.), and *derisory* in the second (*a derisory pay offer, a derisory fee*, etc.). *Derisive* is occasionally mistakenly used for derisory, e.g. **a derisive offer of a purse split at 90 per cent to 10 per cent in favour of the world champion*—*Evening Standard*, 1992.

derring-do. A literary word meaning 'heroic courage, feats of daring'. A phrase born of a misprint, by a process of modern folk etymology it has itself come to be often misspelt as *daring-do*. Its origins and later popularization make an interesting story. Spenser's Glosse to *The Shepheardes Calender*, October (published in 1579) has *In derring doe, In manhoode and cheualrie.* He had taken the word from 16c. prints of Lydgate's *Chronicle of Troy*, where *derrynge do* is misprinted for original *dorryng do*, which echoes *In* dorrynge don *that longeth to a knyght* (= in *daring to do* what appertains to a knight) of Chaucer's *Troilus and Criseyde* v.837. Lydgate also used the phrase as a fully developed noun (e.g. *Chron. Troy* v.136) (*Notes & Queries*, 1962, 369f.). Its currency in modern writers is due to Scott's use of *deeds of such derring-do* (*Ivanhoe*, ch. xxix). Examples (correct): The Colditz Story ... *is a classic tale of wartime derring-do*—*OEC*, 2004; (incorrect) **Patton was to be linked with such 'daring-do' throughout his military career*—*OEC*, 2005.

descant. The noun is pronounced /'dɛskant/ and the verb /dɪs'kant/. See NOUN AND VERB ACCENT 1.

descendant, descendent. In both British and American English the noun is spelt *descendant* and the rarely used, technical adjective meaning 'descending from an ancestor' is spelt *descendent* (*extinct species are replaced by descendent species*).

description. Fowler (1926) deprecated the use of the word as a mere substitute for *kind* or *sort* (*no food of any description; crimes of this description*). As the use is not dealt with in any detail in the *OED* it is not easy to determine how old or how widespread it is. The use has been listed without comment in most smaller dictionaries since at least the 1960s. Examples: *I tried hard to keep talking, but I could not think of a single word of any description*—K. Waterhouse, 1959; *If you sell pottery or trinkets of any description, why would you pay rent for a shop or a market stall . . . when you can market your wares worldwide for a small fee?*—*Observer*, 2005.

descriptive grammar. A term properly used only of scientifically prepared grammars that describe the state of the standard language or regional forms of a given society at a given time, as revealed by a thorough examination and analysis of large quantities of relevant linguistic data. In practice, grammars written before the 20c. were systematically prescriptive or normative, and those written in the manner of *A Comprehensive Grammar of the English Language* (1985), by Randolph Quirk et al., descriptive. The two methods converge, especially as shown in grammars prepared for schoolchildren and for foreigners. The key to the success of the descriptive method is that it must be based on substantial amounts of real (not invented) data. See PRESCRIPTIVISM.

descry. See DECRY, DESCRY.

desert, dessert. 1 Only *desert* in the sense 'an arid waste' is stressed on the first syllable: thus /ˈdɛzət/. The unrelated noun *desert* (usually in the plural *deserts*) 'what one deserves', the noun *dessert* meaning 'the sweet course of a meal', and the verb *desert* meaning 'to abandon' are all stressed on the second syllable: thus /dɪˈzəːt/.

2 The traditional phrase *just deserts* includes *desert* as a plural noun meaning 'what one deserves', e.g. *those who caused great torment to others rarely got their just deserts*. Presumably because the word is not otherwise used as a noun in this meaning, popular wisdom has concocted two new versions of the phrase: *just desserts*, spotted as long ago as 1962 in the *New York Times*, and, less commonly, *just deserves*.

deserter. So spelt, not -or. See -OR.

deservedly. Four syllables. See -EDLY.

déshabillé. This French word, meaning 'a state of being only partly or carelessly dressed', is variously pronounced in English. The most usual pronunciation is probably /ˌdezaˈbiːjeɪ/, but initial /ˌdeɪz-/ is also common. It is also commonly written without accents and pronounced /dɛzəˈbiːl/. The Anglicized variant *dishabille* /dɪsəˈbiːl/ is used more often, according to *OEC* data. As the word came into English in the 17c., it has had plenty of time to settle down, but has not, and is still printed in italics.

desiccated. So spelt (not *dessicated*).

desideratum, something lacking but needed or desired. Generally pronounced /dɪˌzɪdəˈrɑːtəm/, but /-ˈreɪtəm/ is also heard. Plural *desiderata*; see -UM 2.

designedly. Four syllables; see -EDLY.

designer. Since the 1960s a vogue word used first in fashion, etc., to denote goods bearing the name or label of a famous designer, with the implication that they are expensive or prestigious (*designer scarves, labels, jeans*, etc.). The word soon spread into much wider use: *Mr Douglas Hurd, the Home Secretary, . . . turned on 'designer violence' on the* [TV] *screen*—*Times*, 1988; *he remembered thinking to himself: so it's finally happened—designer industrial action*—D. Lodge, 1988. A **designer drug** is a synthetic compound made to simulate an existing illegal 'recreational' drug; **designer stubble** is the 'short, bristly growth on a man's unshaven face . . . purposely cultivated for a supposedly rugged and masculine appearance or to suggest a fashionably casual dishevelment' (*OED*); and a **designer baby** is one whose genetic make-up has been artificially selected by genetic engineering combined with *in vitro* fertilization. All three combinations date from the 1980s. The word can also be used ironically to mock things 'apparently created by a designer, or regarded as fashionable, exclusive, expensive, or conferring status', as in **designer water** for expensive bottled waters and **designer dog** for breeds beloved of celebrities.

desist (verb). Traditionally pronounced /dɪˈzɪst/, but /dɪˈsɪst/ is an acceptable variant. The corresponding noun is usually spelt **desistance** and occasionally **desistence**.

despatch. See DISPATCH.

desperado. Pronounced /-ˈɑːdəʊ/. Plural *desperadoes* (American English also *-dos*). See -O(E)S 4.

despicable. In *The Spoken Word* (1981) Burchfield recommended /ˈdɛspɪkəbəl/, with the stress on the first syllable, i.e. the traditional pronunciation, and that is the only pronunciation shown in the *OED*. But the standard pronunciation nowadays is /dɪˈspɪkəbəl/.

despise. One of the group of English words (*advertise, devise, surprise,* etc.) that must not be spelt with *-ize.* See -ISE 1.

dessert. See DESERT, DESSERT.

destruct. A back-formation from *destruction,* this verb is first recorded in 1958 in its modern sense connected with space missiles. It means 'to destroy (a missile that is malfunctioning or is off course)'. The normal past tense is *destructed.* It is also used as a noun, especially attributively (*destruct button, system,* etc.). See also SELF-DESTRUCT.

destructible. See -ABLE, -IBLE 5, 7.

detail. In British English the stress falls on the first syllable for both the noun and the verb. In American English, second-syllable stressing is in the ascendant for both noun and verb.

détente. Retention of the French accent is desirable. Print in roman.

deter. 1 The present participle *deterring* is pronounced /dɪˈtəːrɪŋ/, but the related noun **deterrent** has medial /-ˈtɛr-/.

2 The *r* is doubled in the inflected forms (*deterred, deterring*) and in the derivatives **deterrence** and **deterrent**.

determinately, determinedly. *Determinately* should not be used to mean 'in a determined or resolute manner': the word required for that sense is *determinedly* (pronounced as four syllables: see -EDLY). *Determinately,* if used at all, should have the sense 'conclusively, finally'. Example (incorrect) **Don't worry, you will. I told you before, I'm not going to lose you again,' Justin said determinately*—*OEC,* 2002.

determiner. A *determiner* is a word that goes before a noun and determines its status in some way, such as *a, the, this, all,* and *such.* A *predeterminer* occurs before another determiner (all *the time*) and a *postdeterminer* occurs after another determiner (*The* only *one*).

detestation. Pronounced /diːtɛˈsteɪʃən/, with the main stress on the third syllable.

detour. Print without the accent of the original French (*détour*) and in roman, and pronounce /ˈdiːtʊə/.

detract, distract. Both words are followed by *from*; but their meanings and syntax are different. *Detract* means 'to take away (a part of something), to diminish', and is generally used without a grammatical object (i.e. intransitively), e.g. *If anything even remotely detracts from my life in a rugby sense it gets binned*—*Irish Examiner,* 2003. *Distract* is used transitively and means 'to divert the attention of' with a person, the mind, etc. as the object, e.g. *This speculation should not distract us from the real issues*—*Daily Record,* 2006. *Detract* sometimes encroaches on *distract,* especially in the expression *detract attention from,* which was an accepted usage in the early 19c. but should now be avoided in favour of *distract attention from.* An example of the unadvisable use: **British pop stars will apparently do anything to simultaneously create publicity and detract attention from their actual music*—*OEC,* 2002.

deuteragonist, the person second in importance to the protagonist in a (Greek) play. The pronunciation recommended is /djuːtəˈragənɪst/. Fowler (1926), by contrast, recommended /djuːtərəˈgəʊnɪst/.

Deuteronomy. Main stress on the third syllable, not the first: thus /djuːtəˈrɒnəmi/.

develop, developable, development. Not *-ope.*

Devil's advocate. A translation (first recorded in 1760) of Latin *advocatus diaboli,* it means 'one who urges the devil's plea against the canonization of a saint, or in opposition to the honouring of any one; hence, one who advocates the contrary or wrong side' (*OED*). In simpler terms it means 'a person who tests a proposition by arguing against it'. It does not mean one who pleads for a wicked person.

devise. Not *-ize.* See -ISE.

deviser, devisor. *Devisor* is a person who devises (i.e. assigns or gives by will) property, and is in legal use only; *deviser* is the agent noun of *devise* in all other senses. See -OR.

devoid. An adjective that from its first recorded use in the 15c. has been used only predicatively, that is after the noun it qualifies, and followed by *of*. Examples: *A very simple style of dress, devoid of ornament or pretension*—W. G. Palgrave, 1865; *The lines are pompous huff and puff—a string of clichés almost devoid of meaning*—*OEC*, 2004. It should not be followed by *from*, nor should it be used absolutely, i.e. without a complement, as in **I think of the times that we live in as culturally and artistically devoid*—*OEC*, 2004.

devolve, devolute. *Devolve* has become a key verb in political discourse in Great Britain since the latter part of the last century. Its three principal uses are as follows: (*a*) you *devolve* powers, authority, etc., *to* someone (*devolve further powers to the Scottish Parliament*); (*b*) power, authority, etc., *devolves on, upon* or *to* someone (*his duties devolved* on *a comrade*); (*c*) an estate, inheritance, benefit, etc., *devolves to* (or occasionally *on*) someone (*the estate had devolved* to *the heir*). The word appears frequently in the form *devolved* to refer to a body or its powers when these have been devolved by a national government (as has happened in the UK in Scotland, Wales, and Northern Ireland): *This is a devolved issue and is the responsibility of the Welsh Assembly Government*—*Times*, 2007. The verb *devolute*, probably back-formed from *devolution* in the 19c., showed tentative signs of life in the late 20c., but has now flatlined.

dexter. See SINISTER.

dexterous. The spelling given preference in the *OED* rather than *dextrous*. However spelt, it is pronounced /ˈdɛkstrəs/, i.e. with the second *e* silent.

diabolic, diabolical. In general, *diabolic* is used with direct reference to attributes of the devil (*Satan . . . merely bent his diabolic brow An instant*—Byron, 1822), while *diabolical* is mainly used in the weakened and colloquial meaning 'bad, disgraceful, awful', describing such things as the weather, road traffic, the performance of a football team, communications, and 'liberties': *Asked our postman about communications between Tunisia and England. He said they were 'diabolical'*—S. Townsend, 1982; *Then, all of sudden, the gendarmes burst in and nabbed the first two blokes they saw who looked like English toffs, which was a diabolical liberty*—*Daily Tel.*, 2004. But during the last four centuries this distinction has been by no means watertight, and the rhythm of the sentence often governs the choice of form. Compare these examples: (diabolic) *Human technology, misused to serve the diabolic purposes of human egoism and wickedness, is a more deadly danger than earthquakes*—Toynbee and Ikeda, 1976; (diabolical) *demonology, the study of devilish phenomena in general and the crime of diabolical witchcraft in particular*—*Canadian Journal of History*, 2001.

diachronic. In linguistics, concerned with the historical development of a language, dialect, etc., as opposed to SYNCHRONIC.

diaeresis (AmE **dieresis**). Plural *diaereses* /-siːz/. Two dots placed over the second of two vowels (as in *naïve, Chloë, Eloïse*), and occasionally in other circumstances (e.g. *Brontë*), to indicate that it is sounded separately. Since the sign is often not on modern keyboards it is often omitted in printed work; and it has also usually been dropped from such familiar words as *aërate, coöperate* (now *aerate, cooperate*). It is, however, still the house style of the *New Yorker*, e.g. *I reëntered the chestnut tunnel*—*New Yorker*, 1987.

diagnose. Properly used to mean 'to make a diagnosis of (a disease, a mechanical fault, etc.)' (*he was able to diagnose the fault at once*), but now often used with a person as object (*a baby who was incorrectly diagnosed as having died before birth, only to be delivered alive, but paralysed, 17 hours later*—T. Stuttaford, 1990).

diagnosis. Plural *diagnoses* /-siːz/.

diagram. The extended and derivative forms have *-mm-* (*diagrammed, diagramming; diagrammatic*), but often *-m-* in American English for the verbal forms. See -M-, -MM-.

dial. In British English usually *dialled, dialling* for the inflected forms, but *-l-* in American English.

dialect is the language form of a region, and varies from the standard language in matters of vocabulary, grammar, and pronunciation. Some dialects are also related to social class and ethnic origin. The words and meanings of many British dialects are recorded in Joseph Wright's *English Dialect*

Dictionary (1896–1905) and in a *Survey of English Dialects* (1962–8), edited by Harold Orton and others. There is a *Linguistic Atlas of England* (1978), edited by Harold Orton and others, and numerous monographs, articles, etc., on or about dialects in general or particular dialects. For the most part dialectal words, meanings, and pronunciations remain in their own geographical area (subject only to the kind of internal linguistic change to which all forms of language are prone), and do not enter the national language. Twentieth-century exceptions to this rule include *elevenses, to give* (someone) *an old-fashioned look, feisty,* and *gobsmacked,* all of which are now part of the standard language; and the colloquial words *cack-handed* and *minger.*

dialectal, dialectic, dialectical (adjectives). Throughout the 19c. all three words were freely used to mean 'belonging to or of the nature of a dialect', but the only one now used in this sense in professional work is *dialectal. Dialectic* and *dialectical* are now confined to the language of logical disputation, and the phrase *dialectical materialism* to a specific theory propagated by Karl Marx and Friedrich Engels.

dialogue. 1 *Dialogue* is not necessarily or 'correctly' the talk of two people, as some usage writers have maintained, misinterpreting its etymology. It is 'conversation as opposed to monologue, to preaching, lecturing, speeches, narrative, or description' (Fowler, 1926). It has nothing to do with Greek δι- 'twice', and is ultimately derived from Greek διάλογος 'conversation' (διά 'through, across'). Cf. DUOLOGUE. In American English, *dialogue* remains the standard spelling with *dialog* as a much less common variant. As a noun, *dialogue* has since the 1960s been something of a vogue word, especially in politics, in the meaning of 'discussion or diplomatic contact between the representatives of two nations, groups, or the like; hence generally, valuable or constructive discussion or communication'. In such contexts it is more or less synonymous with *negotiations* on the one hand and *discussion(s)* on the other. Despite objections from some quarters, it is now well established and useful. When qualified by adjectives such as *constructive, meaningful, real,* etc., it can, however, be tainted by the miasma of cliché.

2 *Dialogue* has a long history as a verb, beginning with Shakespeare (e.g. *Dost Dialogue with thy shadow?,* 1607), but is disliked by some usage writers as part of the present-day hostility in some quarters to verbs believed to have been recently coined from nouns. Example: *The President also rejected reports that the US was having a tough time with China and said the two sides were still dialoguing—Times of India,* 2006.

diamond. Normally three syllables in British English, /'dʌɪəmənd/, but frequently just two, /'dʌɪmənd/, in American English.

diaphanous. See TRANSPARENT.

diarrhoea. So spelt in British English (with *oe* still occasionally printed in the ligatured form œ) but as *diarrhea* in American English.

diastole, in physiology, is pronounced as four syllables, /dʌɪ'astəli/.

dice (noun). In origin (14c.) the plural of *die,* as in *the die is cast,* meaning 'the decision has been taken'). The small cubes with faces bearing 1–6 spots used in games of chance are the *dice* (plural); and one of them is also called a *dice,* e.g. *He had a dice in his pocket.*

dichotomy, a division into two (ultimately from Greek διχοτομία, from διχο- 'asunder' + -τομία used to form abstract nouns from adjectives in -τομος 'cutting', such as *anatomy, lobotomy,* etc.). Since the Greek iota is short, the usual English pronunciation with initial /dʌɪ-/ goes against the etymology, but is nevertheless standard. The word has long-established senses in logic, astronomy, botany, and zoology (essentially 'division into two, bifurcation'), but in the 20c. it came into non-technical use in general contexts to mean a 'division or contrast between two things that are or are represented as being opposed or entirely different' often with implications of contrast and paradox. Examples: *By a dichotomy familiar to us all, a woman requires her own baby to be perfectly normal, and at the same time superior to all other babies*—J. Wyndham, 1957; *The coffee-table featured a couple of Shakespeare texts and a copy of* Time Out—*an intriguing dichotomy, perhaps*—M. Amis, 1973. In most writing *dichotomy* runs the risk of sounding pseudo-academic or pretentious. To avoid that charge, alternatives that could be used include *paradox, contrast, division, split, conflict,* and *dilemma.*

dictate. The noun, usually in the plural (*dictates of conscience*), is stressed on the first syllable, and the verb (*he dictated a letter to his secretary*) on the second. See NOUN AND VERB ACCENT 1.

dictum. Plural *dicta* (rarely *dictums*). See -UM 3.

didn't ought. A remarkable combination of the marginal modal *ought* and the periphrastic negative auxiliary *didn't.* Almost certainly of dialectal origin, it has made its way into novels of the 19c. and 20c. and into informal speech as a typical construction used by rustic or sparsely educated speakers (*I . . . told him he didn't ought to go*—C. M. Yonge, 1854; *And I hope that none here will say I did anything I didn't ought. For I only done my duty*—M. Innes, 1942; *You didn't ought to have let that fire out* (Piggy speaking)—W. Golding, 1954).

die (noun). See DICE.

die (verb). When used with a preposition, the normal constructions are *to die of* a disease, hunger, old age, etc., or *to die from* a wound, inattention, etc., but current usage is somewhat fluid. Numerous examples of each construction and of *to die for* (a cause, object, reason, or purpose), are provided in the *OED.* The informal phrase **to die for**, (or its variant *to die*) meaning '(as if) worth dying for; highly desirable; fabulous, astonishing', originally from American English, is in danger of becoming a cliché. Although it sounds like the gushing, disingenuous hyperbole typical of modern consumer and lifestyle writing, it was first used as long ago as 1898: *Oh! and to 'top off' with, a mince-pie to die for.* Alternatively, it can be viewed more soberly as another example of how English speakers constantly put words such as *awesome, fabulous, marvellous,* etc. into service for their heightened emotional and metaphorical effect, which, paradoxically, diminishes the more the words are used. When used in front of a noun, that is, attributively, *to die for* should be hyphenated: *Excellent Vietnamese fare, including to-die-for softshell crabs—Post* (Denver), 1995.

diesel, named after a German engineer (d. 1913) called R. Diesel, is so spelt.

dietitian. The standard spelling, not *dietician.*

differ. In the sense 'to be unlike or distinguishable', *differ* is almost always followed by *from* (*my interpretation of the passage differs substantially from his*). When it means 'to disagree, to be at variance with' the usual preposition, at least until the end of the 19c., was *with* (*To unite with those who differ with us*—J. H. Newman, 1833; *I differed with him in the conclusion he drew*—J. T. Coleridge, 1869). The second of these is now in relatively restricted use, as *disagree* takes over from it: *Dissanayake . . . had subsequently differed with the President on such issues as the handling of the withdrawal of Indian troops from Sri Lanka—Keesings,* 1990.

different. 1 The commonly expressed view that *different* should only be followed by *from* and never by *to* or *than* is completely untenable in the face of past and present evidence and of logic. Fowler wrote in 1926 that insistence 'that *different* can only be followed by *from* and not by *to* is a superstition'. It is, however, a superstition that refuses to lie down and die. (*a*) *Current use.* The *OED* dates the earliest examples of each construction as *different from* 1590, *different to* 1526, *different than* 1644. In all the varieties of English the *OEC* covers, *different from* is by far the most usual, followed by *different than,* then *different to.* Both British and American English show a marked preference for *different from; different to* is widely used in British and Australian English, and uncommon in American English; *different than* is used frequently in North America but rarely in Britain.

(*b*) *Different from* versus *different to. Different to* is questioned on the premise that we do not say *differ to.* By this argument, all words in the same morphological family should be used with the same prepositions; e.g. we ought to say *according with* (instead of *according to*) because we say *accords with.* Other word families where the preposition changes include *full of* as against *filled with; proud of* as against *pride in.* But in all kinds of circumstances, *different to* is perceived as a perfectly valid alternative, perhaps also influenced by the analogy of *indifferent to,* rather than *indifferent from* or *than,* and by antonyms of *different,* such as *comparable to, equivalent to,* and *similar to.* Examples: (from)

Writing for the web is different from any other kind of writing—*OEC,* 2002 (AmE); *He's no different from my other brother, in the end*—N. Gordimer, 1988 (S.Afr); (to) (rarer in AmE) Road to Perdition *is vastly different to Mendes' engaging debut* American Beauty—*OEC,* 2002 (BrE); *Geoffrey Palmer is a vastly different prime minister to his predecessor*—B. Jesson in *Metro (NZ), 1990.*

(*c*) *Different than.* As previously mentioned, this is a predominantly North American construction, and is often used when *different* affects a subsequent clause: *Farming is different than teaching in that farmers rarely congregate, especially farmers from different countries*—*OEC,* 2004 (AmE); *I was really no different than any other guy in my District*—*OEC,* 2005 (Canad.); (with subsequent clause) *It was an unequal fight, but the outcome was different than one would have expected*—*OEC,* 2002 (AmE); *It was in so many ways entirely different than he could ever have imagined*—Internet website, 2004 (AmE).

There is a strong argument that *different than* is a useful way of avoiding cumbersome wordiness when what follows is a relative clause or a prepositional phrase. Using *different from* in the last sentence above would entail rewriting it as *entirely different from what he could ever have imagined.* To take another example, *the American theatre, which is suffering from a different malaise than ours,* is greatly preferable to *suffering from a different malaise from that which ours is suffering from.* In fact, the use of *different than* here makes it possible to summarize the whole clause *from that which ours is suffering from* in the two words *than ours.* Economy is everything. In the sentence *this year conditions are slightly different than in the past, than* similarly stands in for the verb (*than* they were *in the past*), and has the additional merit of avoiding the unwieldy combination of prepositions that *different from in the past* and *different to in the past* would create. Nevertheless, if you happen to be writing (or speaking) in Britain, and your audience is likely to be irked by *different than,* you may have to resort to wordier formulations or else recast your sentence.

2 *Different* has been informally used since the early 20c. to mean 'out of the ordinary, special', and is used—probably overused—in this way nowadays, despite its being labelled 'colloquial' by the *OED. What a perfectly lovely couch ... Why, it is so beautifully different!*—D. F. Canfield, 1912; *They are always striving to write a piece of copy that will be 'different'*—*Publishers' Weekly,* 1930; *Discover a different holiday combining New Zealand's natural vistas with state-of-the-art accommodation*—*OEC,* 2011.

3 *Different* is commonly found in everyday use as a convenient synonym for more specific words such as *distinct, separate, various,* etc.: *For sociology graduates there are career opportunities in many different areas*—*Edinburgh undergraduate prospectus,* 1993. Though Burchfield decried this use, if the exact meanings of the other words given above are needed, use them; otherwise this application of *different* is useful.

differentia. Plural *differentiae* /-ʃiiː/.

differentiation. **1** See -CIATION, -TIATION.

2 The term was applied by Fowler (1926) principally to pairs of words that at one time or another shared a common meaning in standard English but have now become distinct. For example, among the *OED*'s 18c. quotations for *spiritual* and *spirituous* are these two: *It may not here be improper to take notice of a* wise *and* spiritual *saying of this young prince*—Isaac D'Israeli, 1791–1823; *The Greeks, who are a* spirituous *and* wise *People*—J. Savage, 1703. The linking of each with *wise* indicates that they are interchangeable. In present-day usage they have drawn apart. *Differentiation* has occurred. Similarly, *airship* when first used meant any type of aircraft, whether lighter or heavier than air; later, by differentiation from *aeroplane* (and *airplane*), *airship* became confined to the former kind. *Differentiations* become complete not by authoritative pronouncements or dictionary fiats (as Fowler correctly observed), but by being gradually adopted in speaking and writing. It is the business of a writer of a usage guide to give a clear indication of the stage reached by such *differentiations* in so far as the boundaries and limits can be determined from the available evidence.

Scores of pairs of words that have become partially or fully differentiated are dealt with at their alphabetical places in this book. Judgements are also offered about the rights and wrongs of the attitudes of writers and of members of the general public where controversial areas exist. For example: (fully differentiated in standard English but sometimes confused) *affect/effect, defuse/diffuse, deprecate/depreciate, fortuitous/fortunate, imply/infer, masterful/masterly, prevaricate/procrastinate, refute/deny*; (partially differentiated, with a residual band of overlapping meaning) *administer/administrate, admission/admittance, continual/continuous, mutual/common.*

differently. Normally followed by *from* (*Do percussionists understand music differently from the rest of us?—OEC,* 2005), but, like *different,* also often used with *to* or *than,* e.g. *Children tend to react differently than adults—OEC,* 2002; *Perhaps our minds work differently to the physical world around us*—G. Hartnell, 2004.

differently abled. See ABLE-BODIED, ABLED.

diffuse. See DEFUSE.

diffusible. So spelt, not *-able.* See -ABLE, -IBLE 7.

dig. Of French origin in the 14c., it was conjugated as a weak verb (with *digged* as past tense and past participle) for some three centuries (*all the wels which his fathers seruants had digged in the dayes of Abraham*—Gen. (AV) 26:15; *Also he built towers in the desert, and digged many welles*—2 Chr. (AV) 26:10). Beginning in the 16c. it acquired a past tense *dug* and in the 18c. the same form began to be used for the past participle. The later forms are, of course, now invariable.

digest. The noun is pronounced /ˈdʌɪdʒɛst/, with the stress on the first syllable (*Reader's Digest*), and the verb /dʌɪˈdʒɛst/, /dɪ-/, with the stress on the second. See NOUN AND VERB ACCENT 1.

digraph. Any combination of two letters used to represent a single speech sound, e.g. *dg* in *judge* /dʒʌdʒ/, *gh* in *tough* /tʌf/, *ng* in *long* /lɒŋ/, *ea* in *head* /hɛd/, *ee* in *fleet* /fliːt/, etc. The term is also sometimes applied to ligatures like *æ* as in *æsthetics* (if so printed) and *œ* as in *œuvre.*

dike. See DYKE.

dilapidated. Occasionally thought to be correctly applied only to a *stone* structure that has fallen into disrepair, because its stem relates ultimately to Latin *lapis, lapidem* 'stone'. But even in Latin the verb *dīlapidāre* was used in extended figurative senses apart from the literal sense 'to bring (an edifice) into a state of partial ruin'.

dilatation, etc. This (first recorded *c.*1400) and *dilatator* (1611) are the etymologically correct forms, since the medial element (as also in the verb *dilate*) answers to the Latin *dīlātāre,* from the adjective *lātus* 'broad, wide'. But the shorter unetymological forms *dilation* (1598) and *dilator* (1605) also came into use at an early stage under the influence of patterns like *calculate ~ calculation* (in which *-late* simply represents the Latin first-conjugation past participle termination *-ātum*). In surgery the forms *dilatation* and *dilator* are standard. In lay use (except when the reference is to an operation on a woman's cervix) the dominant forms are *dilation* and *dilator.*

dilatory. Pronounced /ˈdɪlətərɪ/. It should be noted that it is not formed like the words in the preceding entry, but is from Latin *dīlātum,* past participle of *differre* 'to defer, delay'.

dilemma. 1 The traditional pronunciation /dɪˈlɛmə/, with short *i* echoing the short iota in Greek δίλημμα, is now probably less common than initial /dʌɪ-/.

2 The word is correctly used to mean 'a choice between two alternatives both of which are undesirable' (*They were in the dilemma of either violating the Constitution or losing a golden opportunity*). It is widely, but loosely, used to mean simply 'a problem, a difficult choice' (*What to do with one's spare time is a modern dilemma*). See POPULARIZED TECHNICAL TERMS. *Historical note.* The term was first used in the 16c. in rhetoric (and so in logic) to mean 'a form of argument involving an adversary in the choice of two (or, *loosely,* more) alternatives, either of which is (or appears) equally unfavourable to him' (*OED*). The alternatives are commonly spoken of as *the horns of a dilemma,* either of which would impale him.

There are many contexts in the past and at the present time when the line between the strict use and the 'loose' one is very fine, and even non-existent. But when words like *problem* or *difficult choice* fit neatly into such contexts they should be used in preference to 'dilemma'. A range of representative examples: *She was in the dilemma of those who must combine dignity with a bad cold*—M. Innes, 1942; *The dilemma is logically insoluble: we cannot sacrifice either freedom or the organization needed for its defence*—I. Berlin, 1949; *He was caught in a dilemma, a choice between doing a show or going on a much-needed vacation*—D. Halberstam, 1979; *Three corridors: one to the left, one ahead, one to the right ... 'Dilemma. Left, right or centre?'*—D. Bogarde, 1980.

dilettante. Usually pronounced /ˌdɪlɪˈtantɪ/ (di-li-**tan**-ti). Plural either *dilettanti* (pronounced the same as the singular) or *dilettantes.*

dim. For *dim religious light,* see IRRELEVANT ALLUSION.

diminuendo. Plural *diminuendos* (see -O(E)S 4) or *diminuendi* (as in Italian).

dinghy. The pronunciations /ˈdɪŋɪ/ and /ˈdɪŋgɪ/ are both in common use.

dingo (wild Australian dog). Plural *dingoes* or less commonly *dingos.* See -O(E)S 2.

dint. See DENT, DINT.

diocese. Pronounced /ˈdʌɪəsɪs/. Plural *dioceses* /ˈdʌɪəsiːz/ or /ˈdʌɪəsɪsɪz/. The spelling *diocess* was customary from the 16c. to the end of the 18c. and was the only form recognized by Dr Johnson and other 18c. lexicographers. See SEE.

diphtheria. Normally pronounced /dɪfˈθɪərɪə/, irregularly /dɪp-/.

diphthong. Pronounced /ˈdɪfθɒŋ/. The pronunciation with initial /ˈdɪp-/ is highly irregular. The word is properly applied only to a speech sound (very frequent in English) in one syllable in which the articulation begins as for one vowel and moves as for another (as in *coin, loud, fire, sure,* etc.). In professional work it should not be confused with DIGRAPH or LIGATURE.

diploma. The plural is now always *diplomas.* Until the late 19c. the plural form *diplomata* (= state papers) was also used.

diplomat, diplomatist. Both words entered the language at the beginning of the 19c. *Diplomat* is now the more usual of the two, but the reverse was the case throughout the 19c.

direct, directly. Both have been used as adverbs for several centuries (*direct* first recorded *c.*1450, *directly c.*1400), but now *directly* is much the more common. *Direct* is usual when it means 'straight in direction or aspect, without deviation' (*Air NZ flights go direct from Heathrow to Los Angeles; the property is held direct from the Crown; purchasable only from the central office direct*); or 'without intermediaries' (*he appealed over the head of his line manager direct to the chief executive*). The natural form in most of the senses of the adverb is *directly* (*the beginning of a development which was to lead directly to some of his finest war poems; the wind is blowing directly on shore; directly opposite;* (= immediately) *Directly after this, he was taken away.* Only *directly,* not *direct,* can occur immediately before an adjective (*directly responsible for the accident*). In informal contexts *directly* is used as a conjunction = 'as soon as, the moment after' (*Iodine and phosphorus combine directly they come in contact*). In this use *directly* is elliptical for *directly that/as/when.* In dialectal use and in America *directly* has also been used since about the mid-19c. to mean 'shortly, very soon' (*I'll come directly*). It is important to avoid ambiguity in the use of the two words: in *he went direct to Paris* the sense is 'without deviation'; but in *he went directly to Paris* the sense is 'immediately'.

direct object. a noun phrase or noun clause denoting a person or thing that is the recipient of the action of a transitive verb, for example *the dog* in *Jimmy fed the dog.* See also INDIRECT OBJECT.

dirigible. As noun and adjective spelt with *-ible.*

dis-. As a living prefix, it continues to form nouns, adjectives, adverbs, and verbs, expressing negation, indicating the reversal or absence of an action or state, etc. Twentieth-century accessions to the language in *dis-* include *disambiguate* (verb, 1963), *diseconomy* (1937), *disempowerment* (1971), *disincentive* (1946), *disinvestment* (1938), *dispersant* (1944), *disquietingly* (1901). Cf. DE-.

disability, the language of. The language now generally considered suitable to describe and refer to people with different kinds of physical or mental disabilities is very different from what it was only a couple of decades ago. The changes are due partly to the activity of organizations which promote the interests of particular groups with disabilities, and partly to increased public sensitivity to language that might perpetuate stereotypes and prejudices, a sensitivity honed by the phenomenal popularity of the 2012 Paralympic Games in London. Just as most people of goodwill studiously avoid previously established sexist or racist uses of language, so they are more sensitive to the appropriate way in which to talk about people with disabilities.

If you want to use appropriate language, you need not only to avoid words which have been or are being superseded, such as *mongolism* or *backward*, and which are listed below with their more neutral equivalents. You should also try to:

1 avoid using *the* + an adjective to refer to the whole group, as in *the blind, the deaf* and so forth. The reasoning behind this is twofold: that the humanity of people with a disability should not be circumscribed by the disability itself ('the disability is not the person'); and that talking about people with a given disability as a group diminishes their individuality. The preferred formulation these days is 'a person with . . . ' or 'people with . . . ' as in *people with sight problems, people with asthma,* or *people with disabilities.*

2 avoid using words such as *victim, suffer from,* and *wheelchair-bound* which suggest that the person concerned is the helpless object of the disability. Suitable alternatives to *suffer from* are *have, experience,* and *be diagnosed with.* Instead of talking about *victims* you can talk about people who have a particular disability; and instead of *wheelchair-bound* you can say *who use(s) a wheelchair.*

3 eschew words which once related to disabilities and which have now become colloquial, especially as insults, such as *mongoloid, mong, spastic, psycho, schizo,* and so forth.

4 Some of the terms below are better established than others, and some groups with disabilities favour specific words over others. These lists are offered only as a general guide.

Older term	*Neutral term*
able-bodied	non-disabled
asthmatic (noun)	person with asthma
backward	having learning difficulties, having a learning disability
blind	partially sighted, visually impaired
cripple	person with a disability, person with mobility problems
deaf aid	hearing aid
deaf and dumb	profoundly deaf, deaf without speech
deaf mute	profoundly deaf, deaf without speech
diabetic (noun)	person with diabetes
disabled	having a disability
handicapped	having a disability
harelip	cleft lip
to help	to support
invalid	person with a disability
mongol	person with Down's syndrome
spastic	person with cerebral palsy
stone deaf	profoundly deaf

disabled. The word *disabled* came to be used as the standard term to refer to people with physical or mental disabilities from the 1960s onwards, and it remains the most generally accepted term in both British and US English today. It superseded words that are, to a greater or lesser degree, offensive, such as *crippled, defective,* and *handicapped,* and has not yet been overtaken itself by newer coinages such as *differently abled* or *physically challenged.* Although the usage is very widespread, some people regard using the adjective as a plural noun (as in *the needs of the disabled*) as dehumanizing because it tends to treat people with disabilities as an undifferentiated group, defined merely by their capabilities. To avoid offence, a more acceptable term would be 'people with disabilities'.

disassemble, first recorded in 1621, is the standard modern word for 'to take to pieces, to take apart' applied especially to machinery that is being dismantled such as rifles, aircraft, or computers. To *dissemble,* used intransitively, means 'to conceal or disguise one's true feelings or beliefs (*an honest, sincere person with no need to dissemble*); transitively it means 'to disguise or conceal (a feeling or intention)' (*she smiled, dissembling her true emotion*). Historically, there was a homonymous verb *dissemble,* meaning the opposite of *assemble,* but it is effectively obsolete. However, very occasionally *dissemble* is used to mean 'to take apart', and in such a use is likely to be regarded as wrong: *?Every night for the past three months, they have dissembled the furniture—www.BookRags.com,* 2002.

Conversely, *disassemble* is also occasionally used wrongly for *dissemble* in the latter's meaning of 'to disguise one's true feelings'. It was one of President George W. Bush's famous 'Bushisms': *people who were held in detention, people who hate America, people that had been trained in some instances to disassemble—that means not tell the truth—* In a speech of 31 May, 2005.

disassociate. Some usage writers have condemned this variant (first recorded in 1603) of DISSOCIATE. Their strictures are unnecessary, since the *OEC* evidence suggests that writers tend to prefer the shorter form in any case. But in some contexts the longer form may conceivably be more emphatic as the opposite of *associate,* or simply fit the rhythm of the sentence better: Examples: *The Foreign Office at once issued a statement disassociating the Government from the idea—Spectator,* 1988; *M. Sarkozy has gone to great pains to disassociate himself from both M. Chirac's record and his style of government—Independent,* 2007.

disastrous. Be careful not to introduce a fourth syllable: it is not dis-ast-*er*-ous.

disbar. See DEBAR.

disc. *OED* (1896) gave *disk* as 'the earlier and better spelling' but in the second edition (1989) declared that '*disc* is now the more usual form in British English'. In the 20c. there has indeed been a marked preference for *disc* in Britain but for *disk* in America. The division has been lessened by the almost universal spelling of the computer storage device as *disk* (*magnetic disk, disk drive, floppy disk,* etc.). For the time being, however, *disc brake, the sun's disc, compact disc, disc harrow, disc jockey,* etc., remain the standard forms in BrE. For most of these *disk* is the more usual form in AmE.

discernible. The preferred spelling, not *-able.* See -ABLE, -IBLE 7.

***dischord.** Is an incorrect spelling of *discord,* presumably influenced by the spelling of *chord,* and possibly by the existence of a record label spelt with the intrusive, unetymological *h.*

disciplinary. Pronounced /ˈdɪsɪplɪnəri/ or /dɪsɪˈplɪnəri/, i.e. stressing the first or third syllable. The pronunciation with the stressed third syllable rhyming with *fine,* once occasionally heard, now seems to have vanished.

discomfit. Once (from the 13c. onwards) mainly used in the primary sense 'to undo in battle' and 'to defeat or overthrow the plans or purpose of', *discomfit* is now mainly used in the weakened sense 'to disconcert'. It is also often qualified by *rather* (*Bell, conscious of past backslidings, seemed rather discomfited*—William Black, 1872). In this weakened sense it comes close to the etymologically unrelated verb *to discomfort* 'to make uneasy', and in the normal flow of speech it is not always possible—for speaker or hearer—to distinguish them. Examples: (discomfit) *He seemed flustered, discomfited, and this amused me*—W. Styron, 1966; *I should have corrected her, but, discomfited, missed the right moment*—A. Lurie, 1969; (discomfort) *His Section's Mediterranean operations, where his cheerful courage discomforted the Germans and Italians, are dealt with in later chapters*—J. Ladd, 1979; *The show, entitled 'Banality', was eerie, discomforting, and seemed to offend nearly everyone—The Face,* 1990.

disconnection. The standard spelling, not *disconnexion.*

discontent. From Shakespeare's famous lines *Now is the winter of our discontent, Made glorious summer by this sonne of Yorke* (Richard III I.i.1) has been drawn the modern political cliché *a winter of discontent,* first used with reference to industrial unrest in Britain in 1978–9, and recycled in journalese whenever it fits events.

discord. The noun is stressed on the first syllable and the verb on the second. See NOUN AND VERB ACCENT 1.

discotheque. Adopted from French *discothèque* (where it was coined on the model of Fr. *bibliothèque* 'library'), it could have come to mean in English as in French 'a record library, a library of discs'. Instead (first recorded in 1954) we adopted its second French sense, 'a club, party, etc., where (loud) music is played for dancing'. It is, of course, far less common than its truncated form, *disco,* which is rather dated.

discount. The noun is stressed on the first syllable and the verb on the second. See NOUN AND VERB ACCENT 1.

discourse. The noun is stressed on the first syllable and the verb on the second. See NOUN AND VERB ACCENT 1.

discourse analysis. A modern term (first recorded in 1952) for the linguistic analysis of stretches of language with the aim of disentangling the unspoken rituals, strategies, and implications built (unconsciously) into them and the inferences to be drawn from them. A standard textbook on the subject is by Gillian Brown and George Yule (1983).

discreet, discrete. The two words are pronounced the same, and are etymologically 'the same word', i.e. are doublets (Middle English from Latin *discrētus,* past participle of *discernere* 'sift'), but differ widely in meaning. *Discreet* means 'careful and prudent in one's speech or actions, especially in order to keep something confidential or to avoid embarrassment; unobtrusive', e.g. *a discreet touch of rouge. Discrete* means 'individually distinct, separate', e.g. *a telescope powerful enough to resolve galaxies into discrete stars.* The two words should not be confused, as they are in **For practical and cultural reasons, the mortuary facility is located at the far western end of the new wing, where access can be more discrete—OEC,* 2002.

discriminating, discriminative, discriminatory. 1 The first and last call on different meanings of the verb *discriminate.* The verb can mean 'to distinguish, differentiate', particularly the good from the bad in artistic and aesthetic matters, and that meaning is echoed in phrases such as *discriminating tastes, palate, consumer, reader, eye,* etc. Its synonym in this sense is *discerning. Discriminatory* relates to the other meaning of the verb, to the act of discriminating against someone on grounds such as age, race, sex, etc. The two words do not generally overlap, but occasionally *discriminating* is used instead of *discriminatory.* Examples: *luxury marketers are no longer guaranteed that the prestige of their brand will resonate with today's increasingly discriminating and cautious affluent shopper—Art Business News,* 2003; *Highly restrictive and discriminatory legislation in the UK prevented them* [*sc.* female domestic workers] *from leaving abusive employers and seeking new jobs—OEC* (undated); *?Many racially discriminating practices have been researched in education, involving both students (e.g., name-calling) and teachers (e.g., singling children out)—Behavior and Social Issues,* 2005.

2 *Discriminative* is a much less common adjective than the other two. It is occasionally used to refer to behaviour that discriminates undesirably, e.g. *An anti-terrorism bill is due in parliament, but most members of parliament have spoken against it, saying it was discriminative against Muslims—News 24,* 2004. Using it in this way is an unusual choice, since it is mostly used in technical contexts (i) to mean 'able or serving to distinguish', e.g. *perceptual discriminative capacities can be refined or enhanced with training or experience, and can deteriorate with age or disease—Knowledge: Readings in Contemporary Epistemology,* 2000; and (ii) in the compound *discriminative stimulus* in psychology, i.e. a stimulus whose presence reinforces a given behaviour. Occasionally the word is also used instead of *discriminating,* a use which goes back to the 17c. but now sounds a little curious: *?the reader is encouraged to be discriminative and to select materials most relevant to their presentation—OEC* (undated).

discus. Plural *discuses,* not *disci.* See -US 1.

discuss. Anyone reading 19c. fiction should be alert to the use of *discuss,* when used in the context of an item of food or drink, to mean 'to try the quality of, to consume' (*A tall, stout, country-looking man ... busily discussing huge slices of cold boiled beef*—Scott, 1815; *Turner was always to be seen between ten and eleven at the Athenæum, discussing his half-pint of sherry*—G. W. Thornbury, 1861).

discussible. So spelt. See -ABLE, -IBLE 4.

disenfranchise, disfranchise. Both verbs have been in the language for several centuries. At present *disenfranchise* is about ten times more common than *disfranchise.*

Both verbs end in *-ise* not *-ize.* See -ISE 1.

disgruntled has settled into restricted use as an adjective—the older use of *disgruntle* as a finite verb belongs to the past—but it has brought into being in the 20c. the pleasing occasional back-formation *gruntled* (*I could see that, if not actually disgruntled, he was far from being gruntled*—P. G. Wodehouse, 1938) meaning 'pleasing, satisfied, contented'.

disguise. Always so spelt, never *-ize*. See -ISE 1.

dishabille. See DÉSHABILLÉ.

dishevelled (AmE **disheveled**). Pronounced /dɪˈʃɛv(ə)ld/, i.e. with the first syllable rhyming with *dish*, not /dɪsˈhɛv(ə)ld/, i.e. not dis-**he**-veld. It is also one of that delightfully quirky group of words containing negative prefixes that have no opposites: there is no *hevelled*, just as there is no *kempt*. See also DISGRUNTLED.

disinformation, first recorded in 1939 (applied to a German 'Disinformation Service'), is a keyword in modern political vocabulary. At the height of the Cold War (1945–89) the dissemination of concocted false information was one of the most potent and dangerous weapons of governments, and especially of the various intelligence groups, the CIA, the KGB, MI6, etc.

disinterest. This noun has or has had three branches of meaning: **1** that which is contrary to interest or advantage, something against the interest of or disadvantageous to (a person or thing) (recorded from 1662 onwards, but now rare or obsolete): e.g. *All gain, increase, interest ... to the lender of capital, is loss, decrease, and disinterest to the borrower of capital*— Ruskin, 1876.

2 Impartiality (recorded from 1658 onwards and still current, but not in common use): e.g. *We here see Morris working, with entire disinterest, at his work, and caring above all things for fine workmanship—Sat. Rev.,* 1896.

3 Absence of interest, unconcern (recorded from 1889 onwards). The word is most commonly used in this meaning, despite the controversy inspired by the corresponding meaning of **disinterested**. Should you wish to steer clear of this particular usage reef, you could use *lack of interest* instead. Examples: *He misread my quietude ... as either agreement or disagreement. It was neither. Pure, unadulterated disinterest*—C. Achebe, 1987; *Despite British radio's disinterest in new music, and the reduced influence of the music press, I believe real talent will eventually get through*—N. York, 1991.

4 It is worth noting that the notion of impartiality is more often conveyed by the word *disinterestedness* than it is by *disinterest*. Sense 3 is sometimes expressed by the word *uninterest*, but this word has telltale signs of being an example of 'error-avoidance', used because of the controversial nature of *disinterest* 3.

The best course is to avoid using the noun *disinterest* altogether until it has reached safer shores. See UNINTEREST.

disinterested. Not recognized as a problem by Fowler (1926), the use of *disinterested* to mean 'uninterested' had become a matter of fierce controversy by the 1970s and 1980s. In *The Spoken Word* (1981) Burchfield reported that the use 'attracts more unfavourable comment from [BBC] listeners than any other word ... with the possible exception of *hopefully*'. The problem was neatly pointed up by the actor Julian Glover about his mother: *She's also a word pedant, and I hate having inherited this from her. She corrects me firmly about 'disinterested' and 'uninterested'—common but good examples. It's maddening, drives people bananas—Sunday Times Mag.,* 1990.

The word can be approached in three ways: **1** *Etymology.* The prefix *dis-* has a primary function of expressing negation. On these grounds *dis-interested* would in a literal sense mean 'not interested, uninterested'. But *interested* can mean either 'having an interest in, being curious about' (*he was interested in philately*) or 'not impartial' (*an interested party*). As a result, *disinterested* can therefore mean 'not having an interest in' or 'not not impartial, i.e. impartial'. The etymological approach is too fundamental to be helpful.

2 *Historical usage.* In the 17c. and 18c., from Donne to the Junius Letters (1767), *disinterested* meant 'not interested, unconcerned'. This sense then went into abeyance until it was revived in the 20c. (*Oxford, after three successive defeats, are almost entirely disinterested in the Boat Race—Daily Tel.,* 1970). Meanwhile in its second sense, 'impartial, free from self-seeking', *disinterested* has been in unbroken use since 1659. The sense 'impartial' can therefore be said to have had a longer period of continuous use.

3 *Current usage.* (*a*) Without doubt the sense 'uninterested, not interested' is making a strong challenge at the present time. People with an interest in the matter are divided into those who believe that a genuine and useful distinction (*disinterested* = impartial/*uninterested* = not interested) is being eroded, and others who, for whatever reason, have simply not heard the word being used to mean 'impartial', and just regard it as a routine antonym of *interested.*

(*b*) A listing of examples underlines the current strong presence of both meanings (= impartial, unbiased) *His disinterested, scholarly attitude*—K. M. Elisabeth Murray, 1977; *A disinterested approach to the literature of the past can liberate us from being dominated by the anxieties, problems, and even more by the clichés of today*—H. Gardner, 1981; *Many competent and disinterested experts on world poverty often stress the sterility of the East-West confrontation*—*Encounter*, 1981; *a tenacity and sheer steadfastness which must compel admiration ... from the disinterested observer. But of course none of the observers of twelfth-century England was disinterested*—Antonia Fraser, 1988. (= not interested) *'Peanuts, lollies and chocolates,' he muttered in a supremely disinterested voice*—M. Pople, 1986 (Aust.); *A young girl* [*sc.* a nurse, summoned by a patient] *in a green smock came at a disinterested pace*—*New Yorker*, 1987; *Washington ensured that he would appear to be what in fact he was, a republican gentleman disinterested in power*—*TLS*, 1988; *she remains stubbornly neat and unadorned, disinterested in fashion*—Susan Johnson, 1990 (Aust.).

(*c*) The varied pattern of meanings shown in other words in the same family is also bound to have had an effect on the distribution of the conflicting meanings of *disinterested*: thus *disinterestedly* (i) impartially 1711–, (ii) without interest or concern 1941– (e.g. *Instead, she gazes disinterestedly and unblinkingly at her fawning inquisitor and removes a ring from her finger which she toys with absently*—*Q*, 1991); *disinterestedness* = impartiality *a*1682–. In these the 'impartial' sense has the edge.

4 *What does corpus data suggest?* First, the *OEC* and *COCA* show that *disinterested* as a word form is somewhat more frequent than *uninterested* (ratios of 7:5 and 7:6 respectively). But the question is, of those occurrences of the *dis-* form, how many mean 'not interested'? The analysis of *OEC* data I carried out for my book *Damp Squid: the English language laid bare* (2008) suggested that figure was 50 per cent; 40 per cent meant 'impartial' and 10 per cent were ambiguous. Since only half the examples of *disinterested* mean 'not interested', from the ratios given above it follows that to convey that meaning people still use *uninterested* more often than *disinterested.*

5 *Recommendation.* It is clear that semantic change is well under way with this word. There is no reason whatsoever why it should be prevented from having two different meanings; most words do, and its two meanings rarely lead to confusion. However, given the strength of feeling on this issue in many quarters, it is advisable to restrict *disinterested* to its meaning of 'impartial' in any writing that is not informal, or that is likely to be edited or reviewed. There are plenty of other words to hand, such as *indifferent, bored, unconcerned, apathetic,* etc., not to mention *uninterested* itself, which has been in regular use since at least 1772 (*OED*). Examples: *I wouldn't say that—he was totally uninterested in both of us*—G. Greene, 1980; *To viewers who are uninterested in politics, it was worse than the World Cup*—*Observer*, 1990.

disjunctive. In grammar, applied especially to a conjunction (e.g. *but, nor, or*) expressing a choice between two or more words, as *but* in *he is poor but happy,* and *or* in *she asked if he was going or staying,* as against one which has an additive function (e.g. *and*). The distinction is of some importance in determining the number of verbs after compound subjects: (disjunctive) *Neither the binary* nor *the synthetic approach* is *particularly satisfactory;* (copular) *Patience* and *humour* were *Bacon's best weapons.* Cf. COPULAR.

disk. See DISC.

dislike (verb). Constructions with a direct object (*he disliked Picasso's works*) and with a following gerund (*she disliked being absent at any time*) are normal. Occasional examples of a construction with a *to*-infinitive are non-standard: **She was hounded by a fear of imminent poverty that made her dislike to spend any money at all*—B. Guest, 1985; **My irritation is I greatly dislike to see gross ignorance being expressed by purported academics*—*OEC*, 2005.

dislodgement. The preferred spelling in the *OED*, not *dislodgment*, even though the second spelling appears to be commoner.

dismissible. So spelt (*a dismissible offence*). See -ABLE, -IBLE 7.

disorient, disorientate. Both verbs have a long history (*disorient* first recorded in 1655, *disorientate* in 1704) and both are still in use (corresponding to the noun **disorientation**). In most contexts *disorient*, being shorter, is the better form, and it is about three times as frequent in the *OEC* data. Curiously, to judge by the same data, British English shows a marked preference for *disorientate*. As a result, *disorient* may be viewed by some BrE speakers as a pernicious Americanism; conversely, many AmE editors detest the longer form.

dispatch. This is the older form, and the etymologically more correct one. *Despatch* is, in fact, a variant introduced by Dr Johnson in his dictionary of 1755, probably in error, since he always used the form with *-i* in his writing. Either form is correct in modern usage.

dispel means to drive away in different directions, to disperse, and is used literally (*dispel clouds, fog*, etc.) and with generalized abstract nouns (*dispel fear, notions, suspicions*, etc.). It is not idiomatically used with an indivisible entity as object (*dispel an accusation, a rumour*, etc.); other verbs (*rebut, refute*, etc.) are available for such contexts.

dispensable. So spelt. See -ABLE, -IBLE 7.

dispenser. So spelt, not *-or*. See -OR.

disposable. So spelt. See -ABLE, -IBLE 7.

disposal, disposition. In some contexts there is no choice: *His disposition* (= temperament, natural tendency) *is merciful; the disposal* (= the getting rid of) *of the empty bottles is a problem*. The phrase *at one's disposal* no longer freely alternates with *at one's disposition* (as it did from the 17c. to the early 20c.). In most other contexts the choice depends upon the meaning required. If you are in doubt, it is worth remembering that *disposition* usually corresponds to *dispose*, and *disposal* to *dispose of*. So *the disposition of the books is excellent* (they are excellently disposed, i.e. arranged), but *the disposal of the books was soon managed* (they were soon disposed of, i.e. either sold or got out of the way); *the disposition of the shoulders reflected his parade-ground training* (the shoulders were disposed in a military manner), but *the disposal of the body proved impossible* (it could not be disposed of, i.e. buried or concealed).

disproven alternates as a minority variant of *disproved* as past participle, especially in American English, whereas until about the end of the 19c. it was as common. Its continued existence may be influenced by the wide currency in certain circumstances of *proven* beside *proved*. Example: *Gen. Webster's remarks were disproven in gruesome fashion*—*OEC*, 2005 (AmE). See PROVED, PROVEN.

disputable. Stressed either on the first or the second syllable. Second-syllable stressing now seems to be the more usual of the two.

dispute. Both the verb and the noun are stressed on the second syllable. In the 1970s and 1980s, first-syllable stressing of the noun came into prominence in the language of British northern trade-union leaders, but this practice has not established itself in standard English.

dissect is often mistakenly used instead of *bisect*, as when an acquaintance told me that had crossed Wales on roads that 'dissected it'. *Dissect* means 'to cut into pieces', not 'to cut into two', since it is formed on the prefix *dis-*, not *di-*. The first syllable should therefore be pronounced /dɪs-/, i.e. di-**sekt**, not diy-**sekt**, although the second is often heard, probably under the influence of *bisect*.

dissemble. See DISASSEMBLE.

dissimilar. Followed by *to*, less frequently with *from*: (to) *the picture was dissimilar to all the others hanging in the gallery; He underwent a revelation not dissimilar to St Paul's on the road to Damascus*—Godfrey Smith, 1984; (from) *an entirely new style of coinage not dissimilar from the Roman*.

dissimilation. In phonetics, 'the influence exercised by one sound segment upon the articulation of another, so that the sounds become less alike, or different' (Crystal, 1980). In the nature of things this phenomenon is usually observable only after it has happened. It accounts for such words as *pilgrim* (from Latin *peregrīnum* 'one who comes from foreign parts', which in the Romance languages became, by dissimilation of *r* ... *r*, *pelegrin(o)*, whence French *pélerin*); and German *Kartoffel* 'potato', earlier *tartoffel*, where the initial *k* replaced *t* in the 17c. under the influence of the following *t*. Cf. ASSIMILATION; FEBRUARY.

dissociate. First recorded in 1623, slightly later than its variant *disassociate*, it is now the more often used form. Examples: *I was feeling so bad, my self-esteem was squashed like a flea. When I feel like that I completely dissociate from the world. I cannot speak to people*—*OEC*, 2009; *He is at pains to dissociate Reagan's party from the one he helped steer to victory in* 1968—*NY Rev. Bks*, 1990.

dissociation. See -CIATION.

dissoluble, dissolvable. 1 Pronounced /dɪˈsɒljʊbəl/, /dɪˈzɒlvəbəl/.

2 *Dissoluble* is the general word meaning 'capable of being separated into elements or atoms, decomposable'. *Dissolvable* is mainly reserved for contexts in which it means 'make a solution of in a liquid' (*sugar is dissolvable* or *dissoluble in water*), though it also occurs in other senses (*a Chamber dissolvable* or *dissoluble at the Minister's will*). See -ABLE, -IBLE 5.

dissolve. Pronounced /dɪˈzɒlv/.

dissyllable. See DISYLLABLE.

distaff. Originally a cleft stick on which wool or flax was wound in the process of spinning, the word *distaff* came to be used (from the 14c. onwards) as a type of women's work or occupation, and hence, symbolically, for the female sex and the female branch (or line) of a family. Nowadays, the phrase *female line* is preferred in the field of genealogy. Although as late as 1996 Burchfield could write 'it is not unusual to hear the term *distaff side* used by gentlemen in after-dinner speeches or the like', times have changed, even in gentlemen's clubs, and anyone using the phrase in an after-dinner speech today would probably—and justifiably—be pilloried as a chauvinist fossil. Nevertheless, the *OEC* suggests that the phrase lingers on as a rather precious figure of speech, beloved of journalists in search of elegant variation. Example: *It was Ladies Day at Musselburgh yesterday and the distaff side were in the majority at the course*—*Scotland on Sunday*, 2006.

distendible, distensible. For the sense 'capable of being distended', only *distensible* is now in current use. *Distendible* became obsolete in the 18c.

distich. In prosody, a pair of verse lines, a couplet. Pronounced /ˈdɪstɪk/.

distil. After much fluctuation since the word was first recorded in the late 14c., it has now settled down in British English as *distil*, and in American English mostly as *distill*. The conjugated forms in both countries are *distilled, distilling*. See -LL-, -L-.

distinct, distinctive. *Distinct* normally means 'separate, different, not identical' (*the word has several distinct meanings*) and is often construed with *from* (*holiness is quite distinct from goodness*). It also has a range of related senses, e.g. 'unmistakable, decided' (*she had a distinct impression of being watched*). By contrast, *distinctive* means 'distinguishing, characteristic' (*wearing a distinctive dress; the distinctive role of Anglo-Saxon bards*). Fowler (1926) noted that the two words were 'often misused', and the *OEC* data suggests that the two are still occasionally confused. Examples: (distinct) *VW has proven its ability to do product development on the core platforms and keep its various brands distinct*—*Automotive Industries*, 2001; *Global financial traders are now contemplating the distinct possibility that Japan's reflation may be taking hold*—*OEC*, 2003; (distinctive) *Everyone who knew the Temple School will remember the distinctive smell of Freddie's office*—P. Fitzgerald, 1982; *Mark's voice was distinctive, booming and confident*—*OEC*, 2002; *The distinctive feature of his work is, however, a consuming obsession with language*—*Comparative Literature*, 2002; (distinctive instead of distinct) *?BBC Online should be clearly distinctive from commercial offerings*—weblog, 2004; *?Latinos, or Hispanic Americans, constitute the second-largest and most rapidly growing distinctive ethnic group in the United States*—*OEC*, 2001.

distinctly followed immediately by an adjective or adjectival phrase as in *distinctly interesting* was apparently a vogue word between the 1890s and the publication of *Modern English Usage* in 1926. The *OED* cites an American source of 1893: *Now the favourite slang word of literature is 'distinctly'. Heroines are now 'distinctly regal' in their bearing, and there is about the heroes a manner that is 'distinctly fine'.* Fowler was scornful: '*Distinctly,* in the sense *really quite,* is the badge of the superior person indulgently recognizing unexpected merit in something that we are to understand is not quite worthy of his notice: *The effect as the procession careers through the streets of Berlin is described as distinctly interesting.*' Fowler had a point, and he would probably find confirmation of his opinion in more recent use, which often coyly distances the user from what is being said: *That night the singing was distinctly husky and out of tune*—J. B. Morton, 1974; *Religious references ... to the Virgin Mary behaving in a way that is distinctly vampirish have been glossed over*—N. Tucker, 1981; *Young has distinctly craggy features—Glasgow Herald,* 2007.

distract. See DETRACT, DISTRACT.

distrait. This adjective, pronounced in a quasi-French manner as /dɪˈstreɪ/, is used of persons of either sex and of things anywhere along the band of meaning 'not paying attention, absent-minded' to 'distraught'. It entered the language in the 14c. (when it meant 'excessively perplexed or troubled') but it has always resisted Anglicization, even to the extent that when used of females it sometimes retains its French form *distraite* (with the second *t* fully pronounced). Examples: *Mrs Arbuthnot's distrait expression made her look, as Miss Fisher said, quite above the world, but people did as she liked*—E. Bowen, 1935; *He was usually distrait, in pursuit of one of his creative dreams*—R. Church, 1955; *Did he feel pointless, feeble and distrait, Unwanted by everyone and in the way?*—Stevie Smith, 1975.

distribute. The main stress falls on the second syllable, though first-syllable stressing is now increasingly heard in the speech of otherwise standard speakers.

distributive. In grammar means 'referring to each individual of a number or class': **1** Distributive adjectives and pronouns are words such as *each, every, either, neither.* They normally govern a singular verb, e.g. *Each plant, each year and each habitat* is *slightly different and programmed controls will not address these differences—OEC,* 2004.

2 Numerous words are used before nouns relating to time to create distributive expressions: *once, twice, three times, four times,* etc., *a day, a week, a month,* etc. In such phrases *a* can usually be replaced by *every* or *each,* and by *per.*

3 The 'distributive plural' is one that corresponds to individuals separately rather than jointly as shown in the following examples: *we watched the proceedings that led to her resignation with sadness uppermost in our minds* (each person has only one mind); *they wear gowns when the Vice-Chancellor is present* (each person wears only one gown). Such cases display 'distributive plural concord'. But in such contexts a singular noun is often idiomatic, and one could equally say *uppermost in our mind* and *they wear a gown.* In some cases singular concord is obligatory in order to avoid ambiguity: *children under seven must be accompanied by a parent* (only one parent is required).

distributor. So spelt in all uses, not *-er.* See -OR.

distrust, mistrust. It is something of a cliché in lexicography that true synonyms do not exist, that no two words are ever interchangeable in the same context. While that rule does indeed hold good universally, *distrust* and *mistrust* possibly come closer than any other word to being synonyms. Choosing one in preference to the other should therefore not induce stylistic angst. What distinguishes them are some small differences in collocation, and the much higher frequency of use of *distrust,* particularly as a verb, but also as a noun. Examples: (distrust) *However, Plato's distrust of sensory perception led him to reject the visual arts—OEC,* 2002; *blacks, Arabs and other residents of color distrust local politicians and feel disenfranchised—OEC,* 2003; (mistrust) *Russia is mistrusted by many Iranians, who point to a history of hostile relations going back two centuries—OEC,* 2007; *Pornography and a fear of rape play a huge part in girls' mistrust of their* *own bodies*—J. Dawson, 1990. *Distrustful* is also more often used than *mistrustful.*

disyllable. The better spelling, not *dissyllable,* though the spelling with *diss-* 'was universal in the 17-18th c.' (*OED*) in imitation of French *dissyllabe.* (In French the *s* was doubled in accordance with its pronunciation as /dis-/ not /diz-/.) It answers to Latin *disyllabus,* where the prefix *di-* means twice.

ditransitive. A ditransitive verb is one that appears to take two direct objects (without the intervention of a preposition): *he gave the baby a bottle* (= a bottle to the baby); *he resented the author his talent if he had any*—H. Jacobson, 1983. See AS 3(b).

ditto. Plural *dittos.* See -O(E)S 4. Verbal forms *dittoed, dittoes, dittoing.*

diurnal is not an ordinary synonym of *daily* but has special technical meanings especially in medicine and the life sciences. In those fields it means either 'by day', as opposed to *nocturnal* 'by night'; or 'occupying a day', as opposed to *annual, monthly,* etc., e.g. *The literature describes a normal diurnal variation in blood pressure readings—American Family Physician,* 2003. In non-technical contexts, *diurnal* has a quasi-humorous effect, as with many technical words used in this way: *For at least 10,000 years the human race has, at regular and officially sanctioned intervals, abandoned the hard diurnal grind of work and taken to the streets—Guardian,* 2007.

divan. See COUCH. The recommended pronunciation is /dɪˈvan/.

dive. In Britain and in most other English-speaking areas the standard past tense is invariably *dived,* but *dove* /dəʊv/ has been noted in regional use in North American English since the mid-19c. and continues to turn up in fairly standard North American sources today. Nowadays, it also occasionally appears in British English, but should be avoided in any kind of formal writing. A famous early example appears in Longfellow's *Hiawatha.* Examples: *Straight into the river Kwasind Plunged as if he were an otter, Dove as if he were a beaver*—Longfellow, 1855; *He dove in and saved her life*—F. Scott Fitzgerald, *a*1940; *All of the boys dove from the board—OEC,* 2002 (AmE); *Gunfire erupted from either end of the hallway as Graeme finished and the two men dove across the corridor—OEC,* 2005 (BrE).

divers, diverse. The two words were not differentiated in Middle English (both being from Old French, ultimately from Latin *diversus* 'contrary', different, originally 'turned different ways'; cf. *vertere* 'to turn'), but they gradually drew apart. Both words once shared the meaning now confined to *diverse,* i.e. 'varied, unalike', qualifying singular and plural nouns, as in *Why is it so diverse, so varied in its character?*—J. Houston, 1990; *Can a single author cover the diverse techniques of physical biochemistry?—New Scientist,* 1991. *Divers,* pronounced /ˈdʌɪvəːz/, is marked 'archaic or literary' in the *ODO,* and now means 'several, sundry' without the notion of variety: *Evelyn Underhill* (*author of divers fat books on mysticism*)—D. Davie, 1991.

divest. *Divest* has been traditionally used as a rather formal word meaning 'to undress' and, in the reflexive form *divest oneself of,* 'to dispossess oneself of'. In this second meaning it typically refers to rights, powers, etc., or is used as a humorous alternative to 'get rid of': *By about 1900, ... you were generally well-advised to divest yourself of a regional accent if you wanted to rise and get on in the world—Daily Mail,* 2004. These uses were supplemented in the 1950s, first in American English and then elsewhere, by the financial meanings 'to sell off (a subsidiary company)' and 'to cease to hold (an investment)': *We are continually evaluating our asset base to divest assets that are not required for future operations—Lloyd's List,* 2004. The corresponding noun is **divestment**.

divisible. So spelt, not *-able.* See -ABLE, -IBLE 7.

divorcee. First recorded in the early 19c., it is normally pronounced /dɪvɔːˈsiː/. This is the regular spelling in English to refer to a man or a woman who has divorced, but on occasion the French forms *divorcé* (divorced man) and *divorcée* (divorced woman) also occur, and can be useful if a gender-specific term is needed.

dj-. This initial combination of letters was sometimes used in the past as a transliteration of foreign letters having the sound /dʒ/. Numerous words from Arabic, Turkish, and Berber acquired currency in English with initial *dj* (*djebel* 'mountain, hill'; *djinn* 'spirit having power over people'; etc.), but these have all been respelt (normally with initial *j*) in modern English.

djinn. See JINNI.

do.

1 As main verb.
2 As auxiliary.
3 *Don't have = haven't got.*
4 Contracted and uncontracted forms.
5 *I don't think* + clause.
6 *did, does* at head of subordinate phrase.
7 Non-standard uses.
8 Two novel uses.

Do is one of the most complicated verbs in the language. The first step is to distinguish its use as a full verb with multiple meanings from its use as an auxiliary. (Unless otherwise specified, all the examples below are drawn from two novels, namely André Brink's *States of Emergency* (1988) and Anita Brookner's *Lewis Percy* (1989), but they could as easily have been drawn from almost anywhere.) **1** *As main verb.* In practice *do* is used as a main verb much less frequently—the proportions vary from book to book but are of the order 1:10—than it is used as an auxiliary. Examples as a main verb: *we used to do most things together* (= carry out, perform); *anything will do* (= suffice); *I just brought you an article I've done* (= written); *I wanted to bring them up to do you proud* (idiom); *it can't do any harm* (idiom).

2 *As auxiliary. Do* used as an auxiliary is a much more complicated matter, though paradoxically it seems always to fall into place without any particular difficulty. Some of the main types: (*a*) In interrogative and negative contexts followed by a plain infinitive: *Did I somehow dread the prospect of returning?; Do you realize this is the first time you've ever told me anything about yourself?; I didn't know* (*still don't*) *how to cope with the fact*; (with uncontracted negative) *But does not the fate of her small novella demonstrate the futility of such an enterprise?* (*b*) In affirmative, including imperative, statements, with varying degrees of emphasis: *It really did seem as if a better world could still come about; if you do choose me it is a different me you'll have to contend with in future; But do remember, won't you, that we live rather a long way away.* (*c*) With inversion of subject in various circumstances: *Only after what seems to be hours ... do they manage to shake off their pursuers; Such arrested innocence affected him painfully, as did her large eyes; So anxious did this make him that he was determined never to court such condemnation again.* (*d*) In tag questions: *And when you and I talk about history we don't mean what actually happened, do we?*—P. Lively, 1987; *You like Pen, don't you?*—A. Brookner, 1989; *Yet I knew you at once, didn't I?*—ibid. (*e*) contexts in which *do* or *do so* (known as substitutive *do*) refers back to the predicate of a preceding clause, in order to avoid repeating it: *who had married the ungenerous Susan because that was what men did; she might have spent pleasant harmless days, as women of her generation were accustomed to do; if that meant accepting George ... he was perfectly willing to do so.* (*f*) In British English but less commonly in AmE, *do* can also be used intransitively (especially after *have* or a modal verb) to represent an earlier predicate: *We all get on enormously well and have done for the last six weeks*—Susannah York, 1986; *Adults don't believe children but they should* do—TV programme, 1986. (*g*) Fowler (1926) rightly pointed out that *do* must not be used as a substitute for a copulative *be* and its complement: *It ought to have been satisfying to the young man, and so, in a manner of speaking, it did* (read *was*).

3 *don't have = haven't got.* (*a*) 'American writers seem to use the *do* construction in many cases in which Britishers would use *have got*' (Jespersen, 1940). After a complex history in the 19c. (Visser, 1978, pp. 1558ff.), *do* + negative + *have* = *haven't got* became firmly established as American. It is now very commonly used in most other English-speaking countries as well, but still retains a slight American flavour. Examples: (US) *We don't have any beer. Just red wine. Sorry.*—*New Yorker*, 1986; *But I don't have my pack with* me—J. Updike, 1986; *Well, I'm very sorry, but we don't have time for that now* —T. Wolfe, 1987; (outside America) *But you don't have a* car—M. Duckworth, 1986 (NZ); *Bathrooms in the bedrooms. Cocktail bars. Things we don't have*—A. Lejeune, 1986; *we don't have that kind of thing in my house, man*—A. Brink, 1988 (SAfr.)

(*b*) Question: *Have you got a spare room?* Answer: *Yes, we do.* This apparently illogical use of *do*, replacing *have* as the auxiliary verb, arises because the question implicitly being answered is 'Do you have a spare room?' It is a common pattern in AmE and causes less surprise to British visitors than formerly, since it has also become a feature of BrE. Similarly (AmE only), *'You've got to go.' 'No, I don't.'*

4 *Contracted and uncontracted forms.* The contracted forms *don't, didn't,* and *doesn't,* none of which was recorded in print before the later part of the 17c., are now customary in the representation of speech, and are gradually spreading into less formal business writing. It is best to avoid them in descriptive prose, but otherwise it is an individual author's decision whether or not to use them. Examples: (in conversations) *'Doesn't she ever go out, then?' asked Lewis; 'Why don't you do that?'; 'I didn't know what could have happened to you.'*; (uncontracted) *He did not think he could tell her about the stunning monotony of his everyday life; What she lived on Lewis never knew, but money did not appear to be a problem.*

5 *I don't think* + clause. This is so idiomatic that its slight illogicality, once the cause of disapproval, now goes unnoticed. When you say *I don't think I've ever met anyone like you,* you mean to say *I think I've never met anyone like you*; but the second alternative, though possible, is far less natural in ordinary conversation.

6 *did, does* at head of subordinate phrase. This emphasizing use, which, according to Visser (1984), is not recorded before the 18c., is shown in the following examples: *He speaks uncommonly well, does Casaubon*—G. Eliot, 1872; *Never saved a cent, did old Don Juan*—H. A. Vachell, 1899; *It's interesting, she likes the old books, Dickens and Jane Austen, does my old lady*—K. Amis, 1988; *He does have a sense of humour does Mr Marr*—Nigel Williams, 1992.

7 *Non-standard uses.* (*a*) *done* as irregular past tense. This use is common in regional and in uneducated speech in Britain and elsewhere. Examples: *I think it done him good*—M. Twain, 1873; *After what they've done to me, I never could forgive them. And I never done anybody any harm—Listener,* 1969; *'It can be seen that the past tense form* done *is reported by virtually all the schools in the south of the country* [*sc.* Britain], *but that it is less widespread elsewhere* [in Britain]'—J. Cheshire, 1989. (*b*) *don't = doesn't.* This non-standard or dialectal use is illustrated in the following example: *I don't have to tell you, he's not the greatest orator in the world, but that don't—doesn't—it was time to change gears in the third person singular—necessarily make any difference in a criminal trial*—T. Wolfe, 1987. Other examples: *It don't take ten thousand acres here to support one family*—O. W. Norton, 1862; *A man what don't profit from all a woman's telling and hiding the bottles ain't worth the trouble*—K. Tennant, 1946. (*c*) *done* in US dialect. First noted in US records in the early 19c., *done* as a perfective auxiliary or with adverbial force to mean 'already, completely' is recognized as being a colourful regionalism but has failed to make its way into general use. Examples: *He had done gone three hours ago*—US source, 1836; *I don't know what you need with another boy. You done got four*—E. T. Wallace, 1945. (*d*) See DIDN'T OUGHT.

8 *Two novel uses.* (*a*) First recorded in the US in 1970, the meaning 'to eat or drink habitually', has gained considerable currency, especially in the negative, e.g.: *Ellis doesn't do alcohol any longer—Denver Post,* 1994. Closely related to this meaning is the phrase *to do lunch, dinner,* etc., i.e. to meet for the meal specified, especially with a view to doing business, e.g. *They're about honesty, as opposed to that kind of smarmy 'let's do lunch' business deception—OEC,* 2003 (Canad.); *An invitation to lunch might be pitched as, 'Come on, let's do sushi', or 'We have to do some Korean.'—Sunday Tel.,* 1987. (*b*) The very broad meaning, *'to partake of or engage in'* exemplified in phrases such as *I don't do parties* is now used with a wide range of nouns, e.g.: *Don had to explain to her gently but firmly that he didn't 'do' relationships;* D. Bissinger, 1990; *He's never had a boyfriend, he doesn't do boyfriends*—R. T. Davies, 1999; *She is not a people person ... She just doesn't do small talk. If you hang out with her, it feels awkward—NY Times,* 2004.

do (the musical note). Use *doh.*

docile. As recently as 1977, *Everyman's English Pronouncing Dict.* listed /ˈdɒs-/ as an alternative pronunciation for the first syllable, but the only standard pronunciation now in British English is /ˈdəʊsʌɪl/.

Perhaps the most frequent pronunciation in American English is /ˈdɑːsəl/. See -ILE.

dock. In British English, an artificially enclosed body of water for the loading, unloading, and repair of ships (often called a *dry dock*), and also (in plural, also *dockyards*) the whole area concerned with the building, fitting, and repair of ships; but in American English, a ship's berth, a wharf.

doctrinal. The pronunciation /dɒkˈtrʌɪnəl/ is recommended, but in American English /ˈdɑːktrənəl/.

docu-. Sliced from the word *documentary*, the element *docu-* has produced a crop of recently formed words in the entertainment business signifying entertainment that is a mixture of fact and fiction, e.g. *docudrama* (a dramatized documentary film, first recorded in 1961), *docusoap* (1979), *docutainment* (1978).

dodo. Plural *dodos*. See -O(E)S 2.

doe. See BUCK.

do(e)st. If for any reason this form of the verb *do* should be called on in a modern English context, for instance in historical fiction, authors should be aware that it should be spelt *dost* as an auxiliary but *doest* as a finite verb. Examples: *Do'st thou attend me?—Tempest* i. ii. 78; *What doest thou here, Eliiah?*—Kings xix. 9.

dogged. As adjective (= tenacious) always /ˈdɒgɪd/, but as the past tense and past participle of the verb *dog* (*he was dogged by misfortune*) always /dɒgd/, i.e. a single syllable.

doggie is recommended for the noun (pet form for a dog) and **doggy** for the adjective (of or like a dog).

dogma. The old variant plural *dogmata* (answering to the Greek and Latin plural *dogmata*) was frequently used in English from the 17c. to the 19c. but is obsolete now. The ordinary plural is *dogmas*.

doh (the musical note). So spelt, not *do*.

doily, a napkin, so spelt, not *doiley, doyley, doyly, d'oyley, -ie*. In origin it is an eponymous word, named after a 17c. person having the surname Doiley or Doyley who, apparently, kept a linen-draper's shop in the Strand, London.

dolce far niente. This Italian phrase (the individual words mean 'sweet doing nothing') meaning 'pleasant idleness' was placed among 'Battered ornaments' as a 'foreign scrap' by Fowler (1926). It seems a slightly harsh judgement on a serviceable phrase used e.g. by Byron and Longfellow. Modern example: *The Austrians are not as efficient as the Germans, and they know it; they have too much charm, a concern with* dolce far niente—A. Burgess, 1986.

dolce vita. This Italian phrase (literally = 'sweet life') meaning 'a life of pleasure or luxury' was first recorded in English in the 1960s and is particularly associated with people who, for one reason or another, reside abroad. Examples: *It didn't work,* la dolce vita *did not come packed with the detergent inside the new washing machine*—M. French, 1977; *Its expose of the* dolce vita *lifestyle of 30 years ago when it was written has lost its impact—Stage,* 1988.

doll's house. So in British English, but *dollhouse* in American English.

domain. For synonymy, see FIELD.

Domesday (in full **Domesday Book**). Always pronounced /ˈduːmzdeɪ/ and therefore not distinguished in pronunciation from *doomsday*, the day of the Last Judgement.

domestic. 1 In Fanny Trollope's day in the first half of the 19c. and until the mid-20c. *domestic servants* worked for their masters or their mistresses as part of a process called *domestic service.* Such people were also called *domestics* and *servants.* Changes of attitude in the 20c. largely drove these terms out of use, and they have been replaced by a range of terms that are intended to reduce the social divisions once taken for granted: *cleaner, domestic help, live-in companion/cook/housekeeper*, etc.

2 *Domestic partners.* A term sometimes used, especially in American English, for an unmarried couple who are living together, whether heterosexual or homosexual.

domesticity. The pronunciation /ˌdɒmɛˈstɪsɪti/ is recommended, not /ˌdəʊm-/.

domicile. Another word that is pronounced with final /-ʌɪl/ in British English and either /-əl/ or /-ʌɪl/ in American English. Cf. *docile, missile*, etc.

dominatrix, denoting a woman who takes the sadistic role in sadomasochistic activities, is pronounced stressing the third syllable, /dɒmɪˈneɪtrɪks/. For those masochistic enough to need the plural, it can be either the Latinate *dominatrices,* /-ˈneɪtrɪsiːz/ (-**nay**-tri-seez) or the more frequent *dominatrixes.*

domino. Plural *dominoes.* See -O(E)S 1.

donate. This back-formation from *donation,* which earlier in the 20c. was judged to be 'chiefly US', has become established in World English, and is now more or less restricted to contexts of contributing voluntarily to a fund or an institution: *Money donated directly to a foreign organization may not be tax deductible—OEC,* 2005.

done. See DO (verb) 7.

Don Juan. J. C. Wells (1990) comments: 'In English literature, including Byron, and usually when used metaphorically, British English prefers /ˌdɒn ˈdʒuːən/; in imitated Spanish, and generally in American English, /ˈwɑːn/ or /ˈhwɑːn/.'

Don Quixote. Traditionally pronounced /ˌdɒn ˈkwɪksəʊt/, but now frequently, in imitation of Spanish, /ˈdɒn kɪˈhəʊti/.

don't. See DO (verb) 3, 4, 5, 7(*b*).

doomsday. See DOMESDAY.

dos and don'ts. As the *New Hart's Rules* (2005) says, 'The apostrophe is not necessary in forming the plural of . . . words not usually used as nouns.' It is therefore not necessary to insert an apostrophe before the letter *s* when you make them plural (but you keep the apostrophe before the letter *-t* in *don'ts*). Similarly, *fair dos* should be written without an apostrophe.

dossier. Pronounced /ˈdɒsɪə/ and /ˈdɒsɪəɪ/ with about equal frequency. Both pronunciations are acceptable. Cf. CROUPIER.

double. When telephone (or other) numbers or letters of the alphabet are spoken in British English the convention is to pronounce a sequence of two identical numbers or letters in the form *double four, double r*: the number 848266 when read out would end *double six,* and the name *Forrest,* when read out, would be pronounced f-o-*double* r-e-s-t. In American English the equivalents would usually be *six six* and f-o-r-r-e-s-t.

double comparison. From the 14c. onwards double comparatives and superlatives have been used occasionally for emphasis, but since the 18c. they have been regarded by standard speakers as irregular, regional, or illiterate. Shakespeare used the convention repeatedly: *a more larger list of sceptres; his more braver daughter; this was the most unkindest cut of all;* and Jespersen cites numerous examples from the 14c. (Chaucer) to the early 20c. (Compton Mackenzie). The convention is still deeply embedded in local dialects and in the language of children, but not in standard adult speech.

double entendre. This expression, adopted in the 17c. from a French phrase that is no longer current in France, means 'a word or phrase open to two interpretations, one usually *risqué* or indelicate'. The equivalent modern French phrase *double entente,* first recorded in 1895, is rarely used in contemporary English to mean the same.

double genitive. See DOUBLE POSSESSIVE.

double meaning. See OPPOSITE MEANINGS.

double negative. The phrase *double negative* refers to a negative statement containing two negative elements, e.g. *he didn't say nothing,* in which the two negative words are *not* (*n't*) and *nothing.* **1** A plain-speaking shopkeeper explained to an interviewer from the *Sunday Times Magazine* (12 July 1987): *I run a family business and I don't want no hassle.* It is easy to find other examples from various English-speaking areas: *He never did no harm to no one*—BBC Radio 4, *The Archers,* 1987; *'Clouds come up,' she continued, 'but no rain never falls when you want it.'*—E. Jolley, 1980 (Aust.); *I don't give a damn about nobody*—A. Fugard, 1980 (SAfr.). In all these examples the double (or multiple) negative construction is obviously a comfortably natural way of expressing the idea. The double negative emphasizes the negativity and does not cancel it out. There is no ambiguity, and communication is not impeded in any way. But in the 20c. the construction is non-standard.

2 It may surprise some people, for whom the double negative is self-evidently wrong, that repetition of negatives that do not cancel each other out was standard in Old English and Middle English in all dialects.

Thus, in Chaucer: *He* nevere *yet* no *vileyne* ne *sayde In al his lyf unto* no *maner wight*; and, later, in Shakespeare: *And that* no *woman has,* nor neuer none *Shall mistris be of it, saue I alone.* At some point between the 16c. and the 18c., for reasons no longer discoverable, double negatives became socially unacceptable in standard English. Playwrights placed them in the conversation of vulgar speakers, and 18c. grammarians like Lindley Murray roundly condemned them.

3 In present-day English, a special type of double negative construction is used as a kind of understatement, and is perfectly standard, e.g. *it has not gone unnoticed* = it has been noticed. This figure of speech gives an added subtlety to statements. For example, if you say '*I am not unconvinced by your argument*' you are suggesting that you have reservations that are not present in the 'logical' equivalent: '*I am convinced by your argument*'. Similarly, to say '*I am not entirely dissatisified*' suggests that you are satisfied, but only up to a point. In such clauses the complement is often an adjective containing a negative prefix, such as *un-* and *dis-*. Such negative constructions with a positive meaning are eminently acceptable if they are not overused or too intricate.

4 Double negatives also occur, especially in speech, in clauses of the type *You can't not go* (= you have to go), *You shouldn't not eat* (= you should eat). In such cases a negated modal is followed by a negated infinitive, but the meaning is positive, as the respective paraphrases demonstrate.

double passive. See PASSIVE VOICE 6.

double possessive. 1 *Currency.* The currency of the type *a friend of my father's* is not in question. In practice one of its most useful functions is that it enables English speakers to distinguish between the simple types *a picture of the king* (= an actual portrait of him) and *a picture of the king's* (= one owned by him).

Examples: *Aunt Mary was a great admirer of hers*—G. Butler, 1983; *His aunt was a friend of my mother's*—M. Wesley, 1983; *It hardly seemed possible that the Harringtons had believed this story of Barney's*—P. Fitzgerald, 1986; *I am named after an old friend of my father's*—P. Carey, 1988; *Polly told me Gordon's father was an old friend of Mr. Logan's*—*New Yorker,* 1990. Contrast these examples in which the double possessive is not used: *Friedrich Wilhelm Keyl ... became a favourite pupil of Landseer*—*Bodl. Libr. Rec.,* 1987; *A shadowy girl, a niece of her late husband, was invited*—A. Brookner, 1988.

2 *History.* Several types of double possessives emerged in the 14c. and 15c. and have been in use ever since: *A frend of his þat called was Pandare*—Chaucer, *c.*1374; *A yong hors of the Quenes*—1502 in *OED; This was ... a false step of the ... general's*—Defoe, 1724; *I make it a rule of mine*—R. L. Stevenson, 1896.

3 *Limitations.* It will be seen from the examples in (1) that the appositional *of*-phrase must be definite (i.e. not indefinite) and human: *a friend of my mother's* is idiomatic, but *a friend of the British Museum's* is not; *an admirer of hers* is idiomatic, but *an admirer of the furniture's* is not. It will also be observed that the phrase preceding *of* is normally indefinite (a *great admirer, a child of hers,* etc.). The only exceptions are those where the first noun phrase is preceded by the demonstratives *this* or *that* (*this story of Barney's*). It is not easy to explain why such constructions are idiomatic: one can only assert that they are.

See also OF A7, B.

doublespeak. (Also called **doubletalk.**) Both these words denote 'deliberately ambiguous or imprecise language' used as euphemisms or as a deliberate way of deceiving people or obscuring the truth. Its most fertile breeding grounds tend to be politics, big business and the sphere of defence. The term *doubletalk* emerged first (first recorded in 1938), followed by Orwell's *doublethink* (1949), and by *doublespeak* (1957). For similar concepts, see BAFFLEGAB; GOBBLEDEGOOK.

Opposition to the use of doublespeak noticeably increased from the 1970s. Since 1974, in the United States, the National Council of Teachers of English has bestowed a Doublespeak Award as 'an ironic tribute to public speakers who have perpetuated language that is grossly deceptive, evasive, euphemistic, confusing, or self-centered'. Recipients have included Yasser Arafat, several US presidents, the CIA, and the Defense Department. The first award went to a press officer in Cambodia, who, after a US bombing raid, told reporters: *You always write it's bombing, bombing, bombing! It's not bombing! It's air support!* The 1991 award went to the Department of Defense 'for language its spokespersons in Washington and in the military used to gloss over realities of the war in the Persian Gulf. Massive bombing attacks were called "efforts"; warplanes were called "weapons systems" or "force packages"; a bombing mission was called "visiting a site". William Lutz, chair of the NCTE Committee on Public Doublespeak said that buildings and human beings that were the targets of bombing were called "hard" and "soft targets". During their "visits," Lutz said, these "weapons systems" "degraded," "neutralized," "attrited," "suppressed," "eliminated," "cleansed," "sanitized," "impacted," "decapitated," or "took out" targets.'

Obfuscation of language continues to be a major feature of modern life, despite being remorselessly attacked and ridiculed by linguists and others. All of us should be constantly alert to its trickery.

double subject. This is a name for a construction (technically known as 'pleonastic') in which a noun subject is followed by a supporting pronoun as in Longfellow's *The skipper he stood beside the helm.* It has a long history in English, and the *OED* presents examples from *c.*1000 onwards, variously described as 'common in ballad style and now in illiterate speech', 'now only *arch.* (*poet.*) and in uneducated use', and 'now esp. in ballad poetry', and so on. This venerable construction continues to turn up occasionally but only in the special circumstances indicated by the *OED.* Examples: *The Liner she's a lady by the paint upon 'er face*—Kipling, 1896; *From time to time I clean. Mrs Pollypot she don't like cleaning*—M. Wesley, 1983; *My cousin he didn't go to college*—Jessica Williams (citing a second-language-learner), 1987.

double superlative. See DOUBLE COMPARISON.

doublet. A term of etymology meaning either of a pair of words having the same origin but which, for historical reasons, end up as two separate words. Examples: popular Latin **cadentia* (from *cadent-*, participial stem of *cadere* 'to fall' → Old French *cadence* → Eng. *cadence/* → OF *cheance* → Eng. *chance*; medieval Latin *clocca* → OF *cloke* → Eng. *cloak/* → OF *cloche* → Eng. *cloche/* → Middle Low German *klocke* → Eng. *clock*; L *factionem* → OF *faction* → Eng. *faction/* → Eng. *fashion*; L *uncia* ('twelfth part') → Old English *ynce* → Eng. *inch/* → OF *unce* → Eng. *ounce.* There are a great many doublets in English, e.g. *compute/count, dainty/dignity, fragile/frail, pauper/poor, radius/ray, secure/sure, tradition/treason.*

double whammy. The first record of the word *whammy* in the *OED* dates from 1940, but it was popularized from 1951 onwards through the American cartoon strip *L'il Abner. Whammy* means 'an evil influence or hex' and so a *double whammy* means 'a twofold blow or setback', e.g. *And high exchange rates create the double whammy of less revenue from exports and more competition from cheaper imports*—*OEC,* 2004. By a strange reversal of meaning, it is also sometimes used to mean the polar opposite, i.e. a double stroke of luck, as in *the double whammy of Best Film and Outstanding British Film*—*OEC,* 2011.

doubling of consonants with suffixes. The standard treatment of the problem is that in the *New Hart's Rules,* on which the present article is based. See also -B-, -BB-; -C-, -CK-; -D-, -DD-; -LL-, -L-; etc. **1** *Words of one syllable.* Those ending with one consonant preceded by one vowel (not counting *u* in *qu*) double that consonant on adding *-ed* or *-ing* unless it is *h, w, x,* or *y.*

beg *begged* *begging*
clap *clapped* *clapping*
dab *dabbed* *dabbing*
squat *squatted* *squatting*

but

ah *ah-ed* *ah-ing*
tow *towed* *towing*
vex *vexed* *vexing*
toy *toyed* *toying*

This rule also applies to the suffixes *-er* and *-est*:

fat *fatter* *fattest*
glad *gladder* *gladdest*

Monosyllabic words not ending with one consonant preceded by one vowel generally do not double the final consonant (e.g. *clamp, clamped, clamping; squeal, squealed, squealing*). Exceptions are *bused, busing* (carrying people by bus).

2 *Words of more than one syllable.* If the last syllable is stressed, words that end with one consonant preceded by one vowel double the consonant on adding *-ed, -ing,* or *-er, -est* (but not if the consonant is *w, x,* or *y*):

allot	*allotted*	*allotting*
begin	*beginner*	*beginning*
occur	*occurred*	*occurring*
prefer	*preferred*	*preferring*

but

guffaw	*guffawed*	*guffawing*
relax	*relaxed*	*relaxing*
array	*arrayed*	*arraying*

But words of this class *not* stressed on the last syllable do not double the last consonant on adding *-ed, -ing, -er, -est,* or *y* unless the consonant is *l* or *g* (see -G-, -GG-):

audited, -ing	*blanketed, -ing*
balloted, -ing	*bracketed, -ing*
benefited, -ing	*budgeted, -ing*
biased, -ing	*buffeted, -ing*
bigoted	*carpeted, -ing*
chirruped, -ing	*picketed, -ing*
combated, -ing	*pivoted, -ing*
cosseted, -ing	*plummeted, -ing*
crocheted, -ing	*profited, -ing*
ferreted, -ing	*rickety*
fidgeted, -ing	*ricocheted, -ing*
filleted, -ing	*riveted, -ing*
focused, -ing	*rocketed, -ing*
galloped, -ing	*targeted, -ing*
gossiped, -ing	*thickened, -ing*
hiccuped, -ing	*thicker, -est*
leafleted, -ing	*trellised, -ing*
lettered, -ing	*trumpeted, -ing*
marketed, -ing	*visited, -ing*
offered, -ing	*vomited, -ing*

Note: The words most frequently misspelt with a doubled consonant are *benefitted, -ing* (under the influence of *fitted, -ing*), *leafletted, -ing, targetted, -ing,* and *focussed, -ing*; but it is better to keep to the basic rule in these words too. *Inputting, outputting,* and *worshipped, -ing, -er,* on the other hand, always have a doubled consonant in British English, as do *kidnapped, -ing, -er,* but American English often uses a single *p* in *kidnaped, worshiped,* and related forms.

3 BrE generally doubles the last consonant in words ending in *-l* whether they are stressed on the last syllable or not:

annulled, -ing	*initialled, -ing*
appalled, -ing	*instilled, -ing*
bevelled, -ing	*labelled, -ing*
channelled, -ing	*levelled, -ing*
chiselled, -ing	*libelled, -ing*
compelled, -ing	*marshalled, -ing*
counselled, -ing	*modelled, -ing*
dialled, -ing	*panelled, -ing*
dishevelled, -ing	*quarrelled, -ing*
enrolled, -ing	*revelled, -ing*
extolled, -ing	*rivalled, -ing*
fulfilled, -ing	*shovelled, -ing*
grovelled, -ing	*travelled, -ing*
impelled, -ing	*tunnelled, -ing*

Exceptions: *appealed, -ing; concealed, -ing; paralleled, -ing; revealed, -ing.*

Note: In AmE the *-l* is usually not doubled:

	BrE (always)	*AmE* (usually)
cancel	*cancelled*	*canceled*
cruel	*crueller*	*crueler*
dial	*dialled*	*dialed*
duel	*duelling*	*dueling*
fuel	*fuelling*	*fueling*
jewel	*jeweller*	*jeweler*
label	*labelled*	*labeled*
marvel	*marvellous*	*marvelous*
travel	*travelling*	*traveling*

See also -LL-, -L-.

Note: It is not uncommon to find words like *crystallized, swivelled,* and *unravelling* so spelt in standard AmE sources, i.e. as exceptions to standard AmE spelling.

doubt (verb). *I doubt whether he'll come* and *I doubt if he'll come* are the standard constructions when *doubt* is used in the affirmative to mean 'think it unlikely'. When *doubt* is used in the negative to mean 'think it likely', a *that*-clause is normal: *I don't doubt that he'll come.* The logic behind this difference is that when *doubt* is in the affirmative it implies uncertainty in the following clause (which is consistent with use of *whether* or *if*), whereas when it is used in the negative it implies probability in the following clause (which is more consistent with *that*).

This rationale lies behind the objection many people have to the increasing use of *doubt* in the affirmative followed by a *that*-clause or by an object clause without a conjunction. This is commonly regarded as an Americanism, but it is attested in British English use at the end of the 19c. Examples: (with *that*) *Schiller doubted that a poetic measure could be formed capable of holding Goethe's plan*—B. Taylor, 1871; *I doubt that the White House is responsible for this rash of tittle-tattle*—Alistair Cooke, 1981; *I doubt that the okapi which died . . . would agree with Mark Twain that 'Wagner is not as bad as he sounds'*—*Independent*, 1994; (with object clause) *He doubted Ferrari would sue him*—*New Yorker*, 1986; *I doubt there was anything really wrong with him*—Anita Brookner, 1992.

When the main clause is negative or interrogative, *doubt* could also formerly be followed by *but that* (*not doubting but that he would find him faithful; do you doubt but that he will do it?*), but this use is now archaic.

doubtful. 1 The constructions that follow *doubtful* correspond to the pattern outlined for *doubt*, with *whether* and *if* still dominant but a *that*-clause now increasingly common: *It was doubtful if Midge would ever again sleep in their old bedroom*—D. Rutherford, 1990; *It seems doubtful that such an item would have been produced much after c.1550*—J. Litten, 1991.

2 *Doubtful* and *dubious* overlap in meaning but there is a subtle distinction. *Doubtful* implies uncertainty about facts, whereas *dubious* implies suspicion about the value or genuineness of something or someone. *Dubious* is often used ironically of *privileges, honours,* and *distinctions*. To clarify the nuance, let us suggest that if something is of *doubtful quality*, there are good objective reasons for doubting its quality; if it is of *dubious quality*, you are subjectively suspicious about its true quality or worth. The following examples help clarify the differences between the two adjectives and their respective adverbs: (doubtful) *If your tap water is of doubtful quality then you must be prepared to remedy the situation or use rain water instead*—*Practical Fishkeeping*, 1992; *Then meeting Sophie's anxious gaze, she said briskly, 'Now don't look so doubtful'*—M. Bowring, 1993; *'Are you sure?' she said doubtfully*—T. Pratchett, 1990; (dubious) *We still had the dubious privilege of representing two 'resting' actors*—M. Babson, 1971; *The right of people to know the human cost was overruled on the dubious grounds that this information could help the enemy*—*Action*, 1991; *Voters are already dubious about the point of a deputy prime minister*—*Times*, 2007; *Dreaming of luxury, of the quick buck dubiously acquired*—R. Barnard, 1980.

doubtless, no doubt, undoubtedly. Fowler's comment (1926) is still valid: '*Doubtless* and *no doubt* have been weakened in sense till they no longer convey certainty, but either probability (*You have doubtless* or *no doubt heard the news*) or concession (*No doubt he meant well enough; it is doubtless very unpleasant*). When real conviction or actual knowledge on the speaker's part is to be expressed, it must be by *undoubtedly, without* (*a*) *doubt*, or *beyond a* (or *any*) *doubt* (*he was undoubtedly*, etc., *guilty*).'

doubtlessly. Despite its antiquity (first recorded *c.*1440 in the first English-Latin dictionary) this word has always been in the shadow of the more usual adverb *doubtless*, the existence of which in theory makes *doubtlessly* unnecessary. However, some people seem reluctant to use *doubtless* as an adverb, presumably because it does not end in *-ly*, and as a result *doubtlessly* is not uncommon. Its venerable history notwithstanding, highly literate people will consider it at best an oddity, at worst a crass mistake, and so it is best avoided. Examples: *The current argument . . . doubtlessly offers a cogent and easily understood explanation for the current deadlock in East-West relations*—*Washington* Post, 1984; *The overall effect is of a sobriety that can . . . make even Britten's doubtlessly 'greater' War Requiem sound a mite theatrical*—*Independent*, 1994.

dour. The only standard pronunciation in Britain is /dʊə/, rhyming with *tour* not *sour*; but /daʊə(r)/ is common in American English and Australia.

dove (past tense). See DIVE.

dovecote. See COTE.

downmarket. Preferably written as one word, without a hyphen, this chiefly British adjective and adverb 'of or relating to the cheaper part of the market', is now so established in the language that it is surprising to find that its first record in the *OED* is no earlier than 1970.

downsize, meaning 'to reduce in size or scale', is first recorded in the 1970s with reference to the manufacture of smaller and more economical motor cars. In the US in the early 1980s it rapidly acquired what is now its main meaning, in the euphemistic jargon of business management and government, of reducing the personnel of an organization by redundancies and other drastic measures: *The government downsized a lot of public services, like the railways, the Ministry of Works and forestry*—*OEC*, 2003. *Downsize* behaves like a so-called ergative verb in being used as an intransitive with the object made the subject: *The Ryan plant had downsized from 120 to about 60 employees—OEC*, 2004. Its meaning has also been extended in three further ways: (*a*) to refer to moving from where you currently live to somewhere smaller, e.g. *I do like the house, but there comes a time when you have to move on and downsize—Hull Daily Mail*, 2007; (*b*) mainly in American English, as a rather bitter euphemism for being made redundant, e.g. *When John Young was downsized from his job last year, he didn't throw a pity party—OEC*, 2004 (AmE); *I was working on Part II when I was downsized and so spent my extra time and energy on the job hunt—OEC*, 2004 (AmE); and (*c*) again, largely in AmE, as a synonym for 'reduce' in phrases such as, e.g. *Russia must now downsize its ambitions in Latin America because its pockets are no longer so deep—OEC*, 2008. These last two uses are not recommended in British English.

Down('s) syndrome. Named after J. L. H. Down, an English physician (1828-96), the earliest example of *Down('s) syndrome* in the *OED* is from 1961. The spelling *Down's syndrome* predominates in BrE, with *Down syndrome* as an alternative. In AmE the reverse is true. This term has now become standard in medical and lay use as a replacement for the offensive older term *mongolism*, now, thankfully, consigned to the linguistic dustbin. To refer to someone who has *Down('s) syndrome*, the appropriate phrase is *a person with Down('s) syndrome*.

downstairs. Used for both the adjective (*the downstairs loo*) and the adverb (*meet me downstairs when you are ready*). As adjective stressed on the first syllable, but as adverb on the second.

down to. Used in the meaning 'attributable to', the phrase came into general use in the second half of the 20c. Example: *The boom in Gucci and Pucci and ... Lacoste 'names' on clothes, bags, and other ornamentation is all down to the Yuppies—Sunday Tel.*, 1985. Cf. *up to* (s.v. UP 3).

downward(s). The only form of the adjective is *downward* (*in a downward direction*), but *downward* and *downwards* are used interchangeably for the adverb, *downwards* being the more common of the two in British English. Examples: (downward) *And bats ... crawled head downward down a blackened wall*—T. S. Eliot; *Every time he looked downward he grew dizzy*—J. M. Coetzee, 1983; (downwards) *She ferreted in her bag; then held it up mouth downwards*—V. Woolf, 1922; *The fact that commissioners' careers only seem to go downwards after they leave Brussels has a negative effect on morale—EuroBusiness*, 1989.

doyen. See DEAN, DOYEN.

drachm /dram/ is a British weight or measure formerly used by apothecaries, equivalent to one eighth of an ounce (60 grains), or (in full *fluid drachm*) to one eighth of a fluid ounce (60 minims); abbreviated *dr.* See DRAM.

drachma, formerly the chief monetary unit of Greece, before the adoption of the Euro in 2002. Plural *drachmas.*

draft, draught. *Draft,* in origin a phonetic respelling of *draught,* is used for (*a*) a preliminary sketch or version (*to make a rough draft*); (*b*) a written order for payment by a bank; (*c*) a military detachment. A *draftsman* is one who drafts documents. *Draught* is used in all the other common senses (game of *draughts*, air-current, ship's displacement, beer on *draught,* a dose of liquid medicine, *draught-horse*). In American English, *draft* is used for all senses and the game of *draughts* is called *checkers.*

dragoman. For this non-native word (= an interpreter or guide, especially in countries speaking Arabic, Turkish, or Persian) the normal plural is *-mans,* but inevitably *-men* is sometimes used instead.

dram. 1 A small drink of spirits. **2** = DRACHM.

draught. See DRAFT, DOYEN.

drawing. Should not be pronounced with an intrusive *-r-* (/ˈdrɔːrɪŋ/), as if it were spelt *drawring.*

dream. For the past tense and past participle both *dreamt* and *dreamed* are used; *dreamed* is usually pronounced /driːmd/ and *dreamt* /drɛmt/. *Dreamed,* especially as the past tense, tends to be used for emphasis and in poetry. The two forms are equally common in British English as the past tense, but in American English *dreamed* is used more often. As the past participle *dreamed* is more common in both varieties. See -T AND -ED.

drier, drily, dryer, dryly. Apart from being the comparative of the adjective *dry* (*dry, drier, driest*), *drier* is also the far less common spelling for 'a machine, device, or person that dries something'. The recommended and more common spelling is *dryer*, e.g. *blow-dryer, spin dryer, tumble dryer, dryer-up*, which usefully distinguishes the noun from the comparative form of the adjective.

The adverb can be spelt either *drily*, conforming to the spelling rule that a final letter *-y* changes to *-i* before a suffix, or *dryly*. Taking the *OEC* data as a whole, *dryly* is about five times more common nowadays. Though both forms are correct, *dryly* will look odd to many people in Britain, where *drily* is slightly more frequent; in North American English *dryly* predominates. The other derivatives of *dry* are spelt **dryish** and **dryness**.

drink. The only standard past tense is *drank* and for the past participle *drunk*. In past centuries there has been a great deal of fluctuation in the choice of form, and considerable variation is still found in British and American dialects.

drink-driving. A term first recorded in 1964 for the legal offence of driving a vehicle with an excess of alcohol in the blood; hence *drink-driver*. The preferred term in British, Irish, Australian and New Zealand English, it is best written with a hyphen. See DRUNK DRIVING.

dromedary. Now usually pronounced with initial /ˈdrɒm-/. The variant /ˈdrʌm-/ is now seldom encountered.

drouth /draʊθ/, Scottish /druːθ/ is a widespread (Scotland, Ireland, USA) variant of the standard form *drought*, in the two meanings 'dryness of climate' and 'thirst'. A miscellaneous collection of examples: *You might take your death with drouth and none to heed you*—J. M. Synge; *There are flood and drouth Over the eyes and mouth*—T. S. Eliot; *Once in my youth I gave, poor fool, A soldier apples and water; And may I die before you cool Such drouth as his, my daughter*—R. Graves; *while I sit here with a pestering Drouth for words*—S. Heaney; *My heart leaps up with streams of joy, My lips tell of drouth: Why should my heart be full of joy And not my mouth?*—Stevie Smith.

drunk driving. The North American term (first recorded in 1937) for DRINK-DRIVING; hence *drunk driver*. Both are written without hyphens. The synonym *drunken driving* is sometimes used both in American and in British English.

drunk, drunken. 1 In general *drunk* is used predicatively (*judged to be drunk and disorderly; he was drunk when he arrived at the party; she was as drunk as a lord; Napoleon was drunk with success*) and *drunken* attributively (*a drunken brawl; a drunken sleep; a drunken landlord*). See also DRUNK DRIVING.

2 In many contexts there is a semantic distinction: *drunk* implies 'the worse for drink at present', whereas *drunken* is capable of meaning 'often the worse for drink, given to drink'.

dryer, dryly. For the spelling of derivatives and inflected forms of the adjective *dry*, see DRIER, DRILY, DRYER, DRYLY.

dual. The first element in a number of widely used specific collocations of the 20c.: *dual carriageway* (first recorded in 1933), *dual control* (of aeroplanes and motor vehicles, 1913), *dual nationality* (1961), *dual personality* (1905), *dual-purpose* adjective (1914), etc. Fowler (1926) warned against the use of *dual* in general contexts where *two, twofold, double*, etc., are adequate, but this appears to have been a warning about the approach of an imaginary enemy.

dub. Such small words tend to be of several different origins and are apt to have many unrelated meanings. The *OED* records seven distinct nouns and five distinct verbs all written as *dub*. The oldest noun is Scottish and northern, was first recorded in the early 16c. (Gavin Douglas), and means 'a muddy or stagnant pool'. The most recent noun is Jamaican in origin, was first recorded in 1974, and means a remixed version of a piece of recorded popular music'. Perhaps the most widely known use of *dub* as a verb is the most recent one, a phonetic shortening of *double*, first recorded in 1929, and meaning 'to provide (a film, etc.) with an alternative soundtrack, especially in a different language'. The earliest verb use, (*a*1100), 'to confer the rank of knighthood by striking the shoulder with a sword', is known to most speakers, but for obvious reasons rarely used in its literal sense. Instead, it is widely used metaphorically to refer to giving an unofficial name or nickname to someone or something, e.g. *The media dubbed anorexia 'the slimming disease'*.

See -B-, -BB-.

dubbin. The now customary form of the word meaning 'a preparation of grease for softening leather and rendering it waterproof'. It is also used as a verb (past tense and past participle *dubbined*). The older variant *dubbing* (the form preferred by Fowler) seems to have dropped out of use in this meaning.

dubious. See DOUBTFUL.

duck. When used collectively it is often unchanged in form (*a flock*, etc., *of duck*), but in ordinary plural contexts normally *ducks* (*several ducks came for the bread that we threw into the lake*). It is used without the indefinite article as an item of food (*we had duck for dinner*).

due to. **1** The use of *due to* is one of the hottest topics in debates about correct use of language. Before considering why its use is disputed, it is worth looking at the contexts to which nobody objects: (*a*) (= owing or payable to) *Then pay Caesar what is due to Caesar, and pay God what is due to God*—Matt. 22: 21 (*NEB*, 1961); (*b*) (+ infinitive = likely to, supposed to, announced as) *It was due to start at four o'clock, but didn't begin until twenty past*—W. Trevor, 1976; *the train is due to arrive at 12 noon*; (*c*) (= properly owed to) *Herr Wodenfeld hovered on the sidelines exhibiting that cunning deference due to one who had been deposed*—B. Rubens, 1987; (following the verb *to be* = ascribable to) *This development was due directly . . . to the power of advertisement*—E. Waugh, 1932; *part of her happiness, her unaltered sense of her own superiority, was due to a sense of virginity preserved*—A. Brookner, 1988. In all these uses *due* is an adjective with a complement consisting of *to* + noun or a *to*-infinitive.

2 The problem arises when *due to* is used as a fixed prepositional phrase without a preceding noun or pronoun that *due* can be regarded as qualifying and no linking verb such as *be* or *become*, as in *?The train was delayed due to bad weather*. The purist view of the matter is that *There was a delay due to bad weather* is acceptable because *due* qualifies *delay*, whereas *?The train was delayed due to bad weather* is unacceptable because *due* is grammatically unattached.

Due to used as above was described by Fowler (1926) as 'often used by the illiterate as though it had passed, like *owing to,* into a mere compound preposition', and hostility to the construction only emerged in the 20c. In fact, the analogy with *owing to* probably explains the widespread use of the phrase in the potentially controversial way; and since analogy is such a powerful force in language change, it looks as if this use of *due to* is now part of the natural language of the 21c. Those wishing to avoid the tut-tutting of last-ditch pedants can, of course, replace *due to* with the straightforward *because of,* which would work in all the examples below, or the more formal *owing to* and *on account of.*

3 Examples of the contentious use: *Michael . . . hated mathematics at school, mainly due to the teacher*—*Times Educational Supplement*, 1987; *In the past 25 years the population has trebled due to the building programme*—*East Yorkshire Village Book*, 1991; *This kind of lucrative deal went downward in recent years due to the world economic situation*—*Evening Standard*, 2004.

due to the fact that. In this expression *the fact that* is used to turn the prepositional phrase *due to* into a conjunction. It is rather long-winded, awkward in use, and can usually be avoided simply by substituting *because: That this slippage is so slight is due to the fact that* [substitute *because*] *the other Enterprise staff have worked a great deal of extra time*—*Annual Report*, 1993. In some cases, however, substitution does not work well, especially when there is a strong link between *due* and a preceding noun, as in the following example: *The success of the tampon is partly due to the fact that it is hidden*—Germaine Greer, 1970.

dullness, fullness. Use *-ll-*, as in all other words in which *-ness* follows a word ending in *-ll* (*drollness, illness, shrillness, smallness, stillness, tallness,* etc.). But be prepared to find forms with a single *-l-* in 19c. and earlier works: e.g. *which dulness in apprehension occasioned me much grief*—R. M. Ballantyne, 1858.

dumb. **1** *Dumb* has acquired such strong connotations of stupidity and low intelligence that they have swamped its original meaning, 'not able to speak', and to use it in that way is very likely to cause offence. Neutral alternatives, such as *speech-impaired* or *having a speech disorder* are more appropriate.

2 In the late 1990s dumb moved out of its previous twilight existence as a literary verb (*A splendour that dazed the mind and dumbed the tongue*—R. F. Burton, *Arabian Nights' Entertainment,* 1885) with the emergence of the new phrasal verb *dumb down,* meaning 'to make more simple or less intellectually demanding, especially in order to appeal to a broader audience' with pejorative connotations. Used primarily in the fields of broadcasting, education, and the arts, its immediacy of meaning and nuance have made it a standard part of the language: *Successive education ministers have preferred to dumb down exams and glory in vacuous statistics than to deliver real education progress—Express,* 2005. This phrasal verb is also used intransitively (without an object): *I've never believed in this whole idea that you have to dumb down to get an audience—Scotsman,* 2002.

Curiously, the verb to *dumb up,* with the same meaning, first appeared in American English much earlier, in 1927, but is far less common (*The fact that it was a Universal Picture showed, and the whole movie played like it had been dumbed up for the American audience—OEC,* 2004). It can also be used ironically, as when Jeremy Paxman countered criticism that British TV had dumbed down: '*Newsnight has dumbed up and University Challenge has dumbed up,' he insists at the launch of Royal Opera House Cinema. 'We've made the questions harder'—Telegraph,* 2011.

dumbfound(ed). So spelt, not *dumf-,* since it combines *dumb* with *confound.*

dunno /ˈdʌnəʊ/. First recorded in 1842 as a phonetic representation of a reduced form of *do not* (or *don't*) *know,* it is widely used in fiction and plays to represent informal or illiterate speech. It may be acceptable in speech, and in texts or emails between close friends, but should otherwise be avoided. *He was fencing before we come here. Where? I dunno*—M. Eldridge, 1984; '*Now it's back the way it used to be.' 'Why? . . . ' 'Dunno, sweet. Do not know.'—New Yorker,* 1986.

duodecimo (size of book). Plural *duodecimos.* See -O(E)S 6.

duologue, a dramatic piece spoken by two actors. An irregular formation (first recorded in the 19c.) from Latin *duo* or Greek δύο 'two' after *monologue.* Cf. DIALOGUE.

duress /djʊəˈrɛs/ is the only current form (not *duresse*). It originally meant 'hardness', but now survives mainly in the phrase *under duress* 'under compulsion'. Such compulsion to do something against one's will may be by actual imprisonment, but is commonly used more generally (= under a threat of physical violence, etc.).

dustbin (rubbish bin), **dustman** (rubbish collector) are normal terms in British English, but are not common in American English or in other English-speaking areas, except figuratively, e.g. *the dustbin of history.* See RUBBISH.

Dutch. See NETHERLANDS.

duteous, dutiful. Both words were formed in the 16c. and of the two Shakespeare seems markedly to have preferred *duteous,* though he used both (*As duteous to the vices of thy Mistris, As badnesse would desire—Lear* IV.vi.253; *You know me dutifull, therefore deere sir, Let me not shame respect—Troilus* V.iii.72). As time went on, *duteous* (like *beauteous, plenteous*) fell into restricted literary use, while *dutiful* (like *beautiful, plentiful*) became an everyday word.

dutiable. See -ABLE, -IBLE 3 (ii).

dwarf. The traditional plural form in British English is *dwarfs,* but *dwarves* is now increasingly being used, as it has been for a long time outside the UK, perhaps under the influence of J. R. R. Tolkien, who used it regularly. Each plural is found in respected writers from around the Anglosphere. See -VE(D), -VES.

To use *dwarf* to mean simply a very short person is, of course, offensive. To describe people having **dwarfism**, terms suggested on the websites of support groups include the following: *people of restricted growth, people of short stature, people having dwarfism,* and *little people.*

dwell in the sense 'live, reside' (a use first recorded in the 13c. and frequent until the 19c.) is now more or less restricted to literary contexts. For the past tense and past participle *dwelt* (not *dwelled*) is recommended. See -T AND -ED.

dye (verb) has the inflected forms *dyed, dyes, dyeing* to avoid confusion with the conjugational forms of *die* (*died, dies, dying*).

dyke, dike. In the meaning 'embankment', *dyke* is the preferred form, but both are correct. The different word *dyke*, a 20c. informal and offensive word for a lesbian, is also usually so spelt.

dynamic, dynamical. Both words date only from the 19c., but since then *dynamic* has become the much more usual word of the two in its non-scientific meanings of 'characterized by change' (*a dynamic situation*) and 'positive in attitude and energetic' (*a dynamic new marketing manager*). *Dynamical* has become largely restricted to certain technical expressions, especially in the field of dynamics (a branch of physics).

dynamo. Plural *dynamos*. See -O(E)S 6. In origin it is an abbreviation of *dynamo-electric machine*.

dynast, dynasty. Usually for the first and overwhelmingly for the second the opening syllable is pronounced with /ˈdɪn-/ in British English, but with /ˈdʌɪn-/ in American English.

dysentery. So spelt. In British English, stressed on the first syllable: thus /ˈdɪsəntri/. In American English stretched out as four syllables.

-e-. See MUTE E.

e- is a very modern prefix, derived from the word *electronic*, and first recorded in the *OED* from 1990 in its current application (but used in 1988 in the word *e-fit*, a composite electronic image). It is applied especially to nouns denoting the use of electronic data transfer in cyberspace, especially over the Internet (often to distinguish them from their non-electronic counterparts), and to products and services similarly available. Many of the words formed with this prefix are now firmly established, such as: *e-books, e-business, e-commerce, e-learning, e-reader, e-tailer* (someone who retails goods on the Internet), *e-ticket* (an authorization to travel by train or air replacing the conventional printed ticket), and *e-voting* (a system of recording a vote in an election on the Internet or by other electronic means instead of marking a ballot paper). For the moment, it is usual to write these words with hyphens, but no doubt over time some of them will lose it, just as the now universal term *email* has.

each.

1 Singular or plural verb.
2 *each other.*
3 *between each.*
4 *each other's.*
5 *each's.*

1 *Singular or plural verb. Each* is treated as singular (*a*) when it stands by itself as a pronoun subject: *There are only two ties left: each has a thistle pattern*; (*b*) when it comes before a singular noun (e.g. *each house*): *Each group is responsible for its own quality control*—A. Francis, 1986; (*c*) when it is followed by *of* and a plural noun (e.g. *each of the houses*): *each of the three parties has a right to a confidential briefing* (not *have*). *Each* is wrongly used with a plural verb in the following sentence: **I only found out by sheer accident that you, Alan Lloyd and Milly Preston are all trustees, and each* have *a vote*—Jeffrey Archer, 1979 (read *each has* or *all of you have*).

The verb and its complements are in the plural (*a*) when *each* immediately follows a plural pronoun subject (e.g. *we, you, they each*): *We each have our own priorities* (not *has* and not *our own priority*); (*b*) when *each* is not the subject, but is in apposition with a plural noun or pronoun as subject: *the three parties each have a right to a confidential briefing; lettuces cost 75 pence each.*

2 *each other.* A belief that *each other* properly refers to two people and *one another* to more than two is reflected in many contexts: *But Mrs Bentley and Kitty were delighted with each other*—A. Brookner, 1982; *I mean, Stanley and Jessica and I could cry about it. We had one another*—Susan Hill. But the belief was dismissed even by Fowler (1926); historical usage shows that there is no basis for such a restriction; and it is in any case widely ignored, as can be seen from the following departures from the 'rule': (*each other* used to refer to more than two) *Everybody knew each other or about each other*—A. Brookner, 1983; *I sit in one of the smaller theatres at the Young Vic and watch Brecht's characters driving each other into action through the coherence and confidence of their belief and argument*—*Observer*, 2007; (*one another* used to refer to two) *He and Gussy were evidently very fond of one another*—A. N. Wilson, 1978; *There is no such thing as complete harmony between two people, however much they profess to love one another*—A. Brookner, 1984; *We saw one another at weekends but this put a strain on the relationship*—*Sun*, 2007.

3 *between each.* See BETWEEN 3.

4 *each other's.* It is worth noting that the possessive of *each other* is *each other's*, not *each others'*, e.g. *they shared each other's possessions.*

5 *each's.* An uncommon but acceptable use: *The distressing conflict between Catholics and Jews . . . is driven by each's belief that the other is attempting to* [etc.]—*Chicago Tribune,* 1989.

each and every. A tempting phrase, used for emphasis, as Edward VIII (when he was Prince of Wales) found when writing to Mrs Wallis Simpson in 1935: *I love you more & more each and every minute & miss you so terribly here.* But be warned: it is widely reviled by usage pundits ('at best a trite way of providing emphasis, at worst redundant, and generally both', Bill Bryson, 1984) as being a cliché and as unnecessarily wordy. It is probably justifiable to label an example such as *I look forward to seeing each and every one of you* as a cliché—and also as potentially insincere-sounding. It can, nevertheless, provide useful emphasis in examples such as *unfortunately, most* [people] *feel that monitoring must be a complicated and time-consuming process where someone must constantly watch each and every plant,* where it highlights the great size of the task involved. Should you so wish, you can often replace it with *each, every, every single, everyone,* and so forth.

eager. See ANXIOUS.

earl. See TITLES.

early on. This phrase, a kind of back-formation from *earlier on* (itself modelled on *later on*), is first recorded in British English in 1928 and only later in American English. Examples: *'It might have been given him earlier.' . . . 'Well—not too early on, Peter.'*—D. L. Sayers, 1928; *Earlier on, religion had supplied a drug which most of the clergy were quite ready to administer*—V. G. Kiernan, 1990; *I realised very early on that it is no threat at all to our relationship*—*OEC,* 2007. An American correspondent (1989) remarked to Burchfield, 'I'm constantly struck with the immense popularity in the U.S. of the once-exclusive-to-Britain expression "early on". Hardly anyone here can now use the word "early" by itself.' The earliest example of *later on* in the *OED* is from 1882.

earn. The normal inflected form for the past tense, past participle, and participial adjective (*earned income*) is *earned,* e.g. *they earned £200 a week; earned income.* The past participle and past tense are occasionally spelt *earnt,* perhaps because in fast speech this form is often pronounced /ɜːnt/, or by analogy with *learn.* This spelling is not recommended, since people will consider it a mistake, and it is explicitly disallowed by, for example, the *Guardian Style Guide.* Examples: *Ray and Alan Mitchell once worked gruelling hours and earnt good money as contract plumbers in London*—*Independent,* 1992. *Its pretax profits are tipped to be just above the £40.3m earnt at the same time last year*—*Business & Money,* 2007.

See -T AND -ED.

earth. Frequently with initial capital (*Earth*) when considered as a planet of the solar system. In such contexts, like Mars, Venus, etc., it is normally used without the definite article (but *the planet Earth*).

earthen, earthly, earthy. *Earthen* is used only in the literal meaning 'made of earth' (either soil, or clay used as pottery; hence *earthenware*). *Earthly* has two meanings, (*a*) 'of the earth or human life on earth' as opposed to *heavenly,* and (*b*), usually in negative contexts, 'remotely possible or conceivable' (*is no earthly use; there wasn't an earthly reason*). *Earthy* means (*a*) 'of or like earth or soil', and (*b*) 'somewhat coarse or crude'. Typical collocations include *earthen floor, earthen rampart; earthen jar, earthen vessel; the earthly paradise, an earthly pilgrimage; not an earthly* (= no chance); *crystalline rocks occasionally occur in friable form and are then said to be earthy; an earthy taste; strong earthy expressions, earthy humour.*

eastward. As an adjective (*in an eastward direction*), the only form is *eastward.* As an adverb, *eastward* and *eastwards* are both possible, but British English shows a marked preference for *eastwards,* and American English for *eastward.*

easy, easily. *I don't scare easy,* wrote a contributor to the 5 Feb. 1990 issue of the *New Yorker,* thereby drawing attention, as Burchfield noted at the time, to an informal use of *easy* as an adverb which is quite widespread in American English, but less so in British. (What makes Shakespeare's *As easie might I from my selfe depart, As from my soule which in thy brest doth lye* (Sonnet 109, 1600) acceptable, even harmonious, and the American use distinctly informal is a whole subject in itself.) Some set phrases containing *easy* used as an adverb, all of them first recorded in the 19c., are, however, firmly embedded in standard English: *to take it easy* (1867), *to* *go easy* (*on* or *with*, 1850), *easy does it* (Dickens, 1865), *stand easy* (1859), *easy come, easy go* (1832), etc.

Since *easy* functions as an adverb, replacing *easily*, in cases such as the set phrases mentioned above, it is perfectly acceptable to use *easier* and *easiest*, instead of *more easily* and *most easily*: *I decided to take it easier today and will do the same tomorrow*—*OEC*, 2009. In other contexts, however, they have an informal ring, or are American, e.g. *I could associate with them easiest*—*OEC*, 2003 (AmE); *I bleed easy, and I cry even easier*—*OEC*, 2002 (AmE). Choosing between *easier*, etc., and *more easily*, etc., will depend on the formality of what you are writing. But in cases like the following, where *easily* would have to be used if no comparison were being made, *easier* is to my mind clearly wrong, or, at the very least, inelegant: *The castle ... was built on the coast to be easiest supplied by sea and occupies a promontory that juts into the river Dee*—*www.greatcastlesofwales.co.uk*, 2004 (BrE).

eat. The past is spelt *ate* and was usually pronounced /ɛt/ in southern British English, but /eɪt/ is now becoming more common, as it always has been elsewhere in Britain, and is normal in American English and other varieties.

eatable, edible. Both words are used of food that is 'fit to be eaten as food' (a concept which is to an extent culture-dependent), although *edible* is much more frequent in the *OEC* data. But *edible* is the only word of the pair appropriate in contexts where the contrast is with poisonous or harmful (*edible mushrooms, edible snails*). Accordingly, in *we're running out of arable land, drinkable water, eatable fish*, the choice of *eatable* (= fit to eat) is appropriate. In **prepared with a popular variety of eatable leafy vegetable*, the correct choice is *edible*.

eBay. The online retailer's name is spelt with a lower case *e* followed by an upper case letter *b*, and all as one word. At the beginning of a sentence, or in headlines, the *e* looks better capitalized, *Ebay* with lower case *b*, but that spelling is not approved by the company.

ebullient. The pronunciation recommended is /ɪˈbʌljənt/, not /ɪˈbʊljənt/: i.e. with the sound of *pulse* not that of *bull*.

echelon /ˈɛʃəlɒn/, 'a level or rank in an organization or in society' is written without the acute accent it has in French (*échelon*, ultimately from *échelle* 'ladder'). The *e-* is normally pronounced as in *egg*, but can also be as in *hay*. *Echelon* was adopted in English from French in the late 18c. to mean a formation (of various kinds) of troops and still has military applications. It was a natural extension in the second half of the 20c., and originally in the US, to apply the word to civilian grades or ranks, and to speak of 'the higher (or upper) echelons' in any organization. Many commentators, including Gowers (1965, a 'slipshod extension'), have objected to this extended meaning, perhaps because of overuse, but it is here to stay and hard to object to.

echo. Plural *echoes*. See -O(E)S 1.

echoic. In etymology, applied to words brought into being as imitations of the sounds they represent, as *plonk, plop, twang, tweet*. Other terms used for this class of words are *imitative* and *onomatopoeic*.

eco-. The element *eco-* has been abstracted from *ecology* as a highly productive prefix forming numerous combinations, either well established, e.g. *eco-activist* (1969), *eco-friendly* (1989), *eco-warrior* (1987) *ecopolitics* (1973), or on the margins of everyday language, e.g. *eco-catastrophe* (1969), *ecofreak* (1970). It is advisable to consult an up-to-date dictionary such as the *Oxford Dictionary Online* to check whether to hyphenate compounds formed with this prefix.

ecology. There can be few people left who are unfamiliar with what a century ago was a technical word (= the branch of biology which deals with the relations of living organisms to their surroundings) used in tracts about the evolution of humanity and in proceedings of biological societies. A word of comparatively recent origin (the earliest example in the *OED* is one of 1873), and at first, reflecting its Greek origin (Gk οἶκος 'house, dwelling'), normally spelt *oecology* or *oekology*, it has made spectacular progress in the language because of humankind's growing consciousness that the global environment of plants and animals (including human beings) is being placed seriously at risk by industrial pollution, by the destruction of rain forests, and by other factors.

economic, economical. 1 *Economic* is the adjective that refers to anything to do with the subject of *economics*, or to *the economy*, as in *economic policy, growth, crisis, recovery. Economical* means 'careful to avoid waste' or 'providing good value in relation to the amount of money, effort, time, etc. spent'. To illustrate the difference, an *economic rent* is one determined by the laws of supply and demand; an *economical rent* is one that will not overstretch the tenant's resources. Aid to developing countries is *economic aid*, not *economical aid* (though some might argue it ought to be).

Occasionally *economical* is used where the distinction explained above suggests that *economic* is the right choice, but the substitution has little or no effect on meaning, e.g. *all kinds of problems, social, political, economical, and cultural.*

2 There is no consensus about how to pronounce the first syllable of the two words. One can please oneself whether to say /iːk-/ (the more traditional British pronunciation and my preference) or /ɛk-/. Cf. UNECONOMIC, UNECONOMICAL.

economical with the truth, meaning 'saying just as much as is needed or relevant', is a political cliché of our times, recalling earlier notions of Burke and others that 'in the exercise of all virtues, there is an economy of truth'. In its present form it alludes to events of 1986, when the British Cabinet Secretary Sir Robert Armstrong, giving evidence during the 'Spycatcher' trial (in which the British government sought to prevent the publication of a book of that name by a former MI5 employee), referred to a previous statement as follows: *It contains a misleading impression, not a lie. It was being economical with the truth.* The phrase made a huge impact at the time, because it appeared to be a brazen, novel euphemism for lying. It has become a stock part of the language, and is often used, especially in journalism: *Contrast Lord Butler's forensic exposure of intelligence failures this week with the smoothly arrogant evidence in defence of the Iraq dossier presented to the Hutton report last year, and you have a picture, if not of deception, then of men who were being severely economical with the truth—Scotland on Sunday*, 2004.

ecstasy is spelt *-asy*, not *-acy*. It is among the most frequently misspelt words in the language. The drug meaning is usually spelt with a capital, *Ecstasy.*

ecumenical. Now always spelt with an *e-*, not *oec-* (as it was from the 16c. to the 19c., representing Latin *oec-* and Greek οικ-). There is great diversity of opinion about the pronunciation of the first syllable, as between /iːk-/ and /ɛk-/.

-ed and 'd. Sometimes the need arises to add the ordinary adjectival ending *-ed* (as in *a walled garden*) to words normally used as nouns (e.g. *mustachio* → *mustachioed*), or verbs with the same form as nouns (e.g. *shampoo*) that have a fully pronounced final vowel (especially *a, i, o*). Formerly, to avoid the potentially bizarre-looking string of letters *-ioed, -ooed* etc., *'d* was used: *a cupola'd arch, a mustachio'd pirate, a shanghai'd sailor, subpoena'd.* Nowadays, however, the *-ed* ending is added in full, e.g.: *concertinaed, hennaed, mascaraed, mustachioed, pyjamaed, shampooed, shanghaied, subpoenaed.*

The apostrophe should still be used, however, when an initialism adds an inflection, as in *he was KO'd in the fifth round* and *Spike OD'd on barbiturates.* See FEE.

-èd, -éd. 1 Some adjectives have a fully pronounced and uncancellable final *-ed*: e.g. *fair-minded, ragged, warmhearted, wicked, wretched.*

2 In some other words the pronunciation of the *-ed* as a separate syllable, or the merging of it with the preceding syllable, can affect the sense, e.g. *the boy was aged* /eɪdʒd/ *12* but *an aged* /ˈeɪdʒɪd/ *man was sitting on the wall.* See also BELOVED; BLESSED; CURSED.

3 In poetry, convention allows writers, *metri causa* (to keep the meter) to mark as a separate syllable an *-ed* that would not be so pronounced in the ordinary language. In such cases the printers usually print the ending either as *-èd* or as *-éd: In curléd knots man's thoughts to hold*—Sidney (in D. Attridge, 1982); *Till the secret it gives Makes faint with too much sweet these heavy-wingéd thieves*—Shelley (in Palgrave, 1861).

edema. The American English spelling of *oedema* (see OE, etc.).

edgy. The older meaning, 'peevish and irritable', deriving from the idiom *have one's nerves on edge*, is first recorded from 1837, and was used by Kipling and John Buchan among others. Since the 1970s a new meaning, 'at the forefront of ideas, trendy', first attached to the word in US English, has emerged, based on another idiom built round the notion of the edge: *at the cutting edge*. Like *cutting edge* itself, it is in danger of overuse by being applied to things that can hardly be said to challenge the status quo. *Show Euro-cool by dolloping on some good and edgy and far more grown-up crème fraîche instead*—Nigella Lawson, 1998; *Sebastian Coe, having not quite drunk deeply enough of the marketing lexicon, has told us that it* [*sc.* the London Olympics logo] *is 'edgy'. It is nothing of the sort. Edgy would be good—Guardian*, 2007.

edible. See EATABLE.

editress. See -ESS 2, 4. Burchfield described the word as 'still current: e.g. *Alexandra Shulman, my editress at* Vogue, *for giving me a sabbatical*—acknowledgement by C. Lycett Green, 1994'. Since his edition, it has largely withered away.

-edly. 1 *Background to the issue.* 'We accept that this was not the case and unreservedly apologize to—': a standard formula when a newspaper offers apologies to a person whose views have been misrepresented. Count the syllables in *unreservedly* and everyone, I imagine, would say five. *Dickensian insolvency laws match their unembarrassedly Victorian values* (D. Jessel, 1990). Most people, I suppose, would pronounce *unembarrassedly* as six syllables to avoid the unseemliness of a final sequence /-sdli/. *'Oh yes,' says the boy, shamefacedly, 'that's all right.'* Bearing in mind that *shame-faced* is pronounced /-feɪst/, what are we to do with the form in *-edly*? The going begins to look hard.

The problem clearly amused Fowler (1926). He devoted nearly three columns to -EDLY and inserted some seventy cross-references to the article itself, some of them highly idiosyncratic. Of Fowler's seventy, the ones that have stood in the language longest are *advisedly, assuredly*, and *unadvisedly*, all first recorded in the 14c. Further waves of such words came along in the 16c. (*amazedly, ashamedly, deservedly*, etc.), the 17c. (*avowedly, designedly, reservedly, unexpectedly*, etc.), and the 18c. (*animatedly*, etc.). But the great age of *-edly* was the 19c.: no fewer than twenty-one of Fowler's seventy are first recorded then, (including *allegedly*), and under *markedly* the *OED* used to have the comment 'a favourite 19th c. adverb'. Two are not recorded in the *OED* before the 20c. (*painedly, unashamedly*), and *reportedly* (not mentioned by Fowler) is also first recorded in the 20c. Some of those listed by Fowler now seem very abstruse, while ten words that he listed are not recorded in the *OED* at all.

2 *Guidance.* (*a*) Normally *-edly* is pronounced as two additional syllables, even when the *-ed* element is not separately pronounced in the root words. Thus, *markedly* would always have three syllables, and *advisedly, assuredly, deservedly, reservedly*, and *resignedly* would always have four, while the great majority of words beginning with the prefix *un-* would normally have five (*unashamedly, unconcernedly, unreservedly*, etc.). (*b*) Formations from adjectives follow this rule only when *-ed* is pronounced as a separate syllable in the adjective, as in *cold-bloodedly* and *high-handedly* (four syllables) because the adjective already has three, but not, technically, in *shame-facedly* (three syllables), which is, however, also often pronounced with four.

3 There is a residue of *-edly* words in which the problem of pronouncing or not pronouncing the *-ed-* remains. One wonders, for example, how D. H. Lawrence would have pronounced *painedly* in his *England, My England* (1921); and how Browning would have pronounced *starchedly* (in *Red Cotton Night-Cap Country*, 1873); and indeed how the *OED* editors articulated to themselves the forms *admiredly, depressedly, labouredly*, and *veiledly* when they set them down as part of the language. All, however, are spoken too rarely to cause any real problem.

educate has the derivative *educable*. See -ABLE, -IBLE 2, 6.

educationalist, educationist. To denote 'an expert in the methods and science of education' both words are used, and the *OED* makes no distinction between them. In the *OEC* they are almost exactly equal in frequency overall, but *educationalist* is much the more frequent of the two in BrE, while in Indian English *educationist* is widely used. A Google search, however, shows the longer form is more frequent by a large margin. Merriam-Webster suggests that *educationist* is used in BrE to mean 'a professional educator', i.e. a teacher as opposed to a theorist, but the word is often explicitly contrasted with teachers, e.g. *the critics' chorus—which came from parents, teachers and educationists alike—Guardian*, 2008. See -IST, ALIST 2.

-ee[1]. 1 A suffix drawn from Old French words in *-ee, -é*, denoting the recipient of a grant or the like, e.g. *feoffee, grantee, lessee, patentee*, on the model of which many others were made, most of which cannot be construed as 'direct' passives, but denote the indirect object of the corresponding verbs; in *payee* (18c.) 'one to whom something is payable', and *trustee* (17c.), there has been a further (uncontroversial) departure from the usual pattern.

2 The common parallelism between agent-nouns in *-or* or *-er* and nouns in *-ee*, e.g. *lessor* and *lessee, obligor* and *obligee*, led to the general application of the suffix, sometimes risibly, as with *lover* and *lovee* (Richardson), *jester* and *jestee* (Sterne). Many such are nonce words, but others, like *abductee, addressee, amputee* (20c.), *employee, enrollee* (AmE), *escapee, evacuee, examinee, retiree, shortlistee* (someone or something that has been shortlisted for a prize), *standee* (a standing passenger), and *trainee*, look likely to be permanent. It is worth noting that some words in *-ee* have the force of 'one who is —ed' (*employee*) with parallel agent-nouns in *-er* (*employer*); while others are added to intransitive verbs and mean 'one who —s' (*attendee, escapee, standee*).

3 From the 14c. onwards *-ee* had also become the regular representation of French *é* in adopted words like *debauchee* and *jubilee*, and also in similar words from other languages (e.g. *grandee*, Spanish, 16c.). A great deal more about the suffix is set down by Laurie Bauer in his *English Word-Formation* (1983, 243 ff.).

-ee[2]. A suffix (really several distinct suffixes) shown: **1** in diminutives like *bootee, coatee*.

2 (now mostly abandoned in favour of *-i*) in words of Indian origin, *Bengalee, saree*, etc. (but retained in *dungaree, puttee*).

3 irregular in various unexplained circumstances, e.g. *bargee* (17c.), *goatee* (19c.), *jamboree* (19c.), *marquee* (17c.), and *settee* (18c.).

-eer. This suffix (the Anglicized form of French *-ier*, Latin *-ārius, -iārius*) is **1** Appended to nouns meaning 'a person concerned with or engaged in', as *auctioneer* (first recorded in 1708), *mountaineer* (Shakespeare, 1610), *musketeer* (1590), *profiteer* (1912), *volunteer* (1618). A few formations denote inanimate objects, as *gazetteer* (1611). A good many of the words so formed are more or less disparaging, e.g. *pamphleteer* (1642), *profiteer, racketeer* (1928), *sonneteer* (1665).

2 In verbal nouns with the meaning 'the activity of (doing something)', as *auctioneering* (1733), *buccaneering* (1758), *electioneering* (1760). Most of these quickly produced finite verbs as back-formations, e.g. *electioneer* (1789).

effect (noun and verb). See AFFECT, EFFECT.

effective, effectual, efficacious, efficient. All these words mean 'having an effect'. They are distinguished not only by different applications and nuances of meaning, but by frequency of use and level of formality. *Effective* means 'having a definite or desired effect' that is actual rather than theoretical: *an effective way, use, strategy; effective treatment, remedy; effective from 1 January*. *Effectual* is a partial synonym of *effective*, but is rather formal or literary. It often means 'capable of producing the required result or effect' independently of a personal agent, sometimes more in theory than in actuality: *The rich ought to have an effectual barrier in the constitution against being robbed, plundered, and murdered, as well as the poor*—A. Arblaster, 1987; *The rim of my hat, while effectually shading my eyes, did not obstruct my vision*—J. Davidson, 1991. A person cannot be described as *effectual*, but, paradoxically, someone lacking the ability to achieve results is said to be *ineffectual*.

Efficacious also overlaps in meaning with *effective*, but is formal or technical in register, and applies only to things, in particular medicines, treatment, etc. used for a particular purpose. It means 'producing or sure to produce a desired effect': *an efficacious treatment, drug, vaccine, remedy*. Its related noun is **efficacy**, e.g. *a drug of known efficacy*. *Efficient* applies to a person's or thing's capacity to function and produce results with minimum waste or effort: *an efficient use, system, car; efficient* *management, technology*. An *efficient cause* in philosophy is an agent that brings a thing into being or initiates a change.

In modern use, *efficient* is widely used to create compound adjectives, preceded by a noun that defines the scope of the efficiency, notably *energy-efficient* (1972) but also *fuel-efficient, tax-efficient*, etc.

effete entered the language in the 17c. from Latin *effētus* (= that has brought forth young (cf. *foetus*); hence worn out by bearing offspring), applied to animals that had ceased to bear offspring. It rapidly developed the transferred sense '(of a material substance) that has lost its special quality or virtue'; and by the late 18c. was being applied to persons or systems that had lost their effectiveness. Since the 20c. it has sometimes been applied to men as a euphemism for *effeminate* and a coded way of saying *gay: 'Do you mind if I sit down?' asked the young man in effete, accented English*—R. Kee, 1991.

effluvium. The plural is *effluvia*. See -UM 2.

-efied, -efy. See -FY 2.

e.g. is short for Latin *exemplī grātiā* and means 'for example'. To non-Latinists, in other words to most people, it is a source of endless confusion with *i.e.*, which stands for Latin *id est* and means 'that is to say'. To avoid confusion, both should be confined to footnotes or to bracketed information. In running text *e.g.* can be replaced with 'for example' or 'such as', and *i.e.* by 'that is (to say)' or 'namely'. Both should always be printed lower case roman with two points and no spaces.

eggcorn. 1 *Definition.* An 'eggcorn' is a modern linguistic term for 'a word or phrase that results from mishearing or misinterpreting another, with an element of the original being replaced by one which sounds very similar'. Eggcorns must by definition sound similar or identical to the original. They are 'slips of the ear'. But they must also make sense in their own terms. Common eggcorns that sound exactly like their originals (i.e. they are homophones) are *to the manor born* instead of *to the manner born* (from *Hamlet*) and *to tow the line* instead of *toe the line*. Examples that diverge from the original by only one sound are *miniscule* instead of *minuscule* and *on tenderhooks* for *on tenterhooks*.

2 *Origin of the term; key features.* Try saying 'acorn' in a slow, southern-US-states drawl, pronouncing the *c* like a g, and what you come out with will sound like 'egg-corn'. This spelling is recorded by the *OED*, beside more modern examples, in a letter from as far back as 1844: 'I hope you are as harty as you ust to be and that you have plenty of egg corn [*sc.* acorn] bread which I cann not get her[e] and I hope to help you eat some of it soon' (*John Sutter*, A.L. Hurtado, 2006). There are two points to note about this spelling. First, it made complete sense to the writer. Semantically *egg-corn* fits well, because from acorns come trees, as chickens do from eggs; acorns are vaguely egg-shaped; and an acorn in its cup could conjure up the image of an egg in its egg cup.

The second point is that people quite often twist words and phrases into new shapes in a similar way. So widespread is the phenomenon that the linguist Professor Geoffrey Pullum coined this term 'egg corn' [*sic*] in 2003. Since then, the term has become widely used in linguistic discussions, and there is even an online database of examples.

3 Why do *eggcorns* happen? Eggcorns often affect obscure or archaic words or meanings. A good example is the conversion of the original, Shakespearean *in one fell swoop* into *in one foul swoop*. (In *Macbeth* it is actually *at one fell swoop* but *in* ... is much more often used). *Fell* as an adjective no longer exists, and is therefore not meaningful to speakers, whereas *foul* conveys the perceived meaning of the phrase, which often describes undesirable events. In a further eggcornization, the phrase also appears as *in one fowl swoop*.

4 *Uneducated slips or educated guesses?* Eggcorns explain phrases that can, at first sight, look like bizarre mistakes, such as *to all intensive purposes, the Delhi lama, the Dahlia Lama*, (Dalai Lama), *Asparagus syndrome* (Asperger's syndrome), *above/beyond approach* (above/beyond reproach), and countless others. Once one knows about eggcorns, it can be entertaining to listen out and look out for them. To do so is even, perversely, a way of celebrating the playfulness of language. My favourites include *to have a poncho* for something, *the Nuke of the North* (Nanook of the North), *hairy-fairy* and *to go off on a tandem*. While eggcorns do cause mirth, it would be condescending to be superior and view them as signs of poor literacy. Many fit specific phonetic patterns, and illustrate systematic phonetic trends. They also display people's intelligence and ingenuity in making sense of what they hear, which is, after all, what we do all the time.

5 *Different from folk etymology.* It is sometimes unclear what distinguishes eggcorns from FOLK ETYMOLOGY in the latter's sense of 'the process by which the form of an unfamiliar or foreign word or phrase is modified in order to make it seem to be derived from a more familiar word or words'. (Folk etymology accounts for *chaise lounge* from *chaise longue* and *cockroach* from the Spanish *cucaracha.*) The difference is that folk etymologies become a norm, and are collective, whereas eggcorns are individual—which does not prevent them recurring individually time and time again. Eggcorns can even develop their own folk etymology (in its sense of explaining how a phrase arose). Jeannette Winterson reported a delightful example: 'I wasn't surprised to hear the washing machine called "he", but I was surprised by what followed: "My old washing machine, he's given up the goat," he said, in a broad Gloucestershire accent." "The goat?" I replied. "Are you sure?" "Oh, yes," said my neighbour, "ain't you never heard that expression before, given up the goat?" "Well, not exactly . . . where does it come from?" "Ah well," said my neighbour, "in the old days, when folks didn't have much, and mainly worked the land, a man would set store by his animals, especially his goat, and when he come to die, he would bequeath that goat to his heirs, and that is why we say, 'he's given up the goat'" (*Times*, 13 May 2006).

Because they make sense semantically, eggcorns also differ from MALAPROPISMS, which do not, e.g. Mrs Malaprop's 'like an allegory [*sc.* alligator] on the banks of the Nile'.

6 Finally, on a linguistic note, the term *eggcorn* is a rare example of a word that is 'autological', namely a word that is itself a member of or has features of the category it describes. Other examples of autological words are *short* (the word itself is short) and *sesquipedalian* ('having many syllables').

egis is a spelling of *aegis* sometimes used in American English.

ego /ˈiːgəʊ/ or /ˈɛgəʊ/, the *e* as in *eat* or as in *egg*. The plural is *egos*. See -O(E)S 4.

egoism, egotism. 1 The two words are 18c. formations, the first correctly from Latin *ego* 'I' + the suffix *-ism*, and the second from the same elements together with an intrusive *-t-* (unexplained, but perhaps on the false analogy of such words as *idiotism*). As both words are established, the irregular formation of *egotism* is of no importance, and it is in any case the slightly more commonly used term in the *OEC.*

2 The initial *e* of both words can be pronounced as in *egg*, or as in *eat*, as it can in all their derivatives.

3 Philosophers keep the words apart, but less exalted mortals ordinarily do not. For example, in ethics, *egoism* is used for 'the theory which regards self-interest as the foundation of morality', and in metaphysics, 'the belief, on the part of an individual, that there is no proof that anything exists but his or her own mind'.

If one were to claim a distinction between the two words, it could be argued that *egotism* is the general word for excessive self-centredness, vanity, and conceit, whereas *egoism* is a more straightforward preoccupation with the self and an excessive use of *I*. The meanings are, however, so close that they will not stay apart in ordinary usage, nor will those of the corresponding personal nouns, which are about equally frequent: **egoist** and **egotist** (although strictly an *egoist* is someone who subscribes to a type of morality based on the importance of the self and an *egotist* is a self-seeker). The philosophical/everyday distinction does not apply to the adjectives, in descending order of frequency: **egotistical** (four times as frequent as the next), **egoistic**, **egotistic**, and **egoistical** (rather uncommon).

4 Here is a range of examples: (*egoism* and derivatives) *I have never gone out of my way for man, woman, or child. I am the complete egoist*—V. Sackville-West, 1931; *Rationalism in morals may persuade men in one moment that their selfishness is a peril to society and in the next moment it may condone their egoism as a necessary and inevitable element in the total social harmony*—R. Niebuhr, 1932; *There were in man's nature not merely egoistic instincts concerned with self-preservation or the* *good of the Ego*—G. Murray, 1939; *The hero is filled only with himself; in his extreme egoism* [etc.]—E. Fromm, 1976; (*egotism* and derivatives) *Nothing so confirms an egotism as thinking well of oneself*—A. Huxley, 1939; *He was continually talking about himself and his relation to the world about, a quality which created the unfortunate impression that he was simply a blatant egotist*—H. Miller, 1957; *Jasper is sublimely egotistical, and the egotist of course sees himself as self-propagated*—P. Lively, 1987.

egregious. Pronounced /ɪˈgriːdʒəs/, i-**gree**-juhs. Of its two opposed meanings, 'remarkably good, distinguished' (as in Marlowe's *egregious viceroys of these eastern parts* in *Tamburlaine*) and 'remarkably bad, flagrant, outrageous', only the second is now in regular use, e.g. *an egregious example, an egregious waste of time, egregious errors,* etc., although it is also occasionally used to mean 'exceptional, unusual' more neutrally: *The inside is unified and austere, apart from an egregious baroque reredos, with a barrel vault*—J. Sturrock, 1988. The Latin adjective *ēgregius,* formed from *ē* 'out' + *grex, gregis* 'flock', meant 'standing out from the flock' and was almost always used in a favourable sense.

-ei-. The following words are among those spelt with *-ei-* not *-ie-*: *apartheid, beige, ceiling, conceit, conceive, counterfeit, cuneiform, deceit, deceive, either, forfeit, geisha, heifer, heinous, inveigh, inveigle, kaleidoscope, leisure, meiosis, neigh, neighbour, neither, nonpareil, obeisance, perceive, plebeian, receipt, receive, seigneur, seise, seize, seizure, sleight, surfeit, their, weir, weird.* See also I BEFORE E; -IE-.

eighties. See NINETIES.

-ein(e). Until the early part of the 20c. this second element of a number of words was regularly pronounced as two syllables: see CAFFEINE, CASEIN. They are all now simply pronounced as /-iːn/.

either.

1 Pronunciation.
2 Parts of speech.
3 *either* with more than two.
4 Number.
5 *either ... or* should balance

1 *Pronunciation.* Both /ˈʌɪðə/ and /ˈiːðə/ are equally common. Royalists and snobs may wish to note that according to the Queen's private secretary (in 1984), the Queen pronounces the word as /ˈʌɪðə/.

2 *Parts of speech. Either* is used as four distinct parts of speech: as adjective and pronoun, (*a*) = one or the other of two (*either book will serve the purpose; either of* [the two of] *you can go*); (*b*) = each of the two (*In the middest of the street of it, and of either side of the riuer, was there the tree of life*—Rev. (AV) 22: 2; *we sat down on either side of the radiogram, she with her tea, me with a pad and pencil*—J. Winterson, 1985. And as adverb and conjunction, (*a*) = as one possibility (*she ... had chosen not to call herself either Madeleine de Roujay or Madeleine le Freyne*—P. P. Read, 1986); (*b*) = as one choice or alternative (*either come in or go out but don't just stand there*); (*c*) with a negative, and usually placed at the end of a clause or sentence, = any more than the other, for that matter (*if she isn't the right material, she isn't one of that kind, either*—N. Gordimer, 1987; *But then we realized that if this man could attend a television taping without his wife's being any the wiser, perhaps the show's broadcast wouldn't affect her, either*—*New Yorker,* 1992).

3 *either* with more than two. *Either* means essentially 'one or other *of two*', or as *CGEL* expresses it technically (13.39), 'According to the didactic tradition, the use of correlative coordinators is unacceptable when there are three or more conjoins.' A standard unopposable construction is shown in the following: *We can either rely on our children to translate for us or try to catch up*—*Illustr. London News,* 1980. If the number of coordinators is extended to more than two, opinions vary widely about the elegance or even the acceptability of the results. The principle of duality is broken in the following examples: *Either France or Germany or Italy will break ranks in the matter.* In most contexts in formal English, however, it is advisable to restrict *either* to contexts in which there are only two possibilities. But in conversational English, constructions of the type 'a narration of events, either past, present, or to come' is often unavoidable. Cf. Shakespeare's *they say there is Diuinity in odde Numbers, either in natiuity, chance, or death* (1598). Examples of the negative form *neither* followed by more than two alternatives are very common: *neither ABC nor CBS nor NBC has a permanent team in black Africa*—*New Yorker,* 1988.

4 *Number.* In normal circumstances *either* governs a singular verb (*either candidate* [of two] *is acceptable*), but in the type *either* + *of*-phrase (especially in interrogative clauses) the number of the verb often varies 'because of the fundamental plurality of the conception' (Jespersen, 1909–49, ii. 172): e.g. *either of them* [*sc.* the words *friend* and *mistress*] *are enough to drive any man to distraction*—Fielding, 1749; *Are either of you dining with Stewart to-night?*—E. F. Benson, 1911. The same is true of the type *neither* + *of*-phrase: (treated as plural) *I daresay I . . . could have been a more loving mother to you and Jane, but as things are, neither of you require me*—E. Bowen, 1955; *I have written about almost every subject except astrology and economics, neither of which are serious subjects*—P. Howard, 1985; (treated as singular) *Apart from a few minor bruises, neither of them was hurt*—*OEC*, 2010. The informal type *Either John or Jane avert their eyes when I try to take a photograph of them* brings out the fundamental clash between notional and actual agreement. Similarly *If either James or Charles should turn up, offer them a drink.* See also AGREEMENT 6.

5 *either . . . or* should balance. Fowler (1926) suggested that, in 'careful' writing (but not in informal speaking) *either* in *either . . . or* sentences should ideally be placed immediately before the first item being itemized so that the clauses following *either* and *or* are exactly parallel in structure; other usage writers have made the same claim. So, in his example sentence *You are either joking or have forgotten* the clauses are not parallel, because the subject *you* has been left out of the second one, but the clauses are parallel in *Either you are joking or you have forgotten.* In examples such as this, repeating the grammatical subject will, to my mind, make the sentence rather starchy, while leaving it out seems justified by a natural process of ellipsis. But in the following example, also from Fowler (1926), the lack of parallelism between the clauses is more obvious: *Their hair is usually worn either plaited in knots or is festooned with cocks' feathers,* which would be neater as *Their hair is usually worn either plaited in knots or festooned with cocks' feathers.*

-eity. There has been a marked tendency since the second half of the 20c. to replace the traditional /-iːɪtɪ/ (**ee**-i-ti) in the pronunciation of words containing this ending (*deity, homogeneity, spontaneity, etc.*) by /-eɪɪtɪ/ (**ay**-it-i).

ejector. Spelt *-or* not *-er*. See -OR.

eke out. To begin with (16c.) the expression meant primarily 'to make an amount or supply of something last longer by using or consuming it frugally'. Defoe's Robinson Crusoe, for example, commented (1719), *My ink . . . had been gone . . . all but a very little, which I eked out with water.* This construction survives: *Her mother . . . edited 'Aunt Judy's Magazine' to eke out the clerical income*—H. Carpenter, 1985. Fowler (1926) declared this to be the only legitimate construction. 'The proper object is accordingly a word expressing not the result attained, but the original supply. You can eke out your income or a scanty subsistence with odd jobs or by fishing, but you cannot eke out a living or a miserable existence. You can eke out your facts, but not your article with quotations.' From the early 19c., however, *eke out* has also been used to mean 'to manage to make a living with difficulty', the sense to which Fowler objected: *Some runaway slaves . . . contrived to eke out a subsistence*—Darwin, 1845; *He lived with his parents until their death, and thereafter eked out a marginal living as a messenger*—O. Sacks, 1985; *The elder Rossetti eked out a precarious living as a teacher and translator*—A. C. Amor, 1990. It is clear that both constructions are now standard.

elder. 1 As an adjective, *elder* is now confined to the meaning 'senior, of a greater age', e.g. *his elder brother.* Similarly, the superlative form *eldest.* You can say *his elder brother, her sister is the eldest, John is my eldest son,* but you cannot say **John is elder than Paul; *Which one is eldest?*, etc. In these cases, *older* or *oldest* has to be used.

Outside this restricted use of family seniority, *elder* lingers as noun and adjective in a few contexts such as *elders* (*and betters*), meaning people whose age is supposed to command the respect of the young; as the title of lay officers of the Presbyterian Church; the *elder brethren* of Trinity House; the *elder hand* at piquet, and *elder statesman.*

2 The noun *elder* is now quite often used, especially in AmE, by providers of services to older people. It is a useful euphemism which avoids phrases containing words with negative connotations, such as *of the elderly, of old people*, etc. It used most often in this way in the compounds *elder care* and *elder abuse*. Examples: *Various types of elder abuse include neglect, physical abuse, emotional abuse and financial exploitation—California CPA*, 2005; *by 2020 it is estimated that elder care will pose more of a problem at work than childcare, an issue now attracting the Prime Minister's interest—Observer*, 2004 (BrE).

elector. Thus spelt, not *-er*.

electric, electrical. In most contexts *electric* is the automatic choice (*electric blanket, chair, current, fan, heater, kettle, light, razor, shock*, etc.). *Electrical* is reserved for contexts in which the sense is more general, 'relating to or connected with electricity', e.g. *electrical appliances, engineer(ing), problem, storm*. See -IC(AL).

electrocute. This portmanteau word, first recorded in 1889, contains the combining form *electro-* + *-cute* modelled on *execute* (verb). There seems to be an important difference in usage and meaning between British and American English. In the US, where the word was coined to refer to the process of execution by electric current, if you are *electrocuted*, you die. As a result, phrases such as *to be electrocuted to death, to be fatally electrocuted*, etc., are considered a tautology there. In British English, you can suffer an electric shock and refer to the event as being *electrocuted*, and it can also mean, in context, dying from or being executed by electric shock.

eleemosynary. Pronounced as seven syllables, /ˌɛliːˈmɒsɪnəri/ or /-ˈmɒzɪnəri/, e-li-ee-**mo**-si-nuh-ri, or -**mo**-zi-nuh-ri.

elegant variation. In a celebrated essay spread over four pages Fowler (1926) used this expression to describe the way in which 'second-rate writers' and 'young writers' fall into various stylistic traps in their effort to avoid using the same word in a sentence. To illustrate this he first cited examples of avoidable repetition such as *A debate which took wider ground than that* actually *covered by the* actual *amendment itself* (omit either *actually* or *actual*). And for the kind of lapse which was his main target—clumsy attempts at variation—he cited a context from Thackeray (*careering during the season from one great dinner of twenty* covers *to another of eighteen* guests) (use *guests* instead of *covers*, and allow the noun following *eighteen* to be understood). Nowadays, it is to be hoped that experienced copy editors and proofreaders will remove clumsiness of that kind, but the advent of self-publishing means that all too often it remains untouched.

A commonplace method of avoiding repetition is to use a synonym or, especially in journalism, to replace a specific name with an identifying phrase. Thus (from an American periodical) *K. has extraordinary* hair; *the man is nearly sixty years old, and look what* a mane *he's got!* And of the second type (identifying phrases) (cited from the *NZ English Newsletter*, 1991): *A few months ago* she *seemed near death. But* the world's most famous nun *continues her good work. Today* Mother Teresa *announced she is so moved by the plight of the Romanian children she is going to do something about it.* The Nobel Peace prize winner *will open a mission in Bucharest to care for the children.*

There are many other types of elegant, and of inelegant, variation. See also REPETITION.

elegiac quatrain. An alternative name given to the *heroic quatrain* owing to Gray's use of this metre in his *Elegy*. It has four iambic pentameters, rhyming alternately:

> *The Curfew tolls the knell of parting day,*
> *The lowing herd wind slowly o'er the lea,*
> *The plowman homeward plods his weary way,*
> *And leaves the world to darkness and to me.*

elegy. At first (early 16c.) applied to 'a song of lamentation, especially a funeral song or lament for the dead', and this has remained as the principal use of the word in English: notable examples are Milton's *Lycidas* (1637), Shelley's *Adonais* (1821), and Arnold's 'Thyrsis' (1867). But by 1600 the limitation of the word in this manner had partially given way to the sense 'a poem of melancholy reflection', and in particular to all the species of poetry for which Greek and Latin poets (and then English poets) adopted the elegiac metre, or, as in Gray's *Elegy Written in a Country Church-Yard* (1751), wrote ELEGIAC QUATRAINS.

elemental, elementary. *Elemental* refers primarily to the medieval belief in the 'four elements' (earth, water, air, fire) or to the enormous observable power of the elements during storms: hence *elemental* *force, passion, power, struggle,* etc. *Elementary,* by contrast, means 'rudimentary, introductory', as in *elementary book, school, subjects.* But in modern physics *elementary* means 'not decomposable', especially in *elementary particle,* any of several subatomic particles supposedly not decomposable into simpler ones.

elfish, elvish. Both terms are used, and also *elfin,* without any discernible distinction. It is not that one is more established than the others, though *elvish* is first recorded in the 14c. and *elfish* and *elfin* not till the 16c. Spenser and Keats seem to have favoured *elfin,* Coleridge *elfish,* and Chaucer and the Gawain-poet *elvish.* Tolkien revived the obsolete term *elven* (*elven-kin, -tongue,* etc.) in the 20c. One can only suppose that the choice of word is largely a matter of taste.

elicit, illicit. Because they are pronounced identically, /ɪˈlɪsɪt/, they are occasionally confused. *Elicit* is a verb meaning 'to draw out, evoke (an admission, response, etc.)'; whereas *illicit* is an adjective meaning 'unlawful, forbidden'. Examples of wrong use: **Your questionnaire targeted WASPs and illicited a typical reaction—Metro* (NZ), 1989 (read *elicited*); **Whenever I publish a piece such as this it often illicits more questions than it provides answers—OEC,* 2004 (read *elicits*); **Whitfield, the local minister with whom Addie had an elicit affair, arrives at the house to direct her funeral—OEC,* 2002 (read *illicit*).

eligible. *Eligible* means 'fit or entitled to be chosen (*eligible for a pension*)' or 'desirable, suitable' (an *eligible bachelor*). It ends in *-ible,* not *-able,* as is sometimes found.

ellipsis.

1 Definition.
2 Legitimate types.
3 Unacceptable types.
4 Omission of *that* (relative pronoun).
5 In non-standard speech.
6 Punctuation mark.

1 *Definition.* Ellipsis is 'the omission of one or more words in a sentence, which would be needed to complete the grammatical construction or fully to express the sense' (*OED*). It is an important feature of English, in its written and especially in its spoken form. It can be seen in its most elementary form in utterances like *Told you so, Serves you right, Want some?,* and *Sounds fine to me,* in each of which a pronoun has been dispensed with. The primary nature of ellipsis is that it is a process by means of which certain notional elements of a sentence may be omitted if they are clearly predictable or recoverable in context.

2 *Legitimate types.* Ordinary English grammar normally requires the omission of certain elements: (definite article not repeated) *He heard the whirr and* ʌ *click of machinery;* (infinitive marker *to* not repeated before a second infinitive) *I was forced to leave and* ʌ *give up my work at the hospital;* (subject not repeated) *I just pick up wood in a leisurely way,* ʌ *stack it, and* ʌ *slowly rake the bark into heaps;* (infinitive implied though omitted) *Knowledge didn't really advance; it only seemed to* ʌ. In such circumstances insertion of the missing elements is not entirely ruled out if some degree of emphasis is required, but in ordinary declarative or narrative prose, ellipsis is normal. Any substantial piece of writing, when analysed, yields examples of slightly more complicated but still legitimate types of ellipsis, e.g. (from Nicholas Shakespeare's novel *The Vision of Elena Silves* (1989)) *Henriques knew they would eat his tongue for wisdom,* ʌ *his heart for courage and for fertility* ʌ *make their women chew his genitals.* Cf. BE 6.

There are many other types of ellipsis. *CGEL* (1985) needed more than fifty pages to list, illustrate, and label them all (strict, standard, situational, structural, etc., ellipsis). The nature of what can safely be left to be understood is at the heart of the problem. The basic rules allow for a reasonable amount of flexibility in the imaginary wording of the understood parts: e.g. (adjustment of *thought* to *think* after the auxiliary *didn't*) (*'And you thought I was a virgin when I married you?' . . . 'No, I didn't* ʌ'; (adjustment of *felt* to *feel* in the ellipsis) *She hadn't felt fraudulent about it. Nor had there been any reason to* ʌ.

3 *Unacceptable types.* Unacceptable difficulties arise in various circumstances, e.g. if two auxiliary verbs that operate in different ways are placed together. One should not say or write *No state has or can adopt such measures.* Idiom requires *has adopted or can adopt such measures.* When a change of grammatical voice is involved, ellipsis spells danger. A reader cannot be expected to make the necessary adjustment from the active voice to the passive and supply an omitted part of the passive form. One of Fowler's examples (1926) will suffice to support the argument: *Mr Dennett foresees a bright future for Benin if our officials will manage matters conformably with its 'customs', as they ought to have been* (insert *managed*). Comparisons can also produce unacceptable sequences when unwise ellipses are attempted: *The paintings of Monet are as good or better than those of van Gogh* (read *as good as or better than*). Less obviously wrong, perhaps, but best avoided is leaving out an auxiliary which is not the same number (singular/plural) as one that is given: *The ringleader was hanged and his followers* ʌ *imprisoned* (ellipsis of *were*).

4 Omission of *that* (relative pronoun). See THAT (relative pronoun) 2.

5 *In non-standard speech.* Non-standard speech is characterized by the use of many unfamiliar types of ellipsis. For example, American writers such as Michael Doane and E. L. Doctorow underline the nature of a particular way of speaking by employing non-standard ellipses in their speech: (omission of *have*) *Watergate, man, Where you been*?—Doane, 1988; (omission of *do* or *can*) *Well how you expect to get anywhere, how you expect to learn anything?*—Doctorow, 1989.

6 *Punctuation mark. Ellipsis* is also used to mean a punctuation mark consisting of three full points to mark either a pause or the intentional omission of words (for example in quoting).

else. 1 When *else* is combined with an indefinite or an interrogative pronoun the usual possessive form is *anybody else's* (not *anybody's else*, as was the case until the mid-19c.), *who else's* (not *whose else*), *nobody else's* (not *nobody's else*), etc.: e.g. *They look to me like someone else's, to be frank*—P. Lively, 1987; *We never see Lisa from anyone else's point of view*—*OEC*, 2002.

2 When *else* was used with an interrogative pronoun it was possible until about the end of the first quarter of the 20c. to postpone it to the end of the sentence (*What did he say else?*). Now the only available order of words is shown in *What else did he say?*

3 Since the Middle Ages, *else* has been used, sometimes as a quasi-conjunction, to mean 'otherwise, if not': *Strangle her, els she sure will strangle thee*—Spenser, 1596; *The land certainly had ... vomited them out else*—Daniel Rogers, 1642; *and well was it for him that the outburst of his blind fury was over, else he had become an easy prey to his gigantic protagonist*—R. M. Ballantyne, 1858. This use seems now to be archaic, but it does occur occasionally: *Fortunately it* [*sc.* a staircase] *was not spiral, else I would have succumbed to vertigo*—B. Rubens, 1985; *My father was fortunate that my mother's nature was reserved, else he would have found himself out on the road that night*—H. Jacobson, 1986.

elusive, illusive, illusory. 1 *Elusive* is the adjective corresponding to the verb *elude.* Something *elusive* eludes or escapes you, is difficult to grasp physically or mentally: *an elusive enemy, creature, bird; an elusive concept, goal, quality.* Examples: *Yet happiness is an elusive concept, rather like love*—*OEC*, 2002; *if the situation in western Pakistan continues to deteriorate, success will be elusive and very difficult to achieve*—*OEC*, 2009.

2 Something *illusory* is like an illusion, is deceptive and not real. First recorded in 1599, in a letter written by Elizabeth I, *illusory* was joined in 1679 by *illusive*, expressing that same meaning. However, *illusive* has largely withered away in that use, although it occasionally appears. Examples: (illusory) *a Buddhist monk advised him, 'You must first realize the illusory nature of your own body'*—*OEC*, 2003; *Android, being open source, offered them at least the illusory hope that they might maintain control of their business*—*OEC*, 2010; (illusive) *'Tis now a vain illusive show, That melts whene'er the sunbeams glow*—Scott, 1813; *These alterations highlight the immediacy, fluidity, and theatricality of the performance. Admittedly, this sense of immediacy is illusive, since these performance are mediated through the realms of videotape and vinyl*—*OEC*, 2003.

Nowadays, poor, abused *illusive* appears nine times out of ten as a mistake for *elusive.* (The mistake happens, of course, because both words are pronounced /ɪˈl(j)uːsɪv/.) **Sharks up to forty feet are quite common, although when Helen was there they proved to be illusive*—*OEC*, 2005 (read *elusive*).

3 The final word that gets snarled up in this mesh of meanings is *allusive*, the adjective corresponding to *allusion* and used mainly by literary critics, film critics, etc., e.g.: *Although his restless experimentation and complex, allusive style often prove difficult on first reading, his novels possess a complexity and depth that reward the demands he makes upon his readers—OEC*, 2002. It too is occasionally used by mistake for *elusive*: **Give John Kerry this. He's maddeningly allusive—OEC*, 2004 (read *elusive*).

Given the prevailing muddle over the meaning of these words, it is hardly surprising that one has to turn to literary titans to see them used with absolute precision: at a conference in August 2004, Vikram Seth memorably and alliteratively defined writing as 'allusive, elusive, and illusive'.

elvish. See ELFISH.

Elysium. Plural (if needed) *Elysiums*. See -UM 1.

emaciate, emaciation. For pronunciation, see -CIATION, -TIATION 3.

em- and im-, en- and in-. There are several frequent words starting with these prefixes that can technically be spelt either with *e-* or with *i-*. While the two forms of most of these words, e.g. *embed/imbed*, have coexisted over the centuries, and are recognized as variants by the *OED*, by convention the *e-* form is massively more common in the words listed below and in their derivatives. It is therefore advisable to avoid the spelling in *i-*, because most people would consider it a mistake: *embed, encase, encage, enclose, encrust, endorse, endue, enfold, engraft, enmesh, entrench, entrust, entwine, enwrap*. The pair *inure/enure* works the other way round, with *inure* being by far the commoner, which is also true of *ingrained/engrained*. See also IM-; INURE; ENQUIRE.

email (noun and verb), short for *electronic mail*, is a term that has become familiar enough to be spelt as one word, without a hyphen. Its grammatical behaviour follows that of *mail*, i.e. it is a noun and a verb; you can send an *email* and you can *email* messages and people.

emails. Writing and receiving emails is now so much a part of everyday personal and business life that it is worth providing some basic guidance. Generally speaking, emails tend to combine the immediacy of conversation with the formality or semiformality of letter writing, a situation that sometimes makes people uncertain about the appropriate way to express themselves. The main areas of uncertainty concern the opening greeting, signing off, and the style and degree of formality in the message.

1 *Opening greeting.* Using *Dear*—makes an email rather formal. It is appropriate in business, when emailing a new contact, or an established contact with whom you wish to maintain a formal relationship. Whether, and at what point, you switch to a less formal opening is for you to judge, depending on how your relations with the other person are developing. In other contexts, email's affinity with conversation encourages much more casual greetings such as *Hello*— and *Hi*—, as in a hastily written message or in text messaging.

2 *Signing off.* Similarly, to sign off nowadays with *Yours* or *Yours sincerely* is extremely formal in an email, though normal, of course, in a letter. (If you feel the need to write *Yours faithfully* you should be writing a conventional letter with a proper letterhead.) It is quite legitimate to close the email with a simple statement of your name, without any sign-off, but this may strike some people as rather cold. The most commonly used sign-offs nowadays are the informal conversational ones such as *Best wishes, All the best*, and *Best regards*. If their ritualized insincerity makes you uncomfortable, *Thanks* is unlikely to go amiss, particularly if the email is a request of some kind.

3 *Level of formality.* In a professional context, the normal conventions of spelling, grammar, and punctuation should govern what you write. Resist the temptation to be too informal, or to ignore punctuation and capitalization in the way that you might when texting, or to use abbreviations such as *u*, *gr8*, and so forth (*i dont want to go to france this year do u*). A professional email is decidedly not a text message, though, of course, in personal emails if you know someone well enough to be sure they will not be offended, or baffled, by using text conventions, feel free. It goes without saying that you should not write in capital letters, which, by convention, is SHOUTING.

4 *Other issues.* (*a*) As with any piece of writing destined to be read by someone else, you should read through what you have written to check for grammar and spelling. The best way to do this is to print it out before you send, since even spellcheckers will not detect every glitch.

(*b*) Your subject line should ideally tell recipients at a glance what your message is about, and whether it requires any action by them. At the same time, it should be as concise as possible. For example, *Linguistics from Oxford - Available on Inspection* informs the recipient in just six words what the topic is and what action they can take, i.e. order an inspection copy.

(*c*) Emails should ideally be short, so that the content can be read in one screen, without scrolling down. Bullet points and lines between paragraphs help make the information easier to process. If you find that your email is turning into a lengthy e-missive, another way of presenting the information would probably be better, such as an attached text file, chart, etc. Alternatively, a separate email per topic may be a solution.

(*d*) There are many other points to consider when composing an email: for example, never write something you would be embarrassed for people other than the recipient to see, since emails can be forwarded and forwarded again, ad infinitum, and their contents come back to haunt you. However, further advice begins to fall outside the scope of what is strictly language-related, and there are any number of websites you can consult for detailed information about how to make your emails effective, interesting, appealing, and so forth.

emanate. The standard pronunciation of this word is /ˈɛməneɪt/ (**e**-muh-nayt) with a short initial *e*, rather than **ee**-muh-nayt.

embargo. The noun has the plural *embargoes*, and the verb the inflections *embargoes, embargoed, embargoing*. See -O(E)S 1.

embarrass is spelt with two *r*s and two *s*'s.

embarrassedly. See -EDLY.

embed. See EM- AND IM-, EN- AND IN-.

embryo. Plural *embryos*. See -O(E)S 5.

emend. See AMEND.

emigrant, émigré, immigrant, migrant. An *emigrant* is someone who leaves their country to live in another. An *immigrant* is someone who comes as a permanent resident to a country other than their own native land. So the same person is an *emigrant* when passing outward through border control, and an *immigrant* when accepted as a resident member of another country. A *migrant* is (*a*) an animal or bird that migrates, (*b*) (in Australia and NZ) an immigrant. Groups of people working away from their native lands, are often called *migrant workers*, and *economic migrants* are people who travel to work in another country in the hope of a better standard of living. People described as *émigrés*, from French (= having emigrated) are usually political emigrants, the word first having been used to describe those fleeing the French Revolution. The word carries connotations of intellectual or artistic sophistication that the equivalent *refugee* does not: *Austrian émigré Erich von Stroheim.* It is written with the accents, in roman.

eminent refers to people who are famous and respected within a particular sphere (*one of the world's most eminent statisticians*) or to an outstanding quality (*the book's scholarship and eminent readability*). Outlandish though it may seem, some people write *eminent* danger when what they presumably mean is *imminent* danger. It is possible they do this because they pronounce the *e-* and the *i-* at the beginning of the two words similarly. If it means anything at all, 'eminent danger' would be great danger: perhaps that is what these Mrs Malaprops think the phrase means. Something *imminent* is, of course, something about to happen, so *imminent* danger is a danger that is very close at hand.

emolument. See FORMAL WORDS.

emote, a back-formation from *emotion*, means 'to dramatize emotion; to act emotionally'. The word is first recorded in America in 1917, and was for a long time restricted to the language of ballet and theatre critics and to photography: *The female sitter had to emote in some way, either by dressing up or by gazing with drooping head into a bowl of flowers—Amateur Photographer*, 1970; *Just that until a few years ago you could barely talk to strangers, so how are you going to get up and emote in front of an audience?*—L. S. Schwartz, 1989. It has now passed into more general use, but usually with more than a soupçon of sarcasm or humour: *Mr Cameron, emoting about character and DNA while steering clear of policy, is a featherweight in comparison—Telegraph*, 2009; *Mary and Sherlock don't emote all over the place about their feelings—OEC*, 2010.

emotional, emotive. *Emotional* and *emotive* both mean 'connected with or appealing to the emotions', but *emotional* is the word more often used in the neutral sense 'relating to emotions' whereas *emotive* has a stronger sense of 'causing emotion': *In this oppressive society women need the care and emotional support of other women*—A. Wilson, 1988; *The whole subject of removing children from their parents was no less emotive for them than for other members of the community*—R. Black, 1992. *Emotional*, but not *emotive*, also means 'easily affected by emotion' when referring to people: *All of us get elated and emotional as we stroll through a pine grove on a hot summer day when the old trees fill the air with their pungent fragrance*—P. Heselton, 1991. *Emotive* is more commonly used of words or behaviour that tends to arouse emotions, and often qualifies words such as *issue, language, topic*, etc., whereas *emotional* describes feeling and actions that involve emotion in themselves. Contrast *He was just firing a smokescreen of emotive words and phrases*—Gavin Lyall, 1982 with *From a good script will emerge a film in which every scene carries an emotional charge*—J. Park, 1990.

empanel. See IMPANEL. The inflected forms have a doubled consonant in British English (*empanelled, empanelling*), but usually a single *-l-* in AmE. See -LL-, -L-.

empathy, etymologically an adaptation of Greek ἐμπάθεια 'passionate affection', but introduced to English as a translation of German *Einfühlung* at the beginning of the 20c., is a term used in psychology and aesthetics meaning 'the power of projecting one's personality into (and so fully comprehending) the object of contemplation'. In general use it tends occasionally to replace *sympathy* or *feeling for* when those traditional words are sometimes more appropriate: *sympathy* can be felt without the element of personal experience that *empathy* implies. In the following examples (all from non-specialist works), *empathy* is the *mot juste: Seeing our sadness, our empathy with the pain she was surely suffering, she said, 'What's wrong with you all?'*—Angela Davis, 1975; *The empathy of a true friend is what I have lived without for years*—G. Paley, 1980; *We develop empathy as a capacity to share in the experience of others, not just* like *our own but* as *our* own—P. Casement, 1985; *It was a hard life, and Byron recounts it with empathy and gusto*—A. Burgess, 1986. The corresponding adjective is either **empathetic** or **empathic**. The first is about twice as frequent in the *OEC* data, and has the advantage that in form it is a nice parallel with *sympathetic*, whereas for me *empathic* feels as if it is short-changing its meaning.

employee. During the second half of the 19c. *employé* (feminine *employée*) was more commonly used than the anglicized *employee:* the *OED* in 1897 labelled *employee* as 'rare except U.S.'. Now *employee* has completely ousted the French form, which is what Fowler (1926) hoped would happen. In American English the word often used to be spelt *employe*, but that spelling is now rare. Whether spelt with one final *e* or two, it is pronounced as three syllables. The stress can fall either on the second or third. In British English stressing the second syllable is more frequent; in American English, the third syllable is more often stresssed. See -EE[1] 2.

emporium. A rather formal word for a large retail store or a centre of commerce. The more usual plural form is *emporia*, but *emporiums* is also in standard use. See -UM 3.

enamel. The inflected forms show a doubled consonant in British English (*enamelled, enamelling*), but usually a single *-l-* in AmE. See -LL-, -L-.

enamour (US **enamor**). **1** Generally used as the participial adjective *enamoured*, either to mean 'in love' or 'fascinated, enchanted'. The usage question it raises is which preposition should follow it: *of, with*, or *by*. Though all three have good historical precedents, various British and American style guides prescribe *of*. Neither usage nor dictionaries seem to agree with that prescription, however. Merriam-Webster shows *of* and *with* for the second meaning (but only *of* for the first); *ODO* allows all three for both meanings, while the unrevised *OED* (1891) entry shows *of*, and *with* is labelled archaic.

Data from the *OEC* shows that *enamoured of* is still the most common pattern, closely followed by *enamoured with*. Much less frequent than either is *enamoured by*. In both BrE and AmE *of* is used about half the time, but in AmE *with* appears in a higher proportion of all examples than in BrE. Historical data for the whole 20c. suggests *enamoured of* declined, while *enamored with* (i.e. in AmE) increased. Despite the widespread use of *with*, many people feel uncomfortable about it. Conversely, some people find *enamoured of* strange. In the end it boils down to a personal preference that may be influenced by age and location. Examples: *I am not so much enamoured of the first and third subjects*—Dickens, 1866; *Even more perturbing, the king by 1611 was publicly enamoured of Sir Robert Carr*—*ODNB*, 2008; *He is enamored of his profession, but sometimes it gets him in trouble*—*NYT*, 2007; *The press is enamoured with Obama*—*Daily Tel.*, 2008; *But in the end, they came home so enamored with the experience that they made a vow to repeat it every year*—*Boston Globe*, 2008; *Orlando was enamoured by her looks and her long hair*—*Times of India*, 2008.

2 The spelling *enamoured* is more common in all varieties of English, except American, which favours *enamored*, but even in AmE the longer spelling is occasionally used.

en- and in-. See EM- AND IM-, EN- AND IN-.

en bloc. The French phrase *en bloc* 'as a whole' (first recorded in English in 1861), was adopted in English at a somewhat earlier date than BLOC on its own. It is now usually printed in roman in English contexts.

encase. See EM- AND IM-, EN- AND IN-.

enclave. This 19c. French loanword was pronounced in a French manner, /ɑ̃klɑv/, in English until at least the end of the first quarter of the 20c., but is now routinely /ˈɛnkleɪv/.

enclose, inclose. See EM- AND IM-, EN- AND IN-.

encomium. The recommended plural form is *encomiums*, but *encomia* is also in standard use. See -UM 3.

encrust, encrustation. See EM- AND IM-, EN- AND IN-.

encyclopedia, encyclopaedia. The word, which was first recorded in English in the 16c., was adopted from late Latin *encyclopædia*, from a pseudo-Greek ἐγκυκλοπαιδεία, an erroneous form occurring in manuscripts of Quintilian, Pliny, and Galen, for ἐγκύκλιος παιδεία 'encyclical education', the circle of arts and sciences considered by the Greeks as essential to a liberal education. The spelling with final *-pedia* has long been the standard one in American English, while the form in *-ae-*, *encyclopaedia*, was standard in British English. According to *OEC* data, the first spelling is now more than three times as common across all varieties of English, and on an equal footing with the second in British English. The older form with ligature, *encyclopædia*, recommended by Burchfield, is more or less extinct. There is also a marked preference for the adjective to be spelt **encyclopedic**, rather than **encyclopaedic**.

endear. To *endear* someone to someone else means 'to make someone popular with or liked by someone'. The meaning is easy to grasp, but some people get into a bit of a tangle with the grammar. You can *endear yourself* to other people: *she endeared herself to all who worked with her*. Alternatively, a quality someone has, or an action on their part, can *endear* them to other people: *Flora's spirit and character endeared her to everyone who met her*. But to say *his co-operative attitude endeared me to him*, when you mean 'made *me* like *him*', is to describe who likes whom arsy-versy; it should be *his cooperative attitude endeared him to me*.

endeavour (AmE *endeavor*). **1** See PASSIVE VOICE 6.

2 See FORMAL WORDS.

ended, ending. *Statistics for the six months ended* (or *ending*) *31 December*. If the terminal date is in the future *ending* is always used, and *ended* ordinarily when it is past. But it is pedantic to object to *ending* for a past date on the ground that a present participle cannot suitably be used of a past event. If the reference is to the initial date the word is always *beginning*, never *begun*, whatever the date.

endemic, epidemic. An endemic disease is one that is regularly or only found among a particular people or in a certain region; an epidemic disease is a temporary but widespread outbreak of a particular disease. Some scientists, but few laymen, use the terms *enzootic* and *epizootic* when such diseases occur in animals.

end of the day, at the. Already in 1996 Burchfield could refer to this as 'one of the ignoble clichés introduced into the language in the 20c.'. First recorded in 1974, it has, since his day, tightened its stranglehold on certain types of conversation, despite widespread fear and loathing in many quarters, and an energetic campaign by journalist Vanessa Feltz to proscribe it. At the end of the day, all it means is 'when all's said and done'.

endorse, endorsement. 1 The spelling beginning with *en-*, rather than *in-* is the modern norm. The *in-* spelling is, however, sometimes used in legal writing.

2 *Endorse* (literally 'to write on the back of something') has long been used to mean: to confirm a statement or opinion; to write on the back of a cheque or other document for a specified commercial or banking purpose; and (in the UK) to enter details of a conviction for a motoring offence on a driving licence. Since at least the early 20c. it has also been used in the advertising world to mean 'to declare one's approval of a named product, a policy, etc.'. Fowler labelled it 'vulgar in advertisements' in his edition of the Concise Oxford Dictionary, and in 1926 declared its use a 'solecism', but the world has not heeded his complaints.

end product. *End product* and the parallel term *end result* have been subject to criticism from time to time, including that of Gowers (1965), since they contain an element of redundancy, but they are well established and inoffensive. *End product* was at first (Rutherford, 1905) used in chemistry to mean 'a stable, non-radioactive nuclide that is the final product of a radioactive series'. It rapidly made its way into lay use in transferred and figurative senses, especially in the concrete sense 'a finished article in a manufacturing process'.

endue, indue. See EM- AND IM-, EN- AND IN-.

enfold, infold. See EM- AND IM-, EN- AND IN-.

enforceable. Spelt with an *e* after the *c*; see MUTE E.

enfranchise. Always so spelt, not *-ize*. See -ISE 1.

England, English. England is of course merely the part of the island of Great Britain that is not Wales or Scotland, and its land area makes up less than two thirds of the total; but in practice, because the population of England is much greater than that of the other parts, because government has historically centred almost exclusively on London, and for broad historical reasons, the name is often loosely used by English people and others for the whole of Great Britain, a use that is understandably resented in Scotland, Wales, and Northern Ireland. The loose use is not restricted to English people: French *Angleterre*, Italian *Inghilterra*, etc., are sometimes used in the same manner, and when a German speaks of *ein Engländer* he or she is not necessarily excluding the possibility that the person referred to is Scottish, Welsh, etc. It is a natural enough assumption that a person who speaks *English* as his or her native language is *ein Engländer*. For many purposes the wider words are the natural ones. We speak of the *British Commonwealth*, the *British Navy*, *Army*, and *Air Force*; at the Proms we still boast, mainly tongue in cheek, that *Britons* never never never shall be slaves; and *British English* is now the customary term used by all linguistic scholars to distinguish it from American, Australian, etc., English.

The loose use may arise partly from the fact that people in the UK speak the *English* language, and subconsciously conflate the language with the nationality. There have been innumerable patriotic or nostalgic lines of poetry or remarks of one kind or another in which it is not possible to be sure that the author had strict geographical boundaries in mind: e.g. Lord Nelson's famous signal at Trafalgar in 1805 that *England expects that every man will do his duty; England is a nation of shopkeepers*—attributed to Napoleon; *England is the mother of parliaments*—John Bright, 1865; *The English have no respect for their language*—G. B. Shaw, 1916; *There'll always be an England*—popular song in the Second World War. Possibly these contribute; but, whatever the reason for it, the looser use is as regrettable as it is persistent.

engrain. See INGRAINED.

enhance means 'to heighten or intensify (qualities, powers, value, etc.); to improve (something already of good quality)'. In other words, *enhance* is correctly applied to things, values, reputations, etc., but cannot properly be used of people, although it very occasionally is. *The book enhanced his reputation* is correct; *he was enhanced by the publication of his book* is not.

enjambement /ɑ̃ʒɑ̃bmɑ̃/, if Anglicized as *enjambment*, is pronounced /ɪnˈdʒam(b)mənt/. Both spellings are printed in roman. It is used in prosody to mean the continuation of a sentence without a pause beyond the end of a line, couplet, or stanza.

enjoin. **1** *Enjoin* has meanings connected with commanding and issuing instructions, and is typically used in three constructions: (i) you *enjoin* a person *to do* something, (ii) you *enjoin* something *on* a person, and (iii) you *enjoin that* something should happen. Fowler (1926) wrote that the first of these 'is not recommended', but his reasons were not convincing even then and this construction is now too common and useful to be objected to: *The church had enjoined the faithful to say an Ave Maria*—B. Unsworth, 1985; *Does not Islam enjoin upon Muslims that their neighbours should never be threatened by them?*—*OEC*, 2004; *Wilson also left a manuscript autobiography, enjoining that it should not be published*—*ODNB*, 2005.

2 Since the 16c., *enjoin* has also been used in the more or less opposite sense 'to prohibit, forbid (a thing); to prohibit (a person) *from* (a person or thing)'. This use survives principally in law, 'to prohibit or restrain by an injunction': *As the President talked of escalating the battle, Congressman Ron Dellums, along with several colleagues, filed a lawsuit to enjoin the president from widening the war without a declaration of war by Congress*—*OEC*, 2002.

enjoy. The natural and most common sense of the verb is 'to take delight or pleasure in'. From the 15c. onwards, however, it has also been used in a weaker sense to mean 'to have the use or benefit of (something which affords pleasure or some advantage)': e.g. *It* [*sc.* Allworthy's house] *stood ... high enough to enjoy a most charming prospect*—Fielding, 1749; *Animals enjoying a much lower degree of intelligence*—W. B. Carpenter, 1874. From this weaker sense it is an easy step to what the *OED* calls the catachrestic use of *enjoy* with an object denoting something *not* pleasurable or advantageous. This use dates from the 16c. and is shown in expressions like *to enjoy poor health, to enjoy an indifferent reputation*. It is hard to see the logic of this sense but it seems to endure despite its inbuilt self-contradiction. Late 20c. examples of the original senses: *I enjoy very little leisure in the evenings*—P. Fitzgerald, 1978; *Select a sheltered spot which enjoys the sun for most of the day*—*Practical Householder*, 1990.

enmesh. See EM- AND IM-, EN- AND IN-.

enormity, enormousness. **1** *Origins.* First, it is worth recalling that *enormous* is in origin a 16c. adaptation of Latin *ēnormis*, from *ē* 'out' + *norma* 'mason's square, pattern'; and that for some 400 years it stood alongside the shorter form *enorm* (now obsolete) in the same range of meanings. Both words were applied to anything deviating from the norm, whether in behaviour or nature (= disorderly, irregular; wicked, monstrous, outrageous, etc.) or in size (= abnormally large, vast, huge). By the end of the 19c. *enorm* had virtually gone, and *enormous* had but one meaning, 'abnormally large'.

2 Meanwhile the corresponding noun forms *enormity* (15c., from Fr. *énormité*, = deviation from a normal standard of law, morality, etc., and from the late 18c. = hugeness, vastness) and *enormousness* (first recorded in the early 17c. = gross wickedness, and not until the early 19c. = vastness) competed with each other. It seems clear, however, that by the end of the 19c. a fairly clear distinction of meaning existed, or was believed to exist, between the two words. By then *enormousness* meant only 'hugeness of size', and *enormity* only 'extreme wickedness, etc.'. In other words one could speak of, say, *the enormousness of the pyramids*, and also of *the enormity of his crime*; but the two words were not at all interchangeable.

3 Nowadays, careful speakers continue to distinguish *enormousness* from *enormity*. To put it another way, *enormity* is usually restricted to contexts of crime, depravity, wickedness, etc., while large size is indicated by a range of synonymous nouns (*vast extent, hugeness, immensity, enormousness*, etc.). Because of its relative clumsiness, *enormousness* is not the most frequently used of these synonyms. But *enormity* seems to be encroaching on the territory set aside for *enormousness* and synonyms. There are also numerous circumstances in which the notions of wickedness and of hugeness coincide, and it is in these that choosing one or the other becomes more difficult.

4 Examples: (*a*) (*enormity* correctly used to suggest 'some degree of wickedness') *I have got to the stage of disliking Randolph, which is really more convenient than thinking I liked him & constantly trying to reconcile myself to his enormities*—E. Waugh, 1944; *He did not register the enormity of his crime*—H. Jacobson, 1983; (*b*) (*enormity* = largeness (of immaterial concepts)) *Miss Witt . . . frequently impressed upon George Osborne's mind the enormity of the sacrifice he was making*—Thackeray, 1847/8; *I did not know then that one frequently fails to live up to the enormity of death*—A. Brookner, 1990.

5 It is not difficult to find examples of *enormity* used simply to denote great size or extent, and this use is likely to attract criticism in some quarters: *?it was as though one had flown near enough to the sun to realize its monstrous enormity*—S. Sitwell, 1926; *?A wide-angle lens captures the enormity of the Barbican Centre, London's new arts complex which has cost £153m and almost 11 years to build*—*Times*, 1982; *?The enormity of such open spaces momentarily alarms her*—Susan Johnson, 1990 (Aust.).

6 It is recommended that for the present *enormity* should not be used in plain contexts where the physical size of an object is the only feature involved: in other words, one should avoid phrases of the type *the enormity of the pyramids*. It is more difficult to find fault with *enormity* used of the size or immensity or overwhelmingness of abstract concepts, especially when any element of departure from a legal, moral, or social norm is present or is implied, as in *She tried to be a strength for her daughter, but was overwhelmed by the enormity of what was happening to them all*—R. Black, 1992.

enough, sufficient(ly). 1 The distinction is usually one of formality. As a broad rule the plain and vigorous word *enough* is to be preferred. Used as nouns, for example, in the sense 'an adequate amount', in most contexts *enough* is entirely adequate (*there was not enough for both of them*) and *sufficient* unnecessarily formal (*there was not sufficient for both of them*).

2 Grammatical differences begin to emerge when they are used as adjectives (or, in more technical terms, as determiners). In certain circumstances *enough* can be placed either before or after the noun it governs: *he had enough money to buy a car; he had money enough to buy a car*. The post-positioned use is fairly rare, but *sufficient* can never be used in this way. There is a further distinction. As an adjective (or modifier), *enough* will normally serve, but *sufficient* is more idiomatic when a more qualitative point is being made. For example, in the sentence *There will inevitably be concerns that the courts' powers are not sufficient for worthwhile penalties to be imposed—Bristol Evening Post*, 2007, *sufficient* criticizes the inadequacy more strongly than if *enough* had been used.

3 As adverbs, *enough* and *sufficiently* are mainly distinguished by the informality of the first and the relative formality of the second. The main grammatical difference between them is that *enough* is normally placed after the word it qualifies and *sufficiently* before: *he wasn't clever enough to understand the simplest thing; oddities in the judiciary are rare enough to be interesting* (but *sufficiently clever, sufficiently rare*).

enquire, enquiry, inquire, inquiry. From the time that *enquire/inquire* came into English from Old French *enquerre* (modern French *enquérir*) in the 13c. until the early 20c., forms with initial *en-* or *in-* (also in the derivatives) were used with roughly equal frequency and with no difference of meaning. At present the *in-* forms are dominant for all senses in American English, whereas in British English there is a tendency to prefer the *in-* forms for official or formal types of investigation and (to a lesser extent) the *en-* forms for routine or general types of information-seeking. The differences in BrE are seen in these typical collocations: (formal investigation) *inquiry agency; judicial inquiry; public inquiry; a committee to inquire into the allegations*; (general information-seeking) *enquired* *after her health; several enquiries about the job; directory enquiries; door-to-door enquiries.* The distinction is, however, still far from absolute.

In AmE the noun *inquiry* is often pronounced emphasizing the first syllable, i.e. /ˈɪnkwɪri/.

enrol. So spelt, with *-ll-* in the inflected forms (*enroller, enrolled, enrolling, enrolment*). In AmE the usual forms are *enroll, enroller, enrolled, enrolling, enrollment*).

en route. This phrase from French (*en* = in, *route* = road) has been in use since the 18c. It is printed in roman, not italics, and is correctly written as two words, not as one, which commonly happens, especially in US writing. The spellings *on route* and *onroute* are also both mistakes. They are presumably caused because the phrase is pronounced nowadays in an anglicized way as /ɒn ˈruːt/ (on root), whereas it used to be pronounced in a French fashion as /ɑ̃ rut/.

ensure, insure. See ASSURE.

entail. Both the noun and the verb are stressed on the second syllable.

enterprise. Spelt *-ise*, not *-ize*. See -ISE 1.

enthral. So spelt in BrE, with *enthralled, enthralling, enthralment* as the accompanying forms. In AmE the dominant pattern is *enthrall* (also *inthrall*), *enthralled, enthralling, enthrallment.*

enthuse. The credentials of this verb, which is an early 19c. American English back-formation from *enthusiasm*, have been in question for nigh on 150 years and continue to be questioned in some quarters. For some, it even labours under the double burden of being American and being a back-formation, while the *OED* labels it somewhat conservatively as colloquial or humorous. Yet the *OEC* data shows it to be more common in British English than in American; and other back-formations, such as *diagnose* and *edit* do not attract similar disapproval. What the *OEC* data also shows is that *enthuse* is commonly used in writing that is standard in register, rather than informal, especially in the field of news. It is an economical way of expressing the meanings 'show enthusiasm' or 'cause enthusiasm in', and is used with and without an object; you can *enthuse* people, *enthuse* over or about something, or simply *enthuse* (typically with direct speech). Examples: *But military service actually enthused me a lot*—*OEC*, 2004; *I cannot enthuse over the things as Leslie does*—Wilfred Owen, 1912; *She was quite enthused about chemistry*—*OEC*, 2002; *'The sheer scale, height, glam, glitz is just going to be mind-blowing,' enthused Donovan*—*Daily Telegraph*, 2007. Burchfield (1998) rather snootily said 'one day it may be taken out of the drawer marked "Use with caution" and form part of the unopposed vocabulary of the language'. That drawer was pulled open many years ago now.

entourage. This early 19c. loanword from French is still pronounced in a French manner in English: /ˈɒntʊrɑːʒ/ or /ɒntʊ(ə)ˈrɑːʒ/

entrée. In cookery, an *entrée* is usually a dish served between the fish and meat courses, but also, especially in America, the main dish of a meal.

entrench, intrench. See EM- AND IM-, EN- AND IN-.

entrust. See EM- AND IM-, EN- AND IN-.

entwine. See EM- AND IM-, EN- AND IN-.

enunciation. See -CIATION, -TIATION.

envelop (verb). **1** The inflected forms are *enveloped, enveloping.*

2 An older variant spelling with final *-e* (*envelope*), found as late as the 19c., is now obsolete.

envelope (for a letter). **1** The French spelling (*-ppe*) was ignored when the word was adopted in English in the early 18c. (first recorded in 1715), but since the adoption of the word its first syllable has been pronounced either Anglicized as /ˈɛn-/ or in an approximation to French as /ˈɒn-/, rhyming with *pen* and *on* respectively. The Anglicized form /ˈɛn-/ is now dominant and is recommended here.

2 The phrase *to push the envelope* is a bit of a vogue word in business-speak. It means 'to push the boundaries of what is possible or permissible; pioneer, innovate', and has nothing to do with the 'paper container with a sealable flap'. In fact, it is another example of a technical term which has passed into the mainstream—or at least a sidestream—having been popularized by

American author Tom Wolfe in his book about the space programme, *The Right Stuff*, e.g. *these are extremely witty and clever stories that consistently push the envelope of TV comedy.* The *envelope* in question is the *flight envelope*, which is 'the set of limiting combinations of speed and altitude, or speed and range, etc., possible for a particular kind of aircraft or aero-engine'. So, *to push the envelope* in aeronautical slang was to take an aircraft to the very limits of its safe performance.

environs. The pronunciation recommended is /ɪn'vʌɪrənz/. An older pronunciation, /'ɛnvɪrənz/, has been driven out under the influence of the stress pattern and long *i*, (/-ʌɪ-/), of *environment.*

envisage, envision. Broadly speaking, for British and North American speakers the choice between these two synonymous words is dictated by which side of the pond you live on. In British English, to judge by the *OEC* data, *envisage* is six times more frequent than *envision*; according to the same source, in US and Canadian English the proportions are, *grosso modo*, reversed.

Envisage is an early 19c. loanword from French, meaning originally 'look in the face of, look straight at', then 'to view or regard under a particular aspect', and finally its two current meanings: 'to contemplate or conceive of as a possibility or something desirable' (*the Rome Treaty envisaged free movement across frontiers*); and 'to form a mental picture of (something not yet existing or known)' (*he knew what he liked but had difficulty envisaging it*). Fowler (1926) dismissed it as an 'undesirable Gallicism', for no clear reason, other than his general antipathy towards certain beret-wearing, onion-selling words. Gowers (1965) also dismissed it as a 'pretentious substitute'.

Neither of them noticed the arrival, first in Britain (Lytton Strachey, 1921), of the more or less synonymous *envision*, which then went on to flourish in America. Nowadays, it may sound vaguely pretentious, or—which is possibly worse in some quarters—transatlantic, for a British writer to use *envision*. And if one wishes to avoid using either word, ready alternatives exist, according to context, in the shape of *imagine, visualize* and *intend.* Examples: (envisage) *So mother envisaged us all here, gathered round staring down in this ghastly way*—P. Lively, 1989; *she continued to envisage various methods of killing Jack*—I. Murdoch, 1989; *Smith does not envisage bringing in a replacement—Times*, 2006; *I did not envisage it would get as bad as this—Independent*, 2006; (envision) *His blackest hypochondria had never envisioned quite so miserable a Catastrophe*—L. Strachey, 1921; *And the more he envisioned this prospect, the more he was of two minds about it*—M. McCarthy, 1952; *It may be only the stuff of newspaper editorials, of course, to envision a strategy in which the United Nations takes decisive action*—leader in *Sunday Times*, 1990.

enwrap, inwrap. See EM- AND IM-, EN- AND IN-.

Eocene. See MIOCENE.

eon. A frequent American English spelling of British English *aeon.*

epaulette (AmE *epaulet*) is most often pronounced /'ɛpəlɛt/ but variants, e.g. /'ɛpɔːlet/ and /ɛpə'lɛt/, are still commonly heard.

épée (fencing-sword) is spelt, with two accents.

epenthesis. In philology, applied to the phonetic process by which an unetymological sound is added to a given word when it is not present in its antecedent. Examples: *chimney* pronounced as /'ʧɪmbli/, with substitution of /mbl/ for /mn/; *remembrance* pronounced as *rememberance.* Historical examples: *daffodil* from earlier *affodil* (current from the 15c. to the 17c.), from medieval Latin *affodillus* (related to *asphodel*); *empty* from Old English *ǣmtig* (no *-p-*). *Epenthesis* is derived from Greek ἐπένθεσις, from ἐπί 'in addition' + ἐν 'in' + θέσις 'placing'.

ephemeral. Derived from the Greek word ἐφήμερος (= living only a day; short-lived), and first introduced into English in the 16c., *ephemeral* is traditionally pronounced /ɪ'fɛm(ə)r(ə)l/ (i-**fem**-(uh)-r(a)l) with a short second *e*, although the pronunciation with a long *e* /ɪ'fiːm(ə)r(ə)l/ is also valid. Possibly its most famous appearance is in Auden's *Lullaby: Time and fevers burn away Individual beauty from Thoughtful children, and the grave Proves the child ephemeral.*

epic. 1 The traditional use of this word is of a narrative poem celebrating the achievements of some heroic person of history or legend, such as the *Odyssey*, the

Iliad, the *Aeneid*, or Milton's *Paradise Lost*. The term has also frequently been applied to the Old English elegiac poem *Beowulf*. Anything less ambitious, it was felt, did not deserve to be called an epic.

The word has been extended in more recent usage to refer to any major literary work, theatrical performance, or (especially) film, which has some claim to be regarded as exceptional in terms of its length, subject matter, or scale of treatment: *I want very much to see the Birth of a Nation, which is said to be a really great film, an epic in pictures*—Aldous Huxley, 1916; *Meier is still working on his wild, underground epic, Snowball, as well as producing a new Hollywood movie called MM*—*Face*, 1992. It has also gone full circle in developing a new adjectival meaning 'great, heroic': *In his epic landscape of Jerusalem executed in April of 1830, Roberts draws the Holy City in silhouette*—R. Fisk, 1991; *It was from fear of his intellect sinking into torpor that he finally took up the battle against drink. It was an epic struggle, marked by his terrible and yet frequently comic accounts of failure after failure*—*Independent*, 2000.

2 The originally AmE use of *epic* to mean 'particularly impressive or remarkable' is still decidedly informal. Examples: *When ... linguistics professor David Pharies asked 350 sophomores for samples of college slang, here's what he found ... 'Killer' is a compliment, along with 'mint, awesome, prime, epic, golden, [etc.]'*—*USA Today*, 1983; *That's epic, dude*—*Daily Variety*, 2000 (US); *Experiencing an epic car like the GT-R can have such an effect*—*Torque*, 2008 (UK).

epicentre (US epicenter). Some pundits criticize the use of *epicentre* in anything other than its core meaning of 'the point on the earth's surface vertically above the focus of an earthquake'. For instance, one writer cautions: 'Do not use it as a fancy word for "centre", which too many pretentious writers do.' So the question arises: should non-seismologists avoid it at all costs? It depends. In what seems like a legitimate extension of its core meaning, it denotes the central point of something, typically a difficult or unpleasant situation such as epidemics, outbreaks of illness, terrorism, etc., e.g. *the two farms treated as the epicentre for the outbreak of the bird flu*—*Daily Despatch*, 2004. So far, so good: to object to its use in that way seems a trifle pedantic. More debatable, however, is its use to heighten descriptions of creative, cultural or political movements, which seems to be largely a mannerism of British journalism, e.g. *I want to be at the epicentre of youth culture for as long as I care to continue working—Guardian, 2003*. Replacing *epicentre* with *centre of* or *right at the centre of* would not change the meaning of the sentence, and would make it less pompous. Similarly, its use in the following example seems more than a little overblown: *For a month during the spring of 1932 Cairo, Egypt, became the epicentre for debates about the position of Arab music in world music*—*World Music* (*A very short introduction*), 2002.

epidemic. See ENDEMIC.

epigram (literally 'on-writing') has two main meanings: **1** A short poem with a witty or ingenious ending. Baldick (1990) cites an epigram by Herrick which is adapted from Martial: *Lulls swears he is all heart, but you'll suppose By his proboscis that he is all nose.*

2 A concise pungent saying, e.g. *To lose one parent, Mr Worthing, may be regarded as a misfortune; to lose both looks like carelessness*—O. Wilde, 1895. It also formerly meant an inscription on a building, tomb, coin, etc.

epigraph. 1 An inscription, especially one placed upon a building, tomb, statue, coin, etc.

2 A short quotation or pithy sentence placed at the beginning of a work, a chapter, etc., as a foretaste of the leading idea or sentiment in what follows.

episcopalian, belonging or referring to an episcopal church (i.e. one constituted on the principle of government by bishops), especially (with initial capital) the Anglican Church in Scotland and the US, with elected bishops.

epistle. Its commonest use is of the letters of the New Testament (e.g. The Epistle of Paul the Apostle to the Romans). It is sometimes used ironically or whimsically to mean a letter of any kind: *When mischievous gossip columnists were prompted to discuss her age, she put them down with a peremptory epistle to The Times*—*Evening Standard*, 2003.

epithet 1 An epithet is an adjective indicating some quality or attribute (good or bad) which the speaker or writer (or the verdict of history) regards as characteristic of a person or thing, e.g. *Charles the Bold, Ethelred the Unready, Philip the Good, William the Silent,* and many figures (*Alexander, Alfred, Peter, Pompey,* etc.) called *the Great.* An epithet can also be a noun used as a significant title or appellation, e.g. *William the Conqueror, Vlad the Impaler.* These uses continue, particularly with unfavourable connotations. In particular, the word is often used as a euphemism for a term of abuse, particularly in the phrase *racial epithet,* as in the first unfavourable example below. Examples: (favourable) *Geraldine recited some of the traditional epithets used to describe Siva*—G. Vidal, 1978; *How often he would apply the epithet 'de la Marish' to some scene*—L. Whistler, 1985; (unfavourable) *He said it was routine for groups of white men driving by in cars to shout a racial epithet at him—The News Blog,* 2005; *The epithets of liar, racist and worse hurled at the vice president just won't stick—Washington Times,* 1988.

In more casual use, epithet simply means 'description' or 'name': *This is a character who is quite happy to be known by the epithet 'Dopey', having been born with big ears and not much hair—Independent on Sunday,* 2005.

2 For the term *transferred epithet,* see ADJECTIVE 9.

3 The *Homeric epithet* is an adjective (in practice usually a compound one) added to the same thing or person. In Homer we find *the wine-dark sea,* while Hera is repeatedly described as *white-armed,* Athene as *bright-eyed,* and Zeus as *the cloud-gatherer.* From these it is an easy step to the kind of combinations so frequently used by English poets: *Rose-crown'd Zephyrus ... makes the green trees to buss*—Sylvester, 1598; *And still she slept an azure-lidded sleep*—Keats, 1820.

epitome /ɪˈpɪtəmi/. **1** Surprisingly, it is occasionally spelt *epitomy* even in quality newspapers: *You can't help but admire Terence Stamp. Epitomy of the swinging Sixties, heart throb* [sic] *to a generation of women—Observer Food Monthly,* 2002. This spelling is non-standard.

2 It is pronounced as four syllables /ɪˈpɪtəmi/ (i-**pi**-tuh-mee), not e-pee-**tohm**, as one occasionally hears it mangled.

3 Derived from a Greek word of the same spelling meaning 'an incision, an abridgement', it has two main meanings in English: (*a*) a person or thing embodying a quality, class, etc., an embodiment, e.g. *Some delight in abstracts and epitomes* (Dr Johnson); *Adolf Hitler was the epitome of evil; to win a Wimbledon title is regarded by every player as the epitome of success*; (*b*) a summary or abstract, especially of a written work, e.g. *The book ... is not intended to be popular. No doubt a lively epitome will one day be made for general reading*—E. Waugh, 1956.

epoch. 1 See TIME.

2 In 1816 Coleridge wrote of the *epoch-forming revolutions of the Christian world.* Later in the 19c. the adjective *epoch-making* appeared. Lampooned by Fowler (1926) and his successive editors, the word is regularly and often boastfully used to mean little more than 'remarkable, significant' as well as (more appropriately) 'historic'. It is a favourite of journalists and other writers who wish to give a puff to events that others might not think as significant as they do; as Fowler himself wittily put it 'the word is blank cartridge, meant only to startle, & not to carry even so imponderable a bullet as conviction'. Examples: *There were a large number of epoch-making events whose 40th anniversaries were celebrated towards the end of last year, as readers will undoubtedly recall—TES,* 2004; *In Shane Warne's case, it refers to the hex he cast over England's batsmen, following his epoch-making entry into Ashes cricket—Cricinfo News,* 2005.

eponym, originally, a person after whom a discovery, invention, place, institution, etc., is named: for example, Alois *Alzheimer* (1864–1915), after whom Alzheimer's disease is named, and Sir Thomas *Bodley* (1545–1613), who gave his name to the Bodleian Library in Oxford. In current usage, the word *eponym* also denotes the words derived from the name, not only the name-giver. Legions of products, processes, etc., are named after or are believed to be named after particular people: in each case the person concerned, and also the product if it is identical in spelling or pronunciation, is an eponym. Examples: *Braille* (Louis Braille, 1809–52, French inventor), *diesel* (Rudolf Diesel, 1858–1913, German engineer), *mackintosh* (Charles Macintosh, 1766–1843), *Morse* (S. F. B. Morse, 1791–1872, American inventor), *sandwich* (4th Earl of Sandwich, 1718–92).

The word **eponymous** is nowadays used to refer to all manner of products and institutions, as well as to people. Beowulf is the *eponymous* hero of the poem of that name, and Emma is the *eponymous* heroine of Jane Austen's novel *Emma*; the *eponymous* founder of Waterstone's bookshops is Tim Waterstone; and Gordon Ramsay at Claridges is the *eponymous* restaurant of the potty-mouthed celebrity chef.

equal. 1 The inflected forms have *-ll-* (*equalled, equalling*) in British English but usually *-l-* in American English.

2 *The navy is not equal in numbers or in strength to perform the task it will be called upon to undertake: *perform* should be *performing*. See GERUND 3.

3 *This work is the equal, if not better than anything its author has yet done. The word *to* should not be left out: read *equal to, if not better than, anything . . .*

4 *Equal* is often regarded as an absolute that cannot be qualified by words such as *very, more, rather*, etc. According to this view, it is idiomatic to say *almost equal, not equal, less than equal*, or *exactly equal*, but *more equal* is more questionable. In fact, it can mean 'more nearly equal': e.g. *The more to draw his Love, And render me more equal*—Milton, 1667; *the American woman is not the same as other women . . . she is freer in her manners and . . . she is freer because she is more equal*—H. Fairlie, 1976–7. And in its meaning of 'fair, uniform in application or effect; without discrimination on any grounds', it is perfectly legitimate to grade *equal* using *more*, e.g. *a more equal society*. George Orwell's celebrated *'All animals are equal but some animals are more equal than others'* in *Animal Farm* (1945) is often alluded to: e.g. *All victims are equal. None are more equal than others*—J. le Carré, 1989; *The embryo has rights. Are all human beings equal, or are some more equal than others?*—*Sun*, 2005.

equally. Fowler (1926) roundly condemned the quite frequent construction *equally as* (e.g. *Rothwell was equally as thorough when researching the latest and most progressive architectural styles of the day*) as an 'illiterate tautology', and the echoes of his condemnation rumble on. In practice, because one or other word in *equally as* is sufficient on its own, it is desirable in good writing to use an alternative construction. For instance, the previous example can be rephrased as *was equally thorough* or *just as thorough*. To give another example, *the labour crisis has furnished evidence equally as striking* can be rephrased either as *the labour crisis has furnished equally striking evidence*, or as *the labour crisis has furnished evidence just as striking*.

equerry. At court the word is pronounced /ɪˈkwɛri/, but in most other contexts the stress is placed on the first syllable, /ˈɛkwəri/, probably arising from the erroneous idea that the word is connected with Latin *equus* 'horse'. In fact it is derived from French *écurie*, earlier *escurie*, from medieval Latin *scūria* 'stable'. *Equerry* is short for 'gentleman (or groom) of the equerry'.

equilibrium. The recommended plural is *equilibria*. See -UM 3.

equivalence, equivalency. Both forms are in use, the first being much the more common. There is no discernible semantic difference, but there is regional variation: *equivalency* is quite frequent in American English, but uncommon in British English. See -CE,-CY.

era. See TIME.

-er and -est, more and most. This article deals with the forms of the comparative and superlative of adjectives and adverbs, either by inflection (*larger, largest; happier, happiest*) or by using *more* and *most* (*more usual; most unfortunately*). It also deals in outline with the rules for using the various forms available. See also ADJECTIVE 3, 4, ABSOLUTE COMPARATIVE.

1 Adjectives that have *-er* and *-est* forms.
2 *-er* and *-est* in adverbs.
3 Which form to choose.
4 Adjectives forming *-est* but not *-er*.
5 Superlatives in comparisons of two.
6 Novel literary forms with *-er* and *-est*.
7 Combinations.

1 Adjectives that have *-er* and *-est* forms. The adjectives regularly taking *-er* and *-est* in preference to *more* and *most* are:

(*a*) most words of one syllable: *fast, hard, rich, wise,* etc.; but not *right, wrong, French,* etc.
(*b*) words of two syllables ending in *-y* and *-ly*: *angry, early, holy, lazy, likely, lively, tacky* etc.; and corresponding negative forms in *un-* when they exist: *unhappy, unlikely,* etc. Words ending in *-y* change the *y* to *i*: *angrier, earliest,* etc. Sometimes only the *-est* form is used, e.g. *unholiest* but *more unholy.*
(*c*) words of two syllables ending in *-le*: *able, humble, noble, simple,* etc.
(*d*) some words of two syllables ending in *-ow*: *mellow, narrow, shallow,* etc. Some of these inflect with *-er, -est,* or use *more* and *most,* e.g. *more narrow, more shallow.*
(*e*) some words of two syllables ending in *-er*: *bitter, clever, slender, tender,* etc., but not *eager.* In some cases only the *-est* form is used, e.g. *bitterest* but *more bitter.*
(*f*) some words of two syllables pronounced with the accent on the second: *polite, profound,* etc.; but not *absurd, antique, bizarre, secure,* etc., nor the predicative adjectives *afraid, alive, alone, aware,* etc.
(*g*) other words of two syllables that do not belong to any classifiable group, e.g. *common, cruel, pleasant, quiet.*
(*h*) Many other two-syllable adjectives normally use *more* or *most*: *awkward, careful, careless, cheerful, foolish, loyal, sudden,* etc.

Adjectives of three or more syllables require the periphrastic forms with *more* or *most*: *more beautiful/the most beautiful, more interesting/most interesting.*

2 *-er* and *-est* in adverbs. Adverbs not formed with *-ly* from adjectives, but identical in form with them, use *-er* and *-est* naturally: *runs faster, hits hardest, sleeps sounder, hold it tighter*; some independent adverbs, as *often, soon,* do the same; *-ly* adverbs, though comparatives in *-lier* are possible in archaic or poetic style (*softlier nurtured, wiselier said*), now normally appear as *more softly,* etc. The phrase *easier said than done* is a special case, in that there is no equivalent use of the positive *easy.*

3 *Which form to choose.* With adjectives and adverbs of one syllable it is usually less natural to use *more* and *most* when forms in *-er* and *-est* are available, although there are exceptions that are not readily explained: *The job was harder than they thought* sounds less idiomatic in the form *The job was more hard than they thought,* whereas *John had never been gladder to be on Arabella's side* sounds slightly more idiomatic in the form *John had never been more glad to be on Arabella's side.* Many adjectives of two syllables, e.g. *cruel, gentle, handsome, remote,* form comparatives and superlatives both with *-er* and *-est* and with *more* and *most*: *crueller/cruellest, more cruel/most cruel.* For example, the sentences *He was sometimes most cruel to those he loved* and *He was sometimes cruellest to those he loved* are both idiomatic, although the first could mean either 'extremely cruel' or 'most cruel (of all)', in accordance with the different meanings of *most.*

4 Adjectives forming *-est* but not *-er.* Some adjectives besides those described in (1) can occasionally form a superlative in *-est,* used with *the* and serving as an emphatic form, while no one would think of making a comparative in *-er* for them: *the amplest freedom, the awfullest magazine ever, the drollest reason cited,* etc. It is a matter of deciding whether the *-est* form or the *most —* form feels more natural. Adjectives ending in *-ic* (*comic, rustic,* etc.), *-ive* (*active, restive,* etc.), and *-ous* (*famous, odious, virtuous,* etc.) do not have *-er* and *-est* forms except in special circumstances.

5 *Superlatives in comparisons of two. They were forced to give an answer which was not their real answer but only the nearest to it of two alternatives.* This use of *-est* instead of *-er* where the persons or things are no more than two should normally be avoided; the *raison d'être* of the comparative is to compare two things, and it should be allowed to do its job without encroachment by the superlative. *Nearer* should have been used in the example given. But there are exceptions. Use of the superlative is idiomatic in such phrases as *Put your best foot forward; May the best man win* (when only two people are involved). And who would wish to introduce a comparative into Milton's *Whose God is strongest, thine or mine?* See also SUPERLATIVES 2.

6 Novel literary forms with *-er* and *-est.* As a stylistic device, it was once open to writers to extend the use of *-er* and *-est* to many adjectives of more than one syllable that normally take *more* and *most.* Historical examples (listed by Jespersen): *easiliest, freelier, proudlier, wiselier* (all from Shakespeare); *finelier, harshlier, kindlier, proudlier* (all from Lamb); *darklier, gladlier, looselier, plainlier* (all from Tennyson), and Lewis Carroll's *curiouser.* From the 20c. onwards, formations such as *admirablest, loathsomer, peacefullest, wholesomer,* etc., could only be used for comic effect or for some other special purpose.

7 *Combinations.* Jespersen pointed out that an adjective used as the first element of a combination ending in *-ed* is very often in the superlative. Examples: *the sourest-natured dog* (Shakespeare), *noblest-minded* (Shakespeare), *the longest lived* (I. Walton), *the silliest, best-natured wretch* (Swift), *the mildest mannered man* (Byron), *the softest-hearted simpleton* (R. L. Stevenson).

-er and -or. 1 The agent termination *-er* can theoretically be joined to any existing English verb. In practice, many such words (and there are about 100 of them in common use) have *-er* as a termination and others have *-or.* Still others have both forms, often with a different meaning. The *OED* neatly describes the situation: 'The distinction between *-er* and *-or* as the ending of agent-nouns is purely historical and orthographical: in the present spoken language they are both pronounced /ə(r)/, except that in law terms and in certain Latin words not fully naturalized, *-or* is still sounded /ɔː(r)/. In received spelling, the choice between the two forms is often capricious, or determined by other than historical reasons.' Scholarly attempts to account for the distribution of the *-er* and *-or* forms continue to be made (e.g. by L. Bauer in *Trans. Philol. Soc.*, 1990), but the problem remains unresolved. In this book, the most important of the individual words have been dealt with at their alphabetical places. See ACCEPTER, ACCEPTOR; ADAPTER, ADAPTOR; ADVISER, ADVISOR, etc.; -OR.

2 When *-er* is added to verbs ending in *-y* following a consonant, *y* is normally changed to *i* (*carrier, occupier,* etc.), though *flyer* is now more usual than *flier,* and *drier* alternates with *dryer.* The *y* is retained between a vowel and *-er* (*buyer, employer, player,* etc.).

-er and -re. See -RE AND -ER.

eraser. So spelt, not *-or.* See -OR.

ere. Both as preposition and conjunction, *ere* has been clinging to the language with diminishing success for more than a century. It is an outstanding example of the near demise of a word that for centuries, from the Old English period onwards was part of the central equipment of the language. It is now only archaic or poetical. Examples: *And time seemed finished ere the ship passed by*—E. Muir, 1925; *I would give you a gift ere we go, at your own choosing*—J. R. R. Tolkien, 1954; *In that cluster of villages, London by name, Ere slabs are too tall and we Cockneys too few,* [etc.]—J. Betjeman, 1958.

ergative is a term for a type of verb of action or movement in which the same noun can be used as the object when the verb is transitive and as the subject of the same verb used intransitively (without an object), as in *They closed the door/The door closed, I'm cooking the meat/The meat is cooking.* There are many verbs of this type in English, including *change, close, finish, move, open, shut, slide.* Some languages, such as Eskimo and Basque, have a special case for nouns used as the subject of ergative verbs.

ergo. The Latin word for 'therefore' is occasionally used in English, as an alphabetical equivalent of ∴, to precede a logical conclusion. Its most famous occurrence is in Descartes' *Discours de la méthode* (1637), *Cogito, ergo sum,* 'I think, therefore I am': this was facetiously echoed in a famous advertising slogan of yesteryear (1988), 'I think, therefore IBM'. Examples: *The American Colony hotel is in the eastern, ergo Arab, part of the city*—C. James, 1983; *This wine reminds me of Chateau Latour, ergo it is fine wine*—M. Kramer, 1989; *He had not been told about her death; he was not saddened by it; ergo, he was not part of the Literary World*—S. Mackay, 1992.

Eros. In all its uses in English, including (*a*) the name of the well-known statue in Piccadilly Circus, (*b*) = earthly or sexual love, contrasted with *agape,* (*c*) as the name of an asteroid discovered by a German astronomer in 1898, it is pronounced

/ˈɪərɒs/, and thus in this respect has parted company with its Greek original, ἔρως, i.e. /ˈɛrəʊs/ or /ˈɛrəʊz/.

erotica. In practice this word, originally a neuter plural noun in Greek meaning 'erotic literature or art', occurs mostly in contexts where the question of whether it is singular or plural does not arise (e.g. *literature classed under erotica; the erotica industry; the world of erotica*). It is nowadays generally treated as an uncount noun, and therefore any verb it governs is singular, e.g. *Erotica is a form of fantasy*. To use it with a plural verb (*Erotica are much in evidence in the world of videos*) has to be regarded as needless pedantry.

err. Speakers vary considerably in the way in which they pronounce *err, erring,* and *errant,* but in standard English the three words are regularly /əː/, /ˈəːrɪŋ/, but /ˈɛrənt/.

errant. See ARRANT.

erratum. An *erratum* is an error in writing or printing, especially a mistake noted in a list of corrections attached to a printed book. Its plural is *errata*. (They are pronounced /ɛˈrɑːtəm/ and /ɛˈrɑːtə/ respectively.) Accordingly, an *erratum slip* should mean a slip containing one correction, and an *errata slip* one containing several; a list headed *Errata* contains details of more than one correction, and the plural is correctly used in *These errata are of more than usual interest*. Problems arise when *errata* is used as a singular, as it is in publishing, to refer to a list of errors, e.g. *Unfortunately, we have found some minor errors in those amended submissions, and we will be lodging an errata which corrects those errors*. Some usage writers, including Burchfield, insist that this is wrong, and that *errata* should always be plural. If they were right, the verb in the previous example would have to be in the plural, i.e.'which correct', which would be impossible. *Errata* in this use is a shorthand for 'list of errata, errata page', and so forth. Employing the word in that way goes back to the 17c., and should, though somewhat inelegant, be accepted in appropriate contexts. What is indisputably wrong is to create the form *erratas* to refer to several mistakes: e.g. *to check out the erratas of the book* should be *to check out the errata of the book*.

ersatz. This German loanword used as an adjective meaning 'made or used as a substitute, typically an inferior one, for something else', was first recorded in English in 1875 and became much used during the two World Wars. It is sufficiently naturalized to be printed in roman, and pronounced /ˈəːsats/, **uhr**-satz, or /ˈɛːsats/, **air**-satz.

erst, erstwhile. It is always sad to see words of long standing passing into archaism, but these two words, the first of them found already in Old English and the second a Spenserian coinage in 1569, both began to drop out of regular use at some point in the 19c., though *erstwhile* is still not all that infrequent when used as an adjective. *Erst* is an adverb meaning 'formerly, of old', and *erstwhile* is both an adjective (= former, previous) and an adverb (= *erst*). Modern examples of *erstwhile: Jude the Obscure in reverse; erstwhile scholar who transformed himself into a rustic swain*—A. Powell, 1976; *Many erstwhile Green Line travellers were doubtless driving their own cars*—K. Warren, 1980. See QUONDAM; WHILOM.

escalate, escalation, escalator. *Escalate* is a 1920s back-formation from *escalator* (originally a trade name, first recorded in 1900). That it was for a time one of the most overused and therefore unwelcome words in the language, as was its counterpart *escalation,* is suggested by Brian Aldiss's 1980 quote: '"Escalation" was a fashionable word last time I was in London'. It has certainly burst the bounds of meaning that a word for a moving staircase might be expected to impose. Not surprisingly, *escalate* is now rarely used in its primordial meaning 'to travel on an escalator'.

By the 1950s, it had come into regular use to mean 'increase or develop rapidly by stages', especially to move from conventional to nuclear warfare. Typical examples from that time (the first intransitive, the second transitive, i.e. with an object) are: *The possibility of local wars 'escalating into all-out atomic wars'*—*Manchester Guardian*, 1959; *Using tactical nuclear weapons which would be likely to escalate hostilities into a global nuclear war*—*Economist*, 1961.

In more recent use, *escalate* continues to be used in such contexts but has extended beyond them. The things which most typically *escalate* or *are escalated* are wars, violence, tension, situations, prices and cost. Examples: *The police more often came under physical attack and began to respond with a steadily escalating counter-violence—Liberty and Legislation*, 1989; *Her previous calm gave way to terror that escalated until it threatened to overwhelm her*—E. Blair, 1990; *Motoring organisations yesterday urged drivers involved in a road rage encounter to try to keep calm and not to react in a way which could escalate the situation—Herald* (Glasgow), 2000; *As a means of controlling escalating domestic prices and utilising all of China's resources for domestic consumption, Beijing has recently abolished the 8% tax rebates on exports—Lloyd's List*, 2007.

To *escalate* has latterly gained a novel, transitive meaning, which is 'to refer an issue to a manager or superior': *in the event that you need to escalate an issue, our technical staff are ready to help*. It is part of the jargon of IT and of call centres, and best avoided outside those rarefied environments.

Meanwhile, *escalator* still has, of course, its literal meaning (moving staircase), but also a figurative one embodied in *escalator clauses, agreements*, etc. that provide for an increase in prices, wages, etc., to meet specified contingencies. This use was established well before *escalate*, as it were, escalated. Examples: *Labor leaders have never liked cost-of-living 'escalator' contracts, on the grounds that they tie the worker to a fixed standard of living—Time*, 1948; *Cattle prices are subject to escalator adjustment—Farmer & Stockbreeder*, 1960.

escapee. See -EE[1] 2. This remarkable use (instead of *escaper*; cf. *deserter*), which was first recorded in a work of 1875–6 by Walt Whitman, has come in for much adverse comment, but is now entered in all major dictionaries as part of the standard language.

eschscholtzia. The pronunciation recommended is /ɪˈʃɒltsɪə/, not /ɪsˈk-/ or /-ɒlʃə/; and the spelling recommended is as shown (named after J. F. von Eschscholtz, German botanist, d. 1831).

escort (noun and verb). The noun is stressed on the first syllable and the verb on the second. See NOUN AND VERB ACCENT 1.

Eskimo. Plural *Eskimos* (but sometimes just *Eskimo*). See -O(E)S 9. In recent years, the word *Eskimo* has come to be regarded as offensive (partly through the associations of the now discredited folk etymology 'one who eats raw flesh'). The peoples inhabiting the regions from the central Canadian Arctic to western Greenland prefer to call themselves *Inuit* (= plural of *inuk* person). The word *Eskimo*, however, continues to be the only term which can be properly understood as applying to the people as a whole and is still widely used in anthropological and archaeological contexts.

esophagus. The AmE spelling of BrE *oesophagus*.

esoteric. The first letter *e-* can be pronounced as in *egg* or as in *eat*, /ɛsəʊˈtɛrɪk/ or /iːsəʊˈtɛrɪk/.

especial(ly), special(ly). The frontier between these words is not well defined, but it exists. Its fluidity is best illustrated by an anecdote. In the *Telegraph*, 11 Aug. 1990, Burchfield wrote about 'dictionaries *especially* designed to help secretaries with spelling and word-division'. A reader reproved him, insisting that he should have written *specially* instead. Burchfield shrugged off the rebuke in his edition of Fowler thus: 'He was probably right, but the margin between the two words is a narrow and ragged one.' What follows may go some way to suggesting what that 'margin' is.

1 *History*. The contest between the longer and the shorter forms began a long time ago. Both *especial* and *especially* have been in continuous use since about 1400, while *special* and *specially* have had a slightly longer life, both being recorded first in the 13c.

2 *especial* or *special*? Choosing between *special* and *especial* has been simplified in that the first has pushed the second to endangered species status. (*Special* occurs in *OEC* data nearly 400 times as often as *especial*.) *Especial* has an affinity with legal, formal, or technical writing and works as a highly emphatic synonym of *special*, in the meaning 'better or greater than usual': *It* [the tulip bulb] *was received with especial delight in the Netherlands and cultivated with great care—OEC*, 2003.

3 *especially* or *specially*? Each continues to usurp the role of the other, but in the *OEC* data *especially* is about 20 times more common. The differences between them are set out in some detail below; but, as a rule of thumb, if you could use *particularly* in your sentence, then *especially* is the correct choice.

Especially is used (*a*) to single out one person or thing over all others, e.g. *he despised them all, especially Sylvester; I especially thank anyone who has been praying for me*; (*b*) with some verbs, to mean 'very much', e.g. *he didn't especially like dancing*; (*c*) to qualify adjectives and adverbs, = very, e.g. *the sumo wrestlers are not especially tall, but they are especially big.*

Specially means 'for a special or specific purpose' and is used (*a*) to qualify verbs, e.g. *a folder that I've created specially on the desktop of my computer*; (*b*) particularly with participial adjectives, e.g. *specially made; wrap yourself in a world created specially for you by the book you choose.*

Examining one specific collocation, *especially nice*, pinpoints the difference. For example, *an especially nice feature is the guestbook* is part of a larger co-text in which other good points have been mentioned and among which the guestbook stands out. Contrast this with *if you're specially nice to her she might become a real supporter of yours*, which implies that the addressee of the advice has to make a special effort to be nice.

4 Further examples: (especially) *Growers are especially concerned about fields where winter annuals were present*—OEC, 2002; *The transfer of Britain's most sophisticated technologies (especially in laser and micro-computing) ... will have appalling effects on the British economy*—*City Limits*, 1986; *Ancient woods ... are especially important for wildlife*—*Times*, 1982; *I can't say anything especially wise about these paintings*—D. Donoghue, 1991.

In none of those examples would it be appropriate to use *specially* instead of *especially* in formal writing, although it is used more informally, as illustrated in 5 below. (specially) *This fine piano was made specially for us*—*Chicago Tribune*, 1977; *I gathered these specially in bud, because I thought it would be nice to see them open out in the warmth of the house*—D. Madden, 1988; *If it's suitable for your job, try using a plaster repair product as it's specially formulated to be easier to apply and smooth out than conventional plaster*—*Evening Gazette*, 2007.

5 *Either is appropriate.* The meanings of the two words come closest when qualifying an immediately following adjective, as in the following examples in which each word can replace the other, although *especially* is still the more correct, whereas *specially* is more informal. *It's a pretty anonymous mark. Not one I'm specially proud of, either*—P. Lively, 1991; *The function of the criminal law, as we see it, is ... to provide sufficient safeguards against exploitation or corruption of others, particularly those who are specially vulnerable because they are young, weak in body or mind or inexperienced*—T. Newburn, 1992.

6 *Specially* usually encroaches on *especially*, but sometimes *especially* is the offender: *?The fiddler plunged his hot face into a pot of porter, especially provided for that purpose*—Dickens, 1843; *?These Pakistani garments are created especially for the wearer by a joint effort of the women of the family*—A. Wilson, 1988.

espionage. Now always spelt with a single letter *n* (cf. French *espionnage*) and pronounced /ˈɛspɪənɑːʒ/. The word was first recorded in English in 1793 but the ending continues to resist being pronounced in an anglicized way, i.e. as in *heritage.*

esplanade. The pronunciation with final /-eɪd/ is judged by the main authorities to be more common than that with /-ɑːd/. But *promenade* continues to tug it in the opposite direction. See -ADE.

espresso. This form (derived from Italian *caffè espresso*, literally 'pressed-out coffee'), is first recorded in English in 1945. Modern British coffee culture, possibly combined with linguistic snobbery, has largely driven out the variant *expresso*, which was common in the 1950s and reached some sort of apotheosis in the British film *Expresso Bongo* (1959).

Esq. Beginning in the 15c. an esquire was at first 'a young man of gentle birth, who as an aspirant to knighthood, attended upon a knight, carried his shield, and rendered him other services' (*OED*). From the same period onwards, it was also 'a man belonging to the higher order of English gentry, ranking immediately below a knight' (*OED*). As time went on several classes of men became entitled to be called esquires—younger sons of peers, eldest sons of knights; judges, barristers-at-law, and many others. From the mid-16c. it became customary to refer to such people in writing in the form *Andrew Smith, Esquire. Esquire* in such circumstances soon became abbreviated to *Esq., Esqu.*, etc. (*Esq.* is now usual). By the mid-20c., *Esq.* had lost all sense of rank, and was being attached (in correspondence) to the name of any adult male. When *Esq.* is appended to a name, no prefixed title (such as *Mr, Dr, Capt.*, etc.) is used. It should be emphasized that except in one circumstance *Esq.* is hardly used outside Britain, and even there it is moribund. The main exception is that in the US the term is often used by lawyers when referring to or addressing one another in writing. Curiously, in America, *Esq.* is often appended to the names of women lawyers as well as to men.

-esque. A suffix that forms adjectives, it represents French *-esque* or Italian *-esco* (from medieval Latin *-iscus*). It occurs in English in the sense 'resembling the style of', (*a*) in ordinary words, such as *grotesque* (originally = 'resembling a grotto'), *picaresque* (from a Spanish or Italian word meaning 'rogue'), and *picturesque*; (*b*) appended to personal names, as *Audenesque* (20c.), *Browningesque* (19c.), *Disneyesque* (20c.), *Giottesque* (19c.), *Reaganesque* (20c.), etc. It can be seen that adding the alternative suffix *-ian* to the word just listed would produce awkward results. See SUFFIXES ADDED TO PROPER NAMES.

-ess, a suffix forming nouns denoting female persons or animals, was adopted in Middle English from Old French *-esse* (from late Latin *-issa*, ultimately from Greek -ισσα as in βασίλισσα 'queen'; cf. βασιλεύς 'king'). **1** *First arrivals.* The first wave of *-ess* words in English (*countess, duchess, empress, hostess, lioness, mistress, princess*, etc.) were all imported in their entirety into English from French. These words are all deeply embedded in the language.

2 How new *-ess* words were created. The suffix rapidly became a highly productive element in English and was attached to many words that already existed in English from the 14c. onwards, e.g. *Jewess* (14c., Wyclif), *patroness* (15c.), *poetess* (16c., Tyndale), etc.; and it supplanted the older native female suffix *-ster* (which, as a feminine ending, survives only in *spinster*). These new feminine-gender words were formed either by replacing *-er* with *-ess* for (*adulterer/adulteress, murderer/murderess*, etc.) or by adding *-ess* to the stem of the common-gender word (*author/authoress, giant/giantess*, etc.). In some cases a feminine form predates a masculine one, as in *sorceress* (14c., Chaucer) from the common-gender *sorcer* (14c.–1549, now obsolete) before the masculine form *sorcerer* (1526, Tyndale). There were some other refinements, e.g. *governess* (already in Caxton) replacing the earlier *governeresse* and the establishment of the phonetically simplified forms *adventuress* (1754, Walpole; not **adventureress*), *conqueress* (now obsolete), etc. When *-ess* was added to a noun ending in *-der* or *-dor, -ter* or *-tor*, the vowel before the *r* was usually elided, e.g. *ambassadress, wardress; actress, doctress* (now obsolete), *editress, protectress* (16c., J. Foxe), *waitress*.

3 *Middle English to 19c.* From ME until about 1850 the suffix retained its power as a more or less unrestricted means of indicating a feminine agent noun. More than 100 words in *-ess* denoting female persons or animals are listed in the *OED*, many merely fanciful or humorous, many now obsolete, but some still in regular use, e.g. *ambassadress, heiress, mayoress*. (*a*) Except for *lioness* (ME), *tigress* (1611), and to a more limited extent *leopardess* (1567) and *pantheress* (1862), the suffix is not used in any routine way of female animals. (*b*) In *rectoress* (1729) and *vicaress* (1770), both now obsolete, the suffix means 'wife of a —'. (Both words have other meanings as well.) One of the senses of *mayoress* is 'the wife of a mayor'; similarly with *ambassadress*. (*c*) Nonce words, or words of limited currency, e.g. *confectioness* (only 1640), *entertainess* (only 1709), *farmeress* (1672–), *preacheress* (1649–), *professoress* (*c.*1740–), *saviouress* (1553–).

4 Decline and fall of *-ess.* Since the 20c. the feminist and politically correct movements have cut like a scythe through a swathe of *-ess* words in three main groups. (*a*) (Racially sensitive) *Jewess* and *Negress* are regarded as particularly offensive but may occasionally continue to be used among themselves by the groups concerned. (*b*) (Artistic terms) With varying degrees of success, specifically feminine-gender artistic terms like *actress, authoress, editress, poetess, paintress*, and *sculptress* have been replaced by the traditionally male only term, e.g. *actor, author, editor*, on the valid grounds that there is no need for a separate term, any more than there is a continuing need for (say) *interpretress* (18c.), *philosopheress* (17c.), *tutoress* (17c.), all once common and all now obsolete. (*c*) (Occupational terms) Many words relating to jobs, such as *air hostess, manageress, proprietress, stewardess, waitress* have been replaced by gender-neutral alternatives. These can be either the traditional masculine forms, e.g. *manager, proprietor, waiter*, or specially devised terms, such as *flight attendant* (1947, perhaps surprisingly) which has found widespread acceptance, or *waitperson* (1980) which has not. And of course, *shepherdesses* are more at home in pastoral poetry than on modern farms.

5 *A dead suffix.* The suffix *-ess* is probably dead as a productive suffix but there is a central core of *-ess* words (apart from those in (1) above) remaining in use more or less unchallenged, among them *abbess, adulteress, adventuress, ambassadress, ancestress, benefactress, goddess, governess, heiress, instructress, mayoress, ogress, peeress, postmistress, priestess* (but only in non-Christian religions), *procuress, prophetess, protectress, seductress, songstress, temptress.*

essay. As a noun = 'a short composition', it is always stressed on the first syllable; as a rather dated formal word for 'an attempt' it was previously stressed on the second syllable, but is now stressed on the first. As a somewhat dated formal verb, with the broad sense 'to attempt or endeavour to', e.g. *Rufus essayed a smile*, it is always stressed on the second syllable.

-est in superlatives. See -ER AND -EST.

Establishment. *The Establishment*, with a capital letter *E*, refers to 'a group in a society exercising power and influence over matters of policy, opinion, or taste, and seen as self-satisfied and resisting change'. As the journalist Henry Fairlie expressed it in a key article in *The Spectator*, 23 Sept., 1955, it means 'not only the centres of official power—though they are certainly part of it—but rather the whole matrix of official and social relations within which power is exercised'. Others before Fairlie had used the expression in a more or less casual manner: Fairlie brought the term into widespread and continuing use, and helped make it part of the fabric of the language. It is most often used as a blanket term of implied disapproval, denoting people or groups in positions of power about whom the writer or speaker has reservations, e.g. *Steve Earle has never really been a member of the Establishment, either socially or professionally—OEC*, 2004. For something like two decades it was a much overused word, but it has long since settled down as a useful description for any loosely defined influential or controlling group, not necessarily political. When it is qualified, it is not usually written with a capital, e.g. *the business establishment, the educational establishment, the literary establishment, the media establishment*, etc.

estate. 1 *The three estates of the realm* are traditionally in the UK the Lords Spiritual, the Lords Temporal, and the Commons, but the term is occasionally misused to denote the Crown, the House of Lords, and the House of Commons. The standard use dates from the early 15c. and the misuse is first recorded in 1559. The *third estate* (French *tiers état*) was commonly used of the French bourgeoisie before the Revolution, the other two *estates* (clergy, nobility) being seldom spoken of numerically.

2 The *fourth estate* has been applied to the newspaper press since the early 19c., and is attributed to Edmund Burke, which has not been confirmed, but evidence of the use of the phrase in 1821 is given in the *OED*. The phrase *fifth estate* is used with various meanings, which can cause ambiguity: (*a*) as a way of referring to the Internet or to blogs in their capacity to spread news and opinion outside the mainstream media, but also to media itself; (*b*) loosely, for any group of people perceived to have some kind of unofficial power, such as trade unions; (*c*) by mistake for *fourth estate* as a way of referring to the press.

3 Estate car is a general term in British English for a kind of car that has the internal accommodation extended into the rear with a door at the back; it differs in shape from a *hatchback*. The equivalent term in American English is *station wagon*.

esthete, esthetic. Are much less frequent variants spelling of *aesthete, aesthetic* used in American English.

estimate. How you pronounce *estimate* depends on whether you are using it as a noun or a verb. As a noun, e.g. *our first estimates were too low*, it is pronounced /ˈɛstɪmət/ (**e**-sti-muht). As a verb it is pronounced /ˈɛstɪmeɪt/ (**e**-sti-mayt), giving the final vowel its full value. Quite often you hear the verb pronounced **e**-sti-muht, like the noun, but this is incorrect.

estimation. Surprisingly, Fowler (1926) described the phrase *in my estimation* used as a 'mere substitute' for *in my opinion* as 'illiterate', a verdict which is negated by several centuries of use from Chaucer onwards. Examples: *The dearest of men in my estimation*—E. W. Lane, 1841; *It was about this time that Martin took a great slump in Maria's estimation*—J. London, 1909.

estrogen, estrus. The standard American English spellings of BrE *oestrogen, oestrus.*

Estuary English. A once fashionable term, coined in 1984 by a London scholar named David Rosewarne, for a kind of slightly non-standard English adopted as common currency by many people as part of a minor reaction against the norms of standard English. 'The R.P. speaker accommodates "downwards" and the local accent speaker accommodates "upwards",' declared Rosewarne. Some of the features of this middle-ground form of speech are described (and are drawn on here) in Paul Coggle's *Do You Speak Estuary?* (1993). The estuary is the Thames estuary, and the term *Estuary English* refers to a variety of informal, allegedly classless, English spoken in London and some of the Home Counties, especially North Kent and South Essex, and also, it is claimed, in some other southern counties. It is characterized in pronunciation by the use of glottal stops (instead of /t/) in such a sentence as *In Scotland the butter and the water are absolutely outstanding*; and the replacement of /l/ by /w/ in such words as *tall, ballpoint,* and *Maldon*. In *fault* both replacements occur. *Mouth* tends to come out as *mouf* and *anything* as *anyfink*. The choice of vocabulary is important: e.g. *Cheers* instead of *Thank you*, and *mate* tends to replace *friend* (*Me and my mate went to the disco last night:* remember to pronounce the letter *t* as a glottal stop). These are mere specimens of a complex form of speech.

-et (suffix). **1** It occurs naturally as an originally diminutive ending in many words adopted from French at an early date, as *bullet, fillet, hatchet, pocket, tablet,* etc.; these words are now used without any consciousness of their original diminutive sense. *Bullet*, for example, is a 16c. adaptation of French *boulette*, diminutive of *boule* 'ball'; *tablet* is a 14c. adaptation of Old French *tablete* (modern *tablette*), diminutive of Latin *tabula* 'table'.

2 In more recent formations from French in the 16c. and 17c. *-et* represented French *-ette* as well as *-et* (e.g. in *facet, islet*). In even more recent adoptions from French the spelling *-ette* is usually retained (see -ETTE); but shortened forms are shown in BASSINET and in the American English variant *cigaret* of *cigarette.*

et al. An abbreviation of Latin *et alia* (neuter), *et alii* (masculine), or *et aliæ* (feminine), it means 'and other things' or 'and other people' and is used especially to avoid listing a long sequence of names, only the first or the first few being given, as in *Smith, Jones, et al.* It is regularly used in bibliographical citation for works having several authors, and is printed in roman or italic type according to the particular style in use. Special care should be taken not to place a full stop after *et* in the phrase *et al.* It is appropriately used for references to people; for other categories etc. is preferable.

etc. 1 An abbreviation of *et cetera* (which in Latin means 'and other things of the same kind'), it is now in English deemed to mean, (*a*) and the rest; and similar things *and people*; (*b*) or similar things *or people*; (*c*) and so on. Fowler (1926) placed no restriction on the following types: (= and other things) *His pockets contained an apple, a piece of string, etc.*; (= or the like) *'Good', 'fair', 'excellent', etc., is appended to each name*; (= and other persons) *The Duke of A, Lord B, Mr C, etc., are patrons.*

2 By the phonetic process of assimilation, etc., which is properly pronounced /ɛt ˈsɛtərə/, is quite frequently, but wrongly, pronounced as /ɛk ˈsɛt-/. This comes about because no other common word in English begins with /ɛts-/, whereas words beginning with /ɛks-/ abound (*ecstasy, excellence, exclamation*, etc.).

3 Practice varies regarding the punctuation that precedes and follows etc., but in general it is best to treat it as if it were 'and so on', i.e. precede it by a comma when it comes after two or more items already separated by commas (*We need pencils, paper, etc.*), but not when it comes after a single item or two items without a comma (*We need paper etc.; We need some pencils and paper etc.*). It should be followed by a comma when a comma would be used in the case of 'and so on' (*We need pencils, paper, etc., as well as a desk to work on*).

4 Since etc. already means 'and', it is illiterate to write *and* etc. (or & etc.). The form &c, though once common (and used by Fowler in ordinary writing), is now archaic.

-eteria. See -TERIA.

ethnic. The original (15c. onwards) meaning, 'pertaining to nations not Christian or Jewish; heathen, pagan', is now, of course, only historical. Since the mid-19c., and particularly since the mid-20c., it has been applied to a community having common racial, cultural, religious, or linguistic characteristics that distinguish its members. *Ethnic* is typically used to describe clothing, dance, music, and other customs that distinguish such people: *Vegetarian dishes in various ethnic cuisines—Mexican, Thai, Indian, Italian, Japanese, Middle Eastern, etc.—NME*, 1991.

An *ethnic minority* (first recorded in 1945) is a section of a community that forms a minority within a larger community, for example Sikhs, Muslims, and West Indian people in Britain. In a further development of the term, people are described as being (for example) *ethnic Turks* when they are of Turkish origin but living in a country other than Turkey, e.g. *In* The Boat People, *she shows how the ethnic Chinese were targets of government oppression in post-liberation Vietnam—OEC*, 2002.

In recent years, *ethnic* has begun to be used in a somewhat euphemistic way to refer to non-white people as a whole, as in *a radio station which broadcasts to the ethnic community in Birmingham.* Although this usage is quite common, especially in journalism, it is considered by some to be inaccurate and mealy-mouthed and is better replaced by words such as 'black', 'Asian', etc.

ethnic terms. The 20c. was, fortunately, marked by an increasing awareness of the potential hurtfulness of unfavourable ethnic terminology and also by the realization that the problem of racism cannot be legislated away. Some of the terms are too well established to cause any more than wry amusement, though they are unmistakably insulting in origin, e.g. *Dutch courage* (first recorded 1826), *French leave* (1771), and *the English disease* (in economics, 1969). A second group of only playfully hurtful terms includes *Limey* (an Englishman, 1918) and *Pom/Pommy* (1912). A third large group of such terms continues to cause great offence to those to whom they are applied or in the contexts in which they occur: e.g. *dago* (1832), *kike* (1904), *Oreo* (an American black seen as having a 'white' outlook, 1968), *to welsh* (1857, though its connection with Wales is unfounded), *wog* (1929), *wop* (1914), and many much worse ones.

et hoc genus omne. A Latin tag taken from Horace's *Satires*, and used as a learned and sometimes dismissive substitute for etc., referring to people or things. It means 'and the whole of this class or group': *Possibly if Fowler, the tribe of Fowlers,* et hoc genus omne *had received a more unkind critical reception ... —OEC*, 2002.

-ette.

1 Origin.
2 As a diminutive suffix.
3 Imitation and other fabrics.
4 Slightly militant and decidedly unmilitant women.
5 Commercial food names.

1 *Origin.* The suffix was first used to form diminutive nouns, representing the feminine form corresponding to the masculine *-et* (see -ET). The main body of such words joined the language after the 17c., e.g. *chemisette* (1807), *cigarette* (1842), and *pipette* (1839). The basic idea is obviously a small chemise, a small cigar, and a small pipe.

2 *As a diminutive suffix.* The equation of *-ette* with smallness gathered strength in the 19c. The literature of the period is studded with words, not all of them of long duration, like *bannerette* (1884), *essayette* (1877), *novelette* (1820), *sermonette* (1814), and *statuette* (1843). This branch of words tended to weaken in the 20c., but is represented by such words as *dinette* (1930), a small dining-room, *diskette* (1973), a floppy disk, *featurette* (1942) a short feature film, (*kitchenette* (1910), a small kitchen, and *superette* (1938, chiefly US and Antipodean), a small supermarket. Smallness is not quite the meaning in a number of special cases. *Laund(e)rette* (1949), for example, is not a diminutive as such, but is just formed on *launder* (verb) or *laundry*. *Serviette* (15c. onwards) was for centuries exclusively Scottish, was reintroduced into standard English from French in the 19c., and is also not a diminutive. It also lies in the territory designated by A. S. C. Ross and Nancy Mitford as 'non-U'.

3 *Imitation and other fabrics.* Beginning in the 18c., manufacturers began to place the ending on the names of materials intended as imitations of something else. *Muslinette* (1787), was among the first of such terms, followed by *leatherette* (1880), *flannel(l)ette* (1882), *cashmerette* (1886), and others. Some other names of fabrics, not in fact imitations, helped to establish a connection between *-ette* and 'name of a (dress) material'. These include *georgette* (1915), named after Mme Georgette de la Plante, a French dressmaker; *stockingette* (1824), now more commonly written as *stockinet*, and more likely to be, as the *OED* expresses it, 'a perversion of stocking-net'; and *winceyette* (1922), a suffixed extension of the older word *wincey*.

4 *Slightly militant and decidedly unmilitant women.* The most spectacular development of the suffix came at the beginning of the 20c. when (in 1906) female supporters of the cause of women's political enfranchisement in Britain were called *suffragettes*. The suffix thereby acquired a markedly feminist edge which has been partially inherited by later groups of terms applied to women. First came the decidedly unmilitant *majorettes* (1941) and *drum majorettes* (1938), with team names (in N. America and the Antipodes) like *Mercurettes, Pantherettes*, and *Trojanettes*. Particularly in the 1980s, male chauvinistic writers in glossy and satirical journals began to make free use of the suffix in a pejorative manner: the language became peppered with antagonistic terms like *bimbette, editorette, hackette, punkette, reporterette, whizzette*, and *womanette*. This phase has long since passed, but the word *suffragette* will always remain firmly in place as a term of historic importance. Two other words designating classes of women, namely *undergraduette* (1919) and *usherette* (1925), for the most part passed out of use, except in historical contexts, somewhere about 1960. Only *bachelorette* (1965, chiefly Canadian and US), *hackette* (1976) a satirical term for a female journalist first recorded by the *OED* from the British magazine *Private Eye*, and the, sadly and exclusively British, *ladette* from the 1990s ('a young woman who behaves in a boisterously assertive or crude manner') and *chavette*, the female of the chav species, look likely to survive in real usage.

5 *Commercial food names.* In the 1990s American newspapers carried advertisements for a host of such names, e.g. *Clubettes* ('bite-size' crackers), *Creamettes* (a kind of pasta), *Croutettes* (a stuffing mix), and *Toastettes* (a kind of tart). The model for these trade names, which now sound incredibly dated, was possibly the word *croquette* (first recorded in 1706; Fr. *croquette*, prob. from *croquer* 'to crackle under the teeth, to crunch'), 'a fried breaded roll or ball of mashed potato or minced meat', etc.

etymology. 1 *What it is. Etymology* is the study of the history and derivation of words, and *an etymology* is the history of a particular word. Most dictionaries of concise size and larger give detailed accounts of a word's sources, which can be from other English words (e.g. *newspaper*) or from other languages (e.g. *kiosk* via French from Persian).

The word *etymology* comes from a Greek word *etymon* (ἔτυμον) meaning 'true'. However, the etymology of a word represents its original meaning rather than its true meaning in any judgemental sense. Appeals to etymology to defend the use of words against change in meaning (as for example with *decimate*), though commonly made, are usually futile, since few words in the core vocabulary of English now mean what they used to mean.

2 *Where do English words come from?* The great majority of English words can be straightforwardly traced to their roots, as shown in the examples at 5 below. The vast majority of English words (apart from those made from existing English words) are derived from Old English (Anglo-Saxon), from Norse languages, or from a late form of Latin via French words that came into English after the Norman Conquest in 1066. A succinct account of the main sources of English words is given in the *Concise Oxford Dictionary* (1995), ix–xii, to which the reader is referred for further information.

3 *Words with unknown origins.* It is disappointing for many people that the origins of some quite familiar and important words remain obscure or unknown, and are so marked in standard dictionaries (or are said to be of unknown or uncertain origin). For instance, the histories of *boy* and *girl* are unknown before Middle English, and *dog* occurs only once in late Old English as *docga*, but has no identified parallels in the Germanic family of languages (the normal OE word was *hund*, hound). Scores of other mainstream words are of unknown origin, including *boffin, coarse, garbage, nasty, peter out, shandy, trash*, etc., and the same is true of dozens of slang words, such as *bamboozle, caboodle, cagey, clobber, gimmick, jiff, kibosh*, etc.

4 *Folk etymology at work.* A third group of words have substantially changed their form in English under the influence of another English word: e.g. *belfry*, a 15c. adaptation of earlier *berfrey* by association with *bell; bridegroom*, a 16c. alteration of *bridegoom* (from Old English *brȳdguma*, literally 'bride-man'); *shamefaced*, a 16c. alteration of *shamefast*. A more extreme example is Spanish *cucaracha*, which has given us *cockroach* by assimilation with the English words *cock* and *roach*. See FOLK ETYMOLOGY.

5 A fourth group of words have had fanciful explanations foisted upon them. Easily the best example of this phenomenon is *posh*, popularly, but mistakenly, said to be derived from the initials of 'port outward starboard home', referring to the more expensive side for accommodation on ships formerly travelling between England and India. See also FOLK ETYMOLOGY.

6 The *OED* sets out in a classical manner the stages through which the current English form of a given word emerged from its earliest recorded form or forms, together with details of its analogues in related languages; and for loanwords as much information about the spelling, meaning, etc., of the source word as is necessary to explain its passage into and its shape in English. Thus *quick* [Common Teutonic: Old English *cwicu, c(w)uc*, and *cwic, c(w)uc-*, = Old Frisian *quik, quek* (modern Frisian *quick, queck*), etc., etc.]; and *resin* [Middle English *recyn(e), reysen*, from French *résine*, from Latin *rēsīna* (Spanish, Portuguese, and Italian *resina*), cognate with Greek ῥητίνη].

See BACK-FORMATION; BLEND; FACETIOUS FORMATIONS; FOLK ETYMOLOGY.

eulogy, a speech or writing in praise of a person.

euphemism, a mild or vague or periphrastic expression substituted for one judged to be too harsh or direct, e.g. *to pass away* for *to die*. Euphemisms can be viewed positively as words of good omen, or negatively as the avoidance of unlucky or inauspicious words. Numerous examples of both kinds are listed in Burchfield's essay 'An Outline History of Euphemisms in English' in D. J. Enright's *Fair of Speech* (1985).

Key concepts that tend to generate euphemisms are bodily functions (e.g. *point Percy at the porcelain*), sexual activity (e.g. *horizontal jogging*), death (e.g. *pass*), and violence and war. In the Second World War British fighter pilots *bought it* or *went for a Burton* as they crashed and were killed. In the Vietnam war the Americans discovered the calming usefulness of expressions like *pacification* (destruction of villages after evacuation of the inhabitants) and *defoliation* (destruction of forests used by the enemy as cover). In the Gulf War some soldiers were killed by what was chillingly described as *friendly fire*; and destruction brought about by misdirected bombs or missiles was called *collateral damage*. Euphemisms abound, and are frequently mocked, at places of employment. They include fair-sounding titles (e.g. *flight service director* for the chief steward on an aircraft); synonyms for the reduction of staff (*outplacement, restructuring, slimming down, downsizing*).

The word *euphemism*, which is derived from the Greek words εὐφημισμός 'use of an auspicious word for an inauspicious one' and εὔφημος 'fair of speech', was first recorded in English in Thomas Blount's *Glossographia* (1656–81). The use of euphemisms can be traced back to the Middle Ages, but the use of such evasive and concealing (or fair-sounding) terminology has arguably never been more prevalent than it is now.

euphuism, an affected or high-flown style of writing or speaking, originally applied to work (especially of the late 16c. and early 17c.) written in imitation of John Lyly's *Euphues* (1578–80). The name Euphues /ˈjuːfjuːˌiːz/ is derived from Greek εὐφυής 'well-endowed by nature'. The chief features of euphuism include 'the continual recurrence of antithetic clauses in which the antithesis is emphasized by means of alliteration; the frequent introduction of a long string of similes all relating to the same subject, often drawn from the fabulous qualities ascribed to plants, minerals, and animals; and the constant endeavour after subtle refinement of expression' (*OED*). It has no connection with EUPHEMISM.

Eurasian. In the 19c. the word *Eurasian* was normally used to refer to a person of mixed British and Indian parentage. In modern use, however, the term is generally used as a noun and adjective to refer to a person of mixed white-American and SE-Asian parentage. Cf. ANGLO-INDIAN.

Euro-. Shortened to *Eur-* before certain vowels, is one of the more productive combining forms of the end of the 20c., as a linguistic reflection of far-reaching political and economic developments across Europe. The form was first used in the 1950s in hyphenated combinations such as *Euro-African* and *Euro-American*, and in the institutional names *Eurovision* (1951, a network of European broadcasting organizations) and *Euratom* (1956, = European Atomic Energy Community). The first generalized words were *Euro-dollar* (1960, a dollar held outside the US, though not necessarily in Europe), the disparaging *Eurocrat* (= European bureaucrat, 1961), and the not much more favourable *Eurocentric* (= regarded in European terms, 1963). The first uses related to Europe (or Western Europe) generally, and this meaning continues in formations such as *Euromissile* (1979) and *Eurostrategic* (1977), whereas many terms that arose in the 1960s and since refer more specifically to the European Community (now Union) in relation to the UK's potential and later actual membership, especially the notorious *Eurosceptic* (1986) and its antonym *Europhile*, both used as adjectives and nouns, and other irreverent formations including *Eurobabble* (1986, in a US source) and *Eurojargon*.

2 Like many prolific combining forms, *Euro-* has succeeded in detaching itself and forming a word in its own right: *The Euro terrorists announced ... that they had set up a 'Western European Revolutionary offensive*—*Evening Standard*, 1987; *The name Britannia had been dropped from the deal because its nationalistic connotations could have obvious drawbacks in a pan-Euro venture*—*European Investor*, 1990. It has also become the informal name of several European-based sports championships, notably in golf and football. With a lower-case initial *e-*, **euro** has been since 1995 the official name of the common currency adopted by some members of the EU, with coins and notes in circulation since 2002.

evasion, evasiveness. *Evasiveness* is the quality a person has of being *evasive*, whereas *evasion* is the process or result of this quality, or an instance of it: *his evasion of the issue is obvious; he is guilty of perpetual evasion*; but *the evasiveness* (not *evasion*) *of his answers is enough to condemn him. Evasion* has a special meaning in relation to legal obligations, and differs from *avoidance* because it denotes illegality: *He'd been had up for offering bribes to council employees: the whole story had been ridiculous, tales of ... call girls and twenty-pound notes, of tax evasion and porno-movies*—Margaret Drabble, 1977. See -ION AND -NESS.

even (adverb). **1** *Position.* As a general rule *even* should be placed next to the word or words that it governs or qualifies. These examples illustrate its use in some common grammatical patterns: (before an adjective) *doctors must pursue costly and even dangerous investigations; they were disposed to be helpful, even solicitous*; (before a comparative adjective or adverb) *she is talking even louder*; (before a noun) *not a word addressed to me personally—not even a postcard*; (before an adverb) *He himself felt troubled, even slightly humiliated*; (before a finite verb) *he even enrolled in a business studies course to get more organized*; (before a prepositional phrase) *My father was so polite, even in the family.* In some cases *even* qualifies an entire subordinate clause: *Annie Asra was the kind of girl to whom people give a job, even when they didn't originally intend to.*

2 When *even* qualifies a verb formed with an auxiliary or a modal verb (*can, do, have, might,* etc.), it is placed between the auxiliary verb and the infinitive: *He had even managed to laugh at it; I did not even bother to read it.* This is also true when *even* qualifies the complement of the verb: *It might even cost £100.*

3 *Meaning. COD* (1990) says that it is 'used to invite comparison of the stated assertion, negation, etc., with an implied one that is less strong or remarkable (*never even opened* [let alone read] *the letter; does he even suspect* [not to say realize] *the danger?; ran even faster* [not just as fast as before]; *even if my watch is right we shall be late* [later if it is slow]'.

4 In informal contexts involving negatives, *even* sometimes comes at the end of a sentence: *They didn't want anything to eat, or a drink even.*

evenness. So spelt.

evensong. See MORNING.

event. 1 *In the event of* is a somewhat formal prepositional phrase, beloved by insurers and the legal profession, used to mean 'if such and such (should happen)'. It can usually be replaced by a simple *if* (plus verb), but, though often criticized, it can fulfil a useful function in imparting a degree of formality to a statement. 'If there is . . . ' and 'if we carried out . . . ' could replace it in the first and second examples below respectively. It is up to you, gentle reader, to decide what would be lost or gained by doing so: *In the event of a strike, it will not be able to fulfil its contract obligations—Birmingham Post,* 2007; *As I explained to you, it has always been Jeffrey's desire to minimise the risk element in the event of our carrying out the building works—England and Wales High Court (Technology and Construction Court) Decisions,* 2003.

2 In the language of law and business in both British and American English, the phrase *in the event (that),* is used as a conjunction: *Parties should consider at the outset the payment of their advisers' fees in the event that the transaction aborts*—D. J. Cooke, 1993. In other contexts, it too can be replaced by a simple *if.*

eventuality, eventuate. *History.* These words, both first recorded in the 18c., have had a chequered history, especially *eventuate.* Derided by De Quincey (1834) as 'Yankeeish', by Dean Alford (1864) as 'another horrible word, which is fast getting into our language through the provincial press', and by Fowler (1926) as 'flabby journalese', *eventuate* has now settled into a fairly formal, not to say pompous, corner in the language. It is undeniable that *result* or *come about,* or sometimes simply *happen,* are often preferable alternatives: *It had been intended to have educated Saudi women dealing with the public at the exhibition, but . . . this had not eventuated—Times,* 1986; *I hope a sensible result eventuates—Express,* 2002. *Eventuality* is rather more frequently used but has been much less frequently attacked, although it is often a mere, rather inflated, synonym for circumstance, event, or possibility. The phrase *every eventuality,* however, seems like a useful, if rather clichéd, expression. *In certain eventualities this state of things might give rise to grave difficulties*—Lady Herbert, 1878; *Although he had been ordered not to destroy it, Harmel was prepared for the eventuality*—C. Ryan, 1974; *Of course, different situations demand different reactions and one cannot plan for every eventuality*—P. Mann, 1982.

ever. 1 In informal conversation *ever* is sometimes used as an intensifier immediately after an interrogative word such as *who, what, why, when,* etc.: *Who ever can that be?; What ever did you do that for?; Why ever should you think that?* It is important to write the two words separately in sentences like those just illustrated. The single-word forms *whoever, whatever, whenever* mean something different, e.g. *Invite whoever you like; I'll do whatever you want.* See WHATEVER, WHAT EVER; WHEN EVER, WHENEVER; WHOEVER.

2 *Did you ever?* A colloquial phrase meaning 'Did you ever hear or see the like?', it is rare nowadays and has a quaint, old-fashioned, even Victorian flavour: *'And where is she now?' 'In a studio.' . . . 'Did you ever!' said Mrs. Fanshaw—Peel City Guardian,* 1892. A modern example: *What Dad says when he sees Farmer is, 'Well, did you ever?' And what Grandad says is, 'Well, I never!—OEC* (undated).

3 *ever and anon* 'every now and then'. This phrase (first recorded in Shakespeare's *Love's Labour's Lost, Ever and* *anon they made a doubt*) is still very occasionally used in present-day English of a highly literary register: *he ever and anon brought ... a cigarette-end to his lips*—A. Burgess, 1963.

4 *ever so.* An older use after *if* or *though* with the meaning 'at all, in any degree' is now archaic: *Though Sir Peter's ill humour may vex me ever so, it never shall provoke me*—Sheridan, 1777. It is now overshadowed by the same phrase used (since the mid-19c.) in positive contexts as an intensive meaning 'extremely, immensely': *Broken bones sounded ever so unpleasant*—O. Drake, 2001; *He's done ever so well out there. He's a fashion photographer, has his own studio.*—D. Lodge, 1991. This use is largely restricted to conversational English.

5 See FOR EVER.

every. 1 *Singular or plural verb.* (*a*) As a general rule, according to the basic principle of subject-verb agreement, *every* requires a singular verb*: every dog has his day; every man has his price; not every book is worth reading; not every one of these enterprises shows a profit.* The same principle of agreement applies when *every* is repeated in a series of nouns, e.g. *Recognize that every experiment, every program, every drug has plenty of reasons why it shouldn't work—OEC,* 2006; *'We are faced with the Libyan mentality that every tribe, every region, every city has a share in the new government,' Abdel Jalil said—Telegraph,* 2011. (*b*) When *every* modifies two or more nouns joined by *and*, the verb should, technically, be plural, according to the notion that compound subjects conjoined by *and* are plural. That rule has been applied in the following examples: *Every phrase, every line and every stanza are indissolubly welded—M. Gullan,* 1937; *Every single word and meaning of great ancient writers like Geoffrey Chaucer were recorded in the OED*—Robert Burchfield, *US News & World Report,* 1986. However, the more common pattern is for the verb to be singular. The principle at work presumably is that the verb agrees in number with the last stated subject. Examples: *Every shot, every color, every prop, and every costume tells its own story—OEC,* 2001; *And just to make sure we understand that every pint, every glass of wine, and every double whisky is on the taxpayers ... —Telegraph,* 2009.

2 Followed by *their. Their* is nowadays very widely used in order to avoid using the gender-specific *his* in sentences of the type *Every student is expected to meet the standards set forth by their respective school district; Each and every one of my colleagues at the university will express their own opinion.* This construction, which entails 'ungrammatically' referring a plural possessive adjective back to a singular subject induces apoplexy in many purists. Analogous constructions nevertheless have a distinguished historical pedigree, and this construction is infinitely preferable to the long-winded *his or her.* Editors who reel in horror whenever they come across it can always, of course, try to rephrase the sentence, e.g. *All students are expected to ...* In the second example, the problem could be resolved by rephrasing as 'will express an opinion', but something would be lost. Cf. AGREEMENT 6; EACH; EVERYBODY.

3 *Every one. Every one* can refer to people or things, and both words retain their distinct meanings: *When we cut up the apples, every one of them was rotten; My friends are pretty well aware of this, and virtually every one of them has reacted with a certain amount of shock—OEC,* 2002. Written as one word, *everyone* refers only to people: *Just about everyone loves a puppy.*

4 See also EACH AND EVERY.

everybody. First (16–17c., and intermittently until the 19c.) written as two words (*every body*), this pronoun is now always written as one word in its ordinary meaning 'every person, everyone'. (Of course when *body* is a full noun the two words are separated: *Every body was recovered from no man's land by the stretcher-bearers.*) It alternates freely with *everyone* and both words normally require a singular verb. On the type *Has everybody got* their *first course?*, see AGREEMENT 6. The use with a singular (occasionally plural) verb, and with a following plural pronoun or adjective (*they, their,* etc.), has been a feature of the language for more than four centuries. This is the way English naturally operates, despite the obvious clash of number between *everybody* and what follows. For *everybody,* while grammatically singular, is 'notionally' plural in meaning. Examples: *Everye bodye was in theyr lodgynges*—Lord Berners, *c*.1530; *Now this king did keepe a great house, that euerie body might come and take their meat freely*—Sidney, 1580; *Every body else I meet with are full ready to go of themselves*—Bishop Warburton, 1759; *Every body does and says what they please*—Byron, 1820; *Everybody seems to recover their spirits*—Ruskin, 1866; *Everybody has a right to describe their own party machine as they choose*—W. Churchill, 1954; *'There's a bus waiting outside the terminal to take everybody to their hotels,' said Linda*—D. Lodge, 1991.

Cf. EVERYONE.

everyday. When used as an adjective (*an everyday event, everyday clothes*, etc.) meaning 'commonplace, usual; suitable for or used on ordinary days', *everyday* is written as one word. In contexts where it means 'each day' (*she went shopping almost every day*), two words (*every day*) are needed.

everyone. 1 In its regular use as an indefinite pronoun = everybody, it is now invariably written as one word (*living through hard times, as everyone was; everyone was growing leaner and cleaner; you can't please everyone*), but this convention did not fall into place until the 20c. The *OED* (in 1894) gave precedence to *every one*, while Fowler (1926) presented a spirited argument in favour of the linked form.

2 Just as with *everybody*, pronouns and adjectives referring back to *everyone* are often plural, 'the absence', as the *OED* puts it, 'of common gender rendering this violation of grammatical concord sometimes necessary'. Examples: *Every one Sacrifices a Cow or more, according to their different Degrees of Wealth or Devotion*—Dr Johnson, 1735; *Everyone then looked about them silently, in suspense and expectation*—W. H. Mallock, 1877; *Everyone was absorbed in their own business*—A. Motion, 1989; *the classical allegories look like surreal school outings in which everyone got to take their clothes off, and then was sorry*—M. Vaizey, 1991.

Not everyone favours this practice, however: *Well, I'm afraid it's everyone for himself*—R. Hall, 1978 (NZ); *Everyone has his own image of a city—his own image of the Eiffel Tower . . .* —*Art Business News*, 2004.

3 In the expression *every one*, referring to all the people or things in a group, which can be followed by *of* + noun or pronoun, or used on its own, the two words need to be written separately: *The drawings are academical in the worst sense of the word; almost every one of them deserves to be rejected.*

4 Cf. agreement 6; EVERYBODY.

everyplace, a modern American English synonym of *everywhere: She sets them on the floor because everyplace else is taken* (AmE)—Internet website, 2003. Cf. ANY 2(f); SOMEPLACE.

every time used as an adverbial phrase and conjunction, should be written as two words: *It happens every time; Every time they come, there's an argument.* It is increasingly found as one word, both in British and American English, especially on blogs, but this is still incorrect until authoritative dictionaries decide otherwise: **you couldn't help but snicker everytime you looked at them*—*ballet.co.uk*, 2003.

evidence (verb). This uncomfortable verb has been in existence in several senses since the 17c. One of these is the verbal equivalent of the noun, namely 'to serve as evidence, to be evidence of' (*Occurrences evidencing the divinity of Christ*—J. O. Halliwell, 1859). Another is 'to attest' (*This is no reason for doubting their reality, when they are evidenced by Intuition*—F. Bowen, 1864). A third is 'to indicate, manifest' (*The courts eagerly seized on any expressions evidencing this intention*—K. E. Digby, 1876). It is obvious that all three uses occur in contexts which are much more formal than ordinary discourse. It is also apparent that such a verb is at risk of disapproval in any case as part of the traditional dislike of nouns (in this case a noun first recorded in the 14c.) being employed as verbs when other verbs are available. At all events, Fowler (1926) accepted the first meaning as a 'right use' and rejected the third as a 'wrong use'. He left the sense 'to attest' without comment. His arguments in the matter no longer carry any weight. In practice the verb is not common in any of these meanings, but it is legitimately available for all three. Should you wish to use a less portentous word for the meaning of 'indicate, manifest', you have to hand those words themselves and *demonstrate, exhibit, indicate,* and *show*. Examples: *This is not . . . an ideal Universe, as was further evidenced by the eye-crossing patterns of the inlaid marble floor*—Douglas Adams, 1980; *This type of pass* [in basketball] *can be extremely devastating to the opposition, as evidenced by its use in providing the winning scoring opportunity in the final of the Munich Olympic Games*—Hoy and Carter, 1980; *the closer links with the London company were evidenced by the acquisition of LGOC-type buses and equipment*—K. Warren, 1980; *Everything he was and did evidenced distinction*—N. Gordimer, 1990.

evilly (adverb). So spelt.

evince. A learned word, first brought into English in the 17c. in several meanings answering to Latin *ēvincere* (from *ē* 'out' + *vincere* 'to conquer'). Most of these meanings (to overcome, prevail over; to convince; to confute; to constrain; to prove by argument, etc.) flourished for a time in learned work but were obsolete by the end of the 18c. The word is now used mainly in formal English (or, as Fowler put it, by 'those who like a full-dress word better than a plain one') particularly in the arts to mean 'to show, make evident (a quality, a feeling), to show that one has (a quality, a feeling)'. In arty contexts, it is often in the company of other 'full-dress' words, as the last two examples below suggest. Examples: *He had never been inside a church before, but neither then nor on any subsequent visit did he evince the least curiosity*—P. D. James, 1986; *Nobody he passed evinced the slightest interest in him nor seemed to constitute any kind of threat*—J. Leland, 1987; *They constantly evince a smug hermeticism that is graceless and slight—Times,* 1987; *Louis Malle's eponymous 1980 film* [*sc.* Atlantic City] *evinced a more gritty European* vérité, *capturing a bittersweet sense of melancholic despair and a down-at-heel town living on past glories—Architectural Review,* 2002.

evolve. See INVOLVE (verb) 1.

ex-. 1 No difficulties arise when *ex-* meaning 'former(ly)' is prefixed to a single word (*ex-convict, ex-president, ex-wife*); similarly when it is used to mean 'not listed' (*ex-directory*). Fowler (1926) scorned formations in which *ex-* is prefixed to a noun phrase, e.g. *ex-Lord Mayor, ex-Prime Minister, ex-Chief Whip,* on the ground that such persons are not ex-Lords, ex-Primes, etc. Who would dream of thinking so? The eye easily accommodates such expressions, the *ex-* being simply assumed to apply to the whole of the noun phrase. If, however, longer units are felt to be difficult (*ex-trade union leader, ex-Father of the House,* etc.), one can always fall back on *former* instead.

2 See ERST, ERSTWHILE; LATE.

exact is the correct verb to use with the noun *revenge,* to convey the meaning of inflicting revenge. You *exact* revenge *on* someone *for* something. Because *exact* is a verb on the outer reaches of most people's active vocabulary, they often change the phrase to *extract revenge* or *enact revenge.* Until universal usage or dictionaries dictate otherwise, these variants are best regarded as malapropisms. Examples (*exact* correctly used): *Nick, the leader, exacts revenge on Morgan by smashing his bicycle in front of the entire school—DVD Verdict,* 2001; *Robert Carlyle played a terrifying psychopath who exacted revenge for the Hillsborough soccer disaster—Yorkshire Post Today,* 2005; (*extract* wrongly used) **Simply by staying, you extract a revenge of sorts: for so long as you are still in the company, your CEO is not going to be able to forget the embarrassing incident—Financial Times,* 2009; (*enact* wrongly used) **A swift and bloody revenge is enacted by a pair of gamine young women—Guardian* (*Film*), 2009.

exalt, exult. Though unrelated and having different meanings, these two words are sometimes confused because they look and sound similar. *Exalt* (/ɪɡˈzɔːlt/ ig-**zawlt**) means 'to praise highly', and is often used in the participial form *exalted,* referring to people of high or powerful status. *Exult* (/ɪɡˈzʌlt/ ig-**zult**) means 'to feel great joy or triumph', and is common in its adjectival form *exultant.* There are two main ways in which the words are confused. You *exult in* something, and it is in this construction that *exalt* is sometimes wrongly used; *exulted* is also sometimes wrongly used adjectivally when *exalted* is required. Examples: (exalt) *Surrealist artists of more exalted pedigree are also on display—NY Times,* 2007; *If anything, the tendency to* *exalt excellence in sport above excellence in any other field has increased in recent years*—*OEC*, 2005; (exult) *Alice could hardly prevent herself from openly exulting*—Doris Lessing, 1986; *But the growth won't last, and German industry should not be too exultant about it*—*Business Week*, 2005; *The other nobles exulted in Wolsey's misfortune*—*OEC*, 2005; (incorrect use) **Older members of society as well as titled persons enjoy an exulted position of respect*—*OEC*, 2004; **I would exalt in the presence of so many books*—*OEC*, 2005.

excellence, excellency. The first (*c.*1384) comes via French, the second (*a*1400 in the meaning 'excellence') directly from Latin *excellentia*. For several centuries the two words coexisted in the meaning 'the quality of being outstanding', both being used, for example, by Shakespeare. It would be linguistically tidy if one could say that *excellency* is now restricted to its role as a title or form of address for certain high officials, a use first recorded around 1325 in an address to the luckless Edward II. But it still lingers on in some corners as a minority taste in synonyms of *excellence*, e.g. *Standard Bank received a prestigious accolade from the* Euromoney *magazine, in an annual survey on excellency of institutions in their operations*—*Economist* (Namibia), 2004; *Harking back to eighteenth-century theories, some accepted that cultural excellency required racial intermixture but warned that continuing hybridization would inevitably lead to degeneration*—*Oxford Companion to the Body*, 2001; *That the excellencies and subtleties of Neilson's verse depend on the natural speaking voice is apparent from 'May'*—*Quadrant* Magazine, 2002 (Aust.).

except. 1 As a conjunction governing a conditional clause, *except* was continuously in use in the sense 'unless' from the 15c. to the 20c., as in the famous biblical example *Except the Lord build the house, they labour in vaine that build it*—Ps. (AV) 127: 1. Fowler (1926) described it as 'either an archaism resorted to for one or other of the usual reasons, or else an illustration of the fact that old constructions often survive in uneducated talk when otherwise obsolete'.

2 *Except* is frequently used as shorthand (i.e. elliptically) for 'except that' (or, to put it more technically, as a conjunction introducing a statement that is an exception to one just made). Though common in conversation and informal or novelistic writing, it is best avoided in formal style. Examples: *The day he turned 18, Trojan moved into his own council flat in Caledonian Road. Except he didn't like it*—*The Face*, 1987; *the festivities passed off almost painlessly ... Except I forgot the Stilton, the port and the crackers*—*Spectator*, 1987; *They had created the Grand Concourse as the Park Avenue of the Bronx, except the new land of Canaan was going to do it better*—T. Wolfe, 1987 (US).

excepting, excepted. It is not considered good style to use *excepting* as a preposition instead of *except* as in the following examples: **Faith had left all her jewellery, excepting mother's pearl and ruby eternity ring, to Dorothea Shottery*—Susan Hill, 1969; **So far, Mr François has succeeded on all issues excepting one*—*OEC*, 2004. Worse still is to use it followed by a *that*-clause: **I cannot describe it excepting that it was one of the most wonderful things I ever saw or heard in my life*—history website, 2003 (BrE).

Excepting is appropriately used as a preposition in two ways, which mean the opposite of one another. First, *not excepting*, which means 'including', as in *His comprehensive knowledge of the Lakes stood above that of all the men of his time, not excepting Wordsworth*—J. Sloss et al., 1984. An alternative, though less usual, construction is *... Wordsworth not excepted.* Second, in the phrase *always excepting*, and occasionally in *perhaps excepting*, which both mean the same as *except*: *Our newspapers fill themselves with trivia—always excepting that august publication, The FT*—*OEC*, 2000; *It is not unreasonable to define the current and would-be insurgency as the entire population of Afghanistan, perhaps excepting those directly on the United States payroll*—*OEC*, 2009.

The rare use of *excepting* as a true participle or a gerund is also considered acceptable: *He would treble the tax on brandy excepting only*, (or, to mean the opposite *without even excepting*) *that destined for medicine. Excepted* is also sometimes used in post-position without not: *e.g. The men, Marlowe excepted of course, are rather one-dimensional*—*www.DVDVerdict.com*, 2004.

exception. The proverb *the exception proves the rule* is sometimes used to justify the exception, that is, to mean 'this is an exception to the rule'. Strictly speaking, however, what it means can be paraphrased as 'the fact that some cases do not follow the rule proves that the rule applies in all other cases.' The proverb comes from the medieval Latin maxim *exceptio probat regulam in casibus non exceptis* which translates literally as 'the exception confirms the rule in cases not excepted'.

exceptionable, exceptional. These two adjectives relate to different meanings of *exception*. *Exceptional* means 'unusual, not typical', i.e. 'forming an exception' in a favourable sense: e.g. *17th-century Dutch paintings of exceptional quality*. *Exceptionable* means 'to which exception may be taken', 'which is open to objection': *There is nothing intrinsically wrong with, or legally exceptionable about that*—England and Wales High Court (Commercial Court) Decisions, 2004. It is not a common word (there are only a few examples in the *OEC*), and it is very much more often used in the negative form *unexceptionable*, meaning 'not open to objection, perfectly satisfactory'. All the more surprising, then, that *exceptionable* is occasionally found used by mistake for *exceptional*: **The establishment Whigs ... came to argue that resistance was only allowable in exceptionable circumstances, such as those of 1688*—T. Harris, 1993. See also UNEXCEPTIONABLE, UNEXCEPTIONAL.

exchangeable. So spelt. See MUTE E.

excise. 1 Always so spelt, not with *-ize*, in all senses of the noun and of both verbs. See -ISE 1.

2 In the noun and verb in the 'tax' sense, the stress falls on the first syllable, /ˈɛksʌɪz/, **ek**-size; and in the verb meaning 'cut, remove', on the second, /ɪkˈsʌɪz/, ik-**size**.

excitable. So spelt. See MUTE E.

exclamation mark. As F. Scott Fitzgerald said: 'Cut out all those exclamation marks. An exclamation mark is like laughing at your own joke.' Except in poetry, the exclamation mark (!) should be used sparingly. Overuse of exclamation marks in expository prose is a sure sign of an unpractised writer, or of one who wants to add a spurious dash of sensation to something unsensational, or who wishes to underline humour which might otherwise go unrecognized.

There is a range of ordinary circumstances, including the following, in which the use of ! is standard: (*a*) To mark a command or warning: *Go to your room!*; *Be careful!*; (*b*) To indicate the expression of a strong feeling of absurdity, surprise, approval, dislike, regret, etc., especially after *how* or *what*: *What a suggestion!*; *How awful!*; *Aren't they odd!*; *What a good idea!*; *They are revolting!*; *I hate you!*; (*c*) To express a wish, or a feeling of regret: *God save the Queen!*; *I'd love to come!*; *If only I had known!*; (*d*) alarm calls *Help!*; *Every man for himself!*; (*e*) a call for attention *Outside Edith's house, someone knocked. 'Edith!'*; (*f*) to indicate shouting *'You're only shielding her. Shielding her!' His voice rose to a shriek*. Poetical and other literary uses are much more numerous. From *The Oxford Dictionary of Quotations* comes this representative set of 19c. and 20c. examples, which bring out some of the main tendencies: *Nearer, my God, to Thee, Nearer to Thee!* (S. F. Adams, 1805–48); *It did not last: the Devil howling 'Ho! Let Einstein be!' restored the status quo.* (H. Belloc, 1870–1953); *Blow out, you bugles, over the rich Dead!* (R. Brooke, 1887–1915); *Oh, to be in England Now that April's there ... While the chaffinch sings in the orchard bough In England—now!* (R. Browning, 1812–89); *Talk about the pews and steeples And the cash that goes therewith!* (G. K. Chesterton, 1874–1936); *Six days of the week it* [sc. work] *soils With its sickening poison—Just for paying a few bills! That's out of proportion* (Philip Larkin, 1922–85). They represent a wide range of commands, statements, assertions, and wishes.

excusable. So spelt. See MUTE E.

executive, in political discourse, is a noun for one of the three branches of government, of which the others are the *legislative* and the *judicial*. In Britain, it also denotes a rank of civil servant above *administrative* and *clerical*. The most common meaning is, of course, a person with senior management responsibility in a business. Derived from this meaning is the use of the word before another noun (i.e. attributively) to promote anything marketed as suitable for use by executives, i.e. supposedly luxurious or exclusive. In this sense it is now becoming as devoid of real meaning as the word *luxury*, used in the same way. *You can quaff from 'executive bars' ... in 'executive suites' and top up from 'executive ice machines' on 'executive floors' ... We have ... luxuriated over 'executive menus' (smoked salmon is an extra with the 'executive breakfast'), and I once gratefully pocketed my 'complimentary executive gifts'*—Lucinda Lambton, *Listener*, 1989.

As a result of job-title inflation, and to avoid using unimportant-sounding words like *assistant*, *executive* is now routinely prefixed to the titles of relatively humdrum jobs which have no managerial responsibility, such as *customer care executive*.

exercise. Always so spelt, not with *-ize*. See -ISE 1.

exhaustible. So spelt. See -able, -ible 7.

exigence, -cy. *Exigency* is now the more usual and the more natural form of the two by far. Both forms entered the language in the late 16c. and seem to have been equally frequent in their main meanings until about the end of the 19c., by which stage they no longer showed any clear functional differences. See -CE, -CY.

exit (verb). In stage directions the correct style is *Exit Macbeth* (when only one person leaves the stage) and *Exeunt Kings and Banquo* (more than one person). The two forms are respectively the 3rd person singular present indicative and the 3rd person plural present indicative of the Latin verb *exīre* 'to go out'.

-ex, -ix. 1 Naturalized Latin nouns in *-ex* and *-ix*, genitive *-icis*, vary in the form of the plural. The Latin plural is *-ices* /-ɪsiːz/, but there is considerable variation in the English forms. See LATIN PLURALS.

2 The simplest way to present the material is to set it out as a table, listing the most common form (but see the separate entries for most of the words concerned). Where words have alternative plurals, e.g. *vortices, vortexes*, the plural in *-ices* is the preferred form in scientific and technical writing.

Singular	Plural
apex	*apices**
appendix	*appendices**
axis	*axes*
calyx	*calyces* (rarely *calyxes*)
codex	*codices*
cortex	*cortices*
duplex	*duplexes*
helix	*helices*
ilex	*ilexes*
index	*indexes**
matrix	*matrices**
murex	*murices*
radix	*radices*
silex	no plural
simplex	*simplexes*
vertex	*vertices**
vortex	*vortices**

* But usually *apexes* in a metaphorical or non-scientific context, *appendixes* (medicine), *indices* (economics), *matrixes*, *vertexes* and *vortexes* in a metaphorical or non-scientific context.

3 See -TRIX.

ex officio. This Latin phrase meaning 'by virtue of one's office or status' (*the Bursar was a member of the Governing Body* ex officio), is printed in italics and unhyphenated when used before a noun (*the* ex officio *members of the committee*).

exorcize, exorcise. The spelling with final *-ize* is preferable, although that with *-ise* is far more common, as the *OED* remarked as far back as 1894, and as the *OEC* data shows. Perhaps the word *exercise* has had an influence. Nevertheless, the word belongs etymologically with the classic *-ize* words (*baptize*, etc.), being from Greek ἐξορκίζειν (i.e. with zeta), and should be so spelt in editorial styles that prefer the *-ize* ending in other words of the same kind.

exordium. The plural (if ever required) is preferably *exordiums* rather than *exordia*. See -UM 3.

expandable, expansible. The form in *-able* (1926) has now effectively ousted the older, pseudo-Latin *expansible* (first known in Boyle of Boyle's Law, *a*1691), no doubt helped by *expandable* being more easily linked to the base verb. However, *expansible* is still very occasionally used in scientific contexts.

ex parte. A legal Latin phrase meaning 'in the interests of one side only or of an interested outside party'. Printed in italics, and hyphenated when used attributively (*an* ex-parte *affidavit*), as it most commonly is.

expect. Throughout the 19c. the use of *expect* to mean 'to suppose, surmise' came under attack, though this meaning had been in use since the late 16c. The *OED* commented (in 1894): 'Now *rare* in literary use. The misuse of the word as a synonym of *suppose,* without any notion of "anticipating" or "looking for", is often cited as an Americanism, but is very common in dialectal, vulgar or carelessly colloquial speech in England.' Fowler (1926) took a different view: 'Exception is often taken to the sense suppose, be inclined to think, consider probable. This extension of meaning is, however, so natural that it seems needless purism to resist it. *Expect* by itself is used as short for *expect to find, expect that it will turn out that,* that is all.' Fowler's judgement has been borne out by the passage of time. The use is part of standard speech, though it is far less suitable for use in expository prose.

expectorate. In the sense 'to eject, discharge (phlegm, etc.) from the chest or lungs, by coughing, hawking, or spitting', *expectorate* has been used, especially in medical books, since the 17c. Fowler (1926) criticized it for being a 'genteelism', i.e. a polite euphemism, for *to spit,* but since his time the word and the habit have largely become confined to literature. Modern examples (the first of which is in a poem): *Your lips expectorate a stream Of self-igniting gasolene*—C. Raine, 1978; *Captain Anderson walked across the planking and expectorated into the sea*—W. Golding, 1980.

expedience, -cy. Both forms occur, but *expediency* is about eight times more common, according to the *OEC* data. See -CE, -CY. Examples: (expedience) *Burroughs said, 'I am against this board settling for mediocrity and second or third best for the purposes of political expedience.'—Chicago Tribune,* 1990; *the Swansea college's department of philosophy has been riven by allegations of commercial expedience in the awarding of external MA degrees on the moral ethics of medical practices—Independent,* 1991; (expediency) *He did what needed to be done despite the political risk. He stood on principle rather than expediency—Christian Sci. Monitor,* 1990; *Risk assessment is now less rigorous and decisions are being made more on the basis of expediency than public safety—Telegraph,* 2007.

expertise, a loanword (first recorded in 1868) from French, meaning 'expert skill, knowledge, or judgement'. The standard pronunciation is /ˌɛkspəːˈtiːz/ (eks-puhr-**teez**), but in AmE the final syllable is often rhymed with *fleece.* See -ISE 2. It is incorrect to spell the word with a final *-ice,* or *-ize.* The extremely uncommon verb *expertize* (or *-ise*) 'to give an expert opinion (concerning)', is pronounced /ˈɛkspətʌɪz/, **eks**-puhr-tyz.

expletive is an adjective and a noun: both are pronounced /ɪkˈspliːtɪv/, ik-**splee**-tiv, with the stress on the second syllable. The primary meaning is 'filling out a sentence, line of verse, etc.', and the noun denotes a word that does this, typically in verse, without adding any meaning. In more recent use *expletive* as a noun is familiar in the extended sense 'an oath or swear word', a use that goes back to Sir Walter Scott: *We omit here various execrations with which these honest gentlemen garnished their discourse, retaining only such of their expletives as are least offensive—Guy Mannering,* 1815.

exploit is pronounced with the stress on the first syllable as a noun (meaning 'a bold or daring feat') and with the stress on the second syllable as a verb (meaning 'to take selfish advantage of'): /ˈɛksplɔɪt/, (**eks**-ployt), and /ɪkˈsplɔɪt/ (iks-**ployt**) respectively.

explore every avenue, to. See CLICHÉ.

export. See NOUN AND VERB ACCENT 1.

exposé. First recorded in English in 1809 in the current meaning of 'a report in the media that reveals something discreditable' (it had been used earlier in English in the sense 'a recital of facts or particulars'), *exposé* plays a useful role in the language. It is printed in roman, and always written with an acute accent in British English, but sometimes without in American English. The *OED* notes that there is some 19th century evidence for its being pronounced as two syllables corresponding to the spelling *expose,* but current BrE pronunciation is

/ɛkˈspəʊzeɪ/ (ek-**spoh**-zay), stressing the second syllable, while AmE stresses the third.

exposition. Sharply distinguished in meaning from EXPOSÉ. Its main meanings are (*a*) a comprehensive description and explanation of an idea or theory; (*b*) in music, the part of a movement, especially in sonata form, in which the principal themes are first presented; (*c*) in imitation of French *exposition*, a public exhibition. Fowler (1926) decried the last meaning as an unnecessary gallicism, and it is nowadays used in that way chiefly to refer to 19c. exhibitions, and only occasionally to modern ones.

ex post facto is a legal adverbial and adjectival phrase used to mean 'with retrospective action or force' (e.g. *increasing its guilt* ex post facto; ex post facto *laws*). As the *OED* comments, on etymological grounds 'the separation of *postfacto* in current spelling is erroneous'; but the phrase has been regularly written as three words since the 17c. It is printed in italics.

expressible. So spelt. See -ABLE, -IBLE 7.

expresso. See ESPRESSO.

exquisite. The placing of the main stress in this word has steadily changed in standard speech in the last two centuries from the first to the second syllable. Walker (1791) and Daniel Jones (1917) listed only first-syllable stressing. By 1963 Daniel Jones gave preference to first-syllable stressing but commented that the alternative pronunciation was 'becoming very common'. J. C. Wells (1990) reported that 69 per cent of the members of his poll panel opted for /ɪkˈskwɪzɪt/, i.e. for second-syllable stressing.

extant. Once meaning just 'existing', *extant* now means 'continuing to exist, that has withstood the ravages of time' (ancient manuscripts, old churches, fossils, etc., are often described as 'extant', 'the only extant examples', etc.). It can be pronounced with the stress on the second syllable as /ɪkˈstant/, /ɛkˈstant/ (ik-**stant**, ek-**stant**) or on the first, /ˈɛkst(ə)nt/ (**ek**-stuhnt). Like one's faith as far as Elizabeth I was concerned, the choice is a matter of personal conviction that matters little.

extemporaneous, extemporaneously are cumbersome words where the meaning required is along the lines of 'spoken or done without preparation', and seem to be more often used in American English than in British. *Impromptu*, which is about a dozen times more frequent in *OEC* data, means much the same and is somewhat less grandiloquent.

extempore, impromptu. Some people observe a distinction between an *extempore* speech, one that is made without notes (though perhaps prepared to some extent in advance), and an *impromptu* one, which is spontaneously given without preparations of any kind. But the distinction is a fine one: many an *impromptu* speech is only seemingly given off the cuff. In any case, the word *impromptu* is far more common, and more likely to be understood than the rather formal and learned *extempore*, which also has a specific legal meaning.

extend. Dire comments have been applied to some of the uses of this word. There is no difficulty about literal uses where the sense is 'to lengthen or make larger in space or time' (extend a chapter, a sermon, a railway line, a boundary, a term of office, etc.). But objections have been made to metaphorical applications of the word when *give, grant, accord*, etc., would serve as well. Fowler (1926) condemned *extend* used instead of *give* or *accord* as 'a piece of turgid journalese', and claimed that 'native English did not go that way'. '*Extend* in this sense', he said, 'has done its development in America, and come to us full-grown viâ the newspapers—a bad record.' Nowadays, this use is well established, and Fowler's strictures are of purely historical interest. *Extend* has, nevertheless, a slightly formal feel, so one could *offer* congratulations, sympathy, thanks, kindness, an invitation, etc., rather than *extending* them.

extendable, extendible, extensible are all acceptable spellings, the least frequent being *extendible*. *Extendable* is more frequent, is used in general contexts, and is the form recommended in *Garner's Dictionary of Legal Usage*. The most commonly used of the three is *extensible*, largely in computing contexts, because of its appearing in *Extensible Markup Language* (XML) and its offshoots.

exterior, external, extraneous, extrinsic. Etymologically the four words are closely related (from four Latin words meaning respectively 'outside', 'outward', 'external', and 'outward'), but the distinctions they now have reflect their history in English rather than their meanings in Latin. *Outside* is the fundamental meaning of all four; *outward* and *outer* are near-synonyms. Inevitably the description that follows is selective; for a fuller treatment one must turn to the *OED* and also to a good dictionary of synonyms.

1 *exterior* and *external.* Something described as *exterior* encloses or is outermost, while what is enclosed or is inside is described as *interior.* These opposites are often applied to things of which there is a contrasting pair, and with conscious or unconscious reference, when one is spoken of, to the other: an *exterior* door has another inside it; the *exterior* surface of a hollow ball, but not of a solid one, contrasts with the *interior* surface forming the boundary of hollowness within. Remedies, treatments, ointments, etc., applied to the outside of the body are *external* remedies, etc.; such medicaments are usually described as *for external use only.* Acts, appearances, qualities, etc., that are outwardly perceptible are *external. External debt* and *external relations* refer to spheres of operation outside the country concerned. *External evidence* is evidence derived from circumstances or considerations outside or independent of the thing discussed. *External examiners* test students of a college, university, etc., of which they are not members.

2 *extraneous* and *extrinsic.* Something *extraneous* is introduced or added from without, and is foreign to the object or entity in which it finds itself, or to which it is attached. A fly in amber, a bullet in one's shoulder, are *extraneous objects. Extraneous points* are irrelevant matters brought into a debate or discussion to which they do not properly belong. Something *extrinsic* is not an essential and inherent part of something. It is applied, for example, to evidence beyond that afforded by a deed or document under consideration, or to a stimulus not provided by a body, a cell, or some other thing itself, but introduced from without. *Extrinsic* always contrasts with *intrinsic*; in various degrees it also overlaps in meaning with *inessential, irrelevant,* and *superfluous.*

exterritorial. See EXTRATERRITORIAL.

extol (verb). The only spelling in British English (the inflected forms being *extols, extolled, extolling*), and the dominant one (beside *extoll*) in American English.

extract. See NOUN AND VERB ACCENT 1.

extraneous. See EXTERIOR, EXTERNAL, EXTRANEOUS, EXTRINSIC.

extraordinary. The traditional pronunciation in British English is with five syllables (or even four), and only one stress i.e. /ɪkˈstrɔːd(ɪ)n(ə)ri/ (ik-**straw**-d(i)-n(uh)-ri). However the 'spelling pronunciation' as five or six syllables with a secondary stress, /ˌɛkstrəˈɔːdɪn(ə)ri/ (ɛk-struh-**aw**-di-n(uh)-ri) is often heard.

extraterritorial (and derivatives). Now the dominant forms. They stood side by side with synonymous *exterritorial* and derivatives in the 19c., but the longer forms (the first element of which is from Latin *extra* 'outside') have now prevailed.

extravert. See EXTROVERT.

extrinsic. See EXTERIOR, EXTERNAL, EXTRANEOUS, EXTRINSIC.

extrovert meaning 'outgoing and sociable' (also used as a noun to denote such a person), is now the established form in technical and lay use (on the analogy of *introvert* and *controvert*), although *extravert* is etymologically better formed, and was used just as frequently for a time after its introduction by Jung *c.*1915.

exult. See EXALT, EXULT.

-ey and -y in adjectives. 1 (*a*) The normal suffix used to form adjectives from nouns is *-y,* as in *dusty, earthy, messy,* not *-ey.* (*b*) Nouns ending in a single consonant preceded by a single vowel normally double the consonant: *fatty, funny, nutty.* (*c*) Some adjectives are formed from verbs rather than nouns: *chewy, fiddly, runny.*

Doubt arises only (i) when the suffix needs to be appended to nouns ending in silent *e,* such as *chance, noise,* etc. and (ii) in a few special circumstances (see 3 below).

2 Common adjective formations in *-y:* *bony* (from *bone*), *breezy, chancy, crazy, easy, fluky, gory, greasy, grimy, hasty, icy, mangy, nervy, noisy, nosy, racy, rosy, scaly,* *shady, shaky, slimy, smoky, spicy, spiky, spongy, stony, viny* (from *vine*), *wavy, whiny, wiry*. Also recommended are *caky* (not *cakey*), *fluty, gamy, homy, horsy* (not *horsey*), *liny* (= marked with lines), *mousy, piny* (= like, or full of, pines), *pursy* (= short-winded; corpulent), *stagy, whity* (= whitish). The only word in this category that is usually spelt with final *-ey* is *matey*.

3 Special cases. (*a*) When an adjective is formed from a noun that itself ends in *-y*, the adjectival ending is *-ey: clayey* (not *clayy*), *skyey* (not *skyy*). (*b*) *cagey* and *phoney* (beside *cagy* and *phony*) are both of unknown etymology, and do not belong to this group. *Fiddly* is from *fiddle* (verb). (*c*) *holey* (= full of holes) has *-ey* to distinguish it from *holy* (= sacred). (*d*) Adjectives from nouns ending in *-ue* retain the *-e: bluey, gluey* (not *bluy, gluy*). (*e*) The rare adjective *treey* (= abounding in trees) was formed in the 19c.

eye (verb) inflects as *eyeing*, not *eying*. See VERBS IN -IE, -Y, AND -YE 7.

eyot /eɪt/. A variant spelling of AIT.

eyrie (nest of bird of prey). This is the preferred spelling in British English (not *aerie, aery*, or *eyry*), but *aerie* is also used, and is the preferred spelling in American English. It can be pronounced as /ˈɪəri/ (**i**-uh-ri), /ˈʌɪri/ (**I**-ri), or /ˈɛːri/ (**air**-ri). The word is derived from medieval Latin *airea, eyria*, etc., probably from Old French *aire* 'lair of wild animals'. The spelling *eyerie* was favoured by Henry Spelman in his *Glossarium archaiologicum* (1664) by association with *ey* 'egg'. Milton has *Eyries* in *Paradise Lost* vii. 424.

-f. For plurals and inflexions of words ending in *-f* (*dwarf, leaf,* etc.) and *-fe* (*knife, wife,* etc.), see -VE(D), -VES.

façade, facade. Insert the cedilla if your computer allows it, but do not get too upset if you see the word spelt without, which sets pronunciation and spelling at loggerheads: it is the more frequent spelling nowadays and the first one given in *ODO*. *O tempora! O mores!*

facetious formations. Over the centuries many evanescent and some more durable words have been brought into existence as irregularly formed humorous formations. A broad selection from among the hundreds of such words follows, roughly grouped into categories. Containing a pun: *anecdotage* (*anecdote, dotage*), *correctitude* (*correct, rectitude*), *queuetopia* (*queue, Utopia,* coined by Churchill), *sacerdotage* (*sacerdotal, dotage*). English words made to resemble Latin ones: *absquatulate, circumbendibus, contraption, omnium gatherum.* Humorously long: *antigropelos, cantankerous, collywobbles, galligaskin, gobbledygook, panjandrum, skedaddle, spifflicate, splendiferous, spondulicks, supercalifragilisticexpialidocious, transmogrify.* Irreverent familiarity: *crikey* (*Christ*), *gorblimey* (*God blind me*), *gosh* (*God*). Literary nonce words: *chortle, galumph,* etc. (L. Carroll), *grudgment* (Browning), *misogelastic* (hating laughter, Meredith), *nyum-nyum, yogibogeybox,* etc. (J. Joyce). Mock errors: *Eyetalian, highstrikes* (*hysterics*), *trick-cyclist* (*psychiatrist*), *underconstumble.* Pseudo- or mock Latin: *bogus, bonus, cockalorum* (also *hey cockalorum*), *hocus-pocus, holus-bolus.*

face up to. This somewhat clunky-looking phrasal verb was first noted in America and also in Britain in the early 1920s. Since then it has survived a barrage of criticism in Britain (e.g. 'A needless expression, the result of the tendency to add false props to words that can stand by themselves'—Eric Partridge, 1942), but the fury has subsided and the expression (= to accept bravely; to confront; to stand up to) is listed in the *OED* without comment. Examples: *He faced up to the paradox of man*—W. Raleigh, 1920; *Why don't you simply face up to the past?*—K. Ishiguro, 1986; *She has to face up to the fact that Harriet—this incongruously aspiring Harriet—is her own creation*—T. Tanner, 1986; *These are problems which it is a major responsibility of government to face up to*—*Parliamentary Affairs,* 1991.

facile, pronounced /ˈfasʌɪl/ (**fas**-yl) in BrE and /ˈfasəl/ (**fas**-uhl) in AmE, means 'easy, smooth, effortless' with reference to people or what they do, and there is usually, but not always, a derogatory implication of something too easily achieved and of little value. A *facile explanation* does not do justice to the complexities of what it is supposed to explain, and is thus superficial and unconvincing; if someone speaks in a *facile manner,* what they say sounds glib and insincere because it comes too easily. However, in sports writing in particular, especially Irish, *facile* is used with no negative connotations to refer to wins and winners, and means simply 'easy'; and in some other contexts it seems to be used as a term of praise, rather than criticism: e.g. *Charlestown under-14 girls under the management of Tom and Grainne McLoughlin began the season with a facile victory over Aughamore*—*Western Nationalist,* 2004; *A prolific scholar and facile writer, Glenn Feldman risks turning his otherwise fine book into a screed against all who fell short of total moral courage*—*Alabama Review,* 2002. In examples like this last, if no negative connotation is intended, a more neutral or positive synonym such as (for people) *able, accomplished, fluent,* etc. or (with reference to achievements) *effortless, fluent, natural,* etc., will help avoid misinterpretation.

facilitator, though dating from as far back as the 1920s, has a modern ring as a vogue word for a person responsible for the day-to-day management of people and processes; it combines the meanings of *manager, mediator,* and *coordinator.* The grammar can be somewhat forced when the word is used in job titles: a *community facilitator* is an official who promotes community relations, a *workshop facilitator* organizes the resources for a discussion, and a *marriage facilitator* provides counselling to those intending to be married. The word's jargon-like ring is amplified by its appearance in robotic statements such as the following: *Teachers today are facilitators helping children to use their own computer skills to access information—Guardian,* 2007.

facility. *Facility* (from Latin *facilis* meaning 'easy') means 'ease or ready ability to do something, aptitude': *Firstborn children have greater verbal facility, and there is evidence that they have more successful relationships with their teachers—Journal of Genetic Psychology,* 1973. It also has a concrete meaning which proliferated vastly in the 20c., of 'a place, amenity, or piece of equipment provided for a particular purpose': *Other recreational facilities include two lighted tennis courts, a swimming pool and a jogging trail—Philadelphia Inquirer,* 1976; *You don't need a generously proportioned tub to fit a spa or whirlpool bath facility—Do It Yourself,* 1990; *Solihull Council . . . has set out plans to build a 'large' casino at the NEC, although the facility could be built anywhere in the borough—Birmingham Post,* 2007. A common use is in finance and banking, to denote an arrangement such as a loan or overdraft: *If you want credit, a bank facility is usually better value than even a good dealer can offer—Opera Now,* 1990. Cf. FACULTY.

fact. The phrase *the fact that* is sometimes criticized for wordiness. Whether the criticism is justified depends on its different functions. **1** *Impeccable uses.* (*a*) The expression *the fact that* has an important function in enabling clauses to behave like nouns: *Some studies give attention to the fact that non-smokers cannot avoid inhaling smoke when breathing smoky air*—G. Richardson, 1971; *The fact that I am gay is written down in black and white—Gay News,* 1978; *Ethnic minorities will hopefully be tempted into the force by the fact that a black and female PC is given a starring role in the film—Guardian,* 1984; *The fact that Nixon was willing to make his chastisement public suggests . . . that the President at least understands 'the parameters of the problem'—Time,* 1970. When standing at the head of a sentence (as in the second and fourth examples), the words *the fact* can sometimes be omitted without harming grammatical integrity, but a degree of emphasis or focusing is lost. Moreover, nominalizing a clause in that way by simply adding *that* is a somewhat literary device, and may sit uneasily with the style of the sentence. (*b*) *The fact that* also allows a clause introduced by *that* to follow a preposition, as in the first and third examples above. In the first, it would be impossible, for example, to say **give attention to that non-smokers cannot avoid . . .* Nevertheless, sentences including *the fact that* can often be recast and shortened by turning the dependent clause into a noun: *A small group of western European politicians and activists were in Moscow, drawing public attention to the fact that the mayor of Moscow has banned* [read *drawing public attention to a ban by the mayor of Moscow on*] *any Gay Pride march—Independent,* 2007.

2 *Questionable uses.* (*a*) Verbs such as *accept, acknowledge, announce, convince, discover,* etc., that can be complemented by a *that*-clause, do not need to be linked to the clause by *the fact that,* so that the sentence *?We acknowledge the fact that mistakes have been made* can be rephrased as *We acknowledge that mistakes have been made,* and *?They convinced him of the fact that it was right* can be rephrased as *They convinced him that it was right.* (*b*) The phrases *owing to* or *due to the fact that* and *despite the fact that* can normally be replaced by *because* and *although* respectively, thereby producing a more economical and clearer structure.

factious, factitious, fractious. 1 *Factious* is a rarely used and somewhat literary word meaning 'characterized by faction or dissension', e.g. *He hoped that Philip would unite the factious Greek cities into a confederacy and then turn to the great project of invading Persia*—Robin Osborne, 2000. *Fractious,* a much more frequent word, derives from *fraction,* and originally had a similar meaning to *factious,* but now means either 'irritable, peevish', as in *a fractious child,* or 'unruly, difficult to control', as in *Cameron's bag carrier, Major Desmond Swayne, is a regular after his daily dip in the Serpentine. Unlike his boss, who can't iron out creases in an increasingly fractious* *coalition*—*New Statesman*, 2012. Often, one suspects that one word is intended when the other is used. However, since people who are prone to dissent are likely to be unruly as well, and vice versa, it is sometimes hard to be sure. (*fractious* for *factious*?): *In this chapter we have traced the fractious history of relations between ethnic groups in America and the larger 'races' which encompass these*—R. Singh, 2003; (*factious* for *fractious*) We Need To Talk About Kevin *explores the factious relationship between a mother and her son*—*Independent* (Ireland), 2011.

2 *Factitious* refers to things which have been artificially created or developed, e.g. *a largely factitious national identity*. It is an unusual word, most often used in the medical phrase *factitious disorder* or preceding specific illnesses: *Munchausen syndrome. A type of factitious disorder in which you try to appear sick or hurt to gain attention, or you actually harm yourself to receive medical attention*—*www.mayoclinic.com*, 2004; *Many family physicians have had experience with patients whom they suspect of having factitious colic*—American Family Physician, 2001. Though usage guides warn against using it wrongly for fictitious, there is little evidence that it is ever so confused.

factor. 1 The word passed through a phase in the mid-20c. when it became, according to Gowers (1965), a vastly overused substitute for other words he listed: *circumstance, component, consideration, constituent, element, event, fact,* or *feature*. Later commentators echo his disapproval. The word's strict meaning in lay language is 'a circumstance, fact, or influence which tends to produce a result', a meaning first recorded in 1816 in a work by Coleridge. Gladstone used it precisely in that meaning in 1878 in *The first factor in the making of a nation is its religion*, and the next example shows it used in the same way: *Associations have been sought between schizophrenic rates and such factors as maternal age, sibling size, birth order, and season of birth*—A. Clare, 1980. In other contexts, one or other of the words suggested by Gowers could well work, but one has to be sure that they make the meaning clearer. In the first example below the replacement word is vaguer, in the second it is more precise: *The two boys had little in common and there were many factors* [circumstances, things] *that prevented them from becoming friends: caste, upbringing and environment*; [etc.]—M. M. Kaye, 1978; *Because newsreels were becoming a bigger and bigger factor in* [feature of, part of] *American life, Roosevelt would then repeat vital parts of the speech for a newsreel camera*—D. Halberstam, 1979. The *OEC* suggests that *factor* is no longer a vogue or over applied word, so very often it is probably not worth your while to find an alternative.

2 A newish use of *factor* appeared in the 1980s (starting with the *Falklands factor*) and uses a preceding proper noun to specify an event, person, or even brand judged to have a significant effect on people's behaviour in voting, their buying patterns, etc.: *It's true that a lot of our* [*sc.* Hornby's] *best customers are middle-aged men. I call it the Harley-Davidson factor, the same urge that makes them want to own the expensive motorbike they couldn't afford when they were 20*—*Saga Magazine*, 2003; *The TBH* [*sc.* to be honest] *factor is there in Nick Clegg's earnest eyebrows, Cameron's wrinkle-free brow and David Miliband's Primrose Hill mockney*—*Daily Tel.*, 2010. One of the most common compounds of this kind is *wow factor*, something or someone that supposedly overwhelms you with their impressiveness. In fact, it is beginning to sound like a tired cliché: *The Master Plan has the potential to do that and put the 'wow factor' back into Bradford*—*www.thisisbradford.co.uk*, 2003.

3 The phrasal verb *factor in*, meaning 'to include (a factor) in an assessment, plan, etc.', originated in American business speak, but is now also used in Britain; *factor out* is also occasionally found. Examples: *All the political and military variables should be factored in before Israel decides on a response*—*Los Angeles Times*, 1991; *Busy lifestyles have created buildings which have factored out healthy living*—*Guardian*, 2005.

factotum. Plural *factotums*. See -UM 1. Those who make the plural *factota*, as occasionally happens, have at least recognized that the word is Latin, and are declining it. However, the first part, *fac-*, means 'do' and *-tōtum* means 'all, everything', so it is inappropriate to make it plural in this way.

faculty. 1 In some British universities the term is used of a group of departments, etc., which together make up a major division of knowledge (e.g. *Faculty of Anthropology and Geography, Faculty of Biological Sciences, Faculty of Literae Humaniores*).

2 In America it has come to mean 'the staff of an educational establishment', and, as such, is often used without the definite article as a collective noun, with singular or plural agreement. The use of plural agreement has been criticized by American commentators (where singular agreement with collective nouns is viewed as standard) but seems to be well established. The following examples are all AmE, unless indicated otherwise *They had all gone to Swarthmore, then they had all married highly placed faculty or executives of Chubb University*—C. McCullough, 1985; *A prestigious scholar ... would attract top faculty and really put the school on the map*—*Boston Globe*, 1989; *Faculty votes to require all incoming students to own a computer*—*Daily Northwestern* (Ill.), 1995; *Overwhelmingly, our faculty have voted to eliminate a 'rising-junior' proficiency exam*—Composition Studies, 2002; *These activities can further alienate those who already believe that faculty spends too much time on research and not enough time in the classroom*—*OEC*, 2001; *Moitryee retired as a faculty of Bengali from the University of Delhi*—*Times of India*, 2013.

faecal, faeces. The spelling with *-ae-* is standard everywhere, except in NAmer., where **fecal, feces** are the norm.

fag, faggot. 1 Beware. In British English a *fag* is a colloquial word for a cigarette; a piece of drudgery or a wearisome or unwelcome task; and at British public (i.e. private) schools, a junior pupil who runs errands for a senior, for which there is the related verb *to fag*. In AmE, *fag* is a deeply offensive word for a male homosexual.

2 In BrE regional cooking a *faggot* is a ball or roll of seasoned chopped liver, etc., baked or fried. In BrE and also in AmE (in which it is usually spelt *fagot*) it is also a bundle of sticks or twigs bound together as fuel. In AmE *faggot* is also a deeply offensive word for a male homosexual.

fain. A long-standing word in the language (Old English *fægen* 'glad'), it reached some kind of literary climax in the 19c. (*Such scuffling ... as no pen can depict, and as the tender heart would fain pass over*—Thackeray, 1847–8; *I felt my heart grow sick at the sight of this bloody battle, and would fain have turned away*—R. M. Ballantyne, 1858; *Mr. Wegg was fain to devote his attention exclusively to holding on*—Dickens, 1865) and passed into archaism in the 20c.

fair dos. As the *New Hart's Rules* (2005) says, 'The apostrophe is not necessary in forming the plural of ... words not usually used as nouns.' It is therefore not necessary to insert an apostrophe before the letter *s* when you make *do* plural, as in *fair dos.*

fair, fairly (adverbs). **1** The shorter form, in its ordinary sense 'in a fair way', is in common use in a few fixed collocations, e.g. *to bid fair, to fight fair, to play fair, fair between the eyes*. In dialect use and in some areas abroad (esp. in N. America and Australasia) it is used to mean 'completely, fully' (e.g. *It fair gets me down*). In both types *fairly* would not be idiomatic.

2 It should be borne in mind that *fairly* has more than one sense: in a fair manner (*he treated me fairly*); moderately (*a fairly good translation*); to a noticeable degree (*the path is fairly narrow*); utterly, completely (*he was fairly beside himself*). In certain contexts it is sometimes difficult to know whether 'moderately' or 'utterly' is intended; but in speech this possible confusion is prevented by the marked difference in intonation.

fait accompli is generally pronounced in an anglicized manner /feɪt əˈkɒmpli/ (fate uh-**kom**-plee), and is nowadays printed in roman type. The plural is *faits accomplis*, with an *s* added to both words, and pronounced /feɪz ... / (fayz ...) The spelling of this useful shorthand is often mangled as *fate accompli, fait accomplish*, and *fait accomplit.*

faithfully. For *Yours faithfully*, see LETTER FORMS.

fakir /ˈfeɪkɪə/. Now the standard spelling. In AmE, the word not only means a Muslim or Hindu religious ascetic, but also an impostor or swindler. This is no insult to the ascetics, but a 19c. extension of meaning that went from 'street magician' to 'street trader relying on trickery' to 'charlatan': *You can call me quack, you may call me fakir you may call me charlatan—but be sure to call me SOMETHING!*—*Boston Review*, 2003.

fall and *autumn* are used on both sides of the Atlantic as the name for the third season of the year, although in everyday use *autumn* is standard in BrE and *fall* in AmE. *Fall* is a shortening of the phrase *fall of the year* or *fall of the leaf*, and was in British use from the 16c. until about 1800. The word *autumn* dates from the 14c., and comes from Latin *autumnus*, but the ultimate origin is obscure.

fallacy. See PATHETIC FALLACY.

false analogy. See ANALOGY 4, 5.

false friend(s). Not a warning about the fragility of friendship, but a term (derived from French *faux ami(s)*) used by translators and linguists for words that have the same (or a similar form) but different meanings in two or more languages. Some English words derived from Latin or Greek appear in Romance languages with different meanings: for instance, French *actuel* means 'current', Italian *simpatico* means 'likeable', a Spanish *librería* is a bookshop not a library. English and German also have false friends, e.g. *bekommen* means 'to receive' not 'to become', *konsequent* means 'consistent', an *Oldtimer* can be a veteran car, etc. One could even say there are false friends between British and American English, such as *pants, pissed,* and FAG.

falsehood, falseness, falsity all have to do with departure from the truth and overlap in meaning to some extent. *Falsehood* differs from the other two in being a count noun, often a euphemism for a lie, and an uncount noun, 'the state of being untrue'. *Falseness* and *falsity* are used more broadly to mean 'the fact of being untrue, incorrect, or insincere'. In *OEC* data, *falsehood* is twice as frequent as *falsity*, itself four times more frequent than *falseness*. *Falsity* typically associates with *beliefs, claims, propositions* and *statements*, while *falseness* is often applied to what is perceived as empty or insincere. Typical examples: (falsehood) *But a half-truth was a falsehood, and it remained a falsehood even when you'd told it in the belief that it was the whole truth*—A. Huxley, 1939; *As it had always been, truth and falsehood were inextricably intertwined in that statement*—S. Naipaul, 1980; (falsity) *Whatever we verbalize about reality is bound to be false because of the falsity of the premises of the conventional world in which verbalization operates*—Sue Hamilton, 2001; *Only 57 percent recognized the falsity of the statement 'ordinary tomatoes do not contain genes, while genetically modified tomatoes do'*—*Hoover Digest*, 2004; (falseness) *The biggest danger in diplomacy is falseness, dishonesty and lack of credibility*—D. Freemantle, 1988; *the falseness of the culture of celebrity which makes people into Gods and then delights in destroying them*—weblog, 2005.

falsetto. Plural *falsettos*. See -O(E)S 4.

famed. Some commentators censure the use of *famed* ('widely known about, renowned') preceding a noun (i.e. attributively), as in *the famed British director*. They insist that it must only be used attributively followed by *for*, which is the way it was first recorded in the late 16c. by Shakespeare (*As he is famde for mildnesse, peace and praier*—1595). Literary examples in the *OED* entry (1894) after him show a mix of attributive and predicative uses, but the attributive use was marked archaic. Things have changed since then, and *famed* is now widely used to modify a noun, particularly in journalistic writing. *Renowned* or *celebrated* can often replace it in this position, and sound less gushy and trite. Examples: *The English, for example, were famed for their assumptions of innate superiority*—J. Wormald, 1991; *In the cemetery where tens of thousands of soldiers lay, he* [sc. Abraham Lincoln] *delivered his famed address championing 'government of the people, by the people, for the people'*—*Observer*, 2004.

fandango. Plural *fandangos* or *-oes*, the first being more frequent, and in keeping with the original Spanish. See -O(E)S 2.

fan, fanatic. 1 The adjective *fanatic* is about a quarter as frequent as *fanatical* in *OEC* data. (*Fanatic* is, of course, very common as a noun.) Examples: (fanatic) *Apple creates almost fanatic identification, almost entirely through a narrative that started with a single Superbowl ad in 1984*—*OEC*, 2006; (fanatical) *The Rule of the Reformed Carmelites, which St John of the Cross joined, was severe but not fanatical*—L. Gordon, 1988.

2 The abbreviated form *fan*, used to mean 'a keen and regular supporter (of a team, a person, etc.)' and recorded in AmE as early as 1682, became part of the ritual language of baseball in the 19c. and then passed into general use in AmE, BrE, and elsewhere in the 20c. in the senses 'a supporter', 'an admirer' (of people or subjects). Hence *fan letter* (first recorded 1932), *fan mail* (1924), *film fan* (1918), and more recently *fanzine* (1949).

fantasia. (Italian 'fantasy, fancy'.) Now regularly pronounced /fanˈteɪzɪə/, with the stress on the second syllable, though the Italianate pronunciation /fantəˈziːə/ is sometimes used when the word forms part of the title of a particular musical composition.

fantasy, phantasy. In its several meanings the standard spelling now is *fantasy*, reflecting its closer French source, rather than its ultimate Greek source φαντασία. Until at least the end of the 19c. the two spellings were equally frequent. Nowadays, the spelling *phantasy* is mostly confined to psychoanalytic literature.

far.

1 *farther/further*
2 *(so) far from—ing*
3 *far-flung.*
4 *as far as/so far as ... is concerned, goes,* etc.
5 *go so far as to/as far as to*
6 *far and away*

1 For *farther/further,* see FARTHER.

2 *(so) far from—ing.* (used when something is denied and something opposite asserted) This construction headed by *so* and containing an *-ing* form is first recorded in the 17c. and was still current in 1926, when Fowler cited the example *So far from 'running' the Conciliation Bill, the Suffragettes only reluctantly consented to it.* The *so* is now rarely used, but the shorter form *Far from—ing* is still widely current. Examples: *Far from perpetuating the Francophile and mandarin modernist values of his predecessor, Kirk granted more gallery space to contemporary works and invited artists to curate exhibitions—Art in America,* 2003; *So far from being angry, they have cooperated with Blair in embroiling Britain in the Iraq war—Scotland on Sunday,* 2005.

3 *far-flung.* This relatively modern word (first recorded in 1895) features in Kipling's *Recessional* (1897) (*God of our fathers, known of old, Lord of our far-flung battle-line*). Fowler (1926) spoke of 'its emotional value ... as a vogue-word. The lands are distant; they are not far-flung; but what matter? *Far-flung* is a signal that our blood is to be stirred.' The *far-flung Empire* has been replaced by less stirring concepts, but the adjective is still widely used as a useful way of suggesting remoteness and inaccessibility: *We have a number of inhouse petroleum engineers to help us evaluate deals that involve assets in far-flung corners of the world—Herald* (Glasgow), 2007.

4 *as far as/so far as ... is concerned, goes,* etc. (*a*) In adverbial clauses of this kind used to limit the area to which the proposition in the main clause applies, both *as far as* and *so far as* are possible, but the first is many times more frequent: *It's* [*sc.* the TV dinner] *a terrible invention as far as family life is concerned—The New Farm,* 2005; *One of the best action movies around, so far as the action and stunts go—DVD Verdict,* 2000.

(*b*) It was Fowler (1926) who first drew attention to the use of this formula as a kind of preposition with *is/are concerned, goes/go* etc. ellipted, and gave as one of several examples *As far as getting the money he asked for, Mr Churchill had little difficulty.* In the 20c. commentators have criticized this use, which seems to be particularly typical of speech. Despite the fact that it is first recorded, as *MWCDEU* notes, from 1533, and has been used by figures as various as Thoreau and J. F. Kennedy, many people still object to it, so it is best avoided in formal writing.

(*c*) For discussion of the verbosity in certain contexts of *as far as ... is concerned,* see CONCERNED.

5 *go so far as to/as far as to.* In sentences expressing how extreme someone's action is, both formulations are followed by a *to*-infinitive, but *go so far as to* is more frequent than *go as far as to.* Examples: *At Christie's, one buyer even went so far as to set a record for a Matisse print—Art Business News,* 2002; *Throughout his life he collected lavish Catholic icons and even went as far as to wear a clerical collar in public—Criticism,* 2002.

6 *far and away.* An adverbial phrase, first recorded in 1562 (*Ye be better fed then taught farre awaie*—J. Heywood) and nowadays used to emphasize a superlative adjective with the meaning 'by a very long way', e.g. *She* [*sc.* Bette Midler] *delivers line after zinging line in a way that is delightful to behold, and is far and away the best thing in the film—www.futuremovies.co.uk,* 2004. It means the same as *by far,* with which it is sometimes conflated, in a way that is best avoided in writing: *?He said: 'By far and away the bulk of the finance industry's communication is with the UK'*—*Daily Tel.*, 2007.

farce. The word in its sense 'a short dramatic work the sole object of which is to excite laughter' is a 16c. loanword from French (from Old French *farce* 'stuffing'). 'The term, in the latinized forms *farsa, farcia,* was applied in the 13c. to phrases interpolated in the liturgical *kyrie eleison* ... and to passages in French inserted in the Latin text of the epistle at Mass (cf. medieval Latin *epistola farcita*); hence to impromptu amplifications of the text of religious plays, whence the transition to the present sense was easy' (*ODEE*).

faro. This gambling card game is pronounced /ˈfɛːrəʊ/.

farrago /fəˈrɑːgəʊ/. Plural *farragos,* (AmE) *farragoes.* See -O(E)S 4.

farther, further. 1 *Etymology. Farther* is related only coincidentally in form to *far,* although this coincidence seems to have influenced its use. It is in origin a Middle English variant of the older form *further* (Old English *furþor,* usually taken to be the comparative form of *forþ* 'forth'). From ME onwards both *farther* and *further* came to be used as the comparative of *far,* beside the newly formed words *farrer* and *ferrer,* extant from the 12c. to the 17c. After that period the comparative forms *farrer* and *ferrer* remained only in dialects, being superseded in the standard language by *farther* and *further.* Wyclif (*c.*1380) wrote *Sum ferrer and sum nerrer,* and a Scottish work of 1549 has *He vil see ane schip farrer* [= *farther*] *on the seye.* Shakespeare used *farre* once instead of his customary forms *farther* and *further*: *Not hold thee of our blood, no not our Kin, Farre then Deucalion off* (*Winter's Tale*). But he used *further* 199 times and *farther* 47 times apparently without any functional distinction (as well as *farthest* 14 times and *furthest* twice).

2 Distinction between *farther* and *further.* The *OED* (1895) attempted to demarcate the two words, since when many commentators, including Fowler, have tried to do the same. Fowler (1926) said 'the preference of the majority is for *further*; the most that should be said is perhaps that *farther* is not common except where distance is in question.' *CGEL* (1985), expresses the view that the *ar*-forms are chiefly restricted to expressions of physical distance:

The two sets *farther/farthest* and *further/furthest,* which are both adjectives and adverbs, are used interchangeably by many speakers to express both physical and abstract relations. In fact, however, the use of *farther* and *farthest* is chiefly restricted to expressions of physical distance, and, in all senses, *further* and *furthest* are the usual forms found: 'Nothing could be *further* from the truth'; 'My house is *furthest* from the station.' The most common uses of *further* are not as a comparative form of *far* but in the sense of 'more', 'additional', 'later': 'That's a *further* reason for deciding now.' [but not: **a far reason*]; 'Any *further* questions?'; 'The school will be closed until *further* notice.'; 'We intend to stay for a *further* two months.'

3 Examples: (i) Physical distance is involved. (*farther, farthest* as adverbs) *The gulls rose in front of him and floated out and settled again a little farther on*—V. Woolf, 1922; *And farther down the road was the state institution*—Marilynne Robinson, 1981 (AmE); *I began to go farther and farther from the house*—*New Yorker,* 1986; (*farther, farthest* as adjectives) *In The Music Lesson we see two windows of this squares and circles type. Both casements are visible in the farther window, one casement only in the nearer window*—Philip Steadman, 2001 (BrE); *and now the prince is scouring the farthest reaches of the globe for his bride*—J. M. Coetzee, 1977 (SAfr.). (*further, furthest* as adverbs) *I suppose you'll be catching the first boat back—but I shouldn't go further than France*—G. Greene, 1939 (BrE); *My God, what stairs! How much further? My legs ache*—M. Wesley, 1983 (BrE); *As they climbed to the fourth, Veronica knew they could go no further*—B. Rubens, 1987 (BrE); (*furthest* as adjective) *he wanted nothing more ... than to send her off with sixpence to spend at the furthest lolly shop*—M. Eldridge, 1984 (Aust.); *This was the lower fountain, furthest from the house*—A. S. Byatt, 1987 (BrE).

(ii) The notion of actual distance is wholly or partially absent. (*farther, farthest* as adverbs) *'You get a lot farther using your nose than your palate,' Patty says about wine-tasting*—*New Yorker,* 1987; *However, it was so far and no farther*—S. Bellow, 1987; *Kasparov simply saw farther, 'much, much farther', than the machine*—*NY Times Mag.,* 1990; *This production is in fact the one that has gone farthest to date in the integration of acting and music*—*OEC*, 2001 (BrE); (*farther, farthest* as adjectives) *We cannot assume that when sex is invoked no farther explanation is necessary*—*OEC*, 2005 (Aust); *'Why, Lord, no honey!' I told her. 'It's the farthest thing from my mind.'*—Lee Smith, 1983 (AmE). (*further, furthest* as adverbs) *He ... found English currency confusing and the* [taxi] *driver sought to confuse him further*—E. Waugh, 1961 (BrE); *Denning's very subjective report ... further vilified him*—*London Rev. Bks*, 1987; *Silverberg agrees that the film goes furthest astray at the end*—*OEC*, 2002 (Canad.); *But if this movie is supposed to represent an artist at the crossroads of her career, let's pray she opts for the route furthest away from Hollywood in future*—*OEC*, 2004 (BrE); (*further, furthest* as adjectives) *He wrote for booklets containing further particulars of almost every device he saw advertised*—E. Bowen, 1949 (BrE); *It seeks the furthest extension of the educationally valuable among the masses*—*Encounter*, 1987 (BrE); *If the logic is followed to its furthest degree, one day no-one will have the aptitude or the attitude to play Test cricket*—*ABC of Cricket*, 2004 (BrE).

4 *Conclusions*. What *CGEL* (see (2) above) states reflects current usage. Moreover, if *further* was 'the preference of the majority' as Fowler wrote, that preference has only strengthened since his day. According to the *OEC* data: *further* is 33 times more frequent than *farther*. However, *furthest* and *farthest* are much more evenly distributed, the first being a little more than fifty per cent more frequent than the second. In addition, it is worth noting that *farther* and *farthest* are more popular in American English than elsewhere. *Further* has almost entirely replaced *farther* in the meaning 'additional', to the extent that a phrase such as *no farther explanation* in the fifth example at 3 (ii) above sounds odd, although it would not have done so in the past. Conversely, *further* does not seem to be used to denote things that are literally more distant: people write about the *farther shore, side, bank, reaches*, etc., and using *further* would be very unusual.

5 Uses exclusive to *further*. (*a*) Used as a sentence adverb: *Further, shameful as it might be to admit it, the idea of the play had started to interest him rather*—Kingsley Amis, 1958; *Further, he was not given particulars of the grounds for the committee's decision*—P. Leyland et al., 2002. (*b*) In the compound adverb *furthermore* (not †*farthermore*). (*c*) As a verb meaning 'to favour or promote (an idea, scheme, etc.)': *No city has done more than Coventry since the war to further the cause of internationalism*—*Times*, 1973; *There has been greater emphasis by unions upon legislative enactment to further their general objectives*—R. Bean, 1992.

fascination. People are sometimes puzzled by which preposition to put after *fascination*, since *with, for*, and *of* are all used. The choice depends to an extent on which meaning of *fascination* is being invoked, for it can mean either (i) 'the state of being fascinated' or (ii) 'the power to fascinate someone; the quality of being fascinating'. When it means (i), *with* is the most appropriate and frequent: *In recent years, the public's fascination with architecture has grown at an exponential rate*—*Art Business News*, 2001; *From an early age I was always frustrated as my fascination with other languages was doused by drills in sentences one would never use*—*Language Log*, 2003. When it means (ii), the preposition *for* is used in front of the person who is fascinated, while *of* precedes the thing that possesses the quality of being fascinating: *the architecture of Rome and the Mediterranean coastline hold a special fascination for him*—*Apollo*, 2005; *But the perpetual fascination of the human face remains*—*Royal Academy Magazine*, 2005. Sometimes *for* is used instead of *with* in meaning (i), but to some people this seems unidiomatic: *?But nevertheless his sincerity and passion, and his fascination for all aspects of the human condition, good and bad, shine through*—*At the Movies*, 2005.

Fascism, Fascist. 1 Mussolini had not long been in power when Fowler published (1926), and Fowler wondered whether the words would survive and how they were to be pronounced. The pronunciation with medial /-s-/ was occasionally heard before and during the Second World War, but the standard forms have long since settled down with a medial /-ʃ-/. The Italian originals—*fascista*, plural *-ti*, *fascismo*—dropped out of use in English long ago, except in writing about Italian history. The words have initial capitals when they refer to the historical phenomenon, but are otherwise lower case.

2 As the *OED* now notes, *fascist* has been watered down in meaning to provide a convenient, emotive, and somewhat imprecise way of branding anyone 'who advocates a particular viewpoint or practice in a manner perceived as intolerant or authoritarian'. (*Fascism* has undergone the same process.) Both are usually modified by a preceding noun used attributively, and the *OED* has entered *body fascist* (1978) as well as *eco-fascist* (1987) and *health fascist* (1980). *Islamic, Christian, religious, gay* and *cultural fascists* feature in the *OEC* data, but the word is capable of infinite extension. Examples: *She doesn't eat sugar and does yoga at dawn, but not to lose weight. Earl Dittman hears how Gwyneth Paltrow is fighting the body fascists—Big Issue*, 2002; *It'll be fun to see what happens when the tobacco fascists run headlong into the human rights fascists—Canad. Lawyer*, 1997; *The time has come for Catholics and Protestants to respond to the assaults that take place during Lent with the same vigor they have shown in recent years fighting the cultural fascists at Christmastime*—weblog, 2007.

fatal, fateful. The words are etymologically closely related in that they both contained or contain the element *fate*. In times past they shared a number of meanings, and at one time *fateful* meant 'producing or resulting in death'. But the two words are nowadays entirely distinct. *Fatal* alone means 'causing or ending in death', and in this meaning it often associates with *accidents, diseases*, and *injuries*; it also means 'ruinous, ending in disaster', and in that meaning associates with *consequences, blows, errors, flaws*, and *mistakes*, which do not kill, but are nevertheless extremely dire. Its closest synonyms in this meaning are *catastrophic, disastrous, ruinous*.

By contrast, *fateful* refers to things such as events, meetings, decisions and particular periods of time that, in hindsight, can be seen to have had far-reaching consequences, consequences which are usually, but not always, adverse. In general, one does not get confused with the other, but occasionally *fateful* seems to be used inappropriately for *fatal*. Examples: (fatal) *There is some flaw in me—some fatal hesitancy*—V. Woolf, 1931; *Some of his suggestions were indeed harmless; but there was one which from our point of view could be fatal*—H. Macmillan, 1971; *The existence of these private but non-fee-paying schools will have a deeply depressing, if not fatal, effect on other schools in the area*—M. Warnock, 1989; (fateful) *The confusion of patriotism and personalities left behind by the fateful gathering*—J. Galsworthy, 1924; *In summing up 1934 we can see, in the light of what was to come, that it was a fateful year*—J. F. Kennedy, 1940; *He has had an intermittent run of bad luck, from spider bites and knee operations through to that fateful puncture . . . which cost him the race—Bicycle Action*, 1987; (fateful misapplied) *?HMAS Wallaroo was lost only 60 nautical miles west of Fremantle in a fateful midnight collision with the American merchant ship Henry Gilbert Costin on June 11, 1943—Navy News*, 2003; *?But that was the fateful mistake that caused my injury—Combat Edge Magazine*, 2004.

father-in-law. See -IN-LAW.

fathom. Plural can be *fathom* (i.e. unchanged) when preceded by a number, e.g. *six fathom deep*, but it is nowadays usually plural.

faucet. Originally (15c.) 'a tap for drawing liquor from a barrel, etc.', *faucet* survives in technical use (combined with *spigot*) in BrE, but in domestic use has been entirely replaced by *tap*. In AmE *faucet* is in widespread use for an ordinary water tap but its distribution is uneven: '*faucet* is the usual New England name for the kitchen water tap, but *spigot* seems to be coming in from the southward, and *cock* and *tap* are also recorded' (R. I. McDavid, 1977).

fault (verb). Used in the sense 'to find fault with; to blame or censure', *fault* has been in use since the mid-16c. In 1850 Fanny Trollope hinted at the unfamiliarity of the use in Britain at the time: *Her manner . . . could not, to use an American phrase, be 'faulted'*. Some 20c. usage guides, especially in the US (but not Fowler, Gowers, or Burchfield), questioned the validity of the use. In the event, it is not comfortably used to mean 'to blame or censure'; but in the sense 'to find fault with' it is unquestionably standard now: e.g. *Martita wasn't too keen on Fay Compton I gathered* (*though she couldn't fault her perfect diction*)—A. Guinness, 1985.

fauna, flora, meaning respectively the animal and plant life of a given region or period, are collective singular nouns, which means that attendant verbs and determiners are singular, not plural: *Consequently, the eurypterid fauna occurs just below the local Ordovician-Silurian boundary—Jrnl of Paleontogy*, 2005. Use with plural concord is incorrect: **What provides cover to* these *fauna is over 200 species of plants—OEC*, (undated). Their plurals are *faunas* and *floras* (less commonly *faunae* and *florae*). They are Roman goddess names pressed into service for the kingdoms of animals and of plants.

faux ami. The French phrase of which FALSE FRIEND is the translation. Pronounced /fəʊzamiː/, plural *faux amis* (not **faux amies*) pronounced the same. Printed in italics.

faux pas /fəʊ ˈpɑː/. Plural the same, but pronounced /fəʊ ˈpɑːz/. The word is sufficiently a part of English now not to be italicized.

favour, favourable, favourite. The normal spellings in BrE, as against AmE *favor, favorable, favorite.*

fay. See FEY.

fayre. A curiously popular, twee, 'olde worlde' British spelling of *fair* in the sense of 'a gathering of stalls, amusements, etc., usually outdoors' (*a medieval fayre*), or, worse, for *fare* 'food provided by a public house, etc.' (*delicious country fayre*).

faze. A 19c. American English variant of the ancient (but now only dialectal) verb *feeze* 'to drive off, to frighten away'. *Faze* means 'to disconcert, disturb' and is used mainly in negative contexts (e.g. *he was not fazed by the unemployment figures or by other aspects of the recession*). It is now commonly used in informal contexts in BrE as well as in AmE. The word has no connection, etymological or other, with the ordinary word *phase* (stage in a process, etc.), though it is sometimes mistakenly so spelt, e.g. **Far from being phased by the prospect of a potential two weeks in the outback, Linda—who made her name on* Changing Rooms*—was pretty laid back about it all—This is Hampshire,* 2003 (read *fazed*).

fearful, fearsome. *Fearful* in the sense 'frightened, apprehensive' is usually constructed with *of,* (archaic) *to* + infinitive, or with a clause introduced by *lest* or *that* (*fearful of what he would find; made him fearful to act; fearful lest he should fail; fearful that a full-scale attack would not succeed*). It is also used about feelings and circumstances characterized by great fear (*His mother had brought him up to hold priests in fearful reverence*—G. McCaughrean, 1987), and informally like *frightful* to mean 'very great' (*Andrew was tolerantly aware that his mother was a fearful snob*—I. Murdoch, 1965).

Fearsome means 'appalling or frightening, especially in appearance, that should be feared', and is often applied to reputations: *Ichiro continued to regard me with the most fearsome look*—K. Ishiguro, 1986; *Why do swans have this fearsome reputation? A friend who had a flock of them on his lake says they're gentle creatures—Daily Mail,* 2005. They are occasionally confused, with *fearful* being dubiously used for *fearsome*: **He was an enforcer for Arthur Thompson Sr, the Glasgow crime boss, and developed a fearful reputation before they parted company in the 1980s—Sunday Times,* 1985; **He claimed that it* [*sc.* Antarctica] *was cut off from the rest of the world by a region of fire and some others went on to say that fearful monsters inhabited it*—John Long, 2001.

feasible. 1 Spelt *-ible* not *-able.* See -ABLE, -IBLE 7.

2 This word has been in English since the 15c. and derives from French *faire* 'to do'. The problem associated with it lies in its relation to the different meanings of *possible. Feasible* has three uses, all associated with different aspects of possibility. Two have never been at issue, but Fowler (1926) objected to the third, and it has accordingly entered the canon of usage controversies. The three uses of *feasible* are: (*a*) Referring to ideas, projects, etc., 'capable of being done, or carried out': *There was no question that a tunnel was technically feasible, but I wanted to know what the economics would be*—N. Fowler, 1991; *Clearly, it is not feasible to have cameras covering the whole of the track*—Hansard, 1992. (*b*) Referring to implements, devices, processes, etc., 'capable of being used or dealt with successfully': *The sixties should see them* [*sc.* labour-saving devices] *put into commercial production in sufficient quantity to make them financially feasible—Sunday Times,* 1960; *The new semi-automated test could at last make massive screening programmes for cervical cancer economically feasible—New Scientist,* 1991. These two meanings are often hard to distinguish; they are given separately in the *OED* but are combined in *ODO* ('possible or practical to do easily or conveniently'). Perhaps only compilers of dictionaries attempt to see a difference. (*c*) Referring to a theory, proposition, etc., 'able to be the case, likely': *Other feasible explanations focus on the role of monogamy—Jrnl of Sex Research,* 2005; *Even if we dropped the price range we looked at, it was quite feasible it would eventually go beyond our budget—Belfast Telegraph,* 2007.

3 This third and disputed meaning comes closest to being a synonym of *possible* (in its meaning 'able to be the case, likely' rather than 'able to be done') or *probable,* and Fowler insisted that when these words can be substituted without affecting the meaning, they should be. In part he took his cue from the *OED* (1895), which suggested that this meaning was not justified etymologically, despite 'considerable literary authority' starting with Hobbes (1656), but it is now accepted by many dictionaries, including *ODO*.

OEC data suggests that the problem, if it is a problem at all, is rather limited. Used to mean 'likely', *feasible* appears attributively in front of *explanation* (or *answer*), or is preceded by a verb like *be* and followed by a *that*-clause, as in the examples at 2 (*c*) above. In structure, they mirror the examples Fowler gave, unattributed but probably from newspapers: *We ourselves believe that this is the most feasible* [better *probable* (said Fowler)] *explanation of the tradition* and *Witness said it was quite feasible* [better *possible* (said Fowler)] *that if he had had night binoculars he would have seen the iceberg earlier.*

If one follows modern dictionaries, neither of these uses is problematic. If one wishes to avoid the strictures of purists, the alternatives suggested by Fowler in the preceding paragraph should be used, or the word *likely*. My preference would be to retain *feasible* with nouns such as *explanation,* because it means not just 'likely', but also 'plausible, convincing'; but not to use it when followed by a *that*-clause if the meaning covered is possibility or probability rather than practicality.

feature (verb). Fowler tended to be nervous about new uses coming into widespread use in Britain from the general direction of Hollywood. The use of *feature,* he said, 'in cinema announcements instead of *represent* or *exhibit* is perhaps from America ... it is to be feared that from the cinema bills it will make its way into popular use, which would be a pity.' He cited an unattributed example of 1924: *Boys' school and college outfits, men's footwear and under-garments, as well as ..., are also featured.* His words, as so often, went unheeded and the verb is now standard, both with an object, as in the example just given, or without, often being further diluted from the meaning 'to give or have a prominent role' to merely mean 'include' or 'be included', as in Fowler's example: *I was to have my name featured for the first time at the top of the bill*—C. Chaplin, 1964; *Libraries and the youth service feature prominently in many of the local authority cuts—Times,* 1976; *A brutal day in the Alps, featuring five climbs, the longest of which covers over 5,400ft in 12 miles—Sunday Times,* 2007.

February. To pronounce this month as it is spelt, i.e. /ˈfɛbrʊəri/, with both *r*s fully articulated, is, frankly, a bit of a mouthful. Once considered the only standard pronunciation in BrE, it is now often replaced by /ˈfɛbjʊəri/, i. e. converting the first *r* into the initial sound of words like *yell.* The process is called DISSIMILATION. In America, the largest dictionaries report that, despite criticism, dissimilated pronunciations of *February* (i.e. with /-jʊəriː/ or /-jəˌwɛːriː/) are used by educated speakers and are considered standard.

fecal, feces. See FAECAL, FAECES.

fecund. Two pronunciations are possible, /ˈfɛkənd/ and /ˈfiːkənd/. For those who turn to etymology as a basis for the pronunciation of English words, the Latin original (*fēcundus*) has a long *e.* Nevertheless, /ˈfɛkənd/ is the more usual pronunciation of the two among standard speakers and is given first in the *OED.*

federation, confederation, confederacy. It is unrealistic to think that these terms are mutually exclusive, but some indications of their historical applications can be given. The *OED* says: '*Confederacy* now [*sc.* in 1891] usually implies a looser or more temporary association than *confederation,* which is applied to a union of states organized on an intentionally permanent basis.' Specifically the *Southern Confederacy* was the term used for the Confederate States of America, the government established by the

Southern US states in 1860–1 when they seceded from the Union, thus precipitating the American Civil War. *Confederation,* on the other hand, 'is usually limited to a permanent union of sovereign states for common action in relation to externals'. For example, the *Confederation of the Rhine* was the union of all the German states except Prussia and Austria under the protection of Napoleon Bonaparte from 1806 to 1814; and 'the United States of America [is] commonly described as a *Confederation* (or confederacy) from 1777 to 1789, but from 1789, their closer union has been considered a "federation" or federal republic'. A *federation* is 'now chiefly *spec.* the formation of a political unity out of a number of separate states, provinces, or colonies, so that each retains the management of its internal affairs'. Switzerland, USA, Canada, Australia, and Malaysia are examples of federal government, each one differing markedly from the others in constitutional details. Many British people oppose Britain's being included in the push by Eurocrats towards the formation of a federal Europe.

fee (verb). The past tense and past participle are best written *fee'd:* see -ED AND 'D.

feedback is a nice 20c. example of a technical term becoming part of general language, one of what Fowler described as 'popularized technicalities' (see POPULARIZED TECHNICAL TERMS). Defined by the *COD* (1995) as 'the return of a fraction of the output signal from one stage of a circuit, amplifier, etc., to the input of the same or a preceding stage; a signal so returned', *feedback* is also a technical term in biology meaning 'the modification or control of a process or system by its results or effects, esp. in a biochemical pathway or behavioural response'. Round about 1960 the term was adopted by non-specialists and used very frequently to mean 'information about something from the people that have used it or been involved in it, as a basis for improving it', and this has now become an indispensable part of the language, e.g. *The aim of marking is ... to give constructive feedback so that the students' work steadily improves—Electronic Publishing,* 1991.

It is worth bearing in mind, that this 'popularized technicality' is for many people an overused vogue word and a bête noire, and was even banned by the Provost of a university; less potentially irritating alternatives include *comment, criticism, evaluation,* or just plain, old-fashioned *response.*

feel (verb). Occasional, but misguided, opposition has been expressed since the 1950s to the use of *feel* in the intuitive sense 'to think, believe, consider', or, as the *OED* expresses it, 'to apprehend or recognize the truth of (something) on grounds not distinctly perceived; to have an emotional conviction of (a fact)'. The use goes back to Shakespeare (*Garlands ... which I feele I am not worthy yet to weare*—1613), and has been current ever since in standard use. You can safely ignore any objections to its use in this way. Modern examples: *I feel you don't love him, dear. I'm almost sure you don't*—D. H. Lawrence, 1920; *But perhaps it was a little flat somehow, Elizabeth felt. And really she would like to go*—V. Woolf, 1925.

feet. See FOOT (noun).

feint. Since the mid-19c. the usual spelling of the ordinary adjective *faint* in descriptions of stationery printed with light-coloured lines. *Faint* and *feint* are variant spellings of the same word, ultimately from Old French *faint, feint* 'feigned', past participle of *faindre, feindre* 'to feign'.

feldspar /ˈfɛldspɑː/, rather than *felspar.* The first element is from German *Feld* 'field', not German *Fels* 'rock'.

fellahin /-əˈhiːn/ is the plural of *fellah,* an Egyptian peasant. In the 19c. it was usually spelt *fellaheen.*

fellow (in compounds). **1** *Accentuation.* The word *fellow* is, of course, stressed on the first syllable, i.e. /ˈfɛləʊ/. In compounds of *fellow,* when the second element is a noun or verb, the pattern is normally of the type 'secondary stress followed by primary stress' (e.g. ˌ*fellow-*ˈ*travel* (verb), ˌ*fellow* ˈ*traveller*). When the second element is a mere suffix it is unaccented (e.g. ˈ*fellowless,* ˈ*fellowship*).

2 *Hyphenation.* In its meaning 'belonging to the same class or activity' used attributively (before a noun), *fellow* is sometimes hyphenated and sometimes written as a separate word: *fellow citizen* or *fellow-citizen.* There is no general agreement, but the *ODWE* recommends *fellow citizen, fellow feeling, fellow man, fellow traveller.*

The modern tendency is to spell such combinations as two words even when the second element is an agent noun (as in *fellow traveller*) and to add a hyphen to avoid any ambiguity, notably when the combination is a verb: *He has no qualms about saying ... that Oppenheimer was 'a fellow-travelling humanist', and that he behaved with deplorable disloyalty to some of his colleagues*—*Times Higher Education Supplement*, 2004; *He had copied and pasted the words from a fellow blogger who was expressing his alarm at the actions of the Royal Society*—*Guardian*, 2006. But the *-ing* form needs its freedom when it belongs with the following word: *Hatch's lost boy, 28-year-old Kit, sets out to be a cool, round-the-world backpacker and ends up caught uneasily between fellow travelling companions Carlos and Dominique*—*Scotsman*, 2001.

But one must be prepared to find other patterns in printed matter. Such divergence cannot be legislated out of existence.

fell swoop. Usually in the phrase *in* (occasionally *at*) *one fell swoop,* it occurs first in Shakespeare's *Macbeth* (1605): *Oh Hell-Kite! All? What, All my pretty Chickens, and their Damme At one fell swoope?* Except in this phrase, *fell,* an old word meaning 'deadly', is now restricted to poetical or dialectal use; and *swoop* means, of course, a sudden descent, as of a bird of prey. The phrase now means simply 'in a single action', and is by no means restricted to deadly or dangerous actions. Folk etymology tends to play havoc with it, Chinese whispers style, producing many variations, including *foul swoop, fall swoop, fail swoop, full sweep,* and most amusingly, *fowl swoop.*

felo de se /ˌfɛləʊ də ˈseɪ/, /ˌfiːləʊ diː ˈsiː/. A 17c. Anglo-Latin formation, now archaic, or used in legal language, meaning (*a*) suicide; (*b*) a person who commits suicide. The word is derived from L *felō* 'felon' + *dē* + *sē* 'oneself'. The Latinate plural is *felones de se* /ˌfɛləʊniːz də ˈseɪ/, /ˌfiːləʊniːz diː ˈsiː/, but the recommended plural, if needed, is *felos de se*. It is less commonly written with hyphens (*felo-de-se*).

felspar. See FELDSPAR.

female. 1 *Origin.* Adopted in the 14c. from Old French *femelle,* it was almost at once refashioned as *female* to be consistent with its antonym *male,* an etymologically unrelated word. The OF word answers to Latin *fēmella,* a diminutive form of *fēmina* 'woman'. In popular Latin *fēmella* seems to have been used to denote the female of any of the lower animals, as well as retaining its classical Latin (only Catullus) meaning of 'woman, girl'.

2 *Uses.* From the 14c. onwards *female* was used as both noun and adjective, and of human beings and animals: e.g. (adjective) *twelue female children* 1634; *white female slaves* 1841; *female dragon* 1552, *a female scorpion* 1774, *a female salmon* 1870; (noun) *Saturne did onely eate up his male children, not his females* 1652; *The Danish and Swedish laws, harsh ... to all females* 1861; *The females* [*sc.* elephants] *are of greater fiercenesse then the males* 1553; *The stag ... was ... acting as a sentinel for the females* 1847; *The abdomen of the females* [of ants, etc.] *sometimes increases in size* 1881.

3 *Controversy.* Despite the long history of *female* in the sense 'a female person; a woman or girl' with no negative connotations, several 19c. usage guides advised against the use on the grounds that it was unsuitable to apply the same term to animals and to human beings. Even the *OED* (in 1895) said of *female* used as a mere synonym for 'woman' that 'The simple use is now commonly avoided by good writers, except with contemptuous implication.'

4 *Present-day problems.* The *OED* observation holds true in a different way in our gender-sensitive age. Many women object to the use of *female* as a noun, because they feel it is somehow dehumanizing (an online commentator wrote 'it smacks of depersonalization and contempt'—Maeve Maddox, 2009). Such a disparaging or contemptuous attitude is glimpsed by some in sentences such as: *He had no option now but to speak to his landlady in the morning about letting this homeless female have his bed for the night*—M. J. Staples, 1992. The fact is that *female* is most commonly used in natural history, referring to animals, and in medical, scientific, or other impersonal technical writing to refer to humans of the female sex, e.g. *Although females reported higher frequencies of all symptoms except joint pain, none of the differences were statistically significant*—*Archives of Environmental Health*, 2002. To avoid controversy, it is best reserved for that kind of context. The only exception is when a general or neutral term is needed to cover female human beings of all ages, or to avoid the social distinctions still sometimes inherent in *woman* and *lady*: *More than 55 females, from babies to elderly women, have been killed during the first year of the Uprising*—*Spare Rib*, 1989; *We have found that females with male twins are significantly disadvantaged compared to those with female twins or compared to males with male twins*—*Daily Mail*, 2007.

The use of *female* to mean 'a female animal' continues uncontentiously when no separate word (*mare, sow*, etc.) exists.

female, feminine. 1 *The difference.* As adjectives, *female* and *feminine* are generally distinct in meaning and application. *Female* is used (*a*) of the sex that can bear offspring or produce eggs; (*b*) (of plants or their parts) fruit-bearing; (*c*) of or consisting of women or female animals or female plants; (*d*) (of a screw, socket, etc.) manufactured hollow to receive a corresponding inserted part. *Feminine* has more general applications and is usually (but see below) applied only to human beings and not to animals or plants: (*a*) of or characteristic of women or having qualities associated with women; (*b*) in grammar, of words in certain languages (e.g. Old English, Latin, Greek) of a particular class, as distinct from masculine or neuter ones. So much can be gleaned from any standard dictionary. In broad terms *female* is principally used to indicate the sex of a person, animal, or plant, its 'non-maleness'; whereas *feminine* (apart from grammar) is often used of qualities or characteristics regarded as typical of women—beauty, charm, etc. The nouns typically used with each word echo this distinction. One talks of *female athletes, characters* (in fiction and so forth), *friends, officers, patients, roles, students, workers*, and of the *female body, sexuality*, etc.; and of *feminine beauty, form, quality, touch, wiles* and of a man's *feminine side*. In a few cases either word may be used: a *female voice* is one belonging to a woman, whereas a *feminine voice* is distinctively womanlike, and could belong to a man. *Feminine hygiene products* sound gentler and more appealing than *female hygiene products*.

2 Objections to the use of *female*. Some people object to the use of *female* as an adjective, as in *female police officer, female senator*, etc. Their objections are based either on the negative connotations of *female* as a noun, or on the argument that mentioning the sex of the office holder is automatically sexist, unless the sex of the person denoted is relevant in the context. Leaving aside the second argument, which is outside the scope of a book such as this, there is a linguistic parallelism between, for instance, the phrases a *male nurse* and a *female member*, which is lost if you use *woman* attributively instead of *female*, e.g. *woman member*. People do not say a *man member*.

feminine designations. 1 See ARTISTE; CONFIDANT(E); -ESS; -ETTE 4; -MAN; -MISTRESS; -PERSON; -TRIX; -WOMAN.

2 For the great majority of occupational or agent nouns no distinctive feminine term exists: e.g. *chef, chemist, clerk, cook, councillor, counsellor, cyclist, doctor, lecturer, martyr, motorist, nurse, oculist, palmist, president, pupil, secretary, singer, teacher, typist*, etc. There is still an expectation, often subconscious, that some of these offices, etc. will be held by a man (e.g. *chef*), or by a woman (e.g. *nurse, PA*), but this is fast changing.

3 In practice, if the need arises to indicate the sex of an occupational or agent noun, *female, woman, lady*, or *girl* are sometimes used as modifiers, though the last two bring in their wake other problems: e.g. *female/woman doctor, driver, student; lady barrister, doctor*; (US) *girl scout*. The whole question of gender distinctions in occupational and related names is extremely sensitive, verging on explosive. All possible 'solutions' are prone to introduce new inconsistencies or irritate susceptibilities.

feminineness, feminism, femininity. These are the only survivors from a host of formations, all the rest of which have gone to the wall. The *OED* lists the following (with date of first record indicated): *feminacy* (1847), *feminality* (1646), *femineity* (Coleridge, 1820), *feminicity* (1843), *feminility* (1838), *feminineness* (1849), *femininism* (1846), *femininitude* (nonce word, 1878), *femininity* (14c. in Chaucer), *feminism* (1851), and *feminity* (14c. in Chaucer). The abundance of short-lived 19c. formations may simply bear witness to the enthusiasm of the editors of the *OED* and of their contributors for the coinages of their own century. Be that as it may, the existence of such forms throws light on the multiplicity of formative elements (*-eity, -icity, -ility, -ism, -ity,* etc.) that are available for the formation of new abstract nouns. And the disappearance or archaism of some of them (e.g. *feminacy, femininism, femininitude*) illustrates the way in which a language will tolerate only a reasonable number of similarly formed synonyms at a given time.

The only survivors of this group include a word of long standing (*femininity,* 14c.) and two that first came into being in the 19c. (*feminineness, feminism*). *Feminism* stands apart from the others, of course, in having for its main, and now only, meaning 'the advocacy of women's rights on the ground of the equality of the sexes'. It reflects French *féminisme* used in the same sense, and is first recorded in the last decade of the 19c. The other two words are purely abstract nouns with little difference between them to convey 'the fact or quality of being feminine', but *feminineness* is rather rare. Examples: *Put forth each charm And proper floweret of femininity*—Browning, 1868; *I love the feminineness of it* [*sc.* faux fur]; *no man can wear this—Hamilton Spectator,* 1998.

femur. The plural is either *femurs* /ˈfiːməz/ or, particularly in scientific writing, *femora* /ˈfɛmərə/. Cf. Latin *femur, -oris.*

ferae naturae /ˈferaɪ nəˈtjʊəraɪ/. *'The law applies only to animals* ferae naturae; *Rabbits are* ferae naturae; *Rabbits are among the* ferae naturae. The first two sentences show the correct, and the third the wrong use of the phrase, and the three together reveal the genesis of the misuse. *Ferae naturae* is not a nominative plural, but a genitive singular, and means not '"wild kinds", but "of wild kind", and it must be used only as equivalent to a predicative adjective, and not as a plural noun' (Fowler, 1926). Nevertheless the *OED* defines the expression as 'animals living in a wild state, undomesticated animals'. Among the illustrative examples is one where the phrase can be taken to be a genitive singular (*Women are not compris'd in our Laws of friend-ship; they are* feræ naturæ—Dryden, 1668) but may not be; and one (*He evidently viewed himself as the Underwood who alone could do his duty by the* feræ naturæ—C. Yonge, 1873) where it is certainly used as a nominative plural. It is a standard example of a mistaken interpretation of a Latin inflexion, an interpretation which, according to Garner, is established in American legal language.

feral is pronounced /ˈfɛr(ə)l/ or /ˈfɪə-/ according to taste. It means 'wild' (from Latin *fera* 'wild beast' + *-al*) and is commonly applied (i) to animals in a wild state after escape from captivity; (ii) in NZ to animals (esp. deer and goats) brought in from a wild state and farmed; (iii) to human actions reminiscent of wild animals (*the feral grins of the Nazi thugs*); (iv) in the phrase *feral children* to rare cases of children who grow up in the company of animals or otherwise deprived of human society; and (v) depressingly, in Britain in particular, to children and youths behaving in 'a wildly undisciplined and antisocial way'. Anyone who has experience of the last category can hardly doubt that applying the word to such people constitutes a wicked slander against the animal kingdom. Examples: *He was the only one the feral barn cats would allow to touch their kittens—OEC,* 2003; *Romantics agonised over whether or not the feral child has a soul—Sunday Business Post,* 2003; Time *magazine, whose cover story claims our streets are being overrun by disturbed feral youths acting out their misery in drink and crime—Guardian,* 2008; *'Prisoners should carry out work while in jail as part of the process of tackling the growing "feral underclass"', Justice Secretary Ken Clarke said today—Daily Tel.,* 2011.

ferment. See NOUN AND VERB ACCENT.

ferrule, ferule. The ring or cup strengthening the end of a tubular appliance, a walking-stick, umbrella, etc., is a *ferrule* (and is in origin an Old French diminutive form, ultimately from Latin *ferrum* 'iron'); it is also spelt *ferrel.* The flat ruler with a widened end formerly used for beating children is a *ferule* (and is derived from Latin *ferula* 'giant fennel'); it is also spelt *ferula.*

fertile. In 1895 the *OED* gave precedence to the pronunciation /ˈfəːtɪl/ with a short vowel in the second syllable. The standard pronunciation in BrE now is /ˈfəːtʌɪl/ and in AmE /ˈfərtəl/. See -ILE.

fervour. So spelt in BrE; but **fervor** in AmE.

-fest. Beginning in the 19c., but increasingly in the 20c., the German word *Fest* 'festival' made its way into English 'through the front door', as Burchfield put it, as the first element of the word *Festschrift*, beloved of scholars. It is now as firmly established in English as it is in German (Munich's *Oktoberfest*), but as a productive and often colourful suffix with two meanings: (i) an organized festival, often cultural, in celebration of something, and usually capitalized, e.g. *Bookfest Mayfest*, *Summerfest*; (ii) a colourful, slangy way of describing an event, often humorously or satirically. This use started with the American *gabfest* in 1897, and current examples include *slugfest* (a hard-hitting contest, especially in sport), *snoozefest* (anything utterly tedious), and *talkfest* (a disparaging way of referring to a conference or other meeting). It is also quite widely used as an abbreviation of *festival*, particularly in NAmer. Examples: *having given up on Bill Clinton's snoozefest My Life*—*OEC*, (undated); *Look for his latest film, The Wild Dogs, at this year's fest*—*Eye Weekly*, 2002; *on the whole, I don't like the wankfest that constitutes the Turner Prize*—weblog, 2004.

festal, festive. Although *festal* is the older of the two words in the meaning 'relating to a feast, festival, or other joyous occasion', it is now rarely used, *festive* being at least 100 times more frequent. On the rare occasions *festal* appears, it is either literary, or refers to the Christian calendar: *Beethoven's* Missa solemnis ... *was considered suitable for liturgical use on a festal occasion*—*Oxford Companion to Music*, 2002; *At 6.30 pm* [*sc.* on Easter Sunday] *there will be festal evensong*—*Croydon Guardian*, 2005.

fetal. See FOETUS.

fete, fête. *Fete* (without accent), an outdoor function to raise money for charity, is now the standard form. But writing it with an accent is, of course, still correct.

fetid /'fɛtɪd/, less commonly /'fiːtɪd/. The spelling with *-e-* rather than *-oe-* is now the majority spelling. The Latin original is *fētidus*, with a long *e*. The refashioned form *foetidus*, which led to the English form *foetid*, has no etymological justification.

fetish. 1 Until the early 20c. the first syllable was often pronounced like *feet*, but no longer.

2 The word is a 17c. adoption of French *fétiche*, and was originally an African object or amulet having magical power. It is not an African word, though; the French word goes back ultimately to Latin *factīcius* 'factitious'.

fetishes. Fowler (1926) presented a list of grammatical and other linguistic features which, in his opinion, evoked irrational devotion, respect, or hostility, in other words had become *fetishes*. Among 'the more notable or harmful' were (the capitals indicate where in that edition of this book the features were treated): SPLIT INFINITIVE; avoidance of repetition (ELEGANT VARIATION); the rule of thumb for *and* WHICH; pedantry on the foreign spelling of foreign words (MORALE); the notion that AVERSE *to* and DIFFERENT *to* are marks of the uneducated; the dread of a PREPOSITION AT END; the idea that successive metaphors are mixed METAPHORS; the belief that common words lack dignity (FORMAL WORDS). Burchfield (1996) wrote: 'At public and private functions, and in letters, when devotees of Fowler express their opinions to me, these are among the principal items mentioned, together with the incorrect use of classical plurals as singulars (*criteria*, *phenomena*, etc.), the use of *hopefully* as a sentence adverb, and a few other points'. To this list of fetishes can be added the idea that AGENDA and DATA are always plural.

fetus. See FOETUS.

feverish, feverous. Both words entered the language in the 14c. and down the centuries shared the same senses. They also seem to have had approximately equal currency. But *feverish*, used especially to mean 'suffering from a fever' or 'intense, excited' (*feverish activity, a feverish race against time*), has now virtually driven *feverous* out of the standard language. Virtually, but not entirely: there are 14 examples in the *OEC*, all metaphorical, against 2,275 for *feverish*. Example: *but the triumph over neighbours Cavan, and now Meath, have* [*sic*] *ignited a feverous support in the county*—*Sligo Weekender*, 2003.

few. 1 *Few* may be used with or without preceding *a*, although the meaning is slightly different, to the bafflement of many learners of English. *There were few seats left* means there were hardly any (and is negative in implication), whereas *There were a few seats left* means that some were still left (and is positive in implication).

2 As noun and pronoun, *few* is used in a wide range of idiomatic expressions, e.g. *a few of those present, a good few* (BrE, informal, = a fairly large number), *not a few* (a considerable number), *quite a few, many are called but few are chosen, he had had a few* (slang, = a few alcoholic drinks), *for the benefit of the many not the few, the Few* (the RAF pilots who took part in the Battle of Britain). None of these is in the least questionable.

3 For *comparatively few,* see COMPARATIVELY.

fewer, less.

1 The basic rule.
2 *Less than* with numbers.
3 Censured use of *less.*
4 **Number of . . . is few.*

1 *The basic rule.* The starting-point is that according to the rule, infringement of which causes a violent, Pavlovian reaction among the grammatically pure in heart, the comparative adjective *fewer* is used with count nouns, i.e. with nouns that have both a singular and a plural form (*fewer books*); or with collective nouns (*fewer people*). In such constructions *less* is deemed to be incorrect (see 3 below). By contrast, *less* (which is the comparative of *little*) is properly used with uncount nouns. In other words, *fewer* refers to number and *less* refers to quantity; *less* parallels *much,* while *few* parallels *many.*

2 *Less than* with numbers. *Less* is standard when followed by *than* + number + plural noun, for example with distances (*it is less than seventy miles to London*), periods of time (*less than six weeks*), sums of money (*costs less than £50*), or other statistical enumerations. This is because these distances, times, costs, etc., are thought of as composite amounts rather than countable numerical quantities. In phrases like the above, *less* is a pronoun, not an adjective. Supermarket checkouts are perfectly correct if their signs read '10 items or less', and to put '10 items or fewer' is unnecessarily pedantic. Pedantry puts *fewer* in the following example, in which *less* would have been fine: *fewer than 3% of all books published in the U.S. the previous year were translations—Context Magazine,* 2003. Examiners may invite candidates to write a précis of a passage of prose in *fifty words or less.* In some borderline cases it is more idiomatic to use *less* when *fewer* would put an unwelcome emphasis on the individual components rather than the cumulative effect of the total: *unashamedly rejoiced in having had in his house at one time no less than five Nobel Prize winners*—M. Drabble, 1987. Other examples: *unless he read him on consecutive days and for no less than three hours at a sitting*—P. Roth, 1979; *We have had reliable temperature records for less than 150 years—NY Rev. Bks,* 1988. See LESS 3.

3 Censured use of *less.* (*a*) People appreciate clear, simple rules, as set out at 1 above. They provide neat, binary distinctions: this is right; that is wrong. Regrettably, the facts of language, as so often happens, are more complicated than simple, or simplistic, rules allow. First, it is worth pointing out that the use of *less* in front of a count noun goes back to King Alfred the Great in *c.*888 and continued for centuries thereafter; but, as the *OED* (1898) puts it, it is 'freq. found but generally regarded as incorrect'. Second, the injunction against *less* in front of plural count nouns seems to have been launched by one grammarian in 1770, related specifically to *less* in front of numbers, and was tentative rather than dogmatic. Since then it has developed into a rather more extreme and expansive ban.

(*b*) The use of *less* instead of *fewer* in front of plural count nouns is a feature of spoken English, but less so of the standard written language. Analysis of the *OEC* data suggests that *fewer than* followed by a plural noun is five times more frequent than *less than*; and *less than* is prevalent in texts classified as informal. In order to avoid tut-tutting from your readers, or worse still your examiners, it is certainly advisable to review your use of *less* in writing, and to conform to the rules, according to which the following are all wrong: *I shall care about less things*—P. Fitzgerald, 1980; *there will be less 100% loans about*—Chairman of Halifax Building Society, BBC Radio 4, 1987; *We had been given less men . . . to perform a holding action—Paintball Games,* 1989. As a character in Maurice Gee's *Prowlers* (1987) sadly remarks: *'Like', it seems, has taken the place of 'as if'. 'Less' tips 'fewer' out. Less pedestrians, less immigrants.* See LESS 3 (historical note).

(*c*) Comparing English with other languages is invidious, but as an aside it may be worth noting that French, Italian, Spanish and German get by perfectly well by using one word to denote a smaller quantity and number, and thus do not have the *less/fewer* problem e.g. *moins de temps/de gens* (Fr.), *meno tempo/gente* (It.), *weniger Zeit/Leute* (Ger.) = less time/fewer people.

4 **Number of ... is few.* As Fowler pointed out in 1926, neither *less* nor *few* should strictly speaking be used in conjunction with the word *number* as in *The number of thinkers ... who have managed to say anything fundamental or new about translation is very few* (Roy Harris, 1986). A number is *small, smaller,* or *very small,* not *less* or *few(er)* or *very few.*

fey, fay. 1 *Fay* is a literary word for fairy, derived from Old French *fa(i)e,* and related to ModF *fée* 'fairy', and used in the name of the sorceress *Morgan le Faye.* Used attributively (before a noun), it means 'fairy-like': *When she made formal use of figures in her landscapes, they were somewhat mannered, almost fay children*—*Listener,* 1962.

2 The unrelated native word of great antiquity *fey* (Old English *fǣge* 'doomed to die') once meant 'fated to die, at the point of death'. In the 19c., however, a weakened sense developed, 'disordered in mind like one about to die' (*Surely the man's fey about his entails and his properties*—J. Galt, 1823), and then it passed into meaning 'possessing or displaying magical, fairy-like, or unearthly qualities': *A gaze that was not at all fey, but ... remarkably shrewd*—E. Coxhead, 1955; *she's got that fey look as though she's had breakfast with a leprechaun*—D. Burnham, 1969. From there it has developed further in meaning to suggest someone who gives an impression of otherworldliness or mystery, or, if applied to men, of a certain unbecoming lack of masculinity: *Scraggy hair, fey smile, dress like a wet dishcloth. Another example of why being too thin really isn't sexy*—*Times,* 2007, In speech, of course, they are indistinguishable, which accounts for *fay* sometimes being used instead of *fey.* Further Examples: (fay) *They danced and played like forest druids and lyrical fays, changing shape and shifting in a series of brilliant colors*—*OEC,* 2005; *No fay thing would dare cross the threshold; and even if it did, there was plenty of holy water by the door*—*OEC,* 2004; (fey) *The cellist, Robert Morse, portrayed by Zoffany as a somewhat fey young man, seems an unlikely figure of authority*—*Scotland on Sunday,* 2004; (*fay* for *fey*) *?My tour of 'oop north' (there's no way I can pull off this fay Southern poofiness, as I am really one of these people and as is my right, fiercely and unthinkingly proud of my Yorkshireness*—*www.richardherring.com,* 2005.

fez. The inflected forms are (pl.) *fezzes* and (adj.) *fezzed.* See -Z-, -ZZ-.

fiancé /fɪˈɑːnseɪ/, feminine **fiancée**, pronounced the same.

fiasco. Plural *fiascos.* See -O(E)S 6.

fiat. The legal term is pronounced /ˈfiːat/ or /ˈfiat/ and the car (*Fiat*) /ˈfiːət/.

fibre is the spelling in BrE and **fiber** in AmE.

fibroma, a fibrous tumour. The plural is *fibromas* or, especially in technical medical writing, *fibromata.*

fibula. Whether in anatomy (= outer bone between knee and ankle) or in classical antiquity (= brooch or clip), both *fibulae* /-iː/ and *fibulas* are acceptable as plural forms. See LATIN PLURALS.

fictional, fictitious. *Fictional* means 'occurring in fiction', i.e. in a piece of literature, whereas *fictitious* means 'invented, unreal; not genuine'. So *Oliver Twist* is a *fictional* character in Dickens's eponymous novel, and Hercule Poirot is a *fictional* detective created by Agatha Christie. A *fictional* account of something is a description of it in fiction; a *fictitious* account is either an invented story (or a bank account with false personal details used for fraud). However, keeping this distinction watertight sometimes proves difficult. In the following example it is difficult to know if *fictitious* is being used to mean 'invented' or 'from fiction': *Surbiton is home to many famous fictitious characters including Tom & Barbara Good (plus neighbours Jerry & Margot Leadbetter). Terry & June also live here, as does Reginald Iolanthe Perrin. However it is not home to any famous real people*—*OEC* (undated). Conversely, *fictional* is occasionally used when presumably *fictitious* is intended: **this cover of the Stones classic is credited to a mysterious, probably fictional group called Germania, who sound (very approximately) like Bananarama on cheap drugs*—weblog, 2002 (BrE).

fidget. The inflected forms are *fidgeted, fidgeting.* See -T-, -TT-.

fiducial, fiduciary. The second is the ordinary form, *fiducial* being used only in some technical terms in surveying, astronomy, etc.

-fied. See -FY.

field. In the sense 'an area of operation or activity; a subject of study' (*each supreme in his own field; distinguished in many fields*), Fowler (1926) and subsequent critics accused this word of being overused. If one wishes to avoid it, numerous synonyms and near-synonyms exist: (for fields of study) *area, discipline, domain, sphere, subject,* (for areas of operation or responsibility) *area, department, line, province, remit, responsibility speciality,* (sometimes) *territory.* A short selection of these follows, together with brief illustrative examples.

A debate covering a wide area; *fire drill is not my* department; *belongs to the* domain *of philosophy; casuistry is not in my* line; *presumably out of our* province (= not our concern); *in the whole* realm *of medicine; he had selected Roman Law as his* speciality; *useful in his own* sphere; *turn from verified matters to some still unexplored* territory. These also need to be used with care, for fear of avoiding the hackneyed only to adopt an alternative that is precious, stilted, or pompous, as can happen with *bailiwick, territory,* or still worse *métier,* for example.

It is important to keep in mind, however, that there are plenty of contexts in which *field* is the natural and legitimate word. A few examples: *As a Professor of English Literature she had no doubt that the whole field lay within her control*—Angus Wilson, 1952; *Working on him would give me an opportunity to learn something about politics—a field in which, thanks to* Commentary, *I was growing more and more interested*—N. Podhoretz, 1967; *He has . . . made a number of breakthroughs in his field of labour and social welfare*—B. Castle, 1980.

It is also true that *in the field of* is often merely a verbose way of saying *in,* and could be avoided in, for example, *there is much talk about new discoveries in the field of genetics.*

fifth(ly). Both the *-f-* and the *-th* should be clearly sounded, /fɪfθ(li).

fifties. See NINETIES.

figure. 1 Both the noun and the verb are pronounced /ˈfɪɡə/ in British English; similarly with the inflected form *figuring* /ˈfɪɡərɪŋ/. In American English the standard pronunciation of the noun and verb is with medial /-ɡj-/, i.e. /ˈfɪɡjə(r)/. The British pronunciation is sometimes heard in AmE but is usually condemned as substandard. In BrE *figurative* is as often pronounced /ˈfɪɡərətɪv/ as it is pronounced /ˈfɪɡj-/, but the second is standard in AmE.

2 As verb, *figure* (often with *out*) is used, especially in AmE, to mean 'to conclude, think, work out' (*He figured he could write the book in six months*), or with *on* in the sense 'plan' (*he figured on being home by six o'clock*). Also predominantly American is its use to mean 'seem likely or understandable' (*that figures*). Each of these uses is informal. For *go figure,* see GO 2.

figure of speech, refers to any of several recognized linguistic devices used to make language lively or more colourful, such as metaphor and simile. In this book the figures of speech, or terms of rhetoric, are treated at their alphabetical place: see APOSIOPESIS; ASYNDETON; METAPHOR, etc.

fillers are words such as *actually, you know, in fact, really,* and *I mean,* and pause markers such as *er* and *um,* that have little or no propositional meaning and are merely used to help maintain the flow of speech, and sometimes improve sentence balance, in conversational English. Their routine use is quite legitimate, and everyday conversation would be unnatural without them. At the same time, it is clear that too frequent a use of such fillers, particularly the ubiquitous *like,* is undesirable and can be an impediment to communication.

fils. See PÈRE.

finable. See FINEABLE.

final analysis. See ANALYSIS 2.

final clause, in grammar, is a clause that states a purpose, especially when introduced by a formula such as *to, in order to, in order that, in order not to, in the hope that, to the end that, so* (*that*); (expressing apprehension) *that . . . not, for fear* (*that*), *lest.* Such clauses are also called *clauses of purpose.* Examples: *He raised his hand* in order that *the bus might stop; They closed the border post* in order not to *exacerbate* *things further; He confessed everything* in the hope that *he would be forgiven; I have come to you now* so that *you will know that I have not left the country; She walked quickly* for fear that *she would be late for her appointment; Lord God of Hosts, be with us yet,* Lest *we forget,* lest *we forget* (Kipling).

finale has three syllables, /fɪˈnɑːli/. The plural is *finales.*

finalize. Hostility to this formation in *-ize* reached its peak in the 1940s and 1950s: 'As a synonym for *to complete* or *to conclude* it [*sc. finalize*] is superfluous and ugly' (E. Partridge, 1942); 'When I hear of ... things being adumbrated, or visualized, or finalized ... I think of that other aim of this [*English*] Association, "to uphold the standards of English writing or speech"' (N. Birkett, 1953). The word seems to have entered the language in the 1920s in Australia and New Zealand (though the Canadian scholar William J. Kirwin found an isolated example of 1901 in St John's, Newfoundland), but was for a long time regarded in Britain as an 'unwanted Americanism'. Time has moved on, and, though some editors have inherited an ancestral dislike of the word, it is usually only elderly eyebrows that are now raised when the word is used of rules, deals, etc., to mean 'to put into final form'. In the word's favour, it is shorter than its definition just given, and often has a stronger sense of effective conclusion than is conveyed by *complete* or *finish*: *Arrangements have also been finalized for the establishment of a ranching scheme at Jaldesa—Inside Kenya Today,* 1971; *The two companies now have 120 days to finalize an implementation agreement under the terms of the letter of intent—Lloyd's List,* 1995.

fine (noun). The Latinate phrase *in fine* ('in the end') from the 15c. to the 19c. was routinely used to mean 'finally; to sum up; in short', but is now seldom heard, and is described by Garner as 'turgid and legalistic'. Example: *We have, in fine, attained the power of going fast*—Ruskin, 1849. If pronounced, it can be either the anglicized /ɪn ˈfʌɪni/, (in **fy**-ni) or the Latinized /ˈfiːneɪ/(**fee**-nay).

fineable, meaning 'liable to a fine', is more often spelt this way, not *finable.*, though the two have competed throughout their history since the 15c. and 16c. respectively. The spelling with *-eable* contradicts the general rule that words ending in silent *-e* (*fine*) lose it when *-able* is added, but makes the link with the noun *fine* clearer, and avoids possible misreading as **fin**-uhbl.

fine-tooth(ed) comb. See TOOTHCOMB.

finical, finicking, finicky, finikin. Of these, *finical* (first recorded in Nashe in 1592) is the oldest, and it seems to have been a rough-and-ready formation ('probably academic slang', according to *ODEE,* 1966) from *fine* adj. + *-ical.* The others followed at intervals: *finikin* (1661, now obsolete), *finicking* (1741), and *finicky* (1825). It is perhaps best to regard them all as unstable variants of the same word. The only one of the group now commonly used is *finicky,* and it has two main meanings, the first being the more common: (*a*) over-particular, fastidious; (*b*) needing much attention to detail. *The public is less finicky than editors are about length—American Poetry Review,* 2001; *I have one for my Nokia tablets* (*it will produce and run ARM executables*)*—but even that is finicky to setup* [*sic*]—weblog, 2011.

finish (adjective). = rather fine. Best so spelt (see MUTE E) despite the fact that it then becomes identical with the verb.

fiord. See FJORD.

fire (verb). The progress of this word in the sense 'dismiss, sack' from American English slang to everybody's English is of interest in that it started out in AmE (it would seem, from the *OED,* in Dakota) as a phrasal verb, *to fire out,* first recorded in 1885. Fowler (1926) described *fire out* as 'still an Americanism'. Gowers (1965) gave the simple *fire* as the headword and said that it was 'still an American colloquialism, though making headway among us at the expense of the verb to *sack*'. *ODO* labels it 'informal', and defines it as 'dismiss (an employee) from a job'. Its AmE origin seems to have been largely forgotten, and it stands alongside *sack* as a straightforwardly direct term for a disagreeable action.

firm (adverb) is used mainly in two fixed phrases, *stand firm* and *hold firm to.* In all other contexts the natural adverbial form *firmly* is used (*the bracket was firmly attached to the wall*). Despite that, the following cannot be said to be wrong: *the independent Murray-Darling Basin Authority revealed it is sticking firm to the plan to* *cut 2750 billion litres of water a year from irrigation—OEC,* 2012.

first. *first(ly), secondly, lastly.* In such sequences where points or topics are enumerated the choice between *first* and *firstly* is free in modern English, as indeed it has been since at least the 17c. The absence of *firstly* from Johnson's Dictionary (1755), De Quincey's hostility to it in 1847—'First (for I detest your ridiculous and most pedantic neologism of *firstly*)'—, the distaste of 19c. commentators for it, as well as the fact that the Prayer Book, in enumerating the purposes for which matrimony was ordained, introduces them with *First, Secondly, Thirdly,* and other considerations have led to the myth that *firstly* is actually wrong in a sequence *Firstly, ... secondly, ... thirdly, ...* etc. Fowler's judgement, which could aptly be applied to so many things in life, was: 'one of the harmless pedantries in which those who like oddities because they are odd are free to indulge, provided that they abstain from censuring those who do not share the liking'. In practice many different patterns are used: *First, ... second, ... third; First, ... secondly, ... thirdly; Firstly, ... secondly, ... thirdly;* (AmE) *First of all, ... second of all, ... thirdly,* etc. Logic did not and does not come into it. However, it is probably wise to be consistent, and not to use *firstly ... second ... third.* And *second of all* will grate on British eyes and ears (mine, at least), but is standard AmE.

first name. See CHRISTIAN NAME.

firth (noun). Originally (15c. from Old Norse) a Scottish word, introduced into English literary use *c.*1600, it was often in the past (in the work of e.g. Cowper and Tennyson) converted, by the process of METATHESIS, into *frith.* But *firth* is the only standard form now. It means either 'a narrow inlet of the sea' or 'an estuary'.

fisc, fisk. 1 (Usu. spelt *fisc*) in Roman antiquity 'the public treasury; the emperor's privy purse'.

2 In Scottish law, *fisk* (so spelt) is 'the public treasury; the revenue falling to the Crown by escheat'. The word came into English via Old French from Latin *fiscus* 'the imperial exchequer', and is not uncommon in American legal usage. It occurs memorably in Auden's *The Fall of Rome* (1947): *Fantastic grow the evening gowns; Agents of the Fisc pursue Absconding tax-defaulters through The sewers of provincial towns.*

fish. The plural is usually *fish* (*he caught seven fish yesterday; nets full of fish; all the fish in the sea; a pretty kettle of fish*); *fishes* is sometimes used to emphasize a plural rather than a collective concept and to denote kinds of fish (*feed the fishes; food fishes like cod and flounder*). In biblical allusions, *fishes* is used rather than *fish: five loaves and two small fishes.* See COLLECTIVE NOUN.

fisher, fisherman. See ANGLE (noun^2).

fisk. See FISC.

fistic, fistical. Both mean 'relating to boxing, pugilistic', and are facetious formations, dismissed by the original *OED* with the comment 'Not in dignified use'. *Fistic* was first recorded in 1806 and *fistical* in 1767: only *fistic* seems to survive, in humorous or light-hearted use, or in sports, esp. US, writing. Examples: *The late 60s and early 70s spawned an array of fistic talent in the heavyweight division—www.eastside-boxing.com,* 2004; *That screen battle was also the longest fistic encounter in film history—Scotland on Sunday,* 2005.

fistula. The plural is generally *fistulas,* but *fistulae* /-iː/, reflecting the plural form in Latin, is also found in medical and zoological works.

fit (adjective) **1** Fowler considered *fit audience though few,* adapted from Milton's *Paradise Lost,* a hackneyed phrase, but now it would be fairer to call it an allusion whose referent passes generally unnoticed.

2 The British use of *fit* to mean 'sexually desirable' is traced by the *OED* back to 1985, but seems to be a revival of a 19c. usage: *'Better 'en that bird you blagged last night.' 'F*** off! She was fit.'—Observer,* 1985. It has now become a standard part of informal language among people below a certain age, and the phrase *well fit* is all too easy to parody as an example of yoofspeak, as in this 2009 example from the Oxford Twitter Corpus: *He is well fit though* [*sic*] *he is older than me thoughh he is in year 12 xx.* Usually context will distinguish this meaning from 'physically fit', but that wording can be used if there is likely to be ambiguity.

fit (verb). The only past tense, past participle, and participial form in BrE is *fitted* (*they fitted new locks to their doors; he has fitted in well at his new school; fitted carpets*). In certain types of AmE, *fit* is used instead as an alternative, esp. in the senses 'to be of the right size and shape' (*Joan's dresses fit beautifully when she was nine*) and 'to be suitable' (*the name fit him to perfection*). Margaret M. Bryant (1962) commented: 'According to the Linguistic Atlas survey, in New England *fitted,* in the context of "His coat *fit/fitted* me", is more common in cultivated speech, whereas in the Upper Midwest *fit* is preferred by all classes of speakers, and used by 80% of the cultivated speakers'. She concluded that 'both *fit* and *fitted,* like *knit/knitted,* are standard [in the US]'. Examples of *fit* past tense: *the street looked like an improbable setting for such a modest vehicle, but when it pulled up before my grandfather's house it fit in very well*—tr. I. Allende, 1985; *His head fit snugly into his collar like a shell into a canister*—D. Pinckney, 1992; *Many questions were put; none fit.*—*Bull. Amer. Acad. Arts & Sci.,* 1994.

fix (noun). Two originally American uses call for comment. **1** The noun is first recorded in any sense in an American military biography of 1816: *They are in a mighty good fix,* i.e. a position from which it would be difficult to escape. From that meaning it is an easy step to 'a difficulty, dilemma, predicament', and it was so used by Charlotte Brontë in a letter written in 1839: *It so happens that I can get no conveyance . . . so I am in a fix.* Other *OED* examples from the following couple of decades suggest that British writers found it appealing, and it is now an integral part of informal BrE. Examples: *Since she had vowed to remain celibate, she was in rather a fix when her father planned to marry her to the King of Sicily*—B. Cottle, 1983; *The patient will indeed be in a fix from which he may find it hard to extricate himself*—C. Rycroft, 1985.

2 Beginning in the US in the 1930s, a dose of a narcotic drug came to be called a *fix-up* and then a *fix.* The word (only *fix*) reached Britain by the 1950s. Examples: *He needed her as a drug addict needs his fix*—I. Murdoch, 1985; *What do we care where a junkie gets his fix?*—L. Cody, 1986. From drug-taking contexts figurative and transferred uses soon emerged: *Many people seem addicted to exercise and get depressed if they don't get their daily fix*—*Company,* 1985; *The presidency alone had escaped then, and, in their beds at night, all the family members . . . dreamed endlessly of this, the ultimate 'fix' of power*—P. Booth, 1986.

3 *A quick* (or occasionally *cheap*) *fix* is a hasty remedy that deals with a difficulty in the short term; the expression is recorded first in a hyphenated adjectival form from the 1950s, a use which remains common: *Quick-fix reflectors and diffusers, heavy duty bi-pin lampholders*—*Architectural Review,* 1959; *For them conventional war has been lived through and they think nuclear weapons are a cheap fix to deter it*–*Green Magazine,* 1990; *If anyone thinks it will be easy, I would urge them to think again about these quick-fix training gimmicks*—*Stoke Sentinel,* 2007.

fix (verb). This ancient verb (first recorded in the 15c.) has a multitude of senses beginning with the primary one of 'to fasten'. Out of all these, two originally AmE uses call for comment. **1** (Also *to fix up.*) To prepare (food or drink). *You must fix me a drink,* Fanny Trollope said in her *Domestic Manners of the Americans* (1839); and Bret Harte, an American writer, in a work of 1891, wrote *Mother'll fix you suthin' hot.* Examples: (US) *He went to the store to get eggs . . . She fixed his breakfast*—N. Mailer, 1979; *Fix some lemonade*—Anne Tyler, 1983; *We'd just bake a little something, fix up a bowl of punch*—G. Naylor, 1988; (UK) *When I am quite exhausted, go and cook a meal, fix a drink*—N. Bawden, 1981.

2 The informal American expression *to be fixing to* meaning 'to prepare to, intend, be on the point of', which was first recorded in 1716, is still hardly ever encountered outside the US. Examples: *Aunt Lizy is just fixing to go to church*—1854–5 in *OED*; *I-feel-like-I'm-fixing-to-die*—record title, Country Joe and The Fish, 1967; *If you're after Lily, she come in here while ago and tole me she was fixin' to git married*—E. Welty, *a*1983; *I was fixing to turn it down*—*Atlanta,* 1989.

fixation. Used since the 17c. to mean 'the action of fixing (in material and figurative senses)', it quickly made its way into popular use from the language of Freudian theory in the course of the 20c. From meaning 'the arresting of the development of a libidinal component at a pregenital stage, so that psychosexual emotions are "fixed" at that point' (*OED*), it has come to mean simply 'an obsession, an *idée fixe*'. The following preposition can be *on* or *with*, the first being the AmE preference and the second the BrE. Examples: *Cynics predict that Hollywood's fixation on teen girls could fade faster than a high school crush*—*Business Week*, 2004 (US); *The former Northern Ireland Ombudsman also warned that a fixation with past conflicts could threaten the delicate political arrangements established to strengthen reconciliation there*—*Daily Mail*, 2007 (UK). *Fixation* also has technical uses in chemistry and medicine.

fixedly. Three syllables: see -EDLY.

fixedness, fixity. Both words entered the language in the 17c., and both notionally qualify as natural forms when an abstract noun is required for the quality or condition of being fixed (in various senses). There was a sharp decline in the frequency of *fixedness* in the 20c., possibly because of slight uncertainty about the number of syllables in the word (there should always be three), to the point that *fixity* has become the dominant form of the two, outnumbering its rival ten times in the *OEC* data. Examples showing various shades of meaning ('permanence, attentiveness, invariability, steadfast adherence to (a cause), etc.'): (fixedness) *Psychologists even have a special term to refer to the interference of prior knowledge on problem-solving activity: functional fixedness*—*Byte*, 1983; *A film that seemed able to contemplate death ends up by denying even the fixedness of character*—*Independent*, 1990; *This interesting collection . . . deftly explores both the fluidity and the fixedness of ethnic, racial, and sexual identities throughout history and around the world*—*Jrnl of Sex Research*, 2003; (fixity) *Fine eyes, but rather disquieting, she found, in their intent, bright, watchful fixity*—A. Huxley, 1928; *Print-capitalism gave a new fixity to language*—B. Anderson, 1983; *Bhaga-whardi's dreams had no such fixity, but presented ever-changing panoramas and dissolving landscapes to her eye*—O. Sacks, 1985; *What distinguishes perversion is its quality of desperation and fixity*—*NY Times*, 1991. The standard collocation with *purpose* is *fixity of purpose*.

fizz. See -Z-, -ZZ-.

fjord is the more frequent and recommended spelling rather than *fiord*, but both are correct.

fl. See FLORUIT.

flaccid. Can be pronounced /ˈflaksɪd/, or /ˈflasɪd/, which is probably more frequently heard.

flack, flak are homophones. (*a*) *Flak*, meaning anti-aircraft fire, or the shells fired, comes from German *Fl*ieger*a*bwehr*k*anone, literally 'airman-defence-gun', and came into prominence during the Second World War. From the late 1960s onwards the word began to be used as a metaphor to mean '(a barrage of) adverse criticism'. The spelling *flack* is accepted as a variant in British and American dictionaries. (*b*) *Flack* as a noun is a modern AmE slang word (first recorded in 1939 according to Merrriam-Webster and of unknown origin) for a publicity agent. It is mainly used in AmE, but also has some limited currency in BrE and elsewhere. In the mid-sixties by a process of conversion it became a verb as well. Very occasionally the spelling *flak*, appropriate for the first word, is used with the meaning of the second, as in the last example below. Examples: (*flak*: literal) *He dodged the flak, once pulling his parachute from beneath his seat and finding it riddled through with sharp chunks of metal that missed him by only a few inches*—weblog, 2003 (AmE); (= criticism) *The former ASB Bank and Air New Zealand chief executive, who has drawn flak over the years for the bank's interest rate policy and his multimillion-dollar salary*—NZ Herald, 2011; (*flack* = publicity agent) *The Republicans need PR flacks like Brooks to distract voters from their record*—*www.inthesetimes.com*, 2004 (AmE); *Rather than have his PR flacks spin up a new fairytale regarding charity work or orphans in Lesotho, Prince Charles should send Harry to a rehab clinic*—The Unofficial British Royal Family Pages, 2004; (*flack* as verb) *Because kids have gotten so skeptical, companies have countered with more craftiness. They hire cool alpha boys to flack products to their pals*—*Business Week*, 2004 (AmE); (*flak* wrongly used) **He's had the thankless job of working as a flak for Integral Energy in recent years*—*www.crikey.com.au*, 2004.

flagrant is used of an offence or (formerly) an offender: glaring, notorious, scandalous (*a flagrant breach of a contractual agreement*; (archaic) *a flagrant misanthrope*).

Apart from *breach,* it typically modifies the nouns *violation, abuse, disregard* and *foul,* Its etymological meaning (and first meaning in English in the 16c.) is 'flaming, burning' (cf. Latin *flagrāre* 'to burn'). It is now more or less synonymous with BLATANT.

flair in Middle English meant an odour or smell (being originally via Old French from popular Latin *flagrāre,* an altered form of *frāgrāre* (cf. *fragrant*), but this meaning died out. It was borrowed from French again in the late 19c., started to mean 'instinctive discernment', and then developed its modern meaning of 'an instinctive aptitude for doing something well'. Quite often people spell it incorrectly as if it were the unrelated noun and verb *flare,* e.g. **What my model may have lacked in artistic flare it was going to make up for in size*—weblog, 2002.

flak. See FLACK.

flambeau. Plural generally *-x* (pronounced /-z/) rather than *-s*; see -X.

flamenco. Plural *flamencos.* See -O(E)S 4.

flamingo. Plural *flamingos* or *-oes.* See -O(E)S 2.

flammable, inflammable. *Flammable* (1813) and its corresponding noun **flammability** (1646) were revived in modern use (in BrE especially by the British Standards Institution) and used in place of *inflammable* (1605) and *inflammability* (1646). This is in order to avoid the possible ambiguity of the *in-* forms where the *in-* might be taken for a negative. The modern form *flammable* contrasts with the negative form *non-flammable.* As with all such artificial revivals or alterations, the campaign for *flammable/non-flammable* has met with only partial success in lay use.

flan. See TART.

flannel. The inflected forms in BrE are *flannelled, flannelling* (AmE *flanneled, flanneling*); but *flannelette,* a napped cotton fabric imitating flannel. See -LL-, -L-.

flare. See FLAIR.

flat, flatly. The dominant adverbial form is *flatly* (*flatly contradicting his own known views; he flatly refused to come down; rendered flatly into English*), but it is always used figuratively. The shorter form *flat* is used in fixed phrases (*he turned the offer down flat; flat broke*; etc.).

flaunt, flout. *Flaunt* means 'to display ostentatiously' and *flout* 'to display contempt for (the law, rules, etc.)'. *Flaunt* is often wrongly used for *flout,* but not vice versa. The wrong use, which has been particularly prevalent since the 1940s, has not been traced before the 20c. and was not mentioned by Fowler (1926). **1** Correct uses of *flaunt*: *Women should have it both ways—they should be able to flaunt their sexuality and be taken seriously*—E. Wurtzel, 1998; *It has also become more acceptable to flaunt wealth—Guardian,* 2008.

2 Correct uses of *flout*: *Wilde achieved brilliant results at University (Dublin, then Oxford) while lazily flouting the rules—Listener,* 1987; *it is estimated that half a million motorists flout the ban each day—Daily Tel.,* 2007.

3 Illustrating the correct use of both words: *'Your Excellency, let us not flaunt the wishes of the people.' 'Flout, you mean,' I said. 'The people?' asked His Excellency, ignoring my piece of pedantry*—C. Achebe, 1987.

4 Incorrect uses of *flaunt*: *By flaunting these rules, Hongkong and Shanghai have challenged the Bank's authority—Daily Tel.,* 1981; *The union continued its campaign against Sunday trading yesterday, targeting shops which flaunted regulations—Times,* 1989; *If newspapers flaunt the convention, there will be a legislative response—NZ Parliamentary Debates,* 2005; *The fact that a shop so close to the scene of the tragic crash is still flaunting licensing laws will no doubt cause more outrage—Hastings Observer,* 2007.

flautist, flutist. In BrE, *flautist* is customary. In AmE both forms occur, the more usual one being *flutist.* As a matter of historical record, *flutist* (the more natural formation) was first recorded in 1603, and *flautist* (adapted from Italian *flautista*) in 1860.

flavour. So spelt in BrE (also *flavourful, flavouring, flavourless, flavoursome,* but *flavorous*). In AmE, **flavor** is usual for the root word and in all the derivatives.

fledgling, not *fledgeling* is the recommended and more usual spelling both for a young bird that has just fledged, and when used as a modifier, as in *fledgling democracy.*

fleshy, fleshly. From medieval times onwards the two words have been interchangeable in most of their possible senses, but in the 21c. there is generally a clear distinction between them. *Fleshy* primarily means 'having a large proportion of flesh, plump' (*fleshy hands*), '(of fruit) pulpy', or 'like flesh' (*fleshy pink, softness*, etc.). *Fleshly* means 'sensual, carnal, lascivious' (*fleshly desire, lusts*, etc.), or 'unspiritual, worldly' (*not with fleshly wisedome, but by the grace of God*—2 Cor. (AV) 1: 12; *vainely puft vp by his fleshly minde*—Col. (AV) 2: 18).

fleur-de-lis, heraldic lily. This is the recommended spelling, not *fleur-de-lys* (a common variant) or *flower-de-luce* (as sometimes in AmE). The recommended pronunciation is /ˌflɜːdəˈliː/. Plural *fleurs-de-lis* (pronounced like the singular).

flier, flyer. See FLYER, FLIER.

floatation. See FLOTATION.

flor. (abbrev.). See FLORUIT.

flora. See FAUNA, FLORA.

florilegium, an anthology. Plural *florilegia.* See -UM 3.

floruit /ˈflɒrʊɪt/ is a Latin verb (3rd singular perfect indicative of *flōrēre* 'to flourish') meaning 'he or she flourished'. It is used with a date or dates when a writer, painter, etc., is believed to have been alive and working, but the exact dates are not accurately known, e.g. *Arnold Bronckhorst, or Bronckorst or Van Bronckhorst* (floruit *1565–83).* It is set in italic, with a space before the dates, and is often abbreviated to *fl.* (preferably) or *flor.* It is occasionally used as a noun: *The date of each Author's* 'floruit' *is added in the margin*—Liddell and Scott, 1843.

flotation. In the early 19c. *floatation* emerged as a hybrid formation (from the native word *float* + *-ation,* a suffix of classical origin). It was soon joined by the etymologically unjustifiable form *flotation,* introduced to conform with *flotilla, flotsam,* etc., and *rotation.* The spelling *flotation* is now much more frequent for both the financial meaning and the action of floating, although the original spelling is recognized by dictionaries as a legitimate variant.

flotsam and jetsam. The traditional distinction is between goods found afloat in the sea (*flotsam*) and goods found on land after being cast ashore (*jetsam*). *Flotsam* is a rationalized form of Anglo-French *floteson* (modern Fr. *flottaison*); and *jetsam* is a contracted form of *jettison. Flotsam* is first recorded in the early 17c., and *jetsam* in 1570. Although the two words are very strongly associated, in the *OEC* data they occur together only in one third of all examples of *flotsam,* and in two thirds of examples of *jetsam.* In combination or separately either word can refer metaphorically to objects or people viewed as of little value, though *flotsam* is rather more commonly so used. Given the difference in meaning of the words, the last example below strikes an odd note. Examples: *There are cell phones, TVs, toys, gadgets, trinkets, clothes, and appliances—all the flotsam and jetsam upon which America's standard of living now rests—Financial Sense Online,* 2005 (AmE); *Inggs has for some time been collecting detritus and flotsam from an area a short distance from Cape Town where he spends a lot of time—ArtThrob,* 2000 (SAfr.); *Disney's live-action division has a history of releasing cinematic flotsam, but this is one occasion when they have unearthed a rare gem—ReelViews,* 2002 (AmE); *All in all, it's a standard picture of urban despair. Except that this collection of human jetsam contains several specimens of an altogether better-heeled class of lush—Business Week,* 2001 (AmE); *?But like lefties everywhere, clinging to whatever jetsam keeps us afloat, I believe every revolution ere now was betrayed—Backword* weblog, 2005 (BrE).

flounder, founder. 1 *Founder* is the earlier of the two words, and was borrowed into Middle English from Old French *fondrer* ('to collapse, fall in ruins'). The origin of *flounder,* first recorded in 1592, is uncertain, although it may be an onomatopoeic adaptation of *founder,* the combination *fl* at the beginning of a word typically suggesting, as Liberman (2005) puts it, 'unsteady light and quivering motion' as in *flit, flicker, flutter, flip,* etc.

2 These two words are easily confused because they are similar in form and overlap in meaning. The physical meaning of *flounder* is 'to struggle in mud or while wading' and hence 'to stumble or move clumsily'. From these meanings developed two abstract senses 'to show or feel great confusion; to be out of one's depth' and 'to be in great difficulty'. To *founder* physically refers to a ship filling with water and sinking, and in the abstract to a plan, scheme, intention, etc., coming to nothing or failing. Typically, things like economies, careers and negotiations *flounder*, as can people, while things like marriages and relationships *founder*, often *on* something. It is usually *flounder* which is wrongly used instead of *founder*, as in the last two examples below. The following examples are intended to illustrate and clarify the differences. It may also be helpful to bear in mind, as Partridge pointed out, that if something founders 'it breaks down completely ... while one who flounders is still functioning'. Examples: (flounder = struggle as if in mud) *The family physician bucks the case to a psychosomaticist, who flounders in jargon—Time*, 1971; (= show confusion) *'You'll feel better later on,' he floundered*—H. Forrester, 1990; (= be in difficulty) *Despite a financially secure face put forth by executive director Gray Montague, the company was floundering in $800,000 of accumulated red ink—Dance Magazine*, 2005; *In 1979 he left* The New York Times *under controversial circumstances, and his career floundered in the 1980s—Columbia Journalism Review*, 2005. (founder = sink) *I wanted to leave England ... I did not intend to be aboard when that particular Titanic finally foundered in a sea of bureaucracy*—K. Hagenbach, 1980; (= fail) *Without ... help, the marriage may founder, thus providing ... another dire example to romantic young people that 'arranged marriages are best'*—P. Caplan, 1985; *There are concerns that Irish demands for its own commissioner could founder on opposition from Germany and the Benelux countries—Guardian*, 2005; (= come to nothing) *Alfred's quest to obtain a vital set of aerial photographs has foundered in a Kafkaesque comedy of setbacks and misunderstandings—Times*, 2006. (*flounder* used for *founder*) **Creativity, once a hallmark of primary education, floundered on the exams altar—Times Educational Supplement*, 2007; **Bit by bit, season by season, he is removing the remnants of those anguished days when a promising career floundered on the rocks—Scotland on Sunday*, 2005.

flout. See FLAUNT.

flower-de-luce. See FLEUR-DE-LIS.

fluky (adj.) = lucky. Is more commonly spelt without an *e* than with, but both spellings are correct. See -EY AND -Y IN ADJECTIVES 2.

flunkey, a usually derogatory term for a liveried servant or (in extended use) a toady. This is the recommended spelling, not *flunky*. Plural *flunkeys*.

flutist. See FLAUTIST.

fluty. Is more commonly spelt without an *e* than with, but both spellings are correct. See -EY AND -Y IN ADJECTIVES 2.

fly. The noun is used as a collective of any of various small flies or aphids that infest garden or orchard plants, especially *fruit fly, greenfly* (*the roses are infested with greenfly* not *greenflies*).

flyer, flier. *Flyer* is the more common form across all varieties of English. In British English it is the recommended spelling for all senses, and is obligatory for the handbill meaning. In BrE it is used at least twice as often as *flier*, including in the phrase *to get off to a flyer* (= to get off to a flying start). In AmE the two forms are on a roughly equal footing, but in the phrase *to take a flier on* something, meaning to speculate adventurously on something, *flier* is more frequent. *High-flyer* is rather more common than *high-flier* everywhere and should be hyphenated. Examples: (flyer) *Don's customer put flyers up at Carnegie-Mellon University that July—The New Farm*, 2003 (AmE); *Arkell, who got off to a flyer in this year's GP race—Scotsman*, 2001; *I had done an MBA and was considered a high-flyer by my employers. But one day I just decided I could not spend the rest of my life marketing fridges*—William Dalrymple, 2005; *But $350 is just too much for people to take a flyer on—The Hot Blog*, 2008 (AmE); *But maybe the economy will be so bad they'll take a flyer on Obama*—weblog, 2008 (AmE); (flier) *York City manager Terry Dolan stressed the importance of getting off to a flier against Rushden tomorrow—The Press* (York), 2001 (BrE); *And whether we can take a flier on this skinny guy with the strange name and braided ancestry to help us get it back—NYT*, 2008.

fob off is used in two main constructions: **1** (followed by *with* a thing) to deceive into accepting something inferior (*customers have been fobbed off with battery-hen eggs described simply as 'farm eggs'*).

2 (followed by *on* or *upon* a person) to palm or pass off (an inferior thing) (*a well-hyped novel can be fobbed off on readers even though it is poorly written*).

fo'c'sle is a much reduced form of *forecastle* (the forward part of a ship where the crew has quarters). It is one of the few words to have internal apostrophes. The full form as well as the reduced one are both pronounced /ˈfəʊksəl/.

focus. 1 The plural of the noun in general use is *focuses,* and in scientific use most often *foci* /ˈfəʊsʌɪ/.

2 The inflected forms of the verb are according to rule *focused, focuses, focusing,* but forms with *-ss-* are used by many printers and publishers. See DOUBLING OF CONSONANTS WITH SUFFIXES 2.

foetid. See FETID.

foetus, fetus. Medical usage in Britain and the US favours **fetus**, following the word's origin in Latin *fētus* 'offspring' (cf. *effete* from L *effētus* 'that has brought forth young'; hence worn out by bearing children). In AmE this spelling is preferred generally, but *foetus* is still common in non-medical use in BrE, largely because of the misconception that the *-e-* spelling is some kind of Americanism; but *fetus* is gradually taking over. The corresponding adjective is **fetal** in AmE and medical usage, with **foetal** becoming less common in BrE even in general use.

fogey, fogy. The second spelling was formerly the dominant one (Thackeray and Charles Kingsley, for example, wrote about *old fogies,* thereby implying a singular form *fogy*), but with the advent of the *young fogey* in the 20c. the spelling with *-ey* is now the more common of the two. However, the plural *fogies* is more often used than *fogeys,* which is the form corresponding to *fogey.*

föhn, a hot southerly wind on the northern slopes of the Alps. So spelt (rather than *foehn*) and printed in roman. The German original is *Föhn.*

foist is used in two constructions according to the meaning being conveyed: **1** if you *foist* something *on* or *upon* someone, you pass it off as genuine or superior when it isn't (*inferior articles foisted on the general public at exorbitant prices*); if you *foist* something or someone *on* or *upon* someone, you force them to accept an unnecessary or unwelcome thing or person (*she had no desire to have an elderly relative foisted on her*). The most frequently used preposition is *on,* followed by *upon,* and occasionally *onto.* The phrasal verb *foist off* is standard in American English, according to *MWCDEU,* but is unusual in BrE, e.g. *whose woeful activities smack of the same mentality that foisted McCarthyism off on an unwary public*—*OEC,* 2002 (AmE).

2 A rather less common and somewhat old-fashioned meaning 'to introduce surreptitiously or unwarrantably' is followed by *in* or *into* (*he was eventually foisted into the see of Durham; Dylan writes that he detested being foisted into the role as a spokesman for the protest generation and took every opportunity to sabotage that status*). Fowler (1926) cited an example of *foist* being used in a construction which is typical of *fob off* (*The general public is much too easily foisted off with the old cry of the shopman that 'there's no demand for that kind of thing'*) but the *OEC* data does not suggest that this confusion is at all usual.

folio. Plural *folios.* See -O(E)S 4.

folk as an ordinary word for people in general is tending to fall out of use in British English, except in northern England, and Scotland, where it is standard, but it survives strongly in certain specific uses: **1** to suggest a greater degree of affection than *people* does: *Even folk who know little about Scotland have probably heard of the Trossachs*—*Scottish World,* 1989.

2 as the last element in certain compounds and fixed expressions, or qualified by a preceding adjective, e.g. *menfolk, north-country folk, townsfolk, womenfolk.* In general use, however, even these can be somewhat jokey, patronizing, precious, or dated: *What Ursula brought home every week made all the difference to the old folk*—David Lodge, 1991; *The working folk of Lancashire have much in common, of course, with their Yorkshire neighbours*—J. B. Priestley, 1934.

3 in the plural (usually *folks*) to mean one's parents or relatives: *The folks wouldn't like it much*—R. J. Conley, 1986 (AmE).

4 in the singular as an elliptical form of *folk music*.

5 in attributive combinations, some of which are loan-translations from German, e.g. *folk dance, folk dancing, folk memory, folk singer, folk song, folk tale*; and especially *folklore*.

6 *Folks* is also used as a light-hearted form of address to the public by entertainers, and this is sometimes imitated by journalists. *Folks* and the singular form *folk* are still strongly entrenched in AmE in private and public life. Examples: *Yes folks, in 1990, 2,245 people were murdered in the city of New York*—B. Levin, 1991 (BrE); (US examples) *that's all folks!* (the concluding line, written on the screen, of a Warner Bros. cartoon series called *Merry Melodies* from 1930 onwards, according to Nigel Rees, 1990); *now that folks'd had time to go home and have supper, a few more customers had started to come in*—R. J. Conley, 1986.

folk etymology, can mean (i) 'the process by which the form of an unfamiliar or foreign word or phrase is modified in order to make it seem to be derived from a more familiar word or words' and (ii) 'a popular but mistaken account of the origin of a word or phrase'. Examples of (i) are not uncommon and include: *hiccough* (a later spelling of *hiccup* under the mistaken impression that the second syllable was *cough*); *tawdry* (from a silk 'lace' or necktie associated with the East Anglian saint *St Audrey*, much worn by women in the 16c. and early 17c.; the final *t* of 'Saint' wrongly carried across to the name); *under weigh* (an alteration of original *under way*); *Welsh rarebit* (first recorded in 1785 as 'an etymologizing alteration' of the earlier *Welsh rabbit*); and *cockroach* from Spanish *cucaracha*. The classic example of the second kind is the belief that *posh* is formed from the initials of *port out starboard home*, referring to the more comfortable accommodation on ships formerly sailing between England and India. See also ETYMOLOGY; FACETIOUS FORMATIONS.

follow. See AS FOLLOWS.

following has long been used as a participial adjective either qualifying a noun, as in *for the following reasons*, or by itself as a quasi-noun, as in *The following are my reasons*. From this has developed a use of *following* as a preposition independent of any noun: *Used car prices are going up, following the Budget*—*Observer*, 1968. This use was not a problem for Fowler (1926) but Gowers (1965) condemned it in cases where the connection between the two events is 'merely temporal' and the preposition *after* would serve. In the example just given, there is a strong element of consequence, and so the use of *following* is perhaps justified, but this is not so in the example that follows, in which *after* could have been used with no loss of meaning: *Members are invited to take tea in the Convocation Coffee House, University Church, Radcliffe Square, following the meeting*—*AGM announcement, Friends of the Bodleian Library*, 1991. In some cases there is even a possibility of ambiguity with other meanings of *following*: *Police have arrested a man following extensive inquiries.*

font. (in typography) see FOUNT, FONT.

foolscap, a size of folio writing- or printing-paper of a kind that originally bore a watermark representing a fool's cap. The old spelling *fool's-cap* has long since been discarded. Inevitably, the word is sometimes misspelt **fullscap*.

foot (noun). The normal plural *feet* alternates with *foot* when used as a unit of length or height: *She is six feet/foot tall; a plank ten feet/foot long.* When such a phrase is used attributively a hyphen is normally placed between the numeral and *foot; a 12-foot dinghy*. In contexts in which the number of inches is also given, *foot* is more common than *feet*: *C.A.* [a West Indian fast bowler] *is six foot eight.*

foot (verb). The traditional use of *foot* or *foot up* in contexts of reckoning the total of an account, a bill, etc., has passed out of standard use, but has left behind it *to foot the bill* (first recorded in 1819).

footprint. First recorded in the 16c., *footprint* has for several centuries been largely confined to its literal meaning, with only occasional figurative uses (as in Longfellow's 'We can make our lives sublime, and, departing, leave behind us Footprints on the sands of time'—*A Psalm of Life*, 1838). Then in the 1980s it developed a special meaning which is redolent of the times we live in: 'an environmental consequence of human activity in terms of pollution, damage to ecosystems, and depletion of natural resources' (*OED*). A *carbon footprint* is a measure of the carbon emissions of a particular individual, organization, or community. Other frequent compounds with *footprint* include *ecological footprint* and *environmental footprint*, which both refer to a measure of the impact of a person, community, or organization on the environment in terms of resource use, especially expressed as the area of land in hectares required to sustain a prevailing pattern of production and consumption.

for. 1 Used between clauses as a coordinating conjunction, *for* should normally be preceded by a comma or a semi-colon. Examples: *You had best spare her, sir, for she's your son's wife*—Thackeray, 1847/8; *My father was silently upset when I married a Campbell, for perhaps nowhere else as in Scotland are memories so deep*—H. M. Brown, 1986; *I hated walking through the woods; it was gloomy and damp, for the sun could hardly shine through the tops of trees*—*New Yorker*, 1989; *I wanted a setting for my own little life, for I did not think that I should know too many people*—A. Brookner, 1990; *That Yeltsin had called for Gorbachev's resignation only a few days before made the publication of the joint declaration all the more dramatic; for it said, in effect, that whatever their former differences, the signers* [etc.]—*NY Rev. Bks*, 1991. But this 'rule' is sometimes not followed when the linked sentences are fairly short: *The 1941 war had affected him little for he was over forty and his employers claimed that he was indispensable*—G. Greene, 1985; *he did not cry any more for it did not help*—D. Matthee, 1986.

2 In American English a number of verbs can be used with the conjunction *for* to introduce a non-finite clause: *No. I didn't intend for you to find out*—J. McInerny, 1985; *Let's face it, I can't afford for that bike to break down*—*New Yorker*, 1986; *I didn't like for Drew to be back there with him while I was driven like the baggage*—E. L. Doctorow, 1989. In BrE other constructions would be used instead (*I didn't intend that you should find out*, etc.).

foramen /fəˈreɪmɛn/, (anatomy) an opening or hole, esp. in a bone. Plural *foramina* /-ˈramɪnə/.

for- and fore-. A The prefix *for-* occurs in a number of words formed in Old English, such as *forbid*, *forget* and *forgive*, as detailed at B below. It is no longer an active prefix used to form new words. *Fore-* is a native English prefix and is widely used to form verbs and nouns from existing words in the general meanings 'before, in front' with regard both to space and to time. To avoid misspelling words beginning with one or other prefix, it may help to make a mental link between *fore-* and *before*, in order to use *fore-* correctly in words embodying the idea of 'before, in front of', and to remember a common word expressing that idea, such as *forecast* or *forefront*. If a word does not embody that idea, *for-* will be the correct spelling. The phrase 'forgive and forget' may also be a useful aide-memoire for *for-* verbs, as people do not tend to misspell those two words. Particular care needs to be taken with words which have both spellings but with different meanings: see FOREGOING, FOREGONE, FORGO; FORBEAR, FOREBEAR.

B Words with the prefix *for-* fall into two main groups:

1 Those already formed by the end of the OE period: in these the prefix has at least four meanings: away, off, apart (*forget, forgive*), prohibition (*forbid, forfend*), abstention or neglect (*forbear, forbid, forgo, forsake, forswear*), excess or intensity (*forlorn*). *For-* in these cases is related to an Old Germanic prefix whose descendant *ver-* is found in modern German in *vergessen, verlassen, vermissen*, etc. ('forget', 'leave', 'miss').

2 A smaller group, now almost all obsolete, adopted from Old French, where *for-* ultimately represents Latin *forīs* 'outside' (†*forcatch, forfeit*). *Foreclose* belongs in this group and was at first spelt *forclose*, but at a later date was respelt as *fore-*.

C Those with the prefix *fore-* contain a native prefix with the sense 'before' (in time, position, order, or rank). Some of the main types show the following senses: in front (*foreshorten*), beforehand (*foretell, forewarn*), situated in front of (*forecourt*), the front part of (*forearm, forehead*), near the bow of a ship (*forecastle*), preceding (*forebear, forefather, forerunner*).

forasmuch as. If the need should arise to write or print this archaic conjunction, this is the form it should take.

forbear, forebear. 1 *Forbear* is a verb (pronounced with the stress on the second syllable) meaning 'to abstain from, go without' and is usually followed by *to* + infinitive or *from* + verb in *-ing*: *He did not enquire after their progress and Nutty forbore to mention it*—K. M. Peyton, 1988; *Naturally he couldn't forbear from upsetting me*—W. Self, 1993.

Its past form is *forbore* and its past participle is *forborn.*

2 *Forebear* is a noun (pronounced with the stress on the first syllable) meaning 'an ancestor': *Henry Carew had chosen the Church as some of his forebears had done*—T. Hayden, 1991; *An early forebear went to Chicago and made a fortune in the grain business*—*Daily Mail,* 2007. *Forebear* is also used figuratively: *Writing with what at times seems near-compulsive erudition, he details the philosophical and political forebears and descendants of just about every significant thinker whose work has any relevance to science or policy*—*Times Higher Education Supplement,* 2000.

The situation is complicated somewhat by the fact that most dictionaries allow *forbear* as a variant of *forebear,* but the advice here is to maintain the distinction. Those with an eye for such things, and any good editor, will balk at the two being confused.

forbid. 1 The past tense of this verb from the Old English word stock is most commonly *forbade,* but the spelling *forbad* occasionally occurs and is allowable; indeed, it was the form given precedence by the *OED* in 1897. *Forbade* is traditionally pronounced /fəˈbad/ (fuh-**bad**) but the pronunciation /fəˈbeɪd/ (fuh-**bayd**) also occurs and cannot be said to be wrong.

2 One of the central uses of the verb is with *to* + infinitive (*he was forbidden to watch television after 9 p.m.; I forbid you to go*). A construction with *from* + a verbal form in *-ing* has also been used since the 16c., and is now standard, (despite Fowler's objections), though less common than the first construction: *Current laws forbid a company from operating a reactor even after it has been built*—*New Scientist,* 1991. Visser also cites a use of *forbid* followed by an unprotected gerund (*The petition asked the king to forbid villeins sending their children to school*—S. J. Curtis, 1948), and that construction occasionally occurs, but is best regarded as non-standard: *?Remember though that Google's* Adsense *terms strictly forbid you designing web sites purely with the intention of earning* Adsense *income*—*www.articlealley.com,* 2005.

forceful, forcible. 1 The main use of *forceful* is in the meaning 'vigorous, powerful', whereas *forcible* means primarily 'done by or using force'. *Forceful* is used of people as well as actions, whereas *forcible* is used only of actions. Fowler (1926) defined the difference in meaning as follows, and the definition is useful: 'while *forcible* conveys that force rather than something else is present, *forceful* conveys that much as opposed to little force is used or shown; compare *forcible ejection* with *a forceful personality.*' This pair of related words that overlap slightly in meaning are usually kept apart, but sometimes swap places. Examples: (*forceful* correctly used) *it might be easier to ... start again from scratch, crystallizing a lifetime's experience into a hundred forceful pages?*—I. Murdoch, 1976; *He wanted to be forceful—and had an inclination to be yielding*—C. Whistler, 1985; *He was strong and his resources of stamina enabled him to play just as forcefully in the final ten minutes of a game as in the first ten*—S. Studd, 1981; *There will probably be one or two forceful characters who will try to dominate the proceedings*—*Times,* 2001; (*forcible* used correctly) *He favoured the forcible sterilization of criminals, diseased and insane persons, and 'worthless race-types'*—J. R. Baker, 1971; *Section 47 of the National Assistance Act 1948 allows for the forcible removal from their own homes of elderly people who are not mentally ill*—O. Stevenson et al., 1990; *She was lightly mugged and forcibly deprived of some expensive clip-on earrings*—*Independent,* 2002. (*forcible* for *forceful*) *Vaughan has spoken forcibly about the confusion caused by split captains*—*Daily Telegraph,* 2007; (*forceful* for *forcible*) *the contention of the mothers that forceful removal can have both significant short-term and long-lasting harm, particularly for younger children*—*NY Times,* 2008.

2 For the distinction between *forceable* and *forcible,* see -ABLE, -IBLE 4.

forceps. The form ending in *-s* is both singular and plural. Some mistake it for a plural, and create the singular **forcep.*

fore. *To the fore* was originally a Scottish and Anglo-Irish phrase meaning (*a*) (of a person) present, on the spot, within call; (*b*) still surviving, alive; (*c*) (of money) ready, available. The phrase came into English literary use during the 19c., but in standard

English now is used only in the sense 'into view, to the front'. A person is said to have 'come to the fore' when he or she has come into prominence or has become conspicuous for any reason.

fore-. See FOR- AND FORE-.

forebear. See FORBEAR, FOREBEAR.

forecast. After much rivalry between *forecast* and *forecasted* as past tense and participle, the first has carried the day, but by a somewhat smaller margin that that which separates, for example, *broadcast* and *broadcasted*. Many will consider *forecasted* wrong, but it is recognized as valid in some BrE and AmE dictionaries, and there are sound linguistic reasons for its existence, discussed at PODCAST.

Both verb and noun are pronounced with the stress on the first syllable.

forecastle. See FO'C'SLE.

foreclose and its derivative **foreclosure** are spelt with the prefix *fore-* even though they do not contain the idea of 'before'. See FOR- AND FORE- B 2.

foregather. See FORGATHER, FOREGATHER.

forego. See FOR- AND FORE-; FOREGOING; FOREGONE; FORGO, FOREGO.

foregoing meaning 'preceding, previously mentioned' is an adjective corresponding to the verb *forego* 'to precede'. To spell it *forgoing* is a mistake that not even the most liberal dictionaries recognize. Example: *The foregoing is proof that local government is delivering at the regional level—Glasgow Herald*, 2003; **for the forgoing reasons, the application is dismissed—Ontario Superior Court Decisions*, 2004. See also FOR- AND FORE-.

foregone means 'previous, completed' and is used mainly in the expression *foregone conclusion*, meaning 'an easily foreseen or predictable result': *Given the anecdotal evidence—just ask that taxi driver, won't you?—the outcome of such an investigation was a foregone conclusion—Times*, 2001. The spelling *forgone* in this meaning is incorrect. See also FOR- AND FORE-.

forehead. The older pronunciation /ˈfɒrɪd/ rhyming with *horrid* is very much on the decline. The third edition of the *Longman Pronunciation Dictionary* suggests that two thirds of British speakers, especially younger ones, prefer the spelling pronunciation /ˈfɔːhɛd/.

foreign words. 1 Throughout its history, English has borrowed words from other languages, initially Latin, Old French, and Greek, later from dozens if not hundreds of others. The standard issues they raise, together with some instances, recent and otherwise, are: how they are to be pronounced, e.g. *chorizo, macho*; how they are to be spelt, e.g. *bijou, bruschetta, faeces, yoghurt*; in what form they are to be adopted or correctly used, e.g. *criterion, panini, stratum*; what are their plurals, e.g. *curriculum, octopus, referendum*; and, whether they are to be printed in italics or roman, e.g. 'bête noire' (roman) versus *au courant* in italics. For guidance on these matters, see the individual entries throughout the book.

2 Fowler's 1926 article on this topic was titled 'foreign danger', by which he meant mainly the danger posed by people mistaking the meaning of such words. Modern examples of this are *cui bono* and *hoi polloi*. Apart from that issue, it is also important to consider whether one's readers, viewers, or listeners will be familiar with the borrowed word or phrase. If not, it should be avoided. As Fowler said about French words, 'to use ... words that your reader or hearer does not know or does not fully understand ... is inconsiderate and rude'. This is a wise admonition that Boris Johnson would have done well to respect in a Channel Four interview on 24 June 2013, when he paraded the German word *Schwerpunkt* (= focus, main emphasis), although he then glossed it. See also Æ, Œ; FRENCH WORDS; GERMAN; ITALIAN SOUNDS; LATIN PLURALS.

forename. See CHRISTIAN NAME.

forenoon, recorded since the early 16c. in the sense 'the portion of the day before noon', is now falling into disuse. *COD* (1995) labels it *'archaic* exc. *Law* & *Naut.'*, and the OEC suggests it lingers on quaintly particularly in Indian English. Examples: *He employed her on a variety of minor jobs in the forenoon and at lunch time he dismissed her for the day*—N. Shute, 1955; *He had been going there every forenoon for as long as anyone could remember*—A. N. Wilson, 1985; *They devoted the forenoon of Monday giving interviews to media persons—The Hindu*, 2003.

***foresake, *foresaken,** etc. are incorrect spellings of *forsake, forsaking,* etc. See FOR- AND FORE-.

forever, for ever. 1 In World English and American English this adverb is generally written as one word, and that is the only form shown, for example, in the *Merriam-Webster Unabridged.* In British English the spelling rules are in theory more complicated and vary according to the meaning, as explained at 2 below. The simplest recommendation would be for all writers to write it as one word in all contexts, except if they are bound by a style guide which states otherwise. However, writing it as two words could strike readers from other varieties of English than BrE as odd. Conversely writing it as one word may upset some BrE readers. Though there is an argument for using the two-word form in the extended phrases mentioned at 4 below, even in them *forever* is more frequent in *OEC* data.

2 The meanings can be broadly defined as: (i) 'for all future time, permanently' (*he said he would love her for ever/forever*); (ii) used as an exaggeration, 'a very long time' (*it will take forever to wash all these dishes*); (iii) 'incessantly, persistently' (*the children are forever asking for more pocket money; they are forever complaining about the rent*). In type (iii) sentences there is 'a subjective feeling of disapproval of the action described' (*CGEL*). The BrE monolingual dictionaries *ODO* and *Collins* show *forever* as the headword, and *for ever* as an alternative for meaning (i) only, as does *NODWE*. The *Guardian* style guide goes further and suggests *for ever* as the rule for meaning (i). The original 1897 entry in the *OED* labelled *forever* as chiefly US, except for the meaning 'incessantly'.

3 In his 1926 edition of this book, Fowler did not mention the issue. However, the humorous poem *Forever* (1872) by the Victorian poet C. H. Calverley suggests that the question was already in the air well before Fowler's time. It mocks the trend towards joining the two words:

> Forever! passion-fraught, it throws
> O'er the dim page a gloom, a glamour:
> It's sweet, it's strange; and I suppose
> It's grammar.
> Forever! 'T is a single word!
> And yet our fathers deemed it two:
> Nor am I confident they erred;—
> Are you?

Gowers (1965) quoted from that poem, and took the view that *for ever* was safe. Current usage has, however, proved him wrong: in all varieties of English *forever* is now overwhelmingly written as one word, even when it corresponds to meaning (i) described above, and even in BrE.

4 *For ever* is first recorded in the *OED* from *c.*1330. It was used from the dates indicated in various strengthened forms: *for ever and ay* (14c.), *for ever and a day* (mid-16c.), *for ever and ever* (early 17c.), *for evermore* (14c.). *Forever* as one word is first recorded by the *OED* from 1670. Examples: *on the morning they left Pittsburgh forever*—*New Yorker,* 1990. *Is that why they last, why they lodge with some adults for ever?*—*Independent,* 2012 (BrE); *thoughts so precious they were recorded rather than left to float around in the ether of one's mind and eventually vanish forever*—*Theatre People,* 2010 (Aust.).

foreword, preface. *Preface* is the traditional word (first recorded in the 14c.) for an introduction (by the author) to a literary work. *Foreword* is a late-coming word. It was brought into the language by professional philologists in the 19c. to mean simply 'a word or words said before something else' and then 'an introduction (to a literary work)'. Practice varies from book to book and some other terms are also used, e.g. Prefatory Note, Introduction. In the course of the 20c., however, especially for scholarly and technical works, publishers have sometimes favoured the inclusion of both a Foreword (usually written by an authoritative or distinguished person other than the author) and a Preface written by the author. In such cases the Foreword is always placed before the Preface in the preliminary pages.

for free. Originally American, *for free* is now quite regularly used in BrE. Commentators object that it is pleonastic, in other words that *for* is superfluous. In many contexts, it is true, *free* on its own would work perfectly well, but in others it would not, as in the first of the following examples. Use it if it suits your style; avoid it if it doesn't. Examples: *You don't expect to be ill for free*—Godfrey Smith, 1957; *I'd love a research assistant, but you have to pay for them. And most people want me to do things for free!*—C. Tickell, 1991. So too with the originally AmE expression *for real*: *patents have been applied for, and it's for real*—*New Yorker,* 1957. A grammatically similar use, namely *for fair* 'completely, altogether', is restricted to AmE slang: *Then we danced and started on the beer for fair*—J. Kerouac, 1957.

forgather, foregather. The recommended spelling with initial *for-* rather than *fore-* might suggest that it is like other native words in *for-* (see FOR- AND FORE-). In fact it is a 16c. Scottish loanword from Dutch *vergaderen* used in the same sense, i.e. 'to assemble, meet together, associate'. In the *OED* citations the prefix is mainly spelt *for-,* and while the spelling with initial *fore-* is also used, it is not recommended; the word does not mean 'to gather in advance'.

forge has the derivative *forgeable.* See MUTE E.

forget has the derivative *forgettable.* See -T-, -TT-.

forgive has the derivative *forgivable.* See MUTE E.

forgo, forego. Both words are pronounced with the stress on the second syllable. *Forgo* means 'to go without, abstain from'; *forego* means 'to go before, precede' and occurs mostly in the forms **foregoing** and **foregone**. See also FOR- AND FORE- A. Example: *Just last month the firm's board decided to forgo six-figure performance bonuses after coming under political pressure—Daily Tel., 2012.*

forgot, used in BrE as a past participle instead of *forgotten* is now, except in regional speech, a deliberate archaism. It is sometimes used, beside *forgotten,* in AmE.

forlorn hope is an intriguing example of a loanword which has not only been reshaped to fit English, but has also undergone a major shift in meaning. Now used only in the sense 'a faint hope, an enterprise which has little hope of success', it has moved a long way from its first, military meaning. Originally it had nothing to do with the word *hope,* being a 16c. adaptation of Dutch *verloren hoop,* literally 'lost troop' (Dutch *hoop* is cognate with English *heap*). It was first used to mean 'a picked body of men, detached to the front to begin the attack'. Because of their exposed position, casualties and fatalities would inevitably be high, and examples contemporaneous with its use in the military sense show it also being used to mean people in a desperate condition. The current figurative sense, which was first recorded in 1641, may, according to the *OED,* have been wordplay, or simply a misunderstanding.

formal words. In Iris Murdoch's novel *The Message to the Planet* (1989) one of the characters is said to be *capable of solemnity, gravity, even gravitas,* the three nouns clearly representing a subtly ascending ladder of solemnness. The example may serve as an introduction to the notion that pairs or groups of nearly synonymous words, and the choices between them made by writers and speakers, are at the heart of the language. All modes of writing and speaking are marked by their level of vocabulary. At a surface level *peruse,* one can see, is a more formal word than *read, purchase* is more formal than *buy, luncheon* more formal than *lunch, purloin* more formal than *steal,* and *evince* more formal than *show.* The preference for one of these rather than the other is a matter of conscious contextual choice. Part of the distinction lies in the contrast between words of native origin and synonyms of (ultimately) classical origin: thus (with the native word placed first) the pairs *ask/enquire, bear/carry, begin/commence, drink/imbibe, gift/donation, hide/conceal,* etc. At other times it is just a matter of the contrast between a shorter word and a longer one: (none of them native words) *brave/valiant, pay/emolument, try/endeavour,* etc. And in practice the choice is rarely just between two words.

In his article 'The Five Clocks' (*Internat. Jrnl Amer. Linguistics,* 1962), Martin Joos identified five degrees or keys of style, which he called *frozen, formal, consultative, casual,* and *intimate.* His distinctions remain broadly true. The first may be observed, for example, in legal documents, the formal in (say) a philosophical monograph or in the pages of (say) the *London Review of Books,* and so on down to the intimate informality of the conversation of families and friends. The distinctions in the end are infinitely complex and not properly definable, but, as a working hypothesis, and no more than that, Joos's classification of degrees of linguistic formality is a good starting point. The subject is further developed in G. W. Turner's *Stylistics* (1973), who comments *inter alia* 'but five is an arbitrary number of steps to cut in a gradation from slang to ceremony'.

format. **1** The noun, in the 19c. and until about 1930 always /ˈfɔːmaː/, is now always pronounced /ˈfɔːmat/.

2 In computing the inflected forms of the verb are *formatted, formatting;* see -T-, -TT-.

former, latter. **1** These two words are used individually or contrastively (as *the former* and *the latter*) to refer to the first and second respectively of two people or things previously mentioned; in this role they are used attributively (before a noun) or, more usually, absolutely (with no noun following): *He had to be either a woman or a cross-dresser. His money was on the former*—J. Leavell, 2004; *My aunt advised me to steer clear of street scenes and go for parish churches or country houses. As a keen enthusiast of architecture, I went for the latter category*—*Derby Evening Telegraph,* 2005.

2 For the meaning of *former* contrasted with *latter,* there are several points of usage to consider: (*a*) In their contrastive uses, *former* and *latter* are more often used without a following noun: *The relationship between capitalist and non-capitalist modes is one of exploitation, in which the former creams off the surplus from the latter*—T. Cubitt, 1988. They are occasionally used attributively (*No one mentioned the latter point and only four teachers the former*—D. Pimm, 1988), but care needs to be taken in these cases to avoid possible ambiguity with the 'having been previously' meaning of *former*: the sentence *I am sure the former view will prevail* needs its context to clarify whether it is an earlier view or the first of two views that is intended. (*b*) *Former* (in particular) and *latter* should only be used in writing when they are close to what they refer back to, so that the reader is not forced to search back in order to establish the identity of the persons or things referred to. The following example probably stretches most readers' memory to its limit: *The most likely scenario is that The Devil Lady will strike you one of two ways: a rather plain, uninvolving exercise in tedium and excess, or a pleasant surprise that more than repays its meager asking price. If you experience the former reaction, you have wasted a nontrivial sum of cash, while the latter reaction means you are in for an inexpensive treat*—*DVD Verdict,* 2004. (*c*) Most usage guides insist that when more than two people or things are involved, *former* and *latter* should not be used; either *first* and *last* should be used, or the sentence should be rephrased. Usage shows, however, that in fact *latter* is much more often used in this way than in combination with *former.* There seems to me no principled reason why a sentence such as the following should be amended, since it is eminently clear to whom *the latter* refers. *Though her bibliography includes Hecht, Snyder, and Daiches, she omits the latter's first name*—*Modern Language Notes,* 1957. One could of course rephrase it as *Daiches' first name.* Possibly more objectionable is the use of former as in *there are three sorts of recruits ... The former of these probably joined with a view to an eventual captaincy*—*TLS,* 1949 where there is only a single noun, not a list. (*d*) When *former* and *latter* refer to something in the plural, they are regarded as plural in turn, and verbs are in the plural: *The former describe events which are possible if not mundane, while the latter are metaphors*—J. Empson, 1989.

formidable. The established pronunciation is with the main stress on the first syllable, but second-syllable stressing is often heard in British English, and a limited opinion poll by J. C. Wells (2008) revealed a slight preference for *formídable* in BrE, though not in AmE.

formula. As regards the two possible plural forms, *formulae* and *formulas,* the traditional distinction is that *formulas* should be used in general writing and *formulae* /-liː/ (-lee) in mathematical and scientific contexts, but analysis of the *OEC* data shows that *formulas* is increasingly the dominant form in both technical and general uses.

forte. There are two distinct though etymologically related words with this spelling: **1** the noun meaning 'a person's strong point' (from French, ultimately from Latin *fortis* 'strong') is generally pronounced /ˈfɔːteɪ/ or /ˈfɔːti/, (**faw**-tay or **faw**-ti). Some people still use the older pronunciation /fɔːt/ (**fawt**), and insist that it is the only correct one. The plural is *fortes.*

2 The adjective and adverb *forte* come from Italian *forte* (= strong, loud) and are an instruction in music to play a passage loudly or strongly. It is pronounced in an anglicized manner as /ˈfɔːti/ (**faw**-ti) or in a more Italian manner as /ˈfɔːteɪ/ (**faw**-tay). It is also used as a noun meaning such a passage, and the plural is again *fortes.*

forth. The phrase *and so forth* is a less common and somewhat more literary alternative for *and so on*, used after the enumeration of items that could be continued but, since the point has been made, need not be. It is worth retaining as a language curio some of Burchfield's remarks on the matter. 'My impression is that *and so forth* is the option usually chosen by foreigners when they read their conference papers in English, reflecting their own formulas, *und so weiter, et ainsi de suite,* etc. . . . I pointed out to Professor John Bayley that he had used *and so forth* (*Shakespeare was a playwright, actor, and so forth*) and that his wife, Iris Murdoch, on the same occasion had used *and so on.* Dame Iris felt that there was a slight and probably definable distinction, probably arising from the buried assertiveness of *forth* in phrases like *go forth, set forth,* and so on.'

forties. See NINETIES.

fortissimo. When used as a noun (= a passage of music to be played very loudly) the plural is either *fortissimos* or (as in Italian) *fortissimi.*

fortuitous. 1 *The issue.* Many people object to *fortuitous* used as a high-falutin' synonym for *fortunate.* Fowler (1926) first noted this use, condemning it as a malapropism, brought about 'through mere sound'. He cited *I must say I should not have expected so fortuitous a termination of a somewhat daring experiment,* where, clearly, writerly pretension has replaced a simple word with a flowery one. Later critics followed Fowler in their condemnation, a condemnation echoed by one of Burchfield's friends in 1987: 'How sad it will be to lose "fortuitous" to the Visigoths.' The next sections discuss whether the word has indeed been looted and pillaged.

2 *Original meaning.* The word entered the language in the mid-17c., with the meaning 'that happens or is produced by chance, accidental'. The Cambridge Platonist Henry More wrote about *the fortuitous concourse of Atoms,* Addison of *fortuitous Events,* and Walter Scott of *a fortuitous rencontre.* For them, and for later writers, *fortuitous* meant 'by chance, by fortune', in keeping with the Latin roots of the word, *fors* 'chance' and *forte* 'by chance'. The derivatives *fortuitously, fortuitousness,* and *fortuity* also established themselves, always in contexts involving accident or chance: *Wiles, Trech'ry, Lies, Guilt, Flattery, Deceit, Like Atoms here fortuitously meet,* wrote Bishop Thomas Ken in 1711. Charles Reade, in *The Cloister and the Hearth* (1860), remarked that *one of the company, by some immense fortuity, could read.*

This meaning persists, as exemplified in: *His presence is not fortuitous. He has a role to play; and you will see him again*—A. Brink, 1979; *Quite fortuitously, Morse lights upon a set of college rooms which he had no original intention of visiting*—C. Dexter, 1983.

3 *An intermediate meaning: = 'happening by lucky chance'.* Things stood as described above until the middle of the 20c. Then something happened. From about 1920, and increasingly from about the middle of the century, the word began to be used as a near-synonym for *fortunate.* The relevant *OED* entry was unrevised at the time of drafting this, so examples are lacking, but even so this development in meaning seems easy to understand. Events that are remarked upon as happening by chance will often have fortunate outcomes, and so the link between something happening by chance, and happening by a *fortunate* chance was forged. A recent example is *She called for help—to her party's health spokesman, . . . with whom, most fortuitously, she had been dining minutes earlier—Guardian,* 2007. This use, which has been around for many decades now, is accepted by several dictionaries, including *ODO*, which defines it as 'happening by a lucky chance'.

4 = *'fortunate'.* This was the use that Fowler was the first to comment on. It, like the previous one, is well established, and is recognized in Merriam-Webster, but many other dictionaries do not include it. This is the meaning that will ruffle feathers the most. An argument in its favour is that it actually often conveys rather more than the obvious synonyms *lucky* and *fortunate.* Examples (from *MWCDEU*): *This circumstance was a fortuitous one for Abraham Lockwood*—J. O'Hara, 1965; *But from a cost standpoint, the company's timing is fortuitous—Business Week,* 1982; *The opening of his firm had come at an extremely fortuitous time—Atlantic Monthly,* 1984.

5 *Advice and ambiguity.* If you use *fortuitous* or its derivatives to mean anything other than 'coincidental', or 'happening by a lucky chance', you will upset some people's sensibilities. On a less emotional plane, you may also create sentences that are highly ambiguous. Because of the overlap of the three meanings discussed, it is impossible to tell if the sentence *The dossier was fortuitously found by a Labour staffer—Independent*, 2007, means that the discovery was a mere coincidence, a fortunate coincidence, or merely fortunate. As Burchfield commented: 'When an intrusive meaning contains a seed of ambiguity, it is advisable to stay with older ones.'

forum has two possible plural forms, *forums* and *fora*, the second reflecting the word's Latin origin. The first is several times more frequent in *OEC* data, and is preferable for all meanings other than 'a public square in an ancient Roman town or city'. However, *fora* is quite often used as the plural in technical or formal, particularly legal, writing, e.g. *Subsequently, in international fora, the United States opposed measures designed to promote economic and social rights*—International Human Rights in Context, 2000. When used as the plural of 'an Internet site where users can post comments about an issue', it creates a piquant discord between the ultramodern and the ancient, or is utterly pretentious, depending on your point of view: e.g. *They may well also seek advice from other crackers, through online fora or in chatrooms—OEC*, 2009. See -UM 3.

forward(s). 1 As adjective the standard spelling is *forward* (*forward movement, forward play* [in cricket], *sufficiently forward in walking; a very forward child for his age, a rather forward* [= presumptuous] *person*, etc.).

2 *forward* as adverb. (*a*) The distinction applying to other *-ward/-wards* pairs, e.g. *upward/upwards, northward/northwards*, namely that BrE prefers the form ending in *-s* for the adverb, while NAmer English prefers the shorter form, does not apply to *forwards*. The *OEC* data suggests that *forward* is more than 20 times more frequent than it overall, and is the preferred form in all varieties of English, including BrE. British and Irish English are the remaining strongholds of adverbial *forwards*, but even in those varieties *forward* is respectively 15 times and ten times more common.

(*b*) *Forward* is generally preferred in combination with verbs indicating movement, e.g. *lurch, lunge, leap, spring, surge*, etc. In many fixed expressions and phrasal verbs *forward* is obligatory: *bring forward* (= move; propose), *come forward* (= volunteer oneself), *look forward to, put forward* (= propose). And, of course, in the much maligned phrase *going forward*, e.g. *The critical question going forward will be whether average temperatures are above or below normal during the period.*

(*c*) In other meanings also there is a marked preference for *forward*: ('to the front, into prominence') *Hugh stepped forward. 'It's me, don't be frightened.'*—Mary Wesley, 1983; *Then Nigel Carew drew his sabre and thrust it into the hand of his youthful son and pushed him forward*—T. Hayden, 1991; ('in advance, ahead'); *Civilian volunteers from the town carried sacks of grenades forward to the men in action*—J. Ladd, 1979; ('onwards so as to make progress') *Rossi expressed surprise that the Commission was 'apparently no further forward than in 1984'*—C. Rose, 1990; *He had continually to be looking at his watch and calculating whether they were forward enough*—G. E. Evans, 1993; ('towards the future, continuously onwards') *The overall feeling is that the Jockey Club is genuinely concerned with helping the industry move forward—Independent*, 1989.

3 *forwards* as adverb. The set expression *backwards and forwards* is preferred in all varieties of English to *backward and forward*, except in AmE, where the two versions are equally frequent: *the door kept swinging backwards and forwards*—A. Brookner, 1984; *Roll your shoulders, backward and forward, 10 times*—American Fitness, 2004. Otherwise, the most common use of *forwards* is to denote physical movement towards the front: *single-celled organisms are propelled forwards in the water—New Scientist*, 1971; *Then he leaned forwards and touched Colin's forearm*—Ian McEwan, 1981; *The opponent sees the opening and moves forwards to sweep or punch you*—D. Mitchell, 1991. In all these examples *forward* would be at least as natural. Note, however, the following example in which the use of *forwards* denotes literal physical action in contrast with the 'volunteer' meaning of *come forward*: *It was Amelia who came forwards*—K. Newman, 1990.

foul (adverb). The normal adverbial form is *foully*, pronounced with two *l*s. Adverbial *foul* survives only in *foul-mouthed* and in *to fall foul of*, whereas it was common from the Middle English period onwards: *Ye wil nat fro your wyf thus foule* [= foully] *fleen?* (Chaucer, 1385); *Our Allies have . . . played us foul* (Lord Nelson, 1799).

foulard, a thin soft material of silk or silk and cotton, or an article made of this, is now often pronounced /fuːˈlɑːd/, i.e. with the final consonant pronounced. The *OED* (1897) gave precedence to a French-type pronunciation /ˈfuːlɑː/ for this 19c. loanword from French.

founder. See FLOUNDER.

fount, font. These are the traditional British and American spellings respectively of the term meaning 'a set of printing type of one size or face'. *Font* is now also used in BrE, and has largely ousted *fount*. Both words are only remotely connected with *fount* meaning 'fountain, source' (see FOUNT, FOUNTAIN) and *font* meaning 'a basin for water in a church'. *Font* in the typographical meaning comes from French *fonte*, from *fondre* 'to melt, cast', and *fount* is a variant.

fount, fountain. *Fount* is a poetical and rhetorical back-formation (Shakespeare, 1594) from *fountain* (cf. *mount/mountain*), and means a source or a stream: *if streams did meander level with their founts* (Macaulay, 1830); *By Kedron's brook, or Siloa's holy fount* (W. M. Praed, *a*1839). Apart from such literary uses the word is also used in the popular phrases *the fount of all wisdom, knowledge*, etc., which are also often found as *font of all wisdom*, etc.

four. In the 19c. the phrase *on* or *upon all fours* replaced the 16c. *on* or *upon all four*, namely the extremities (either the four legs of a quadruped or the legs and arms of a child). A homily of 1563 refers to *A bruit beast, creeping upon all foure*, and the Bible (Lev. (AV) 11: 42) has *Whatsoeuer goeth vpon all foure*. The added *-s* is shown in: *Edward . . . could perceive him crawling on all-fours* (Scott, 1814). The phrase is most common in its literal use (= on hands and knees) but has also retained, particularly in BrE and in legal language, the metaphorical meaning of 'to present an exact analogy or comparison (with); be compatible with': e.g. *Mr. McArthur says the case at bar is on all fours with the Sykes case*—Decisions of the Ontario Superior Court of Justice, 2004; *A prisoner is dragged on all fours, like a dog. In so doing, his captors appear to put America on all fours with Saddam Hussein*—weblog, 2004 (BrE). The variant *on fours with* is also used.

foyer. The standard pronunciation in BrE is /ˈfɔɪeɪ/ (**foy**-ay), and in AmE /ˈfɔɪər/ (**foy**-uhr). In both varieties the word is occasionally pronounced /ˈfwɑːjeɪ/ in imitation of French.

fracas is pronounced /ˈfrakaː/ (**frak**-ah) in BrE and /ˈfreɪkəs/ (**fray**-kuhs) in AmE. Its plural in BrE is *fracas*, pronounced /-kaːz/ (-kahz), and *fracases* in AmE.

frack, fracking. 1 The adjective *frack* is a variant of *freck*, both extinct and from Middle English *frek*, Old English *frec*, meaning 'eager, impetuous' and related to *freak*.

2 Particularly in AmE, but also, according to *OEC* data, in NZE, *fracking* and *frackin'* are used as euphemisms for the F-word, which is unfortunate for proponents of the much-disputed technology. Anti-fracking protesters in Britain holding placards reading 'frack off' are punning on this well-established use: *And the design that was replaced was pretty fracking lovely already*—weblog, 2003 (NZE); *Honestly, wherever I go in my nightmares, Hello frackin' Kitty is there, waiting*—*OEC*, 2007 (AmE).

3 The verb *frack* and the verbal noun *fracking* are derived from the *frac-* part of *fracturing* in the earlier (1948) term *hydraulic fracturing*. They refer to 'the process of fracturing subterranean rock by the injection of water into existing fissures at high pressure, usually in order to facilitate the passage of some fluid (especially oil or gas) through an otherwise impermeable barrier': *We've also drilled and cased our first Utica Shale well, which is below the Marcellus, and plan on fracking it in about a month*—*OEC*, 2010; *This is no time to lift the fracking ban; it's time to make it permanent*—*NYT*, 2011.

fractious. See FACTIOUS, FACTITIOUS, FRACTIOUS.

fraenum. See FRENUM.

fragile. Like many other adjectives ending in *-ile* (e.g. *docile, facile, fertile, futile*, etc.), *fragile* is now always pronounced in BrE with final /-ʌɪl/. It was not always so.

In John Walker's *Pronouncing Dictionary* (1806) and in the *OED* (1897) only /-ɪl/ was given; but by 1932 A. Lloyd James in *Broadcast English* admitted only /-ʌɪl/. In AmE the standard pronunciation is with /-əl/.

fragmentary. Is preferably pronounced /ˈfragməntəri/ stressing the first syllable, but second-syllable stress is also heard.

framboesia, the medical name for yaws. So spelt, and pronounced /framˈbiːzɪə/. In AmE spelt **frambesia**.

Frankenstein is the title of a Gothic tale of terror by Mary Shelley (1818). It 'relates the exploits of Frankenstein, an idealistic Genevan student of natural philosophy, who discovers ... the secret of imparting life to inanimate matter. Collecting bones from charnel-houses, he constructs the semblance of a human being and gives it life' (*OCELit.*, 1985). The monster thus created inspires loathing in whoever sees it, and eventually turns upon its creator before destroying itself. So, *Frankenstein* is the name of the creator of a monster and not of the monster itself, which has no name. Since at least 1838, however, the name has been used to suggest 'something that becomes terrifying or destructive to its maker', as if it referred to the monster and not its creator. This use is recognized in dictionaries and is so much part of the language that to criticize it or try to correct it, as some do, is as pointless as insisting that 'blood, sweat, and tears' should be corrected to Churchill's original 'blood, toil, tears and sweat': *Its laboratories in Brittany ... have invented a way of messing around with the bacteriological process in order to produce a Frankenstein of cheeses*—*Independent*, 2002. The phrase *Frankenstein's monster* is quite widely used, in addition to Frankenstein on its own: *Did the EU effectively create a Frankenstein's monster when it stitched a handful of moribund legacy currencies to the Deutschmark to create the euro?*—*Sunday Business Post*, 2004. Frankenstein food, a semi-humorous informal way of describing genetically modified food, dates from the late 1980s. Use of *Frankenstein* in this way has led to Franken- being used as a prefix, particularly in Frankenfoods, but also with other words, to suggest danger or terror, e.g. Frankenfish for the snakehead. Examples: *Early Danish studies suggest these effects will turn out to be beneficial and that GM crops actually boost numbers of local wild birds and insects. So much for Frankenstein foods*—*Observer*, 2003; *Europeans have never liked genetically modified organisms, or GMOs. The products—nicknamed 'Frankenfoods'—have been banned in Europe for the past five years*—*www.inthesetimes.com*, 2003.

frantically (adverb) is now the usual form, not *franticly*, even though the latter has been in the language for two centuries longer (1549 compared with 1749) than the former.

fraught is an interesting example of a word gradually shifting in nuance over a long period, making its modern meaning seem far removed from its original one. In late Middle English (15c.) there was a verb *fraught* (related to *freight*) meaning 'to load with cargo' (borrowed from Middle Dutch *vrachten*, from *vracht* 'ship's cargo'). *Fraught* was also the past participle of this verb. In time the verb died out, but the past participle continued in use to mean 'laden, equipped' with something, either literally or metaphorically: *The writings of Plinius ... being fraught with much fabulous matter*—Francis Bacon, 1605; *I would you would make vse of that good wisedome whereof I know you are fraught*—Shakespeare, 1608. Over time, it came to be generally unpleasant rather than useful things that *fraught with* described (*This measure, which, by your own admission, is fraught with danger*—W. H. Ainsworth, 1840), and that continues to be true today. *Fraught* followed by *with* constitutes over two thirds of *OEC* examples, e.g. *fraught with danger/difficulty/problems/uncertainty*. In the 19c., compound adjectives started to appear, *danger-fraught*, *pain-fraught*, etc.; finally, in the 20c., people started to use the word adjectivally, without any preposition or complement, in its meaning of 'distressed, distressing; stressed, stressful', e.g. *there was a fraught silence*; *she sounded a bit fraught*. The *OED* notes this use first from 1966, but Ben Zimmer has found examples dating back to 1925. Despite objections from some quarters when this novel use was taking off in the 1960s, it is now a standard part of English.

free. See FOR FREE; FREE GIFT; FREE REIN; FREE WILL.

-free is a suffix used in dozens of common words such as *acid-free* (paper), *alcohol-*

free, duty-free, fat-free, hands-free, interest-free, smoke-free, tax-free. A hyphen should separate it from the word it is joined to, i.e. *alcohol-free* not **alcohol free* or **alcoholfree, hands-free* rather than **handsfree* or **hands free,* etc.

free gift, an expression first recorded in 1899 (*The 'taster',* a free gift bestowed of yore in order to retain the ... goodwill of regular but temporarily impecunious customers) is standard in the language of marketing and sales for 'an object given away without charge as part of a sales promotion exercise'. It refuses to go away despite the repeated objections of critics to its self-evident tautology.

free rein. The image behind the phrase *give free rein to somebody* is from horse riding, and the *rein* referred to is the strip of leather used to control a horse's (or child's) movements. Nowadays the spelling *free reign,* with an image taken from kingship, is widespread everywhere, and is almost as common in North American English as the original spelling. While the *reign* spelling constitutes an interesting example of *folk etymology,* its appearance in printed matter will no doubt cause reactions ranging from a wry, smug smile to thunderous, apoplectic rage among readers au fait with the origin of the phrase. Whatever the case, any moderately literate subeditor ought to be able to prevent examples like the following creeping into print: **Those offenders would have been arrested and brought to justice far sooner, rather than having a free reign to reoffend—Express,* 2007.

free verse. See VERS LIBRE.

free will should be written as two words, not one, and should only be hyphenated when used attributively (*his free-will hypothesis*; but *I did it of my own free will*). Used attributively the form *freewill* (one word, no hyphen) is also sometimes used (*freewill offering*).

French words.

1 Preliminary remarks.
2 Phonological assimilation.
3 The general process of assimilation.
4 Degrees of anglicization.

1 *Preliminary remarks.* French words have flowed into English since the late Old English period. The process has never ceased, but there were two periods of intense intake: the Norman Conquest and the years after (the result of cultural imperialism), and the Age of Classicism (18c.), when movements in science and philosophy exposed lexical gaps in English which were filled by French words, (much as the computing industry and the media in France are absorbing English terms at the moment). With regard to imports since those periods, the role of French as the former language of international diplomacy is clearly significant; and so are certain national stereotypes, particularly that of the perceived sophistication of the French in matters sensual and artistic (art, literature, food, wine, and sexuality). Part of the attraction of French was that it filled lexical gaps in English, and also that the 'otherness' of French made it possible to refer to facts and situations which English-speakers, reflecting no doubt the moral codes of the 19c., preferred to leave unmentioned in English, e.g. *affaire de cœur* (first recorded in English in 1809), *crime passionnel* (1910), and *ménage à trois* (1891).

2 *Phonological assimilation.* The great majority of French loanwords are so firmly established that they are pronounced as English words with no hint of foreignness: thus *button, glory, ounce, place, prime, uncle,* etc. It is a general rule, however, that words borrowed from one language to another tend for a time, sometimes a long time, to remain in a kind of no man's land, especially when they contain sounds for which there is no exact equivalent in the host language. Uncertainty prevails until the pronunciation of the adopted word is adjusted in order to fit into the phonetic arrangements and accentual system of English. Some words remain partially or permanently in a zone of incomplete adaptation.

3 *The general process of assimilation.* Words that are not fully assimilated are usually pronounced in something like a French manner, and may also be printed in italic (as shown at 4 (a)). A typical example of the process of adoption is the noun *abandon.* First recorded in English in 1822, it was pronounced /abɑ̃ːˈdɔ̃/, or thereabouts, throughout the remainder of the 19c. and at least as late as 1917 (the date of publication of the first edition of Daniel Jones's *English Pronouncing Dictionary*). Some time after that it acquired its current anglicized pronunciation, aided by the existence of the already assimilated verb. It was italicized in Ruskin (1851) but printed in roman type in Joyce's *Ulysses* (1922). By the 1930s it seems to have been treated as an ordinary English word by everyone. Hundreds of French loanwords had a similar history between the time of their adoption in English and their complete assimilation. Others are in the process of being assimilated.

4 *Degrees of anglicization.* The degree of anglicization of words and phrases adopted from French varies from person to person or from group to group, and any classification is likely to be vulnerable in some respect. With that proviso, the following groupings may be useful:

(*a*) Pronounced in a French manner (with the modifications listed below) and printed in italic. In such words the routine deviations from French include: introduction of diphthongs where French has none; marked stressing of syllables where French has little or none; total or partial elimination of nasalization; introduction of the 'schwa' sound /ə/ for unaccented vowels. Examples include *affaire de cœur, crime passionnel, enfant terrible, esprit de corps, ménage à trois, nom de guerre, pièce de résistance, soi-disant, soixante-neuf.*

(*b*) Fully anglicized and printed in roman type (the bracketed dates are those of the first record of each word in English): *baroque* (1765), *bizarre* (1648), *blasé* (1819, Lord Byron), *brunette* (1713), *cachet* (*a*1639), *clairvoyant* (1671), *éclair* (1861), *façade* (1654), *gigolo* (1922), *mayonnaise* (1841), *son et lumière* (1957), *tour de force* (1802).

(*c*) Printed in roman, but retaining partial elements of French pronunciation (final letter not pronounced, etc.): *billet-doux, camembert* /-bɛː/, *déjà vu, escargot* /-ɡəʊ/, *laissez-faire, nom de plume, sobriquet* /-keɪ/, *touché, tournedos* /-dəʊ/.

(*d*) In literary and scholarly work, Gallicisms are scattered about like grain (the bracketed dates are those of the first record of each word in English): *à merveille* (1762), *arrière-pensée* (1824), *au fond* (1782), *au pied de la lettre* (1782), *esprit d'escalier* (1906), *point d'appui* (1819), *roman-fleuve* (1936). These expressions, and many others like them, are not in everyday use among standard speakers, but will be pronounced in a French-sounding way, and be printed in italic.

There is no doubt that un-English sounds will continue to be anglicized in expressions like *tête-à-tête* and *tour de force*: and that French words like *blasé, chic,* and *naïve,* for which there are no English synonyms with exactly the same shade of meaning, will continue to be used in the years ahead. And there is also no doubt that printers and publishers will disagree about which of them is to be printed in italic type and which not. See GALLICISMS.

frenum /ˈfriːnəm/ (**free**-nuhm), in anatomy, a fold of mucous membrane or skin, especially the one under the tongue, checking the motion of the part to which it is attached, is nowadays the more common spelling than *fraenum*. Plural *frena* /-nə/.

frequentative. Frequentative verbs are formed with certain suffixes to express repeated or continuous action of the kind denoted by the simple verb. The chief frequentative suffixes in English are *-er* (answering to Old English *-rian*), e.g. *chatter, clamber, flicker, glitter, slumber;* and *-le* (answering to OE *-lian*), e.g. *crackle, dazzle, paddle, sparkle, wriggle.* Frequentative verbs are found in many other languages, e.g. Latin, Russian.

fresco. The plural *frescoes* is preferable and more common, but *frescos* is also correct. See -O(E)S 2.

friar, monk. A *friar* is a member of any of certain religious orders of men, originally in the 13c. and esp. the four Roman Catholic mendicant orders (Augustinians, Carmelites, Dominicans, and Franciscans), in former times living entirely on alms and doing good works in the community. A *monk* can include these, but is strictly speaking a member of a religious community of men living under certain vows, especially of poverty, chastity, and obedience, seeking salvation through their vows and their secluded way of life.

fricative. In phonetics, denoting a consonant made by the friction of breath in a narrow opening (cf. Latin *fricāre* 'to rub'). In English, for example, /f/ and /v/ are labiodental fricatives; /θ/ and /ð/ are dental fricatives; and /s/ and /z/ are alveolar fricatives. They contrast with *stops* (see STOP (noun)), such as /b/ and /p/.

Friday. *Friday,* being the first day of the week alphabetically, is chosen to make this point, which also applies to the other six. The suppression of *on* in adverbial phrases with days of the week (*See you Friday; He normally eats fish Fridays*) has spread to BrE from America, but the use remains informal in Britain, especially in the singular. Only an American would say or write that something 'happened Tuesday' instead of 'happened last Tuesday', or to give a real example: *When Goosen took his family to dinner here Tuesday night, not a single person asked for an autograph*—*Houston Chronicle*, 2005.

friendlily, friendly (adverbs). Used to mean 'in a friendly manner, with friendship', *friendly* is recorded in the *OED* from *Beowulf* onwards until the mid-19c. (e.g. *Some of the men marry three wives, who in general live friendly together*—James Cook, 1771–84), but has almost entirely dropped out of use. The alternative form *friendlily*, first recorded in the work of Rochester in the late 17c., is available but, because of its awkward-sounding ending *-lily*, is not often used. Examples: *'By the same token,' went on Callie, friendlily smiling, 'I'm afraid I must ask you, Arthur, to take your boots off'*—E. Bowen, 1945; *The women ... still addressed him friendlily*—W. Trevor, 1980; *All this was friendlily presented*—Roy Jenkins, 1991. Similarly infrequent are other adverbs formed from adjectives ending in *-ly* such as *holily, jollily, lovelily*, and *sillily*.

frier. See FRYER.

frith. See FIRTH.

frizz. See -Z-, -ZZ-.

frock was originally a male garment, especially the mantle of a monk or priest (hence to *unfrock*), then the *smock-frock* that was the overall of an agricultural labourer, and finally the *frock-coat* that was for many years the uniform of the man-about-town. Discarded by men, the word came back into favour as a synonym of *gown* or *dress* for women or girls in the 19c. It remains in use, but *dress* or *gown* are the more usual terms, especially those with designer labels, while use of the word *frock* often betrays an ironic or facetious intention. But *posh frock* is a standard collocation in BrE, e.g. *The loss of her posh frocks also meant Naomi was left with nothing to wear to her birthday party*—*www.femalefirst*, 2005.

frolic (verb). The inflected forms are *frolicked, frolicking*. See -C-, -CK-.

from. Avoid the mixture of styles shown in the type *he was chairman of the board from 1979–1985*; read ... *from 1979 to 1985* or ... *between 1979 and 1985*.

from whence, from hence. These and analogous phrases have been widely criticized on the grounds that *from* is redundant, since the words *whence, hence*, etc. themselves already contain that idea. **1** *from whence. COD* 1990 baldly says, 'Use of *from whence* (as in *the place from whence they came*), though common, is generally considered incorrect.' But *from whence* has a long and distinguished history in direct and indirect questions and as a conjunctive phrase introducing a relative clause. Many historical examples are cited in the *OED*, including: (interrogative = from what place or source?) *From whence these Murmurs, and this change of Mind?*—Dryden, 1697; *My wife, as I'm a Christian. From whence can she come?*—Goldsmith, 1773; (indirect question) *Thys felowe, we knowe not from whence he ys*—Tyndale, 1526; *No man can say from whence the greater danger to order arises*—F. Harrison, 1867; (relative or conjunctive uses) *I will lift vp mine eyes vnto the hilles: from whence commeth my helpe*—Ps. (AV) 121: 1; *The quarter from whence the following lucubration is addressed*—Swinburne, 1887. Similar (though fewer) examples are cited for the other phrases (*from thence*, etc.).

The phrase with *from* continues to be used as a conjunction in modern writing, although *whence* on its own is more frequent: *Father ... puts me excitingly on his shoulder from whence I lord it over the world*—P. Lively, 1987; *Dark clouds had gathered over the hills to the north, from whence came the lucky changeling folk in times long past*—S. Koea, 1994 (NZ); It should go back as close as possible to the spot from whence it came—*Daily Tel.*, 2007. The best policy, perhaps, is to use the simple word *whence*. Or, unless one wishes to be formal or literary, to rephrase in a more natural way, e.g. *to the spot it came from* in the last example.

2 *from hence*. Numerous historical examples of the pleonastic phrase *from hence* in the *OED* stretch from the 14c. to the 19c.: e.g. (of place) *Richard, not farre from hence, hath hid his* head—Shakespeare,

1593; *From hence I was conducted up a staircase to a suite of apartments*—W. Irving, 1820; (of time) *From hence Ile loue no Friend*—Shakespeare, 1604; (= as a result) *From hence he has been accused, by historians, of avarice*—Goldsmith, 1771. But the phrase has virtually dropped out of the living language and can only be used as a conscious archaism.

frontier. In BrE the standard pronunciation is /ˈfrɒntɪə/ and in AmE the stress is commonly placed on the second syllable.

fruition. Through false association with *fruit,* the figurative sense the 'state or process of bearing fruit' has become imposed on *fruition* as the 20c. proceeded, and is now in standard use. This word's original meaning (first recorded in the 15c.) was 'enjoyment, pleasurable possession' (ultimately from Latin *fruitiōnem,* noun of action formed from *fruī* 'to enjoy'). In the late 19c., through association with *fruit,* it was interpreted to mean 'coming into fruit' and then 'realization, fulfilment'. Despite the carping of generations of pundits, this last meaning, esp. in the phrase *to come to fruition,* is entirely valid.

frustum. (In geometry) plural *frustums* or, less commonly, *frusta.*

fryer. The better spelling (not *frier*) for 'a person who fries; a vessel for frying (fish, etc.)'.

fuchsia. Spelt with *-chs-* (not *fuschia*), but pronounced /ˈfjuːʃə/ (**fyoo**-shuh). The awkward spelling comes from the name of the 16c. German botanist Leonhard Fuchs, after whom the plant is named.

fucus (type of seaweed). Pronounced /ˈfjuːkəs/; plural *fuci* /ˈfjuːsʌɪ/.

fuel (verb). The inflected forms are *fuelled, fuelling* (AmE *fueled, fueling*). See -LL-, -L-.

fugacious is a 17c. formation from Latin *fugax, fugācis* 'prone to run away', from *fugere* 'to flee', the same verb as in the tag *tempus fugit.* Its main use is in biology, esp. botany, to describe 'organs or parts that fall off once they have served their purpose': *Flowers of Sisyrinchium are regarded as fugacious and bee-pollinated—Jrnl of the Torrey Botanical Society,* 2003. In the meaning 'fleeting, not lasting long', it features in books that claim to expand one's vocabulary but merely list words that will baffle most people. It is rather rare, even in literary or journalistic use: *an extremely complicated and fragile post-conflict situation composed of an unstable and fugacious network of key players*—Julian Warczinski, 2005.

fugue. The parts are *fugues, fugued, fuguing.* A composer of fugues is a *fuguist.* The corresponding adjective and adverb are **fugal** and **fugally**.

-ful. The right plural for such nouns as *cupful, handful, mouthful, spoonful, teaspoonful,* etc., is *cupfuls,* etc., not *cupsful,* etc. See CUPFUL; PLURALS OF NOUNS 9.

fulcrum. Pronounced /ˈfʊlkrəm/ or /ˈfʌl-/. Plural either *fulcra,* especially in technical writing, or *fulcrums,* particularly in its metaphorical meaning 'a thing that plays a central or essential role': *And, as he was one of the fulcrums of the Maori cultural renaissance of the early 1970s, his place in our history is the same—New Zealand Listener,* 2004. See -UM 3.

fulfil. Spelt with a single final letter *l* in BrE with the inflected forms *fulfilled, fulfilling.* In AmE either *fulfill* or *fulfil* (inflected forms as in BrE). The corresponding noun is **fulfilment** in BrE and either *fulfillment* or *fulfilment* in AmE. See -LL-, -L-.

full (adverb). In the phrase *full well* (*you know full well that I told you*), *full* is being used as an adverb in a way that was once quite standard but is now confined to this phrase, to phrases such as (*hit him full in the face*), and is embodied in Shakespeare's *Full fadom fiue thy Father lies.*

ful(l)ness. Spell as *fullness,* but be prepared to find *fulness* in 19c. and earlier works (e.g. *in the fulness of his heart*—R. M. Ballantyne, 1858). Cf. DULLNESS.

full stop. 1 *In sentences.* The full stop is also called the *point* or *full point* by printers and editors, and *period* in NAmer English. Its main use is to mark the end of a sentence that is a statement (as in this sentence). This applies to sentences which are not complete statements or which contain ellipsis, as in the examples below. For rhetorical or other effects a 'sentence' is frequently broken up into separately punctuated parts: *Culloden is Scott's watershed. And it is largely absent from his fiction.* Also, *It was as though Hungary was not another place but another time, and therefore inaccessible. Which of course was not so—*

P. Lively, 1987. Much more adventurous departures from the norm are now commonplace and have been for some time, dramatically so in the opening of Dickens's *Bleak House*: *London. Michaelmas term lately over, and the Lord Chancellor sitting in Lincoln's Hall. Implacable November weather—Bleak House,* 1852–3.

2 *In abbreviations and contractions.* (*a*) The full stop is also used in abbreviations and contractions, although this use is diminishing, partly as a matter of printing style and partly because many abbreviations have become more familiar and no longer need identification. The traditional distinction is that abbreviations are written with full points (e.g. *I.o.W.* = Isle of Wight) while most contractions (namely words with the middle part omitted, e.g. *Dr* = Doctor), are written without. Though arguably a useful distinction, it has been eroded, so that shortenings of various kinds are printed and written without full stops, e.g. *BBC, etc, ie, IoW, Mr, Ms, pm* (= post meridiem), *St* (= Saint or Street), etc.

(*b*) The style recommended here involves dropping full stops in initialisms that are all capital letters (e.g. *BBC, NNW* = north-north-west, *TUC*), in many contractions (*Dr, Mr,* etc.), and in acronyms that are pronounced as words (e.g. *Anzac, Nato*), but retaining them in lower-case initialisms such as *a.m., e.g.,* and *i.e.* and in shortened words such as *Oct.* (= October), *Tues.* (= Tuesday), and *Visc.* (= Viscount). In mixed styles the tendency now is to omit points, as in *DPhil, MLitt,* and *GeV* (= gigaelectronvolt). The important point, however, is to be consistent within a particular piece of writing or printing, e.g. *a.m./p.m.* and *am/pm, St.* and *St, D.Phil.* and *DPhil,* and so on. Some shortenings have a greater need of full stops to avoid possible ambiguity with other words in some contexts, e.g. *a.m.* (= ante meridiem), *no.* (= number).

3 If an abbreviation with a full stop comes at the end of a sentence, another full stop is not added when the full stop of the abbreviation is the last character: *Bring your own pens, pencils, rulers, etc.* but *Bring your own things* (*pens, pencils, rulers, etc.*).

4 Full stops are routinely used between units of money (*£11.99, $27.50*), before decimals (*10.5%*), and between hours and minutes (*10.30 a.m.*; AmE *10:30 a.m.*).

5 The *New Hart's Rules* provides detailed guidance on the numerous subtleties attendant on the printing or omission of full points: e.g. *4to, 8vo, 12mo,* etc. (sizes of books), points of the compass, names of well-known reference works (*OED, DNB,* etc.), names of books of the Bible, and so on. See CONTRACTIONS 1.

fulsome. (Pronounced /fʌlsɛm/ by the *OED* (1898 but now always /ˈfʊl-/.) **1** If you receive *fulsome praise,* should you be wholeheartedly grateful to the praisers or question their sincerity? That is the heart of the question about this particular adjective. First formed in the 14c. from *full* + *some* (the Old English suffix present in *handsome, wholesome,* etc.), this word has acquired and then largely lost many senses, among them '(of food) tending to cloy or surfeit'; 'foul-smelling' (possibly from *foul* + *-some*). For more conservative speakers, its proper meaning is defined at considerable length by the *OED*: 'Of language, style, behaviour, etc.: Offensive to good taste; *esp.* offending from excess or want of measure or from being 'overdone'. Now chiefly used in reference to gross or excessive flattery, over-demonstrative affection, or the like.' First recorded in 1663, this disparaging meaning is a legacy of several older disparaging senses of the word.

It seemed secure until the second half of the 20c., when some people began to use *fulsome* in a favourable sense, thereby elevating *fulsome praise* from toadying, fawning flattery into 'high praise'. An age-old semantic process, in which a word loses its negative connotations, has gained a new recruit. The process seems to be more advanced in American than in British English, understandably, in view of the former's predilection, as perceived at least by British speakers, for over-the-top expressions of sentiment. For a British audience, it is best to retain the word's conventional connotations, because the adverse meaning is still much alive and there is a danger of unfortunate misunderstanding. For example, the following could sound like a wish for crocodile tears: *Critics, who insist the Pope has not gone far enough in apologising, will be expecting him to express fulsome remorse—Irish News,* 2006. Other examples showing the positive and disputed meaning of *fulsome* include: *I'm grateful for this very friendly and very fulsome introduction*—B. Hays (US Congressman), 1968; *I got a very fulsome apology from the President of Iraq*—President Reagan, quoted on NBC News, 19 May 1987. Useful alternatives to *fulsome* in the 'favourable' sense include *lavish, generous, enthusiastic, effusive, exuberant, copious, glowing,* and *extravagant.*

2 *Fulsome* is also occasionally used to mean 'full-figured' (of a woman's figure) by fashion writers who, correctly as it happens, but anachronistically, analyse the word as consisting of *full* and *-some*: e.g. *I am warned that these particular cassocks will only fit either the exceptionally petite or the handsomely fulsome—Daily Tel.,* 1985. The somewhat analogous use of *fulsome* in the following example harks back to the word's original meaning of 'abundant, plentiful': *the legendarily flamboyant singer sporting a fulsome moustache—Manchester Music,* 2012.

3 It almost goes without saying that the spelling *fullsome,* though historically attested, is nowadays incorrect.

fun. This modernish noun (first recorded in 1699 in a 'cant' or slang dictionary and stigmatized by Johnson as 'a low cant word') has long hovered on the brink of adjectival status (*It was really fun*) and more recently has taken a step further in informal attributive uses such as *We had a fun time* or *That would be a fun thing to do.* It still has a way to go, however, since it cannot yet be qualified by intensifying adverbs such as *very* or *extremely* (use of *great fun* instead gives away the noun's disguise). In informal English, especially AmE, its status as a quasi-adjective is signalled by its use with *so,* e.g. *That was so fun; He is so fun.* In standard English it also lacks the comparative and superlative inflections that a single-syllable adjective normally has, although *more fun* as in *This sounds more fun* is legitimate. *Funner* and *funnest* have appeared in youth slang in AmE and are now found in BrE too, albeit usually in a humorous form: *She is also looking forward to the camaraderie of her country's locker room. 'Teams', she said, 'are so much funner.'—Guardian,* 2004.

function. To say that such and such a thing 'is a function of' such another or such others is a POPULARIZED TECHNICAL TERM: *A man's fortitude under given painful conditions is a function of two variables*—L. Tollemache, 1876; *Mifune's top billing is a function of his stature in Japanese cinema, not the centrality of his role in the film—DVD Verdict,* 2005. Its use in this way is typical of those who, as Fowler described them, 'feel that the use of an ordinary word for an ordinary notion does not do justice to their vocabulary or sufficiently exhibit their cultivation'. Whereas the first example at least talks about two variables, all the phrase means in the second example is 'is a result of'. The definition of the mathematical sense of *function* in *COD* 1995 may be found useful: 'a variable quantity regarded in relation to another or others in terms of which it may be expressed or on which its value depends (*x is a function of y and z*)'.

fungus. The recommended plural is *fungi,* pronounced /ˈfʌŋgʌɪ/ or /ˈfʌndʒʌɪ/. *Funguses* is rarely used. The most frequent adjectival form is **fungal**, *fungous* and *fungoid* being rather rare. *Fungus* itself is sometimes used attributively before a noun, as in a *fungus infection.*

funnel (verb). The inflected forms in BrE are *funnelled, funnelling,* but in AmE usu. *funneled, funneling.* See -LL-, -L-.

funny. In some contexts, e.g. *he's rather funny,* it can be unclear whether the meaning is: (*a*) amusing, comical (*a funny story, film, line*); (*b*) strange, perplexing, hard to account for (*a funny look, it's a funny old world, she's funny that way*). Since the 1930s (first recorded in a late novel by Ian Hay), sense (*a*) has come to be called *funny-ha-ha* and sense (*b*) *funny-peculiar,* and people may ask 'Do you mean funny ha-ha or funny peculiar?' My impression is that this question is not often asked nowadays, which suggests either that the ambiguity does not often arise, or that the question is rather old-fashioned. In American English, sense (*a*) is also called *ha-ha funny.*

furore. (An outbreak of public anger or excitement). Pronounced generally as three syllables in BrE, /ˌfjʊ(ə)ˈrɔːri/ (fyoo-(uh)-**raw**-ri), alternatively as two, /ˌfjʊ(ə)ˈrɔː/ (fyoo-(uh)-**raw**). The word is spelt **furor** in AmE and pronounced as two syllables, stressing the first, /ˈfjʊ(ə)rɔː/ (**fyoo**-(uh)-raw).

further. See FARTHER, FURTHER.

furze, gorse, whin. All three words are synonymous (yellow-flowered shrub of the genus *Ulex*), but *furze* is chiefly restricted to BrE and *whin* is chiefly a Scottish and northern counties word. *Gorse* is used throughout the English-speaking world.

fuse. There are two distinct words: **1** (first recorded in 1644) a device for igniting a bomb, etc.; derived from Italian *fuso*, from Latin *fūsus* 'spindle', (hence) a spindle-shaped tube originally used for a bomb, etc. Usually spelt **fuze** in AmE.

2 (first recorded in 1884) a device or component for protecting an electric circuit; the verb *fuse* from L *fundere, fūs-* 'to melt', used as a noun.

fused participle. See POSSESSIVE WITH GERUND.

fuselage. Introduced from French at the dawn of aviation, it can be pronounced /ˈfjuːzəˌlɑːʒ/ (**fyoo**-zuh-large) in a quasi-French way, or with the last syllable rhyming with *ridge*.

-fy. 1 English verbs in *-fy* are derived from or as from French verbs in *-fier* (Latin *-ficāre*), e.g. *beautify* (16c.), *classify* (18c.), *countrify* (17c.), *dandify* (19c.), *demystify* (20c.), *gentrify* (20c.), *horrify* (18c.), *pacify* (15c.), *speechify* (18c.). There has been some fluctuation in the spelling of the infinitival forms (*-ify/-yfy*) and also of the derivatives (*countryfied/countrified, dandyfied/dandified*, etc.). For these well-established words the recommended spelling is *-ify, -ified, -ifying.*

2 A small group of words have *-efy* in the infinitive and therefore *-efied, -efying* in the inflected forms, e.g. *liquefied, -efying* from *liquefy; stupefied, -efying* from *stupefy.*

3 The recommended spelling suggested in section 1 has hardly affected the spelling of similar, but humorous or trivial, formations that have decorated English since the late 16c., e.g. *bullify* (18c., = to make into a bully), *Frenchify* (16c.), *ladify/ladyfy* (17c.), *truthify* (17c.). The *-ee-* in *Yankeefied* (19c.) and the *-ey* in *cockneyfied* (19c.) naturally remain unchanged, i.e. the ending is not converted in them to *-ified.*

g. See GREEK G.

gabardine This is the recommended and usual spelling, not *gaberdine* for a smooth durable cloth or a raincoat made from it. The spelling *gaberdine* is the one used with historical reference to the smock worn by almsmen and beggars, and by Jews on the Elizabethan stage, as in Shakespeare's *Merchant of Venice* I.iii.111 (Shylock): *You call me misbeliever, cut-throat, dog, And spit upon my Jewish gaberdine.*

Gaelic usually /ˈgeɪlɪk/ but sometimes /ˈgalɪk/. Any of the Celtic languages spoken in Ireland, Scotland, and the Isle of Man. There are two main varieties of these languages. The term *Brythonic* (or *Brittonic*) describes the language brought to Britain by the bearers of that variety of primitive Celtic speech known as *P-Celtic,* one of the branches of the primitive Celtic group of languages. The *Q-Celtic* group differed from them in that in them the Indo-European /kw-/ sound remained, whereas in the *P-Celtic* group this sound became /p/. Irish Gaelic, Scottish Gaelic, and Manx Gaelic belong to the Q-Celtic or Goidelic group, whereas Welsh (and also the Celtic of Cornwall and Brittany) belongs to the P-Celtic or Brythonic group. Cf. e.g. Irish Gaelic *ceathair* and Welsh *pedwar* 'four'.

gag (in the parliamentary sense). See CLOSURE 2.

gage is the spelling of the obsolescent word meaning 'a pledge, a challenge, etc.' and of the abbreviated form of the *greengage plum.* In American English it is a recognized but not common variant of *gauge* meaning 'measure', usually as a noun and only rarely as a verb, but *gauge* must be spelt with an *-au-* in BrE.

gainsay. This ancient verb (first recorded *c.*1300) meaning 'to deny, to speak or act against' lay firmly in the standard language for nearly 600 years but seems to have fallen into relative disuse at some point in the 19c. It is now encountered mostly in a handful of set phrases, such as *there is* etc. *no gainsaying, to be impossible to gainsay,* in rather formal writing. The third-person present indicative form *gainsays* is usually pronounced /-seɪz/, not /-sɛz/, unlike *says.*

gala (a festive occasion). Pronounced /ˈgɑːlə/ (**gah**-luh), though the traditional pronunciation, as shown in the *OED* (1899) and as used in the Durham Miners' Gala, is /ˈgeɪlə/ (**gay**-luh). The dominant pronunciation in American English is /ˈgeɪlə/, but /ˈgalə/ is also common.

gallant. The ordinary pronunciation, when the word means 'brave', is, of course, /ˈgalənt/. But when used in the sense 'attentive to women, amorous' and as the related noun 'a ladies' man, lover', for example in historical or romantic fiction, the stress changes to /gəˈlant/.

galley. The plural is *galleys.*

Gallic, Gallican, Gaulish, French. *Gallican* is an ecclesiastical word, relating to the ancient church of Gaul. It is also used in palaeography of a certain kind of script. *Gaulish* means only 'of the (ancient) Gauls', and, even in that sense, is less usual than *Gallic. Gallic* is also much used as a refined synonym in some contexts for *French.* It means not simply 'French', but 'characteristically', 'delightfully', 'distressingly', or 'amusingly French', 'so French you know', etc.; or again not 'of France', but 'of a typical French person'. We do not normally speak of Gallic wines or trade or law or climate, but we do of Gallic shrugs, in particular, and of Gallic charm, flair, pride and wit. If *Gallic* is used for *French* without any implication of the kinds suggested, it is merely an attempt at ELEGANT VARIATION.

Gallicisms. Fowler (1926) used this term to describe what he called 'borrowings of various kinds from French in which the borrower stops short of using French words without disguise'. While acknowledging their established contribution to English vocabulary, he gave a warning not to use them as a kind of affectation derived from their foreignness. He was thinking particularly of type (b) below.

The term *Gallicisms* here covers French words or idioms that have been adapted to a larger or smaller extent in the process of adoption into English, or have been adopted element by element in a literal and often unidiomatic manner. The asymmetry of such linguistic borrowing is a well-known phenomenon in all languages. It is relatively rare for a word or phrase taken into language A from language B to retain *precisely* the same meaning or range of meanings as those of the original language and to maintain the equivalence as time goes on. Some examples of the various types of Gallicisms: **1** *Fully adapted words.* French words which have been adapted to suit the ordinary conventions of English, e.g. by dropping accents or by substituting English verbal endings, etc.: *actuality* (Fr. *actualité*), *redaction* (Fr. *rédaction*), Middle English *striven* (Old French *estriver*) → *strive.*

2 *Loan translation or calques.* That is, expressions adopted from French in a more or less literally translated form, e.g. *castle in Spain* (*château en Espagne*); *gilded youth* (*jeunesse dorée*); *give furiously to think* (*donner furieusement à penser*); *jump* or *leap to the eye*(*s*) (*sauter aux yeux*); *success of esteem* (*succès d'estime*); *a suspicion* (*of*) = a hint (of) (*un soupçon*); *that goes without saying* (*cela va sans dire*).

3 *Mismatches.* These include (*a*) French-looking words for which there is no equivalent in French (e.g. *epergne*, dinner-table ornament), or which have acquired a meaning in English not paralleled in French (e.g. *papier mâché,* literally 'chewed paper'; the French equivalent is *carton-pâte).* (*b*) 20c. mismatches: The now ubiquitous item of bedding which became available in the 1960s in Britain under the name of a *continental quilt* is now generally referred to as a *duvet* which in French means 'a sleeping bag', the French term being *couette* (which has the same Latin root as *quilt*). A *cagoule* in French is either a monk's hood or a child's balaclava, and never 'a hooded thin windproof garment worn in mountaineering, etc.' (the French for this garment being a *K-way*). *Fromage frais,* now available in British supermarkets, is in fact *fromage blanc—fromage frais* being a fresh, unmatured cheese. The term *mange-tout* denotes a type of green bean to French native speakers, who know the currently fashionable pea as *pois-gourmand.*

See FRENCH WORDS.

gallop (verb). The inflected forms are *galloped, galloping.* See -P-, -PP-.

gallows. Now usually treated as a singular noun, i.e. 'set up a gallows, a gallows was set up, etc.'. In Old English the singular *galga* and the plural *galgan* were both used for 'a gallows', the plural having reference presumably to the two posts making up the apparatus. From the 13c. onwards the plural *galwes* and its later phonetic developments have been the prevailing forms. Since the 16c. *gallows* has normally been treated grammatically as singular, with a new (and rarely used) plural *gallowses.*

galop /ˈgaləp/, the dance, is spelt with only one *l.* Historical novelists beware: as a verb, the inflected forms are *galoped, galoping,* with a single *p.* See -P-, -PP-.

galore. A loanword, adopted in the 17c. from Irish *go leór* 'to sufficiency, enough', which is always placed after the word it qualifies (*whisky galore; there is talent galore here*).

galosh (an overshoe), usually in plural *galoshes.* So spelt, not *golosh*(*es*).

galumph (verb). One of Lewis Carroll's delicious inventions, a portmanteau word perhaps with some reminiscence of *gallop* and *triumphant,* now usually meaning 'to gallop heavily; to bound or move clumsily or noisily': *Viola ... had slept through the stifled cries of her parents beneath the bedclothes when Beyle* [*sc.* a bulldog] *was galumphing round their room*—C. Mackenzie, 1930.

gambade (a horse's leap). If this French form of the word is used, the plural is *gambades.* If the Spanish form *gambado* is used, the plural is *gambados.*

gambit. A gambit is 'a chess opening in which a player sacrifices a piece or pawn to secure an advantage'. In general contexts the idea of sacrifice has largely gone, and the word is used simply to mean 'an opening move in a conversation, meeting, set of negotiations, etc.'. It is a routine example of a POPULARIZED TECHNICAL TERM.

Perhaps inevitably, the unwitting or the unread use *gambit* when what they mean is *gamut*, e.g. **The acting was excellent, the cast portraying the whole gambit of emotions with great conviction.* To warn readers of this book against such a slip is, I am sure, entirely redundant.

gambol (verb) (skip or frolic playfully). The inflected forms are *gambolled, gambolling* (in AmE frequently with a single *-l-*). See -LL-, -L-.

gamesmanship. See BRINKMANSHIP; -MANSHIP.

gamp. In the UK an informal, rather dated word for an umbrella, especially a large unwieldy one. Named after Mrs Sarah Gamp, who habitually carried a large cotton umbrella, in Dickens's *Martin Chuzzlewit* (1844).

gamut. In music, *gamut* properly means 'the note G at the pitch now indicated by the lowest line of the bass staff'. (The word is formed from medieval Latin *gamma* (= the note G) + *ut*, the first of six arbitrary names forming the hexachord (*ut, re, mi, fa, sol, la*); these were said to be taken from the initial letters of a sequence of Latin words in the office hymn for St John the Baptist's day.) It was later extended to mean 'the whole series of notes used in medieval or modern music', and this has given rise to the generalized meaning 'the whole series or range or scope of anything' which chiefly occurs in the expression *run* (or *go through the*) (*whole/full*) *gamut* (= experience the whole range of), as in the infamous remark by Dorothy Parker about Katharine Hepburn's acting running 'the gamut of emotions from A to B'. Beware of confusing *gamut* idiomatically with *gauntlet*: **No need to run the gamut of residents parking until next January*—*Times*, 2007. See also GAMBIT.

gamy. (having the flavour or scent of game left till high). So spelt, not *gamey.* See -EY AND -Y IN ADJECTIVES 2.

gang agley. A traditional Scottish idiomatic phrase meaning '(of a plan, etc.) to go wrong'. It is occasionally used in standard English as a half-remembered remnant from Burns's poem 'To a Mouse' (1785): *The best laid schemes o' mice an' men Gang aft a-gley.*

ganglion. The recommended plural form is *ganglia,* not *ganglions.*

gantlet is a variant of GAUNTLET in American English, especially in the idioms *run the gantlet* and *throw down the gantlet.*

gaol, gaoler, the traditional and treacherous spellings in the UK, are now under severe and probably unstoppable pressure from *jail, jailer,* which are dominant in most other parts of the English-speaking world, and outnumber them several dozen times in the *OEC* data. Both words come from French, but from different varieties: *gaol* from *gay(h)ole* (13c.) from Anglo-Norman French *gaole,* and originally pronounced with a hard *g,* as in *goat; jail* from *jaiole* (16c.) from Old French *jaiole. Jail* and its derivatives mercifully simplify spelling: they are analogous to *bail, fail, mail,* etc., and avoid the historical misspelling 'goal', noted as long ago as the 16c. In practice the agent noun is hardly used: it has been almost entirely replaced first by *warder* and later by *prison officer.* But note: *Tiny radiator grille like a gaoler's spyhole*—J. Barnes, 1991; *alone in a house which was empty except for parents who were now gaolers*—A. Brookner, 1991.

gap. This much-favoured word for a 'difference, especially an undesirable one, between two views or situations', now very frequently qualified by a preceding noun, shows no sign of weakening or passing out of fashion. Among the compounds listed in the *OED* are *credibility gap* (first recorded in 1962), *export gap* (1952), *gender gap* (1969) *generation gap* (1962), and *technology gap* (1967). Since the 1980s the practice of students taking a break from full-time education in order to travel and gain experience of the world between school and university has been institutionalized in the term *gap year.*

garage. The standard British pronunciation is /ˈgærɑːʒ/ (**ga**-rahzh). A minority of standard speakers say /ˈgærɪdʒ/ (**ga**-rij) or transfer the main stress to the second syllable: /gəˈrɑːʒ/ (gə-**rahzh**) or /gəˈrɑːdʒ/ (gə-**rahj**). The dominant pronunciation in AmE is /gəˈrɑʒ/, followed by /gəˈrɑdʒ/.

garbage. See RUBBISH.

Garden. For *the Garden* in Greek philosophy, see ACADEMY.

garrotte (verb and noun). The standard spelling for the word to do with killing by strangulation. In AmE the dominant spelling is **garrote**, pronounced either /gəˈrɒt/ or /gəˈrəʊt/, but forms with one *r* or with two *t*s are also used.

gas. **1** The plural of the noun is *gases,* while the inflected forms of the verb are *gases, gassed, gassing.*

2 It is the most usual word in AmE for petrol, gasoline.

gaseous. The dominant pronunciation now in British English is /ˈgasɪəs/, the first syllable as in *gas.* Daniel Jones (1917) recommended /ˈgeɪzɪəs/ (which is now defunct), and gave /ˈgɛɪsɪəs/ as a variant, but the pronunciation with initial /ˈgeɪs-/ (**gays**-) is now not often heard. In American English /ˈgaʃəs/ (**gash**-uhs) is an option.

gasoline, volatile liquid from petroleum, especially (chiefly AmE) petrol; not *gasolene.*

-gate. A hugely prolific suffix taken from the name *Watergate* (q.v.) from 1973 onwards and used to denote an actual or alleged scandal in some way comparable with the Watergate scandal of 1972. It has been a godsend to journalists eager to add the frisson of juicy scandal to short eye-catching headlines. Most such formations are very short-lived, but a couple that may still have some resonance today are: *Dianagate* (1989, referring to secretly recorded conversations between the Princess of Wales and her friend James Gilbey), and *Monicagate* (1998, referring to a sexual scandal involving Monica Lewinsky and President Bill Clinton). Much more recent (2012) are *Plebgate,* in the UK, referring to words the then Conservative Chief Whip Andrew Mitchell was alleged to have used to police, and *Benghazigate,* in the US, to criticize how the US Administration dealt with the murder by terrorists of its ambassador to Libya. While most formations add *-gate* to a proper name of a person or place, it can also be attached to other nouns, e.g. in Britain *pastygate* (2012, referring to the outcry at the Chancellor's decision to impose 20% VAT on hot pasties) and *piegate* in Australia (2012, when a government minister swore at the shop-owner selling him a pie).

gateau, a loanword from French meaning 'a rich cake', has the plural form *gateaux,* or occasionally *gateaus,* both endings being pronounced /-əʊz/ (-ohz). The circumflex accent of the original French *gâteau* is no longer used in English.

gaucho (S. Amer. cowboy). Plural *gauchos.* See -O(E)S 4.

gauge. So spelt, not *guage.* See GAGE.

Gaulish. See GALLIC.

gauntlet. The only spelling in British English for the word meaning (*a*) 'a stout glove' and 'a challenge' (especially in *throw down the gauntlet*); and (*b*) also for the separate word (of Swedish origin) in the phrase *run the gauntlet* 'pass between two rows of people and receive blows from them, as a punishment or ordeal'. Sense (*b*) is often spelt **gantlet** in American English.

gay. **1** *Current meaning. 'There is no historical case for homosexual ownership of "gay". So can we have our word back, please.'*—Paul Johnson, 1995. This typifies the reaction of many people to this seismic and politically willed change in the use of language. Rarely has it been so obvious that ostensibly linguistic anxieties—in this case, over a dated meaning of a not particularly frequent word—are a cloak for much darker sociological concerns. One could with justification replace the phrase 'our word' in the quotation above with 'our prejudices'.

From the 1970s onwards, the homosexual community made it clear that *gay* was preferable to the medicalized *homosexual* or any of the host of slang insults including *fag, faggot, fairy, homo, pansy,* and *queer.* The *OED* has citations charting the development of the new meaning from the 1920s onwards, but some of them are rather ambiguous. It is only in citations from the 1940s that the equation of *gay* with 'homosexual' becomes unmistakable, as in this entry from Kenneth Williams's 1948 diary: *Met a charming young RAF fellow there obviously gay who played Debussy's* Bergamasque *with more understanding than I've heard for many a day.*

The historical basis for this use of *gay* is sometimes sought in earlier meanings:

(17c.) 'addicted to social pleasures and dissipations' (as in *gay dog* and *gay Lothario*) and (19c.) '(said of a woman) leading an immoral life, living by prostitution'. But these older and hardly favourable meanings constitute dubious precedents. Whatever its exact origins, the modern meaning is certainly here to stay, and dictionaries of current English tend to list it first of the several meanings of *gay*. In the *OEC* data it outnumbers *homosexual* many times over.

2 *As a noun. Gay* is also used attributively in the meaning 'intended for, used by, or associated with homosexuals' (as in *gay bar, gay marriage, gay politics*), and as a noun: *my own dear mother, who has grey hairs, who at one time admitted to so little knowledge even of marital sex that I supposed I had been conceived in her sleep, now refers with familiarity and deference to gays*—H. Jacobson, 1983; *It seems that the people who are most adamant about gays not getting married are guys like Newt Gingrich. He left his* [critically ill] *wife for his 25-year-old intern—Eye Weekly*, 2005. Unlike the adjective, the noun *gay* usually denotes men only, and the phrase *lesbians and gays* (or the other way round) is used to indicate clearly that both sexes are meant: *an organisation that campaigns for the rights of lesbians, gays and transsexuals—Guardian*, 2007. While *gays* as a plural noun is widely used and accepted, the singular *a gay* is rather uncommon, and potentially disparaging.

3 *A new derogatory meaning.* Finding the door bolted firmly against it, prejudice slips in through a skylight. While the word *gay* was being enlisted in the fight for equality, a new, slang meaning of 'foolish, stupid' or 'insipid, unimpressive' was developing, thereby putting old prejudice in a new bottle: *'It looks terrific on you.' —'It looks gay.'*—J. Kimberly, 1978. This meaning is now quite widespread, especially in the US, and is offensive, despite disingenuous claims that the two meanings are not related. Efforts to disguise the offensiveness have even led to the creation of the pseudo-euphemism *ghey*.

4 *The older meaning.* The traditional meaning of *gay* ('lighthearted and carefree') is of course still alive, if somewhat ailing. The dominance of the current main meaning is illustrated in the first example below. And while context may often prevent any possibly titterworthy misinterpretation, even the second and third examples below oblige readers to perform something of a linguistic double-take. Gay *should now only be used in the context of homosexuality, 88 percent of the editors agreed—Righting Words* (US), 1987; *She had lived a very gay life in London, when she was on the stage*—Nina Bawden, 1991; *But she disobeyed him, brought the baby out, and he had never found her so gay, so welcoming*—Marina Warner, 1992; *As an elementary-school music teacher, I have deplored for years the homosexual adoption of the word gay ... The beautiful "Have Yourself a Merry Little Christmas" declares, "make the Yuletide gay," which I changed to "it's a special day" to keep even first graders from nudging one another*—B. Sikes. Cf. HOMOSEXUAL.

gazebo (a small building, especially one in the garden of a house, that gives a wide view of the surrounding area). Plural *gazebos*. The word was formed in the 18c., and is thought to be a humorous derivative of *gaze* (verb) treated as if it were a Latin verb with a future tense in *-ebo*, meaning 'I will gaze (at the view)'.

gelatin /ˈdʒelətɪn/, the normal form in chemical use (including photography) and in American English in all uses, but *gelatine* /-iːn/ is the more usual form in British English in contexts of the preparation of food.

gemma (in certain plants). Plural *gemmae* /-miː/ (-mee).

gender. Since the 14c. the word has been primarily a grammatical term, applied to groups of nouns designated as masculine, feminine, or neuter. During all these centuries, however, as the *OED* shows, it has also been used as a term meaning 'the sex of a person' (e.g. *His heyres of the masculine gender of his body lawfully begotten*—1474; *Of the fair sex ... my only consolation for being of that gender has been the assurance it gave me of never being married to any one among them*—Lady M. W. Montagu, 1709). The *OED* (1899) labelled this sense 'Now only jocular', but as the updated entry puts it: 'In the 20th cent., as *sex* came increasingly to mean sexual intercourse, *gender* began to replace it (in early use euphemistically) as the usual word for the biological grouping of males and females.' Since the 1960s this secondary meaning has come into much more frequent use, especially among feminists, to denote 'the state of being male or female as expressed by social or cultural distinctions and differences, rather than biological ones'. In other words, *gender* in this sense is often counterposed to *sex*, which is a biological given. Many new compound expressions have been created, including *gender bias, gender difference, gender discrimination, gender equality, gender gap, gender identity, gender imbalance, gender model, gender politics, gender role, gender-specific*, and *gender stereotype*; and academic disciplines now include the field of *gender studies*.

See also GRAMMATICAL GENDER.

gender-neutral language. This topic can be summarized under three main headings, which are dealt with in detail at the relevant entries in this dictionary. (*a*) The choice of non-gender specific nouns denoting professions and roles, e.g. *actor* not *actress, manager* not *manageress*, etc.; see FEMININE DESIGNATIONS; SEXIST LANGUAGE. (*b*) The now largely discarded use of *he, him, his*, etc. with indefinite reference to cover people of both sexes; see HE OR SHE. (*c*) as a corollary of (*b*), the often hotly debated issue of using *they, them, their*, etc., with singular reference, in order to avoid the unwieldy *he or she, him or her, his or her*, etc.; see AGREEMENT 6; HE OR SHE; THEY, THEIR, THEM.

genealogy. The existence of scores of words ending in *-ology* (*psychology, sociology*, etc.) traps some people into pronouncing and even spelling as if it too ended in *-ology*. It is derived ultimately from Greek γενεά 'race, generation' + -λόγος 'that treats of'. See -LOGY.

-general. For the plurals of such compound nouns as *Attorney-General, Lieutenant-General*, see PLURALS OF NOUNS 9.

generalissimo. Plural *generalissimos*. See -O(E)S 8.

generator. So spelt, not *-er*.

generic names and other allusive commonplaces. Burchfield (1996) shortened Fowler's much longer original entry on this topic, adding some further literary allusions. Burchfield's entry follows, untouched; it is interesting to note that many of the allusions will be obscure to most modern readers, and some are likely to be found only in classic literature. When Shylock hailed Portia as *A Daniell come to iudgement,* he was using a generic name in the sense here intended; the *Historie of Susannah* (from the Apocrypha) was in his mind. We do the same when we talk of a *Croesus* or a *Jehu* or a *Hebe* (daughter of Zeus and Hera) or a *Nimrod* or of *Bruin* (name of the bear in *Reynard the Fox*), *Chaunticleer* (in Chaucer's *Nun's Priest's Tale*), and *Reynard.* When we talk of *a Barmecide feast,* of *Ithuriel's spear,* of *a Naboth's vineyard,* of *being between Scylla and Charybdis,* of *Procrustean beds,* or *Draconian measures,* or *an Achilles heel,* we are using allusive commonplaces (to the *Arabian Nights, Paradise Lost,* the Bible, and classical antiquity). Some writers revel in such expressions, some eschew them, some are ill provided with them from lack of reading or imagination; some esteem them as decorations, others as aids to brevity. They are in fact an immense addition to the resources of speech, but they ask to be used with discretion. This article is not intended either to encourage or to deprecate their use; they are often in place, and often out of place; fitness is all. An allusion that strikes a light in one company will only darken counsel in another: most audiences are acquainted with the qualities of *a Samson, a Sancho Panza*, and *a Becky Sharp*, fewer with those of *a Count de Saldar* (Meredith's *Evan Harrington*) or *a Silas Wegg* (Dickens's *Our Mutual Friend*), and fewer still with those of *the Laputans* (in *Gulliver's Travels*) and *Ithuriel's spear.*

For examples of allusions of one kind or another see DEVIL'S ADVOCATE; FRANKENSTEIN; ILK; IRRELEVANT ALLUSION.

genesis. Spelt with an *e* after the *n* (cf. *genitive*).

genie /ˈdʒiːni/, a spirit of Arabian folklore. Plural *genies* or *genii* /ˈdʒiːnɪʌɪ/.

genitive. See APOSTROPHE B, D, E; OBJECTIVE GENITIVE; 'S AND -S' OF-POSSESSIVE.

genius, (person of) consummate intellectual power. Plural *geniuses* (*genii* only for 'spirit of place').

Genius is one of those nouns like *fun, magic,* and *rubbish,* which are rapidly spreading their wings as adjectives of a sort. *Genius* doesn't have all the qualities of a standard adjective—you can't modify it with *very, more,* etc., although you can use *most—,* but it often appears in informal writing in the phrases *genius idea, move, touch.* This seems to be a further extension of its use to modify nouns denoting professions and vocations, as in *genius artist, inventor, scientist,* etc. Some people wince at this new use, so for the time being it is best confined to informal writing, despite being a colourful addition to the lexicon of English. Examples: *the extraordinary documentary on genius artist Moebius—OEC* (undated); *Then, out of nowhere this genius idea flashed through my head—OEC,* 2008 (BrE); *Casting Carol Burnett as Sue's mom seemed like a genius move, but they never came close to leveraging her talents—DVD Verdict,* 2011 (AmE); *As you will soon find out, even the most genius plans involving potatoes and heavy drinking can fail—OEC,* 2004 (AmE).

genre. This originally French word is nowadays generally pronounced /ˈʒɒnrə/ (**zhon**-ruh), in an anglicized way, less often /ˈʒɒ̃rə/ with a nasalized vowel in line with its French pronunciation. Pronouncing the *g* like the *j* in *just* is not recommended.

gens /dʒɛnz/ (in Roman history and in anthropology). Plural *gentes* /ˈdʒɛntiːz/.

genteel. Its primary meaning is 'affectedly or ostentatiously refined or stylish', but it is often used ironically to mean 'of or appropriate to the upper classes'.

genteelly, the correct spelling of the adverb corresponding to GENTEEL.

gentle art, the. This phrase, long favoured by anglers as an affectionate description of their pursuit, was used ironically by the American painter James McNeill Whistler in his title *The Gentle Art of Making Enemies* (1890). The oxymoron was what made it effective. Fowler (1926) complained of it as a bit of a cliché, but it has continued to thrive. Examples: (in titles) *The Gentle Art of Verbal Self-Defense*—advt in *Reason* (US), 1991; (general contexts) *Hype is an American word for the gentle art of getting a tune into the pop charts without actually selling any records—Sunday Times,* 1968; *There's a gentle art to Indian cooking but it doesn't have to be labour-intensive—Observer,* 2006.

gentleman. Thanks to the erosion of class distinctions, *gentleman* has largely fallen out of use as an indicator of social class (= 'a man of good social position, especially one of wealth and leisure'), except vestigially in the phrase *gentleman farmer.* It remains most commonly in use either as a polite form of address: *Ladies and Gentlemen; Gentlemen* (when only males are present); and as a deferential way of referring to an adult male: in an audience, *the gentleman in the second row* (à la David Dimbleby on *Question Time*); *the Right Honourable Gentleman opposite* (in the House of Commons and the House of Representatives); referring to a visitor, customer, or client: *There's a gentleman at the door who says he is an old friend of yours.* An agreement which is binding in honour but not legally enforceable is still a **gentleman's agreement** (the commoner spelling, though *gentlemen's agreement* is also correct). But men (and women) using public lavatories have been subjected to an enforced drop in status, with the replacement of the sign *Gentlemen* by mere *Men.* As Burchfield (1996) lamented: '*Gentleman* was once a key word in social rankings: it now lies in the straitened circumstances of formulaic phrases, modes of address, and courtly titles.'

gentlewoman. In Fowler's day, in the lost worlds of Victorian and Edwardian society, *gentlewoman* could still be used as a synonym for 'lady', denoting a woman of good birth or breeding. As late as 1932 Rosamund Lehmann could still speak of a *distressed gentlewoman* (meaning 'an impoverished woman of good birth'), but nowadays the word would only be used in historical contexts, or ironically: *Caroline . . . remembered as a clever, courageous, kind and courteous gentlewoman—South Australian History,* 2002; *Underwear, as anyone au fait with the night-time antics of the Hilton/Spears/Lohan generation will attest, is an unnecessary part of a young gentlewoman's wardrobe in the modern age—Sunday Review,* 2007.

genuflection, a bending of the knee. Normally spelt so, the Latinate *genuflexion* being now rather unusual. See -XION.

genuine. 1 See AUTHENTIC.

2 The standard pronunciation is /dʒɛnjʊɪn/. In America the pronunciation with final /-ʌɪn/ is widespread but non-standard: 'the second [pronunciation], with the final syllable rhyming with *sign,* occurs chiefly among less educated speakers, esp. older ones. [It is also] sometimes used deliberately by educated speakers, as for emphasis or humorous effect' (*Random House Webster's College Dict.*, 1991). In Britain it is also often heard, especially in regional English, but is still considered non-standard.

genus. The standard pronunciation is /ˈdʒiːnəs/, rhyming with *genius*, though /ˈdʒɛnəs/ is frequently heard. Plural *genera* /ˈdʒɛnərə/ (**je**-nuh-ruh).

geographic(al). Both forms have a long history (*geographic* first recorded in 1630 and *geographical* in 1559). The *OEC* data shows that usage across the English-speaking world is evenly divided (if the magazine title *National Geographic* is excluded), but with a slight preference for the longer form, except in the US, where the shorter form is twice as common. The same data shows the longer form to be more frequent in all uses in the UK in a ratio of 3:1. In the US, usage to form compound words is divided: Webster's Third (1986 printing) lists the compounds *geographical biology, botany, coordinate, distribution, latitude, longitude, mile, point, position* as headwords; and *geographic race, terrapin, tongue, tortoise, variation.* From this evidence it would appear that the choice is made according to the preferences expressed in different academic disciplines. But other indeterminable factors may be at work.

geometric(al). As with GEOGRAPHIC(AL), both forms have a long history (*geometric* first recorded in 1630 and *geometrical* in 1552). The shorter form is more common in a 3:1 ratio across the English-speaking world as a whole; in British English it is somewhat more frequent than *geometrical*, but massively so in North American usage. The only fixed phrase in which *geometric* is almost invariable is *geometric mean*. Otherwise, a comparison of how the alternative forms collocate suggests that *geometric* is by far the preferred choice when the meaning is 'characterized by or decorated with regular lines and shapes', e.g. *geometric design, motif, pattern, shape.* Webster's Third (1986 printing) lists *geometrical clamp, construction, optics, pitch, radius* as headwords; but *geometric design, isomerism, lathe, mean, plane, progression, series, spider, stairs, tortoise, unit.* See also ARITHMETIC(AL) PROGRESSION.

geriatric is the normal, semi-official term used in Britain and the US when referring to the health care of old people (*a geriatric ward; geriatric patients*). When used outside such contexts, it typically carries overtones of being worn out and decrepit and can therefore be offensive if used to refer to people, as in *the photographer's bemused, bright-colour studies of the geriatric residents of San City.* In fact, it may be seen as insulting to old people if used of anything else other than them, e.g. *the US is full of geriatric coal-fired power stations.* See also ELDER.

German, a member of the Germanic group of languages (which includes English, Dutch, Swedish, and Danish) of the Indo-European family, the national language of Germany and Austria and one of the official languages of Switzerland. Like English, German has many dialectal forms. The standard language is called *High German* (*Hochdeutsch*). *Low German* (*Plattdeutsch*) is a comprehensive name used by philologists for Dutch, Frisian, Flemish, and some dialects within Germany itself. The words *High* and *Low* are merely geographical, referring to the southern, or mountainous, and the northern, or low-lying, regions in which the two varieties developed.

English has adopted a fair number of words from German, many of them in scientific and technical fields, including (showing the first date of record in English) *abseil* (1923), *allergen* (1911), *angst* (1922), *blitz* (1940), *diesel* (from a surname, 1894), *dirndl* (1937), *histamine* (1912), *kindergarten* (1852), *poltergeist* (1848), *quartz* (1676), *rucksack* (1853), *schadenfreude* (1895), *waltz* (1781). In German, by custom, all nouns have a capital letter (so *Angst*, etc.), but the capital is not normally carried over into English except in proper names (*Gestapo, Nazi*, etc.). As is the way with loanwords, the sounds of the original language, except when they exactly match English, are often modified to a greater or lesser extent. But just as often the sounds of the original language are retained in English even though the spellings are visibly 'foreign'. Thus, because Ger. *w* is pronounced /v/ and Ger. *eu* is pronounced /ɔɪ/ we pronounce *Wagner* /ˈvɑːgnə/ and *Freud* /frɔɪd/. Further examples showing the preservation in English of the original German sounds: *Beethoven* (first syllable) /ˈbeɪt-/, not /ˈbiːt-/, *Junker* /ˈjʊŋkə/, *Mainz* /mʌɪnts/, *Mozart* /ˈməʊtsɑːt/, *poltergeist* /ˈpɒltəgʌɪst/ (and /ˈpoʊltərˌgʌɪst/ in American English), *Riesling* /ˈriːslɪŋ/, *sauerkraut* /ˈsaʊəˌkraʊt/, *Schiller* /ˈʃɪlə/, *Volkslied* /ˈfɒlksliːt/.

gerrymander (originally US), to manipulate election districts unfairly so as to secure disproportionate representation; formed from the name of Elbridge Gerry, governor of Massachusetts in 1812 when the word was coined. As his surname was pronounced with initial /g/ not /dʒ/, *gerrymander* was pronounced with a 'hard' *g* throughout the 19c. in Britain, and still by some people in America. But the only pronunciation in Britain now is with /dʒ/, and this too is the dominant form in America. In both countries it is sometimes spelt **jerrymander**, which emphasizes its pronunciation but cuts it off from its etymological roots.

gerund.

1 Latin gerund and gerundive.
2 English gerund and participle.
3 Choosing gerund or infinitive.
4 Gerund and possessive.

Terminology. Many modern grammars avoid the term *gerund,* preferring the more neutral description '*-ing* form', or 'verbal noun'. The adjective corresponding to *gerund* is **gerundial**.

1 *Latin gerund and gerundive.* The distinction lies in Latin grammar not in English. The Latin gerund is a distinctive form of a verb functioning as a noun and is declinable: thus *amāre* 'to love' has the gerunds *amandi* 'of loving', *amando* 'by loving', *amandum* 'the act of loving'. It corresponds to the English verbal noun *loving.* In Latin, *difficultas navigando* means 'difficulty in sailing', *ars legendi* 'the art of reading', and *hic locus idoneus est dormiendo* 'this is a suitable place for sleeping'. From the same stem as *amandi,* etc., is formed in Latin an adjective *amandus* 'lovable', and in Latin grammar this is called the gerundive (or gerund-adjective). It is also often called a passive verbal adjective. The phrase *vir laudandus,* containing the gerundive of the verb *laudāre* 'to praise', translates as 'a man to be praised, a laudable man'. The Latin gerundive usually contains or implies a sense of obligation or necessity. English *agenda* is a Latin neuter plural gerundive, from the verb *agere,* 'to do', and means literally 'the things to be done'.

2 *English gerund and participle.* The English gerund is identical in form but not function with the active present participle. *Jogging* is a present participle in *he was jogging when we last saw him,* and a gerund in *jogging is a popular form of exercise.* Examples: (present participle) *girls on bicycles with gowns* billowing *behind them*—A. S. Byatt, 1985; *So we turned away, left them* guarding *nothing in particular*—W. Golding, 1985; (participial adjective) *My mother and I sat and talked, in a* musing *way*—V. Ackland, 1985; (simple gerund) *Mr Justice Curlewis also ruled out* caning *as a penalty*—B. Levin, 1985. Sometimes an *-ing* form can be interpreted as either a gerund or a participial adjective: a *flying machine* is either 'a machine for flying in' (gerund) or 'a machine that flies' (participial adjective).

3 *Choosing gerund or infinitive.* There is usually no choice between the rival types 'word (+ preposition) + gerund' and 'word + *to*-infinitive or plain infinitive': you are obliged to say *she* avoided marrying *me* (not 'to marry me') and *I* have decided to stick *to my original intention* (not 'I have decided sticking'). Some words, however, permit a choice. For example, *The directive* aims at ensuring *open passage through borders* is idiomatic; but so is *Much imagination has gone into the project, which* aims to attract *half a million visitors a year.* Also (see RATHER), both of the following examples are idiomatic: *She bestowed her activity,* rather than letting it be harnessed *to anyone else's needs*—A. Brookner, 1988; Rather than try *to improve our own appeal to those whose votes we must win, it is suggested we should do a deal of some sort with the Alliance*—*London Rev. Bks,* 1988. So too are both of the following: *Stella* began rolling her head *to and fro upon the pillow*—I. Murdoch, 1983; *Edith felt the hairs on the back of her neck* begin to crepitate—A. Brookner, 1986.

4 *Gerund and possessive.* See POSSESSIVE WITH GERUND for discussion of the difference between the formulations *I don't like his coming here* and *I don't like him coming here.*

gesticulation, gesture. Both words ultimately answer to Latin *gestus* 'action', related to *gerere* 'to carry'. *Gesture* entered English in the 15c. and at first meant 'manner of placing the body, posture, deportment'. By the 16c. it had come to mean 'movement of the body and limbs as an expression of thought or feeling' (its main current sense). The present-day sense 'an action to evoke *a friendly response'* is an early 20c. borrowing from French *geste* with the same meaning. From the time it entered the language in the 17c., *gesticulation* has had just one primary sense, 'the making of lively or energetic motions with the hands or body esp. as an accompaniment to or in lieu of speech'. In so far as the two words share this sense, it is the degree of animation that governs the choice, *gesticulation* indicating a more theatrical movement of the arms or the body.

get. 1 *Supposed overuse.* Burchfield, referring to his 1930s schooldays, wrote: 'the teachers were hostile to this small and useful verb: we were constantly asked to rewrite sentences containing *get* by substituting another verb in its place (*fetch, obtain, earn,* and a multitude of others). The exercises ... left one wondering if *get* could ever be used in an acceptable manner.' A similar fatwa was enforced by my teachers in the 1960s. But any dictionary will demonstrate that *get* is indispensable in scores of idiomatic phrases, particularly phrasal verbs: *get along with, get away with, get down, get down to, get even with,* etc. *Get* also has a range of natural uses in which it passes virtually unnoticed: *get one's feet wet, flattery will get you nowhere, get going, get the upper hand,* etc.

That *get* is an overused word to be avoided in good English is a schoolmasterish superstition, endorsed neither by Fowler (1926) nor by Gowers (1965). Idiomatic phrases involving *get* are best regarded as neutral in register, while alternatives are either markedly formal or appropriate to the written register: contrast e.g. *We got along fine* with *We were on good terms,* and *What are you getting at?* with *What are you suggesting* [or *implying*]*?*

The same holds true when *get* is used instead of more precise synonyms for its many meanings, e.g. *arrive, become, buy, catch, collect, obtain, receive.* There is no advantage in *I received a letter this morning* over *I got a letter this morning* nor in *She's gone to collect her post* over *She's gone to get her post.*

2 *have got = 'possess'.* Fowler wrote that '*have got* for *possess* or *have* is good colloquial English but not good literary English', and Gowers noted that '*I have it* and *he has it* are clear statements, but if we elide we must insert *got* to avoid the absurdity of *I've it* and the even greater absurdity of *he's it.*' In negative contexts and questions, British English *have* (or *had*) *not got* and *have* (or *had*) *you got?* are as common as (and somewhat less formal than) *do* (or *did*) *not have,* and *do* (or *did*) *you have?*, but the second alternative is the usual form in American English.

3 See GOTTEN.

4 For *have to be, have got to be,* see HAVE 4.

5 See AHOLD.

get-at-able meaning 'accessible, attainable', is recorded from 1799, and is now more common than the older *come-at-able* (1687). English allows many unwieldy formations, and these are notable examples. They are more quickly understood when written with hyphens. *Unputdownable,* however, is written without them.

geyser. In the *OED* (1899) precedence was given to the pronunciation /ˈɡeɪsə/ (**gay**-suh) for both senses (hot spring; apparatus for heating water), with /ˈɡʌɪsə, -zə/ (**gy**-suh, -zuh) as variants. Time has moved on. J. C. Wells (1990) recommends /ˈɡiːzə/ (**gee**-zuh) for both meanings in standard English, but '/ˈɡʌɪzə/ (if at all) particularly for the meaning "hot spring"'. In America and NZ the bathroom heater sense is not used and the pronunciation is uniformly /ˈɡʌɪzə(r)/.

-g-, -gg-. Words ending in *g* preceded by a single vowel double the *g* before a suffix beginning with a vowel, even in unstressed syllables: *wagging, sandbagged, zigzagged, shaggy*; *bootlegging, nutmegged*; *digging, priggish*; *froggy, leapfrogged, logging*; *humbugged, mugging.*

ghat, (in India) a mountain pass, steps to a river. So spelt, not *ghât, ghát, ghaut.* Pronounced /ɡaːt/.

ghetto. The recommended plural is *ghettos,* but *ghettoes* is also correct. See -O(E)S 2.

ghey. See GAY, 3.

ghillie, gillie (Scottish), a man or boy attending a person hunting or fishing, has a hard initial /ɡ/. The spelling *ghillie* is more frequent in *OEC* data than *gillie.*

ghoul, ghoulish. Pronounced /ɡuːl(ɪʃ)/ rhyming with *fool(ish),* not *owl(ish).*

gibber (verb), **gibberish. 1** Both with initial /dʒ/ not /g/. (It is worth noting that the *OED* (1899) gave only /g/ for the initial sound of *gibberish.*)

2 See JARGON.

gibbous (convex, protuberant, etc.). Pronounced /ˈgɪbəs/.

gibe, gybe. See JIBE

gift (verb). In 1996 Burchfield noted that *gift* 'despite its antiquity (first recorded in the 16c.) and its frequent use, especially by Scottish writers, since then, . . . has fallen out of favour . . . and is best avoided'. *OEC* data suggests that it continues to be uncommon. In fact, it is relatively more frequent in British than American English, and is used mostly in news and sport. However, the odium it incurs among editors, particularly across the pond, is disproportionate to its frequency, so it is wise to avoid it in writing for a US audience. It is disliked on three grounds: as a verb from a noun; as tainted by association with the meretricious language of advertising (e.g. *The Genesis Program is a National Down Payment Assistance Program that provides homebuyers with FREE GIFT MONEY . . . Genesis will gift up to $22,500*); and as the usurper of perfectly serviceable words such as 'present, give, bestow, donate'.

Objections to it as an instance of 'verbing' can be dismissed on historical grounds. The association with advertising will strike some people but not others. In order to decide whether it has usurped the role of other words, it is necessary to consider its four different meanings: (i) 'to give (something) as a gift, especially formally or as a donation or bequest': *the company gifted 2,999 shares to a charity*; (ii) 'to present (someone) with a gift or gifts': *the queen gifted him with a heart-shaped brooch*; (iii) 'to endow with (something)': *humanity is gifted with a moral sense*; (iv) the informal sports use, 'to inadvertently allow (an opponent) to have something': *the goalkeeper gifted Liverpool their last-minute winner.*

The definitions given above demonstrate by their wording that other verbs can replace *gift*: in (i) *give, donate,* or *bequeath*; (ii) *present*; (iii) *endow.* Replacing 'gifted' with 'donated' in *the company gifted 2,999 shares to a charity* might make it infinitesimally more formal. In *the queen gifted him with a heart-shaped brooch* there is a rather naff clash between the regal topic and the language used. Using 'endowed with' instead of 'gifted with a moral sense' sounds more formal and ponderous—but then, perhaps it should. In essence, whether one chooses to use *gift* or alternatives in those three meanings is a matter of formality, tone of voice, individual sensibility—and possibly specific editorial guidelines (the *Guardian* outlaws it other than in the next meaning).

Which brings us to the fourth, largely British, meaning. It has no obvious synonym and it is hard to see how to replace it in e.g. *Gary Neville gifted Arsenal their equalizer.*

See also FREE GIFT.

gigolo. Pronounce this 20c. loanword from French with initial /ʒ/ or /dʒ/. Plural *gigolos.* See -O(E)S 7.

gild the lily. It has often been pointed out that this firmly established idiom (= to try to improve what is already beautiful) is a not quite accurate rendering of Shakespeare's line in his *King John* (IV.ii.11): *To gilde refined Gold, to paint the Lilly; To throw a perfume on the Violet,* [etc.]. See MISQUOTATIONS.

gill. The separate words meaning 'the respiratory organ in fishes' and 'a ravine' are both pronounced /gɪl/. Those meaning 'a unit of liquid measure' and 'a female ferret' are pronounced /dʒɪl/. The female first name, whether spelt *Jill* or *Gill,* is pronounced /dʒɪl/.

gillie. See GHILLIE, GILLIE.

gillyflower. Pronounce with a soft initial /dʒ/.

gimbals (plural noun). Pronounced with soft initial /dʒ/.

gimmick, a 20c. word (first recorded in an American *Wise-Crack Dict.* of 1926) of unknown origin. In our publicity-conscious and heavily politicized age the word surged into common use after about 1950, and now is widely applied to any trifling or ingenious device, gadget, idea, etc., that catches the public eye but is regarded as likely to be short-lived, unsound, etc., as time goes by. Seldom has such an unpromising word made its way into the central core of the language so swiftly and so successfully.

gimp. In any of its meanings, deeply insulting, unpleasant, or otherwise, (a stupid person, a person with a physical disability, a sadomasochistic sexual partner, a trimming, a fishing-line), spelt *gimp* not *guimp* or *gymp* and pronounced with hard initial /g/.

gingerly. **1** Though its etymology is not absolutely settled, it seems pretty certain that *gingerly* has nothing to do with *ginger* the spice and hair colour. The *OED* plausibly suggests that it is a 16c. adaptation of an Old French word *gensor, genzor* (variously spelt), properly comparative of *gent* 'noble', but used also as a positive, 'pretty, delicate', + *-ly*. The first uses of *gingerly* as an adverb had the meaning 'elegantly, daintily (chiefly with reference to walking or dancing)'.

2 Unlike hundreds of adjectives ending in *-ly* (*bankerly, beggarly, comely, fatherly, friendly, portly*, etc.) *gingerly* works as an adjective and adverb. And it does so without changing form, which confuses some people about which part of speech constitutes its essence. In fact, it nearly always functions as an adverb (= in a careful or cautious manner) and very, very rarely as an adjective (= showing great care or caution). Examples: (adverb) *He descends gingerly from the cab—New Yorker,* 1990; *and they start gingerly to shift timbers and bricks*—P. Lively, 1991; (adjective) *Decision-makers must now, therefore, treat with* [*sic*] *this evidently explosive situation in a gingerly fashion—Guardian* (Trinidad), 2005.

Giotto, Giovanni. See ITALIAN SOUNDS.

gipsy. See GYPSY.

gird (verb). The normal past tense, past participle, and participial adjective forms are *girded.* But the variant form *girt* was in use in the 19c., and still appears as a self-conscious archaism, especially in passive or adjectival constructions, and, most memorably, in the Australian national anthem: *The doctor . . . girt on a cutlass . . . and . . . crossed the palisade*—R. L. Stevenson, 1883; *But still they set her up in the pose of the Madonna, girt in a sky-blue mantle for the family photo—Quadrant* Magazine, 2005 (Aust.); *Australians all let us rejoice, For we are young and free; We've golden soil and wealth for toil; Our home is girt by sea*—Australian national anthem.

girl. **1** Maud, the heroine in Anita Brookner's *Incidents in the Rue Laugier* (1995), *had learnt all the lessons she was supposed to have learnt, knew that girls were no longer to be addressed as girls but as women.* This passage reflects the fact that since the 1960s feminists have objected to the word *girl* as applied to adult females, and have had a large measure of success. In fact, few words are capable of raising some women's hackles as much as *girl* used in this way. Conservatives may say that using it thus is usually harmless and jokey; feminists might argue, in contrast, that it is disempowering and infantilizes women. It is certainly undeniable that there is often a huge gender gap between the connotations of *girl* and those of *boy* (and their respective derivatives) when applied to adults: *his boyish charm* versus *the film is a bit girlie*; *boys will be boys* versus *he's a big girl's blouse.* Since it is potentially so very contentious a word, it is better to be extremely cautious about making use of it. Some recommendations follow.

2 (*a*) Nouns which include it, such as *newsgirl, weathergirl, working girl* (two meanings), *girl Friday,* and *career girl,* can be replaced by more neutral words: *newsreader, weather forecaster, working woman/ sex worker, office assistant,* and *career woman.* (*b*) Avoid using it to refer to any woman in a job or role, for instance *the woman who helps us out in the shop* rather than *the girl* . . . (*c*) Although the word is still used informally by some women to refer to exclusive groups of women (*a night out with the girls; Come on, girls! Let's show them we are more than cheerleaders with sticks*), not all women are happy with this use of it. Using *the girls* is perhaps less contentious if the women concerned are youngish and there is an explicit parallel with *the boys.*

3 One area where it still seems to be used consistently is in the popular press, in expressions such as *glamour girl, page-three girl, cover girl, It girl,* and so forth. That it continues in use there supports the argument that the word can be patronizing or demeaning. Of course, men of various ages still have *girlfriends*, while a young man may go out with his *girl.* And the word survives uncontroversially in film, song, and book titles such as *Gregory's Girl* (1981), Helen Gurley Brown's *Sex and the Single Girl* (1962), or *Diamonds are a girl's* *best friend* (Leo Robin, 1949). In general use, however, *woman* or *young woman* are preferable, particularly when contrasted with *man*.

girly is the more common spelling by far, but *girlie* is also used, and is not wrong.

girt. See GIRD (verb).

given name. See CHRISTIAN NAME.

given (that). *Given* is used as a preposition, and both it and *given that* are used as subordinating conjunctions. They operate in a similar manner to *considering* (*that*), *granted* (*that*), and a few others. The crucial point is that, in such constructions, *given* and the other words like it are free of the need to be attached to a particular subject, and so cannot be viewed as the verb in a participle clause. In other words, they are not unattached participles.

Examples of these uses go back to the 19c. (e.g. *Given a reasonable amount of variety and quality in the exhibits, an exhibition ... is sure to attract large numbers—Manchester Examiner,* 1885) and form part of standard English everywhere. Examples: (preposition) *He didn't think that, given her ambitions and temperament, she would enjoy it*—A. West, 1984; *There are doubts over the quality of the player he will be able to attract, given the uncertainty hanging over the north London club—Daily Tel.*, 2007; (*given* as subordinating conjunction) *Given what the boy's father was like, they had all been prepared for something roughish*—I. Murdoch, 1962; *Given how busy the Spanish monarchs were in the 1480s, it's a wonder they gave Columbus any notice at all—Chicago Tribune*, 1988; *(given that* as subordinating conjunction*) The biggest savings would come through rationalisation given that roughly two-thirds of the cost is attributable to teachers' salaries—TES*, 1990; *Given that the government shies away from a graduate tax, student loans are the next best way of making sure that students who benefit from higher education foot some of the bill—Economist*, 1991.

glacial, glacier. The standard pronunciations in BrE are /ˈgleɪsɪəl/ (**glay**-sɪ-uhl) and /ˈglasɪə/ (rhyming with *brassiere*) respectively; in AmE, /ˈgleɪʃəl/ and /ˈgleɪʃər/.

glacis (bank sloping down from a fort). Pronounced in BrE /ˈglasɪs/ or /-si/, in AmE /glaˈsi/ or /ˈglasi/.

gladiolus. 1 Pronounced /gladɪˈəʊləs/. The pronunciation recommended by the *OED* in 1899, namely /glaˈdʌɪələs/, is now obsolete. In classical Latin (Pliny) the word, which is a diminutive of *gladius* 'sword', had four short syllables, but this pattern has not been carried over into English.

2 The recommended plural is *gladioli* /-lʌɪ/. *Gladioluses* is too clumsy; *gladiolus,* i.e. the same form as the singular, is used in some plant catalogues, but has nothing to commend it. The problem can of course be circumvented altogether by using the conversational plural *glads.*

gladsome. See -SOME. In continuous use from the 14c. to the 19c., it is now restricted to hymns, literary contexts, or used as a deliberate archaism. Example: *She heads straight for him and gives him a gladsome embrace and a kiss on the cheek*—T. Stoppard, 1993 (stage direction).

glamour. 1 The corresponding adjective is **glamorous**. Some people mistakenly suppose that *glamorous*, dropping the *u* before the *r*, is an American only spelling and therefore spell the word **glamourous.* In fact, *glamorous* is the correct spelling on both sides of the pond and everywhere else, while **glamourous* is universally a mistake. See also -OUR AND -OR.

2 *Glamour* with *-our* is dozens of times more frequent than the ending in *-or,* which is very rarely used outside American English, and even there is not at all common.

3 The word, which was brought into general literary use by Walter Scott *c.*1830, was originally Scottish, and etymologically was an alteration of the word *grammar* with the sense ('occult learning, magic, necromancy') of the old word *gramarye.* It then passed into standard English with the meaning 'a delusive or alluring charm', and, nearly a century later (in the 1930s), was applied to the charm or physical allure of a person, especially a woman, first in AmE and then in BrE and elsewhere.

glance, glimpse. 1 *Noun: standard use.* A *glance* (usually followed by *at*) is a brief look at something or someone, whereas a *glimpse* (usually followed by *of*) is what is seen by taking a glance. Examples: (glance) *He cast a doting glance at his* *wife*—M. Underwood, 1973; *There were glances of frustration as balls went astray and half-chances failed to be converted—Independent,* 1999; (glimpse) *The automatic roof light gave me a quick glimpse of two men*—A. Ross, 1970; *Here's a possible glimpse of the future: it's the year 2030, our landfill rubbish dumps are full . . . —Leicester Mercury*, 2004.

2 *Problems.* It was Fowler (1926) who noted that the two different but related meanings could be confused, e.g. 'a glimpse at the map will show why . . . ' (read *glance at*). The *OEC* shows this confusion still happening: e.g. **A glimpse at the world's trouble spots is enough to delineate the scale of the problem—Sunday Herald,* 2001; **He stole glimpses at the picture all morning—OEC* (undated).

To complicate matters, while the normal preposition after glimpse is *of,* it is also followed by *at,* particularly in American English. While this use (presumably influenced by *look at*) goes back at least as far as Jane Austen ('I had only a glimpse at the child' in a letter of 1798), many readers will find it unusual, though it can hardly be considered non-standard: *?With only nine days to go before their big day, we are getting a glimpse at Prince William and Kate Middleton's wedding program—CNN* transcripts, 2011.

3 The verbs differ in meaning in the same way as the nouns. *Glimpse* takes a direct object whereas *glance* requires a preposition: *He glanced down at the face of his gold Rolex*—W. Wager, 1970; *I wanted to glimpse the buildings, monuments and streets from which the nightmares of the past century had been unleashed—Daily Tel.*, 2004. The verb meanings can be confused too, as in **Just to glimpse at the long list of Kick It Out's sponsors should tell you a lot*—weblog, 2004 (BrE).

glassful. In the plural, care should be taken to distinguish *glassfuls* from *glasses full.* A *glassful* is an amount contained in a glass, and *three glassfuls* (e.g. of water) means three times this amount, though not necessarily held in three glasses. *Three glasses full* (of water) means three different glasses each full of water. Note that there is no form *glassesful.* See also -FUL.

glimpse. See GLANCE.

-glish. See SPANGLISH.

glissade. Pronounced /glɪˈsɑːd/.

global. From the 17c. to the 19c. it simply meant 'spherical, globular'. Beginning in the late 19c., in imitation of French *global,* it acquired the meaning 'pertaining to or embracing the totality of a number of items, categories, etc.; all-inclusive' (e.g. *The global sum of £300 million looked like the result of bargaining with the Treasury—Ann. Reg. 1947,* 1948; *A 'global' picture can be obtained from the use of such techniques as Rorschach—Brit. Jrnl Psychology,* 1952). In the course of the 20c. it became widely used to mean 'worldwide, involving the whole world', especially in military and environmental jargon: thus *global war(fare); global village* (coined by Marshall McLuhan in 1960 in recognition of the fact that new technology and communications have effectively 'shrunk' world societies to the level of a single village); and especially *global warming,* a term that became established in the 1980s to mean 'a gradual increase in the overall temperature of the earth's atmosphere generally attributed to the greenhouse effect caused by increased levels of carbon dioxide, CFCs, and other pollutants'.

In computer technology from the 1960s onwards, *global* means 'operating on the whole of a file or program', so that a *global change* made to an item is one that affects every occurrence of that item.

glossary, dictionary, vocabulary. A *glossary* is an alphabetical list of the technical words used in a specific subject or text, with explanations. *Glossaries* are usually of modest length, e.g. those of the British Standards Institution (of aeronautical terms, highway engineering terms, etc.), and those appended to the texts in series like those of the Early English Text Society and the Scottish Text Society. A *dictionary* is usually a much more ambitious work, though sometimes, when restricted to the terminology of a specified subject, *dictionary* and *glossary* are virtually interchangeable terms. A *vocabulary* supplies the reader of a book in a foreign language (e.g. a school edition of Latin texts) with the English equivalents of the foreign words used in it. A *glossary* selects what is judged to be obscure; a *vocabulary* assumes that all is obscure. *Vocabulary* also means the whole stock of words used by those speaking a given language, by any set of persons, or by an individual.

glue. The inflected forms and derivatives are spelt *glues, glued, gluing;* and **gluey**.

glycerine /ˈglɪsəˌriːn/. So spelt in BrE, but usually **glycerin** /-rɪn/ in AmE. In scientific writing the synonymous term *glycerol* is customary.

gn-. In nearly all current English words initial *gn* is pronounced /n/ with the *g* silent, though it is clear that in native words like *gnat* and *gnaw* the *g* was sounded until the 17c. The main exceptions are *gnocchi,* a 19c. loanword from Italian, which is sometimes pronounced with initial /nj/; and *gnu* (from a Bushman language in S. Africa), which is also sometimes pronounced with initial /nj/, beside the normal pronunciation /nuː/. All such words of Greek origin (*gnomic, gnostic,* etc.) are pronounced with the *g* silent.

gneiss (metamorphic rock). This 18c. loanword from German is now always pronounced /nʌɪs/, with the initial *g* silent.

go (noun). Plural *goes.* See -O(E)S 3.

go (verb). Six uses of the verb are worth commenting on. **1** *goes without saying.* Though few people are aware of the fact, *goes without saying* (first recorded in English in 1878) is a naturalized Gallicism (see GALLICISMS 2). Linguistic eurosceptics opposed to the use of such loan translations can replace it with *needless to say, need hardly be said, of course,* etc.

2 *go* + bare infinitive. This was the primary construction in English until the 17c., e.g., in Shakespeare's *Winter's Tale, Ile* go see *if the Beare bee gone; I must* go buy *Spices for our sheepe-shearing.* It survives as a normal construction in American English (*hide and* go seek), but in British English is used in only a few fixed expressions, such as *he can* go hang *for all I care, to* go get (chiefly US), and the relatively recent US *go figure* (1980). In Britain the normal constructions are of the type *go and* + infinitive or *go* + *to*-infinitive. Examples of *go* + bare infinitive: *I'll go put your lovely flowers in water*—J. Updike, 1986 (US); *Go look in the mirror—New Yorker,* 1986. Occasional examples turn up outside N. America as late as the 19c. (natural uses) and in the 20c. (probably as conscious Americanisms): *'Very true,' said I, 'let us go fetch it.'*—R. M. Ballantyne, 1858; *'Sweetheart, I'm ravenous. Go call us a cab.'*—Maggie Gee, 1985 (UK).

3 *go* + *and.* The combination *go* + *and* + infinitive often has special meanings: (*a*) an 'inchoative' function, suggesting beginning the action indicated in the infinitive: *She ... said she would go and turn the sprinkler off herself—New Yorker,* 1986; *He packed the sacks with goods for Kaliel to go and sell*—D. Matthee, 1986 (SAfr.); (*b*) as an instruction: *It's late, child ... Go and get some sleep*—J. M. Coetzee, 1977 (SAfr.); *Tell them, go and beg in the marketplace*—A. Desai, 1988 (India); (*c*) used informally or conversationally to mean 'to be so foolish, unreasonable, or unlucky as to—'. *You say you're my best friend but then you go and pull shit like this—OEC,* 2004 (AmE); *You herd cattle all day, you come to despise them, and pretty soon ... you have gone and shot one*—G. Keillor, 1990; *And, fool that I am, I've gone and done it again, provoking much the same reaction*—weblog, 2003 (BrE). These constructions are standard in all varieties of English.

4 *go* = say. The use in question here is illustrated by: *Butch and I were discussing this problem, and Butch goes, 'But you promised you'd do it.' Then I go, 'Well, I changed my mind.'—Chicago Tribune,* 1989. This use is seen by Sara Tulloch (1991) as occurring mainly 'in young people's speech ... (usually in the present tense, reporting speech in the past)'. She sees it as 'an extension of the use of *go* to report a non-verbal sound of some kind expressed as an onomatopoeic word or phrase, as in "the bell went ding-dong" or "the gun went bang", perhaps with some influence from nursery talk (as in "ducks go quack, cows go moo")'. It is indeed common in children's speech and especially (but not only) in America: *In school Friday our teacher held up a note and goes to Amy, 'Did you pass this note?' And Amy goes, 'Who, me?'*—dialogue in strip cartoon in *Chicago Sun-Times,* 1988.

An intermediate stage between onomatopoeia and reported speech is found in Dickens's *Pickwick Papers* (1836): *He was roused by a loud shouting of the post-boy on the leader. 'Yo- yo-yo-yo-yoe,' went the first boy. 'Yo-yo-yo-yoe!' went the second.*

5 *go for it.* The American cox in the Oxford boat in the 1987 Boat Race had the slogan *Go for it* on the back of his rowing shirt. He thus drew attention to the arrival in Britain of this popular American phrase of the 1980s, which has now become standard in BrE as well. Examples: *I told her about Scott* [*sc.* a boyfriend]. *Eileen said, 'Go for it, Andrea.'*—*New Yorker*, 1986. It is probably an extension of the use of *go* + *for*, as in *I could go for you in a big way, kid* (= be enthusiastic about, be enamoured of).

6 *not go there* is a way of suggesting that a subject should be avoided. It can either be a warning to someone else, *don't (even) go there*, or a statement that the speaker will avoid the topic, *we won't (even) go there*. This idiom, first recorded in the 1990s, is vivid but highly informal: *Don't talk about my childhood. Don't even go there. You know nothing!*—fiction website, 2004 (AmE); *There's also the question of bovine flatulence in NZ, but I won't go there*—weblog, 2003 (NZ).

gobbledegook. (Also spelt **gobbledygook**, which is the more common spelling in American English, while in British English *gobbledegook* is slightly more frequent.) **1** This highly expressive and dismissive term, first recorded in America in 1944, describes writing that is (i) incomprehensible to non-specialists (and possibly to specialists too), and (ii) complete and utter nonsense, e.g. *You insult my intelligence by trying to put gobbledy-gook like that over me*—P.G. Wodehouse, 1951. It was almost certainly coined as a representation of a turkey cock's gobble. The *OED* defines it as 'official, professional, or pretentious verbiage or jargon', which gives it plenty of latitude. But while long-windedness and overuse of technical terms are certainly necessary conditions, they are not sufficient: *gobbledegook* must also be directed to a general reader or listener in whom it produces complete bafflement.

The following passage from an American policy document about transport plans (as reported in a Chicago newspaper of 1995) shows *gobbledegook* in its most virulent form. The opacity of technical terms such as 'conformity determinations'; unusual word choices such as 'solicit' and 'supplemental'; the ungainly syntax, for example 'respectively' referring to five different items all surround readers with a dense blanket of verbal fog from which few will emerge. *While EPA [the Environmental Protection Agency] will solicit comments on other options, the supplemental notice of proposed rulemaking on transportation conformity will propose to require conformity determinations only in the metropolitan planning areas (the urbanized area and the contiguous area(s) likely to become urbanized within 20 years) of attainment areas which have exceeded 85 percent of the ozone, CO, NO 2, PM-10 annual, or PM-10 24-hour NAAQS within the last three, two, one, three, and three years respectively.* Presumably, the statement made good sense to members of the EPA. Its accuracy is not in question. The fault lies in its inability to make any sense to the general public to whom it was addressed.

2 Authentic *gobbledegook* emerges in the abyss between the type of technical language used in the example just cited, and its comprehension by the general public. In contrast, among professionals working within particular disciplines, such as computing, economics, or linguistics, the use of technical terms (which some people will judge to be jargon) is quite legitimate, not to say essential. In some domains, especially law, complex language arises from a need to achieve detailed precision and to avoid the ambiguity or uncertainty that can result from using everyday language. For example, it is necessary to know the meaning of the words *lien* and *demurrage* if one is to understand the following passage (from a legal newsletter of 1988): *The Commercial Court has held that where a shipowner exercises a lien on cargo for demurrage due, he can claim demurrage for the further period of delay caused by his own exercise of the lien.* The words themselves are not replaceable by simpler terms.

3 Fields of activity where *gobbledegook* flourishes include academia, the social services, welfare, insurance, human resources, taxation, banking, local government, politics in general, and the NHS. Nevertheless, the clarity of some public documentation has improved noticeably since the 1980s, partly as a result of decisive action by Margaret Thatcher's government, and the work of the Plain English Campaign and similar organizations. Since there are as yet no helplines for the problem, anyone worried that their writing might be infected could consult any of the many forums or blogs dealing with plain English, or detoxifying books such as Sir Ernest Gowers' *The Complete Plain Words* (1954 and later editions),

Richard C. Wydick's *Plain English for Lawyers* (1979 and later editions), Cutts and Maher's *Gobbledygook* (1984), Martin Cutts' *The Oxford Guide to Plain English* (2nd edition, 2004).

4 As a hopefully inspiring coda to the discussion, the following from the arts pages of a newspaper shows that *gobbledegook* is not confined to the world of 'suits' and officialdom: *In some ways, the notion of longevity has become eccentric, or proposed as simply an example of historical signage: the breadth of Proust's fiction, for example, or the gravitas of Henry Moore's sculpture. Culturally we tend to be more focused on the neurasthenic effects of the short-term, than the vista of the long term. Within an increasingly secular and fragmentic [sic] society, the notion of sacred or civic art has been replaced by a culture of commentary and reaction to a culture, in fact, which is more linked to topicality than to longevity—Independent,* 2003.

The newspaper's own chief copy-editor commented a few days later: 'I won't try to translate that into plain English. Anyone who thinks that they can is cordially invited to have a go.' It appears that no one ever did.

See also BAFFLEGAB; JARGON; OFFICIALESE; PLAIN ENGLISH.

god, God. Whether or not one believes in a divine supreme being, it is conventional to capitalize the word *God* when it refers to 'the creator and ruler of the universe and source of all moral authority' in monotheistic religions—Christianity, Islam, Judaism, etc., and in phrases associated with that meaning: thus *God the Father*; *the Trinitarian God of Christian worship*; *God forbid, God's gift to women*; *to play God*, etc. When the word refers to a deity, an image of a deity, or in its metaphorical meanings, it is written with a lower case initial *g*. Thus, *wooden gods from the Congo*; *false gods*; *don't make money your god*; *the fashion victims for whom he is a god*; *he dialled the number and, the gods relenting, got through at once*, etc. Most style guides recommend that pronouns and adjectives referring to the monotheistic God should be written with a lower case g, as in the Bible and the Book of Common Prayer: *And God called the light Day, and the darkness he called Night.*

God's acre (a churchyard) is modelled on German *Gottesacker.* It is properly 'God's seed-field', in which the bodies of the departed are 'sown' (1 Cor. 15: 36-44) in hope of the resurrection.

Goidelic. See GAELIC.

gold(en). For objects made in part or whole of gold, the shorter form is now usual (*gold ring, gold watch*). *Golden* more commonly means 'coloured or shining like gold' (*golden hair, golden retriever, golden syrup*), and is the form preferred in figurative uses (*golden age*). But the distinction is far from complete. There are plain indications, if not of gold itself, then certainly of wealth, in the phrases *Golden Fleece, golden goose,* and the widespread use of *golden* to refer to financial inducements in phrases such as *golden handcuffs, handshake, parachute.*

golliwog. This is the standard spelling for the word, first used as *Golliwogg* in 1895, and now only used in historical or collecting contexts, for 'a black-faced brightly dressed soft doll with fuzzy hair' or for the once very popular badges produced for most of the 20c. by Scottish jam makers Robertson's.

golosh. See GALOSH.

good (adverb). In continuous use from the 14c. to the 18c., it dropped out of standard use *c.*1800, and now survives mainly in non-standard use, especially in American English. Examples: *But it didn't work too good, because you still managed to get a coffee break out of it—New Yorker,* 1991; *Like I said, the rent's all paid. I'm looking after the place good*—Maurice Gee, 1994 (NZ).

good and. Used colloquially to mean 'completely', it has been in common use in American English since about the 1880s and elsewhere at a slightly later date. Examples: *When I was good and drunk I tried to start a conversation with the other people in the bar*—Nigel Williams, 1985; *Only I'm good and tired of watching high-quality people fuck up in practical life*—S. Bellow, 1987; *Leave when you are good and ready—Time Magazine,* 2004. See HENDIADYS.

goodbye. Always spelt as one word in BrE. The plural of the noun is *goodbyes.* The AmE variant **good-by** has pl. *good-bys.*

good will, good-will, goodwill. The spelling as one word is more common in all varieties of English than *good will* as two separate words. The latter is an option when the meaning is 'wishing well to a person, cause, or idea'; but *goodwill* is normal when it means 'the established reputation of a business regarded as a quantifiable asset'. The hyphenated spelling is not very common, and should only be used before another noun (i.e. attributively), e.g. *goodwill ambassador, gesture,* etc., but the single-word form is much more frequent in this position, e.g. *goodwill ambassador, gesture,* etc.

google. Here is one of the key words of our age (in more than one sense of the word *key*), vertiginously rising within a short space of time (the first record in the *OED* is of 1999) from nowhere to almost global familiarity, even to those who are not computer-literate. *Google,* it hardly needs to be said, is the proprietary name of an Internet search engine, ranked by its supporters alongside inventions such as the wheel and the microchip in its usefulness. To *google* is to search for information on the Internet using a search engine, and like other verbs based on everyday activities derived from proprietary terms (*hoover, xerox,* etc.) it has a small initial letter when used in this way, because a verb cannot be registered as a trademark. For this reason, most modern dictionaries include the word as a verb only, which is both intransitive and transitive: one can *google* something sought (*Met this woman last night at a party and I came right home and googled her—New York Times,* 2001) or one can simply *google.* No doubt in time the word will give rise to other extended and figurative uses as well. The adjective **googleable**, 'capable of being found by an internet search' is already listed in the *ODO.* Not yet listed are the two amusing derivatives **googleganger** and **doppelgoogler**, the first of which is rather more common. Both refer to a person whose name is the same as your own, and references to whom are mixed in with references to yourself when you do an Internet search for your own name. The origin of both is the originally German *doppelgänger,* a double of a living person, and *googleganger* was voted the Macquarie Dictionary word of the year in 2011.

gormandize. See GOURMANDISE.

gorse. See FURZE.

gossip. The inflected and derived forms are *gossiped, gossiping; gossiper; gossipy.*

got. This past tense and past participle of *get* is as productive as the verb as a whole. (*a*) (slightly informal) used with a *to*-infinitive meaning 'to have an opportunity to': *This was considered a bonus for me, because I got to sit in the front*—F. Kidman, 1988 (NZ); *Mark and his mother had moved to Holland when he was just four months old, meaning he never got to meet his dad—Mirror,* 2004. (*b*) (non-standard in BrE) *got to* ellipitically for have got to = must: *We just got to live. Isn't that so?*—A. Fugard, 1980 (SAfr.); *'We got to help these people,' he says, 'any way we can'—Newsweek,* 1990. (*c*) *got to be* (slightly informal) (i) meaning 'came round to being': *It got to be 11 p.m. We left the way we had come—New Yorker,* 1989; (ii) meaning 'has to be': *what's got to be the most pleasurable prog-rock to come along in a decade—Musician,* 1991 (US). (*d*) (non-standard in BrE) *got* elliptically for *have got* meaning 'possess': *What you got in that jar, Alvie?*—M. Eldridge, 1984 (Aust.); *I can't get my head around it, Sharon. Suddenly I got three fathers—at least—Times,* 1987 (preview of the TV programme *EastEnders*).

gotten. 1 Few language traits mark out someone as American more readily than their natural use of *gotten* as an alternative to *got* as the past participle of *get.* This use has spread to Australia and New Zealand, as some of the examples below will show. Although it was historically in regular use in Britain, *gotten* had become defunct (except in *ill-gotten*) in southern Britain, but the *OEC* data suggests that its use is now increasing there. In American English, it tends to be used particularly when the meaning is 'have (or has) obtained or acquired', i.e. when it denotes coming into possession. When it denotes the fact of possession now, *got* is used. The difference can be seen by comparing the two sentences *We have gotten an apartment in Manhattan,* which means we have recently acquired it, and *We have got an apartment in Manhattan,* which means we have one available to us (as well as a house in Boston, for example). Modern British English uses *got* in both cases, with consequent occasional ambiguity. Examples: *An army friend . . . had gotten us tickets for a Tchaikovsky extravaganza*—Philip Roth, 1979; *Have you* *gotten your paper the last couple of Sundays?—New Yorker,* 1986; *I'd only gotten about 4 hours of sleep the night before*—weblog, 2005 (Canad.)

2 *Gotten* is also often used when the meaning is 'have (or has) become, come, developed, etc.', i.e. when the idea of progression is involved: *Has my reputation in town gotten that bad?*—T. Winton, (AusE) 1985; *This last year and a half I've gotten to fill out a lot of forms*—J. Updike, 1986; *People in the USA have gotten much healthier in the past 30 years—USA Today,* 1988; *It had gotten too quiet in the neighborhood*—T. McGuane, 1989; *It's strange that I still haven't gotten used to it over the past fifteen years*—fiction website, 2004 (AmE); (gotten used to) *Been sewn up for a long time and the locals have gotten used to the idea*—T. Winton, 1985 (Aust.); *Joe had not gotten used to Astrid's friends*—T. McGuane, 1989.

gourd (fleshy fruit or its shell). Both /gʊəd/ and /gɔːd/ (**goo**-uhd, gawd) are standard.

gourmand, gourmet. 1 The history of the two words is known but has left us with a curious legacy. *Gourmand* entered the language in the 15c. in the sense 'a glutton'. From the mid-18c. it also acquired the meaning 'one who is fond of delicate fare; a judge of good eating', and was so used by Coleridge, Darwin, Charlotte Brontë, among others. *Gourmet* entered the language in the early 19c. and has always been used only to mean 'a connoisseur in the delicacies of the table'. The preference of conservative speakers is to restrict the favourable sense (a judge of good eating) to *gourmet,* and to apply *gourmand* only to those for whom quantity is more important than quality, e.g. *Such places are more gourmand than gourmet, tied up with the wrong kind of greed and a vulgar desire to impress—Observer Food Monthly,* 2005. In practice, however, *gourmand* is most often used as a synonym of *gourmet,* e.g. *The carefully cooked ideas behind Slow Food are beginning to appeal to people outside gourmand circle—OEC,* 2004. *Gourmet* is frequently used attributively (*a gourmet meal*), whereas *gourmand* cannot be so used.

2 *Gourmand* is either Anglicized as /ˈgʊəmənd/ or /ˈgɔːmənd/, or pronounced in a French manner as /ˈgʊəmɑ̃/. *Gourmet* is always /ˈgʊəmeɪ/ or /ˈgɔːmeɪ/. Neither word is italicized.

gourmandise. This is the recommended form for the noun (= the habits of a gourmand; indulgence in gluttony) and has the advantage of clearly showing the word's derivation from *gourmand.* For the verb (= to eat or devour voraciously), *gourmandize* seems to be the most common spelling, but *gourmandise, gormandize,* and *gormandise* are also correct.

governor-general. The plural form recommended is *governor-generals,* but *governors-general* is still current as an acceptable variant. See PLURALS OF NOUNS 9.

gradable, gradability, gradience. The useful concept of *gradability* in grammar and semantics was first extensively used by Quirk et al. (1972) and by Lyons (1977), and has passed into general currency. A particular set of words can be seen as forming a continuum of size, degree, vulnerability, etc.: thus *few, little, much,* and *many* are *gradable* in that they do not represent a fixed number, quantity, size, etc. By contrast, words like *single* and *married,* or *male* and *female,* cannot be seen in terms of *gradience*: one is either single or married, male or female. Most adverbs and adjectives are *gradable* (*pretty, rich; slowly, patiently*) in that it is a matter of judgement what constitutes prettiness, richness, etc. They have comparative and superlative forms, and can be modified by intensifiers such as *extremely, so, very,* etc. Others are only controversially *gradable,* e.g. *perfect, unique*(*ly*). See also ADJECTIVE 4; UNIQUE.

graduate (verb). There is no problem about its ordinary intransitive sense (*he graduated from Yale in 1984; she graduated last year*). The particularly American English transitive type *he graduated Yale in 1984* is often criticized and is best avoided. In AmE the word is not restricted to the completion of a university degree: it is also used for the completion of a high-school course.

Graecism, Graecize, Graeco-. See GRECISM, GRECIZE, GRECO-.

graffiti. The word is, strictly speaking, a plural (Italian) form, and therefore ought to require plural agreement. Burchfield insisted that it did, but nowadays many dictionaries accept it both as a mass noun (like *confetti, data, spaghetti*) used collectively with singular agreement, and as a plural count noun. Examples: (mass noun) *what graffiti there* was *would be written largely in Latin—Independent on Sunday,* 1998; *The main concern was the impression graffiti* creates *of the district*—website, 2004; (count noun) *The inscription on the fire engine in New College cloisters is written in Latin and so* are some of *the graffiti you find chalked on the walls of Oxford lavatories*—J. Morris, 1978;

The word comes from the Italian *graffio,* 'a scratch'. Before the 1960s it was mainly art historians and archaeologists who used the word to describe drawings or writing scratched on the walls of ancient classical ruins. In their work they unfailingly distinguished the singular form *graffito* and the plural form in *-i.* The singular form is still available to refer to a single instance: *A graffito in the fourth-floor women's bathroom in the University library—Daily Northwestern,* 1991.

Using *graffiti* as a mass noun or a plural count noun is nowadays generally acceptable, but the same does not apply to its use as a singular, as in *'I don't need drugs' the T-shirt graffiti proclaims—Observer,* 1981. Many people object to this; but using the singular *graffito* could sound rather precious or overpedantic. It all depends on the context and the audience. That the word causes, and will continue to cause, confusion (if not verbal anxiety) is clear.

-gram. 1 A long-standing suffix (ultimately representing Greek γράμμα 'something written') in many English words, including *anagram, diagram, epigram, mammogram,* and *telegram.*

2 Since the late 1970s the suffix has combined with various words to produce a wide range of (mostly humorous) formations based on *telegram,* 'denoting a message delivered by a representative of a commercial greetings company, especially one outrageously dressed to amuse or embarrass the recipient'. Examples (some of which are respelt when used as proprietary terms) include *kissogram* (*Kissagram*), the best-known of them all; and *strippergram* (*Strip-a-Gram*).

grammar, as the *ODO* defines it, is 'the whole system and structure of a language or of languages in general, usually taken as consisting of syntax and morphology (including inflections) and sometimes also phonology and semantics.' At the risk of simplifying enormously, this is what linguists generally understand by the term, and they see their task as describing it scientifically and objectively, not judgementally. While this book's *raison d'être* is self-evidently to provide guidance on matters of style and usage, the word 'grammar' is only ever used in it in the meaning just defined.

For the general public, however, the word mostly has a crucially different meaning: 'a set of actual or presumed prescriptive notions about correct use of a language'. That umbrella provides cover for a wealth of criticism as 'bad grammar' of many aspects of language that fall well outside the range of the technical definition, including spelling, changes to the meaning of words, jargon of different kinds, nouns being used as verbs, the use of 'fillers', and verbs ending in *-ize/-ise.*

Grammar, in modern terms, is a branch of *philology* (the older term) or *linguistics* (the usual current term). Other components or branches of linguistics include: *etymology*: the origin, formation, and development of a word: OE *æcer* is the etymon of modE *acre*; *morphology*: deals with the internal structure of word forms; the word *enrichment* consists of three *morphemes,* namely *en-* + *rich* + *-ment; orthography*: correct or conventional spelling; the study or science of spelling; *phonology*: the study of sounds in a language; *semantics*: the branch of linguistics concerned with meaning and change of meaning; *syntax*: the grammatical arrangement of words, phrases, and clauses, showing their connection and relation; *word formation*: the way in which compound words are formed from simpler elements, e.g. *musicology* from *music* (noun) + the combining form *-ology.*

See also DESCRIPTIVE GRAMMAR; PRESCRIPTIVISM.

grammatical agreement. See AGREEMENT.

grammatical concord. See AGREEMENT.

grammatical gender. In the earliest form of our language, called Old English or Anglo-Saxon (*c.*740 to 1066), nouns fell into three classes, masculine, feminine, and neuter, i.e. were distinguished by their grammatical gender. Thus *stān* 'stone' was masculine, *giefu* 'gift' was feminine, and *scip* 'ship' was neuter. The definite article and most adjectives varied to accord with the gender of the accompanying noun. This system was lost by the end of the 11c. by which time, among other factors, the distinctive unstressed vowel endings, which were one of the mainstays of the system, had weakened to the neutral sound schwa, /ə/. Grammatical gender is an essential element of ancient languages like Latin and Greek, and also of numerous modern languages. The absence of grammatical gender in English is one of the many reasons why some English speakers have considerable difficulty in mastering the major languages of Western Europe.

gram(me). The shorter form is now customary (abbreviated g, not g., *gm*, or *gr*) for the sense 'fundamental unit of mass in the system of cgs (centimetre, gram, and second) units'. So *kilogram* (= 1,000 grams), *milligram* (one-thousandth of a gram), *microgram* (one-millionth of a gram), etc.

grand compounds. It is recommended that the following current English compounds of family, etc., names should be written as follows: (ranks) *grand duchy, grand duchess, grand duke*; (family relationships) *grand aunt, grandchild, grandad, granddaughter, grandfather, grandma, grandmam(m)a, grandmother, grand nephew, grand niece, grandpa, grandpapa, grandparent, grandsire* (an archaic word for *grandfather*), *grandson, grand uncle*; (miscellaneous) *grand jury, grand master* (chess), *Grand National, grand opera, grand piano, Grand Prix, grand slam* (sport, bridge), *grandstand, grand total, grand tour* (sightseeing tour), *grand unified theory* (physics). For family terms an initial capital should be used at the beginning of letters (*Dear Grandpa*, etc.) and also in mid-letter (*Will you tell Grandma, please, that I loved her presents*). In chess circles *grandmaster* is very frequently written as one word.

grande dame. This term for an influential woman within a particular sphere was borrowed from French in the 18c. and is now sufficiently naturalized to be printed in ordinary roman type. The phrase is often used in a possessive structure (*grande dame* + *of* + noun) as in *A ... hugely acclaimed portrayal of feminism's grande dame, Virginia Woolf*—*Sunday Express*, 2004. It is also occasionally used to refer to places and institutions: *Louise Nicholson transfers the idea to the grande dame of New York's museums, the Met*—*Apollo Magazine*, 2005.

granny. The more usual spelling (rather than *grannie*). See -IE, -Y.

granted. Like GIVEN and CONSIDERING, *granted* can be used independently of the subject of the sentence in such a way that it does not become an 'unattached participle': (i) as a marginal preposition, e.g. *And, granted the initial assumptions ... I think it stands the test*—A. White, 1965; (ii) in the form *granted (that)*, as a subordinating conjunction, e.g. *I enjoy ... knowing that if you're really ill, someone's there to run down and buy that medicine* (*granted that most men really don't get how to take care of women when they're ill*)—weblog, 2008 (India); and (iii) informally, as a sentence adverb, e.g. *Granted, it was not hard to interest a security man, who apart from a regular soldier had the most boring job on earth*—T. Keneally, 1985.

gratis. The dominant standard pronunciation in British and American English seems to be /ˈgratɪs/ (**grat**-is). An alternative in AmE is /ˈgreɪtɪs/ (**gray**-tis), and in BrE a third possibility, /ˈgrɑːtɪs/ (**grah**-tis), is also used, especially in the colloquial phrase *free, gratis, and for nothing*.

gratuity is a rather grand word for 'tip', and is often found on restaurant menus and bills. In British English it also refers (without the same pretension) to a special payment awarded to employees on retirement or to members of the armed forces, police, etc., on discharge.

gravamen /grəˈveɪmɛn/, a chief ground of complaint. Plural *gravamina* /grəˈvamɪnə/.

gravel (verb). The inflected forms are *gravelled, gravelling*; *gravelly* (in AmE the first two but not the third often written with a single *-l-*).

graven is a past participle form of the archaic verb *grave*, 'to engrave, carve', kept alive in set phrases, especially the biblical phrase *graven images*.

gray was once a standard spelling in BrE but is now unusual. However, it is the standard spelling in AmE, although *grey* is also used. In all other varieties of English, except East Asian, *grey* is the usual spelling.

greasy. In its literal sense 'smeared with grease' always /ˈgriːsi/ (**gree**-see); when applied to an obsequiously oily person, can also be /ˈgriːzi/ (**gree**-zee).

great. For *the great Cham, the Great Unwashed,* see SOBRIQUETS.

Grecian. This adjective has steadily retreated before *Greek,* and is now idiomatically restricted to architecture (*Grecian columns*), facial outline (*Grecian nose*), a soft low-cut *Grecian slipper,* and references to *Grecian urns,* Keatsian or otherwise. *Greek* is elsewhere the natural word (*Greek alphabet, chorus, language,* etc.).

Grecism, Grecize, Greco-. The now more common spelling for these words, not *Graecism,* etc.

Greek g. Words containing *g* derived from Greek gamma (γ) are of three kinds: **1** The small group [in which *g* is silent in English (*gnome* = 'aphorism', *gnomic, gnomon* (on sundial), *gnosis, gnostic; diaphragm, paradigm, phlegm*).

2 A larger group (before a consonant or the vowels *a, o*) in which it is always 'hard', i.e. /g/ (*glaucoma, Greek; galaxy, demagogue, gonorrhoea*).

3 A large group of words in which the *g* happens to fall before *e, i,* or *y.* The English natural tendency to pronounce *g* 'soft', i.e. as /dʒ/, in such cases has been partially prevented by standard speakers who are familiar with the derivation of the words in question. In the following list the standard current pronunciation is given first, followed by variants.

anthropophagi	/g/ or /dʒ/
antiphlogistic	/dʒ/
autogyro	/dʒ/
demagogic	/-ˈgɒgɪk/
demagogy	/-ˈgɒgɪ/
geriatric(s)	/dʒ/
gerontology	initial /dʒ/, final /-dʒ-/
gymnastic(s)	/dʒ/
gynaecology	initial /g/, final /dʒ/
gypsophila	/dʒ/
hegemony	/g/ or /dʒ/
hemiplegia	/dʒ/
isagogic	first *g* hard, second *g* /dʒ/
laryngitis	/dʒ/
meningitis	/dʒ/
misogynist	/dʒ/
misogyny	/dʒ/
paraplegia	/dʒ/
paraplegic	/dʒ/
pedagogical	/-ˈgɒdʒ-/ or /-ˈgɒg-/
pedagogy	/-ˈgɒdʒ-/ or /-ˈgɒg-/
pharyngitis	/dʒ/
phlogiston	/dʒ/
syzygy	/dʒ/

Note: *gynaecology* and its derivatives were very commonly pronounced with initial /dʒ/ in the first third of the 20c., but from about 1930 only with /g/.

greenhouse effect. This important but much misunderstood term is defined by the *ODO* as follows: 'the trapping of the sun's warmth in a planet's lower atmosphere, due to the greater transparency of the atmosphere to visible radiation from the sun than to infrared radiation emitted from the planet's surface'. On earth the increasing quantity of atmospheric carbon dioxide from the burning of fossil fuels, together with the release of other gases, is causing an increased greenhouse effect and leading to global warming. A greenhouse effect involving CO_2 is also responsible for the very high surface temperature of Venus.

Cf. *global warming* (see GLOBAL).

greenness, the quality of being green, is spelt with two *ns.*

Green Paper. A publication issued by a British government department setting out various aspects of a matter on which legislation is contemplated, and inviting public discussion and suggestions. In due course it may be followed by a WHITE PAPER, giving details of proposed legislation. The first Green Paper was issued in 1967. (*Hutchinson Encycl.,* 1990).

grey. In an unusually long note the *OED* (1901) said 'an enquiry by Dr. Murray in Nov. 1893 elicited a large number of replies, from which it appeared that in Great Britain the form *grey* is the more frequent in use, notwithstanding the authority of Johnson and later Eng. lexicographers who have all given the preference to *gray*'. In Britain a century later, *grey* is the only current form.

greyhound. The word goes back to Anglo-Saxon times, and it is known that the first element is unconnected with *grey.* Its ultimate etymology is uncertain, though it seems to answer to an Old Norse *grøy* meaning 'bitch'. The word is often spelt **grayhound** in AmE.

grievous (/ˈgriːvəs/) is occasionally pronounced with an extra vowel /ˈgriːvɪəs/, presumably by analogy with the many common adjectives that end in *-ious*, such as *devious, glorious, previous, serious*, etc. It is also sometimes spelt to match, as *grievious.*

griffin, griffon, gryphon. *Griffin* (also spelt *griffon,* and, e.g. by Lewis Carroll, *gryphon*) is a mythical creature with an eagle's head and wings and a lion's body'. *Griffon* is (*a*) a dog of a small terrier-like breed, and (*b*) (in full *griffon vulture*) a large vulture. All three are variants of the same Old French word, derived ultimately from Greek γρύψ.

grill, grille. There is nowadays a clear distinction between these two spellings. *Grill* denotes the cooking device for radiating heat downwards; a meal cooked using this device (e.g. *a mixed grill*); and a restaurant (*the Savoy Grill*). A *grille* is a metal grid protecting the radiator of a motor vehicle, or a latticed screen separating e.g. customers from staff in a bank. Occasionally *grill* is used when *grille* is meant: **small windows covered by heavy steel grills—Contemporary Review*, 2003.

grimace. For both noun and verb first-syllable stressing seems the more common, but the second syllable can also be stressed. Take your pick.

grimy. So spelt, not *-ey*. See -EY AND -Y IN ADJECTIVES 2.

grisly, grizzly. Though quite different in meaning, these two words are sometimes confused. *Grisly,* of Old English origin, means 'causing horror or disgust', as in *grisly murder, discovery, scene, footage,* etc. *Grizzly* means 'grey or grey-haired', and comes ultimately from the French *gris* 'grey'. It is chiefly used of the *grizzly bear,* but also in contexts such as *He had a grizzly gray beard.* In British English *grizzly* can also describe a whining or complaining child, and comes from the verb *grizzle,* meaning to sulk or cry, e.g. *He was very grizzly and unsettled—until I bought a baby sling and started to carry him round with me—Mother & Baby,* 1988. The most common mistake is for the spelling *grizzly* to be used when *grisly* is correct, as in **two grizzly murders.*

groin is a physiological or architectural term, and **groyne** (AmE **groin**) is a low wall or timber framework built out from a seashore to prevent beach erosion.

grosbeak /ˈgrəʊsbiːk/. The *s* is fully pronounced.

grotto. Plural *grottoes* or *grottos* See -O(E)S 2.

group names of animals (a pride of lions, etc.). See PROPER TERMS.

grovel. The inflected forms are *grovelled, grovelling*; in AmE often written with a single *-l-*. See -LL-, -L-.

groyne. See GROIN.

gruelling is the spelling in BrE, but **grueling** in AmE.

gruntled. See DISGRUNTLED.

Gruyère (name of district in Switzerland). The cheese name is so spelt.

gryphon. See GRIFFIN.

guano (fertilizer). Pronounced /ˈgwɑːnəʊ/. Plural *guanos.* See -O(E)S 4.

guarantee, guaranty. For the verb, the only correct form is *guarantee.* For the noun, *guaranty* is now practically confined to American English, either in proper names (*Pension Benefit Guaranty Corporation*) or in legal and commercial writing only, to denote an undertaking to pay a debt if the person or party primarily responsible defaults.

See WARRANTY.

guerrilla with two *r*s and two *l*s is the recommended spelling in English (thus, as it happens, reflecting the original Spanish spelling), not *guerilla.* The spelling *guerrila* with two *r*s and a single *l* is occasionally found, and is recognized by the *OED* as correct. Pronounced /gəˈrɪlə/, the same as *gorilla.* **Guerrilla marketing** is advertising that uses unconventional, and low-cost marketing techniques aimed at obtaining maximum exposure for a product. Because *guerrilla* and *gorilla* sound the same, it is sometimes misspelt **gorilla marketing*; or deliberately spelt that way as a pun.

guess. The informal use of *I guess* meaning 'I think it likely, I suppose' (e.g. *I guess I'd better tell you everything*) developed in America in the late 18c. from the standard use of the phrase meaning 'it is my opinion or hypothesis (that)'. Throughout the 19c. and for much of the 20c. its Americanness was quite marked and was frequently commented on, for example by Byron and Sir Walter Scott. Although the phrase may still sound somewhat transatlantic to some people in Britain, and is still much less common there than in the US, *I guess* may now occur anywhere in the English-speaking world. Examples: *No, I guess it was Candy I told*—J. Steinbeck, 1937; *'You're too romantic,' he said . . . 'I guess I am.'*—D. Eden, 1955; *You remember them now?* George. *Yes, I guess so, Martha.*—E. Albee, 1962; *I guess you're supposed to think to yourself that you're in a garden*—R. Ingalls, 1985; *I guess this is my bed and I have to lie on it. Wash the sheets, plump up the pillows and try to make the best of it*—weblog, 2005 (BrE).

Using *I guess* as a tag at the end of a statement is still characteristic of North American English: *He would have been watching the returns in the Senate elections I guess*—A. Broinowski, 1973; *It's about a meter and a bit under water—about three or four feet, I guess?*—weblog, 2005 (Canad.).

guesstimate. This popular little portmanteau word (*guess* + *-timate*, from *estimate*) usefully suggests a figure based on a mixture of guesswork and reasoning, and adds dignity, if not credibility, to what might otherwise be dismissed as 'back of an envelope' calculations. Like other informal words which have never fully shaken off their less than noble origins, it is older than one might suspect, being first recorded from 1936, in the US, after which it was for many years confined within inverted commas. The verb arrived in 1942, also in the US. Both noun and verb follow the pronunciation of *estimate*, i.e. /ˈgɛstɪmət/ (**ges**-ti-muht) and /ˈgɛstɪmeɪt/ (**ges**-ti-mate) respectively. The spelling with two *ss* is rather more common than *guestimate*, but both are correct.

guest, as a noun, has developed a wide range of uses in which payment may or may not be involved (as it is with *paying guests* and *guest workers*). The development of attributive uses (before a noun) that go well beyond the core meaning of *guest* may be seen in *guest beer, guest blogger, guest editor, guest speaker, guest star, guest worker, guest writer*, and others. Some people object to the common use in the entertainment industry of the word as a verb, e.g. *He guested on the show two weeks ago*. This originally AmE meaning has been around for at least 70 years, and seems like a useful shorthand for 'appear as a guest'.

guillemot. Pronounced /ˈgɪlɪmɒt/.

guilloche (architectural, etc., ornament). Pronounced /gɪˈlɒʃ/.

guillotine (in parliament). See CLOSURE.

guimp. See GIMP.

guipure (linen lace). Pronounced /gɪˈpjʊə/.

gullible (easily cheated). So spelt, not *-able*.

gumma /ˈgʌmə/ (soft swelling, usually of syphilitic origin, in connective tissue). Plural either *gummas* or *gummata*.

gunwale (upper edge of ship's side). Pronounced /ˈgʌnəl/. Sometimes spelt *gunnel*.

Gurkha. So spelt.

gusseted (adjective). So spelt. See -T-, -TT-.

guts. Its meaning of 'courage' or 'determination' has been occasionally commented on by usage writers, who have considered it coarse or shocking. It is true that it was first recorded in the English Dialect Dictionary in 1887 and listed in an 1893 book about slang; frequent use since then in phrases such as *to have the guts to do something, it takes guts, to lack the guts*, etc., suggest that it has largely shaken off its informal tag and should be avoided only in the starchiest of formal prose. It has the advantage over synonyms such as *courage, pluck*, etc. of placing emotion in its bodily location, while being less vehement, and potentially masculinist, than *balls*. A literary example of the word in this metaphorical sense is: *I hate the idea of causes, and if I had to choose between betraying my country and betraying my friend, I hope I should have the guts to betray my country*—E. M. Forster, 1951.

gutta-percha /ˌgʌtəˈpəːtʃə/. Note /-tʃ-/ not /-ʃ-/.

guttural (from Latin *guttur* 'throat'). **1** So spelt, not *gutteral*.

2 In non-technical language, '(of a consonant) produced in the throat or by the back of the tongue and the soft palate', and applied particularly to certain throaty sounds in the German language. Phoneticians do not use the term, but divide these sounds into *pharyngeals* (e.g. the *h* in Arabic *Ahmed*) and *velars.* Thus English *k* is a voiceless velar plosive and *g* is its voiced equivalent. The voiced velar fricative /ɣ/ is typical of Spanish, e.g. *agrio* /ˈaɣrjo/ 'sour'; and the voiceless velar fricative /x/ is found in Ger. *ach* 'oh' and Scottish *loch* 'lake'. (Ger. '*ich* 'I' has the voiceless palatal fricative /ç/.)

guy (noun). **1** *Current use.* In his 1965 edition of Fowler's, Gowers confidently proclaimed: 'The noun in Britain means someone of grotesque appearance.' Even if his statement was true then, half a century on that meaning seems to be stone dead, and the word—in Britain as elsewhere—is the most widely used informal synonym of 'man'. In fact, it seems to have ousted long-established informal British alternatives such as *chap,* which now has a dated ring, and *bloke,* which is tainted by the overtones of stereotypical masculinity inherent in *blokeish* and *blokeishness.* Examples: (of males) *Take a look at them. All nice guys. They'll finish last*—L. Durocher, 1946 (US); *Half jokingly, he* [*sc.* Bing Crosby] *asked that his epitaph read, 'He was an average guy who could carry a tune'*—*Newsweek,* 1977; *I'm just as romantic as the next guy, and always was*—J. Lennon 1980; (of females; chiefly NAmer.) *She was a regular guy, a good sport and a fine actress*—1982 in *American Speech,* 1983.

2 *History.* In the meaning 'man', *guy* is often viewed as American in origin, but the earliest examples of its use in this way are British. It comes ultimately from the first name of the Gunpowder Plot (1605) conspirator Guy Fawkes. His name was transferred to an effigy ostensibly of him in ragged clothing burnt on a bonfire on 5 November, a use first recorded in the *OED* from 1806. From that literal meaning developed the use (1836) of the word to describe someone dressed outlandishly (*He was such an old guy in his dress*—*Tom Brown at Oxford,* T. Hughes, 1861). The first record of its use to denote a man in general is from 1847, in the rather louche British *The Swell's Night Guide,* where it is clearly slangy. It first appeared in a US source in 1896, and has since gone from strength to strength.

3 *'Guys', 'You guys'* as a form of address. While singular *guy* generally refers to an adult male, in the plural it is widely used, in American English above all, but also elsewhere, to address groups of males, groups of males and females, exclusively female groups, and, in writing, people in general: *You guys all belong in the same ballpark*—*Observer,* 1970; *The new meaning ... which still may evoke masculine images in some women, is nonetheless positive, especially since guys permits one to refer to numbers of a group without reference to their sex*—*Word,* 1985; [a man addressing his two daughters] *You guys are dwelling and brooding. A great thing right now would be exercise*—*New Yorker,* 1993; *Do you guys get a show over there called Little Britain?*—*www.twitchfilm.net,* 2005.

This use has interpersonal advantages but in certain circumstances may be contentious. It is arguably friendlier than a straightforward 'you'. Indeed, it has been suggested that it is the equivalent of the genial southern US 'you all, y'all'. However, there are limits to its social appropriateness: being informal, it presupposes that the people addressed are known to the person addressing them. So, in more formal situations, such as a restaurant, even some men may baulk at being invited to their table with a 'Your table is ready, guys.' More contentious is its use to address mixed groups. Though many people seem to accept it without demur as a standard part of everyday language, others find it objectionable on the grounds that it subsumes women under an inherently masculine term. An additional argument adduced is that the reverse is not true: you could not address a mixed group by an inherently feminine word such as 'girls'. In contrast, others argue that in this plural use the word has effectively been desexed: that it functions as a sort of gender-neutral pronoun. Whichever line of argument one accepts, the important point is to be aware that this form of address can upset people for reasons of gender politics, not to mention age or social status.

gybe (noun and verb). The sailing term is spelt thus in British English, but **jibe** in AmE. See also GIBE, GYBE, JIBE.

gymnasium. 1 Plural (for preference) *gymnasiums*; but *gymnasia* is also widely used. See -UM 3.

2 In Germany (pronounced /gʏm'naːzi̯ʊm/), Scandinavia, and Central Europe the word has an additional sense, 'a school that prepares pupils for university entrance'.

gymp. See GIMP.

gyn(a)ecology. 1 See GREEK G (especially the note).

2 Spelt with *-ae-* in BrE and *-e-* in AmE.

gyp. (*a*) In the British informal expression *give someone gyp*, can also be spelt **gip**. (*b*) In its rare, originally and chiefly informal US meaning of 'swindle', it is always spelt *gyp*. The inflections of the related verb are *gypping, gyps, gypped*. (*c*) As the name of a college servant, *gyp* belongs to Cambridge and Durham, not Oxford (where the regular term is *scout*).

gypsy, gipsy. The recommended spelling now is *gypsy,* The spelling *gipsy* (which was given priority in the *OED,* 1901) is gradually being ousted. The term has both ethnic and general reference: either to a member of dark-skinned nomadic people of Hindu origin and associated with Egypt or a person who adopts a similar style of life. The word was originally *gipcyan,* short for Egyptian, because Gypsies were popularly supposed to have come from Egypt. *Gypsy* is capitalized when it refers to the people, and written *gypsy* (with small initial letter) in the generalized meaning 'a free spirit'. The derivative is **gypsyish**.

gyre (noun and verb). The standard pronunciation of the word is /dʒʌɪə/, with an initial 'soft' g, but Burchfield mentioned the survival of gramophone records in which the poet W. B. Yeats recites his well-known lines with a 'hard' *g* in the word: *To watch a white gull take A bit of bread thrown up into the air; Now gyring down and perning there* (1920); *O sages standing in God's holy fire ... Come from the holy fire, perne in a gyre* (1928).

gyves (fetters, shackles). This archaic word is pronounced /dʒʌɪvz/, with a 'soft' initial *g*.

h. 1 The sound of *h* (aitch) at the beginning of words such as *have* and *house* and in the middle of words such as *ahead* and *behave* is known technically as a 'voiceless glottal fricative'. In Britain, the presence or absence of this sound in speech is one of the key factors in the social evaluation of an individual's use of language or, as the *OED* expressed it, it 'has come to be regarded [in Britain] as a kind of shibboleth of social position'. The then Archbishop of Canterbury, George Carey, (*Time*, 2 Sept. 1991) described how he had been brought up in a working-class family in the East End of London. 'At the age of 17½,' he said, 'I discovered the letter *h* in the English language, which, you know, isn't much known among the English working class.' In practice large numbers of people in Britain go through life blissfully unencumbered by the need to distinguish between such pairs of words as *hedge/edge, hill/ill,* and *high/eye.* While it makes no difference to their ability to communicate effectively, or to their happiness, it does, sadly, cause some people to make unfavourable inferences about their education or intelligence: there can be no doubt that George Carey would not have risen to such ecclesiastical heights had he continued to drop his aitches.

2 While it is true that /h/-lessness is characteristic of non-standard speech, standard speakers would do well to notice that certain function words (e.g. *has, have, had*), pronouns, and pronominal adjectives lose /h/ in unstressed non-initial contexts in rapid speech: *she shoved him into her car* /ʃiː ʃʌvd ɪm ɪntʊ əː kaː/, *you should have heard him* /juː ʃʊd əv həːd ɪm/. Until about the beginning of the 20c., words containing *wh (where, whistle; nowhere,* etc.) were regularly pronounced with the /hw/ intact by a majority of RP (Received Pronunciation) speakers in England, and regularly too in Scotland, Ireland, and America. But *COD* 1995, by entering only /w/ for all such words, drew attention to the fact that the aspiration of *h* in such circumstances has largely disappeared from standard English in England (but not in the speech of some Scots). As a result, *whales* and *Wales* are both pronounced /weɪlz/, *whit* and *wit* /wɪt/, and so on.

3 On the use or non-use of aspiration in such cases as *a(n) habitual, a(n) historic,* see A, AN 3(b); HABITUAL; HISTORIAN; HISTORIC; HISTORICAL. See also AITCH; HUMOUR; VEHEMENT, VEHICLE.

habitual is still preceded in writing by *an* rather than *a* in about 25 per cent of cases. See A, AN 3(b).

habitude was in continuous regular use from the 15c. to the 19c. in several meanings in which it competed with *habit* (manner of being or existing, a customary or usual mode of action, etc.) Since then it has fallen on lean times, and is now confined to the more florid corners of prose. Examples: *Shows them the main-spring of the play, The moral tragedy revealing, And country habitudes, country ways*—A. Cronin, 1979; *What would impede such a transformation, or slow it down? To my mind, nothing but inertia, bureaucracy, habitudes that have built up for years and have implanted in their bearers a fear of anything that is new*—*Sydney Morning Herald Webdiary*, 2002.

habitué (a habitual visitor or resident). This French word is nowadays printed in roman and pronounced /həˈbitjʊɛi/ in an Anglicized manner. In writing it is still widely preceded by the determiner *an* instead of *a,* which suggests a pronunciation with the *h* silent. The accent should be retained, despite the widespread use of the form **habitue.* Also to be avoided is the form **habituee,* possibly modelled on words such as *employee,* but illogical, since there is no verb **habitu* to which the *-ee* suffix can legitimately be added.

háček /ˈhatʃɛk/. The regular (but in Britain little-known) term for the diacritical mark ˇ

placed over letters to modify the 'natural' sound in some Slavonic and Baltic languages. It is a Czech diminutive of *hák* 'hook'.

hackneyed. Spelt *-eyed*, not *-ied*.

hackneyed phrases. It is impossible to draw a firm line between hackneyed phrases and clichés: they are species of the same genus. They are at the same time endearing and irreplaceable, and maddening and replaceable. Used sparingly, they pass unnoticed, or even add a touch of quality, in novels, short stories, journalism, and some other kinds of writing. But, as Fowler put it: 'their true use when they come into the writer's mind is as danger-signals; he should take warning that when they suggest themselves it is because what he is writing is bad stuff'.

Many hackneyed phrases are allusions to famous passages in literature or politics: *to be or not to be* (Shakespeare); *not with a bang but a whimper* (T. S. Eliot); *the wind of change* (H. Macmillan). Others are drawn from possibly less well-known or half-remembered sources: *a consummation devoutly to be wished* (Shakespeare's *Hamlet*); *conspicuous by ... absence* (from a speech of 1859 by Lord John Russell, *Among the defects of the Bill, which were numerous, one provision was conspicuous by its presence and another by its absence*); *he had the defects of his qualities* (cf. *Vauvenargues has the defects of his qualities*, J. Morley, 1878). Some are of Biblical origin: *the writing on the wall* (Swift, referring to the story of Belshazzar's Feast in Dan. 5); *a multitude of sins* (Peter 4:8); *For ye suffer fooles gladly, seeing ye your selues are wise* (2 Cor. 11:19). A diminishing number are drawn from classical sources: *O tempora, O mores!* (O what times, O what habits!—Cicero); *et hoc genus omne* (and the whole of this class—Horace); *in vino veritas* (Truth comes out in wine—Pliny).

These are but a small selection from a virtually limitless list. Cf. CLICHÉ.

had.

1 *had better.*
2 *had have.*
3 *had rather.*

1 *had better.* See BETTER 1, 2.

2 *had have.* This occurs with unreal (or unfulfilled) propositions in the past, constructed either with *if* (or an equivalent construction) as in the sentence *If I had have known, I would have said something* or with a verb expressing an unfulfilled intention, such as *wish*: *I wish you'd have kept quiet.* Though now associated with dialect and informal usage, the construction can be traced back in print to the 15c., e.g. *Had not he have be* [= been], *we should never have returned*—Malory, 1470–85; *The sayd kyng had not so sone have returnyd*—J. Style, 1509; *'If the fire hadn't have gone out,' he mused*—J. F. Wilson, 1911 (US). The matter was discussed in the journal *English Today* (1986), and the main conclusions were that the construction represents the type 'unreal conditions in the past', and that it is often written with either *had* or *have* in contracted form (thus *If I'd have gone* or *If I had've gone*). 'There is a problem with past unreal,' commented Professor Frank Palmer, 'because it needs to mark past tense twice, once for time and once for unreality. English does not have past-past forms, so instead introduces the verb "have".' The several contributors agreed in thinking that the construction was now common. One contributor called it the 'plupluperfect', another the 'pluplupast'. Another pointed out the type '*had* + schwa + past participle' as shown in the first part of a sentence in Galsworthy's *Strife* (1909), *If we'd a-known that before, we'd not a-started out with you so early.* There is also the type *had of*, as in the example cited in *MWCDEU* from F. Scott Fitzgerald's *The Great Gatsby* (1925): *It was four o'clock in the morning then, and if we'd of raised the blinds we'd of seen daylight.* For those with access to *DARE*, numerous regional American examples of the various types are given at *have* v[1] and v[2].

3 *had rather.* The type *I had rather* (or in its reduced form *I'd rather*) is as idiomatic as *I would rather/I'd rather.* In historical terms it was formed on the analogy of the now archaic type *I had liefer* 'I should hold it dearer': *I had rather err with Plato than be right with Horace*—Shelley, 1819; *I had rather gaze on a new ice age than these familiar things*—J. Winterson, 1985.

haemo-, hæmo-, hemo-, a combining form from Greek αἷμα 'blood', found in words such as *haemorrhage* and *haemophilia.* In BrE usually written as *haemo-* (the digraph *æ* has now been virtually abandoned), and in AmE as *hemo-*. Hence *haemoglobin*/US *hemoglobin*. See Æ, Œ.

haemorrhage. So spelt in BrE (note the two *r*s), but as **hemorrhage** in AmE. See Æ, Œ.

hagiography, hagiolatry, hagiology. All are pronounced with initial /hag-/, i.e. with a 'hard' *g*. See GREEK G.

hail-fellow-well-met (adjective phrase). Written with three hyphens. e.g. *Arnold was very cheerful in a hail-fellow-well-met sort of way.*

***hair-brained.** See HARE-BRAINED.

hairdo. Plural *hairdos.*

haitch. To pronounce the letter *h* in this way has long been considered a mark of ignorance or illiteracy, despite the fact that in certain parts of the United Kingdom that pronunciation has always been standard. It appears that in the inexorable move towards making British English more demotic, such a pronunciation is now favoured by people born in the eighties and later, and will, presumably, in time prevail, unspeakably uncouth though it may appear to older RP speakers.

hale, in the phrase *hale and hearty,* comes from an Old English word *hāl* meaning 'whole'. The spelling *hail and hearty* is a mistake.

half. 1 When *half* (*of*) is used with a singular or uncount noun it is followed by a singular verb or pronoun: *half of the country* is *employed in agriculture; she took half a bag of mushroom compost and spread* it *under the roses.* When *half* (*of*) is followed by a plural noun, a plural verb (or plural pronoun) is required: *half* (*of*) *the members of Nato* have *been deploying military aircraft; half the folks round here* have *never taken their children south of Nottingham.* Occasionally, by the principle of 'notional agreement', the type '*half* (*of*) + non-count noun' can properly be used with a plural verb: *Nearly half (of) the population* lose *at least half their teeth before they reach the age of 40.*

2 In some phrases concerned with quantities, measures of time, etc., the position of *half* is variable in relation to the following *a* or *an*, e.g. *I'll have half a pint* (no hyphen) or *I'll have a half-pint* (with a hyphen). In most cases, however, the type *half a year, half a million dollars,* etc., is more usual.

3 The tendency in speech to insert a redundant *a* in contexts such as *a private meeting which lasted* a half *an hour* is best avoided in writing; *half an hour* is all that is required.

4 Most compound nouns and adjectives prefixed by *half-* are hyphenated, e.g. *half-time, half-century, half-life; half-baked, half-hearted, half-naked.* But a few are not, especially *halfway* and *halfwit.* It is best to check in an up-to-date dictionary such as *ODO.*

5 *half-yearly* is preferable to *biyearly,* which is ambiguous: see BI-.

6 *halfpennyworth.* Survives, since the disappearance of the coin, as a colloquial term for 'a negligible amount' (especially after a negative: *doesn't make a halfpennyworth of difference*). Pronounced /ˈheɪpəθ/, and sometimes written as *ha'p'orth.*

7 *half-brother, half-sister.* See -IN-LAW 3.

half-rhyme. See RHYME 2.

hallelujah. See ALLELUIA.

hallo. See HELLO.

Halloween /haləʊˈiːn/. Pronounced hal-oh-**een**, the spelling without the apostrophe is now much more common than *Hallowe'en,* thereby disguising the etymology of *-e'en* as a shortening of *even* = evening.

halo. The plural can be *halos* or *haloes,* the first being rather more frequent. See -O(E)S 2.

handful. Plural *handfuls.* See -FUL.

handicap. The inflected forms are *handicapped, handicapping.* See -P-, -PP-.

handicapped is first recorded in the early 20th century referring to a person's mental or physical disabilities. In British English it was the standard term until relatively recently, but like many terms in this sensitive field its prominence has been short-lived. It has been superseded by more recent terms such as *disabled,* or, when referring to mental disability, *having learning difficulties* or *learning-disabled.* In

American English, however, *handicapped* remains acceptable. Its figurative use seems uncontentious, e.g. *The acting is handicapped by Gibson's need to show religious rapture*—*OEC*, 2004 (BrE); *Also players have been handicapped by the lack of indoor facilities*—*OEC*, 2004 (NZ).

handkerchief. The recommended plural is *handkerchiefs*, not *-chieves*.

handsome. Applied equally to men and women of striking appearance ('beautiful with dignity', Dr Johnson, 1755) since the 16c., but now, when applied to women, tending to be used only of such as are middle-aged or elderly. Examples: *Today* good-looking ... *Tomorrow they'll be talking about what a* handsome *woman she is*—T. Wolfe, 1987; *Mrs Gorbachev is a stylish, handsome woman with an intense and intelligent manner*—*Time*, 1988; *Barbara Bush is what she is: 63. Sturdy. White-haired ... Handsome. (That's the word that reporters, struggling for an adjective to describe a woman who dares not to be glamorous, have unanimously settled on.)*—*Chicago Tribune*, 1988.

hang (verb). The recommendation is to use *hanged* as past tense and past participle of capital punishment and in old-fashioned oaths of the kind *I'll be hanged if I'll do that*; otherwise *hung*. The distinction goes back ultimately to the existence of two Old English verbs (*hōn*, past tense *heng*, past participle *hangen*; and *hangian*, past tense *hangode*, past participle *hangod*) and an ON one (*hengjan*, a causal transitive verb). A full account of the subsequent history and entanglements of these three verbs in Middle English and in later centuries is set down in the *OED*: in brief, *hung* became established in literary English in the late 16c., with *hanged* largely restricted to the sense 'kill by hanging' and in oaths. In practice, a wide range of writers use *hung* in descriptions of executions. This use is not mistaken, just less usual in standard English, although those who have had it drummed into them since childhood that *hanged* should always be used in the grisly sense may raise an eyebrow.

hanger-on. The plural is *hangers-on*.

hanging participles. See UNATTACHED PARTICIPLES.

hara-kiri /ˌharəˈkɪri/. Spelt with a hyphen is the form that corresponds most closely to the original Japanese. The variant *hari-kari* is old-established, and still quite common, *hari-kiri* less so.

harass. 1 Few things are more likely to displease traditional RP speakers in Britain than to hear *harass* pronounced with the main stress on the second syllable, i.e. as /həˈras/. John Walker (1806), the *OED* (1898), Daniel Jones (1917), *COD* (7th edn. 1982) gave only first-syllable stressing. But second-syllable stressing (also in *harassment*) is dominant in American English and, since about the 1970s, seems to be the pattern favoured by younger speakers in Britain, where dictionaries now recognize both as standard.

2 Note that the word is spelt with one *r*, unlike *embarrass*.

harbour. So spelt in BrE, but as **harbor** in AmE. See -OUR AND -OR.

hardly.

1 *hardly ... when/than.*
2 *without hardly.*
3 *no* + noun + *hardly.*
4 *can't hardly*

1 *hardly ... when/than.* In sentences of the type *Hardly had the party begun, when the police arrived*, it is generally accepted that *when* is the correct conjunction, not *than* (i.e. *?Hardly had the party begun than the police arrived*). It was Fowler (1926) who first lighted on the issue, classifying *hardly ... than* among 'corruptions', caused, as he said, by analogy; and it is indeed a syntactic blend formed on the analogy of *no sooner ... than.* The *OED* example is from a highly respectable source, the *Cambridge Modern History*: *Hardly had the Council been re-opened at Trent ... than Elizabeth was allying herself with the Huguenots*—F. W. Maitland, 1903. Jespersen (1909–49, vol. vii) added three more examples from the works of minor 20c. writers. Fowler himself judged the construction to be 'surprisingly common', which it may well have been in his day, but now it certainly seems not to be. Neither construction is exactly frequent in the *OEC* data, but *hardly ... when* crops up about six times more often than *hardly ... than.* Should *hardly ... than* be avoided, then? As always, it depends on whether your readers are likely to be grammatical martinets, or sloppy liberals, happy just to go with the flow of language flux. Change it if you will, but the fault, if fault it be, is a venial one. Examples: (when) *Indeed, hardly had he set foot in Antigua when he was reported to have talked about sailing alone around the world*—*This is Hampshire*, 2003; (than) *But hardly had New Labour been elected, than the euro began to cause problems for the Blair administration*—*Sunday Herald*, 2000. Cf. BARELY; SCARCELY 1.

2 *without hardly*. See WITHOUT 3.

3 *no* + noun + *hardly*. Fowler (1926) considered this construction (exemplified in '*I had no qualifications hardly, and realised the importance of taking up training that was offered*'—*Yorkshire Post Today*, 2005) unacceptable. It seems typical of speech, as in the example noted, where it is thrown in as an afterthought. In writing it is advisable to change such constructions to e.g. *I had hardly any qualifications* . . .

4 *can't hardly*. The *OED* gives the example *I couldn't hardly tell what he meant*, and considers the negative in 'can't' superfluous. The premise behind the *OED* statement is that since *hardly* is a negative, the sentence therefore constitutes a double negative. But *hardly* is not a full negative; rather, it often acts to weaken the force of negation in the sentence. *Can't hardly* is typical of informal American speech and writing, and of fictional renderings of informal speech. In other kinds of prose, it should be edited out. Examples: *But now we really got a beast, though I can't hardly believe* it—W. Golding, 1954 (Piggy speaking); *No, Sweedon can't write anything. He can't hardly write his own pawntickets*—P. Fitzgerald, 1990; *Of course I said yes and I can't hardly wait!*—personal weblog, 2005 (AmE).

hard words. In one meaning, this is a semi-technical term for what it immediately suggests, long and difficult words that are often derived from Latinate rather than English sources, such as *rebarbative* (= repellent) and *nugatory* (= futile, trifling).

It is worth reflecting that the first English dictionary, Robert Cawdrey's *A Table Alphabeticall of Hard Usual English Words* (1604), contained a mixture of 'hard' and of 'usual' words. A typical sequence of twelve words chosen at random contains only 'usual' words: *halaluiah, hallucinate, harmonie, hautie* (= haughty), *hazard, herault* (= herald), *heathen, hebrew, hecticke, hemisphere, helmet, hereditorie* (Cawdrey was not concerned with strict alphabetical order). But there are some 'hard' words among the 2,500 words listed and glossed, e.g. *agnition* (acknowledgement, from Latin *agnōscere*, to recognize), *carminate* (to card wool, from L. *cārmināre*, with the same meaning), *combure* (to burn up, from L. *combūrere*, with the same meaning), etc., all of them now lost from the language.

hare-brained. Usually spelt *hare-* (or without a hyphen, *harebrained*). *Hairbrained* is a variant, first recorded in 1581. In the *OEC* data the word is spelt *hair-brained* in roughly a quarter of cases. Many people will regard it as a mistake, although the *OED* recognizes it as a legitimate variant.

harelip. See CLEFT LIP.

harem. The established spelling in English of this Arabic word. In British English the stressed syllable varies between /ˈhɑːriːm/ and /hɑːˈriːm/ (**hah**-reem, hah-**reem**); in AmE the first syllable is stressed, pronounced either as in *hair* or as in *hat*.

haricot. Pronounced /ˈharɪkəʊ/.

hark back to, harken back to, hearken back to. 1 *Hark, harken*, and *hearken* all mean 'to listen'. (*Hearken* is a 16c. variant of the earlier *harken*). *Hark* was used with various particles in the language of hunting (*hark on, hark forward*) and in the 19c. *hark back* developed the meaning of hounds retracing their steps to find a lost scent again. From this came the current metaphorical use 'to return to some earlier point in a narrative, discussion, or argument' (*He has to hark back again to find the scent of his argument*—Robert Louis Stevenson, 1882) and the related meaning 'to evoke an older style or genre' (e.g. *paintings that hark back to Constable and Turner*). The standard and most common formulation everywhere is *to hark back*. However, in North America, the variants *harken back* and *hearken back* (first recorded in 1900) are well established, and between them outnumber *hark back* in US and Canadian English. Many British English speakers are likely to regard this as a mistake, but it is recognized in *ODO*, and in American dictionaries. Examples: (hark back) *Mohammad*

Rassim's works also hark back to the towering achievements of Bronze Age Iraq—Art in America, 2004 (AmE); *I ended up standing next to Bono at the end of the record and he was fantastic. I've seen him a few times since and we always hark back to Band Aid—Observer*, 2004 (BrE); (harken back) *In the original Battle of Angels, this character was named Cassandra, again harkening back to Greek mythology—DVD Verdict*, 2005 (AmE); (hearken back) *it felt as if most participants were hearkening back to their old club days, when they underwent the same routine on the dance floor—OEC*, 2002 (Canad.)

2 Occasionally, *hark on* is used by mistake for *harp on* to convey the meaning 'to write or speak persistently and tediously about a topic'. The confusion between the two verbs, which in the *OEC* is largely confined to British journalistic sources, could well be due to the fact that if someone *harks back* to something, they may well be tempted to go on about 'the good old days' at tedious length: *One problem was that cricket didn't strike Yankees as being very democratic. Two old codgers harking on about long summer days back home could hog the crease all afternoon—Observer*, 2005

harmonium. Plural *harmoniums*. See -UM 1.

harp on (verb). See HARK BACK TO, HARKEN BACK TO, HEARKEN BACK TO, 1.

hart. See BUCK.

hash. In BrE this is the normal name for the symbol #, for example on a telephone keypad. In the US and elsewhere it is called either the *number sign*, in contexts such as *question #2*; or the *pound sign*, on telephone keypads or when used as a symbol for pounds of weight, e.g. *2# of sugar*. You may briefly impress some of your friends by telling them that the technical name for this symbol is the **octothorp**, but it is not widely used.

hashish. Pronounced variously as /ˈhaʃiːʃ/ (**ha**-sheesh), /ˈhaʃɪʃ/ (**ha**-shish), and /haˈʃiːʃ/ (ha-**sheesh**).

hashtag. As a noun, it refers to the use of the hash symbol (#) in front of a word or phrase on social media sites such as Twitter, to identify and group messages on a specific topic. When used as a verb, the inflections are *hashtagging, hashtagged*, e.g. *Kim posted a close-up on Instagram of the towering white Giuseppe Zanotti heels she wore today during their outing, hashtagging the designer, Kanye and 'CruelSummer'—OEC*, 2013.

hautboy, hautbois. Standard authorities recommend /ˈəʊbɔɪ/ for these archaic variants of *oboe*.

hauteur (haughtiness). Pronounced /əʊˈtəː/ and printed in roman.

have. 1 *No legislation ever* has *or ever* will affect *their conduct*. For this common mistake, see ELLIPSIS 3.

2 In constructions of the type *Some Labour MPs* would have preferred to have wound up *the Session before rising*, the second *have* (i.e. the perfect infinitive) is strictly speaking redundant, and the sentence can be rephrased as '*Some Labour MPs* would have preferred to wind up *the Session before rising*' with no loss of meaning. This type of construction is, however, very common, and in many cases emphasizes the fact that the event, situation, etc. described did not happen. Compare the first example that follows, where to me editing seems allowable, though not essential, with the second, where it does not: *The filmmakers would have done well to have openly acknowledged the elusive nature of their quarry—OEC*, 2004; *Given a particular piece, 'Diamond Head', for example, there would be 160 numbered as part of an American Edition, 125 as part of a Museum Edition and 125 as proofs. All of the images were evidently identical, and the 'multiple editioning' was simply a ploy to keep the numbers relatively low on all of the pieces in circulation. Otherwise, each would have to have been numbered from a total edition of 410—Art Business News*, 2002.

3 For *don't have* = 'haven't got' see DO 3.

4 *have* (*got*) *to*. When the sense is 'must' a fairly clear distinction is made between habitual necessity (*I have to wear contact lenses*) and immediate necessity (*I've got to catch a plane at 3 p.m.*). In interrogative constructions the type *Do you have this book in stock?* is somewhat more common in American than in British English; while the type *Have you got this* *book in stock?* is customary in BrE but unusual in AmE. UK examples: (have to) *He knew . . . that in order not to lose control irretrievably of his life he had to hold on to his job*—W. Boyd, 1981; (have got to) *'I have got to go & see de Valera about it next month.' 'Got' is the operative word*—E. Waugh, 1952; *Don't you listen to anything I say? It's* got *to be away by tomorrow*—W. Boyd, 1981.

5 For the use of a redundant or intrusive *have* in certain types of past clauses, see HAD 2.

haver. One of the pleasurable aspects of English is the way in which some regional uses become part of standard language. This verb is a case in point. In Scotland it means (*a*) to talk garrulously and foolishly (first recorded in 1721), and (*b*) to hesitate, to be slow in deciding (1866). At some point in the mid-20c. sense (*b*) emerged in standard English use and is now well established. Sense (*a*) is still anchored in the north.

havoc. 1 For *wreak havoc, wrought havoc,* etc., see WREAK.

2 If the verb is ever called on its inflected forms are *havocked* and *havocking.*

he. We expect *he* to be used only as a subject, and *him* only as the object of a verb or preposition. (The same applies to other personal pronoun pairs, e.g. *I/me, she/her,* etc.) The two sections of this entry suggest that things are not as straightforward as the grammatically tidy-minded would have us believe. **1** The long-drawn-out battle between *he* and *him* after the verb *to be* has been partly resolved in favour of *him,* especially *that's him* (not *that's he*). But in slightly more extended constructions, particularly when the pronoun is followed by a *who-* (or *that-*) clause, *he* is still the norm in standard prose, e.g. *Foucan is the original Free Runner as it was he who created and named the sport*—*www.iofilm.co.uk,* 2003. Technically ungrammatical, and unacceptable in formal writing, but not uncommon in informal speech, and in representations of it, is the type using *him* instead of *he* as the first item of the coordinated subject of the sentence, e.g. *Him and Ruihi were clearing out up north to live on a Maori marae*—N. Virtue, 1990. There is, however, evidence from more than one corpus showing that in coordinated subjects including a name, use of *he* + name is by far the more common structure. See also CASES 2.

2 The following citations show the use of *he* where *him* is expected. Burchfield castigated them as 'an indication of genuine illiteracy', which is rather condescending to the respected authors of the first two. The use of *he* in the following examples can be explained by hypercorrection (first example), an underlying finite clause (second example), and the confusion often caused when a pronoun is the object of a preceding verb or preposition but also the subject of the following clause (final three examples): *The orderly precision of the custody arrangements between he and Sylvia*—M. Golden, 1989 (US); *Once Mrs Delaney stood over him and asked plaintively was there any chance of he and Gina reconciling*—T. Keneally, 1985; *Any contact with Flora would have to include he who was keeping an eye on her*—B. Rubens, 1987; *David Hirst wants he and other tenants to take over the management of their council block in south London*—*Sunday Times,* 1989; *To he that hath shall it be given*—letter to *Independent,* 1991 (ludicrously misquoting Matt. 13: 12).

3 For the now outmoded use of *he* to mean 'anyone', see HE OR SHE.

head (verb). When *head* means to 'move in a particular direction', there is a choice between the structures *to be heading for* and *to be headed for.* The first is commoner across the English-speaking world, the second is the majority use in American English, but is also used elsewhere. Examples: (heading for) *I rather think Rhoda is heading for a row with Ann*—George Bernard Shaw, 1903; *Now that Martha Stewart may be heading for jail, we'll see how her company's holding up*—*CNN transcripts,* 2004 (AmE); (headed for) *Where is he headed for, anyway?*—H. Crane, 1922 (AmE); *Without corrective action, the company was headed for extinction*—*England and Wales High Court Decisions,* 2000.

headline language. The need for brevity in headlines leads to uses that are not characteristic of English generally. Prepositions, articles, auxiliary verbs, and some other parts of speech are often omitted altogether or used in modified ways. Nouns are run together attributively like verbal dominoes, e.g. *baby heart swap drama*. Paradoxically, the damage to the language is probably non-existent. Readers simply regard headlines as blackboard pointers: the real message lies below. Certain syntactic patterns are typical of headlines, such as combinations of nouns (as in the example above); use of the present continuous tense with no auxiliary, *Councillor planning action over go-go girl affair claim—Evening News* (Edinburgh), 1994; use of the simple present: *Sex cinema blaze man pleads guilty—Independent*, 1995; and use of a *to*-infinitive to denote future time: *Hundreds to face recall for breast cancer tests—Sunday Express*, 2013. Puns, as the most concise form of written humour, feature prominently in headlines, e.g. *Sugar is no sweet talker—Sunday Express*, 2013, referring to Sir Alan Sugar.

headmaster, headmistress, head teacher, etc. To avoid referring to the sex of the person in charge of a school, many people, especially teachers, refer to the *head* or the *head teacher*. (In American English, *principal* is similarly gender-neutral.) *ODO* and *CED* give *head teacher* as two words, but people often run them together as *headteacher*, on the model of *headmaster*. To my mind it still looks distinctly odd, but that is surely because I have not seen it as often as *headmaster*: then, 'How use doth breed a habit in a man'. For those who enjoy such terms, *school leader* is also admirably gender-free.

headquarters can legitimately be used either as a singular (*a large headquarters*) or as a plural (*the firm's headquarters are in London*). The singular more often denotes the physical premises and the plural the institution in its broader sense.

head up. The verb on its own is still much more common than *head up* with objects such as *inquiry, committee, investigating team*, or *department*. This enhanced phrasal verb first emerged in N. America ('the haven of energetic phrasal verbs') in the 1940s, and is now commonly used in Britain as well, particularly in 'the enhanced language of personnel departments anywhere', for example in job advertisements.

healthful, healthy. The Atlantic divide deepens into an abyss with these two words: some American editors get into a complete lather about their use, to the bemusement of British speakers. Stateside, such people insist that the only correct word to convey the meaning 'conducive to health' is *healthful*, and that *healthy* can never, never ever, be so used. One should therefore, they claim, speak of *healthful eating, food, diets, lifestyles, meals*, etc. The supposed distinction is a completely artificial one, invented by the American usage writer Alfred Ayers in 1881. Tenaciously upheld by a few North Americans, it has never made any inroads in Britain, and defies actual usage everywhere. It is true that *healthful* is the older word (1398), but age does not guarantee rectitude in words (any more than it does in people). *Healthful* originally meant 'conducive to health'; it acquired the meaning 'full of health' in the 16c. (interestingly, its first citation in the *OED* is by Coverdale). *Healthy* came on the scene in the 1550s, and from early on had both meanings. The *OEC* data shows that across the English-speaking world *healthy* is roughly 70 times more common than *healthful*, and 40 times more frequent even in the latter's North American heartland. Three quarters of the occurrences of *healthful* are from US sources, and elsewhere it is vanishingly rare, except in Canada. In Britain it occurs (e.g. *When healthful living and moral character were equated, good sexual hygiene meant abstaining from all sexual activities—Oxford Companion to the Body*, 2001) but will strike most people as a bit of an oddity. It cannot be used in the extended or metaphorical meanings of *healthy*, and could not replace it in e.g. *healthy competition, a healthy debate, relationship, respect, scepticism*, etc.

hearken back to. See HARK BACK TO, HARKEN BACK TO, HEARKEN BACK TO, 1.

heaved, hove. There are two forms, *heaved* and *hove*, for the past tense and past participle of *heave*, but in practice they are kept fairly strictly apart. In most ordinary senses of the verb ('lift, haul, utter (a sigh), throw, etc.') the normal form is, as it has been since the 16c., *heaved* (*heaved a bag of coal on to the lorry; heaved a sigh; he heaved and was sick*). When the sense is 'come into view' the normal form is *hove: she hove around the Minister's flank with the effect of an apparition*—T. Keneally, 1980; *Other families' nurses ... quailed when we hove in sight*—P. Lively, 1987. In nautical language the dominant past form is *hove* (*the cable can be hove in; the ship* *hove to; the boat remained hove-to; the anchor was hove up*). In a moment of aberration, the *Independent* (22 Aug. 1991) treated *hove* as an infinitive: **You never feel that Dr Mengele might suddenly hove into view.* Similar confusion about what part of speech *hove* is seems a particularly journalistic malaise, and leads to sentences like these: **He had seen 60 hove into sight, and assumed that must mean he was no longer up to it—Scotland on Sunday*, 2002; **the festival's* [*sc.* Glastonbury's] *immense acreage of tents, marquees, cars and people hoves into view—Sunday Times*, 2005.

Hebraism, Hebraist, Hebraize are the usual forms, not *Hebrewism*, etc.

hecatomb. Pronounced /ˈhɛkətuːm/, but in AmE /-təʊm/. The word has no connection with *tomb:* it is derived from Gk ἑκατόμβη, properly 'an offering of a hundred oxen', from ἑκατόν 'hundred' + βοῦς 'ox' (but even in Homer meaning simply 'a great public sacrifice' not necessarily confined to oxen).

hectare. This metric unit of land measurement is usually pronounced /ˈhɛktɛː/ (**hek**-tair) when it is used in Britain, but both it and /-ɑː/ (-ar) are commonly heard in English-speaking countries that have officially adopted the term.

hectic. The current meaning, familiar to everyone, is 'full of incessant or frantic activity' as in *Back at work after a hectic, but highly enjoyable, long weekend*—weblog, 2004. But *hectic* was originally a medical term, 'relating to or affected by a recurrent fever typically accompanying tuberculosis', and often described symptoms of flushed cheeks and hot, dry skin. (It comes ultimately from the Greek ἑκτικός 'habitual'). The medical meaning, which may surprise some readers, lingers on in literary contexts such as *The hectic face on the thin neck rose too sharply out of the collar of a silk blouse*—A. Brookner, 1990. As a historical footnote, at the time Fowler was writing, the word was just developing its modern meaning. Fowler objected to it as 'a vogue-word', popularized by journalists, and questioned the new metaphorical extension on etymological grounds. Subsequent usage commentators mentioned it purely because Fowler had; now it can be viewed as a nice example of how usage often overrides etymological niceties.

hecto-. See CENTI-.

hedonic, hedonism, hedonist. The first syllable can be pronounced to rhyme with *heed* or *head*. The first pronunciation reflects the words' origins in Greek ἡδονή (hēdonē) 'pleasure', with its long *e* sound (eta).

hegemony. Pronounced /hɪˈdʒɛməni/ or /ˈ-gɛməni/, i.e. with a soft or hard g, and stressing the second syllable. First syllable stress seems also to be an option in American English. See GREEK G.

hegira, denoting Muhammad's departure from Mecca in AD 622 and used for dates in the Muslim era, is pronounced /ˈhɛdʒɪrə/ (**hej**-i-rə) in British English and in AmE more commonly as /həˈdʒʌɪrə/ (hə-**jiy**-rə). The spelling *hejira* is occasionally found.

heifer. So spelt.

heinous. The traditional pronunciation is /ˈheɪnəs/, rhyming with *famous*, but /ˈhiːnəs/ (**hee**-nəs) is also heard and recorded in British dictionaries.

heir. 1 The first half of Tennyson's line from his *Locksley Hall* (1842), *I the heir of all the ages, in the foremost files of time*, was classified by Fowler (1926) as a hackneyed phrase, but the allusion, if ever made now outside Eng. lit. circles, would most probably be unrecognized.

2 An *heir apparent* is an heir whose claim cannot be set aside by the birth of another heir. An *heir presumptive* is an heir whose claim may be set aside if an *heir apparent* is born. *Heir apparent* is often used now of a person seen likely to succeed the present incumbent as head of a political party, a business firm, etc.

hel-. This sequence of letters in words that have an immediately following vowel is pronounced /ˈhɛl-/ in *helical, helichrysum, helicon, helicopter, heliport*, etc.; but /hiːl-/ in *helianthus, heliograph, heliolithic, heliotrope, helium*, and *helix*. Those in the first group all answer to Greek ἕλιξ 'something in spiral form'; while all in the second group except *helix* answer to Greek ἥλιος 'sun'.

helix /ˈhɛːlɪks/. Pronounced /ˈhiːlɪks/. Plural *helices* /ˈhɛlɪsiːz/, occasionally *helixes*.

hellebore. Pronounced /ˈhɛlɪbɔː/, with three syllables.

Hellene, Hellenic, are the noun and adjective respectively referring to the people and culture of Greece, ancient and modern. They are normally used in the context of the history, literature, and archaeology of Greek lands. *Hellene* is pronounced /ˈhɛliːn/ (**hel**-een) and *Hellenic* is pronounced most commonly as /hɛˈlɛnɪk/ (he-**len**-ik) but also /ˈhɛliːnɪk/ (he-**lee**-nik).

hello, hallo, hullo. This word had many historical forms as forebears (e.g. *hollo, holloa, hollow; holler; hillo*(*a*), before settling down into its three modern variants, *hello, hallo,* and *hullo.*

Hello is by far the most usual spelling in the *OEC* data, and is first recorded in 1883, and, used as an answer to a telephone call, in 1892 (Kipling). The other two are in a tiny minority. *Hallo* is more common in Australian English sources than elsewhere, and *hullo* more common in British English ones, and now the least usual spelling, despite being the first recorded. The plural form is *-os.*

Hallo is first recorded (as a shout to call attention) in 1864. *Hullo* is first recorded in Thomas Hughes's *Tom Brown's School Days* (1857), and, used as an answer to a telephone call, in a book by one C. H. Chambers published in 1900. *Halloo* as noun and verb has mostly been restricted to hunting circles, = (to shout) a cry to urge on the dogs. No one seems to mind that there are so many possible variants, including the *'Allo, 'allo* that British policemen are popularly portrayed as saying when they come across something or someone suspicious.

helmet. The corresponding adjective is **helmeted**. See -T-, -TT-.

help (verb). **1** *Help* is one of the oldest words in English, going back to the time of King Alfred (9c). It has two principal meanings in current English: 'to assist' (Can I help you?) and 'to prevent' (I can't help it). These two apparently unrelated sets of meanings are connected by the use of *help* in the context of dealing with disease and misfortune, in which the interrelation between providing help and preventing suffering is clearer. Three issues may arise with *help,* the first connected with the 'assist' meaning, the second and third with the 'prevent' meaning.

2 *Help* followed by bare or *to*-infinitive. Many speakers and learners of English must ask themselves at some point whether they should write *help someone to do something* (as in *He helped me* to dig out *my driveway*) or *help someone do something* (as in *He helped me* dig out *my driveway*). The construction with the bare infinitive developed from the Middle English period onwards. Many writers, including Shakespeare and Marlowe, allowed both constructions, but it is noteworthy that Shakespeare used the bare infinitive only when *help* was itself preceded by *to*: *The day will come that thou shalt wish for me* To *help thee curse this poisonous bunch-backed toad—Richard III* i.iii.247. In fact, one governing factor, past and present, is the natural reluctance to allow the sequence *to help* + *to*-infinitive, that is, to repeat *to.* This reluctance means that the bare infinitive is usually chosen in such cases, but not always; no doubt formality and literariness also have an influence, as in: *She allowed Pearl to help her to stack up her hair*—I. Murdoch, 1983; *This scheme aims to help us to continue working later in our lives by eliminating age discrimination*—business website, 2003 (BrE). Otherwise, the structure with the bare infinitive is preferred in everyday written and spoken English. Examples: (*to* omitted) *The purpose is as much to help the actors discover their roles as to work out cinematically effective moves—Daily Tel.,* 1970; *I had helped her carry it to her bedroom*—Garrison Keillor, 1986 (AmE); *Twice she had asked him to help her attach her stockings to her garter straps while she combed her hair or did her nails*—fiction website, 2005 (AmE); (*to* included) *where he helped to look after German prisoners of war—Brit. Med. Jrnl,* 1986; *The levees were helping to aggravate the problem they were meant to solve—New Yorker,* 1987; *His words helped me to laugh and feel very pretty*—fiction website, 2003 (AmE).

3 *Can't help doing, cannot but do, can't help but do.* These three constructions (and their various tenses, e.g. *couldn't help doing,* etc.) mean broadly the same, and all are current: e.g. *Bertrand* could not help venting *his frustration upon Madeleine*—P. P. Read, 1986; *The frailty of man without thee* cannot but fall—*Book of Common Prayer,* 1549; *He* could not help but feel *going home would put an end to this adventure*—S. Johnson, 1993 (Aust.). This last construction, which is probably a blend of the first two, is not recorded before the end of the 19c., first in the work of the Manx writer Hall Caine (*She could not help but plague the lad*—1894). Possibly because of being a relative newcomer, it has attracted criticism by usage pundits, which can nowadays be completely ignored, especially since it is the most widely used. The only point worth noting is that the three constructions have rather different frequencies and levels of formality. *Cannot help but do* is by far the most widely used (generally in the form *can't* when in the present tense); next comes *cannot help doing*, also usually shortened to *can't*; least frequent, and most formal or academic, is *cannot but do*, predominantly with the full form *cannot*: e.g. *Since words arrive to us always already endowed with meanings, Meursault cannot but make value judgments and interpretations each time he speaks, or each time, equally, when he remains silent*—M. Aristodemou, 2000 (BrE).

4 Also much (and fruitlessly) debated have been sentences in which, as the *OED* notes, *cannot* is replaced idiomatically by *can* after a negative expressed or implied. The *OED* lists four 19c. examples of this construction, including these: *Your name shall occur again as little as I can help, in the course of these pages*—Cardinal Newman, 1864; *I did not trouble myself more than I could help*—C. H. Spurgeon, 1879. Fowler (1926) objected to such constructions as illogical, but they are an idiomatic part of English.

helpmate, helpmeet (a helpful companion or partner, usually a husband or wife). Of these two legitimate spellings, the first is now the usual, though *helpmeet* (first recorded in 1673, hyphenated *help-meet*, in a Dryden play) is slightly older than *helpmate* (1715). *Helpmeet* was created when people ran together the two separate words *help meet* in the King James Bible, Gen. 20, 2:18, where it is related how God decided to create a companion for Adam: 'I will make him an help meet for him', i.e. a help suitable for him. It is easy to imagine people hearing the phrase read in church, and parsing it as a single word. Then folk etymology intervened to turn it into *helpmate*. An interesting example of the lasting influence of the Bible and of people's linguistic inventiveness.

hemi-. See DEMI-.

hemiplegia. Pronounced /ˌhɛmɪˈpliːdʒə/ (hemee-**plee**-juh) See also GREEK G.

hemistich (half a line of verse). Pronounced /-stɪk/.

hemo-. See Æ, Œ; HAEMO-, HÆMO-, HEMO-; HAEMORRHAGE.

hence. 1 For *from hence*, see FROM WHENCE.

2 *hence why*. By far the most common use of *hence* is in the meaning 'as a consequence; for this reason', i.e. as a connecting adverb, typically in technical, formal, or academic writing. It can occupy different positions in the sentence or clause, and is often used in front of a noun phrase. When it is the first word in a sentence, it should be followed by a comma. Examples: *Hence, he is apt to allow others to make decisions for him*—*Feminism and the History of Philosophy*, 2002; *Here too, wildlife is plentiful, though many species are nocturnal and hence difficult to spot*—*OEC*, 2004; (before noun phrase) *This is now rare in indigenous British working-class families but often occurs among immigrants—hence their impressive record of social mobility*—*Sunday Times*, 2005.

Recently, the formula *hence why* has started to be used, particularly in informal British and American English, e.g. *It's a miracle of modern technology, and a highly technical gadget—hence why I was attracted to it*—weblog, 2005 (BrE); *With no internet (hence why I haven't been online all weekend), I went to where I thought the Media Services/IT office was*—weblog, 2009, (AmE). Online comments show that it annoys or puzzles many people. In the examples cited the phrase is clearly tautological, because *hence* can be rewritten as 'which is why' and we therefore have 'which is why why'. In slangy speech it may be acceptable as sloppy shorthand; in writing, it should be given short shrift.

hendecasyllable (a line of eleven syllables; from Gk ἕνδεκα 'eleven'). A measure widely used in Greek and Latin verse, especially by Catullus, and later in Italy and Spain. It has never been common in English poetry, but note, for example: *If mine eyes can speake to doe heartie errand* (Philip Sidney's *Arcadia*, 1580s); *I beholding the* *summer dead before me* (Swinburne's *Hendecasyllabics,* 1866).

hendiadys /hɛn'dʌɪədɪs/, a figure of speech in which a single complex idea is expressed by two words connected by a conjunction (in English always *and*) instead of subordinating one to the other. The word was formed in late Latin from the Greek phrase ἓν διὰ δυοῖν 'one by means of two'. English examples include *nice and cool* (instead of *nicely cool*), and *good and ready* (instead of *completely ready;* see GOOD AND). The term should not be applied to expressions like *might and main, spick and span, whisky and soda,* etc., in which the parts are of equal standing, and neither is subordinate in sense to the other.

henna (verb). The inflected forms are *hennas, hennaed,* and *hennaing.* See -ED AND 'D.

he or she. 1 *The issue.* In English, explicit grammatical gender is chiefly confined to the third-person singular personal pronouns and determiners, *he, she, it, his, hers, its,* etc. From earliest times until about the 1960s it was unquestionably acceptable to use the pronoun *he* (and *him, himself, his*) with indefinite reference to denote a person of either sex, especially after indefinite pronouns and determiners such as *anybody, anyone, each, every,* etc., after gender-neutral nouns such as *person, individual,* and *speaker,* and in fixed expressions such as *every man for himself* and *one man one vote.* The feminist movement has greatly intensified sensitivities in this area, and alternative devices are now usually resorted to. When a gender-neutral pronoun or determiner (i.e. one that is free of grammatical gender) is needed, the options usually adopted are the plural forms *they, their, themselves,* etc., or *he or she* (*his or her,* etc.).

2 *They, their, them,* etc. The following are typical examples of plural forms referring back to singular grammatical subjects: Each *client should take the advice of* their *estate agent, who will take into account the style of the property,* [*etc.*]*—Real Property Guide* (Edinburgh), 1995; Anyone *who involves* themselves *in such issues does so for* their own *salvation—Big Issue,* 1998. Many people still object to this workaround, considering it ungrammatical, and it is a hotly debated issue in editorial forums. But in fact it is not new, being a revival of a practice dating from the 16c. and common in 19c. literature (*Whenever* a person *says to you that* they are *as innocent as can be in all concerning money, look well after your own money, for* they are *dead certain to collar it, if* they can—Dickens, 1853). It is also not entirely free of its own problems. (i) While some accept the plural after an indefinite antecedent, they would baulk at rewriting *The tragedy of a depressive's position is that he or she remains frozen in front of the mirror* as ... *they remain frozen* ... (ii) Following nouns are inappropriately put in the plural: *Ultimately* someone *will lose their* lives *over this—Edinburgh Herald & Post,* 2002 (Are they cats?). (iii) Treatment is inconsistent, plural nouns being followed by *his or her,* where *their* would be logical: *Instead they relied on* farmers' *ability to follow the market and decide the best future for* his or her *farm—OEC,* 2003.

3 *He or she, his or her,* etc. This has the advantage of avoiding the grammatical objection to *they,* etc. referring to a singular subject, e.g. *Now,* every *farmer with a GPS map of* his or her *field operations has the information just waiting to be mined—Successful Farming Magazine,* 2004. However, if the text requires repeated *he or she, his or her,* etc. the effect can be rather tiresome: *The potential user, if he or she already possesses hardware, may also be able to take the systems with him or her.* And, as with *they, their,* etc., inconsistency often lies in wait: *I cannot urge this bargain version too strongly on* anyone *who loves this work, even if* he or she *already has another performance in* their *collection—Gramophone,* 1995. (The last two points also apply to the formulation *he/she, his/her,* etc.)

4 *Alternative strategies.* (i) The sentence can be rephrased, for example by couching the whole thing in the plural. By this stratagem the last example above becomes ... *on* all those *who love this work, even if* they *already have another performance in* their *collection,* although the loss of singular focus can sometimes blur the sense. (ii) The generic 'you' can be used, where appropriate, e.g. *Each client should take the advice of their estate agent* could become 'As a client you should take the advice of your estate agent'. But this will only work in writing where it is appropriate to address the reader directly. (iii) *S/he.* This goes some way to redressing what is often perceived as a masculinist bias in English, but its disadvantage is that it does not have associated forms, and so recourse must be had to *him or her, his or her* etc. As Burchfield commented: 'The problem is an old one, and various methods of avoiding the use of a backward-referring *he* have been in use over the centuries. The only change is that the process has been greatly accelerated in recent times.'

5 *Artificial devices.* Composite forms such as *hesh, uself,* etc., have not found general currency, partly because they are difficult or impossible to say and are only possible in writing.

6 *Themself.* This reflexive pronoun, first recorded in the 14c. and corresponding to the singular gender-neutral use of *they,* has re-emerged in recent years, is occasionally found, and is likely to become more common, but at present is not generally accepted as part of standard English. Examples: *It is not an actor pretending to be Reagan or Thatcher, it is, in grotesque form, the person themself*—I. Hislop, 1984; *Someone in a neutral mood can devote themself solely to problem solving*—*Independent*, 1995.

her. 1 *Case.* For questions of *her* or *she,* see SHE 2, 3. Cf. HE 1, 2.

2 For questions of *her* and *hers* (e.g. *her and his tastes differ*), see ABSOLUTE POSSESSIVES.

3 For *her* and *she* used in personifications (*the Queen Elizabeth II made* her *stately way past the Needles; Switzerland has zealously guarded* her *neutrality in the* 20c.; *Britain stood alone in 1940 after* she *had lost* her *European allies during the blitzkrieg*), see PERSONIFICATION. It is important not to use both *it/its* and *she/her* in the same passage, as in *The United States has given another proof of* its *determination to preserve* her *neutrality.*

4 *Her* is sometimes used as part of a coordinated subject: e.g. *He's slashing bracken along the boundary fence and* me *and* her *go there to get kindling*—M. Eldridge, 1984 (Aust.); Her *and Kitty didn't have much to do with each other anymore*—N. Virtue, 1990. For comment on this, see HE 1.

herb. The standard AmE pronunciation is with a silent letter h, which preserves an older BrE pronunciation that died out in the 19c.

here. 1 The normal agreement rules apply in most cases when *here's/here are* are used (*here's my ticket/here are my children*). But in speech such a sentence as *Here's some flowers for you* is idiomatically acceptable.

2 The types *this here friend of mine* and *these here bicycles,* with *here* in mid-position, are found only in non-standard speech; but *here* in post-position is standard (*your friend here, these bicycles here*).

hereby, herein, hereof, hereto, heretofore, hereunder, herewith. The first and last are the strongest survivors in this group of threatened words (*I hereby promise never to smoke again; Herewith I enclose a cheque for my subscription*). The others, especially as used in legal language, are rapidly being replaced by plain English expressions (substituting *by this means, in this matter, of this,* etc.).

hereditary. The *OEC* data suggests that *a hereditary* is about seven times more common than *an hereditary.* See A, AN 3(b).

hero. Plural *heroes.* See -O(E)S 1.

heroic. 1 *OEC* data suggests that the type *a heroic act, performance, struggle,* is about ten times more frequent than *an heroic* . . . See A, AN 3(b).

2 Some uses in literature and prosody call for comment: (*a*) *heroic poetry,* epic poetry. Such poetry normally uses a specified type of line: the hexameter in classical Greek and Latin, the alexandrine in French, the hendecasyllabic line in Italian, and the iambic pentameter in English. (*b*) The *heroic couplet* is a rhymed pair of iambic pentameters, a scheme favoured by Chaucer in the 14c. and characteristic of much late 17c. and 18c. poetry.

> *And bathed every veyne in swich licour*
> *Of which vertu engendred is the flour*
> Chaucer, *General Prologue*
>
> *How happy is the blameless vestal's lot!*
> *The world forgetting, by the world forgot.*
> Pope, *Eloisa to Abelard*

(*c*) The *heroic* (or *elegiac*) *quatrain* or *heroic stanza* is not used in epic poetry, but is so called because it uses the English heroic line: four pentameters rhyming *abab*, as in Gray's *Elegy written in a Country Church-Yard* (1751), or *aabb*.

Can storied urn or animated bust
Back to its mansion call the fleeting breath?
Can honour's voice provoke the silent dust,
Or flatt'ry soothe the dull, cold ear of death?

See ELEGIAC QUATRAIN.

heroin, heroine (both pronounced /ˈhɛrəʊɪn/). One of the features of English is the existence of homophones like *heroin* (the drug, first recorded in 1898 and at first pronounced /hɪˈrəʊn/, stressed on the second syllable), and *heroine* (first recorded *c.*1659). The two are very rarely confused, but when they are, *heroine* is wrongly used for *heroin*, as in the thought-provoking *The aim is to help heroine addicts break their habit.*

herring pond. From the 16c. to the 19c. *the herring pond* was used as a humorous term for an ocean, the sea, especially the North Atlantic ocean. The phrase is now practically extinct, having been replaced by 'the pond', but still occasionally surfaces. Examples from post-19c. sources: *I hope you will pay us another visit when you next 'cross the herring pond'*—E. Waugh, 1945; *Judging by the widespread grief of the British public following Arthur Miller's death, we still take a lively interest in writers from across the herring pond*—*Cherwell Magazine*, 2005.

hers. See ABSOLUTE POSSESSIVES.

hesitance, hesitancy, hesitation. All three words are first recorded in English in the early 17c., but since then *hesitation* has far outstripped the others, especially *hesitance*: in the *OEC hesitation*, singular and plural, occurs nearly 10,000 times, *hesitancy* (singular and plural) roughly 1,000, and *hesitance* a mere 200. A not-always observed residual distinction is that *hesitancy* indicates a tendency to indecision, whereas *hesitation* denotes the fact or action of hesitating. Examples: (hesitancy, hesitance) *An examination of the client's hesitance, however, indicates that he is not at all sure about the terminology and that he may simply be echoing the wording of the charge*—J. Citron, 1989; *He was reluctant to begin and his hesitancy made her look questioningly at him*—T. Hayden, 1991; (hesitation) *He had driven the Deputy Director … half mad with his hesitation, his recycled arguments for accepting and not accepting*—D. Bloodworth, 1978; *Women have trouble communicating in a 'male' language and the result is hesitations, false starts, and so on*—D. Cameron, 1992. *Hesitation* is the form mostly used in the idiomatic phrases *not have a moment's hesitation* and *without hesitation*, though *hesitancy* is occasionally also used: *When Granpa asked me what I wanted for my fifteenth birthday I replied without a moment's hesitation, 'My own barrow'.*—Jeffrey Archer, 1991; *He answered clearly and without hesitation*—business website, 2004.

heteronym, a word having the same spelling as another, but a different sound and meaning, e.g. *moped* /məʊpt/ verb past tense and *moped* /ˈməʊpɛd/ noun; *refuse* /ˈrɛfjuːs/ noun and *refuse* /rɪˈfjuːz/ verb; *used* /juːst/ 'accustomed' and *used* /juːzd/ 'made use of'.

hew has two past participles, *hewn* and *hewed*, the first being much commoner in both British and American English. More precisely, the *OEC* data suggests: (*a*) in the traditional meaning of 'chop, cut', *hewn* is slightly more frequent in the perfect tenses and massively more common in passive constructions, and when used adjectivally (e.g. *roughly hewn*); (*b*) in the largely American phrase *hew to* (= adhere to), *hewed* is the preferred form for both perfect and passive. Examples: (hewn) *the planks, or 'chynes', were cut to size for me, so I can't claim to have hewn the wood myself*—Robert Leggatt, 2005 (BrE); *the Californian has hewn a voice for the philosopher-poet in contemporary American verse*—*Believer Magazine*, 2005 (AmE); *By the end there is a rickety, roughly hewn bridge between them*—*Guardian*, 2004 (BrE); *the Obama administration, which has hewn to a much more pro-Israeli line in the run up to next year's presidential election in the United States*—*Daily Tel.*, 2011; (hewed) *After the tree had been chopped down the part to be hewed was cleared of limbs and also peeled*—*OEC* (undated); *But in the general election, McCain has hewed closer to Penn's advice*—*Time Magazine*, 2008; *His house was built of hewed cottonwood logs, which he hauled fourteen miles*—*OEC* (undated).

hexameter, a metrical verse line of six feet, used especially in Greek and Latin epic poetry (*dactylic hexameters*), and imitated in modern languages, esp. in German, Russian, and Swedish verse (Baldick, 1990), and occasionally in English, e.g. in A. H. Clough's *The Bothie of Tober-na-Vuolich* (1848): *This was the/final re/tort from the/ eager, im/petuous/ Philip.*

hiatus. A technical term in linguistics and prosody used to mean a break between two adjacent fully pronounced vowels forming two successive syllables, e.g. *the eye, Noel, Eloïse,* i.e. expressions in which elision or diphthongization does not occur. Both in this technical sense and in the general meaning 'pause or break in continuity' the plural is *hiatuses,* not the occasionally found **hiati*. See -US 2.

Hibernian as adjective and noun means 'of or concerning Ireland; a native of Ireland', is found in historical contexts, but nowadays is most commonly found in names, e.g. *the Royal Hibernian Academy.* The related *Hiberno-* (a combining form, as in *Hiberno-English*), is restricted to technical, especially linguistic, contexts.

hiccup. 1 The inflected forms are *hiccuped, hiccuping.* See -P-, -PP-.

2 The variant *hiccough,* also pronounced /ˈhɪkʌp/, was formed in the 17c. under the mistaken impression that the second syllable was *cough.* Its spelling is an unnecessary complication, and it is a minority spelling nowadays, despite its long history.

hide (verb). The past tense is now always *hid* and the past participle *hidden, hid* being archaic or poetical when used as the past participle, e.g. *The Iuy which had hid my princely Trunck*—Shakespeare*; I don't love you anymore I don't think I ever did And if you ever had any kind of love for me You kept it all so well hid*—Annie Lennox & David Stewart, 1989.

hierarchic(al). *Hierarchical* is the older form and is about forty times more frequent in *OEC* data. *Hierarchic* is a rare and somewhat self-conscious choice.

high, highly. *High* functions as an adverb in e.g. *most surfaces were piled high with magazines; feelings were running high.* In this adverbial function it could theoretically overlap with the adverb *highly,* but it only does so in the collocations *to rate, rank, figure, score high/highly*: *Johnny Depp's performance in the movie is rated high by critics; My partner Karin went for deep fried mozzarella with tomato and garlic ... which she rated highly.* In the *OEC* data, *highly* is much more common with *rate* and *rank, high* is much more common with *score,* and the two are equally balanced with *figure. Highly paid* in front of a noun, e.g. *highly paid executives,* is much more frequent than *high paid.*

hight. The past participle (from the 14c.) of the Old English verb *hatan* 'to call' is an archaism for 'called, named', likely to be encountered only in older works: *Childe Harold was he hight*—Byron, 1812.

hike (noun). It seems quaint now that Burchfield (1996) could write that this word in the meaning 'an increase (in prices, wages, etc.)' was 'mainly restricted to N. America'. First recorded in 1931 in the US, it is now a staple of BrE journalism, particularly on financial topics: e.g. *the group had been able to pass on most of the price hikes to its customers in the past year, and it was expecting to do so again*—*FT*, 2011. It is worth bearing in mind, however, that some newspapers' style guides proscribe it absolutely.

hillo(a). See HELLO.

him. In standard English, *him* should not be used as the first item in a coordinated subject, although it often is in informal speech and representations of it, e.g. *Him and Carol lived too high, kept buying stuff they couldn't nohow afford*—Truman Capote, 1965. See also HE 1.

Himalayas. There seems no good reason to abandon the traditional English pronunciation /hɪməˈleɪəz/, stressed on the third syllable, or the traditional form (plural in -*s*), in favour of the cultish form *Himalaya,* pronounced /hɪˈmɑːlɪə/, though it is true that the Nepalese word *Himalaya* is derived from Sanskrit *hima* 'snow' + *ālaya* 'abode', and has /ɑː/ not /ə/ in the second syllable.

him or her. See HE OR SHE.

himself has two primary roles: (*a*) as a reflexive (*He was talking about himself; John was looking at himself in the mirror; He made himself a cup of coffee*), and (*b*) to emphasize a male denoted by a noun or pronoun (*Marcus hoped simply to avoid* *being touched himself; He told me himself*). *Himself*, unlike *he*, is still quite often used as a pronoun referring to people in general, possibly because the alternative *himself or herself* is rather long-winded, and *themself* following a singular subject is not fully accepted. Examples: *while it is still true that knowledge is something each person can achieve only for himself*—J. Annas, 2003 (BrE); *Cunningham lets each viewer decide for himself what the dance means, or what it is about*—*Dance Magazine*, 2002 (AmE); *Each looks to himself only, and no one troubles himself about the rest*—*American Jrnl of Economics and Sociology*, 2002.

The delightful use of *himself* to mean (as the *ODO* quaintly puts it) 'a third person of some importance, especially the master of the house' is mainly Irish: *I'll mention it to himself; Himself and Bimbo were at the fryer*—R. Doyle, 1991 (Ir.). See also HE OR SHE; MYSELF; THEMSELF.

hind (noun). See BUCK.

hindsight. At first used to mean the backsight of a rifle, since the last quarter of the 19c. it has become a pleasing abstract word meaning, as Gowers (1965) put it, 'the quality that finds expression in being wise after the event'. It is written as one word, without a hyphen, and the collocation *in hindsight* is about twice as frequent as *with hindsight*. A cliché one might think of avoiding is 'Hindsight gives 20/20 vision' and variations on that theme.

hinge (verb). The *The Oxford Dict. for Writers and Editors* recommends, as does *ODO*, *hingeing* for the present participle (to bring out the pronunciation), but the *OEC* data shows that the slightly odd-looking *hinging* is much more frequent in practice.

hippo. Plural *hippos*. See -O(E)S 6.

hippocampus (zoology and anatomy). Plural *hippocampi* /-pʌɪ/.

hippogriff (fabulous monster). The recommended spelling (but *hippogryph* is also found).

hippopotamus. The recommended plural is *hippopotamuses*, not *-potami* /-mʌɪ/.

his. 1 From Old English onwards, but especially between about 1400 and 1750, and still occasionally (plainly as an archaism), *his* has sometimes been placed after a noun (esp. a proper noun) instead of the possessive *'s*; similarly *her* and *their*, where appropriate. Examples: *to such as will vouchsafe to reade the saide Sir Thomas More his aunswere*—*Harpsfield's Life of More*, 1558; *And this we beg for Jesus Christ his sake*—*Book of Common Prayer*, 1662; *In examining Æneus his Voyage by the Map*—Addison, 1712. Despite the distinguished history of such uses it was and is a mistake to interpret possessive *'s* as a reduced form of *his*.

2 *A graceful raising of* one's *hand to* his *hat*. For the use of *his* to refer back to *one's*, see ONE.

3 Modern practice tends to frown on male-oriented sentences like *Where your child gets* his *income determines how much tax* he *owes* (*USA Today*, 1988); and to favour the type *Each player, alone on* his or her *part, was embarrassed whenever* he or she *became lost* (J. Updike, 1988), or to use *they* with singular reference. See also HE OR SHE.

his or her. See HIS 3; HE OR SHE.

Hispanic. In the US *Hispanic* is the standard accepted term, as adjective and noun, to refer to Spanish-speaking people living there. Other, more specific, terms such as *Latino* and *Chicano* are also used where occasion demands. Examples: *For some students, especially Hispanic females, perceived gender roles affect career choice*—*OEC*, 2004 (AmE); *About 20 percent of the Bay Area market is composed of Hispanics*—*OEC*, 2000 (AmE). See also CHICANO.

hisself. Since the 14c. there has been a tendency to treat *self* as a noun (= person) and to place possessive pronouns and adjectives in front: thus *to thine own self be true* and, in the *OED*, *his owne self* (1406), *his very self* (1826), etc. A by-product of this process is the emergence of the dialectal form *hisself* usually written as one word.

historian. In writing, *OEC* data suggests that *historian* is still preceded by *an* rather than *a* in about a fifth of cases. See A, AN 3(b).

historic. 1 Its primary meaning is 'famous or important in history or potentially so' (*a Norman castle on that historic spot; the historic figure of the Warrior Queen* [*sc.* Boudicca]; *we travelled to the historic breakthrough point* [of the Channel tunnel]). As William Safire noted in 1992, 'Any past event is *historical,* but only the most memorable ones are *historic.*' But the distinction is not watertight, and the words overlap in some collocations, in particular, as the *OEC* data shows, in the collocations *historic background, context, documents, record*: *Extinct volcanoes are those that have not erupted in historic time, whereas active volcanoes have been seen to erupt*—M. A. Summerfield, 1991; *It may involve the use of relevant historic documents*—R. Brooks, 1993. It is, however, advisable to remember that many people uphold the distinction as absolute, and therefore to choose carefully.

2 In grammar, **historic present** is the technical term to denote narrative that is put in the present tense for dramatic effect, although it is describing events in the past. The intended effect is well summed up in: 'The speaker, as it were, forgets all about time and imagines, or recalls, what he is recounting, as vividly as if it were now present before his eyes' (Jespersen, 1909–49, part iv). Examples: *She had no notion of how welcome she would be. But Raymond opens the door before she can touch the bell, and he hugs her around the shoulders and kisses her twice* —A. Munro, 1989; *'Then she slams into me,' he continued, gesturing, 'and suddenly I'm in the world of things beyond myself.'*—*New Yorker,* 1991.

As exemplified above, the device is often used in fiction (and non-fiction) narrative, and particularly in spoken narrative, as in the second example. Indeed, many modern novels are written entirely in the historic present, while in others it is used as an occasional stylistic emphasizer. It is a particular favourite of TV and radio historical narrative, in an attempt to inject immediacy into the recounting of events, but arguably overuse there has largely deprived it of its dramatic effect, and it has become a mere genre convention. The historic present has been used in English since at least the 13c. and, debatably, even in Old English.

3 The *OEC* data suggests that *a historic* . . . is about twice as common as *an historic* . . . See A, AN 3(b).

historical. 1 A word of quite general meaning: 'of or concerning history; belonging to the past, not the present; from the historian's view; etc.' The *OED* is a dictionary 'on historical principles'. Historical events are portrayed in several of Shakespeare's plays. Historical fiction is the genre for which Hilary Mantel scoops up prizes. *Roland's famous legendary death is a very easy perversion of his historical death*—E. A. Freeman, 1871; *Historical linguistics is the study of the developments in languages in the course of time*—R. H. Robins, 1964; *Walker provides a useful historical perspective on the moral panic surrounding videos*—*Sense of Cinema,* 2001 (Aust.).

2 *Historical* is occasionally used (but mostly during the 19c.) in the same way as *historic* (sense 1) but this use is to be discouraged. Also a few linguistic scholars use *historical present* instead of *historic present,* but more perhaps by inadvertence than by conviction.

3 The *OEC* data suggests that *a historical* . . . is three times more frequent than *an historical* . . . See A, AN 3(b).

hither. Except in archaic or deliberately archaizing use, this ancient word (used already in Old English) and its correlative *thither* are restricted in modern use to the fixed phrases *hither and thither* and *hither and yon* (in various directions, esp. in a disorganized way). Examples: *the European children who rush hither and thither, shrieking in French or English*—P. Lively, 1987; *Cozzens discusses these topics relying, for the most part, on reports in the mass media, his own experience, and data gathered hither and yon*—*OEC,* 2003. *Hither* is also still very much alive in the expression *come-hither* 'enticing, flirtatious' (first recorded in 1900): *Her eyes are so wide, so innocent until they narrow with 'come hither' malice*—*OEC,* 2003.

HIV. Since the abbreviation stands for 'human immunodeficiency *virus',* it is tautological to speak of the *HIV virus.* But, tautologous or not, the phrase is now well established.

hoard (stock or store) and *horde* (large group) are homophones, and are sometimes confused. Usually *hoard* is mistakenly used for *horde*: e.g. *It does not involve hoards* [read *hordes*] *of customers parking in the streets*—G. Jones, 1987.

hoarhound. See HOREHOUND.

hobnob (verb). The inflected forms are *hobnobbed, hobnobbing.* See -B-, -BB-.

hobo. Dictionaries recognize both *hoboes* and *hobos* as correct plurals, the second being rather more frequent despite being listed second by dictionaries. See -O(E)S 2.

hodgepodge. See HOTCHPOTCH.

hoe (verb). The inflected forms are *hoes, hoed, hoeing.*

hoi polloi. 1 *'hoi polloi'* or *'the hoi polloi'*? This phrase is a somewhat derogatory way of referring to 'the masses, the common people'. Nowadays printed in roman rather than italic, it comes from the Greek οἱ πολλοί, which translates literally as 'the many'. When first used, seemingly by Dryden, it was actually written in Greek preceded by the word 'the', i.e. *the* οἱ πολλοί, as it was also by Byron and Wordsworth. The first transliteration into English script, as 'the oi [*sic*] polloi', appears in a James Fennimore Cooper book of 1837.

Despite this impressive literary pedigree, *the hoi polloi* has been criticized by usage commentators and traditionalists on the grounds that 'the' is redundant, because *hoi* already means 'the'. Such an argument rather misses the point: once established in English, expressions of this kind are subject to the rules and conventions of English. The formulation *the hoi polloi* is more frequent in the *OEC* data, but not hugely so. You may leave the article out if you wish, but there is no obvious advantage in doing so. And if you do, some may interpret the omission as linguistic snobbery, misguided pedantry, or even unwholesome one-upmanship. As Burchfield said, 'who is prepared to correct W. S. Gilbert's lines from *Iolanthe*: *'Twould fill with joy, And madness stark the* οἱ πολλοί (a *Greek remark.*)?' Examples: (without *the*) *Alcibiades might have thought himself above hoi polloi, but none of the competitors* [in the Olympic Games] *in his day sought artificial aids to bolster their prowess*—B. Levin, 1992; *We learn ... that by appearing for a photo call and chat with hacks in a local pub, the second in line to the throne is in touch with hoi polloi—Sunday Herald*, 2007; (with *the*) *Our days among the hoi polloi ended the moment we were requested to join the Recorder Orchestra. We were plucked from obscurity and thrust into the limelight—SX News National*, 2004 (Aust.); *the appeal of this blue-collar megastar extends far beyond the hoi polloi—OEC*, 2003 (AmE).

2 By a strange reversal of its original meaning, *hoi polloi* has, since the 1950s, been used to mean 'high society, the upper crust'. Substantial evidence of this use was presented in vol. ii (1991) of *DARE*, and a more recent example is *Unless the issue impedes their spending habits, the hoi polloi could care less if people are starving, nations are warring, or bombs are dropping. Their money is a barrier to human interaction—OEC*, 2004 (AmE). The use is not confined to American English, e.g. *I know our Terry's much too grand for the likes of us nowadays—too busy consorting with the hoi polloi at all those literary soirees*—S. Mackay, 1992. I remember hearing the word used in this meaning as far back as the mid-1960s, and it seems well established. It is not, however, acknowledged by dictionaries.

hoist was originally a variant past participle of the now obsolete verb *hoise*, meaning the same as modern *hoist*. Both *hoist* and *hoised* were current at the turn of the 16c.: *For tis the sport to haue the enginer Hoist with his owne petar* [i.e. blown up by his own bomb]—Shakespeare, 1604; *they ... hoised vp the maine sail to the winde*—Acts (AV) 27: 40. At the same time *hoist* was already in use as a verb in its own right: *Let him take thee, And hoist thee vp to the shouting Plebeians*—Shakespeare, 1606.

holey (full of holes). The *e* is retained to distinguish it to the eye from *holy*.

Holland. See NETHERLANDS.

hollo, holloa, holler, hollow. See HELLO.

home, house. The complexities of these two words in the literal sense 'one's dwelling-place' cannot be set down here except by repeating what the *OED* states: 'Also (chiefly in later use) a private house or residence considered merely as a building'. Examples (from the *OED*): *More houses (or 'homes' as a house is kindly called here) are needed*—A. Ross, 1955 (Aust.); *Her three ... sons were shot to death in their home*—*Globe & Mail* (Toronto), 1968. It is usual to say *in the privacy of one's own home* rather than *one's own house*, and estate agents tend to prefer *home* as having a more personal sound. In American English, *home* is used much more freely where in British English *house* would be used: *In Beverly Hills and Bel Air, we saw the homes (never called houses) of Jane Withers, Greer Garson, and Barbra Streisand*—*Guardian*, 1973.

home in on, hone in on. Which of these sentences is correct? *A teaching style which* homes in on *what is important for each pupil* or *A teaching style which* hones in on *what is important for each pupil*? Where you live in the English-speaking world is likely to affect your opinion. In particular, editors and readers in the US may well consider *home in* a mistake, while the opposite applies in Britain. Who is right? *Home in* is a metaphor, from *home* used as a verb to describe how a missile or aircraft is directed to a target, as in: *The other helicopter located the dinghy by homing in on the bleeping of the emergency distress call.* To *hone* means 'to sharpen a knife with a whetstone', or 'to improve a skill or talent'. Across the English-speaking world, *home in* is about 70% more frequent than *hone in*. But there is a noticeable contrast between BrE and AmE. In AmE, *home in* makes up about 55% of occurrences of both, but in BrE the picture is rather different. Of the total pie, 85% are examples with *home in*.

ODO calls *hone* a mistake, as does the *Collins English Dictionary*. The *OED*, however, does not. Instead it notes that it is 'originally US', and gives the earliest example from 1965. On the other side of the pond, *MWCDEU* suggests that it 'seems to have become established in American usage'. The *hone in* variant has been around for nearly half a century and is used in many parts of the English-speaking world. Some dictionaries list it without comment; others warn against it. If you use it, you will probably not be misunderstood, but bear in mind that some people will consider it a mistake; others will come to the same conclusion if you use *home in*. To avoid the problem, why not use *focus on*, *concentrate on*, *zero in on*, or any other synonym that suits your context?

homely. The connotations of this word as applied to a person (usually a woman) are favourable in British English, in which it means 'simple, unpretentious' but disparaging in American English, in which it means 'unattractive, dowdy': *Homely and welcoming, owners Doug and Karen Richards have gone out of their way to ensure visitors are immediately put at their ease*—*Cornish Guardian*, 2005; *A homely woman with an apron on answers the door*—A. Drai, 2002 (AmE).

homeo-. See HOMO-, HOMOEO-, HOMEO-.

home page, homepage. (The initial page displayed to a visitor of a website or intranet site, typically containing introductory information and links to other parts of the site.) There is no consensus about writing this as two words or one. The *OED*, *ODO*, and *ODWE* give it as two, as does Merriam-Webster online and the AP stylebook. But many people write it as one, as does the Guardian style guide, and the *OEC* data shows use in practice is evenly split. If you are not bound by specific editorial guidelines or house style, you can please yourself, but perhaps writing it as two words is the safer option for the time being.

homey, homy (adjective) (suggesting home; cosy). The dictionaries give conflicting advice about the spelling. Some give preference to *homey*, and others to *homy*. It is not a matter of great moment either way. My own preference is for *homey*.

homo (noun) /ˈhəʊməʊ/. An offensive abbreviation of *homosexual*. Plural *homos*. See -O(E)S 6. See also GAY.

homo-, homoeo-, homeo-. These two prefixes are derived from two different Greek words: *homos* (ὁμός) meaning 'same', and homoios (ὅμοιος) meaning 'of the same kind'. This difference in meaning is reflected in the English words based on them, e.g. *homosexuality* denotes sexual attraction towards the *same sex* and *homoeopathy* denotes treatment of disease by using small doses of drugs that have the *same kind* of effect as the disease itself. The combination *-oeo-* is now more usually reduced to *-eo-* in British English, e.g. *homeopathy*, and this shorter spelling is standard in American English.

In these compounds the short *o* of the Greek originals is not uniformly retained in English. In general, words in *homo-* are pronounced either hom- or hohm-, whereas words in *hom(o)eo-* are more usually pronounced hom-, but there is a lot of variation. *ODO* gives the following pronunciations: hohm only: *homocentric*, *hom(o)eopath*; hohm, then hom: *hom(o)-*

eopathy, homoerotic; hom, then hohm: *hom(o)eostasis, homomorphic, homophobia, homosexual, homograft, homograph, homophone*; hom only: *homogeneous, hom(o)eotherm, homologue, homonym*.

homogeneous, homogenous. *Homogeneous* is a general word meaning 'of the same kind' (*a strategy that identifies homogeneous subgroups of people based on common defining characteristics—Amer. Jrnl of Health Studies*, 2002). It is pronounced /hɒməʊˈdʒiːnɪəs/, with the main stress on the third syllable. It is often confused with the scientific word *homogenous* /həˈmɒdʒənəs/, stressed on the second syllable, and formerly used in biology to mean 'having a common descent', but now superseded by *homogenetic*. This confusion has become so widespread that some dictionaries, including *ODO*, now recognize *homogenous* as a legitimate variant of *homogeneous*. It seems likely that the verb *homogenize*, 'to make homogeneous', also stressed on the second syllable, has influenced the use of *homogenous* in this meaning. An example showing *homogenous* used in this way: *?In doing so, they produced a much more homogenous and orthodox form of narrative than that of the legendary tales themselves*—Essays & Studies, 1991.

homograph, a word spelt like another but having a different meaning or origin, e.g. *pole* (piece of wood or metal), derived from Old English *pāl*, and *pole* (as in *North Pole, South Pole*), derived from Gk πόλος. Homographs need not have the same pronunciation, e.g. *lead* (to guide) and *lead* (a heavy metal), respectively /liːd/ and /led/.

homonym is a generic term for a word having the same spelling or sound as another but a different meaning. Homonyms identical in spelling include *calf* (young bovine animal), derived from Old English *cælf*; and *calf* (fleshy hind part of the human leg), derived from Old Norse *kálfi*. And those identical in sound but not in spelling include *tail* (of an animal), derived from OE *tægl*; and *tale* (narrative), derived from OE *talu*. Examples of the first type are called *homographs*, and those of the second *homophones*. Cf. HETERONYM.

homophone, a word having the same sound as another but a different meaning, origin, or spelling. Homophones are a major feature of English, to the bafflement of many of its spellers, and the delight of punsters. A short list (in which the examples assume each word is pronounced in RP): *air/heir, aloud/allowed, cue/queue, heal/heel, hear/here, hoard/horde, pair/pare/pear, peak/peek/pique, pore/pour, rains/reins/reigns, site/sight/cite, stationary/stationery, their/there, vain/vein*. Near-homonyms like *affect/effect, descent/dissent, eminent/imminent* also abound in the language. Robert Bridges wrote a classic paper on homophones (SPE Tract ii, 1919) and included lists of them divided into classes: the total number of words listed was 1,775. His main conclusion was that English was exceptionally burdened by them.

homosexual. Still often used in some formal contexts (news bulletins, law courts, etc.), but in other contexts potentially burdened with disapproval, and generally replaced by *gay* in ordinary use, e.g. *gay couple, community, group, man, marriage, relationship, rights, sex*, etc. There is no agreement about the pronunciation of the first *o*. Many people use the same vowel as in *homage*; just as many people use the sound of *home*. The popular belief that the *homo-* in *homosexual* comes from Latin *homo* 'man' is mistaken. See also HOMO-, HOMOEO-, HOMEO-.

homy. See HOMEY.

Hon. Also **hon**. That this prefix may be an abbreviation of either *honourable* or *honorary* is a source of some confusion to people outside Britain. It stands for *honourable* in reports of debates in the House of Commons, where members may not be referred to by name, except by the Speaker, but must be called *the honourable member for* . . . (*honourable and gallant* if a member of the Armed Forces, *honourable and learned* if a lawyer). It stands for *honorary* when prefixed to the holder of an office (*Hon. Secretary, Hon. Treasurer*, etc.) and indicates that he or she is unpaid. As an abbreviation of *honourable* it is also a courtesy title of the sons and daughters of viscounts and barons and of the younger sons of earls, as well as the holders of certain high offices, especially Puisne Judges in England and Lords of Session in Scotland. (Privy Councillors and peers below the rank of marquess are *right honourable*; so are Lords Justices of Appeal, the Lord Mayor of London, the Lord provost of Edinburgh, and a few other civic dignitaries; marquesses are *most honourable* and a duke *his grace.*) *The Hon.,* when used as a courtesy title, requires the person's first name or initial, not his or her surname alone (*the Hon. James* or *J. Brown,* not *the Hon. Brown*); a common mistake is to suppose that the first name is unnecessary before a double-barrelled surname. The same rule applies to the prefixes REVEREND and SIR.

There is a great deal of variation in English-speaking countries outside Britain. For details readers will need to consult e.g. *Debrett's Correct Form.* The American practice is described by Bryan A. Garner (1987) as follows: '*Honorable* is a title of respect given to judges, members of the U.S. Congress, ambassadors, and the like. It should be used not with surnames only, but with complete names (e.g. *The Honorable Antonin Scalia*) or with a title of courtesy (e.g. *The Honorable Mr. Scalia*). The abbreviation *Hon.* should be used only in mailing addresses.'

hone in on. See HOME IN ON, HONE IN ON.

honeyed, honied. The first of the two is recommended for both literal and figurative meanings, e.g. *honeyed duck breast, honeyed words.*

honorarium (a payment made for professional services that are provided nominally without charge). Either *honorariums* or *honoraria* is acceptable as the plural, but the formal nature of this word causes the second to be rather more common. See -UM 3.

honorary. See HON.

honour. 1 So spelt in British English, but **honor** in American English.

2 *it is a custome More honourd in the breach, then the obseruance.* In context (*Hamlet* i.iv.16) it means a custom that one deserves more honour for breaking than for keeping; but it is generally quoted in the mistaken and very different sense of dead letter or rule more often broken than kept, e.g. *Those two sections of the Act are honoured much more in the breach than in the observance—NZ Parliamentary Debates,* 2004.

honourable. 1 So spelt in BrE, but **honorable** in AmE.

2 See HON.

hoof. For the plural form, both *hoofs* and *hooves* are permissible, but *hooves* seems now to be the dominant form throughout the English-speaking world. Cf. ROOF.

hope (noun). The *OED* gives examples of *hopes* used in a singular sense, especially in the phrase *in hopes* (e.g. *I was in hopes you would have shown us our own nation*—Addison, 1702). Phrases containing *hopes* of the type *in the hopes of, in hopes of, in the hopes that, in hopes that,* are now much more characteristic of, though not exclusive to, American English, (e.g. *He never said a kind word to them, and they worked like dogs in hopes of hearing one*—G. Keillor, 1989). In British English the usual equivalent is *in the hope of* (or *in the hope + that*-clause), e.g. *They* [*sc.* emails] *are sent randomly to consumers, in the hope that someone will divulge their banking details—BBC News,* 2004.

hope (verb). Fowler (1926) vehemently rejected the use of *hope* in the passive followed by an infinitive, e.g. *A luncheon at which the Queen is hoped to be present,* which occurs mainly in British English news writing. As he pointed out, the construction is based on analogy with *expect*: *I expect the Queen to be present* can be passivized as *the Queen is expected to be present,* but there is no corresponding structure capable of passivization for *hope,* i.e. **We hope the Queen to be present.* Most usage guides ignore Fowler's strictures, and so can you. This passive construction is not in any case very common: the construction with *it is hoped* (*that*) is much more frequent, e.g. *A luncheon at which it is hoped that the Queen will be present,* and available to be used by anyone who shares Fowler's distaste for the use.

hopefully. It is hard to think of another word which has provoked such revulsion and condemnation. The complete story of that revulsion is too complex for an article of this length. What follows consists of some basic facts and a modest recommendation. **1** *Current status.* Opinions of the word vary enormously. The *OED* merely notes, dispassionately if rather coyly, 'Avoided by many writers'; but as recently as March 2013 the editor of the *Independent* seemed incensed by *hopefully* being used twice in its 'wrong sense' in a single report on the *Today* programme, while the *Telegraph style book* rather jingoistically calls it 'another ignorant Americanism'. In the other camp stand many dictionaries, the Associated Press stylebook, which decriminalized the word via a tweet in April 2012, and the *Guardian* style guide, which concludes 'Why some people are upset by "hopefully we will win" and not "sadly we lost" is a mystery'. Among whatever audience you are writing for, there are bound to be people who detest this word, as opposed to the majority, who will probably pass over it without comment. You might therefore wish to consider how important the opinion of the detesters is: if you are writing a journalistic article, the irritation of the few will probably not impinge on you (but the opinion of your Editor may); but if it is a research paper, business report, civil service memo, etc. for presentation to someone who you know is a language faddist, caution is the watchword. In speech, feel free to use it with gay abandon.

2 *Uncontroversial use.* First, *hopefully* has been used since the 17c. as an adverb of manner meaning 'in a hopeful way'. Apart from the now proverbial misquotation 'It is better to travel hopefully than to arrive' (Robert Louis Stevenson actually wrote 'To travel hopefully is a better thing than to arrive.'), any number of examples exist: *We ... are that posterity to which you hopefully addressed yourself*—A. Burgess, 1963; *Tam* [*sc.* a dog] *followed her, gazing hopefully upwards*—P. Lively, 1989; *Now she's looking hopefully around, as if she's eager to get burned again*— *New Yorker*, 1993.

3 *Controversial use.* The following examples illustrate the use to which, since at least 1962, some people have objected: *I want a bigger range to choose from and hopefully this role will help me*—S. Stone, 1989; *He is buried with his mammy and hopefully they are together—Sunday Mirror*, 2007. Used in this way, *hopefully* functions as a 'sentence adverb' or a 'sentence adjunct'. Rather than modifying a specific verb or verbs, it expresses a writer's or speaker's attitude to the content of what they are writing or saying. Yet we routinely use a host of other sentence adverbs without raising an eyebrow, for instance *confidentially, fortunately, frankly, happily, interestingly, sadly, seriously, surprisingly, unhappily*, etc: *Unhappily, there are times when violence is the only way in which justice can be secured* (in which *Unhappily* = it is an unhappy fact that); *Frankly, I do not wish to stop them* (= in all frankness, to speak frankly); *Seriously, David, it is people like you who keep us all motivated* (= in all seriousness, to speak seriously).

4 *Supposed grounds of objection.* (*a*) *Ambiguity.* It has been argued that *hopefully* can create ambiguity. Bill Bryson (1984) suggested that Stevenson's 'It is a better thing to travel hopefully than to arrive' could now be interpreted in either meaning. In his edition of *The Complete Plain Words*, Sir Bruce Fraser adduced 'Our team will start their innings hopefully immediately after tea' as a confusing example. But in these cases the ambiguity is a chimera. In the first example, the position of *hopefully* links it firmly to 'travel'. Fraser's example is presumably made up to prove his point; if *hopefully* were being used as a sentence adverb, in writing it would in all likelihood come first, and in speech intonation and stress would make the intended meaning clear.

(*b*) *Irregularity.* Within the class of sentence adverbs, *hopefully* is sometimes perceived to be irregular. Many sentence adverbs such as *astonishingly, curiously, remarkably*, etc. can be paraphrased as *It is* + adjective + *that*, e.g. 'it is astonishing, curious, remarkable that ... '; sentence adverbs such as *frankly, honestly, seriously* can be paraphrased as 'to speak frankly, honestly, seriously/to be frank, honest, serious with you'. *Hopefully* cannot be paraphrased in this way: *'it is hopeful that'. It is akin to *happily* and *thankfully*, in that its adjective form cannot take the impersonal construction. English is full of irregularities to which nobody objects; to criticize this one on the grounds of syntactic irregularity seems like a pseudo-scientific way of justifying a prejudice.

(*c*) *It is foreign.* One of its earliest critics suggested that it was a slapdash translation of the German *hoffentlich*, but produced no evidence to substantiate the claim. The word's supposed German origin now seems to have become part of urban myth. We are perfectly happy to use other loan translations, such as 'superman' (from German) and 'it goes without saying' (from French). It is hard to dismiss the suspicion that the antipathy towards *hopefully*, at least originally, channelled anti-German feeling. And in Britain such hostility has often been strengthened by covert or overt anti-Americanism.

(*d*) *Aesthetics.* The word has been frequently lambasted, for instance as 'ambiguous and obscure, as well as illiterate and ugly'. Obscurity, illiteracy, ugliness, and similar judgements are purely subjective.

5 *History of disputed use.* According to the evidence of the *OED* entry (not updated at the time of writing this), after an isolated use in 1932, *hopefully* emerged as a sentence adverb in the 1960s, appearing in the *New Yorker* as early as 1965: *We asked her when she expected to move into her new apartment, and she answered, 'Hopefully on Tuesday'.* However, according to research cited in *MWCDEU*, it was well established as a sentence adverb in the 1930s, and its first use in this way dates as far back as 1702. This is in line with Burchfield's statement that 'the present-day widespread use of sentence adverbs is no more than an acceleration of a much older process', and he quotes the *OED* entry for *seriously* with an example of 1644 drawn from the diary of Richard Symonds, who marched with the royal army during the Civil War: *Except here and there an officer* (*and seriously I saw not above three or four that looked like a gentleman*).

Burchfield wittily summed up the hostility to *hopefully*: 'Suddenly, round about the end of the 1960s, and with unprecedented venom, a dunce's cap was placed on the head of anyone who used just one of them—*hopefully*—as a sentence adverb.'

horde. See HOARD.

horehound (herbaceous plant). So spelt, not *hoarhound*.

horrid, etc. **1** The older (16–19c.) sense, 'bristling, shaggy, rough' (reflecting the primary sense of Latin *horridus*) is now extinct, but watch out for *horrid spears, mountain peaks, thickets*, etc., in earlier literature.

2 An ascending order of unpleasantness might perhaps begin with *horrid* (the least emphatic of the 'disagreeable' group of words: *horrid little* boy), and go on with increasing degrees of severity to *horrible* (of accidents, weather, etc.) and *horrifying* (arousing horror). *Horrendous* and *horrific* may once have added an extra degree of disagreeableness to what is being described, but have arguably lost much of their power to shock through overuse in speech, popular fiction, film, and broadcasting.

3 *OEC* data suggests that in writing both *horrendous* and *horrific* are still sometimes preceded by *an* rather than *a*; *horrendous* in a little over 10% of cases and *horrific* in a little over 20%. See A, AN 3(b).

horsey, horsy (devoted to horses). The first is the much more common spelling, though both are correct. See -EY AND -Y IN ADJECTIVES 2.

hospitable. Formerly pronounced with the stress on the first syllable, as in the *OED* entry of 1899, but second-syllable stressing is now the norm.

hospitalize (send or admit a patient to hospital). *Hospitalize* is a pantomime villain of the lexical troupe: its appearance invariably leads to loud hisses and raucous boos from editors and assorted word-lovers. Nor does its advanced age (it was first recorded in 1901) shield it from such unmerciful attacks. Outside strictly medical or nosocomial contexts, use it at your peril, particularly in Britain; but even elsewhere it may well get the bird. Certainly, *hospitalize* does not seem to be enjoying 'an old age serene and bright' (Wordsworth). See also -IZE, -ISE IN VERBS.

host (verb). *Host* as a verb has attracted criticism since it started to be widely used in the second half of last century. For many years it was banned by the *AP Stylebook*, as it still is by the *Telegraph style book*. The first ground for criticism is its presumed status as a back-formation from the noun; but it has been around as a transitive verb since the 16c. A second ground seems to be the extension of its 'core' meaning (i) 'to receive (any one) into one's house and entertain as a guest; to be the host at a party, dinner, etc.' from the personal to the public sphere by the addition of two new meanings: (ii) 'to introduce a television or radio programme, a show, etc.' and (iii) 'to organize an event to which others are invited and make all the arrangements for them'. It is hard to see what all the fuss is about. Dictionaries have long since recognized the new meanings (as well as the computing meaning exemplified in *Columbia University currently hosts some 400 websites*); the verb is widely used across the English-speaking world; it has the advantage of expressing lengthier verb phrases in one word. The worst that can be said about it is that it may be overused (*Oscar awards hosted by* ...). Nevertheless, as Burchfield put it, 'do not be surprised if the use is greeted with a certain *froideur*'. Should you wish to avoid it, synonyms are offered after the examples below. But, as will quickly be seen, they will not work in every case; which suggests that the verb *host* is often indispensable. Examples: (meaning (i)) *Afterwards, we went to an aftershow party hosted by our record company—Observer*, 2005 (BrE); *a charity dinner hosted by Egypt's first lady—Forbes*, 2009 (AmE); (meaning (ii)) *They've seen Ozzy sparring with his kids on TV while his wife hosts an especially awful TV show—OEC*, 2005 (AmE); *For the past year, I have hosted an award-winning weekly national radio program, webcast, and broadcast to an audience of over 50,000 weekly—OEC*, 2005 (Aust.); (meaning (iii)) *When China hosted the Asian Games, the whole country had to shoulder the expenses for the infrastructure and hosting costs—OEC*, 2001 (AmE); *Opening the same night, The Art Gallery of Calgary hosts several exhibitions focusing on newly created works by Calgary artists—FFWD Weekly*, 2001 (Canad.). Synonyms: (i) give, hold, act as host at, play host at, throw (ii) compère, emcee (AmE), front, introduce, present (iii) hold, organize, play host to, stage.

hostler. The usual NAmer spelling of OSTLER. There, apart from its normal use ('a person who takes care of horses, esp. at an inn'), it also means 'a person who services trains, buses, etc., or maintains large machines'.

hotchpot, hotchpotch. The most common spelling throughout the English-speaking world for 'a confused mixture' is *hodgepodge*, and in North America it is the norm. In contrast, in British English *hotchpotch* is found twice as often in the *OEC* as *hodgepodge*. Both words are variants of *hotchpot*, which comes, via Norman French, from French *hochepot* (*hocher* = 'shake' + *pot* = 'pot'), referring to a dish of mixed ingredients, or a kind of stew. The spelling *hotchpot* is now restricted to being the standard spelling in law for 'the reunion and blending of properties for the purpose of securing equal division especially of the property of an intestate parent'.

hotel. See A, AN 3 (c).

Hottentot, the origin of which is not known for certain, is first recorded in the late 17c. as a name applied by white Europeans to the *Khoekhoe* group of peoples of South Africa and Namibia. It is now regarded as offensive when referring to people and should always be avoided in favour of *Khoekhoe* or the names of the particular peoples, such as the *Nama*. The only acceptable modern use for *Hottentot* is in the names of animals and plants, such as the *Hottentot cherry*.

houmous, houmos. See HUMMUS.

houri. Pronounced /ˈhʊərɪ/.

house. See HOME, HOUSE.

houseful. Plural *housefuls*. See -FUL.

housewife. The shortened pronunciation /ˈhʌzɪf/, is standard for the sense 'a case for needles, thread, etc.'

hove. See HEAVE.

how. 1 For *as how*, see AS 7.

2 *How come?* (in interrogative constructions = How did or does it come about (that)?). This colloquial American phrase was first noted in the mid-19c., and is now international, with barely a trace of its American heritage. (My German stepmother's Teutonic grammar stopped her ever quite mastering it, and she always used her own poetic version, 'How comes it ... ?') Some examples: *How come you weren't there? Were you taking some kind of examination or something?—New Yorker*, 1988; *'How come you're still thin?' she asked with amusement*—A. Munro, 1989; *The night he got back I'd said, 'So what's the deal? How come you're home so soon?*—F. Barthelme, 1991.

however. 1 *How ever* or *however.* When *ever* is used as an intensifier immediately after interrogative words such as *what, who, how,* as it often is in informal conversation (*Why ever did you do that?*), it should never be joined up to the pronoun in written English. So *How ever are you going to manage?* is right, and *However are you going to manage?* is wrong. See EVER 1.

2 *But ... however.* See BUT 6.

3 *Beginning a sentence. However* meaning 'nevertheless' has many possible positions in a sentence. If it is placed at the beginning, it should be followed immediately by a comma: *I should be angry if the situation were not so farcical. However, I had a certain delight in some of the talk*—W. Golding, 1980. This use is to be distinguished from *However* used at the beginning of a sentence as an ordinary adverb meaning 'no matter how': *However confident he may be that he has outgeneralled a woman, a man likes to have reassurance on the point from a knowledgeable third party*—P. G. Wodehouse, 1973.

4 The placement of *however* (= 'nevertheless') depends on the nature of the sentence in which it appears: there is no single correct position. The following examples (drawn from standard sources) demonstrate that it is a matter of judgement, not of exceptionless rules. The choice of position depends on the word being emphasized, which is usually the one immediately before *however*. It is important to remember, too, that *however* in mid-sentence is enclosed within commas, and at the end of a sentence is preceded by one. Examples: (early in sentence, after a noun phrase subject) *Susie is only one of five admitted last night. Two of these, however, are on medical wards; The man himself, however, was not greatly put out by the experience.* (mid-sentence, after a clause) *As time passed, however, I slowly began to see the originality of the resistance you offered; How complete a rescue operation can be mounted, however, is quite another matter.* (at end of sentence) *Lanzmann's tone over-generalizes, however; The luridity of her confessions isn't confined to self-revelation, however.*

5 *Disparaged uses.* Two uses of *however* are generally considered stylistically suspect: as a simple substitute for but, e.g. *?It was hoped that New HAG rents could be pooled to equalize rents, however a recent review has concluded that this will not be possible*; and allowing a sentence to run on when *However* should have started a new sentence, e.g. *?Resources for doing so are not available, however, the matter will be reviewed at a later date.*

Huguenot. Better pronounced /ˈhjuːɡənəʊ/ than /-nɒt/.

hullo. See HELLO.

human (noun). The canard that *human* is only an adjective and that *human being* must be used for the noun is found in some older usage books (though not Fowler, 1926) and is still believed by some people, despite Burchfield's attempt (1996) to scotch it. *Human* as a noun is supported by the weight of usage going back to the 1500s, and more modern examples include: *There rose before his inward sight the picture of a human at once heroic and sick*—William Golding, 1954; *The human got in and, still holding the box with exaggerated care, placed it on its knees*—T. Pratchett, 1992; *Sorry, dear, I forgot that you humans need to eat every day*—J. Slater, 2003.

humankind, as a way of referring to the whole human race, is first recorded from 1560: *O fading humane kinde, How vaine and how vncertaine is thys transitory life.* Thereafter it was an occasional variant of *the human race* or *mankind,* often written as two words, e.g. in Dryden's translation (1697) of Vergil: *Let my Body have, The last Retreat of Human Kind, a Grave.* The term had something of a revival in the early 20c., notably in T. S. Eliot's oft-quoted line from *Four Quartets, Human kind Cannot bear very much reality.* Nowadays, it is a serviceable gender-neutral word to denote the human race, and avoids the irritation that using *mankind* often causes. Nevertheless, the *OEC* data, which is largely 21c., shows it to be less common than *mankind.* Examples: *One single species—humankind—is putting the Earth at risk—BBC Wildlife,* 1990; *For as long as humankind has been on earth we've looked to the skies and asked this question—are we alone in this universe?—CNN transcripts,* 2008. See also MANKIND.

humbug (verb). The inflected forms are *humbugged, humbugging.* Also *humbuggery* (noun). See -G-, -GG-.

humerus. Plural *humeri* /-rʌɪ/.

hummus /ˈhʊməs/, **humus** /ˈhjuːməs/. The first is a very moreish paste whose main ingredients are ground chick-peas and sesame seeds; the second is the organic constituent of soil. Alternative spellings for the food include *houmous, houmos* and *humous.*

humour. 1 'The pronunciation of the *h* is only of recent date, and is sometimes omitted' (*OED* 1899). This is no longer true in Britain, though the pronunciation with silent *h*, i.e. /ˈjuːmə(r)/, may well be encountered in AmE.

2 The US spelling is **humor**. The derivatives are spelt **humoresque, humorist,** and **humorous** both in BrE and AmE; but contrast **humourless** (BrE) and **humorless** (AmE).

hung. See HANG (verb).

huntress. See -ESS 5.

hyaena. See HYENA.

hybrids, etymologically speaking, are words composed of elements belonging to different languages. In the last quarter of the 19c., as the study of etymology quickened, and as fascicles of the *OED* began to appear, it became apparent that English contained a large number of words that had been 'irregularly' formed, i.e. not in accordance with the rules that were being established by the great linguistic scholars of the day. Fowler (1926), as a considerable classical scholar and lexicographer, devoted a long article entitled 'hybrids and malformations' to identifying words which were in his view malformed, going so far as to call some of them 'abortions'. Certain classes of words he found to be acceptable. For example, the medieval practice of clapping 'native' English prefixes like *be-* and native suffixes like *-ness* on to foreign loanwords was accepted as a 'natural' process: thus *bemuse, besiege, genuineness, nobleness,* and so on, all containing a native affix joined to a French stem, were not condemned as hybrids. Similarly exempt from criticism were words such as *readable, breakage, fishery,* and *disbelieve,* in which an English word has been joined by one of the foreign elements that are living affixes in English: clearly *-able, -age, -ery,* and *dis-,* though of Latin-French origin, are all part of the family now, and their etymology is irrelevant in any discussion of hybrids.

Arguments about hybrids apply only to words formed in the 19c. and 20c. A particular target of Fowler's was English words created by mixing two classical languages (e.g. *television*) or by adding a classical suffix to an English word (e.g. *speedometer*). Typical examples include the following, all of which Fowler mentioned, except *television*:

amoral: coined in the 19c. from Greek ἀ- (privative prefix) and *moral,* a word of Latin origin.

bureaucracy: coined as French *bureaucratie* in the 18c. by a French economist from *bureau* and Gk -κρατία 'rule', and adopted in English in the 19c.

coastal: coined in the 19c. from Eng. *coast* and the Latin-derived suffix *-al.*

gullible: coined in the 19c. from English *gull* 'to deceive' and the Latin-derived suffix *-ible.*

speedometer: formed in the 20c. from English *speed* and the combining form *-ometer,* ultimately from Gk μέτρον measure'.

television: formed in the 20c. from Greek τῆλε 'far', and *vision,* a word of Latin origin. As Burchfield put it: 'If such words had been submitted for approval to an absolute monarch of etymology, some perhaps would not have been admitted to the language. But our language is governed not by an absolute monarch, nor by an academy, far less by a European Court of Human Rights, but by a stern reception committee, the users of the language themselves. Homogeneity of language origin comes low in their ranking of priorities; euphony, analogy, a sense of appropriateness, an instinctive belief that a word will settle in if there is a need for it and will disappear if there is not—these are the factors that operate when hybrids (like any other new words) are brought into the language.' Wise words indeed.

See BARBARISMS; METANALYSIS.

hyena. Nowadays overwhelmingly written with *-e-*, but *hyaena,* i.e. the Latin spelling, is still found and correct.

hyperbaton /hʌɪˈpəːbətɒn/. A figure of speech in which the logical order of words or phrases is inverted, especially for the sake of emphasis, e.g. *this I must see;* (Shakespeare's *Othello) Nor scarre that whiter skin of hers, then snow.*

hyperbola. /hʌɪˈpəːbələ/. A particular kind of plane curve, it generally has the plurals *hyperbolas* and occasionally *hyperbolae,* /liː/.

hyperbole /hʌɪˈpəːbəli/. A figure of speech for an exaggerated statement not meant to be taken literally, e.g. *a thousand apologies.* If a plural is required, to mean instances or examples of the use of *hyperbole,* it is *hyperboles,* e.g. *Chandler's similes* *and sarcastic hyperboles ('a white-straw garden hat with a brim the size of a spare tire') are full of attitude in the contemporary New York sense*—*Jacket Magazine*, 2002. In a mistaken excess of classicism, occasionally the plural *hyperbolae* is used: **Classical academics who are not generally prone to hyperbolae referred to him as 'undoubtedly the greatest general of his race and probably of antiquity'*—weblog, 2005. *Hyperbolae* is a perfectly correct plural of the geometric HYPERBOLA, in addition to the anglicized *hyperbolas*.

hypercorrection is a modern (20c.) term for the application of a grammatical feature to contexts in which it is not appropriate. Typical examples are (i) the use of a pronoun form *I*, *he*, etc., instead of *me*, *him*, etc., as a grammatical object, e.g. *It is time for you and I to have a talk* on the analogy of *It is time you and I had a talk*, and (ii) use of *as* instead of *like* as a preposition, e.g. *He talks as a fool*, influenced by *as* when used as a conjunction: *He talks as a fool talks*.

hyper-, hypo- *Hyper-* means 'above; beyond normal' (thus *hyperactive, hypersensitive*); whereas *hypo-* means 'under; below normal' (thus *hypotension*, abnormally low blood pressure; *hypothermia*, the condition of having an abnormally low body temperature). In most compounds the prefixes are pronounced in a similar manner, and spoken context may not always make the meaning clear.

hypernym. In linguistics, the superordinate term in a semantically related group of words, e.g. *insect* is a hypernym of *bee*, *wasp*, *fly*, *spider*, etc. Cf. HYPONYM.

hyphens. In print, a hyphen is half the length of a dash; unlike the dash, it has the purpose of linking words and word elements rather than separating them. Beyond this apparently simple rule, in the world of real usage, lies chaos (Fowler's word, 1926), especially when use of the hyphen is governed by discretion, context, or taste rather than by clear-cut rules. Confusion can be increased by differences between American and British usage, and between different house styles. In general, the hyphen is on the wane, even in British English, partly because it is often felt to look cluttered, fussy, and old-fashioned (and, frankly, because most people know little and care less about some basic rules). For the 6th edition of the Shorter Oxford Dictionary (2007), the editors removed hyphens from 16,000 words. This amputation particularly affected compound nouns: some became two words, which is the British preference, e.g. ice-cream → ice cream, pot-belly → pot belly, test-tube → test tube; some became one word, which is the American preference, e.g. chick-pea → chickpea, low-life → lowlife, water-borne → waterborne. Compare *end point* in British and *endpoint* in American English.

To check the hyphenation of individual words, the best policy is to use an up-to-date dictionary of your variety of English (i.e. British, Canadian, etc.). For more complex decisions, detailed information on the fundamental principles is given in the *New Hart's Rules*, and individual words are listed in *the Oxford Dictionary for Writers and Editors*. The following paragraphs can do no more than describe the main uses of the hyphen, beginning with the more routine and ending with the least straightforward.

1 *Creating a single unit of meaning.* To join two or more words so as to form a single noun, verb, adjective, etc., e.g. *co-worker, dry-clean, get-at-able*, and words having a grammatical relationship which form a compound, e.g. *load-bearing, punch-drunk*. The routine use of the hyphen to connect two nouns is diminishing in favour of one-word forms, especially when the elements are of one syllable and present no problems of form or pronunciation, as in *birdsong, eardrum*, and *playgroup*, and in some longer formations such as *figurehead, nationwide*, and even (despite the clash of vowels) *radioisotope*, which is entered in this form in the *OED*. However, a hyphen is often necessary to prevent a pile-up of consonants or vowels which could make a word difficult to read, e.g. *co-opt, fast-talk, take-off.* When there is a choice between spelling as one word with hyphen and as two words, the second option is now widely favoured, especially when the first noun acts as a straightforward modifier of the second, as in *filling station, house plant*, and *sword dance*. But there are different house styles in publishing and journalism in many of these cases.

2 *Phrases in front of nouns.* To clarify the meaning of a phrase that is normally spelt as separate words, when it is used attributively (before a noun): *an up-to-date record*; *the well-known man*; but *the* *record is up to date*; *The man is well known*. It is not necessary to insert a hyphen between an adverb of manner and an adjective (or past participle used adjectivally), e.g. *a highly competitive market, a statistically significant figure, prettily furnished rooms, brightly painted walls*. Compound adjectives consisting of an adjective and a verb participle are always hyphenated, whether they come before a noun or not, e.g. *double-breasted, good-looking, short-sleeved*.

3 *With prefixes*. (*a*) Many words containing a prefix are written without a hyphen, e.g. *antenatal, outdo, predetermine, recapture, underestimate*, etc. But a prefix coming before a name or designation is hyphenated, e.g. *anti-Christian, ex-husband*. There is no satisfactory way of dealing with the type *ex-Prime Minister*, in which the second element is itself a compound, except to rely on the tendency of readers to use their knowledge of the world to choose the natural meaning, i.e. 'former Prime Minister' (which makes sense) rather than 'Minister who was once Prime' (which is nonsense). A second hyphen, e.g. *ex-Prime-Minister*, is not recommended. (*b*) To avoid ambiguity by separating a prefix from the main word, e.g. to distinguish *re-cover* (= provide with a new cover) from *recover* and *re-sign* (= sign again) from *resign*.

4 *In lists*. To represent a common second element in all but the last word of a list, e.g. *two-, three-, or fourfold*.

5 *To avoid misinterpretation*. To clarify meanings in groups of words when the associations are not clear or when several possible associations may be inferred. This is the area that involves the greatest initiative and discretion on the part of the writer, and it is also the area to which Fowler devoted most of his attention. The best way of offering guidance is to give examples in which careful hyphenation prevents misunderstanding: *The library is reducing its purchase of hard-covered books*; *Twenty-odd people came to the meeting*; *The group was warned about the dangers of extra-marital sex*; *There will be special classes for French-speaking children*; *He was a public-school boy* (not *a public schoolboy*).

6 *With phrasal verbs*. When an adverb or preposition combines to create a new meaning, e.g. *buy out, get out, hand over, pay out, warm up, wind up*, it is a common enough mistake to insert a superfluous hyphen, probably because some nouns derived from phrasal verbs are hyphenated, i.e. *a get-out clause, a warm-up, a wind-up*. But even with such nouns usage is not consistent, because some are written as one word, e.g. management *buyout, handover* of power, massive *payout*.

7 *Avoid creating words with multiple hyphens*. Burchfield suggested that phrases such as *early-nineteenth-century poets* can always be written as *poets of the early nineteenth century* instead, which, though longer, is probably easier for readers to process. Similarly with many other multi-hyphenated words. In 1989 Philip Howard said that he followed a similar course; instead of *a nuclear-weapon-free world* he would opt for *a world free of nuclear weapons*. Hyphenating should not become burdensome.

8 *In printing*. The hyphen is also used in printing to divide a word that comes at the end of a line and is too long to fit completely. The principle here is a different one, because the hyphen does not form a permanent part of the spelling. Printers have sets of rules about where to divide words; for example, between consonants as in *splen-dour* and between vowels as in *appreci-ate*, and words of one syllable should not be divided at all, even quite long ones such as *queues* and *rhythm*.

hypo-. See HYPER-, HYPO-.

hypocoristic *Hypocoristic forms* or *hypocoristics* are pet names, nursery words, or diminutives. The majority of them have distinctive endings. Examples: *-er*: *rugger, fresher* ('freshman'); *-o*: *ammo* ('ammunition'), *arvo* ('afternoon', AustE); *-s*: *Babs* ('Barbara'), *preggers* ('pregnant'), *Twickers* ('Twickenham'); *-y, -ie*: *Aussie, baddy, bicky* ('biscuit'), *Katie, sickie* (a day taken as sick leave when one is not ill), *Susie, sweetie*. See also -IE, -Y.

hyponym. In linguistics, a specific term in relation to its superordinate term: e.g. *daffodil, rose*, and *crocus* are hyponyms of *flower*; *robin, thrush*, and *finch* are hyponyms of *bird*. Cf. HYPERNYM.

hypothecate, hypothesize. If the meaning required is 'to frame a hypothesis' the better verb to use is *hypothesize,* a word that has been in standard and widespread use since the 18c. *Hypothecate* is an old-established legal verb whose primary meaning is 'to pledge without delivery of title or possession', especially in the context of taxation in which the money raised is used for a special purpose: *An alternative scheme for financing the NHS involves the removing of finance from general taxation and the introduction of a health stamp or hypothecated tax*—P. Hardy, 1991. But *hypothecate* was used to mean 'hypothesize' as long ago as 1832, and is recognized in this meaning by the *OED,* while Webster's Third goes so far as give it its own entry as a homonym of the legal verb. One is therefore free to use it if one will, but it may puzzle readers: e.g. *to this hypothecated 'missing link' Haeckel in 1867 gave the name Pithecanthropus, years before such a creature was found—OEC,* 2001.

hypothesis. Plural *hypotheses* /-siːz/.

hypothetic(al). The shorter form *hypothetic,* first recorded in the 17c., is still occasionally used, especially in American English.

hysteric(al). Both adjectives have been in use since the 17c. *Hysterical* is now massively more frequent, but the shorter form is still occasionally used, e.g. *the image of the hysteric, melancholy genius—OEC,* 2001.

I. 1 *I* or *me*? In accordance with strict grammar, we expect *I* to be used only as a subject, and *me* only as the object of a verb or preposition, e.g. *I like him*, and *he likes me*, or *he came with me*. (The same applies to other personal pronoun pairs, e.g. *he/him, she/her*, etc.). But *me* is also often used in cases where *I*, according to traditional grammar, is correct, as discussed below. As a result, in certain contexts many people are confused about which form to use, and this has led to a proliferation of the hypercorrect use of I where me is correct because the pronoun is governed by a verb or preposition. The best known case, between you and I, is discussed at the entry for *between.*

As grammatical object. One type which clearly seems the result of hypercorrection is the use of *I* as in **Honestly if one day I should marry, I'll insist that my in-laws live in their own house far away from my husband and I*—M. Tlali, 1989. The specific syntactic pattern in which this occurs is when a personal pronoun or name precedes *and I* in a phrase which is the object of a verb or preposition. Further examples: e.g. **I think she disapproved of Beth and I, just quietly*—S. Johnson, 1990; **'What is it?' asked Lempriere. 'Part of you and I,' said Septimus*—L. Norfolk, 1991; **after seeing Mary and I lingering over a late breakfast*—*Chicago Tribune Mag.*, 1991. The fault can be seen by removing the first pronoun or name: in the first example that would produce **far away from I* and in the second **I think she disapproved of I*. (It is, of course, possible that the writers of some of these examples were making a point about their characters by having them speak hypercorrect language.) It is, however, also worth pointing out that *I* as verb or prepositional object has good historical precedents, as explained at BETWEEN 1.

As grammatical subject. With examples such as *me and Frances/Frances and me flew to Paris* or *Her and me/Me and her flew to Paris*, there is a clear distinction between speech and writing. While these formulations violate strict grammar, they are normal in informal speech. It goes without saying that they will be avoided in any kind of formal writing.

2 It is a minor curiosity that *I*, of all the pronouns, is the only one that must always be written with a capital. As the older forms *ic, ich, ik*, etc., gave way to the reduced form *i* during the Middle Ages, the new form was generally written as *i* or *y*, and was often merged by the scribes with the verb or auxiliary it governed. With the advent of printing in the late 15c. the new form *I* soon established itself as the only standard form, though instances of small *i* can be found as late as the 17c.

-i¹. 1 For plurals with this ending, see LATIN PLURALS 3, 4; -US.

2 Words of Italian origin ending in *-e* or *-o* have plurals in *-i*. The *-i* is for the most part retained as the English plural of words adopted from Italian, e.g. *cognoscenti* pl., *cognoscente* sing., *dilettanti* pl., *dilettante* sing.

-i². A termination used in the names of certain Near Eastern and South Asian peoples, e.g. *Bangladeshi, Bengali, Iraqi, Israeli, Pakistani.* See also -EE² 2.

iambic, the adjective corresponding to *iambus* (plural *iambuses*), in prosody, a foot consisting of one short or unstressed followed by one long or stressed syllable, the best-known measure in ancient Greek and modern English poetry. Examples: *They also serve who only stand and wait* (Milton); *The woods are lovely, dark, and deep, But I have promises to keep, And miles to go before I sleep* (R. Frost).

-ian. See SUFFIXES ADDED TO PROPER NAMES.

i before e. The traditional spelling rule 'i before *e* except after *c*' should be extended to include the statement 'when the combination is pronounced *-ee-*'as in *believe, brief, fiend, hygiene, niece, priest, shield,* *siege*, etc.; but *ceiling, conceit, receipt, receive*, etc. The rule can then helpfully be extended by adding 'except when the word is pronounced *-ay-* (*beige, freight, neighbour, sleigh, veil, vein, weigh*, etc.)'. A further exception: a few words that are pronounced with *I* are regularly spelt with *ei: eiderdown, Eisteddfod, height, kaleidoscope, sleight.* So too are *either* and *neither* (however pronounced). There are some further special cases: inflected forms, e.g. *holier; occupier; carried, defied;* and proper names, e.g. *Leicester, Leigh, Reith;* but *Piedmont.* There are also several familiar words that do not obey the simple rule as qualified. The spelling of these must simply be learnt by heart: e.g. (all with *ei*) *caffeine, codeine, counterfeit, foreign, forfeit, heifer, heir, leisure, protein, seize, their.* For longer, unanalysed lists, see -EI-; -IE-.

ibidem is a Latin word meaning 'in the same place'. Usually encountered in reading lists or bibliographies abbreviated as *ibid.* or *ib.*, it means 'in the same book, chapter, or passage' and is used to avoid repeating a bibliographic reference, e.g. R. Whiston, *Cathedral Trusts and their Fulfilment*, pp. 2–4 ... *ibid.*, pp. 10–12. It is printed in italic, and, if pronounced at all, is generally pronounced /ˈɪbɪdɛm/ rather than /ˈɪbʌɪdɛm/. It is to be carefully distinguished in meaning from IDEM.

-ible. See -ABLE, -IBLE.

-ic(al) (adjectival suffix). **1** There are three main categories:

(*a*) only an adjective ending in *-ic* is currently used (e.g. *alcoholic, basic, dramatic, linguistic, patriotic, plastic, public*); (*b*) only an adjective ending in *-ical* is currently used (e.g. *chemical, practical, radical*); and (*c*) adjectives ending in *-ic* and *-ical* are both used often with a difference in meaning (e.g. *classic/classical, comic/comical, economic/economical, historic/historical*) but sometimes with no difference in meaning (e.g. *geographic/geographical, lexicographic/lexicographical, problematic/problematical*).

Pairs that represent a difference in meaning are discussed as separate entries. When there is no difference in meaning, choice is often determined by the shape of words in the same phrase, or by overall sentence rhythm. In some cases, the *OEC* data suggests that there may be regional distinctions: for instance in AmE *geographic* is markedly more common than *geographical.*

2 With one exception, all these adjectives, whether they end in *-ic* or *-ical* or either, form adverbs in *-ically* (*basically, dramatically, geometrically, practically*, etc.). The exception is *public*, which has an adverb form *publicly.*

icon, iconic. 1 The original meaning of *icon*, 'a devotional painting on wood of Christ or a saint in Byzantine Christian art', has been all but obscured—except in specialist use or as a vague memory—by modern uses first in the language of media and marketing and then in computing. From the 1950s in America and soon after in Britain, *icon* has acquired an extended meaning 'a person or thing regarded as a representative symbol, or as worthy of admiration or respect'. The word is often qualified in a way that specifies the relevant domain: in 2000, for example, the press referred to *Hollywood's female gay icons Jodie Foster, Susan Sarandon and Jamie Lee Curtis—Sunday Mail.* Other frequently occurring phrases are *American, cultural, fashion, feminist, rock* and *style icon.*

Icon is often derided for the promiscuous ease with which it can be applied to a person, place or product, regardless of how great or lasting their influence may be. A search on Google news on the day I drafted this entry threw up—I use the word advisedly—nearly seven hundred million hits. Supposed icons included Edinburgh's Royal Blind School building, a restaurant in New York, folk singer Woody Guthrie, elderly French rocker Johnny Halliday, an Egyptian footballer, Tiffany & Co. Jewellers, and, as *shoe* or *style icon*, Victoria Beckham. (One begins to wonder if there is more cachet in not being an icon than in being one.) It is as well to remember that Greek and Russian icons are the object of intense veneration, if not outright worship. Readers will have their own views on the veneration Mrs Beckham or any of the others is due.

2 In computing, an *icon* is familiar in a more physical transfer of meaning as a symbol or graphic representation on a VDU screen of a program or function.

3 The increased use of *icon* has been outstripped by that of **iconic**. Previously a word of limited currency in the sense 'relating to or of the nature of an icon', it denoted in particular the conventional style of victorious athletes as depicted in ancient Greek statuary. From the 1970s it has come to be applied predominantly to a person or institution considered to be important or influential in a particular social or cultural context, and collocates with words such as *brand, building, figure, image,* and *status.*

It is widely criticized as being overused, particularly in the language of marketing and journalism, and overuse has quickly robbed it of its original impact. A Guardian columnist cynically suggested that '"iconic" has become a synonym for "vaguely familiar if you're particularly interested in that sort of thing"' (Harry Pearson, 29 April, 2011). Beware therefore of redundant uses in which *iconic* is a meaningless 'filler' that tells the reader nothing because the thing described is familiar enough already (or in need of rather more explanation for the benefit of the ignorant than a vogue word will achieve): *A passenger ferry collided with a pleasure boat under Sydney's iconic harbour bridge yesterday—Independent,* 2007. Even worse is the unintentional absurdity produced by the common phrase *iconic image,* in which the writer seems blithely unaware of what an *icon* originally is: *The opening scene of Ingmar Bergman's 1957 masterpiece is one of the most iconic images in cinema history—Empire,* 2002. An 'iconic image' is equivalent to a 'symbolic symbol' and no one would, in all seriousness, write such a thing. It is not pedantic to insist on this kind of awareness, but respectful of the ways in which precise and graphic old meanings underlie more generalized modern usage.

4 The spelling ikon is occasionally used when the meaning is religious (*The ikon of our Lady of Tsarskoe Selo is a sentimental painting of the Virgin with Christ*).

-ics. 1 There are a few names of arts or branches of study ending in *-ic* that are invariable: the main ones are *logic, magic, music, physic* (the art of healing), and *rhetoric.* Otherwise the overwhelmingly normal ending for such words is *-ics: acoustics, classics, economics, ethics, mathematics, metaphysics, obstetrics, paediatrics, phonetics, physics, politics, statistics,* and scores of others. *Dialectic* and *dialectics* are used interchangeably when they mean 'the art of logical disputation'. In a few cases, different endings create different meanings: *ethic* 'a set of moral precepts (*the work ethic*)' differs from *ethics,* which has a wider meaning; similarly *metaphysic* 'a system of metaphysics' has a much narrower application than *metaphysics;* a *statistic* is 'a statistical fact or item', not the name of the subject.

2 Grammatical number of *-ics.* The primary rule is that *-ics* words used strictly for the name of a subject (*Economics, Ethics,* etc.) govern a singular verb, e.g. *Economics is her main area of expertise.* But when used more generally, and especially when preceded by determiners such as *his, the, such,* etc., a plural verb is called for: *the economics of lending vast sums of money to Third World countries are difficult to understand; such ethics are abominable.* Another class of nouns correspond to adjectives ending in *-ic* or *-ical* and always govern a plural verb: *heroics are out of place; hysterics leave me cold; heroics are out of place here.*

ictus (in prosody). Rhythmical or metrical stress. Plural same or *ictuses.*

idem. Printed in italic, is a Latin word meaning 'the same person'. Usually encountered in reading lists or bibliographies, and sometimes abbreviated as id., it is used to avoid repeating an author's name when works by the same author are cited successively, e.g. Marianne Elliott, *Partners in Revolution,* 1982; *idem, Wolfe Tone,* 1989.

ideologue, ideology, ideological are sometimes misspelt *ideal-. Ideology* and *ideologue* follow the pattern of the French words *idéologie* and *idéologue,* themselves based on the Greek ἰδέα (idea) 'form, pattern' + λόγος (logos) (denoting discourse or compilation). All three can be pronounced with initial /ʌɪ/ or /ɪ/, unlike *ideogram* and *ideograph,* which both have initial /ɪ/ only.

ideology. The first recorded use of the word was in 1798, when it meant 'the science of ideas'. Its main current meanings, 'the system of ideas at the basis of an economic or political theory (*Marxist ideology*)', and the manner of thinking characteristic of a class or individual (*bourgeois ideology*)' came into being at the end of the 19c.

id est. See I.E.

idiom. The word *idiom* has several meanings. The most important in the study of language, and for dictionary makers in particular, is defined as 'a group of words established by usage as having a meaning not deducible from those of the individual words' e.g. *to have one's head in the clouds. Idiom* can be seen as a major force and one of the most difficult aspects to master in any language. Exact definitions of the term vary from scholar to scholar, but the concept is often extended beyond the definition given above to cover a range of features of English which are in some way not predictable, or otherwise anomalous. These include: (prepositions) *we tamper* with, but *we meddle* in; (binomials) *odds and ends, part and parcel, neither here nor there;* (formulae and fixed phrases) *when all is said and done, how do you do?;* (ungrammatical at first sight) *it's me, how's tricks?, how's you?*; (obsolete or archaic words in familiar phrases) chop *and change, in a* trice, *at one* fell *swoop;* (idioms in the sense defined above) *to blow hot and cold, once in a blue moon, to rain on someone's parade.*

Another, less technical, meaning of *idiom* is 'a form of expression natural to a language, person, or group of people', e.g. *he had an ear for Manchester idiom.* The adjective **idiomatic** draws on both these meanings in denoting what is natural and customary in the use of a language. Fowler (1926) attached great importance to *idiom* ('grammar and idiom are separate categories'), so that a mode of expression can be idiomatic or grammatical or both or neither. Fowler's various examples are still valid and useful: *It was not me* and *There is heaps of material* are idiomatic but ungrammatical, *The distinction leaps to the eyes* and *a hardly earned income* are grammatical but unidiomatic, *He was promoted captain* and *She all but capsized* are both grammatical and idiomatic, and *You would not go for to do it* is neither. See also PHRASAL VERBS.

idiosyncrasy is occasionally misspelt with a final *-cy*. The mistaken spelling is presumably by analogy with such pairs as *aristocracy/aristocratic* and *democracy/democratic,* unlike **idiosyncracy/idiosyncratic.* The final element of *democracy* and so forth derives from Greek κράτος 'power, rule', whereas the separate elements of *idiosyncrasy* come from Greek ἰδιο- 'own, peculiar' + σύν 'together' + κρᾶσις 'mixture, combination', so its etymological meaning is 'a peculiar mixing together'. As Burchfied rather testily put it: 'It is not suggested that everyone should be a walking etymologist, but simply that people should learn to spell correctly.'

idle (verb). In various intransitive senses the verb has been an ordinary part of the standard language since the 16c. It was also first recorded in the late 18c. in the transitive sense 'to cause to be idle'. The *OED* provides examples of both types from good sources. In the 20c. the engine of a motor vehicle is said to *idle* (i.e. an intransitive use) when it is just 'ticking over' and the vehicle is not in motion. Since about the 1960s the transitive branch has been strengthened by being commonly used, except in British English, (*a*) of sports players made idle by injury, etc. (*a spring training in which Ramirez was idled by a sore hamstring*—Baseball Digest, 2001), and (*b*) of workers, machinery, etc. made idle for whatever reason (*LTV often hired outside contractors for some jobs, then idled workers on their payroll—Houston Chronicle,* 2005).

idyll. Probably in order to differentiate it from *idle* and *idol,* the word is now usually pronounced /ˈɪdɪl/ with a short initial *i.* But there are some who say /ˈʌɪd(ə)l/, and some (esp. in America) who spell the word **idyl**. The word answers to Latin *idyllium,* Greek εἰδύλλιον, but it has gone its own way in English as far as the length of the first syllable is concerned.

i.e., abbreviation of *id est.* **1** The full form *id est* is not usually either written or said, except as an affectation or facetiously.

2 *i.e.* means 'that is to say', and introduces another way (more comprehensible to the reader, driving home the writer's point better, or otherwise preferable) of putting what has already been said. It does not introduce an illustrative example, for which E.G. is the proper formula.

3 By its nature, it is preceded by a punctuation mark, usually a comma. It is not normally followed by a comma unless the sense requires one, as when a parenthesis immediately follows: (no comma) *He attacked reactionaries, i.e. those whose opinions differed markedly from his own;* (comma needed) *He attacked reactionaries, i.e., it would seem, those whose opinions* [etc.].

4 It is normally written as lower case and in roman.

-ie-. The following words are among those spelt with *-ie* not *-ei-: achieve, adieu,* *aggrieve, Aries, befriend, belief, believe, besiege, bier, bombardier, brief, brigadier, cashier, cavalier, chandelier, chief, fief, field, fiend, fierce, friend, frieze, grenadier, grief, grievance, grieve, grievous, handkerchief, hygiene, lief, liege, mien, mischief, mischievous, niece, piece, piecemeal, pier, pierce, priest, relief, relieve, reprieve, retrieve, review, shield, shriek, siege, sieve, species, thief, thieve, tier, tierce, tiercel, wield, yield.* See also -EI-; I BEFORE E.

-ie, -y (in pet names and diminutives). See HYPOCORISTIC. There is sometimes a free choice between *-ie* and *-y*, except that *-y* is always used in the pet names *baby, daddy, ducky* (darling), *granny, hubby, mummy,* and *sonny;* in the diminutives *bunny* (rabbit), *doggy, fatty, goody, hanky, kitty, piggy, pinny, missy, nappy, teddy,* and *tummy.* In a number of words associated with Scotland (*beastie, kiltie, laddie, lassie,* etc.) *-ie* is the preferred form. Unless you have to conform to a particular house style or style guide, it is a good idea to check the spelling in a dictionary such as *ODO,* which currently gives the following: (*-y* only) *bobby* (policeman), *buddy* (friend), *Froggy* (French person, informal, derogatory), *nanny, puppy, telly* (television), *Tommy* (British soldier, old-fashioned)*;* (*-ie* only) *auntie, bookie* (bookmaker), *charlie* (a fool, cocaine)*, clippie* (bus conductress, old-fashioned), *cookie* (biscuit), *dearie, goalie, Mountie* (in Canada), *nightie, postie* (postman), *rookie, walkie-talkie*; (*-ie,* and also *-y*) *girlie, hottie, kiddie, sweetie.* The plural of all of these ends in *-ies.* The familiar forms of personal names follow similar patterns, but there can be no question of insisting that one or another form is the 'preferred' one: the choice is simply a matter of agreement between the persons concerned. As a rough guide the following (of *-ie* and *-y* names) seem to be the more usual: *Amy, Annie, Betty, Billy* (but *Billie* if female), *Bobby* (but *Bobbie* if female), *Charlie* (or *Charley*), *Dicky, Eddie, Elsie, Fanny, Freddy, Georgie* (Georgina), *Ginny* (Virginia), *Jamie, Jeanie, Jenny, Jerry, Jessie, Johnny, Katie, Kitty, Milly, Molly, Nelly, Paddy, Patsy, Peggy, Polly, Reggie, Sally, Sandy, Sophie, Susie, Teddy, Tommy, Willie, Winnie.*

if. 1 *If* is followed by the subjunctive form *were* (instead of *was*) when the condition it introduces is hypothetical or impossible to fulfil, as in *If I were younger, I'd travel the world. Was* is used (i) informally in such cases (*If I was younger, I'd travel the world*), and (ii) to indicate past tense in which the condition had been capable of fulfilment (*If I was younger, I wasn't any wiser*). Use of the subjunctive form *be* (instead of *am, is,* or *are*) is now decidedly old-fashioned: *If this be true, all is not lost.* See SUBJUNCTIVE MOOD.

2 *If* and *whether* are both used to introduce noun clauses as in *Tell me if/whether you can come,* but *whether* is regarded as somewhat more formal and is preferable in avoiding possible ambiguity; in the sentence just given, a possible interpretation, though not the natural one, when *if* is used is 'If you can come, tell me (some other thing)'.

3 *If* and *though* are both possible in constructions of the type *a cheap, if/though risky method,* although again there is sometimes a small risk of ambiguity in the use of *if.*

4 *If* is sometimes used in a clause without any continuation, either as a way of making a strong assertion or as a polite request. This use is normally limited to conversation: *Well, if that isn't the best thing I've heard since I was home*—C. Mackenzie, 1919; *'I've got to leave this morning; so if you'll make out my bill, please?'*—C. Dexter, 1983; *'There's your tea. Drink it.' ... 'If I could have another lump of sugar.'*—G. Greene, 1988.

if and when. It was the Fowler brothers who first attacked this phrase, in *The King's English* (1906). They supported their argument with six examples drawn from undated issues of *The Times* and one (which they found defensible) from Gladstone. 'Many writers', they said, seem to have persuaded themselves that neither "if" nor "when" is any longer capable of facing its responsibilities without the other word to keep it in countenance.' Fowler (1926) cited eleven more examples—they are unattributed but seem to be from newspapers. So, there can be little doubt that the construction was in common use in the first quarter of the 20c. It is listed in the *OED* with the rubric 'in reference to a future time but with a strong element of doubt'. *CGEL* (1985) treats it as 'a stereotyped expression weakening the expectation (conveyed by *when* alone) that the condition in the clause will be realized', and mentioned *as and when* and *unless and until* as 'other institutionalized conjoinings of conjunctions'. Those who wish to uncouple the pair and use only *if* or only *when* are free to do so. While it is true that *if* alone (when there is doubt) or *when* alone (when there is no doubt) would often serve, there are contexts in which a point needs to be made about both the likelihood of the event happening and its timing: *Many drugs will be given if and when needed, probably with no obvious rhythm*—J. M. Waterhouse et al., 1990. The 'conjoined' pair undoubtedly reinforces the element of doubt, which makes it popular with lawyers, because at the very least it makes the same point doubly effective: *But it is not a breach of contract for a party to misconstrue it. The breach, if any, occurs only if and when its misunderstanding of its own responsibilities leads it to fail to perform a contractual obligation*—*OEC* (undated). Cf. AS AND WHEN.

-ified, -ify. See -FY.

ignoramus. Formerly a law term from the Latin word meaning 'we do not know', and used in law to mean 'we take no notice of (it)'; but from the 17c. onwards used simply as a noun to mean an ignorant person. In view of the derivation of the word its plural form can only be *ignoramuses* (not *ignorami*): it has nothing to do with Latin nouns ending in *-us*. See -US 5.

I guess. See GUESS.

-ile. Words ending in *-ile* (*docile, domicile, facile, fertile, fragile, missile, mobile, prehensile, servile, sterile, tactile, virile,* etc.) are usually pronounced with /-ʌɪl/ in BrE and with /-ɪl/ or /-əl/ in American English. The division seems not to have become clear-cut until about 1900. Before that date the dominant pronunciation of these words in British English as well as in AmE, was with a short *i*, that is /-ɪl/ or /-əl/. The main exceptions are *automobile* and *imbecile,* which are usually pronounced with final /-iːl/ in both varieties, and *profile*, pronounced as /-fʌɪl/, as, with some variation, are the statistics terms *decile, percentile,* and *quartile.*

ilex. Plural *ilexes.* See -EX, -IX 2. It means both the common holly and the holm oak.

ilk. This is a word that has aroused passions among usage commentators, though few others, while the meaning they—and James Murray—objected to must now be considered part of mainstream English. For most people the issue will be a conundrum; to understand it a bit of history may help. Only then will the futility of misdirected pedantry become clear. In origin *ilk* is an adjective meaning 'same' (Old English *ilca*), but in ordinary contexts it gradually retreated before *same* (of Old Norse origin) during the Middle English period and vanished from standard English. In Scotland, beginning in the 15c., the phrase *of that ilk* emerged and meant 'of the same place, territorial designation, or name', chiefly in the names of landed families, in which case convention suggests that it should be capitalized, since it forms part of a title, e.g. *Moncreiffe of that Ilk, Wemyss of that Ilk* = Moncreiffe of Moncreiffe (a place), Wemyss of Wemyss (a place). In the late 18c., by analogy with the misunderstood Scottish use, *ilk* began to be used to mean 'family, class', and, by further extension 'kind, sort'. The *OED* (1899) has a string of examples of these uses from 1790 to 1973, described as 'erroneous', because the only 'correct' meaning was in the titles of landed families.

There can be few people left so committed to antiquarian etymology as to be irritated by the 'incorrect' use; nevertheless, objecting to this 'new' (in heavily inverted commas) use, has become part of the folk tradition of usage bugbears. The only feature of *ilk* worth commenting on is that in general use it often has rather negative connotations: it as if it embodies some of the contempt with which its original referents, the landed few, all too often viewed their social inferiors. Fortunately for *ilk*, it has strayed from the aristocratic salons onto the broad highway of English. Its origins constitute a mildly interesting fact, but hardly a compelling argument against its modern use. Examples: *Rambo and Rocky and their ilk are the mere tip of a vast iceberg*—*Encounter*, 1987; *I'm being flippant. Irresponsible in the well-known propensity of my ilk*—K. Amis, 1988; *Other attempts to lampoon the secret agent genre aren't as successful. In the wake of Austin Powers and its ilk, that vein has been bled dry*—*ReelViews*, 2002 (AmE).

ill. There are one or two anomalies in the use of the word. As an adjective it is most commonly used predicatively and is followed by *with* (*he was ill with pneumonia*). But in the broad sense 'out of health' it can also be used attributively (*he was an ill man when I last saw him; mentally ill people*).

It can also be used to mean 'faulty, unskilful' (*ill taste; ill management*); and it is found in many idioms (*do an ill turn to; ill at ease*), proverbs (*it's an ill wind that blows nobody any good*), and, as an adverb, is used to form many adjectival compounds (*ill-behaved, ill-considered, ill-mannered*). In many attributive contexts, *ill* is unidiomatic and is replaced by *sick: a sick child* is more usual than *an ill child;* and *sick leave* and *sick pay* cannot be replaced by *ill leave* and *ill pay.* By contrast with *ill, sick* is used primarily to mean 'vomiting or tending to vomit', in British English that is. To underline the anomalies of the two words a person can *look ill* and then *go sick* (i.e. to report sick). The above comments apply mainly to British English. There is considerable overlapping of meaning and idiom in the other English-speaking countries. In some of them *ill* and *sick* have no difference of primary meaning: *ill* is just the more formal word of the two. In N. America, if the meaning required is 'vomiting', the usual phrase is *sick to* (or *at*) *one's stomach.*

illegal, illegitimate, illicit, unlawful. The four words have similar workloads to their antonyms *legal, legitimate, licit,* and *lawful,* and their meanings and applications can be deduced from them: see LEGAL. The main difference is that *illicit* is much more commonly used than *licit.* In phrases like *illicit love affair* it 'carries moral overtones in addition to the basic sense "not in accordance with or sanctioned by law"' (Garner, 1987).

illegible, unreadable. In current use the distinction is crystal-clear, and confusion does not seem to occur: as Fowler put it 'the *illegible* is not plain enough to be deciphered; the unreadable is not interesting enough to be perused'.

illicit. See ELICIT; ILLEGAL.

illiteracies. 'There is a kind of offence against the literary idiom that is not easily named' (Fowler, 1926). He described them as *illiteracies* ('their chief habitat is in the correspondence columns of the press'). Time has moved on; moods have changed. On the one hand, few would be arrogant or foolhardy enough to use the word *illiterate* (except perhaps behind closed doors); on the other, scientific understanding of the complexity and subtlety of grammar and usage has advanced enormously. Some of the items unequivocally marked by Fowler as illiterate are now generally described by dictionaries as 'disputed' or 'informal': these are marked with an asterisk below. Readers of the present book will find comments and advice on many of the words, constructions, etc., that Fowler judged to be illiterate. Some of his list (rearranged in broad alphabetical order) follows for its historical interest:

absolute adjectives qualified (*almost, quite, *rather unique, more preferable*); **aggravating* for *annoying*; present tense, etc., after *as if* and *as though* (*It looks as if we are winning* or *shall win*); *between ... or* used for *between ... and* (*The choice is between glorious death or shameful life*); *however, whatever, whoever,* etc., used interrogatively (*However did you find out?* for *How ever did you find out?*; etc.); *individual* for *person*; **like* as a conjunction; *me* etc. for *my* etc. in gerund construction (*instead of me being dismissed*); negative after *should not wonder* (*I shouldn't wonder if it didn't come true yet*); **re* in unsuitable contexts (*the author's arguments* re *predestination*); *same, such,* and *various* used as pronouns (*have no dealings with such*; etc.); split infinitives used too frequently; *think to* = *remember to* (*I did not think to tell them when I was there*); **write* with direct personal object (*though she had promised to write him soon*).

Gowers (1965) added three more examples of illiteracies: *I* for *me* when in company (*Between you and I*); *likewise* as a conjunction (*Its tendency to wobble ... likewise its limited powers of execution*); **neither* with a plural verb (*For two reasons neither of which are noticed by Plato*).

illogicalities. For examples of unintended or idiomatic illogicalities, see BECAUSE C; BUT 4; DO 5; MUCH 2 . A stray example of an unintended illogicality on a notice in a public park: *Any person not putting litter in this basket will be liable to a fine of £5.* Those who have no litter must, it seems, go and find some or face a fine.

illume, illuminate, illumine. The first, a poetical shortening of *illumine,* which was used by Shakespeare and many later writers, is now entirely restricted to literary use (e.g. *The lamp illumed only the surface of the desk and one of Lucas's hands*—I. Murdoch, 1993). The third is also for the most part a literary word, and is used mainly in the senses 'to light up; to make bright' and 'to enlighten spiritually'.

The normal word in these and other literal and figurative senses is *illuminate.*

illusion. See DELUSION.

illusive, illusory. See ELUSIVE.

illustrative. The standard pronunciation in Britain is /ˈiləstrətɪv/, but the form with second-syllable stressing, which is the only pronunciation given in the *OED* (1899), is still used often enough and is also the preferred form in the standard American dictionaries.

im-. See EM- AND IM-, EN-AND IN-. The words, not there mentioned, that regularly have *im-*, not *em-*, are *imbrue* (a literary word = stain (one's sword, etc.)), *imbue* (saturate, etc.), *impale,* and *imperil.*

image. The word is old (13c.) and over the centuries has developed a wide range of meanings. In the late 1950s it began to be used in an entirely new way by advertising companies to mean 'the impression, preferably favourable, that a person, institution, or product creates in the public'. The word is now a part of everyday language, not just that of advertisers and marketers, but it was criticized as a vogue word in the 1960s by various commentators, including Gowers in his edition of this book. Today, it features particularly in the collocations *new image, public image, positive* or *negative image, brand image,* and *image problem.* In our world of smoke and mirrors, however, it is worth quoting what Gowers wrote in 1965, both for its elegant form and for its witty content: 'This at least is clear: that though we may not care nowadays very much about the gift of seeing ourselves as others see us, we put a high value on persuading others to see us as we see ourselves.'

imaginable is spelt without an *e* in the middle. See MUTE E.

imbalance. It is a minor curiosity that a noun meaning 'absence of balance' seems not to have been called for until the 19c. and that the corresponding verbs *disbalance* and *unbalance* are also 19c. words (except for an isolated 16c. example of *unbalance* (verb)). Ophthalmologists were the first to use the noun *imbalance* (in 1898) but from this technical use the word has branched out in the 20c. and is now used generally in many subjects and contexts. A typical example: *Teaching implies an imbalance of knowledge, otherwise it would not be necessary*—B. Bergonzi, 1990.

imbecile. See -ILE. BrE /ˈɪmbɪsiːl/, AmE /ˈɪmbəsəl/.

imbed. See EM- AND IM-, EN-AND IN-.

imbibe. See FORMAL WORDS.

imbroglio /ɪmˈbrəʊliːəʊ/ (im-**broh**-lee-oh). Plural *imbroglios.* See -O(E)S 4.

imbrue. See IM-.

imbue. See IM-. For construction, see INFUSE.

I mean. See MEAN (verb) 3.

imitate has the derivative form **imitable**, meaning 'able to be imitated'.

immanent. Some things never change. And if they don't, it is often for an obvious cause. Nearly a century ago, Fowler (1926) suggested that people would easily confuse this word, largely used, as he said, by 'divines and philosophers', with *imminent. Immanent,* 'means 'indwelling, inherent; (of the Supreme Being) permanently pervading the universe (opposed to *transcendent*)', and is derived from Latin *in* + *manēre* 'to remain'. Those who misspell *imminent* as *immanent* because the words are identical in all but one sound are clearly neither divines nor philosophers: e.g. **For these individuals, it is only in the face of immanent danger that the neurological systems that govern anxiety become active*—*OEC* (undated).

immediately has been occasionally used informally as a conjunction (= immediately after), especially in British English, since the early 19c. According to *MWCDEU,* this construction is not common in AmE, and some commentators consider it a mistake. Examples: *I started writing* Jill *immediately I left Oxford*—P. Larkin, 1983; *He vowed to call her immediately he had a story that would interest* her—L. Grant-Adamson, 1990; *Immediately I heard the front door I switched off his computer*—N. Williams, 1992.

immense. Ebullient Welsh rugby commentator Jonathan Davies, MBE, often extols stellar performances, especially by the 'Man of the Match', with this word. His use of it in this way might sound idiosyncratic, but is shared by others and seems to have a very long history. *Immense* apparently flourished from the 1760s until the end of the 19c. in the meaning 'superlatively good' (e.g. *You look like a crown prince ... Perfectly immense*—F. M. Crawford, 1883), but Fowler declared in 1926 that it had 'lost its freshness and grown stale'. Were he alive to hear Jonathan Davies, he would have to revise his view. Examples: *'What is happening is immense for east London,' Gold says. The Olympics are 'bringing the pride back to this part of the world'*—*Washington Post*, 2012.

immigrant. See EMIGRANT.

imminent. See EMINENT; IMMANENT.

immoral means 'not conforming to accepted standards of morality; morally wrong (especially in sexual matters), wicked' by contrast with *amoral,* which means 'not concerned with or outside the scope of morality; having no morals'. In general the two words are used in different contexts. But there are some contexts which make it hard to distinguish between the meaning 'morally wrong' of *immoral* and the meaning of 'having no moral principles' of *amoral.* For example, in *The scientific developments grabbing the most headlines are those often perceived as amoral or unethical, such as sheep cloning or fertility treatments*, which meaning does the author intend? The proximity to 'unethical' suggests that *immoral* is the better choice, since *immoral and unethical* is a standard collocation. In the following example, however, it seems much clearer that *immoral* is the more apt word, given the definitions above. We can hardly suppose that Bill Clinton did not know he was breaking moral codes: *Clinton was good for America because he did so little. And he did so little because he spent most of his time defending his own repeated amoral behaviour*—weblog, 2004. The following examples highlight the distinction between the two words admirably: *Children are first amoral ... then enter a pre-moral stage, when social and authoritarian factors are the main restraints*—M. E. Wood, 1973; *Simon criticised Jesus for allowing such an immoral woman to touch him*—R. Cooper, 1990.

immovable. 1 Is spelt without an *e* in the middle, not *immoveable.* See MUTE E.

2 It has a wide range of applications in the broad sense 'that cannot be moved'. When the sense required is 'that cannot be removed, esp. from office' the word to use is *irremovable.*

immune. A person is said to be (*a*) *immune to* an infection (i.e. resistant to, protected from or against); or (*b*) *immune from* some undesirable factor or circumstance (i.e. exempt from, not subject to). But the division is not clear-cut; in some contexts *from* is idiomatically used in type (*a*), and *to* in type (*b*). Examples: (to) *Each country will be concerned to maintain the invulnerability of its submarine-based strategic missiles, which are essentially immune to attack from land-based weapons*—*Scientific American*, 1972; *A situation could arise where harmful bacteria, having become immune to disinfectants, survive to cause illness which cannot be treated by antibiotics*—R. North, 1985; *Anywhere that remains immune to fashion is to be lauded*—*Times*, 2004; (from) *Those who have a commitment to the Christian faith are not thereby immune from depression*—M. Batchelor, 1988; *The laws affecting the common land were supervised by Down Drivers, themselves not immune from prosecution*—M. Lister, 1988; *Real diamonds have a quite distinctive, soapy texture to the surface and are immune from water*—F. Forsyth, 1989; *Royal grants may also explain why some churches ... enjoyed unusually extensive rights of sanctuary which developed into privileged zones immune from secular authority*—W. Davies, 2003.

immunity in non-medical contexts means 'freedom or exemption from an obligation, penalty, or unfavourable circumstance'. Like immune, it is followed by *to* or *from.* By contrast, *impunity* has the much more limited sense 'exemption from punishment or from the injurious consequences of an action' (especially in the phrase *with impunity*). It is not generally followed by *from.* According to Gowers (1965) the two words were sometimes confused, but the *OEC* data shows that they generally keep apart. Only in the rather tautological phrase *impunity from prosecution* is *impunity* used when *immunity from prosecution* is more appropriate.

impact (noun and verb). The noun is stressed on the first syllable, the verb on the second. **1** *Noun.* This noun, first recorded in the late 18c., means literally 'the action of one body coming forcibly into contact with another', and metaphorically, from the early 19c. onwards, 'the effect of one thing or person upon another; an impression (especially in the phrase *to make an impact (on)*'. The figurative sense seems to have been sparingly used until the mid-20c.; and at that point it passed into widespread use and ran into opposition ('why not use *effect, impression, ability to impress*, etc., instead?'). The wave of hostility has now receded, all the more so as no permanent damage seems to have been done to the words that, for a time, it seemed to threaten.

2 *Verb.* Hostility to the verb, however, continues unabated, in part because it is (wrongly) perceived as a modern back-formation from the noun. In fact, used transitively ('to press closely into or in something'), the verb has a pedigree going back to about 1600, i.e. it is older than the noun: e.g. *The seed of this hearbe remooveth the tough humours bedded in the stomacke, how hard impacted soever they be*—P. Holland, translating Pliny. Intransitive uses first appeared in the 20c.: e.g. *Something impacted with a soft thud against Lingard's temple*—Seamark (pseudonym), 1929. In 1962 it was reported that a Soviet space rocket had *impacted onto the Moon's surface.* A few years earlier figurative uses of the verb had begun to proliferate: e.g. *The Magazine ... is not the place for consideration of national or international events except in so far as they impact on Oxford*—*Oxford Mag.*, 1956. By the 1980s it was a vogue verb, but voices were being raised against it, and have continued to be. The Usage Panel of the *Harper Dict. of Contemporary Usage* (1985) contemptuously rejected the transitive use shown in the sentence *High school publishing is a tough market and is being impacted by declining enrollments.* Their verdicts were uncompromising: 'an ugly verb from a noun'; 'another barbarism'; 'this is bureaucratese and ought to be rejected'. They were wrong to describe it as a noun forcibly turned into a verb in the 20c. (see above). But there is no mistaking the hostility they and others have shown towards the verb. Nevertheless, it seems part of standard AmE, particularly in technical and business language, though much less used elsewhere. Those of us whose teeth it sets on edge are always free to use *affect, influence, have an effect on*, or *endanger, threaten, risk*, etc., when the consequences are unfavourable. Examples: *Increased satisfaction can also translate into increased student evaluations, which can directly impact the instructor's career*—*NACTA Journal*, 2003 (AmE); *The downturn in the US economy had already impacted transatlantic air travel and the events of 11 September simply compounded the problem*—*www.motleyfool.co.uk*, 2001 (BrE).

impactful is a word often derided for its overuse in marketing, advertising, and related fields, even moving someone to say online 'I could never love someone who uses the word "impactful".' Those who bridle at the use of the verb *to impact* will find this derived adjective doubly repellent. But a case can be made for its usefulness. Its *ODO* definition as 'having a major impact or effect' shows that it actually has two meanings. In one, it is synonymous with *effective*, which could replace it in contexts such as: *I think the FM radio ads are the most impactful. Or at least amusing*—weblog, 2005. To express the meaning 'having a major impact', in contrast, it is arguably a useful shorthand for the whole clause that would have to be used instead of it in examples like: *'Laura Mackie has produced some of BBC Drama's most impactful serials over the past year,' says Jane Tranter*—BBC press release, 2004. Use it if you wish, but be aware of the health warning it comes with.

impale. See IM-.

impanel. 1 See EM- AND IM-, EN-AND IN-. *Empanel* is the usual form in British but *impanel* in American English.

2 However spelt at the beginning of the word, the inflected forms are usually *-panelled, -panelling* in BrE and *-paneled, -paneling* in AmE. See -LL-, -L-.

impassable, impassible. See -ABLE, -IBLE 4. Though unrelated in origin, these words are sometimes confused because they are pronounced similarly. *Impassable* means 'that cannot be traversed', referring to roads, stretches of countryside, etc. Its second syllable is pronounced as in *pass. Impassible* is a learned word used in theological discourse to mean 'not subject to suffering', e.g. *Aquinas accepted Aristotle's view that God cannot change and is impassible. He can act, but nothing can act upon him*—*Internet Encycl. of Philosophy*, 2004. Its second syllable is pronounced as in *passive*, which, like it, ultimately comes from *pass-*, the past participle stem of Latin *patī* 'to suffer'. The spelling *impassible* is mistakenly used in examples such as **dirt roads, which become nearly impassible during wet weather—OEC*, 2005. Confusion does not seem to happen the other way round.

impasse. A word much used, but with no settled pronunciation. The World English version of *ODO* gives /am'pɑːs/, /'ampɑːs/ in that order, while J. C. Wells (1990) gives pride of place to /am'pɒːs/. *ODO*'s American version gives /'ɪmpas/ or /ɪm'pas/ in that order, as does Merriam-Webster online. Some speakers also try to retain the French nasalized /ã/ of the first syllable.

impeach. In legal contexts, usually but not always historical, in BrE it means 'to charge with a crime against the State, esp. treason'. In AmE it means 'to charge (the holder of a public office) with misconduct'. What it does not mean in either variety is 'to dismiss from office'.

impel. The inflected forms are *impelled, impelling*. See -LL-, -L-.

impenitence, impenitency. Both words have been used for about four centuries with no perceptible difference of meaning. *Impenitence* is rare, but *impenitency* is rarer still. See -CE, -CY.

imperialism. In the 19c. (when it came into being) the word simply reflected the British politics of the time. It meant essentially 'the principle or spirit of empire', seen for the most part as a benevolent process. In the 20c. it came to be used disparagingly, first by the Communist bloc of the outside forces which they believed to be ranged against them, i.e. the Western powers; and then, conversely, to refer to the imperial system or policies of the USSR in the countries over which it held sway. *Imperialism* now seems to be largely a historical concept, though the word is still used in political writing of the continuing or potential imperial policies of certain countries. *Cultural imperialism* is the attempt to impose social or cultural characteristics, such as language, on other nations, typically to further the political and commercial interests of the imposer: *A list in which Anglo-American films so outnumber the rest of the world is, in my opinion, a list based on arrogant cultural imperialism: believing English-language culture far superior to all others is the real elitism—Guardian*, 2007.

imperil. 1 See IM-.

2 The inflected forms are *imperilled, imperilling* (AmE *imperiled, imperiling*). See -LL-, -L-.

impersonal verb. Now, a verb used only in the third person singular without a particular subject, e.g. *it is snowing; when it rains; it makes no difference*. Once a rich class of verbs originally (in Old English) governing either an accusative or a dative case. Examples of past uses: *What boots it with incessant care To tend the homely slighted shepherd's trade ... ?* (Milton) 'What good does it do ... ?'; *him listeth* 'he is pleased'; *methinks* 'it seems to me'.

impetus. The rarely needed plural is *impetuses*, not **impeti*.

impinge. The recommended and standard present participle is *impinging*, without the *-e-*.

implement (verb). The corresponding noun has existed in its ordinary sense since the 15c. As a verb it came into use first in Scottish legal language at the beginning of the 19c. in the now widespread sense 'to complete, carry into effect (a contract, agreement, etc.); to fulfil (an undertaking)'. As early as 1841 it was subject to grotesque censure: 'To implement, meaning to fulfil, is likewise derived from the barbarous jargon of the Scotish [*sic*] bar'—Irving, *Elements of English Composition*, 1841. By the mid-20c. the verb had come to be used, it would seem, by every committee, board, and governing body in the land. It has now passed through the usual stages that await any new verbs: a nervous welcome ('pedantry', said Fowler in 1926), widespread use ('why can't they use the traditional words *carry out, effect, fulfil*, etc.?'), followed by acceptance (the present attitude). Note that the noun has only one main stress, /'ɪmplɪmənt/, while the verb has a secondary stress on the final syllable, /'ɪmplɪˌmɛnt/.

implicit comparative. The term used in *CGEL* (1985) for what here is called the ABSOLUTE COMPARATIVE.

impliedly. This adverb, which appears most often in legal writing, is pronounced as four syllables, /ɪmˈplʌɪɪdli/. See -EDLY.

imply. See INFER.

impolitic. The corresponding adverb is *impolitically* rather than *impoliticly.*

import (noun and verb). The noun is stressed on the first syllable, /ˈɪmpɔːt/, and the verb on the second, /ɪmˈpɔːt/. See NOUN AND VERB ACCENT 1.

important, importantly. 1 Usage issues which once aroused strong feelings can now feel as obscure as the finer points of Byzantine theology. The choice between *more* etc. *important* and *more* etc. *importantly* is one such. Preceded by *more* or *most,* both words comment on the sentence or clause containing them, e.g.: *However, perhaps more important/importantly, in the history of Indian architecture, it holds a unique place.* Both work perfectly well; as Burchfield (1996) wrote, these uses 'must now be considered standard and useful acquisitions to the language'. Objections formerly raised to *importantly* can safely be ignored. Choose whichever you prefer, and whichever reads better in your specific context. Examples: (important) *But most important of all, we begin by giving you the training you need—Scientific American,* 1973*; More important, Mr Deng gave China a new revolutionary vision in the decade of reform from 1978—Economist,* 1991; (importantly) *In Nigeria he is at the more liberal end of the Christian spectrum. More importantly, he is in the front line of relations between Christianity and Islam—Times,* 2007; *and, most importantly, soon after the birth of his daughter he is referred to as Honorary Secretary of the Donhead branch of the British Legion—Bodl. Libr. Rec.,* 1986.

2 *Byzantine details.* The use of *more* etc. *importantly* was criticized on the grounds that it modified nothing in the sentence. But in fact it behaves like other SENTENCE ADVERBS in commenting on the whole proposition. It was also criticized on novelty grounds; yet it is probably older than the adjective use, going back at least to 1919, while the adjective use goes back at least to 1932 (T. S. Eliot). Finally, it was criticized on the grounds that *more important* was sufficient. *More important,* etc. is glossed by the *OED* as a 'kind of sentence adjective'; and in *CGEL* is described as a 'supplementive adjective clause'. In other words, it too functions very much like a sentence adverb, although grammatically it may be analysed differently.

impostor. This spelling retains the original Late Latin shape of the word, is recommended in Garner, and is the preferred form—just—in BrE, according to *OEC* data. However, across the English-speaking world as a whole, usage is pretty finely balanced between *impostor* and *imposter.*

impracticable, impractical. 1 These two words have related meanings but are used differently, and appear in different collocations. *Impracticable* means 'impossible to carry out, not feasible' and normally applies to a specific procedure or course of action: *poor visibility made the task difficult, even impracticable; in addition, the passage of 16 years from the date of the events in question meant that it was wholly impracticable—indeed impossible—to mount an adequate defence.* Although it is the older word (17c.), *impracticable* is much less frequent than *impractical,* is more formal in style, is used more in British English than American, and in BrE occurs particularly in the field of law. In general *impractical* (a more recent word, first recorded in the mid-19c.) means 'not adapted for use or action' (*impractical high heels*); referring to an idea or course of action 'not sensible or realistic' (*Don't think that this is just an impractical ideal*); applied to people, 'lacking the ability to do practical things' (*Paul was impractical and dreamy*). Increasingly, *practical* is displacing *practicable* in the meaning of 'feasible', particularly in AmE. Examples: (impracticable) *It was a memorable statement of the ascetic viewpoint at its most unpleasant and impracticable*—Peter Brown, 1988; *It would be impracticable to provide full-time security in cemeteries—Birmingham Post,* 2003; (impractical) *I have always been ridiculously impractical ... I cannot repair a fuse*—F. Howerd, 1976; *Her plans were so impractical that someone like me was necessary to point this out*—A. Brookner, 1987; *If she lost her licence it would have a catastrophic effect ... It would be totally impractical for her to use public transport—Essex Chronicle,* 2007.

2 Fowler (1926) favoured *unpractical* rather than *impractical* as the opposite of *practical.* Usage has largely ignored his preference: *unpractical* is outnumbered dozens of times over. However it is occasionally used, and some people make a distinction between people being *unpractical* and ideas or schemes being *impractical,* as in G.K. Chesterton's *There has arisen in our time a most singular fancy: the fancy that when things go very wrong we need a practical man. It would be far truer to say, that when things go very wrong we need an unpractical man—What's Wrong with the World,* 1910. A modern example is: *They reveal more clearly than any other source his erratic and unpractical temperament, contrasted with the methodical care that characterizes his method of poetic composition—ODNB,* 2003.

impregnable is an example of the quirkiness of English spelling. An alteration of Middle English *imprenable* (from Old French) 'not able to be taken' (cf. Fr. *imprenable*). 'The *g* was evidently in imitation of the *g* mute in *reign, deign,* and the like' (*OED*). In other words, etymologically it has nothing to do with *pregnancy* or *impregnate.*

impregnatable refers to a female capable of being made pregnant or to a material that can be impregnated with another substance.

impresario /ɪmprɪˈsɒːrɪəʊ/. Plural *impresarios.* See -O(E)S 4.

imprescriptible. A legal term meaning '(of a right) that cannot be taken away by (negative) prescription, i.e. one that is not invalidated by lapse of time'.

imprint (noun and verb). The noun (e.g. the *imprint page* of a book) is stressed on the first syllable, /ˈɪmprɪnt/, and the verb (e.g. *He'd always have this ghastly image imprinted on his mind*) on the second, /ɪmˈprɪnt/. See NOUN AND VERB ACCENT 1.

impromptu. 1 As a noun, has the plural *impromptus.*

2 See EXTEMPORE.

improvable is correct, not *improveable.* See MUTE E.

improvise is one of the group of words that can never be spelt as *-ize.* See -ISE 1.

impuissant. Normally pronounced /ɪm ˈpjuːɪs(ə)nt/ in English, but it can also be /ɪmˈpwiːsənt/.

impunity. See IMMUNITY.

in. 1 Use of *in* instead of *for* with reference to past time (*We have not spoken in more than a year*) has spread from American to British English. It is used in contexts that are explicitly or implicitly negative, and as such is a revival of an older English use: *To Westminster Hall, where I have not been ... in some months*—Pepys, 1669. More recent examples are: *Mark had never been near his house in a year*—C. Mackenzie, 1924; *The first bridge across the Bosphorus in 2,300 years ... is now being built—Daily Tel.,* 1971; *The ostensible reason for their first trip to London in several years was a new album—Evening Standard,* 2003.

2 In meanings to do with place, in certain contexts AmE uses *on* or *at* where BrE uses *in*: *a store on Fifth Avenue*/*They are all in school now.*

3 INASMUCH AS, IN ORDER THAT, IN ORDER TO, IN SO FAR AS, and IN THAT are discussed at their alphabetical places.

inacceptable. This 19c. alternative to *unacceptable* has never been widely used, but it still occurs, and is correct.

inadvertence, inadvertency. Both are used with no apparent difference of meaning, but *inadvertence* is by far the more common. Typical examples: (inadvertence) *But whether the failure was due to inadvertence or to incompetence there could be no doubt that the penalty for it was a most severe one—Times,* 1992; (inadvertency) *This is the moment of truth ... our truth can no longer be hidden away in the dark recesses of inadvertency or neglect—Times,* 1991.

in- and un-. 1 *General observations.* (*a*) Both prefixes are used to make negative forms of adjectives and nouns; *in-* is Latin in origin and is no longer active in making new words, whereas *un-* is English in origin and is a living prefix. Historically, some words have had both in- and un- forms, and the historical pattern is untidy. For example, *inarguable* and *unarguable* (both first recorded in the late 19c.) are still fighting it out, though *unarguable* has the upper hand. By contrast, *inability* (first recorded in the 15c.) and *unability* (also 15c.) both remained in common use from the 15c. to the 18c., at which point *unability* inexplicably dropped out. But *unable* (*c.*1380) was never challenged by an unrecorded *inable,* so that we are left with the asymmetrical pair *inability/unable.* (Other such assymetrical pairs are listed at 3). (*b*) A number of *un-* and *in-* forms are now being challenged by forms with the prefix *a-* (*amoral, apolitical,* etc.); and, in a continuing way, by NON-.

2 *Uncertain cases.* Fowler (1926) wrote 'There is often a teasing *un*certainty—or *in*certitude' about these two prefixes. Nearly a century later choice between them normally poses no problem for mother-tongue speakers of English, though they would be hard put to it to explain why they use one form and not another. Everyone knows that *instability* corresponds to *unstable,* and that *imbalance* corresponds to *unbalanced.* The number of words which cause doubt (e.g. *inarguable* and *unarguable*) is not large. Current examples are *unadvisable/inadvisable, incommunicative/uncommunicative, unconsolable/inconsolable,* and *undecipherable/indecipherable,* the second of each pair being much the more frequent. Sometimes differences of meaning determine the choice of form: e.g., *inhuman* (= brutal, unfeeling) and *unhuman* (= non-human); *immoral* and *unmoral* are not synonymous.

3 *Current asymmetrical pairs.* (*a*) adjective/noun pairs: *unable, inability; uncivil, incivility; unequal, inequality; unjust, injustice; unquiet, inquietude.* (*b*) *un-* words ending in *-ed*: *uncompleted, incomplete; undigested, indigestible; undisciplined, indiscipline; unreconciled, irreconcilable; unredeemed, irredeemable; unseparated, inseparable.* (Note: the only indisputable *in- -ed* word is *inexperienced.*) (*c*) *un-* words ending in *-ing: unceasing, incessant; uncomprehending, incomprehensible; undiscriminating, indiscriminate.*

4 *Historical comments.* (*a*) Negative *in-* seems to be no longer a living prefix in English, though it was until the 19c.: thus *inacceptable, inadvisable, inappeasable, indecipherable,* and *insanitary* were all first recorded in the 19c. (*b*) Negative *in-* has never been prefixed to words that already begin with *in:* forms like *ininformed, inintelligible,* and *inintentional* are unacceptable. (*c*) The following list contains a representative selection of words that have occurred in the past, and are listed in the *OED,* in both *un-* and *in-* forms. An indication is given of which of the two forms is more current; also an indication of the date of first record of the prevailing forms. *acceptable, un-* (15c.); *advisable, in-* (19c.); *alterable, un-* (17c.); *communicative, un-* (17c.); *completed, un-* (16c.); *consolable, in-* (16c.); *controllable, un-* (16c.); *decipherable, in-* (19c.); *describable, in-* (18c.); *digested, un-* (16c.); *discriminating, un-* (18c.); *distinguishable, in-* (17c.); *edited, un-* (19c.); *escapable, in-* (18c.); *essential, in-* (17c.); *frequent, in-* (16c.); *navigable, un-* (16c.); *sanitary, in-* (19c.); *substantial, in-* (17c.); *supportable, in-* (16c.); *surmountable, in-* (17c.). The puzzling distribution of the forms is confirmed by this list, in which thirteen words begin with *in-* and ten with *un-*. None of the words is of native origin; and it is to be noted that all centuries between the 15c. and the 19c. are represented as the time of first record of the recommended forms. Ours is indeed an unregulated and richly endowed language.

inapt, inept, etc. Something that is *inapt* is inappropriate or unsuitable; something or someone that is *inept* lacks skill or is clumsy. Contrast *a more inapt name for a boy than Cruz I cannot imagine* with *the referee's inept handling of the match was heavily criticized.* These two adjectives tend not to get confused, but raise other questions. (*a*) While *inapt* is by far the more common form, *unapt* also exists and is not wrong (in fact, Fowler recommended it), but generally only appears in historical prose, often followed by *for* or by a *to*-infinitive: *I . . . have a brain so entirely unapt for every thing of that kind—Tristram Shandy,* 1765; *I have, too, a sort of spiritual gaucherie which makes me unapt to participate in any rite*—C. S. Lewis, 1955. (*b*) Second, *inapt* has two noun derivatives, *inaptness* and *inaptitude,* but they are not interchangeable. The first tends to be applied to something's lack of suitability, e.g. *as a result of the inaptness of his theory, in which there is no space for radical choice among conflicting values*—weblog, 2004. *Inaptitude* tends to be applied to people's unsuitability for doing or inability to do something, e.g. *in spite of all this he shows a singular inaptitude for grasping so simple an idea as the following—OEC* (undated). (*c*) To express someone's lack of skill, or even bungling, *ineptitude* with an *e* is the normal word, e.g. *One unfortunate example of artistic ineptitude was the production of a stove, by one of Tatlin's associates, which though elegant in silhouette had a tendency to explode in the* *faces of the peasants in whose homes it was installed*—weblog, 2004. However, there are *OED* examples of inaptitude used historically in this way. Thus, sentences like the following, to which the obvious reaction is that *ineptitude* must be meant, cannot categorically be labelled mistakes, but to avoid the suspicion that they are, *ineptitude* is the better choice: *?They use their medieval picture of the Jew (this they borrowed from the Christians) to cover up their inaptitude, unwillingness and jealousy of others*—*OEC*, 2002.

inarguable is not as uncommon as I had supposed before examining the *OEC* and other corpora. The data in them suggests that there is a strong US preference for *inarguable*, and an equally strong BrE one for *unarguable*, which appears frequently in legal contexts, while *inarguable* is used in general contexts. *The right of the Jews to their land was an inarguable commonplace in his own day*—*First Things* magazine, 2005 (AmE).

inasmuch as. This rather formal conjunction is conventionally printed as two words, though it is quite often seen as four. It has two meanings: 'to the extent that, in so far as' and 'in view of the fact that, since'. Fowler (1926) accused it of 'pomposity' if used in the second meaning, and many later commentators have seconded his disapproval. Nevertheless, it is quite widely used in this way, particularly in American legal discourse, where it can add a certain *je ne sais quoi* of *gravitas*. Examples: (to the extent that) *In as moche as ye have done it vnto won of the leest of these my brethren; ye have done it to me*—Matt. 25: 40 (Tyndale); *Inasmuch as she could be pleased, the idea of this marriage pleased her*—C. Blackwood, 1977; (since) *I am unable to reply that I am much the better for seeing you, Pussy, inasmuch as I see nothing of* you—Dickens, 1870; *Inasmuch as Gray was Perdita's father, he was to be treated with a reasonable degree of respect*—B. Guest, 1985.

in back of. See BACK 2.

in behalf of. See BEHALF.

incage, encage. The second is the usual, if rare, form. See EM- AND IM-, EN- AND IN-.

incarnate. 1 As adjective it is pronounced /ɪnˈkɒːnət/ and means (*a*) embodied in flesh, especially in human form (*he is the devil incarnate*), and (*b*) represented in a recognizable or typical form, extreme (*stupidity incarnate, formality incarnate*).

2 As verb it is pronounced /ˈɪnkɑːneɪt/ or /ɪnˈkɑːneɪt/ and means (*a*) to embody in flesh, and (*b*) to put (an idea, etc.) into concrete form. It is often used in religious discourse. In other kinds, it could usually be replaced by *embody*, if one so wished. Examples: *From a Buddhist perspective we find ourselves incarnated in the human realm of samsara*—*OEC*, 2004 (AmE); *The characters of the heroines, both perfectly incarnated by the lead actresses, form an interesting contrast with each other*—*Senses of Cinema*, 2002 (Aust.).

incase, encase (verb). The second is the standard form now. See EM- AND IM-, EN- AND IN-.

in case. See CASE 3.

incentivize (verb). Verbs ending in *-ize* tend to be Marmite words: you love them or loathe them, and many people find *incentivize* extremely unpalatable. Burchfield described it as being on 'the fringe of the language, mostly in business contexts', and, happily for its detractors, that is where it has stayed. *OEC* data shows also that it is most widely used in the US, and very little elsewhere. The *OED* first records it from 1968, in the British *Guardian* newspaper. An argument in its favour, or against it, according to taste, is its multiple meanings: (i) to motivate or encourage someone, especially an employee or customer by providing an incentive (usually financial); (ii) to make a product or service more attractive by offering an incentive for purchase or participation (iii) broadly, without being specific about the nature of the incentive, to encourage or motivate. The following examples illustrate those meanings, and their sources suggest the fields and context in which the word adds its special flavour: (i) *We also incentivized those new employees by offering stock options that gave them an ownership stake in the new company*—*MX Business Strategies for Medical Technology Executives*, 2002 (AmE); (ii) *We . . . have already introduced a number of innovative offers aimed at attracting new custom to rail; they also showed that we need to continue to incentivise advance purchase and* *thus guarantee seat reservation—Modern Railways*, 1997 (BrE); (iii) *Imagine, we'll be able to incentivize people to produce work in the public domain—ExtremeTech Magazine*, 2003 (AmE).

inchoate /ɪnˈkəʊeɪt/. **1** *Meaning.* It derives from Latin *inchoātus*, past participle of *inchoāre* 'to begin'. If we leave aside its specific legal meaning, it originally meant 'just begun, at an early stage' and, by a natural extension, 'not yet organized, rudimentary'. Since what is rudimentary is likely also to lack structure, particularly in the stock phrase *inchoate anger*, the word started to be used to mean 'disorganized' or 'chaotic' from the early 20c. Usage commentators have disliked this extension of meaning, but it has been accepted by the *OED* since 1993. Examples: ('rudimentary') *It was obviously necessary that we should continue our still inchoate discussion over a drink*—D. M. Davin, 1975; *She is not allowed to express her real, if inchoate, feelings for Robert Marlin*—T. Tanner, 1986; *As the pace of industrialization quickened in the 1890s ... new social groups emerged and focused an inchoate but widespread discontent—Canad. Jrnl of History*, 2002; ('incoherent') *Haddon writes with an unrestricted access to his characters' inchoate thoughts, a direct line to their deepest sensual experiences*—Scotland on Sunday, 2005; *the first signs of widespread opposition, even an opposition that remains, for now, politically inchoate—World Socialist* website, 2000.

2 *Misuses.* (i) Under the influence of *incoherent* there is a slight danger that some people will be tempted to spell the word *incohate*: *the heated exchanges of those who have made the year of culture in 2008 an incohate, ill-thought vista*—weblog, 2006. (ii) The prefix *in-* is not a negative implying an antonym *choate*. However, there is a disputed legal term *choate*, meaning complete or valid, which has been in use for many decades. *Choate* is also, though rarely, used to mean 'coherent': *A walk around the camp reveals the difficulties they must have had in presenting a united, choate vision—Daily Tel.*, 2012. (iii) The following look like malapropisms 'for incoherent with, incandescent with', and 'chaotic' respectively: **Syria and Iraq have proved almost inchoate with rage at the fearful imagery of their biggest single source of water being stemmed for a solid month—Observer*, 1990; **The protesters at Genoa, inchoate and unfocused though they may be, ... can be considered the heroes of today's society—Scotland on Sunday*, 2001.

incidence. The *incidence* of a disease or crime is how often it happens, e.g. *an increased incidence of cancer*. It is quite distinct from *incident*, but confusions between the two words do happen. (i) *Incidence* is not a sophisticated synonym for *incident*, and should not be so used, as in **In another incidence, this time while at High Greave, he is alleged to have 'fixed it' for him to extend a car park—Yorkshire Post*, 2005. (ii) It is sometimes wrongly used when *instance* would be correct. In this quote by Baroness Neville-Jones, it is presumably the journalist transcribing rather than the noble Lady who made the mistake: **This is another incidence of the failure of the Government to safeguard sensitive information and yet another example of a lapse in discipline—Daily Tel.*, 2008. (iii) The plural *incidents* seems to be sometimes used by mistake for *incidence*: *?a number of articles about increasing incidents of accidental deaths in the public hospital system in the state of New South Wales—World Socialist*, 2004.

incident. The freeing of *incident* from its traditional role as an adjective meant that in the 20c. it began to be widely used as a synonym for 'event' or 'occurrence'. Gowers (1965) thought it was overused, and disliked its official use during the Second World War to describe any bombing raid, 'however disastrous its consequences'. In his view, *incident* correctly referred only to minor events, but that restriction ceased to be true long ago, and the word has become elastic. It encompasses events as serious as terrorist bombings, border raids, leaks of radiation from nuclear power stations, right down to minor muggings, domestic arguments, affrays at public houses, etc. Such elasticity gives the word vagueness, and thus potential as a euphemism, and its status as such is shown by the inverted commas round it in many of the *OED* quotations, e.g. *One impotent little man from Clapham, who was insolent to the Maharani, received for his pains a dismissal from the Civil Service for having made an 'incident'*—L. Broomfield, 1937. *In IT, the phrase security incident begins to sound like a euphemism: The average UK business now has roughly one security incident a month and larger ones around one a week—The Register*, 2004.

incidentally. 1 This is the only acceptable spelling in current standard English. The form *incidently*, in use from the 16c. to the 19c., derived from *incident* used as an adjective, but the modern examples of *incidently* probably reflect poor spelling skills or poor editing, not philological nicety. Do not use it. Example: **Viruses, incidently, remained* hors concours *throughout, it being doubtful whether they are living—New Scientist,* 1989.

2 Fowler's comment on *incidentally* as a sentence adverb, which is as acidulous as it is misguided, can mostly be ignored: '[*incidentally*] is now very common as a writer's apology for an irrelevance. Naturally, those who find it most useful are not the best writers.' (It is ironic that he used one sentence adverb, 'naturally', to dismiss another.) *Incidentally* is used to add a further comment to, or a remark apparently unconnected with, the current topic, and is equivalent to 'by the way'. It can be placed at the beginning or end of the clause, or after the subject. Examples: *Incidentally, in theory he must still owe me fifty pounds or* so—C. P. Snow, 1934; *Langmuir, incidentally, was the first scientist in private industry to win a Nobel Prize*—K. Vonnegut, 1981; *Words commonly used in the Dales just two generations ago were now a mystery to many young people. Attercop, which, incidentally, translates as 'spider', and blashy, which means 'wet weather', have evidently long gone—Independent,* 2007.

incise (cut into, engrave). Always so spelt, not *-ize*. See -ISE 1.

incisor. So spelt, not *-er*.

incline. The verb is stressed on the second syllable, /ɪnˈklʌɪn/, and the noun on the first, /ˈɪnklʌɪn/. See NOUN AND VERB ACCENT 1.

inclose. *Enclose* is the usual form. See EM- AND IM-, EN-AND IN-.

include, comprise. Many usage commentators insist that a rigid distinction separates these two verbs, as follows. The grammatical subject of both these verbs is the totality of something. The difference is that *comprise* must be used when all the components of the totality are mentioned, and that *include* cannot be so used. Thus, the University of Oxford *includes* All Souls, Christ Church, St John's College, and Somerville College; but it *comprises* All Souls, Christ Church, St John's College, Somerville College, and more than 30 other colleges, as well as several permanent halls. This leads to the distinction that one cannot legitimately say that the University of Oxford *comprises* All Souls, Christ Church, St John's College, and Somerville College; in such a context only *includes* is correct.

In practice, the two words are used in the way usage writers say they should be. Occasionally *include* is used when, according to the distinction, *comprise* is appropriate: *The 630 job losses include 300 in Redcar and 330 in Port Talbot—The Times,* quoted in Bryson (1984). However, it is worth remembering first that Fowler (1926) did not maintain this absolute distinction: his wording allowed for the possibility that *include* covers all parts of the whole: 'there is no presumption (though it is often the fact) that all or even most of the components are mentioned'. Second, he was objecting to a different problem: the mistaken, and possibly pretentious, use of *comprise* in place of *include*, as in 'The German forces . . . exceed twenty-three corps; this number does not comprise the corps operating in the Masurian Lakes.' The following modern example suggests that *comprise* is still very occasionally used in this way: *The Knights' injury list also comprises Hallas' fellow former Great Britain tourist Lee Jackson, who has a back problem, and Aussie stand-off Jonny Firth, who is out indefinitely after surgery on a torn bicep* [*sic*], *as well as long-term absentees Carl Stannard and Matt Blaymire*—The Press, 2003.

incognito /ɪnkɒgˈniːtəʊ/. (Printed in roman, not italic) The plural form of the noun (though rarely needed) is *incognitos.* The inflexions of the donor language, in this case Italian, have long since been abandoned in English: thus *a young incognito, this actress from London.* When the word is used adverbially (*they travelled incognito*) no change of form is called for. Contrast the fixed phrase (from Latin) *terra incognita* in which the L feminine ending is retained.

incoherent. See INCHOATE.

incommunicado /ˌɪnkəˌmjuːnɪˈkaːdəʊ/. Always spelt with two *ms* in English, despite the spelling of the Spanish original (*incomunicado*).

incommunicative. The usual form now is *un-*. See IN- AND UN-.

incomparable /ɪnˈkɒmpərəbəl/. Is stressed on the second syllable. Cf. COMPARABLE 1.

incompetence, incompetency. In lay language the two are not distinguished, except that *incompetence* is used dozens of times more often. Cf. COMPETENCE. In legal language, according to Garner (1987), 'The best advice is to reserve the *-cy* form to contexts involving sanity or ability to stand trial or to testify, and to use the *-ce* form when referring to less than acceptable levels of ability.' How closely such a distinction is observed in legal writing in Britain I do not know. Once one form has been chosen, however, it is important to use it consistently, and not to change from one to another in a given passage.

incompleted. The usual form now is *uncompleted* (but *incomplete*). See IN- AND UN-.

in connection with. See CONNECTION 2.

inconsequent is a rare word meaning 'not following naturally; lacking logical sequence'. For example, a disconnected argument could be described as *inconsequent*: *Careful of his three little horses, and always ready in an emergency, he yet preserves the gay, inconsequent nature of a very young child—OEC* (undated).

inconsiderateness, inconsideration. Both words came into the language in the 16c. and have remained synonymous since then, chiefly in the senses 'thoughtlessness (resulting from lack of consideration)' and 'lack of consideration for others'. In practice *lack of consideration* is used more commonly than either of them.

inconsolable, un-. The first is now the favoured form. See IN- AND UN-.

incontrollable, un-. The second is now the favoured form. See IN- AND UN-.

increase. The noun, pronounced /ˈɪnkriːs/, and the verb, pronounced /ɪnˈkriːs/, fall into the normal pattern for such pairs. See NOUN AND VERB ACCENT.

incrust, encrust. *Encrust, encrustation* and *encrustment* are the usual forms . See EM- AND IM-, EN-AND IN-.

incubator. Spelt *-or*, not *-er*.

incubus. The much more common plural is *incubi* /-bʌɪ/, but *incubuses* is also correct. Cf. SUCCUBA, SUCCUBUS.

inculcate. Derived from Latin *inculcare* 'to stamp in with the heel' (cf. L *calc-, calx* 'heel'), 'tread in', 'cram in', this verb has traditionally been used to mean 'to endeavour to instil (a view, a subject, a habit, etc.) by persistent instruction'. The usual prepositions governing the indirect object, according to *OEC* data, are *in, into,* and, mostly in archaic contexts, *upon.* Examples: *These words deserve to be inculcated in our minds; It is an interesting and demonstrable fact, that all children are atheists and were religion not inculcated into their minds, they would remain so; The doctor inculcated upon the minds of the students the duty of endeavouring to be something more than mere practitioners.* A less standard construction, *to inculcate* (a person) *with* (an idea, habit, etc.), takes the verb further from its roots and its traditional meaning. It was roundly condemned by Fowler (1926) and, with varying degrees of hostility, by some later usage writers. Examples: *A passer-by saved him, formed a close friendship with him, and* inculcated him with *his own horrible ideas about murdering women; The glorification of criminality, the idea that scholastic excellence is race-treason, all of that—it all adds up to a giant disadvantage for black kids* inculcated with it *from youth.* Though criticized, this use is common and unobjectionable.

incur. The inflected forms are *incurred, incurring.* See -R-, -RR-.

indecipherable. See IN- AND UN-.

indefeasible, indefectible. The distinction between these two rather uncommon words may perhaps best be kept in mind by associating them respectively with *defeat* and *deficit.* Particularly in law and philosophy, that which is *indefeasible* is not liable to defeat, i.e. (of claims, rights, etc.) that cannot be lost or annulled. That which is *indefectible* is not liable to fail, end, or decay. Examples: (indefeasible) *The people have a right, an indisputable, inalienable, indefeasible divine right to that most dreaded and envied kind of knowledge, I mean of the characters and conduct of their rulers*—John Adams, 1765; (indefectible) *though the eternal truths depend upon God for their existence as their primary cause, they are no less indefectible, that is,* *they are unchangeable in their substantial being—Stanford Encycl. of Philosophy*, 2005.

indefinite article. See A, AN.

indent. The verb, pronounced /ɪn'dɛnt/, and the noun, pronounced /'ɪndɛnt/, show the usual contrasting pattern for such pairs. See NOUN AND VERB ACCENT.

independence, independency. The *-cy* form is now restricted, mostly in historical contexts, to the meanings, (*a*) congregationalism (used since the 17c. of 'that system of ecclesiastical polity in which each local congregation of believers is held to be a church independent of any external authority', (*b*) an independent or autonomous state. In all other contexts *independence* is the usual word. It occasionally occurs as a synonym of *independence,* and cannot be said to be wrong, but it is rather odd: *a student will be incapable of actively participating in the academic world otherwise, especially given its guided independency*—weblog, 2011; *In the end, it would help to uphold the central bank's independency—Jakarta Post*, 2002.

index. In general use the normal plural is *indexes;* but in scientific language and in mathematics *indices.* See LATIN PLURALS.

Indian. In British English an Indian is first and foremost a native or national of India, or such a person born in and resident in the UK or elsewhere. To refer to the original inhabitants of the US, *Indian* and *Red Indian* are now regarded as old-fashioned and inappropriate, and more reminiscent of stereotypical images of the Wild West than of contemporary America. *American Indian,* or preferably *Native American,* should be used instead.

indict, indictable, indictment. *Indict,* meaning 'to accuse formally', is pronounced /ɪn'dʌɪt/ (in-**diyt**), and the same pronunciation applies to *indictable* and *indictment.* To confuse matters, there is an archaic homophone *indite* 'to compose, write', probably best known as the title of a Handelian anthem 'My heart is inditing', a title taken from the opening line of Psalm 45 in the AV, *My heart is inditing a good matter.* Because of their identical pronunciation, it is not uncommon for *indite* and *inditement* to be mistakenly used instead of *indict, indictment*: **The novel indites the centuries-old African tradition for its role in the torture, enslavement, and destruction of women—Concise Oxford Companion to African American Literature,* 2002; **it is obviously a terrible inditement of our so-called society that the mentally ill wander our streets with no-one to care for them*—weblog, 2003.

indifference, indifferency. For all practical purposes the former has driven out the latter, though they were equally common, with more or less matching meanings, from the 16c. to the 19c.

indigenous Australians. See ABORIGINAL, ABORIGINES.

indigestible is the usual form for 'not digestible', while *undigested* is usual for 'not digested'. See IN- AND UN-.

indirect object. An indirect object is a person or thing named as the recipient of the direct object of a transitive (or more strictly, ditransitive) verb. In Latin and Greek the indirect object is recognizable, as it once was in English, by being in the dative, while the direct object is in the accusative. The English dative now having no separate form, the indirect object must be otherwise identified, usually by the fact that it stands between the verb and the direct object (e.g. *Hand* me *that book*), and, if it is to follow the direct object, must be replaced by a prepositional phrase (e.g. *Hand that book* to me). Variations are (1) when no direct object is expressed, as in *You told me yourself;* (2) when the direct object is a pronoun and is allowed to precede, as *Give it me!*; *I told it you before* (but not *I told the story you before*); (3) when the indirect object comes after a passive verb, as *It was told me in confidence.* Note: Variation (2) is non-standard, and should be *Give it to me!* and *I told you that* (or *about it*) *before.* Variation (3) is now distinctly archaic. A speaker would now be more likely to say *it was told to me in confidence,* or *I was told it in confidence.*

indirect question. In grammar, an indirect question reports what someone has asked, as opposed to a direct question, which uses the person's exact words, often in inverted commas, and using the word order typical of questions. For example, '*What do they want to do?*' is a direct question and its indirect form is *I asked them what they wanted to do.* As in the previous example, indirect questions consist of a 'reporting' verb, usually *ask,* or more formally *enquire,* followed by a clause reporting the question. That clause uses the word order used in statements, and does not use the auxiliary 'do/does/did' etc. The tense of the verb in a direct question often needs to change in the indirect question, and the pronouns may need to as well: *'How long have you been waiting?'* becomes *I asked him/her/them how long he/she/they had been waiting*; and *'When will you go, Mary?'* becomes *I asked Mary when she would go*. When the direct question calls for an answer 'yes' or 'no', the indirect form is introduced by *if* or *whether*: (direct) *Do you want to go for a walk?*/(indirect) *I'll ask them whether they want to go for walk.* Since indirect questions follow the word order of statements they are not followed by a question mark; it is non-standard to write, for example, **I asked them what did they want to do?* or **Tell me how old are you?*

indiscreet, indiscrete. The first of these homophones (both pronounced /ɪndɪˈskriːt/) is the common word meaning 'not discreet, lacking discretion'; and the second is the much less common word meaning 'not divided into distinct parts'. Cf. DISCREET, DISCRETE.

indiscriminating. To express the idea of 'lacking or failing to exercise good judgement or taste' the normal adjective is *undiscriminating.* However, *indiscriminating,* though rather less frequent, does occur and is correct, if unusual. Examples: *The first is an undiscriminating public, primarily in industrialised countries, who support animal rights because it costs them nothing in terms of their personal lifestyle—Man in Nature,* 2004; *it makes for perfect family fare—but only if the children are young enough to be indiscriminating about what they're seeing—ReelViews,* 2002.

indispensable. Spelt *-able,* not *-ible.* See -ABLE, -IBLE 7.

indisputable. 1 Stressed on the third syllable.

2 This is the standard form for the adjective *indisputable;* but *undisputed* (adj.). See IN- AND UN-.

indissoluble (adjective). The pronunciation favoured by the *OED* (1900), namely with second-syllable stressing, has now given way to /ɪndɪˈsɒljʊbəl/, i.e. with the stress on the third syllable.

indite. See INDICT.

indoor, indoors. The adjective is *indoor* (e.g. *indoor games*), a shortening of earlier *within-door.* The adverb is *indoors* (e.g. *he went indoors at sunset*), representing earlier *within doors.*

indorse, indorsement. Variants of the more usual ENDORSE and *endorsement.* See EM- AND IM-, EN-AND IN-.

induction. See DEDUCTION.

inedible, uneatable. The dividing line between the two words can be traced from the definitions below, but is best understood by means of the examples shown. *Inedible* has two aspects: it refers to plants, animals etc. that cannot be eaten, either because they are inherently poisonous or harmful, or because they have been made so; it also refers to food that is disagreeable or impossible to eat because of the way it has been prepared or cooked. *Uneatable* in nearly all cases has only this second meaning, and is several times less frequent than *inedible.* (In fact, in the *OEC* data, half the examples are versions of the Wilde quote given below.) For the forms, see IN- AND UN-. Examples: (inedible) *Arnolds rules out overpicking and forest management practices, because both edible and inedible mushrooms have declined and all types of mature forests show similar drops—www.Realclimate.org,* 2005 (AmE); *Mulching also assures that light does not reach the tubers; potatoes exposed to light turn green and produce a toxin that renders them inedible—Mother Earth News,* 2003 (AmE); *The English country gentleman galloping after a fox—the unspeakable in full pursuit of the uneatable—A Woman of No Importance,* 1893; *I assumed this was a peace offering, probably one of her inedible fruit cakes that had been the cause of the W.I.'s unpleasant altercation with Trading Standards*—weblog, 2005 (BrE); (uneatable) *it was a typically minimalist 'gourmet' spread of undercooked steak and uneatable entrée*—weblog, 2004 (Aust.)

inedited, unedited. The first is still occasionally used by some textual editors, but *unedited* is the more usual term in general literary use. See IN- AND UN-.

ineffective, ineffectual, inefficacious, inefficient. For distinctions, see EFFECTIVE.

inept. See INAPT.

inequity, iniquity. These two words are related in form, meaning, and derivation. *Inequity* is the opposite of *equity* and means 'inequality, unfairness, injustice': *He believes that politicians need to tackle the inequities that divide society—TES,* 2007. *Iniquity* means 'grossly immoral or unjust behaviour': *It is easy for a well-fed English woman like myself to ... protest about the iniquity of racial prejudice*—M. & L. Hoy, 1991. Confusion happens in both directions. Sometimes *iniquity* is used when *inequity* is meant: **I suggest this iniquity be removed as soon as possible—Daily Tel.,* 1992. The set phrase *a den of iniquity* sometimes becomes *a den of inequity,* which sounds rather like the City, but is not, presumably, what is meant: **The notion that Dublin is a den of inequity and there are no drugs anywhere else is not true—Carlow Nationalist,* 2005.

inescapable, inessential. These are the standard forms now, not *un-*.

inexactitude, inexactness. Neither of these derivatives of *inexact* is common, but the first is the more frequent. This is no doubt because Winston Churchill employed it in the expression *terminological inexactitude,* which has now become a set phrase, possibly reinvigorated when it was used by US Secretary of State Alexander in 1983: 'That's not a lie. It is a terminological inexactitude. Also, a tactical misrepresentation.' Fowler (1926) had originally included it as an example of 'polysyllabic humour', but nowadays it is used allusively, with or without humorous intent. The Churchill quote is: *It* [*sc.* the employment of indentured Chinese labour on the Rand] *cannot in the opinion of His Majesty's Government be classified as slavery in the extreme acceptance of the word without some risk of terminological inexactitude.* The background is that Churchill, as Parliamentary Under-Secretary of State for the Colonies, addressed the House of Commons on 22 February 1906 as spokesman of a government that had just won an overwhelming victory in an election in which denunciation of their predecessors for having sanctioned 'Chinese slavery' had played no small part.

inexpressive is now the more usual term rather than *unexpressive.* But *unexpressed* (adjective) is the established form. See IN- AND UN-.

infectious. See CONTAGIOUS.

infer. 1 The inflected forms are *inferred, inferring;* **inferable** is commoner, but **inferrable** is also correct; *inference* has only one *r.*

2 *Meaning.* The frontier between *infer* and *imply* has been ferociously patrolled by the border guards of usage since the early 20c. It was Gowers in his 1965 revision, rather than Fowler, who first included it with the note 'misuse of *infer* for *imply* is sadly common'. The recommendation here is to maintain the distinction set out below: otherwise one risks eternal stylistic damnation. But the facts are less straightforward, as shown in 3 and 4 below. The uncontentious use of infer is to mean 'deduce or conclude from facts and reasoning', by contrast with *imply,* which means 'strongly suggest the truth or existence of (something not expressly asserted), to insinuate or hint'. Using *infer* to mean that is controversial, and not generally recognized in dictionaries. As the *ODO* usage note puts it:

'In the sentence *the speaker implied that the General had been a traitor, implied* means that the speaker subtly suggested that this man was a traitor (though nothing explicit was actually stated). However, in *we inferred from his words that the General had been a traitor, inferred* means that something in the speaker's words enabled the listeners to *deduce* that the man was a traitor.'

In a more humorous vein, A. P. Herbert in *What a Word!* (1935) drolly pinpointed the difference: 'If you see a man staggering along the road you may *infer* that he is drunk, without saying a word; but if you say "Had one too many?" you do not *infer* but *imply* that he is drunk.' It is, according to this interpretation, all a question of viewpoint and of logic. For the most part the distinction is carefully observed, but every now and then some writers (and speakers) stray across the meaning border, almost always by using *infer* where *imply* is preferred.

3 Examples: (*imply* correctly used) *Vast stretches of abandoned concrete underfoot imply that someone once had plans for the land—New Yorker,* 1986; *She's doing the* *bartending for money, her nonchalance implies*—M. Atwood, 1989; *It is a shocking departure from the procedures of good governance apparently designed to skirt Cabinet approval and the oversight that implies*—*Daily Mail*, 2007; (*infer* correctly used) *One might infer, from Judy's appearance, that her business rather lay with the thorns than the flowers*—*Dickens*, 1853; *You would have been able to infer from the room alone the nature of those who lived in it*—D. M. Davin, 1979; *No reference to any living person is intended or should be inferred*—S. Bellow, 1987; *Rose inferred from the letters that Sinclair was in love with Gerard*—I. Murdoch, 1987; (*infer* dubiously used for *imply*) *I can't stand fellers who infer things about good clean-living Australian sheilas*—*Private Eye*, 1970; *These were the ones who had made a slightly sulky entrance (inferring rebellion), and had then proceeded to sit on the floor*—M. Bracewell, 1989; *She was 'flabbergasted' when complaints were made that she had taken financial advantage of him by inferring they had an 'exclusive relationship'*—*Express*, 2004.

4 *Border disputes.* The borderline between *imply* and *infer* is often questioned, and with a certain justification. It should be kept in mind that the *OED* gives unquestionable examples of *infer* used to mean 'to lead to (something) as a conclusion; to involve as a consequence: said of a fact or statement; sometimes, of the person who makes the statement', with excellent supporting evidence from the 16c. to the 19c. (and some less impressive 20c. examples). There is also evidence that lawyers and judges sometimes use *imply* in contexts which seem plainly to call for *infer.* Garner (1987) cites three examples of *imply* in contexts where a layman would have expected *infer*, for example: *The requirements of the rule are met if such an intention may be clearly* implied *from the language.* Linguistic attitudes tend to change as time goes on. *OED*'s historical meaning may well become one of the natural uses of *infer* at some point in the 21c. The aberrant legal use of *imply* may also come to be regarded by all parties concerned as legitimate. Meanwhile they remain minefields and should be avoided.

inferable /ɪnˈfəːrəb(ə)l/. Stressed on the second syllable.

inferior. Because it is not a true comparative it, like *superior*, cannot be used in comparative constructions with *than:* thus *X is inferior to Y* (not *than Y*). In a phrase like *inferior wine* the meaning is 'inadequate' rather than 'less good'.

inferiority complex. See COMPLEX.

inferno. Plural *infernos.* See -O(E)S 4.

inferrable is an alternative, correct, but rather less common, spelling of *inferable.*

infinitely. Used hyperbolically, *infinitely* means 'to an indefinitely great extent' (*he is infinitely cleverer than I am*). When smallness rather than largeness is in question, *infinitesimally* is the better word (*the chances that a nuclear weapon will spontaneously explode are infinitesimally small*).

infinitive. 1 It is not practicable to set down here a full account of all the ways in which the infinitive form of verbs functions in English. First, though, some obvious points. The infinitive is the simple uninflected form of a verb, and is the form under which verbs are listed in dictionaries. An infinitive is frequently preceded by the particle *to* (*I am going* to cut *the hedge tomorrow*), in which case it is generally known as a *to*-infinitive, the term used throughout this book whenever it is mentioned. But there are also many circumstances in which the form without *to* (called the bare infinitive) is either optional or obligatory. The split (or cleft) infinitive, i.e. an infinitive with an adverb or adverbial phrase inserted between *to* and the verbal part, as in *you have* to really watch *yourself*, has been a matter of intense public debate since at least the 1860s. See SPLIT INFINITIVE.

2 The *to*-infinitive is related in a complex way to the verbal/nominal form in *-ing*, i.e. the gerund. For a basic account of some of the similarities and differences between the two constructions, see GERUND 3.

3 The *to*-infinitive. Some of its features: (*a*) When a second infinitive is used after a *to*-infinitive, the second (and third, etc.) example is not necessarily preceded by *to.* Contrast *'can be induced* to move *or* to change *its orientation'* with '*I prefer not* to live *and* work *in the same room.* (*b*) A number of formulaic phrases, the descendants of older and longer constructions, are in frequent use: e.g. *so to speak, to tell the truth, to put it mildly, to be honest, to say the least, come to think of it, to hazard a guess.* (*c*) Miscellaneous uses: (in which *to* = in order to) *She sat down to wait for him;* (at the head of a clause) *'To be frank with you,' she said, 'I don't believe it'*; (*to* at end of sentence with an infinitive implied but omitted) *Knowledge didn't really advance, it only seemed to; he has to make a decision but doesn't know how to;* (accusative + a *to*-infinitive) *he often took groups of students to see the work.* See also FOR 2.

4 *The bare infinitive.* It is often optionally used after the verbs DARE, HELP, and NEED, but often with a slight change of emphasis. But its use after modal verbs (CAN, MAY AND MIGHT, *must, shall,* etc.) and after comparatives and superlatives (BETTER, *had better, best, had best,* RATHER *than,* etc.) is obligatory; e.g. *Peter said he thought he* had better push *on; Bertrand preferred to go to a restaurant* rather than eat *alone.* A select list of some other common uses of the bare infinitive: (after *let* + object) Let him enjoy *his ignorance;* (after *is* and *was*) *All they want to do* is hide *in the kitchen; All he had to do* was take *his seat;* (after *why* and *why not*) Why suppress *it?*; Why not drop *in at the surgery and let me write out a prescription for you?*. For the mainly American English use of *come* and *go* + a bare infinitive, see these verbs.

infinitude was gently dismissed by Fowler (1926) as a 'needless variant' of *infinity,* but he judged that 'Milton [the first recorded user of the word] and Sterne, however, will keep it in being for poets to fly to and stylists to play with when *infinity* palls on them.' In lay language (as distinct from that of mathematics and photography) the two words seem to have been more or less interchangeable till the late 19c. Nowadays, however, *infinitude* is a rare choice, and *infinity* is over twenty times more frequent in the *OEC. ODO* defines *infinitude* merely as 'the state or quality of being infinite', as exemplified in *the infinitude of space; the infinitude of God's mercy.* This use is typical of religious and humanities writing. But *infinitude* is also used rhetorically, like 'an infinity of', as an exaggeration meaning 'an infinite number of': *As one did one's wonderful duty one could forget that one's legs were aching from the infinitude of the passages at Windsor*—L. Strachey, 1921; *'Well . . . ,' he said, looking with an infinitude of regret and reluctance at his newspapers*—J. Krantz, 1982; *the choices multiply into an infinitude of decisions that seem like they might determine the course of our children's lives*—Spiked Magazine, 2008.

infirmity. *The last infirmity of noble minds* is a MISQUOTATION. The passage in Milton's *Lycidas* reads *Fame is the spur that the clear spirit doth raise* (*That last infirmity of noble mind*) *To scorn delights, and live laborious days.*

infix. See TMESIS.

inflammable. See FLAMMABLE.

inflatable. So spelt, not *-eable.* See MUTE E.

inflection (Also **inflexion**). The general name for a suffix, etc., used to change the form of a word in order to express tense, number, comparison, etc., as *-ed, -ing, -s, -er* in *jumped, hunting, books, bigger.* Either spelling may also be used for the sense 'a modulation of the voice'. See -XION, -XIVE.

inflict, afflict. Both words are concerned with the suffering of unpleasant things, but they have different standard constructions. *Inflict* has the unpleasantness as object, and *afflict* has the victim. Using Fowler's (1926) somewhat gruesome examples, the respective constructions are: *he inflicted plagues* on (also upon) *them, he afflicted them* with *plagues; plagues were inflicted* on *them, they were afflicted* with (also by) *plagues.* Examples: (afflict) *He knew also that the greater part of the ills which had afflicted him were due, indirectly, in chief measure to the influence of Christian teaching*—S. Butler, 1903; *Such commentaries afflicted Australia with a burden of original sin*—*OEC,* 2004; *Most commanders would have been afflicted with convenient deafness at that moment, but Davout rounded on the speaker at once*—R. Butters, 1991; (inflict) *It was he who had inflicted an appendectomy of doubtful necessity on Harry forty-two years ago*—R. Goddard, 1990; *Further, that a harm, emotional as well as economic, was inflicted on the* victim *is, we think, obvious*—*OEC* (undated).

Fowler gave examples of the words' being muddled, and this still seems to happen: *?how such a gentleman was inflicted with the pain of cancer I will never understand*—*Waterford News and Star,* 2004. Although *inflict* was historically used in the way just exemplified, *afflicted* is the better choice according to current norms.

infold. *Enfold* is the recommended form. See EM- AND IM-, EN- AND IN-.

inform is a formal equivalent of *tell* and is in fairly restricted use: e.g. *the detective informed him of his rights; a station announcement informed us that the next train would arrive in ten minutes.* A customer, taxi, visitor, etc., might be *asked* or *told* to wait; it would not be idiomatic to say, for example, *Please inform Mr Jones to wait outside for five minutes.* In other words, dictionaries do not recognize the construction *inform* + someone + *to*-infinitive, although it quite often occurs, e.g **If management knows how well or badly a reporting unit is operating, they can inform investors to avoid surprises—OEC,* 2001. The formulaic uses of *inform* in commercial, official, etc., letters (*I am obliged to inform you; I have the honour to inform you,* etc.) 'are generally unnecessary preludes to giving the information provided' (Gowers, 1965), but such phrases nevertheless persist.

informant is a neutral term, (*a*) one who gives information; (*b*) specifically, the regular term for a person from whom a linguist, anthropologist, etc., elicits information about language, culture, etc. An *informer,* by contrast, is a person who informs against another person or other persons, e.g. to the police, i.e. is a term with sinister overtones.

infringe. 1 The inflected forms are *infringed, infringing;* also *infringeable.*

2 'Latin scholars, aware that both *frango* and *infringo* are transitive only, will probably start with a prejudice against [*infringe*] *upon;* but Latin is not English, as some of them know' (Fowler, 1926). The earliest uses of *infringe* in English (16c.–early 18c.) showed the verb used only transitively. But from about the 1760s constructions of *infringe* with *on* or *upon* gradually became established (alongside transitive ones) and are now commonplace: the sense is 'encroach; trespass' (e.g. *the measure threatens to infringe upon and restrict our right to travel in certain countries*). The older use survives, of course: it is still possible to use *infringe* with *right, law, patent, copyright, rule,* etc., as direct object, as it has been since the 16c.

infuse. The verb's oldest meaning (15c. onwards) was 'to pour in'. Very soon afterwards it acquired the transferred and figurative meanings 'to instil, insinuate' (e.g. *to infuse new life into a community*). When using the word in its physical meaning, you can *infuse* (a plant, herb, etc.) in a liquid in order to extract its properties, or (by a linguistic process that Fowler called 'object-shuffling') you can *infuse* (a liquid) by inserting something in it. The figurative meanings of *infuse* behave in corresponding ways: you can *infuse* (a quality or attribute) *into* a person or thing or you can *infuse* (a person or thing) *with* a quality or attribute. This use has been in existence since the 16c., and has good supporting evidence in the *OED.* Despite objections from some past critics, it follows that *infuse with* and *imbue with* are alternative standard constructions in the types *the self-respect with which the troops had been infused* (or *imbued*); *he infused* (or *imbued*) *his troops with self-confidence.* Further examples: *Joanna Trollope's latest delicious novel . . . focuses on two men, lifelong friends of sixty-something, whose younger women infuse them both with seemingly eternal vigour—She,* 1989; *He did his best to infuse good humour into his voice*—H. Forrester, 1990.

-ing. 1 *Picking up my Bible, the hill seemed the only place to go just then*—J. Winterson, 1985; *Packing to leave, her fingertips had felt numb on contact with her belongings*—M. Duckworth, 1986. For liberties of this kind, see UNATTACHED PARTICIPLES.

2 For the difference between participles in *-ing* and the gerund, see GERUND 2.

3 *Then we had our old conversation about the house being haunted*—C. Rumens, 1987. For such mixtures of participle and gerund, see POSSESSIVE WITH GERUND.

4 *In all probability he suffers somewhat, like the proverbial dog, from his having received a bad name*—cited in Fowler, 1926. For the need or no need of *his* and other possessives in such contexts, see GERUND 4.

5 *She bestowed her activity, rather than letting it be harnessed to anyone else's needs*—A. Brookner, 1988; *It seemed better to come and talk to someone here, rather* *than to continue to write letters*—Francis King, 1988. For the competing types *rather than* + *-ing* and *rather than* + infinitive, see RATHER 3.

6 *As well as closing the railway, it should make the Danube impracticable for traffic*—cited in Fowler, 1926; *Just like Dolly to usurp the mourning function as well as presuming to treat the evening as a normal evening party*—A. Brookner, 1985. On the use of *-ing* forms after *as well as,* see WELL A 1.

ingénue First recorded in English in Thackeray's *Vanity Fair* (1848), it is still often printed in italics as being not a fully naturalized word. It is also pronounced in Britain in a manner roughly resembling the French original, i.e. as /ãʒeɪ'njuː/. The accent is sometimes omitted.

ingrained is the normal spelling for the adj. meaning (*a*) deeply rooted, inveterate, (*b*) (of dirt, etc.) deeply embedded. And the finite verb *ingrain,* meaning (*a*) to implant (a habit, belief, etc.) ineradicably in a person, (*b*) to cause (a dye, etc.) to sink deeply into something, is usually so spelt (not *engrain*).

ingratiate. The standard syntax of this 17c. Latinate loanword meaning 'to make oneself agreeable to someone by flattering or trying to please them' is reflexive (with *oneself* etc.), optionally followed by the preposition *with*: *The child glared at me so fiercely that I tried to ingratiate myself by asking who was her favourite composer*—M. Dibdin, 1991; *Now, the troubled musician, who was jailed during the summer for possessing drugs, would appear to be keen to ingratiate himself with the Goldsmith family*—*Daily Tel.*, 2011. There are, however, many historical precedents for a directly transitive use, e.g. *This ... might ingratiate Hadad with Pharaoh*—Sir Isaac Newton, *a*1727, and the *OEC* contains several examples, (not to mention several showing that some users of the word have only a very approximate idea of what it means.) Often, as in the first example below, the transitive construction stands for 'endear to'. *Ingratiate* is also often used absolutely, i.e. without an object, as in the second example. *?Her first records with John Lennon didn't exactly ingratiate her to Beatle fans with their feedback-drenched, primal scream freak-outs*—music reviews website, 2004; *'Good' behaviour designed to placate and to ingratiate*—A. Storr, 1972.

inherent. In standard English either /ɪn'hɛrənt/ or /ɪn'hɪərənt/ is acceptable. J. C. Wells (1990) reports that his poll panel of RP speakers showed a 66% preference for the first of these.

inheritor. A person who inherits is so spelt, not *-er*. In accordance with the trend towards using unsexed or gender-neutral words, it also refers to women, and the specifically feminine archaic forms *inheritress* and *inheritrix* are used only in literary prose, and then but rarely.

in hopes of, in hopes that. See HOPE (noun).

inhuman. See UNHUMAN.

iniquity. See INEQUITY, INIQUITY.

initial (verb). The inflected forms are *initialled, initialling* (AmE *initialed, initialing*). See -LL-, -L-.

initialisms. See ACRONYM 2.

-in-law. 1 The plural of *-in-law* formations, e.g. *brother-in-law,* is typically *brothers-in-law,* i.e. *-s* is added to the first word in the formation.

2 *-in-law* Formerly *-in-law* was also used to designate those relationships which are now expressed by *step-*, e.g. *son-in-law* [formerly] = *stepson, father-in-law* [formerly] = *stepfather.*

3 The word *in-laws* referring to one's relations by marriage is hyphenated.

inlay. 1 The noun is stressed on the first syllable and the verb on the second. See NOUN AND VERB ACCENT 1.

2 The past tense and past participle of the verb is *inlaid.*

inmesh. *Enmesh* is the usual form. See EM- AND IM-, EN-AND IN-.

innavigable is a rare variant of *unnavigable.* See IN- AND UN-.

innings. In cricket, *innings* is both singular (*the first innings*) and plural (*the best of his many innings*). In baseball, the singular form is *inning* and the plural *innings.*

innit. See TAG QUESTION 3.

innocence, innocency. Both words were more or less equally current from the 14c. to the 19c., but *innocency* is now rare except in readings of Psalm (AV) 26: 6: *I will wash mine hands in innocencie: so will I compasse thine Altar, O Lord.*

innocent of. This standard expression (*entirely innocent of the crime with which he was charged*) has also been informally used since the early 18c. in a semi-humorous way to mean 'free from, devoid of': e.g. *The Sermon ... was quite innocent of meaning*—J. Wesley, 1743; *The windows are small apertures ... innocent of glass*—J. Colborne, 1884; *His skull-cap was innocent of decoration*—G. Durrell, 1954.

innuendo. 1 For the plural both *innuendoes* and *innuendos*, are correct. See -O(E)S 2.

2 The word was first (16–18c.) used as a formula to introduce a parenthetical remark commenting on or elucidating what had just been said or written, = 'meaning, to wit, that is to say'. This use was derived from Latin *innuendō* 'by nodding at, pointing to, meaning', ablative gerund of *innuere* 'to nod to, mean', in medieval Latin used to introduce a parenthetic clause. Skeat's *Etymological Dict.* quotes an example from Thomas Blount's *Glossographia* (1674): *he* (innuendo, *the plaintiff*) *is a thief.* From this use, it ultimately came to mean any disparaging allusive remark or hint.

inoculate. Spelt with one *n*, not *inn-*.

in order that.

1 Types of construction.
2 Examples
3 Subjunctive in negative sentences.
4 Alternatives to *in order that.*

1 *Types of construction.* Historically, *in order that* has been rather more restricted in the grammatical construction that follows than has the less formal alternative *so that*. Fowler, writing in 1926, regarded the use of (i) the subjunctive (*in order that nothing be forgotten*) as archaic; (ii) the modal verbs *may* and *might* as the regular construction (*in order that nothing might be forgotten*); (iii) *shall* and *should* as permissible in some contexts (*in order that nothing should be forgotten*); (iv) *can, could, will,* and *would* as 'undoubtedly wrong' (*in order that nothing can be forgotten/in order that nothing would be forgotten,* etc.). It is doubtful whether Fowler was correct about usage even in his own day. Today, with electronic language data available to check our intuitions about language, the facts are: (i) that the subjunctive is increasingly used and is therefore by no means archaic; (ii) the modal verbs, including *can* and *could, shall* and *should* (though rarely *will* and *would*), as well as *may* and *might*, are freely used when the context calls for them, although the *could, should,* and *would* forms are more common in each pair; (iii) that in order to avoid problems about which construction to use, many people resort to the alternative *in order for ... to ...* (see 4 below).

2 *Examples.* A variety of examples of usage over the last ninety years or so will illustrate the grammatical range of this phrase: (*a*) (may, might) *Stabilisation of wages is an urgent necessity in order that the industry might enjoy continued peace*—*World's Paper Trade Review*, 1922; *A suitable block-and-tackle is essential in order that the boat may be hauled far enough up the shore to be safe from 'rafting' ice*—*Discovery*, 1935; *The staff is committed to developing a genuine curiosity and love of learning in order that every child may be able to stretch and build upon their talents*—*Croydon Guardian*, 2004.

(*b*) (can, could) *The motor should be wound up fully for each record played, in order that the turntable can rotate at its normal and even speed*—P. A. Scholes, 1921; *The Telematics Programme ... looks at users' needs and requirements in order that entire networks can talk to each other ready for 1992*—*Practical Computing*, 1990; *Poor old cockerel ... was also going to be 'cut' later that day in order that an offering could be made once more to Muniapa, God of the forest*—fishing website, 2002.

(*c*) (shall, should) *In order that he shall be said to make a moral judgement, his attitude must be 'universalisable'*—A. E. Duncan-Jones, 1952; *He faces obstinately towards the future rather than the past, resolving to unmask the worst in order that it should not come to pass*—C. Welch, 2001; *A new trial of Mooney should be had in order that no possible mistake shall be made in a case where a human life is at stake*—history website, 2003.

(*d*) (do) *I can only hope that such methodology will be adopted by teachers new to media work in order that learning about the media does not become a bookcover* [*sic*] *here and a story-board there with little attempt at a coherent conceptual context*—*Times Educational Supplement*, 1990.

(*e*) (subjunctive) *It is necessary to overcome this stability in order that a chemical reaction take place*—*Chemical Reviews*, 1952; *In order that he be regularly scared by Authority, he should present himself every six months to the Service's Legal Adviser*—J. Le Carré, 1989; *Another recent development in fouling is where the opposition is fouled well away from the scoring zone and each subsequent foul is perpetrated by a different player in order that yellow cards be avoided*—news website, 2003.

3 *Subjunctive in negative sentences.* Use of the subjunctive is often awkward in negative constructions but examples are found, mostly in American but occasionally also in British English: *Paulin vacillates in his claims in order that he not have to meet the responsibilities of arguing any of them out*—*London Review of Books*, 1990 (BrE); *We asked him to remove the pictures that violated trademark, in order that we not be sued*—weblog, 2005 (AmE).

4 Alternatives to *in order that.* When the subject of the purpose clause (i.e. the clause introduced by the word *that* of *in order that*) is the same as that of the main clause, the alternative and simpler expression *in order to* is available. Thus, the first example in 3 above would become: *Paulin vacillates in his claims in order not to have to meet the responsibilities of arguing any of them out.* When it is not the same (as in most of the examples given above), the looser construction *in order for* + noun/pronoun + *to*-infinitive has become much more common. Thus, the second example in 3 above would become *We asked him to remove the pictures that violated trademark, in order for us not be sued.*

in order to. From the 16c. to the 19c. used as a complex preposition meaning 'with a view to the bringing about of (something), for the purpose of (some prospective end)': e.g. *A meeting ought ... to be called ... in order to a regular opposition in parliament*—Burke, 1773; *In order to the existence of love between two parties, there must be a secret affinity between them*—E. M. Goulburn, 1869. The only standard use now is a construction (first recorded in 1711) with a following *to*-infinitive, with essentially the same meaning, i.e. 'with the purpose of doing, with a view to': e.g. *Rozanov ... had taken a sharp right-hand turn in order to avoid going along the road*—I. Murdoch, 1983; *in order to make the material manageable, he divides it into three parts*—*Jrnl RSA*, 1986; *The High Court lawsuit highlights the lengths insurance firms are willing to go to in order to protect their reputation and their clients*—*Daily Tel.*, 2007.

It is occasionally claimed that *to*, rather than *in order to*, is all that is needed, and it is true that *to* is much the more commonly used of the two, and is often less formal: e.g. *the voice used by the daughter to bully her mother*—P. P. Read, 1986; *the path takes an unscheduled turn to miss a big tree*—C. K. Stead, 1986; *over half the members of Nato have been deploying military aircraft to relieve the African drought*—*Times*, 1986; *I went there to find the largest rose in the world*—*Western Mail*, 2007. There is clearly room for both constructions. It is hard to pin down reasons for the choice of the longer form, apart from its greater formality. The presence of a different kind of *to*-infinitive in the vicinity (see the *Telegraph* example above) may sometimes be a factor, as will considerations of rhythm and emphasis.

in petto is an Italian phrase (*petto*, from Latin *pectus* 'breast') meaning 'privately, in a person's mind or heart; in secret'. It was adopted in this sense in literary English in the 17c. but is nowadays rarely used. But, by confusion with *petty*, it has been repeatedly used in English since the early 19c. to mean 'in miniature, on a small scale', by authors such as e.g. Kipling in *Kim* (1901), *He represents* in petto *India in transition*; also Disraeli, T. E. Lawrence, and others. This meaning is recognized by the *OED*, although, if one were to insist on etymological purity, the correct phrase for 'in miniature' is the Latin *in parvo*: *It is for him to ensure that a Cabinet committee is the Cabinet* in parvo, *a microcosm of the Cabinet itself*—*Harold Wilson*, 1976.

input (noun and verb). **1** Both the noun and the verb are now stressed on the first syllable, though previously the verb was stressed variously. The past and past participle are recognized in the *ODO* as either *input* or *inputted.* According to the *OEC* data, the first is several times more common than the second, which suggests that many people find *inputted* somehow anomalous or discordant. Nevertheless, there are sound linguistic reasons for the existence of *inputted*, which are discussed at PODCAST. The present participle is *inputting*. See -T-, -TT-. The Spelling *imput*, though historical for the verb, is no longer recognized as correct.

2 The history of the noun gives a fascinating insight into how threatened words can take on a new lease of life as circumstances change. What is now very much a vogue word, in certain contexts, once tottered on the brink of extinction. To the original editors of the *OED* in the 19c. the word looked doomed except in Scotland, where it meant 'a contribution, a sum put in': *Ilka ane to be liable for their ain input*—Sir Walter Scott, 1818 (*ilka ane* = 'each one'; *ain* = 'own').

3 According to the *OED* examples, the word first appeared in something approaching its very expansive modern meaning of 'what is put in, taken in, or operated on by any process or system' in a Royal Society paper of 1893: *the quantity of blood which passes from them* [*sc.* large systemic veins] *into the right ventricle (which we may refer to as the 'input' of the heart), in a given time, is diminished.* The word then acquired specialist uses in electronics and economics, but it was really the advent of computers that gave it muscle; and from the language of computers *input* made its spectacular entry into the everyday vocabulary of psychology, linguistics, and related subjects, and then into the language at large, used of data, information, effort, etc. Many usage commentators have damned it as being overused, particularly when it means 'a contribution of work or information' (*her input on issues was appreciated*). Whether one uses it in this meaning is a personal decision, and many alternatives are available.

inquire, enquire. See ENQUIRE.

in regard to. See REGARD 1.

in respect of, in respect to. See RESPECT.

insalubrious, unsalubrious. Both are well-established but infrequent words meaning '(of climate or place) unhealthy', but the first is about ten times more frequent. See IN- AND UN-.

insanitary, unsanitary. Sanitation is a 19c. concept: the word itself was first recorded in 1848, and other words in the family also made their first appearance in that century (*insanitary* 1874, *unsanitary* 1871, *sanitary* 1842, *sanitate* 1882, *sanitize* 1836). Of the negative adjectives *unsanitary* is by far the more common of the two in all varieties of English., while *insanitary* is used, if at all, mainly in British English. There is no difference in meaning between them. See IN- AND UN-.

inside of. Used of a period of time (*inside of a week* = in less than a week), this colloquial expression is first recorded in an American work of 1839. From AmE it has gradually made its way into other forms of English, though its Americanness is apparent. The *OED* also records the closely related, but now rather old-fashioned, phrase *the inside of* 'the middle or main portion of a period of time', labelled *'colloq.'* and first recorded in 1890. Examples: (inside of) *Renny won a fiver off me because he made friends inside of the month*—M. de la Roche, 1940 (Canad.); *I'll be between the sheets inside of half an hour, old man*—A. Fullerton, 1954; *There too, faces were sometimes painted with 'any kind of paint that you could rub off inside of a few days'*—*Christmas Mumming in Newfoundland*, 1969; (the inside of) *Why, I can't even keep a man faithful to me for the inside of a month*—C. Isherwood, 1939; *At first Isabel had only meant to stay away for the inside of a week*—L. P. Hartley, 1955.

insidious, invidious. Both words suggest harmful results, but despite their similarity tend not to confused, except in one specific phrase. *Insidious* (from Latin *insidiae* 'ambush') means 'proceeding in a gradual, subtle way but with very harmful effects': *An insidious form of sexism pervades most biographies of famous women, a tendency to treat women's work as peripheral to their lives*—*Ms*, 1973. Something described as *invidious* (from Latin *invidia* 'envy') is likely to upset someone: *I hope it is not invidious ... to single out here the museums for mention*—*Oxford University Gazette*, 1984. If someone is said to be in an *invidious position*, their position is unenviable, often because they are caught in a dilemma: *This puts the conscience-driven*

Soyinka in an invidious position. As a Nobel prizewinner, he has access to international platforms where he can speak out against such atrocities. But he also wants to pursue his own work, live his own life—*Sunday Herald*, 2000. *Invidious* also refers to comparisons that are unfair or that discriminate unjustly: *This decrees that a company cannot make fraudulent claims or invidious comparisons with another product*—*BMJ*, 2004. It is in this meaning that *insidious* is most often wrongly used: **That plays right into the hands of those Christian anti-Semites . . . who make insidious comparisons between a 'loving' Christianity and a 'cruel' Judaism*—*First Things Magazine*, 2003.

insightful. First recorded in a work by John Galsworthy in 1907, and meaning, 'having or showing a deep knowledge and understanding; perceptive', this inoffensive-seeming adjective has had more than its fair share of brickbats thrown at it, and possibly suffers from its latent connection with the *insight* of psychology and psychoanalysis. It is particularly popular in American English, and is most often used in the arts, humanities, and religious fields. The worst that can be said about it is that it can be something of a critics' reach-me-down, and overuse may have worn it a trifle threadbare. Examples: *She created a film which was memorable, intriguing and moving, a warm and insightful reconstruction of a vanished age*—*Listener*, 1982; *It was a wonderful insightful exhibition*—*Modern Painters*, 1988. *Sales people must be emotionally literate, pick up signals from clients and be insightful about their own emotions*—*Daily Tel.*, 2007.

insignia. In origin it is the Latin plural form of *insigne* 'mark, sign, badge of office', which is itself a noun use of the neuter singular of the adjective *insignis* 'distinguished'. In two of its uses it has had an uncomfortable history since it entered the language in the mid-17c. (*a*) *Insignia* as plural (= badges or distinguishing marks of office) (*they pulled down all the insignia of royal state*). (*b*) Used incorrectly (according to the *OED*) as sing. with *insignias* as its plural: *In his hand he bore a slender white wand, the dreaded insignia of his office.*—Washington Irving, 1832; *I saw not a single racer at Sestrière bearing an insignia that seemed out of place*—*Times*, 1971. (*c*) *insigne* (singular) 'badge, ensign, emblem', pronounced /ɪnˈsɪgni/: *The men of Lord Louis Mountbatten's South-eastern Asia command wore it* [*sc.* the figure of a phoenix] *as an insigne in World War II*—W. R. Benét, 1948; *pieces here and there of old Wehrmacht and SS uniform, tattered civilian clothes, only one insigne in common, . . . a painted steel device in red, white and blue*—T. Pynchon, 1973. Type (*a*) is the only one of the three in standard use in BrE. Type (*b*) is marked as 'fully standard' in American dictionaries. *Insigne* is rare and its use likely to cause bewilderment.

insist takes several constructions in current English in the meaning 'to assert as a demand': you can *insist on* something (or *on doing* something); you can *insist that* something *be* done (subjunctive with *that* optionally omitted) or that something *should* be done; or you can simply insist, with no grammatical complement. Examples: *They insisted on spending ages there wandering around choosing a book each*—*Yorkshire Post*, 2002; *Henry had not wanted to bring Louisa on the expedition but she had cried to go, and the adults insisted that she not be left behind*—L. Clarke, 1989; *Tony insisted that she accompany him to a meeting of the Literary Society*—A. S. Byatt, 1985; (*that* omitted) *There were nights when she seemed so forlorn that he insisted she sleep over in the spare room at the back*—R. McCrum, 1991; (with *should*) *The family received me very warmly and Signora Ugolotti insisted that I should have something to eat*—W. Newby, 1991; (no complement) *OK, since you insist, I'll tell you the answer*—*Language Log*, 2004.

in so far as. This compound subordinator has been in use since the 16c. (it has the rare distinction of being treated twice in the *OED*), and is still common. The *OED* has it as four words, but other standard authorities (including *CGEL*, 1985) use *insofar as*, which is the more common form in all varieties of English, and as frequent as the four word form in British English. Hyphenated *in-so-far as* is rather rare. It normally means 'to the extent that'. Examples: *Enforcement, insofar as salaries are concerned, is costing nothing*—*Times*, 1969; *The exercise of reviewing his life was proving monstrous in so far as it revealed the places in which it had gone irredeemably wrong*—A. Brookner, 1988. *Insofar as I had thought at all about what Italians did on vacation, I imagined the inhabitants of the cities joyfully rushing towards the provinces for the *whole of August*—*Times*, 2004. It is a somewhat formal phrase, and can sometimes be replaced without loss of meaning or dislocation of syntax by *so far as*, or *as far as*. It is also used in contexts where it does not really mean 'to the extent that', in which case it can be replaced by *though, since*, or some other simpler conjunction.

insouciance, insouciant. Opinion has opted for a fully Anglicized pronunciation for these words: /ɪnˈsuːsɪəns/, /ɪnˈsuːsəɛnt/. It is rare to hear, i.e. /ɛ̃sʊsjɑ̃ːs/, /ɛ̃sʊsjɑ̃/.

inspector is spelt *-or* not *-er*. The specifically feminine equivalent *inspectress* is now rarely used outside period or historical contexts, although it appears in the job title *housekeeping inspectress* in AmE.

inst. Formerly used in business letters, this abbreviation of *instant* (*your letter of the 6th inst.*) means 'of the current month'. Nowadays the name of the month is used instead (*your letter of 6 June*).

instability. See IN- AND UN-.

install is now the recommended form, rather than *instal.* The inflected forms are *installed, installing,* but **instalment** (AmE normally **installment**). See -LL-, -L-.

instance. 'The abuse of this word in lazy periphrasis has gone far,' says Fowler (1926), 'though not as far as that of *case.*' He cited two examples of which this is one: *The taxation of the unimproved values in any area, omitting altogether a tax on improvements, necessarily lightens the burden* in the instance of *improved properties.* As Fowler suggested, the phrase should here be replaced simply by *on.* Whether the battering by Fowler and others has brought it about or not, it is now quite hard to find examples of *in the instance of,* though they do occasionally occur, e.g. *teachers exhibited prejudice against non-heterosexual sexualities that would not be tolerated in the instance of a racial or gender issue*—*MediaCulture Jrnl*, 2005. The best policy is to refrain from using this particular phrase, but to continue to use the word *instance* in its other dictionary-listed senses, e.g. 'an example or illustration of' (*just another instance of his lack of consideration*), 'a particular case' (*that's not true in this instance*); also the phrases *for instance,* and the rather formal *at the instance of* 'at the request or suggestion of (a person)': *I was there at the instance of Mrs. Shuttlethwaite*—T. S. Eliot, 1950.

instigate at one time had rather negative connotations, and meant 'to foment, provoke (especially antisocial or discreditable acts)', with such an act as its grammatical object, e.g. *What he and they called levying war was, in truth, no better than instigating murder*—Thackeray, 1852; *Observers said his comment implicitly suggested that Mr Gusmao had deliberately instigated the present violence to dislodge the premier*—*Daily Tel.*, 2006. But for at least the last quarter of a century it has also been used to mean 'institute, start, set up', as was noted by Burchfield in 1996 by means of the next two examples: (from a 1991 letter written by a prison governor) *Re improvement objectives*—*I have made a start on the above ... The first change is to instigate a full induction programme*; (from a Treasury circular dated 16 May 1991) *Departments ... should ensure that all staff are made aware of their obligations under the legislation, and instigate appropriate actions to ensure compliance.* While these examples certainly smack of bureaucratese, the meaning has gone from strength to strength, and is recognized by *ODO*. The legal phrase *to instigate proceedings* may also have played its part in this shift. Whatever the case, the negative connotations are absent in many contexts, and all manner of things can be instigated, such as investigations, reviews, campaigns, inquiries, processes and policies. The word also seems particularly popular in British English: *The objective of this new phase is to ... instigate legal, policy and institutional reforms at the country level*—*Lloyd's List*, 2007; *The scam has already been the subject of a Welsh television documentary, instigated by Richard's early research*—news website, 2003 (BrE). If one wishes to avoid it, synonyms such as *institute, initiate, launch, establish, inaugurate, encourage,* etc. are available. There is also a construction with a personal object, which, though recognized by *ODO*, some will find a step too far: *Another group drove civilian vehicles and distributed weapons to the people, instigating them to kill the American troops*—weblog, 2004 (AmE). *Incite* would be better in this context.

instil, instill. 1 The spelling with double *ll* is the norm in AmE and Canada, while in BrE single *l* is standard, but double *ll* is also quite widely used. Elsewhere the two forms are in competition, with Irish, Indian, Australian, and NZ English showing some preference for the shorter form. The inflections are *instilled, instilling*. See -LL-, -L-.

2 The word's non-physical meaning is 'to gradually but firmly establish (a feeling, idea, attitude etc.) in a person's mind', the feeling, idea etc. being the grammatical object of the verb. It is followed by *in* rather more often than *into*: *Many noted the significance the new Prime Minister has given in recent days to the values and morals that were instilled in him while he was growing up in Fife*—*Scotsman*, 2007; *They believed, quite wrongly, that to instil a sense of guilt into me would ultimately be for my good*—R. Hitchcock, 1989. Fowler (1926), was adamant that only this syntax was possible; his insistence was inspired by his concerns about what he called 'object-shuffling confusion': 'You can inspire men with hope,' he said, 'or hope in men; but you can only instil it into them, not them with it.' The unrevised entry for the *OED* to which he went for authority contained a single 1644 example from Milton with the structure *with*, sternly labelled 'obsolete' and 'rare': *instilling their barren hearts with conscientious slavery*. Whether one takes Milton as a model or not, the use of the construction *instil* + person + *with*, though not common, continues in modern English, and even appears to have support from high-placed politicos: *During the war my mother and brother and I went to Norfolk, and there I was instilled with a love of the countryside*—*Sunday Express Mag.*, 1986; *In his speech yesterday, Mr Cameron said youngsters had to be instilled with a greater sense of responsibility and taught respect for authority*—*Daily Tel.*, 2007.

instinct (noun and adj.). The noun is stressed on the first syllable, /ˈɪnstɪŋ(k)t/, but the rather formal or literary adjective meaning 'imbued or filled with (a quality, especially a desirable one)' is stressed on the second, /ɪnˈstɪŋ(k)t/, e.g. *If you read this chronicle very carefully, you will find that it is instinct with the concepts of state-craft and attitudes to the Prince of the renaissance*—BBC History, 2004.

instinct, intuition. See INTUITION.

instinctive, instinctual. Gowers (1965) considered *instinctual* a superfluous word, and jibed 'perhaps the psychologists wanted a word of their own'. First recorded in 1924, and then often taken up, it is true, in works of psychology, *instinctual* is the less common of the two words, but is still quite often used. The normal, everyday word you and I would use is *instinctive*. But we would probably do so in its meanings 'done without conscious thought' (*an instinctive distaste for conflict*) and to describe people who are 'naturally talented, without necessarily being trained' (*an instinctive chef*). Those extended meanings have largely overridden the meaning 'related to or prompted by instinct', which is why *instinctual* is deemed necessary. Modelled on other forms such as *conceptual* and *habitual*, it seems to have an extra authority not shared by the more generalized word *instinctive*. *Instinctual* is often used in technical contexts such as psychology and psycholinguistics, and in academic writing, which are its proper domain. However, it also seems to be competing with *instinctive* in the latter's meaning of 'done without conscious thought', when it will often sound portentous, if not pretentious. Examples: (*instinctual* in academic writing) *For Snow, therefore, the differences between the behavior of boys and girls instantiate instinctual differences between the sexes*—*Art Bulletin*, 2002; *the ritual is an indirect expression of an instinctual impulse that the sufferer had repressed and which therefore could not be discharged in a straightforward manner*—*Freud, A Very Short Introduction*, 2001; (arguably pretentious) *'I'm trying to make the personal-networks group ebb and flow into other parts of Motorola like an amoeba, so that I don't know where their people end and mine start,' she says. 'It's not instinctual in a high-testosterone culture'*—*Fast Company* Magazine, 2000.

institute, institution. For concrete uses of the words, namely (*a*) a society or organization instituted to promote some literary, scientific, artistic, professional, or educational object, or (*b*) a building in which the work of such a society is carried on, there is no formal distinction between the two words. That a particular society has *institute* or *institution* in its title is one of the glorious accidents of English; the important point is to use the right word when referring to the body concerned. The earliest *institute* mentioned in the *OED* is the *Mechanics' Institute* (established 1823), and others listed include the *Royal Institute of British Architects* (founded 1834) and the *Royal Archaeological Institute* (1843). Of *institutions* the earliest mentioned in the *OED* is the *Royal Masonic Benevolent Institution* (founded 1798), but it is clear that various benevolent and charitable institutions existed from the beginning of the 18c. Other early institutions included the *Institution of Civil Engineers* (1818) and the *Smithsonian Institution* (Washington, DC, 1830). Typical examples of the two forms: *Taylor Institution* (Oxford, opened 1848); *Women's Institute* (first in Canada 1897; then in various other countries in the early 20c.); *British Standards Institution* (UK national standards body, 20c.); *Institute for Advanced Studies* (at Princeton Univ., NJ, founded 1933). Since the early 19c. *institution* has also been widely used for well-established and much loved national customs, (sporting) events, constitutional concepts, etc. Thus cricket, the Grand National, the monarchy, Yorkshire pudding, Wimbledon, the Trooping of the Colour, the Chelsea Flower Show, the last night of the Proms, chicken tikka masala, and a host of other aspects of life in Britain are said to be *national institutions.* The impermanence of such public recognition, however, is shown by the fact that in 1926 Fowler included the Workhouse and capital punishment in his list of such institutions.

in-store, instore. Thanks to the hypertrophy of supermarkets and hypermarkets, it now seems possible to fulfil all the functions of human life (excluding, so far, procreation, birth, death and burial, but one never knows) under the roof of a single emporium. Owners of such are justifiably proud of all the facilities offered, including *in-store tastings, pharmacies, bakeries, opticians, seminars,* even *chaplains.* To describe these delights, hyphenated *in-store* is ten times more frequent in the *OEC* data than *instore,* and is the spelling recommended here. Such is the power of shopping that the standard idiom *in store* (= about to happen) can now be found spelt as one word: **The Sunday Herald sports team pick their highlights from the last 12 months and look ahead to what's instore for 2002*—*Sunday Herald,* 2001.

instruct (verb). The derivatives are **instructor** (not *-er*) and (now rare) **instructress**.

insubstantial, first recorded in 1607, is about ten times more frequent in the *OEC* data than *unsubstantial* (mid-15c.). There is no clearly definable difference between them, since they both can mean 'not having physical existence' and 'lacking solidity or substance'. Shakespeare used both in the same scene of *The Tempest*: *The great Globe it selfe, Yea, all which it inherit, shall dissolue, And like this insubstantiall Pageant faded Leaue not a racke behind*—iv. i. 155; *Welcome then, Thou vnsubstantiall ayre that I embrace*—iv. i. 7.

insupportable, first recorded in 1530, is more common in the *OEC* data than *unsupportable* (1586), but only in a ratio of 12:10, and both words are in any case somewhat rare. Both can mean 'unendurable' and 'unjustifiable'. *Unsupportable* seems to collocate particularly with *claim,* and with related words such as *assertion, assumption, allegation,* while *insupportable* collocates with words such as *burden, debt, nuisance.* This suggests that *unsupportable* leans towards meaning 'unjustifiable' and *insupportable* towards 'unendurable'. Examples: (insupportable) *Joyce* [*sc.* James Joyce] *had become an insupportable burden, and, it seemed to her, an ungrateful one*—*TLS,* 2010; *Although two nineteenth-century authorities suggest that cheques may also be drawn on an interest-bearing account, this view is insupportable in modern law*—*Modern Banking Law,* 2002; (unsupportable) *the unsupportable claim that the United States was always construed as plural before the Civil War and always as singular afterward*—*Language Log,* 2005; *Another way in which absolute libertarian arguments fail is in the utterly unsupportable notion that we can stop people from behaving politically*—*The Hot Button,* 2003.

insure. See ASSURE. See also EM- AND IM-, EN-AND IN-.

insusceptible, first recorded in 1603, is slightly less frequent than *unsusceptible* (1692), though neither is in common use.

intaglio /ɪnˈtalɪəʊ/ or /ɪnˈtɑːlɪəʊ/. Plural *intaglios.* See -O(E)S 5. *Intaglio* is opposed to *relief* as a name for the kind of carving in which the design, instead of projecting from the surface, is sunk below it. Cf. Italian *intagliare* 'to cut into'.

integral. As a noun it has little if any currency outside mathematics, and is stressed on the first syllable. As an adjective (= necessary to the completeness of a whole; forming a whole) in British English it is preferably pronounced with the stress on the first syllable, i.e. /ˈɪntɪgrəl/, but second-syllable stress is also common, i.e. /ɪnˈtɛgrəl/.

intelligent, intellectual. While an *intelligent* person is one who is 'quick of mind; clever, brainy', an *intellectual* lives on a higher plane of abstract thought. The range of ability covered by the word *intelligent* is considerable, from that of a child seeming to have acquired skills ahead of the normal time to the kind of person, Fowler said in 1926, 'we most of us flatter ourselves that we can find in the looking-glass'. Wayward people in the dock are often described by prosecuting counsels as '*intelligent* but . . . '. A dog that performs a particular act, e.g. fetches a thrown stick, may be described as *intelligent.* An *intellectual* is a being apart, someone with rare special insights, such as, say, Isaiah Berlin, or, come to that, Karl Marx. *Intelligent people* are dispersed through the nation. They may or may not be ham-fisted or impractical; they are simply too busy protecting society from anarchy to claim immunity from the acquisition of ordinary skills. *Intellectuals* are a distinguished but impermanent minority; they normally speak like archangels, or philosophers, or political scientists, usually in several languages, and have original views about the arts and about the diverse ways of humankind, but often cannot cut a slice of bread straight or drive a car. Their reputations, like their opinions, come and go.

intelligentsia. A key word in 20c. political vocabulary, it was first formed in pre-revolutionary Russia to refer disparagingly to the educated middle classes. Nowadays it is used generically to mean 'intellectuals or highly educated people as a group, especially when regarded as having cultural or political influence'. It is usually in the form *the . . . intellegentsia,* with a qualifying adjective, especially one of nationality or class, intervening, e.g. *the Russian, American, liberal, Jewish, left-wing intelligentsia.* It can have both singular and plural concord, like other collective nouns, i.e. *But the intelligentsia also* bears *some responsibility, since* it privileges its *own experience over that of the common people—History Today,* 2003; *Not only did the left-wing intelligentsia* dislike *uppity lower-middle-class arrivistes:* they *positively discouraged the most deprived working-class people from rejecting their 'roots'—City Journal* (New York), 2002.

intend. The typical standard constructions for this verb include: + *to*-infinitive, with or without an intervening direct object, (*we intend to go, we intend our message to be peaceful*); + *-ing* form (*we intend going*); with a *that*-clause (*we intended that you should go*). In the passive, it is followed by *for* in the meaning 'be meant or designed for' (*These are intended for children*). The following two constructions, particularly common in North American English, must for the moment be considered non-standard: (i) *intend* + *for* + object + *to*-infinitive, e.g. **Nature never intended for us to remember everything—Art Journal,* 2001 (AmE) (read *intended us to remember everything,* or *that we should remember everything*); (ii) *intend* + *on* + *-ing* form, e.g. **Always be sure to research the keyphrases you intend on using—OEC,* 2005 (AmE) (read *you intend using*).

intense, intensive. Historically *intense* (*c.*1400) and *intensive* (1526) have intertwined and overlapped. It was Fowler (1926) who first enshrined the distinction between them in the canon of usage issues. He considered *intensive* a 'popularized technicality' used inappropriately in contexts where *intense* was preferable. The details of his objections need not concern us here; what is true, however, is that in certain uses the demarcation between the two words is fuzzy. In very broad terms, *intense* can often relate to subjective responses—emotions and how we feel about something—while *intensive,* in the meaning of 'very thorough, vigorous' tends to be more objective. So, *an intensive course* describes a course designed to cover a lot of ground in a short time; but *an intense course,* describes how someone felt about it. According to this distinction, *intense negotiations* would be marked by tension and emotional excitement, while *intensive negotiations* would be thorough and probably concentrated into a short period of time. But the distinction is not as clear-cut as that.

When the thoroughness of an activity or its concentration into a short time is highlighted, that is when the words compete. Their definitions suggest this jockeying for position: *intense* = 'highly concentrated'; *intensive* = 'concentrated on a single subject or into a short time; very thorough or vigorous'. What follows is a list of many of the collocations in which they compete, with some representative examples, and comments where appropriate. Fastidious readers will no doubt be able to make up their own minds about the merits of one or other word.

(*a*) *Intense* is the norm. The following words normally collocate with *intense*, whereas collocation with *intensive* could be seen as anomalous: *competition, debate, fighting, pressure, scrutiny, workout.* (i) *The retail sector is reeling from intensive competition—OEC,* 2003. This reads like a straightforward case of *intensive* invading *intense's* collocational space. (ii) *The escalating riots and protests in China have provoked alarm in Beijing. The official establishment is engaged in an intensive debate on how to defuse the growing discontent—World Socialist* (website)—2004. *Intensive* here suggests the debate was indeed urgent and concentrated. (iii) *After a year-and-a-half of intensive scrutiny in the press, Wen Ho Lee is a free man—CNN* transcripts, 2000. Something lasting a year and a half can hardly be considered 'concentrated into a short time'. But this example may foreground the focus on a single topic mentioned in the definition of *intensive*. (*b*) *Intense* is in the majority, but *intensive* is also very frequent: *lobbying, negotiations, preparations.* There often seems little to choose between them. *The Canadian government has been the target of intense lobbying for stronger copyright legislation in recent months—First Monday Journal,* 2005; *Plans to allow financial institutions to provide conveyancing services were abandoned in 1994 following intensive lobbying by the legal profession—Sunday Business Post,* 2003; *It followed a week of intense round-the-clock negotiations with Walker Morris partner David Hinchliffe at the firm's Leeds office—OEC,* 2004; *The revised plan followed intensive negotiations conducted by UN special envoy Alvaro de Soto with the two leaders in the past three days—Irish Examiner,* 2002. (*c*) *Intensive* is more common preceding a mention of a short period. In these cases it is often unclear whether *intense* means 'highly concentrated' or 'emotionally demanding': *It's a hardcore though friendly environment designed to address your writing-related issues in an intense three-day immersion—Philadelphia Weekly,* 2004; *the newest entrants to the 51st Highland Regiment are halfway through an intensive six-week course that is the equivalent of nine months' regular training in the TA—Scotland on Sunday,* 2005. (*d*) *Intense* is surely wrong. There is a specialist meaning of *intensive* in farming, i.e. 'aiming to achieve maximum production in a limited area'. Very occasionally *intense* is used instead: *Intense farming is one of the nastiest institutions this century has produced—OEC* (*undated*).

intensifier, a class of adverbs that amplify or add emphasis to a gradable adjective, e.g. *greatly obliged, highly intelligent, perfectly reasonable;* or that have 'a general lowering effect' from an assumed norm, e.g. *barely intelligible, relatively small.* Also a class of adjectives that have emphasizing, amplifying, or downtoning force, e.g. *a sure sign, a true scholar, utter nonsense; a close friend, a complete fool; a feeble joke.*

intensive. See INTENSE.

inter (verb). The inflected forms are *interred, interring.* See -R-, -RR-.

inter- is a prefix meaning 'between, among' (*intercity, interlinear*) or 'mutually, reciprocally' (*interbreed*); as opposed to *intra-*, which is a prefix forming adjectives, and has the meaning 'on the inside, within' (*intramural, intravenous*).

inter alia is Latin for 'among others' when 'others' are things. If the rules of Latin are to be carried over to English, when persons are referred to the correct form is *inter alios.* In practice, however, it is best to restrict *inter alia* to things (e.g. *he said,* inter alia, *that* . . .), and to use *among others* when referring to people. Printed in roman.

intercalary. The main authorities recommend second-syllable stressing, i.e. /ɪnˈtɛːkələrɪ/, but /ɪntəˈkalərɪ/ is also permitted. Second-syllable stressing is standard for the verb *intercalate.*

intercept. The agent-noun is *interceptor* (not *-er*).

interchange. The verb is stressed on the third syllable and the noun on the first.

interchangeable. Spelt, with the final *-e* of *interchange,* in order to retain the soft *g.*

intercourse, in the meaning *sexual intercourse,* was first recorded in 1798 and was uncommon before the 20c. It has now completely overshadowed the earlier use of *intercourse* 'social communication or dealings between individuals, nations, etc.'

(first recorded in 1494) to the extent that in older passages such as the following it runs the risk of smutty *double entendre*: *Those with whom time and intercourse have made us familiar*—Dr Johnson, 1751; *We looked forward to years of unchanged intercourse*—Charles Dickens in a letter of 5 Aug. 1852.

interdependence, interdependency. There is no difference of meaning, but *interdependence* is much more frequently used. See -CE, -CY.

interdict. The noun bears the main stress on the first syllable, and the verb on the third.

interestingly. It is curious that its use as a SENTENCE ADVERB, first recorded in the 1960s, has escaped censure, unlike *hopefully*. It is often qualified by *enough*. Example: *Interestingly, what exercises Lord Chalfont is not the existence of nuclear weapons, an existence which, he says, cannot be repealed*—M. Amis, 1987.

interface. In 1901, when the relevant section of the *OED* was issued, *interface* was virtually a new word. The earliest example was one of 1882, and the word had only the concrete sense 'a surface lying between two portions of matter or space, and forming their common boundary'. In 1976, when volume ii of the *OED* Supplement was published, a transformation had occurred. Computers had arrived, and so too had Marshall McLuhan. Now, an interface was, on the one hand, 'an apparatus designed to connect two scientific instruments, devices, etc., so that they can be operated jointly' and, on the other, 'a point where interaction occurs between two systems, processes, subjects, etc,'. Its vogue status was assured as it was applied ever more widely to the relations between business development and marketing systems, lecturers and students, unions and management, and other areas of public life; in fact, any system could be found to have *interfaces*: *The issue of insanity as a defense in criminal cases . . . is at the interface of medicine, law and ethics*—*Scientific American*, 1972. As noun and verb *interface* became an instant vogue word in the 1960s. As Burchfield put it: 'One of the keywords of the 20c. had made its grand and noisy entrance, and was heckled and censured by those who had no taste for it.' McLuhan was also responsible for the first use of *interface* as a verb, meaning 'to come into interaction with', first recorded in 1967, and a corresponding use in computing and electronic technology soon followed.

Nowadays the word has, through overhandling, lost some of its gloss, but not its ability to irritate. As noun, it is, of course, standard in IT language, in *user, computer, web*, etc. *interface*, and half its appearances are in this field. In other arenas it seems to have lost none of its pretentiousness, e.g. *In spatial terms the foyer constitutes a generous public interface, being triple height and glazed at both ends*—*Architecture Australia* Magazine, 2001. As a verb, it seems particularly at home in American English. Some of its non-technical applications are their own best parodies: '*For many people, their lifestyle helps them interface with cheese more often,' she says*—*Dairy Field*, 2004 (AmE); *The plot follows János as he interfaces with his family members*—*Movie Martyr*, 2001 (AmE). In businesspeak, it has become a bit of a cliché to describe interpersonal relations: *According to Clague, those things include any job that involves working directly with the client, project management, and interfacing with suppliers*—*Fast Company* Magazine, 2004 (AmE). More familiar (and usually more precise) alternatives, such as (for the noun) *boundary, contact, link, liaison, meeting point, interaction*, and (for the verb) *communicate, have contact with, interact*, even *talk to* are readily available to cater for the general meanings.

interior. See EXTERIOR 1.

interlocutor /ɪntəˈlɒkjʊtə/, a person who takes part in a dialogue or conversation. So spelt, not *-er*.

interlope /ɪntəˈləʊp/, **interloper** /ˈɪntə ləʊpə/. So pronounced, i.e. with contrasting stressing.

interlude. Can be pronounced either as /-luːd/ or as /-ljuːd/ (-lood, -lyood).

interment, the burial of a corpse, is, of course, to be distinguished from *internment*, the confinement of people for political or military reasons. The two generally keep their own company, but occasionally *internment* tragicomically replaces *interment*, e.g. **her Requiem Mass and the internment of her remains in Ballyheane cemetery*—*Western People*, 2003.

intermezzo /ɪntəˈmɛtsəʊ/. Both *intermezzi* /-tsi/ and *intermezzos* are correct as plurals.

intermission, an interval between parts of a play, film, concert, etc. Originally (19c.) an Americanism, but now probably as widely used in Britain as the traditional word *interval.*

in terms of. 1 *A usage bugbear.* This much-debated and much-criticized three-word sequence is a complex preposition, joining such long-established sequences as *in front of, in place of; in common with, in compliance with; in exchange for; in relation to.* Given the critical battering it has received, it is best treated with some degree of caution. It was called 'a vague all-purpose connective' by the usage writer H. P. Guth in 1985, and 'it encounters a good deal of criticism when used to speak of one ill-defined thing *in terms of* another equally vague and ill-defined' (*Columbia Guide to Standard American English,* 1993). It was even extravagantly described in 1993 by the Oxford philosopher Michael Dummett as representing 'the lowest point so far in the present degradation of the English language'. Examples cited by Dummett include (from 'broadcasters and military and governmental spokesmen'): *We have made great progress in terms of the balance of payments* (rewrite, says Dummett, as *The balance of payments has improved*); *Our troops have been highly successful in terms of advancing into enemy territory* (read *Our troops have advanced deep into enemy territory*).

2 *Particularizing uses.* How did this complex preposition come into being? The *OED* reveals that it has been in use since the mid-18c. as a mathematical expression 'said of a series ... stated in terms involving some *particular* (my emphasis) quantity', and illustrates this technical use by citing examples from the work of Herbert Spencer (1862), J. F. W. Herschel (1866), and other writers. From this technical use came at first a trickle and, after the 1940s, a flood of imitative uses by non-mathematicians to mean 'with regard to the aspect or subject specified': e.g. *The impact of Ibsen ... did much to revitalize the degenerate English theatre and force it to think in terms of living ideas and contemporary realities*—J. Mulgan and D. M. Davin, 1947. And it is a simple matter to collect examples of *in terms of* which have been written, like the previous example, by people who are not 'broadcasters or military or governmental spokesmen': *He deals with the* converso *judaizing world in terms of its social and religious rituals, births, marriages, deaths, leading to the establishment of the Inquisition*—*Bull. Hispanic Studies,* 1990; *Rameau ... conceived his music precisely in terms of timbres, types of attack, degree of sostenuto*—*Country Life,* 1990; *Justifying space in terms of material wealth is as ridiculous as saying that man went to the Moon merely to be able to return with velcro zips and non-stick frying pans*—*New Scientist,* 1991; *The dating of his novels in terms of when they were written rather than when they were published is often uncertain, since in the upheavals of exile some were not published chronologically*—*NY Rev. Bks,* 1991.

In all these examples, this complex preposition works as a useful particularizing device and objecting to it may seem unreasonable. Nevertheless, the last example shows that it often insinuates itself into sentences in which the thought could have been expressed more concisely, e.g. *It is difficult to establish when his novels were written as opposed to published, since ...*

3 *Dubious uses.* As with the examples cited in section 1, and the last example above, many sentences containing *in terms of* can, and should, be recast, as this next example from the business world illustrates: *the effect would be significant in terms of potential impact on earnings.* It says the same thing twice. It should be cut down to size as *the effect on potential earnings would be significant.* Readers will no doubt find it easy to supply other examples of this kind.

4 = *'concerning, as regards'. In terms of* is often condemned as being 'a vague all-purpose connective', and that criticism could be applied to the following examples: *When John Major emerged as a possible candidate to lead the Conservative party, one was struck by his engaging artlessness in terms of class*—*Daily Tel.,* 1991; *Let's face it*—*in terms of artistic talent, Emin isn't fit to wipe Monet's backside*—*Cherwell Mag. Online,* 2005. In both cases *as regards* could, as it often can, be used instead, though the only obvious benefit of doing so is the saving of one word (and the peace of mind of your more prickly readers). Other alternatives include *as for* and, if you wish to be more forceful, *when it comes to*. This complex preposition is also often used at the beginning of a sentence, particularly in speaking, as a means of highlighting the theme of the clause: *In terms of acquisitions, WestFarm Foods does not see them as a critical growth strategy—Dairy Field*, 2003. While this is a very useful device, it also is open to the criticism that the thought could be expressed as ... *does not see acquisitions as critical to* ..., but rephrasing would lose the emphasis.

The conclusion must be, assess with a critical eye any sentence in which you write *in terms of*, and decide whether it makes your point easier to understand, or merely long-winded and cumbrous.

intern. In the US and Canada (on occasion elsewhere) the term (sometimes spelt *interne*) for a recent medical graduate, resident and working under supervision in a hospital as part of his or her training. It is stressed on the first syllable. The equivalent terms in Britain are *houseman, house physician*, and *house surgeon*.

internecine. Pronounced /ɪntəˈniːsaʌɪn/ and used in English to mean 'mutually destructive', it is a rare example of a word whose meaning changed thanks to a lexicographer. Classicists will know that its 'true' meaning is 'characterized by great slaughter', a meaning found in some 17–19c. contexts, including Samuel Butler's *Hudibras* (1663). The word is an adaptation of Latin *internecīnus*, from *interneciō* 'general slaughter, massacre', from *internecāre* 'to slaughter': the element *inter-* in Latin words meaning 'to kill' did not carry its usual sense of 'mutual, reciprocal'. Johnson in his *Dictionary* (1755) mistakenly interpreted the adjective to mean 'endeavouring *mutual* destruction', and thus set the word on its way to its only current meaning. It is used in this sense not only of battles between warring factions, but also, more trivially, of boardroom or other internal battles in business circles or other walks of life. *He was on edge, engaged in flaming rows, head-blasting music mayhem and internecine squabbling with his garage band compadres Crazy Horse—NME*, 1991.

Internet. BrE style guides tend to recommend lower-case *i*, while AmE ones, *NODWE*, and this book favour a capital.

internment. See INTERMENT.

interpersonal. Recorded once in 1842, and reintroduced in 1938 by the psychologist H. S. Sullivan (1892–1949), *interpersonal* was once restricted to the language of psychology to describe behaviour between people in any encounter. From there it has become part of the standard vocabulary of anyone concerned with how people get on with each other, and in business and recruitment good *interpersonal skills*, or the ability to deal effectively with other people, are an indispensable attribute in any candidate's CV.

interpretative, interpretive. In standard British English the traditional (and recommended) form is *interpretative* (formed on the stem of Latin *interpretātus*), thus analogous with *authoritative, qualitative*, and *quantitative*. But the shortened form *interpretive* is now more common in all varieties of English, except BrE. For further discussion of the matter, see -ATIVE, -IVE; PREVENTIVE.

Examples: (interpretative) *Some of deconstruction's avowed interpretative misreadings of literature—Brit. Jrnl Aesthetics*, 1986; As *Dr John Coiley, keeper of the museum ... says: 'If you're not interpretative, the general visitor won't learn anything.'—TES*, 1990; *You may be wondering why I am rabbiting on about interpretative processes when the theme of this article is how to build a bracket clock— Practical Woodworking*, 1990; (interpretive) *A converted wartime building, it will provide an interpretive base from which visitors can enjoy extensive views of the saltmarshes—Bird Watching*, 1986; *He ... is working at present on a project to develop a network of marine wardens and interpretive centres*—E. Wood et al., 1988; *Chinese culture ... has undergone major interpretive phases in recent decades—Dædalus*, 1991.

interregnum. The plural *interregnums* is more frequent than *interregna*, and both are correct. See -UM 3.

interstice /ɪnˈtəːstɪs/, an intervening space. A word that is most commonly found in the plural form *interstices* /ɪnˈtəːstɪsiːz/ or /-sɪz/. It appears in a famously opaque definition of Dr Johnson's: 'network n.s. Any thing reticulated or decussated, at equal distances, with interstices between the intersections'.

interval. See INTERMISSION.

intestinal. Most authorities recommend placing the stress on the second syllable, i.e. /ɪnˈtɛstɪnəl/. But third-syllable stressing, with lengthening of the stressed vowel, i.e. /ɪntɛˈstʌɪnəl/, is gaining ground, at least in BrE.

in that. In the nature of things, because of the multiplicity of ways in which *in* and *that* are separately used, it is not easy to find the conjunction *in that* in the *OED,* but it is there, defined as 'in the fact that; in its being the case that; in presence, view, or consequence of the fact that; seeing that; as, because', and illustrated by six quotations from the 15c. to the 19c., including this one from Shakespeare's *2 Henry VI* (1593): *Let him dye, in that he is a Fox.* It would seem to be a very flexible conjunction. Jespersen (1909–49, iii) provided further examples (16–19c.) and described *in that* as 'literary rather than colloquial'. He also reminded us that some scholars think 'that *that* in this group is the demonstrative pronoun *that* with omission of the conjunction'. Curme (1931) repeated the point by asserting that the type *He differed from his colleagues* in that *he devoted his spare time to reading* was the equivalent of *He differed* in that: *he devoted his spare time to reading.* He also believed that *Acts* (AV) 10: 33 *and thou hast well done,* that *thou art come* would perhaps be now rendered as '*in that you have come* or more simply *in coming*'. (In fact, the corresponding passage in the *NEB* is crassly banal: *it was kind of you to come.*) *CGEL* (1985) paid little attention to *in that:* it simply called it a 'complex subordinator' and left it unillustrated.

In view of all this listing of uses of *in that*—its true force seems to baffle or not baffle the experts in turn—it is not easy to decide whether much value should be placed upon Fowler's insistence in 1926 that *in that* is wrongly used for simple *that* in several sentences that he cites, including *The legislative jury sat to try the indictment against Mr Justice Grantham* in that *during the Great Yarmouth election petition he displayed political bias.* Perhaps one should say that the jury is still out on that one. What one can say is that *in that* clauses are not uncommon, and that the meaning of *in that* is amply covered in the *OED.* Witness, for example, this sentence by Henry Cecil Wyld in his *History of Modern Colloquial English* (3rd edn, 1936): *M.E. spelling ... is to a certain extent phonetic,* in that *there is often a genuine attempt to express the sound as accurately as possible.* As that example and following ones show, *in that* is a part of everyday usage, and means rather more than a simple *because*: *They work like disks* in that *they can be partially erased—Management Computing,* 1990; *it is an inescapable truth that the petroleum industry is subject to a rigid technical constraint,* in that *a large proportion of inventories are tied in the supply system—Oxford Institute for Energy Studies,* 1990; *The vessels ... are unusual* in that *they have no engine room, being powered by ten diesel-driven alternator packs connected to the main switchboard—Ships Monthly,* 1991.

in the circumstances. See CIRCUMSTANCE.

intimidate. You can *intimidate* someone so that they do what you want, or so that they refrain from doing what you don't want them to do. In the first case it is clear that the structure is *intimidate* + object + *into* + *-ing* form/noun, e.g. *And they try and intimidate employees into keeping their mouth shut; The press is heavily controlled and intimidated into self-censorship.* But what of dissuading someone from doing something through intimidation? Fowler (1926) considered it unidiomatic to use *intimidate* followed by a direct object + *from.* It is, however, the standard construction and is an obvious example of analogy at work, i.e. deter from, dissuade from, *prevent from,* etc. It seems preferable to the structure with direct object + *out of,* which is presumably influenced by *scare out of, terrify out of,* etc. Examples: *Threats, however implicit or subtle, have no place in a process of conflict resolution. They will certainly not intimidate the Government from doing its duty—Irish Examiner,* 2005; *And yet the bully-boys try to intimidate people out of saying it*—weblog, 2004.

into, in to. 1 The two words should be written separately when the sense is separate, most commonly when *in* is a full adverb and *to* is an infinitive marker and means 'in order to'. Examples: (*in to*) *People dropped in to see him; The maid looked in to ask if they wanted coffee; the Secretary of State, George Shultz, slipped in to replace Reagan;* (+ noun) *he accompanied her in to dinner;* (*into,* esp. expressing motion or direction) *I was reduced to staring into the water; The desire to know can degenerate* *into mere trickery; The Highway Code can be taken into account; He wants to put his hand into hers.* In the first group it would be wrong to conjoin *in* and *to* (e.g. *People dropped into see him*); and in the third group to let them stand apart (e.g. *I was reduced to staring in to the water*).

2 The modern use (1960s onwards) of *into* to mean 'involved in, knowledgeable about' (*he is into Zen*) is still suitable only for distinctly informal contexts.

intra-. See INTER-.

intransigent. The recommended pronunciation is /ɪnˈtransɪdʒənt/, but /-ˈtranz-/, /-ˈtrɑːns-/, and /-ˈtrɑːnz-/ are all permissible. The word came into English from French in the 1880s and was for some time pronounced in a French manner and often spelt (as in French) *intransigeant.*

intransitive (adjective). In sentences of the type *they lit a fire,* the verb *lit* is **transitive** in that it has an object (*a fire*). By contrast, in the sentence *they arrived at noon,* the verb *arrived* has no direct object and is called *intransitive.* Numerous verbs, e.g. *to lie, to seem,* are always used intransitively. Other verbs have both transitive and *intransitive* uses: e.g. (transitive) *he played the piano;* (intransitive) *she plays well.* Thus the presence or absence of a direct object determines whether a verb (or sense of a verb) is transitive or *intransitive.* Many verbs can appear to govern two objects, a direct one and an indirect one (*they gave her an apple*). These are called DITRANSITIVE verbs.

intrench. See EM- AND IM-, EN-AND IN-.

intrigue (verb). **1** The inflected forms are *intrigues, intrigued, intriguing.*

2 *The (non-)issue.* Readers may be surprised to discover that this word raises any issues, apart from spelling. The issue it raises can be safely ignored, but the word's history provides an interesting excursus on how meanings evolve, and on how people in general, not usage pundits, help them evolve. The main current meaning of *intrigue* is 'arouse the curiosity or interest of', e.g. *he's an intriguing character.* This meaning is first attested from 1894, but it clearly flourished so vigorously thereafter that Fowler (1926) declared it to be a literary critics' word 'of no merit whatever except that of unfamiliarity to the English reader' and a Gallicism. Fowler could not see why *fascinate, mystify, interest,* and *pique* were not adequate for the task: he might also have mentioned *absorb, captivate, charm, enchant, enthral, transfix.* After him, several critics poured scorn on the word in its newly acquired meaning, including Partridge in 1957: 'Such words as ... "to be intrigued" for "deeply or much interested" ... have degenerated from definite sense to indefinite nonsense.' But none of the near-synonyms mentioned quite captures the shades of meaning suggested by *intrigue,* since something which *intrigues* us puzzles and fascinates us at the same time, and impels us to find out more. Hence the word's usefulness. It would be difficult and pointless labour to replace it in most of the following examples: *As an artist, I am intrigued by this idea*—*Art Business News,* 2005; *Even more intriguing than the sociology of fashion is its psychology*—*Observer,* 1974; *She created a film which was memorable, intriguing and moving*—*Listener,* 1982; *We are in turn sympathetic, intrigued, shocked, entertained—but oh the yearning for the world she magically conjured*—A. Huth, 1992.

3 *Previous history. Intrigue* is a standard example of a word of long standing (first recorded in 1612) that was adopted from French into English initially in the main meaning it had in its language of origin, namely 'to trick, deceive, cheat', e.g. *He that trusteth to a Greeke, Shall be intreaged, and still to seeke.* It then branched out in various ways, especially in the direction of erotic intimacy ('to carry on a secret amour') and of underhand plotting ('to employ secret means to bring about some desired end'): *He had intrigued with a Vestal virgin*—J. A. Froude, 1879; *They tell me that the Queen is now intriguing with Mirabeau*—G. Morris, 1791. This last meaning, of course, still coexists with the meaning discussed at 2.

introit. The pronunciation /ˈɪntrɔɪt/ (two syllables) is ousting the older pronunciation with three /ɪnˈtrəʊɪt/.

introvert. See EXTROVERT.

intrusive r is the insertion of the sound of an unwritten *r* between one vowel sound and another, as in *draw-r-ing* for *drawing* and *umbrella-r-organization* for *umbrella* *organization*. Though much criticized, it is common even in received pronunciation and follows the pattern of linking *r* in words ending in an *r* that is only pronounced when a vowel follows, as in *far away*. See LAW AND ORDER; LINKING R.

intrust. See EM- AND IM-, EN-AND IN-.

intuit (verb). An 18c. back-formation from *intuition*, it seems to be largely the preserve of writers, literary critics, and those concerned with the workings of the mind, such as philosophers and psychologists. *Intuit* turns up frequently, for example, in the works of Iris Murdoch and of A. S. Byatt. Examples: *Jenkin did not say any of this, but Gerard intuited it behind some clumsy expressions of sympathy and was irritated*—I. Murdoch, 1987; *As Browning was six years younger than his wife Elizabeth Barrett, he may well have feared that he would one day act as the wife intuits her husband will act*—*N&Q*, 1989; *Maud decided she intuited something terrible about Cropper's imagination from all this*—A. S. Byatt, 1990.

intuition, instinct. Most of Fowler's (1926) elegant, original entry, retained verbatim by every editor since then, follows in section 1. Section 2 is an edited version of Burchfield's comment, with examples added. **1** The word *intuition* being both in popular use and philosophically important, a statement of its meaning, adapted from the *OED*, may be welcome. The etymological but now obsolete sense is simply inspection (Latin *tuērī* 'to look'): *A looking-glass becomes spotted and stained from their only intuition* [i.e., if they so much as look in it]—O. Feltham, 1627–77. With the schoolmen it was 'The spiritual perception or immediate knowledge, ascribed to angelic and spiritual beings, with whom vision and knowledge are identical': *St Pauls faith did not come by hearing, but by intuition and revelation*—J. Taylor, 1660.

In modern philosophy it is 'The immediate apprehension of an object by the mind without the intervention of any reasoning process': *What we feel and what we do, we may be said to know by intuition*—J. Priestley, 1782; or again (with exclusion of one or other part of the mind) it is 'Immediate apprehension by the intellect alone', as in *The intuition by which we know what is right and what is wrong, is clearer than any chain of historic reasoning* (W. E. H. Lecky, 1865), or 'Immediate apprehension by sense', as in *All our intuition takes place by means of the senses only* (tr. of Kant, 1819).

Finally, in general use, it means 'Direct or immediate insight', as in *Rashness if it fails is madness, and if it succeeds is the intuition of genius* (J. A. Froude, 1879). How closely this last sense borders on *instinct* is plain if we compare *A miraculous intuition of what ought to be done just at the time for action* (N. Hawthorne, 1851) with *It was by a sort of instinct that he guided this open boat through the channels* (William Black, 1873). One of the *OED*'s definitions of *instinct*, indeed, is: 'intuition; unconscious dexterity or skill'; and whether one word or the other will be used is often no more than a matter of chance.

2 In psychological and philosophical terms, the differences between the two words remain important and continue to be topics for perpetual discussion. To laypeople it matters little whether *intuition* is restricted to 'angelic and spiritual beings'. Rather, they perceive it as a valuable faculty possessed by human beings alone, and proverbially by women, meaning 'immediate apprehension by the mind *without reasoning*'. *Instinct*, by contrast, is 'an innate, typically fixed pattern of behaviour in animals in response to certain stimuli', e.g. *the homing instinct*; and a similar property in human beings to act without conscious intention. Animals cannot reason, it is argued, but have only *instincts*; human beings have both *instincts* and *intuitions*.

Distinctions as clear-cut as those stated above mean that the two words follow their own logic in general use, as the *OEC* data shows, but occasionally overlap. In particular, as grammatical subjects both words *tell* and *guide* people and *suggest* what to do; and as grammatical objects people can *possess, lack, trust*, or *hone* either. As superior, if not 'angelic and spiritual', beings, mothers, the *OEC* suggests, have both *instincts* and *intuitions*, but journalists exist on a simpler plane, being associated only with *instinct*. Readers might enjoy pondering whether one word can replace the other in the examples that follow. (intuition) *A student's intuition moves far more swiftly than can an instruction manual, and I believe that self-tuition is the finest form of education*—R. Brindle Smith, 1986; *Whatever that small voice of intuition was telling her about her destiny, common-sense decreed that the Prince already had a full hand of potential suitors*—A. Morton, 1993; *Decisions based on guesses and intuition are often horribly wrong*—*Golf Digest*, 2004; (instinct) *Blythswood Square, once home of the infamous poisoner Madaleine Smith, and latterly, numerous other ladies with hearts of loose change and the instincts of a blushing tarantula*—E. Chisnall, 1989; *Running out was totally unprofessional, but she had acted purely on instinct*—J. Evans, 1993; *In general you have to trust your own instincts. If something sounds too good to be true then it invariably is*—*Sunday Business Post*, 2001.

intwine. See EM- AND IM-, EN-AND IN-.

inure, enure. The second form of the word has some currency in law in the sense 'to take effect, to come into operation', but even in law the form *inure* is the more usual of the two (*the damages must inure to the exclusive benefit of the widow and children*—Garner, 1987). In its other senses, especially in the passive followed by the preposition *to*, 'to accustom (a person) to something unpleasant', *inure* is the normal spelling.

inveigle. The recommended pronunciation is /ɪnˈveɪgəl/ rather than /ɪnˈviːgəl/, but both pronunciations are in standard use.

inventor. So spelt, not *-er*.

inventory. Pronounced /ˈɪnvəntəri/ in BrE, and /ˌ-tɔri/ in AmE, and by some BrE speakers who don't know any better.

inversion. 1 In grammar, *inversion* is the process by which the normal order of words is reversed. The normal order in English is subject/verb/object (SVO) or subject/verb/complement (SVC). This is reversed in questions (*Do you play football on Saturdays?*) or by putting the complement (or part of it) first in the sentence, often for emphasis (*On Saturdays, we play football*).

2 For native speakers such *inversions* are for the most part routine and pass virtually without notice. Some of the conditions in which *inversion* is usual or standard are:

(*a*) In the formulaic setting down of direct speech: *'Hey!'* shouted Mrs. House, *who sat inside with her jumpsuit around her knees*—*New Yorker*, 1992. But this is optional: *'I was out in the orchards a while back,'* Milton said—W. Trevor, 1992.

(*b*) To give prominence to a particular word or words, a technique often known as 'fronting': Trusting *she had been, she who had been reared in the bosom of suspicion*—M. Drabble, 1987; Deprived *all the rest of us are*—D. Lessing, 1988; Most notable *among the Bodleian's Gibson manuscripts are two volumes of collections for the edition of Camden's* Britannia—*Bodl. Libr. Rec.*, 1992.

(*c*) To obtain contrast or parallelism: To Laura, Mrs. Laughlin said, *'Mr House loves birds. He builds them houses in his spare time.'* To him, she said, *'You'll have to cultivate a taste for squirrels.'*—*New Yorker*, 1992.

(*d*) After negatives: *Yet never before* had I seen *anything so scarlet and so black*—J. M. Coetzee, 1990; *she said she wouldn't come to the party, nor* did she; *As Ernst Mayr has pointed out, seldom* can biology boast *the certainty of absolute laws*—*Dædalus*, 1986.

(*e*) In sentences led by an adverb or an adverbial phrase: *Up* stood Joe—M. Bail, 1975; *Up and down the stoep* struts Klein-Anna mastering the shoes— J. M. Coetzee, 1977.

(*g*) After *so*, particularly when followed by an adjective, as in the second example: *So* didst thou travel *on life's common way*—Wordsworth; *He had hardly been aware, so nervous* was he, *of what he had been saying*—P. Carey, 1988.

(*h*) Mostly in informal contexts, in a delayed anaphoric *do/did* or *is/was/were* clause: *One of life's battlers,* was Raelene—M. Eldridge, 1984; *She enjoyed a laugh,* did Lilian—M. Drabble, 1987.

(*i*) In conditional clauses which omit the conjunctions *if* or *whether*: Were this done, *we would retain a separate Bar with skill*—*Times*, 1986; *Statistically, afterworlds*—be they *Christian, Greek, Pharaonic—must be populated almost entirely by children*—P. Lively, 1987.

(*j*) In certain kinds of comparative (followed by *than*) clauses: *Poland's power structure included neither more nor fewer Jews than* did the power structure *in Rumania or in Hungary*—*Dædalus*, 1987.

(*k*) Poetical inversion: His soul *proud science never taught to stray*—Pope; *But uglier yet* is the Hump *we get From having too little to do*—Kipling.

3 Fowler (1926) provided a list of examples to show that inversion is often 'ugly, and that resort to it is the work of the unskilful writer'. His examples come from a flowery journalistic style which used inversion in inappropriate contexts. It has largely vanished, but is not entirely dead: He it was that *scored more goals than anyone else in the World Cup*—S. Barnes, *Times,* 1987 (It was he who). Another typical modern inversion is putting the complement before the verb: Great literature it's not, *but ... it's short, pithy*—*The Face,* 1987 (It's not great literature). Whether such inversions as these last ones serve any useful purpose is, of course, debatable.

inverted commas. See QUOTATION MARKS.

investigative. In BrE this is normally stressed on the second syllable, /ɪn'vɛstɪgətɪv/, with the fourth syllable pronounced indistinctly as a schwa. In AmE it is pronounced with a secondary stress, making /-geɪtɪv/ rhyme with *native*. This looks likely to be another word whose British pronunciation will give way to an American one, as *resource* and *research* already have.

investigator. So spelt, not *-er.*

investor. So spelt, not *-er.*

invidious. See INSIDIOUS, INVIDIOUS.

invite (noun). A classic example of a word that seems to have been in continuous use beside *invitation* since the mid-17c. but has never quite made its way into uncriticized neutral use. It must have been known to Dr Johnson but he excluded it from his *Dictionary* (1755). It is also not listed in 'a new edition' (1863) of Charles Richardson's *Dictionary*. It was admitted to the *OED* (1901), labelled *colloq.* Fowler (1926) said that 'it has never, even as a colloquialism, attained to respectability; after 250 years of life, it is less recognized as an English word than *bike*.' Getting on for a century later, dictionaries such as *ODO, Macmillan,* and *Collins* concur in marking it 'informal'. Examples: *Is it just an invite from the colonel for a working week-end?*—*Listener,* 1968; *The four detectives didn't await an invite into the house*—G. F. Newman, 1970; *He scoffs, indicating the dodgier invites entreating his attendance at this or that launch*—*Sunday Express Mag.,* 1987; *He knows a particularly good printer who did the invites for his cousin's wedding*—*Precision Marketing,* 1989.

invoke (verb). The corresponding adjective is **invocable** (not *invokable*).

involve (verb). **1** Use a short o, i.e. /ɒ/, in words ending in *-olve* (*absolve, dissolve, evolve, resolve, revolve, revolver,* etc.).

2 Several critics have censured the use of *involve* to mean 'include as a necessary or integral part' (*the work involves travelling*) and when it means 'to cause to participate' (*we want to involve the whole community*). Before condemning such uses of the verb, frequent though they are, readers are advised to bear in mind that in the 600 years since it entered the language, *involve* has been current in numerous reflections and extensions, including figurative ones, of the original meanings of Latin *involvere* 'to wrap up, envelop, entangle'. It is all a matter of the degree of envelopment or entanglement. Examples: (= envelop) *I saw Fog only, the great tawny weltering fog, Involve the passive city*—E. Barrett Browning, 1856; (= intertwine) *Our misfortunes were involved together*—L. Sterne, 1768; (= beset) *The numerous difficulties in which this question is involved*—B. Jowett, 1875; (= entangle in a difficulty of some kind) *Mr. Muller had been involved in financial difficulties*—A. W. W. Dale, 1898; (= to contain explicitly) *Every argument involves some assumptions*—B. F. Westcott, 1892; (= to include or affect in its operation) *It will be held a worthy subject of consideration what are the political interests involved in such accumulation*—Ruskin, 1857. The idiomatic nature of *No other vehicle was involved,* as the police (and journalists) describe a one-vehicle accident, can hardly be questioned. Nor can that of *He was involved with* [i.e. was having an affair with] *the hotelier's wife,* or of *He became deeply involved in the conspiracy at an early stage.* Something of the primary sense of the word has survived in each of these examples.

Nevertheless, a word of caution should be added. It is a tainted word in the sense that it is widely believed that other words are available to replace it. Some typical examples of uses rejected in other usage guides: *A collision took place involving a private motor vehicle and a lorry* (between); *There was no reduction last year in the number of cases involving cruelty to horses* (of); *Everyone involved in the demonstration* (taking part in); *The cost involved would be excessive* (omit *involved*). It is easy to become *involved* in an argument about such substitutions and rewritings. The best advice, perhaps, is to use the verb sparingly and with reasonable caution.

inward, inwards. The correct form for the adjective is inward (*inward investment, journey, migration*), but inward and inwards are both used for the adverb, with a preference for inwards in British English and *inward* in North American English. Occasionally *inwards* is used by mistake as an adjective. Examples: *Our instructor starts us on snowplough turns (with the tips of the skis pointing inwards)—Observer*, 1978 (BrE); *Do not let your knees collapse inward; keep them in line with the second toe—Men's Fitness*, 2003 (AmE); **I hear how expanding Heathrow will increase income from tourism and inwards investment—Croydon Guardian*, 2003.

inwrap. The more usual form is *enwrap*. See EM- AND IM-, EN-AND IN-.

iodine. Pronounced either as /ˈʌɪədiːn/ or /-dɪn/; AmE /ˈʌɪədʌɪn/ or /-dɪn/.

-ion and -ment. As formative elements in English, the relationship is complex. Superficially, it is clear that some verbs form nouns of action in *-ion*: thus *abolish → abolition, inflict → infliction*, and *pollute → pollution*; while others form nouns of action in *-ment*: e.g. *achieve → achievement, assign → assignment, manage → management*, and *punish → punishment*. This is a useful distinction as far as it goes. The neatness of such a relationship, however, is misleading and will not stand up to historical examination. Some of the formations are not governed by arrangements in English but by the forms that already existed in Old French. There are various chronological considerations (see below). And a small number of the contrasting forms stand side by side in the language but with differences of meaning. Note, first, that whereas *abolishment* and *abolition* and *admonishment* and *admonition* exist, they have unequal currency in current English. The lack of parallelism is brought out also by the non-existence of *inflictment* and *pollutement* on the one hand, and the non-existence now of *punition* on the other (though it was in use from the 15c. to the 19c.).

Two main waves. Nouns of action in *-ment* entered the language in two main periods: (i) (from Anglo-French) *abridgement, accomplishment, commencement*, etc.; (ii) in the 16c., (from French verbs) *banishment, enhancement*, etc.; (from native verbs) *acknowledgement, amazement, atonement*, etc. New formations in *-ment* after the 16c. are relatively rare except for words beginning with *en-* (e.g. *enlightenment*, 17c.) or *be-* (e.g. *bedevilment*, 19c.). The affix has scarcely been drawn on in the 20c.

Differences of meaning. A small number of verbs have corresponding nouns of action in both *-ion* and *-ment*. Thus *commit* corresponds both to *commission* (first 15c.) and *commitment* (17c.); and *excite* corresponds both to *excitation* (15c.) and *excitement* (17c., but its main current sense not until the 19c.). Both pairs of nouns have followed their own complicated tracks as the centuries passed, as a glance at the *OED* will show. All that one can say is that these paths have been asymmetrical.

-ion and -ness. Not surprisingly, the relationship of pairs of words in *-ion* and *-ness* differs from that of -ION AND -MENT in several respects. First, *-ness* is the suffix commonly attached to adjectives to form nouns expressing a state or condition: e.g. *bitter → bitterness, dark → darkness, dry → dryness, persuasive → persuasiveness*. In this function it vies with formations in *-ity*: e.g. *certain → certainty* (occasionally *certainness*), *serviceable → serviceability* (occasionally *serviceableness*). Secondly, *-ness*, unlike *-ment*, is still a living suffix, with at any rate the capability of being added to any new adjective. Thirdly, a reasonable number of the possible pairs have come to be used with different meanings, the forms in *-ion* likely to denote 'the act or process of—', and those in *-ness* more likely to denote 'the quality of being —'. Compare, for example, the following pairs: *abstraction ~ abstractness, consideration ~ considerateness, correction ~ correctness, indirection ~ indirectness*. The subtlety of the relationship between seemingly similar affixes is nowhere more clearly seen than in the groups briefly discussed in this and the article on -ION AND -MENT. The wonder is that, by and large, the correct choice of the possible forms is made by standard speakers, for the most part naturally with unawareness of the lexical complexities involved. See CONCISENESS.

Iran. Pronounced /ɪˈrɒːn/ and /ɪˈran/ and in AmE sometimes also /ʌɪˈran/.

Iranian. The more common British pronunciation is /ɪˈreɪnɪən/, but in AmE /ɪˈrɒːnɪən/ seems to be more usual. A pronunciation with initial /ʌɪ-/ is also found in AmE.

Iraq. The standard pronunciation in BrE is /ɪˈrɑːk/; hence (a native or inhabitant) *Iraqi* /ɪˈrɑːki/. In AmE /ɪˈrak/ and /ɪˈraki/ seem to be more usual; also, less commonly, with initial /ʌɪ-/.

irascible. So spelt, not *-able*. See -ABLE, -IBLE 8.

Irene. The name of the Greek goddess of peace is always pronounced as three syllables, /ʌɪˈriːni/: it is derived from Gk εἰρήνη 'peace'. Traditionally, when used as a Christian name in English, it was pronounced in the same manner, that is with three syllables. But nowadays most Irenes call themselves /ˈʌɪriːn/.

iridescent. So spelt (being from Latin *īris, īrid-* 'rainbow'), not *irri-*.

iron. For *the Iron Duke, Lady, Maiden*, see SOBRIQUETS.

iron curtain. First recorded in 1794 of a curtain of iron which could be lowered as a safety device between the stage and the auditorium in a theatre, it soon (1819–) began to be used of any impenetrable barrier. Its classic use in the 20c. was of 'a barrier to the passage of information, etc., at the limit of the sphere of influence of the Soviet Union'. The phrase was first used in this sense in 1920 by Mrs Philip Snowden (*We were behind the 'iron curtain' at last!*), but the *locus classicus* was a speech by Winston Churchill at Westminster College, Fulton, USA in 1946 (*From Stettin, in the Baltic, to Trieste, in the Adriatic, an iron curtain has descended across the Continent*). With the dismantling of the Berlin Wall in 1989, and the breaking up of the Soviet Union, the phrase has lost its usefulness except as a potent reminder of a major confrontation between the great powers for nearly half a century.

ironic, ironical. 1 *Ironic* or *ironical*? The longer form is dozens of times less frequent than the shorter one. Factors governing its choice seemingly include the rhythm of the sentence and the shape of adjacent words. Both mean (*a*) using or characterized by irony, i.e. relying for its effect on a contrast between the apparent and the intended meaning of a *word, smile, look, laugh*, etc.: e.g. *If there was anything ironic in my meaning, it was levelled at your readers, not at you*—Horace Walpole, 1788; *She gave an ironical laugh as she looked at Guy*—O. Manning, 1977. (*b*) that uses or is addicted to irony: *Ostrowski was dignified, Lelewel ironical and inflexible*—W. H. Kelly, 1848.

2 Both words are now increasingly used to mean simply 'odd, strange, paradoxical', particularly in the phrase *it is ironic that*, a use with which many people have found and still find fault. The word became a usage superstar after Canadian singer Alanis Morissette had a huge hit with a song entitled '*Ironic*' (1995). Its lyrics consist of supposedly ironic situations, almost none of which could be considered *ironic* in any traditional sense. Ms Morissette consequently came in for flak over her misuse of the word. For example, '*It's like rain on your wedding day*' may be disappointing, distressing, or just plain unlucky, but whether it is ironic or not depends on the circumstances. It might conceivably be ironic if, let us suppose, the bride and groom lived in a part of the country which had the highest rainfall, and had specifically arranged to get married in a church in an altogether different region which was famous for being dry. While the song may not constitute a crash course in the finer points of literary terminology, it is a comprehensive catalogue of the uses to which *ironic* can now be put in its vague, watered down newer meanings. As Burchfield wrote almost 20 years ago, 'This weakened use looks as if it has come to stay.' In any case, since IRONY is such a complex topic, as the entry on it in this book suggests, it is hardly surprising that people have attached different meanings to it. *ODO* sums up this new use rather neatly: 'happening in a way contrary to what is expected, and typically causing wry amusement because of this.'

Further examples: *It is paradoxical, 'ironical' as people say today, that the constitution should bestow this power on someone who laments constitutionitis in others*—*Observer*, 1987; *It is ironic that such a beautiful orderly house should be the setting of our messy little farce*—Simon Mason, 1990; *It is somewhat ironic that the two British politicians whose deaths received the widest and most sympathetic coverage last year were hereditary peers. At a time when the Blair Government is anxious to destroy all the political influences of the hereditary peers, people were reminded of the tremendous role they had played in public life*—*Contemporary Review*, 2002.

ironically. This adverb, frequently followed by *enough*, is now widely used as a sentence adverb (or disjunct, to use a technical term), meaning not much more than 'strangely (enough), paradoxically (enough)'. It seems to have emerged into widespread use from the 1940s onwards, although the earliest *OED* example is by Edith Wharton from 1907: *He had done very little with the opportunity ... What he had done with it ... had landed him, ironically enough, in the ugly impasse of a situation from which no issue seemed possible.* It is subject to the same criticisms as the adjective, but is recognized in this 'weakened' use by the *OED*. These uses, which are well established despite frequent criticism of them, perhaps contain an echo of the concept of dramatic irony, in which an audience is made aware of an act or circumstance that affects the action on stage (or screen) in a way that is unknown to one or more of the participants in the drama. Should you wish to eschew it in writing, *paradoxically*, *curiously*, *unexpectedly*, and *coincidentally* may fit the bill. Examples: (ironically) *Ironically the bombing of London was a blessing to the youthful generations that followed*—I. and P. Opie, 1969; *Less than 0.002 per cent of ... muscle proteins comprise dystrophin, which was why it was overlooked. Ironically, its discoverers believe it is the largest protein molecule in the body*—*Times*, 1987; (ironically enough) *That caged rebuked question Occasionally let out at clambakes or College reunions, and which the smoke-room story Alone, ironically enough, stands up for*—W. H. Auden, 1945; *Ironically enough, the Israeli role in both remains crucial—thus underlining how relevant the idea of 'linkage' is, whatever cynical use Saddam Hussein has tried to make of it*—*Sanity*, 1991.

ironist (one whose works or conversation is characterized by an ironic tone) is the kind of casual formation that could have come into existence at any time since the 16c. (from Gk εἴρων 'dissembler, user of irony' + *-ist*) when IRONY itself came into the language. In fact it is first found in a work of 1727 by Alexander Pope and others.

iron out. The 17c. sense of *iron* (verb) 'to smooth or press with an iron' was occasionally represented as a phrasal verb (*iron out*) in the 19c., but *iron out* started to be used much more frequently in figurative contexts in the 19c. and 20c., especially of the smoothing out of differences of viewpoint. There are limits to its sensible use, if one accepts that the metaphor is not entirely dead. It is not very stylish to speak of ironing out bugs in a new computer (*The new computer was delivered ... last week ... Ironing out the bugs will probably take until the new year*—*Guardian*, 1971), and incongruous to speak of *ironing out bottlenecks* (as Gowers pointed out in 1965).

irony. It should be borne in mind that there are several kinds and degrees of irony. The word was taken into English from Latin *īrōnīa*, from Greek εἰρωνεία, at the beginning of the 16c. in two main senses: (*a*) A figure of speech in which the intended meaning is the opposite of that expressed by the words used; usually in the form of laudatory expressions used to imply condemnation or contempt; (*b*) (in its etymological, ultimately Greek, sense) dissimulation, pretence, especially with reference to the feigned ignorance practised by the Greek philosopher Socrates as a means of confuting an adversary. Type (*b*) is also called *Socratic irony*. A third type, (*c*), is called *dramatic irony* in which the audience or reader knows more about the outcome of a play or an epic poem than the character or characters do because the author has, as it were, taken the audience or reader into his confidence at an early stage. *Dramatic irony* is first recorded in 1907 (in a work by Walter Raleigh, first holder of the chair of English literature at the University of Oxford). It was used as a literary device in Greek drama: as Fowler (1926) expressed it, 'all the spectators ... were in the secret beforehand of what would happen. But the characters, Pentheus and Oedipus and the rest, were in the dark; one of them might utter words that to him and his companions on the stage were of trifling import, but to those who hearing could understand were pregnant with the coming doom.' *Dramatic irony* is much used of certain episodes in *Beowulf*: *The well-known hymn on the loyalty and harmony reigning among the Danes which, in view of the poet's intimations of Hrothulf's treachery ... may be considered as a fine piece of dramatic irony*—A. Bonjour, 1950.

These three types of irony are often further subdivided. Baldick (1990), for example, adduces *verbal irony* (a trivial example is the type *What a lovely day* said when it is actually raining), *structural irony, tragic irony,* and *cosmic irony* in addition to the three types mentioned above. Katie Wales (1989) cites various kinds of *literary irony* from the works of Shakespeare, Fielding, Hardy, Henry James, and Ford Madox Ford. These types and distinctions are matters for professional students of English literature. A typical example: *Irony is often said to be a figure in which the true sense contradicts the literal meaning. But in Swift's subtler irony the meaning need not be opposite exactly, and can be very elusive*—A. Fowler, 1987. The subtle weaving and unravelling of irony in literature and in life are matters of infinite gradations, and no amount of terminology will encompass them all or receive universal acceptance.

irrecognizable, un-. Both were first used in the early 19c. but *unrecognizable* is now the regular form.

irreducible. So spelt, not *-able.* See -ABLE, -IBLE 8.

irrefragable. Stress the second syllable, /ɪˈrɛfrəɡəbəl/.

irrefutable. The traditional pronunciation is /ɪˈrɛfjʊtəbəl/, i.e. stressed on the second syllable, but the form with third-syllable stressing, /ɪrɪˈfjuː-/, is gaining ground.

irregardless raises two questions: does it exist? and should you use it? Despite many people's objections that 'it is not a word', dictionaries, including the *OED,* record it, and it has been in existence since at least 1912. In origin almost certainly a blend of *irrespective* and *regardless,* it has been criticized since its earliest days, and objections to it include the fact that it is a double negative, because it adds the negative prefix *ir-* to a word which already has the negative suffix *-less.* Compared to *regardless* and *irrespective* it is uncommon, and seems to be most at home in North America. Should you use it? Not unless you are of a masochistic bent, for most people will berate you as an illiterate for doing so. It is decidedly non-standard, but nevertheless creeps in to otherwise earnest contexts, e.g. *?This bill will give all couples the same legal rights irregardless of their sexual orientation or marital status*—weblog, 2004 (NZ); *?Hence, in a competitive market . . . only efficient owners and efficient behaviour would be able to survive, irregardless of how the initial distribution of ownership took place—Amer. Jrnl of Economics and Sociology*—2002.

irrelevance, irrelevancy. Both are used with no distinction in meaning, but *irrelevance* is much the more usual of the two. See -CE, -CY.

irrelevant. The *OED* (1901) commented, 'A frequent blunder is *irrevalent.*' It is not that frequent now, but can occasionally be found in print.

irrelevant allusion. It was Fowler (1926) who categorized as 'irrelevant' the allusions discussed below. He thought that those who used them were showing off their superficial knowledge, with scant regard for appropriateness to the context. It is very likely, though unprovable, that fewer people nowadays than in Fowler's time, or even Burchfield's, recognize these phrases as allusions to specific texts: they are surely perceived merely as set phrases, or even clichés. With that in mind, I have left what Burchfield wrote intact, as follows, for readers to enjoy its mordant, academic humour. 'One of the frailties to which we are all prone from time to time is to make an unnecessary allusion to a familiar, often literary, phrase or line. Thus, a writer in the 29 July 1991 issue of the *New Yorker*: *When Switzerland talks about 'being Europe' instead of about 'servicing Europe', you know that there has been a sea change in the way Europeans think about who they are, and what they are, and where they are.* This is, of course, a half-remembered, gauche allusion to Shakespeare's *The Tempest, Nothing of him that doth fade, But doth suffer a Sea-change Into something rich, and strange: Sea-nimphs hourly ring his knell.* Sea changes happen in the context of sea nymphs, not in landlocked Switzerland. Instances of such irrelevance or semi-relevance are not difficult to find. Who has not heard someone say *There is method in my madness* when the madness is not such but merely a surface appearance of irregularity? The allusion is, of course, to Polonius' *Though this be madness, yet there is method in't.* A trade-union strike in early winter automatically produces the headline *A winter of discontent?* in the tabloids, half-echoing Richard III's *Now is the winter of our discontent, Made glorious summer by this sonne of Yorke.* How many times has *light* been described as *religious* as well as *dim,* echoing the passage in Milton's *Il Penseroso, And storied windows richly dight, Casting a dim religious light*? How often has Marcellus' line in *Hamlet, Something is rotten in the state of Denmark,* been echoed down the centuries, when the context is merely something local (far from Denmark) that has a suggestion of moral or social decay? And how often have you said, when leaving a disappointing party or theatrical performance, *Home James, and don't spare the horses* when the vehicle is in fact a car? Our minds are half-filled with irrelevant allusions and with HACKNEYED PHRASES and literary allusions. We live in a world of reduced quotations with the quotation marks removed'.

irremovable. See IMMOVABLE 2.

irreparable /ɪˈrɛpərəbəl/. Loss, damage, or harm that cannot be rectified or made good is *irreparable,* e.g. *I have 13 of the 19 possible side effects which can come from being in contact with sheep dip. Exposure to sheep dip has done my nerves irreparable damage—The Ecologist,* 2001. By contrast, a material object that is badly damaged or badly worn is *unrepairable* (stressed on the third syllable). The adjective irrepairable appears in the *OED* meaning both 'that cannot be physically repaired' and 'irreparable'. Both meanings are marked obsolete. When irrepairable is used nowadays, it seems to be a mistake, e.g. *If it turns out that the allegations are indeed unfounded, irrepairable damage to the reputation of those involved has been done*—weblog, 2006 (AmE).

irreplaceable. So spelt, not *-placable.*

irrepressible, irresistible. So spelt, not *-able.* See -ABLE, -IBLE 8.

irrespective(ly). Dictionaries and grammars do not agree on how to classify *irrespective.* The *ODO* calls it an adjective followed by *of,* meaning 'not taking into account; regardless of', and lists *irrespectively* without definition as its corresponding adverb. The *OED* (1900) says that *irrespective* 'is now chiefly in adverbial construction, qualifying a verb expressed or understood; = *irrespectively.* Const. *of.*' By contrast, Jespersen, *CGEL,* and other grammars treat *irrespective of* as a group preposition or a complex preposition, or as an element introducing a concessive clause (e.g. *irrespective of cost, irrespective of the fact that*). There is no quarrel about usage, just a difference of opinion about terminology, and there is a lot to be said for analysing it as a complex preposition. However, if one follows the *OED* analysis of the phrase as adverbial, one might be tempted to use *irrespectively of,* which does indeed quite often happen. Although that use has a historical pedigree, it sounds distinctly odd and unidiomatic. The use of *irrespectively* on its own as an adverb of manner to mean *disrespectfully* has one 17c. citation in the *OED* and is marked obsolete. Its use in the last example below must therefore be classed as either pretentious or illiterate: Examples: (irrespective of) *People sometimes judge actions to be right irrespective of their consequences*—A. J. Ayer, 1972; *He is fed only to suit his mother's convenience, irrespective of whether he is hungry or not*—A. Storr, 1972; *A great deal of time and energy is given to ensuring that opportunities are given to all boys irrespective of sporting ability—Croydon Guardian,* 2004; (irrespectively of) *The security service must play a role of service to the state and society, irrespectively of the political alignment in Poland*—BBC Summary of World Broadcasts 13 Sept., 1989; *In this case, they are unlikely to judge that the competitor has this atypical attribute, irrespectively of whether they rely on the explicit ad information* [etc.]—*Jrnl Consumer Research,* 1991; (= disrespectfully) **Tyler is my wonderful boyfriend who you irrespectively placed outside—OEC,* 2005.

irresponsible. So spelt, not *-able.* See -ABLE, -IBLE 8.

irresponsive, unresponsive. *Unresponsive* is the standard choice, *irresponsive* very much a minority taste, but perfectly correct.

irreversible. So spelt, not *-able.* See -ABLE, -IBLE 8.

irreversible binomials is the technical term in linguistics for a very interesting and highly idiomatic group of pairs of words which are traditionally linked by *and* or *or* and consist of two words which either have similar, mutually reinforcing, meanings, or are related in other formulaic ways, and whose order cannot be reversed. Gowers (1965) christened them with the now politically incorrect term 'Siamese twins', for want of a suitable technical name.

Examples: (*a*) (used mostly for emphasis) *airs and graces, alas and alack, bag and baggage, betwixt and between, bits and pieces/bobs, fit and well, leaps and bounds, lo and behold, rant and rave, in any shape or form.* These are technically tautological but totally idiomatic. (*b*) Others are fixed collocations, either because one of the components is used in an archaic sense and would not now be understood by itself, or because the combination has acquired a meaning different from that of either component alone. Examples: *at someone's beck and call, chop and change, fair and square, fast and furious, hue and cry, kith and kin, with all one's might and main, odds and ends, part and parcel, go to rack and ruin, no rhyme or reason, spick and span.* (*c*) Others again consist not of synonyms but of associated ideas. Examples: *bill and coo, bow and scrape, bright-eyed and bushy-tailed, flotsam and jetsam, huff and puff, hum and haw, a lick and a promise, loud and clear, nuts and bolts, smoke and mirrors, spit and polish, thick and fast, ways and means.* Or consist of opposites or alternatives: *cut and thrust, fast and loose, hit and miss, hither and thither, by hook or by crook, through thick and thin, to and fro.*

There are various other types, but the examples cited above will perhaps suffice to show that such linked phrases are a significant feature of the language. See COLLOCATION.

irrevocable. Stressed on the second syllable, /ɪˈrɛvəkəbəl/.

irridescent. For this mistaken spelling, see IRIDESCENT.

is.

- **1** The remarkable double *is.*
- **2** *is* and *are* between sentence elements of different number.
- **3** incorrect ellipsis of *is.*
- **4** *is* after a compound subject.
- **5** *is what, is how* following a statement.
- **6** *is* or *has nothing to do with.*
- **7** — *is* —.
- **8** Postponed and repeated *is.*
- **9** *is all.*

1 The remarkable double *is.* For discussion of phrases of the kind *the challenge is, is . . . , the conclusion is, is . . . , the thing is, is . . . ,* etc. See REPETITION 2.

2 *is* and *are* between sentence elements of different number. For example, *more nurses is/are the next item on the agenda.* See AGREEMENT 7; ARE, IS; BE 1.

3 incorrect ellipsis of *is.* See BE 6 (where the example given happens to be of *was,* but the same principle applies).

4 *is* after a compound subject. See AGREEMENT 3 for examples of a composite subject seen as a single concept (e.g. *tarring and feathering*) followed by a singular verb.

5 *is what, is how* following a statement. Within certain limits, and usually in informal contexts, *is how, is what* may follow a preceding statement: (is how) *He is one of God's special children, is how I look at* it—Lee Smith, 1983; (is what) *He's a fucking operator, is what I think*—T. Wolfe, 1987; *One never knows with these lefties, is what I always say*—A. Brink, 1988; *You're wicked, is what you are*—M. Doane, 1988; *You step up to him and you cart him all over the park, is what you* do—S. Fry, 1990.

6 *is* or *has nothing to do with.* The *OED* partially deals with the problem in two entries, which between them make it clear that *to have to do with* means 'to have dealings with, to have relation to' and is an idiom of some antiquity: e.g. *He wolde not haue to doo with svche myscheuous men*—R. Eden, 1555; *Away, I haue nothing to do with thee*—Shakespeare, 1605; *I nevuer had any thing to doe with the said Duke*—J. Wadsworth, 1630; *It has nothing to do with the purpose—Fraser's Mag.*, 1830; *All law has to do with pleasure and pain*—B. Jowett, 1875.

The phrase *to be nothing to* is registered in the sense 'to be insignificant compared to some other person or thing' (*But all this is nothing to that which they both suffered for their conscience*), but there is no sign of *is nothing to do with.* It is perplexing to find that this use of *is* for *has* is neglected in some major works of reference, but help is at hand in Jespersen (1909–49, vii, § 15.83). First, he gives examples of *has,* including one from Shakespeare's *Venus and Adonis* (*Beautie hath naught to do with such foule fiends*) and another from Dickens's *Nicholas Nickleby* (*that has nothing to do with his blustering just now*). And then he goes on to say that 'in recent use we find also *is, was,* instead of *has, had.* Perhaps this may have started with the rapid pronunciation of *has* (*what's that to do with me?*) which was interpreted as *'s = is*; at any rate it is now extremely frequent in colloquial English.' Examples: *Besides, what I have had is nothing to do with it*—D. Jerrold, 1846; *This is nothing to do with your life*— H. S. Merriman, 1896. Fowler (1926) made out a stirring case for the recognition of the type with *is:* 'Most of us, when we have occasion to repel an impertinent question, and are not in the mood for weighing words in the scales of grammar, feel that *That is nothing to do with you* expresses our feelings better than *That has* etc.; that is to say, the instinctive word is *is,* not *has.'*

Despite the strength of Fowler's feeling about the matter, the *OEC* data shows that *it is nothing to do with* remains a minority choice, outweighed more than a dozen times over by *it has nothing to do with.* Moreover, its stronghold seems to be British English, and it is rare elsewhere. A few examples: (has nothing to do with) *The stark fact is that the Constitution has nothing whatever to do with issues of sexual morality*—R. Bork, 1990 (AmE); *The intellectual dishonesty that saturates the Whitney has nothing to do with lack of scholarship—Connoisseur,* 1990 (AmE); *Animal phobias have nothing to do with physical danger—Daily Tel.,* 1991 (BrE); *I'm often told that anti-Semitism has nothing to do with racism—TES,* 1991 (BrE); (is nothing to do with) *My settlement was nothing to do with the loss of salary—Sunday Business Post,* 2003*; Oliver Stone's The Doors was nothing to do with the music and everything to do with the lifestyle—Film Inside Out,* 2000; *GM crops are nothing to do with tackling hunger and everything to do with expanding corporate control of agriculture and food—Socialist Worker,* 2003.

7 — *is* —. This is apparently a modern type used for emphasis with the force of 'really, after all'. Examples: *A job's a job, that was the* thing—M. Gee, 1985; *It wasn't exactly* The Old Man and the Sea, *but reading was reading and he was probably too old, at fifteen, to accept her censorship*—M. Leland, 1987; *She worried about Colin's wrist in the cast but a trip out was a trip out, and the day mustn't be spoiled*—N. Virtue, 1990. A different kind of emphasis or insistence is the double repetition of a noun in a formulaic type established by Gertrude Stein's *Rose is a rose is a rose is a rose: There is only one art form common to all sorts and conditions of people: the poster ... a hoarding is a hoarding is a hoarding—Guardian,* 1970.

8 Postponed and repeated *is.* This somewhat informal type has been in use since the early 19c. Examples: *He's a sad pickle is Sam!*—M. Mitford, 1828; *And Miss Rose got awfully angry, and she's clever, is my Miss Rose*—G. Meredith, 1861; *Yes, he is true to type, is Mr Heard*—R. Knox, 1932.

9 *is all.* Used at the end of a sentence, often reinforcing the regret or sadness of the statement just made, this idiomatic expression sounds dialectal in origin, but is now found in standard (esp. American) fictional sources: *'Looks like you're into purple,' he says to her ... 'It's my favorite color, is all,' she says—New Yorker,* 1987; *No one's interested, is all.*—M. Doane, 1988; *Sometimes,' says Tillie, 'God just wants to make sure He's got your attention, is all.'—New Yorker,* 1989; *'I don't know why you always spite me by loving that house so.' 'I don't say I love it. I was born there, is* all.'—J. Updike, 1993.

isagogic. For pronunciation, see GREEK G.

-ise. 1 This spelling is compulsory in the following words, most of which are derived from French (especially from the French past participle ending *-is*). All are pronounced with final /-ʌɪz/. *advertise, advise, apprise, arise, chastise, circumcise, comprise, compromise, demise, despise, devise, dis(en)franchise, disguise, enfranchise, enterprise, excise, exercise, franchise, improvise, incise, merchandise, prise (open), revise, supervise, surmise, surprise, televise.*

2 *-ise* is also compulsory in a few French loanwords that are pronounced with final /-iːz/: *chemise, expertise, reprise.* It is also compulsory in the noun *premise,* and in *promise* (noun and verb).

3 On the general question of the spelling of verbs ending in the sound /-ʌɪz/, see -IZE, -ISE IN VERBS.

4 For the coining of verbs in *-ize,* see -IZE, -ISE IN VERBS.

island, isle. Etymologically speaking, appearances can be deceptive. *Isle* is not a shortened form of *island*: in fact the two words are etymologically unconnected. *Island* comes from Old English *ī(e)gland,* later *īgland,* from OE *ī(e)g* 'island'+ *land. Isle* was originally written *ile* or *ille,* and was a loanword from Old French words with the same spelling, themselves a reduced form of Latin *īnsula*. The present spelling *isle* began to be used from the 15c. onwards, the *s* being inserted in reference to Latin *īnsula*. The spelling *iland* (found e.g. in Spenser, and the AV) followed suit by introducing an *s*, and the modern spelling was established as the norm by 1700.

-ism and -ity. 1 *-ism* is a prolific, still potent, suffix (representing French *-isme*, Latin *-ismus*, Greek -ισμός) in English, forming (*a*) nouns of action from verbs; a typical example is Greek βαπτίζειν 'to baptize', βαπτισμός 'baptism': similarly English *criticize* ~ *criticism*, *plagiarize* ~ *plagiarism*, etc.; (*b*) similarly formed, expressing the action or conduct of a class of persons, but with no accompanying verb, e.g. *heroism*, *patriotism*; (*c*) forming the name of a system of theory or practice, religious, political, etc., e.g. *Buddhism*, *Judaism*; (*d*) a subclass of (*c*) forming class names for doctrines or principles, e.g. *agnosticism*, *atheism*, *Communism*, *realism*; (*e*) forming terms denoting a characteristic feature, esp. of language, e.g. *Gallicism*, *Scotticism*; (*f*) a pathological condition, e.g. *alcoholism*, *Parkinsonism*; (g) in the second half of the 20c. forming 'politically correct' terms such as *ableism* (prejudice against disabled people by able-bodied people), *speciesism* (prejudice or discrimination of one species over another, esp. of the human species in the exploitation of animals): see POLITICALLY CORRECT. The suffix is so prevalent in English words that, since the 17c., it has often been used as a noun in its own right: e.g. *The proletarian Isms are very much alike*—G. B. Shaw, 1928; *Democracy could become more dynamic than Fascism or Communism or any other ism or ideology*—J. S. Huxley, 1944.

2 *-ity* is a rich formative element in nouns expressing a state or condition, (*a*) from adjectives of various kinds, e.g. *absurd* ~ *absurdity*, *curious* ~ *curiosity*, *modern* ~ *modernity*; (*b*) specifically forming abstract nouns from comparatives, e.g. *inferiority*, *majority*, *minority*. It does not follow that all adjectives have a corresponding abstract noun in *-ity*: thus *furious* but no **furiosity* (the asterisk is conventionally used here to indicate non-existent formations), *flat* but *flatness*, not **flatity*. Also the relationship between pairs that do exist is not, in word-formation terms, always exactly the same: thus *voracious*, if it followed the model of *curious*, would produce not *voracity* but **voraciosity*; *grave* loses its *-e* and becomes *gravity*; *divine* with a long second syllable produces *divinity* with a short one, but both *obese* and *obesity* have /iː/ in their second syllable.

3 The absence of firm rules has meant that over the centuries pairs of *-ism* and *-ity* words have come into the language, usually with different meanings. Thus *community* and *Communism* share the basic notion of Latin *commūnis* 'common', but are widely different in meaning. There are many such pairs in the language, some of which are treated at their alphabetical place in this book, e.g. *barbarism*, *barbarity*; *fatalism*, *fatality*; *humanism*, *humanity*; *Latinism*, *Latinity*; *legalism*, *legality*; *liberalism*, *liberality*; *modernism*, *modernity*; *realism*, *reality*; *spiritualism*, *spirituality*. The differences of meaning are more or less self-evident.

4 The *OEC* shows that dozens of words ending in *-ity* were coined in the 20c. including the much-maligned Eurojargon *subsidiarity* (formed as a rendering of German *Subsidiarität* in 1936, not as a direct formation on the adjective *subsidiary*) and *additionality*. See also -TY AND -NESS.

issue (noun). Vehement objections are often raised to the use of *issue* (often in the plural) in contexts where it is probable that the word *problem* would previously have appeared, e.g. *a small number of users are experiencing connectivity issues*. This trend seems to be a development from *issues* being employed, originally in 1980s AmE, to mean 'emotional or psychological difficulties', e.g. *emotions and intimacy issues that were largely dealt with through alcohol*. Some people see both this psychological application and the broader one as unnecessary euphemism: an *issue* somehow sounds more positive than a *problem*, more easily capable of resolution.

Others insist that the proper meaning of *issue* is restricted to 'a topic of interest or discussion', as in *The issues which arise are issues of principle*; *No amount of appeals to the government for education reforms will resolve the fundamental issues at stake*. However, if *issues* are defined as 'topics of interest or discussion' they will often be questions that need to be decided, and, as the *OED* puts it, 'the decision of which involves important consequences', e.g.

And scientific progress is a force that's apt to create, rather than solve, thorny ethical issues; For at its heart this election has highlighted the thorny, divisive issue of what that flag stands for. From there it seems a short step for *issue* to invade the semantic territory of *problem.*

Whatever the reasons for this burgeoning use of *issue,* it seems unstoppable. Pessimists and purists will decry it as namby-pambyism and pedants will call it 'bad grammar'; the majority will bow to linguistic peer pressure. Cf. ADDRESS.

issue (verb). Construed with *with,* and having the meaning 'to supply, esp. officially' (*issued them with passports*), this use of *issue* has passed from strong condemnation to acceptance (at least in BrE) in the course of the 20c. It is interesting to look back to the comment in Fowler (1926): 'The military construction, to issue a person with a thing (*The Company was issued with two gas-masks per man*), on the analogy of *supply* and *provide,* though much popularized by the war, is not to be recommended.' This use is said to be not current in AmE, but it turns up occasionally: e.g. *People in Russia's second city—hit by severe food shortages—are issued with coupons which entitle them to basic foodstuffs at subsidized state prices*—Chicago Tribune, 1991. In such circumstances the normal construction in AmE is *issue* + a direct object.

issue (noun and verb). The pronunciation /ˈɪʃuː/ is recommended, rather than /ˈɪsjuː/.

-ist, -alist, etc. **1** *-ist* forming agent nouns from verbs in *-ize,* e.g. *baptist* ~ *baptize, dogmatist* ~ *dogmatize,* answers to French *-iste,* Latin *-ista,* and Greek -ιστής, and is richly productive in English. There are several types: (*a*) Forming a simple agent noun and usually having an accompanying verb in *-ize* (see above, also *antagonist, apologist, evangelist,* etc.) and an accompanying abstract noun in *-ism* (*antagonism,* etc.); (*b*) designating a person devoted to some art, science, etc., e.g. *archaeologist, economist, dramatist, philologist;* (*c*) designating an adherent of some creed, doctrine, etc., e.g. *atheist, Buddhist, Calvinist, hedonist;* (*d*) modern formations of various kinds, e.g. *balloonist, cyclist, fetishist, finalist.*

2 Most of the *-ist* words have one undisputed form. The main exceptions (with the preferred form placed first) follow. Where neither form is labelled, e.g. educationalist, educationist, both are equally acceptable. *accompanist, accompanyist* (?obs.); *agriculturalist, agriculturist; constitutionalist, constitutionist* (obs.); *conversationalist, conversationist* (?obs.); *diplomat, diplomatist* (?obsolesc.); *educationalist, educationist; egoist, egotist; horticulturist, horticulturalist* (not in *OED* but current since at least 1863); *pacifist, pacificist* (obs.); *separatist, separationist* (obs.); *voluntarist, voluntaryist* (obs.). Note. *Tobacconist* is an irregular late-16c. formation from *tobacco* + *-ist* with insertion of an unetymological *-n-*.

isthmus /ˈɪsməs/. The plural is *isthmuses.*

it.

1 Customary uses.
2 *it* used to highlight a sentence element.
3 Anticipatory *it.*
4 Pleonastic *it.*
5 *it* as a 'prop' in statements of time, etc.
6 *It's I/It's me.*

This article aims to record some of the central uses of the pronoun *it* on the assumption that they are mostly 'known' to native speakers but not in any critically analysed manner. For further uses of *it,* which are very numerous, readers will need to consult the *OED* and *CGEL.*

1 *Customary uses.* To state the obvious first, the pronoun *it* occurs most commonly as subject (*It was an unremarkable incident*), as object (*he took her hand and kissed it*), and as object after a preposition (*she seemed to have forgotten about it*). Its functional forms are the possessive *its* (*the main thrust of any story is to be found in its incidentals*); the abbreviated form *it's* = 'it is' (*It's just for half an hour*); the interrogative *is it?* (*'Where the hell is it?' she said, all patience gone*); the negative interrogative *isn't it?* (*Sickening, isn't it, how we stick together?*); and *it isn't* as an ordinary negative (*It isn't here*).

2 *it* used to highlight a sentence element. *It* is used to introduce an element that is being emphasized or highlighted (the so-called 'cleft' sentence). Various types are shown in the following examples: *Our lives are not worth living* → *It is we whose lives are not worth living; We laughed at you* → *It was we who laughed at you; I met him on Monday* → *It was on Monday that I met him; I've not come to discuss*

Henry but Poppet, your wife → *It isn't Henry I've come to discuss. It's Poppet, your wife.*

3 Anticipatory *it.* 'When the logical subject of a verb is an infinitive phrase, a clause, or sentence, this is usually placed after the verb, and its place before the verb is taken by *it* as "provisional" or "anticipatory" subject' (*OED*). (*a*) An infinitive phrase: *It was difficult to know to what level Moyra would be able to rise*; (*b*) With a clause introduced by *that* expressed or understood (especially frequent with the passive voice in *it is said, believed,* etc., *that*): *It was said that it was a matter of attitude*; *Wasn't it true that we didn't hit it off at first?* When such a *that*-clause is introduced by *it is appropriate, crucial, essential,* etc., the *that*-clause has a *should* construction or a verb in the subjunctive: *it is crucial that you* (*should*) *be home by four.*

4 Pleonastic *it.* In ballads and in rhetorical passages of prose *it* has traditionally been used pleonastically after a noun subject: *The raine it raineth euery day*—Shakespeare, 1601; *This piteous news so much it shocked her*—Wordsworth, 1798. Outside the higher forms of literature this type (e.g. *The bird it flapped its wings and flew off*) is now non-standard or dialectal.

5 *It* as a 'prop' in statements of time, etc. *It* is especially common in statements as to the time of day, season of the year, distance to or from a place, the state of the weather, and so on: *It was morning. Outside, it was cold and sunny; it's three miles from Abingdon.* This impersonal use of *it* is sometimes called a 'prop *it*'.

6 *It's I/ It's me.* For the competing types *It's I* and *It's me,* see CASES 2.

It should perhaps be noted that the majority of the examples in this article have been taken for convenience from Simon Mason's novel *The Great English Nude* (1990) and from 1992 issues of *The New Yorker,* but they could have been drawn from almost any other standard source.

Italian sounds. Loanwords from Italian fall into the usual three broad categories: those still pronounced to resemble the original Italian (*pizzicato, scherzo*), those sometimes pronounced in a largely Anglicized manner (*intaglio, intermezzo*), and those that are fully acclimatized (*umbrella, volcano*). English speakers normally recognize that the vowels of words in the first and second categories are to be pronounced in a 'continental' (i.e. tense, not lax or diphthongal) manner. There is rather less public knowledge of the consonantal sounds of Italian where these differ from English consonantal sounds. Phoneticians can detect subtle differences of aspiration, voicedness, and so on, between the way in which Italian and English speakers pronounce *b, d, f, g,* etc., but these need not concern us here. The consonants that cause difficulty are as follows (the IPA symbols represent the standard Italian pronunciations):

c and *cc* before *e* and *i* = /ʧ/: *cicerone, Cinzano, arancia 'orange', capriccio*
cch = /k/: *Ponte Vecchio*
ch = /k/: *Chianti*
ci before *a, o, u* normally = /ʧ/: *ciao!, cioccolata*
g and *gg* before *e* and *i* = /ʤ/: *generalissimo, viaggio* 'journey'
gh = /g/: *ghetto*
gi before a, o, u normally = /ʤ/ *Giotto, Giovanni*
gl = /lj/: *seraglio*
gn = /nj/: *bagno* 'bath', *signor, gnocchi*
gu = /gw/: *Guelph*
sc before *e* and *i* = /ʃ/ *Fascisti* 'Fascists'
sch = /sk/: *scherzo*
sci before *a, o, u,* normally = /ʃ/: *sciolto* 'loose'
z = /ts/: *scherzo*
zz normally = /ts/: *pizzicato*
zz occasionally = /dz/: *mezzo*

italics. These are *a style of sloping type, like this,* indicated in handwritten or typewritten matter by a single underlining. Italic type is conventionally used in English in a wide range of circumstances, a reasonably full account of which is set down in the *New Hart's Rules,* pp. 20–5, and elsewhere. The more important types are as follows:

Book titles: *David Copperfield, To the Lighthouse.*
Play and film titles: *Hamlet, Gone with the Wind.*
Works of art: Leonardo da Vinci's *Last Supper,* Picasso's *Guernica.*
Long poems which are virtually books in themselves: *The Faerie Queen, Paradise Lost,* and any other poems divided into books or cantos.
Names of periodicals, newspapers, etc.: *London Review of Books, Times Literary Supplement.*
Names of ships (preceded by 'the' in roman type): the *King George V,* the *Ark Royal,* HMS *Dreadnought.*

Stage directions in plays: *Exeunt Don Pedro, Don Iohn, and Claudio.*

Foreign words and phrases which are not fully naturalized in English: *amour propre, jeu d'esprit, ne plus ultra, Weltanschauung*

Words, phrases, or letters mentioned by name: 'The word *loyally* has three *l*s; the sentence adverb *frankly* is the equivalent of the phrase *to be frank.*'

As a method of emphasizing (a device to be used sparingly): 'Oh come now, it can't be *that* bad.'

As a method of distinguishing: 'The question is not whether indexing *can* be automated but whether and why it *should* be.'

itch (verb). **1** Used transitively in the sense 'to cause to itch', *itch* is recorded from the 16c. onwards in all manner of writing, but in BrE it is restricted to informal contexts. It seems to be still standard in AmE. Examples (all the BrE ones being rather literary): *The thick super-salty water of the Mediterranean, which tires and itches the naked eye*—Roy Campbell, 1951 (BrE); *The dice already itch me in my pocket*—L. MacNeice, 1951 (BrE); *I heard those [fruit] flies are coming to hide under your bed tonight—to itch you!*—*New Yorker*, 1990; *the stone seat, whose grittiness pressed through his trousers, itching his thighs*—A. Huth, 1991 (BrE).

2 A more down-market transitive use, restricted to AmE, is 'to scratch (an itchy part of the body)', as in: *Don't itch your leg. You can't do that on stage*—*Chicago Tribune*, 1991.

-ite as an adjective ending is derived chiefly from Latin past participles in *-ītus, -itus,* in which the *i* could be long or short, e.g. *ērudītus* 'erudite', *compositus* 'composite'. The length of the *i* in Latin has long ceased to affect the pronunciation of the English derivatives. The short *i* in *apposite* and *opposite* follows the Latin; that in *definite* does not. The long *i* in *bipartite* and *erudite* follows the Latin; that in *recondite* does not. The separate suffix *-ite* (originally from Greek -ίτης) seen in *anthracite, dynamite, Jacobite*, etc., is always pronounced /ʌɪt/ in English.

its, it's. Just a reminder that *its* is the possessive form of *it* (*the cat licked its paws*) and that *it's* is a shortened form of *it is* (*It's raining again*) or *it has* (*It's come*). See IT 1.

-ity. See -ION AND -NESS; -ISM AND -ITY.

-ize, -ise in verbs. 1 First, we shall put aside verbs which must always be spelt with *-ise*: *advertise, advise*, etc. A list of these is provided s.v. -ISE 1. The American spelling of *analyse, catalyse*, etc., as *analyze, catalyze*, etc., is also a separate matter: see -YSE, -YZE.

2 *Spelling*. (Whatever is said here applies not only to the verbs themselves, but also to derivatives, e.g. *pauperize(d), -ization*. References to *-ize* only should be taken to cover *-ise* too.) The primary rule is that all words of the type *authorize/authorise, civilize/civilise, legalize/legalise,* where there is a choice of ending, may be legitimately spelt with either *-ize* or *-ise* throughout the English-speaking world, except in America, where *-ize* is always used. Oxford University Press and other publishing houses prefer *-ize*; Cambridge University Press and others prefer *-ise*.

The reason there is a choice is that the *-ize* ending, which corresponds to the Greek infinitive ending -ίζειν (Latin *-izāre*), and regardless of whether the particular verb existed in Greek in the same form, has come into English in many cases via Latin and French sources, and in French the spelling has been adapted to *-ise*. A key word showing this line of descent is *baptize*, which answers to Greek βαπτίζειν and Latin *baptīzāre*. But the French opted for *baptiser* and many English writers and publishers have followed suit by writing the word as *baptise*, as with hundreds of other formations of this type. The non-American public are generally aware of the choice, but often mistakenly regard the *-ize* ending as an Americanism; and they find it especially hard to countenance in words which do not have corresponding nouns in *-iz*ation but other forms in which the letter *s* features, such as *criticize* (*criticism*), *hypnotize* (*hypnosis*), and *emphasize* (*emphasis*).

3 *A history of controversy*. As Burchfield (1996) expressed it, there is a 'widespread current belief that new formations of this kind are crude, overused, or unnecessary'. Objecting to *-ize* verbs is nothing new, though: it goes back to at least 1828. Words pilloried in the 19c., include *Americanize, demoralize, deputize*, and *jeopardize*. Today they seem entirely uncontentious, as do a host of indispensable words with centuries-old pedigrees: e.g. *authorize* (first recorded in the 14c.), *characterize* (16c.), *civilize* (17c.), *fossilize* (18c.), *immortalize* (16c.), *memorize* (16c.), *patronize* (16c.), *sterilize* (17c.), *terrorize* (19c.). Nor do people generally object to rather more recent formations such as *computerize* (1960), *deindustralized* (1940), *industrialized* (1882), and *privatize* (1959 in its modern meaning). It seems, then, that the novelty of words ending in *-ize/-ise* may have a major bearing on their acceptability. But the novelty is often an illusion: people still dislike *hospitalize*, though it has been in use for over a century, being first recorded in the *OED* from 1901. The dates of other still disliked words are as follows: *finalize* (1922), *incentivize* (1968), *marginalize* (1970 in its modern meaning, 1822 in a different one), and *prioritize* (1954). One begins to wonder whether it is not the words themselves that irritate, but rather their users, or their typical contexts—business language, officialese, etc.

4 *Size of the issue.* Any feeling that the language is being swamped by new formations in *-ization* and *-ize* is not supported by the facts. For example, the 1997 *Oxford Dictionary of New Words* entered fewer than ten out of a total vocabulary of 2,000 words. A trawl in the *OED* for *-ize* words recorded there as created since 1970 produces the earth-shattering total of . . . two, both of them technical terms: *anonymized* (medicine) and *defamiliarize* (literary criticism).

5 *Verdict.* (i) English already has a large number of established words ending in *-ization* and *-ize* which pass without comment. Any anxieties about new *-ize* verbs have to be set against the long history and distinctive usefulness of such formations. (ii) Often verbs ending in *-ize* are economical: a single word encapsulates a more complex idea, e.g. *synthesize* 'to produce (a compound, especially an organic compound) by synthesis; *securitize* 'to convert (assets, especially loans) into securities, usually for the purpose of raising capital by selling them to investors'. For that reason, they are very useful in technical fields. (iii) Some newcomers are one-offs or extremely restricted in use (e.g. *Zambianize*); others will fall by the wayside as the phenomenon they describe becomes irrelevant or of historical interest only, e.g. *Stalinization, Finlandization.*

Some few will flourish, and the creasing of brows, or even gnashing of teeth, over them will no doubt continue.

jabot. Pronounced /ˈʒabəʊ/.

jackal. Pronounced either /ˈdʒakɔːl/ or /ˈdʒakəl/.

jacket. Retain single *t* in the extended forms *jacketed, jacketing*. See -T-, -TT-.

Jacobean, Jacobin, Jacobite. These adjective and noun forms, ultimately from Latin *Jacobus* 'James', have been used as sobriquets of several different groups of people or things. *Jacobean* is used as adjective and noun with reference to the reign (1603–25) or times of James I, and, in particular, to an architectural style which prevailed in England in the early part of the 17c. The commonest use of *Jacobins* (the name earlier given in France to Dominican friars) is for the group of revolutionaries formed in Paris in 1789 and so named because they used to meet in what was once a Dominican convent. The commonest use of *Jacobites* is for adherents of James II after his abdication in 1688, or of his successors, the Old Pretender, James Francis Stuart, and the Young Pretender, Charles Edwards Stuart, otherwise known as 'Bonny Prince Charlie'. *Jacobites* is also a rather literary description occasionally used by writers for devotees of the works of Henry James (1843–1916).

jaggedly. Three syllables. See -EDLY.

jail, jailer, etc. are now more common than *gaol, gaoler* in BrE and are the dominant spellings in AmE. They are generally the preferred spellings, except in historical contexts in which the *gaol-* forms might be more appropriate.

jamb (side-post of doorway, etc.). Pronounced /dʒam/ to rhyme with *lamb*.

janissary, a member of the Turkish Sultan's guard, is the form most writers use, rather than *janizary,* which is the form given precedence in the *OED* (1900). The first syllable is stressed: /ˈdʒanɪs(ə)ri/.

jargon.

1 *Jargon* and its synonyms: *argot, cant,* etc.
2 Etymologies.
3 Definitions.
4 The use and misuse of *jargon*.

1 *Jargon* and its synonyms: *argot, cant,* etc. Over the centuries this word and its numerous near-synonyms have been used in a number of ways to describe types of speech or writing rejected from normal standard English as being unintelligible, restricted in use, inarticulate, or unfamiliar. Because it is one of the commonest words so used, it is the most suitable heading for an article describing the main distinctions between the words in this group. The words are *argot, cant, dialect, gibberish, idiom, jargon, lingo, lingua franca, parlance, patois, shop, slang,* and *vernacular.*

2 *Etymologies.* It may be best, first, to consider the etymology of each of these terms before assigning meanings to them. The bracketed dates indicate the centuries in which the various words were first recorded. *Argot* (19c.), *jargon* (14c.; as a pejorative term 17c.), *parlance* (16c.), and *patois* (17c.) are French; *dialect* (16c.) and *idiom* (16c.) are immediately from French, but ultimately from Greek (διάλεκτος 'discourse, way of speaking'; 'language of a district'; ἰδίωμα 'peculiar phraseology'); *cant* (16c.) and *vernacular* (17c.) are from Latin (cf. L *cantāre* 'to sing'; *vernāculus* 'domestic, indigenous', from *verna* 'home-born slave'); *lingo* (17c.) is probably from Portuguese *lingoa* but may be a corrupt form of *lingua* (*franca*); *lingua franca* (17c.) is Italian and means 'Frankish tongue'; *gibberish* (16c.), *shop* (this sense 19c.), and *slang* (18c.) are English, the first from the verb meaning 'to chatter incoherently' + the ending *-ish* of *English, Scottish, Danish,* etc., the second a particular application of the ordinary word *shop,* and the third of unknown origin.

3 *Definitions.* The thirteen words and their present-day meanings: *argot,* the peculiar phraseology of a group or class, originally that of thieves and rogues. At first applied only to such groups in France, it is now broadly used as a synonym for *slang*: *He has an ear for Glaswegian argot—OEC,* 2001.

cant: see CANT.

dialect: see DIALECT.

gibberish: nowadays, unintelligible or meaningless speech or writing; historically, blundering or ungrammatical language; inarticulate chatter, especially in a language not understood by the person describing it as such.

idiom: a fixed phrase established by usage and having a meaning not deducible from those of the individual words in the expression, e.g. *to keep a straight face; to sow one's wild oats*. See also IDIOM.

jargon has several meanings: the inarticulate utterance of birds; a term of contempt for something (including a foreign language) that the listener does not understand; and especially any mode of speech abounding in unfamiliar terms, or peculiar to a particular set of persons, e.g. the specialized vocabulary of bureaucrats, scientists, or sociologists. See 4 below.

lingo: a contemptuous designation for foreign speech or language (*I can't speak their beastly lingo*); also, for language peculiar to some special subject and not intelligible to the listener or reader.

lingua franca: (*a*) a language adopted as a common language between speakers whose native languages are different, e.g. Latin in medieval Europe, Arabic in the Near East, Malay in South-East Asia, English in many parts of the world. (*b*) earlier, and now only in historical contexts, a mixture of Italian with French, Greek, Arabic, and Spanish, used in the Levant. See CREOLE; PIDGIN.

parlance: a particular way of speaking, especially as regards choice of words, idiom, etc. Though originally from French, the word is no longer current in modern French. In practice, *parlance* must always be accompanied by a defining word or phrase, e.g. *in racing parlance, in the parlance of postmodernists, in common parlance.*

patois: the language of the ordinary people in a region, differing fundamentally from the standard language, and generally of a lower status; also, more loosely, a variety of language specific to a particular group. Although originally used to designate popular modes of speech in France, it is now used to refer to many other languages, including varieties of English: *Jamaican patois, Cockney patois.*

shop: occurs chiefly in the phrase *to talk shop,* to talk about one's work or business out of working hours.

slang: see SLANG. See also BACKSLANG; RHYMING SLANG.

vernacular: the indigenous language of a particular country (*Latin gave way to the local vernaculars in France, Italy, Spain,* etc.). It is also sometimes applied to ordinary, as distinct from formal or literary, English. In America, Black English, a mode of speech widespread among black speakers, is now often called Black English Vernacular (BEV), or African American Vernacular English (AAVE).

4 The use and misuse of *jargon.* (*a*) No one has any quarrel with the use of *jargon* to mean 'the inarticulate utterance of birds', especially since it occurs mainly in literary sources from Chaucer to Longfellow.

(*b*) Nor do arguments break out when the term is applied, as, since the 17c., it often has been, to hybrid speech arising from a mixture of languages (e.g. *A mingled dialect, like the jargon which serves the traffickers on the Mediterranean and Indian coasts*—Dr Johnson, 1755).

(*c*) *Academic jargon.* Writers of technical and scientific works and authors of scholarly monographs are entitled to expect their readers to master the specialized terminology of their subjects. Scholarship has its own intricate rules and conventions, and user manuals theirs. In the passages that follow each of the writers doubtless hopes that what he has written will be understood, even though none of the passages is written in 'plain English'.

(The kind of 'Eurospeak' used at international linguistic conferences) *As an example of a common development in both genetically and areally closely related languages one could take the grammaticalisation of embraciation in declarative sentences in German, Dutch and Frisian*—A. Danchev, 1991. (The language of computer user manuals) *When the SET FORMAT TO SCREEN has been issued, an ERASE will clear the screen of all information that was previously on it, will release all the GETS . . . and will reset the coordinates to 0,0. When the SET FORMAT TO PRINT has been issued, an EJECT will do a page feed and reset the coordinates to 0,0—DBASE II User Manual,* 1985. (Semiotics) *Moreover, nearly all the non-verbal signs usually rely on more than one parameter; a pointing finger has to be described by means of three-dimensional spatial parameters, vectorial or directional elements, and so on*—U. Eco, 1976. (Literary criticism) *This view of the text ... has been seriously challenged in recent years, mainly by structuralist and semiological schools of criticism. According to these, the text has no within, beneath or behind where hidden meanings might be secreted. Attention is instead focused exclusively on the processes and structures of the text and on the ways in which these produce meanings, positions of intelligibility for the reader or the specific effects of realism, defamiliarisation or whatever*—T. Bennett, 1982. (Philosophy) *he suggests that someone with my realist views about the qualitative properties of experience ought to allow for the possibility of inverted spectra, thus pulling apart content and qualia. I think myself, in opposition to this, that inverted spectrum cases are precisely cases in which representational content is changed, so that it fits qualitative character*—C. McGinn, 1991.

But many scholars are dismayed by the employment of obscure terminology in academic writing. Thus, for example, the distinguished American philosopher John R. Searle (in *Bull. Amer. Acad. Arts & Sci.*, 1993): 'There is supposed to be a major debate ... going on at present concerning a crisis in the universities—specifically, a crisis in the teaching of the humanities ... Though the arguments are ostensibly about Western civilization itself, they are couched in a strange jargon that includes not only *multiculturalism* but also such terms as *the canon, political correctness, ethnicity, affirmative action,* and even more rebarbative expressions such as *hegemony, empowerment, poststructuralism, deconstruction,* and *patriarchalism.*' Some of these terms have become part of the mainstream, since Searle wrote, but readers will no doubt be able to suggest others to fit the bill.

(*d*) Repetitive jargon is a feature of live commentaries on sports and games: e.g. (Rugby football) *players left on the deck; hoisting one deep into Scotland's territory; the little chip and chase;* (Association football) *sick as a parrot; over the moon; take each match as it comes; that's what football is all about;* (Snooker) *the jaws of the pocket; get his cue arm going; the rub of the green; he failed to develop the black.* For some people, the sheer familiarity and predictability of such language add to the pleasure of the occasion. Others crave for more flexibility. At worst the linguistic sin of the playing field and the games room provides amusement for sophisticated couch potatoes.

(*e*) A steep downward path leads to the often mystifying jargon of various kinds of sociological writing. The Holroyds in Cyra McFadden's *The Serial* (1977) present us with what has been called *psychobabble*—rosy enriched spontaneous pseudo-comfortable language reflecting the intricacies of their lives in an idyllic landscape known as Marin County in California (*Marin's this high-energy trip with all those happening people; Harvey and I are going through this dynamic right now, and it's kinda where I'm at. I haven't got a lot of psychic energy left over for social interaction.*).

(*f*) Worst of all is the kind of jargon employed as an obfuscating technique in bureaucratic and political contexts. One of its most distinguished critics, Sir Ernest Gowers, attacked it relentlessly in his book *Plain Words* (1948) and in the expanded version called *The Complete Plain Words* (1954). Everyone must be aware of the danger by now. In the latest edition (2014), the author's great-granddaughter Rebecca Gowers has magisterially updated the original, restored its unpatronizing tone, removed the infelicities of previous revisions, and identified several modern-day horrors of long-windedness and obfuscation. Every kind of pomposity and inelegance is surveyed, analysed, and 'translated'. Civil servants, politicians, lawyers, diplomats—indeed, anyone who has to address the general public in some official or business capacity—should have the latest version of the book at hand. Genuine communication in such areas of life has never been more important.

jarl. Pronounced /jɑːl/, with the initial sound of *yew*.

jasmine. The three-syllabled by-form *jessamine* /ˈdʒɛsəmɪn/ was common in literary use in the 19c. (and earlier): *And the jessamine faint, and the sweet tuberose*—Shelley, 1820; *All night has the casement jessamine stirr'd*—Tennyson, 1855. But *jasmine* (first recorded in Lyte, 1578) continues to be the normal term in botanical parlance.

jazz. See -z-, -zz-.

jehad. See JIHAD.

jejune. 1 Now usually pronounced /dʒɪˈdʒuːn/, with short first vowel, and stressed on the second syllable. Fowler (1926) suggested stressing the first syllable, 'by recessive accent', as he put it, and making it rhyme with *tea*, but his view has long since been overtaken by events.

2 Derived from Latin *jējūnus* 'fasting', the word first (17–18c.) meant 'without food' in English; then, in transferred use, '(of concrete things, land, water, food, etc.) thin, meagre, unsatisfying'; and, more or less simultaneously, 'unsatisfying to the mind, dull, insipid, etc.: said of thought, feeling, action, etc., and especially of speech or writing' (*OED*). Towards the end of the 19c., by a somewhat surprising association of ideas, *jejune* acquired the sense 'puerile, childish, naive' as if it were connected with Latin *juvenis* 'a young person' or French *jeune* 'young', or so some authorities say.

The *OED* lists examples of the new use from 1898 onwards, including the following: *Is anybody ... now so jejune as not to realise that the state ownership of the deadweight of present nationalised industries must prevent Labour governments from being able to follow ... their social policies?—Economist,* 1975. A more recent example is: *Nonetheless, it'd be jejune to discard the weight of the experience—OEC,* 2005. *WDEU* cites further examples of the new use from H. L. Mencken (1920) and from various journalistic sources. On the other hand, in an essay in *The State of the Language* (1980), Kingsley Amis famously railed against the use ('my favourite solecism of all time'). It seems unlikely that French *jeune* or Latin *juvenis* had anything to do with the matter. A semantic shift from 'unsatisfying, insipid' to 'puerile' is not intrinsically improbable in a word that is in any case rather rare. In the circumstances, those who wish to use the word at all are advised to use it in its traditional meanings, at least for the present. For the newer meaning there are several, less ambiguous options: *puerile, childish, infantile, juvenile.*

je ne sais quoi. This expression, meaning literally 'I don't know what', is first recorded in one of the earliest monolingual English dictionaries, Blount's 1656 *Glossographia.* Since then it has become a standard, if somewhat high-falutin', part of English, to refer to an indefinable quality. Despite its long residence in English, the phrase should still be printed in italic. If a more prosaic synonym is what you are looking for, *a certain something* should fit the bill.

jerrymander. See GERRYMANDER.

jessamine. See JASMINE.

jetsam. See FLOTSAM AND JETSAM.

jettison. In maritime law (since the 15c.) it means 'the action of throwing goods overboard, especially in order to lighten a ship in distress'. Since the 19c. it (and also the corresponding verb) has been used of the action of throwing out or discarding any unwanted object (or idea, etc.).

jeu d'esprit. Plural *jeux d'esprit,* with the *x* left silent. See -X .

Jew (and related words). **1** A Jew is a person of Hebrew descent or one whose religion is Judaism. Jewish people live in many countries in the world. Citizens of modern Israel, many of whom are not Jewish, are called *Israelis.* The biblical *Israelites* were descendants of the Hebrew patriarch Jacob, whose alternative name was 'Israel'. The ancient language of the Israelites was *Hebrew,* which was spoken and written in ancient Palestine for more than 1,000 years. By *c.*500 BC it had come greatly under the influence of Aramaic, which largely replaced it as a spoken language of the Jewish people. It was revived as a spoken language in the 19c., with the modern form having its roots in the ancient language but drawing words from the vocabularies of European languages, and is now the official language of the State of Israel (*Oxford Reference Dict.,* 1986).

2 Since the 17c. the word *Jew* has sometimes been offensively applied to persons considered to be parsimonious or to drive hard bargains in trading. The stereotype, which is now deeply offensive, arose from historical associations of Jews as moneylenders in medieval England. The verb *jew* (or *jew down*) has also been recorded in use since the early 19c. to mean 'to cheat or overreach, in the way attributed to Jewish traders or usurers; to drive a hard bargain'. The need to abandon such unenlightened language is accepted by all well-meaning people, and it is to be hoped that the 21c. will see these uses drop out altogether. An account of the controversial history of the word, as noun and as verb, may be found in R.W. Burchfield's book *Unlocking the English Language* (1989).

3 The normal adjective is **Jewish**. To use the form *Jew* attributively or as an adjective (e.g. *Jew boy, agenda* etc.) is now very offensive, though it was not originally so.

jewel. The inflected forms are *jewelled, jewelling,* and *jeweller* (in AmE usu. with *-l-*). See -LL-, -L-.

jewellery. Pronounced /ˈdʒuːəlri/. The pronunciation /ˈdʒuːləri/, with the last two syllables pronounced as in *foolery,* is considered non-standard. The spelling **jewelry** is sometimes used in BrE, and is the usual form in AmE.

Jewess, now has derogatory overtones for racial reasons and because of gender sensitivity, and should be avoided, although Jewish people are said to use it among themselves. This habit of claiming exclusive rights to the use of particular words and denying them to outsiders is an intriguing modern linguistic paradox. The word *Jewess* has in fact been in continuous use since the 14c., and, until the 20c., seems to have had no adverse connotations. The current taboo status of the word is implied in the following example: *The antiquated language is even sharpened by a reference to an Ashley daughter-in-law as a 'Jewess'*—A. Hollander, 1990. See NEGRESS.

jibe, gibe, gybe. Spelling and meaning are in a pretty pickle here, because these three words are pronounced exactly the same (i.e. are homophonous). The mainly American meaning 'agree' largely contents itself with one spelling only, namely *jibe*; but the meaning 'taunt' as a noun or verb is spelt both *jibe* and *gibe,* while the sailing term ('change course by swinging the sail across a following wind') is *gybe* or *jibe,* according to whether one is sailing in British or American waters. Matching meaning to spelling: (*a*) ('taunt') both *jibe* and *gibe* are correct, the first being far commoner, although most historical *OED* quotations show *gibe*: *'It wouldn't be responsible to make promises I can't keep. That's Nick Clegg's job,' he jibes—Daily Tel.,* 2011; *Spalding, whose time in Glasgow was stormy, directs a few jibes at Scotland's cultural shibboleths—Scotland on Sunday,* 2002; *In one day and night, he gibed, 'all those who had any power and authority were wiped out'—OEC,* 2003 (Indian); *Where be your gibes now? your gambols? your songs?—Hamlet;* (*b*) (the sailing term) *gybe* is the preferred form in British and *jibe* in American English: *But halfway through a slightly wobbly but adequate gybe, my instructor Beth called out from behind me—OEC,* 2005 (BrE); *I'll have to jibe, a far riskier maneuver that puts the stern of the boat through the wind—New York Times,* 2011; (*c*) ('agree, be in accord') the standard spelling is *jibe.* Webster's Third recognizes *gibe* as an alternative, but people may well see it as a mistake: *On the whole, the remix is cleaner than the original, jibing well with the other compositions—www.pitchfork.com,* 2004 (AmE).

jihad /dʒiˈhɑːd/. Now the normal spelling in English, rather than *jehad,* for this Arabic word meaning 'a holy war undertaken by Muslims against unbelievers in Islam'. Note that the pronunciation shown here rhymes the last syllable with *hard,* but that syllable is generally pronounced like *had.* The same observation applies to the derivatives **jihadi** (Plural the same, or more usually *jihadis*) and **jihadist**.

jingles. Not to be confused with the short verses or songs in radio or TV advertisements, this is the term Fowler used for 'the unintentional repetition of the same word or similar sounds'. The danger of such 'jingles' is that through their unwitting yet intrusive sound-play they may deflect your readers—especially those who 'subvocalize' what they read, i.e. say the words silently in their head—from the sense of what you write. Fowler's examples included: *The sport of the air is still far* from *free* from *danger; Mr Leon Dominian has* amassed *for us a valuable* mass *of statistics; Most* of them *get rid* of them *more or less completely; I aw*aited *a bel*ated *train; Hard-working folk should participate in the pl*easures *of l*eisure *in goodly m*easure. If you unintentionally use such jingles when speaking, you may well be lightheartedly teased (e.g. *You're a poet but don't know it*). A second read of the text at draft stage—preferably aloud, if you have the privacy to do so—or a read by someone else, will help ensure that such stylistic blemishes are noticed and removed from your final version.

jingo. **1** This dated word, whose modern descendants are **jingoism** and **jingoistic** (= extreme patriotism, especially a warlike foreign policy, and the attitude supporting it, respectively), has an intriguing backstory. It was first used in the late 17th century as a conjuror's word, commanding something to appear (*hey jingo!*). The phrase *by jingo* first appeared in a 1694 translation of Rabelais, standing for the French *Par Dieu* ('by God') and then became popular as an informal exclamation (e.g. *By jingo, there's not a pond or slough within five miles of the place but they can tell the taste of—She Stoops to Conquer*, 1773). Its heyday was in the late 19c. when a popular song was adopted by those supporting the sending of a British fleet into Turkish waters to resist Russia in 1878. The chorus ran: 'We don't want to fight, yet by Jingo! if we do, We've got the ships, we've got the men, and got the money too'.

2 This use generated the noun *jingo* (e.g. *The Jingo is the aggregation of the bully. An individual may be a bully; but, in order to create Jingoism, there must be a crowd—Gentleman's Mag.*, 1881), which is still very occasionally found today. Its plural is preferably *jingoes*, but *jingos* cannot be said to be wrong: *The 'khaki election' of 1900 (fought after the supposed defeat of the Boers in South Africa) rang hollow even to the jingos who won it*—Colin Matthew, 2000.

jinni. This word for a spirit in Arabic or Muslim mythology was Europeanized as the *genie* of magic lamp and pantomime fame. It comes from the Arabic *jinnī*, singular, plural *jinn*. In English, both *jinni* and *jinn* are used as the singular, and the plural can be *jinn* or *jinns*. The same is true of the variant spellings *djinni* and *djinn*. Examples: (*jinni*) *In some contexts, he's described not as a fallen angel but as the most powerful jinni, a form of lesser spirit—Slate* (online magazine), 2005; (*jinn*: singular) *the defendants believed that Naila had been possessed by a jinn, which had been sent from Pakistan by Naila's parents—Daily Tel.*, 2012; (*jinn*: plural) *Many stories are about spirits, called jinn, who are believed to play tricks on humans beings who are traveling alone in the desert—Countries and their Cultures*, 2004; (jinns) *The 25-year-old believed that jinns frequently possessed people and that they used their victims to do their work—Daily Tel.*, 2012.

jiu-jitsu. The spelling that seems to predominate in American English of JU-JITSU.

jockey (noun). Plural *jockeys.*

jockey (verb). Inflected forms are *jockeyed, jockeying, jockeys.*

joined-up. The original meaning referring to handwriting with linked characters has been applied as a metaphor in BrE since the 1980s to suggest coherence and consistency of thought and action. It is most often used to modify the nouns *thinking, government*, and *approach*, and is particularly associated with the 'New Labour' governments of 1997 and 2001. It became something of a journalistic cliché at that time, but has largely fallen from favour in recent years. *To dumb down the assessment of doctors is not joined up Government—Daily Tel.*, 2007.

joke (verb). The archaic meaning of 'to poke fun at', first recorded in Smollett, has surfaced again in recent very colloquial uses such as *don't joke me* = don't kid me. This use is appealing, but for the moment is non-standard.

jollily, jolly (adverbs). As an informal, if rather old-fashioned, substitute for *very* (*a jolly good hiding; you know jolly well*) the adverb is *jolly*; in other uses (*he smiled jollily enough*), it is *jollily*, or, if this is felt to be too clumsy, *in a jolly* (*enough*) *way*. See FRIENDLILY, FRIENDLY; -LILY.

journalese. *It is sad ... to find [him] guilty of such journalese as 'transpired'—Athenæum,* 1893. The word *journalese* is first recorded from 1882, and ever since has been used to describe (and implicitly criticize) the more hackneyed or formulaic uses of language associated with newspaper writing. Many words and uses are, indeed, typical of the language of newspaper articles, and particularly of newspaper headlines. Some examples are *probe* for 'investigation' or 'investigate': *Hong Kong missing millions* probe; *quiz* for 'interrogate': *Police* quiz *councillors over expenses fraud*; *swap* for 'transfer' in the medical sense: *Baby heart swap drama*; and 'love-child' to refer to a child born from an illicit affair: *Prince Albert of Monaco has* love-child. Certain syntactic patterns are also highly typical of journalese: (headlines presented in the style of speech in a novel) *'Time to end excess in the City', says David Cameron;* (frequent use of the present tense in headlines) *Former bank manager* pleads *guilty*; (frequent use of a *to*-infinitive referring to future time) *Prime Minister* to visit *India*; (combinations of nouns in headlines) *Councillor planning action over* go-go girl affair claim. While these lexical and syntactic choices are not confined to newspaper writing, they occur more often there than in other genres.

journey. Plural *journeys.*

joust. 1 *Spelling.* The historical spelling for this word from the 13c. to about 1800 was predominantly *just:* it is derived from Old French *juster* from late Latin *iuxtāre* 'to approach, come together' (cf. L *iuxtā* 'near together'). Cf. the cognate word *adjust.* Nevertheless most early English dictionaries (including Johnson's, 1755) listed both forms, while Walter Scott and some other 19c. authors preferred *joust.* The only current spelling is, of course, *joust.*

2 *Pronunciation.* When written as *just* the word seems to have been pronounced /dʒʌst/ in the 19c. For the form *joust* the standard pronunciation (as given by Daniel Jones) in 1917 was /dʒuːst/. By 1932 A. Lloyd James (*Broadcast English*) recommended /dʒaʊst/, and this pronunciation has now entirely supplanted the older /dʒuːst/ in BrE, but that pronunciation can still be heard in AmE.

Jubilate (or jubilate) (noun), the hundredth psalm; a call to rejoice. Pronounced (in an Anglicized manner) /dʒuːbiˈleiti/ or (in a Latinate manner) /juːbiˈlɑːtei/.

judgement. Both spellings are in use, and both are correct. The *OEC* shows that in most varieties of English *judgment* is by far the commoner form. Exceptions to this trend are Indian and Irish English, where the two forms are more or less equally frequent. In BrE *judgement* is somewhat more common in general use, but *judgment* is dominant in legal contexts. The presence or absence of *-e* is not, therefore, a matter of correctness, but just one of convention in various publishing houses.

judging by, judging from, used to mean 'if we are to judge by', are now used at the head of a subordinate clause loosely connected to a preceding or following main clause. The construction is common and accepted in all varieties of English: (judging by) *Judging by what happened Monday, only the courts can now block the dodge engineered by politicians; judging by Google News this is a story that people as far as Malaysia are interested in;* (judging from) *Judging from his wan appearance, however, it was clear that the show had taken its toll—OEC,* 2005. The danger is that these two phrases will be perceived by some as UNATTACHED PARTICIPLES. If the threat seems real, fall back on *if we are to judge by.*

judicial, judicious. These two words, both derived from the Latin word *jūdex* meaning 'judge', are easily confused although their current meanings are very distinct. The first has to do with judges, law courts, and legal judgements, whereas *judicious,* in most of its uses, means simply 'sound in discernment and judgement, sensible, prudent'. A *judicial inquiry* is one that is conducted by properly qualified legal officers; a *judicial separation* is a separation of two spouses by the decision of a court. In Scotland a *judicial factor* is an official receiver. By contrast, *judicious* is usually found in such sentences as these: *They made judicious use of the time available; a judicious plan of action; a tale should be judicious, clear, succinct.* Examples: (judicial) *Administrative and judicial authority still rested with the gentlemen Justices of the Peace, chosen from among the landowners*—G. M. Trevelyan, 1946; *They resolved not to seek judicial review.* (judicious) *Popularity had been cheaply purchased by the judicious distribution of dried apricots and jelly cubes*—M. Drabble, 1967; *The Lalpukur school had always believed in a judicious mixture of practical and theoretical knowledge*—A. Ghosh, 1986; (*judicial* incorrectly for *judicious*) **Many a country gentleman restored his depleted fortunes by a judicial alliance, marrying no doubt for love but prudently falling in love where money was.* Overlap of meaning can legitimately occur in contexts where a judge is deemed to have made not merely a *judicial* decision (i.e. one in accordance with the law) but a *judicious* one, i.e. one that is wise and discerning when all factors, including legal, social, and political ones, have been taken into account. But the example above does not have that justification.

ju-jitsu. Now the regular spelling in English (also *jiu-jitsu* and *ju-jutsu*). The word is a 19c. loanword from Japanese *jujutsu* (pronounced /dʒʊdʒɪtsʊ/, from *ju* (Chinese *jeu* 'soft, yielding') + *jutsu* (Chinese *shu, shut* 'science').

jumbo. Plural *jumbos.*

jump (verb). The rather old-fashioned phrase *jump to the eye(s)* 'to be obvious or prominent' is a Gallicism (cf. French *sauter aux yeux*), and, according to the *OED,* Fowler (1926) was the first to notice this. Examples: *the Banquo scene in 'Macbeth'—a scene which jumps to the eye—was overlooked*—G. Goodwin, 1929; *Things jump to the eyes of the reader of this passage which have yet been ignored*—M. D. George, 1931.

juncture. A *juncture* means 'a coincidence of events producing a critical or dramatic moment': *This I take to be as bad a Juncture as ever I observed. The King and his new Queene minding their pleasures at Hampton Court. All people discontented*—Pepys' *Diary*, 1662; *We do appear to be at a crucial juncture, to say the least—Musical Times*, 2000; *Candidates come and go, but as the people of Taiwan we collectively stand at a historical* [*sic*] *juncture—Taipei Times*, 2004. The *OED* citations show it being used since the 17c. in collocations such as *at this juncture of time* and *the present critical juncture of things*; the *OEC* data shows that it is still often used in combination with the adjectives *critical, crucial, particular, important, historic(al),* and the like. The set phrase *at this juncture* is first recorded in 1874, and is the context for the word in 75% of examples. It is appropriate when one is talking about a critical or dramatic moment; but to use it merely to mean 'now' or 'at this point', as often happens in legal language, runs the risk of sounding long-winded and pompous. Examples: *The last thing she wanted at this juncture was to be under an obligation to Wilcox*—D. Lodge, 1988; *It is vital, at this juncture, that the government does not give in to bullying by arms companies—Morning Star*, 2007; *the defendants are unable to elaborate further on this point at this juncture, but reserve the right to do so following disclosures—England and Wales High Court Decisions*, 2005.

junior. See ABSOLUTE COMPARATIVE.

junta. This Spanish loanword is best now anglicized as /ˈdʒʌntə/, though the pronunciation with initial /ˈhʊ-/ is often heard in BrE and is more or less standard in AmE. The erroneous form *junto,* once common, is now obsolete.

jurist. 'In BrE, this word is reserved for those having made outstanding contributions to legal thought and legal literature. In AmE, it is rather loosely applied to every judge of whatever level, and sometimes even to nonscholarly practitioners who are well respected . . . The most common error in AmE is to suppose that *jurist* is merely an equivalent of *judge:* "We find no constitutional question concerning the validity of Charles Milton's conviction and sentence of death about which reasonable *jurists* [read *judges*] could differ"' (Garner).

juror. A member of a jury is a *juror.* The term *juryman* is fast disappearing, and *jurywoman* is almost extinct except in occasional historical references.

just (verb and noun). See JOUST.

just (adverb). **1** When it means 'a little time ago', *just* is used differently in British and American English. In BrE the usual construction is with a perfect tense formed with *have*: *I have just arrived home,* but in AmE the verb is normally a simple past form: *I just arrived home.* Some BrE speakers regard this American use with distaste. Care also needs to be taken to avoid misunderstanding, since *just* can also mean 'only, simply' as in *They are just good friends.* So a sentence such as BrE *I have just seen my brother* and, even more, AmE *I just saw my brother* can mean either 'I have recently seen my brother' or 'I have seen my brother and no one else' (or, perhaps, 'I have seen my brother and have done nothing else'). In speech, intonation will usually clarify the meaning, but in written English the difficulty may need to be resolved by rephrasing.

2 The phrase *just now* has several meanings, some of which are specific to certain regions of the English-speaking world. The main possibilities are: with past reference (= a short time ago) *What was it you were saying just now, child?*—E. Jolley, 1985; with a present continuous tense, (= at this moment) *The Fife rain is lashing and bashing my hut just now*; with a simple present (= for the time being, right now), generally with a negative: *I don't want to decide just* *now*; note that the positive use is characteristically Scottish: *I have my home in Britain just now—Express* (Scottish edition), 2007; in South African and Indian English, *just now* is used with a future tense to mean 'very shortly, in a little while': *Yes, yes, just now I will have a dialogue with you* (Ind).

3 The many standard uses and meanings of *just* in all varieties of English include the following: = exactly (*just what I need, that's just right*); = a little time ago (*I have just seen him getting into a car*); = simply, merely (*we are just good friends, not lovers; it just doesn't make sense*); = barely, no more than (*he just managed to reach the airport in time; just a minute*); = positively (*it is just splendid*); = quite (*not just yet*); *informal* = really, indeed (*won't I just tell him!*); in questions, seeking precise information (*just how did you manage?*). The last of these uses, *just* in questions, was originally American (where it was first recorded in 1884) but has now come into general use: *I am beginning to wonder just how far these people are willing to go. Just* on its own can also be used colloquially to mean 'it's just that': *Not that it mattered, just a fellow liked to know*—K. Amis, 1988*; I don't know why I'm telling you all this really. Just I wouldn't want to see you do something you might regret*—P. Lively, 1991. This use is best avoided in any writing style that is not informal.

kadi. See CADI.

Kaffir. In a South African context, the word *Kaffir* is first recorded (as *Caffre*) by the eminent Elizabethan editor Richard Hakluyt in 1599. It was originally an innocuous designation both for people belonging to the Nguni subdivision of the Bantu family, including the Xhosa (and sometimes the Zulu), and for their languages. Under apartheid it became a racially abusive word to describe any black person, and in South Africa its use is now actionable. Although it survives in the names of flora native to South Africa, such as the *Kaffir lime* and the *Kaffir lily*, it is always a racially abusive and offensive term when used of people. The word, which comes from the Arabic *kāfir* 'infidel', is also used by some Muslims as a derogatory way of describing non-believers.

Kaiser. A term in almost daily use while H. W. Fowler was preparing *Modern English Usage*: he therefore commented on its pronunciation. It is now a rarely used term, except in historical contexts concerning the Holy Roman Empire, the Austrian and the German emperors, etc. Whether the term is used of the head of ancient empires or in the name *Kaiser Bill* (Kaiser Wilhelm II, Emperor of Germany 1888–1918), it is pronounced /ˈkʌɪzə/.

kale, kail. Etymologically, these are Scottish and northern-counties variants of the southern word *cole*, a general name for various species of brassica, especially of the curly variety, including colewort, borecole, and cabbage. *Kale* is grown as a crop (especially for animal feed) throughout Britain. In the spelling *kail* (less commonly *kale*) the word is Scots for (*a*) certain kinds of curly brassica, (*b*) a broth or soup in which cabbage is a principal ingredient. A *kailyaird* is a cabbage garden, a kitchen-garden. The *Kaleyard* (or *Kailyard*) *School* is a name applied to a group of 19c. fiction writers including J. M. Barrie (1860–1937) and S. R. Crockett (1860–1914), who described local town life in Scotland in a romantic vein and with much use of the vernacular.

kalendar, kalends. See CALENDAR; CALENDS.

kangaroo. Plural *kangaroos*. For the parliamentary sense, see CLOSURE.

karat, AmE variant of *carat* (a measure of the purity of gold).

kartell. See CARTEL.

kedgeree, now the usual spelling of a word spelt in many different ways (*kidgeree, khichri*, etc.) since it was first recorded in English in the 17c. It is a loanword from Hindi. The stress is on the first syllable, /ˈkɛdʒəri, -iː/.

keelson /ˈkiːlsən/, a line of timber fastening a ship's floor timbers to its keel. Now the preferred spelling and pronunciation, not *kelson* /ˈkɛlsən/.

keep (verb). Used as a transitive verb, *keep* + object + *from* + *-ing* is normal English and means 'prevent someone from doing something': *Jimmie ... was glad that distance and duty kept Mr Neville from visiting him more than twice*—T. Keneally, 1972; *His hands held flat over his ears as if to keep his whole head from flying apart*—M. Amis, 1978. The *OED* records 19c. British examples of *keep from* used intransitively to mean 'to restrain or contain oneself from' + an *-ing* clause: e.g. *Nor was Louis able to keep from turning pale*—C. Yonge, 1870. This use once sounded distinctly archaic on the British side of the Atlantic, but it is flourishing in N. America, and now sounds acceptable, if slightly, transatlantic to British ears: (AmE. examples) *Maria cut the wheel to the left, to keep from hitting the cans*—T. Wolfe, 1987; *He thinks we should all come ... to listen to some ... old university professor rabbit on about how to keep from going stale*—M. Atwood, 1990; (BrE examples) *Sabriel* *had to bite her fist to keep from laughing*—*OEC*, 2001; *'How do I get to buy food and keep from starving' he once said*—*OEC*, 2009.

kelim. See KILIM.

kennel (verb). The inflected forms are *kennelled, kennelling* (AmE *kenneled, kenneling*). See -LL-, -L-.

kerb. The standard spelling in BrE of the word meaning a stone edging to a pavement or raised path. In AmE spelt **curb**.

kerosene, paraffin, petrol, petroleum. *Kerosene* in the US (where it is sometimes spelt *-ine*), Australia, and NZ is a fuel oil suitable for use in domestic lamps and heating appliances. The corresponding term in Britain is *paraffin. Petroleum* (popularly shortened to *petrol*) is a hydrocarbon oil found in the upper strata of the earth, refined for use in internal-combustion engines, etc.; in the US called **gas** or **gasoline**.

ketchup is the established spelling in Britain. See CATCHUP.

Khedive. Pronounced /kɪˈdiːv/.

Khoikhoi (also **Khoekhoe**). Pronounced with both syllables rhyming with *boy*. This term should always be used in preference to *Hottentot*, which is offensive. See HOTTENTOT.

Khrushchev, Nikita Sergeevich, Soviet statesman (1894–1971). The man who turned banging shoes on rostrums into a diplomatic weapon, as he did at the UN in 1960, would presumably not be pleased that his name in the *OEC* is as often incorrectly spelt with a *Kr-* as it is correctly, with a *Khr-*.

kibbutz /kɪˈbʊts/, a communal farming settlement in Israel. In the plural *kibbutzim* /ˌkɪbʊtˈsiːm/ the stress falls on the last syllable.

kibosh. In the phrase *put the kibosh on something*, of disputed origin, the spelling shown is much more frequent than the spelling **kybosh**, which is more frequent in British English than elsewhere.

kid (noun). Used to mean 'child', despite its long history (first clearly recorded in the 17c.), it is still somewhat informal and should be restricted to such contexts (*he's only a kid; his wife and kids; spend the day with the kids; school kids; kids' stuff;* etc.). The verb *to kid*, meaning 'to trick or tease', is early 19c. and possibly derived from this noun; it has the same level of informality.

kidnap. The inflected forms are *kidnapped, kidnapper, kidnapping,* except that in AmE forms with a single *-p-* are sometimes used. See -P-, -PP-.

kidney. Plural *kidneys.*

kilim is the more frequent spelling for this flat-woven rug or carpet, rather than *kelim.*

kiln. Now normally pronounced /kɪln/, but the *OED* (1901) gave precedence to /kɪl/, with the final *n* silent, and Daniel Jones (1917) noted that 'The pronunciation /kɪl/ appears to be used only by those connected with the working of kilns.' The *SOED* (1993) assigns /kɪl/ to Scotland.

kilo. Plural *kilos*. See -O(E)S 6.

kilometre (AmE ***kilometer***). There is considerable variation in the placing of the stress. In BrE the stress is traditionally placed on the first syllable, /ˈkɪləmiːtə/, and this pronunciation is recommended. But /kɪlˈɒmɪtə/ is also common. In English-speaking countries other than Britain, including the US, second-syllable stressing seems to be dominant, possibly under the influence of *barometer, speedometer,* etc. Other metrical units (e.g. *centimetre, millimetre, kilogram, kilolitre*) are always stressed on the first syllable.

kilo-, milli-. In the metric system, *kilo-* means multiplied, and *milli-* divided, by 1,000; *kilometre* 1,000 metres, *millimetre* 1/1,000 of a metre. Cf. CENTI-; DECA-.

kilt, as worn by Scotsmen. So spelt, not *kilts.*

kiltie, a wearer of the kilt; a soldier in a Highland regiment. So spelt, not *-y.*

kimono, meaning 'long loose Japanese robe', has the plural form *kimonos*, or occasionally (as in Japanese) *kimono.* See -O(E)S 7.

kin. As noun = one's relatives or family (*he seems to have neither kin nor country; he's no kin of mine*), now a rather old-fashioned word except in the phrases *next of kin, kith and kin.* It is also found in predicative use 'passing into *adj.*' (as the *OED* expresses it): *We are kin; we have the same blood in our veins.*

kind (noun).

> **1** Ordinary uses.
> **2** *these kind of.*
> **3** *this kind of* (a).
> **4** Adverbial *kind of.*
> **5** *kind of a.*

1 *Ordinary uses.* In the ordinary sense 'type, sort, variety', the normal use is shown in phrases such as *a new kind of soap powder; a nashi is a kind of pear; the rock formed a kind of arch; nothing of the kind; people of every kind.*

2 *these kind of.* Beginning in the 14c., phrases of the type *these kinds of trees,* though themselves continuing in standard use, produced a strangely ungrammatical variant: *these* kind *of trees.* As the *OED* expresses it, 'The feeling that *kind of* was equivalent to an adj. qualifying the following noun, led to the use of *all, many, other, these, those,* and the like, with a plural verb and pronoun, when the following noun was plural, as in *these kind of men have their use.*' This illogical type is now exceedingly common in colloquial contexts: e.g. *She was used to these kind of smells in the night-time bedclothes*—M. Duckworth, 1960; *I memorized it for these kind of occasions*—J. McInerny, 1988. Should you wish to avoid a formulation which might be open to criticism, alternatives available are *these kinds* (or *sorts*) *of* and *of this kind* (or *sort*). Examples: *I knew I couldn't work with these kinds of people*—*OEC,* 2007.

Conservatives can be every bit as ideologically lethal as liberals when ballots of this kind are placed in their hands—*White House Studies,* 2003.

3 *this kind of* (*a*). When followed by a singular noun, the correct form is *this kind of house,* not *this kind of* a *house.*

4 Adverbial *kind of.* Adverbial *kind of* turns up in informal contexts (now especially in AmE) in the types *I kind of thought you weren't coming; She kind of wasn't listening* (in which *kind of* is a 'downtoner' in *CGEL's* terminology), meaning 'I rather thought ... ', 'She wasn't listening carefully'. Examples: *and, for the record, I kind of liked Tom Cruise in the role*—*OEC,* 2003; *My communication with the world has always been through my music. I guess certain other social attributes have kind of passed me by*—*OEC,* 2002.

5 *kind of a.* This slightly more complex type appears in: *I was always kind of a second-level jack-of-all-trades*—*OEC,* 2003; *This is one of the worst case scenarios. It's kind of a doomsday scenario*—*OEC,* 2003. The BrE equivalent would read ... *a kind of* ... Historically the AmE construction is a reduction of a long-established type, ... *a kind of a* ... Examples: *I haue the wit to thinke my Master is a kinde of a knaue*—Shakespeare, 1591; *I ... thought myself a kind of a monarch*—Defoe, 1719; (a tautologous use) *Dash is a sort of a kind of a spaniel*—Miss Mitford, 1824.

The phrases described in 2 and 4 should not be used in standard language of reasonable formality, but both form a natural part of informal speech. Type 5 is restricted to AmE. See SORT.

kinda. As part of a widespread tendency in the last century to link reduced forms of *of* (and *have,* etc.) to the preceding word in writing, so as to reflect informal speech, *kinda, shoulda,* etc., are sometimes printed in place of *kind of, should have,* etc.: *I know it's crass and kinda cheesy*—*OEC,* 2011. These reduced forms are strictly excluded from formal writing.

kindly. 1 (adverb). Fowler (1926), logically if somewhat pedantically, objected to the 'misplacement' of *kindly* in such a sentence as *Authors are kindly requested to note that Messrs X only accept MSS. on the understanding that ... ,* when the writer should have said *Will authors please note ... ,* since it is not Messrs X who are being kind. As a type of polite request, the use to which Fowler objected now feels distinctly dated, as does the formula *will ... kindly refrain from + -ing*: *Will passengers kindly refrain from smoking.* Nowadays, the formulations *thank you for + -ing* or *thank you for not + -ing* tend to be used: *Thank you for driving slowly. Kindly* is undebatably used to express polite thanks (*she kindly offered to babysit for us*), and as a forceful, exasperated, or ironic command (*kindly behave yourself; kindly acknowledge this letter;* (*will you*) *kindly leave the room*). It is important to note that in this second use it cannot be moved about in a sentence. *Kindly leave me alone* and *Kindly don't make a fuss* are idiomatic; *Leave me alone, kindly* and *Don't kindly make a fuss* are not.

2 (adjective). Of course, *kindly* is also often used as an adjective (*a kindly word, a kindly policeman*).

3 *kindlily.* This adverb (first recorded in the 19c.) is recorded in dictionaries, but its clumsiness ensures that it is not often used: in practice it gives way to *in a kindly manner/way,* etc.

kinema. See CINEMA.

king. The types *King of Arms* and *King at Arms* have both been used in heraldry since the 16c. as a title of a chief herald of the College of Arms, but the first has now established itself as the designation of those who still hold such offices: Garter, Clarenceux, and Norroy and Ulster; in Scotland, Lyon.

kinsfolk, meaning one's relatives, is first recorded from *The Paston Letters* in the mid-15c. The *OEC* shows that the variant **kinfolk**, which first appeared in 19c. AmE, is nowadays the more common of the two. Although both words are already conceptually plural, an *-s* is sometimes suffixed to either form, even by First Ladies: *I had asked Mrs. MacArthur and her son, and the Ambassador and all the kinfolks, to stop by the White House*—Lady Bird Jonson, 1964. Despite its folksy charm, this use is likely to be considered incorrect by many.

kitty-corner(ed). See CATER-CORNERED.

knee. The adjective from *knock knees, broken knees,* etc., can now be safely spelt *kneed* (rather than *knee'd*); so **knock-kneed** (adjective). See -ED AND 'D.

knee-jerk. This popularized technical term (= a sudden involuntary kick caused by a blow on the tendon just below the knee when the leg is hanging loose) has endeared itself to politicians, debaters, etc., used attributively in the figurative sense 'predictable, automatic, stereotyped', as in *knee-jerk reaction, response, decision, liberal*: Example: *That is what's so damning about the knee-jerk opposition of so many anti-war liberals, it's based in animus, not logic—OED,* 2003.

kneel (verb). From the evidence of the *OEC,* it is clear that in all English-speaking countries *knelt* is far more common than *kneeled.* Though more than half of the examples of *kneeled* are AmE, in BrE it is used most often in formal genres or fiction, as in: *And he kneeled down and cried with a loud voice*—T. S. Eliot, 1935. The *OED* (1901) noted that 'the past tense. and participle *knelt* appear to be late (19th c.) and of southern origin'. See -T AND -ED.

knickers. In British English, a woman's or girl's undergarment covering the body from the waist or hips to the top of the thighs and having leg-holes or separate legs. In AmE, short for **knickerbockers**, loose-fitting breeches gathered at the knee or calf; also, a boy's short trousers.

knick-knack. So spelt, not *nick-nack.*

knife. The plural of the noun is *knives,* but the inflected forms of the verb *knife* are *knifes, knifed,* and *knifing.*

knight. 1 For *knight of the road,* see SOBRIQUETS.

2 The plurals of *knight bachelor* and *knight errant* usually have *-s* after the first element (*knights bachelor,* etc.), but *Knight Hospitaller,* when used (they are also called *Knights of St John,—of Rhodes,—of Malta*), normally has *-s* after both elements. The plural of *Knight Templar* is either *Knights Templars* or *Knights Templar.*

knit. The past tense and past participle form for the dominant sense of the verb, namely 'to make a garment, etc., with knitting needles', is of course *knitted,* e.g. *knitted jumpers, sweaters, scarves,* etc. In figurative phrases such as *closely/close, tightly/tight knit* only *knit* is possible. In other figurative uses both forms are possible. Examples: *Beneath knitted brows his eyes seem to fix on a point in the distance—Apollo,* 2004 (UK); *Dedicated cinephiles knitted their brows to suss out subtext, while casual moviehounds munched popcorn—Bright Lights Film Jrnl,* 2004 (US); *The red-orange beard, knit brow, and clenched mouth at the centre of the composition insist on a determined presence and artistic temperament—Art Resources,* 2004 (US); *He narrowed his eyes as his charred-beam brows knit together—The Thirteenth Heir,* 2003 (UK).

knock-kneed. See KNEE.

knock up. Care needs to be taken with this phrasal verb, which in British English means 'to wake by knocking on the door' and in AmE (and increasingly in BrE too) means 'to make pregnant'. In intransitive use, to *knock up* is to practise tennis strokes before the start of formal play, and a **knock-up** is a period of practice.

knoll. The recommended pronunciation in British and American dictionaries is /nəʊl/, rhyming with *droll*, although the pronunciation /nɒl/, rhyming with *doll*, is often heard. Words with the diphthong /-əʊ-/ include *droll, poll* (voting), *roll, stroll, toll*; while those with the monophthong /-ɒ-/ include *doll, loll, moll, Poll* (parrot).

knot. This is a unit of a ship's or aircraft's speed equivalent to one nautical mile (approx. 2,025 yards or 1,852 metres) per hour. It is not a measure of distance, even though it is often loosely so used: e.g. *the ship went ten knots an hour*, where *an hour* is, strictly speaking, superfluous. Originally a *knot* was 'a piece of knotted string fastened to the log-line, one of a series fixed at such intervals that the number of them that run out while the sand-glass is running indicates the ship's speed in nautical miles per hour; hence, each of the divisions so marked on the log-line, as a measure of the rate of motion of the ship (or of a current, etc.)'. As a matter of curiosity, the *OED* lists three examples of the loose use from unimpeachably (if somewhat old-fashioned) nautical sources, Anson's *Voyages* (1748), Cook's *Voyages* (1772–84), and Marryat's *Peter Simple* (1833).

knout (scourge used in imperial Russia). Pronounced /naʊt/, not /nuːt/ or /kn-/.

know. Now strikingly overused, especially in non-standard speech: **1** In the form of a rhetorical question, (*Do you*) *know what I mean?* Examples: *I get confused. You know what I mean?—OEC*, 2002. In rapid speech the question is often reduced to something like *know't I mean?*

2 In *you know*, as a conversational filler. Examples: *A. They're supposed to be, you know, sexy. B. That's all right, but all men are the same, after one thing, but sometimes, you know, it can be wonderful—Listener*, 1965; *People get the wrong idea, thinking we might be, you know, glamorous or brilliant or something—Sunday Times*, 1974. It is a marked feature of informal conversation and unscripted speech. A Swedish scholar, Britt Erman, in her *Pragmatic Expressions in English* (1987), analysed the commonest of such expressions—*you know, you see,* and *I mean*—used in conversations between educated speakers. She concluded that *you know* has a number of useful interpersonal functions. It is often used to introduce background information (such as a parenthesis), or extra clarification or exemplification. It is also often used to finish off an argument, or to mark the boundary between one topic or manner of speaking and another. While all this is true, the fact remains that a conversation peppered too frequently with *you knows*, however closely the function of the expression is analysed, is also likely to be judged inept.

know-how. After a period in the 1950s, when its lexical respectability was called into question in Britain, *know-how* has come to be accepted in all English-speaking areas as an indispensable term for technical expertise or practical knowledge. The word was first recorded in print in AmE in 1838, but did not come into widespread use until about a century later.

knowing. Used in the sense 'from what I know about (a person)' or short for 'knowing (a person) as I do', it is now frequently used in a formulaic way to emphasize the truth of the statement it qualifies. Examples: *'What are you doing today?' 'Lunching with Lalige. Some shopping. We won't lunch till late, knowing her'*—M. Wesley, 1983; *I think her intention right now is to live for a very, very long time. And knowing her, she will—OEC*, 2007. It is one of a number of admissible 'unattached participles'. Cf. JUDGING BY.

knowledgeable. Is spelt with an *-e* after the *-g*.

kopje. This older spelling (from Dutch *kopje*) for a small hill has been entirely replaced in South Africa by **koppie** /ˈkɒpi/. But *kopje* is still the customary spelling outside South Africa.

Koran. Pronounced /kɔːˈrɑːn/ or /kəˈrɑːn/. Frequently also written **Quran** and occasionally **Qur'an** as a closer transliteration of the Arabic original.

kosher. Pronounced /ˈkəʊʃə/, to rhyme with *coast* not /ˈkɒ-/.

kowtow, pronounced /kaʊˈtaʊ/, to rhyme with *cow*, entirely replaced *ko-tow*, pronounced /kəʊˈtaʊ/, at some point in the 20c.

kraal. The pronunciation is given as either /krɑːl/ or /krɔːl/ in South African dictionaries, but in British English it is pronounced /krɑːl/.

kris (Malay or Indonesian dagger). Now the preferred spelling. Formerly also *crease, creese, kreese.*

krona, krone. **1** *krona* (plural *kronor*) is the chief monetary unit of Sweden; and *krona* (plural *kronur*) that of Iceland.

2 *krone* (plural *kroner*) is the chief monetary unit of Denmark and of Norway.

Krushchev. See KHRUSHCHEV.

kudos /ˈkjuːdɒs/, AmE /ˈkuːdɑs/, meaning 'glory, renown', usually in connection with a particular event or achievement, is a 19c. adoption (originally university slang) of Gk κῦδος in the same sense. Like *glory* and *renown*, it is an UNCOUNT(ABLE) NOUN, which means that in standard usage it has no plural nor is it used with the indefinite article *a*. However, the final *-s* is sometimes misinterpreted as marking a plural (e.g. *She deserves so many kudos for her bravery in this movie—OEC,* 2002) of a meaning 'honourable mention for a particular achievement'. For that reason, a back-formation, *kudo,* has emerged since about 1940, e.g. *With every kudo its writers achieve, more visitors flock to the site—OEC,* 2004. It is true that back-formations caused by misinterpretation of a final *-s* can be found: e.g. asset (*assets*, from Norman-French *assetz,* mistakenly taken as plural), *cherry* (from Old French *cherise,* taken as plural), *pea* (from *pease,* taken as plural). But this is an old, discarded process. No other word of Greek origin (*bathos, chaos, pathos,* etc.) has suffered such an undignified fate. It is impossible to deny that the use of *kudos* as a plural and of *kudo* as a singular is widespread; it is equally impossible to affirm that it is desirable or elegant.

kukri (curved knife). Pronounced /ˈkʊkri/. Plural *kukris.*

kybosh. See KIBOSH.

Kyrie eleison. Of the numerous variant pronunciations, the *OED* gives precedence to /ˈkɪərɪeɪ ɪˈleɪɪzɒn/. It is derived from Greek Κύριε ἐλέησον and means 'Lord, have mercy'.

label. The inflected forms are *labelled, labelling* (AmE *labeled, labeling*). See -LL-, -L-.

labial. Literally 'of the lip', in phonetics it means '(of a consonant) requiring partial or complete closure of the lips (e.g. *p, b, f, v, m, w*; (of a vowel) requiring rounded lips (e.g. *oo* in *moon*)'. Of these consonants, *f, v* are labio-dental (only one lip is used to form the sound), and *m, p, b* are bilabial; *w* is a labio-velar semivowel, involving lip-rounding, while the sound (i.e. /w/) is made at the velum.

labium. Plural *labia*. See -UM 2.

laboratory. The standard pronunciation in BrE now is /lə'bɒrət(ə)rɪ/, stressed on the second syllable. In 1902 the *OED* gave only first-syllable stressing for the word, with the last four syllables all unstressed. In AmE the word is stressed on the first syllable and the last two syllables are pronounced like *Tory*.

labour. The standard spelling in BrE (AmE **labor**). Hence **Labourite**, a member or follower of the Labour Party. In Australia, *labour* is the usual spelling except, curiously, in the official name of the Australian **Labor Party** (and **Laborite**). See BELABOR.

lac. See LAKH.

lace. The related forms are *lacier, laciest, lacily, laciness.*

laches /'latʃɪz/. In law, it means 'a delay in performing a legal duty, asserting a right, claiming a privilege, etc. It is a singular noun (derived from Old French *laschesse* (modern *lâchesse* 'cowardice, laxness'), ultimately from Latin *laxus* 'lax'): e.g. *Laches is* [not *are*] *pleaded as a defence.*

lachrymose (and related words, e.g. **lachrymal**). Now always spelt with *lachry-* though this group of words all answer to Latin *lacrima* 'tear' (and derivatives, e.g. *lacrimāre* 'to weep'). The *ch* of the current spelling of this and the related words is due to the medieval Latin practice of writing *ch* for *c* before Latin *r*; cf. *anchor, pulchritude, sepulchre.* The *y*, in medieval Latin a mere graphic variant of *i*, has been retained in modern English from the mistaken notion that *lacrima* is an adoption of Greek δάκρυμα.

lack (verb). The use with *for* meaning 'to be short of something' (used mainly in negative constructions) seems to have originated in American English, in which it is more frequent than elsewhere, and spread to British English during the 20c. Examples: *Here's hoping he'll never lack for friends*—M. Twain, 1892; *In terms of hardware capabilities, the models lack for very little*—*The Register*, 2004.

lackey. So spelt generally. *Lacquey* is an archaic spelling that occasionally resurfaces.

lacrim-. See LACHRYMOSE.

lacuna. Both *lacunae* /-niː/ and *lacunas* are correct plurals, but the first, Latin plural is several dozen times more often used, presumably because the word itself is a learned one.

laddie. So spelt, e.g. *he's just a wee laddie*. See -IE, -Y.

lade (verb). The past participle *laden* is all that remains of the ancient verb *lade* (recorded in *Beowulf*) except for the fossilized phrase *bill of lading* for the document that the master of a ship gives to the consignor as a receipt for his cargo. In some of its remaining applications, *laden* vies with the much more natural word *loaded*: *Its final conclusion was that a 'dynamic combination of laden wagon, and track features on the bridge' caused the accident*—*Sunday Times*, 2005; *the torture of the prisoners by making them pull loaded wagons back and forth*—*Sports Factor*, 2001. But in others, it adds a certain colour and *je ne sais quoi* that *loaded* does not possess: e.g. *the boughs of* *the tree were laden with apples; the cart was laden with sacks of corn; heavily laden buses.* It is also used in the sense '(of the conscience, spirit, etc.) painfully burdened with sin, sorrow, etc. (*a soul laden with the sin which he had committed*)'. The word may have a literary or archaic feel, but it is still widely used.

ladleful. Plural *ladlefuls.* See -FUL.

lady. 1 The division of usage between *lady* and *woman* is complex and is caught up in issues of social class, if not gender politics. In George Meredith's *Evan Harrington* (1861), the heroine, Rose Jocelyn, is rhetorically asked, *Would you rather be called a true English lady than a true English woman, Rose?*, and it is still the case that *lady* denotes social standing and refinement and is the female equivalent of *gentleman,* whereas *woman* is the normal word that is generally neutral in tone but in some contexts can sound over-direct or discourteous (*Which of you women is Mrs Jones?*). The more affectionate connotations of *lady* also make it characteristic of children's language.

As well as its use as a title, *lady* is used in certain fixed expressions, such as *lady of the house, the Ladies* (or *Ladies'*, a women's public lavatory), a *ladies' man,* the *Ladies' Gallery* at the House of Commons, and others, and in the form of address *ladies and gentlemen.* In American English, though hardly at all in British English, *lady* has developed an informal meaning rather like *dame,* both as a form of address (*Where are you going, lady?*) and in third-person reference (*She's some lady*). In designations of profession, *lady* now sounds impossibly condescending (as in *lady doctor*), and has given way to *woman* (as in *woman doctor*) although this too is now considered sexist in implying that doctors are typically male and only as an exception female. As a general rule, *lady* comes across as being socially and historically loaded, and the more neutral *woman* is preferable despite its occasional bluntness of tone.

2 *Lady* is also used as of right in certain titles. The style *Lady Jones* is proper only for a peeress below the rank of duchess or a baronet's or knight's wife or widow. The style *Lady Mary Jones* is appropriate for a daughter of a duke, marquess, or earl. The style *Lady Henry Jones* is used for the wife or widow of the younger son of a duke or marquess. A *Lady Mayoress* is the wife or other chosen female consort, e.g. a daughter, of a Lord Mayor. Much fuller information about the correct use of such titles is available in the latest version of *Debrett's Correct Form.*

See also FEMININE DESIGNATIONS; GENTLEWOMAN.

lady-in-waiting. Plural *ladies-in-waiting.*

laid, lain. See LAY AND LIE.

laissez-aller, -faire, -passer. Meaning 'absence of restraint', 'non-interference' and 'a permit or pass' respectively are preferably written with a hyphen and printed in roman. The preferred spelling is *laissez-*, not *laisser-*, although the latter is the current spelling in French. The phrase *laissez-faire* comes from the maxim of the 18c. French proponents of free trade, *laissez faire et laissez passer* 'let them do [whatever] and let them pass'.

lakh. In India, = 100,000, is most often spelt as shown, but the variant **lac** is also occasionally used.

lam (thrash, etc.). So spelt (not, as sometimes until the 18c., *lamb*). The inflections are *lams, lamming, lammed.*

lama, llama. A Tibetan or Mongolian Buddhist monk is a *lama.* A *llama* is a South American ruminant, used as a beast of burden: **Wakefield also rears chickens, sheep, ducks and lamas—This is Wiltshire,* 2003.

lamentable. Pronounced /ˈlaməntəbəl/, with stress on the first syllable; in AmE also with the main stress on the second syllable (as in the noun and verb *lament*).

lamina. Plural *laminae* /-niː/.

lampoon, libel, etc. There is often occasion to select a term for an intended-to-be hurtful or embarrassing attack (even if light-hearted) on a person, a group, etc. A *lampoon* is a satirical attack on a person, institution, etc. A *libel* is a published statement damaging to a person's reputation; contrasted with a *slander,* which is a false oral defamatory statement damaging to a person's reputation (Cf. LIBEL, SLANDER (nouns)). Other terms for satirical or 'witty' statements, parodies, etc., that are potentially hurtful to those to whom they are addressed, but are mostly judged to be part of life's rich tapestry, include *pasquinade* (now rare), a lampoon or satire, originally one displayed in a public place (Italian *pasquinata,* from *Pasquino,* a statue in Rome on which abusive Latin verses were annually posted); *skit,* a light, usually short, piece of satire or burlesque; and *squib* (now rare), a short satirical composition, a lampoon. See SATIRE.

lamprey. Plural *lampreys.*

landslide, landslip. The original term (17c.) for 'the sliding down of a mass of land on a mountain or cliff side' was *landslip.* From the mid-19c. the preferred term in America was *landslide*; and before the end of the 19c. it was also being used, in the US and elsewhere, to mean a sweeping electoral victory. *Landslide* is probably the more usual term now in the literal sense in BrE as well as AmE. In NZ both terms are familiar, but warning road signs about them usually just say DANGER. SLIP, or the like.

landward, landwards ('towards the land'). The adjectival form everywhere is *landward* (*a landward breeze*); in Scotland it is also used specifically to mean 'rural, in or of the country as opposed to (a particular) town'. As an adverb, *landwards* and *landward* compete in British English (*sail landwards*), but *landward* is standard in AmE. In Scotland, *landward* as an adverb can be used to mean 'in, toward, or in the direction of the country as opposed to the town'.

lantern, lanthorn. The second of these, commonly found in 16-19c. literature (e.g. *this lanthorn doth the horned moon present*—Shakespeare, 1590; *Fishing up a lanthorn he turned the light on her face*—G. C. Davies, 1873) is probably due to popular etymology, lanterns having formerly been almost always made of horn.

lapel. Pronounced /lə'pɛl/. The adjective is **lapelled** (also in AmE beside **lapeled**), e.g. *your average velvet lapelled, brilliantined, bike-chained ted is now over 60*—Jonathan Meades, 2004,

lapis lazuli. /'lapɪs 'lazjʊlʌɪ/ (**la**-zyoo-ly), though many people pronounce the second word /'laɛzjʊli/ (-lee).

Lapp. Although this term is still widely used and is the most familiar to laypeople, the indigenous people widely known by this name consider it somewhat offensive and prefer *Sami.* The name *Samiland* for the area they inhabit is not yet fully established.

lapsus calami, lapsus linguae. Printed in italic, and pronounced /ˌlapsəs 'kaləmʌɪ/ (**lap**-suhs **ka**-luh-my) and /'lɪŋgwʌɪ/ (**ling**-gwy), these are rather literary phrases for a slip of the pen and of the tongue respectively. If a plural of *lapsus* is called for, it is *lapsus,* pronounced /'lapsuːs/, not **lapsi.* See -US 2.

larboard. See PORT.

large, largely (adverbs.). *Large* is used idiomatically as an adverb only after the verbs *bulk* and *loom,* (although *largely* is very occasionally used, presumably through a type of hypercorrection), and in the set phrase *by and large.*

largesse. Contrary to one of Fowler's verdicts, it is clear that *largesse* is now the natural form not *largess,* as Fowler recommended in 1926. While the latter is still quite widely used, particularly in American English, and is correct, the former is at least twice as frequent there, and several times more frequent elsewhere.

largo, a musical instruction. Used as a noun (= a largo passage or movement) the plural is *largos.* See -O(E)S 4.

larva /'lɑːvə/. Plural *larvae* /-viː/.

laryngeal. In this and other words in which *-ng-* is followed by *e* or *i* the *g* is 'soft': thus /lə'rɪndʒɪəl/, *laryngitis* /larɪn'dʒʌɪtɪs/. Otherwise it is 'hard': e.g. *laryngoscope* /lə'rɪŋgəskəʊp/.

larynx, organ forming air passage to lungs. Plural *larynges* /lə'rɪndʒiːz/.

laser. We are all so familiar with the word now—*laser beam, laser printer, laser-guided bomb,* etc.—that it is easy to forget that it is a recent coinage (1960) and that it is an acronym (formed from the initial letters of '*l*ight *a*mplification by the *s*timulated *e*mission of *r*adiation'). It was modelled on the slightly earlier word *maser* (1955), which itself is a combination of the initial letters of several words ('*m*icrowave *a*mplification by *s*timulated *e*mission of *r*adiation'). Lasers are optical masers.

lassie. The diminutive form, commonly used in Scotland, of *lass* is so spelt (not *-y*). See -IE, -Y.

lasso. A word of Spanish origin (Spanish *lazo,* cognate with *lace*), it is pronounced /la'suː/. As noun its plural is almost always *lassos,* but *lassoes* is also correct. The verbal forms are *lassoed, lassoes, lassoing.* The noun and verb are often pronounced /'lasəʊ/ in AmE. See -O(E)S 2.

last. 1 *last/lastly.* In listing a sequence of points or topics *lastly* is preferable when other *-ly* adverbs are used, e.g. *First(ly), . . . secondly, . . . thirdly, . . . lastly* (or *finally*). See FIRST.

2 *at long last* (formerly also *at the long last*). Described in the *OED* (1902) as 'Now *rare',* the phrase has long since come back into common use: *At long last I am able to say a few words of my own*—King Edward VIII, 1936 (abdication speech); *Someone answers the phone at long last*—J. Aiken, 1971.

3 *last/latest.* In such a context as *In his latest book, Dr A . . .* , it is clear that Dr A has written earlier books and that he is still alive and may well write others. If the statement runs *In his last book, Dr A . . .* , the meaning could be the same, or it could also imply that this was the final book written by Dr A before he died. It is obvious, therefore, that if there is any danger of contextual ambiguity some word other than *last* should be used.

4 *the last analysis.* See ANALYSIS 2.

late. Used attributively after *the* and in front of a person's name, or noun indicating their office or profession, to show that they are 'singing with the angels'. **1** There are no hard-and-fast rules about how recent the death has to be for *the late* to be appropriate. To speak of 'the late Queen Victoria' would be palpably absurd. But what about referring in 2004 to 'the late president John F. Kennedy', who had been assassinated 41 years previously: *'I'm not running to be a Catholic president. I'm running to be a president who happens to be Catholic.' Democrat John Kerry . . . quoting the late president John F. Kennedy—CNN* transcripts, 2004? It has been suggested (*MWCDEU*) that using the tag in this way is a mark of respect, which may well be true. It is, however, strictly speaking redundant when any reader can be assumed to know that the person named is no longer with us.

2 Dictionaries recognize that *the late president, a late colleague,* etc. can mean not only 'deceased' but also 'former'. However, since the presumption will be that the first meaning is intended, it is generally better to avoid ambiguity by using *former,* or any of its synonyms. This substitution is particularly recommendable when the person so named will be unknown to most people. For synonyms of *former* of differing levels of formality or archaism, see ERST, ERSTWHILE; EX-; ONE-TIME; QUONDAM; SOMETIME; WHILOM.

3 The set phrases *late, great* and *late, lamented* are often best avoided as sounding trivial or insincere.

later on. First recorded from 1882, it was once criticized on the grounds that *on* is redundant, but is now perfectly standard. Cf. EARLY ON.

lath /lɑːθ/, a flat strip of wood, has plural *laths* /lɑːθs/, less commonly /lɑːðz/.

lather, as noun and verb, is most commonly pronounced /'lɑːðə/ in BrE, but also /'laðə/, which is the standard pronunciation in AmE.

lathi /'lɑːtiː/ (**lah**-tee), in India, a long, heavy iron-bound bamboo stick used as a weapon, especially by police, has the plural *lathis.*

Latin plurals (or Latinized Greek plurals). Detailed guidance is given in separate entries at their alphabetical place for Latin words that are in regular use in English. A few general features are worth noting. **1** No simple, all-encompassing rule can be given for when to use one of two rival forms, e.g. *referendums, -a.* (*a*) Some common words regularly retain the Latin plural, e.g. *bases, crises, oases, theses* (not *basises, crisises, oasises, thesises*). Some others exhibit both the original Latin form and the anglicized one, e.g. *atria/atriums, cacti/cactuses, lacunae/lacunas.* There is a tendency for the Latinate form to be used in more scientific, technical, or formal writing, and the anglicized form elsewhere. In an age when formal knowledge of Latin rules is fading fast, it is not surprising that there should be a general movement towards the use of English plurals like *crematoriums* (rather than *-oria*), *cruxes* (rather than *cruces*), *encomiums* (rather than *-mia*), *forums* (rather than *fora*), *gymnasiums* (rather than *-sia*), *referendums* (rather than *-da*). Choosing to use the Latin plural form when an English one is available can smack of pretentiousness or pomposity. Telling your friends about the different *aquaria* you have visited may force them to stifle a giggle, but for a marine biologist would be entirely appropriate. Talking of *online fora* creates a resounding dissonance of meaning and form.

(*b*) There is a further group for which the Latin plurals are more or less obligatory: not to use them represents a serious stepping out of line. The plurals of *alga, corrigendum, desideratum, nucleus, stratum,* are regularly *algae, corrigenda, desiderata, nuclei, strata.*

(*c*) A vulnerable group is that in which the classical plural ended in *-ata:* thus *lemma*/pl. *lemmata, miasma*/pl. *miasmata, stigma*/pl. *stigmata.* It would not be surprising if the forms in *-ata* fell into disuse in the 21c. except in special circumstances.

(*d*) Specialists in the disciplines to which they relate use other 'irregular' Latin plurals consistently and correctly, although laypeople may have difficulty: e.g. *apex/apices, codex/codices, corpus/corpora, cortex/cortices, genus/genera, helix/helices, matrix/matrices, radix/radices, vortex/vortices.*

(*e*) For a very small group of words, the choice of plural form depends on the subject field: e.g. *appendixes* in surgery and zoology but *appendices* in books. In scientific work *foci, formulae, indices,* and *vortices* are regularly used, but in general writing the ordinary plural forms in *-s, -es* are more usual.

2 Some originally plural nouns, or plural forms of singular nouns, of classical origin have tended over the years to be treated as singular nouns in English. See e.g. AGENDA; BONA FIDE(S); CRITERION; DATA; ERRATUM; MEDIA; PHENOMENON; STRATUM.

3 With a few exceptions too firmly rooted to be dislodged (e.g. *Adelphi*), Latin plurals in *-ī* are generally pronounced like the letter *i* not the letter *e*: e.g. *fungi, gladioli, narcissi, nuclei, radii.* But *bacilli* and *stimuli* can be pronounced either way.

4 Most Latin words in *-us* form their plural in *-i*, but some, such as *prospectus*, do not. See -US. It is a mistake to write, for example, *hiati, ignorami, octopi.* See also -EX, -IX; -TRIX; -UM.

Latin pronunciation. Those who are interested in the details of standard English usage are very often curious to know how the Romans pronounced the Latin language in the classical period. The standard work on all these troublesome matters (how *ae, au, c, eu, g, oe, s, th, u* consonant, *y*, etc., were pronounced) is W. Sidney Allen's *Vox Latina* (2nd edn, 1978). His book is partly dependent on John Sargeaunt's paper 'The Pronunciation of English Words Derived from the Latin', SPE Tract iv (1920). The various types of pronunciation of Latin words—Classical (Ciceronian), Italian (Dantean), Continental (Chaucerian), and English (Shakespearean)—together with advice on the pronunciation of numerous legal phrases (*de jure, amicus curiae, ultra vires,* etc.), may be found in H. A. Kelly's paper 'Lawyer's Latin: *Loquenda ut Vulgus?*, in *Journal of Legal Education* 38 (1988), pp. 195–207. In the present book the recommended pronunciations of English words and phrases adopted from Latin are given under the individual words. The great majority of them differ markedly from the way in which the same words were pronounced in classical Latin.

-latry, representing Greek -λατρεία 'worship', is shown in *idolatry,* a 13c. loanword from Old French (ultimately a reduced form of Greek (New Testament) εἰδωλολατρεία). In English the formative element meaning 'worship of' is *-olatry.* It has been widely put to service since it was first used in *Mariolatry* (1612), 'excessive reverence for the Virgin Mary'. Words containing it that are still in use include *bardolatry* (worship of the 'Bard of Avon', 1901), *bibliolatry* (excessive reverence for the mere letter of the Bible, 1763), and *statolatry* (excessive devotion to the State, 1851). The suffix was particularly productive in the 19c. and lent itself to facetious formations like *babyolatry* (1846), and *lordolatry* (1846). The corresponding agent-nouns end in *-ater*: *bardolater, bibliolater, idolater,* etc.

latter survives almost solely in *the latter,* as pronoun or adjective, which provides with *the former* a pair avoiding undesirable repetition of one or both of the previously mentioned people or things. **1** Like *the former,* it should, in theory, only be used of the last *of a pair* (of persons, ideas, etc.), as in: *the Russians could advance into either Germany or Austria—they chose the latter option; the President appoints the Prime Minister and, on the latter's advice, the rest of the government.* The criticized use of *latter* to refer to the last of more than two antecedents is shown in: *His three previous novels are 'Blood Test', 'Over the Edge' and 'When the Bough Breaks', the latter of which won ... the Edgar Allan Poe Award*—*Chicago Tribune,* 1988. Despite the objections of purists, however, the evidence suggests that *latter* is more often used thus than in the prescribed way.

2 Like *the former,* it should be placed close to the word or idea to which it refers so as not to mystify the reader. Fowler (1926) cites just such a mystifying passage: *The only people to gain will be the Tories and the principal losers will be the working-class voters whose interests the Labour Party is supposed to have at heart. It is a very poor compliment to the intelligence of the latter* [which, in heaven's name?] *to believe, as many Labour members seem to do, that their support of the Labour cause will be all the more ardent if their interests are thus disregarded.*

laudable, laudatory. The first means 'commendable, praiseworthy' (*he carried out his plan with laudable firmness*). *Laudatory* means 'expressing praise' (*a politician from one party is not likely to speak in a laudatory manner about a politician from another party*). The two words are not interchangeable, but are occasionally confused. Examples: (laudable) *What was laudable about her politics was her passion to become involved*—M. Forster, 1988; (laudatory) *One wounding review is liable to be more memorable than ten laudatory notices*—R. Berthoud, 1987; (*laudatory* by mistake for *laudable*) **so they can help the federal government in its ongoing, highly laudatory attempts to reach 100 percent compliance*—*www.futurepundit.com,* 2005.

laudanum, the analgesic and decadent poets' favourite tipple can be pronounced with the first syllable as in *lord* or *god.*

lavabo /lə'vɑːbəʊ/ or /-'veɪbəʊ/ has a range of meanings from 'the ritual washing of the celebrant's hands at the offertory of the (Roman Catholic) Mass', to (usually pronounced /'lavəbəʊ/) 'a washing-trough used in some medieval monasteries'. The Roman Catholic rite (in its Latin form) is accompanied by the saying of Ps. 26:6, beginning *Lavabo inter innocentes manus meas* ('I will wash my hands in innocence'). The plural is *lavabos.*

lavatory. In the early 20c. perhaps the dominant plain-speaking word for a WC (both the fixture itself and the room) was *lavatory,* but it has mostly given way now to other words, in BrE especially the euphemistic *loo* (the usual middle-class word) and *toilet* (the name councils deemed appropriate for mere 'men' and 'women' before then closing such houses of easement as part of austerity measures). Were it up to me, I would encourage use of the plain-speaking word *thunderbox,* but I fear this is a vain wish. For a description of the general distribution of the various terms, see TOILET.

laver[1], edible seaweed. Pronounced /'lɑːvə/; but /'leɪvə/ is also in standard use.

laver[2], washing basin. Pronounced /'leɪvə/.

law and order. Careful speakers will be at pains to avoid inserting an 'intrusive' /r/ between *law* and *and,* so as not to produce the pronunciation parodied as 'lorandorder'. That pronunciation, however, is easily explainable by the desire to avoid a hiatus between the vowels of *law* and *and* (/ɔː/, /a/), a systematic phenomenon known as INTRUSIVE R. See also LINKING R.

lawful. See LEGAL.

lay and lie. 1 *Verbs.* These two words cause confusion even to native speakers of English because their meanings are related and their forms overlap. *Lay* is a transitive verb, i.e. it takes an object, and means 'to place on a surface, to cause to rest on something'; its past form and past participle are both *laid.* Examples: *Please* lay *it on the floor; The teacher* laid *the book on the desk; They had* laid *it on the floor; Babies should be* laid *down to sleep on their backs. Lie* is intransitive—in other words, it cannot be used with a grammatical object—and means 'to rest or be positioned on a surface'; its past form is *lay* (i.e. identical with the present form of the other verb), its present participle is *lying,* and its past participle is *lain*. Examples: *Go and* lie *on the bed; She went and* lay *on the bed; He is* lying *on the bed; The body had* lain *in the field for several days.* In the 17c. and 18c. the alternation of *lay* and *lie* seems not to have been regarded as a solecism, and the intransitive use of *lay* in fact goes back as far as the 14c. But ever since the confusion was first noted in the late 18c., generations of grammarians and schoolteachers have tried to eradicate it. Nowadays, some people still consider confusing one with the other to be, as Burchfield charmingly put it, 'certain evidence of imperfect education'; alternatively, it 'is accepted in regional speech as being a deep-rooted survival from an earlier period'. Certainly it is not uncommon in speaking; it should, however, be avoided in any kind of formal writing. The most common mistakes are using *lay* for *lie*, *laid* for *lay* (past of *lie*), and *lain* for *laid*: (*lay* for *lie*) **We are going to lay* (read *lie*) *under the stars by the sea—Sun*, 1990; **Laying* (read *lying*) *back some distance from the road ... it was built in 1770 in the Italian style—Fulham Times*, 1987; (*laid* for *lay*) **It was very uncomfortable and painful especially when I laid* (read *lay*) *down to sleep—Mirror*, 2003; (*lain* for *laid*) **Standing in a semicircle, we had lain* (read *laid*) *all our uniforms and possessions at our feet*—C. Jennings, 1990.

2 *Nouns.* The various strands of meaning of the two nouns are clearly separated except in one case: British and Irish English favour *the lie of the land*; other Englishes, especially American English, normally favour *the lay of the land.* The division is not absolute, however, as is shown in Muriel Spark's *Symposium* (1990): [a butler speaking] *'I am explaining to our young man,' said Charterhouse, 'the lay of the land for the forthcoming dinner.'*

BrE and AmE share various other senses of the nouns: e.g. both use *lay* for the sexual sense, e.g. *a good lay, an easy lay*, etc., a term coined in the US and used as long ago as 1955 by Graham Greene; and both choose *lie* for 'the position of a golf ball when it is about to be struck'.

lay-by, written with a hyphen, plural *lay-bys*. An interesting example of how a seemingly straightforward word can have different meanings in different parts of the English-speaking world. In Britain it refers to an area at the side of an open road where vehicles may stop; a similar arrangement on a canal or railway. In Australian, New Zealand, and South African English it refers to a system of paying a deposit to secure an article for later purchase: *you could secure it by lay-by.*

lay figure, a dummy or jointed figure of a human body, has no connection with any of the English words *lay*, but is derived (18c.) from Dutch *led* (now *lid*) 'joint, limb'.

layman, layperson. In accordance with the trend towards replacing words ending in *-man* to avoid the charge of sexism, intentional or otherwise, *layperson* (1972), plural *laypeople* or (less often) *laypersons*, is widely used, to denote both non-clergy and non-experts: *in layperson's terms; scholars and educated laypeople alike.* This trend is particularly evident in American English. Nevertheless, even there, the traditional *layman* is still the more frequent term: cf. CHAIR, CHAIRPERSON; SEXIST LANGUAGE.

lb., pound, pounds (weight), is an abbreviated form of Latin *lībra* 'pound'.

LCD. Strictly speaking, to talk about an *LCD display* is a pleonasm, since the *D* already stands for display: *l*iquid *c*rystal *d*isplay. However, this classic case of tautology misleads nobody.

leach, leech. As homophones, this pair are easily confused. A *leech* is a bloodsucking worm, of the kind that Humphrey Bogart found himself covered with in *The African Queen* (they were actually rubber in the film). Someone described as a *leech* sponges on others (*they are leeches feeding off the hard-working majority*) and this use has a related verb (*he's leeching off the abilities of others*). To *leach* means to remove a substance from soil by the action of water (*the nutrient is quickly leached away*), and has an intransitive use (*pesticides and fertilizers that leach into rivers*). Examples of confusion: **I didn't want it to leech into my own work—Bookslut.com*, 2004; **what your small business computer consulting company can do to protect itself against freeloaders and other time and financial leaches—Article Alley*, 2005.

leadership came into being in the 19c. in two main senses: (*a*) the dignity, office, or position of a leader (*Tartars under the leadership of their khan*). (*b*) ability to lead (*the person appointed will be expected to have outstanding leadership qualities*). These were joined by a third sense, = leaders, in the 20c. (*a dinner for the heads of the Senate Committees and the Leadership on both sides and their wives*—Mrs L. B. Johnson, 1964; *They have refrained from making declarations that the union's policy is not in the best interest of the membership or that the leadership has failed to implement the policy*—cited in Gowers, 1965. Gowers objected to its use as an example of 'abstractitis', instead of the concrete *leaders*, but it is well established and should only be avoided if one's context might leave it unclear which meaning of this triune word is intended). Cf. MEMBERSHIP; READERSHIP.

leading question. In law, a *leading question* is a question which suggests to a witness the answer which he or she is to make. 'In Anglo-American law such questions are generally permissible only on cross-examination' (Garner, 1987). Laypeople often employ the term to mean, as Garner puts it, 'a question showing hostility or posed just to embarrass or take unfair advantage', or simply one designed to elicit further information. In that sense, the expression has become a POPULARIZED TECHNICAL TERM. It has developed also to mean something like 'pressing question'. Examples: (legal use) *A leading question is one which in some ways suggests the answer. The reason for the rule arises from a concern that the witness, who in many instances favours the party who calls him or her, will readily agree to the suggestions put in the form of a question rather than give his or her own answers to the questions*—*Decisions of the Ontario Superior Court of Justice*, 2004; *The applicant's barrister may not 'lead' by asking questions which suggest a certain answer. If a barrister does ask leading questions, the respondent's barrister may interrupt and object*—*Sunday Business Post*, 2003; (lay use) *Begin your exchange with an 'I' message: 'I'm concerned', 'I'm confused', or 'I'm frustrated'. Also acceptable as a leading question: 'What the heck is going on?'*—*Selfhelp* magazine, 2004; (= pressing question) *Following the end of the First World War, the leading question in the mining industry was whether or not the state would return the coal mines to their pre-war owners*—K. Laybourn, 1990.

lead, led. The verb meaning 'to go in front' is, of course, pronounced /liːd/ and its past tense is *led*, pronounced /lɛd/. A common mistake is to use *lead* for the past form and pronounce it /lɛd/ in speech, probably on the false analogy of *read*: **His idea was the one that lead to the solution of the mascara mystery*—*Chicago Sun-Times*, 1990. There are several hundred examples of the phrase *has* (or *have*) *lead to* in the *OEC*, including this one: **At times undemocratic practices have lead to a breakdown in trust*—current affairs weblog, 2004. The chemical element *lead*, pronounced /lɛd/, is of quite separate origin; the associated verb and its parts (*leaded, leaden*, etc.) all have /lɛd/ as their first syllable.

leaf. As noun, the plural is *leaves*. As verb, the inflected forms are *leafs, leafed, leafing* (*she was leafing through the book*), all pronounced with /f/ not /v/.

-leafed, -leaved. 1 Dictionaries recommend /liːft/ for the first and /liːvd/ for the second, but in practice the distinction is perhaps less neatly observed.

2 As the second element of combinations, *-leaved* is the standard word for plants and trees: *broad-leaved, large-leaved, narrow-leaved, purple-leaved*, etc. But not always: e.g. *a vigorous sword-leafed fern*—A. S. Byatt, 1990. Doors and gates are also *two-leaved*. But in older literature (down to that of the 19c.) there is much fluctuation between *leafed* and *leaved* in contexts where the meaning is simply 'having leaves or foliage' and especially when there is no qualifying prefixed word (*Bamboos ... sending from every Joint sprouts of the same form, leafed like Five-fingered Grass*—J. Fryer, 1698; *Three lilies, slipped and leaved*—C. Boutell, 1864). See -VE(D), -VES.

leaflet (verb). The inflected forms are *leafleted, leafleting*; also **leafleteer**. See -T-, -TT-.

lean (verb). The past tense and past participle are either *leaned* (normally pronounced /liːnd/ but sometimes /lɛnt/) or *leant* /lɛnt/. *Leaned* is the preferred form in all varieties of English, while *leant* is used more in British English than it is elsewhere. Examples: (leaned) *Georgia Rose ... leaned forward and blew out every one of her candles*—L. Smith, 1983 (US); *I leaned sideways just a little, but enough*—M. Pople, 1986 (Aust.); *Syl smiled back at me and leaned* *across and took my hand*—A. T. Ellis, 1987 (UK). (leant) *Colin leant back in his chair, balancing on the two rear legs*—A. Judd, 1981 (UK); *so she leant back on the pillow*—S. Johnson, 1990 (Aust.); *His tone was weary, and he leant his head down on one hand*—I. Murdoch, 1993 (UK). See -T AND -ED.

leap (verb). **1** The past tense and past participle are either *leaped* (pronounced either /liːpt/ or, in BrE, /lɛpt/) or *leapt* /lɛpt/. The second spelling is the more frequent in all varieties of English. Examples: *Medicinal discovery, It moves in mighty leaps, It leapt straight past the common cold And gave it us for keeps*—P. Ayres, 1976; *he leapt awkwardly from the car*—*New Yorker*, 1988; *The dad-of-two suffered a near fatal motorcycle accident when a deer leapt on to his bike*—*Mirror*, 2007; *A man was recovering in hospital yesterday after he leaped into a bog to save a blind horse from drowning*—*Liverpool Daily Post*, 2007. See -T AND -ED.

2 The rather old-fashioned and rare phrase *to leap to the eye* (= be obvious or striking) may, like *jump to the eye(s)* (see JUMP), be a Gallicism. Cf. French *sauter aux yeux*.

learn (verb). **1** The past tense and past participle are either *learned* (pronounced /ləːnt/ or /ləːnd/) or *learnt* /ləːnt/. The *OEC* data shows that in British English and many other varieties *learnt* is relatively common both as the past tense and the participle. In North American English, however, these uses are rather uncommon. Using the form in *-ed* is therefore always a safe choice, whoever you may be writing for. Examples: (learned) *I learned ... that had I been free to dive and swim ... I should not have known the love of my mother and father*—P. Bailey, 1986 (UK); *The good chess player ... has learned to reconsider ... the overall situation after each step*—B. Bettelheim, 1987 (US); *Charlie learned .... that if he called for a vote he was bound to win*—*New Yorker*, 1987. (learnt) *Trained as a sculptor, Perry learnt pottery at evening classes*—*The Face*, 1987 (UK); *a point that few of my bright young officers seem to have learnt at school*—B. L. Barder, 1987 (UK); *The Ministry of Defence and the Treasury will agree to finance equipment projects worth more than £30 billion this week, ... The Times has learnt*—*Times*, 2007. See -T AND -ED.

2 In the sense 'to impart knowledge, to teach', *learn* has been in use since about 1200 and only gradually descended from acceptability. In 1902 the *OED* described this use as 'Now *vulgar*'. It is a classic example of a meaning that seemed ordinary and unexceptionable to writers like Caxton, Spenser, Bunyan, and Samuel Johnson (1755), but that fell into disfavour *c.*1800 and is used now only by non-standard speakers and in representations of the speech of such people. Typical examples: *if she knows her letters it's the most she does—and them I learned her*—Dickens, 1865; *We asked whether he had learned the instrument at school ... 'No. He learned it himself and now he's learning me.'*—*Times*, 1974; *Children use 'learnt' for 'taught' ('I learnt the game in Germany, and when I came here I learnt it to Susan and Carol.')*—I. Opie, 1993.

learned. As past tense and past participle of LEARN (verb) it has always one syllable. Used as an adjective (*a learned journal; my learned friend*) it always has two, /ˈləːnɪd/ (**ler**-nid).

learnedly. Three syllables. See -EDLY.

learning difficulties refers to 'difficulties in acquiring knowledge and skills to the usual level expected of those of the same age, especially because of mental disability or cognitive disorder'. First recorded in a US source from 1921, this term became common in the 1980s to describe a wide range of conditions including DOWN('s) SYNDROME, dyslexia, and the complaint known as *attention deficit disorder*. In emphasizing the difficulty experienced rather than any perceived deficiency in the individual, it is not demeaning in the way that *mental handicap* and related terms are, and is standard in official contexts in the UK. **Learning disability** is the standard accepted term in North America.

lease (noun). In most varieties of English, *a new lease of life*, and *a new lease on life* are more or less equally frequent. In North American English, however, the first is very much a minority choice, and in British English the second is.

least. 1 Use *less*, not *least*, when contrasting only two things: *I'm not sure which of the two of you is the less* (not *the least*) *irresponsible.*

2 Fowler (1926) lighted on a rather subtle, if not pedantic, point concerning *least*. *Least of all* means 'especially not' and should therefore logically only be used in negative constructions: *Nothing fazes him, least of all his dodgy heart, which he considers merely a blip on a perfect landscape*. *Most of all* means 'especially' and should be used only in positive constructions and in questions: *Active politicians, most of all those burdened with heavy domestic responsibilities, are often little known abroad*. Fowler (1926) suggested that the two sometimes get swapped around, and the *OEC* has examples of that still happening, e.g. **If nothing is sacred, most* (read *least*) *of all Nature, then we create the potential for the perfect kind of storm*—*Daily Tel.*, 2011. *Least of all* is more complicated. The following sentences can hardly be considered wrong; though not containing a negating word, the idea in them is nevertheless negative: *?It's obvious that Hollywood has ceased to respect anyone's intelligence, least of all ours*—*DVD verdict*, 2004; *?Dumbest scene: Every one in which we're supposed to believe that anyone, least of all John Corbett, could fall for that dump of an asexual woman*—*IndieLondon Film Reviews*, 2004. See also MUCH 2.

leave, let. *Leave* is well on its way to forcing out *let* in certain idiomatic uses, especially in *leave/let be* (*Will you leave/let me be? I'm trying to work*); *leave/let go* (*Please leave/let go of the handle*); and above all in *leave/let alone* when it means 'to refrain from disturbing, not interfere with' (*I'll leave/let you alone to get on with it now; to leave/let well alone*). *Leave alone* is the only possibility when the meaning is 'not to have dealings with' (*I wish you'd leave the matter alone*), and *let alone* is still dominant in the meaning 'still less, not to mention' (*They never buy a newspaper, let alone read one*), and is several dozen times more frequent than *leave alone*, which is occasionally found, especially in Indian English (e.g. *There was simply no understanding, or acknowledgement, of historic wrongs, leave alone present ones*—*The Hindu*, 2003) but may well read slightly oddly to some people.

lectern. see PODIUM.

lecturership, lectureship. The older form (17c.) of the two and the more common is *lectureship*, but the University of Oxford still retains the longer form (first recorded in the late 19c.).

led. See LEAD, LED.

leech. See LEACH, LEECH.

leeward. Pronounced /ˈliːwəd/ by lay speakers, but /ˈluːɛd/ in nautical circles. It means on or towards the side sheltered from the wind (as opposed to *windward*). It is invariable in form (not *-wards*) as adjective, adverb, and noun.

leftward(s). The only form of the adjective is *leftward* (*a leftward glance*; *in a leftward direction*). For the adverb, both *leftward* and *leftwards* are used. As with other adverbial pairs of this kind, e.g. *backward(s), downward(s), forward(s)*, American English shows a marked preference for the shorter form, British English for the longer.

legalese, a comparatively recent term (first recorded in 1914) for the complicated technical language of legal documents. Inevitably opinions differ about its usefulness. A correspondent to *The Times* in February 1990 diatribed that 'in almost every walk of life language is used as much as a form of magic as a way of conveying meaning ... The evocatively archaic cadences of the liturgy are ... intended to endow syntax with arcane significance, nouns, verbs and adjectives with the binding power of a spell ... Most people terminate their letters with adverbs which have little or no relation to those virtues of truthfulness and sincerity which they claim to possess, and the use of language in a basically irrational way to create feelings of awe and respect is as justifiable as the wig of a judge or the mitre of a bishop.'

Be that as it may, the 20c. has witnessed a broad movement towards the simplification of the language of legal documents. A useful short description of *legalese* is provided by Bryan A. Garner, an American scholar, in his *Dict. Modern Legal Usage* (1987): '*Legalese* itself has, throughout the history of Anglo-American law, been a scourge of the legal profession. Thomas Jefferson railed against statutes "which from verbosity, their endless tautologies, their involutions of case within case, and parenthesis within parenthesis, and their multiplied efforts at certainty, by *saids* and *aforesaids*, by *ors* and *ands*, to make them more plain, are really rendered more perplexed and incomprehensible, not only to common readers, but to the lawyers themselves." (quoted in D. Mellinkoff, *The Language of the Law* (1963) 253).

'... For a humorous epitome of legalese, the following nineteenth-century example is without equal: "The declaration stated, that the plaintiff theretofore, and at the time of the committing of the grievance thereinafter mentioned, to wit, on, etc., was lawfully possessed of a certain donkey, which said donkey of the plaintiff was then lawfully in a certain highway, and the defendant was then possessed of a certain wagon and of certain horses drawing the same, which said wagon and horses of the defendant were then under the care, government, and direction of a certain then servant of the defendant, in and along the said highway; nevertheless the defendant ... then ran and struck with great violence against the said donkey of the plaintiff, and thereby then wounded, crushed, and killed the same,' [etc.]." *Davis* v. *Mann,* [Exch. 1842] 10 M. & W. 546, 152 Eng. Rep. 588.

'Other manifestations of legalese commonly appear. One aspect of it is its compressedness: "The question here is whether service of citation was proper in the face of a writ of error attack on a default judgment." Another is ceremoniousness, which arguably has a place in some legal instruments: "In testimony whereof, I have hereunto subscribed my name and affixed my seal, this 24th day of June, in the year of our Lord, one thousand nine hundred and eighty five."'

Garner's verdict is that simplification is desirable: 'The ... effect of the passage just quoted [the one about the donkey], and other passages throughout this work [*sc.* Garner's own book] should purge readers of any affection for or attraction to legalese.'

Legal language has become complex and difficult for the lay person to understand because of a need to be both precise and comprehensive in the points made; nonetheless, there is now a vigorous campaign in progress, led (in the UK) by the Plain English Campaign and (in the US) by the Plain English Forum and others, to simplify legal language in everyone's interests. This should ultimately avoid situations such as the one described by Tom McArthur in the *Oxford Companion to the English Language* (1992), 595, when 'in 1983, an English court ordered a law firm to pay £93,000 damages for unintentionally misleading a client by using "obscure" legal language in a letter of advice'.

legalism, legality. The first means '(1) formalism carried almost to the point of meaninglessness; a disposition to exalt the importance of law or formulated rule in any department of action; or (2) a mode of expression characteristic of lawyers' (Garner). (Examples of Garner's second definition are found in LEGALISMS). *Legality* means principally, 'lawfulness, conformity with the law'. Examples: *Unbending legalism was the rock upon which both the ethics and politics of the colonist were built—Daily Chron.*, 1901; *We cannot advance United States interests if public officials ... resort to legalisms, word games—NY Times*, 1987; *The call for a return to 'strict and complete legalism' must be rejected as the fairy tale that the legal reformation taught it was—Quadrant* Magazine, 2004.

See -ISM AND -ITY.

legalisms. Garner (1987) assembled a list of the circumlocutions, formal words, and archaisms that are characteristic of lawyers' speech and writing. 'Little can be said by way of advice except that generally lawyers ... are best advised to avoid them. It must be granted, however, that there may be those rare contexts in which the legalistic is preferable to the ordinary term.' Selected items from Garner's list (the legalistic term first the ordinary term following in brackets):

abutting (*next to*); *anterior to* (*before*); *at the time when* (*when*); *be binding upon* (*bind*); *be empowered to* (*may*); *during such time as* (*during*); *for the reason that* (*because*); *in the event that* (*if*); *in the interest of* (*for*); *per annum* (*a year*); *per diem* (*a day*); *prior to* (*before*); *pursuant to* (*under, in accordance with*); *subsequent to* (*after*); *the reason being that* (*because*).

David Lodge catches the nature of certain kinds of legal language in the following passage from his *Paradise News* (1991): The text was written in typical legal jargon designed to cover every possible eventuality—*to purchase, sell, bargain, or contract for, encumber, hypothecate, or alienate any property, real, personal or mixed, tangible or intangible ...*

legal, lawful, legitimate, licit. '*Legal* is the broadest of these terms [*sc. legal, lawful, licit*], meaning either (1) "of or pertaining to law, falling within the province of law", or (2) "permitted, or not forbidden, by law". These two senses are used with about the same frequency. *Lawful* and *licit* share with *legal* sense (2), "according or not contrary to law, permitted by law". The least frequently used of these terms is *licit. Lawful* is quite common: "In March 1977, the company posted a notice on the bulletin board that contained a *lawful* statement on the solicitation and distribution of materials." *Lawful* should not be used in sense (1) of *legal,* however, as here: "The judgment must be affirmed if there is sufficient evidence to support it on any *lawful* [read *legal*] theory, and every fact issue sufficiently raised by the evidence must be resolved in support of the judgment"' (Garner, 1987). *Legitimate* belongs in the same group in that it frequently means 'lawful', but its meanings branch out in other directions as well, among them: (of a child) born of parents lawfully married to each other; (of an argument, viewpoint, etc.) logically sustainable; (of a sovereign) having a genuine claim to the throne; constituting or relating to serious drama as distinct from musical comedy, revue, etc.

legible, readable. English has several pairs of words (e.g. *legal/lawful, regal/kingly*), one from Latin the other from English, that ostensibly mean the same thing but that are well differentiated in use. *Legible,* of course, means 'clear enough to read easily' referring to handwriting, print, etc.). *Readable* can be used to mean the same, but is much more frequently used to mean 'interesting or pleasant to read'. Both words are used in the first meaning in combination with *barely, clearly, easily.* Cf. ILLEGIBLE, UNREADABLE.

legitimate (adjective). See LEGAL, LAWFUL, LEGITIMATE, LICIT.

legitimate, legitimatize, legitimize. Pronounced /lɪˈdʒɪtɪmeɪt/ (li-**ji**-ti-mayt), *legitimate* (1533) is the oldest of these three. Long without a rival in the sense 'to render lawful, legal, or legitimate', it gradually retreated before *legitimatize* (first recorded 1791), and, especially, *legitimize* (first recorded 1848). The oldest word of the three is now much less often encountered than it once was, and *legitimatize* has not greatly prospered, although it is still occasionally found. For better or worse, *legitimize/-ise,* despite the public antipathy to words ending in *-ize* is, the *OEC* data suggests, about four times more frequent in all varieties of English, including BrE. In AmE *legitimate* is hanging on more convincingly, but *legitimize* is still three times more common even there. It is the only verb of the three used to mean 'to make (a child) legitimate'. The derivative **legitimation** is rather more frequent that **legitimization**. Examples: (legitimize) *You ... forget the very people who legitimize your authority*—C. Achebe, 1987; *This exhibition helps legitimize the last quarter century's most incontrovertible cultural phenomenon*—*Sunday Herald,* 2000; *She raised the present action* [in 1827] *that the defender, having been born a bastard in England, where the ... subsequent marriage of the parents does not legitimize offspring, therefore should be held to be a bastard still*—*Times,* 2007; (legitimate) *My companion had up his sleeve something that would legitimate his employing my Christian name*—J. I. M. Stewart, 1974; *They support doctors' professional status by legitimating them as medical experts*—*Language in Society,* 1990; *Citizens of the New World sought to legitimate young democratic nations by recalling a grander, classical past*—C. Freeland, 2003; (legitimatize) *He also challenged the Palestinian electorate to legitimatize the peace process with Israel*—*Tech Central Station,* 2005 (US).

leisure. Pronounced /ˈlɛʒə/ in BrE. An older variant with a long first syllable, namely /ˈliːʒ-/, is the one most frequently heard in AmE.

leitmotif, pronounced /ˈlʌɪtməʊtiːf/, is now the more usual spelling in English, not *-motiv* (cf. German *Leitmotiv*), but both are correct. The derived adjective is **leitmotivic**.

lemma, /ˈlɛmə/ (from Greek λῆμμα, plural λήμματα) is the technical term in lexicography and linguistics for a lexical item as it is presented in a dictionary entry, for the sake of clarity and economy. For example, the verb *loan* in this dictionary is the *lemma,* which is in some ways an abstraction from and subsumes the different word forms the verb can take, i.e. *loan, loans, loaning, loaned.* The anglicized plural *lemmas* is more commonly used than the classical *lemmata* /-mətə/ (-muhtuh).

lend. 1 See LOAN (verb).

2 Used as a noun meaning 'a loan' in Scotland, in northern dialects of England, and, colloquially, in NZ. Examples: (16c. onwards examples from Sc. and northern sources cited in the *OED*); *Do ye think Mr. Awmrose could gie me the lend of a nicht-cap?*—J. Wilson, 1826 (Sc.); *Could you give me the lend of a bob?*—F. Sargeson, 1946 (NZ); *Just ringing this feller to ask if I could have a lend of his gun*—J. Howker, 1985 (UK).

lengthways, lengthwise. From its first recorded use in the late 16c. until the present time the first of these has been used only as an adverb (*a hollow tube split lengthways*), never as an adjective. During the same period, *lengthwise* has been used as an adverb (*in a straight line lengthwise on the front of each seat*) interchangeably with *lengthways*; and also, more recently (first recorded 1871) as an adjective (*the driver was sleeping in a doubled-up lengthwise position*). There is a very marked preference for *lengthwise* in NAmer. English and for *lengthways* in BrE.

Cf. LONGWAYS, LONGWISE.

lengthy. Before the 19c. used only by American writers and therefore, it was asserted, to be held at arm's length. In 1812 Southey remarked, *That, to borrow a transatlantic term, may truly be called a lengthy work.* And in 1827 Walter Scott wrote, *The style of my grandsire . . . was rather lengthy, as our American friends say.* It is now in everyday use throughout the English-speaking world, meaning 'at unusual length, often with reproachful implication, prolix, tedious'. Not a person in a thousand would regard it as anything other than an ordinary English word.

lenience, leniency. Both words came into the language in the late 18c., and at several removes derive from the Latin lēnis, 'soft, mild'. The *OED* defines *lenience* as 'lenient action or behaviour; indulgence', and *leniency* as 'the quality of being lenient', but in practice there is little to divide them except that *leniency* is many, many times more frequent. Modern examples: (leniency) *Ellis said the then minister for finance, Albert Reynolds, pleaded with the bank for leniency on his behalf — Sunday Business Post,* 2000; (lenience) *Mr Naismith said he was surprised at the apparent lenience of some of the sentences—The Press* (York), 2000. See -CE, -CY.

lese-majesty. 1 Now normally so written (without accents and in roman) and pronounced /liːz ˈmaʒɪsti/ (leez **maj**-is-tee). If written in the French form *lèse-majesté* it should logically be pronounced in a French way, but usually comes out in a modified manner, approximately /leɪz ˈmaʒɛsteɪ/.

2 The term no longer has any legal force in English (having been replaced by *treason*). It is most commonly applied to presumptuous or offensive behaviour—originally towards the sovereign (the French word is derived from Latin *laesa majestas* 'hurt or violated majesty', i.e. of the sovereign people). Nowadays it is usually applied to any action that can be viewed as undermining the dignity or reputation of a public figure. Examples: *Flying the flag upside down is 'lese-majesty', which means insulting the Crown, and is theoretically still a crime in the UK—OEC* (undated); *In the days when Montagu Norman or Lord Cromer governed the Bank of England it would have been lese-majesty for the press to give them nicknames but now that 'Steady Eddie' is common parlance, I suspect we need a name for Mervyn King when he shuffles up the Threadneedle Street corridor next year—Scotland on Sunday,* 2002; *They do for gardening, he says, risking the ultimate lese-majesty, what Delia Smith's* How To Cook *did for cooking—Sunday Herald,* 2002.

less.

1 *nothing less than.*
2 *much less, still less.*
3 *less, fewer; no less, no fewer.*
4 *less, lesser.*

1 *nothing less than.* Use of this phrase to mean 'anything rather than' (= Fr. *rien moins que*) is now only historical: *Who, trusting to the laws . . . expected nothing less than an attack*—Scott, 1827.

2 *much less, still less.* For the illogical use of *much less* instead of *much more,* see MUCH 2.

3 *less, fewer; no less, no fewer.* (*a*) The stigmatized use of *less* instead of *fewer* is also dealt with under FEWER, LESS. Here are some additional examples of incorrect uses found in standard sources: (heading) *A Million Less School Leavers Won't Mean A Million Less Jobs* (but *fewer* in the text); *School leavers. Over the next few years you're going to see a lot fewer of them—Independent Mag.,* 1988 (*you're going to see a lot less of them* would have changed the meaning); *a traffic expert who believes that the answer, paradoxically, lies in building less roads, not* *more*—*Listener*, 1988; *There were less people about, as the weather was chilly*—N. Virtue, 1988. In all of these examples *fewer* is the technically correct word.

A further example of an idiomatically acceptable use (cf. FEWER, LESS 2): *She liked to pray for not less than fifteen minutes*—S. Faulks, 1989 (i.e. for a period of time seen as a unit). Another borderline case: *The police surgeon, and no less than three outside doctors who were called in, confirmed the opinion of Marzillian*—I. Murdoch, 1989. This is the most vulnerable area—contexts forcing writers or speakers to choose between *no less than* and *no fewer than*—and the choice often depends on whether the notion of plurality or that of quantity is dominant. Clearly Iris Murdoch here felt *no less than* to be preferable, and who is to contradict her? A routine correct use to end with, showing a clear distinction between the two words: *Indira Gandhi supported sterilisation in the belief that fewer children meant less poverty*—*Times,* 1991.

(*b*) *Historical note.* The account given above (and under FEW 1, 2, 3) refers to current attitudes towards the use of *less* and *fewer.* It should be borne in mind, however, that there is ample historical warrant for the type *less roads, less people,* etc. Such uses originate from the Old English construction of *lǽs* adverb (quasi-substantive) with a partitive genitive. In OE, King Alfred the Great's *lǽs worda* meant literally 'less *of* words'. When the genitive plural case vanished at the end of the OE period the type *less words* took its place, and this type has been employed ever since: e.g. *there are few Vniuersities that haue lesse faultes than Oxford*—Lyly, 1579. Hostility to the use emerged in the 18c., but 'folk memory' of the medieval type has ensured that there has been no break in the use of the type which has been branded as 'incorrect'.

(*c*) It is of interest to set down the way in which the problem of *less* and *fewer* is presented in *CGEL,* a standard descriptive grammar of current English: (§5.24) 'There is a tendency to use *less* (instead of *fewer*) and *least* (instead of *fewest*) also with count nouns: *You've made* less *mistakes than last time.* This usage is however often condemned. *No less than* is more generally accepted: No less than *fifty people were killed in the accident.*'

4 *less, lesser.* See LESSER.

-less. 1 A hyphen is necessary when the suffix is added to a noun ending in *-ll*, e.g. *wall-less, will-less,* in order to avoid the ungainliness of three consecutive letter *l*s, but not when appended to one ending in a single *-l*, e.g. *soulless, tailless.*

2 This suffix forming adjectives was already strongly established in Old English (spelt *-leas*); it stood beside the separate adjective *leas* governing a genitive, as *firēna leas* 'free from crimes'. The first element of such compounds was always a noun (e.g. *wīflēas* 'without a wife'). The separate adjective *leas* did not survive in Middle English, but the suffix *-lieas* (which became our *-less*) attached to nouns created a virtually limitless class of words. Examples (with date of first record); *aimless* 1627, *endless* OE, *homeless* 1615, *landless* OE, *lawless* ME, *penniless* ME, *pitiless* ME, *restless* OE, *timeless* 1560. In many instances the noun to which the suffix was attached was a noun of action, coinciding in form with the stem of the corresponding verb, and some of the adjectives so formed had the sense 'not to be —ed', 'un—able' (rather than *devoid of*), e.g. *countless* (1588), *numberless* (1573). On the supposed analogy of these words, the suffix became appended to many verbs, e.g. *abashless* (1868), *dauntless* (1593), *resistless* (1586), *tireless* (1591), *weariless* (1430). But of all such formations only *countless, dauntless, numberless,* and *tireless* survive. As a living suffix *-less* can be appended now only to nouns, and not, except fancifully, to verbs.

lesser. Formed from *less* + *er*, this word is technically a double comparative. Fowler (1926) was at pains to distinguish it from *less,* and in contemporary use there is still occasional confusion, as illustrated below. Apart from its use in animal and plant names (e.g. *lesser spotted woodpecker*), it means (*a*) 'not so great or important as the other or the rest' (e.g. *he was convicted of a lesser assault charge; they nest mostly in Alaska and to a lesser extent in Siberia; the lesser evil*) and (*b*) 'lower in rank or quality' as in *lesser beings, lesser mortals, a lesser man than* . . . , etc. Occasionally it is used where *less* is the obvious choice. Compare *Other factors of lesser importance include* . . . where *of lesser importance* means 'of secondary importance' with **Lower scores indicated lesser* (read *less*) *importance placed on religion.* It is also used by mistake for *less* in front of past participles used adjectivally, and in front of compound adjectives: **one of the better and lesser seen Italian crime films*; **a second, lesser well-known plot.*

lest. 1 *Lest* is used in two ways (both paralleling uses of Latin *ne*): (*a*) As a negative particle of intention or purpose, meaning 'in order to avoid something undesirable'. Examples: *Forge your work as true as you can, least it cost you great pains at the Vice*—J. Moxon, 1677; *Look to the Purser well, lest he look to himself too well*—J. R. Leifchild, 1855; *Lord God of Hosts, be with us yet, Lest we forget, lest we forget*—Kipling, 1897; *Her head swings back and forth, lest she leave a listener untouched*—*New Yorker*, 1987; *it is a place where I don't go often, lest I be jostled*—M. Spark, 1988. (*b*) To introduce a clause after verbs of fearing, or phrases indicating apprehension or danger, (often replaceable by *that*). Examples: *Lady Catherine grew frightened, lest her infanta should vex herself sick*—H. Walpole, 1750; *Fearing lest they should succumb*—*Punch*, 1881; *And she also felt slightly nervous lest the large house should suddenly disgorge many other hidden residents*—M. Drabble, 1988.

2 *Lest* is a mainstay of the subjunctive in English, as can be seen from the examples in 1(*a*), and from the proverbial *judge not lest ye be judged* (the AV text Matt. 7:1 does not actually include *lest*: *judge not, that ye be not judged*). The subjunctive is identifiable only in the third person singular anyway, and with the verb *to be*, as in the Muriel Spark example above. In 1(*b*), *lest* is normally followed by *should*. Fowler considered the use of *will* or *would* wrong, as in the following example, but in practice both are rarely used: *Knos and I became agonised with anxiety lest next time he would leave it too late*—C. Day Lewis, 1960.

3 *Lest* is occasionally used with the indicative, particularly in past tenses, but this construction is unusual. Examples: *He was anxious lest Nunn was absent, or dead*—M. Frayn, 1965; *which is precisely why Westminster does everything it can to hold onto us and deny us what is rightfully ours lest it loses its Scottish oil cow*—*Guardian*, 2011.

let. 1 It is obvious that any pronoun following *let* and preceding an infinitive, e.g. *let me go*, should be in the objective case (*me, him, her*, etc.) and not the subjective (*I, he, she*, etc.), since it is the object of *let*. Nevertheless, mistakes occur most often when there are two pronouns joined by *and* or when the pronoun is followed by a clause with *who*: **Let you and I say a few words about this unfortunate affair* (read *Let you and me* ...); **Let he who did this be severely punished* (read *Let him who* ...).

Historical note. The *OED* cites examples from the 17c. to the 19c. in minor literary works: e.g. *Let we* [1485 *lete vs*] *hold us together till it be day*—*Malory's Arthur*, 1634; *Awhile Let thou and I withdraw*—Southey, 1795. These cannot be used as evidence to support erroneous constructions of this type in present-day English.

2 The type '*let us* (or *let's*) + infinitive', in which *let us*/*let's* is an imperative marker, is well established in the standard language (*let's hold more* chat—Shakespeare, 1588; *Let us begone from this* place—Dickens, 1840). Innovatory colloquial variants, irregular in form, have been brought into the language in America (and thence elsewhere) in the 20c.: e.g. *Let's you and I take 'em on for a set*—W. Faulkner, 1929; *Let's you and me duck out of here*—J. D. Macdonald, 1950. These, and also the absurd *let's us* (e.g. *Let's us go too*), are many distant suburbs away from formal standard English. In grammatical terms, *let's*, in these constructions, is simply being treated as a quasi-modal pronounced /lɛts/, with *'s* no longer perceived as a reduced form of *us*. When *let us* is used to introduce a firm request it must always be written as two words: *Let us go then, you and I, When the evening is spread out against the sky.*—T. S. Eliot, 1917.

3 The negative of *let's* is *let us not* (the most formal), *let's not* and *don't let's*, and, an unexpected type, *let's don't*, which is largely confined to spoken AmE (e.g. *But let's don't go too far here. Let's don't get into politics when things have not been proven at all*—*CNN* transcripts, 2004).

4 See LEAVE.

let's. See LET 2, 3.

letter forms. 1 Many of the more formal formulas for writing letters that were noted by Fowler (*Your obedient servant, Yours respectfully*, etc.) have disappeared even from business letters and the letter pages of the more traditional newspapers.

So too has the practice of addressing colleagues by their surnames only (*Dear Jones*). And the habit of writing letters itself is in decline. The standard forms of opening are: (*a*) to individuals in a company or organization who are known to you, or whose names you know: *Dear Mr Smith/Mrs Jones/Ms Brown*, or (more informally) *Dear John/Jane*. The corresponding conclusion is normally *Yours sincerely* (with capital Y), or, in the case of people the writer knows well, *With kind regards, With best wishes*, or some variant or combination of these. Since about the 1960s it has also been common practice in some quarters to use the first name and surname, e.g. *Dear Mary Smith*, a use which annoys some people; (*b*) in personal correspondence more intimate forms such as *My dear John, My dearest Jane, My darling Jim*, etc., are used, with an appropriate conclusion such as *Yours ever, All love*, etc.; (*c*) in business and other more formal contexts the inclusive *Dear Sir or Madam* is recommended, or one of the following, if you happen to know that it corresponds to the sex of the recipient, *Dear Sirs/Sir/Madam*, with the conclusion *Yours faithfully* or (somewhat less formally) *Yours truly*.

2 In private correspondence, Americans tend to reverse the order of words used at the end of letters (*Sincerely yours, Cordially yours, Very truly yours*) or to write simply *Sincerely, Cordially*, etc.

3 *Historical note.* Epistolary style has varied considerably over the centuries. The broad pattern has been of movement away from extreme formality to relative informality. The following examples show typical opening and closing greetings from the 15c. to the 20c. Inevitably they give only a surface impression of the main styles used at various periods.

(*a*) From the Paston Letters, a collection of over 1,000 family letters written by members of a Norfolk family from about 1420 until soon after 1500: (1441) *Ryth worchipful hosbon/Yourrys, M. Paston*; (1445) *To myn welbelovid son/By yowre modre, Angneis Paston*; (1449) *Trusty and weel beloved cosyn/Be youre cosyn, Elisabeth Clere*; (1454) *To hys wurchypfull brodyr Jon Paston/Be yowre pore brodyr, Wyllyam Paston.*

(*b*) John Keats (1795–1821): (to Leigh Hunt, 1817) *My dear Hunt ... Your sincere friend John Keats*; (to his brother George, 1819) *My dear George ... Your most affectionate Brother John Keats*; (to Fanny Brawne, 1820) *My dearest Fanny ... Ever yours affectionately my dearest—J.K.*

(*c*) Evelyn Waugh (1903–66): (to Tom Driberg, 1937) *My Dear Tom ... Yours Evelyn (Waugh)*; (to his daughters Teresa and Margaret, 1953) *My Darling Daughters ... Your loving papa E.W.*; (to Sir Maurice Bowra, 1959) *Dear Maurice ... Yours ever Evelyn*; (to Constantine Fitzgibbon, 1964) *Dear Mr FitzGibbon ... Yours sincerely E. Waugh.*

4 For forms of address in special cases such as bishops or members of the nobility, readers should consult the latest edition of a work such as *Debrett's Correct Form*.

leukaemia. So spelt in BrE, but **leukemia** in AmE.

level. 1 (noun) Several critics since the 1960s, in particular Gowers (1965), take issue with the overuse, as they perceive it, of this noun to indicate 'a rank or position in a hierarchy', usually with a qualifying adjective or attributive noun, e.g. *at national/local/international level, at Council/village level.* According to the *OED*, Aldous Huxley was an early adopter: *Examples of non-violence on the governmental level are seldom of a very heroic kind*—*Ends and Means*, 1937. The phrase 'by government' would have worked equally well in Huxley's specific context. Similarly, the following could be rewritten as shown in brackets: *discussions at Cabinet level* (*in Cabinet*); *at the regional level* (*regionally, in the regions*); *full consultation with users at the national level* (*nationally*). It is a matter of judgement whether the word conveys anything at all in such phrases; for it to do so, the larger context would surely have to refer somewhere to other 'levels' of whatever is being described.

What seems clear is that these and similar phrases are standard in corporate or government speak, and part of the reliance of that discourse on formulas and clichés. Often, they can be viewed as longhand adverbs defining the field of reference, e.g. *at a regional level* = regionally, *at a personal level* = personally, etc., and as such their only fault is long-windedness. Distinctly more dubious is the widespread use of *on many levels, on various levels*, etc., e.g. *the stories can be read and enjoyed on at least two levels; this made for engaging viewing, the works accessible on many different levels, their meaning continually shifting, always eluding complete understanding.* Such adjuncts may sound grandiose, and even give the impression their writers have considered an issue in depth and from every angle. But, 'on a personal level', I can never avoid the lingering suspicion that they are merely the blether of critics, who, if challenged to define those levels, would be floored.

2 (verb) The inflected forms are *levelled, levelling* in BrE, and *leveled, leveling* in AmE.

level playing field, denoting a situation in which everyone has a fair and equal chance of succeeding, is first recorded by the *OED* in a US source from 1979, having appeared sporadically in AmE sources from the 1920s onwards. It was a vogue phrase of the 1980s and 1990s, and can now be regarded either as a dreaded cliché or as a rather useful idiom. Whatever one's view, it has taken on a life of its own. Not only has the verb *level*, converted from the adjective *level* of the original, been selected to play: in current usage many other adjectives, such as *fair/economic/political* substitute for it, and many different verbs show off their kicks. All in all, it is a highly testosteronic metaphor. Examples: *That is not a level playing field. It is not even just a home-field advantage. It is like asking their competitors to play ball in a swamp—Washington Journalism Review*, 1990; *One of several suggestions was that BSkyB might be broken up to level the playing field—Business & Money*, 2007; *Let's start by closing the loopholes that allow IPO favoritism to imbalance the financial playing field*—A. Huffington, 2002; *But Howard Stringer, the Briton now in charge of the company, also told the New York Times that 'the playing field has changed'—Guardian*, 2009.

leverage. 1 The first syllable is pronounced /ˈliːv-/ in BrE but /ˈlɛv-/ in AmE.

2 *Noun.* First noted in 1724 referring to a system of levers in an 'Engine' for raising water, in the 19c. the word acquired (i) the meaning of the mechanical advantage gained by use of a lever. From there it was a mere hop, skip, and jump to (ii) the metaphorical meaning of 'the power to accomplish something through influence', recorded by the *OED* as used first by Gladstone in his *Studies on Homer* (*The leverage of this straightforward speech ... produces an initial movement towards concession on the part of the great hero*—1858) but probably in use in that sense well before then. From the mid-20c. the word developed a narrow range of technical financial meanings.

3 (*A widely disliked*) *verb.* The *OED* records the verb first from 1937 in a physical sense, and from 1971 in its financial sense of 'to use borrowed capital for (an investment), expecting the profits made to be greater than the interest payable' as in a *leveraged buy-out.* Many editors detest another use of the verb, in a way parallel to (ii) above, to mean 'to use something to maximum advantage', widely used in AmE (less so elsewhere) particularly in business, computing, and military speak, e.g. *Google also understands the capacity of the Web to leverage expertise—Fast Company magazine*, 2003; *So we're leveraging our strong regional relationships to build national ties—Brandweek*, 2000. It has even figured in *Forbes* magazine's list of 'jargon madness'. Presumably, hostility to the word has multiple causes: it is an example of verbing; it is perceived as being overused; it is jargonistic; it can also be somewhat vague. Furthermore, it may induce the editorial anxiety often caused by words when they first move out of their original, limited, technical sphere into wider use. In short, one to be used with extreme caution.

lexicon. The plural is *lexicons.*

Leyden jar. The first word is pronounced /ˈlʌɪdən/.

liable, apt, prone, likely. The differences between these are implicitly clear to mother-tongue speakers, but are hard for learners of English to grasp, particularly because in some contexts the words are interchangeable. What distinguishes them is (i) frequency, *likely* occurring many times more often than the other three combined; (ii) whether they have neutral or negative connotations; and (iii) specific syntactic patterns. What follows can only highlight some salient features of these near-synonyms. **1** *liable, apt, prone* + *to*-infinitive. (In descending order of frequency in this structure.) (*a*) To say that someone is *liable* to do something or that something is *liable* to happen does not necessarily mean that it is a habit, merely a future probability. The event described is, however, often undesirable, as in the last two examples below: *The relationship between gold and alchemy allows Lyly to suggest that the pursuit of gold is liable to make people behave foolishly—Early Modern Literary Studies,* 2002; *The ambitious young male executive appears particularly liable to suffer from neglecting his home life—Intercity,* 1989; *At one time people accepted that if they went skating they were liable to fall and might get hurt—Manchester Online,* 2003.

(*b*) To say that someone is *apt* to do something or something is *apt* to happen means that it is likely, and also suggests that it is a habit or a tendency, as in the first two examples below. The event can be neutral, or it can be undesirable, as in the last example: *thousands of scantily clad Westerners who are apt to indulge in public displays of affection—Daily Tel.,* 2008; *she . . . began to finger an old Christmas decoration that the cat was apt to play with*—M. Bracewell, 1989; *Given that it's the exam season, I'm apt to be distracted by just about anything*—weblog, 2005; *Such conflation of EC and public international law is nonetheless apt to mislead*—J. Kriger, 2001. In the last two examples *liable* could just as easily be used.

(*c*) If something or someone is *prone* to do something, usually something undesirable, they have a tendency to do it, and it has probably happened before. In this use the word could often be replaced by *liable.* Examples: *The structures are prone to collapse in the region's frequent earthquakes, often burying occupants in the rubble—Plate Tectonics,* 2004; *Although the elderly are more prone to develop anemia, older age is not of itself a cause of the condition—American Family Physician,* 2000.

2 *liable to, prone to* + noun/verbal noun in *-ing.* *Liable* and *prone,* unlike *apt,* can be followed by the preposition *to* and then by a prepositional object, which can be a noun or a verbal noun in *-ing.* Examples: *The affected children themselves are liable to behavioural problems such as temper tantrums—Journal of the Royal Society of Medicine,* 1980; *pigs being notoriously skittish and liable to overheating due to their lack of sweat glands —The Red Men,* 2007. In this structure *liable to* often has the meaning 'subject to (a penalty)': *Anyone convicted of giving away examination papers to candidates will be liable to two years in jail—Daily Tel.,* 1982.

Prone to is very much more often used with a noun object than *liable to,* typical nouns being *disease, problems, infections, depression, attacks.* It is also very frequently used with a verbal noun in *-ing,* and this structure is nearly as common as *prone* + *to*-infinitive. Examples: *This is fortunate because a number of breeds . . . are prone to eye disease and should be carefully watched—Animals* magazine, 2001; *Large areas of the reserve are prone to flooding during the winter—Plant Life UK,* 2004; *All willows are fast growing and short-lived, and their wood is notably weak and prone to breaking—Doityourself.com,* 2003.

3 *liable* used instead of *likely.* In some dialects in BrE and frequently in AmE, *liable* is used in place of standard English *likely.* Examples of the type *'Tis very liable he's* [*sc.* a wounded pheasant] *a-croped into one o' these here hovers* [*sc.* shelters] are listed in the *Eng. Dialect Dict.* US examples: *Norman Hunter's new record . . . is liable to stand unmolested for many years—NY Evening Post,* 1903; *Boston is liable to be the ultimate place for holding the convention*—H. W. Horwill, 1935.

4 *likely* + *to*-infinitive is more neutral than the other words in fitting well into favourable as well as unfavourable contexts. It is also nearly twenty times more common than the other three put together: *A plan to help young home-buyers is likely to be announced within the next week—Times,* 1973; *For the parents of teenagers who are likely to have encounters with the police, the teenage years can be a nightmare—BBC Parenting,* 2004. None of the three other words would be appropriate in these examples.

liaise /lɪˈeɪz/ (verb). Originally Services slang (first recorded in 1928, as having been uttered in 1916 by Admiral Lord Fisher), this back-formation (= to establish cooperation, form a link) from the long-established noun *liaison* attracted much criticism from purists at first, but has survived and is now part of everyday (especially spoken) BrE. It is much less common in NAmer. English.

liaison /li'eɪzən/ *or* /-ɒn/ became fully Anglicized at some point in the early 20c.; before that the final syllable was pronounced in a manner resembling French /ɔ̃/. The word is variously pronounced in America: (in probable order of frequency) /'liːəzɒn/, /lɪ'eɪzɒn/. William Safire (1981) made fun of the pronunciation of the word by President Reagan and others as /'leɪəzɒn/. It is somewhat curious that the noun has been used since the early 19c. in the sense 'an illicit sexual relationship', but that the corresponding verb *liaise* is restricted to military and business contexts and cannot properly be used of an amorous relationship. *Liaison* is occasionally used as a verb, but is not recognized by the *OED*, and will generally raise eyebrows.

liana (a climbing plant) is pronounced /lɪ'ɒːnə/, and the variant **liane** is pronounced /lɪ'ɑːn/.

libel (verb). The inflected forms are *libelled, libelling, libellous*, etc., in BrE, but usually with a single medial *-l-* in AmE. See -LL-, -L-.

libel, slander (nouns). The first is a published false statement damaging to a person's reputation, whereas *slander* is a malicious, false, and injurious statement spoken about a person. In popular usage the terms are often used interchangeably. In law, what started out in the 17c. as a clear distinction has now become more complicated, depending on how far the word *published* can be extended to cover email, Internet websites, and other forms of electronic (as distinct from print) media of communication. Anyone who is in doubt about the likelihood of infringing the law should not merely rely on dictionary definitions of the two words, but should take legal advice before setting down in writing, whether in print or on the Internet, broadcasting, or simply uttering potentially hurtful statements about an identifiable person. In recent years courts have awarded very large sums of money to persons, especially those in public life, who have successfully brought actions alleging defamation, libel, etc., including comments made on social media such as Twitter.

liberal. As an adjective it was originally (from the 14c. onwards) applied to an occupation, education, or area of study worthy of or suitable for a person of noble birth or superior social status, and was the opposite of *servile* or *mechanical*'. Cf. Latin *liber* 'free'. In medieval times such education was divided into two main groups—the quadrivium (arithmetic, geometry, astronomy, and music) and the trivium (grammar, rhetoric, and logic). The idea that a university course should be restricted to students of gentle birth, and that it should have a set range of subjects offered to all students, has long since been abandoned. But the word *liberal*, as applied to *education*, still retains the residual sense 'directed to a general broadening of the mind; not restricted to the requirements of technical or professional training' (*OED*). In AmE the *liberal arts* are 'academic college courses providing general knowledge and comprising the arts, humanities, natural sciences, and social sciences' (*Random House Webster's College Dict.*, 1991).

libretto. The plural of this Italian word (diminutive of *libro* 'book', literally 'a little book') can be either *librettos* or the Italian plural *libretti*. The first is more frequent. See also -O(E)S 4.

licence, license. In BrE the first is the only spelling for the noun (AmE **license**), while the second is the normal form for the verb in both countries. Thus, in BrE, *motor vehicle licence, poetic licence; to license one's car, licensing hours*. Hence also *licensed premises, licensed restaurants* (implying that they have a licence to serve alcoholic liquor), and (now a rather old-fashioned word) *licensed victuallers* (see VICTUAL). Occasionally one encounters *licenced* instead of *licensed* in such circumstances (rationalized, it is alleged, as being formed from the noun rather than from the verb), but this is a case of special pleading.

lichee. A variant spelling of the more usual LYCHEE.

lichen. The more common pronunciation is /'lʌɪkən/ as in *liken*, but /'lɪtʃən/ is also common in BrE (though not in AmE). The word ultimately comes from Gk λειχήν.

lichgate. See LYCHGATE.

licit. See LEGAL, LAWFUL, LEGITIMATE, LICIT.

lickerish is the better form (rather than *liquorish*) of the adjective that means **1** lecherous.

2 fond of fine food. It is a 16c. variant of the Middle English word *lickerous,* which is itself in origin an Anglo-French variant of *lecherous.* The word is not etymologically connected with *liquor.*

licorice is a variant of LIQUORICE, a black root extract used as a sweet.

lie (verb), be prostrate. See LAY AND LIE.

lie (verb), speak falsely. The inflected forms are *lies, lying, lied.*

lie (noun), position. See LAY AND LIE.

lien, a right to keep possession of property belonging to another person until a debt owed by that person is discharged, is pronounced /liːn/ or /ˈliːən/.

-lier. For comparative-adverb forms, see -ER AND -EST 3.

lieutenant. Normally pronounced /lɛfˈtɛnənt/ in BrE, and /luːˈtɛnənt/ in AmE. The British navy, on the other hand, omit the /f/ in the first syllable: thus /lɛˈtɛnənt/, /ləˈt-/. It is difficult to explain where the *f* in the British pronunciation comes from. Probably, at some point before the 19th century, the *u* at the end of Old French *lieu-* was read and pronounced as a *v,* and then later as an *f.*

life. The plural is always *lives* (e.g. Johnson's *Lives of the English Poets,* 1779–81), except that the plural of the artistic term *still life* is *still lifes.*

life cycle, first recorded in 1855 in the biological sense 'the sequence of stages through which an individual organism passes from origin to as a zygote to death', is a classic example of a POPULARIZED TECHNICAL TERM. As early as 1915 it was applied to the course of human existence from birth through childhood and to old age and death (e.g. *Here he is, only in middle age, and his life is over— . . . no new fields to conque r . . . So while he is not out of a job . . . the very nature of the life-cycle in America is such that he feels like an old man*—Margaret Mead in 1949, describing the modern man). Since the 1960s the word has been widely used of the pattern of economic or business development shown in a country, a business firm, etc., specifically when the pattern is one of a distinguishable cycle of events, e.g. *In principle the task of the project manager is to plan, organize and lead a group of people to complete a project life cycle*—S. A. Bergen, 1990. It is as well to check whether the simple word *life* is adequate before drawing on either of these transferred uses of *life cycle,* as using it in non-cyclic contexts can easily sound unnecessarily portentous: *?You can change the look at any time and know that the long hair has a limited life cycle.*

lifelong, livelong. The first, pronounced /ˈlʌɪflɒŋ/, is a combination of *life* and *long,* and means 'lasting or continuing for a lifetime'. The second, pronounced /ˈlɪvlɒŋ/, is a combination of *lief* adjective, 'dear, beloved', and *long,* and is an emotional intensive of *long,* used of periods of time (*the livelong day, night,* etc.). It was first recorded in the 15c., and is now in restricted (poetical and rhetorical) use.

lifestyle. 1 Is written as one word, without a hyphen.

2 Used in 1929 by the psychotherapist Alfred Adler (1870–1937) to denote 'a pattern of reactions and behaviour that is established in childhood and remains characteristic of an individual', the term quickly became extended to mean generally 'a way or style of living' (e.g. *The mass-media . . . continually tell their audience what life-styles are 'modern' and 'smart'*—*Guardian,* 1961). The extended sense has often been assailed ('obnoxious', 'an unnecessary and clumsy excrescence on the language', etc.) but has flourished. Of course, if the simple *life,* or the traditional phrase *way of life,* would in context adequately convey the required meaning, one of these should be used instead. (Indeed, the *Telegraph* style book decrees that the latter must always be used in preference to *lifestyle.*) In recent years it has been absorbed into marketing jargon to mean 'relating to the way in which one lives (or chooses to live) one's life, especially with regard to quality of life', or to describe a publication, a product, advertising, etc., designed to appeal to consumers by association with a *lifestyle* regarded as desirable, glamorous, or attractive. In these meanings it is attributive (i.e. coming before a noun): *The latest lifestyle choice for the vibrant elderly is the 'retirement village'*—*Independent,* 1995; *The company seeks to be what Ms. Hilfiger calls a 'lifestyle brand', with one-stop shopping and old-fashioned service*—*NYT,* 2001.

ligature. See DIGRAPH; DIPHTHONG.

light (noun). **1** For *dim religious light,* see IRRELEVANT ALLUSION.

2 *in light of, in the light of.* Both phrases work as complex prepositions meaning 'in view of; with the help of knowledge accorded by some fact' (*Performance on period instruments ... has allowed us to hear much music as the composer, in the light of modern research, is thought to have intended it; In light of what you've told us, we have decided to leave earlier*). The shorter form is the standard in NAmer. English, but is also used in BrE, where the longer form is more common. Both phrases also share the meaning 'against the background of X, taking X into account': *We have to read Chaucer's poetry in the light of the social changes going on in the fourteenth century; Discouraged by horrible reviews, he returned to his trademark technique, a sad bit of irony, especially in light of Magritte's contempt for the nostalgic.*

light (verb). In British English the past tense is usually *lit* (*he lit the fire at 7 pm last night*), as also the past participle (*he had lit his pipe before he noticed the no-smoking sign; frontiers and border checkpoints are always well lit*). When used attributively or as an adjective the standard form is *lighted* (*a lighted cigarette*), except when it is qualified by an adverb (*a well-lit room, a badly lit cellar*). In AmE the same pattern exists, but one is more likely to encounter *lighted* in contexts where in BrE *lit* is more or less obligatory: *She lighted a candle and turned off the lamp—* New Yorker, 1987; *At night the parking lot is badly lighted—New Yorker,* 1987; *the explosion occurred immediately after he had lighted a cigarette—Daily Northwestern* (Evanston, Illinois), 1991.

lightning (electrical discharge in the sky) must always be spelt as shown. *Lightening,* by contrast, is the *-ing* form of the two verbs *lighten* (to reduce the weight of; to brighten up), e.g. *the task of lightening the burdens of taxpayers.* The spelling with *-e-* is widely used mistakenly for the natural phenomenon.

like.

1 As a conjunction.
2 As a preposition.
3 Used as a filler, parenthetically.
4 Introducing reported speech.
5 Idiomatic phrases.

1 *As a conjunction.* (*a*) *The issue. Like* is used as a preposition in the sentence *Please try to write like me* and as a conjunction in the sentence *Please try to write like I do.* Fowler (1926) cited the following sentence from Charles Darwin (1866): *Unfortunately few have observed like you have done.* The Great Schoolmaster's view of this and analogous sentences was expressed with characteristic verve: 'Every illiterate person uses this construction daily; it is the established way of putting the thing among all who have not been taught to avoid it; the substitution of *as* for *like* in their sentences would sound artificial. But in good writing this particular *like* is very rare.' The *OED* (1903) cited examples of *like* used as a conjunction from the works of Shakespeare, Southey, William Morris, Jerome K. Jerome, and others, but added the comment: 'Now generally condemned as vulgar or slovenly, though examples may be found in many recent writers of standing.' Jespersen lists Keats, George Eliot, Dickens, and Shaw, among many others, as having used it.

(*b*) *A persistent shibboleth.* It is unclear exactly when *like* as a conjunction became *verboten,* but it was already mentioned by Noah Webster as 'improper and vulgar' in 1790, and various 19c. commentators depreciated it. Its status has been debated many times since then. A modern authority, *CGEL* (1985), slightly disguises the problem by speaking of 'clausal adjuncts' and 'semantically equivalent phrasal adjuncts', but the verdict is nevertheless much as before. Constructions such as *Please try to write as I do* and *Please try to write like me* are standard; but *Please try to write like I do* is described as being only in informal use, and especially in AmE. Thus, throughout the 20c., the mood was condemnatory, as it still is in many usage guides. The use of *like* as a conjunction has been dismissed as 'illiterate', 'vulgar', 'sloppy', or, in the coded language of modern grammarians, 'informal'. That unrivalled snob Evelyn Waugh spoke for his generation of writers, and for some people still, when he said of Henry Green's *Pack My Bag* (1940): 'Only one thing disconcerted me ... The proletarian grammar—the "likes" for "ases", the "bikes" for "bicycles", etc.'

(*c*) *Some recurring patterns.* Burchfield reconsidered the matter by examining the works of 'many recent writers of standing',

British, American, and from further afield, and the results are still of interest: four main conjunctional uses of *like* emerged.

(i) First, quite frequently, with repetition of the verb used in the main clause, or with the pro-form *do* replacing it, and bearing the sense 'in the way that': *They didn't talk like other people talked*—M. Amis, 1981; *Gordon needs Sylvia like some people need to spend an hour or two every day simply staring out of the window*—P. Lively, 1987; *I'm afraid it might happen to my baby like it happened to Jefferson*—*New Yorker*, 1987; *The retsina flowed like the Arno did when it overflowed in 1966*—*Spectator*, 1987. This use, which, Burchfield claimed, owes something to the song 'If you knew Susie like I know Susie', is common in all English-speaking countries, and, in his words 'must surely escape further censure or reproach. Naturally, though, we may continue to use other constructions if we wish to, and in good company: *She changed wallpapers and lampshades the way some women changed their underwear*—A. N. Wilson, 1986'.

(ii) Secondly, it is frequently used in all sources to mean 'as if, as though', especially with link verbs such as *look, feel sound*: *It looks like it's still a fox*—*New Yorker*, 1986; *She acts like she can't help it*—L. Smith, 1987 (US); *I wanted him born and now it feels like I don't want him*—E. Jolley, 1985 (Aust.). It should also be borne in mind that this use is still widely disliked, and is banned, for instance, in the *Guardian* style guide. Sentences where a negation precedes *like*, e.g. *Well, it isn't like you don't know,* still have a markedly transatlantic ring in BrE.

(iii) Thirdly, it is interchangeable with *as* in all English-speaking countries in a range of fixed, informalish phrases of saying and telling: *Send for your copy now. Like we said it's free*—*Globe & Mail* (Toronto), 1968; *Like you say, you're a dead woman*—M. Wesley, 1983; *Well, like I told you, I work with him upstairs*—P. Ackroyd, 1985; *Like I said, I haven't seen Rudi for weeks*—T. Keneally, 1985.

(iv) Fourthly, it is increasingly used in contexts where a comparison is being made. In these it has the force of 'in the manner (that), in the way (that)': *You call us Mum and Dad like you always have*—M. Wesley, 1983; *How was I to know she'd turn out like she did?*—C. Burns, 1985 (NZ); *Like Jack and Jill came down the hill, Dilip also rolled down the box-office in 'Karma'*—*Star & Style* (Bombay), 1986.

It would appear that in many kinds of written and spoken English *like* as a conjunction is standard and unremarkable. Despite that, if you are writing for an extremely fastidious or conservative audience, when *as* (or *as if* or *as though*) can be substituted for *like*, use these alternatives, which are absolutely safe: *They didn't talk as other people talked*; *Now it feels as if I didn't want him.*

2 *As a preposition.* (*a*) The use of *like* to make a comparison between one thing or action and another, especially in idioms and similes, is unquestioned: *drink like a fish*; *sell like hot cakes*; *if it walks like a duck and quacks like a duck, it is a duck*; (in written sources) *one of those frilly little wooden stations like gingerbread houses*—A. Carter, 1984; *He saw the sunlight leave the grass like an eye suddenly closed*—P. Ackroyd, 1985; *The Pope was confined like a prisoner in the Vatican*—R. Strange, 1986.

(*b*) Sometimes questioned is its use in place of *such as* in the meaning 'of the class of, for example', e.g. *a subject like philosophy*. Objections rest on the claim that in such a sentence prepositional *like* is ambiguous because it could just as easily mean 'resembling' as 'for example'. However, in practice it is hard to find examples which are genuinely ambiguous, since larger context or one's knowledge of the world will suggest the correct interpretation: it would be perverse to interpret the title of Kingsley Amis's novel *Take a Girl Like You* (1960) as meaning 'a girl resembling you'.

(*c*) Hypercorrect use of *as* instead of *like.* Because the use of *like* as a conjunction has been so widely and persistently condemned, writers and editors sometimes avoid it even when it would be correct. A couple of examples cited in *MWCDEU* and an *OEC* example illustrate: *He was built* as *a swordfish*—Ernest Hemingway; *New York,* as *most major cities, has found that the general public is very apathetic*—*NYT*, 1970; *but he will nevertheless consider the profit of the entrepreneur as robbing him of what is his, in particular because he,* as *most people, does not readily understand its substance and origin*—*Amer. Jrnl of Economics and Sociology*, 2002.

(*d*) Logically misleading uses of *like.* The things being compared by means of *like* have to be in the same category. Infringing this rule does not make a statement incomprehensible or ambiguous, but it does make it clumsy. In *Like all group labels [sc.* Freeze artists], *many artists who were included in international shows dedicated to young British artists neither counted themselves part of it nor necessarily actively disassociated themselves—Tate Museum papers,* 2004, artists are being compared to labels. The problem can be removed by rephrasing as 'As with all group labels . . . '.

3 *Used as a filler, parenthetically.* As nobody who is not a hermit can have failed to notice, *like* is now widely used to qualify a preceding or following word, phrase, or clause. The older use, which generally followed whatever it qualified, was first noted in Fanny Burney's *Evelina* (1778): *Father grew quite uneasy, like, for fear of his Lordship's taking offence.* Further examples are cited in the *OED* from works by Scott, Lytton, De Quincey, Arnold Bennett, and other well-known writers. The modern use of this 'filler' or 'discourse particle' typically puts it in front of what it refers to. As Burchfield (1996) said: 'As an occasional device it was unexceptionable. By the mid-20c., however, its use as an incoherent and prevalent filler had reached the proportions of an epidemic.' Many people below the age of, say, twenty-five, or rather more if they are American, seem incapable of constructing a single affirmative sentence without at least one *like* in it. One devoutly hopes that the unfortunates hooked in early life will be able to kick this American verbal drug as they mature, but the signs are not good: weaning them off this addiction looks as unlikely as eliminating crack cocaine.

It is no doubt true, as highly technical academic papers have suggested, that it is not merely a 'meaningless' filler, that it has its own complex rules, and that it fulfils subtle interpersonal functions. However, it is just as true that its overuse will cause listeners outside the speaker's immediate circle, wider social group, or age cohort to ignore the content of the message completely, to assume that the speaker is little short of brain-dead, or, in extreme cases, to wish they had a discreet firearm to hand. A range of typical examples (in many of which it is being used as a sign of unsophisticated speech): *Naa, I was all into that last year, but like I don't really think it's so relevant now*—M. du Plessis, 1983; *I'll say goodbye, like, and send you a message, like, somehow or other, when she turns up, like*—P. Bailey, 1986; *The Blitz? Like right in London?*—M. Pople, 1986; (waitress speaking) *The crowd here is hard to define. Like, they're pretty rich—New Yorker,* 1987; *Like, I just got this journal in the mail from this microtonal music society—Melody Maker,* 1988; *Hayley was pleased. 'That's him. He's, like, got her hypnotized.'*—Maurice Gee, 1990.

4 *Introducing reported speech.* Those who object to the use of *like* described in the previous section will object as, if not more, strenuously to its use in the construction *to be + like,* as in *He was so young he was from the generation of human beings who use the word 'like' to mean 'said'. 'I'm, like, "You've got to be kidding"' was one of his expressions—New Yorker,* 1991. They may be even more horrified to discover that the *OED* (2010) has added this meaning under the following rubric: '*colloq.* (orig. *U.S.*). *to be like*: used to report direct speech (often paraphrased, interpreted, or imagined speech expressing a reaction, attitude, emotion, etc.); to say, utter; (also) to say to oneself . . . Frequently in the historic present . . . Often used to convey the speaker's response to something, or to introduce segments of an ongoing conversation between two or more speakers. Sometimes also used to introduce a gesture or facial expression evocative of the speaker's feelings'. The *OED* examples include the following, the earliest being from the lyrics of a Frank Zappa song: *She's like* Oh my God—F. Zappa & M.U. Zappa, *Valley Girl* (song), 1982; *And I was just like,* [*making a face*]—*Amer. Speech* 65, 1990; *When it came to the contract he cut it back a quarter, so I'm like, whatever, it's still more than what I was asking for—Daily Tel.* (Sydney, Austr.), 2008.

5 *Idiomatic phrases.* Used adverbially in a number of colloquial phrases, e.g. *like anything, like blazes, like crazy* (20c., = like one who is crazy), *like fun* (archaic), *like mad.* These belong only in informal writing or speech. Examples: *Carsons' mill is blazing away like fun*—Mrs Gaskell, 1848; *The horse . . . went like blazes*—De Quincey, 1853; *They wept like anything to see Such quantities of sand*—L. Carroll, 1872; *We . . . heard our fellows cheering like mad*—W. Forbes-Mitchell, 1893; *There she was, beating them with her umbrella like crazy*—J. Osborne, 1957; *Skate was with him like always*—M. Doane, 1988.

like (noun). In 1988 Burchfield was upbraided for writing *Who has not seen the likes of the following?.* He turned to the *OED* to justify himself, and noted with satisfaction that the use of *likes* as a plural noun was listed there with illustrative examples from 1787 onwards (as an alternative to *the like of*), including *2,500 [copies sold] in five months is a good sale for the likes of me* from Browning (1872). This use is also shown in e.g. Penelope Lively's: *that's a luxury for the likes of me—Moon Tiger*, 1987, and is the more frequent form.

like (verb). **1** *I would like* vastly outnumbers *I should like* (in practice, the abbreviated form *I'd like* neutralizes the distinction in any case, especially in the spoken language). The extended type *I would have liked* is used in two distinct constructions: (*a*) *I/he*, etc., *would have liked* + *to*-infinitive: *I would have liked to pause there*—T. Keneally, 1980; *He would have liked to run*—I. McEwan, 1987. (*b*) *I/he.* etc., *would have liked* + *to have* + past participle: *I would have liked to have met James's mother*—A. Brookner, 1983; *She would have liked to have asked them*—B. Rubens, 1987. (*c*) In both such types *should* is sometimes used with a first-person pronoun. Examples: *I should have liked to spare you this*—T. S. Eliot, 1939; *I should have liked to talk to Maurice*—A. Brookner, 1982; *I should have liked to have enjoyed this more*—ibid. The examples in (*b*) and the last one in (*c*) could equally well have used the present infinitive in the subordinate clause without loss of meaning or time reference. An alternative construction is *I should like* + *to have* + past participle, e.g. *I should like to have enjoyed this more.*

2 *like for* + object + *to*-infinitive. This cracker-barrel use (not in the *OED*) seems, mercifully, not to have spread its wings far outside America. Examples: *He told Highridge he would like for the writer ... to be his guest for dinner*—T. Wolfe, 1987; *I'd like very much for you to meet him*—*New Yorker*, 1988. The *Amer. Dialect Dict.* (1944) lists examples from 1888 to 1943, mostly from southern States, but it is not so regionally restricted now.

3 *like to, liked to.* Formed on *like* (adjective), it was first recorded in the 15c. in the Paston Letters in the sense 'seem'. It survived in regional use in BrE until about 1800 before becoming archaic or obsolete, but survives in AmE, chiefly in compound tenses, with the meaning 'to look like or be near to doing (something)'. Examples from US sources: *The evening liked to have been a tedious evening*—J. A. Benton, 1853; *She liked to fainted just* now—J. E. Cooke, 1854; *Then when we got him abroad he liked to kick our brains* out—1938 in *Amer. Dialect Dict.*; *I like to had a fit*—M. K. Rawlings, 1939; *Well, the icing was rancid. I took a big bite and like to died*—M. Grimm, 1989.

-like. In occasional or less familiar formations, and when the first part ends in *-l*, or *-ll*, a hyphen is used: *eel-like, owl-like, cell-like, mill-like; cat-like, cartoon-like, zombie-like.* But established *-like* compounds are normally written as one word, e.g. *childlike, lifelike, statesmanlike.*

likeable is the more frequent spelling everywhere, except in AmE, where **likable** is more frequent and given as the first form in dictionaries, but *likeable* is also quite widely used. See MUTE E.

likely. 1 Freely used as an adjective: *it is not likely that they will come; a likely story;* (followed by a *to*-infinitive) *he is not likely to come now.*

2 As an adverb it is often qualified by another adverb, especially *more, most, quite,* or *very* but just as often stands without an adverbial prop in AmE, a tendency which is also spreading in BrE: *It is possible to predict that within a few years the microfiche likely will move into the study and home*—*Publishers' Weekly*, 1971; *I ... caught myself trying to calculate how maybe he'd brought it on, why likely he'd had it coming*—T. R. Pearson, 1993; *While the population has likely increased in the past couple of decades, many researchers point out that the animals are still in jeopardy*—*Defenders of Wildlife*, 2004.

likewise. Like *also*, *likewise* is used as an adverb and not a conjunction in standard English: *Go and do likewise; They likewise prefer reading.* Where it might be a conjunction, it normally needs the support of a genuine conjunction such as *and*: *A heated window, and likewise rear wipers, are essential.* Fowler (1926) cited *Its tendency to wobble and its uniformity of tone colour, likewise its restricted powers of execution* as an example of what to avoid (he actually called it an 'illiteracy'). On the other hand, it is correctly used when placed as an 'additive conjunct' (*CGEL*'s term) at the head of a sentence: e.g. St *Paul's Cathedral is one of the most easily recognizable sights of London. Likewise the Eiffel Tower is one of the most easily recognizable sights of Paris.*

-lily. 1 For reasons of euphony, adverbs in *-lily* formed from adjectives in *-ly* now seldom occur. For some examples, see FRIENDLILY. As Fowler (1926) remarked, 'It is always possible to say *in a masterly manner, at a timely moment,* and the like, instead of *masterlily, timelily.*'

2 Presumably for the same reason, a number of adjectives ending in *-ly* often or usually remain unchanged when used as adverbs: GINGERLY, *jolly soon, a kindly thought and kindly said.*

3 A few *-lily* adverbs are listed as current English in *COD* (1995), e.g. *holily, jollily, sillily, uglily,* but all of these are formed from words in which *-ly* is part of the word stem and not the usual adjectival ending.

limbo (The word referring to a West Indian dance in which a dancer bends low in order to pass under a bar is a different word.). Apart from its religious meaning 'the supposed abode of the souls of unbaptized infants, etc.', *limbo* can refer to an uncertain period of awaiting a decision or resolution, (e.g. *the legal battle could leave the club in limbo until next year*), or a state of neglect or oblivion (e.g. *these prisoners are in limbo: no one is responsible for their welfare*). It is most often used in the phrase *in(to) limbo,* and to insert *a* before the word is unnecessary unless *limbo* itself is postmodified, e.g. *?'I'm living in a limbo here,' says 41- year-old Susan—Irish Examiner,* 2002; but *millions of other immigrants around the world who may go to sleep in their own beds but live in a limbo of expired documents and steely bureaucracies—AlterNet.org,* 2004. Nor should it be used to mean simply a period between two other events, e.g. *?the limbo between Christmas and the resumption of normal life in early January.* The plural, if required, is *limbos.* See -O(E)S 4.

limey. The adjective corresponding to the white caustic alkaline substance *lime* is *limy*; that corresponding to the fruit called *lime* is *limey. Limey* as an AmE slang term for a person from Britain arose from the enforced consumption of lime juice in the British navy.

limited (adjective). A *limited* (or *limited liability*) *company* is one whose owners are legally responsible only to a limited amount for its debts. It does not imply that the number of members is limited.

limn (verb). Encountered in works about miniature portraits and in palaeography, the base-form is, like *solemn,* pronounced with the *n* silent. The inflected forms are *limns* /lɪmz/, *limned* /lɪmd/, *limner* /ˈlɪmnə/, and *limning* /ˈlɪmɪŋ/ or /ˈlɪmnɪŋ/. It is a curiosity that the 'Painter and Limner' has since 1702 been the title of the official painter of the royal household in Scotland. It is nowadays an unpaid post imposing no obligation to produce works of art for the monarch.

linage /ˈlʌɪnɪdʒ/ is the correct spelling for the word meaning 'the number of lines in printed or written matter'; contrasted with *lineage* /ˈlɪnɪɪdʒ/ 'lineal descent, ancestry'.

linchpin, originally a pin put through the end of an axle to keep the wheel in position, is mostly used in its figurative sense 'a person or thing indispensable to an organization', e.g. *nurses are the linchpin of the NHS.* It is spelt *linch-* in preference to *lynch-,* and as one word.

lineage. See LINAGE.

lingerie. In BrE pronounced in an approximately French manner as /ˈlãʒərɪ/ or /-riː/; in AmE most commonly as /ˌlɑnʒəˈreɪ/ or /-ˈriː/. But the pronunciation of the word is still very unstable in all English-speaking countries.

lingo. The plural is *lingos.* For some related words, see JARGON.

lingua franca. For some related words, see JARGON.

linguistic engineering is a term sometimes used for the process by which a group, an institution, government, etc., tries to control the language used by the public, on the assumption that language controls thought and attitude. It has been a feature of totalitarian societies, such as the Soviet Union and Maoist China, and Orwell's Newspeak is its most celebrated literary incarnation. The term is also sometimes used as a way of disparaging milder attempts to change everyday language, such as the use of *partner* to cover all kinds of relationship, the use of *chair* or *chairperson* and other gender-neutral language. The beneficial side of linguistic engineering is shown in the introduction of a medical term like *Down's syndrome* instead of *Mongolism* and similar adjustments to the way people with disabilities are described. Its sinister nature is shown by the Chinese government's insistence on removing the word Tibet from imported dictionaries and any kind of reference work.

linguist, linguistics. First used in the early 19c. to mean 'the science of languages, linguistic science', it gradually overtook and then almost totally replaced the term *philology* in universities in the second half of the 20c. The Karl Marx of linguistics is Ferdinand de Saussure (1857–1913), the French-speaking Swiss linguistic scholar, and the key work is his *Cours de linguistique générale* (first published in 1916, compiled from the lecture notes of his students). He established the primary distinction between a *synchronic* approach (seeing a language as a state at a particular point in time) and a *diachronic* (historical) one. He also perceived language as having two dimensions, which he called *langue* (the systems and totality of a given language) and *parole* (the act of speaking, individual speech). Linguistics has inevitably broken up into subdivisions, such as sociolinguistics, computational linguistics, psycholinguistics, and applied linguistics. Like many academic disciplines it has opposing schools of thought, often with their own battery of complex terminology.

The term *linguist,* first introduced in 1593, in general usage describes someone skilled in the use of language, particularly foreign languages, e.g. *a gifted/talented/brilliant/French linguist.* The word is also applied to someone who works in the field of linguistics, e.g. *a professional/computational/historical linguist.* It is in theory ambiguous, but in practice rarely so, and the term *linguistician* (1895) to refer to professional linguists only has never really caught on.

linking r. Many English speakers do not pronounce the final written *r* of the many words which have it, such as *weather, richer, floor,* and *pour* when such words occur in isolation or are followed by a word beginning with a consonant: accordingly, /pɔː/ and *pour cups of coffee* /ˈpɔː ˈkʌps . . . /. *Linking r* is the term for the phenomenon of the /r/ being pronounced when followed by a word beginning with a vowel, e.g. *pour out* /ˈpɔːr ˈaʊt/. The linking *r* is always used by non-rhotic standard speakers in such expressions as *a pair‿of gloves, wouldn't hear‿of it, feather‿edge.* Cf. INTRUSIVE R.

links (golf-course). The word has the same form as a singular noun and as a plural one: *a suburban links; there are numerous links within easy reach of the city.*

Linnaean, of the Swedish naturalist Carolus Linnaeus (1707–78). But spelt *Linnean* in the *Linnean Society* (London).

liny (marked with lines, wrinkled). Spelt as shown, not *liney.*

liquefaction, liquefied, etc. Spelt as shown, not, as quite often happens, *liquifaction, liquify,* etc. Reading this word inevitably recalls Herrick's *Whenas in silks my Julia goes Then, then* (*methinks*) *how sweetly flows That liquefaction of her clothes.* See -FY 2.

liqueur. Pronounced in BrE /lɪˈkjʊə/ and in AmE usually /lɪˈkəːr/.

liquid. An old-fashioned term used by some phoneticians in the classification of speech sounds for the apico-alveolar sounds /r/ and /l/. Also applied by some writers to the sounds denoted by the letters *m* and *n.*

liquorice /ˈlɪkərɪs, -rɪʃ/. In BrE the normal spelling of the word meaning a black root extract used as a sweet; AmE **licorice**.

liquorish. An occasional misspelling of *liquorice.* For its proper, if rare, meaning, see LICKERISH.

lira /ˈlɪərə/, formerly the monetary unit of Italy, and still that of Turkey, has plural *lire* (in English pronounced the same as the singular).

lissom. The standard spelling, not *lissome.*

lit. See LIGHT (verb).

litany, liturgy. 1 The first is 'a series of petitions for use in church services and processions, usually recited by the clergy and responded to in a recurring formula by the people; specifically, that contained in the Book of Common Prayer'. The second is 'public worship in accordance with a prescribed form' embracing many individual prayers and petitions e.g. *Byzantine, Orthodox, Catholic Liturgy.* It is tempting to suppose that the initial *lit-* in each word has the same derivation, but it hasn't. *Litany* is ultimately from Greek λιτανεία 'prayer', from λιτή 'supplication'; whereas *liturgy* answers to Greek λειτουργία 'public service, public worship', from (recorded only in compounds) λεῖτος 'public'.

2 *Litany* is frequently used for 'a tedious recital or repetitive series' seen as resembling a form of religious ritual (e.g. *a litany of complaints, failures, lies, problems, woes*). Occasionally *liturgy* is questionably used in this sense: *?Heidegger was by no means the only twentieth-century intellectual to subscribe to an inexhaustible liturgy of anxieties about modernity and the perils of city life*—*TLS*, 2011.

litchi. See LYCHEE.

lite was first used in advertising in the 1960s to denote a product, especially beer, lower in weight, calorie content etc. than the standard ones. Since then this simplified spelling variant of *light*, often placed after the noun it qualifies, has become a usefully humorous or dismissive way of characterizing more abstract notions as superficial or lacking in seriousness: *I am the happy feminist, the feminist who likes men, the feminist lite*—*Playboy*, 1992; USA Today *is still dogged by the perception among many would-be advertisers and the media elite that it remains News Lite, a triumph of marketing over substance*—*Newsweek*, 1992; *That is why the worldwide ascendancy of lite anti-Americanism is a dangerous trend. And not only for Americans*—*New Perspectives Quarterly*, 2003.

literally. 1 *The issue.* 'My grandfather, King George VI, who had literally been catapulted onto the throne'—Prince Edward as quoted in *Private Eye*, 1998. Few words have the potential to cause such mirth. Fewer still have such a capacity to raise so many hackles. In mid-August 2013, the media in Britain and elsewhere were agog with the news that the *OED* had caved in to the persistent 'misuse' of *literally* by supposedly giving it a new definition.

The *OED*'s alleged change of heart provoked heated debate because it appeared to authorize a usage which had been widely ridiculed, by members of the public as well as by usage pundits, and to reverse entirely the meaning of the word. For it is clear to anyone that George VI was not propelled from a medieval siege machine. Still less is it the case that when sports commentator Jamie Redknapp characterized Wayne Rooney as 'literally on fire' the fire brigade was called on to douse the overpaid Liverpudlian. Those two examples are, therefore, literally nonsense according to the traditional meaning of the word as defined by the *OED*: 'In a literal, exact, or actual sense; not figuratively, allegorically, etc.' According to this definition, 'literally catapulted' should have been 'figuratively catapulted' or 'metaphorically catapulted'.

2 *The original meaning.* As just defined above, it is first recorded from *c.*1429, is alive and well, and is often used with the verbs *take* and *mean*. Examples: *She often became very angry with me for taking her literally*—*New Yorker*, 1973; *The expression 'class warfare' was meant analogically, not literally, by Marx and Engels*—*Marx's Revenge*, 2004. It is also still used to show that the metaphor or image following it is to be taken in its literal sense: *Found guilty of treason, he is tortured, and his right arm cut off . . . How can he possibly fend for himself at all, let alone manage quite literally single-handed for 30 years?*—*Tokyo Weekender*, 2001.

3 *The disputed meaning.* (*a*) *It is not new.* Using *literally* to mean the opposite of what it is 'supposed' to mean is nothing new. Round the turn of the 19c. it had come to the attention of the *OED* editor Henry Bradley, who accordingly added a note to his 1903 entry: 'Now often improperly used to indicate that some conventional metaphorical or hyperbolical phrase is to be taken in the strongest admissible sense'. He gave this 1863 example: *For the last four years I literally coined money*—F. A. Kemble. But, as *MWCDEU* points out, Dickens had previously used it in *Nicholas Nickleby* (1839), when the unforgettably abominable Wackford Squeers recaptures the luckless Smike: '"Lift him out", said Squeers, after he had literally feasted his eyes in silence upon the culprit.' The latest version of the *OED* takes this use back a further 70 years: *He is a fortunate man to be introduced to such a party of fine women* *at his arrival; it is literally to feed among the lilies*—F. Brooke, 1769. Similar usage was criticized in Webster in 1909, and pounced on by Fowler in 1926: 'We have come to such a pass with this emphasizer that where the truth would require us to insert with a strong expression "not literally, of course, but in a manner of speaking", we do not hesitate to insert the very word that we ought to be at pains to repudiate.' His shudder of reproof finds echo in a slightly earlier quotation by Rose Macaulay (1922): *The things 'they' say! They even say . . . that 'literally' bears the same meaning as 'metaphorically' ('she was literally a mother to him,' they will say)*.

(*b*) *It is a logical evolution.* The second meaning defined in the *OED* is: 'Used to indicate that the following word or phrase must be taken in its literal sense, usually to add emphasis', e.g. *Every day with me is literally Another To-morrow; for it is exactly the same with Yesterday*—Pope, 1708; *What punishment has he suffered? Literally none*—'Junius', 1769. The key word here is 'emphasis', as foreshadowed by Fowler's 'emphasizer'. From emphasizing non-metaphors *literally* has bit by bit passed to emphasizing metaphors and figures of speech, as it was already doing in the quotation from Pope. This historical development explains how the word has apparently reversed its meaning. In fact it has done no such thing but has been absorbed into the metaphor. Once it is analysed as part of the verbal image and not as external to it, the use makes good linguistic sense, and can often be reinterpreted in the way suggested by Fowler and the current *OED*, that is to say, as equivalent to 'practically, virtually; as good as'. In the light of that definition, examples such as the following make perfect sense: *And with his eyes he literally scoured the corners of the cell*—V. Nabokov, 1960; *Many in this group think they can ignore depreciation as they are buying the car new and literally running it into the ground*— *Money Paper*, 1987.

4 *Dos and don'ts.* (*a*) *Use your judgement.* Knowing that your readers may have the screaming abdabs (dated British English for 'have a fit') if they read *literally* prefacing a metaphor in the ways described above, you might want to avoid using it altogether. Otherwise, I urge you to reread what you have written so as to avoid hilarity or ridiculousness you did not intend, as in: *'OMG, I literally died when I found out!' No, you figuratively died. Otherwise, you would not be around to relay your pointless anecdote*—*Herald-Times* (Bloomington, Indiana), 2008.

(*b*) There are also contexts in which *literally* is inserted in a trite semi-apologetic way that seemingly seeks to overcome a fear that the reader will not believe what is said, carrying a 'please believe me' or 'I'm not kidding you' tag: *Thus the Prime Minister, the chief executive of the British Government, had literally no idea that he lacked the means to do what he wanted*—*Independent*, 2006. The same applies to *You'd start in the morning and it would literally go on till late at night*—J. Gathorne-Hardy, 1984. In both *literally* adds nothing to the sense and is redundant.

Similarly, although *literally* often collocates with *impossible* and *unthinkable,* it is hard to see what it adds in examples like these: *For millions of the unemployed, it is literally impossible to find a job*—*Economic Policy Institute*, 2003. (Could the thinking behind this, if there is any, be that to say finding a job is 'impossible' is merely a figure of speech, whereas now it has become true in fact?) Similarly: *But when you say it's literally unthinkable that we would default on the payment of a bond, why? Tell our viewers what might happen if we did that*—*CNN* transcripts, 2011. To say that something is *unthinkable* means it is out of the question, it is absurd; but to say that it is 'literally unthinkable' is a contradiction in terms, since someone clearly has already thought about it enough to raise it as a possibility.

As a postscript, the revised *OED* definition (September 2011) is almost word for word (i.e. 'literally') the same as the 1903 definition quoted at 3 above. What has changed is that (i) the synonyms 'completely, utterly, absolutely' have been added, which justify examples like the last two in the preceding paragraph; and (ii) that the weight of modern usage has been acknowledged by changing Bradley's note 'improperly used' to: 'Now one of the most common uses, although often considered irregular in standard English since it reverses the original sense of *literally* ("not figuratively or metaphorically").' Perhaps all the fuss in 2013 was literally a storm in a teacup.

literary words. The notion that certain words are more suitable for verse and literary prose than for the ordinary language held sway from the earliest times until the first part of the 20c. Fowler (1926) touched on the matter when he remarked '[A literary word] is one that cannot be called archaic, inasmuch as it is perfectly comprehensible still to all who hear it, but that has dropped out of [everyday] use and had its place taken by some other word except in writing of a poetical or a definitely literary cast.' He had in mind such words as *eve* (for *evening*), *gainsay* (for *deny*), and *visage* (for *face*). He might easily have added words like *ere, erstwhile, perchance,* and other WARDOUR STREET words.

Fowler's view is no longer valid. Poetry and writing 'of a definitely literary cast' have become democratized and no longer necessarily contain an element of specialized vocabulary. As Katie Wales points out in her *Dictionary of Stylistics* (1989), 'literary language can be different and yet not different from "ordinary" or non-literary language; there is, as it were, a "prototype" of literary language, and also numerous variants. But it is the impossibility of defining it in any simple way that is its most defining feature.' The chronological arrangement of Philip Larkin's *Oxford Book of Twentieth-Century Verse* (1973) underlined the change of attitude that occurred as the century progressed. In the early part of the century Thomas Hardy could write *Did her gifts and compassions* enray *and* enarch *her sweet ways With an aureate* nimb?' (my emphases). Many poets of the 1930s, including Auden and MacNeice, ventured into plainer or even informal language. Kingsley Amis wrote lines such as these: *The journal of some bunch of architects Named this the worst town centre they could find.* Now there are no words designated 'for literary use only', but also none that are banned from poetic or literary use. Witness lines like the following: *The butcher carves veal for two* (Hugo Williams); *The stars, the buggers, remained silent* (Brian Patten); *They fuck you up, your mum and dad* (Philip Larkin); *Size isn't everything. It's what you do That matters* (Wendy Cope). The frontiers have been abolished, and, as a result, the classification of literary words has largely passed out of the sphere of lexical enquiry into that of literary theory.

literature. Though the word itself is old—it was first recorded in the 14c. in the now-obsolete sense 'acquaintance with "letters" or books'—the usual modern sense, 'literary productions as a whole', dates only from the 18c. Before the 19c. was over the word had been pressed into service to mean printed matter of any kind, especially leaflets, brochures, etc., used to advertise products or provide information and advice: *In canvassing, in posters, and in the distribution of what, by a profane perversion of language, is called 'literature'—Daily News,* 1895. Gowers (1965) disliked this extended sense, and worried that it would diminish the primacy of the central sense, i.e. 'written work valued for superior or lasting artistic merit'. That meaning has not been undermined in any way, despite also being in competition with the sense 'the material in print on a given subject' (*there is a considerable literature on anabolic steroids*).

litotes. 1 Generally pronounced stressing the second syllable /lʌɪˈtəʊtiːz/ (ly-**toh**-teez) /lɪˈtəʊtiːz/ (li-**toh**-teez), but also with first-syllable stress, as shown in the *OED* (1903) /ˈlʌɪtəʊtiːz/ (**ly**-toh-teez).

2 *Meaning.* A rhetorical figure or trope in which an assertion is made by means of understatement or denial of an opposite. It has been a marked feature of English from earliest times. *Beowulf,* for example, has many instances: e.g. *gūð-werig,* literally 'war-weary' but by litotes 'dead'; *nō þæt ȳðe byð tō beflēonne,* lit. 'that is not easy to escape from', by litotes 'that is impossible to escape from'. An example from the AV is St Paul's declaring that he was '*a citizen of no mean city*' (Acts 21:39). Typical modern examples include: *not a few,* a great number; *it was nothing* (used by a successful performer, examinee, etc., to downplay the achievement); *not unwelcome* (a polite way of saying 'very welcome'); *not uncommon,* quite common; *not bad, eh?,* (after an anecdote or mild boast). *Litotes* is the opposite of HYPERBOLE or overstatement. Cf. also MEIOSIS.

litre is the BrE spelling, **liter** the AmE one.

liturgy. See LITANY.

livable is the preferred form in NAmer. English, and **liveable** in BrE. The first conforms to the standard rule for MUTE E.

-lived. In *long-lived, short-lived* the second element is pronounced /-lɪvd/, with a short stem vowel, in BrE, but usually with a long vowel in AmE. The pronunciation with a short stem vowel is presumably a product of the 20c. as the *OED* (entries of 1903 and 1914 respectively) recommends /-lʌɪvd/ for both words.

livelong. See LIFELONG, LIVELONG.

livid. *Livid* is derived from Latin *līvidus* 'slate-coloured; discoloured by bruises or chafing'. Dictionaries list the senses (first recorded in the 17c.) (*a*) of a bluish leaden colour, and (*b*) discoloured as by a bruise, literally black and blue. It was also used to suggest an unhealthy pallor, as in the gothic novelist Ann Radcliffe's *The light glared upon the livid face of the corpse—The Italian*, 1797. But the meaning most likely to be encountered in everyday life (still marked *colloq.* or *informal* in some dictionaries) is 'furiously angry' (first recorded in 1912). The *OED* says of this meaning 'as if pale with rage', and the original idea behind the extended meaning was indeed one of ashen-faced anger. However, because anger is often associated with a flushed complexion, *livid* has also been interpreted as meaning 'red', 'red-faced', or simply 'vivid'. This use has been criticized, and can certainly produce ambiguity, since it can be unclear if *livid red* is pale or intense. Examples: (= furiously angry) *She was furious with me for ruining her tax-free investment. Livid.—Wall St. Jrnl*, 1987; *Further communications . . . culminated in Shelley's most livid screech of rage against his father*—R. Christiansen, 1988; (= discoloured, of a scar) *A huge, livid, recently healed scar ran along the right side of his face*—P. Abrahams, 1985; (= vivid) *?My attention is seized by a young man with a pitbull and livid red face, swigging lager and belching—Daily Tel.*, 2007; *?I should have asked for the livid red curry sauce to be just a smidgen hotter, but that was my fault—The Press* (York), 2000; (ambiguous use) *She slapped him, hard, her own palm stinging in response and a livid red mark blossoming across his cheek—Forbidden Love*, 2005.

llama. See LAMA.

-ll-, -l-. 1 Words in final *-l* are usually treated differently from those ending in most other final consonants in that, in BrE, in inflected forms, the *-l* is doubled irrespective of the position of the accent. By contrast, in AmE, final *-l* is usually left undoubled in such circumstances. For details, see DOUBLING OF CONSONANTS WITH SUFFIXES 2. Exceptions: before *-ish, -ism,* and *-ist,* final *l* is not doubled (e.g. *devilish, liberalism, naturalist*); and before *-able,* the *-l* is usually doubled both in BrE and AmE (e.g. *annullable, controllable, distillable*).

2 The 20c. witnessed much shuffling and reshuffling of *-l* and *-ll* in the simple form of a good many verbs. A fairly safe guide is to use *annul, appal, befall, distil, enrol, enthral, extol, fulfil, install,* and *instil* in BrE, and *annul, appall, befall, distill, enroll, enthrall, extol, fulfill, install,* and *instill* in AmE. But, truth to tell, no firm rule can be applied. All of these words except *annul* and *befall* may turn up with either *-l* or *-ll* in good sources in either country.

3 Before *-ment,* the usual spellings are *annulment, enrolment, enthralment, extolment, fulfilment, instalment,* and *instilment* in BrE; and *annulment, enrollment, enthrallment, extolment, fulfillment, installment,* and *instillment* in AmE. But forms with single *-l-* are often found in good AmE sources for the words listed here with *-ll-*.

4 The doubling rule does not apply when the *l* is preceded by a double vowel or a vowel + consonant, e.g. *ai, ea, ee, oi, ow, ur,* as in *failed, squealed, peeled, boiled, howled, curled.* Another exception is *paralleled, -ing.*

5 Derivatives and compounds of words ending in *-ll* sometimes drop one *l*: so *almighty, almost, already, alright, altogether, always*; *chilblain, skilful, thraldom, wilful.* The AmE equivalents of the last four are *chilblain, skillful, thralldom, willful* (the last three alternating with forms in *-l-*).

6 See DULLNESS, FULLNESS.

Lloyd's, society of underwriters in London (hence *Lloyd's list, Lloyd's Register*), not *Lloyds* or *Lloyds'*. But *Lloyds Bank* (no apostrophe).

loadstar. See LODESTAR.

loadstone. See LODESTONE.

loaf. The plural of the noun is *loaves.* The third person singular present indicative of the verb is *loafs.*

loan (verb). Sentences of the type *we once loaned a Protestant lady a pamphlet by an eminent Catholic divine,* i.e. *loan* used as a ditransitive verb, and *the stalls are barrack chairs loaned for the occasion,* i.e. *loaned* used as past participle in a passive construction, were well established in standard English in the 19c. The *OED* placed no restriction on their currency. Fowler (1926), on the other hand, declared that the verb *loan* 'has been expelled from idiomatic southern English by *lend,* but was formerly current, and survives in U.S. and locally in U.K.' It is still true to say that to convey the literal meaning of 'grant someone something temporarily on the understanding that it will be returned' *loan* is comparatively rare in BrE, but it does occur. In this meaning, according to *MWCDEU,* in AmE it is 'entirely standard . . . and includes literature but not the more elevated kinds of discourse'.

There are two contexts in which *loan* as a verb is widely used in BrE: when it is a bank or some other institution lending money, often in a business context (e.g. *The gas industry is using a major part of its profits to benefit the PSBR by loaning money to Government*); and when a work of art or something of value or significance is lent by one institution, owner, etc.

Examples: *Delaney told him he could loan him $50 a week*—T. Keneally, 1985 (Aust); *the . . . problem was how to stretch the small amount of money he had been loaned by Herr Pfuehl*—A. Desai, 1988 (India); *The Development Bank of Southern Africa . . . loaned R650-million for the purpose—Panorama,* 1991 (SAfr.); *The coach was restored . . . and is loaned now to charity organisations to help with fund-raising—Lancaster Guardian,* 1987 (UK); *It is part of the Christ Church plate in the treasury showcase, which also displays many items loaned by parishes within the diocese—Christ Church Oxford: A Pitkin Guide,* 1991 (UK); *Family and friends loaned money and helped her to buy the former Muslim girls school—www.thisisbradford.co.uk,* 2003 (UK); *Within days, she had signed a document confirming that she wanted to loan him £16,000 interest free—www.thisishampshire.net,* 2004 (UK).

loanword is the technical term for a word borrowed from another language with little or no adaptation, e.g. *blitz* (from German), *locale* (from French), and *kiosk* (from Turkish). A **loan translation** is a word or phrase translated literally, i.e. word for word, from another language: *loanword* itself is a loan translation of German *Lehnwort,* while *lose face* is a loan translation of Chinese *diū liǎn. Loanword* is now usually written as one word (no hyphen, not two words).

loath /ləʊθ/, averse. Preferably spelt as shown, not *loth,* though that too is correct. In theory both are to be pronounced to rhyme with *both,* but are often pronounced to rhyme with *clothe.* As a result they are quite often confused with the verb *loathe* /ləʊð/, to hate, which, apart from its different spelling, has a fully voiced *th.* (The *-oa-* spelling is obligatory in *loathsome,* which derives from the verb.) Examples of confusing the two: (*loathe* used for *loath*) **The young seventies family man . . . was loathe to purchase the same car that his fifty-five-year-old father might own*—B. Elton, 1991; (*loath* used for *loathe*) **I loath reading a review that tells me more about the critic than what they are critiquing*—D. Poland, 2003.

locale. This noun meaning 'a scene or locality, especially with reference to an event or occurrence taking place there' (*COD* 1995) was adopted in the 18c. from French in the form *local,* and respelt in the early 19c. (Walter Scott and others) as *locale* to indicate that the stress lay on the second syllable, /ləʊˈkɑːl/. Cf. MORALE.

locate is recorded first in the American colonies in the early 17c., and has now achieved global use, despite repeated criticism. The intransitive use to mean 'to establish oneself or itself in a place, to settle' (e.g. *numerous industries have located in the area*) is more or less confined to N. America. In this and other uses in AmE the stress normally falls on the first syllable, /ˈləʊkeɪt/, as against second-syllable stressing in BrE.

Various uses of the verb have become established in other English-speaking areas. The central senses in Britain are (*a*) to discover the exact place or position of (*to locate the enemy's gun emplacements; She had located and could usefully excavate her Saharan highland emporium*—M. Drabble (*OMEU*)); and (*b*) in the passive, to be situated (*a supermarket located in the outskirts of the city*). This second use is sometimes viewed as unnecessary, since the sentence just quoted would mean the same without it, but it is too well established to cause most people any qualms.

locative (/ˈlɒkətɪv/, **lo**-kuh-tiv). In languages expressing relationships by means of inflections, the case of nouns and pronouns expressing location; cf. Latin *locus* 'place'. Many Indo-European languages have or had such a case, typified by Latin *domī* 'at home', *rūrī* 'in the country', *Romae* 'in Rome', *Corinthī* 'at Corinth'. Modern English does not have a locative case, the locative idea being introduced by a preposition (*at, in, on*).

loch, lough (both pronounced with a guttural final sound as /lɒx/ or in anglicized form as /lɒk/), respectively the Scottish and Irish words for 'lake'.

loculus, in zoology and botany a small separate cavity. Plural *loculi* /-lʌɪ/. In practice the anglicized form *locule* is much more often used.

locum tenens is the Latin phrase, literally 'one holding a place' of which *locum* is an abbreviation. According to Burchfield, all the locums he had ever met pronounced the phrase /ˌləʊkəm ˈtɛnɛnz/, with a short /ɛ/ in the first syllable of *tenens.* But standard dictionaries tend to give precedence to /ˈtiːnɛnz/. The plural, if it should be needed, is *locum tenentes*; and the position of such a deputy is a *locum tenency* (not *-ancy*).

locus. Usually pronounced (e.g. in mathematics and biology, and in many legal phrases) as /ˈləʊkəs/, with plural *loci* /ˈləʊsʌɪ/. In the phrase *locus classicus* it is as frequently pronounced /ˈlɒk-/, i.e. with the short *o* of the Latin original. The plural is *loci classici,* with both words ending in /-sʌɪ/.

lodestar. The recommended spelling, not *load-*.

lodestone. The recommended spelling, not *load-*.

lodgement. The action of depositing or lodging something. More often spelt as shown, not *lodgment,* except that the latter spelling is given precedence in US dictionaries. Cf. JUDGEMENT.

loggia (gallery, arcade). Can be pronounced /ˈləʊdʒə/ or /ˈlɒ-/ the first syllable having the *o* of *load* or *log.* The first is more common in AmE. The plural is normally *loggias* or rarely, when discussing an Italian building, *loggie* /ˈlɒdʒeɪ/, in line with the Italian original word.

logion /ˈlɒgɪɒn/, a saying attributed to Christ. Plural *logia* /ˈlɒgɪə/.

-logue. Principally **1** forming nouns denoting talk (*dialogue, prologue*) or compilation (*catalogue*).

2 Words ending in *-logue.* The equivalent AmE words are often, but not always, spelt with final *-og* (*analog, catalog, dialog,* etc.).

-logy, a combining form which normally has *o* as the combining element: thus *archaeology, tautology, zoology,* etc. The principal exceptions are *genealogy* (answering ultimately to Greek γενεαλογία 'tracing of descent') and *mineralogy* (from *minera*(*l*) + *-logy*). The incorrect forms **geneology* and **minerology* are often heard. Cf. -OLOGY.

lonelily. This rare adverb was pressed into service by Matthew Arnold to give him a ten-syllable line (*The weird chipping of the woodpecker Rang lonelily and sharp; the sky was fair* 1852), but in ordinary prose it is too awkward to use and is replaced by 'in a lonely way'. See -LILY.

longest word. The innocent question 'What is the longest word in the English language?' can only be sensibly answered by saying that the longest words in the largest dictionary of English, namely the *OED,* are *pneumonoultramicroscopicsilicovolcanoconiosis* (a made-up word of 45 letters, coined in 1935 in imitation of medical terminology and alleged to mean 'a lung disease caused by the inhalation of very fine silica dust'); *supercalifragilisticexpialidocious* (34 letters, 'fantastic, fabulous', 1964); *floccinaucinihilipilification* (a humorous word of 29 letters invented by William Shenstone in 1741 meaning 'the action or habit of estimating as worthless'); and *antidisestablishmentarianism* ('opposition to the disestablishment of the Church of England', 28 letters, early 20c.). None of these has ever really been a proper nine-to-five word, although *supercali* etc. has occasionally been used to express the utter fabulousness of something. In the real world, but in a very limited technical sphere, the following contestants from the *OED* qualify as spectacularly long: *pseudopseudohypoparathyroidism* (30 letters, a genetic disorder), and the astounding adverb *spectrophotofluorometrically* (28 letters).

longevity. Pronounced /lɒnˈdʒevɪti/, not /lɒŋˈg-/ (lon-**je**-vi-tee, not long-**ghe**-vi-tee).

longitude. The pronunciation recommended is /ˈlɒndʒɪtjuːd/ rather than /ˈlɒŋgɪ-/. The form *longtitude* (modelled on *latitude*), with the first *t* fully pronounced dates back at least to the early 19c. but is nevertheless incorrect.

long-lived. See -LIVED.

long variants. Fowler (1926) argued at length that 'The better the writer, the shorter his words', though he admitted that the 'statement needs many exceptions for individual persons and particular subjects'. He set down three main types of words in contrastive pairs: (i) where two forms or close relations of the same word are equally available and the longer form is chosen; (ii) where a short form exists and a longer form is made by the addition of a suffix such as -*atable*, -*en*, or -*ize*; (iii) where a longer form exists but bears a different meaning.

Examples of types (i) and (ii) include (with the date of first record indicated): *administer* 14c./*administrate* a1639; *assertive* 1562/*assertative* 1846; *contumacy* 14c./*contumacity* 15c.; *cultivable* 1682/*cultivatable* 1847; *damp* (verb) 1564/*dampen* c.1630; *doubt* 13c./*dubiety* c.1750; *educationist* 1829/*educationalist* 1857; *epistolary* 1656/*epistolatory* 1715 ('erroneous formation', *OED*); *experiment* (verb) 1481/*experimentalize* 1800; *perfect* (verb) c.1449/*perfectionize* 1839 ('rare', *OED*); *preventive* 1639/*preventative* 1654–66; *quiet* (verb) 1526/*quieten* 1828.

Many of these words are discussed at their alphabetical place. It is more or less self-evident that the first words of the pairs are usually to be preferred, though *dampen*, *preventative*, and *quieten* have wide currency at the present time. What stands out is that the first words of the pairs are all recorded earlier than their contrasted forms, a fact that draws attention to the fluctuating fortunes of various suffixes over the centuries. What feels comfortable in one century does not necessarily feel as comfortable in another.

Examples of type (iii) include: *advance* (noun)/*advancement; alternate*/*alternative; correctness*/*correctitude; definite*/*definitive; distinct*/*distinctive; estimate* (noun)/*estimation; intense*/*intensive; prudent*/*prudential; reverent*/*reverential; simple*/*simplistic*. These are discussed under the words in their dictionary place unless they are too familiar to need discussion.

Fowler listed a fourth type in which he preferred the longer form: *pacifist* 1906/*pacificist* 1907; *quantitive* 1656/*quantitative* 1581; *authoritive* (not listed in any dictionary)/*authoritative* 1605; *interpretive* 1680/*interpretative* 1569. Of these the longer forms are still recommended, except for *pacifist* (which is now the only usual form of the word).

longways, longwise. Both words have been in the language since the 16c., but both are now rather infrequent in comparison with *lengthways, lengthwise*, both of which have also been in use since the 16c.

loo. See TOILET.

look (verb).

1. Non-standard uses.
2. *look* + *to*-infinitive.
3. *look* + adverb or adjective.
4. *look like* + clause.

Several uses call for comment.

1 *Non-standard uses.* Various idiomatic uses of *look* are confined to particular parts of the English-speaking world. For example, *look you* (also variants), found in Fluellen's vocabulary in Shakespeare's *Henry V* and still in use in Wales. Secondly, the predominantly AmE *looky here* and variants (the spelling reflects the level of speech being represented), a folksy extension of the imperative phrase *look here!* Examples: *Looka-here, Dr. Hare, I don't have a picture at this time*—*Black Scholar*, 1971; *'Hey, Lewis!' Bobby sits straight up. 'Looky there! Get it!'*—L. Smith, 1983; *'Looky here, looky here,' he chanted. The tall SP man stared up at the photograph*—B. Moore, 1987. Thirdly, the colloquial AmE form *lookit* (first recorded in 1917), used only in the imperative, with the meaning 'Listen!' or 'Look at (something)': *Oh, isn't that the classiest, darlingest little coat you ever saw! . . . Lookit the collar. And the lining!*—T. Dreiser, 1925; *And lo, look-it there . . . a woman playing two machines at once*—E. Leonard, 1985.

2 *look* + *to*-infinitive. (*a*) In the meaning 'to expect', this construction has been in continuous use since the 16c. but is now unusual. Examples: *In these last wordes that euer I looke to speake with you*—Thomas More, *c.*1513; *By whom we look to be protected*—Hobbes, 1651; *Two lovers looking to be wed*—A. E. Housman, 1896; *I shall hereafter look to be treated as a person of respectability*—T. Huxley, 1900. (*b*) Now widely used in all varieties of English, especially in news, business and sports language, but still perceived by some to have an AmE taint, is an extension of the earlier type to include the idea of hoping, intending, or aiming to do something. It is often used in the continuous form *looking* + *to*-infinitive. Examples: *most people are looking to improve their living standards*—*New Statesman*, 1988; *The home team will be looking to get a result against the visitors next Saturday*—*Times*, 1988; *The council had been looking to take ownership of the historic Moat for a number of years*—*Kildare Nationalist*, 2003; *We always look to incorporate as many health components as possible into any new product or when improving existing products*—*Dairy Field*, 2001. (*c*) A third use of *look* + *to*-infinitive means 'to seem to the view, to appear, to look as if'. The *OED* illustrates it from works by Edmund Burke (1775) and other later writers. Examples: *A little hat that looked to be made of beaver*—C. Russell, 1890; *The Queen looked to be in good health*—*Graphic*, 1893; *The owl looked to be encircled by six cloaked hit-men*—J. E. Maslow, 1983. This type is now quite common.

3 *look* + adverb or adjective. An interesting example of how what is considered grammatical changes over time. The *OED* lists numerous examples of adverbs following intransitive *look* in the senses (*a*) 'to direct one's eyes in a manner indicative of a certain feeling', and (*b*) 'to have the appearance of being; to seem to the sight'. Examples: (*a*) *Wherefore looke ye so sadly to day?*—Gen. (AV) 11: 7, 1611; *The man look'd bloodily when he spoke*—R. Carpenter, 1642. (*b*) *The skies looke grimly*—Shakespeare, 1611; *The world looked awkwardly round me*—Defoe, 1719; *On the whole ... things as yet looked not unfavourably for James*—Macaulay, 1849. The only adverb that can still idiomatically be used is *well* (e.g. *you look well* = you appear to be in good health), and even here it is arguable that *well* is an adjective (= healthy). In the sense 'to have the appearance of being', adjectives are normal: e.g. *to look black, blue, cold, elderly, foolish, small, vain*, etc.

4 *look like* + clause. *Look like* introducing a clause (a construction first used in AmE but now widespread) is still eschewed in some quarters. Examples: *Don't it look to you like she would of asked us to stay for supper?*—M. Mitchell, 1936; *Looks like your child's birthday is news again this year*—*Guardian*, 1973; *It makes you look like you're late*—H. Hamilton, 1900. Further examples are given at LIKE 1(c) (ii).

loom (verb). For *loom large*, see LARGE, LARGELY.

Lord. The younger sons of a duke or a marquess are known by the courtesy title of *Lord*, followed by their first name and surname, e.g. *Lord Edward Fitzgerald.* A letter addressed to such a person should begin *Dear Lord Edward*, but the surname should be added if the acquaintanceship is slight (*Debrett's Correct Form*). For *lord* used as an undress substitute for *marquess, earl, viscount*, see TITLES.

Lord Bacon. This incorrect mixture of styles bestowed on Francis Bacon (1561–1626) by Macaulay in an essay that appeared in the *Edinburgh Review* in July 1837 still appears. The appropriate styles are *Bacon, Francis Bacon, Lord Verulam*, and *Viscount St Albans.* In literary criticism the only styles used are the first two.

Lord's is the name of a cricket ground in London. *Lords* (preceded by *the*) is a conventional shortening of *House of Lords*, the British Upper House of Parliament.

lose, loose (verbs). The everyday verb meaning 'to be deprived of something' is, of course, spelt with only one letter *o*. Possibly because *lose* is pronounced like *choose*, there is a common tendency to write that meaning with two letter *o*s. The much rarer verb *loose* means (*a*) to release, set free (e.g. *the hounds have been loosed*), (*b*) to untie or undo (e.g. *the ropes were loosed*), (*c*) to relax one's grip (e.g. *he loosed his grip suddenly*), and (*d*) (usually with *off*) to fire (e.g. *he loosed off a shot at the vehicle*). A typical mistaken sentence is **That company is performing very poorly, loosing money all over the place*—weblog, 2010. Such a mistake would probably not be picked up by spellcheckers, since *loose* and its inflections are valid words.

lose out. 1 This apparently harmless phrasal verb, first used in mid-19c. AmE, has attracted a certain amount of criticism in Britain, partly because of its transatlantic birthplace, partly because *out* looks like (but is not) one of those dreaded prepositions one must not end a sentence with. Examples of the flak directed at it are: 'The American tendency is to burden every verb with a preposition that adds nothing to its meaning (*win out, lose out, face up to,* etc.)'—Orwell, 1947; 'The monstrous proliferation of redundant prepositions in the ever more popular usages "check up on", "lose out to", "meet up with"'—*Times*, 1973; and the correspondent who in 1988 asked Burchfield 'Why, in England, is *lose* now losing to *lose out?*' (Presumably he or she did not really mean to suggest that Scotland, Wales, and Northern Ireland were exempt from the trend.)

2 Unless you happen to agree with these visceral criticisms, you may safely ignore them: they rather miss the point that *lose out* often conveys shades of meaning absent from *lose*. Its two core meanings can be summarized as (*a*) 'to be deprived of an opportunity, be disadvantaged' and (*b*) 'to be beaten in competition'. It can be used on its own, or followed by *on* in the first meaning and *to* in the second. Examples: *We are going to lose out unless the Government are prepared to do a tremendous public relations job for the tourist industry*—*Guardian,* 1971; *'Quality is going to be one of the benchmarks we are going to access.' 'We are very mindful of that and we don't want to lose out on quality.'*—*ABC Rural Online*, 2004; *The popular press, thrown off balance and uncertain of its role, lost out to the heavies and the provincials*—*Author*, 1971. In none of these examples, I would suggest, does *lose* on its own do the same job.

loth. See LOATH.

Lothario /lə'θɑːrɪəʊ/. Plural *Lotharios.* See -O(E)S 9. For obvious reasons, the word now tends to appear on its own, rather than in the traditional collocation *gay Lothario.*

lot, lots. 1 The phrases *a lot of* and *lots of* are used interchangeably with singular (uncount or mass) nouns and plural nouns: *a lot of time/lots of time*; *a lot of chairs/lots of chairs.*

Although both occur in the works of well-known writers such as Galsworthy and Winston Churchill and 19c. authors cited in the *OED* such as the poet A. H. Clough and Carlyle, the *OED* entry (admittedly unrevised since 1903) labels the use *colloquial*, while *ODO* calls it *informal.* To say that it is neutral in register would be more accurate: it is used freely in nearly all kinds of writing, except academic writing. (Merriam-Webster Online recognizes this by giving it no label.) If one wishes to avoid it, alternatives include *much, many, a great many, a great deal of,* etc. The frequent use of *a lot of* and *lots of* in speech is underlined by the presence in many modern works of the contracted forms *lotta* and *lotsa*: (lotta) *No, I'm a lotta things, but I ain't crazy*—*Coast to Coast* (Aust.), 1969; *He did ... a lotta community theatre work in Houston*—*Ritz,* 1989; (lotsa) *The Notting Hill Carnival was lotsa fun for seven days and nights*—*It,* 1971.

2 See ALOT.

lotus. Plural *lotuses.*

loud, loudly. In certain restricted circumstances *loud* is used as an adverb, as it has been since Old English, instead of *loudly.* Apart from set phrases such as *loud and long* and *loud and clear,* it is preferred as the comparative, rather than *more loudly* (e.g. *Because he's snoring louder than the TV*). Otherwise, the strictly correct adverb is *loudly*: e.g. *complaining loudly about his treatment, talking/laughing/shouting loudly.* However, *loud* is often used with verbs such as *talk, say, laugh, scream, yell,* etc., particularly in conversation, and to use *loudly* could in many cases sound precious.

lough. See LOCH.

lour (of the sky, etc.), to look dark and threatening; (of a person) to frown, look sullen. This verb, which is sometimes spelt *lower,* is pronounced /'laʊə/, like *tower.* It is first recorded in the 13c. and is probably of native origin but happens not to be found in Old English. To avoid confusion with *lower,* it is best spelt like the headword here. The verb *lower* (to cause to descend) is pronounced /'ləʊə/, rhyming with *mower,* and is etymologically unrelated to *lour*; it is a derivative of the adjective *low* (Middle English *lāh*, from Old Norse *lágr*).

louvre. Spelt as shown in BrE (AmE **louver**).

lovable spelt as shown is the more common form everywhere, and generally given as the standard in dictionaries, though **loveable** is also correct and slightly more often used in BrE than the shorter form.

love. From its earliest use in the 16c. the phrase *to make love* (often followed by *to*) meant simply 'to pay amorous attention (to)'. At some point in the mid-20c. it came to have only the restricted and very precise meaning 'to have sexual intercourse (with)', and the older meaning was forced out. When reading 16-19c. literature one must simply bear in mind that *making love* means no more than 'paying amorous attention': e.g. *Demetrius ... Made loue to Nedars daughter*—Shakespeare, 1590; '*who's had the —impudence to make love to my sister! cried Harry*—G. Meredith, 1861.

lovey. An affectionate form of address in Britain (*Ruth, lovey, are you there?*). Spelt as shown (not *lovy*) and so conforming with the reduplicated form *lovey-dovey.* It can also be spelt *luvvy* or *luvvie.* See LUVVIE.

Low Countries. See NETHERLANDS.

lower, lour. See LOUR.

low hanging fruit. Sometimes ridiculed as one of the more overripe outgrowths of business and management speak, this phrase is not particularly common outside those spheres. It can be defended as an exceptionally vivid, immediately graspable metaphor, whose freshness has not yet withered on the vine. That said, it is still likely to figure high on many people's list of rancid management bovine scatology, and what precisely it means is often rather vague. *Discovering and developing new drugs is getting more difficult and expensive. The low-hanging fruit has been plucked*—*motleyfool.co.uk*, 2003; *I see us going forward by addressing three key areas. We must continue to cultivate our low-hanging fruit such as properties like Harry Potter*—*Black Enterprise*, 2002.

low, lowly. The first can function either as an adjective (*a low neckline, a low moon,* etc.) or an adverb with a wide range of verbs (*to aim low, to fly low, to hang low, to lie low,* etc.). The second is most commonly used as an adjective (*of lowly station, a lowly position in the firm*); as an adverb (= to a low degree; in a low voice; etc.) it is occasionally used instead of *low* in the phrase *lowly paid.*

lucre (derogatory word for 'financial profit or gain'). Spelt as shown both in BrE and in AmE (not *lucer*).

luggage. See BAGGAGE.

lunging, present participle of the ordinary verb *lunge.* Spelt as shown, rather than *lungeing.* But for the separate verb *lunge* 'to train or exercise a horse with a lunge (a long rope)', use *lungeing* as the *-ing* form.

lustre. Spelt as shown in BrE (AmE **luster**).

lustrum (period of five years). Plural *lustra* (less commonly *lustrums*).

lusus naturae, a freak of nature. Pronounced /ˈluːsəs nəˈtjʊəriː/ or /-ˈtjʊərʌɪ/.

luvvie. This entertaining, if less than respectful, informal, and originally British word for 'an actor or actress, especially one who is particularly effusive or affected' is best spelt as shown, rather than *luvvy.* It is a specialized offshoot of the affectionate form of address *lovey,* supposedly often used by theatricals. The earliest *OED* citation is from the *Guardian* of 2 June, 1988, quoting the omnipresent Stephen Fry: *Acting in a proper grown-up play, being a lovie, doing the West End, 'shouting in the evenings', as the late Patrick Troughton had it.* It is particularly used in the press, and on blogs, and is quite often a light-hearted way of referring to actors and actresses, with no disparaging connotations.

luxuriant, luxurious. These two adjectives, both connected with the word *luxury* (in turn derived from the Latin word *luxus* 'abundance') have invaded each other's semantic space many times during and since the 17c. In strict terms *luxuriant* is primarily used of vegetation and means 'lush, profuse', as R. M. Ballantyne showed in his *Coral Island* (1858): *the trees and bushes were very luxuriant. Luxurious,* on the other hand, means 'extremely elegant or expensive; sumptuous', something that is brought out in the same book of

Ballantyne's: *Altogether this was the most luxurious supper we had enjoyed for many a day.*

Keeping the two words apart is difficult not only for modern-day speakers. The *OED* lists (*a*) 17–19c. examples of *luxuriant* 'misused' for *luxurious,* e.g. *It was a splendid apartment ... luxuriant to a degree*—C. Gibbons, 1885; and (*b*) 17–19c. examples of *luxurious* used for *luxuriant,* e.g. *Their villages are situated in the midst of the most luxurious groves*—R. Southey, 1826. However, confusing one with the other is always and everywhere regarded as a mistake and the best policy is to keep the two words apart, as Ballantyne did.

It is worth noting that in certain contexts *luxurious* has largely been replaced by *luxury* used attributively (e.g. *luxury apartment, coach, cruise,* etc.). This use has been going for much longer than might be supposed: the *OED* notes, for example, Osbert Lancaster, Shaw, and Noel Coward respectively as the first source for *luxury coach* (1936), *luxury cruise* (1941), and *luxury liner* (1933). Through overuse, particularly by estate agents and property developers (*luxury flat, luxury apartment,* etc.), the word has largely been eviscerated of any real meaning, and indicates merely that the sellers of the item so described are attempting to hypnotize customers into paying a premium (aka inflated) price.

-ly. 1 A number of articles in this book suggest that there is often a fine idiomatic line to be drawn between adjectives and adverbs, and also between 'flat' adverbs, i.e. those that do not add the adverbial suffix *-ly,* and their corresponding forms that do add it: see e.g. CLEAN, CLEANLY; CLEAR, CLEARLY; CLOSE, CLOSELY; DEAR, DEARLY; DIRECT, DIRECTLY; HIGH, HIGHLY; IRRESPECTIVE(LY); LARGE, LARGELY; LOUD, LOUDLY; PRETTY; QUICK; RIGHT, RIGHTLY; SURE, SURELY; TIGHT, TIGHTLY; UNCOMMON; WIDE. Mother-tongue speakers for the most part instinctively know which form is appropriate in a given context. But for foreign learners of the language, and mother-tongue speakers not much exposed to standard language, the going is more difficult. For such groups the addition of *-ly* to an adjective must seem the obvious way of forming an adverb, since the majority of adverbs do indeed end in *-ly* and correspond to a clearly related simple adjective: *angry/angrily, mere/merely, usual/usually,* etc. But the application of any such simple rule, that is to regard the addition of *-ly* as the only way of turning an adjective into a word meaning 'in the manner of, after the style of, etc.', ignores the quirks and quiddities of English.

It is not necessary to assemble here specimens of unidiomatic uses in which *-ly* is missing where it is wanted or is present when it is not needed, as numerous examples are to be found in the entries listed above, as well as in others. Standard speakers also need no special guidance about the difference of meaning between such types *as he had arrived late* and *he had arrived lately.* But there are always special cases which may surprise even the most articulate of readers, as for instance the humorous use of the double adverb MUCHLY and the transatlantic use of THUSLY. Three examples of adverbs lacking the notional *-ly* illustrate the point: *I burrow* deep *into my notebook; He took a great leap and landed* square *on the glossy back* [of a horse]; *Leo would be the first to concede that he had spread himself too* thin.

2 For uncertainty over the pronunciation of some of the more unusual participial adverbs formed on the same model as *determinedly, reservedly,* etc. see -EDLY.

3 For *first(ly),* see FIRST.

4 Considerations of sound and meaning make it desirable to avoid placing two *-ly* adverbs in succession when their function in the sentence is different. Thus *We are utterly, hopelessly, irretrievably, ruined* is acceptable because each of the *-ly* adverbs has the same relation to *ruined,* and the opening of W. H. Auden's *Prime* (1951) is poetically adverbial and adverbially poetical *Simultaneously, as soundlessly, Spontaneously, suddenly As, at the vaunt of the dawn, the kind Gates of the body fly open.* But the following jar on the eye and ear (or in Burchfield's gloriously unmusical phrase 'show slightly uneuphonious contiguities'): *Many of the manuscripts were until comparatively recently in the keeping of Owen's family—English,* 1987; *he reverts to it* (*apparently disbelievingly*) *on several occasions—Encounter,* 1987. Appearing relatively recently, Kyra represented change—New Yorker, 1987. The good news is that the dairy industry has pooled its efforts to combat food-safety issues, largely successfully—Dairy Field, 2000. The cruder type *Soviet* *industry is at present practically completely crippled* is avoidable by substituting *almost* for *practically.*

Lyceum. For the meaning in Greek philosophy, see ACADEMY. Plural *-eums.* See -UM 1.

lychee (a sweet fleshy fruit) /ˈlʌɪtʃiː/. In descending order of frequency, the spellings are *lychee, litchi, lichee,* the first outnumbering the next two together. In AmE the pronunciation /ˈliːtʃiː/ (**lee**-chee) is given preference over the pronunciation shown above.

lychgate /ˈlɪtʃgeɪt/ meaning 'a roofed gateway to a churchyard', should be spelt *lych-* and as one word, rather than *lich-,* although the latter is still accepted as a variant. The word is derived from the Old English *līc* meaning 'corpse' + *gate,* because the gateway was formerly used at burials for sheltering a coffin until the clergyman's arrival.

lynchpin. See LINCHPIN.

lyric (noun), 'in the modern sense, any fairly short poem expressing the personal mood, feeling, or meditation of a single speaker (who may sometimes be an invented character, not the poet). In ancient Greece, a lyric was a song for accompaniment on the lyre and could be a choral lyric sung by a group . . . Among the common lyric forms are the sonnet, ode, elegy, . . . and the more personal kinds of hymns' (C. Baldick, 1990). From about the third quarter of the 19c., but more particularly since the time of the following example, *lyric* or *lyrics* have also been the usual terms for the words of a popular song or a musical *On July 8 Edgar Leslie, the prolific and most successful lyric writer in America, arrived in London—Melody Maker,* 1927.

lyric, lyrical (adjectives). The border between the two words is slightly porous, but *lyric* is the more usual adjective when referring to the type of poetry described in LYRIC: *lyric form, poem, poetry, poet, verse.* (It also describes a particular kind of operatic voice, e.g. *lyric soprano, baritone.*) *Lyrical* can be used in the poetic meaning, as in Wordsworth's title *Lyrical Ballads* (1798), but is rather less frequent. Unlike *lyric,* which is purely a classifying adjective, *lyrical* is qualitative, e.g. *the intensely lyrical violin concerto.* But perhaps its most common use is in the stock phrase expressing enthusiasm e.g. *he waxed lyrical about the performance.*

ma'am. See MADAM.

macaroni. In current English it has only one sense (a tubular variety of pasta) and no plural form. In the historical (18c.) sense 'a British dandy affecting Continental fashions', its plural is *macaronies.*

machinations. Pronounced /ˌmakɪˈneɪʃənz/ or /ˌmaʃ-/.

machismo, a show of masculinity, can be pronounced /məˈtʃɪzməʊ/ or /məˈk-/. The first is in line with the original Spanish and could therefore be considered preferable.

macho /ˈmatʃəʊ/, AmE /ˈmætʃ-/ can be used as a synonym of MACHISMO, but is more commonly used as an adjective meaning 'masculine in an exaggerated way'. It is occasionally pronounced /ˈmakəʊ/, which sounds bizarre.

mackintosh, a waterproof coat. Now so spelt (despite the surname of its inventor, Charles Macintosh, a Scottish chemist, 1766–1843, having no letter *k*). The shortened form *mac* (no point) is almost always used instead.

Mac-, Mc-. The major British dictionaries (and other works of reference) place all such names, whether they are spelt with *Mac-* or *Mc-*, at the notional alphabetical place of *Mac*: so the order of the following is *Maccabees, McCarthyism, mace, McNaughten rules, macrame.* By contrast, some American dictionaries list *Mac-* names under *Mac,* but *Mc.* names between *Mb* and *Md.* In a standard American dictionary published in 1991, the entry for James Ramsay *MacDonald* is 26 pages away from that for *McCarthyism.*

macula /ˈmakjʊlə/, a dark spot in the skin. Plural *maculae* /-liː/.

madam, madame. 1 As a nowadays rather formal or respectful way of addressing or referring to a woman (*Dear Madam*; *Can I help you, Madam?*; *Madam Chair(man)*) the spelling without *-e* is appropriate. It is also (in BrE) an informal term for a precocious or conceited girl or young woman (*a right little madam*); and it is the term for a woman brothel-keeper. When addressing royalty the shorter form *ma'am* /mam/ should be used.

2 *Madame,* pronounced /məˈdɑːm/ (plural *Mesdames* /meɪˈdɑːm/), is the right form of address to a woman belonging to any foreign nation (substituted e.g. for German *Frau* or Dutch *Mevrouw*), if the correct local term is unknown to the speaker or writer, e.g. *Madame Mao, Madame Ceaušescu. Madame* is also used (less frequently than *madam*) as the term for a woman brothel-keeper.

3 The pronunciation /ˈmɒdəm/ used by assistants in fashion shops at the beginning of the 20c. now seems to be obsolete (except in humorous or period use). Fowler (1926) called it 'odd', and suggested that it was 'perhaps due to a notion that French *Madame* is more in keeping with haunts of fashion than English *Madam.*'

Madeira. Spelt with a capital both as the geographical name and when referring to the fortified wine.

madness. See IRRELEVANT ALLUSION.

maelstrom. Pronounced /ˈmeɪlstrəm/, and originally from a Dutch word meaning 'whirlpool', referring to a mythical whirlpool in the Arctic Ocean off the west coast of Norway.

maenad, a female follower of Bacchus, not *me-*. Pronounced /ˈmiːnad/.

maestro. Pronounced /ˈmʌɪstrəʊ/ (**my**-stroh). The plural is much more often *maestros* than the Italianate *maestri* /ˈmʌɪstri/ (**my**-stree).

Mafia /ˈmafɪə/. Its central meaning is 'an organized international body of criminals, operating originally in Sicily, now also in mainland Italy and in the US'. But it is also widely used of any group regarded as having hidden powerful (not necessarily sinister) influence (*the literary mafia, the academic mafia*, etc.). In this transferred sense a small initial (thus *mafia*) is used. A member of the *Mafia* is a **Mafioso** /mafɪˈəʊsəʊ, mɒ-/, plural *Mafiosi* /-si/.

Magdalen(e). 1 In the name of the Oxford *(-en)* and Cambridge *(-ene)* colleges, pronounced /ˈmɔːdlɪn/.

2 In the full biblical name *Mary Magdalene*, of Magdala in Galilee (Luke 8: 2), *Magdalene* is generally pronounced /ˈmagdəlɪn/ and occasionally /ˌmagdɛˈliːni/ (mag-duh-**lee**-nee).

maggoty. So spelt. See -T-, -TT-.

Magi. See MAGUS.

magic, magical (adjectives). The two words compete with one another in all the main senses, 'relating to magic', 'produced by or as if by magic', and 'wonderful', although in certain fixed expressions such as *magic carpet, magic circle, magic lantern*, and *magic square* only *magic* is used. When used in its descriptive role, *magic* still behaves more like a noun than an adjective, which is to say that it cannot be preceded by *very, extremely*, etc., and does not have a comparative; otherwise, *magic* and *magical* are often interchangeable, however close or remote the connection with magic and related phenomena: *In the evenings, when the afterglow makes the whole valley magic*—J. Ashe, 1993; *She had not been kissed for over two years and it was magical*—P. Wilson, 1993. In the second half of the 20c. *magic* came to be used informally in the attributive position or by itself (*Magic!*) as a term of enthusiastic commendation, simply meaning 'wonderful, exciting', e.g. *It's magic!; The food* (or *concert, exhibition*, etc.) *was magic.*

magma. The plural is *magmas*, no longer *magmata.* The corresponding adjective is **magmatic**.

Magna Carta, Magna Charta. The name of the famous charter of 1215 is pronounced /ˈmagnə ˈkɑːtə/ however it is spelt. The recommended spelling of the second word is *Carta*, although *Charta* was at one time quite common and is still occasionally found. It is worth noting, as reported by Gowers (1965), that 'In a Bill introduced in 1946 authorizing the Trustees of the British Museum to lend a copy to the Library of Congress, *Charta* was the spelling used. But when the Bill reached committee stage in the House of Lords, the Lord Chancellor (Lord Jowitt) moved to substitute *Carta* and produced conclusive evidence that that was traditionally the correct spelling. The amendment was carried without a division; so *Carta* has now unimpeachable authority.'

magneto /magˈniːtəʊ/ is a shortened form of *magneto-electric machine.* Its plural is *magnetos.* See -O(E)S 6.

magnum opus, from the Latin neuter of *magnus* 'great' + *opus* 'work', refers to a work of art, music, or literature that is regarded as the most important or best that its creator has produced. The *OED* attributes its first use to Boswell: *My Magnum Opus, the Life of Dr. Johnson … is to be published on Monday, 16th May*—letter of 19 April, 1791. *Opus* can be pronounced with a short or long *o*, /ˌmagnəm ˈəʊpəs, ˈɒpəs/, and the plural is more often the hybrid Latin-English *magnum opuses* than the strictly correct Latin *magna opera* /ˌmagnə ˈəʊpərə, ˈɒpərə/. It is also found in the form *opus magnum*: *I quoted St. Thomas Aquinas from his opus magnum Summa Theologia—Calgary Herald*, 2001; *Cardew's magna opera to this day are two large, Cage-influenced indeterminate scores from the 1960s—OEC* (undated).

magus /ˈmeɪgəs/. Plural (as in *the three Magi*) *magi* /ˈmeɪdʒaɪ/. The word has travelled to us from Old Persian via Greek and Latin, and originally denoted a member of a priestly caste.

maharaja(h), formerly, an Indian prince, can be spelt with or without a final *h.* With capital initial when used as a title. The wife of a *maharaja* was a *maharanee.*

mahout, an elephant-driver or keeper in India. Pronounced /məˈhaʊt/.

maiolica /məˈjɒlɪkə/, **majolica** (also pronounced /məˈdʒɒlɪkə/). Renaissance Italian enamelled earthenware. Art historians generally use the anglicized spelling, *majolica,* only for Victorian or later pieces.

Example: *In Italy interest in porcelain often takes second place to that of maiolica and Renaissance and Baroque ceramics—Antique Collector,* 1990.

major. In origin the comparative of Latin *magnus* 'great', *major* is sometimes used in contrast with *minor* (e.g. *a major road* in contrast with *a minor road; the two major political parties and several minor ones*), and as a synonym of *greater (the major portion of his speech* the greater portion), but it is not a true comparative in English in that it cannot be followed by *than.*

Repeated criticisms have been made against using *major* as an absolute adjective equivalent to *main, principal, important,* etc., but it is difficult to see how any of these near-synonyms could be idiomatically substituted for *major* in most contexts in which *major* is used, or what the benefit of such a substitution is. *Major* may not be a true comparative in English, but it is implicitly one in a way that *main, principal,* etc. are not. The word has also been criticized as being overused to such an extent that it has lost much of its meaning, and is often modified by *very,* a use which is best avoided, e.g. *?Second, from the early 1980s, firms benefited from a very major reduction in the corporate tax rate.*

major-domo, chief steward of a great household. Plural *major-domos.* See -O(E)S 4.

major-general, an officer in the British army next below a lieutenant-general. Plural *major-generals.*

majority. This word raises two issues. **1** = 'the greater number or part'. *An informed minority of the 'public' was opposed to escalation, while the majority* was *rather malleable in its opinion—Canad. Jrnl of History,* 2000; *The vast majority* have *now come to terms with their destiny—Encounter,* 1987.

As these examples show, when the word is used in this meaning the verb can be either singular or plural, depending on whether the people or things concerned are thought of as a group or as individuals. *Majority* is routinely used in the plural in this meaning, particularly when modified: *Majorities in various countries are, of course, critical of American foreign policies*—weblog, 2004. *Enmity between Hindus and Muslims led the British to partition British India, creating East and West Pakistan, where there were Muslim majorities—OEC,* 2004.

2 *majority of* + noun. *Majority* in this use means 'the greater number' of people or things, and the noun following *of,* together with its related verb, is generally plural: *A majority of them come from the Scheduled Castes—Times of India,* 1972; *The majority of school buildings are dilapidated and decaying—Encounter,* 1987; *I fully accept that the vast majority of kids in South Woodham are good*—news website, 2004. Uses with uncount nouns (*the majority of the work; the majority of the time*) are disliked by critics who insist that only plural nouns or collective nouns such as *group, population, public,* etc. which denote a collection of individuals, can be used: *Gillray, in common with the vast majority of his public, did not want to take the Jacobin side*—M. Billig, 1991; *They are simply out of touch with the majority of the electorate and have been for many years—Bolton Evening News,* 2003. However, the use with uncount nouns is widespread and must be considered standard grammatically, even if undesirable stylistically. In many cases the simpler *most of* can easily replace it, e.g. *He spent the majority of* (read: *most of*) *his working life as a schoolteacher*—television news, 1996. Similarly, the standard phrase *the vast majority of* has been criticized as overused, wordy, and easily replaceable by *most,* e.g. *The vast majority of music* [read: *most music*] *is execrable in quality*—arts website, 2004.

majorly The *OED* and Merriam-Webster assign three meanings to this word, all originally American. The first two listed here are uncontentious, but the third often causes worries over its correctness or appropriateness: (*a*) as an adverb of degree, 'to a great extent', e.g. *Doug Doretti, president of the company, said last night: 'If this keeps happening it will majorly affect us.'—Guardian,* 1997; (*b*) meaning 'largely, in the main', e.g. *The conclusions of the writers, however, are majorly unsupportable, illogical, unknowledgeable and inconsistent—NY Law Jrnl,* 1971; (*c*) as an intensifier modifying an adjective, 'really, very' e.g. *It was a real bachelor pad, majorly slimy—Montreal Gazette,* 1995. The *Corpus of Contemporary American* shows that the word is used mainly in magazine writing, and hardly at all in academic prose, while the word's contexts in the *OEC* data are clearly informal. Comments on the Merriam-Webster website are critical of it, suggesting it is 'slang' or even 'Valley Girl talk' in the 'really' meaning, which has spread to other areas of the English-speaking world. It is best avoided in any kind of formal or serious prose. Examples: *However, there are some majorly cool bits here and there—www.bit-tech.net,* 2005 (BrE); *'People majorly screwed up' she says of the treatment she received when she was diagnosed with stage 4 ovarian cancer in 1994—The Advocate,* 2001 (AmE).

make-believe, make-belief. The verbal phrase *to make believe* 'to pretend to do something' (formed in the 14c. on the model of Old French *faire croire*) yielded the nouns *make-believe* and *make-belief* in the early 19c. *Make-believe* happens to precede *make-belief* by some 20 years and is the standard spelling, while *make-belief* (the word not the action) is rather uncommon.

Malapropisms denotes 'the mistaken use of a word in place of a similar-sounding one, often with an amusing effect'. It must be the only term for a widespread linguistic phenomenon derived from a fictional character, namely Mrs Malaprop, in Sheridan's *The Rivals* (1775), whose name itself is derived from the adverb and adjective *malapropos* (= inappropriate, inopportune, from French *mal à propos,* 'not to the point'). When challenged about her use of *hard words which she don't understand,* she protested *Sure, if I reprehend anything in this world, it is the use of my oracular tongue, and a nice derangement of epitaphs.* She was producing misshapen recollections of the words *apprehend, vernacular, arrangement,* and *epithets.* Fowler (1926) believed that such Malapropisms 'pass the bounds of ordinary experience and of the credible'. In his view, Malapropisms normally come as 'single spies, not in battalions, one in an article, perhaps, instead of four in a sentence, and not marked by her bold originality, but monotonously following well beaten tracks'. Whether it is a case of 'single spies' or 'all the time', many readers will probably have their own favourites. Examples: *One, a head of English, could not explain the function of an* intransigent [intransitive] *verb and advised me to 'forget it'*—letter in the *Sunday Times,* 1988; *She's a child* progeny [prodigy], *a* vivacious [voracious] *reader—gets through 15 books a* week—oral source, 1989; *When she* [*sc. our daily*] *heard our Gloucester house was haunted, she uttered the immortal line, "You'll have to get the vicar in to* circumcise [exorcize] *it.'*—J. Cooper, 1991.

male. Both *male* and *masculine* entered the language from Old French (ultimately from Latin *masculus)* in the 14c. and gradually adopted different roles more or less parallel to those of FEMALE and FEMININE. *Male* (adjective) is used (*a*) of the sex that can beget offspring by fertilization or insemination; (*b*) (of plants or their parts) containing only fertilizing organs; (*c*) of or consisting of men or male animals, plants, etc. (*the male sex; a male-voice choir; male kennels*); (*d*) (of parts of machinery, etc.) designed to enter or fill the corresponding female part (*a male screw).* As noun, 'a male person or animal'. *Masculine* is (*a*) applied to qualities associated with men, manly, vigorous (not merely describing the fact of being male); (*b*) in grammar, of words in certain languages (e.g. Old English, Latin, Greek, German) of a particular class, as distinct from feminine or neuter ones. In the 20c. *male* was incorporated in the terms *male chauvinist* (first recorded in 1970) 'a man who is prejudiced against women', and *male menopause* (1949) 'a crisis of potency, confidence, etc., said to afflict men in middle life'.

male chauvinism, male chauvinist. See CHAUVINISM.

malignancy, malignity. The first formally corresponds to *malignant* and the second to *malign. Malignancy* is a Latinate word brought into the language in the 17c. and is now used 90 per cent of the time in the medical sphere. However, it is also still used in the general sense 'the state or quality of being malignant', in which meaning it is interchangeable with *malignity. Malignity,* much the older word of the two, was first used in the 14c. to denote 'the condition or quality of being malign, malevolent, or deadly'. From the 17c. to the 19c., like *malignancy,* it was applied to malignant or life-threatening medical conditions, but has now given way in this sense to *malignancy.* The spelling **malignance**, as an alternative to *malignancy* in its non-medical meanings, is correct but unusual. Examples: *Those same theologians typically underestimated the malignancy of many streams of thought in the contemporary West—First Things* magazine, 2005; *'The spirit of allusion,' one critic has written recently, 'is at the furthest remove from envious malignity'—*

Art Bulletin, 2004; *'It* [*sc.* a book] *is', he says, 'very inspiring—a desire for ecological change with no ego or malignance and no messianic tendencies'*—*Sunday Times*, 2006.

malign, malignant. The shorter form was adopted from French in the 14c. and has gradually retreated before the later word (first in 16c.) *malignant. Malign* is used mostly of things that are evil in their nature or effects, and occasionally of diseases (fevers, syphilis, etc.). *Malignant* is the normal word applied to diseases or conditions (esp. cancerous tumours) that are life-threatening. It is also used to designate any aspect of life that is characterized by intense ill will, or to a person or persons keenly desirous of the suffering or misfortune of another person, or of others generally. Cf. BENIGN, BENIGNANT.

mall. In the senses 'a sheltered walk or promenade' and 'an enclosed shopping precinct' the pronunciation /mɔːl/ is increasingly being used in Britain now rather than /mal/, as it has been for some time in America, Australia, etc. But /mal/ is still obligatory in the London place-names *The Mall, Chiswick Mall,* and *Pall Mall.*

mamilla /maˈmɪlə/ (AmE **mammilla**), the nipple of a woman's breast. Plural *mamillae* /-liː/.

mamma /ˈmamə/, a milk-secreting organ of female mammals. Plural *mammae* /-miː/.

man. From the time of the earliest records of English until the second half of the 20c. *man* could be used without comment to mean 'a human being (irrespective of sex or age)'. (In Old English the main words distinctive of sex were *wer* 'a man' and *wif* 'a woman'.) The use is embedded in hundreds of traditional expressions (e.g. *Man cannot live by bread alone*; *Man proposes, God disposes*; *Every man for himself*; *Time and tide wait for no man*; *as good as the next man*), and in the works of our greatest poets and philosophers. However, in the light of modern sexual-political sensibilities, it is no use protesting that in Old English the word referred not only to an adult human male, but also to a human being irrespective of sex and that it doesn't necessarily contain implications of male supremacism. The word's historical ambiguity is its downfall, and some men as well as some women consider it an unacceptable outward sign of male dominance. There are alternatives available, though none is completely without awkwardness: *person* or *one* for *man* in the countable sense (*One cannot live by bread alone*; *as good as the next person*), and *humanity* or *humankind* for *man* in the collective sense (*Humankind cannot live by bread alone*). As these examples suggest, however, such substitutions can sound rather contrived, and it will take time for them to sound completely natural. But in everyday language there is every reason to respect gender sensitivities in language, unless one can be sure (and how could one?) that nobody will be offended by the generic use of *man.* See also HUMANKIND; SEXIST LANGUAGE.

manageress. See -ESS 4.

mandamus /manˈdeɪməs/. This term for a particular kind of judicial writ, which is a nominalization of Latin *mandamus* 'we command', has the plural *mandamuses.* See -US 5.

mandarin. The word meaning (*a*) (with capital initial) the official language of China, and (*b*) a high-ranking Chinese official (also in transferred use), is regarded by some authorities as a separate word from *mandarin,* a kind of orange, and they are therefore given separate entries in some dictionaries. But it is possible that both are derived from the same Sanskrit original, the fruit being so named in the 18c. from the yellow of the mandarins' costumes.

maneuver. AmE variant of MANOEUVRE.

mangel, mangel-wurzel, mangold. This root vegetable used as cattle fodder has mythical status, enshrined in names such as *The Wurzels,* a British West-Country folk group, and *Wurzel Gummidge,* a scarecrow in the children's books and TV series of the same name. It has an interesting etymology. The alternative forms result from changes within the German language. The original German *Mangold-wurzel,* is a combination of *Mangold* 'beet, chard' and *Wurzel,* root'. The altered form *Mangelwurzel,* due to association with *Mangel* 'want', was sometimes taken to mean 'root of scarcity'.

mango. The plural is either *mangoes* (preferably) or *mangos.* See -O(E)S 2.

mangy. Spelt as shown. See -EY AND -Y.

-mania. The *OED* reports that about two thirds of all the words with this suffix of Hellenistic Greek origin were formed in the 19c. The suffix has an unfavourable connotation in words such as *dipsomania, egomania, kleptomania, nymphomania,* in which it indicates compulsive, pathological behaviour. But it also has favourable connotations of enthusiasm in many cases, e.g. *balletomania, bibliomania.* Many of the words that make use of it are short-lived, or refer only to the historical period in which they were created. Who now remembers *turtlemania* (the craze for Teenage Mutant Ninja Turtles, fantasy characters, beginning in the late 1980s), still less the one-off *Queenomania* (support for George IV's estranged wife Queen Caroline)? And who will remember, or was indeed swayed by, *Cleggmania,* the 'very brief, very British, Lego-scale version of Obama-mania that swept the land for a matter of weeks during the 2010 election campaign' (referring to enthusiasm for the British politician Nicholas Clegg)? The suffix, however, continues to provide journalists with a useful bit of kit for headlines.

manic depression, manic depressive. Despite being terms with which many people are familiar, both are generally felt to be negative by people experiencing the condition and those working with them. A less loaded term which is being increasingly used in medical and psychiatric circles is *bipolar disorder,* or *bipolar affective disorder.* People with the condition can be referred to simply as *bipolar,* or as having *bipolar disorder.* See also BIPOLAR DISORDER.

Manichaean, Manichean. Pronounced /ˌmanɪˈkiːən/ (ma-ni-**kee**-uhn), this adjective denoting an extreme dualistic view of the world or of events (e.g. *a Manich(a)ean view, struggle, division*) is written with a capital and can be spelt in either of the ways shown, though the spelling *-ean* is more frequent.

manifesto. Plural *manifestos.* See -O(E)S 7.

manifold (adjective). **1** Pronounced /ˈmanɪfəʊld/ rather than /mɛnɪ-/, i.e. the first syllable rhymes with *man,* not *men.* It means 'various', or 'having many different forms or elements', e.g. *the implications of this decision were manifold; the appeal of the crusade was manifold.* Although once also spelt *manyfold,* this spelling is nowadays best avoided, e.g. *?The issues are manyfold—The Mac Observer,* 2011.

2 The adverbial meaning 'by many times' is normally conveyed by the spelling *manyfold,* but the spelling *manifold* is also used. However, it may be regarded as a mistake by some people. Examples: *While the number of sites has doubled and the total membership has increased manyfold, the pattern of distribution of members, as shown in Figure 1, is basically the same—First Monday,* 2007; *The welcome we received was overwhelming but ... the hospitality extended to us was ... repaid manifold—Times,* 2001.

manikin, mannikin, mannequin. Strictly speaking, the spellings *manikin* or *mannikin* denote (i) a jointed model of the human body used in anatomy or in art as a lay figure; (ii) rather disparagingly, a very small man (e.g. *he is not at all a manikin, but a well-proportioned human being*). Both are 16c. loanwords, derived from the Dutch *mannekijn,* diminutive of *man,* meaning 'little man'. The spelling *mannequin* refers to (i) a dummy used to display clothes and (ii) a person employed to model clothes. It too derives from Dutch, but in this case came into English via French. Since *mannequin* is often pronounced in the same way as *man(n)ikin* (it can also be pronounced /manɪkwɪn/), it is not surprising that the simpler spelling is occasionally used to cover its meanings too, and that use is recognized in dictionaries. It is nevertheless sensible to maintain the distinction. Examples: *Never mind the clothes—you need only look at the mannequins in shop windows to feel obese; If actresses became mannequins, mannequins also became actresses who played new roles with each dress they modeled; Basic life support training was defined as training in cardiopulmonary resuscitation using a manikin; She wasn't blinking and it made her look like a manikin.*

Manila, in the Philippine islands, is spelt as shown. The recommended spelling for the hemp and the paper is *manila,* not *manilla* or *Manil(l)a,* but all of these forms are still found in standard sources.

manipulable, manipulatable. The first is older (1881) and is several times more frequent in the *OEC* and other corpora. Both are used for things which can be easily handled in the physical sense, but only *manipulable* occurs in phrases such as *easily manipulable* to describe people who are pliable.

mankind. 1 Stressed on the second syllable when it means 'the human species', and on the first in its rarely used meaning 'male people, as distinct from female'.

2 In its generic sense 'the human species', it is now often replaced by HUMANKIND. See also SEXIST LANGUAGE.

-man, man-. Just as *man* as a generic for human being is deeply suspect for many people, so words containing the same three letters as a prefix or suffix have had the spotlight of the language police shone on them. **1** *As suffix.* Occupational terms ending in *-man* (e.g. *anchorman, chairman, craftsman, houseman* = male or female hospital doctor, *ombudsman, spokesman*) raise two issues: (i) whether they should be avoided in favour of a gender-neutral alternative (e.g. *police officer*), even if the person concerned happens to be male; and (ii) whether it is appropriate to use the feminine form (e.g. *spokeswoman*), if it exists. The prevailing orthodoxy suggests, at least in written language, that in either case a gender-neutral form should be used, unless the sex of the person concerned is relevant, or is present in the co-text, e.g. *he was a keen sportsman.* At the same time, it is wise to avoid formulations which easily risk making the whole enterprise of gender-neutral language look ludicrous: e.g. *The poor work person blames the tools*—a comment by one Asst Prof. John Kupetz in *The Daily Northwestern* (Illinois), 1991, instead of the traditional proverb *A poor workman blames his tools.*

The whole area is a potential minefield, but there are a number of unsexed designations which are now established if one wishes to make use of them and so avoid being labelled an unreconstructed sexist or quaintly last-century. Alternatives—some more established than others—are listed below. See also FEMININE DESIGNATIONS; -PERSON; SEXIST LANGUAGE.

gendered	*gender-neutral*	*plural*
barman	bartender	bartenders, bar staff
businessman	businessperson	businesspeople
chairman	chair, chairperson	chairpersons
clergyman	vicar, priest	the clergy
fellow countryman	compatriot	compatriots
fireman	firefighter	firefighters
foreman	supervisor	supervisors
freshman	fresher	freshers
juryman	juror, member of the jury	jurors, members of the jury
layman	layperson	laypeople, the laity
policeman	police officer	police officers
salesman	salesperson	sales staff
spokesman	spokesperson, representative	spokespeople, representatives
sportsman	sportsperson, athlete	sportspeople, sportsmen and sportswomen, athletes

2 *As prefix.* There are fewer words containing *man-*, and they seem to be less of an issue. Some alternatives are suggested as follows: *manhour* → *person-hour; manmade* → *artificial, manufactured; manpower* → *staff, employees, the workforce* (according to context); *to man* → *to operate, to staff,* etc.

manner. The phrase (*as if*) *to the manner born* is now commonly used to mean 'naturally at ease in a given situation'. The phrase is taken from Shakespeare, *Hamlet* i.iv.17. (*Though I am native here And to the manner born, it is a custom More honoured in the breach than the observance*), where it means 'destined by birth to follow a custom or way of life'. The *OED* shows that the spelling *to the manor born* goes back at least to 1847, and provides many later examples of this spelling. It is used either in the same meaning as *to the manner born,* or punningly to convey the idea of someone 'born into, naturally suited for, or readily taking to upper-class life'. Some people will consider using the *manor* spelling in the first meaning a mistake, but it is a mistake with a good pedigree. Examples: (unimpeachable) *The English replacements ... fitted in to the England machine as to the manner born*—*Scotland on Sunday,* 2005; (questionable by some) *?a tremendously charismatic pianist, and a Beethoven player to the manor born*—*MV Daily,* 2004; (knowingly (?) punning) *Upper-class accents can be learned; Baroness Blackstone, a Labour life peeress whose mother was a dancer, sounds to the manor born*—R. Critchfield, 1990.

mannikin. See MANIKIN, MANNIKIN, MANNEQUIN.

manoeuvre /mə'nuːvə/. So spelt in BrE as noun and verb. The inflected forms are *manoeuvred, manoeuvring.* But **AmE maneuver** (inflected *maneuvered, maneuvering*).

manpower. See MAN-, -MAN 2; SEXIST LANGUAGE.

manqué. Pronounced in a quasi-French manner /'mɒ̃keɪ/. In the meaning 'having failed to become what one might have been', *manqué* is placed immediately after the noun it qualifies, e.g. *a poet manqué,* and is printed in roman. It should be written with its accent in printed material (though in electronic media it often lacks it). The spelling *manquee* with two letter *e*s is wrong, although *manquée* with an accent could be, and very occasionally is, used of a woman.

-manship. In the many widely used terms containing this suffix describing (i) a particular skill or knowledge (*craftsmanship, salesmanship, statesmanship,* etc.); and (ii) a personal or interpersonal attitude of mind (*brinkmanship, gamesmanship, one-upmanship*), the *-man-* element does not appear to be perceived as sexist, since alternatives have not been created.

mantra, originally a term in Hinduism and Buddhism for a word or phrase repeated as an aid to meditation, is now used much more often in the extended sense 'a statement or slogan repeated frequently', with connotations of tedium or scepticism: *Doctors are not allowed to speak to the press directly: it's the managers who hold the line, learn the key-words, repeat the magical mantra 'No operations have been cancelled' and spin the agenda—Daily Tel.,* 2007; *This is the same mantra that politicians of every stripe have recited over the decades—The Australian,* 2004.

manuscript. Abbreviated MS (/ˌɛm'ɛs/) in singular (*MS Bodley 34*), and MSS (/ˌɛm'ɛsɪz/) in plural. Occasionally written lower case.

manyfold (adverb). See MANIFOLD.

Maori. A number of things have happened within New Zealand to the word *Maori* since about 1980. As part of an ambitious race-relations policy, attempts have been made to persuade non-Maoris to adopt the pronunciation and morphology of the word in the Maori language itself, and to respell the word either as *Māori* (with macron) or as *Maaori.* In the Maori language the word is pronounced /'mɑːɔri/, (**mah**-o-ri) i.e. as three syllables with the first vowel long. A small number of non-Maoris have adopted this pronunciation, but the majority of non-Maori speakers continue to say /'maʊri/, as does everyone outside New Zealand. The spelling *Māori* and the use of the word as an uninflected plural in order to accord with the conventions of the Maori language are shown in *The Oxford History of New Zealand Literature* (1991). It is too early yet to see whether these new conventions will prevail. Examples from this book: *The 1980s ... ended in a sesquicentennial year full of reminders, for most Māori and many Pākehā, of long-standing injustices still to be remedied—*T. Sturm; *There has been a written form of Māori since 1815—*J. McRae. From an earlier book (with an unmarked plural but without the macron): *For years Maori have struggled to secure public recognition of rights based on their understanding of the treaty—*C. Orange, 1987.

maraschino. Now often pronounced with a *sh* sound rather than the more traditional /marə'skiːnəʊ/, with a *k* sound, which is in line with the Italian pronunciation. Plural *maraschinos.* See -O(E)S 4.

marathon. 1 This now familiar word for a long-distance race and, by extension, for any other long-drawn-out test of endurance, was introduced in the first revived Olympic Games at Athens in 1896. The modern race is one of 26 miles 385 yards (42 km 352 m), usually through the streets of a large modern city. The circumstances of the run on which the modern event is based are disputed. The *OED*'s description is as follows: 'Herodotus records that Pheidippides ran from Athens to Sparta to secure aid before the battle [between the Greeks and the Persians], but the race instituted in 1896 was based on a later less sound tradition that Pheidippides ran from Marathon to Athens with news of the Persian defeat.'

2 For modern formations in *-athon* based on marathon, see -ATHON.

marginal, marginalize. 1 *Marginal* originally referred to writing that was literally in the margin of a page in *marginal notes*, and then to anything on the brink or edge of something else, such as *marginal plants* on the edge of a body of water. In the 20c. it developed the sociological meaning 'isolated from or not conforming to the dominant society or culture; belonging to a minority group' and then, as an extension of this, the more general meaning 'of minor importance, insignificant'. Examples: *Until recently, children's books were regarded as marginal, less than serious as literature*—J. Briggs, 1989; *His reputation was at best that of a marginal poet*—P. Zweig, 1984. Some commentators object to its being used to mean simply 'small, slight, insignificant' e.g. *a marginal effect on, a marginal improvement in*, and so forth. While it is true that this is an extension of a technical use, and can therefore be seen as slightly pompous or pseudo-scientific, it is well established and is best viewed as a POPULARIZED TECHNICAL TERM.

2 To the editors of the *OED* around the turn of the 20c., *marginalize* meant no more than 'to write marginal notes upon', and they marked it 'rare'. Since then it has been so transformed that the 1991 edition of the *Oxford Dictionary of New Words* described it (or, more precisely, its derivative **marginalization**) as 'one of the main social buzzwords of the eighties'. Increased awareness of the rights of underprivileged groups and minorities has given the word its new lease of life in the meaning 'to treat (a person or group of people) as marginal and therefore unimportant'. Inevitably, it is disliked by many on several counts: as an *-ize* verb; as a bit of a vogue word; and because of its sociological implications. Yet suitable replacements do not immediately leap to mind in the following examples: *Society, taking its lead from the media and its politicians, begins to reject a whole class and marginalizes them in the job market*—C. Phillips, 1987; *It is not yet clear that the church's long years of marginalisation in our national life have been ended*—*Independent*, 1990; *You work with what are often called 'marginalized' people, such as African-Americans and people of color*—*Bomb*, 1992.

marginalia /ˌmɑːdʒɪˈneɪlɪə/ (mar-ji-**nay**-li-uh) 'marginal notes' is a plural noun and must obviously govern a plural verb (*the marginalia in this manuscript* are *of considerable interest*). The following example mistakenly uses the singular: **And manuscript marginalia in miscellanies similarly* suggests *readers drawn from a wide cross section*—*Criticism*, 2000. Should a singular ever be needed, to refer to a single marginal note, it is *marginale*, not *marginalium*.

marijuana /ˌmarɪˈhwɑːnə/ is by far the more frequent spelling, rather than *marihuana*, which, however, mirrors the original Mexican Spanish word. The form with *-j-* appears to be an adaptation within English, according to the *OED*.

markedly. See -EDLY.

marriageable. Spelt with *-ge-*; see MUTE E.

marshal (verb). The inflected forms are *marshalled, marshalling*, but in AmE usually *marshaled, marshaling*. See -LL-, -L-.

marten, martin. The first, a weasel-like carnivore, is to be distinguished from the second, any of several swallows of the family Hirundinidae.

marvel (verb). The inflected forms are *marvelled, marvelling*, but in AmE usually *marveled, marveling*. See -LL-, -L-.

marvellous. Spelt as shown in BrE, but usually **marvelous** in AmE.

Mary. The plural is *Marys*, e.g. *the two Marys, several Bloody Marys*, etc. Ordinary nouns ending in consonant + *y (analogy, company*, etc.) have plural in *-ies*, but this rule does not apply to names. See PLURALS OF NOUNS 6.

masculine. See MALE.

Masorah, a body of traditional information and comment on the text of the Hebrew Bible. Spelt as shown, not the many variants.

massacre (noun and verb). So spelt in both BrE and AmE. The inflected forms are *massacres, massacred, massacring*.

massage. Pronounced /ˈmasɒːʒ/ or /-ɒːdʒ/. In AmE, *massage* is given second-syllable stressing. The corresponding agent nouns **masseur** and **masseuse**, by contrast, are stressed on the second syllable: thus /məˈsəː/, /məˈsəːz/. To avoid embarrassment, verbal or physical, it is as well to remember that a *masseur* is, or should be, a man, and a *masseuse* a woman.

massive in its various extended senses (*massive amount, attack, cut, increase, investment, overdose,* etc.) was accused by Gowers (1965) of being an overused vogue word, but is now standard. Any decent thesaurus will provide synonyms, if required.

mass noun, in this book is not a synonym of UNCOUNT NOUN. Instead, it denotes a smaller class of nouns such as *bread, wine, medicine,* which are usually uncount nouns but can be count nouns when they refer to types or amounts of something, e.g. *some bread/artisan breads, less wine/French wines.* See also COUNT NOUNS.

masterful, masterly. 1 Put simply, the issue is this: can *masterful* be used to mean 'extremely skilful, having the skill of a master', or is that meaning the exclusive territory of *masterly*? Fowler (1926) it was who first issued the diktat that *masterful* must not mean 'extremely skilful'. Usage commentators ever since have attempted to erect a Berlin Wall between the two words, but the 'skilful' meaning has consistently outfoxed the guards and taken shelter with *masterful.* (It, according to the purists, should only ever mean 'powerful and able to control others'.)

The facts of actual use are otherwise. Most of the examples of *masterful* in the *OEC* show it used in the 'skilful' sense. A comparison of the nouns associated with both words shows that *masterful* is more frequent in many collocations where the diktat would forbid it, e.g. *masterful/masterly display, handling, grasp.* Readers can decide for themselves if they approve of this use and wish to follow suit: the historical note at 2 may give them food for thought. It is also worth noting that the preference for *masterful* is stronger in North American English than in British English. The following are a few typical examples: (masterly) *The heart of the concert was some positively thrilling playing from the Grimethorpe Colliery and Black Dyke Bands, best of all when combined in Elgar's masterly Severn Suite*—*Daily Tel.,* 2007; *Akin to Turkish novelist Orhan Pamuk's masterly portrayal of his home city*—*The Hindu,* 2005; (masterful: 'acceptable' meaning) *Masterful was certainly what Pinky was: right from the moment when she had given him a smart tap on the nose, and shouted in his ear, 'Shall we get engaged?'*—J. Bayley, 1994; (masterful: disputed meaning) *Mackay's evocation of small community life in New Zealand almost a century ago is masterful*—fiction reviewer in *Spectator,* 1992; *Technically, Sher is in masterful control of his part*—theatre critic in *Sunday Times,* 1991.

2 *Historical note.* (*a*) From the 14c. to the present day *masterful* (i) has been used of persons (occasionally of animals) who are imperious, self-willed, or domineering; or of actions that are high-handed, despotic, or arbitrary; (ii) from the 15c. to the present (with, according to the revised *OED,* some falling-off in the 19c.) it has also been used in the 'skilful' sense. (*b*) From the 16c. to the 18c. *masterly* was used to mean 'imperious, domineering', but became obsolete in this sense at some point in the second half of the 18c. From then on its only meaning has been that of the disputed sense of *masterful,* as in *a masterly piece of work.*

A further fact may have some bearing on the rise and rise of *masterful*: its corresponding adverb is the natural formation **masterfully**, in regular use since the 14c. But adding the normal adverb suffix to *masterly* produces the ungainly *masterlily,* which would be avoided. The *OED* cites instances of *masterly* itself used as an adverb since the 14c. but labels it rare.

3 Both words can, inevitably, appear sexist to those who make it their business to be annoyed by trivia. A decent thesaurus will help them out of their misery.

mat, an AmE variant of MATT.

materialize. This verb is first recorded as having been used by Addison in 1710 and its earliest meanings were transitive (with an object): to *materialize* an idea was to realize it and to *materialize* a spirit was to make the spirit appear. Its intransitive use, now more familiar, dates from the late 19c., still in the context of spiritualism: *The . . . ghosts . . . gave dark séances and manifested and materialized*—*Harper's Magazine,* 1884. From there it is a small step to the transferred sense 'to come into existence'. First in the US in the 1880s and soon afterwards in Britain too (*Year after year passed and these promises failed to materialise*—*Blackwood's Mag.,* 1891) this meaning easily established itself and is accepted as standard by dictionaries. Nevertheless, it has been criticized since the early 20c., partly on the grounds that it is an inflated way of saying 'happen', 'be fulfilled', 'become available', etc. (Fowler, with typical forthrightness, called it an 'abomination'.) Modern examples: *Plans do not always materialise in the anticipated* way—B. Pym, 1982; *The alimony her ex-husband was supposed to pay her never materialized*—R. Deacon, 1988; *He denied the accusations and threatened legal action that has yet to materialize*—*Mirror*, 2007. This use is so common that objection to it is futile. It may, however, be worth ensuring, as Bryson (1984) observes, that the verb refers to the appropriate noun. In *Hopes of a patriotic rally failed to materialize* it is the rally rather than the hopes that was not realized.

materiel. Used in English since the early 19c. to mean 'material and equipment used in warfare (as distinct from personnel)', it has been naturalized and is printed in ordinary roman type without the accent on the first *e* of the original French *matériel*. The open *e* in the last syllable /məˌtɪərɪˈɛl/ differentiates it in speech from *material*.

matey. This largely British and Australian adjective and noun is generally spelt as shown, rather than *maty*. The derivative noun is rather more often **mateyness** than **matiness**.

math. The AmE abbreviation of MATHEMATICS; in BrE always *maths*.

mathematics. As the name of a subject always construed with a singular verb (*Mathematics is a difficult subject*). But when used to mean 'the use of mathematics in calculations, etc.', a plural verb should be used (*The mathematics of the launching of the spacecraft are extremely complicated*). See -ICS 2.

maths. See MATH.

matinee. The acute accent of the original French *matinée* is nowadays generally dropped, but to spell it with the accent is, of course, correct.

matiness. See MATEY.

matins. Usually with a singular verb. **1** The first of the seven canonical hours of the breviary, properly a midnight office, but sometimes 'anticipated' by being recited in the afternoon or evening before, or recited instead at daybreak.

2 The order for public morning prayer in the Church of England since the Reformation. See MORNING. In both senses the word is sometimes spelt **mattins** (and 16-17c. *mattens*), and this spelling is given precedence in the *Oxford Dict. of the Christian Church*, ed. F. L. Cross (1957), but is not generally used by the Church.

matrix /ˈmeɪtrɪks/. The plural is most commonly the Latin *matrices* /ˈmeɪtrɪsiːz/, far outnumbering *matrixes* in written sources, possibly because the fields in which the word is used are technical. See -EX, -IX 2.

matt, dull, without lustre. Spelt as shown, not *mat*, in BrE. The more usual spellings in AmE are either **mat** or **matte**.

matter. The phrase *no matter who* is sometimes affected by the confusion affecting *whom*, leading to mistaken formulations such as *But no matter whom the manufacturer, a general purpose lens is still, in many ways, attempting to be all things to everyone*—*OEC*, 2003. See WHO AND WHOM.

maty. See MATEY.

matzo /ˈmatsəʊ/, unleavened bread. Dictionaries generally recognize **matzoh** as a variant. Plural *matzos, matzohs*, or *matzoth* /-əʊt/.

maunder (verb). 'to talk in a dreamy or rambling manner; to move or act listlessly or idly' is a word of obscure origin (perhaps imitative?) first recorded in the 17c. It is not related to the verb *meander*, though the superficial resemblance of the two words has not escaped the notice of amateur etymologists.

mausoleum. The standard plural is *mausoleums*, but the far less frequent Latin plural *mausolea* is also used, despite its possible pretentiousness, particularly in British sources. See -UM 3.

maven, an expert or connoisseur, is an informal term (derived from Yiddish) that is familiar in North America; it is much less familiar elsewhere, but is making headway: *Hathaway plays Andy Sachs, a total novice who learns fast, changes from a sloppy dresser into a fashion maven and ends up winning the respect of her boss*—*Sunday Life*, 2006; *Lord Bell, the Tory peer and advertising maven, argues that all the classic*

British television ads —for Hovis , Heineken and Hamlet—rested on the notion of self-deprecation—*Guardian*, 2005.

maxilla. Plural *maxillae* /-iː/.

maximum. In technical and formal writing the plural is *maxim*a, which far outnumbers the workaday plural *maximums*. See -UM 3.

may and might. 1 *Present or future possibility.* Referring to present or future possibility, *may* and *might* are both used, but, in theory, with *may* the possibility is more open and with *might* it is more tentative or remote: (may) *The ACLU may have a strong case—Economist*, 1980; *The cyclists may use up to 6,000 calories during a race—Times*, 1983; (might) *The news that the Met season might have to be cancelled ... is an annual threat—Listener*, 1980; *Some players get a 'buzz' from the game* [of *Space Invaders*] *and that might explain why they become addicted—Times*, 1983.

2 *May* = present, *might* = past? Traditionalists insist that one should distinguish between *may* as the present tense and *might* as the past tense in expressing possibility: *I may have some dessert if I'm still hungry; she might have known her killer*. However, this distinction has long since been neutralized, and *may* and *might* are generally acceptable in either case: *she may have visited yesterday; I might go and have a cup of tea*. The difference is often in the degree of tentativeness, as described at 1 above.

3 Potentially ambiguous *may have.* The distinction between *may* and *might* can become significant when they are followed by *have* + past participle. (*a*) If at the time of writing or speaking it is not known whether an event or circumstance was actually the case, then either can be used. For example, a news item in the *Oxford Times* began: *Six prize-winning Shetland ponies stolen from a field near Chalgrove may have been sold at Reading market.* The headline immediately above it read *Stolen ponies might have been sold.* Here the two forms are effectively interchangeable.

(*b*) However, if it is known for a fact that the event or circumstance was not the case, then *might have* should be used. This applies in statements in which an unfulfilled condition is introduced by *if*, (or where there is inversion, as in the *Guardian* example below): **Shane acknowledges that without the help of close friends, he may not have survived the downward spiral he was in—This is Wiltshire*, 2005. Now imagine the headline 'Shane may not have survived'. It suggests the possibility that Shane did not survive, whereas in fact he did. Further examples: **A mentally ill man may not have committed suicide had he been kept in hospital, rather than been discharged to be cared for in the community* [but he did commit suicide]—*Guardian*, 1990; **If Apple had licensed Windows for its computers instead of insisting on its own operating system, it may not have squandered the lead built up with the launch of the Macintosh in 1984* [but it did squander it]—*Independent*, 2006.

(*c*) *CGEL* (1985) relegates this issue to a footnote: 'There is a tendency for the difference between *may* and *might* (in a sense of tentative or hypothetical possibility) to become neutralized ... This neutralization occasionally extends, analogically, to contexts in which only *might* would normally be considered appropriate: e.g. "An earlier launch of the lifeboat *may* [= might] *have averted* the tragedy." The fact that sentences such as this occasionally occur is a symptom of a continuing tendency to erode the distinctions between real and unreal senses of the modals.'

4 *That's as may be.* This chiefly BrE phrase means 'that may or may not be the case' and implies that whatever has just been said can be disregarded: *Once again 'our Tone'* [*sc.* Tony Blair] *is attempting the 'right or wrong this is what I truly believe' line of defence. Well that's as may be Tone but, right or wrong I don't believe you—and that's what I truly believe*—weblog, 2004. The ancestor of this phrase, *be as be may*, where the first *be* is subjunctive (cf. Spanish *sea como sea*) goes back at least as far as Chaucer, and *as may be* clearly contains the modal verb *may* + *be*, not the adverb *maybe*. Despite its widespread use in that latter form, the two words are best kept separate.

maybe. 1 Meaning 'perhaps', in origin a 14c. shortening of *it may be*, is such a familiar part of current standard English that it comes as a surprise to discover that it fell out of use in the 19c. to an extent that caused the *OED* (1906) to label it 'archaic and dialect'. It still has a somewhat informal air about it, and would be avoided in the most formal styles or writing, but it is now used in a wide range of contexts, written and spoken, and shares all the grammatical flexibility of *perhaps*. In AmE data in the *OEC*, it and *perhaps* are equally frequent, but in BrE data *perhaps* is as yet much more frequent. *Maybe a shotgun was all he had*—A. Munro, 1987; *Maybe if one of them had been sick that morning their father might not have gone to work. Maybe they should have ... said something at breakfast to delay him*—*New Yorker*, 1992; *I think maybe that's what Setanta were trying to go for*—*Guardian*, 2007.

2 Note that *may be* is spelt as two words when it is a combination of the modal verb *may* and the verb *be*: compare *Maybe that's no bad thing* and *That may be no bad thing*. Beware of mistakenly joining the words when they are used compositionally: **That maybe* (read *may be*) *all we can do*. For the mistaken spelling *that's as *maybe*, see MAY 4.

Mc-. See MAC-, MC-.

me. 1 See also I 1.

2 There are many contexts in spoken or informal written English in which *me* is the normal form, and to use *I* would sound inappropriately formal. (*a*) At the head of clauses introduced by conjoined subjects *me* is very common in informal conversation, but will be considered non-standard by some and is best avoided in other kinds of speech. It should not be used in writing, except to convey the authentic flavour of speech. Contrast *Senator Christopher Dodd of Connecticut and I met with President Bashar al-Assad for more than two hours*—*Boston Globe*, 2007; *I think that Brian and I would agree that we produce scholarly works when we translate*—*ABC, The Book Show*, 2007 with *Me and the lads have been wintering down here in Morocco*—*London Rev. Bks*, 1988; *Me and my deputies sometimes would be out riding, and we'd see a barn and think, That looks like a good place to hide*—A. Wilkinson, 1992. Of course, in standard or formal speech or writing the structure *X and I* is used. (*b*) *It's me*, in answer to the question *Who is it?*. (*c*) In answer to the question *Who's there?*, the natural answer is *Me*, not *I*. (*d*) After *as* and *than*, *I* is much more formal than *me* and more typical of written style. Examples: (as) *Jim would have run the farm as good as* me—M. Eldridge, 1984; *I sensed that he was as apprehensive as I about our meeting after seven years*—J. Frame, 1985; (than) *I hit her as hard as I could. She was taller than* me—M. Wesley, 1983; *He was taller than I, so that I had to stand a little to the rear*—B. Rubens, 1985. (*e*) When agreeing with someone else's affirmative or negative statement, *me too* or *me neither* are invariably used; and one usually replies *not me* rather than *not I*. Examples: *'Let's talk about each other, that's all I'm interested in at the moment.' 'Me too,' says Tom*—P. Lively, 1987; *'Oh no, I couldn't stand it!' 'Me neither!'*—R. McAlpine, 1985. In the well-known lyrics *Did you think I'd crumble? Did you think I'd lay down and die? Oh, no,* not I, *I will survive*, the phrase *not I* stands out as unusual, but is enforced by the refrain *I will survive*.

3 In representations of informal speech, *me* frequently takes the place of the possessive pronoun *my*. Examples: *That's him all right. He's got me coat and hat. That's him*—J. P. Donleavy, 1955; *I'll just go and clean me teeth*—*Encounter*, 1981; *These might do for me dad*—G. McGee, 1984.

4 For the use of *myself* instead of *me*, see MYSELF.

meagre. Spelt as shown in BrE, but in AmE usually **meager**.

mealie (or, from Afrikaans, **mielie**). Used chiefly in the plural form *mealies* (or *mielies*) as a South African name for maize, Indian corn. The singular form occurs chiefly in compounds, e.g. *mealie-cob, mealie-field, mealie meal*.

mean (verb). **1** When it means 'to intend', *mean* can be followed by a *to*-infinitive (when the speaker intends to do something): *I meant to go*, by an object + *to*-infinitive (when the speaker intends someone else to do something): *I meant you to go* and, more formally, by a *that*-clause with *should*: *I meant that you should go*. Use of *mean for* + object + *to*-infinitive, e.g. *I meant for you to go*, which is not uncommon in informal AmE, is non-standard.

2 For (*Do you*) *know what I mean?*, see KNOW 1.

3 *I mean.* This is often legitimately used to introduce an explanation of what has just been stated, e.g. *But he was a marvellous butler. I mean, if you went there he'd welcome you in the most graceful and polite and proper way*—*New Yorker*, 1986; *Courage to buy and courage to sell—I mean, maybe the real courage is in the keeping, before you sell*—R. Rofihe, 1990. In conversation it is increasingly heard as a sentence filler, with very little propositional meaning, rather like *you know* (see KNOW 2): *Well I mean a lot of these things that are happening, well they just don't quite ring true*—G. Chapman et al., 1972; *'It's not really expensive. I mean, it only costs a pound.' 'It seems, sort of, a lot. I mean, when it used to cost only forty pence. I mean, where will it all end?'* And it is all too easy to point to extremes that no one would consider standard, e.g. *You know, like, uh, hey, man, I mean, cool, huh?*—L. Woidwode, 1992.

meander. See MAUNDER.

meaningful. The journalist and literary critic Philip Howard wrote in 1978 that 'ongoing situations and meaningful dialogues are two popular pieces of jargon ... at present'. It was in the 1960s and 1970s that the word, though first used in 1852, enjoyed such a vogue that it started to attract unfavourable criticism, and was viewed as a massive cliché. Now, several decades later, the word has lost much of its capacity to irritate, but still raises the question: in certain contexts does it mean very much at all? *Meaningful* in one sense is the opposite of *meaningless*, i.e. 'having meaning', as in *meaningful elements in a language* and *words likely to be meaningful to pupils.* It is also used to describe communication that is non-verbal but pregnant with significance, as in a *meaningful look, glance, smile*, or *pause*.

But in phrases such *as meaningful discussions, negotiations, conversation, debate*, etc. it can justifiably be criticized as adding nothing, for in any negotiation or discussion surely some kind of meaning must be exchanged. And how could a *conversation* not have meaning? These phrases, in particular the potentially groan-inducing *meaningful dialogue*, are best avoided and adjectives such as *fruitful, productive*, etc. used instead. And when it is importance rather than meaning that is the issue, alternatives such as *important, major*, and *effective* should be considered: *It will take time for these changes in strategy to have a meaningful influence on financial performance*—*Birmingham Post*, 2007. As a postscript, it is worth noting that the *OED* lists *meaningful relationship* as a compound noun and defines it as 'a romantic association based on a strong emotional or intellectual attachment (especially as opposed to a relationship based principally on sexual attraction)'.

means is ostensibly a plural noun in form, but in some circumstances may be construed either with a plural or a singular verb, like the small group of nouns that work in this way, e.g. *crossroads, gallows, headquarters*, (golf) *links*. **1** When the meaning is 'financial resources', *means* is plural: *Their means are somewhat limited.* When the meaning is 'a way or method' it can operate as a singular noun (preceded by a determiner such as *a, any*, or *every*) or as a plural noun (preceded by a plural-marking word such as *all, many, several*, etc.): *They remained for her* a *means, and not an end, a bargaining power rather than a blessing*—Margaret Drabble, 1967; *Derek and I drove down there and shut off the whole barn, preventing* all *means of getting in or out*—J. Hadwick, 1991; *In those days gondolas were cheap and* a *perfectly normal means of transport*—*Mail on Sunday*, 2001. When *means* is preceded by *the*, the following verb can be either singular or plural, depending on whether a single 'way or method' or several are concerned: *Moreover, the means by which this end is achieved* are *remarkable*—M. Foot, 1986; *When I first travelled to England in 1960, the normal means* was *by boat*—*Daily Tel.*, 2003.

2 The dual role of *means* in the 'way, method' sense is a survival of an earlier time, when both the singular *mean* and the plural *means* were used: e.g. *Baptisme is necessarie as a meane to saluation* (C. Sclater, 1611); *Let us consider it as a mean, not as an end* (T. Balguy, 1785). The singular use has disappeared, but the construction, attached to the plural, has survived.

meantime, meanwhile. 1 Both words can be used on their own as adverbs or in the phrases *in the meantime, in the meanwhile*. From the 16c. to the 19c. *meantime* was as common as *meanwhile* as an adverb (e.g. *The ladies, meantime, were on* *the* qui vive—1842; *Meantime where was Lord Palmerston?*—1879). Nowadays, the *OEC* data suggests that *meanwhile* is at least twenty times more frequent across Englishes, and *meantime*, though not common, is more frequent in AmE than elsewhere. Conversely, *in the meantime* is well over one hundred times more frequent than *in the meanwhile*. Examples: *The telephone will . . . redial the number you last called, even if you've hung up in the meantime*—*Which?*, 1987; *Meantime, melt the remaining butter in a saucepan*—D. Smith, 1978; *The animals Mrs Murray cares for are always returned to the wild if possible. Meanwhile, they stay at her study centre*—*Times*, 1986; *In the meanwhile, I'll just lie here, flat on my back, fingering my perfect bones*—J. Shute, 1992.

2 From the 14c. to the 19c., *meantime* and *meanwhile* were both written as two words, but they are nowadays always written as one. Accordingly, examples like the following will be judged as misspelt: **So in the mean time I'm catching up on some reading and blogging*—weblog, 2005.

3 *Meanwhile* is commonly used in journalism and especially broadcasting as a means of resuming a main theme after a digression or aside. It is the equivalent of phrases like *while we are on the subject* or *and another thing*. The next two examples show that the journalists using it were very aware of its nuances: *When we* [*sc.* journalists] *begin our final paragraphs with 'meanwhile', we are usually* (*and a bit shamefacedly*) *trying to get away with a disgraceful non sequitur*—*New Statesman*, 1964; *Meanwhile, as we say in the trade, Motherwell* [*sc.* a Scottish football team] *go bottom* [*of the league table*]—D. Lynam, BBC TV, 14 March 1987. The use may owe its origins to the catchphrase *Meanwhile, back at the ranch*, one of the most memorable captions in silent Westerns of the 1930s, used to introduce a subsidiary plot. It made its way into later Westerns like *Champion the Wonder Horse* (1956), promoted from caption to voice-over. The phrase is now used in its full form as a sort of folk allusion, and has also generated the use of *meanwhile back* . . . introducing a range of adjuncts. Example: *Meanwhile, back at the ranch, the transport system is in chaos, there's a full-scale law and order crisis and the NHS is a basket case*—*Sun*, 2002.

4 According to *MWCDEU*, some American commentators dislike *meantime* as an adverb, and *in the meanwhile*. Both are standard, but as noted at 1, much less common than *meanwhile* and *in the meantime*.

measles. Most commonly construed as a singular (*Measles is decidedly infectious*) but occasionally as a plural, and also, especially in some regional forms of English, with *the* (e.g. *The measles have left him feeling weak*).

measurements. *A blank white eight-by-eleven sheet can look as big as Montana if the pen's not so hot*—G. Keillor, 1989. It is worth noting that in such double measurements the smaller number is usually placed first in AmE and the larger in BrE. Oxford lexicographers once upon a time copied illustrative examples on to 6″ × 4″ slips, but our colleagues in America called them 4″ × 6″ slips. Compare also the colloquial military *four-by-two* '(in Brit.), the cloth attached to a pull-through (for cleaning a rifle)'; and *two-by-four* '(originally and chiefly US) a post or batten measuring 2 inches by 4 in cross-section'.

meatus /mɪˈeɪtəs/, (anat.) a channel or passage in the body or its opening. Plural same (pronounced /mɪˈeɪtuːs/) or *meatuses*. See -US 2.

medal. 1 The inflections and derivatives are *medalled, medalling*, **medallist** (AmE usually *medaled, medaling*, **medalist**). See -LL-, -L-.

2 Vociferous objections have been raised, particularly in Britain, against the use of *medal* in sporting circles as an intransitive verb, e.g. *Holland have only medalled three times at the world outdoor championships*—*Irish Examiner*, 2005. (There was a massive spike in searches for the word in the *OED* around the time of the 2012 London Olympics as people tried to discover if this use was legitimate.) Objections are largely based on the perception that it is both a dastardly Americanism and an egregious example of the newfangled craze for verbing. The *OED*'s first citation for the verb is from none other than Thackeray in 1860 (*Irving went home medalled by the king*—*Cornhill Mag.*) and the Cambridge University literary magazine *Granta* published this in 1890: *In that year it was decided that both crews should be medalled, the winners with silver, the losers with bronze.* Admittedly the meaning here is 'to be decorated with a medal' rather than to win one. That decried intransitive use the *OED* (2001) labels 'now chiefly US sport', and shows it first in an isolated 1865 example, and then in a 1979 example from the *Washington Post*: *Our women are coming along beautifully—they've medaled well recently*. The *OED*'s reservation noted above should now be removed, since the verb is as commonly used in BrE sports journalism as it is in AmE. Detested by some, it has become a fixture of sporting language.

media in its modern meaning 'channels of mass communication such as newspapers and broadcasting regarded collectively', often preceded by *the*, has long been treated as a plural noun: *When the media* report *events there must always be a line, an angle, a spin*—B. Morrison, 1998. It is increasingly used, especially by the media themselves, as a collective noun allowing plural or singular agreement. Use with singular agreement is disliked by some people: *The British media at its finest is the best in the world*—Tony Blair on BBC Radio, 1998. *Media* is also recorded in the *OED* as a count noun, i.e. usable with *a*, and having a plural, from as far back as 1927, e.g. *Often urged on by a mass media that magnified the public danger, politicians tried to answer the ... call for protective action*—C. Townshend, 2002. Perhaps the best advice is, if in doubt, use the plural; and avoid *a media* and the plural *medias*.

medieval, mediaeval. The second is now rapidly passing out of use in favour of the shorter version, which is much more often used.

mediocrity. Pronounced /miːdɪˈɒkrɪti/, the first syllable rhyming with *mead*.

Mediterranean is spelt with one *d*, one *t*, and two *r*s, as its derivation from the Latin words *medius* 'middle' and *terra* 'land' reminds us.

medium. When the meaning is 'one who claims to be in contact with the spirits of the dead', the plural is always *mediums*. In all other senses, *mediums* and *media* are both in use, except that MEDIA (newspaper/broadcasting sense) has its own pattern of behaviour. See -UM 3.

meerschaum Spelt as shown, with *-sch-* not *-sh-*. The first syllable rhymes with *near*, the second can be pronounced /-əm/, /-ɔːm/, or /-aʊm/ (-uhm, -awm, -owm).

meet (verb). On its own, *meet* can be used transitively (*I met him yesterday*) and intransitively (*we met yesterday*). Idiomatically one meets *with* a circumstance rather than a person, typically something unpleasant or unwelcome; or one meets with a response or reaction, again often unfavourable (*This may not meet with the approval of the parents; Her appointment as chief vet met with sniffiness among some farmers*). Now *meet* is increasingly used with the link word *with* (or *up with*, based on *meet up*) when people are involved, typically in contexts involving prolonged discussion or dealings (*the people who will be meeting with the Secretary of State; A few weeks later I met up with them again*). This is far from being a new use: it is recorded in the *OED* from the 13c. in the sense both of a planned encounter, and of a casual or accidental one, as in the following examples: *An appointment to meet with the others of his company at the sign of the Griffin*—Scott, 1828; *'Tis ... rare to meet with persons, who can pardon another any opposition he makes to their interest*—D. Hume, 1740. It is true to say however that *meet with* has become fashionable again in contexts of intentional or arranged meeting under the influence of AmE, and tends to be used in contexts where plain *meet* was once more usual. Anyone wishing to leave the preposition out is, of course, at liberty to do so. Example: *the American national security adviser, Gen. James L. Jones, met with top Pakistani officials here in the capital*—*NYT*, 2009.

mega. This is an unusual example of a prefix taking on (since the 1980s) a life of its own as an independent word. It can be used as an adjective, meaning 'very large; huge' (*he has signed a mega deal to make five movies*) and 'excellent' (*it will be a mega film*). It can occasionally be used predicatively, e.g. *The implications are mega*. It also functions as an adverb meaning 'extremely': *It has never been my ambition to be mega famous or mega rich—I've just wanted to make a living*—*People*, 2007. It is still somewhat informal in style.

mega-. This prefix, representing Greek μεγα-, combining form of μέγας 'great', was drawn on repeatedly in the 19c. to form new words, both technical and scientific (*megalith, megalomania, megaspore, megavolt,* etc.) and general (*megaphone*). It continues in widespread use (*a*) in scientific and technical terms denoting a million (times), i.e. 10^6, as in *megaparsec* and *megadeath* (meaning one million deaths in nuclear warfare); (*b*) in computing language, meaning 2^{20} (1,048,576), as in *megabyte, megapixel;* and (*c*) to denote anything of great size, excellence, or importance, e.g. *megahit, megamerger, megastar, megastore,* etc. As in all the examples shown, words with this prefix are not hyphenated and are written as one unit.

meiosis /mʌɪˈəʊsɪs/ (my-**oh**-sis), plural *meioses* /-iːz/, derived from Greek μείωσις 'lessening', is a rhetorical device in classical and later literatures, and in ordinary speech and language, in which circumstances, a predicament, or any event is intentionally understated, e.g. describing something outstanding as 'rather good'. A literary example is found in *Romeo and Juliet* where Mercutio describes his *mortall hurt* as *a scratch, a scratch.* A special form of *meiosis* using negative understatement is called LITOTES.

-meister. From German *Meister* ('master'), since the 1970s *-meister* has been pressed into service, especially in AmE, as the second element in various, mostly transparent, compounds, to denote a person who is a master of, or strongly associated with, the first element, e.g. *Paul* [McCartney] *was always a closet schmaltzmeister* (*'Michelle')*—L. Bangs, 1975. Probable one-offs noted in the *OED* examples include *newsmeister, pubmeister,* and *groove-meisters;* given entries in their own right are *schlockmeister* ('master of shoddy entertainment'), *spinmeister* (= spin doctor), and *webmeister* (= webmaster). Other examples in the *OEC* include *horrormeister* and *blogmeister.*

melodeon. Spelt as shown, also **melodion.**

melodrama. 'In early 19th century use, a stage-play (usually romantic and sensational in plot and incident) in which songs were interspersed, and in which the action was accompanied by orchestral music appropriate to the situations. In later use the musical element gradually ceased to be an essential feature of the "melodrama", and the name now denotes a dramatic piece characterized by sensational incident and violent appeals to the emotions, but with a happy ending' (*OED,* 1907). The term is also now applied to cinema and TV productions of a similar type; and to a series of incidents, or a story, true or fictitious, resembling what is represented in a melodrama.

membership had two established uses before the 20c.: (*a*) (first recorded in 17c.) the condition or status of a member of a society or organization (*the oath of membership required fidelity*); (*b*) (19c.) the number of members in a particular organization (*a large membership is necessary*). A third sense, simply = 'members', especially in the language of trade unions, was described by Gowers (1965) as 'now rife and corrupting other words' (e.g. *Her acceptance of this role has . . . given enormous pleasure to the membership*—B. Grant, 1990) on the grounds that it replaced the concrete 'members' with the abstract. Its use is normally restricted to official or reporting contexts. Cf. LEADERSHIP; READERSHIP.

membraneous /mɛmˈbreɪnɪəs/, **membranous** /ˈmɛmbrənəs/. Both are adjectives corresponding to the noun **membrane**. The second is several times more frequent than the first.

memento, a souvenir, or a reminder of someone or something, should not be converted into *momento,* which obscures the word's origins as the imperative (i.e. *remember!*) of the Latin verb *meminisse* 'to remember'. Nevertheless, the *OED* includes it without comment as a variant (first recorded 1600), and *MWCDEU* cites an example from 1853 in a letter from the first editor-in-chief of Merriam-Webster dictionaries, no less. Despite that, many people will consider it wrong, and in the case of **memento mori** (literally 'remember (that you have) to die') referring to something such as a skull kept as a reminder of one's mortality, almost grotesquely wrong. Both *mementos* and *mementoes* are correct as the plural, the first more often used than the second in AmE, while in BrE the opposite is true. See -O(E)S 2.

memorabilia (plural noun), souvenirs of memorable events, people, etc. It should always be treated as a plural. Incorrect examples (from American newspapers 1994–5): *The memorabilia on the walls includes a magazine cover of an outlaw he* *killed in Miami; Older memorabilia, however, is more difficult to come by.*

memorandum. The recommended plural is *memoranda,* but *memorandums* is also in standard use. See -UM 3. Beware of falling into the trap of regarding *memoranda* as a singular and consequently speaking of *these memorandas.*

memsahib. See SAHIB.

ménage, the members of a household, is written in roman, but normally retains its French accent and its not fully Anglicized pronunciation, i.e. /meiˈnɑːʒ/ (may-**nahzh**). The euphemism *ménage à trois* referring to a love triangle should be italicized. It is often misspelt *ménage à *trios.*

mendacity is habitual lying or deceiving, and **mendicity** is the practice or habit of begging.

meninges /mɪˈnɪndʒiːz/, the three membranes that line the skull. Singular *meninx* /ˈmiːnɪŋks/.

meningitis /mɛnɪnˈdʒʌɪtɪs/. See GREEK G.

menstruum /ˈmɛnstrʊəm/, a solvent, or a liquid medium. Plural generally *menstrua* /-strʊə/, occasionally *menstruums.* See -UM 3.

-ment. For differences between this suffix and *-ion,* see -ION AND -MENT. Nouns in *-ment* are almost all formed on verbs: *merriment* is only an apparent exception (it was formed on an obsolete verb *merry* 'to make merry'); *oddment* is a genuine exception. In words like *garment, raiment,* and *testament,* the *-ment* is not a suffix but is part of the stem of the word.

mental. Yesterday's euphemisms sometimes become today's insults, and *mental* is a case in point. Its use in compounds such as *mental hospital* and *mental patient* is first recorded at the end of the 19th century and became the normal accepted term in the first half of the 20th century. Now, however, it is regarded as certainly old-fashioned, if not offensive. The most usual acceptable alternative is *psychiatric,* which has already generally replaced it in official use. The particular terms **mental handicap** and **mentally handicapped**, though widely used a few decades ago, have fallen out of favour in recent years and have been largely replaced in official contexts by less demeaning terms such as LEARNING DIFFICULTIES.

Mephistopheles /mɛfɪˈstɒfɪliːz/. The adjective is either *Mephistophelean* or *Mephistophelian* /ˌmɛfɪstəˈfiːlɪən/.

merchandise. As a noun, pronounced with final /-ʌɪz/ or sometimes with /-ʌɪs/, *merchandise* belongs to that group of words that must always be spelled *-ise.* As a verb it is pronounced with final /-ʌɪz/ and more often spelt with final *-ise* than with final *-ize.*

merino. Plural *merinos.* See -O(E)S 4.

merit (verb). The inflected forms are *merited, meriting.* See -T-, -TT-.

merriment. See -MENT.

Messrs. As this abbreviation is now unusual, the description of the term in *Debrett's Correct Form* (1976) may be found useful: 'The use of the prefix "Messrs." (a contraction of the French Messieurs), as the plural of "Mr.", is becoming archaic for commercial firms in Britain, Australia and New Zealand, but is still generally used by the professions, especially the law. It is not generally used in Canada or in the United States. For those who prefer to use the term "Messrs.", this is restricted to firms with personal names, e.g. Messrs. Berkeley, Stratton & Co. . . . It is never used in the following instances: (*a*) Limited Companies. (*b*) Firms which do not trade under a surname, or the surname does not form the complete name. e.g. The Devon Mechanical Toy Co., . . . John Baker's School of Motoring. (*c*) Firms whose name includes a title, e.g. Sir John Jones & Partners. (*d*) Firms which bear a lady's name, e.g. Josephine Taylor & Associates.' In most modern work *Messrs* is printed without a full point.

Some examples: *Messrs Hodder & Stoughton; Armour Glass . . . similar to that made by Messrs. Pilkington Bros. in this country; Thanks to Messrs McCaskill and Fish with their TV weather forecasts.*

messuage, house with outbuildings (a legal term). Pronounced /ˈmɛswɪdʒ/.

meta-. Especially since the second half of the 20c. this prefix has been borrowed from *metaphysics* and applied to other words with the meaning 'of a higher or second-order kind': a *metalanguage* is language used to describe language, *metafiction* is a form of fiction in which the author sets out to parody literary conventions, and *metadata* is data that describes and gives information about other data.

metal (noun) and **mettle** are in origin the same word. From the late 16c. onwards *mettle* began to move apart as a separate word used only in figurative senses, especially '(of persons) ardent or spirited temperament; spirit, courage'. Meanwhile *metal,* while still current in figurative uses in the 16c. and 17c., especially in the sense 'the "stuff" of which a person is made, with reference to character', gradually became more or less restricted to metallic substances (e.g. industrial metals; also, road metal).

metal (verb). The inflected forms are *metalled, metalling* (but usually *metaled, metaling* in AmE). See -LL-, -L-.

metallurgy. The only pronunciation given in the *OED* (1907) showed the stress on the first syllable. *COD* (1990) gives precedence to second-syllable stressing. This tendency to adopt an antepenultimate stress pattern in four-syllable words is a marked feature of 20c. English. Cf. *despicable, disputable, pejorative,* etc. In AmE first-syllable stressing is still normal for *metallurgy.* The same patterns apply to **metallurgist**.

metamorphosis. The *OED* (1907) gave only /mɛtəˈmɔːfəsɪs/, i.e. stressed on the third syllable. *COD* (1990) added /ˌmɛtəmɔːˈfəʊsɪs/ as a permissible variant. In either case the plural form *metamorphoses* ends with /-iːz/.

metanalysis (philology). Reinterpretation of the division between words or syntactic units: e.g. *adder* from Old English *nǣdre* by analysis in Middle English of *a naddre* as *an adder.*

metaphor. 1 Fowler's lengthy essay on this subject in the first edition of this book (1926) can be consulted in the *Oxford World Classics* edition. Readers may also wish to consult K. Wales, *A Dictionary of Stylistics* (1989) with the works cited in it under the entry for *metaphor.*

2 Perhaps the two best-known figures of speech are the *metaphor* and the *simile.* They differ only in form: a *simile* is a fanciful comparison introduced by *like* or *as* while a *metaphor* directly equates the image with the person or thing it is compared to. Straightforward examples: (metaphor) *True to the signal, by love's* meteor *led, Leander hasten'd to his Hero's bed*—G. White, 1769; (simile) *Th' Imperial Ensign ... Shon* like a Meteor *streaming to the Wind*—Milton, 1667.

3 Ordinary language abounds in simple, often dead or invisible, metaphors. Figurative uses of language e.g. in this *neck* of the woods, the *mouth* of the river, a *blanket* of fog, are often metaphors, while many set idioms and proverbs are also metaphors, e.g. no *smoke* without *fire,* throw out the *baby* with the *bathwater,* get the *green light, off the wall,* etc. can be regarded as metaphors.

4 A type of metaphor that always invites derision is the *mixed metaphor,* in which two (or more) incompatible images are combined. Examples (all but the last two from the letter pages of *The Times*): *He has been made a sacrificial lamb for taking the lid off a can of worms*; *In coal mines, mice are used as human guinea pigs*; *Why do the dear old Labour party persist in burying their heads in the sand, parroting tired old formulae?*; *In a debate on shipping and the merchant fleet ...* [*he*] *called for a level playing field*; *The grass roots are pretty cheesed off*—*BBC Radio* news, 1999; *Europe's Central Bank should take its head out of the sand and call a spade a spade*—*Wall Street Journal*, 2001.

metaphysical (adjective). See METAPHYSICS.

metaphysics. 1 As the name of a branch of philosophy, *metaphysics* has had an adventurous history and important consequences. Since at least the 1c. AD it was applied (as Greek τὰ μεταφυσικά) to the thirteen books of Aristotle dealing with questions of 'first philosophy' or ontology. They were in fact τὰ μετὰ τὰ φυσικά 'the things (works) after the Physics', in other words the works that in the received arrangement followed the treatise on natural science known as τὰ φυσικά 'the Physics'. In the 18c. the Greek word was falsely interpreted as 'beyond what is physical', and *metaphysics* came to be widely used to mean 'the science of things transcending what is physical or natural'. The adjective *metaphysical* followed suit.

2 *Metaphysical* was adopted by Dr Johnson as the designation of certain 17c. poets (Donne, Cowley, and others) addicted to poetical conceits and far-fetched imagery.

3 *Metaphysics,* like other subject-names ending in *-ics,* is plural in form but is construed as a singular (see the first sentence in 1).

metathesis. (phonetics) The transposition of sounds or letters in a word. Examples include the transposition of the *p* and *s* in *hasp* (cf. Old English *hæpse*); the *s* and *k* in non-standard *ax*(*e*) 'ask' (OE *āscian*); the *r* and *i* in *third* (OE *þridda*) and *thrill* (OE *þȳrlian*); the *r* and *u* in *curled* (ME *crolled, crulled*). For a modern example, see IRRELEVANT.

meter. The normal spelling in both BrE and AmE for an instrument for recording the amount of gas, electricity, etc., used. Also **parking meter**. Also, the standard spelling in AmE of the words spelt METRE in BrE meaning a unit of length and the rhythmical pattern of poetry.

-meter, combining form. **1** Forming nouns denoting measuring instruments (*barometer, speedometer*).

2 (prosody) Forming nouns denoting lines of poetry with a specified number of measures (*pentameter, hexameter*). Cf. METRE[2].

method. For *method in* (*his,* etc.) *madness,* see IRRELEVANT ALLUSION.

methodology. Business or academic speak and officialese love long-winded synonyms. A *methodology* is not a mere *method.* It is either 'the branch of knowledge that deals with method generally or with the methods of a particular discipline' or it is 'a system of methods used in a particular area of study or activity', in other words, something that is scientific or scholarly: *A reconsideration of the problem how the logical analysis of scientific procedure* (*methodology*) *is related to deductive logic—Methodology of Social Science,* 1944; *Consumers must demand labeling and independent safety testing using methodology that consumers can trust—Co-op Connection,* 1993. A *method* is simply a 'procedure for accomplishing something' and, as the dictionary suggests, it is 'especially a systematic or established one'. The word *methodology* is prostituted in contexts such as the following where *method* or *methods* would suffice: *Given these principles of andragogy, experiential learning can be an effective methodology for teaching adults—NACTA Jrnl,* 2004; *Some investors also question the methodology used by some analysts to make recommendations—BBC News,* 2004.

meticulous. 1 The word entered the language in the 16c. in the sense of Latin *meticulōsus* 'fearful, timid' (cf. Latin *metus* 'fear', *metuō* 'regard with awe'). But this use was short-lived and thinly evidenced, and has not been found since the 17c. For whatever reason, the word reappeared in the early 19c., but used to mean 'over-careful about minute details, over-scrupulous' (e.g. *The decadence of Italian prose composition into laboured mannerism and meticulous propriety*—J. A. Symonds, 1877), a use scorned by the Fowler brothers in *The King's English* (1906). They included it in a list of 'stiff, full-dress, literary, or out-of-the-way words'. At some point in the 20c. the over-carefulness element of the meaning dropped out, and the word is now routinely used simply to mean 'careful, punctilious, scrupulous, precise'. It is a useful word, together with its derivatives **meticulously** and **meticulousness**. Examples: *He also set down with meticulous care an exact itinerary of Stillman's divagations*—P. Auster, 1985; *He'd read it all up beforehand, in the most meticulous manner*—J. Gloag, 1986; *Utz had planned his own funeral with meticulous* care—B. Chatwin, 1988; *Meticulous, obsessional scholars whose lives are dedicated to their work*—A. Storr, 1988.

2 Dictionaries show the first syllable rhyming with *mitt.*

metonymy, a figure of speech in which an attribute or property is used to refer to the person or thing that has it. When we call Queen Elizabeth *the Crown,* we use metonymy. Similarly, *the White House* for the American presidency; *the stage* for the theatre; and *the pen is mightier than the sword* as a way of saying that the written word has more power than war. Cf. SYNECDOCHE.

metope (architecture, part of a Doric frieze). Generally pronounced as two syllables, /ˈmɛtəʊp/ occasionally as three, /ˈmɛtəpi/ as in the orginal Greek μετόπη.

metre[1]. The spelling in BrE of the metric unit of length equal to about 39.4 inches. AmE **meter**.

metre[2]. Any form of poetic rhythm, determined by the number and length of feet in a line. AmE **meter**.

metropolis. The plural is *metropolises,* not the pseudo-Latin *metropoli.*

metrosexual, a blend of *metropolitan* and *heterosexual,* is a word that was created by journalist Mark Simpson in 1994 to describe men whom the *OED* defines as follows: 'A man (esp. a heterosexual man) whose lifestyle, spending habits and concern for personal appearance are likened to those considered typical of a fashionable, urban, homosexual man.' A considerable talking point in 1990s and a bit of a vogue word, it now seems to have settled down as an apt noun and adjective to describe the ongoing social trend of more and more heterosexual men becoming born-again shoppers and obsessive self-groomers. Examples: *Metrosexuals also love more fashionable suits teamed with the vivid (some might say lurid) Paul Smith shirts—Business Review Weekly,* 2003 (Aust.); *For starters, we are becoming a nation of metrosexuals. British girls are getting their beauty tips out for the boys who are now collectively spending £959 million on first date grooming*—Sarah Modlock, 2005 (BrE).

mettle. See METAL (noun).

mews. This originally British word for 'a row or street of houses or flats that have been converted from stables or built to look like former stables' is in origin the plural of *mew* 'a cage for hawks'. It is now usually construed as a singular (*an expensive apartment in a fashionable mews*). In the plural, like headquarters, it is invariable (*The mews of London . . . constitute a world of their own*—H. Mayhew, 1851). Fowler (1926) recommended *mewses* as a plural, but his recommendation has not found favour.

mezzanine. Pronounced /ˈmɛzəniːn/ or /ˈmɛtsə-/, a low storey between two others (usually between the ground and first floors).

mezzotint. Pronounced /ˈmɛtsəʊ-/, though the Italian original *mezzotinto* is pronounced /mədz-/.

miasma /mɪˈazmə/, /maɪ-/, an archaic word for an infectious or noxious vapour. Plural *miasmata* /-mətə/ or *miasmas.*

mic. According to the *OEC* evidence, this abbreviation for *microphone,* first recorded from 1961, now seems to be as frequent as, if not more frequent than, the older *mike,* first recorded in 1911. Despite its appearance, it is pronounced like the name *Mike.*

mickle and **muckle** are merely variants of the same word, and the not uncommon proverb *Many a mickle makes a muckle* is, strictly speaking, a corruption of the original, despite the fact that it is hallowed by usage and everyone understands it in the same sense as the original. The original formulation is *Many a little makes a mickle* (first recorded in the 17c.), in which *mickle* means 'a large sum or amount'. (*Pickle* has been used occasionally in place of *little.*) The *mickle . . . muckle* version arises from the mistaken notion that, rather than being variants, *mickle* and *muckle* have opposite meanings, the *mickle* representing 'a small amount'. An ancestor of the folk-altered formulation is first found in the phrase *Many mickles make a muckle* in 1793 in the work of George Washington.

micro- continues to be a combining form of limitless power. Hundreds of *micro*-compounds are already entered in the *OED,* including a great many first recorded in the 20c., e.g. *microclimate, microdot, microfiche, microfilm, microform, micromanage, microsurgery, microwave.*

mid- meaning 'the middle of', is normally joined by a hyphen to the following word, e.g. *in mid-September*; *at mid-term.* According to *New Hart's Rules,* however, *mid* can also be treated as an independent adjective and not hyphenated in combinations such as *the mid nineteenth century.* Note that when the noun attached to *mid-* is in attributive position (before another noun), two hyphens are needed: *a mid-nineteenth-century church.* Note also that *mid-air* is spelt with a hyphen whatever its position in the sentence, despite Fowler's preference (1926) for *mid air.*

midriff denotes the front of a man or woman's body between the chest and the waist, e.g. *Her friend . . . was wearing a sprayed-on dress that showed her pants and midriff—Bridget Jones's Diary,* 1996. It comes from Old English *midrhif,* = mid +

rhif ('belly'). Folk etymology occasionally turns it into the entertaining **midrift*: *However, the entire look is ruined by his refusal to unbutton the coat, which means it's gathered up in an aesthetically displeasing fashion around his midrift—Guardian,* 2005. More mistakenly creative still is **mid drift*: *The mid drift area is located below the chest and above the waist—www.livestrong.com,* (undated).

midst is most commonly used as a noun in the fixed phrases *in the midst of* 'among, in the middle of', *in our* (or *their,* etc.) *midst* 'among us (or them, etc.)'. As a preposition = *amidst,* it is now rare. Example: *'Midst brightly perfumed water-flowing Eighteenth-century silks*—E. Sitwell, 1924.

midwifery. In standard use in BrE now mostly pronounced as four or three syllables, /ˈmɪdˌwɪf(ə)ri/, but it is only relatively recently that the second syllable has settled down as /-wɪf-/. The *OED* (1907) gave priority to /ˈmɪdwʌɪfri/, and also listed /ˈmɪdɪfri/ (with the *w* silent). In AmE, usage is divided but /-waɪf-/ is commonly used for the second syllable.

mielie. See MEALIE.

might. See MAY AND MIGHT.

mighty as an adverb has been in use in English since about 1300 (*þair blisced lauerd ... þat ... was ... Sa mighti meke* 'Their blessed Lord who was so exceedingly meek'), and has continued to flourish in AmE at all levels except the most formal. In British and other Englishes it is also used in non-formal writing, though less often than in AmE: *As I say, I had mighty little to complain of*—J. Buchan, 1926; *Trolls are slow in the uptake, and mighty suspicious about anything new to them*—J. R. R. Tolkien, 1937; *Heating the greenhouse ... can be a mighty expensive proposition—Practical Gardening,* 1986; *Another key disadvantage of the policy is that it is mighty risky to implement—BBC news,* 2004.

migraine. In BrE the standard pronunciation is /ˈmiːɡreɪn/, but /ˈmaɪ-/ is also very commonly heard. In AmE, /ˈmaɪɡreɪn/ is standard.

migrant. See EMIGRANT.

mikado. Plural *mikados.* See -O(E)S 7.

mike (microphone). See MIC.

mil = one-thousandth of an inch, i.e. 0.0254 millimetre, as a unit of measurement for the diameter of wire, etc. 'The use is discouraged' (*Oxford Dict. for Science Writers and Editors,* 1991). It is printed without a full point.

mileage, milage. The first is the recommended spelling.

milieu. According to the *OED,* it was George Eliot who, in a letter of 1854, first used this borrowing from French as a chic way of referring to a physical, social, or cultural environment: *I could no more live out of my milieu, than the haddocks I daresay you are often having for dinner.* It can be pronounced with stress on the first or second syllable, /ˈmiːljəː, mɪˈljəː/ (**meel**-yuhr, mil-**yuhr**), and is printed in roman. There are two spellings for the plural: the anglicized *milieus* or the French *milieux,* both of which can be pronounced like the singular or as /-ljəːz/. The *OEC* data shows that the *-s* plural predominates in AmE (it is also recommended by Garner), while *milieux* predominates in BrE. Elsewhere the two forms are level-pegging. See -X.

militate, mitigate. 1 Because of their similar shape and sound, these verbs are sometimes confused. *Mitigate* is a transitive verb meaning 'to make less severe', and is applied to usually undesirable situations or effects, e.g. *drainage schemes have helped to mitigate the problem of flooding. Militate* is intransitive and means 'be a powerful factor in preventing', e.g. *these disagreements will militate against the two communities coming together.*

2 *Types of confusion.* (*a*) Possibly because neither word is part of people's core vocabulary, *mitigate against* is often mistakenly used in place of *militate against.* This originally US malapropism is of very long standing, goes back at least to 1893, numbers Faulkner among its users, and is entered in the *OED* with no indication of its doubtful status. It has been a usage chestnut for several decades, at least since Gowers' 1965 edition of this book. Although it is now widespread, it will still be regarded by many people as a mistake, as will the next two. (*b*) Rather more frequent, and not generally noted by commentators, is the use of *mitigate* with the superfluous *against* instead of the transitive *mitigate* on its own. (*c*) Very occasionally *militate* on its own is used transitively by mistake for *mitigate*.

Examples: (*mitigate* correctly used) *The King's eventual course of action did nothing to mitigate the conspirators' difficulties*—A. Fraser, 1979; *A great yellow sun like a runaway balloon shone from a deep blue sky, and a cooling breeze from the lagoon mitigated the heat*—L. Wilkinson, 1992; (*militate against* used correctly) *The housing styles, narrowness of the streets and the location of the district . . . all militate against Neustadt becoming an environmentally attractive area overnight*—R. Rolley, 1990; *The impact of such a new development on the regional and local press in the UK strongly militates against its adoption*—*England and Wales High Court Decisions*, 2005; (*mitigate against* instead of *militate against*) **But the time factor may have mitigated against that course*—*Times*, 1977; **The high 'operational tempo' of the Armed Forces and the 'unrelentingly demanding' operations in Afghanistan are combining to 'mitigate against Special Forces recruitment', Brig. Richard Dennis warned*—*Daily Tel.*, 2011; (*mitigate against* instead of transitive *mitigate*) **He said the party planned to talk to colleagues in the South African Development Community (SADC) to seek help in mitigating against the threat*—*Daily Tel.*, 2009; (*militate* used transitively for *mitigate*) **Sex workers remain and continue to be one of the main sources of the spread of HIV/AIDS. So anything that can militate the spread should be welcome*—*Times* (Zambia), 2005.

3 A further standard use in addition to those mentioned at 1 is worth noting. It is the use of *militate* intransitively followed by *in favo(u)r of*, to mean 'to exert influence or to campaign for' and 'to be an argument in support of': *The non-market institutions that militate in favor of greater income equality—trade unions, the public sector, regulatory constraints on financial speculation—took it on the chin*—*New Republic*, 1992; *The court also found that the situation of the applicant's family, although difficult, was not a circumstance that could militate in favour of his release*—*Oxford Reports on International Law*, 2000.

millenarian /ˌmɪlɪˈnɛːrɪən/, of or relating to, believing in, the millennium (in the theological sense of Christ's second coming). The apparent inconsistency in spelling (*-n-*, *-nn-*) results from the fact that *millenarian*, like *millenary*, is derived from Latin *millēnī*, the distributive form of *mille* 'thousand'. See MILLENNIUM.

millenary. Now for the most part pronounced /mɪˈlɛnəri/ in BrE, though the *OED* (1907) gave only /ˈmɪlɪnəri/, and the *COD* did not admit the second-syllable stressing until 1982. AmE favours the form with first-syllable stressing.

millennial, millennium. Note that both are spelt with *-nn-*, not *-n-*. Both are 18c. formations from Latin *mille* 'thousand' + *annus* 'year', on the analogy of *biennium, triennium*, etc. The plural *millennia* is many times more frequent than *millenniums*, though it makes sense to use the latter when the word means 'thousand-year anniversary', e.g. *Indians are used to parties, having probably celebrated more millenniums than any other civilization in history*—*Pattaya Mail*, 2000. See -UM 3.

milli-. See KILO-.

milliard (= one thousand million). Borrowed from French in the 18c., and originally used to refer to French contexts, this word is now used with historical reference, and only very occasionally to refer to modern, particularly EU, realities, e.g. *an 8-milliard Euro loan*. It has also been used figuratively, e.g. *milliards of deities* (1990) but this use is exceedingly rare. Otherwise, the word is entirely superseded by BILLION.

mimic (verb). The inflected forms are *mimics, mimicked, mimicking*. See -C-, -CK-.

mind (verb). An absolute or intransitive use of *mind* or *mind you* in the imperative, calling attention to or emphasizing what the speaker is saying, is noted by the *OED* from the late 18c. onwards, with examples from Coleridge, Browning, and some other sources. Examples (at beginning of statement) *Mind, he wasn't here these last years, scarcely*—J. Gardam, 1985; *Mind, you may feel that sort of thing is passing you by*—P. Lively, 1987; (at end of statement) *It's his Navy too, mind*—V. O'Sullivan, 1985; *Well, all right, but you aren't to do anything, mind*—D. Lessing, 1988; (in form *mind you*) *Mind you, if you think she behaved strangely, you should have seen me*—M. Amis, 1984; *Mind you, I don't know who the mother was*—A. L. Barker, 1987.

mine. 1 For *either my or your informant must have lied* or *either your informant or mine must have lied,* see ABSOLUTE POSSESSIVES.

2 In present-day English, *mine* cannot be used immediately before the noun it qualifies except humorously (*mine host*) or with a historical purpose. Historically it could be so used if the following noun began with a vowel or *h* (*mine ease, mine heart*). Before a noun the normal form of the possessive pronoun is, of course, *my.* From the 13c. onwards, and still archaistically, *mine* has been placed immediately after the noun it modifies (e.g. *O lady Venus myne!*—Lydgate, *c.*1402; *For doting, not for louing pupill mine*—Shakespeare, 1592). Its natural modern use, however, is as a pronoun: e.g. *She held out her hand, which I clasped in both of mine; Irvan suddenly tilted his head toward mine; these qualities, even to myself, are indisputably mine.*

mineralogy is formed, probably based on French *minéralogie,* from *minera*(*l*) + -LOGY. Like GENEALOGY, therefore, the ending should not be written *-ology.*

mini-. This combining form of *miniature* (reinforced by the first letters of *minimum*) first appeared in 1936 and, especially since the 1960s, has been in great demand to designate things, tendencies, etc., that are very small of their kind, or reduced in complexity. A great number of *mini-* combinations were brought into use in the 20c., e.g. *minibike, mini-budget, minicab, mini-crisis, mini-recession, miniskirt,* etc. The *OED* records several dozen as fully established, as well as illustrating examples of what are probably one-offs such as *mini-minded* (= small-minded) and *mini-odysseys.* As these last two examples suggest, the hyphen is used when a new combination first appears, but once a word is established it tends to be written without one. A by-product of the popularity of this prefix is the etymologically incorrect form *miniscule* for MINUSCULE.

minimum. The more commonly used plural is *minima,* generally in scientific and technical writing, whereas *minimums* appears in other kinds of writing. See -UM 3.

miniscule. This altered spelling of MINUSCULE, influenced by the idea of smallness inherent in the *mini-* element, first occurred in the 19c., perhaps surprisingly, in contexts where the term had its technical sense referring to a particular kind of script, or to lower-case letters. Since then, it has gone on to firmly establish itself, and is recognized in many dictionaries, including the *OED,* as a variant. Nevertheless, a minority of people will consider it a mistake, so it should be avoided in writing for certain kinds of readers. Conversely, it is so well established that, though I have no evidence, I would not be surprised if some people objected to the original spelling as a mistake. Examples: *with more than thirteen thousand entries spread across more than twenty-five hundred double-column pages of miniscule type*—*New Yorker,* 1986; *He . . . peered at the miniscule handwriting*—F. King, 1988; *I was taken through events in miniscule detail*—C. Burns, 1989.

minister. The *COD* (1990) definition 'a member of the clergy, especially in the Presbyterian and Nonconformist Churches' is correct as far as it goes, but the matter is complex and requires fuller treatment. 'A person officially charged to perform spiritual functions in the Christian Church. As a general designation for any clergyman, it is used especially in non-episcopal bodies. In the Book of Common Prayer it usually means the conductor of a service who may or may not be a priest. A Minister is also one who assists the higher orders in discharging their functions, and in this sense the Deacon and Subdeacon at High Mass are known as the "Sacred Ministers". In yet another sense, the word is used semi-technically of one who "administers" the outward and visible signs of a Sacrament. Thus should a layman baptize in a case of necessity, he would in that case be the "minister" of the Sacrament' (*Oxford Dict. of the Christian Church,* 1957). Cf. PASTOR; PRIEST.

minority. 1 For the most part the word stands at the opposite end of the field to MAJORITY or in relative contrast to it. Of a political party or other group, often followed by *of,* it means 'a smaller number or part (*a minority of MPs voted for the restoration of capital punishment*)'. *Minority government* is that in which the ruling party has received fewer votes than those given to the other parties together, a common state of affairs in 20c. Britain. A member of a committee or other body who has found little support for his or her views is said to be *in the minority*. Like *majority*, it is treated as a collective noun, with either singular (rather more often) or plural verb concord: *In Latin America for instance,* a *white minority* dominates *the political scene—New Internationalist* (magazine) 2004; *Mr Cameron will express his concern for the rights of millions of Christians, especially in Egypt, where the Coptic minority* say they are *facing increasing persecution—Daily Tel.*, 2012.

2 In one respect, however, *minority* has gone its own way, namely in its widespread current use referring to any relatively small group of people who differ, or perceive themselves to differ, from others in the society of which they are a part in race, ethnic origin, language, religion, political persuasion, sexual orientation, disability, or any other distinguishing feature that may give rise to legal, social, economic, or political discrimination and disadvantage: *Flaubert always sides with minorities, with 'the Bedouin, the Heretic, the philosopher, the hermit, the Poet'*—J. Barnes, 1985; *Among specific measures provided for in the convention were the launch of at least one radio station and a television network broadcasting in minority languages—Keesings*, 1990. In this meaning *minority* has become flexible in use, giving rise to apparently paradoxical collocations such as *growing* or *increasing minority* (i.e. increasing in numbers and therefore becoming less rather than more truly a minority): *Mixed race youngsters are the city's fastest-growing minority group—Express*, 2007. But this is not a startlingly new linguistic development: cf. *We are a minority; but then we are a very large minority*—Burke, 1789.

3 Running parallel to the word's increased prominence in certain kinds of discourse is the use of *minority* as a quasi-adjective meaning 'of, for, or appealing to a minority of people', frequently with connotations of 'serious, intellectual' (as opposed to 'popular, mass'): *Drummond once told me that Radio 3 broadcasts to about 30 minority tastes, each of which is characterised by its intense dislike of the other 29—Daily Tel.*, 1992.

4 When I was growing up, the first syllable was generally pronounced with a short *i*, which was the only pronunciation given in the 1989 2nd edition of the *OED*. Since then the AmE pronunciation rhyming with *mine* has become dominant in BrE.

Minotaur can be pronounced as /ˈmʌɪnətɔː/ (**my**-nuh-taw) or /ˈmɪn-/, the latter being the only one shown in the original *OED* entry (1907).

minus. *Minus* has been used as a marginal preposition = 'short of, having lost; without' (*they arrived back minus their tracksuits*) since the early 19c.: e.g. *My gun was found to be minus bayonet and ramrod—U.S. Mag. & Democratic Rev.*, 1839; *The Englishman got back to civilization minus his left arm—Review of Reviews*, 1903; *I hope he comes minus his wife—CGEL*, 1985. It is perfectly standard.

minuscule /ˈmɪnəskjuːl/ (but until about the mid-20c. almost always /mɪˈnʌskjuːl/). **1** Etymologically speaking, the word should be spelt with two letter *us*, since the first part relates to Latin *minus*. But see MINISCULE.

2 In palaeography, 'a small letter, as opposed to a capital or uncial; the small cursive script which was developed from the uncial during the 7th–9th centuries; also, a manuscript in this writing'.

minutiae (plural noun), precise, trivial, or minor details. **1** Dictionaries recognize several pronunciations, so choice is a matter of personal taste. The first and last syllables vary. The *OED* gives preference to a Latin pronunciation for the last syllable, with variation of the first syllable, /mʌɪˈnjuːʃɪʌɪ/, /mɪˈnjuːʃɪʌɪ/, (my-**nyoo**-shi-iy, mi-**nyoo**-shi-iy), and then gives the same variation in the first syllable but with the ending pronounced -shi-ee, /mʌɪˈnjuːʃiiː/, /mɪˈnjuːʃiiː/.

2 The singular form, rarely called for, is *minutia*, e.g. *This is an example of how good life has become for the privileged classes— . . . that we must sift through every minutia of our lives to find something unsatisfying about it—Daily Californian*, 1998. Three uses of different forms of the word are not generally recognized as standard: (*a*) the not uncommon use, esp. in AmE, of *minutia* as a plural (presumably as if it were the plural of a Latin second declension noun ending in *-um*), e.g. **The amount of care and consideration John Vanderslice puts into the minutia of his records is beyond impressive*—US website, 2004;

(*b*) *minutiae* as a singular—**Yet with every minutiae of the bid under scrutiny, the benefit of assurances from those politicians vying for power can do no harm—The Cherwell Mag.*, 2005 (these two uses go back to the late 17c., and are not labelled incorrect in the *OED*); and (*c*) the plural form *minutias*.

Miocene. One of a family of geological epoch names ending in *-cene* (*Holocene, Pleistocene,* etc.), all irregularly formed from classical elements, but long since established and uncancellable. The periods covered by the terms are: *Holocene*, 0.01 (million years ago); *Pleistocene*, 2; *Pliocene*, 5; *Miocene*, 24; *Oligocene*, 38; *Eocene*, 55; *Palaeocene*, 65. The word *Miocene* was coined in 1831 by the distinguished scientist William Whewell (1794–1866) from Gk μείων 'less' + καινός 'new, recent'. So too was *Eocene* from Greek ἠώς 'dawn' + καινός; and, at various dates, several other scientific words. Fowler (1926) described these geological words as 'monstrosities'. ('The elements of the word [*sc. Miocene*] are Greek, but not the way they are put together, nor the meaning demanded of the compound.')

mis-. Words formed with this prefix do not require a hyphen, even when the stem of the word begins with *s:* thus *misbehave, miscarriage, miscount, mismanage, misshapen, misspelling, misspent,* etc. An exception is *mis-sell* (= to sell wrongly or inappropriately) and its inflections *mis-selling* and *mis-sold,* which might be misread without the hyphen.

misandry (*miso-* + ἀνδρ-, ἀνήρ 'man') means 'hatred of men', and is the newest (1885) in a series of nouns describing dislike of some or all of one's fellow human beings. The related adjective is **misandrist** (1952). A *misanthrope* is a person who hates fellow human beings. A *misogynist* is a person who hates women, and *misogyny* means 'hatred of women'. A *misogamist* is a person who hates marriage, and *misogamy* means 'hatred of marriage'.

misanthrope. See MISANDRY.

miscegenation, mixture of races, is an irregular formation (in the 19c.) from Latin *miscēre* 'to mix' + *genus* 'race' + *-ation.* There is no classical precedent for a combining form *misce-* from *miscēre.*

miscellany. In BrE now always pronounced /mɪˈsɛləni/ (mi-**sel**-uh-nee), though earlier in the 20c. (e.g. in the *OED,* 1907; Daniel Jones, 1917) first-syllable stressing was preferred, as it still is in AmE /ˈmisəˌleɪni/ (**mi**-suh-lay-nee).

mischievous. The spelling of the word as *mischievious* and the pronunciation /mɪsˈtʃiːvɪəs/ (mis-**chee**-vi-uhs) are both incorrect. The correct pronunciation is /ˈmɪstʃɪvəs/ (**mis**-chi-vuhs).

misdemeanour. AmE **misdemeanor**.

miserere, misericord. The first is an alternative word, first recorded in 1801 in this use, and still occasionally found, for the regular form *misericord,* /mɪˈzɛrɪkɔːd/ (mi-**ze**-ri-kord). They denote the ledge, projecting from the underside of a hinged seat in a choir stall, that gives support to someone standing and is often embellished with carvings providing a fascinating insight into medieval myth and symbolism. The standard use of *miserere* is referring to Psalm 51 or music written for it. It is pronounced /ˌmɪzəˈrɛːri/ or /ˌmɪzəˈrɪəri/ (mi-zuh-**rair**-i, -**ri**-uh-ri).

mislead. The past tense and past participle are both *misled.*

misnomer. A *misnomer* is the misapplication of a name or term to something or someone inappropriate or undeserving, especially if it creates a misleading impression: *My name of Epic's no misnomer*—Byron, 1819; *Morning sickness is a misnomer—it can strike at any time—Guardian,* 2000; *'Copy cat' is a misnomer because cats never copy anybody*—C. Van Vechten, 1996. It originated as a legal word meaning 'a mistake in naming a person or thing'. Acts of Queen Victoria's reign were riddled with the proviso 'no misnomer or inaccurate description ... shall hinder the full operation of this Act'. It was, characteristically, a lawyers' escape route.

As often happens with underused words, usage put it to work among laypeople, who employed it to mean 'the application of a wrong name' in any context, which is the meaning current today (as in the above examples). Now it is in danger of being watered down further in contexts that are not about the applicability of a name: *A Christianity without peace would be a misnomer*—C. Stevens, 2004 (what is meant is 'contradiction in terms'). And in the following example (where it is clear in other ways that the writer's reach has exceeded his or her grasp) the word is being misapplied to mean 'misconception': *But there are also a lot of misnomers about this documentary, concepts that must be debunked and debased before really understanding what Blank and Gosling have fashioned*—*DVD Verdict*, 2005.

misogamist, misogamy, misogynist, misogyny. See MISANDRY.

misogynist, misogyny. See GREEK G.

misprints. In his *Esprit de Corps: Sketches from Diplomatic Life* (1957), Lawrence Durrell describes the perils of printing the *Central Balkan Herald* in wartime Serbia. 'The reason for a marked disposition towards misprints was not far to seek; the composition room, where the paper was hand-set daily, was staffed by half a dozen hirsute Serbian peasants with greasy elf-locks and hands like shovels.' Among the headlines Durrell cites were: *Minister fined for kissing in pubic*; *Wedding bulls ring out for princess*; *Britain drops biggest ever boob on Berlin.* And various gems from the text of news reports: e.g. *In a last desperate spurt the Cambridge crew, urged on by their pox, overtook Oxford.*

OCELang. (p. 121) lists some traditional examples of misprints: 'On many occasions, editions of the AV have contained misprints which have led to their receiving special names, such as the *Wicked Bible* (1632), so called because the word "not" was omitted in the Seventh Commandment, making it read *Thou shalt commit adultery*; the *Vinegar Bible* (1717), so called because the Parable of the Vineyard became *The Parable of the Vinegar*; and the *Printer's Bible,* where a misprint makes the Psalmist complain that *printers have persecuted me without cause,* as opposed to *princes.*'

misquotations. Many stock metaphors, proverbs, and catchphrases are based on altered forms of literary quotations. The proverb *Every dog has his day* is based on a 16c. adage translated from the Dutch humanist Erasmus (1500) and was given currency by a line spoken by Shakespeare's Hamlet: *Let Hercules himself do what he may, The cat shall mew, and dog will have his day*—Shakespeare, *Hamlet,* v.i.286. The idiom *to escape* by *the skin of one's teeth* is an altered form of the Authorized Version of Job 19:20: *I am escaped* with *the skin of my teeth.* Thus, just as folk etymology can alter the shape of words, so their very popularity can subtly alter literary quotations. Since these misquotations are hallowed by usage, it would be a rather vulgar act of pedantic one-upmanship to correct anyone using them. Only when the allusion is given as a quotation is it important to reproduce it literally. The list below gives the canonical form of the quotation, and the popular variant in brackets.

In the sweat of thy *face* shalt thou eat bread (not *by* nor *brow*)—Gen. 3:19.

I am escaped *with* the skin of my teeth (not *by*)—Job 19:20.

To gild refined gold, to *paint* the lily (not *gild the lily*)—Shakespeare, *King John.*

A goodly apple rotten *at the heart* (not *to the core*)—Shakespeare, *Merchant of Venice.*

An *ill-favoured* thing, sir, but mine own (not *poor*)—Shakespeare, As *You Like It.*

I will a *round* unvarnished tale *deliver* (not *plain ... relate*)—Shakespeare, *Othello.*

But yet I'll make assurance *double* sure (not *doubly*)—Shakespeare, *Macbeth.*

Tomorrow to fresh *woods* and pastures new (not *fields*)—Milton, *Lycidas.*

That last infirmity of noble *mind* (not *The ... minds*)—ibid.

They kept the *noiseless* tenor of their way (not *even*)—Gray, *Elegy Written in a Country Church-Yard.*

A little *learning* is a dangerous thing (not *knowledge*)—Pope, *Essay on Criticism.*

The best laid *schemes* o' mice an' men (not *plans*)—Burns.

Water, water, every where, *Nor any* drop to drink (not *and not a*)—Coleridge, *The Rime of the Ancient Mariner.*

Power tends to corrupt, and absolute power corrupts absolutely (not *Power corrupts*)—Lord Acton, letter of 1857.

My dear, I don't give a damn—M. Mitchell, *Gone with the Wind,* 1936. Compare Clark Gable's words in the 1939 film version: *Frankly, my dear,* I don't give a damn!

I have nothing to offer but *blood, toil, tears and sweat* (not *blood, sweat, and tears*)—W. S. Churchill, Hansard, 1940.

If she can stand it, I can. *Play it!* (not *Play it again, Sam*)—H. Bogart, *Casablanca* (1942 film).

misrelated clauses, constructions, etc. An American correspondent submitted to Burchfield numerous examples of such infelicities, which are worth preserving for amusement's sake. A selection follows: *The Pope wore a full-length white coat Saturday to protect against the biting wind in his speech in Punta Arenas* (? a windy speech); *Fluent in German, his position at the university was professor in ... Germanic languages and literatures* (a position can hardly be fluent); *Dean lived in Fairmount with an aunt and uncle through his teens after the death of his mother at age 9* (? the youngest mother in history). Despite the vigilance of sub-editors, correspondents, and others involved, such awkwardnesses are bound to occur from time to time in the torrid world of newspapers. Modern examples are commented on regularly in Michael Quinion's weekly newsletter from *www.worldwidewords.org*. For similar syntactic blunders, see UNATTACHED PARTICIPLES.

Miss. *The Misses Jones* is the old-fashioned plural, occasionally used when formality is required, e.g. in printed lists of guests present, etc.; otherwise the type *the Miss Joneses* is now usual.

misshapen, misspelling, misspent. See MIS-.

missile. In BrE /'mɪsaɪl/, in AmE /'mɪsəl/. See -ILE.

-mistress. As a second element it occurs in only a few words, all of them contrasting with words in *-master*: e.g. *headmistress* (first recorded in 1872), *housemistress* (1875), *paymistress* (1583), *postmistress* (1697), *quartermistress* (1917), *schoolmistress* (*a*1500), *stationmistress* (1897), *taskmistress* (1603). The *OED* lists no feminine equivalents of *bandmaster, choirmaster, grand master, harbour master.*

mitigate. See MILITATE, MITIGATE.

mitre. So spelt in BrE; in AmE usu. **miter**.

mixed metaphor. See METAPHOR 4. Further examples: *The chief economist of the Commonwealth Bank ... said it was an impressive and comprehensive package, although judgment would have to be withheld until the nuts and bolts of the reforms were digested—Australian*, 1991; *One day, when he's in charge of finance or foreign affairs, those lions and tigers will come home to roost. Stephen smiled. His boss was renowned for the mixture of his metaphors*—R. McCrum, 1991; *I became aware that very frequently important objects were not brought forward because the committee was seen to have no teeth*—letter in *Independent*, 1992.

mixed race. When used attributively in front of a noun, it should be hyphenated, e.g. *Mr Obama's appeal is partly his own mixed-race backstory—Guardian*, 2008. Contrast this with the following, which is not hyphenated: *This and other paintings portraying subjects of mixed race underscore the role of the artist in confirming and preserving their identity and achievements—Art in America*, 2005.

mizzen, mizen (naut.). The spelling with two *zz*s is rather more frequent, and reflects better the word's origin from Italian *mezzana*, 'mizzensail' but *mizen* is also found and is correct.

-m-, -mm-. Single-syllable words containing a simple vowel (*a, e, i, o, u*) before *m* normally double the consonant before suffixes beginning with a vowel (*rammed, hemmed, dimmest, drummer*) or before a final *-y* (*Pommy, tummy*); but remain undoubled if the stem contains a diphthong (*claimed*), doubled vowel (*gloomy*), or a vowel + consonant (*alarming, balmy, squirmed, wormy*). Words of more than one syllable ending in *m* (e.g. *emblem, maximum, pilgrim, venom, victim*) rarely have vowel-led suffixes; but when they do the final *m* is normally left undoubled (*emblematic, maximal, pilgrimage, venomous, victimization*). Exceptions are words that end in what is perceived as a word in its own right (*bedimmed*) or that end in *-gram* (*diagram: diagrammatic, monogram: monogrammed*).

mnemonic /nɪ'mɒnɪk/. Note that the first *m* is not pronounced. Both the spelling **pneumonic* and its associated pronunciation /njuː'mɒnɪk/ (nyoo-) are incorrect. A device to help one remember a set of related information or facts, often in the form of a memorable sequence of words whose first letters match the first letters of the words constituting information to be remembered, e.g. *Richard Of York Gave Battle In Vain* as a mnemonic of the order of the colours of the spectrum: red orange yellow green blue indigo violet; *All Cows Eat Grass* as a reminder of the spaces of the bass clef ACEG; *No Plan Like Yours To Study History Wisely* as a reminder of the royal families of England: Norman, Plantagenet, Lancaster, York, Tudors, Stuarts,

Hanover, Windsor; and the rhyme *In fourteen hundred and ninety two Columbus sailed the ocean blue* as a reminder of a famous date.

The word was first recorded in English (from Greek μνημονικός 'mindful') in the 18c. (adjective) and the 19c. (noun).

mobile. Both the adjective (= movable) and the noun (= decorative structure) are pronounced /'məʊbʌɪl/ in BrE. In AmE the adjective is usually pronounced to rhyme with *noble,* and the noun is pronounced /'məʊbiːl / (**moh**-beel). It is worth remembering that the device called a **mobile** or **mobile phone** in Britain is usually a **cell phone**, **cellular phone**, or simply **cell** in AmE.

mobocracy (*a*) mob rule; (*b*) a ruling mob. An excellent example of an irregular formation (first recorded in 1754) that has been admitted to the language without serious disapproval and is still flourishing. It is formed from *mob,* itself a shortened form of Latin *mobile vulgus* 'the movable or excitable crowd', after *democracy.* Cf. OCHLOCRACY.

moccasin. Spelt as shown, with two *cc*s and one letter *s.*

mocha (variety of chalcedony; coffee). Now usually pronounced /'mɒkə/ in BrE, though earlier in the century (*OED,* 1907; Daniel Jones, 1917) the pronunciation /'məʊkə/ was customary, as it still is in AmE.

modal verb. *Modal* (or, more fully, modal auxiliary) *verbs* are used in front of other verbs to express those verbs' mood, which, in the linguistic sense, distinguishes statements, commands, suppositions, questions, and so on. The principal modal verbs are *can, could, may, might, must, ought, shall, will.* They behave in special ways, of which the most important are (i) that they form questions and negatives without the use of *do* (*Can I go?*; *You may not leave*), and (ii) their third-person singular forms do not add *-s* (*She will*; *It must*). A group of other verbs that share some of these features, such as *dare* and *need,* are sometimes called *semi-modal.* Note that *be, do,* and *have,* which behave somewhat differently, are not classed as modal verbs but as ordinary auxiliary verbs.

model (verb). The inflected forms are *modelled, modelling* (AmE usually *modeled, modeling*). See -LL-, -L-.

modulus (math.). Plural *moduli* /-lʌɪ/. See -US 1.

modus operandi, pronounced /ˌməʊdəs ɒpə'randiː, -dʌɪ/ (**moh**-duhs opuh-**ran**-dee, -dy), from Latin 'way of operating', refers to a way of doing something usually perceived as undesirable, or even criminal, and is a favourite phrase of fictional detectives, who often abbreviate it as *MO* /ɛm əʊ/. The plural if required is *modi operandi* /ˌməʊdi ɒpə'randi, ˌməʊdʌɪ ɒpə'randʌɪ/. This poor phrase, described by Garner as 'often a highfalutin substitute for method' suffers the double indignity of frequent misspelling, particularly as **modus operandum* or **operendi,* and of being MONDEGREENed as **mode of operandi.* If people must use it, they should at least endeavour to spell it correctly. It is printed in roman.

modus vivendi, pronounced /ˌməʊdəs vɪ'vɛn-diːˌ -dʌɪ/ (**moh**-duhs vi-**ven**-dee, -dy) from Latin 'way of living', but more often it means an arrangement to help parties in a dispute coexist peacefully. Plural *modi vivendi* /ˌməʊdi vɪ'vɛndiː, ˌməʊdʌɪ vɪ'vɛndʌɪ/. Like *modus operandi,* often grossly misspelt. Printed in roman.

mogul is always spelt as shown in its extended sense 'an important or influential person', e.g. *media, movie, music,* etc. *mogul.* In its historical sense 'any of the Muslim rulers of N. India in the 16c.–19c.', it is now usually spelt *Mughal* after Arabic, Persian *mugul, mugal* 'Mongol'.

moiety. A legal and literary word for 'a half'. Plural *moieties.*

moire, moiré are alternative spellings as both noun and adjective for the patterned appearance of watered silk or for the material itself. The first is pronounced /mwɑː(r)/, the second /'mwɑːreɪ/.

mold. See MOULD.

mollusc is the standard spelling in BrE, and is also used in AmE, but rather less than **mollusk**, which is given priority in dictionaries.

molt. See MOULT.

momentarily. In BrE it means only 'for a moment, briefly' (*He wondered* *momentarily if he had crossed into the wrong lane*). In AmE it may also mean 'at any moment, soon' (*This is your Captain speaking. Please fasten your seat belts as we shall be taking off momentarily*). The American sense is first recorded in the late 1860s. The AmE pronunciation, with the main stress falling on *-árily,* has made major inroads in BrE, where traditionally the main stress was on the first syllable.

moment in time. See AT THIS MOMENT IN TIME.

momently (adverb) has had a precarious hold on the language since, in its primary sense 'from moment to moment', it was first recorded in use in a work of 1676. It has also been used to mean 'at any moment, on the instant', and 'for the moment; for a single moment'. To judge from the available evidence this last sense seems to be the prevailing one now, but the word is a rare bird even in literary sources. Examples: *Thoughts ... look at me With awful faces, from the vanishing haze That momently had hidden them*—George Eliot, 1868; *A wild white face that overtops Red stretcher blankets momently*—Philip Larkin, 1964; *You acknowledged, however momently (that infinite moment) that at least what I claim is true*—A. S. Byatt, 1990.

momento. An occasional, not recommended, variant of MEMENTO: e.g. *And the London frowsty Casino, a momento of which I enclose*—Dylan Thomas, 1951.

momentum in scientific writing has the plural *momenta* for the meaning 'the quantity of motion of a moving body'. For the metaphorical meaning, 'the impetus gained by a process or course of events' the plural *momentums* tends to be used, e.g. *You just have to constantly monitor markets, which have their own strange momentums—Sunday Herald,* 2001. See -UM 3.

monarchal, monarchial, monarchic, monarchical. All four adjectives entered the language within a generation of one another *c.*1600; all have been used in the broad senses 'of, belonging to, or characteristic of a monarch', 'ruled by a monarch', 'that advocates monarchy as a form of government'; all four are still listed in the major dictionaries of current English. The *OEC* data shows that *monarchical* outnumbers *monarchic* 7 to 1, *monarchial* is occasionally used in journalism and academic writing, and *monarchal* is vanishingly rare. Examples: (monarchical) *He maintained a monarchical sensitivity in matters of protocol*—M. Meyer, 1967; *the House of Commons, many of whose members have been agitating for months for a reduction in monarchical privilege—Times,* 1992; (monarchic) *But Burke was not defending or advocating a return to an aristocratic or monarchic order—The American Conservative* (magazine), 2003; (monarchial) *Monarchial displeasure is not lightly to be incurred—Observer,* 1981; *he* [*sc.* a resort developer in the Bahamas] *was sometimes criticized for operating in a monarchial style—NYT,* 1988.

Monday. See FRIDAY.

mondegreen is the word created in 1954 by the American writer Sylvia Wright to describe the common phenomenon of a 'misunderstood or misinterpreted word or phrase resulting from a mishearing, especially of the lyrics to a song'. An often quoted example is the reinterpretation of the line 'Excuse me while I kiss the sky' in Jimi Hendrix's 1967 song *Purple Haze* as 'Excuse me while I kiss this guy'. It illustrates the mistaken analysis of word boundaries that is typical of mondegreens. Sylvia Wright coined the term because, as she explained it: 'When I was a child, my mother used to read aloud to me from Percy's *Reliques*, and one of my favorite poems began, as I remember: Ye Highlands and ye Lowlands, Oh, where hae ye been? They hae slain the Earl Amurray, And Lady Mondegreen.' The exact words of the ballad are 'Ye highlands, and ye lawlands, Oh! quhair hae ye been? They hae slaine the Earl of Murray, And hae laid him on the green'.

moneyed (adjective). Spelt as shown, not *monied.*

moneys (plural noun). See MONIES.

-monger. Used as a second element in compounds, *-monger* has produced a few common words meaning simply 'one who trades in (the item specified in the first element)': thus *costermonger* (first recorded in 1514, from *costard* apple), *fishmonger* (1464), *ironmonger* (1343). Somehow these have remained untainted by the limitless class of *-monger* words (the *OED* records over 300) which, from the mid-16c. onwards, have been created to describe someone who carries on a contemptible or discreditable 'trade' or 'traffic' in what is denoted by the first element. Thus, for example, *gossip-monger* (1836), *scandal-monger* (1721), *scaremonger* (1888), *war-monger* (1590), *whoremonger* (1526).

mongol, mongolism, mongoloid. Terms formerly applied to people with or to the condition of DOWN('S) SYNDROME, and now obsolete because they are regarded as demeaning and offensive.

mongoose, a small flesh-eating civet-like mammal: a word derived from Marathi *mangūs*. Its plural is *mongooses*.

monies. The plural of *money* used to mean 'sums of money' should be *moneys* according to standard spelling rules (cf. *donkeys, monkeys*). But in legal and accountancy parlance from at least the mid-19c. the irregular form *monies* has taken hold and now seems uncancellable, being several times more common than *moneys*. Examples (from three different countries): *Certain monies had been put aside for them*—A. Brookner, 1988; *The government has done just the opposite by giving Maori Affairs monies to the other departments*—S. Jackson in *Metro* (NZ), 1988; *Some of the bond monies are exempt because of their funding sources*—*Arizona Republic*, 1988.

monk. See FRIAR.

monkey (noun). Plural *monkeys*.

monkey (verb). The inflected forms are *monkeys, monkeyed, monkeying*.

monocle. An interesting example of a loanword which is not easily recognized as such. It was borrowed from French in the mid-19c. and is derived ultimately from late Latin *monoculus* 'one-eyed'.

monologue and *soliloquy* are parallel terms (= 'speaking alone') of Greek and Latin origin respectively. Both denote a single person's action; *soliloquy* generally refers to speaking one's thoughts aloud regardless of any hearers, particularly in a play, whereas *monologue* means speech that is meant to be heard and is used especially of the discourse of a talker who monopolizes conversation, or to describe a performance or recitation by a single actor or speaker, often contrasted with dialogue.

Monseigneur /mɒnsɛ'njəː/, a title or form of address used of or to a French-speaking prince, cardinal, archbishop, or bishop. Plural *Messeigneurs* /mɛsɛ'njəː/. Literally 'my lord' from French *mon* 'my' + *seigneur* 'lord'.

Monsieur /mə'sjəː/, a title or form of address used of or to a French-speaking man, corresponding to *Mr* or *Sir*. Plural *Messieurs* /mɛ'sjəː/. Literally 'my lord' from French *mon* 'my' + *sieur* 'lord'.

Monsignor /mɒn'siːnjə/ or /-'njɔː/, a title or form of address used of or to various Roman Catholic prelates. Plural *Monsignori* /-'njɔːrɪ/ or, more often, *Monsignors*. An Italian loan translation of French MONSEIGNEUR.

mood. It may save misconceptions to mention that the grammar word has nothing to do with the native (i.e. Old English) word meaning frame of mind, etc.; it is merely a variant of *mode*, and refers to 'a form or set of forms of a verb in an inflected language, serving to indicate whether the verb expresses fact, command, wish, conditionality, etc. ... The principal moods are known as indicative (expressing fact), imperative (command), interrogative (question), optative (wish), and subjunctive (conditionality)'. English moods are expressed through MODAL VERBS or the SUBJUNCTIVE.

moot (adjective). A *moot point* or *moot question* is a debatable or undecided one. The word, which is of Old English origin, should not be confused with *mute* 'silent', as quite often happens in speech, e.g. **mute point*, but less so in writing. Especially in AmE, *moot* is also used predicatively to mean 'having little or no practical relevance; academic', e.g. *But the choice may become moot as the pressure mounts to ban a class of drugs once called the greatest thing since sliced bread*—*www.healthtalk.ca*, 2004. This use is best avoided in BrE contexts, since the word is most likely to be misinterpreted as 'debatable' rather than 'irrelevant'.

moral, morale (nouns). Fowler (1926) treated the issue of how to spell these words at great length. That was because in the years following the First World War *morale*, in the meaning 'mental attitude or bearing', was a word very much in people's minds (e.g. *the morale of the troops*). But they were unsure whether to spell it *morale* (an early 19c. respelling preserving the sound of the French word and distinguishing it from the other meanings of English *moral*) or *moral*, reintroduced towards the end of the 19c. for this meaning on the grounds that *morale* was artificial and not the form of the word in this meaning in French. Over time, *morale*, together with its French-like pronunciation /məˈrɑːl/ (mo-**rahl**) which Fowler recommended, has won the day, and few people will know that there was ever a problem. However, the story gives a curious twist to the history of the continuous interaction between these two great languages.

moratorium. The recommended plural is *moratoriums*, which is rather more frequent than the Latinate *moratoria*. See -UM 3.

more. 1 *Historical note.* In origin from Old English *māra* (adjective), comparative of *micel* 'big', its subsequent history is too complicated to be dealt with here. Suffice it to say that until about 1600 it was often contrasted with *mo* (from OE *mā*, comparative of *micle* 'much'): *mo* was used with plural nouns and *more* with uncount nouns. Thus, in Shakespeare, *and let's first see moe ballads* (*Winter's Tale*), but *is there more toil?* (*Tempest*). The *mo/more* distinction dropped out during the 17c. and survives only in some regional forms of English.

2 *To form comparatives.* The use of *more* before comparatives (*more hotter*) is now regarded as non-standard, but was standard use in earlier centuries (*and his more braver daughter could control thee—Tempest*). In comparative constructions that are legitimate, *more* is used with adjectives of three syllables or more (e.g. *difficult, memorable*), with many adjectives of two syllables (e.g. *afraid, awful, harmless*), and with adverbs ending in *-ly* (e.g. *highly, slowly*). In certain circumstances even monosyllabic adjectives can take *more*: (i) when two adjectives are compared with each other, e.g. *More dead than alive*; (ii) for stylistic reasons, e.g. *This was never more true than at present*. For more details on comparisons see -ER AND -EST.

3 It is broadly true that *more* should not be used with absolute adjectives like *complete, equal, unique,* but that in practice they often are: see ADJECTIVE 4.

4 Verb agreement after *more than one*. Despite its plural appearance, this phrase is normally followed by a singular verb: e.g. *more than one journalist* was *killed* (not *were*). But if the phrase is couched in the form *more* + plural noun + *than one*, or if *more than one* is followed by *of* and a plural noun or pronoun, the verb is plural: *more doctors than one* attend *each patient*; *If more than one of these contracts* are *played, all the payments are made—Card Game Rules*, 2004; *It's no coincidence that more than one of these* have *been edited by David Crystal: good man!*—weblog, 2005; (incorrect singular) **Since starting this blog, more than one of these individuals has told me that things are different in Bermuda*—weblog, 2004.

5 *Fossilized uses.* (*a*) As adjective *more* was once (14-19c.) commonly used to qualify the designation of a person with the sense 'entitled to the designation in a greater degree': e.g. *A more heretike than either Faustus or Donatus*—Reginald Scot, 1584. This use survives only in the phrase (*the*) *more fool* (*you*, etc.). (*b*) Historically (OE to the early 19c.) (*the*) *more* was used to mean 'greater in degree or extent': e.g. *for our more safety*—Thomas Heywood, 1632; *to make the miracle the more*—Southey, 1829. This use survives only in the phrase (*the*) *more's the pity*.

6 For difficulties arising from some uses of *much more* and *much less*, see MUCH 2.

7 For *more important, more importantly*, see IMPORTANT, IMPORTANTLY.

mores /ˈmɔːriːz/ or (esp. AmE) /-eɪz/. In origin the plural of Latin *mōs* 'manner, custom', *mores* refers to 'the normative conventions and attitudes embodying the fundamental moral values of a particular society' and is normally construed as a plural in English (e.g. *Its conservative mores* forbid *most citizens from owning satellite dishes or maintaining Internet connections*). Singular agreement is incorrect: *Social mores* *regulates *the joke field, not copyright—TechDirt*, 2011.

morning. *Morning Service, Morning Prayer, Matins* are alternative terms (the first of them unofficial) for the order of public morning prayer in the Church of England. The corresponding service in the evening is officially called *Evensong,* less commonly *Evening Service.*

morphia is an old-fashioned term still occasionally found for *morphine.*

morphology, linguistically speaking, is the study of the structure and form of words. It includes both inflection, that is, how words assume different forms according to their grammatical function, e.g. *come, comes, came,* etc.; and derivation, that is, how one word is formed from another, e.g. *unhelpful* contains three elements (called morphemes) *un-*, a negating prefix, *help,* the noun, and *-ful,* a suffix used to form adjectives from nouns. The word itself is well-travelled, being based on ancient Greek μορφή 'form' + *-o-* + *-logy,* but was first created in Germany (by Goethe) as *Morphologie* and came into English via French *morphologie.*

mortgagee, is technically, and somewhat confusingly for laypeople, the lender of a mortgage, usually a bank or building society, rather than the person who takes out the mortgage. A *mortgagor,* with a 'soft' second g, is the debtor in a mortgage.

mosquito. Plural *mosquitoes.* See -O(E)S 1.

most, as noun, adjective, and adverb, has innumerable uses and many historical oddities: a few observations must suffice. **1** Avoid using *most* when a contrast is being made between two people or things: e.g. *of the two dictionaries this is the more* (not *most*) *useful.*

2 It is not necessary to repeat *most* when two adjectives joined by *and* follow (e.g. *one of the most brilliant and successful people in America*).

3 Instances of *most* + the superlative form of adjectives (*most cleverest*) are now non-standard, but from the 15c. to the 19c. were standard: e.g. *With the most boldest, and best hearts of Rome*—Shakespeare, 1601; *One of the most wretchedst Spectacles in the World*—W. Penn, 1683; *I was always first in the most gallantest scrapes in my younger days!*—T. Hardy, 1878. In superlative constructions that are standard, *most* is used with adjectives of three or more syllables (e.g. *notable, convenient*), with many adjectives of two syllables (e.g. *evil, dreadful, stylish*), and with adverbs ending in *-ly* (e.g. *blatantly, nearly*). It may also for stylistic reasons be used with monosyllabic (single-syllable) adjectives: e.g. *That was the most cruel thing you could have said.* For more details on comparisons see -ER AND -EST.

4 The two types of superlatives can co-occur without awkwardness: e.g. *Beyond these tropes may lie the profoundest fears and most appalling lusts; one of the deepest and most sensitive studies I've yet read.*

5 *Most* modifying an adjective frequently has an intensive rather than a superlative function: e.g. *a most remarkable woman; this most fashionable garment.*

6 Like *more, most* is not normally used with absolute adjectives, but for stylistic reasons it sometimes is: *That's the most perfect thing I've ever seen*—V. O'Sullivan, 1985 (NZ). See ADJECTIVE 4.

7 A rogue elephant is the double or strengthened superlative *(the) mostest,* first recorded in Britain in an 1887 dictionary of Kentish dialect ('*The mostest that he's bin from home is 'bout eighteen miles*') but now having a particularly US ring to it because of its often quoted use by a Confederate commander in the Civil War who, when asked how he won his battles, replied 'Git thar furst (or *furstest* in some versions) with the mostest men'. It is used only in humorous contexts. Examples: *The world's biggest choir, hugest pigeon flock, mostest balloon let-goers*—*Evening Post* (NZ), 1995; *Now each park is trying to outbid the other to get the biggest, baddest and mostest roller coaster*—*Denver Post,* 1995.

8 For *most important(ly),* see IMPORTANT, IMPORTANTLY.

9 *most all, most any . . . , most every . . . , most always,* etc. In this meaning, in use since the 16c. first in Scotland and now chiefly in British dialects and in AmE, *most* (often written *'most*) is a shortening of *almost* and therefore a distinct word, though often treated together with the main meanings of *most* in dictionaries. When used in speech and non-formal writing, it is considered standard in AmE by *MWCDEU* in the constructions listed at the head of this section: *I 'most met my death climbing up just now*—S. Merwin and W. K. Webster, 1901; *Most anybody can play*—S. Greenbaum and J. Whitcut,

1988; *Dewey knew no fear, would just roar on into most any species of difficulty*—T. R. Pearson, 1991.

'most (= almost). See MOST 9.

mostest. See MOST 7.

mostly. Readers of texts from the 17c. to the early 19c. will now and then encounter *mostly* used to mean 'in the greatest degree, to the greatest extent': e.g. *It* [*sc.* the epithet] *was applied to those Things which were mostly esteemed,* 1754; *the person whose society she mostly prized*—J. Austen, 1818 (*WDEU*). But this second sense is no longer current: *most* is used instead.

mother. For the *Mother of Parliaments,* see SOBRIQUETS.

mother-in-law. See -IN-LAW.

Mother's Day. In Britain, another name for *Mothering Sunday,* the fourth Sunday in Lent, traditionally a day for honouring mothers with gifts. In America, *Mother's Day* is an equivalent day on the second Sunday in May.

motif /məʊ'tiːf/ is an example of a French word that English has borrowed not just once, but twice. It was borrowed in the 14c. in the meaning that we now spell **motive**, i.e. a factor that causes someone to act in a certain way. French *motif* was then borrowed again in the mid-19c. to denote some of the specialist meanings it had developed in French, to refer to a dominant or recurring distinctive theme or feature in an artistic or musical work. The spelling *motive* can also convey these meanings, e.g. *The entire work grows organically from the opening horn motive,* but the *motif* spelling is much more often used.

mot juste. Usage has moved on since Fowler (1926) described *mot juste* as 'a pet literary critics' word, which readers would like to buy of them as one buys one's neighbour's bantam cock for the sake of hearing its voice no more'. He complained that it was to be found neither in French dictionaries nor in English ones. The lexicographers in Oxford and elsewhere have done their work, and have established that it entered English from French near the beginning of the 20c.: *Here and throughout we have conspicuously the* mot juste, *not one too many and each where it will tell*—*Nation* (NY), 1912. It is, however, still sufficiently literary or special to be italicized.

There does, however, appear to be a disparity of usage between the two languages. French dictionaries mention the expression only in so far as it illustrates a precise sense of *juste. Mot juste* is thus not considered to be a compound in French and means nothing more than its literal translation—i.e. the right word, where right = correct.

motorcade. See CAVALCADE.

motto. The plurals *mottoes* and *mottos* are equally frequent and equally correct. See -O(E)S 2.

mould The AmE spelling is **mold** for all three common words so spelt (shape, fungous growth, loose friable earth, and three corresponding verbs).

moult. AmE **molt**.

mouse. 1 *Noun.* Unless we are very young children, we all know that we use *mice* to refer to more than one of these adorable rodents. But when we want to refer to more than one computer *mouse,* is it correct to say *mice* or *mouses*? You may sometimes hear *mouses,* but people seem to prefer the standard *mice.*

2 *Verb.* (*a*) In its most frequent meaning, i.e. 'to use a mouse to move or position a cursor on a computer screen' (*simply mouse over any item on the list*) the verb is pronounced like the noun. (*b*) When it means 'to hunt for mice', it can also be pronounced /maʊz/ with a final *z* sound.

3 Among the myriad unexpected pronunciations of British place names is that of *Mousehole* (in Cornwall) as /'maʊzəl/.

mousey. See MOUSY.

moustache, mustache, mustachio. Historically, English spellings of this hairy 'excrement' (= 'growth'), as Shakespeare called it, have been as varied as the styles of the appendage itself, but they have now settled down to the three shown. All come ultimately from the Greek μύσταξ, μυστακ- ('moustache') through different intermediary languages. *Moustache* and *mustache* came from French in the 16c.; the first is the norm in BrE and is pronounced /mə'stɑːʃ/, stressing the second syllable; the second is the norm in AmE, though *moustache* is also used, and is often stressed on the first syllable. The respective adjectives are **moustached** and **mustached**. *Mustachio* /mə'stɑːʃɪəʊ/ (muh-**stah**-shi-oh), often in the plural, is a slightly earlier loanword, imported from Italian *mostaccio* via Spanish *mostacho* in the 16c. Nowadays it usually refers to a particularly splendid or abundant moustache, e.g. *This face possessed huge mustachios, appendages unknown to the Maya race—OEC* (undated). The most common adjective to describe someone possessing the hirsute 'excrement' is **mustachioed**, which is often incorrectly but understandably spelt **moustachioed,* a form not recognized in dictionaries.

mousy is the recommended spelling and is more frequently used than *mousey,* which is, however, also correct.

movable. Spelt as shown; except that **moveable** is preferred for legal work.

movie. For British people of an older generation, to use this word to describe a film sounds ludicrously and affectedly American; for younger people and film buffs it is, inevitably, the norm.

mow (verb), to cut down grass, hay, etc. The past participle, when used as an adjective, is *mown* (*the mown,* not *mowed, grass; new-mown,* etc.); as a true past participle both forms are permissible (*he had mowed,* or *mown, the lawn yesterday*).

MP, M.P., Member of Parliament. Normally now printed without full points. So *MPs* (plural), *MP's* (possessive singular), *MPs'* (possessive plural).

Mr, Mrs Now usually printed without points: *Mr and Mrs Smith.* In AmE the points are generally kept: *Mr. and Mrs. Smith.*

MS. See MANUSCRIPT.

Ms, Ms. /mɪz/. This title is now used without a full point in BrE, but with one in AmE. Perhaps surprisingly, the use of this artificial blend of *Mrs* and *Miss* was mooted as long ago as 1901, but it was in the 1950s in American business correspondence that people started to use it before a woman's name when the addressee's marital status was unknown or irrelevant. It was enthusiastically taken up by feminists in the 1970s and was at first greeted with derision and hostility by certain sections of society. The heat has long since gone out of the controversy and *Ms* is now standard everywhere in official or business correspondence. When *Ms* is used the style to be followed is: (on the envelope) *Ms*(.) *Fiona Jones*; (at the beginning of a formal letter) *Dear Ms*(.) *Jones*; the plural is *Mss*(.) or *Mses*: e.g. *the undeniable attractions of Mss Harker and Kensit.*

much. 1 For the use of *much* rather than *very* with passive participles (*much obliged, much aggrieved,* etc.), see VERY 2.

2 *much more, much less, still more, still less.* Fowler (1926) analysed these phrases with precision: 'used . . . to convey that a statement that is being made or has been made about something already mentioned applies more forcibly yet to the thing now to be mentioned'. *The principles,* much more *the practice, need a good deal of scrutiny. I didn't even see him,* still less *talk to him. Much/still more* is used when the grammatical form of the sentence is positive, and *much/still less* when it is negative. Difficulties arise when the form is positive but the sense is negative, as with adjectives in *un-* and words like *difficult.* In sentences like *It is difficult to establish all the facts,* much less *to reach a conclusion,* Fowler argued that *much more* is strictly needed, not *much less,* because of the ellipsis involved, as shown in brackets: *It is difficult to establish all the facts, much more* (*is it difficult to*) *reach a conclusion.* Similarly, in the sentence *I confess myself altogether unable to formulate such a principle,* much less *to prove it,* the underlying meaning is 'I confess that I am unable to formulate such a principle, let alone prove it.' Each context must be considered on its merits, but if you are tempted to use a *much less* construction after a preceding statement that is plainly or by implication negative, consider whether using *much more* is more appropriate or recasting the sentence using *let alone.*

muchly, used to mean 'much, exceedingly', is surprisingly durable (it was first recorded in the 17c., in poetry, though it is not listed in Johnson's *Dict.,* 1755), but it is now only a humorous variant of *much* (e.g. *thank you muchly for the chocolates*). The *OED* entry tracks its descent from seriousness to jokiness, and it was already being used jokily in 1881. A modern example: *Much of it is muchly much of a muchness, but occasionally . . . there is a song which* *might just be played again if the rest of your collection is lost in a bizarre gardening accident—Evening Standard,* 1999.

mucous, mucus. The first is the adjective, and is the spelling to use in compound medical terms such as *mucous cell, gland, membrane,* etc.; the second is the noun (= a slimy substance secreted by a gland).

muezzin, Muslim summoner to prayer. Pronounced /muːɛzɪn/.

Mughal. See MOGUL.

mulish (obstinate; mule-like) is spelt as shown, not *muleish.*

multi-, from Latin *multus* 'much, many', is a prefix in a great many words of different vintages, some taken directly from Latin, such as *multifarious* (1593), others created from English elements, e.g. *multiculti* (1989). Treatment of hyphenation varies considerably, but in general the more established and more frequent a word is, the more likely it is to be written without a hyphen, e.g. *multimillionaire, multipurpose, multistorey.* Adjectives consisting of *multi-* prefixed to an adjective also tend to be written without a hyphen, e.g. *multicoloured, multicultural, multidimensional, multidisciplinary, multifaceted,* unless there would be an awkward combination of vowels, i.e. *multi-ethnic* rather than *?multiethnic.* A hyphen also tends to be used in adjectives consisting of *multi-* prefixed to a noun, e.g. *multi-agency approach, multi-channel television, multi-party democracy,* etc. In other cases, it is advisable to use a single dictionary as a consistent style guide.

mumps. Usually treated as a singular (*mumps is common in young children*). In some regions in Britain and abroad it is sometimes used with the definite article *the* (e.g. *When I was sick with the mumps ... my mother found one* [*sc.* a balloon] *at the bottom of the steamer trunk*—M. Atwood, 1989).

Munchausen is generally anglicized and simplified thus from the German spelling *Münchhausen* (the surname of a historical character), in **Munchausen's syndrome** and **Munchausen's syndrome by proxy**. The pronunciation recommended is /ˈmʌntʃaʊzən/.

Muses. 'Greek deities of poetry, literature, music, and dance; later also of astronomy, philosophy, and all intellectual pursuits. Throughout antiquity the prevailing conception of Muses follows Hesiod's *Theogony.* Muses approach the poet on Helicon and give him sceptre, voice, and knowledge. Hesiod is also responsible for the canonical number of nine ... In late Roman times the Muses were differentiated according to their function ... Calliope is Muse of the heroic epic, Clio of history, Euterpe of flutes, Terpsichore of lyric poetry (dance), Erato of lyric poetry or hymns, Melpomene of tragedy, Thalia of comedy, Polyhymnia of the mimic art, and Urania of astronomy. These functions and names vary considerably and names of other Muses are known. Daughters of Zeus and Mnemosyne, the Muses sing and dance at the festivities of Olympians and heroes, often led by Apollo' (*Oxford Classical Dict.,* 2nd edn, 1970).

must (noun). **1** Use of the verb as a noun to mean 'a necessity or compulsion' goes back to Ben Jonson, and was used by other dramatists of his day: *Do you say you must arrest sirha: away with him to the iayle, ile teach you a tricke for your must—Every Man in his Humor,* 1598. Another example: *In uttering these three terrible musts, Klesmer lifted up three long fingers in succession*—G. Eliot, 1876.

2 Beginning in America in the 1890s, but only becoming widespread from the 1940s, is its more trivial use to mean 'something highly recommended or not to be missed'. It passed through a period of about four decades when it was usually printed within quotation marks, and this convention is still sometimes followed, e.g. *No. 1 on the list of 'musts' from the publishers surveyed was to find the right artist—Art Business News,* 2001. *Must* long ago moved a stage further by being used attributively (before a noun): *A dream place at the edge of Bosphorus, between Europe and Asia—a must experience!.* Latterly, in combination with any verb to hand, e.g. *must-see, -buy, -watch, -hear, -attend, -visit,* etc. ad nauseam, it has been co-opted as a cliché in the remorseless, repetitive litany of consumerist phrases advertising not just products but experiences: *The King George is, self-evidently, a royal occasion, one of the 'must-see' races—Observer,* 2007; *The site* (*a must-bookmark for iPhone and iPod Touch owners*)*—PC World* (magazine), 2009.

mustache(d), mustachio(ed). See MOUSTACHE.

mute e. 1 The letter *e* is 'mute' or silent at the end of words such as *excite, move, sale,* and *rare.* Adding suffixes to words of this kind raises the question of whether the final *e* should be kept (as it is in *changeable*) or dropped (as it is more usually, e.g. in *excitable* and *mauvish*). For example, if we wish to derive an adjective in *-ish* from the noun *mule,* do we write *muleish* or *mulish*? The answer is 'obviously' *mulish.* But if we wish to form a verbal noun from the verb *singe* the answer is 'obviously' *singeing,* not *singing,* because the latter is the verbal noun formed from the verb *sing.*

2 There are three basic spelling patterns. The following examples are representative, not exhaustive. (*a*) The *e* is consistently dropped with suffixes beginning with a vowel or the letter *y*, as in *change → changing, cleave → cleavage, clique → cliquish, conservative → conservatism, dose → dosage, love → lovable, love → loving, mouse → mousy, move → movable, nose → nosy* (also *nosey*), *race → racist, retrieve → retrieval.*

(*b*) The *e* is retained for specific reasons: (i) When it preserves the 'soft' sound of a preceding *c* or *g*, as in *gauge → gaugeable, marriage → marriageable, notice → noticeable, outrage → outrageous.* (ii) When it distinguishes the root from another word e.g. *dye → dyeing* versus *die → dying.* (iii) When the suffix begins with a consonant, as in *acknowledge → acknowledgement* (also *acknowledgment*), *change → changeling, hire → hireling, judge → judgement* (also *judgment*), *like → likely.* (iv) Verbs ending in *-oe* regularly retain the *e* when *-ing* is added, e.g. *canoe → canoeing, hoe → hoeing, shoe → shoeing, tiptoe → tiptoeing.*

(*c*) Derived forms optionally retain the *-e*, in parallel with forms without the *-e*, as a visual reminder of the pronunciation of the vowel of the root word. For example, *likable* and *sizable* look odd to BrE people. Sometimes, as with AGEING, AGING, BrE and AmE usage differs markedly. Examples: *age → ageism/agism, bloke → blokeish/blokish,* HINGE *→ hingeing/hinging, like → likable/*LIKEABLE, *mile → milage/mileage, nice → niceish/nicish, rate → ratable/*RATEABLE, *sale → salable/*SALEABLE.

For further information about particular cases, e.g. the use of both *ageing* and *aging, judgement* and *judgment, mileage* and *milage,* readers should consult them at their alphabetical places.

For similar problems with adjectives ending in *-y* and verbs ending in *-ye*, see -EY AND -Y IN ADJECTIVES; VERBS IN -IE, -Y, AND -YE 7.

mutual. 1 *The (supposed) issue.* Discussion of the correct meaning and use of *mutual* is first known from 1770, and long ago established itself as part of what can justly be called the canon of usage issues. Evelyn Waugh classically drew attention to this more than two-centuries-old issue in a letter of 13 November 1950 to Louis Auchinloss, an American lawyer and writer: 'Apart from that, your misuse of 'mutual' (tricky word best left alone if you aren't happy about its precise meaning . . .) I have no criticisms.' What is the nature of the 'misuse'? And is it really one? The strength of feeling is unmistakable in the following examples from well-known usage manuals:

(*a*) Henry Alford, *The Queen's English,* 1864: 'What is *"mutual"*? Much the same as *"reciprocal".* It describes that which passes from each to each of two persons . . . And *mutual* ought never to be used, unless the reciprocity exists. "The *mutual love* of husband and wife" is correct enough: but "a *mutual friend* of both husband and wife" is sheer nonsense.'

(*b*) Richard Grant White, *Words and Their Uses,* 1871: '*mutual* for *common,* an error not infrequent now even among educated people'.

(*c*) H. W. and F. G. Fowler, *The King's English,* 1906: 'Every one knows by now that *our mutual friend* is a solecism. *Mutual* implies an action or relation between two or more persons or things, A doing or standing to B as B does or stands to A . . . *Our mutual friend* is nonsense; *mutual friends,* though not nonsense, is bad English, because it is tautological. It takes two to make a friendship, as to make a quarrel, and therefore all friends are mutual friends, and *friends* alone means as much as *mutual friends.*'

(*d*) *Fowler's Modern English Usage,* 1926: 'it follows that *our mutual friend Jones* (meaning Jones who is your friend as well as mine), & all similar phrases, are misuses of *mutual* . . . In such places *common* is the right word, & the use of *mutual* betrays ignorance of its meaning.'

From these statements it will be abundantly clear that in the usage manual tradition (reflected by Evelyn Waugh in 1950) *mutual* is correctly used only when it means 'reciprocal'.

2 *The true picture.* There is another tradition, not to be ignored, and it is set down in the *OED*. It presents two broad strands of meaning, both of them in use for a very long time. This great dictionary shows that the meaning 'reciprocal', i.e. the uncensured sense of *mutual,* has been in continuous use since 1513. But it also shows that the other sense of *mutual,* namely 'held in common or shared between two or more parties', has also been in unbroken use since 1600 (Shakespeare). In 1907, when the relevant fascicle of the *OED* was issued, the editors added the comment 'Now regarded as incorrect', almost as if the Fowler brothers had dropped in on them when the entry was being prepared. Abundant evidence was presented in the *OED* for the phrases *our mutual friend* (first in 1658, i.e. long before Dickens gave his novel that title), *our mutual acquaintance* (1723), *our mutual opinion of Pope* (1820), and numerous others.

3 *Recommendations.* Although *MWCDEU* aptly comments 'it is about time the matter was laid to rest', some people will still insist that to use *mutual* in the sense of 'common' is wrong. The contest between the two main meanings of the word thus remains still unresolved, but one can say with reasonable certainty: (*a*) *Mutual* used to mean 'reciprocal' is, of course, acceptable, e.g. *Wilde and Yeats reviewed each other's work with mutual regard*—R. Ellmann, 1986; *That was my genuine feeling and until Lord Tonypandy's memoirs appeared last week I had every reason to believe that the feeling was mutual*—M. Foot, 1986. (*b*) So too are phrases of the type *a mutual friend, a mutual acquaintance,* in which *common* might be ambiguous, implying vulgarity, e.g. *We met ... at a dinner party at a mutual friend's apartment*—P. Monette, 1988. (*c*) *Mutual* is also acceptable in many other sentences with the meaning 'pertaining to both parties', e.g. *of mutual benefit to both the Scots and the English*—D. Stewart MP, BBC Radio 4, 1977; *No camaraderie exists between mother and daughter, no sympathy born out of mutual suffering*—J. Berman, 1987; *They could discuss mutual problems*—*Information World,* 1987. (*d*) But if it is possible idiomatically to use *common* (without its meaning of 'vulgar' getting in the way) or *in common* (in constructions of type (*c*)), it may be advisable to do so, if your audience or readership is likely to cavil, e.g. *They could discuss problems they had in common.*

See RECIPROCAL.

my. 1 For *my or your informant,* etc. (not *mine*), see ABSOLUTE POSSESSIVES.

2 The use of *my* as an exclamation, especially at the beginning of a statement, though possibly originally Scottish, and perceived as particularly American is used in all English-speaking areas, including Britain. The *OED* cites illustrative examples of the use from 1707 onwards. Modern examples: *Have you met him? Oh my!*—M. Wesley, 1983 (UK); *My, don't we look pretty*—H. Beaton, 1984 (NZ); *Oh my! My memory is shocking these days*—E. Jolley, 1985 (Aust.); *My, you're a deep one, thought Angela, not sufficiently taken in*—D. Potter, 1986 (UK); *My, but I was scared*—M. Grimm, 1989 (US); *I pointed to a pile of bird drawings. He went through them. 'My, you do this well.' I shook my head*—P. Saenger, 1991 (US).

Myanmar. The military authorities in Burma have promoted the name *Myanmar* as the official name for their state since 1989; *Burma* is often preferred by people who oppose the current government.

myriad. 1 *Meaning.* Is used to mean a countless number of things, e.g. *As I walked along Broadway it began to light up with myriads of coloured electric bulbs*—Charlie Chaplin, 1964. It is by nature a rhetorical exaggeration, so to use it when the numbers involved are not that large cheapens it; often it seems to mean little more than 'a large range': Accessorize *sells earrings, bracelets, necklaces, bags and hats in a myriad of colours which will help complete your beach wardrobe*—*The Press* (York), 2001.

2 *A disputed use.* Rather inexplicably, *myriad* has become a usage issue for certain people. The word is quite legitimately, and with good historical precedent, used in three syntactic patterns (dates of first known use in the *OED* in brackets): (i) as a plural noun: *myriads of stars* (1555); (ii) as a singular noun + *of*: *a myriad of stars* (1609); (iii) as a sort of adjective, or quantifier: *a myriad stars, myriad stars* (1735). Some people insist that the noun uses are incorrect. (*MWCDEU* points out that the first usage book to proscribe them dates from as recently as 1996, but I suspect that the issue had surfaced long before then.) My advice is that you can safely use the word in any of the ways shown above, unless, of course, the person who objects is your boss, editor, or anyone whose opinion might affect you materially. Modern examples: (noun) *Crystals are made of myriads of layers of atoms (or equivalent), and each layer builds upon the layer below*—R. Dawkins, 1991; *Three teleconferences about Sars sandwiched between a myriad of delayed patients waiting an hour in the office*—*Guardian*, 2003. (adjective) *Acting as a walking/talking A-Z, directing traffic, dealing with accident victims and domestic disputes are several of the myriad activities that absorb police personnel*—M. Brogden, 1991; *Tyres, brakes, state of alertness, and above all attitude towards risk are among the myriad relevant factors that bear on the outcome*—*Times*, 1998.

3 On a historical note, it is worth remembering that *myriad* goes back ultimately to a Greek word meaning 'ten thousand' (Greek μυριάς, μυριαδ-, from μυρίος 'countless', μυρίοι 'ten thousand'), and that the sense 'ten thousand' was to some extent current in English from the 16c. to the 19c. ('Chiefly in translations from Greek or Latin, or in reference to the Greek numerical system', *OED*.)

myself. 1 The normal and uncontroversial uses of *myself* are as an emphatic form of *I* (*I began to feel guilty myself; I myself couldn't see him as a worker*); and as a reflexive form of *me* (*in a room by myself; I managed to restrain myself*). There is also an obsolete use, with *myself* placed initially as a simple subject, chiefly in poetry (e.g. *Myself when young did eagerly frequent Doctor and Saint*—E. FitzGerald, 1859) which need not concern us.

2 There are also some very frequent other uses to which objections have been raised since the late 19c.: (i) when *myself* is the subject of a verb: *It wasn't that Peter and myself were being singled out*—F. Weldon, 1988; *My friends and myself do not find it a great problem*— *Paintball Games*, 1989; (ii) when *myself* is the object of a verb: *they hauled Barry and myself in for questioning; Several of the ultra-popish bishops . . . had denounced the Bible, the Bible Society, and myself*—G. Borrow, 1842; and (iii) when *myself* is the object of a preposition: *Palme Dutt's nervousness communicated itself to Isaac and myself*—N. Williams, 1985; *'the rift between myself and Lord Hailsham is unseemly and ought to be ended,' Judge Pickles said*—*Times*, 1987; *I have submissions also on the position as regards costs as between myself and Dr Jarman, but I will leave that for the moment*—*England and Wales High Court Decisions*, 2000.

3 All three uses have long historical pedigrees, including, as the *OED* shows, Bunyan, Richardson, Dr Johnson, Scott, Hardy, Ruskin, and many others, and Burchfield (1996) described such uses as 'beyond reproach'. From the examples given above it is clear that *myself* is often part of a group of names or nouns. Another reason for its use instead of *me* may be that *me* is considered by the speaker too brusque or direct, while *I* may be thought of as placing too egocentric an emphasis on the speaker. Some people might also use *myself* because they consider it in some way more elegant or refined. Whatever the reasons, it is perfectly acceptable if used in the ways illustrated above. The use which the style guides tend to agree should be avoided is exemplified in 'how inspirational and uplifting your publication is for someone such as myself' (quoted in *languagelog*, 5 September 2005) and 'a rather interesting enigma manifested itself, one which I hope you can elucidate for myself.' (quoted in *MWDCEU*).

'n (or **'n'**), colloquial shortening of *and*. Recorded occasionally in the 19c. and early 20c. (the *Radio Times* mentions a one-step dance called *By 'n' Bye* in 1923), *'n* or *'n'* became common in the second half of the 20c. especially under the influence of the phrase *rock 'n' roll:* e.g. *cut 'n' paste, down 'n' dirty, drum 'n' bass, fish 'n' chips, good 'n' ready, pick 'n' mix.* Phrases with this abbreviation are sometimes written with hyphens (*sex-'n'-violence*, etc.).

naff (adjective). This originally BrE word meaning, 'tasteless, vulgar, lacking in style; inept' seems to have slipped into general use at the end of the 1960s. It may be an adaptation of several similar-sounding regional words meaning 'inconsequential, stupid; unpleasant, objectionable', or it may have come from the coded slang Polari formerly used by British gay men. *OEC* data suggests *naff* is also used in Aust. and NZ English, and very occasionally in AmE. Examples: *I didn't want it* [*sc.* a television series] *to look naff and corny. It had to trigger memories and be funny but it also had to be cool—BBC* (press release), 2002; *Jeremy has a ghost-like presence in the novel, and I don't mean that in the naff sense that he haunts people but he's showing us the way in which the past constantly reaches forward into the present—ABC* (radio interviews), 2009.

naiad /ˈnʌɪad/. The plural is generally *naiads* or, rarely, *naiades* /ˈnʌɪəˌdiːz/.

naïf /nʌɪˈiːf/ or /nɑːˈiːf/. Though recorded in English as an adjective from the 16c. onwards and as a noun ('artless person') from the late 19c., it has practically been ousted by NAIVE in all main uses as an adjective, though it is still occasionally used to refer to a deliberately unsophisticated style of painting, etc. It is still used, and useful, as the noun to denote an artless or unsophisticated person. It should be printed in roman, ideally with a diaeresis over the letter *i*, but more often appears without. Examples: (noun) *Gladwell is not some art naïf who skated into the gallery, he's a guy who is represented by Sherman Galleries—The Art Life*, 2005 (Aust.); (adjective) *Tort is a naif artist who paints a magical world—Art Business News*, 2004.

nail. *To hit the nail on the head* ('to do or say exactly the right thing') is now the standard form. From the *OED* it seems that *to hit the right nail on the head* was the usual idiom in the 18c. and 19c., even though the form without *right* was standard in the 16c. and 17c. The variation was wittily utilized by a *Times* obituarist to produce a phrase that deserves to be recycled: *In controversy he may not always have hit the right nail, but he hit it on the head, and hit it very hard*—9 April 1935.

naive (or **naïve**) is pronounced in a quasi-French fashion /nɑːˈiːv/ or /nʌɪˈiːv/ (nah-**eev** or ny-**eev**). In origin the feminine form of the French adjective *naïf*, it has become so anglicized that it is more often printed without its diaeresis than with. Its grammatical gender in French is ignored in English—in other words it applies to both sexes. The corresponding nouns are spelt in a bewildering variety of ways: the most frequent is the completely anglicized **naivety**, which is the most frequent in all forms of English, except North American; next comes **naivete**, keeping the French shape of the word, but without accents, which is the most frequent spelling in NAmer.; about as often used as each other and frequent in NAmer. but not elsewhere, are the betwixt and between English and French, **naiveté**, and the fully French **naïveté**. Least used of all in the *OEC* is **naïvety**. One can only say *chacun à son goût. Naivety* is pronounced /nɑːˈiːvti or nʌɪ-/, and the others are /nɑːˈiːvteɪ/ or nʌɪ-/.

Nama. The *Nama* people are one of the Khoikhoi peoples of South Africa and SW Namibia. They have in the past been called *Hottentot* (actually a somewhat broader term), but that is now obsolete and offensive and *Nama* is the standard accepted term. See also HOTTENTOT; KHOIKHOI.

name (verb). **1** *you name it.* A formula used after a list of people, things, etc., to indicate that further listing is unnecessary. It is first found in print in the 1960s. Examples: *Whatever they choose to say, Directors, DG, Higher Command, War Cabinet, Prime Minister, you name it, I'm not sending my units back into Europe*—P. Fitzgerald, 1980; *Brunch minus the first hour, the one with just drinks in it, and minus too no doubt wine, beer, brandy, you name it and we're not going to get it*—K. Amis, 1988.

2 *named after, for, from* (someone). There is good evidence for each of these constructions in standard sources at intervals from the 15c. onwards, but the third is now rare. It is often assumed that *named for* is standard in AmE, and unknown elsewhere, but that is a false assumption. In the *OEC* data, across all varieties of English both are used, but *named after* is the preferred form by a very large margin, except in American English. Even there, however, *named after* is in a ratio of 4:3 with *named for* in the *OEC* data, while in *COCA* data, *named for* is just slightly more frequent. Some examples: (named for) *At one time he* [*sc.* Peter Van Rensselaer] *owned thousands of acres in this region and the city of Rensselaer is named for him*—G. Ade, 1930 (US); *Which Canadian city is named for a Royal Navy captain and great explorer from Kings Lynn, Norfolk?—Liverpool Daily Post*, 2007 (UK); (named after) *Wellington, who, as we all know, has a boot named after him—Printing World*, 1976 (UK); *So they're named* [*sc.* the Tea Party] *after a tax revolt, but they don't know anything about taxes—CNN* transcripts, 2010 (US).

names and appellations. **1** Certain types of proper names receive detailed treatment in specialized dictionaries: e.g. *English Place-Names* (Eilert Ekwall), the *BBC Pronouncing Dictionary of British Names* (G. E. Pointon), *English River names* (Ekwall), *English Place-Name Elements* (A. H. Smith), *British Surnames* (P. H. Reaney), *English Christian Names* (E. G. Withycombe). There are also innumerable monographs on such matters and learned journals devoted to the collection and description of particular types of names.

2 For a brief historical account of the use of personal names and designations, especially from the 18c. to the early 20c., one may turn to R. W. Chapman's essay 'Names, Designations and Appellations' (SPE Tract xlvii, 1936). For brief descriptions of some modern conventions in the use of titles and forms of address, see ESQ.; MADAM; MS. The general tendency in the 20c. is to settle for informality except in formal correspondence and on grand occasions (e.g. garden parties at Buckingham Palace, the opening of parliament). For adjectival formations of the type *Aesopian, Audenesque, Borrovian, Platonic,* etc., see SUFFIXES ADDED TO PROPER NAMES.

3 For names of groups of animals, etc. (*a pride of lions, a charm of finches,* etc.), see PROPER TERMS.

4 For names of people after whom a discovery, invention, product, process, etc., is called, see EPONYM.

5 Non-Americans continue to be mildly amused by the American habit of adding II, III, etc., to the names of descendants of persons of the same name. From a March 1992 American newspaper: *Other than her husband, she leaves three sons, the Rev. Raymond II, Silas and Mark; a daughter, Ann Semotan III, and 10 grandchildren.*

6 Every now and then correspondence breaks out in newspapers about curiosities of nomenclature, e.g. the frequent use of certain types of first names (women's names from flowers: *Fleur, Flora, Lily, Marigold, May, Rose, Rosemary, Veronica,* etc.); the aptness of some surnames to the occupation of the owner of the name (e.g. *Mr Veale,* a butcher; *Mr Coffin,* an undertaker; *Mr Churchyard,* a vicar). Such correspondence is a paradisal garden for the amateur collector of unexpected connections.

naphtha. So spelt. Pronounced /ˈnafθə/, not /ˈnap-/.

napkin, according to Fowler (1926), Nancy Mitford, and others, 'should be preferred to *serviette*' (the latter word being judged to be a genteelism). As a totally separate matter, in Britain a baby wears a *nappy* (hypocoristic form of *napkin*) and in America a **diaper**.

narcissus. On grounds of euphony, the plural form *narcissi* /-sʌɪ/ is recommended rather than *narcissuses*.

narghile, oriental tobacco-pipe. Pronounced /ˈnɑːgɪleɪ/, i.e. as three syllables.

nary ('not a, not a single'). Markedly American from the mid-18c. onwards until some point in the 20c., when it began to appear in British works. Except in regional AmE sources, it is almost always used in the form *nary a* + noun: e.g. *The traffic diminishes, the mangrove forests are dense and there's nary a tacky tourist shop in sight*—weblog, 2005. In origin it seems to be an extended respelling of *ne'er a* = 'never a'.

nasal. In phonetics, describes a sound pronounced with the breath passing through the nose, e.g. as represented by *m, n, ng,* or French *en, un.*

native. 1 It requires a certain amount of skill to avoid the seen and unseen tripwires stretched across uses of this word. *He is a native of Leeds, of Yorkshire, of England* are all acceptable as factual statements about where a person was born. *He speaks Italian like a native* also has no derogatory connotations, although *native speaker* is now often replaced by *mother-tongue speaker.* There are scores of plants and animals in the former British colonies whose names are qualified by *native* on the grounds that they are similar to analogues in the British Isles but do not belong to the same species or genus, e.g. in Australia, *native bear* (koala), *native cat* (marsupial cat), *native oak* (casuarina). In New Zealand, *native bush* is the ordinary term for woods or forests made up of indigenous trees and shrubs. When, however, *native* is applied to the original or usual inhabitants of a (formerly) colonized country, difficulties begin to arise.

2 Throughout the 19c. and in the first decades of the 20c. it was acceptable, indeed customary, for British writers such as Mary Kingsley, R. M. Ballantyne, and E. M. Forster to speak of West Africans, Pacific Islanders, and Indians as *natives,* usually implying social or cultural inferiority. Such uses are now offensive. In uses that are clearly humorous, there is less objection to *native*: *New York in the summer was too hot even for the natives.* Otherwise, it is better to use more neutral terms such as *original inhabitant.*

Native American. Originally used as a noun to denote a member of any of the native Indian peoples of the Americas or West Indies, this has since about the 1950s been the term preferred by the indigenous inhabitants of the US. It has largely replaced *Indian* and *American Indian* in any serious contexts. It is sometimes written with a small initial *n,* and is also used as a compound adjective. Examples: (original meaning) *Peru is inhabited by the Spaniards, who conquered it, and the native Americans*—*Royal Eng. Dict.,* 1775; (modern uses) *Investigators have identified five distinct mitochondrial lineages ... in modern Native Americans*—*High Country News,* 2000; *The polarities of the Ghost-Dance songs are part of the heritage of modern Native American literature*—*Native American Writers,* 2010.

natter. This everyday informal word in Britain, usually meaning (as verb) 'to chatter idly' and (as noun) 'aimless chatter', is not widely used in AmE. It seems to be an alteration of the earlier dialectal verb *gnatter* (of uncertain origin) which, besides the sense 'to chatter', like *natter* could also mean 'to grumble'. The emergence of the word from restricted dialectal use to general UK use seems to have happened during the Second World War.

nature. Fowler (1926) criticized as verbose the use of the word *nature* in two constructions, and his criticism was amplified by Gowers (1965). Those constructions are its use (i) in noun phrases such as *the serious nature of the allegations* where it replaces the abstract noun *seriousness*; and (ii) in the construction *of a* + adjective + *nature,* e.g. *allegations of a serious nature,* where it stands for the simple adjective *serious.* Such circumlocutions are typical of formal registers, particularly legal writing, and could, it is true, often be shortened. But it does not follow that all periphrastic uses of *nature* are to be avoided: the *OED* disproves such blanket assumptions in its presentation of the phrases *of* (a certain) *nature,* and *of* or *in the nature of.* Examples: *With other Particulars of the like Nature*—Addison, 1711; *Your desires are to me in the nature of commands*—Fielding, 1749; *A plan of this* *nature*—Blackstone, 1765; *It was not in the nature of things that popularity such as he ... enjoyed should be permanent*—Macaulay, 1854; *Most of his public acts are of a ceremonial nature—London Calling* (cited in Webster's Third, 1961). In one's own writing, the best policy is to consider each potentially periphrastic use of *nature* on its merits and to use such constructions sparingly. Cf. CHARACTER.

naughties. See NOUGHTIES.

naught, nought. **1** *naught*: now (in both BrE and AmE) an archaic or literary word meaning 'nothing'. It survives chiefly in the phrases *come to naught* 'to end in failure', *set at naught* 'place no value on', and *all for naught* 'all for nothing'. The spelling *nought* is also used in this meaning and these phrases, though rarely in AmE.

2 *nought* (in BrE) means principally 'the digit 0' (as in the game called *noughts and crosses*; '0.5' pronounced as 'nought point five'). The variation in spelling is not a modern accident, but descends from Old English.

nauseated, nauseating, nauseous. **1** *Nauseating, nauseated.* As participles of the verb *nauseate, nauseated* and *nauseating* both have physical and figurative meanings: 'affected by/causing the physical desire to vomit' and 'disgusted/disgusting'. The *OEC* data shows clearly that they differ greatly in the proportion of physical to figurative use. While *nauseated* is slightly more often physical, esp. in collocation with *feel* and *dizzy*, than metaphorical, *nauseating* is practically always metaphorical (i.e. 'disgusting'). Examples: (physical) *I got out of bed, but felt dreadfully giddy, nauseated and then panic stricken.—Daily Tel.*, 1990; *He woke up to the nauseating smell of burning skin and a roaring sound—FlyPast,* 1991; (figurative) *The duo ... await a wave of laughter from the crowd, but there is only a nauseated silence—See Magazine*, 2002 (CanE); *What a nauseating little Miss Perfect you are*—R. Goddard, 1993; *Most anecdotes associated with Diogenes consistently depict him as a nauseating and narcissistic sociopath—First Things* (magazine), 2004 (AmE).

2 *Nauseous.* (*a*) This word (1613), which antedates the verb *nauseate,* is a usage issue in AmE, but nowhere else. There, to cut a long story short, since the 1950s usage commentators have been busy perpetuating the myth that *nauseous* can mean only 'causing nausea' and never 'suffering from nausea, feeling sick to one's stomach', for which, according to this pseudo-rule, *nauseated* is the only correct word. To judge from online comments, this shibboleth causes considerable confusion, not to say angst, among ordinary users of American English.

(*b*) The simple facts of the matter are (i) that currently *nauseous* is roughly twice as frequent as *nauseated* in *OEC* data overall, and 40 per cent more frequent than it in AmE. (In the *COCA* American data the two words have roughly equal frequency); (ii) most examples of *nauseous* refer to the physical meaning, i.e. feeling like vomiting; (iii) historical, figurative meanings are still alive, but infrequent: referring to unpleasant flavours or smells, and to anything the speaker finds disgusting or distasteful; (iv) the *OED* labels the disputed meaning originally US, and gives the earliest citation from a Kingston, Jamaica newspaper of 1885, and the first US example from the *Chicago Tribune* of 9 May 1927. As *MWCDEU* says 'Any handbook that tells you that *nauseous* cannot mean "nauseated" is out of touch with the contemporary language.'

Examples: (physical) *When a toadlicker licks the toad his mouth and lips will become numb and he will feel intensely nauseous—Times,* 1991; *Stephen Wright had been standing on the edge of the railway platform feeling nauseous and did not spot the train speeding towards him—Daily Tel.,* 2012; (metaphorical) *local people complained of 'sickening, disgusting and nauseous' smells from the animal rendering factory—This is the Lake District,* 2004; *In the event, parliament proceeded with a nauseous display of collective royalist sycophancy and mourning for Britain's past imperial grandeur—World Socialist Website,* 2002.

nautilus, cephalopod or shell. Plural *nautiluses* or *nautili* /-lʌɪ/.

naval, navel, are both pronounced /ˈneɪvəl/. The first, meaning 'pertaining to the navy' is derived from Latin *nāvālis* (from *nāvis* 'ship'), and the second, 'a small depression in the centre of the belly', from Old English *nafela* (cf. German *Nabel*).

nay. **1** As an adverb it is curiously persistent (first recorded in this use in the mid-16c.) as a sometimes rhetorical, sometimes archly humorous way of emphasizing a more appropriate word than one just used to mean 'or rather': *one could not but notice how theatrical, nay operatic, the whole adornment of the church was—Oxford Mag.*, 1991; *He grips my hand in public, nay brandishes it. 'We're a team,' he cries—*Alan Bennett, 1988.

2 As a noun, *nay* means principally 'a negative vote': *they counted 20* ayes and *16* nays.

né (or **ne**). Is now used to indicate the original name of a man who changed his name at some point in his life, e.g. *Andy Warhol (né Warhola), Fred Astaire (né Austerlitz) from Omaha.* Like the feminine form NÉE, it is also occasionally used of things to mean 'formerly known as': *The* Morning Star (*né* Daily Worker, *as it was in May 1945*) *proved that some things have not changed—Pick of Punch,* 1985; *the tabloid (né broadsheet) Times—London Rev. Books,* 2004. See also NÉE.

near (adverb). **1** In most of its adverbial uses *near* is completely natural (*the time drew near; near at hand; the bomb dropped near to their home; as near as one can say*). But it is becoming progressively rarer in the meaning 'almost, nearly', though still found, esp. in AmE in phrases such as *not near as* + adjective/adverb, e.g. *not near as bad/often/much; to be near dead; for damn well near a century.* In such circumstances *nearly* is the natural form.

2 An exception to this general rule is that *near* can be added freely as a prefix to any adjective to create a hyphenated compound adjective, e.g. *near-flawless.* In practice, while others are created as the need arises, only a small group of these compound adjectives is commonly used, e.g. *near-perfect, near-fatal, near-total, near-complete.* Combinations which can be used both attributively and predicatively should be hyphenated in the first case but not in the second. e.g. *near-perfect weather, the weather was near perfect.* Examples: *The capsule's attitude would have to be near-perfect* [*sic*] *when the rockets fired, or the angle of re-entry would be affected—*J. Glenn, 1962; *No doubt the injuries from a near-fatal accident this year in his native Jamaica had an effect on him—www.chartattack.com,* 2004; *Contrast and color are near perfect, and there are just enough small blemishes to remind us that this was a low-budget film—DVD Verdict,* 2011.

near by, nearby. As an adjective it should be written as one word (*a nearby hotel*), but as an adverb normally as two (*at a hospital near by*).

neath, beneath. Used only in dialects or in poetry since it first appeared in print in the 18c.

nebula. The recommended and rather more frequent plural form is *nebulae* /ˈnɛbjʊliː/, not *nebulas,* though it too is correct.

necessaries. See NECESSITIES.

necessarily. The nowadays dominant pronunciation in BrE, which has been influenced by American practice, is with the stress on the third syllable /ˌnɛsəˈsɛrɪli/; Wells (3rd ed.) shows that two thirds of BrE speakers prefer it. First-syllable stress /ˈnɛsəs(ə)rɪli/ is given priority in dictionaries, and is sometimes advocated by older speakers, but whether they always use it themselves is questionable. In *The Spoken Word* Burchfield urged BBC broadcasters to avoid the American stress pattern. The book was published in 1981, which shows that the trend towards third-syllable stress in BrE goes back at least as far as then.

necessities, necessaries. At one stage earlier in the 20c. it seemed to some authorities that *necessaries,* not *necessities,* was the word to use when the meaning required was 'any of the basic requirements of life, such as food, warmth, shelter, etc.'. This use of *necessaries* had been current since the 14c. (*ȝe shal haue bred and clothes, And other necessaries i-nowe—*Langland, 1377) and was still favoured in the 19c. (*an island which was so prolific and so well stored with all the necessaries of life—*R. M. Ballantyne, 1858). But *necessities* has a similar history from the 15c. onwards. A typical example: *Sufficient for many things more than the necessities of life—*E. Du Bois, 1799. After much locking of horns between the two words, *necessities* has clearly emerged as the stronger of the two in this concrete sense, and *necessaries* is now mostly confined to literary or legal discourse: (necessaries) *I assembled* *the necessaries, including a homemade chicken stock and fresh basil from the greenhouse.*—New Yorker, 1998; (necessities) *The possibilities of bulk ordering of whole ranges of hospital equipment and necessities, such as blankets and linen, were realized early in the development of the scheme*—A. Bevan, 1952.

nectar. As a remarkable demonstration of the richness, not to say redundancy, of English vocabulary, the *OED* lists no fewer than eight corresponding adjectives having the broad sense 'of the nature of, sweet as, nectar': *nectareal* (first recorded in 1648), *nectarean* (1624), *nectared* (*c*.1595), *nectareous* (1657), *nectarian* (1647), *nectarine* (1611), *nectarious* (1710), and *nectarous* (1667). Famous writers—among them Crashaw, Milton, Gay, Pope, Smollett, and Tennyson—made their choices, but no single form emerged as the dominant one, which is in any case an academic question, since with rare exceptions the words do not exist outside the realms of classic literature, or, in the case of *nectareous,* botany.

née (or, in modern printing, often **nee**). From the French word meaning 'born', the traditional use is to add it to a married woman's name after her surname to indicate what her maiden name was, e.g. *Mrs Ann Jones, née Smith.* This remains the standard use. (The type *Mrs Ann Jones, née Ann Smith,* i.e. with the first name added after *née,* has been criticized on the absurd grounds that people are born with a surname but not a first name; such criticism can obviously be ignored.) The use of *née* as an explanation of a pseudonym or stage name (the type *Diana Dors née Diana Mary Fluck*) is also now perfectly standard. Moreover, the word is now used, often tongue-in-cheek, after the current name or title by which not only people but places and things are known. (Though strictly speaking *née* should only be used of women, it is also applied to men, which indicates how far it has become naturalized in English. Sticklers will, naturally, abhor this use.) Examples: *Mrs Agnes Childe was* née *O'Byrne, of Ratsey and O'Byrne, ship's chandlers*—A. Price, 1982; *The flight attendant,* née *stewardess, singsongs over the loudspeaker*—William Safire, 1981; *Slimehead ... and fellow latecomer Chilean sea bass* (née *Patagonian toothfish*) *have been virtually eliminated from much of their range*—*U.S. News and World Rep.,* 2001; *For over a decade the Nova Scotia native* (née *Richard Terfry*) *has been storytelling in verse over twanged-out beats*—*OEC,* 2005.

See NÉ.

need (verb). **1** Like *dare, need* can behave in two ways: as an ordinary verb and as a modal auxiliary verb sharing some of the characteristics of the main modals such as *can, might,* etc. As an ordinary verb, *need* is regular and can be followed by a simple object (*We need more bread*), a verbal noun (*The cupboard needs cleaning*), or a *to*-infinitive (*They need to see for themselves*). As a modal verb, it has certain grammatical restrictions: (i) it is only used with a so-called 'bare' infinitive without *to* (*I'm not sure you need answer*); (ii) it is only used in the negative, or in phrases with a negative implication, and in questions without *do* (*You need not answer; Need I answer; I need hardly add ...*); and (iii) the third person singular form is *need* without the addition of *s* (*He says she need not answer*). In many cases the modal meaning can equally be expressed by using *need* as an ordinary verb, e.g. *He says she does not need to answer.*

Some examples: (*a*) (modal use) *One need interrupt the narrative no further than to say this*—A. N. Wilson, 1984; *The Landlady need never know*—J. Frame, 1985; *But need she lie? Was he just a boy?*—M. Leland, 1985; *Nothing that need embarrass you. Not at this stage*—A. Lejeune, 1986; *It need not only be children who can enjoy guessing games*—*Spectator,* 1988; *Contemporaries do not conveniently die at the same time, nor need they all be dead before we write the history of their exploits*—M. Inwood, 2000. (*b*) (ordinary use) *which was what he needed to do if his feelings were to be relieved*—C. K. Stead, 1984; *the Bar and the judiciary need to know what is being proposed*—*Counsel,* 1987; *she acted as if Strawberry needed to be cuddled*—*New Yorker,* 1988; *That's the area that one needs to be a little careful about*—*CNN news transcripts,* 2002.

2 *X needs + -ing/to*-infinitive/*-ed.* When used as an ordinary verb to mean 'stand in want of', *need* can be followed by either a verbal noun (which is more common in speech) or a passive *to*-infinitive (*The car needs washing/to be washed*). A third type, *The car needs washed,* is either American regional dialect, or Scottish, and is disliked by some people: *I walked round the cottage* *to see what needed done*—C. Burns, 1989 (UK); *When you see one* [*sc.* a dog] *drag its butt on the ground like that, it needs wormed, Otis*—T. McGuane, 1989 (US).

See also NEEDS MUST, MUST NEEDS.

needle. The commonplace phrase *like looking for a needle in a haystack* is a 19c. variant of the much older phrases *like looking for a needle in a meadow, in a bottle* (i.e. a *bundle* or *truss*) *of hay.*

needs must, must needs. 1 Preceding or following the modal verb *must, needs* is in origin an adverb (Old English *nȳdes, nēdes*) meaning 'of necessity, necessarily'. Both phrases survive in modern literary use, *must needs* being much more frequent, e.g. *Even if we dislike the processes, we must needs excrete and eat*—A. Storr, 1979. *Needs must* is sometimes used in the same way as a deliberate archaism, for instance to give the prose of historical fiction a patina of antiquity, e.g. *Now they were nearly upon me and I needs must move to keep myself from the mud flying off the hooves of their beasts*—*The Circle of Ceridwen*, 2004.

2 Much more common is *needs must* on its own, or preceded by *if*, to mean 'it is necessary or unavoidable': *'I'm pleased you have adapted yourself to our work ethic so readily.' Larkin shook his head. 'Needs must.'*—M. Waites, 1998; *its new compact five-door X-Trail is designed more for the road than the ruts. But if needs must it is quite capable of zipping across the nearest field*—*The Press* (York), 2001. This version of the phrase is probably a shortening of the proverb *Needs must when the devil drives* [and variants], which goes back at least to the early 16c.: *He must needes go, whom the dyuel dryueth.*—Thomas More, 1532. In this context, the word *needs* is often taken to be a plural noun.

ne'er. A literary (chiefly poetical) shortening of *never*, in regular use since the 13c., but now rarely used except in the compound *ne'er-do-well*, a good-for-nothing person.

negation. 1 For problems arising from double or multiple negation, see DOUBLE NEGATIVE.

2 Fowler (1926) classified various types of construction in which negative and affirmative statements occur in parallel clauses, and emphasized how important it was not to let the negativity of the first clause carry over into the second. Examples, followed by suggested improvements: No lots *will therefore be put on one side for another attempt to reach a better price,* but must *be sold on the day appointed* (read *but all must be sold*); (with negative inversion in first clause) *Nor* is it expected *that tomorrow's speech will deal with peace,* but will be confined *to a general survey of* . . . (read *It is expected* . . . *will not deal*). To which may be added the following example in the proofs of a 1992 institutional report: *We greatly regret that —— decided that for personal reasons he would have to give up the chairmanship, but that he intended to remain an active member of the committee* (the final *that*-clause is in danger of being qualified by *We greatly regret*). The advice remains sound.

3 When the grammatical subject of a negative sentence contains the word *all*, ambiguity may result. For example, an American agony aunt tried to reassure a married woman who was upset because her husband wanted to sleep in a separate bed by saying *All married couples do not sleep together.* The advice should have been *Not all married couples sleep together.* It should be noted, however, that this unrecommended construction has many historical precedents. Jespersen (1909–49, v. 472) cites numerous examples, including the following: *I maintained that certainly all patriots are not scoundrels* (Boswell); *But all men are not born to reign* (Byron); *All Valentines are not foolish* (Lamb); *All our men aren't angels* (H. G. Wells). As Jespersen says, 'very often *all* is placed first for the sake of emphasis, and the negative is attracted to the verb'.

4 It is desirable not to multiply negatives to the extent that clarity is endangered. For two examples of over-negatived sentences, see NOT 5.

5 For the ambiguity that can arise when a negative clause precedes one beginning with *because*, see BECAUSE C.

6 For other problems concerning negation, see BUT 7; CANNOT 2, 3; HARDLY 3, 4.

negative. Originally and chiefly in radio communication, for reasons of clarity, *negative* was widely adopted from about the

1950s to replace or reinforce *no*. Examples: *'Any result of my application for the return of my typist?' 'Negative,' said Mr Oates*—E. Waugh, 1961; *I shook my head. 'Negative,' I said*—P. Cleife, 1972; *'Do you see any friendlies around?' 'Negative.'*—T. Clancy, 1987. Cf. AFFIRMATIVE.

negligee, négligée. The first spelling with the accents dropped is now standard in printed work, though *négligée* is also correct. However spelt, the word is usually pronounced /ˈnɛglɪʒeɪ/.

negligible. Spelt as shown, not *negligeable* nor *negligable*. (cf. French *négligeable*).

negotiate. One of Fowler's lost causes. In 1926 he strongly attacked its use in 'its improper sense of tackle successfully', but this extended sense (originally used in hunting in the mid-19c.) is now routine in contexts of a person who succeeds 'in crossing, getting over, round, or through (an obstacle, etc.) by skill or dexterity'. The word is usually pronounced /nɪˈgəʊʃɪeɪt/ rather than /-ˈgəʊsɪ-/.

Negress is no longer used (*Blacks all over the world find the term 'Negress' offensive*—*TLS*, 1974). The standard terms now are *black* (or *Black*) and (in America) *African American*. See -ESS 4; JEWESS.

Negro. Plural *Negroes*. See -O(E)S 1. A term that is only used with historical reference, or among black people themselves. The standard terms are **African-American** (in AmE) and **black** (or **Black**). See AFRICAN AMERICAN; BLACK.

neighbourhood. It is inadvisable to use the cumbrous periphrasis *in the neighbourhood of* (a sum or figure) when *roughly* or *about* would serve equally well.

neither.

1 Pronunciation.
2 Word class of *neither*.
3 *Neither* (. . .) *is* or *neither* (. . .) *are*?
4 Verb agreement after *neither* . . . *nor*.
5 Position of *neither* . . . *nor*.
6 *Neither* . . . *or*.
7 *Neither* as quasi-conjunction.
8 *Neither* replacing *nor*.
9 Redundant *neither* reinforcing preceding negative.

1 *Pronunciation*. The two pronunciations /ˈnʌɪðə/ and /ˈniːðə/, rhyming with *driver* and *cleaver* respectively, are about equally common in British English. Both are correct, though many British people consider only the first right. AmE dictionaries give the second as the standard pronunciation, and the first as a variant. See also EITHER 1.

2 Word class of *neither*. *Neither* belongs to four different word classes. It can function either as a determiner-cum-pronoun, or as an adverb-cum-conjunction. As a determiner-pronoun it means 'not the one nor the other (of two things)': *Neither child knew the answer*; *Neither wanted to stay*; *Neither of them is right*. When more than two items are involved, *no* is preferable for the adjective and *none* for the pronoun, although *neither* tends to be used informally especially for the pronoun.

3 *Neither* (. . .) *is* or *neither* (. . .) *are*? Normally, *neither* as adjective or pronoun governs a singular verb: *Neither* was *exactly English*—D. J. Enright, 1955; *Neither of these figures* illuminates *the case against* Trident—D. Steel, 1985; *Neither of the two answers* is *satisfactory*—*Dædalus*, 1987. Disregard of this rule is likely to be taken as a grammatical mistake, although historically it is well established, and in the structure *neither of* (+ plural) a plural verb is sometimes used to emphasize the plurality of the statement as a whole: *I daresay I . . . could have been a more loving mother to you and Jane, but as things are, neither of you* require *me*—E. Bowen, 1955; *I have written about almost every subject except astrology and economics, neither of which* are *serious subjects*—P. Howard, 1985. It is salutary to bear in mind Jespersen's principle concerning 'the fundamental plurality of the conception [of *either* and *neither*]' (see EITHER 4) in certain circumstances; and also the principle of attraction exemplified in *Do you mean to say neither of you know your own numbers?* (H. G. Wells, 1905), where strict application of the rule would require third person singular *knows*, but the verb's proximity to *you* changes it to *know*.

4 Verb agreement after *neither* . . . *nor*. If both subjects are singular and in the third person, the verb should normally be singular and not plural, e.g. *Neither its chairman, Sir Frederick Dainton, nor its chief executive, Kenneth Cooper*, is *planning any dramatic gestures*—*Times*, 1985. There are historical precedents for the use of a plural verb in such circumstances, but what was acceptable in the 18c. and 19c. may be questionable in the 21c., e.g. *Neither search nor labour are necessary*—Johnson, 1759; *Neither painting nor fighting feed men*—Ruskin, 1874; *But neither Baker nor Bush are needed for that*—*Newsweek*, 1991. *CGEL* also asserts (10.41) that the type *Neither he nor his wife have arrived* is more natural in speech than the type *Neither he nor his wife has arrived.* A plural verb is required if either of the subjects (especially the second one) is plural: e.g. *Neither the Conservative figures nor the evidence of Labour's recovery since 1983* produce *any sense of inexorable movement in political fortunes*—*Times*, 1985.

Fowler (1926), in an unusually stretched-out passage, commented on the difficulties that can arise as regards the choice of verb form: 'Complications occur when, owing to a difference in number or person between the subject of the *neither* member and that of the *nor* member, the same verb-form or pronoun or possessive adjective does not fit both: Neither you nor I (was?, were?) chosen; Neither you nor I (is?, am?, are?) the right person; Neither eyes nor nose (does its?, do their?) work; Neither employer nor hands will say what (they want?, he wants?)'. Rephrasing eliminates the problem: *You are not the right person, and neither* (or *nor*) *am I.*

5 Position of *neither ... nor.* In good writing *neither* in *neither ... nor* sentences should be placed immediately before the first of the items being listed. The type *Which neither suits one purpose nor the other* should be rewritten as *Which suits neither one purpose nor the other.* Cf. EITHER 5. In the following example *neither* should have followed *interview* not preceded it: *Students who neither interview on campus nor through SLAC still have a chance to attract the attention of businesses*—*Oberlin College Observer*, 1990.

6 *Neither ... or.* When a negative has preceded, a question often arises between *nor* and *or* as the right continuation, and the answer to the question sometimes requires care. However, there is a problem in that the *OED* cites abundant literary evidence from the 16c. to the 19c. for *neither ... or*: e.g. *Neither on the one side or on the other*—Burke, 1757; *Neither rabbits at Coniston, road-surveyors at Croydon, or mud in St. Giles's*—Ruskin, 1864; *Wasn't it true that he neither knew anything or could do anything?*—G. W. Dasent, 1874. The matter must be left to the discretion of the reader, but it is advisable to use only *neither ... nor* in one's own writing, since many will consider it the only correct formulation.

7 *Neither* as quasi-conjunction. This use, in which *neither* is preceded by another negative and means 'nor yet' or 'and moreover ... not', is labelled 'Now chiefly Caribbean' in the *OED.* Examples: *There was now no respite neither by day nor night for this devoted city*—Southey, 1827; *Christianity abrogated no duty ... neither for Jew nor Gentile*—H. Coleridge, 1849. Fowler sagely commented 'This use is best reserved for contexts of formal tone.'

8 *Neither* replacing *nor.* When *nor* follows a negative statement (not necessarily one with *neither*) and introduces a different grammatical subject, it can be replaced by *neither*: *Becky is killed accidentally. The police don't care much; neither does Henry's wife*—*Publishers Weekly*, 1974.

9 Redundant *neither* reinforcing preceding negative. Fowler (1926) gave as his example '*I don't know that neither*' which he described as 'formerly idiomatic though colloquial'. By contrast, the *OED* records the same phenomenon with an impressive array of illustrative examples from the 16c. to the 19c., and comments 'nonstandard in later use', which comment is borne out by the last example below. Examples: *There were no books neither*—Disraeli, 1844; *Lady Edbury would never see Roy-Richmond after that, nor the old lord neither*—Meredith, 1871; *Bliddy right we don't. And it's not a very fair one neither! I mean d'yi see that?*—*More Rab C. Nesbitt Scripts*, 1992.

nem. con. In his book *Unlocking the English Language* (1989) Burchfield described how Dr C. T. Onions (of the *OED*) and Fowler quarrelled about the definition of *nem. con.* Dr Onions said it meant 'with no one dissenting' (= Latin *nemine contradicente*), and Fowler insisted that it meant 'unanimously'. Onions was right, since, apart from dissenting voices, there may be abstentions. Printed in italic.

neologism. A neologism is a new word or new sense of a word. The main nine types of neologism, together with examples, are listed in *OCELang.* (1992). Nearly all neologisms are formed from elements already in the language. *OCELang.* mentions *googol* and *Kodak* as rare examples of words formed *ex nihilo.*

nepenthes /nɪˈpɛnθiːz/, a drink or drug 'capable of banishing grief or trouble from the mind' (*OED*), is mentioned in the Odyssey (Greek adjective νηπενθές). The word was taken into English in the 16c. (Lyly) and was immediately joined by an unetymological *s*-less form **nepenthe** (Spenser), also trisyllabic, /nɪˈpɛnθiː/. Both forms are still in use, with *nepenthe* probably the more usual of the two in literary work and **Nepenthes** the standard spelling to refer to the genus of pitcher plants.

nereid (a mythological sea nymph). Pronounced /ˈnɪərɪɪd/.

nerve-racking. British and US dictionaries give preference to this spelling, and show **nerve-wracking** as a permissible variant. However, the *OEC* data suggests that across all types of English, the spelling with *w* is the more frequent one, esp. in British English. In AmE *COCA* data shows that *-racking* is somewhat more frequent, while in *OEC* data it is slightly less frequent.

-ness. For the distinction between the words *abstraction* and *abstractness,* and between *sensibility* and *sensibleness,* and similar pairs, see -ION AND -NESS; -TY AND -NESS.

It is worth noting that *-ness* is a strong living suffix (used especially to form nonce words). Burchfield noted numerous examples of such formations that are either not in the *OED* or are marked as rare: e.g. *accidentalness* (I. Murdoch, 1989), *energizedness* (*New Yorker,* 1986), *familyness* (*Newsweek,* 1992), *unimpressedness* (*New Yorker,* 1990).

nestle, nestling. The *-t-* is always silent in verbal senses. As a noun, *nestling* ('a bird that is too young to leave its nest') may also be pronounced with the *-t-* intact.

Net. As a shortening of *Internet,* in *the Net,* the word is spelt with a capital initial letter.

net. In the commercial sense ('not subject to deduction') the spelling *net* is standard and many times more frequent than **nett,** which is recognized as a variant in British dictionaries, but not in Webster's Third. *Nett* is used chiefly in British, Irish and Australian English, according to *OEC* data.

Netherlands, Low Countries, Holland, Dutch. *The Netherlands* is now the official name for the Kingdom of Holland (*Queen of the Netherlands, The Netherlands Ambassador,* etc.), though formerly Holland was only part of *The Netherlands,* or *The Low Countries* (which included what is now Belgium and Luxembourg). The language spoken in *The Netherlands* is *Dutch;* and *Dutch* is the adjective used of the people there, and also in certain familiar phrases ranging from the quaint to the disagreeable and reflecting older attitudes or practices, e.g. *Dutch cap* (a contraceptive pessary, first recorded in 1922), *Dutch courage* (bravery induced by drinking, 1826), *Dutch treat* (one in which each person present contributes his or her own share, 1887), *to go Dutch* (ditto, 1914), *double Dutch* (gibberish, 1789), etc. (The word for a costermonger's wife, immortalized in Albert Chevalier's *My Old Dutch,* is different: it is an abbreviation of *duchess.*)

neuroma. Plural either *neuromas,* or (somewhat pedantically) *neuromata.*

neurosis. Plural *neuroses* /-siːz/.

never. 1 *CGEL* 1985 (8.112) lists a use of *never* as 'a negative minimizer': *You will never catch the train tonight* = 'You will not under any circumstances catch the train tonight'. And it also points out that 'in nonassertive clauses *ever* (with some retention of temporal meaning) can replace *never* as minimizer, [especially] in rhetorical questions: "Will they (n)ever stop talking? Won't they ever learn?"' In some circumstances *never* may be used as a simple substitute for *not:* e.g. *I never knew you felt like that* (= 'I didn't know'); *he never used to* (= 'he didn't used to'). Uses of *never* = 'not (at all)', with little or no temporal sense, are particularly common in Irish English: e.g. *'That's never true,' exclaimed Mrs Riordan. 'How can you say such things on the anniversary of his going?'*—J. Leland, 1987; *'You're never going to cut hay in this weather?' asked Conor*—ibid.

2 *never ever* (sometimes separated by a comma). This emphatic adverbial phrase is, surprisingly, labelled 'colloquial' by the *OED.* Examples: *She continued, a little too vehement. 'I've never, ever been bored.'*—M. Gee, 1985; *It seems odd but I never ever saw the meat truck on its way back to*

Huntington—L. Maynard, 1988 (US); *How much that he never would have known he was capable of experiencing, never ever*—N. Gordimer, 1990 (SAfr.).

3 The adverbial phrase *never so* prefixed to adjectives or adverbs in concessive or conditional clauses with inversion of subject and verb denoting an unlimited degree or amount is recorded from the 12c. onwards. It is common in the Bible (*a showre of heauenly bread sufficient for a whole host, be it neuer so great*—Translators' Preface, para 4), Shakespeare, and in various sources until the late 19c. (*Were the critic never so much in the wrong, the author will have contrived to put him ... in the right*—Swinburne). It is now archaic, though occasionally used as a stylistic device: *There are certain spells that can prevent the life departing from a body, be it never so abused*—T. Pratchett, 1983.

4 *Never!* (as an expression of denial and surprise). This use, first recorded in the 18c. in Goldsmith (e.g. *My approbation of such a choice! Never!*—*Vicar of Wakefield*, 1766) is still commonly encountered (e.g. *'There's a fellow ... a gun—a pistol.' 'Never!'*—N. Bentley, 1974).

nevertheless, nonetheless. These are variants as adverbs meaning 'in spite of that, all the same', the first being about twice as frequent in the *OEC* data. The form *nonetheless* is nowadays preferred to *none the less*, which is, however, also correct. *Nevertheless* should always be written as one word. Examples: *Garway was not elected but nevertheless worked to prevent the final rupture between the City and the king*—*ODNB*, 2007; *This text, predictably fulsome in its praise, is nevertheless valuable for its personal insights into Sir Henry's travels, daily habits, and sayings*—*ODNB*, 2007; *The characteristics of his style, nonetheless, remained essentially the same*—*Oxford Companion to Western Art*, 2001; Parmalat *began with the development of a seemingly ordinary but nonetheless revolutionary product—the world's first shelf-stable milk*—*Dairy Field* (magazine), 2001. It is worth distinguishing those uses of *nonetheless* from *none the less* as three separate words when it is equivalent to *no less*: *Stories none the less heroic for being hackneyed remind us that the Republic was founded on a tyrannicide*—G. K. Chesterton, 1925.

news. From the 16c. to the 18c. *news* 'tidings' was construed either as a plural or a singular noun, but since the early 19c. it has normally been treated as a singular (e.g. *News is what a chap who doesn't care much about anything wants to read*—E. Waugh, 1938).

next. 1 *the next three*, etc. In most contexts *next* precedes the noun it governs when it means 'the one (of two or more) immediately following thing, occasion, etc.' (*the next three, the next time, the next chapter*, etc.). But there are circumstances in which it may legitimately follow the noun or stand in predicative use, e.g. *on Friday next, follow next in order, it would be next to impossible.*

2 *next Friday, Saturday*, etc. Care needs to be taken in referring to a future day of the week, since usage differs. For some people, *next Friday* means the coming Friday of the current week; for others, *next Friday* always means the Friday of the coming week, and to denote Friday of the same week *this Friday* would be used. When making an arrangement, organizing a meeting, etc., for 'next Friday' it is advisable to add the date of the Friday that is meant, or clarify matters in some other way. For example, if the Friday of the week following is meant, you may say *Friday week, a week Friday, a week come Friday, a week on Friday*, or *a week next Friday*. As a separate matter, *next June, next Monday*, etc., can be used without a preposition (*let's make a start next June*); but if *next* is put after the noun, idiom requires a preposition (*the meeting will take place on Monday next*).

nexus. While the plural of this word is technically spelt the same as the singular, reflecting the word's Latin origins, *OEC* data suggests that people tend to use the anglicized *nexuses*. The Latinate *nexi* is incorrect, since the word forms its Latin plural in *-us*, not in *-i*.

Nicaea, Nicea. Though both are correct, the first spelling is more frequent for the name of the place (now Izmir in Turkey) where the Council of Nic(a)ea (AD 325), in the reign of the Emperor Constantine, adopted the **Nicene Creed**.

nice. 1 *An overused word?* (*a*) The meanings to do with precision and fine distinctions (as in *a nice point* or *distinction*) arose in the 16c., and are still in use, but they are now swamped by the generalized favourable meaning 'agreeable, pleasant, attractive' or, of a person, 'kind, good-natured': *All her furniture is second-hand and rather nice*—J. Rose, 1990; *I have three children of my own now and I thought it would be nice to surprise them with the sugar mice on the tree, and also the chocolate cat*—C. Cookson, 1990.

The *OED's* first record of this meaning is from lines by the actor-playwright David Garrick (*He speaks like a Lady for all the World, and never swears as Mr. Flash does, but wears nice white Gloves*—1747), who was a pupil and friend of Dr Johnson; *MWCDEU* suggests that this use was current in Johnson's circle.

(*b*) Whatever its ultimate origin, it has been repeatedly criticized since the 19c. Fowler rather sexistly pooh-poohed it as 'too great a favourite with the ladies, who have charmed out of it all its individuality and converted it into a mere diffuser of vague and mild agreeableness'. Well before him, Jane Austen put criticism into the mouth of a male character in *Northanger Abbey*: *'I am sure,' cried Catherine, 'I did not mean to say any thing wrong; but it is a nice book, and why should not I call it so?' 'Very true,' said Henry, 'and this is a very nice day, and we are taking a very nice walk, and you are two very nice young ladies. Oh! it is a very nice word indeed!—it does for every thing.'—Northanger Abbey*, *a*1817.

(*c*) Many synonyms, often more apposite and stronger in meaning, are available (*good, pleasant, enjoyable, fine, agreeable, satisfying*, etc.) and it may well be better to use them in any serious writing, but in conversation *nice* has established itself too well and too idiomatically for cautionary advice to have any real point. The *BNC* shows that it is over eight times more frequent in speech than in writing: *I thought the shoulder of lamb would be much nicer and it looked nice and fresh!*—conversation recorded in the *BNC*, 1992. And it is impossible to imagine any other word in British comedian Bruce Forsyth's catchphrase 'Nice to see you! To see you, nice!'. As *MWCDEU* puts it: 'There is certainly nothing wrong with an effort to get college freshmen to use a wider variety of adjectives in their writing, but there is also nothing inherently wrong with *nice* in its generalized use.'

2 This word is also the great *cause célèbre* of meaning change in English. In medieval and Renaissance literature, *nice* (derived from Latin *nescius* meaning 'ignorant') has a wide range of generally unfavourable meanings such as 'foolish, stupid' and 'wanton'. In its current incarnation in the *OED*, the adjective meanings are divided into 12 major categories, and 39 subcategories, many of them long since obsolete. The word's first, now dead, meaning of 'foolish, silly, simple', applied to people, dates from *c*.1300, and remains in some of the Romance languages. Before acquiring its modern use, as described at 1, the word developed in zigzag fashion, adopting meanings ranging from 'ostentatious', and 'elegant' to 'lazy'; as the *OED* puts it: 'The semantic development of this word from 'foolish, silly' to 'pleasing' is unparalleled in Latin or in the Romance languages. The precise sense development in English is unclear.'

3 *Nice and* ... is used idiomatically as a sort of adverb = 'satisfactorily' to intensify a positive adjective (*I hope it will be nice and fine; nice and early* = nicely early). This is a kind of HENDIADYS that is well established in conversation and in a conversational style of writing: *Talk to her in your best, professorial manner, make her think how nice and kind you are*—Nina Bawden, 1989; *Pour the warm water from the teapot into the cup you're going to use, so that the cup gets nice and warm too*—weblog, 2004 (Aust.) The *OED* traces this use back to the end of the 18c. with a quotation from Fanny Burney: *Just read this little letter, do, Miss, do—it won't take you much time, you reads so nice and fast—Camilla*, 1796.

4 The derived adjective is *niceish*: see MUTE E.

niche. The usual and preferred pronunciation in BrE is /niːʃ/ (neesh) in the French manner, although the anglicized form /nɪtʃ/ (nich) is also heard, and that is the preferred form in AmE. In business jargon, *niche* (always pronounced neesh) means 'a specialized section of the market'.

nickel, (*a*) a malleable metallic element, and (*b*) a US five-cent coin, is spelt as shown in BrE, not *nickle*; the latter is an accepted spelling in AmE. The inflected forms of the corresponding verb are *nickelled, nickelling* in BrE, and usually *nickeled* and *nickeling* in AmE.

nick-nack. An acceptable, but far less frequent, variant of *knick-knack.*

nickname. 1 In origin an *eke-name* 'an additional name', with the initial *n* falsely carried over by METANALYSIS from the preceding indefinite article *an* (as also, for example, in *newt*).

2 A *nickname* is a familiar or humorous name given to a person, place, thing, etc., instead of or as well as the real name. Examples are legion. A selected few: *Beantown* (Boston, Mass.); *Dicky Bird* (famous cricket umpire); *Dog Star* (the star Sirius); *Jolly Roger* (pirates' flag); *La Stupenda* (Joan Sutherland, soprano); *Pompey* (Portsmouth, especially its football team); *Sally Army* (Salvation Army); *Silicon Valley* (an area south of San Francisco); *tin Lizzie* (model T Ford); *Tommy* (*Atkins*) (British soldier(s)); *Windy City* (Chicago). Some nicknames are regularly preceded by the definite article (e.g. *The Sally Army* but *Silicon Valley*). No simple rule governs the matter. A modern, journalistic trend involves taking the names of celebrities and combining them, either for a single person, e.g. *SuBo* and *J.Lo* for singers Susan Boyle and Jennifer Lopez, *SamCam* for Samantha Cameron, or for couples, e.g. *Brangelina* for Brad Pitt and Angelina Jolie.
See SOBRIQUETS.

nidus. The plural recommended is *nidi* /-ʌi/, rather than *niduses.*

niece. One of the most commonly misspelt words in the language.

niggardly. This expressive, though not very frequent, word, probably of Scandinavian origin, describes someone who is mean or miserly (*he accused the Government of being unbelievably niggardly*) or an amount that is meagre and given grudgingly (*niggardly allowances from the Treasury*). It has absolutely no historical connection with the N-word, but because of the similarity of sound, its negative meaning, and the fact that it lies outside some people's vocabulary, it has been perceived in the US as a racial slur. As a result, it is now widely avoided there. *OEC* data shows that it is much more frequent in BrE than elsewhere, and its use there has not so far caused a similar brouhaha; nevertheless, even there it may be prudent to use it only with people of whose literacy one can be quite certain.

nigger. One would have to be resident on Mars not to know that the N-word is the most taboo word in the English language. The current *OED* note expresses the situation admirably: 'This term is strongly racially offensive when used by a white person in reference to a black person. In written Black English and written representations of spoken Black English, however, there are usually not the same negative connotations. Recently the term has been reclaimed by some black speakers and used with positive connotations in various senses (esp. in the form *nigga*). However, even among black speakers, use of the word is problematic because of its potential to give offence, as is clear from the following, from a black speaker: 1995 N.Y. Times 14 Jan. i. 7 "The prosecutor, his voice trembling, added that the 'N-word' was so vile that he would not utter it. 'It's the filthiest, dirtiest, nastiest word in the English language,' Mr. Darden said."' Cf. NEGRO.

nigh. See WELL-NIGH.

nightie, nighty, a nightdress. The first is the recommended and much more frequent spelling.

nihilism. The word is usually pronounced with the *h* silent, i.e. as /ˈnʌɪɪlɪz(ə)m/ **ny**-i-liz(uh)m in BrE, with /niː-/ as a variant in AmE. Similarly **nihilist**.

nimbus (halo of a saint, etc.; a raincloud). Plural *nimbi* /-bʌɪ/ or *nimbuses.* See -US 1.

nimby. Plural *nimbys* or *nimbies.* A slogan that became an acronym that became a word that begat another word. The *OEC* data suggests that this originally US slogan-cum-acronym is nowadays as often or more often used in BrE. Standing for 'not in my back yard' it generally refers to people who object to the siting of something they dislike in their own neighbourhood, while not objecting to similar developments elsewhere. In this meaning it is often used as an attributive adjective, as in the last example below. The derivative **nimbyism** stands for the attitude adopted by *nimbys.* First recorded in 1980, for a while *nimby* was a vogue word, but now seems to have settled down as a standard part of English. Spelling in the *OED* quotations varies between *Nimby, NIMBY,* and *nimby,* but in the *OEC* data the last is standard. Examples: *It's an attitude referred to in the trade as NIMBY—'not in my* *backyard'*—*Chr. Sci. Monitor*, 1980; *every new road . . . , will be met by the thunderous coalition of young eco-warriors and middle-aged Nimbies*—*Independent*, 1997; *David Cameron himself has boldly warned his party that it can no longer be the home of the nimby vote*—*Guardian*, 2006.

nineties (and **twenties, thirties,** etc.). These words do not require an apostrophe (*the 'nineties,* etc.) when used for the years 0–9 of a decade, and still less for those of a person's life. Nor is an apostrophe needed in decades expressed in Arabic numerals, *the 1920s* (not *the 1920's*), *the 1930s, the 1990s,* etc.

nite. As a humorous spelling of *night,* it turns up, for example, in the work of the 19c. American humorist Artemus Ward (C. F. Browne), but was not commonly used in advertisements and neon signs (*nite club, nite life,* etc.) until the 1930s (later in BrE). It should not be used in general writing.

nitre. Spelt as shown in BrE, but as **niter** in AmE.

-n-, -nn-. The same rules as regards doubling of consonants apply to the letter *n* at the end of a word as apply to other final consonants. (i) Single-syllable words containing a simple vowel (*a, e, i, o, u*) before *n* normally double the consonant before suffixes beginning with a vowel (*tanned, penned, sinning, donnish*) or before a final *-y* (*sonny, funny*); (ii) the consonant remains undoubled if the stem contains a diphthong (*raining*), doubled vowel (*soonest*), or a vowel + consonant (*scorned, damnable, burning*). (iii) Words of more than one syllable follow the rule for monosyllables if their last syllable is accented, but otherwise do not double the *n*: accordingly *japánned* and *begínner;* but *wómanish, túrbaned, awákening, tobógganist, cóttony.*

no. 1 *As determiner.* = *'not a, not any'.* (*a*) Though hallowed by some eight centuries of usage, *no* accompanied by other negatives is now only dialectal or non-standard: e.g. *Don't try to con me with no such talk*—G. Ade, 1896; *He's not going to be put in no poorhouse*—*Listener,* 1968; *'Clouds come up,' she continued, 'but no rain never falls when you want it.'*—E. Jolley, 1980 (Aust.).

(*b*) We normally have the choice of placing the negative *not* with a verb or of using *no* with another element in the sentence without change of meaning: e.g. *I can't see any footprints/I can see no footprints.* But, as *CGEL* 10.58 points out, such pairs of sentences can often show a difference of meaning: e.g. *He is not a teacher* denotes that his occupation is not teaching (i.e. he is a banker, accountant, etc.); but *He is no teacher* indicates that he lacks the skills needed to be a good teacher.

(*c*) Misleading commas in adverbials containing *no.* Adverbial phrases containing *no* which negate the main verb in a clause must not be separated off by commas from the word they belong to as though they were mere parentheses. In other words, the information they contain is a crucial part of the meaning of the clause and is not merely supplementary. The rule only needs to be stated to be seen as sensible, for it is clear that it is as illogical to write *He will, under no circumstances, consent* as to write *He will, never, consent,* or *He will, not, consent.* Another example reinforces the point: *her knowledge that, under no circumstances, will her father return to Spain* (omit the commas). It is worth adding that it would often be better in these negative adverbial phrases to resolve *no* into *not . . . any* etc.: *We are assured that the Prime Minister will, in no circumstances and on no consideration whatever, consent* ('will not in any . . . or on any . . . '—or omit the commas, at the least); *Proposals which, under no possible circumstances, would lead to any substantial, or indeed perceptible, protection for a home industry* ('which would not lead under any . . . ' or 'which would under no possible circumstances lead . . . ').

(*d*) *Qualifying a gerund in the predicate, denoting the impossibility of the action specified.* Historical examples: *There is no healing of thy wounde*—*Bible* (Geneva), Nahum, 1560; *Do what they might, there was no keeping down the butcher*—W. Irving, 1820; *There's no accounting for tastes, sir*—Thackeray, 1850. Modern examples: *There was no denying that without Arabic I should not have been able to take charge of the boat*—W. Golding, 1985; *there was no knowing what a badly brought-up creature like that might not chop to pieces*—K. Amis, 1988.

2 *As adverb.* Uses of the adverb worthy of comment are: (*a*) = 'not'. Now only a Scottish use (where it may be a reduced form of *nocht* 'nought' in origin): e.g. *Oh, my dear, that'll no dae!*—R. L. Stevenson, *a*1894; *Who says the Scots are a dour lot? No' us anyway!*—Inverness newspaper, 1973.

(*b*) *whether or no.* Expressing the negative in an alternative choice, possibility, etc., this is now a rather dated or self-conscious alternative to *whether or not,* e.g. *A frog he would a-wooing go, Heigh ho! says Rowley, Whether his mother would let him or no*—traditional nursery rhyme, *c.*1809; *It was a half-baked eloquence . . . But half-baked or no, David rose to it greedily*—Mrs H. Ward, 1892; *In January, whether the shop were open or no was a matter of no great importance*—J. Bowen, 1986.

(*c*) In the representation of certain kinds of speech, especially of non-mother-tongue speakers, *no?* is often used as a tag question: *We all have families, no? We all need the family, also.*—M. Gee, 1985 (Frenchman speaking); *'Funny,' she added in an afterthought, 'that they sent it to me, no?'*—A. Desai, 1988 (context in India); *Can you not see, no?*—M. du Plessis, 1989 (Afrikaner speaking).

3 *As noun.* (*a*) The recommended plural is *noes* (*The noes have it,* the negative voters are in the majority). See -O(E)S 3. (*b*) When used to mean 'an utterance of the word *no,* a denial', the word *no,* by convention, is nowadays usually printed in roman and without surrounding quotation marks: e.g. *he would not take no for an answer; in answer to his question she gave a solemn no.*

noblesse /nəʊˈblɛs/. Use italics, especially in the phrase *noblesse oblige* /ɒˈbliːʒ/ 'privilege entails responsibility'.

nobody, no one. (*a*) Like *anybody* and *anyone, nobody* and *no one* are interchangeable in most contexts, e.g. *whether this was true or not nobody* (or *no one*) *can say for certain; No one* (or *Nobody*) *took a photograph.* (*b*) *Nobody* and *no one,* like other indefinite pronouns (see ANY), are frequently, though not without ferocious resistance from certain linguistic Luddites, followed by the plural pronouns *they, them,* or *their*: e.g. *Nobody wants to hear that* their *hero isn't a hero; No one likes to be turned out of quarters where* they *have lived comfortably for many years.* This kind of perfectly natural construction, which relies largely on notional agreement and is recorded in the *OED* from the 16c. onwards, is still being questioned in the 21c. by dinosaur editors wishing to justify their blinkered, ahistorical pedantry.

no-brainer should be written as shown, i.e. with a hyphen, not as two separate words, or joined up as one. First recorded from a US source in 1959, this informal term meaning 'an idea or choice that involves hardly any mental effort', while still most frequent in AmE, is used in other national varieties. It is particularly found in informal and semi-informal styles, such as blogs, sports writing, computing, and news. *If this was the first Christmas it would be a no-brainer as to what the three kings would turn up with at the manger. Forget the gold, frankincense and myrrh. It would be iPods, Play Stations and MP3s, or similar technomiracles*—*Irish News,* 2006.

nodus /ˈnəʊdəs/, a knotty point. Plural *nodi* /-dʌɪ/.

***nom de guerre*, nom de plume, pen name, pseudonym.** Here is a pretty kettle of fish and a quirky illustration of how English can borrow words from French (*nom de guerre*), invent them as if it had borrowed them (*nom de plume*), return them to the lender, and even translate these pretend-imports (*pen name*). (*a*) *Nom de guerre* (literally 'name of war', first recorded in English in 1680) is current French for an assumed name, but is far from universally intelligible to English-speakers, most of whom assume that, whatever else it may mean, it surely cannot mean 'pseudonym' or 'nom de plume', such as 'George Orwell' for Eric Arthur Blair. In fact, it has a broader range than its French original, is rarely used of writers' assumed names, and covers names assumed for various dubious reasons such as espionage and terrorism. Printed in italic. (*b*) *Nom de plume* was formed in English (first recorded in 1850) from the three corresponding French words (literally 'name of pen'); it apparently exists in French but was reimported from English. It is printed in roman type. (*c*) *Pen name* is a 19c. English translation of the faux-French *nom de plume.* It is generally written as two separate words. (*d*) This leaves *pseudonym,* which is a 19c. adaptation of French *pseudonyme* (from the Greek base *pseudo-* 'false' combining form + *-onym* 'name' combining form); cf. HOMONYM, SYNONYM, etc. It covers more than just literary assumed names, but is the most widely used for literary disguises. Of the four, *pseudonym* is the most frequently used; then in descending order *pen name, nom de plume, nom de guerre.*

nominal. For this as the adjective of *noun,* see NOUN.

nominative. The grammatical word is always pronounced /ˈnɒmɪnətɪv/, with /ə/ (uh) in the third syllable. The adjective connected in sense with **nominate** and **nomination** (e.g. *partly elective and partly nominative*) normally has /-eɪt-/ for its third syllable.

non-. Of all the negative prefixes (cf. A-1; DE-; DIS-; IN- AND UN-; UN-), none has thrived as abundantly as *non-*. Around us in so many everyday words, it is easily overlooked but repays investigation. **1** *History.* Though many current words with this prefix are relatively recent, native words formed with it, the *OED* explains, are found from the late 14c., many of them suggested by pre-existing Anglo-Norman or French formations. Until about the middle of the 17c. compounds with *non-* were mostly of a special or technical kind, but thereafter the prefix became less restricted and began to be prefixed freely to nouns, adjectives and adverbs, participles, and verbal nouns. Many new formations arose from the political and religious movements of the 17th and 18th centuries, e.g. *nonconformist* n., *non-resistance* n.

2 *A versatile prefix.* (*a*) The fact that *non-* can prefix so many different parts of speech contributes to its wide spread, e.g. (with nouns) *non-aggression* (1903); *non-arrival* (1665); *non-disclosure* (1897); *non-event* (1936); *non-fiction* (1909); (with adjectives) *non-assertive* (1842 in its grammatical meaning); *non-flammable* (1961); *non-returnable* (containers) (1903). Prefixed to verbs it creates adjectives that describe in a single word the benefits of certain products: *non-crease* (1936); *non-iron* (1957); *non-skid* (1905); *non-stick* (pan, etc., 1958).

(*b*) *Productive because non-judgemental.* A second reason for its prevalence is that it simply denotes the opposite of whatever it attaches to: *non-biological* washing powder, *non-edible* plants. It is in the interests of manufacturers to describe products as *non-biodegradable,* thereby purporting to state a mere fact; environmental campaigners make a value judgement with *unbiodegradable.* This contrast between *non-* and *un-* affects several word pairs; contrast *non-British,* meaning not from Britain, with *un-British,* meaning disagreeably out of step with whatever value or idea the writer describes or espouses. A similar dichotomy differentiates the following, to mention just a few: *non-academic/unacademic, non-Christian/unchristian, non-scientific/unscientific, non-sporting/unsporting, non-traditional/untraditional.*

3 *Hyphenation.* No hard-and-fast rule can be stated. As with other hyphenation questions, BrE favours inserting hyphens, while AmE favours omitting them. The *OED* puts hyphens in all its compounds, but *ODO* does not (e.g. *non-art/nonart, non-living/nonliving*). The dilemma does not arise with old-established words where *non-* is hardly felt to be a separate prefix at all, e.g. *nondescript, nonentity, nonsense, nonplussed,* etc.

nonce. In origin from Middle English *for than anes* (unrecorded) = for the one, altered by wrong division (cf. *a newt* for *an ewt*), it survives only in the old-fashioned phrase *for the nonce* 'for the time being, for the present occasion'; and in the compound *nonce word,* coined by James Murray himself, to denote a word only used on one occasion, e.g. *finneganswaked* in Anthony Burgess's *Inside Mr Enderby* (1963), 'the intermittent drone was finneganswaked by lightly sleeping Enderby into a parachronic lullaby chronicle'. This word has no connection with the homonymous slang word for a sexual offender.

nonchalant, nonchalance. Pronounced /ˈnɒnʃələnt/, /ˈnɒnʃələns/, i.e. as English words, but with /ʃ/ not /ʧ/.

non-count nouns. See COUNT NOUNS; MASS NOUN.

none. 1 *As pronoun.* It is a mistake to suppose that the pronoun is singular only and must at all costs be followed by singular verbs or pronouns. It should be borne in mind that *none* is not a shortening of *no one* but is the regular descendant of Old English *nān* (pronoun) 'none, not one'. At all times since the reign of King Alfred the choice of plural or singular in the accompanying verbs, etc., has been governed by the surrounding words or by the notional sense. When individuality is being emphasized, or when *none* refers to something that cannot be plural, a singular form is used: *a fear which we cannot know, which we cannot* *face, which none understands*—T. S. Eliot, 1935; *She is rather difficult to describe physically, for none of her features is particularly striking*—D. Lodge, 1962; *Except in the eye of God, none of these people was very interesting*—F. Tuohy, 1984; *I waited on, in the hope of further customers, but none was in the offing*—C. Rumens, 1987; *None of this was a matter of treachery*—P. Wright, 1987. When collectivity is the dominant notion, a plural form is used: *we were forced to develop arts organizations in places where there were none*—*Dædalus*, 1986; *None of our fundamental problems have been solved*—*London Rev. Bks*, 1987; *She also says that though she had many affairs, none were lighthearted romances*—*New Yorker*, 1987; *None of these situations exist here*—*Independent*, 2003.

Verdict: use a singular verb where appropriate but if the notion of plurality is present a plural verb has been optional since the OE period and in some circumstances is desirable. The type *None of them have finished their essays* is better than the clumsy ... *has finished his or her essay.*

2 *As adverb.* First recorded as an adverb in the 12c. but the earliest types of use have not survived in modern English. In the sense 'by no means, not at all', *none* (adverb) was common from the 17c. to the 19c. (e.g. *After some questioning, by which he saw that I was none informed regarding the page*—J. Galt, 1824); and remains in use in *none too* followed by an adjective (especially forming compounds). *I was none too sure of it*—A. Hope, 1896; *This none-too-accurate article on the DAE*—*Amer. Speech*, 1941; *it was seen as a none-too-subtle power-grab*—*OEC*, 2009.

nonentity is best written as a single, unhyphenated word. In the past it was occasionally written as two words, but more often with a hyphen, especially in the philosophical meaning 'something which does not exist, a non-existent thing'. Nowadays, the hyphenated form will be considered wrong in most contexts.

nonetheless, none the less. See NEVERTHELESS.

non-flammable. See FLAMMABLE.

nonplus /nɒn'plʌs/. **1** This verb, meaning 'to surprise and confuse (someone) so much that they are unsure how to react' hides its Latin origins and is also a venerable example of 'verbing'. It comes from the 16c. noun *nonplus*, now only very occasionally used, meaning originally 'a state in which nothing further can be said or done'; thence 'the state of being confused and surprised'; it is a combination of L *non* + *plus*, literally 'not more'. The past participle is spelt *nonplussed* about ten times as often as with a single *-s-*, in line with the rule that words of more than one syllable ending in vowel + consonant double that consonant if the last syllable is stressed (contrast *audited*). The *nonplused* spelling is largely confined to AmE, and recognized by Webster's Third, but not by the *OED* nor by *ODO*.

2 In NAmer. English a new use has developed in recent years, meaning 'unperturbed'—more or less the opposite of its traditional meaning—as in *he was clearly trying to appear nonplussed.* This new use probably arose on the assumption that *non-* was the normal negative prefix and must therefore have a negative meaning. It is not considered part of standard English, and is not common even in the AmE component of the *OEC*. Nor is it recognized by dictionaries—yet. Nevertheless, online comments about the word on the Merriam-Webster dictionary website suggest that many Americans take the word to mean this. Examples: (noun) *Reduced to a perfect nonplus, McCoy half-rose from his chair*—J. M. Dillard, 1989 (AmE); (verb in traditional meaning) *Control is a dominant theme in her work, but when I ask why, Haynes appears nonplussed. They are about relationships, she replies repeatedly*—*Independent*, 2012 (BrE); (verb in reverse meaning) *Scouting major Lawton is nonplused. He says that while he believes 'someone can be gay and it's totally cool', it's against what Scouting believes*—*Gay Opinion* blog, 2003 (AmE).

non-restrictive clauses. See RESTRICTIVE CLAUSES.

non-rhotic. See RHOTIC.

nonsense. Despite Gowers' (1965) insistence that such uses were unidiomatic, the alternative use of *nonsense* as a count noun (i.e. with *a* or in the plural) to mean 'a ridiculous notion or idea' became standard in the 20c. especially in BrE, and particularly in legal language. These uses are largely unknown in AmE. Examples: *I* *daresay I shall go on scribbling one nonsense or another to the end of the chapter*—Sir Walter Scott, 1803. *Everyone said, 'Lyne made a nonsense of the embarkation.'*—E. Waugh, 1942; *I would do everything I could to ensure the nonsenses of NHS finances are exposed*—*Croydon Guardian*, 2004.

non sequitur /nɒn 'sɛkwɪtə/, a conclusion that does not logically follow from the premise or premises (from Latin, literally 'it does not follow') is written as two separate words, unhyphenated, and printed in roman. Thus: *It will be a hard winter, for holly-berries* [which are meant as provision for birds in hard weather] *are abundant.* The reasoning called *post hoc, ergo propter hoc* is a form of *non sequitur.*

non-U. See U AND NON-U.

no one, no person, nobody. Spelt as shown (no hyphen). Contrast the sense in *No one person was guilty.* See NOBODY.

no place, noplace. As adverb (also sometimes written with a hyphen) meaning 'nowhere', fairly firmly restricted to informal use in AmE: e.g. *You're going no place until Herb gets here*—M. Pugh, 1969.

no problem used in certain situations in response to 'thank you', 'thanks', etc. irritates some people like nobody's business. Critics are often very literal-minded (i.e. 'By saying this are you suggesting that there might have been a problem?') or they take issue with the informality of the response, insisting that phrases such as 'You're welcome', 'It's a pleasure' are preferable. A third line of attack, by people who write about appropriate language in business, is that the phrase contains two negative words and therefore creates a negative impression of the speaker.

Nothing that can be said here will cause the phrase to be used less. Moreover, it is worth pointing out that social situations of the kind in which it occurs often involve formulaic language, and it can be argued that *no problem* is just a more recent formula which people over a certain age have not yet got used to. As often turns out to be the case after investigation, the reviled phrase has been around longer than one might suppose. According to the *OED*, Martin Amis used it in his 1973 *Rachel Papers.* John Osborne, in the 20 June 1992 issue of *The Spectator,* called it 'peoplespeak' and gave an example of a different but related use: *Last week, on doctor's orders, I telephoned a pathology factory to organise a blood test. 'No problem.' How can they possibly know until I've had it? But I do hope they're right.* One assumes he deliberately missed the point, that it was the test, not the result, that was *no problem.*

nor. **1** The primary use of *nor* is as a coordinator after *neither* e.g. *neither my grandmother nor my grandfather had much formal education; his reassurance had in a way been neither here nor there at the time; unable to understand anything, neither what she had just seen nor the support of his expression,* or other negative or implied negative (e.g. *that is not why I want to marry Bertrand nor why he wants to marry me*). As the examples show, the words following *neither* . . . *nor* can be nouns, noun phrases, adverbial phrases, or clauses of various types.

2 On the type *Neither Anabel nor Mark are in London* (M. Wesley, 1983), see NEITHER 4.

3 *neither* . . . *nor* . . . *nor. Nor* can be used to introduce a third or further item: e.g. *Neither rain, nor cold, nor obscure polling places could keep voters from their civic duty yesterday* (referring to the US presidential election of Nov. 1992); *But the comment that receives the heartiest agreement concerns neither the war, nor the earthquake, nor the crime rate*—*Observer Mag.,* 1992.

4 *CGEL* (13.36) points out that in non-correlative sentences containing a negative in the first element *neither* and *nor* are sometimes interchangeable: e.g. *They never forgave him for the insult, neither* (or *nor*) *could he rid himself of the feelings of guilt for having spoken in that way.*

5 *Nor* is occasionally used when there is no negative present or implied in the first clause. Such constructions were formerly more common (16–19c. in the *OED*, e.g. *His Age and Courage weigh: Nor those alone*—Dryden, 1697) than they are now. But the construction is still standard though rather formal: e.g. *Practically all the sovereign rights and powers of the smaller political units—all of them that are significant enough to be worth absorbing—have been absorbed by the federal unit;*

nor is this all—*Ludwig von Mises Institute*, 2009.

6 The correlative construction *nor . . . nor*, once common (e.g. *Nor Bits nor Bridles can his Rage restrain*—Dryden, 1697), is now only archaic or poetical.

7 Correlative constructions of the type *either . . . nor* and *neither . . . or*, being on the face of it illogical, should be avoided. But see NEITHER 6.

normalcy. *MWCDEU* states that *'Normalcy* became a notorious word during the 1920 Presidential election, when Warren G. Harding proclaimed that what the country needed was a return to the "normalcy" of the days before World War I.' (As the same source points out, it was widely believed that Harding had simply and incorrectly made the word up.) Since then its notoriety has come and gone in AmE, but lingers in BrE, where **normality** is the customary word. It may surprise people that the competing abstract nouns *normalcy, normality,* and *normalness* all entered the language at approximately the same time, in the middle of the 19c. The surprise is perhaps reduced when it is noticed that the adjective *normal* itself, though recorded in the 17c. in the sense 'rectangular', did not acquire its modern everyday meaning until about 1840.

Of the three, *normalness* has hardly taken on at all. Across all varieties of English, *normality* is the more frequent form. *Normalcy* is rare (and disliked) in BrE, but in NAmer. (especially US) English it is the more frequent form. Elsewhere, *normality* outstrips *normalcy* by varying margins, except in Indian and East Asian English, where *normalcy* is, as it were, the norm.

Examples of *normalcy*: *partly in order to tidy up, tidy the room and restore it to normalcy*—A. Desai, 1988 (Indian); *such a surfeit of civility and normalcy from people who will pay with cash instead of cheques or credit cards in the morning*—F. Kidman, 1988 (NZ); *Every effort is made to suggest that a certain 'normalcy' prevails, that relations remain roughly as they were*—*Dædalus*, 1992. And an example of the standard BrE form *normality*: *The morning passed slowly, uneventfully, and with a beguiling normality*—A. Brookner, 1989.

northward(s). As adjective before a noun (*in a northward direction*) always *northward*. As adverb either *northward* (*he travelled northward*) or *northwards* (the latter form esp. in BrE).

nosey, a variant of NOSY.

nostrum. Plural *nostrums,* not *nostra.* See -UM 1.

nosy. The adjective, 'inquisitive', etc. and the verb are preferably spelt as shown. The verb inflections are *nosies, nosying* (or *noseying*), *nosied.*

not.

1 Normal uses.
2 Printing *not* or *n't*.
3 *not all/all . . . not.*
4 *not unnoticed, not ungrateful*, etc.
5 Confusion caused by repeated *nots*.
6 Superfluous *not*.
7 *not only . . . (but (also)).*
8 *Not I* or *not me*? Case of following pronoun.
9 *not but.*
10 Unusual placement of *not*.
11 *better not, best not.*
12 *whether or not.*

1 *Normal uses.* These include the types (i) 'auxiliary verb + not + bare infinitive' (*I do not believe that Shelley could have written these lines; one should not rule out the possibility*); (ii) negation of an adjective or noun (*appearances that are and are not identical; I'm not a tyrant*); (iii) *not* followed by an adverb (*not entirely, not merely, not really, not simply, not sufficiently, not surprisingly*). (iv) It can negate a clause (*I'll do it, not that I don't think you're perfectly capable of dealing with it*). (v) It is frequently used in association with *but* (*Shelley's sonnet is not a specific critique but at most an 'indirect response'*) and with *even* (*No, that is arrogant and not even true*); see also *not only . . .* (*but* (*also*)), 7 below.

2 Printing *not* or *n't.* In formal prose it is traditional to print *not* in full, rather than contracting it to *-n't* when joined to a preceding auxiliary or modal verb (e.g. *we cannot, do not, should not,* etc.) This rule is now less rigorously applied than it used to be, and whether to apply it depends very much on individual and house editorial styles. In conversations and other informal contexts in fiction the reduced forms are almost always printed: e.g. *It wasn't true; I don't suppose it was difficult; he couldn't keep his eyes off it; so that she* *shouldn't see his distress; you can't mourn for unborn grandchildren; They wouldn't want anyone to know.* It is also a trend in modern business writing to use contracted forms, but in academic work they are often avoided.

3 *not all/all ... not.* Depending on their respective positions in the clause, *not* in conjunction with *all* might create ambiguity. Fowler (1926) cited the best-known example, Shakespeare's *All that glisters is not gold* (from *The Merchant of Venice* II. vii. 66). This and analogous constructions are sometimes viewed as not strictly logical, since Shakespeare's phrase 'ought' to mean 'everything that glisters is not gold', and non-native speakers it seems may interpret it in that way. Technically, this is an issue of what is termed the 'scope' of the negation: in such constructions the scope of the negative *not* is, unusually, extended backwards to include the subject of the clause, so that the meaning is equivalent to 'Not all that glisters is gold' (i.e. some things that glister are indeed gold).

It would be futile to try to change the proverb now, but caution is desirable when in other contexts *not* immediately precedes *all*. (Similar problems can arise with any of the 'universal' pronouns and determiners, *each, every, everybody,* etc.) Thus *Not all children of five can recite the alphabet* means that only some of them can. *All children of five cannot recite the alphabet* can (just) mean the same, but is in danger of being treated as meaning 'No children of five can recite the alphabet'. An American columnist, James J. Kilpatrick, in the *Chicago Sun-Times* (10 Mar. 1991) cited several ambiguous uses of *all, everybody,* etc. ... *not* from AmE sources, including the following: *All television Westerns haven't ridden off into the sunset; Everybody in America is not a good person and everybody in politics is not a good person; Every woman does not aspire to be a mother; All the people living around local courses are not golfers.*

4 *not unnoticed, not ungrateful,* etc. By means of a device known technically as litotes, it is a well-established practice to use *not* with negative adjectives, adverbs, and past participles, to imply the affirmative term: *at length Not unamaz'd, she thus in answer spake*—Milton, 1667; *We say well and elegantly, not ungrateful, for very grateful*—tr. Erasmus, 1671; *Not unclever but importunate*—Earl Malmesbury, 1794; *It is ... certainly true—and has not gone unnoticed—that the language* [etc.]—T. Tanner, 1986. This type of double negation attenuates the strength of the implied affirmative: to say that something is *not unwelcome* means that it will be quietly and grudgingly welcomed rather than being rapturously greeted with riotous huzzahs and fireworks.

The 18c. grammarian Lindley Murray was perhaps the first to distinguish such repeated negatives from DOUBLE NEGATIVES (which he roundly condemned): 'Two negatives, in English, destroy one another, or are equivalent to an affirmative ... "His language, though inelegant, is *not ungrammatical*"; that is, "it is grammatical"' (*English Grammar,* 1795, cited from an edn of 1824, p. 172). Fowler (1926) acutely noted that 'the very popularity of the idiom in English is proof enough that there is something in it congenial to the English [*sc.* British] temperament, and it is pleasant to believe that it owes its success with us to a stubborn national dislike of putting things too strongly.'

5 Confusion caused by repeated *not*s. In some types closely related to those in the previous section, *not* is slightly (or startlingly) confusing, so that one is required to do, as it were, some mental arithmetic to work out the intended meaning: e.g. (slightly) *Not that watching the 'park' at work has not been every bit as interesting as watching the subjects which we have set off to investigate—Spectator,* 1988; (startlingly) *This is not to say that I do not think that some of the dissents are not preferrable* [*sic*] *and not to publish them would hurt everyone—Bull. Amer. Acad. Arts & Sci.*, 1988.

6 Superfluous *not. Not* is sometimes introduced in a subordinate clause as an echo of an actual or virtual negative in the main clause in a way that may seem at first sight superfluous, e.g. *I shouldn't wonder if it* didn't *turn to snow now.* This is not uncommon in unscripted speech, and can be interpreted as a way of reinforcing the uncertainty expressed in the main clause by the use of *not, nobody,* or a negated adjective, as in the next examples: *Nobody can predict with confidence how much time may* not *be employed on the concluding stages of the Bill; He is unable to say how much of the portraiture of Christ may* not *be due to the* *idealization of His life and character; I shouldn't be surprised if the Secretary of State* didn't *agree with the trade union about this.* In writing, inserting such a *not* can sometimes make the writer express the opposite of what he or she intended: *It is hard not to conclude that there was not a cynical and calculating element to the performance—Independent,* 2006 (read: *that there was a cynical and calculating element* . . .).

7 *not only* . . . (*but* (*also*)). *Not only* out of place, said Fowler (1926), is 'like a tintack loose on the floor; it might have been most serviceable somewhere else, and is capable of giving acute pain where it is'. Or, as it is less colourfully expressed in *OMEU* (1983): '*Not only* should always be placed next to the item which it qualifies, and not in the position before the verb. This is a fairly common slip, e.g. *Katherine's marriage not only kept her away, but at least two of Mr. March's cousins* (C. P. Snow); *kept not only her* would be better. If placing it before the verb is inevitable, the verb should be repeated after *but* (*also*), e.g. *It not only brings the coal out but brings the roof down as well* (George Orwell).' Examples of correct placement (including cases where the second correlative *but* (*also*) is idiomatically omitted): *To deliberately change anything requires* not only *courage* but *the greatest motivation*—C. Burns, 1985; *He was proof that a breakthrough into the new world was* not only *possible, it was a fact*—D. Malouf, 1985; *men who* not only *rhymed Moon with June* but also *thought they were spelt the same way—Sunday Times,* 1987. *Rowers* not only *face backward, they race backward—New Yorker,* 1988; Examples of incorrect placement cited by Fowler (1926): Not only *had she now a right to speak,* but *to speak with authority* (she had now a right not only to speak); Not only *does the proportion of suicides vary with the season of the year,* but *with different races* (the proportion of suicides varies not only with).

8 *Not I* or *not me*? Case of following pronoun. According to the *OED,* when *not* emphasizes a pronoun after a negative statement, or in a reply, it is traditionally followed by the subjective case of a pronoun, and this statement is, no doubt, historically true: *He is no Witch, not he*—Dekker et al., *c.*1625; *He didn't care for himself—not he*—Thackeray, 1847–8; *They are not to be 'had' by a bit of worm on the end of a hook* . . . *not they!*—J. K. Jerome, 1889.

In literary contexts the subjective case is still often used: e.g. *Not I, not I, but the wind that blows through me!*—D. H. Lawrence, 1917; *And so it is my mother who's told the lie, not he*—N. Gordimer, 1990; *But I don't like it either; I just put up with it. Not he*—A. Brookner, 1991; *This woman is a skeleton, not I*—J. Shute, 1992. However, these last three examples clearly show how the use of the subjective case marks these sentences as almost self-consciously literary: in the written examples below, the objective case reads much more naturally. And in conversation, use of the subjective case would sound starchily affected. '*You were all in the same room together, were not you?' 'No, indeed, not us.'*—J. Austen, 1811; *She should be here, not me, it's a good setting for her*—M. Wesley, 1983; *It wasn't that she hated living in Johannesburg. Many did of course. Not her*—M. du Plessis, 1989; *He shook his head. 'you're wrong. Not her.'*—A. Billson, 1993.

See CASES 5.

9 *not but.* (*a*) *Meaning 'only, merely, just'.* From the 14c. to the 16c. *not but* stood side by side with *nobbut* (from *no* adverb + *but* conjunction). At that point *nobbut* gradually retreated into dialect use and is now so restricted: *I nobbut wanted to know if they'd gotten him cleared?*—Mrs Gaskell, 1855; *It's nobbut Thursday, isn't it? Well it seems like months*—J. B. Priestley, 1929. *Not but* as an adverbial phrase became obsolete in the 16c., but re-emerged (? only in the US) in the 20c.: *When I was not but eight, I wrote a poem named 'God's Garden'*—L. Smith, 1983 (US); '*She's not but twenty-three,' Cobb said to his stepfather. 'You think she's into capital gains and tax shelters?'—New Yorker,* 1988; *when she spotted her father with his men not but a hundred yards off—Rein of Blood,* 2002 (US). (*b*) *not* . . . *but. Mrs Fraser's book, however, is* not *confined to filling up the gaps in Livingstone's life* . . . but *it deals most interestingly with her father's own early adventures.* In such sentences the subject must not be repeated (or, as here, be taken up by a pronoun). The above sentence is easily made right by omitting it.

10 Unusual placement of *not.* (*a*) *'Splitting' an infinitive. Not* is routinely used before a *to*-infinitive, negating all that follows it: *But he preferred not to torture himself with the specific knowledge*—A. N. Wilson, 1986; *Lisa was enrolled in the Church of England in order not to give offence*—P. Lively, 1987; *She tried not to watch Oscar count out his farthings*—P. Carey, 1988. But, not uncommonly, *not* is placed between ('splits') the *to* and its infinitive. This has the effect of emphasizing the negation of the verb in question. *It was wrong to not love them*—P. Carey, 1985; *a perfect morning to not read 'Moby Dick'*—New Yorker, 1986; *I thought about how good it would be to not have Christmas but to be off in a room by myself*—D. Vaughan, 1986; *My advice to any woman who earns the reputation of being capable, is to not demonstrate her ability too much*—M. Spark, 1988.

(*b*) *In subjunctive clauses.* From about 1400 until the 19c. *not* was frequently placed immediately before a finite verb in the indicative mood: e.g. *I not doubt He came aliue to Land*—Shakespeare, 1610. This use has now lapsed but it survives in certain kinds of subjunctive clauses (especially in AmE): e.g. *Aunt Clara preferred that I not ransack the memories of her mother and Uncle Eugene*—D. Pinckney, 1992 (US); *McCain quickly asked that he not be considered*—*Time*, 2000. See SUBJUNCTIVE MOOD 3(d).

11 *better not, best not.* The use of these phrases without a preceding *had* or *'d* (cf. better 2), is sometimes found in standard colloquial use in Britain, but is much more common in North America, Australia, and New Zealand. Examples: *I don't know what you're saying, but it better not be about me*—B. Oakley, 1985 (Aust.); *'Better not tell Willy what?' says Willy*—J. Elliott, 1985 (UK); *Well, I better not hear any complaints about how American tourists are staying away*—T. Clancy, 1987 (US); *I was about to double up for a good laugh. 'Better not,' Arnez said. 'Better not.'*—D. Pinckney, 1992 (US); *'I better not right now, Louise,' said Dan*—*New Yorker*, 1992. In the UK, *best not* (a reduced form of the much older idiom *I/you* etc. *had best not*) is the more usual colloquial construction. Examples: *Charlotte said, 'Best not fall in the marsh in them.'*—J. Gardam, 1985; *if you want to play Greta Garbo, best not do it with a journalist present*—*Scotland on Sunday*, 2003.

12 *whether or not.* See WHETHER 2.

See also BECAUSE C. For *cannot* (*help*) *but*, see BUT 7; HELP (verb) 3.

notary public. Plural *notaries public.*

nothing. For *is* or *has nothing to do with*, see IS 6.

noticeable. Spelt as shown, not *noticable.* See MUTE E.

notional agreement (Also called **notional concord**). Strict grammatical agreement (or concord) is essential in most circumstances in standard English, but there are some contexts in which this strictness is overridden and what linguists call 'notional agreement' occurs. This is when the verb agrees in number with the idea or 'notion' contained in the subject noun or pronoun, e.g. *The* jury *reached* their *decision; but* no one *hates it*, do they?, in both of which the subject is implicitly plural. Such notional agreement accounts for some of the cruxes of grammatical dispute. See also AGREEMENT 5, 6, 7.

not to worry. There are two intriguing things about this phrase. The first is the unique way it uses the *to*-infinitive as a quasi-imperative (related to the type *Laura told her not to worry*—E. Jolley, 1980). Historically, this structure was preceded by the word *please*, e.g. *please not to mention that again*—G. Eliot, 1872. In its modern form without *please* this idiom first emerged in BrE (see 1958 example below). The second point is that when this Britishism was taken up in AmE, it was criticized by usage commentators there, in a reversal of the usual trend for Brits to dislike Americanisms. According to the *OEC* data, the phrase is now as often used in AmE as in BrE, and is also used in other varieties of English. It is not a completely set idiom, in that it allows a small range of other verbs, e.g. *fear, fret*, etc. Examples: *Not to worry. By the time he ... had finished with me ... I'd be doing long division*—*Daily Mail*, 1958; *'Not to worry, no hero or anti-hero is killed off,' he continued*—*NYT*, 2011 (US); *the sense that they might have created unrealistically high expectations for their next album. Not to fear: Jaga have created unreal studio versions of their new material*—*Eye Weekly* (Toronto), 2005.

nought. See NAUGHT 2.

noughties. There has never been universal consensus about what to call the first decade of the 21c. Proposals made before or during include *aughts, zeros, two* *thousands*, and *oh ohs*. Now that we are well into the second decade, the issue is fading from relevance, but the *noughties* (proposed in 1989) is the word that seems to have taken the firmest root in BrE. (In AmE it is hampered by the fact that *nought* is far less used than in Britain.) The alternative spelling **naughties** is rather less common. And possibly neither has flourished because, as the BBC put it on the very first day of the new millennium, when spoken '"noughties" still sounds like a word East End villains might use to describe imprisonable activities or even worse a polite, middle-class code for the reproductive organs'. Examples: Desperate Housewives *has been the ratings hit of the year, and probably of the naughties—so far—www.crikey.com.au*, 2005; *Tonight will see the live climax of The Big Reunion, the hit reality show about 1990s and noughties bands reforming—Guardian*, 2013.

noun. **1** *Proper nouns* name particular people or things of which there is usually only one example (*Darwin*), places (*Paris*), months (*January*), days (*Friday*), etc., and are always written with a capital initial letter. All other nouns (*bottle, diary, fate, hand, happiness, marriage*, etc.) are *common nouns*. Common nouns, in turn, are categorized as *concrete* when they refer to physical things and beings (*bread, flower, man, tiger*) and *abstract* when they refer to ideas, qualities, or states (*cost, greed, helpfulness, philosophy, sleep*). Some nouns are concrete and abstract in different meanings, e.g. *cheek* is concrete when it refers to part of the face and abstract when it means 'impertinence'. See also ABSTRACT NOUNS; COUNT NOUNS; NON-COUNT NOUNS.

2 Two adjectives exist to describe anything to do with nouns—*nominal* (first recorded in this sense *c*.1430) and *nounal* (1871). The objection to the traditional form *nominal* is that it is a word much used in other meanings. This led some grammarians to favour the ill-formed word *nounal*. In practice, however, *noun* by itself is sufficient in attributive use (*noun classes, noun clause, noun phrase*, etc.), and this form should be used whenever possible. If a 'real' adjectival form is called for (e.g. to contrast with *adjectival, adverbial*, etc.), then *nominal* is recommended.

noun and verb accent, pronunciation, and spelling. When, for historical reasons, a word does double duty as a noun and a verb, English has from almost the earliest times shown a strong tendency to differentiate the two by pronunciation, as in *use* (noun with final voiceless /s/, verb with final voiced /z/). Since the letter *s* can be pronounced as a voiced or voiceless consonant, the distinction does not need to be reflected in the spelling, but with other letters it does, e.g. *bath* (noun)/*bathe* (verb), *calf* (noun)/*calve* (verb). A large number of two-syllable nouns and verbs are also distinguished by the placing of the stress, the normal pattern being to stress nouns on the first syllable and verbs on the second, e.g. *áccent* (noun), *accént* (verb); *cómpound* (noun), *compóund* (verb). The following lists are illustrations of the main types and are not intended to be exhaustive.

1 Two-syllable nouns and verbs distinguished by the placing of the stress (normally on the first syllable for the noun, and the second syllable for the verb): *accent, commune, compound, concert, conduct, confine(s), conflict, conscript, consort, contest, contract, contrast, convert, convict, decrease, defect, dictate, digest, discord, discount, discourse, escort, export, extract, ferment, import, imprint, incline, increase, indent, inlay, insert, insult, produce, prospect, record, reject, suspect, transfer.*

2 Such pairs are sufficiently numerous to make it seem that the distinction might be a regular one. However, it should be noted that RP has any number of pairs in which the stress falls in the same place in both noun and verb (e.g. *cómpost* (noun and verb), *concérn, cóncrete, consént, diréct, dislíke, displáy*), so that it is impossible to assume that the matter is governed by simple rules. There are other pairs in which the pattern is still changing, e.g. see PRESAGE.

3 Pairs of nouns and verbs distinguished by the nature of the final consonant. (*a*) Spelt the same: *abuse, close* (noun, cathedral close), *excuse, grease* (verb sometimes /griːz/), *house, misuse, mouth, use.* (*b*) With change of spelling: *advice/advise, bath/bathe, belief/believe, breath/breathe, calf/calve, cloth/clothe, glass/glaze, grass/graze, grief/grieve, half/halve, life/live, loss/lose, practice/practise* (BrE), *proof/prove, relief/relieve, safe/save, sheath/sheathe, shelf/shelve, strife/strive, thief/thieve, teeth/teethe, wreath/wreathe.*

nouns as verbs. See CONVERSION 1, 3; VERBING.

nouveau riche in the form shown can refer either to a single person who has recently acquired wealth or to the whole class of such people. There is also a plural form *nouveaux riches,* pronounced the same as the singular. Both are printed in roman. The singular and plural spelling should be kept rigorously distinct, not betwixted and betweened as in the last two examples below. In the 19c. this word, meaning literally 'new rich', was a coded and somewhat dismissive way of differentiating those, often aristocrats, who had inherited wealth from those who had merely acquired it. Nowadays it is often a neutral statement of fact with no such condemnatory overtones. Examples: (singular) *You never pass by the white and modern mansion of a nouveau riche*—E. Bulwer-Lytton, 1828; (plural) *The society of the Second Empire—the courtesans, the financiers, the foreign adventurers, the nouveaux riches*—T. Aronson, 1978; *a class of nouveau riche keen for the goddesses to intercede and protect their business interests*—S. Broughton et al., 2000; **China*'s *fast-growing class of nouveaux riche—Asian Economic News,* 2001; **But I've witnessed the nouveau riches using coupons and racking up frequent flyer miles—Business Pundit,* 2003.

novecento. See TRECENTO.

now (adjective). Adjectival or attributive uses are recorded in standard sources from the 15c. onwards (e.g. *The dreadful treatment of the now king*—Burke, 1793), but were falling into disuse by the end of the 19c. The adjectival use was revived in the 1960s in the sense 'modern, fashionable, up-to-date' with reference to the allegedly exciting innovations of that time (e.g. *Even a poet as now as Dylan has two kinds of female character in his imagery*—G. Greer, 1970). This use is now firmly established, especially in BrE, in the kind of breathless, fey, vacuous language one associates with puffery and self-aggrandisement of various orders: *R&B star Ms Dynamite said the new recording was 'totally different' from its predecessors. She said: 'Musically, it is very now. Very current. I really like it—Irish Examiner,* 2004.

no way. See WAY 1.

nowt. This northern English dialectal variant of *nought* 'nothing' made inroads into colloquial standard English during the 20c., especially in the phrase *There's nowt so* (or *as*) *queer as folk* (e.g. *Patrick went back to reflecting how there was nowt as queer as folk*—K. Amis, 1988). Genuinely dialectal uses of the word also turn up in speech and writing in national sources: *Getting owt for nowt, it's useless*—a Tynesider speaking on BBC Radio 2; *Well I tell you, there's nowt that's cheap if you want fruit*—J. Winterson, 1985 (Lancashire speaker in context). See also OWT.

nth. Pronounced /εnθ/. In mathematics, *n* is used to indicate an indefinite number, that is, a number that is contextually determined (e.g. *Even an* n-*dimensional series of such terms ... is still denumerable*—B. Russell, 1903; *Relations ... are accordingly named dyadic, triadic,* (*or, for* n *terms,* n-*adic*)—E. Bach, 1964). From the mid-19c., by a natural extension of meaning, *to the nth power* or *degree* came to mean 'to any required power; hence fig. to any extent, to the utmost'. Fowler (1926), in his spirited way, rejected the extended use as a 'popularized technicality' and 'wrong', but his view has not prevailed, and the lay application of *nth* is now standard: e.g. *The Neapolitan ... is an Italian to the nth degree.*

nubile. Ancient lechers who leer at female flesh which they cliché as *nubile* might be shocked by the original meaning of this word, for making 'honest women' of the objects of their desire is usually the last thing on their mind. Used in English in its classical Latin (*nūbilis*) meaning 'marriageable; of an age suitable for marriage' since the 17c., the word degenerated into 'sexually attractive' in the second half of the 20c., and this later sense is now the dominant one.

nuclear. The generally accepted pronunciation is /ˈnjuːklɪə/. The oft-derided pronunciation as if it were spelt *nuc-u-lar* (cf. *circular, particular, secular,* etc.) is well documented in America and is particularly associated with several leading politicos, including Eisenhower and George 'Dubya' Bush. *MWCDEU* provides a well-argued and thorough analysis of the phonological reasons for certain speakers' pronouncing the word as *nuc-u-lar,* and says they 'have succumbed to the gravitational tug of a far more prevalent pattern', since there is only one other reasonably common word that ends in unstressed /-klɪə(r)/, namely *cochlear,* and several that end in *-ular* (see above); but it admits that those who adopt President Eisenhower's form 'are likely to draw some unfriendly attention from those who consider it an error'.

nucleus /ˈnjuːklɪəs/. Plural *nuclei* /-lɪʌɪ/, rather than *nucleuses*.

number (as a grammatical concept). See AGREEMENT.

number, as a noun of multitude in the structure '*a number of* + pl. noun', normally governs a plural verb in both BrE and AmE because the plural noun is regarded as the 'head' of the noun phrase and therefore as the real subject: *A number of books by ballerinas have been published lately—New Yorker*, 1987; *Fortunately, a number of strategies* are *available to mitigate problems caused by severe weather—OEC*, 2004. By contrast, the structure '*the number of* + pl. noun' normally governs a singular verb, because the head of the noun phrase is *number*: *The number of MPs has increased—Daily Tel.*, 1987; *As the number of people in the water rises, so do the odds that attacks will occur—BusinessWeek*, 2001.

numeracy is a word coined by the Committee on Education presided over by Sir Geoffrey Crowther in 1959. The committee defined it as 'not only the ability to reason quantitatively but also some understanding of scientific method and some acquaintance with the achievements of science'. Clearly there was a need for such a word, and it, together with **numerate**, long ago settled into the standard language.

numerals. The writing and printing of figures and numerals is a highly specialized matter: for detailed guidance readers are referred to the *New Hart's Rules*. In general, numerals are used in more factual or statistical contexts and words are used (especially with numbers under a hundred) in more descriptive material: *I have lived in the same house for twelve years*; *The survey covers a period of 12 years*. Some selected examples (drawn mostly from *Hart*) must suffice here. **1** *Words or figures.* Figures should be used when the matter consists of a sequence of stated quantities: *Figures for September show the supply to have been 85,690 tons, a decrease in the month of 57 tons. The past 12 months show a net increase of 5 tons*; *The smallest tenor suitable for ten bells is D flat, of 5 feet diameter and 42 cwt.* This applies generally to all units of measurement—tons, cwt., feet, as above, also of area, volume, time, force, electrical units, etc.

Separate objects, animals, ships, persons, etc., are not units of measurement unless they are treated statistically: *A four-cylinder engine of 48 b.h.p. compared with a six-cylinder engine of 65 b.h.p.*; *The peasant had only four cows*; *A farm with 40 head of cattle.*

In descriptive matter, numbers under 100 should be in words; but write *90 to 100,* not *ninety to 100.* Write as words in such instances as: *With God a thousand years are but as one day*; *I have said so a hundred times.*

2 *Numerals generally.* Insert commas with four or more figures, as *7,642* and *525,500*; write dates without commas, as *1993*; omit commas in figures denoting pagination, column numbers, and line numbers in poetry; also in library shelf-marks, as *Harleian MS 24456.* In decimals use the full point, as *7.06*; and write *0.76,* not *.76.* Similarly in writing the time of day: *4.30 p.m.* and, with the 24-hour clock, *00.31, 22.15.* In references to pagination, dates, etc., use the least number of figures possible; for example, write *30–1, 42–3, 132–6, 1841–5, 1990–1*; but write e.g. *10–11,* not *10–1; 16–18,* not *16–8; 116–18,* not *116–8*; *210–11,* not *210–1*; *314–15,* not *314–5* (i.e. for the group 10–19 in each hundred). The numbers from one to ten should always be written in full. Do not contract dates involving different centuries, e.g. 1798–1810 not 1798–810.

In collective numbers: either *from 280 to 300*; or *280–300*; not *from 280–300* (which shows a mixture of styles). Do not begin a sentence with an Arabic numeral. Thus write *Eighty-seven Coalition aircraft attacked targets near Baghdad on Monday,* not *87 Coalition aircraft* ... It is also desirable to avoid placing arabic figures next to each other in this manner: *The theatre can accommodate 700, 450 of whom are in the stalls.* Reword as ..., *of whom 450 are in the stalls.*

See also AD; BC; BILLION; DATE 2.

numerous. Fowler (1926) was adamant that *numerous* is solely an adjective, i.e. meaning 'great in number' (*received* *numerous gifts*) or 'consisting of many' (*a numerous family*). Dictionaries, however, and usage guides, not to mention Thackeray, disagree: like VARIOUS, it can occasionally function as a pronoun in the structure *various* + *of* + plural, typically in informal style. Examples: *Mr. Mick ... brought numerous of his comrades with him*—Thackeray, *Barry Lyndon*, 1844; *An additional struggle that these carers I have named, and numerous of their colleagues, are enduring*—*Queensland Parl. Debates*, 1995; *I cannot begin to imagine how much offence this has caused numerous of your viewers throughout the country*—weblog, 2004.

nuncio. Plural *nuncios*. See -O(E)S 5.

nursling. Now the recommended spelling, rather than *nurseling*.

nurturance, 'emotional and physical nourishment and care', used instead of the verbal noun **nurturing**. Introduced in 1938 in the technical language of psychologists, the word is still largely confined to technical and scientific books and journals, and is most often found in AmE. A modern example: *Compared to girls, boys are also less likely to receive warmth and nurturance*—*Internat. Jrnl of Men's Health*, 1992.

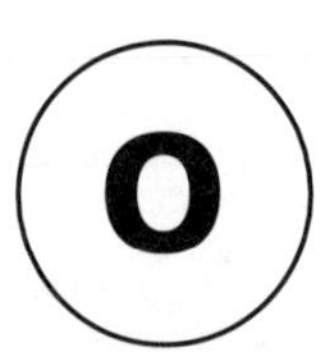

-o is a suffix used to combine words. On the analogy of Greek combinations in *-o* (e.g. λευκόχλωρος 'pale green'; cf. λευκός 'white'), and their adaptations and imitations in Latin, late or medieval, like *Gallograeci, Anglosaxonicus*, etc., *-o-* has come to be the usual connecting vowel in English combinations of various kinds: in ethnic names, as *Anglo-Saxon, Indo-European*, etc.; in scientific terms generally, as *electromagnetic, psychotherapy*. Typical examples of *-o* appended to the stems of English words of classical origin include *chloro-, cirrho-, pneumo-; dramatico-, economico-, historico-, politico-*. Two main developments have occurred in English: **1** The creation of imitative (i.e. non-classical) formations within English, e.g. *cottonocracy, meritocracy; gasometer, speedometer* (a notorious example, *speed* being a word of native origin).

2 The emergence of curtailed words in *-o* such as *chromo* (short for *chromolithograph*), *dynamo* (short for *dynamo-electric machine*), *electro* (short for *electro-plate, -plating*), *photo* (short for *photograph*).

-o. For the plural forms of nouns ending in *-o*, see -O(E)S.

oaf. Plural *oafs.* The plural form *oaves* occurred sporadically in the 19c.

O and Oh. There is no exceptionless rule in the matter, but the usual practice is to use *O* (especially in poetry) when a name being addressed or invoked follows, and when it is not separated by punctuation from what follows, and to use *Oh* as an independent exclamation, followed by a comma or exclamation mark. Examples: (O) *O mighty Caesar!*; *O Death, where is thy sting?*; *O little town of Bethlehem*; *O that I had wings like a dove.* (Oh) *Oh, snatch'd away in beauty's bosom*; *Oh! the professions; oh! the gold; and oh! the French* (Darwin); *Oh, how do you know that?*

oarlock. See ROWLOCK.

oasis /əʊˈeɪsɪs/. Plural *oases* /-siːz/.

oath /əʊθ/. Plural *oaths* /əʊðz/.

obbligato. Note that this musical term of Italian origin has *-bb-*. Plural *obbligatos.* See -O(E)S 4.

obeisance. Pronounced /ə(ʊ)ˈbeɪsəns/ (oh/uh-**bay**-suhns) The stressed syllable *-beis-* rhymes with *base*, i.e. it is not pronounced as two syllables, /-ˈbeɪɪs-/.

obelus, a dagger-shaped reference mark in printed work. Plural *obeli* /-lʌɪ/.

obiter dictum, an incidental remark. Plural *obiter dicta.*

object (verb). In its prevailing current sense 'to have an objection to, disapprove of', *object* is frequently followed by *to* + noun (phrase) (*he objected to capital punishment*) and *to* + gerund (see below). In the 19c. and early 20c. it was also commonly construed with *to* + infinitive. Examples: (with a *to*-infinitive) *whether I would object to give the ladies the benefit of my assistance*—W. Collins, 1860; *we object to pass Sundays in a state of coma*—Gissing, 1892; (with *to* + gerund) *Would the lady object to my lighting the pair of candles?*—Dickens, 1865; *Battle was being given to the front door, which objected to opening on principle*—E. Bowen, 1969.

objection. The pattern is the same as that for OBJECT (verb). Examples: (with a *to*-infinitive) *he had no great objection, but also no great wish, to fight*—C. Kingsley, 1853; *Cecil's objection to go through with it*—G. B. Shaw, 1911; (with *to* + gerund) *I have no objection to doing it myself*—G. B. Shaw, 1911.

objective genitive. The ordinary possessive genitive is shown in *John's dog* (i.e. John has a dog), *the world's oceans* (the world has oceans). A subjective genitive is shown in *Thackeray's novels* (i.e. those he wrote), *the girl's decision* (the girl has decided). An objective genitive is shown in *the boy's murder* (= the murder of the boy). Further examples of the objective genitive: *a London cultural policy just before the* [Greater London] *Council's abolition*—*Essays & Studies*, 1987; Kennedy's *in* Kennedy's assassination *is an objective genitive* —S. Greenbaum, 1996.

objector. So spelt, not *-er*.

objet d'art. Plural *objets d'art* (like the singular, pronounced /ɒbʒeɪ 'dɑː/). Printed in italics.

obligate. The verb *obligate* in non-legal use is almost always used in the passive (*be obligated, feel obligated*, etc.) followed by *to* + a noun (phrase) or by a *to*-infinitive, and it is now less common in BrE than *obliged.* It is a routine example of a word that was once (17–19c.) standard in BrE but has retreated somewhat, while remaining common (beside *obliged)* in AmE and to some extent elsewhere. Examples: (active) *The Truman Administration devised a policy that obligated the United States to come to the aid of all 'free peoples who are resisting attempted subjugation by armed minorities'.*—*New Yorker*, 1990; (passive) *President Ford is obligated early next month to report to Congress on the 'progress' of negotiations looking toward a Cyprus settlement*—*NY Times*, 1975; *After the divorce she felt obligated and guilty to both her parents and her child*—B. Ripley, 1987 (US); *it was the last thing I wanted, but I felt obligated*—R. Scott, 1988 (NZ); *we will be obligated also to recommend educational and communications strategies that can overcome* [etc.]—*Bull. Amer. Acad. Arts & Sci.*, 1992; *We've felt obligated to be part of it in the past, but we're very glad to see East Riding pulling out. I can totally understand why*—*Yorkshire Post Today*, 2004.

oblige (verb). See OBLIGATE.

oblique (noun). The oblique stroke (/) in print or writing is used between alternatives (e.g. *and/or*), in fractions (e.g. *3/4*), in ratios (e.g. *miles/day*), in Internet addresses (*http://public.oed.com/whats-new/*), and to show the line breaks of the original when successive lines of poetry are run on as a single line ('Whose woods these are / I think I know, / His house is in the village, though.). *Oblique* is a BrE term for what is also called a *slash, forward slash*, or in editing and printing a *solidus*. For problems it can cause see AND/OR and this extract from a letter (11 Oct. 1992) by a friend of Burchfield's in the diplomatic service: 'FCO-speak [*sc.* Foreign and Commonwealth Office], or rather FCO-write, is currently ... littered with the oblique stroke or slash, entailing constant ambiguity—is it an indolent substitute for "or", or "and", or "I don't know which and can't be bothered to decide between them"?'

oblivious. 1 Derived from Latin *oblīviōsus* 'forgetful, unmindful', *oblivious* was used from the 15c. onwards for just on four centuries only in its Latin sense (e.g. *Gods memory is not so oblivious, that it can so soone forgett this covenaunt*—J. Bell, 1581; *The slow formality of an oblivious and drowsy exchequer*—Burke, 1780). This sense survives (often followed by *of*), but is less prominent now than it was a century or so ago. Examples: *Never before ... has a great painter been completely oblivious of the style, or styles, of his time*—K. Clark, 1949; *Oblivious of any previous decisions not to stand together ... the three stood in a tight group*—D. Lessing, 1985.

2 In the mid-19c., by a normal process of semantic change, it came to be used in the sense 'unaware of, unconscious of' (with *to* much more often than *of*). The *OED* (1904) firmly labelled this new sense *erroneous.* Fowler (1926) dutifully accepted the Dictionary's verdict, and cited numerous examples of the 'erroneous' sense. Time has moved on, and the 'new' (1854) sense now forms part of the orthodox vocabulary of every educated person. Examples: *I stayed indoors all day for several days, oblivious to the damp heat of Falmouth*—C. Day Lewis, 1960; *He would ... look up at the startled faces of his company entirely oblivious of any offence that might have derived from his choice of expressions*—A. N. Wilson, 1984; *Up till this point she had been as oblivious to her surroundings, she might as well have been alone*—P. Farmer, 1987; *you are just as likely to get your eye poked out by an elbow whilst the owner is yapping away on his/her mobile, completely oblivious to their surroundings*—J. Schembri, 2011.

oboe. See HAUTBOY. A player of the instrument is an *oboist.*

obscene. In the 20c. when attempts were repeatedly made to define the nature and desirable limits of obscenity, that is of lewdness, in books, films, etc. (always by extending the limits), the word gathered strength in its other main meaning, 'highly offensive or repugnant' (of violence, famine, accumulation of wealth, etc.). Some people initially objected—and some probably still do object—to this second meaning as a rhetorical or even hysterical overstatement and a debasement of the word's true value. It is true that in its frequent collocations with *amount, profit, salary,* and *wealth* it means little more than 'ridiculously or outrageously high or large', and sometimes seems to be nothing more than a ritualized criticism of the wealthy or well paid, justified or otherwise, depending on one's politics. Both strands of meaning in fact go back to the late 16c. Shakespeare being the first recorded source for the extended meaning. Examples: (= lewd) *Our later writers are saucy rather than obscene—Athenæum,* 1899; *Appeal Court judges ruled ... that not only sex, but drug addiction, made a book obscene and depraved—Daily Tel.,* 1964; *The obscene is whatever touches nerves, whether of desire or loathing, which society, usually in the person of one of its most susceptible members, such as Mrs Mary Whitehouse, deems better left untouched*—A. Burgess, 1988. (= highly offensive) *Something in the very robustness of Germany's economy seemed to the terrorists and their sympathizers profoundly obscene—Time,* 1977; *The idea of these old women being walled up and told what to do by a superstitious parson was* (*Tibba allowed herself the modernism*) *obscene*—A. N. Wilson, 1982; *His pay was branded 'utterly obscene' amid calls for him to quit and drop his name from the company—Daily Mirror,* 1992.

observance, observation. Both words are of long standing in the language (*observance* first recorded in the 13c., and *observation* in the 14c.) and both have impeccable etymological origins in Latin, the first being originally a noun denoting a state or condition ('regard, reverence, etc.') and the second a noun of action from Latin *observāre* 'to observe'. In practice the words are not interchangeable and are not generally confused since they correspond to different branches in meaning of the verb *observe* ('to see or notice' and 'to follow or adhere to'). *Observance* is the word normally used in connection with respecting rules, carrying out duties and obligations, and performing formal customs and rituals (e.g. *observance of the speed limit*) whereas *observation* is the equivalent in the more physical senses of seeing and perceiving, has the special countable meaning 'a remark or comment', and is used in special combinations such as *observation car* (on a train, chiefly AmE) and (military) *observation post.* Fowler decried at length the use of *observance* for *observation* as a journalistic verbal tic, tending to undermine this well-established distinction (e.g. *His early poetry, the product of exalted sensation rather than of careful observance*—1926 in Fowler). He also spotted *observation* used for *observance* (e.g. *The British Government has failed to secure the observation of law and has lost the confidence of all classes*—1926 in Fowler). Such uses of the words as synonyms are not mistakes so much as rarities, e.g. *Her baby's motionless observance of me observing his mother must have woken her*—B. Neil, 1993.

obsess has been used since the 16c. as a transitive verb in its modern meaning of 'preoccupy', often in the passive with *obsessed* as a quasi-adjective: *Modern society is obsessed with romanticizing ancient societies—Times,* 1980. In that use, the preposition following it is much more often *with* than *by*. In the later part of the 20c. there emerged, first in AmE (1977) and later in BrE, in which it can still sound slightly alien, a new intransitive use of *obsess* to mean 'to be preoccupied or unduly worried (about something)', usually followed by *about* or *over*: *The only way to go about judging your work is not to obsess too much over it—Times,* 1998. This intransitive form also appears with no complement: *You're obsessing! I want you to stop it right now!—China Post,* 1996.

obsolete (verb). In the 17–19c. in standard use in the sense 'to render obsolete; to discard', this verb has dropped out of use in BrE, but remains in use (or was revived) in North America. Examples: *Our precoated steel failed to obsolete the glass TLC plate—Sci. Amer.,* 1975; *A dual-density orthotic, one whose construction obsoletes the typical foam slab found in ordinary boots—Backpacker* (magazine), 1991 (US).

obstetric, obstetrical (adjectives). The shorter form is much the more usual of the two in a ratio of 5:1. *Obstetrical* is used mainly in AmE. The formation of both words is in fact irregular: a midwife is *obstetrix, -īcem,* so that the 'regular' form would be the awkward-sounding *obstetricic.* But only pedantry would take exception to *obstetric* at this stage.

occasion. Spelt as shown. For some reason it is one of the most frequently misspelt words in the language.

occiput, the back of the head. Pronounced /'ɒksɪpʌt/, the last syllable rhyming with *putt.*

occur. The inflected forms are *occurred, occurring.* See -R-, -RR-.

occurrence /ə'kʌrəns/. In BrE RP the stressed second syllable is pronounced like the first syllable of *current.* In AmE that stressed syllable is the same as in *occur,* /əː/, a pronunciation which is regional in BrE.

ocellus /ɒ'sɛləs/, simple (as opposed to compound) eye (of an insect). Plural *ocelli* /-lʌɪ/.

ochlocracy /ɒk'lɒkrəsi/, a baffle-your-friends kind of word for 'mob rule'. Cf. Gk ὄχλος 'crowd'.

ochre, name of a yellow pigment. Spelt **ocher** in AmE. See -RE AND -ER. Hence **ochrous** (adjective) (sometimes **ochreous**), AmE **ocherous.**

octavo /ɒk'tɑːvəʊ, -'tʌɪ-/. Plural *octavos*: see -O(E)S 4. Abbreviated *8vo.*

octocentenary, octocentennial. Of these two forms for the eight-hundredth anniversary of an event, the first is the preferred form in Britain, and the second the more usual form in other English-speaking countries. See CENTENARY 2.

octodecimo, a book based on 18 leaves, 36 pages, to the sheet. Also called *eighteenmo.* Abbreviated *18mo.* Plural *octodecimos*: see -O(E)S 4.

octopus. The only correct plural in English is *octopuses.* The Greek original is ὀκτώπους, -ποδ- (which would lead to a pedantic English plural form *octopodes*). The plural form *octopi,* which is occasionally heard (often jokingly), though based on modern Latin *octopus,* is misconceived. See LATIN PLURALS; -US 4.

octosyllabics. The usual name of the eight-syllable rhyming iambic metre used in *Hudibras, The Lay of the Last Minstrel,* etc.: *The way was long, the wind was cold, The Minstrel was infirm and old; ...*

octothorp. See HASH.

oculist. See OPHTHALMOLOGIST.

-odd. Appended to a number, sum, weight, etc., to mean 'roughly, or somewhat more than' (e.g. *forty-odd members*) it should be written with a hyphen in order to avoid ambiguity; compare the above with *forty odd members* (of the Society of Eccentrics?).

ode. 'In reference to ancient literature (and in some early uses of the word in English), a poem intended or adapted to be sung; e.g. the Odes of Pindar, of Anacreon, of Horace. *Choral Odes,* the songs of the Chorus in a Greek play, etc.; spec. a short Old English poem, esp. *The Battle of Brunanburh.* In modern use: A rhymed (rarely unrhymed) lyric, often in the form of an address, generally dignified or exalted in subject, feeling, and style, but sometimes (in earlier use) simple and familiar (though less so than a song)' (*OED*). *The Battle of Brunanburh* is no longer called an ode, but a 'panegyric poem'. Among the most famous odes in English literature are 'Ode on a Grecian Urn' (Keats, 1819), 'Ode to a Nightingale' (Keats, 1819), and 'Ode to the West Wind' (Shelley, 1819).

odour, odorous. The slightly genteel word *odour* (instead of *smell*) is so spelt in BrE but as **odor** in AmE. In both countries the corresponding adjective is spelt **odorous.**

odyssey. Plural *odysseys.*

oe, œ, e. See Æ, Œ. There is a broad tendency in AmE, and much less so in BrE, to simplify *oe* to *e.* The following lists show the dominant spelling in each country of some common words in this group:

BrE	AmE
oedema	*edema*[1]
Oedipus	*Oedipus*
oenology	*enology*[1]
oesophagus	*esophagus*
oestrogen	*estrogen*
oestrus	*estrus*[1]

Also in medial position:

amoeba[2]	*amoeba*[2]
fetid	*fetid*
fetus[3]	*fetus*[3]
homeopathy[3]	*homeopathy*[3]

1 Also *oe-* 2 Also *-e-* 3 Also *-oe-*

The earlier forms (esp. in the 19c.) *oecology, oeconomy,* and *oecumenical* have now been entirely replaced by *ecology, economy,* and *ecumenical* in both forms of English.

-o(e)s. At one time or another we probably all have doubts about the plural of words which in the singular end in *-o*. Unfortunately, there is no simple rule stating that all such plurals end in *-oes*: if there were, *heroes* would 'look' fine, and so would *potatoes*; but *egoes* and *Eskimoes,* for example, would not. Conversely, if the rule stated that all such words ended in *-os, curios* would 'look' fine, and so would *cantos, memos,* and *ratios*; but *heros* and *potatos* would not. When in doubt about particular words, all one can do is follow the practice of one's favourite dictionary. It is, however, probably the case that most nouns ending in *-o* follow the normal pattern of simply adding *-s* to form their plural. The number of those which only ever form it in *-oes* is quite small (see 1 below), and there is a rather larger group for which both forms are correct (see 2 below). **1** Exclusively *-oes*. The following words, which are completely naturalized as English invariably have the plural *-oes*: *buffaloes, calicoes* (but also *calicos* in AmE), *dominoes, echoes, embargoes, heroes, mosquitoes, Negroes, potatoes, tomatoes, torpedoes, vetoes.*

2 Either *-os* or *-oes*. A large group of others have either *-os* or *-oes* as their plural forms. Recommendations for many of them are given at their alphabetical place in the present book. While both forms are possible, the *OEC* data suggests that different words have different preferences. For example *cargoes* is many times more frequent than *cargos,* but *halos* is rather more frequent than *haloes*. With such words one is therefore free to choose the form one feels more comfortable with. Alternatively, one can see which spelling is given first in a dictionary: *archipelago, banjo, cargo, desperado, dodo, fandango, flamingo, fresco, ghetto, grotto, halo, innuendo, lasso, mango, memento, motto, peccadillo, pedalo, portico, salvo* (discharge), *tornado, tuxedo, vertigo, virago, volcano.*

3 A small group of monosyllables take *-oes*: so *goes, noes* (as in 'the noes have it').

4 Exclusively *-os*. Many words of the kind whose plural is seldom wanted or is restricted to special uses have *-os*. Many of these are treated at their alphabetical place. It is worth noting that many of them come from Italian, Spanish, or Latin, and that many of the Italian ones are musical terms: (Italian) *casinos, dados, dittos, fiascos, imbroglios, impresarios, infernos, maraschinos, manifestos, pistachios, portfolios, s(c)iroccos*; (musical terms) *adagios, allegros, arpeggios, concertos, contraltos, crescendos, diminuendos, dos* (the musical note), *intermezzos, largos, librettos, obbligatos, oratorios, piccolos, pizzicatos, solos, sopranos, trios*; (Latin) *credos, egos, farragos, folios, limbos, octavos, placebos, provisos, quartos, rectos, sextos, versos*; (Portuguese) *albinos, commandos*; (Spanish) *boleros, caballeros, fandangos, flamencos, gauchos, guanos, major-domos, merinos, olios, palmettos, paramos, patios, pesos, pim(i)entos, sombreros, tobaccos.*

5 When a vowel or the letter *y* precedes the *-o* in the singular, *-os* is the usual plural, probably because of the bizarre look of *-ioes,* etc. This also applies to some of the words in the previous category, such as *adagios, arpeggios,* etc.: so *bagnios, bamboos, cameos, curios, embryos, intaglios, kangaroos, mustachios, nuncios, radios, rodeos, scenarios, seraglios, studios, videos.*

6 Abbreviations always have *-os*. Truncated words, usually made by dropping the second element of a compound or the later syllables, always have *-os*: so *altos, demos, dynamos, hippos, homos, kilos, magnetos, memos, photos, pianos, pros* (professionals), *rhinos, stylos, typos.* The same rule applies to nouns such as *saddos* and *weirdos,* formed from adjectives, and to Aust. abbreviations such as *ambo, arvo,* etc.

7 Alien-looking words and comparatively recent loanwords have *-os*: so *calypsos, gigolos, kimonos, magnificos, merinos, mikados, moroccos, shakos, silos, stilettos, torsos, tyros.*

8 Polysyllabic words tend to have *-os*: so *armadillos, clavicembalos, generalissimos, Punchinellos.*

9 Proper names have *-os*: so *Lotharios, Martellos, Neros, Romeos*; similarly with ethnic names, as *Eskimos, Filipinos*. Also *Tornados* (fighter aircraft).

of.

A *Fowler's observations and pronouncements.* 'Straying' in the use of *of*, said Fowler in 1926 in typically combative style, 'is perpetual, and the impression of amateurishness produced on an educated reader of the newspapers is discreditable to the English Press.' From newspapers of the time, but not identified and therefore no longer recoverable, Fowler classified seven uses of *of* which he called 'crimes of grammar'. (Modern journalistic writing is generally afflicted with other verbal mannerisms.) His comprehensive, detailed discussion is here abridged for the modern reader's sake, and some categories have been omitted.

1 *Overview.* The preposition *of* is one of the key words in structuring phrases and sentences in English, and it is sometimes possible to make a slip in usage that can give the wrong meaning. Problems usually occur in extended sentences and consist of either adding an *of* where it is not wanted (or where another preposition is called for) or leaving out an *of* where it is needed to clarify the sense. Examples taken from a wide range of sources.

2 *Of* is the wrong preposition. This happens usually at a point in a long sentence where *of* is meant to refer back to an earlier part of the sentence but is in fact the wrong choice, influenced by another *of* close by which has nothing to do with it: *He will be in the best possible position* for *getting the most out of the land and* of *using it to the best possible advantage* (the preposition wanted is *for* not *of*); *The magistrate commented* on *the nuisance of street-collections by means of boxes, and* of *the scandal of a system under which a large proportion of the money given goes for the expenses of collection* (the preposition wanted is *on* not *of*).

3 Needless repetition of *of*. There are two patterns involved here. (*a*) Sometimes an *of* is inadvertently inserted in echo of an earlier *of* which in fact belongs to a different phrase or clause within the sentence: *It could be done* without *unduly raising the price of coal, or* of *jeopardizing new trade. Jeopardizing* is governed by *without*, not by price. (*b*) In other cases, a repeated *of* is not incorrect but unnecessary: *A series of problem contracts and* of *bad debts does not explain the situation*; *On the one hand there are the conventional rules of good manners and* of *correct behaviour*. This is a question of style, not syntax.

4 Essential *of* wrongly omitted. The other principal error lies in omitting an *of* when it is essential to convey the intended meaning: *The banning of meetings and the printing and distribution of leaflets stopped the agitation* (*of* should be put in before *the printing* to show that the ban applied to printing and distribution as well); *He has mapped the development of the animal's nervous system and its behaviour* suggests mapping of the behaviour, whereas the intended meaning is that he mapped the development of that behaviour, so the sentence should read *He has mapped the development* of *the animal's nervous system and* of *its behaviour*.

5 *In parallel structures. Of* should also be repeated in constructions with *both* when the position of *both* requires a parallel sequence: *There are teachers with low standards who think a mere pass at whatever grade is a feather in the cap both* of *themselves and* of *their pupils* (alternatively, one could put ... *a feather in the cap of both themselves and their pupils*, but the result would be awkward).

B 1 *of* for *have, 've*. In the spoken language the auxiliary verb *have* when unstressed (in such phrases as *could have, might have, would have*) is normally pronounced /əv/ and so, often, is *of*. It needed only the keen ears of children and of other partially educated people, to misinterpret /əv/ = *have* as being 'really' one of the ways of saying *of*. The erroneous use (first recorded in 1837) is found in all English-speaking countries. Typical examples (in each of which the speech represented is that of a child or of a poorly educated adult): *Well, you should of buyed some* *cigarettes for yourself so it's your own fault*—S. Mackay, 1984 (UK); *My friend Gladys wouldn't of wanted you to come here nosing*—N. Virtue, 1988 (NZ); *An' Edward might of been dying*—P. Lively, 1989 (UK); *Firecracker must of lifted a rock or something. Didn't see it hit*—C. Tilghman, 1991 (US).

2 Splitting of the *of*-genitive. Elisabeth Wieser (in *English Studies* 1986) described a little-noticed phenomenon which she called 'the splitting of the *of*-genitive'. In such constructions the governing noun is divided from its *of*-genitive by any of various elements. The use appears to be widespread in all varieties of English. Examples: *The remnant* that exists in my memory *of a book read and admired years ago*—P. Lubbock, 1921; *The dubbing* into British English *of Fellini's 'La Dolce Vita' was a tour de force*—A. Burgess, 1980; *With the rise* to power *of the National Socialists*—D. M. Thomas, 1981; *There was a glint* in his eye *of the charming Continental rascal*—G. Mikes, 1983.

3 Type *of an evening.* The chiefly AmE type *he works* nights; *she plays cards* Thursdays (*see* ADVERB 4) is a concise way of expressing the general English type *of an evening, of a Sunday afternoon,* though this latter type now sounds literary or archaic. A typical example: *All the intellect of the place assembled of an evening*—Carlyle, 1831. Until the 19c. the type *of nights, of mornings* was also possible: e.g. *Dice can be played of mornings as well as after dinner*—Thackeray, 1849.

4 *A final word.* Dwight Bolinger (*World Englishes* vii, 1988) reminded us that as a function word like *of* 'occurs in increasingly cohesive and stereotyped larger assemblies [i.e. multiplies the ways in which it is idiomatically used], its nuclear sense begins to fade, and eventually it turns into a kind of grammatical particle'. It then begins to be replaced by other prepositions, e.g. *about.* Bolinger cited numerous examples from radio broadcasts of the period 1982–8 in which *about* is used where *of* would have been expected, e.g. *There was none of the awareness about drugs that we have now; I'm perhaps a little more conscious about that; The Vietnamese are downright disdainful about Chinese cookery; Pierre Salinger thinks that* [President] *Kennedy was wary about television.* The broad sense of the preposition in such contexts is 'on the subject of', and, at least in AmE, in uses like these *about* is beginning to sound the more natural of the two. Bolinger also cited examples of other replacements: *enamoured of* → *enamoured with* (cf. *in love with*), *free of* → *free from* (e.g. *It's free of/from contaminants*).

It begins to look as if preposition replacement is becoming an occasional but significant feature of the language. Powerful analogies are strewn about everywhere waiting to be seized upon.

of a. Observed so far only in AmE sources is the colloquial type adj. + *of a* + noun, e.g. *wouldn't be that difficult of a shot*—L. Trevino, 1985 (during a TV interview). *MWCDEU* 1989 cites numerous examples (including the one by Trevino) from informal oral sources, e.g. *How big of a carrier force?*—J. Lehrer, 1986 (TV newscast). The type may possibly be a slowly evolving extension of a much older quasi-nominal use of the adj. *considerable*: e.g. (from *DARE,* 1985) *This morning about 6 o'clock considerable of a shock of an earthquake was felt in Boston*—1766 source.

of course. See COURSE.

off. 1 In its prepositional use 'from the charge or possession of', *off* construed especially with *take, buy, borrow, hire,* and the like is, according to the *OED,* now colloquial despite the antiquity (mid-16c. onwards) of the construction. One no longer buys a car *off* a stated person but *from* a person. Typical examples of the older use: *A villager had come . . . to know whether Blincoe 'would take a goose off him'*—C. James, 1891; *She admitted borrowing the 1l. off the plaintiff*—*Daily News,* 1897. A modern example: *He would borrow money off loads of people but never be able to pay it back* —*This is Wiltshire,* 2005. Cf. OFF OF.

2 The vowel sound /ɔː/ in *off,* which was standard at the beginning of the 20c., has now given way, except in the speech of a select group of elderly grandees, to /ɒ/. I have only ever met one ordinary citizen who used the old-fashioned pronunciation, over thirty years ago, and that person was then already in late middle age.

offence (noun). So spelt in BrE, but as **offense** in AmE.

offer has the inflections *offered, offering.* See -R-, -RR-.

office (noun). In AmE the ordinary word for a doctor's surgery, e.g. *The doctor's office, which occupied the two front rooms of his house, was cool and high-ceilinged—New Yorker*, 1990.

office (verb). The noun *office* has been used intermittently as a verb, in various senses, now mostly obsolete, since the 15c. Shakespeare, for example, used it to mean 'to appoint to an office' in *The Winter's Tale* (*So stands this Squire Offic'd with me*). The verb is no longer extant in British English but is not uncommon in North American use, in the sense 'to have an office' or, followed by *with*, 'to share an office'. Some US commentators dislike it, but it is in any case largely confined to business speak. Examples: (advertisement) *Chance for high grade realtor to office with lawyer—Atlantic Monthly*, 1936; *Mr. Mardian spoke of a man who 'officed in that same agency'—NY Times*, 1973.

official (adjective) means 'of or relating to an office or its tenure (*official duties*)' or 'properly authorized (*an official fellowship at Magdalen College*; *the official attendance was 47,000*)'. *Officious*, by contrast, means 'asserting authority aggressively or intrusively' (*an officious fussy little clerk*; *an officious waiter*). It is part of the canon of usage that the two words should not be confused, but in any case there is no clear evidence to suggest that they ever are. See OFFICIOUS.

officialese. 1 (*a*) *Definition.* The term, first recorded in 1884, is used, almost always pejoratively, to refer, as the *OED* puts it, to 'the formal and typically verbose language considered characteristic of officials or official documents; turgid or pedantic official prose'.

Adjectives describing it in the illustrative examples in its original *OED* entry include *crabbed, jolting,* and *dry*; to those, no doubt many of us would add some less refined but more expressive epithets.

(*b*) *A 20c. example.* Wry comments about the unsuitability, unattractiveness, or impenetrability of official memoranda and the terminology of groups of officials turn up all the time. The attitude is one of bemusement or of horror. A passage from a column by Theodore Dalrymple, a regular contributor to *The Spectator,* may be taken as representative:

'I'm beginning to wonder whether I still speak modern English, or whether, approaching middle age, the language of my youth and education has become an archaic and somewhat quaint dialect. Last week, I read a review in the *British Medical Journal* . . .

'The pages of the *BMJ* are as Edward Gibbon, however, compared to the language used during meetings by the new managers of the NHS. To attend one of these meetings is to enter a world in which people are not busy: they are 'fully occupied operationally'. When these meetings have lasted more than three hours, the chairman does not say, 'It's late and I am bored', he says, 'I'm conscious of the time.' Up and down the country, in all our hospitals, members of committees are fully occupied operationally, identifying and then defining live issues, which of course can only be approached multidisciplinarily, utilising a pool of resources (that is to say, employees).'

Despite vigorous campaigns by groups committed to the use of Plain English, examples of such double Dutch are still all too easy to find. And despite the just quoted gibberish being a couple of decades old, it is impossible not to suspect that the use of such language has played and still plays a role in the problems that the British NHS persistently faces. It is, however, arguable that such language is typical of the management speak which infests private as well as official bodies, rather than *officialese* as defined.

(*c*) *A 21c. example.* Another feature of *officialese* is its fascination with dressing up banal ideas in full-dress language, as the following from a 2010 Scottish Government policy document on designing streets illustrates: 'Streets have important public realm functions beyond those related to motor traffic. They are typically lined with buildings and public spaces and, whilst facilitation of movement is still a key function, they normally support a range of social, leisure, retail and commercial functions'. Streets have shops, offices, and parks on them. Who knew?

2 *Gowers' view.* (*a*) Fowler (1926) had no entry on *officialese*; it was Gowers (1965) who first created the entry, some of which is retained in the current one. As a high-flying mandarin who had worked in a wide range of civil service posts during his long career, he had no doubt been exposed to more than his fair share of *officialese*. The definition he offered was '*Officialese* is a pejorative term for a style of writing marked by peculiarities supposed to be characteristic of officials.' He continued, 'If a single word were needed to describe those peculiarities, that chosen by Dickens, *circumlocution*, is still the most suitable. They may be ascribed to a combination of causes: a feeling that plain words sort ill with the dignity of office, a politeness that shrinks from blunt statement, and, above all, the knowledge that for those engaged in the perilous game of politics, and their servants, vagueness is safer than precision. The natural result is a stilted and verbose style, not readily intelligible—a habit of mind for instance that automatically rejects the adjective *unsightly* in favour of the periphrasis *detrimental to the visual amenities of the locality*.'

(*b*) *Officialese* versus *legalese*. Gowers made a valid distinction: 'This reputation, though not altogether undeserved, is unfairly exaggerated by a confusion in the public mind between *officialese* and what may be termed *legalese*. For instance a correspondent writes to *The Times* to show up what he calls this "flower of circumlocution" from the National Insurance Act 1959; it ought not, he says, to be allowed to waste its sweetness on the desert air. *For the purpose of this Part of this Schedule a person over pensionable age, not being an insured person, shall be treated as an insured person if he would be an insured person were he under pensionable age and would be an employed person were he an insured person.*

'This is certainly not pretty or luminous writing. But it is not officialese, nor is it circumlocution. It is legalese, and the reason why it is difficult to grasp is not that it wanders verbosely round the point but that it goes straight there with a baffling economy of words. It has the compactness of a mathematical formula. Legalese cannot be judged by literary standards. In it everything must be subordinated to one paramount purpose: that of ensuring that if words have to be interpreted by a Court they will be given the meaning the draftsman intended. Elegance cannot be expected from anyone so circumscribed. Indeed it is hardly an exaggeration to say that the more readily a legal document appears to yield its meaning the less likely it is to prove unambiguous. It is fair to assume that if the paragraph quoted were to be worked out, as one would work out an equation, it would be found to express the draftsman's meaning with perfect precision.'

(*c*) An exquisite flower of *officialese*. Gowers quoted the extract below from a London evening newspaper, and then condensed its bloated 47 words to a slimline 16: '*Discussing Anglo-American talks on the Barnes Wallis folding-wing plane, a Ministry spokesman said: "The object of this visit is a pooling of knowledge to explore further the possibility of a joint research effort to discover the practicability of making use of this principle to meet a possible future NATO requirement, and should be viewed in the general context of interdependence." Or,* (*our version*): *"This visit is to find out whether we can, together, develop the folding wing for NATO."*'

3 See BAFFLEGAB; GOBBLEDEGOOK; PLAIN ENGLISH.

officious formerly had a meaning in diplomacy oddly different from its ordinary one. Until roughly the turn of the last century, an *officious* communication meant much what a lawyer still means by one 'without prejudice'; it was to bind no one, and, unless acted upon by common consent, was to be as if it had not been. Corresponding to the French *officieux* (unofficial), it was the antithesis of *official*, and the notion of meddlesomeness attached to it in ordinary use was entirely absent. But the risk of misunderstanding was obvious, and the use is now obsolete.

off of is still strongly present in informal speech in Britain but is considered undesirable in any writing other than informal. The *OED* gives numerous examples of the use, beginning with one in Shakespeare's *2 Henry VI* (A [= I] *fall off of a tree*), and also: *About a furlong off of the Porters Lodge*—Bunyan, 1678; *I'd borrow two or three dollars off of the judge for him*—M. Twain, 1884. In AmE, the *OEC* data shows that *off of* is widespread in writing such as news and sports reporting, fiction, and blogs. *MWCDEU* provides copious evidence of its use in respectable sources and summarizes: 'If it is part of your personal idiom and you are not writing on an especially elevated plane, you have no reason to avoid *off of*.' US examples: *the night Wayne came at Randolph with a hammer to pull him off of Mary*—M. Golden, 1989; *the collection of virtually all older artifacts* *and most modern ones—pulled out of chapels, peeled off of church walls, removed from decayed houses,* [etc.]—S. Greenblatt in *Bull. Amer. Acad. Arts & Sci.*, 1990; *She had a way of moving her head to pitch it* [*sc.* her hair] *about, a way of sweeping it off of her face with her fingers*—T. R. Pearson, 1993.

offset. The verb means 'to counterbalance' or 'to compensate for' and apart from a couple of technical uses has had a limited range until fairly recently. Now, with climate change in everyone's thoughts, it has taken on a new lease of life as the word that eases the conscience over carbon emissions caused by environmentally unfriendly activities: *Whitehall has adopted the fashionable habit of carbon offsetting—effectively paying penance for the contribution made by transatlantic flights, hotel air conditioning and cars to wrecking the ozone layer. Tree planting schemes are a particular favourite*—*Observer*, 2005. The past tense and past participle are usually *offset*, the base form, in line with *set* as an irregular verb. However, as happens with a small group of other verbs containing an irregular verb as a sort of suffix (*broadcast, input, podcast,* etc.), *offset* is also sometimes treated as a regular verb, particularly in AmE, e.g. *But there were also benefits that offsetted this added Tax, namely not having to serve in the Muslim armies*—weblog, 2011 (US). The corresponding compound noun is **carbon offset**. See also PODCAST.

offspring. From the 16c. to the early 19c. a plural form *offsprings* was current (e.g. *the widows and the offsprings of the poorer, the indigent clergy,* 1756), but since then this ancient word (found already in Old English) has been invariable in form (*These are the offspring of Italian parents; the son tried to become the worthy offspring of his famous father*). The *OED* marks *offsprings* as 'now rare', but many editors will consider it a mistake. The word should not be hyphenated.

oft, recorded in standard use from the Old English period onwards, survives as a single word only in special contexts or in literature: e.g. *Do this, as oft as ye shall drink it, in remembrance of me*—*Bk of Common Prayer*; *What oft was thought, but ne'er so well expressed*—Pope, 1711. It is often prefixed to a past participle to create a compound adjective, in which case it should be hyphenated, e.g. *oft-repeated, oft-quoted, oft-cited,* etc.

often. The *OED* (1904) gave only the pronunciation /ɔːfən/ rhyming with *orphan*, but since then the vowel has almost universally been replaced by /ɒ/ as in *not* and a spelling pronunciation with medial /t/ has also emerged in standard speech. This alternation between pronouncing the medial /t/, and not pronouncing it was, according to the *OED*, commented on as far back as the 16c.; Elizabeth I seems to have enunciated the word without, although that pronunciation seems to have been avoided by careful speakers in the 17c. Fowler (1926) considered pronouncing the *t* hypercorrection, which he dismissed rather cattily as follows: '... is practiced by two oddly assorted classes—the academic speakers who affect a more precise enunciation than their neighbours ... & the uneasy half-literates who like to prove that they can spell by calling *hour* ... howr'. Nowadays many standard speakers use both /ˈɒfən/ and /ˈɒftən/, and it is hard to say which is the more common of the two. For the loss of *t* after *f* compare *soften.*

oftener, -est. Theoretically the comparative and superlative forms of *often* but in practice much less common than *more often* and *most often.*

oh. See O AND OH.

OK. 1 *Origins.* (*a*) Shortly after the first appearance of what is possibly the only universally recognized English word, competing theories about its origin had already begun to flourish, as illustrated in this *OED* note: 'Other suggestions, e.g. that O.K. represents an alleged Choctaw word *oke* "it is" (actually the affirmative verbal suffix *-okii* "indeed, contrary to your supposition"), or French *au quai,* or Scottish English *och aye,* or that it derives from a word in the West African language Wolof via slaves in the southern States of America, all lack any form of acceptable documentation.'

(*b*) Its true source has long since been established beyond any reasonable doubt by the indefatigable labours of the American scholar Allen Walker Read. (For the word's full history, readers should consult Allan Metcalf, *OK: The improbable story of America's greatest word,* 2011). In fact, it is most unusual etymologically, since we know both who created it and when.

The background to its invention was the craze in Boston in late 1838 for using initialisms not unlike those of modern texting: e.g. *R.T.B.S* (remains to be seen), *I.S.B.D.* (it shall be done), *S.P.* (small potatoes, i.e. insignificant), *O.K.K.B.W.P.* (one kind kiss before we part) and so forth. This universal word was born on Saturday 23 March 1839, in the *Boston Morning Post*, and its midwife was the paper's editor, Charles Gordon Greene. The word was based on the initial letters of *orl* (or *oll*) *korrect*, a humorous alteration of 'all correct'. (Greene had previously used *O.R.* for *all right*). *O.K.*, as Metcalf explains, was then popularized first by its association in the presidential election campaign of 1840 with 'Old Kinderhook', the nickname, derived from the name of his hometown, of Democrat candidate and current president William Van Buren; and, later, by the widespread but mistaken belief that it had been used by President Andrew Jackson to approve documents.

2 *Spelling.* The most common spelling is *OK*/*ok* (but usually upper case), followed by the spelt-out form *Okay*/*okay*. The spelling with full points as **O.K./o.k.** is far less frequent than either of those, except in product names. Apostrophes are used before the verb inflections when the word is spelt in the form *OK*, e.g. *OK's*, *OK'd*, and *OK'ing* . The last, however, is rare, because of its awkward look (at first glance it can look like a proper name) and is usually replaced by the *okaying* form. The *okays*, *okayed* inflections of the verb are nearly as frequent as the abbreviated forms. *OK* has very wide currency in the spoken and written language, despite repeated onslaughts by naysayers. As *MWCDEU* puts it, it 'is widely used ... on all levels of writing except the stodgiest'.

okapi. Plural unchanged or *okapis*.

old. 1 For the distinction between *older*, *oldest*, and *elder*, *eldest*, see ELDER.

2 For the *Old Lady of Threadneedle Street*, see SOBRIQUETS.

olde. Used as an archaism, originally commercially, later also often ironically, for *old*, sometimes with other words spelt archaistically, e.g. *Olde English(e)* and especially *olde-worlde*. It is interesting to note the *OED's* first example from an AmE source, and the example below from *Finnegan's Wake*. Examples: *We shall ... show ... the character of 'the old fogy', or 'ye olde fogie', as he at present exists—U.S. Democratic Rev.*, 1852; *A glass of Danu U'Dunnell's foamous olde Dobbelin ayle*—J. Joyce, 1939; *A lot of olde realle beames in Amersham and a lot of olde phonie cookynge too—Good Food Guide*, 1959; *The interior is old but not olde worlde, the medieval oak beams have been left ... without ... horse brasses and warming pans—Guardian*, 1972.

olden. First recorded in the 15c., in a fixed phrase equivalent to the modern *in olden days*, this word has gradually fallen into disuse except in that expression and in its variant *in olden times*. Use of the word on its own is now markedly literary, e.g. *All he could see was a single sandy suede shoe ... : the olden hushpuppy of R.C. Squires*—M. Amis, 1995. Its origin is uncertain, but it has been suggested that the suffix *-en* may represent a fossilized Old English inflexion of *old*.

olio. Plural *olios*. See -O(E)S 4.

-ology. See -LOGY. New, sometimes temporary, formations in *-ology* are coined all the time. Examples that have not established themselves include *coupology* (study of the plotting of coups), and *tegestology* (1960, the study and collection of beer mats). The language seems to welcome such words as temporary passengers, so long as they get off at the next station. Somewhat more established forms include *Ripperology* (1976, investigation into the crimes of Jack the Ripper) and *ufology* (1959, the study of UFOs). The word as an entity in its own right achieved a certain notoriety in Britain thanks to a 1980s advertisement in which a Jewish grandmother says to her grandson who has achieved his only exam pass in sociology 'You get an ology, you're a scientist'. Perhaps surprisingly, it was first used in this way as long ago as 1811: *She ... was therefore supposed to understand Chemistry, Geology, Philology, and a hundred other ologies*—E. Nares, *Thinks I to myself*.

Olympiad, Olympian, Olympic. 1 *Olympiad.* 'In its earliest use (Pindar, Herodotus) it refers to the [Olympic] games themselves or to a victory in the games; only later does it come also to signify the period between celebrations; and only much later still, in Latin, does the second sense become the principal one' (W. Sidney Allen, 1992). In English the earliest recorded use (Trevisa, 1398) is the period between the ancient games, used by the Greeks for the computation of time. The sense 'a quadrennial celebration of the ancient Olympic Games' is first recorded in the late 15c. (Skelton). The Olympic Games were revived in Athens in 1896, and the term *Olympiad* was first recorded of these in 1907. It is often used in this last meaning, e.g. *With the 3 Olympics under her belt so far and with the '96 Games, she would become one of a very select band to make 4 Olympiads—Swimming Times*, 1994.

2 *Olympian.* (*a*) This word is a tree with two etymological branches. (i) In the branch that comes from the classical Latin *Olympius*, the adjective refers to Mount Olympus, in NE Greece, traditionally the home of the Greek gods, and thus 'heavenly, celestial'; (ii) the other branch comes from the post-classical Latin *Olympianus*, referring to Olympia in the Peloponnese, the site of the ancient Greek games. Shakespeare, Milton, and others used this adjective for the ancient Greek games (*the Olympian games*), and it is still occasionally so used (e.g. *We have a need to speak out on behalf of our Canadian Olympian Champions* ... [*robbed*] *of an Olympic Gold Medal—Ottawa Sun*, 2002), but the dominant use historically is in meaning (i), e.g. *Olympian Zeus, god, goddess*, etc. From that meaning developed the sense of 'aloof; superior or condescending in manner', e.g. *The book is not helped by the Olympian tone of many of its* obiter dicta—*Eng. Today*, 1993.

(*b*) Outside classical scholarship, the noun *Olympian* is now most often used to mean 'a competitor in the modern Olympic Games': *McDonalds's* ... *wanted to launch a new campaign involving a series of sports paying tribute to past Olympians—Chicago*, 2002.

3 *Olympic.* In modern use it principally refers to the games of ancient Greece or those of modern times. The games themselves are frequently called the *Olympics* (as well as the *Olympic Games*).

omelette. The normal spelling in BrE (rather than *omelet*), whereas **omelet** is the more usual form in AmE.

omission of relatives, etc. A characteristic feature of English speech and writing, current since at least the 13c., is the construction of relative clauses without the 'normal' introductory *that* (or *whom*, etc.). Some grammarians treat the matter as the omission of a relative pronoun or of the conjunction *that*; but see CONTACT CLAUSES. Examples: (omission of a relative pronoun) *I do loue a woman* ... *and shee's faire* ʌ *I loue*—Shakespeare, 1592; *In the day* ʌ *ye eate thereof, then your eyes shalbee opened*—Gen. 3: 5 (AV), 1611; *This is a spray* ʌ *the Bird clung to*—Browning, 1855; *She is engagingly grateful for the good luck* ʌ *she has had*—D. Davie, 1982; (omission of the conjunction *that*) *Direct mine Armes,* ʌ *I may embrace his Neck*—Shakespeare, 1591; *It may be* ʌ *they will reuerence him*—Luke 20: 13 (AV), 1611; *We were sorry* ʌ *you couldn't come*— *a*1912; *I felt* ʌ *I should have gone to the tradesmen's entrance*—G. Greene, 1980.

The two 20c. examples just cited have a natural feel about them, i.e. the omission of the conjunction *that* passes unnoticed. But things do not always go so smoothly. Examples showing that omission can produce forced constructions: *Keating made it plain yesterday* ʌ *he did not accept the thesis* ʌ *swinging voters can be spooked into voting for Labor by* [etc.]—*Aust. Financial Review*, 1993; *A practical argument for Australian action is* ʌ *the British themselves may yet seek a future in Europe. Britain is not demanding* ʌ *Australia remain a constitutional monarchy—it accepts* ʌ *the choice rests with Australia—Weekend Aust.*, 1993.

omit. The inflected forms are *omitted, omitting*. Cf. -T-, -TT-.

omnibus (vehicle). Now entirely supplanted by the shortened form *bus*, but if it is used in, for example, historical contexts the plural is *omnibuses*, not the pseudo-Latin *omnibi*. (The word is not a Latin noun ending in *-us*, but a Latin inflexion of the adjective *omnis*, and means 'for all'). Since the late 1920s the terms *omnibus book, volume*, etc., have been commonly used for a volume containing several novels, etc., previously published separately.

omniscience, -scient. The recommended pronunciation of *-sc-* in these words is /sɪənt/ rather than /ʃənt/.

omnium gatherum. A mock Latin formation, first recorded in 1530, for 'a miscellany or strange mixture (of persons or things)'.

on. **1** For *on all fours,* see FOUR. For *on to, onto,* and *on,* see ON TO, ONTO. For *on* and *upon,* see UPON. For *on* and *in* a street, see IN 2 (and below, 2).

2 North American (also elsewhere, but not standard in British English) use of *on* where *in* is standard in Britain: (place) *My father, may he rest in peace, had a dry-goods store on Gesia Street*—I. B. Singer, 1983; *'I've lived on Eagle Street fifty-five years,' Mike said*—*New Yorker,* 1986; *I head north on University Avenue*—M. Atwood, 1989; *The street Logan lived on was tranquil, shaded by an impressive congregation of sturdy trees*—M. Golden, 1989; (time; BrE prefers *at* but *on* is increasingly used) *On weekends she would play disk jockey like that for hours*—*New Yorker,* 1987. But cf. BrE *on Monday, Tuesday, Boxing Day,* etc.

-on. Plural of words derived directly or indirectly from Greek or modelled on Greek words and having in English the termination *-on*: **1** Some may, and often or always do, form the plural in *-a*: so *asyndeton,* AUTOMATON, CRITERION, GANGLION, *hyperbaton, noumenon, organon, parhelion,* PHENOMENON.

2 Others seldom or never use that form, but fall in with the normal English plurals in *-s*: so *cyclotron, electron, lexicon, neutron, oxymoron, proton, skeleton.*

3 In others again, the substitution of *-a* for *-on* to form the plural would be a blunder, their Greek plurals being, if they are actual Greek words, of some quite different form, and *-s* is the only plural used in English: such are *anion* (19c.), *archon, canon, cation* (19c.), *cotyledon, pylon, siphon.*

on account of. See ACCOUNT.

on behalf of. See BEHALF.

on board, onboard. Which is correct? It depends on the meaning and grammatical function. To talk about passengers on a ship or plane, you should write *on board* as two words: *the plane crashed with twenty people on board.* You should also write *on board* in non-literal phrases like *to take something on board* and *to bring someone on board.* In those examples, *on board* functions as an adverbial phrase. When the phrase is used as an adjective, for talking for example about a piece of equipment or computer fitted into a car, boat, plane, or other vehicle (*onboard DVD players for the kids*), some dictionaries hyphenate it *on-board,* while others write *onboard* as a single word. The *OEC* data suggests that *onboard* is used more than twice as often as *on-board.* There follow some 'correct' and 'incorrect' examples, according to the distinction made above. It is worth noting, however, that, possibly as a result of *online* being generally written as one word, *onboard* is far more often written that way even in the cases where it is suggested above that it should be two. Perhaps dictionaries have some catching up to do, which would make *onboard* parallel with *online.* Examples: (adjectival) *He read in the onboard sensors that the ship was swinging back around for another pass*; (adverbial, as two words) *She just caught me by the collar as I was sinking along with the ship and she hauled me on board*; (adverbial, not recognized by dictionaries as a one-word form, and not recommended) *Some 220 passengers were onboard at the time*; *When a major brings him onboard and gives him room to work, watch out.*

one.

1 Writing of *anyone, no one,* etc.
2 The type *one of, if not the finest, poem*; *one of the finest, if not the finest, poem.*
3 The type *one of those who need(s).*
4 *One in/out of ten women has/have.*
5 Impersonal or generic *one*; replacing *I.*
6 Possessive with impersonal *one.*
7 Mixtures of *one* with *he, you, they, my,* etc.

1 Writing of *anyone, no one,* etc. The written forms recommended are *anyone* (see ANY 2); EVERYONE; NO ONE; SOMEBODY, SOMEONE.

2 The type *one of, if not the finest, poem*; *one of the finest, if not the finest, poem.* The difficulty here is that people can easily be trapped into writing a mixture of two constructions. *One of the finest poems* is normal and so is *the finest poem,* but they should not be used together in writing in the way indicated above, although such mixed constructions sound natural in speech. Fowler (1926) cited several examples, pointing out acutely that these mixed constructions result from the desire to economize on words by using ellipsis. One of the examples he used was 'One of the finest, if not the finest, poem of an equal length produced of recent years'. However, as he explained, if the phrase introduced by *if not* is left out, grammatical nonsense results. Removing it from the first formulation above, i.e. *One of, ~~if not the finest,~~ poem of an equal length* . . . , produces **One of poem* . . . ; removing it from the second, i.e. *one of the finest, ~~if not the finest,~~ poem* . . . produces **One of the finest poem* . . . . Strictly grammatical sentences are produced in such cases by a simple rearrangement of the elements: *one of the finest poems of an equal length produced in recent years, if not the finest.*

3 The type *one of those who need(s).* As explained at AGREEMENT 8, it is normal to follow this and analogous phrases with a plural verb, pronoun, etc. (*regarding those rather than one as the antecedent*), unless particular attention is being drawn to the uniqueness, individuality, etc., of the *one* in the opening clause, in which case a singular verb is called for (plural verb in the subordinate clause). The same alternation between singular and plural applies also to *one of the things/considerations/*etc. *that* . . . *OEC* data suggests a preference for singular for both types of construction. *She was one of those women who make an enchanted garden of their childhood memories*—A. Brookner, 1990; *Oh, he's one of those people who need a nurturing older woman to listen to their woes*—A. Nelson, 1992 (US); *That*'s one of the things that happen to you—*Twitchfilm*, 2005; (singular verb in the subordinate clause) *He's one of those Yanks who wants to be really English, you know*—A. Motion, 1989; *'Don't you think,' said Bernard, 'that Hawaii is one of those places that was always better in the past?'*—D. Lodge, 1991; *Yes*, one of the things that makes the Lethal Weapon series special is the humor—*DVD Verdict*, 2000 (US).

4 *One in/out of ten women has/have.* The same consideration applies to phrases of this kind as to those in the previous section. According to strict grammatical analysis, the verb should be singular, since the subject is one, but plural agreement is as common, if not more so. Plural agreement is presumably influenced by the proximity of a number to the verb (i.e. proximity agreement comes into play) and by the idea that the group as a whole is the focus of the sentence. *OEC* data suggests a marked preference for the plural: (plural) *Fewer than one in ten US and Canadian households* use *cloth diapers*—*Mothering* (magazine), 2005 (US); (singular) *Only one in ten retained fire stations in Derbyshire* is *fully staffed in a situation which is stretching firefighters to the limit and could be putting people's lives at risk*—*Yorkshire Post*, 2002.

5 Impersonal, or generic *one*; replacing *I*. In the following examples two subtly different aspects of the pronoun are exemplified: *One is often forced to confess failure*; *One knew better than to swallow that.* In the first, *one* may be called an *impersonal pronoun*, standing for, the average person, or the sort of person we happened to be concerned with, or anyone of the class that includes the speaker. It does not mean a particular person, and in many ways corresponds to French *on* or German *man*. In the second, *one* is neither more nor less than a substitute for *I*: in that context it is often used ironically or with a sense of social superiority (see below). The distinction between the second and third types is often a fine one—indeed there is much overlapping. The use of *one* to mean *'any person', 'I'*, or *'me'* is often regarded as an affectation, although English does not always have a ready alternative. It is probably true to say that the more *one* is associated with *'I'* or *'me'*, the greater the affectation. A range of examples illustrating one or other type, or in some cases both: *The Caterpillar murmured—'One doesn't pretend to be a Christian, but as a gentlemen one accepts a bit of bad luck without gnashing one's teeth'*—H. A. Vachell, 1905; *Lady Seal* . . . *had told Anderson it* [*sc.* the bombardment] *was probably only a practice. That was what one told servants*—E. Waugh, 1942; *How to persuade the* Telegraph *that* . . . *one was a man of immense culture?* (*saying 'one' when you mean 'I' would do for a start, I decided*)—F. Johnson, 1982; *you must realize that there are risks that one doesn't take*—N. Gordimer, 1987; *This performance commanded attention; at times* . . . *it brought one's blood to a boil*—*Chicago Tribune*, 1988; *One knew immediately that he was a bad lot*—C. Phipps, 1989; *a highly readable classic that nevertheless got into the Guinness Book of Records for having been rejected 69 times before publication. One wonders why, does not one?*—*Fortune*, 1990 (US).

6 Possessive with impersonal *one.* What are the proper pronouns and adjectives to use after impersonal *one*? Impersonal *one* always can, and now usually does, provide its own possessive etc.—*one's, oneself,* and *one*. Thus *One does not like to have* one's *word doubted; If one fell,* one *would hurt* oneself *badly*. At various times in the past, and still often in AmE, the above sentences would run *One does not like to have* his (or even 'their') *word doubted; If one fell,* he *would hurt* himself *badly*. This tendency is now fast disappearing in AmE because of concern over sexual bias, and the BrE pattern of using *one* etc. is tending to be used in AmE too.

7 Mixtures of *one* with *he, you, they, my,* etc. These are all ill-advised, especially when they occur in the same sentence. Examples (with remedies): *As* one *who vainly warned* my *countrymen that Germany was preparing to attack her neighbours,* I *say that* ... (Replace *my* by *his,* let *I* stand); *To listen to his strong likes and dislikes* one *sometimes thought that* you were *in the presence of a Quaker of the eighteenth century* (Replace *you were* by *one was*); *As one walks ... down any street in Nashville one can feel now and again that* he has *just glimpsed* [etc.]—*New Yorker,* 1986 (Replace *he has* by *one has*); *Yet one can now see that it was the usages of the newly literate which have prevailed, so that* you cannot help *but feel* [etc.]—*English Today,* 1988 (Replace *you cannot help* with *one cannot help*).

An example of an 'unmixed' (i.e. standard) type: *If one has no base on which to formulate probing questions, can one actually give informed consent?*—*Dædalus,* 1986.

one another. See *each other* s.v. EACH 2.

one-time should be written as shown, with a hyphen, in both its meaning (i) 'former' (e.g. *a one-time actor*) and (ii) relating to a single occasion (e.g. *a one-time charge*). From which it follows that this example is incorrect: **One of the most exceptional artists to buck this trend was one time Marvin Gaye attachment Tammi Terrell*—*BBC Popular Music Reviews,* 2004.

one word or two or more. At any given time, English contains elements that are written together (or with a hyphen) by some writers, and as separate elements by others, influenced by personal taste or by geographical location. The editorial committees of publishing houses come and go and make their decisions in these matters as is their right. But there is no superfamily of scholars and writers—such as an academy or linguistic politburo—with the power to impose uniformity on everyone. As a result, the custom of this publishing house or that is to encourage *their* house-style: *to get under way* or *to get underway; straight away* or *straightaway; any more* or *anymore; common sense* or *common-sense* or *commonsense; loanword* or *loan-word* or *loan word*. In some cases a difference of meaning governs the way in which the parts are written (see e.g. EVERYONE and *every one*). More often the choice is just a matter of custom or fashion. An attempt has been made in the present book to make recommendations in such matters, especially but not only, for writers, printers, and the general public in the UK. Further marriages or divorces of such word elements are bound to happen in the future. It is salutary to remember that, for example, *any thing* was generally written as two words until the 19c., in the AV, by Milton, Addison, Richardson, Jane Austen, etc. Our language is a restless one: none of its components is static or wholly governable.

ongoing (adjective). First recorded in 1841, this adjective gained such widespread currency in the 1950s and beyond that it quickly attracted criticism as a vogue word particularly in the phrase *an ongoing situation,* as a cliché on a par with *at the end of the day, in this day and age,* etc. 'The phrase *ongoing situation* should be avoided at all times [on the BBC],' Burchfield declared in *The Spoken Word* (1981), suggesting that 'It signals a person's linguistic impoverishment.' That particular cliché seems to have faded away, and the word is widely used in many standard collocations (e.g. *ongoing investigation, process, effort, problem*), but can justifiably be slated as padding that adds little or nothing to the noun it qualifies: after all, if a problem is not resolved, it is by definition *ongoing*. More meaningful adjectives or adjectival phrases that suggest themselves are *persistent, continuing, current, in process,* etc. Preferably to be avoided is the inflated phrase *on an ongoing basis,* typical of business speak and officialese (e.g. *Honeywell, like many of our associates in the business world, is looking for potential strategic combinations on an ongoing basis*—*The Chief Executive* magazine, 2000), which could be stated in one word as *always, continually, regularly,* etc. If you have to use the word, it is best not hyphenated as *on-going.*

on line, online, on-line. When referring to computing and the Internet, how should this be written? The simplest solution is to write it as one word whether it is an adjective (*online banking, community, game, service, shopping,* etc.; *the article is online*) or an adverb (*shoppers would rather pick up the phone than do business online; apply, chat, go, shop, vote,* etc. *online; available, popular, published,* etc. *online*). This is the style that *ODO* endorses. As an adjective, it should never be written as separate words. To complicate matters, as an adverb, however, there is justification for doing so, since it can be viewed as an adverbial phrase no different from e.g. *in line, on time, in full,* etc. Some people prefer to write it this way (e.g. *People who can't tell what the vegetables are in their box can look them up on line*), but most people write it as one word. Apart from uses in the digital sphere, the phrase also appears in collocations such as *bring, come, get on line,* meaning 'to come or be put into operation', e.g. *EKPC plans to get all the generators on line this summer; new power plants coming on line are built for gas rather than coal or nuclear; you should be able to bring new oil fields on line. ODO* and some other dictionaries write this use also as a single word, but you are free to write it as two in order to keep the distinction from the digital meaning. In any event, the hyphenated form *on-line* is to be discouraged for both parts of speech, in accordance with the modern trend to avoid hyphenation when not strictly necessary.

only (adverb) **A** *The Issue.* **1** *Ambiguity in writing.* The position of *only* is one of the major unresolved topics of discussion in English usage. The upshot is that logical position, i.e. association with the word to which *only* most closely refers, is not always consistent with naturalness, which generally favours a position between the subject and the verb. *CGEL* (1985, 8.117) states that the natural intonation of a sentence containing an early-placed *only* will normally ensure that there is no ambiguity. In written English, however, it is quite another matter. In its written form the following sentence could be interpreted in three different ways: *John could only see his wife from the doorway* could imply (*a*) he could not talk to her; (*b*) he could not see her brother; or (*c*) he could not see her from further inside the room, depending on whether the main sentence stress is placed (*a*) on *see,* (*b*) on *wife,* (*c*) on *doorway.* In order to eliminate any possible ambiguity, meanings (*b*) and (*c*) could be written as *John could see only his wife from the doorway,* and *John could see his wife only from the doorway.*

2 *A light-hearted practice example.* Readers may like to experience how the placement of *only* affects meaning by using the single sentence that in a single lesson gave the writer Marghanita Laski and her classmates at preparatory school the ability for ever to use *only* correctly, that is to say, in its 'logical' position. The single sentence was *The peacocks are seen on the western hills.* The exercise was to place *only* in every possible place in the sentence (Only *the peacocks are seen; The peacocks are* only *seen,* etc.). Clearly the meaning changes with each new placing.

3 *Recommendation.* (*a*) In written English, the logical position of *only* should be respected when serious (rather than notional or theoretical) ambiguity would otherwise result, especially in contexts such as legal language in which precision is more important than a pleasing style: *The public interest is properly served only where companies pursue the traditional goal of profit maximisation*—J. E. Parkinson, 1993. In that example it would be more natural but also ambiguous to place *only* before *properly.* In a long article on the subject, Fowler made a case for allowing 'illogical' positioning in a sentence such as *He only died a week ago,* which is a great deal more natural and stylistically satisfactory than *He died only a week ago.* In general usage, the most natural position of *only* is where it always has been, between the subject and its verb, and invariable insistence on logical position sacrifices naturalness to pedantry.

(*b*) *Grammars and usage both support this approach.* (i) Jespersen (1909–49, vii) is quite explicit: 'Purists insist on placing *only* close to the word it qualifies, but as a matter of fact it is by most people placed between subject and verb, and stress and tone decide where it belongs.' One of his several examples neatly brings out the problem: [a journalist speaking] *I have only been married once. I mean I have been married only once*—G. B. Shaw, 1934. (ii) *Examples.* The view that a reader can be expected to supply the necessary intonation or make immediate contextual adjustments when *only* is allowed to drift to a front position in a sentence is supported by the following examples, in all of which *only* is placed at a distance from the element(s) which it limits: *I was ... made to attend a Catholic businessman's luncheon (where I only got wine by roaring for it)*—E. Waugh, 1958; *Boris doesn't eat shanks so, of course, I only cook them when he is away on circuit*—E. Jolley, 1985 (Aust.); *Those days, you only applied to one college*—*New Yorker*, 1986; *garments which Hartmann thought should only be worn by students or those of indeterminate age*—A. Brookner, 1988; *the Soviet flag only flew on official buildings*—*London Rev. Bks*, 1989; *Until I grew up, and she came to live with Uncle Roy and Aunt Deirdre, I only saw Granny at carefully spaced intervals*—A. N. Wilson, 1990; *He says he only took the job because the neon sign always cheers him up*—J. Barnes, 1991; *I'm afraid I only seem to have five pounds*—P. Lively, 1991; *I only wanted to work with vocalists*—BBC Popular Music Reviews, 2004.

The placing of *only* takes us to a front-line battle which has been raging for more than 250 years. It would be perverse to ignore the evidence provided by so many of our best writers when they are prepared to allow *only* to make an early entrance in a sentence and leave common sense to work out the meaning.

B *Historical Background.* **1** *Origin of the shibboleth.* The first grammarian known to have commented on the placing of *only* is Robert Lowth (1762): 'The Adverb, as its name imports, is generally placed close or near to the word, which it modifies or affects; and its propriety and force depend on its position. [*footnote*] Thus it is commonly said, "I *only* spake three words": when the intention of the speaker manifestly requires, "I spake *only* three words."' Numerous other grammarians followed suit and urged their readers to pay regard to the placing of *only*.

2 *Historical examples of varying placements.* The *OED* (3rd edn) editors give numerous examples of each of three different placings and limit themselves to commenting about (*c*) as shown there: (*a*) Preceding the word or phrase which it limits (illustrative examples from *a*1325 to 2002), e.g. *To distinguish ... that which is established because it is right, from that which is right only because it is established*—Johnson, 1751; *It is true, I have been only twice*—T. Harral, 1805); (*b*) Following the word or phrase which it limits (examples from *c*.1350 to 2000), e.g. *What belongs to Nature only, Nature only can complete*—J. Brown, 1763; *In one only of the casements*—Lytton, 1838); (*c*) 'Placed away from the word or phrase which it limits, esp. preceding the main verb. Frequent in speech, where stress and pauses eliminate ambiguity; often avoided by careful writers' (examples from 1483 to 2001), e.g. *When Beasts were only slain for Sacrifice*—Dryden, 1697; *I only asked the question from habit*—Jowett, 1875; *I've been seeing a much older man who says he only wants to be friends*—*Bella* (magazine), 1988).

3 *Fowler's view.* Fowler (1926) presented the case for the acceptance of the 'illogical' placing of *only* in such a sentence as *He only died a week ago*: since 'the risk of misunderstanding [is] chimerical, it is not worth while to depart from the natural'. He thought it reasonable that 'a reader should be supposed capable of supplying the decisive intonation' to bring out the meaning, and argued strongly that only 'one of the modern precisians who have more zeal than discretion' would wish to write *He died only a week ago*. His insistence was expressed in colourful language: 'the pedants who try to forward it [*sc.* a tendency shown by a language to eliminate illogicalities as time passes] when the illogicality is only apparent or the inaccuracy of no importance are turning English into an exact science or an automatic machine; if they are not quite botanizing upon their mother's grave, they are at least clapping a strait waistcoat upon their mother tongue, when wiser physicians would refuse to certify the patient.'

He further argued that there were many longer sentences in which it is important to 'get [an] announcement of purport made by an advanced *only*'. A precisian, he argued, is bound to insist on an orthodox placing of *only* in the following sentence: *It would be safe to prophesy success to this heroic enterprise only if reward and merit always corresponded.* Fowler claimed that the sentence 'positively cries out to have its *only* put early after *would.*' He concluded: 'there is an orthodox position for the adverb, easily determined in case of need; to choose another position that may spoil or obscure the meaning is bad; but a change of position that has no such effect except technically is both justified by historical and colloquial usage and often demanded by rhetorical needs.'

3 *Conjunction.* The word *only* works also as a conjunction in sentences such as the following, in which it means 'except that, but': *he is still a young man, only he seems older because of his careworn expression; the place was like school, only better.* This use has been criticized since the 19c. as dialectal or too informal for writing. The *OED* shows that the word has been used in this way since the 14c., e.g. *For, brethren, ye have been called unto liberty; only use not liberty for an occasion to the flesh, but by love serve one another*—Gal. 5:13 (AV); *I ... would like to catch the trick in his style—only I fear its thinking*—V. Woolf, 1920. Readers can no doubt decide for themselves if a usage more than six centuries old is to be avoided.

onomatopoeia (adjective **-poeic**): 'name-making'. The formation of names or words from sounds that resemble those associated with the object or action to be named, or that seem suggestive of its qualities: *atishoo, babble, cuckoo, croak, ping-pong, puff-puff,* and *sizzle* are probable examples. The word is also used of sequences of words whose sound suggests what they describe, as in Tennyson's *Myriads of rivulets hurrying thro' the lawn, The moan of doves in immemorial elms, And murmuring of innumerable bees.*

on to, onto. 1 *On to* or *onto*? (*a*) The complex preposition *onto* written as one word (instead of *on to*) is recorded from the early 18th century and has been widely used ever since, but is still not wholly accepted as part of standard British English (unlike *into*, for example). Many style guides still advise writing it as two words. However, *onto* is more or less the standard form in US English and in the specialized mathematics sense. (b) It is important to maintain a distinction between the two words functioning as a complex preposition, in which case *onto* is allowable, and the use of *on* as an independent adverb followed by the preposition *to*: *she climbed* on to (*or* onto) *the roof* but *let's go* on to (*not* onto) *the next point*, in which the adverb *on* forms part of a meaning unit, or phrasal verb, with *go*. It should also be noted that *They drove* on to *the beach* would normally mean 'They continued the journey until they reached the beach' but could also mean 'They drove their vehicle to a position on the beach'; whereas *They drove* onto *the beach* could only mean 'They drove their vehicle to a position on the beach'. (*c*) Further examples. In these *on* is used as a full adverb before *to* and is therefore written separately: *It was some time before she cottoned on to what he meant; We must walk on to Keswick; Each passed it on to his neighbour; Struggling on to victory.* See UPON.

2 *To be on to somebody/something.* In all varieties of English, these two phrases are more often written with *on to* separately: *Everybody has been on to that for some time*—J. C. Lincoln, 1911; *I can't help feeling that he's on to us ... That he knows about us*—J. Osborne, 1959; *But if Palmer can break free of his genre's clichés and pitfalls, he might be on to something*—*OEC*, 2004; *Could they be onto something?*—*Manchester Music*, 2002.

3 *A historical note.* (*a*) Written as two words, *on to* is first recorded as a complex preposition in 1581 (*I haue stept on to the stage ... contented to plaie a part*) and has been in continuous use since then. In all the following examples except the 1992 one, *onto* could be used, e.g. *He subsided on to the music-bench obediently*—Mrs H. Ward, 1888; *French windows opened from the breakfast-room on to the terrace and large walled garden*—P. Lively, 1981; *A tear trickled on to the pillow*—A. Brookner, 1991; *An important determining factor here was the need to ensure that the paint had dried completely on one side of the sheet before moving on to the other*—*Bodl. Libr. Rec.*, 1992; *my knees gave way and I collapsed on to the seat opposite*—A. Billson, 1993. (*b*) Written as one word, *onto* is first recorded as a preposition in 1715 (*[A] place gutted away by the rain down onto Mr. Wiswells land*) and has been in continuous use since then (e.g. *He jumped down onto the rubbish*—C. S. Lewis, 1954; *There is nothing in the room to hold onto*—D. Hirson, 1986 (SAfr.); *He sank down once again onto his footstool*—A. Brookner, 1989; *He advanced onto the verandah*—I. Murdoch, 1989; *The blue sky threw its light down onto the fields below*—L. Norfolk, 1991; *Once again paper will disappear, this time onto optical discs like CD-ROM and CD-I*—*Logos*, 1992).

onward, onwards. As an adjective the shorter form is obligatory (*resuming his onward journey*). As adverb both *onward* and *onwards* are used (*from the tenth century onward(s)*); the longer form is more frequent throughout all varieties of English, and five times so in BrE, but the shorter form is about twice as frequent in AmE.

oolite (a sedimentary rock). Pronounced as three syllables, /ˈəʊəlʌɪt/.

opacity, opaqueness. Both mean 'the quality or state or an instance of being opaque' and both are used in concrete as well as in abstract senses. *Opacity* is the preferred form in various technical senses in physics, philosophy, etc.

op. cit. (Latin *opere citato*), an abbreviation meaning 'in the work already cited'. It is normally preceded by the name of the author and set out thus in roman: Bloomfield, op. cit., pp. 54–5.

operculum (flaplike structure covering gills of fish). Plural *opercula*. See -UM 2.

ophthalmologist, optician, optometrist, oculist. An *ophthalmologist* is a person who makes a scientific study of the eye, its structure, functions, and diseases; especially a medical practitioner specializing in the diagnosis and treatment of the eye. An *optician* (also called an *ophthalmic optician* and nowadays often an *optometrist*) is a person qualified to test the eyes and prescribe and supply spectacles and contact lenses. A *dispensing optician* is a person who supplies and fits spectacle frames but is not qualified to prescribe lenses. An *oculist* is a somewhat old-fashioned term for an *ophthalmologist*. In America, one is more likely to go to an *optometrist* for the testing of eyesight and prescribing of 'eyeglasses', but the synonym *optician* is also used. The term *ophthalmologist* is used in the same way as in Britain.

opinion. For *climate of opinion*, see CLIMATE.

opportunity. One *takes the opportunity*, or *an opportunity*, or *every opportunity*, to do something, or, less commonly, *of* doing something (*the opportunity of going over the papers*). Constructions of *opportunity* followed by *for* + gerund are more difficult to find (*opportunities for procuring advantages to ourselves*), but examples of *opportunity* followed by *for* + noun (phrase) are reasonably frequent (*provided an opportunity for greater leisure*).

oppose has the derivative **opposable**, as in *opposable thumbs*. See -ABLE, -IBLE 7.

opposite. As adjective, *opposite* 'having a position on the other or further side', is construed either with *to* (*two persons directly opposite to each other*) or with *from* (*on the opposite side of the river from that on which his house stood*). When used as a noun, *opposite* is construed with *of* (*Ariel is the extreme opposite of Caliban*). *Opposite* may also be used as a preposition (*they sat down opposite each other*), in which case it is a shortening of *opposite to*.

opposite meanings, words of. A minor curious feature of English is the coexistence at a given time of apparently opposite meanings under the umbrella of the same, or what appears to be the same, word. The phenomenon occurs, for example, in the verb *to cleave,* which means (*a*) to stick fast to (*Rose's mouth was dry, her tongue cleaving to the roof of her mouth*) and (*b*) to split or sever something (*You can cleave the log in two with an axe*). With *cleave* the two are different words etymologically, but another example is the single verb *dust*, meaning (*a*) remove the dust from or (*b*) sprinkle with a powdered substance (*I broke the vase I had been dusting; roll out on a surface dusted with icing sugar*). A more notorious example is *bad* being used also to mean 'good, excellent' in US slang (*I say read these poets of the Seventies. They got something bad to say.*) Words with this feature are called 'contronyms' or 'autoantonyms'. Other examples are *oversight* and *sanction*. See also CHUFFED (= pleased/displeased) for a word that is a contronym only in dialect terms.

optative. Can be pronounced /ɒpˈteɪtɪv/ (op-**tay**-tiv) stressing the first syllable, or stressing the second, /ˈɒptətɪv/ (**op**-tuh-tiv).

optician. See OPHTHALMOLOGIST.

optimal, optimum. For a little over a century (both words entered the language in the late 19c.) these words have been vying with each other as adjectives in the sense 'best or most favourable (under given conditions), most satisfactory'. The *OEC* data shows *optimal* to be more than twice as frequent, but otherwise there is little difference between the words, and they enter into the same collocations, e.g. *optimal/optimum alignment, dosage, configuration, temperature,* etc. Neither word is appropriately used as a substitute for a simple *best*, as in *although such lies will secure you many inquiries, none of the dates are likely to go well. An optimum strategy is to go for exaggeration.*

optometrist. See OPHTHALMOLOGIST.

opus. For a musical composition and in the phrase *magnum opus* the recommended pronunciation is /ˈəʊpəs/ with a long *ō*. The plural is either *opera* /ˈɒpərə/ or *opuses* /ˈəʊpəsɪz/.

opuscule (minor musical or literary work) /əˈpʌskjuːl/. Plural *opuscules*. **Opusculum**, plural *opuscula*, is also used in the same sense: see -UM 2.

or. 1 Verb agreement after *or*. (*a*) *Singular subjects.* When the subject is a set of alternatives each in the singular, however many the alternatives, and however long the sentence, the verb must be in the singular. Examples: *Costs ... will only be awarded when the behaviour or stance of one or other party is in some way unreasonable*—*Counsel*, 1987; *One had to ... admit that a paint or steel company or a salt or coal mine was no place for the late Herr Baumgartner's widow*—A. Desai, 1988. Occasionally notional agreement leads to an incorrect plural verb being used: *The effect of anti-racist casting may not be that which the playwright intended but ... it may not be that which the actor or director intend either*—*Listener*, 1988.

(*b*) *Mixed or plural subjects.* When both or all subjects are plural, obviously the verb is plural. When one subject is singular and the other plural, the verb is also plural, irrespective of whether it comes second or first. Examples: The words or order militate *against such an interpretation*—*Modern Banking Law*, 2002; *This works particularly well where* your spouse or children have *little or no income*—*Beyond Numbers* (magazine), 2005.

(*c*) *Person of the verb with pronouns different in number.* If alternative pronouns separated by *or* differ in number, the nearest prevails: e.g. *Were you or he there?*; *Was he or you there?* (To avoid the awkwardness of *was* elliptically referring to *you* in the second example, give the verb twice: *Was he, or were you, there?*).

2 See also EITHER 5; NEITHER 6; NOR 7.

-or is the Latin agent noun ending corresponding to English *-er*: compare *doer* and *perpetrator*. English verbs derived from the supine stem of Latin ones—i.e. especially most verbs in *-ate*, but also many others such as *act, credit, invent, oppress, possess, prosecute, protect*—usually prefer this Latin ending to the English one in *-er*. Some other verbs, e.g. *conquer, govern,* and *purvey,* not corresponding to the above description also have agent nouns in *-or* owing to their passage through French or because of some other circumstance. Compare the following: *corrupter* and *corrector*; *deserter* and *abductor*; *dispenser* and *distributor*; *eraser* and *ejector*. From some verbs come alternative forms, e.g. *adapter/adaptor*, both of which are valid spellings for the human and mechanical meanings; in other cases the *-er* spelling is for laypeople's use and the *-or* for the lawyers, e.g. *abetter/abettor, accepter/acceptor, deviser/devisor*, etc. See also ACCEPTER; ADAPTER; ADVISER; CASTER; -ER AND -OR.

oral. See AURAL; VERBAL.

orate (verb) can mean either simply 'to deliver an oration' or, in humorous or disparaging use, 'to speechify, to hold forth pompously or at length'. Although the word is based directly on the Latin verb *ōrāre* ('to speak, plead, pray'), it looks like a back-formation, and the *OED* notes that 'The word is only rarely attested before the second half of the 19th cent. when it was apparently re-formed after e.g. *oration* n., *orator* n. (perhaps first in the U.S ...).' The *OED* and the *OEC* show both the straightforward and the disparaging uses. Examples: (straightforward) *Four actresses, who ... obtained better salaries for orating at Carlisle-house*—*Town & Country Mag.*, 1780; *I never became an orator. People do not orate in England as they do in America*—G. B. Shaw, 1905; (disparaging) *Kerry is an old-fashioned senatorial blowhard, with a tendency to 'orate'*—*www.reason.com*, 2002; *A drumroll and a blare of trumpets accompany Hun Sen's arrival. He then proceeds to orate. And orate*—*OEC* (undated).

oratio obliqua, recta ('bent speech, straight speech'). These are the Latin names respectively for reported and direct speech. See REPORTED SPEECH.

orator. So spelt, not *-er*. See -OR.

oratorio. Plural *oratorios*. See -O(E)S 4.

orbit has the derivatives **orbital**, *orbited, orbiting*. See -T-, -TT-.

orchid, orchis. The first is the familiar (greenhouse) 'epiphytic plant of the family Orchidaceae, bearing flowers in fantastic shapes and brilliant colours, [etc.]' (*COD*), grown outdoors in temperate and tropical regions. The *orchis* is 'any orchid of the genus *Orchis*, with a tuberous root and an erect fleshy stem having a spike of usu. purple or red flowers; any of various wild orchids' (*COD*). Plural *orchids* (for both words), but usu. *orchises* for *orchis*. Both words are originally from Greek ὄρχις 'testicle' (with reference to the shape of its tuber).

order (noun). **1** See IN ORDER THAT; IN ORDER TO.

2 *of the order of* is a COMPOUND PREPOSITION meaning 'in the region of, somewhere about' (*the average flow through the gorge is of the order of 2,000–3,000 cubic metres per second*). It is a POPULARIZED TECHNICAL TERM from a more complex use of the term in mathematics.

order (verb). The construction *ordered* + object + past participle (often expressed in the passive) is first recorded in 1781 in AmE (*These things were ordered delivered to the army*—J. Witherspoon) and has been predominantly American ever since: BrE normally requires the insertion of *to be* before the past participle. Further examples: *My bill was introduced by Senator Williams of Oregon, read by title, and ordered printed*—J. H. Beadle, 1873; *twelve other neighborhood people testified in court that they ... would feel horrible if the jury ordered them* [*sc.* church bells] *unplugged*—*New Yorker*, 1990; *An 11-year-old English girl allegedly left alone when her mother went on a holiday in Spain was ordered kept in the care of local authorities yesterday*—*Dominion* (Wellington, NZ), 1993.

orderly. See -LILY. The word is used only as an adjective (*behaved in an orderly manner*), never as an adverb The notional adverbial form *orderlily* does not exist.

ordinance, ordnance, ordonnance. An *ordinance* is 'an authoritative order'; *ordnance* is 'a branch of government service dealing esp. with military stores and materials; *specif.* artillery'; and *ordonnance* is 'a plan or method of literary or artistic composition; an order of architecture' (*The most conspicuous qualities of the style are these: ordonnance, or arrangement and structure, precision in the use of words, and relevant intensity*—T. S. Eliot, 1936; *the dead figure ... is not exaggerated and achieves a monumental 'ordonnance' which is nearly classical*—*Burlington Mag.*, 1938). **Ordnance Survey** is an official UK survey organization, originally under the Master of the Ordnance, preparing large-scale detailed maps of the whole country.

oread (mountain nymph in Greek and Roman mythology). Pronounced /ˈɔːrɪad/.

oriel. See BAY WINDOW.

orient, orientate (verbs). **1** *Which to use.* In the perverse way in which such things can happen, these two verbs have the same origin (French *orienter* 'to place facing the east') but came into competition with one another in the second half of the 20c. The key difference between them is that *orient* is more frequent in a ratio of 7:1 in all meanings across all varieties of English, including British (in which the ratio drops to 2:1). In AmE *orientate* is almost unheard of, occurring in a mere 3 per cent of cases. The *OED* notes '*Orientate* is commonly regarded as an incorrect usage in American English', and even if it is not regarded as incorrect it will be viewed as anomalous, or as a pointless longer variant of *orient*.

2 *History and examples.* The shorter form emerged in the 18c. (first cited in *Chambers Cyclopaedia* of 1728) and the longer one, in the same sense (as in the French original), in the 19c. (1848), both with the meaning 'to face or cause to face east' specifically in relation to the east-west alignment of churches. Both words then went in identical directions and developed the same extended senses: 'to place in any particular way with respect to the cardinal points of the compass'; and, figuratively, 'to ascertain one's "bearings"'. In particular both words are frequently used as participial adjectives (*oriented, orientated*). Their semantic parallelism is brought out clearly by the collocations they share in the *OEC*, (*a*) Preceded by an adverb: *academically, religiously, vertically, visually oriented/orientated*; (*b*) Preceded by a noun (to which it should be hyphenated): *business-, community-, family-, service-oriented/orientated.* But when adverbs denoting position or orientation follow the past participle, only *oriented* is used, e.g. *oriented horizontally, perpendicularly, obliquely, north, east,* etc.

Further examples: (orient(ed)) *Man needs relations with other people in order to orient himself*—R. May, 1953; *He can begin the next big step . . . of becoming emotionally more independent of his parents and oriented instead towards the outside community and its ways of doing things*—B. Spock, 1955; *In a youth-oriented society for a woman to grow old means to run the risk of being ignored*—A. Hutschnecker, 1981; *Email is more interactive, more oriented to exchange; the pleasure of reading and writing is produced through the interrelationality and reciprocity of the epistolary mode*—*Text*, 2003; *The four similar buildings are oriented differently, so that from any given vantage point, they demonstrate a dramatic diversity*—*Architecture Week*, 2000; (orientate(d)) *In a language like Malagasy it is also possible to orientate the predicate with respect to what in French would be a circumstantial complement*—E. Palmer, 1964; *Kant's own philosophy was undeniably orientated towards problems that lay at the heart of the philosophical enterprise*—P. Gardiner, 1988; *It was very much a London-orientated magazine*—N. Sherry, 1987; *Despite the fact that the game has been marketed as if it's a family orientated adventure title*—*Gamepower Australia*, 2002; *Even those routes that are orientated towards business travellers are still competing with existing services to other airports, making it harder and harder for the carriers to get bums on seats*—*Scotland on Sunday*, 2004.

In the face of the evidence, what is one to do? If one uses *orientate,* one maintains a largely BrE form which is out of step with international English usage. On the other hand, for many it will be the preferred and natural form.

originator. So spelt, not *-er*. See -OR.

orison (prayer). Pronounced /ˈɒrɪzən/.

Orleans, New. Pronounced /ɔːˈliːənz/. But some prefer to stress on the first syllable: /ˈɔːlɪənz/.)

ornament. The noun is pronounced /ˈɔːnəmənt/ with an obscure vowel (schwa) in the final syllable. The verb, by contrast, normally has a clear /ɛ/ in the final syllable.

ornithology, etc. In Greek the *i* is long, but in English words derived from Greek ὀρνῑθο- (*ornithophile, ornithorhyncus,* etc.) a short *i* is now usual.

orography, oropharyngeal etc. Two different formative elements yield words in *oro-*: (*a*) Greek ὄρος 'mountain' (e.g. *orogeny* or *orogenesis,* the formation of mountains; *orography,* the branch of physical geography dealing with the formation of mountains); (*b*) Latin *ōs, ōr-* 'mouth' (e.g. *oronasal, oropharyngeal*).

orotund. This delightful and underused word was proscribed by Fowler because it is an 'irregular' 18c. reduction of the classical Latin (Horatian) phrase *ōre rotundō* 'with round, well-turned speech' (literally 'with round mouth'). Almost onomatopoeically, it can mean either 'resonant and imposing' referring to a person's voice (think Mr Carson in *Downton Abbey*), or 'pompous or pretentious' referring to a style of verbal expression. Examples: *When more emotion was needed, the volume was turned up, or the elocution became more orotund*—*New York Metro*, 2004; *There, speaking in orotund tones, the Court announces that 'Liberty finds no refuge in a jurisprudence of doubt.'*—*FindLaw's Writ*, 2003; *An orotund Tory in pinstripes boomed out that he never expected to see the day when he would stand shoulder to shoulder with Tatchell and cry revolution*—*Guardian Unlimited*, 2005; *a curious historical paradox that dictates declarations of crisis should always be written in slow, orotund prose that declares emergency and demands urgency but does so at the slowest possible pace and with maximum ambiguity*—*Scotland on Sunday*, 2005.

orthopaedic. So spelt in BrE, but usually as **orthopedic** in AmE.

osculate, osculatory. (Cf. Latin *osculārī* 'to kiss'.) Since the 17c. (the verb) and the 18c. (the adjective) these words have been used in several technical senses (in geometry, anatomy, biology, etc.) with the central meaning of 'being, or coming into contact with, some specified thing'. As a noun an *osculatory* is 'a painted, stamped, or carved representation of Christ or the Virgin, formerly (18–19c.) kissed by the priest and people during Mass'. During this period, and still (just), the verb and adjective have occasionally been called on in humorous contexts in place of the natural words *kiss* and *kissing*. Examples: *The two ladies went through the osculatory ceremony*—Thackeray, 1849; *As against this, there are several scenes devoted to the osculatory prowess of the upper-class*—*The Hindu*, 2002; *None of that endless schlepping up and down the country, pressing sweaty palms with the hoi polloi and osculating sprogs*—*Me Three* (magazine), 2005.

ostler. Pronounced /ˈɒslə/. A term used 14–19c. (and still with historical reference) for a man who attended the horses at an inn. The word is a phonetic respelling of *hosteler, hostler* (and thus etymologically related to *hostel* and *hotel*), representing the historical pronunciation with *h* mute. See HOSTLER.

other.

1 *each other* and *one another*.
2 *on the other hand*.
3 Objections to *other* as adverb in *other than*.
4 *of all others*.
5 *other* or *others*.
6 *a whole other* + noun.
7 Archaic irregular word order.

1 *each other* and *one another*. See EACH 2.

2 *on the other hand*. For the difference between this and *on the contrary* see CONTRARY 2.

3 Objections to *other* as adverb in *other than*. When *other* is a pronoun or adjective in *other than*, its use is straightforward and causes no comment: *I'd never known anything other than hard times*—D. Dears, 1974. Objections have been raised to *other than* when *other* is forced into the role of adverb (which it does not otherwise have), and Fowler (1926) regarded it as 'ungrammatical and needless' when a genuine adverb, *otherwise*, is available; so in the following example he would have urged use of *otherwise than* in place of *other than*: *Other than at football matches or on coach journeys, people sing less spontaneously than in previous generations*—T. Portsmouth, 1992. However, the grammar of *other than* is not always so clear-cut, as the following example shows: *I married her . . . but it never even occurred to me that our marriage would be other than a marriage in name only*—A. Roudybush, 1972. Is *other* here an adjective linked to *marriage* or an adverb linked to *be*? (The answer is a bit of both.) In BrE it is common and generally unexceptionable, and often more idiomatic than the awkward alternative *otherwise than*, but readers should be aware of the caveat attached to it in more pedantic circles. Major American dictionaries just list the adverbial use of *other* in *other than* without comment and give routine illustrative examples (e.g. *not being able to sell the product other than by reducing the price*—Webster's Third, 1961; *We can't collect the rent other than by suing the tenant*—*Random House Dict.*, 1987). *MWCDEU* (1989) illustrates the use of *other than* followed by various parts of speech and in various constructions, and concludes that in some of them it is being treated as a compound preposition. 'All of these uses are standard English,' it declares.

4 *of all others*. A fading use cited in the *OED* from Steele (1711) (*This Woman, says he, is of all others the most unintelligible*), and several other sources (e.g. *In Birmingham, the very place, of all others, where it is most likely to be of real* service—J. Morley, 1877). The phrase was called an 'illogicality' and a 'sturdy indefensible' by Fowler (1926), who cited as an example *You are the man of all others I wanted to see* (a mixture, according to Fowler, of *You are the man of all men* etc. and *You are the man I wanted to see beyond all others*). If you use the phrase you will be regarded as swimming against the tide. Further example: *But how could Israel, the nation which of all others understood the horror of mass murder, have allowed the Palestinians of Sabra and Chatila camps . . . to have been murdered*—R. Fisk, 1990.

5 *other* or *others*. Used as a pronoun, *other* was formerly often (and still occasionally) an uninflected plural: *A body of men whom of all other a good man would be most careful not to violate*—Berkeley, 1713; *I know two other of his works*—J. H. Newman, 1844; *Petite teenage girls . . . often perform and record Paganini's caprices, concertos and other of his works with exceptional virtuosity*—*Strad*, 1990; *In her youth R. knew Werner von Braun and other of the German scientists who came to the United States after the war*—weblog, 2003.

The now normal form *others* is recorded from the 16c. onwards: e.g. *Loans from the citizens of London and others of her subjects*—H. Hallam, 1827; *In others of his sermons*—H. H. Milman, 1868; *I want to compare the will with others of the same period—NY Rev. Bks*, 1991; *Some typefaces look larger than others of the same size because their* x-height, *the height of the lowercase* x, *is higher—PC Computing*, 1992.

6 *a whole other* + noun. This informal use of *a whole other* + noun to mean 'an entirely different, separate or additional . . . ' seems to have begun life in AmE: *He had a family, a whole other life, in Florida*—J. Silber, 1991; *I thought she was going to come up with a whole other kind of animal, but this was just as good*—J. Hecht, 1992; *But tonight, it's a whole other story for some Hollywood stars who have had a rough few weeks—CNN transcripts*, 2005.

7 *Archaic irregular word order. Other* is called a postdeterminer by modern grammarians in that it normally follows other determiners, including (sometimes) numerals (*our other neighbours*; *several other places*; *four other people*; *the other end*; but *the other two men in the room*). It is worth recalling that from the OE period until the 19c. *other* was often placed in a manner that seems strange or impossible now: e.g. *The kynge of Fryse, & other his prysoners*—Caxton, *c.*1489; *amonge other his good qualities*—N. Harpsfield, 1558; *hee stayed yet other seuen dayes—Gen.* 8:10 (AV), 1611; *With other the great men of Scotland*—J. H. Burton, 1864.

otherwise. 1 *The (now dead and buried) issue.* 'A definite outrage on grammatical principles' was Fowler's verdict in 1926 on the structure *economic or otherwise,* i.e. the use of an adjective + *or* (or *and*) + *otherwise.* He was the first grammarian to note this use, and fulminated at great length against it. His examples included: *There are large tracts of the country,* agricultural and otherwise, *in which the Labour writ does not run*; *No further threats,* economic or otherwise, *have been made.* He said that 'none of them would be less natural if the offending expressions were rewritten thus: *some agricultural and some not* / *No further economic or other threats*'. But the language has moved on, and in any case the pattern condemned by Fowler dates back to 1425, is now in standard use, and has been extended to cover other parts of speech (preceding the *or* or *and*) as well.

2 *Current use.* The current *OED* glosses the phrase as '(following a noun, adjective, adverb, or verb, to signify a corresponding word, thing, idea, etc., of opposite or alternative meaning) or the converse'. Examples: *Mrs. Lidderdale's dread . . . was that her son would acquire a West country burr, and it was considered more prudent, economically and otherwise, to go on learning with his grandfather and herself*—C. Mackenzie, 1922; *I do not question the eruption at Santorini . . . but the supposed connection of the underwater survey with the historicity or otherwise of the Atlantis myth—Listener*, 1966; *12,000 Cowley workers enjoyed* (*or otherwise*) *an enforced holiday because of a strike by plant attendants at the car assembly factory—Oxford Times*, 1973; *It's the balance of foods you eat that is healthy or otherwise—Which?*, 1989; *The blameworthiness or otherwise of another party bears no relation to the issue of the instant trader's diligent pursuit of safety—Statute Law Rev.*, 1991.

otiose. This rather learned or highfalutin synonym for 'redundant, superfluous', comes from the Latin *ōtiōsus*, 'idle, useless, superfluous'. I have only once in my entire life heard it uttered (perhaps I should get out more, or else move in more refined circles), and that by a senior figure at *OUP*, who pronounced it /ˈəʊtɪəʊz/ (**oh**-ti-ohz). Alternatives are /ˈəʊtɪəʊs/ (**oh**-ti-ohs) or /ˈəʊʃɪəʊs/ (**oh**-shi-ohs), which is given preference in AmE dictionaries.

ottava rima. Pronounced /əʊˈtɑːvə ˈriːmə/ and printed in roman. An Italian stanza of eight eleven-syllabled lines rhyming abababcc, pioneered by Boccaccio in the 14c. and employed by Tasso, Ariosto, and other Italian poets. It was introduced into English by Thomas Wyatt (1503–42). The English version as used by Byron in *Don Juan,* as well as by Keats, Shelley, Yeats, and others, has iambic pentameters but in other respects follows the Italian model.

Whate'er his youth had sufferd, his old age
With wealth and talking made him some amends;
Though Laura sometimes put him in a rage,
I've heard the count and he were always friends.
My pen is at the bottom of a page,
Which being finished here the story ends;
'Tis to be wish'd it had been sooner done,
But stories somehow lengthen when begun.
(Byron, 1818)

ought (noun). Since the mid-19c. *ought* has sometimes been used as a colloquial corruption of *nought*, e.g. *a half smeared-out game of oughts and crosses*—G. A. Sala, 1861; *'But did they find a rifle on Sutton?' 'Yep. Thirty-ought-six.'*—D. Anthony, 1972; *Strawberry Bill had played left field for Toronto in ought eight when Francis played third*—W. Kennedy, 1979; *Sir William Walton was born in nineteen ought two*—announcer on Radio WNIB (US), 29 Mar. 1993. It probably arose from a misdivision of *a nought* as *an ought*.

ought (verb). **1** This modal verb has a complicated history but in its normal uses now it is followed by a *to*-infinitive: *Two people advised me recently ... that I ought to see a doctor*—T. S. Eliot, 1950; *But oughtn't I first to tell you the circumstances?*—ibid, 1950; *You ought to have a cooked breakfast, these cold mornings*—D. Lodge, 1988; *If Canada should disintegrate ... what ought the U.S. to do?*—*Wall St. Jrnl*, 1990. *Ought* is peculiarly liable to be carelessly combined with auxiliary verbs that differ from it in taking the plain infinitive without *to*. *Can and ought to go* is right, but *ought and can go* is wrong. *We should be sorry to see English critics suggesting that they ought or could have acted otherwise*: insert *to* after *ought*, or write *that they could or ought to have acted*. See ELLIPSIS for similar difficulties. The negative equivalent is *ought not to* (or, as a contracted form, *oughtn't to*). The *to* is optional in ellipses: *Yes, I think I ought* (*to*). It is also optional in informal non-assertive contexts (*non-assertive* is the term used in *CGEL*): e.g. *They ought not* (*to*) *do that sort of thing*; *Oughtn't we* (*to*) *send for the police?* But the more natural standard expressions are *They oughtn't to do that* or *They shouldn't do that*; and *Shouldn't we send for the police?*

2 See DIDN'T OUGHT.

3 *hadn't ought.* Only found in dialectal use in parts of Britain and America: e.g. *Did you do that? You hadn't ought* (= ought not to have done it).

our.

1 *our* or *ours*.
2 *our* editorial and ordinary.
3 *our, his.*

1 *our* or *ours.* A difficulty can arise when *our* is used in conjunction with another qualifying word as in *The NATO and our troops*; *Our and the NATO troops.* A better alternative is *The NATO troops and ours*, but not **Ours and the NATO troops.* See ABSOLUTE POSSESSIVES.

2 *our* editorial and ordinary. The editorial *our*, like *we* and *us* of that kind, should not be allowed to appear in the same sentence as, or in close proximity to, any non-editorial use of *we*, etc. In the following extract, *our* and the second *we* are editorial, while *us* and the first *we* are national: *For chaos it is now proposed to substitute law, law by which* we *must gain as neutrals, and which in* our *view, inflicts no material sacrifice on* us *as belligerents.* We *do not propose to argue that question again from the beginning, but ...*

3 *our, his. Which of us would wish to be ill in* our *kitchen, especially when it is also the family living room?* If a possessive adjective were necessary, *his* and not *our* would be the right one, or, in our gender-conscious age, *his or her*. People of weak grammatical digestions, unable to stomach *his*, have a means of doing without the possessive altogether: why not simply *the kitchen*, here? Grammatical concord requires that the possessive pronoun following *which of us* should be in the singular: using *their* would not only breach it, it would also confusingly introduce yet another grammatical (3rd) person.

-our and -or. As in American English *color* versus British *colour*. **1** *The main patterns.* What follows is a heavily reduced description of the main patterns.

It is a simple matter, first, to set down a representative list of words that are now regularly distinguished in the two countries, BrE, followed by (AmE): *behaviour* (*behavior*), *candour* (*candor*), *colour* (*color*), *harbour* (*harbor*), *honour* (*honor*), *labour* (*labor*), *neighbour* (*neighbor*), *parlour* (*parlor*), *splendour* (*splendor*), *valour* (*valor*).

The above list could easily be more than doubled by including *arbo*(*u*)*r*, *clamo*(*u*)*r*, etc. and it might be tempting to conclude that for every British *-our* the Americans write *-or*. Any such 'rule', however, is contradicted by a number of factors. For one thing, both countries use only *-or* as a terminal element in a wide range of abstract nouns (e.g. *error, horror, pallor, stupor, terror, torpor, tremor*), agent nouns (e.g. *actor,* *governor, orator, sailor;* see also SAVIOUR), and others of miscellaneous origin (e.g. *ambassador, anchor, bachelor, emperor, liquor, mirror, matador*). And for another, both countries regularly use *-our* in a number of words of diverse origin (e.g. *contour, glamour,* (also *glamor* in AmE), *paramour, tambour, vavasour* (but often *vavasor* in AmE)).

2 *History.* Anyone who is really determined to pursue the history and distribution of such spellings as *colour/color* and *valour/valor* in BrE and AmE should turn to the *OED* entries for *-or* and for *-our* (as well as to the entries for the individual words themselves); and also to an article by C. M. Anson in *Internat. Jrnl Lexicography,* spring 1990. Three main historical factors govern the emergence of the various present-day spellings: (*a*) the adoption of Latin words ending in *-or* via Anglo-Norman (where they were spelt *-our*); (*b*) the later post-Renaissance adoption of *-or* words direct from classical Latin; (*c*) a steady adoption in America in the first half of the 19c., esp. by Noah Webster, of *-or* in all the main abstract nouns of the type *colo*(*u*)*r, hono*(*u*)*r*, etc. A radical solution lies close at hand, namely to adopt the spelling *-or* in all nouns listed or implied in the first list given above. There is some movement in this direction in Australia, and Canadians are for the most part free to choose whichever spelling they prefer. But everyone knows that such a change would be regarded by Britons as a kind of linguistic cleansing, something not to be contemplated in any circumstances. And, of course, there is always a great deal to be said for national pride concerning long-held traditions. See also -ER AND -OR; -OR.

3 Even those nouns that in BrE regularly end in *-our* (see above), as opposed to AmE *-or,* e.g. *clamour, humour, odour, rigour, valour, vapour, vigour,* have adjectives ending in *-orous,* not *-ourous,* in all varieties of English: thus *glamorous, humorous,* etc. Particularly in BrE and Canadian English, failure to apply this rule leads to **glamourous, *humourous,* etc. Derivatives in *-ist, -ite,* and *-able,* on the other hand, mostly retain the *-our-*: so *behaviourist, colourist* (but note *humorist*), *Labourite, favourable,* and *honourable.* Derivatives in *-ation* and *-ize* are usually spelt, both in BrE and AmE, with *-or-*: so *coloration, invigoration; deodorize, glamorize, vaporize.*

ourself. The standard reflexive form corresponding to *we* and *us* is **ourselves** (as in *We are going to enjoy ourselves*), but a form *ourself* is recorded from the 14c. onwards in uses corresponding to *we* when used of a single person (*I loved your father, and we love ourself*—Shakespeare, *Hamlet,* iv. vii.40). The form is occasionally found in modern English, particularly in contexts like the following, in which it refers to the spiritual or psychological aspects of people in general, as in the first three examples, or to a group regarded collectively: *She tells us things about ourself*—Martin Amis, 1991; *The one person who will never leave us, whom we will never lose, is ourself—Communion,* 2002; *By performing some form of penance, prayaschitta, we can rid ourselves of the sense of feeling bad about ourself—Hinduism Today,* 2003; *We see ourself as the biggest club in Britain, with a stadium to match—Today,* 1992. This use is not very common, and can be regarded as standard, if specialized. However, the use of *ourself* when it does not have the implications mentioned should be regarded as non-standard, e.g. **We are going to restrict ourself to the crimes.*

ours, our. See OUR 1.

out (preposition). *Out* is primarily an adverb, but its use as a preposition instead of the customary *out of* has a long history: the *OED* lists examples from the mid-13c. to the 20c. (e.g. *When you haue pusht out your gates the very Defender of them*—Shakespeare, 1607). At the present time *out of* is the standard form, but *out* on its own is also common in a highly restricted use, in contexts of *looking, going,* and other verbs involving motion, etc. *out the door* or *the window.* Examples: *To drive with the left arm out the window—Amer. Speech,* 1962; *She looked out the window ... at all the other houses—Southerly,* 1967 (Aust.); *We looked out the window at the snow—New Yorker,* 1986; *But Grandfather was out the door*—M. Pople, 1986 (Aust.); *Now he looked past Bacon, out the bay window behind him*—T. Wolfe, 1987 (US); *I drove out the gates and left them open behind me, swinging in the wind*—S. Koea, 1994 (NZ); *I grew up in the 70's too and yes our parents kicked us out the door—Guardian* (*Comment is Free*), 2010.

out (verb, adjective). **1** *Verb.* As a verb, *out* goes back to Old English in various meanings, 'to drive out or expel', 'to disable', '(of news or information) to become known', 'to disclose or speak out', and others. In the 1990s, the last meaning was extended further, namely 'to reveal the homosexuality of (a prominent or famous person)': *She 'outs' dozens as bi* [= bisexual]*—instead of exclusively straight or gay—The Face*, 1996. The process is called **outing**. The verb is now used to mean 'to disclose private, often controversial or damaging information about a person, institution, etc.', e.g. *At his 80th birthday party, he officially 'outed' himself as a member of the Communist party for 50 years—Daily Tel.*, 1991; *Patients were brazenly stalked and 'outed'—their names emblazoned on picket signs—Rolling Stone*, 1993; *She threatened to out him as father of her child—Total Film*, 2002.

2 *Adjective. Out* in the meaning 'openly or publicly gay or bisexual' is first recorded in the *OED* from 1977. It probably derives from the use of the phrasal verb *to come out* with the meaning of 'to reveal publicly one's homosexuality'. It can be used both predicatively and attributively, although the latter appears to be more frequent. Examples: *It may remind gay viewers of out playwright Edward Albee's* Who's Afraid of Virginia Woolf? *(written some 60 years later), but there's absolutely nothing gay about the play, McKellen insists*—The Advocate, 2001; *If you're gay or lesbian and out, you may well also find it in your interest to support this, but there's nothing essentially homosexual about it—www.barbelith.com*, 2004.

outcome is a word that easily leads to tautologous constructions: e.g. *The outcome of such nationalization would undoubtedly lead to the loss of incentive and initiative in that trade.* The outcome of nationalization would *be* loss; *nationalization* would lead to loss.

outdoor is used only as an adjective (*outdoor games*); **outdoors** is an adverb (*the concert was held outdoors*) or a noun (*the great outdoors*).

outfit. The inflected forms are **outfitter**; *outfitted, outfitting* in both BrE and AmE.

out-Herod (verb). Shakespeare was responsible for introducing this type of verb in which *out* is prefixed to a proper noun: *I could haue such a Fellow whipt for o'er-doing Termagant: it out-Herod's Herod. Pray you auoid it—Hamlet.* It was no more than a casual expression, related to similar formations of his own in which the second element of the *out*-compound is not a proper name: *out-frowne false Fortunes frowne—King Lear; He hath out villain'd villanie—All's Well that Ends Well.* The type produced a flood of imitative formations, especially in the 19c. ('a few instances are found in the 17th c., esp. in Fuller, and in the 18th c. in Swift; but the vast development of this, as of so many other Shaksperian [*sic*] usages, belongs to the 19th c., in which such expressions have been used almost without limit' (*OED*, 1903).) Among the numerous examples listed in the *OED* are *to out-Alexander Alexander* (J. Wolcott, 1800)*, to out-Milton Milton* (Lowell, 1870), and *to out-Zola Zola (Literary World,* 1887); and the related type (ordinary nouns, not proper names) *to out-devil the devil* (B. H. Malkin, 1809), *to outmonster the monstrosities* (E. Blunden, 1930), and *to outrainbow the rainbow* (H. MacDiarmid, 1956). The type is shown in a weakened form when the object of the verb does not repeat or echo it, e.g. *Out-heroding the French cavaliers in compliment and in extravagance* (1809 in *OED*).

out of. See OUT (preposition).

output (verb). The past tense and past participle can be either *output* or *outputted.* The first is somewhat more frequent, and three quarters of the examples of the second are from AmE. The use of *outputted* is in line with what happens to verbs such as *broadcast* and *input,* which contain an irregular verb, but are themselves viewed as regular by many people, probably because they are seen to be derived from nouns, as is discussed further at PODCAST. The present participle is *outputting.* See -T-, -TT-.

outside of. As a compound preposition *outside of* is used, especially in AmE, in two main senses: (*a*) exterior to, outside: *These books are . . . distributed outside of the U.S.A. and Canada by Academic Press—Nature,* 1975; *People in show business refer to those outside of it as 'civilians'*—S. MacLaine, 1987; *I remember an industrialist who, outside of presidential earshot, voiced stinging criticism of certain budget proposals*—B. and E. Dole, 1988; (*b*) with the exception of: *Outside of a slightly* *annoying tendency to call all female customers 'Hon', everything about Mr. Blume inspires confidence*—*New York*, 1972; *Outside of an unfortunate sermon in which he confused the words for charity and diarrhea, causing some tittering behind fans, he never put a foot wrong with his hosts*—W. Sheed, 1985; *Outside of the wound, I'd say primarily traumatic shock*—R. Ludlum, 1990. In most circumstances, however, uncompounded *outside* is sufficient, and is overwhelmingly the normal use in BrE.

outward, outwards. As an adjective, the only legitimate form is *outward* (*the outward journey, his outward appearance*). As an adverb (*one eye is turned outward*) *outward* is the more frequent form in NAmer. English, but *outwards* is more frequent in British, Austr. and NZ English.

outwit. The inflected forms are *outwitted, outwitting.*

over. 1 Since the later part of the 19c. there has been a strong tradition in American newspapers and in some American usage guides of absolute, unconditional, almost maniacal hostility to the use of *over* with a following numeral to mean 'in excess of, more than' (e.g. *a little over £50, a distance of over 700 yards*). It is useful for editors and writers of other varieties of English to be aware that the anxiety continues (and, to judge by some editorial forums, can almost induce nausea or hyperventilation): *The national view is a graphic composite of local reports across the country from over 50* (*Oops! Make that 'more than' 50*—*I'm almost 'over' 50*) *reporting stations*—columnist in *Chicago Sun-Times*, 1989; *Not perfect yet:* 'over *150,000' AIDS deaths should have been* more than, *used with all figures except ages*—W. Safire, 1992. The AP Stylebook notes '*More than* is preferred with numerals', but *MWCDEU* cites numerous examples of the use and concludes: 'There is no reason why you need to avoid this usage.' In Britain, *over* has been used with a following numeral without restriction or adverse comment throughout the same period. And the usage itself extends back to Old English. No voices have been raised in Britain or N. America against phrases of the type *over forty* (*years of age*). Examples: *These four sons were all over forty but they were treated as babies by their parents*—P. Kavanagh, 1948; *She was a little over twenty, very graceful and witty and cunning*—G. Greene, 1969.

2 For the use of *over* as a prefix in adjectives such as *overambitious*, compared with *overly ambitious*, see OVERLY.

overall. 1 *Pronunciation.* As a noun (= two kinds of garment), it is stressed on the first syllable: /ˈəʊvərɔːl(z)/. As an adjective the stress falls mainly on the first syllable and as an adverb on the third, but the stress is variable in context: thus /ˈəʊvərɔːl(z)/ or /ˌəʊvərˈɔːl/.

2 *Parts of speech.* As a noun, an *overall* (in BrE) is a coat-like garment worn over one's clothes as a protection against stains, etc.; *overalls* are protective trousers, dungarees, or a combination suit worn by workmen, etc. (always construed with a plural verb). As an adjective it is always used in the attributive position, e.g. *the overall pattern, the overall effect.* It is also used as an adverb, e.g. *Overall, the performance was excellent.*

3 Hostility to the use of the adjective (and by implication the adverb as well) surfaces from time to time, the argument being that *overall* is overused, and that a range of synonyms (*aggregate, comprehensive, general, total, whole*, etc.) is available. Its use was decried by Gowers (1965) as a vogue word. Since then it has settled into standard use and is among the 1,000 most frequent words in the language. It is still advisable, however, to be on one's guard against using it when it contributes nothing to the sense: e.g. *The overall growth of London should be restrained; That would be a meaningful step towards defusing the demographic time bomb and easing the overall pension situation in the UK.*

overestimate, underestimate. In a wallchart on the plays of Shakespeare published with the *Independent* newspaper in 2007, the text included the assertion *his contributions to the world of theatre and to language cannot be underestimated.* Faint praise indeed! Because these two words are often used in negative or quasi-negative contexts, there is a danger of losing track of logic and using the wrong word, usually *underestimate* when *overestimate* is required. It is an observable fact that this substitution is widespread and happens in the specific syntactic patterns *cannot + underestimate/be underestimated* and *it is impossible/difficult to underestimate.* Attempts, especially on the *Language Log* website, to explain in linguistic terms why this seeming illogicality is so common are subtle and ingenious: nevertheless, whoever notices such a substitution may well consider it a slip of the tongue or pen. A similar reversal of meaning also happens with *overstate/understate.* Examples: **It is almost impossible to underestimate the importance of rugby to the South African nation in terms of its self-esteem on the world stage*—quoted in *Language Log*; **We can't underestimate the impact of the Wall Street Journal. We didn't know how impactful that article would be*; *'*It is difficult to understate the immense impact that this would have across the communion, and particularly in England,' he said*—*Daily Tel.*, 2007.

overflow has past tense and past participle *overflowed.*

overfly. The inflected forms are *overflies, overflew,* and *overflown.*

overlay, overlie. The past tense and past participle of *overlay* are respectively *overlaid* and *overlaid,* while those of *overlie* are respectively *overlay* and *overlain.* Both *overlay* and *overlie* also seem to be used in geology for the sense 'lie over or upon (e.g. of a stratum resting directly upon another)' (*the Palæozoic rocks do not appear to be overlain by recent marine deposits*—J. Ball, 1885; *At the edges of the cross section, we see a sequence of magnetized sedimentary blankets overlaying the crust*—P. J. Wyllie, 1976).

On the other hand, the sense 'to cover the surface (of something) with a coating, etc.' requires *overlay* (e.g. *wood overlaid* (not *overlain*) *with gold; they overlaid* (not *overlay*) *the walls with hessian*). And so do figurative extensions: e.g. *A habit of obedience overlaid the tumultuous desires and suppressions of her young daughter*—M. Keane, 1937; *Her anger was overlaid with bewilderment*—D. Welch, 1943; *This kind of insight overlays the patterns of his works, and the enjoyment of his art is as much the enjoyment of the overlay as it is of the patterns themselves*—*TLS*, 1975.

overly (adverb). **1** *Origins and current spread.* (*a*) Despite having been coined in Old English, and being quoted in the works of the 11c. Archbishop of York Wulfstan, this adverb then vanished off the radar for several centuries. As the *OED* puts it: 'After the Old English period, rare (outside Scotland and North America) until the 20th cent'. The first modern *OED* example dates, intriguingly, from an 1806 work of Irish fiction. The American corpus *COHA*, consisting of a selection of American books from 1810 onwards, shows two isolated examples in the 1820s, sporadic examples for the rest of the 19c., and then a steady increase decade by decade throughout the 20c. (*b*) Burchfield (1996) stated 'Until about the 1970s, and in some quarters still, regarded as an Americanism' and it is probable that for many conservative British speakers (me included) the word still wears a baseball cap, if not a Stetson. The *OEC* data shows, however, that it is now as widely used in BrE as in AmE, and has spread throughout the English-speaking world.

2 *Criticism and alternatives.* As *MWCDEU* points out, American criticism of the word dates back to the 19c., when its users were described as vulgar or unschooled. Criticism has continued. Partridge (1942) declared that '*over* . . . or *excessively* is preferred in British usage'; Bill Bryson (1984) opines that 'making *over* into *overly* is a little like turning "soon" into "soonly"'. The popularity of *overly* can in part be attributed to some people's insistence that any adverb has to end in *-ly*, but the question remains: is there anything inherently wrong in using it? If you think there is, then of course the best policy is to replace it with *over* prefixed to the adjective in question, e.g. *overambitious, overconfident* etc., rather than *overly ambitious, confident* etc. (Such words, if they are not of historical standing, are often hyphenated.) The *OEC* data shows that the ten adjectives that are the most frequent collocates of *overly* are more widely used in that pattern than in the prefixed form with *over* . . . , e.g. *overly ambitious* rather than *overambitious,* but it is hard to see what influences that preference in the case of those adjectives.

3 *Examples.* It is worth noting how often *overly* is used in contexts where there is a negation, and how often it qualifies adjectives relating to emotions. Examples: *The Manitoba Minister of Agriculture is not overly impressed with the horsemen's woes*—*Globe & Mail* (Toronto), 1968; *That same novel is now with Macmillan. I am not* *'overly' hopeful*—B. Pym, 1977; *Fitzpatrick's male adversary is an impassioned, overly emotional man*—*Times*, 1985; *she was so overly agreeable and pleasant that there had to be a reason for it*—J. Hecht, 1992 (US); *Since 1989, nearly 100 cases of overly lenient sentences have been referred by the Attorney General to the Court of Appeal*—*Times*, 1993; *She is not overly cheerful about the future of British drama*—M. Geare, 1993.

overseas. Now the customary word (rather than *oversea*) for both the adverb (*he was sent overseas for training*) and the adjective (*overseas postage rates*), though at least until the early 20c. *oversea* was the usual form for the adjective.

oversight is potentially ambiguous, since it can mean 'unintentional failure to notice or do something' (*he had simply missed Parsons out by an oversight*), and that meaning also has an uncount use (*was the mistake due to oversight?*); or it can mean 'the action of overseeing something' (*effective oversight of the financial reporting process*). In practice, ambiguity is rare, since the two meanings appear in rather different contexts, but occasional examples can lead to puzzlement, e.g. *Congressional oversight has proliferated*—*Time*, 1977.

over the time. See OVER TIME.

overthrowal. The noun-forming suffix *-al* came into wide favour in the 19c. (see -AL 2) and *overthrowal* 'the act of overthrowing' (first recorded 1916) seems to have come into being as a kind of afterthought. It was first admitted to the *OED* in 1933, is used primarily in current AmE, has found a place in Webster's Third, while smaller dictionaries find no place for it, and it is aspersed by Garner. *Overthrow* as a noun can easily replace it. Examples: *I don't see his regime lasting more than 18 months before an overthrowal*—*Washington Post*, 1979; *As far as his own century was concerned, Buero* [*sc.* Buero Vallejo, a Spanish playwright] *did not purely raise questions pertaining to the overthrowal of Francoism but of totalitarian structures per se*—Susan Willis-Altamirano, 2001.

over time means 'as time passes; by degrees during a (usually long) period of time' (e.g. *I lost my fire over time Always playin' one more hand for one more dime*—Joni Mitchell; *Players developed characters over time, accumulating skills, equipment, and treasure*—*New Yorker*, 2007). The curious, mostly AmE phrasing *over the time* is to be avoided: **The original configuration of the sub-notebook has changed a little over the time*—*www.xbitlabs.com*, 2005.

overtone, undertone. In their metaphorical uses both have the implication that there is more to a statement, undertaking, etc., than meets the eye. In music, an overtone is 'a musical tone which is a part of the harmonic series above a fundamental note, and may be heard with it'.

Overtone is therefore an apt metaphor for suggesting that a word, etc., has implications over and above the plain meaning (e.g. *'Artificial' cannot be used without an overtone of disparagement*). *Undertone* is not a technical term in music. An *undertone* is rather an unexpressed or underlying feeling (and again roughly matches the musical meaning 'a subdued tone of sound'): *Welsh's scabrous comedy of alcoholic manners is full of dark undertones*—*Sunday Times*, 2006.

ovum. The plural is *ova*. See -UM 2.

owing to is not inserted here because it is misused, but to give readers an assurance that it is as often as not a suitable substitute for *due to* (a phrase which still attracts adverse criticism in some of its uses). *Owing to* has two main meanings: (*a*) (as a predicative adjective) caused by; attributable to (*the cancellation was owing to ill health*); (*b*) (as a complex preposition) because of (*the trains were delayed owing to a signals failure*). Its use in sense (*b*) is particularly recommended. A literary example: *Owing to its length, my hair tends to fall forward in two curves on the temples*—S. Bellow, 1987. The wordy phrase *owing to the fact that* can usually be avoided: use a conjunction such as *because* instead.

owl-like. See -LIKE.

owt represents 'a variety of English regional and Scots pronunciations of *aught*' (= anything). First recorded in ?1746, in northern English it is the indefinite, negative, and interrogative pronoun corresponding to NOWT. Examples: *Owt's possible, any bloody thing*—E. W. Hildick, 1977; *You never wrote us or owt, while I was inside, did you?*—D. Glazier, 1992; *Why* *aren't you saying owt? Because you're soft as pigshit, that's why!*—C. Birch, 2003.

ox. The plural is *oxen*, but the plural of the idiom *dumb ox*, meaning a stupid person, is usually *dumb oxes*.

Oxford comma. What follows owes a considerable debt to the *New Hart's Rules*. **1** *Definition.* The so-called 'Oxford comma' is an optional comma that follows the penultimate item in a list of three or more items and precedes the words 'and' and 'or': *We sell books, videos, and magazines.* It is known as the 'Oxford comma' because it was traditionally used by printers, readers, and editors at Oxford University Press. However, the style is also used by other publishers, both in the UK and elsewhere. It is also widely known as the 'serial comma', as well as the 'Harvard comma'.

2. *Examples and usefulness.* Examples of the Oxford comma are: *mad, bad, and dangerous to know*; *a thief, a liar, and a murderer.*

The general rule is that it should be used consistently, or not at all. In the preceding three examples the Oxford comma could easily be removed without affecting meaning (though it does serve the function of suggesting pauses in reading). However, the Oxford comma can help to avoid ambiguity, particularly when any of the listed items are compound terms joined by *and*, and it is sometimes helpful to the reader to use an isolated serial comma for clarification even when the convention has not been adopted in the rest of the text.

In *These items are available in black and white, red and yellow, and blue and green,* leaving the comma out after *yellow* could suggest five different options, four of them being single colours, rather than the three options actually available. In *cider, real ales, meat and vegetable pies, and sandwiches,* the absence of a comma after *pies* would imply something unintended about the sandwiches, namely that they are meat and vegetable. In the next example, it is obvious from the grouping produced by the commas that the Bishop of Bath and Wells is one person, and the bishops of Bristol, Salisbury, and Winchester are three people: *the bishops of Bath and Wells, Bristol, Salisbury, and Winchester.* If the order is reversed to *the bishops of Winchester, Salisbury, Bristol and Bath and Wells* then the absence of the comma after *Bristol* generates confusion: is the link between Bristol and Bath rather than Bath and Wells?

3 *Ambiguity it cannot resolve.* The omission of the Oxford comma can also provide unintended humour, sometimes scabrously so. A supposedly direct quote from the *Times*, talking about a Peter Ustinov documentary, said: 'highlights of his global tour include encounters with Nelson Mandela, an 800-year-old demigod and a dildo collector'. Of course, any ambiguity is strictly theoretical, not real (a computer might be fooled, but not a human being). But in any case, inserting the Oxford comma would not truly remove the ambiguity. As it currently reads, *encounters with Nelson Mandela, an 800-year-old demigod and a dildo collector* is ambiguous because it is unclear if what follows the comma is in apposition to Mandela, i.e. describes him, or whether those two nouns continue the list. However, inserting the comma to give *encounters with Nelson Mandela, an 800-year-old demigod, and a dildo collector* does not resolve the problem, since *an 800-year-old demigod* could still be read as appositive. In the rare cases like this where ambiguity might be caused, rephrasing is the best option, e.g. *encounters with Nelson Mandela, with an 800-year-old demigod, and with a dildo collector.*

Finally, it is worth noting that the AP style guide, the *Economist*, the *NYT*, the *Wall Street Journal*, and the *Times*, (note the Oxford comma in that list) do not use the serial comma.

oxymoron. 1 The word derives from two Greek words opposed in meaning (Greek ὀξύμωρον, formed from ὀξύς 'sharp' + μωρός 'dull') and denotes 'a figure of speech in which apparently contradictory terms appear in conjunction': e.g. *a cheerful pessimist*; *harmonious discord.* Longer examples: *And faith unfaithful kept him falsely true*—Tennyson, 1859; *And yet ninety-nine-point-nine per cent of the time Middlehope* [*sc.* a village] *is madly sane, if you'll permit the paradox*—E. Peters, 1978; *He gets out of it by saying that he used to think 'interesting Canadian' was an oxymoron, but that Eric was obviously an exception*—M. Atwood, 1990.

2 The name is properly used of a deliberate literary device, and should not be used to mean simply an accidental or casual contradiction in terms: **Robert proves why it's no oxymoron to be known as a creative producer*—*Take One* (magazine), 2003; **The divide is between man-centered worship (surely an oxymoron) and God-centered worship*—*religious website*, 2004. In neither of these sentences is there an *oxymoron* in the proper sense: *contradiction in terms* is what is required. The offence is even worse when the contradiction is not contained within a single term at all: **It seems like an oxymoron, but rock has benefited enormously from singers who really shouldn't have been singing*—*Pitchfork Media album reviews*, 2004. The word wanted here is *paradox*.

pace (preposition). Derived from Latin, and first used in English in the 19c., it is the ablative singular of Latin *pax* 'peace', and means 'With due deference to (a named person or authority); despite'. Latin *pāce tuā* or *pāce vestrā* mean 'with all due respect to you'; (with the noun in the genitive) *pāce Veneris* means 'if Venus will not be offended by my saying so'. In English *pace* is used chiefly as a courteous or ironic apology for a difference of opinion about to be expressed. *COD* 1995 gives precedence to /ˈpɑːtʃeɪ/, but the word is also pronounced /ˈpeɪsi/. It is almost always printed in italic, to avoid confusion with homographs, and its use is restricted to works in which Latinisms are likely to be recognized. Examples: *I do not believe,* pace *Peirce and Derrida, that it is signs all the way down, and that,* pace *Dennett, there is no distinctive human intentionality, and that,* pace *almost everyone, thinking is fundamentally linguistic—Computers & Humanities*, 1995.

pachydermatous. Brought into English in the 19c. in zoological works to mean 'thick-skinned' (of certain animals, including the elephant and the rhinoceros, from Greek παχύς 'thick' + δέρμα 'skin'), it was quickly applied, sometimes playfully, to persons regarded as 'thick-skinned, not sensitive to rebuff, ridicule, or abuse'. Modern examples: *Can I be sincere without wounding people less pachydermatous than myself?*—H. Nicolson, 1934; *Edward laughed. His happiness had made him pachydermatous*—L. P. Hartley, 1961.

pacifically. In spoken English, it is not uncommon for this adverb, from the adjective *pacific*, to replace *specifically*. It is true that apart from the initial letter *s* of the latter, the two are pronounced identically; but surely it is also true that people who mistakenly say *pacifically* know the adjective *specific*, and, if asked, would be able to form its corresponding adverb correctly. It is also odd that people use this adverb at all formed as it is from a somewhat unusual adjective. Perhaps they hear *specifically* as *pacifically*, because people saying it do not stress the /s/. In any event, it is a mystery to me why this substitution should happen (I look forward to a flurry of letters enlightening me with a linguistic explanation). Since the substitution is a feature of speech, written examples are not easy to find, while most instances of *pacifically* show it used correctly. Example: *Although Motorways are pacifically designed to deal with cars going quickly in a straight line the cops have decided to put cameras in on the M4—dooyoo.co.uk* (discussions), 2005.

pacifier is the usual word in AmE for a baby's dummy.

package. Used for 'the packing of goods' and for 'a bundle of things packed in a receptacle', the noun has been part of the standard language for many centuries. In the course of the 20c., first in AmE and then in all English-speaking areas, it developed figurative senses, and in particular 'a set of proposals, terms, commercial products, etc., offered or agreed as a whole', as in *package deal, offer, proposal,* etc. Any set of agreements, proposals, transactions, travelling arrangements, etc., can now be described as a *package*. The more obviously physical slang metaphor for a man's genitals is surprisingly recent, being first recorded from an oral source in 1987 and from a written one in 1993.

paean (a song of praise or triumph). So spelt in BrE (in AmE also **pean**).

paed(o)-. A number of words containing this element (from Greek παῖς, παιδ- 'child') are more often spelt with *-ae-* in British English and most other varieties, but with *-e-* in North American English: thus *paediatrics/pedia-, paedophile/pedo-*, etc.

paid past tense and past participle of PAY.

paillasse. See PALLIASSE.

painedly. See -EDLY.

pair. 1 When used to mean (*a*) a set of two persons or things regarded as a unit (*a pair of eyes; a pair of gloves*), and (*b*) an article consisting of two equal parts which are joined together (*a pair of binoculars, clippers, jeans, pincers, pyjamas, scissors, shears, trousers*, etc.), the phrase is normally construed with a singular verb or demonstrative adjective (e.g. *pass me that pair of scissors; there's a pair of gloves in the drawer*). If *a pair of* is omitted, a plural pronoun or verb is required: e.g. *those gloves, scissors*, etc., *need replacing.*

2 Used as a collective noun, *pair* can take a singular verb according to strict grammatical agreement, or a plural verb according to notional or proximity agreement: either *a pair of crocodiles* were *basking beside the river or a pair of crocodiles* was *basking* [etc.]. See AGREEMENT 5.

3 Number contrast for *gloves, pyjamas, scissors*, etc., can only be made by using them with *a pair of*: thus *a pair of binoculars* = one object, and *two pairs of binoculars* (not *two binoculars*) = two objects.

4 The phrase *a pair of twins* is common enough in speech (= one set of two babies born at a single birth), but should be avoided if there is any risk of ambiguity (as at a convention of twins).

5 The plural form *pairs* is desirable after a numeral (e.g. *seven pairs of jeans*). The type *seven pair of jeans* is non-standard in BrE but standard in AmE.

pajamas. See PYJAMAS.

palace. The second syllable is pronounced /-ɪs/ in BrE according to the *OED*, but /-əs/ is favoured by J. C. Wells (2008), and is given by the *OED* as the AmE pronunciation. The same divergence of opinion is found in two major American dictionaries, those of Random House and Merriam-Webster. Usage is obviously divided: but Christopher Robin's Alice would only half-rhyme with the second.

palaeo-. More frequently spelt as shown in BrE (only rarely printed with the digraph *æ* as *palæo-*), but *paleo-* in AmE.

Palaeocene See MIOCENE.

palatal. A term used in phonetics of a sound made by placing the front of the tongue against the hard palate (e.g. *y* in *yes*). *Palatalization* is the process of rendering palatal, e.g. of changing the nature of a consonant in certain circumstances by articulating it with the front of the tongue raised towards the hard palate. This is an essential part of the [ʃ, ʒ] sounds in English words such as *she* and *measure*, being additional to an articulation made between the blade and the alveolar ridge.

palindrome (from Greek παλίνδρομος 'running back again'), a word, verse, or sentence that reads the same when the letters composing it are taken in the reverse order. Edward Phillips's dictionary (1706) cited as an example *Lewd did I live, & evil I did dwel* (which doesn't quite work today). Greek, Latin, and English examples are cited in A. J. Augarde's *The Oxford Guide to Word Games* (2003), e.g. *Roma tibi subito motibus ibit amor* (attributed to Sidonius 'Your love, Rome, will suddenly come to you through these stirrings to action'); *Able was I ere I saw Elba* (attributed to Napoleon); and numerous others, including some that are much more complex than these.

palladium, in literary use, a safeguard or source of protection, rather than the atomic element. Plural *palladia.* See -UM 2.

palliasse. Now the established spelling, pronounced /ˈpalɪas/. Cf. French *paillasse* (from *paille* 'straw').

Pall Mall (name of street in London). Now pronounced /ˌpalˈmal/. Formerly also /ˌpɛlˈmɛl/.

pallor. So spelt in both BrE and AmE.

palmetto (small palm tree). Plural *palmettos.* See -O(E)S 4.

palpable (adjective) corresponds to the verb *palpate*, to examine (especially medically) by touch. It means (*a*) that can be touched or felt, especially in technical, medical use, and (*b*) (readily perceived by the senses or mind. Sense (*a*) dates from the 14c. and is most memorably illustrated in Osric's verdict to Hamlet, *a hit, a very palpable hit*, during the fatal duel at the end of Shakespeare's *Hamlet.* Further example:

Two fifths of the head are palpable above the brim—M. F. Myles, *Textbk Midwives*, 1985.

Sense (*b*) dates from the 15c., and is illustrated in the *OED* by examples from the works of Hooker, Pepys, Byron, and numerous others. Modern examples: *This problem (so individual in its origins) takes palpable public shape in the fiction*—C. G. Wolff, 1977; *Othello's crisis of identity becomes palpable when 'seeming' ceases to be synonymous with 'being'*—*Studies in Eng. Lit.* (University of Tokyo), 1990; *the tension—friendly tension—in the room was palpable*—*Atlantic*, 1991.

pamphlet. See BROCHURE.

panacea /panəˈsiːə/, a universal remedy, a remedy reputed to heal all ailments. It cannot be used with reference to a single illness (*a panacea for measles* is not idiomatic), and is most frequently used in negative contexts or ironically (of another person's proposal) of wide-ranging suggestions for the solution of (especially social or economic) problems. It is derived from Greek πανάκεια 'all-healing', from παν- 'all' + ἄκος 'cure'. Examples: *To . . . deaden the pain of neuralgia, the early Victorian panacea of laudanum was prescribed*—D. Thomas, 1979; *Kipling reminds us often that work is the only panacea for most of life's ills*—M. Pafford, 1989; *her approach to the high life . . . is tempered with this decade's unrealistic just-say-no panacea*—*Details* (US), 1991.

pandemonium. Coined by Milton in the form *Pandæmonium* (= place of all demons) in his *Paradise Lost* (1667), it is a striking example of a word that has made its way from the higher realms of literature into everyday use, always now meaning '(place of) uproar'.

pandit. See PUNDIT.

panegyric. Now pronounced /panɪˈdʒɪrɪk/. *Panegyric*, ultimately from the Greek adjective πανηγυρικός means 'a public eulogy', and was formed from παν- 'all' + ἄγυρις = ἀγορά 'assembly', i.e. a eulogy fit for a public assembly or festival.

panel. The inflected forms are *panelled, panelling* (AmE *paneled, paneling*). See -LL-, -L-.

panful. The plural is *panfuls*. See -FUL.

panic (noun and verb). The inflected forms are *panics, panicked, panicking,* and *panicky*. See -C-, -CK-.

panini. In Italian this is a plural form (just like *spaghetti*) as the *-i* ending shows. The singular *panino* in Italian denotes a bread roll, and is the diminutive of *pane* = bread, loaf. In English-speaking culture, the word usually refers to a small flat loaf, often served toasted. Although *panini* is plural in Italian, it has long been interpreted (since 1985 according to the *OED*) as singular in English, and has its own plural *paninis*. By all means, use the singular if you are an Italian scholar or like to uphold the racial purity of loanwords. But to ask for a *panino* may sound like pedantry, one-upmanship, or worse still, a criticism of the provider's English.

pantaloons, pants. 1 *Pants* (first recorded in 1835 in America as an abbreviation of *pantaloons*) became in Britain a colloquial and 'shoppy' term for 'drawers', and then for 'underpants, panties, or shorts worn as an outer garment'. Now the word is mainly used to mean underpants or knickers in the UK, and trousers or slacks (for men or women) in America, but the distinction is not an absolute one. Several idiomatic phrases, generally of US origin, containing the word *pants* are now common currency, the interpretation of *pants* depending on where one is from, e.g. *to bore the pants off, to be caught with one's pants down, to get into someone's pants, by the seat of one's pants*. The use of *pants* to mean 'rubbish', especially in the phrase *a load* (or *pile*) *of pants*, is British: *A Liberal Democrat stunned his fellow peers when he dismissed a landmark report on the future of the historic environment as 'a load of pants'*—*Independent*, 2000.

2 The distinction between BrE and AmE usage may occasionally cause problems, though probably less so nowadays than at the time of this quotation: *I heard an American student at Cambridge University telling some English friends how he climbed over a locked gate to get into his college and tore his pants, and one of them asked in confusion, 'But how could you tear your pants without tearing your trousers?'*—N. Moss, 1973.

3 *Pantaloons* (first recorded in the 17c.) in the days of Evelyn and Samuel Butler was the name given to fashionable breeches worn by men at the time. By the late 18c. the word was applied to 'a tight-fitting kind of trousers fitted with ribbons or buttons below the calf', and, in the course of the 19c. in America, became extended to close-fitting trousers in general. The word *pantaloon* is now largely restricted (written with a capital *P*) to a foolish old man who is the butt and accomplice of a clown in a pantomime (cf. Shakespeare's *The leane and slipper'd Pantaloone, With spectacles on nose, and pouch on side, His youthfull hose well sau'd, a world too wide, For his shrunke shanke*, from *As you like It*). This disparaging use is a distant echo of its origins in the Italian Commedia dell'Arte as the name for a stock character, *Pantalone*, whose name derives from the patron saint of Venice, *Pantaleone*.

paparazzo, an Italian loanword, refers to a freelance photographer who relentlessly pursues celebrities, often very intrusively, to get photographs of them for sale to the media. The word comes from the fictional photographer *Paparazzo* in Fellini's 1959 film *La Dolce Vita* and first appeared in English in 1961. Note that the only doubled letters are the *zz*s. The plural, as in Italian, is *paparazzi*. Since these feral snappers usually hunt in packs, the plural is far more often used than the singular, e.g. *most of the paparazzi of the time photographed in black-and-white—Art Business News*, 2001. As a result of the word's appearing more often as *paparazzi*, that form has a long history (since 1981) of being interpreted as a singular, e.g. *?suddenly she was being tailed by a paparazzi who desperately wanted a close-up snap shot—HecklerSpray*, 2005. The *OED* records this without comment, but for many people it constitutes a mistake. To be on the safe side, it is wise to use *paparazzo* for a single specimen of these greedy invaders of privacy. Occasionally *paparazzi* also seems to be interpreted as a collective noun and accordingly used with incorrect singular verb agreement: **I was actually thinking that Michelle Obama will be the one that the paparazzi takes the most pictures of, you know, detailing, you know, her every outfit—CNN* (transcripts), 2008. Cf. PANINI.

papier mâché. The accents in *mâché* are essential, but the phrase is printed in roman.

papilla, papula. The plural forms are *papillae, papulae*.

papyrus /pəˈpʌɪərəs/. Plural *papyri* /-rʌɪ, -riː/, or occasionally *papyruses*. See -US 1.

para-. Two prefixes of different origin are used in forming English words: (*a*) the first is the Greek preposition παρά 'alongside of, beyond', as in *parable, paradigm, paradox, paragraph, parallel, paramedical, paramilitary*, and *paraphrase*; and (*b*) the second is from French *para-* from Italian *para-*, from *parare* 'to make ready, prepare, defend from, shelter', from classical Latin *parāre* 'to prepare', as in *parachute, parapet, parasol*; cf. French *parapluie*.

parable, 'a (usually realistic) story or narrative told to convey a moral or spiritual lesson or insight'. The forty allegorical parables attributed to Jesus of Nazareth provide the traditional models in Christian literature. Modern examples, as Baldick (1990) mentions, include Wilfred Owen's poem 'The Parable of the Old Man and the Young' (1920), which relates a biblical story to the 1914–18 war; and a longer prose parable, John Steinbeck's *The Pearl* (1948).

paradigm /ˈparədʌɪm/, with the last syllable rhyming with *dime*, in technical use denotes a model or pattern of some kind; in grammar, it means 'a representative set of inflections of a noun or verb', and so the paradigm of *come* is *come* (base form), *comes* (third person singular present), *came* (past tense), *come* (past participle), *coming* (present participle), and that of the Old English verb *bidan* (to wait) is *bidan* (base form), *bitt* (3rd person singular present indicative), *bad* (3rd person singular past tense), *bidon* (plural past tense) *biden*, (past participle). In linguistics it means 'a set of linguistic items that form mutually exclusive choices in particular syntactic roles', e.g. *English determiners form a paradigm: we can say 'a book' or 'his book' but not 'a his book'*. From these meanings has developed the meaning 'a world view underlying the theories and methodology of a particular scientific subject', e.g. *The publication of Chomsky's* Syntactic Structures *provided a new paradigm for linguistics—Language*, 1975. In non-technical contexts it has become a somewhat portentous or vogue word where *example* or *model* or *pattern* might be more straightforward choices, e.g. *Perhaps, he suggests, Victorian scholars sanitised the past to create in the occupation of Britain a paradigm for the British Empire—Times*,

2007. In particular, *paradigm shift*, 'a conceptual or methodological change in the theory or practice of a particular science or discipline; (in extended sense) a major change in technology, outlook, etc.' is often used in contexts that do not do justice to its *gravitas*: *Michael Mann typically makes a stylish brand of crime movie, sometimes accomplishing the paradigm shift into colorful film noir*—*Flak* magazine, 2004. The corresponding adjective **paradigmatic** is pronounced sounding the -*g*- fully /ˌparədɪɡˈmatɪk/.

paradise. An extraordinarily large number of adjectival forms have been created for the word *paradise: paradisaic* (first recorded 1754), *paradisaical* (1623), *paradisal* (1568), *paradisean* (1647), *paradisiac* (1632), *paradisiacal* (1649), *paradisial* (1776), *paradisian* (1615), *paradisic* (*a*1723), and *paradisical* (1649). Of these, modern use favours first *paradisiacal*, followed by *paradisal*, then *paradisical*. Alongside these uses stand attributive uses of *paradise* itself in certain fixed expressions, e.g. *paradise crane, duck, fish, flycatcher*.

paragoge, the addition of a letter or syllable to a word in some contexts or as a language develops (e.g. *t* in *peasant*; cf. French *paysan*). It is pronounced as four syllables, /parəˈɡəʊdʒiː/.

parakeet is now the normal spelling in BrE, but **parrakeet** is also sometimes found in AmE.

parallel. Exceptionally among verbs ending in *-l* (see -LL-, -L-) *parallel* does not double the *l* in inflected forms (*paralleled*, etc.); the anomaly is due to the *-ll-* of the previous syllable. The same applies to the corresponding noun **parallelism**.

parallelepiped, one of the longest words possibly recalled from geometry lessons at school, should be pronounced /ˌparəleləˈpɪpɛd/ or /-ˈpʌɪpɛd/.

paralogism, illogical reasoning. Pronounced /pəˈralədʒɪzəm/.

paralyse. So spelt in BrE, but **paralyze** in AmE.

paralysis. Plural *paralyses* /-siːz/.

parameter. A mathematical and scientific term with several highly technical meanings, in the course of the 20c. it became perceived by the general public as broadly meaning 'a constant element or factor, esp. serving as a limit or boundary'. This meaning has attracted criticism over several decades (e.g. 'frothy and shallow') and is still at a controversial stage, the stage at which usage manuals attach the word 'loosely' to the popular meaning, while mathematicians smile knowingly and exclude the word from their social vocabulary. The mathematical and computer science uses are too technical to define and illustrate here, but examples of non-technical uses lie readily to hand: *There are parameters to these recollections which may not be immediately apparent: the world of learning... and the war*—D. M. Davin, 1975; *Given a few early broadly defined parameters within which any reasonably sensitive adult works with an individual child* (*e.g. enthusiasm, patience* [etc.])—R. Cameron, 1986; *Lewis's refusal to accept her standards, her parameters, she regarded as threatening*—A. Brookner, 1989. Anyone feeling uneasy about *parameter* has a wide choice of near-synonyms to choose from: *border, boundary, criterion, element, factor, limit, scope, term, term of reference*, etc; one or other of these is often more suitable in context.

paramo (high treeless plateau in tropical South America). Plural *paramos*. See -O(E)S 4.

paranoia. It is strange to think that this familiar word (answering to Greek παράνοια) was regularly spelt *paranœia* (with *œ* usually printed as a ligature) for most of the 19c. The corresponding adjective **paranoid** (first recorded in 1902) many times more frequent than **paranoiac** (1885), though both are in use (also as nouns). **Paranoic** (adjective) is also very occasionally used.

paraphernalia. In origin a plural noun, being the neuter plural of medieval Latin *paraphernālis*, short for *paraphernālia bona*, the 'personal property' (*parapherna*) which a married woman was in law entitled to keep. By the early 18c. it had developed the more general sense 'miscellaneous belongings, especially the equipment needed for a particular activity (*drills, saws, and other paraphernalia necessary for home improvements*) and later 'trappings associated with a particular institution or activity that are regarded as superfluous' (*the rituals and paraphernalia of government*). Since the mid-18c. the word has been used with both singular and plural verb agreement, according to whether it is conceived as an uncount noun or alternatively as a plural or collective noun. Modern examples: *A doctrine that aimed to restore religious practice to New Testament standard inevitably rejected the* whole *paraphernalia of medieval veneration of the saints*—*Rev. Eng. Studies*, 1990; *the executive position is today surrounded by often useless paraphernalia which* does *little more than ... reflect her ... standing in the company*—*Times*, 1992; *Painting paraphernalia ...* abound—*Observer Mag.*, 1993.

paraplegic. Pronounced with a 'soft' g, /parəˈpliːdʒɪk/.

parasitic, parasitical. The first is over ten times more frequent than the second and has both literal and metaphorical meanings, while the second is only ever used as a metaphor. Examples: (parasitic) *This parasitic castle life had left my funds comparatively intact*—P. L. Fermor, 1986; *Budgies often scratch ... Sometimes it's because they have a parasitic problem*—*Fast Forward*, 1990; (parasitical) *For Freud, sociology and the other social sciences are parasitical on psychology*—P. Gay, 1985; *I am keen on police checks on people working with vulnerable adults. But who is doing the police checks? Yes—another hateful, skinflint, parasitical private agency*—*Guardian*, 2002. Both words use *on* (or *upon*) before a prepositional object, as in the example about Freud above.

parataxis (grammar, 'a placing side by side'). The placing of phrases or clauses one after another, with no linking word(s) to indicate coordination or subordination, e.g. *It's ten o'clock, I have to go home*; *Tell me, how are you?*; *I couldn't keep my eyes open, I was so tired* (examples from Bloomfield 1933, *COD* 1995, and *CGEL* 1985, respectively). Such **paratactic** constructions have been a feature of English from the OE period onwards: readers who are interested in pursuing the matter should consult Mitchell's *Old English Syntax* (1985), ch. 5.

parcel (verb). The inflected forms are *parcelled, parcelling* (AmE usually *parceled, parceling*). See -LL-, -L-.

parenthesis. 1 Plural *parentheses* /-siːz/.

2 (*a*) *Parenthesis* is a term denoting an aside or extra remark that is added to a sentence; it is normally marked off by brackets, commas, or dashes, and the rest of the sentence is grammatically complete without it. Parentheses can be single words, phrases, or whole clauses. The essence of a parenthesis is that it interrupts the flow of a sentence, generally in order to explain or elaborate on something just written. Because they are interruptions, parentheses are best kept fairly short.

(*b*) The most memorable use of the word *parenthesis* occurs in W. S. Gilbert's *The Gondoliers* (1889), Act II: *'Take a pair of sparkling eyes, Hidden, ever and anon ... Take a tender little hand, Fringed with dainty fingerettes, Press it—in parenthesis;—Take all these, you lucky man—take and keep them, if you can!'* It shows one of the common ways in which a parenthetic remark is printed, namely between dashes. But there are other ways: (between commas) *In Italian, a language he had been told was the same as Rumanian, he asked to be directed to the British Legation*—O. Manning, 1960; (in brackets) *He and Moira* (*then a milkman's pretty daughter*) *grovelled together long and effectively enough to cause the eventual birth of their son Rick*—T. Winton, *Shallows*, 1985; (dashes again) *On Thursday I come back from work to an empty house—Kate is spending the night at a girlfriend's house again—and the stillness and solitude calm me down*—A. Lambert, 1989; *Once, I told one of the men to do something, and he—my father, that is—asked me what it would be like if I couldn't order men around any more*—D. Leon, 2006.

3 For the various shapes of printed parentheses, see BRACKETS. In printing terminology, *parentheses* mean 'round brackets' (as opposed to e.g. square brackets).

parenthetic, parenthetical. The longer form *parenthetical* is much more often used, both in specialist and non-specialist writing, than *parenthetic*, which tends to be confined to highly formal or academic writing.

pariah. For the pronunciation the *OED* (1905) gave precedence to /ˈpɛːrɪə/, Daniel Jones (1917) to /ˈparɪə/, and *COD* (1990) to /pəˈrʌɪə/. There is no doubt that, after much experimentation and hesitation, the word has now settled down, as *COD* indicates, to rhyme with *Isaiah*.

pari passu. Frequently encountered in academic and legal work, this Latin adverbial phrase means 'at an equal rate of progress, simultaneously and equally'. It is derived from Latin *pār, pari-* 'equal' + *passu* ablative of *passus* 'step'. The dominant pronunciation in BrE is /pɑːri'pasuː/. Printed in italics.

Parkinson. The medical condition known as *Parkinson's disease* was first so called in 1877 (one year earlier in France as *maladie de Parkinson*) and was named after James Parkinson (1755–1824), English surgeon and palaeontologist. It is also often shortened to *Parkinson's*. The whimsical 'law' known as *Parkinson's Law* ('work expands to fill the time available for its completion') first appeared in print in 1955 and was propounded by C. Northcote Parkinson (1909–93), English historian and political scientist.

parlance. See JARGON 3.

parliament. Better pronounced /'pɑːləmənt/, not /'pɑːlɪəmənt/.

parlous. This syncopated form of *perilous* came into use in the 14c. and stood side by side with it in similar contexts and with much the same geographical distribution until the early 20c., when unmistakable signs of decay began to show. Fowler (1926) described it as 'a word that wise men leave alone'. *ODO* labels it *archaic or humorous.* It is a sad fate for a long-serving word. It can still be safely used, however, in fairly formal circumstances with a very limited range of collocates such as *state* (*the economy is in a parlous state*), *situation* (*He first rescued a parlous situation in the west midlands by raising the siege of Lichfield, then sacked Birmingham*), *condition, position*, and the like, and *finances*. But *perilous, dangerous, hazardous*, and other undisputed words are preferable in most other circumstances.

Parmesan, the cheese, is spelt with a capital *P* and pronounced with the medial *s* as /z/.

paronomasia. From Greek παρονομασία 'a play upon words which sound alike', this rhetorical term has been used in English since the 16c. for serious (as opposed to banal or embarrassing) examples of wordplay or punning. The best known of all (though concealed in English) is perhaps that of Matt. 16: 18 *thou art Peter, and vpon this rocke* [Greek πέτρα 'rock'] *I will build my Church.* See PUN.

parricide, patricide. The first of these, which was first recorded in the 16c., has a wide range of meanings: one who murders either parent, or other near relative; also, the murderer of a person considered specially sacred as, for example, being the ruler of a country; also, one who commits the crime of treason. It is also used for any of these crimes themselves. In the same century *patricide* entered the language for the specific person or crime 'the murderer of/the murder of one's father'. The words are etymological doublets: *parricide* is from the Latin type *parricīda*, by Quintilian, thought to be for *patricida* (cf. Latin *patrem* 'father', *-cīda* 'killer'). *Patricide* neatly parallels *matricide, fratricide,* and *sororicide* to form a set of transparently distinguishable terms.

parsing. 1 The resolution of a sentence into its component parts and the assigning of names (noun, verb, adjective, adverb, conjunction, etc.; subject, predicate, etc.) to each part of speech and to each component. See PARTS OF SPEECH.

2 In extended use in computational linguistics, *parse* is 'to analyse (a string [of characters]) into syntactic components to test its conformability to a given grammar' (*OED* 2, 1989)—a simple definition of an extremely complex process.

partake. In origin a 16c. back-formation from the earlier *partaker* (= *part-taker*, rendering Latin *parti-ceps*), it has come to be a somewhat formal, usually intransitive, verb meaning 'to take a part in, to share in some action or condition' (*we need to partake in each other's joys*); and especially (with *of*) to have a share of portion of (food or drink) in the company of others or of another person' (*Your papa invited Mr. R. to partake of our lowly fare*—Dickens, 1865). The notion of sharing with others, i.e. of receiving only a due part of the food being served, is considered crucial by some conservative usage guides, but the *OED* shows that this idea is not always present. The issue is to do with style, or to put it more scientifically, linguistic register: to use *partake of* to mean simply *eat* or *drink* runs the risk of sounding faintly ludicrous, if not Mills and Boonish, as in Eric Partridge's example: 'Being alone, I consoled myself with partaking of a glass of stout.'

part and parcel. A convenient alliterative collocation that has found favour with English-speakers since the 15c. From the 15c. to the 19c. *parcel* was used to mean 'a constituent or component part', and, while it can no longer be used in that way, the sense survives uniquely in this alliterative phrase. The expression, let it be noted, means not just 'a part' but 'an essential part' (of something). Occasionally it is egg-corned to *part and partial*, e.g. **I mean this is part and partial of why things are so broken in Washington—COCA*, 2007.

Parthian shot is now synonymous with *parting shot*, i.e. they both mean 'a remark or glance, etc., reserved for the moment of departure'. The allusion is to the custom of the ancient Parthian horsemen (Parthia was an ancient kingdom in W. Asia, within the borders of modern Iran) of confusing their enemy by shooting arrows into their ranks while in real or pretended flight. The actual term *Parthian shot* (first recorded in 1902 in this meaning) is comparatively recent, although there is a citation from 1842 in a less developed sense (referring to an action rather than a remark) and another for *Parthian glance* from 1859, while the allusive use dates to the 17c. in less fixed expressions. The first examples of *parting shot* are from the end of the 19c.: *That was a parting shot he took at you, by jingo!*—J. Payn, 1888. This is now the standard form of the phrase, although *Parthian shot* (note the capital *P*) is still very occasionally used: *'Anyway,' he offered a Parthian shot, 'I don't know why you bother. You hate vegetarian food.'—Sunday Times*, 2005.

partially, partly. 1 These two long-established adverbs—*partially* first recorded in the 15c. and *partly* in the 16c.—have shared the sense 'in part' from the beginning. The only clear semantic difference between them is that from the 15c. until about 1800 *partially* (like French *partialement*) also meant 'in a partial or biased manner, with partiality', a sense that *partly* could not share.

2 Fowler (1926) attempted to make a distinction in principle between *partially* and *partly* by defining *partially* as contrasted with *completely* (i.e. = to a limited degree) and *partly* as contrasted with *wholly* (i.e. = as regards a part and not the whole). His illustrations based on this criterion were *It is partly wood; This was partly due to cowardice* and *a partially drunken sailor; his partially re-established health*, which in all cases show idiomatic uses that are not readily replaced by the alternative word. So if we say, for example, *The room is partly panelled*, we mean that only part of the room is meant to be panelled, whereas if we say *The room is partially panelled*, we mean that the panelling has still to be completed.

3 Fowler's rubric still works up to a point, but the meanings shade into each other and current usage reflects this: (partially) *I partially solved my money problems by being paid ten shillings to play regularly at the Black Horse*—A. Burgess, 1987; *A partially built shopping centre, for instance, will adversely affect the tenant's business*—R. Walker, 1993; *His new view was partially blocked by castle turrets and a gray stone drawbridge*—fiction website, 2005; (partly) *Her untidy blonde fringe partly covered her eyes*—J. G. Ballard, 1988; *The door to Suzy's bedroom was wide open and her partly clothed body was spreadeagled on the bed*—T. Barnes, 1991; *The strategy was only partly successful—Oxford Companion to Aust. History*, 2001.

4 A study of current usage suggests the following further observations: (*a*) *Partly* is used when it is balanced by a further *partly* or followed by some other link phrase such as *but also*, and many instances of its occurrence fall in this category: *She was shaking all over*, partly *because she was so angry with Oliver and* partly *because she was so afraid*—N. Bawden, 1989; *Maria jeered caustically, driven* partly *by masochism* but also *by a need to lash out*—J. Bauling, 1993. But *partially* occurs occasionally in this role, although it sounds rather less idiomatic: *In practice there were innovations*, partially *because of the perceived need to reduce the influence of headmen, and* partially *because British officials naturally governed on the basis of their own training and inclinations*—J. D. Rogers, 1987.

(*b*) *Partly* is preferred when it qualifies an adjective or participial adjective that is also qualified in some other way: *Her dislike of him was of course ...* partly based upon a sense that *he disliked her*—I. Murdoch, 1980; *This is* partly attributable to the increased opportunity for *away travel which has increased the contact between rival groups of supporters*—D. Waddington, 1992.

(*c*) *Partly* is also much preferred when followed by a reason or cause introduced by *because, due to, on account of, as a result of,* and so on (the *OEC* has over ten times as many examples of *partly because* as examples with *partially because,* which sounds far less idiomatic): *I had chosen a homebirth* partly *for that reason*—*Mothering Magazine,* 2002; *The new class arose* partly because *almost all modern judges were educated in law schools staffed by professional law teachers*—*Quadrant Magazine,* 2003; *?Things quieted down,* partially because *no one could come up with a line to top it*—*Eye Weekly,* 2005.

(*d*) *Partially,* rather than *partly,* is normally used to qualify words describing physical disability such as *blind* and *deaf,* e.g. *Nor can they sell glasses for children under 16 or to registered blind or partially sighted people*—*Which?,* 1985.

(*e*) Both words are used to qualify judgemental and evaluating words such as *responsible, to blame, true,* etc., but *partly* is rather more common in this use.

5 In sum, Fowler's rule and the other observations will serve if a rule is needed and you are unsure which to choose; but usage is inconsistent and the alleged distinctions in meaning do not always work in practice.

participles. 1 For unattached participles, see UNATTACHED PARTICIPLES.

2 For the absolute construction, see ABSOLUTE CONSTRUCTION.

3 For fused participles, see POSSESSIVE WITH GERUND.

4 *Kinds of participle.* There are two kinds of participle in English: the present participle ending in *-ing* as in *We are* going, and the past participle ending in *-d* or *-ed* for many verbs and in *-t* or *-en* or some other form for others, as in *Have you* decided?; *New houses are being* built; *It's not* broken.

5 *Initial participles.* Participles are often used to introduce subordinate clauses that are attached to other words in a sentence, e.g. *Her mother,* opening *the door quietly, came into the room*; Hearing *a noise, I went out to look*; Born *in Rochdale, he spent most of his life in the area.* Participles in initial position, as in the last two examples, are acceptable grammatically but when overdone can produce a poor style, especially when the participial clause bears little causal or other relation to the main one: Being *blind from birth, she became a teacher and travelled widely.*

Fowler (1926) identified the use of initial participles as a stylistic mannerism of newspapers, and rather fancifully described it as follows: 'In these paragraphs, before we are allowed to enter, we are challenged by the sentry, being a participle or some equivalent posted in advance to secure that our interview with the C.O. (or subject of the sentence) shall not take place without due ceremony.' His examples included: *Winner of many rowing trophies, Mr. Robert George Dugdale, aged seventy-five, died at Eton; Found standing in play astride the live rail of the electric line at Willesden . . . Walter Spentaford, twelve, was fined 12s. for trespass.* The type to which Fowler objected seems now to be less common, at least in the quality press. Contrast these sentences (drawn from issues of *The Times* and the *Sunday Times*) in (*a*) where the subject is delayed, as in Fowler's examples, and those in (*b*), the more common type, where the subject is highlighted by being placed first: (*a*) *Having filled the Tate with various enormous metal 'vessels', Sir Anthony Caro is moving still closer to nautical areas; Trailing Minnesota, two games to nil, the Braves were on the verge of extinction in game three.* (*b*) *Fred Overton, thought to be the last survivor of the Channel tunnel project halted in 1923, has died aged 87.*

6 Certain participles, such as *considering, assuming, excepting, given, provided, seeing, speaking* (of), etc., have acquired the status of prepositions or conjunctions, and their use in a grammatically free role is well established: *'Speaking of money,' said Beryl, 'do you mind my asking what you did with yours?'*—A. Munro, 1987. Recent additions to the list are the semi-floating forms *that said* and *having said that: We're just one big happy family. But having said that, it's a family unlike your family because I don't pretend to be something I'm not*—*X-Press Online,* 2004.

7 Placing of the stress and changing of the pronunciation can distinguish a past participle (or adjective derived from the participial stem) from a verb having the same spelling. A standard example is *consummate* (adjective), usually stressed on the second syllable, /kən'sʌmət/, as against *consummate* (verb), which is always stressed on the first, /'kɒnsəmeɪt/. Similarly *dílute* (adjective) but *dilúte* (verb); and the archaic adjective *frústrate* contrasted with the verb *frustráte* (in BrE). A second group distinguishes the part of speech by placing the obscure vowel /ə/ in the final syllable of the adjective but /-eɪt/ in the final syllable of the verb. Examples: *animate* (adjective) /'anɪmət/ but *animate* (verb) /'anɪmeɪt/; similarly, *deliberate* (adjective) /-ət/ but *deliberate* (verb) /-eɪt/; and numerous other pairs of adjectives and verbs including *articulate, degenerate, designate, desolate, elaborate, legitimate, moderate, separate*, and *subordinate*. See also NOUN AND VERB ACCENT, and most of the above words at their alphabetical places.

particoloured (**particolored**, US). Best spelt without a hyphen, and not as **party-colo(u)red*. The first element appears to be a respelling of *party* (adjective.), first recorded in the 14c. in the sense 'variegated' (*She gadereth floures, party white and rede*—Chaucer, *c*.1386), ultimately from Latin *partītus* 'divided', past participle of *partīre* 'to part, divide'. *Party* is still used as an adjective in heraldry, said of a shield divided into parts of different tinctures, and is preserved in the compound *party wall*.

particular. Frequently used for emphasis, especially after the demonstrative pronouns *this* and *that* (*he didn't like that particular tax; in this particular instance*) to the point that it has attracted adverse comment ('an unnecessary reinforcement', 'can often be left out, to the benefit of the sentence'). Up to a point such criticism is just, but it should be borne in mind that there are some contexts, especially (but not only) after a negative, when the adjective supplies legitimate emphasis (e.g. *He had no particular reason for being there as far as I could tell; She didn't write that particular essay but many others just as good*).

partisan. Generally, a zealous supporter of a party, cause, etc.; specifically, a guerrilla in wartime. It is usually pronounced /pɑːtɪ'zan/ in BrE, with the main stress on the last syllable; but in AmE first-syllable stressing is favoured, and is also heard in BrE. The word was adopted from French in the 16c., and the French word in turn was an alteration of Italian (Tuscan) dialect *partigiano*, from Latin *pars partem* 'share, part' + a suffix answering to Latin *-iānus*.

partitive. As noun, a word, form, etc., denoting a part of a collective group or quantity (e.g. *any, some; half, portion*). The word is most familiar in *partitive genitive*, a genitive used to indicate a whole divided into or regarded as parts, expressed in modern English by *of* as in *most of us, half of the ground*. The partitive genitive is a common feature of inflected languages: e.g. Latin *Plato totius Graeciae doctissimus fuit* 'Plato of all Greeks was the most learned': OE *pæs landes sumne dǣl* 'a part of the land'; *scipa fela* 'many (of) ships'.

partly. See PARTIALLY.

partner is an alteration of *parcener* 'partner, joint heir', from Anglo-Norman French *parcener*, based on Latin *partitio*(*n*-) 'partition', due to association with *part*, and is first recorded *c*.1300. Its wide scope includes bridge partners, tennis partners, partners in crime, business partners, and sexual partners. The reason it is mentioned here is its meaning of 'either member of a married couple or of an established unmarried couple', which, as the *OED* puts it, is 'Now increasingly used in legal and contractual contexts to refer to a member of a couple in a long-standing relationship of any kind, so as to give equal recognition to marriage, cohabitation, same-sex relationships, etc.'. It is also increasingly used in general language.

While many people find it useful precisely because it makes no comment about the legal status of the partnership or the sex of the person so described, others see it as the work of the thought police, if not the Devil, forcing people to replace 'husband', 'wife', 'spouse' with what they view as a PC term. But there is no ban on using those words if one so wishes. In addition, *partner* seems a more dignified and neutral word in long-standing but unmarried mature relationships than *boyfriend, girlfriend*, or the tabloidish *fiancé*(*e*) (when the people concerned are not engaged), and the mawkishly contrived *significant other*. Nor is it purely a concoction of political correctness: Milton used *partner of my life*, and this phrase is found in later writers, though *partner* on its own in this modern meaning is a 20c. development.

parts of speech. In 1990, an Oxford undergraduate, immediately before his final examinations, in which he was eventually placed in Class I, asked Burchfield what he called 'an embarrassing question': could Burchfield please explain to him the difference between an adjective and an adverb? Burchfield supplied the essential facts and referred him to *CGEL* (1985). The episode is a startling reminder that we live in an age when it can no longer be assumed that even a well-schooled person is capable of analysing sentences into their named parts and units. It is also an age when the linguistic analysis of sentences by professionals has reached a stage of complexity that puts their work beyond the reach of ordinary people.

In broad terms the central parts of speech named in the first modern English grammar, namely William Bullokar's *Bref Grammar for English* (1586), were those used from earliest times of Latin grammar. The same is true of other English grammars written between 1586 and the end of the 18c. A change of attitude came about in the later part of the 19c. and especially in the 20c. Modern professional grammarians endeavour to analyse and describe English grammar in terms of its own features, with negligible reference to the grammar of Latin or of other languages. In the present book, for the benefit of the general reader, the traditional terminology used by Burchfield is retained as far as possible, while trying to import into relevant entries the discoveries and insights of modern linguistics.

The main parts of speech used in this book are as follows: noun, verb, auxiliary verb, adjective, adverb, pronoun (including demonstrative and possessive pronouns), determiner, preposition, conjunction, article (definite and indefinite), interjection, and numeral. Most of the regular terms are treated at their alphabetical place, but the auxiliary verbs (i.e. *be, do,* and *have*) and the modals (*can/could, may/might, must, shall/will, should/would*) are treated as main entries.

party. Quite separate from various uses in law (*guilty party, third party,* etc.), *party* preceded by the indefinite article (e.g. *a pious party, an aggrieved party*), has come to be used informally (the *OED* in 1905 labelled the use *low colloquial* or *slang*) to mean 'a person': and more vaguely 'the person (defined by some adjective, pronoun, etc.)'. This second use (which seems to be commoner in AmE than in BrE) was described by the *OED* in 1905 as 'Formerly common and in serious use; now shoppy, vulgar, or jocular, the proper word being *person'.* The descent of the word into mercantile or other types of informality seems to have occurred during the 19c. Modern examples: *I don't know who the injured party is here*—R. Carver, 1986; *I've known this party for three years now and I hardly know him at all*—D. Goodis, 1986; *June had taken Imogen from her—'What a stout little party'—and settled down for the interview with Imogen on her knee*—J. Trollope, 1990; *She was staring right at the window, and the man's face was staring right at her. What party is he looking for, do you suppose?'*—*New Yorker*, 1992.

party. See PARTICOLOURED.

pasquinade. See LAMPOON.

passable /ˈpɑːsəbəl/ means 'barely satisfactory' (a *passable performance*) or 'able to be passed' (of a road, mountain pass, etc.). *Passible* /ˈpasɪbəl/, occasionally used by mistake for *passable,* is a theological term meaning 'capable of suffering', ultimately from Latin *patī, pass-* 'to suffer'. See -ABLE, -IBLE 5.

passed. See PAST.

passible. See PASSABLE.

passionate. As used in advertising and the business world, *passionate* has long since passed into the realm of cliché. The meaning 'ardent, extremely enthusiastic' dates to the 16c. and was used for example by Hobbes (*Cicero,* (*a passionate defender of Liberty*)—*Leviathan*, 1651) and satirized by Kingsley Amis (*His wife... was frequently described as passionate without it being revealed what she was passionate about or at*—*I like it Here*, 1958). The collocation *be* + *passionate* + *about* is now widely used and abused by companies as a mantra of their professionalism, as the following quotes from websites illustrate: *At the new General Motors, we are passionate about designing, building and selling the world's best vehicles; We are passionate about helping you succeed* (Cox, Costello & Horne, UK accountants); *We are passionate* *about taking on immense challenges that matter to our clients and, often, to the world* (McKinsey & Company). Such uses have been cleverly satirized by David Mitchell, whose skit on the subject can be found on the Internet. Obviously it is more rewarding to do business with someone who is enthusiastic about what they do, and enthusiasm can be contagious; but ultimately one cannot avoid the suspicion that for many companies to say they are *passionate* about something amounts to nothing more than saying 'this is what we do'.

passive voice.

1 Overview and recommendation.
2 Grammar and terminology.
3 Standard uses.
4 In scientific writing.
5 Criticized uses.
6 The double passive.
7 Passive of *avail oneself of.*

1 *Overview and recommendation.* Despite a generalized view, a superstition almost, among some editors that the passive voice is to be avoided under any circumstances, it supplies a useful means of achieving a different focus on an event from that provided by the active voice. (Imagine how undramatic Churchill's 'Never in the field of human conflict was so much owed by so many to so few' would be in the active voice.) The many legitimate and irreproachable uses of the passive are described in 3. Additionally, in scientific writing the passive is seen as a crucial means of achieving objectivity. However, overuse of the passive in formal non-scientific writing often leads to wordiness, or worse, as 5 (b) and 6 illustrate. If you find yourself writing a passive sentence which does not fit any of the patterns outlined at 3, ask yourself if you could just as easily express it in the active. In particular, you should ask yourself if you are evading personal ownership of the event, opinion, or statement you are writing about.

2 *Grammar and terminology.* (*a*) *France beat Brazil in the final* is 'active' and *Brazil were beaten by France in the final* is its 'passive' equivalent. In the first, *France* performs the action of the verb, and its grammatical object *Brazil* is affected by the action. In the second, the grammatical object of the active sentence has become the subject of the passive verb *was beaten* and the subject of the active sentence is expressed as an 'agent' (the person or thing who does the action) introduced by the preposition *by*. Sentences containing an active form of the verb are in the 'active voice'; those containing a passive verb form are in the 'passive voice'.

(*b*) Passive forms of verbs consist of the appropriate tense of *be*, and the past participle of the main verb (*beat* in the above example). In many passive sentences the agent (i.e. *France*) is not expressed. Our example sentence could be rewritten as *Brazil were beaten in the final.* Sentences of that kind are called 'agentless passives'. The agentless passive is a useful device in the circumstances discussed at 3 below.

(*c*) In written English only about half the notional forms of passives occur with any frequency (*is taken, was taken, will be taken, may be taken, has been taken, is being taken*, etc.); in spoken English other parts of the paradigm occur somewhat more frequently (*may have been taken, may be being taken*), and even the most extended forms (*has been being taken, may have been being taken*) are occasionally used in spoken English without causing undue inconvenience to the listener.

3 *Standard uses.* (*a*) Passive verbs allow you to describe the same event as in an active sentence from a different viewpoint: our example sentence makes *France* the topic of the sentence, the thing you are going to talk about, while its passive version makes *Brazil* the topic. Since it is usually the first element in a sentence that introduces your topic, passive verbs allow you to highlight the person or thing affected by the action, rather than the doer of the action. They also make it possible to concentrate on the process rather than on the participants.

(*b*) There are perfectly valid reasons for using a passive verb form. (i) The agent is unknown: *President Kennedy was assassinated in Dallas; Bring the pesticide material in for identification and disposal if the label has been removed from its container*. (ii) It is not important who or what the agent is: *Additionally, all penetrations, such as electrical outlets and light switches, should be carefully sealed; All my life I have been told I am nothing. That I will always be a lowlife, scum, a peasant.* (iii) The agent has already been mentioned. *They were shooting everybody. I felt a pain in my shoulder and a man told me I was hit.*

(iv) It is obvious or easily deduced who or what the agent is: *He speaks of the case of a young student who is being treated for depression; Charged with sedition, Blake was tried and acquitted the following year.* (v) People in general are the agents: *Adult beetles can be obtained from several sources; It has not been explained, however, why Swedish social democrats chose to do this.* (vi) It is tactful or politic not to mention the agent: *I don't oppose all wars. My grandfather signed up for a war the day after Pearl Harbour was bombed*—Barack Obama, as Senator, 2 October, 2002. (vii) You report an opinion or statement but wish to avoid saying whose opinion or statement it is. The passive is often used with verbs such as *accept, agree, allege, announce, claim,* etc., either in an 'impersonal passive', with 'it' as the subject, or with the person or thing referred to in the report as the subject of the verb: e.g. *it has been alleged that many officers in the Colorado City Police Department are practicing polygamists/Many officers in the . . . are alleged to be practicing polygamists.*

(*c*) While some of the examples above could be rewritten actively, there is often no clear advantage in doing so. In (i) to rephrase *if the label has been removed from its container* as *if someone has removed the label from its container* inappropriately shifts the focus from the label to the agent. Similarly in (ii) to rewrite as *All my life, people have told me I am nothing* shifts the focus away from the person expressing his or her feelings of inadequacy.

4 *In scientific writing.* In scientific writing the passive voice is much more frequent than in ordinary expository or imaginative prose: e.g. *the cultures were fixed with 4% paraformaldehyde* rather than *I/we fixed the cultures with* [etc.]; similarly, *when DNA molecules are placed on a gel; an electron is scattered once every 1,000 molecules.* In ordinary prose true passives are relatively uncommon—usually not more than two on an average page of a book. In scientific work they are a main constituent even though concerted attempts have been made to encourage scientists to use the passive less, and, as reported in the *Cambridge Guide to English Usage* (2004), research showed that a large group of professionals surveyed preferred technical writing with a lower density of passive forms.

5 *Criticized uses.* (*a*) For a long time it has been a staple of usage guides and clear writing manuals and courses that the passive is to be avoided wherever it can be (or that you should avoid the passive wherever you can). Additionally, grammar checkers, such as that in Word, will flag all passives as checkworthy. As one of his six rules for avoiding muddled writing, Orwell wrote 'Never use the passive where you can use the active' (*Politics and the English Language,* 1946). Fowler (1926) had an entry entitled 'passive disturbances' with four categories, of which only one, the 'double passive' (see 6 below) is still relevant. To those four categories Gowers (1965) added one of his own, which he called the 'impersonal passive'. By this, he meant sentences such as *It is believed that no action should be taken; It is felt that your complaint arises from a misunderstanding.* As a senior civil servant no doubt he saw many such examples in correspondence that came his way, so that he was led to write that 'the impersonal passive . . . is a construction dear to those who write official and business letters'. 'It is reasonable enough in statements made at large,' he continued, giving the example *It is understood that the wanted man is wearing a raincoat and a cloth cap,* 'but when one person is addressing another it often amounts to a pusillanimous shrinking from responsibility.' What Gowers was referring to are the impersonal passive report structures mentioned at 3 (vii). The use or avoidance of such passives depends on the level of formality being aimed at and often on the wisdom of accepting personal or group responsibility for the statement that follows. While it is undoubtedly true that the use of such structures sometimes amounts to a shirking of responsibility, they are also a useful tool for writers wishing or forced to distance themselves from the opinion expressed. The official who wrote Gowers' second example may have had good reason not to put himself (as it probably was) in the firing line for taking a wrong decision.

(*b*) The *Oxford Guide to Plain English* (1995) provides several real-life examples of clumsily phrased passive sentences which would be better with active verb forms. They also illustrate how the passive in business or official letters can lead to other inelegant, wordy, and unnecessarily pompous phrasing. One example is enough to illustrate this: *We have been asked by your home insurers to obtain your written confirmation that all their requirements have been completed by yourself* is clearer, friendlier, and more personal as *Your insurers have asked us to obtain your written confirmation that you have completed all their requirements.*

6 *The double passive.* (*a*) In constructions such as *the satellite is scheduled to be put into orbit in March* or *a vast natural garden, which has to be seen to be believed,* a passive verb is comfortably followed by a passive infinitive. In *a review tribunal is required to be reviewed itself after the first year* the double passive begins to obtrude, though the construction is still acceptable. Some grammarians (including Fowler) have condemned constructions in which passive uses of *attempt, begin, desire, endeavour, hope, intend, order, propose, purpose, seek, threaten,* and a few others, are immediately followed by a passive infinitive, e.g. *But the weapons were the pretext on which the invasion was sold to a lot of people in this country, and was attempted to be sold to the people of the world; no greater thrill can be hoped to be enjoyed.* Such constructions are awkward because they have no active counterpart, **they attempted the pretext to be sold;* **We hope no greater thrill to be enjoyed* and should be avoided in favour of sentences in the active voice, or else be rewritten. The *OED* provides historical examples of the double passive with some of these verbs, e.g. *The evils that were intended to be remedied—Bk of Common Prayer,* 1662; *all classes were threatened to be overwhelmed in one universal ruin—Picture of Liverpool,* 1834; *Persons who have any interest in lands which are sought to be registered can lodge a caution with the registering officer—Law Times,* 1891. There are also modern examples of the condemned group of verbs: e.g. *Other records . . . were taken to Moscow and their contents have been begun to be made available to Western researchers only in the last five years—Chicago Tribune,* 1990. But they are relatively uncommon.

(*b*) A related remnant of this kind of construction (but with ellipsis of *to be*) remains in standard use in AmE: *this is the first time in 30 years a person has been ordered deported for fascist activities—NY Times,* 1982. This use is first recorded in AmE in 1781: see ORDER (verb).

7 Passive of *avail oneself of.* See AVAIL 3, 4.

past. *Passed* is the past tense and past participle of the verb *pass: We passed a police car; The time has passed.* The related adjective, preposition, and adverb are all *past: for the past three hours; We drove past a police car; She hurried past.* The form *past* is also a noun: *living in the past.*

past master. The *OED* says that the use of the expression to mean a person who is especially adept in an activity, subject, etc., 'may have arisen partly in allusion to the expertise which results from having passed through such an office as master of a Freemasons' lodge, etc. Sometimes it simply alludes to the expertise resulting from having passed the necessary training to qualify as 'master' in any art, science, or occupation.' It is no longer written as *passed master.*

pastor is now used, especially in AmE, as the term for or title of a clergyman or clergywoman in charge of a nonconformist church, especially a Lutheran or Methodist one (occasionally also a Roman Catholic one). In 1989 an American correspondent collected a large number of clippings about services, funerals, etc., conducted by pastors in the state of Illinois. The word occurred as a title (*Fourth Presbyterian Church, John M. Buchan, Pastor*), and as a general descriptive term (*the Roman Catholic pastor of St Norbert parish; The Rev. Samuel Solomon was pastor of the African Methodist Episcopal Church in Gary*). The term was sometimes qualified by words indicating rank (*Pastor Emeritus, associate pastor*). In news reports, obituaries, and other reasonably extended pieces, the word *minister* alternated freely with the word *pastor.*

pastorale. Now usually pronounced as three syllables, /pastəˈrɑːl/, but occasionally as four /-li/. The plural is *pastorales* (formerly alternating with *pastorali*).

past tense. It is of interest to note here (as *CGEL* 4.16 points out) that in certain circumstances the past tense may legitimately be used with reference to past and future time: **1** In indirect speech, e.g. *Did you say that you had* (or *have*) *a house to let?/How did you find out that I was* (or *am*) *the owner?* Such 'backshifts' are optional. Note also *'What did you say your name* *was?' 'Jones.'* (G. Greene, 1980). A past tense is used retrospectively with reference to future time in such a sentence as *My pupils will be annoyed that they mistook the time of your lecture and therefore missed it.*

2 What *CGEL* calls the 'attitudinal past': e.g. *Do/Did you want to come in now?*

3 The hypothetical past is used in sentences like the following: *It's time we left to catch the train*; *If you tried harder, you would probably win the game* (the implication being that you probably won't try harder).

pâté /ˈpateɪ/ (BrE), /paˈteɪ/ (AmE). Printed in roman. The accents are obviously needed to distinguish the word from *pate* (= the head) and *pâte* (= the paste of which porcelain is made, pronounced /pɑːt/ (paht)), which is printed in italic.

patella /pəˈtɛlə/, the kneecap. Plural *patellae* /-liː/.

paten, patten. Both pronounced /ˈpat(ə)n/. The first is the now usual spelling of the word for the shallow dish on which the bread is laid at the celebration of the Eucharist; a *patten* is a (now disused) term for a shoe or clog specially shaped for walking above wet or muddy ground.

patent 1 (noun) (= authority giving a person the sole right to an invention). In BrE pronounced either /ˈpeɪtənt/ or /ˈpatənt/. So also in *Patent Office*, and in the phrase *letters patent* (in which *patent* is an adjective). In AmE for these uses /ˈpatənt/ is standard. In *patent leather* my impression is that /ˈpeɪtənt/ is the more usual of the two pronunciations in BrE, but /ˈpatənt/ in AmE.

2 As adjective and adverb when *patent*(*ly*) means 'evident(ly), obvious(ly)' (*it was a patent lie*; *it was patently true*) the pronunciation is usually /ˈpeɪt-/ in BrE but in AmE it alternates with /pat-/. Clearly the pronunciation is unsettled, and resort to the Latin and French words lying behind the English ones does not help to resolve the problem.

pathetic fallacy, the attribution of human feelings and responses to inanimate things, especially in art and literature. The term was introduced into the language by John Ruskin in his *Modern Painters* (1856).

patina. This loanword from Italian refers to (i) the film of green produced on copper by oxidation, (ii) the attractive sheen on old furniture produced by age and polishing, and (iii) the impression of something (*he carries the patina of old money and good breeding*). In BrE generally the first syllable is stressed (as it is in Italian) **pa**-ti-nuh, but AmE dictionaries give preference to second-syllable stress, puh-**tee**-nuh, as many British antiques experts also seem to do.

patio. Plural *patios.* See -O(E)S 4.

patois. Pronounced /ˈpatwɑː/ (**pat**-wah), plural *patois* /-z/. Printed in roman. See JARGON 3.

patricide. See PARRICIDE.

patriot. The pronunciations /ˈpatrɪət/ and /ˈpeɪt-/ are equally current in BrE at present. For the derivative **patriotic**, initial /ˈpat-/ with a short *a* is preferred by nearly 80 per cent of BrE speakers, according to Wells (3rd edn), but younger speakers tend towards the alternative. For **patriotism** the preferred pronunciation seems to be that with initial /ˈpat-/. In AmE all three words have initial /ˈpeɪt-/.

patrol. The inflected forms are *patrolled, patrolling* in both BrE and AmE. See -LL-, -L-.

patron. 1 *Patron* is pronounced /ˈpeɪtrən/ and *patroness* /ˈpeɪtrəˌnɛs/, but the derivatives **patronage** and **patronize** both have initial /ˈpat-/ in BrE. In AmE initial /ˈpeɪt-/ is usual for all four words.

2 See CLIENT.

patroness was in regular use from the 15c. to the 19c., principally in the senses 'a woman who promotes social functions, as balls, bazaars, etc.' and 'a female patron saint', but is now less used. In the wake of the quest for gender-neutral language, it does not, however, seem to have suffered as much attrition as other specifically feminine terms (e.g. *authoress, poetess*). For example, the phrase *patroness of the arts* and related phrases outnumber the gender-neutral *patron of the arts* applied specifically to a woman. See -ESS.

patten. See PATEN.

pawky. First recorded in the 17c. in Scotland and northern dialects in the sense 'artful, sly', from the 19c. onwards the word has been applied to varieties of humour judged to be typical of the Scots: 'having a matter-of-fact, humorously critical outlook on life, characterized by a sly, quiet wit' (*Concise Scots Dict.*, 1985).

pay. In its ordinary senses the past tense and past participle are, of course, *paid.* The nautical verb *pay,* meaning 'to smear or cover with pitch, tar, etc., as a defence against wet', is of quite different origin and has *payed* as its past tense and past participle.

pay off. See PHRASAL VERBS.

PC, pc. Now just as likely to mean *political correctness* as *police constable, Privy Counsellor,* or *personal computer.*

peaceable, peaceful. Both words joined the language in the 14c. and there is a substantial overlap of meaning. In general, *peaceable* means (*a*) 'disposed to peace, not quarrelsome' (*the inhabitants are simple, peaceable, and inoffensive*), and (*b*) (*less commonly*) 'free from violence or disorder, characterized by peace' (*to do one's duty is not easy in the most peaceable times; peaceable, non-violent behaviour*). *Peaceful* is much the more common of the two words, and means (*a*) 'characterized by peace, tranquil' (*a peaceful country scene*), and (*b*) not violating or infringing peace (*peaceful coexistence*). Examples: (peaceable) *From the moment of the child's birth the unity with its mother can never be completely peaceable*—P. Roazen, 1985; (peaceably) *The baby lay peaceably in his carrycot, and was pleased to be joggling gently along*—J. Trollope, 1989; *here is proof that people with very different traditions can live peaceably together*—P. Ustinov, 1990; (peaceful) *The nights were peaceful and black*—L. Erdrich, 1988; (peacefully) *The water shone peacefully*—E. Jolley, 1981.

peak, peek, pique. Since all three words sound the same and all function both as nouns and verbs, muddling them is perhaps inevitable. A *peak* is the highest point of something, and if something *peaks* it reaches its highest point. A *peek* means 'a quick or furtive look' and *to peek* means to 'look quickly or furtively'. *Pique* is irritation resulting from a slight; if something *piques* your curiosity, it arouses it, and if you feel *piqued,* you feel resentful. Probably, deep down in our mental lexicons we all store this knowledge about these words, but in writing it is all too easy to bang down the wrong one. The main villain of the piece seems to be *peak,* perhaps because it is the most common of the three. It often replaces *peek* (noun) in the collocations *have a peek, sneak a peek, take a peek.* With the verb such substitution seems less frequent, but does occasionally happen, e.g. **I kept peaking at my watch*—weblog, 2007. *Peak* as a verb is also used where *pique* is correct, as in the last two examples below. Beware: spellcheckers cannot spot these confusions. Examples: (*peak* for *peek*) **Of those that do switch off* [*sc.* their phones], *22 per cent still can't resist having a peak at their work emails over the weekend*—*Daily Tel.*, 2010; **The idea of sneaking a peak at a Web page before clicking on the link eventually came to fruition*—*PC World,* 2011; (*peak* for *pique*) **It peaked my curiosity enough to buy the CD today during lunch*—weblog, 2005; **Two aspects of Hox genes have peaked the interest of phylogeneticists*—*American Zoologist,* 2001.

peccadillo. The plural *peccadilloes* is rather more frequent than *peccadillos,* and both are correct. See -O(E)S 2.

pedagogue. First recorded in the 14c. with the meaning 'teacher, instructor', by the end of the 19c. it had often come to be applied in a contemptuous way to teachers judged to be pedantic, dogmatic, or severe. It is rarely spelt *pedagog* even in AmE, and is in common use in the US usually without any implication of fussiness or pedantry, whereas in BrE there is very often a contemptuous, sardonic, or satirical tone to its use. Examples: *The master, a dryish Scotsman whose reputation as a pedagogue derived from a book that he had written*—*Sci. Amer.*, 1955; *Renowned pedagogue Nelita True will be the recipient of the Achievement Award*—*Amer. Music Teacher,* 2002; *Georges de Beauvoir also thought teachers were low-minded pedagogues*—L. Appignanesi, 1988 (BrE); *Of his postgraduate training: 'We learned by the principle of Wackford Squeers, a somewhat underrated pedagogue'*—*BMJ,* 2002.

pedagogy, the science of teaching. The pronunciation recommended is /ˈpɛdəˌgɒdʒɪ/, with a 'soft' second *g.* Similarly in **pedagogical** /-ˈgɒdʒɪkəl/. But see GREEK G. In AmE *-gog-* is also pronounced with a long *o.*

pedal. 1 The inflected forms of the verb are *pedalled, pedalling* (but usually *pedaled, pedaling* in AmE). See -LL-, -L-.

2 The mistaken spelling *back-peddle* (noun and verb) is not uncommon, as shown in the following example from an issue of the *Independent: Croatia . . . accepted the EC declaration with alacrity, while insisting that it would not back-peddle on the issue of full independence from Yugoslavia.* See PEDLAR.

pedantry. Fowler's classic statement of 1926 is still relevant: '*Pedantry* may be defined, for the purpose of this book, as the saying of things in language so learned or so demonstratively accurate as to imply a slur upon the generality, who are not capable or not desirous of such displays. The term, then, is obviously a relative one; my pedantry is your scholarship, his reasonable accuracy, her irreducible minimum of education, and someone else's ignorance. It is therefore not very profitable to dogmatize here on the subject; an essay would establish not what pedantry is, but only the place in the scale occupied by the author; and that, so far as it is worth inquiring into, can be better ascertained from the treatment of details, to some of which accordingly, with a slight classification, reference is now made. The entries under each heading are the names of articles; and by referring to a few of these the reader who has views of his own will be able to place the book in the pedantry scale and judge what may be expected of it. There are certainly many accuracies that are not pedantries, as well as some that are; there are certainly some pedantries that are not accuracies, as well as many that are; and no book that attempts, as this one does, to give hundreds of decisions on the matter will find many readers who will accept them all.'

Some of the main entries in which elements of pedantry are discussed in this book are as follows: Choice of words: FORMAL WORDS; LITERARY WORDS; POLYSYLLABIC HUMOUR; SAXONISM; WARDOUR STREET. Grammar: AGREEMENT; CASES; ELLIPSIS; PREPOSITION B; SPLIT INFINITIVE; UNATTACHED PARTICIPLES; VERBLESS SENTENCES. Pronunciation: ESTUARY ENGLISH; GREEK G; PRONUNCIATION. Punctuation: AMPERSAND; APOSTROPHE; BRACKETS; COLON; COMMA; DASH; EXCLAMATION MARK; FULL STOP; HYPHENS; ITALICS; QUESTION MARK; QUOTATION MARKS; SEMICOLON. Sensitivity: -ESS; ETHNIC TERMS; FEMININE DESIGNATIONS; LINGUISTIC ENGINEERING; POLITICALLY CORRECT; U AND NON-U. Spelling: I BEFORE E; MUTE E; SPELLING. Style: ELEGANT VARIATION; U AND NON-U.

peddler. See PEDLAR.

pedigree. The corresponding adjective is **pedigreed**, not *pedigree'd.*

pedlar, the traditional term for an itinerant seller of small items, is losing ground rapidly before the AmE spelling **peddler**, especially in the context of the peddling of drugs (in which it is virtually the only spelling). Examples of the contrasting spellings: *a cafeteria called informally the Saigon, a place for poets, drug-pedlars and speculators, not professors' daughters*—J. le Carré, 1989; *We've been missing the independent Senegalese venders in mid-town lately: except for watch peddlers . . . the venders . . . seem to have vanished*—*New Yorker*, 1989.

ped(o)-. See PAED(O)-.

pee. Since the introduction of decimal currency in Britain in 1971 the spelling *pee* has come into widespread use to represent the pronunciation of the initial letter of 'penny'. Example: *May I trouble you for forty-two pee?*—R. Rendell, 1974. The pronunciation as /piː/ is disliked by people who prefer /ˈpɛni/ as singular and /pɛns/ as plural.

peek. See PEAK, PEEK, PIQUE.

peewit /ˈpiːwɪt/. Spelt as shown, rather than *pewit* (q.v.).

peignoir. Pronounced /ˈpeɪnwaː/.

pejorative. Stressed on the (long) first syllable, thus /ˈpiːdʒərətɪv/, in the *OED* (1905) and Daniel Jones (1917), the word is now normally stressed on the second syllable, thus /pɪˈdʒɒrətɪv/.

pekoe (black tea). Pronounced /ˈpiːkəʊ/. (The *OED*, 1905, recommended /ˈpɛkəʊ/.)

pellucid. See TRANSPARENT.

pelta, a small light shield used by the ancient Greeks and Romans. Plural *peltae* /-iː/.

pelvis. The 'natural' plural now is *pelvises*, but in medical and scientific work *pelves* /-viːz/ is widely used.

penates (Roman household gods). Pronounced /pɪˈnɑːtiːz/.

pence, pennies. Both *pence* and *pennies* have existed as plural forms of *penny* since at least the 16c. The two forms now tend to be used for different purposes: *pence* refers to sums of money (*five pounds and sixty-nine pence*) while *pennies* refers to the coins themselves (*Such items could then be bought for a few pennies*) and has metaphorical uses. Even though in British decimal coinage the 1p coin is stamped 'one penny', *pence* rather than *penny* is often used as the singular (e.g. *the chancellor will put one pence on income tax*). This usage is disliked by some but will pass unnoticed by most.

penchant. Still pronounced in a French manner, /ˈpɑ̃ʃɑ̃/, in English.

pencil (verb). The inflected forms are *pencilled, pencilling* in BrE, but often *-iled, -iling* in AmE. See -LL-, -L-.

pendant, pendent, pennant, pennon. The spellings of the first two are quite often confused, *pendent* being incorrectly used for the item of jewellery. The meanings of the four words are as follows: *pendant* is a noun meaning a hanging jewel or the shank and ring of a pocket-watch; also, in nautical language, a short length of rope fixed on the main- and foremasts of a square-rigged ship, used for attaching tackles; also, any length of rope used as a means of purchase to a distant object; *pendent* is an adjective meaning (over)hanging; *pennant* is a nautical word (sometimes written *pendant* but always pronounced 'pennant') for a narrow tapering flag used for signalling or for some other specified purpose; *pennon* is principally a long narrow flag, used especially as the military ensign of lancer regiments. In the 15c. and 16c. *pennon* was also used for a long, coloured streamer flown from the mastheads or yardarms of warships on occasions of state or national importance, and they are said to have been 'on occasions as much as 60–80 feet in length' (*Oxford Companion to Ships and the Sea*, 1976).

pendente lite, 'during the progress of a lawsuit', is written in italic, and pronounced /pɛnˌdɛnti ˈlʌɪti/.

pending has been used as a preposition or quasi-preposition since the 17c. to mean 'during, throughout the continuance of' (*pending these negotiations*); and since the 19c. also to mean 'while awaiting, until' (*a final decision cannot be taken pending his trial; pending her return*). These prepositional uses are to be distinguished from *pending* used as a predicative adjective, when it means 'awaiting decision or settlement' (*The printing of the first edition is still pending, because final production details have not been worked out*), or 'soon to come into existence' (*patent pending*). A *pending tray* is, of course, a tray for documents, letters, etc., awaiting attention.

pendulum. Plural *pendulums* (from the 17c. to the 19c. occasionally *pendula*). See -UM 1.

penetralia (innermost shrines or recesses) is a plural noun. It is in origin the neuter plural of Latin *penetrale*, from *penetralis* 'interior, innermost'.

peninsula is the noun (*the Spanish Peninsula*) and **peninsular** the corresponding adjective (*the Peninsular War*). They are best kept strictly apart. The type *the Peninsula War* could be justified by regarding *Peninsula* as an attributive use of the noun; but the type *the Spanish Peninsular* is clearly wrong.

penman should be used only with reference to handwriting, not to the writing of books or articles. The second sense, 'an author, a writer', flourished from the 16c. to the 19c., but is now an affectation.

pen name. See NOM DE GUERRE.

pennant. See PENDANT.

pennon. See PENDANT.

penny. The plural for the separate coins is *pennies* (*he had four pennies in his pocket*), but for a sum of money is *pence* (*an increase of 50 pence*). See also PEE. In North America a one-cent coin is often called a *penny*, plural *pennies.* See also PENCE, PENNIES.

pension, used in the sense 'a French boarding-house' has not been anglicized (though it has been used in English since the 17c.) and is pronounced in a French manner, /pɑ̃sjɔ̃/. Printed in italic.

pentameter, a verse of five feet. One of the commonest metres in traditional English poetry is the *iambic pentameter,* i.e. a line consisting of five feet each containing an unstressed syllable followed by a stressed one: Enfórced to séek some cóvert ních at hánd. In classical Latin and Greek, *pentameter* is 'a form of dactylic verse composed of two halves each of two feet and a long syllable, used in elegiac verse'.

penult /pɪˈnʌlt, ˈpɛnʌlt/. Frequently used in phonetics, = the last but one (syllable). Thus *referendum* /rɛfəˈrɛndəm/ has its main stress on the penult. The *pen-* part of the word answers to Latin *paene* 'almost'.

penultimate. William Safire (*NY Times Bk Rev.*, 7 June 1981) reported instances in American newspapers of *penultimate* mistakenly used to mean 'ultimate, final', as if the element *pen-* simply added emphasis to the adjective *ultimate.* Burchfield had another from the *Chicago Sun-Times*, 23 Nov. 1988: *'These are the penultimate in quality scarves,' she said* [to a customer]. *'Well, then, show me the better line,'* [the customer cruelly said]. *'This* is *the better line', she responded.* This marketing malapropism seems unlikely to catch on. See PENULT.

people, persons. 1 Since the mid-19c. debate has continued about whether it is correct to use the word *people* when it is preceded by a numeral *or* by determiners (*many, several, a few, these, those,* etc.), or *persons.* Use with people has been part of standard English for many centuries: *But right anon a thousand peple in thraste*—Chaucer, *c.*1386; *These people saw the Chaine about his necke*—Shakespeare, 1590; *And many giddie people flock to him*—Shakespeare, 1593. Jespersen (1909–49, ii) cites *two people dying* from a 1722 work by Defoe, and *three thousand people* from Disraeli's *Lothair* (1870). Modern examples: *Twenty million people suffer from rheumatism each year*—V. Bramwell, 1988; *Four out of five people thought that fresh fruit and vegetables should be labelled—Which?*, 1989; *a great many people feel that a hug can make their day—Chicago Tribune*, 1991; *People have been debating abortion for decades, and two people cannot resolve this issue—Daily Northwestern* (Illinois), 1991. Clearly these types are legitimate and have been for a long time, though there happens to be no specific entry for them in the *OED.*

2 Competing with them, however, has been the specifically plural form *persons.* The *OED* cites *Fyftene persons* from a 14c. romance called *Richard Coer de Lion* and also a series of later examples, e.g. *more than ouer ninety and nine iust persons*—Luke (AV) 15: 7, 1611. In Shakespeare we find *Time trauels in diuers paces, with diuers persons* (1600); *Eight Wilde-Boares rosted whole at a breakfast and but twelue persons there* (1606).

3 In the US, attempts have been made to impose the rule that the plural of *person* must be *persons,* and this rule is still ingrained in many people's mind. The vagueness of the rule, however, emerges from the following comment in the *Harper Dictionary of Contemporary Usage* (2nd edn, 1985): 'The basic difference between *persons* and *people* is that *persons* is usually used when speaking of a number of people who can be counted and *people* is used when speaking of a large or uncounted number of individuals.' The Associated Press long ago ruled that *people* could be used in all circumstances, and *persons,* whether preceded by a numeral or not, is tending in both BrE and AmE to yield to *people,* and to retreat into somewhat restricted, mostly (semi-)legalistic use: e.g. in notices in lifts, banks, police reports (e.g. *killed by a person or persons unknown*). The following AmE examples illustrate the formal or stilted contexts in which *persons* tends to be used: (extract from a Federal Savings Bank notice) *It is also the Board of Directors' view that these provisions should not discourage persons from proposing a merger*; (from a Movie Ratings Guide) *R* (*Restricted*). *Persons under 17 not admitted unless accompanied by parent or adult guardian*; (brochure of a religious sect) *Open to all persons: prior membership in a twelve-step group is not required*; (advertisement) *the Chinese banquet dinner is only suited for a group of at least eight persons.*

per. It has long been stated as a rule not to use this Latin word when an English equivalent exists and is idiomatic: it is supposedly better, for example, to say that *the salary is £25,000 a year* rather than *£25,000 per year.* It seems that it was William Cobbett who first took offence at the use of *per* with English words, but the rule is now irrelevant or moribund. In commercialese, to say that a parcel is to travel *per rail* or *per* + name of delivery firm was a long-established commercial convention, but is now archaic. In correlative statements of the type '— head — week', it is clearly better (on grounds of euphony) to use *per* rather than the indefinite article: *£200 per head per week,* though there are notable exceptions, especially *an apple a day keeps the doctor away.* In a number of fixed phrases in which the accompanying word is also Latin, *per annum, per capita, per diem,* etc., and also in *per cent,* clearly *per* must be kept. *Per* also seems the natural choice in scientific and numerical contexts: to insist on its replacement by *a, each,* etc. in the following examples would be less idiomatic. Finally, in AmE, *per* is often used in the same way as *as per,* i.e. 'according to', as in the last example below: *It contains between 100 and 1,000 atomic particles per cubic centimetre—New Scientist,* 1959; *The recipe will serve 4 to 6 portions and that works out at less than 1 oz. of flour and 4 oz. of sugar per portion—Woman's Illustrated,* 1960; *I think twelve tablets per calf, then six every eight hours after that*—J. Herriot, 1974; *Fifteen minutes per baby, per breast, at specific intervals*—M. Roberts, 1983; *They can also bat in the happy knowledge that bouncers are restricted to one per over*—Willis and Lee, 1983; *This is my chore, per our agreement—New Yorker,* 1991.

See also *as per* s.v. AS 9.

peradventure. The word has been used in English for so long (first recorded as an adverb in the 13c. and as a noun in the 16c.) that it is somewhat surprising to find that it has stepped down a rung into archaism, deliberate or otherwise, or even further into the world of humour. Examples of its use as adverb meaning 'perhaps' can be found, but for the most part only in somewhat atmospheric or humorous contexts or in some English-speaking countries abroad. As a noun meaning 'uncertainty; conjecture', it survives in the fossilized phrase and variants *beyond (a, all, any) peradventure,* meaning 'without a doubt', especially in legal parlance. Examples: *Where else* [except in Ghana] *in the English-speaking world will you still hear the word 'peradventure', meaning 'perhaps', used in current speech?—Times,* 1982; *Peradventure they were the only two windows in the house*—B. Breytenbach, 1984 (SAfr.); *it is absolutely clear beyond peradventure that prior to the expiration of the applicable period of limitation ...—High Court of Austr. transcripts,* 2000. See WARDOUR STREET.

per capita. Properly meaning 'by heads' (in law), 'among a number of individuals in equal shares (relating to a form of inheritance in cases of intestacy). Opposed to *per stirpes*' (*OED*). *Per capita* (printed in roman) is now a standard way in English of saying 'for each person or head (of population)'. But *capita* is plural in Latin, so literally translated the phrase means 'per heads'. Fowler (1926) accordingly regarded this use of *per capita* as 'a modern blunder, encouraged in some recent dictionaries'. Attitudes have changed, and *per caput* is now rare, and when used exhales a stale whiff of pedantry. Examples: (per capita) *During the same period, per capita personal consumption rose 15 percent in terms of constant prices—Dædalus,* 1990; (per caput) *It may be argued that the per-caput cigarette consumption is not a good measure of the cigarette consumption in young women—Lancet,* 1976.

per cent. 1 *One word or two? Per cent* is traditionally written as two words in BrE but as one word (**percent**) in AmE. However, the single-word form is now widely used in BrE. In attributive use (i.e. before a noun), it is normally written with a hyphen in BrE: *a 12 per-cent increase.*

2 *Verb agreement.* The type '30/40 etc. per cent of + noun' normally governs a singular verb if the noun is a collective or an uncount noun and a plural verb if the noun is an ordinary plural. Examples: *Fifteen per cent of the* electorate has *yet to make up its mind—Daily Tel.,* 1987; *35 per cent of an officer trainee's* time *on the one year course* is *academic—Daily Tel.,* 1987; *50 per cent of children with nut allergies also* react *to egg—Observer,* 2007. But the choice of concord is often governed by which element of the construction is felt by the writer or speaker to be dominant. Many people would have written the first example in the form 'Fifteen per cent of the electorate have yet to make up their mind(s)'.

3 *Words or figures? Symbol or word?* The New Hart's Rules is very straightforward on the matter: 'Generally speaking, figures should be used with units of measurement, percentages, ...' and gives the example '10 per cent of all cars sold'. The *OEC* data shows that, as in the examples just given, words are far less often used even at the beginning of a sentence. *Hart* also advises 'Note that *per cent* rather than % is used in running text.' The latter rule is often ignored in scientific or humanistic writing containing many percentages.

4 In AmE, but not in BrE, *percent* is also used as a noun, an alternative to *percentage* (*a large percent of the population*).

percentage. 'The notion has gone abroad that a percentage is a small part' (Fowler, 1926), and he went on to remind readers that whereas 'a part is always less than the whole, a percentage may be the whole or more than the whole'. The use to which Fowler objected, citing copious examples from newspapers of his day which indicate that it was a vogue word, was in conjunction with the word *only*, as in his example 'It is none the less true that the trade unions represent only a percentage of whole body of railway workers.' However, such uses do not appear common currently, and his advice now smacks slightly of pedantry. Generally, the word is only used in contexts containing figures expressed as percentages, or implying them. It is true that occasionally in examples such as the next the word is cast entirely adrift from its numerical moorings and means merely 'some' or 'an indeterminate, possibly small, portion or number': *Although a percentage of the faculty has rallied to his side, I suspect most have better records than Churchill* [*sc.* an academic]—weblog, 2005. It is sometimes suggested that it is desirable to modify the word by adjectives like *small, tiny, large.* The more relevant point, it seems to me, is that if the context does not deal with figures, the word can be dispensed with altogether: e.g. *a large percentage* (read *very many*) *of the professional books appearing in America or Britain represent small adjustments . . . of an immediately current idea—London Rev. Bks,* 1987; *out of reach of all but the tiny percentage of the people* (read *the very few, the tiny minority of people*) *who are themselves involved in the new economic activity—New Yorker,* 1991.

perchance is the kind of word that immediately summons up a recollection of its most celebrated occurrence (*To die to sleepe, To sleepe, perchance to dreame: I* [= Aye] *there's the rub*—Shakespeare, 1602) and, to the layperson, of not much else. The word in fact has a rich literary history from the 14c. onwards, and it began to fall into an archaistic or purely poetical mode only at some point in the 19c. It was often more or less interchangeable with *peradventure,* which has suffered a similar fate. See WARDOUR STREET.

père. Added to a surname to distinguish a father from a son, especially when both are well known, and printed in italic, e.g. *Amis père* (= Sir Kingsley Amis) and *Amis fils* (= Martin Amis).

peremptory means 'admitting no denial or refusal' and not (perhaps by confusion with *perfunctory*) 'abrupt, sudden'. A *peremptory decision* is not one that has been hastily reached but one that is definitive. Occasionally the two words seem to be confused as in, e.g. *if the corpses were not on such a busy route, they would probably be left. If they were near crevasses they would be pushed into them in the most peremptory of burial—Daily Tel.,* 2007. The word is normally pronounced with the stress on the second syllable, although an older first-syllable stress survives in legal usage. J. C. Wells (1990) notes that 'both stressings are in use among English lawyers' (we must presume that Welsh, Scots, and Northen Irish lawyers use only one pronunciation).

perfect (adjective). **1** 'There is a prescriptive tradition forbidding the use of *very* or the comparative with intensifying adjectives like *perfect, absolute, unique,* and also with the corresponding adverbs (*perfectly, absolutely, uniquely*)' (*CGEL,* 1985, 7.4n.). The statement is in general true: some grammarians from Lindley Murray (1795) onwards have ruled out *more perfect, most perfect,* etc., as 'improper', but the more sophisticated authorities have noted that in certain circumstances rigid application of the rule is mere pedantry. The *OED* noted that the adjective *perfect* is 'often used of a near approach to such a state [of complete excellence], and hence is capable of comparison'. Numerous examples of comparative uses are cited in the *OED* from good 14–19c. sources, including one from Shakespeare (1597) (*Our men more perfect in the vse of armes*) and one from Leigh Hunt (1841): *The perfectest prose-fiction in the* *language.* Gowers (1965) cites G. M. Trevelyan on Lady Jane Grey: *As learned as any of the Tudor sovereigns, this gentle Grecian had a more perfect character than the best of them.*

The rule must therefore be modified to read something like this: in most circumstances *perfect* is used as an absolute adjective, but there are somewhat rare occasions when the speaker has in mind a near approach to such a state and a comparative adjective or the adverb *very* may be appropriately used with it. It can, of course, legitimately be governed by *almost* and *so.* Examples: *What figure is more perfect than the sphere?*—W. Golding, 1965; *She knew she had an almost perfect manner with subordinates*—R. West, 1977; *Maybe not purity but he seemed so perfect and so unreal, in a way*—C. Achebe, 1987.

2 As a curiosity, the phrase *a perfect stranger* is idiomatic, but it cannot be rephrased so that *perfect* is used predicatively (as *a stranger he is perfect*). In *a perfect stranger* the adjective is called a 'non-inherent' one, and is one of a class of adjectival phrases that cannot be re-expressed predicatively (e.g. *a firm friend,* but not *as a friend he is firm*).

3 The tendency, at least in BrE, to give the second *e* its full value in a hideous spelling-pronunciation, i.e. /ˈpəːfɛkt/, looks set to oust the traditional /ˈpəːfikt/. To grasp the full horror of this cuckoo-in-the-nest pronunciation, try mentally re-recording Lou Reed using it in *Perfect Day.*

perfect (verb). The stress is on the second syllable, thus distinguishing the verb from the adjective, where it falls on the first.

perfectible. So spelt, not *-able.* See -ABLE, -IBLE 8.

perfect infinitive, i.e. the type *to have done,* etc. **1** In its simplest form it is used after the verbs *appear* and *seem.* Examples: *she appeared to have encouraged him; GEC appears to have taken a firm grip on the project; that seemed to have been an isolated event; a fist-sized water bug that seemed to have fallen from the sky.* In each case the reported event had occurred before the time of the statement itself. If the appearing and seeming occur at the same time as the event that is being reported a present infinitive is used instead: *Herr Schmidt appeared to be internationally important; they seemed to get to know one another quickly.*

2 For the types *should/would have liked to have met, should/would have liked to meet,* see LIKE (verb) 1. See also HAVE 2.

3 The type *Jane was very sorry to miss you when you called* is preferable to *Jane was very sorry to have missed you when you called,* but both types occur frequently.

perforce. Used from the 14c. first as a phrase meaning 'by the application of physical force' and from the 16c. as an adverb meaning 'by constraint of circumstances, of necessity', the word has largely fallen out of use except in formal, legal, or literary contexts. Examples: *We sat and listened, perforce, and the pure notes shivered the motes of dust from the kitchen shelves*—F. Weldon, 1988; *Since Harvey had perforce moved in with his mother he had not shaved*—I. Murdoch, 1993.

perfume (noun and verb). Both words are normally stressed on the first syllable. This appears to be the result of a tidying-up process in the 20c., as the *OED* (1907) gave only second-syllable stressing for the verb, a pronunciation which the current *OED* gives as an alternative in BrE, and as the main pronunciation in AmE.

perhaps. In everyday relatively formal speech this common adverb is normally pronounced /pəˈhaps/. In relaxed or informal speech, and especially in rapid speech, it is often pronounced /pəˈraps/ or /praps/ or even /paps/ in standard English, though many speakers would rather die than admit it.

perimeter. Figurative uses recorded in the *OED* started in the 17c. (Ben Jonson), but are not plentiful thereafter. Its extension from the traditional geometrical, military, and (civil) airport meanings denoting the extremes or limits of a subject, topic, etc., is first noted towards the end of the 19c. but seems to have intensified in the last third of the 20c., thus coinciding with the period during which *parameter* broke loose from its technical and scientific straitjackets. The two events would seem to be connected. Occasionally, as in the last example below, one suspects either word would fit. Modern figurative examples: *The perimeter of her own life was shrinking*—J. Urquhart, 1986 (Canad.); *Patrick smiled* *at me, yet with his old Pinch hauteur, a just perceptible curl of the upper lip just so you'd know what the perimeters of his new tolerance were*—J. C. Oates, 1996 (US); *?The spectrum of opinion is always restricted by the fact that the right blasts the atmosphere with gaseous rhetoric so inane and outrageous that they define the perimeter of the debate*—weblog, 2006.

period. For near-synonyms, see TIME. For the punctuation mark, see FULL STOP 1. For its use in abbreviations and contractions, see FULL STOP 2, 3.

periodic, periodical. The first is only an adjective and is largely restricted to technical and scientific contexts, especially in the expressions *periodic acid, decimal, function,* and *table.* Also, in grammar, a *periodic sentence* is one consisting of a main clause, followed by 'several clauses, grammatically connected, and rhetorically constructed'. An example is given by Ogilvie and Albert in their classic *Practical Course in Secondary English* (1913): 'The various methods of propitiation and atonement which fear and folly have dictated, or artifice and interest tolerated in the different parts of the world, however they may sometimes reproach or degrade humanity, at least show the general consent of all ages and nations in the opinions of the placability of the Divine nature.' Note that the main statement is completed only at the end of the sentence.

In the sense 'appearing or occurring at regular intervals' *periodic* has ousted *periodical* in technical and non-technical language. If it does appear, it seems always to be used predicatively, e.g. *Updates tend to be periodical—depending on the product.* It is the only word of the two to be used as a noun (= a newspaper, magazine, etc., issued at regular intervals).

peripeteia /ˌpɛrɪpɪˈtʌɪə, -ˈtiːə/. An Aristotelian rhetorical term (from Greek περιπέτεια 'a falling round, a sudden change') for a sudden change of fortune or reverse of circumstances (in a tragedy, etc., or in everyday life), e.g. in *The Merchant of Venice*, the downfall of Shylock, when Gratiano repeats to him his own words, *O learned judge*, and Shylock's case collapses.

periphrasis. Plural *periphrases.* A rhetorical term for a roundabout way of saying something, a circumlocution, e.g. to refer to Shakespeare as *the Bard of Avon.* Circumlocutory phrases (e.g. *be of the opinion that* = think, believe; *in close proximity* = near(ly)) lie strewn about in the language and must be used with caution to avoid accusations of prolixity or windbagging. As Fowler remarked in 1926, '"The year's penultimate month" is not in truth a good way of saying "November".'

perk. See PERQUISITE.

permanence, permanency. 'One of the pairs (see -CE, -CY) in which the distinction is neither broad and generally recognized, nor yet quite non-existent or negligible' (Fowler, 1926). In practice *permanence* is much the more common of the two words. Both share the meaning 'the quality of being permanent'. When *permanency* is used, it often means 'the state of being permanent' or 'something permanent'. But there is no clear-cut distinction between the two words. Examples: (permanence) *His determination, which he now estimated to have the size and permanence of an ice cube, began to grow even smaller*—B. Byars, 1981; *Its* [sc. a memorial's] *construction was touched with grace, its stark and solid geometry with permanence*—*Newsday* (US), 1991; *There is a sense of invulnerable permanence at General Motors*—*Fortune* (US), 1992; (permanency) *The new world view fundamentally altered long established notions about the permanency of the continents and the ocean basins*—*Sci. Amer.*, 1974; *Permanency is also associated with marriage, and a person in a temporary position cannot marry and remain in the household without moving into a permanent position*—*Man*, 1983; *A stranger is not a permanency. One can easily shed a stranger*—G. Greene, 1988.

permissible. Spelt as shown, not *-able.* See -ABLE, -IBLE 8.

permit. 1 The inflected forms of the verb are *permitted, permitting.*

2 When *permit* is used as a noun the stress falls on the first syllable, and as a verb on the second. See NOUN AND VERB ACCENT 1.

3 The verb is normally transitive (*permit the traffic to flow again*) but can also be used absolutely (*traffic permitting*), and also intransitively with *of,* when it means 'to admit, to allow for' (*the rule permits of certain exceptions*). Cf. ADMIT 1; ALLOW 3.

pernickety (= fussy, fastidious) is a 19c. word of Scottish origin (its etymology beyond that cannot safely be postulated) which has spread to all English-speaking areas. In North American English, since the beginning of the 20c., it has alternated in standard colloquial use with the form with an intercalated *s*, namely **persnickety** (e.g. *That archetype of persnickety Yankee tool-makers*—R. Stein, 1967), but outside AmE *pernickety* is the form generally used.

perorate (verb). This rarely used high-brow verb (= to speak at length) sounds like a back-formation from *peroration* (the noun which was first recorded in the 15c.). It is in fact a natural formation in the 17c. from the past participle stem of Latin *perōrāre*: *But that alternation is significantly unbalanced, for the bosses always speak longer than the workers; they perorate happily, while the workers sweat and stutter; their style is conventionally eloquent, while that of the workers is halting and at times aphasic*—*Context* (magazine), 2003.

perpetrate, perpetuate are verbs that are sometimes confused. *Perpetrate* means 'to commit (a harmful, illegal, or immoral action)', as in *a crime has been perpetrated against a sovereign state*, whereas *perpetuate* means 'to make continue indefinitely', as in *a monument to perpetuate the memory of those killed in the war*. Each is incorrectly used for the other in the following examples: **For example, violence perpetuated by adolescents is a major problem in our society* (read *perpetrated*)—*OEC*, 2004; *Yet the Attorney General's prosecutors and the High Court judgment continue to perpetrate the myth that the massacre was spontaneous* (read *perpetuate*)—*OEC*, 2003.

perplexedly. Four syllables: see -EDLY.

per pro, per proc. See PP.

perquisite, an incidental benefit attached to one's employment. This is the formal word used only in e.g. business correspondence, noticeboard announcements, legal or tax cases, etc., whereas the once informal, now standard, equivalent *perk* is the only form most people ever use in speech. *Perquisite* is not to be confused with *prerequisite* (noun and adjective), (something) required as a precondition.

persiflage. 1 After more than two centuries of use in English, the word is pronounced /ˈpɜːsɪflɑːʒ/, i.e. is still not fully anglicized in pronunciation but it always appears in roman type.

2 It means 'light banter or raillery'. Hannah More defined it in 1799 as *The cold compound of irony, irreligion, selfishness, and sneer, which made up what the French ... so well express by the term* persiflage. Perhaps friendly teasing and levity are the main ingredients of the word as it is now used. In French the noun was formed from *persifler* 'to tease', from the intensive prefix *per-* + *siffler* 'to whistle' + *-age*.

persistence, persistency. Both words entered the language in the 16c. and are still in theory interchangeable in the senses 'the action or fact of persisting' and 'the quality of persisting or being persistent'. Whatever the reason (? a preference for the shorter word), *persistence* is scores of times the more common of the two. Examples: (persistence) *The opening phrase continued to echo in my mind with an obstinate throbbing persistence*—L. Durrell, 1957; *By sheer persistence he'd achieved what at first seemed inaccessible*—E. North, 1987; (persistency) *agelessly silent, with a reptile's awful persistency*—D. H. Lawrence, 1921; (used of insurance policies) *Motorists Life said it has revised its commission schedule and added a persistency bonus program*—*Investment Dealers' Digest* (US), 1991. See -CE, -CY.

persnickety. See PERNICKETY.

person (noun). **1** For the plural *persons*, see PEOPLE.

2 *So now one person can start their own magazine*—*The Face*, 1991: an extreme (and easily avoidable) example of the increasingly popular, and acceptable or unacceptable according to taste, types: anyone *who wants to improve* their *writing may attend the course* and Everyone *was absorbed in* their *own business*. See AGREEMENT 6; ANY 1(a).

-person (as a gender-neutral element). **1** At first to the bemusement of some, and then to the amusement, and even to the despair, of a few, in the 1970s feminists began to use, and then to insist that others use, *person* or, where appropriate as a second element, *-person* (e.g. *draughtsperson, salesperson, spokesperson*) instead of *man* or *-man*. This movement was reflected in language, first with the coining of the emblematic *chairperson* (1971), followed throughout the 1970s by other new *-person* coinages, and seems to have reached a point of maximum intensity by the 1990s. See CHAIR, CHAIRPERSON.

2 Although coining these words was in principle a laudable attempt to reduce the sexism considered to be enshrined in the language, their use in practice, as demonstrated by the *Oxford English Corpus*, has spread rather more slowly than might have been expected. One reason for this may be that people are reluctant to adopt forms that, while more 'politically correct', are linguistically more awkward or cumbersome. In some cases they sound deliberately contrived or ironic or even fundamentalist, as in *fisherperson, clergyperson, henchperson,* or *snowperson.* One solution has been to use a different word, such as *firefighter* instead of both *fireman* and *fireperson,* and *police officer* instead of *policeman* or *policewoman*. People are also finding other ways of expressing the professions and roles concerned: for instance, instead of referring to someone as a *barman* or *barperson* (let alone *barmaid*), one hears *a member of the bar staff* or that someone *works behind the bar.*

3 It is also interesting that the most widely used forms according to the *OEC* data, namely *spokesperson* and *chairperson,* come from the public arena and are often used in official and news documents. Even so, *spokesman/-men* is about five times as frequent as *spokesperson/-people* in the *OEC*, while *spokeswoman/-women* is a third more frequent. These last two are often used when the name of the person is mentioned, presumably because to use the gender-neutral term *spokesperson* in such cases strikes many writers as a bit of an oxymoron. But it is interesting to note that both are also often used when no name is mentioned, in which case it would be easy and appropriate to use the gender-neutral term. The list below gives the 'top ten' most widely used *-person* compounds in the *OEC* in descending order of frequency. As can be seen, all but three of them are 1970s creations.

4 There is a marked preference for forming the plural of these *-person* words with *-people,* but the strength of the preference varies from word to word. For instance, *spokespeople* is only slightly more frequent in *OEC* data than *spokespersons, sportspeople* is about twice as frequent as *sportspersons,* while *salespeople* is more than ten times as frequent as *salespersons.* It is unclear what factors influence these disparities.

spokesperson	1972
chairperson	1971
salesperson	1971
layperson	1972
sportsperson	1909
businessperson	1834
foreperson	1973
craftsperson	1976
congressperson	1972
tradesperson	1886

5 The substitution of *person* for *man* in other ways, e.g. in *personhandle, personpower,* and *gingerbread person,* still shows little sign of being taken seriously and leads to such facetious suggestions as *personhole* (for *manhole*), *Personchester* (for *Manchester*), and *chairperdaughter* (= a female *chairperson*), but none of these has taken root except as anecdotal items at the dinner table. Common phrases such as *the man in the street* and *every man for himself* still hugely outnumber *the person in the street, every person for themselves,* etc.

6 It is noteworthy that there is a marked tendency for the *-person* combinations to be applied mainly to women, leading to such pairs as *spokesman* (male)/*spokesperson* (female). Many of the occupational terms (*draughtsperson, salesperson,* etc.) occur in job advertisements to attract applications from either sex. Such innovations in the language as have occurred since the 1970s can now be clearly seen as one aspect of the POLITICALLY CORRECT movement. The arguments about them will no doubt continue in the 21c., but are far less vociferous than they previously were.

persona. **1** The plural is somewhat more often anglicized as *personas* than the Latin *personae* /-niː, -nʌɪ/. In compounds such as *dramatis personae, personae non gratae,* etc., the Latin plural is of course invariably used. Printed in roman.

2 In current use, *persona* has acquired two special meanings and a generalized one that draws on both. (*a*) 'a character deliberately assumed by an author in his or her writing' comes from the Latin *persona* whose primary meaning was 'a mask, esp. as worn by actors'. It also meant 'a character in a play, a dramatic role', and '(with no idea of deception) the part played by a person in life, a role, character'. Ezra Pound, in a work of 1909 called *Personae,* introduced the term to literary criticism, where it has settled down to mean 'the assumed identity or fictional "I"... assumed by a writer in a literary work: thus the speaker in a literary poem, or the narrator in a fictional narrative' (C. Baldick, 1990). (*b*) In a separate 20c. development, *persona* was employed in Jungian psychology to mean 'the set of attitudes adopted by an individual to fit himself or herself for the social role seen as his or hers; the personality an individual presents to the world'. This sense is first recorded in English in 1917. (*c*) In the non-technical sense, 'an aspect of the personality as shown to or perceived by others'. The psychological resonance of these uses makes *persona* a more powerful word than (say) *identity*, or *image*, and the development is a useful one. Examples: (*a*) *The outstanding example is Burns, whose ability to assume different poetic personae... is one of his most individual characteristics*—*TLS*, 1989; *Does he intend to stick with one character or will he develop another persona?*—*Bolton Evening News*, 2003; (in Jungian sense) *The stiff upper lip, the persona of the English gentleman, is a particularly appropriate mask for the schizoid person to adopt*—A. Storr, 1968; (*c*) (in generalized meaning) *Despite his assertion that he is merely a machine, Warhol constructs a carefully-crafted persona that he markets relentlessly*—*Modern Painters*, 1989; *James Spicer, his military persona now well to the fore, ignored the question and picked up the phone*—M. Hamer, 1991.

persona grata. a person, especially a diplomat, acceptable to certain others. Printed in italic and pronounced /pɜːˈsəʊnə ˈgrɑːtə/. Plural *personae gratae* /-iː, -ʌɪ/. Its antonym is *persona non grata* /nɒn/ or /nəʊn/.

personally. 1 There is a use of *personally* to which many usage guides object, and that is in conjunction with personal pronouns, particularly *I*, as in the examples below. It often comes before the pronoun, as in the second example. The objection to it is that it is supposedly redundant: if someone says *I personally think* ..., who else could be doing the thinking if not the *I* involved? This seemingly redundant use appears in conversational or informal passages in standard sources: Examples: *I am personally very gratified that the Committee has seen fit to make this recommendation*—C. P. Snow, 1934; *Well, you'd better get on, then... Personally, I'm going to wait until Fiver and Pipkin are fit to tackle it*—R. Adams, 1973; *I personally would like to see fewer groups*—S. Biko, 1978. It has a useful emphatic function, but because of the black mark against it it is best avoided in any kind of serious prose that presents a point of view or an argument.

2 The other standard uses are uncontentious: (*a*) to mean that something was done by or to someone in person and not through an agent or deputy (*The writ was served on the defendant personally at his residence*; *I welcome the decision though I was not personally involved*); (*b*) individually rather than as a group: *every pupil is known personally*; (*c*) in a private rather than public or professional capacity: *nothing had gone well personally or politically.*

personalty. Used only in law, one's personal property or estate (as opposed to *realty*).

personification. is 'the attribution of a personal nature or human characteristics to something non-human, or the representation of an abstract quality in human form'. It occurs partly as a natural or rhetorical phenomenon (see the Keats quote below) and, in English, partly as a result of the loss of grammatical gender at the end of the Anglo-Saxon period. In Old English a pronoun used in place of a masculine noun was invariably *he*, in place of a feminine noun *heo* (= she), and in place of a neuter noun *hit* (= it). When the system broke down and the old grammatical genders disappeared, the obvious result was the narrowing down of *he* to refer only to a male person or animal, *she* to a female person or animal, and *it* to nearly all remaining nouns. At the point of loss of grammatical gender, however, *he* began to be applied 'illogically' to some things personified as masculine (mountains, rivers, oak trees, etc., as the *OED* has it), and *she* to some things personified as feminine (ships, boats, carriages, utensils, etc.). For example, the *OED* cites examples of *he* used of the world (14c.), the philosopher's stone

(14c.), a fire (15c.), an argument (15c.), the sun (16c.), etc.; and examples of *she* used of a ship (14c.), a door (14c.), a fire (16c.), a cannon (17c.), a kettle (19c.), and so on. At the present time such personification is comparatively rare, but examples can still be found: e.g. *Great Britain is renowned for* her *stiff upper lip approach to adversity*; *I bought that yacht last year:* she *rides the water beautifully*; (in Australia and NZ) she's *right*; she's *jake*; she's *a big country*, etc; and in certain rural British dialects, such as Somerset, doors, tools and any inanimate object one is working on, repairing, etc. are generally referred to as 'he'.

Personification has long been used as a literary device, especially in poetry: e.g.

> *Ay, in the very temple of delight*
> *Veil'd* Melancholy *has her sovran shrine.*
> (Keats, 1819)

In the ordinary language, personified uses of words are widespread and so familiar that they pass virtually unnoticed. Proverbs are fertile territory for such uses (*Brevity is the* soul *of wit*; *the wish is* father *to the thought*); and such ordinary metaphors as *the* heart *of the matter* and *the* mouth *of the river* are used all the time.

personnel. Pronounced /pəːsəˈnɛl/. First in French and, from about the 1830s, in English the word came to be used, especially in the armed services, of the human as distinct from the *materiel* or material equipment (of an institution, undertaking, etc.). It seems not to have been widely favoured outside the armed forces until the second half of the 20c. Then all self-respecting large firms had *personnel departments, personnel managers*, etc., and this is the name by which this function is still known by those who find the cant phrase 'human resources' odious. Its use preceded by a numeral (e.g. *one copy to every twenty-five personnel*) has little to commend it, but occasionally occurs in reasonably standard sources.

persons. See PEOPLE.

perspective. 1 *Perspective* is well established in the meaning of 'point of view', as in: *from our perspective this is a sensible proposal.* Nowadays it is increasingly common to encounter phrases where *perspective* is wrongly replaced by *prospective*: **from our prospective this is a sensible proposal.* Though there are historical precedents for *prospective* being used in this way, it is best to avoid doing so, as many people, especially British speakers, will regard such a use as a mistake.

2 In the type '*new perspectives*—(a subject)', the usual preposition is *on* (not *of*). Thus 'Three Perspectives on Canada's Future' in *Dædalus*, 1988; *Perspectives on Thomas Hobbes*, ed. G. A. J. Rogers and Alan Ryan, 1989.

perspicacious, perspicacity, perspicuous, perspicuity. These two groups of words, part of the vast influx of Latin-derived words in the 16c. and 17c., are generally restricted to highly formal or literary contexts. Despite some historical overlap of meaning, the clear current distinction between them is generally observed. *Perspicacious* means 'having a clear and ready insight into something', and its corresponding noun is almost always *perspicacity* rather than *perspicaciousness*. *Perspicuous*, on the other hand, means 'easily understood, clearly expressed, (of a person) expressing things clearly', and its corresponding noun is *perspicuity* much more often than *perspicuousness* . (For current purposes, let us gloss over the fact that since the 17c. *perspicuity* has often been used to mean 'discernment, insight' by distinguished writers including Charles Dickens, and since the 16c. *perspicuous* has also been used to mean 'discerning, perspicacious' by eminent writers including Swinburne). Since all these words usually flow from the pens of the highly literate, confusion does not appear to be common, but when it happens, *perspicuous*, etc. mistakenly replaces *perspicacious*, etc. Examples of standard uses: (*perspicacious* and derivatives) *He went through the photographs. But it didn't take much perspicacity to tell that some . . . were missing*—R. Rendell, 1983; *How much Edith longed for my wholehearted commitment to her I was not perspicacious enough to see*—R. Manning, 1987; *I was not overjoyed to recognise myself as the cuckold of the piece, an idiotic Hamlet betrayed . . . by his own lack of perspicacity*—S. Mason, 1990. (*perspicuous* and derivatives) *I am always willing to run some hazard of being tedious in order to be sure that I am perspicuous*—Adam Smith, 1776; *People . . . will get a lot out of Soames's careful and perspicuous accounts of what is living and what is dead in the work of Russell's successors*—*London Rev. Bks*, 2005; *He wrote with perspicuity* *and vigour, in a prose style commended by Hazlitt as 'plain, broad, downright English'*—M. Drabble, 2000; (dubious uses of *perspicuous*, etc.) **In some ways, this was a particularly perspicuous comment, since it drew together the two themes . . . that I have claimed Richard explored separately in his video and commentary*—*Jrnl of Popular Film and Television*, 2002; **The thing is, if the subjects are making it up—pretending or acting for the camera—if you have any perspicuity at all, you can see through it*—*Take One* (magazine), 2003; *Tony Blair, with his usual perspicuity, predicted that when Poland joined the European Union, 13,000 Poles would move to Britain*—*OEC* (undated).

persuade. See CONVINCE.

persuasion. When Matthew Arnold declared in 1879 that *Men of any religious persuasion might be appointed to teach anatomy or chemistry*, he was using *persuasion* without irony or humour in one of its traditional senses (first recorded in the early 17c. in a work by John Donne). The senses 'belief or conviction' or 'a religious belief, or the group or sect holding it (*of a different persuasion*)' are nowadays less often used meanings of the word. For, since the 1860s, the word has acquired other meanings, namely (i) 'a school of thought, esp. in politics', usually with a modifying word (e.g. *His political satires would have galled Tories, . . . and could hardly be read by persons of that persuasion with such complete enjoyment*—G. Saintsbury, 1888), and (ii) humorously 'a group or collection linked by a shared characteristic, quality, or attribute. Esp. in early use in *of the—persuasion*: of a (specified) nationality, occupation, inclination, etc.' (e.g. *She said she thought it was . . . a gentlemen of the haircutting persuasion*—F. Anstey, 1885; *A sinister moustache of the toothbrush persuasion*—R. Hichens, 1902). In modern use the most frequent adjectives preceding it when it is not humorous are *different, political, religious, sexual*, and when it is humorous (although the list is in principle infinite) *female* and *male*. Since the word sometimes implies humour or irony examples such as the following could be misinterpreted, so the word is best avoided in such contexts: *Sampson has even found a psychoanalyst of the sturdily Freudian persuasion*—*TLS*, 1990. Further examples: *In Galicia, men of all political persuasions wear beards*—*Daily Tel.*, 2011; *Today, I am pathetically grateful to be able to sit and type on the train. This is only possible because the poor sod jammed in beside me is a very slim young person of the female persuasion*—weblog, 2008.

pertinence, pertinency. The first is standard; the second has all but disappeared. Examples: (pertinence) *One essay, 'patriotism and Sport', has a particular pertinence today, in a world of fighting football fans*—M. Coren, 1989; (pertinency) *But let that pass; he will not fail to see the pertinency of the question, I think*—*OEC* (undated).

perturbedly. Four syllables: see -EDLY.

peruse is a somewhat formal word with a long literary history and many fine shades of historical meaning. What concerns us here is its use to mean 'to read', and the thoroughness of the reading so denoted. Historically, *peruse* has sometimes meant 'to examine closely' (e.g. *I think nine people out of ten who have perused the evidence would agree that it fully substantiates the conclusions*—*Times*, 1911) and sometimes 'to go through (a text) in detail to check or correct' *He* [*sc.* Churchill] *always carefully perused and corrected the drafts, often supplying inimitable Winstonian touches*—M. Soames, 1998. Since the early 20c., the notion has arisen that it can only mean 'to read (something) in a thorough and careful way'. However, this is not now, and never has been, the case. As the *OED* currently puts it: 'Modern dictionaries and usage guides, perhaps influenced by the word's earlier history in English, have sometimes claimed that the only 'correct' usage is in reference to reading closely or thoroughly . . . However, *peruse* has been a broad synonym for *read* since the 16th cent., encompassing both careful and cursory reading; Johnson defined and used it as such. The implication of leisureliness, cursoriness, or haste is therefore not a recent development, although it is usually found in less formal contexts and is less frequent in earlier use . . . The specific sense of browsing or skimming emerged relatively recently, generally in ironic or humorous inversion of the formal sense of thoroughness.'

In current use, therefore, it covers the whole spectrum of reading, from skimming to going through with a fine-tooth comb; adverbs often specify the degree of thoroughness. On its own, it can be a straightforward, if somewhat precious, synonym for 'read'. However, since there is a widespread prejudice against using it to mean merely 'to read' or 'to skim', unless you are being literary or ironic, why not use those words if that is what you mean? Examples: *Whatever is common is despised. Advertisements are now so numerous that they are very negligently perused*—Dr Johnson, 1759; *I am always incorrigibly interested in the behaviour of the 'human animal', and look forward to perusing divers effusions of your lively pen*—K. Amis, 1946; *Also take some time and carefully peruse the specification chart comparing the different models—Guns* (magazine), 2003; *Having been made welcome we perused the menu—Pattaya Mail,* 2001; *Perusing its promotional materials, you might get the idea the pharmaceutical industry is a nonprofit research operation out to save the human race—The Nation,* 2003. See also FORMAL WORDS.

pervert. The noun is stressed on the first syllable, and the verb on the second. See NOUN AND VERB ACCENT 1.

peso (chief monetary unit of several Latin American countries). Pronounced /ˈpeɪsəʊ/. Plural *pesos.* See -O(E)S 4.

petal. The inflected forms and combinations are **petalled** (adjective) but **petaloid** (adjective) and **petaliferous** (adjective). **Petalless** is normally written without a hyphen, and **petal-like** normally with one. See -LL-, -L-.

Peter Principle. A humorous term of profound significance, propounded in 1968 by the Canadian-born US scholar Laurence J. Peter (1919–90), for the principle that members of a hierarchy are promoted until they reach the level at which they are no longer competent.

petite /pəˈtiːt/. This adjective is in widespread use in English (normally only as shown, in its grammatically feminine form), and has been for more than two centuries. Being so naturalized, it is printed in roman type.

petitio principii /pɪˌtɪʃɪəʊ prɪnˈsɪpɪʌɪ, prɪŋˈkɪp-/, from Latin, literally 'laying claim to principle', is a logical fallacy in which a conclusion is taken for granted in the premise; begging the question. Fowler cited as examples the assertion that foxhunting is not cruel, since the fox enjoys the fun; and that one must keep servants, since all respectable people do so. See BEG THE QUESTION.

petrol(eum). See KEROSENE.

pewit. See PEEWIT. The form *pewit,* sometimes pronounced /ˈpjuːɪt/ rhyming with *cruet* (e.g. in Tennyson's 'Will Waterproof', 1842), was common from the 16c. to the 19c., and is still a recognized variant.

ph-. These first two letters of the word *phone* have in effect become a productive prefix and word-forming element, and have been used to create four 20c. and 21c. portmanteaus, of which three are now very well known. It will be intriguing to see how many more are created in the near future. **Phishing**, first recorded in 1996, is a punning alteration of *fishing,* denotes the fraudulent practice of sending emails purporting to be from reputable companies in order to 'angle' for the recipient's personal information, such as passwords and credit card numbers, online. **Phablet**, a blend of *ph(one)* + *(t)ablet* apparently first coined in 2010, was voted the word of 2012 'least likely to succeed' by the American Dialect Society. They seem to have misjudged, since the term is now used by the general public and by the manufacturers of these smartphones, which have a screen intermediate in size between that of a typical smartphone and a tablet computer. **Phubbing**, a blend of *(ph)one* and *(sn)ubbing,* refers to the discourtesy of ignoring someone you are with because you are using your mobile phone or similar device. It is unusual in that it was wilfully created, brainstormed into existence on 22 May 2012 by a group of language experts, writers, and the like, as part of a marketing campaign by Macquarie dictionaries. It then went viral through social media, and, presumably, by the time you read this, will either have faded from view as a passing fad, or become completely established. Finally, a now largely forgotten term, **phreaking**, provided the model for the creation of *phishing.* First recorded centuries ago in technology terms (1971), it refers to the action of hacking into telecommunications systems, especially to obtain free calls, and is a blend of *phone* and *freak* in its sense 'a bizarrely abnormal person or thing'; there may also be play on the words *free call.*

phablet. See PH-.

phaeton. The *OED* (1907) gave priority to a three-syllabled pronunciation, i.e. /ˈfeɪ-ɪ-tən/, and so did Fowler in 1926. This pronunciation is still favoured in AmE, but the word is normally pronounced as two syllables in BrE, i.e. /ˈfeɪtən/.

phalanx. In its ordinary sense '(in Greek antiquity) a line of battle' its plural is normally *phalanxes*. In anatomy ('any of the bones of the fingers or toes') the pattern is usually *phalanx* singular, *phalanges* plural /fəˈlandʒiːz/.

phallus. The layman's plural form is *phalluses* (less commonly *phalli*), but in the technical language of medicine and botany it is more usually *phalli* /-laɪ/.

phantasy. See FANTASY.

Pharisee. The usual adjective is **Pharisaic**, though **Pharisaical** is also used. Both are commonly misspelt with an intrusive letter *i*, **Pharisiaic*(*al*). The corresponding abstract noun in *-ism* is **Pharisaism** /ˈfarɪseɪɪzm/ (less commonly **Phariseeism**).

pharmacopoeia. The final two syllables are pronounced /-ˈpiːə/. Always so spelt in BrE, but commonly as *-peia* in AmE.

pharyngitis. The medial -g- is 'soft', /-dʒ-/.

pharynx. The recommended plural is *pharynges* /faˈrɪndʒiːz/. The corresponding adjective is **pharyngeal** /farɪnˈdʒiːəl/ or, very rarely, *pharyngal* /faˈrɪŋgəl/. In phonetics the adjective means '(of a speech sound) articulated in the pharynx', and is normally spelt *pharyngeal* and pronounced /faˈrɪndʒəl/.

phenomena. See PHENOMENON.

phenomenal. In the early 19c. the word was first used to mean 'of the kind apprehended by (any of) the senses'. This meaning and the related noun **phenomenalism**, continued to be used in philosophy to denote the doctrine that human knowledge is confined to the appearances presented to the senses. In the way in which the lay public like the sound of a new word but overlook its strict technical meaning, *phenomenal*, by the middle of the 19c., had come to be used as a general epithet of high praise, meaning 'of the nature of a remarkable phenomenon; extraordinary, remarkable, prodigious'. This use has long since settled in as part of the standard language (*phenomenal growth, success, talent*, etc.).

phenomenon. **1** *Recommendations*. Despite everything that is said below, it is still wise to fall in with majority usage and (i) make *phenomena* rather than any other form the plural of *phenomenon* and (ii) to avoid using *phenomena* as a singular. Despite the historical pedigree of both deviations from the norm, they are still only borderline acceptable in any kind of serious prose. If others in your particular sphere habitually use such minority forms, you too are at liberty to do so: but bear in mind that someone, somewhere, will apply a red pen, notional or otherwise, to them.

2 *A phenomena?* Some people, including me, wince perceptibly on hearing or seeing *phenomena* used as a singular (*This natural phenomena occurs more during the summer because* [etc.]), while those who use it thus are blissfully unaware that they are upsetting the likes of me. What is to be done? To pose a question that will sort the prescriptive sheep from the descriptive goats, should this use be reviled as crass ignorance or accepted as a now institutionalized mistake? The answer to the first part of that question is 'no'; the answer to the second, as suggested previously, is 'only up to a point'.

3 *Etymology and plural forms.* (*a*) *Etymology. Phenomenon* comes via classical Latin *phaenomenon* from the ancient Greek φαινόμενον, usually in plural τὰ φαινόμενα 'things that appear, appearances, phenomena, celestial phenomena' used as a neuter noun of the present participle φαινόμενος 'appearing, apparent (to the senses or mind)'.

(*b*) *Plural forms.* (i) Since ancient Greek neuter nouns ending in -ον (*-on*) form their plurals in -α, the philologically impeccable plural of *phenomenon* is therefore *phenomena*, e.g. *Scientists endeavor to explain all phenomena in naturalistic ways*. However, the *OED* lists without comment both *phenomenas* and *phenomenons* as plurals. The first recorded from as long ago as 1635, the second from 1693. And as Howard (1978) notes, 'English grammar evolves with majestic disregard for the susceptibilities of classical scholars.'

(ii) *phenomenons.* Merriam-Webster gives *phenomenons* as the plural in the meaning 'an exceptional, unusual, or abnormal person, thing, or occurrence'. While it could make linguistic sense for that specific meaning to develop its own inflection (cf. *dumb oxes* at OX), according to the *OEC* evidence the form *phenomenons* is very much a minority choice (not to mention that Word underlines it as a mistake). Moreover, in most cases it does not reflect the 'exceptional' meaning: the second example following shows this meaning, but the first embodies merely the meaning of 'observed occurrence': *Droughts are not sudden phenomenons like cyclones or earthquakes; they can be seen to be building up for months—www.AsiaWeek.com,* 2000; *One of the all-time phenomenons of video games, this game ensured that the Gameboy became the greatest selling console of all time—OEC,* 2004.

(iii) *phenomenas.* Even rarer as a plural is *phenomenas,* which is puzzling: many people use *phenomena* as a singular, and therefore one might expect the regular (in English) plural *phenomenas* to crop up frequently. The fact that it does not often occur supports the supposition that *phenomena* is perceived by users either as a collective noun or as one with an identical singular and plural.

(iv) *phenomenae.* Inevitably, some people interpret the singular *phenomena* as Latin, and therefore create the bogus plural *phenomenae* (e.g. the title of a medical research paper *Biological applications of localised surface plasmonic phenomenae*).

4 *phenomena* as singular. As I observed in *Damp Squid: the English language laid bare* (2008), and as confirmed by the current *OEC,* only about 10 per cent of occurrences of this form correspond to a use that is demonstrably singular, as indicated by *a, this,* etc., e.g. *This is clearly a 20th century phenomena*—S. Kreis, 2001 (AmE). However, there are many examples in which it is impossible to tell whether the form refers to one or several, e.g. *and we should be on the alert for any phenomena that might contribute to the detection of advanced civilizations elsewhere—OEC* (undated). Possibly such grammatically indeterminate examples contribute to the uncertainty over the status of the form, as the *Cambridge Guide to English Usage* (2004) suggests. It also refers to research from 1979 showing that between 80 and 90 per cent of young Australians think of *phenomena* as singular. No doubt the same is true in other countries. That book seems likely that *phenomena* as a singular is more frequent than written sources suggest, because, at least in material edited by someone else, it will have been changed, while in speech obviously editing does not happen.

philately. First recorded in English in 1865 (one year earlier, as *philatélie,* in French), it is one of the best-known of the numerous terms meaning 'the hobby of collecting (some specified objects)'. Cf. *cartophily* (first recorded in 1936) 'the collecting of cigarette-cards', and *deltiology* (1947) 'the collecting of postcards'. *Philately* is an artificial formation from Greek φιλ(ο)- 'loving' + ἀτέλεια 'exemption from tax or charge', the second element being regarded as a passable equivalent of *free* or *franco,* which were formerly stamped on prepaid letters. The plainer words *stamp collecting* and *stamp collector* are often preferred to the 'official' terms *philately* and *philatelist.*

-phile /fʌɪl/ (from Greek φίλος 'loving') is now the usual combining form (rather than *-phil* /fɪl/) forming nouns and adjectives denoting fondness for what is specified in the first element (*bibliophile, Francophile,* etc.).

philharmonic. Technically speaking, this word is a loan translation: it is based on the Italian *filarmonico,* 'that loves or practises music', and is a fusion of the Greek prefix *philo-* + *harmonic.* The standard pronunciation in BrE is generally with a silent *h* after the *l,* but, possibly under the influence of AmE pronunciation, or of the speak-as-you-spell school of thought, the *h* is now quite often pronounced in BrE as well.

Philippines. So spelt. The islands are inhabited by *Filipinos.*

philogynist, the little known opposite of *misogynist,* i.e. a person who likes or admires women, is pronounced /fɪˈlɒdʒɪnɪst/ with a 'soft' *g.*

philology. First used in the 17c. in the sense 'love of learning and literature' it gradually became narrowed in sense in BrE to mean 'the study of the structure and development of language or of a particular language or language family'. **Comparative philology**, i.e. the study of parallel features in a related language family, became established in Britain in the course of the 19c. *Philology* in the linguistic sense never became established in the US. There, and since about the middle of the 20c. also in the UK, the dominant form for the study of the structure and development of language, etc., has been LINGUISTICS.

philosophic(al). *Philosophical* is several times more frequent than the shorter form, which occurs predominantly in AmE. Both forms of the word are used in many of their possible applications, except that most people would say *'he took a philosophical* [i.e. sensibly calm or unperturbed] *view of* [some setback]' rather than *'he took a philosophic view,* etc.' In the names of societies, transactions, proceedings, etc., the longer form is also dominant.

philtre, -ter, a love potion. Spelt with *-tre* in BrE and with *-ter* in AmE.

phishing. See PH-.

phlegm. The *g* is unsounded in *phlegm* and **phlegmy**, but is fully pronounced in **phlegmatic**.

phlogiston. The pronunciation recommended is /flə'dʒɪstən/ with a 'soft' *g*.

Phoebe, Phoenician, phoenix. All three are regularly spelt with *-oe-* (not *-e-*) both in BrE and AmE.

phone. This abbreviated form of *telephone* (noun and verb) is not preceded by an apostrophe.

phoney (adjective) is generally spelt **phony** in North American English, and *phoney* in BrE. Elsewhere the two forms compete on a nearly equal footing.

photo. The plural of this abbreviation of *photograph* is *photos.* As a verb, the inflections are *photos, photoing, photoed.*

phrasal verbs.

1 Definition and examples.
2 Syntactic patterns.
3 Levels of formality.
4 Objections.
5 Necessary and unnecessary hyphens.
6 Recommendation.
7 Brief history of the type and the term.

1 *Definition and examples.* A phrasal verb is a combination of a verb with an adverb or preposition (or both) such as *come about, draw up, put up with,* and *work out.* Phrasal verbs have meanings that cannot be directly deduced from the individual words (much to the bafflement of learners of English) and they often have several meanings and grammatical patterns. For example, *run up* has three distinct meanings in the sentences *She ran up to meet them, She ran up debts,* and *She ran up the flag.* In these examples *up* is an adverb, and in the last two the objects *debts* and *flag* are governed by the verb *ran.*

An entertaining illustration of the versatility of this class of verbs was provided by Tom McArthur (*English Today,* April 1989). 'Revolutionaries', he said, 'can *bring down* or defeat a government, then *bring in* or introduce new laws, *bring off* or clinch deals with foreign countries, *bringing on* or creating new problems, while journalists *bring up* or raise awkward questions about the revolution and later *bring out* or publish books about it.'

2 *Syntactic patterns.* Phrasal verbs formed with adverbs can be either transitive (*He drew up a chair*) or intransitive (*A taxi drew up*). Phrasal verbs formed with prepositions are transitive (*I must go through some papers*). When the object of a phrasal verb is a pronoun, it normally comes between the verb and a following adverb, e.g. *He took up my references* but *He took them up.* This pattern can occur with noun objects as well, though not in all cases: *I'll put up the shelf* could be converted to *I'll put the shelf up,* whereas *She heads up a team,* cannot be converted to *She heads a team up,* although *up* is an adverb in both cases.

3 *Levels of formality.* Phrasal verbs constitute a highly productive area of current English, and a staple of the language (as Dr Johnson pointed out; see 7 below). They range from the informal or slangy to the 'neutral', but are rarely, if ever, formal. Examples of neutral phrasal verbs include *bring up* (i.e. children), *get up,* and *put on.* Their respective single-word forms *raise/rear, arise,* and *don* all are considerably more formal, if not literary. In some cases phrasal verbs are neutral alternatives to neutral single words, e.g. *take off* (= mimic) or *work out* (= solve). In other cases they provide an informal alternative to a single word which is in itself neutral, such as *chill out* or *veg out* for 'relax'. Clearly the more scabrous ones (*sod off, bugger off, piss off* and the like) provide an affective intensity which their synonyms cannot. In yet other cases phrasal verbs provide a handy means, which cannot be said to be 'informal', of economically encapsulating a more complex idea in two words, e.g. *bottom out* (= level out at the lowest point), *factor in* (= include in an assessment or survey), and *talk up* (= stress or exaggerate the importance of). Finally, while there are phrases or words which adequately 'translate' many phrasal verbs, a lot of meaning and connotation would be lost in translation, e.g. the notorious *sex up* (= present in a more lively way) and *dumb down* (= simplify, make simpler).

4 *Objections.* Objections to phrasal verbs generally criticize (i) their alleged informality, or inappropriateness to written styles, and (ii) the redundancy of the adverb or preposition used. Objection (i) can be countered to an extent by the remarks at 3 above. It is also true that academic or formal writing tends to use fewer phrasal verbs than fiction, news, or spoken language. Examples of the alleged redundancy include verbs censured by Gowers (1965) such as the combinations *meet up with* (= meet), *visit with* (= visit), *lose out* (= lose), and *miss out on* (= miss). Where is the gain, he asked, in the particle-supported phrases *pay off* 'prove profitable', *rest up* 'rest', *drop off* (= drop, fall; 'It is expected that by that time the usual afternoon temperatures of about 90° will have started to *drop off*')? While it is true that on a very literal reading the adverb/preposition can seem redundant, it often serves a subtle emphasizing or interpersonal function.

5 *Necessary and unnecessary hyphens.* Phrasal verbs produce noun derivatives of two types: (i) the verb precedes the adverb/preposition, e.g. *breakdown, feedback,* and *lie-in*; (ii) the adverb/preposition precedes the verb, e.g. *backdrop* and *outcome.* Nouns of the first kind sometimes have a hyphen, e.g. *check-in, tie-in, lie-in, sleep-in.* Phrasal verbs themselves should never be hyphenated, as in the incorrect **So we can't* cover-up *any imperfections* (advt in *Sunday Times Mag.*).

6 *Recommendation.* Use them with gay abandon, but be cautious in formal prose. In particular, (i) guard against the use of phrasal verbs that you know or suspect to be relatively recent formations or that seem too clever by half, unless the one in question seems to add an element of intensification or a dimension of meaning not present in the verb without its adverb. If you find for example *check on* preferable to *check up on,* by all means use the shorter form. And if you are writing anything, you might want to assess your use of phrasal verbs, while bearing in mind that their alternatives may introduce a note of starchiness or formality; (ii) do not place a hyphen in a phrasal verb. But keep in mind also that phrasal verbs are a long-established and essential component of the language, useful, difficult for foreigners, but not cancellable or removable by edict or decree.

7 *Brief history of the type and the term.* (*a*) The earliest example known to Burchfield was *to give up* = 'to surrender', which is recorded in 1154: *[He] sende efter him & dide him* ȝyuen up *ðe abbotrice of Burch—OE Chron.,* annal for 1132. The type thrived in the centuries that followed: *And downe fro his neke he it* [*sc.* a mantle] *lete, It* covyrd ouer *his kne—Ipomedon,* a 15c. romance; *They came forth out of all the townes... and* closed *them* in [= shut in, confined] 1 Macc. (AV) 7: 46, 1611; *Ye whiles* sleep in [= sleep late] *on a morning*—a Scottish writer, 1827. (*b*) Dr Johnson provided a classic and perceptive description of the type in the Preface to his *Dictionary* (1755) but did not actually use the term *phrasal verb.* The term was said by Logan Pearsall Smith (1923) to have been suggested to him by Dr Bradley, i.e. the lexicographer Henry Bradley (d. 1923). Johnson's words are worth quoting for their typical elegance of expression and the light they throw on phrasal verbs of his day, some of which to us seem archaic. 'There is another kind of composition more frequent in our language than perhaps in any other, from which arises to foreigners the greatest difficulty. We modify the signification of many verbs by a particle subjoined; as to *come off,* to escape by a fetch; to *fall on,* to attack; to *fall off,* to apostatize; to *break off,* to stop abruptly; to *bear out,* to justify; to *fall in,* to comply; to *give over,* to cease; to *set off,* to embellish; to *set in,* to begin a continual tenour; to *set out,* to begin a course or journey; to *take off,* to copy; with innumerable expressions of the same kind, of which some appear wildly irregular, being so far distant from the sense of the simple words, that no sagacity will be able to trace the steps by which they arrived at the present use. These I have noted with great care; and though I cannot flatter myself that the collection is complete, I believe I have so far assisted the students of our language, that this kind of phraseology will be no longer insuperable; and the combinations of verbs and particles, by chance omitted, will be easily explained by comparison with those that may be found.'

phreaking. See PH-.

phth-, -phth-. The *ph* is best always sounded as /f/, whether initially, as in *phthalic acid, phthisis*, or in other parts of the word, as in *diphtheria, diphthong, naphtha*, and *ophthalmology.* In the latter group the spelling pronunciation with /-p-/ is logical and not uncommon, but repellent to some classicists.

phubbing. See PH-.

phylloxera. The pronunciation recommended is /fɪˈlɒksərə/. In AmE /fɪlɑkˈsɪərə/ seems to be more usual, but both pronunciations occur in both AmE and BrE.

phylum /ˈfʌɪləm/. The plural of this taxonomic term is *phyla.* See -UM 2.

physic is an archaic word for (*a*) a medicine (a *dose of physic*); (*b*) the art of healing, medicine (*Medicine has long been divided into two departments, Physic and Surgery*—J. Thomson, 1813). It was adopted in Middle English from Old French *fisique*, ultimately from Greek φυσική (ἐπιστήμη) 'the knowledge of nature'.

physiognomy. The *g* is usually silent. The primary sense is 'the cast or form of a person's features'. It was also once in widespread use to mean 'the art of judging character and disposition from the features of the face or the form and lineaments of the body generally'.

physiologic(al). The longer form *physiological* rather than *physiologic* is much the more common form, but the shorter form is used in, and is practically confined to, AmE. Cf. GEOGRAPHIC(AL).

pianist. Pronounced /ˈpɪənɪst/ in BrE, but predominantly /pɪˈanɪst/ in AmE. Another example of the often subtle ways in which BrE and AmE differ.

piano. The musical instrument is pronounced /pɪˈanəʊ/, whereas the musical direction (= performed softly) is pronounced /ˈpjɑːnəʊ/. The plural of the noun is *pianos.*

piazza. Usually pronounced in English in an Italianate manner, as /pɪˈatsə/, when it refers to a square, and printed in roman. The plural is very rarely *piazze*, as in Italian, and usually *piazzas.* In AmE, when used to mean 'the veranda of a house', the plural is always *piazzas*, and the pronunciation can be /pɪˈazə/.

pibroch, an air on the bagpipes (*not* the instrument itself). Pronounced /ˈpiːbrɒx/, with the final sound like that in *loch*, or with final /k/.

picaresque. (Ultimately from Spanish *picaresco* 'roguish', from *pícaro* 'a wily trickster'.) The earliest Spanish picaresque novels, that is fiction dealing with the adventures of an (amiable) rogue, date from the 16c. In English, the genre is associated particularly with 18c. writers such as Daniel Defoe, Henry Fielding, and Tobias Smollett. The picaresque style is characterized by social satire and realistic descriptions of scenes from low life. The type is represented in English by *Moll Flanders, Jonathan Wild, Tom Jones*, and other classic works. Curiously the term itself was apparently slow to come into use in English: the first record of its use is by Walter Scott in 1829.

piccolo, the smallest flute. Plural *piccolos.* See -O(E)S 4.

pickaxe. For the spelling of the second element, see AXE.

picket (verb). The inflected forms are *picketed, picketing.* See -T-, -TT-.

picnic. The inflected forms are *picnicked, -cking, -cker.* See -C-, -CK-.

pidgin, a simplified language containing vocabulary and grammatical elements from two or more languages, used for communication between people who do not have a language in common. Cf. CREOLE. A pidgin differs from a creole in that it is essentially a trading language and is not the mother tongue of a given speech community. The word is probably a Chinese corruption of the English word *business*, and has no connection with *pigeon*, though both words are pronounced /ˈpɪdʒɪn/.

pie. See TART.

piebald, skewbald. A *piebald* animal (especially a horse) is one having irregular patches of two colours, especially black and white. A *skewbald* animal has irregular patches of white and another colour (properly not black).

pièce de résistance /ˌpjɛs də reɪˈzɪstɒ̃s, pjɛs də rezistɑ̃s/. The accents and the italic type are obligatory. Plural *pièces de résistance*, pronounced the same as the singular.

pied-à-terre /pjeɪdɑːˈtɛː/. The hyphens are essential; printed in roman. Plural *pieds-à-terre* (pronunciation unchanged).

pietà, a picture or sculpture of the Virgin Mary holding the dead body of Christ on her lap or in her arms. An Italian word, from Latin *pietās*, dutifulness, piety, it should be written and printed with the accent, which is often omitted. Printed in roman and pronounced /pɪeɪˈtɑː/.

pigeon (English). Now disused in favour of PIDGIN (English).

pigmy. See PYGMY.

pigsty. Plural *pigsties.*

pilau /pɪˈlaʊ/. The prevalent form in BrE for this 'Middle Eastern or Indian dish of spiced rice or wheat with meat, fish, vegetables, etc.', beside *pilaff* /pɪˈlaf/ and *pilaw* /pɪˈlɔː/. AmE dictionaries give precedence to **pilaf** or **pilaff**. The word is of Turkish origin.

pilfer (verb). The inflected forms are *pilfered, pilfering.* See -R-, -RR-.

pilot (verb). The inflected forms are *piloted, piloting.* See -T-, -TT-.

pimento (small tropical tree), **pimiento** (sweet pepper). Plural *pimentos, pimientos* respectively. See -O(E)S 4.

pinch. The idiomatic expression *at a pinch* 'in an emergency, if necessary', which is standard in BrE, becomes in AmE *in a pinch.* Examples: *It could carry two passengers easily, three at a pinch*—M. R. D. Foot, 1966; *And then Danchkovsky looked in. In a pinch he could be called famous*—*New Yorker*, 1989. In the 19c. either phrase could be used in either country, but now *at a pinch* is virtually unknown in AmE, while *in a pinch* is only occasionally used in BrE.

Pindaric, of or pertaining to the work of the Greek poet Pindar (518–438 BC), a writer of choral odes. Pindar's odes 'are written in regular stanzas, either in a series of strophes on the same plan or in a series of triads, each consisting of strophe, antistrophe, and epode' (*Oxford Classical Dict.*), using three main classes of metre. The Pindaric odes of English imitators have 'an unfixed number of stanzas arranged in groups of three, in which a strophe and antistrophe sharing the same length and complex metrical pattern are followed by an epode of differing length and pattern' (C. Baldick, 1990). English writers of Pindaric odes include Thomas Gray ('The Progress of Poesy', 'The Bard', both 1747) and Abraham Cowley ('Pindarique Odes', 1656). Others, including Dryden and Pope, wrote poems that resemble the model set by Pindar, expressing 'exuberant heated ideas and passionate feelings in appropriately loose and (relatively) free rhythms' (Alastair Fowler, 1987).

pinion (verb). The inflected forms are *pinioned, pinioning.* See -N-, -NN-.

pinkie is the Sc. and AmE word for the little finger (sometimes spelt **pinky** in America). The adjective *pinky* 'tinged with pink, pinkish' must always be spelt with *-y.*

pinna (a part of the outer ear of mammals). Plural *pinnae* /-niː/.

pinny (colloquial shortening of *pinafore*). So spelt. Plural *pinnies.*

pipy, like, or having, pipes, not *pipey.*

piquant. Pronounced /ˈpiːkənt/ or /-kɒnt/.

pique. See PEAK, PEEK, PIQUE.

pis aller /ˌpiːz aleɪ/, a course of action followed as a last resort, is printed in italics.

piscina. Pronounced /pɪˈsiːnə/. For both the sense 'fish-pond' and 'stone basin for disposing of water used in washing the chalice, etc.', the plural is either *piscinae* /-niː/ or *piscinas.* Printed in roman.

pistachio /pɪˈstɑːʃɪəʊ/. Plural *pistachios.* See -O(E)S 4.

pistil. The inflected forms are **pistillary, pistillate, pistilliferous,** and **pistilline** (adjs.).

pistol (small firearm). The inflected verbal forms are *pistolled, pistolling*; also *-l-* in AmE.

pistole /pɪˈstəʊl/. The regular spelling for a former Spanish gold coin.

piteous, pitiable, pitiful. All three words share the broad sense 'arousing pity'; *piteous* and *pitiable* share the sense 'deserving pity'; and *pitiable* and *pitiful* share the sense 'evoking mingled pity and contempt'. But that is as far as the synonymy goes. *Piteous,* the least common of the three words, can also mean 'wretched'. *Pitiful* alone is used in the meaning 'absurdly small or insignificant', as in *The state pension has been reduced to a pitiful sum.*

The history of the three words, all of which were first recorded in Middle English, is very tangled, and readers of older literary works must be prepared to find that the historical senses are more diverse than the present-day ones. Examples: (piteous) *What did I do this time? Helen looked piteous*—M. Binchy, 1988; (pitiable) *How she had suffered for him, for her poor pitiable ridiculous father*—M. Drabble, 1987; *He wanted to say, 'I'm sorry ...' as if to a pitiable innocent victim*—I. Murdoch, 1987; *What was coming into being was a sort of pity. Owen seemed to me pitiable, unshriven*—A. Brookner, 1990; (pitiful) *In the centre of the profitless lawn a pitiful tube squirts water to a height of a couple of feet*—J. D. R. McConnell, 1970; *His blindness now struck her as utterly pitiful*—M. Forster, 1988; *He had been a thorn in the Empire's side for many years, and he had eluded their pitiful armies again and again*—fiction website, 2006.

pixel(l)ated, pixil(l)ated. The adjective *pixilated* is a 19c. AmE word derived from *pixie,* originally meaning 'bewildered or confused' (literally 'led astray by pixies'), and informally 'drunk'. Another word entirely is *pixellated,* a technical term for a digital image that has been distorted into component areas (*pixels*) in order to conceal the identity of the person being shown. However, as *ODO* acknowledges, the spelling *pixilated* is also used in that meaning. *Pixelated* is the more common spelling in AmE and *pixellated* in BrE, while *pixillated* with double *l* is not very common at all.

pixie (small fairy). So spelt, not *pixy.*

pizzazz. Of all the variants, *pizazz, bezazz, pazzazz,* etc., this is the most widely used. See -Z-, -ZZ-.

pizzicato. Pronounced /pɪtsɪˈkɑːtəʊ/. Plural *pizzicatos.* See -O(E)S 4.

placard. Both as noun and as verb pronounced /ˈplakɑːd/.

placate. The pronunciation recommended is /pləˈkeɪt/, though the *OED* (1907) gave precedence to /ˈplekeɪt/.

-place. See *anyplace* (s.v. ANY 2(f)); EVERYPLACE; NO PLACE; SOMEPLACE (AmE equivalents of *anywhere, everywhere, nowhere,* and *somewhere*).

placebo. Plural *placebos.* See -O(E)S 4.

plague. The inflected forms are *plagues, plagued, plaguing.*

Plain English. The current drive for plain English grew out of the consumer movement and the demand for fair dealing. It insists on clarity as well as accuracy and is opposed to convoluted, obfuscating language in official, legal, and commercial documents. It wages war on language typified by the use of such words as *aforesaid, heretofore,* and *thereto,* and argues that inflated announcements such as *Encashment of a foreign currency may incur a processing fee* may be stated more effectively as *We may charge you to change your foreign money.* Similarly, *He hails from a multidelinquent family with a high incarceration index* is better expressed by *Other members of his family have been or are in jail.* Throughout the English-speaking world attempts are now being made, sometimes by the official groups themselves and sometimes by their linguistic opponents, to bring about the demise of bureaucratic language (see GOBBLEDEGOOK) and DOUBLESPEAK that characterize, discredit, and diminish much of the documentary language of our age. Though great progress has been made in some areas, and in some arms of government, the tendency to backslide is ever-present. The struggle will no doubt continue, following in the tradition of Sir Ernest Gowers (through his book *The Complete Plain Words,* 1954 and later versions), Rudolph Flesch, and Jeremy Bentham in earlier periods.

plan (verb). The more usual construction is with a *to*-infinitive (*The government plan to close them and redeploy their workers*—*Times,* 1986), but a construction with *on* + gerund also occurs with no change of meaning, especially in AmE: *Do you plan* *on staying with Muriel forever?*—A. Tyler, 1985.

planet. In order to emphasize that something is superlative, the best, the most whatever it may be, it seems no longer enough merely to call it the best in the world: fashion dictates that it has to be the best *on the planet*, which, supposedly, conveys a stronger impression of its superlativeness, or else, in certain contexts, sounds rhetorically inflated and hollow. Examples: *Still, he would have to be the most incompetent guy on the planet to mess up such jaw-dropping source material*—*Eye Weekly* (Toronto), 2005 (Canad.); *Being as Ecuador is the most bio-diverse country on the planet, this task took me all day*—*www.newfarm.org*, 2004 (AmE); *Turturro is able to take Eddie Izzard—one of the funniest men on the planet—and put him in a purely serious role*—*Twitchfilm*, 2005 (BrE)

planetarium. Plural rather more often *planetariums* than *planetaria*. See -UM 3.

plaster. The inflected verbal forms are *plastered, plastering*. See -R-, -RR-.

plastic. Now always /'plastɪk/, though earlier in the 20c. it passed through a phase in some quarters of being pronounced /'plɑːstɪk/.

plat du jour (a dish specially featured on a day's menu). Usually pronounced in a semi-Gallic fashion, /ˌplɑː dy 'ʒuːə/. Plural *plats du jour*, pronounced the same as the singular. Normally printed in italic.

plateau. For the plural, some dictionaries give *plateaux* first, while others give *plateaus*, which is three times more frequent in the *OEC*. Both are correct and are pronounced with final /z/. AmE tends to stress the second syllable, BrE the first. The verb inflections are *plateaus, plateauing, plateaued*. See -X.

plateful. Plural *platefuls*. See -FUL.

plate glass. Write as two words unhyphenated; but hyphenated when used attributively (*plate-glass window*).

platonic love. In his *Symposium*, the Greek philosopher Plato (*c.*429–347 BC) declared that love of a beautiful person can lead us to the love of wisdom and of the 'form' of beauty itself (*Oxford Classical Dict.*). As it was thus originally used, there was no specific reference to women. First recorded in English in 1631 (Ben Jonson), *platonic love* from the beginning was 'applied to love or affection for one of the opposite sex, of a purely spiritual character, and free from sensual desire' (*OED*). The *OED* has a large number of quotations from Jonson onwards to illustrate this sense. It also provides evidence for the meaning 'applied to affection for one of the same sex'. Now normally printed with lowercase initial *p*.

platypus. Plural *platypuses*, not **platypi*. See -US 4.

playwright. So spelt. A *wright* is a maker or builder; the word is not related to the verb *to write*. For the formation, cf. *shipwright*.

plc, PLC. An abbreviation of *Public Limited Company*. The name was proposed in 1973 and brought into being in the Companies Act of 1980.

plead. The past tense and past participle in standard BrE are *pleaded*, but *pled* and *plead* /plɛd/ occur in America, Scotland, and some dialects in the UK beside *pleaded*.

In law courts a person charged with an offence can *plead guilty, plead not guilty*, or *plead insanity*, but in normal circumstances cannot *plead innocent*.

please. 1 The ordinary imperative or optative use of *please* by itself (*Will you come in, please?*) is a reduced form of *may it* (*so*) *please you*. It was first recorded in the 17c., but was not known to Shakespeare, whose shortest form is *please you*.

2 The somewhat antiquated type *Please to return the book soon* (i.e. *please* + a *to*-infinitive) had been in use since the 17c. but is now no longer used. One of its earliest uses is in Milton's *Paradise Lost*: *Heav'nly stranger, please to taste These bounties which our Nourisher...hath caus'd The Earth to yield*. A modern example: *Please to go over there and sit next to your friends*—T. J. Binyon, 1988 (a foreigner speaking).

plebiscite. 1 The older BrE pronunciation /'plɛbɪsɪt/ has given way to /-sʌɪt/, which is standard in AmE.

2 A *plebiscite* is most commonly used of a direct vote of the electors of a State (almost always one abroad) on a fundamental constitutional matter. For example, the word was applied in 1852 to the ratification of the *coup d'état* in December 1851 in France, conferring the imperial crown upon Napoleon III. A *referendum* is usually the referral of an important specific issue to the electorate for a direct decision by a general vote, e.g. the vote which led to the admission of the UK into the then European Common Market in 1974.

plectrum is a Latin word, and therefore can form the Latin plural *plectra*, or the Anglo-Saxon *plectrums*. Since it is mostly guitar picks that the word denotes, to use *plectra* in such contexts would be absurd: *If you refer to your collection of tortoiseshell guitar picks as plectra, the rest of your rock group are going to make merciless fun of you*—*Lingua Franca* (transcripts), 2002. The learned plural is appropriate in contexts of classical music (e.g. harpsichords) and in botany and zoology. See -UM 3.

Pleistocene. See MIOCENE.

plenitude. First recorded in the 15c. (= the condition of being full), and, since the 17c., in the sense 'plentifulness, abundance', it is now little used except in high-sounding prose. From the 17c. onwards it has occasionally, under the influence of *plenty*, been written as *plentitude*, but this form is not recommended.

plenteous, plentiful. Several adjectives in *-eous*, e.g. *beauteous, bounteous*, and *plenteous*, are more likely to be encountered in 19c. and earlier literary works than in any 20c. context. The normal and natural word for 'abundant, copious, etc.' is *plentiful*.

plenty. **1** *Noun/pronoun. Plenty* is historically and in essence a noun. It came into English from Latin (via Old French) *plēnitas* (cf. Latin *plēnus* 'full') in the 13c., and has had a continuous and varied presence in the language since then (*compliments in plenty; plenty of errors; in plenty of time; we have plenty*; etc.). Examples of its use as noun (especially followed by *of*, and paralleled by *a lot of* and *lots of*) and as quasi-pronoun (*plenty more*): *There were parties every night and plenty of rooms for friends*—R. Whelan, 1985 (US); *There's plenty more at University Press Books/New York where that came from*—*New Yorker*, 1986; *There were still plenty of cars hurrying up and down, though no pedestrians but themselves*—K. Amis, 1988; *Money brings deceit... as he had plenty of opportunity to observe in Newport or in New York society*—J. Bayley, 1988; *Plenty of excuses are offered*—*Independent*, 1989; *The two orchestral* Nocturnes *have plenty going for them*—*Gramophone*, 1990; *The very stylish, smoky-toasty-vanilla signature of oak is all over this wine from first sniff to finish, but there is plenty more, built round a core of deep, blackberry-raspberry fruit*—*Wine & Spirits* (US), 1991.

2 *Adjective.* (*a*) Yet almost from the beginning it was used predicatively as a quasi-adjective. Examples: *If Reasons were as plentie as Blackberries, I would giue no man a Reason vpon compulsion*—Shakespeare, 1596; *Mosques are plenty, churches are plenty, graveyards are plenty, but morals and whisky are scarce*—M. Twain, 1869; *Both* [quartz and cinnabar] *were plenty in our Silverado*—R. L. Stevenson, 1883. As the *OED* notes, 'This use was commonly criticized by grammarians from Johnson down to the early 20th cent.' Such uses are hard to find in standard 20c. sources: the natural word to use in such circumstances is *plentiful*.

(*b*) In the 19c., attributive uses of *plenty* (i.e. short for *plenty of*) came into widespread currency in regional forms of English, both in the UK and overseas. The *OED* provides evidence from a range of regional or non-standard sources, e.g. *Although there are plenty other ideals that I should prefer*—R. L. Stevenson, 1878; *The water they brought was a little thick... but Dad put plenty ashes in the cask to clear it*—Australian source, 1899; *When all dem fellas gambling and heap up plenty money, we bawl out 'Police!'*—*Sunday Express* (Trinidad), 1973; *There's plenty places where people have died*—R. Anderson, 1982 (UK). This use is best considered informal.

3 *Adverb.* From the 1840s onwards, *plenty* has also been much used, most frequently in non-standard American contexts, as an adverb meaning (i) 'abundantly, very' and (ii) 'quite, amply', preceding an adjective which is followed by *enough*. Modern examples: (i) *I'll bet you got Irving Thalberg plenty worried*—B. Schulberg, 1941; *Tell her he's plenty mad*—B. Byars, 1981 (UK); *The 'young daughter' here was seventeen and plenty nubile*—*New Yorker*, 1984; *It's hard to be completely sure just by looking. But he seems plenty dead to me*—R. Silverberg, 1985; *I was plenty scared myself, not to mention ticked off*—R. Banks, 1989; *I frowned* *at my mother plenty—New Yorker*, 1990; (ii) *This quintessential teen flick is plenty dumb enough to serve as a fanfare for the official arrival of summer—Tucson Weekly*, 1992; *Shier should, of course, have been plenty big enough to take all this in his stride—The Australian*, 2000.

4 *Conclusion*. Uses of *plenty* as an adjective (whether predicative or attributive) and as an adverb are rare in standard BrE, but are well established in informal (and especially in non-standard) contexts in AmE. They stand at the frontier of acceptable standard English and could well move into the standard zone in the 21c.

pleonasm is a 16c. loanword in English from Latin *pleonasmus*, from Greek πλεονασμός 'excess', from πλεονάζειν 'to be superfluous'. As a rhetorical device, 'the use of more words in a sentence than are necessary to express the meaning' is a necessary feature of poetry and of ornate prose. In this book, however, we are not concerned with rhetorical pleonasm, but rather with expressions and grammatical constructions that contain an element or elements of redundancy. They are treated under many heads, e.g. DOUBLE COMPARISON; DOUBLE SUBJECT; PREFERABLE 2; REDUNDANCY; TAUTOLOGY.

plesiosaurus. Plural *plesiosauri* /-rʌɪ/ or *plesiosauruses*. In practice more commonly called a **plesiosaur** /ˈpliːsɪəsɔː/, with a normal English plural in *-s*.

plethora. 1 *Meaning*. A *plethora* is in principle 'an excessive supply, an overabundance; an undesirably large quantity' of something rather than merely an abundance of it. Some commentators object to its use in this second sense, but it is widely, if sometimes a tad pretentiously, used in that way. As the *OED* pronounces: 'Originally in pejorative sense... Subsequently, and more usually, in neutral or favourable sense: a very large amount, quantity, or variety'. Given some people's objections, and the possibility of ambiguity between the favourable and unfavourable senses, if you intend it favourably to mean 'abundance, great variety, profusion, wealth, etc.', any of those synonyms may be preferable. Examples: (= overabundance) *We are... suffering under a plethora of capital*—F. Marryat, 1835; *a superfluity of over-detailed materials and a plethora of contradictory conjectures*—K. Hara, 1920; (neutral to favourable sense) *Of races there was a plethora; indeed no fewer than 400 matches took place in 1876—Encycl. Britannica*, 1911; *She was a flower among flowers, a unique and exotic bloom in the midst of this plethora of blossoms*—M. W. Bonanno, 1985.

2 *Concord*. When *a plethora of* is followed by a plural noun the dependent verb can be singular or plural according as the noun phrase is thought of as a single unit or a collection of separate entities: (plural concord) *And let's not forget the plethora of California organizations that consistently* honor *all that dairy has to offer—Dairy Field* (magazine), 2003; (singular concord) *Looking at the nonfiction category, a plethora of books* looks *at the current state of affairs*—weblog, 2004.

3 *Pronounced* /ˈplɛθərə/. Contrast the long vowel quantities in the medieval Latin original *plēthōra* (from Greek πληθώρα 'fullness, repletion').

pleura (membrane lining the thorax and enveloping the lungs). Plural *pleurae* /-riː/.

plexus. Plural same (but pronounced /-uːs/) or (more commonly) *plexuses*. See -US 2.

Pliocene. See MIOCENE.

plosive (noun). See STOP (noun).

plough is the normal BrE spelling. AmE **plow**.

plunder. The inflected verbal forms are *plundered, plundering*. See -R-, -RR-.

plurality. See MAJORITY.

plurals of nouns.

1 Words ending in *-ics*.
2 Words ending in *-f, -fe*.
3 Words ending in *-o*.
4 Words ending in *-s*.
5 Words ending in *-us*.
6 Names, etc., ending in *-y*.
7 Irregular plurals.
8 Animal names.
9 Compounds.
10 Letters, figures, and abbreviations.
11 Plural concord, though singular in form.
12 Plural forms only.
13 Foreign plurals.

1 Words ending in *-ics*. See -ICS 2.

2 Words ending in *-f, -fe*. For plurals of nouns ending in *-f* (*dwarf, hoof, leaf*, etc.) and *-fe* (*knife, wife*, etc.), see -VE(D), -VES. The plural of *still-life* is *still-lifes*.

3 Words ending in *-o*. See -O(E)S.

4 Words ending in *-s*. (*a*) Names of illnesses (*AIDS, measles*, etc.). (*b*) CORPS, INNINGS, NEWS are treated as singular nouns. (*c*) Names of games (*billiards, darts, deck quoits*, etc.) are normally treated as singular nouns (but *billiard table, he threw a dart, a deck quoit*, etc.). (*d*) Proper names (*Athens, the Thames*, etc., other than *the United States*, which can have singular or plural verb agreement) are always treated as singular nouns. (*e*) For surnames ending in *-s*, the plural is *-es* (*the Joneses, the Rogerses, the Simmses*).

5 Words ending in *-us*. See -US.

6 Names, etc., ending in *-y*. Proper names ending in *-y* have plurals in *-ys*: *the two Germanys*; *three Marys in the class*; *the Kennedys*. Note also *lay-bys, stand-bys, the 'if onlys', treasurys* (= treasury bonds).

7 *Irregular plurals*. (*a*) Mutation plurals: *foot/feet, goose/geese, louse/lice, man/men, mouse/mice, tooth/teeth, woman/women*. Also *brother*/(occasionally) *brethren* (with irregular plural ending). (*b*) Irregular plurals: *child/children, ox/oxen*.

8 *Animal names*. These normally have the regular plural: *cat/cats, elephant/elephants, hawk/hawks*, etc. When regarded collectively some animal names remain unchanged in the plural: e.g. *they were in the country shooting duck*; *they had an excellent haul of fish*. The following names of animals and fish are unchanged in the plural: *bison, cod, deer, grouse, salmon, sheep, squid, swine*.

9 *Compounds*. Compound words formed from a noun and an adjective, from two nouns connected by a preposition, or from a personal noun followed by an adverb, normally form their plurals by a change in the chief word: e.g. ***Attorneys-General, **courts martial, **Governors-General, **Poets Laureate; aides-de-camp, commanders-in-chief, fleurs-de-lis, men-of-war, **sons-in-law; listeners-in, passers-by*. In the words marked with a ** this rule is often ignored (so *Attorney-Generals*, etc.). They are being drawn towards such exceptionless plural compounds as *forget-me-nots* and *ne'er-do-wells*. Compounds consisting of a verb + an adverb normally have *-s* at the end: *call-ups, close-downs, knockouts, push-ups, stand-ins*. Words ending in *-ful* add *-s* at the end: *cupfuls, mouthfuls, spoonfuls* (see -FUL). Note also *gin-and-tonics, whisky-and-sodas* (not *gins-and-tonic*, etc.).

10 *Letters, figures, and abbreviations*. All types were once normally written with *'s*: *two VC's, the 1990's*, etc. Increasingly now the apostrophe is being dropped in the following types: *B.Litts, MBAs, MPs, QCs, the sixties, the 1960s*. But after letters of the alphabet referred to as such an apostrophe is usual: *dot your i's, mind your p's and q's*.

11 *Plural concord, though singular in form. Cattle, people* (the corresponding singular is *person*), *police, poultry, vermin*.

12 *Plural forms only*. (*a*) Names of instruments and tools: *bellows, binoculars, clippers, forceps, glasses, pincers, pliers, scissors, shears, tongs* (construed with a plural verb). (*b*) Names of articles of dress: *braces, briefs, flannels, jeans, knickers, pants, pyjamas* (US *pajamas*), *shorts, slacks, suspenders, tights, trousers* (all construed with a plural verb).

13 *Foreign plurals*. Apart from those dealt with under LATIN PLURALS, -O(E)S, -UM, -US, and -X, there are numerous common English words of foreign origin that regularly or frequently have a plural form other than the ordinary English type in *-s*. These are dealt with at their alphabetical places: CONCERTO, CRITERION, LIBRETTO, PHENOMENON, etc.

plus. First adopted in the 17c. from Latin *plus* 'more' and used as a quasi-preposition, i.e. in a manner that did not exist in Latin. To begin with, and still primarily, it was used in English as the oral equivalent of + (as opposed to minus, or −). In the 20c. it has gone from strength to strength as a quasi-preposition in the sense 'with the addition of, and also' (e.g. *A cup of Epps's cocoa and a shakedown for the night plus the use of a rug or two and overcoat doubled into a pillow*—J. Joyce, 1922; *There . . . was a . . . plane waiting plus an army scout car and a guard of soldiers*—E. Ambler, 1974).

Even more striking, and causing widespread ripples of dismay among purists, is the use of *plus* from about the 1960s (first in America) as a conjunction meaning 'and furthermore, and in addition'. Examples: *You can fly an airplane . . . and command a ship. Plus you ride horses*—T. Clancy, 1987; *I'm a pianist, but I feel all thumbs today. Plus which I've got a cold.*—*New Yorker*, 1987. This use persists in informal contexts, and is now joined by an adverbial use in which *Plus*, often followed by a comma, leads a new sentence which is only loosely connected to the previous one. Examples: *'So I'll quit romanticizing him. Plus, he never got to go on any road trips*—B. Ripley, 1987; *When you have to take a hot-water bottle to bed even after Memorial Day something is very wrong. Plus, the neighbor's dog was putting me over the top*—*New Yorker*, 1990. *Plus* used both as a quasi-preposition and as an adverb occurs frequently in advertisements (e.g. *20% off everything—plus no deposit; salary £50K—plus you will have a luxury company car*), and in informal contexts of various kinds, but should be excluded from contexts requiring any degree of formality.

p.m. As an abbreviation of Latin *post meridiem*, it is normally written in the form *3.15 p.m.* (or *pm*; in AmE *3:15 p.m.*). When the exact hour is given, *4 p.m.* is sufficient rather than *4.00 p.m.*, etc. See A.M.

pocket. The inflected forms of the verb are *pocketed, pocketing*. See -T-, -TT-.

pocketful. Plural *pocketfuls*. See -FUL.

podagra (gout of the foot). Pronounced /pɒˈdagrə/.

podcast. 'A digital audio file of speech, music, broadcast material, etc., made available on the Internet for downloading to a computer or portable media player'. Like many 21c. and 20c. coinages, this is a portmanteau word, a combination of (*i*)*Pod* and (*broad*)*cast*. Though coined only in 2004, the word has quickly become an established part of English. When used as a verb, its past tense is sometimes written as *podcasted* rather than *podcast*. (*ODO* does not acknowledge this, but *Collins English Dictionary* does.) This alternation between forms is not unique: it occurs also with *broadcast(ed), forecast(ed), input(ted), offset(ted)* and *output(ted)*. Verbs consisting of a prefix and an irregular verb, like the five just mentioned and *podcast*, often inflect like regular verbs, rather than like the irregular verbs they contain. Pinker (1994) argues convincingly that this happens because people instinctively analyse these verbs as derived directly from nouns; and nouns converted to verbs have separate entries in the mental lexicon. In other words, in speakers' minds verbs from nouns behave like regular verbs. You are therefore free to choose whichever past form sounds better to you, while bearing in mind any known sensitivities in your audience.

podium /ˈpəʊdɪəm/. Plural *podiums* or, much less usually, *podia*. See -UM 3. It is as well to be aware that in both BrE and AmE *podium* is a platform or rostrum (e.g. for a speaker or an orchestral conductor), but exclusively in AmE it also means 'lectern'. A *lectern* is a stand for holding a book (usually the Bible) in church, or a similar stand for a lecturer, etc.

poetess. See -ESS. The generic term *poet* is now overwhelmingly used of both male and female writers of verse, and examples of *poetess* are not frequent.

In a standard textbook, Alistair Fowler (1987) discusses the work of the *New England poet Emily Dickinson*. *OCELit*. (1985) uses *poet* throughout for women writers of verse: e.g. *Hemans, Mrs Felicia Dorothea . . . a precocious and copious poet; Sappho . . . a Greek lyric poet.* But cf. *Sappho . . . 6th century B.C. Greek lyric poetess of Lesbos*—*Collins Eng. Dict.*, 1986. Further examples from the *OEC: I aspired to be Gertrude Stein . . . or some poetess tragically and forlornly trying to scrape some piece of misery off the sole of my soul*—R. Barr, 1989; *For Sylvia Plath, an American poetess living in England, it was sometimes her mother . . . who sat on her typewriter and prevented her from believing in her work*—*Raritan*, 1990.

poeticisms. By these are meant modes of expression that are thought (or were once thought) to contribute to the emotional appeal of poetry but are unsuitable for plain prose: 'To most people nowadays, I imagine,' says T. S. Eliot, '*poetic diction* means an idiom and a choice of words which are out of date and which were never very good at their best.' Poeticisms are not favoured even by poets any more. The revolt against them advocated by Wordsworth in his preface to *Lyrical Ballads* has gone to lengths that would have surprised him. Nevertheless injudicious writers of prose are still occasionally tempted to use them as tinsel ornaments. See WARDOUR STREET.

poetic, poetical. In a great many contexts the choice of form is a personal matter, there being no clearly designated differences of meaning. Sentence rhythm is perhaps a factor governing the choice. *Poetical* also seems to be more restricted to the meaning 'of, belonging to, or characteristic of poets or poetry' and 'written in verse', meanings which *poetic* expresses more often, as well as more often expressing the meaning 'elevated or sublime in expression' On occasion *poetical*, but not *poetic*, can have a disparaging connotation. Whatever the reasons, *poetic* is the more common of the two words in a ratio of 17:1. There are, however, a few fixed collocations, e.g. *The poetical works of—*; *poetic diction*; *poetic justice*; *poetic licence.* Examples: (poetic) *The second* [*sc.* programme] *has two young people looking at the sunset and describing it both in poetic cliché and in scientific terms—TES*, 1991; *One of the finest poetic examples from the late sixteenth century is Shakespeare's Venus and Adonis—Jrnl Royal Mus. Assoc.* 1988; *He allowed the music room to breathe, suffusing the Rimsky-Korsakov finale with poetic sensibility—MV Daily*, 2009; (poetical) *The affluence and comprehension of our language is... displayed in our poetical translations of Ancient Writers*—Dr Johnson, 1779; *Significantly a 'maker', the Anglo-Scottish word for poet, suggests the poetical craft—N.Y. Rev. of Books*, 1997; *Panthea, the Spirit of Nature (1849) was a poetical romance of little merit—ODNB*, 2001.

Poet Laureate. Plural either *Poets Laureate* or *Poet Laureates.* See PLURALS OF NOUNS 9.

point in time, at this. The South African writer Andre Brink, in his *States of Emergency* (1988), drew attention to the unnecessary use of this popular 20c. phrase when shorter and more direct synonyms are available: *if it could be amplified by a political dimension to involve what was happening in the country right now* (*the actual phrase they used was 'at this point in time'*). Like *at this moment in time, at the end of the day*, and *in this day and age*, it is the kind of phrase that calls out for the attention of copy editors and journalistic sub-editors.

point of view (first recorded in the early 18c.; cf. French *point de vue*) is freely interchangeable with *standpoint* (19c., modelled on German *Standpunkt*) and *viewpoint* (mid-19c.). The run of the context governs the choice of word.

polemic, polemical. The noun is *polemic* 'a controversial discussion, argument, or controversy, esp. over a doctrine, policy, etc.' **Polemics** (plural in form but functioning as a singular) is 'the art or practice of controversial discussion'. The corresponding adjective is usually **polemical** and only rarely **polemic**.

policewoman, a female member of a police force, especially one holding the rank of constable: hence the abbreviation *WPC*, woman police constable (in the UK). Laypeople are tending to use the gender-neutral term *police officer* (or *officer* for short) when addressing or referring to such a person.

policy. There are two separate words. The word meaning 'course of action, etc.' is from Old French *policie*, from Latin *polītīa* from Greek πολιτεία 'citizenship, government'. The second *policy* meaning 'a contract of insurance' is from French *police* 'bill of lading, contract', from medieval Latin *apodissa, apodixa*, from Greek ἀπόδειξις 'evidence, proof'.

politically correct. At some point in the 1980s, first in the US and soon afterwards elsewhere, the term *politically correct* (abbreviated *PC, P.C.*) began being used to mean, as the current *OED* defines it, 'conforming to a body of liberal or radical opinion, esp. on social matters, usually characterized by the advocacy of approved causes or views, and often by the rejection of language, behaviour, etc., considered discriminatory or offensive'. It, and the corresponding noun phrase **political correctness**, gathered up notions which had gradually evolved during the previous half-century or so. In crude terms, the aim of the liberal-minded crusaders was to persuade the community at large to abandon earlier prejudices and suppositions in certain broadly designated areas of life, and to substitute a whole range of new vocabulary for expressions which were alleged to be false, hurtful, discriminatory, sociologically dangerous, or inept in some other way. The public reaction ranged from widespread acceptance of some of the attitudes and the attendant vocabulary to amusement and even to downright hostility. Typical of the antipathy was a leader in the *Sunday Times* (20 October 1991) attacking *political correctness* in the following manner: 'Something is rotten in the United States of America and it threatens the whole basis of that great society's role as protector of the free world and inspiration for those who yearn to be free. American politics is being corrupted and diminished by the doctrine of Political Correctness which demands rigid adherence to the political attitudes and social mores of the liberal-left, and which exhibits a malevolent intolerance to anybody who dares not comply with them.'

Among the first major works of reference to deal with the new terms *political correctness* and *politically correct* was *OCELang.* (1992): 'The phrase is applied, especially pejoratively by conservative academics and journalists in the US, to the views and attitudes of those who publicly object to: (1) The use of terms that they consider overtly or covertly *sexist* (especially as used by men against women), *racist* (especially as used by whites against blacks), *ableist* (used against the physically or mentally impaired), *ageist* (used against any specific age group), *heightist* (especially as used against short people), etc. (2) Stereotyping, such as the assumption that women are generally less intelligent than men and blacks less intelligent than whites. (3) "Inappropriately directed laughter", such as jokes at the expense of the disabled, homosexuals, and ethnic minorities... Both the full and abbreviated [i.e. *PC*] terms often imply an intolerance...of [opposing] views and facts that conflict with their "progressive orthodoxy".'

Humorous aspects of the PC movement were set down in *The Official Politically Correct Dictionary and Handbook* by Henry Beard and Christopher Cerf (1992). It is interesting to note that some of the terms derided there are now routinely used in certain restricted contexts: *differently abled* (disabled), *nonwaged* (unemployed, now generally *unwaged*), *physically challenged* (disabled), *significant other* (lover, sexual partner, etc.); and a range of more or less transparent words in *-ism*: *ableism, ageism, lookism, sizeism, weightism,* etc.

The *OED* labels *politically correct* as 'sometimes depreciative'; it would be truer to change 'sometimes' to 'regularly'. The phrase provides opponents of whatever initiative, point of view, or language they so describe with a handy tag through which to discredit supporters, as emerges rapidly from examples e.g. *Gilbert and George's antiquarian bent has often been seen by a politically correct art world as evidence of a suspicious conservatism—Royal Academy* magazine, 2004; *And the film's ultimate resolution is watered-down, politically correct treacle about Muslims and Christians getting along and worshipping in peace—www.shakingthrough.net,* 2005. While some of the dogmas or widely enforced orthodoxies of *political correctness* should always, like any dogma or orthodoxy, be questioned, many of them are not linguistic but rather habits of thought. It is to my mind clear that certain changes in the use of language wrought by this trend are beneficial. See also FEMININE DESIGNATIONS; MS; PERSON; SEXIST LANGUAGE.

politics is construed as a singular noun when used to mean 'the art or science of government' (*Politics is a popular subject at many universities*), but normally as a plural when used to mean 'a particular set of ideas, principles, etc., in politics' (*what are their politics?*). See -ICS 2.

polity is (*a*) a form or process of civil government or constitution; (*b*) a society or country as a political entity. It should not be confused with *policy* 'a course or principle of action'.

polloi. See HOI POLLOI.

polypus /ˈpɒlɪpəs/ (a small benign growth, a polyp). Plural *polypi* /-pʌɪ/ or *polypuses.* See -US 4.

polysyllabic humour is a marked characteristic of many a comedian and journalist. It was also resorted to by numerous popular writers of the past, typified by W. S. Gilbert: *Merely corroborative detail, intended to give artistic verisimilitude to an otherwise bald and unconvincing narrative* (1885).

There is no shortage of 20c. polysyllabic humour: e.g. *£17.10s., the cost of their passage, may not be a healthy or proper contract, but it cannot in the opinion of His Majesty's Government be classified as slavery in the extreme acceptance of the word* *without some risk of terminological inexactitude*—W. S. Churchill, 1906.

I test my bath before I sit,
And I'm always moved to wonderment
That what chills the finger not a bit
Is so frigid upon the fundament.
Ogden Nash, 1942

Supercalifragilisticexpialidocious!—title of a song in the Walt Disney film *Mary Poppins* (1964).

Words you've never used
And have always wanted to—
Get them in quickly.
Dight in dimity
Enlaced with lazy-daisy
In fishnet fleshings . . .
Jalousies muffle
Criminal conversation—
Discalced and unfrocked
Ithyphallic, perforate—
A case of jactitation.
(D. J. Enright, 1993)

Fowler (1926) compiled 'a short specimen list of long words or phrases that sensible people avoid'. The implication was that they were all examples of polysyllabic humour: (*a*) Proper names. *Batavian* Dutch; *Caledonian* Scottish (Fowler said 'Scotch'); *Celestial* Chinese (as in *Celestial Empire*); *Hibernian* and *Milesian*, both meaning 'Irish'. Of these only *Caledonian* and *Hibernian* are still in common use. (*b*) Ordinary nouns and adjectives: *cachinnation* 'laughter', *culinary* (adjective) 'kitchen', *diminutive* 'small', *epidermis* 'skin', *equitation* 'horse riding', *esurient* 'hungry', *femoral habiliments* 'trousers (breeches)', *fuliginous* 'sooty', *matutinal* 'morning', *minacious* 'threatening', *olfactory organ* 'nose', *osculatory* (adjective) 'kissing', *pachydermatous* 'thick-skinned', *peregrinate* 'travel'. The clock has moved on. *Culinary* and *diminutive* are everyday words now. The humour has disappeared from many of the other expressions, along with the expressions themselves. The *COD* (1990) lists nearly all of them (*minacious* has dropped by the wayside) without any qualificatory labels. The only words labelled 'jocular' or 'archaic' or both are *esurient, habiliments*, and *peregrinate*. Nevertheless Fowler's list is still worth bearing in mind. The natural course in neutral contexts is to choose the familiar rather than the unfamiliar word. Clarity is better than opacity, unless obscurity is the whole point of the context.

See OSCULATE; PACHYDERMATOUS.

pommel. The noun means 'a knob, esp. at the end of a sword-hilt; also, the upward projecting front part of a saddle', and is pronounced /ˈpʌməl/ in BrE. The corresponding verb means 'to strike repeatedly esp. with the fist', and is normally spelt **pummel**, pronounced the same as the noun, instead of *pommel*. The inflected forms of both spellings of the verb are *pummelled, pummelling* (or *pommelled*, etc.) in BrE, but usually *pummeled, pummeling* (or *pommeled*, etc.) in AmE.

poncho (South American cloak). Pronounced /ˈpɒntʃəʊ/. Plural *ponchos*. See -O(E)S 4.

pond. Used light-heartedly for the sea, especially the North Atlantic Ocean, since the mid-17c. Cf. HERRING POND. A modern example: *It is telling that Jackie Collins, born British, wrote thin, amoral novels when she was resident here . . . but huge, earnest tomes which even started to feature safe-sex warnings when she took up residence across the pond*—J. Burchill, 1993.

pontifex. Plural *pontifices* /pɒnˈtɪfɪsiːz/. See -EX, -IX.

pontificate, to be pompously dogmatic (first recorded in this sense in 1922), has now replaced *pontify* (first recorded in the same sense in 1883).

poof /pʊf, puːf/ is a largely BrE offensive term for (*a*) an effeminate man; (*b*) a male homosexual. It is sometimes written as *pouf* and also as *poove*, pronounced /puːv/. The slangy synonym **poofter** was first used in Australia at the beginning of the 20c. but is now used elsewhere. Its added syllable and extra plosive *t* give it greater vehemence, appropriate no doubt to Australian straight talking.

poor. The pronunciation is variable: either /pʊə/ or /pɔː/.

poorly. Apart from its routine uses as an adverb in the senses of poor (*he came out of the affair poorly; she performed poorly*), *poorly* is in widespread, ever so slightly informal, use as a predicative adjective in BrE meaning 'unwell' (*she looked poorly after the game of squash; her husband had been poorly for months before he died*).

poorness. See POVERTY.

popular etymology. See ETYMOLOGY; FOLK ETYMOLOGY.

popularized technical terms. When Fowler was preparing *Modern English Usage* he remarked that 'the term of this sort most in vogue at the moment of writing (1920) [was] *acid test*'. In scientific use it meant 'the testing for gold by the use of nitric acid'. In transferred use it had acquired the broad sense 'a severe or conclusive test', a use perhaps popularized by Woodrow Wilson in 1918 (*The treatment accorded Russia by her sister nations in the months to come will be the acid test of their good will—Times*, 9 Jan. 1918), though this figurative use occurred earlier in the same decade. The emergence of such popular extensions of meaning may be designated as 'something lost, something gained'. And so it is with numerous other technical and scientific terms that passed into lay use in the 20c., in the process losing something of the import of the original expression but nevertheless adding something of value to non-specialized language: see e.g. the entries for *allergy, climax* (sexual sense), *clone, complex, feedback, fixation, function, parameter, persona*, and *syndrome*. The process is as old as the language itself. The technical terminology of specialized subjects has at all times passed into general use. Lexicographers once tended to look upon the emerging new uses as 'weakened' or even 'trivial' senses, but tend to remove the qualifications as time goes on. A handful of examples that have made their way from specialized subjects into general use: law (*leading question, special pleading*); logic (*dilemma*); mathematics (*arithmetic/geometric progression; to the nth degree*); physics (*quantum jump* or *leap*).

Porch. For *the Porch* in philosophy, see ACADEMY.

porpoise. Pronounced /ˈpɔːpəs/. The second syllable does not rhyme with *poise*.

porridge was formerly frequently treated in Scotland as a plural noun (*and put butter in* them).

portcullis. Plural *portcullises*. The corresponding adjective is **portcullised**. See -S-, -SS-.

portfolios. Plural *portfolios*. See -O(E)S 4.

portico. Plural *porticoes* or *porticos*. See -O(E)S 2.

port, larboard. The two words mean the same, but *port* has been substituted for *larboard* (the earlier opposite of *starboard*) because of the confusion resulting when orders were shouted from the too great similarity between *larboard* and *starboard*.

portmanteau. The recommended plural, particularly for the linguistic meaning, is *portmanteaus* /-əʊz/, not *portmanteaux*, since this is a completely naturalized word in that sense. The *OEC* data suggests that the *-x* form almost always applies to the item of luggage. See -X.

portmanteau words. 1 A *portmanteau word* (for short, a *portmanteau*), also known linguistically as a *blend*, is a word derived by combining portions of two or more separate words, e.g. *motel* (= *motor* + *hotel*), *Oxbridge* (= *Oxford* + *Cambridge*), *smog* (= *smoke* + *fog*). The numerous examples from the *OED* suggest that the trend for creating blends began in the 19c., but really took off in the 20c. Nowadays, such formations are exceedingly common, and are one of the major ways of creating terms to denote new technologies, fashions, sports, methods of entertainment, etc. A few modern examples: *advertorial* (= *advertisement* + *editorial*), *Bollywood* (= *Bombay* + *Hollywood*), *blog* = *weblog* (= *web* + *log*), *bromance* (= *bro-*(*ther*) + *romance*), *ginormous* (BrE, informal = *giant* + *enormous*), *infomercial* (= *information* + *commercial*), *labradoodle* (= *labrador* + *poodle*), *Mockney* (BrE, humorous = *mock* + *cockney*), *netiquette* (= (*the*) *net* + *etiquette*), *phablet* (= *phone* + *tablet*), *podcast* (= *iPod* + *broadcast*). See -AHOLIC; -ATHON; BURGER.

2 The term derives from Lewis Carroll's explanation of one of the words he invented for *Jabberwocky* in *Through the Looking-Glass* ('Twas brillig, and the slithy toves Did gyre and gimble in the wabe'): *Well, 'slithy' means 'lithe and slimy'... You see it's like a portmanteau—there are two meanings packed up into one word.* To understand the image one has to remember that a portmanteau is typically a stiff leather case hinged at the back to open into two equal parts. The most enduring *portmanteau word* Carroll created is *chortle* (presumably = *chuckle* + *snort*).

posh. See ETYMOLOGY 5.

position (noun). See -TION.

position (verb). The use of *position* as a verb meaning 'put or arrange (someone or something) in a particular or appropriate place or way' has met with some criticism, usually from those who object to any verb made 'relatively recently' from a noun (in this case the 'verbing' started in the early 19c.). But *position* has a useful role (in physical and abstract contexts) that is not fulfilled by *place, put,* or *pose,* as the following examples show: *he pulled out a chair and positioned it between them; she positioned herself on a bench; Uniformed constables had been positioned to re-direct traffic*—J. Wainwright, 1979. And in the marketing sense, it is indispensable: *Ricoh is positioning itself as a high-end data collection device for style-conscious executives and dot-commers—DigitalFoto,* 2000.

position of adverbs. See ADVERB 5. For split infinitives and false adjustments made by writers because of an irrational fear of the splitting of other sentence elements, see SPLIT INFINITIVE (where a history of attitudes towards the splitting of the particle *to* and its following infinitive may also be found). It should be noted that Fowler's classic articles POSITION OF ADVERBS and SPLIT INFINITIVE, which are now mainly of historical interest, were first published in SPE (Society for Pure English) Tract xv (1923) and simply reprinted in *MEU* in 1926.

possessive. See ABSOLUTE POSSESSIVES; APOSTROPHE B, D, E; OBJECTIVE GENITIVE; 'S AND OF-POSSESSIVE.

possessive pronouns and adjectives. 1 See the warning given under APOSTROPHE D5, and the reminder s.v. ITS, IT'S.

2 Distinguish *their* (possessive adjective) from *they're,* a contracted form of *they are* (e.g. *They're off to Birmingham tomorrow*); and distinguish *your* (possessive adjective) from *you're,* a contracted form of *you are* (e.g. *you're not my friend*).

possessive with gerund. 1 *The issue.* (*a*) A 'gerund' (nowadays generally called a 'verbal noun', also 'the *-ing* form') is the verb form ending in *-ing* that functions as a noun, for example *smoking* in the phrase *no smoking* and in the sentence *Smoking damages your health.* It is distinguished from the identically formed participial adjective (*a smoking chimney*) and participles used to form continuous tenses (*The chimney is smoking*).

(*b*) Because verbal nouns are part of a verb as well as being nouns, they retain characteristics of verbs in their grammatical behaviour. For example, the constructions *They do not like* us *smoking in the house* (non-possessive) and *They do not like* our *smoking in the house* (possessive) are both established in ordinary usage, although the second, in which *smoking* is treated as a full noun, is sometimes preferred in more formal writing.

(*c*) The possessive construction is well established, and has been used by reputable authors from the 17c. onwards. Its correctness has been hotly debated by grammarians since the mid-18c., with some approving it and others condemning it. Fowler (1906, 1926) rejected the non-possessive type as 'grammatically indefensible', since the construction defies simple grammatical analysis, but the basis of his argument lay in Latin rather than English grammar and has rightly been questioned since (notably by the Danish linguist Otto Jespersen, 1860–1943). Fowler's term for the phenomenon was 'fused participle', and his comments on the subject and Jespersen's response are discussed at 4 below.

2 *Current practice.* In current use, certain patterns are discernible, although, as *MWCDEU* points out, a single author can use both patterns in the same document (a letter by Lewis Carroll). One motive may be that using the possessive stresses the noun-like quality of the phrase that follows, and views the phrase as a whole, whereas the non-possessive stresses the verbal action. Whatever the reasons, the choice of construction is mostly resolved along the following lines: (i) The possessive with gerund is frequently used when the word before the *-ing* form is a proper name or personal noun (e.g. *Andrew, sister, baby*), but less so when the name is an organization: *One cannot say that* Kafka's marvelling at mundane accomplishments was not genuine—*London Rev. Bks,* 1987; I was now counting on my father's being able *to make some provision somehow*—V. Mehta, 1987; *wondering if he should be angry . . . about* May's sleeping *with him and then throwing him out, about his* grandfather's having left *no message or sign for him but a field of junked* *cars*—C. Tilghman, 1991; *There is no question of* Gazprom cutting off *supplies in Russia—Independent*, 2007. But there are many exceptions and the choice is a highly personal one: e.g. *Preserving his reputation depended upon* Housman disguising *his real nature*—R. P. Graves, 1979; *how could she think of the* baby being born *in the house*—A. S. Byatt, 1985; *Sylvia stopped saying how exciting it was* Gordon being *so much in demand*—P. Lively, 1987. (ii) When the noun is non-personal, is part of a phrase, or is in the plural the possessive is normally not used. (In any case, plural, nouns ending in *-s* will be indistinguishable from a possessive when spoken): e.g. *They turned a blind eye to* toffee apples going *missing*—J. Winterson, 1985; *Then we had our old conversation about the* house being *haunted*—C. Rumens, 1987; *many will question the wisdom of* government departments straying *into competitive commercial areas—Daily Tel.*, 1987; *I'm not averse to* others making *good money or big profits—Western Morning News*, 2007. (iii) With personal pronouns, where there is a difference of form, (i.e. other than with *her*) usage is evenly divided, but the possessive is more usual at the start of a sentence: (possessive) *Then it became empty and the question had arisen of its being sold*—I. Murdoch, 1958; *Fancy his minding that you went to the Summer Exhibition*—A. N. Wilson, 1978; *'Is it all right?' he asked, needing reassurance. 'My coming to your party?'*—B. Rubens, 1987; *Their Aunt Martha had been remarkably circumspect on the subject of their leaving her house so soon after arriving*—fiction website, 2005. (non-possessive) *You're talking rather loudly, if you don't mind me saying so, Claudia*—P. Lively, 1987; *There can be no question of you disturbing the clerks*—P. Carey, 1988; *There would be something so despicable about him blustering ahead with a palpably unsound argument*—C. Chambers, 1992. (iv) With indefinite pronouns usage is divided, but the non-possessive form is now dominant: (possessive) *There are many sound reasons, then, for* everyone's wanting *to join in this new Gold Rush—Encounter*, 1988; *Mrs Longo has nothing against* anyone's being *Japanese, of course—New Yorker*, 1988. (non-possessive) *he didn't think for a time of* anybody clawing at *his back*—D. A. Richards, 1981 (Canad.); *should we not primarily be looking on Aids as a symptom of* something having *gone fundamentally wrong with our attitudes to sexuality?—Daily Tel.*, 1987; *There is nothing wrong with* everyone knowing *your public key, but they should verify that it is yours—Linux Journal*, 2005.

3 *Conclusion.* The possessive with gerund may be on the retreat, but its use with proper names and personal nouns and pronouns persists in literary and formal writing. When the personal pronoun stands in the initial position it looks certain that the possessive form will be preferred for a long time to come: e.g. *His being so capable was the only pleasant thing about the whole dreadful day*—E. Jolley, 1985 (Aust.); *'My being here must embarrass you,' she says—New Yorker*, 1986. The substitution of *Him* and *Me* would considerably reduce the formality of the sentences. For most mother-tongue speakers the choice is instinctive, determined by personal preference and the style or level of formality of the speaking or writing concerned.

4 *Historical note: the fused participle.* (*a*) In a classic battle in SPE (Society for Pure English) Tracts xxii (1925), xxv (1926), and xxvi (1927), Fowler and the grammarian Otto Jespersen disputed the merits of the type *Women having the vote reduces men's political power.* Fowler asserted that *women having* was 'a compound notion formed by fusion of the noun *women* with the participle *having*', called it a fused participle, and condemned it. He contrasted it with the legitimate types *Women having the vote share political power with men* (in which *having* is a true participle) and *Women's having the vote reduces men's political power* (in which the subject is the verbal noun or gerund *having (the vote)*, and *women's* is a possessive case attached to a noun). He went on to cite a number of newspaper examples in which the subject is separated from its fused participle by a subordinate clause or clauses, e.g. *New subsections giving the Board of Trade power to make regulations for permitting* workmen *who are employed under the same employer, partly in an insured trade and partly not in an insured trade*, being treated .... 'It need hardly be said,' he added, 'that writers with any sense of style do not, even if they allow themselves the fused participle, make so bad a use of the bad thing as is shown above to be possible.'

He went on to claim that 'a dozen years ago' (he meant when he was writing *The King's English*, 1906) it was not very easy to collect instances of the most elementary form of the fused participle, i.e. that in which the noun part is a single word, and that a pronoun or proper name. He then went on to cite a dozen examples, 'culled without any difficulty whatever from the columns of a single newspaper', including the following: *It is no longer thought to be the proper scientific attitude to deny the possibility of* anything *happening* (anything's); *I quite fail to see what relevance there is in* Mr Lloyd George *dragging in the misdeeds of*... (George's); *The reasons which have led to* them *being given appointments in these departments* (their). All such sentences he regarded as 'grammatically indefensible' because 'the words defy grammatical analysis'. He then resorted to Latin grammar to support his view.

(*b*) Jespersen (SPE Tract xxv) vigorously defended the construction condemned by Fowler. He gave numerous examples of its use by writers from Swift to Shaw, said that Fowler's 'article is a typical specimen of the method of what I call the instinctive grammatical moralizer', and criticized Fowler for believing in the validity of Latin parallels ('Each language surely has a right to be judged on its own merits'). Jespersen's examples were of two types: (i) the common-case of nouns denoting living beings (e.g. *what is the good of a* man being *honest in his worship of dishonesty*—G. K. Chesterton; *no chance of the* lady coming *back*—A. Bennett). (ii) pronouns (e.g. *that accounts for* them bein' *away all night*—J. Galsworthy; *I set my heart on* you coming *out to Spain*—C. Mackenzie). He thought that with an indefinite pronoun (*anybody, no one*, etc.) 'the common-case construction is now the general rule' (e.g. *He insists on* no one knowing *about the experiment*). He concluded that the construction represented 'the last step of a long line of development, the earlier steps of which... have for centuries been accepted by everybody. Each step, including the last, has tended in the same direction, to provide the English language with a means of subordinating ideas which is often convenient and supple where clauses would be unidiomatic or negligible.' Fowler in his rejoinder (SPE Tract xxvi) admitted that he had underestimated the extent of its use, but was otherwise unshaken.

possible. It was formerly permissible to construct *possible* with a following *to*-infinitive in the sense 'able, capable', i.e. the type 'the broken toy was possible to be mended': e.g. *Firm we subsist, yet possible to swerve*—Milton, 1667; *The only offence against him of which she could accuse herself, had been such as was scarcely possible to reach his knowledge*—J. Austen, *a*1817. This must once have seemed as natural as the type *it is/was possible* + *to*-infinitive (e.g. *it is not possible to distinguish one from the other*), in which *it* is used in an anticipatory or impersonal manner. Fowler (1926) expressed the matter succinctly: *'But no such questions are* possible, *as it seems to me,* to arise *between your nation and ours; No breath of honest fresh air is suffered to enter, wherever it is* possible to *be excluded.* These are wrong. Unlike *able,* which ordinarily requires to be completed by an infinitive (*able to be done, to exist,* etc.), *possible* is complete in itself and means without addition *able to be done* or *occur.* The English for *are possible to arise* and *is possible to be excluded* is *can arise, can be excluded'.*

postdeterminer. See DETERMINER.

post hoc, ergo propter hoc, from Latin, 'after this, therefore due to this': a common logical fallacy of confusing consequence with sequence. On Sunday we prayed for rain; on Monday it rained; therefore the prayers caused the rain. *Post hoc* by itself means 'after the event' and is printed in roman type: *this rhetoric offers a post hoc justification for the changes.*

posthumous /ˈpɒstjʊməs/, i.e. the *h* is silent as well as being etymologically intrusive. The English word is derived from Latin *postumus* 'last, late-born', which in late Latin was mistakenly attributed to *humus* 'the earth'.

postilion, postillion. The first is the spelling given first by several dictionaries, but the second is more often used, for the unsuspecting retainer whose unhappy lot it is, traditionally and apocryphally, to be struck by lightning. Pronounced /pɒˈstɪlɪən/.

postmaster general. The traditional plural is *postmasters general.* Cf. PLURALS OF NOUNS 9. The office was abolished in the UK in 1969.

postmistress, a woman in charge of a post office. See -ESS 5; -MISTRESS.

postmodernism. 'A late 20th-century style and concept in the arts, architecture, and criticism, which represents a departure from modernism and is characterized by the self-conscious use of earlier styles and conventions, a mixing of different artistic styles and media, and a general distrust of theories'. The noun and its related adjectives **postmodern** and **postmodernist** do not need to be hyphenated, and are rather more often written without than with hyphens.

postprandial, as in a *postprandial speech*, one given after dinner or lunch, is now mainly in formal or humorous use. Cf. Latin *prandium* 'a meal'. The word does not need to be hyphenated, and the solid form is the more common of the two, although the hyphenated form often appears. Examples: *What do people prefer for their pre- and post-prandial drinks?—House & Garden*, 1990; *The best is for last—a postprandial stroll along the edge of Battery Park City—NY Woman*, 1990; (caption) *Rest for the wicked: the master of the house takes a post-prandial nap in the library—National Trust Mag.*, 1992.

potato. Plural *potatoes*. See -O(E)S 1.

poteen, in Ireland, an illicit spirit, usually distilled from potatoes, is given as the standard form in the *OED*, along with many variants, including *potheen* and *potcheen*, which are still used. The anglicized pronunciation is /pɒ'tiːn/; the more Irish one is /pɒ'ʧiːn/.

potence, potency. In general contexts where the sense is 'power, the quality or state of being potent' the usual word is *potency*. In technical uses the two terms have gone their own way: *potence* is favoured in certain uses in watchmaking and as a particular movement of soldiers, etc., marching; while *potency* is used of the male ability to achieve orgasm in sexual intercourse, and in certain specific senses in homeopathy, genetics, pharmacology, etc. See -CE, -CY.

potful. Plural *potfuls*. See -FUL.

pother. **1** *Pronunciation*. Walker's *Critical Pronouncing Dict.* (1791) gave only /'pʌðər/, i.e. rhyming with *other, brother, mother, smother*; the *OED* (1908) gave both /ɒ/ and /ʌ/ forms in that order; while Daniel Jones (1917) gave only the form with /ɒ/. Later standard dictionaries give only /ɒ/. As the *OED* remarks, the current pronunciation 'appears to be a 19th c. literary innovation, after the spelling, and perh. influenced by association with *bother*.'

2 The word emerged in the late 16c. in the sense 'disturbance, commotion', but its etymology is unknown. The similar-sounding word *bother* was first recorded in the 18c. in the works of Irish writers (T. Sheridan, Swift, Sterne). It is 'doubtless of Anglo-Ir. origin, but no plausible Irish source can be adduced; possibly an Irish pronunciation of *pother*' (*ODEE*).

potter (verb), to work or occupy oneself in a desultory but pleasurable way (*he likes pottering around in the garden*), is commonly used in BrE. The AmE equivalent verb is **putter**.

poverty, poorness. *Poverty* is the usual noun corresponding to *poor* in its meanings to do with lack of wealth or lack of things regarded like wealth (e.g. *poverty of inspiration*) and *poorness* is not so used in modern English. *Poorness* is at least a thousand times less frequent, and if used at all refers to 'deficiency in some desirable quality or evaluation'. In practice, the further the dominant sense of 'lacking wealth' is departed from, the more does *poverty* give way to *poorness*: e.g. *Poverty is no excuse for theft; the poverty* (not *the poorness*) *trap; the poverty* (or *poorness*) *of the soil; the poorness* (rather than *the poverty*) *of the harvest; the poorness of his performance.*

pp (or **p.p.**) is now widely regarded as an abbreviation of Latin *per pro* 'for and on behalf of', and is used against a principal's (Jane Bloggs) typed name when his or her secretary or other agent (John Doe) is signing on her or his behalf. The formulation would therefore be *John Doe pp Jane Bloggs*. By others it is regarded as an abbreviation of Latin *per procurationem* (hence the abbreviation *per proc.*) 'through the agency of', in which case it should appear against the signature of the agent or proxy rather than the principal: *pp John Doe*. Though this is without doubt the true origin of the abbreviation, now that Latin is not so widely understood as it was in Fowler's day, *per pro* is much more usually understood to be the phrase for which *pp* stands. I am told that the abbreviation is not used in either sense in the US, where *Signed by X in Y's absence* or *Dictated but not read* are usual. *Dictated by Y but signed in his* (or *her*) *absence* is a commoner variation on this theme in the UK.

-p-, -pp-. **1** Monosyllabic (single-syllable) words containing a single vowel (*a, e, i, o, u*) before *p* (i) normally double the consonant before suffixes beginning with a vowel or before a final *y* (*trapped, stepped, ripped, dropped, cupped, puppy*); (ii) but the *-p* remains single if the stem contains two successive vowels (*leaper, sleepy*), or a vowel + a consonant (*carping, helped, chirping, romped, pulped*).

2 Words of more than one syllable (i) follow the rule for monosyllables if their last syllable bears the main stress (*entrapped*, but *outleaped*). They also double the *-p* if, like *handicap, kidnap*, and *bebop*, the final syllable is fully pronounced, as opposed to the obscure vowel, i.e. /ə/, in *gallop*, or if, like *horsewhip* and *sideslip*, they are compounded with a monosyllable. (ii) The main exceptions are *worshipped, worshipper*, etc. (but often *worshiped*, etc., in AmE), and (occasionally in AmE) *kidnaped, kidnaper*, etc.

Examples that follow the rules:

(-p-) *chirruped, enveloping, filliped, galloper, gossipy, hiccuped, scalloped, syrupy, turnipy, walloping.*

(-pp-) *bebopper, equipped, handicapped, horsewhipping, kidnapper, kneecapped, shipping, sideslipped, worshipper.*

practicable, practical. **1** The negative forms are *impracticable* (first recorded in the mid-17c.), *unpracticable* (1647, now rare and unusual), *impractical* (1865), and *unpractical* (1637). Of these, *impractical* is tending to encroach on the territory of *impracticable*: see IMPRACTICABLE, IMPRACTICAL.

2 Since Fowler's time (1926) at least, commentators have attempted to set clear boundaries between the two words and have warned against confusing them. (*a*) The primary meaning of *practicable* as applied to steps, means, solutions, etc., is 'feasible, able to be put into effect or practice successfully', e.g. *Schemes which look very fine on paper, but which, in real life, are not practicable; The result of any election by an annual meeting shall be announced as soon as practicable by the person presiding over the election.* It has the secondary meaning of 'usable', e.g. *Signal processing can let you understand the information in a signal, transform it into a practicable form, or use it to synthesize information.*

(*b*) The adjective *practical* has several meanings, and in its sense of 'feasible' ((ii) below) largely overlaps with *practicable*: (i) *practical* means 'concerned with practice or use rather than theory (*Lexicography is more of a practical than a theoretical art; there are two obvious practical applications of the research*); (ii) referring to ideas, plans, methods, etc. 'likely to succeed or be effective in real circumstances; feasible': *neither of these strategies is practical for smaller businesses; meantime we would welcome any practical suggestions of ways in which this can be done*; (iii) additionally, applied to people it means 'sensible and realistic in approach' and 'skilled at manual tasks' (*I'm merely being practical—we must find a ground-floor flat; Steve'll fix it—he's quite practical*), and applied to things it means 'suitable for a particular purpose' (*a practical, stylish kitchen*).

(*c*) The two words share certain collocations, such as *step* and *solution*, which highlight their subtly different emphases. A *practicable* solution is one which can be put into effect, but nothing is being said about its effectiveness, or the ease of putting it into effect. A *practical* solution, in contrast, is one which is well suited to the problem, and will probably be both successful and easy to implement. Fowler (1926) phrased the difference thus: 'it is true that the practicable is often practical & that the practical is nearly always practicable; but a very practical plan may prove owing to change of circumstances impracticable, & a practicable policy may be thoroughly unpractical.'

(*d*) In actual usage, people still draw on *practicable* to mean 'feasible', but there are severe limitations on its use. First, it is far more common in BrE than in other varieties, and it is particularly used in legal contexts. Secondly, in AmE it is almost unused, being outnumbered several dozen times over by *practical*. In general language, *practicable* seems to be very much on the wane, and *practical* is used in its stead.

practically. The meaning 'in a practical manner', as opposed to *theoretically* or *formally*, has been in use since the 16c., e.g. *Questions which are theoretically interesting to thoughtful people and practically* *interesting to every one*—*Manchester Examiner*, 1886; *Yet how was this undertaking to be practically achieved?*—B. Duffy, 1987; *At tertiary level there are . . . options for students: the colleges offer an educational programme of six semesters . . . and are practically oriented*—*European Sociological Rev.*, 1991.

In the course of the 18c. it developed a tributary sense 'virtually, almost', and now the tributary is at least as broad as the main stream and is part of standard English. Examples: *The application was supported by practically all the creditors*—*Law Times*, 1891; *When he returns to his department just before lunch he finds the building practically deserted*—A. Brink, 1988; *Her mother smiled practically all the time, for no understandable reason*—P. Ustinov, 1989.

practice, practise. In standard BrE, *practice* is invariably used for the noun and *practise* for the verb. In AmE, *practice* is the dominant spelling of both noun and verb; but *practise* is also used by some writers for both parts of speech.

pratique (licence to have dealings with a port). Pronounced /ˈpratiːk/ or /ˈpratɪk/.

pre-. In compounds whose second element begins with *e* or *i* a hyphen is normally used: *pre-eminent, pre-empt, pre-ignition*. In others the hyphen is not necessary, but is generally used in the following circumstances: if the compound is one made for the occasion; if *pre-* comes before a capitalized name, or a date; or if any peculiarity in the form of the resulting compound might prevent its being instantly recognized as a combination of *pre-* with another element: (no hyphen) *prearranged, predetermine, prenatal, preoccupy, preschool*; (with hyphen) *pre-position* (to distinguish from *preposition*, the part of speech), *Pre-Raphaelite, pre-tax* (without the hyphen it could look like a word rhyming with *relax*), *pre-1990s*.

precautionary measure. Often hauled before the magistrates of usage as a persistent offender in the field of pleonasm, and sentenced to being curtailed to *precaution*, this phrase is too hardened to be reformed. In any case, the punishment suggested does not seem proportionate.

precede is the spelling of the word meaning 'to come or go before in time, order, etc.' (*in the word* money, y *is preceded by a vowel*); and *proceed* that for the word meaning 'to make one's way, to go on' (*he paused and then proceeded to demolish his opponent's arguments*).

preciosity, preciousness. These two words overlap to an extent when describing the quality of 'being affectedly refined in matters of taste, language, etc., esp. in the choice of words', although *preciousness* is the more frequent of the two. (The use of *preciosity* in this way was suggested by French *préciosité*, a sense derived from Molière's *Les Précieuses ridicules* (1659), a comedy in which ladies frequenting the literary salons of Paris were satirized.) If there is a difference, it is that *preciosity* focuses on verbal affectation, whereas *preciousness* can be applied to other kinds. *Preciousness* is also the abstract noun corresponding to all the main general senses of the adjective *precious* (of memories, metals, stones, etc.). *Preciosity* once had the meaning 'great worth, value' but this is now largely obsolete; it can also be used in the plural to mean 'valuable things'. Examples: (preciosity) *The only novel to meet with general popularity, though exhibiting the growing preciosity of Meredith's style, was* Diana of the Crossways—*OCELit.*, 2000; *This is a formidably intellectual study, not without its preciosities, but clarifying fundamental ideas in European thought*—*Greece & Rome*, 1991; *Humor is welcome in this short novel, which can verge on preciosity*—*NYT*, 2012; *The preciosity of these resources, one of them being water, is perhaps the most important element to our survival and well-being*—*Windsor (Ontario) Star*, 2004; *Preciosities such as galena and mica sheets were put to decorative use, and there was lapidary work as well*—*Amer. antiquity*, 2004; (preciousness) *Fray veers almost too closely to the edge of preciousness, with a sense of rubato that borders on the cloying—if not really crossing into it*—weblog, 2010; *Despite the occasional air of preciousness, the album boasts a surprising sturdiness*—*Eye Weekly*, 2005; *I've also let go of my preciousness about work . . . Since then I've become more sociable*—*www.indielondon.co.uk*, 2004

precipitancy, precipitateness can both be used to denote 'hastiness, rashness', i.e. the quality of being *precipitate*.

precipitate. 1 The verb is pronounced /prɪˈsɪpɪˌteɪt/ (secondary stress on final syllable) and the adjective /prɪˈsɪpɪtət/ (obscure vowel in final syllable).

2 See PRECIPITOUS, PRECIPITATE.

precipitous, precipitate. 1 *The classic distinction.* (*a*) *precipitous.* The core, literal meaning of *precipitous* is 'sheer like a precipice; dangerously high or steep', e.g. *a half-buried beck where you can scramble past still pools... along precipitous ledges lined with wild yew trees—National Trust Mag.*, 1992. Derived from this is a metaphor to describe a change for the worse in a situation or condition, i.e. meaning 'dramatic'. This meaning is often invoked by words such as *decline, drop*, and *plunge*, e.g. *A number of factors might be responsible for such a precipitous decline, including overzealous lepidopterists who have ignored signs asking them to leave the beleaguered butterfly alone—Discover*, 1992.

(*b*) *precipitate.* In its core meaning refers to an action that is 'hasty, rash, not thought through', or one that is 'headlong, violently hurried', e.g. *His precipitate action was clearly calculated to make life harder rather than easier for the PLO*—D. McDowell, 1990; *One can't help wondering whether rumours of his precipitate departure might not be wishful thinking—Sunday Herald*, 2001.

2 *The issue.* The two adjectives were freely interchangeable for most of the period between the 17c. and the 19c., but by Fowler's day (1926), the distinction outlined above seems generally to have applied. He consequently objected to the use of *precipitous* as a synonym of *precipitate*, i.e. meaning 'rash', citing the following examples in which, according to him and the distinction, *precipitate* would have been the better word: *Are the workers justified in taking the* precipitous *action suggested in the resolution?; The step seems a trifle rash and* precipitous *when one remembers the number of banking and commercial failures that* [etc.]. Subsequent commentators have followed his lead.

3 *Current usage and recommendation.* The distinction advocated by Fowler and his successors was hazy, historically speaking, and, if it was largely observed in his day, has since been largely eroded. It is easy to see why. Because a metaphorical decline or drop that is *precipitous*, i.e. steep, is also likely to be headlong and violently hurried, *precipitous* is now often used instead of *precipitate*; in fact, the latest revision of the *OED* cross-refers three of its four meanings to *precipitate*. At the same time, in the *OEC precipitous* is roughly thirty times more frequent than *precipitate*, which is hardly used at all, while the literal meaning of the former is far outweighed by its metaphorical uses. Similarly, *precipitously* is several times more frequent than *precipitately*. Some traditionalists will no doubt object to these uses, so if you plump for *precipitous(ly)* where *precipitate(ly)* is traditionally canonical, it is wise to be very sure of your grounds for doing so. Examples of *precipitous*: (historical) *The attempts of some have been precipitous*—Sir T. Browne, 1646; *I should be censur'd for being too precipitous*—T. Shadwell, 1689; (modern) *There are important lessons from the outcome of the referendum and we need to consider them in the cold light of day rather than jumping overrapidly into any precipitous conclusions—Daily Mail*, 2004; *And I'm concerned about any precipitous withdrawal of our troops that would jeopardize the success that we've made—CNN* (transcripts), 2011; *Rather than drift along until a calamity galvanizes the world, and especially the United States, into precipitous action, the time to act is now—NYT*, 2011; examples of *precipitate* (historical) *Our senses are not in fault, but our precipitate judgments*—J. Glanvill, 1661; *Which, as no other evidence is particularly specified, makes me fear that this horrid execution has been a little precipitate*—Adam Smith, 1759; (modern) *He jumped too hastily to his conclusion. He ought not to have been so precipitate. He ought to have made inquiries—Tort Law*, 2003; *It is good that all these questions are being raised; indeed, far from being precipitate, Mr Cameron, I would argue, has been slow—Daily Tel.*, 2012.

precis /ˈpreɪsi/. The accent of the original French (*précis*) need no longer be retained in the English word. As a noun, its plural is *precis*, pronounced /-siːz/, (-seez). The verb inflections are *precises* /-siːz/, *precising* /-siːɪŋ/, *precised* /-siːd/.

preciseness, precision. *Preciseness*, though the earlier of the two words in the sense 'exactness, accuracy' is now moribund, being outnumbered by *precision* more than three hundred times in the *OEC* data, and in a similar proportion in *COCA*. The main distinction now is the common use of *precision* (but not *preciseness*) as an attributive noun in the sense 'marked by or having a high degree of accuracy (*precision instruments, precision timing*)'.

predeterminer. See DETERMINER.

predicate. 1 The corresponding *-able* adjective is **predicable**: see -ABLE, -IBLE 3(v).

2 The verb is pronounced /ˈprɛdɪˌkeɪt (secondary stress on final syllable) and the noun /ˈprɛdɪkət/ (obscure vowel in final syllable).

3 The verb *predicate*, which is derived from Latin *praedicāre* 'to cry in public, to proclaim', means (*a*) to assert or affirm as true or existent; (*b*) (followed by *on*) to found or base (a statement, etc.) on (e.g. *a new conception of reality is . . . predicated on dissatisfaction with formalist literature*—*TLS*, 1973). It should not be confused with the verb *predict* (derived from Latin *praedicere*) 'to foretell', though it should be noted that the *OED* lists examples from 1623 to 1996 of *predicate* used mistakenly for *predict.*

predominantly, predominately. Both words mean 'in a predominant manner' and both have a long history: *predominantly* is first recorded in 1681 and *predominately* in 1594, but the latter was rare before the 19c. In the early 21c. *predominantly* is overwhelmingly the commoner of the two words and is the one recommended. Examples: (predominantly) *Clinton had seized the opportunity to talk past the predominantly black audience in the room and deliver a message to white America*—*Seattle Times*, 1992; *The gutsy mayor won . . . in the predominantly White city*—*Ebony*, 1993; (predominately) *Eastview, Ont., a predominately French-speaking, low-income suburb of Ottawa*—*Gaz.* (Montreal), 1992. It is worth noting that the old adjective *predominate* (first recorded in 1591, probably modelled on such adjectives as *moderate, temperate*) is now virtually extinct, having given way to *predominant* (first recorded in 1576).

preface. 1 For *preface* and *foreword*, see FOREWORD.

2 For *preface* and *prefix* (verbs), see PREFIX.

prefer. 1 The inflected forms of the verb are *preferred, preferring* (see -R-, -RR-); but all other formations containing the base *prefer* (*preferable, preference, preferential*, etc.) have a single *r*.

2 *prefer that.* In AmE, a subordinate *that*-clause after *prefer* frequently has its verb in the subjunctive: e.g. *He prefers that the shoes be ready*—*New Yorker*, 1986; *Aunt Clara preferred that I not ransack the memories of her mother and Uncle Eugene*—D. Pinckney, 1992.

3 *prefer* + *to*-infinitive or with *-ing* form. Both constructions are used but the first is much the more frequent: (+ *to*-infinitive) *I prefer to be alone here*—O. Manning, 1955; *Most of them preferred to stand, to move about, gracefully*—G. Vidal, 1967; *I prefer not to live and work in the same room*—C. K. Stead, 1986; *But he preferred not to torture himself with the specific knowledge* [etc.]—A. N. Wilson, 1986; (+ *-ing* form) *He* [*sc.* a parrot] *has never said anything but prefers watching TV*—M. Kington, 1985.

4 Limits on *prefer . . . to.* When *prefer* is followed by a pair of alternatives, the normal construction is with *to* (*she preferred honey to marmalade; he preferred walking to jogging*). When the object is an infinitive a rigid adherence to this rule could sometimes be calamitous, e.g. producing the impossible construction *I prefer to die to to pay blackmail* (rewrite as *I prefer to die rather than pay blackmail*). People avoid this problem by using a clause led by *rather than: Bertrand . . . preferred to go to a restaurant . . . rather than eat alone*—P. P. Read, 1986. It should be added that *prefer . . . than* in such contexts without *rather* is disapproved of by some commentators, and does seem ungainly to the extent that it separates alternative objects with *than* instead of *to* (one does not say **I prefer beer than wine*). The sentence *He would prefer to die than hear the jeers of people rejoicing at his downfall* is arguably better with *rather than.*

preferable. 1 The stress normally falls on the first syllable, /ˈprɛfərəbəl/, but stress on the second, based on the verb, is also heard, and disliked by many.

2 Sometimes the double comparative form *more preferable* is used. The word *more* is of course unnecessary, since *preferable* by itself means 'more desirable (than)'. Like other comparatives, it is therefore intensified by *far, much, infinitely,* etc. (e.g. *far/much/infinitely more pleasant*) but not by *more,* e.g. *After a hundred and eighty* [skips] *an unclear head seemed much preferable to more skips*—K. Amis. It is worth noting that **much more preferable* occurs about half as often as *much preferable.* Presumably, in people's mental grammars *much* preceding an adjective is automatically associated with the comparative form; preferable doesn't look like a comparative, so *more* is inserted to make it conform to the paradigm.

prefigure. For the pronunciation, see FIGURE 1.

prefix. 1 Both the noun and the verb are usually stressed on the first syllable: thus /ˈpriːfɪks; as the pronunciation of the verb, /priːˈfɪks/ is still sometimes heard.

2 In grammar, a *prefix* is an additional element placed at the beginning of a word to adjust or qualify its meaning: e.g. *be-, ex-, non-, re-* in *befog, ex-servicemen, non-smoking, reopen.* Cf. SUFFIX.

3 *Prefix* (verb) is normally transitive in the sense 'to provide (something) as a beginning or introduction' (e.g. *Contributors are requested to prefix a synopsis to their articles*). But the type *to* —— *their articles with a synopsis* requires *preface* as the verb or needs to be re-expressed (e.g. *to place a synopsis at the beginning of their articles*).

prejudgement, prejudgment. The spelling without medial *-e-* is many times more frequent than that with, as is the case with *judg(e)ment.* The word is most often used in the legal meaning of 'before judgment', e.g. *prejudgment interest,* rather than in the meaning 'prejudice'. It would make eminent sense to write that first meaning as *pre-judgment,* but in accordance with the trend to limit hyphens, it is more often written without one.

prejudice. In the meanings 'bias' and 'partiality', it is generally followed by *against* and *in favour of* respectively (*prejudice against foreigners/in favour of marriage*). The use of the preposition *toward(s)* instead of *against* is not uncommon. While in theory it is ambiguous, i.e. does it mean 'sympathy' or 'antipathy', in practice context shows that it usually accompanies the negative meaning of *prejudice,* e.g. *We hope the resolve and commitment in tackling racism in football will be just as effective in countering prejudice towards people seeking sanctuary in Scotland.* However, using *against* eliminates any possibility of ambiguity.

preliminary. See QUASI-ADVERBS.

prelude. Both the noun and the verb are now pronounced with the stress on the first syllable, /ˈprɛljuːd/ (AmE usually /ˈprəɪluːd/). But the *OED* reports that /prɪˈljuːd/was indicated for the verb in the early part of the 19c. by 'all the verse quotations and the dictionaries down to *c.*1830'. See NOUN AND VERB ACCENT.

premier. 1 In BrE the normal pronunciation is /ˈprɛmɪə/ (prem-i-uh), with the first syllable short. In AmE the dominant pronunciation is /priˈmɪ(ə)r/ (pri-mee-uh), with the stress on the i.

2 The main meaning of the noun is 'a prime minister or other head of government'; in Canada it denotes the chief executive officer of a provincial government (with a capital initial letter when used as a title).

3 As an adjective *premier* is enjoying a period of great popularity in the meaning 'first in importance, order, or position': *Hypersonic flight has become the premier area for aerospace research in the United States—Mechanical Engineering,* 1991; *It would be nice to chew the fat with Silver Falls's premier tourist attraction*—N. Stewart, 1990 (Canad).

premiere. Now fully established as a noun (= the first performance or showing of a play or film) and as a verb (= to give a premiere of). According to the *OED,* the noun is first recorded in English in 1877, and the verb in 1927. The pronunciation in BrE is /ˈprɛmɪˌɛː/, and probably the dominant one in AmE is /prɪˈmiər/. It is generally now printed in roman without the accent of the original French (*première*).

premise, premiss. As noun, (*a*) In logic, a previous statement from which another is inferred (often spelt *premiss* in BrE, a spelling I have known to be greeted with incredulity by AmE speakers). Plural *premises* (or *premisses*). (*b*) In the plural form *premises*, a house or building with its grounds and appurtenances. As verb, *premise* is generally pronounced /ˈprɛmɪs/, especially in meaning (i), though it may rhyme with *surmise* in the other meanings. It means (i) to base an argument, theory, or undertaking on (*the reforms were premised on our findings*); (ii) to posit as a *premise* (*one school of thought premised that the cosmos is indestructible*); (iii) (rarely) to say or write by way of introduction (*I will premise generally that I hate lecturing*). The verb is always spelt with *-ise*, not with *-ize*.

premium. Plural *premiums*. See -UM 1.

prep. See ABBREVIATIONS 2.

prepared to. Bombarded as he was by official documents of many kinds, Sir Ernest Gowers developed a distaste for formulaic phrases such as *is not prepared to, is not in a position to,* and *does not see his way to*. 'Such phrases as these are no doubt dictated by politeness, and therefore deserve respect. But they must be used with discretion' (cited from the 1986 revised edition of *The Complete Plain Words*.) He condemned such examples as *he was not prepared to disclose the source of his information; I am prepared to overlook the mistake* 'as wantonly blurring the meaning of prepare' (Gowers, 1965). '*Prepared to*', he added, 'should be reserved for cases in which there is some element of preparation, e.g. *I have read the papers and am now prepared to hear you state your case*.'

But Gowers' literalistic argument was based on an unworkable distinction which ignored the role of idiom in such matters. Whatever influence Gowers may have had in Whitehall, it has not touched the rest of the world, where *prepared to* and *not prepared to* are regularly used in the simple meanings 'willing to' and 'unwilling to'.

Examples: *I came here to place it before a body of persons of European distinction. I am not prepared to discuss it with an irresponsible young woman*—G. B. Shaw, 1939; *Mr Baker stressed... that the US and its allies were not prepared to compromise on 'full' membership of Nato for Germany after unification*—*Guardian*, 1990; *That suggests the rethink is motivated by the belief that more local authorities would be prepared to remove bad teachers*—*TES*, 1990; *If non-executives are to carry out their duties properly, they must be prepared to blow the whistle*—*Independent*, 1991.

prepone. This opposite of *postpone*, i.e. to bring forward in time, deserves to be more widely used than it is. First quoted as an apparently contrived invention in 1913 in the *NYT*, it is now a feature particularly of Indian English. Examples: *For the benefit mainly of the legal profession in this age of hurry and bustle may I be permitted to coin the word 'prepone' as a needed rival of that much revered and oft-invoked standby, 'postpone'*—J. J. Trenon; *[The] transport minister... decided to ask schools to prepone their examinations and start summer vacations in April in view of a transport crisis*—*Times of India*, 2001.

prepositions.

A Definition.
B No preposition at end: history of a myth.
C Cases in which a preposition may or must end a clause or sentence.
D Anecdotes.
E Selected historical examples of stranded prepositions.
F Final verdict.

A *Definition*. For those who have forgotten the elementary terminology of grammar, here is a standard definition of the term *preposition*: 'a word governing (and usually preceding) a noun or pronoun and expressing a relation to another word or element, as in: "the man *on* the platform", "came *after* dinner", "what did you do it *for*?"'. See also COMPOUND PREPOSITIONS. J. C. Nesfield's *Manual of English Grammar* (1898) gave as his examples: *I put my hand* on *the table*; *A bird* in *the hand is worth two* in *the bush*; *He is opposed* to *severe measures*. And Nesfield reminded his readers that two prepositions are often needed: e.g. *The mouse crept out* from under *the floor*; *The rabbit escaped by running* in to *its hole*. The noun or pronoun that follows a preposition is a 'prepositional object' (or 'prepositional complement'). Besides nouns and pronouns, the objects of prepositions can also be adverbs (*By* | far *the best*), phrases (*The question of* | how to do this *is difficult*), and clauses (*He told every one of* | what we had heard). (Examples from Nesfield.). Because what follows a preposition is grammatically its object, the objective form of a pronoun, where it differs from the subjective form, must always be used: *believe in* him; *between* us; *for* them. This is especially important when two pronouns are linked by *and* or *or*: *between you and* me (not *I*); *a gift from my brother and* me (not *I*); *asked if there was any chance of* him (not *he*) *and Gina reconciling.*

B *No preposition at end: history of a myth.*

1 One of the most persistent myths about prepositions in English is that they properly belong before the word or words they govern and should not be placed at the end of a clause or sentence.

(*a*) *Dryden invented the ban.* Apparently Dryden set the myth going. In his *Defence of the Epilogue* (1672) he cited a line from Ben Jonson's *Catiline* (1611), *The bodies that those souls were frighted from*, and commented, 'The Preposition in the end of the sentence; a common fault with him, and which I have but lately observ'd in my own writings.' At some later date, it is believed, Dryden made a partial attempt to remove end-placed prepositions from his other prose works. In a note on this passage in the Everyman edition, George Watson comments that 'Each instance of the solecism was corrected by Dryden for the second edition (1684) of the essay *Of Dramatic Poesy.*' A Dryden scholar whom Burchfield consulted, Dr Derek Hughes, reported, however, that he hadn't found any evidence that Dryden conducted a more general purge of his early prose. 'He certainly did not tidy up the famous description in the Preface to *Annus Mirabilis* of "the faculty of imagination in the writer, which like a nimble Spaniel, beats over and ranges through the field of Memory, till it springs the Quarry it hunted after".'

(*b*) *Grammarians created the myth.* The myth became entrenched, though the grammarians were inclined to treat the stranding of prepositions simply as a matter of informality rather than of error. Robert Lowth in his *Short Introduction to English Grammar* (1775), for example, after citing several examples from Shakespeare (e.g. *Who servest thou* under?'—*Henry V*; *Who do you speak* to?—*As You like It*) and Pope (*The world is too well-bred, to shock authors with a truth, which generally their booksellers are the first that inform them* of—Preface to his poems), concluded: 'This is an idiom, which our language is strongly inclined to: it prevails in common conversation, and suits very well with the familiar style in writing: but the placing of the preposition before the relative, is more graceful, as well as more perspicuous; and agrees much better with the solemn and elevated style.'

Fowler turned to Ruskin's *Seven Lamps of Architecture* (1849) and reported that: 'In the text of the *Seven Lamps* there is a solitary final preposition to be found, and no more; but in the later footnotes they are not avoided (*Any more wasted words . . . I never heard of. / Men whose occupation for the next fifty years would be the knocking down every beautiful building they could lay their hands on*).' The natural inference, Fowler decided, would be: 'you cannot put a preposition (roughly speaking) later than its word in Latin, and therefore you must not do so in English.'

(*c*) *Some disputed the myth.* Alford (1864) regarded the placing of prepositions at the end as something that 'is allowable in moderation, but must not be too often resorted to'. Henry Sweet (1891) set down various circumstances in which what he called 'detached prepositions' are 'liable to be dissociated from their noun-words not only in position, but also in grammatical construction, as in *he was thought of*, where the detached preposition is no longer able to govern the pronoun in the objective case because the passive construction necessitates putting the pronoun in the nominative. Prepositions are also detached in some constructions in connection with interrogative and dependent pronouns and adverbs, as in *who are you speaking of?*, *I do not know what he is thinking of*, *where is he going to?*, *I wonder where he came from*; such constructions as *of whom are you speaking?* being confined to the literary language . . . Although detached prepositions approach very near to adverbs, yet they cannot be regarded as full adverbs for the simple reason that those prepositions which are otherwise never used as adverbs, such as *of*, can be detached with perfect freedom.'

2 *The myth debunked.* The myth of the illegitimacy of deferring prepositions had clearly been destroyed by the end of the 19c., as the quotations from Alford and Sweet have shown. Modern grammars simply recognize that 'Normally a preposition must be followed by its complement, but there are some circumstances in which this does not happen' (*CGEL* 9.6).

C *Cases in which a preposition may or must end a clause or sentence.* **1** In categories 2–4 and 6 following, prepositions may, and usually do, come at the end of the clause or sentence. In categories 5 and 7, they must come at the end.

2 *Relative clauses.* Examples: *I certainly don't know any that I'm attracted to*—A. Lurie, 1965; *The Falls on the Peregrine River was nothing like the waterfalls you see pictures of*—A. Munro, 1993. More formally: *I wanted a window seat from which I could watch the road she would come along*—G. Greene, 1980 [contains both an undeferred (*from*) and a deferred (*along*) preposition]; *We found an Italian restaurant, or rather we went in search of one of which I had already heard*—A. Brookner, 1990.

3 *Wh*-questions (i.e. questions in which *what, where, which, who,* and other pronouns and conjunctions beginning with *wh* are used). Examples: *What should we talk about?*—P. Lively, 1987; *Who is it you are smiling at so beautifully?*—P. Lively, 1987; *He said, 'What do you want an old dump like this for?'*—S. Bellow, 1987; *What do you want to go there for?*—J. Hecht, 1992.

4 *Indirect questions.* Examples: *No one had said whom I reported to*—D. Davie, 1982; *Nowadays insolence is what you survive by*—*London Rev. Bks*, 1987; *Budget cuts themselves are not damaging: the damage depends on where the cuts are coming from*—*Spectator*, 1993.

5 *Exclamations.* Examples: *What a shocking state you are in!*

6 *Infinitive clauses.* Examples: *he still had quite enough work to live on*—P. Fitzgerald, 1980; *In our forays we spent our time looking for V-shaped branches to make catapults with*—*Encounter*, 1981; *Arafat is a difficult figure with whom to come to terms*—*New Perspectives Quarterly*, 2005.

7 *Phrasal verbs and set phrases.* With phrasal verbs, the prepositional particle is an integral part of the meaning, and cannot be detached from the verb itself (hence the famous Churchill anecdote mentioned below). The same is true of set phrases, as in the last two of the examples that follow: *They must be entirely reliable and convinced of the commitment they are taking on*—*TES*, 1987; *Even the dentist was paid for*—*New Yorker*, 1987; *What did Marion think she was up to?*—J. Barnes, 1980; *She looks out the window and says a bit of poetry and they know who has gone by*—*New Yorker*, 1987; *the conflict would be hard to live with if* [etc.]—*London Rev. Bks*, 1981; *Laszlo was made a fuss of by both teachers and fellow students*—P. Lively, 1987; *Daddy never had any savings to speak of*—D. Lodge, 1991

D *Anecdotes.* **1** *A preposition pile-up.* A correspondent in SPE (Society for Pure English) Tract xv (1923) quoted a context in which deferred prepositions are used in an absurd (but perfectly understandable and parsable) manner: [Sick child] *I want to be read to.* [Nurse] *What book do you want to be read to out of?* [Sick child] *Robinson Crusoe.* [Nurse goes out and returns with *The Swiss Family Robinson.*] [Sick child] *What did you bring me that book to be read to out of for?* The child's answer has since been enhanced with an extra preposition in a version which entails the nurse going downstairs to get the book: *What did you bring me that book to be read to out of up for?*

2 *An apocryphal Churchillian phrase.* Winston Churchill is supposed to have made this marginal comment against a sentence that clumsily avoided a prepositional ending: *This is the sort of English up with which I will not put* (cited by Gowers, 1948). In fact, there is no evidence that Churchill used such a phrase (though he may of course have agreed with the sentiment), which has since become legendary.

3 *A humorous debunk.* (Courtesy of *reddit.com,* via Catherine Soanes on *blog.oxforddictionaries.com*) A snobbish English teacher was sitting in an Atlanta airport coffee shop waiting for her flight back to Connecticut, when a friendly Southern belle sat down next to her. 'Where y'all goin' to?' asked the Southern belle. Turning her nose in the air, the snob replied, 'I don't answer people who end their sentences with prepositions.' The Southern belle thought a moment, and tried again: 'Where y'all goin' to, bitch?'

E *Selected historical examples of stranded prepositions.* Anyone who is in any doubt about how often over the centuries prepositions were placed at the end of clauses or sentences may wish to browse in the *OED* entries for *about, by, for, from,* etc., used as prepositions, or in Jespersen (1909–49, iii. 10.2-6). The following examples are drawn from these two sources: they represent only a tiny fraction of the examples provided in these two places alone. *Me lihtide candles to æten bi* (*OE Chron.*, 1154); *This thinge the whiche ye ben about* (Chaucer, *c*.1385); *The most of them . . . attempt . . . vnlawfull meanes to liue by* (P. Stubbes, 1583); *I would haue* *told you of good wrastling, which you haue lost the sight of* (Shakespeare, 1600); *The worke which himselfe and Paul went about* (D. Rogers, 1642); *Many stories of the lady, which he swore to the truth of* (Fielding, 1749); *The grass it fed upon* (H. Martineau, 1832); *What is a clock good for?* (*P. Parley's Ann.*, 1840); *I am far from saying that merit is sufficiently looked out for* (A. Helps, 1847–9); *Which eye can you see me upon?* (R. Hunt, 1865); *Resolutions which perhaps no single member in his heart approves of* (J. Bryce, 1888).

F *Final verdict.* In many circumstances, except in formal writing, as detailed at D, it is standard to place the preposition at the end of a clause or sentence, and in some cases it is obligatory. Placing the preposition before the word that is its object dramatically increases the formality of the sentence; contrast the standard and formal formulations of these sentences, taken from the examples already listed: *What should we talk about/About what should we talk?; No one had said whom I reported to/No one had said to whom I reported; he still had quite enough work to live on/he still had quite enough work on which to live.* Sometimes a stranded preposition at the end of a sentence may make the sentence anticlimactic; on the other hand, to invariably put the preposition in front of its object will result in a starchy, stilted, formal style that is only suitable in certain contexts.

prerequisite. Now occasionally misused for *perquisite*: e.g. *If she is not released, perhaps she could be treated to the same prerequisites enjoyed by the inmates of Parkhurst prison—Independent,* 1991. A *perquisite* (generally shortened to *perk*) is an incidental benefit attached to one's salary, etc., a customary extra right or privilege; a *prerequisite* is something required as a precondition.

presage. Both noun and verb are generally stressed on the first syllable: thus /ˈprɛsɪdʒ/. The verb may also be pronounced with the stress on the second syllable, i.e. /prɪˈseɪdʒ/.

prescience, prescient. The usual pronunciations now in BrE are /ˈprɛsɪəns/ and /ˈprɛsɪənt/, whereas the *OED* (1909) gave only /ˈpriːʃɪəns/ and /ˈpriːʃɪənt/, which are still used in AmE.

prescribe, proscribe. One main meaning of *prescribe* is 'to lay down as a course or rule to be followed'. Another main meaning is 'to issue a (medical) prescription or recommend a specified (medical) treatment'. It should be carefully distinguished from *proscribe* in its sense 'to reject or denounce (a practice, etc.) as dangerous, antisocial, etc.; to condemn, outlaw'. An easy-to-remember distinction is that a prescribed book is one that is set down for special study (e.g. *'Beowulf' was among the prescribed texts for the final examination*), whereas a proscribed book is one that is prohibited or banned (e.g. Salman Rushdie's *The Satanic Verses* (1988) was *proscribed*).

prescriptivism. In the *OED* this linguistic term is defined as follows: 'The practice or advocacy of prescriptive grammar; the belief that the grammar of a language should lay down rules to which usage must conform'. It is first found in 1953. The corresponding adjective **prescriptive** is first recorded, in its linguistic sense, in a 1933 work by the great linguist Otto Jespersen: it is contrasted with *descriptive* and equated with *normative.* Since the terms *prescriptive* and *descriptive* and their derivatives now occur in almost every informed discussion of English usage, it is interesting to quote from Burchfield's book *The English Language* (1985) a short passage describing the nature of each. Readers can make up their own minds about his suggestion that there is no clear boundary between the two approaches. 'In the present century [*sc.* 20c.], starting more or less with the work of Ferdinand de Saussure, emphasis has been placed much more firmly than hitherto on language as it is used rather than on how experts say that it should be used. There is no clear boundary between the doctrines of prescriptivism and those of descriptivism, much more an attitude of mind. Prescriptivists by and large regard innovation as dangerous or at any rate resistible; descriptivists, whether with resignation or merely with a shrug of the shoulders, quickly identify new linguistic habits and record them in dictionaries and grammars with [little or] no indication that they might be unwelcome or at any rate debatable. Prescriptivists frequently use restrictive expressions like *loosely, erroneously, sometimes used to mean, falsely, avoided by careful writers,* and the like ...' Whether dictionaries are prescriptive or descriptive is an issue that constantly surfaces, and the contrast between the two approaches informs much, if not all, discussion of usage. See DESCRIPTIVE GRAMMAR.

presentiment can be pronounced either /prɪ'zɛntɪm(ə)nt/ or /-'sɛn-/, in other words with a voiced or unvoiced medial *s*, i.e. as *z* or *s*.

presently. There are two meanings which serve well to illustrate the interactions of British and American English. The older of the two current meanings, 'at the present time, now', dates from the 15c. and is still the dominant meaning in AmE. In BrE it had been largely overtaken by the second meaning, also 15c., 'in a while, soon', but the older meaning has re-established itself under American influence. This second meaning became weakened at an early date (by the 17c.) from the third, now obsolete, meaning 'immediately' to 'in a little while, soon'.

Examples: (*a*) (= now) *Mr. William O'Brien, solicitor, Dumfries, for the accused, said Mr. Savage was presently unemployed, his last employment being a year ago*—*Dumfries Courier*, 1978; '*We are presently climbing through 30,000 feet on our way to our cruising altitude of 37,000 feet,' says the pilot*—*Chicago Tribune*, 1991 (the journalist who wrote the article regarded this as a misuse of *presently*).

(*b*) (= in a little while, soon) *'A very curious one, as you shall see presently,' replied Jack*—R. M. Ballantyne, 1858; *Presently, seeing Ralph under the palms, he came and sat by him*—W. Golding, 1954; *Muriel waited for an hour... Her feet hurt and she was thirsty. Presently she set off to walk back to her lodgings*—H. Mantel, 1986. There is much criticism of the use of sense (*a*) both in America and in Britain because of the risk of ambiguity, but in practice the context normally makes it quite clear which sense is intended. Alternatives that avoid any possible ambiguity are *at present, now*, or *currently* in the older meaning and *soon, shortly, in a while, imminently*, in the newer one.

(*c*) (= immediately). This sense flourished between the 15c. and the 18c. but is now obsolete. Historical examples: *the Master and the Boat-swaine Being awake, enforce them to this place; And presently, I pre'thee.*—Shakespeare, 1610; *The poor woman... no sooner looked at the serjeant, than she presently recollected him*—Fielding, 1749.

present tense. The natural and most frequent use of the present tense is in contexts of present time, whether actual (*he wants to know now; the door is open*) or habitual (*Paris is the capital of France; he has his pride; the clock strikes every half-hour*). It is also used of past events (*A British writer wins the Nobel Prize*—newspaper headline) and of future events (*When do* [= *will*] *you retire?; the Paddington train for Didcot leaves at 9.15 pm; term ends tomorrow*). For the *historic present*, see HISTORIC 2.

present writer, the (or **present author,** etc.). The phrase *the present writer* is used from time to time instead of *I* or *me* by writers whose name appears at the head or end of an article or other work in order to introduce a personal opinion or fact. Fowler called the phrase a *Coa vestis* (transparent garment of fine silk made in antiquity at Kos), and dismissed it as 'irritating to the reader'. But it is used by the great and the good and seems a harmless enough convention. Cf. *your columnist, your reviewer* (as used by journalists). Examples: *Like the present writer, Stevenson, Davenport, and Cousland had family connections with the Catholic Apostolics and hence greater ease of access to source material*—C. G. Flegg, 1992. But passions can run high in the matter. In the 30 November 1989 issue of the *Independent*, the late journalist Miles Kington wrote: *We agree that if we are writing in the first person, we will use the word 'I' and not nauseating expressions such as 'your humble author', 'my very good self', 'the present writer', 'a person not a million miles from myself'*, [etc.]. And note also *the journalist feels no need to avoid using the first-person singular, 'I' or 'me', when necessary. He doesn't have to pretend he is someone else, with coy references to 'the present author'* (N. Bagnall, 1993). So perhaps caution is required after all.

Presidents' Day. The third Monday in February, a legal holiday in most of the states of the US, commemorating the birthdays of George Washington and Abraham Lincoln. Often erroneously printed with an apostrophe before the *s* or without an apostrophe at all.

prestidigitator, -tion. Formal or humorous words for a juggler, a conjuror/

juggling, conjuring. Adopted from French. *prestidigitateur/prestidigitation* ('quick-fingeredness') in the mid-19c.

prestige. **1** Adopted in the 17c. from French in its original sense of 'illusion, conjuring trick', *prestige* lost this sense, as it did in French, in the course of the 19c. and gained the favourable meaning 'glamour, reputation derived from previous achievements, associations, etc.'. Etymologically the word answers to Latin *praestīgia* 'a delusion, illusion', usually in the feminine plural form *praestīgiae* 'illusions, juggler's tricks', from *praestringere* 'to bind fast' (*praestringere oculōs* 'to blindfold'; hence 'to dazzle the eyes').

2 Surprisingly, the French-mimicking pronunciation /prɛˈstiːʒ/ has persisted though, according to the *OED* (1909), an Anglicized pronunciation /ˈprɛstɪdʒ/ also existed at the beginning of the 20c. Cf. *vestige*, the pronunciation of which has been totally Anglicized.

prestigious. A striking example of a word which has lost its original negative connotations ('deceptive, illusory, in the manner of a conjuror's trick': see PRESTIGE) and became the adjective corresponding to the noun *prestige* in the course of the 20c. The new, and now virtually the only current, meaning 'having or showing prestige' was first noted in Joseph Conrad's novel *Chance* (1913). As the century proceeded, it appeared sporadically in journalistic sources, and then, against stiff opposition, in standard literary works. It also went through a period of wavering between the pronunciations /prɛˈstiːdʒɛs/ and /prɛˈstɪdʒəs/ before the latter became dominant, although the former is still a standard variant in AmE, and is occasionally heard also in BrE, presumably influenced by the pronunciation of the noun. *Prestigious* is often replaced by *prestige* used attributively (*prestige car, group, location, model, ware*, etc.), but it remains part of the day-to-day standard language. (The less euphonious form *prestigeful* (first recorded in 1936) has never really taken off,) The misspelling **prestigeous* is surprisingly common.

prestissimo, presto. When used as nouns, both have *-os* as their plural. See -O(E)S 4.

presume. See ASSUME.

presumedly. Four syllables if used: see -EDLY. But it is better to use *presumably* or another synonym.

presumptive. For *heir presumptive*, see HEIR 2.

presumptuous. Beware against using the once valid (15c.–early 19c.) by-form *presumptious*. An example of the mistaken form: *I thought it would be very presumptious of me to quote from myself as an epigraph*—*Times Saturday Rev.*, 20 July 1991.

pretence. The usual AmE spelling is **pretense**.

preterite. In AmE often **preterit**. In English grammar, the better form is *past*, e.g. '*jumped* is the past tense of *jump*'.

pretty was once in regular use as an ironical adjective: *a pretty mess you have made of it; things have come to a pretty pass*. It is also used, especially in informal contexts, as an adverb meaning 'fairly, moderately' (*the performance was pretty good; he did pretty much what he liked*), but only when qualifying another adverb or an adjective. Otherwise the adverb is *prettily* (*she dresses prettily; she arranged the flowers very prettily*).

prevaricate, procrastinate. Because their meanings, or at least the implications of their meanings, overlap, the first has absorbed some of the meaning of the second. Strictly speaking, to *prevaricate* (derived from Latin *praevāricārī* meaning literally 'to walk crookedly') is 'to speak or act evasively', whereas to *procrastinate* (derived from Latin *cras* meaning 'tomorrow') is 'to put off or delay'. Examples: *She prevaricated, wanting the story verified or denied before sharing it with him*—L. Grant-Adamson, 1989; *Coleridge never arrived, and early in January the now beleaguered Southey decided that his endlessly procrastinating friend must be brought back from London*—T. Mayberry, 1992. But since you might *prevaricate* in order to *procrastinate, prevaricate* too now generally has implications of delaying. Indeed, the *OED* now declares that the meaning 'to behave evasively or indecisively so as to delay action; to procrastinate' is the usual sense of *prevaricate*, as in *Mr Mandelson... said European leaders would not listen to Britain while it prevaricates over whether to play a full role in the EU*—*Daily Tel.*, 2003.

prevent. There are three competing constructions when the verb *prevent* is followed directly or indirectly by a gerund in *-ing*. All three are legitimate, but the third type is largely falling into disuse. (*a*) *prevent* + object + from + *-ing* (*OED* 1663–): *tanks are being prevented from entering the center of the city*—*New Yorker*, 1989; *Cushla was only just quick enough to grab Colin's arms to prevent him from belting Restel across the head*—N. Virtue, 1990. (*b*) *prevent* + object + *-ing* (*OED* 1688-): *Muscle relaxants could prevent an actual seizure recurring*—R. D. Laing, 1985; *the Government now has an enormous challenge on its hands if it is to prevent its new environmental awareness backfiring in its face*—J. Porritt, 1989. (*c*) *prevent* + possessive + *-ing* (*OED* 1841-): *his shoes were locked up to prevent his running away*—P. Fitzgerald, 1986.

See POSSESSIVE WITH GERUND 3.

preventable, -ible. The first is recommended; the second is in any case rare: see -ABLE, -IBLE 3.

preventive, preventative. Both words entered the language in the 17c. and have been fighting it out ever since. The shorter form is nearly three times as frequent as the longer in the *OEC*, and is the preferred form in medical contexts, e.g. *preventive medicine, care, treatment, medication*, etc., though *preventative* is also used with those collocates. Outside medical contexts, both are used, *preventive* again being more frequent, e.g. *preventive measure, war, detention, action, intervention*, etc.

Some examples: (preventive) *Two days later university students demonstrated outside the palatial mansion of the President for the release of Professor Okola from preventive detention*—B. Head, 1989; *Although many preventive measures do improve health, they are not without risks and costs and in fact seldom reduce medical expenditure*—*BMJ*, 1989; *Is that service backed up with driver evaluations and preventive maintenance to reduce accident losses and downtime?*—*Industry Week* (US), 1990; *Preventive medicine may be more effective if problem-based learning programmes are established in place of the traditional methods of education*—*Physiotherapy*, 1990. (preventative) *If we happen to live near an airport... apart from the usual preventative measures such as double glazing and noise insulation to our homes, there is nothing we can do but try our best to live with it*—*Internat. Health & Efficiency Monthly*, 1990; *The All England Club had agreed to co-operate with the ban* [of a spectator from major tennis tournaments]. *In the end, no such preventative measures were necessary*—*Times*, 1993.

Both words are also used as nouns, *preventative* being more frequent in *OEC* data: (preventive) *And ask about... ivermectin—the heartworm disease preventive you give to your dog once-a-month*—*Outdoor Life* (US), 1990; *Best wrinkle preventive around: a good sunscreen with an SPF of 15 or higher*—*Homemaker's Mag.* (Toronto), 1993; (preventative) *Merck's has been overflowing for more than a decade... with preventatives, mainly enzyme inhibitors, which 'block' or thwart many kinds of diseases*—*Kiplinger's Personal Finance*, 1991 (US).

See -ATIVE, -IVE.

previous. For the construction in *will consult you previous to acting*, see QUASI-ADVERBS.

pride. The common proverb *Pride goeth* (or *goes*) *before a fall* is one of several reductive versions of Prov. 16: 18, *Pride goeth before* [= *precedes*] *destruction: and an hautie spirit before a fall.* Several other variants, e.g. *Pride must have a fall* (Johnson, 1784), are listed in standard dictionaries of proverbs.

prie-dieu. Plural *prie-dieux*, pronounced the same as the singular. See -X.

priest. A priest is **1** an ordained minister of the Roman Catholic or Orthodox Church, or of the Anglican Church (above a deacon and below a bishop), authorized to perform certain rites and administer certain sacraments.

2 an official minister of a non-Christian religion (*COD*, 1995). Women who are ordained ministers of the Anglican Church are also called *priests* (the word *priestess* being used only of female priests of non-Christian religions). Cf. MINISTER; PASTOR.

priestess. See -ESS 5; PRIEST.

prima donna. 1 The first word is pronounced /ˈpriːmə/ but in AmE sometimes /ˈprɪmə/.

2 The plural is generally *prima donnas* when referring to lead female opera singers, and always when referring to drama queens. Sometimes the Italian plural *prime donne* /ˌpriːmeɪ ˈdɒneɪ/ is used to refer to the operatic species. The related adjective, meaning 'self-important and temperamental' is best spelt with a hyphen as **prima donna-ish** to make it easier to relate to its root.

prima facie. In BrE normally pronounced /ˌprʌɪmə ˈfeɪʃiː/. In AmE there are several competing pronunciations: /ˈprɪmə/ *or* /ˈprʌɪmə/ *or* /ˈpriːmə/, /ˈfeɪʃiːiː/ *or* /ˈfeɪʃiː/.

primarily. In the *OED* (1909) stressed only on the first syllable: thus /ˈprʌɪmɛrɪli/. But now, under AmE influence, increasingly stressed on the second syllable: thus /prʌɪˈmɛrɪli/.

Primate /ˈprʌɪmeɪt/. **1** any animal of the order Primates /prʌɪˈmeɪtiːz/, the highest order of mammals, including tarsiers, lemurs, apes, monkeys, and man.

2 an archbishop. The ordinary plural for both senses is *primates* /ˈprʌɪmeɪts/, i.e. is not pronounced like the name of the zoological order.

primer. The word meaning 'an elementary or introductory book' is always pronounced /ˈprʌɪmə/ in Britain, but /ˈprɪmə/ in America, New Zealand, and sometimes in Australia. It is interesting to note that the *OED* (1909) gave priority to the form with a short stem vowel. The form with /ɪ/ is preserved in Britain when the word is used of a size of type.

primeval. Now the dominant, and recommended, form, not *primaeval.*

princess. As an independent word, usually stressed on the second syllable: thus /prɪnˈsɛs/. When used as a title (*Princess Diana, Princess Margaret*) it has an initial capital and is stressed on the first syllable: thus /ˈprɪnsɛs/.

principal, principle. 'Confusion of the two', Burchfield olympianly opined, 'betrays inadequate instruction at an early age.' Or lack of practice, or a poor memory, or… (fill in as appropriate). Only the first is an adjective (= first in rank or importance), though it can also be a noun (= a head, ruler, or superior; also, numerous other senses including 'a capital sum as distinguished from interest'). The second is a noun only, and means 'a fundamental truth or law as the basis of reasoning or action (*arguing from first principles*); (in plural) rules of conduct (*a person without principles*)'. The only weedy mnemonic I can offer to console the educationally deprived is that the *principal* dancer of a ballet company is the first dancer, just as the letter *a* is the first letter of the alphabet.

prioritize. 1 *Hostility towards.* The first citation for this word in the *OED* is from 1954, and it is interesting to note that from the outset it was associated with bureaucratese: *Now they* [*sc.* 'finalize' and 'concretize'] *seem… to be firmly embedded in the speech of government workers, along with 'civilianize'… and 'prioritize' (give preferential rating to)—Reno Evening Gaz.*, 9 Nov. Almost thirty years later, 'A word that at present sits uneasily in the language', was Burchfield's comment in the 1982 supplement to the *OED*. In the more than thirty further years since his remark, *prioritize* seems to have made itself rather comfortable, nay, has even got its feet firmly under the table. And though its feet are indeed under it, that table is now less likely than before to be in boardrooms, government buildings, universities, or barracks: the word has spread outside those jargonistic confines. Many commentators think that such a spread is undesirable ('It is a bureaucratic word, best avoided in most types of writing,' Trask, 2001). But is it?

2 *Usefulness of. Prioritize* is a double whammy for purists: it ends in *-ize*, and is formed from a noun. But I would argue for its usefulness: like many other *-ize* words, it says in a single word what otherwise would take several, as the following definitions of its meanings make abundantly clear: transitively (i) 'designate or treat (something) as being very or most important' (*the department has failed to prioritize safety within the oil industry*); (ii) 'determine the order for dealing with (a series of items or tasks) according to their relative importance' (*age affects the way people prioritize their goals*); and, (iii) intransitively, in the same meaning as (ii) (*A hot file forces you to prioritize because you have to select which things will be included—Wall St. Jrnl*, 2004). The word has become a mainstay of self-help (*How to prioritize your time/ projects/life*, etc.), and for that reason can seem a bit shop-soiled. On the other hand, most of the synonyms one will find in a thesaurus are long-windedly phrasal, e.g. *bring/call/draw attention to, focus attention on, highlight, point up, foreground, put/lay stress on, give an emphasis to,* etc. And of course, they do not mean quite the same thing. Avoid it in writing if it really irritates you (for it is in any case not the kind of word you or I ordinarily drop into conversation); just be certain you are not gaily leaping on the bandwagon of prioritizeophobia.

3 *Spelling and prepositional use. Prioritize* outnumbers *prioritise* ten to one in AmE; the opposite applies in BrE. Elsewhere, other than in Canadian English, the spelling with *-ise* is more frequent. The occasional spelling *priorize,* which would nonsensically mean 'to make earlier', is not recognized in dictionaries. It may be influenced by e.g. the Spanish and Portuguese for 'prioritize', *priorizar*; or simply by the trend towards economy in language; or, then again, by Johnsonian ignorance, pure ignorance. The normal preposition governing whichever noun is less of a priority is *over,* but *above* is also used: *The second issue currently confronting local government unions is* Best Value, *which seeks to prioritise service quality over cost reduction—Capital and Class,* 2002; *From the opening scene ... spectators are at the mercy of Anderson's desire to prioritize sound over image—Jrnl of Popular Film and Television,* 2001; *I suspect the point people were trying to make was that the police need to prioritize violent crime above chasing down traffic offences—Celebrating Mediocrity* (weblog), 2005.

prior to. As a complex preposition used instead of *before,* it has attracted much criticism. Fowler (1926) suggested that it should only be used 'in contexts involving a connexion between the two events more essential than the simple time relation, as in *Candidates must deposit security prior to the ballot*'. In such contexts *prior to* means 'as a necessary preliminary to', as it does in the next example: *It is important to eliminate all weeds, especially perennials, prior to planting—OEC,* 2004. *Prior to* used in technical or formal writing is appropriate in register. Elsewhere it is best replaced by the simple *before,* e.g. *Thorpe is interviewed on devolution and electoral reform, prior to the 1974 general election*—weblog, 2005. Conservative style guides, such as the *Telegraph style book,* ban it outright.

Priscian. The colourful phrase *to break* (or *knock*) *Priscian's head* (or *pate*) means 'to violate the rules of grammar' (representing Latin *diminuere Prisciani caput*). It had a long history in English from Skelton (*c.*1525) onwards, but is now a rarity. Priscian's *Institutiones grammaticae* (early 6c. AD) was the most voluminous grammar of his time, and was influential throughout the Middle Ages.

prise (verb), 'to force (something) open or out by leverage', is occasionally written as **prize** in World English. While that is the standard spelling in AmE, elsewhere it is likely to be regarded as a mistake, despite having many historical precedents. Rather more common in AmE than either spelling is **pry** used in exactly the same way. Examples: (prise/prize) *Then, with a joint prizing, the lock finally snapped*—C. Dexter, 1983 (UK); *We did not speak again or look at each other till the chest was prized open and the lid raised—New Yorker,* 1991. (pry) (All US) *Marilyn pried her hand from her father's and slipped beneath the bed to board a little boat*—P. Burke, 1989; *The girl pried the lid from the shoebox*—T. Drury, 1992.

Pry is an early 19c. shortening of *prise, prize* (verb), 'apparently through confusing the final consonant with the *-s* of the 3rd pers. sing. present' (*OED*).

pristine. 1 The *OED* (1909) gave only /ˈprɪstɪn/, i.e. with a short /ɪ/ in the second syllable, but /ˈprɪstiːn/ is now usual. The stress is variable, and the second syllable is sometimes pronounced /-stʌɪn/.

2 Before the 20c. the sense of the word in English usually reflected that of Latin *pristinus* (belonging to olden times, antique, ancient, not new), and at the turn of the century most uses of the word were commendatory. *The translators ... have happily preserved for us the pristine simplicity of our Saxon-English*—Disraeli, 1841. It is a short step from the notion of 'in its original state' to 'untouched, unspoilt' and thence simply 'fresh and clean as if new', the meanings acquired by the word in the 20c. Although objected to by language purists, the developed meaning is well established alongside the original one, especially in the collocations *pristine white* and *in pristine condition: The pitch, as ever, looked in pristine condition at kick-off—Press* (York), 2001;

This was deliberately not the pristine white gallery space—*ArtThrob*, 2003.

privacy. The *OED* (1909) gave only /ˈprʌɪvəsi/ as the pronunciation, i.e. with /ʌi/ as in *private* in the first syllable. Since then /ˈprɪvəsi/ has supplanted it as the dominant form in Britain (cf. *privilege*, etc.), but the older pronunciation is still the usual one in English-speaking countries abroad, including America.

privative /ˈprɪvətɪv/. In grammar, designating particles or affixes that express privation or negation. The *a-* of *amoral* and *aseptic* (see A-[1]) and the *in-* of *innocent* (cf. Latin *nocēre* 'to hurt') and *inedible* are privative, whereas the *a-* of *arise* and the *in-* of *insist* are not.

prize. See PRISE.

pro (professional). See ABBREVIATIONS 2. Plural *pros*: see -O(E)S 6.

probe (noun). *The Russian probe was not able to measure the lower 25 kilometres of the Venusian atmosphere*, reported *The Times* in 1968. It was a newish (1953) use of the word *probe.* The primary sense (from the 16c. onwards) of *probe* was a blunt-ended surgical instrument for exploring the direction and depth of wounds and sinuses. The early-20c. extension of the word to mean a small device, especially an electrode, used for measuring, testing, etc., and the mid-20c. extension to mean an unmanned exploratory spacecraft for obtaining information about the nature of planets and other bodies in outer space are natural uses of the word, and entered the language unopposed. Less well received by some has been the widespread, mainly journalistic, use of *probe* to mean a penetrating investigation, e.g. *Despite evidence that Hunt may have broken the ministerial code, Cameron has refused to order a probe by the independent adviser on ministerial interests, Alex Allan*—*New Statesman*, 2012. Its overuse trivializes and dumbs down, by avoiding the weightiness of 'inquiry' (the *Telegraph style book* bans it *tout court* in that meaning). Its appeal to journalists, however, lies largely in its brevity and therefore its suitability for use in headlines. See HEADLINE LANGUAGE.

problematic, -atical. The shorter form is a score or more times the more common of the two in both BrE and AmE sources, and the two words overlap collocationally very little. See -IC(AL).

proboscis /prəˈbɒsis/: the medial *c* is generally silent, though pronouncing the word with it is recognized as a US variant in some dictionaries. The plural is *proboscises* /-isiːz/ or (esp. in zoological work) *proboscides* /-ɪdiːz/. The forms reflect Greek προβοσκίς, προβοσκίδος, 'an elephant's trunk'. Its use to mean the human nose is merely humorous.

proceed. So spelt. Contrast *procedure* and PRECEDE.

process (noun). The *OED* (1909) gave precedence to /ˈprɒsɛs/, i.e. with a short vowel in the first syllable, but /ˈprəʊsɛs/ is now standard in BrE. The standard pronunciation in AmE is with /ɒ/.

process (intransitive verb), to walk in procession, is a back-formation from *procession.* It is pronounced /prəˈsɛs/. The unconnected verb *process* meaning 'to treat (food, esp. to prevent decay); to deal with (data, etc.)' is pronounced like the noun (see PROCESS (noun)).

proclitic refers to a word pronounced with so little emphasis that it becomes merged with the stressed word that follows it, e.g. in some forms of regional English down to the first half of the 19c., *chill* from *ich* 'I' + *will*; also, in modern English, *at* in *at home*, pronounced /təʊm/.

procrastinate. See PREVARICATE.

proctor. So spelt, not *-er.*

procuress, a woman who makes it her trade to procure women for prostitution. The word was first recorded in this sense in the 18c. See -ESS 5.

proem, a preface or prelude to a literary work, is pronounced /ˈprəʊem/. The corresponding adjective is **proemial** /prəʊˈiːmɪəl/. It came into Middle English from Old French *pro(h)eme*, ultimately from Greek προοίμιον, used in the same sense.

professedly. Four syllables: see -EDLY.

professor. In BrE, a holder of a university chair, a university academic of the highest rank. In AmE, a university teacher who has the rank (in ascending order of seniority) of *assistant professor, associate professor*, or *professor.*

professorate /prɛˈfɛsərət/ and **professoriate** /ˌprɒfiˈsɔːriət/. Both words have been used since approximately the mid-19c. to mean either (*a*) the office of a professor; professorship, or (*b*) the professorial staff of a university. Both are much more widely used in AmE than in BrE; in AmE the second form is sometimes spelt without the final *e* (*professoriat*).

proffer (verb). The inflected forms are *proffered, proffering*. See -R-, -RR-.

prognosis. Plural *prognoses* /-siːz/.

program, programme. 1 (noun). There is no doubt that the standard spelling in BrE, except in computer language, is *programme* and in AmE *program* (all senses). In World English, the first is the more frequent spelling, but the second is also used outside the field of computing. *Programme*, however, was not always the BrE standard. The word, which is derived from Greek πρόγραμμα 'a public written notice', was taken into English in the 17c. in the form *program*, and was the form regularly used by Walter Scott, Carlyle, and numerous other 19c. writers. One could reasonably have expected this spelling of the word to have survived in standard British use after the model of *anagram, cryptogram, diagram*, etc. Instead, from about the beginning of the 19c., the French spelling *programme* was adopted, and gradually established itself except in the US. In computer work in all English-speaking countries, the spelling *program* is routinely used for 'a series of coded instructions to control the operation of a computer'.

2 (verb). The inflected forms in BrE for all uses (including those in computer work) are *programmed, programming*; in AmE either *programed, programing* or with medial *-mm-*.

progress. In BrE the noun is pronounced /ˈprəʊgrɛs/ and the verb /prəˈgrɛs/. See NOUN AND VERB ACCENT 1. In AmE the dominant forms show the same stress patterns, but the noun is normally pronounced with a short vowel in the first syllable. When used transitively to mean 'to cause (work, etc.) to make regular progress' (e.g. *Welders to be trained to make more tack items to allow them to progress their own work to completion—Observer*, 1978) the verb was previously pronounced /ˈprəʊgrɛs/ in Britain, but is now pronounced like the verb in its intransitive meanings.

progression. See ARITHMETICAL, GEOMETRICAL PROGRESSION.

prohibit. In the sense 'to forbid, stop, or prevent (a person)' + a verbal construction, the historical sequence is as follows: (*a*) (first recorded in 1523) + *to do* a thing (e.g. *The patients . . . are peremptorily prohibited to bathe on Sundays*—C. Lucas, 1756; *Marshal Oyama prohibited his troops to take quarter within the walls*—cited, and disapproved of, by Fowler, 1926). (*b*) (first recorded in 1840) + *from doing* something (e.g. *There is no Act . . . prohibiting the Secretary of State for Foreign Affairs from being in the pay of continental powers*—Macaulay, 1840). Type (*b*) is of course now the standard construction, but type (*a*), though far less frequent, is still found, e.g. *Because British law then prohibited skilled workers to leave the country, many Scotch-Irish laborers found their way to the United States through Canada—OEC*, 2004 (US).

project. In BrE the normal pattern is /ˈprɒdʒɛkt/ for the noun and /prɛˈdʒɛkt/ for the verb. See NOUN AND VERB ACCENT 1. In other English-speaking countries the noun is often pronounced /ˈprəʊdʒɛkt/, but the type with a short vowel in the first syllable is also found, especially in America.

prolegomena. A plural noun meaning 'introductory observations on a subject'. The singular, which is rarely used, is *prolegomenon* (from Greek προλεγόμενον, neuter of the present participle passive of προλέγειν 'to say beforehand').

prolepsis. Plural *prolepses* /prəʊˈlɛpsiːz/ *or* /-ˈliːp-/. A rhetorical and grammatical term derived from Greek πρόληψις 'anticipation'. It is used in English in four main senses: **1** The anticipation and answering of possible objections in rhetorical speech, e.g. a passage beginning *I know it will be said that* . . .

2 The representing of a thing as existing before it actually does or did so, as in Hamlet's exclamation when he was wounded, *I am* dead *Horatio.* Also in Keats's poem *Isabella* (1820):

> *So the two brothers and their* murdered *man*
> *Rode past fair Florence.*

i.e. the man who was afterwards their victim.

3 The foreshadowing of events which take place at a later stage in the narrative, e.g. in the OE poem *Beowulf* the mention of the harmony at the court of Hrothgar is accompanied by a warning of treachery to come:

Heorot innan wæs
freondum afylled; nalles facenstafas
þeod-Scyldingas þenden fremedon.
(Heorot within was filled with friends; not
yet then had the Scylding people
resorted to treachery.)

4 In informal English, contexts in which 'a noun phrase is positioned initially and a reinforcing pronoun stands "proxy" for it in the relevant position in the sentence' (*CGEL* 1985, 17.78, where the construction is actually called *anticipated identification*). Example: *That* man *you spoke about, I saw* him *again this morning.* Other sources use *prolepsis* of different constructions, e.g. 'the anticipatory use of adjectives, as in *to paint the town red*' (*COD*, 1990). Cf. also Shakespeare's *Timon of Athens* IV.iii:

when Ioue
Will o'er some high-Vic'd City, hang his poyson
In the sicke *ayre*:

The air is not 'sick' until Jove introduces his poison into it.

prolific. 1 The adjective is in common use, but there is no consensus about its derived noun. The possibilities are *prolificacy* (first recorded, according to the *OED*, in 1756), *prolificalness* (1699), *prolificity* (1718), and *prolificness* (1678). None slips easily off the tongue, but corpora show that the first is, while still rare, the most common, and the last two are rarer still, while *prolificalness* is not used at all. Substitutes such as *fertility, fruitfulness*, and *productiveness* are often better solutions.

2 *Prolific* is derived from the Latin word *proles* meaning 'offspring', and is properly applied to someone or something that produces either offspring or something compared to offspring such as writings, works of art, etc. Like many adjectives in English (e.g. *a generous gift, a thoughtful present*), it is often transferred from the producer to the thing produced (e.g. *a prolific output* as well as *a prolific writer*), and objections to this use that are sometimes made (e.g. Gowers, 1965) are hard to justify, although alternatives such as *abundant* and *numerous* are available to those who are inclined to be cautious in such matters: *McGonagall ... had just had his prolific collection of bizarre poems translated into Russian, Chinese, Japanese and ... Thai—Times,* 1977.

prologue. The word is often spelt **prolog** in AmE.

promenade. Pronounced /-ɑːd/, not /-eɪd/ in BrE. In AmE, /-eɪd/ is the dominant pronunciation.

Promethean. Stressed on the second syllable: /prɛˈmiːθɪən/.

promiscuous. Its more general meaning 'demonstrating an unselective approach, undiscriminating' has been practically obliterated by its dominant meaning 'having frequent and diverse sexual relationships, esp. transient ones'. However, the first meaning still surfaces occasionally, e.g. *For some weeks I read systematically through these* [sc. articles] *to satisfy my somewhat promiscuous intellectual curiosity—OEC,* 2000. The derived noun **promiscuity** covers all meanings and is dozens of times more frequent than **promiscuousness**.

promise (verb). In the sense 'assure, assert confidently' (i.e. not expressing a future undertaking, etc.), *promise* is used only in the spoken language, and only then in the phrase *I promise you.* Examples: *Why that's nothing more than a trick of the candlelight, Rosanna. I promise you, there's no blood on the crucifix.—Islands* (NZ), 1985; *They were some bozo individuals, I promise you—New Yorker,* 1986; *'Hey, you're making that up.' 'No, it's true, I promise you.'*—M. du Plessis, 1989 (SAfr.); (Hannah) *You mean the game books go back to Thomasina's time?* (Valentine) *Oh yes. Further ... really. I promise you. I* promise *you.*—T. Stoppard, 1993. The use is recorded in the *OED* with 15–19c. examples.

promisor. So spelt in legal language, but *-er* in ordinary use.

promissory. So spelt, not *-isory.* The stress falls on the first syllable.

prone. 1 For the sense 'disposed or liable, esp. to a bad action, condition, etc. (*is prone to bite his nails*)', see LIABLE 2.

2 In the meaning 'lying down', strictly speaking it means 'face downwards', but often it is used merely to mean 'lying horizontally'. Cf. SUPINE.

pronounceable. So spelt. See -ABLE, -IBLE 2.

pronouncedly has four syllables. See -EDLY.

***pronounciation.** An all-too-common misspelling and mispronunciation of PRONUNCIATION.

pronouns. 1 *Types of pronouns.* Once set down these are instantly recognizable. (*a*) personal pronouns: *I, me; we, us; you; he, him; she, her; it; they, them.* The subjective forms are given first, the objective second. Where only one form is given it does double duty. (*b*) possessive pronouns: *mine, yours, his, hers, its, ours, theirs.* (*c*) reflexive pronouns: *myself, yourself, himself, herself, itself, oneself; ourselves, yourselves, themselves.* (*d*) demonstrative pronouns: *this, that; these, those.* (*e*) indefinite pronouns: *all, any, both, each, either, none, one; everybody, nobody, somebody; everyone, no one, someone,* etc. (*f*) relative pronouns: *that, which, who, whom, whose; whatever, whichever, whoever, whosoever,* etc. (*g*) interrogative pronouns: *what, which, who, whom, whose.*

There are also a number of reciprocal pronouns (*each other, one another*); and also a number of non-standard or regional forms, e.g. *hisself, themself, theirselves, yous*(*e*). Articles on many of the pronouns are found at their alphabetical places, e.g. HE; I; ME; MYSELF. See also AS; BUT; CASES. In these articles major points of disputed pronominal uses are presented, and in particular the case of pronouns (e.g. *It's goodbye from Delia and I; her and John are responsible for this*). Most disputed uses arise from the fact that, unlike nouns, most pronouns have both a subjective and an objective form. Defaulters are perhaps expressing a yearning for a normalization of the rules affecting both nouns and pronouns.

2 *The role of pronouns.* A pronoun is a 'word used instead of and to indicate a noun already mentioned or known, esp. to avoid repetition'. The definition is sound for most ordinary pronominal uses, so long as 'noun' is taken to include 'noun phrase', and so long as it is understood that the antecedent does not have to be the exact semantic and morphological equivalent of the pronoun itself. *CGEL* (1985) cites examples illustrating these two points: *The man* invited *the little Swedish girl* because *he* liked *her* (2.44); *The clean towels* are in the drawer if you need *one* [= 'a clean towel'] (12.15). Jacques Barzun, in a work published in 1985, claimed that 'there can be no proper link between a proper name in the possessive case and a personal pronoun: "Wellington's victory at Waterloo made him the greatest name in Europe" is all askew, because there is in fact no person named for the *him* to refer to.' But substitute *his* for *him* and the difficulty disappears. Even with *him* retained the reader (or listener) would have no difficulty in making the necessary morphological adjustment.

3 *Avoiding ambiguity.* It is clearly desirable that an anaphoric (backward-looking) or cataphoric (forward-looking) pronoun should be placed as near as the construction allows to the noun or noun phrase to which it refers, and in such a manner that there is no risk of ambiguity. Fowler (1926) cited a number of newspaper examples in which the antecedent was too far away for safety or in which ambiguity was possible. A more recent example: *He knew something she didn't. He knew that two students were missing. A boy and a girl. Whether together or otherwise was not yet clear. They had last been seen standing by* her *car.* [Whose car?]—G. Butler, 1992. An example in which a character in a play's uncertainty about the antecedent of the pronoun *he* is used for humorous effect: (Septimus) *Geometry, Hobbes assures us in the* Leviathan, *is the only science God has been pleased to bestow on mankind.* (Lady Croom) *And what does* he *mean by it?* (Septimus) *Mr Hobbes or God?*—T. Stoppard, 1993.

pronunciamento /prəˌnʌnsɪəˈmɛntəʊ/. An interesting example of a distinction in meaning being reflected in variant spellings of a Spanish loanword. The spelling shown is an adaptation of Spanish *pronunciamiento,* dropping the second *i* of the original. It tends to be used when the meaning is 'pronouncement' (e.g. *the somber pronunciamento of America's Greatest Living Playwright watching his first masterpiece triumph once again*); when the context is Spanish or Latin American politics, and the meaning is 'proclamation of allegiance' or 'coup', the Spanish spelling tends to be used (e.g. *On 1 January 1820 General Rafael Riego staged a pronunciamiento in the south of Spain that led to the reestablishment of the 1812 Cadiz constitution*—W. Fowler, 2000). In the first meaning the word is not italicized, but in the second, *OED* examples show that it is, as an unassimilated loanword. Plural *pronunciamentos*: see -O(E)S 8.

pronunciation.

1 Introductory.
2 Some modern changes in RP in BrE.
3 Disputed pronunciations.
4 Words containing a short *o* in stressed syllables.
5 Proper names.

1 *Introductory*. Guidance on pronunciation given in this book follows the system of the International Phonetic Alphabet (IPA), and, in particular, that version of it used in the *Oxford Dictionary of English* (2010). It is based on the pronunciation of educated adults in the south of England, i.e. is the version of English usually called *Received Pronunciation* (RP) (or *Received Standard*). In most respects, *Received Pronunciation* coincides with the version called *Modified Standard*, i.e. the version spoken by educated speakers who have modified the pronunciation system they used at an earlier date in some other region of Britain or in an overseas English-speaking country, so that the differences pass almost unnoticed by standard speakers. No judgement is intended on deviation from such pronunciations: the pronunciations themselves are merely a generally agreed norm. A great deal of information is provided where relevant about (*a*) pronunciations in standard AmE, and (*b*) about changes of stress and of particular sounds in the course of the 20c. in BrE. See e.g. (*a*) LEISURE, LIEUTENANT, LIQUEUR, -LIVED; (*b*) GYN(A)ECOLOGY, METALLURGY, PARIAH.

2 *Some modern changes in RP in BrE*. These changes have happened over the last half century or more. (i) Under AmE influence, adverbs ending in *-arily* now mostly bear the main stress on the *-ar-* (*necessarily, primarily*, etc.). See -ARILY. (ii) A number of words ending in *-ies* (e.g. *rabies, scabies*), formerly pronounced as /-ɪiːz/, i.e. with a two-syllabled ending, are now pronounced with one, i.e. /-iːz/. (iii) Scientific words ending in *-ein*(*e*) (*codeine, protein*, etc.), formerly having a two-syllabled ending, now have a monosyllabic one, i.e. /-iːn/. (iv) The /ɔː/ that was dominant at the beginning of the century in words such as *cross* and *loss* has almost entirely given way to /ɒ/. (v) In words ending in *-eity* (*deity, homogeneity, spontaneity*, etc.) /iː/ has been widely replaced by /eɪ/.

3 *Disputed pronunciations*. These are numerous. Many are dealt with in this book at their alphabetical places. Examples include *apartheid, centrifugal, cervical, communal, contribute, controversy, decade, despicable, dilemma, dispute* (noun), *dissect, distribute, envelope, extraordinary, forehead, formidable, harass, homosexual, kilometre, privacy, recondite, sheikh, sonorous, subsidence, zoology*. It should be borne in mind that the number of such words probably does not differ in any significant way from that at any given time in the past from Old English onwards. It is worth noting, for example, that one of the earliest dictionaries to recommend pronunciations, John Walker's *Pronouncing Dictionary* (1791), added numerous comments in support of his recommendations for particular words, e.g. under *Envelope*: 'This word signifying the outer case of a letter is always pronounced in the French manner by those who can pronounce French, and by those who cannot the *e* is changed into an *o*. Sometimes a mere Englishman attempts to give the nasal vowel the French sound, and exposes himself to laughter by pronouncing *g* after it, as if written *ongvelope*.' And under *Gymnastick*: 'In this word and its relatives we not unfrequently hear the *g* hard, because forsooth they are derived from the Greek. For the very same reason we ought to pronounce the *g* in *Genesis, geography, geometry*, and a thousand other words, hard, which would essentially alter the sound of our language.'

4 Words containing a short *o* in stressed syllables. These are evenly divided between those always pronounced with /ɒ/ and those always pronounced with /ʌ/, e..g. /ɒ/ *brothel, column, compact, constant, honest, lozenge, mongoose*; /ʌ/ *brother, colour, company, constable* (sometimes /ɒ/), *honey, dozen, mongrel*. The combination *ov* is normally now pronounced /ɒv/ in **Covent Garden, *Coventry, *hovel, *hover, novel*, and *sovereign*; but /ʌv/ is still very occasionally heard in those marked with an asterisk.

5 *Proper names.* Many proper names have a traditional pronunciation not easily inferred from their spellings. A few examples are given below, but the list merely skims the surface of a huge problem. For authoritative guidance on hundreds of others, readers are referred to J. C. Wells's *Longman Pronunciation Dictionary* (2008), and especially the *BBC Pronouncing Dictionary of British Names* (2nd edn by G. E. Pointon, 1983). *Althorp* (Northants) /'ɔːltrəp/; *Beauchamp* /'biːtʃəm/; *Beaulieu* /'bjuːli/; *Belvoir* (place in Leics.) /'biːvə/; *Caius* (Cambridge college) /kiːz/; *Cherwell* /'tʃɒːwəl/; *Cholmondeley* /'tʃʌmli/; *Cockburn* /'kəʊbən/; *De'ath* (surname) /di'aθ/; *Fiennes* /fʌɪnz/; *Glamis* /glɒːmz/; *Harewood* (Earl and House) /'haːwʊd/; *Home* (Earl) /hjuːm/; *Keynes* (family name) /keɪnz/; *Keynes* (in Milton Keynes) /kiːnz/; *Leveson-Gower* /'luːsən 'gaʊə/; *Magdalen(e)* (the colleges) /'mɔːdlɪn/; *Marjoribanks* /'mɒːtʃbaŋks/; *Ruthven* /'rɪvən/; *Sandys* /sandz/; *Walthamstow* /'wɔːlθəmstəʊ/; *Waugh* /wɔː/; *Wemyss* /wiːmz/; *Whewell* /'hjuːəl/; *Woburn* (Abbey) /'wuːbəːn/; *Wrotham* /'ruːtəm/.

propaganda is a 17c. loanword from Italian, derived from the modern Latin title *Congregatio de propaganda fide* 'congregation for propagating the faith', at first a committee of Cardinals of the Roman Catholic Church having the care and oversight of foreign missions, and later (late 18c.) applied to any association or movement for the propagation of a particular doctrine. In this extended sense it was sometimes treated as a neuter plural (= efforts or schemes of propagation) with singular *propagandum.* The dominant current sense (usually derogatory), 'the systematic propagation of selected information to give prominence to the views of a particular group; also, such information', is first recorded in the early 19c., but took off spectacularly in the 20c. The misspelling **propoganda* is one of the 100 most common spelling mistakes.

propel. The inflected forms are *propelled, propelling.* See -LL-, -L-.

propellant (noun) is something that propels. It is reasonably familiar to the general public in the sense 'a substance used as a reagent in a rocket engine to provide thrust' (*COD*). The corresponding adjective, which is much less frequent, is **propellent** 'propelling; capable of driving or thrusting (a space vehicle, etc.) forward'.

propeller, the only standard spelling in BrE for a revolving shaft with blades used to propel a ship or aircraft, etc. Sometimes spelt **propellor** in AmE.

proper terms. The following list of terms for groups of animals, etc., is reprinted from *The Oxford Encyclopedic Dictionary* (1991), Appendix 22. Terms marked † belong to 15th-c. lists of 'proper terms', notably that in the *Book of St Albans* attributed to Dame Juliana Barnes (1486). Many of these are fanciful or humorous terms which probably never had any real currency, but have been taken up by Joseph Strutt in *Sports and Pastimes of England* (1801) and by other antiquarian writers.

a †shrewdness of apes
a herd or †pace of asses
a †cete of badgers
a †sloth or †sleuth of bears
a hive of bees; a swarm, drift, or bike of bees
a flock, flight, (*dial.*) parcel, pod (= small flock), †fleet, or †dissimulation of (small) birds; a volary of birds in an aviary
a sounder of wild boar
a †blush of boys
a herd or gang of buffalo
a †clowder or †glaring of cats; a †dowt (= ?do-out) or †destruction of wild cats
a herd, drove, (*dial.*) drift, or (*US* & *Austral.*) mob of cattle
a brood, (*dial.*) cletch or clutch, or †peep of chickens
a †chattering or †clattering of choughs
a †drunkship of cobblers
a †rag or †rake of colts
a †hastiness of cooks
a †covert of coots
a herd of cranes
a litter of cubs
a herd of curlew
a †cowardice of curs
a herd or mob of deer
a pack or kennel of dogs
a trip of dotterel
a flight, †dole, or †piteousness of doves
a raft, bunch, or †paddling of ducks on water; a team of wild ducks in flight
a fling of dunlins
a herd of elephants

a herd or (*US*) gang of elk
a †business of ferrets
a charm or †chirm of finches
a shoal of fish; a run of fish in motion
a cloud of flies
a †stalk of foresters
a †skulk of foxes
a gaggle or (in the air) a skein, team, or wedge of geese
a herd of giraffes
a flock, herd, or (*dial.*) trip of goats
a pack or covey of grouse
a †husk or †down of hares
a cast of hawks let fly
an †observance of hermits
a †siege of herons
a stud or †haras of (breeding) horses; (*dial.*) a team of horses
a kennel, pack, cry, or †mute of hounds
a flight or swarm of insects
a mob or troop of kangaroos
a kindle of kittens
a bevy of ladies
a †desert of lapwing
an †exaltation or bevy of larks
a †leap of leopards
a pride of lions
a †tiding of magpies
a †sord or †sute (= suit) of mallard
a †richesse of martens
a †faith of merchants
a †labour of moles
a troop of monkeys
a †barren of mules
a †watch of nightingales
a †superfluity of nuns
a covey of partridges
a †muster of peacocks
a †malapertness (= impertinence) of pedlars
a rookery of penguins
a head or (*dial.*) nye of pheasants
a kit of pigeons flying together
a herd of pigs
a stand, wing, or †congregation of plovers
a rush or flight of pochards
a herd, pod, or school of porpoises
a †pity of prisoners
a covey of ptarmigan
a litter of pups
a bevy or drift of quail
a string of racehorses
an †unkindness of ravens
a bevy of roes
a parliament or †building of rooks
a hill of ruffs
a herd or rookery of seals; a pod (= small herd) of seals
a flock, herd, (*dial.*) drift or trip, or (*Austral.*) mob of sheep
a †dopping of sheldrake
a wisp or †walk of snipe
a †host of sparrows
a †murmuration of starlings
a flight of swallows
a game or herd of swans; a wedge of swans in the air
a herd of swine; a †sounder of tame swine, a †drift of wild swine
a †glozing (= fawning) of taverners
a †spring of teal
a bunch or knob of waterfowl
a school, herd, or gam of whales; a pod (= small school) of whales; a grind of bottle-nosed whales
a company or trip of widgeon
a bunch, trip, or plump of wildfowl; a knob (fewer than 30) of wildfowl
a pack or †rout of wolves
a gaggle of women (*derisive*)
a †fall of woodcock
a herd of wrens

prophecy /ˈprɒfɪsi/ shows the spelling and pronunciation of the noun. The corresponding verb is **prophesy** /ˈprɒfɪsʌɪ/.

prophetess. See -ESS 5.

proportionable, proportional, proportionate. The first is virtually extinct, but very occasionally turns up (e.g. *a racially conscious society divided into racial and ethnic groups, each entitled as a group to some proportionable share of resources, careers, or opportunities—Race and Racism,* 2001) The second and third are close synonyms, and it is not easy to tease out the distinctions between them, other than that *proportional* is more than twice as frequent; what follows are pointers. (*a*) Both modify a few semantically similar nouns, e.g. *increase, reduction, decrease,* but *proportionate* is less common in such collocations. (*b*) Both also occur in the structure noun

+ *proportional/proportionate to* + noun, but in that structure the noun following *proportionate to* is much less likely to denote measurement: contrast *proportional to the number, amount, size, square, distance,* etc. with *proportionate to the aim, risk, threat, offence, seriousness, crime,* etc. (*c*) *Proportional* is the only possible choice in several fixed collocations, e.g. *proportional compasses* (US *dividers*), *proportional spacing, proportional representation*; (*d*) *proportionate,* rather than expressing a numerical ratio, often suggests 'appropriateness in respect of quantity, extent, degree', as is shown by collocations such as *necessary and proportionate, reasonable and proportionate,* etc. *Proportional,* in contrast, is the obvious choice in financial, numerical, scientific, etc. contexts. Finally, while *proportional representation* is a specific electoral system in which each party gains seats in proportion to the total number of votes it receives, usually by means of a form of transferable vote, *proportionable representation* means representation of a group in appropriate relation to its size.

Examples: (proportional) *By 1979 all the beds and hospital places, which were provided up to the prescribed national levels proportional to the catchment population, had been opened*—D. Tomlinson, 1991; *Some evidence exists in favor of a larger proportional reduction in juvenile, as compared to adult, survival in deteriorating conditions—Ecology,* 2000; *equality is reached when a state's share of income is exactly proportional to its share of population—Economic Geography,* 2004; (proportionate) *The United States does not have the vote that is proportionate to its funding—CNN* (transcripts), 2004; *The Tribunal could have adopted a much more proportionate response—Spiked Online,* 2004; *Disclosure of information should be necessary and proportionate to the aim it seeks to achieve—England and Wales High Court Decisions,* 2004; *The difficult but crucial central issue about the whole operation is whether it was proportionate to the threat posed—Guardian,* (*Comment is Free*), 2010.

proposition (noun). It is worth recording that Fowler (1926), writing at a time when the sense 'a matter or problem which requires attention (e.g. *a tough proposition, an attractive proposition, a business proposition*)' was widely felt in Britain to be an intrusive Americanism, sternly remarked, 'it is resorted to partly because it combines the charms of novelty and length, and partly because it ministers to laziness.' He wanted *proposition* to 'be brought back to its former well defined functions in Logic and Mathematics, and relieved of its new status as Jack-of-all-trades'. His advice, his admonitions, and his numerous illustrative examples (more than twenty, in contexts where, it was claimed, *proposal, task, undertaking, possibility, prospect, enterprise,* etc., would have been more suitable) have all gone unheeded. The noun continues to be widely used in ordinary contexts in precisely the manner that Fowler found objectionable. Examples: *'Call this a store?' he would say. 'Call this a paying proposition?'*—A. Tyler, 1980; *For a quizzical, curious mind . . . adequate explanations are too thin to suffice and tinkering with the possibilities becomes an enticing proposition*—D. Shekerjian, 1990; *Altering an alloy composition calls for relatively large orders, but to adjust slightly the temper of a work-hardening sheet alloy is a more feasible proposition—Professional Engineering* (UK), 1992. The corresponding verb was first recorded in America in the 1920s in two main senses: (*a*) to make or present a proposition to (someone), e.g. *While being propositioned by Lord Beaverbrook about becoming the film critic of the* Evening Standard, *I nervously filled in a yawning silence by telling this anecdote*; (*b*) to make a suggestion of sexual intercourse to (someone), especially in an unsubtle way: *she had been propositioned at the party by a subeditor with bad breath.* These senses, especially (*b*), now form part of the ordinary fabric of the language.

proprietor. So spelt, not *-er.*

proprietress. See -ESS 5.

propylaeum /ˌprɒpɪˈliːəm/ (entrance to a temple; specifically the entrance to the Acropolis in Athens). Plural *propylaea* /-ˈliːə/.

pros and cons, reasons or considerations for and against a proposition, etc., is written without apostrophes.

proscenium. Plural normally *proscenium,* rarely *proscenia.* The first syllable can be pronounced either /prəʊ-/ or /prə-/. See -UM 3.

prosciutto. This Italian word for a type of cured ham is pronounced /prəˈʃuːtəʊ/

(pruh-**shoo**-toh). The correct spelling is with the letter *i* before the *u*, not the other way round as often seen on menus. (On Google, this misspelling outnumbers the correct spelling.) It may help to recollect which vowel comes first if you remember that in *fascist*, another Italian word, the same combination of letters - *sci* - is similarly pronounced as a *sh* sound, /ʃ/.

proscribe. See PRESCRIBE.

prosecutor (person who prosecutes, especially in a criminal court). So spelt, not *-er*.

prosecutrix. A female plaintiff, especially a rape victim, who brings a charge against someone. For the plural, see -TRIX.

proselyte. The noun means 'a person converted, esp. recently, from one opinion, creed, party, etc., to another'. In World English the corresponding verb (= to convert (a person) from one belief, etc., to another) is **proselytize, proselytise**. In AmE the verb is either **proselytize** or occasionally **proselyte**.

prosody. Traditionally, and still today, its primary sense is 'the theory and practice of versification' and, in particular, 'the laws of metre'. The corresponding adjective is **prosodic** /prəˈsɒdɪk/; and 'one skilled or learned in prosody' is a **prosodist** /ˈprɒsədɪst/. In linguistics, since 1949 in the theories of J. R. Firth and his followers, *prosody* has established itself with the meaning 'a phonological feature having as its domain more than one segment'. The *OED* adds a note: 'Prosodies include the class of "suprasegmental" features such as intonation, stress, and juncture, but also some features which are regarded as "segmental" in phonemic theory, e.g. palatalization, lip-rounding, nasalization.' The concept of 'semantic prosody' outlined by the late Professor John Sinclair (1991) suggests that some words regularly associate with semantic sets of words in such a way as to convey a particular attitudinal meaning. For example, things that *set in* are always undesirable.

prosopopoeia /prɒsəpəˈpiːə/. In use in rhetoric since the 16c. as the direct descendant of Greek προσωποποιία 'personification', it means principally 'a figure in which an inanimate or abstract thing is represented as being able to speak'. As a rhetorical device it was known already to the Anglo-Saxons (though not under that name). In the Old English poem The *Dream of the Rood*, for example, the True Cross speaks:

> *þæt geara iu, (ic þæt gyta geman)*
> *þæt ic wæs aheawen holtes on ende,*
> *astyrede of stefne minum ...*
> (It was long ago (I still remember it)
> that I was cut down at the edge of the forest,
> moved from my trunk ...)

The device is also employed in the OE riddles, and in many a poem in later centuries.

prospect (noun). Regularly stressed in all its senses on the first syllable. The corresponding verb (= to explore a region for gold, oil, etc.) is stressed on the second syllable (thus /prəˈspɛkt/). See NOUN AND VERB ACCENT 1.

prospective is an adjective describing a likely future event or situation, as in *prospective students*, and *prospective changes in the law*. For its use in phrases where *perspective* is the appropriate word, see PERSPECTIVE.

prospectus. The plural is *prospectuses* (notwithstanding the Latin plural *prospectūs*). The plural **prospecti* is mistaken pedantry, since the Latin word is fourth rather than second declension. See -US 2.

prosper. The inflected forms are *prospered, prospering*. See -R-, -RR-.

prostate (gland). See note at PROSTRATE.

prosthesis /ˈprɒsˈθiːsɪs/ (an artificial limb, etc.). The plural is *prostheses* /ˈprɒsˈθiːsiːz/.

prostrate (adjective). **1** Care should be taken to distinguish *prostrate* from *prostate*. The second (in full *prostate gland*) is a gland surrounding the neck of the bladder in men and male mammals. It is often used incorrectly as in **prostrate (gland), prostrate cancer*, etc.

2 The adjective means (strictly) 'lying face downwards', but also, more generally, 'lying horizontally', and, in transferred use, 'overcome, esp. by grief or exhaustion'. It is stressed on the first syllable: thus /ˈprɒstreɪt/. For the corresponding verb the stress moves to the second syllable: thus /prɒˈstreɪt/. Cf. SUPINE. Examples of the adjective: *Among those often listed as alpines or rock plants are a number of prostrate or low-growing perennials or shrubs*—*Garden Answers* (UK), 1990; *Gavin Hastings had charged upfield and at a subsequent ruck Carminati clambered in and stamped twice on the prostrate John Jeffrey*—*Independent on Sunday*, 1990; *He was obsessed . . . by the prostrate, naked, and callipygous corpse in the foreground*—*NY Rev. Bks*, 1991.

protagonist. 1 *Technical meaning.* In Greek drama the protagonist (πρωταγωνιστής, from πρῶτος 'first' + ἀγωνιστής 'an actor') is the chief personage in a play, (often also the name by which the play is known, as with Sophocles' *Oedipus Rex*), and this single sense is maintained in all scholarly work on Greek drama. The *deuteragonist* (δευτεραγωνιστής) and *tritagonist* (τριταγωνιστής) take parts of second and third importance.

2 *First extended meaning and Fowlerian strictures.* (*a*) Dryden seems to have been the first user of the term in English: in the preface to 'An Evening's Love' (1671) he wrote *'Tis charg'd upon me that I make debauch'd Persons . . . my protagonists, or the chief persons of the drama.* Many writers since Dryden have used the word *protagonist* thus to mean 'the leading character in a play, poem, novel, film, etc.', e.g. *As 'Hiawatha', this man* [*sc.* Ayenwatha] *became the protagonist of the historically confused epic poem of that name by Henry Wadsworth Longfellow*—C. Mann, 2005. Since a narrative work of art can have more than one principal character, the word is often used in the plural, e.g. *The two protagonists, the cuckoo and the nightingale, present a series of antithetical statements about the power of love, in which the cuckoo finally gains the edge*—*Dict. of National Biography*, 1993.

(*b*) Fowler (1926) was the first person to flag this word as a usage issue; one of the uses to which he passionately objected was the plural. It is understandable that as a distinguished classical scholar he should cleave to the original, technical meaning, but usage has long since made the plural standard. On the grounds that, again in Greek drama, there is only one *protagonist*, he also objected to the word being preceded by *chief, leading, main, principal*, etc.: e.g. *Price's "Smiley" is Dr David Audley, the chief protagonist of 17 previous novels*—*Oxford Today*, 1990. Such uses are well established, and while strictly speaking they could be viewed as tautological, it is unlikely that anyone nowadays will view them as such.

3 *Second extended meaning.* Since '*All the world's a stage . . .*', with hindsight it seems inevitable that the word should become one of what Fowler termed 'popularized technicalities' and come to mean '*the main figure, or one of the most prominent figures, in any situation*': e.g. *This year the season has been characterized by the duel between the McLaren and Ferrari teams whose protagonists are Senna and Prost*—*Ronda Iberia* (Iberia Airlines), 1990. *By then most of the original protagonists had gone their separate ways and the Salon itself was divided and no longer held in much esteem*—*Oxford Companion to Western Art*, 2001.

4 *Third, wider still and wider, meaning.* Early in the 20c., speakers and writers, ignoring the etymology of the word, seem to have perceived *protagonist* as being formed on the Latin prefix *pro*- 'for, in favour of' and therefore to have thought of the word as meaning 'a proponent, advocate, supporter (of a cause, idea, etc.)', as opposed to an antagonist. A. P. Herbert commented on this in his *What a Word!* (1935): *I have heard with horror . . . that the word 'protagonist' is being used as if it were pro-tagonist—one who is for something, and opposed to ant-agonist, one who is against it.* Further example: *These may be worthy views but they are not those of a true protagonist of the arts*—*Scotland on Sunday.*

5 *Recommendation.* It is easy to see how the development of meanings happened once the word had come into the ordinary vocabulary of people who knew nothing of the nature of Greek drama. In the arts, the *protagonists* are the chief actors in a play or the main characters in a work of fiction, poem, film, etc. In politics the *protagonists* are prominent 'players'. In such contexts, and also in business, trade, banking, etc., *protagonist* may properly be used of those who hold opposing views on important matters. Such *protagonists* will often be called *chief, leading, main*, or *principal*, though such uses have a whiff of tautology about them. One should, however, be slightly cautious about stretching the word further than that to mean someone who is *for* a specified belief or set of beliefs, i.e. taking the element *pro-* as the equivalent of that used in, for example, *pro-choice* or *pro-life*. Despite the age of this use (1896), some people will still find such a use inappropriate, if not mistaken. Several standard alternatives readily offer themselves, e.g. *advocate, champion, partisan, proponent*, and *supporter*.

protasis /ˈprɒtəsɪs/. The clause expressing the condition in a conditional sentence, e.g. the *if*-clause in *If I can come I will* or *I will come if I can*. Cf. APODOSIS. Plural *protases* /-siːz/.

protean (adjective). The *OED* (1909) gave only first-syllable stressing (/ˈprəʊtɪən/), and this pronunciation is still preferred by some standard speakers. Also stressed on the second syllable, /prəʊˈtiːən/. The word is the adjective corresponding to *Proteus*, in Greek mythology a sea-god able to take various forms at will. Despite being based on a proper name, *protean* should not be written with an initial capital.

protector. So spelt, not *-er*. See -OR.

protégé /ˈprɒtɛˈʒeɪ/. In this and the corresponding feminine form **protégée**, the accents should be retained. Both are printed in roman.

protest. 1 The noun is stressed on the first syllable and the verb on the second. See NOUN AND VERB ACCENT 1.

2 The transitive use of the verb in the sense 'to protest against (an action or event); to make the subject of a protest' has been widely accepted in AmE throughout the 20c. and has made such inroads in other English-speaking areas that it now outnumbers the alternative constructions *protest against* and *protest at*. In BrE this transitive use and *protest against* are equal in frequency. But it is far from being a natural use in BrE. Note however that *protest* is transitive in BrE in the sense 'to assert or maintain', typically with *innocence* as the object. Some examples: *Anatoly Koryagin, who has been imprisoned for protesting the use of psychiatry for political purposes*—*New Yorker*, 1987; *But I must protest this latest twist from law*—*USA Today*, 1988; *The ruin of Belfast's Black Mountain protested by the local community*—*Independent*, 1991; *At the core really is the 'ownership' of cricketers, an issue which had emerged during a previous World Cup when the Indian players protested the use of their images by sponsors*—*sports website*, 2005 (BrE).

protestant. In its religious sense always written with an initial capital and pronounced /ˈprɒtɪstənt/. In its very rare non-religious use to mean simply 'a protesting person, an objector', it is sometimes pronounced with the stress on the second syllable. But *protester* is, of course, the normal word.

protester. More often spelt as shown than *-or*, which is also correct.

prototype. See -TYPE.

protractor (geometrical instrument). So spelt, not *-er*.

provable. So spelt, not *proveable*. See MUTE E.

proved, proven. Middle English developed two distinct infinitives from Old French *prover* (ultimately from Latin *probāre*), namely *proven* and *preven* (or *preoven*). In standard British English *prove* alone survives with past tense and past participle *proved*. In Scotland and some northern dialects of England the pattern *preve*, past participle *proven* survived, the past participle being usually pronounced /ˈprəʊvən/. Cf. *cleave/cloven, weave/woven*. In Scots law the verdict *not proven* is a central concept. In the rest of the UK the form *proven*, usually pronounced /ˈpruːvən/, was occasionally used beside *proved* in non-legal contexts both as a past participle and as an attributive adjective, e.g. *His love of precise dates and proven facts*—N. Shakespeare, 1989. Over the last few years, the frequency of *proven* in BrE has dramatically increased as a result of its repeated use in advertising both attributively and otherwise, e.g. *proven health benefits, scientifically proven to reduce wrinkles*.

In AmE *proven* is standard in both parts of speech. The *OEC* data shows, however, that even in AmE *proved* is more frequent in the present perfect, i.e. *have/has proved*, as it is also in World English, except for Canadian, where *proven* dominates. In BrE *proved* is more than six times more frequent. Examples, all from BrE unless indicated otherwise: (*proved*: past participle) *Four cheeses were chosen to spearhead the consumer packs, and initial results have proved positive—Grocer*, 1988; *Attempts at winning environmental controls... have so far proved of only limited effectiveness—Natural World*, 1988. (*proven*: attributive adjective) *Anchor's proven track record with aerosol products led to the introduction of... a non-dairy dessert topping—Grocer*, 1988; (past participle) *That Uncle was a susceptible and sometimes hallucinated reader is proven by his enthusiasm for the books he urged on me*—S. Bellow, 1987 (US); *Medical science has utterly proven the case in this issue—Sunday Times*, 1987; *in the United States... conducting necessary seroprevalence studies has proven politically problematic—Dædalus*, 1989 (US); *The story would have been reported very differently if Jade had accidentally taken other tablets that could also have proven fatal—www.spiked-online.com*, 2004.

See DISPROVEN.

provenance, provenience. The first, borrowed from French, is the standard form for 'a record of ownership of a work of art or an antique, used as a guide to authenticity or quality'. In general its pronunciation is anglicized as /ˈprɒv(ə)nəns/ (**prov**-nuhns), though antique dealers delight in giving it a one-upmanship French twist as /prɒvˈnɑ̃ns/. *Provenience*, (stressed on the second syllable) is an occasional variant, found particularly in AmE.

provided (that), providing (that). In sentences of the type *Provided that/ Providing that he had a good book to read, he did not mind how much it rained* the phrases *provided that/providing that* are compound subordinate conjunctions introducing conditional clauses. In slightly less formal contexts *that* is often omitted, and then *provided/providing* may be regarded as quasi-conjunctions. All four types have a long history in English, as the *OED* shows: *provided that*, illustrative examples from *c.*1460 onwards; *provided* 1604–; *providing that* 1423–; *providing* 1632–. Some modern examples: (provided (that)) *Provided, only provided, that it not be that one, or anything like it*—M. Bradbury, 1987; *In summer he will show visitors around the chapel provided he likes their faces and they are not wearing shorts—Linguist*, 1992; (providing) *It works well enough providing I keep my blanket round me*—J. Winterson, 1987; *Kids are actually as tough as old boots. Providing they're fed and watered and have at least one primary attachment figure, they tend to survive—Metro* (NZ), 1988. In such contexts, and in those given in the *OED*, the meaning ranges from 'on condition that', 'on the undertaking that', or 'in case that' to 'if only'.

province. For synonyms, see FIELD.

proviso. Plural *provisos*. See -O(E)S 4.

provost. In the names of the officers of the military police often pronounced /prɒˈvəʊ/ (after French. *prévôt*), AmE /ˈprəʊvəʊ/. In all other senses /ˈprɒvəst/.

prowess /ˈpraʊɪs/. The standard pronunciation makes the first syllable rhyme with *now*, not with *dough*.

prox. Abbreviation of PROXIMO.

proximo (abbreviation **prox.**) formerly used in commercial letters = 'of next month' (*the seventh proximo*). It is a shortened form of Latin *proximo mense* 'in the next month'.

prude has the derivative **prudish** (not *prudeish*). See MUTE E.

prurience, pruriency. Both denote the lip-smacking, prying, gossipy, gloating interest in the sexual affairs of others to which the British tabloids so admirably cater, but *prurience* is by far the more common of the two, whereas *pruriency* is rather uncommon. See -CE, -CY.

pry. The intransitive verb *pry*, meaning 'to inquire impertinently (into something secret or private)', is first recorded in the 14c. and is of unknown origin. It is distinguished from the dialectal and AmE verb (first found in print in the 19c.) of the same spelling, meaning 'to force open or out by leverage'. See PRISE.

PS (abbreviation of *postscript*). A second postscript is *PPS*, and a third *PPPS*. No one, except in jest, writes more than three postscripts.

ps-. The *OED* (1909) described the dropping of the *p* sound as 'an unscholarly practice often leading to ambiguity or to a disguising of the composition of the word'. Fowler (1926) hoped that 'With the advance of literacy the pronunciation of the *p* in words beginning thus is likely to be restored except in *psalm* and its family, e.g. in the compounds of *pseud*(*o*)- and such important words as *psychical* and *psychology.*' Nothing of the kind has happened and all English words beginning with *ps* (e.g. *psalm, pseudonym, psittacosis, psychiatry, psychopath, psychology*) are now pronounced with initial /s/, not /ps/.

pseudonym. See also NOM DE GUERRE. In the realms of literature and film, *pseudonyms* have been adopted for many reasons: to conceal the author's identity: e.g. 'Junius': Letters 1769–72; to conceal the sex of the writer: e.g. Acton Bell (real name Anne Brontë); Currer Bell (Charlotte Brontë); Ellis Bell (Emily Brontë); George Eliot (Mary Ann Evans); to distinguish one's professional from one's literary work: e.g. Lewis Carroll (C. L. Dodgson); to distinguish different genres of the same author's work: e.g. Barbara Vine (i.e. Ruth Rendell); Robert Galbraith (i.e. J.K. Rowling); to disguise one's foreign origin: e.g. Joseph Conrad (Teodor Josef Konrad Korzeniowski); to replace what was regarded as a less memorable name: e.g. Mark Twain (Samuel Langhorne Clemens).

Pseudonyms are perhaps most commonly of all adopted by actors and film stars for various reasons, such as to make a name more memorable, to avoid ethnic associations, or to avoid a family connection perceived as unfair. *Pseudonyms* in these cases are known as *stage* or *screen names*: e.g. Fred Astaire (Fred Austerlitz); Michael Caine (Maurice Micklewhite); Cary Grant (Alexander Archibald Leach); Marilyn Monroe (Norma Jean Baker); Nicolas Cage (Nicolas Coppola).

psychic, psychical. The second of these, used in the sense 'relating to the soul or the mind, as distinguished from *physical*', is much the earlier of the two adjectives. The earliest example of *psychical* in the *OED* is one of 1642 from the work of the Cambridge Platonist Henry More (1614–87). *Psychic,* by contrast, has not been found in print before 1836. Both words survive but are not generally interchangeable, and *psychic* is much the more frequent of the two in the meaning defined above. The shorter form is generally preferred in matters to do with the occult (telepathy, clairvoyance, etc.), although the collocation *psychical phenomena* is occasionally used instead of *psychic phenomena,* and the collocation *psychical research* is rather more often used than *psychic research. Psychic* is obligatory when applied to a bid in bridge 'that deliberately misrepresents the bidder's hand'. Examples: *Consequently, exile is experienced as dislocation, both physical and psychic*—*MELUS*, 2003; *From psychoanalysis too we learn that we avoid psychic pain only to pay dearly for it in other ways*—*Psychoanalysis Down Under*, 2001; *one of the terms which has been used in order to integrate physiological, psychical, and social aspects of the human body*—*Jrnl of Sex Research*, 2001.

psychological moment. A curious little byway of English: a loan translation based on a mistranslation. Curiouser and curiouser. This phrase (= the most appropriate time for achieving a particular effect or purpose) is a loan translation of the French *le moment psychologique.* It arose in French during the German siege of Paris in 1870. French journalists used the phrase to render the German phrase *das psychologische Moment* through confusing masculine *der Moment* 'moment (of time)' with neuter *das Moment* 'operative factor, momentum'. The phrase then passed into English journalistic use in its non-original meaning, and has tenaciously remained in the language, albeit at the margins. Examples: *Politicians also sometimes talk about the psychological moment, meaning the time at which something is best done. When they do so they fail to realise that the phrase originally meant something completely different*—*BMJ*, 2001; *the Napoleon-like stroke of the old Provisional Committee in resuming control at the psychological moment saved the situation for the country at large*—*OEC* (undated).

psychosis. Plural *psychoses* /-siːz/.

pt-. The *OED* (1909) expressed a preference for the *p* to be fully pronounced in all such Greek-derived words (*pterodactyl, Ptolemaic, ptomaine,* etc.), but implied that a silent *p* was acceptable in the fanciful misspelling *ptarmigan* (derived from Gaelic *tarmachan*). But, as in words beginning with *pn-* and *ps-*, the *p* is now always silent, despite the fact that it is pronounced in all the relevant words in French, German, and other European languages.

pub. See ABBREVIATIONS 2.

publicly. What a (delightfully or infuriatingly) wayward language English is. Adjectives ending in *-ic* form their adverbs in *-ically,* e.g. *automatically, basically,* *specifically*, etc. By analogy, therefore, *publically* should be the standard, but, alas, it is not: the non-conformist *publicly* is. While the *OED* recognizes *publically* without demur, many readers will not be so gracious. Avoid.

pucka. See PUKKA.

pucker. The inflected forms are *puckered, puckering.* See -RR-, -R-.

pudenda, pudendum are both used with the same meaning, but the first is plural, the second is singular. See -UM 2.

puisne. Pronounced /ˈpjuːni/, like *puny.* Both are derived from French *puis né* 'born afterwards', hence 'inferior'. A **puisne judge** is a judge of a superior court inferior in rank to chief justices.

puissant (a literary or archaic word meaning 'mighty, powerful'). The pronunciation recommended is /ˈpwiːsənt/ (**pwee**-suhnt), but /ˈpjuːɪsənt/ (pyoo-) is also used.

pukka (genuine). Formerly a catchword of British celebrity chef Jamie Oliver, and spelt as shown, not *pucka, pukkah.* See SAHIB.

pulley (noun). The plural is *pulleys.*

pullulate. Pronounced /ˈpʌljʊleɪt/.

pummel (verb). See POMMEL.

pun. A standard account of puns—the good, the bad, and the indifferent—is provided in Tony Augarde's *Oxford Guide to Word Games* (1984), especially pp. 204–15. Puns have been used in Western countries from earliest times. Aristotle approved of them in some kinds of writing. Pope Gregory I (*c.*540–604) famously described English slaves as *Non Angli, sed angeli* 'not Angles, but angels'. Shakespeare is said to have used about 3,000 puns in his plays, among them Mercutio's dying words in *Romeo and Juliet*: *aske for me to morrow, and you shall finde me a graue man.* Catherine Winkworth, in *Punch* 18 May 1844, set down the message General Sir Charles Napier supposedly sent after he had conquered the Indian province of Sindh in 1843—*Peccavi* (Latin, I have sinned). These are celebrated examples. Each one of us has a store of private puns and the ability to make new ones. Rhetoricians like them and give them fancy names (see PARONOMASIA). Journalists like them, especially in headlines (see HEADLINE LANGUAGE). Schoolchildren adore the near-puns built into riddles: (Question) *What is an ig?* (Answer) *An Eskimo house without a loo.* Puns will doubtless continue to be a feature of the language in the centuries that lie ahead.

punctilio. Plural *punctilios.* See -O(E)S 4.

punctuation. See AMPERSAND; APOSTROPHE; BRACKETS; COLON; COMMA; DASH; EXCLAMATION MARK; FULL STOP; HYPHENS; ITALICS; QUESTION MARK; QUOTATION MARKS; SEMICOLON.

punctum (in biology). Plural *puncta.* See -UM 2.

pundit. The normal transliteration of the Hindi original is *paṇḍit,* and this spelling (without the subscript dots) is used in printed work, with a capital initial when prefixed to the name of a learned Hindu (*Pandit Nehru*). But *pundit* and **punditry** are used in general contexts, and are the only spellings admissible when the reference is to a (non-Indian) learned expert or teacher.

punter. *Our choice of venue is usually the Mermaid Restaurant, where punters can dine al fresco at white plastic tables, rain or shine, in season or out—Daily Tel.*, 1992. This meaning of *punter*, 'a customer or client', developed in the 1960s from an older meaning 'a gambler; a backer of horses' (1860), i.e. a customer of a bookmaker, by way of several underworld slang meanings including 'an accomplice in a crime', 'a victim of a swindle', and then 'a client of a sex worker'. In the 1980s and 1990s it became a more salubrious vogue word, and even achieved enough respectability to be used in more highbrow contexts: *For the punters, it may not be all bad: alternative bookings [at Covent Garden] could include leading foreign dance and opera companies—BBC Music Magazine,* 1999. Despite continued use, however, it is already beginning to sound like yesterday's buzzword, and is still labelled 'colloquial' by the *OED*: *With wide, muscular shoulders, V-shaped screens and deep-set lamps, it's exactly the sexy, sporting car Alfa needs to lure in the punters—Arena,* 2002. The older meanings continue to be used, as do two other words having the form *punter*: 'someone who propels a punt on a river' (1814) and 'someone who punts a football' (1887).

pupa. Plural *pupae* /ˈpjuːpiː/.

pupil(l)age. The spelling with a single *-l-* is AmE; that with two is BrE.

purée (pulped vegetables, fruit, etc.). It is desirable to retain the accent for both noun and verb, but not fatal if one does not. The inflected forms of the verb are *purées, puréed, puréeing*. Pronounced /ˈpjʊəreɪ/.

puritanic, puritanical. Both words came into use in the 17c. The shorter form is now extremely rare, the normal words being *puritanical* or **puritan** (adjective). Examples: (puritanic) *They were also not fond of other aspects of the puritanic restrictiveness of the Soviet culture*—*Contemporary Rev.*, 2000; (puritanical) *Both [D. H.] Lawrence and Catherine came from puritanical, conventional and smothering families*—J. Meyers, 1990 (US); *Gould's aesthetic was uncompromisingly puritanical and severe, yet his playing is never cold or dispassionate*—*London Rev. Bks*, 1992.

purlieus used instead of 'surroundings' is generally journalistic, pretentious, or tongue in cheek, e.g. *It was as a humorous writer that Coren flourished, constructing a netherworld of the satirical, the lunatic and the surreal, all vaguely anchored in Coren's own domestic purlieus of Cricklewood*—*Daily Tel.*, 2007. It is normally found in the form *purlieus*, with the final letter *-s*. Though dictionaries show *purlieux* on the French model as a legitimate plural, in the *OEC* data it makes nary an appearance. The word itself was not borrowed from French in its current form, and the *-lieu* spelling is a development based on the earlier Anglo-Norman *puralee*, and influenced by the French *lieu*. See -X.

purport. 1 The noun is stressed on the first syllable, /ˈpəːpɔːt/, and the verb on the second, /pəˈpɔːt/. See NOUN AND VERB ACCENT 1.

2 *The noun.* Its normal meaning, 'the ostensible meaning of something; the sense or tenor (of a document, speech, etc.)', causes no problems. *In contrast to the position in some other jurisdictions no explicit provision is made in relation to statements of negative purport*—*Blackstone's Q&A: Evidence*, 2003; *No one would go into the details of the latest meeting which they described as a brotherly gathering, however hints as to its purport were abundant*—*Jakarta Post*, 2001; *Despite the letter's obscure anagram ... its purport is clear: a confession of love from Olivia*—*Oxford Companion to Shakespeare*, 2001.

2 *The verb.* (*a*) *History.* Uses of the verb are more complicated, and opinions vary widely about the acceptability of some of the 20c. constructions. First, a few words on its history. It first appeared in the 16c., used transitively in the senses 'have as its purpose; express' (e.g. *I ... enclose copies of letters ... purporting some of the above facts*, 1780). This construction is no longer idiomatic. A transitive use with a relative clause, however, first recorded in 1693, is still standard (e.g. *It purports that some one from Oxfordshire ... applied to the College of Arms to have his title recognised*, 1858). Constructions in which *purport* is followed by an infinitive, and meaning '(of a document, book, etc.) to profess or claim by its tenor', first appeared towards the end of the 18c. and are still valid (e.g. *This epistle purports to be written after St. Paul had been at Corinth*, 1790; *The Declaration which purported to give them entire freedom of conscience*, 1849; *A letter purporting to have been written by you*, 1870). Less idiomatic is such a construction headed by (the name of) a person (e.g. *Jack Downey ... who purported to accompany the presidential party and to chronicle its doings*, 1884).

(*b*) *Fowler's objections.* Fowler (1926) watched these traditional constructions being further extended in the newspapers of his day, and did not like what he saw, especially developments in the use of *purport* with a following passive infinitive: e.g. *Many extracts from speeches purported to have been made by Mr Redmond are pure fabrications*; He judged that *supposed* would have been the better word in each case. He also thought that *purport* itself should not be used in the passive. And he believed that the subject of *purport* should only in rare circumstances be a person.

3 *Present-day constructions of the verb.* The main present-day types are shown in the following examples: *The revolutionary intellectual purports to believe ... that the utopian ideal of unalienated existence can only be realised through violent struggle*—P. Fuller, 1986; *He even hesitantly claimed a near-sighting of his own, recalling that he had seen 'what purported to be a saucer phenomenon'*—R. Ferguson, 1991;

The paper purporting to demonstrate cold fusion is a case in point—*New Scientist*, 1991; *Those who purport to describe educational issues should not promulgate miseducative stereotypes*—*TES*, 1991; *More recently, the Family Court of Australia held in contempt a layman who falsely purported to be a lawyer*—D. Pannick, 1992; *Set in what was purported to be modern-day California, it was about a family of lively young nowsters who dressed in flowery jumpers*—J. and M. Stern, 1992.

4 *Conclusion*. It would appear that the language has largely admitted some uses of *purport* not recorded in the *OED* and others that were disliked by Fowler. It is a classic example of a verb continuing to vie for space with its near-synonyms, e.g. *allege(d), claim, have the appearance of being, repute(d)*, and *suppose(d)*, and having a mixed reception from standard speakers as the linguistic battle takes its course.

purpose (noun). For *clauses of purpose*, see FINAL CLAUSE.

purposefully, purposively, purposely. 1 *Basic distinctions*. A careful examination of dictionary definitions of these three words and of the corresponding adjectival forms of the first two will throw light on some of their differences, but reveals also much overlapping of meaning and use. The sturdiest of them all is *purposely* 'on purpose, by design', which entered the language in the 15c. (e.g. *he purposely avoided all reference to his ex-wife*). Both *purposeful* 'having a definite purpose in mind; resolute' and *purposefully* are mid-19c. creations. So too is *purposive* 'serving or tending to serve some purpose', while the adverb *purposively* is a 19c. word (1878–). *Purposive* was taken over by psychologists in the 1880s with the meaning 'relating to conscious or unconscious purpose as reflected in human and animal behaviour or mental activity', and it is in psychological work that the word principally turns up (e.g. *The behaviourists, with the exception of Tolman, rejected purposive explanation, because they avoided all reference to consciousness, subjectivity, ideas, or mind*—*Oxford Companion to the Mind*, 1987).

2 *Overlaps of meaning*. While the core distinction between the two words is that *purposely* can be paraphrased as 'on purpose' and *purposefully* as 'for a particular purpose', *purposefully* is nowadays often used to mean simply 'on purpose'. The *OED* does not recognize this, but *ODO* does. For some people this use will jar; others it will leave totally unperturbed. In fact, in many examples with *purposefully* it is impossible to tell which meaning is intended; hence the interchangeability of the two words. *Purposively* being an infrequent, rarefied, academic, or legal word, such problems do not usually arise, although it is occasionally used where *purposely* would seem the more obvious choice. If vacillating between *purposely* and *purposefully* in your own writing, ask yourself whether 'on purpose' would convey the same meaning. If so, the first option is the better one.

3 Examples of *purposeful, purposefully* in their core meaning: (purposeful) *During the hour... they had transformed a restless bunch of chewing, pencil-tapping, fidgeting, chattering, inattentive bundles of undirected energy with an attention span of about 10 seconds into a purposeful class*—*TES*, 1990; *Prussia's civil service and even that of France were models of purposeful efficiency compared with Britain's patronage recipients down to the Age of Reform*—W. D. Rubenstein, 1991; (purposefully) *He proceeded... to fashion for himself... a course all his own, made up of Latin, French and English with a special view to following words from one language to another, until one saw dimly how language worked and how purposefully it drifted*—W. Sheed, 1985; *Skeins of wild geese moving purposefully across the sky*—*Gourmet* (US), 1990; (*purposefully* used like *purposely*) *As with Oslo, it purposefully avoids all the fundamental issues, like settlements, Jerusalem, borders, refugees, international law and human rights*—*The Nation*, 2003; *Hillenbrand purposefully avoids some of the more arcane data surrounding racing and gambling, and avoids breathless prose and hyperbole when it comes to describing the horse*'s *athletic achievements*—*Sunday Business Post*, 2001; (*purposively* used like *purposely*) *There was evidence that this particular US citizen had cooperated with the guerrillas and purposively led us astray*—*Sense of Cinema*, 2002.

pur sang. Adopted from French in the mid-19c., this adjectival and adverbial phrase meaning 'of the full blood, without admixture, genuine' is often used after a noun, e.g. *It is in fact possible to be a* *sociologist* pur sang *and not a black* (*white, yellow, piebald, Scots, Croat, Methodist, Muslim*, etc., etc.) *sociologist*—*TLS*, 1975. Printed in italic.

pursuant. The phrase *pursuant to* is regarded by modern grammarians as a complex preposition and by an older school (including the editors of the *OED*) as a QUASI-ADVERB. It is more or less restricted to law, and means 'under, in accordance with', e.g. *Appellant is a state prisoner incarcerated in the Louisiana State Penitentiary... pursuant to a 1964 aggravated rape conviction*—B. A. Garner, 1987.

pursuivant. Now conventionally Anglicized to /ˈpəːsɪvənt/, but at the beginning of the 20c. normally pronounced with a medial /w/, /ˈpəːswɪvənt/.

purulent. Pronounced /ˈpjuːrʊlənt/.

purveyor. So spelt, not *-er*.

putsch. This word for a violent attempt to overthrow a government, comes via German from Swiss-German. It is a metaphorical extension of its meaning in that dialect of 'knock, thrust, blow'. It rhymes with *butch*, not with *Dutch*. Printed in roman and with a lower-case *p*.

putrefy (to go rotten). So spelt, not *-ify*.

puttee /ˈpʌti/, strip of cloth wrapped round each leg as part of army uniform. Spelt as shown, though derived from Hindi *paṭṭī*.

putter. See POTTER.

pyaemia (type of blood-poisoning). So spelt, but AmE **pyemia**.

pygmy. For etymological reasons (cf. Latin *pygmaeus*, Greek πυγμαῖος (adjectives) 'dwarfish', from a Greek measuring word πυγμή [*pygmē*] meaning 'the length from the elbow to the knuckles'), this is the better and now generally used spelling, rather than *pigmy*. The word is capitalized when referring to peoples, e.g. *Possibly the ancestors of the Pygmies* (*Mbuti, Twa, and Mbenga peoples*), *who are short-statured, forest-dwelling groups of Central Africa*, but not when used metaphorically, e.g. *intellectual, political, moral pygmy*.

pyjamas. The standard spelling in BrE, but **pajamas** in AmE.

pyorrhoea (dentistry). So spelt in BrE, but **pyorrhea** in AmE.

pyramidal. Pronounced /pɪˈramɪdəl/.

pyrrhic¹, of a victory won at too great a cost to be of use to the victor, is named after Pyrrhus of Epirus, who defeated the Romans at Asculum in 279 BC but sustained heavy losses. Written and printed with a lower-case *p*.

pyrrhic² (noun and adjective). Used of a metrical foot of two syllables, both of which are short (in Greek) or light (in English). Thus *tune and* in | *When in* | *disgrace* | *with For* | *tŭne aňd* | *men's eyes* (Shakespeare's Sonnet 29). Some prosodists, however, regard *pyrrhic* as an unsafe concept in the scanning of English verse. For example, the line just given could be interpreted as | *When in dis* | *grace with* | *Fórtŭne aňd* | *mén's* | *éyes* |, or as | *Whén ĭn* | *dĭsgráce* | *wĭth Fór* | *tŭne ánd* | *mén's éyes* |.

qua /kweɪ/. This useful word, nowadays printed in roman, is in origin the ablative feminine singular of Latin *qui* 'who'. One of its several meanings in Latin is 'in virtue of the fact that'. It was adopted in English in the 17c. as a useful link word (it is variously described as an adverb, a preposition, and a conjunction in standard English dictionaries) meaning 'in the capacity or character or role as'. Fowler (1926) thought that it should be restricted to contexts in which 'a person or thing spoken of can be regarded from more than one point of view or as the holder of various coexistent functions, and a statement about him (or it) is to be limited to him in one of these aspects: *Qua lover he must be condemned for doing what qua citizen he would be condemned for not doing*; the lover aspect is distinguished from another aspect in which *he* may be regarded. The two nouns (or pronouns) must be present, one denoting the person or thing in all aspects (*he*), and the other singling out one of his or its aspects (*lover*, or *citizen*).' *WDEU* (1989), on the other hand, cites several examples in which *qua* is used between two identical nouns as 'a somewhat more emphatic synonym of *as*', e.g. *a key to any one poem* qua *poem*—L. MacNeice, 1941. It also cites examples of the less common type in which qua does not occur between repeated nouns, e.g. *It cannot, qua film, have the scope of a large book*—J. Simon, 1974.

Both descriptions are sound, as the following string of examples from good 20c. sources will show: *Earth closets, too. Do they exist* qua *earth closets? No*—K. Mansfield, 1920; *the presence of actual words is apt to confuse any estimate of the evocative power of the music qua music*—C. Lambert, 1934; *Qua phonetician, de Saussure has no interest in making precise the notion of species*—R. S. Wells, 1947; *Look at the sky... What is there so extraordinary about it? Qua sky?*—S. Beckett, 1956; *I don't think that 'Hard Times' is a particularly good novel* qua *novel, whatever it may be as a social document*—*Broadcast*, 1977; *James Kirkup's poem about Jesus... is... an indefensibly bad poem qua poem*—*London Rev. Bks*, 1981; *Dressed in an Armani suit... and espadrilles, he plays a cop* qua *existential hero*—*Literary Rev.*, 1989. As to assigning it to a part of speech, *qua* seems to coexist as a conjunction and an adverb but hardly as a preposition. And as to usage, *as* is often the better choice of word, *qua* word.

quad. See ABBREVIATIONS 2.

quadrate. Stressed and pronounced the same as adjective and noun but differently as verb: thus (adjective and noun) /ˈkwɒdrət/; (verb) /kwɒˈdreɪt/.

quadrennium, a period of four years. The Latin original is *quadriennium*, but the first *i* has been lost in English under the influence of other 'period of X years' words, such as *decennium, millennium, septennium*. So too **quadrennial** adjective.

quadriga (chariot drawn by four horses harnessed abreast). Now normally pronounced /kwɒˈdriːɡə/, but, earlier in the century (*OED*, 1904; Fowler, 1926) only /-ˈdrʌɪɡə/. Plural *quadrigae* /-ɡiː/.

quadrille. Now always pronounced /kwəˈdrɪl/, but, earlier in the century (*OED*, 1904; Fowler, 1926) and still in AmE, optionally also /kəˈdrɪl/.

quadrillion, a thousand raised to the fifth (or formerly, especially in BrE, the eighth) power (10^{15} and 10^{24} respectively).

quagmire. The pronunciations /ˈkwɒɡmʌɪə/ and /ˈkwaɡ-/ are both current.

quality. 1 For 'has the defects of his qualities', see HACKNEYED PHRASES.

2 The corresponding adjective is **qualitative** /ˈkwɒlɪtətɪv/. The rarely used form **qualitive**, though of long standing, and recorded in the *OED*, is liable to be viewed as incorrect. See -ATIVE, -IVE. Cf. QUANTITATIVE.

qualm. Pronounced /kwɑːm/, no longer optionally as /kwɔːm/.

quantitative has been fighting it out with the now almost never used **quantitive** for more than three centuries, and is the outright winner; the shorter form, though of long standing and recorded in the *OED*, is liable to be viewed as incorrect. See -ATIVE, -IVE.

quantum. In physics a *quantum* (plural *quanta*: see -UM 2) is a 20c. term for 'a minimum amount of a physical quantity which can exist and by multiples of which changes in the quantity occur' (*OED*). A **quantum jump,** which can be small or large, is simply 'an abrupt transition between one stationary state of a quantum system and another'. In popular use, since the 1950s, and, from the 1970s, in the form **quantum leap,** the phrase has been gleefully and endlessly used in general contexts to mean 'a sudden large increase'. It is one of the most striking POPULARIZED TECHNICAL TERMS of the 20c.

quarrel (verb). The inflected forms are *quarrelled, quarrelling* (AmE usually *quarreled, quarreling*). See -LL-, -L-.

quarter. 1 *Hyphenation.* Common compound nouns formed with *quarter* are written as follows in BrE, according to *ODO*: (i) two words: *quarter day, quarter note, quarter pipe, quarter sessions*; (ii) one word: *quarterback, quarterdeck, quartermaster*; (iii) hyphenated: *quarter-final, quarter-hour* (but more commonly *quarter of an hour*), *quarter-light* (in a car), *quarter-pounder, quarter-sawn, quarter-tone* (musical interval).

2 In phrases of time, value, etc., there is considerable flexibility of idiom: *a quarter of an hour, a quarter to eleven* (AmE *a quarter of eleven*, and, regionally, *a quarter till eleven*), *with nearly quarter of an hour to spare, a quarter past eleven* (AmE *a quarter after eleven*), *quarter-past eleven, be there by quarter to* are all (except the bracketed AmE ones) standard in BrE. So are *for a quarter of the price, for quarter of the price, for a quarter the price*, and *for quarter the price.*

quarter (verb). The inflected forms are *quartered, quartering.* See -R-, -RR-.

quarto. Plural *quartos.* See -O(E)S 4.

quasi. The recommended pronunciation is /ˈkweɪzʌɪ/, not /ˈkwɑːzi/.

quasi-adverbs. A smallish group of adjectives are idiomatically used in such a manner as almost to fall into the broad class of adverbs. They are therefore called quasi-adverbs, and by some grammarians complex prepositions (because they are invariably followed by a simple preposition). Some of the main quasi-adverbs are *according to, contrary to, irrespective of, preliminary to, preparatory to, previous to, prior to, pursuant to, subsequent to.* The type is shown in *he was rolling up his sleeves preparatory* (not *preparatorily*) *to punching the other boy; He did it contrary* (not *contrarily*) *to my wishes* (note that neither *different from* nor *opposite to* can be used in this manner). Further comments may be found under some of the words at their alphabetical place. See also DUE TO; OWING TO.

quat. This sequence of letters has multiple pronunciations. It is /kwɒt/ in *quatrain* and *squat.* In unstressed initial position (*quaternary, quaternion*) it is /kwət-/, except that in *quatorze* it is /kət-/. In *quatercentenary* and *quattrocento* it is /kwat-/. In *aquatic* it is normally /-kwat-/. In *quatorzain* and *quatrefoil* it is usually /ˈkat-/.

quatercentenary. See QUAT, and CENTENARY 2.

quatorzain, quatrain, quatrefoil. See QUAT.

quattrocento (Also **Quattrocento**) /ˌkwatrəʊˈtʃɛntəʊ/. The style of Italian art of the 15c., i.e. 1400–99. See QUAT; TRECENTO.

queer. The updated *OED* summarizes the current status of this word, first used to mean 'homosexual' in AmE in 1914: 'Although originally chiefly derogatory (and still widely considered offensive, especially when used by heterosexual people), from the late 1980s it began to be used as a neutral or positive term (originally of self-reference, by some homosexuals; e.g. *Queer Nation*) in place of *gay* or *homosexual*, without regard to, or in implicit denial of, its negative connotations. In some academic contexts it is the preferred adjective in the study of issues relating to homosexuality (e.g. *Queer theory*).'

querist, a questioner, a person who asks questions. This word, first recorded in the 17c., has now passed into extremely restricted, mostly literary, use.

question.

1 See LEADING QUESTION.
2 For the order of words in indirect questions (*He asked what he was to do*, etc.), see INDIRECT QUESTION.
3 See BEG THE QUESTION.
4 For *the question as to*, see AS 11 (c).

question mark. The mark of interrogation in English, represented by the sign ? **1** Its ordinary use is shown in the following examples: *What time is it?; What does the word* empathy *mean?; Ah, did you once see Shelley plain, And did he stop and speak to you And did you speak to him again?* The next word should normally begin with a capital letter.

2 The question mark should not be used after indirect questions, although there is a modern tendency to insert one unnecessarily in sentences like the following, e.g. *He asked why I was there; He asked whether I would come with him; I was asked if I would stay for dinner.*

3 The question mark and the exclamation mark (*!*) are normally easily distinguishable in function, e.g. *How often does it happen?; How seldom it happens!* Sometimes, especially in popular writing, the two are combined for emphasis: *How often must I tell you?!*

4 A question mark may be placed before a word, etc., whose accuracy is in doubt, e.g. *Thomas Tallis (?1505–85); Phnom Penh is the capital of Cambodia (?Kampuchea).*

5 A question mark is not needed after certain types of requests, e.g. *Would passengers now on platform 2 please move to platform 3 if they wish to join the 8.50 train for Reading and intermediate stations.*

6 A tag question (e.g. *He's much taller now,* isn't he?) must always be followed by a question mark.

questionnaire. Now almost invariably pronounced with initial /kw/, not the old-fashioned /k/, which reflected the word's French provenance. The main stress falls on the last syllable.

queue. The inflected verbal forms are *queues, queued, queuing* (or *queueing*).

quiche. See TART.

quick has a long history in standard use as an adverb (first recorded in the 13c. and used, for example, by Shakespeare, Milton, Locke, and Dickens), but now has restricted currency (the *OED* says 'now usually considered less formal than *quickly*, and found chiefly in informal or colloquial contexts, often in standard constructions'). It is often used for the comparative and superlative forms, e.g. *She ran quickest.* Examples of a thin line of current uses: *Get out quick!; the 'get-rich-quick' society; quick-frozen food;* (message on clothes) *Kiss Me Quick.*

quid (slang, = one pound sterling). The plural is unchanged (*it cost me five quid*), except in the phrase *quids in*, 'to be in a financially advantageous position'.

quiescence, quiescency. Both words entered the language in the 17c., and mean the same, but *quiescence* has always been the dominant word of the two. See -CE, -CY.

quiet (verb). In the sense 'to reduce to quietness, to soothe (a person, an emotion, a disturbance, etc.)', *quiet* has been used transitively since the 16c. (e.g. *The unexpectedness of this departure from the routine at first disquieted but then quieted us all*—M. Lindvall, 1991; *Bishop regularly quiets the butterflies by reassuring himself that his new job is no different, really, from the old one*—*NYT Mag.*, 1992). From the late 18c., chiefly in North America, it has also been used intransitively, usually followed by *down* (e.g. *And sometimes, at night, when everything had quieted down . . . he would lie supine and evoke the one and only image*—D. Nabokov, 1986; *I didn't last that long as a rowdy drunkard, and when I switched to opiates at least I quieted down*—*New Yorker*, 1992; *After the raucous pounding (the boys beating on the door) quieted, she emerged into the dim light but nothing had changed*—*Amer. Poetry Rev.*, 2001).

As one of the later *-en* verbs from adjectives, *quieten* emerged in the early 19c. as a transitive verb and in the late 19c. as an intransitive one (commonly with *down*). It has not had an easy journey: 'To "quieten" the children is not English,' said a writer in *The North British Review*, 1844; 'quieten, whether as transitive or as intransitive, is a superfluous word,' said Fowler in 1926. But, in BrE at any rate, *quieten* is now a commonplace verb (used either transitively or intransitively) and any stigma attached to it for something like a century has gently disappeared. Examples: *Bapaiji related the story in outraged tones, rocking the baby to make it quiet, while Dhunmai quietened down herself*—B. Desai, 1988; *Arnica also helps to calm and quieten the upset child*—*Health Shopper*, 1990; *By the time this issue of* The Linguist *reaches our Members, business activity in the UK and other parts of Europe will have quietened down for the summer months*—*Linguist*, 1993.

quiet (noun), **quietness, quietude.** The first is much more commonly used than the others, and *quietude* the least often of the three. *Quiet* means principally 'silence, stillness, tranquillity' (*the quiet that sometimes precedes a storm; a period of peace and quiet*). *Quietness* is 'the condition of being quiet or undisturbed' (*the quietness of a congregation at prayer*). *Quietude*, a formal synonym of *quietness*, means 'the state or condition of being quiet, peaceful, or calm' (*the Coventry Canal (of more interest today to the industrial archaeologist than to the lover of rural quietude)*—C. Dexter, 1989; *Their two and one-half acres retain a bucolic quietude*—*Angeles* (US), 1991).

quincentenary. See CENTENARY 2.

quire. See CHOIR.

quit (verb). The past tense and past participle are either *quit* (especially in AmE) or *quitted*.

quite. 1 *Quite* (*so*). This somewhat dated, somewhat formal way of expressing agreement with a previous affirmative statement is characteristically BrE, e.g. *'The Minister should have resigned.' 'Quite.'*; *'No takers,' I said. 'Quite. By the way, I'm sorry to say "quite" all the time but . . . my work lies amongst Americans and they expect Englishmen to say it.'*—K. Bonfiglioli, 1976. My impression is that it has virtually been ousted by the omnipresent ABSOLUTELY.

2 *Quite a* + noun. Used with a noun preceded by the indefinite article, *quite* traditionally meant 'completely, entirely': e.g. *You are a humourist . . . Quite a humourist*—J. Austen, 1816. This use has dropped out of the literary language, but survives as an informal way of suggesting that something is notable, remarkable, impressive, etc., sometimes ironically: e.g. *We had us a party last night—quite a party*—D. Divine, 1950; *It had been quite a week and I wanted a day of relaxation*—R. Crossman, *a*1974. This intensifying use is also seen in the set phrase *quite something*: e.g. *It's quite something to be the target of a whole Guardian editorial but it would have been helpful if there had been some justification*—*Guardian*, 2012.

3 *quite* = 'completely' and 'fairly'. (*a*) The most important modern development of *quite*, however, is its use as a 'downtoner' to mean 'to a moderate degree, fairly'. This use emerged in the 19c. but became established, especially in BrE, in the 20c. As a result, *quite* can mean either 'completely' or 'fairly'. In *Alan quite approves of my literary efforts* (N. Williams, 1985), the meaning is 'really does approve'. But in *the social archaeologist quite often needs to use the techniques of the locational analyst* (*Geographical Jrnl*, 1983) the meaning is 'fairly often'.

(*b*) The sense 'somewhat, fairly' normally occurs with 'gradable' adjectives (those that may be modified by *more, less*, or *very*) and their corresponding adverbs, i.e. words such as *cheap(ly), good (well), bad(ly), interesting(ly)*, etc: e.g. *the book is quite interesting; the music was at times quite loud; he was quite generous with his money.*

(*c*) By contrast, when used with adjectives that are 'non-gradable' and express all-or-nothing concepts (e.g. *different, excellent, impossible*, and their corresponding adverbs), *quite* means 'completely, totally': e.g. *it would be quite impossible for me to know you*—E. Jolley, 1980; *It's very hard to imagine a child growing up with quite different beliefs*—P. Fitzgerald, 1986; *You needn't feel at all awkward about approaching other publishers. In fact, I think you were quite right to*—*London Rev. Bks*, 1988.

(*d*) However, this distinction is not watertight, and examples can readily be found (especially with adverbs) which either leave the choice of meaning unclear or suggest a meaning somewhere between the two extremes: e.g. *I'm bound to own that it was quite nice being telephoned by lots of young ladies*—*Times*, 1986. (How nice?) *It was quite awkward for me to arrange to come here* (P. Fitzgerald, 1986). (How awkward?). In speech, intonation usually clarifies the difference between *quíte nice* (= reasonably nice, but I've known better) and *quite níce* (= very nice). In writing only the surrounding context can unlock the precise meaning of such sentences.

(*e*) The use of *quite* with a verb is much more common in BrE than in AmE, and can have either the stronger meaning (*I quite agree* = I agree entirely; *We quite understand* = we understand completely) or the weaker meaning (*They'd quite like to come* = they wouldn't mind coming). Interpretation depends entirely on the type of verb.

4 *quite* = 'very, really'. This is standard in AmE, which could be confusing for BrE speakers: e.g. *You've no intention of coming back?' 'I'm quite sorry, but no, I have not.'*; *That is why we took quite seriously these particular clauses with regard to biosecurity, and we do so now*; *Rachel is going to stay with her brother for a few days which I think is quite positive*; *It is often quite beneficial to decide on a school first and then look for housing after.*

quiz. See -Z-, -ZZ-.

quoin, quoit. *Qu-* pronounced as *k*, /kɔɪn/, /kɔɪt/, or as /kw-/.

quondam. This Latin word meaning 'former(ly)' has been used in English as adverb and adjective since the 16c., but is hardly ever encountered now except as an attributive adjective applied to persons. Printed in roman. Examples: *The memory of her quondam fiancé on his knees*—S. Mackay, 1984; *she saw all male members of her quondam department as persecutors*—A. S. Byatt, 1990. Cf. ERST, ERSTWHILE; LATE.

quorum, the number of members whose presence is needed to make proceedings valid. Plural *quorums.* See -UM 1. The derived adjective **quorate** is chiefly BrE, e.g. *Are we quorate?*; *the decision of a quorate general meeting.*

quota, a share, the number allowed, etc. Plural *quotas.*

quotation marks (also called *inverted commas*). The placing of quotation marks varies from publishing house to publishing house, and each system has its own validity. What follows is adapted from the *New Hart's Rules*. Within the space of this short article it is impossible to lay out all the complexities of the topic, since different styles are followed in, and within, different countries; what follows summarizes the most important aspects. **1** *General.* It is useful to bear in mind that BrE and AmE usage in particular differ over the use of single and double quotation marks, and over the position of commas in relation to quoted material. See 3 and 4(a)(ii) respectively.

2 *Introducing quotations and direct speech.* (*a*) When quoted speech is introduced, interrupted, or followed by a reporting verb such as *said, shouted, whispered*, etc., the interpolation is usually separated from the speech by commas: *'I wasn't born yesterday,' she said.*; *'No,' said Mr Stephens, 'certainly not.'*; *A voice behind me says, 'Someone stolen your teddy bear, Sebastian?'*

(*b*) A colon may also be used before the quoted speech, typically to introduce more formal speech, or speeches of more than one sentence: *Rather than mince words she told them: 'You have forced this move upon me.'*; *Peter Smith, general secretary of the Association of Teachers and Lecturers, said: 'Countries which outperform the UK in education do not achieve success by working teachers to death.'*

(*c*) Very short speeches do not need introductory punctuation: *He called 'Good morning!'*; neither does a quotation that is fitted into the syntax of the surrounding sentence: *He is alleged to have replied that 'our old college no longer exists'.*

(*d*) The words *yes* and *no* and question words such as *where* and *why* are enclosed in quotation marks where they represent direct speech, but not when they represent reported speech or tacit paraphrasing: *She asked, 'Really? Where?'*; *He said 'Yes!', but she retorted 'No!'*; *The governors said no to our proposal.*

3 *Quotations within quotations.* When a quotation occurs within a quotation, in BrE the inner quotation is put in double quotation marks if the main quotation is in single marks (or vice versa, which is the practice especially in newspapers, and uniformly in American practice): BrE *'Have you any idea', he asked, 'what a "gigabyte" is?'*; AmE *"Have you any idea," he asked, "what a 'gigabyte' is?"*. If another quotation is nested within the second quotation, revert to the original mark, either single-double-single or double-single-double.

4 *Relative placing of quotation marks and other punctuation.* BrE tends to follow the maxim that 'All signs of punctuation used with words in quotation marks must be placed *according to the sense.*' (*a*) *Placement of commas.* (i) When quoted speech is broken off and then resumed after reporting verbs such as *she said, laughed,* etc., a comma *within* the quotation marks represents any appropriate punctuation in the original passage. Accordingly, if someone's words were *Go home to your father,* which has no punctuation, those words would be quoted as: *'Go home', he said, 'to your father.'* Note that the comma *follows* the quoted words. In contrast, if someone said *Go home, and never come back.* this would be quoted as *'Go home,' he said, 'and never come back.'* Here the first comma is *within* the quotation marks because it is part of the original direct speech. Note also the position of the full stop, *within* the quotation marks, in both versions.

(ii) In US practice, commas and full stops are set *inside* the closing quotation mark regardless of whether they are part of the quoted material (note the double quotation marks in the US examples): *No one should 'follow a multitude to do evil', as the Scripture says. / No one should 'follow a multitude to do evil'.; He believed in the proverb 'Dead men tell no tales'.* American: *No one should "follow a multitude to do evil," as the Scripture says.; No one should "follow a multitude to do evil."; He believed in the proverb "Dead men tell no tales."*

(iii) This is also often the style in much modern British fiction and journalism. In the following extract from a British novel the comma after 'suggest' is enclosed within the quotation marks even though the original spoken sentence would have had no punctuation: *'May I suggest,' she said, 'that you have a bath before supper?'* Traditional British style is: *'May I suggest', she said, 'that you have a bath before supper?'*

(*b*) *Placement of full stops.* (i) When a grammatically complete sentence is quoted, the full stop comes *within* the closing quotation mark. Direct speech reading originally *It cannot be done. We must give up the task.* would then be quoted as *'It cannot be done,' he concluded. 'We must give up the task.'* (or *"...give up the task."* in US). In particular, when a long sentence is quoted, introduced by quite a short phrase, it is better to attach the closing point to the long sentence: *Jesus said, 'Do not think that I have come to annul the Law and the Prophets; I have come to fulfil them.'* (But in US, *"... to fulfil them."*)

(ii) When the quoted sentence ends with a question mark or exclamation mark, they come *within* the closing quotation mark, with no other mark outside the quotation mark—only one mark of terminal punctuation is needed: *He sniffed the air and exclaimed, 'I smell a horse!'*

(iii) When the punctuation mark is *not* part of the quoted material, as in the case of single words and phrases, place it outside the closing quotation mark: *Why does he use the word 'poison'?* When a quoted sentence is a short one with no introductory punctuation, the full stop is generally placed *outside* the closing quotation mark: Cogito, ergo sum *means 'I think, therefore I am'. / He believed in the proverb 'Dead men tell no tales'. / He asserted that 'Americans don't understand history', and that 'intervention would be a disaster'.*

5 *Quotation marks round poetry, titles of works, place names.* (*a*) 'Displayed' (i.e. printed on a separate line from preceding prose) quotations of poetry and prose take no quotation marks. But when the line of poetry runs on with the prose, or when a number of quotations follow one another and it is necessary to distinguish them, then quotation marks are to be used. (*b*) Use quotation marks and roman (not italic) type for titles of short poems, short stories, and songs: 'Raindrops Keep Falling on my Head'; 'The Murders in the Rue Morgue'. (*c*) Use quotation marks for titles of chapters in books, articles in periodicals, and the like: *Mr Brock read a paper entitled 'Description in Poetry'.* But omit them when the subject of the paper is an author: e.g. *Professor Bradley read a paper on Jane Austen.* (*d*) Quotation marks may be used to enclose an unfamiliar or newly coined word or phrase, or one to be used in a technical sense: *'hermeneutics' is the usual term for such interpretation; the birth or 'calving' of an iceberg'.* (*e*) They are often used as a way of distancing oneself from a view or claim, or of apologizing for a colloquial or vulgar expression: *Authorities claim* *to have organized 'voluntary' transfers of population; I must resort to a 'seat of the pants' approach.* Such quotation marks should be used only at the first occurrence of the word or phrase in a work. Note that quotation marks should not be used to emphasize material. (*f*) They should not be used around the names of houses or public buildings: *Chequers, the Lamb and Flag.*

quote (verb) has the derivative **quotable**. See MUTE E. The formulaic pair *quote... unquote* used in dictation to introduce and terminate a quotation is first illustrated in the *OED* in 1935, in a letter by e. e. cummings.

quotes (plural noun). In copy-editing departments, printing houses, etc., *quotes* is used as the abbreviated form of 'quotation marks'. See ABBREVIATIONS 2 (b).

quoth. See ARCHAISM. In origin it descends from Old English *cwæð* 'he said' (past tense of *cweþan* 'to say'). When used, for example in historical novells, it is always placed before the subject, e.g. *Quoth an inquirer, 'Praise the Merciful!'—Browning,* 1884. Now pronounced /kwəʊθ/.

Qur'an. Now a frequent spelling in English of KORAN.

q.v. Abbreviation of (Latin) *quod vide* 'which see'.

r. See INTRUSIVE R; LINKING R.

rabbet /ˈrabət/ (carpentry). The AmE and etymologically more faithful spelling of BrE REBATE.

rabbit (noun). For *Welsh rabbit* (or *rarebit*), see WELSH RABBIT.

rabbit (verb). The inflected forms are *rabbited, rabbiting.* See -T-, -TT-.

rabies. Now always pronounced as two syllables, /ˈreɪbiːz /, but the *OED* (1904) and Fowler (1926) gave it as three, /ˈreɪbɪiːz /. See PRONUNCIATION 2 (ii).

race. In its ethnic sense 'a tribe, nation, or people, regarded as of common stock', *race* entered the language in the late 16c. and had considerable uncontroversial currency until the 20c. (*the British race, the German race, the Tartar race,* etc.). Now, as *OEDS* (1982) remarks, 'The term is often used imprecisely; even among anthropologists there is no generally accepted classification or terminology.' In practice, the word has retreated rapidly and is now largely replaced by such words as *nation, people*(*s*), and *community.* As a minor curiosity, the ultimate origin of the word *race* is obscure. We know that it was adopted from French *race* (earlier *rasse*) *c.*1570, and that it had entered French from earlier Italian *razza.* Cognates exist in most European languages (Spanish *raza*, German *Rasse*, etc.) but etymologists have found no pre-14c. evidence for the word in any European language.

raceme, racemose. Pronounced /ˈrasiːm/, /ˈrasɪˌməʊs/.

rachitis (rickets). Pronounced /rəˈkʌɪtɪs/.

racial /ˈreɪʃəl/. Formed in English in the 1850s by tacking the suffix *-ial* on to *rac*(*e*), the word swiftly gathered momentum in the 20c. as it was used to qualify such words as *prejudice, discrimination, equality, minority, conflict, segregation,* and *tension.*

racialism, one of the key words of the 20c., entered English at the beginning of the 20c., some thirty years before the term *racism,* which has almost entirely superseded it, and is more than 200 times more frequent than it is in the *OEC* data. Both terms are used of discriminatory behaviour by authorities or groups (governments, police, employers, etc.) against people on grounds of colour, religion, or nationality. What can be called 'linguistic racism' is typified by the use of derogatory terms for ethnic groups. The phenomenon is by no means confined to white English-speaking people: name-calling seems to be a universal phenomenon.

rack in *rack and ruin* means 'destruction' and is normally so spelt in this phrase in BrE. One of nine nouns and seven verbs with the same spelling, it is a spelling variant of *wrack* (Old English *wræc*) 'damage, disaster, destruction', and the spelling with an initial *w* is accepted in dictionaries. This *rack* is not etymologically related to the *rack* = framework, that = instrument of torture, that = an awkward gait of a horse, a *rack* of lamb, nor to the verb *rack* in *rack one's brains,* and numerous others, although that idiom too may be spelt *wrack one's brains.* The word of the same sound meaning 'seaweed' is spelt *wrack.* All the complexities of this exceedingly complicated word cannot be set down here: spare an hour (at least) to consult a large dictionary, especially the *OED.*

racket is the recommended spelling for the bat used in tennis, squash, etc., rather than **racquet** (cf. French *raquette*), but if your instinct leads you to prefer *racquet,* no one is going to quarrel with you about it. The game played by two or four persons in a four-walled court is always written as **rackets** in BrE but usually as **racquets** in AmE. The unrelated word **racket** meaning (*a*) a disturbance, (*b*) a fraudulent scheme, has no variant spelling.

racoon is the customary spelling in BrE for this furry North American nocturnal carnivore, but **raccoon** in AmE. The word was first adopted in the 17c. from a Native American language (Algonquian).

raddle. See RUDDLE.

raddled, the usual spelling of the adjective applied to a person, meaning 'aged- or fatigued-looking'.

radiance, radiancy. The second is now extremely rare, but is occasionally drawn on for metrical, rhythmical or other stylistic reasons. See -CE,-CY.

radiator. So spelt, not *radiater.*

radical as noun and adjective is always spelt as shown in its main meanings. The noun **radicle** is (*a*) the part of a plant embryo that develops into the primary root; (*b*) a rootless subdivision of a nerve or vein (*COD*). The adjectival form of *radicle* in sense (*a*) is *radical.*

radio. 1 (noun). Plural *radios.* See -O(E)S 5. To the puzzlement, it seems, of some people, *radio* gradually replaced *wireless* from about 1920 onwards, i.e. during the period when 'wireless' broadcasting turned into a worldwide industry. The word *wireless,* when used at all now in this meaning, is humorous or deliberately quaint. See also WIRELESS.

2 (verb). The verb has the inflected forms *radioes, radioed, radioing.*

radius. The recommended plural is *radii* /-dɪʌɪ/, not the rarely used, especially in AmE, *radiuses.*

radix /ˈreɪdɪks/ *or* /ˈradɪks/. The plural is *radices* /-dɪsiːz/ or *-ixes.* See -EX, -IX.

railroad (noun) is the customary term in AmE for BrE *railway.* In AmE, **railway** is sometimes used of the track on which trains run but not of the system of transportation itself. In both countries *railroad* is used as a verb to mean 'to pressurize or coerce into a premature decision', etc.

raise, rear (verbs). The first is especially common in AmE of the cultivation of plants (*to raise corn*), the breeding and rearing of livestock (*to raise cattle*), and of the bringing up of children (*to raise children*); but *rear* is also used of livestock and children (*to rear a child*), and *bring up* of children (*to bring up a family of four*). In BrE, *raise* is sometimes used in all three senses, but the more usual terms are *to cultivate* or *to grow* (plants), *to rear* (animals), and *to bring up* (children).

raise, rise (nouns). An increase of salary is called a *raise* in AmE and a *rise* in BrE.

raise, rise (verbs). In almost all of their numerous senses, *raise* is transitive (*raise prices, raise money, raise an army, raise an objection, raise hopes,* etc.) and *rise* is intransitive (*he rose to his feet, prices have risen, he rose from the ranks, to rise in arms,* etc.). It is worth noting, however, that historically (15–18c.) *raise* was interchangeable with certain senses of *rise* in BrE, and that such uses persist in some regional forms of AmE (*the Mississippi is raising; the prices of rent have raised 10 per cent in the last two years*).

raison d'être /ˌreɪzɒ̃ ˈdɛtrə/. This loanword from French (literally 'reason for being') is printed in italics, and with the circumflex accent on the letter *e.* Plural *raisons d'être* (pronunciation the same as singular). Since the phrase means not merely 'reason' but 'a purpose or reason that accounts for or justifies or originally caused a thing's existence' (*COD*), it does not make a great deal of sense to modify it with words such as *main, primary,* etc., e.g. *?The main raison d'être for the 'new police' was crime prevention by regular patrol.*

Raj (preceded by *the*), a historical term meaning 'British sovereignty in India', is pronounced /rɑːdʒ/.

Rajput, a member of a Hindu soldier caste, is now spelt as shown, not *Rajpoot.* Pronounced /ˈrɑːdʒpʊt/.

Raleigh. Sir Walter *Raleigh* (or *Ralegh*; he never used the spelling *Raleigh* himself) is believed to have pronounced his surname as /ˈrɔːli/, but his name is now commonly pronounced either as /ˈrali/ or /ˈrɑːli/. The place name in North Carolina is /ˈrɔːli/. *Raleigh* bicycles are /ˈrɔli/ in AmE and /ˈrali/ in BrE.

rallentando (musical direction). For the plural both *rallentandos* and *rallentandi* (/-di/) are correct. The choice depends on how Italian and technical one wishes to be.

Ralph. The pronunciation /reɪf/, now decreasingly heard, is a survival from the

17c. spelling *Rafe*. The usual pronunciation now is /ralf/, except in the name of the composer Ralph Vaughan Williams.

ramekin /ˈramɪkɪn/. This is the recommended spelling, not *ramequin*.

rancour. So spelt in BrE, but **rancor** in AmE. The corresponding adjective is **rancorous** in both varieties.

random. The long-established meaning of *random* that everybody knows is 'done or happening without method or conscious decision': *here are some random thoughts.* The newer meaning, 'odd, unusual, or unexpected', can strike people above a certain age as novel and alien. As a result, it is still informal in tone. First appearing in the 1970s, it is now well established among people below a certain age, especially in the US: *you are so incredibly random!*; *I find it impossible to not laugh at such a random guy.* In those examples, *random* functions as an adjective. People also use it as a noun, to mean someone who is somewhere by chance, or who is not part of a particular group: *randoms are a fundamental ingredient at any good party.*

ranunculus. The plural is either *ranunculuses* or *ranunculi* /-lʌɪ/.

rapport. An unusual example of a word that has become un-anglicized in pronunciation in the 20c. after having the final *t* fully pronounced at an earlier stage (Walker, 1791; *OED*, preferred form, 1904). The only current pronunciation is /raˈpɔː/.

rapt. In origin (15c.) from Latin *raptus*, past participle of *rapere* 'to seize', *rapt* first meant 'taken or carried up to or into heaven'; then (16c., among other senses) 'fully absorbed, engrossed (*listen with rapt attention*)'. In colloquial Australian, it is used on its own to mean 'delighted': *Hoyer ... said he'd be 'rapt to be invited to train with them'*—*Mercury* (Hobart), 1986. The spelling *wrapt*, though of considerable antiquity, was and is incorrect. The homophone *wrapped*, past tense of *wrap*, which is first recorded in the 14c., is unrelated. It is a sheer coincidence that *wrapped up* in *He is* wrapped up *in his work* means 'engrossed'.

rarefaction (from Latin *rārēfacere* 'to make less solid, rarefy') has better etymological credentials than the less common noun *rarefication*, since there is no Latin verb **rārēficāre*.

rarefaction, rarefy. So spelt (in contrast with *rarity*), and pronounced /ˈrɛːrɪ-/.

rarely. 1 Used by itself, i.e. without an accompanying (*if*) *ever* or *or never*, this negative adverb (= not often) has some interesting idiomatic uses, from the obvious (*He rarely leaves home now*) to others that are less obvious: (front-placing followed by subject-verb inversion) *Rarely had I seen such a mess*; (front-placing = 'on rare occasions', without causing subject-verb inversion) *Rarely, aggression is not premeditated.*

2 The standard uses with *ever* or *never* are (i) *rarely if ever* and (ii) *rarely or never* (which is also occasionally reversed as *never or rarely*). Criticism has been levelled at (iii) *rarely or ever* (by confusion of 'rarely if ever' and 'rarely or never',), though illustrated by examples in the *OED* from 1692 onwards; and (iv) *rarely ever*, though illustrated by *OED* examples from 1679 onwards, and supported by a British and an American example in *MWCDEU* (2002): *and the thieves are rarely ever caught*—R. Blythe, 1969; *I rarely ever think about the past*—*New Yorker*, 1971. In *OEC* data, formulation (i) is the most frequent, more often with commas, i.e. '*rarely, if ever,*' than without. Next is (iv), *rarely ever*, which can be considered an intensive form of *rarely* (cf. *never ever*). Less frequent than either is (ii), *rarely or never*, while (iii) *rarely or ever* is extremely infrequent, though used in an example by business and marketing guru Seth Godin. In practice, any of them can be used, though those who have a mind to may quibble at types (iii) and (iv), particularly (iii). Examples: (i) *When walking down the street Sam Endicott is a man who rarely, if ever, gets recognized*—*Stylus* (magazine), 2005; (ii) *Of Indian respondents, 32% rarely or never ate meat compared with less than 2% of other ethnic groups*—*BMJ*, 2001; (iii) *It turns out that the way the EPA computes mileage means that the typical Prius driver will rarely or ever achieve the mileage posted*—weblog (Seth Godin), 2005; (iv) *These things are rarely ever explored outside the confines of the Catholic church*—*Independent*, 1989.

raring to do. The informal expression *to be raring to* (*go*, etc.) 'to be extremely eager to (do something)' made its way into the standard language from AmE or from English dialects at the beginning of the 20c. The infinitive *to rare* from which *raring* derives is a variant of *rear*, as applied to a horse rising on its hind feet. Those who use the form *?rearing to do*, which many will consider wrong, are nevertheless correct in making the horsey connection. Examples: *He's laid it on that the preacher makes some inflammatory remarks . . . so that the congregation . . . will be rarin' to go*—J. Tyndall, 1971; *John Patten, the education secretary, was described by his aides as 'raring to go' after throwing off the viral infection that put him in hospital last month*—*Times*, 1993; *?First back on the pitch for the second half of this terrific game the boys in blue were rearing to go and the fans were as eager, waiting for the final score to dictate who would return for the final*—*Laois Nationalist*, 2003.

rase. See RAZE.

rat-catcher. A rat-catcher was originally a person employed to rid farm buildings, houses, etc., of rats and other rodents. Much later (early 20c.) the word was used to denote informal attire in the hunting-field rather than the black covert coat worn by riders to hounds who, although regular subscribers to the Hunt, do not aspire to pink. In its original sense the word is now only used outside officialdom. Most British rats now meet their doom at the hands of a local-authority official with the designation of *pest control officer* or *rodent operator*.

rateable. Despite the usual rules described s.v. MUTE E, *rate* (verb) has the derivative form *rateable* rather than *ratable* (lest the word should be momentarily connected with *rat*).

rather.

1 *rather than* + *-ing* form or infinitive.
2 *would rather, 'd rather*.
3 After comparatives.
4 Subject-verb inversion.
5 Emphatic use.
6 *had rather*.

1 *rather than* + *-ing* form or infinitive. The phrase *rather than* has two main meanings which shade into each other: (i) 'in preference to', and (ii) 'instead of'. When a noun follows there is little difficulty: *I suggested beer rather than wine*. With other parts of speech certain difficulties arise: (*a*) With pronouns, the case of the pronoun following *rather than* is normally the same as the word preceding *rather than*: *I wanted to see her rather than him*; *She, rather than he, decided to come*. (*b*) With verbs, an *-ing* form is used after *rather than* when the meaning tends towards 'instead of': *When she voiced her grievances quietly and calmly, rather than* screaming *them, her family paid attention to her for the first time*—M. Herbert, 1989; *Shareholders are greedy, that's why they buy shares rather than* blowing *their excess earnings on flashier cars or champagne*—weblog, 2004. (*c*) When the balance is between individual words and not phrases or clauses, the forms used before and after *rather than* tend to match: *In the video Jones is, in the main,* observing *rather than* advocating *the ruthless antics of the hard men*—*Daily Mirror*, 1992; *Mr Cameron admitted using the drug, but escaped the most serious punishment because he only* smoked *it, rather than* traded *in it*—*Independent*, 2007; *For decades afterwards, successive leaders attempted to* utilise, *rather than* destroy, *the Peronist bequest*—*Spiked Online*, 2004; When an infinitive follows, it can be either a bare infinitive, as in the previous example, or a *to*-infinitive, as in *The press . . . has a responsibility* to elevate *rather than* to degrade *them*—*Bull. Amer. Acad. Arts & Sci.*, 1987. (*d*) When the meaning is more to do with preference and rejection than with parallel alternatives, and so especially after the verb *prefer* itself, an infinitive (with or without *to*) is more natural after *rather than*: *Better to part with what they must now, rather than* lose *more later*—M. Shadbolt, 1986; *Many Vietnamese soldiers preferred to kill themselves rather than* be captured—*Independent*, 1989; *Key executives will resign rather than* face *negative media attention*—*Dollars and Sense Magazine*, 2003. (*e*) A mixed style, with an infinitive before and a verbal noun after *rather than,* is less natural in contexts based clearly on preference rather than alternatives: *?I can't believe any sane parent would send their kids to a camp that actually advocates that their kids should* kill *themselves rather than* being *gay*—weblog, 2005.

2 *would rather, 'd rather*. The full and the contracted forms both express preference and therefore may (but need not) be followed by a comparative construction beginning with *than*: *I'd rather read a* *book than watch television; he would rather not join the committee; I felt lucky to make it out of the country alive and would rather boil my testicles than risk returning*—*Sunday Times*, 2006.

3 *After comparatives.* After a comparative form such as *better, more,* etc., *than* and not *rather than* is the preferred construction, although *rather than* is sometimes more natural when the two parts of the construction are far apart in the sentence: *It is better to give way and let them have what they want rather than standing up for the rule of law*—R. Muldoon, 1986.

4 *Subject-verb inversion.* In certain circumstances, some writers are moved to reverse the natural subject/verb order after comparatives, including *rather*. Fowler (1926) s.v. *inversion* judged that such link inversions are 'so little necessary as to give a noticeable formality or pomposity to the passage'. He cited as an example *His book is not a biography in the ordinary sense; rather is it a series of recollections culled from*...(read *it is rather, it is instead*). The construction is still occasionally found, e.g. *This is not in any way politicising the thing, rather am I stating what I believe to be a fact*—*Waterford News and Star*, 2003.

5 *Emphatic use.* A particularly BrE use of *rather*, now very old-fashioned, is as an emphatic response to a question, when it means 'Indeed, assuredly' (e.g. *Did you enjoy your holiday?*—*Rather!*) In such cases the main stress falls on the second syllable: thus /rɑːˈðəː/.

6 *had rather.* See HAD 3.

ratio Plural *ratios*. See -O(E)S.

ratiocination The recommended pronunciation is /ˌratɪɒsɪˈneɪʃən/ rather than /ˌraʃɪ-/. Similarly with related forms.

ration. Now always pronounced /ˈraʃən/ in BrE though the *OED* (1904) gave precedence to /ˈreɪʃən/, while commenting that the form with /a/ was 'usual in the army'. Both pronunciations are common in standard AmE.

rationale. At the beginning of the 20c. this word (which is the neuter of the Latin adjective *ratiōnālis*) was pronounced as four syllables: /raʃəˈneɪli/. At some point in the century, probably under the influence of the French loanwords *locale* and *morale* (there is no French *rationale*), it became routinely pronounced as three syllables: /raʃəˈnɑːl/.

rationalize in the sense 'to make (a business, etc.) more efficient by reorganizing it to reduce or eliminate waste of labour, time, or materials' (*COD*) is less than a century old: the first example in the *OED* is dated 1926. Gowers (1965) disliked it as a 'vogue word'. While it is still used and standard in this meaning, the more current vogue word is *restructure*. *Rationalize* nowadays is most often used in its psychological sense, 'to explain or justify (one's behaviour or attitude) to oneself or others with plausible but specious reasons, usually unwittingly', e.g. *Unfortunately, often people use therapy to rationalize current behaviors instead of trying to change them*—*The Black Table*, 2003.

ratline /ˈratlɪn/, usually in the plural (any of the small lines fastened across a sailing ship's shrouds like ladder rungs, *COD*), is now the customary spelling, not *ratlin* or *ratling*.

rattan /raˈtan/, climbing palm, walking-stick, is the recommended spelling of this Malay loanword, not *ratan*.

ravel (verb). **1** The inflected forms are *ravelled, ravelling* (AmE often *raveled, raveling*).

2 This is an example of a word capable of having two opposite meanings: 'to entangle or become entangled'; (often followed by *out*) 'to disentangle, to unravel'. Both senses have been in existence for several centuries without causing confusion, though *unravel* is now the more usual word for the second sense. Two literary examples: (= entangle) *Those wild, unhappy, self-defending Few, If not destroy'd in Time, will ravel all the Clew*—Defoe, 1706; (= disentangle) *Must I rauell out My weau'd-vp follyes?*—Shakespeare, 1593.

raze, rase. In the sense 'to destroy, to tear down' the word is now normally spelt *raze* (especially in *the building was razed to the ground*), not *rase*, notwithstanding that it entered the language *c.*1400 from Old French *raser* (from *rās-*, past participle stem of Latin *rādere* 'to scrape', etc.). Contrast the history of *erase*, formed in the early

17c. from *e-* (prefix form of *ex-* before some consonants) + the same Latin base as that of *raze*.

re. Pronounced either /riː/ or /reɪ/ (ree, ray), it is in origin the ablative of Latin *rēs* 'thing, affair'. *Re* (often in the form *in re*) has been used in legal documents before case names (e.g. *In re Rex v. Smithers*) for more than a century, and from there has made its way into commercial correspondence and into office memoranda in the sense 'with regard to, with reference to, etc. (your enquiry, note, etc.)'. Some authorities have objected to it. In particular, A. P. Herbert in his *What a Word!* (1935) ridiculed *re* in this example: *We herewith enclose receipt for your cheque £4 on a/c* re *return of commission* re *Mr. Brown's cancelled agreement* re *No 50 Box Street top flat.* Fowler (1926) was equally antagonistic and cited several examples with distaste: e.g. *Dear Sir,—I am glad to see that you have taken a strong line re the Irish railway situation./Why not agree to submit the decision of the Conference re the proposed readjustment to the people so that they alone can decide?* There can be no objection to its use as an introductory preposition, which, with its following noun or noun phrase, announces the subject of the correspondence, memo, etc., that follows. 'Its conciseness makes it well-nigh irreplaceable' (Garner, 1987). In other contexts, while equally useful as a synonym of 'about', it does run the risk of sounding like Councilspeak or legalese, e.g. *I saw the deputy head re the incident.*

re(-). In words beginning with *re-*, the prefix of repetition, a hyphen is unnecessary (e.g. *reaffirm, recharge, regroup, reinterpret, reopen, reshape, reuse*) except (*a*) in words in which the second element begins with *e* (e.g. *re-edit, re-entry*); (*b*) to distinguish words containing this prefix from words spelt the same but having a different meaning (e.g. *re-collect* to collect again, but *recollect* to remember; *re-count* to count again, but *recount* to narrate; *re-cover* to cover again, but *recover* to return to health; *re-creation* creation over again, but *recreation* pleasurable activity; *re-form* to form again, but *reform* to make or become better, to improve). Similar prefixes such as *pre-* behave in the same way.

're. Used as a reduced form of *are*, plural present indicative of *be*, it has been commonplace after personal pronouns in the representation of speech, or for metrical reasons in verse, from the time of Shakespeare onwards (thus *they're, we're, you're*). What seems to be a 20c. innovation, particularly outside Britain, is the use of 're after plural nouns and after *there* and *what*. Examples: *'Things're bad, though,' Pell said... 'Recession.'*—T. Winton, 1985 (Aust.); *My cards're in my desk*—M. Cope, 1987 (SAfr.); *'There're oyster catchers too,' said Eric defensively*—A. T. Ellis, 1990; *What're you spying on him for?*—N. Gordimer, 1990 (SAfr.); *What're you doing?*—*New Yorker*, 1990; *When're we going to see Charles?*—B. Anderson, 1992 (NZ).

reaction. 1 *History.* In chemistry since the early 19c. used to mean 'the action of one chemical agent *on* another, or the result of such action'. In physiology and pathology since the late 19c. used to mean 'the response made by the system or an organ *to* an external stimulus'. Some authorities have therefore argued that *reaction* may only be used as a response *to* something that had acted *on* it. But the word did not begin its life in the language of chemists and medical practitioners.

The word had been used figuratively in general contexts at a much earlier date. Sir Thomas Browne, for example, used it in his *Religio Medici* (1643) to mean 'resistance exerted by something in opposition to the impact or pressure of something else': *It is the method of Charity to suffer without reaction.* Charles Wesley in vol. v of his *Works* (1771, edn of 1872) used it to mean 'reciprocal action': *A continual action of God upon the Soul, and a re-action of the Soul upon God.* Numerous other writers (cited in the *OED*) brought it about that *reaction* came to be used with various prepositions—e.g. *against, on,* and *upon*—particularly in the senses 'resistance; something exercised in return on something else'. Also, since 1792, the word had been employed in political language to mean 'a tendency to oppose change'.

2 *Current usage.* This is the general picture before 1900. In the 21c. the word continues to be used in various specialized ways by technical and scientific writers: these uses lie outside the scope of this book. In general use, two main branches of meaning flourish: (*a*) 'a response (to an event, a statement, etc.); an action or feeling that expresses or constitutes a response' e.g. *The public reaction was no greater than the response . . . to the death of the Princess of Wales—Historian,* 2002; (*b*) 'a tendency to oppose change or to advocate a return to a former state of affairs, especially in politics' (*COD*): e.g. *The show's overarching theme is the familiar battle between progressive modernists and the forces of reaction—NYT,* 2007. There is also a marked tendency, especially by media interviewers, to use the word to mean 'immediate response', 'first impression': e.g. *What was your reaction when you were notified that the mother of the sixteen-year-old was suing you?—Interview,* 1990.

3 *Recommendation.* If we leave aside technical language, a simple enough rule is to restrict *reaction* to contexts in which the idea of a response to some previous action, event, stimulus, etc., is present. But cross-questioners in general, and media interviewers in particular, will doubtless persist in using *reaction* in its weakened sense of 'immediate impression' when a handful of other words (*impression, judgement, opinion, response, view,* etc.) is available.

readable. See LEGIBLE.

readership is used in the world of 21c. newspapers and magazines to mean either 'the total number of (regular) readers of a periodical publication', or 'all such readers considered collectively'. Cf. LEADERSHIP; MEMBERSHIP.

real (adverb). Used only as an intensifier (= very) with an immediately following adjective or adverb (*real nice, real slow; real soon*), it is non-standard or at best very informal in England, but more acceptable in Scotland and in America. The standard adverb in most contexts is, of course, *really* (e.g. *Are you really coming tomorrow?; I am really sorry*). Some US examples: *Stay around till she gets back, she'd be real sorry to miss you—New Yorker,* 1987; *You look real nice today, Carla—New Yorker,* 1987; *Lester is real alone*—B. Ripley, 1987.

real (adjective). **1** As an adjective *real* tends to be wildly overused in an intensifying role equivalent to adjectives such as 'significant, important, strong': *It may be too late to halt the brain drain and decline in morale unless the Government shows a real commitment to research—Daily Tel.,* 1992; *There are real conflicts of interest and viewpoint—Whole Earth,* 2000. Collocations in which it is often used without adding anything much to the meaning are *real difference, threat, danger, change, challenge.* In such contexts a more exact word, such as *strong* in the first example and *significant* in the second, can be more effective. To adapt Gowers' verdict (*Complete Plain Words,* 1954), if a difference is always qualified by *real,* a difference by itself becomes a poor filleted thing.

2 *For real* is an informal expression of AmE origin dating from the 1950s and is used in questions to express surprise or to question the truth or seriousness of what one has seen or heard, or in affirmative statements for emphasis: *Are these guys for real?; Global warming is for real*—farming website, 2004.

realm. For synonymy, see FIELD.

-re and -er. One of the great differences separating the spelling of BrE and AmE is that in many words BrE opts for *-re* and AmE for *-er* (in many cases preserving an earlier spelling from which BrE has since departed): e.g. *calibre, caliber; centre, center; fibre, fiber; goitre, goiter; litre, liter; louvre, louver; lustre, luster; manoeuvre, maneuver; mitre, miter; nitre, niter; ochre, ocher; reconnoitre, reconnoiter; spectre, specter; theatre, theater.* The contrast is, however, not totally systematic. For one thing, words such as *acre, involucre, lucre, massacre, mediocre, nacre,* and *ogre* are so spelt in both forms of English: the presence of *-er* would turn the preceding *c* or *g* into a 'soft' variety. Moreover there is a group of words that are always spelt with final *-re* in America as in Britain: e.g. *antre* (cave, cavern), *cadre, double entendre, euchre, oeuvre.* And some American publications opt for *-re* spellings in at least some words: e.g. *Through his sombre eyes, the pharmacist examined her face—New Yorker,* 24 Dec. 1990. One important distinction: BrE distinguishes poetic *metre* and *metre* used as the unit of length from the electricity, gas, and parking *meter*; in AmE the only spelling used for each of these is *meter.*

rear (verb). See RAISE, REAR.

rearing to do. See RARING TO DO.

rearward(s). As adjective and noun always *rearward* (*a rearward view; to the* *rearward of the castle*). As adverb both forms are used (*to move obliquely rearward; the unfit were taken out of the front line and moved rearwards*).

reason. Various studies of the construction *the reason*...(*is*) *because* leave no doubt about its frequency, especially in contexts where several words or a clause separate the two elements, and particularly in the work of illustrious 17c. and 18c. writers (Pepys, Wycherly, Pope, etc.). In the 20c. the construction appeared with unquestionable frequency all over the English-speaking world in many kinds of writing (letters and novels by Robert Frost, P. G. Wodehouse, Ernest Hemingway, William Faulkner, etc.). Some further modern examples: *The only reason an individual is a suspect in a crime is because he's probably guilty*—letter in *Chicago Tribune*, 1988; (with *why* intervening) *the reason why she painted so many flower pieces in the early Thirties was because she was at the time having an affair with Constance Spry*—J. R. Taylor, *Times*, 1988; *Part of the reason that I don't feel any need to break out of romantic fiction, is because I know I can if I want to*—*More* (NZ), 1988; (straightforward examples of *the reason* ... *is because*) *The reason I wrote the check is because I was the only one who could sign it, because the account was in my name*—*Daily Northwestern* (Evanston, Illinois), 1989; *The reason for this was because the director wished to create an atmosphere of gritty realism*—B. Elton, 1991; *The reason I like The Beatles is because they remind me of Chuck Berry*—Q, 1991. Despite repeated criticisms since the 18c. of these constructions on grounds either of logic or grammar, they are well established. To substitute *that* in the examples above, while it would content the grammarians, would in many cases sound less natural.

See also BECAUSE B.

reason why. 1 As verb, *reason* 'to question, discuss' has frequently been followed by an object clause led by *what, why*, etc., or with *why* absolutely, since the 16c., most famously in Tennyson's poem 'The Charge of the Light Brigade' (1855), *Their's* [*sic*] *not to reason why, Their's but to do and die.*

2 As noun, *reason* has been idiomatically construed with *why* at the head of a subordinate clause since the 13c. (*Ancrene Riwle*). Typical examples: *Aske me no reason why I loue you*—Shakespeare, 1598; *Is there any reason in you ... why I sh^d respect you any more than the very Ethiopians?*—Bishop Hall, 1633. The construction remains valid in the 21c., e.g. *It is well established in international law that obligations cannot be imposed upon a State without its consent. There is no reason why this principle ... should not also be applied to unilateral declarations*—*Max Planck Encycl. of Public International Law*, 2007; *The first and most obvious reason why those in management care about the stock market is that they typically have a monetary interest in the company*—*Investopedia*, 2003. But the border into redundancy is crossed, which produces patently poor style, if *reason, why*, and *because* all form part of the same sentence, especially in close succession, as in the first following example: *The* reason why *everyone is doing it is* because *it's getting ratings*—CNN (transcripts), 2000; *The* reason *I wrote about it then was* that *it was what was going on at the time, and the* reason, *I think*, why *I write about the war now is* because *it isn't what is going on at the time*— F. Wyndham, *London Rev. Bks*, 1988. Replace *because* by *that* in both cases.

rebate (carpentry). If the BrE spelling *rebate* is used, pronounce it /ˈriːbeɪt/. The spelling *rabbet* is pronounced /ˈrabət/.

rebec (musical instrument) /ˈriːbɛk/. So spelt, not *rebeck*.

rebel. 1 The noun is stressed on the first syllable and the verb on the second. See NOUN AND VERB ACCENT 1.

2 The inflected forms of the verb are *rebelled, rebelling*. See -LL-, -L-.

rebound, redound. 1 *Rebound* is pronounced with the stress on the first syllable as a noun (e.g. *on the rebound*) and with the stress on the second syllable as a verb.

2 The image with the verb *rebound* is of something bouncing back, and with *redound* it is of a tide or wave flooding back (from Latin *redundāre* 'surge', from *re(d)-* 'again' + *unda* 'a wave'). When circumstances *rebound on* someone they have a harmful effect on the person responsible for them: *The allegation may rebound on the party making it*—J. Kendall, 1992. In some uses, however, the *rebounding* can be directed elsewhere: *The strategy of encouraging, supporting and protecting deliberate non-payers is deeply flawed, as it* *will rebound on the most vulnerable—Marxism Today*, 1990. When a circumstance *redounds to* someone's advantage or credit, it contributes to it: *Each piece of field research aims at achieving a 'scoop' which will redound to the anthropologist's credit*—I. M. Lewis, 1992; *Some of these* [*sc.* ideas] *have implications for the growth of tourism, which will redound to the benefit of all states—Montserrat Reporter*, 2004. Contrary examples of both words occur occasionally (*The moderate majority of Turks must realise it will rebound to their credit if they show magnanimity—Independent on Sunday*, 2006), but the distinction between the notions of harm (*rebound on*) and advantage (*redound to*) generally holds good and is worth observing.

rebus (a puzzle) /ˈriːbəs/. Plural *rebuses*. See -US 5.

rebut. The inflected forms are *rebutted, rebutting*. See -T-, -TT-.

receipt, recipe. From the 14c. until shortly after the end of the 19c. *receipt* (from Anglo-French *receite*, from Latin *recepta*, feminine past participle of *recipere* 'to receive') was a formula or prescription of the ingredients needed for some preparation, especially in medicine and cookery (e.g. *I have put up two bottles of the gillyflower water for Mrs. Sedley, and the receipt for making it, in Amelia's box*—Thackeray, 1847/8). From about 1400, *receipt* was also used to mean 'an amount of money received', and from the beginning of the 17c. 'a written acknowledgement of money received (i.e. one of its main current senses). Meanwhile *recipe* (from Latin *recipe* 'take', 2nd person singular imperative of *recipere* 'to receive') from the late 16c. meant a formula for a medical prescription, and from the early 18c. a statement of the ingredients and procedures needed for the preparation of a dish in cookery. The overlapping of spellings and meanings came to an end in the 20c. At some point after the 1920s, *receipt* became almost entirely restricted to its two main current senses (the act or an instance of receiving something; an acknowledgement of money received), while *recipe* now means principally a formula for preparing food, and transferred applications (*a recipe for disaster*, etc.). Keep in mind when reading Victorian or earlier literature that *receipt* and *recipe* are liable to turn up in a confusing manner in any of the present-day senses of each word. *Receipt* is, of course, pronounced /rɪˈsiːt/ and *recipe* /ˈrɛsɪpɪ/.

receive. A key word supporting the simple rule of spelling '*i* before *e* except after *c*'. See I BEFORE E.

received pronunciation. See RP.

recess (noun and verb). The *OED* (1904) gave only /rɪˈses/ as the pronunciation of both, i.e. with the stress on the second syllable, and this remains the dominant pattern, but /ˈriːsɛs/, which is the standard AmE, is being increasingly used for the noun.

recessive accent. Fowler's term (1926) for a process that is mostly of historical interest. **1** *Definition.* The term is defined by the *OED* as 'stress transferred towards or on to the first syllable of a word'. It should be borne in mind that English is a Germanic language, and that 'the primitive Germanic language developed a stress accent which fell upon the first syllable of all words . . . Thus in Old English we find the stress on the first syllable of all simple words, and in most compound words: *wórd* word, *stā́nas* stones, *lúfiende* loving, *sī́þfæt* journey, *ándġiet* sense . . . '(A. Campbell, *Old English Grammar*, 1959). This simple 'rule', however, has to be modified because OE nouns and verbs formed from prepositional adverbs prefixed to the stem came to have different stress patterns, the nouns being stressed on the first syllable and the corresponding verbs on the second. Examples of such doublets: *ándsaca* 'apostate', *onsácan* 'to deny'; *bī́genga* 'inhabitant', *begā́n* 'to occupy'.

2 *Historical examples.* In practice the accentual patterns of OE words are more complicated than these two 'rules' would indicate. But the essential point about the *recessive accent* is that, from the Norman period onwards, the large contingents of French, Latin, and Greek words that poured into the language became subject to the accentual rules of the receiving language. For example, the accent in French loanwords tended to move towards the first syllable. In Chaucer's General Prologue, the metre shows that *natúare* and *coráge* were stressed on the second syllable: *So priketh hem nature in hir corages.* But these two words, and many others (e.g. *château, garage, menu, plateau, tableau,* *village; charlatan, nonchalant*) are now stressed on the first syllable.

See also RECONDITE.

3 *Stable patterns.* At the present time the stress patterns of the majority of English words drawn from French, Latin, or Greek, as well as those of native origin, are relatively stable, but they are not simple. Some two-syllabled words are stressed on the first syllable (*ínvoice, wíndow*) and others on the second (*alóne, arríve*). Similarly with three-syllabled words: (first syllable) *báchelor, quántity*; (second syllable) *eléven, impórtant*; (third syllable) *magazíne, understánd*. There are four types of four-syllabled words: (first syllable) *cáterpillar*; (second) *rhinóceros, unfórtunate*; (third) *circulátion, diplomátic*; (fourth) *aquamaríne, misunderstánd*. The complications in longer words are even more marked, with a goodly proportion of them having secondary stresses as well as primary stresses: e.g. *in,feri'ority, ,indis'tinguishable, im,penetra'bility*. Moreover, many of these patterns are true only when the words are pronounced in isolation. The stress is often moved in the rhythmic pattern of particular contexts: thus *,thir'teen, but 'thir,teen steps*; *,after'noon*, but *'after,noon tea*.

4 *Unstable accents.* In a number of words two conflicting tendencies have been or are being shown over recent years. In one group the accent has moved or is moving (sometimes only in qualified circumstances) in a recessive manner, that is to say, backwards. In the second group the movement is, in contrast, forwards. The following table numbers syllables from left to right, as it were, 1 being the first syllable, 2 the second.

Many of these words are treated at their alphabetical place in the dictionary. The list is far from complete but from the examples listed it looks as if the recessive process is less common than the opposite one.

recessive		
cervical	2→1	
contribute	2→1	
distribute	2→1	
doctrinal	2→1	(AmE)
laboratory	2→1	(AmE)
subsidence	2→1	
progressive		
applicable	1→2	
aristocrat	1→2	increasingly in UK
centrifugal	2→3	
clematis	1→2	
communal	1→2	increasingly in UK
controversy	1→2	
decade	1→2	
despicable	1→2	now standard BrE
disciplinary	1→3	
exquisite	1→2	
formidable	1→2	now standard BrE
harass	1→2	now standard BrE
hospitable	1→2	now standard BrE
integral	1→2	(AmE)
lamentable	1→2	

réchauffé. The two French accented letters should be retained and the word printed in italics, for this noun, meaning a dish of warmed-up food left over from a previous meal, and its related adjective. The word comes from French *réchauffer* 'to reheat', and is occasionally applied metaphorically to something that is rehashed or derivative, e.g. *Set in a recognisable contemporary Ireland, and played with an impressively straight face, Stew comes heavily wreathed in the* réchauffé *aromas of British TV sketch soups—Sunday Times*, 2004.

recherché. The word is more acclimatized than *réchauffé* and is normally printed in roman type, but with the French accent on the letter *e* retained.

recidivist Pronounced /rɪ'sɪdɪvɪst/.

recipe. See RECEIPT.

reciprocal (grammar). *Each other* and *one another* are reciprocal pronouns, but they have limitations of use. Thus *Each could see the other in the distance* is idiomatic, and so is *They could see each other in the distance*, but the notional passive equivalent **Each other could be seen in the distance* is not. Both reciprocal pronouns may be used as possessives. Note the position of the apostrophe: e.g. *They got in each other's way*; *The prisoners stole one another's cigarettes*. See EACH 4.

reciprocal, mutual. What follows largely reproduces Fowler's 1926 entry. It is worth struggling through its slightly antiquated prose style to achieve a sort of miniature enlightenment. 'To the difficulties presented by MUTUAL itself must be added that of the difference between it and *reciprocal*. *Mutual* regards the relation from both sides at once: *the mutual hatred of A and B*; never from one side only: *not B's mutual hatred of A*. Where *mutual* is correct, *reciprocal* would be so too: *the* *reciprocal hatred of A and B*; but *mutual* is usually preferred when it is possible. *Reciprocal* can also be applied to the second party's share alone: *B's reciprocal hatred of A. Reciprocal* is therefore often useful to supply the deficiencies of *mutual*. A, having served B, can say 'Now may I ask for a reciprocal [but not for a mutual] service?' Two parties can take mutual or reciprocal action, and the meaning is the same; one party can take reciprocal, but not mutual, action. *Mr Wilson said: 'I trust your Government saw in the warmth of the greetings accorded to his Royal Highness the manifestation of friendly goodwill which the people of the United States hold for those of Britain. Believing in* the reciprocal friendship of the British people *it will be my aim in the future to* ...' In this passage, *mutual* could not be substituted for the correct *reciprocal*; if, however, the words had been not 'of the British people', but 'of the two peoples', *mutual* would have been as good as *reciprocal*, or indeed better. But it must be added that, since it takes two to make a friendship, which is essentially a mutual or reciprocal relation, to use either adjective is waste.'

recitative Pronounced /ˌrɛsɪtəˈtiːv/.

reckon. 1 The inflected forms are *reckoned, reckoning*. See -N-, -NN-.

2 In 1992, in a conversation with an American, Burchfield used *reckon* to mean 'consider, think, be of the opinion' with *that* (in fact he omitted the *that*) before a reporting clause (the sentence was of the type *I reckon it's time to go now*). The American rejected the use as 'cowboy English', which Burchfield took to mean countrified or regional (American) English. He would have said *I guess* or *I think* himself. Burchfield went into the matter and it seems that the construction was in formal literary use in England from the early 16c. onwards, e.g. *Men woulde not recon that hee coulde haue right to the realme*—More, 1513; *For I reckon, that the sufferings of this present time, are not worthy to be compared with the glory which shall be reuealed in vs*—Rom. (AV) 8: 18, 1611. Its literary use seems to have persisted in Britain until the late 19c., e.g. *I reckon, said Socrates, that no one ... could accuse me of idle talking*—Jowett, 1875. With the omission of the relative pronoun *that*, it seems since then to have dropped a rung and become just part of the spoken language in Britain (*ODO* labels the use 'informal', but other British dictionaries list the meaning without a restrictive label), in the Antipodes (the Macquarie dictionary labels it 'colloquial') and in certain parts of the US (especially southern and midland States; Merriam-Webster labels the use 'chiefly dialect'). Some representative examples: *I don't reckon I've had a fare there for more than ten years*—I. Shaw, 1977 (UK); *I reckon he couldn't have been more than eighteen*—M. du Plessis, 1989 (SAfr.); *They* [*sc.* his students] *all reckon he's pretty amazing*—S. Johnson, 1990 (Aust.); *D'y'reckon it's still breathing?*—B. Anderson, 1992 (NZ). The sharp drop in formality between the 16–19c. examples and the 20c. ones is very noticeable. *Reckon* in this sense seems to be a rollercoaster word with many ups and downs in status in the 20c. and more likely to come.

reclaim (verb). The main derivatives are **reclaimable** and **reclaimer**, but **reclamation**.

recognizance. Stressed on the second syllable, /rɪˈkɒgnɪzəns/. Less frequently, also spelt **recognisance** in BrE.

recollect, remember. 1 First, *recollect*, pronounced /ˌrɛkəˈlɛkt/, 'to remember' is to be distinguished from **re-collect** (with hyphen), pronounced /ˌriːkəˈlɛkt/ 'to collect again', though the two words have the same origin. See RE(-).

2 In most contexts *recollect* means 'to succeed in remembering', and implies a search in the memory or the recalling of something temporarily forgotten. But the distinction is not an absolute one, and it shares with *remember* much of the territory of the ordinary sense 'to call or bring back to one's mind'.

recommend. Traditional constructions of this transitive verb include those shown in the following types: (*a*) (with direct object) *He recommended Miss Jones for promotion.* (*b*) (in the passive + a *to*-infinitive) *The committee is being recommended to approve the proposals.* (*c*) (followed by a *that*-clause: with *should*) *I recommend that you should stay at the George and Dragon*; (with a subjunctive in the dependent clause) *If you go looking for her, I don't think I can recommend you attend*—N. Shakespeare, 1989; *One of the observers from the International Commission of Jurists ... had recommended she be approached*—

N. Gordimer, 1990; *Under a plea agreement, both sides recommended that he serve 27 to 33 months in prison—NYT,* 2010. (*d*) less frequently, (ditransitive) *Let me recommend you a little of this pike!*—Disraeli, 1826; *Can you recommend me a nice hotel?—Times,* 1985.

recondite. The recommended pronunciation is that with the stress on the first syllable, i.e. /ˈrɛkəndʌɪt/. But traces of an old dispute have been transmitted down the ages, leaving second-syllable stressing as a possible alternative, /rɪˈkɒn-/. That sides were being taken as early as the 18c. is shown in the following extract from Walker's *Pronouncing Dict.* (1791): 'Dr. Johnson, Dr. Ash, Dr. Kenrick, Mr. Nares, Mr. Scott, Mr. Fry, and Entick, accent this word on the second syllable; Mr. Sheridan and Bailey on the last ... A few words of three syllables from the Latin, when anglicised, without altering the number of syllables, have the accent on the same syllable as in the Latin, as *Opponent, Deponent,* &c.; but the general inclination of our language is to place the accent on the first syllable, as in *Manducate, Indagate,* &c.'

reconnaissance. Now completely anglicized, i.e. /riˈkɒnɪsəns/.

reconnoitre. So spelt in BrE, but **reconnoiter** in AmE.

record. The noun is stressed on the first syllable and the verb on the second. See NOUN AND VERB ACCENT 1.

recount /rɪˈkaʊnt/, to narrate, is to be distinguished from *re-count* (noun) /ˈriːkaʊnt/, a counting again, and *re-count* (verb) /riːˈkaʊnt/, to count again.

recourse. See RESORT.

recover, re-cover, recreation, re-creation. See RE(-).

recriminatory (adjective). Pronounced /rɪˈkrɪmɪnətəri/.

recrudescence, ultimately from the classical Latin verb *recrūdēscere,* of wounds 'to break open afresh', and of sedition, fighting, etc., 'to break out again'. In its original medical use in English it meant 'the breaking out again of a disease, etc., after a dormant period', e.g. *For a few hours after there was a recrudescence and exacerbation of all the foresaid Symptoms*—G. Thomson, 1665. In transferred uses it was for a long time restricted to contexts in which some undesirable or unwanted setback or circumstance has occurred. The Fowler brothers (1906) noted its journalistic use outside these bounds, and in the first edition (1926) of this book Fowler fulminated against its application to the recurrence of something agreeable or neutral, calling it 'disgusting'. However, his disgust has not prevented this rather infrequent and literary word also being applied to facts and events viewed as neutral or even beneficial, as the *OED* recognizes, although it is rather more often applied to what is considered undesirable. Examples: *But now there has been a recrudescence of violence—The Australian,* 2004; *That apart it is at least possible that any recrudescence of Kurdish nationalism following the liberation of Iraq might place the Turkish government under an obligation to protect its own interests in the north—Contemporary Rev.,* 2002; *One reaction has been the recrudescence of earlier notions of social justice, with those drawing on the Catholic and left traditions coming together—OEC,* 2001.

recto. 1 Plural *rectos.* See -O(E)S 4.

2 See VERSO, RECTO.

rector. In the Church of England the incumbent of a parish where all tithes formerly passed to the incumbent, as compared with a vicar, an incumbent of a parish where tithes formerly passed to a chapter or religious house or layman. Since the passing of the Tithe Act 1936 tithes have no longer been payable to any parish priest, but the designation *rector* is preserved where it previously existed; in all other parishes the incumbent is a *vicar. Rector* has a different meaning in some other churches; and the word is also used for the head of some schools (especially in Scotland), universities, and colleges.

recur /rɪˈkəː/ (verb). **1** The inflected forms are *recurred, recurring.* See -R-, -RR-.

2 The stressed vowel in *recurred* and *recurring* is pronounced /əː/, but in *recurrence, recurrent* it is /ʌ/.

recusancy, recusance. *Recusancy* is the form generally used (stressed on the first syllable).

reddle. See RUDDLE.

Red Indian, redskin. These terms have fallen into disuse, being considered racially offensive, in favour of *Native American.*

redingote is an interesting example of lexical Channel-hopping between Britain and France. It is an early 18c. French corruption of English *riding-coat,* which was brought back into English before the end of the 18c. as a term for various fashionable coats.

reduce (verb). **1** The corresponding adjective is **reducible**. See -ABLE, -IBLE 8.

2 After *reduce to* and *be reduced to* the gerund, not the infinitive, is idiomatic: e.g. *He was reduced to retracting* (not *to retract*) *his statement.*

reductio ad absurdum. 'A method of proving the falsity of a premise by showing that the logical consequence is absurd; an instance of this' (*COD*). A *reductio ad absurdum* of the theory that the less one eats the healthier one is would be 'Consequently, to eat nothing at all gives one the best possible health.' It is a not uncommon mistake to write the last word as **absurdam.* Printed in italics.

redundancy. Actual or concealed redundancy, in the sense of the use of more words than are strictly necessary to convey meaning, occurs with great frequency in English. One type is shown in Muriel Spark's novel *The Only Problem* (1984): '*she is lively and vital enough to be a member of a terrorist gang.' 'Lively and vital,' said Harvey, 'lively and vital—one of these words is redundant.*' Here the redundancy is debatable. More understandable are examples arising from unfamiliarity with the extended form of an acronym or with the mechanics of a foreign language: e.g. *ATM machine* (*ATM* = automated teller machine) *HIV* virus (*HIV* = human immunodeficiency virus); the *hoi polloi* (*hoi* is the Greek definite article); *LCD* display (*LCD* = liquid crystal display); *OPEC* countries (*OPEC* = Organization of Petroleum Exporting Countries); *SALT* talks (*SALT* = Strategic Arms Limitation Talks). Less defensible are phrases such as sworn *affidavits* (an affidavit is a written statement confirmed by oath); and *safe haven* (a haven is a place of refuge, which implies safety).

Careless examples, for which it is hard to find an excuse, are phrases such as *10a.m. in the morning, an armed gunman, a new recruit, RSVP requested,* and *a free gift.* Indefensible redundancy occurs in the following (the words within brackets should have been omitted): *We cannot dodge* (*out from under*) *the social consequences of our actions—Daily Tel.,* 1980; *One should not assume that because a critical mass of women on campus has been reached* (*that*) *their place is in any way guaranteed—Univ. of Chicago Mag.,* 1992.

See PLEONASM.

reduplicated words. The language is saturated with reduplicated words of various kinds. Most of them seem to represent a natural impulse to emphasize by repetition. They are of varying vintages and they illustrate various kinds of word formation. For example, *ding-dong* and *helter-skelter* are first found in print in the 16c., *hocus-pocus* and *hoity-toity* in the 17c., *chin-chin* and *namby-pamby* in the 18c., *argy-bargy* and *bye-bye* in the 19c., and *arty-farty* and *heebie-jeebies* in the 20c. Some of them show reduplication by simple change of the initial consonant(s), e.g. *hanky-panky, harum-scarum, higgledy-piggledy, teeny-weeny.* Others result from a change of vowel in the second element, e.g. *dilly-dally, ding-dong, shilly-shally, tip-top.* Others again simply result from a repetition of the first element, e.g. *bye-bye, chop-chop, puff-puff.* The great majority of them are familiar to most people, but, for example, some of those that occur in Shakespeare's works now properly need to have glosses attached to them, e.g. *And such a deale of skimble scamble stuffe* (nonsensical) (*1 Henry IV*); *In hugger mugger to inter him* (secrecy) (*Hamlet*); *That hugs his kickie wickie heare at home* (beloved wife) (*All's Well*).

re-enforce. See REINFORCE.

reeve (a wading bird). See RUFF.

reeve (verb) (nautical). To thread or fasten a rope. Past tense and past participle either *rove* or *reeved.*

refection (meal). An extremely literary or formal word.

refectory. The recommended pronunciation is with the stress on the second syllable, though in some monasteries the stress is placed on the first.

refer (verb). The inflected forms are *referred, referring.* See -R-, -RR-.

referable. Unlike the inflected forms of the verb *refer,* this adjective is most often spelt with a single *-r-*, in which case it should in theory be pronounced with the stress on the first syllable /ˈrɛfərəbəl/ in order to fit the rule for the doubling of final *r* when a suffix is added. However, most people probably pronounce it stressing the second syllable, whether they spell it *referable* or its much less frequent variant **referrable.** See -ABLE, -IBLE 3(vii); -R-, -RR- 2.

reference (noun). **1** Until quite recently, compendious works of reference were normally called *reference books, works,* etc. Now, especially in publishing houses, the dominant term seems to be *reference* alone: e.g. *His work will long remain a basic reference for anyone working on Titian—TLS,* 1989.

2 Since about the 1920s the word *reference* has become established as the customary word for a (usually written) report produced by a referee; a testimonial.

reference (verb). To *reference* something has a precise technical meaning in the field of bibliography, and a more general one. The technical meaning is 'to provide a book or article with citations for the sources of information mentioned' as in: *each chapter is referenced, citing literature up to 1990.* From this has developed a broader meaning of 'to mention or refer to': *one British Computer Society paper is referenced on page 35 of the White Paper.* Using the word in this somewhat broader way to mean that something is mentioned, often with a precise indication of where it is mentioned, is perfectly legitimate. But using it as a supposedly stylish replacement for the simpler *refer* or *mention,* as in *the media referenced our association in almost 40 articles,* is merely modish, and may well irritate people alert to the nuances of language.

referendum, referring to the electorate on a particular issue. Plural *referendums* rather than *referenda,* though the latter form is widely used. See -UM 3.

refill. The noun is stressed on the first syllable, and the verb on the second.

reflectible. Use *reflexible.*

reflection, reflexion. The etymological spelling with *x* is the earliest (14c., from French *réflexion*), but as the centuries passed it was gradually supplanted by that with *ct,* and is now archaic. See -XION, -XIVE.

reflective, reflexive. These are now not merely variants, but two distinct words. *Reflective* is used to mean principally '(of a surface) giving a reflection or image'; and '(of a person, disposition, etc.) thoughtful, given to meditation'. *Reflexive* is most often a grammatical term exhibited in such pronouns as *I wash* myself *in warm water, he made them* himself, *she* herself *is no angel, he came to the party by* himself, i.e. where the reflexive pronoun and the subject are the same entity. It is also used of an action performed as a reflex, without conscious thought, e.g. *reflexive anti-Americanism.*

reflector. So spelt, not *-er.*

reflexible, capable of being reflected. Not *reflectible.*

reflexive. See REFLECTIVE.

reform, re-form. The verb *reform* (with the stress on the second syllable) means 'to improve by removing faults'. *Re-form* (with hyphen) means 'to form again'. See also RE(-).

refractor. So spelt, not *-er.*

refrangible, that can be refracted, is now the current form, rather than *refractable.*

refrigerator. So spelt, not *-er.*

refuse. The noun is stressed on the first syllable, and the verb on the second. See NOUN AND VERB ACCENT 1.

refutable. Second-syllable stressing, i.e. /rɪˈfjuː-/, in line with the verb, is standard. Cf. IRREFUTABLE.

refutal. A common word 17–19c., *refutal* is now extremely rare, occurring 5 times in the *OEC* to *refutation*'s 1,869.

refute. The traditional meaning (first recorded in the 16c.) is 'to prove (a statement, opinion, allegation, accusation, etc.) to be false; to disprove by argument'. When T. S. Eliot (in *Murder in the Cathedral*) wrote *If you make charges, Then in public I will refute them,* and when Rebecca West wrote *The case against most of them must have been so easily refuted that they could hardly rank as suspects,* both writers could be assured that their use of *refute* was beyond reproach. At some point in the second half of the 20c., however, traditionalists began to notice that people outside an educated social divide were beginning to use *refute* as a simple synonym of *deny*. In 1986 an enraged (and supremely snobbish) person wrote to the letters editor of the *Spectator*: 'In Mr Chancellor's [*sc.* previous Editor of the magazine] day someone who didn't know the difference between "refute" and "deny" wouldn't have been employed by the *Spectator* as an office cleaner, let alone as a television critic.' In the 1980s the police, trade union leaders, and other sternly honest authorities were forever *refuting* (that is, *denying*) allegations of brutality, malpractice, dishonesty, and so on. The skirmishing continues. The likelihood that the new use represents a legitimate semantic shift is rejected by the traditionalists, who insist that it is wrong to use it simply as an alternative for *deny* or *repudiate* (or in some cases *reject* or *dispute*), which imply straightforward rejection without argument, as in *?I refute Mr Bodey's allegation that it is our policy not to observe publication dates* (read *reject*); *?Bernice . . . refuted a magazine report in which her son said he preferred the University of Miami* (*Fla.*) *over the Wildcats* (read *dismissed*). Burchfield wrote: 'Those who have no idea what a semantic shift might be like the sound of *refute*, and will continue to use it in its partially standard new way. I have an uneasy feeling that the new sense will begin to sound normal in the 21c.—but not yet.' He was correct, to the extent that *ODO* and the *OED* both recognize this use, while attaching a suitable caveat to it. As regards its normality, it will sound normal to those who normally use it in this way, and aberrant to those who do not. However, there is one syntactic pattern that will still seem unsettling to many, namely using *refute* to mean *deny* and following it with a *that*-clause, e.g. *While economics professor Fred Gottheil admitted that the nation is experiencing an economic dip, he refuted that the economy is in a recession*—quoted in *Language Log*, 2004.

regalia. In its main sense 'the emblems or insignia of royalty; the crown, sceptre, and other ornaments used at the coronation of a king or queen', *regalia* must always be construed as a plural noun. Since the early 17c. the word has also come to be used (in the plural) in the transferred sense 'the decorations or insignia of an order', i.e. of mayors, Freemasons, senior military officers, etc. Etymologically such transferred uses are inaccurate, but it is too late now to try to dislodge them. A typical example: *I . . . answered a knock on my door only to find a stormtrooper dressed in RSPCA regalia standing there*—letter to the *Spectator*, 1993.

regard. 1 *In complex prepositions.* Despite their obvious wordiness, the complex prepositions (in descending order of frequency) *with regard to, in regard to,* and *as regards,* are often used, in addition to *regarding,* to introduce a statement (e.g. in business letters, beginning *With regard to your letter of 2 May* . . .). In general writing, these complex prepositions can be used at the beginning of a sentence or, more typically, in mid-sentence, e.g. *He also acted as almoner and adviser to Douglas of Cavers with regard to the annual distribution of alms to the poor*—K. M. E. Murray, 1977; *As regards the customer, the bank has to be aware of two main requisites*—*Modern Banking Law*, 2002. The *OED* shows these phrases in older use, e.g. *I speak with regard to sensible things only*—Berkeley, 1713; *In regard to the matter . . . he had, no doubt, been misled*—*Monthly Rev.*, 1792; *The world was believed fixed until . . . it was found to change its place with regard to them*—W. R. Grove, 1842. They are all in standard use, but should be used sparingly and with discretion: sometimes they are merely a turgid, formal-sounding synonym for a simpler preposition, e.g. *Data are lacking, however, with regard to effects of vitamin E on the inflammatory immune response* (read *about*).

2 **with regards to.* Historically, *with regard to* and *in regard to* have varied considerably in form, e.g. *in regard* of, at *regard* of. It is, therefore, possibly unsurprising that the further, still incorrect, variation **with regards to* is now quite widely used, particularly in speech. (In *OEC* data, which is written, *with regard to* in any sentence position is still seven times more frequent.) There is an obvious explanation for the use of **with regards to.* In speech, people do not use the noun *regard* as an independent lexical item in the singular, since it is slightly formal and more typical of the written register. However, the plural *regards,* in the meaning 'best wishes' is used, e.g. *give my regards to Daphne.* Until dictionaries say otherwise, it is best to stick to *with regard to.*

regardless can be used both as an adjective (*A man who had been openly regardless of religious rites*—G. Eliot, 1863) and as a quasi-adverb (*although my voice was cracked and vanishing, . . . I struggled on regardless*—S. Mason, 1990).

regenerate. As a verb pronounced /rɪ'dʒɛnəreɪt/, and as an adjective /rɪ'dʒɛnərət/.

regime. No accent. Printed in roman, except in the phrase *ancien régime,* which requires the accent. Though fully anglicized in spelling, still pronounced in a quasi-French fashion.

regime change is a pair of words that chance might throw together at any time; the earliest occurrence found by the *OED* editors happens to be from 1925, and the phrase was used originally of a peaceful change of government. Events at the start of the 21c. brought it forcibly to our attention and have even given it a deep aura of euphemism, since what it means in practice is the violent overthrow of a foreign government by a power which regards that government as hostile. It therefore joins the stock of politically sanitized expressions alongside *collateral damage, ethnic cleansing,* and others. The phrase is also quite widely used, sometimes somewhat knowingly, outside political contexts, e.g. *Tom Stern says the movie was plagued with budget cuts shortly before it was finished when 20th Century-Fox underwent a regime change*—*DVD Verdict,* 2005 (US); *To make this regime change in our hearts possible, God sent his son Jesus into the world to die, bringing us forgiveness if we trust in him*—*Northern Rivers Echo,* 2003 (Aust.)

regimen. Now mainly restricted to its medical sense, 'a prescribed course of exercise, way of life, and diet'. Some doctors use *regime* instead. Example: *a feeding regimen that takes no account of the baby's needs is likely to be experienced as frustrating*—Dædalus, 1993.

region. For synonymy, see FIELD.

register. 1 The agent noun corresponding to the verb *register* is **registrar**, and in Cambridge University **registrary**.

2 In Britain, **register office** is the official term for 'a State office where civil marriages are conducted and births, marriages, and deaths are recorded with the issue of certificates' (*COD*). The unofficial term **registry office** is also in widespread use.

regnal, regnant. The *-gn-* as in *magnify,* etc., not as French, nor as in *poignant.*

regress. The noun is stressed on the first syllable, i.e. /'riːgrɛs/, and the verb on the second, i.e. /rɪ'grɛs/. See NOUN AND VERB ACCENT 1.

regret (verb). The *t* is doubled in inflected forms (*regretted, regretting*) and in *regrettable.* See -T-, -TT-.

regretful, regrettable. 1 Fowler (1926) cited three examples in which *regretful,* properly meaning 'feeling or showing regret' and applied to people, is misused for *regrettable* 'causing regret', which is applied to actions. One of his examples was *Sir Newton Moore's resignation of the Premiership of Western Australia was a regretful surprise to Australians in London.* Though not common, this muddling of the two still occasionally happens: **Allison worried that her patience with Shirley might one day give out and that she would do something deeply regretful*—M. Carlson, 2011.

2 The adverbs **regretfully** and **regrettably** should be used only in senses corresponding to those of the correct uses of the adjectives. Both adverbs are now being commonly used as SENTENCE ADVERBS, and unfortunately, since the 1960s, *regretfully* has sometimes been used where *regrettably* (= I regret to say, it is a pity that) properly belongs, e.g. ?*Regretfully, that is no ground for leniency towards him*—*New Statesman,* 1976; ?*Regretfully, many measures employed in the social sciences have important limitations that fundamentally affect the findings of the study*—*Child Sexual Abuse,* 2001. Regrettably, the *OED* records this use (first cited from as far back as 1945) with no comment or caveat.

regulable is the recommended form of the adjective (= capable of being regulated) corresponding to *regulate,* not *regulatable.*

regularly. All four syllables should be pronounced, i.e. /'rɛgjʊləːli/, rather than as three syllables, as if the word were spelt 'reguly'.

regulatory. In BrE there seems now to be a slight preference for third-syllable stressing, /rɛgjʊˈleɪtəri/ (reg-yoo-**lay**-) over first-syllable stress /ˈrɛgjʊlətəri/ (**reg**-yoo-luh-), which is given first in Merriam-Webster.

regulus (impure metallic product). Plural either *reguluses* or *reguli* /-ˈlʌɪ/.

reign, rein. The first is to do with royalty (the period during which a sovereign rules, etc.), and the second is a narrow strap used to guide or check a horse or child. The now widespread and incorrect use of *reign* (instead of *rein*) in the phrase *give (free) reign to* is deeply regrettable. Examples: **They say that if they are given free reign to invest and produce they will grow richer—New Yorker*, 1987; **Under these measures, highly productive tenant farmers were given reign to new, independent operations—Dædalus*, 1990. Cf. FREE REIN.

reinforce, re-enforce. The ordinary form (*rein-*) has been so far divorced from the simple verb (formerly *inforce* or *enforce*, now always the latter) that it no longer means to enforce again, as when a lapsed regulation is revived. For that sense *re-enforce* should be used; see RE(-).

reject. The noun is stressed on the first syllable, i.e. /ˈriːdʒɛkt/, and the verb on the second, i.e. /rɪˈdʒɛkt/. See NOUN AND VERB ACCENT 1.

rejoin, re-join. See RE(-). Both in its meaning 'to say in answer, retort' and 'to join again' the verb *rejoin* does not usually need a hyphen. One is required only in contexts where it would otherwise not be clear that the 'join again' meaning is intended.

relate (verb). This long-established word (first recorded in Caxton) has enjoyed a period of great popularity since the second half of the 20c. in a sense derived from the jargon of social workers, namely 'to have an attitude of personal and sympathetic relation to'. Examples: *Group formation such as takes place in the classroom tends to be adult-centered and dependent upon the varying ways children relate to the teacher—Childhood Education*, 1950; *Married people can still relate—Guardian*, 1971; *The best medicine was a person to relate to—Big Issue*, 1998.

-related. This has flourished since the 20c. as the second element of compound adjectives: e.g. *AIDS-related disease; a smoking-related lung problem; oil-related employment.* A hyphen is customary but is not obligatory in all cases: e.g. *vivid sketches linking a child's inattention at school to the gang-and-drug related shoot-outs he witnesses at home—Dædalus*, 1993.

relation, relationship, relative (nouns). Their history as terms of kindred is set out in the *OED*. *Relation* 'a person related to one by blood or marriage' was the first to come on the scene (1502); as an abstract noun meaning modern English 'relationship' it is first recorded *c.*1485. *Relative*, as a term of kinship, is first recorded in 1650. *Relationship* in its normal present-day sense 'the fact or state of being related' is first recorded in 1724, and shortly after in Pope's *Dunciad*, (*a*1744).

2 In their meaning 'a person related by blood or by marriage' *relation* and *relative* are both idiomatic in the plural. For some reason, however, *relation* is the normal choice in the explicit context of wealth: *He resented... the mother who had inconsiderately died and left him a poor relation—*J. Symons, 1978. The state of a person's connection with relations or relatives is his or her *relationship*, which is also used in the wider context of people's dealings with one another: *How difficult and unnatural are in-law relationships!—Daily Tel.*, 1970; *You need to consider the quality of the relationship which exists between your son and the teachers, your son and his peers, and between you and the teachers—Where*, 1972. In modern use, *relationship* has a sexual connotation which should always be borne in mind when using this word: *She can't forgive me for leaving and I've had to accept that our relationship's finally over—Woman*, 1991. Consequently, *relation* is often preferred to denote the way things (especially concepts and ideas) relate to each other: *It's now apparent that there's a positive relation between body mass index and the risk of acute coronary events in people with known coronary artery disease—BMJ*, 2003. It is also the normal choice in meanings to do with activities and procedures, as in *business relations*, and is the only choice in fixed expressions such as *in relation to* and *bear some* (or *no* etc.) *relation to*. The plural form *relations* typically has political connotations, as in *good relations, diplomatic relations, foreign relations*, etc.

relative clause, a subordinate clause that is attached to a main clause by a relative pronoun or adverb (*that, which, who,* etc.), e.g. *This is the house* that Jack built.

relatively. Like COMPARATIVELY, *relatively* has been in standard use before a following adjective since the early 19c. as a 'downtoning' adverb meaning 'fairly, somewhat', without any real notion of relativity or comparison, e.g. *Justice... denied to the relatively poor* (1825); *worth the relatively small sum... paid for them* (1884); *The natural question to pursue is whether the Chinese state has been able to maintain control in this relatively open geopolitical region—Dædalus,* 1993.

relative pronouns. See the separate words: THAT; WHAT; WHICH; WHO; WHOM; WHOSE. See also OMISSION OF RELATIVES.

relay, re-lay. It is necessary to distinguish *relay* /ˈriːleɪ/, /rɪˈleɪ/ 'to receive (a message, broadcast, etc.) and transmit it to others' (past tense and past participle *relayed*) from *re-lay* /riːˈleɪ/ 'to lay again' (past tense and past participle *relaid*). See RE(-).

relevance, first recorded in the 18c., is far more frequent than the older form **relevancy**, (16c.), which seems to flourish more in North American English than elsewhere. Examples: (relevance) *Though the facts of Rembrandt's education and training are well-known, their relevance to his approach to self-portraiture has not been considered*—H. P. Chapman, 1990; *My primary criticism is that the relevance of the volumes to L2 acquisition and language pedagogy is not emphasized—Language in Society,* 1991. (relevancy) *We understand what the search engines really mean when they tout their size, freshness, or relevancy—Online* (magazine), 2003.

reliable. It will come as a surprise to many that, according to the *OED* (1908), this word (and by inference also **reliability**), though first recorded in 1569, came into common use only from about 1850, and at first perhaps occurred more frequently in American works than in British ones. It is now, of course, in standard use everywhere, as is also *reliability*. Earlier objection to the word was based on the belief that *reliable* ought to mean 'able to rely' rather than 'able to be relied on'. As Alford (1864) expressed it: '*Reliable* is hardly legitimate. We do not *rely a man,* we *rely upon a man*; so that *reliable* does duty for *rely-upon-able*. "*Trustworthy*" does all the work required.'

relict /ˈrɛlɪkt/ now has only technical senses in geology and ecology and, archaically, the meaning 'widow' (followed by *of*), by contrast with **relic**, which has a wide range of meanings (a surviving custom, part of a deceased saint's body, etc.).

relievo /rɪˈliːvəʊ/. Also in the Italian spelling *rilievo* /riːˈljeɪvəʊ/. Plural *-os.* Cf. BAS-RELIEF.

religious. For *dim religious light,* see IRRELEVANT ALLUSION.

remain. 1 Fowler (1926) rightly rejected as 'a ridiculous tautology' the phrase *continue to remain.* He judged it to be 'surprisingly common', and cited three examples, presumably from newspapers of his day, of which the following are two: *And yet through it all I continue to remain cheerful; It is expected that very soon order will be restored, although the people continue to remain restive.* He would be horrified to learn that the ridiculousness continues to this day in phrases such as the following: *The report also focused on why the relationship will continue to remain mutually beneficial for both countries; While the US will continue to remain a hotspot for Indian professionals, Russia, Germany, France and the Netherlands will also become important destinations.* If one substitutes *be* for *remain* there is nothing objectionable in such sentences, which suggests that *remain* has lost any dynamic quality and is acting as a kind of intensive form of *be,* as in the letter formulas discussed next.

2 *I remain.* As part of the concluding formula of a letter, *I remain* was in frequent use from about 1600 to some point in the 20c., but now is rarely encountered. Examples: *I will ever remain Your assured friend Charles Percy* (1600); *I remain, my dear friend, Affectionately yours, WC.*—Cowper, 1793; *Here is my letter done, and I remaining yours always sincerely, E.F.G.*—E. FitzGerald, 1873.

remember. See RECOLLECT 2.

reminisce (verb) is a back-formation (first recorded in 1829) from the noun *reminiscence.*

remise. As verb and noun in law and in fencing, pronounced /rɪˈmiːz/ according to *COD* and the *New SOED,* but as /rɪˈmʌɪz/

according to some other dictionaries, especially American ones.

remit. 1 The inflected forms of the verb are *remitted, remitting,* and the verb is stressed on the second syllable. The related adjective meaning 'able to be remitted' is either **remissible** or **remittable**, with different meanings.

2 *Remit* (noun), 'the task or area of activity officially assigned to an individual or organization' or an item submitted for consideration at a conference, etc., is pronounced either as /ˈriːmɪt/ or /rɪˈmɪt/ in Britain, but generally as /ˈriːmɪt/ elsewhere. See NOUN AND VERB ACCENT.

3 Of the related nouns, **remittance** is right for the sending of money, **remittal** for referring a case from one court to another, and **remission** for all other senses.

remonetize. Pronounced /riːˈmʌnɪtʌɪz/.

remonstrate (verb). The only pronunciation given in the *OED* (1908) was that showing the stress on the second syllable, but it is now always pronounced /ˈrɛmənstreɪt/, i.e. stressed on the first syllable. The corresponding noun **remonstrance** is stressed on the second syllable.

remunerate, remuneration are more formal words than *pay* and *payment* and are chiefly used of the higher salaries in business firms. To be avoided at all costs is the metathesized form *renumeration* (for *remuneration*): it occurred, for example, of all unfortunate places, in the 25 Aug. 1992 issue of *The Times* in an advertisement for the vacant post of General Secretary of the Association of University Teachers. Let it never be said that educational standards are slipping.

Renaissance (with a capital *R*) is the customary word for '(the period of) the revival of art and literature under the influence of classical models in the 14c.–16c.' With a small *r* it is used both of artistic and of other kinds of revival, e.g. *the remarkable renaissance of the once moribund Russian oil industry.* The anglicized form **Renascence** (or *r-*) is an infrequent variant used in the same meanings.

rendezvous /ˈrɒndeɪvuː/, /-dɪvuː/. The plural is the same, but pronounced /-vuːz/. As verb the inflected forms are *rendezvouses* /-vuːz/, *rendezvoused* /-vuːd/, and *rendezvousing* /-vuːɪŋ/.

renegade is now the only current form of the word, but *renegado* (the Spanish original) will still be encountered in historical novels.

renouncement, renunciation. From the beginning (*renouncement* 15c., *renunciation* 14c.) the second of the two words has been dominant, and *renouncement,* not having developed an independent meaning (cf. *pronouncement* and *pronunciation*), is now rarely used.

rep (textile fabric). This spelling is recommended, not *repp* or *reps*: the French original is spelt *reps,* pronounced /rɛps/.

repa(i)rable. *Reparable* /ˈrɛpərɛbəl/ is used almost only of abstracts such as *loss, injury, mistake,* which are to be made up for or to have their effects neutralized; *repairable* sometimes is used in that way also, but chiefly of material things that need mending. The negatives are *irreparable,* but *unrepairable.* See IN- AND UN-.

repeat (noun). The use of *repeat* to mean 'the repetition of a radio or television programme which has already been broadcast', and its attributive use in compounds such as *repeat fee, repeat performance,* have tended to give additional prominence to the word *repeat* and slightly less prominence to *repetition.* As a result there has emerged a marked tendency to use *repeat* where formerly *repetition* would have been the automatic choice even in the meaning 'the act of repeating' (as distinct from 'a thing repeated'), which is the meaning historically more closely associated with *repetition* than with *repeat*: *Rare sturgeon valued at £670 were stolen from Syon Park last weekend, in a repeat of robberies committed last year—Croydon Guardian,* 2003. *Repeat* is also common in attributive position in medical contexts, with the meaning 'further or repeated': *Strangely, it was decided that a repeat investigation was not required and I was allowed to go on caring for the patient throughout her stay—*A. Morton-Cooper, 1990.

repel (verb). The inflected forms are *repelled, repelling.* See -LL-, -L-.

repellent, repellant. The first of these is recommended for all senses, as noun or adjective.

repellent, repulsive. *Repulsive* is the stronger of the two words, implying physical recoiling rather than just a feeling of disgust: *I was given some repulsive food which, by the end of the second day, I trained myself to eat*—B. Aldiss, 1991; *It's hard to imagine a more repellent group of people*—*Sunday Herald*, 2000.

repertoire, repertory are in origin the same word, being the French and English equivalents of Latin *repertōrium* 'an inventory, a catalogue'. Both can refer to 'the stock of dramatic or musical pieces which a company or player knows or is prepared to perform', and to 'the whole body of items that are regularly performed', e.g. *classical, operatic, orchestral, varied repertoire*, but in both those meanings *repertoire* is rather more frequently used. In the extended use, 'a stock of skills or types of behaviour that a person habitually uses', *repertoire* is far and away the more frequent and natural choice, e.g. *repertoire of moves, techniques, dishes, jokes, skills, anecdotes*, etc. *Repertory*, besides having those meanings, is also specifically a type of theatrical organization in which the plays performed by a company are changed at regular short intervals: hence *repertory company, player, theatre*, etc., and the abbreviated form *rep.*

repetition.

1 Juxtaposed repetitions of words in different grammatical functions.
2 *The problem is is*; *The important thing is is*, etc.
3 Repetition for rhetorical effect.
4 Undesirable repetition.

1 *Juxtaposed repetition of words in different grammatical functions.* (*a*) Chance repetition of words is a natural feature of English. Sometimes it happens because the repeated words are just part of the ordinary way in which verbs work: e.g. *Of course he too had had a choice and still had one*—I. Murdoch, 1989; *The way in which we do do such things*—BBC Radio 4, 1990. At other times it occurs because the same word is used twice with different functions: e.g. *The heart wasn't beating... Whoever he was, the chap had had it*—M. Innes, 1956; *She brings with her her daughter Elizabeth-Jane*—M. Drabble, 1985; *They're all married, said her mother. Not that that would bother most people nowadays*—P. Lively, 1989; *such publicity as there was was left to the chairman and senior editors*—P. Howard, 1990; *He's out back in the darkroom. He'll be in in a minute*—N. Virtue, 1990. The phenomenon is not new: *Harry could forgive her her birth*—G. Meredith, 1861. Nor, of course, is it restricted to BrE sources: *the front page* [of the newspaper] *was missing and all there was was columnists and the lifestyle section*—G. Keillor, 1990 (US).

(*b*) Any awkwardness residing in such repetitions is normally passed over as something that is inevitable and unavoidable. If there is any question of loss of clarity a comma is inserted between the repeated words: e.g. *And while we're at it, it wasn't me with the fedora at Bea's sweet-sixteen*—M. Richler, 1980. In spoken English, in such slightly convoluted circumstances, a pause is often inserted between the repeated words: e.g. *We are getting people who had a right to be out* [pause] *out*—W. Waldegrave, BBC 1 News, 1990. Jespersen's *Modern English Grammar* draws attention to a spectacular example of word repetition in Addison's *Spectator* (May 1711). In reply to an article about the increasing use of *that* for *which* in the early eighteenth century, a pseudonymous writer called 'That' submitted an ironic reply: 'My lords! with humble submission, *That that* I say is this: *that that that that* gentleman has advanced, is not *that, that* he should have said to your Lordships.' It takes a little working out but the meaning comes through.

2 *The problem is is*; *The important thing is is*, etc. (*a*) Back to the twenty-first century. Common or garden repetition has been joined in quite recent times by a remarkable domino-type repetition of *is*, which some would say has become an epidemic. It occurs typically, though not exclusively, in spoken English, and mainly in sentences beginning with 'topic' phrases such as *The problem is, The question is, The thing is*, etc., often with an adjective inserted, e.g. *The amazing/freaky/funny/key* etc. *thing is is.*

(*b*) The American linguistic scholar the late Professor Dwight Bolinger, first consciously noticed the reduplicated use of *is* in a speech by a former president of the Linguistic Society of America as long ago as 1971: *My real feeling is, is that there is...* This example could, one can suppose, have been the result of a momentary hesitation, in other words what is known as a 'production error'. But Bolinger, by then alerted to the construction, noted that it was breaking out everywhere, mostly in radio or television broadcasts, often with no perceptible pause between the first and second uses of *is*: e.g. *The problem is, is that*... (a Californian radio station, 1978); *The other problem is is on the demand side* (as against the supply side) (ditto, 1985). Sometimes the repetition is disguised or deflected by a change of tense, which makes it all the more incongruous: *The strange thing was, is that*... (1981); *Some of the problems in loading the structure was is that*... (1985). As long ago as the 1980s a correspondent from West Yorkshire, Mr James A. Porter, wrote to Burchfield to say that he had encountered this type of construction on the BBC 'scores of times': e.g. *The question is, is if the merger goes ahead, will*...? (David Owen, BBC, 30 August 1987); *But isn't that the problem, is that*... (BBC Radio 4 on a radio call-in with Nick Ross, 6 Nov. 1990). Further BBC examples of that vintage follow, while many readers will no doubt have noted the trend for themselves: *The curious thing about it is that, is*... (Peter Barnes, BBC 1, 29 July 1990); *My message is to the government, is*... (G. Kaufman, BBC 1, 25 Aug. 1990). Luminaries such as President George Bush and President Obama have been criticized for their use of the doppelgänger *is*, or the 'reduplicative copula' as it has been christened by Shapiro and Haley (2002).

(*c*) This 'pleonastic' doubling or repetition of *is* is clearly a marked and possibly permanent feature of modern spoken English. There are even examples of triple *is*. It is noteworthy that in many examples there is no perceptible pause, or 'prosodic boundary' before the second occurrence. A copytaker transcribing double *is* would often, I think, be tempted to insert a comma between the two occurrences or silently omit the second *is* as being otiose or 'a mistake'; the same applies to copy-editors. In view of its frequency, it is impossible to view this construction as a production mistake, or, as Burchfield put it, 'just some kind of unguarded syntactic stuttering'. It is also worth distinguishing between structures of the type *The problem is is*, where genuine reduplication is taking place, and pseudo-cleft sentences (i.e. those beginning with a *wh-* word, generally *what*, introducing a noun clause), where the whole noun clause is the grammatical subject of the second *is*, e.g. *What the question is is if this was simply a blowing over of ground water on the surface and we see a tailing off of seismicity*—*CNN* (transcripts), 2004; *How serious the problem is is less important than how serious it feels to them*—quoted in *Language Log*, 27 June, 2004.

3 *Repetition for rhetorical effect.* Repetition of words and sounds is entirely uncontentious and can be extremely effective in some other circumstances, e.g. (*a*) when done for rhetorical effect: *Looking at the far sandhills, Wiliam Bankes thought of Ramsay: thought of a road in Westmorland, thought of Ramsay striding along a road by himself hung round with that solitude which seemed to be his natural air*—V. Woolf, 1927; *For she could regard me without strong emotion—a familiar shape, a familiar face, a familiar silence*—M. Robinson, 1981; *Long grey iron trains, the compartments jammed with people all the way, long long waits in grey steel-vaulted stations*—S. Bedford, 1989; (*b*) in the type *there are kings and kings*. See AND 5.

4 *Undesirable repetition.* Certain other kinds of (mostly unintentional) repetition are undesirable. For example: (*a*) (awkward repetition of small words such as *of* or *with*, or of terminations such as *-ly*): *it is vital to advise gardeners* of *the importance* of *properly disposing* of *their grass cuttings*; *Taken up* with *warfare* with *an enemy*; *He lived* practically exclusively *on milk*. (*b*) Accidental repetition of the same or a similar-sounding word, e.g. *The Japanese democracy are* affronted *at what they regard as an* affront *to their national dignity*; *The cure for that is clearly the* alternative *vote or the second ballot, the former* alternative *being the more preferable*; *Anonymity seems to be a peculiar delight to writers on naval* matters, *though perhaps necessity has something to do with the* matter; *The features which the* present *Government in this country* presents *in common with representative and responsible government are few and formal*. The moral is simple: read through what you have written before it is committed to print.

repetitional, repetitionary, repetitious, repetitive. Of these four adjectives, first recorded in 1720, 1720, 1675, and 1756 respectively, the first two are, while technically still available for use, now vanishingly rare, while *repetitive* is at least 10 more frequent than *repetitious* in the *OEC*. *Repetitious*, of AmE origin, is used particularly of speech or writing characterized by unnecessary or tiresome repetition: it tends to be a judgement of the performer of the task and implies an avoidable tedium, e.g. *The story is both repetitious and predictable—New York Metro*, 2004. *Repetitive* is often a more objective word and can sometimes mean simply 'occurring repeatedly' (*A quiet but repetitive clicking noise caught his attention—Interesting Times*, 2003) and at others refers to tasks and duties that are unavoidably tedious, e.g. *Brain injury rehabilitation is a slow, repetitive, boring process that plays out over many years of dedicated effort—Psychology Today*, 2001. Consider the neutral use of *repetitive* in *repetitive DNA*, a form of DNA that contains multiple copies of a particular gene in each cell; and *repetitive strain* (or *stress*) *injury* or *RSI*, the name given to a medical condition affecting some individuals after prolonged periods of keyboarding.

replace. The corresponding adjective in *-able* is spelt **replaceable**, not **replacable*.

replenishment, repletion. The first means 'a fresh supply' or the act or process of replenishing'; whereas *repletion* means 'the action or fact or condition of being replete, i.e. filled up, stuffed full, or crowded'. *Repletion* is rather literary, except in medical writing, where it is often used to mean 'the act or process of replenishing', e.g. *The use of selenium repletion in cancer patients to normalize selenoprotein levels—Alternative Medicine Review*, 2004.

replete. The primary sense is 'supplied with in abundance, stuffed with' (*a purse replete with £10 notes*); but, beginning in the 17c. and still, it is sometimes used where *complete* is more appropriate (*a medieval library replete with a chained-Bible table and a few manuscripts*). Quite full and abundantly full (*replete*) are not the same as characteristically containing or supplied with (*complete*). To take another example, *A two-storey retirement home, replete with pool, bar and stuccoed façade—Independent*, 2006. Attractive as these amenities doubtless are, we can safely assume that there is only one of each.

replicate. The word has been in use in various senses (e.g. to reply, to repeat, to fold back) from the 16c. onwards, but it spread its wings in the 20c., especially in various technical senses in biology, computer science, etc., in the broad senses 'to reproduce or give rise to a copy of itself', 'to imitate', and 'to copy exactly'. It is best avoided in non-scientific writing, as it may sound unnecessarily technical when so many general words (*to be modelled on, to imitate, to duplicate, to reproduce, to repeat*, etc.) are available to express the same ideas.

reportage. This French loanword is still only semi-anglicized in pronunciation, /rɛpɔːˈtɑːʒ/, though /rɪˈpɔːtɪdʒ/ is also used. Its older senses 'repute; gossip' have been dropped and now it means 'the reporting of events for the press or for broadcasting, especially with reference to reporting style' (*SOED*), or an instance of this. Examples: *One hard lesson we all learned during the Gulf war of 1991 was that to avoid myopic reportage, we need comprehensive eyewitness journalism—Guardian*, 2003.

reported speech. Direct speech in its printed form is conventionally placed within quotation marks: *'Here I have a suggestion which you might think about, Jane,' said Mr Pickering*—A. Brookner, 1993. Had the same statement been expressed in indirect or reported speech it would have been printed as *Mr Pickering said to Jane that he had a suggestion that she might think about.* A change of tense is often involved in reported speech as well as other minor changes. Thus, the direct speech statement '*I believe you should sell this place and make a move across the river. You will be quite comfortable there.*' (ibid.) would become in reported speech *Mr Pickering said that he believed she should sell her place and make a move across the river. She would be quite comfortable there.*

See also INDIRECT QUESTION.

repp. See REP.

reprimand. Both noun and verb are stressed on the first syllable. The older, third-syllable stressing for the verb, is not incorrect, but is unusual.

reproducible. Spelt *-ible*, as shown.

reps. See REP.

repulsive. See REPELLENT.

reputable. Stressed on the first syllable, /ˈrɛpjʊtəbəl/, unlike the noun **repute**, which is stressed on the second.

reredos. Plural the same. It is pronounced as two syllables in BrE, /ˈrɪədɒs/ (**reeuh**-doss). In AmE it is variously pronounced as /ˈrɛrəˌdɑːs/ (**re**-ruh-daws), /ˈrɪ(ə)rə-/ (**ri**(uh)-ruh-), and /ˈrɪr-/.

rescind (verb). The corresponding noun is **rescission**, pronounced /rɪˈsɪʒən/. **Rescindment** is occasionally found, but Garner calls it 'a needless variant'.

research (noun). Traditionally stressed on the second syllable in BrE and on the first in AmE. But /ˈriːsəːtʃ/ is now increasingly and irritatingly heard also in BrE, although Wells (2008) shows an 80% preference among BrE speakers for first-syllable stressing, rising to 95% among university teachers.

reservedly. Four syllables. See -EDLY.

resignedly. Four syllables. See -EDLY.

resile (verb) /rɪˈzʌɪl/. An uncommon word meaning 'to withdraw from a course of action', e.g. *Bill Cash, unofficial leader of the rebels, told the Commons, 'I will not in any way resile from the objections that I have to the* [Maastricht] *treaty*—newspaper report, 24 July 1993.

resilience, resiliency. The two words are not clearly distinguished in sense, but the first is much the more common of the two. Cf. -CE, -CY.

resist (verb) makes **resistible**. See -ABLE, -IBLE 8.

resistance. *Resistance to* idiomatically governs an *-ing* participle, not an infinitive, i.e. *she put up no resistance to being led away* rather than *There is powerful national resistance to see such assets leave Slovenian control.*

resister, one who resists, contrasted with **resistor**, a device having resistance to the passage of an electrical current.

resoluble, resolvable (capable of being resolved). The first is archaic in the meaning 'capable of being resolved'; instead it is used in AmE to mean 'able to be dissolved again', which would be written hyphenated in BrE. Both are stressed on the second syllable. The corresponding negatives are, in descending order of frequency, *irresolvable* /ɪrɪˈzɒlvəbəl/, *unresolvable*, and the very infrequent *irresoluble* /ɪrɪˈzɒljʊbəl/.

resolution (in prosody). The substitution in a metrical foot of two shorts for a normal long. Thus a spondee – – by resolution becomes a dactyl – ⏑⏑ or anapaest ⏑⏑–.

resolve (verb). See INVOLVE 1.

resolvedly. Four syllables. See -EDLY.

resort, re-sort. The first has a wide range of meanings as noun and verb, and is pronounced /rɪˈzɔːt/. The second means 'to sort again or differently' and is pronounced /riːˈsɔːt/. See RE(-).

resort, resource, recourse. 1 Fowler (1926) cited a number of examples showing confusion in the use of these three: e.g. *She will not be able to do so . . . without resource to the sword* (recourse, resorting, resort); *Surely he was better employed in plying the trades of tinker and smith than in having resource to vice* (recourse). These examples underline Fowler's doggedness in identifying such evidence, but if such confusion still occurs, it is really rather rare: *The current draft Local Plan which takes us up to 2011 shows that our predicted needs can be met without resource to any major greenfield development*—*This is Hampshire*, 2003 (read *without recourse*).

2 The three words all have to do with finding help or support and are usually clearly distinguished from one another by the typical phrase patterns in which they operate: (resort) *as a last resort, in the last resort* (after French *en dernier ressort*); *without resorting to*; *to resort to*; *a holiday resort*; (resource) *a valuable resource*; *without resources*; *at the end of one's resources*; *one's own resources* (one's personal capabilities); *a person of many resources*; (recourse) *to have recourse to*; *one's usual recourse*; *without recourse* (a formula used by the endorser of a bill, etc., to disclaim responsibility for non-payment).

3 In general, *resource* denotes what one adopts for help or support whereas *recourse* denotes a process or avenue of finding support. There is an area of possible confusion in the overlap between *to resort to* (especially in the past, *to have resorted to*) and *to have recourse to*: *More than 100 governments had resorted to torture or the maltreatment of prisoners*—*Keesings*, 1990; *Crazed individuals who wreak appalling* *acts of terror have recourse to the same self-justifying arguments*—*Times*, 2006.

One normally *resorts* to things in extreme circumstances and has *recourse* to them more routinely.

resource. Pronounced slightly more often as /rɪˈzɔːs/ than as /rɪˈsɔːs/. In BrE the stress used always to fall on the second syllable, but recently the favoured AmE first-syllable stressing is, sadly, gaining ground.

respect. The complex prepositions *in respect of, in respect to, with respect to* and the simple preposition (or present participle) *respecting* are all listed in the *OED* with extensive historical evidence from literary works, e.g. *Item, shee is not to be fasting in respect of her breath*—Shakespeare, 1591; *After this, the Colony enjoy'd a perfect Tranquillity with Respect to the Savages*—Defoe, 1719; *He could not agree with him respecting the price*—M. Edgeworth, 1802; *She had struck him, in respect to the beautiful world, as one of the beautiful, the most beautiful things*—H. James, 1904. Despite a certain amount of hostility or discouragement shown by some usage guides, all four expressions have continued in use. Examples: *Any allowance for relief at the higher rate in respect of interest on loans within MIRAS will be withdrawn*—*Financial Times*, 1991; *Miami of today . . . cannot compare to the Milwaukee of 100 years ago in respect to the proportionate numbers of immigrants or their apartness in the larger culture*—*NY Times Bk Rev.*, 1991; *All stressed the need to reaffirm a position within the Labour Party against revisionism, particularly with respect to public ownership*—*Twentieth Century Brit. History*, 1991; *If . . . they are unable to reach any consensus of opinion respecting the things of the mind that ought to form the center of education*—*Jrnl Higher Educ.*, 1999.

respectively is correctly used when the sense required is 'each separately or in turn, and in the order mentioned' (e.g. *Iraq and Syria have been ruled by small minorities* (*Sunni Arabs and Alawite officers respectively*)—*Internat. Affairs*, 1991; *The product is a joint venture by Rudy Rucker, a science fiction writer, and John Walker, who are employed respectively as 'mathenaut' and 'virtual programmer' by the computer-aided design specialist Autodesk Inc.*—*New Scientist*, 1991. Fowler (1926) cited numerous examples in which *respectively* is used tautologically (e.g. *He wants the Secretary for War to tell the House in what countries they are at present stationed, and the numbers in each country respectively* (*each* is adequate) or unintelligibly (e.g. *The writing-room, silence-room, and recreation-room, have respectively blue and red arm-chairs*). He added a comment: 'The simple fact is that *respective* and *respectively* are words seldom needed, but that pretentious writers drag them in at every opportunity for the air of thoroughness and precision they are supposed to give to a sentence.' His comments are sound but their present-day relevance is uncertain.

respite (noun). The *OED* and *ODO* both give precedence to the pronunciation /ˈrɛspʌɪt/ for BrE, with the more old-fashioned /ˈrɛspɪt/ as a variant. In AmE, the alternatives are /ˈrɛspət/ and /rɪˈspʌɪt/.

resplendence, resplendency. Both are rare, but the first is the more often used.

responsible. So spelt, not *-able*. See -ABLE, -IBLE 8.

restaurant. In standard BrE the final *t* is generally sounded, but the word is also pronounced in a quasi-French manner, /ˈrɛstərɒ̃/.

restaurateur, a restaurant owner, borrowed directly from French (1793) is spelt as shown. The spelling *restauranteur* (with internal *n*), though increasingly common, is incorrect and is not recognized by dictionaries.

restive is used particularly of a horse that stands still or moves backwards or sideways and refuses to go forward; of a refractory child; or of a discontented army, or any other group of people harbouring a grievance. The word makes contact with *restless* when the meaning required is no more than agitated or fidgety, because of loss of sleep (*a restless night*), boredom (*unemployment left him listless and restless*), a poor performance of a play, etc. (*the audience was becoming increasingly restless*), or some other unsettling circumstance. *Restive* most often suggests that potentially hostile or disruptive action seems likely to occur, while *restless* is more often a kind of explanatory word, implying that there is a reason (lack of sleep, an unhappy relationship, a lacklustre concert, etc.) leading to the behaviour in question.

restrainedly. Four syllables. See -EDLY.

restrain, re-strain. See RE(-).

restrictive appositives, non-restrictive appositives. See APPOSITION 2.

restrictive clauses. The main discussion of these and of **non-restrictive clauses** will be found s.v. THAT (relative pronoun), but it may be helpful, as an aperitif, to set down here the definitions of the terms in standard sources.

Restrictive clauses are relative clauses 'delimiting the meaning or reference of a modified noun phrase or other element' (*SOED*, 1993). Leech and Svartvik (1975) cite the following pair of sentences to bring out the distinction: [1] *Children* who learn easily *should start school as early as possible*; [2] *Children,* who learn easily, *should start school as early as possible.* 'In [1] the relative clause is restrictive and tells us *what kind* of children ought to start school early. In [2], where the relative clause is non-restrictive, the speaker is talking about all children in general . . . The clause does not in any way limit the reference of *children.*'

S. Greenbaum offers the following definition (*OCELang.*, 1992): '*A restrictive relative clause* (also *defining relative clause*) is a relative clause with the semantic function of defining more closely what the noun modified by the clause is referring to. In the sentence *My uncle who lives in Brazil is coming to see us*, the relative clause *who lives in Brazil* restricts the reference of *my uncle*. The restrictive modification would distinguish this uncle from any others who might have been included. A *non-restrictive relative clause* (also *non-defining relative clause*) adds information not needed for identifying what a modified noun is referring to. The sentence *My uncle, who lives in Brazil, is coming to see us* contains the non-restrictive relative clause *who lives in Brazil.* This clause provides information about the uncle, but his identity is presumed to be known and not to need further specification. Non-restrictive relative clauses are usually separated from the noun phrases they modify by parenthetical punctuation (usually commas, but sometimes dashes or brackets). In speech, there may be a pause that serves the same function as the parenthesis.' When these are taken together it emerges that a *non-restrictive relative clause* can normally be recognized because of its parenthetical punctuation or its spoken equivalent—pauses in the flow of speech.

restroom. See TOILET.

result. The word is pushing into the territory of not just an outcome (of some action, game, etc.) but a favourable or desirable outcome. The earliest examples found so far are from the 1920s and show the word in the plural: e.g. *take some of those pamphlets with you to distribute aboard ship. They may bring results*—E. O'Neill, 1922. More recently, *result* has firmly established itself in this meaning in the singular, and not only in the language of footballers and their managers: e.g. *They tried hard to get a result but rain stopped play and the game ended in a draw*—television news broadcast, 1993; *And the shares paid me dividends along the way. Result!*—*www.MotleyFool.co.uk*, 2005.

résumé /ˈrɛzjʊmeɪ/. In BrE written as shown (with accents, in roman) and normally meaning 'a summary'. In AmE, often without the first accent or with no accents (*resumé, resume*), used also to mean 'a summary', but more specifically and frequently 'a brief account of a person's education, qualifications, and previous experience', equivalent to a **CV** (*curriculum vitae*) in BrE.

resurrect. See BACK-FORMATION.

retable (a frame or shelf enclosing decorated panels or revered objects above and behind an altar). Pronounced /rɪˈteɪbəl/ (ri-**tay**-) in BrE, and also /ˈriːteɪbəl/ (**ree**-tay-) in AmE. The form **retablo**, plural *retablos*, pronounced /rɪˈtɑːbləʊ/ (ri-**tah**-bloh) is equally frequent.

reticent. Since it entered the language in the 1820s, along with the related noun **reticence**, its standard meaning has been 'reserved; disinclined to speak freely'. There is incontrovertible evidence that it is now also regularly used to mean 'reluctant *to act*', and is dragging the noun along in the same direction. (This use seems to have been originally AmE, and is first noted from 1875.) The syntax of this meaning is normally + *about* + *-ing* verb form, or + *to*-infinitive. Examples: *Zhang Liang says he understands Western reticence about introducing genetically altered organisms into the environment*—*New Scientist*, 1993; *And other than that I'm slightly reticent to talk* *about it*—weblog, 2005 (which sounds decidedly tautological if one adheres to the older meaning of the word). Many will still consider this newer use non-standard, but it has an air of inevitable semantic shift about it: the *OED* records it without comment.

retina. In technical work the plural is usually *retinae* /-niː/, but in non-technical writing and speaking *retinas*. See LATIN PLURALS.

retiral, meaning 'retirement from office', is hardly used outside Scotland. Example: *There is also a huge group of doctors who are on the verge of retiral or resignation, and are simply hanging on to see if this new contract will deliver improvements—Scotland on Sunday*, 2003.

retractation, retraction. The second is the customary word as the noun corresponding to all the main senses (withdraw a statement, etc.) of the verb *retract*, except that *retractation* is properly used with direct or indirect reference to the title of a book written by St Augustine 'containing further treatment and corrections of matters treated in his former writings' (*OED*); and also (beside *retraction*) to mean 'recantation of an opinion, statement, etc., with admission of error' (*OED*).

retrieve (noun). Apart from special uses in the training of gun-dogs, and in some American games (e.g. volleyball), hardly used now except in the collocations *beyond retrieve, past retrieve*. The customary noun for all the main senses is **retrieval**.

retro-. For long pronounced either as /ˈrɛtrəʊ/ or /ˈriːtrəʊ/. At some point in the 20c. the pronunciation with a short /e/ virtually drove out that with /iː/ in all the relevant words, and now /ˈriːtrəʊ/ is rarely heard.

retroussé (adjective). (of the nose) Turned up at the tip. Printed in roman, retaining the acute accent of the original French.

rev (verb). The inflected forms are *revs, revved, revving*.

reveille /rɪˈvali/. So spelt. Printed in roman.

revel. The inflected forms of the verb are *revelled, revelling*; also **reveller**. In AmE usually written with a single *l*. See -LL-, -L-.

Revelation. The last book in the New Testament was called *The Revelation of S. Iohn the Diuine* in 1611, and the singular form *Revelation* remains in standard use to this day. In popular use the plural form *Revelations* is common.

revenge (verb). See AVENGE.

Reverend is abbreviated *Revd* (in BrE, with no point) or, with increasing frequency, *Rev.* (with point). It means 'deserving reverence', as contrasted with *reverent* 'feeling or showing reverence'. Archbishops are *Most Reverend*, bishops are *Right Reverend*, and deans *Very Reverend*; archdeacons are not *Reverend* but *Venerable*. The correct form of address to a member of the clergy is *The Revd* (or *The Rev.*) *J. Smith* (or with the first name in full). To describe such a person as *Rev. Smith* or to speak of such a person as *Reverend Smith* or *the Reverend* is incorrect, at least in standard use in Britain. The *Shorter Oxford* (1993) expresses it as follows: 'It is commonly considered unacceptable to use *Reverend*... with a surname alone (rather than with a forename, initial, other title, or some combination of these) or without preceding *the*: thus *the Reverend Joseph Brown, the Reverend J. B. Brown, the Reverend Dr Brown*, but not (*the*) *Reverend Brown*, and not *Reverend* as a form of address, either spoken (*Hello, Reverend* (*Brown*)) or to begin a letter (*Dear Reverend* (*Dr Brown*)).' Actual usage is variable, but members of the clergy are quite rightly adamant about the need to keep to the older conventions while recognizing that in our age of receding Christian belief those who break with tradition are usually deeply respectful but quite simply ignorant of protocol.

In AmE scant regard is paid to the conventions of BrE in the matter, to judge from the following examples: *There really was something between her and Reverend Propper?*—J. Updike, 1988; *Reverend Samuels led the congregation in a prayer for Jackie Robinson*—M. Golden, 1989; *Reverend Knox decided he could join the staff on those terms*—G. Keillor, 1991; *The Reverend Cutcheon gave an address before the celebration began—New Yorker*, 1992. If a person is at the same time a minister or chaplain and (say) a professor, the correct style is *The Revd Professor James Jones*. The complications of how to address ordained members of religious orders in the Church of England, archbishops of the Church of Ireland, bishops of the Episcopal Church in Scotland, and so on, lie outside the scope of this book. For the procedures, *Debrett's Correct Form* (1970 or later printing) is an excellent guide.

reverent, reverential. Fowler's differentiation of the two words is somewhat gnomic: 'Between *reverent* and *reverential* the difference is much the same as that between *prudent* and *prudential, reverential* being as applicable to what apes reverence as to what is truly instinct with it, while *reverent* has only the laudatory sense'. While he criticized *reverential* for being the longer word, there seems to be something in what he said about 'aping reverence'. The two words share certain noun collocations, such as *reverent(ial) awe, attitude, hush, silence* on a more or less equal footing. However, the collocations for which *reverential* is rather more frequent (*tone*), or the only one of the two (*whisper, homage, worship, biography, atmosphere, manner*) perhaps hint at the slightly artificial, possibly unctuous, nature of any reverence so described. Contrast *The kids have taken a somewhat reverent tone when talking about Pete. He has become the ultimate hero to them* and *I lost count of the number of times this band was earnestly recommended to me, in reverential tones*. In the first the reverence is sincere; in the second it is being mocked.

reversible. So spelt (also **irreversible**), not *-able*. See -ABLE, -IBLE 8.

reviewal had wide currency in the 19c. when nouns in *-al* were popular, but in most contexts now *review* (noun) is used, and *reviewal* is extremely unusual.

review, revue. The former has numerous senses including the following: a general survey or assessment of a subject, policy, etc.; a display and formal inspection of troops; a published assessment of the value, interest, etc., of a book, play, etc.; part of the title of a regular journal (e.g. *The Review of English Studies*). A *revue* is simply a theatrical entertainment consisting of a series of short sketches and songs, i.e. has only one sense. *Review* is occasionally used instead of *revue*, but the two words are best kept apart in the manner indicated above.

revolutionary, revolutionist (nouns). The form in *-ist* is first recorded as a noun with the meaning 'an advocate of or participant in revolution' in 1710 and was the standard word until the mid-19c. *Revolutionary* is first recorded in a 1795 translation from French, and presumably calques the French use of *révolutionnaire* as a noun. It is now the standard form, while *revolutionist* is in comparison rather infrequent, e.g. *I have always been an evolutionist rather than a revolutionist—Daily Tel.*, 1996.

Rev., Revd. See REVEREND.

revue. See REVIEW.

rhapsodic, rhapsodical. In classical literature a rhapsody (Latin *rhapsōdia*, from Greek ῥαψῳδία) was an epic poem or part of one, e.g. a book of the Iliad or Odyssey, suitable for recitation at one time. From this came the use of the word in English (16–19c.) to mean a literary work consisting of miscellaneous or disconnected pieces; and (from the late 19c.) a free musical composition in one extended movement, usually emotional or exuberant in character. From the mid-17c. onwards the word also stepped outside literary forms to be used of an exaggeratedly enthusiastic or ecstatic expression of feeling. All this from the *OED*. In past times *rhapsodic* and *rhapsodical* were used as adjectives corresponding to the literary senses of **rhapsody**. Now they are increasingly restricted to mean exaggeratedly enthusiastic, or to musical contexts, with *rhapsodic* being much the more common of the two. Examples: (rhapsodic) *By the same token, critics wax rhapsodic about* The Cook, the Thief [etc.] *because its images* [etc.]—M. Medved, 1992; *Their interpretation has a freedom of tempo and rubato that brings a rhapsodic quality to the music—Strad*, 1992; *When Barry Diller . . . speaks of his Apple PowerBook, a laptop computer, he grows rhapsodic—New Yorker*, 1993. (rhapsodical) *People write rhapsodical volumes about the glories awash on Chesapeake Bay—the skipjacks, the oyster tonging—* V. Tanzer, 1989.

Rhenish (of the River Rhine). Pronounced /ˈrɛnɪʃ/ rather than /ˈriːn-/.

rhetorical questions are questions posed purely for effect with no expectation that they will be answered, e.g. *Who do they think they are?* Though such questions are interrogative in form, they often imply a forceful negation, e.g. *What has it got to do with you?* (= it has nothing to do with you); *Where do you think you're going?* (= you're not going anywhere). Rhetorical questions are often employed as a more striking substitute for a statement. The assumption is that only one answer is possible, and that if the hearer is compelled to make it mentally himself it will impress him more than the speaker's statement. So *Who does not know ...?* for *Everyone knows*; *Was ever such nonsense written?* for *Never was* etc.

rhino. Plural the same or *rhinos*. See -O(E)S 6.

rhinoceros. Plural the same (*a herd of rhinoceros*) or *rhinoceroses*.

rhombus. Plural *rhombuses* (preferred) or *rhombi* /-bʌɪ/.

rhotic. Of a form of English, especially Scots and AmE, that retains historical /r/ in medial and final position (Arthu*r*, fo*r* fea*r*, ha*r*der). The state or condition of being *rhotic* is **rhoticity** or **rhotacism**. RP is notable for its lack of rhoticity, i.e. is a non-rhotic form of English.

rhyme, identity of sound between words or the endings of words, a marked feature of verse. **1** The word entered English in the 13c. in the form *rime* (from Old French *rime*) and this spelling (or *ryme*) remained dominant until the early 17c. when, through etymological association with the ultimate source, via Latin *rhythmus*, the Greek ῥυθμός, the spelling *rhyme* began to be used. Gradually the new spelling established itself and *rhyme* is now the prevailing form. In Coleridge's *The Rime of the Ancyent Marinere* (1798) *Rime* means a rhyming poem.

2 The rhyming element may be a monosyllable (*feet/seat, love/above*), known as a 'masculine rhyme', two syllables (*rabble/babble, guessing/blessing*), known as a 'feminine rhyme' or 'double rhyme', three syllables (*glamorous/amorous*), known as a 'triple rhyme', or more. *Half-rhyme* is much favoured by certain poets, e.g. Hopkins and Owen: *shell/shall, fronds/friends, hitting/hurting*. More complex types also occur: e.g. *sisterhood/good, Christ/sacrificed, room there/loom there/doom there*.

rhyme royal. A term in prosody meaning a metre in stanzas of seven iambic pentameters rhyming ababbcc. Chaucer's *Clerk's Tale* is a typical example:

This sergeant cam unto his lord ageyn,
And of Grisildis wordes and hire cheere
He tolde hym point for point, in short and pleyn,
And hym presenteth with his doghter deere.
Somwhat this lord hadde routhe in his manere,
But nathelees his purpos heeld he stille,
As lordes doon, whan they wol han hir wille; ...

rhyming slang, a type of slang (originally Cockney) in which a word is replaced by words or phrases which rhyme with the word substituted. When such phrases become familiar they are often used with the rhyming word omitted, e.g. *take a butcher's* (*butcher's* is short for *butcher's hook* = look). Examples are first found in Cockney in the early 19c. They include: *apples and pears* (stairs, first recorded in 1857), *dog (and bone)* (phone, 1961), *plates (of meat)* (feet, 1887), *porky (pie)* (lie, 1981) *rock of ages* (wages, 1937), *round the houses* (trousers, 1857), *Sweeney Todd* (Flying Squad, 1938), *titfer* = *tit-for-tat* (hat, 1930), *trouble and strife* (wife, 1929). In practice they are seldom explained, e.g. *Goethe never spoke... All through the afternoon not a dickybird, Barley said*—J. le Carré, 1989. It is simply assumed that the reader knows that *dickybird* (first recorded in this sense in 1932) is rhyming slang for 'word'.

rhythmic, rhythmical. The two forms have coexisted for nearly four centuries, and in most contexts (except in physical geography, where the shorter form is favoured) are technically interchangeable, though the first is roughly 20 times more frequent in *OEC* data. In practice, the choice looks instinctive and arbitrary, and must have to do with personal preference and the shape of the sentence in question. In William Thomson's classic work *The Rhythm of Speech* (1923) *rhythmical* seems to be used throughout (*Each of the series is organically rhythmical*). By contrast, Fowler (1926) uses both forms in his article on *rhythm*: *Rhythmic speech or writing is like* *waves of the sea; A sentence ... is rhythmical if, when said aloud,* [etc.]. D. Attridge, in *The Rhythms of English Poetry* (1982), keeps to *rhythmic* throughout his book (*Part of the rhythmic character ... of any line stems from the placing of word and phrase boundaries; the same unconscious immediacy with which we respond to some rhythmic patterns*). Recommendation: use whichever form seems natural, but be consistent.

See -IC(AL).

rick (noun and verb), a sprain; to sprain. So usually spelt, rather than *wrick*. Both words are relatively recent (verb late 18c., noun mid-19c.). They seem to be of dialectal origin.

rickety. So spelt, not *-etty*. See -T-, -TT-.

ricochet. The spelling and pronunciation recommended are: *ricochet* /ˈrɪkəʃeɪ/; *ricocheted* /ˈrɪkəʃɛɪd/; and *ricocheting* /ˈrɪkəʃeɪɪŋ/. Cf. CROCHET; CROQUET.

rid. The past tense and past participle are now normally *rid* rather than *ridded*. Particularly in AmE the active past, e.g. *the system did not exclude people who qualified but also ridded it of elements of fraud,* occurs sporadically, as does the present perfect, e.g. *El Salvador has ridded itself of its indigenous currency for the greenback, too.* But when the past participle is used passively the only possible form is *rid*: e.g. *I thought myself well rid of him.*

Riesling. Pronounced /ˈriːzlɪŋ/ or /ˈriːs-/, but not /ˈrʌɪ-/ as in *rye*.

right, rightly. 1 *Right* is used as an adverb meaning 'in the right or proper way' with a number of verbs, notably *do right, go right* (as in *Nothing went right*), *guess right, spell something right, treat someone right,* and in the phrase *right or wrong* (*His faith in the screenplay is what guided him, right or wrong*). Generally, however, especially when the adverb precedes the verb or qualifies an adjective, *rightly* is the more natural choice: *incapable of acting rightly; he thought, rightly or wrongly, that his manager was less than sympathetic; One of them was rightly furious as the escaper had whipped ... his overcoat*—A. Miller, 1976; *These practices were rightly banned generations ago*—weblog, 2004; *I love many of his designs and think he rightly deserves his status as one of the greatest architects*—*A Daily Dose of Architecture,* 2004. *Rightly* is commonly used with *so* to express approval for something described by a preceding word or clause: *She was angry, and rightly so.* It is also part of a set idiom in the phrase *if I remember rightly.*

2 *Right* is also idiomatic in the meanings 'directly, immediately' or 'completely' in phrases such as *right away* and *right now,* and in uses such as *I'll be right with you* and *Turn it right off.* The emphatic *Right on!,* used since the 1920s as an expression of enthusiastic agreement or encouragement, is still mostly restricted to AmE.

3 (*a*) In an older use now considered archaic (but see below) in standard BrE (but still in use dialectally, e.g. *right nice,* and in regional AmE), *right* means 'very, extremely' without any notion of rightness in the judgemental sense: *I was right glad ... to see your writing again*—Coleridge, 1800; *Miz Wilkes is right sensible, for a woman*—M. Mitchell, 1936; *My husband reports from Iraq that he's right glad the Aussies aren't leaving*—weblog, 2004 (US). In BrE it remains in standard use only in certain titles and forms of address, such as *Right Honourable, Right Reverend,* and *Right Worshipful.* But *right* has been used informally since the 1960s in BrE as an intensifying adjective in the sense 'utter, complete': *You look a right clown*—I. Murdoch, 1978. (*b*) Older literary examples. The *OED* lists examples from the 13c. to the 20c., including the following: (with adverbs) *The portrait of him she loved right dearly*—Disraeli, 1826; *The 'proofs' of the Blake book are coming in ... The illustrations look right well*—W. B. Yeats, 1891; *Cale was doing right well for himself*—P. Mallory, 1981; (with adjectives) *I should be right sorry To have the means so to be venged on you*—B. Jonson, 1611; *I did not feel right comfortable for some time afterwards*—M. Twain, 1869. From these examples, and from other evidence, it is clear that *right* was at one time in good literary use.

rightward(s). As adjective always *rightward* (*a rightward movement*). As adverb either *rightward* or, especially in BrE, *rightwards* (*the car drifted rightwards after hitting a puddle*).

rigour. So spelt in BrE, but **rigor** in AmE. The corresponding adjective is **rigorous** in both BrE and AmE. In the Latin phrase *rigor* *mortis* the spelling *rigor* is obligatory in both countries. See -OUR AND -OR.

rilievo. See RELIEVO.

rime. See RHYME 1.

ring. The conjugation of the verb (used of bells, telephones, etc.) is stable, the past tense being *rang* and the past participle *rung.* The unrelated verb *ring* 'to make or draw a circle round; to put a ring on (a bird, etc.)' has past tense and past participle *ringed.*

ringleted. So spelt, not *-etted.* See -T-, -TT-.

riot (verb). The inflected forms are *rioted, rioting.*

rise. See RAISE, RISE (nouns and verbs).

ritardando (musical direction). For the plural both *ritardandos* and *ritardandi* are correct. The choice depends on how Italian and technical one wishes to be.

rival (verb). The inflected forms are *rivalled, rivalling.* In AmE often *rivaled, rivaling.* See -LL-, -L-.

rive (verb) (archaic or poetic) /rʌɪv/, to split. Past tense *rived,* past participle *riven* /ˈrɪvən/.

rivet. The inflected forms have a single *t* (*riveted, riveting, riveter*). See -T-, -TT-.

road, street, etc. Of the many different names we give to thoroughfares for vehicles, *road* is the most comprehensive. The *New Shorter Oxford* (1993) defines it as 'A path or way between different places, usually one wide enough for vehicles as well as pedestrians and with a specially prepared surface. Also, the part of such a way intended for vehicles.' It was the natural word for British long-distance highways such as the Great North Road and the Great West Road, and for what we used to call the Dover Road, the Portsmouth Road, and the Bath Road, until in the second half of the 20c. we resorted to a numerical system and called them respectively the A2, A3, and A4.

A *street* is originally a paved way—from Latin *via strata.* According to the laws of Henry I a street 'was to be sufficiently broad for two loaded carts to meet and for sixteen armed knights to ride abreast' (Ekwall; *Street-Names of the City of London,* 1954). It was the name bestowed by the Anglo-Saxons on the great roads of the Roman occupation—Ermine Street, Watling Street, and others. Its current meaning is 'A public road in a city, town, or village usually running between two lines of houses or other buildings; such a road along with the pavements and buildings on either side' (*New SOED*).

The history of the two words and of the words *lane, avenue, crescent, gate, row, place, terrace, rise, vale,* and some others is extremely complicated. Over the centuries thoroughfares have repeatedly changed their nature. For example, as Ekwall points out: 'In medieval London records a distinction between *street* and *lane* is fairly well kept up in street-names. But the difference between a comparatively narrow street and a comparatively wide lane might be slight, and there are cases of vacillation between *street* and *lane* in street-names ... [Thus] Paternoster Row was *Paternosterstrete* 1307 ff., *Paternosterlane* 1321–35, finally Paternoster Row from 1334 on ... New Street (1185 ff.) was superseded by *Converslane* (1278 ff.) and by Chancery Lane.' A 'place' was originally 'an open space in a town, a market-place'. Now, it is a small square or a side-street, especially a cul-de-sac, lined with houses' (*New SOED*). In London, *Grosvenor Place* and *Portland Place,* for example, might now be called 'streets' with perfect propriety. Similar 'anomalies' can be found in any major city in Britain. *Way,* as the name for a road, is as old as Fosse Way and Icknield Way. It has been preserved in *highway* and *railway,* and has been revived in the 20c. in *motorway.*

Certain fixed phrases have become established over the centuries: thus *No Through* Road, but *One Way* Street; *Cross*roads, but Street *corners*; *Rule of the* Road, but *High*way *Code*; *Keep in* Lane, but *Dual Carriage*way; *Major* Road *Ahead,* but *Clear*way.

No short article can do justice to the historical circumstances lying behind the names given to our streets and roads and avenues. There were no avenues in the village in which Burchfield lived. But he waxed poetical in writing 'among the names given to the "streets" of this quiet corner of the world are *All Saints Lane, Hobby Horse Lane, Bradstocks Way, Church Street, High Street, Tullis Close, The Green, Harwell Road, Drayton Road,* and *Milton Road.* Each name has an establishable history. And so it is in towns, villages, and cities up and down the country.'

rob (verb) is used principally to mean 'to steal from' (*rob a bank, a jewellery shop*); also followed by a personal object + *of* + indirect object (*robbed her of her jewels*). The old use (13c. onwards) meaning 'to steal' (*he robbed money from the till*) is falling into disuse and should be avoided (even though it was used by Joyce in *Finnegans Wake*: *Robbing leaves out of my taletold book*).

robust. 1 Deriving ultimately from the Latin *rōbur* ('oak' and hence 'strength, vigour') and used in English since the 15c. to describe people and things as 'strong and hardy', it is widely used to refer to immaterial things, particularly in economic contexts, e.g. *a robust economy, market, performance, recovery*, etc. The more abstract sense of 'uncompromising and forceful' (e.g. *Scientists tend to take a robust view of truth and are impatient of philosophical equivocation*—R. Dawkins, 2003) is arguably rather overused, and is a clichéd, facile choice when someone is cornered and has to defend themselves, as in: *ministers were last night preparing a robust defence of Government economic performance*; *a rather more robust rebuttal of the allegations against her*. Synonyms which can deliver you from the tyranny of cliché include *assertive, forceful, forthright, rigorous, spirited*, and *vigorous*.

2 The word has its stress on the second syllable, although first-syllable stress is sometimes heard, perhaps on the analogy of RECESSIVE ACCENT shifts in *dispute, romance*, and other words.

robustious. 'In common use during the 17th century. In the 18th it becomes rare, and is described by Johnson (1755) as "now only used in low language, and in a sense of contempt". During the 19th it has been considerably revived, especially by archaizing writers.' (*OED*) Fowler (1926) described it as 'One of the words whose continued existence depends upon a quotation (*Hamlet* III. ii.10)'. In practice *rumbustious* (first recorded in 1778), a corrupted form of it, has almost totally replaced it.

rock, stone. In BrE a small piece of rock capable of being thrown is normally called a *stone* (or a *pebble*); in AmE the word used in this sense (as well as for a mass of stone forming a cliff, etc.) is a *rock* (or a *pebble*), but not a *stone*.

rococo. See also BAROQUE. A 19c. loanword from French (in which language it was a playful alteration of *rocaille* shellwork) meaning **1** (of) a late baroque style of decoration prevalent in 18th c. continental Europe, with asymmetrical patterns involving scrollwork, shell motifs, etc.

2 referring to literature, music, architecture, and the decorative arts, it is used, much like *baroque*, to mean 'extravagantly or excessively ornate'. Examples: *He continues to contrive ever more rococo and outlandish preparations—New Yorker*, 2008; *Banville* [*sc.* author John Banville] *savors the opportunity to indulge the bloviating confessor's every rococo ejaculation and alliterative incantation—Village Voice*, 2003.

3 Note the spelling with single letter *c*s. The word is often written with an initial capital in art-historical works.

rodent operator. See RAT-CATCHER.

rodeo. Plural *rodeos*. Pronounced either /ˈrəʊdɪəʊ/ (**roh**-di-oh) or /rə(ʊ)ˈdeɪəʊ/ (ruh/roh-**day**-oh).

rodomontade. Not *rho-*.

roe. See BUCK.

roentgen (unit of ionizing radiation). So spelt in English (also *röntgen*), though named after Wilhelm *Röntgen* (died 1923), German physicist. Pronunciation now normally anglicized to /ˈrʌntʤən/, though /ˈrəːn-/ is equally acceptable.

roguish. So spelt. See MUTE E.

role (actor's part, etc.) is the more frequent spelling nowadays, but **rôle** is also valid.

romance. Both the noun and the verb can bear the stress on the second syllable: /rɛʊˈmans/ or on the first, i.e. /ˈrɛʊmans/.

Romania. Now the official spelling of the name of the country which has also historically been spelt *Rumania* or *Roumania* in English-language contexts.

Roman numerals are used with decreasing frequency but are still customary in certain circumstances: e.g. for the names of monarchs (*George VI*); for the preliminary pages of books; for acts and scenes in plays (*Romeo and Juliet* II.iii);

sometimes for the numbering of issues of learned journals; on old clocks and watches; on some almanacs; and, most visibly nowadays, to represent dates that follow the copyright symbol in the credits of cinema films and television productions.

The series runs as follows: (lower case) i, ii, iii, iv, v, vi, vii, viii, ix, x, etc. (note the positioning of i in iv and vi); (capitals) I, II, III, IV (or less often IIII), etc. Arabic 30 = xxx, 40 = xl (or less often xxxx), 42 = xlii, 49 = xlix; 50 = l (or L), 90 = xc, 99 = xcix: 100 = c (or C); 500 = D, 1,000 = M.

The main principle governing the system is that if a numeral is followed by another numeral of smaller value, the two are added together (LI = 51); if it is preceded by one of lower value the smaller numeral is deducted from the larger one (IV = 4). Accordingly, 1990 was written MCMXC (i.e. M = 1,000 + CM = 900 (1,000-100) + XC = 90 (100-10) = 1990). 1999 had to be written MCMXCIX, not MCMIC and still less MIM, as was also suggested, because a smaller value is followed by a higher value at the next available level; for those who reject the subtraction principle altogether as a late and inauthentic compromise, 1999 had to be written MDCCCCLXXXXVIIII. Since the turn of the millennium, the element of subtraction has been reduced and the problems have eased (the year of publication of this 4th edition is MMXV). Multiples of a thousand are indicated by a superior bar: thus $\bar{\text{V}}$ = 5,000, $\bar{\text{X}}$ = 10,000, $\bar{\text{C}}$ = 100,000.

Romansh /rɛʊ'manʃ/. Name given to a Rhaeto-Romanic dialect, especially as spoken (by some 40,000 speakers) in south-east Switzerland. (Variant spellings are also used in some publications: *Ru-*, *Rou-*, *-ansch*.)

rondeau. 1 'A medieval French verse form also used by some late 19th-century poets [e.g. Austin Dobson] in English. It normally consists of 13 octosyllabic lines, grouped in stanzas of five, three, and five lines. The whole poem uses only two rhymes, and the first word or phrase of the first line recurs twice as a refrain after the second and third stanzas. The standard rhyme scheme (with the unrhymed refrain indicated as R) is *aabba aabR aabbaR*' (Baldick, 1990).

An example:

On London stones I sometimes sigh
For wider green and bluer sky;—
Too oft the trembling note is drowned
In this huge city's varied sound;—
'Pure song is countryborn'—I cry.

Then comes the spring,—the months go by,
The last stray swallows seaward fly;
And I—I too!—no more am found
On London stones!

In vain!—the woods, the fields deny
That clearer strain I fain would try;
Mine is an urban Muse, and bound
By some strange law to paven ground;
Abroad she pouts;—she is not shy
On London stones!

(Austin Dobson 'On London Stones', 1876)

2 Pronounced /'rɒndəʊ/. Plural *rondeaux*, with the final letter pronounced /z/. See -x.

rondel. 'A medieval French verse form related to the triolet and the rondeau. In its usual modern form, it is a 13-line poem using only two rhymes in its three stanzas. It employs a two-line refrain which opens the poem and recurs at lines 7 and 8, the first line (or, in a 14- line variant, both opening lines) also completing the poem. The rhyme scheme—with the repeated lines given in capitals—is thus *ABba abAB abbaA(B)*. There is no fixed metre. This form was adopted by some poets in England in the late 19th century, including Austin Dobson and W. E. Henley' (Baldick, 1990).

An example:

Love comes back to his vacant dwelling,—
The old, old Love that we knew of yore!
We see him stand by the open door,
With his great eyes sad, and his bosom swelling.

He makes as though in our arms repelling
He fain would lie as he lay before;—
Love comes back to his vacant dwelling,—
The old, old Love that we knew of yore!

Ah, who shall help us from over-spelling
That sweet forgotten, forbidden lore!
E'en as we doubt in our heart once more,
With a rush of tears to our eyelids welling,
Love comes back to his vacant dwelling.

(Austin Dobson 'The Wanderer', 1880)

rondo (music). Plural *rondos*.

röntgen. See ROENTGEN.

roof. The standard plural form in BrE is *roofs*, but there is an occasional, and recognized, minority form *rooves*, which will disturb many people. It is a classic example of a disputed plural, something that was brought out by a correspondent to *The*

Times: 'Almost daily now I am troubled by the sound of "rooves". Is there any hope of a cure?' Cf. HOOF.

room. Both pronunciations /ruːm/ and /rʊm/ are standard, the first being by far the dominant one of the two.

roomful. Plural *roomfuls*. See -FUL.

roost. For *rule the roost*, see RULE.

root (noun). (philology) One of those ultimate elements of a language that cannot be further analysed, and form the base of its vocabulary (*OED*). For example, the word *unhistorically* can be shorn of its various affixes, *un-*, *-ic*, *-al*, and *-ly*, each of which modifies the root *-histor-*. Now *-histor-* answers to Greek ἵστωρ 'knowing, learned, wise man' (cf. Greek ἱστορία 'history'). The irreducible root is *histor*, which can still be accounted for by referring it to the hypothetical earlier Greek form *Ϝίδτωρ, from *Ϝιδ, ἰδ- ' to know', which is the assumed base or root of the English words *idea*, *vision*, *wit*, etc. The etymological network is valid, though the task of constructing such networks is a relatively modern achievement, beginning in an acceptable form in the late 18c. and early 19c.

root, rout (verbs). Several separate verbs with these spellings are involved. The *OED* identifies two verbs spelt *root* and pronounced /ruːt/ (like *boot*), and no fewer than eleven (most of them northern English or Scottish, and five of them obsolete) spelt *rout* and pronounced /raʊt/ (like *bout*). For example, *root* (v.)[1] can mean (of plants) to take or strike root', and *root* (v.)[2] can mean 'to poke about, to rummage'. There is coincidence of meaning, namely 'to poke about, to rummage', in *root* (v.)[2] and *rout* (v.)[9]. What all this amounts to is that it largely depends on where you live whether you say *root about* or *rout about* for the sense 'to rummage' and *root out/up* or *rout out/up* for the sense 'to find by rummaging'. From the web of meanings and derivations for the other senses one can say with reasonable certainty that to *root for* (i.e. 'encourage a team by applause') is largely restricted to American slang; that the sense '(of pigs) to turn up the ground with the snout while searching for food' is *root* in standard southern English and *rout* in many dialects of English.

Roquefort is pronounced /ˈrɒkfɔː/, i.e. is only partially anglicized.

roquet (in the game of croquet) is pronounced /ˈrəʊkeɪ/. The final *t* remains silent in the verbal forms *roqueted* /ˈrəʊeɪd/ and *roqueting* /ˈrəʊeɛɪɪŋ/. In practice the sound in the last syllable of *roquet* is often /ɪ/-, hence /-ɪd/, /-ɪɪŋ/—rather than /eɪ/.

rosary, rosery (rose garden). The first is the older word (from the 15c. in the *OED*), based on Latin *rosārium*; and *rosery* is a mid-18c. formation (after *nursery*, etc.). But in ordinary use *rose garden, bed, border* are now the more usual terms. (The most prominent sense of *rosary* is of course the religious one.)

roster. An 18c. loanword from Dutch *rooster* 'grating, gridiron, table, list' (from the appearance of paper ruled with parallel lines). It was for long mainly a military word for 'a list or plan exhibiting an order of rotation', and in such circles was normally pronounced like *roaster*, i.e. as /ˈrəʊstə/. This pronunciation survives, but in ordinary use /ˈrɒstə/ is standard.

rostrum. Plural preferably *rostrums* for the platform for public speaking, but *rostra* in the zoological meaning. See -UM 3.

rotten. 1 The corresponding noun is **rottenness** (so spelt).

2 For *something rotten in the state of Denmark*, see IRRELEVANT ALLUSION.

rouble (monetary unit of Russia). So spelt in BrE, but **ruble** in AmE.

roué (a debauchee) /ˈruːeɪ/. With accent, not italic.

rouleau (a cylindrical packet of coins). Printed in roman. Plural *rouleaux* with the final letter pronounced /z/. See -X.

round. See AROUND.

roundel. 'An English version of the rondeau, devised by A. C. Swinburne for his collection *A Century of Roundels* (1883). It is a poem of eleven lines using only two rhymes in its three stanzas of 4, 3, and 4 lines. Lines 4 and 11 are formed by the repetition of the poem's opening word or phrase as a refrain, which may be rhymed with lines 2, 5, 7, and 9. The rhyme scheme (with the refrain represented as R) is thus *abaR bab abaR*, or, with a rhyming refrain, *abaB bab abaB*. The term was at one time a synonym for a rondeau or rondel' (Baldick, 1990).

An example (Swinburne's 'The Roundel'):

A roundel is wrought as a ring or a starbright sphere,
With craft of delight and with cunning of sound unsought,
That the heart of the hearer may smile if to pleasure his ear
A roundel is wrought.

Its jewel of music is carven of all or of aught—
Love, laughter, or mourning—remembrance of rapture or fear—
That fancy may fashion to hang in the ear of thought.

As a bird's quick song runs round, and the hearts in us hear
Pause answer to pause, and again the same strain caught,
So moves the device whence, round as a pearl or tear,
A roundel is wrought.

rouse. See AROUSE.

rout (to poke about). See ROOT, ROUT.

route. Normally pronounced /ruːt/, but sometimes in military use, especially in *route march*, pronounced /raʊt/, rhyming with *clout*, which is also the preferred pronunciation of a third of US speakers, according to Wells (2008).

rout, route (verbs). These two verbs (respectively 'to put (an enemy force) to flight' and 'to send or direct along a specified course') share the spelling *routing* as their *-ing* form, but context generally prevents ambiguity. Occasionally the spelling *routeing* is used, especially in BrE.

rowan (mountain ash). Normally pronounced /ˈrəʊən/ (**roh**-uhn), but /ˈraʊən/, the first syllable rhyming with *cow*, is also common and is standard in Scotland.

rowel (verb). The inflected forms are *rowelled, rowelling* in BrE, but usually *roweled, roweling* in AmE. See -LL-, -L-.

rowing boat is the customary form in BrE, and **rowboat** in AmE.

rowlock. Pronounced /ˈrɒlək/, occasionally /rʌlək/. The North American equivalent word is **oarlock**.

royal we. See WE 4.

RP, is the abbreviation of **received pronunciation**, which is also known as **received standard**. **1** *Definition and alternative terms.* (*a*) These are the names given to the form of speech associated with 'educated speakers' in the southern counties of England and broadly used as a model for teaching English to foreign learners. As Henry Sweet pointed out in *The Sounds of English* (1908), *RP* (which he called *Standard English*) is 'a vague and floating entity', and 'like all living languages, [it] changes from generation to generation'. Like Standard French, he asserted, '[it] is now a class-dialect more than a local dialect. [Its] best speakers... are those whose pronunciation, and language generally, least betray their locality.' Despite the considerable loss of prestige suffered by *RP* in the later 20c., Sweet's last observation is still to some extent true. *RP* can claim the advantage of being considered the least 'regional' pronunciation within British English, and can therefore be used as some kind of standard, though taking it as a standard raises all sorts of thorny sociolinguistic, sociological, and even political questions. The analogous term in the US for a variety of pronunciation lacking particularly marked regional characteristics is **General American**.

(*b*) The terms *received pronunciation* and *received standard* are not the only ones used: it is also known 'as the spoken embodiment of a variety or varieties known as *the King's English, the Queen's English, BBC English, Oxford English,* and *Public School English*... It is often informally referred to... as a *BBC accent* or a *public school accent*; and... *as talking proper* or *talking posh*. In England, it is also often referred to simply as *Standard English*' (*OCELang.*, 1992). It has always been a minority accent in Britain, and is at present spoken by an estimated 3–4% of the British population. The adjective most frequently applied to *RP* by speakers of *General American* is *clipped*, though this is not necessarily a term of disapproval. Speakers of many other overseas varieties of English, and non-*RP* speakers in Britain, freely use the words *posh, la-di-dah,* and *very English* of *RP* accents, with varying degrees of admiration or hostility.

2 *RP notation and assumptions.* (*a*) *Notation.* Except when explicitly giving the pronunciation of American or other overseas words, or words from other regions of the UK, this book presents in the

International Phonetic Alphabet the sounds and phonetic assumptions of *RP* speakers, even though it must be admitted that there is no fixed circumference to this variety of speech and much fluctuation within it. The pronunciations given are normally those of the *COD* (1990), and apart from listing alternative pronunciations (where they exist within *RP*), specific recommendations are also sometimes made. Great reliance has been placed on the evidence presented in J. C. Wells's *Longman Pronunciation Dictionary* (1990), a standard work of great distinction. For older, discarded pronunciations, John Walker's *A Critical Pronouncing Dictionary* (1791 and 1806 edns), the relevant sections of the first edition of the *OED* (1884–1928), and Daniel Jones's *An English Pronouncing Dictionary* (1917) have all been consulted.

(*b*) *Assumptions.* Among the assumptions taken for granted in this notation is that *RP* speakers still favour /əʊ/ in *goat, show*, etc.; /ʌɪ/ in *fine, light*, etc.; /a/ in *trap, bad*, etc.; /ɪ/ in the final syllable of *early, gently*, etc., though there has been a marked movement in *RP* towards /i/ (as in *General American* and some other overseas forms of English); and it is regarded as axiomatic that /ɔː/ is now a virtually extinct pronunciation in words such as *loss, off*, etc., having been replaced by /ɒ/.

(*c*) For convenience and simplicity a bracketed (r) in the pronunciation of words such as *after* has not been used: that is, *RP* is presented as fully NON-RHOTIC. Again, for the sake of simplicity, words such as *little* /ˈlɪtəl/ and *rhythm* /ˈrɪðəm/ are treated as having a fully syllabic final element, though the matter is debatable.

3 *Further reading.* There are numerous classic books, essays, and articles on the nature of *RP*, among them that by Henry Sweet (see above); in various works by H. C. Wyld, including *A History of Modern Colloquial English* (1920; enlarged edn 1936); in A. C. Gimson's *An Introduction to the Pronunciation of English* (1962 and later edns); in J. C. Wells (see above); and in Tom McArthur's *Oxford Companion to the English Language* (1992). In this dictionary there are numerous articles, treated at their alphabetical place, on 20c. changes in *RP*, disputed pronunciations, and other matters to do with pronunciation. See PRONUNCIATION.

-r-, -rr-. **1** *The basic rules.* (*a*) Monosyllabic words containing a single vowel (*a, e, i, o, u*) before *r* (i) normally double the consonant before suffixes beginning with a vowel or before a final *y* (*barring, stirring, currish* [*sc.* like a cur], *furry*); (ii) but it remains undoubled if the stem contains two successive vowels (*nearing, chairing, boorish*). (*b*) Words of more than one syllable follow the rule for monosyllables if their last syllable bears the main stress (*preferred* but *proffered, interring* but *entering, abhorrent* but *motoring*).

2 *Exception.* The group of verbs ending in *-fer* is not subject to strict rules in the corresponding adjectival forms ending in *-able*. See -ABLE, -IBLE 3 (vii). Those that transfer the accent in the adjective to the first syllable are regularly spelt with a single *r* (*preferable*, (*in*)*sufferable*). But when the adjective bears the stress on the second syllable, as it often does in *conferable, inferable, referable*, and *transferable*, application of the rule given above would seem to require *-rr-*. See INFER 1; REFERABLE.

rubbish. In BrE *rubbish* is the generic term for waste material placed in *dustbins*, plastic bags, wheelie bins, or other containers, and collected at regular intervals by *dustmen* for conveyance to a designated *tip*. At some tips, or other collecting points, *skips* (large metal containers) are placed in which householders may deposit separated loads of garden refuse, paper, cardboard, DIY waste, used clothing, etc., and a *bottle bank* for recyclable bottles. In AmE, domestic rubbish is called **garbage** or, in certain categories, **trash**, and a dustbin is called a *garbage can* or *trash can*. In American newspaper reports, however, the terminology is somewhat fluid: several terms are sometimes used, seemingly synonymously, in the same report, e.g.: *Coyotes . . . at night scoot into town and raid the* garbage cans—*New Yorker*, 1988; *He said the amount represents the saving the city would realize by separating* recyclable trash *from waste trucked to area* dump sites—*Chicago Sun Times*, 1988; (headline) *A Lot of Rubbish. With* dumps *filling up fast, America is finally embracing the new* garbage *ethic*—*US News & World Report*, 1990; *The inclusion of so many new materials in Chicago-area recycling programs means that less* trash *is being sent to* garbage dumps. *Usually, a separate truck comes for* yard waste *and a* garbage truck *makes a run to pick up* nonrecyclable trash—*Chicago Tribune*, 1991.

In May 1988 a retired American lexicographer wrote to Burchfield to say that he liked to think that he did not use the various terms as synonyms. To him, 'garbage = orange and grapefruit rinds, eggshells, leftover food; what one puts in a garbage pail/can, usually covered, in the kitchen or outside the kitchen door. It has a bad odor. trash = what I throw into a wastebasket: letters, envelopes, newspapers, junk mail, broken toys; as in trash can. rubbish = stuff thrown out of the attic and garage; mown grass, tree limbs. Empty tin cans go out with the garbage, but I could also consider them trash. I'm sure there is much overlapping in the use of these words, even if I don't consider them synonyms.'

A casual collection of examples from other English-speaking countries suggests that *garbage* is becoming the main generic term outside BrE: *We all dashed to the bins with our garbage*—M. Pople, 1986 (Aust.); *I was replacing a wheel on our garbage can*—*Personality* (Durban), 1988; *the area being too poor for there to be any garbage that could be thrown in to enrich it*—A. Desai, 1988 (Ind.). But the distribution of terms for *rubbish* of various kinds (of the literal sort, that is, apart altogether from figurative and transferred uses as well as verbs) would be a profitable subject for a Ph.D. thesis or a section in a linguistic atlas.

ruble. See ROUBLE.

ruddle. The usual spelling of the word for a kind of red ochre used to mark sheep; also for the corresponding verb. **Raddle** and **reddle** are regional variants.

ruff /rʌf/, a wading bird, *Philomachus pugnax*, has **reeve** /riːv/ as its feminine form.

rug, carpet. These two words, which are often used as synonyms (see below), are by no means always interchangeable. When the place of origin is given it usually seems to be a matter of taste whether one or the other word is used, e.g. *Kilim carpet/rug, Oriental carpet/rug, Persian carpet/rug. Carpet* is the normal, probably exceptionless, word used in *stair carpet, wall-to-wall carpet*, and *magic carpet.* Figurative extensions include *on the carpet; to sweep a thing under the carpet* (or *rug*); *to pull the rug out from under someone*: flexibility is possible only in the second of these. Of combinations, *carpet-bagger, carpet bombing*, and *carpet slippers* are always so called: *rug* could not be substituted. Similarly with numerous less well-known combinations in *rug.*

An American correspondent of Burchfield's told him that a shop selling rugs and carpets informed him that the primary difference was one of size: 'Anything 9′ × 12′ or larger is a carpet, anything smaller than that is a rug.' It seems unlikely that this is a general rule. One kind of rug is not a floor covering, namely a *travelling rug*, i.e. a kind of blanket used for warmth on a journey or as a ground cover at a picnic. And such a rug is not made of 'shaggy material or thick pile' as indoor rugs and carpets are.

ruination, the act of bringing to ruin, the state of being ruined, is a derivative (first recorded in 1664) of the once-common (16–19c.) but now obsolete verb *ruinate* (which answers to med Latin *ruīnātus*, past participle of *ruīnāre*, i.e. is not like *botheration, flirtation*, and *flotation*, which are HYBRIDS).

rule. 1 *For the exception proves the rule*, see EXCEPTION.

2 *to rule the roost*, to have full sway or authority. First recorded *c.*1400 in the unexplained form *to rule the roast*, which lasted until the 19c. before being replaced at some point by to *rule the roost*. The later expression was first recorded in 1769 but does not seem to have become dominant until a later date, probably *c.*1900.

Rumania. See ROMANIA.

rumbustious. See ROBUSTIOUS.

rumour. So spelt in BrE, but **rumor** in AmE.

rung (past participle). See RING.

runner-up. Plural *runners-up.*

ruridecanal (pertaining to a rural dean). Pronounced /ˌrʊərɪdɪˈkeɪnəl/ (-di-**kay**-nuhl).

russety. So spelt, not *russetty.* See -T-, -TT-.

Russian. Since 1991 definitions of the word have had to be changed. The *OED* (2011) defines the primary senses of the noun as '**1** A native or inhabitant of Russia or (more widely) its former empire, or the former Soviet Union; a person of Russian nationality.

2 The Slavonic language of Russia; the official language of the (former) Soviet Union.'

-s. 1 For the use of *-s* to form adverbs from nouns (e.g. *he works nights, we nip off to her place afternoons*), see ADVERB 4.

2 The normal plural ending of nouns, namely *-s* (*boys, cars,* etc.), should never be preceded by an apostrophe (the type *video's for rent* is wrong, though such uses are often found in shops). See APOSTROPHE B3.

3 For the plurals of abbreviations and numerals (*MAs, the 1990s*), see APOSTROPHE C1.

's. 1 For *for conscience' sake*, etc., see SAKE.

2 For *Achilles', Burns's,* etc., see APOSTROPHE D 2, 3, 4.

3 For the types *the sentence's structure* and *the extent of the frame-up*, see 'S AND S' AND OF-POSSESSIVE.

4 For the type *a friend of my mother's*, see DOUBLE POSSESSIVE.

Sabbatarian, a strict sabbath-keeping Christian (for whom the sabbath is a Sunday) or a Jewish person (for whom the sabbath is a Saturday).

sabbatical. As adjective it is still sometimes used of observances, etc., appropriate to the sabbath. But its main use is of leave granted at agreed intervals to a university teacher for study or travel, originally every seventh year. Also as noun, a period of sabbatical leave.

sabre. So spelt in BrE, but usually as **saber** in AmE.

saccharin, saccharine. Though either spelling is technically correct for the 'sweet-tasting synthetic compound used in food and drink as a substitute for sugar', and dictionaries list them as alternatives, usage distinguishes them clearly. *Saccharin* is generally used for the sugar substitute, while *saccharine* is the majority spelling when the word is used metaphorically of things that are sickly sweet or sentimental: e.g. *John Waters' refusal to buy into the conventional social constructs that underlie and inform most of the saccharine films we endure—Senses of Cinema,* 2005. Using the other spelling for each sense is not, however, incorrect, but merely unusual.

sack (noun) dismissal and *sack* (verb) to dismiss have been used in English since the first half of the 19c. but are still not in formal use. The phrase *to give* (a person) *the sack* may be a calque on an earlier (but now obsolete) French phrase *donner son sac* (e.g. *on lui a donné son sac*). The modern French equivalent is (for the noun) *renvoi,* and for the phrase *renvoyer quelqu'un* or *mettre* (or *flanquer*) *quelqu'un à la porte.* Cf. FIRE (verb).

sacrarium (sanctuary of a church). Plural *sacraria.* See -UM 2.

sacrilegious, the adjective formed from **sacrilege**. So spelt, and pronounced /ˌsakrɪˈlɪdʒəs/. It is sometimes misspelt by confusion with *religious,* but the words have different origins. *Sacrilegious* is ultimately from Latin *sacrilegus* 'one who steals sacred things', from *sacer, sacri-* 'sacred' + *legere* 'take possession of'; while *religious* is from L *religiōsus,* from *religiō* 'religious fear, religious feeling, a religious practice', etc.

saga. A word that has gone on acquiring new senses. In English it was first applied to 'any of the narrative compositions in prose that were written in Iceland or Norway during the Middle Ages' (*OED,* with its earliest example taken from a work by George Hickes, 1709). From the mid-19c. it began to be applied to any narrative having the real or supposed characteristics of the Icelandic sagas, especially a novel or series of novels recounting the history of a family through several generations (Galsworthy's *Forsyte Saga* is a well-known example). From the Icelandic sense also came a spate of applications of the word to mean merely 'a legendary story, an orally transmitted story': in 1903, for example, an Anglo-Saxon scholar, L. F. Anderson, wrote anachronistically of the sagas known to the *Beowulf*-poet. This use was doubtless partly after German *Sage.* In the course of the 20c. *saga* has also come to be applied (some would say 'loosely') to any long and complicated account of a series of (ordinary) events. Burchfield (1996) recalled that his Old Norse tutor in the early 1950s was saddened by all the extended senses of the word: he felt that it properly belonged only to the Icelandic sagas. But it is clear that, for the moment at any rate, the boundaries between the various senses remain stable and unthreatened.

sage. Often applied playfully to a wise person. *Harrap's Book of Nicknames* (1990) lists ten writers upon whom the nickname *sage* has been bestowed, including *the sage of Baltimore* (H. L. Mencken), *the sage of Chelsea* (Thomas Carlyle, who moved from Scotland to Cheyne Walk, Chelsea in 1834), and *the sage of Monticello* (Thomas Jefferson). See SOBRIQUETS.

sago. Plural *sagos.* See -O(E)S 4.

Sahara Desert. One of the pleasant ironies of language is that exotic foreign place names are not thought of as having a self-evident meaning, but are simply taken to be the names of particular places. In Arabic the word *Sahara* (actually, in transliterated form, *ṣaḥrā*) means 'desert'. It has been argued therefore that we should speak only of *the Sahara* and never of *the Sahara Desert.* Arabists are certainly entitled to follow such a restriction, but the less well informed of us will doubtless continue to speak of *the Sahara Desert* from time to time.

sahib. Pronounced /ˈsɑːhɪb/ or /sɑːb/. (in colonial India) A polite form of address used by Indians to an Englishman or other European man. A *pukka sahib* was a true gentleman; and *memsahib* was the equivalent term of respect for a married European woman.

said. 1 *The said* —. In legal documents phrases such as *the said witness* and *the said meeting place* are traditional and are beyond reproach. In non-legal contexts (e.g. *regaling themselves on half-pints of lager at the said village hostelry*), such uses verge on being humorous.

2 *said he* (or *I*, etc.). This inversion of the natural order (*he said*) is often resorted to as a stylistic variation and is unobjectionable, e.g. *'Oh,' said a man to me, when the news had penetrated our circle of acquaintance, 'I hear they're actually giving you money for it.'*—H. Mantel, 1993. This is immediately followed by a passage in which the *said* formula precedes the direct statement: *Said another, 'Do you know—have you any idea—how many books are published in the course of a year?'* This construction is also acceptable: in the context one *said* formula balances the other. What is debatable, however, is the journalistic convention of using the second type as an eye-catching device, e.g. *Said a Minister: 'American interests are not large enough in Morocco to induce us to...'* See INVERSION 2(a).

3 Substitutes for *said.* These are innumerable, depending on the nature of the context. In Iris Murdoch's *The Green Knight* (1993), for example, direct speech is usually presented without any kind of *he said* formula, e.g. *'Once upon a time there were three little girls—'*; *'Oh look what he's doing now!'*; *'And their names were—'* (etc.). Here the dashes and the quotation marks make it clear that more than one speaker is involved. Much less common in this book are the types *Clement said* and, especially after direct speech, the type *said Lucas.* Substitutes for *said* are infrequent, but the following words are among those that occur: *called, continued, cried out, exclaimed, intervened, murmured, repeated, replied,* and *went on.* There are numerous examples of *said* + an adverbial phrase, e.g. *said in a low voice, said in a soft confidential tone.* The pattern is a little different in William Boyd's *The Blue Afternoon* (1993) in that the type used after the passage of direct speech always seems to be that shown in *Carriscant said* (rather than *said Carriscant*). His substitutes for *said* include *asked, began, declared, muttered,* and *shouted.* Boyd also uses numerous phrases of the type *said* + an adverbial phrase, e.g. *he said petulantly*; *he said almost light-heartedly.* Doubtless other authors, other patterns.

sailor. In the sense a seaman or mariner, always so spelt. But the normal agent noun *sailer* exists for use in such contexts as *She* [*sc.* a ship] *is a slow sailer.* Cf. also the Australasian *trailer sailer,* a small sailing vessel, usually one between 5 and 8 metres in length.

Saint. The customary abbreviations are now **St** (without point) or **S.** (with point). Plural *Sts* or *SS* (no points). In alphabetical arrangement always place under *Saint,* not under *St.*

sake. *For appearances' sake, for Christ's sake, for God's sake, for Heaven's sake, for Pete's sake, for old times' sake* illustrate the obligatory use of the possessive apostrophe in such phrases. In *for conscience'/conscience's sake, for goodness' sake,* and *for convenience'/convenience's sake* the apostrophe is as often left out as it is put in. In AmE, **sakes** is sometimes used in place of *sake*: e.g. *'Shush, for God's sakes!' warned my mother*—L. S. Schwartz, 1989; *I suppose that's hearsay, but, for heaven's sakes, it's hearsay from the guy who did the shooting*—*New Yorker,* 1993.

salable. See SALEABLE.

salad days (one's raw youth) is one of the phrases whose existence depends on a single literary passage (*My Sallad dayes, When I was greene in iudgement, cold in blood*—Shakespeare, 1606. It does not necessarily follow that present-day users of the phrase are aware of its source.

saleable seems to be the natural spelling, despite flouting the MUTE E rule, though *salable* is a US alternative.

salivary (adjective). Now pronounced either as /sə'lʌɪvəri/ or /'salɪvəri/. The corresponding Latin word was *salīvārius.*

Salonica /sə'lɒnɪkə/ is the former English name for *Thessaloníki,* the second largest city in Greece. Its Latin name was *Thessalonica.*

saloon. As the first element of compounds (*saloon car, saloon deck, saloon pistol, saloon rifle*) it is not normally joined to the second element by a hyphen.

salve. The Latin greeting meaning 'hail!' may be pronounced /'salveɪ/ or /'salviː/.

salvo (simultaneous firing of guns). Plural *salvos* rather more often than *salvoes.* See -O(E)S 2.

sal volatile. Pronounced /ˌsal və'latɪli/.

same. 1 *A historical note.* Its use as a substitute form preceded by *the, that* or *this* has been noted by the *OED* in literary sources from the 14c. onwards, e.g. *Watermen haunt the waters, and fishes swim in the same*—P. Stubbes, 1583; *In the instant that I met with you, He had of me a Chaine, at fiue a clocke I shall receiue the money for the same*—Shakespeare, 1590; *That was a temple... Farre renowmed... Much more then that, which was in Paphos built, Or that in Cyprus, both long since this same*—Spenser, 1596; *But he that shall endure vnto the end, the same shall be saued*—Matt. (AV) 24: 13, 1611; *Her lute-string gave an echo of his name. She spoiled her half-done broidery with the same*—Keats, 1819.

2 At some point, probably during the 19c., the use dropped out of serious literary work and into the realms of legal usage and commercialese, in the latter often with *the* omitted. Fowler (1926) cited numerous journalistic examples, presumably of his own day, in which he judged *same* or *the same* to be misused, e.g. *Having in mind the approaching General Election, it appears to me that the result of same is likely to be as much a farce as the last; I can only confirm the statement of the transfer, but the same will be made slowly.*

3 *Present status.* (*The*) *same* is rare nowadays, even in commercialese: e.g. *We thank you for your order of 9 December for — and we shall supply same as soon as fresh stock has come in.* Garner (1987), while admitting that (*the*) *same* was very frequent in legal writing (e.g. *The informer told the officer that a white male would usually load the buyer's car with marijuana at a residence and then deliver same to buyer*), nevertheless urged lawyers to use the appropriate pronoun (*it, him, them,* etc.) instead. *WDEU* (1989) cited several examples of (*the*) *same* from 20c. letters and periodicals and judged it to be 'often simply a mark of an informal style'. Opinion, it is clear, is divided. In such circumstances the best advice that can be offered to readers is to fall back on ordinary pronouns to do the backward glancing, and leave (*the*) *same* to legal writers, to works of business, and to contributors of informal articles to such periodicals as *Esquire* and the *Saturday Review* (US).

same as. When used as an attributive adjective *same* is usually construed with *as.* There are several types of construction, among them: (*a*) where *as* introduces a clause, e.g. *Entering college at the same age* *as Fletcher had entered six years earlier*; (*b*) followed by a noun or noun phrase, e.g. *Other rules ... point in the same direction as the first rule of the order*; (*c*) followed by an adverb, e.g. *I again consulted your magnificence, and you gave the same answer as before.* (Examples from the *OED*.) Less commonly *the same* is construed with *that* or without a relative pronoun, e.g. *It's the same textbook* (*that*) *I used when I was an undergraduate.*

same like used as an adverbial phrase meaning 'just like' or 'in the same way as' is first recorded in 1898 and has remained non-standard or jocular since then. Examples: *'See no evil, hear no evil, think no evil. Same like the monkeys,' observed Sergeant Percy Bond*—A. Christie, 1959; *I have rich friends, same like you*—I. Murdoch, 1980.

samite (medieval silk fabric). Pronounced /ˈsamʌɪt/ or /ˈseɪm-/.

samurai. Pronounced /ˈsamʊrʌɪ/ or /ˈsamjʊ-/. Plural the same.

sanatorium. This is a modern Latin word, first recorded in 1839, and formed from Latin *sānāre* 'to cure, heal'. It is the customary word in BrE for an establishment for the treatment of invalids, especially of convalescents or the chronically ill; also (in BrE) a room or building for sick children at a boarding school, etc. (abbreviation *the san*). This form of the word is also current in AmE, but alternates there with **sanitarium** (first recorded in 1851), a quasi-Latin form derived from Latin *sānitas* 'health'. The occasional hybrid of the two *sanitorium* is a mistake. The plural of both *sanatorium* and *sanitarium* is either *-iums* or *-ia*. See -UM 3.

sanction (noun). The principal modern meaning, in the plural, is economic action taken by a state or alliance of states against another or others, usually to enforce a violated law or treaty. It goes back to 16c. and 17c. technical uses in law and ethics concerned with specific penalties enacted in order to enforce obedience to the law or to rules of conduct. The main secondary sense, 'approval or encouragement given to an action, etc.', surfaced in the 18c. and still sits happily beside the other, despite the fact that the two senses are virtually the opposite of one another.

sanction (verb). By contrast with the noun, *sanction* (verb), from its first use in the late 18c. until the mid-20c., had only one primary set of senses, namely 'to authorize, countenance, or agree to (an action, etc.)'. Since the 1950s it has gained a secondary sense, 'to impose sanctions upon (a person, etc.); to attach a penalty or reward before making valid'. This use, though now well over half a century old, is still far from common. Examples: *Georgina Dufoix, the only politician so far sanctioned for allowing the Palestinian guerrilla chief ... into France last week*—*Independent*, 1992; *But he was sanctioned for bookkeeping violations and barred from securities trading*—*Black Enterprise*, 2004.

sandal (verb). The past participle and participial adjective are *sandalled* (but usually *sandaled* in AmE.)

sand-blind. First recorded in the 15c., it is probably a corrupt form of unrecorded Old English *samblind* half-blind (Old English *sam*, corresponding to Latin *semi-*, meant 'half'). When the prefix lost its force, the word was perceived as being *sand-blind*, as famously shown in Shakespeare's *Merchant of Venice* (1596): *This is my true begotten Father, who being more then sand-blinde, high grauel blinde, knows me not.* Note also Dr Johnson's definition (1755): 'Having a defect in the eye, by which small particles appear to fly before them'. The word survives locally and in verse, e.g. *Hope ... Led sand-blind Despair To a clear babbling wellspring And laved his eyes there*—W. de la Mare, 1938.

's and -s' and of-possessive. 1 *The issue.* A friend of Burchfield's, an inspector of quarries, drew a questioning ring round the *'s* in a sentence he had found in an article about safety in quarries: 'It had been known for some time that the shovel's brakes were faulty.' Shouldn't it be 'the brakes of the shovel'?, he asked. He had encountered the problem of the type *the water's edge*: that is, whether to opt for an *of*-construction rather than a possessive apostrophe when the noun in question is an inanimate one. The rival constructions are the outcome of a morphological schism some 900 years ago. In Anglo-Saxon a wide variety of nouns referring to animates (human and animal), to materials, and to abstract qualities all had the power to 'possess', and this capacity was usually expressed by means of the genitive case (usually, but not always, *-es*). In the centuries that followed, some nouns, especially those denoting living things, continued to express the genitive by adding *'s* while most others came to be re-expressed as prepositional genitives.

2 *Some guidelines.* The use of *'s* and *-s'* to form respectively singular and plural possessive forms of nouns (*a woman's hat; their friends' house; the dog's dinner*) is commoner with nouns that represent humans or animals, as in the examples just given; in other cases the alternative construction with *of* is more usual: *the petals of the flower; the windows of the house.* There are, however, notable exceptions to this general rule:

(*a*) nouns denoting time or space: *a day's journey; a stone's throw; at arm's length.*

(*b*) in a number of fixed expressions (in which the possessive noun is often in effect personified): *at death's door; out of harm's way; in his mind's eye; for heaven's sake.*

(*c*) nouns denoting vessels or vehicles: *the car's wheels; the ships' masts; the plane's engines.*

(*d*) names (or common nouns) for countries and large places: *Russia's tourist industry; London's homeless; the region's wildlife.* In all these cases there is probably an element of personification, making the nouns concerned 'honorary' living things.

3 Apparent exceptions also occur in uses that are not really possessives at all but denote a looser relationship: *the soil's productivity; the painting's disappearance.* (Compare uses in relation to people, such as *Napoleon's defeat; John's concentration.*)

4 Conversely, the type of construction with *of* known as a 'partitive genitive', e.g. *a glass of water; a dose of salts*, cannot be expressed with a form in *'s* (**a water's glass; *a salts' dose*).

5 It should be noted that some *'s* and *-s'* forms with human or animal nouns cannot be converted into *of* forms, usually because the relationship is not simply possessive: *the man's reward; the boys' explanation; Sophie's revelation.*

6 For the type *a friend of my father's*, see DOUBLE POSSESSIVE.

7 Burchfield (1996) deduced from the evidence available to him 'that the *'s* genitive for inanimate nouns is commoner now than it was a century ago, though it and the *of*-construction are not free alternatives. The reason for the shift in this direction lies deeply buried in a long-drawn-out historical process.' Further examples: *I always seem to be sitting up in bed at the day's end*—J. Barnes, 1980; *at the sea's edge its appearance was oily*—J. Fuller, 1983; *He jogged down-hill to the water's edge*—M. Wesley, 1983; *all scattered along the sandy mud by a high tide which had bored up the river's mouth*—C. Burns, 1989.

sanguine, sanguinary. Both words derive from the Latin word *sanguis* (stem *sanguin-*) meaning 'blood'. *Sanguine* (/ˈsaŋgwɪn/, **sang**-gwin) originally meant 'blood-coloured'; then in medieval and later physiology, it was descriptive of one of the four 'complexions' (the other three being melancholic, phlegmatic, and choleric) and supposed to 'be characterized by the predominance of the blood over the other three humours, and indicated by a ruddy countenance and a courageous, hopeful, and amorous disposition'. In its later, more general meaning 'optimistic or positive, especially in an apparently bad or difficult situation', *sanguine* is somewhat recherché and much less frequent than its synonyms *hopeful* and *optimistic.* Sanguinary (/ˈsangwɪn(ə)ri/, **san**-gwin-(uh)-ri) is a similarly refined word, and means 'accompanied by blood' or bloodthirsty. Examples: *The company is especially sanguine about its prospects in the Middle East, where it expects to sell $14 billion worth of aircraft from now to 2030—OEC*, 2012; *From a financial markets standpoint, I am troubled that things are diverging dramatically from previous sanguine expectations—OEC*, 2003; *a series of ruthless and sanguinary wars against the western Indians—OEC*, 2003; *there are few more gruesome and sanguinary spectacles than a Tory leadership struggle: one lasting eight months is uncharted territory—a marathon of fear, loathing and betrayal—Scotland on Sunday*, 2005.

Sanhedrin (highest court of justice in ancient Jerusalem) is the correct form (from late Hebrew *sanhedrīn*, from Greek συνέδριον 'council', from σύν 'together' + ἕδρα 'seat'), though a pseudo-Hebrew form in *-im* has been a rival spelling in English from the 16c. onwards and is given as an alternative in *ODO*. The word can be pronounced /ˈsanɪdrɪn/, /sanˈhiːdrɪn/, or /sanˈhɛdrɪn/ (**san**-i-drin, san-**hee**-drin, san-**he**-drin).

sans. 1 In phrases of French origin (e.g. *sans-pareil* 'not having its like'; *sans peur* 'fearless', *sans souci* 'without care or concern') *sans* must always be pronounced in a French manner, /sɑ̃/.

2 When used in ordinary English contexts, often with direct allusion to Shakespeare's famous context in *As You Like It* (1600) (*Second childishnesse, and meere obliuion, Sans teeth, sans eyes, sans taste, sans euery thing*), the Anglicized pronunciation /sanz/ is customary. Example: *The result was a high-quality recording, sans commercials*—A. Hailey, 1979.

Sanskrit. So spelt, not *Sanscrit.*

Santa Claus. First recorded in the *New York Gazette* in 1773 and for long mainly restricted to the US, the term is derived from a Dutch dialectal form *Sante Klaas* (cf. Dutch *Sint Klaas*), Saint Nicholas. It is now virtually synonymous in English with *Father Christmas.*

sapid. Unlike its negative *insipid, sapid* ('palatable; not vapid or uninteresting') lives out its precarious life an extremely rare esoteric word. Examples: *The aromatic dish, a kind of thick red stew, was just as sapid as it smelled*—P. Roscoe, 1988 (Canad.); *The most prized wines were those that were . . . infused with a sapid delicacy*—M. Kramer, 1989 (US).

sapient /ˈseɪpɪənt/, wise; of fancied sagacity. Mostly found used ironically in the higher realms of literature, it is not an everyday word. Examples: *Nor bring, to see me cease to live, Some doctor full of phrase and fame, To shake his sapient head and give The ill he cannot cure a name*—M. Arnold, 1867; *Polyphiloprogenitive The sapient sutlers of the Lord Drift across the window-panes In the beginning was the Word*—T. S. Eliot, 1919.

saponaceous, literally 'of, like, or containing soap; soapy' from modern Latin *sāpōnācēus* from Latin *sāpō, sāpōnis* 'soap', is a word that will thrill some by its rarity. It has sometimes been used humorously or sarcastically to mean 'unctuous, flattering, ingratiating', notably by Thomas Gray in a letter written after he declined the Poet Laureateship, a use referenced by Tony Harrison. Examples: *Tho' I very well know the bland emollient saponaceous qualities both of Sack and Silver*—Thomas Gray, letter of Dec. 19, 1757; *This so-called synodical judgment was, no doubt, a well-lubricated form of words, but it was so oily, so saponaceous, that no one could grasp it*—*Daily Tel.*, 1864; *There should be no successor to Ted Hughes. 'The saponaceous qualities of sack' Are purest poison if paid poets lose Their freedom as PM's or monarch's hack*—T. Harrison, *Laureate's Block*, 1999.

Sapphics. Lyric verses written in the sapphic stanza of four lines of the form –⏑–––|⏑⏑–⏑–⏑ (3 times), –⏑⏑–⏓ (once), named after Sappho (7–6c. BC), the female lyric poet of Lesbos. The stanzaic form has been imitated, sometimes not quite successfully, by a number of English poets including Sidney, Watts, Swinburne, and Ezra Pound. Examples:

All the night sleep came not upon my eyelids,
Shed not dew, nor shook nor unclosed a feather,
Yet with lips shut close and with eyes of iron
Stood and beheld me.

(Swinburne)

Breathing softly, wrapped in a shawl of daylight,
Trusting blossom loveliness brought to being,
Too small yet to lift up your head or turn round,
I will stay with you.

(Francis Warner)

sarcoma (tumour). Plural nowadays usually *sarcomas* rather than the etymologically correct Greek *sarcomata* /sɑːˈkəʊmətə/.

sarcophagus (stone coffin). Plural usually *sarcophagi* /-gʌɪ/ rather than *-uses.*

sardine (young pilchard) is pronounced /sɑːˈdiːn/. The unrelated word *sardine,* a precious stone mentioned in Rev. 4: 3, is pronounced /ˈsɑːdʌɪn/.

sardonic. A 17c. loanword from French *sardonique*, it answers ultimately (with change of suffix) to Greek σαρδάνιος, used by Homer and others as the descriptive epithet of bitter or scornful laughter. In late Greek, Σαρδόνιος 'Sardinian' was substituted for σαρδάνιος, the notion being that facial convulsions resembling horrible laughter, usually followed by death, resulted from eating a Sardinian plant.

sari, plural *saris,* is the more common form in English-language publications, though *saree* is still often found in English-language newspapers in India and elsewhere.

sartorial is derived from Latin *sartor* 'tailor', and means (*a*) relating to a tailor or tailoring; (*b*) relating to clothes, or style of dress. Though Fowler considered its use an example of puerile and tiresome pedantic humour, it, and its related adverb **sartorially**, can be used facetiously, but often facetiousness is not an ingredient of either word in modern use. Examples, facetious or otherwise: *Wherever he goes, the Prime Minister adapts sartorially to the country in which he finds himself—Scotland on Sunday*, 2005; *Looking down at my own unpainted feet—the chapped heels resembling slabs of Parmigiano—topped by tatty jeans, I realised that I was seriously sartorially challenged. The only requirement I have ever made of my attire is that it be flame-retardant—OEC* (undated); *Palestinian sources disclosed that two suits had been packed, indicating that he* [*sc.* Yasser Arafat] *might yet use his sartorial style at the ceremony on the White House lawn to demonstrate his transformation to statesman—New Yorker*, 1993; *The true legacy of 1969-70 to 1993 is . . . the courage, on the part of women, to write the narratives, sartorial and otherwise, of their daily lives—New Yorker*, 1993.

Sassenach /ˈsasənax/ *or* /-nak/. A derogatory term in Scotland and Ireland for an English person. Cf. Gaelic *Sasannach* and Irish *Sasanach,* from Latin *Saxones* 'Saxons'. Cf. Gaelic *Sasunn*, Irish *Sasana* 'England'.

sat, combined with the auxiliary *be* in place of a progressive tense (i.e. *she is/was sat,* instead of *she is/was sitting*), has become a topic of interest because of its increasing use: it raises the question of what is 'standard'. The *OED* entry for *sit* (not fully updated) shows that this use stretches back to Old English (earliest citation, Anglo-Saxon Chronicle for 922), and the editors of the entry (1911) labelled it 'dialectal'; the latest citation they showed (1864) was from a book of Lancashire rhymes and clearly dialectal. So much for the history. For many people from a large part of the North and part of the West of England, it continues to be the normal formulation, and they might well be offended to hear it described as 'dialect'. What has changed is that, as the *OEC* data suggests, its use has spread well beyond its traditional regional confines; though still a predominantly British construction, it is also found in other varieties, including AmE, Australian, NZ, and Irish English. Unsurprisingly, it appears above all in texts classified by the *OEC* as not being formal or technical, especially in blogs, news, and sports writing. Many of the British newspaper examples are from Northern papers, often directly quoting what people said. However, even a paper as starchy as the *Telegraph* occasionally slips it in, as in the last example below. For the moment it is likely to raise eyebrows in some quarters, so is best avoided in any kind of writing where formal standard English would be expected. Examples: *I can't help thinking of that Tim sat there juddering his leg up and down*—K. Amis, 1988; *Now, I'm sat in a nice car, my husband at my side*—A. Duff, 1990 (NZ); *now, as a result of a conference débâcle, you are sat on the back benches with nobody wanting to sit next to you*—B. Elton, 1991; *It means that if people are sat here waiting a long time they will see new things each time they look at it—This is Wiltshire*, 2004; *Both Mr Swinney and Mr Russell were sat near the First Minister as he misled parliament by claiming that the £546 million college budget increased this year—Daily Tel.*, 2012. For a parallel phenomenon, cf. STOOD.

satanic is first recorded in Milton's *Paradise Lost* (1667).

satiety. Pronounced /səˈtʌɪɪtɪ/, rhyming with *variety.*

satire. The many-branched entry in the *OED* sets out the history of the word (first recorded in English in 1509) and is a primary guide to the ramifications of the noble art of satire in the ancient world of Aristophanes, Juvenal, Horace, and others and in the modern equivalent world of such writers as Pope, Swift, and Samuel Butler (*Hudibras*). The novel became a powerful vehicle for social satire in the 19c. (Dickens, Thackeray, et al.) and has continued in this role in the 20c. (Evelyn Waugh, Kingsley Amis, et al.). Beginning in the 1960s, satire took on a new dimension. Merciless mockery of established figures and ideas became part of the world of popular entertainment. In Britain it began with the satirical revue *Beyond the Fringe* (1960) and a television programme called *That Was The Week That Was.* The programme ran its course, but its irreverent, reputation-lancing tone lived on and has been inherited by many BBC radio or TV programmes, such as *Have I got News for You* or *The News Quiz.* Hardly any institution, group, or individual lies beyond the reach of such ridicule. Society survives. Cf. LAMPOON.

satiric, satirical. As Fowler (1926) remarked, 'the line of demarcation between the two [forms] is not always clear'. What is clear, however, is that though both collocate with certain nouns, such as *comedy, novel, verse,* and *wit,* the second form is several time more frequent in World English, according to *OEC* data: in BrE *satiric* is rarely used, and is more common in AmE, though even there less frequent than *satirical.* Both are of long standing in the language: *satiric* was first recorded (as an adjective) in 1509 (as a noun in 1387), and *satirical* some twenty years later.

satiric, satyric. The two spellings represent two different and unconnected words: *satyric,* which is in learned or literary use only, means of satyrs, and especially, in *satyric drama* (a form of Greek play), having a satyr chorus. See SATIRIC, SATIRICAL.

satrap, pronounced /'satrap/, refers historically to a provincial governor in the ancient Persian empire, and in modern contexts refers to any subordinate or local ruler or person of influence, usually with unfavourable connotations of corruption, toadyism, etc., e.g. *In former days there was far more influence exercised over the Australian by Ken Cowley, his* [*sc.* Rupert Murdoch's] *local satrap—Quadrant* (magazine), 2004; *There is a complex and shifting web of alliances and rivalries involving local satraps, militia commanders and tribal leaders—World Socialist,* 2002.

Saturday. For the adverbial use (*shall see you Saturday*), see FRIDAY.

Saturnalia /ˌsatə'neɪlɪə/. In Roman antiquity, *Sāturnālia,* neuter plural of the adjective *Sāturnālis* 'pertaining to Saturn', was always construed as a plural. In English, especially in the transferred sense 'a period of unrestrained licence and revelry', it has often been perceived as a singular, e.g. *This was the beginning of a perfect saturnalia of tail-cutting and other operations* [*among the lambs*]—R. Haggard, 1899. Thus reinterpreted, a permissible plural is *saturnalias,* but it looks strange to the trained eye. Modern examples: *The sexual revelries began, a continuous saturnalia*—A. Greeley, 1986 (US); *Mind and body are preparing for war. The body, during the waking hours, with its regimes, its saturnalias of self*—M. Amis, 1991.

sauté. The accent of this originally French word is generally retained in all its parts of speech, i.e. as adjective (lightly fried), noun, and verb, though spelling it without the accent is also correct. As verb, its inflections are *sautés, sautéing* and *sautéed* or *sautéd.* AmE tends to write the infinitive without the accent, BrE with, and both varieties often omit the accent in inflected forms.

savanna(h) (grazing plain in subtropical regions). The form without *-h* is twice as frequent in AmE in *OEC* data as the form with; in BrE, the form with *-h* outnumbers the one without three to one. The seaport in E. Georgia and river of that name are spelt *Savannah.*

save. When used as a preposition (*no ornaments in the room save a crucifix*) and a conjunction (*I cannot remember anything about his appearance save that he had a morning coat*; *A small liqueur glass... empty save for a tiny drop*) it has an air of archaism or formality about it. It can often be replaced by *except* or *but.*

saviour, savour, savoury. So spelt in BrE, but as **savior**, **savor**, and **savory** in AmE. See -OUR AND -OR.

saw (verb) has past participle *sawn* and *sawed,* the first being standard in BrE, the second in AmE. The past tense is invariably *sawed.* This difference in use is reflected in AmE *sawed-off shotgun* and BrE *sawn-off shotgun.*

Saxonism. 'A semi-technical term for: (1) The use of, and preference for, expressions of Anglo-Saxon origin. (2) A word or other expression of Anglo-Saxon origin or formed on an Anglo-Saxon or Germanic model, often contrasted with *classicism,* as in *foreword* with *preface, folkwain* with *omnibus.* Saxonisms are generally the outcome of a purist and nativist approach to the language. The aim behind many deliberately created forms has been to create compounds and derivatives to replace foreign borrowings; the device is rooted in the Old English practice of loan-translating words: *benevolentia* as *welwilledness* or *wellwillingness*; *trinitas* as *thriness* threeness ... Saxonism has resurfaced only occasionally. In the 16c., it was a reaction to inkhorn terms; in his translation of the Bible, John Cheke used *hundreder* and *gainrising* instead of *centurion* and *resurrection* ... The most enthusiastic 19c. Saxonizer was William Barnes [1801–86], English dialectologist and poet, who wished to turn English back into a properly Germanic language ... His work is now largely forgotten and where remembered is usually seen as quaint and unrealistic' (*OCELang.*, 1992).

Most of Barnes' Saxonisms were not registered in the *OED*: such artificial words were mostly omitted on principle. Among these were *bodeword* commandment, *earthlore* geology, *gleecraft* music, *tastecraft* aesthetics, and *wondertoken* miracle. But *birdlore* was included, and dialectal words that he used such as *dew-bit* a small meal before the regular breakfast, and *gil[t]-cup* buttercup. As Fowler (1926) remarked, 'The wisdom of this nationalism in language—at least in so thoroughly composite a language as English—is very questionable.'

say. 1 Except as a poeticism, the noun survives only in such phrases as *to have a say* (to have an opportunity to influence developments and policy) and *to have one's say* (to have an opportunity for stating one's opinion or feelings).

2 The use of the verb's imperative to introduce a hypothesis or an approximation (*Let us meet soon—say next Monday*; *You will need some cash—say £20*) is an established idiom.

3 The participial phrase *having said that* has acquired a grammatically free status similar to phrases introduced by *considering, seeing,* etc. (see UNATTACHED PARTICIPLES). The participle does not always relate to the grammatical subject of the sentence; it does in the first example but not in the second: *Having said that, I must say her depiction of what happened made me view Polanski with much more 'critical' eyes*—D. Poland, 2003; *There are times when the film ... goes for the teen market with a lot of bad language and some silly, toilet humour. But having said that there are some clever in-jokes and many funny cameos*—film review website, 2004.

This grammatically loose structure is generally acceptable (especially in spoken English), but should be avoided in more serious or academic writing.

4 The ordinary pronunciation of *says* (3rd person present indicative) is /sɛz/. It is therefore odd that from the mid-19c. *sez* should have been repeatedly used in representations of uneducated speech, especially in the phrase *sez you* (= so you say).

sc. is the abbreviation of the Latin *scilicet* (derived from *scīre licet* 'one may understand or know') for 'to wit, that is to say' and is used to introduce an explanation of a difficult or unclear term. Printed in italics. Examples: (explaining a term already used) *The policy of the NUT* (*sc.* National Union of Teachers); *The Holy Ghost as Paraclete* (*sc.* advocate); (introducing a word, etc., that was omitted in the original as unnecessary, but is thought to require specifying for the present audience) *Eye hath not seen nor ear heard* (*sc.* the intent of God). This abbreviation is used repeatedly in this book. See also VIZ.

scalawag. The preferred AmE spelling of BrE SCALLYWAG.

scald (medieval Icelandic poet). See SKALD.

scallawag. An unusual AmE variant spelling of SCALLYWAG.

scallop. This is the recommended spelling (pronounced /ˈskɒlɛp/ or /ˈskaləp/), not *scollop.* The verb has inflections *scalloped, scalloping*; see -P-, -PP-.

scallywag. The word emerged in American politics in the 1840s and is of unknown etymology. Its usual spelling in BrE is *scallywag,* but the word is spelt in various ways in AmE including *scalawag* and *scallawag.*

scaly (having many scales or flakes). So spelt, not *-ey.*

scam. The noun ('a fraud') and the verb ('to swindle'), whose etymology is not known, are both originally US slang, and first recorded in 1963. They are now widely used in World English, and are marked by many dictionaries as 'slang' or 'informal' but are often employed in contexts that are not informal, such as news, communications from banks, etc. Derivatives and inflections double the final *m*, i.e. *scamming, scammed,* **scammer**.

scampi (large prawns) is a plural noun. When used in the sense 'a dish of these' it is sometimes treated as a singular. The word is derived from Italian *scampo* 'shrimp', plural *scampi.*

scandalum magnatum. The second word is the genitive plural of Latin *magnas* 'a magnate', not a participial adjective agreeing with *scandalum.* The phrase (now disused) means the utterance or publication of a malicious report against a dignitary. The plural is *scandala magnatum.* Printed in italic.

scant, scanty. First taken into Middle English from Old Norse in the mid-14c., *scant* flourished as noun, adjective, adverb, and verb for several centuries before it became restricted to literary, or, in some of its senses, to dialectal contexts. Such limitations applied first to the noun, and in time to the adverb and the verb. Criticized by Fower (1926) as a literary word, used instead of *scanty* only by those with 'no sense of incongruity', it is now much more frequent than the longer form, and standard in familiar collocations, e.g. *scant attention, regard, evidence, consolation, information, respect, reward,* and (echoing Hamlet's mother Gertrude) *scant of breath.*

-scape. Based on *landscape* (first recorded in 1598 and borrowed from Dutch *landschap*) and *seascape* (1799), a number of formations in *-scape* made their way into the language in the 19c. (e.g. *cityscape, cloudscape, roofscape*) and the 20c. (e.g. *dreamscape, lunarscape, mindscape, moonscape, soundscape*).

scapula (the shoulder-blade). Plural generally *scapulae* /-iː/, though *scapulas* is also correct.

scarce (adverb) was often used instead of the fuller form *scarcely* in ordinary adverbial contexts until about the end of the 19c. (e.g. *I ran as I never ran before, scarce minding the direction of my flight, so long as it led me to the murderers*—R. L. Stevenson, 1886), but is hardly ever encountered now except in poetry. It has frequently been called on by 20c. poets to qualify a participial adjective used attributively (e.g. *In the scarce-glimmering boles*—E. Blunden, 1922; *I match that child with this scarce-changed old man*—W. de la Mare, 1951).

scarcely. 1 *scarcely . . . than.* The standard construction is *scarcely . . . when . . .*: *Scarcely had he begun when Claverhouse ordered him to rise*—A. Boyle, 1990; The construction with *than* is not uncommon and is perhaps suggested by the analogy of *no sooner . . . than . . .*: *But scarcely had he begun to investigate these new, if somewhat less adventurous, hunting-grounds, than the entire party was 'summoned back to Hobarton by Sir John'*—I. Tree, 1991. The *OED* at the entry *than* cites an example of 1867 (see HARDLY 1), and Fowler (1926) cited another example (*Scarcely was the nice new drain finished than several of the children sickened with diphtheria*), but the constructions *Scarcely . . . when* or *Scarcely . . . before are preferable.* Cf. BARELY.

2 In common acceptable use, however, is the type *scarcely* + comparative adjective or adverb + *than.* Examples: *There could scarcely be a less promising environment for an amphibian than the desert of central Australia*—D. Attenborough, 1988; [*The*] *bill encourages 'bare bone' policies—providing scarcely more coverage than Medicaid*—*Village Voice* (US), 1992.

3 *scarcely* with negatives. *Scarcely* is not a negative as such, as will be seen from the pair of sentences *he scarcely mentioned the subject/he didn't mention the subject.* But, like *barely* and *hardly,* it has a negative force without being grammatically negative, and another negative should be avoided in the same sentence unless it is in a following subordinate clause, as in the following examples: *There is scarcely an aspect of the race that is not rife with meaning*—*New Yorker,* 1989; *There has scarcely been a time since the Russian Revolution when the American right was not fretting about the number of 'tenured radicals' . . . installed at American universities*—R. Hughes, 1993 (US).

scarf. In its ordinary sense of a long strip of material worn round the neck, the plural is either *scarves* (the form recommended here) or *scarfs.* The plural of the unrelated word *scarf,* meaning a joint or notch in timber, metal, etc., is *scarfs.*

scarify. There are two separate verbs. The first, pronounced /ˈskarɪfʌɪ/, has existed since the 15c. in various technical and figurative uses in the basic sense 'to scratch, to make incisions in'. The second, pronounced /ˈskɛːrɪfʌɪ/, was irregularly formed in the late 18c. from *scare* (verb) + *-ify,* perhaps after *terrify,* and means 'to scare, frighten'. This second verb is classified as *colloq.* in the *COD* (1995) and *colloq.* (orig. *dial.*) in *SOED* (1993).

scavenge, scavenger (verbs). The noun *scavenger* is a 16c. altered form of earlier *scavager,* with an intrusive *n* as in *messenger, passenger.* It yielded the verb *scavenger* and (as a back-formation) *scavenge* in the 17c. Parallels to the first of these (i.e. verbal uses of nouns) are commonplace, e.g. *to bicycle, to mountaineer, to soldier.* At about the end of the 18c., *scavenger* (verb) more or less dropped out of use, leaving *scavenge* to hold the field.

scena (music). Pronounced /ˈʃeɪnə/. As plural *scene* /ˈʃeɪneɪ/ reflects the word's Italian origin, but *scenas* is often used. Printed in roman.

scenario. 1 Usually pronounced /sɪˈnɑːrɪəʊ/ in BrE and /-ˈnɛːrɪəʊ/ in AmE, but there is much variation in both countries. Its plural is *scenarios*: see -O(E)S 5.

2 The word came into the language from Italian in its original meaning of 'an outline of the plot of a play, ballet, novel, etc.' in the 1870s, and thence in the meaning 'a film script' in the first quarter of the 20c., when cinema was becoming established. From the 1960s a new meaning exploded into use, initially referring to an outline of an imagined situation or sequence of events, especially the development of a hypothetical future world war, and hence an outline of any possible sequence of future events and a scientific model or description intended to account for observable facts.

From there it started to be used in the weakened sense of any supposed or imagined series of events, or even of a static situation: *How then do we decide which class to assign a couple to where he is a builder and she is a secretary* (*not that uncommon a scenario*)*?*—R. Symonds, 1988; *The entire education scenario is a joke—Liverpool Daily Echo,* 2007. Every kind of circumstance, situation, relationship, train of events, etc., can be called a *scenario,* and it has become something of a vogue word or cliché, particularly in the phrases *worst-case scenario* and *nightmare scenario.* Such uses of *scenario* are regarded by some with suspicion, and it is arguable that in the first example above it could be replaced by *situation* or left out altogether, and in the second that it is vague and meaningless. However, in its right place, when the imagined events or circumstances form a related sequence and are therefore comparable to the elements of a storyline, the word can be a useful one. Some typical examples: *With regard to the second scenario* (*redistributing libraries' costs to other entities, such as computer centers and research departments*)*, there is little that one outside the academic community can say—Logos,* 1990; *Taking this scenario one step further, Hamlet himself becomes Edward de Vere, the seventeenth Earl of Oxford—Atlantic,* 1991; *Road tolls are slowly edging their way on to the political agenda, and already two scenarios can be painted—Independent,* 1992; *At first, I thought the stentorian snores were part of the script, then that one of the actors had accidentally fallen asleep* (*a highly enjoyable scenario*)*—Times,* 1994. Nevertheless, a wise writer uses the word sparingly.

scene. At first, in the 1950s, restricted to the language of beatniks and their informal followers in the senses 'an area of action or interest (*not my scene*)' and 'a way of life' (*well-known on the jazz scene; a bad scene*), the word gradually made its way, at first mockingly and later just informally, into the speech of the general public.

scenic. Pronounced /ˈsiːnɪk/ in BrE and also usually in AmE. But the variant /ˈsɛnɪk/ also exists in AmE, and is dominant in some other English-speaking countries.

sceptic. Pronounced /ˈskɛptɪk/. So spelt in BrE, but as **skeptic** in AmE. The word is to be distinguished from *septic* /ˈsɛptɪk/, contaminated with bacteria.

sceptre. So spelt in BrE, but as **scepter** in AmE.

schedule. The traditional standard pronunciation /ˈʃɛdjuːl/ is still dominant in BrE, but the AmE pronunciation with initial /ˈsk-/ is increasingly heard, and is, inevitably, the preferred pronunciation of younger people.

schema (a synopsis, etc.). Pronounced /ˈskiːmə/. The plural is rather more often *schemas* than the etymologically correct Greek plural *schemata* /-mətə/.

scherzando, scherzo. These musical terms, from Italian, can have anglicized plurals *scherzandos* and *scherzos*, or, probably less often, the Italianate *scherzandi* and *scherzi*.

schism. The *OED* (1910) had only /ˈsiz(ə)m/ but since then, except among the clergy, this pronunciation has been joined, if not quite replaced, in general use by the form with initial /ˈsk-/. Similarly in the derivatives **schismatic** and **schismatical**.

schismatic, schismatical. As adjectives the first is usual, the second infrequent. The noun ('a holder of schismatic opinions') is always *schismatic*. See also SCHISM.

schist (geology). Pronounced /ʃɪst/.

schizoid, schizophrenia, schizophrenic. To use these words outside their medical context in a metaphorical way, e.g. *Gibraltar's schizophrenia continues to be fed by colonial pride*, is nowadays felt to be offensive.

schnapps /ʃnaps/. Spelt as shown.

scholium (marginal note in a manuscript) /ˈskəʊlɪəm/. Plural *scholia* /-lɪə/. See -UM 2.

school (of fish, etc.), **shoal**. The two words are etymologically one (from a Middle Dutch word) and are equally unconnected with the ordinary word *school* (which is derived from Latin *schola*). Both *school* and *shoal* are current and are used without difference of meaning.

schwa /ʃwɑː/ (shwah). In the phrase '*a* moment *a*go' in unemphatic BrE speech, the two unstressed vowels in italics are pronounced identically. The technical name for this sound is *schwa*, and its symbol is /ə/ in the International Phonetic Alphabet. Not only letter *a* can be pronounced /ə/: the italicized letters in the following show it represented by other written vowels: numb*e*r, th*e*, *o*bey, c*o*mmit, s*u*ccess, pict*u*re. The fact that letters *a*, *e*, *o*, and *u* can all be pronounced as a *schwa* explains many widespread spelling mistakes, such as **relevent*.

sciagraphy (art of the perspective of shadows, used in architectural drawing). Pronounced /sʌɪˈagrəfi/. Spelt as shown or as **skiagraphy**. The first element corresponds to Greek σκιά 'shadow'.

scilicet. Pronounced /ˈsɪlɪsɛt/ (**sil**-), or /ˈsʌɪlɪsɛt/ (**syl**-), or by Latinists /ˈskiːlɪkɛt/ (**skeel**-). Printed in italics. See SC.

scimitar /ˈsɪmɪtə/. So spelt. From French *cimeterre* or Italian *scimitarra*. The word is of unknown origin.

scintilla. Mostly used in the singular (*not a scintilla of doubt*), but if a plural is called for use *scintillas*.

scion /ˈsʌɪən/. So spelt in BrE and AmE in the sense 'descendant of a (noble) family'. When used to mean 'a shoot of a plant, etc.' often spelt **cion** in AmE.

scirocco. See SIROCCO.

scission. Pronounced /ˈsɪʃ(ə)n/.

scissors /ˈsɪzəz/ is construed as a plural noun (*the scissors are in the study drawer*), except in specialized senses in high-jumping (*the ordinary scissors is the least effective of the four styles*), wrestling, and rugby football.

sclerosis /sklɪəˈrəʊsis/ (hardening of body tissue). Plural (if needed) *scleroses* /-siːz/.

scone, originally a Scots word, probably derived from Dutch, has two possible pronunciations: the first rhymes with *gone*, the second *tone*. In US English the second is more common. In British English the two differing pronunciations traditionally have different regional and class associations, the first being associated with the north of England and Scotland, while the second is associated with the south and with middle-class affectation. It is the pronunciation once considered genteel that Hyacinth Bucket would insist on, but according to Wells (3rd edn), 65% of British respondents prefer the pronunciation rhyming with *gone*. *Scone*, a village in central Scotland, the site of the coronation of Scottish kings, is pronounced /skuːn/.

scope. For synonyms, see FIELD.

score (noun) (= 20). The phrase *three score (years) and ten*, as a traditional way of describing one's allotted lifespan, is probably fading fast, if the *OEC* is anything to go by. Though no doubt most people would think of it as somehow biblical, it is not from the AV: it antedates it by 76 years, appearing in Coverdale's version of Psalm 90: 10, as 'The days of our age are three-score years and ten'. Often enough *three score* is used on its own, as it has been since the 15c.: *Frank Roe was part of the racing scene in Ireland for over three score years and you could not meet a nicer person at the races—I'll vouch for that*—*The Kingdom*, 2003. When followed by *of, a score* normally governs a plural verb: *a score of customers were waiting at the door.* Formerly *score* preceded by *a* was often treated as a numeral adjective (e.g. *I form'd a score different plans*—Sterne, 1768).

scoria /ˈskɔːrɪə/ is a singular noun, plural *-iae* /-ɪiː/; but, as the meaning of the singular and of the plural is much the same (cf. *ash* and *ashes, clinker* and *clinkers*), it is no wonder that the singular is sometimes wrongly followed by a plural verb (*The scoria were still hot* etc.), or that a false singular *scorium* is on record.

scotch (verb). The verb that currently means 'to quash, destroy, bring to nothing' (e.g. *to scotch once and for all any lingering doubts or rumours*) has no connection with the adjective referring to people and things from Scotland and is not, unlike the verb *welsh,* a racial slur. It was probably influenced by *scotch* (verb), which answers to a noun (first recorded in the 17c.) meaning 'a block placed under a wheel, etc., to prevent moving or slipping'; hence (for the verb) 'to render inoperative'.

Scotch, Scots, Scottish. It is not possible to set down here all the complications of this somewhat sensitive group of words. The adjective *Scotch,* in origin a contracted variant of *Scottish,* 'had been adopted into the northern vernacular before the end of the 18th c.; it [was] used regularly by Burns, and subsequently by Scott' (*OED*). But 'since the mid-19th c. there has been in Scotland a growing tendency to discard the form altogether, *Scottish,* or less frequently *Scots,* being substituted' (*OED*). *Scots* is also a longstanding variant of *Scottish.* The outcome is that all three adjectives are still current, but *Scotch* is the least frequent and survives mainly in certain collocations, e.g. *Scotch broth, Scotch egg, Scotch mist, Scotch terrier, Scotch tweed, Scotch whisky,* and a few others, or on the lips of unsuspecting American tourists. *Scots* is the term regularly used of the form of English spoken in (especially Lowlands) Scotland. It also occurs in the names of certain Scottish regiments. But the all-embracing general adjective meaning 'of or relating to Scotland, its history, its day-to-day life, or its inhabitants' is *Scottish.* These are middle-class preferences. 'Paradoxically,' A. J. Aitken reports in *OCELang.* (1992), 'for working class Scots the common form has long been *Scotch*...and the native form *Scots* is sometimes regarded as an Anglicized affectation.'

Scot, Scotsman, Scotchman, etc. As nouns, *Scot* and *Scotsman/Scotswoman* are preferred by middle-class English-speakers in Scotland, but outside Scotland, and especially outside the UK, *Scotchman* and *Scotchwoman* are still widely used. See SCOTCH, SCOTS, SCOTTISH.

Scotticism, Scotticize. The forms with *-tt-*, rather than *-t-*, are recommended.

scoundrel has the derivative **scoundrelly** (adjective). See -LL-, -L-.

scourge. I was puzzled to hear this word pronounced /skɔːdʒ/ (skawj) by a BrE speaker instead of /skəːdʒ/ (skerj). It is, as it turns out, an alternative AmE pronuncation.

scout, gyp, skip. College servants at Oxford, Cambridge, and Trinity College Dublin, respectively.

scrannel (thin, meagre). First recorded in Milton's *Lycidas* (1637), *Their lean and fleshy songs Grate on their scrannel Pipes of wretched straw.* Now used chiefly as a reminiscence of Milton's context, usually with the sense 'harsh, unmelodious', e.g. *His scrannel music-making*—W. H. Auden, 1951.

scrimmage, scrummage. The form with *-u-* is obligatory (or more usually just *scrum*) in rugby, that with *-i-* in more general use ('a brawl, a confused struggle') and as a technical term for a particular sequence of play in American football.

scriptorium. Plural *scriptoria* (for preference) or *scriptoriums.* See -UM 3.

scrum(mage). See SCRIMMAGE.

scull, skull. The single-handed oar has initial *sc-*, the cranium *sk-*. Both words entered the language in the Middle English period, but they are not etymologically related.

sculpt, sculpture (verbs). Adopted in the mid-19c. from French *sculpter, sculpt* may now be perceived as a back-formation from *sculptor.* It far outnumbers the older verb *sculpture,* a 17c. example of 'verbing' first found in John Evelyn's diary. The *OEC* data suggests that as a verb *sculpture* is largely confined to the physical art of working stone, while *sculpt* can be both literal and metaphorical: thus pillars can be *beautifully sculpted* or (less often) *sculptured,* but only the first applies to human faces, bodies, and lips.

sculptress. The regular feminine equivalent of *sculptor,* in use since the 17c. (Evelyn), but now tending to be put aside in favour of the gender-free word *sculptor.* See -ESS 4.

scutum /ˈskjuːtəm/. (zoology) Plural *scuta.* See -UM 2.

sea change. An intensifying variant of *change,* which has outgrown its Shakespearean origins. See IRRELEVANT ALLUSION.

seamstress, sempstress. The first of these is now the standard form, the second rare, though occasionally still encountered. The first is pronounced /ˈsiːmstrɪs/ the second /ˈsɛmstrɪs/.

seance, séance. The word is rather less often spelt with an accent than without. It is also pronounced with varying degrees of anglicization, as /ˈseɪɒns/, /-ɒ̃s/, or /-ɑːns/.

sear, sere. Several words are involved: *sear* for the verb meaning 'burn' or 'char', and the corresponding noun (mark produced by searing); *sere* for the noun meaning 'a catch of a gunlock'; for the ecological noun meaning 'a series of plant communities'; and for the adjective meaning 'dried up, withered'. In past centuries the adjective was often spelt *sear*: e.g. *I haue liu'd long enough, my way of life Is falne into the Seare, the yellow Leafe*—Shakespeare, 1605; *The rude materialities of life in this sear generation*—N. P. S. Wiseman, 1837.

seasonable, which is a relatively rare word, means 'usual for or appropriate to a particular season of the year', e.g. *Hot weather is seasonable for August; he loved the seasonable mince pies that his aunt cooked at Christmas.* It was formerly used also to mean 'opportune, well-timed'. **Seasonal,** by contrast, means 'occurring at or associated with a particular season', e.g. *sheep-shearing is seasonal work; the seasonal migration of geese; the farming year and its seasonal activities.* Sometimes *seasonable* is used where *seasonal* is appropriate, e.g. **seasonable climbing vegetables.* The opposites of these two words can both mean 'unusual for the time of year' when referring to the weather, e.g. *unseasonable/ unseasonal weather, rain,* etc., but only *unseasonable* has the additional meaning of 'occurring at the wrong time, inopportune', e.g. *You are apt to be pressed to drink a glass of vinegary port at an unseasonable hour* (S. Maugham).

seated. See SIT (verb).

second. 1 The *second chamber* of some parliamentary democracies is the upper house in a bicameral parliament.

2 *second-hand.* There is much variation in the use of the hyphen. *COD* (1995) opts for *second hand* for the hand recording seconds in a watch or clock; *second-hand* for the adjective meaning not new (*second-hand clothing*) and the adverb meaning at second hand, not directly (*she always buys second-hand*); and *second hand* in such phrases as *heard only at second hand.* But the adjective and adverb are very commonly written as one word (*secondhand*).

3 *second of all.* An Americanism based on the general English phrase *first of all,* e.g. *First of all he's not my Roosevelt, and second of all we don't have to discuss these things while we're eating*—L. S. Schwartz, 1989.

4 *second* (verb). When it means to transfer temporarily to other employment or another post, the stress falls on the second syllable: /sɪˈkɒnd/ (si-**kond**). But when it means formally support or endorse (a motion, nomination, etc.), the stress falls on the first syllable: /ˈsɛkənd/ (**se**-kuhnd).

secretive. Now normally pronounced /ˈsiːkrɪtɪv/, i.e. stressed on the first syllable, though the *OED* (1911) gave only the form with the stress on the second syllable, /sɪˈkriːtɪv/.

sect. Adopted in Middle English from Old French *secte* or Latin *secta,* from *sect-* past participle stem of *sequi* 'to follow', its dominant meaning is 'a body of people subscribing to views divergent from those of others within the same religion; a party or faction in a religious body' (*SOED*). Hence, over the centuries, often applied by Anglicans to various Nonconformist groups (Quakers, Methodists, etc.), and by Roman Catholics to Protestant groups, and, outside religion, to the followers of a particular philosopher or school of thought.

sedilia /sɪˈdɪlɪə/, a series of usually canopied and decorated stone seats, usually three in number, placed on or recessed into the south side of the choir near the altar for use by the clergy. The singular if required, is *sedile*, /sɪˈdʌɪlɪ/.

see, bishopric, diocese. A *bishopric* is the office belonging to a bishop; a *diocese* is the district administered by a bishop; a *see* is (the chair that symbolizes) a bishop's authority over a particular *diocese*. A *bishopric* is conferred on, a *diocese* is committed to, a *see* is filled by, such and such a person: *my predecessor in the see; all the clergy of the diocese; hoping for a bishopric.*

seeing is frequently used as a quasi-conjunction, usually followed by *that* + a clause, to mean 'considering that, inasmuch as, because' (*seeing that you do not know it yourself*). Colloquial equivalents are *seeing as, seeing as how*: these are normally restricted to informal contexts, e.g. *Seeing as how you're always short of £sd, I thought you could maybe earn a bit*—S. Gulliver, 1974.

seek (verb). See PASSIVE VOICE 6(a).

seem (verb).

1. The pleonasm shown in *These conclusions, it seems to me, appear to be reached naturally* should be avoided.
2. *can't seem* + infinitive. See CANNOT 3.
3. See PERFECT INFINITIVE 1.

seigneur etc. Spellings entered in the *COD* (1995): *seigneur, seignior; seigneurial, seignorial; seigniorage, seignorage; seigniory, seigneury.* In each pair the first is normally the preferred form. The pronunciation in all begins with /seɪn-/ followed by /j/ (i.e. the *y* sound). Differences in meaning or use exist but are too complicated to be given here: see the *OED.*

seise, seisin. Pronounced /siːz/, /ˈsiːzɪn/. The words are sometimes (but less often) spelt *-ze, -zin,* and belong etymologically to the ordinary verb *seize.* But in the legal phrases *to seise a person of,* i.e. put him in possession of, and *to be seised of,* i.e. to possess, the *-s-* spelling is usual.

seize (verb). See SEISE, SEISIN.

seldom. 1 (adjective). Used since the 15c., seemingly without break, but now more or less restricted to literary contexts, e.g. *My seldom night terrors*—W. Golding, 1959; *With her small seldom smile*—Edmund Wilson, 1961 (in Webster's Third).

2 (adverb). Used in emphatic phrases, some now rare or obsolete, e.g. *seldom ever* (10c., still current); *seldom or ever* (18–19c., obsolete); *seldom(,) if ever(,)* (17c., still current); *seldom or never* (14c., still current). Examples: (seldom ever) *I seldom ever dreamed of Lolita as I remembered her*—V. Nabokov, 1955; (seldom or ever) *The Players seldom or ever throw out the Voice with any Vehemence*—A. Murphy, 1752; (seldom(,) if ever(,)) *The pettish Israelites (a people seldom if ever, pleased with God's present Providencies) who murmured under Moses*—W. Sclater, 1653; *Surrey backwoodsmen seldom, if ever, call much upon the rock-climbing or bog-defying wherewithal of their 4-w-d off-roaders*—*Daily Tel.*, 1991; *A strong, confident exposition of the last movement completes an interpretation which has seldom, if ever, been surpassed on record*—*Gramophone*, 1992; (seldom or never) *Also in wynter selden or neuer pytte water fresyth*—Trevisa, 1398; *those that doe dye of it, doe seldome or neuer recouer*—Shakespeare, 1606; *Around 80 per cent of Spaniards identify themselves as Catholics but two-thirds seldom or never attend church*—*Daily Tel.*, 2011.

selector. So spelt, not *-er*.

self. Formerly in commercial use as a substitute for *myself* or *oneself*, and in particular when written on a cheque or counterfoil: e.g. *He drew a cheque for a hundred pounds to self on Friday*—G. Heyer, 1935; *He turned back the counterfoils . . . The uppermost . . . was marked 'Self', a withdrawal of four hundred pounds*—C. Watson, 1967. Though attested since the mid-18c., its use in non-commercial contexts is now merely humorous or fairly informal, especially in the ironic reminder 'note to self'. Examples: *Mr. H. and self agreed at parting to take a gentle ride*—Dr Johnson, 1758; *As both self and wife were fond of* *seeing life . . . we decided a trip to Baden Baden would be a nice change for us*—J. Astley, 1894; *Drunks black out, remember nothing; A.A.* [*sc.* Alcoholics Anonymous] *requires memory, the acknowledgement of actions' effects on self and others, then apology and atonement*—B. Holm, 1985 (US); *Memo to self: even if you don't think you're going to win, write a speech*—weblog, 2002; *Note to self: don't ever forget suntan lotion again, I'm so burnt!*—*OEC*, 2004.

See MYSELF.

self-. Such compounds are unlimited in number. The principal types are (*a*) those in which *self-* is in the objective relation to the second element (*self-abandonment, self-betrayal*, etc.); (*b*) used with verbal nouns (*self-searching, self-understanding*, etc.); (*c*) with agent-nouns (*self-educator, self-seeder*, etc.); (*d*) with nouns of state or condition (*self-awareness, self-mastery*, etc.); (*e*) with adjectives (*self-analytical, self-protective*, etc.); (*f*) with the participial *-ing* form (*self-serving, self-defeating*, etc.), and numerous others. Occasionally such compounds are unnecessarily formed where the second element would suffice by itself. Writers should pause before writing *self-conceit*(*ed*), for example, in contexts where *conceited* by itself would suffice. Similar considerations apply to *self-assurance, self-complacent, self-confidence*, and some other *self*-compounds. The rule is quite simple: make a lightning decision about whether the *self*-adds anything essential to the proposed second element of a compound. It usually does (e.g. *self-addressed, self-defence, self-service*), but occasionally does not.

self-deprecating, -deprecation, -depreciation. See DEPRECATE, DEPRECIATE 3.

self-destruct. In the 1960s the extended form *self-destruct* appeared, used intransitively to refer to a device that is preset to destroy itself by exploding or disintegrating, and by extension to people who in some way damage or destroy themselves physically or mentally, or their reputations, by their actions and habits: *the idea of DVDs that self-destruct after a few plays*—*The Hot Button*, 2002; *the family is already on the point of self-destructing through jealousy and squabbling*—*Senses of Cinema*, 2003; *the ward represented by Paul Sutherland until he self-destructed as a Conservative candidate in the recent election*—*Eye Weekly* (Toronto), 2003. Like *destruct, self-destruct* is also used as a noun, especially attributively (*self-destruct device, mechanism*, etc.).

selfie. Voted Oxford Dictionaries Word of the Year 2013, this term for a 'photograph that one has taken of oneself, typically one taken with a smartphone or webcam and uploaded to a social media website' (e.g. *occasional selfies are acceptable, but posting a new picture of yourself every day isn't necessary*) goes at least as far back as 2002, but did not achieve prominence until much later. The phenomenally rapid growth which words can enjoy thanks to the Internet and social media is illustrated by the 17,000% increase in the use of *selfie* between October 2012 and October 2013. The spelling in *-ie* is more frequent than that in *-y*, and also highlights the word's Australian origin: the diminutive *-ie* ending appears also in *barbie* (barbecue), *firie* (firefighter), *tinnie* (can of beer) and *rellie* (relative).

semantics (noun) (construed, like *politics*, etc., as a singular). Its primary sense, the branch of linguistics concerned with all aspects of meaning, was adopted in English in the 1890s from French *sémantique* (M. Bréal, 1883), and has now replaced the slightly earlier term *semasiology*. The subject is now a highly sophisticated one beyond the reach of anyone but specialized linguistic scholars. But one aspect of historical semantics can be glimpsed from some elementary examples where fundamental changes of meaning have occurred over the centuries. The original meaning is given in brackets after each example; full details are set out in the *OED*. Examples: *buxom* (obedient, compliant); *deer* (an animal, a beast); *effete* (no longer fertile, past producing offspring; cf. *foetus*); *elaborate* (to produce by effort or labour); *horrid* (rough, bristling); *meat* (food); *meticulous* (timid, fearful); *treacle* (any of various medicinal salves). Since the 1940s, *semantics* and the corresponding adjective **semantic** have passed into general language in a much weakened use: in examples such as *quibbling over semantics may seem petty stuff* and the following ones, the word always carries a suggestion that such concern with meaning is somehow trivial or irrelevant. Examples: *Almost daily in the press briefing, whenever a newsman raises his hand to ask for clarification of some mealy-mouthed statement: 'I am not going* *to debate semantics with you,' the spokesman replies*—K. Hudson, 1978; *President Bush is now endeavoring to redress the looming embarrassment of Social Security's obligation to pay more than it will take in. The semantic argument about whether this shortfall constitutes a crisis, a problem, or a banana daiquiri is pointless*—OEC, 2005; *Bah! This is just semantics. If we are to accept that all acts are selfish, then we're going to have to make a distinction between two kinds of selfishness*—weblog, 2008.

semaphore. Pronounced /ˈsɛmɛfɔː/ with a short *e* in the first syllable, *e* despite the fact that the first element answers to Greek σῆμα 'sign, signal'.

semi- is the most active and versatile of the prefixes meaning 'half' (the other two being *demi-* and *hemi-*) in forming compounds, which are innumerable, especially with adjectives and participles as the second element. The earliest of these compounds in English is *semicircular* (1432–50) and *semi-mature* (*c*.1440). In so far as a pattern is discernible at all, the prefix is extensively employed in technical terminology (e.g. *semiconductor, semidiameter, semigroup*), but it is preferred to *demi-*, *hemi-*, and *half-* in many ordinary words as well (e.g. *semi-automatic, semicircle, semi-conscious, semi-detached, semifinal, semi-professional, semi-skilled*). It is worth noting that the *e* in *semi-* is short, despite being long in the Latin original (*sēmi-*). In AmE the words above spelled with hyphens would not have them. It is necessary, however, to retain hyphens when two letter *i*s would clash, e.g. *semi-invalid*.

semicolon. 1 This name of the punctuation mark consisting of a dot placed upon a comma (;) is first recorded in Ben Johnson's grammar of *a*1637. The semicolon is the least confidently used of the regular punctuation marks in ordinary writing, and the one least in evidence to anyone riffling through the pages of a modern novel. But it is extremely useful, used in moderation. Its main role is to mark a grammatical separation that is stronger in effect than a comma but less strong than a full stop. Normally the two parts of a sentence divided by a semicolon balance or complement each other as distinct from leading from one to the other, in which case a COLON is usually more suitable.

2 (*a*) The semicolon separates two or more clauses which are of more or less equal importance and are linked as a pair or series: *To err is human; to forgive, divine./The temperate man's pleasures are always durable, because they are regular; and all his life is calm and serene, because it is innocent./Never speak concerning what you are ignorant of; speak little of what you know; and whether you speak or say not a word, do it with judgement.* (*b*) It is also used as a stronger division in a sentence that already contains commas: *What has crippled me? Was it my grandmother, frowning on my childish affection and turning it to formality and cold courtesy; or my timid, fearful mother, in awe of everyone including, finally, me; or was it my wife's infidelities, or my own?*—A. Lambert, 1989. (*c*) In a list where any of the elements themselves contain commas, use a semicolon to clarify the relationship of the components: *They pointed out, in support of their claim, that they had used the materials stipulated in the contract; that they had taken every reasonable precaution, including some not mentioned in the code; and that they had employed only qualified workers, all of whom were very experienced.* This is common in lists with internal commas, where semicolons structure the internal hierarchy of its components: *I should like to thank the Warden and Fellows of All Souls College, Oxford; the staff of the Bodleian Library, Oxford; and the staff of the Pierpont Morgan Library, New York.* (*d*) Since it can be confusing and unattractive to begin a sentence with a symbol, especially one that is not a capital letter, the semicolon can replace a full point: *Let us assume that* a *is the crude death rate and* b *life expectancy at birth;* a *will signal a rise in . . .*

semivowel. In English phonetics the term applied to the sounds /j/ (normally spelt *y*, as in *young*) and /w/, i.e. to sounds intermediate between a vowel and a consonant.

sempstress. See SEAMSTRESS.

senarius /sɪˈnɛːrɪəs/. A (Greek or Latin) verse consisting of six usually iambic feet, especially an iambic trimeter. Also called an *iambic senarius*. Plural *senarii* / -rɪiː, -rɪʌɪ/.

senator. So spelt, not *-er*.

senatus /sɛˈnɑːtəs/, the governing body or senate of certain universities, especially in Scotland. The plural, if required, is *-tuses* or *-tus* /-tuːs/, not *-ti*. See -US 2.

senhor, senhora, senhorita. Portuguese and Brazilian titles. Pronounced in English /sɛnˈjɔː/, /sɛnˈjɔːrə/, /sɛnjəˈriːtə/.

senior. 1 For the *Senior Service*, see SOBRIQUETS.

2 The relatively recent phrase **senior moment** (1996) is a way of describing a short period of forgetfulness or confusion, such as might be experienced by an elderly person. It is best kept for informal contexts, since some people will consider it demeaning and ageist. Often, it is used by speakers of themselves, e.g. *I tell you, I had a bit of a senior moment yesterday! I only bloody left a bag of shopping outside!*—weblog, 2005 (UK).

sennight (from Old English *seofon nihta* 'seven nights'). An archaic word for a week.

señor, señora, señorita. Spanish titles. Pronounced in English /sɛnˈjɔː/, /sɛnˈjɔːrə/, /sɛnjəˈriːtə/.

sensational entered the language in the literal sense 'of or pertaining to or dependent upon sensation or the senses' in the mid-19c. and almost immediately acquired the exaggerated meanings 'aiming at violently exciting effects; calculated to produce a startling impression'. Since then these extended senses have to all intents and purposes driven out the literal one, especially in newspaper reportage (*a sensational upset at Wembley*), in advertisements (*sensational bargains in the New Year sales*), and in contexts of informal praise (*she looked sensational in her new dress*).

sense (noun). The phrase **sense of humour** means 'the faculty of perceiving and enjoying what is ludicrous or amusing'. It happens not to be recorded (in the *OED*) before the 1880s but it seems likely that it was in use at an earlier date. It is often, perhaps most often, used in negative contexts of someone who seems not to recognize the humorous side of things (*he lacks a sense of humour; he has no sense of humour*).

sense (verb). It is worth noting that the current meaning 'to be or become vaguely aware (of something), to detect subconsciously (*I sensed a hardness in his tone*)' is first recorded (according to the *OED*) in 1872, and was sufficiently 'modern' for Fowler (1926) to find it irritating. The verb entered the language much earlier (late 16c.) with the meaning 'to perceive (an outward object) by the senses; also, to feel (pain)', and some other specific meanings (e.g. 'to expound the meaning of'). But the chief modern use is as noted above. There are also technical uses in philosophy ('to have a sense perception of') and in technology of a machine, instrument, etc., able to detect something (e.g. *In general particle detectors operate by sensing the ionization of atoms caused by the passage of a charged particle*—*Sci. Amer.*, 1978).

sensibility, sensitivity. The nouns *sensibility* and *sensitivity* are not synonyms, though they occasionally overlap. *Sensibility* does not correspond to *sensible* (in its familiar meaning 'having common sense') at all and chiefly denotes (often in the plural) a person's delicate finer feelings: *Walter was a little hurt at this since he did most of the cooking at their place, but Zimmerman was too upset to worry about Walter's sensibilities*—B. Elton, 1992. *Sensitivity* has a wider range of meanings concerned with physical or emotional reactions of various kinds, and can be paraphrased straightforwardly as 'being sensitive'. If people exhibit *sensitivity* to something, they show themselves to be *sensitive* to it; if they exhibit *sensibility*, they display the ability to appreciate and respond to complex emotional or aesthetic influences. Contrast *American officials have exhibited growing sensitivity to cultural property issues* with *Valerio's work exhibits an almost religious sensibility, one that seems to accept the Christian notion that the eternal realm can be viewed through the veil of ordinary visible reality.* Further examples: *My reference to it was simply a tease, and all the more tempting given Victor's known sensitivity on the point*—*Climber and Hill Walker*, 1991; *This book's greatest strength is its sensitivity to Kissinger the man*—*Scotland on Sunday*, 2004.

sensible, sensitive, susceptible. In certain uses, in which the point is the effect produced or producible on the person or thing qualified, the three words are near, though not identical, in meaning. *I am sensible of* [*sc.* not unaware of] *your kindness, sensitive to ridicule, susceptible to beauty.* Formerly *sensible* could be used in all three types of sentence; but its popular meaning as the opposite of *foolish* has become so predominant that we are no longer intelligible if we say *a sensible person* as the equivalent of *a sensitive* or *a susceptible person*, and even *sensible of* is counted among LITERARY WORDS though perhaps surviving as a formulaic phrase for the opening of highly formal speeches: *I am deeply sensible of the honour you have done me*... The difference between *sensible of* and *sensitive to* is roughly that you are *sensible of* something when you apprehend it with emotional consciousness and are *sensitive to* something when you react to it with strong emotional feeling, the words 'consciousness' and 'feeling' characterizing the difference between the two. However, *sensible of* now sounds extremely old-fashioned, and a more likely choice of words is *conscious of* or *aware of*, although these admittedly denote intellectual rather than emotional perceptions. With *of* the meaning of *susceptible* is different: it is equivalent to 'admitting or capable of': *A passage susceptible of more than one interpretation; an assertion not susceptible of proof.*

sensitize is a word first made for the needs of Victorian photographers and made irregularly. It should have been *sensitivize*. One might as well have omitted the adjective ending of *fertile, immortal, liberal*, and *signal*, and say *fertize, immortize, liberize*, and *signize*, as omit the *-iv(e)-* of *sensitive*. The photographers, however, made their bed, and we must all lie in it. At this distance of time we must just accept the shorter form. The *OED* (section issued in 1912) included only *sensitize* (e.g. *Education, while it sensitises a man's fibre, is incapable of turning weakness into strength*, 1880), not *sensitivize* (nor *sensize*). Nor does any other modern dictionary include the more regular form. There is no possibility of turning the etymological clock back.

sensorium (area of the brain). Plural *-ia* (recommended) or *-iums*. See -UM 3.

sensual, sensuous. 1 The second of these is thought to have been expressly formed by Milton (in 1641) to convey what had originally been conveyed by the older *sensual* (first recorded *c.*1450) but had become associated in that word with the notion of undue indulgence in the grosser pleasures of the senses, especially carnal pleasure. At any rate Milton's own phrase *simple, sensuous, and passionate* in describing great poetry as compared with logic and rhetoric has had much to do with establishing one meaning of *sensuous*, i.e. 'relating to or affecting the senses rather than the intellect'. In other words, *sensuous* is supposedly the more neutral word of the two, while *sensual* generally has more than a hint of gratification, voluptuousness, or sexuality.

2 The following examples maintain this distinction for those who wish to stick to the supposed rule: (sensual) *Modigliani appreciated Kisling for what he was, a sweet-natured, high-spirited, sensual young man*—J. Rose, 1990; *The Hindu god of love, Kama, is the husband of Rati, the goddess of sensual desire*—P. Allardice, 1990; *A good slow, deep, seductive, sensual, sexual kiss can be the very thing that sends someone over the edge in my opinion*—weblog, 2005; (sensuous) *All the sensuous elements of the previous years have been banished; colour has been reduced to a severe combination of browns, dull greens and greys*—J. Golding, 1988; *The passage exemplifies the distancing effect of simile, and the more sensuous effect of metaphor*—E. Black, 1993.

3 In practice, the meanings are too close, and *sensuous* has long since gone the way of *sensual* and developed a second meaning, 'attractive or gratifying physically, especially sexually': *He looked forward to this drink, the first of the day, with a sensuous desire*—B. Vine, 1987; *There was something extremely sensuous about having a man dry her hair, especially this man*—A. Murray, 1993. *Sensuous* retains its 'neutral' meaning in uses that are primarily to do with aesthetics, for example in the context of music or poetry: *Cesti's great gift was for melody: sensuous and eminently singable*—G. Abraham, 1985. It should be borne in mind, however, that in some contexts, when a faculty is being distinguished that is not rational or logical or intellectual, but one simply pertaining to the senses, then either *sensual* or *sensuous* may be safely used.

sentence. Fowler (1926) had no doubts about the nature of a sentence: '*sentence*, in grammar, means a set of words complete in itself, having either expressed or understood in it a subject and a predicate, and conveying a statement or question or command or exclamation. If it contains one or more *clauses*, it is a *complex sentence*; if its subject consists of more than one parallel noun etc., or its predicate of more than one verb etc., it is a *compound sentence*; if its subject or predicate or verb (or more) is understood, it is an *elliptical sentence*... Simple sentences: *I went* (statement); *Where is he?* (question); *Hear thou from heaven* (command); *How they run!* (exclamation). Complex sentence: *Where he bowed there he fell down dead.* Compound sentences: *You and I would rather see that angel; They hum'd and ha'd.* Elliptical sentences: *Listen; Well played; What?* Two sentences (not one): *You commanded and I obeyed.*'

Modern grammarians, by contrast, are nervous about defining the traditional terms of grammar ('Neither of these terms [*sc. sentence* and *grammar*] can be given a clear-cut definition', *CGEL*, 1985), but usually end up by providing working definitions: 'Sentences are units made up of one or more clauses. Sentences containing just one clause are called *simple*, and sentences containing more than one clause are called *complex*' (Leech and Svartvik, 1975). '*Sentence*. The largest unit of language structure treated in traditional grammar; usually having a subject and predicate, and (when written) beginning with a capital letter and ending with a full stop' (*Oxford Dict. Eng. Grammar*, 1994).

Set down here are some of the main types of written English sentences. Similar examples can be found in any other well-written source.

Simple. *Culloden is Scott's watershed.*
Compound. *Fiction and history are kindred forms.*
Complex. *If history is about dates, then* Cousin Bette *is self-evidently an historical novel.*
Long complex. *In 1854 and 1855, Dickens was also showing signs of overwork (the strain, not the work itself, was unusual) and was often angry, even to helplessness, at the turn of public events: progress in education, sanitation, social reconciliation, scant enough, was further impeded by the Crimean war (an excuse to defer home legislation), while the conduct of the war itself seemed increasingly criminal, with an army before Sebastopol virtually abandoned by the government and destroyed less by the enemy than by disease, lack of supplies, and general incompetence (it was another humiliation, felt deeply and not by Dickens alone, that the French ordered these things better, as was bitterly obvious to observers in the Crimea).*

Verbless or otherwise incomplete sentences (stylistically acceptable in context). *She only spoke to me once about her private life and that's what I've told you. As I remember it*—G. Greene, 1980; *They ate what was in front of them. While it was hot*—M. Drabble, 1987; *Max played ping-pong with the children. Then records*—*Encounter*, 1987; *Dionysiac release? I suppose so. A rehearsal for the release of seeds. An invisible embrace. The motion of the mountainside*—H. Brodkey, 1993; *Still, it had been a good party. An unforgettable party, actually. And still was*—A. Huth, 1992.

sentence adjective. See IMPORTANT.

sentence adverb. 1 *Introduction.* In an issue of *The Times*, coastguard Peter Legg, senior watch officer at Dover, was reported as saying *Frankly we don't want them.* He was referring to Channel swimmers and the hazard they present to shipping in the world's busiest waterway. His use of *frankly*, meaning 'if I may speak frankly', draws attention to one of the most bitterly contested of all the linguistic battles fought out in the last decades of the 20c. This unofficial war against certain uses of adverbs ending in *-ly* broke out in the late 1960s. Its chief focus was the adverb *hopefully*. The adverb was regarded as acceptable when it meant 'in a hopeful manner', as in *to set to work hopefully*, i.e. its traditional use since the 17c.; but not acceptable when used to mean 'it is hoped [that], let us hope', as in *We asked her when she expected to move into her new apartment, and she answered, 'Hopefully on Tuesday'*.

Burchfield (1996) suggested that in the 20c. there had been 'a swift and immoderate increase' in the currency of *-ly* adverbs used to qualify a predication or assertion as a whole. The *-ly* adverbs concerned include *actually, basically, clearly, frankly, hopefully, interestingly, normally, regrettably, strictly*, and *thankfully*. Suddenly, as he put it 'round about the end of the 1960s, and with unprecedented venom, a dunce's cap was placed on the head of anyone who used just one of them—*hopefully*—as a sentence adverb'.

2 (*a*) *Definition.* The traditional definition of an adverb is that it is a word that modifies the meaning of a verb, an adjective, or another adverb, as in, for example, *he shook his head sadly*. However, another important function of some adverbs is to comment on a whole sentence, either expressing the speaker's attitude or classifying the discourse. For example, in *sadly, he is rather overbearing, sadly* does not mean that he is overbearing in a sad manner: it expresses the speaker's attitude to what is being stated. Sentence adverbs (also called sentence adverbials or disjuncts) are adverbs or adverbial phrases that express a writer's or speaker's attitude to the content of the sentence in which it occurs (such as *frankly, obviously*), or place the sentence in a particular context (such as *technically, politically*). It is only the first kind that are in any way contentious.

(*b*) *Typical examples.* Typically, *-ly* sentence adverbs begin a sentence and are marked off from what follows by a comma, although they can also occur elsewhere: *Unhappily, there are times when violence is the only way in which justice can be secured* (in which *Unhappily* = it is an unhappy fact that); *Agreeably, he asked me my name and where I lived* (= in a manner that was agreeable to me); *Frankly, I do not wish to stop them* (= in all frankness, to speak frankly); *Well, that won't happen at Pringle's, hopefully as they say. Hopefully* (= it is to be hoped). These examples are drawn, respectively, from T. S. Eliot's *Murder in the Cathedral* (1935), a 1987 issue of the *New Yorker*, Brian Moore's *The Colour of Blood* (1987), and David Lodge's *Nice Work* (1988). A reasonable cross-section of English writing, it would seem. Such sentence adverbs do not necessarily stand at the beginning of sentences: *Aldabra Island in the Indian Ocean, where man 'has thankfully failed to establish himself'—Times*, 1983; *Competitions in Australia, regrettably, have a very different history, and have frequently led to less satisfactory results—Architecture Australia* (Magazine), 2002.

3 *History.* Clearly, the former debate over the legitimacy of *hopefully* as a sentence adverb branches out far beyond the domain of the actual word itself. The second edition of the *OED* has entries for *hopefully, regretfully, sadly, thankfully*, and perhaps one or two others, used as sentence adverbs. It draws attention to their unpopularity among 'some writers'. Most of the illustrative examples given in the dictionary to support the constructions are drawn from works written since the late 1960s. What the 20c. evidence in these entries fails to bring out is that the present-day widespread use of sentence adverbs is no more than an acceleration of a much older process. The *OED* entry for *seriously* (sense 1) has an example of 1644 drawn from the diary of Richard Symonds, who marched with the royal army during the Civil War: *Except here and there an officer* (*and seriously I saw not above three or four that looked like a gentleman*). It is clear that *seriously* does not directly qualify *saw*, but the whole of the sentence that follows it. In 1872 Ruskin, in *The Eagle's Nest*, used the same adverb in the same manner: *Quite seriously, all the vital functions . . . rise and set with the sun.* In both examples, *seriously* is an elliptical use of the phrase *to speak seriously*. The *OED* also cites a 1680 example of *strictly* from the work of the printer Joseph Moxon, qualifying (as it says) a predication or assertion as a whole' (= strictly speaking: *This whole Member is called the Moving Collar, though the Collar strictly is only the round Hole at* a. Other pre-20c. adverbs used to qualify a sentence are not difficult to find: e.g. *Frankly, if you can like my niece, win her* (Lord Lytton, 1847).

4 *Conclusion.* Since at least the 17c., certain adverbs in *-ly* have acquired the ability to qualify a predication or assertion as a whole. Such adverbs are all elliptical uses of somewhat longer phrases. In the last third of the 20c., this little-used and scarcely observed mechanism of the language attracted attention, specifically in the shape of *hopefully*. Any number of adverbs in *-ly* have come into common use as sentence adverbs. Conservative speakers, taken unawares by the sudden expansion of an unrecognized type of construction, exploded with resentment that in some cases still lingers on. Hackles are still raised by *thankfully, regretfully*, and, above all, *hopefully*. This may be because, unlike the others, there is no phrasal basis corresponding to *it is clear that* (for *clearly*) or *to be frank* (for *frankly*). Whatever the reason, sentence adverbs of the kind described are an integral part of English usage and should be used without fear of criticism. See HOPEFULLY.

sentinel (verb). *Sentinel* has the derivatives *-elled, -elling* (AmE *-eled, -eling*); see -LL-, -L-.

septenarius /ˌsɛptɪˈnɛːrɪəs/. Plural -rii /-rɪʌɪ/. Also called a **septenary** /ˈsɛptɪn(ə)ri, -ˈtiːn(ə)ri/. In prosody, a verse of seven feet (often printed as two lines), especially a trochaic or iambic tetrameter catalectic, commonly used in medieval works in verse such as the *Ormulum,* in ballads, and by Wordsworth (1800): *A slumber did my spirit seal; I had no human fears: She seemed a thing that could not feel The touch of earthly years.*

septic. See SCEPTIC.

septicaemia, blood-poisoning. So spelt (but AmE **septicemia**).

septillion, formerly the seventh power of a million (10^{42}); (originally US) now, the eighth power of a thousand (10^{24}).

septingentenary. See CENTENARY 2.

septum (anatomy, botany, zoology). Plural *septa.* See -UM 2.

sepulchre. So spelt, but AmE **sepulcher**. See also WHITED SEPULCHRE.

seq., seqq. The singular and plural forms respectively of Latin *sequens* 'the following', and, in the plural, of *sequentes, -tia* 'the following (lines, etc.)', *sequentibus* 'in the following places'. Also, more fully, *et seq.* Now generally replaced by *f., ff.,* and *etc.*

sequelae /sɪˈkwiːliː/ (plural noun). A medical word meaning a morbid condition or system following a disease' (cf. Latin *sequi* follow'). The singular *sequela* /-ə/ is rarely used.

sequence of tenses refers to the pattern of tenses in a sequence of verbs within a sentence. If a simple statement such as *I'm afraid I haven't finished* is put into indirect speech by means of a reporting verb such as *said, thought,* etc., the tense of the reported action changes in accordance with the time perspective of the speaker: *He said he was afraid he hadn't finished.* However, the tense of the reported verb can stay the same if the time relative to the speaker is the same as that relative to the person reported, in what Fowler (1926) called 'vivid' sequence: *She likes beans* can be converted either to *She said she liked beans* or to *She said she likes beans,* and *I won't be here tomorrow* can be converted either to *He said he wouldn't be here tomorrow* or to *He said he won't be here tomorrow.*

But creative writers can play with the conventions, as the following examples taken from Iris Murdoch's *The Green Knight* (1993) show: *This dog business* will end *in tears, said Jane. Louise who also thought that it* would end *in tears, said,* '[etc.].' Other normal patterns are shown in: (past tense followed by present tense) *She thought, this is the end of happiness, darkness begins here*; (past tense imperfect followed by present tense) *Bellamy was saying, 'Are you all right?'*; (past tense followed by a mixture of tenses) *She thought: something awful has happened and the children know it.*

seraglio /səˈrɑːljəʊ/. Plural *seraglios.* See ITALIAN SOUNDS; -O(E)S 5.

serai (= caravanserai). Pronounced /sɛˈrʌɪ/.

seraph. Plural *seraphim* /-fɪm/ or *seraphs.*

sere. See SEAR, SERE.

serendipity was coined by Horace Walpole in 1754 after the title of a fairy tale, *Three Princes of Serendip.* (*Serendip* is said to be a former name of Sri Lanka (Ceylon).) It originally meant 'the faculty of making happy and unexpected discoveries by accident', e.g. *It was not till some weeks later, when by the aid of Serendipity, as Horace Walpole called it—that is, looking for one thing and finding another—that the explanation was accidentally found*—E. Solly, 1880. However, that meaning has long since been eclipsed by its modern meaning, rarely used before the 20c., of the occurrence and development of events by chance in a happy or beneficial way, e.g. *a fortunate stroke of serendipity.*

The corresponding adjective **serendipitous** is sometimes used to mean 'occurring by (especially fortunate) chance, fortuitous'.

sergeant, serjeant /ˈsɑːdʒənt/. Normally in military and police contexts spelt *sergeant* (hence *sergeant-major*), but in older use often written as *serjeant.* 'The spelling *serjeant* is now usually restricted to legal and ceremonial offices, exc. in historical and in certain official contexts' (*New SOED*).

serial comma. See OXFORD COMMA.

seri(ci)culture (silkworm industry). The longer form (adopted in the 1890s from French *séricicultur*e; cf. Latin *sēricum* 'silk') and recommended by Fowler (1926) never really caught on and has now been abandoned in favour of *sericulture*, pronounced /ˈserɪ-/.

series. 1 Spelt the same as singular and as plural.

2 Regularly pronounced as three syllables until the early 20c. (the *OED* gave preference to the three-syllabled form in 1912), like several other words ending in *-ies* in the singular, it is now always pronounced as two syllables, the second one being simply /-iːz/.

serif (typography), a slight projection finishing off a stroke of a letter as in T contrasted with **T**, is now always so spelt, not *cerif* or *seriph.*

serious, seriously. Relatively new and still somewhat informal uses of the adjective, as in *serious money, serious shopping,* and of the adverb, as in *seriously rich,* have now firmly established themselves as part of the language. The adjective use spans two *OED* definitions ('intense, determined' and 'impressive in quantity or extent'), and a long historical development has resulted in these two meanings taking shape. The use of *seriously* as an intensifier equivalent to 'very, extremely', e.g. *seriously good, bad, cool, rich,* etc. was originally US (1970), but is now widespread. Examples (all UK): *For serious shopping you need to return to the less frenetic streets of Recoleta—Travel Intelligence,* 2005; *Try the Gamekeeper's tea (venison, duck and pheasant pâté with toast) at this seriously good tea shop—Observer,* 2005; *America's seriously wealthy step up the pressure on Obama—Independent,* 2010.

serjeant. See SERGEANT.

serum (fluid that separates from clotted blood, antitoxin). Plural generally *sera,* but *serums* is also allowable. See -UM 3.

service (verb). A surprisingly late addition to the language (first recorded in Stevenson's *Catriona,* 1893), it was used at first only in the sense 'to be of service to, to provide with a service'. In the course of the 20c. it has become established in certain specific senses and now is a normal word for 'to perform routine maintenance on (a motor vehicle, etc.)'; 'to pay interest on (a debt)'; '(of a male animal) to copulate with (a female animal), to serve'; etc.

serviceable. So spelt. See -ABLE, -IBLE 3 (iii).

serviette. 1 The main American dictionaries add the label 'chiefly Brit.' to this word, but the label presumably means 'not the customary word in AmE' as the word is common enough in several major English-speaking countries outside Britain.

2 See NAPKIN.

sesquicentenary. See CENTENARY 2.

sestet, the last six lines of a sonnet.

sestina /sɛˈstiːnə/, plural *sestinas,* a poem of six 6-line stanzas and a 3-line *envoi,* linked by an intricate pattern of repeated line endings. Chiefly an Old Provençal, Italian, and French form, but occasionally copied in English, notably by Sidney in his *Arcadia* (1590), by Kipling in his 'Sestina of the Tramp Royal' (in *The Seven Seas,* 1896), and by W. H. Auden in his 'Paysage Moralisé' (1933).

sett is still a common variant spelling of *set* meaning (*a*) a badger's burrow; (*b*) a granite paving block. Cf. the final *-tt* in MATT.

seventies. See NINETIES.

Sèvres (porcelain made in this suburb of Paris). Pronounced /ˈsɛvrə/.

sew (verb). Past tense *sewed,* past participle *sewn* or *sewed. Sewn* is the majority form, though *sewed* is occasionally used in AmE, including in the phrasal verb *to sew up* 'to bring something to a favourable conclusion' or 'achieve exclusive control over something': *Had Bush won the debates, he likely would have sewed up the election immediately, under vote-by-mail—The Nation,* 2004 (AmE); *it looks like she has Celebrity Big Brother all sewn up—OEC,* 2006 (BrE).

sewage. In strict usage *sewage* is the waste matter conveyed in sewers, and **sewerage** is a system of or drainage by sewers.

sexcentenary (noun). A six-hundredth anniversary or the celebration of one. Also as adjective. See CENTENARY 2.

sexist language. 1 As indicated in numerous articles in this book, e.g. -ESS; FEMININE DESIGNATIONS; HE OR SHE; HIS; MAN; -MAN; and -PERSON, feminists and others sympathetic to their views, from about the 1970s onwards, have attacked what they, and many others, take to be male-biased terminology of every kind and have scoured the language for suitable evidence and for gender-free substitutes. Their argument hinges on the belief that many traditional uses of the language discriminate against women or render them 'invisible' and for these reasons are unacceptable. Perhaps the most obvious older reference works on the subject are *The Handbook of Non-Sexist Writing for Writers, Editors and Speakers,* ed. C. Miller and K. Swift (1981) and *The Non-Sexist Word-Finder: A Dictionary of Gender-Free Usage* by R. Maggio (1988). Both books had mixed receptions.

2 *Some landmarks.* Since the 1980s, many official style guides (including Judith Butcher's *Copy-editing,* 3rd edition, Cambridge, 1992) have included advice on how to avoid sexist language. To provide rough indicators of the development of feminist views on gender-free language it is interesting to set down in chronological order details of some decisions and discussions that have taken place in various English-speaking countries since 1988:

In 1988 Cambridge University dons voted to eliminate sexist language from the university's *Statutes and Ordinances.* In 1988 the Style Manual of the Commonwealth of Australia (4th edn) included a detailed chapter, divided into 49 sections, setting out ways of avoiding sexist language. In 1989 the General Synod of the Church of England debated a report on the need to introduce non-sexist language into the liturgy. In 1989 a revised version of the Bible substituted *one* for *man* in such contexts as Psalm (AV) 1: 1 *Blessed is the* man *that walketh not in the counsell of the vngodly.* Cf. the *NEB* (1970) *Happy is the* man *who does not take the wicked for* his *guide.* In 1990 Radio New Zealand considered it unacceptable to say *fisherman, crewman, clergyman, actress, bridesmaid, maiden voyage, manhole, masterpiece, nobleman, mothering, mother tongue,* or *motherland.* (Certain of these are, to my mind, clearly of the kind that bring into disrepute perfectly laudable attempts to make language less biased.) In 1990 the mayor of Los Angeles, Tom Bradley, banned sexist terms from city reports. His mandated changes included *maintenance holes* for *manholes, people* or *humanity* for *mankind, staffed* for *manned,* and *chairperson* for *chairman.*

3 *Some revealing examples.* When reviewing the *Handbook* of Miller and Swift, the Irish writer the late Brigid Brophy complained about the 'leaden literalness of mind' of M & S (as she called them) and 'their tin ear and insensibility to the metaphorical contents of language'. Other female writers show in their works that they prefer to ignore the advice of feminists. Witness, for example: *'It's every* man *for* himself *till tea-time'*—she *raised her voice*—Elizabeth Jolley, 1985; *She was the* mastermind—mistressmind—*behind a deception that was going to rake in some considerable . . . profit*—Colin Dexter, 1989; *In the* master *bedroom, Ruth announces that she will throw away all her mother-in-law's shoes*—Sarah Gaddis, 1990 (US).

4 *An academic view.* In *English Today* (Jan. 1985) the dialect and sociolinguistic scholar Jenny Cheshire concluded: 'There is a built-in masculine bias in English, and this does have very serious implications for both the women and the men who use the language. And this bias will not disappear unless there is some measure of conscious reform in the language.' Such conscious reform as there has been since she wrote appears to have come about in many cases through the usage of sensible people acknowledging the wisdom of removing inbuilt sexist bias (despite the groans and ridicule of others, including Burchfield); at the same time, certain uses (i.e. banning *masterpiece*) have not caught on precisely because they appear inspired by an almost jihadist strand of feminism and defy common sense.

sext. A very modern portmanteau verb, combining *s(ex)* + *(t)ext,* to refer to the activity of sending sexually explicit images or messages via mobile phone. Often used as the verbal noun **sexting**, and seemingly a craze among some people despite the fact that it can lead to all sorts of embarrassments. Examples: *one in nine Brits sext their partner every day, a new survey has found*; *Cell phone smut: the growing trend in high schools, sexting.*

sextet. An alteration of SESTET after Latin *sex* 'six'.

sextillion. Originally (especially in BrE), the sixth power of a million (10^{36}). Now usually (originally AmE), the seventh power of a thousand (10^{21}).

sexto, a size of book or page in which each leaf is one-sixth that of a printing sheet. Plural *sextos*: see -O(E)S 4.

sez. Curiously used as a conventional spelling of *says* (which, of course, is in fact pronounced thus) in slang contexts.

sf-. A combination of initial letters found only in loanwords from Italian, e.g. *sforzando* (music), *sfumato* (painting).

sg-. A combination of initial letters, found only in loanwords from Italian, e.g. *sgraffito* /sgraˈfiːtəʊ/ (form of decoration on ceramic ware). Plural *sgraffiti* /sgraˈfiːti/.

shade, shadow. The difference in form is etymologically one of declension: *shade* descends from the nominative singular of Old English *sceadu,* and *shadow* represents the oblique case (Old English *sceadwe*) of the same noun.

shag. 1 Although this verb is still labelled 'coarse slang' by the *OED,* the fact that it has lost some of its pariah status arguably echoes a widespread relaxation of sexual taboos in some sections of English-speaking society. The *OED*'s 'coarse' is an apt comment on the word's unloveliness, an unloveliness which has not, however, prevented it from becoming borderline acceptable in informal contexts, and even being used in respectable magazines and newspapers. The deliberately provocative, tongue-in-cheek 1999 film title 'Austin Powers: The Spy who Shagged Me' can perhaps be seen as a seminal moment (pun intended) in the word's development. (Its origin is unknown, although the *OED* posits a connection with an obsolete verb meaning 'toss about'.) Its heartland is Britain and the Antipodes, although it occasionally occurs in other varieties, including AmE. It comes as a surprise to find that the earliest *OED* citation, earlier even than one in Grose's 1788 *Classical Dictionary of the Vulgar Tongue,* is from one of Thomas Jefferson's memorandum books for the year 1770. The noun is much more recent, being first recorded in Eric Partridge's 1937 *Dictionary of Slang and Unconventional English.* It is fair to say, as some of the following examples suggest, that the world is divided between those who use the word not at all, or only with the most intimate friends, and those for whom it is standard vocabulary, even a mark of bravado. It goes without saying that the warning to use it with extreme caution will be superfluous for the former and disregarded by the latter.

Examples: *I am unsure if you will print the word 'shagging', but it is used on this programme* [*sc.* River City, a TV programme] *with monotonous regularity*—(presumably from a letter to) *Scotland on Sunday,* 2003; *Basically my brief was to see who Nicole Kidman was shagging—what she was doing, poking through her bins and get some stuff on her—NZ Herald,* 2011; *And he* [*sc.* a BBC radio presenter] *took a swipe at Radio 1 DJ Sara Cox, whose Breakfast Show slot he used to present in the 1970s, for her 'crude' language. 'Sara Cox talks about "shagging", a word I wouldn't dream of using in public. She's coarse and unpleasant—very "yesterday"'—Yorkshire Post Today,* 2003.

2 It is as well to be aware that there is a possibly defunct verb meaning 'wander about aimlessly', e.g. *The Princess is getting too grown-up to be shagging around Broadway, and... she is now going to public school*—Damon Runyan, 1938. Related to this is the informal US baseball idiom *to shag flies,* meaning 'to chase for fly balls', e.g. *For some, the ultimate celebrity fantasy would be practicing chip shots with Tiger Woods, shagging flies with New York Yankees' Derek Jeter or...—Brandweek,* 2000 (US).

Shakespeare. Now universally spelt as shown, but in the early decades of the 20c. *Shakspere* was the more usual form, and was recommended by the *OED* (1913) and by Fowler (1926). The corresponding adjective (and noun) may be written as **Shakespearian**, the older but less frequent form, or **Shakespearean**.

shako /ˈʃeɪkəʊ/, a cylindrical peaked military hat with a plume. Plural *shakos*: see -O(E)S 7.

shall and will.

A The traditional rule.
B The reality.
C Conclusion.
D History.

What follows is mainly drawn from *The Oxford Guide to English Usage* (1993), but with different examples inserted.

A *The traditional rule.* Simply put, the traditional rule is as follows.

1 (*a*) *I shall, we shall* express the simple future, e.g. *In the following pages we* shall *see good words ... losing their edge* (C. S. Lewis); *'I* shall *have to wear my old coat,' she said apologetically* (A. Brookner). This is especially true in questions, when the use of *will* would either change the meaning or would be unidiomatic: e.g. *I'll put the back rest up for you,* shall *I?* (P. Lively); 'Shall *we have a cup of tea?' he asked* (A. Brookner). (*b*) *I will, we will* express determination or insistence on the part of the speaker, e.g. *'I don't think we* will *ask Mr. Fraser's opinion,' she said coldly* (V. S. Pritchett); *I* will *invite them to tea!* (A. Brookner).

2 For the second and third persons, singular and plural, the position is reversed. (*a*) *You, he, she, it,* or *they will* express the simple future, e.g. *Seraphina* will *last much longer than a car. She'll probably last longer than you* will (G. Greene); Will *it disturb you if I keep the lamp on for a bit?* (S. Hill); *Presently Claudia says, 'What* will *you do when the war's over?'* (P. Lively). (*b*) *You, he, she, it,* or *they shall* express intention or determination on the part of the speaker or someone other than the actual subject of the verb, especially a promise made by the speaker to or about the subject, e.g. *In future you* shall *have as many taxis as you want* (G. B. Shaw); *One day you* shall *know my full story* (E. Waugh); Shall *the common man be pushed back into the mud, or* shall *he not?* (G. Orwell). Type 2(*b*) is no longer common, but the usage is enshrined in people's consciousness in the shape of the Fairy Godmother's promise to Cinderella: *You* shall *go to the ball.*

3 The two uses of *will* just described and one of those of *shall* are well illustrated by: '*I* will *follow you to the ends of the earth,' replied Susan, passionately. 'It* will *not be necessary,' said George. I am only going down to the coal-cellar. I* shall *spend the next half-hour or so there.'* (P. G. Wodehouse) The distinction between types 1 and 2 can also be seen in many well-known literary contexts, e.g. (type 1(*a*)) Shall *I compare thee to a summer's day?* (Shakespeare); (types 1(*b*) and 2(*b*)) *I* will *not cease from mental fight, Nor* shall *my sword sleep in my hand* (Blake).

B *The reality.*

1 It is unlikely that the rule ever had its foundation in real usage, although it may have applied to some people some of the time. In practice, *shall* and *will* are today used more or less interchangeably in statements (though not in questions).

(*a*) In everyday language *I will* and *we will* are generally used for the simple future, e.g. *I* will *be a different person when I live in England* (J. Rhys); *'*Will *I be there?' I enquired. 'No, darling. You wouldn't enjoy it.'* (A. Brookner). To use *shall* in ordinary conversation and writing, even in BrE, runs the risk of sounding quaint, affected, or pedantic. (*b*) In any case, more often than not the distinction is rendered irrelevant by the use of contracted form *'ll*, e.g. *I*'ll *book a table at Francesco's; 'I*'ll *come in after church and give you a hand,' said Miss Lawlor; 'We*'ll *be going on later for bridge,' she explained; They*'ll *cook and clean for a week before a party.* (*c*) It is worth noting that in all English-speaking countries pure future uses are often expressed by *be going to* rather than by *shall, will, 'll,* e.g. *For myself, I*'m going to *become a sober citizen. A son of toil* (P. Lively); *Nobody* is going to *examine your coat* (A. Brookner); *I*'m going to *teach him people are more important than money* (M. Gee).

2 In the standard English of countries outside the UK, the absence of *shall* and the omnipresence of *'ll* and *will* are even more marked than in BrE, and in the United States *shall* is largely unknown, e.g. *We*'ll *be in touch; I*'ll *cope with him in my office;* (J. Updike, 1986, US); *I*'ll *fill up while you get your keys; 'I hope you do it, Jack.' 'I* will.' (M. Gee, 1992, NZ); *Every hundred paces we*'ll *call out; 'We* will *not be going to the veld today ...' she told them* (D. Matthee, 1986, SAfr.).

3 *Shall* survives mostly (*a*) in first-person questions or suggestions, e.g. Shall *we dance? On a bright cloud of music* shall *we fly?* Shall *we dance?* Shall *we then say 'Goodnight' and mean 'Goodbye'—The King and I;* Shall *I help you to try again?*—B. Jagger, 1986; Shall *we take our drinks to the bedroom?' she said softly*—J. Francome, 1990. (*b*) In certain formulaic or set expressions, e.g. *one Abstract Expressionist* who shall remain nameless; *Both arguments are,* shall we say, *imaginative;* As we shall see, *though, this is a crucial question.* (*c*) In legal drafting, where it means 'must, has a duty to', e.g. *The landlord shall maintain the premises.* (This use has been brought into question by some legal authorities in the US because of its alleged ambiguity.) (*d*) In the contracted negative form *shan't,* e.g. *Have no fear ... I* shan't *throw in the towel,*

I promise you. But even in BrE this is not common, and it is very rare in AmE. (*e*) In the English of England (but not of Britain as a whole), *shall* half-survives, albeit tending to sound old-fashioned and affected, in commands and assurances (*Yes, you* shall *take some eggs back to your aunt*—C. Harvey, 1992) and in questions seeking information rather than making a request, (*And where* shall *you be while I'm hobbling all over the castle?*—*OEC*, 2005), but *will* (or sometimes *can*) is just as common, especially in speech, and is more natural. In Scotland, *will* is used in the first person even in requests (Will *I help you with your bags?*).

C *Conclusion*. The supposed rule is a dead letter in speech, and in most kinds of writing. It is broadly true that *shall* and *should* have largely retreated in the standard language even as used in England. In other English-speaking areas, *shall* and *should* have been almost totally replaced by *will* and *would*, or by the reduced forms *I'll*/*we'll*. There is not much doubt that *will* will win, and *shall* shall lose, in the end.

D *History*. The history of these modal verbs and of their contracted forms is immensely complicated and cannot be satisfactorily summarized here. For such detailed information it is necessary to turn to such standard authorities as the *OED* and Jespersen (1909–49, iv). The long article in Fowler 1926, which closely follows his article 'Shall and Will, Should and Would in the Newspapers of To-day' in SPE Tract vi (1921), is a classic, but it too narrowly insists on the preservation of fast-fading traditional distinctions (though he did describe the time-honoured type *I will be drowned, no-one shall save me* as 'too good to be true'). See also SHOULD AND WOULD.

shambles. In general use now invariably treated as a singular noun, and used mainly as an informal word for 'a mess, a muddle' (*their marriage was a shambles*). The word has a colourful history. From its Old English senses 'a stool, a footstool' and 'a table or counter for displaying goods for sale', it came to mean specifically 'a table or stall for the sale of meat'. (In the Shambles in York, the projecting sills below the ground-floor windows where meat was once displayed suggest a continuation of the Old English meaning.) The word was then applied to the slaughterhouse from which the meat came, and, from the 16c. onwards, any scene of blood and carnage. It was not until the 1920s that the weakened sense 'a scene of disorder, a mess' emerged in AmE. The chiefly BrE informal derivative **shambolic**, 'chaotic, disorganized', is first recorded from 1970 in the *OED*, but is certainly older, as is acknowledged by the *OED* note 'reported to be in common use in 1958'.

shamefaced, now the invariable form, is a 16c. alteration of the older word *shamefast* (cf. *steadfast*), in which the *-fast* element reflects an Old English adjectival suffix.

shamefacedly. Pronounced as three or four syllables. See -EDLY.

shampoo. The inflected forms are *shampoos, shampooed, shampooing*.

shanghai. The recommended inflected forms are *shanghais, shanghaied, shanghaiing*. See -ED AND 'D.

shan't. From the 17c. onwards *shall not* has been frequently written in the contracted forms *sha'nt, shann't, sha'not, shan't*, etc. Of these, *shan't* survives in standard southern English as the regular contracted form, but is seldom used outside England. See SHALL AND WILL.

shanty. Two separate words are involved:
1 A crudely built hut; hence **shanty town**, a poor or depressed area of a town, consisting of shanties. This word was first recorded in N. America in 1820 and seems to be from Canadian French *chantier* 'the headquarters at which woodcutters assemble after their day's work'.

2 A song, especially one sung by sailors while hauling ropes, etc. Said to be a corruption of French *chantez*, imperative of *chanter* 'to sing'. First recorded in 1856. Formerly in BrE and still usually in AmE spelt **chantey** or **chanty** (plural *-eys* or *-ies*).

shape. The common phrase *in any shape or form* is plainly pleonastic but enjoys wide currency as a formulaic emphatic variant of *in any way, at all* (e.g. *not on offer in any shape or form*).

shard /ʃɑːd/. A broken piece of pottery, a potsherd. This is a native word derived from Old English *sceard*. The alternative spelling **sherd** /ʃəːd/ is much less often used.

sharif, a Muslim leader, is a word of Arabic origin. It is etymologically unrelated to the English word *sheriff,* which is derived from Old English *scīr-gerēfa,* literally 'shire-reeve'.

sharp as an adverb is correctly used to mean punctually (*seven o'clock sharp*) or abruptly (*the van pulled up sharp; turn sharp right*). But in most other contexts it cannot replace **sharply** (e.g. *share prices dropped sharply during the afternoon; opinions were sharply divided about the matter*).

shat seems to be the most common past tense and past participle, rather than *shit* or *shitted.* The alternation between weak and strong verb past forms has existed since Middle English, but *shat* first appeared only in the 20c. (*Cowface looked as though she'd shat herself*—H. Beaton, 1984; *the jay covered the square pedestal with twigs and leaves and shat on the head and arms*—*New Yorker,* 1990). The Australian and NZ phrase *to be shitted off* is vulgar slang for to be annoyed or irritated.

shave (verb). The past tense and past participle are *shaved.* But the participial adjective form is usually **-shaven** *(a clean-shaven man in his twenties*).

she. 1 For *she* (and *her*) in personifications, see PERSONIFICATION. See also HE OR SHE; HER 3.

2 The use of *she* rather than *her* after the verb *to be* follows the same pattern as that of *he* rather than *him* (see HE 1). Examples: (she) *And don't fear that it is she who might convert you*—P. P. Read, 1986; *If anyone could write about the narcissistic personality, it was she*—*New York Rev. Bks,* 1987; (her) *Phone rings at 8.07 . . . it must be her, no one else would call at such a time*—*The Face,* 1987; *She comes down the basement stairs sideways, . . . so you always know it's her*—*New Yorker,* 1987. In such circumstances *she* is the more formal of the two.

3 After *than, she* is the more formal of the two pronouns, but both are in standard use. Examples: (she) *On the whole the men are . . . more formal and authoritarian in tone than she*—M. Butler, 1987; (her) *I'm not really fatter than her, am I?*—M. Duckworth, 1960 (NZ); *He's a million times better than her*—M. Bail, 1975 (Aust.). See CASES 3.

4 Examples of the nominative *she* used wrongly for *her* after a preposition or in other respects in the objective position: *this uncombed stick-limbed fellow . . . who had finally cracked the defences of she whom Harvey Fig had dubbed 'our pocket Venus'*—P. Carey, 1988.

s/he is a written form, used by some writers since the 1970s as a nominative singular third person pronoun including both sexes in an attempt to redress gender imbalance in language. Example: *A child's sexual orientation is determined before s/he enters school—Amer. Educator,* 1978. It has not been as widely adopted as it might have been, perhaps because of its self-evident artificiality, or perhaps because for some it is a positive discrimination step too far. It is also possible that uncertainty about how to read it out contributes: is it 'he or she', which defeats the purpose, or is it 'she stroke he', which most men will feel uncomfortable with?

sheaf. The noun has plural *sheaves.* The corresponding transitive verb meaning 'to make into sheaves' is **sheave**. See -VE (D), -VES.

shear (verb) has past tense *sheared* in its ordinary current senses (*we sheared our sheep last week; a machine sheared the bar into foot-lengths; the pressure from above sheared the rivets*). The normal past participle is *shorn* (*the sheep had been shorn; his shorn locks; shorn of one's authority*), except in contexts of metal-cutting (*a bar of wrought iron needed to be sheared across*). The more usual past tense in Australian and NZ sheep-shearing sheds is *shore.*

sheave (verb). See SHEAF.

sheep. Plural same.

sheikh. This is the recommended and most frequent spelling, pronounced /ʃeɪk/. Less common variants are **shaykh**, **shaikh**, and **sheik**, in that order. The pronunciation /ʃiːk/ is also common.

shelf /ʃɛlf/. The plural is *shelves* /ʃɛlvz/ and the corresponding verb is **shelve** /ʃɛlv/. The compound **shelf-ful** is best written with a hyphen; plural *shelf-fuls.*

shellac. As verb has the inflected forms *shellacs, shellacked, shellacking.*

shell-less, shell-like. Spelt as shown, with hyphens. See -LESS 1.

Shelta, sheltie. The first is the name of an ancient hybrid secret language used today by Irish and Welsh travellers and gypsies; *sheltie* (rather than *shelty*) is a Shetland pony or sheepdog.

shereef, sherif are variant spellings in English of SHARIF.

sheriff. Over the last few centuries a number of abstract nouns have been used for 'the office or post of sheriff': *sheriffalty* (first recorded in the 16c.); *sheriffdom* (16c. in this sense; 14c. in the sense 'district under the jurisdiction of a sheriff'); *sheriffry* (17c.; rare); *sheriffship* (15c.); *sheriffwick* (15c.; also 16c. in the sense 'district under the jurisdiction of a sheriff'); and *shrievalty* (16c.). The official term is the last of these, despite the disadvantage of not immediately announcing its (valid) etymological connection with *sheriff.*

shew, show. As the *Oxford Writers' Dict.* (1990) says 'use *show* except in Scottish law, and biblical and Prayer Book citations'. Pronounced /ʃəʊ/ (also in the first element of *shewbread*), however spelt.

shibboleth. 1 It is in origin the Hebrew word (*šibbōleṯ* 'ear of corn') used by Jephthah as a test word by which to distinguish the fleeing Ephraimites (who could not pronounce the *sh*) from his own men the Gileadites (Judges 12:4–6). Their inability to lisp cost them dear; the ensuing slaughter makes modern massacres sound like a tea party: 'and there fell at that time of the Ephraimites two and forty thousand'. From this, from the 17c. onwards, it was used for any word or sound which a person is unable to pronounce correctly; hence a word or sound used to detect foreigners, or persons from another district. That use is now archaic.

2 By extension, since the mid-20c., it has been used to mean 'a moral formula held tenaciously and unreflectingly, especially a prohibitive one; a taboo' and 'an entrenched (political) belief or dogma'. Examples: *Room for Debate asks: How can we tell the difference between a sound principle of English and a made-up shibboleth?—NYT,* 2012; *You are a dinosaur—you're an old Marxist—if you challenge these new shibboleths of the neo-liberal age—Workers Online,* 2001; *Instead, he spouted standard liberal shibboleths about solving our problems through federal programs and a higher minimum wage—New York Post,* 2006.

shier. See SHY.

shillelagh. So spelt. Pronounced /ʃɪˈleɪlə/ or /-li/.

shine (verb). The past tense and past participle forms are normally *shone* /ʃɒn/, AmE /ʃəʊn/, when the verb is intransitive, but in its transitive meaning 'to polish, make bright', *shined* is standard. In intransitive uses, *shined* is also quite common in AmE; except in the 1989 and 1990 (US) examples, speakers of standard BrE would use *shone* instead, but *shined* is also found, though not recommended, in BrE, as in the last example below: *Her shiny black paint shined in the sun—Black World* (US), 1974; *I asked him if it shined in the sunlight—*M. Doane, 1988 (US); *The car is a red Mercedes, newly shined—*S. North, 1989 (UK); *I have my shoes shined by a man who says he will pray for my wife and family—*J. Cheever, 1990 (US); *his hair was combed and flattened down with bay rum until it shined—*N. Virtue, 1990 (NZ); *It occurred to me that this was not a reflection from his glasses or his crown, no matter how much they shined—*D. Pinckney, 1992 (US); *If McEnroe's light shined brightly, it also shined briefly—BBC Sport,* 2004.

shingles (acute viral inflammation), like other illnesses ending in *-s* (*measles, mumps,* etc.) is normally treated as a singular noun (*shingles is an unpleasant disease*), but if the emphasis is perhaps more on the resulting blisters than on the illness itself a plural verb may be used instead.

ship. 1 In the proverb *Do not spoil the ship for a ha'porth of tar, ship* represents a dialectal pronunciation of *sheep.* The original literal sense was 'Do not allow a sheep to suffer for the lack of a trifling amount of tar'. Tar was used as a protection against flies and maggots.

2 See BOAT.

-ship. See BRINKMANSHIP; LEADERSHIP; MEMBERSHIP; READERSHIP; RELATION, RELATIONSHIP, RELATIVE.

shoal. See SCHOOL.

shoe (verb). The inflected forms are *shoes, shoeing,* and *shod* /ʃɒd/.

shoo-in. The informal noun *shoo-in* first appeared with the sense 'a person or thing that is certain to succeed' in the 1930s and comes from an earlier North American use of the term referring to the winner of a rigged horse race. The *shoo-* element is obscure in meaning, coming as it does from an earlier US slang phrasal verb, *shoo in,* 'allow a racehorse to win easily'. As a result, through folk etymology many people transform it to *shoe-in,* which accounts for 35% of occurrences in the *OEC.* In an online poll by *OUP,* respondents were evenly divided over which spelling they favoured. Nevertheless, for the time being dictionaries only recognize *shoo-in.* Examples: *Meanwhile, Philip Seymour Hoffman is considered a near shoo-in for an Oscar nomination for 'Capote,' in which he plays gay author Truman Capote—CNN* (transcripts), 2005; *Everyone thought Real* [*sc.* Madrid] *were shoo-ins for their 25th league title, particularly as they were playing lowly Tenerife—Guardian Unlimited,* 2003.

shoot, shute (nouns). See CHUTE.

shop (noun). For the talk called *shop,* as compared with *cant, slang,* etc., see JARGON 3.

shop (verb). In AmE, since the 1950s, but not in BrE, the verb has been used transitively (as well as in the traditional intransitive uses) to mean 'to shop at (a store); to examine goods on sale (in a shop)': e.g. *One man who had shopped the entire store complained that he hadn't found what he was looking for*—S. Marcus, 1974. The informal transitive use 'to inform on (someone)' is chiefly BrE.

short-lived. See -LIVED.

shorts. See PANTALOONS.

should and would. See also SHALL AND WILL. As with *shall* and *will, should* has been largely driven out by *would* as a modal verb but still survives in certain uses. The most that can be offered in the small compass of this article is to provide a few observations supported by examples.

1 *Prevalence of contracted forms.* In conversational English, the contracted forms *I'd, you'd,* etc., are often used in simple statements instead of the full forms, so that the *should/would* distinction is not an issue: *I*'d *be delighted to join you*—K. Amis, 1988; *I'd sooner do it at home, thank you*—M. Gee, 1992; *That*'d *teach her mother to be selfish*—R. Billington, 1988; *This particular one is limited to 400 so you*'d *better hurry if you want one—BBC Popular Music Reviews,* 2004. But in meanings to do with obligation or likelihood (see 3 below) the full form *should* has to be used.

2 Usual or obligatory *would.* (*a*) As a modal verb used to state a condition or proposition, *would* is obligatory with *you, he, she, it,* and *they,* and more usual than *should* even with *I* and *we*: *They would like to stay; I would think so; I wouldn't exactly say.* (*b*) *Would* is the only option when asking a question or making a request: Would *you do me a favour?;* Would *you bring the children?;* Would *you tell them to wait, please?* (*c*) *Would* has to be used when referring to unfulfilled conditions and hypotheses: *Ordinarily, I would have chosen an empty table*—B. Aldiss, 1991; *How they* would *respond at such a time is anyone's guess*—M. Amis, 1987; *She* would *put off thinking till she had the tea in her hand*—R. Billington, 1988. (*d*) *Would* also expresses habitual action in the past (*These he would produce with a flourish during our Wednesday- and Sunday-evening sessions*—W. Self, 1993) and the future in the past (*She realised they would have to come back at some point and face the music—Yorkshire Post Today,* 2001).

3 Obligatory *should. Should* has to be used (*a*) when obligation or likelihood is being expressed: *Now I think we should bring down the curtain on this little episode, and go to bed*—A. Browning, 1992; *The letters, which should have arrived at patients' homes today, ask them to seek advice and counselling—York Press,* 2002; *Patients with diabetes should have tighter limits placed on blood pressure—BMJ,* 2003. (*b*) in constructions expressing a condition where it and the grammatical subject are inverted: *You will find plenty of wood for a fire should you need one*—fishing website, 2002.

4 Optional *should.* In the following cases *should* is markedly more formal, and very much less frequent than *would* or *'d,* and may even be perceived as affected. (*a*) With the first person pronouns *I* and *we*, *should* can be used before verbs of liking, e.g. *be glad, be inclined, like, prefer*, e.g. *'Would you like a beer?' 'I* should *prefer a cup of coffee, if you don't mind'; 'I* should *like one of these, says Claudia*—P. Lively, 1987; *It is a rule that has stood me in very good stead in many a complicated matter, and in the absence of further advice I should be inclined to stick to it now*—*Daily Tel.*, 2009. For the types *should have liked to/would have liked to*, see LIKE (verb) 1(*a*–*c*). (*b*) *Should* is still current in tentative statements of opinion, with verbs such as *guess, imagine, say,* and *think*. *I* should *imagine that you are right; I* should *say so; I* should *have thought you'd got used to that principle by now; I* should *say that there is not only increasing public awareness of the problems of smoking and its long-term consequences to the health of smokers, but* [etc.]—*Hansard*, 1992.

should of. See OF B.1.

shovel (verb). The inflected forms are *shovelled, shovelling* in BrE but frequently *shoveled, shoveling* in AmE. See -LL-, -L-.

show (verb). For the spelling, see SHEW. The past tense is *showed* and the past participle normally *shown* (*the book was shown to him*) but occasionally *showed*, though not when the participle is passive, e.g. *Have you showed it to Thomas Blackhall?*—G. Butler, 1992; *Mr Marr hadn't showed up at any of the places where he should have been*—N. Williams, 1992; *I didn't see it happen but realised almost immediately the card was gone, must have showed panic by standing to shake out the pleats of my long skirt*—B. Neil, 1993.

shred (verb). For the past participle *shredded* and *shred* were used as acceptable alternatives until the 20c., but *shred* is now much less commonly used.

shrievalty /ˈʃriːv(ə)lti/. See SHERIFF.

shrink. The standard BrE past tense is *shrank* /ʃraŋk/, although *shrunk* /ʃrʌŋk/ is also used, and, though less common, is regarded as a standard alternative in AmE and is recognized in the Austr. English Macquarie Dictionary. The past participle is *shrunk* /ʃrʌŋk/ or (especially as attributive adjective) *shrunken* /ˈʃrʌŋkən/: *has shrunk, is shrunk* or *shrunken*; *her shrunken cheeks*. The contrast between the customary forms of the past participle and participial adjective is neatly brought out by these examples from adjacent pages in an issue of the *Guardian*: *For the entire race the margin between them has stretched and shrunk; Among the shrunken white community which has steadied at around 100,000 . . . there are few conspicuous signs of . . . racist attitudes.*

shrivel. The inflected forms are *shrivelled, shrivelling* in BrE but frequently *shriveled, shriveling* in AmE. See -LL-, -L-.

shy (adjective) has the derivatives *shyer, shyest, shyly, shyness, shyish*. The verb makes **shier** (shying horse). See DRIER; VERBS IN -IE, -Y, AND -YE.

Siamese twins. See CONJOINED TWINS; IRREVERSIBLE BINOMIALS.

sibilants are FRICATIVES 'produced by forcing the air stream through a groove-shaped opening between the tongue and the roof of the mouth, e.g. [s] in *sin*; [z] in *zoo*; [ʃ] in *shop*; [ʒ] in *pleasure*' (Hartmann and Stork, 1972).

sibling, an ancient word for a relative (a sense obsolete by the end of the 15c.), was reintroduced by anthropologists in the first decade of the 20c. with the meaning 'each of two or more children having one or both parents in common'. It is a kind of POPULARIZED TECHNICAL TERM, and usefully fills a lexical gap by providing a gender-neutral term for 'brother or sister': *Small groups drifted through the classroom: mothers and fathers, large numbers of children—Edward's pupils along with older and younger siblings*—P. Lively, 1990. The word is also common in the expression *sibling rivalry*: *Moses . . . shows more than a hint of sibling rivalry in his attitude to his brother Aaron*—C. Raphael, 1972. The word also has a figurative or transferred use, e.g. *The line dividing the Kevin Street Sinn Fein organisation and its terrorist sibling, the Provisional IRA, is almost invisible*—*Daily Tel.*, 1972.

sic, printed in italics, is the Latin word for 'so, thus', and is added in square (or occasionally round) brackets after a quoted word or phrase about which the reader might have doubts, because of a misspelling (which the quoting writer does not want to correct) or some other error of use: *The*

Abbey PR office phoned to issue a statement: 'Abbey is committed to providing it's (*sic*) *customers with good service, and we apologise if on this specific occasion we fell below our high standards'—Liverpool Daily Echo*, 2007, drawing attention to rather than silently correcting an incorrect apostrophe. (But if the Abbey office issued the statement by telephone, the error must have been in the newspaper's own transcription in any case.) It should not be used as a supercilious comment on the quoted writer's style or supposed looseness of grammar, as in the following example: *I probably have a different sense of morality to* [*sic*] *most people—Chicago Tribune*, 1994, quoting Alan Clark. Further examples: *his* [an inventor's] *crudely written notice declaring that it 'dose* [*sic*] *the work of a press that would cost £10,000'—Spectator*, 1994.

sick. See ILL.

sidle, the verb, is a back-formation from *sideling*, an obsolete form of *sidelong* 'inclining to one side; oblique'.

siege. So spelt; also *besiege*. Both are words for which the good old *i before e* rule works.

sienna, the pigment and its colour of yellowish-brown (*raw sienna*) or reddish-brown (*burnt sienna*), is so spelt despite its origin (from *Siena*, with a single letter *n*, a city in Tuscany).

sieve. So spelt.

sight unseen, without previous inspection. This phrase, an 'absolute construction', first recorded in America in the 1890s, is now well established in the main forms of English everywhere. Examples: *I've always hated that phrase, haven't you, Paola, sight unseen, it's a tautology or something near, it simply means* unseen, *doesn't it?*—A. S. Byatt, 1990; *A friend writes: I acquired, sight unseen, a piece of land just outside Lynchburg.—New Yorker*, 1990.

signal (verb). The inflected forms are *signalled, signalling* in BrE but frequently *signaled, signaling* in AmE. See -LL-, -L-.

signatory is now the usual spelling (not *signatary*) for both the noun and the adjective.

significant other is a POPULARIZED TECHNICAL TERM, taken up as a non-gender-specific way of referring to 'a person with whom someone has an established romantic or sexual relationship'; in other words, as a synonym for *partner* in the same sense. First cited in the *OED* from 1940 as a social psychology term denoting 'any person with great influence on the behaviour, self-opinion, etc., of another (especially of a child)' it is still used with this meaning, especially in the plural, and can be useful as an umbrella term for a group of people who are connected in various ways to the person to whom they are significant, as in the first two examples below. More common, however, is its use in the romantic sense, which the *OEC* suggests flourishes largely in North American English. Brought to a wider audience by its appearance in the title of a novel by Armistead Maupin, it somehow combines politically correct earnestness with mawkishness in a way that makes it hard—for me at any rate—to use without large, virtual quotation marks. Examples: *Ask clients about the level of support they are getting from their significant others regarding exercise—American Fitness*, 2005; *One such was a chart on which each interviewee was asked to represent graphically his relationships with significant others—Doing Research on Crime and Justice*, 2000 (BrE); *Put this baby on at your next dinner party or whenever your significant other wants to go salsa dancing, and you should win a few friends who will demand to borrow this at the earliest opportunity—BBC Popular Music Reviews*, 2004.

signifier (and related words in linguistics). The Swiss scholar Ferdinand de Saussure (1857–1913) introduced the French terms *signifiant* 'a physical medium (as a sound, symbol, image, etc.) expressing meaning, as distinct from the meaning expressed (the *signifié*)', and emphasized the arbitrary relationship between the linguistic sign and that which it signifies. These French words are sometimes replaced in scholarly work by their Latin equivalents *significans* and *significatum*; and also, commonly, by the English words *signifier* and *signified*. The last two are also often used in the critical terminology of modern literary theory. Examples: *The bond between the signifier and the signified is arbitrary*—W. Baskin (tr. de Saussure), 1960; *He has only to offer the Signifier, 'Lie'—which could mean 'tell an un-truth'—for Othello to snatch the Signified, 'lie with'—Dædalus*, 1979; *This novel understands that it is politics—torture, suffering, deprivation—which* *reminds us that our signifier-shaped existence is more corporeal than textual*—T. Eagleton, 1994. Meanwhile non-linguists, i.e. nearly everyone else in the English-speaking world, are content with the traditional terms *word* (or *phrase,* etc.) and *meaning* (or *sense,* etc.).

signor, signora, signorina. Italian titles. Pronounced in English /ˈsiːnjɔː/, /siːnˈjɔːrə/, /siːnjəˈriːnə/.

Sikh. Normally pronounced /siːk/ in English and /sɪk/ in Hindi.

silex /ˈsʌɪlɛks/ (kind of glass). See -EX, -IX.

sillabub. See SYLLABUB.

sillily. One of the few current *-lily* adverbs, but rather uncommon all the same. See -LILY.

silo. Plural *silos.* See -O(E)S 7.

silvan. See SYLVAN.

simian. Pronounced /ˈsɪmɪən/ with a short /ɪ/ in the stem, despite the long stem vowel in Latin *sīmia.*

similar. It should be followed by *to,* not *as* (though it was formerly also construed with *with*). Examples: (obsolete use) *A legend of similar import with that of the death of Hercules* (1832 in *OED*); (standard use) *It seemed to me that she was acknowledging an emotion similar to my own*—C. Rumens, 1987; (non-standard use) *Wolverton Seconds showed similar form as their seniors in their two home games*—*Oxford Guide to Eng. Usage,* 1993.

simile. 1 'Part' as Burchfield (1996) put it, 'of the spiritual nourishment of writers and esp. of poets', similes are 'figure[s] of speech involving the comparison of one thing with another of a different kind, as an illustration or ornament' (*COD,* 1995). They turn up in profusion at all periods and are normally introduced by *as* or *like.* Some examples chosen at random by Burchfield: *Blue as the gendarmerie were the waves of the sea* (E. Sitwell); *Soft as rain slipping through rushes, the cattle Came* (E. Blunden); *She on the earth, with steadfast sight, Stood like an image of the Muse* (R. Pitter); *Then I turn the page To a girl who stands like a questioning iris By the waterside* (C. Day Lewis). Observe the spelling and weep for the thousands of students of English literature who persist in writing about 'similies'. Contrast METAPHOR.

2 *Similes* are not the preserve of literati and poets: there are dozens in ordinary language that are long-standing stock phrases, e.g. (*as*) *drunk as a lord,* (*as*) *fit as a fiddle,* (*as*) *high as a kite, as rich as Croesus,* and some rather more recent ones such as *like a bear with a sore head,* (*as*) *cheap as chips, as sharp as a tack,* and a whole panoply of the kind *as much use as a chocolate teapot, as much use as an ashtray on a motor bike, as useful as a lawyer in a foxhole,* and many variations on the same theme.

simple. Note the post-positioning of the adjective in the legal term *fee simple,* an inherited estate, unlimited as to the category of heir, as against *fee tail,* which imposes limits.

simpleness, simplicity. See -TY AND -NESS.

simplistic. A word of surprising modernity (first recorded in its modern sense in the late 19c.; slightly earlier of medicinal plants or simples). It adds a connotation of excessive or misleading simplification to the ordinary adjective *simple.* Examples: *She's quite right . . . It is simplistic to speak of malice*—T. Stoppard, 1976; *Unfortunately, Morris . . . seems to dismiss his* [*sc.* Pope John XXIII's] *courageous attempts at reform as being naive and simplistic*—*Atlantic,* 1991. Care should be taken not to use *simplistic* in contexts where *simple* is adequate by itself, e.g. *We have got to take things back down to a more simplistic* (read: *simple* or *basic*) *level. Pensions . . . are essentially a life decision. Everything we do makes it more complicated*—*Birmingham Post,* 2007. Similarly, *oversimplistic* and *overly simplistic* are hopelessly pleonastic, since the notion of excess is already contained in the word *simplistic*: **However, such comparisons are oversimplistic, particularly in view of the fact that St John's wort is associated with only about half the incidence of adverse effects of a conventional antidepressant*—*BMJ,* 2000; *a spokesman for Tesco defended the company's decision not to take part, saying the MSC rating was 'overly simplistic'*—*Scotsman,* 2014.

simulacrum. Pronounced /sɪmjʊˈleɪkrəm/. Plural overwhelmingly *-cra,* though *-crums* is also correct. See -UM 3.

sin (verb). The phrase *to sin one's mercies* 'to be ungrateful for one's blessings or good fortune' is found in 19c. literature (beginning with Scott's *Redgauntlet*, 1824), and was familiar to Fowler (1926) and Gowers (1965), but now seems largely to have dropped out of use. An isolated example: *Sometimes I speak hard things about my profession. I sin my mercies, as the Scots say*—E. Linklater, 1929.

since. 1 For the clumsy use of *since* after *ago*, see AGO.

2 For the type *P.S. Since writing this your issue of today has come to hand*, see UNATTACHED PARTICIPLES.

sincerely. For *Yours sincerely*, etc., see LETTER FORMS 1, 2.

's incongruous. Fowler's term for 'S AND -S' AND OF-POSSESSIVE.

sinecure. Most BrE and AmE dictionaries show the first syllable rhyming either with *sign* or *sin*.

sine die. If uttered rather than read, more likely to be pronounced in a Latinate way /ˌsɪneɪ ˈdiːeɪ/ (**si**-nay **dee**-ay) than the older anglicized /ˌsʌɪnɪ ˈdʌɪiː/ (**sy**-ni **dy**-ee) or /ˈdʌɪ/ (dy). Of course, outside legal or academic circles, 'adjourned indefinitely' or 'with no appointed date' are more likely to be used. Printed in italics.

sine qua non, an indispensable condition or qualification, is pronounced /ˌsɪneɪ kwɑː ˈnəʊn/, though several variant pronunciations are also current, e.g. /ˌsʌɪnɪ/ or /ˌsɪni kweɪ ˈnəʊn/ or /ˈnɒn/. Uncertainty about the pronunciation, not to say the meaning, no doubt causes the vast majority of people never to use the phrase and to use an English equivalent instead. Printed in italics.

sing (verb). The past tense is *sang* (formerly, especially in the 18c. and 19c., often *sung*) and past participle *sung*. *Sung* for the past tense is occasionally used nowadays, especially in speech, but in writing is considered non-standard.

Singalese. See SINHALESE.

singeing (burning lightly). So spelt to distinguish it from *singing* (uttering musical sounds). See MUTE E.

single most. A correspondent pointed out to Burchfield that in strict terms *single* is tautologous when followed by *most* + an adjective and noun, as in the type *the single most valuable player in the team*. Example: *I've had mini-relationships and then gone for... 12 months without sex... and it has been the single most important growing time for me as a woman*—*NY Herald Tribune*, 1991. However, the tautology does no harm, and is a useful way of emphasizing the superlative it precedes.

singular -s. The instinctive feeling that a noun ending in *-s* is by nature plural has caused a good number of 'false' singular forms to come into being in the past, e.g. *caper* (the herb; earlier *capers*, from Old French *caspres*, modern French *câpre*, Latin *capparis*); *cherry* (from Old Norman French *cherise*, taken as a plural, modern French *cerise*); *pea* (from earlier *pease*, apprehended as a plural), *succour* (from Old French *sucurs*, *socours*, modern French *secours*). *Riches*, from French *richesse*, is now always treated as a plural. For aspects of the same phenomenon, cf. also FORCEPS; GALLOWS; KUDOS.

Sinhalese. A member of a people living chiefly in Sri Lanka or their Indic language. Formerly also *Sing(h)alese* and other variants.

sinister in heraldry means left (and *dexter* right), but with the contrary sense to what would naturally suggest itself, the left (and right) being that of the person bearing the shield, not of an observer facing it.

sink (verb). **1** The past tense is now overwhelmingly *sank* rather than *sunk*.

2 For the past participle the longer form *sunken* is no longer used as part of a compound passive verb: *a ship would have been, will be, was, sunk*, not *sunken*. As adjectives both *sunk* and *sunken* are used and their distribution is not easy to determine. The most that can be said is that *sunken* is often used to mean 'submerged' (*a sunken ship*), 'fallen in, hollow' (*sunken cheeks, sunken eyes*), and often 'below the normal level' (*sunken garden, sunken porch*). *Sunk* is the form normally chosen for technical expressions such as *sunk fence, sunk initial, sunk key, sunk panel, sunk relief* (for the meanings consult an unabridged dictionary), but *sunken* is also used in some of these.

3 Used predicatively with the verb *to be* and meaning 'in a hopeless position' the only form used is *sunk* (e.g. *'Hell!' thought Mr R., 'we're sunk!'*).

sinus. Plural *sinuses* (despite the fact that the Latin plural is *sinūs*). See -US 2.

Sioux. Pronounced /suː/. Plural unchanged and pronounced the same or, optionally, /suːz/.

siphon. This spelling is recommended and very much more frequent than *syphon* for both noun and verb. See Y AND I.

Sir, a titular prefix to the forename of a knight or baronet. Thus *Sir William Jones,* or, contextually, just *Sir William.* People who are unaware of the correct procedure sometimes use the erroneous form *Sir Jones.* A further hazard: a double- or treble-barrelled surname should not be used instead of first name and surname: thus *Sir Cave-Browne-Cave* cannot be written for *Sir Robert Cave-Browne-Cave.* The same conventions apply to the corresponding female prefix **Dame**.

sirloin. A spurious but standard spelling of what should have been **surloin* (cf. *surname*) from a hypothetical Old French form **surloigne,* variant of *surlonge* (the modern French word for 'sirloin' is in fact *aloyau*). It is the upper (cf. French *sur* 'above') and choicer part of a loin of beef. From the 17c. onwards evidence has survived falsely attributing the 'knighting' of a loin of beef to Henry VIII, James I, and Charles II. The mistaken spelling **sirlion* occurs very frequently; whether this is a typo or folk etymology, it is impossible to tell.

sirocco. More often spelt so in English, as it is in French. Plural *siroccos*: see -O(E)S 4. The Italian spelling **scirocco** (the source of the English word) seems to be less used in English, except in contexts referring specifically to Italy.

sister, a senior female nurse, especially one in charge of a hospital ward. The equivalent AmE term is **head nurse**.

sit (verb). The standard past tense is *sat*: see SAT. The corresponding participial adjective is **seated**: *the seated part of the stadium; two-seated vehicles; please be seated.*

situation. A useful noun for expressing the sense 'a set of circumstances, a state of affairs', especially when preceded by a defining adjective, e.g. *the financial, industrial, military, political situation.* The placing of a noun immediately before *situation* should normally be resisted: *a crisis situation* adds nothing to *a crisis*; *a bankruptcy situation* adds nothing to *bankruptcy*; similarly in *the conditions had deteriorated to virtually a no-visibility situation,* the word *situation* is arguably redundant. On the other hand, *hostage situation* is a convenient short way of saying 'a situation in which hostages have been taken' because *hostage* is not already a word equivalent in itself to a 'situation'. See ONGOING; -TION.

sixteenmo. In printing, the English reading of the symbol 16mo, which also represents the Latin-derived term *sextodecimo.*

sixties. See NINETIES.

sizeable, sizable. The first is the more common spelling in World English, and the preference for it is particularly pronounced in British and Irish English, whereas AmE much prefers *sizable.* See MUTE E.

sjambok. (in S. Africa) A rhinoceros-hide whip. Pronounced /ˈʃambɒk/.

skald (medieval Scandinavian poet), **skaldic** (adjective). Recommended spellings, not *sc-*.

skeptic. See SCEPTIC.

skewbald. See PIEBALD.

ski. As Burchfield (1996) recalled, in his boyhood (1930s) it was very commonly pronounced /ʃiː/, as in Norwegian, the language from which the word was adopted; but now always /skiː/. The plural of the noun is *skis*; and the inflected forms of the verb are *skis, skied, skiing.* The related noun ('one who skis') is **skier**.

skiagraphy. See SCIAGRAPHY.

skier, skyer. For 'one who skis', use *skier.* For 'a high hit (in cricket)', use *skyer.*

skilful. So spelt in BrE, but usually **skillful** in AmE. See -LL-, -L- 5, and SKILL-LESS.

skill-less. Best hyphenated as shown to avoid the ungainliness of three consecutive *l*s. Similarly *bell-less, hill-less, shell-less,* etc.

skin. *With the skin of my teeth.* See MISQUOTATIONS.

skip (college servant). See SCOUT.

skull. See SCULL.

skul(l)duggery. An interesting example of a word changing meaning, location, and spelling. *Skulduggery* with one letter *l* is originally a US word (1867), an adaptation of the earlier Scots word *skulduddery* ('obscenity'), whose origin is unknown. It therefore has nothing to do with skulls, but folk etymology has decided that there is a connection. Dictionaries recognize both spellings, which occur with equal frequency in the *OEC* data; BrE shows a marked preference for *skulduggery*, and AmE for *skullduggery*.

skyer. See SKIER.

slander. See LIBEL (noun).

slang can be defined as 'a type of language consisting of words and phrases that are regarded as very informal, are more common in speech than writing, and are typically restricted to a particular context or group of people'. **1** The term *slang* is first recorded in the 1750s, but it was not used by Dr Johnson in his *Dictionary* of 1755 nor entered in it as a headword (he used the term *low word*, with implications of disapproval). Nonetheless, the notion of highly informal words or of words associated with a particular class or occupation is very old, and this type of vocabulary has been commented on, usually with disfavour, for centuries. More recently, the development of modern linguistic science has led to a more objective assessment in which slang is seen as having a useful and specific purpose when used in the right context.

2 Drawing the line between colloquial language and slang is not always easy; slang is at the extreme end of informality and usually has the capacity to shock. In English slang often has associations of class or occupation, so that many slang words have their origins in cant (the jargon of a particular profession or group), e.g. *flog, prig, rogue*); criminal slang (*bogus* = fake, *broad* = female companion, *drag* = inhalation of tobacco smoke, *nick* = to steal); racing slang (*dark horse, no-hoper, hot favourite*); military slang (*bonkers* = crazy, *clobber* = beat or defeat, *flog* = sell, *ginormous* = huge); and most recently computing slang (*hacking* = breaking into networks, *surfing* = browsing on the Internet). Other words stay largely within their original domain of usage, such as drugs slang (*flash* = pleasant sensation from a narcotic drug, *juice* = a drug or drugs) and youth slang (*blatantly* = definitely, *wicked* = excellent).

3 Slang words are formed by a variety of processes, of which the following are the main ones: (*a*) established words used in extended or special meanings: *flash* and *juice* in the previous paragraph, *awesome* = excellent, *hooter* = nose, *take out* = kill. (*b*) words made by abbreviation or shortening: *fab* from *fabulous*, *pro* from *professional*, *snafu* (= *situation normal: all fouled/f***d up*). (*c*) rhyming slang: *Adam and Eve* = believe, *Brahms and Liszt* = pissed (drunk), *butcher's* (*hook*) = look. (*d*) words formed by compounding: *airhead* = stupid person, *couch potato* = person who lazes around watching television, *snail mail* = ordinary mail as opposed to email. (*e*) merging of two words: 'portmanteau' words such as *ditsy* = *dotty* + *dizzy*, *ginormous* = *gigantic* + *enormous*. (*f*) backslang, in which the spelling or sound of words are reversed: *yob* from *boy*, *slop* from *police*. (*g*) reduplications and fanciful formations: *heebie-jeebies, okey-doke*. (*h*) words based on phrases or idioms: *bad-mouth* = to abuse, *feel-good* as in *feel-good factor*, *in-your-face* = aggressive, *drop-dead* = extremely (beautiful etc.), *must-have* = essential, *one-night stand* = brief sexual encounter, *to die for* = extremely desirable. (*i*) loanwords from other languages: *gazump, nosh, shemozzle* from Yiddish, *kaput* from German, *bimbo* from Italian (= little child). (*j*) words taken from dialect or regional varieties: *manky* = dirty, *minging* = foul, both from Scottish; *dinkum* = genuine, right, Australian and New Zealand.

4 Slang uses are especially prevalent in areas in which direct language is regarded as taboo or unsocial, such as death (*to kick the bucket, to hand in one's nosebag, to snuff it*), sexual functions (*to have it off, to screw*), and excretion (*to dump, to sit on the throne*).

5 Slang is by its nature ephemeral, and relatively few words and uses pass into standard use. Examples of these include *bogus, clever, joke*, and *snob* (all classed by

Dr Johnson as 'low words'). Conversely some words that were once standard have passed into slang (e.g. *arse, shit, tit*).

6 The first work to record English slang was published as B.E.'s *Dictionary of the Canting Crew* in 1699. Modern works include Eric Partridge's famous *Dictionary of Slang and Unconventional English* (1937; most recently edited by Paul Beale, 2002), *The Oxford Dictionary of Slang* (edited by John Ayto, 1998), *The Slang Thesaurus* (2nd edition, edited by Jonathon Green, 1999), and the *Cassell Dictionary of Slang* (also edited by Jonathon Green, 2000).

7 As a vivid illustration of how many words and phrases considered slang when first recorded quickly become part of informal general language, and of how some die a death, there follows a short list selected by Burchfield in 1996 of words labelled 'slang' in the range A–C in *The Oxford Dictionary of New Words* (ed. Sara Tulloch, 1991): *ace* (fantastic), *Adam* (a designer drug), *airhead* (stupid person), *angel dust* (an hallucinogenic drug), *awesome* (marvellous, great), *bad* (excellent), *bad-mouth* (to abuse someone verbally), *bimbo* (attractive but unintelligent young woman), *bonk* (an act of sex; to have sex), *bottle* (courage, guts), *brill*(*iant*) (fantastic, great), *chase the dragon* (to take heroin), *couch potato* (person who spends leisure time passively, mostly watching television and videos), *cowabunga* (an exclamation of exhilaration), *crack* (form of cocaine), *cred* (credibility, reputation), *crumblie* (an old or senile person). See RHYMING SLANG.

slash. See OBLIQUE.

slate (verb). One of its main senses in BrE is 'to criticize severely, to scold' (*he was slated by his constituency party for voting against the amendment*). By contrast the word is used in AmE to mean 'to write or set down for nomination or appointment' or 'to schedule or designate (*slated a meeting of service chiefs for the following afternoon*)'. The context will normally make it clear which meaning is intended, but clearly care is called for, especially in interpreting headlines such as *Summit meeting slated.*

slave has the derivative **slavish**. See MUTE E.

slay (verb). Though poetic and rhetorical in BrE, it is still in ordinary use in AmE, for violent killing. The mainly American use is sometimes carried over into UK newspapers (*Serial killer slays seven young men*). The past tense is *slew* and past participle *slain.* In the secondary slang sense 'to overwhelm with delight, to convulse with laughter' the past tense is usually *slayed* (*the comic scene simply slayed them*).

sledgehammer is spelt as one word as noun and verb, not **sledge hammer*, nor **sledge-hammer.*

sled, sledge, sleigh. *Sled* is the mainly AmE word for 'a vehicle on runners for conveying loads or passengers especially over snow, drawn by horses, dogs, or reindeer, or pushed or pulled by one or more persons' (*COD*), and *sledge* the BrE equivalent. A *sleigh* is 'a sledge, esp. one for riding on, rather than conveying loads, and drawn by horses or reindeer' (*COD*).

sleight (as in *sleight of hand*). Pronounced /slʌɪt/, it is related to *sly* as *height* is to *high.* Journalists in a hurry and bloggers, beware: it is all too easy to write it incorrectly as **slight of hand*, e.g. **He's an old-fashioned type of scrum-half, with good deception and slight of hand and an outstanding kicking game—The Press* (York), 2004. Correct example: *This is a nice bit of sleight of hand, confusing correlation with causation—TechDirt*, 2012.

slew (noun)[1]. This is the correct spelling of the informal word for a large group of things or people, originally US, and from an Irish word, e.g. Fugitive Pieces *was perhaps the decade's most celebrated novel about the Holocaust, winning a slew of awards including the Guardian and Orange prizes—The Age*, 2009, not **They responded to the defense secretary with a slue of press releases, documents and conference calls—CNN* (transcripts), 2006.

slew (noun)[2]. An AmE variant of *slough,* 'bog, swamp', pronounced /sluː/.

slew, slue (verb). The first is now the normal spelling for this word in its sense 'to turn or swing forcibly from its ordinary position'.

slier, slily. See SLY.

***slight of hand.** For this misspelling, see SLEIGHT.

slime has the derivative **slimy**. See MUTE E.

sling, slink. The standard past tense and past participle are *slung* and *slunk*. *Slinged* and *slinked*, occasionally found, must be considered dialectal.

slither, sliver are often confused, especially in newspapers. *Slither* is overwhelmingly a verb meaning 'to slip or slide unsteadily', whereas *sliver* is a noun meaning 'a thin narrow piece cut off a larger piece', e.g. *a sliver of cheese*. The more common mistake is to put *slither* for *sliver*: **A shave here and a slither* (read *sliver*) *of metal there can make all the difference to a bell—Guardian*, 1999. While *ODO* marks this misspelling merely 'informal', those who notice it will surely consider it a mistake. Very rarely is the swap the other way round: **Scan the surface like a hawk for tiny succulent slivering* (read *slithering*) *fish—www.indianest.com*, 2002.

sloe-worm. See SLOW-WORM.

slogan. From the 16c. to the 19c. this word of Gaelic origin meant 'a war-cry or battle cry; *spec.* one of those formerly employed by the Scottish Highlanders or Borderers, or by the native Irish, usually consisting of a personal surname or the name of a gathering-place' (e.g. *The isle of Clareinch was the slogurn or call of war, proper to the family of Buchanan*—W. Buchanan, 1683). The less specific sense 'the distinctive note, phrase, cry, etc. of any person or body of persons' overlapped with the older sense in the 19c., and has now itself been replaced by the modern meaning 'a motto associated with a political party or movement or other group, or a short and striking or memorable phrase used in advertising'. Throughout the 20c. and in the 21c. slogans have become commonplace in politics, charities, and advertising: e.g. *Ban the bomb*; *Make Poverty History*; *No Child Born to Die*; *Vorsprung durch Technik*. See also ADVERTISING, LANGUAGE OF.

slosh. See SLUSH.

slough. The noun meaning 'bog, swamp' is pronounced /slaʊ/. The separate word *slough* meaning (as noun) 'a part that an animal casts' and (as verb) 'to cast or drop off' is pronounced /slʌf/. A cautionary note: many Americans pronounce the 'swamp' noun /sluː/ and spell it *slew*.

slow, slowly. The primary distinction, namely that *slow* is an adjective (*take the slow train to Oxford*) and *slowly* is an adverb (*the yachts moved slowly out of the harbour*), is almost always followed in practice. But there are exceptions. In days gone by literary examples of *slow* used as an adverb abound: *But oh, me thinkes, how slow This old Moon wanes*—Shakespeare, 1590; *I hear the far-off Curfeu sound... Swinging slow with sullen roar*—Milton, 1632; *As the stately vessel glided slow Beneath the shadow*—Byron, 1812; *We drove very slow for the last two stages on the road*—Thackeray, 1848. In current English the normal adverb for general purposes is *slowly* (*We drove slowly down the road*; *She slowly closed the door*). The literary uses of *slow* as an adverb died out in the 19c., and in current usage it is confined to the expression *go slow*, to compounds such as *slow-acting* and *slow-moving*, and to occasional informal uses, e.g. *It was easy to drive slow and look into lighted uncurtained windows*—L. Ellmann, 1988. The comparative and superlative forms *slower* and *slowest* are, however, regularly used as well as *more slowly* and *most slowly*: *Neurotransmitters make the heart beat faster or slower—Scientific American*, 1974; *In congested motorway traffic, I always appear to be in the lane moving the slowest—Daily Mail*, 2002.

slow-worm (small legless lizard). Formerly also *sloe-worm*. It is not directly related to either *sloe* or *slow* but is derived from Old English *slā-wyrm*, the first element of which is of uncertain origin.

sludge. See SLUSH.

slue. See SLEW, SLUE (verb); SLEW[1] (noun).

slur (verb). The inflected forms are *slurred*, *slurring*. See -R-, -RR-.

slush, sludge, slosh. *Sludge* is usually applied to something relatively thick and less liquid, e.g. to wet clinging mud or slimy deposits, whereas *slush* more typically describes thawing snow or melting ice. *Slosh* (in its related uses) is a verb meaning 'to move with a splashing sound', and *slush* as a verb can be used in this way too, e.g. *there was water slushing around in the galley*; *water in the boat sloshed about under our feet*.

sly has the inflections and derivatives *slyer, slyest, slyly, slyness, slyish* (not *slier*, etc.). Contrast DRIER; FLYER, FLIER.

smart. We may or may not be smart ourselves, but we live in a very 'smart' world. *Smart* referring to a device or machine 'appearing to have a degree of intelligence; able to react or respond to differing requirements, varying situations, or past events; programmed so as to be capable of some independent action' and specifically 'containing a microprocessor' is most familiar to us in *smartphones*. The use defined above dates back to 1948 and is now all around us in applications as diverse as *smart bombs* (1970), *smartcards* (1980), *smart fabrics* (1991), and *smart meters* (1974).

smell (verb). **1** Both *smelled* and *smelt* are used for the past tense and past participle, but the first is rather more frequent in the *OEC* data. Other than in North American English, where *smelt* is rare, the two forms have roughly equal frequency in all varieties of English. See -T AND -ED. Examples: *Although he no longer smelled of sick his appetite was poor*—A. Brookner, 1988; *They* [*sc.* dogs] *smelt, especially when wet*—*Good Housekeeping*, 1989; *Barry has smelled it on winos after they've been on a three-week binge*—*New Yorker*, 1988; *And then he smelled something, and that wasn't his fault, was it?*—G. Keillor, 1991 (US).

2 When used intransitively to describe the quality of a smell, the verb is normally followed by an adjective, not an adverb: *Hort's house always smelled so good*—*New Yorker*, 1988; *He smelled the cup of water and it smelled putrid*—*Community Development Jrnl*, 1988. When it is used to mean 'stink', however, an adverb of manner is the norm: *the prison cell smelled abominably. Smell* is also commonly followed by an *of*-phrase: *I settled down on the leather seat that already smelled of orange peel*—M. Pople, 1986 (Aust.); *The wood smelled of beeswax*—A. S. Byatt, 1990. Had a qualifying word been inserted in either of these sentences it would undoubtedly have been an adverb, not an adjective (*smelled* strongly *of orange peel*; *smelled* faintly *of beeswax*).

smite. This ancient verb (past tense *smote*, past participle *smitten*), after centuries of use from Anglo-Saxon times onwards, and a prominent percussive role in the Old Testament, has now fallen into disuse or is reserved for literary contexts (*And it came to pass, that at midnight the* LORD *smote all the firstborn in the land of Egypt*—Exod. 12:29 (AV); *When he saw Tissy moving about the quiet rooms of his house*... *his heart smote him*—A. Brookner, 1989). Its most frequent use is as the participle *smitten*, 'infatuated, fascinated'. The preposition following can be either *with* or *by*, the first being about twice as common overall. When the object of the fascination is a person, *with* is much more often used than *by*; when the object is inanimate, the pattern is the opposite: *Yvan is smitten with Charlotte*; *Roberts happens upon Grant's bookstore and is smitten with his English charm*; *a successful engineer/entrepreneur smitten by the film bug*; *it turns out that Angela is smitten by Dave*.

smog. So familiar and widely used is this word that it is easy to overlook that it is a portmanteau, and a deliberate creation, formed in 1905 from *smoke* + *fog* by Dr H. A. des Vœux, Hon. Treasurer of the Coal Smoke Abatement Society, in one of the most enduring blends of the 20c. Apart from its literal use it is also used in figurative contexts, to describe something, often deliberately contrived, that prevents clear understanding, e.g. *In his several visits to Moscow in the 1920s, he found a thickening smog of terror and lies*—*Quadrant* (magazine), 2005; *Such bold and clear statements of truth are like breaths of fresh air in a culture choked by the smog of relativism*—*Southern Appeal*, 2005.

smoky, smokey. The first is about ten times more frequent in the *OEC* data.

smoulder (burn slowly, etc.). So spelt in BrE, but often as **smolder** in AmE.

snail-like. For the hyphen, see -LIKE.

snaky, snakey. The first is rather more frequent than the second, and is to be preferred. See -EY AND -Y IN ADJECTIVES.

snapshot is an interesting example of a word which has a more vivid life as a metaphor than in its literal meaning, which is any case another metaphor. Originally (1808) a 'snap shot' was 'a quick or hurried shot taken without deliberate aim, especially one at a rising bird or quickly moving animal'. Then (1890) it became a metaphor, denoting 'an informal photograph taken quickly with a small hand camera', e.g. *an album of family snapshots*. Now, in the era of digital phones and cameras, that meaning sounds a trifle quaint, and the word is mainly used to mean 'a brief look or summary', e.g. *I asked President Masaryk... if he could give me a snapshot of the difference between what he found when he came to Prague in 1918, and what he has the satisfaction of seeing now—Observer*, 1928; *The first half of the exhibition provides an enlightening snapshot of workshop practices in renaissance Florence—Apollo*, 2005.

sneak (verb). **1** *Early beginnings.* Its origins are shrouded in mystery. First recorded in print in the 16c., it seems to have emerged from some uncharted dialectal area and made its way swiftly into the language of playwrights: *A poore vnminded Outlaw, sneaking home*—Shakespeare, 1596; *I hope he will not sneake away with all the money*—Dekker, 1604; *Where's Madrigall? Is he sneek'd hence?*—Jonson, 1625. From the beginning, and still in standard BrE, the past tense and past participle forms are *sneaked*. Modern UK examples: *I bet every father in the land sneaked out of the house to get an eyeful of that Miss Jane Russell*—P. Bailey, 1986; *I sneaked into his workroom—Spectator*, 1987.

2 *A new past form.* Just as mysteriously, in a little more than a century, a new past tense and past participle form **snuck** has crept and then rushed out of dialectal use in America, first into the areas of use that lexicographers label as non-standard, and, more recently, has reached the point where it is a virtual rival of *sneaked* in many parts of the English-speaking world, and is recognized as standard in AmE. There is evidence of *snuck* sneaking into BrE in a big way as well, though probably here it would be regarded as informal. The progress of *snuck* can be seen fairly clearly in the following chronologically arranged set of examples: *He grubbed ten dollars from de bums an den snuck home—The Lantern* (New Orleans), 1887; *They had all snuck in and were having a good time, making trouble*—J. T. Farrell, 1932 (US); *So I snuck off to the park and had a good read—Oz*, 1969; *This Crisp, he snuck over into the Blood's territory to make that mark—New Yorker*, 1986; *He had snuck through the orchards like a deserter*—J. Urquhart, 1986 (Canad.); *It* [*sc.* bad luck] *had snuck up on him from behind as it always did—Metro* (NZ), 1988; *While I was groaning at my reflection in the bathroom mirror he snuck out of the flat*—A. Billson, 1993 (UK).

3 *An unparalleled form.* What the future holds for *snuck* is unpredictable. Meanwhile no one has satisfactorily accounted for its origin: there is no other verb in the language with infinitive *-eek* or *-eak* and past forms *-uck*. Consider the following verbs in /-iːk/: *creak, freak, leak, peak, peek, reek, seek, squeak, streak, wreak*, also *shriek*. None of them has shown any sign of following the path of *sneak* by acquiring a new past tense and past participle form.

snivel (verb). The inflected forms in BrE are *snivelled, snivelling*, but in AmE often *sniveled, sniveling*. See -LL-, -L-.

snuck. See SNEAK (verb).

so.

1 Phrases treated elsewhere.
2 *so long* (as formulaic farewell); *and so to—*.
3 *I so don't want to go*.
4 The explanatory *so*.
5 *so* with superlatives and absolutes.
6 *so* as conjunction.

1 *Phrases treated elsewhere.* For *ever so*, see EVER 4; for *so far from, so far as*, see FAR 2; for *and so forth/and so on*, see FORTH; for *quite so*, see QUITE 1; for *so to speak*, see INFINITIVE 3(*b*); SUPERIORITY.

2 *so long* (as formulaic farewell); *and so to—*. (*a*) *so long* used colloquially for 'goodbye' or '*au revoir*'. The once popular view that this is an adaptation of *salaam* is without foundation. It is merely a special combination of *so* and *long*, and it has been in use according to the *OED* since 1865. English is richly endowed with farewell formulas, varying greatly in their degree of formality: *adieu; bye(-bye); see you; be seeing you; see ya; ta-ta*; etc.

(*b*) *And so to a division, and so to dinner*, etc. This formula for winding up the account of a debate or incident, borrowed directly or indirectly from Pepys, is apt to become addictive. 'It is wise to abstain from it altogether' (Fowler), or at any rate to use it sparingly.

3 *I so don't want to go.* In modern slang, originally in AmE and now quite common also in informal BrE, possibly popularized by the TV series *Friends*, *so* as an intensifier has been extended into roles that stretch standard grammar, i.e.: (i) meaning 'extremely, characteristically' and modifying a noun or noun phrase, or an adjective or adjectival phrase or adverb which does not usually admit comparison: *Oh, please, you know. God, you're so the opposite! I mean, you write that absolutely fabulous television show*—Woody Allen, 1979; *African models are so last year—Independent*, 2004; *Or, as 12-year-old Olivia puts it: 'Dad, you are so yesterday'—Scotland on Sunday*, 2005; (ii) meaning 'definitely, decidedly' and modifying active verbs, frequently in negative constructions: *Oh thank you, Josh, I so need lessons from you on how to be cool—Clueless*, 1994; *We so don't have time—Buffy the Vampire Slayer*, 1996; *It's the sort of slangy, informal use of* so *you might hear a teen of the MTV set employ, as in: 'Omigod, I would so marry Carson Daly if he asked me'—Brill's Content*, 2000; (iii) in the phrase *so not* = emphatically not, e.g. *We guess communism just got buried in the rubble there somewhere. And those Ceauşescus? So not missed—Salman Rushdie*, 1999; *You've seen the carousel and it's so not cool to be seen here if you're over nine years old*—J. M. Czech, 2005.

These usages are youthful (or would-be-young) and appealing, but cannot yet be considered standard.

4 The explanatory *so*. Type: *He could not move, he was so cold*. The second clause is equivalent to a sentence beginning with *for* or *because*, and the idiom is mainly, but not only, spoken. In such sentences it is clear to the listener that the second clause provides an explanation of the first and no conjunction is needed to link them.

5 *so* with superlatives and absolutes. *So*, when it qualifies adjectives and adverbs, means to such a degree or extent; it is therefore not appropriately applied to a superlative, as in *The difficult and anxious negotiations in which he has taken* so *foremost a part in Paris*; or to an absolute, as in *It is indeed a privilege to be present on* so *unique an occasion*.

6 *so* as conjunction. Earlier commentators and grammarians have been unhappy about treating *so* on its own as a conjunction, i.e. allowing that it could connect two clauses, as in *There is no clear record of the debates within the federal government, so the political dynamics of such delay are only conjecture—Dædalus* (US), 1989. Their contention was that *so* had to be followed by *that* in order to qualify as a 'proper' conjunction. It is true that the practice in standard English as late as the 19c. was to use *so that* to introduce clauses describing result or logical consequence ('result clauses'), or as a synonym for 'in order that' in 'clauses of purpose': (purpose) [*They*] *had conveighed their shippes in to the havens, so that he could not fight with them on the sea*—1548 in *OED*; *We will spend our evenings . . . at our own lodgings, so that we may be found—c.*1760 in *OED*; (result) *The turf roof of it had fallen in: so that the hut was no use to me*—R. L. Stevenson, 1886. Constructions using *so* alone are recorded from medieval times, but were no more than sporadic. First in America in the 19c., and gradually elsewhere, *so* alone has gradually established itself in standard use, especially in spoken English. In the face of the evidence it seems clear that standard speakers now feel that the use without *that* is entirely unobjectionable. When used in this way, *so* normally follows a comma, but the punctuation is sometimes altered so that it leads a sentence.

Examples of *so* alone: (purpose) *I'll knock . . . and peep round the door When I come back, so you'll know who it is*—R. Frost, 1913 (US); *Shovelling coal up the back of the chimney, throwing it on so it would burn for hours*—C. P. Snow, 1951; *My husband . . . kept his head down so he would not have to see the barn—New Yorker*, 1986; *Tom passed the binoculars to Jamie so he could see that it was an allosaurus attacking two stegosaurs—Dinosaur Cove*, 2010; (result) *My father had been a minor diplomat, so as a child I had lived in France, Turkey and Paraguay*—G. Greene, 1980; *The wind blew straight into his nose and mouth so he had to turn away for a moment to breathe*—M. Gee, 1985; (after a full stop) *But work is scarce, especially in winter. So he watches a lot of TV, soaps*, [etc.]—*New Yorker*, 1989.

sobriquet /ˈsəʊbrɪkeɪ/ is the recommended and more often used spelling, not *soubriquet*. Print in roman, not italics.

sobriquets. Under this heading are grouped together fifty or so out of the limitless number of NICKNAMES or secondary names that have become so firmly attached to particular people, places, or things, as to be intelligible when used instead of the real or primary name. Even now, for example, who in Britain would fail to recognize the reference in *the Iron Lady*? But, like any other word, sobriquets can be restricted to certain eras, and to particular genres or social groups. How many people would nowadays be baffled by the reference in *the Bard of Avon* or *the Maid of Orleans*? A selective list, some topical, others dated or historical, based on Burchfield's (1996) list, follows:

Albion (England); *alma mater* (one's university); *Athens of the North* (Edinburgh); *Auld Reekie* (Edinburgh); *Auntie* (BBC); *Bard of Avon* (Shakespeare); *Beefeater* (Yeoman of the Guard); *Big Apple* (New York); *Black Country* (industrial west Midlands); *Black Death* (14c. plague); *Black Maria* (prison van); *Black Prince* (eldest son of Edward III); *Blighty* (Britain, used by British service personnel abroad); *Buck House* (Buckingham Palace); *City of Dreaming Spires* (Oxford); *Cœur de Lion* (Richard I); *Elia* (Charles Lamb); *Emerald Isle* (Ireland); *Garden of England* (Kent); *Gherkin* (30 St Mary Axe, Swiss Re Building, London); *Great Cham* (Samuel Johnson); *Great Wen* (London); *Iron Duke* (Wellington); *Iron Lady, Iron Maiden* (Lady Thatcher); *Jack Tar* (sailor, RN) *John Bull* (Englishman); *Kiwi* (New Zealander); *knight of the road* (highwayman; tramp); *La-La Land* (Hollywood); *Latin Quarter* (hub of Paris's intellectual life); *Left Bank* (artistic district of Paris); *Maid of Orleans* (Joan of Arc); *Mother of Parliaments* (British Parliament); *Old Nick* (devil); *Old Lady of Threadneedle Street* (Bank of England); *Pom(my)* (British migrant to Australia or New Zealand); *Sage of Chelsea* (Carlyle); *Senior Service* (navy); *Spaghetti Junction* (Gravelly Hill motorway intersection, Birmingham, UK); *sport of kings* (horse racing); *staff of life* (bread); *Stars and Stripes* (US flag); *Swan of Avon* (Shakespeare); *The Thunderer* (*The Times*); *Tinseltown* (Hollywood); *Tommy* (*Atkins*) (British soldier(s)); *Uncle Sam* (USA); *Union Jack* (British flag); *Virgin Queen* (Queen Elizabeth I of England); *Warrior Queen* (Boadicea, Boudicca); *Windy City* (Chicago); *Wizard of the North* (Walter Scott).

For a much fuller treatment, see e.g. B. Freestone, *Harrap's Book of Nicknames and Their Origins* (1990), and L. Urdang, *A Dictionary of Names and Nicknames* (1991).

socage (feudal tenure of land). So spelt, rather than *soccage*.

so-called is traditionally used, often rather scornfully, before a name or description to signal doubt about whether the thing or person so described is entitled to the description, as in *this so-called work of art*. In more recent usage, and now quite commonly (especially in technical contexts), it is used merely to call attention to the description, without implying that it is incorrect, (e.g. *the so-called 'generation gap'*). Strictly speaking the quotation marks are not needed, but their use or omission is just a matter of taste. When used predicatively (after a verb) *so called* is compositional and normally explanatory rather than judgemental, and it is therefore printed as two words: *Prayer plants are so called because the leaves fold upwards as if in prayer*.

soccer (formed irregularly from As*soc*iation football + -*er*). Now the only spelling, though *socker* was often used in the last decade of the 19c. Most words having *cc* before *e, i, y* are pronounced with /-ks-/: *accept, eccentricity, success, accident, flaccid, coccyx*. The only exceptions, apart from *soccer*, seem to be *baccy* and *recce*, where the /-k-/ is taken over from *tobacco* and *reconnaissance* respectively.

social media. This noun denoting websites and applications that enable users to create and share content or to participate in social networking can be treated as singular or plural as regards verbs following it: (singular) *As far as social media goes, it depends on what kind of business you have—StartUp Nation*, 2011; *And that is the other area social media works well: brand building—SEObook*, 2009; (plural) *If we use the 'recreational' analogy, we may come up with better answers for education, in which social media play a role—Rough Type*, 2012; *I attribute this to the transparency, connectedness, and immediacy that social media offer—BusinessWeek*, 2009.

sociolinguistics. A term introduced in the late 1930s for a subdivision of linguistics which may be defined briefly as 'the study of language in relation to social factors'. By studying such linguistic features as *h*-dropping (omitting the initial *h* when pronouncing *hay, horse*, etc.), the full pronunciation of postvocalic /r/ (as in *bar, heart*, etc.), the glottal stop (e.g. in the pronunciation of *butter* as /ˈbʌˀə/ and *pattern* as /ˈpaˀɛn/), kinship terms, certain grammatical constructions (e.g. the double negative in *I didn't see nothing*), and many other aspects of, especially, non-standard pronunciation, grammar, and vocabulary, sociolinguists have established a broad stratification of types of English. Pioneering scholars in the subject include Peter Trudgill in Britain (e.g. his *Sociolinguistics: An Introduction*, 1974) and William Labov in the United States (e.g. in *The Social Stratification of English in New York City*, 1966). The subject is now a routine part of university courses in linguistics, and the annual output of books and papers about it is formidable. Taken out of context some of the assertions of sociolinguists have been fiercely contested in that they seem to claim that all varieties of English, standard, regional, uneducated, inner city-based, are of equal value, aesthetically and linguistically (e.g. 'All varieties of a language are structured, complex, rule-governed systems which are wholly adequate for the needs of their speakers'—Trudgill, 1974). The great debate continues.

It hardly needs to be said that the aim of the present book is to identify the main elements of standard English in the UK, both those that are stable and those that are in process of changing, with numerous observations on standard American English, and with passing comments on differences of substance in the other main varieties of English in countries where English is spoken as a first language.

sociologese. 'We live in a scientific age, and like to show, by the words we use, that we think in a scientific way': thus Gowers in the second edition (1965) of this book. He then went on to attack what he called *sociologese*, i.e. a style of writing supposedly typical of sociologists 'characterized by verbosity and jargon' (as the *OED* has it). He built up his argument: 'Sociology is a new science concerning itself not with esoteric matters outside the comprehension of the layman, as the older sciences do, but with the ordinary affairs of ordinary people. This seems to engender in those who write about it a feeling that the lack of any abstruseness in their subject demands a compensatory abstruseness in their language. Thus, in the field of industrial relations, what the ordinary man would call an informal talk may be described as a *relatively unstructured conversational interaction*, and its purpose may be said to be *to build, so to speak, within the mass of demand and need, a framework of limitation recognized by both worker and client*. This seems to mean that the client must be persuaded that, beyond a certain point, he can only rely on what used to be called self-help; but that would not sound a bit scientific.'

Sociologese is an easy target and one that 'has been frequently targeted, not least by Gowers himself, while admitting that 'there are of course writers on sociological subjects who express themselves clearly and simply'. Among Gowers' examples of over-dense sociological language, all unattributed, is the following: (in the field of industrial relations) *The technique here reported resulted from the authors' continuing interest in human variables associated with organizational effectiveness. Specifically, this technique was developed to identify and analyse several types of interpersonal activities and relations, and to provide a method for expressing the degree of congruence between two or more of these activities and relations in indices which might be associated with available criteria of organizational effectiveness.* But it is worth stating that there is a difference between sociology written for sociologists (which this is) and sociology intended for a wider readership (if there is such a thing).

For further comments on related matters, see GOBBLEDEGOOK; JARGON; OFFICIALESE. A useful book on this general field is Walter Nash's *Jargon: Its Uses and Abuses* (1993).

socker. See SOCCER.

socle (plinth supporting a column, etc.). Pronounced /ˈsəʊkəl/.

Socrates. Pronounced /ˈsɒkrətiːz/ in English despite the long *o* in Greek Σωκράτης.

soft is primarily an adjective. After centuries of idiomatic use as an adverb (beside the 'regular' form *softly*) it had become mostly poetic and archaic by the end of the 19c.: *There is sweet music here that softer falls Than petals from blown roses on the grass*—Tennyson, 1833; *Sleep soft, beloved!*—E. B. Browning, 1850; *The wanderer . . . Halts on the bridge to hearken How soft the poplars sigh*—Housman, 1896. It may still be used in a few combinations (*soft-spun, soft-tinted*), but for all practical purposes it has lost its primary power as an adverb.

soften. In the *OED* (1913) only /ˈsɔːfən/, but now regularly /ˈsɒfən/ with a short stem vowel.

soi-disant. Pronounced /ˌswɑːdiːˈzɒ̃/ in a quasi-French manner, and printed in italics. Gowers (1965) protested that English is well supplied with words of similar meaning, and usage seems to agree with him: *soi-disant* is much less often used than e.g. *self-proclaimed, self-styled* and *so-called.*

sojourn. In standard BrE pronounced /ˈsɒdʒ(ə)n/, /-dʒəːn/, or /ˈsʌdʒ-/ with equal acceptability. In AmE the second syllable can also be stressed. The word's level of formality is wittily highlighted by the following remark in David Lodge's novel *Nice Work* (1988): *'You seem to have acquired a very utilitarian view of universities, from your sojourn in Rummidge,' said Professor Penrose, who was one of the very few people Robyn knew who used the word sojourn in casual conversation.*

solarium /səˈlɛːrɪəm/. Plural *solariums* or *solaria* /-rɪə/. See -UM 3.

solemnness. With two *ns*, the recommended form, if needed, which it rarely is, instead of *solemnity*, not **solemness.*

Solicitor General. Capitals, no hyphen. Plural *Solicitors General.*

solidus /ˈsɒlɪdəs/. Plural *solidi* /ˈsɒlɪdʌɪ/. See OBLIQUE.

soliloquy. See MONOLOGUE.

solo. Plural *solos*; see -O(E)S 4; in Italian music *soli* /ˈsəʊli/.

so long = goodbye. See SO 2.

soluble, solvable have as opposites *insoluble, unsolvable*: see IN- AND UN-. Substances are *soluble* (or *dissolvable*), not *solvable*; problems are *soluble* or *solvable.* See also DISSOLUBLE; RESOLUBLE.

sombre. So spelt in BrE, but **somber** in AmE.

sombrero (broad-brimmed Mexican hat). Plural *sombreros*: see -O(E)S 4.

some. 1 As the central meaning of *some* (determiner) is 'an unspecified amount or number of' (*some cheese, some apples; some of them*), the word has been regarded with suspicion when used either as an understatement to express admiration of something notable, or ironically to express disapproval or disbelief, e.g. *This is some party* (= a fine party); *That's some example he sets us* (= a 'fine' example, ironically); and *'They're some geologists,' he added with unwilling admiration* (= remarkable). Such uses are recorded from 1808 onwards in the *OED*, most famously by Winston Churchill in a speech in 1941: *When I warned them* [*sc.* the French government] *that Britain would fight on alone whatever they did, their Generals told their Prime Minister and his divided Cabinet: 'In three weeks England will have her neck wrung like a chicken.' Some chicken! Some neck!* But despite all the examples (including the Churchillian one), and the span of time involved, the use still seems to be informal and, as it were, on probation, in standard BrE.

2 In AmE *some* is used adverbially to mean 'to some extent', as in *She thought about it some*, in the same way that *any* is used to mean 'at all' (*You haven't aged any*), and is occasionally used with the meaning 'somewhat' to qualify an adjective: *We had done been feeding it* [*sc.* a horse] *for two-three days now by forced draft . . . and it looked some better now than when we had brung it home*—W. Faulkner, 1940; *An old worker . . . turned the handle and tried it with a few roots. Asked what he thought of it he said with conviction: 'It's some stiff, maaster.'*—G. E. Evans, 1956; *He's going to be some pissed off when he finds out about this*—M. Machlin, 1976. Adverbial *some* is not used in BrE.

3 When *some* is used before a number, that number should be an approximate or rounded one: *A row over the seating of the wives of a Gulf VIP held up a British Airways flight from Milan for almost three hours, resulting in some 50 fellow passengers missing connections—Guardian,* 2007.

4 The phrase *some of us* may be treated as a first-person or a third-person phrase depending on the degree of involvement by the speaker or writer: *Some of us want to change our plans* includes the speaker whereas *Some of us want to change their plans* excludes or at least distances the speaker from the intended change of plans. The choice only arises when a personal or possessive pronoun or adjective (here *our* and *their*) follows in the sentence.

-some. 1 Adjectives ending in *-some* (ultimately representing Old English *-sum,* a suffix used to form adjectives from nouns) entered the language at widely different periods. Among the Old English and Middle English words, those still in use include *buxom* (Old English *buhsum*), *cumbersome, fulsome, handsome, irksome, loathsome, noisome, wearisome, wholesome,* and *winsome,* but the casualty rate has been high. In the 16c. appear *awesome, brightsome, darksome, gruesome* (later revived by Walter Scott), *quarrelsome, tiresome,* and *troublesome* among others; numerous others have subsequently fallen by the wayside. Of later date are *adventuresome* 18c., *bothersome* 19c., *cuddlesome* 19c., *fearsome* 18c., and *lonesome* 17c., all still current, but many others were just short-lived formations, and the 19c. in particular was the heyday of new adjectives with this prefix (91 according to the *OED*) including *clipsome* fit to be clasped, *dabblesome* given to dabbling, and *duelsome* inclined to duelling. Only *flavoursome* and *worrisome* have outlived their era. See also AWESOME; GLADSOME.

2 Old English *-sum* was also used after the smallest numerals in the genitive plural to form nouns meaning 'a group of (so many)': *twosome, threesome, foursome* (in all of which *-some* is pronounced /səm/). In recent times in AmE (occasionally elsewhere) *-some* has been affixed to larger numbers, with full pronunciation as /-sʌm/ , to mean 'about, approximately'. Though often written without one, it is better with a hyphen: e.g. *Me, I like the .45 Colt, but I been shooting that little baby for twenty-some years*—T. Clancy, 1987; *a silver-haired Catholic priest at the head of it* [*sc.* a coffin] *with a teen-age acolyte in a white smock, and forty-some mourners*—*New Yorker,* 1988; *Of our thirty-some days together so far, some have been better than others*—G. Keillor, 1989; *Forty-some hours since she had seen Charles, or heard from him*—*New Yorker,* 1989; *The book has been translated into, I forget what it is, 60 some languages*—*CNN, In the Money,* 2005.

somebody, someone. 1 For the general question of using *they, their,* etc. after singular indefinite pronouns like *somebody,* see AGREEMENT 6; ANY 1(*a*). See also the examples at the end of this entry.

2 It is a matter of curiosity that the relevant section (1885) of the *OED* treats *anybody* as a main entry but merely subsumes *anyone* under that for *any.* This is not just a historical accident: from the Middle English period onwards *anybody* (or *ani-body* etc.) was a fully fledged indefinite pronoun, whereas *anyone* (as distinct from the type 'any one of the two will suffice') does not appear until 1711. It is quite otherwise with *somebody* and *someone,* which have been in constant parallel use since the beginning of the 14c. Both stand as main entries in the *OED.*

3 There follow some additional examples from diverse sources of the modern tendency to use a plural pronoun with backward reference to the technically singular indefinite pronoun *someone*: *The extreme irritation one always feels when* someone *proves to be more percipient than one has decided* they *shall be*—A. S. Byatt, 1967; *For* someone *to dream about* their *own death is a . . . sign that it is soon to come about*—Oxford student's essay, 1985; *The woman at the door shouted back at him, 'It's* someone *for Florrie.' Well, tell* them *to go upstairs.'* (only one caller)—R. Rive, 1990 (SAfr.). The trend seems irreversible.

some day, someday. Until the beginning of the 20c. this phrase was normally written as two words. Now, corpus data suggests that it is more often written as a single word, particularly in AmE, while in other varieties the two spellings are in more equal competition. British dictionaries tend to show it as two words, American as one. When the meaning is 'at some time in the indefinite future', the conjoined form *someday* is more often used, but the spelling as two words also persists, e.g. *someday we must talk about accreditation and the graduate school*—*Dædalus,* 1988; *he likes writers and wants to be one someday*—J. McInerney, 1988; *If the weather keeps cooling off I might even be inspired to cook a meal some day soon!*—weblog, 2013 (NZ). When *day* retains its meaning as a discrete unit of time, the words are separate, e.g. *the debate will be held on* some day *to be agreed;* some day *or other.*

someone. See SOMEBODY.

someplace. 1 See ANY 2(*f*); EVERYPLACE.

2 The adverb *somewhere,* i.e. the normal form in BrE, is still widely used in AmE (e.g. *A television technician with a belt full* *of toys came out of the nave on his way somewhere*—*New Yorker*, 1988). In AmE (rarely elsewhere) *someplace* surged into prominence in the second half of the 20c.: e.g. *she can get a good job herself someplace and they can get married*—L. Smith, 1983; *If this discourse is not someplace in the culture, it is a rather tall order for us to try to invent it here*—*Dædalus*, 1988; *as if she had pushed off someplace else in her head*—N. Virtue, 1988 (NZ); *Somebody pulled in a trailer so they would have someplace to sleep tonight*—*CNN* (transcripts), 2007.

somersault. The several older variant spellings, *somersaut, somersalt, summersault*, etc., have now been discarded in favour of *somersault.*

-something. Starting in AmE but now universally, *-something* has been appended to multiples of *ten*, especially *twenty* to *fifty*, as an adjective and noun to indicate the approximate age of a person. Cf. -SOME 2. It is best written with a hyphen before *-something*. Examples: *At the time of its creation, the show was nothing more than a college rock-opera by a twenty-something composer*—*DVD Verdict*, 2003; *Country Music legend Dolly Parton played to a sell-out crowd of crazed forty-somethings in Dublin's Point Theatre at the weekend*—*Showbiz Ireland*, 2002.

sometime, some time. *Sometime*, spelt as one word, is an indefinite adverb with two main meanings: (*a*) chiefly used in the sense 'former(ly)' of a person who once held office (*sometime Lord Mayor of Oxford*) or a building which has changed its function (*the old Ashmolean Building, sometime the headquarters of the OED*). When used as an adjective (*a sometime Fellow of Balliol College, Oxford*; *his sometime colleague*) it must be written solid. Cf. LATE; (*b*) When the contextual meaning is 'at some future time' the two words are normally run together (e.g. *Let's talk about them sometime. Not just now*—P. Lively, 1987; *Presumably, they will be released on DVD sometime in the near future*—*Bright Lights Film Journal*, 2002). When *some* and *time* both retain their separate meaning, 'a certain amount of time', most people write the elements separately (e.g. *Some time after this interview, it happened that Mr. Cuff... was in the neighbourhood of poor William Dobbin*—Thackeray, 1847/8; *We'll need some time to consider the matter*). But this neat distinction is not always observed. Compare the following example (= a certain amount of time) with the Thackerayan one above: *his* [*sc.* Kieslowski's] *last film* No End, *which caused the Polish authorities collective heartburn and took sometime to achieve distribution*—*Times* 19 May 1988. Using a joined-up form to represent an adjective + noun has nothing to commend it.

sometimes, some times. The common adverb of frequency *sometimes* is written as one word: *I sometimes like my coffee black. Some* and *times* are spelt as two words when they retain their separate meanings, 'certain times', normally as a noun phrase: *There are some times when you don't want to be surprised; But it's not so great if your income varies considerably, and you're likely to overpay at some times, but not others.*

somewhen. This potentially useful compound adverb has had a phantom-like existence for nearly two centuries, usually coupled with *somehow* or *somewhere*, e.g. *I shall write out my thoughts more at length somewhere, and somewhen, probably soon*—J. S. Mill, 1833; *I cherished the belief that somehow and somewhen I should find my way to Oxford*—J. C. Masterman, 1975. At no time has it been in common use.

somewhere. See SOMEPLACE 2.

sonant. In phonetics, 'a consonant that can be either syllabic or non-syllabic; a continuant or nasal, as /l̩,m̩,n̩, ŋ̍,r̩/' (*SOED*).

songstress. Interestingly, a female designation that is commoner than its male counterpart, *songster*. Beloved of journalists, presumably because it sounds more 'artistic' than singer, but also because it implies that the person writes her own songs. It is a historical curiosity that *songster*, of which *songstress* is the derivative, originally meant a female singer, so, etymologically speaking, *songstresses* are doubly female. See -ESS.

son-in-law. See -IN-LAW.

sonnet. A poem consisting of 14 lines (of 11 syllables in Italian, generally 12 in French, and 10 in English), the English ones being arranged in three main patterns, the Petrarchan (or Italian), the Shakespearean, and the Miltonic. Further details of the main types can be found e.g. in the *Oxford Companion to English Literature* and in Baldick's *Concise Oxford Dictionary of Literary Terms*

(1990). Examples of each of the three types:

Petrarchan

The world is too much with us; late and soon,
Getting and spending, we lay waste our powers:
Little we see in Nature that is ours;
We have given our hearts away, a sordid boon!
This sea that bares her bosom to the moon;
The winds that will be howling at all hours,
And are up-gathered now like sleeping flowers;
For this, for everything, we are out of tune; [octave]
It moves us not.—Great God! I'd rather be
A Pagan suckled in a creed outworn;
So might I, standing on this pleasant lea,
Have glimpses that would make me less forlorn;
Have sight of Proteus rising from the sea;
Or hear old Triton blow his wreathed horn.
(Wordsworth)

Note. The Petrarchan sonnet has a break in sense between the octave and the sestet, two rhymes only in the octave, arranged abbaabba, and two, or three, other rhymes in the sestet variously arranged, but never so that the last two lines form a rhymed couplet unless they also rhyme with the first line of the sestet.

Shakespearean

Let me not to the marriage of true minds
Admit impediments. Love is not love
Which alters when it alteration finds,
Or bends with the remover to remove.
O, no! it is an ever-fixèd mark,
That looks on tempests and is never shaken;
It is the star to every wandering bark,
Whose worth's unknown, although his height be taken. [octave]
Love's not Time's fool, though rosy lips and cheeks
Within his bending sickle's compass come;
Love alters not with his brief hours and weeks,
But bears it out even to the edge of doom.
If this be error, and upon me proved,
I never writ, nor no man ever loved.
(Shakespeare)

Note. In the Shakespearean sonnet, though the pause between the octave and the sestet is present, the structure consists less of those two parts than of three quatrains, each with two independent rhymes, followed by a couplet again independently rhymed—seven rhymes as compared with the Petrarchan four or five.

Miltonic

When I consider how my light is spent,
Ere half my days, in this dark world and wide,
And that one talent which is death to hide
Lodged with me useless, though my soul more bent
To serve therewith my Maker, and present
My true account, lest he returning chide,
'Doth God exact day-labour, light denied?'
I fondly ask. But Patience, to prevent [octave]
That murmur, soon replies: 'God does not need
Either man's work or his own gifts; who best
Bear his mild yoke, they serve him best. His state
Is kingly: thousands at his bidding speed,
And post o'er land and ocean without rest;
They also serve who only stand and wait.'
(Milton)

Note. Of the Miltonic sonnet, which follows the Petrarchan in the arrangement of the octave, the peculiarity is that the octave and the sestet are worked into one whole without the break of sense elsewhere observed.

soprano. Plural *sopranos* (see -O(E)S 4) or, less commonly, *soprani* /-ni/.

sorceress. See -ESS.

sort (noun). **1** In the ordinary sense 'a group of things etc. with common attributes; a kind', the normal use is shown in phrases such as *a fear of the right sort, the rosettes are of two sorts, nothing of the sort, he is some sort of doctor, all sorts of people watch football.*

2 *these/those sort of.* From the 16c. onwards, *sort* has been used collectively, preceded (illogically) by *these* or *those*, e.g. *Inchoatives . . . are those sort of Verbs which express a gradual proceeding in any action*—E. Phillips, 1671; *'Those sort of rules are all gone by now,' said Mr. Arabin*—Trollope, 1857; *These sort of people are only interested in lining their pockets*—J. Leland, 1987. Not unexpectedly, the plural form *these/those sorts of* is also used, e.g. *He . . . did an infinity of those sorts of things which were not professionally required of him*—T. Hook, 1825; *To afford her apartment in New York, she often took these sorts of library fellowships*—*New Yorker*, 1989. The type *these/those sort of* should now be used only in informal contexts. See KIND (noun) 2.

3 Adverbial *sort of.* Since the late 18c., *sort of* has been used adverbially in somewhat informal contexts to mean 'in a way or manner; to some extent or degree; somewhat'. Examples: *I'll sort of borrow the money from my dad until I get on my own feet*—G. B. Shaw, 1903; *It just happened, sort of, and we couldn't either of us help it*—M. Laski, 1952; *I knew sort of underneath that I did want to do it*—J. Gathorne-Hardy, 1984; *The Shorewalkers looked sort of like mountain natives*—*New Yorker*, 1986; *I can't reproduce the way he talks... but he just sort of zooms off*—J. Barnes, 1991.

sotto voce. Pronounced /ˌsɒtəʊ ˈvəʊtʃeɪ/ in English, and printed in roman.

soubriquet. See SOBRIQUET.

soufflé /ˈsuːˌfleɪ/. Printed in roman. The accent is obligatory (at least in printing). Without it, the word turns into an archaic medical term, also from French, meaning literally 'breath', referring to 'a low murmuring or blowing sound heard through a stethoscope'.

sough (verb) (make a sound as of wind in trees, usually encountered in the form *soughing*) and (noun). Both words may be pronounced as either /saʊ/ or /sʌf/. The first of these is recommended. The unrelated words *sough* noun (= boggy or swampy place) and verb (= face a ditch with stone) have only one pronunciation, /sʌf/.

soulless. So spelt, no hyphen.

sound bite, a short pithy extract from a recorded interview, speech, etc. that is selected for broadcasting because of its effectiveness or appeal. Dictionaries show it as two words, which is how it most often appears in *OEC* data; less frequently, it is written solid. This term, and also *spin doctor* (a senior political spokesman or -woman presenting political views in a favourable light), and *photo opportunity* (an opportunity for media photographers to take pictures of well-known people) emerged in the US, but rapidly spread to other parts of the English-speaking world.

soupçon /ˈsuːpsɒn, -sɒ̃/. See GALLICISMS 2.

sow (verb) (scatter or plant seeds, etc.). The past tense is *sowed* and the past participle either *sown* (the more usual form in a ratio of over 7:1 in the *OEC*) or *sowed*.

spadeful. Plural *spadefuls*. See -FUL.

spam. This noun for one of the major irritations of Internet life, i.e. 'irrelevant or unsolicited messages sent over the Internet, typically to large numbers of users, for the purposes of advertising, phishing, spreading malware' etc. is probably so named with specific reference to a 1971 sketch from the British television series *Monty Python's Flying Circus*, set in a café where Spam was served as the main ingredient of every dish, and featuring a nonsense song whose lyrics consist chiefly of the word 'Spam' repeated many times over, at times interrupting or drowning out other conversation. The final letter *m* of *spam* is doubled in front of inflections and suffixes beginning with a vowel, e.g. *spamming, spammed, spammers*.

Spanglish. Another portmanteau, a blend of *Span(ish)* + *(En)glish*, first recorded from 1967 in English (though a Spanish form, *espanglish*, emerged earlier) and used to describe the hybrid language combining words and idioms from both Spanish and English, used in certain Latin American countries and by some Hispanics in the US. It is one of the most often mentioned of many terms for hybrid languages combining English with another language, in which *-glish* acts as a combining suffix: *Chinglish* (1957), *Hinglish* (*Hindi* + *English*, 1967), *Singlish*, with two meanings (*Sinhala* + *English*, 1972; *Singapore* + *English*, 1984). Predating all of these is the humorous *Yinglish* (*Yiddish* + *English*, 1951), a blend of English and Yiddish spoken in the United States or a form of English containing many Yiddishisms.

spastic (adjective). This term, used since the 18c. of certain medical conditions (especially cerebral palsy) characterized by spasmodic movements of the limbs, was ignorantly and offensively used by some people in the 1970s and 1980s as a term of abuse directed at anyone judged to be uncoordinated or incompetent. Also as noun. The abusive use has compromised the normal use of the word to an extent that makes it considered too offensive now. Phrases such as 'having cerebral palsy' for the adjective and 'person with cerebral palsy' for the noun are now standard.

spats (gaiters). Short for *spatterdashes*: see ABBREVIATIONS 2(*a*).

spavined /ˈspavɪnd/ (adjective), not *-nned*. See -N-, -NN-.

-speak. Orwell's terms *Oldspeak* (standard English) and *Newspeak* (a sinister artificial language used for official communications), which he used in *Nineteen Eighty-Four* (1949), gave the English-speaking world a new formative element *-speak* denoting 'a particular variety of language or mode of speaking characteristic of a group or field of activity'. They have since been joined by many others, the most common of which are *doublespeak, management-/business-/corporatespeak, marketingspeak* and *geekspeak*. This suffix can now be combined more or less at will, usually with nouns, to denote and implicitly criticize the language of any group, or even prominent persons (e.g. *Eurospeak* (laughable euphemism and sterile bureaucratese emanating from EU institutions), *Bushspeak* (fractured syntax). Less common formations which are transparent in context are *e-speak, Washingtonspeak, consultantspeak, lawyerspeak, Netspeak*, and *Greenspeak*.

spec = speculation. So familiar is the phrase *on spec*, 'as a gamble, on the off chance' that it is worth pointing out that it stands for speculation in the sense of a business venture, and was originally used on its own, first by none other than the US President John Adams in 1794: *Many merchants have already made a noble spec. of the embargo by raising their prices.*

special. See ESPECIAL(LY), SPECIAL(LY).

speciality, specialty. Fowler (1926) suggested that these two words 'seem to cry out for different roles', but any specialization that has happened since is purely geographical. Both words share the same two meanings, i.e. (*a*) a special pursuit, product, operation, etc., to which a company or a person gives special attention; (*b*) a special feature, characteristic, or skill. (There is also a technical sense of *specialty* in law: an instrument under seal; a sealed contract.) In those two meanings, *specialty* is the preferred AmE form, and *speciality* the favourite in British, Irish, and Indian English, though in BrE *specialty* is not far behind. Elsewhere, *specialty* prevails. Examples: *We had eaten nothing with the champagne except a small dish of potato crisps, a speciality from the island of Maui, thick and gnarled like tree bark*—D. Lodge, 1991; *She considered dog issues her specialty*—T. Drury, 1991; *Al Roker, of Channel 4 News, m.c.'d, and since his specialty is weather, not music, he probably isn't to blame for the selection*—*New Yorker*, 1992.

specially. See ESPECIAL(LY), SPECIAL(LY).

specialty. See SPECIALITY.

specie /spiːʃi/ is coin money as opposed to paper money.

species /ˈspiːʃiːz/, prissily /ˈspiːs-/, is unchanged in the plural. The *OED* (1914) gave a three-syllabled pronunciation, thus /ˈspiːʃɪiːz/, as a legitimate variant (cf. *-ies*), but this form dropped out of use at some later date.

specifically. See PACIFICALLY.

specious. Like its Latin original (*speciōsus*), English *specious* began (in the 14c.) its life meaning 'fair or pleasing to the eye'. From then until about 1800 it is safe to assume that in most contexts *specious* maidens, boys, buildings, flowers, birds, and so on are being praised for their handsomeness, beauty, brilliance, etc. But overlapping with the favourable sense, from about the beginning of the 17c., a qualification began to apply: having a fair or attractive appearance, yes, but in reality devoid of the qualities apparently possessed. From there it was an easy step to the general senses 'superficially plausible, but actually wrong' (e.g. *a specious argument*), and 'misleading in appearance, especially misleadingly attractive' (e.g. *the music trade gives Golden Oldies a specious appearance of novelty*). The implications of deceit are now so strong, that *specious* is often mistakenly used instead of *spurious*, also from Latin, in this case *spurius* = illegitimate, false. A specious claim is one that is attractive but insubstantial whereas a spurious claim is one based on a false premise. Similarly, logic can be *completely spurious*, but to call it **completely specious* stretches the adjective too far.

specs, = spectacles (for the eyes). First recorded as *specks* in 1807 and as *specs* in 1826. See ABBREVIATIONS 2(*b*).

spectator. So spelt, not *-er*. Stressed on the second syllable.

spectre. So spelt in BrE, but usually as **specter** in AmE. See -RE AND -ER.

spectrum. Plural usually *spectra*. See -UM 3.

speculator. So spelt, not *-er*.

speculum. Plural usually *specula*. See -UM 3.

speed (verb). The past tense and past participle forms are *sped* when the basic meaning is 'go fast' (*cars sped past; he had got into his car and had sped off down the road*). For other senses of the verb and for the phrasal verb *speed up*, the past tense and past participle are normally *speeded* (*up*), e.g. in the intransitive sense '(of a motorist, etc.) travel at an illegal or dangerous speed' (*he speeded up and went through the traffic lights at 60 mph; the process of reform must be speeded up*). *Sped* is often preferred in AmE in this second group (*I sped my pace to catch up*) but is less idiomatic, even informally, in BrE.

spell (verb). Throughout this book *spelt* is used as the past tense and past participle of this verb. The form *spelled* is widespread, and more frequent especially in AmE, and also when the meaning is 'explained in detail', as in *spelled out*, and in the sense 'mean or have a as result', e.g. in such collocations as *spelled disaster, trouble, the end of/for . . . , the death of . . . , doom*, etc. See -T AND -ED. Examples: (spelt) *men who not only rhymed Moon with June but also thought they were spelt the same way*—*Sunday Times*, 1987; (spelled) *She was very handsome, but she spelled trouble*—S. Bellow, 1987; *Bech tried to . . . inscribe the names, spelled letter by letter*—*New Yorker*, 1987; *This is spelled out by Langland in two passages*—*English*, 1988; *Lil took it as an omen, sure that such an occurrence spelled bad luck*—S. Mackay, 1992.

The past tense of the unrelated (mainly AmE) verb *spell* 'to relieve or take the place of (a person) in work, etc.' is always *spelled*: *That night Jake stayed on the sofa in the living room, spelling Olivia at her mother's side*—*New Yorker*, 1994.

spel(l)icans. See SPILLIKINS.

spelling.

1 An outline history.
2 Spelling reform.
3 The relationship of English spelling and pronunciation.
4 Commonly misspelt words.
5 House style.
6 Double and single letters for consonantal sounds.
7 Cross-references.
8 Miscellaneous rules and mistakes.

1 *An outline history.* From the time of the earliest records of English in the 8c. until now the conventions governing the spelling of words in the language have changed radically several times. This sketch cannot do justice to what is in fact an absorbing story. Before 1066, and going back to the 8c., spelling was governed by the use of a combination of the roman alphabet and of a limited number of symbols from the earlier runic alphabet, including æ 'ash', þ 'thorn', ð 'eth', and ƿ 'wynn' (w). Everything set down on parchment, etc., was written or (on wood or stone) carved by hand. Manuscripts containing the texts of poems, sermons, proverbs, and so on, were copied and recopied, often with striking illustrations, and with many of the letters having shapes characteristic of particular monasteries or particular areas. Scribal conventions were by any standard strict. Spelling variation tended to reflect dialectal differences of pronunciation, but in general terms spelling was rule-governed in a manner not matched in the next period, namely 1066 (Norman Conquest) until 1476 (first printed book). The Old English texts that have come down to us can be said to show the closest relationship between sound and symbol of any period of the language. A typical passage:

Leofan men, ʒecnaƿað þæt soð is: ðeos ƿorold is on ofste, 7 hit nealæcð þam ende

(Beloved people, know what the truth is: this world is in haste, and it approaches its end. (Wulfstan (d. 1023), *Sermo Lupi ad Anglos*))

Note the use of some runic letters and the absence of French loanwords.

Norman scribes brought their conventions and their words with them and works written down in the period 1066–1476 reflect the habits of the new regime. Thus in Chaucer's *Anelida and Arcite* (14c.):

> *Singest with* voice memorial *in the shade,*
> *Under the* laurer *which that may not* fade
> (Singest with memorial voice in the shade,
> Under the laurel which may not fade)

Note the marked French influence on the vocabulary. Chaucer frequently used *qu-* in French loanwords (*quarter, querele* 'quarrel', etc.) and also in native words that were spelt with *cw-* in Old English (*quake* 'shake', *qualm* 'plague', *quelle* 'kill', etc.).

With the advent of printing, Caxton and the early printers in England adopted the spelling patterns of the late Middle English period and substantially rendered them immobile, though allowing more trivial variation than is permitted today. Such 'trivial variation' (see below) was permissible in all printed work of the period until the appearance of the increasingly sophisticated and influential dictionaries of the 17c. and 18c. The influence of 17c. and 18c. schoolmasters was also important in the emergence during this period of a national standard of spelling.

At this time spelling was not random or haphazard, but during the period 1476 to (say) 1755 (Johnson's *Dictionary*) moderate variation was permitted. Thus in Caxton's *Reynard the Fox* (1481) 'profit' is spelt *prouffyte* and *prouffyt*, 'peace' is spelt *pees* and *peas*, 'way' is spelt *waye* and *weye*, and 'opened' is spelt *opend* and *opened*. In Shakespeare's works a similar amount of relatively minor variation was admitted in the printed texts: 'Even a cursory glance will show that the spelling is by no means consistent, and a word appearing in one form in a given line may appear with a different spelling only a few lines later—or even within the same line' (Vivian Salmon in Stanley Wells et al., *Shakespeare: The Complete Works*, original-spelling edn, 1986).

Variation is one thing; systematic spelling changes quite another. The period from 1476 to 1776 (American Independence) 'is the time when initial *fn* (Middle English. *fnēsen*, modern English *sneeze*) and *wl* (Middle English *wlatsom* loathsome) disappeared from the language; when *gh* or *f* took the place of earlier *h* or ȝ (yogh), pronounced /x/ in final position or before another consonant, as in *cough* (Middle English *coȝe*), *enough* (Old English *genōh*), *fight* (Old English *feoht*), and *plight* (Old English *pliht*). The old runic letter *thorn* (þ) drifted in the way it was written until it so resembled the letter *y* that it had to be abandoned in favour of *th*...' (these together with details of numerous other changes of spelling in this period are given in Burchfield's book *The English Language*, 1985, especially pp. 144–8).

Changes in pronunciation in this period are even more important. The 'Great Vowel Shift' was mostly at an end before Caxton's first book came off the press, but its reverberations are central to an understanding of what happened later. This is not the place to give details of all the sound changes that occurred during these three centuries. Suffice it to say that phonetic disturbances of a major kind occurred and most of them were not accompanied by changes in the spelling system. The result is that modern English spelling falls well short of being a reliable guide to the pronunciation of a sizeable number of English words. (Readers who wish to pursue the matter further should turn to any of several standard works on the subject, including Barbara Strang's *A History of English*, 1970.)

2 *Spelling reform.* The notorious inconsistencies of English spelling are described in numerous articles in this book (see below for a partial list). They are of such an order that it is tempting to think that they could be legislated away. All such attempts have so far failed for three main reasons. First, the absence of a single competent linguistic authority empowered to make such fundamental changes; secondly, reform, if radical, would automatically place millions of books, newspapers, etc., out of the reach of the general public until they were reprinted in the new spelling system; and thirdly, the insuperable difficulty of the existence of divergent pronunciations throughout the English-speaking world. Whose standard English would qualify as the model for the respelling of the whole language, that of Britain, the USA, or (as a compromise) Canada or Australia?

There are numerous other difficulties. For example, spelling reform, if carried out at any more than a superficial level, would conceal the connectedness of word families that are divided only by the positioning of the stress. Consider the confusion that would arise if the spelling of the following pairs of words were adjusted to reflect the contrasting pronunciations of the key sounds in each: *adore/adoration, electric/electricity, fraternal/fraternize, history/historical, malign/malignant, mode/modular, nation/national, photograph/photography, sign/signature.* Furthermore, it is widely accepted that where systematic differences of spelling occur between two varieties of English, namely British and American (e.g. in obvious pairs of the type *centre/center, humour/humor, aesthetic/esthetic, catalogue/catalog,* etc.), the risk of misunderstanding is minimal.

Burchfield's broad conclusion, after setting down considerably more evidence than is presented here, is given on p. 145 of his book *The English Language* (1985): 'The English spelling-system is best left alone, except in minor particulars. Attempts to simplify or respell the language are likely to be unavailing for a long time to come.'

3 *The relationship of English spelling and pronunciation.* In general terms, written English has remained relatively static since the invention of printing in the late 15c., but spoken English, in its received form, has changed repeatedly since then. Loanwords have also been adopted from languages which have different spelling systems. As a result the sound /f/, for example, can be represented by a number of different spellings, e.g. *f* (*firm*), *gh* (*rough, draught*), *ff* (*bluff, offer*), and *ph* (*philosophy*). The letter *h* can be silent (*honour*) or fully pronounced (*hand*). The sequence -*ough* can be pronounced /ʌf/ (*tough*), /aʊ/ (*plough*), /əʊ/ (*dough*), or /ə/ (*borough*), and in up to six other ways. The sound /s/ can appear written as *c* (*cinder*), *s* (*send*), *sc* (*scent*), *ps* (*psalm*), *ss* (*assist*) or *sw* (*sword*); conversely the letter *s* can be pronounced as /s/ (*seven*) or /z/ (*is*). Occasionally it is silent (*aisle, demesne, island*). The digraph *ch* represents /k/ in *chasm*, /ʧ/ in *chain*, /ʃ/ in *charade*, or /x/ in *loch*. The trigraph *sch* is pronounced differently (in BrE) in *eschew* /sʧ/, *schedule* /ʃ/, *schism* /s/, and *school* /sk/. All such variations can be accounted for historically.

4 *Commonly misspelt words.* It is of interest to speculate about the amount of dislocation to the spelling system that would occur if English dictionaries were either out of reach or (as when Malory or Sir Philip Sidney were writing) did not exist. For instance, when writing private letters (in which spelling is thought not to 'matter' as much as it might in other circumstances) or in the stressful atmosphere of the examination room, the likelihood of misspellings increases at once. A list of the 100 most often misspelt words based on *OEC* data includes the following select thirty: *accommodation, aggressive, appearance, assassination, bizarre, cemetery, committee, disappoint, ecstasy, friend, glamorous, idiosyncrasy, interrupt, irresistible, knowledge, liaise, lollipop, millennium, noticeable, pavilion, pharaoh, possession, publicly, receive, religious, siege, successful, surprise, tongue, unforeseen.*

5 *House style.* The 'house' style of printers and publishers varies from one to another. Where acceptable variants exist a choice must be made and should be adhered to throughout a given publication. The conventions of the Oxford University Press are set down in *The Oxford Dictionary for Writers and Editors* (1990). Thus it states: *absinth*, the plant; *absinthe*, the liqueur; *acknowledgement*, not *-ledgment*; *baptize*, not *-ise*; *Czar*, etc., use *Ts-*; *Djakarta*, Indonesia, use *J-*; *equinoctial*, not *-xial*; *feoff*, use *fief*.

6 *Double and single letters for consonantal sounds.* If a list were made of the many thousands of words whose spelling cannot be safely inferred from their sound, the doubtful point in perhaps nine-tenths of them would be whether some single consonantal sound was given by a single letter, as *m* or *t* or *c*, or by a double letter, as *mm* or *tt*, or two or more, as *sc* or *cq* or *sch*. A*cq*uiesce and a*q*ueduct, bivoua*c* and bivoua*ck*ing, Bri*t*ain and Bri*tt*any, co*mm*i*tt*ee and co*m*i*t*y, *c*rystal and *ch*rysalis, i*n*oculate and i*nn*ocuous, insta*ll* and insti*l*, ha*r*ass and emba*rr*ass, leve*ll*ed and unpara*ll*e*l*ed, perso*n*ify and perso*nn*el, s*ch*edule and s*h*ed, *sc*ience and *s*ilence, ti*c* and ti*ck*, are examples enough. The use of double letters (*tt* etc.) or two letters (*ck* etc.) to give a single sound is due sometimes to the composition of a word, as when *in-* meaning 'not' and *nocens* 'harmful' are combined to make *innocent*, sometimes to the convention by which the sound of a previous vowel tends to be of one kind (long *a, e, i, o, u*) before a single letter and of another (short *a, e, i, o, u*) before two, and sometimes to other factors in word formation, perhaps philologically explicable, but less obvious than in compounds like *innocent.*

Among the rules are those that govern the doubling or not of a word's final consonant when suffixes are added in inflexions or word formation. Directions are given for the various consonants under the articles -B-, -BB-, and so on, to be found in their alphabetical places.

Two more questions of single and double letters are of importance. In forming adverbs in *-ly* from adjectives in *-l* or *-ll*, neither a single nor a triple *l* is ever right; *full, purposeful, especial,* and *dull*, have adverbs *fully, purposefully, especially,* and *dully*. And in forming nouns in *-ness* from adjectives in *-n* both *n*s are retained—*commonness, rottenness, plainness*, etc. *Solemn*, with its silent *n*, needs hardly to be excepted: both *solemnness* and *solemness* are permissible, but the first of these is recommended as being the better visual form.

7 *Cross-references.* Various points are discussed in short special articles throughout the book; and many words whose spelling is disputed will be found with or without discussion at their alphabetical places. The following collection of references may serve as a survey of likely mistakes and of readers' uncertainties.

For the rule *'i before e except after c'*, see I BEFORE E.
For such words as *judg(e)ment, lik(e)able, mil(e)age, pal(e)ish, wholly*, see MUTE E.
For the plural of words in *-o*, see -O(E)S; many individual words also have their own entry.
For the plural of words in *-y*, see PLURALS OF NOUNS 6.
For *cipher, siphon; gypsy, pygmy, syllabub; silvan/sylvan, tire/tyre, tiro/tyro*, etc., see Y AND I, and the words themselves.
For *Aeschylus/Æschylus, Oedipus/Œdipus; archaeology/archeology, diarrhoea/diarrhea, homoeopathy/homeopathy, oenology/enology, paediatrics/pediatrics*, etc., see Æ, Œ.
For *tying, dyeing, denied, paid, buys, copied*, etc., see VERBS IN -IE, -Y, AND -YE.
For *concertinaed/-a'd, hennaed/-a'd, mustachiod*, etc., see -ED AND 'D .
For the choice of *-ize* or *-ise* as the normal verb ending for the relevant class of verbs, see -IZE, -ISE IN VERBS. For a list of words in which *-ise* is obligatory, see -ISE.
For the plural of *handful, spoonful*, etc., see -FUL. The choice is often not between *handfuls* and *handsful*, but between *handfuls* and *hands full.*
For adjectives ending in *-ble*, see -ABLE, -IBLE.
For inflexions of verbs in *-c* like *mimic* and *picnic*, see -C-, -CK-.
For pairs like *enquiry* and *inquiry*, see ENQUIRE, ENQUIRY, IN-; INQUIRE, ENQUIRE.
For adjectives like *bluey, clayey, holey, mousy, stagy*, see -EY AND -Y IN ADJECTIVES.
For *for(e)bear, for(e)go, forswear*, etc., see FOR- AND FORE-.
For *cooperate/co-op-/coöp-*, etc., *pre-eminent* etc., *recollect* and *re-collect, recount* and *re-count*, etc., see CO-; PRE-; RE(-).
For *formulae -las, hippopotamuses -mi*, see LATIN PLURALS.
For *burnt -ned, leapt -ped*, etc., see -T AND -ED.
For *by and by, by the by, by-election*, etc., see BY, BY-, BYE.
For *classified, countrified*, etc., see -FY.
For *into in to*, see INTO; for *onto on to*, see ON TO.
For *corrector, deserter*, etc., see -OR.
For *behavio(u)r, labo(u)r*, etc., see -OUR AND -OR.
For *clamorous, honourable, humorous*, etc., see -OUR AND -OR.
For *Dr/Dr., a.m./am*, etc., see FULL STOP 2.
For *Dickens's/Dickens', Venus'/Venus's*, see APOSTROPHE D2, 3.
For *preferred, referable*, etc., see -R-, -RR-.
For the *seventies*, etc., see NINETIES.

8 *Miscellaneous rules and mistakes.* (*a*) The writing of the very common *anti-* 'against' instead of the rarer *ante-* 'before' (e.g. writing *antichamber, antidated* for *antechamber, antedated*) is to be carefully avoided.

(*b*) Verbs in *-cede, -ceed*, are so many and so much used, and the causes of the difference are so far from obvious, that mistakes are frequent and a list will be helpful: *cede, accede, antecede, concede, intercede, precede, recede, retrocede, secede*, to which may be added *supersede*; but *exceed, proceed, succeed.* The commonest mistake is to write *preceeding* for *preceding.*

(*c*) Adjectives and nouns in *-ble, -cle, -tle*, etc., make their adverbs and adjectives not by adding *-ly* or *-y*, but by changing *-le* to *-ly*: *humbly, singly, subtly, tangly, treacly.*

(*d*) Adjectives in *-ale, -ile, -ole*, add *-ly* for their adverbs: *docilely, vilely, solely*; but *whole* makes *wholly.*

(*e*) Of adjectives in *-(e)rous* some never use the *e*, such as *cumbrous, disastrous, idolatrous, leprous, lustrous, monstrous, wondrous*; some always have it, such as *boisterous, murderous, obstreperous, slanderous, thunderous.*

(*f*) *Silent letters.* One of the frustrations facing learners of English as well as first-language speakers is the number of silent letters, all arising from some quirk or other of the history of the relevant words. Thus *g* in *gnarled, gnaw, gnu*, etc.; *gh* in *might, sight*, etc.; *k* in *knight, knob, know*, etc.; *l* in *calm, palm*, etc.; *p* in *psalter, psychology*, etc.; *ptarmigan, pterodactyl*, etc.; *s* in *aisle, island*, etc.; *w* in *wrangle, write*, etc.

(*g*) *q* without *u.* Contrary to standard spelling, English has a handful of words containing an initial *q* without a following *u*. The few words involved fall into three classes: loanwords from Arabic (*qasida* 'elegiac poem', *Qatar*, State in Persian Gulf); loanwords from languages other than Arabic (from Chinese, *qi* 'life force'; from Eskimo, *qiviut* 'underwool of arctic musk ox'); artificial formations (*Qantas*, Australian airline; *Qiana*, a US trade name for nylon).

Spenserians (prosody). The metre of *The Faerie Queene*, often used by later poets, especially by Byron in his *Childe Harold*. It consists of eight five-foot iambic lines, followed by an iambic line of six feet, rhyming ababbcbcc.

A Gentle Knight was pricking on the plaine,
Y cladd in mightie armes and siluer shielde,
Wherein old dints of deepe wounds did remaine,
The cruell markes of many a bloudy fielde;
Yet armes till that time did he neuer wield:
His angry steede did chide his foming bitt,
As much disdayning to the curbe to yield:
Full iolly knight he seemd, and faire did sitt,
As one for knightly giusts and fierce encounters fitt.

sphere. See FIELD.

sphinx. Plural *sphinxes*. The earlier (17–19c.) alternative plural *sphinges* /ˈsfɪndʒiːz/ is now obsolete.

spill. The past tense and past participle (also participial adjective) are either *spilt* or *spilled*. It would appear that *spilt* was the more favoured of the two until the end of the 19c., but according to *OEC* data now *spilled* is nearly ten times more frequent in World English. BrE appears to be the bastion of *spilt* (though even there *spilled* is commoner for both forms), which lingers on as a far less frequent alternative in all varieties of English, even AmE. In the idiom *to cry over spilt milk*, *spilt* is more frequent, except in AmE; in *spill the beans*, *spilled* predominates in the same proportion as overall. Examples: (spilled) *The vision of spilled parcels hit her harder than she expected*—D. Malouf, 1985 (Aust.); *I was given the job because I never spilled any of the valuable stuff*—P. Bailey, 1986 (UK); *He nearly spilled his drink*—J. Updike, 1988 (US); *which could equally be the reaction to hot coffee being spilled over somebody's knee*—H. Hamilton, 1990 (UK). (spilt) *Where the pubs were . . . forlorn establishments of spilt beer and Formica tables*—R. MacNeil, 1989 (Canad.); *The lounge boy . . . left too much change on the table and a puddle where he'd spilt the Coke*—R. Doyle, 1990 (Ir.); *She has never had much faith in therapy—all that crying over spilt milk*—*Atlantic* (US), 1992; *It spilt on his leg*—*Independent*, 1992 (UK); See -T AND -ED.

spillikins, spel(l)icans (plural noun). *Spillikins* is the recommended form. Also *spillikin* for the singular (= splinter of wood, bone, etc.).

spin (verb). The regular past tense and past participle forms are now *spun*. Before the 20c. *span* was commonly used for the past tense but it is now an unusual minority form. It occurs famously in the rhyme attributed to John Ball, an unruly priest involved in the Peasants' Revolt of 1381, 'When Adam delved and Eva span, Who was then the gentleman'. Examples: (span) *The other two . . . were swept half across the room before they span aside, one either way*—E. Peters, 1978; *He put the book back in the shelf and span the celestial globe gently*—C. Phipps, 1989; (spun) *my mother spun daydreams as easily as she mixed the turkey's mash*—M. Eldridge, 1984 (Aust.); *The other man spun towards the sound, gun extended, ready to fire*—A. Lejeune, 1986; *The wheels spun up spray as we drove back to the farm*—*Encounter*, 1988; *I didn't get a chance to try it again because I was spun round, and dragged back*—A. Billson, 1993.

spin doctor. See SOUND BITE.

spindrift (spray blown along the surface of the sea), a Scottish variant of *spoondrift* (from *spoon*, in sailing, to run before wind and sea + *drift*), has now replaced the 'correct' form.

spinet (a small harpsichord). Pronounced /spɪˈnɛt/ or /ˈspɪnɪt/. In AmE usually stressed on the first syllable.

spinney (in BrE, a small wood, a copse). Plural *spinneys*.

spiny, not *spiney*. See MUTE E.

spiraea /spʌɪˈriːə/ (rosaceous shrub). So spelt in BrE, but often as **spirea** in AmE.

spiral (verb). The inflected forms are *spiralled, spiralling* in BrE, but often *spiraled, spiraling* in AmE. See -LL-, -L-.

spirit (verb). The inflected forms are *spirited, spiriting.* See -T-, -TT-.

spiritism. Coined in the 1850s as an alternative to *spiritualism* (also first recorded in the 1850s in the sense 'the belief that the spirits of the dead can hold communication with the living'), it has lost ground since and is now far less often used than the longer term. **Spiritualism** is the usual term for this sense, and also for the philosophical sense 'the doctrine that the spirit exists as distinct from matter, or that spirit is the only reality'.

spit. The past tense and past participle of the verb meaning 'to eject saliva from the mouth' are regularly *spat* in Britain, but in AmE either *spit* or *spat.* Examples: (spat) *'Kidnapped,' my aunt spat out*—G. Greene, 1988; (spit) *I was so mad I could have spit*—*New Yorker*, 1989; *He spit. Then he jumped, from one rock to the next... until he was gone*—M. Sumner, 1993 (US). The unrelated verb *spit* meaning 'to impale on a spit' has past tense and past participle *spitted.*

spitting image is an interesting example of how a misunderstanding can become part of standard language: it is ultimately a misinterpretation of *spit and image* (and variants such as *spit and fetch, spit and picture*), fashionable in the late 19c. as an extension of the earlier and original 19c. phrase *the very spit of* (1825). This in turn produced the dialectal (and then standard) phrases *spitten image* (first recorded in 1910), *spittin' image* (1901), and *spitting image* (1929). The standard phrase now is *spitting image,* but echoes of the earlier forms remain, as in some of the following 20c. examples: *You are a queer fellow—the very spit of your father*—T. Hook, 1836; *He would be the very spit and fetch of Queen Cleopatra*—G. A. Sala, 1859; *He's jes' like his pa—the very spittin' image of him!*—A. H. Rice, 1901; *A nice-behaved young gentleman, and the spitten image of his poor mother*—A. Bennett, 1910; *In another twenty years... she would be her mother's spitting image*—H. S. Walpole, 1929; *Spitten image of his dad, little Alf is, isn't he, Reg?*—W. Holtby, 1936; *The son's the dead spit of the old man*—A. Upfield, 1953; *Look at this, Father, appeared last Friday on Sister Philomena, the very spit and image of the nail marks in the palms of Our Blessed Lord*—H. Mantel, 1989; *And no man should grieve because he isn't the spit and image of Tom Cruise*—*Parade Mag.* (US), 1990.

splendiferous. See FACETIOUS FORMATIONS.

splendour. So spelt, but **splendor** in AmE. See -OUR AND -OR.

split infinitive. Few other grammatical issues have become such a cultural meme. As Fowler put it: 'The English-speaking world may be divided into (1) those who neither know nor care what a split infinitive is; (2) those who do not know but care very much; (3) those who know and condemn; (4) those who know and approve; (5) those who know and distinguish'. The aim here is to convert to the fifth category anyone included in the first four.

1 *Definition.* The base form of an infinitive is shown in *to love,* with the verbal parts preceded by the particle *to.* When these two elements are 'split' by an adverb or adverbial phrase (e.g. *to madly love, to really and truly love*) or other word or words the construction is called a *split infinitive.* In Latin such a construction was impossible because infinitives (*amāre* 'to love', *crescere* 'to grow') were indivisible and not preceded by a grammatical particle. The type *My mother taught me to be always prepared* is not a split infinitive. It would become one only if phrased as *My mother taught me* to always be *prepared.* Another type sometimes falsely taken to be a split infinitive is that containing *to* + insertion + verb in *-ing.* e.g. *I mean it's not as if I'm going* to be actually risking *my life*—K. Amis, 1988.

2 *A brief history.* (*a*) The standard work on the history of English syntax, F. Th. Visser's *An Historical Syntax of the English Language* (4 vols., 1963–73), states that the earliest examples of split infinitives date from the 13c.; but the construction was not widely used between the 13c. and the 15c. (for example, there are only two examples in Chaucer).

(*b*) Typical historical examples: (i) (adverb between *to* and the infinitive; note that *forto, for to* frequently = *to* in Middle English) *What movede the pape of Rome* to thus accepte *mennes persones*—Wyclif, *c.*1380; *To enserche sciences, and* to perfitly knowe *alle manere of Naturals þinges*—*Secreta Secretorum, c.*1400; *it longiþ* forto not oonly bigynne ... *but it longiþ* [etc.]—R. Pecock, *c.*1443; (ii) (a noun, pronoun, or noun phrase inserted) *heo cleopode him to alle his wise* for to him *reade*—Layamon, *c.*1250; *being moche redier* forto suche writings lette *and* distroie *þan* [etc.]—Pecock, *c.*1445; (iii) (two or more words between *to* and its infinitive) *A kyng owith not* to... ouer oft haunte *the company of his sugetis*—Prose version of *Secreta Secretorum, c.*1425; forto iustli and vertuoseli do *a dede contrari to goddis comaundement*—Pecock, *c.*1449.

(*c*) Visser goes on to say that 'From about the beginning of the sixteenth century to about the last decades of the eighteenth century the use of the split infinitive seems to have been as it were tabooed in the written language.' Nevertheless he cites four examples from the 16c. Burchfield had no difficulty in finding several examples of the avoidance of split infinitives in three 16c. lives of Sir Thomas More (e.g. *I am ready* obediently to conforme *my self to his graces commandements*—Roper, ?1557). There were no split infinitives in any of these three Lives.

(*d*) The split infinitive seems to have come back into favour at the end of the 18c.: e.g. *I know not how I should be able* to absolutely forbid *him my sight*—F. Burney, 1778; *To sit on rocks to muse o'er flood and fell,* To slowly trace *the forest's shady scene*—Byron, 1812; *She wants* to honestly and legally marry *that man*—Hardy, 1895.

3 *Current attitudes.* There can be no doubt that journalists in parts of the national press, many respected writers, and average people are reluctant to split infinitives in writing. Thus in Peter Carey's *Oscar and Lucinda* (1988): *He was never ashamed* publicly to bear *witness.* When the late Bernard Levin, wrote in the *Times* (24 Oct. 1991) *he* [a former political prisoner] *was in Vilnius* to formally close down *the headquarters of the Lithuanian KGB,* the use called for special comment in the Diary pages two days later. In a leading article in the 18 May 1992 issue of *The Times* it was stated that 'The most diligent search can find no modern grammarian to pedantically, to dogmatically, to invariably condemn a split infinitive.' These light-hearted comments highlighted the irrational nervousness that many people feel: they imagine that, by splitting an infinitive, they are breaking a terrible taboo. A quarter of a century on, depending on the publication concerned, many modern-day editors and subs are more relaxed; the *Economist* Style Guide neatly sums up this approach 'Happy the man who has never been told that it is wrong to split an infinitive: the ban is pointless. Unfortunately, to see it broken is so annoying to so many people that you should observe it.' Stephen Pinker (1994) expresses a modern linguistic and commonsensical approach: 'forcing modern speakers of English... not to split an infinitive because it isn't done in Latin makes about as much sense as forcing modern residents of England to wear laurels and togas'. However, the millions of people who use the grammar checker in Word will still find split infinitives flagged for their attention.

4 *Avoiding the split infinitive.* (*a*) First, much evidence points towards the reality of the feeling that it is 'wrong' to split infinitives. Examples showing an adverb placed immediately before the particle *to* are not uncommon: e.g. *I had no wish* actually to read *it*—C. Rumens, 1987; *I want* briefly to examine *three elements of the picture*—*Senses of Cinema,* 2002. Less commonly the adverb comes after the verb: e.g. *Party leaders have simply refused* to attempt seriously *to come to terms with the new situation*—*Parl. Aff.*, 1986.

(*b*) On the other hand, avoiding split infinitives can lead to results that are unnatural, stylistically poor, ambiguous, or misleading: *Rhys considers it unwise to attempt* radically to alter *taxes on large cars, as proposed by Labour*—*Autocar and Motor,* 1990; *It should be the Government's task* quietly to advocate *such a comprehensive strategy with our American allies*—*Times,* 1998; *I know too that* repeatedly to drink and drive *is a profound and serious matter*—*Independent,* 2007. In these examples the natural position of the adverbs *radically, quietly,* and *repeatedly* is after the word *to,* and in the first case the important connection between *radically* and the verb it qualifies (*alter*) is compromised; in the second, *quietly* and *advocate*; are similarly affected; and in the third, the sensible alternative is to recast the sentence and avoid the problem altogether (*I know too that repeated drink-driving is a profound and serious matter*). It is arguable in these cases that the adverb, or adverb phrase, is more strongly associated with the verb than is the purely functional particle *to.*

In some cases, the adverb even becomes attached to the wrong verb: *It was in Paris that the wartime alliance began finally to break up*—television broadcast, 1998. The intended meaning is that the process of breaking up entered its final phase, not, as suggested by the order shown, that it finally began.

5 *Unproblematic split infinitives.* (*a*) Examples abound of most of the categories of split infinitives that Visser found in works of earlier centuries. As can quickly be seen, to recast any of the following to avoid splitting would often make them stilted and pedantic, even the last one, where four words intervene between *to* and its verb: *David . . . questing her attention, allowed one eyelid* to minimally fall—A. Brookner, 1984 (UK); *it led Cheshires* to finally abandon *publishing fiction at all*—B. Oakley, 1985 (Aust.); *For your safety and comfort we do ask you* to please stay *in your seats*—British Airways flight attendant, 1986; *Everything he had written seemed* to just deliberately and maliciously draw *attention to the fact that* [etc.]—B. Elton, 1991.

(*b*) The commonest type is that in which an adverb, especially intensifying adverbs such as *actually, even, ever, further, just, quite, really, utterly,* is inserted between *to* and the infinitive: e.g. *The goal is* to further exclude *Arafat*—*US News & World Rep.*, 1986; *Spring, the season she had been able* to utterly ignore—J. Urquhart, 1986 (Canad.). Occasionally, for stylistic reasons or other special effects, adverbial phrases are inserted, not just a single adverb: e.g. To suddenly, after all these years, *fire them*—P. Carey, 1982 (Aust.); *a willingness* to not always, in every circumstance, *think the very best of us*—P. Roth, 1987.

(*c*) The negative adverbs *never* and *not* are often inserted in AmE, less commonly in BrE: e.g. *a perfect morning* to not read *'Moby Dick'*—*New Yorker*, 1986; *Many professional players hope* to never play *there again*—*American Way*, 1987; *The only unforgivable sin is* to not show up—G. Keillor, 1991.

6 *Questionable split infinitives.* The only, not very compelling, argument against split infinitives is when they jar for some reason. This argument shifts the issue from grammar to style, but is only valid when the adverb can be placed naturally in another position or when the split is a lengthy one: *We talked about how everything was going to suddenly change*—N. Williams, 1985 (defensible on grounds of emphasis, perhaps, but the normal order is *We talked about how everything was suddenly going to change*); *You two shared a curious dry ability to without actually saying anything make me feel dirty*—P. Roth, 1987 (split here for effect); *Lectures . . . were introduced in the Middle Ages only because it was not possible to affordably type lecture notes for students*—*Independent*, 2006. This is one that truly jars stylistically (not to mention historically) because of the long adverb: better to put the adverb at the end of the phrase: *not possible to type lecture notes for students affordably*.

7 *Recommendation.*, The prejudice against the split infinitive, though relatively recent in the broader context of the history of English, has a considerable weight of opinion behind it. The split infinitive is, therefore, best avoided, especially when it is stylistically awkward. But it is not a major error nor a grammatical blunder, and it is acceptable, even necessary, when considerations of rhythm and clarity require it.

spoiled, spoilt. In World English both forms are used for the past tense, past participle, and participial adjective of *spoil* (verb) with similar frequency, except in AmE and Canadian English, in both of which *spoilt* is rather unusual. See -T AND -ED.

spokesman See -PERSON 3.

spondee (prosody). A foot (– –) consisting of two long or stressed syllables as in the last two words of the following line: *And one with trembling hands clasps his cold head*—Shelley, 1821.

sponge has the derivative **spongeable** with an *e*, to keep the *g* soft, but **spongy** and the inflection **sponging** are very much more frequent than the forms with an *e*, though both types are correct.

spontaneity. The traditional pronunciation with final /-iːɪtɪ/ (-**ee**-i-ti) has now been superseded by that ending in /-eɪɪtɪ/ (-**ay**-i-ti). See -EITY. The parallel derivative **spontaneousness** is nowadays vanishingly rare.

spoondrift. See SPINDRIFT.

spoonerism, nowadays generally written with a lower-case first letter, is formed from the name of the Revd W. A. Spooner (1844–1930), Dean and Warden of New College, Oxford. The type is illustrated by Anthony Burgess in his *Inside Mr Enderby* (1963): *But* A Sale of Two Titties *had struck Lady Fennimore as something like calculated insolence.* 'The eponymous Spooner was reputed to make errors of this type,' remarks *OCELang*; 'and a number of utterances are quoted as "original spoonerisms": a *well-boiled icicle* (a well-oiled bicycle), *a scoop of Boy Trouts* (a troop of Boy Scouts), and *You have hissed all my mystery lectures and tasted a whole worm.* It seems likely that these transpositions were exaggerated inventions by his students.' The term is now applied to normally accidental transpositions of any sounds, e.g. *a pea flit* for *a flea pit.* But some Spoonerisms are less than accidental: e.g. W. H. Auden is said to have referred to Keats and Shelley dismissively as *Sheets and Kelly.*

spoonful. Plural *spoonfuls.* See -FUL.

spouse, pronounced /spaʊz/ or /spaʊs/, has over the centuries been used to mean either a married woman in relation to her husband or a married man in relation to his wife. Being gender-neutral, it is a useful term in law and in rules, regulations, etc. where the person denoted might be male or female. Once considered a rather formal word, its usefulness has led to its being used in non-formal and journalistic language, e.g. *Good working relationships are difficult to come by, as most filmmakers know. Sometimes adding a spouse to the mix is not necessarily a good thing—Film Threat,* 2004; *about 5,000 foreign spouses from 57 countries filed for work permits—Taipei Times,* 2001. Because of the increase in unmarried relationships in certain societies, the word, or its adjective *spousal,* has come to apply, for example in family law, also to people living together but unmarried. In such contexts, although the phrase *married spouse* reads like a tautology, it is not one when contrasted with 'unmarried spouses'.

spring (verb). The past tense is normally *sprang,* but quite often *sprung* (especially in AmE): *And then his hands sprung loose from the handle*—P. Carey, 1988 (Aust.). The past participle is always *sprung.*

spry. The *-y* is retained in its inflected forms and derivatives: *spryer, spryest; spryish, spryly, spryness.* Contrast DRIER; FLYER, FLIER.

squalor. So spelt, not *squalour.* See -OUR AND -OR.

squeeze. The standard past tense and past participle are *squeezed* (*she squeezed out a tear; he was squeezed into a corner*). The non-standard or dialectal form *squoze* is used occasionally for the past tense. Ronald Reagan used *squoze* at a press conference in August 1985 when commenting on a small skin cancer: *I picked at it and I squoze it and so forth and messed myself up a little.* The *OED* cites numerous examples of *squoze,* beginning with one of 1844 and including the following from Malcolm Lowry's *Ultramarine* (1933): *He just sort of* squoze *the rabbit.*

squib. See LAMPOON.

squirearchy. This spelling is recommended rather than *squirarchy.* Similarly, **squirearch(ical)**.

squirrel (verb). The verb inflections, i.e. in *squirrelling* funds *away* to keep them out of the hands of incompetent governments, double the letter *l,* as is the norm in BrE to give *squirrelling, squirrelled,* but keep it single in AmE.

-s-, -ss-. 1 The general rules for the doubling or not doubling of final consonants are given at DOUBLING OF CONSONANTS WITH SUFFIXES. With certain caveats, the basic rule is that single-syllable words and words of two or more syllables stressed on the last syllable double the last consonant when a suffix is added, e.g. *begging, preferring.* Since very few monosyllables or longer words stressed on the last syllable end in a single *s,* it is hardly necessary here to do more than draw attention to specific cases. In the following words there is wide variation in practice among printers and publishers, but the forms recommended here are in almost every case those with a single *s*: *atlases; biases, biased, biasing; boluses; bonuses; buses, bused, busing; canvas*: see CANVAS, CANVASS; *focuses, focused, focusing* (but see FOCUS); *gases,* but *gassed, gassing; incubuses; minuses; nimbuses; orchises; pluses; portcullised; trellised, trellising; yeses.*

Words ending in *-ss* naturally retain the *ss* in the plural: *abysses, busses* (= *kisses*), *congresses, crosses,* etc.

3 *Nonplus* has the inflections *nonplussed, nonplussing* (all three words stressed on the second syllable).

4 A hyphen is needed to avoid a succession of three *s*'s: Inverness-shire, mistress-ship. For *misshapen*, etc., see MIS-.

St. For whether to write *St Peter* or *St. Peter*, see FULL STOP 2; SAINT.

stadium. The anglicized plural *stadiums* is much more frequent than the Latinate *stadia*. The latter is appropriate when talking of classical antiquity, and is also quite widely used in BrE in modern sporting contexts, but rarely in AmE in this way. See -UM 3.

staff. 1 (*a*) a pole (plural *staffs*, or historically *staves*); (*b*) (music) a set of lines on which music is written (plural *staffs* or *staves*); (*c*) a body of persons employed in a business, etc. (plural, if required, = such bodies of employees of various businesses, *staffs*). See STAVE (noun).

2 For *staff of life*, see SOBRIQUETS.

stag. See BUCK.

stage has derivatives **stagily, staginess, stagy**.

stain(ed) glass. It is all too easy to poke fun at the idiosyncrasies of estate agents' language, and since it is all too easy, I see no reason to refrain. I cannot count the number of times while I have been house hunting that my interest has been aroused by mention in the brochure or blurb of **stain glass* in a window or door. A delightful feature, but one best spelled properly as *stained glass*.

stalactites, stalagmites. The first hang down from the roof of a cave, etc.; *stalagmites* are deposits rising from the floor of a cave, etc. Both words are stressed on the first syllable in BrE. In AmE the dominant pronunciation is with the stress on the second syllable.

stamen. Plural *stamens*. The plural of the Latin original, namely *stamina*, has moved into English in a different sense.

stanch. See STAUNCH.

stand (verb). In BrE candidates *stand* for office; in AmE they *run* for it. See also STOOD.

standard English. Because the term appears often throughout this book, and can be somewhat controversial in certain circles, it is worth clarifying what exactly it means here. First, *standard* contrasts with *non-standard*, which is also widely used throughout this book, rather than *substandard*. Which is to say, that if something is judged not to be standard, that judgement does not in any way suggest inferiority, merely difference: it highlights the fact that a word, phrase, or spelling is appropriate in some, even many, contexts, and inappropriate in others. Standard language considered in that way is the kind of language one would be happy to write, for example, in the non-technical sections of a report or to put in a CV or résumé, or for journalists to use in a newspaper, in the knowledge that nothing in its style would draw unwarranted attention to itself. It is also the kind of language one would expect to hear and not baulk at in factual radio and TV programmes, and the news.

Peters (2004) suggests three useful yardsticks by which to define standard language: it is neutral as regards register or level, as regards region, and as regards social class. Under the first heading, that means it is not taboo, informal, colloquial, or slang on the one hand; on the other it is neither highly literary, nor recherché, nor jargonistic. Therefore the *f-word* and *betimes* are non-standard by that definition. Under the second heading, it means that the language will be understood universally, and is not confined to a particular region: that excludes *snicket* (North of England for 'alleyway') and Australian *arvo* ('afternoon'). Under the third heading, it means that, for example, contrary to the snobbishness of the preposterous U and non-U distinction, *serviette* and *napkin* are both standard and of equal value. Inevitably, and truistically, the boundaries between standard and non-standard are not eternal: it is possible that fairly soon 'sat' and 'stood' instead of 'sitting' and 'standing' will become part of standard English, and nobody will turn a hair. But that has not yet happened.

Given its historical genesis within these islands, this book's main aim is to identify and describe the principal elements of standard written English in Britain, often by contrasting them with non-standard, dialectal, extra-British, archaic, or obsolescent features. Mention is made of the pronunciation of words (especially the positioning of the stress) about which someone in the English-speaking world might conceivably have doubts. The standards of other Englishes, especially American English, are contrasted with BrE, but inevitably standard speakers in the United States, Canada, Australia, New Zealand, South Africa, and elsewhere will need to interpret the recommendations made here in the light of their own experience. Many other major English-speaking countries have guides which give prominence to their own usage, for example *Merriam-Webster's Concise Dictionary of English Usage* (2002, mainly concerned with AmE), and Nicholas Hudson's *Modern Australian Usage* (1993). It is remarkable how often the problems they discuss are the same as those dealt with in this book; but points of detail and emphasis may well be different.

standpoint. See POINT OF VIEW.

stanza in prosody is 'the basic metrical unit in a poem or verse consisting of a recurring group of lines (often four lines and usually not more than twelve) which may or may not rhyme' (*COD*). In lay use sometimes called a VERSE.

state. The initial letter is conventionally capitalized when it means 'an organized political community under one government' (*the United States of America, the State of Israel*), or a constituent unit of a federal nation (*the State of Virginia*; *crossing the State border*); also when the word is used attributively in this sense (*State documents, a State visit*), and when it means 'civil government' (*Church and State, the Secretary of State for Northern Ireland*). In other contexts use a lower-case *s* (*a police state, the welfare state*).

stationary, stationery. The adjective (= not moving) *-ary*; the noun (= writing materials) *-ery*. If it is not too babyish, thinking of the *-er* in *paper* for *stationery*, which is made of paper, may help.

statistic (noun) in the sense 'a statistical fact or item' is a well-established back-formation from **statistics**, the name of the science.

statistic, statistical (adjectives). Both adjectives are of similar age (late 18c.) when applied to **statistics**, but the longer form has for all practical purposes driven out the shorter one.

statist, statistician. Both entered the language in the sense 'one who deals in statistics' in the early 19c., but the longer form has prevailed and *statist* /ˈsteɪtɪst/ now means someone who supports the idea of **statism**.

status. 1 Pronounced /ˈstəɪtəs/ despite the fact that the stem vowel was short in the Latin original. The pronunciation /ˈstatəs/ is sometimes used in AmE.

2 The Latin plural *statūs* is not used in English, the regular form being *statuses*. See -US 2.

statutable is a very rare near-synonym, first used in the mid-17c., for **statutory**, meaning 'prescribed, authorized, or permitted by or in accordance with statute' and 'legally punishable'.

staunch /stɔːntʃ/. This spelling is used both for the verb meaning 'to restrain the flow of blood' and for the adjective meaning 'trustworthy, loyal'. The variant form **stanch**, pronounced /stɑːntʃ/ (stahnch) is preferred in AmE for the verb.

stave (noun). (*a*) = STAFF 1(*b*); (*b*) each of the curved pieces of wood forming the sides of a cask, etc.; (*c*) a stanza of a poem; (*d*) an alliterating letter in a line of Old English verse. Plural of each, *staves*.

stave (verb) has the alternative forms *staved* and *stove* for the past tense and past participle. Both are used in the various senses of the verb, but *staved off* is standard as the past tense of *stave off* 'to avert or defer (danger or misfortune)'.

stem (noun). In etymology and word formation, the main part of a noun, verb, etc., to which elements may be added to make new words. Thus *ship* forms *shipment, shipshape, shipwreck*, etc., by adding postfixed elements, and *airship, warship*, etc., by adding prefixed elements. The stem *ship* also forms *ships, shipped, shipping* by the addition of inflections.

stem (verb). So well established in all varieties is the phrasal verb *stem from* = to derive from or take origin from, that it is a surprise to discover that Gowers (1965) objected to it on the grounds that British people using it valued it purely for its novelty. First noted from 1932 in the *OED* (but there is an earlier example in the *COHA*), it is now widely used in World English. Examples: *Part of Pastor Spratt's charisma stemmed from his time spent as an advertising manager for Rathbone's Wrought Iron*—J. Winterson, 1985 (UK); *Investment-driven* *growth stemming from technological catch-up is an incomplete . . . explanation of Japanese economic history during the Showa era*—*Dædalus* (US), 1990.

stemma (a family tree; a line of descent). The plural is *stemmata*.

stencil. The inflected forms are *stencilled, stencilling,* but often *stenciled, stenciling* in AmE. See -LL-, -L-.

step-. See -IN-LAW.

stereo /ˈsterɪəʊ/, plural *stereos*.

sterile. The *OED* (1916) admitted both /ˈstɛrʌɪl/ and /-ɪl/ in that order. Now the only standard pronunciation in BrE is that with /-ʌɪl/, while AmE favours a short vowel in the second syllable (in practice a schwa). See -ILE.

sternum. Plural generally *sterna* in technical or scientific writing and *sternums* otherwise. See -UM 3.

stewardess, for a female steward on an aircraft is now decidedly old-fashioned, not to mention suspect as regards its political correctness. Now replaced by **flight attendant**. See -ESS 4.

stichomythia /stɪkəʊˈmɪθɪə/. In verse plays, an interchange of short speeches consisting each of a single line. Common in ancient Greek plays. Modern examples may be found in Molière's *Les Femmes savantes* III.v, and in Shakespeare's *Richard III*, IV.iv: Elizabeth: *But how long shall that title euer last?* Richard: *Sweetlie in force vnto her faire lyues end.* Elizabeth: *But how long farely shall her sweet life last?* Richard: *As long as heauen and nature lengthens it.* Elizabeth: *As long as hell and Richard likes of it.* [etc.] The word is Greek, from στίχος 'line' + μῦθος 'speech, talk'.

sticking place, point. In the context in Shakespeare's *Macbeth* I.vii (*But screw your courage to the sticking place, And wee'le not fayle*) *place* is the word used. The phrase *sticking point* is first recorded in this sense in 1826, and in its common modern sense, 'the limit of progress, agreement, etc.', not until the 1960s. In *Macbeth* the reference (according to the *OED*) seems to be to the screwing-up of the peg of a musical instrument until it becomes tightly fixed in the hole.

stigma. Has two plural forms, the Greek *stigmata* /ˈstɪgmətə/, sometimes (especially in AmE) /stɪgˈmɑːtə/ and the ordinary *stigmas*. Which is preferable depends on the shade of meaning. In the Christian sense, 'marks corresponding to those left on Christ's body by the crucifixion', *stigmata* is standard, and is also often used medically to mean 'a visible sign or characteristic of a disease' (e.g. *knee deformities or other stigmata of childhood rickets*). In the botanical meaning, namely the part of a pistil that receives the pollen during pollination, *stigmas* is rather more frequent, but *stigmata* is also used; in the metaphorical meaning 'a mark of disgrace', *stigmas* is standard, e.g. *Twenty years later, such social stigmas have disappeared.* See LATIN PLURALS.

stiletto. Plural *stilettos*. See -O(E)S 7.

still and all. A resilient, rather casual adverbial phrase, first recorded in 1829, and used, much more commonly, since the 1920s, and suitable in informal contexts. Examples: *Still and all, if you see something I haven't, let me know*—R. Moore, 1978; *Still and all, you might have worked out all right*—T. Clancy, 1987; *Still and all, something had undeniably changed*—*Encounter*, 1988.

still less. For confusion between this and *still more*, see MUCH 2.

still life. The correct plural is *still lifes.*

still more. For confusion between this and *still less*, see MUCH 2.

stimulus. In *OEC* data, the plural is overwhelmingly (nearly a thousand times) more often written as *stimuli*, the word's Latin plural, the ending being pronounced either like *lie* or *lee*. *Stimuluses* is sometimes used, particularly in writing about economics, but is not recognized by dictionaries. See LATIN PLURALS.

stimy, stimie. Archaic spellings of STYMIE.

stink. The past tense is *stank*, occasionally *stunk*. The past participle is *stunk*.

stoep. In South Africa, a terraced veranda in front of a house. Pronounced /stuːp/.

stoic, stoical. Fowler (1926) posited an ingenious semantic and syntactic distinction between these two; unfortunately, usage has not conformed to his hypothesis. As with other *-ic*/*-ical* pairs, one is markedly more frequent—in this case, *stoic*, in a ratio of 4:1. Both enter into a very small number of mutual collocations, such as *stoic/stoical acceptance, resignation*, the first in each case being the commoner form. When it refers to the ancient philosophical sect, *Stoic* should be capitalized, as adjective or noun, e.g. *the Stoic philosopher Epictetus; Stoics sought to free themselves from bodily concerns by philosophical contemplation*.

stomach. See BELLY.

stomacher (formerly, an item of women's dress). Many 18c. and 19c. dictionaries list /ˈstʌmətʃə(r)/ as the pronunciation of this word, but it is now normally pronounced with /-kə/.

stone (noun). **1** See ROCK.

2 *to leave no stone unturned* is a tiresome cliché for 'to try all possible means'.

stone (adverb). Combinations in which *stone* has metaphorical force have been used for centuries: e.g. *stone-blind*, as blind as a stone, 14c.; *stone-cold*, 16c.; *stone-dead*, 13c. A more recent development is the use of *stone* as a mere intensive = very, completely. It is not easy to pin down exactly when this happened, but such uses are now commonplace, especially in AmE. Examples: *The Irish were stone courageous*—T. Wolfe, 1987; *He was stone angry, as if he had been brawling with some upstart stranger who got him with a lucky punch*—R. Scott, 1988 (NZ); *People . . . got stone drunk and cruised through red lights*—G. Keillor, 1989.

stood, used, like SAT, with the auxiliary *be* in place of a progressive tense (i.e. *she is/was stood*, instead of *she is/was standing*), presumably has a regional distribution in BrE similar to *sat*, but if it has, its history seems so far to have gone unrecorded in the *OED*. Its existence in modern regional use is not in question, but its precise spread has not been established. J. Cheshire et al. (1989) conclude that it and the similar use of *sat* 'are now becoming characteristic of a general nonstandard or semistandard variety of English'. The types of register in which it appears are the same as for *sat*, and, just like *sat*, it appears often in journalism from the North of England reporting what people said. It seems to be very much a spoken form, and is best avoided in any kind of standard formal prose. Examples: *She was stood in front of the mantelpiece trying to think of the name for the clock*—A. Bennett, 1981 (Yorkshire); *'But that's not the half of it.' Uncle Simon sat forward. 'Do you know what he did when he was stood there face to face with the priest, the man who positively identified him?*—G. Patterson, 1988 (NIr.); *And she'd pay the driver, and she'd be stood there, on the soiled concrete footpath*—A. Duff, 1990 (NZ); *My husband was stood on the opposite side of the pits*—*Cycling Weekly*, 1993.

stop (noun). In phonetics, a word widely used for 'a speech sound which is the result of a complete closure tract' (Hartmann and Stork, 1972). Within the broad class of stops there are several subclasses, with much variation of terminology, e.g. *simple stop* (*p* in *pin*), *complex stop* (*pˀ* in French *pain* bread), *labial stops* (p, b), *alveolar stops* (t, d), *velar stops* (k, g), and *glottal stop* (ˀ). A different classification distinguishes *voiced stops* (*b, d, g*), in the production of which the vocal cords are brought into play, from *voiceless stops* (*p, t, k*) in which they are not. Some scholars use the term *plosive* instead of *stop*.

stops. See APOSTROPHE; BRACKETS; COLON; COMMA; DASH; EXCLAMATION MARK; FULL STOP; HYPHENS; ITALICS; QUESTION MARK; QUOTATION MARKS; SEMICOLON.

storey. Plural *storeys*. In AmE the word is usually spelt **story**, with plural *stories*. Contrast BrE *three-storeyed house* and AmE *three-storied house*.

A **storied** window, urn, shrine, etc., is one ornamented with historical or legendary events: it is formed from the ordinary word *story* (= narrative, etc.).

stove (past tense). See STAVE (verb).

Strad. See ABBREVIATIONS 2(*b*).

straight away. *Straight* (which is in origin an adjectival use of the medieval past participle of *stretch* and is not etymologically related to its homonym *strait*) is first recorded in conjunction with *away*—as two separate words—in 1662: *some prisoners were hurri'd streight away to their Quarters*. As an adverbial form it stayed that way, as two separate words, until the beginning of the 20c. Then, perhaps under the influence of the fast fading adverb *straightway*, it began to be written as one word. In 1923, for example, the *Daily Mail* reported that a horse called Evander had been badly hurt and was 'straightaway' withdrawn from a race. A character in Marghanita Laski's *Tory Heaven* (1948) followed with *I said straightaway... that I'd like to be a landagent.* The *OEC* data suggests that the two-word form is holding its own: it is nearly five times more frequent than the single-word version.

straight-faced (expressionless). By a strange reversal in the direction of the normal confusion between *straight* and *strait*, this is sometimes incorrectly spelt **strait-faced*. Cf. STRAIGHT, STRAIT.

straight-laced. See STRAIGHT, STRAIT 2.

straight, strait. 1 These are in origin entirely separate words with their own complex histories, but in some uses their different spellings now overlap. *Straight* (not curved or bent) is from a medieval adjectival use of the past participle of Middle English *strecchen* 'to stretch'. *Strait* (tight, narrow) is from Middle English *streit*, from Old French *estreit* 'tight, close, narrow' (also as noun, 'strait of the sea'), from Latin *strictus* 'drawn together, tight', past participle of *stringere* 'to draw or bind tight'.

2 While there is generally no hesitation about how to spell the verb **straighten** in clauses such as *he straightened up* (= he stood up straight), there are some words and phrases that create problems. The spellings we suggest are: **straitjacket**, **strait-laced** (puritanical), and **straitened circumstances,** but **straight and narrow**. The form *straightjacket* is sanctioned by some dictionaries, including *ODO*, and has presumably arisen through FOLK ETYMOLOGY, with people interpreting the jacket as one which keeps your limbs straight, rather than one that confines them, which is the meaning of *strait* in this context. A similar process seems to have created the alternative spelling *straight-laced*, also accepted by some dictionaries. What is not yet accepted, and will be viewed by most people as a mistake, is to write **straightened circumstances*. See also STRAIGHT-FACED.

3 *Straight* is, however, now the most commonly used form in the phrase *the straight and narrow* ('the honest course of action'), it being understood in the sense 'honest, morally correct'; the older form *strait and narrow*, in which *strait* itself means 'narrow' (thereby producing a hendiadys similar to *nice and easy*), has largely gone out of use. The *straight and narrow* version is an elliptical version of *the straight and narrow path*, deriving ultimately from the biblical 'Because strait is the gate, and narrow is the way which leadeth vnto life, and few there be that finde it', Matt. 7: 14 (AV).

4 *Straight* meaning 'heterosexual' was originally a US slang term, first recorded in 1941. Since then it has come to be widely used in this meaning, and, though marked 'informal' in *ODO*, is in many contexts the neutral term, the natural counterpart of *gay*, rather than the more formal *heterosexual*.

strappado (old form of torture). Plural *strappados*. See -O(E)S 4.

strategic, strategical. The first is scores of times more frequent than the second.

strati-, strato-. Such formations in which the main stress falls on the first element are normally pronounced in BrE with /a/ not /eɪ/. Thus *stratiform, stratigraphic(al)*; *stratocirrus, stratocumulus, stratosphere*, etc. In AmE, *stratocirrus, stratocumulus*, and other compounds of this kind usually have /eɪ/ in the first element.

stratum /ˈstrɑːtem/ or sometimes /ˈstreɪtəm/. This is a Latin singular word, whose Latin plural is *strata*. The *OED* lists three 18c. examples of *strata* used as a singular, with plural *stratas*, and one 19c. example of *stratums* used as a plural. Such aberrant forms are not infrequently found in modern writing, particularly when the word applies to a social or economic level. While it is true that other Latin plurals such as *agenda* and *candelabra* now function as singular nouns, *strata* treated as a singular has not yet unequivocally achieved that status. *MWCDEU* quips that '*Strata* is a Latin plural with ambitions to become an English singular.' At the moment, there is no good reason to further its ambitions, and the traditional *-um* (singular) and *-a* (plural) distinction should be insisted on, not least because many people will consider deviations from it a mistake. Examples: (correct) *The Reformation diffused the* *text of the Old Testament in previously untouched strata of the population*—*Bull. Amer. Acad. Arts & Sci.*, 1987; *While people in various economic strata are apt to feel an acute shortage of time, those with money are able to buy some time in numerous contexts*—*OEC*, 2003; (incorrect) **This is a film where a forgotten strata of society will see themselves authentically represented on a screen for the first time'. The key question, however, is whether the strata is worth representing*—*Scotland on Sunday*, 2004; **The issue of how journalism is bankrolled now sits high in the consciousness of everyone in the top stratas of the news business*—*Sydney Morning Herald*, 2000.

stratus /ˈstrɑːtəs/ or /ˈstreɪtəs/ in BrE, and /ˈstreɪtəs/ or /ˈstretəs/ in AmE, a continuous horizontal sheet of cloud. Plural *strati* /-tʌɪ/.

street. See ROAD.

street cred(ibility). See CREDENCE, CREDIT, CREDIBILITY 4.

strew. The past tense is *strewed* and the past participle and participial adjective overwhelmingly *strewn*, *strewed* being quite rare.

stricken, struck. *Stricken* as an alternative past participle to *struck* dates back to Old English. The *OED* (1919) labelled it 'archaic' except in legal use; Fowler (1926) considered it a cliché, and Burchfield (1996) also thought it archaic. The *OEC* data casts doubt on those views. **1** (*a*) As with the contrasting participles *hanged/hung*, the alternation *stricken/struck* seems to embody a difference of meaning. In passive constructions, whatever someone is *stricken with* has to be unpleasant or undesirable, e.g. *stricken with* (less often *by*) *cancer, grief, guilt, fear*, etc. It is impossible to be *stricken with* something neutral or positive, whereas you can be *struck* by a *thought, similarity, contrast*, etc., or by someone or something's *beauty*. Similarly, you cannot be **struck with grief, guilt, fear*, etc. (*b*) Far from being archaic, the word is a staple of modern, particularly BrE, journalism, somewhat more often used as a participial adjective before a noun, but also as a true passive. It is routinely used to describe ships, vessels, aircraft etc. that have been seriously damaged or put out of action. Whether one considers this latter use a cliché is a matter of personal taste. Examples: *There's the dashing hero, a former pilot stricken with impending blindness who stoically refuses to be pitied*—*Screen Online*, 2003; *Stricken with remorse, they weep for the rest of their lives*—*Apollo*, 2004; *Clothing is often sent to stricken areas, but its transport is expensive and its storage can be difficult and costly*—*BMJ*, 2005; *HMS Invincible rescued two Frenchmen from their stricken yacht while taking part in exercises in the Mediterranean*—*www.NavyNews.co.uk*, 2000. (*c*) Apart from the uses just described, stricken occurs almost as often as the second element of compound adjectives, the commonest of which are *poverty-stricken, grief-stricken, panic-stricken, drought-stricken, cancer-stricken* and *famine-stricken*.

2 In AmE legal use *stricken* continues to be used as the past participle when something is to be *struck* from the record: *Over strong objections from the prosecutor, Sybil R. Moses, Judge William J. Arnold ordered the question stricken*—*NYT*, 1978. This usage is condemned by Garner.

stride (verb). In theory, and according to dictionaries, this verb inflects like *ride*, i.e. its past tense is *strode* and its past participle *stridden*. However, the *OEC* data suggests that, while the present perfect tense of the verb is in any case rarely used, *strode* is the form most often used, and *stridden* is rare. Its rarity as an actual past participle is underlined by its rather desperate use in the popular magazine *The Face* (Nov. 1987): *Great strides are being strode in the cultivation of pre-teen female engineers.* Whether *has/have/be* etc. *strode* grates on one's ears will largely depend, I suspect, on one's age.

stride (noun). **1** In North American English the phrase *to take* (*something*) *in stride* is standard, rather than the World English *to take* (*something*) *in one's stride*.

2 The slang use of *strides* for 'trousers' is British and Australian, e.g. *The Oxford University candidate was to be seen in T-shirt and khaki strides*—M. Amis, 1973.

strike (verb). The past tense is *struck* (*the ship struck a rock*) and the most widely used past participle is also *struck* (*the house was struck by lightning*). But see STRICKEN, STRUCK.

string (verb). The normal past tense and past participle are *strung* (*they strung him up after a fair trial; his clothes were strung* *out on the line to dry*). A *stringed instrument* (in which *stringed* is formed from the noun *string*) is one having strings, but if the strings need renewing it will be *restrung*.

strive (verb). The standard past tense is *strove* and past participle *striven*; *strived* is also used for both, but is rather less frequent as the past tense than *strove* in all varieties of English, and on a par with *striven* as a participle, especially in AmE. Examples: *Her father... had been a uniformed policeman... who strived to make his beat a safe one for all*—D. Koontz, 1984 (US); *On the one hand, she'd never strived for celebrity*—*Musician* (US), 1991; *As surely as the painters of the nineteenth century strived to capture the city and people of Paris, so photographers in this century have been drawn to futuristic New York*—*Portfolio Mag.* (UK), 1991; *We've strived to lead the way in offering you the tools you need*—*Money* (US), 1993.

stroma (biology). Plural *stromata*.

strophe. A group of lines forming a section of a lyric poem (*COD*).

strow (verb). Formerly common, it is now only a by-form of *strew* (verb). Example: *Put it all back real neatly and strow it with old leaves and things*—A. S. Byatt, 1990.

struma (medicine). Plural *strumae* /ˈstruːmiː/.

strung. See STRING (verb).

stubbornness. So spelt, with *-nn-*.

stucco. Plural *stuccos* or less commonly *stuccoes*. As verb, *stuccoes, stuccoed, stuccoing*. See -O(E)S 2.

studio. Plural *studios*. See -O(E)S 5.

stupefy. So spelt (cf. *liquefy, putrefy, rarefy*), not *-ify* (cf. *dignify, gratify, modify*, etc.).

stupor. So spelt, not *stupour*. See -OUR AND -OR.

sty (noun) (pen for pigs, on eyelid). Plural *sties*.

stylo (= stylograph). Plural *stylos*. See -O(E)S 6.

stymie. Now the regular spelling of the word in golf and in transferred senses, not *stimy* or *stimie*. As verb, the inflected forms are *stymies, stymied, stymieing*.

subduedly. Kipling used the word in his novel *The Light that Failed* (1891): *Maisie was crying more subduedly*, and it still occasionally crops up. Pronounced as three syllables, not four, as *-ed* is part of the stem, not a separate syllable. See -EDLY.

subject. For synonyms in sense theme etc., see FIELD.

subjective genitive. See OBJECTIVE GENITIVE.

subjunctive mood. The subjunctive mood is one of the great survivors of an earlier state of English grammar. Its complexity over the centuries is such that the standard reference work on historical English syntax by F. Th. Visser (4 vols., 1963–73) devoted 156 pages to the subject (Visser called it the 'modally marked form') and listed more than 300 items in its bibliography. What follows here is necessarily merely an outline of the present-day situation, with a few backward glances at earlier conventions.

1 *Its grammar.* (*a*) The subjunctive is a verbal form or mood expressing hypothesis, usually denoting what is imagined, wished, demanded, proposed, exhorted, etc. Its main contrast is with the indicative mood. It is recognizable in modern English only in the third person singular present tense by the absence of a final -s (*If you want to irritate D., then suggest glibly that she* see *a sports psychologist*; *God save the Queen!*) and in the use of *be* and *were* instead of the indicative forms *am/is/are* and *was* (*Believing it to be fundamental that they* be *fully counselled by a professional of their own choice*; *Blanche almost wished that it* were *winter again*).

(*b*) Contrast the use of the indicative mood in *'It is important that he* makes *friends,' said Fibich*; *I do wish he* was *coming too.* And consider also contexts in which the verbal form is the same in the subjunctive and the indicative mood: *We cannot talk as if the other parties* were *demons*; *He asked that I* do *him the courtesy of...*

2 *Present-day currency.* The subjunctive mood was common in Old English and until about 1600. Examples are harder to find in the period 1600–1900 but it became remarkably prevalent in the 20c., first in AmE and then in other forms of English, including BrE, as the examples at 3 (*a*) below illustrate. In many dependent clauses *should* + infinitive is used instead without discernible change of meaning. The type with *should* is at least as common (e.g. *The report recommends that access to patent information* should be *widened and improved*). And so is the use of the indicative in similar constructions (e.g. *If Mr Ward is 'between airlines' let someone suggest that he* looks *towards Britain—Weekend Guardian*, 1990).

3 *Typical patterns.* (*a*) After *if* (or *as if, as though, unless*) in hypothetical conditions: *Each was required to undertake that if it* were *chosen it would place work here—Times*, 1986; *It was as if Sally* were *disturbed in some way and was translating this disturbance into the habit of thought*—A. Brookner, 1986 (UK); *His voice strained as though he* were *walking on a wire above a pit of sharks*—fiction website, 2003 (US). In this type the indicative can also be used, i.e. *was* instead of *were* in all the examples above, but the subjunctive conveys the hypothetical sense more forcefully.

Notes. (i) Usage seems to be changing in phrases such as *if I were you, if it were up to me*, etc. People often say *if I was you* and *if it was up to me*, but the subjunctive is preferable in writing.

(ii) In the Brookner example above the change from *were* to *was* indicates a shift of mood after *and*. Visser (§839) cites parallel examples from Old English onwards, e.g. *If Colonel Camperfelt be in Town, and his Abilities are not employ'd another Way* [etc.]—Steele, 1712.

(*b*) In *that*-clauses following a verb connoting suggestion, wish, etc. (e.g. *demand, insist, pray, propose, recommend, suggest, wish*). For more conservative British writers this use still has a distinctly transatlantic feel; in all cases it can be replaced by a construction with *should*, and often by the indicative. Examples: *Your situation demands that either Kooti* be *nobbled or Whitmore nullified*—M. Shadbolt, 1986 (NZ); *Fundamentalist Islam . . . decrees that men and women* be *strictly segregated—Listener*, 1988 (UK); *She declined a seat beside Charles on the sofa. She insisted Jane* sit *there*—B. Anderson, 1992 (NZ); *It was suggested he* wait *till the next morning*—M. Ondaatje, 1992 (Canad.); *He'd insisted his brother* return *home*—fiction website, 2002 (US).

Note. When *insist* has the sense 'assert, state forcefully' (and not 'demand') the ordinary indicative mood is needed: *Collins insists he* has *no regrets about any aspect of his career—Scotland on Sunday*, 2002.

(*c*) *were* or *be* placed at the head of a clause with the subject following in an inverted construction (rather formal). Examples: Were *I to get drunk, it would help me in the fight*—J. Updike, 1986; *Statistically, afterworlds*—be *they Christian, Greek, Pharaonic—must be populated almost entirely by children*—P. Lively, 1987; *There was a real risk of his suffering inhumane and degrading treatment* were *he to return to India—London Review of Books*, 2004.

(*d*) In negative constructions, *not* (or *never* etc.) is normally placed before the subjunctive verb (and this position identifies the subjunctive status of verbs in the first and second persons as well as the third): *One essential quality for a holiday novel is that it not* be *too light*—Frederic Raphael, 1988 (UK); *Mr. Radley insisted that he not* be *sent to an asylum*—literature website, 2002 (US). In uses of this kind the negative form makes the subjunctive mood transparent in other persons than the third singular: *I recommend that we not* approve *this letter—CNN* (transcripts), 2005.

Note. This construction is routine in AmE, but less common elsewhere.

(*e*) Subjunctives preserved in an array of fossilized clauses or sentences expressing a wish 'whose realization depends on conditions beyond the power or control of the speaker . . . and consist in short formulae of praise or prayer, in invocations, supplications, blessings, curses, oaths and imprecations' (Visser §841): *be that as it may; so be it; bless my soul; come what may; far be it from me to; God forbid (that); God bless you; God save the Queen*, etc.; *heaven forbid/forfend (that); heaven help us; So help me (God); Thy kingdom come, thy will be done; long live the Queen*, etc.; *perish the thought; the powers that be; serve you right; so be it; suffice it to say that; woe betide.*

(*f*) The fixed phrase *as it were*. In the sense 'in a way, to a certain extent' the phrase is invariable: *Having to ask permission,* as it were, *to see her friends*—A. Lurie, 1985; *Suddenly,* as it were *overnight, the weather became hot and sultry*—A. Brookner, 1986.

4 *General comments.* In BrE the subjunctive mood is most likely to be found in formal writing or speech (apart from some of the formulaic uses listed in 3(*e*) above), and particularly (the so-called *mandative subjunctive*) after the verbs listed at (*b*) and semantically related nouns and adjectives such as *demand, essential, important, insistence, proposal, suggestion, vital,* and *wish.* But it is seldom obligatory, and indeed is commonly (?usually) invisible because the notionally subjunctive and the indicative forms are identical.

submerge (verb). The adjective ('capable of being submerged') corresponding to this verb is **submersible** rather than *submergible.*

submissible (adjective), able to be submitted, and **submittable** are both used.

subpoena /səb'piːnə/. So spelt (but occasionally **subpena** in AmE). Plural *subpoenas,* not **subpoenae.* Verb inflections, *subpoenas, subpoenaing, subpoenaed*: see -ED AND 'D.

subscribe. *Ascribe* and *subscribe* are sometimes confused. If you *ascribe* a quality to a person or group of people, you think it is typical of them, as in *tough-mindedness is a quality commonly ascribed to top bosses.* If you *subscribe to* a belief, view, or idea, you agree with it: *we prefer to subscribe to an alternative explanation.* It is incorrect to give this meaning to *ascribe to,* as in **which theory do you ascribe to?*

subsidence. The traditional pronunciation /səb'sʌɪdəns/, with the stress on the second syllable, is recommended. But the form with initial stress, namely /'sʌbsɪdəns/, under the influence of *residence* and *subsidy,* is also common in standard speech.

sub specie aeternitatis. Pronounced /sʌb 'spiːʃiː ɪˌtəːnɪ'tɑːtɪs/ (sub **spee**-shee i-tur-ni-**tah**-tis) or /sʊb 'spiːsiː/ (sub **spee**-see), and printed in italics, this is a modern Latin phrase first recorded in the *Ethics* of the 17c. Dutch philosopher Spinoza and used chiefly in philosophical or academic writing. It means literally 'under the aspect of eternity', i.e. viewed in relation to the eternal; in a universal perspective: *The work of art is the object seen* sub specie aeternitatis*; and the good life is the world seen* sub specie aeternitatis. *This is the connection between art and ethics*—Wittgenstein.

substantial, substantive. Both words mean 'of substance', but they have become differentiated to the extent that *-ial* is now the word in general use for real, of real importance, sizeable, solid, well-to-do, etc., and *-ive* (apart from its dated meaning in grammar) is chiefly used in special senses: in parliamentary procedure *a substantive motion* is one that deals expressly with a subject in due form; in law *substantive law* (that which is to be enforced) is so called to distinguish it from *adjective law* (the procedure for enforcing it); in the Services *substantive* is used to distinguish rank or office that is permanent from one that is acting or temporary. Where *substantive* is used in a non-technical way, it refers more to what something consists of, e.g. *This finding moves beyond rhetoric and provides substantive evidence that fathers have an important and measurable impact on the well-being of their adolescent children*—*Fathering*, 2003. *Substantial* discussions are lengthy and wide-ranging ones, whereas *substantive* discussions deal with important topics.

substitute (verb). The normal uncontroversial sense (construed with *for*) is 'to put (someone or something) in place of another' (*sacrifice could not be substituted for duty; the local priesthoods, who substituted their own favourite god for Re*—examples from the *OED*).

Beginning in the 17c., and running parallel to the normal sense, were transitive (often passive) uses in which the sense is 'replace': *Double Pica* [a typeface] ... *was ... substituted by a new Letter* (1770); *Good brandy being substituted by vile whiskey* (1863, US); *Miss Hughes substituted Miss Oliver* (1867). The use went out of favour to the point that the *OED* (1917) commented 'Now regarded as incorrect', and it was heavily criticized by Fowler (1926). The use has, however, fully re-established itself, and the *OED* now notes that it is part of current standard English. Examples: *The ecclesiastical principle was substituted by the national, the Empire and the Papacy by the Communes*—cited in Fowler, 1926; *If potatoes substitute bread, what is going to substitute potatoes? is a question every German will have to ask himself*—cited in Fowler, 1926; *The tribunal concludes that British Rail's proposal to compensate ... at rates of four, five and six per cent are inadequate and substitutes them with levels of five, 7½ and 10 per cent*—*Daily Tel.*, 1974. Repeatedly football commentators announce that a specified tired-looking player is about to be *substituted* (i.e. replaced) by a fresh-looking player on the bench (or, in the active voice, *X substituted Y just before half-time*). Anyone who objects to this use can simply use *replace* instead.

subtle. The corresponding adverb is **subtly**, not **subtlely*, in accordance with the rule that adjectives ending in *-le* form adverbs by transforming that ending to *-ly*; cf. *gentle, gently*.

succinct. The *-cc-* is pronounced /ks/, as in *accent, success* etc. Contrast *succour* /ˈsʌkə/.

succour, as noun and verb, is generally spelt as shown in World English, but as **succor** in NAmer. English.

succuba /ˈsʌkjʊbə/, **succubus** /ˈsʌkjʊbəs/. Plural *succubae* /-biː/, *succubi* /-bʌɪ/. For centuries equally acceptable terms for a female demon believed to have sexual intercourse with sleeping men (the male equivalent being *incubus*), but *succubus* is the more usual word now.

such. Before embarking on this article it will be as well to bear in mind that this simple-looking word has had many branches and intricacies of meaning and construction from Anglo-Saxon times onwards. Since the majority of these are not mentioned in what follows, let us begin by citing a few examples of incontestably legitimate uses, all from standard 20c. sources: *our hands are quite unsuited to such fragility; We laugh in this country for such strange reasons; Fortunately for Owen, such an event was to hand; there will be no such sermon given next Tuesday; her mind refused to bring any such memory forward; a very profitable company such as British Telecom; Its prey are other small creatures such as frogs and lizards; I was proud of his being accepted at such a good school; It should be of such a nature as to command credibility; The one such marsupial we saw; shapeless dresses made of such materials as emerald silk moiré.* From these alone one can see that *such, such a(n), such as, no such,* and so on, have a multitude of idiomatic uses that do not call for comment in a usage manual.

1 *such* followed by the relative pronouns *that, which, who*.
2 Emphatic *such*.
3 *Such as* followed by personal pronoun.
4 *such as* or *like*.

1 *such* followed by the relative pronouns *that, which, who.* The *OED* gives a chain of examples from Anglo-Saxon times to 1888 but judged that by 1915 (when the relevant section was issued) the type was 'Now rare and regarded as incorrect'. Typical examples: *Such suffering Soules that welcome wrongs*—Shakespeare, 1601; *These ... seemed to him ... such which he never thought ... would be seriously opposed*—J. Strype, 1709; *Such of his friends that had not forsaken him*—Goldsmith, *a*1774; *Only such intellectual pursuits which are pleasant*—S. Grand, 1888. Fowler, in one of his moments of antagonism to the *OED*, objected that 'It is not in fact very rare.' Such constructions in the 20c., he said, 'are due either to writers' entire ignorance of idiom or to their finding themselves in a difficulty and not seeing how to get out of it'. He then cited ten examples from unassigned (but obviously journalistic) sources and rewrote several of them, e.g. *The Roumanian Government contends that it has only requisitioned* such things of which *there is abundance in the country* (such things as are abundant, *or* as there is abundance of). Whatever the reason, such uses seem to have disappeared from sight. In most constructions of this type modern idiom prefers *such ... as*.

The standard sources of grammatical evidence (Jespersen, Curme, *CGEL*, etc.) provide no parallel examples, either, though they give examples of idiomatic sentences in which *such* functioning as either a predicative or an attributive adjective is followed by a *that*-clause of result: *There is* such *confusion* that *I can't collect my thoughts; The confusion is* such that *I can't collect my thoughts;* and others with the insertion of the indefinite article (in which *such a* becomes adverbial): *She is* such a *good lecturer* that *all her courses are full; There was* such a *large crowd* that *we couldn't see a thing.*

2 Emphatic *such.* The type *He's such a nice man* is widespread in spoken English, but less common in expository prose. Varying degrees of emphasis are shown in: *It was such a fine evening; His misbehaviour* *was such a bore; She has such beautiful manners.* A literary example from an American author: *Papa was, he still is, such a dude*—S. Bellow, 1987. Again, *such* (*a*) is adverbial.

3 *Such as* followed by personal pronoun. Janice Elliott was following a long tradition in her novel *The Italian Lesson* (1985) when she used the subjective form of the pronoun: *Such as* he *are never popular with hotels.* But outside literary sources it is more natural to regard *such as* as a preposition and to follow it with *me, her, him,* etc., rather than *I, she, he,* etc. (regarding *such as* as a conjunction with the continuation understood as *such as I am,* etc.) Historical examples: (*a*) *Others such as* he—Shakespeare, 1611; *It is not fit for such as* we *to sit with the rulers*—Scott, 1819; *Death was not for such as* I—C. Brontë, 1847. (*b*) *while such as* her *die*—Swift, 1710–13; *Did ever man have such a bother with himself as* me?—H. G. Wells, 1900; *they were not bad, for such as* her—R. Macaulay, 1920. (Some of the examples drawn from Jespersen.)

4 *such as* or *like.* (See LIKE 2(*b*).) Opinion is neatly divided about the merits of *like* or *such as* used to introduce examples of a class. There is abundant evidence for *like* to be used when only one item, person, etc., is specified (*a writer like Tennyson*), and equally abundant evidence for *such as* to be used in the same way (*Many large gold coins, such as the doubloon*). The choice is often governed by the meaning: if the sense required is 'resembling' then *like* is preferable. And there is much to be said in favour of *such as* when more than one example of a class is mentioned: *All of the cat kind,* such as *the lion, the tiger, the leopard, and the ounce*—Goldsmith, 1774; *Writers* such as *Theophrastus and La Bruyère*—*Mirror,* 1779.

suchlike. 'Whether as adjective (barley, oats, and suchlike cereals) or as pronoun (schoolmasters, plumbers, and suchlike) [suchlike] is now usually left to the uneducated, *such* being used as the adjective and *the like* as the pronoun' (Fowler, 1926). Some voices are still raised, with diminishing levels of condemnation, but most dictionaries now simply list the two uses of the word as part of the standard language. The adjective and the pronoun have been in continuous use since the 15c.: it seems unlikely that they will be abandoned now or left to the mercy of any special group.

Sudan, Sudanese. Now the normal spellings in English, not *Soud-*.

sudarium (cloth for wiping the face), **sudatorium** (hot-air or steam bath), not being household words in English, retain their Latin plurals in *-ia.*

suddenness. So spelt, with *-nn-*.

suede. The accent of its original (French *Suède* 'Sweden') is now usually omitted when the word is used to mean 'leather of kidskin'. Printed in roman.

suffice. *Suffice it to say he was not best pleased.* This established form of the phrase, used to make your meaning clear while withholding information for brevity's or discretion's sake, includes the word *it* (known technically as a dummy subject). In that form, the phrase is an example of the SUBJUNCTIVE: the verb form *suffice,* without the normal third-person *-s* ending, marks the subjunctive and is equivalent in meaning to 'let it suffice', and *it* is the impersonal grammatical subject (as in *it is raining*). However, the winds of change are buffeting the little word *it* clean away, so that nowadays it is just as common to hear and see *suffice to say* (for example, by British broadcaster and writer Jeremy Paxman, on the BBC programme *University Challenge*). Nearly half the examples in the *OEC* are of that form. Although the form without *it* is attested historically, it seems likely that the truncated modern version is a reinterpretation of the syntax rather than a re-emergence of an older form. Subjunctives are rare outside certain fixed phrases, *suffice it* includes inversion, and most people probably have difficulty parsing the phrase correctly, which is why they change it. The whittling away of *it* is also an interesting example of economy of language in action. Be that as it may, the shorter form is now acceptable and correct, though some will still prefer the longer.

sufficient(ly). See ENOUGH.

suffix. In grammar, a *suffix* is a word or element added at the end of another word to adjust or qualify its meaning, such as *-ation* (*confirmation, privatization*), *-ing* (*driving, soldiering*), and *-itis* (*appendicitis*). Some suffixes are created artificially from the end part of words to form similar types of word with different reference, e.g. *-aholic* (from *alcoholic*, forming *workaholic* etc.) Cf. PREFIX.

suffixes added to proper names. **1** The suffix most commonly used to form nouns and adjectives relating to people's names (writers, artists, composers, thinkers, philosophers, etc., or founders of dynasties) is *-an* or *-ian*. An encomium in the *London Review of Books* illustrates how this works: *his best efforts took him from . . . an aesthete's and illustrator's art to an account—more Proustian, or Powellian, than Swiftian—of the morals and manners of the Swinging London that ever was and isn't any more.* Also used is the suffix *-esque*, as the *OED* has it 'representing French *-esque*, adapted from Italian *-esco* . . . In Italian derivatives in *-esco* are formed *ad libitum* on names of artists, and French and English writers on art have imitated this practice'. Current examples include *Audenesque, Browningesque, Caravagg(i)esque, Chaplinesque, Disneyesque*, and *Turneresque*. See also -ESQUE.

2 The habit of appending *-esque, -(i)an*, or *-ic* to the names of authors to indicate resemblance appears not to have begun until the 16c. (*Virgilian* is first recorded in 1513, *Platonic* in 1533), and then only rarely. The names of a few well-known classical writers are first recorded in adjectival form in 17c. sources: *Aristotelian* in 1607, *Ovidian* 1617, *Pindaric* 1640, *Plinian* 1649, *Ciceronian* 1661, and *Ptolemaic* 1674. Of English names, *Drydenian* is even recorded during his own lifetime (1687). In the 18c. it was not unusual for such formations to be used very soon after the death of the writer concerned—thus *Gibbonian* 1794, *Johnsonian* (by Boswell) 1791, *Richardsonian* 1786—but, unless the *OED* records are faulty, most formations of this kind are not found until much later: *Fieldingesque* 1931; *Ouidaesque* ('marked by extravagance or lack of restraint') 1909. *Shakespearian* is not recorded before 1755. The choice of suffix seems to be mostly governed by euphony, but names that end in *-aw* or *-ow* normally have the Latinate terminations *-avian* (*Shavian*) and *-ovian* (*Borrovian*) given to them. Thoreau becomes *Thoreauvian*. Some classical names have generated a cluster of adjectival forms since the 17c.—for example *Ptolemy*—but one of them (in this case *Ptolemaic*) usually settles down as the customary form.

3 There is one oddity. An unaccented final syllable of a name is normally lengthened and stressed when the adjectival form is made: thus *Beethoven* but *Beethovenian*, Jane *Austen*, but *Austenian* /-iːn-/.

suffragette. See -ETTE 4.

sugar has derivatives **sugared** and **sugary**. See -R-, -RR-.

suggest (verb). In his book *The Changing English Language* (1968) Brian Foster cited a sentence spoken by the actor Albert Finney in a BBC *Face to Face* programme in 1962: *The headmaster suggested I went to drama school.* He might alternatively have said *The headmaster suggested I go to drama school*, or else *The headmaster suggested* [that] *I should go to drama school.* 'Usage', Foster concluded, 'is in a somewhat fluid state.' The evidence supports this view. What can be said, however, with some degree of certainty is that *suggest* (and a few other words) now very commonly generate a subjunctive form in a following *that*-clause (in so far as this form is distinguished from the indicative equivalent: see SUBJUNCTIVE MOOD), especially in North America but increasingly elsewhere. *CGEL* (16.32) cites as alternatives *People are demanding that she should leave/leave/leaves* [especially BrE] *the company.* It would be the same if *suggesting* had been used instead of *demanding*. Some of the main patterns are shown in the following examples, all from standard sources:

(*a*) *suggest* (or *suggestion*) + *that*-clause: *If you want to irritate D., then suggest glibly that she* see *a sports psychologist—Times*, 1990; *including the suggestion that colleges and the General Board* be *invited to consider whether ways of reducing academic pressures on students can be identified—Oxford Today*, 1993 (UK).

(*b*) *suggested* + *that*-clause: *She suggested . . . that Harry* turn *bisexual and* get *a chauffeur as well*—P. Carey, 1981 (Aust.); *He suggested that they* went *into the church at the end of the road*—A. S. Byatt, 1990 (UK); *After tea he suggested that she* have *a lie down until dinner*—R. Rive, 1990 (SAfr.); *It was suggested he* wait *till the next morning*—M. Ondaatje, 1992 (Canad.).

In the BrE examples and in some of the others a simple indicative verb or the type *should* + infinitive would have been equally idiomatic (see SUBJUNCTIVE MOOD, 3(*b*)).

As Foster remarked, 'Usage is in a somewhat fluid state.'

suggestible. So spelt, not *-able*. See -ABLE, -IBLE 8.

suggestio falsi /sə,dʒɛstɪəʊ 'falsʌɪ/. Plural *suggestiones falsi* /-ɪəʊniːz/. The making of a statement from which, though it is not actually false, the natural and intended inference is a false one; an indirect lie. Example: *It is rare to find a positively verifiable untruth in a school brochure: but it is equally rare not to find a great many* suggestiones falsi, *particularly as regards the material comfort and facilities available*—J. Wilson, 1962. Cf. SUPPRESSIO VERI.

suitor. So spelt, not *-er*.

sullenness. So spelt, with *-nn-*.

sulphur. The traditional BrE spelling is *sulphur* and the AmE spelling is **sulfur**. In chemistry and other technical uses, however, the *-f-* spelling is now the standard form for this and related words in British as well as US contexts, and is increasingly used in general contexts as well.

sumac (an ornamental tree). This spelling is given for the headword in *ODO* with the variant **sumach**. Corpus data suggests that the spelling *sumac* is much more often used. Pronounced /'s(j)uːmak/ or /'ʃuː-/ (**s(y)oo**-, **shoo**-).

summersault. See SOMERSAULT.

summon, summons. 1 A *summons* is a call to appear before a judge or magistrate. Plural *summonses*.

2 As a transitive verb, *summons* means (in law) to serve with a summons. In ordinary use the normal form of the verb is *summon* (*the boy was summoned to the headmaster's study; the chairman summoned the members to a meeting*).

Sunday. For the adverbial use (*Sunday* = *on Sunday*), see FRIDAY.

sung. See SING (verb).

sunk, sunken. See SINK (verb).

super-. As a living prefix in English, 'super- first appears about the middle of the 15th c.; it became frequent in Elizabethan times, and in the 17th c. it was very widely used' (*OED*). In the 20c. it has continued to be a prolific formative element. Among the formations of modern times (the dates are those of first record in the *OED*) are: *supercharge* (verb) (1919), *supercluster* (astronomy, 1930), *superconductor* (1913), *supercontinent* (geology, 1963), *super-duper* (1940), *super-ego* (1924), *superfluorescence* (physics, 1966), *superhighway* (1925, 1975 in telecommunications sense), *superman* (1913), *supermarket* (1933), *superpower* (1921), *supersonic* (adjective) (1919), *superstar* (1925), *superstore* (1965), and numerous other general, technical, and scientific words.

***supercede.** For this misspelling, see SUPERSEDE.

superficies (geometry). Five syllables, /ˌs(j)uːpə'fɪʃɪˌiːz/. Plural the same.

superior. Because it is not a true comparative it, like *inferior*, cannot be used in comparative constructions with *than*: thus *X is superior to its rivals* (not *superior than*). The equivalent comparative phrases are *better than, greater than*, etc. In the language of marketing, and sometimes in general social contexts, *superior* is used as a kind of blind or absolute comparative (= above the average in quality) (*a superior bungalow; made of superior leather; a very superior box of chocolates*).

superiority. Fowler's term for the use of a slang expression preceded by a distancing or defensive comment implying that in normal circumstances the speaker would not deign to use such an expression himself or herself. Such distancing remarks are also used to preface technical terms, and include *as it were; as they/people say; as . . . might say; as the . . . say; to use the jargon; not to mince matters; not to put too fine a point upon it; so to speak; to call a spade a spade; to put it bluntly*; and also the use of inverted commas. Examples: *I never sensed the sweep of a story arc, as screenwriters say; He seized my hand in what the lover of a cliché would call an 'iron grip'; He's eight years old, and as Keynes might say, his marginal propensity to save is low; For all I know the boy selling dusters could have been, as they say, 'casing the joint'; 'Hopefully,' as people say, it will not rain on Sunday; These sort of protesters do not* (*to put it bluntly*) *pee in the street.*

superlatives. 1 For various uses of superlatives, see ADJECTIVE 3.

2 In general it is a sound rule that confines the use of comparative forms of an adjective to contexts in which two entities are being compared, and reserves superlative forms for comparison of three entities or more. But the English language is not a totally restrictive system. Jespersen (1909–49, vii.11.61) remarked that 'it is important to insist on the fact that in ordinary usage the superlative does not indicate a higher degree than the comparative, but really states the same degree, only looked at from a different point of view'. Whatever the explanation, seemingly illogical uses of the superlative occur from time to time in impeccably standard sources. Examples (the first three drawn from Jespersen ii.7.772): *to prove whose blood is* reddest, *his or mine*—Shakespeare, 1596; *whose God is* strongest, *thine or mine*—Defoe, 1720; *She was the* youngest *of the two daughters*—J. Austen, 1816; dinghy, dingey. *The first is* best—H. W. Fowler, 1926. Clearly there is a ragged edge at the rim of any strict rule, but the general pattern should normally be adhered to, and exceptions left only to the truly great or to literary or linguistic licence.

supersede. Under the influence of *accede, cede, intercede,* etc., *supersede* (ultimately from Latin *supersedēre* 'to sit above, be superior to') is frequently, but mistakenly, spelt *supercede.* Examples: **Somewhere down the line, you are superceded by another load of players—Independent on Sunday* (headline), 1990; **a thoroughly nasty little conflict that illuminated our news bulletins for a while before it was superceded by that far greater conflagration in the Gulf—Spectator,* 1992. It is worth noting that the word appeared first as *superceder* in Old French and only later as *-seder*; and that in English, forms with medial *c* have been recorded since the 15c. It was also often written as *supercedere* in medieval Latin, according to the *OED.*

superstitions. Among the most enduring of the superstitions or myths about our language are these: sentences should not begin with *and* or *but*; sentences should not end with a preposition; and infinitives should not be 'split'. For further examples of such beliefs, see FETISHES.

supervise. So spelt, not *supervize.* See -ISE.

supervisor. So spelt, not *-er.*

supine. 1 (adjective) lying face upwards, as opposed to *prone,* lying face downwards.

2 (noun) A Latin verbal noun used in the accusative case in *-um* with verbs of motion (*eo Romam servos emptum* 'I am going to Rome to buy slaves') or in the ablative in *-u* (*mirabile dictu* 'wonderful to relate'), especially to express purpose.

3 *Pronunciation.* The grammatical term is pronounced with the stress on the first syllable, /ˈs(j)uːˌpʌɪn/. Similarly now with the adjective, but it has not always been so: the *OED* (1917) gave preference to second-syllable stressing, and Daniel Jones (also 1917) gave only second-syllable stressing for it. Cf. RECESSIVE ACCENT.

supplement. The noun is always stressed on the first syllable, /ˈsʌplɪmənt/, with a SCHWA in the last syllable. Most dictionaries show the same stress pattern for the verb, but with the last syllable pronounced /-mɛnt/, which is also occasionally stressed /sʌplɪˈmɛnt/.

supposedly. Four syllables. See -EDLY.

suppositious, supposititious. These rather uncommon words both entered the language in the 17c. and for a long period shared the sense 'fraudulently substituted for the real thing or person'. Nowadays the longer word is the one used in this sense (*The various publications . . . include the numerous supposititious works bearing Geminiani's name—OED,* 2004), while *suppositious* is normally used to mean 'hypothetical, conjectural' (*We might take a small cottage outside Dublin . . . Not that I imagine that the atmosphere of our suppositious cottage could . . . become more unpleasant to you than the atmosphere you are at present breathing.*—J. Joyce, 1905). *Supposititious* is derived from Latin *suppositicius* '(fraudulently) put in place of another', from *suppōnere,* which has a wide range of senses including 'to place under' and 'to suppose'. The shorter form is partly a shortened form of *supposititious,* partly directly from *supposition.*

suppressio veri /səˌprɛʃɪəʊ ˈvɪːərʌɪ/. Plural *suppressiones veri* /-ɪəʊniːz/. A misrepresentation of the truth by concealing a fact or facts which ought to be made known. Example: *It would not be easy to* *find a more flagrant case of* suppressio veri *than this omission . . . of any reference to the notorious Rohling scandal*—M. Hay, 1950. Cf. SUGGESTIO FALSI.

suppressor. So spelt, not *-er*. See -ER AND -OR; -OR.

supreme. See ADJECTIVE 4.

surcease (noun and verb). A literary word of some antiquity (noun 16c., verb 15c.) for 'cessation, respite' and 'to cease'. Now rarely used (especially the verb), except in AmE. Some examples of the noun possibly reflect the well-known context in Shakespeare's *Macbeth* (1605), *If th' Assassination Could trammell vp the Consequence, and catch With his surcease, Successe.* Modern (noun) examples: *The movies were low-cost balm and surcease for large audiences during the Depression*—A. Miller, 1987; *S. Rado coined the term 'pharmacothymia' to describe the disorder in which drugs are taken to find surcease from intolerable psychic pain*—E. A. Grollman, 1988; *The sculptured forms piled overhead, one into another without surcease*—A. Dillard, 1989.

sure, surely (adverbs). **1** The dominant adverb of the two by far is *surely*, and especially in its use as an appeal to likelihood or reason. Examples of standard uses of *surely*: *it was surely here, if anywhere, that he became the 'Poet'*; *the protester is surely honour-bound to show that he knows what he's talking about*; *those* [*sc.* performance indicators] *for dons will surely be easy to agree on*; *Tim was old enough, surely, to come and go as he pleased?*; *The only question to be asked . . ., surely, is what can be salvaged from the wreck*; *what was not wanted by its owner surely does not belong to anybody?*; *Not just for irony's sake, surely?* One of its commonest uses is in the phrase *slowly but surely*, when the meaning called for is 'so as to be certain to achieve or reach a result or end': *These things are slowly but surely coming about*—1912 in *OED*. All of the types cited above are part of general English, i.e. are not primarily associated with any specified region in the English-speaking world.

2 By contrast, *sure* used as an adverb is relatively uncommon in BrE. It exists in the time-honoured semi-proverbs *as sure as eggs is eggs* and *as sure as God made little apples.* It has also been used since the beginning of the 19c., first in Britain and then elsewhere, as (part of) an affirmative response (19c. examples are given in the *OED*): *'Is that a fact?' 'Sure,' murmured Archibald—P. G. Wodehouse, 1914; If it had been a request to chop off one's right hand one would have said, 'Sure.'*—Mrs. L. B. Johnson, 1963; *I asked if you could finish your lunch, and they said sure, no hurry*—R. Stout, 1975. But most adverbial uses of *sure* are strongly associated with America, and to a lesser extent with Ireland. Witness the following examples: *Parts of it were pretty, sure*—A. Lurie, 1969 (US); *You sure were one sweet kid*—TV programme, *Cagney & Lacey*, 1987; *Sure how old are you, both of you?*—M. Leland, 1987 (Ir.); *A chemical fire. You worry about those, sure, said Clerk*—*New Yorker*, 1988.

3 Two useful sets of distinctions are given in *CGEL* (1985). The first group (7.56n.):

Surely, she's right. (Persuasive: 'you surely agree')
Sure, she's right (AmE = agreement: 'of course')
Sure, she's right. (IrE = asseveration: 'I assure you')

And the second (8.100), as responses to requests:

(*a*) *Please get me the file on Robert Schultz.*
Certainly
Sure (esp. AmE informal)
Surely (esp. AmE).

(*b*) *Are you willing to help her?*
(*Yes*) *certainly*
Sure (esp. AmE informal)
Surely (esp. AmE).

surety. The standard pronunciation is with three syllables, /ˈʃʊərɪtɪ/, but the main dictionaries also list two-syllable /ˈʃʊətɪ/.

surly. A 16c. altered form of earlier (first recorded 14c.) *sirly*, from *sir* + *-ly*. The earliest sense was 'lordly, magnificent', but this sense gave way in the 17c. to the modern meaning, 'bad-tempered and unfriendly, morose'. The corresponding adverb is **surlily**, but it is usually avoided (in favour of 'in a surly manner' or the like) on grounds of euphony: see -LILY.

surmise (noun and verb). So spelt. See -ISE. While the verb is always stressed on the second syllable, and the noun usually is, the noun can also have first-syllable stress.

surprise. 1 (noun and verb) So spelt. See -ISE.

2 For the pleonastic type of phrase *I shouldn't be surprised if* + a negative in the subordinate clause, see NOT 5.

surprisedly. Four syllables. See -EDLY.

surveillance. The pronunciation recommended is /sɜːˈveɪləns/, but /sɜːˈveɪ(j)əns/ is still valid though gradually falling into disuse. The related verb *surveil* is mostly AmE; its inflections are *surveilling, surveilled.*

survey. The noun is stressed on the first syllable and the verb on the second. See NOUN AND VERB ACCENT 1.

surveyor. So spelt, not *-er.* See -OR.

survivor. So spelt, not *-er.* See -OR.

susceptible. **1** For the spelling, see -ABLE, -IBLE 8.

2 See SENSIBLE, SENSITIVE, SUSCEPTIBLE.

suspender. In British English a *suspender* is a device fastened to the top of a stocking or sock to hold it up; and a **suspender belt** is 'a woman's undergarment consisting of a belt and elastic suspenders to which the tops of the stockings are fastened' (*New SOED*). In North American English, *suspenders* is the ordinary word for what in British English are called *braces.*

suspense, suspension. Formerly the two words were interchangeable in several senses, but no longer. *Suspense* in most of its uses is 'a state of anxious uncertainty or expectation', especially in the phrase *to keep in suspense* 'to delay informing (someone) of urgent information', and, used attributively, as in *suspense novel, suspense thriller.* In bookkeeping a *suspense account* is one in which items are entered temporarily before allocation to the correct or final account. *Suspension* has numerous unshared senses, especially (*a*) the act of suspending or the condition of being suspended; (*b*) the means by which a (motor) vehicle is supported on its axles; (*c*) attributive in *suspension bridge,* a bridge with a roadway suspended from cables supported by structures at each end (e.g. the Humber Bridge at Hull and the Golden Gate Bridge at San Francisco).

suspicion (noun). See GALLICISMS 2.

suspicion (verb). Apart from a stray 17c. example, this verb has been recorded since 1834, principally in AmE sources, in the representation of non-standard, regional, or facetious language instead of the synonymous *suspect.* Typical examples: *Our nineteen-year-old son, which he's home from Yale on his midyears and don't suspicion that his folks are rifting*—S. J. Perelman, 1946; *I suspicioned what she was, but I didn't have no proof*—D. Shannon, 1973. Presumably drawing on his Arkansan origins, President Clinton used the word in a speech in 1993 (cited by William Safire in the *NY Times Mag.*, 5 Sept. 1993): *The only thing that I can tell you is that everything I ever suspicioned about the way the Federal Government operates turned out to be true, plus some.*

sustain (verb). This old verb, taken into the language from Old French in the 13c., has or had many senses (to succour, support; to uphold the validity of; to keep in being; etc.), some of which have survived and some not. The only controversial one is 'to undergo, experience, have to submit to (evil, hardship, or damage)'; and even then only the linking of *sustain* with a particular injury (a broken limb, or the like). Dean Alford (1864), as part of a lament about the deterioration of the language ('Its fine manly Saxon is getting diluted into long Latin words not carrying half the meaning') gave a series of examples from newspapers to support his view ('We never *eat* but always *partake*'; 'No man ever *shows* any feeling, but always *evinces* it'; etc.). His paragraph on *sustain* is filled with passion: 'In the papers, a man does not now *lose his mother*: he *sustains* (this I saw in a country paper) *bereavement of his maternal relative.*' Alford comments: '*to sustain* a bereavement, does not properly mean merely to undergo or suffer a loss, but to behave bravely under it'. And then adds: 'Men never break their legs, but they always *"sustain a fracture"* of them.'

The *OED* (1918) seemed to take the same view ('In modern journalistic use (orig. U.S.) to suffer the injury of (a broken limb, or the like)'). Fowler (1926) was cautious about its use in the restricted sense: 'Nevertheless, *sustain* as a synonym for *suffer* or *receive* or *get* belongs to the class of *formal words,* and is better avoided .' Such uses of *sustain* are now just listed without comment in modern dictionaries (*sustain injuries, bruises,* etc., as well as *sustain losses,* etc.). Perhaps the bluntest comment is that of *The Times Guide to English Style and Usage* (1992): '*sustain* a broken leg is pompous: just break a leg. Sustain injuries is acceptable, as is sustain losses.'

sustainedly. Four syllables. See -EDLY.

svelte. This French loanword has been used in English since the early 19c. to mean '(of persons, especially women, occas. ironically of men, also occas. of animals) slim, slender, willowy'. Examples: *The Matron led the way, lovely, smiling, svelte, and graceful*—Miss Braddon, 1887; *There is a plush green carpet and a svelte grey cat with silky fur*—P. Carey, 1981; *Marlin Fitzwater* [President Bush's chief spokesman] ... *whose physique has ranged from svelte to portly in the last few years*—*Chicago Sun-Times*, 1991; *Foremost among these* [*sc.* animated short films] *is the story of a svelte, psychosexual, sci-fi assassin—Aeon Flux—Wired (US)*, 1993. Since the early 20c. it has also been used to mean '(of edifices, cities, vehicles, etc.) elegant, graceful'. Examples: *And first the cities of north Italy I did behold, Each as a woman wonder-fair, And svelte Verona first I met at eve*—E. Pound, 1909; *Is our svelte hired limousine at the door?*—N. Marsh, 1974.

Swan of Avon. See SOBRIQUETS.

swap (= exchange) is the recommended form, not *swop.*

swat (verb), to crush (a fly) with a sharp blow. So spelt. *Swat* is in origin a 17c. regional variant of *squat*, to squash, flatten. Cf. SWOT.

swathe[1] (noun) /swɛɪð/ is the more common World English spelling for this word, originally meaning 'a row or line of grass, corn, or other crop as it falls or lies when mown or reaped' but now generally used metaphorically to mean 'a broad strip or area of something' and by extension 'a large proportion of something', e.g. *A shortage of dentists is afflicting huge swathes of Yorkshire*; *Because he does not want to alienate a wider swathe of voters*. The spelling *swath*, pronounced /sweɪð/ or /swɒθ/ is preferred in North American English, and is a variant elsewhere.

swathe[2] (verb and noun), to bind or enclose in bandages or garments; a bandage or wrapping. Always so spelt. Pronounced /sweɪð/.

sweetie, a term used in BrE for confectionery of various kinds (= US *candy*). Also (in general English) *colloq.*, a likeable person; *sweetie-pie*, a term of endearment (especially as a form of address).

swell (verb). In most of its uses the past tense is *swelled* (*after he tripped on a loose paving-stone his ankle swelled up*) and the past participle *swollen* (*his left ankle had swollen after the game*). The participial adjective is normally **swollen** except in the phrase *swelled head* (beside *swollen head*). The *OED* has examples of *swelled* and *swollen* for the past participle and attributive adjective existing side by side in past centuries; and also of *swoll* as a by-form for the past tense until the 19c. before it became restricted to dialectal or illiterate use (*me ankles swoll so, and I 'ad dizzy spells*—illiterate speaker in A. S. Byatt's *Still Life*, 1985). It is broadly true that as past participle *swollen* implies harmful or undesirable swelling (*the river was swollen and running level with its banks*), whereas *swelled* has more neutral connotations (*the audience was swelled by the arrival of two coachloads of tourists*).

swim (verb). The past tense is now always *swam* and the past participle *swum*, but do not be surprised to see *swam* used for the past participle in earlier texts: *Who, being shipwrecked, had swam naked to land*—Dr Johnson, 1750. Also *swum* for the past tense as late as the 19c. (*who turn'd half-round to Psyche as she sprang To meet it, with an eye that swum to thanks*—Tennyson, 1847).

swine. In AmE 'a pig' (*He was sweating like a swine*—*New Yorker*, 1993). In BrE, *swine* is used formally as a collective noun, but in the main the animals are called *pigs* rather than *swine*. In colloquial use, *swine* (plural *swines*) also = (*a*) a term of contempt for a person; (*b*) a very difficult or unpleasant thing.

swing. Past tense and past participle now regularly *swung*, though *swang* was often used for the past tense by writers until the early 20c. (*and Silenus swang This way and that, with wild-flowers crowned*—*Wordsworth*, 1828; *His arms dangled rather than swang*—H. Belloc, 1912).

swinging, the ordinary present participle and adjective from *swing* is distinguished from *swingeing* by the retention of the final *-e* of *swinge* (verb) in the latter (*swingeing cuts in the armed forces*).

swivel (verb). The inflected forms are *swivelled, swivelling,* but usually *swiveled, swiveling* in AmE. See -LL-, -L.

swop. See SWAP.

swot (verb and noun). In *colloq.* BrE, to study assiduously; a person who swots. Cf. SWAT. Both *swat* and *swot* are pronounced /swɒt/, and both are first recorded in the mid-19c. *Swot* is in origin a dialectal variant of *sweat.*

syllabication, syllabification, the division of words into syllables. Both forms are used by lexicographers and linguists.

syllabub. So spelt, not *sillabub.*

syllabus. *OEC* data suggests that there is a strong preference for *syllabi* /-bʌɪ/ in North American and Indian English, and for *syllabuses* in BrE and in most other areas of the English-speaking world.

syllepsis /sɪˈlɛpsɪs/ (Greek σύλληψις, = taking together), plural *syllepses* /-siːz/. '*Gram. & Rhet.* A figure of speech in which a word, or a particular form or inflection of a word, is made to cover two or more functions in the same sentence whilst agreeing grammatically with only one (e.g. a sing. verb serving as predicate to two subjects, sing. and pl.), or is made to apply to two words in different senses (e.g. literal and metaphorical)' (*New SOED,* 1993).

Examples: (*a*) *She has deceiv'd her father, and may thee*—Shakespeare, 1604 (*deceive* understood between *may* and *thee*); *He works his work, I mine*—Tennyson, (*work* (verb) understood between *I* and *mine*); *She's a lovely, intelligent, sensitive woman who has and continues to turn around my life in a wonderfully positive way*—Woody Allen, reported in *The Times,* 1992 (*turned* understood between *has* and *and*); *his avowal of Christianity could have* (*and perhaps did*) *damage his career—Times,* 1995 (*damaged* understood between *have* and (*and*...). Constructions of this type are now regarded as ungrammatical.

(*b*) *Here, thou, great Anna! whom three realms obey Dost sometimes counsel take—and sometimes tea*—Pope, 1712–14; *She... went home in a flood of tears and a sedan chair*—Dickens, 1836–7; *the small fire, over which toast could be made with the help of a long fork and much patience—London Rev. Bks,* 1987; *Sir Geoffrey Howe, who had arrived in a limousine, the editor of the Daily Telegraph, who had arrived in a motor-boat, and Dave Nellist, who had arrived in an anorak*—M. Parris, 1991.

Cf. ZEUGMA, but note that 'the term *syllepsis* is frequently used interchangeably with *zeugma,* attempts to distinguish the two terms having foundered in confusion' (Baldick, 1990).

syllogism. '*Logic.* A form of reasoning in which a conclusion is deduced from two given or assumed propositions called the premises, which contain a common or middle term that is absent from the conclusion' (*New SOED,* 1993). A syllogism of the simplest form is: *All men are mortal; Socrates is a man; Therefore Socrates is mortal.* The predicate of the conclusion (here *mortal*) is called the *major term,* and the preliminary proposition containing it the *major premise.* The subject of the conclusion (here *Socrates*) is called the *minor term,* and the preliminary proposition containing it the *minor premise.* The term common to both premises (here *man*) is called the *middle term.* There are several types of syllogism and only a small proportion of them are valid.

sylvan rather than *silvan,* is by far the more common spelling now, though *silvan* corresponds more closely to Latin *silva* 'wood'. Examples: *Sylvan meant savage in those primal woods Piero di Cosimo so loved to draw*—W. H. Auden in *Woods*; *The sauna belongs to a private house, both designed by David Salmela on a sylvan Minnesota site—Architectural Review,* 2002.

symbolic, symbolical. There is no difference of meaning but the shorter form is overwhelmingly the more frequent. See -IC(AL). Examples: (symbolical) *the occultism of symbolical Masonry*—J. McManners, 1990; (symbolic) *On the day before Easter, there is a symbolic burning of a cloth-draped wooden statue of Judas*—C. Hammerschlag, 1988; *Because they were symbolic of his psychoanalytic work, Freud was more than ready to share his 'archaeological' interests with patients*—B. Bettelheim, 1990; *The symbolic 'black rooster'* (*Gallo Nero*) *which is affixed to every Chianti bottle—Q Rev. Wines,* 1991.

symbology, the science or study of symbols. First recorded in the 19c., this word is irregularly formed, but the 'correct' form **symbolology* has not been used.

sympathetic. Used to mean 'tending to elicit sympathy or to induce a feeling of rapport', this sense of *sympathetic* was too freshly minted for Fowler to approve of it in 1926 (the first recorded example of the sense in the *OED* is one of 1900). But it is now in unopposed and widespread use. Examples: *The true Don Juan . . . is . . . not a 'sympathetic' part*—M. Beerbohm, 1900; *Macbeth . . . is not made sympathetic, however adequately his crime may be explained and palliated, by being the victim of a hallucination*—cited in Fowler, 1926; *Being a lover of the south, I personally found it* [*sc.* a novel] *more sympathetic*—*Listener*, 1965; *Despite the sympathetic portrayal of his father in these anecdotes, Lawrence turned against him after the death of his mother*—J. Meyers, 1990.

symposium /sɪmˈpəʊzɪəm/. Plural more often *symposia* than *symposiums*, though both are correct. See -UM 3.

synaeresis /sɪˈnɪərɪsɪs/. (US **syneresis**). Plural *synaereses* /-siːz/. The making of two separate vowel sounds into one, as when *aerial* moved from /eɪˈɪərɪəl/ (four syllables) to /ˈɛːrɪəl/ (three syllables), and the ending *-ein* in some scientific words, e.g. *protein*, moved from /-ɪɪn/ (two syllables) to /-iːn/ (one syllable). Its opposite is DIAERESIS.

synchronic (adjective). Concerned with or describing the state of a language, culture, etc., at one particular time or period, past or present, without regard to historical development, as opposed to DIACHRONIC.

syncope /ˈsɪŋkəpi/. A grammatical term for the shortening of a word by the omission of a syllable or other part in the middle. Examples include *idolatry*, *pacifist*, and *symbology* for †*idololatry*, *pacificist*, and **symbolology* as well as the careless pronunciation of *deteriorate* as four syllables instead of five.

syndrome /ˈsɪndrəʊm/, a medical word for a set of symptoms, and, in extended use, a characteristic combination of opinions, emotions, behaviour, etc., is in origin, like *syncope*, a three-syllable word, i.e. /ˈsɪndrəmi/. English dictionaries, including the *OED* (1918), indicated three-syllable pronunciation, either as the only one or as a variant, until well into the 20c. It was still listed as an alternative pronunciation in the seventh edition of the *COD* in 1982. Now universally two-syllable, on the model of *aerodrome*, *hippodrome*, *palindrome*, etc. Its extended use is generally acceptable, but not when *syndrome* is simply a synonym for *factor* or *aspect*, i.e. a single circumstance rather than a set of circumstances coming together, which lies at the heart of its meaning: *?Perhaps the improved performance at Boots is due to 'new broom syndrome'?*—business news website, 2004.

synecdoche /sɪˈnɛkdəki/. A figure of speech in which a more inclusive term is used for a less inclusive one or vice versa, as a whole for a part (*England beat South Africa by four wickets*, i.e. the England and South Africa cricket teams) or a part for a whole (*a fleet of fifty sail*, i.e. fifty sailing ships). Cf. METONYMY.

synonymity, synonymy. There is work for both words, the first (infrequently used) meaning 'synonymousness', and the second (the more general word) meaning the state of being synonymous (i.e. the same as the longer word), but also a system or collection of synonyms, and an article or treatise on synonyms.

synonyms. It is now universally recognized that no exact synonyms exist in a given language. In other words there is no pair of words of which one of the pair can be substituted for the other in all circumstances. Fowler himself made the point neatly in 1926: 'Synonyms in the widest sense are words either of which in one or other of its acceptations can sometimes be substituted for the other without affecting the meaning of a sentence; thus it does not matter (to take the nearest possible example) whether I say a word has "two senses" or "two meanings", and *sense* and *meaning* are therefore loose synonyms; but if "He is a man of sense" is rewritten as "He is a man of meaning", it becomes plain that *sense* and *meaning* are far from perfect synonyms.' The word *synonym* is therefore unavoidably used of words of approximately the same meaning 'but having a different emphasis or appropriate to a different context (as *serpent, snake*; *Greek, Hellene*; *happy, joyful*; *kill, slay*), or having a different range of other senses (as *ship, vessel*; *tube, pipe*)' (*New SOED*).

It is not practicable to provide a full list of all the articles in which the subject of synonymy or near-synonymy arises: they occur on almost every opening of this book. It must suffice to say that there are scores of relevant articles dealing with such matters as the differences, sometimes clear-cut and sometimes not, between such words as *feasible, possible,* and *probable*; *historic* and *historical*; *legible* and *readable*; and *masterful* and *masterly.*

synopsis. Plural *synopses* /-iːz/.

syntax. See GRAMMAR.

synthesis. Plural *syntheses* /-iːz/. Cf. ANALYSIS.

synthesize (verb), to make a synthesis of, has virtually replaced *synthetize,* used in the same sense. Both words entered the language, according to the *OED, c.*1830. The *OED* (1918) described *synthetize* as 'the correct form' (i.e. etymologically).

syphon. See SIPHON.

syrupy. So spelt, not *syruppy.* See -P-, -PP-.

systematic, systemic. The ordinary word in lay language for 'methodical; done or conceived according to a plan or system' is *systematic.* The second word used to be reserved for certain technical uses in physiology (of or concerning the body as a whole), horticulture (of an insecticide entering a plant by its roots or shoots and passing through the tissues), and grammar (M. A. K. Halliday's term for a method of analysis based on the conception of language as a network of systems determining the options from which speakers choose in accordance with their communicative goals—*New SOED*). Since *systemic* is now used more broadly to mean 'relating to or affecting a system as a whole (rather than to a part of it)', it is often used in relation to *systemic problems* and *systemic failures* in organizations and to, er, systems, e.g. *And even marginally more serious proposals are far from convincing. First they rest on the assumption that there can be technical solutions to what are essentially systemic problems—Ecologist,* 2000. Most dictionaries give priority to the pronunciation /sɪˈstɛmɪk/ (sis-**tem**-ik) with /-ˈstiːm-/ (-**steem**-) as an alternative.

systole (physiology). Pronounced as three syllables, /ˈsɪstəli/.

syzygy (astronomy, etc.). Pronounced /ˈsɪzɪdʒɪ/. See GREEK G.

tabes (emaciation). Pronounced /ˈteɪbiːz/.

table (verb). In BrE to *table* a motion means 'to place it on the agenda'. In AmE it means 'to put aside (a bill, a motion) for an indefinite period'.

tableau. Plural several times more frequent in the *OEC* data as *tableaux* (pronounced /-ləʊz/ or like the singular) than *tableaus.* See -X.

table d'hôte, a meal consisting of a set menu at a fixed price, as opposed to an *à la carte* (adverb and adjective), ordered as separately priced items from a menu, not as part of a set menu. Printed in roman with the circumflex accent of the French original. See also À LA CARTE.

tablespoonful. Plural *tablespoonfuls.* See -FUL. But in practice the usual formula is of the type *take three tablespoons of*...

taboo. Stress on the second syllable whether as noun, adjective, or verb. The word is now occasionally written as *tabu* to reflect more accurately the Tongan original. The inflected forms are *taboos, tabooed* and *tabooing.* The related Maori word **tapu** is pronounced /ˈtɑːpuː/ in NZ English.

tabula rasa /ˌtabjʊlə ˈrɑːzə/. Plural, if required, *tabulae rasae* /ˌtabjʊliː ˈrɑːziː/. Printed in italic.

tactile, tactual. These two adjectives meaning 'of, connected with or perceptible by the sense of touch' were rivals from the time they entered English in the 17c. Currently, in ordinary use, *tactile* is the usual and much more frequent word, e.g. *vocal and visual signals become less important as tactile signals intensify*; *she had a distinct, almost tactile memory of the girl fleeing. Tactual* is largely confined to philosophical works, or is very occasionally used, like *tactile,* to mean 'designed to be perceived by touch', for the benefit of people with visual impairments. Examples: *Information, when disseminated verbally, may benefit the auditory learners, but not the visual, tactual, or kinesthetic learners—Amer. Jrnl of Pharmaceutical Education,* 2000; *Visual and tactual sense-data do this directly, the others indirectly, as explained above—Knowledge: Readings in Contemporary Epistemology,* 2000.

taenia /ˈtiːnɪə/ (US **tenia).** Plural *taeniae* /-nɪiː/ or *taenias.*

tag question. 1 This is the grammarians' name for a question added at the end of a statement and acting as a reinforcement rather than seeking an answer, e.g. *You will do this for me,* won't you?; *She has been to America,* hasn't she?; *I don't need an umbrella,* do I?. In each case the verb in the main statement has been changed into an equivalent question; if the statement is positive the tag is negative, and vice versa, although a positive tag can follow a positive statement in the type *You heard it too,* did you?. The tag question is a prominent feature of English grammar and one that is difficult for foreign learners of English, who often resort to simplified formulas to achieve the same result. There are also regional variations within Great Britain and Ireland (see below), and degrees of emphasis and changes of intonation in certain kinds of confirmatory and peremptory tags. The scholarly literature on the whole subject is considerable: the examples that follow can only palely reflect the work done by numerous grammarians.

2 There follows a series of examples showing regional, social, and other variants on the standard type of tag question: *It's a glorious day,* isn't it?*—CGEL,* 1985 (confirmatory); *Students are human too,* aren't they? (as part of a possibly confrontational argument); *That's a bloody good reason,* innit?—J. Wainwright, 1973 (representing the speech of an uneducated person); *When will the taxi get here?—We'll know when it gets here,* won't we? (peremptory tag); *I work here,* don't I?—BBC TV *Eastenders,* 1987 (peremptory); *Do you know Lord Astor has made a statement to the police saying that these allegations of yours are totally untrue?* (M. Rice-Davies:) *He would,* wouldn't he? (satirical tag); *Surely a man must be kind to a man whose life he has saved,* isn't it?—Irish speaker in I. Murdoch, 1989 (formulaic tag used in some forms of Irish English); *You're going home now,* isn't it?—A. R. Thomas, 1994 (replacing person reference in some forms of Welsh English); *You are going tomorrow,* isn't it?—B. B. Kachru, 1994 (ditto, in South Asian English); *After all, the culprits had to be found,* not so?—A. Brink, 1988 (SAfr.) (verb not used in tag); *There must be thousands,* no? *said Don Miguel*—South American speaker in N. Shakespeare, 1989; *You're at university,* yes?—A. R. Thomas, 1994 (N. Wales).

3 While that list of examples could be greatly extended, one thing that is worth highlighting is the expansion of *innit.* A colloquial version of *isn't it,* first recorded from 1959, in that function it requires the presence of the verb *be* in the preceding statement, e.g. *That's a bloody good reason,* innit? Additionally, in certain varieties of World English, notably South African and Indian, *isn't it* can be equivalent to 'aren't you', 'isn't he', 'wasn't I', etc., inviting agreement, approval, and so forth. *The de Mussy fellow and that Portuguese chap, they are good swimmers,* isn't it?—B. Mukherjee, 1993. Related to that use is the use of *innit* as an all-purpose, weakened filler, (stereo)-typically associated with the speech of young British Asians, and not echoing the presence of *be* in the preceding statement: *I like fresh air,* innit—H. Kureishi, 1991; *I've just got to get off my arse one day* innit?—R. Graef, 1992; *I definitely wouldn't snog her—she's a mum,* innit?—*Smash Hits,* 2003.

take (verb). See BRING 1.

talc (verb). The inflected forms are *talced, talcing.* The corresponding adjective **talcy** is normally so spelt.

talented. It is a chastening thought that the adjective *talented,* endowed with talent or talents, came in for severe treatment in the early 19c. Coleridge, in his *Table Talk* (1832), commented 'I regret to see that vile and barbarous vocable *talented* stealing out of the newspapers into the leading reviews and most respectable publications of the day.' And in the Jan. 1988 issue of the journal *English Today* it was reported that Carlyle, 'notorious for his eccentric style, had been criticized by his friend James Sterling . . . for inventing such unnecessary new words as "environment", "visualised", and "talented".' Carlyle accepted the criticisms: 'With unspeakable cheerfulness I give up *talented*: indeed, but for the plain statement you made, I could have sworn such a word had never, except for parodistic, ironical purposes risen from my inkhorn or passed my lips.' (In fact Sterling was not quite accurate: Carlyle seems to have invented the word *environment* but not the other two.) Sterling's objection to *talented* was based upon the belief that an adjective in *-ed* could not properly be formed from a noun (a verb *talent* in the sense required had existed in the 17c. and 18c. but was obsolete by the 1820s). But cf. (with the earliest recorded dates given in each case) *bigoted* (1645), *leisured* (1631), *moneyed* (1457), and *skilled* (1552), all formed from nouns + *-ed.*

talent, genius. In 1899, in the *OED,* Henry Bradley summed up the familiar contrast thus: 'It was by the German writers of the 18th c. that the distinction between "genius" and "talent", which had some foundation in Fr. usage, was sharpened into the strong antithesis which is now universally current, so that the one term is hardly ever defined without reference to the other. The difference between *genius* and *talent* has been formulated very variously by different writers, but there is general agreement in regarding the former as the higher of the two, as "creative" and "original", and as achieving its results by instinctive perception and spontaneous activity, rather than by processes which admit of being distinctly analysed.'

talisman. Since the word has nothing to do with the English word *man,* the plural is *talismans,* not *talismen.* It came into English in the 17c. from any of three languages (French, Spanish, or Portuguese) which had derived it from an Arabic word connected with late Greek τέλεσμα 'a consecrated object'.

talkative. Fowler (1926) reminded us that this is the only word in *-ative* in which this element has been appended to a non-Latin, i.e. a native word. See -ATIVE, -IVE.

talus[1] /ˈteɪləs/, ankle-bone. Plural *tali* /-lʌɪ/. Derived from Latin *tālus* 'ankle' in the 17c.

talus[2] /ˈteɪləs/, slope of a wall, etc. Plural *taluses*. Adopted from French in the 17c.

-t and -ed. Problems arise in a number of irregular verbs which have competing forms for the past tense and/or the past participle. They differ often in not only having rival forms in *-t* and *-ed* but also in some cases having a different vowel sound before the termination (e.g. *leapt* and *leaped*). Nor is it possible in every case to say in what circumstances the final sound is /t/ or /d/, even when the word is spelt with *-ed*. The distribution of the variant forms in Britain and in English-speaking countries abroad cannot for the most part be determined precisely, though in most of the verbs Americans show a marked preference for the forms in *-ed*. The main verbs affected are listed below. Further details of each are to be found under the individual words themselves at their alphabetical place.

bereave: *bereft, bereaved*; *beseech*: *besought, beseeched*; *burn*: *burnt, burned*; *cleave*[1]: *cleft, cleaved*; *dream*: *dreamt, dreamed*; *dwell*: *dwelt, dwelled*; *earn*: (*earnt*), *earned*; *kneel*: *knelt, kneeled*; *lean*: *leant, leaned*; *leap*: *leapt, leaped*; *learn*: *learnt, learned*; *smell*: *smelt, smelled*; *spell*: *spelt, spelled*; *spill*: *spilt, spilled*; *spoil*: *spoilt, spoiled*; *toss*: (*tost*), *tossed*.

See also LEARNED.

tantalize means more than just 'tease or torment', as is shown by the word's origins in the treatment meted out to the legendary Phrygian king Tantalus, who was forced to stand in water which receded when he tried to drink and under branches that drew back when he tried to pick the fruit. The word is therefore best used when it retains an element of torment caused by something offered and then withdrawn, although this cannot always be as explicit or obvious as it was for Tantalus. It occurs most often in the adjectival form *tantalizing* or the adverbial form *tantalizingly*: *Foremost among their key sources was a man whom the authors still tantalizingly refuse to name*—*Time*, 1974; *There are tantalizing hints of a personal love story, but there is no development or continuity*—J. Culler, 2000.

Taoiseach (Prime Minister of the Irish Republic). Pronounced /ˈtiːʃəx/ (**tee**-shukh), with the final consonantal sound, technically a voiceless velar fricative, being that of Scottish *loch*. But both words are often pronounced with an anglicized /-k/ instead of /-x/.

Taoism. Pronounced /ˈtaʊɪzəm/, rhyming with *Maoism*. (For an elaborate discussion of the way in which this pronunciation emerged from Chinese *dào* 'way', see Michael Carr's note in *Dictionaries* 12 (1990), 55–74.)

tapu. See TABOO.

target (noun). It is instructively piquant to see how linguistic history, like other histories, can repeat itself, though whether as tragedy or farce only time will tell. In his 1965 edition of this book, Gowers, clearly disheartened by the way in which enthusiastic bureaucrats had been using it in post-WWII reconstruction, lambasted the word: 'After the second world war this word was much used to express the quantitative result hoped for from some enterprise such as the output of a manufacturing concern or the amount subscribed for some public or charitable purpose. To an exceptional degree it has shared the experience of most popular metaphors of being "spoilt" by use in a way flagrantly incongruous with its literal meaning. Targets, it is said, must be "pursued vigorously"; to be "within sight" of one and to "keep fully abreast" of it are, it seems, positions that practically guarantee success, and when a target is "doubled" the implication that it will be twice as difficult to hit goes unquestioned. But then, as Lord Conesford has remarked, "those who thus describe their ambitions never seem to entertain the faintest hope of actually hitting their targets, even when these are overall or even global ones; in their most optimistic moods they speak of 'reaching' or 'attaining' the target, an achievement which, since the bow and arrow went out of use, has never been rated very high."' How ironic, then, that in British politics in 2014 the target-mania of the previous decade or so is still very much in evidence: in early 2014 there was concern that many British A&E departments were yet again failing to meet their target of no more than four hours' waiting time.

target (verb). The inflected forms are *targeted, targeting*. See -T-, -TT-.

tarmac (verb). The inflected forms are *tarmacked, tarmacking*. See -C-, -CK-.

tarry (verb), to linger, is pronounced /ˈtarɪ/; and the unconnected adjective *tarry*, smeared with tar, /ˈtɑːrɪ/.

tarsus (bones forming ankle and upper foot, etc.). Plural *tarsi* /-sʌɪ/.

tart. What precisely is a *tart* as distinct from a *pie*? On both sides of the Atlantic a *tart* is more likely to be sweet than savoury, with a fruit, jam, custard, etc. filling. A *pie* can contain meat or fish, or it can have a fruit filling. A tart is generally an open pastry shell (though *Merriam Webster's Collegiate Dict.*, 10th edn, 1993, gives as one definition 'a small pie made of pastry folded over a filling'). A pie usually has a pastry crust covering the filling in its pastry or biscuit shell. In Britain a *mince pie* is a small individual round pie filled with mincemeat (i.e. a mixture of dried fruit and spices, etc.) rather than of minced meat. When reading books from earlier centuries it is well to keep in mind that various dishes, covered with a crust or not, and containing either a sweet filling or meat, fish, or vegetables, might turn up (*jam tart, strawberry tart*; *eel tart, veal tart*, etc., beside *goose pie, pigeon pie, eel pie*; *pumpkin pie*, etc.). A *pasty* is a pastry case more or less semicircular in shape with a savoury (or, less often, sweet) filling; a *turnover* is like it, but with a fruit or jam filling. A *flan* is a pastry or sponge base with a sweet or savoury topping, and a *quiche* is a tart or flan with a pastry base and a rich custard filling flavoured with bacon, onion, cheese, vegetables, etc.

In *The Times Cookery Book* by K. Stewart (1972) the chapter on pastries and pies gives savoury recipes first in this order: steak and kidney pie, Cornish pasties, quiche Lorraine, bacon and mushroom flan, French onion tart, chicken and mushroom vol au vents, and cheese tartlets. The sweet recipes follow: lemon meringue pie (which has a meringue rather than a pastry top), apricot tart, plum flan with almonds, strawberry and cream cheese tarts, apple and blackberry pie, etc.

Tartar, Tatar. A Tartar was originally 'a member of the combined forces of central Asian peoples, including Mongols and Turks, who under the leadership of Genghis Khan (1202–27) overran much of Asia and eastern Europe and later established a far-reaching and powerful empire in central Europe' (*New SOED*, 1993). *Tartar* was also the name of their language. The preferred ethnological term, ultimately derived from Turkish, is now *Tatar*. A Tatar is now defined as 'a member of a group of Turkic peoples probably originating in Manchuria and Mongolia and now found mainly in parts of Siberia, Crimea, the N. Caucasus, and districts along the River Volga' (*New SOED*). *Tatar* is the name of the Turkic language of these peoples.

tassel (verb) (provide with a tassel or tassels). The inflected forms are *tasselled, tasselling*; in AmE frequently *tasseled, tasseling*. See -LL-, -L-.

tasty is now restricted to mean '(of food) pleasing in flavour, appetizing', a meaning first recorded in the 17c. Its additional 18c. and 19c. sense 'characterized by or displaying good taste' (*My... waistcoat... is a much more tasty thing than these gaudy ready-made articles*—Thackeray, 1862) has now entirely given way to **tasteful** (itself first recorded in this sense in the 18c.). The antonym **tasteless** can be used in either of the senses '(of food) without taste or flavour' or 'devoid of good taste, lacking in discrimination'.

Tatar. See TARTAR.

tattler, a prattler, a gossip. Thus spelt, unlike the 18c. (1709–11) periodical *The Tatler*.

tattoo (verb). The inflected forms are *tattooed, tattooing*; **tattooer**. See -ED AND 'D.

tautology. Ultimately from Greek ταὐτολογία 'the repeating of what has been said' (from ταὐτό 'the same' + -λογία 'saying or speaking'), *tautology* has been used in English since the 16c. to mean 'the repetition (esp. in the immediate context) of the same word or phrase, or of the same idea or statement in other words; usually as a fault of style' (*OED*). Among the illustrative examples in the *OED* is one of 1686: *The Taedium of Tautology is odious to every Pen and Ear*. Odious, indeed, provided that the repetition has gone unnoticed or unintended by the writer or speaker. Tautological phrases such as *free gift, in this day and age, new innovation*, and *lonely isolation* can be condemned at once. So can the use shown in a report 'by Our Foreign Staff' in *The Times* (9 Sept. 1994): *The Cold War came to a* final close *in Germany yesterday with the withdrawal of the last British* *soldier from West Berlin.* For other examples of tautologous expressions or clauses, borderline (the *hoi polloi*, etc.) or otherwise, see PLEONASM; REDUNDANCY. Fowler (1926) cited numerous examples of clumsily inbuilt tautology, including the following: *The wool profits were* again *made the subject of* another *attack by Mr Mackinder last night* (omit either *again* or *another*); *May I be permitted to state that the activities of the Club are not* limited only *to aeronautics?* (*limited* and *only* are tautological; read *limited to*, or *directed only to*).

These warnings given, *tautology*, as a rhetorical device, can be turned to advantage. Simple repetition is a feature of innumerable well-known literary contexts: e.g.

Alone, alone, all, all alone,
Alone on a wide wide sea!
(Coleridge, 1798)

Keeping time, time, time,
In a sort of Runic rhyme,
To the tintinabulation that so musically wells
From the bells, bells, bells, bells.
Bells, bells, bells—
From the jingling and the tinkling of the bells.
(Poe, 1849)

Whether the term *tautology* is nowadays ever employed to describe such skilful use of repetition is, however, extremely doubtful.

taxi (noun). Plural *taxis*.

taxi (verb). The inflected forms are *taxis, taxied, taxiing* (not *taxying*).

teasel (plant of the genus Dipsacus). Is mostly spelt as shown, but **teazel** and **teazle** are also correct.

teaspoonful. Plural *teaspoonfuls*. See -FUL. But in practice the usual formula is of the type *take two teaspoons of*...

tec. See ABBREVIATIONS 2.

techno-. The word *technology* (from Greek τεχνολογία, systematic treatment of grammar, etc., now the mechanical arts and applied sciences collectively), and also its main derivatives, *technological*, etc., joined the language in the 17c. But it was not until the 20c. that *techno-* became a free-flowing formative element, forming compounds mostly of self-evident meaning, e.g. *technobabble* (first recorded in 1987), *technochat, technocracy* (1919), *technocrat* (1919), *techno-freak* (1973), *technomania* (1969), *technophobia* (1965), *technostress, technothriller*, most of them occurring in the technical language of computing and other high-technology areas. Other formations refer to types of synthesized electronic music, e.g. *technopop* (1980) and *technorock* (1983), and have led to the independent word *techno*, used as an adjective and a noun: *This listener expected a jazz/techno hybrid—Milk Factory*, 2004.

techy. See TETCHY.

Te Deum. Most often pronounced /ˌtiː ˈdiːəm/ rather than /ˌteɪ ˈdeɪəm/.

teem (verb)[1], to be full of or swarming with (*the sea is teeming with fish*), is derived from Old English *tēman* 'to give birth to'. It is not etymologically related to TEEM (verb)[2].

teem (verb)[2], (of water, rain) to flow copiously, to pour (*it was teeming with rain*), came into English in the 14c. from Old Norse *tœma* 'to empty'. Its earliest sense in English was 'to empty (a vessel, etc.)'. The application to water, rain, etc., seems to have come from dialectal use into the standard language in the early 19c.

teenager, a person from 13 to 19 years of age. The term seems to have been with us for ever, but the earliest recorded example (in an American source) is one of 1941. To begin with, it was printed with a hyphen as *teen-ager* (and still is in some publications). The word is sometimes loosely used of any adolescent, without strict regard to age, particularly one judged to be behaving in an unsocial manner. The family of *teen-* words, all derived from the *-teen* of *thirteen*, etc., includes **teenage** (adjective and noun) and **teenaged** (adjective), the latter being far less often used than the former, and more frequent in North American English than elsewhere.

teetotaller. So spelt (but in AmE frequently **teetotaler**); but **teetotalism** in both BrE and AmE. See -LL-, -L-.

tele-. From Greek τηλε-, combining form of τῆλε 'afar, far off', *tele-* has become one of the great formative elements of words in modern English. The notion of distance in its various senses is built into all words containing *tele-*. Those that have emerged have for the most part been formed without regard to etymological 'correctness'; that is to say, they combined an originally Greek prefix with words not of the same origin.

Thus *telecast* was based on *broadcast*; *telecommunication* was formed first in French in 1932 at a conference in Madrid (where the official language happened to be French); *telegenic* (adjective) was modelled on *photogenic*; *tele-lens* combines a Greek prefix with a word of Latin origin; *teleprinter*, *teleprompter*, and *teletext* were coined simply by clapping *tele-* on to *printer*, *prompter*, and *text*. Blends include *televangelist* (*tel*(*evision*) + *evangelist*) and *Telex* (*tele*(*printer*) + *ex*(*change*)).

Great technological developments over the centuries are mirrored in the use of *tele-* as a formative element: *telescope* (first recorded in 1648), *telegraph* (1794), *telegram* (1852), *telephone* (in the modern Alexander Graham Bell sense, 1876), *telepathy* (1882), and *television* (1907). One wonders what new central concept will be captured in new uses of *tele-* in the 21c. Meanwhile the limitless class of *tele*-words is joined, almost daily, it would seem, by more members, e.g., since 1980, by such words as *telebanking* (1981), *telebetting* (1983), *telemarketing* (1980), *teleshopping* (1981), *teleworking* (1984).

televise (verb). So spelt, with *-ise* not *-ize*, in BrE and AmE. It is a back-formation from *television*.

temerarious. First introduced into English by Thomas More in 1532 ('reckless, rash', from Latin *temerārius* in the same sense), it and also the adverb in *-ly* are now only in restricted use. Examples: *In temerariously excluding Wilfred Owen from the* Oxford Book of Modern Verse ... *Yeats made clear that for him poetry ... cannot find its end in pity*—R. Ellmann, 1967; *One conversation ... involved my temerarious claim that if you focus attention on finding well-defined answers, then you're not doing research*—J. L. Casti, 1989.

template. Now spelt as shown, not *templet*, though *templet* was the dominant spelling in the 17–19c., and *-plate* is 'pseudo-etymological' based on *plate*. The word is probably a derivative of *temple*, 'a device in a loom for keeping the cloth stretched'. The second syllable can be pronounced like *plate*, or simply as *-plit*.

tempo (music). The plural is either *tempos* or *tempi* /-piː/.

temporal, temporary. From the 14c. to the 19c. *temporal* shared with *temporary* the sense 'lasting only for a time'. Conversely, at various periods, *temporary* shared some of the senses of *temporal* (details in the *OED*). The central meaning of *temporal* now is 'of worldly as opposed to spiritual affairs, secular'. Hence the distinction between the *temporal* (civil) and the *spiritual* (ecclesiastical) authorities and the division of the House of Lords into *Lords Temporal* (lay peers) and *Lords Spiritual* (bishops).

temporary, temporarily. The first of these is pronounced as four syllables, /ˈtempərəri/; in AmE there is a secondary stress on the *-ar-*. The second word has five syllables and until recently was regularly pronounced in BrE with the stress on the first syllable, /ˈtɛmpərərɪli/, but is now almost as often /tɛmpəˈrɛːrɪli/, i.e. the regular pronunciation in AmE. See -ARILY.

temptress. see -ESS 5.

tend (verb)[1] (aphetic form of *attend*). A word of several meanings derived from *attend*. The main standard use in BrE is the transitive one, 'to take care of, look after (a person, esp. an invalid, animals esp. sheep, a machine)': *tend the sick, tended their flocks, tend a machine*. One use that has drifted out of dialectal or American English into occasional use in standard English is *tend to* meaning 'to give attention to, attend to'. Examples: *But mainly both global brands have tended to their own focused businesses—The Register*, 2005.

tend (verb)[2] (from Old French *tendre* 'to stretch', from Latin *tendere*). This common verb meaning 'to be apt or inclined, have a tendency' is used only intransitively: *he tends to lose his temper; she tended to do what her parents advised; the argument tends only in one direction*.

tenderhooks. See TENTERHOOKS.

tendinitis, tendonitis (inflammation of a tendon). Both spellings are correct, though dictionaries put *tendinitis* first, and it seems to be the preferred spelling in medical writing. The source word medieval Latin *tendo* has accusative singular *tendinem* or *tendōnem*.

tenet (dogma, doctrine). Daniel Jones (1917) gave /ˈtiːnɛt/ as his preferred pronunciation of the word. Fowler (1926) preferred the variant with a short /ɛ/ in the first syllable. The dominant pronunciation now is the one recommended by Fowler, though some modern dictionaries still list both types.

tenor. 1 So now spelt, not *-our*, in all senses in both BrE and AmE.

2 See MISQUOTATIONS.

tenses. 1 Certain points requiring care are discussed under AS 8; HAD 2; HAVE 2; HISTORIC 2; LEST; PERFECT INFINITIVE; SEQUENCE OF TENSES; SHALL AND WILL; SUBJUNCTIVE MOOD; and further articles cross-referenced in these.

2 To these may be added a few trifles which draw attention to some minor aspects of the English tense system: *Will that be all, Miss?*—T. S. Eliot, 1939 (servant to employer: future formula used of present time); *'They'll be rehearsing for the fête on Saturday,' Sylvia says*—M. Duckworth, 1986 (future form used to describe something actually taking place in the speaker's presence); *Next week she reveals the horrors of her recent experiences in a psychiatric ward—Truth* (NZ), 1986 (present tense of future time in an announcement).

tenterhooks. The idiom *on tenterhooks*, 'in a state of suspense or agitation because of uncertainty about a future event', usually with the verb *to be* (*He was on tenterhooks waiting for his directors' decision*) is correctly spelt as shown, not **tenderhooks*. A *tenter* was a wooden framework on which cloth was stretched after being milled, so that it would set or dry evenly and without shrinking, and antique prints and paintings sometimes show fields on the outskirts of towns covered, as it were, with cloth being processed in this way. *Tenterhooks* were hooks that held the cloth firmly and tautly in place on the tenters; hence the idiom, first used in the form *on the tenterhooks*, by Smollett, in 1748. As the word is obsolete, folk etymology has transformed it into **tenderhooks*, a form not accepted in dictionaries but quite often encountered.

tercentenary. See CENTENARY 2.

tercet /'təːsɪt/ (prosody). A set or group of three verse lines, especially one of those in TERZA RIMA, or half the sestet in some Petrarchan sonnets (see SONNET).

teredo /tə'riːdəʊ/ (bivalve mollusc). Plural *teredos* /-dəʊz/, occasionally *teredines* /tɛ'riːdɪniːz/ (the word is derived from Latin *terēdō*, plural *-ines*).

-teria (also **-eteria**), a suffix (originally and chiefly US) derived in the 1920s from *cafeteria* by analysis of its constituents as *café* + *-teria*, but not one that has formed many standard words. Examples are *danceteria* (night club), *washeteria* (self-service laundry).

term. 1 For *major, minor, middle term* in logic, see SYLLOGISM.

2 See IN TERMS OF.

terminal (noun), **terminus.** The first has several meanings, among them 'a station at the end of a railway line; a departure and arrival building at an airport; a device for entering data into a computer or receiving its output'. A *terminus* (plural usually *termini* /-nʌɪ/ or occasionally *terminuses*) is the term often used in Britain for the station at the end of a railway or bus route (but not the passenger building at an airport), as well as being a technical term in mathematics and architecture. In AmE, and to an increasing extent in BrE, the terms *terminal* and *terminus* are used interchangeably for the final stop of any passenger journey by train, bus, or aeroplane.

terminate. 1 This has **terminable** (not *-atable*) as its corresponding adjective; and **terminator** (not *-er*; see -OR) as its corresponding agent noun.

2 In the basic senses 'to bring to an end' (e.g. *terminated her pregnancy; terminate an agreement*) and 'to come to an end' (e.g. *this service terminates at Paddington, London*), *terminate* is sometimes (as shown in the examples) the natural idiomatic word. But in most contexts in which either of these senses is required, *end, finish,* or *stop* are more suitable words.

terminological inexactitude. See INEXACTITUDE.

terminus. See TERMINAL (noun).

Terpsichore (muse of dancing). Pronounced /təːp'sɪkəri/. See MUSES.

terrain is most often used to mean 'a tract of country considered with regard to its natural features; in military use especially as affecting its tactical advantages.' When it is used figuratively, the context often reflects one or other of these two images, e.g. *the muddy terrain of partisan politics; the emotional terrain covered is wild, unexpected, unexplained.* To use it figuratively as a substitute for *territory, domain, field,* etc. without such connotations is arguably a trifle precious.

terrible, terribly have gone the way of other words of this type, such as *awful/ awfully, dreadful/ dreadfully, frightful/ frightfully.* Like them, *terrible* intensifies something by definition bad (*a terrible mistake*) and *terribly* intensifies adjectives and other adverbs generally (*terribly important/ not terribly good*). Informally, *terrible* is used disparagingly with neutral nouns (*a terrible speaker/What a terrible name to give a baby!*). However, the adjective and adverb retain their literal meanings 'horrifying, horrifyingly' in contexts such as *a terrible cry, terrible consequences,* and *terribly disfigured.* By contrast, *terrific* when used with neutral nouns is not disparaging but approving (*a terrific meal/a terrific speaker*).

tertium quid /ˌtəːʃɪəm 'kwɪd/. A Latin phrase, apparently rendering Greek τρίτον τι 'some third thing', and meaning *sensu stricto* 'something indefinite or left undefined related in some way to two definite or known things, but distinct from both' (*New SOED*). An alloy of two metals or a chemical compound made from two elements might be called a *tertium quid.* But the phrase has been used to mean 'any third thing of a group of three' (the notion of indefiniteness being lost): in other words a third alternative or a middle course. Browning used it as the heading of book iv of *The Ring and the Book,* in which views are set forth about the culpability of the murderer Guido which are neither those of the 'Half-Rome' who have defended him in book ii nor those of 'The Other Half-Rome' who have condemned him in book iii. A new connotation was given to the expression when Kipling wrote a story called 'At the Pit's Mouth' (1888) beginning *Once upon a time there was a Man and his Wife and a Tertium Quid;* and the meaning 'the third party in an eternal triangle' is likely to be suggested by it. Some recent examples: Webster's Dictionary of English Usage *is a tertium quid, combining the virtues of the report and the pronouncement without their vices, and it is therefore a new breed of usage guide*—*English Today,* 1991; *Possibilities are opened up for another kind of Western, a secondary Western dealing with that New Man, the American tertium quid*—*Twenty Twenty,* 1991. Printed in roman.

terza rima /tɛːtsə 'riːmə/ (prosody), 'third rhyme' (printed in roman). A verse form invented by Dante Alighieri in his *Divina Commedia* (*c.*1320) and followed by many English poets, among them Byron, Shelley, and Browning. It consists of a sequence of TERCETS rhyming aba bcb cdc ded, etc. Dante's lines consisted of five iambic feet with an extra syllable (hendecasyllabic lines). The English poets mostly wrote in iambic pentameters. The essential point of the rhyming scheme is that the second line of each tercet provides the rhyme for the first and third lines of the next, thus producing an effect of unending continuity. An example from Byron (1819), with three tercets and a line:

Oh! more than these illustrious far shall be
The being—and even yet he may be born—
The mortal saviour who shall set thee free,
And see thy diadem, so changed and worn
By fresh barbarians, on thy brow replaced;
And the sweet sun replenishing thy morn,
Thy moral morn, too long with clouds defaced,
And noxious vapours from Avernus risen,
Such as all they must breathe who are debased
By servitude, and have the mind in prison.

tessera (square block in mosaics, etc.). Plural *tesserae* /-riː/.

testatrix /tɛ'steɪtrɪks/ (feminine equivalent of *testator*). For plural, see -TRIX 3.

test match. Originally (examples in the *OED* from 1862 onwards) one of a series of cricket matches between England and Australia. In the 20c., at various points, the term came to be used of official representative cricket matches between any of the major cricketing countries; and, since the 1920s (first in South Africa) of international rugby matches (except that in rugby football circles such matches are for the most part just called *internationals*).

tetchy. This spelling is more usual than *techy.* The word is more or less synonymous with *testy,* meaning 'irritable, peevish'. *Touchy,* on the other hand, most often means 'apt to take offence, oversensitive' rather than 'irritable', but potential or actual irritability lies at the heart of all three words.

tête-à-tête. The accents and hyphens are obligatory, but the word is normally printed in roman, not italics. Plural the same, or *tête-à-têtes*, pronounced like the singular.

tetralogy. A group of four related plays, speeches, operas, etc.; *spec.* (*Gk Antiq.*) a series of four dramas, three tragic and one satyric, performed in Athens at the festival of Dionysus. (*New SOED*)

tetrameter (prosody). A line of four metrical feet, as in Coleridge's *Christabel* (1816): e.g. *A little child, a limber elf, Singing, dancing to itself.*

text (verb). **1** The meaning most familiar to people today, namely 'to send a text message' (see TEXT MESSAGE) has revived this formerly obsolete verb, first cited in 1564, and used later in the 16c., by Shakespeare among others, to mean 'to write in large or capital letters': *Yea and text underneath, here dwells Benedick the married man—Much Ado about Nothing,* 1600. In its modern meaning, the *OED* dates the first citation to 1998.

2 *Text* or *texted* as past? (*a*) People are often confused about how to say or write the past tense and past participle of this verb. If it conformed to the pattern of regular verbs in English, as newly created verbs do, its past tense and past participle would be *texted.* (Dictionaries do not explicitly state this, because they do not show inflections for regular verbs, but they imply it in examples showing the past.) However, at least in speech, the form *text* is often used, and some people have even commented that *texted* sounds wrong. What is the explanation?

(*b*) My conclusion is that the explanation must be phonetic. I shall state the argument, which is slightly technical, as briefly as I can. (i) New verbs in English are always regular, i.e. they add the suffix *-ed* to create their past forms. (ii) At the same time, there are many common verbs with identical present and past forms, e.g. *cut, put, set* (and *fit* in AmE). *Text* as a past form would fit that pattern, thereby making it 'legitimate', but including it among those irregular verbs still does not explain why it should be an exception to a universal rule in the first place. (iii) The answer must lie in other words which end in the identical sound cluster /kst/. Other than in the very common word *next,* that sound cluster is most commonly found in the past forms of verbs ending in the letter *x* in their base form, e.g. *annexed, artexed, banjaxed, Botoxed, climaxed, detoxed, faxed, flexed, foxed, hoaxed, vexed,* and over 100 others listed in the *OED.* Such verbs therefore constitute a substantial group in the mental lexicon, which could influence how people deal with *text.* (iv) If we take *vex* from this group as our example paralleling *text,* the base form ends with the sound /ks/ and the past adds the /t/ sound, which for the verbs in this group represents the past tense morpheme *-ed* (as it does for other verbs ending in unvoiced consonants, e.g. *ducked, stopped*). It seems, then, that when *text* is used as the past tense or participle, the final /t/ sound is being interpreted as this morpheme, as if the present tense of the verb were *tex.* This phenomenon seems less irregular if one bears in mind that *text* is often pronounced /tɛks/ in any case, with the final /t/ sound dropped.

3 *Recommendation.* For the time being, avoid writing *text* as the past tense or past participle. At some stage, dictionaries may acknowledge the weight of usage, and accept it.

text message. A *text message* (usually abbreviated to *text* for short) is a 'written message which is transmitted electronically, especially a short, keyed message sent from one mobile phone to another, or via the Internet'. The limitations of the screen format of earlier generations of mobile phone have given rise to ingenious conventions for abbreviating the written language and reducing the awkwardness of the miniature environment in which the message appears. Some of these use existing abbreviations such as the ampersand (&) and the 'at' sign (@). Others employ phonetic substitutions, such as 'l8' (= late), '2nite' (= tonight), 'thx'(= thanks), 'u' (= you), 'soz' (= sorry) and 'lol' (= 'laughing out loud', but often mistakenly and notoriously interpreted as 'lots of love') . Concerns that this practice might corrupt use of language more generally are misconceived; such practices are as old as writing itself, and because they are a response to the restrictions of the medium they do not normally extend beyond it. It is also worth noting that analogous abbreviations are used in other languages such as French, German, Italian, Spanish, etc.

textual, textural. The first means 'of, in, or concerning a text of any kind (*textual emendation, textual criticism*)'; whereas *textural* means 'of or belonging to texture (of paint, fibres, music, etc.)'. The writer of the following sentence chose the wrong word: *He seems to be moving into popular journalism, and away from textural criticism.*

thalamus. Plural *thalami* /-mʌɪ/.

Thalia. See MUSES.

than.

1 *than* and *prefer.*
2 Part of verb after *rather than.*
3 *different than.*
4 *other than.*
5 *barely . . . than, hardly . . . than, scarcely . . . than.*
6 *than* as conjunction and preposition.
7 Reflexive pronouns after *than.*
8 *than* and inversion.
9 *than* after non-comparatives.
10 Miscellaneous standard uses of *than.*

1 *than* and *prefer.* For the criticized use of *than* after *prefer,* see PREFER 4. Correct use of *prefer* followed by *rather than*: *I* preferred *to write, to explore the world of imagination,* rather than *to mix with others*—J. Frame, 1984.

2 Part of verb after *rather than.* Infinitive or gerund, etc., after *rather than.* See RATHER 3.

3 *different than.* See DIFFERENT 1.

4 *other than.* On the competing merits of *other than* and *otherwise than,* see OTHER 3. Evidence for the validity of various uses of *other than* (with *other* employed in more than one part of speech) continues to turn up. Examples: *it became clear that there was nothing other than social niceties to be shared*—M. Sutherland, 1974 (NZ); *the United States . . . will have no other choice than to reduce the costs of its overseas commitments*—*Dædalus,* 1987; *We were seen as . . . unable to conceive of any interpretation other than Hollis' being guilty*—P. Wright, 1987; *there were now no people other than the tall, silent, courteous white-uniformed servants*—F. King, 1988.

5 *barely . . . than, hardly . . . than, scarcely . . . than.* See BARELY; HARDLY 1; SCARCELY 1.

6 *than* as conjunction and preposition. In the type *Diana has better manners than I, than* is a conjunction, implying the ellipsis of *have* after *I.* By contrast, in the type *Diana has better manners than me, than* is a preposition followed by the objective form *me.* The second type is much less formal than the first. In practice, there is no distinction between the two types when the word after *than* is the same in the nominative case as in the objective, e.g. *He was shorter than Bertrand; He's older than you; Everything that lives in the sea has had a longer evolutionary history than anything on land.* Sometimes, in order to bring out that *than* is thought of as a conjunction, the 'implied' clause is written out in full: e.g. *I'll have to say this for them—they all feel better* than I do; *She has long black hair and is thinner* than I am; *He was a few years older* than I was; *his attitude was kind and generous to those less endowed* than he was. See also CASES 3; ME 2(*d*).

7 Reflexive pronouns after *than.* One means of avoiding the problem of whether to use a nominative or an objective pronoun after *than* (see 6 above) is to use a reflexive pronoun instead, but the result is often rather less than satisfactory. Examples: *One of the most encouraging performances came from Darren Cook . . . against senior athletes with far more experience than himself*—*Grimsby Gaz.,* 1986; *Yes, I have one brother, five years, less one month, younger than myself and fifty times more successful*—conversation in Oxford, 1987; *It had often seemed as though the people in the poems were more real to the old man than himself and his brother Michael*—*Encounter,* 1989.

8 *than* and inversion. *No tariff-armed nation has got better entry for its potatoes to the U.S.A. market* than has Ireland; *The visit will be much more direct in its effect upon the war* than could be any indiscriminate bombing of open towns. Such inversions, deprecated by both the previous editors, are now rare. See INVERSION 2(*h*).

9 *than* after non-comparatives. Such originally Latin words as *inferior* and *superior, junior,* and *senior,* are not true comparatives and therefore cannot be construed with *than.* See SUPERIOR.

10 Miscellaneous standard uses of *than.* The following examples illustrate uses that would pass unnoticed as part of the ordinary standard language. They are drawn from a wide range of standard sources of the period since 1980. *More than 50 per cent of the members of the entertainment-industry-related unions are out of work; When no more than a lad he acquired this socially objectionable habit; Lanzman presses his Polish peasants far harder than he does the Nazis; He tended to look sideways, probably because he could see more clearly with one eye than with the other; They know that few things are better for them than amity; The extreme irritation one always feels when someone proves to be more percipient than one has decided they shall be; He loved wrecking even more than getting possession; It is possible to be better off out of work than in work; One need interrupt the narrative no further than to say this; You know better than to be late; Pat had been more involved than the others; The recent amnesty should be seen more as Solidarity's triumph than as the government's free initiative; I think I spoke no more harshly than was deserved; Girls are thought to need less food than boys; As if I were more absolutely my particular self than ever; There was nothing more important than that he get to Epsom for the start of the card.*

They underline the virtual necessity of the presence of a comparative (*more, less, better, harder,* etc.) in the vicinity of *than.* And they go some way to confirming that uncontroversial uses of *than* are far more numerous and more significant than constructions of the type *Diana has better manners than me* (see 6 above).

-th /θ/ **and -th** /ð/. Monosyllabic nouns ending in *-th* after a vowel sound sometimes differ in the pronunciation of the plural forms, i.e. vary between /θs/ and /ðz/. It is necessary to consider only those words whose plurals are in regular use, which excludes *dearth, ruth, sloth,* and many others. The common words *mouth, oath, path,* and *youth* all sound the plural as /ðz/, not /θs/. The equally common words *berth, birth, breath, death, fourth, girth, growth, myth,* and *smith* always have /θs/ in the plural form. Others again fluctuate between /θs/ and /ðz/, e.g. (/θs/ recommended) *cloth, heath, hearth, lath, wraith;* (/ðz/ recommended) *bath, sheath, truth.* It should be added that the verbs or verbal nouns connected with *bath, breath, cloth, mouth, sheath, teeth,* and *wreath* have /ð/, namely *bathe, breathe, clothe, mouthing, sheathe, teething,* and *wreathe.* Cf. also *northern, southern, smithy,* and *worthy,* all with /ð/.

thankfully. The ordinary adverbial use (= with thankfulness; in a thankful manner), which goes back to Anglo Saxon times, has continued in use over the centuries: e.g. *He accepted thankfully all my presents*—Defoe, 1725; *the Pacific Islands, which are not members of ANZUS, thankfully shelter under the ANZUS umbrella*—R. Muldoon, 1986; *Then, 'until Friday,' said Mrs Marsh, and shut the door thankfully behind her*—A. Brookner, 1992. Since the 1960s it has been joined by constructions in which *thankfully* is a SENTENCE ADVERB (= let us be thankful (that); fortunately), as in *Thankfully his injuries were not serious.* Modern example: *Thankfully, what Britain has always done best is weird stuff—Guardian,* 2012. The new use has not attracted the same level of criticism as that given to similar uses of *hopefully,* and must be considered standard.

thanks to. A correspondent wrote to Burchfield in 1988 complaining about the use of *thanks to* in such contexts as these: *Thanks to the hurricane, millions of trees were destroyed.* 'What is wrong with *because of* or *due to*?' he asked. The *OED* supplies the answer. Since the 17c. the phrases *thanks to* and *no thanks to* have been used positively or adversely or ironically, the first to mean 'thanks are due to' or 'owing to, as a result of', and the second 'no credit to, not because or by reason of'. A positive use of *thanks to*: *Thanks to better budgeting, I haven't been overdrawn since early 2003*—finance website, 2005. An ironic example: *Thanks to the rank stupidity of Steve Gillery's bride-to-be, he had to hold his stag night on Saturday morning and rush off to the ceremony during half-time in the afternoon*—M. Gist, 1993. Cf. the assertive use of *thank you very much* in: *I've got him now. Urhh! I know all I need to know about him, thank you very much*—K. Amis, 1988.

thank you. 1 In origin short for *I/we thank you,* it has inevitably produced a number of equivalent phrases showing varying degrees of formality and emphasis. In very formal circumstances it can be lengthened to *thank you so much,* or *thank you very much,* sometimes with the addition of *indeed* for good measure. *Thanks* is a shade less cordial than *thank you,* and *many* and *best* and *a thousand* *thanks* and *thanks awfully* are frequent elaborations of it. *Much thanks* is archaic, surviving through our familiarity with *For this relief much thanks* (the sentinel Francisco in *Hamlet*), and now only used humorously. The colloquial variant *Thanks a lot* has also become popular. If an acknowledgement of thanks is felt to be needed it will be *Don't mention it, Not at all,* or *You're welcome.*

2 A noticeable tendency to write *Thank you* as one word has emerged recently in private letters and also, for example, on bills at restaurants (*Thankyou for your lovely present; Thankyou for dining with us*). The standard form is still *Thank you* (two words), but when the formula is used as a noun it can, according to the *OED*, be written as one word, or hyphenated (*We send our thank-yous*), and when used attributively, (*a thank-you letter*) a hyphen is essential.

that (demonstrative pronoun). **1** It might be useful to begin the treatment of the multifaceted word *that* by setting down a series of examples of the word used pronominally in an entirely usual way. All are drawn from standard sources of the 1980s and 1990s. As can be seen, many of these examples are formulaic or idiomatic, and this is shown in roman.

It goes deeper than that; *Something worth a lot of money,* that's for sure (informal); *It's the first to the store,* is that it?; *'You write clever stuff in* Varsity *and* Granta ...*don't you?* 'Something like that,' *said Tony; She had not meant it so, but it could have been read* like that; *That's the way it ought to be; A different kind of excitement from that roused by the park; All right, that's what she meant; So Boston stopped asking questions, while he was sober,* that is; What was all that about?; *She was innocent: that is all anybody has ever been able to draw out of him; What benefactor will continue voluntarily to sponsor that?; He didn't say that, or anything like it; Upsy a bit, dear,* that's a good girl; *He's a good officer*...*It's just he talks too much,* that's all; *She had a small, pretty face,* I'll give you that; *Hey, great work there, Toddie! Hey, look at that!* That's my boy (informal); *Too much of an easy touch,* that's me (informal); *Because if that happens, then I will be just like you*—isn't that so?; *Now how the hell did you manage that? You really are a one; The witnesses,* if they could be called that, *continued to repeat that they knew nothing; Their eyes tangled. 'I said "love", dammit.' 'Ah. That. I thought you said that.'; She cleared her throat to speak but* left it at that; *'He wasn't a straightforward man, Francis'.* 'That he wasn't.'

What stands out from these examples is that *that* used as a demonstrative pronoun is overwhelmingly anaphoric, i.e. directs the attention back to a word, statement, or circumstance mentioned previously. It may also be used formulaically: e.g. *that's it, that is* (*to say*), *that's all,* etc.

A somewhat uncommon anaphoric use—postponement of *that* to the end of a statement—is worth noting: e.g. *a neat comeuppance for the Japanese, that*—*NY Times,* 1990; *It all seemed a bit* [*too*] *good to be true, that*—N. Virtue, 1990; *'Well, you poor girl,' said Margaret, and Wendy added, 'Hard on a young person, that.'*—A. Brookner, 1993. This somewhat quirkish, but still standard, construction does not seem to be dealt with in the *OED.*

2 It is well to remember that all these uses of the pronoun *that* have a history of their own and are all likely to be encountered in pre-20c. contexts: e.g. *Look to me*... *That is look on me, and with all thine eyes*—Jonson, 1625; *'Very well,' cried I, 'that's a good girl.'*—Goldsmith, 1760; *A man began to scream, and that so loud that my voice was quite drowned*—J. Wesley, 1772; *Do you, my dear K, have them sent to me, that's a darling*—T. Arnold, 1849; *What do you think I would give to be your age, and able to draw like that!*—Ruskin, 1884.

3 *at that. The only seats available were at the back, and very uncomfortable at that.* This convenient use, described by the *OED* as 'orig. U.S. colloq. or slang', is first recorded in 1830, and is probably extended from such phrases as *cheap at that, dear at that* (*price*).

that (demonstrative adjective). The simple demonstrative adjective *that* is distinguished from the definite article *the* in that it *points out* something as distinct from merely *singling out* something. Some standard modern examples: *I don't feel that kind of attraction—lust you would call it; If I were he, I should keep an eye on that young man; What the painter intended to do was to introduce everything into that small space; That simple, honest, trusting marriage that had been theirs before Maria had appeared; Why did you take that picture* *of me?; It wasn't a nature reserve, that Ark of ours.* This type goes back to the earliest period of Middle English.

A subdivision of the same type, in which *that* is used to indicate quality or amount, and correlates with *that, as,* etc., was once common, but was archaic or unfashionable by the end of the 19c. Examples: *From me, whose loue was of that dignity, That it went hand in hand, euen with the Vow I made to her in marriage*—Shakespeare, 1602; *With that cunning and dexterity as is almost imperceavable*—Milton, 1648; *An Error of that Magnitude, that I cannot but wonder*—I. Walton, 1678; *He ... struck her ... with that heaviness, that she tottered on the marble floor*—Dickens, 1848. Fowler (1926) cites an unattributed example: *He has that confidence in his theory that he would act on it tomorrow.* But he admits that the type was 'formerly normal English'.

that (demonstrative adverb). Use of *that* as an adverb preceding an adjective or adverb, in phrases of the type *I was* that *angry,* i.e. 'so angry, very angry', and its negative counterpart, *things aren't really* that *bad, it wasn't* that *long ago,* has been slipping into and out of standard language since it was first recorded in the 15c. As *MWCDEU* points out, it was condemned by Alford in the mid 19c. and several later commentators followed suit. Echoing this disapproval, in 1912 the *OED* labelled the affirmative use as 'Now *dial.* and *Sc[ottish]*' and the negative as 'colloq[uial]'.

Usage has moved on, but some affirmative uses may still be considered informal, whereas negatives (or interrogatives) have been standard for quite some time, as the following examples show: *It's not* that *easy in a place like Sheffield*—*Spare Rib,* 1977; *'Shut up,' says Claudia ... 'It's not* that *funny'*—P. Lively, 1987; *The questioning attitude that comes naturally at student age is not that easily abolished*—*Listener,* 1987; *You and your brother, you're not really that alike, are you* —*Encounter,* 1989; *Do they think the American people are* that *stupid?*—*CNN* (transcripts), 2007. In contrast, some affirmative uses had and still have an informal ring, e.g. *I was on my guard for a blow, he was* that *passionate*—Dickens, *Bleak House* (the character speaking uses slightly informal language); *I've been that worried. I thought I'd lost you*—D. Lodge, 1988. But others seem completely standard, e.g. *The CGI* [*sc.* computer-generated imagery] *is unbearable. The werewolves look almost cartoonish, it's* that *bad*—*OEC,* 2004; *'We're really striving for fair prices for every farmer and every buyer. It's* that *simple,' McDowell says*—*Rural Cooperatives,* 2004. The slightly different use of adverbial *that* followed by a result clause is unusual in standard writing, e.g. *I was that ashamed I didden know w'ere to look*—D. L. Sayers, 1937. Cf. ALL THAT.

that (conjunction). **1** Kinds of clause attached by *that* (conjunction). The conjunction *that* is legitimately used to join a subordinate clause to a preceding verb or its parts in the manner shown in the following examples: (preceded by a finite verb) *They understood* that *this was an errand of mercy;* (infinitive precedes) *I would hate to feel* that *we were corrupting you;* (past participle precedes) *He had taken it for granted* that *any compatriot of Louis Pasteur must have seen a needle or two;* (verb *to be* precedes) *It wasn't* that *Peter and I were being singled out;* (*that* repeated when introducing a second subordinate clause) *He later discovered* that *it was St. Lucy's Day, and* that *this was a ceremony associated with its celebration;* (*that* (conjunction) followed by *that* (demonstrative adjective)) *he realized* that that *sprint was all that was left.* In every such *that*-clause the sentence out of which it is made or completed by prefixing *that* must be in the form of a statement, not a question, command, or exclamation. Sentences like the following type are best rephrased: *Crises, international or national, arise so rapidly in these days* that *who can say what a few years may bring forth?* (replace *who* by *no one* and delete the question mark). A *that*-clause may sometimes, in a rather forced manner, occupy the first position in a sentence: e.g. That *any compatriot of Louis Pasteur must have seen a needle or two he had taken for granted;* That *England would win was hoped for.* But such reversals of the natural clause order are not common, and indeed are not possible in some of the examples cited in the first paragraph above.

2 Omission of the conjunction *that* is standard, not only in informal contexts, e.g. *They understood* (*that*) *this was an errand of mercy; I would hate to feel* (*that*) *we were corrupting you.* But self-evidently it must be retained in some of the examples cited in the first paragraph above. When the conjunction *that* is part of the correlative pairs *so ... that, such ... that, now that* (or *so that*, etc.), it is normally retained in formal writing but is sometimes omitted in informal contexts, e.g. *What would he do now* (*that*) *he had missed him in Toulouse?; The heat was up so high* (*that*) *almost everyone took off their coats. That* may not be omitted, however, if a phrase or clause intervenes between the verb and it, e.g. *I am saying, am I not,* that *I no longer loved Kioyoko.*

that (relative pronoun).

1 *that* or *who* referring to people?
2 *That* omitted as relative pronoun.
3 Definition of the terms 'restrictive' and 'non-restrictive'.
4 Is *that* obligatory in 'restrictive' clauses?
5 *That* more idiomatic than *which*: special cases.
6 Examples.

1 *that* or *who* referring to people? (*a*) 'How many well-educated people have you heard say *Those are the people* that *attended the play?*'—thus a gloomy correspondent to a major newspaper, echoing a widely held belief that *that* as a relative pronoun should never be used when the antecedent is human. What in fact is the rule in such cases? A human antecedent is normally followed by *who* (rather than *that*) in a restrictive clause (*But it was I* who *got away to the steps up to the morning room*). An inanimate antecedent naturally calls for *that* (or *which,* as appropriate): *an electric blanket* that *knows how to warm various parts of the body; the bus* that *bore us away. That* is often used in contexts in which the antecedent is animate but not human (*a white poodle* that *sported a red hair bow*), and also in contexts where the antecedent is human but representative of a class (*a baby* that *cries in unsocial hours; a fellow* that *sells a bracelet is not necessarily interested in people*). *That* can also replace *who* (or *whom*) when the reference is non-specific, as in *The person* that *I saw was definitely a woman.*

(*b*) Down through the centuries, *that* has often been used with a human antecedent. Chaucer, Langland, and Wyclif are all cited in the *OED* using *that* in this way, and examples are also given from writers in each of the later centuries. Modern literature abounds with writers who keep to the rule that only *who* is appropriate when the antecedent is human (whether a specified person or one representative of a class). Thus, from Penelope Fitzgerald's *The Golden Child* (1977): *And the vast, patient public*... who *would soon be filing across the Museum courtyard to proffer their money at the entrance; The Russians have made a very considerable loan to Garamantia* [name of a fictitious country], who *is anxious to develop her agriculture; I know that there are some people in the service* who*'d rather not have them let in at all; a wonderfully good representation of the sea by a people* who *had never beheld it.*

(*c*) *Summary.* Normally use *who* as the relative pronoun following a human antecedent and *that* (or *which*) following an inanimate antecedent. Either *who* or *that* may be used when the antecedent is animate but not human, or when the antecedent is human but representative of a class. In contexts containing a double antecedent, of which the first is human and the second inanimate, *that* is naturally required (*he answered accusingly*... *as though it was she and not the drug* that *had done it*).

2 *That* omitted as relative pronoun. One of the most capricious features of our language is the way in which some seemingly necessary elements may be omitted without loss of meaning or dislocation of syntax. From the 13C. onwards the relative *that* has been omissible in a variety of circumstances. Modern examples: *It reminded him of the Exhibition* ʌ *he was going back to*—P. Fitzgerald, 1977; *and that lipstick* ʌ *she used to put on*—H. Mantel, 1985; *it was your geography* ʌ *caused the doubt*—T. Stoppard, 1993. For further discussion of this phenomenon and additional examples, see CONTACT CLAUSES; OMISSION OF RELATIVES.

3 *Definition of the terms 'restrictive' and 'non-restrictive'.* Take two sentences or parts of sentences from Anita Brookner's *A Family Romance* (1993): *with the ball-point pen which my father had bought for me in a curiously shaped department store; This sharpness of gaze gave her an air of vanity, which I dare say was justified.* The first contains what is known as a 'restrictive' clause led by *which.* In it *which* could have been replaced by *that* without any change of meaning and without offending any rule of syntax. The second contains a 'non-restrictive' use of *which* preceded by a comma, and that comma is obligatory (as is a comma to close off the non-restrictive clause if it is followed by something else, e.g. *A new edition of the book, which has taken ten years to write, is published today*). In the first sentence the *which*-clause defines and gives essential information, telling us exactly which pen is meant; and *that* would have done the same work just as well. In the second example, the *which*-clause provides additional information as a kind of parenthetic aside. In other words it is a non-restrictive clause. *That* is not generally used, and is best avoided, in non-restrictive clauses.

4 Is *that* obligatory in 'restrictive' clauses? (*a*) The short answer is a qualified no, since it depends to an extent on where you live. In AmE *which* is not generally used in restrictive clauses, and that fact is then interpreted as the absolute rule that only *that* may introduce a restrictive clause. In BrE, one might say in a typically British compromise, either *that* or *which* may be used in restrictive clauses, as the examples at 6 (*a*) and (*b*) illustrate. However, it has to be added that many British people, including editors and even those who teach language and writing skills, believe that *that* is obligatory. And the most pervasive editor of all, the grammar checker in Microsoft's Word, will pull you up whenever you use *which* to introduce a restrictive clause.

(*b*) The division of labour between the relative pronouns is far from being an absolute one. In 1926 Fowler wisely observed: 'The relations between *that, who,* and *which,* have come to us from our forefathers as an odd jumble, and plainly show that the language has not been neatly constructed by a master-builder who could create each part to do the exact work required of it, neither overlapped nor overlapping; far from that, its parts have had to grow as they could.' He went on to stress that not all writers observe the distinction between restrictive clauses (which he called *defining clauses*) and non-restrictive clauses (which he called *non-defining clauses*): 'The two kinds of relative clauses, to one of which *that* and to the other of which *which* is appropriate, are the defining and the non-defining; and if writers would agree to regard *that* as the defining relative pronoun, and *which* as the non-defining, there would be much gain both in lucidity and in ease. Some there are who follow this principle now; but it would be idle to pretend that it is the practice either of most or of the best writers.' AmE usage has largely put Fowler's recommendation into practice.

5 *That* more idiomatic than *which*: special cases. *That* is the more natural and idiomatic choice in speech (as is leaving the relative pronoun out altogether, as at 2). In addition, *that* is more usual (i) when *which* already occurs earlier in the sentence in another role (*Which is the house that you bought?*); (ii) after indefinite pronouns such as *anything, everything, nothing,* and *something* (*There is something that I forgot to mention*); (iii) after a construction with the impersonal *it* (*It is the new one that we want*).

6 *Examples.* All are drawn from standard modern sources: (*a*) 'restrictive' *that*-clauses: *Everything* that *lives in the sea has had a longer evolutionary history than anything on land; it was Labour Party politics* that *captured his youth; boundaries* that *one would like to see kept distinct have blurred; the great new glass tower* that *housed Eldorado Television.*

(*b*) 'restrictive' *which*-clauses: *he is described frequently . . . in terms* which *will set your teeth on edge; the villa in Italy . . .* which *she and Arthur were being pressed to visit; She was coming from the Rhodesian girls' school* to which . . . *she was sent because her father had grown up in Salisbury; He sat there with one foot on a fruitbox to support the leg* on which *the guitar rested; the procedures . . . are those* into which *young ladies are to be inducted; the legal and political anomalies* which *exclusion of the Catholics has given rise to.*

(*c*) 'non-restrictive' *which*-clauses preceded by an obligatory comma, and closed by one where applicable: *She held out her hand,* which *I clasped in both of mine; Baxandall makes it sound not just boring but unnecessary,* which *is severely to misunderstand our intention; his company plane, a Citation jet,* which *he uses to visit his stores; my father's last illness,* which *she persisted in seeing as a fantasy and betrayal; You bought a Depression bargain,* which *I tipped you off to; Besides him being a poodle,* which *is not one of your heroic breeds of dog; Dickinson's contract,* which *has four years to run, would be paid in full; the concomitant of ownership,* which *is the right to alienate property.*

the.

1 *The* in titles of books, etc.
2 With names of illnesses.
3 The type *Prime Minister Cameron*.
4 Pronunciation.
5 *by the hundred*, etc.
6 Omission of a second *the*.
7 *the* with two nouns and a singular verb.

For some other uses of *the*, see DEFINITE ARTICLE.

1 *The* in titles of books, etc. In ordinary contexts *The* should always be retained when it is part of the title of a book, poem, journal, etc.: *The Times, The Old Curiosity Shop, The Lay of the Last Minstrel, The Doctor's Dilemma, The Merry Wives of Windsor, The Oxford English Dictionary, The Chicago Manual of Style.* It should be borne in mind, however, that some familiar titles are reduced forms of the original ones: for example, Shakespeare's *Hamlet* was originally *The Tragedie of Hamlet Prince of Denmarke. The* is usually omitted or reduced to lower-case romans 'the' in abbreviated forms of titles: e.g. the *OED*; *Merry W.* or even *M.W.W.*; *Lay of Last Minstrel.* Kingsley Amis (*Spectator*, 6 Sept. 1986) maintained that the type *Harold Robbins, whose* The Storyteller *shows* was 'not English': he insisted that the language does not tolerate a possessive followed by the definite article. Write *Robbins, whose novel* The Storyteller ... instead, he suggested. Not everyone agreed. In practice there is considerable variation. In a single issue (autumn 1994) of *Letters* (the journal of the Royal Society of Literature), for example, were found: *Kenneth Tynan once wrote in the* New Yorker; *J. R. R. Tolkien's* Lord of the Rings; *Trollope's* The West Indies and the Spanish Main; *Devlin's* The Judge; *Izaak Walton's* Compleat Angler.

All five examples either broke Amis's Law or simply omitted the *The* of the original title.

2 *With names of illnesses.* See MEASLES; MUMPS.

3 The type *Prime Minister Cameron.* This construction, in place of the more traditional *the Prime Minister*, i.e. with omission of *the* before an occupational title and the addition of a person's surname, sometimes also with the first name, is embedded in AmE and becoming more so in BrE. It is especially common in journalistic work. Examples: *Vocalist Bjork, meanwhile, has taken her first acting role in a television play*—*Melody Maker*, 1988; *Two recent publications, the report of the National Commission on children ..., and a more popular work, by economist Sylvia Ann Hewlitt, suggest* [etc.]—*Dædalus*, 1993; *That means it's very detrimental to overseas investment in creative sectors, something Prime Minister Cameron said he wants to see more of*—*The Register*, 2012.

4 *Pronunciation.* The definite article is the most common word in the language. Yet it is remarkable how many speakers ignore the traditional rule that, while it is pronounced /ðə/ before a word beginning with a consonant (*the tree* /ðə triː/), it is /ðɪ/ before a word beginning with a vowel (*the adverb* /ðɪ ˈadvəːb/) and /ðiː/ when stressed.

5 *by the hundred*, etc. *Ashcroft began enforcing a rule that required non-U.S. citizens to notify the federal government whenever they move. Change of address cards have been pouring into the government office* by the hundreds *of thousands.* Fowler insisted that 'the idiomatic English is *by the hundred thousand*; *by hundreds of thousands* will also pass, but with the plural *the* is not used. So also with *dozen, score*, etc.' However, his rule is widely flouted.

6 Omission of a second *the.* The definite article is normally dispensed with before the second of two nouns joined by *and*: *The distortion and innuendo to which several of your correspondents have resorted*; *They throw valuable light on the ethos and attitudes of the ruling elite.* But it should be noted that a second *the* may be inserted (for emphasis or other contextual reasons) in such sentences. The same considerations do not apply to the second of two adjectives. For example, *the black and white penguins* has a different meaning from *the black and the white penguins*, and *the red and yellow tomatoes* (one group) is likely to differ in meaning from *the red and the yellow tomatoes* (two separate groups).

7 *the* with two nouns and a singular verb. A composite subject of the type *'the* + noun + *and* + noun', if thought of as a single theme, may be followed by a singular verb. See AGREEMENT 3. Examples: The innocence and purity *of their singing* comes *entirely from their identification with the character*—B. Levin, 1985; The respect and freedom *that money can buy* has *made me not one jot happier than in my former years of penury*—B. Rubens, 1985; The power and wealth *of the United States* is *a natural source of envy*—*Daily Tel.*, 1987.

theatre. So spelt in BrE, but usually **theater** in AmE. See -RE AND -ER.

thee, objective case of the pronoun *thou*, has very little currency now (having been effectively replaced by *you*) except in verse surviving from older times (*Hail to thee, blithe Spirit!*—Shelley, 1820; *Dost thou love me, cousin? . . . I have loved thee long*—Tennyson, 1842), in humorous or regional verse (*Dreamin' of thee! Dreamin' of thee*—E. Wallace, 1900), and in biblical contexts (*Get thee behinde me, Satan*—Bible (Geneva), Matt., 1560). It is also used as nominative case (a use unaccounted for) by Quakers (*Perhaps thee has noticed the point in our* Friends Journal *on February 15*—*Friend*, 1964).

their. 1 Fowler (1926) was among those who objected to the use of *their* in contexts that call 'logically' for *his* (though this use of the masculine gender to cover both is now contentious) or *his or her*. Examples: *But does anyone in* their *heart really believe that Ireland is only that?*; *no one can be easy in* their *minds about the present conditions of examination.*

The issue is unresolved, but it begins to look as if the use of this plural third person determiner to refer back to a singular pronoun is now passing unnoticed by standard speakers (except those trained in traditional grammar) and is being left unaltered by some copy editors, though among many it is a bone of contention. Its value lies in its being gender-neutral and avoiding the inherent sexism of *his* and the cumbersomeness of *his or her*. Examples: *I feel that if someone is not doing* their *job it should be called to* their *attention*—an American newspaper, 1984; *Everyone was absorbed in* their *own business*—A. Motion, 1989; *A mission statement that is sufficiently bland to encompass everyone's conception of* their *role in the university is of little use to anyone*—*Dædalus*, 1993.

2 This possessive personal determiner is to be carefully distinguished from *there* (adverb, noun, and interjection) and *they're* = 'they are'.

theirs. How many teachers at all levels need to point out daily that the correct spelling of *theirs* (and *ours, yours*) is not *their's* (etc.)? The misconception about the spelling is not all that surprising, perhaps, when one recalls the memorable lines from Tennyson's *Charge of the Light Brigade* (1855), *Their's not to make reply, Their's not to reason why, Their's but to do and die.* In compound subjects connected by *and*, the correct form is (e.g.) *Our children and theirs went on holiday together*, not **Theirs and our children went on holiday together.*

theirselves. 'From the 14th c. there has been a tendency to treat *self* as a noun (= person, personality), and substitute *their* for *them* . . . This is prevalent dialectally, but in literary Eng. has place only where an adj. intervenes, as *their own, sweet, very selves*' (*OED*). Example of a use of *theirselves*: *But they've only got theirselves to thank for it, I'm afraid*—P. Lively, 1991. See HISSELF.

them. 1 As the *OED* says, it is 'often used for "him or her", referring to a singular person whose sex is not stated, or to *anybody, nobody, somebody, whoever*, etc.'. Example: *Nobody else . . . has so little to plague them*—C. Yonge, 1853.

2 Its use as a demonstrative pronoun, permissible in standard sources from the 15c. onwards, is now only dialectal or non-standard except in the humorous type *them's my sentiments.* Examples: *Them be my two children*—L. J. Jennings, 1877; *Them as says there's no has me to fecht*—J. M. Barrie, 1891; *We're out here to do justice and keep the peace. Them's my sentiments*—E. M. Forster, 1924.

3 As a demonstrative adjective, *them* has been downgraded in the 20c. (it is first recorded in the late 16c.) and now is only dialectal or non-standard. From the late 16c. to the 19c. it seems to have been in standard use. Examples: *I hope, then, the agent will give you encouragement about them mines*—M. Edgeworth, 1809–12; *Them ribbons of yours cost a trifle, Kitty*—S. Lover, 1842; *I've done all them skirting boards, but me back's not what it was*—J. Winterson, 1985; *I didn't know much about planes in them days*—P. McCabe, 1992.

themself. The normal emphatic and reflexive form of *they* and *them* is, of course, *themselves.* The *OED* reports standard uses of the alternative form *themself* from the 14c. to the 16c., but then it seems to have lost its grip on the language and disappeared from sight. A remarkable byproduct of the search for gender-neutral pronouns, *themself* re-emerged in the 1980s. It is a minority form, but one that turns up from time to time in Britain, North America, and doubtless elsewhere. The plural form *themselves* is also used in this way, but the effect is if anything more awkward: *It may be best, however, to confess to someone who will never meet her boyfriend, ... just in case that third party got tremendously drunk at a party themselves, and blurted it out to someone else*—*Independent*, 1998. The final battle for a set of gender-free pronouns will probably be fought over *themself*, but it is hard to see what could comfortably replace it in the following examples: *It is not an actor pretending to be Reagan or Thatcher, it is, in grotesque form, the person themself*—I. Hislop, 1984; *I think somebody should immediately address themself to this problem*—A. T. Ellis, 1987; *After all, how could anyone defend themself against the soft-focus sleaze of a show like 'A Current Affair'?*—*Chicago Sun-Times*, 1991; *a principal who desires to acquire the tobacco for use or consumption by themself or other persons at their expense*—Canadian legal context in *English Today*, 1994.

then. Two uses, one adjectival the other adverbial, call for comment. **1** (adjective) Murmurs are occasionally heard against the type *the then Bishop of London* (= the person who was the Bishop of London at the time), especially if a hyphen has been inserted between *then* and the noun that follows. But *then* has been used to modify a noun continuously since the late 16c. It is now often used also in front of an adjective or participial adjective (*the then astronomical sum, the then floundering Paramount studios*). It is hard to see why anyone should object to this use, since it is both economical and clear. In both uses, hyphens are unnecessary, and most writing avoids formulations such as **Japan's then-embryonic biotechnology industry*; **a conclusion of then-White House Counsel Fred Fielding*.

2 Tail-end *then* (adverb). *Then* is frequently used, at least in BrE, 'as a particle of inference, often unemphatic or enclitic' (*OED*), sometimes merely as part of a formulaic farewell greeting, e.g. *As Lucas continued to stare at the window, Clement said, 'Well, goodbye then.'*—I. Murdoch, 1993; *I say. That time already? Good-night, then*—B. Neil, 1993; *He rose from his chair, patting his pockets, and said, 'So, well, I'll be off, then.'*—idem, 1993. It is also often used as the final element of an interrogative sentence: e.g. *'Not too much trouble getting here, then?' asked my father genially*—A. Brookner, 1993. It is also used as a stronger 'particle of inference' when the implied meaning is something like 'in that case': e.g. *What had she sat next to him for in the first place, then?*—M. Eldridge, 1984 (Aust.).

thence is a formal or literary word meaning 'from a place or source previously mentioned' or 'as a consequence': *At first, bishops were regarded as equals of the people, but gradually they took upon themselves arbitrary powers. Thence arose the rigid distinction between clergy and laity*—S. Kreis, 2001; *These boxes are shipped from Varna to Whitby and thence to Carfax*—M. Drabble, 2000. Use of *from* before *thence*, despite its evident tautology, is established and idiomatic: *From thence he made his way to Egypt*—D. Ford et al., 2002. The word is no longer used in spoken English.

See also FROM WHENCE.

theoretic, theoretical. As adjectives the two forms have coexisted in the language since the 17c., but *theoretical* is several dozen times more frequent than *theoretic*. The latter, if used on its own, features mainly in AmE. The longer word forms compound adjectives such as *games theoretical* or *information theoretical*, etc., relating to the theory so mentioned i.e. games theory, information theory, etc.

thereabout(s). One of the medieval compound adverbs in *there-* that survive in common use without hint of any archaism, the others being *thereby, therefor*(*e*), and *thereupon*. The form with final *-s*, which is recorded from about 1400 onwards, is now the more usual of the two (*it all changed in 1970 or thereabouts*; *there or thereabouts*). The casualty rate of adverbs in *there-* is high (see THEREAFTER; THEREAT; THEREFOR), and one wonders how many of these words will still be in regular use in the centuries ahead.

thereafter. One of several traditional adverbs in *there-* now restricted to formal use, especially in legal documents or ceremonial language. It was first recorded in Old English (King Alfred). Other formal words in *there-* include *therein* (first recorded in OE), *thereof* (OE), *thereto* (OE), and *theretofore* (*c.*1350).

thereat. One of several adverbs in *there-* now falling or fallen into disuse after centuries of routine service in the language. It was first recorded in Old English. Other archaistic words in *there-* include *therefrom* (first recorded *a*1250), *thereinto* (*a*1300), *thereon* (OE), *thereout* (OE), *therethrough* (*c.*1175), *thereunto* (*c.*1300), *therewith* (OE), and *therewithal* (*a*1300). *Thereanent* (*c.*1340) is an archaic Scotticism.

therefor. An adverb now mainly in legal use, stressed on the second syllable, and meaning 'for that object or purpose, for that reason, for it'. Examples (from the *OED*): *He shall supply a copy of such report... on payment of the sum of one shilling therefor* (1885); *The ill-used crew promptly refused to do any more in her, and were, of course, clapped in jail therefor* (1899). Other examples (from Garner, 1987): *We are not unmindful of the sound and salutary rule, and of the obvious reasons therefor*; *The plaintiff discharged union cutters and shop foremen without just cause therefor.*

therefore. The most resilient of all the adverbs in *there-* and part of the central core of English since the 12c. Unlike THEREFOR it is always stressed on the first syllable, and can be placed in various positions in a sentence, including the beginning. **1** (*a*) In short sentences and in constructions in which *therefore* is associated with a particular word or phrase, it is not necessary to separate it with commas: *Would I please therefore oblige her by using the musical notation provided—Guardian*, 1986; *The relationship of patronage was therefore complex*—R. Greene, 1993. (*b*) When commas are used, *therefore* becomes parenthetical and its force tends to be spread over the whole sentence in the same way as *however* (though with opposite meaning): *Although, therefore, the element of surprise could not come into play on this occasion, the enemy were forced to withdraw; I trust, therefore, that you will accede to this request; It's unsurprising, therefore, that the most expensive restaurant meal of all time—costing over £44,000—was served here last year—Observer Food Monthly*, 2002.

2 When *therefore* comes at the beginning of a sentence, a following comma is optional and depends on the flow of the sentence: *You're not here as a solicitor... Therefore, you're entitled to call some other solicitor*—J. Wainwright, 1972; *The pound was falling against the Deutschmark. Therefore it was necessary to leave the ERM; Therefore I wear my 'power suit', I call it, if I have to go to a board in the conference room on the top floor with senior officials*—G. Kirkup et al., 1990. When it is immediately followed by a subordinate clause, it is more likely to be separated by a comma: *Therefore, when a battery shows signs of diminishing power and range effectiveness, it makes sense to replace it*—B. Smithson, 1988.

there is, there are. Before launching into a sentence beginning with *there* + a part of the verb *to be*, one must decide whether the following subject is actually or notionally singular or plural. In most circumstances no difficulties arise. Thus: *There* is *a spider in the bath;* but *There* were *many who disagreed with the speaker.* The choice is more difficult when the subject is more complicated than in these two examples. When the number of the following noun is more complex, choice is normally determined by what follows immediately; for example, *There* is *a pen and three sheets of paper on the desk* sounds more natural than *There* are *a pen and three sheets of paper on the desk.* Amounts regarded as a unit are also treated as singular: *There is £5000 in my account* (equivalent to 'the sum of £5000'). Use of *there is*, or more often *there's*, as an invariable formula regardless of number is often found but is only acceptable informally: There's *35 branches throughout the country. But for every big, dumb move like this,* there's *half a dozen small, smart details.*

Note. In constructions of these kinds, *there* is described by some scholars as *introductory* and by others as an *existential*, an *anticipatory*, or a *dummy* subject.

there you are. This colloquial expression of regret, reluctant acceptance, resignation, etc., always preceded by *but*, has been in common use since the mid-19c. and its currency remains unquestioned. Examples: *It's a pity we have to shoot so many of them but there you are*—L. P. Hartley, 1953; *The* *conversation was a bit one-sided mind, devoted as it was to the morality of laying waste the African rain-forests to make chairs for tourists, but there you are*—A. Coren, 1991; *I felt ridiculous of course, but there you are*—S. Wall, 1991.

there you go. An exceedingly common conventional phrase used by persons bringing a meal in a restaurant or an item or items bought in a shop, delivering the post, etc. Preceded by *but* it is also sometimes used instead of *but there you are* (see THERE YOU ARE). Examples: *So we trooped off to a nearby public toilet, not the most salubrious of venues, but there you go*—R. Elms, 1988; *There yeh go, he said.—Keep the change*—R. Doyle, 1991; *Evan handed over her change. 'There you go then.'*—B. Anderson, 1993.

thesaurus. Pronounced /θɪˈsɔːrəs/ (thi-**saw**-ruhs) stressing the second syllable, not the first. The plural is either *thesauruses* or *thesauri* /-ʌɪ/, the second being rather more frequent. See -US 1.

these. See KIND (noun) 2; SORT (noun) 2.

thesis. 1 For the sense 'dissertation', the plural is *theses* /ˈθiːsiːz/.

2 In Greek and Latin verse *thesis*, pronounced /ˈθiːsɪs/ or /ˈθɛsɪs/, is the term for an unstressed syllable or part of a metrical foot (as opposed to ARSIS).

they, their, them. 1 *one, anyone, everybody, nobody,* etc. followed by *they, their, them.* Over the centuries, writers of standing have used *they, their,* and *them* with anaphoric reference to a singular pronoun or noun, and the practice has continued into the 21c. to the point that, traditional grammarians aside, such constructions are hardly noticed any more or are not widely felt to lie in a prohibited zone. Fowler (1926) disliked the practice ('few good modern writers would flout the grammarians so conspicuously') and gave a number of unattributed 'faulty' examples, including the following: *The lecturer said that* everybody *loved* their *ideals*; Nobody *in* their *senses would give sixpence on the strength of the promissory note of that kind.*

The evidence presented in the *OED* points in another direction altogether. From the 16c. onwards *they* has often been 'used in reference to a singular noun [or pronoun] made universal by *every, any, no,* etc., or applicable to one of either sex (= "he or she")'. The examples cited by the *OED* include: Every Body *fell a laughing, as how could* they *help it*— Fielding, 1749; *If* a person *is born of a...gloomy temper...* they *cannot help it*— Chesterfield, 1759; Nobody *can deprive us of the Church, if* they *would*—W. Whewell, 1835; *Now,* nobody *does anything well that* they *cannot help doing*—Ruskin, 1866. Similar constructions are presented in the *OED* for *their* (from the 14c. onwards) and *them* (1742–). All such 'non-grammatical' constructions arise either because the notion of plurality resides in many of the indefinite pronouns or because of the absence in English of a common-gender third person singular pronoun (as distinct from *his* used to mean 'his or her' (now politically *verboten*) or the clumsy use of *his or her* itself).

Modern examples of *they, their,* and *them* used with singular reference may be found in this book in the articles for several of the indefinite pronouns, and also in the separate articles for THEIR and THEM. The process now seems irreversible.

2 *Muddles with collective nouns.* Consistency is essential. *The government* is *pressing ahead with* its *policy of privatization* is acceptable, and so (at least in BrE) is *The government* are *pressing ahead with* their *policy of privatization.* A mixture of numbers, e.g. *The government* is *pressing ahead with* their *policy of privatization,* should not be allowed to stand.

thief. Plural *thieves.* See -VE(D), -VES.

thimbleful. Plural *thimblefuls.* See -FUL.

thin has the derivative **thinness**.

thing. For the idiom *another thing coming,* see THINK (noun).

thingumajig, thingumabob, thingummy are the chief survivors of a large number of 18–19c. variants.

think (verb). **1** After *think, that* is usually omitted; see THAT (conjunction) 2.

2 For the transfer of negativity from *I don't think* to the following clause, see DO 5.

3 *think to* + infinitive. This construction, meaning 'to expect', is an old one (e.g. *I neuer thought to heare you speake againe*—Shakespeare, 1597). It survives to this day, though in some contexts its meaning is 'remember' rather than 'expect' (*Did you think to ask him for his address?*).

4 *no thinking man.* 'One of the bluffing formulae, like *It stands to reason* and *with respect,* that are intended to put the reader's or listener's back up and incline him or her to reject the view that is being presented'. While Gowers (1965) was able to write that, and Burchfield to repeat it in 1996, what is rather more likely to put many people's back up these days is the use of *man.* If the phrase is to be used at all, it had better be *no thinking person.*

think (noun). This late-coming word (not recorded until 1834, though the corresponding verb is Old English) is labelled *colloq.* in the *New SOED* (1993). It is commonly used in such sentences as *Have a think about it,* and *You have another think coming* 'you are greatly mistaken'. This last idiom is the original (1898), and always mirrors an expressed or implicit 'if you/he/etc think(s) . . . ', e.g. *If he thinks he will be blissfully free of directives and paperwork, he has another think coming*—*Independent,* 2002. Because the sound at the end of *think* and the beginning of *coming* is identical, i.e. /θɪŋk/ and /k-/, the word boundaries have been reanalysed as /θɪŋ/ /k-/, which produces *another thing coming.* Many people will consider that a mistake, although it is nearly as old (1906) as the original.

thinkable (adjective). This word, meaning 'able to be deemed real or actual; capable of being thought' seems not to have entered the language until the early 19c., some 450 years after its much more common antonym *unthinkable*: *A crash is a moment of panic when events are out of control and outlandish predictions become thinkable*—*Economist,* 1991.

thirties. See NINETIES.

this (demonstrative adjective). **1** The simple demonstrative adjective *this* is used 'to indicate a thing or person present or near (actually or in thought), esp. one just mentioned' (*OED*). Some standard modern examples of ordinary uncontentious uses: *I wanted to enjoy this room; Only in this way can one hope to reconstruct the physical landscape of the time; The allies endorsed this hegemony because they stood to benefit from it; At this time it was Bodley's custom to remain in London; He wasn't particularly active in this respect; Both this house and No. 45 will be converted.*

2 There is a long tradition in English of using *this* instead of *these* in concord with 'a numeral expression denoting a period of time taken as a whole (. . . usually = 'just past or completed')' (*OED*). Examples: *Within this three houres will faire Iuliet wake*—Shakespeare, 1592; *The silence has kept my own heart heavy this many a day*—Ruskin, 1867; *This last six months*—L. Oliphant, 1883. It is a small example of the way in which a lack of formal agreement is justified by the concept of notional agreement.

3 In narrative writing or speech, *this* is now used to refer in a familiar manner to a person, place, object, etc., not previously mentioned (usually taking the place of an indefinite article). The type seems to have emerged first in AmE in the 1920s. Examples: *He had this driver called Reg Whelan, father of seven*—T. Keneally, 1980; *He had this great little Nagra portable recorder for the birdcalls*—*New Yorker,* 1986; *She asked me to do this play for Icelandic television . . . It's about this girl. Her parents live in a huge house*—*Melody Maker,* 1988; *There was this man who trained his dog to go around the corner to Bud's Lounge with a dollar bill under his collar*—G. Keillor, 1989.

this (demonstrative adverb). Like *that* (see THAT (demonstrative adverb)), *this* is used in the sense 'to this extent or degree', very much in the manner of an intensive. Examples: *Perhaps this much of Plato is enough for one letter*—Ruskin, 1877; *I have a stack of telegrams this thick*—*Boston Sunday Herald,* 1967; *I haven't been this excited about farming for 25 years*—*The New Farm,* 2004; *Could 1950s Cambridge students really have been this pretentious?*—*Future Movies,* 2004; *Cycling surely hasn't been this popular in Britain since pre-internal combustion engine days*—*Guardian,* 2012.

this (demonstrative pronoun). This common pronoun is used to indicate 'a thing or person present or near (actually in space or time, or ideally in thought, especially as having just been mentioned and thus being present to the mind' (*OED*). Some typical modern examples from standard sources: *Am I going to undertake this just* *to oblige him?; What had I done to deserve this?; The result of all this was to re-open in Edith's mind the question...; One need interrupt the narrative no further than to say this; I started to wonder—could I be making this up?; All college scarves are like this anyway; Should governments do more, or ought this to be left to the private sector?.* The test of the validity of *this* is that it must be crystal-clear to what it refers. It is comparatively easy to slip into the fault of leaving it unclear precisely what the antecedent is.

thither. See HITHER.

-th nouns. There are large numbers of well-established words ending in *-th* with corresponding adjectives, verbs, etc., as *breadth* (cf. *broad*), *dearth* (cf. *dear*), *depth* (cf. *deep*), *growth* (cf. *grow*), *health* (cf. *whole*), *length* (cf. *long*), *tilth* (cf. *till*), *truth* (cf. *true*), *warmth* (cf. *warm*), *wealth* (cf. *well* or *weal*), *width* (cf. *wide*). Long ago, however, *-th* ceased to be a significant living suffix for new nouns. Horace Walpole coined *blueth, gloomth,* and *greenth,* but to no avail. *Blowth* 'a blossoming', *mowth* 'a mowing', and *spilth* '(an instance of) spilling' came into the language in the 17c. but are now dialectal, archaic, or obsolete. Ruskin's coinage *illth* (antonym of *wealth*) has achieved only the most limited currency.

those. See KIND (noun) 2; SORT (noun) 2.

tho, tho', informal (especially in AmE) or poetic spellings of *though*; the spelling *tho* is also useful shorthand in text messaging. Examples: *Tho' much is taken, much abides*—Tennyson, 1842; *Tho all the good food and wine and reefer was gone now*—*Black World,* 1973; *Tho' the trip's less than a mile it's still a dreary bore*—*NY Times,* 1982.

thou. See THEE.

though. 1 For the choice of *though* or *although,* see ALTHOUGH, THOUGH. In concessive clauses led by *although* or *though,* the former is almost always used by conservative writers. For example, Anita Brookner in her novel *A Family Romance* (1993): (p. 119) *I thought I detected a change in her,* although *I had not seen her for some weeks*; (p. 120) *Quite possibly,* although *this seemed grotesque to me, Dolly was in love*; (p. 121) *I saw that Dolly despised us,* although *she would never have admitted as much, even to herself*; (p. 135) *and* although *I wanted to cry and sob my eyes were quite dry and my face composed*; (p. 140) *it was my mother who was her true friend,* although *she had the company of the church ladies on Monday evenings.* In the sense 'and yet' the shorter form is used: (p. 120) *These* [*glances*] *were indulged without mercy,* though *unaffectedly.* And the shorter form is compulsory after *even*: (p. 163) *but I should be quite content to watch,* even though *it might mean seeing the equivalent of one of those television programmes my mother so enjoyed.* But see ALTHOUGH, THOUGH 3, for the Scottish *even although.*

2 For *as though,* see AS 8.

thought shower. See BRAINSTORM, BRAINSTORMING.

thral(l)dom. Both spellings are correct. See -LL-, -L- 5.

thrash, thresh. Originally variants of the same word, now with pronunciations and spellings differentiated. To separate grain is *thresh,* to flog is *thrash. Thrash* is the usual spelling of figurative and transferred uses, e.g. to thrash one's opponents (in a game of cricket, etc.), to thrash out a problem. But both spellings are found for the senses 'to move one's limbs about violently' and 'to toss and turn (in bed)' (followed by *about*).

Threadneedle Street, Old Lady of. See SOBRIQUETS.

threaten (verb). For its use as a double passive, see PASSIVE VOICE 6(*a*).

three-peat (Also **threepeat**). An unappealing neologism (an altered form of *repeat*) of the late 1980s mainly in North American English: used both as a noun (= three consecutive victories in a (championship) series, originally in basketball), and a verb (to win a given contest three times in succession).

three-quarter(s). The noun expressing a fraction is *three-quarters* (usually hyphenated). In a rugby football team a *three-quarter* is one of two, three, or four players (*three-quarters*) positioned between the *half-back* and the *full-back.* When used attributively the form without final *-s* is obligatory: *the three-quarter line* (in rugby football), *three-quarter length* (coat, etc.), *three-quarter face* (in photography, the aspect between full face and profile), etc. Cf. *billiards* but *billiard ball, billiard table.*

threnody /ˈθrɛnədi/, a song of lamentation. The standard form, rather than *threnode* /ˈθrɛnəʊd/ (altered on model of *ode*).

threshold. Spelt with a single letter *h* (contrast *withhold*), but pronounced both /ˈθrɛʃəʊld/, or, with medial /h/ inserted, /ˈθrɛʃhəʊld/.

thrice. From about 1200 a regular word for 'three times', but now only archaic or poetical.

thrive (verb). The regular or 'weak' form *thrived* has won the centuries-old battle between irregular or 'strong' *throve* as past tense and *thriven* as past participle, which are now rarely used, largely in BrE, and have an aura of archaism.

throes. So spelt, as in *to be in the throes of*, to be struggling with the task of. Keep it carefully apart from *throws* 'propels' and *throws* (plural noun) (*allowed three throws with the javelin*).

through. 1 The construction *to be through with* something, meaning to have finished it, to be tired of it, etc., while more frequent in North American English than elsewhere, is part of World English and has a long history, e.g. *We were born into good society; and we are through with it: we have no illusions about it, even if we are fit for nothing better*—G. B. Shaw, 1934; *When will we be through with the events now happening in the world?—Art Business News*, 2001 (US); *I thought you were through with that terrible, childish tendency to scream over everything!—OED*, 2005 (BrE); *a comparison between what cohorts of one generation will pay in taxes before they're through with their mortal coils, and what other generations will pay—The Republic* (newspaper), 2004, (Canad.). The construction *be* + *through* + verbal noun, meaning to have finished doing something, is typically AmE: *'I'm through eating,' said my father, pushing his plate away—L. S. Schwartz*, 1989; *Kids don't need a shower and a brainwash when they're through watching it* [*sc.* a family film]—*DVD Verdict*, 2002.

2 The convenient AmE use of *through* to mean 'up to and including' (*Monday through Friday*) is familiar to standard speakers of BrE but is not often used by them except as a conscious Americanism. Examples: *they range from regimes of explicit rules and organizations at one end of the spectrum through private networks and informal conventions at the other—Dædalus*, 1991; *an eight-week summer program for disadvantaged children ages three through five*—ibid. 1993.

thru, an occasional non-standard AmE spelling of *through.* Examples: *I see the thing thru, alone*—e. e. cummings, 1917; *When she wuz little and she had stuttered thru a sentence—Black World*, 1971; *Available for S types right thru to Mk 10s it retails for 26 notes—Hot Car*, 1977. The spelling has a history of its own in the 20c. in American spelling-reform circles, but the American public has rejected it except in informal circumstances (private letters, memos, etc.) and in the traffic term *thruway* (= expressway).

thunderer. For *The Thunderer* = *The Times*, see SOBRIQUETS.

Thursday. For the adverbial use, see FRIDAY.

thus is a word with an awkward role in modern English. Used sparingly and appropriately, it is highly effective, whereas when overused it can seem stilted and affected. In any case, it brings with it an air of formality, forcing other words to sit up straight and stop misbehaving. It has two basic meanings, (i) 'in this way', and (ii) 'accordingly, therefore'. In the first meaning, it is placed in the same position as 'in this way' would be, but sits more comfortably before a verb or participle: *He persistently declines to extend to the Press that assistance* (*such as circulating in advance scripts of major speeches, or sticking to the text of speeches thus pre-released*) *which so greatly facilitates newspaper production—Church Times*, 1976. It is probably in this first meaning that it sounds most starchy, and can often be softened to 'in this way'.

In the second meaning, it can follow the word order used with *therefore*, except that if it begins a sentence it often seems clumsy: *Thus the parents, in conversation at home, are able to identify themselves with the place and people under discussion—Where*, 1972. In some uses, *thus* combines the two meanings: *He attempts to defamiliarize and deconstruct the text and thus account for its persuasive power—Review of English Studies*, 1984. Given its usefulness in linking ideas, it is hardly surprising that it occurs most often in technical and formal writing.

thusly (adverb). Despite *ODO*'s recognizing this word as an informal variant of *thus* in its meaning 'in this way', the following quote aptly illustrates the bemused derision with which many BrE speakers are likely to greet it: *Thusly—a word I picked up in Massachusetts and will give this single outing—if you are in that South Atlantic coaling station* [etc.]'—C. Freud in *The Times* (3 Aug. 1989). But its naturalness is more or less unquestioned in AmE (it was first recorded in the *OED* in an American source of 1865), and a string of examples lie in the Merriam Webster files. Their usage guide (1989) declares that '*thusly* is not now merely an ignorant or comic substitute for *thus*: it is a distinct adverb that is used in a distinct way in standard speech and writing.' Since the late Clement Freud's comment, the word has spread its joyous hilarity into BrE and other varieties. Examples: *The division of responsibilities evolved thusly, with the help of a business consultant who enabled them to focus on specific areas—Art Business News*, 2002 (US); *It will work thusly: you send us your suggestions, we'll collate the top ten* (*most popular, or just ones we like*) *and hold a poll to determine the winner—The Register*, 2004.

thyme. Though ultimately from Greek θύμον, it seems to have had initial /t/ from the time of its adoption (15c.) in English from French. It was frequently spelt *tyme* or *time* in former times (15–18c.). By contrast, some scientific words derived ultimately from Greek θύμον, as *thymene, thymidine, thymine, thymol*, always have initial /θ/ in English.

-tiation. See -CIATION, -TIATION.

tibia /ˈtɪbɪə/. Plural *tibiae* /-bɪiː/; also *tibias*, even in technical or academic writing. The stem vowel is short in English, despite the *ī* in its etymon, Latin *tībia.* See LATIN PLURALS.

tidal (adjective). The formation was called into question by Fowler (1926) in his most puristic mood as being a modernish (1807) welding of the adjectival suffix *-al* to a noun of native origin (*tide*), a process not elsewhere paralleled. But the word is now, of course, essential and uncancellable. See -AL 1.

tidbit. See TITBIT.

tigerish, tigress. So spelt.

tight, tightly. The first is primarily an adjective, but it overlaps with *tightly* in some adverbial uses, e.g. in the imperative phrase *hold tight!*, and immediately after a few verbs. Thus, drawn from standard modern sources: *but, from what I know of them, they won't sit tight*; *Well, goodnight. Sleep tight*; *like something that had been wound tight and suddenly released. Tight* (adverb) also occurs in a few adjectives, e.g. *tight-fisted, -fitting, -lipped.*

tike. See TYKE.

tilde. A mark (˜) put over a letter, e.g. over a Spanish *n* to indicate that it is to be pronounced /nj/, as in *señor*; and over a Portuguese *a* or *o* to indicate nasalization, as in *São Paulo.*

till, until. The early history of the two words in medieval English, as set down with great thoroughness in the *OED*, is complicated. It is not true, for example, that *till* is a shortened form of *until*: in fact *till* is the earlier of the two. Though they are often interchangeable, there are differences. The *COD* states that *'Until* is used especially at the beginning of a sentence', and *until* is fractionally more formal than *till*, especially in speech. This might account for the fact that *until* occurs much more frequently than *till* in edited prose (including fiction). In practice *until* is six times more likely than *till* to turn up in such work (according to a standard dictionary of word frequency).

Some typical examples of each word, all drawn from standard modern sources: (till) *Wait till you see what I've been doing*; *don't you dare even look at anybody till I get back*; *I could live here forever, he thought, or till I die.* (until) *The runic signature in the Fates was not found until 1888*; *This process will go on until election day*; *Many of the manuscripts were until comparatively recently in the keeping of Owen's family*; *This would continue for hours until he reached a more advanced stage*; *It used to be widely believed that in Britain one is innocent until proved guilty.* The evidence tends to confirm that *till* is sometimes the informal equivalent of *until*, but also that in many contexts the two words are simply interchangeable without affecting the stylistic level. Finally it should be noted that some authorities urge their readers not to use a third form, namely *'til*. In fact it is an informal 20c. contraction of *until*, and may be used in informal contexts.

See UNTIL 2.

tilth An ordinary noun in Old English (*tilþ*) corresponding to the verb *tilian* 'to labour', (by 1200) 'to cultivate land'. It has retained its place in agricultural and horticultural language ever since. Some recent examples: *Settle instead for a sprinkling of blood, bone and fishmeal . . . once you've dug over the ground and are ready to break it down to a finer tilth prior to sowing—Amateur Gardening,* 1990; *As last season's mulch breaks down, it adds tilth to the soil—Harrowsmith,* 1993. For similar formations, see -TH NOUNS.

timbre /ˈtambrə/ or, in a French manner, especially by musicians and critics, /ˈtɛ̃brə/. Adopted from French in the mid-19c. in the sense 'the distinctive character or quality of a musical or vocal sound apart from its pitch and intensity', but still not fully anglicized in pronunciation. Printed in roman.

time. Under this word, as the most general term, it may be useful to some readers to list some of its near-synonyms. Of the six following words each is given a simple definition (based partly on those in the *New SOED*) with a view merely to suggesting the natural relation between them. Though each is often used in senses here assigned not to it but to another (or not mentioned at all), the words *aeon, cycle, date, epoch, era,* and *period* form a broadly based series when they are used in their primary senses.

An *aeon* is an immeasurable period of time.

A *cycle* is a period in which a connected series of events or phenomena is completed, usually as part of a repeating succession of similar periods.

A *date* is the identifiable or stated point of time (day, month, year, etc.) at which something occurs, has occurred, or will occur.

An *epoch* is the beginning of a distinctive period in the history of something or someone.

An *era* is a period of history characterized by a particular state of affairs, series of events, etc.

A *period* is a portion of time characterized by the same prevalent features or conditions.

A *time* and an *age* are often interchangeable with all or most of the above, but are less precise in meaning. Cf. also the terms *duration,* JUNCTURE, *moment, occasion, season, span, spell,* and *term,* all of which, in some of their uses, refer to divisions of time. Note that *in time* means, among other things, 'not (too) late', whereas *on time* means 'punctually, on the dot'.

timeous /ˈtʌɪməs/ (**ty**-muhs) (adjective), in good time, used in Scottish English and some varieties of African English. This is the better spelling, rather than *timous.* Similarly the adverb **timeously**.

times. Preceded by a cardinal numeral and followed by a number or expression of quantity (6 *times 4 = 24*; *an animal of ten times my strength*), *times* has been used as an agent of multiplication since at least the 14c. and is still, of course, in current use. Followed by an adjective or adverb in the comparative degree it is for the most part used only in an additive way (*a cathedral is usually at least five times larger than any parish church*). Though the *OED* gives a 19c. example of the type *ten times less* (*Men who had ten or twenty times less to remember*—Gladstone, 1876) and the type occurs from time to time in the 20c., it is better to assume that *times* normally implies multiplication, and to restrict its use to contexts in which multiplication is plainly intended.

timpani /ˈtɪmpəni/ (plural noun), a set of kettledrums. So spelt, rather than *tympani.* See TYMPANUM.

tin. This ordinary word in BrE for 'an airtight sealed container made of tin plate or aluminium for preserving food' stands beside *can. Can* is the word generally used in BrE for the container when the contents are liquid (*a can of beer*). When the contents are solid, *tin* is more usual (*a tin of beans*; *a tin of peaches*) but *can* is used for this too in AmE. Notice *tinned fruit* but *a canning factory.*

tinge (verb). Both *tingeing* and *tinging* are used for the participle, both are correct, and they occur with equal frequency in the *OEC,* but the second has the drawback of potentially being read as if it were pronounced with a hard *g* /ˈtɪŋɪŋ/. Cf. HINGE (verb).

tinker (verb). The *OED* entry shows that figurative uses of the verb (= 'to occupy oneself about something in a desultory or aimless way') were normally construed with *at* in the 19c., but from the 20c. with *with*. Examples: *The public were tired of government which merely tinkered at legislation* (1880); *Nobody is prepared to tinker with a social structure that has withstood every kind of outside pressure—Times*, 1955; *Whatever moral doubts there may be about tinkering with nature, the biotechnology revolution will not be stopped in its tracks—Oxfam News*, 1990; *Some of the alterations suggest little more than ideological tinkering with the wording—TES*, 1991.

Tinseltown. See SOBRIQUETS.

-tion. Fowler (1926) rightly ridiculed the excessive use of abstract nouns ending in *-tion*, and cited an unattributed but presumably journalistic example: Speculation *on the subject of the* constitution *of the British* representation *at the Washington* inauguration *of the League of* Nations *will, presumably, be satisfied when Parliament meets, but there is a certain nervousness at the* suggestion *that Mr Lloyd George will go over there as chief of the British* delegation. Anyone with half an ear would find such a succession of *-tion* words objectionable. But Fowler's general point is a sound one.

Two of the most overused words in *-tion* in the 20c. are *position* and *situation*. Examples (from the 2nd edn, 1965): *The* situation *in the industry has reached a tragic* position; *They based this opinion largely on the* position *of the company's financial* situation; *The Trades Union Congress should call a halt to the* situation; *We ought to be told the present* position *on this matter*; *The* position *in regard to unemployment has deteriorated*; *At the moment the political* situation *in Malta is in a strange* position. The sentences call out for recasting (e.g. *The industry is in a sorry state*, etc.). In fact relentless attacks on such turgid sentences seem to have had a beneficial effect. The following is from *The Times Guide to English Style and Usage* (1992):

> *position* like situation, an empty, overworked word as in "the unemployment position is unchanged". Try to rephrase such sentences. However, when preceded by an adjective ("a strong position") or a participial form ("a bargaining position"), it is acceptable. For "in a position to", "able to" or "can" are preferable.
>
> *situation* avoid. Even a quote using this vacuous word is probably waffle and not worth inclusion. The word *situation* cannot be rescued by being propped up by an adjective, as in "classroom situation", let alone the *banned* "crisis situation". As for ongoing situation, no-win situation and chicken-and-egg situation . . . !

Doubtless recruits on other newspapers are, or used to be, given the same or similar advice.

tip (noun). See RUBBISH.

tipstaff. Plural *tipstaffs* (not *tipstaves*).

tiptoe. The inflected forms of the verb are *tiptoes, tiptoed, tiptoeing* (the *-ing* form does not follow the usual rule that a final silent *e* is dropped when adding endings that begin with a vowel). For the noun, both *on tiptoe* and *on tiptoes* are used, and, especially in North Amererican English, *on one's tiptoes*.

tirade. Usually pronounced /tʌɪˈreɪd/ in BrE, but commonly /ˈtʌɪ-/ (i.e. stressed on first syllable) in AmE. Variants with a short /ɪ/ in the first syllable are also used by some standard speakers in both countries.

tire (of a wheel). See TYRE.

tiro (a novice). See TYRO.

tissue. The pronunciation /ˈtɪʃuː/ is recommended, rather than /ˈtɪsjuː/.

titbit, tidbit. The first is the customary spelling in Britain, and the second in North America. The word entered the language in the 17c., chiefly in the forms *tyd bit, tid-bit* (from Eng. dial. *tid* adjective tender, nice, special).

titillate means 'to excite' (*Some interesting titles to titillate your literary tastebuds*), and often has sexual overtones (especially in the noun derivative **titillation**), whereas *titivate* is a now somewhat dated word meaning 'to adorn or smarten' (*Striking abstract paintings titivate the otherwise bare walls*; *someone to titivate her hair*). *Titivate* is occasionally used by mistake for *titillate* (although the reverse mistake does not occur): **Even now twelve heartfelt pages are titivating the senses of a Dead Letter superintendent—Dylan Thomas*, 1933.

titles. Some of the ground has already been covered, e.g. in the article NAMES AND APPELLATIONS, in other articles cross-referred to therein, and in THE 1. The complex difficulties of the correct designations of members of the nobility, bishops and archbishops, lord mayors, lady mayoresses, the Chief Rabbi, the Pope, ambassadors, and so on can only be safely resolved by consulting the current editions of *Debrett's Correct Form, Who's Who* (of the country concerned), *The Dictionary of National Biography,* and so on. Further detailed guidance is that provided to their journalists in *The Times Guide to English Style and Usage* (1992). Fowler (1926) wrote a 21-line piece deploring the emergence 'in the last twenty or thirty years' of the prefixes *Marquis, Earl,* and *Viscount,* and also of *Marchioness* and *Countess* in place of *Lady* ('that used to be good enough for ordinary wear'), and by this means neatly sidestepped most of the central issues. The holders of titles know how they should be addressed, on the envelope, at the head of a letter, and face to face. They are doubtless amused (or irritated) by some of the forms adopted by people who are unaware of the correct procedures.

TLA. Short for *three-letter acronym.* See ACRONYM 4.

tmesis. Plural *tmeses* /'tmiːsiːz/. (grammar) The separation of parts of a compound word by an intervening word or words, known technically as an 'infix' or 'infixes', used particularly in informal speech. The process is seen clearly in words such as *hoo-bloody-ray, im-bloody-possible,* etc. Words of this kind are the only examples in English of the linguistic process of 'infixation', which also occurs with other expletives, such as *bleeding, flaming, flipping, frigging, fucking,* etc., e.g. *abso-freakin-lutely, fan-bleeding-tastic.* Such creations are often hyphenated. The word is derived from Greek τμῆσις 'a cutting'.

to. The uses of the preposition *to* and of the infinitival particle *to* are discussed under several headwords in this book. For phrases of the type *she gave it to Elizabeth and I* (correctly *me*) and *to we* (correctly *us*) *lexicographers,* see CASES 6 and I 1. For the type *to fervently believe,* see SPLIT INFINITIVE. For the type in which *to* is placed in final position (e.g. *I learned what to put in my mouth and what not to*), see INFINITIVE 3(*c*). For the circumstances in which it is used between the verbs *dare, help,* and *need* and a following infinitive, see DARE; HELP; NEED. A new use of the preposition *to,* replacing traditional *of,* now emerging in AmE, might be called the relational *to*: e.g. *interviewing a woman who neighbors said they believed was a girlfriend* to *the fired employee*—*Chicago Tribune,* 1987; *He's married and the father* to *a son*—ibid., 1989.

Finally, the preposition *to* used to mean 'at' is recorded in the *OED* from Old English times onwards but is now only dialectal in Britain and only in non-standard use in AmE. Examples: *On Cantwarabyrig VII myneteres . . . to Hrofceastre*—a 10c. charter; *I haue heard say there is to Mountferrat . . . a deuoute & holy place*—a romance of *c.*1500; *Lucy Passmore, the white witch to Welcombe*—C. Kingsley, 1855; *In Somerset . . . it is correct to say 'I bought this to Taunton'*—R. Jefferies, 1889; *We could do something in the afternoon. Were you ever to the Botanic Gardens?*—New Yorker, 1977.

tobacco. Plural *tobaccos.* See -O(E)S 4.

tobacconist. See -IST, -ALIST 2.

toboggan makes *toboganer, tobogganing, tobogganist.* See -N-, -NN-.

today, tomorrow, tonight. Forms with a hyphen (*to-day,* etc.) were listed as alternatives in editions of the *COD* down to and including the 7th edn of 1982. They were dropped in the 8th edn of 1990. The lingering of the hyphen in these words in much printed work of the 20c. is a very singular piece of conservatism, but now it has virtually disappeared from sight in all three words.

to die for. See DIE.

together. See ALL TOGETHER, ALTOGETHER.

together with. See AGREEMENT 4.

toilet. *At least the children are told how to hold their knives properly and get walloped if they call the lavatory the toilet.* This example from Joanna Trollope's novel *A Passionate Man* (1990) neatly introduces the sociological problem about what was once called the *water closet.* There are many synonyms in all the main English-speaking countries, and the choice of word normally depends on what is judged to be the sociological level, age, etc., of the person addressed. A wide range of terms forms part of the passive vocabulary of most people, but not all of them are used in practice. On the evidence available, *toilet* is the first choice of the majority of people in Britain, while *lavatory* (now fading) and *loo* (especially) are the favourites of the chattering classes. There are many polite evasions (*the geography of the house, the facilities,* etc.), numerous dialect words (e.g. *netty* in the North Country), and many slang words (e.g. *the bog, khazi*). A public lavatory is often called a *public convenience* in BrE, with separate sections once labelled *Ladies* and *Gents* but now all too often *Men* and *Women,* or with signs indicating which is which.

In AmE the dominant word (in houses, public places, on aeroplanes, on long-distance buses, etc.) seems to be *restroom,* and, when the facilities are divided, *men's room* and *ladies room. Bathroom* and *washroom* are also common. *Toilet* is known but hardly ever occurs in print except when used attributively (*toilet attendant, toilet seat*) and in the phrase *public toilets.* There are also numerous slang words (*can, john,* etc.), and euphemisms (*comfort station, powder room,* etc.). Not uncommonly several of these synonyms are used in the text of the same newspaper article: e.g. (a 150-word report of the arrest of a man charged with smoking marijuana in the lavatory of a Continental Airlines flight from Chicago to Newark, NJ, in 1988) *bathroom, restroom, john,* and *lavatory. John* was the word used by the accused. *Water closet, WC,* and *privy* are known in both countries but are now used less and less. *Latrine* is a communal lavatory in camping sites, military barracks, etc.

token. The idiomatic phrase *by the same token* has been a convenient connective since the 15c. (Paston Letters) and is nowadays confined to meaning 'for the same reason; in the same way'. It is important that there should always be some clear causal or consequential connection between the original statement and the consequent assumption. Some modern examples: *There was little evidence to substantiate the gossip and, by the same token, there was little to disprove it; It is convenient to claim that what goes on in other countries is no business of ours and by the same token that foreigners should keep their noses out of what happens inside our borders; The writers might never quite get at what they believed was Giacometti's essence, but by the same token Giacometti was not going to go off on some completely different tangent and thereby get away from the writers—Mod. Painters,* 1992. The idiom is less appropriately used to introduce a parallel or additional circumstance rather than a causally related one: *Style is a heady compound of instinct, experience and context: what cuts a dash in the Masai Mara won't necessarily do the trick in Mayfair. By the same token* (read: *At the same time*), *while style is nailing a kind of timelessness, it has to look modern—Times,* 2006.

tomato. Plural *tomatoes.* See -O(E)S 1. No single word has the power to symbolize the differences between NAmer. and BrE pronunciation as this, a symbol created and universalized in Ira Gershwin's lyrics for the 1937 song 'Let's call the whole thing off': You like potato and I like potahto | You like tomato (/tə'meɪtəʊ/) and I like tomahto (/tə'mɑːtəʊ/|) Potato, potahto, Tomato, tomahto | Let's call the whole thing off.

tome. A large heavy book, not just a book of any size.

Tommy (Atkins). See SOBRIQUETS.

tomorrow. See TODAY.

ton, prevailing mode or fashion. Though used in English since the 18c. it is still not fully naturalized: printed in italics and pronounced /tɔ̃/.

ton (weight) and **tun** (the cask, vat, and wine measure) are both pronounced /tʌn/. They were originally the same word (from Old English *tunne,* from medieval Latin *tunna*), but became differentiated in the 17c.

tondo (a circular painting or relief). Plural *tondi* /'tɒndi/.

tonight. See TODAY.

tonne (a metric ton equal to 1,000 kg.; = approx. 2,205 lb.). In both BrE and AmE pronounced /tʌn/, i.e. the same as the ordinary word *ton* (= 2,240 lb. avoirdupois).

tonsil. The derivatives are spelt **tonsillectomy, tonsillitis, tonsillotomy**. See -LL-, -L-.

tonsorial has nothing to do with tonsils, but is instead a useful word for those who need an adjective referring to hairdressers or hairdressing (cf. Latin *tonsor* 'a barber'). Generally used light-heartedly or tongue firmly in cheek, e.g. Bald *is the story of young Andrew Wood... who is going* *prematurely bald. He's worried that his lack of tonsorial splendor will have a negative effect on his romantic endeavors*—*DVD Verdict*, 2009; *he ridicules the sartorial and tonsorial preferences of Southern Baptists*—*First Things* (magazine), 2004.

too.

1. With passive participles.
2. At the beginning of a clause.
3. As an intensifier.

1 *With passive participles. Too* is the normal word used to qualify an adjective or adverb to denote excess: *The house is too large; I spoke too soon.* It should not be used to qualify a participial adjective when this could not idiomatically be qualified by *very: She was too tired* is idiomatic because *tired* has acquired the role of an ordinary adjective, but *She was too affected by their criticisms* is less satisfactory because *affected* is still regarded as part of a verb. In this case a better alternative is *She was too much affected by their criticisms* or *She was excessively affected by their criticisms.*

2 *At the beginning of a clause.* Placed at the beginning of a clause and meaning 'in addition; moreover, furthermore', *too* had a long and untroubled history from Old English until the 17c. (e.g. *Too, we profess our selves the Redeemed of the Lord*—J. Shute, 1641), at which point it became rare or obsolete, only to be revived in the 20c., chiefly in AmE. Examples: *She's had her novel published this year; but too, she's written some interesting articles on acupuncture— cited in CGEL,* 1985; *she was a veteran of the Friday shooting incident and, too, she had Fleurier, the patron, on her side*—T. Winton, 1985 (Aust.); *He told me a man needed sex. But I didn't want to. He got like that. But, too, he was a charmer*—*New Yorker*, 1988.

3 *As an intensifier. Too* has many standard (though informal) uses as an intensifier: e.g. *It's too good of you* (= very good, extremely good); *I'm not too sure that you're right* (= *not at all sure*); *'This boy is not an athletic type.' 'Too true!'*. Note, also, the mainly AmE type *'I don't know what you're talking about.' 'You do too.'* (= you certainly do).

toothcomb. If your imagination has ever been troubled by the surreal vision of someone combing his or her teeth, or if you have wondered what a *toothcomb* is, and what mania could drive anybody to comb teeth, wonder no more. There is no such thing (except in zoology, referring to a group of procumbent lower front teeth). The forms *toothcomb* and *fine toothcomb* come from a misdivision of the noun *fine-tooth comb,* meaning a comb with very fine, close-set teeth. In modern standard English the versions *fine toothcomb* and even *toothcomb* on its own are largely acceptable (though not in the *Guardian* style guide, and possibly others), if nightmarishly implausible. There is even a verb, *to toothcomb.* The correct spelling is, for the time being, still the most frequent. Examples: *Sister Margaret Locker, A&E manager, said: 'The inspectors ran a fine-tooth comb over the whole department*—*The Press* (York), 2003; *A novel which has been picked over with toothcombs, in search of clues to 'The Mystery'*—*TLS*, 1972; *And even those who have gone through the figures with a fine fiscal toothcomb are still unsure that they can work out how it will all work*—*Scotland on Sunday*, 2004; *We can toothcomb the statistics, scowl over the double counting, curl a lip at florid rhetoric*—*Guardian Unlimited*, 2005.

tormentor. So spelt, not *-er*.

tornado. The plural *tornadoes* is several times more frequent than *tornados,* though both are correct. The plural of the fighter plane of that name is *Tornados* only. See -o(e)s 2, 9.

torpedo. Plural *torpedoes.* See -o(e)s 1. The inflected forms of the verb are *torpedoes, torpedoed, torpedoing.*

torpor. So spelt. See -our and -or.

torso. Plural *torsos.* See -o(e)s 7.

tortoise. The prestige pronunciation is /ˈtɔːtəs/. The spelling pronunciation with final /-ɔɪz/ is, however, recognized in *ODO.*

tortuous, torturous. The first means 'full of twists, turns, or bends' (*a tortuous route with many hairpin bends*) or '(*fig.*) indirect, circuitous, devious' (*a tortuous argument, mind, policy,* etc.). *Torturous,* a fairly rare word, is the adjective corresponding to *torture* and means 'involving or causing torture' (*a torturous execution, hours of torturous anguish*). The two sets of meanings almost come together in the following extract: *There was some debate* *about the pictures used to accompany this article, but it was nothing compared to, say, the torturous negotiations that preceded the Kylie Minogue story in the June issue of this magazine—The Face,* 1994. But it seems certain that *tortuous*(*ly*) fits the context better in the following examples: *Sam did as he was instructed as Deborah torturously rolled her way back towards him*—B. Elton, 1991; *Turow spoke last night . . . giving a detailed synopsis of the 'torturous path' that led him to be a practicing lawyer and author—Daily Northwestern* (Chicago), 1992.

torus. Plural *toruses* or, less commonly, *tori* /ˈtɔːrʌɪ/. See -US 1.

tost. An archaic literary form of the past tense and past participle of *toss* (verb): *Wretch that long has tost On the thorny bed of Pain* (Gray); *these stormtost seas* (Carlyle). See -T AND -ED.

total. The adjective makes *totally* (adverb), *totality* (noun), *totalizator* (noun). The inflected forms of the verb are *totalled, totalling* (but usually *totaled, totaling* in AmE): see -LL-, -L-.

to the manner born. See MANNER.

tother. Formed in Middle English as *þe toþer* ('the tother') by a misdivision of earlier *þat oþer* ('the other'), *tother* (also *'tother, the tother*) has delightfully persisted in use until the present day as a regional or occasionally humorous variant of *the other*. The phrase *tell tother from which* 'to tell one from another' also surfaces from time to time.

touchy. See TETCHY.

toupee (wig) /ˈtuːpeɪ/. So spelt, not *toupée, toupet.* Printed in roman.

tourniquet. Pronounced /ˈtʊənɪkeɪ/, not /-kɛt/.

tow- and towing-. The usual forms in the more important compounds now are *tow bar* (also *towbar*), *towline, tow net, towpath,* and *tow rope* (also *towrope*), rather than *towing bar,* etc.

toward, towards. 1 As prepositions, in the *OEC* data, *toward* is at least twice as frequent in AmE as *towards.* In other varieties of English, *towards* is more frequent, though *toward* is also used, and in BrE the preference for *towards* is in a ratio of 9:1. Routine examples: (UK) *Madeleine . . . led her guests towards Edmond*—P. P. Read, 1986; *Miles Harrier was making his way . . . towards their rendezvous*—M. Bracewell, 1989. (US) *'I'd hate to see you be so unforgiving toward me,' she said—New Yorker,* 1989; *There is a new policy toward risk that is at least as important to American society as tort— Dædalus,* 1980.

2 *Towards* is normally pronounced /təˈwɔːdz/ or /twɔːdz/ in BrE. The variant /tɔːdz/ also occurs in rapid speech. There is a similar wide spread of pronunciations in AmE.

towel (verb). The inflected forms are *towelled, towelling,* but usually *toweled, toweling* in AmE. See -LL-, -L-.

trachea. In BrE usually pronounced /trəˈkiːə/, but sometimes /ˈtreɪkɪə/. Plural *tracheae* /-iːiː/, or, less frequently, *tracheas.* In AmE usually /ˈtreɪk-/. In the derivatives **tracheostomy** and **tracheotomy**, the first vowel is usually /a/ in BrE and /eɪ/ in AmE.

trademarks. Reference to proprietary names in print—by journalists, novelists, or lexicographers—can lead to protests from the owners of the trademarks. They are concerned to defend their rights to the word registered as a trademark; its use with a lower-case initial suggests that it is the generic name of the item. Every vacuum cleaner is not a *Hoover,* nor ball-point pen a *Biro,* not all sticky tape is *Sellotape,* nor jeans all *Levi's,* and if this is implied, the trademark holder is in danger of losing the value, as measured in sales, of his trademarked product. Proprietary names are of more than usual concern to lexicographers, not only because they are often the subject of protracted and complicated correspondence. Besides this, dictionary entries are consulted by the Registrar of Trade Marks at the Patent Office in London, and by his analogues in other countries, and the registration of such terms is sometimes delayed or brought into question because, among other factors, a given dictionary shows a term without indication of its proprietary status.

The preferred expression in the *OED* for the names of these marks is 'proprietary name'. It is used as a synonym of 'trade name', 'trademark', and 'trade term', notwithstanding the fact that the four expressions are not synonymous in legal and business language. Proprietary names should properly be entered in dictionaries with a capital letter in the lemma (e.g. *Bovril*). If in literary works or other sources systematically read for the *OED* such names are used with a lower-case initial letter, the entry also contains the uncapitalized form (e.g. *Bovril* ... Also *bovril*). It should not be assumed that such a term, once registered, remains a trademark indefinitely. *Cellophane, jeep,* and *linoleum* are examples of words which no longer have proprietary status. In 1962 *thermos* ceased to be a trademark in the US, and Canada followed suit in 1967, but it remains a trademark in Great Britain. Disputes between publishers and owners of trademarks are matters for lawyers.

trade union (not *trades union*). Plural *trade unions.* But *Trades Union Congress,* abbreviation *TUC.*

trade wind. Write as two words.

traditionalist, traditionist. The second is now only very rarely used.

traffic (verb). The inflected forms are *trafficked, trafficking*; also *trafficker* (noun). See -C-, -CK-.

tragedienne. Rarely used other than to refer to historical actresses. Printed in roman and spelt without the accent of the French original *tragédienne.*

tragedy. Used in English since the Middle Ages of a play or other literary work, ancient or modern, in which the principal figure or figures fall from grace or are killed, *tragedy* has been applied since the early 16c. to any dreadful calamity or disaster in real life. This extension of its meaning away from a strictly literary application has had its critics, but it is well established and essential, e.g. Wilde's 'All women become like their mothers. That is their tragedy. No man does. That's his.' Given that disasters and calamities occur, it is not surprising that almost half of the occurrences of the word in the *OEC* data are from news reports. Nevertheless, it can be overused and hyperbolic, e.g. *With his* [*sc.* a basketball player's] *best supporting cast yet, falling for an eighth straight time in the first round would be viewed as a tragedy—Basketball Digest,* 2004. For these lesser setbacks other terms are available. Moreover, the word can be justifiably criticized for emphasizing the emotional impact of any disaster instead of concentrating on its causes and what actually happened. As *MWDCEU* puts it: 'We recommend that you use it thoughtfully.'

tragic, tragical. The same caveat applies to the word *tragic* as to TRAGEDY. The form *tragical* is scarcely used at all, other than in references to *The Tragical History of Doctor Faustus* and *The Tragical History of Romeus and Juliet,* the forerunner of Shakespeare's play.

traipse (verb), to tramp or trudge wearily. It emerged in the 16c. and is of unknown origin. The favoured spelling used to be *trapes,* but no longer.

trait. The pronunciation with silent final *t,* mirroring the original French, is nowadays less frequent than that with the *t* pronounced.

trammel (verb). The inflected forms are *trammelled, trammelling* in BrE, but usually *trammeled, trammeling* in AmE. See -LL-, -L-.

tranche, 'a portion of something, especially money', is spelt with a final letter *e,* as shown, not **tranch.* It can be pronounced in a semi-anglicized way as /trɑːnʃ/, the *a* as in *car,* or nasalized in a French manner /trɑ̃ʃ/, but should not be pronounced like *haunch.*

tranquil (adjective). The derivatives have *-ll-* in BrE: **tranquillity, tranquillize, tranquillizer, tranquilly** (adverb). But AmE usually has *-l-* in the first three of these. See -LL-, -L-.

transcendence, transcendency. The second spelling is virtually extinct.

transcendent(al). These words, with their many specialized applications in philosophy, are for the most part beyond the scope of this book; but there are popular uses in which the right form should be chosen. **1** The word that means surpassing, of supreme excellence or greatness, etc., is *transcendent,* and the following is wrong: **The* matter *is of transcendental importance, especially in the present disastrous state of the world.* See LONG VARIANTS for similar pairs.

2 The word applied to God in contrast with IMMANENT is *transcendent.*

3 The word that means visionary, idealistic, outside experience, etc., is *transcendental.*

4 The word applied to Emerson and his 'religio-philosophical teaching' is *transcendental.* Note also the 20c. cult of **Transcendental Meditation**, a method of detaching oneself from problems, anxiety, etc., by silent meditation and repetition of a mantra (*COD*).

transexual. See TRANSSEXUAL.

transfer. 1 Noun *tránsfer,* verb *transfér*: see NOUN AND VERB ACCENT.

2 The inflected forms of the verb are *transferred, transferring.* Derivatives include **transferrer**, but **transferable** (see -ABLE, -IBLE 3(vii)), **transference**, **transferee**, and **transferor**. See -R-, -RR-. Of *transferrer* and *transferor,* the first is the general agent noun, a person or mechanism that passes something on, and the second a legal term for the person who conveys his or her property to another, the *transferee.*

transfixion, the state of being transfixed. So spelt, not *transfiction,* which refers to a subgenre of fiction involving transsexuals.

transgressor. So spelt, not *-er.*

tranship, transhipment. Acceptable, but not recommended, variants of transship, transshipment.

transient, transitory. Both words mean 'brief, fleeting', with *transient* conveying rather more strongly the notion of people or things 'passing through' while *transitory* denotes temporary situations that are more static: *The highly transient nature of the casual labour force in hotels and catering, and the low attachment to work of many casuals . . . mean that the unions' task will scarcely be an easy one*—B. Casey, 1988; *In traditional critical study, questions about politics were rarely felt important since politics engaged with transitory activities*—T. Healy, 1992. *Transient* has special meanings in music, philosophy, electricity, and nuclear physics, and *transitory* has a special meaning in law. The noun **transience** is generally preferable to the more cumbersome word **transitoriness**.

transistor. So spelt, not *-er.*

transitive verb. See INTRANSITIVE (adjective); DITRANSITIVE.

translator. So spelt, not *-er.*

transliterate, means 'to replace the letters or characters of a word with the corresponding letters in another alphabet'. Words may be transliterated, for example, into the Roman alphabet from their originals in Greek, Russian, Chinese, Japanese, Arabic, and so on. The result is a *transliteration,* which preserves the form of the original, as distinct from a *translation,* which gives the equivalent word (often unrelated in form) in another language. Thus Greek πτερόν is transliterated into roman letters as *pteron* (cf. *pterodactyl*) and translated as 'wing'.

translucent. See TRANSPARENT.

transmit (verb). The inflected forms are *transmitted, transmitting,* and the agent noun **transmitter**. Also **transmittal** (noun). See -T-, -TT-. Related forms are **transmissible** and **transmittable**: see -ABLE, -IBLE.

transmogrify. See FACETIOUS FORMATIONS.

transparence, transparency. The words are interchangeable when the meaning is 'the quality or state of being transparent', but the form in *-ence* is nowadays rather unusual. In the photographic sense (= a slide), and in several other specialized senses, *transparency* is the only possible form.

transparent, and the near-synonyms *diaphanous, pellucid, translucent. Transparent* is the general word for describing what is penetrable by sight (lit. or fig.) or by light, and it can replace any of the others unless there is some point of precision or of rhetoric to be gained. The three near-synonyms have the rhetorical value of being less common than *transparent,* and therefore appear more often in literary work, *pellucid* being the rarest of the three. As regards precision, the following definitions of the words' narrower senses are offered, and to each are appended some appropriate nouns, and the adjective or participle that seems most directly opposed. The only one of the four capable of bearing the figurative sense 'obvious' is *transparent.*

Something *diaphanous* is so insubstantial, thin, or gossamer-like that it does not preclude sight of what is behind it; *fabric, gown, veil, mist*; opp. *shrouding.* Whatever is *pellucid* does not distort images seen through it; *sky, water, prose*; opp. *turbid.* Something *translucent* does not bar the passage of light but diffuses it, for instance like frosted glass; *skin, quartz, plastic, tortoiseshell*; opp. *opaque.* Anything that is *transparent* does not obscure sight of what is behind it and transmits light without diffusion, or, figuratively, can easily be seen through or understood; *glass, attempt, procedure*; opp. *obscure, unclear.*

transpire. 1 *Etymology and historical development.* The word was brought into English from French in the 16c. in the technical sense 'to emit as vapour'. The French word was derived from modern Latin *tran(s) spīrāre,* from Latin *trans-* 'through' + *spīrāre* 'to breathe'. The English word was immediately applied to the process by which plants exhale watery vapour through the surface of the leaves; and, in the 17c., came also to mean '(of a liquid) to escape by evaporation; (of moisture) to give off through the skin (of an animal or human being)'. From these meanings it was just a short step (in the 18c.) to the figurative sense 'to become known by degrees, to leak out'. Dr Johnson did not like the new use: he defined it as 'to escape from secrecy to notice' and commented 'a sense lately innovated from France, without necessity'. This figurative sense of *transpire* has remained in the language since the 17c. though it is often said to be 'formal'. Examples: *The conditions of the contract were not allowed to transpire*—J. A. Froude, 1856; *But then, to our surprise, it transpires that he doesn't think much of our critics, either*—D. J. Enright, 1966; *Yaddo, it transpired, had been under FBI surveillance for some time*—I. Hamilton, 1982; *Unfortunately he died soon afterwards . . . Though the blow was softened when it transpired that he'd left her several million francs*—S. Faulks, 1989.

2 *The criticized meaning.* Meanwhile in the late 18c., first in America, *transpire* began to be used in the sense 'to occur, happen, take place': e.g. *There is nothing new transpired since I wrote you last*—A. Adams, 1775; *Transpire . . . 3. To happen or come to pass.*—*Webster's Dict.,* 1828; *Few changes—hardly any—have transpired among his ship's company*—Dickens, 1848. The use was condemned in vitriolic terms by the American writer Richard Grant White in his book *Words and their Uses* (1870). And he concluded: 'There is a very simple test of the correct use of *transpire.* If the phrase *take place* can be substituted for it, and the intended meaning of the sentence is preserved, its use is unquestionably wrong; if the other colloquial phrase, *leak out,* can be put in its place, its use is correct.' The *OED* (1914) firmly marked the sense 'to occur, happen, take place' as incorrect, while presenting a string of 'misused' examples. It said that the misuse evidently arose 'from misunderstanding such a sentence as "What had transpired during his absence he did not know"'. Fowler (1926) spoke of 'the notorious misuse of this word . . . in making it mean happen or turn out or go on'. And so we have another example of a long drawn-out battle between competing senses, one seen as logical and etymologically sound, and the other as a 'monstrous perversion' (Richard Grant White, 1870) and a 'notorious misuse' (Fowler, 1926). It is still described as a disputed use by the *COD* (1995), and can be criticized as a long-winded, jargonistic, and unnecessary substitute for *occur* or *take place,* Nevertheless, this meaning is frequent: about half the citations in the *OEC* data are for this contentious use.

3 *Verdict.* If you are tempted to use *transpire* to mean 'to happen, occur' it will be greeted by many people with varying degrees of disapproval and by others with equanimity. The safest course is to leave the word to botanists, biologists, and physicists in their learned journals, or at most to restrict it to contexts in which it means 'to emerge, become clear'.

4 *Foonote.* As a matter of interest, the modern French word for 'perspire' is *transpirer.* And this French verb is also used to mean '(*secret, projet, détails*) come to light, leak out'. The phrase *rien n'a transpiré* means 'nothing came to light, nothing leaked out *or* transpired'.

transsexual. The better spelling, rather than *transexual,* despite the old models of *transcribe* (from Latin *transcrībere*; cf. Eng. *scribe*), *transept* (from Latin *trans-* + *septum*), etc.

transship, transshipment. The better forms, rather than those with a single medial *-s-*. Both words are better hyphenated *trans-ship, trans-shipment,* but in practice the solid forms are more frequent.

trapes. See TRAIPSE.

trapezium. Plural either *trapezia* or *trapeziums.* See -UM 3. As a trap for the unwary, it means a quadrilateral with only one pair of sides parallel in BrE, while in AmE it means a quadrilateral with no two sides parallel. On the other hand, a *trapezoid* means a quadrilateral with no two sides parallel in BrE, while in AmE it means a quadrilateral with only one pair of sides parallel. Vigilance is called for.

trash. See RUBBISH.

trauma. The pronunciation recommended is /ˈtrɔːmə/, rather than /ˈtraʊmə/; but /ˈtraʊmə/ is more usual in AmE. Plural (in medical use) *traumata,* (in lay use) *traumas.*

travail, travel. 1 The first is pronounced /ˈtraveɪl/ and the second /ˈtrav(ə)l/.

2 Used as a verb, *travail* has the inflected forms *travailed, travailing* in both BrE and AmE. By contrast, *travel* makes *travelled, travelling* (and also **traveller**) in BrE, but usually has forms with a single *-l-* in AmE.

treachery is a general term meaning a violation of faith or trust, a betrayal; a person who betrays something entrusted to him or her is **treacherous. Treason** is specifically violation by a subject of allegiance to the sovereign (or in countries without a monarch to the State); the corresponding adjective is **treasonable**, and the agent noun is **traitor**.

treble. See TRIPLE.

trecento /treɪˈtʃɛntəʊ/. (Rather less often with a capital initial.) The style of Italian art and literature in the 1300s (1300–99), i.e. what we call in English 'the fourteenth century'. Similarly *quattrocento* (the 1400s, i.e. our fifteenth century), *cinquecento* (the 1500s, i.e. our sixteenth century), and so on down to *novecento,* the style of Italian art and literature in the twentieth century (1900–99). In Italian a capital initial is obligatory in all such uses, and this practice is sometimes followed in English-language studies of Italian art and literature of these periods. In all general contexts Italian follows the same rules as English: *il quattordicesimo secolo, il quindicesimo secolo,* ... *il ventesimo secolo,* the fourteenth century, the fifteenth century, ... the twentieth century.

trefoil. The *COD* (1995) and the *New SOED* (1993) give preference to the pronunciation with a short *e,* namely /ˈtrɛfɔɪl/, rather than /ˈtriːfɔɪl/. The standard dictionaries of AmE give their preferences in the opposite order.

trek (verb). **1** The inflected forms are *trekked, trekking.* The agent noun is **trekker**.

2 The verb normally retains an element of arduousness in its uses (*the boy had to trek two miles to school each day*), as a kind of folk memory of the 19c. South African use of the word to mean 'to migrate or make a long journey with one's belongings by ox wagon'. It is not merely a synonym of *go, walk.* Similarly with the noun *trek.*

trellis (verb). The inflected forms are *trellised, trellising.* See -S-, -SS-.

tremor. So spelt. See -OUR AND -OR.

trepan /triˈpan/ (verb). Formerly, to perforate the skull as a surgical operation. The inflected forms are *trepanned, trepanning.* See -N-, -NN-.

trephine /trɪˈfʌɪn/ or /-ˈfiːn/ (noun). An improved form of the original instrument, the TREPAN. The word *trepan* is first recorded *c.*1400, and *trephine* in 1628. *Trephine* was originally *trafine,* and, according to its inventor, John Woodall, was formed from Latin *trēs fīnēs* 'three ends'.

trial balloon is a loan translation (see LOANWORD) of the French *ballon d'essai* (plural *ballons d'essai*) adopted in English in 1858 in the sense 'an experimental project or piece of policy put forward to test its reception'. The loan translation *trial balloon* is first recorded from 1939 in a US source, and is now the standard expression, *ballon d'essai* being rather rare and literary. If used, it is italicized. Examples: *A good deal of Hume's theory of belief is rather a* ballon d'essai *than meant altogether seriously*—Mind, 1942; *The launching of such a controversial* ballon d'essai *naturally had its impact in Moscow*—J. Haslam, 1997; *While some might suspect Google's foray into the UK market is merely a trial balloon, and that an entrance into the US market is inevitable, I certainly wouldn't hold my breath*—*SeoBook,* 2012 (US); *Because what appears to be an off-the-record, after-dinner, thinking-aloud aside ... may be a well thought-out trial balloon, floated to start a* *debate and score a few points—The Hindu*, 2003 (India).

tribunal. Pronounced /trʌɪˌbjuːn(ə)l/ or /trɪ-/.

tricentenary. See CENTENARY 2.

triceps. The form *triceps* works as both a singular and plural noun: *the triceps on his left arm; a pair of bulging triceps*. The singular *tricep* is a back-formation and is incorrect. See also BICEPS; FORCEPS.

triclinium /trʌɪˈklɪnɪəm, trɪ-, -ˈklʌɪn-/ (Roman antiquity). Plural *triclinia*. See -UM 2.

tricolour (a flag of three colours, especially the French national flag of blue, white, and red). So spelt in BrE and pronounced /ˈtrɪkələ/. In AmE usually spelt **tricolor** and pronounced /ˈtraɪˌkʌlər/.

triforium (gallery or arcade in a church). Plural *triforia*. See -UM 2.

trigger (verb). The inflected forms are *triggered, triggering*. See -R-, -RR-.

trill (phonetics). Especially, in certain regional varieties of BrE, pronunciation of *r* with vibration of the tongue. The term is also applied to the rolled *r* in Italian and the uvular *r* in German.

trillion. It normally means now a million million (1,000,000,000,000 or 10^{12}) both in AmE and BrE. Formerly, in BrE, it meant a million million million (1,000,000,000,000,000,000 or 10^{18}). See BILLION.

trilogy. In ancient Athens there were dramatic competitions at which each dramatist presented three plays, originally giving successive parts of the same legend; the extant *Agamemnon, Choephoroe,* and *Eumenides,* of Aeschylus formed a trilogy, and, with the addition of the lost *Proteus,* a TETRALOGY. Later trilogies were connected not necessarily by a common subject, but by being works of the same author, presented on the same occasion. In modern use the word is applied to a work such as Shakespeare's *Henry VI,* comprising three separate plays, or to a novel, etc., with two sequels.

trimeter (prosody). A line of three measures, especially preceded by a defining word (*iambic trimeters, trochaic trimeters,* etc.). | *Hígh̆er* | *stíll ănd* | *hígh̆er* | is a trochaic trimeter.

trio. Plural *trios*. See -O(E)S 4.

triolet. /ˈtriːə(ʊ)lɛt/, /ˈtrʌɪəlɛt/. A poem of eight (usually eight-syllabled) lines rhyming abaaabab, the first line being repeated as the fourth and seventh, and the second as the eighth. An example (entitled 'How Great my Grief') from Thomas Hardy:

How great my grief, my joys how few,
Since first it was my fate to know thee!
—Have the slow years not brought to view
How great my grief, my joys how few,
Nor memory shaped old times anew,
Nor loving-kindness helped to show thee
How great my grief, my joys how few,
Since first it was my fate to know thee?

And another, more light-hearted example (G. K. Chesterton) with a slightly different rhyming scheme:

I wish I were a jelly fish
That cannot fall downstairs:
Of all the things I wish to wish
I wish I were a jelly fish
That hasn't any cares,
And doesn't even have to wish
'I wish I were a jelly fish
That cannot fall downstairs'.

triplet (prosody). Applied to the occasional use, in rhymed-couplet metres, of three lines instead of two to a rhyme; common among the heroic couplets of Dryden and some 18c. poets. An example from Dryden's *Religio Laici* (1682):

Or various Atom's, interfering Dance
Leapt into Form (the Noble work of Chance,)
Or this great All was from Eternity;
Not ev'n the Stagirite himself could see;
And Epicurus Guess'd as well as He
As blindly grop'd they for a future State,
As rashly Judg'd of Providence and Fate:

Triplets occurring among heroic couplets are sometimes marked by a brace, as, for example, in Pope's *Essay on Criticism* (1711):

Musick resembles Poetry, in each }
Are nameless Graces which no Methods teach. }
And which a Master-Hand alone can reach. }

triple, treble. If the musical sense of *treble* is put aside, and also specialized senses in betting, darts, and baseball, the two words are as often as not interchangeable. But there are differences. Though either can be adjective, verb, or noun, *triple* is rather more common for the verb in all varieties of English (especially in intransitive uses, in the sense 'to become three times as many' (*The editorial staff had tripled and was producing issues 250 pages thick—Columbia Journalism Review*, 2003) and the adjective (*I was starting to get triple vision and wondering how you did that with only two eyes*—I. Banks, 1990). Both words are used in the meaning 'three times as many', as in *treble/triple the number* and *treble/triple the size*. In the adjectival use *treble* is perhaps increasingly being used to refer to amount (= three times as much), and *triple* to plurality (consisting of or involving three items or people), though the distinction is far from absolute.

A few examples will point up some of the differences. Others will underline their interchangeability. (treble) *treble hook* (having three prongs); *a treble brandy*; *Treble the money would not buy it now*; *It sells for treble the price of whale oil*; *Think of a number and treble it*; *The newspaper has trebled its circulation*. (triple) *triple agent* (espionage); *triple alliance*; *triple century* (cricket); *triple crown* (in sporting events); *a triple (heart) bypass*; *a triple threat* (= a threat of three different kinds); *a triple-layer sponge cake*; *her triple role as headmistress, gym instructor, and music teacher*; *a triple whammy*; *The firm's income tripled last year*.

tripod. Walker (1791) listed a form with a short *i* as a variant pronunciation, i.e. /ˈtrɪpɒd/, but preferred the form with a long *i*, i.e. /ˈtrʌɪ-/. Fowler (1926) thought that the form with a short *i* was 'now certainly often heard, and is now not unlikely to prevail'. Walker's preferred form has prevailed, not Fowler's, and /ˈtrʌɪpɒd/ is now the only standard form. Cf. *tripodal* adjective /ˈtrɪpədəl/.

triptych. Pronounced with final /-k/.

triumphal, triumphant. *Triumphal* is a classifying adjective only, meaning 'in honour of a victory', and is properly used of a celebration (*a triumphal march, parade, procession*) or of a monument erected to celebrate a victory (*triumphal arch*). *Triumphant* is a qualitative adjective, i.e. it is more descriptive, and means either 'victorious' (*two of their triumphant Cup team*) or 'feeling or expressing jubilation after a victory or achievement', e.g. *O come, all ye faithful, joyful and triumphant*; *'I thought so,' said Gray, with a small triumphant laugh*—S. Faulks, 1993.

The *OED* entries show that the two words have sometimes been used interchangeably in the past (e.g. *triumphal* = 'victorious' by Gavin Douglas in 1513; and *triumphant* = 'in honour of a victory' by several writers from 1531 to 1876), but the distinction is nowadays generally observed.

The two words can occasionally occur in the same context: a *triumphal* entry into a captured city is one in which victory is celebrated with all the appropriate pomp and circumstance, while a *triumphant* entry might refer to the same event, but emphasizing the jubilation involved. Such entries are usually *triumphant* for the victors, but not for the vanquished. Occasionally the words are confused: **The unique building, which is a Georgian triumphant arch with an octagonal gazebo on top* (read *triumphal*); **Well, earlier today, Nawaz Sharif tried to make a triumphal return to Pakistan. It didn't quite turn out the way he had hoped* (read *triumphant*).

triumvir /trʌɪˈʌmvə/ or /ˈtrʌɪəmvə/. Plural either *triumvirs* or, less commonly, *triumviri* /-rʌɪ/. See LATIN PLURALS. But **triumvirate** (set of triumvirs) /trʌɪˈʌmvɪrət/ is now more usual than either plural.

trivia (things of little consequence). A 20c. word (first recorded in Logan Pearsall Smith's title *Trivia* in 1902), adopted from the modern Latin plural of *trivium* (= 'a place where three ways meet' in classical Latin), it comes via the medieval sense of a three-part education in grammar, rhetoric, and logic as a division of the liberal arts. It is now used both as a singular and a plural noun: *Besides, trivia has its importance too. Or to put it another way, trivia have their importance too—Sunday Times*, 26 Feb. 1978. In practice it is most frequently used as an uncount noun: *Picture to yourself a monstrous skip crammed with trivia: singularly ununique childhood memories*, [etc.]—J. Barnes, 1991; *Listeners bored with election trivia might prefer to hear music while watching the swingometers with the sound turned down—Classic CD*, 1991. In such contexts the pronouns and verbs used with *trivia* do not reveal its number.

-trix. 1 For words in *-trix* that are not agent nouns with a male correlative in *-tor*, see CICATRICE; MATRIX. Cf. also -EX, -IX.

2 Since the 15c. a number of words in *-trix* have been formed to signify the female equivalent of agent nouns in *-tor*. The most important of these have been *administratrix* (first recorded in the 17c.), *aviatrix* (20c.), *directrix* (17c.), *dominatrix* (16c., then obsolete, revived in the 20c.), *editrix* (20c.), *executrix* (16c.), *heritrix/heretrix* (16c.), *inheritrix* (16c.), *mediatrix* (15c.), *narratrix* (19c.), *oratrix* (15c.), *prosecutrix* (18c.), *testatrix* (16c.). The *OED* record of these feminine derivatives is uneven, and it is not possible to make safe statements about (*a*) their currency at a given time, (*b*) the currency of notional or actual rival forms in *-ess*, (*c*) the distribution down the centuries of the 'regular' plural forms in *-ices* or the Anglicized ones in *-ixes*. It seems clear, however, that, except in legal language, *-trix* forms are rather infrequent. Of the above (leaving one or two of the legal terms aside) only *dominatrix, editrix*, and *executrix* have any currency.

3 *Plurals*. The notionally regular plural form of each of these *-trix* words, or at any rate those formed between the 15c. and the 18c., is *-ices*, and such forms are indeed found (*executrices, heretrices, mediatrices, prosecutrices*, etc.) at various times; but there has been a marked tendency over the centuries to use the Anglicized forms in *-ixes* instead, and this tendency seems likely to continue in so far as there is any future at all for words in *-trix*. When the plural forms in *-ices* occur the main stressing pattern of the equivalent male word is sometimes retained and sometimes not. The pronunciations given in the *New SOED* (1993) are as follows:

(stress unchanged) *executor* /ɪɡˈzɛkjʊtə/, *executrix* /ɪɡˈzɛkjʊtrɪks/, and *executrices* /ɪɡˈzekjʊtrɪsiːz/.
(stress changed) *mediator* /ˈmiːdɪeɪtə/, *mediatrix* /miːdɪˈeɪtrɪks/, and *mediatrices* /miːdɪˈeɪtrɪsiːz/.
(stress variable) *prosecutor* /ˈprɒsɪkjuːtə/, *prosecutrix* /ˈprɒsɪkjuːtrɪks/ *or* /-ˈkjuː-/, and *prosecutrices* /prɒsɪˈkjuːtrɪsiːz/.

No wonder such plural forms tend to be avoided.

troche (small medicated lozenge). This altered version of the long obsolete word *trochisk* (from French *trochisque*, ultimately from Greek τροχίσκος 'small wheel') is pronounced /trəʊʃ/ in BrE and /ˈtrəʊkiː/ in AmE.

trochee (prosody) /ˈtrəʊkiː/ (**troh**-kee). A foot consisting of one long or stressed syllable followed by one short or unstressed syllable, i.e. – ◡, as in *manner* or *body*.

trolley. So spelt (not *trolly*). Plural *trolleys*.

troop (verb). *Trooping the colour* is the orthodox modern term for a ceremonial mounting of the guard, but in the early 19c. examples in the *OED* it was *colours* that were trooped.

troop, troupe. In BrE a *troop* is an artillery or armoured unit of soldiers, or a group of Scouts; a *troupe* is a company of actors or acrobats. A **trooper** is a private soldier in a cavalry or armoured unit (whence the phrase *to swear like a trooper*), and, in America and Australia, a mounted police officer, while a **trouper** is a member of a theatrical company, or, by extension, a reliable, uncomplaining person. *I don't think you're selfish at all. In fact, Maisie, I think you're a proper trouper*—D. Francis, 1976.

troublous (adjective). An archaic or literary word for 'full of troubles; disturbed (*troublous times*)'. In most contexts, *troubled* or *troublesome* are the more appropriate words.

trough. The only standard pronunciation in the UK now is /trɒf/, though Daniel Jones (1917) recommended /trɔːf/, gave /trʌf/ as a former variant, and added a note saying (somewhat mysteriously) 'Bakers often say trau.'

trousers. Always construed as a plural noun (*his new trousers were given to him by his sister*); but, when used attributively and in compounds, the word loses its final *-s*: e.g. *trouser leg, trouser pockets, trouser suit*.

trousseau. The plural form recommended is *trousseaus*, but *trousseaux* is also used. See -x. Both plural forms are pronounced with final /-z/.

trout. Plural usually the same. But *old trouts* for the derogatory informal term.

trow. Markedly archaic, but if used it should be pronounced /trəʊ/ both as noun (= belief) and verb (= believe). The noun is now rarely used.

truculence, truculency. The first entered the language in the 18c. and the second in the 16c. They have been used as synonyms since the 18c. (= the condition or quality of being truculent), but *truculency* has now all but vanished. For pronunciation, see TRUCULENT.

truculent. The *OED* (1915) gave precedence to /ˈtruːk-/ in the first syllable, and also in *truculence* and *truculency*, but the only standard pronunciation now is /ˈtrʌkjʊlənt/.

true and false etymology. The English language, perhaps more than any other, has from its earliest times onwards drawn loanwords from many other languages—Latin, Greek, French, Italian, Dutch, and so on—and has usually respelt the adopted words so that they 'fitted in with' English conceptions of what constitutes properly established native models of spelling, prefixation, suffixation, conjugation, and so on. Some of the incoming words have undergone changes to the point that they seem to the amateur to be directly related to similar-sounding words of native origin (see e.g. *belfry* s.v. ETYMOLOGY 4). Many words of native origin were respelt at a later stage because of all kinds of spurious associations with similar-sounding words: e.g., from the list below, *crayfish, forlorn hope, greyhound, island, shamefaced, slow-worm.* Readers who wish to avoid some of the more obvious misconceptions about the origins of some of the commonest words in the language may find the following list a useful starting-point. Really determined readers should pursue them in *The Oxford Dictionary of English Etymology* (1966) or in its Concise version (1986), or indeed in any standard dictionary of moderate size. The words given are mere signposts to a huge and complicated subject. The words in small capitals are the few that happen to be treated at their alphabetical places. See also the articles ETYMOLOGY and FOLK ETYMOLOGY.

AMUCK, not Eng. *muck*
andiron, only by sound-association with Eng. *iron* (and *fire-iron*)
apparel, not Latin *parō* 'provide oneself with'
arbour, not Latin *arbor* 'tree'
barberry, not Eng. *berry*
belfry, not Eng. *bell*
blindfold, not Eng. *fold*
bliss, not Eng. *bless*
bound (*homeward,* etc.), not Eng. *bind*
Boxing Day, not pugilistic
bridal, not an adjective in *-al*
bridegroom, not Eng. *groom*
BRIER pipe, not Eng. *brier* (prickly bush)
bum (buttocks), not a contraction of Eng. *bottom*
buttonhole (verb), not *hole* but *hold*
catgut, not made from the intestines of a cat
cinders, not Latin *cineres* 'ashes'
cockroach, not Eng. *cock* or Eng. *roach*
comity, not Latin *comes* 'companion'
convey, not Latin *vehō* 'carry'
cookie (biscuit, etc.), not Eng. *cook*
COT(E), separate words
court-card, a corruption
CRAYFISH, not Eng. *fish*
curtail, not Eng. *tail*
cutlet, not Eng. *cut*
dispatch, not French *dépêcher*
egg on, not *egg* but *edge*
EQUERRY, not Latin *equus* 'horse'
errand, not Latin *errō* 'wander'
fall asleep, not Eng. *fall* but OE *fēolan* 'penetrate into (sleep)'
farouche, not Latin *ferox* 'fierce'
FOREBEARS, = fore-beërs
FORLORN HOPE, not *forlorn* nor *hope*
FUSE (for igniting explosive), from Latin *fūsus* 'spindle'
GINGERLY, not Eng. *ginger*
GREYHOUND, not Eng. *grey*
humble pie, a pie made from the *umbles* (intestines of a deer)
incentive, not Latin *incendō* 'set on fire'
ingenuity, modern sense by confusion of *ingenious* with *ingenuous*
island, respelt by association with *isle*
Jerusalem artichoke, not *Jerusalem* but *girasole* (sunflower)
LITANY, LITURGY, first syllables unconnected
MOOD (grammar), = *mode,* not *mood* (temper)
old dutch, not *Dutch* but *duchess* (see NETHERLANDS)
pen, pencil, unconnected
PIDGIN, not Eng. *pigeon*
POSH, not *p*ort *o*utward *s*tarboard *h*ome
PROTAGONIST, Greek πρῶτος 'first', not Latin *pro-* 'for'
recover, not Eng. *cover*
river, not Latin *rivus* 'river'
run the gauntlet, not *gauntlet* (glove) but 17c. *gantlope* (see GAUNTLET)
SAND-BLIND, not Eng. *sand*
scissors, not Latin *scindō sciss-* 'cleave, tear apart'
shamefaced, not Eng. *-faced* but *-fast*
SLOW-WORM, not Eng. *slow*
sorrow, sorry, unconnected
vile, villain, unconnected
walnut, unconnected with Eng. *wall*
WATERSHED, neither a store of water nor a place that sheds water
Welsh rabbit, not *rare bit* nor *rarebit*

truffle. Both the *OED* (1915) and Daniel Jones (1917) allow the vaguely French-sounding variant /ˈtrʊf(ə)l/ (the French equivalent is actually *truffe*), but it is now always pronounced /ˈtrʌf(ə)l/, at least in standard BrE. American dictionaries list /ˈtruː-/ as a permissible variant.

truly. See LETTER FORMS.

trumpet (verb). The inflected forms are *trumpeted, trumpeting.* See -T-, -TT-.

trunkful Plural *trunkfuls.* See -FUL.

trustee, trusty. The first, which is stressed on the second syllable, is 'a person or member of a board given control or powers of administration of property in trust with a legal obligation to administer it solely for the purposes specified' (*COD*). The second, which is stressed on the first syllable, is an archaic adjective meaning 'trustworthy' (*a trusty steed*) or 'loyal (to a sovereign)' (*my trusty subjects*); and also a noun (with plural *trusties*) meaning 'a prisoner who is given special privileges for good behaviour'.

truth. The recommended pronunciation of the plural *truths* is with final /ðz/, but /θs/ is also standard. See -TH (θ) AND -TH (ð).

try and, try to. 1 Arguments continue about the validity of *try and* followed by an infinitive instead of *try to,* 'To be used only in informal contexts', 'grammatically wrong' are among the verdicts of some writers on English usage. Fowler's judgement in 1926 was much more lenient. After briefly setting out the facts he concluded: '*try and* is an idiom that should not be discountenanced, but used when it comes natural.' He also made out a sort of case for the semantic distinctiveness of *try and* constructions. A Scandinavian scholar, Åge Lind, has examined a group of fifty modern English novels of the period 1960–70 and found that *try to* was likely to occur in certain syntactic conditions, *try and* in others, and that in some circumstances the choice seemed not to be governed by any particular reason. 'If a subtle semantic distinction exists it does not seem to be observed,' he concluded. Whatever critics say about the legitimacy or otherwise of the *try and* construction, it is an integral part of English.

2 *Try* has parallels in *come* and *go,* which can also be followed by *and* + verb instead of by a *to*-infinitive: *You will come* and *see us sometimes, won't you?; Do go and thank him; Try and survive, try and live with the system*—G. Seymour, 1983. Some people consider this use more informal than the construction with *to,* and it also has the effect of placing the weight of meaning less on *try* and more on the following verb (compare the balance of meaning in *Try* to *survive . . .*). It is most common in the present and future tenses, and especially in the imperative (as mentioned above, and in e.g. *So let's not try* and *be too funny, eh?*—T. Lewis, 1992), and there are occasions when *and* is the more likely or natural choice: (i) when *try* is already preceded by *to,* e.g. *Jack didn't stop to try* and *work it out*—A. Masters, 1991; *Seoul promised yesterday that it would continue to seek a diplomatic solution to the crisis and that it would be holding talks with both Russia and China to try* and *find a means of resolving the dispute—Scotland on Sunday,* 2002; (ii) in casual or formulaic commands and invitations, e.g. *Turn yer light out and try* and *get some sleep*—H. Innes, 1991; and (iii) in expressions of challenge or defiance, e.g. *Don't try* and *frighten me*—Thackeray, 1847; *Just you try* and *stop me*—J. Barnes, 1992).

But these are tendencies only, and many contrary examples can be found: *That girl was going to try* to *put the blame on her, she could tell*—S. Shepherd, 1988; *They had to try* to *find out for themselves what went on inside the secretive home—OEC,* 2005.

3 When *try* is in the negative, *to* and *and* occur more interchangeably in the same types of construction (for example, in commands), but *and* is noticeably more informal: *Don't try* and *change the subject!*—M. Dibdin, 1989; *Don't try* to *deny it*—S. Howard, 1993; *So Herbie didn't try* and *jump in the car before I could lift him*—conversation recorded in British National Corpus, 1991; *They should not try* to *be fair to other countries—New Scientist,* 1991.

4 (*a*) The construction with *and* is not available after any other form of *try,* i.e. not after *tries, tried,* or *trying.* Try to substitute *tried and* etc. for *tried to* etc. in the following: *They tried* to *warn us; What were you trying* to *tell me?; What if she tries* to *ring you?; I . . . paced around and tried* to *absorb all the details*—A. Brookner, 1986. (*b*) But it is available in tenses formed by auxiliary or modal verbs + the simple form of *try*, e.g. *I* could *try* and *make my own films*—film website, 2003; *We* might *try* and *get back later today*—weblog, 2004. (*c*) A construction with *to* is also obligatory when *try* is followed by a negative proposition: *Try* not to *hang things too close, too high, or too far apart*—M. Gilliatt, 1992 (not **Try and not hang things too close* . . .).

5 *Conclusion*. From all this evidence we must conclude that choice between *try to* and *try and* is largely a matter of spontaneity, rhythm, and emphasis, especially in spoken forms. Generally speaking, *try and* is somewhat more casual in effect, and is especially idiomatic in speech, whereas there are often good reasons for preferring *try to* in more formal contexts. But usage is fluid, and is likely to remain so.

tryst. This archaic word for a date, an assignation is normally pronounced /trɪst/ now, though the *OED* (1915) gave only /trʌɪst/. The main AmE dictionaries give preference to the form with a short vowel.

tsar. BrE dictionaries favour the form *tsar*, with **czar** (and, in *ODO*, **tzar**, which is rather infrequent) as alternatives. AmE ones favour *czar*, with *tsar* as variant. Some BrE style guides positively proscribe *czar*, and the AP Stylebook does the same with *tsar*. The spelling *tsar* (which is closer to the Russian form) is more common in most varieties of English, particularly BrE, than *czar*, which is preferred in North American English. In the extended meaning of an official with special powers in some designated domain, such as a *drugs tsar/czar* or an *intelligence tsar/czar*, both spellings are used depending on which is favoured in the variety of English concerned. Whichever way it is spelt, the word has an initial capital when used with the personal name of a Russian ruler, e.g. *Tsar Alexander II*. Pronounced /zɑː/ or /tsɑː/.

-t-, -tt-. 1 (*a*) Monosyllabic words containing a simple vowel (*a, e, i, o, u*) before *t* normally double the consonant before suffixes beginning with a vowel (*batted, wetter, fitted, forgettable, cutter*) or before a following *y* (*witty, nutty*); (*b*) but the *t* remains undoubled if the stem contains a diphthong (*baiting, flouting*), doubled vowel (*sooty*), or a vowel + consonant (*fasted, nested, bolting*).

2 Words of more than one syllable follow the rule for monosyllables if their last syllable is accented, but otherwise do not double the *t*: thus *regretted*; but *balloted, benefited, bonneted, buffeted, combatant, cosseted, discomfited, fidgeted, pilotage, trumpeter*. It is inconsistent to double the *-t-* in the past tenses of two- or three-syllabled words, though such forms as *benefitted, cossetted, plummetted*, and *targetted* are not infrequently found in standard sources.

3 The recommended forms for three special cases (especially in the language of computers) are *formatting, formatted*; *inputting, inputted* or *input*; *outputting, outputted* or *output*.

tub. For *the Tub*, see ACADEMY.

tubercular, tuberculous. Before 1882, in which year the tubercle bacillus was discovered, the two words were used interchangeably to mean 'of the nature or form of a tubercle' and 'in reference to tuberculosis (or tubercular consumption)'. Since then, in medical use, *tuberculous* has been restricted to the second of these meanings and *tubercular* to the first. But in lay use the adjectives continue to be used without distinction of meaning, though *tubercular* is markedly the more common of the two words. *Tubercular* has also been used as a noun since the mid-20c. meaning 'a person having tuberculosis' (e.g. *In 1949 Orwell left the Isle of Jura to enter a convalescent home for tuberculars at Cranham in Gloucestershire*—I. Hunter, 1980).

tuberose (noun). (botany) This plant of the agave family, *Polianthes tuberosa*, is pronounced /ˈtjuːbərəʊz/. It is sometimes erroneously written as *tube-rose*, pronounced /ˈtjuːbrəʊz/.

Tuesday. For (*on*) *Tuesday*, see FRIDAY.

tulle. Pronounced /tjuːl/.

tumbrel, tumbril. The first spelling is recommended.

tumefy. So spelt, not *tumify*.

tumour. So spelt in BrE, but **tumor** in AmE. See -OUR AND -OR.

tumulus /ˈtjuːmjʊləs/. Plural *tumuli* /-lʌɪ, -liː/.

tun. See TON.

tunnel (verb). The inflected forms are *tunnelling, tunnelled* in BrE (also **tunneller** noun), but usually *tunneling, tunneled* (and *tunneler*) in AmE. See -LL-, -L-.

tu quoque (rhetoric; from Latin, literally 'you too'). An argument which consists in retorting a charge upon one's accuser. A standard example is the medical rejoinder *Physician heal thyself.*

turban. The corresponding adjective is **turbaned**. See -N-, -NN-.

turbidity, turbidness. The first is standard, the second virtually extinct.

turbid, turgid. The first means '(of a liquid) cloudy, unclear', and '(of a writer's style) confused, obscure'; whereas *turgid* means 'swollen, distended', and '(of language) inflated, bombastic'.

turbine. Most British dictionaries give /ˈtəːbʌɪn/ first and /ˈtəːbɪn/ as a permissible variant, whereas most standard American dictionaries reverse the order. (The *OED* (1915) gave only the form with /-ɪn/ and Daniel Jones (1917) gave preference to the same.)

Turco-. The normal combining form of *Turkish*, not *Turko-*. Thus *Turcocentric, Turcophilia*, etc.; *Turco-Russian discussions.*

Turcoman. A now mostly discarded variant of TURKOMAN.

tureen. Pronounced /tjʊˈriːn/ rather than /təˈriːn/ since the word has moved away from its earlier form *terrine* (ultimately from Latin *terra* 'earth'). The spelling *tureen* is possibly modelled on the place name *Turin.* In AmE the first syllable is usually pronounced /tə-/.

turf. In the senses 'a piece of turf cut from the ground (used with other pieces to make a lawn)', and 'a piece of peat cut for fuel', the plural is usually *turves.* But *turfs* is also a standard form. See -VE(D), -VES, ETC.

turgid. See TURBID.

turkey Plural *turkeys.*

Turkish. See TURCO-.

Turkoman. Plural *Turkomans.*

turnipy. So spelt. See -P-, -PP-.

turnover. See TART.

turps. See ABBREVIATIONS 2.

turquoise. The recommended pronunciation in BrE is /ˈtəːkwɔɪz/, but /-kwɑːz/ is sometimes heard (in imitation of the French equivalent word). In AmE, /ˈtərkɔɪz/ seems to be the dominant form, i.e. without medial /w/.

turret. The corresponding adjective is **turreted**. See -T-, -TT-.

tussore. (in full **tussore silk**) This spelling, pronounced /ˈtʌsɔː/, is the one given first in BrE dictionaries, with **tussah** /ˈtʌsə/ as a variant; the opposite applies in AmE dictionaries. The spelling *tussar* is the most frequent in Indian English sources in the *OEC*, and, as the *OED* notes, that spelling is one of the variants that represent most accurately the original Hindi (and Urdu) *tasar*, adopted as a loanword in English in the 16c.

tutoress. See -ESS 4.

tweet. 1 Considering that this noun and verb onomatopoeically represent a high-pitched birdcall, it is possibly surprising that both parts of speech are unknown before the 19c., though the interjection *tweet*, or more precisely Scots *tueit*, dates back to 1550. However, such avian lore is rendered largely irrelevant by the modern meaning.

2 A *tweet* is, of course, a posting made on the social networking service Twitter. Each posting is in the form of a text-based message of up to 140 characters. *To tweet* is to create such a posting. Noun and verb both date to 2006. The verb has rapidly acquired its own fully fledged syntax (forgive the pun): (intransitive) *She talks about her own life, but she's just as likely to tweet about budget cuts and Keynesian economics*; (transitive) *She tweeted a picture of them smiling at the camera; email us, tweet us, go to our blog, and find us on Facebook*; (introducing a clause) *He tweeted that he would be willing to take a lie detector test*; (with direct speech) *The president tweeted: 'After you vote, tell your Facebook friends "I voted."'*; (ditransitive) *The Communications Director tweeted us the following.*

twenties. See NINETIES.

twilight, twilit. The noun *twilight* is frequently used to describe another noun, e.g. *twilight hour, years, the Twilight Zone* (TV series), etc. The form *twilit* comes from the 19c. verb *to twilight,* first used by Keats, according to the *OED.* It should only be used when the meaning is 'lit by or as by twilight' (*a twilit sky*). Otherwise, *twilight* should be used, and should replace *twilit* in the following example: **He looked forward to a gentle decline into an eccentric and amiable dotage, his twilit years untroubled by chore or challenge—OEC,* 2004.

Twitter. The social media website is written with a capital first letter. The verb, meaning 'to talk rapidly in a trivial way' is not, of course. In the early days of *Twitter* there was some uncertainty about whether the verb to denote making a posting on *Twitter* was *twitter* (lower case) or *tweet. Tweet* is now standard, while *twitter* is likely to sound odd, or even disparaging.

-ty and -ness. (Including some abstract nouns in *-ety* and *-ity.*) **1** (*a*) Most English adjectives can form nouns by adding the still active (originally Old English) suffix *-ness,* and these nouns denote either a state or quality (*cleverness, happiness*) or an instance of a state or quality (*a kindness*).

Though any adjective may be formed into a noun on occasion by the addition of *-ness,* the nouns of that pattern actually current are substantially fewer than those made from Latin adjectives with *-ty, -ety,* or *-ity* as their English ending. (*b*) The suffix *-ty* represents via Old French a Latin noun ending *-tas* or *-itas,* and is very common in English (e.g. *honesty, notoriety, prosperity, sanity, stupidity*); some forms also denote an instance of the quality in the way that some *-ness* nouns do (*an ability, an ambiguity, a curiosity, a fatality, a subtlety, a variety*). (*c*) In most cases parallel nouns in *-ness* (*ableness, curiousness, honestness,* etc.) are not normally used, but in other cases a form in *-ty* has developed a special meaning or a sense of remoteness from the adjective that leaves room for an alternative in *-ness,* e.g. *casualty/casualness, clarity/clearness, crudity/crudeness, enormity/enormousness, ingenuity* (from *ingenious*)/*ingenuousness* (from *ingenuous*), *nicety/niceness, purity* (with sexual overtones)/*pureness, preciosity* (used of literary or artistic style)/*preciousness, speciality/specialness.*

2 The following are a few types that have not been cited above, but are notable in some way. (*a*) Some words in *-ty* for which there is no companion in *-ness,* the Latin adjective not having been taken into English: *celerity, cupidity, debility, fidelity, integrity, lenity, utility.* (*b*) Some of the few words in *-ness* that are as much used as those in *-ty,* or more, though the *-ty* words exist: *falseness, ponderousness, tenseness, unctuousness.* (*c*) Some adjectives of Latin origin that might have been expected to have forms in *-ty* in fact do not, and *-ness* forms are used instead: *crispness, facetiousness, firmness, largeness, massiveness, naturalness, obsequiousness, pensiveness, proneness, robustness, rudeness, seriousness, tardiness, tediousness, tenderness, vastness, vileness.* (*d*) If there is also a *-tion* word, derived from the verb, this naturally signifies the process, and the *-ty* word, derived from the adjective, the result: e.g. *liberty* and *liberation, multiplicity* and *multiplication, profanity* and *profanation, satiety* and *satiation, variety* and *variation.* But sometimes these pairs develop by usage a sharper differentiation: e.g. *integrity* and *integration, sanity* and *sanitation.* (*e*) As the *OED* points out, such words as *difficulty, faculty, honesty, modesty,* and *puberty* represent Latin formations in which the suffix *-tās* is directly added to a consonantal stem. The number of these in English is very small.

tyke, tike. In its current senses (= a mischievous little child, etc.) the more usual spelling is *tyke,* not *tike.*

tympanum /ˈtɪmpənəm/ (the eardrum). Plural *tympana* /-nə/: see -UM 3. Cf. TIMPANI (plural noun).

type. Be careful to distinguish the modern AmE attributive use of the word (= *type of,* with ellipsis of *of*), as in *The 110C systems may be used with virtually any type projector,* from the use of *-type* with a preceding defining word, as in *California-type barbecues; Fifties-type social realist films.* The first of these sounds forced and calls for the attention of a copy editor. The second is a natural use.

-type. Dictionary definitions of various technical terms in which *-type* is the second element should enable readers to work out the meaning of most of the contexts in which the word appears on the page before them. Thus, from the *New SOED* (1993):

antetype, a preceding type, an earlier example. (But this word is now rare and *prototype* can normally be used instead.)

antitype. **1** Something which a type or symbol represents. **2** A person or thing of the opposite type.

archetype. **1** The original pattern or model from which copies are made. **2** In Jungian psychoanalysis, a primordial mental concept inherited by all from the collective unconscious. **3** A pervasive or recurrent idea or symbol in legend, etc.

prototype. The first or primary type of something, the original of which a copy, imitation, representation, derivative, or improved form exists or is made.

typo. Whether used to mean a typographical error or a typographer, the plural is *typos.* See -O(E)S 6. See also ABBREVIATIONS 2.

typographic, typographical (adjectives). Both forms are current and both are of respectable antiquity (*-ic* 18c., *-ical* 16c.). The longer form is much the more usual of the two in all varieties of English, except AmE, where the shorter form is not much less frequent. See -IC(AL).

tyrannic, tyrannical (adjectives). The shorter form, recorded in use from the 15c. to the 19c., is now rarely used in comparison with *tyrannical.* See -IC(AL).

tyrannize (verb). The transitive type *this attempt to coerce and tyrannize us* seems to be coming back into standard use since the first edition of this book (1926) appeared, when Fowler regarded it as a solecism. The traditional construction is *tyrannize over* (*us*). Examples of the various types: *She tyrannised over the older woman in all their personal relations*—D. Lindsay, 1987; *the priests know nothing, but pretend to know much and tyrannise over the common people*—*New Scientist,* 1992; *The camps were largely tyrannized by a volunteer cadre of prisoners named kapos by the Nazis*—*NY Times Bk Rev.,* 1992; *We can use it to tyrannize ourselves, to live in the future instead of in the present,* [etc.]—M. Williamson, 1992.

tyrant. The original Greek sense of the word is so far alive still that readers must be prepared to encounter it, especially when the context is of an absolute ruler in a Greek city-state. Neither cruel nor despotic conduct was essential to the Greek notion of a tyrant, who was simply an absolute ruler owing his office to usurpation. The word connoted the manner in which power had been gained, not the manner in which it was exercised; despotic or 'tyrannical' use of the usurped position was natural and common, but incidental only.

tyre, tire (of a wheel). The first is the standard spelling in BrE, and the second in AmE.

tyro (a novice) is by far the more common spelling, rather than **tiro**, which is an occasional and correct variant. See Y AND I. Plural *tyros*: see -O(E)S 7.

Tyrrhenian. So spelt, as in *Tyrrhenian Sea,* part of the Mediterranean separating Sicily and Sardinia, from the Italian mainland.

u. Anyone who believes that there is a simple relationship between a given letter and the way in which it is pronounced should glance at what follows. It will be self-evident that the pronunciation of the letter *u* varies according to the circumstances in which it occurs. The list makes no claims to completeness, and the pronunciations given are limited to those of standard BrE.

1 /ʌ/ *ugly, under, undo*; /ʊ/ *butcher, Jungian, pulpit, put*; /uː/ *fruit, June, rule, ruminate*; /ə/ *circus, ukulele* (second *u*); /juː/ *amuse, unit, university*; /ju/ *fraudulent* (second *u*), *uranium* (first *u*), *uvular* (second *u*); /ʊə/ *usual* (second *u* + *a*); /aʊə/ *flour, sour*. Note also: /gw/ *guano*; /kw/ *equal, quite*; /sw/ *suave*; (silent) *guarantee, fatigue, opaque*.

2 *Special cases*. In the 20c. the retreat of the palatalized /sj-/ in *Sue* (now usually /suː/, *suit, supreme, super*, etc.; but its retention (in BrE) in *assume*; also /-zjuː/ in *presume, resume*.

U and non-U. First, it needs to be said, for the sake of accuracy, that *U*, as a simple abbreviation for 'upper class (esp. in linguistic usage)' was introduced by A. S. C. Ross, a professor of linguistics, in a 1954 issue of the learned journal *Neuphilologische Mitteilungen*, and, together with its antonym *non-U* ('not upper class'), was turned into a cult by Nancy Mitford when she included the essay in a book of essays that she edited in 1956 called *Noblesse Oblige*. The intention was to identify expressions and modes of behaviour which marked off the aristocracy (or upper class) from hoi polloi. This national game entertained snobs for decades but is little played now, in a less class-conscious age. The subject had fascinated Nancy Mitford long before Alan Ross wrote his article. For example, in ch. 4 of her largely autobiographical novel *The Pursuit of Love* (1945):

Uncle Matthew: 'I hope poor Fanny's school (the word school pronounced in tones of withering scorn) is doing her all the good you think it is. Certainly she picks up some dreadful expressions there.'

Aunt Emily, calmly, but on the defensive: 'Very likely she does. She also picks up a good deal of education.'

Uncle Matthew: 'Education! I was always led to suppose that no educated person ever spoke of notepaper, and yet I hear poor Fanny asking Sadie for notepaper. What is this education? Fanny talks about mirrors and mantelpieces, handbags and perfume, . . .

Aunt Emily: . . . (All the same, Fanny darling, it is called writing-paper you know—don't let's hear any more about note, please.)

Any bald list of U and non-U expressions tends to be misleading: the contextual nuances and qualifications need to be examined item by item. But a list (mostly drawn from Ross and/or Mitford) follows, out of historical interest.

U	non-U
bike	*cycle*
false teeth	*dentures*
—	*God Bless* (when saying goodbye)
house	*home*
lavatory, loo	*toilet*
looking-glass	*mirror*
luncheon (in middle of day)	*dinner*
pudding	*sweet, dessert*
rich	*wealthy*
scent	*perfume*
be sick (or *vomit*)	*be ill*
Sorry? (when something is not clearly heard)	*Pardon?*
table napkin	*serviette*
vegetables	*greens*
writing-paper	*notepaper*

The mood of the language game did not escape the gentle satirical eye of John

Betjeman. His poem 'How to Get On in Society' (1954) lampoons the pretensions of the Hyacinth Buckets ('It's pronounced "Bouquet"!') of his day. It does so sociolinguistically, by bringing together words that are genteel (*requisites*), informal (*kiddies*) and non-U (*toilet*); and sociologically, by referring to things aristos supposedly despised, such as fish knives, cruets, and faux fires.

Phone for the fish-knives, Norman,
As Cook is a little unnerved;
You kiddies have crumpled the serviettes
And I must have things daintily served.

Are the requisites all in the toilet?
The frills round the cutlets can wait
Till the girl has replenished the cruets
And switched on the logs in the grate.

It's ever so close in the lounge, dear,
But the vestibule's comfy for tea
And Howard is out riding on horseback
So do come and take some with me.

Now here is a fork for your pastries
And do use the couch for your feet;
I know what I wanted to ask you—
Is trifle sufficient for sweet?

Milk and then just as it comes, dear?
I'm afraid the preserve's full of stones;
Beg pardon, I'm soiling the doileys
With afternoon tea-cakes and scones.

The potentially sinister social exclusiveness behind the *U and non-U* distinction has lost much of its power since people turned their attention to more pressing aspects of language use, such as those that are considered to perpetuate stereotypes and discrimination of many kinds.

ukase (arbitrary command). This Russian loanword has become completely anglicized, and is pronounced /juː'keiz/ (yoo-**kayz**). Printed in roman.

ulna. Plural *ulnae* /'ʌlniː/.

ult. See ULTIMO.

ultima /'ʌltɪmə/. In linguistics, the last syllable of a word, as al*ways*, decor*um*. Contrast ANTEPENULT; PENULT.

ultimatum. Plural *ultimatums* (for preference), which is twenty or so times more frequent in the *OEC* than *ultimata*, which, frankly, sounds ridiculous and hypercorrect. See -UM 3.

ultimo. Also abbrev. as *ult.* Formerly, but now rarely, used in commercial letters, meaning 'of last month' (*your letter of the 12th ult.*). Cf. Latin *ultimō mense* 'in the last month'. See COMMERCIALESE.

ultra, originally a Latin preposition and adverb meaning 'beyond', was adopted as an English noun (plural *-as*) and adjective in the early 19c. It was initially a shortening of the French *ultra-royaliste*, a term for extreme monarchists, and then came to be applied generally in English to extremists and their views. In current use it can work as a noun (*ultras in the animal rights movement*), but is more often used as a prefix to intensify the adjective it is attached to, e.g. *ultra-conservative, ultra-modern*. When it has this intensifying meaning it is often hyphenated, but when used in established scientific adjectives such as *ultramicroscopic, ultrasonic, utlraviolet*, etc., it is written as one word.

ultra vires (beyond one's legal authority). Pronounced /ʌltrə 'vʌɪəriːz/ (**ult**-ruh **vy**-reez).

ululate (verb). This word for 'to howl' was imitative or onomatopoeic in Latin (*ululāre*) and is more easily pronounced /'ʌljʊleɪt/ (**ul**-yuu-layt) than its dictionary alternative, the unpronounceable /'juːljʊleɪt/ (**yuul**-yuu-layt).

-um. For general remarks on the plural of Latin nouns adopted in English, see LATIN PLURALS. Those ending in *-um* are numerous and call for special treatment. The Latin plural being *-a*, and the English *-ums*, four selections follow of nouns (1) that now always use *-ums*, either as having completed their naturalization, or for special reasons; (2) that show no signs at present of conversion, but always use *-a*; (3) that vacillate, sometimes with a differentiation of meaning, sometimes in harmony with the style of writing, and sometimes very much according to the writer's inclination; and (4) nouns that raise issues peculiar to themselves. Further comments may be found at the individual entries shown in small capitals in the following lists.

1 Plurals in *-ums* only. Those marked † are not Latin nouns, and the *-a* plural for them would violate grammar as well as usage:

albums, antirrhinums (and other plant names), *asylums, †begums, †conundrums, delphiniums, Elysiums, †factotums, †harmoniums, laburnums, lyceums, museums, nasturtiums, nostrums, †panjandrums, pendulums, †quorums, †Targums* (also *Targumim*), *†vade-mecums, †variorums, vellums.*

2 Plurals in *-a* only: *bacteria* (and many other scientific terms), *corrigenda, desiderata, effluvia, errata, fraena, labia, opercula, opuscula, ova, palladia, phyla, pudenda, puncta, quanta, sacraria, scholia* (and other learned words of this kind), *scuta, septa, solaria, triclinia, triforia, vascula, vela, vexilla, viatica, vivaria.*

3 *Words with either plural.* (i) In many cases, the plural in *-a* is used in technical, scientific, or legal contexts, or in discussions of classical civilization, where it is entirely appropriate, while the *-ums* form is used by laypeople; e.g. *aquarium, gymnasium, minimum.* (ii) Outside such contexts, however, in a few words the Latinate plural jars stylistically, or seems too formal, pedantic, or hypercorrect; this, in my view, is true of *forum* and *ultimatum.* (iii) Words which are themselves rather formal and unlikely to be used much outside scholarly, academic, or medical contexts, very much favour the *-a* plural, e.g. *scriptorium, sensorium, simulacrum, tympanum.* (iv) With yet other words there seems little to choose stylistically between the two forms, for example *consortium, symposium,* but using the Latin plural pays homage to the word's origins, and may convey a slightly more academic or formal tone.

Where one form is markedly more frequent in *OED* data than the other, the more common form is bracketed; an = sign shows roughly equal frequency.

aquarium (*-ums*), *atrium* (*-a*), *compendium* (=), *consortium* (*-a*), *continua* (*-a*), *cranium* (*-a*) (*-ums* in jocular use for heads), *curricula* (*-a*), *dictum* (*-a*), *emporium* (*-ums*), *encomium* (*-ums*), *equilibrium* (*-a*), *exordium* (*-ums*), *florilegium* (*-a*), FORUM (*-ums*), *frustum* (*-ums*), *fulcrum* (*-ums*), *gymnasium* (*-ums*), *honorarium* (*-a*), *interregnum* (*-ums*), *mausoleum* (*-ums*), *maximum* (*-a*), *minimum* (=), *momentum* (*-a*), MEDIUM (*-ums* in spiritualism; *-a* of the newspaper, etc., world), *memorandum* (*-ums*), *menstruum* (*-a*), *millennium* (*-a*), *moratorium* (*-ums*), *planetarium* (*-ums*), *plectrum* (*-ums*), *podium* (*-ums*), *premium* (*-ums*), *proscenium* (*-ums*), *referendum* (*-ums*), *rostrum* (*-a*), *sanatorium* (=), *scriptorium* (*-a*), *sensorium* (*-a*), *serum* (*-a*), *simulacrum* (*-a*), *spectrum* (*-a*), *speculum* (=), *stadium* (*-a* in ancient-world contexts; *-ums* for modern sports grounds), *sternum* (*-a*), *symposium* (*-a*), *trapezium* (*-ums*), *tympanum* (*-a*), *ultimatum* (*-ums*), *vacuum* (*-ums*).

4 The following raise issues peculiar to each and are discussed at their alphabetical place: ADDENDUM; AGENDA; CANDELABRUM; DATA; ERRATUM; STRATUM.

umbilical. Pronounced /ʌm'bɪlɪk(ə)l/, stressed on the second syllable, less commonly /ʌmbɪ'lʌɪk(ə)l/, with stress on the third syllable and with the diphthong /ʌɪ/ in that syllable.

umbilicus. The plural of *umbilicus* is generally *umbilici* /-sʌɪ/, since it is a medical word, rather than *umbilicuses*: see -US 1. The same double pattern found in *umbilical* applies to its pronunciation.

umbo (shield boss, knob, etc.). Plural rather more often *umbones* /ʌm'bəʊniːz/, as in Latin, than *umbos.*

umbra. Plural either *umbras* or *umbrae* /-briː/.

umlaut. Pronounced /'ʊmlaʊt/ (**uum**-lowt).

'un. Sometimes written without the apostrophe, it represents a rendering in colloquial standard of dialectal forms of two different personal pronouns, *him* (*the ladies liked 'un*—P. Hill, 1977) and *one* (*those striped uns* [sc. roses] *have no smell*—G. Eliot, 1859).

un-. 1 For the asymmetry of many *un-* and *in-* forms (e.g. *unstable* but *instability*), see IN- AND UN-.

2 For the cancelling negation of the type *not uncommon* see NOT 4.

3 Danger of ellipsis after *un-* words. *Untouched* means 'not touched', but with the difference that it is one word and not two, a difference that in some circumstances is important. In *I was not touched, and you were* the word *touched* is understood to be repeated, and does not carry the *not* with it. But in *I was untouched, and you were,* the ellipsis does not work in the same way: *un-* cannot be detached as *not* was in the other example. In the following example (cited by Fowler, 1926): *Dr*

Rashdall's scholarship is unquestioned; most of his writings and opinions on ecclesiastical matters are, what is meant is that most of them are questioned, not unquestioned. Ellipses, like computer commands, work with mechanical logic, and must be treated with caution.

unabashedly, unadvisedly. Five syllables. See -EDLY.

unanimous. See NEM. CON.

unapt, inapt, inept. See INAPT.

unarguable. See IN- AND UN-.

unartistic, inartistic. These words, neither of them frequent, share the meanings 'Not possessing artistic value, tasteless' referring to works of art, and 'devoid of artistic talent' referring to people. More or less exclusive to *unartistic*, which is the less frequent word, seems to be the meaning 'not concerned with or relating to art'. Examples: *Robinson decried one of the favourite tricks of architects, the clipping and aligning of trees, as 'barbarous, needless, and inartistic; It is impossible to entirely acquit this otherwise excellent conductor of the charge of an undue and very inartistic exaggeration for the sake of effect; It was the most unartistic house imaginable and there was a dreadful pergola that hung over the front door; artists have to do unartistic things to put food on the table.* See IN- AND UN-.

unashamedly. Five syllables. See -EDLY.

unattached participles. 1 (*a*) Some grammarians call them dangling, hanging, or misrelated participles. Fowler (1926) called them unattached participles, and cited an example from a letter: *Dear Sir, We beg to enclose herewith statement of your account for goods supplied, and* being desirous *of clearing our Books to end May will* you *kindly favour us with cheque in settlement per return, and much oblige.* The reply ran, *Sirs, You have been misinformed. I have no wish to clear your books.* The mistake in the first letter was to attribute the desire to the wrong person.

(*b*) *In unscripted speech.* Such failures to look ahead and consider the grammatical compatibility of the following clause are exceedingly common, especially in unscripted speech. Lord Belstead, speaking on BBC Radio 4 in January 1988 about his own role after the resignation of Lord Whitelaw as Leader of the House of Lords, said, *Being unique, I am not going in any way to imitate him.* He did not intend, we presume, to imply that he was himself unique. A commentator on *World at One* (BBC Radio 4) at the end of May the same year spoke of the Reagan/Gorbachev summit meeting: *After inspecting a guard of honour, President Reagan's motorcade moved into the centre of Moscow.* In December, 1987, Richard Ingrams wrote about the house in which he grew up: *Now demolished, I can call it to mind in almost perfect detail.* Obviously the entire motorcade did not inspect the Russian troops, and Mr Ingrams had not been demolished.

(*c*) *In writing.* Naturally, such misrelated clauses are not restricted to unscripted speech: *Picking up my Bible, the hill seemed the only place to go just then*—J. Winterson, 1985; *While serving... as a sentry outside St James's Palace, on an extremely hot day in 1980, the Queen Mother sent an equerry down who instructed my partner and I* [*sic*] *to perform our duties on the opposite side of the road which was shaded and much cooler*—letter in *Independent*, 1991; *While serving in the RAF in North Africa the cockroaches and other creatures baked in the bread provided an interesting gauge as to how long the recipient had served out there*—letter in *Independent*, 1993.

2 Distinguished from *considering* (*that*), *providing* (*that*), etc. (*a*) Fowler went on to approve of sentences in which certain participles have acquired the character of (marginal) prepositions or subordinating conjunctions, and can stand before a noun or a clause without disturbing the logicality or grammatical soundness of the sentence: Talking of *test matches, who won the last?*; Considering *the circumstances, you were justified*; Roughly speaking, *they are identical*; allowing for *exceptions, the rule may stand.* His judgement was surely right. In such examples the participial form is now normally seen to be in harmony with what follows. Modern examples come easily to hand: Knowing *my mother, this is her way of punishing us*; 'Speaking of *money,' said Beryl, 'do you mind my asking what you did with yours?'*. Somewhat more debatable is the use in scientific work of *using* as a semi-unattached participle: Using *carbon monoxide, his hiccups were cured for 30 minutes, but they came back again* (the writer, not his patient's hiccups, used carbon monoxide). See also BASED (ON); CONSIDERING; GIVEN (THAT); GRANTED; JUDGING BY.

(*b*) *Further subordinating conjunctions: historical.* Some of the other key words in constructions of this type are *assuming, barring, excepting, owing to* (first recorded as a prepositional phrase in the work of Sir Walter Scott), *provided, providing, seeing,* and *supposing.* Some of them can also be used with *that,* with an added touch of slight formality: *Even* assuming that *the Socialist government was seriously committed ... all this could only be accomplished ...* Many of the constructions are traced back to earlier centuries by the *OED.* For example, *considering* construed as a preposition with a simple object is found as early as the 14c.: *And gentilly I preise wel thy wit ...* considerynge *thy yowthe* (Chaucer). *Provided* (*that*) and *providing* (*that*) construed as quasi-conjunctions have also been used for several centuries.

(*c*) *Further subordinating conjunctions: modern.* Examples of the various key words of this type are strewn about in books, journals, and newspapers in every part of the English-speaking world: Considering *his gene pool, Sean Thomas Harmon is probably among the better-looking babies born Monday—Chicago Tribune,* 1988; Given *bad light ... a nervous enemy firing this way and that may do most of our work for us*—M. Shadbolt, 1986 (NZ); Granted, *it was not hard to interest a security man, who apart from a regular soldier had the most boring job on earth*—T. Keneally, 1985 (Aust.); Granted *that any interpretation is partial ... nevertheless there is a difference ... between* [etc.]—D. Lodge, 1992. It is a remarkable fact that criticism—and ridicule—of unattached participles did not begin until about a century ago.

3 *Criticism is a modern phenomenon.* Historical grammarians—Jespersen, Visser, and others—and the *OED* cite clear examples from the Middle Ages onwards. A small selection must suffice: *Tis giuen out, that sleeping in mine Orchard, A Serpent stung me*—Shakespeare, 1602; *Having applied a smelling-bottle to her nose, the blood began to revisit her cheeks*—Smollett, 1748; *Meeting some friends and singing with them in a palace near the Hague his pen fails him to express his delight*—R. L. Stevenson, 1887. Scores of other examples have been dredged up from the past.

4 *Further examples.* To conclude, here is an elementary example of a correctly attached participle: *Looking at Jim, I remembered the first time I had seen him—Encounter,* 1988. And here are further examples of incorrect or questionable uses: *Being a vegan bisexual who's into Nicaraguan coffee picking and boiler suits, you could safely assume that I vote Labour—Private Eye,* 1988; *By giving this youngster the chance to repair and race old cars, he's not tempted to steal new ones*—Home Office advt in *Times,* 1989; *Mentioning* [= when I mentioned] *a love of folk music, Mynors immediately produced a set of the most beautiful original broadside ballads for me to look at—Times,* 1989; *Driving near home recently, a thick pall of smoke turned out to be a bungalow well alight while the owner and neighbours watched helplessly—Oxford Times,* 1990; *Watching the President struggle with the crisis in Lithuania, the answer appears to be yes—NY Times,* 1990; *Yesterday, after conferring with my senior national security advisers and following extensive consultations with our coalition partners, Saddam Hussein was given one last chance*—statement by President Bush in *Chicago Tribune,* 1991. It must be admitted that unattached participles seldom lead to ambiguity. They just jar.

See ABSOLUTE CONSTRUCTION; MISRELATED CLAUSES.

unavowedly. Five syllables. See -EDLY.

unaware(s). *Unaware* is a predicative adjective usually followed by *of* (*he was unaware of her presence*) or *that* + clause (*I was unaware that you had moved to Brussels*); and, archaically in BrE, an adverb (*A Zephyr ... gathering round her unaware Fill'd with his breath her vesture and her veil*—R. Bridges, 1885–94). *Unawares* is only an adverb, especially meaning 'unexpectedly' (*he stumbled on them unawares; the question took him unawares*) or 'inadvertently' (*dropped it unawares*).

unbeknown, unbeknownst are grammatical and stylistic oddities. Though technically adjectives, they are used almost exclusively in the prepositional phrase *unbeknown(st) to someone.* While *unbeknownst* has the patina of archaism, it is two centuries newer than *unbeknown* (1636), being first known from an 1848 letter of Mrs Gaskell. And even the *OED* is at a loss to find analogies for an *-st* added to an adjective.

No matter. Both forms are current throughout the English-speaking world, and are not restricted to formal contexts. *Unbeknownst* is more frequent, and is preferred in AmE, while BrE prefers the shorter form. Fowler (1926) regarded them as 'as out of use except in dialect or uneducated speech or in imitations of these', but his view has long ceased to be accurate. Very occasionally they are used in a rather WARDOUR STREET English style as highfalutin synonyms of *unknown*, e.g. *for some unbeknown(st) reason*. Examples: *Unbeknownst to Mr. Semetis, Mrs. Clinton was navigating some dire financial straits—NYT*, 2008; *I was advised that, unbeknown to me, there were additional reporting requirements—Daily Tel.*, 2007.

unbend (verb). Fowler (1926) pointed out the minor linguistic curiosity that this verb belongs to the select band of contronyms, i.e. words having diametrically opposed meanings, like *sanction*. It can mean 'to become less formal, or strict' (*you could be fun too, you know, if you'd only unbend a little*). By contrast, the participial adjective *unbending* normally means 'unyielding, inflexible; austere' (*she knew how unbending her father was*), though it can be used in the literal sense ('not stooping') as well (*the tall old foreigner stood erect and unbending*).

unbias(s)ed. The form with a single *s* is recommended; that with *ss* is rare in comparison. See -S-, -SS-.

uncharted, unchartered. In its literal use, *uncharted* denotes an area of land, sea, space, etc. not mapped or surveyed: *the plane landed on a previously uncharted islet; an uncharted region of space*. From this comes its metaphorical use, especially with *territory* and *waters*, e.g. *The stakes are terribly high as operators enter uncharted territory in the broadband world*. In both literal and figurative meanings, **unchartered* is wrongly used in approaching one tenth of cases, e.g. **In that sense, the Lisbon agenda is sailing into unchartered waters—BBC News*, 2004.

uncia (copper coin in Roman antiquity). Plural *unciae* /ˈʌnsiiː/.

Uncle Sam. See SOBRIQUETS.

uncommon. The old slang or colloquial use as an adverb = remarkably (*an uncommon fine girl*), first recorded in 1794, has completely died out, English outside the dialogue of period novels.

unconcernedly, uncontrolledly. Five syllables. See -EDLY.

uncooperative, uncoordinated. Both words are now written solid, i.e. without a hyphen or diaeresis. See CO-.

uncount(able) nouns. See COUNT NOUNS; MASS NOUN.

under (preposition). For distinctions, see BELOW; BENEATH; UNDERNEATH.

underestimate. See OVERESTIMATE.

underlay, underlie. The past tense and past participle of *underlay*, meaning 'to place something under something else, in order to support it', are both *underlaid* (e.g. *a beautiful collection of songs featuring soaring string work underlaid by metal drumming; I took vengeful joy in the smattering of boos that underlaid the applause, though*). The past tense and past participle of *underlie*, meaning 'to be situated under' and 'to be the basis of', on the other hand, are *underlay* and *underlain* respectively (e.g. *the principles of justice and retribution that underlay the beliefs of Anglo-Saxon rulers in the eighth century; the policy considerations that have underlain the courts' attitudes to certain types of claimant*). Cf. OVERLAY.

underneath (preposition). From earliest times in competition with *below*, *beneath*, and *under*, this word is tending to be restricted to its literal sense, 'directly beneath or covered by' (*underneath the arches of the bridge; he wore a bullet-proof vest underneath his uniform*). Figurative uses of the word have tended to drift into archaism (*Philosophy, thou canst not even Compel their causes underneath thy yoke*—Coleridge, 1822) and are now uncommon. As Fowler (1926) expressed it, 'its range is much narrower than that of *under*, being almost confined to the physical relation of material things (cf. 'underneath the bed' with 'under the stimulus of competition').' See BELOW; BENEATH.

understatement. See LITOTES; MEIOSIS.

under the circumstances. See CIRCUMSTANCE.

undertone. See OVERTONE.

under way, underway. It may well surprise the uninitiated that these unassuming eight characters (or nine with a space) cause intense linguistic anxiety to some people, but indeed they do, as a Google search will quickly reveal. But first, before the explanation, a little historical aside. **1** *A loan-translation from Dutch.* (*a*) Though some people mentally connect it with German *unterwegs*, the phrase is an adaptation of the Dutch *onderweg*, with a similar meaning to the German. In the mid-18c., ships, away from their moorings, were said to be *under way*: *To prevent which, we do agree, that when Under-way they shall not separate—A Voyage to the South-Seas*, 1743.

(*b*) *Folk etymology working intelligently.* About forty years later some people connected with the sea cleverly and logically but mistakenly associated the phrase with the weighing of anchors and used *under weigh* instead. They were followed by myriads of writers, including Thackeray (*But though the steamer was under weigh, he might not be on board, Vanity Fair*, ch. 67). This older variant seems virtually to have disappeared, though it was used by Anthony Burgess in his *Little Wilson and Big God* (1987): *arrangements were already under weigh.*

(*c*) *Two words becoming one.* For nearly two centuries, writers, whether of the *way* or the *weigh* camp, regularly wrote the expression as two words, *under way* or *under weigh*: Captain Marryat, Washington Irving, Byron, Carlyle, and many others. Then something happened. The mysterious gravitational force that in earlier centuries had dragged a great many other adverbs together (*any* + *way* → *anyway*) struck again. Ships, projects, experiments—almost anything—from the 1930s onwards began in some circles to get *underway*. Uncle Sam was partly to blame but so was John Bull in the form of some celebrated writers—Martin Amis and William Boyd, for instance. From the latter: *They walked arm-in-arm into the club where the dance was underway*. And from a 1987 issue of the *NY Rev. Bks*: *America's declared foreign policy of fostering stability ... in Central America might at last get underway.*

2 *What is the issue? Under way* is an adverbial phrase, like hundreds of others consisting of preposition + noun, e.g. *under canvas, under consideration, under cover*, and perhaps most relevantly, *under sail*. The matter is complicated semantically because there is also a rare adjectival use, noted for example in Webster's Third, 'occurring, performed, or used while traveling or in motion', used primarily in military or naval parlance, e.g. *underway period, replenishment, training*, etc. This is written joined up, as was recognized in the AP Stylebook. However, in late 2013 the AP Stylebook decreed that *underway* as a single word was correct also in the adverbial use.

3 *What do dictionaries say?* They disagree. The 1986 *OED* update rubrics the single-word adverbial form as 'the phrase *under way* ... taken as one word'. On the other hand, the *New SOED* (1993) gives it precedence over the unjoined form. As noted, Webster keeps the two forms separate. Other dictionaries play it safe and show the adverbial as two words, sometimes giving one word as an alternative; or the reverse. Up-to-date ELT dictionaries give the single-word form, which makes sense for learners. The Telegraph Style Book prescribes two words. In short, confusion reigns. Quoi faire?

4 *Recommendation.* Follow your nose or your gut, whichever is the more prominent organ. Those who must abide by a specific style guide or house style must abide by it; those who need not will be guided by instinct and habit. Personally, to write the adverbial as one word strikes me as odd. But that is merely ingrained convention. A recent parallel for compressing an adverbial into a single word is to be found in *online*, now generally recognized. On the other hand, my guess is that most people would balk at *undersail* as one word: clearly frequency has an influence. Though they are different parts of speech, at one time the pronouns *some body, no body*, and *every body* were two words. History sometimes divides and then joins states. So too with words.

underwhelm (verb). An artificial, but successful, mid-20c. humorous adaptation of *overwhelm*. It means 'to leave unimpressed, to arouse little or no interest in', and has wide currency in standard English sources everywhere. Examples: *Both the prose and the play are underwhelming—TLS*, 1972; *I have always been slightly* *underwhelmed by Boyle's films, slick entertainments with a populist component but little of that complex, lingering after-taste that comes with enduring art*—*New Statesman*, 2012.

undeservedly, undesignedly. Pronounced as five syllables. See -EDLY.

undiscriminating is several times more frequent than *indiscriminating*, though both are of similar 18c. vintage. See IN- AND UN-.

undisguisedly. Five syllables. See -EDLY.

undistinguishable. Now somewhat rare in comparison with its slightly younger cousin *indistinguishable*. See IN- AND UN-.

undistributed middle. In logic, a fallacy resulting from the failure of the middle term of a syllogism to refer to all the members of a class in at least one premise. See SYLLOGISM.

undoubtedly. See DOUBTLESS.

uneatable. See INEDIBLE.

uneconomic, uneconomical. Broadly speaking, the shorter, more frequent form means both 'unprofitable' (*the closure of uneconomic pits*), and 'constituting an inefficient use of money or other resources, wasteful' (*It would be hugely uneconomic to build a whole new network*), though these two meanings tend to merge. The longer form means only the second (*the old buses eventually become uneconomical to run*). As can be seen either word would work in the last two examples. See ECONOMIC, ECONOMICAL.

unedited, inedited. See INEDITED.

unequalled. So spelt in BrE, but usu. *unequaled* in AmE. See -LL-, -L-.

unequivocal. The standard adverb corresponding to this adjective (in use since the late 18c.) is *unequivocally*. However, the form **unequivocably** also makes sporadic appearances (in 1 per cent of cases) in respectable sources, e.g. *this blue combines with the rooftop letters to unequivocably signal the presence of MoMA QNS* [*sc.* Museum of Modern Art, Queens]—*Architectural Review*, 2002. Before rejecting it out of hand as a slip of the tongue or pen, one should note the existence of the adjective *unequivocable*, from which it derives. That adjective (first recorded 1921) is recognized in the *OED* with the note 'irregular', meaning unetymologically created by adding *-able* to the truncated *unequivoc-*. Etymological correctness apart, it is probably best edited out of any writing, since to 99.999 per cent of people it will look and sound like a crass mistake.

unescapable (first recorded in 1614, John Donne) is now vanishingly rare in comparison with *inescapable* (first recorded in 1792). See IN- AND UN-.

unessential (first recorded in 1656) is still used interchangeably with *inessential* (first recorded in 1677) in about 25 per cent of all occurrences. See IN- AND UN-.

unexceptionable, unexceptional. See EXCEPTIONABLE. These two words are the precise opposites of their positive forms *exceptionable* and *exceptional*. *Unexceptionable* means 'with which no fault can be found, entirely satisfactory' (*The idea is unexceptionable, indeed worthy of applause*), whereas *unexceptional* means 'not out of the ordinary, run-of-the-mill' (*The food was unexceptional plain pub fare*). The distinction just described between the two words is almost always maintained nowadays, despite the fact that *unexceptional* on its first appearance (Fanny Burney, 1775) and in the 19c. meant exactly the same as *unexceptionable*. Sometimes, however, the two are confused: **But it's the unexceptionable nature of Pi's theorising, its commonplace and modish ordinariness, that so disappoints*—*London Rev. Bks*, 2002 (read *unexceptional*); **While this would seem to be an unexceptional educative goal, being 'critical' often seems to mean adopting a hostile, distanced relationship to the mass media*—*Jrnl of Popular Film and Television*, 2002 (read *unexceptionable*).

unfeignedly. Four syllables. See -EDLY.

unfollow means 'to stop tracking (a person, group, or organization) on a social media website or application' e.g. *never unfollow someone just because they unfollowed you!*

unfriend as a transitive verb, meaning 'to remove (someone) from a list of friends or contacts on a social networking website' is, of course, a thoroughly modern meaning first noted from 2003. However, the verb itself is of venerable antiquity, being first recorded in a letter written by the 17c. cleric and writer Thomas Fuller: *I Hope, Sir, that we are not mutually Un-friended by this Difference which hath happened betwixt us.* There can be no doubt that Fuller would have been perplexed by the transient, trivial nature of 'friendships' that can be terminated with a keystroke: *I wrote 'your' instead of 'you're' on a post and she corrected that so I unfriended her—Sunday Times,* 2012. The alternative *defriend* is also used, but less frequently.

ungula (hoof, claw). Plural *ungulae* /ˈʌŋgjʊliː/.

unhuman, inhuman. Both words have been in use for centuries (*unhuman* since the 16c., *inhuman* 15c.) in a range of similar meanings clustered round the broad sense 'not characteristic of the behaviour, appearance, etc., of a human being'. The modern distinction is that, apart from being over 100 times more frequent, *inhuman* is generally used to mean 'lacking human qualities of compassion and mercy; cruel and barbaric' (e.g. *the inhuman treatment meted out to political prisoners; inhuman conditions*); also, but less often, to mean 'not human in nature or character' (*the inhuman scale of the dinosaurs; Over the ruins of the castle rose an unearthly wind, carrying with it an inhuman wail.*). In contrast, *unhuman* conveys only the second meaning, e.g. *artificial intelligence is best when it remains slightly unhuman and slightly alien.*

uninterest. This relatively uncommon word (it is not even listed in *COD* 1995) is first recorded in 1890 and is used only in the sense 'lack of interest, indifference'. Modern examples: *She had no idea... whether all men went through periods of uninterest*—S. Faulks, 1989; *In undergraduates it tends to produce uninterest or rejection when compulsory—English,* 1991. Cf. DISINTEREST.

uninterested see DISINTERESTED.

Union Jack (also **union jack**). As the *SOED* expresses it, '(*a*) orig. & properly, a small British Union flag flown as the jack [*sc.* a small national flag usu. flown from the bow] of a ship; later & now usu., a Union flag of any size or adaptation, regarded as the national flag of the United Kingdom; (*b*) US (*union jack*) a jack consisting of the union from the national flag.' Some people have pedantically insisted that the term *Union Jack* may be used only in naval contexts, and that *Union flag* is the correct term to use for the national flag of the UK. However, this appears not to be the case, as the Flag Institute notes: 'It is often stated that the Union Flag should only be described as the Union Jack when flown in the bows of a warship, but this is a relatively recent idea. From early in its life the Admiralty itself frequently referred to the flag as the Union Jack, whatever its use, and in 1902 an Admiralty Circular announced that Their Lordships had decided that either name could be used officially. Such use was given Parliamentary approval in 1908 when it was stated that "the Union Jack should be regarded as the National flag".' It is therefore perfectly legitimate to use the term that most people have always used.

unique. 1 *The issue. Unique* is one of a handful of words, including *hopefully*, that give rise to very strong feelings about 'correct' use, a use which has been debated by usage commentators for well over a century. How often has it been said that something or someone is either unique or not unique? To put it grammatically, according to this notion, *unique* is not a gradable adjective: it does not have a comparative *more* unique, and it cannot be intensified by the kind of adverbs that modify other adjectives, e.g. *comparatively, rather, somewhat, very.* Like the word *perfect*, in this view it is regarded as absolute in sense. The question is: does this view hold water?

2 *The 'absolute' meaning.* This can be defined as 'being the only one of its kind; unlike anything else', e.g.: *Throughout these fluctuations of fortune, Edith's unique teaching style was getting more finely honed—Medau News,* 1986; *the unique and infrequently seen portrait of Sidney from the Upper Reading Room frieze—Bodl. Libr. Rec.,* 1986; *Hopkins's inner ear is awash with an infinite and exquisite sense of unique vocal patterns—TLS,* 1987. Clearly, in this use the intensifiers and comparatives mentioned previously would not work. On the other hand, it is perfectly possible for people and things to be *nearly* or *almost* or *perhaps* unique, and for the word to be modified by adverbs denoting an extreme such as *absolutely, completely,* and *utterly.*

3 *The 'incorrect' meaning.* (*a*) The word is also used to mean 'particularly remarkable, special, or unusual'. As such it is gradable, as some of the following examples demonstrate, and behaves grammatically like its synonyms *remarkable, special,* etc. All modern monolingual dictionaries recognize this meaning, usually with a warning. Examples: *'Toad Hall,' said the Toad proudly, 'is an eligible self-contained gentleman's residence,* very *unique*—K. Grahame, 1908; *Our Insti is a* very *unique place, not only bridging the gap between Christians and Jews but also between academics and clergy*—*New Yorker,* 1993; *Some design choices become* so *unique that they border on the eccentric and make a property difficult to sell*—*Chicago Tribune,* 1995; *I imagine that would be a* fairly *unique experience for you*—film review website, 2004.

(*b*) Possibly the specious use of the word in advertising and marketing, which offer *unique advantages, challenges, features, flavours, insights, opportunities,* etc. ad nauseam has cheapened it, at the same time as strengthening the prejudice against its gradable use. Some examples follow, the *Country Life* example being particularly awkward: *a unique blend of Scottish heather honey and rare old malt whisky; Almost the* most *unique residential site along the south coast*—advt in *Country Life,* 1939; *All these diverse atmospheres merge together beautifully to create a most delightful and unique East Lindsey market town*—P. Furlong, 1989.

4 *Origin.* Latin *ūnicus* yielded French *unique* (and Spanish, Portuguese *único,* Italian *unico*) 'single, sole, alone of its kind', and in those languages the word is still mainly restricted to contexts in which oneness is implied (e.g. French *sens unique* 'one-way road', *fils/fille unique* 'only son/ daughter'). The French word made its way into English at the beginning of the 17c., at first narrowly restricted to mean 'single, sole, solitary' (e.g. *He hath lost . . . his unic Son in the very flower of his age, c.*1645). The *OED* points out that it was 'regarded as a foreign word down to the middle of the 19th c., from which date it has been in very common use, with a tendency to take the wider meaning of "uncommon, unusual, remarkable"'.

5 *Recommendation.* In an 1818 edition of Dr Johnson's dictionary, it was described by the editor as 'an affected and useless term of modern times'. A certain amount of hostility still lingers. That makes it advisable, outside the hyperbolic world of advertising and marketing, to use it with caution in its 'remarkable, unusual' meaning, for which those and many other synonyms are readily available. Copy editors of serious or formal prose may still be well advised to query such uses for as long as the controversy about its acceptability continues.

United Kingdom is a political and administrative term, short for the *United Kingdom of Great Britain and Northern Ireland;* from 1801 until 1922 it referred to Great Britain and Ireland.

unities. The *unities,* or *dramatic unities,* are the unity of time, the unity of place, and the unity of action. In the past the terms were sometimes said to be derived from Aristotle's *Poetics,* but this is only partially true, as Baldick points out in his *Concise Oxford Dict. Literary Terms* (1990): 'In fact Aristotle in his discussion of tragedy insists only on unity of action, mentioning unity of time in passing, and says nothing about place.' These principles of dramatic composition were formulated by English and continental writers of the 16c. and 17c. According to Baldick, Jean Mairet's *Sophonisbe* (1634) was the first French tragedy to observe the *unities.* Mairet and others believed that a play should have a unified action, without subplots, and should represent the events of a single day within a single setting. But certain variations were permissible: 'The place the stage represented was allowed to shift from one point to another within a larger area: a palace or even a city' (*OCELit.,* 1985). The dramatic *unities* were not widely favoured by English dramatists of the period. For example, Shakespeare adopted them only in *The Tempest* and *The Two Gentlemen of Verona.*

university. At some point in the 20c. the word began to be used without the definite article. 'After I went to school I went to the university,' wrote an elderly professor to Burchfield in 1986, 'not to university'. Example of the more modern use: *Kolya, who resents the fact that I went to university instead of doing national service*—C. Rumens, 1987. In AmE, *to/at the university* is the normal construction when the reference is non-specific, i.e. the older convention is retained there.

unlawful. See ILLEGAL.

unlearned, unlearnt. 1 In contrast with the verb *learn*, *unlearnt* for the past tense and past participle is rather unusual; *unlearned* is far more frequent, e.g. *A natural born cook perhaps, but friends say Ken . . . has never quite unlearned his passenger ship habits—Better Homes and Gardens Mag.*, 2002.

2 *Unlearned* used adjectivally has three syllables (/ʌnˈlɜːnɪd/) when it means 'not well educated' (*he appealed to an unlearned audience as well as to sympathetic scholars*) and two when it means 'innate, not having to be learned' (*an unlearned behaviour pattern*).

unless and until. A modern 'strengthened' extension of *until* (the words *unless and* are often omissible without discernible loss of meaning). Fowler (1926) expressed doubts about its legitimacy, but, by citing numerous examples of its use, drew attention to its frequency. The *OED* provides further examples from standard sources beginning with the following: *We should as a rule stick to that pronunciation unless and until we find another native whose speech we have reason to think is more characteristic*—Daniel Jones, 1937. More recently the phrase has also appeared in the forms *unless or until* and *until and/or unless*: *Until and unless he discovered who he was, everything was without meaning*—D. Potter, 1986; *Iraq . . . announced that it would honor the cease-fire ordered by the UN Security Council, until or unless the other belligerent, Iran, violated it—Chr. Sci. Monitor*, 1987; *Membership of the House of Commons is still the only legitimate qualification for real power in Britain and likely to remain so unless or until our national identity is totally submerged in Europe—Spectator*, 1991. As *CGEL* (13.38) points out, phrases of the type *as and when*, *if and when*, and *unless and until* 'weaken the expectation' and, as such, need no defence.

See AS AND WHEN; IF AND WHEN.

unlike (adjective, preposition etc.). **1** (*a*) *Unlike* functions (i) as an adjective meaning 'not like' (*utterly unlike in temper and tone*) or 'dissimilar' (*animals as unlike as the bear and the lion*), and (ii) as a preposition meaning 'dissimilar to' (*a man wholly unlike anyone she had met before*) or 'uncharacteristic of ' (*it is unlike him to be late for work*). (*b*) Fowler (1926) criticized the position of *unlike* in the following example: '*M. Berger, however, does not appear to have—unlike his Russian masters—the gift of presenting female characters.* As with many negatives, the placing of *unlike* is important; standing where it does, it must be changed to *like*; *unlike* would be right if the phrase were shifted to before "does not appear".' While his suggestion may read better, there is no real ambiguity in the example as it stands.

2 (*a*) Informally *unlike* is used as a quasi-adverb followed by a preposition: *Unlike with fax messages you can edit and re-use the text of e-mails once they arrive on your computer—Times*, 1998. This use has had its critics (Fowler among them), and some people may still object to it, despite its economy. In more formal contexts, such combinations can usually be replaced by wordier alternatives such as *in contrast to* or *as distinct from*, or simply by using *unlike* without the preposition (i.e. *with* in the above example). (*b*) Sometimes, however, one has to be careful not to omit the preposition, as to do so can lead to a false comparison: *I am pleased to say that unlike most DVDs, both of the commentaries included on this Special Edition are worthy of a listen.* What is being compared here are DVDs and commentaries, whereas the comparison intended is between DVDs. Insert *with* before *most*, or to avoid the informal tone of *unlike* followed by a preposition, reword the example '. . . unlike those of most DVDs, the commentaries . . .'.

unlike (verb). The adjectival use of the participle *unliked*, i.e. 'not liked', dates to the 16c. The full verb is first recorded in a novel by Richard Sheridan's mother, Frances (*My heart is not in a disposition to love . . . I cannot compel it to like, and unlike, and like anew at pleasure*—1761) and this use continues, e.g. *I don't think he is unliked (if he is at all) because of his nationality.* Much more common is the social media use, i.e. 'withdraw one's liking of a web page or posting on a social media website that one has previously liked': *I cut about 300 of my 400 friends and unliked about 20–30 pages.* Cf. UNFOLLOW, UNFRIEND.

unparalleled. Note the position and number of the letters *l*.

unpractical. See IMPRACTICABLE, IMPRACTICAL, 2.

unputdownable, 'so engrossing that one cannot stop reading', first recorded as used by Raymond Chandler, is unusual in being formed from a phrasal verb. While previous formations on the same model have fared badly (e.g. *un-come-at-able*, first recorded in 1694 and characterized by Dr Johnson as 'a low, corrupt word', *un-get-at-able*, first recorded in 1862 and equally homespun), it flourishes. Best written as one word, to avoid the quandary of where to put a hyphen or hyphens.

unravel (verb). The inflected forms are *unravelled* and *unravelling* in BrE, but *unraveled* and *unraveling* in AmE. See RAVEL (verb).

unreadable. See ILLEGIBLE.

unreligious, unlike *irreligious*, excludes the latter's implications of sin, blasphemy, etc., and means 'indifferent or hostile to religion'. It is therefore a synonym of *non-religious* in one of the latter's meanings. *Strongly religious voters were very likely to vote Republican. Unreligious or not-very-religious voters were very likely to vote Democratic*—*Power Line weblog*, 2002.

unrepairable. See IRREPARABLE.

unreservedly, unrestrainedly. Five syllables. See -EDLY.

unrivalled. So spelt in BrE, but *unrivaled* in AmE.

unsanitary. See INSANITARY.

unseasonable, unseasonal. See SEASONABLE .

unsolvable differs from *insoluble* in being limited to the meaning of the English verb *solve*, and not covering, as *insoluble* does, various meanings (*dissolve* as well as *solve*) of the Latin verb *solvere*. *Insoluble* has been the standard word for '(of a difficulty, question, problem, etc.) not soluble' since the Middle Ages, and for 'incapable of being dissolved in a liquid' since the early 18c. On the other hand, *unsolvable* is a relative newcomer (early 19c., once also in a dictionary of 1775) in its primary sense of 'not able to be solved'.

unthinkable. From the 15c. onwards, *unthinkable* has been in standard use in the philosophical sense 'unable to be imagined or grasped in the mind, unimaginable'. This sense is still current. By the beginning of the 20c., however, it was beginning to be used in various extended ways, applied, for example, to courses of action that were regarded by the speaker or writer as unacceptable or too horrible to contemplate (civil war, extreme action by terrorists, etc.) or just highly unlikely or undesirable. Fowler (1926) denounced all such extended uses: 'anything is now unthinkable from what reason declares impossible or what imagination is helpless to conceive down to what seems against the odds (as that Oxford should win the boat-race), or what is slightly distasteful to the speaker (as that the Labour Party should ever form a Government)'. Fowler's condemnation of these extended or weakened was in vain. Modern dictionaries simply record such uses as part of the standard language.

Examples: *In these circumstances the removal of British troops was unthinkable*—C. Allen, 1990; *What we would spend abroad without a qualm is unthinkable extravagance at home*—M. Duffy, 1991; *Margaret Thatcher give up? Unthinkable*—N. Wyn Ellis, 1991; *The ambition became a compulsion, failure literally unthinkable*—R. Ferguson, 1991; *The notion that you should give a new [television] channel a particular qualitative charge and invite it to be different in particular ways is almost unthinkable today*—*Independent*, 1992; *We have achieved in North America, Western Europe, and Japan a 'zone of peace' within which it is fair to say war is truly unthinkable*—A. and H. Toffler, 1994 (US). An element of the unimaginable resides in all of them: the link with the traditional uses of the word is not entirely broken.

until. 1 *until, till.* See TILL.

2 *until* or *till* for *before* or *when.* In the following type, *until* (or *till*) is sometimes said to be unidiomatically used for *before* or *when*: *In one of the city parks he was seated at one end of a bench, and had not been there long until a sparrow alighted at the other end.* The *OED* comments on this type: 'Formerly and still dial. and in U.S. used after a negative principal clause, where *before* (or *when*) is now substituted in Standard English.' The last example given is one of 1756: *I was not long set till Margaret came to see me.* But the *OED* gives no examples of this type, and it would seem best to reserve judgement about the construction until more evidence of its existence is found.

3 *unless and until* (and variants). See UNLESS AND UNTIL.

4 *until such time as*. This phrase can, particularly in legal and contractual language, be effective in emphasizing uncertainty about an outcome, but it should not be made to serve as a more verbose alternative to the simple word *until*, which it is, arguably, in *Such noisy groups of youngsters ... need to be broken down into smaller groups each controlled by a responsible competent leader or instructor until such time as they become mature canoeists*—*Canoeist*, 1991.

unto is an archaic variant of the prepositions *to* and *until*. It survives mainly in fixed phrases (*do unto others; faithful unto death; take unto oneself*), and is often followed by *-self/selves* pronouns, especially *itself*: e.g. *Readers ... may well wonder ... whether each religious group dealt with in the separate chapters is unique unto itself*—*Bull. Amer. Acad. Arts & Sci.*, 1993; *no one is permitted to be a law unto himself, and no religion is permitted to be a law unto itself*—*OEC*, 2002.

unvoiced (phonetics). See VOICED (adjective).

up.

1 Complexity.
2 *up to date.*
3 *up to, down to.*
4 *up and* (+ verb).

1 *Complexity*. This most complicated word requires great subtlety of treatment in dictionaries. It is used as adverb, preposition, adjective, noun, and verb, and with great diversity within each part of speech. A syndicated column in some major American newspapers in 1994 (reproducing a letter to the *Reader's Digest* some 25 years earlier) provides an amusing introduction to some of the idiomatic uses of the word:

'We've got a two-letter word we use constantly that may have more meanings than any other. The word is *up*. It is easy to understand *up*, meaning toward the sky or toward the top of a list. But when we waken, why do we wake *up*? At a meeting, why does a topic come *up*? And why are participants said to speak *up*? Why are officers *up* for election? And why is it *up* to the secretary to write *up* a report? The little word is really not needed, but we use it anyway. We brighten *up* a room, light *up* a cigar, polish *up* the silver, lock *up* the house and fix *up* the old car. At other times, it has special meanings. People stir *up* trouble, line *up* for tickets, work *up* an appetite, think *up* excuses and get tied *up* in traffic. To be dressed is one thing, but to be dressed *up* is special. It may be confusing, but a drain must be opened *up* because it is stopped *up*. We open *up* a store in the morning, and close it *up* in the evening. We seem to be all mixed *up* about *up*. In order to be *up* on the proper use of *up*, look *up* the word in the dictionary. In one desk-sized dictionary, *up* takes *up* half a column; and the listed definitions add *up* to about 40. If you are *up* to it, you might try building *up* a list of the many ways in which *up* is used. It may take *up* a lot of your time, but if you don't give *up*, you may wind *up* with a thousand.'

All these and many more are treated in our standard dictionaries. For some discussion of a few of them (*give up*, etc.), see PHRASAL VERBS.

2 *up to date*. This phrase should be written as three words unhyphenated, except when it is used as an attributive adjective; then it is hyphenated: *you are not up to date; bring the ledger up to date*; but *an up-to-date model*.

3 *up to, down to*. These phrases often have distinct meanings: e.g. (*up to*) not more than (*you can have up to five*), less than or equal to (*sums up to £10*), occupied with or busy with (*what have you been up to?*); (*down to*) having used up everything except (*down to their last tin of rations*). But both can mean 'until': cf. *up to the present; from Elizabethan times down to the nineteenth century*. In such contexts the choice of *up to* or *down to* depends on the vantage point of the speaker. Cf. DOWN TO.

4 *up and* (+ verb). Followed by a verb, *up and* means 'do (something) suddenly or unexpectedly' (*he just upped and vanished; she upped and married her cousin; suddenly the division ups and marches to Aldershot*). An early use is recorded in R. L. Stevenson's *Treasure Island* (1883): *And you have the Davy Jones's insolence to up and stand for cap'n over me!*

up and down. 1 *Meaning 'north' and 'south'.* In geographical terms, *down* means south and *up* means north, and so you go *up* to Scotland from London and *down* to

Atlanta (Georgia) from Chicago. A conventional exception to this straightforward logic occurs with capital or major cities; for example, it used to be customary to speak of going *up* to London from whatever direction, and *down* when travelling away from it, as the examples at 2 show. Nowadays, it seems likely, but is difficult to establish, that people speak of going *up* to London, *over* to London, *down* to London, as appropriate, depending on the location of the starting point. In particular, distance often makes the geographical logic the most important, so that someone from e.g. Newcastle, York, or Edinburgh would probably go *down* to London—unless subjectively they felt which is unlikely, that they were going to a more significant place than their home city.

2 *Historical note.* As Gowers wrote in 1965, reflecting the use of an earlier generation (he was 85 at the time): 'The use of *up* for a journey to London and *down* for one from it preceded the adoption of those expressions by the railways. Perhaps the idea of accomplishment latent in *up* made it seem the right word for reaching the more important place. Geographical bearing was immaterial; going north from London was no less *down* than going south. "At Christmas I went down into Scotland," wrote Lord Chancellor Campbell in 1845, "and, crossing the Cheviots, was nearly lost in a snowstorm." "You don't mean to say," said Miss La Creevy, "that you are really going all the way down into Yorkshire this cold winter's weather, Mr. Nickleby."

'The railways conformed. They gave the name *up-line* to that on which their trains arrived at their London terminal and *down-line* to that on which they left. When a railway was built without any direct connexion with London the up-line was that on which trains ran to the more important terminus.' British Rail South West Region confirmed (1995) that the same terminology is still used, i.e. the trains arriving at mainline stations travel on the *up-line* and those leaving mainline stations travel on the *down-line*. Cross-country journeys sometimes require different terms.

3 *In relation to Oxford and Cambridge.* To a member of these universities *up* means in residence. An undergraduate goes *up* at the beginning of term and remains *up* until he or she goes *down* at the end of it (unless he or she has the misfortune to be *sent down* earlier). But this special use relates only to the universities, not to the cities. Someone travelling to Oxford or Cambridge would use *up, down, over* to Oxford (or Cambridge), whichever is geographically appropriate.

upcoming (adjective). One of Burchfield's most hard-line correspondents remarked (July 1994) that '*upcoming* seems to be ousting the perfectly serviceable *forthcoming* [in British English]'. The *OEC* data suggests that this originally American use of the word (first recorded in the *OED* in this sense in 1959, in a letter by Aldous Huxley) has fully settled in to English-speaking countries outside the US, but it has not yet ousted *forthcoming* entirely. Nevertheless it does seem to be almost as frequent as *forthcoming* in most varieties, except BrE, and is very much more frequent in North American English. It just seems irresistible to some writers in certain contexts from time to time. Examples: *Guinness Peat Aviation . . . angrily rejected its merchant banks' advice to sell its shares at little more than $20 a share in its upcoming flotation—Economist*, 1992; *And in real life, Doucett will appear in an upcoming 'pictorial' in Playboy—Globe & Mail* (Toronto), 1993; *he told last week of the spectator who telephoned Selhurst Park to enquire about Wimbledon's upcoming game—Spectator*, 1995.

upmost. See UTMOST.

upon. 1 For (*up*)*on all fours*, see FOUR.

2 According to the *OED* 'The use of the one form or the other [*sc. on* or *upon*] has been for the most part a matter of individual choice (on grounds of rhythm, emphasis, etc.) or of simple accident, although in certain contexts and phrases there may be a general tendency to prefer the one to the other.' The choice seems almost wholly arbitrary, and there is no saying why one has taken root in some phrases and the other in others: *once upon a time, row upon row of seats*; but *on no account, have it on good authority*; *Kingston upon Thames, Burton-upon-Trent*; but *Henley-on-Thames, Newark-on-Trent.*

uppermost. See UTMOST.

upside (preposition). *He was not a person looking for love in all the wrong places, but it was something that just slapped him upside the head—Chicago Tribune*, 1990 (of a space pilot in Star Wars); *No, he did not.*

Never did. And if he did, he would have gotten a frying pan upside his head—*Newsweek*, 1995 (ex-wife of the American footballer O. J. Simpson, denying in a TV interview that he had ever slapped her). This thoroughly American use of the preposition *upside*, which is almost always construed with a verb meaning 'hit' (*go, slap*, etc.) and *head*, seems to have been first noted in the late 1970s (*OED*) in the language of US African Americans, and to have spread from there to other forms of informal AmE.

upward(s). 1 As adjective the standard form is *upward* (*an upward movement of the voice; upward mobility*). As adverb the normal but not invariable form in BrE is *upwards*, but in AmE mostly but not invariably *upward*.

2 *upwards of* (rather less often *upward of*). First recorded in 1721 (*OED*) in the sense '(rather) more than', it remains in standard use (*there were upwards of a hundred people at the wedding reception*). Occasionally, according to the *OED* and to dialect sources, it is used to mean '(rather) less than' in some regions in England. Occasionally also when *upwards of* is used of a large figure it means no more than 'approximately' (*upwards of £250,000*), but it is best to assume that the meaning is '(rather) more than' unless there is contextual evidence to the contrary.

Uranus. Dictionaries vary in showing the stress on the first syllable, i.e. /ˈjʊərənəs/ (**yoo**-ruh-nuhs), preferred in AmE, or on the second, i.e. /jʊˈreɪnəs/ (yoo-**ray**-nuhs), which is sometimes avoided for euphemistic reasons.

urinal. The dominant pronunciation in BrE is that with the second syllable bearing the main stress, i.e. /jʊˈrʌɪn(ə)l/, but the form with first-syllable stressing, i.e. /ˈjʊərɪn(ə)l/ is also standard, and is the only one in standard use in AmE.

us (pronoun). **1** Its normal uses as the objective form of the pronoun *we* (sometimes in its reduced form *'s*) are unremarkable: *They despise us; Let's look in at the party* . . . *We needn't stay long; Both of us write books; Have you ever seen two giggling angels* . . . *like us?; he looks down upon us country people; it's only us*.

2 It can legitimately be used instead of *we* in certain circumstances. Thus *you are as well-informed as us* (more formally *as we* (*are*)). For other examples, see CASES; WE. In colloquial use it can also be used instead of *me* (*Done your homework, Oakley? Give us a look at it*).

3 The most common misuse is shown in *Us country boys have to stick together* (read *We country boys* . . .).

4 A minor optional type is shown in *So it's been strange, us being in England because of me* (*our being* would be equally acceptable). See OUR; WE; POSSESSIVE WITH GERUND.

-us. The plurals of nouns in *-us* can cause problems. **1** Most are from Latin second-declension words, whose Latin plural is *-i* (pronounced /ʌɪ/); but when that should be used, and when the English plural *-uses* is better, has to be decided for each separately; see LATIN PLURALS and the entries for individual words (CIRRUS; DISCUS; FUNGUS; LOCUS; UTERUS; etc.).

2 Many are from Latin fourth-declension words, whose Latin plural is *-ūs* (pronounced /-uːs/); but the English plural *-uses* is almost always preferred, as *prospectuses*. The Latin ending *-ūs* is occasionally seen in a few of the rarer words, e.g. *lusus, meatus, senatus*. Words of this class, which must never have plural in *-i*, are *afflatus, apparatus, conspectus, hiatus, impetus, lapsus, nexus, plexus, prospectus, sinus, status*.

3 Some are from Latin third-declension neuters, whose plurals are of various forms in *-a*; so *corpus, genus, opus*, have the plural *corpora, genera, opera*, which are almost always preferred in English to *-uses*.

4 *Callus, octopus, platypus, polypus*, and *virus*, nouns variously abnormal in Latin, can all have plural *-uses* and usually do; for any alternatives, see CALLUS; OCTOPUS; PLATYPUS; POLYPUS; VIRUS.

5 Some English nouns in *-us* are in Latin not nouns, but verb forms, etc.; so *ignoramus, mandamus, mittimus, non possumus*; for these, as for the dative plural *omnibus* and the ablative plural *rebus*, the only possible plural is the English *-uses*.

6 Some English nouns in *-us* are not Latin words at all: e.g. *caucus* (perhaps Algonquin), *rumpus* (probably fanciful).

usable. Much more often spelt as shown than **useable**, but both spellings are correct.

use (verb). **1** Pronounced /juːz/ as a transitive verb (*use your discretion*), past tense *used* /juːzd/ (*she used him for her own ends*). Things become more complicated when *used to* refers to what happened or existed in the past but no longer does.

2 *In affirmative statements.* In these *used to* poses little difficulty. The past tense form *used* is followed by a *to*-infinitive. Because *used to* and *use to* sound identical, i.e. /juːstuː/, unstressed /-tə/, the second is sometimes incorrectly used, for example in the kind of puerile, sub-literary fiction which floods the Web. Examples: *I know what you're thinking, Patrick, and I used to think it too*—K. Amis, 1988; *I used to joke bleakly that he had run off with my Muse*—*Guardian*, 1990; *As a teenager he'd used to wander up there and clamber around*—M. du Plessis, 1989 (SAfr.); (incorrect *use to*) *'You know we use to do that all the time,' he said*—online fiction website, 2005.

3 In negative statements: *used not to, didn't use to* or **didn't used to.* (*a*) Because *used to* traditionally works as a semi-modal, negatives can be formed without using *did* as the auxiliary, e.g. *I used not to play.* This type is however rather formal or old-fashioned. The form *usedn't* (or *usen't*) is also found in casual English but is less suitable in more formal contexts. Examples: *You usen't to be like that*—A. Christie, 1964; *The Mistress usedn't to sleep well at night*—A. Christie, *Poirot Loses a Client* (n.d.); *He used not to sweat like that*—I. Fleming, 1964; *She used not to be so censorious of others' behaviour*—T. Barnes, 1991.

(*b*) But *used to* also functions as a regular lexical verb, using *did*, e.g. *I didn't use to play.* In addition, the type **I didn't used to play* is frequent, in which the past aspect indicated by *did* is doubled in the past marker *-d* of *used* itself. The grammatically correct construction is *didn't use to*, but this is less frequent in *OEC* data than the 'anomalous' **didn't used to.* Despite its higher frequency, purists may well consider the latter incorrect. Examples: (*didn't use to*) *'It didn't use to be that way,' Manuel said*—*New Yorker*, 1986; *Another discernible difference between then and now is that they didn't use to snatch mobile phones at gunpoint*—*Guardian*, 2008; (**didn't used to*) **Prostate cancer... didn't used to be a problem*—*Times*, 1995. **Simple words like 'living room' come out of her mouth with a twang we didn't used to hear from the pop princess*—*TMZ.com*, 2006.

4 *In questions.* (*a*) The same trio of options as for negatives is available: *Used she to play?*, *Did she use to play?*, and **Did she used to play?* The first, like the corresponding negative, is formal and unusual. The second is grammatically correct; the third is anomalous. Examples: *And how did you use to get on with the Labor Council?*—*Workers Online*, 2002. **What time did she used to return?*—L. Thomas, 1972. (*b*) The negative/interrogative type *Use(d)n't people to...* is also found, especially in spoken English and in informal letters, and arguments rage as to whether it is 'better' than the type *Didn't people use(d) to...?* Restructuring of the sentence is often the way out. *People used to... didn't they?* is perhaps the best way to avoid the problem.

(The problem of whether *use*(*d*) *to* is an anomalous verb or a lexical verb is discussed by Eric Jørgensen in *English Studies*, 69 (1988); some of the examples are taken from that article.)

5 *Used to* can also, of course, be used with *be, become, get*, etc. and a following noun, pronoun, or verbal noun to mean 'accustomed to, familiar with': *she had got used to the sissy... thin-blooded climate of Auckland*—D. M. Davin, 1986; *He still isn't used to her being old enough to drive*—*New Yorker*, 1988.

usherette. See -ETTE 4. A late-20c. example: *What the hell are you holding that torch for as if you were a bloody usherette?*—A. N. Wilson, 1990.

uterus. Plural *uteri* /-rʌɪ/ in medical parlance, *uteruses* in non-technical use. See -US 1.

utilize. This mid-19c. loanword from French *utiliser* has led a precarious life for a century and a half beside *use* (continuously in use since the 13c.). In virtually all contexts where one or the other word is needed to cover the sense 'to bring into service', *use* is the more satisfactory word. But a case can be made out for *utilize* when the required sense is 'to make practical use of, to turn to account'. The boundary is nevertheless a murky one and it is not all clear why *utilize* is preferred to *use* in the following examples: *utilizing the electric kettle and the little packets provided*—A. Thomas Ellis, 1990; *Levy utilizes eight Bodleian manuscripts; Katzenelenbogen utilizes, inter alia, Bodleian MS. Opp. 34, while Chavel relies heavily on Oxford Corpus Christi College Heb. MS. 165—Bodl. Libr. Rec.*, 1992.

utmost, uttermost. Both are used to mean 'most extreme, greatest', e.g. of the *ut(ter)most importance,* but *utmost* is much more commonly used in this meaning. *Upmost* is a somewhat rare adjective and a variant of *uppermost.* It refers to the position of something, as in *the upmost layer.* Through a process of folk etymology it is sometimes incorrectly used instead of *utmost*: e.g. **with the upmost care,* instead of *with the utmost care; *to do your upmost,* instead of *to do your utmost.*

uvula. Pronounced /ˈjuːvjʊlə/. Plural *uvulae* /-liː/ or *uvulas.*

vacation is in America the ordinary word for what in BrE is called a *holiday*. In Britain it is not so used except (often abbreviated to *vac.*) for the interval between terms in the law courts and universities. The corresponding word for Parliament is *recess*. Used as an intransitive verb meaning 'to take a vacation' (*they always vacation in Miami*), *vacation* is mostly restricted to AmE.

vacillate. So spelt, not *vacc-*. Pronounced /ˈvasɪleɪt/.

vacuity, vacuousness. The two forms have coexisted for more than three centuries, but *vacuity* has always been the dominant one of the two.

vacuum. Plural (in ordinary use) *vacuums*; (in scientific use) *vacua*. See -UM 3.

vade mecum (modern Latin, literally 'go with me'), a handbook, guidebook, etc., carried constantly for ready reference. Pronounced /vɑːdɪ ˈmeɪkəm/. Plural *vade mecums*.

vagina. Invariably pronounced /vəˈʒʌɪnə/. The adjective *vaginal* is /vəˈdʒʌɪn(ə)l/ in BrE but /ˈvadʒɪn(ə)l/ in AmE. Plural (in ordinary use) *vaginas*, (in medical use) *vaginae* /-niː/.

vainness. So spelt, with *-nn-*.

valance (a short curtain round the frame or canopy of a bedstead, etc.). Pronounced /ˈvaləns/, and spell with *-ance*, not *-ence*, thus distinguishing it from the unconnected words VALENCE, VALENCY.

valence, valency. In chemistry, in the form *valence* (e.g. in C. A. Coulson's 1952 book *Valence*), used for 'the power or capacity of an atom or group to combine with or displace other atoms or groups in the formation of compounds; a unit of this' (*New SOED*, slightly abridged). The dominant form in BrE for this phenomenon seems to be *valency*; in AmE *valence*. But scientists often cross linguistic barriers, and the geographical distribution of the two forms cannot be pinned down neatly.

valet. The noun is pronounced either /ˈvalɪt/ or /ˈvaleɪ/; in AmE also /vəˈleɪ/. The verb, now also commonly used in the sense 'to clean, esp. the inside of, a motor vehicle', has past tense and past participle *valeted* /ˈvaleɪd/ or /ˈvalɪtɪd/, in AmE also /vəˈleɪd/, and present participle *valeting*.

valise. In BrE pronounced /vəˈliːz/, now archaic except as a term for a soldier's kitbag. In AmE pronounced /vəˈliːs/, a small piece of hand luggage.

Valkyrie. Pronounced with the stress either on the first syllable, i.e. /ˈvalkɪri/ or on the second, i.e. /valˈkiəri/. Plural *-s*.

valley. Plural *valleys*.

valour, valorous. For spellings see -OUR AND -OR. The noun is spelt **valor** in AmE.

van Dyck, Van Dyck, Vandyke, vandyke. The name of the Flemish painter Anthony *van Dyck* (1599–1641) was Anglicized to (Sir Anthony) *Vandyke* while he lived in England. The derived noun and adjective are usually spelt *Vandyke* (so *Vandyke beard, Vandyke brown*). But in the sense 'a painting by van Dyck' (*there are several van Dycks in Buckingham Palace*) it is perhaps best to preserve the original Flemish spelling of the name.

vanguard. See AVANT-GARDE.

vanity. 1 *Vanity* is occasionally used in its old sense of futility, waste of time, without any of its modern implication of conceit (*I haue seene all the workes that are done vnder the Sunne, and behold, all is vanitie, and vexation of spirit*—Eccles. 1: 14).

2 The appurtenances of this wicked world that the candidate for Confirmation in the Church of England is required to renounce together with the devil and all his works are its pomps and *vanity*, not, as often misquoted, *vanities*.

vapidity, vapidness. The first is several times more frequent than the second to denote the quality of emptiness and triviality.

vapour. For the spelling of the word itself, see -OUR AND -OR. Allied words are best spelt *vapourer, vapourings, vapourish, vapourless, vapoury*; but *vaporific, vaporize* (*-zation, -zer*), *vaporous* (*-osity*). For the principle, see -OUR AND -OR.

variability, -bleness. The first is nearly one thousand times more frequent than the second, and many of the handful of citations for the latter echo the biblical 'with whom is no variableness, neither shadow of turning' (Jas. 1: 17).

varia lectio /ˈvɛːrɪə ˈlɛktɪəʊ/, a variant reading. Plural *variae lectiones* /ˈvɛːrɪʌɪ ˈlɛktɪəʊniːz/. Printed in italic.

variance. *It *is utterly at variance from the habit of Chaucer*. Idiom demands *with*, not *from*.

variant. In writing about language, a *variant* is a legitimate form or spelling of a word that differs from the main one. For example, *judgment* is a variant of *judgement*.

varicose. Pronounced /ˈvarɪkəʊs/ or /-əs/ or /-z/.

variegated. The *OED* (1916) gave it five syllables, i.e. /ˈvɛərɪəgɛɪtɪd/, but it is now usually pronounced as four, i.e. /ˈvɛərɪgeɪtɪd/, except in AmE, in which the pronunciation with five syllables is the dominant one.

variorum, when used as a noun, has plural *-ums*; see -UM 1. The word is a compendious way of saying *editio cum notis variorum*, and means an edition of a work that contains the notes of various commentators on it. *Variorum* is a genitive plural in Latin, not the neuter nominative singular that a bookseller took it to be when he offered **a good variorum edition including variora from MSS. in the British Museum*.

various is like *certain, few, many, several, some*, etc., in that it can be used both as an adjective and as a pronoun followed by *of*, as in *He gave me various of his books*. In the first edition of this book (1926), Fowler took issue with this pronoun use, while Burchfield (1996) stated that it was unidiomatic in BrE, but what Burchfield said is now debatable. The use had been recorded occasionally since the later part of the 19c. in AmE sources, according to him, and according to *MWCDEU* it appeared in Bartlett's 1887 *Dictionary of Americanisms*. While the unrevised *OED* entry (1916) for *various* does not include it, it appears elsewhere in the *OED* twelve times, both in its earliest citation (*Apologies for various of the great doctrines of the faith*—Cardinal Newman, 1850) and most often in notes to revised entries made by editors from 2000 onwards. Those suggest that it is quite established in BrE, which is borne out by the fact that in *OEC* data it occurs with a higher frequency in BrE sources, especially legal writing, than in AmE ones. However, against that has to be set the fact that its frequency is a mere fraction of that of the analogous *several of*; that it doesn't to my mind sound as idiomatic as the latter; and that in many cases the wording *of* and its following determiner could be dispensed with altogether, as in all the recent examples that follow: *it can be seen that there is scope, not only for overlap between various of the sections of the Act, but for repugnance as well*—*England and Wales Court of Appeal Decisions*, 2000; *but he and various of his colleagues met Wittgenstein on an occasional basis*—*Wittgenstein, A Very Short Introduction*, 2001 (UK); *And there also are going to have to be constraints on various of our programs*—*CNN* (transcripts) 2013 (US); *It was referred to by various of your Honours in the judgments in Patterson, to which detailed reference will be made*—*High Court of Australia* (transcripts), 2001.

varlet, a menial or rascal (historically 'an attendant on a knight'), is now used only archaizingly or humorously.

vasculum (botanist's specimen case). Plural *vascula*. See -UM 2.

vastly. In contexts of measure or comparison, where it means by much, by a great deal, as is *vastly improved, a vastly larger audience*, *vastly* is still in regular use. Where the notion of measure is wanting, and it means no more than 'exceedingly, extremely, very' as in *I should vastly like to know, is vastly popular*, it was fashionable in the 18c. (e.g. *The City . . . was vastly full of People*—Defoe, 1722; *This is all vastly true*—F. Burney, 1782; *A'nt you* *come vastly late?*—Sheridan, 1799), but became less common as time went on, and is now archaic.

vast majority. See MAJORITY 2.

vaudeville. The recommended pronunciation is /ˈvɔːdəvɪl/, rather than /ˈvəʊd-/.

've. Abbreviated form of *have*. Since the 18c. (according to the *OED*) often joined to a previous word, especially a modal verb or a personal pronoun, in the representation of speech. Examples: *I've a good mind to take the tram*—F. A. Guthrie, 1885; *You would've thought at least she could've cut the bobbles off*—M. Forster, 1986; *Can't've been a nightmare, then, can it?*—P. Barker, 1991.

-ve(d), -ves, etc. from words in *-f* and *-fe*. Corresponding to the change of sound discussed in -TH (θ) AND -TH (ð) that takes place in the plural, etc., of words ending in *-th*, like *truth*, there is one both of sound and of spelling in many words ending in *-f* or *-fe*, which become *-ves, -ved, -vish*, etc. As the change is far from regular, and sometimes in doubt, an alphabetical list follows of the chief words about which some doubt may exist, showing changes in the plural of the noun and in the parts of the verb and in some derivatives (d.). When alternatives are given, the first is recommended.

beef. Pl. *beeves* fattened bulls or cows, *beefs* kinds of beef; d. *beefy.*
calf. Pl. *calves*; v. *calve*; d. *calfish.*
dwarf. Pl. *dwarfs* or *dwarves*; v. *dwarf*, pa. t. *dwarfed*; d. *dwarfish, dwarfism.*
elf. Pl. *elves*; d. *elfin*; *elvish, elfish.*
half. Pl. *halves*; v. *halve.*
handkerchief. Pl. *handkerchiefs.*
hoof. Pl. *hooves* or *hoofs*; v. *hoof, hoofed, hoofing*; d. *hoofy.*
knife. Pl. *knives*; v. *knife, knifed, knifing.*
leaf. Pl. *leaves*; v. *leaf, leafs, leafed, leafing*; *-leaved*; d. *leafy.*
life. Pl. *lives*; v. *live*; *-lived*; d. *lifer.*
loaf. Pl. *loaves.*
oaf. Pl. *oafs*; d. *oafish.*
proof. Pl. *proofs*; v. *prove*, pa. pple *proved/proven.*
roof. Pl. *roofs* or *rooves.*
scarf. Pl. *scarves* or *scarfs.*
scurf. d. *scurfy* having scurf; *scurvy* paltry, mean.
self. Pl. *selves*; d. *selfish.*
sheaf. Pl. *sheaves*; v. *sheave*; adj. *sheaved.*
shelf. Pl. *shelves*; v. *shelve.*
staff. Pl. *staffs*, (mus. etc.) *staves*; v. STAVE.
thief. Pl. *thieves*; v. *thieve*; d. *thievery, thievish.*
turf. Pl. *turves* or *turfs*; v. *turf*; d. *turfy.*
wharf. Pl. *wharves* or *wharfs*; d. *wharfage*, (Aust. and NZ) *wharfie.*
wife. Pl. *wives.*
wolf. Pl. *wolves*; v. *wolf, wolfs, wolfed*; d. *wolfish, wolvish.*

vehement, vehicle. The *OED* (1916) gave priority to an *h*-less pronunciation of both words, but included forms with the *h* fully pronounced as legitimate variants. In standard English now the *h* is never pronounced, as it is not also in *vehicular*.

velamen /vɪˈleɪmən/, an enveloping membrane of an aerial root of an orchid. Plural *velamina* /-mɪnə/.

velar (adjective). (phonetics) Of a sound: articulated with the back of the tongue against or near the soft palate, especially in the pronunciation of /k/, /g/, and /ŋ/. Cf. GUTTURAL; PALATAL.

veld (open country in southern Africa). Pronounced /vɛlt/ in the UK, but /fɛlt/ in South Africa. Sometimes still written in the older form *veldt*.

vellum (fine parchment). Plural *vellums*. See -UM 1.

velum /ˈviːləm/, a membrane. Plural *vela* /-lə/. See -UM 2.

velvet has derivatives **velveted**, **velvety** (adjectives). See -T-, -TT-.

venal, venial. These words are so alike in appearance that they are occasionally confused in spite of their being so unlike in meaning, possibly because their meanings both have to do with forms of transgression. *Venal* means 'able to be bribed, corrupt' (from Latin *vēnum* 'thing for sale') and is used of people and their actions; *venial* means 'pardonable' (from Latin *venia* 'pardon') and refers in Roman Catholic teaching to minor or pardonable sins as distinct from mortal sins which bring eternal damnation. Though they mostly keep apart, occasionally *venal* intrudes incorrectly, as in **Gluttony is a venal sin in Catholicism.* Examples: *Both the Indian and Pakistani governments are weak regimes that are beholden to extreme chauvinist and fundamentalist forces and that uphold the privileges of corrupt and venal ruling elites—World Socialist Website*, 2001; *the presumption that all politicians must be venal, lazy or incompetent—Scotland on*

Sunday, 2005; *Only in a very unusual and venial case of this kind would the tribunal be likely to regard as appropriate any order less severe than one of suspension*—England and Wales High Court decisions, 2005.

vendor, vender. *Vendor* is the customary spelling in BrE in the legal sense 'the seller in a sale, esp. of property', and in the sense 'a vending machine'. In AmE, *vender* is often used in both these senses.

venery. The word meaning 'sexual indulgence' is distinct in origin from that meaning 'hunting'. Both are pronounced /'vɛnərɪ/. Both are now archaic.

venison. The *OED* (1916) and Fowler (1926) gave pride of place to the pronunciation /'vɛnz(ə)n/ (two syllables). But this has now been supplanted by three-syllabled forms, either /'vɛnɪs(ə)n/ or /-z(ə)n/.

venturesome, venturous. See ADVENTUROUS.

venue. Pronounced /'vɛnjuː/. This term, once common in the sense 'a thrust or hit in fencing' (obs.—*OED*), and still used in law as the place appointed for a jury trial (especially *lay the venue, change the venue*) has largely taken over from *rendezvous, meeting place, setting*, etc. as the place where an event (a concert, a race meeting, etc.) is scheduled to take place.

veranda(h). Both are correct and more or less equally frequent in use.

verbal. This common adjective has several established senses including: **1** Of the nature of a verb (*verbal noun*).

2 Concerned with or involving words only rather than things or realities (*Opposition between these two modes of speaking is rather verbal than real*—B. Jowett, 1875).

3 Consisting or composed of words (*the verbal wit and high-flown extravagance of thought and phrase which Euphues had made fashionable*—J. R. Green, 1874).

4 Expressed or conveyed by speech instead of writing; oral (*The archbishop believed that a verbal agreement was all which would be demanded of him*—J. A. Froude, 1877).

All four senses have a long history of recorded use (1, 3, 16c.– ; 2, 17c.– ; 4, late 16c.–), but since the late 19c. some usage commentators have drawn attention to the possible ambiguity of sense 4, and have expressed a preference for *oral* in such contexts. Perhaps the best policy for the present is to restrict *verbal* in sense 4 to a few fixed phrases (e.g. *verbal agreement, contract, evidence*); but use *oral* in most other circumstances when a formal distinction is contextually called for between a spoken and a written statement. It is worth noting that the *oral tradition* believed to have preceded the writing down of ancient poetry (Greek, Old English, etc.) is always so called, never the *verbal tradition, verbal composition*, etc.

verbal noun, verbal substantive. A noun in *-ing* formed as the present participle of a verb and used as a noun (e.g. *smoking* in *smoking is forbidden*).

verbatim. Pronounced /vəː'beɪtɪm/, not /-'bɑːt-/.

verbing. A non-technical name for the act or practice of using nouns as verbs, e.g. *to medal, to leverage, to interface*, etc., and an example itself of the phenomenon it denotes. Though *verbing* is a particularly modern bugbear, the word itself dates back to 1766. Cf. VERBS FROM NOUNS.

verbless sentences. The occasional use of verbless sentences in radio and television broadcasts is acceptable: e.g. *This report from Paul Reynolds; And so for the main points of the news again.* Sentences that lack a verb or are in other ways 'incomplete' are often found in good fiction, used as stylistic devices of various kinds, as afterthoughts or re-expressions, as a way of avoiding extensive listing, to represent broken thoughts, and so on. Examples of various types: *Friday morning. By tube to a lecture at the London School of Economics*—*Encounter*, 1981; *It asserts itself as impassive, impenetrable, enigmatic. Alluring*—M. Leland, 1987; *That way, they can work out their aggression. Once a year*—*New Yorker*, 1987; *'So,' my mother said. 'Maybe that's what this is. Just a coincidence.'*—*New Yorker*, 1987; *Made her want to weep sometimes. And not so much for her as for the kids. Their future. If you could call it that*—A. Duff, 1990 (NZ). For further examples, see SENTENCE.

verb. sap. (also **verbum sap., verbum sat**) Abbreviation of a Latin phrase variously given in full as *verbum sapienti sat est*, or *verbum satis sapienti*, both of which mean 'a word is enough for the wise person'. Both these Latin tags were formerly widely used, esp. in the 19c., to introduce or conclude a statement, implying that further explanation or comment is unnecessary or unadvisable, but are now practically extinct, except in modern collections of Latin phrases. Their approximate modern equivalent is *A word to the wise.* The *OED* considers *verbum sap.* to be a combination of *verbum sat est* and *dictum sapienti sat est*, both of which are used by Plautus, the latter also by Terence. An early 20c. example: *But*—Verbum sap! *Beware the atmosphere and the testing* [*sc.* of wine] *to which you are invited*—*Vistas of Sicily*, 1925.

verbs from nouns. Throughout its history, English has made selective use of its power to press nouns into service as verbs, a process going by the technical name of CONVERSION (where examples are given), and non-technically of VERBING. Despite the calmness with which Henry Alford greeted such new verbs in his book *The Queen's English* (1864) ('I do not see that we can object to this tendency in general, seeing that it has grown with the growth of our language, and under due regulation is one of the most obvious means of enriching it'), cries of anguish are almost invariably heard when a fresh example of conversion is noticed. Thus: 'The collapse of the tongue that Milton spoke into various mutant babbles is proceeding apace. We were told by one of the Post Office robots trained to handle enquiries that our request for further details of one of their services should be "attentioned" on the application form' (*Oldie*, 7 Jan. 1994). *Attention* (verb) is not registered in dictionaries yet and may well remain as part of the personal vocabulary of the 'office robot' in question. What cannot be questioned, however, is the legitimacy of the process of linguistic conversion, as the verbs from nouns *to question, to knife, to quiz, to pepper, to service, to access, to premiere*, and *to text* demonstrate.

verbs in -ie, -y, and -ye sometimes give trouble in the spelling of inflexions and derivatives. The following rules apply to the normally formed parts only, and are merely concerned with the question whether *-y-*, *-ie-*, or *-ye-* is to be used in the part wanted. **1** *-ay*: *plays, played, playing, player, playable* is the model for all except *lay, pay*, and *say*, and their compounds (*inlay, repay, gainsay*, etc.), which use *-aid* instead of *-ayed. Allay, assay, bay, belay, decay, delay, essay, flay, okay, relay, sway*, etc., follow *play* (thus *allayed, assayed*, etc.).

2 *-ey*: *conveys, conveyed, conveying, conveyer* (one who conveys), *conveyable.* All follow this type, except that *purvey, survey*, have *purveyor, surveyor*, and *convey* has *conveyor* for the machine.

3 *-ie*: *ties, tied, tying.* Other words in this group (*die, lie* (tell an untruth), *vie*) follow this type, and also for the most part have no *-er, -or*, or *-able* forms in common use. *Hie* has either *hieing* or *hying* as its present participle.

4 *-oy*: *destroys, destroyed, destroying, destroyer, destroyable.* This pattern is followed by *annoy, cloy, deploy, employ, enjoy, toy*, etc. There appear to be no exceptions.

5 *-uy*: *buy, guyed, buying, buyer, buyable. Buy* (and its compounds, e.g. *overbuy*) and *guy* are the only two verbs in this group.

6 *-y* after consonant: *tries, tried, trying, trier, triable; denies, denied, denying, denier, deniable; copies, copied, copying, copier, copiable.* Neither number of syllables, place of accent, nor difference between *-y* /i/ and *-y* /ʌɪ/, affects the spelling of the inflected forms. But see DRIER; FLYER; SHY.

7 *-ye*: *dyes, dyed, dyeing, dyer, dyable; dyeing* is so spelt to avoid confusion with *dying* from *die* (cf. *singeing*). *Eyeing* is also recommended, rather than *eying*, because it more obviously preserves the connection with *eye.*

verdigris. Though adopted from Old French *vert de Grece* (cf. modern French *vert-de-gris*) as early as the 14c., its pronunciation in English is still unsettled. The possibilities are (in order of preference) /ˈvəːdɪgriː/, /-griːs/, and /-grɪs/. All three pronunciations are listed in the standard BrE and AmE dictionaries, but not in the same order. The final element has no connection with the word *grease.*

verger (church official). So spelt except in St Paul's Cathedral in London and

Winchester Cathedral, where the 17c. variant spelling *virger* is still used.

veridical (adjective). Apart from its technical use in psychiatry, '(of visions, etc.) coinciding with or representing real events or people', *veridical* has little currency now except in formal language, = truthful; true or faithful to an original.

verify. For inflexions, see VERBS IN -IE, -Y, AND -YE 6.

verily will not be forgotten as long as the Gospels are read, but outside biblical contexts it has rarely been used except rhetorically since the end of the 19c.

veritable had a strong presence in the language from the 15c. to the 17c., but then fell out of use until it was revived as a Gallicism in the 19c., especially used intensively = 'deserving its name'. It is a journalistic favourite because of the slightly breathless way it is sometimes used to highlight the noun that follows. Examples: *They had a succession of governors who were veritable brigands*—A. Harwood, 1869; *At Rochefort there was . . . a veritable hail of tiles, slates*, etc. *blown off the roofs*—*Standard*, 1897; *The book is a veritable encyclopedia of great sentences*—*Writer's Digest* (US), 1988; *Tree ferns from the humid forests of Tasmania, Chilean firebushes, the dove tree from China . . . these secret gardens are a veritable Noah's Ark of fabulous, rare plants*— *Garden*, 1991; *she lost no time in establishing a veritable spider's web of an old-girl network*—*Gourmet* (US), 1992.

It is not used in English, as *véritable* is in French, to mean 'authentic, genuine (of leather, pearls, tears, anger, etc.)'.

vermeil. Pronounced /ˈvəːmeil/ rather than /-mɪl/.

vermilion is the preferred spelling, but *vermillion* is also standard.

vermin. In each of its senses, especially 'mammals and birds injurious to game, crops, etc.; vile or despicable persons', usually treated as a plural (e.g. *these vermin infest everything; such vermin as them are a danger to the community*). But it is capable of being used as a singular: e.g. *You vermin!* (addressed to one person). There is no plural form *vermins*.

vermouth. In BrE usually stressed on the first syllable, i.e. /ˈvəːməθ/, and in AmE always on the second, i.e. /vərˈmuːθ/.

vernacular. For *vernacular, idiom, slang*, etc., see JARGON.

verruca /vɛˈruːkə/. Plural (in ordinary use) *verrucas*; (in scientific use) *verrucae* /-kiː, -siː/.

verse has several meanings, including (*a*) a poetical composition, poetry (*wrote many pages of verse*); (*b*) a metrical line in a poem that conforms with the poem's rules of prosody (in ordinary use called a *line*); (*c*) a STANZA of a poem; (*d*) each of the short numbered divisions of a chapter in the Bible.

versify. For inflexions, see VERBS IN -IE, -Y, AND -YE 6.

vers libre /vɛːr ˈliːbr(ə)/. Also called *free verse*. Printed in italic. Versification or verses in which different metres are mingled, or prosodic restrictions disregarded, or variable rhythm substituted for definite metre. Perhaps now the dominant form of verse. An example (taken at random from the *London Review of Books*, 6 Apr. 1995):

The table was a wreck.
Bleared glasses stood
Half-empty, bottoms stuck to wood.
Cigarette stubs:
Ashes:
Bits of bread:
Bottles leaning,
Prostrate,
Dead.
A pink stocking: a corkscrew:
A powder puff: a French-heeled shoe:
Candle-grease.
A dirty cup.
An agate saucepan, bottom up.

The reviewer of the poet's work commented: 'The . . . description of the end of the party is full of details, but the short lines level them all into throwaways, as if only short stabs at speech were possible, as if syntax was beyond all human hope. The very colons are full of despair . . .' Well, reviewers have to say something, don't they? There are many examples of *vers libre* in the work, for example, of Ezra Pound and T. S. Eliot.

verso. Plural *versos*. See -O(E)S 4.

verso, recto. The *verso* is the left-hand page of an open book or the back of a printed sheet of paper or manuscript, as opposed to the *recto*.

vertebra /ˈvəːtɪbrə/. Plural *vertebrae*, pronounced /-breɪ/ or /-briː/.

vertex, highest point, angular point of triangle, etc. Plural generally *vertices* /ˈvəːtɪsiːz/, occasionally *vertexes*.

vertigo. After at least two centuries of fluctuation, *vertigo* seems to be always pronounced now as /ˈvəːtɪgəʊ/. Formerly also stressed on the second syllable, which was pronounced as either /-ˈtiːgəʊ/ or /-ˈtʌɪgəʊ/. Plural *vertigos* or *vertigoes*. See -O(E)S 2.

vertu. See VIRTU.

very, much. 1 (*a*) The uses of *very* and *much* as intensifying adverbs are for the most part complementary. *Very* qualifies adjectives and adverbs (*very large, very slowly*), whereas *much* qualifies past participles that are used as adjectives (*a much enlarged edition; They were much criticized; a much enfeebled Soviet Union*).

(*b*) There is a grey area including words that are strictly speaking past participles but have come to be treated as full adjectives, notably words of feeling such as *annoyed, pleased, tired, worried*, etc., and words with a strong adjectival element such as *sheltered* (*a very sheltered upbringing*) and *involved* (*He is very involved in charitable work*). These are now more naturally qualified by *very* than by *much*. When the verb element is uppermost, *much* is preferred; we would for example speak of a *much honoured* dignitary rather than a *very honoured* one, of *much needed* reforms rather than *very needed* ones. At the heart of this grey area lie words such as *respected*, in which the adjective and verb emphasis is infinitely variable: if we say *a much respected politician* we stress the process, whereas if we say *a very respected politician* we assess the effect.

2 It is worth adding that *much* can itself be qualified by *very*; consequently any of the words we have been reviewing that can be intensified by *much* can be more strongly intensified by *very much* (e.g. *very much criticized, very much enlarged*).

3 Some types of participial adjective are conventionally qualified by intensifying words other than *much* and *very*, e.g. *injured* (and similar words such as *burnt, scarred*, etc.) is qualified by *badly* or *seriously, bungled* by *badly* or *severely*, and *outnumbered, outvoted*, etc. by *heavily*.

4 In a relatively recent development, *very* is used to qualify nouns that have assumed the role of adjectives: for example, a song might be called *very sixties* (characteristic of the 1960s), and a building might be called *very art deco* (built in that style).

-ves. See -VE(D), -VES, etc.

vesica /ˈvɛsɪkə/. The bladder. Plural *vesicae* /-kiː/ or /-siː/. The *OED* (1917) gave only /vɪˈsʌɪkə/, a pronunciation still current, with others, in AmE. Cf. Latin *vēsīca*. The derivatives **vesical** adjective, **vesicle** noun have a short /ɛ/ in the (stressed) first syllable.

vest. In BrE a *vest* is an undergarment worn on the upper part of the body, equivalent to AmE *undershirt*. In AmE a *vest* is the term for what in BrE is called a *waistcoat*. In former times (17–19c.), *vest* was used for a variety of men's and women's garments. At the present time, in addition to the primary senses given above, an athlete's top garment is sometimes called a *vest*; and in AmE the term is also used for a short sleeveless woman's jacket.

vet (noun) is a well-established abbreviation (see ABBREVIATION 2) of *veterinary surgeon*, and in AmE of *veteran*. From the first of these has come the main two senses of *vet* (verb), namely 'to examine or treat (an animal)'; and the more frequent 'to examine (a scheme, a preliminary draft, a candidate, etc.) carefully and critically for errors or deficiencies'.

veto. Plural *vetoes*. See -O(E)S 1. The inflected parts of the verb are *vetoes, vetoed, vetoing*.

vexillum /vɛkˈsɪləm/ (a military standard, etc.). Plural *vexilla* /-lə/. See -UM 2.

via /ˈvʌɪə/ (also /ˈviːə/ in AmE, and increasingly in BrE). Used as a preposition = 'by way of' (*London to Sorrento via Naples*) it is in origin the ablative of Latin *via* 'way, road'. As such it was formerly printed with a circumflex accent and in italic (thus *viâ*). Despite earlier objections by some critics, it is now routinely used to mean 'through the agency of' (e.g. *most people buy a home with a mortgage via a building society*) and 'by means of' indicating the mode of transport or transmission (e.g. *via rail; via email/the Internet/satellite/Twitter*, etc. Examples: *It would in theory be possible to provide five more services with national coverage via satellite*—*Rep. of the Committee on the Future of Broadcasting*, 1977; *As a former Agony Aunt, I do know that many people find comfort in discovering, via pages in newspapers and magazines, that others share their dilemmas*—C. Rayner, 1995; *By listening to Friends' opinions, we will be more successful at promoting membership of the organisation to other graduates via the mailing*—memo from the Development Office of the Univ. of Oxford, 1995.

viable. This 19c. loanword from French first had the sense '(of a fetus or newborn child) capable of maintaining life; cf. French *vie*', but soon began to be used from time to time in figurative and extended ways, e.g. *What we have here is a romance in embryo; one, moreover, that never attained to a viable stature and constitution* (1883). It was not until the 1940s, however, that it became a vogue word applied to any concept, plan, project, proposition, etc., judged to be workable or practicable, especially economically or financially. Like all vogue words it (and its corresponding noun **viability**) has been repeatedly put to the sword by protectors of the language, but half a century on it still remains widely in use. Attitudes change slowly and it is probably advisable for the present to use other, well-established terms instead (e.g. *feasible, practicable, sustainable, tenable, workable*), at least until the stigmas of fashionableness and overuse cease entirely to be attached to *viable*.

viaticum /vʌɪˈatɪkəm/ (Eucharist given to a person near death). Plural *viatica* /-kə/. See -UM 2.

vibrato (music). Pronounced /vɪˈbrɑːtəʊ/. Plural *vibratos*: see -O(E)S 4.

vibrator. So spelt, not *-er*.

vicar. See RECTOR.

vice (noun) (clamping device). So spelt in BrE, but **vise** in AmE.

vice /ˈvʌɪsi/ (preposition), in the place of, in succession to (*appointed Secretary vice Mr Jones deceased*). In origin the ablative of Latin *vix, vic-* 'change'.

vice- /vʌɪs/ is the same word as the preceding one, but used as a combining form meaning 'acting as a deputy or substitute for' (*vice chancellor, vice president*) or next in rank to (*vice admiral*). Dictionaries differ over whether such compounds should be hyphenated.

vicegerent /vʌɪsˈdʒɛrənt/ is a wide-ranging term derived from medieval Latin *vicegerens* (from Latin *vix, vicem* 'stead, office, etc.' + *gerens* present participle of *gerere* 'to carry, hold'), meaning a person appointed to discharge the office of another. Since the 16c. it has specifically been used to mean 'a ruler, priest, etc., regarded as an earthly representative of God; in particular, the Pope'. In Oxford, Pembroke College has a Vicegerent, corresponding to the Vice-Master, Vice-President, Vice-Principal, etc., of other colleges. *Vicegerent* should not be confused with *viceregent*, a rather rare term for the deputy of a regent (to a sovereign).

viceregal is the usual term for 'of or relating to a viceroy', not *viceroyal*, though the latter had some currency in the 18c. and 19c. In Australia and New Zealand, *viceregal* is used of a Governor-General.

vice versa derives from a Latin phrase 'the position being reversed', from the same word as *vice* (preposition) (see VICE) + *versa*, ablative feminine past participle of *vertere* 'to turn'. The first word can be pronounced as two syllables or one, vys or, more correctly, as **vy**-si, and the phrase should be written as two words and printed in roman.

vicious circle. In logic, *circle* and *vicious circle* mean the same—the basing of a conclusion on a premise that is itself based on this conclusion. Or, as the *New SOED* (1993) defines it, the fallacy of proving a proposition from another that rests on it for proof. The following is an example: That the world is good follows from the known goodness of God; that God is good is known from the excellence of the world he has made. More generally, it is used to mean 'a sequence of reciprocal cause and effect in which two or more elements intensify and aggravate each other, leading inexorably to a worsening of the situation', e.g. *they were caught in a vicious circle—in low-paid jobs because they were women, while the jobs were low-paid because women did them.* The phrase *vicious spiral* is used in a similar way. The opposite of a *vicious circle* is a *virtuous circle* (1903), namely 'a recurring cycle of events, the result of each one being to increase the beneficial effect of the next', e.g. *Lower prices result in more demand for a firm's products, which can in turn allow it to achieve even more economies of scale. This virtuous circle of lower costs leading to competitive advantage can result in a small number of firms gaining a dominant position in the market-place—Principles of Marketing,* 2000.

victual. Almost always in the plural form **victuals**, pronounced /ˈvɪt(ə)lz/. A rather old-fashioned or rustic word for food, provisions. Hence **victualler** (AmE **victualer**), someone who supplies victuals; and, in BrE, **licensed victualler**, an innkeeper licensed to sell alcoholic liquor. The corresponding verb *victual* is also pronounced /ˈvɪt(ə)l/; its inflected forms are *victualled, victualling* (in AmE both usually with *-l-*). See -LL-, -L-. *Victual* (noun) entered the language in the 14c. as a modified form of Old French *vitaille(s)* (modern French *victuailles*) and was respelt in the 16c. to accord with late Latin *victuālia*, neuter plural of the adjective *victuālis*, from Latin *victus* 'nutriment, food'. The modern pronunciation of *victuals* reflects the earlier spelling of the word.

vide. Pronounced /ˈvɪdeɪ/, /ˈviːdeɪ/ or /ˈvʌɪdɪ/ (**vi**-day, **vee**-day, **vy**-di); literally 'see' (imperative). It is used in referring a reader to a passage in which he or she will find a proof or illustration of what has been stated, and should be followed by something in the nature of chapter and verse, or by the name of a book or author. But for this purpose *see* will usually do as well as *vide*, and *see above* (or *below*) as well as *vide supra* (or *infra*), and *above* and *below* are superfluous if a page is mentioned. There is, however, no convenient English equivalent of *quod vide* (abbreviated, q.v.) literally 'which see'.

videlicet /vɪˈdɛlɪsɛt/ (adverb) (from Latin, from *vidēre* 'to see' + *licet* 'it is permissible') is now rare, the abbreviation *viz.* being used instead (or the English equivalent word *namely*). For its meaning, see VIZ. See also SCILICET.

vie, 'to compete for superiority', has inflexions *vies, vied, vying.*

view is used in two well-established and current idioms and another which, though common until the early 20c., has now effectively dropped out of use. They are *in view of, with a view to,* and *with the* (or *a*) *view of.*

In view of means 'taking into account, or not forgetting, or in consideration of', and is usually followed by a noun expressing circumstances that exist or must be expected: *In view of the readiness she showed to help him with his research, all was forgiven; In view of these facts, we have no alternative but to recommend your dismissal.*

With a view to means 'with the aim or object of attaining, effecting, or accomplishing (something)', and is usually followed by a gerund or verbal noun in *-ing*: *We should pledge to hold a referendum to seek a mandate for fundamental renegotiation of our position in Europe, with a view to recreating a European partnership of sovereign nations—Daily Tel.,* 2007. In less elevated organs a construction with *in order to* (+ infinitive) is often preferable. (In the 18c. and the 19c. the more usual construction was with an infinitive (*with a view to become*...), but such constructions have now dropped out of favour.)

With the (or *a*) *view of* is a once-standard complex preposition (common in the 18c. and 19c.) meaning 'with the object or design of (doing something)': *With a view of ascertaining more accurately the nature of the sun.* It has now effectively been replaced by *with a view to.*

viewpoint. See POINT OF VIEW.

vigour. So spelt in BrE but as **vigor** in AmE. The corresponding adjective is spelt **vigorous** in both countries. See -OUR AND -OR.

vilify. For inflexions, see VERBS IN -IE, -Y, AND -YE 6.

villain, villein. These two words present a remarkable example of the severance of an original single word into two separate ones, neatly distinguished in both meaning and spelling. **1** First it should be emphasized that neither *villain* nor *villein* is etymologically related to *vile* 'disgusting, base'. The latter is derived from Latin *vīlis* 'cheap, base'; while the other two are medieval forms of Old French *villein*, ultimately from Latin *villa* 'country-house, farm'.

2 Of the two branches of the medieval senses of the word *villain*/*-ein*, (*a*) a low-born base-minded rustic, and (*b*) one of the class of serfs in the feudal system, the first by the late 16c. had worsened in meaning to 'an unprincipled scoundrel' (more or less regularly spelt *villain* from the 17c. onwards), and the second gradually slipped into historical use as the feudal system was replaced by capitalism (and is now regularly spelt *villein*). The adjective corresponding to *villain* was often spelt *villanous* from the 16c. to the 19c. but is now always **villainous**. For the pair, cf. *mountain*/*mountainous*.

-ville. Used as a terminal element since the 19c. (the *OED* includes an isolated 16c. example) to form the names of fictitious places or concepts denoting a particular quality suggested by the word to which it is appended. Recorded examples, some of which now sound rather dated, include *Dullsville*, *Geeksville*, *Hicksville*, *Mediaville*, and *Nowhereseville*.

vinculum (algebra and anatomy). Plural *vincula* /ˈvɪŋkjʊlə/.

viola. The musical instrument is pronounced /vɪˈəʊlə/ and the flower /ˈvʌɪələ/.

violoncello. So spelt (not *-lin-*; it is an Italian diminutive of *violone* a double-bass viol). The recommended pronunciation is /vʌɪələnˈʧɛləʊ/. Its plural is *violoncellos*. In practice the instrument is usually just called a *cello*.

virago. Pronounced /vɪˈrɑːgəʊ/. Plural *viragos* or *viragoes*. See -O(E)S 2.

viral. To those not in tune with the Internet Age, anything that is *viral* will sound rather unhealthy, if not distinctly grubby. To everyone else, it is a term of praise. **Viral marketing** is a term describing marketing that relies on the rapid spread of information amongst customers and potential customers by word of mouth, email, social media, etc., thereby constituting a PR person's dream: maximum exposure at no financial cost. If something, not necessarily commercial, *goes viral* it is massively or endlessly copied and forwarded on the Internet, especially in social media. (In other words, people who should be otherwise gainfully employed steal a few minutes of their employers' or their own time to propagate something of usually doubtful relevance or importance.) Examples: *Many of the new games are viral, meaning that they permit players to spread the games by e-mail to friends—NYT*, 2001; *Their petition also went viral, gathering half a million signatures in a few weeks*—A. Boyd, 2004.

virement, a regulated process of transferring funds (especially public funds) from one financial account to another. The word, taken from French in the early 20c., has now been fully anglicized in pronunciation as /ˈvʌɪəmənt/, although the French-sounding /ˈvɪəmã/ is current still.

virger. See VERGER.

Virgil (Roman poet). The more frequent and recommended spelling rather than *Vergil*. In Latin the poet's name was Publius Vergilius Maro.

Virgin Queen. See SOBRIQUETS.

virile. Now always pronounced /ˈvɪrʌɪl/ in standard speech in BrE, and /ˈvɪrəl/ or /ˈvɪrʌɪl/ in AmE. It is worth noting that the *OED* (1917) listed four pronunciations for the word, giving forms in which both *i*s vary between /ɪ/ and /ʌɪ/

virtu (as in *articles*/*objects of virtu*, i.e. beautiful objects of exquisite workmanship). This spelling, a loanword from the Italian *virtù*, and the spelling *vertu*, from the French, are both used. Pronounced /vəːˈt(j)uː/ and printed in roman.

virtual. This adjective has existed in English since the mid-14c. in a variety of meanings, but 20c. computer technology gave it an entirely new set, which is now the most widely used one, beginning in 1959 with the sense 'not physically existing as such but made by software to appear to do so', as in **virtual memory**. This use was then extended to computerized or digitized simulations of something, particularly in **virtual reality** (1987) 'a computer-generated simulation of a lifelike environment that can be interacted with in a seemingly real or physical way by a person, esp. by means of responsive hardware'. That sense also applies to things such as *virtual images* and *virtual world*. In a further expansion of meaning since 1982, *virtual* also applies to activities carried out or data accessed or stored by means of a computer, especially over a network, instead of by more traditional methods, such as *virtual business, community, tour, learning, library*. Examples: *Internet connectivity promises to reduce knowledge workers to independent telecommuters, interacting in a virtual corporate environment—Business Economics*, 2000; *The idea is to scale this up and bind virtual corporations that coalesce very quickly in internet time for a project—Bombay Times*, 2000; *Writing open-source code that becomes widely used and accepted serves as a virtual business card—First Monday Jrnl*, 2000.

virtue. The semi-proverbial phrase *to make a virtue of necessity* has a long history: it was first found in Chaucer as a rendering of Old French *faire de necessité vertue* and of Latin *facere de necessitate virtutem*. The emphasis varies in its two main senses: (*a*) to derive benefit or advantage from performing an unwelcome obligation with apparent willingness; (*b*) to submit to unavoidable circumstances with a good grace. The sainted first editor of this book remarked that it is 'often applied to the simple doing of what one must, irrespective of the grace with which one does it'. This may well be true, but no printed evidence was provided. Over the centuries the indefinite article has sometimes been omitted from the phrase, and (15–16c.) *necessity* was sometimes replaced by *need*.

virtuoso. The anglicized plural *virtuosos* is more frequent than the Italianate *virtuosi* /-siː/ or /-ziː/, and both are correct.

virtuous circle. See VICIOUS CIRCLE.

virus. Plural *viruses*. See -US 4. A **computer virus** is 'an unauthorized self-replicating [computer] program that can interfere with or destroy other programs, and can transfer itself to other systems via disks or networks' (*New SOED*). It is the electronic equivalent of a microbiological virus.

It is malicious in intention, unlike a *bug*, which is an unintentional flaw in a program. See also VIRAL.

visa (endorsement on a passport). This early 19c. loanword from French *visa* (from Lat. *vīsa*, neuter plural of the past participle of *vidēre* 'to see') has replaced *visé*, the more common of the two words in the second half of the 19c. and early 20c.

visage. Pronounced /ˈvɪsɪdʒ/. See COUNTENANCE.

vis-à-vis (preposition). Pronounced /viːzɑːˈviː/. Though its original meaning is 'face to face' in French and English (e.g. *His master dived down to him, leaving me* vis-à-vis *the ruffianly bitch*—E. Brontë, 1847), it is far more commonly used now to mean 'in relation to' (e.g. *British farmers' views* vis-à-vis *the Common Agricultural Policy*) and 'as compared with' (e.g. *the advantage for US exports is the value of the dollar* vis-à-vis *other currencies*). Printed in roman.

viscount /ˈvʌɪkaʊnt/, a British nobleman ranking between an earl and a baron, often contextually with a place name attached (*Viscount Montgomery of Alamein*). The title, dignity, or rank of a viscount is a *viscountcy*. See TITLES.

vise. See VICE (noun).

visé See VISA.

visibility, visibleness. The second was formerly in more frequent use than many *-ness* words with predominant partners in *-ty*. The current prevalence of *visibility* in the sense 'the possibility of seeing (a motor vehicle, a vessel, etc.) in adverse weather conditions' has driven out *visibleness* in other senses as well. Since the 1950s *visibility* has acquired wide currency in the figurative sense 'the degree to which something impinges upon public awareness': e.g. *From a business standpoint, the visibility Carl receives during the Olympic Games can enhance his value to the companies—Observer*, 1984. It retains its currency and may be counted among VOGUE WORDS.

visible, visual. *Visible* means 'that can be seen by the eye; *visual* broadly means 'concerned with, or used in seeing' (*visual aid, visual display unit*). The *visual arts* (painting, sculpture, etc.) are concerned with the production of the beautiful or the startling in *visible* form. The differentiation (as far as it goes) of *visible* and *visual* is worth preserving. For instance, the wrong word is used in the descriptive phrase *Diagnosis by visual symptoms*; the method of diagnosis is *visual*, but the symptoms are *visible*.

vision, in the sense of statesmanlike foresight or political sagacity, enjoyed a noticeable vogue some years ago and still flourishes. *Where there is no vision the people perish* (Prov. 29: 18) is perhaps what makes the word tempting to politicians who wish to be mysteriously impressive; at any rate they are much given to imputing lack of *vision* to their opponents and implying possession of it by themselves when they are at a loss for more definite matter. More recently the word has been commandeered by others, from multinationals to local government, who wish to bamboozle with words, as a supposedly **visionary**, quasi-ecstatic way of expressing what is often merely a plan or idea, half-baked or otherwise, e.g. *The BBC's Director-General Mark Thompson today outlined a new vision for programmes and content focused on 'excellence'—BBC* press releases, 2004.

visit (verb). Few expressions are more likely to signal American provenance than the phrase *visiting with* someone (*We visited with our elder daughter at Easter*). This phrasal verb had some currency in the UK in the second half of the 19c. (the *OED* cites an 1850 example in a letter written by Euphemia ('Effie') Ruskin, and an 1872 one from George Eliot's *Middlemarch*), but seems to have become largely confined to AmE throughout the 20c. It should be borne in mind that in AmE *visit with* usually means no more than 'call on (someone) for a friendly chat'. *Visit,* used by itself without *with,* has abundant currency in America.

visitor. So spelt, not *-er,* except in Daisy Ashford's small comic masterpiece *The Young Visiters* (1919).

visit, visitation. *Visitation,* once a formal word for visiting, as in the Prayer Book Service for the Visitation of the Sick, is now little used except for official *visits* of inspection, especially ecclesiastical, by someone in authority, and for an affliction attributed to divine or other supernatural agency. *Visitation* is also used in some parts of America (beside *viewing* and *visiting*) for the paying of last respects to the dead in the day or days between death and burial (*Visitation at Felician Sisters Provincial House Friday 10 a.m. to 7 p.m.*). In legal AmE *visitation* also refers to the right granted by a court to a divorced parent to visit a child that is in the custody of the other parent.

visor not *vizor* is the preferred spelling everywhere for this word in all its main senses (part of helmet, peak of cap, sunshield in car, etc.).

visual. See VISIBLE.

vitamin. Pronounced /ˈvɪtəmin/ in BrE, but /ˈvaɪtə-/ in AmE (and also frequently in some other varieties of English).

vitellus (yolk of egg). Plural *vitelli* /-lʌɪ/. See -US 1.

vitrify. For inflexions, see VERBS IN -IE, -Y, AND -YE 6.

vitta (botany, zoology). Plural *vittae* /ˈvɪtiː/.

viva[1]. See VIVA VOCE.

vivace (music, in a lively, brisk manner). Pronounced /vɪˈvɑːʧeɪ /.

vivarium (enclosure for keeping animals in their natural state). Pronounced /vʌɪˈvɛːrɪəm/. Plural *-ia* /-ɪə/: see –UM 2.

vivat. See VIVA², VIVAT, VIVE.

viva², vivat, vive. Pronounced /ˈviːvə/, /ˈvʌɪvat/, and /viːv/, these are respectively the Italian, Latin, and French for 'long live ——'. All may be expressed in the plural (*vivano* /ˈviːvənəʊ/, *vivant* /ˈvʌɪvant/, *vivent* /viːv/) when the object is plural, e.g. French *vivent les vacances!* 'hurrah for the holidays!'. But some French authorities at any rate regard *vive* as invariable, e.g. *Vive les gens d'esprit.* All three verbs can be used as nouns in English, with plural *-s* (e.g. *the repeated vivas of the vast crowd*).

viva voce /vɑɪvə ˈvəʊʧəɪ/ or /ˈvəʊʧiː/, from Latin, literally 'with the living voice', an oral examination for an academic qualification. Often shortened to *viva,* and the shortened form is frequently used as a verb (*Most of the candidates vivaed are on the borderline between one class and another*).

vive. See VIVA².

vivify. For inflexions, see VERBS IN -IE, -Y, AND -YE 6.

viz. /vɪz/. Abbreviated form of VIDELICET (*z* in its medieval shape being the usual symbol of contraction for *-et*). As is suggested by its usual spoken substitute *namely, viz.* introduces especially the items that compose what has been expressed as a whole (*For three good reasons,* viz. 1 . . . , 2 . . . , 3 . . .) or a more particular statement of what has been vaguely described (*My only means of earning, viz. my fiddle*). It is preceded by a comma and printed in roman, sometimes without a full point, but *viz.* is the form recommended here. Care should be taken to distinguish *viz.* from I.E. and SC.

vizor. See VISOR.

vocabulary. See GLOSSARY.

vocal chords, vocal cords. See CHORD, CORD 2.

vocation. See AVOCATION.

vogue word. 1 The word *vogue* is a 16c. adoption of French *vogue* 'rowing, course, success', from Italian *voga* 'rowing, fashion', from *vogare* 'to row'. In the broad senses 'fashion, acceptance, currency, prevalence' it has had wide currency in English ever since. The *OED* examples show a range of concepts, activities, etc., that have been *in vogue* at various times and in sundry places since the 16c.: the study of medals, austere doctrines, travelling in a carriage, prodigality, mountaineering, tartan shawls, moustaches, waltzing, burlesque, etc. Curiously, except for an isolated 17c. example (*Pox on your Bourdeaux, Burgundie . . . no more of these vogue names . . . get me some ale*) the *OED* entry reveals that the application of *vogue* to words and names is predominantly a 20c. phenomenon. In the first edition (1926) of this book, Fowler introduced the concept of *vogue words* in the following manner: 'Every now and then a word emerges from obscurity, or even from nothingness or a merely potential and not actual existence, into sudden popularity . . . Ready acceptance of vogue-words seems to some people the sign of an alert mind; to others it stands for the herd instinct and lack of individuality . . . on the whole, the better the writer, or at any rate the sounder his style, the less will he be found to indulge in the vogue-word.'

2 (*a*) The attitude of writers of usage guides has been consistently hostile: e.g. '*Vogue words* wander in and out of journalism and can become instant clichés. They are as likely to deaden a story as to enliven it. The only safe rule is to beware of them. Current examples: backlash, bombshell, bonanza, brainchild, charisma, Cinderella of, consensus, crunch, escalate, facelift, lifestyle, mega-, persona, prestigious, quantum leap, rationale, trauma(tic), viable' (*Times Guide to English Style and Usage,* 1992). It is interesting to ponder which of the above words from a quarter of a century ago can still be classed as 'vogue' words.

(*b*) 'There are two reasons for avoiding a vogue word while the vogue lasts. First, any reader who has noticed the recent frequency of its occurrence will be irritated by it. Secondly, the usual result of its being used by many writers on every possible occasion is that its meaning becomes exceedingly vague' (M. Dummett, 1993).

3 Usage guides have also stressed the ephemerality of vogue words, e.g. 'The borrowed Russian words *glasnost* and *perestroika* were vogue words a short time ago, and *infrastructure, ecosystem, caring, share,* and *senior citizen* are vogue words today' (K. G. Wilson, *Columbia Guide to Standard American English,* 1993).

4 Vogue words come and go. They are as it were like baggage on an airport carousel, sometimes visible, sometimes not, appearing, disappearing, and reappearing. Some vogue uses arise because they are associated with events of particular public interest (such as *yomping* = marching over heavy terrain, used by Royal Marines in the Falklands war of 1982, and hardly used since). Many arise in the domains of business, government, and IT. Many of them are treated at their alphabetical places in the book, and others in the entries for CLICHÉS, and POPULARIZED TECHNICAL TERMS. See also -ATHON; -SPEAK; -VILLE.

A list of some of the vogue words and phrases of recent times follows: *at the end of the day; at this moment* (or *point*) *in time; ball game* (*a different,* etc.); *best practice; bleeding-edge; bottom line; buy-in; cutting edge; community* (*the Muslim,* etc.); *engage* (v.); *high-end; impact* (v.); *interface* (v.); *kick-start* (v.) (*to—the economy*); *learnings; lifestyle; ongoing; -oriented* (e.g. *market-oriented*); *off-message; paradigm; parameter; quantum jump/leap; resonate; robust; syndrome; target; track record; unacceptable; visibility* (e.g. of a product, etc., in the public awareness); *vision* (meaning 'plan' or 'idea').

voiced (adjective) (phonetics). Uttered with vibration or resonance of the vocal cords, as opposed to *unvoiced* or *voiceless*. Voiced consonants include *b, d, g, th* /ð/, *v*, and *z*. Their unvoiced or voiceless equivalents are *p, t, k, th* /θ/, *f*, and *s*.

voicemail, denoting the electronic system of storing messages from telephone callers, and such a message, is now normally spelt as one word.

volcano. Recommended plural *volcanoes*, rather than *volcanos*. See -O(E)S 2.

volley. Plural *volleys*. For verb inflexions, see VERBS IN -IE, -Y, AND -YE 2.

volte-face. Pronounced /vɒlt'fas/ or /'fɑːs/.

voluntarily. Pronounced (in older and conservative use) /'vɒləntərɪlɪ/, but in AmE (and increasingly in BrE) /vɒlən'tɛːrɪlɪ/, i.e. stressed on the third syllable. See -ARILY.

vomit (verb). The inflected forms are *vomits, vomited, vomiting*. See -T-, -TT-.

vortex (whirlpool, etc.). Plural *vortexes*, but usually *vortices* /tɪsiːz/ in scientific and technical use. See -EX, -IX 2.

vouch. See AVOUCH.

wage, wages (weekly pay). *Wages* is normally used in the plural (*Their wages are still too low; What are the wages for the job?*). The biblical *For the wages of sinne is death* (Rom. 6: 23) is the sole survivor of a once common (14–early 18c.) construction with a singular verb. But *wage* (singular) is also used (*What sort of wage is he paid?*), and in some circumstances is obligatory (*wage earner; a wage cut; minimum wage*).

wagon, waggon. The form with a single *-g-* is recommended, but *waggon* is also used by some printing houses in Britain.

wait (verb). See AWAIT.

waitperson, waitron. Two coinages of the 1980s as 'common-gender' forms to replace *waiter* and *waitress,* i.e. a person, male or female, who serves at table in a hotel, restaurant, etc. The collective term *waitstaff* (*Waitstaff full and part time. Inquire within*—sign in the window of a restaurant in Chicago, 1992) has also been used in AmE since about the same time. *Waitron* is said to have been formed with *-on,* as in *automaton,* as a contemptuous judgement of waiting at tables as a mindless, robotic activity before it was taken up as a gender-neutral term. Neither *waitperson* nor *waitron* is widely used.

waitress. Under attack from some quarters as an unnecessary 'sexist' term, but it remains in normal standard use. See -ESS 4.

waive (verb) means 'refrain from insisting on or using (a right, claim, opportunity, legitimate plea, etc.)' (*COD*), and is derived from an OF verb meaning 'to allow to become a waif, to abandon'. Correct use: *Let us waive the formalities and proceed with the business of the meeting.* It has had a rich and varied history in English since the 13c. But in the early 19c. it began to be confused with the homonym *wave* (verb) and used in phrasal verbs to mean 'to put (a person or thing) aside, away, off with or as with a wave of the hand', e.g. *He says* Fabrication *was 'written in the belief that the factual details are matters not to be waived aside'—Quadrant,* 2004. Such uses are to be avoided.

wake (verb), **waken** (verb). See AWAKE.

wallop makes *walloped, walloping, walloper.* See -P-, -PP-.

walnut. In origin from Old English *walhhnutu* 'nut of the (Roman) foreigner', the first element being the same as that in *Welsh* (Old English *Welisc,* from *wealh, walh* 'foreigner' + *-isc).* It has nothing to do with *wall* (Old English *weall*). See TRUE AND FALSE ETYMOLOGY.

wantonness. So spelt, with *-nn-*.

wapiti (a North American deer). Pronounced /ˈwɒpɪti/. Plural *wapitis.*

war. *And yee shall heare of warres, and rumors of warres* (Matt. 24: 6) is the correct quotation (not *war,* not *rumour*). See MISQUOTATIONS.

Wardour Street (or **Wardour Street English**). The phrase is a fascinating historico-linguistic curiosity. Wardour Street in London's Soho was once occupied mainly by dealers in antique and imitation-antique furniture. This fact gave rise to the expression *Wardour-street English,* nowadays little used but once applied to the pseudo-archaic diction affected by some writers, especially of bad historical novels (*To the difficulty of following Borgese's Wardour Street diction* (*'Bread and wine needs a man to fight and die'; 'Us enchants he, but eke frightens'*) *Sessions adds that of hearing the words—New Yorker,* 1976). The term is first recorded in 1888, and it was applied to certain uses (especially those placed in the wrong century) of such expressions as the following, beloved of earlier generations of historical novelists. Some of these are treated at their alphabetical places: *anent; a-* as in *aplenty; belike;* BETIMES; *eke* (= also); *ere; erst* (*while*); *haply*; *hither*; *howbeit*; *nay*; *oft*; *peradventure*; *perchance*; *quoth*; some *there-* compounds (e.g. *-from*); *thither*; *to wit*; *trow*; *twain*; *ween*; *what time* (= when); *whilom*; *wight* (= a person); *withal*; *wot*; *yea*; *yon*; *yore* (only in *of yore*).

Nowadays the use of language inappropriate to a given historical period is more likely to work in the other direction, particularly in TV period dramas. Twitting the scriptwriters of *Downton Abbey* for anachronistic modern turns of phrase became something of a pastime among the chattering classes.

See also ARCHAISM, and for a fuller discussion of *Wardour Street English*, Michael Quinion's article at *www.worldwidewords.org/weirdwords/ww-war1.htm.*

-ward(s). Most words ending in *-ward(s)* are used as adverbs, adjectives, and nouns. In BrE the *-s* is usually present in the adverb (*backwards, downwards*) but not in the adjective (*a backward glance, in a downward direction*). In most circumstances AmE seems to prefer the forms without *-s* for the adverbs. The nouns, which are really absolute uses of the corresponding adjectives, tend to follow the adjectives in being without *-s* (*looking to the eastward*). See also the separate entries for many of these words: AFTERWARD(S); FORWARD(S); ONWARD(S); TOWARD(S); ETC.

warp (noun). The *warp* is a set of parallel threads stretched out lengthwise in a loom. The threads woven across and between them are the *woof* or *weft*. The fabric that results is the *web*.

warranty is the term used in various branches of law (e.g. property law, contract law, insurance law) defining and delimiting certain kinds of covenants, contracts, and insurance risks. See GUARANTEE. In origin they are 'the same word', the spelling with initial *w* coming from Anglo-Norman *warantie*, a dialect variant of *guarantie*, modern French *garantie*.

washroom. See TOILET.

wash up in BrE means to wash (crockery and cutlery) after use, to wash the dishes. In AmE it means to wash one's face and hands.

wassail. Pronounced /ˈwɒseɪl/, /ˈwɒs(ə)l/ or /ˈwa-/.

wast. See BE 4.

wastage is partially differentiated from *waste* in that it tends to be restricted to mean (*a*) the amount wasted; (*b*) loss by use, wear, erosion, or leakage; (*c*) (preceded by *natural*) the loss of employees other than by forced redundancy (especially by retirement or resignation). In most contexts *wastage* should not be used simply as a LONG VARIANT of *waste:* thus *waste* not *wastage* in *to go to waste, a waste of time, a waste of words, a boggy waste*; *waste disposal unit, wasteland, waste-pipe*, etc.

wastepaper basket is the normal word in BrE for a basket into which waste paper is thrown, as against **wastebasket** in AmE.

Watergate. The name of a building in Washington, DC, containing the headquarters of the Democratic Party, which was burgled on 17 June 1972 by persons connected with the Republican administration, an event that led to the resignation of President Richard M. Nixon in 1974. It was the immense brouhaha over this event that gave English the prolific suffix -GATE so widely used to create words referring to actual or alleged scandals of other kinds, e.g. *Monicagate, Plebgate, Rebekahgate* (Rebekah Brooks), etc.

wave (verb). See WAIVE (verb).

wax (verb). Its primary meaning 'grow larger, increase' (as opposed to *wane*) leads naturally to the sense 'pass into a specified state or mood, begin to use a specified tone'. In this meaning a following modifier must be an adjective not an adverb (*He waxed enthusiastic* [not *enthusiastically*] *about Australia*). Correct use: *When the Roman soldiers were asked to take part in the Claudian invasion of 43, they waxed indignant*—A. Fraser, 1988.

way. 1 Among uses originating in AmE in the 20c. and initially given somewhat reluctant currency in BrE are *no way* (in colloquial contexts) = it is impossible, it can't be done (e.g. *He said he wouldn't start up a gang today—no way—New Yorker*, 1975); *way too* + adjective (e.g. *Stuart struggled with the suitcases, which were way too heavy for him, she thought—New Yorker*, 1987; *Jack? Nah, he's way too smart. You know Jack*—A. Billson, 1993 (UK)); *the way* + clause, in which *the way* is treated as if it is a conjunction (e.g. *They'd assumed we'd run away to the army, the way three or four boys on our street had done*—N. Williams,

1985 (UK); *You help women the way people help dogs they're training to do tricks*—J. Hecht, 1991 (US)).

2 *under way, underway*. See UNDER WAY, UNDERWAY.

waylay. Has the inflexions *waylays, waylaid, waylaying*.

ways. *We've come a ways in journalism, too,* wrote the American word maven William Safire in 1994, meaning (he said) 'we've come pretty far, but not too far', as distinct from 'a long way' if his meaning had been 'we had come really far'. In March 1994 the American Secretary of State Warren Christopher said that an overall peace agreement in Bosnia was *a ways down the road*. It was hard to say how far down the road peace was. Tom Wolfe in his *Bonfire of the Vanities* (1987) wrote *I was standing out in the street a little ways*; and T. R. Pearson in his *Cry Me a River* (1993) wrote *concealed completely from me his pangs and his anguishments which surely went a ways towards confirming the wisdom of seeking Ellis's help*. Clearly *a ways* gives no more than an approximate indication of the distance a person, process, etc., has travelled along a particular route, and it may be qualified by an adjective (*good, great, little, long,* etc.). Use of this plural form *ways* in this meaning was once standard in BrE: the *OED* lists BrE examples from 1588 onwards including the following: *Not that I hope . . . to live to any such Age as that neither—But if it be only to eighty or ninety: Heaven be praised, that is a great Ways off yet*—Fielding, 1749; *Falmouth . . . is no great ways from the sea*—Byron, 1809. But it is now only dialectal in BrE.

-ways. See -WISE.

we.

1 Normal uses.
2 Wrong case.
3 Indefinite *we*.
4 The royal *we*.
5 Addressing the sick and some others.

1 *Normal uses. We* has an indefinite range of reference, so that care is sometimes needed to avoid misunderstanding. In its primary meanings it can denote any of the following: (i) you (singular or plural) and I, (ii) you and I and some others, or (iii) I and some others (but not you: *We are going now, but don't you hurry*). Some other languages make these distinctions. Examples of normal uses of the first person plural *we* (including examples of *we* merged with reduced forms of accompanying auxiliary verbs): *We needn't stay long; We're going to a civic reception; We've still got plenty of time; we three girls; We Europeans rode the streets in cars; we neither of us; we both of us.*

2 *Wrong case. We* is sometimes mistakenly used for *us* in the objective case, presumably as a case of hypercorrection. Examples (drawn from standard sources): *that is good news for* we *who watch; a brassiere showing Jane Russell saying 'For* we *full-figured gals'; Australia's monarch-in-waiting has been sprayed with insecticide, like* we *mere mortals; Perhaps this product is best suited to* we *cloth-capped northerners*. Read *us* in each case. (It is worth noting that the *OED* (1921) cited similar examples from standard sources from *c.*1500 to 1890.)

3 Indefinite *we*. *We* is often used indefinitely in contexts in which the speaker or writer includes those whom he or she addresses, his or her contemporaries, family, fellow citizens, etc. Examples: *There is nothing we receive with so much reluctance as advice; What do we, as a nation, care about books?; In ordinary life we use a great many words with a total disregard of logical precision; We have to get our production and our earnings into balance.*

4 The royal *we*. The *OED* gives examples from the Old English period onwards in which *we* is used by a single sovereign or ruler to refer to himself or herself. The custom seems to be dying out: in her formal speeches Queen Elizabeth II rarely if ever uses it now. (On royal tours when accompanied by the Duke of Edinburgh *we* is often used by the Queen to refer to them both; alternatively *My husband and I.*)

History of the term. The *OED* record begins with Lytton (1835): *Noticed you the* we*—the style royal?* Later examples: *The writer uses 'we' throughout—rather unfortunately, as one is sometimes in doubt whether it is a sort of 'royal' plural, indicating only himself, or denotes himself and companions*—*N&Q*, 1931; '*In the absence of the accused we will continue with the trial. He used the royal 'we', but spoke for us all*—J. Rae, 1960. (The last two examples clearly overlap with those given in 3.) It will be observed that the term 'the royal *we*' has come to be used in a weakened, transferred, or jokey manner. The best-known example came when Margaret Thatcher informed the world in 1989 that her daughter-in-law had given birth to a son: *We have become a grandmother,* the Iron Lady said with blatant delusions of grandeur. A less well-known American example: interviewed on a television programme in 1990 Vice-President Quayle, in reply to the interviewer's expression of hope that Quayle would join him again some time, replied *We will.*

5 *Addressing the sick and some others. We* is often used informally, and nowadays in an unacceptably patronizing fashion, instead of *you* by a nurse or other medical person when addressing a patient: e.g. *A young doctor came... 'Well, Mrs Orton, how are we?'.* A playful use of this convention is shown in the following example: *'We don't want to drop, do we?' 'I don't know what we're talking about,' Muriel said. 'Our head hurts.'*—H. Mantel, 1986. Used similarly in various other contexts: (a hairdresser speaking to a customer) *Do we have the hair parted on the left as usual, sir?*; (an army officer addressing a recruit) *Not quite professional soldier material, are we?*

weave (verb). **1** This verb has two sets of past tense forms corresponding in origin to two separate verbs. The past tenses are generally kept distinct, but occasionally criss-cross.

2 When the meaning is (i) 'to create fabric' the standard past tense and participle are the irregular forms *wove* and *woven* respectively, e.g. *the web the spider wove; textiles woven from linen or wool; woven shawls.* When the meanings are (ii) 'to move repeatedly from side to side' and 'thread one's way through or past obstructions' the standard past tense and participle are the regular *weaved,* e.g. *they weaved in and around the traffic.* In general this distinction is observed in writing, but, presumably because people see the verb as a single strand rather than two, crossovers regularly occur. Nevertheless, it is advisable to keep the distinction, particularly with the literal sense of 'creating fabric', for which *weaved* is likely be viewed as a mistake, less so for figurative uses. *Wove* for meaning (ii) is quite widespread for *weaved,* and less likely to raise eyebrows.

3 Examples: (a) meaning (i), literal: (*wove,* past tense) *A man wove bamboo to build a wall for a hut*—*OEC,* 2013 (US); (*woven,* past participle) *When we left for Tennessee, all the knitting was done. I had even woven in the ends*—*OEC,* 2012; figurative (*wove,* past tense) *She returned to Sierra Leone and wove a love story in and around the twin horrors of civil war and the scars left on its survivors*—*OEC,* 2013 (US); (*woven,* past participle) *You stole the money, and you have woven a plot to lay the sin at my door*—G. Eliot, 1861 (UK). meaning (i), literal (*weaved,* past tense) *They *weaved a variety of baskets made from natural fibres using a technique that has been practiced for thousands of years*—*OEC,* 2013 (SAfr.); figurative *?The corporation officials weaved a strange argument that convinced no one*—*OEC,* 2013 (India). (b) meaning (ii) (*weaved,* past tense) *Then they got on to the little scooter and weaved down the lane*—J. Winterson, 1987 (UK); *Andrew found Ruth, and the two weaved their way to the car*—R. Rive, 1990 (SAfr.); (*wove,* past tense) *?They wove off* [on their bicycles] *through the theatre crowd, bending and bowing together*—A. S. Byatt, 1985 (UK); *?She wove her way among the crowd, bumping into people, being bumped into*—M. Ramgobin, 1986 (SAfr.).

4 Although some standard dictionaries treat them as a single verb, there are two distinct words. *Weave*[1] (past tense *wove,* past participle *woven*) is of native origin (Old English *wefan*); *Weave*[2] (past tense *weaved,* irregularly but frequently *wove,* past participle *weaved*) entered the language in the 16c., ultimately deriving from Old Norse *veifa.*

web. See WARP (noun).

weblog. See BLOG.

website, web site. Dictionaries are in disarray over the preferred spelling: *web site* (*OED*), *website* (*ODO,* Collins), *Web site* (Merriam-Webster), *website,* also *web site* (Macquarie), to name just a few. Internet users, however, vote with their fingers, and show a clear preference for the solid form.

Web, the, referring to the World Wide Web, the information system on the Internet, is written with an initial capital letter. *World Wide Web* itself is written as three words, and often abbreviated to *WWW.*

wed. Outside certain familiar collocations (e.g. *wedded bliss, wedding breakfast, With this ring I thee wed*), the Old English verb *wed* long ago fell out of everyday use: try saying 'We are wedding next March' to see what I mean. When the *OED* entry was first published (1926), the editors considered it dialectal or literary. That same year Fowler noted 'the need of brevity in newspaper headings is bringing into trivial use both the verb instead of *marry*... & the short instead of the long p.p.' (i.e. *wed* instead of *wedded*). Both trends he mentioned have continued consistently: the word is still de rigueur in the popular press (but irretrievably naff in more serious journalism; see the *Guardian* quote below); and it is also tending in this meaning towards a verb with the single form *wed* as past tense and past participle instead of the historical *wedded*, except in figurative uses, as noted below. Examples: *He did wed one of his regular girlfriends... in a Wicca ceremony—Sky Mag.*, 1991; *The millionaire drummer has slapped a no-sex ban on their relationship until they wed—Daily Mirror*, 1992; *Matthew's graduate companion... proposes a night's dissipation—'one last bachelorly bout before we wed the stern bride of the future'*—G. Swift, 1992; *until a messy divorce allowed him to wed archaeologist Jacquetta Hawkes—Guardian*, 1994; *No one had to dwell on the ugliness of his policies if he were treated as a cartoon, sleepily wed to Cruella De Ville—Spy* (US), 1994.

In the phrase *to be wedded to*, meaning to be deeply or obstinately attached to an idea, belief, etc., both *wedded* and *wed* are used, but *wedded* is very much more frequent. When the meaning is 'to combine two things', *wedded* is the norm as the past participle. *The main conference agenda does not include any reference to the Big Society even though the Prime Minister remains wedded to the idea—Daily Tel.*, 2011; *'This electorate is not wed to either party, and they do not like the deeply ideological bent of this particular administration,' Davis says—Guardian unlimited*, 2004; *inspirational or downright bizarre lyrics wedded to competent, workmanlike music—Bright Lights Film Jrnl*, 2004.

Wedgwood. So spelt, not *Wedge-*.

Wednesday. For the type *Can you come Wednesday?*, see FRIDAY.

ween (verb) (= think, suppose). A WARDOUR STREET word.

weft. See WARP (noun).

weigh. For *under weigh*, see UNDER WAY.

weird. So spelt. See -EI-.

Welch. See WELSH.

well (adverb).

A *as well as; as well... as.*
B The preliminary or resumptive *well.*
C *well* as an intensifier.

A *as well as; as well... as.* **1** *Straightforward constructions.* Undisputed constructions are those in which the phrase simply means (*a*) 'in as good, satisfactory, etc., a way or manner as': e.g. *She affected... to listen with civility, while the Hydes excused their recent conduct, as well as they could*—Macaulay, 1849; (*b*) with weakened force, passing into the sense of 'both... and', 'not only... but also': e.g. *Our churchmen have become wealthy, as well by the gifts of pious persons, as by... bribes*—Scott, 1828. (Type (*b*) seems archaic.)

2 *Potential issues.* There are three main areas in which the grammatical status of *as well as* has been called into question. (*a*) When *as well as* means 'in addition to' (e.g. *He must irrevocably lose her as well as the inheritance—G. O. Curme*, 1931) or 'and not only' (e.g. *It was obvious that* he *had been consulted as well as I*—G. Greene, 1965) the question arises whether a following pronoun should be in the subjective case, as in the Graham Greene example, or in the objective, i.e. *me*. In the first case it is being used as a conjunction, agreeing with the preceding pronoun *he*; more commonly, however, it is treated as a preposition, in which case the example would read... *as well as me.*

(*b*) *Following verb singular or plural.* Grammatical agreement calls for a singular verb to accord with the subject noun or noun phrase preceding *as well as* if it is in the singular. The standard construction is illustrated in the following examples, particularly in those in which commas are used fore and aft to bring out the parenthetical nature of the subordinating phrase or clause after *as well as*: *To talk as her thoughts came, as well as to wear her hair as it grew,* was *a special privilege of this young person*—G. Meredith, 1861; *This sheep, as well as the long-tailed Damara sheep and the small black-headed Persian,* is *very popular—SAfr. Panorama,* 1989; *He believes that tutor as well as pupil* benefits *from the arrangement*—*Oxford Today*, 1990. Some might have been tempted to use a plural verb in such constructions, i.e. to replace *benefits* by *benefit*, and so on, but they would have been ill-advised to do so. Nevertheless such plural constructions do occur from time to time: e.g. (cited by Jespersen) *When a man enlists in the army, his soul as well as his body* belong *to his commanding officer*—J. A. Froude, 1884.

(*c*) In most circumstances *as well as* may be idiomatically followed by an *-ing* form, e.g. (the first example cited by Jespersen) *as you're a Trinity scholar as well as being captain of the eleven*—E. F. Benson, 1916; *Just like Dolly to usurp the mourning function as well as presuming to treat the evening as a normal evening party*—A. Brookner, 1985.

Fowler (1926) argued, however, that in certain circumstances the *-ing* form is better replaced by a verb form that parallels the verb form used in the introductory clause. He cited several examples (with suggested improvements) including this one: '*His death leaves a gap* as well as creating *a by-election in Ross and Cromarty* (Read *creates*).' This construction still occurs, typically when an auxiliary or modal verb such as *have* and *will* precedes: *I'm sure the children* will learn *a lot from the project* as well as enjoy *themselves getting stuck in to the mud and planting the bulbs*—*Bolton Evening News*, 2003). So there is room for disagreement in sentences containing *as well as* followed by an *-ing* form. Each case must be judged on its merits.

B The preliminary or resumptive *well*. What the *OED* calls the preliminary or resumptive use of *well*, tantamount to a plea for a moment's grace to gather one's thoughts, is for most of us a reflex response to the stimulus of any question. Those taking part in broadcast discussions would add to the pleasure of listeners if they would try to curb it, although it would be unreasonable to expect them to abandon altogether such a natural item of speech. It should also be borne in mind that the use of *well* in a resumptive manner has been a feature of the language from the Anglo-Saxon period onwards.

C *well* as an intensifier. In many varieties of English, people below a certain age now quite commonly use *well* to emphasize any adjective: *she is well thick*; *Jack said he was well chuffed*; *this is a well cool bar*; *a technology now well familiar*. Using *well* like this is still markedly informal even in speech, and should be avoided in any kind of serious writing. It is, nevertheless, a logical extension of some old-established ways of using *well* for emphasis.

well and well-. For combinations of *well* and a past participle, e.g. *well-made*, *well-received*, there is widespread uncertainty about whether the two parts should be hyphenated or left separate. In fact the matter is easily resolved. If a participle with *well* is attributive (*a well-aimed stroke*) a hyphen is normally used in order to clarify the unity of the sense; but if the participle is predicative (*the stroke was well aimed*) a hyphen is not required. This is not an arbitrary rule; it follows from acceptance of the principle that hyphens should be used only when a reader is helped by their presence. Cf. *up to date* s.v. UP 2. See HYPHENS 2.

well-nigh (adverb) (very nearly, almost wholly or entirely) has been in continuous use since the Old English period. Burchfield (1996) gloomily prognosticated that 'it looks as if it is drawing towards archaism or becoming restricted to literary use' but his prophecies have not come true. Though not exactly a word on everyone's lips, it is firmly established, particularly in the collocations *well-nigh impossible*, and with many other negative adjectives beginning *un-/im-/in-/ir-*, and in *well-nigh perfect*. Dictionaries spell it with a hyphen, to underline its nature as a compound adverb, and this is the better spelling (rather than the unusual solid form **wellnigh*), though spelling as two words, *well nigh*, is frequent. Examples: *His journey toward anti-intellectualism was well-nigh complete by this time*—R. Ferguson, 1991; *If your country is the size of a postage stamp, your population is unsophisticated and your borders are well-nigh indefensible, you need luck*—*Economist*, 1992.

Welsh. In past times *Welch* was a frequent variant of *Welsh*, but *Welsh* is now standard for all uses of the noun and the adjective except in the name of the *Royal Welch Fusiliers*. Other Welsh units, including the *Welsh Guards*, are spelt with final *-sh* in the word *Welsh*. For the origins of the word *Welsh*, see WALNUT.

welsh (verb). Used at first (since the mid-19c.) to mean 'to swindle (a person) out of money laid as a bet' (especially in racing parlance), and later (since the 1930s), followed by *on*, 'to fail to carry out one's promise to (a person); to fail to honour (an obligation)'. The word has understandably not gone down well in Wales and among Welsh people in America and elsewhere. Some writers have tried to take the sting out of it by spelling it *welch*, and the *OEC* data suggests that this form is used in a ratio of 4:7 against *welsh*. In the interests of good-neighbourliness, it would be as well, particularly for English people, to use the tactful spelling. However it is spelt or pronounced, etymologists have not been able to determine its derivation. It must not be assumed that the name of the people and the verb *welsh* are the same word. Our language abounds in homonyms (e.g. *light* not heavy, and *light* not dark; (Egyptian) *mummy* (Arabic origin) and *mummy* (= mother)).

Welsh rabbit. This dish, originally of simple cheese on toast but nowadays often embellished with other ingredients, is first recorded with *rabbit* spelt like the animal, in 1725. In Mrs Hannah Glasse's *The Art of Cookery* (1747), on the same page, she also called what reads like an almost identical recipe a *Scotch rabbit* (a wording which appears in some later sources), not to mention the somewhat less frugal *English rabbit*, to which wine was added. In the same century, the lexicographer Francis Grose defined *Welsh rabbit* in his *Classical Dict. of the Vulgar Tongue* (1785) as 'bread and cheese toasted' and added, 'i.e. a Welch rare bit'. The *OED* first records the spelling with *rarebit* as one word in 1787, though there is no evidence of the independent use of *rarebit* in other contexts. In modern use, *OEC* data, other corpora and Google searches show that the spelling *rarebit* is now considerably more frequent; Google ngrams shows that it started to take off from the 1880s. Nevertheless, the original spelling with its attendant pronunciation is also still quite widely used, despite the fact that those in the *rarebit* camp may consider it pedantic or old-fashioned; conversely, for some people *rarebit* will sound pretentious or affected. Its dominance is presumably aided by the fact that it makes it clear there is no meat in the dish, which is an advantage when it appears, as it quite often does, on menus. The origin of the name must remain a mystery: it is not thought to be Welsh in origin, there is no rabbit in it, and neither cheese nor toast is rare. Half-parallels included *Bombay duck*, which is dried fish, not a duck, *Scotch woodcock*, which contains no dead game birds, and *toad-in-the-hole*, which encases no amphibians.

wen. For *the Great Wen*, see SOBRIQUETS.

were. For the use of *were* as a subjunctive form (*as it were, wished that it were winter again, were this done*, etc.), see SUBJUNCTIVE MOOD.

werewolf /ˈwɛːwʊlf/. The recommended spelling (not *werwolf*) and pronunciation (not /ˈwɪə-/), like *ware*. Plural *werewolves*. The Old English form was *werewulf* and the first element is thought to be based on *wer* meaning 'man'.

wert. See BE 4.

westernmost. See -MOST.

westward(s). See -WARD(S).

wet. The past tense and past participle forms are either *wet* or *wetted*. The shorter form seems to be on the retreat except in familiar contexts (e.g. *she's wet the bed; while coming ashore from the lifeboat they wet all their clothes; after they had wet their whistles*). Meanwhile *wetted* seems to be favoured in most 'free' uses of the verb and in many forms of English, particularly as the past participle (as in the second and fourth examples) in order to denote the completed action of *wetting* as against the simple adjective *wet*: e.g. *perspiration wetted those few strands of hair that fell against his broad forehead*—D. A. Richards, 1981 (Canad.); *In the square, the statues, roofs and monumental buildings were wetted slick*—B. Moore, 1987 (Ir./US); *Two weeks ago a heavy rain had leaked through the ceiling and wetted the box—NY Rev. Bks, 1987; with her clothes wetted and her pockets full of big round stones*—A. S. Byatt, 1990 (UK).

wh. In words beginning with the digraph *wh* the pronunciation depends on regional and social factors. In Received Pronunciation and some other accents in England and Wales it is usually /w/ with no aspiration or minimal aspiration, but in general American, in Canadian, and in Scottish and Irish English it is usually /hw/. Australian,

New Zealand, and South African English mostly follow RP, but in these countries and sometimes in England one encounters varying (usually only faintly audible) degrees of aspiration, especially in circumstances in which minimal pairs happen to occur (*whales/Wales, white/Wight, Whig/wig*, etc.).

wharf. Plural either *wharves* /wɔːvz/ or *wharfs* /wɔːfs/. See -VE(D), -VES.

wharfinger (owner or manager of a wharf). This flavoursome if unusual word is pronounced /ˈwɔːfın(d)ʒə/, the *-inger* element as in *Ninja*.

what.

1 Verb agreement.
2 Singular *what* and plural *what*.
3 *what* doing double duty.
4 *what* wrongly paralleled by *and which* or *but which*.
5 *It's dashed hot, what?*
6 'Pseudo-cleft' sentences led by *what*.
7 *what* as relative pronoun.

1 *Verb agreement.* (*a*) Fowler (1926) was in an unusually dogmatic mood when he discussed phrases of the type *what* (relative pronoun) + singular verb + a second verb followed by a plural complement, e.g. *what really worries me is the numbers.* As he wrote: 'In each of the examples to be given it is beyond question that *what* starts as a singular pronoun (= that which or a thing that), because a singular verb follows it; but in each also the next verb... is not singular but plural. He went on to give a dozen quotations in each of which, he said, *are* should be replaced by *is.* Here are three of them: *What is required* are *houses at rents that the people can pay*; *What seems to be needed, and what, I believe, public opinion calls for,* are *stringent regulations to restrict the sale*; *What strikes the tourist most* are *the elegant Paris toilettes.* The plural verbs are due to the influence of a complement in the plural, and the grammatical name for such influence is *attraction.*' (See AGREEMENT 2b.)

(*b*) Later studies of the matter have confirmed that Fowler's 'rule' is followed by many writers: e.g. *I know it's awful, the noise, keeping us all awake, but what really worries me* is *the numbers*—N. Bawden, 1987; *What bothered him* was *drivers who switched lanes without signalling*—*New Yorker*, 1989. In such cases, it is arguable that a noun phrase such as *the circumstance of* or *the fact of* should be understood after the main verb; it is not the numbers as such that cause the worry in the first example or the drivers as such that cause the bother in the second, but the fact of what they represented or were doing.

(*c*) But the phenomenon of 'attraction' is strong, and there is an understandable tendency to let it take its course in certain circumstances. In the competing type, i.e. *What upsets me most* are *the numbers,* attention is being focused on the plural noun complement. That happens also in e.g. *What concerns me* are *the number of construction projects that are delayed*—*The Press* (York), 2004. Each context will need to be judged on its merits, but for the sake of simplicity it is better to adhere to Fowler's rule than to make it subject to qualifications.

2 Singular *what* and plural *what.* (*a*) In each of the quotations in the preceding section (*b*), the writer made it plain, by giving *what* a singular verb, that he or she conceived *what* in that context as a singular pronoun. But the word itself can equally well be plural: *I have few books, and what there* are do *not help me.* In this sentence, *what* refers back to *books,* and so its plural status is clear. When *what* refers forward, the choice is less obvious: *We seem to have abandoned what seem/seems to us to be the most valuable parts of our Constitution.* Fowler (whose example this is) had another useful rule in these cases: if *what* can be resolved into *the—s that,* with—*s* standing for the plural noun later in the sentence to which *what* refers forward, the verb governed by *what* should be plural. In the example just given, *what* can be resolved into *the parts of our Constitution that,* and the verb should therefore be *seem* (plural), not *seems.*

(*b*) If the relative clause introduced by *what* comes at the head of the sentence, the same rule can be followed if *what* can be resolved into *that which*: *What* (= *that which*) is *required* is *faith and confidence, and willingness to work.* This principle is much less secure, however, since *what* in the example given (Fowler's again) can as easily be resolved as *the things which* (plural): *What* (= *the things which*) are *required* are *faith and confidence, and willingness to work.* Here there is clearly a choice, and naturalness and rhythm will often be decisive; the important point is that the choice between singular and plural should be consistent throughout the sentence, and that a singular verb immediately after *what* should not be followed by a plural verb later on: **What* is *required* are *faith and confidence, and willingness to work.*

(*c*) Further examples from Fowler, with their corresponding rewrites, will help clarify the issue: *The Manchester City Council, for what* was *doubtless good and sufficient reasons, decided not to take any part* (read *were;* for reasons that were); *No other speaker has his peculiar power of bringing imagination to play on what* seems, *until he speaks, to be familiar platitudes* (read *seem;* on sayings that seem); *What* provoke *men's curiosity* are *mysteries, mysteries of motive or stratagem; astute or daring plots* (read *provokes . . . is;* that which provokes—rather than the things that provoke).

3 *what* doing double duty. Subtle problems occur in sentences in which *what* appears only once when it should be repeated. In other words, it is used in one construction, and is then meant to be 'understood', and to govern a second dissimilar construction. Fowler (1926) gave four examples of such anomalies and emphasized that there was no single easy way of correcting such misfits. Here are three of them: *This is pure ignorance of what the House is* and its *work consists of* (and what its); *Mr —— tells us not to worry about Relativity or anything so brain-tangling, but to concentrate on what surrounds us,* and we *can weigh and measure* (and can be weighed and measured); *Impossible to separate later legend from original evidence as to what he was,* and said, *and how he said it* (and what he said). Attentive readers will no doubt be able to root out more modern examples of this phenomenon.

4 *what* wrongly paralleled by *and which* or *but which.* (*a*) When a relative clause introduced by *what* is followed by further relative clauses joined by a conjunction such as *and* or *but,* the *what* should be repeated when it refers to something other than at its first occurrence: *There is a definite mismatch between what universities are producing and what industry is wanting—Daily Tel.,* 1971. In this example, the first *what* refers to one thing and the second *what* to another, and both are needed.

(*b*) But the temptation to use a second *and what* or *but what,* or worse still, *and/but which* should be resisted when this would have the same grammatical status (as subject or object in its clause) and reference, since the first *what* is adequate to sustain the sense: **Nobody is going to object to* what *is a popular measure* and which *will help those most in need* should be rewritten as *Nobody is going to object to what is a popular measure and will help those most in need.* Alternatively it could be rewritten as *Nobody is going to object to what is a popular measure which will help those most in need,* where *a popular measure* becomes the antecedent of *which.*

As Fowler (1926) colourfully put it, referring to an analogous sentence: 'A want of faith either in the staying power of *what* (which has a good second wind and can do the two laps without turning a hair) or in the reader's possession of common sense has led to this thrusting in of *which* as a sort of relay to take up the running.' An example he gave illustrates the potential ambiguity caused by *and what.* If in the following sentence *We are merely remembering what happened to our arboreal ancestors,* and which *has been stamped by cerebral changes into the heredity of the race* (and has been stamped), you replace *and which* with *and what,* the result is that '*what happened*' and '*what has been stamped*' might be thought to be different things, whereas they are clearly one and the same thing.

5 It's dashed hot, *what*? This use of *what?* at the end of an affirmative sentence as an 'interrogative expletive', as the *OED* called it, surely strikes us nowadays as rather 'period', or Wodehousian. It is intriguing that the first example in the *OED,* from Fanny Burney's diary for 19 December 1785, fell, affectedly or otherwise, from the lips of George III: *He said,—'What? what?'—meaning, what say you? . . . ' . . . it is not possible. Do you think it is?—what?'* A 20c. example: *they do tend to insist when they can on dealing with the fellow they're used to, even if he's a poor old antique like me, what?*—K. Amis, 1988.

6 'Pseudo-cleft' sentences led by *what.* A standard type of what are technically known as 'pseudo-cleft' sentences begins with a noun clause introduced by *what* followed by the complement: *What you need most is a good rest.* Very often the complement clause is an infinitive, with or without *to*: *What I'm going to do to him is have his guts for garters.* Burchfield identified and dismissed as 'unattractive and inelegant' a special sub-type of pseudo-cleft sentence in which the infinitive is replaced by a finite verb, e.g. *Anyway, with this piece, what Gounod did was he went and put words to that silent part that was never meant to be exposed*—M. du Plessis, 1989 (SAfr.); *and she was bound to fall out so what Jimmy Sr did was, he went into the dunes and found a plank*—R. Doyle, 1991 (Ir.). These examples sound typical of speech, and natural. They may, Burchfield suggested, faintly reflect the type in which the actual words used by one person are reported by another, e.g. *What Dorothy said was 'My mother's on the phone.'* (*CGEL* 14.29).

7 *what* as relative pronoun. From the Old English period until the 19c. *what* was in standard use as a relative pronoun meaning 'that, who, or which', but the use is now non-standard: *I was the only boy in our school what had asthma*—W. Golding, 1954; *Boy, the guy what thought it up sure was a smart one*—G. Keillor, 1985.

what ever, whatever.

1 One word or two?
2 In questions and exclamations.
3 The indefinite use.
4 Dismissive '*Whatever*'.
5 The intensifying use: *no ... whatever.*
6 The conditional-concessive use and the artful comma.
7 Superfluous *that.*

1 *One word or two.* It is only, strictly speaking, correct to write *what ever* as two words in the circumstances explained at 2 below.

2 *In questions and exclamations.* In phrases of the type *What ever did you do that for?* (equivalent to 'What on earth did you do that for?'), the two words should be written separately. See also EVER 1. Despite the tendency to join the two words together in literary works from the 14c. to the 19c., they should no longer be spliced, since such phrases place heavy emphasis on *ever*, intimating that the speaker has no notion what the answer will be.

3 *The indefinite use.* *Whatever* functions as an indefinite relative pronoun or adjective used in statements or commands, in which case it is written as one word: *Whatever* [pronoun] *you're up to during the snowy season, a wonderful warm woolly makes the perfect winter wear*—*Hair Flair*, 1992; *They make it harder to discuss differences openly, and to take a stand against racism whenever and in whatever* [adjective] *form it arises*—*Times*, 2007. It is also used elliptically (with the relevant noun omitted) in informal uses such as: *People want a kind of more adult conversation instead of just talking about a policy, be it tuition fees or foundation hospitals or whatever*—*Scotland on Sunday*, 2003.

4 Dismissive '*Whatever*'. The relatively recent, informal spoken use of *whatever* as a dismissive response to what someone has just said is equivalent in effect to 'if you say so', 'have it your own way', 'fine', or, more passive-aggressively, 'Do I care?'. Originally US, and first noted from 1973, it is now used more widely, particularly by the 'yoof'. The following *OED* citations show its development from reluctant acceptance of what has been said to downright boredom and cynicism. Whatever, *equivalent to 'that's what I meant'. Usually implies boredom with topic or lack of concern for a precise definition of meaning*—*U.S. Secretary of Defense, Public Affairs 10*, 1973; *When someone responds 'whatever', he or she seems to be saying 'I'm amenable to anything. I'll defer to you.' But in my experience, when a person says 'whatever', he or she is really saying, 'I don't want to take any responsibility'*—*San Francisco Examiner*, 1982; *Feed any of these guys a full-scale briefing ... and you'd get the same response: 'Yeah, right. Whatever, man, whatever'*—*Platoon*, 1986; *If someone came running to say he'd just seen Jesus preaching on the steps of the 72nd Street subway stop, most New Yorkers would reply, 'Whatever'*—*Village Voice*, 1998.

5 The intensifying use: *no ... whatever.* *Whatever* is also written as one word in negative statements, when, as an adverb (= at all) it has the effect of emphasizing the noun it follows, and is interchangeable with *whatsoever*: *There is no reason whatever not to seize this opportunity and practice with greater and greater exertion*—Buddhist website, 2000.

6 *The conditional-concessive use and the artful comma.* (*a*) In sentences of the type *She looks pretty whatever she wears; I am safe now, whatever happens; whatever you do, don't lie,* the clauses introduced by *whatever* indicate 'a free choice from any number of conditions'.

(*b*) Sometimes it might not be clear if a clause beginning with *whatever* is conditional-concessive or indefinite. For example, *Whatever they have done they are leaving* could be taken to mean (i) (indefinite) 'they are leaving (intransitive) irrespective of what they have done', or (ii) (the conditional-concessive interpretation) 'they are leaving (transitive) whatever it is they have done'. A well-judged comma distinguishes the two for those (rather few, I suspect) who still have an eye for such subtleties. Meaning (ii) is indicated by not separating the two clauses with a comma, since *whatever* belongs to and is part of both, as the grammatical object both of 'leave' and of 'done'; and meaning (i) is indicated by inserting a comma, i.e. *whatever they have done* [pause], *they are leaving.* Admittedly this places a great burden on the shoulders of a single comma, but this Hercules of the punctuation world shoulders equally heavy burdens in relative clauses. A further example from Fowler's original edition may help highlight the difference: *Sir Edward Grey has no reason to be displeased with this sequel and, whatever responsibility he may have, he will no doubt accept gladly.* It is the responsibilities he will gladly accept; therefore, deleting the comma is essential.

7 Superfluous *that.* Fowler (1926) pointed out that constructions of the type *whatever* (or *whatsoever*) + noun (or noun phrase) + *that*-clause are incorrect in that *whatever* by itself already contains the relative *that*: to insert a later *that* is unnecessary. Omission of the roman-type *that* in the following examples would set matters right: (Fowler) *His cynical advice shows that whatever concession to Democracy* that *may seem to be involved in his words may not be of permanent inconvenience*; (current) *We all have a sense of humor about whatever level* that *we're at—Film Threat,* 2003.

when. See IF AND WHEN.

whence. The word has a long (13–19c.) history in the language used in various routine ways, e.g. (in an indirect question) *He inquired whence the water came*—M. Edgeworth, 1802; *From whence I did then conclude... that Wine doth not inspire Politeness*—Swift, 1731–8; *From whence have we derived that spiritual profit?*—Dickens, 1853; (*from whence* = from the place from which) *Let him walke from whence he came*—Shakespeare, 1590. See also FROM WHENCE.

At some point in the 19c. attitudes changed: *whence* came to be more or less restricted to formal or literary use, and *from whence* to be regarded as an old-fashioned expression better replaced by *where ... from.* The outcome is that Tennyson's *O babbling brook... whence come you?* (1855), for example, is now seen to be a quaint poetic way of saying 'where do you come from?' There is no going back. *Whence* (and to a greater extent *from whence*) is no longer a routine word in frequent use. But words come and go, and *whence* may well come back into routine use at some point in the future. Meanwhile here are two modern examples from standard British and American sources: *He has also, of course, a passport which nails him for who he is and whence he comes*—P. Lively, 1987; *On learning whence she hailed... he was briefly enchanted to meet somebody he took to be an ideological bird of a feather*—*New Yorker,* 1987.

when ever, whenever. When used as an interrogative adverb in phrases of the type *When ever did you say you were sorry?, when ever* (always written as two words) is merely an emphatic extension of *when.* See EVER 1; WHAT EVER, WHATEVER 2. (*When did you ever say you were sorry?* is a variant of the same type.) *Whenever* is the right form for the ordinary conjunction, e.g. *ring whenever you have a chance.*

whereabouts (noun). Towards the end of the 18c. *whereabouts,* plural in form, replaced the earlier noun *whereabout,* or rather the two forms stood side by side until the mid-19c. at which point *whereabout,* singular in form, began to disappear. The only trouble is that standard authorities and the printing world at large do not agree about its number. One authority (1970) said bluntly '*Whereabouts* takes the singular'. So did another (1962): 'Even if the reference is to several persons, each with a different whereabouts, a singular verb is still used: "She has a brother and two sisters, but their whereabouts is unknown."' Standard dictionaries for the most part settle for a formula that recognizes that the noun is plural in form but is construed either as a plural or a singular noun. Burchfield examined a large body of newspaper and other evidence, British and American, of the period 1988 to 1994. If cases where the number is left undetermined are excluded (e.g. *In Scotland... the erectors of signposts seem reluctant to reveal to the motorist the precise whereabouts of Dumfries*), his mini-corpus revealed that of the four possible constructions (of those in which the writer had to make a choice of number in the following verb) there was a clear preference for a plural verb. The examples that follow are drawn from this mini-corpus: **1** One person or thing + a singular verb: *Colleen's whereabouts* was *kept secret*; *Five months later, the whereabouts of the purse and its contents* remains *a mystery*; *Its whereabouts* was *never revealed*; *The exact whereabouts of its new home* has *yet to be determined.*

2 One person or thing + a plural verb: *His current whereabouts* were *not disclosed*; *He did not call his wife, Felicidad, whose whereabouts* are *not known*; *His whereabouts* are *definitely known.*

3 More than one person or thing + a singular verb: *the whereabouts of the remaining two paintings* is *unknown*; *the whereabouts of two,* [names given], is *unknown*; *the whereabouts of three others* was *unknown.*

4 More than one person or thing + a plural verb: *by early Friday the whereabouts of the raiders still* were *unknown*; *The nuns left suddenly and a spokeswoman said their whereabouts* were *a mystery*; *Israel refuses to release any of its Arab prisoners until the whereabouts of six of its servicemen* are *known.*

Types 2 and 4 were more frequent than types 1 and 3, but all four must be regarded as standard.

whereby. One of the diminishing number of *where*-compounds still in common use. It is especially useful in attaching an explanatory statement to a noun or noun phrase. Examples: *'Acceptance in lieu', whereby heirs give a picture to a museum to pay off capital transfer tax, has also been kind to the National Gallery—Antique Collector*, 1990; *Schemes whereby such patients can quickly get such medicines direct from the pharmacist... will be promoted and extended—BMJ*, 2003.

where- compounds. A small number of these are still in free general use, though chiefly in limited applications, with little or no taint of archaism. These are WHEREABOUTS, *whereas* (in contrasts), *whereby, wherever, wherefore* (as plural noun in *whys and wherefores*), *whereupon* (in narratives), and *wherewithal* (as noun). The many others—*whereabout, whereat, wherefore* (adverb and conjunction), *wherefrom, whereof, whereon, wheresoever, wherethrough, whereto, wherewith,* and a few more—have given way, though to different degrees, in both the interrogative and the relative uses either to the preposition with *what* and *which* and *that* (*whereof* = of what?, what... of?), or to some synonym (*wherefore* = why). Apart from their use in certain formulaic legal documents, words in this second group should be resorted to only in very formal contexts or as a matter of pedantic humour.

where ever, wherever. As for WHEN EVER, WHENEVER.

wherefore. It has been pointed out over and over again that when Juliet cries out from the balcony *O Romeo, Romeo, wherefore art thou Romeo?* she is asking not *where* he is but *why* or *for what purpose* or *on what account*. Shakespeare uses *wherefore* in such a manner more than a hundred times (and also as a noun: *in the why and the wherefore is neither rime nor reason* (1590)). And so frequently did other writers from the 13c. to the 19c., But it did not deter a headline writer in a 1988 issue of the *Sunday Times* from placing the headline *Wherefore art thou, biographer* above a letter written by Anthony Holden who had published a new biography of the Prince of Wales and had allegedly gone to ground away from journalists.

wherein. As conjunction and adverb labelled 'formal' in some dictionaries, but surprisingly widespread nevertheless. Some examples (mostly from 'informal' sources): *Biamping. Method of powering speakers wherein each drive unit of a speaker is powered by a separate channel of an amplifier—What Hi-Fi?*, 1991; *Australia's cultural isolation constitutes a comedic time-capsule, wherein Britain's exported* *vaudeville tradition has been preserved long after its extinction back in Blighty*—*Guardian,* 1994.

wherewithal. As noun (always preceded by the definite article) recorded since the beginning of the 19c. and curiously persistent in the sense 'the means, the resources, especially pecuniary resources'. Examples: *To supply him with the wherewithal to pay for the defence of the border*—*Eng. Historical Rev.,* 1917; *You don't need the intellectual wherewithal to function in society*—S. Pinker, 1994.

whether. 1 For *whether* and *that* after *doubt,* see DOUBT (verb).

2 *Whether or no(t). Whether he was there or was not there* easily transforms by ellipsis into *Whether he was there or not,* and that by transposition into *Whether or not he was there. Whether or no he was there* is not so easily accounted for, since *no,* unlike *not,* is not ordinarily an adverb (see NO 2(b)), but this phrase has been in use since the 17c. From the evidence it is clear that *whether or no* is now rather rare and extremely legalistic or formal. Examples: (whether or not) *He had not made it plain whether or not I would be welcome on the bus*—F. Weldon, 1988; *his face seemed familiar in a way which made you forget to ask whether or not you judged it good-looking*—J. Barnes, 1989; (whether or no) *J. L. Austin, in a British Academy lecture, has recently argued that whether or no determinism be the case, it is certainly contrary to what is suggested by ordinary language and ordinary thought*—*Free Will: A Very Short Introduction,* 2003. Whichever form is used, such a doubling of the alternative as the following should be avoided: *But clearly, whether or not peers will* or will not *have to be made depends upon the number of the Die-Hards.* Omit either *or not* or *or will not.*

3 *Whether* is often repeated as a clearer pointer than a bare *or* to an alternative that forms a separate clause, particularly when the distance between *whether* and *or* is great: *You must decide yourself whether each new Beaver* [*sc.* junior Scout] *should be asked to pay for his scarf and woggle, or whether these should be provided by the Colony*—J. Deft, 1983.

4 *the question (of) whether* + clause. When a clause introduced by *whether* relates to a preceding word such as *matter, issue, problem,* or *question, whether* can follow directly or be introduced by *of*: *Senator Ervin said the* issue of whether *the subpoenas were continuing was 'a difference in a teapot'*—*Times,* 1973; *The whole* question whether *women actually are more pacific by nature is not the subject of the present book*—A. Fraser, 1988; *This . . . goes some way to answering the* problem of whether *there is free will in heaven*—*Christis Magazine,* 2004.

which. 1 For the use of *which* (normally preceded by a comma) as a relative pronoun at the head of restrictive and non-restrictive clauses, see THAT (relative pronoun) 4, 5, 6.

2 *Which* leading a clause or sentence of affirmation. This type, in which, sometimes almost as an afterthought, a new clause or sentence (often one of direct comment on a state of affairs just described) is introduced by *which,* is now increasingly common, especially in spoken English. The type is not new (the *OED* gives examples from the 14c. onwards), but it has become more frequent than hitherto. Examples: *He does Mr Rabinowitz's teeth,* which *is super*—N. Williams, 1985; (starting a new sentence) *It was as though Hungary was not another place but another time, and therefore inaccessible.* Which *of course was not so*—P. Lively, 1987. A more extreme example from a 1995 book review: *What is missing from* You Will Learn to Love Me *is the kind friend—a voice we can trust.* Which *brings us back to the original question of what binds our sympathies to a character.* These examples are close to the type (18–19c.) condemned by the *OED* as 'in vulgar use, without any antecedent, as a mere connective or introductory particle' (e.g. *If anything 'appens to you*—which *God be between you and 'arm—I'll look after the kids*—*Daily Chron.,* 1905).

4 *Referring to people.* 'Now only dialectal except in speaking of people in a body, the ordinary word being *who* or (as relevant) *that*' (*OED*). Examples: *Yow* which *I haue loued specially*—Chaucer, *c.*1386; *O God,* which *art author of peace, and louer of concorde*—*Book of Common Prayer,* 1548–9; *A couple of women . . . one of* which *. . . leaned on the other's shoulder*—Goldsmith, *a*1774; *His mother had ten children of* which *he was the oldest*—*Scribner's Mag.,* 1899.

5 *and which.* 'And which or but which should not be used unless the coming *which*-clause has been preceded by a clause or expression of the same grammatical value as itself' (Fowler, 1926). This is a simple but safe rule. In the following, the first *which* is the subject of its clause; the second is the object of the verb *found*: *In contrast Peake's use of elevated language has a childlike quality which is appropriate given that the protagonist, Titus, is a boy,* and which *I found endearing*—(read ... *is a boy, which I found* ...).

6 *That* preferable to *which.* When the preceding clause to which the relative pronoun refers contains an indefinite pronoun (e.g. *anything, everything, nothing, something*), or an inanimate noun qualified by a superlative adjective, *that* is normally preferable to *which.* Examples (from the *Oxford Guide to Eng. Usage*, 1993): *Is there* nothing *small* that *the children could buy you for Christmas?*; *This is the* most expensive *hat* that *you could have bought.* But there are exceptions: e.g. *there was* nothing ... which *distinguished him from any other intelligent young Frenchman studying law*—P. P. Read, 1986.

while (noun). See WORTH.

while. (conjunction). **1** *While* and *whilst* mean the same thing, and work in the same way grammatically. *Whilst* is far less frequent, tends to be more formal, is used particularly in BrE, and is relatively uncommon in AmE.

2 (*a*) The principal use as a conjunction is in the meaning 'during the time that' (*They had begun drinking while he prepared to cook*); 'at the same time as' (*He enjoyed drawing while he was being read to*). Such temporal uses have been dominant since the Old English period, so much so that some writers on English usage concluded that other uses are improper (see below). At least since the 16c., however, contrastive or concessive senses have emerged, in which *while* means 'although' or 'whereas'. Thus *CGEL* (15.20) contrasts *He looked after my dog* while I was on vacation (temporal) and *My brother lives in Manchester,* while my sister lives in Glasgow (concessive).

(*b*) Eric Partridge in his *Usage and Abusage* (1942) condemned the use of *while* to mean 'although' in no uncertain terms: '*while* for *although* is a perverted use of the correct sense of *while,* which properly means "at the same time as", "during the same time that".' But this indefensible remark was counterbalanced by a quotation from the work of A. P. Herbert which draws attention to the danger of confusion between the temporal and the concessive senses: *The Curate read the First Lesson while the Rector read the Second.* Such contrived, if amusing, examples apart, the temporal, concessive, and contrastive uses of *while* (or of *whilst*) do not create ambiguity.

(*c*) Examples: (concessive) *while domestic happiness is an admirable ideal, it is not easy to come by*—T. Tanner, 1986; (contrastive) *We are told that our institutions should concentrate on their business of education while being told also that they should do more to contribute to economic development and direct public service*—H. H. Gray, 1988 (US); (temporal) *Whilst it's in the computer it's stored*—S. Hockey, lecture in Univ. of Oxford, 1981.

3 *While* and *whilst* are often used elliptically, i.e. omitting subject and main verb, as shown bracketed in these examples: *Dinner ladies helping with playground supervision have been jostled and abused while* (they were) *trying to tackle unruly pupils—Daily Tel.*, 1983; *While* (he was) *still working for the restaurant in 1956, he began his franchising career—Money*, 1985. In such sentences *while* (or *whilst*) is usually temporal (as in both these examples), rarely concessive; when concessive it tends to come before the main clause, e.g.: *More recent evidence, whilst not addressing this issue directly, tends to suggest that this desired relationship is still important*—J. Finch, 1989.

4 A sentence such as the following is incorrect: **While being in agreement on most issues, I would like to challenge one in particular.* The omission is misconceived since the full form is *while I am* and not *while I am being*; correct *while being* to '*while I am in agreement*' or to '*while in agreement*'.

whilom /ˈwʌɪləm/. The last two letters represent a remarkable survival of the Old English dative plural ending *-um* (Old English *hwīlum* 'at times, at some past time'). *Hwilom* formed part of the normal vocabulary of writers down to the 19c. (e.g. Scott and Carlyle), but now belongs to the category of words known as WARDOUR STREET. Typical uses: (as adverb) *The wistful eyes which whilom glanced down . . . upon the sweet clover fields*; (as adjective) *General Doppet, a whilom Medical man.* See also LATE. Twentieth-century examples (the first of which is for a nonce adjective *whilomst*): *He saw these things in the whilomst moment when the Navajos were making merry with the Choctaws*—H. Miller, 1939; *Hidden in the tall marsh grass of the coastal lowland, the whilom seaport that once rivaled Philadelphia was remarkable*—W. Least, 1982.

whilst. See WHILE (conjunction).

whin. See FURZE.

whine (noun and verb). The corresponding adjective is rather more often **whiny** than **whiney**. The present participle and participial adjective form is **whining**.

whinge (verb) has the inflexion *whingeing.*

whir, (make) continuous buzzing sound. The spelling **whirr** is as frequent as that shown, but *whir* is the more usual form in AmE. The inflected forms of the verb are *whirred, whirring* in all varieties of English.

whisky, whiskey. The first is the usual spelling in BrE (*Scotch whisky*) and in Canada (plural *whiskies*), and the second the normal spelling in Ireland and USA (plural *whiskeys*).

whit (= a least possible amount: usually in negative contexts), a 16c. word derived ultimately from an Old English form meaning 'a thing or creature of unknown origin', is commonly used in both BrE and AmE in several phrases (often with the verbs *care* and *matter*) of which the most frequent is *not a whit,* (= not at all, by no means), or its variant *no whit.* Said by Fowler (1926) and Gowers (1965) to belong to the vocabulary of WARDOUR STREET, it seems to have escaped from archaism into standard use. Examples: *This much ballyhooed Andrew Lloyd Webber musical is fun—if you're not bothered by theatre that cares not a whit for words and contains not one ghost of an idea—New Yorker,* 1991; *the embodiment of a proprietorial dream no whit less obsessive than Gatsby's own*—A. Coren, 1995; *Desmond had not one whit of experience in running a newspaper—Sunday Business Post,* 2002.

Whit. *Whit Sunday* (or *Pentecost*) is the seventh Sunday after Easter; hence *Whit Monday. Whitsun* and *Whit* are frequently used as informal shortenings of *Whitsuntide,* the weekend including *Whit Sunday. Whit Sunday* answers to Old English *Hwīta Sunnandæg,* lit. 'white Sunday', probably from the white robes of the newly baptized at Pentecost.

white (adjective) **1** The term *white* has been used to refer to the skin colour of Europeans or people of European extraction since the early 17c. In modern contexts terms which relate to geographical origin rather than skin colour are preferred: hence the current preference in the US for AFRICAN AMERICAN rather than *black* and *European* rather than *white.* See also CAUCASIAN.

2 *White* has the derivative forms **whitey** (adjective) 'whitish' (rarely *whity*) and the derogatory **Whitey** (noun) 'a white person (as seen by black people)', white people collectively'. The plural of the noun is *Whiteys.*

whited sepulchre. A person so described is a hypocrite, or, as the *OED* quaintly put it, 'one whose fair outward semblance conceals inward corruption'. Derived from Matt. 23:27, in Wycliffe's Bible expressed as 'sepulchris whitid' and in the AV in its current form: *Woe unto you, scribes and Pharisees, hypocrites! for ye are like unto whited sepulchres, which indeed appear beautiful outward, but are within full of dead men's bones, and of all uncleanness.* Though not among the most common of biblical quotations outside religious discussion, it is still in use, e.g. *'Binge drinking is consumerism with sick on its shoes.' As ever we get the society we deserve. Instead of pointing the finger at yobs we should perhaps inspect our own whited sepulchres—www.boris-johnson.com,* 2005.

white(n) (verbs). The shorter form is first recorded in Old English meaning 'to become white; to make white', and, by *c.*1200, 'to cover or coat with white'. *Whiten* appeared in the early 14c. with the second and third of these meanings, and acquired the sense 'to become white' in the 17c. This longer form is the more usual one now in the primary senses 'to make white' and 'to become white'. But **white out**, rather than *whiten out,* is the usual phrasal verb when the sense required is 'to obliterate a mistake with white correction fluid', and 'to lose colour vision before losing consciousness', e.g. *He tried to raise his head, and his sight whited out entirely; I bolted for the door and whited out as I hit the street.*

White Paper. In the UK and some other countries, an official document that expresses government policy on an issue. It is usually preparatory to the introduction of a parliamentary bill. Its name derives from its having fewer pages than a government 'blue book', and therefore needing no blue paper cover (*Hutchinson Encycl.*, 1990).

whither. *Whither* was in unbroken standard use as adverb and conjunction from Old English times until the 19c. but then began to retreat into archaism. In the meaning 'to what place or state' it is highly literary, or deliberately archaizing; in its meaning of 'what is the future of' (e.g. *Whither modern architecture?*) it is highly rhetorical.

But these 20c. examples show that *whither* has not disappeared yet: (title of article) *Whither Islamic Economics,* in *Islamic Q*, 1988; *I write, now, from my bed, whither Dr Felton has banished me*—M. Roberts, 1990; *The United States . . . is having an increasingly disagreeable time in the Horn of Africa, whither it went, nine months ago, to facilitate the distribution of food for a few, perhaps two, months*—*Newsweek*, 1993. And churchgoers are accustomed to its use in the Bible, e.g. *The winde bloweth where it listeth, and thou hearest the sound thereof, but canst not tel whence it commeth, and whither it goeth*—John 3:8.

whitish. So spelt, not *-eish*.

whizz (noun and verb). The recommended spelling, not *whiz*. Hence *whizz-bang, whizz-kid* (but the forms with *-z-* are also commonly used). The inflected forms of the verb are *whizzes, whizzed,* and *whizzing*. See -Z-, -ZZ-.

who and whom.

1 Introductory remarks.
2 Recommendation.
3 Conflicting views.
4 A historical note.
5 Current practice.
A Legitimate uses of *who*.
B Questionable uses of *who*.
C Legitimate uses of *whom*.
D Questionable uses of *whom*.

1 *Introductory remarks.* (*a*) *Who* is a relative pronoun (*The woman who saw you*) and an interrogative pronoun (*Who is there?*), and *whom* is, formally, its 'objective' form (*The woman whom you saw/Whom did you see?*). In these uses *who* (or *whom*) refers to a person or to several people, but it is only as a relative pronoun that *who* can refer to an animal (*the cat who lived in the palace*) or to an organization regarded in terms of its members (*The committee, who meet on Friday, . . .*).

(*b*) *Who*, in strict grammatical terms, is used only as the subject of its clause or sentence, *whom* as the object, as in the bracketed sentences above. In practice, *whom* is in terminal decline and is increasingly replaced by *who* (or *that*), especially in conversational English, in which in most circumstances it would be inappropriately formal. (This is not a new development; examples can be found from Shakespeare onwards; see 4). In the examples given in (*a*), it would be more natural to say *Who did you see?*, and in the one before it *The woman who you saw*, or *The woman that you saw*, or to leave out the pronoun altogether and say *The woman you saw*. In the same way, while Dame Iris Murdoch, in her novel *The Green Knight* (1993), actually wrote *Was there anyone now* whom *she could decently ask?*, outside literature *whom* would be replaced by *who, that,* or left out.

2 *Recommendation.* Despite exceptions, the best general rule is as follows: *who* will work perfectly well in conversation (except of the most elevated kind) and in informal writing, except in certain kinds of relative clause discussed at 5 C (*a*) below, which in any case are a feature of writing, not of speech. (Conversely, ungrammatical *whom* used in the ways illustrated at 5 D (*b*) should be carefully avoided.) However, for any kind of loftier discourse (by lawyers, especially in AmE, formal lectures, speeches, presentations, etc.) and in writing for academic purposes or for publication, it is advisable to follow the traditional rules.

The numerous examples and comments in **5** are offered to be read through at leisure to help readers fully grasp the issues involved in choosing one word or the other.

3 *Conflicting views.* There are three approaches to the modern use of *who* and *whom*.

(*a*) First, some see the use of *whom* as moribund or at best as socially divisive: '"To whom do you wish to speak?" is usually regarded as formal (in some circles superformal or superpolite), indeed almost as something frozen, archaic, stifling, or artificial. Indeed, a conversation might be killed right there' (A. S. Kaye in *English Today*, 1991). '*Whom* has outlived *ye*, but is clearly moribund; it now sounds pretentious in most spoken contexts... why insist on clinging to *whom*, when everyone uses *who* for both subjects and objects?' (S. Pinker, *The Language Instinct*, 1994). In humorous vein: '*Whom* is a word invented to make everyone sound like a butler' (Calvin Trillin).

(*b*) Others say or imply that the retreat of *whom* is regrettable (the examples happen to be from fiction but are revealing): 'In *The Archers* on the other hand, no one leaves the "m" off "whom"' (L. Ellman, 1988). '"I don't know whom else to ask." The elder of the two policemen, Butterworth, noticed that she had said "whom" and decided that she was a credible witness' (A. Brookner, 1992).

(*c*) Thirdly, there are the deadpan ('scientific') views of professional grammarians: '*Who* has an objective case *whom*... for which, however, the uninflected *who* is substituted in the spoken language, as in *who*(*m*) *do you mean?*' (H. Sweet, *A New English Grammar*, 1891). 'In objective use, *who* is informal and *whom* is formal. The distinction is parallel to that between *who* and *whom* as relative pronouns. Similarly, interrogative *whom* functions like relative *whom*, except that interrogative *whom* strikes most people as even more formal than relative *whom*' (*CGEL* 6.38, 1985).

4 *A historical note.* (*a*) It is not just moderns who are wrong-footed by the difference between *who* and *whom*. There is abundant evidence in historical sources of departure from the normal subjective/objective relationship of *who*/*whom*. One need look no further than Shakespeare and the Bible: who *wouldst thou strike?*—Shakespeare, 1591; Albany. *Run, run, O run.* Edgar. *To* who *my Lord?*—Shakespeare, 1605; *But* whom *say ye that I am?*—Matt. (AV) 16: 15. (Contrast the *NEB*'s who *do you say I am?*)

(*b*) The *OED* lists numerous examples (15–20c.) of the breakdown of formal grammatical rules governing *who* and *whom*, including: (i) (*who* used '*ungrammatically*' for *whom*) *A great Prince* who *I forbeare to name*—Monmouth, 1641; *Not being able to ask exactly who he liked*—R. S. Surtees, 1858; *Just over half... of our sample* who *we assessed as working class concurred*—Times, 1984. (ii) (*whom* used ungrammatically for *who*) *I counsel... all wise... men, that they doo not accompany wyth those* whom *they know are not secret*—T. North, 1557; *Comparing the... humble epistles of S. Peter, S. James and S. John*, whom *we know were Fishers, with the glorious language... of S. Paul*, who [*sic*] *we know was not*—I. Walton, 1653; *A strange unearthly figure*, whom *Gabriel felt at once, was no being of this world*—Dickens, 1837; *He saw the man* whom *he knew must be the King*—R. H. Benson, 1906.

5 *Current practice.* **A** Legitimate uses of *who*: (*a*) (*who* as subject relative pronoun referring back to a person) *women* who *had once talked of love now talked only of sexual harassment*—M. Bradbury, 1987; *His father had had a brother, an older brother,* who, *he let it be known, had dominated him cruelly*—J. Updike, 1987; *I could not be close to anyone* who *I thought was rejected by God*—V. Mehta, 1988. (*b*) (*who* as interrogative pronoun) *'You mean Loseby?'* 'Who *do you think I mean?*'—C. P. Snow, 1979; *'But* who's *to blame?' asked Madeleine.*—P. P. Read, 1986; *'We've got Sir Luke Trimingham.'* 'Who?' *asked Henry. 'The acting knight, that's who,' said Gill*—M. Bradbury, 1987; Who *else did I know?*—C. Rumens, 1987. (*c*) (*who* introducing an indirect question) *The sight of him raised the obvious question of* who *was going to restrap his leg*—T. Keneally, 1985; *She wanted to ask* who *he was*—*New Yorker*, 1987; *May I ask* who's *speaking?*—C. Rumens, 1987. (*d*) (*who* with preposition at the end of the sentence) Who *do you think you're speaking* to?—W. McIlvanney, 1985; Who's *she talking* to? *Has she got a visitor?*—P. Lively, 1987; 'Who *does he deal* with?' *Fred asked*—*New Yorker*, 1987; *After all, what did she know of his life,* who *he went to bed* with—I. Murdoch, 1993.

B Questionable uses of *who*: In these cases, strict adherence to grammar calls for *whom*. Although *who* sounds more natural in speech, and in most kinds of writing, purists are entitled, grammatically speaking, to insist on *whom* in examples such as the following, even though their authors clearly chose not to use it: *not knowing who is sitting with* who *in the T.V. room*—E. Jolley, 1985 (Aust.); *Christ, who went for* who *first?*—V. O'Sullivan, 1985 (NZ); *'The country is behind us.' 'Behind* who? *The unions do not want this demonstration.'*—B. Moore, 1987; *There's a woman called Kristin Johannesdottir* who *I really admire*—*Melody Maker*, 1988.

C Legitimate uses of *whom*: Though *whom* is unquestionably legitimate in the next three sub-categories, it is markedly formal. (*a*) (*whom* as object after a preposition) In these cases, it is a matter of fine judgement whether to use the structure preposition + *whom* immediately following, or to put the preposition at the end, as in the examples in 5 A (*d*). Readers might like to experiment with rephrasing the following examples to move the preposition to the end, in order to make up their own minds and to appreciate the difference in formality. Where words such as *some, many, few* are followed by *of whom*, as in the V. Seth example that follows, *whom* seems obligatory. *These were people* to whom *no civic monuments would ever be erected*—W. McIlvanney, 1986; *They ... argue about a man called Simpkins* of whom *the poet is jealous*—*Encounter*, 1987; *The grand ramp, too, was crowded with pilgrims from all over India, many* of whom *had just arrived by special trains*—V. Seth, 1993; *Lord Jenkins likened this stance to countries ... 'who in the two world wars have waited to see which side was winning before deciding* with whom *to ally themselves'*—*Times*, 1999. (*b*) (*whom* as object in relative clause) *Was there anyone now* whom *she could decently ask?*—I. Murdoch, 1993. (*c*) (*whom* as interrogative pronoun) *But* whom *should we support in the present fluid situation?*—*Bull. Amer. Acad. Arts & Sci.*, 1990.

D Questionable uses of *whom*: (*a*) (*whom* with preposition at the end of the sentence) This is an uneasy combination of the styles of 5 A (*d*) and 5 C (*a*) and is best avoided. *There were other people* whom *I would have liked to speak* to—G. Butler, 1983; *an astronomical fee for this young man*—whom *I guarantee three-quarters of you have never heard* of—*Dædalus*, 1986. (*b*) (*whom* used ungrammatically for *who*) This often happens when verbs such as *think, believe, claim, say*, etc. come between the relative pronoun and the verb it governs, e.g. *the baronet* whom *Golitsin claimed had been the target for homosexual blackmail*—P. Wright, 1987. In that example *whom* should be *who*, because it is grammatically the subject of the clause, i.e. *who had been the target*, rather than being the object of *claimed*. The following examples are of a similar kind: *further alienation of the people* whom, *whether he likes it or not, have his fate in their hands*—*Times*, 1984 (who have his fate); *In late 1982, officers of the Royal Ulster Constabulary shot dead six people* whom *they said were armed members of the Irish Republican Army*—*Economist*, 1988 (who were armed members); *Although married with three children, he is demanding £5,000 from the elderly woman* whom *he says has ruined his life*—*Sunday Times*, 1990 (who has ruined); *far more hostile to Diana* whom *she believes betrayed the Prince of Wales*—*Independent Mag.*, 1993 (who betrayed). Despite the antiquity and prevalence of this construction it is best avoided. In all such constructions, *who* is still the better form. See also WHOSE.

whodunnit, whodunit /huːˈdʌnɪt/ is a humorous formation, from a 'phonetic' respelling of *who done it?*, a non-standard form of *who did it?* (For similar deliberate misspellings that have become words, compare *bovver, eejit, yoof*). First recorded in 1930, it is still widely used as an informal term for a story, play, etc., about the detection of a crime, especially a murder. The spelling with a single letter *n* is about twice as common as that with two, *whodunnit*, which is more popular in BrE than elsewhere.

who else's. See ELSE 1.

who ever, whoever, whomever, etc. **1** The same distinction applies as to *what ever* and *whatever*, *whoever* being written as one word when it is an indefinite relative pronoun equivalent to 'whatever person' used in statements or commands (*Whoever wants it can have it*) and when the meaning is 'regardless of whom' (*Whoever it is, I don't want to see them*). *Who ever* is written as two words when *ever* is used as an intensifying word and the expression as a whole is equivalent to *who on earth*, usually in direct questions: *Who ever are those people?*. See EVER 1.

2 The objective form *whomever* still occurs but it can sound formal or affected in general contexts: *To impose his will on whomever he sees comfortably settled*—M. Beerbohm, 1920. In some cases it is wrongly (hypercorrectly) used: **ready at once to relax with whomever came to hand*—A. Brookner, 1992; **Accepting the poverty it entailed, he* [*sc.* Socrates] *appears to have spent all his time in unpaid discussion with whomever would join with him*—E. Craig, 2002. In each case *with* governs the whole following clause, *came to hand* and *would join with him*; the pronoun is the subject of the clause and should therefore be *whoever*.

3 *Forms.* Subjective: *whoever, whosoever* (emphatic), *whoe'er* (poetic), *whoso* (archaic), *whose'er* (poetic). Objective: *whomever* (chiefly literary), *whoever* (wrong case but standard), *whomsoever* (chiefly literary), *whomsoe'er* (poetic), *whomso* (formal or obsolete). Possessive: *whosever* (formal and rare), *whoever's* (standard in modern English), *whosesoever* (archaic or obsolete).

whole other. For the North American phrase *a whole other*, see OTHER 6.

wholesale, wholescale. *Wholesale* has been in use as a noun since the 15c. in its commercial sense, and since the 17c. as an adjective in its metaphorical sense of 'unlimited, indiscriminate' (e.g. *Those wholesale Criticks, that . . . cry down all Philosophy*—S. Butler, 1664) and is nowadays often applied to negative things such as *destruction, slaughter, privatization*, etc. The version *wholescale*, based on *whole* + *scale*, though recorded in the *OED* from 1960 onwards in respectable sources, is rarely used, and may well be viewed as a slip of the tongue or pen because of that very rarity, e.g. *But I do think that baseball caps should be banned wholescale, merely on the grounds of taste*—weblog, 2005; *The wholescale Cabinet cull when McConnell entered office was never sustainable long term*—*Scotland on Sunday*, 2002.

wholly (adverb). So spelt, not *wholely*.

whom. See WHO AND WHOM.

who's is a shortened form of *who is* (*Who's coming to the party?*) and *who has* (*Who's been reading the proofs?*) It is occasionally carelessly used instead of *whose*: e.g. *'Conor,' called Vaun, humping a churn of milk. 'Who's turn to deliver?'*—J. Leland, 1987.

whose. Human or inanimate antecedent. **1** No problems arise in questions: in these *whose* always refers to a person: e.g. Whose *book is this?; 'Can you give me his phone number please?'* 'Whose?' *'The landlord's.'*—C. Rumens, 1987.

2 It is quite another matter in relative clauses. The twists and turns of grammatical teaching from the 18c. onwards produced the folk belief that while *whose* was the natural relative pronoun when the antecedent was human, or at a pinch was an animal, it should not be used with an inanimate antecedent. The *OED* (1923), by contrast, demonstrated that in all kinds of circumstances from medieval times onwards *whose* had been used as a simple relative pronoun with an inanimate antecedent. Fowler (1926) was at his most vehement in attacking the rigidity and the prevalence of the folk belief: 'in the starch that stiffens English style one of the most effective ingredients is the rule that *whose* [as a relative pronoun] shall refer only to persons.' After citing some examples of *whose* used with an inanimate antecedent (including an example of *whose* as an objective genitive in the opening lines of Milton's *Paradise Lost*: *Of man's first disobedience, and the fruit Of that forbidden tree,* whose *mortal taste Brought death into the world*), he concluded his article by declaring: 'Let us, in the name of common sense, prohibit the prohibition of *whose* inanimate; good writing is surely difficult enough without the forbidding of things that have historical grammar, and present intelligibility, and obvious convenience, on their side, and lack only—starch.'

3 *Past and present usage.* (*a*) The *OED* lists numerous examples of *whose* inanimate, including the following: *I could a Tale vnfold,* whose *lightest word Would harrow vp thy soule*—Shakespeare, 1602; *Mountains on* whose *barren brest The labouring clouds do often rest*—Milton, 1632; *The clock,* whose *huge bell . . . may be heard five leagues over the plain*—Southey, 1807; *There were pictures* whose *context she understood immediately*—I. McEwan, 1981.

(*b*) To which may be added: (i) (with person as antecedent) *She was not the only child* whose *parents were divorced*—N. Gordimer, 1987; (ii) (with animal as antecedent) *The exhaust from the car irritates the lion,* whose *head rolls from side to side*—*New Yorker*, 1987; (iii) (with inanimate antecedent) *An aged ferrysteamer*...whose *captain was a White Russian princeling*—R. Sutcliff, 1983; *a deeply disturbing book*...whose *message will remain with you*—S. Hill, 1986; *He looked up again at the tank* whose *huge cannon seemed to be pointing at him*—P. P. Read, 1986; *bought on an Access card* whose *credit limit has already been exceeded*—*Daily Tel.*, 1987; *It is a malady* whose *effects seem relatively independent of changes in the language in which they are experienced*—*TLS*, 1987; *Anne heaved her cases up to the front doors through* whose *glass panels she could make out a broad lobby*—S. Faulks, 1989.

(*c*) Taken together they demolish the folk belief that *whose* must always have a personal antecedent. But it would be equally wrong to suggest that equivalent *of which* constructions are being driven out. Readers may indeed prefer to read *of which* instead of *whose* in several of the examples in (*b*) (*the captain of which; the message of which*; etc.). In fact it is likely that *of which* constructions outnumber those with *whose* when the antecedent is inanimate, especially in essays and monographs. The *OED* (1923) was on target in its definition of *whose* 'in reference to a thing or things (inanimate or abstract). Originally the genitive of the neuter *what* ...; in later use serving as the genitive of *which* ..., and usually replaced by *of which*, except where the latter would produce an intolerably clumsy form.'

why. 1 Plural *whys* (in the phrase *the whys and the wherefores*).

2 See REASON WHY.

wide. It should be borne in mind that there are a good many circumstances, mostly in fixed phrases, in which, though *widely* is theoretically the needed form, *wide* is the idiomatic form. Thus *wide apart, wide awake, open one's eyes wide, wide open, is widespread*, are all idiomatically required (not *widely apart*, etc.); and there are many more.

-wide. This familiar formative element, found, for example, in *citywide, countrywide, nationwide, statewide*, and *worldwide*, is now used productively in a great many combinations, e.g. *But there's much more involved in creating enterprisewide applications than mastering Notes*—*PC Week*, 1992; *We may be approaching a point where, on an economywide basis, layoffs may become counterproductive*—*Chicago Tribune*, 1993. Contrary to the spelling in those examples, if the word is not one of the well-established ones mentioned earlier, hyphenation is preferable, e.g. *campus-wide, enterprise-wide, economy-wide, EU-wide, industry-wide, UK-wide, university-wide*, etc.

wide(-)awake. He is *wide awake*; but when used attributively, *a very wide-awake person*.

widely. See WIDE.

wife. Plural *wives*. See -VE(D), -VES.

Wi-Fi. Dictionaries list this word in the spelling shown here, i.e. with a hyphen and both words given an initial capital, because the word (short for *Wi*reless *Fi*delity) is a trademark. This is the form in which it should be, and generally is, written rather than any of the many variations, e.g. *WiFi, wi-fi, wifi, Wifi*, etc.

wight (a person). A WARDOUR STREET word.

wilfing is the name for the habit, or addiction, of being diverted from the Internet search one originally undertook to all manner of other sites, with no particular purpose in mind. It is a verb acronym derived from the question '*W*hat was *I* looking *f*or?', and usefully describes the trance-like state of pointless website-hopping the Internet so easily induces. Though most common as the verbal noun shown, it exists in other forms: *Shopping is the online activity most likely to make users wilf. Men are more likely to admit to being wilfers than women*—*Daily Tel.*, 2007.

wilful. So spelt in BrE, but as either **willful** or **wilful** in AmE.

will (noun). We owe to the German language a relatively small but important group of phrases of the type *the will to* + verb or noun. To judge from the *OED, the will to live* (reflecting German *der Wille zum Leben*) and *the will to power* (German *der Wille zur Macht*) entered the language in the late 19c. These were joined by others in the 20c., e.g. *will to art* (German *der Wille zur Kunst*) an innate human drive towards artistic creation, *will-to-be, will to believe*.

The expressions are mostly derived from Nietzschean philosophy and from analytic psychology as part of the description of instincts and internal drives that govern human behaviour.

will (verb). One needs an advanced course in Old English and the history of the language to understand the origin and development of what are now taken to be two separate verbs, namely the *will* that operates as a flexionless auxiliary with a bare infinitive (*the judge adjourned the case and* will give *his verdict tomorrow*) and the *will* that conjugates in the normal way (*wills, willing, willed*; formerly also *willest*) and corresponds to the noun *will* 'the faculty of conscious and deliberate choice of action (*he has a* will *of his own*)'. For the auxiliary *will*, see SHALL AND WILL. The full verb *will* has several meanings, including, as the *COD* reminds us, 'to have as the object of one's will; intend unconditionally (*what God* wills; willed *that we should succeed*)'.

willful. See WILFUL.

wimmin. This semi-phonetic spelling, which dates back to the first quarter of the 18c. as a representation of non-standard speech, was used early in the 20c. as an ironical term for 'women' (e.g. '*Wimmin's a toss up,' says Uncle Penstemon*—H. G. Wells, 1910). It was adopted by feminists in the 1980s to avoid the ending *-men*. In Britain the word was particularly applied to the women protesters camped outside an American airbase at Greenham Common in Berkshire. In America it has been used since the late 1970s, but generally has achieved only a limited currency in writing by or about feminists, and also in ironic contexts. Examples: *The Women*'s *Center and the Department of African-American Student Affairs are sponsoring a fireside on 'Black Wimmin*'s *sexuality and its impact on sister-to-sister relationships'*; *Anyone, Roisin. That includes adolescent boys, wimmin, transgender hang gliders, and people of all ethnic, religious, social, political backgrounds and persuasions*—*Sunday Business Post*, 2004.

wind (verbs). The verb meaning to twist, coil, go on a circular course, etc. (pronounced /wʌɪnd/ (wiynd), past tense *wound* /waʊnd/ (wownd)) is unconnected with the verb meaning to exhaust the breath (*wind* /wind/, past tense *winded* /ˈwɪndɪd/). The archaic meaning of that verb, namely to sound a wind instrument, especially a bugle, by blowing can be pronounced /wʌɪnd/ rather than /wɪnd/, with past tense and past participle either *winded* or *wound* /waʊnd/ (*But scarce again his horn he wound*—Scott).

windward is invariable (not *-wards*) as adjective, adverb, and noun. It means (on) the side from which the wind is blowing (as opposed to LEEWARD).

wine, wire. The corresponding adjectives are respectively **winey** and **wiry**.

wireless, as an adjective, refers to the technology that allows the transmission of data between computers or other networked devices or over a mobile phone network without the use of wires. As a noun for a radio, it is now extremely dated, or else whimsical, but it has been given a new lease of life as the noun for the technology described above, e.g. *The second step is to help create the right policy and regulatory environment for broadband, and satellite, and wireless.*

-wise, -ways. 1 Modern use of *-wise*. Somewhere about 1940, chiefly in informal contexts, but also in more serious ones, *-wise* began to be tacked on to nouns (including verbal nouns in *-ing*) with the broad meaning 'as regards, in respect of'. The habit began in America and continues to be commoner in AmE than in other forms of English. Burchfield opined that 'Some speakers treat it with mild disdain, or with a shrug of the shoulders as if to say that its use in this way is inevitable, painful or too clever by half though it is.' On the other hand, it is often useful shorthand for 'as regards, in respect of'. Occasionally it is used redundantly, or could be rephrased, e.g. *We were late time-wise, but so was everyone else* (remove *time-wise*); *until things get better business-wise* (until business gets better). Words created using it are sometimes hyphenated, sometimes not. Some examples: *John Robert Russell, 13th Duke of Bedford . . . in twelve TV performances, was the greatest,* successwise, *among the aristocrats*—*Spectator,* 1958; Acting-wise, *I like Katharine Hepburn, Joanne Woodward, Judy Garland and, of course, Marilyn*—*Gossip* (Holiday Special), 1981; *They all kept up with me,* drinkingwise—*New Yorker,* 1993.

2 *A historical note.* As a terminal element of adverbs, *-ways* was originally a use of the genitive of the ordinary noun *way*. From the 12c. onwards such adverbs were formed, sometimes with by-forms ending in *-way*. This class of words includes *alway(s), anyway(s), crossway(s), endway(s),* and *sideway(s),* not all of which have survived. Parallel to this group of words were many with the same first element but with *-wise* (from Old English *wise* 'way, manner, fashion') as their ending, e.g. *anywise, crosswise, edgewise,* and *sidewise*. The two types made contact, and came to be thought of by some as two forms of the same word. Dr Johnson (in his Dictionary s.v. *Way* 25) went further and said that '*Way* and *ways* are now often used corruptly for *-wise*', and this statement, as the *OED* pointed out, 'has probably led many to prefer *-wise* to *-ways* or *-way* on the ground of supposed correctness'.

As a result of these word-forming processes, spread out over many centuries, the use of *-ways* and *-way* as free-forming adverbial suffixes had come to an end by the 20c. But most of the well-established forms have survived, *e.g. anyway, breadthways, crossways, edgeways, lengthways, sideways,* and *widthways*. While *-way(s)* as a free-forming terminal element died away, *-wise*, meaning 'in the manner of', has continued to thrive as it has done since the 14c. Some examples: *Priests sitting with their legs tucked up,* tailor-wise, *in the attitude of Buddha—Cornhill Mag.,* 1885; *Her mass of chestnut hair parted* Rossetti-wise *in the middle*—R. Macaulay, 1923; *It . . . swerved out of control and came* crabwise *down the middle lane and hit my lorry—Times,* 1963; *dangling his arms beside his hips and rolling his head* idiotwise—J. McInerney, 1985.

3 Distribution of forms in *-way, -ways,* and *-wise*. To judge from the *COD* (1990) the commoner adverbs of these types still in use are as follows: *anyway* (archaic *anywise*); *breadthways, breadthwise; clockwise; contrariwise; crabwise; crosswise,* var. *crossways; edgeways,* var. *edgewise; endways,* var. *endwise; lengthways,* var. *lengthwise; likewise; nowise,* var. *noway; otherwise; sideways,* var. *sidewise; slantwise; widthways, widthwise.*

wish (verb). Freely used with a direct object to mean 'to want, desire' from Old English times onwards, the type was described by the *OED* (1928) as 'Now *dial.*; superseded in standard English by *wish for*, or colloq. in certain contexts by *want*'. Typical examples: *Would you* wish *a little more hot water, ma'am?*—Dickens, 1854; [*The maid*] *flew into a rage, and wanted to know if I* wished *a month*'s *notice*—W. R. H. Trowbridge, 1901. But *WDEU* (1989) regards the use as 'certainly standard' (in America), citing some insubstantial evidence in support: e.g. *a majority of employees wished a union shop—Current Biography,* 1948.

wishful. Now archaic is the use of *wishful* followed by a *to*-infinitive, e.g. *I was wishful to say a word to you, sir* (Dickens, 1852). The word is archaic in the sense '(of a person) wishing, desirous' used in other constructions, e.g. *Wishful from my soul That truth should triumph* (R. Browning, 1875). The word is now largely restricted to the phrase *wishful thinking* and derivatives, used to mean impracticable ideas and impractical wishes. *Wishful thinking* is a relatively new term: the earliest example in the *OED* is one of 1932. Its status as a word extinct outside that phrase has led to the folk-etymology version **wistful thinking,* which should be avoided.

wisteria /wɪsˈtɪərɪə/, any plant of the genus *Wisteria*, is much the commoner form, not *wistaria*, even though most authorities say that it was named after Casper Wistar (1761–1818), an American anatomist. (*The R.H.S. Gardeners' Encycl. of Plants & Flowers,* 1991 printing, lists only *Wisteria*.)

wit (verb). Except for the phrase *to wit* (= that is to say; namely) and the derived adverbs **wittingly** and **unwittingly**, this verb (= to know) survives chiefly in the 1st and 3rd singular present *wot* (especially in T. E. Brown's often quoted remark (1892) *A garden is a lovesome thing, God wot!*). See WARDOUR STREET.

witenagemot /ˈwɪtənəgəˌməʊt/. The name of an Anglo-Saxon national council (lit. 'a meeting of wise men').

with. See AGREEMENT 4.

withal (adverb), moreover, as well, etc. A WARDOUR STREET word.

withe /wɪθ, wɪð, wʌɪð/, a flexible shoot of willow or osier used for tying a bundle of wood, etc. This form (plural *withes*) is as acceptable as **withy** /ˈwɪði/, plural *withies*.

(Note that the Bible (1611) has the plural form *withs*: *And Samson said vnto her, If they binde mee with seuen greene* withs... *then shall I be weake*—Judg. 16: 7.)

withhold. Spelt with two *hs*, not *withold.*

without.

1 = *outside.*
2 As conjunction = *unless.*
3 Repetition after *or.*
4 *without hardly.*

1 = *outside.* Both as adverb (*listening to the wind without; clean within and without*), as preposition (*is without the pale of civilization*), the word retains this meaning; but it is no longer for all styles, having now a literary or WARDOUR STREET sound that may be very incongruous or even ambiguous. Awareness of this older meaning of *without* is essential, for example, in this passage written by the Irish poet Cecil Frances Alexander (1818–95): *There is a green hill far away,* Without *a city wall, Where the dear Lord was crucified, Who died to save us all.*

2 As conjunction = *unless.* Once (14–17c.) in standard literary use (e.g. *Such a one, as a man may not speake of,* without *he say sir reuerence*—Shakespeare, 1591), this type was described by Johnson in his Dictionary (1755) as 'not in use' (he cited two examples from the work of Sir Philip Sidney). It has subsequently become restricted to regional speech in the UK and Ireland, and is also liable to turn up in the sense 'without its being the case that' in regional speech in America and elsewhere. Examples: *Everything she looked at was that child... She couldn't lie with that man without she saw it*—F. O'Connor, 1955; *Man can put up with only so much without he descends a rung or two on the old evolutionary ladder*—E. Albee, 1962; *the silly bitch can't even keep the fire going without I have to rouse on her*—M. Eldridge, 1984 (Aust.); *The top copy for the customer, the carbon for ourselves. You couldn't do business without you keep a record of receipts*—W. Trevor, 1994.

3 *without hardly.* Example: *The introduction of the vast new refineries has been brought about quickly, silently, and effectively, and* without *the surrounding community* hardly *being aware of what was happening.* Again, like sense 2, this is non-standard, in that it represents a joining of a negative word and an approximate negative, i.e. is dangerously close to being a double negative. It is the kind of construction that should not appear outside the setting down of informal speech. Trollope should not have used the phrase in *It seemed to her as though she had neglected some duty in allowing Crosbie's conduct to have passed away* without hardly a *word of comment on it between her and Lily.* The standard English for *without hardly* is *almost without.* But the use continues to turn up now and then: e.g. *They manage to weave together without hardly ever touching*—*New Musical Express,* 1992.

with regard(s) to. See REGARD.

witticism. An ingenious hybrid formation coined by Dryden in 1677 from *witty* (adjective) after *criticism.*

wizard. For *Wizard of the North,* see SOBRIQUETS.

wizened (adjective). The survivor of three adjectival forms (the other two being *wizen* and *weazen*) meaning 'thin and shrivelled'. It was originally (16c.) restricted to Scottish texts but is now a general English word. All three words answer ultimately to an Old English verb *wisnian* 'to shrivel'. *Wizen* (first recorded in the 18c.) is a clipped form of *wizened,* while *weazen* (19c.) is what etymologists call an 'altered form' of *wizen* (adjective).

wolf. Plural *wolves.* See -VE(D), -VES.

woman. A great deal about the currency and distribution of this word has already been said s.v. FEMALE 3,4; FEMININE DESIGNATIONS 3; GENTLEWOMAN; WIMMIN. See also -WOMAN; WOMYN. For the sense 'women in general', **womankind** (rather than the occasionally found *womenkind*) is the favoured word now. **womenfolk** is also occasionally used in this sense (e.g. *The Prime Minister's ice-breaker appeared to have worked perfectly as he wooed the doughty womenfolk of Middle Britain yesterday*—*Independent,* 2000) but just as often it is used to describe the women of a particular household, family, social group, etc., e.g. *The ambassador's glamorous ex-mistress Gloria Swanson did not crash the party, as the womenfolk of both families had feared*—*History Today,* 2003. The 20c. phrase *women's liberation* (and the shortened form *women's lib*), is less often heard, but there is no slackening in the use of the term *women's rights* (coined in the 17c.), especially with reference to the legal entitlement of women to the same terms as men in conditions of employment, in the selection of candidates as MPs, etc. And *women's studies*, academic studies concerning women's role in society, history, etc., has become a central option in the degree syllabuses of universities and in writing in general.

-woman. There has been a noticeable drop in the use of compounds in *-woman*, mostly because genderless equivalent terms such as *police officer* for *policewoman* are being used. But many such terms remain in common use, including the following (*policewoman* among them) which are all listed in the *COD* (1990) without restrictive labels of any kind: *airwoman, chairwoman, charwoman, horsewoman, kinswoman, needlewoman, oarswoman, policewoman, saleswoman, servicewoman, spokeswoman, tradeswoman, washerwoman*.

womyn (plural noun). A word coined by feminists to replace *-men* as a sequence of letters in the word *women*. A headline in a 1991 issue of an American newspaper: *How to 'Do' the Michigan Womyn's Music Festival.*

wonder (verb). **1** For *I shouldn't wonder if it didn't rain*, see NOT 5.

2 *wonder whether/if.* In formal style sometimes construed with a subjunctive in the dependent clause: e.g. *Hilliard wondered whether Barton were not right after all*—S. Hill, 1971; *Watching her departing figure... he wondered whether he were any happier*—A. Brookner, 1989; *they had never had a serious conversation, and she wondered if that were wrong*—idem, 1992.

wonder child, wonderkid. See WUNDERKIND.

won't. From a welter of contracted forms of *woll not* = *will not* (among them *wonnot, woonnot, wo'nt*, some of them recorded as early as the 15c.), *won't* emerged in the 17c. as the standard one, the others now being dialectal or obsolete. Cf. DON'T; SHAN'T.

wont(ed). *Wont*, the past participle of an obsolete verb *won* (Old English *gewunian*, past participle *gewunod*) 'to accustom oneself to', is still used as a predicative adjective (*as he is wont to do*). The participial origin of the word having been forgotten, *wont* was used as a verb (*Talbot is taken, whom we wont to feare*—Shakespeare, 1591) and acquired a past participle of its own, *wonted*. In its other parts the verb is no longer used, but *wonted* survives as an attributive adjective (*he showed his wonted skill*). There is also a noun *wont* (*as is his wont*). The traditional pronunciation /wʌnt/, rhyming with *runt* and useful in differentiating this word from *won't* (= will not), has been preserved in AmE (as one of at least three standard pronunciations), but not in BrE, in which the standard pronunciation is /wəʊnt/, rhyming with *won't*.

woodbine (BrE wild honeysuckle, AmE Virginia creeper) is the standard modern form, not the ancient spelling *woodbind*, formerly just as often used and likely to be found in older writing. It echoes the word's derivation from Old English *wudubind(e)* (= 'wood' + 'bind'), recorded as far back as the Lindisfarne Gospels.

woodenness. So spelt, not *woodeness*.

woof. See WARP (noun).

wool has, in BrE the derivatives **woollen, woolly**, and in AmE **woolen, woolly** (also **wooly**).

word division. See HYPHENS 5.

word order. 1 The legitimate inversion of subject/verb/complement order is treated in numerous articles in this book (see especially INVERSION). Some typical examples follow: *Only in the dream-sequence, where he debates with the devil*, is he *triumphant*—K. Muir, 1987; *Nor* am I pretending *that there can be only one legitimate interpretation*—idem, 1987; *Only in recent times* have they insisted on *and begun to receive justice*—*Dædalus*, 1988; *Rarely* do they remind *the stranger that they have the privilege of living in one of the world's most dramatic environments*—ibid., 1988; Beats there a heart amongst us *so jaded... that it has failed to be touched... by the sound of Roy Orbison?*—*The Face*, 1989.

2 Unfortunately, however, unintended humour is often brought about by the careless ordering of words, often, as can be seen in these next examples, from the slapdash placement in writing of adverbial phrases in the position that is natural in speech, but unintentionally hilarious in writing. Some typical examples follow (they happen to be from American newspapers, but similarly inept examples could doubtless be found in newspapers anywhere in the English-speaking world): *One of the biggest supporters of Schoolfest was Carolyn Blount, who donated the $21.5 million complex* along with her husband, Winton; *'His humility and his courage are something we will always remember,' said coach Bill McCartney, commenting publicly about Aunese's* death for the first time; *She strongly disapproves of our living together* for religious reasons; '*Sure enough, somebody at the San Diego hospital* where she was born erroneously *had typed in "male"*'; *She did not want her last name* used to protect her daughter's identity.

work (verb). Perhaps the most important development to have happened to this polysemous verb (from Old English *wyrcan*) is the virtual disappearance of its true past tense and past participle *wrought* (Old English *worhte*; *geworht*). Richly documented in the *OED* from Anglo-Saxon times onwards, *wrought* began to be challenged by *worked* in the 15c., and *worked* is now the normal form except in a limited range of literary collocations (*she wrought changes, miracles, a revolution; carefully wrought research,* etc.), and in senses which denote 'fashioning, shaping, or decorating with the hand or an implement'. Of course anyone who reads the Bible or pre-1900 literary works is familiar with *wrought*: e.g. *And by the hands of the Apostles, were many signes and wonders wrought among the people*—Acts (AV) 5: 12; *A splendid cover...of tapestry richly wrought*—Cowper, 1784. One notable survivor is the participial adjective *wrought* in *wrought iron*. Another reasonably common residual use is the adjective *wrought-up*, agitated or excited: e.g. *I got so wrought up watching that trembly little fellow that I started cheering him on*—*New Yorker*, 1987.

For the phrases *work/wrought havoc* see WREAK.

workaday. Since the Middle Ages, *workaday, workday,* and *working day* have all been used as nouns meaning 'a day on which work is done (as distinct from a holiday or a day off)'. The distribution of the three forms before the 20c. is not easily determinable, but at the present time it would seem that as nouns *workaday* is obsolete, while *workday* and *working day* are still very much in use in all forms of English. As an attributive adjective *workaday* means (*a*) ordinary, everyday; humdrum, routine; (*b*) characteristic of, used on days at work. In AmE, *workday* also means the period of time in a day during which work is performed (*an eight-hour workday*). In BrE, *working day* would be the preferred term in this sense.

worldly. Take care not to write it as *wordly*, a common mistake.

World Wide Web. See WEB.

worn-out humour. Burchfield wrote: 'There is nothing so tired as a tired joke, nor so unamusing as an overused piece of facetious wordplay. However hilarious a pun or a deliberate misquotation was on first (or even second and third) hearing, it can outstay its welcome. To a new generation the jolly turns of phrase that amused our parents and grandparents seem laboured—and, what is worse, we have heard them before, and more than once. It is not the great comic writers of the past who now make us groan—*The Diary of a Nobody* and *Tristram Shandy*, Evelyn Waugh and P. G. Wodehouse, Damon Runyon and Ogden Nash will surely never lose their savour. But how worn out are such jests as *Don't do anything I wouldn't do*; such toasts as *Down the hatch*; such parodies as *to —— or not to ——*; such oxymorons as the *gentle art* of doing something ungentle, or the *tender mercies* of a martinet; the insufferability of such truisms as *he does not suffer fools gladly*; such needless euphemisms as *pushing up daisies*; such sobriquets as *his nibs* and *trick cyclist*; all these, and many more, are overdue for a long rest, if not permanent banishment from the language.' We have been warned. See also CLICHÉ; HACKNEYED PHRASES; IRRELEVANT ALLUSION; POLYSYLLABIC HUMOUR.

worry. Has inflexions *worrying, worries, worried.*

worsen. The *OED* has an interesting note on the word's history: 'The word [first recorded *c.*1225 but with no record of use between 1670 and 1806] is common in dialect (see *Eng. Dial. Dict.*) and was introduced to literature *c.*1800–1830 (by writers like Southey and De Quincey) as a racy vernacular substitute for *deteriorate* and the like.' 'Racy' it no longer is: just a routine verb playing an ordinary part in the standard language.

worsened words. Changes in the meaning of words often reflect the value or values of what they stand for. Over the course of history a great many words have developed positive connotations or, conversely, have lost their pejorative ones: e.g. *boy* (fettered person → male servant → male child), *meticulous* (over-scrupulous → very careful, accurate), PRESTIGE, and PRESTIGIOUS. An even larger number have gone in the opposite direction, i.e. have worsened in meaning.

Colonialism was once seen as a benevolent process. 20c. events led to *colonialism* and *imperialism* becoming deeply suspect concepts. *Appeasement*, after five centuries of use in contexts denoting pleasure or satisfaction, moved into pejorative territory in the 1930s when Neville Chamberlain embarked on a foreign policy of conciliation by concession. *Collaboration* and *collaborator* took on sinister connotations during the Second World War. In several words a specific sexual sense has all but effaced earlier general meanings, e.g. *erection, arousal*, and *intercourse*. *Sleaze* and *sleazy* are no longer applied to the flimsiness of textiles but to instances of moral turpitude, especially in regard to financial transactions and sexual affairs of a scandalous nature. *Egregious*, once capable of meaning 'towering above the flock, remarkable' now normally means 'outstandingly bad, flagrant', i.e. remarkable in a bad sense.

These linguistic processes, sometimes known as 'amelioration' (bettering) and pejoration (worsening) are immensely complicated, as the *OED* reveals in its treatment of thousands of upwardly mobile, downward-sliding, and sideways-moving words. The only certainty is that all three processes will continue inexorably and often for long periods unnoticed by the majority of a given community. Readers may wish to pursue the history of some ordinary words such as *buxom, candid, crafty, genteel, knave, lewd, sad, silly, specious*, and *villain* to see the way in which the language treats its own components. C. S. Lewis's *Studies in Words* is a mine of information about some of these words. Fuller treatment of them all is available in the *OED*.

worser. This double comparative has a long literary history beginning in the late 15c.: e.g. *Chang'd to a worser shape thou canst not be*—Shakespeare, 1591; *I find she is A diuell, worser then the worst in hell*—J. Ford, 1633; *For I, e'en I, the bondsman of a worser man was made*—W. Morris, 1887; *Some gals is better, some wusser than some*—E. Pound, 1959; *The people oh Lord Are sinful and sad Prenatally biassed Grow worser born bad*—S. Smith, 1975.

The *OED*'s verdict (1928) on the status of the word is still about right: 'The word was common in the 16th and 17th c. as a variant of 'worse', in all its applications. In modern use, it is partly a literary survival (esp. in phrases like *the worser part, sort, half*), partly dial. and vulgar.' Its 'vulgar', i.e. colloquial, use is illustrated by the following examples: *Your poor dear wife as you uses worser nor a dog*—Dickens, 1835; *That's my new word. Yeah, it's gonna be worser. You know, worse to worser*—*Interview* (US), 1990. For the analogous *lesser*, see LESSER.

worship has the forms *worshipped, worshipper, worshipping* in BrE, but often *worshiped* etc. in AmE. See -P-, -PP-.

worst. The idiomatic phrase *If the worst come(s) to the worst* has been in standard use in Britain since the late 16c. In AmE the usual form lacks the definite article, i.e. *if worst comes to worst*; and sometimes *worse* is used instead of the first *worst* or even instead of both.

worsted. Another word whose spelling hides a nasty secret, to the possible despair of learners of English and the unwary: pronounced /ˈwʊstɪd/ (**wuus**-tid).

worthwhile, worth-while, worth while. This word was sufficiently novel in Fowler's day for him to call it a 'vogue' word in this book's first edition (1926). It is an application of *worth* with a following noun (*worth the time, money, effort*, etc.) to the noun *while* meaning 'time', as in *a long while ago*, and abbreviates the phrases *worth the while* (14c.) and *worth one's while* (17c.). Though Fowler and Gowers objected at length to certain uses, the only issue that need concern us here is spelling.

In theory, like other compound adjectives such as *well(-)respected*, used predicatively *worth while* could be written separately (*the experiment was worth while*), and be written hyphenated when used attributively (a use first emerging at the end of the 19c.), i.e. *a worth-while experiment*. In practice, it is overwhelmingly written as one word in both functions, negating Burchfield's distaste for the use of the single-word form in the predicative position.

-worthy. Used as a combining form producing adjectives meaning (i) deserving (*blameworthy, noteworthy*), (ii) suitable or fit for (*airworthy, newsworthy, roadworthy*). Best written without a hyphen. They all seem so obvious. But a very large number of such compounds have fallen by the wayside since they came into the language. Among the casualties (with the date of first record indicated) are the following: *deathworthy* 13c., *faith-* 16c.; *fame-* 17c.; *fault-* 16c.; *honour-* 16c.; *labour-* 17c.; *laugh-* 17c.; *love-* 13c.; *mark-* 19c.; *name-* 16c.; *pains-* 17c.; *sale-* 16c.; *scorn-* 17c.; *song-* 19c.; *thank-* 14c.; *wonder-* 17c.; *worship-* 16c.

And among the survivors, some of them first used in the 20c. century or the 19c., are: *airworthy* 19c.; *battle-* 19c.; *blame-* 14c.; *hate-* 20c; *news-* 20c.; *note-* 16c.; *praise-* 16c.; *road-* 19c.; *sea-* 19c.; *trust-* 19c. Among the newer arrivals that look like staying is *cringeworthy* (1977).

would. See SHOULD AND WOULD, where some of the main distinctions are set down, especially the dominance of *would* or *'d* even with the first-person pronouns *I* and *we*. For *would of* = *would have*, see OF B. 1.

wove (past participle and adjective). Instead of *woven* the usual form for these parts of *weave* (verb)[2] (of fabrics etc.), *wove* is used to mean 'Of paper: made on a wire-gauze mesh so as to have a uniform unlined surface' (*New SOED*). So *wove mould, paper*, etc.

wove (past tense). See WEAVE (verb).

wow factor. See FACTOR 2.

wrack. See NERVE-RACKING; RACK.

wraith. Plural *wraiths* /reɪθs/. See -TH /θ/ AND -TH /ð/.

wrapt, wrapped, rapt. See RAPT.

wrath, wrathful, wroth. The first two are literary words for extreme anger and extremely angry respectively, and are normally pronounced in BrE /rɒθ/ and /ˈrɒθfʊl/; but /rɔːθ/ is also standard in both words. *Wroth*, pronounced /rəʊθ/ or /rɒθ/, is an archaic predicative adjective, especially in the phrase *wax wroth*, meaning angry (e.g. *Then the old man Was wroth, and doubled up his hands*—Tennyson). In AmE, /raθ/, /ˈraθfʊl/, and /rɔːθ/, respectively, are the usual standard pronunciations. As these words recede into the mists of archaism, their differences are seen more hazily, and *wroth* is often used for the noun.

wreak most commonly means 'cause (a large amount of damage or harm', above all in the collocation *wreak havoc*. That phrase raises two questions: how to spell it correctly, and whether its past tense and past participle are *wreaked* or *wrought*.

1 The correct spelling is, of course, *wreak*, despite the not infrequent appearance, even in the most reputable journalistic organs, of **wreck havoc* (presumably through folk etymology) and the baffling and plain daft *reek havoc*, e.g. **the foot and mouth outbreak wrecking havoc on sporting events like rugby and horse-racing in the UK and parts of Europe—Scotsman*, 2001; **But during a burst of energy he could reek havoc on the house—Daily Tel.*, 2006. Subeditors please take note.

2 (*a*) *Wreak* is nowadays a regular verb, which is to say that its past tense and participle are *wreaked*, e.g. *The teenagers had, however, wreaked havoc in the house*—weblog, 2007 (SAfr.). Is *wrought havoc* therefore wrong? Yes and no. As a past tense in the phrase *wrought havoc* it is perfectly correct. It is not, however, the correct past tense of *wreak*, because it actually comes from a different verb. It is in fact the now archaic or literary past tense of the verb *work* in its meaning of 'to cause, produce' (as in *The beer had wrought no bad effect upon his appetite*—Dickens, 1841). The collocation *to work havoc* is well established and historical, but is nowadays far less often used than *to wreak havoc*. And, as the *OED* states, 'the past tense *wrought* is common (though it is often interpreted as the past tense of *wreak*)'.

(*b*) As regards the relative frequencies of *wreaked* and *wrought*, *OEC* data shows that *wreaked* is rather more frequent as the past tense and past participle, but that *wrought* is equally frequent when the participle follows the noun. Further examples: (*wreaked*: past tense) *In recent years Hollywood wreaked havoc on the silver screens of the world in a succession of natural disaster flicks—E: The Environmental Magazine*, 2005 (US); (past participle) *The fateful earthquake had wreaked havoc on it*—*Contemporary Review*, 2000 (UK); (participle following noun) *But the havoc wreaked by the floods is a rude reminder that governance leaves a huge gap in our progress report*—*Times of India*, 2007. (*wrought*: past tense) *A freak tide wrought havoc on one of Australia's biggest barramundi farms*—*ABC PM* (transcripts) (Aust.); (past participle) *the fast-spreading virus that has wrought havoc with the nation's computers could release a malicious code*—*Yorkshire Post Today*, 2003 (UK); (participle following noun) *Black's doc on the sad state of Jamaica isn't subtle, but it is essential viewing for anyone concerned about the havoc wrought by economic globalization*—*Eye Weekly* (Toronto), 2002 (Canad.).

wreath. Plural *wreaths* pronounced either /riːðz/ or /riːθs/. The corresponding verb **wreathe** is pronounced /riːð/. See -TH /θ/ AND -TH /ð/.

wrick. See CRICK.

write. The transitive AmE use with the recipient as the grammatical object is shown in the following example from the *New Yorker*: *I had written my mother about all this* (1987). This construction was formerly standard in BrE ('frequent from *c*.1790' says the *OED*), but it is now in restricted use unless accompanied by a second (direct) object, as in *I shall write you a letter as soon as I land in Borneo*. In old-fashioned commercial correspondence the types *We wrote you yesterday*; *Please write us at your convenience* were often used, but nowadays *to* would normally be inserted before *you* and *us*.

writ large. In the ever-popular, usually figurative, phrase *writ large*, first recorded in the 17c. (*New Presbyter is but Old Priest writ large*—Milton), *writ* is an otherwise obsolete past participle of *write*. *OED* examples of *writ large* and other phrases containing *writ*: *The man was no more than the boy writ large, with an extensive commentary*—G. Eliot, 1866; *This year's Defence White Paper . . . is last year's writ quietly*—*Times*, 1959; *In a curious way he's* [*sc.* Sir Isaac Hayward's] *an amalgam, writ small, of Attlee, Morrison and Bevin*—*Observer*, 1961; *Every project has success writ large all over it*—*Author*, 1994.

wrong (adverb) like *right*, exists as an adverb alongside *wrongly*. It is used with a limited number of words and means roughly 'incorrectly', or 'astray', as in *We guessed wrong* and *I said it wrong*, and the informal *Don't get me wrong*. In the first two cases *wrongly* could also be used, but the effect would be somewhat ponderous. *Wrongly* is appropriate in the more general meaning 'in error' or 'in the wrong way', and is obligatory when it precedes the verb, adjective or participle it refers to. (= in error) *It arrived at Heathrow as mishandled luggage, having been wrongly off-loaded in Rome from a flight from Australia to London*—*Daily Tel.*, 1972; (= in the wrong way) *The court was told the machine had been wrongly calibrated at the police station*—*OEC*, 2003. Note that in the expression *go wrong*, *wrong* is probably not an adverb but an adjective complement of the subject as with *become* and similar verbs, e.g. *There are more ways of going wrong than of going right*—Herbert Spencer.

Cf. RIGHT.

wroth. See WRATH.

wrought. See WORK (verb).

wry. The various extended forms are *wryer*, *wryest*, *wryly*, rather than *wrier*, etc.

wunderkind. This loanword from German (literally 'wonderchild') first cited in Shaw (1891), is pronounced, according to the dictionaries, /ˈvʊndəːkɪnd/ in a semi-Germanic manner. Judging by the *OEC* data, it is holding its own very well against the loan translations *wonder child* and *wonderkid*, than which it is much more frequent. Being a noun, in German it is written with a capital letter, but this convention no longer applies to the English word. It is printed in roman, and the German plural *wunderkinder* /-kɪndə/ is slightly more frequent than the anglicized *wunderkinds*.

-x, as plural of French loanwords. For many words in *-eau* and *-ieu* adopted from French, we still write the plural with *-x* as an alternative to the English *-s*. Sometimes we pronounce that spelling with /z/, as in standard English plurals, but if we want to be truer to a word's origins, we often do not. Regularizing all such plurals to a compulsory final *-s*, though theoretically desirable, seems likely to be a long-drawn-out process. It seems that we appreciate the look of final *-x* as a plural marker, perhaps as a reminder that these words came from French. The choice of one form depends to an extent on personal preference, and dictionaries generally give both forms; the trends noted below, based on the *OEC*, are merely that: trends.

(*a*) plural more often *-s*, though *-x* also used: *adieu, trousseau, plateau.*

(*b*) plural more often *-x*, though *-s* also used: *bandeau, beau, château, flambeau, plateau, rondeau, rouleau, tableau.*

(*c*) special cases: (i) *bureaus* is by far the preferred form in AmE, *bureaux* in BrE, and everywhere, naturally, as the plural of *bureau de change*; (ii) *milieus* is preferred in AmE, *milieux* in BrE; (iii) *portmanteaus* for the linguistic sense is preferable; *-x* is used for the item of luggage; (iv) *purlieus* is the norm; (v) the *-x* of the plurals *jeux d'esprit, prie-dieux,* and often of *milieux,* is left unpronounced; the *-x* of *rouleaux* is pronounced.

xenophobia, meaning 'irrational dislike of foreigners', is a combination of Greek ξένος ('stranger, foreigner') + *phobia*, the *x* in English representing the Greek letter xi. Because the first element is pronounced /zɛnə-/, spelling sometimes follows suit as ?*zenophobia*. Though the *OED* records that spelling, many will consider it a mistake. The same applies to the derivatives **xenophobe** and **xenophobic**.

Xerox, a proprietary term for a make of photocopier, should be spelt with a capital *X*. As a verb, however, it is spelt *xerox.*

-xion, -xive. A small group of nouns drawn from Latin nouns (classical, ecclesiastical, medieval, etc., Latin) ending in *–iō, -iōnem,* have been spelt either *-xion* and *-ction* in English at one time or another; similarly some adjectives in *-xive* and *-ctive.* No doubt influenced by the spelling of related verbs (*connect, deflect,* etc.), and by the many nouns ending in *-tion*, current usage prefers *-ction/-ive* (e.g. *deflection/-ive, connection/-ive, genuflection, inflection*), but *-xion* is the only ending in use for *complexion, crucifixion,* and the highly literary *transfixion.*

Xmas. In this abbreviated form of *Christmas,* which is first recorded in the 18c., *X* represents the first letter (chi) of the Greek word for Christ, namely Χριστός. Its convenience accounts for its common use in commercial printing and in personal letters and diaries, but in spoken English it is usually pronounced like 'Christmas' rather than as 'ex-mass', though the latter pronunciation is not uncommon.

X-ray. Spelt with capital *X* and hyphen.

-y. For the suffix used in making adjectives from nouns (*racy*, etc.), as it affects spelling, see -EY AND -Y IN ADJECTIVES. For the diminutive suffixes *-y* (*Johnny*) and *-ie* (*bookie, doggie*, etc.), see HYPOCORISTIC.

Y'all. See YOU-ALL.

y and i. There are a few words in which *i* and *y* are interchangeable (for these, publishing houses usually adopt a house spelling), a few others in which BrE practice differs from that of AmE, and a handful containing the letters in successive syllables making it difficult to remember which is *i* and which is *y*. The main words involved are (those in small capitals are treated in separate articles):

cider; CIPHER; GYPSY; LYCHGATE; PYGMY; *sibyl*; SIPHON; STYMIE; SYLLABUB; SYLVAN; TYRE, TIRE; TYRO; *wych elm*.

Yankee. The mistaken practice of applying this term, and also its shortened form *Yank*, to any citizen of the USA persists in Britain and in many other English-speaking countries. *Yankee* was originally the nickname of those who lived in New England; at its most comprehensive a hundred years later it was extended contemptuously by the Confederates during the American Civil War to all soldiers of the federal armies. The derivation of the word has been the subject of much discussion and no agreement.

yclept. An archaic or jocular word meaning 'called (by the name of)', a direct descendant of Old English *gecleopod*, past participle of *cleopian* 'to call, name'.

ye (definite article). Sometimes written as *y*[e]. A pseudo-archaic form of *the* (as in *Ye Olde Tea-Shoppe*), in which *y* is the descendant of a 14c. handwritten form of the Old English and Middle English runic letter *þ* (thorn), which had come to resemble the letter *y*. *Ye* is pronounced /jiː/ like the pronoun *ye*, but is 'properly' /ðiː/, and in any case is just a variant of the definite article.

yeah /jɛː/. The conventional spelling of a shortened form of *yes*. It occurs in speech with greater frequency than is realized by many standard speakers. It is also used in the phrase *Oh yeah?* to express incredulity.

year. A possessive apostrophe is needed in expressions of the type *five years' imprisonment* (contrast *a year's imprisonment*) and *in two years' time*.

yellowhammer. The latest view on the etymology of this bird name is that the second element *-hammer* is perhaps from Old English *amore* (name of an unidentified bird, but with cognates in some other Germanic languages), possibly conflated with Old English *hama* 'covering, feathers'. The full name *yellowhammer* has not been found before the mid-16c., and then only in the form *yelambre*.

yen (Japanese currency unit). Plural the same.

yeoman. The ancient phrase *yeoman('s) service* means 'efficient or useful help in need', e.g. *Percy Brown has done yeoman service in painstakingly documenting the architecture of India in his book* Indian Architecture: Islamic Period—*The Hindu*, 2003. The *OEC* data suggests that the phrase, first recorded in *Hamlet* (1604) and in sporadic literary use ever since, is now far more widely used outside the UK, especially in India and the US, than within. The standard spelling is without the apostrophe.

yes (noun). Plural *yeses*. See -S-, -SS-.

yet, still (adverbs). **1** These two adverbs were once more interchangeable than they are now. The sentence *Mrs. Throckmorton was shot in her apartment last night, and the bullet is in her yet* (1988, US) where *yet* denotes continuity of action up to the time in question, would be acceptable, especially informally, in the US and Scotland, but in most Englishes elsewhere *still* would be used and the word order would be different: ... *and the bullet is still in her.* Generally, *yet* is used to mean 'up to this time' or 'up to then' in a question or after a negative: *Is she 21 yet?*; *She wasn't yet 18*; *Have they arrived yet?*; *They haven't arrived yet* (or *haven't yet arrived*); *I hadn't yet decided what to do.* Note the position of *yet* in these examples.

2 It is worth noting that questions of the type *Is it raining yet?* in Scotland could be ambiguous, equivalent both to the question 'Has it started to rain yet?' and to 'Is it still raining?'. In conversation, intonation would normally clarify the meaning, with the *yet* accented.

3 A usage note in *The Amer. Heritage Dict.* (3rd edn, 1992) identifies an informal use of *yet* that is not current in Britain: 'In formal style *yet* in the sense "up to now" requires that the accompanying verb be in the present perfect, rather than in the simple past: *He hasn't started yet,* not *He didn't start yet.'* In other words, in informal AmE a past tense formed with *do* is sometimes used in negations and questions, e.g. *Did they arrive yet?*

4 In affirmative contexts, *yet* is a more formal alternative to *still* in the following types of phrase, normally with *be, have to,* or a modal verb such as *can*: *We'd better do it while there is yet time*; *I have yet to receive a reply*; *I can hear her yet.*

5 (conjunction). Formerly the presence of the conjunction *yet* often led to the reversal of word order. Example: *Though ye haue lien among the pots,* yet shall yee bee *as the wings of a doue*—Ps. (AV) 68: 13. Such inversions would now be regarded as archaic.

Yiddish (adaptation of Ger. *jüdisch* 'Jewish') is 'a vernacular used by Jews in or from central and eastern Europe, based chiefly on High German with Hebrew and Slavonic borrowings, and written in Hebrew characters' (*New SOED*). English (especially AmE) has adopted many words and phrases from Yiddish over the last century or so, some very often used, others less so, e.g. *bagel, chutzpah* (audacity); *klutz* (clumsy or inept person); *kvell* (to boast, gloat); *mazuma* (money); *need it like a hole in the head* (have no need for); *nosh* (food); *schlemiel* (clumsy person, fool); *schlep* (to haul, drag; to go reluctantly or with effort); *schmuck* (contemptible person); *shtoom* (silent); *What's with you?* (What's the matter?).

yodel. The inflected forms are *yodelled, yodelling,* but usually *yodeled, yodeling* in AmE. See -LL-, -L-.

yog(h)urt. Both *yoghurt* and *yogurt* are correct spellings for this word (borrowed from the Turkish *yoğurt* in the early 17c.), which has been spelt in many guises historically before settling down to its two major current variants. Many dictionaries list *yogurt* as the main form with *yoghurt* as a variant (thought the Macquarie gives priority to *yoghurt*). The *h*-less version is by far the preferred form in North American English, the other spelling being rare, while *yoghurt* is several times more frequent in BrE, and Australian and NZ English. Elsewhere the two forms are more closely matched. Generally pronounced /ˈjɒgət/ in BrE, while in AmE (and also in Australian and NZ English) the first syllable is pronounced /ˈjəʊg-/.

yoke is a wooden crosspiece fastened over the necks of two oxen, etc.; *yolk* is the yellow internal part of an egg.

yon, yore. See WARDOUR STREET.

you. For the mixture of *you* and *one* in the same sentence, see ONE 7.

you-all (Also in abbreviated form *y'all*). Best written with the hyphen to make it clear that it is the plural pronoun form. Used at all social levels in certain Southern states in the USA for *you* (either singular or plural, but predominantly plural; 'always with a plural meaning by those to whom the form is native, although often misunderstood as a singular by outlanders' (*CGEL*)). There is lively debate about whether *you-all* can be singular, but that it can be is suggested by the use in certain areas of the 'doubly' plural form *all y'all.* Examples: (y'all) *Yes, Doctor. You'll be in the breakfast room. Y'all have a nice day*—J. S. Borthwick, 1982; *The only reason I can't do that is I would then be laundering y'all's money, which I can't do*—*Chicago Tribune,* 1988. (you-all) *You-all certainly is used as singular in the Ozarks*—*I have heard it daily for weeks at a time*—*Amer. Speech,* 1927; *In almost a score of years of residence in North Carolina I have never heard anyone say 'you all', unless the plural was definitely and* *distinctly intended*—ibid., 1944; *'Don't forget to get you-all some beer!' Ruth calls out to the men*—S. Gaddis in *New Yorker*, 1990; (all y'all) *So all y'all who call yourselves a man, sit down and do your homework—define the meaning of being a man—Youth Outlook*, 2004.

you're is a contraction of *you are* (e.g. *You're a member of the Senior Common Room, aren't you?*) to be distinguished from the identical-sounding possessive word *your*.

yours. 1 The possessive pronoun *yours* is spelt this way (*this book is yours*), never as *your's*. Similarly, *hers, its, ours,* and *theirs* have no apostrophe. In compound subjects connected by *and*, the correct form is *your*, not *yours*, e.g. **For both* yours *and our sanity, here is the definition of SMTP according to Webopedia* (read *your and our*)—*Register*, 2001. See ABSOLUTE POSSESSIVES.

2 See also LETTER FORMS.

yourself. There are two ways of using *yourself* to which nobody will object, and one which some people will criticize. The innocuous uses are: (*a*) as a reflexive pronoun, e.g. *did you hurt yourself? help yourself to some cake, Tim*; (*b*) to emphasize the word *you*: *you are going to have to do it yourself; did you do it yourself?* Staff who deal with the public, in businesses such as restaurants, call centres, and the like, quite often use *yourself* in a rather different way, as a substitute for *you*: *is this soup for yourself? is the appliance for yourself, sir?* Using *yourself* in this way should be avoided in any kind of formal writing, and is considered wrong by some people even in speech. Arguably, however, it fulfils a useful function in the situations mentioned. *Yourself* sounds more formal and less direct than *you*, and is thus perceived as more polite. Cf. MYSELF 3.

yous, youse. Standard English lacks an explicitly marked plural form of *you* that would correspond to French *vous*, German *ihr*, Spanish *vosotros/as*, etc. However, regional and dialectal usage fills this gap in many areas of the English-speaking world, especially in parts of Ireland, Scotland, and Northern England, and in some American, Australian and NZ English. These forms are marked variously in dictionaries as 'colloquial', 'not standard', etc., and are generally stigmatized, as 'low-prestige' or 'uneducated' by those who do not use them, among whom they may well create an unfavourable impression. While they are to be avoided in any writing other than the informal, or that reproduces speech, to those who use them they are as natural and unremarkable as the Scottish 'amn't I', the Yorkshire 'it were grand' and the Australian 'g'day'. Some examples: *Youse kids makes me tired*—S. Crane, 1893 (US); *Say, yous guys, this is fellowworker McCreary*—J. Dos Passos, 1930 (US); *Look here, Ray, It's the least I can do for youse*—E. Jolley, 1985 (Aust.); *What sort of caper yous buggers coming at now?*—V. O'Sullivan, 1985 (NZ); *Ah jist want tae tell youse a' that thae folk sayin' the weans* [*sc.* children] *ur no' gettin learned gude at the schule ur talkin' mince* [*sc.* nonsense]—*Scotland on Sunday*, 2002.

youth /juːθ/. Plural *youths*, pronounced /juːðz/. See -TH /θ/ AND -TH/ð/. Its primary sense is a young male person. It may also mean collectively 'young people (of both sexes)' (*the youth of the country*). In the plural form *youths* it is used only of males, frequently disapprovingly (*the youths in the estate are well known to the police*).

-yse, -yze. In a small group of words with these endings the standard spelling in BrE is *-yse* (*analyse, catalyse, dialyse, paralyse,* etc.), and in AmE *-yze (analyze,* etc.).

zed. The usual pronunciation of the letter *z* in BrE and elsewhere, while *zee* is standard in AmE. See also ZZZS.

zeitgeist /ˈzʌɪtgʌɪst/. This 19c. loanword from German meaning 'the spirit of the age' is first recorded in a letter of Matthew Arnold's. It is sufficiently assimilated into English not to need the initial capital letter of German nouns, and to be written in roman. The adjective **zeitgeisty** was not in the *OED* at the time of writing, but is marked informal in *ODO*. It seems to be predominantly BrE, and is a firm journalistic favourite, e.g. *The idea of 'respect' in politics seemed so zeitgeisty a couple of years ago but today it's almost a dirty word—Guardian, Comment is Free*, 2008.

zenith. Pronounced /ˈzɛnɪθ/ in BrE, but with initial /ˈziːn-/ in AmE.

***zenophobia, *zenophobic.** For these misspellings see XENOPHOBIA.

zero. 1 Several dictionaries allow both *zeros* and *zeroes* for the plural of the noun. The first is about twice as frequent in *OEC* data.

2 The verb inflections for *zero* (*in* (*on*)) are *zeroes, zeroing, zeroed*.

3 For the circumstances in which the numeral '0' is pronounced 'zero', see NOUGHT.

zero-derivation. See CONVERSION.

zeugma (Greek, = yoking). 'A rhetorical figure by which a single word is made to refer to two or more words in a sentence, esp. when applying to them in different senses' (*New SOED*, 1993), e.g. *he lost his hat and his temper*. See SYLLEPSIS.

zigzag. The inflected forms are *zigzagged, zigzagging;* but *zigzags*. See -G-, -GG-.

zinc. When a final letter *-c* has to be doubled before an inflection beginning with a vowel, it becomes *-ck-* to retain the hard sound of the *-c*, e.g. *panicking*. However, the inflected and derived forms of *zinc* are an exception, producing *zinced, zincic, zincite, zincification*, etc.

zoology. In 1921 the *OED* gave only /zəʊˈɒlədʒi/, the first syllable rhyming with *woe*. That pronunciation in standard in AmE, but in BrE has almost entirely given way to /zuːˈɒlədʒi/, as if the word were spelt *zoo-ology*.

zwieback (a kind of rusk). A word of German origin (in German literally 'twice-baked') for which no settled pronunciation has been achieved in English. In BrE it is pronounced /ˈzwiːbak/, /ˈzwʌɪbak/, or /ˈtsviːbak/; in AmE any of several pronunciations are current, /ˈswiːbak, ˈswʌɪ-, ˈzwiː-, ˈzwʌɪ-, -bɑk/.

zythum /ˈzʌɪθəm/. A kind of malt beer drunk in ancient Egypt, is included merely to give this book a sense of an ending, and as a gift to Scrabblers. As the *OED* says, 'Much of the word's continuing use is due to its status as the last word listed in several dictionaries'. However, it is not the final word. See ZZZS.

-z-, -zz-. 1 Very few standard words end in a single letter *-z* preceded by a vowel or vowels, namely *biz* (as in *the music biz*), *fez, squiz* (Australian and NZ 'a look'), and *quiz*. Inflections or derivatives of these words double the final letter *-z* when the added suffix begins with a vowel, e.g. *fezzed, quizzing*.

2 A tiny group of words can be written with single or double final *-z*: *friz(z), swiz(z)*, and *whiz(z)*.

See also PIZZAZZ; WHIZZ.

zzzs. A shorthand way of writing the informal expression for 'sleep', *zeds*, as in to *catch a few zeds*, or *zees* in AmE, e.g. '*What the hell, we'll go first class and you can catch some zeds on the flight!' he says—www.theregister.co.uk*, 2004 (UK); *Working hours are longer here, and for many, Sunday is their only day off, which is often spent just catching up on missed zzzs*—weblog, 2005 (UK).